THE INTERNATIONAL STANDARD BIBLE ENCYCLOPAEDIA

Michael Angulo

THE INTERNATIONAL STANDARD BIBLE ENCYCLOPAEDIA

JAMES ORR, M.A., D.D., GENERAL EDITOR

JOHN L. NUELSEN, D.D., LL.D.

EDGAR Y. MULLINS, D.D., LL.D.

ASSISTANT EDITORS

MORRIS O. EVANS, D.D., PH.D., MANAGING EDITOR

MELVIN GROVE KYLE, D.D., LL.D., REVISING EDITOR

VOLUME I

A—CLEMENCY

WM. B. EERDMANS PUBLISHING CO.

GRAND RAPIDS, MICH.

Reprinted, November 1986

ISBN 0-8028-8045-2

PREFACE

In presenting to the public in completed form the volumes which comprise THE INTERNATIONAL STANDARD BIBLE ENCYCLOPAEDIA it is fitting that an explanation should be given of the reasons for the appearance of so comprehensive a work, of its distinctive character and aims, and that some mention should be made of the principles by which the Publishers and Editors have been guided in its preparation.

Most readers are aware that the last twenty years have been marked on both sides of the Atlantic —but in Britain chiefly—by a remarkable productivity in dictionaries and encyclopaedias of the Bible. Prior to that time the need of a new departure in Bible dictionaries had become acutely felt. The age was one of transition, of vast and rapid progress in knowledge, and the old aids to the study of the sacred Book no longer satisfied. The movement then already in process has gone forward steadily since, with the result that something like a revolution has taken place in our knowledge of Biblical antiquity and still more in the prevailing methods of approaching and dealing with Biblical subjects. While thus new needs have been created, the task of those entrusted with the preparation of new dictionaries and encyclopaedias of the Bible has been rendered increasingly difficult. It is a byword that things in theology are just now very much in flux. The old landmarks are disappearing or at least are being considerably shifted. The Bible is passing through the ordeal of a remorseless and revolutionary criticism, and the singular fact is that conclusions which decades ago would have been condemned as subversive of all faith in its authority are now naturalized in large sections of the Church as the last and surest results of scholarship, to question which is well-nigh to put one's self beyond the pale of consideration—almost as if one denied the Copernican theory of the universe.

The impulse to meet these new conditions has given rise, as above stated, to the preparation of numerous Biblical dictionaries and encyclopaedias, the chief of which have already taken their places as standard works in this department of scholarship. It is in no spirit of rivalry to these existing works that the present Encyclopaedia is produced. Able and scholarly as these earlier undertakings are, it is believed that there is room for yet another work of the kind, conceived on distinct lines, embodying the best scholarship and newest knowledge, yet somewhat less technical in character than the existing larger works, adapted more directly to the needs of the average pastor and Bible student, and therefore serving a purpose which the others do not so adequately fulfil. There are other considerations which have had weight in determining upon a production of this new work.

As its title indicates, this Encyclopaedia aims at being "International." On the one hand, it may be claimed that, because it has been produced on American soil, and in considerable part under American care, it has been able to draw from a wider area, and to incorporate the fruits of a fuller and more representative American scholarship, than is possible in any British work; while on the other hand its connection through its chief editor with the Old World enables it to reap not less the benefits of some of the best learning of Britain and its Colonies, as well as of the Continent of Europe. How far this has been accomplished will appear farther on.

The choice of the word Encyclopaedia as the principal one in the title of this work has also been made with a definite purpose. While very complete in its definition of words and terms as a dictionary, the larger function of the work planned by its projectors was to group and arrange data and information after the manner of an encyclopaedia. It will be observed, therefore, that the latter term more accurately describes the completed work.

An important question in connection with a new reference work of this kind is the attitude to be assumed by its writers toward matters fundamental to the newer learning, in so far as the latter deals with the structure, critical treatment, inspiration, and authority of the Bible. Scholarship alone cannot be the deciding factor here, for the scholarship of different minds leads to widely different conclusions, determined often by the ultimate presuppositions on which the treatment of a subject is based. The spirit so widely prevalent in our day which rejects the idea of the supernatural in nature and history, and the criticism which proceeds on that basis, must reach entirely different results from those attained by that attitude of mind and heart which reverently accepts a true revelation of God in the history of Israel and in Christ. It is the former spirit which eviscerates Christianity of most of the vital truths which the Church, resting on Scripture, has always regarded as of its essence. With such a spirit, and with the treatment of Biblical subjects resulting from it, the present Encyclopaedia disclaims all sympathy. In fact, its general attitude may be described as that of a reasonable conservatism. In harmony with most, though not all, recent works of the kind, this Encyclopaedia is positive and constructive in New Testament criticism and doctrine; on the other hand, while acknowledging the rights of a reverent Old Testament criticism, and welcoming any aids which such criticism may bring to the better understanding of the sacred Word, it differs from most of these ultra-modern works either in declining to accept the views of, or in adopting a more cautious attitude toward, the advanced Wellhausen school. Notwithstanding, the aim throughout has been to secure fairness of statement of all subjects on which marked differences of opinion prevail, and in such cases—e.g., Baptism, the Eucharist, questions of church government, theories of criticism, etc.—it has been provided that the divergent views be presented in separate articles, each article being prepared by a leading exponent of the view set forth therein.

In harmony with the practical and authoritative character of the Encyclopaedia the greatest pains have been taken to secure comprehensiveness and completeness in its presentation of all Biblical matters, and in its fulness of typical Scriptural references on all subjects dealt with. In scope the work embraces the Old and New Testaments and the Apocrypha, together with all related subjects of Language, Text, Literature (apocalyptic, apocryphal, sub-apostolic, etc.), Archaeology, historical and religious environment—whatever, in short, may throw light on the meaning and message of the sacred Book. The aim has been that nothing great or small conducing to this end shall be omitted. History of peoples and religions, Ethnology, Geography, Topography, Biography, Arts and Crafts, Manners and Customs, Family Life, Natural History, Agriculture, War, Shipping, Ritual, Laws, Sects, Music, and all else pertaining to the outer and inner life of the people of the Bible, and therefore throwing light upon the meaning of the original writers, are amply and minutely treated. Proper names are explained and their occurrences in the Bible and Apocrypha noted. Large space has been devoted to the meanings and uses of the more ordinary, as well as of rarer and obsolete, English words with special reference to their Hebrew and Greek originals and to the variations of usage in the Authorized Version and the Revised Versions. Careful attention has been given to the figurative uses of words in connection with all subjects where such uses occur. This feature alone of the Encyclopaedia will render it of special value to ministers, teachers, and the rank and file of students of the Bible.

Such being the general character and design of the Encyclopaedia, its preparation was entrusted to a staff of Editors and assistants whose scholarly attainments and known sympathy with the objects to be attained furnished a guarantee that these plans would be effectively carried out in the completed work. As General and Consulting Editor the Publishers secured the services of the Reverend Professor James Orr, D.D., of the United Free Church College, Glasgow, Scotland, and with him were conjoined as Associate Editors the Reverend President Edgar Y. Mullins, D.D., of the Southern Baptist Theological Seminary, Louisville, Kentucky, and the Reverend Bishop John L. Nuelsen, D.D., of the Methodist Episcopal Church, now of Zurich, Switzerland. The duties of Managing Editor were committed to the Reverend Morris O. Evans, D.D., of Cincinnati, Ohio; on him and his corps of skilled assistants has fallen the onerous task of seeing the work carried safely through the press. To the General and Managing Editors fell the preparation of the necessary lists of subjects and their grouping and classification; then, in conjunction with the Associate Editors, the assignment of these to suitable contributors. In this connection special care was exercised to give the work a genuinely international and representative character, not only by selecting contributors distinguished in their several departments from both sides of the Atlantic, and from the British Colonies and the Continent, but by seeing that these were chosen from the various sections of the Christian Church and, moreover, that in so far as possible the writers should be those altogether qualified to produce the most satisfactory articles possible on the subjects assigned to them within the space allotted. In all, nearly two hundred contributors, many of them scholars of the highest rank, have been employed upon this work during the past six years. Over one hundred of these contributors are residents of the United States, about sixty of Great Britain and Continental Europe, and the rest, of Canada, Syria, India, Australia, and other countries. Inspection of the Index of Contributors will show how largely all Churches in the respective countries are represented in this Encyclopaedia. Anglicans, Baptists, Congregationalists, Lutherans, Methodists, Presbyterians, with those of still other communions, diverse in name but united in the faith of the one Lord and Saviour Jesus Christ and laboring in the interests of His Kingdom, have all willingly lent their aid in the production of this truly ecumenical work. Valued assistance also has been unstintingly rendered by a number of Jewish authors. A large proportion of the writers are scholars engaged in professorial work in leading Universities, Seminaries, and Colleges—a fact which greatly enhances the responsible and representative character of their contributions.

It is not possible, and the attempt would be invidious, to particularize the share of the several writers in a work which is the product of so many scholarly pens. An examination of the Encyclopaedia itself will reveal to the most critical eye such a wealth of scholarly articles as has seldom been made available to those in need of such a work. It will be sufficient to say that it was desired at the outset by the promoters of this Encyclopaedia that special prominence should be given to Archaeology and the most recent findings of Exploration, in their bearings on the Bible, and on the lands and civilizations with which Biblical history is connected (Egypt, Babylonia, Assyria, Palestine, Hittites, etc.). How fully this end has been attained is seen in the fact that a large number of the foremost authorities on Archaeology are contributors to these pages. In this connection deep regret must be expressed for the severe loss sustained to Biblical knowledge in general and to this Encyclopaedia through the lamented death, while the work was progressing, of Colonel C. R. Conder, whose acquaintance with Biblical Archaeology and Palestinian Topography, equaled by few and surpassed by none, made his services of such special value. It is, however, a gratification that, before his decease, Colonel Conder had completed most of the articles for the Encyclopaedia assigned to him.

In the treatment of the wide range of subjects opened up by the Natural History of the Bible, with kindred subjects relating to the Geology, Mineralogy, Agriculture, Trades and Industries, etc., also the Topography of Palestine, this Encyclopaedia is largely indebted to Palestinian contributors whose names occupy prominent places in the list. However, the Birds of the Bible are dealt with by a noted American writer, Mrs. Gene Stratton-Porter, whose stories and bird books have charmed multitudes of people all around the world. The abundant articles on Eastern customs, food, trades, marriage, family relationships, etc., are principally the work of American contributors.

Embracing in the two Testaments well-nigh every species of literature, the Bible gives rise, even in external respects, to a multitude of questions which it is required of an adequate Encyclopaedia to answer. Such are questions of language, of manuscripts, of text, of internal arrangement, of the growth of the Canon, of Versions, of vicissitudes of literary history, then of chronology as framework, of diversity of contents, leading up to history and biography; all finally merging in the wider questions with which criticism proper has to deal. It is the aim of the present work to yield reliable and satisfactory information on all these important subjects. In several articles, such as "Religion in Ancient Greece," by Dr. A. Fairbanks, of the Museum of Fine Arts, Boston, Massachusetts, and "The Roman Empire and Christianity," by Dr. S. Angus, the aim has been to give the true perspective and atmosphere to the Bible history. It is of the first importance that the reader should realize the background and salient features of that history—have a clear conception of the mythological systems and ancient world-powers with which Christianity had to contend and which it was destined to supplant. Several illustrations also will be found to serve the same end.

The center of interest in the Bible must ever be the Lord Jesus Christ, to the consideration of whose life and teaching, as enshrined in the Gospels, and to the significance of whose Person, mission, and saving work, as further unfolded in the Epistles, large space in this Encyclopaedia is necessarily devoted. It was with great diffidence, and a deep sense of the responsibility of the task, that the principal article on Jesus Christ was undertaken by the General Editor. The treatment of the subject is guided by the conviction that, while critical discussion cannot be ignored, a simple and straightforward presentation of the narrative of this transcendent life, in its proper historical and chronological setting, is itself the best antidote to the vagaries of much current speculation, and the endeavor is made to give the article throughout a character which will render it informatory and helpful to the average Biblical student. The same author is responsible for the articles on the Bible and on Criticism. On the latter subject, however, another article from a different standpoint is appended to the one by the General Editor.

The articles on the greater doctrines and on doctrinal and ethical themes generally, as drawn from both Old and New Testaments, cover a wide range, and in all of these several departments of Biblical learning most painstaking effort has been put forth with such results as an examination of the Encyclopaedia itself cannot fail to reveal.

It is essential to a good encyclopaedia that in addition to its scholarly execution it possess distinctive outstanding features for the convenience and information of those who consult it. This Encyclopaedia is particularly characterized by the following features:

I. **Fulness.** It has been the design of the Editors that every word in the Bible and the Apocrypha having a distinct Scriptural meaning should appear in this work; and also that all the doctrines of the Bible, the principal terms of Biblical criticism and related subjects of profane history, biography, geography, social life of the peoples, and the industries, sciences, literature, etc., should be included and given proper treatment. A much greater number of words and subjects are defined and treated in this Encyclopaedia than in any other work of its kind, as will be seen by comparison.

II. **Authority.** In order that those who use such a work may be assured of its trustworthiness it is necessary that the subject-matter should be identified with its authors. Therefore every article in this Encyclopaedia, of sufficient length to be regarded as more than a mere definition or notice, appears over the signature of its author. Items of less than one hundred words are not signed, as so many signatures to short and relatively unimportant paragraphs would serve no valuable purpose, but would give a monotonous appearance to a page. It will be noted that the authors responsible for all the major subjects were selected and requested to write upon those particular themes because of their marked ability and recognized authority in the special departments of Biblical learning to which their articles belong.

III. **Accessibility.** More frequently than otherwise those who consult an encyclopaedia desire to obtain information on only one or two points in an article and have neither the time nor inclination to read it throughout its entire length. To aid such busy readers, therefore, a uniform division of articles by the employment of headings and subheadings has been adopted. The principal divisions of articles are indicated by captions in bold-faced italics. Subordinate to this first class of divisions appears a secondary class of numerical headings known as cut-in heads, the text-matter being indented for their insertion. An illustration of these two headings follows:

II. The Ordinance.—The "seats of doctrine," i.e. the Scripture texts which must be employed for determining every essential part of the teaching of Scripture regarding the second sacrament of the Christian church, are the words of institution recorded in Mt **26** 26–28; Mk **14** 22–24; Lk **22** 19.20; 1 Cor **11** 23–25. Valuable statements, chiefly concerning the proper use of the sacrament, are found in 1 Cor **10** 15 ff; **11** 20 ff. That these texts are controverted is no reason why a doctrine should not be established from them. No doctrine of the Christian religion could be established, if every text of Scripture had to be withdrawn from the argument, so soon as it had become controverted. Jn **6** 32–59 does not treat of this ordinance, because (1) the ordinance must be dated from the night of the betrayal, which was considerably after the Lord's discourse at Capernaum; (2) because this passage speaks of "eating the flesh," not the body, of the Son of man, and of drinking "his blood," in such

1. Source and Norm of the Doctrine of the Eucharist

The cut-in heads are followed by a third class of subject divisions indicated by plain Arabic numerals enclosed in parentheses as follows: (1), (2), (3). The reader will be further aided by a fourth class of subdivisions composed of the letters of the alphabet arranged in the following style: (*a*), (*b*), (*c*), etc. In a few exceptional instances other special methods of subdividing articles have been provided to suit particular cases. The principal divisions and subdivisions of each leading article appear in tabulated form as an outline or analysis immediately preceding the article itself, so that one may observe at a mere glance the general method of treatment of any particular subject, and also the relative place in the article in which any feature is located.

IV. **Illustrations.** A large number of pictures, maps and charts, particularly adapted to illustrating the text, serve the purposes both of instruction and embellishment. While some of the illustrations are necessarily copied or redrawn from familiar subjects, by far the larger number are reproductions of recent photographs. Many of these latter were obtained by the Publishers through their own special representatives who either made the photographs themselves or collected them from many available sources at great outlay of time and money. The Editors and Publishers are under special obligation to many authors and interested friends who have procured from others or loaned from their own private collections many rare pictures which have been used. Among others who have thus unselfishly aided in the production of this work special mention should be made of the following persons: the Reverend A. E. Breen, D.D., of Rochester, New York; Professor Albert T. Clay, of Yale University; Professor A. E. Day, of the Syrian Protestant College, Beirut, Syria; Professor A. C. Dickie, Manchester, England; the Reverend William Ewing, D.D., Edinburgh, Scotland; Dr. Arthur Fairbanks, Director of the Museum of Fine Arts, Boston, Massachusetts; the Reverend M. G. Kyle, LL.D., Professor in Xenia Theological Seminary, Xenia, Ohio; Dr. E. C. Richardson, Librarian at Princeton University; the Reverend Professor George L. Robinson, of McCormick Theological Seminary, Chicago; the Reverend Professor G. H. Trever, D.D., of Gammon School of Theology, Atlanta, Georgia; and Mrs. W. J. Williams, Cincinnati, Ohio.

V. **Maps.** At some places in the text maps are used for illustration. The colored maps, which comprise an atlas, are grouped at the close of the fifth volume for convenience in reference. They have been drawn under the immediate supervision of the Reverend Professor George L. Robinson, of McCormick Theological Seminary, Chicago. The index, which precedes the atlas, renders the location of all identified places easy.

VI. **Cross-References and Indexes.** Although the alphabetical arrangement of an encyclopaedia enables one using it readily to locate its principal subjects, it is possible to obtain all the information concerning any theme only by an acquaintance with all the articles in which that theme appears. A system of cross-references extensively used throughout this work leads the reader to the various articles which give information on any given theme or subject. A little overlapping or repetition has occasionally been allowed to save readers the trouble of referring too frequently from one article to another. To aid further those who use this work to locate immediately any fact or particular contained in the Encyclopaedia there are seven indexes as follows: I. Contributors; II. General Subjects; III. Scripture Texts; IV. Hebrew and Aramaic Words; V. Greek Words; VI. Illustrations; VII. Index to the Atlas.

In the pronunciation of proper names and English words the international character of the work has not been overlooked. Great care has also been exercised in view of the doubts and difficulties attaching to the derivation of proper names. The American Standard Edition of the Revised Version of the Bible, copyright 1901 by Thomas Nelson & Sons, New York, by consent of the owners of the copyright, has been made the standard English text of the Biblical quotations and references where not otherwise indicated; the writers, however, have enjoyed full liberty in the use of other versions or in giving their own translations and paraphrases.

The Editors and Publishers have not spared time, painstaking care or expense in their efforts to produce an Encyclopaedia in every way adequate to the exacting requirements of teachers in colleges and theological seminaries and Bible schools, clergymen, and all others who desire to be familiar with the Holy Scriptures and those themes of doctrine, criticism, and scholarship which are directly related to them.

PREFACE, REVISED EDITION

The necessity of issuing another large edition of THE INTERNATIONAL STANDARD BIBLE ENCYCLOPAEDIA affords the opportunity to bring the ENCYCLOPAEDIA abreast of the most recent work in archaeology in Bible lands and thus make it not only the latest, but also the most complete, work of its kind before the English-reading public. Within the fourteen years since its publication there have been discoveries which have given back to the world little known, and sometimes wholly unknown, ancient civilizations.

Here in the Preface can only be enumerated the extended articles which present new material. Since the first edition, further researches have added greatly to our conception of the Empire of the HITTITES; and the painstaking labors of German philologists have turned our minds away from the military glory to the strange development of the civilization and literature. A scientific chronology of POTTERY has disclosed the culture of both Canaanite and Israelite Palestine. The researches of Vincent, Albright, and Garstang have made the early civilization of the JORDAN VALLEY an open book. The work at Jericho, begun by Sellin and Watzinger, is slowly revealing the history there. BETHEL and SHILOH have given us some glimpses into the story of the Patriarch Jacob and of the setting up of the Tabernacle in the land. The tragic narrative of the CITIES of the PLAIN, subjected to the most searching scientific tests, is now corroborated at every point; and the location of those cities definitely fixed at the lower end of the Dead Sea. OPHEL gives us the secrets of the Jebusite castle and the Zion of David's day; GIBEAH of Saul, the "house" of Israel's first king; BETH-SHEAN, the temple of Ashtaroth in which the trophies of Saul and Jonathan were hung; and MEGIDDO, the Gibraltar of "the Bridge of Nations." CAPERNAUM has shown us the foundations of the very synagogue in which our Lord preached; KIRIATH-SEPHER furnishes indubitable evidence of the Conquest and the cultural DATE of the EXODUS. And now UR of CHALDEES amazes with its revelations. In all this, wherever Biblical history is definitely touched, it is corroborated.

Besides the revision of this long list of articles on archaeological subjects, some other articles of the first edition have been found to be inadequate and earnest effort has been made to bring them up to the high standard set by the Editors and Publisher. Alternative views also have been presented on still other subjects, and thus a number of new contributors have been added to the distinguished list in former editions. It is the aim of the Publisher to present the latest and best product of Biblical scholarship in this Revised Edition of the ENCYCLOPAEDIA.

To this end it has now been made to reflect fully the doctrines of the Christian faith presented in the very words of Scripture and formulated in the historic faith of the great body of Christendom; to catch also the spirit of the historic records of the Old and the New Testaments; and to set forth both the doctrines and the spirit in the light of archaeological research as presented at the date of issuing this Revised Edition.

LIST OF ABBREVIATIONS

I. GENERAL

ℵ	Codex Sinaiticus
A	Codex Alexandrinus
Ab	*'Ābhōth, Pirḳē*
acc.	according
ad loc.	at the place
AHT	*Ancient Hebrew Tradition*
AJSL	*American Journal of Semitic Languages and Literatures*
AJT	*American Journal of Theology*
Akk	Akkadian
al. (*alii*)	others
Alex	Alexandrian
Am PEFSt	*American Palestine Exploration Fund Statement*
Am Tab	Tell el-Amarna Letters
Amurru	Clay, *Amurru, the Home of the Northern Semites*
anc.	ancient
Ant	Josephus, *Antiquities*
AOF	Winckler, *Altorientalische Forschungen*
Ap Lit	Apocalyptic Literature
Apoc	Apocrypha
Apos Const	Apostolical Constitutions
app.	appendix
Aq	Aquila
Arab.	Arabic
Aram.	Aramaic
art.	article
ARV	American Standard Revised Version
ARVm	American Revised Version, margin
AS	Anglo-Saxon
Assyr	Assyrian
*	theoretical or unidentified forms
AT	*Altes Testament*
AV	Authorized Version (1611)
b.	born
B	Codex Vaticanus
Bab	Babylonian
BDB	Brown, Driver, and Briggs, *Hebrew and English Lexicon of the OT*
Bez	Bezold, *Catalogue of the Cuneiform Tablets in the Ko(u)yunjik Collection of the British Museum*
Bib.	Biblical
BJ	Josephus, *Jewish Wars*
Bk	Book
BR	Robinson, *Biblical Researches*
BS	*Bibliotheca Sacra*
BST	*Bible Student and Teacher*
BTP	G. A. Smith, *Book of the Twelve Prophets*
BW	*Biblical World*
C	Codex Ephraemi
c, cir	*circa*, about
CAG	Smith, *Chaldean Account of Genesis*
Can	Canaanite
CAp	Josephus, *Against Apion*
CC	Covenant Code
CE	*Cyclopedia of Education*
cf	compare
ch(s)	chapter(s)
CH	Code of Ḫammurabi
Chald	Chaldaic
CH (*St P*)	Conybeare and Howson, *St. Paul*
CI	*Corpus Inscriptionum*
CIG	*Corpus Inscriptionum Graecarum*
CIL	*Corpus Inscriptionum Latinarum*
CIS	*Corpus Inscriptionum Semiticarum*
cod., codd.	codex, codices
comm(s).	commentary, commentaries
COT	Schrader, *The Cuneiform Inscriptions and the OT*
CRT	Craig, *Assyrian and Babylonian Religious Texts*
d.	died, denarius (penny)
D	Deuteronomist, or Codex Bezae
D_2	Later Deuteronomistic editors
DB	Smith, *Dictionary of the Bible*
DCA	*Dictionary of Christian Antiquities*
DCB	*Dictionary of Christian Biography*
DCG	Hastings, *Dictionary of Christ and the Gospels*
Did	*Didache*
disc.	discovered
doct.	doctrine
DOG	*Deutsche Orientalische Gesellschaft*
E	Elohist
E_2	Later additions to E
E.	East
EB	*Encyclopaedia Biblica*
ed, edd	edition, editions
Eerd *St*	Eerdmans, *Studien*
Egyp	Egyptian
Einl	*Einleitung*
Enc Brit	*Encyclopaedia Britannica* (11th ed)
enl.	enlarged
ep., epp.	epistle, epistles
EPC	Wiener, *Essays in Pentateuchal Criticism*
ERE	Hastings, *Encyclopaedia of Religion and Ethics*
ERV	English Revised Version
ERVm	English Revised Version, margin
esp.	especially
ET	English translation

et al.	and others
EV	English Versions of the Bible
expl.	exploration
Expos	*The Expositor*
Expos T	*Expository Times*
f, ff	following (verse, or verses, page, etc)
fem.	feminine
fig.	figurative(ly)
fl.	flourished
Fr.	French
fr	from
fr.	fragment
ft.	foot, feet
gal(s).	gallon(s)
GAP	Buhl, *Geographie des alten Palästina*
GAS	Smith, *Modern Criticism and the Preaching of the OT*
GB or Ginsburg's Bible	Ginsburg, *New Massoretico-Critical Text of the Hebrew Bible*
GBA	Winckler, *Geschichte Babyloniens u. Assyriens*
gen.	genitive
Ger.	German
GGA	*Göttingische gelehrte Anzeigen*
GGN	*Göttingische gelehrte Nachrichten*
GJV	Schürer, *Geschichte des Jüdischen Volkes* (4th ed)
Gr	Greek
GVI	Stade, *Geschichte des Volkes Israel*
H	Law of Holiness (Lev **17–26**)
HA	*Hebräische Archäologie* (Benzinger; Nowack)
HCM	Sayce, *Higher Criticism and the Monuments*
HDB	Hastings, *Dictionary of the Bible* (five volumes)
HDB, 1 vol	Hastings, *Dictionary of the Bible* (single volume)
HE	Eusebius, *Historia Ecclesiastica*
Heb	Hebrew
Hel	Hellenistic
Hex	Hexateuch
HGHL	Smith, *Historical Geography of the Holy Land*
HI	Kuenen, *History of Israel to the Fall of the Jewish State*
Hiph.	Hiphil
Hithp.	Hithpael
HJ	*The Hibbert Journal*
HJP	Schürer, *History of the Jewish People in the Time of Jesus Christ*
Hor Heb	Lightfoot, *Horae Hebraicae*
HPM	McCurdy, *History, Prophecy and the Monuments*
HPN	Gray, *Studies in Hebrew Proper Names*
ib or ibid	same place
ICC	*International Critical Commentary*
id	same person or author
ideo.	ideogram
IJG	Wellhausen, *Israelitische und jüdische Geschichte*
IL	Stevenson, *Index-Lexicons to OT and NT*
impf.	imperfect
infra	below
in loc.	in the place cited
inscr.	inscription
intrans.	intransitive
intro(s)	introduction(s)
introd.	introductory
J	Jahwist
J$_2$	Later additions to J
JAOS	*Journal of the American Oriental Society*
JBL	*Journal of Biblical Literature and Exegesis*
JD	Jastrow, *Dictionary of the Targumim, Talmudim and Midrashic Literature*
JDT	*Jahrbücher für deutsche Theologie*
Jeh	Jehovah (Yahweh)
Jerus	Jerusalem
Jew Enc	*Jewish Encyclopedia*
Jos	Josephus
jour.	journal
JPT	*Jahrbücher für protestantische Theologie*
JQR	*Jewish Quarterly Review*
JRAS	*Journal of the Royal Asiatic Society*
KAT	Schrader, *Die Keilinschriften und das Alte Testament*
KB	*Keilinschriftliche Bibliothek* (Schrader, editor)
Ḳ^{e}rē and K^{e}thībh	See art. TEXT OF THE OT
KGF	Schrader, *Keilinschriften und Geschichtsforschung*
Kim	Ḳimḥi
l., ll.	line, lines
lang.	language
Lat	Latin
LB	Thomson, *The Land and the Book*
LBR	Robinson, *Later Biblical Researches*
l.c. or loc. cit.	in the place cited
lect	lecture
lex.	lexicon
lit.	literature, or literally
LOT	Driver, *Introduction to the Literature of the OT*
LOTB	Clay, *Light on the OT from Babel*
LTJM	Edersheim, *Life and Times of Jesus the Messiah*
LXX	Septuagint
m or mg	margin
Maim	Maimonides
masc.	masculine
Masp	Maspero, *Dawn of Civilization*
MDO-G	Winckler, *Mitteilungen der Deutschen Orient-Gesellschaft*
ME	Middle English
Midr	Midrash
Mish	Mishna
mod.	modern
M S	Moabite Stone
MS(S)	Manuscript(s)
MT	Mas(s)oretic Text. See art. TEXT OF THE OT
N.	North
n.	note
n.d.	no date
NHB	Tristram, *Natural History of the Bible*
NHWB	Levy, *Neuhebräisches und chaldäisches Wörterbuch*
NKZ	*Neue Kirchliche Zeitschrift*
no.	number
N.O.	Natural Order
NT	New Testament
obs.	obsolete
obv.	obverse
OC	*Transactions of the International Congress of Orientalists*
OE	Old English
OHL	*Oxford Hebrew Lexicon;* see *BDB*
OLZ	*Orientalistische Literatur-Zeitung*
om.	omitted
Onk	Onḳelos (Targum)
Onom or *OS*	Eusebius, *Onomasticon—Onom Sacr*
OP	Wiener, *Origin of the Pentateuch*
op. cit.	in the work quoted
OT	Old Testament
OT (Sept or LXX)	Swete, *OT in Greek according to Sept*
OTJC	Smith, *OT in Jewish Church*

P or PC	Priestly Code
P_2	Secondary Priestly Writers
Pal	Palestine
PAOS	*Proceedings of the American Oriental Society*
par.	paragraph
‖	parallel
part. or ptcp.	participle
pass.	passive
PB	*Polychrome Bible*
PEF	*Palestine Exploration Fund Memoirs*
PEFSt	*PEF Quarterly Statement*
Pent	Pentateuch
Pers	Persian
Pesh	Peshito, Peshiṭṭā
PHI	Wellhausen, *Prolegomena to the History of Israel*
Phili(s)	Philistine(s)
Phoen	Phoenician
pl., plur.	plural
PN	Cheyne, *Complete List of the Proper Names in the OT and NT*
POT	Orr, *The Problem of the Old Testament*
PRE	Hauck-Herzog, *Realencyklopädie für protestantische Theologie und Kirche*
pref.	preface
prim.	primitive
prob	probably
ps(s)	psalm(s)
PS	Wiener, *Pentateuchal Studies*
PSBA	*Proceedings of the Society of Biblical Archaeology*
Pseudep	Pseudepigrapha
PTR	*Princeton Theological Review*
qt.	quoted by
q.v.	which see
R or red.	redactor or editor
r. or √	root
RB	*Revue biblique*
RE	See *PRE*
rev.	revised, or reviewed
RGG	Schiele-Zscharnack, *Religion in Geschichte und Gegenwart*
Rom	Roman
RP	*Records of the Past*
RS	*Revue sémitique*
RV	Revised Version (English and American)
RVm	Revised Version, margin
S.	South
s.	shilling
Sam	Samaritan
SBE	Müller, *Sacred Books of the East*
SBL	Wiener, *Studies in Biblical Law*
SBOT	*Sacred Books of the Old Testament*
Sch-Herz	*The New Schaff-Herzog Encyclopedia of Religious Knowledge*
SCOT	Wright, *Scientific Confirmation of the OT History*
sec.	section
Sem	Semitic
Sept or LXX	Septuagint
ser.	series
Sin	Sinaitic
sing.	singular
SK	*Studien und Kritiken*
sq.	square, or the following
StBD	*Standard Bible Dictionary*
subst.	substantive
s.v.	under the word
SWP	*Memoirs of the Survey of Western Palestine*
Syr	Syriac
t	times
Talm	Talmud
text.	textual
Tg(s), Targ(s)	Targum(s)
TLZ	*Theologische Literaturzeitung*
TMH	J. Dahse, *Textkritische Materialen zur Hexateuchfrage*
tr	translation, or translate
tr^d	translated
tr^s	translations
TR	*Textus Receptus* of the NT. See art. TEXT OF THE NT
trans	transitive
Treg.	Tregelles
TS	*Theologische Studien und Kritiken*
TSBA	*Transactions of the Society of Biblical Archaeology*
TT	*Theologisch Tijdschrift*
U	*Untersuchungen*
ut supra	as above
v.	versus
V	Codex Venetus
ver	verse
vs	verses
VS, VSS	version, versions
Vulg	Vulgate (Jerome's Latin Bible, 390–405 AD)
v.v.	vice versa
W.	West
WAE	Wilkinson, *Ancient Egyptians*
WAI	*Western Asiatic Inscriptions*
WCH	Wellhausen, *The Composition of the Hexateuch*
WGA	Wright, *Grammar of the Arabic Language*
WH	Westcott and Hort, *The New Testament in Greek*
WZ(KM)	*Wiener Zeitschrift für die Kunde des Morgenlandes*
Z	*Zeitschrift*
ZA	*Zeitschrift für Assyriologie und verwandte Gebiete*
Zahn *NT*	Zahn, *Introduction to the New Testament*
ZATW	*Zeitschrift für alttestamentliche Wissenschaft*
ZDMG	*Zeitschrift der Deutschen Morgenländischen Gesellschaft*
ZDPV	*Zeitschrift des Deutschen Palästina-Vereins*
ZK	*Zeitschrift für Keilschriftforschung*
ZKW	*Zeitschrift für kirchliche Wissenschaft*
ZNTW	*Zeitschrift für neutestamentliche Wissenschaft*
ZWT	*Zeitschrift für wissenschaftliche Theologie*

II. BOOKS OF THE BIBLE

OLD TESTAMENT

Gen	Genesis	2 K	2 Kings	Cant	Canticles, or Song of Solomon	Am	Amos
Ex	Exodus	1 Ch	1 Chronicles	Isa	Isaiah	Ob	Obadiah
Lev	Leviticus	2 Ch	2 Chronicles	Jer	Jeremiah	Jon	Jonah
Nu	Numbers	Ezr	Ezra	Lam	Lamentations	Mic	Micah
Dt	Deuteronomy	Neh	Nehemiah	Ezk	Ezekiel	Nah	Nahum
Josh	Joshua	Est	Esther	Dnl	Daniel	Hab	Habakkuk
Jgs	Judges	Job		Hos	Hosea	Zeph	Zephaniah
Ruth		Ps	Psalms	Joel		Hag	Haggai
1 S	1 Samuel	Prov	Proverbs			Zec	Zechariah
2 S	2 Samuel	Eccl	Ecclesiastes			Mal	Malachi
1 K	1 Kings						

APOCRYPHA

1 Esd	1 Esdras	Wisd	Wisdom of Solomon	Ep Jer	Epistle of Jeremy	Bel	Bel and the Dragon
2 Esd	2 Esdras	Sir, or Ecclus	Sirach, or Ecclesiasticus	Three	Song of the Three Holy Children	Pr Man	Prayer of Manasses
Tob	Tobit	Bar	Baruch	Sus	Susanna	1 Macc	1 Maccabees
Jth	Judith					2 Macc	2 Maccabees
Ad Est	Additions to Esther, or Rest of Esther						

NEW TESTAMENT

Mt	Matthew	2 Cor	2 Corinthians	1 Tim	1 Timothy	2 Pet	2 Peter
Mk	Mark	Gal	Galatians	2 Tim	2 Timothy	1 Jn	1 John
Lk	Luke	Eph	Ephesians	Tit	Titus	2 Jn	2 John
Jn	John	Phil	Philippians	Philem	Philemon	3 Jn	3 John
Acts		Col	Colossians	He	Hebrews	Jude	
Rom	Romans	1 Thess	1 Thessalonians	Jas	James	Rev	Revelation
1 Cor	1 Corinthians	2 Thess	2 Thessalonians	1 Pet	1 Peter		

III. PSEUDEPIGRAPHA

Apoc Bar	Apocalypse of Baruch, Syriac (2 Baruch in Charles)	En (Slav)	Enoch, Slavonic Book of (Book of the Secrets of Enoch, 2 Enoch in Charles)
Apoc Bar (Gr)	Apocalypse of Baruch, Greek (3 Baruch in Charles)	Jub or Bk Jub	Jubilees, Book of
Asc Isa	Ascension of Isaiah	Ps Sol	Psalms of Solomon
Asm M	Assumption of Moses	Sib Or	Sibylline Oracles
En	Enoch, Ethiopic Book of (1 Enoch in Charles, *Apoc and Pseudep*)	XII P	Testament(s) of the Twelve Patriarchs

See also arts. APOCALYPTIC LITERATURE; APOCRYPHA.

NOTE.—In the references to the Apocrypha and Pseudepigrapha, no uniform attempt at completeness has been made.

KEY TO ENGLISH PRONUNCIATION

ā	as in fate	ō	as in old
ä	" " far	ô	" " orb
â	" " fare	o	" " not
a	" " fat	ó	" " obey
ạ	" " fall	oi	" " oil
ȧ	" " senate	o͞o	" " noon
ch	" " *church*	o͝o	" " book
dū	" " verdure	ou	" " sound
ē	" " me	sh	" " *ship*
é	" " event	th	" " *thing*
e	" " met	th	" " *this*
ẽ	" " ever	tū	" " culture
g	" " *go*	ū	" " use
ī	" " *ice*	û	" " urn
i	" " pin	u	" " but
n	" " man	ú	" " unite
ṇ (*ng* sound)	" " single	y	" " *yet*
ñ	" " cañon (kan'yun)		

SCHEME OF HEBREW TRANSLITERATION

VOWELS (CONTINENTAL VALUES)

LONG					SHORT					VERY SHORT				
ָ	ֵ (ֵי)	ִ (ִי)	ֹ (וֹ)	וּ	ַ	ֶ	ִ	ָ	ֻ	ְ	ֱ	ֲ	ֳ	ַ (furtive)
ā	ē	ī	ō	ū	a	e	i	o	u	ᵉ	ĕ	ă	ŏ	ᵃ

NOTE.—In particular cases, where a distinction should be made between a naturally long and a tone-long vowel, the signs ʌ and ‾ are used, respectively. In other cases the macron (‾) is used to indicate "full" writing (i.e. with ו or י) rather than the actual quantity, of which such writing is ordinarily a sign. In some instances ī represents ָי, whether the י is consonantal or vocal in origin. Where *sh*ᵉ*wā'* (:) is not sounded it is not represented. Where the vowel is not marked, it is understood to be short.

To represent the definite article *ha-* (or *hā-*) is used without indicating the doubling of the following consonant where this occurs. In other instances where it is necessary to separate a prefix from a stem a hyphen is employed. See also art. ALPHABET.

CONSONANTS (ENGLISH VALUES)

א	' (soundless)	*'āleph*	ח	ḥ (guttural h)	*ḥēth*	פּ	p	*pē*
בּ	b	*bēth*	ט	ṭ (intense t)	*ṭēth*	פ ף	ph (=f)	
ב	bh (=v)		י	y	*yōdh*	צ ץ	ç (almost ts)	*çādhē*
גּ	g	*gīmel*	כּ ךּ	k	*kaph*	ק	ḳ (intense k)	*ḳōph*
ג	gh (aspirated g)		כ ך	kh (=Ger. ch)		ר	r	*rēsh*
דּ	d	*dāleth*	ל	l	*lāmedh*	שׂ	s	*sīn*
ד	dh (=th in *the*)		מ ם	m	*mēm*	שׁ	sh	*shīn*
ה	h	*hē*	נ ן	n	*nūn*	תּ	t	*tāw*
ו	w (or v)	*wāw(vāv)*	ס	ṣ	*ṣāmekh*	ת	th (as in *thing*)	
ז	z	*zayin*	ע	ʿ(a peculiar guttural)	*ʿayin*			

PRONUNCIATION OF HEBREW NAMES IN THE ENGLISH BIBLE

General rule.—Usage in the pronunciation of Hebrew names in English has developed after the analogy of Greek and Latin proper names, without any regard for the pronunciation of the Hebrew originals, either as represented in the Masoretic Text or as theoretically reconstructed.

Spelling.—The spelling of these names, especially of the best known, deviates widely from any system of uniform transliteration that can be devised. Its evolution must be traced through the attrition of the Greek and Latin endings in the Vulgate forms, based in turn on the Septuagint versions. Thus "Solomon" and "Moses" have retained Greek endings that have no counterpart in the Hebrew *sh*ᵉ*lōmōh* and *mōsheh;* "Gomorrah" and "Gaza" have an initial vowel that represents the closest approximation that the Greek alphabet furnished for the peculiar guttural ע, elsewhere represented by a rough breathing or *h* (as in "Hebrew," "Hai"). The second *r* in "Gomorrah" is likewise due to the Greek spelling ῤῥ and not to the Hebrew ר. The loss of an *h* in Aaron (*'ahărōn*) and of *h* in Isaac (*yiçḥāḳ*) must be explained in the same way. The first vowel in each of the words "Solomon," "Samuel," "Sodom," "Gomorrah," "Pharisee," "Debir," and similar words, takes the place of a practically soundless *sh*ᵉ*wā'*, which had no exact equivalent in Greek. In form, then, the Hebrew names in the Bible are to all intents and purposes Greek.

Accentuation.—The accentuation, however, is based on the Latin scheme, never on the Hebrew or Greek. That is to say: the last syllable is never accented; the second last is, if long, or if the word has only two syllables; the third from the end is accented in all other cases. Thus in each of the following names the accent differs from that of the Hebrew: Deb'o-rah (*d*ᵉ*bhōrāh'*); Ab'i-dan or A-bi'dan (*'ăbhīdhān'*); Dan'iel (*dānī'ēl'*); Sol'o-mon (*sh*ᵉ*lōmōh'*); Sod'om (*ṣ*ᵉ*dhōm*); Sam'u-el (*sh*ᵉ*mū'ēl'*); Ke'naz (*ḳ*ᵉ*naz*); A-bed'ne-go (*ʿăbhēdh-n*ᵉ*ghō'*); Che'mosh (*k*ᵉ*mōsh*); De'bir (*d*ᵉ*bhīr*). It will be noticed that in many of these words the syllable accented in English is not a syllable at all in Hebrew, but a part of a syllable in which there is no vowel but a mere breath.

Vowels.—In determining the length of a vowel, etymology must be ignored and position in a word considered. Thus, in general, a vowel that closes a syllable is long, whereas one followed by a consonant in the same syllable is short. English models seem to be followed in this matter and the concepts "long" and "short" carry with them the qualitative changes customary in English. Thus short *a* is pronounced as in "cat," and not as a merely less drawn-out *ā*. Authorities differ on the pronunciation of *ai* in Scriptural names (e.g. "Sinai"); thus the *Imperial Dictionary* prefers *ā*, Webster and others *ī*. *i*-final is always long (as in Cozbī, Cushī, Malachī, and Zimrī).

Consonants.—Each of the consonants, excepting *c*, *s*, and *t*, has but a single sound, its ordinary English sound. *g* is always hard, as in "go," excepting in the word "Bethphage," which has been more thoroughly Graecized than Old Testament words. *th* is pronounced as in "thin"; *ch* as *k*, excepting in the name "Rachel," where it has the sound heard in the word "church"; *ph* is sounded *f*. *c*, *s*, and *t* are governed by the English rules. *c* is always hard (sounded as *k*) except before *e*, *i*, and *y*. Thus "Cinneroth" has the soft sound (*s*). *s* as an initial vowel of a word or syllable is sounded as in the word "sit." Between two vowels or at the end of a word after *e*, *l*, *m*, *n*, or *r* it is pronounced as *z* (e.g. "Moses" [pronounced "mozez"], "Solomon," "Israel" [*s* soft, but oftenest given as *z*, "Isaac" [*s* as *z*]). The tendency to pronounce *si* and *ti* in obscure positions as *sh* is recognized by some, but this combination is not common in Biblical names. The pronunciation of *t* before *th*, as in "Matthew," is by some authorities disposed of by assimilating the *t* to the *th*.

Conclusion.—Though Hebrew scholars have recently displayed a tendency to permit the pronunciation of the Hebrew according to the Masora to influence that of Bible names in English by giving preference to forms that show the greatest resemblance to the Hebrew (as in the name "Bezaleel," Hebrew *b*ᵉ*çal'ēl*, pronounced in English "bē̆-zăl'ē̆-ĕl" or "bĕz'à-lēl," former preferred), we must bear in mind that though these names are derived from the Hebrew they are spelled as if derived from Latin or Greek, accented as if Latin, and pronounced so far as separate letters are concerned as if native English words.

GREEK PRONUNCIATION

Form		Name	Transliteration	Eng. Pronunciation	Phonetic Value
Α	α	ἄλφα	alpha	*al'fa*	*a* in "far," "man"
Β	β	βῆτα	beta	*bā'ta*	*b*
Γ	γ	γάμμα	gamma	*gam'a*	*g* in "go"
Δ	δ	δέλτα	delta	*del'ta*	*d*
Ε	ε	ἒ ψιλόν	epsilon	*ep'si-lon*	*ĕ* in "set"
Ζ	ζ	ζῆτα	zeta	*zā'ta*	*dz* in "adze"
Η	η	ἦτα	eta	*ā'ta*	*ä* (German) or *e* in "prey"
Θ	θ	θῆτα	theta	*thā'ta*	*th* in "thin"
Ι	ι	ἰῶτα	iota	*ē-ō'ta*	*i* in "pique," "pin"
Κ	κ	κάππα	kappa	*kap'a*	*k*
Λ	λ	λάμβδα	lambda	*lam'da*	*l*
Μ	μ	μῦ	mu	*mōō; mü*	*m*
Ν	ν	νῦ	nu	*nōō; nü*	*n*
Ξ	ξ	ξῖ	xi	*ksē; zī*	*ks*=*x*
Ο	ο	ὂ μικρόν	omicron	*om'i-kron*	*ŏ* in "obey"
Π	π	πῖ	pi	*pē*	*p*
Ρ	ρ	ῥῶ	rho	*rō*	*r*
Σ	σ ς	σίγμα	sigma	*sig'ma*	*s* in "see"
Τ	τ	ταῦ	tau	*tou*	*t* in "ten"
Υ	υ	ὖ ψιλόν	upsilon	*ūp'si-lon*	*u* (French and Welsh) or German *ü*
Φ	φ	φῖ	phi	*fē*	*ph*=*f*
Χ	χ	χῖ	chi	*khē* (kh=Ger ch)	*ch* (German and Welsh)
Ψ	ψ	ψῖ	psi	*psē*	*ps*
Ω	ω	ὦ μέγα	• omega	*ō'me-ga*	*ō* in "so"

α, ι, and υ are sometimes long, sometimes short.

The diphthongs are:

αι as in "aisle"
ει as in "eight"
οι as in "toil"
αυ as *ou* in "out"
ευ and ηυ as ε or η+υ, hence roughly speaking=*ĕü* or *āü* (no exact equivalents in Englich)
ου as in "group"
υι as in "quit"

and the following so-called improper diphthongs ᾳ, *āi*, ῃ, *ēi*, ῳ, *ōi*. The second vowel is called "**iota** subscript," and is not sounded in pronouncing these forms, which equal *ā*, *ē*, and *ō*, respectively.

Consonants.—The consonants are in general equal to their English equivalents, except that a single γ, *g*, is always hard; ζ, *z*, is a *dz*-sound as in "a*dz*e," rather than the simple *z* as in "*z*eal"; θ, *th*, is always the surd aspirate as in "*th*in," never pronounced like the *th* of "*th*is"; σ, ς, *s*, is always a sibilant as in "so," never the *z*-sound as in "ease"; χ, *ch*, is a strong palatal aspirate like *ch* of German "I*ch*," "Bu*ch*," or the Welsh "ei*ch*," "uw*ch*," etc. A special note must be made of γ, *g*, preceding a palatal (κ, *k*, γ, *g*, χ, *ch*), as in this case the first *g* is nasalized, e.g. ἄγγελος, *ággelos*, is pronounced "a͂ggelos" ("aṇ'ge-los"). It might be noted further that an initial ρ, *r*, is always aspirated.

Transliteration.—In this Encyclopaedia it has been the practice to transliterate letter for letter: α = *a*, β = *b*, etc; even the gamma nasal has been so transliterated instead of using an ṇ or g̃ character. Further, the long forms of *a*, *i*, and *u* have not been indicated, and ᾳ, ῃ, ῳ, have been transliterated as *ā*, *ē*, *ō*, respectively, since the "iota subscript" was not pronounced in sounding the diphthongs (e.g. αἱρέω, *hairéō*, but αἰτίᾳ, *aitía*). Only the rough and not the smooth vowels are indicated.

Accentuation.—The Greek has three accents: (1) the acute (′), as in θεός, *theós* = a rising pitch in the voice; (2) the grave (‵), as in τὸν θεόν, *tón theón* = a falling pitch in the voice; (3) the circumflex (ˆ), as in τοῦ θεοῦ, *toú theoú* = a rising and falling pitch in the voice. The grave occurs only on the last syllable and is merely a way of indicating that other words follow (in the same clause or sentence) a word which has an acute accent on the final syllable, e.g. τό, *tó* ("the"), but when followed by another word, τὸ ἔργον, *tó érgon* ("the work"). The Greek accent was originally a musical or pitch accent rather than a stress accent as in English, and the acute, grave, and circumflex accents were doubtless differentiated. In indicating the accents in this Encyclopaedia, however, the stress alone is considered, and all accents are so indicated, whether acute, grave, or circumflex; e.g. τὸ ἔργον ποιῶ is transliterated *tó érgon poiṓ* and not *tò érgon poiô*.

THE INTERNATIONAL STANDARD BIBLE ENCYCLOPAEDIA

A

A.—See Aleph; Alphabet.

AALAR, ā′a-lär. See Allar.

AARON, âr′un, sometimes pronounced ar′on (אַהֲרוֹן, *'ahărōn*—LXX **'Ααρών**, *Aarōn*, meaning uncertain: Gesenius suggests "mountaineer"; Fürst, "enlightened"; others give "rich," "fluent." Cheyne mentions Redslob's "ingenious conjecture" of *hā-'ārōn*—"the ark"—with its mythical, priestly significance, *EB* s.v.): Probably eldest son of Amram (Ex **6** 20), and according to the uniform genealogical lists (Ex **6** 16–20; 1 Ch **6** 1–3), the fourth from Levi. This however is not certainly fixed, since there are frequent omissions from the Heb lists of names which are not prominent in the line of descent. For the corresponding period from Levi to Aaron the Judah list has six names (Ruth **4** 18–20; 1 Ch **2**). Levi and his family were zealous, even to violence (Gen **34** 25; Ex **32** 26), for the national honor and religion, and Aaron no doubt inherited his full portion of this spirit. His mother's name was Jochebed, who was also of the Levitical family (Ex **6** 20). Miriam, his sister, was several years older, since she was set to watch the novel cradle of the infant brother Moses, at whose birth Aaron was three years old (Ex **7** 7).

1. Family

When Moses fled from Egypt, Aaron remained to share the hardships of his people, and possibly to render them some service; for we are told that he pleaded inability and God sent Aaron to aid in his mission to Pharaoh and to Israel, and that Aaron went out to meet his returning brother, as the time of deliverance drew near (Ex **4** 27). While Moses, whose great gifts lay along other lines, was slow of speech (Ex **4** 10), Aaron was a ready spokesman, and became his brother's representative, being called his "mouth" (Ex **4** 16) and his "prophet" (Ex **7** 1). After their meeting in the wilderness the two brothers returned together to Egypt on the hazardous mission to which Jehovah had called them (Ex **4** 27–31). At first they appealed to their own nation, recalling the ancient promises and declaring the imminent deliverance, Aaron being the spokesman. But the heart of the people, hopeless by reason of the hard bondage and heavy with the care of material things, did not incline to them. The two brothers then at God's command made appeal directly to Pharoah himself, Aaron still speaking for his brother (Ex **6** 10–13). He also performed, at Moses' direction, the miracles commanded by God unto Moses (Ex **7** 9–10). With Hur he held up Moses' hands, in order that the 'rod of God might be lifted up,' during the fight with Amalek (Ex **17** 10.12).

2. Becomes Moses' Assistant

Aaron next comes into prominence when at Sinai he is one of the elders and representatives of his tribe to approach nearer to the Mount than the people in general were allowed to do, and to see the manifested glory of God (Ex **24** 1.9.10). A few days later, when Moses, attended by his "minister" Joshua, went up into the mountain, Aaron exercised some kind of headship over the people in his absence. Despairing of seeing again their leader, who had disappeared into the mystery of communion with the invisible God, they appealed to Aaron to prepare them more tangible gods, and to lead them back to Egypt (Ex **32**). Aaron never appears as the strong, heroic character which his brother was; and here at Sinai he revealed his weaker nature, yielding to the demands of the people and permitting the making of the golden bullock. That he must however have yielded reluctantly, is evident from the ready zeal of his tribesmen, whose leader he was, to stay and to avenge the apostasy by rushing to arms and falling mightily upon the idolaters at the call of Moses (Ex **32** 26–28).

3. An Elder

In connection with the planning and erection of the tabernacle ("the Tent"), Aaron and his sons being chosen for the official priesthood, elaborate and symbolical vestments were prepared for them (Ex **28**); and after the erection and dedication of the tabernacle, he and his sons were formally inducted into the sacred office (Lev **8**). It appears that Aaron alone was anointed with the holy oil (Lev **8** 12), but his sons were included with him in the duty of caring for sacrificial rites and things. They served in receiving and presenting the various offerings, and could enter and serve in the first chamber of the tabernacle; but Aaron alone, the high priest, the Mediator of the Old Covenant, could enter into the Holy of Holies, and that only once a year, on the great Day of Atonement (Lev **16** 12–14).

4. High Priest

After the departure of Israel from Sinai, Aaron joined his sister Miriam in a protest against the authority of Moses (Nu **12**), which they asserted to be self-assumed. For this rebellion Miriam was smitten with leprosy, but was made whole again, when, at the pleading of Aaron, Moses interceded with God for her. The sacred office of Aaron, requiring physical, moral and ceremonial cleanness of the strictest order, seems to have made him immune from this form of punishment. Somewhat later (Nu **16**) he himself, along with Moses, became the object of a revolt of his own tribe in conspiracy with leaders of Dan and Reuben. This rebellion was subdued and the authority of Moses and Aaron vindicated by the

5. Rebels Against Moses

miraculous overthrow of the rebels. As they were being destroyed by the plague, Aaron, at Moses' command, rushed into their midst with the lighted censer, and the destruction was stayed. The Divine will in choosing Aaron and his family to the priesthood was then fully attested by the miraculous budding of his rod, when, together with rods representing the other tribes, it was placed and left overnight in the sanctuary (Nu **17**). See Aaron's Rod.

After this event Aaron does not come prominently into view until the time of his death, near the close of the Wilderness period. Because of the impatience, or unbelief, of Moses and Aaron at Meribah (Nu **20** 12), the two brothers are prohibited from entering Canaan; and shortly after the last camp at Kadesh was broken, as the people journeyed eastward to the plains of Moab, Aaron died on Mount Hor. In three passages this event is recorded: the more detailed account in Nu **20**, a second incidental record in the list of stations of the wanderings in the wilderness (Nu **33** 38.39), and a third casual reference (Dt **10** 6) in an address of Moses. These are not in the least contradictory or inharmonious. The dramatic scene is fully presented in Nu **20**: Moses, Aaron and Eleazar go up to Mount Hor in the people's sight; Aaron is divested of his robes of office, which are formally put upon his eldest living son; Aaron dies before the Lord in the Mount at the age of 123, and is given burial by his two mourning relatives, who then return to the camp without the first and great high priest; when the people understand that he is no more, they show both grief and love by thirty days of mourning. The passage in Nu **33** records the event of his death just after the list of stations in the general vicinity of Mount Hor; while Moses in Dt **10** states from which of these stations, viz. Moserah, that remarkable funeral procession made its way to Mount Hor. In the records we find, not contradiction and perplexity, but simplicity and unity. It is not within the view of this article to present modern displacements and rearrangements of the Aaronic history; it is concerned with the records as they are, and as they contain the faith of the OT writers in the origin in Aaron of their priestly order.

6. Further History

Aaron married Elisheba, daughter of Amminadab, and sister of Nahshon, prince of the tribe of Judah, who bore him four sons: Nadab, Abihu, Eleazar and Ithamar. The sacrilegious act and consequent judicial death of Nadab and Abihu are recorded in Lev **10**. Eleazar and Ithamar were more pious and reverent; and from them descended the long line of priests to whom was committed the ceremonial law of Israel, the succession changing from one branch to the other with certain crises in the nation. At his death Aaron was succeeded by his oldest living son, Eleazar (Nu **20** 28; Dt **10** 6).

7. Priestly Succession

Edward Mack

AARONITES, âr′on-īts (לְאַהֲרֹן, *le-'ahărōn*, lit. "belonging to Aaron"): A word used in AV, but not in the revised versions, to translate the proper name Aaron in two instances where it denotes a family and not merely a person (1 Ch **12** 27; **27** 17). It is equivalent to the phrases "sons of Aaron," "house of Aaron," frequently used in the OT. According to the books of Josh and Ch the "sons of Aaron" were distinguished from the other Levites from the time of Joshua (e.g. Josh **21** 4.10.13; 1 Ch **6** 54).

AARON'S ROD (Nu **17** and He **9** 4): Immediately after the incidents connected with the rebellion of Korah, Dathan and Abiram against the leadership of Moses and the priestly primacy of Aaron (Nu **16**), it became necessary to indicate and emphasize the Divine appointment of Aaron. Therefore, at the command of Jehovah, Moses directs that twelve almond rods, one for each tribe with the prince's name engraved thereon, be placed within the Tent of the Testimony. When Moses entered the tent the following day, he found that Aaron's rod had budded, blossomed and borne fruit, "the three stages of vegetable life being thus simultaneously visible." When the miraculous sign was seen by the people, they accepted it as final; nor was there ever again any question of Aaron's priestly right. The rod was kept "before the testimony" in the sanctuary ever after as a token of the Divine will (**17** 10). The writer of He, probably following a later Jewish tradition, mentions the rod as kept in the Holy of Holies within the ark (He **9** 4; cf 1 K **8** 9). See Priest, III.

Edward Mack

AB (אָב or אַב, *'ābh* or *'abh*, the Heb and Aram. word for "father"): It is a very common word in the OT; this art. notes only certain uses of it. It is used both in the singular and in the plural to denote a grandfather or more remote ancestors (e.g. Jer **35** 16.15). The father of a people or tribe is its founder, not, as is frequently assumed, its progenitor. In this sense Abraham is father to the Israelites (see, for example, Gen **17** 11–14.27), Isaac and Jacob and the heads of families being fathers in the same modified sense. The cases of Ishmael, Moab, etc, are similar. The traditional originator of a craft is the father of those who practise the craft (e.g. Gen **4** 20.21.22). Sennacherib uses the term "my fathers" of his predecessors on the throne of Assyria, though these were not his ancestors (2 K **19** 12). The term is used to express worth and affection irrespective of blood relation (e.g. 2 K **13** 14). A ruler or leader is spoken of as a father. God is father. A frequent use of the word is that in the composition of proper names, e.g. Abinadab, "my father is noble." See Abi.

Ab in Gen **45** 8 is an Egyptian word meaning "inspector," i.e. "vizier," of Pharaoh. This word the Hebrew writer transliterated Ab and properly so, but the English translator translated it as though it were the Hebrew word meaning "father" instead of transliterating it, or else translating it as "vizier" (Kyle, *Moses and the Monuments*, 28).

Willis J. Beecher

AB (אָב, *'ābh*): The name of the fifth month in the Heb calendar, the month beginning in our July. The name does not appear in the Bible, but Jos gives it to the month in which Aaron died (*Ant*, IV, iv, 6; cf Nu **33** 38).

ABACUC, ab′a-kuk (Lat *Abacuc*): The form given the name of the prophet Habakkuk in 2 Esd **1** 40.

ABADDON, a-bad′on (אֲבַדּוֹן, *'ăbhaddōn*, "ruin," "perdition," "destruction"): Though "destruction" is commonly used in translating *'abhaddōn*, the stem idea is intransitive rather than passive—the idea of perishing, going to ruin, being in a ruined state, rather than that of being ruined, being destroyed.

The word occurs six times in the OT, always as a place name in the sense in which Sheol is a place name. It denotes, in certain aspects, the world of the dead as constructed in the Heb imagination. It is a common mistake to understand such expressions in a too mechanical way. Like ourselves, the men of the earlier ages had to use picture language when they spoke of the conditions that existed after death, however their picturing of the matter may have differed from ours. In three instances Abaddon is parallel with Sheol (Job **26** 6; Prov **15** 11; **27** 20). In one instance it is parallel with death, in one with the grave and in the remaining instance the parallel phrase is "root out all mine increase" (Job **28** 22; Ps **88** 11; Job **31** 12). In this last passage the place idea comes nearer to vanishing in an abstract conception than in the other passages.

Abaddon belongs to the realm of the mysterious. Only God understands it (Job **26** 6; Prov **15** 11). It is the world of the dead in its utterly dismal, destructive, dreadful aspect, not in those more cheerful aspects in which activities are conceived of as in progress there. In Abaddon there are no declarations of God's lovingkindness (Ps **88** 11).

In a slight degree the OT presentations personalize Abaddon. It is a synonym for insatiableness (Prov **27** 20). It has possibilities of information mediate between those of "all living" and those of God (Job **28** 22).

In the NT the word occurs once (Rev **9** 11), the personalization becoming sharp. Abaddon is here not the world of the dead, but the angel who reigns over it. The Gr equivalent of his name is given as Apollyon. Under this name Bunyan presents him in the *Pilgrim's Progress*, and Christendom has doubtless been more interested in this presentation of the matter than in any other.

In some treatments Abaddon is connected with the evil spirit Asmodeus of Tobit (e.g. **3** 8), and with the destroyer mentioned in Wisd (**18** 25; cf 22), and through these with a large body of rabbinical folklore; but these efforts are simply groundless. See APOLLYON. WILLIS J. BEECHER

ABADIAS, ab-a-dī'as (Gr **'Αβαδίας**): Mentioned in 1 Esd **8** 35 as the son of Jezelus, of the sons of Joab, returned with Ezra from the captivity; and in Ezr **8** 9 called "Obadiah the son of Jehiel."

ABAGARUS, a-bag'a-rus. See ABGARUS.

ABAGTHA, a-bag'tha (אֲבַגְתָא, *'ăbhaghᵉthā'*, perhaps meaning "fortunate one"): One of the seven eunuchs, or "chamberlains," of Xerxes mentioned in Est **1** 10. The name is Persian, and is one of the many Pers marks in the Book of Est.

ABANAH, ab'a-na, a-bā'na (אֲבָנָה, *'ăbhānāh* [Kᵉthībh, LXX, Vulg]), or **AMANA** (אֲמָנָה, *'ămānāh* [Ḳᵉrē, Pesh, Tg]; AV **Abana** [ARVm Amana], RV ABANAH [RVm Amanah]): Mentioned in 2 K **5** 12, along with the PHARPAR (q.v.), as one of the principal rivers of Damascus. The reading Amana (meaning possibly the "constant," or perennial stream) is on the whole preferable. Both forms of the name may have been in use, as the interchange of an aspirated b (bh = v) and m is not without parallel (cf Evil-merodach = Amil-marduk).

The A. is identified with the Chrysorrhoas ("golden stream") of the Greeks, the modern Nahr Baradā (the "cold"), which rises in the Anti-Lebanon, one of its sources, the Ain Barada, being near the village of Zebedani, and flows in a southerly and then southeasterly direction toward Damascus. A few miles southeast of *Suk Wady Barada* (the ancient Abila; see ABILENE) the volume of the stream is more than doubled by a torrent of clear, cold water from the beautifully situated spring *'Ain Fijeh* (Gr πηγή, *pēgē*, "fountain"), after which it flows through a picturesque gorge till it reaches Damascus, whose many fountains and gardens it supplies liberally with water. In the neighborhood of Damascus a number of streams branch off from the parent river, and spread out like an opening fan on the surrounding plain. The Barada, along with the streams which it feeds, loses itself in the marshes of the Meadow Lakes about 18 miles E. of the city.

The water of the Barada, though not perfectly wholesome in the city itself, is for the most part clear and cool; its course is picturesque, and its value to Damascus, as the source alike of fertility and of charm, is inestimable. C. H. THOMSON

ABARIM, ab'a-rim, a-bā'rim (עֲבָרִים, *'ăbhārīm*): The stem idea is that of going across a space or a dividing line, or for example a river. It is the same stem that appears in the familiar phrase "beyond Jordan," used to denote the region E. of the Jordan, and Hellenized in the name Peraea. This fact affords the most natural explanation of the phrases 'the mountains of the Abarim' (Nu **33** 47.48); 'this mountain-country of the Abarim' (Nu **27** 12; Dt **32** 49); Iye-abarim, which means "Heaps of the Abarim," or "Mounds of the Abarim" (Nu **21** 11; **33** 44). In Nu **33** 45 this station is called simply Iyim, "Mounds." It is to be distinguished from the place of the same name in southern Judah (Josh **15** 29). The name Abarim, without the article, occurs in Jer (**22** 20 RV, where AV translates "the passages"), where it seems to be the name of a region, on the same footing with the names Lebanon and Bashan, doubtless the region referred to in Nu and Dt. There is no reason for changing the vowels in Ezk **39** 11, in order to make that another occurrence of the same name.

When the people of Abraham lived in Canaan, before they went to Egypt to sojourn, they spoke of the region east of the Jordan as "beyond Jordan." Looking across the Jordan and the Dead Sea they designated the mountain country they saw there as "the Beyond mountains." They continued to use these geographical terms when they came out of Egypt. We have no means of knowing to how extensive a region they applied the name. The passages speak of the mountain country of Abarim where Moses died, including Nebo, as situated back from the river Jordan in its lowest reaches; and of the Mounds of the Abarim as farther to the southeast, so that the Israelites passed them when making their détour around the agricultural parts of Edom, before they crossed the Arnon. Whether the name Abarim should be applied to the parts of the eastern hill country farther to the north is a question on which we lack evidence. WILLIS J. BEECHER

ABASE, a-bās': The English rendition of שָׁפֵל, *shāphēl* (Job **40** 11; Ezk **21** 26), and of its derivative שְׁפַל *shᵉphal* (Dnl **4** 37) = "bring down," "debase," "humble"; of עָנָה, *'ānāh* (Isa **31** 4) = "abase self," "afflict," "chasten self," "deal harshly with," etc; and of ταπεινόω, *tapeinóō* = "to depress"; **fig.** "to humiliate" (in condition or heart): "abase," "bring low," "humble self" (Phil **4** 12). The word is always employed to indicate what should be done to or by him who nurtures a spirit and exhibits a demeanor contrary to the laudable humility which is a natural fruit of religion. Such a person is warned that the most extravagant audacity will not daunt Jehovah nor abate His vengeance (Isa **31** 4), and good men are exhorted to employ their powers to bring him low (Job **40** 11; Ezk **21** 26). If men are not able to curb the arrogant, God is (Dnl **4** 37); and He has so constituted the world, that sinful arrogance must fall (Mt **23** 12 AV; Lk **14** 11 AV; **18** 14 AV). FRANK E. HIRSCH

ABATE, a-bāt′: Used six times in OT for five different Heb words, signifying "to diminish," "reduce," "assuage"; of the Flood (Gen **8** 8); of strength (Dt **34** 7); of pecuniary value (Lev **27** 18); of wrath (Jgs **8** 3); of fire (Nu **11** 2).

ABBA, ab′a (ἀββᾶ, אַבָּא, *'abbā'*, Hebraic-Chald, "Father"): In Jewish and old-Christian prayers, a name by which God was addressed, then in oriental churches a title of bishops and patriarchs. So Jesus addresses God in prayer (Mt **11** 25.26; **26** 39.42; Lk **10** 21; **22** 42; **23** 34; Jn **11** 41; **12** 27; **17** 24.25). In Mk **14** 36; Rom **8** 15, and Gal **4** 6 ὁ πατήρ, *ho patēr*, is appended even in direct address, in an emphatic sense. Servants were not permitted to use the appellation in addressing the head of the house. See Delitzsch on Rom **8** 15; cf G. Dalman, *Gram. des jüd.-paläst. Aramäisch*, etc, § 40, c. 3. J. E. Harry

ABDA, ab′da (עַבְדָּא, *'abhdā'*, perhaps, by abbreviation, "servant of Jeh"): (1) The father of Adoniram, King Solomon's superintendent of forced labor (1 K **4** 6). (2) A Levite mentioned in the statistical note in Neh (**11** 17). This "Abda the son of Shammua" is in the partly duplicate passage in 1 Ch (**9** 16) called "Obadiah the son of Shemaiah."

ABDEEL, ab′dē-el (עַבְדְּאֵל, *'abhde'ēl*, "servant of God"): The father of Shelemiah, one of the officers whom King Jehoiakim commanded to arrest Baruch, the scribe, and Jeremiah the prophet (Jer **36** 26).

ABDI, ab′dī (עַבְדִּי, *'abhdī*, probably by abbreviation "servant of Jeh"): A Levite, father of Kishi and grandfather of King David's singer Ethan (1 Ch **6** 44; cf **15** 17). This makes Abdi a contemporary of Saul the king. (2) A Levite, father of the Kish who was in service at the beginning of the reign of Hezekiah (2 Ch **29** 12). Some mistakenly identify this Abdi with the former. (3) A man who in Ezra's time had married a foreign wife (Ezr **10** 26). Not a Levite, but "of the sons of Elam."

ABDIAS, ab-dī′as (2 Esd **1** 39 = Obadiah): One of the Minor Prophets. Mentioned with Abraham, Isaac, Jacob and the Minor Prophets who shall be given as leaders to the "nation from the east" which is to overthrow Israel (cf Obadiah).

ABDIEL, ab′di-el (עַבְדִּיאֵל, *'abhdī'ēl*, "servant of God"): A Gadite who lived in Gilead or in Bashan, and whose name was reckoned in genealogies of the time of Jotham, king of Judah, or of Jeroboam II, king of Israel (1 Ch **5** 15–17).

ABDON, ab′don (עַבְדּוֹן, *'abhdōn*, perhaps "service"; Ἀβδών, *Abdōn*):

(1) A judge of Israel for eight years (Jgs **12** 13–15). The account says that he was the son of Hillel the Pirathonite, and that he was buried in Pirathon in the land of Ephraim. No mention is made of great public services rendered by him, but it is said that he had seventy well-mounted sons and grandsons. So far as we can judge, he was placed in office as a wealthy elderly man, and performed the routine duties acceptably. Very likely his two next predecessors Ibzan and Elon were men of the same type.

An effort has been made to identify Abdon with the Bedan mentioned in 1 S **12** 11, but the identification is precarious.

A certain importance attaches to Abdon from the fact that he is the last judge mentioned in the continuous account (Jgs **2** 6—**13** 1) in the Book of Jgs. After the account of him follows the statement that Israel was delivered into the hands of the Philistines forty years, and with that statement the continuous account closes and the series of personal stories begins—the stories of Samson, of Micah and his Levite, of the Benjamite civil war, followed in our English Bibles by the stories of Ruth and of the childhood of Samuel. With the close of this last story (1 S **4** 18) the narrative of public affairs is resumed, at a point when Israel is making a desperate effort, at the close of the forty years of Eli, to throw off the Philistine yoke. A large part of one's views of the history of the period of the Judges will depend on the way in which he combines these events. My own view is that the forty years of Jgs **13** 1 and of 1 S **4** 18 are the same; that at the death of Abdon the Philistines asserted themselves as overlords of Israel; that it was a part of their policy to suppress nationality in Israel; that they abolished the office of judge, and changed the high-priesthood to another family, making Eli high priest; that Eli was sufficiently competent so that many of the functions of national judge drifted into his hands. It should be noted that the regaining of independence was signalized by the reëstablishment of the office of judge, with Samuel as incumbent (I S **7** 6; I S **2** 27–28). This view takes into the account that the narrative concerning Samson is detachable, like the narratives that follow, Samson belonging to an earlier period. See Samson.

(2) The son of Jeiel and his wife Maacah (1 Ch **8** 30; **9** 36). Jeiel is described as the "father of Gibeon," perhaps the founder of the Israelitish community there. This Abdon is described as brother to Ner, the grandfather of King Saul.

(3) One of the messengers sent by King Josiah to Huldah the prophetess (2 Ch **34** 20); called Achbor in 2 K **22** 12.

(4) One of many men of Benjamin mentioned as dwelling in Jerus (1 Ch **8** 23), possibly in Nehemiah's time, though the date is not clear.

Willis J. Beecher

ABDON, ab′don (עַבְדּוֹן, *'abhdōn*, perhaps "service"): One of the four Levitical cities in the tribe of Asher (Josh **21** 30; 1 Ch **6** 74). Probably the same with Ebron (in AV "Hebron") in Josh **19** 28, where some copies have the reading Abdon. Now called Abdeh, a few miles from the Mediterranean and about fifteen miles south of Tyre.

ABED-NEGO, a-bed′nē-go (Heb and Aram. עֲבֵד נְגוֹ, *'ăbhēdh neghō*; Dnl **3** 29, עֲבֵד נְגוֹא, *'ăbhēdh neghō'*): According to many, the *nego* is an intentional corruption of Nebo, the name of a Bab god, arising from the desire of the Heb scribes to avoid the giving of a heathen name to a hero of their faith. The name, according to this view, would mean "servant of Nebo." Inasmuch as *'ăbhēdh* is a tr of the Bab *'arad*, it seems more probable that *nego* also must be a tr of some Bab word. The goddess Ishtar is by the Babylonians called "the morning star" and "the perfect light" (*nigittu gitmaltu*). The morning star is called by the Aramaeans *nogah*, "the shining one," a word derived from the root *negah*, the equivalent of the Bab *nagu*, "to shine." Abed-nego, according to this interpretation, would be the tr of Arad-Ishtar, a not uncommon name among the Assyrians and Babylonians. Canon Johns gives this as the name of more than thirty Assyrians, who are mentioned on the tablets cited by him in Vol. III of his great work entitled *Assyrian Deeds and Documents*. It means "servant of Ishtar."

Abed-nego was one of the three companions of Daniel, and was the name imposed upon the Hebrew Azariah by Nebuchadnezzar (Dnl **1** 7). Having refused, along with his friends, to eat the provisions of the king's table, he was fed and flourished upon pulse and water. Having successfully passed his examinations and escaped the death with which the wise men of Babylon were threatened, he was appointed at the request of Daniel along with his companions over the affairs of the province of Babylon (Dnl **2**). Having refused to bow down to the image which Nebuchadnezzar had set up, he was cast into the burning fiery furnace, and after his triumphant delivery he was caused by the king to prosper in the province of Babylon (Dnl **3**). The three friends are referred to by name in 1 Macc **2** 59, and by implication in He **11** 33.34.

R. DICK WILSON

ABEL, ā'bel (הֶבֶל, *hebhel;* Ἄβελ, *Ábel;* WH *Hábel;* etymology uncertain. Some tr "a breath," "vapor," "transitoriness," which are suggestive of his brief existence and tragic end; others take it to be a variant of Jabal, *yābhāl,* "shepherd" or "herdman," Gen **4** 20. Cf Assyr *ablu* and Bab *abil,* "son"): The second son of Adam and Eve. The absence of the vb. *hārāh* (Gen **4** 2; cf ver 1) has been taken to imply, perhaps truly, that Cain and Abel were twins.

1. A Shepherd

"Abel was a keeper of sheep, but Cain was a tiller of the ground," thus representing the two fundamental pursuits of civilized life, the two earliest subdivisions of the human race. On the Heb tradition of the superiority of the pastoral over agricultural and city life, see *Expos T,* V, 351 ff. The narrative may possibly bear witness to the primitive idea that pastoral life was more pleasing to Jeh than husbandry.

2. A Worshipper

"In process of time," the two brothers came in a solemn manner to sacrifice unto Jeh, in order to express their gratitude to Him whose tenants they were in the land (vs 3.4. See SACRIFICE). How Jeh signified His acceptance of the one offering and rejection of the other, we are not told. That it was due to the difference in the material of the sacrifice or in their manner of offering was probably the belief among the early Israelites, who regarded animal offerings as superior to cereal offerings. Both kinds, however, were fully in accord with Heb law and custom. It has been suggested that the LXX rendering of **4 7** makes Cain's offence a ritual one, the offering not being "correctly" made or rightly divided, and hence rejected as irregular. "If thou makest a proper offering, but dost not cut in pieces rightly, art thou not in fault? Be still!" The LXX evidently took the rebuke to turn upon Cain's neglect to prepare his offering according to strict ceremonial requirements. διέλῃς, *diélēs* (LXX in loc.), however, implies נתח (נָתַח), *nāthaḥ* (*nattaḥ*), and would only apply to animal sacrifices. Cf Ex **29** 17; Lev **8** 20; Jgs **19** 29; 1 K **18** 23; and see COUCH.

3. A Righteous Man

The true reason for the Divine preference is doubtless to be found in the disposition of the brothers (see CAIN). Well-doing consisted not in the outward offering (**4** 7) but in the right state of mind and feeling. The acceptability depends on the inner motives and moral characters of the offerers. "By faith Abel offered unto God a more excellent [abundant, *pleiona*] sacrifice than Cain" (He **11** 4). The "more abundant sacrifice," Westcott thinks, "suggests the deeper gratitude of Abel, and shows a fuller sense of the claims of God" to the best. Cain's "works [the collective expression of his inner life] were evil, and his brother's righteous" (1 Jn **3** 12). "It would be an outrage if the gods looked to gifts and sacrifices and not to the soul" (*Alcibiades* II.149E.150A). Cain's heart was no longer pure; it had a criminal propensity, springing from envy and jealousy, which rendered both his offering and person unacceptable. His evil works and hatred of his brother culminated in the act of murder, specifically evoked by the opposite character of Abel's works and the acceptance of his offering. The evil man cannot endure the sight of goodness in another.

4. A Martyr

Abel ranks as the first martyr (Mt **23** 35), whose blood cried for vengeance (Gen **4** 10; cf Rev **6** 9.10) and brought despair (Gen **4** 13), whereas that of Jesus appeals to God for forgiveness and speaks peace (He **12** 24) and is preferred before Abel's.

5. A Type

The first two brothers in history stand as the types and representatives of the two main and enduring divisions of mankind, and bear witness to the absolute antithesis and eternal enmity between good and evil.

M. O. EVANS

ABEL, ā'bel (אָבֵל, *'ābhēl,* "meadow"): A word used in several compound names of places. It appears by itself as the name of a city concerned in the rebellion of Sheba (2 S **20** 14; cf 18), though it is there probably an abridgment of the name Abel-beth-maacah. In 1 S **6** 18, where the Heb has "the great meadow," and the Gr "the great stone," AV translates "the great *stone of* Abel."

ABEL-BETH-MAACAH, ā'bel-beth-mā'a-ka (אָבֵל בֵּית מַעֲכָה, *'ābhēl bēth ma'ăkhāh,* "the meadow of the house of Maacah"): The name appears in this form in 1 K **15** 20 and 2 K **15** 29. In 2 S **20** 15 (Heb) it is Abel-beth-hammaacah (Maacah with the article). In ver 14 of that chapter it appears as Beth-maacah, and in vs 14 and 18 as Abel.

In 2 S it is spoken of as the city, far to the north, where Joab besieged Sheba, the son of Bichri. In 2 K it is mentioned, along with Ijon and other places, as a city in Naphtali captured by Tiglath-pileser, king of Assyria. The capture appears also in the records of Tiglath-pileser. In 1 K it is mentioned with Ijon and Dan and "all the land of Naphtali" as being smitten by Benhadad of Damascus in the time of Baasha.

In the account in Ch parallel to this last (2 Ch **16** 4) the cities mentioned are Ijon, Dan, Abel-maim. Abel-maim is either another name for Abel-beth-maacah, or the name of another place in the same vicinity.

The prevailing identification of Abel-beth-maacah is with *Abil,* a few miles W. of Dan, on a height overlooking the Jordan near its sources. The adjacent region is rich agriculturally, and the scenery and the water supply are especially fine. Abel-maim, "meadow of water," is not an inapt designation for it.

WILLIS J. BEECHER

ABEL-CHERAMIM, ā'bel-ker'a-mim (אָבֵל כְּרָמִים, *'ābhēl kᵉrāmīm,* "meadow of vineyards"): A city mentioned in the RV in Jgs **11** 33, along with Aroer, Minnith, and "twenty cities," in summarizing Jephthah's campaign against the Ammonites. AV translates "the plain of the vineyards." The site has not been identified, though Eusebius and Jerome speak of it as in their time a village about seven Roman miles from the Ammonite city of Rabbah.

ABEL-MAIM, ā′bel-mā′im (אָבֵל מַיִם, *'ābhēl mayim,* "meadow of water"). See ABEL-BETH-MAACAH.

ABEL-MEHOLAH, ā′bel-mḗ-hō′lah (אָבֵל מְחוֹלָה, *'ābhēl m^e ḥōlāh,* "meadow of dancing"): The residence of Elisha the prophet (1 K **19** 16). When Gideon and his 300 broke their pitchers in the camp of Midian, the Midianites in their first panic fled down the valley of Jezreel and the Jordan "toward Zererah" (Jgs **7** 22). Zererah (Zeredah) is Zarethan (2 Ch **4** 17; cf 1 K **7** 46), separated from Succoth by the clay ground where Solomon made castings for the temple. The wing of the Midianites whom Gideon pursued crossed the Jordan at Succoth (Jgs **8** 4 ff). This would indicate that Abel-meholah was thought of as a tract of country with a "border," W. of the Jordan, some miles S. of Beth-shean, in the territory either of Issachar or West Manasseh.

Abel-meholah is also mentioned in connection with the jurisdiction of Baana, one of Solomon's twelve commissary officers (1 K **4** 12) as below Jezreel, with Beth-shean and Zarethan in the same list.

Jerome and Eusebius speak of Abel-meholah as a tract of country and a town in the Jordan valley, about ten Rom miles S. of Beth-shean. At just that point the name seems to be perpetuated in that of the Wady Maliḥ, and Abel-meholah is commonly located near where that Wady, or the neighboring Wady Helweh, comes down into the Jordan valley.

Presumably Adriel the Meholathite (1 S **18** 19; 2 S **21** 8) was a resident of Abel-meholah.

WILLIS J. BEECHER

ABEL-MIZRAIM, ā′bel-miz′rā-im (אָבֵל מִצְרַיִם, *'ābhēl miçrayim,* "meadow of Egypt"): A name given to "the threshing floor of Atad," E. of the Jordan and N. of the Dead Sea, because Joseph and his funeral party from Egypt there held their mourning over Jacob (Gen **50** 11). The name is a pun. The Canaanite residents saw the *'ēbhel,* "the mourning," and therefore that place was called *'ābhēl miçrayim.*

It is remarkable that the funeral should have taken this circuitous route, instead of going directly from Egypt to Hebron. Possibly a reason may be found as we obtain additional details in Egyp history. The explanations which consist in changing the text, or in substituting the North Arabian *Muçri* for *Miçrayim,* are unsatisfactory.

WILLIS J. BEECHER

ABEL-SHITTIM, ā′bel-shit′tim (אָבֵל הַשִּׁטִּים, *'ābhēl ha-shiṭṭīm,* "the meadow of the Acacias"): The name appears only in Nu **33** 49; but the name Shittim is used to denote the same locality (Nu **25** 1; Josh **2** 1; **3** 1; Mic **6** 5). The name always has the art., and the best expression of it in English would be "the Acacias." 'The valley of the Acacias' (Joel **3** 18 [**4** 18]) is, apparently, a different locality.

For many weeks before crossing the Jordan, Israel was encamped in the roundout of the Jordan valley, N. of the Dead Sea, E. of the river. The notices in the Bible, supplemented by those in Jos and Eusebius and Jerome, indicate that the camping region was many miles in extent, the southern limit being Beth-jeshimoth, toward the Dead Sea, while Abel of the Acacias was the northern limit and the headquarters. The headquarters are often spoken of as E. of the Jordan at Jericho (e.g. Nu **22** 1; **26** 3.63). During the stay there occurred the Balaam incident (Nu **22**–**24**), and the harlotry with Moab and Midian (Nu **25**) and the war with Midian (Nu **31**), in both of which Phinehas distinguished himself. It was from the Acacias that Joshua sent out the spies, and that Israel afterward moved down to the river for the crossing. Micah aptly calls upon Jehovah's people to remember all that happened to them from the time when they reached the Acacias to the time when Jehovah had brought them safely across the river to Gilgal.

Jos is correct in saying that Abel of the Acacias is the place from which the Deuteronomic law purports to have been given. In his time the name survived as Abila, a not very important town situated there. He says that it was "sixty furlongs from Abila to the Jordan," that is a little more than seven English miles (*Ant,* IV, viii, 1 and V, i, 1; *BJ,* IV, vii, 6). There seems to be a consensus for locating the site at *Kefrein,* near where the wady of that name comes down into the Jordan valley.

WILLIS J. BEECHER

ABEZ, ā′bez: Used in AV (Josh **19** 20) for EBEZ, which see.

ABGAR, ab′gar, **ABGARUS,** ab-gā′rus, **ABAGARUS,** a-bag′a-rus (Ἄβγαρος, *Ābgaros*): Written also Agbarus and Augarus. A king of Edessa. A name common to several kings (toparchs) of Edessa, Mesopotamia. One of these, Abgar, a son of Uchomo, the seventeenth (14th?) of twenty kings, according to the legend (*HE,* i.13) sent a letter to Jesus, professing belief in His Messiahship and asking Him to come and heal him from an incurable disease (leprosy?), inviting Him at the same time to take refuge from His enemies in his city, "which is enough for us both." Jesus answering the letter blessed him, because he had believed on Him without having seen Him, and promised to send one of His disciples after He had risen from the dead. The apostle Thomas sent Judas Thaddeus, one of the Seventy, who healed him (*Cod. Apoc. NT*).

A. L. BRESLICH

ABHOR, ab-hor′: "To cast away," "reject," "despise," "defy," "contemn," "loathe," etc. (1) Tr[d] in the OT from the following Heb words amongst others: בָּאַשׁ (*bā'ash*), "to be or to become stinking" (1 S **27** 12; 2 S **16** 21); גָּעַל (*gā'al*), "to cast away as unclean," "to loathe"; cf Ezk **16** 5 AV; קוּץ (*kūç*), "to loathe," "to fear" (Ex **1** 12 m; 1 K **11** 25; Isa **7** 16); שָׁקַץ (*shākaç*), "to detest" (Ps **22** 24); תָּאַב (*tā'abh*), תָּעַב (*tā'abh*), "to contemn" (Dt **23** 7); דֵּרָאוֹן (*dērā'ōn*), "an object of contempt," "an abhorring" (Isa **66** 24; Dnl **12** 2 m). (2) Tr[d] in the NT from the following Gr words: *bdelússomai,* which is derived from *bdéō,* "to stink" (Rom **2** 22); *apostugéō,* derived from *stugéō,* "to hate," "to shrink from" (Rom **12** 9).

A. L. BRESLICH

ABI, ā′bī (אֲבִי, *'ăbhī*): The name of the mother of King Hezekiah, as given in 2 K **18** 2. Most naturally explained as a contraction of Abijah ("Jehovah is a father," or "is my father"), found in the ‖ passage in 2 Ch **29** 1. The spelling in the oldest tr[s] seems to indicate that *'ăbhī* is not a copyist's error, but a genuine contracted form. She is spoken of as the daughter of Zechariah, and was of course the wife of Ahaz.

ABI, ā′bī, in the composition of names (אֲבִי, *'ăbhī,* "father"): The Heb words *'ābh,* "father," and *'āḥ,* "brother," are used in the forming of names, both at the beginning and at the end of words, e.g. Abram ("exalted one"), Joah ("Jehovah is brother"), Ahab ("father's brother"). At the beginning of a word, however, the modified forms *'ăbhī* and *'ăḥī* are the ones commonly used, e.g.

Ahimelech ("king's brother") and Abimelech (by the same analogy "king's father").

These forms have characteristics which complicate the question of their use in proper names. Especially since the publication in 1896 of *Studies in Hebrew Proper Names*, by G. Buchanan Gray, the attention of scholars has been called to this matter, without the reaching of any perfect consensus of opinion.

The word *'ăbhī* may be a nominative with an archaic ending ("father"), or in the construct state ("father-of"), or the form with the suffix ("my father"). Hence a proper name constructed with it may supposably be either a clause or a sentence; if it is a sentence, either of the two words may be either subject or predicate. That is to say, the name Abimelech may supposably mean either "father of a king," or "a king is father," or "a father is king," or "my father is king," or "a king is my father." Further, the clause "father of a king" may have as many variations of meaning as there are varieties of the grammatical genitive. Further still, it is claimed that either the word father or the word king may, in a name, be a designation of a deity. This gives a very large number of supposable meanings from which, in any case, to select the intended meaning.

The older scholarship regarded all these names as construct clauses. For example, Abidan is "father of a judge." It explained different instances as being different varieties of the genitive construction; for instance, Abihail, "father of might," means mighty father. The woman's name Abigail, "father of exultation," denotes one whose father is exultant. Abishai, "father of Jesse," denotes one to whom Jesse is father, and so with Abihud, "father of Judah," Abiel, "father of God," Abijah, "father of Jehovah." See the cases in detail in Gesenius' *Lexicon*.

The more recent scholarship regards most or all of the instances as sentences. In some cases it regards the second element in a name as a verb or adj. instead of a noun; but that is not important, inasmuch as in Heb the genitive construction might persist, even with the verb or adj. But in the five instances last given the explanation, "my father is exultation," "is Jesse," "is Judah," "is God," "is Jehovah," certainly gives the meaning in a more natural way than by explaining these names as construct clauses.

There is sharp conflict over the question whether we ought to regard the suffix pronoun as present in these names—whether the five instances should not rather be tr[d] Jehovah is father, God is father, Judah is father, Jesse is father, exultation is father. The question is raised whether the same rule prevails when the second word is a name or a designation of Deity as prevails in other cases. Should we explain one instance as meaning "my father is Jesse," and another as "God is father"?

A satisfactory discussion of this is possible only under a comprehensive study of Bible names. The argument is more or less complicated by the fact that each scholar looks to see what bearing it may have on the critical theories he holds. In the *Hebrew Lexicon* of Dr. Francis Brown the explanations exclude the construct theory; in most of the instances they treat a name as a sentence with "my father" as the subject; when the second part of the name is a designation of Deity they commonly make that the subject, and either exclude the pronoun or give it as an alternative. For most persons the safe method is to remember that the final decision is not yet reached, and to consider each name by itself, counting the explanation of it an open question. See NAMES, PROPER.

The investigations concerning Sem proper names, both in and out of the Bible, have interesting theological bearings. It has always been recognized that words for father and brother, when combined in proper names with Yah, Yahu, El, Baal, or other proper names of a Deity, indicated some relation of the person named, or of his tribe, with the Deity. It is now held, though with many differences of opinion, that in the forming of proper names many other words, e.g. the words for king, lord, strength, beauty, and others, are also used as designations of Deity or of some particular Deity; and that the words father, brother, and the like may have the same use. To a certain extent the proper names are so many propositions in theology. It is technically possible to go very far in inferring that the people who formed such names thought of Deity or of some particular Deity as the father, the kinsman, the ruler, the champion, the strength, the glory of the tribe or of the individual. In particular one might infer the existence of a widely diffused doctrine of the fatherhood of God. It is doubtless superfluous to add that at present one ought to be very cautious in drawing or accepting inferences in this part of the field of human study. WILLIS J. BEECHER

ABIA, a-bī'a, **ABIAH,** a-bī'ah: Variants for ABIJAH, which see.

ABI-ALBON, ab-i-al'bon, ā'bi-al'bon (אֲבִי עַלְבוֹן *'ăbhī 'al^ebhōn*, meaning not known. Gesenius infers from the Arab. a stem which would give the meaning "father of strength," and this is at worst not quite so groundless as the conjectures which explain *'al^ebhōn* as a textual misreading for *'ēl* or *ba'al*): Abi-albon the Arbathite was one of David's listed heroes (2 S **23** 31), called Abiel the Arbathite in 1 Ch **11** 32. Presumably he was from Beth-arabah (Josh **15** 6.61; **18** 22).

ABIASAPH, a-bī'a-saf, ab-i-ā'saf (אֲבִיאָסָף, *'ăbhī-'āṣāph*, "my father has gathered"): A descendant of Kohath the son of Levi (Ex **6** 24; 1 Ch **6** 23.37 [8.22]; **9** 19). In Ch the name is אֶבְיָסָף, *'ebhyāṣāph*, which seems to be a mere variant spelling. The Sam version has the same form in Ex. The list in Ex terminates with Abiasaph, who is to be regarded as the contemporary of Phinehas, the grandson of Aaron. The two lists in 1 Ch **6** lead up to the prophet Samuel and the singing companies which David is said to have organized. The list in 1 Ch **9** leads up to the Korahite porters of the time of Nehemiah. Apparently all the lists intentionally omit names, just names enough being given in each to indicate the line.

WILLIS J. BEECHER

ABIATHAR, a-bī'a-thar, ab-i-ā'thar (אֶבְיָתָר, *'ebhyāthār*, "father of super-excellence," or, "the super-excellent one is father." With changed phraseology these are the explanations commonly given, though "a father remains" would be more in accord with the ordinary use of the stem *yāthar*. The pious Abiathar was still conscious that he had a Father, even after the butchery of his human relatives):

The Scriptures represent that Abiathar was descended from Phinehas the son of Eli, and through him from Ithamar the son of Aaron; that he was the son of Ahimelech the head priest at Nob who, with his associates, was put to death by King Saul for alleged conspiracy with David; that he had two sons, Ahimelech and Jonathan, the former of whom was, in Abiathar's lifetime, prominent in the priestly service (1 S **21** 1–9; **22** 7 ff; 2 S **8** 17; **15** 27 ff; 1 Ch **18** 16; **24** 3.6.31). See AHIMELECH; AHITUB.

1. The Biblical Account

Abiathar escaped from the massacre of the priests at Nob, and fled to David, carrying the ephod with him. This was a great accession to David's strength. Public feeling in Israel was outraged by the slaughter of the priests, and turned strongly against Saul. The heir of the priesthood, and in his care the holy ephod, were now with David, and the fact gave to his cause prestige, and a certain character of legitimacy. David also felt bitterly his having been the unwilling cause of the death of Abiathar's relatives, and this made his heart warm toward his friend. Presumably, also, there was a deep religious sympathy between them.

Abiathar seems to have been at once recognized as David's priest, the medium of consultation with Jehovah through the ephod (1 S **22** 20–23; **23** 6.9; **30** 7.8). He was at the head of the priesthood, along with Zadok (1 Ch **15** 11), when David, after his conquests (1 Ch **13** 5; cf 2 S **6**), brought the ark to Jerus. The two men are mentioned together as high priests eight times in the narrative of the rebellion of Absalom (2 S **15** 24 ff), and are so mentioned in the last list of David's heads of departments (2 S **20** 25). Abiathar joined with Adonijah in his attempt to seize the throne (1 K **1** 7–42), and was for this deposed from the priesthood, though he was treated with consideration on account of his early comradeship with David (1 K **2** 26.27). Possibly he remained high priest emeritus, as Zadok and Abiathar still appear as priests in the lists of the heads of departments for Solomon's reign (1 K **4** 4). Particularly apt is the passage in Ps **55** 12–14, if one regards it as referring to the relations of David and Abiathar in the time of Adonijah.

There are two additional facts which, in view of the close relations between David and Abiathar, must be regarded as significant. One is that Zadok, Abiathar's junior, is uniformly mentioned first, in all the many passages in which the two are mentioned together, and is treated as the one who is especially responsible. Turn to the narrative, and see how marked this is. The other similarly significant fact is that in certain especially responsible matters (1 Ch **24, 18** 16; 2 S **8** 17) the interests of the line of Ithamar are represented, not by Abiathar, but by his son Ahimelech. There must have been something in the character of Abiathar to account for these facts, as well as for his deserting David for Adonijah. To sketch his character might be a work for the imagination rather than for critical inference; but it seems clear that though he was a man worthy of the friendship of David, he yet had weaknesses or misfortunes that partially incapacitated him.

The characteristic priestly function of Abiathar is thus expressed by Solomon: "Because thou barest the ark of the Lord Jehovah before David my father" (1 K **2** 26). By its tense the verb denotes not a habitual act, but the function of ark-bearing, taken as a whole. Zadok and Abiathar, as high priests, had charge of the bringing of the ark to Jerus (1 Ch **15** 11). We are not told whether it was again moved during the reign of David. Necessarily the priestly superintendence of the ark implies that of the sacrifices and services that were connected with the ark. The details in Kings indicate the existence of much of the ceremonial described in the Pent, while numerous additional Pentateuchal details are mentioned in Ch.

A priestly function much emphasized is that of obtaining answers from God through the ephod (1 S **23** 6.9; **30** 7). The word ephod (see **1 S 2** 18; 2 S **6** 14) does not necessarily denote the priestly vestment with the Urim and Thummim (e.g. Lev **8** 7.8), but if anyone denies that this was the ephod of the priest Abiathar, the burden of proof rests upon him. This is not the place for inquiring as to the method of obtaining divine revelations through the ephod.

Abiathar's landed estate was at Anathoth in Benjamin (1 K **2** 26), one of the cities assigned to the sons of Aaron (Josh **21** 18).

Apart from the men who are expressly said to be descendants of Aaron, this part of the narrative mentions priests three times. David's sons were priests (2 S **8** 18). This is of a piece with David's carrying the ark on a new cart (2 S **6**), before he had been taught by the death of Uzza. "And also Ira the Jairite was priest to the king" (2 S **20** 26 ERV). "And Zabud the son of Nathan was priest, friend of the king" (1 K **4** 5 ERV). These instances seem to indicate that David and Solomon had each a private chaplain. As to the descent and function of these two "priests" we have not a word of information, and it is illegitimate to imagine details concerning them which bring them into conflict with the rest of the record.

No one will dispute that the account thus far given is that of the Bible record as it stands.

2. Critical Opinions Concerning Abiathar

Critics of certain schools, however, do not accept the facts as thus recorded. If a person is committed to the tradition that the Deuteronomic and the priestly ideas of the Pent first originated some centuries later than Abiathar, and if he makes that tradition the standard by which to test his critical conclusions, he must of course regard the Biblical account of Abiathar as unhistorical. Either the record disproves the tradition or the tradition disproves the record. There is no third alternative. The men who accept the current critical theories understand this, and they have two ways of defending the theories against the record. In some instances they use devices for discrediting the record; in other instances they resort to harmonizing hypotheses, changing the record so as to make it agree with the theory. Without here discussing these matters, we must barely note some of their bearings in the case of Abiathar.

For example, to get rid of the testimony of Jesus (Mk **2** 26) to the effect that Abiathar was high priest and that the sanctuary at Nob was "the house of God," it is affirmed that either Jesus or the evangelist is here mistaken. The proof alleged for this is that Abiathar's service as priest did not begin till at least a few days later than the incident referred to. This is merely finical, though it is an argument that is gravely used by some scholars.

Men affirm that the statements of the record as to the descent of the line of Eli from Ithamar are untrue; that on the contrary we must conjecture that Abiathar claimed descent from Eleazar, his line being the alleged senior line of that family; that the senior line became extinct at his death, Zadok being of a junior line, if indeed he inherited any of the blood of Aaron. In making such affirmations as these, men deny the Bible statements as resting on insufficient evidence, and substitute for them other statements which, confessedly, rest on no evidence at all.

All such procedure is incorrect. Many are suspicious of statements found in the Books of Ch; that gives them no right to use their suspicions as if they were perceptions of fact. Supposably one may think the record unsatisfactory, and may be within his rights in thinking so, but that does not authorize him to change the record except on the basis of evidence of some kind. If we treat the record of the times of Abiathar as fairness demands that a record be treated in a court of justice, or a scientific investigation, or a business proposition, or a medical case, we will accept the facts substantially as they are found in S and K and Ch and Mk. WILLIS J. BEECHER

ABIB, ā′bib (אָבִיב, *'ābhībh*, young ear of barley or other grain, Ex **9** 31; Lev **2** 14): The first month of the Israelitish year, called Nisan in Neh **2** 1; Est **3** 7, is Abib in Ex **13** 4; **23** 15; **34** 18; cf Dt **16** 1. Abib is not properly a name of a month, but part of a descriptive phrase, "the month of young ears of grain." This may indicate the Israelitish way of determining the new year (Ex **12** 2), the year beginning with the new moon nearest or next preceding this stage of the growth of the barley. The year thus indicated was practically the same with the old Bab year, and presumably came in with Abraham. The Pentateuchal laws do not introduce it, though they define it, perhaps to distinguish it from the Egyp wandering year. See CALENDAR. WILLIS J. BEECHER

ABIDA, a-bī′da (אֲבִידָע, *'ăbhīdhā'*, "father of knowledge," or "my father knows"): A son of Midian and grandson of Abraham and Keturah (Gen **25** 4; 1 Ch **1** 33). **Abidah** in AV in Gen.

ABIDAH, a-bī′dah: Used in AV in Gen **25** 4 for ABIDA, which see.

ABIDAN, a-bī′dan (אֲבִידָן, *'ăbhīdhān*, "father is judge"): Abidan, son of Gideoni, was a "prince" of the children of Benjamin (Nu **2** 22; **10** 24). He was chosen to represent his tribe at the census in the wilderness of Sinai (Nu **1** 11). When, on the erection, anointing and sanctification of the Tabernacle, the heads of Israel offered, Abidan offered on the ninth day (Nu **7** 60.65).

ABIDE, a-bīd′: OE word signifying progressively to "await," "remain," "lodge," "sojourn," "dwell," "continue," "endure"; represented richly in OT (AV) by 12 Heb and in NT by as many Gr words. In RV displaced often by words meaning "to sojourn," "dwell," "encamp." The Heb and Gr originals in most frequent use are יָשַׁב, *yāshabh*, "to dwell"; *μένω*, *ménō*, "to remain." "A. [sit or tarry] ye here" (Gen **22** 5); "The earth a. [continueth] forever" (Eccl **1** 4); "Who can a. [bear or endure] the day?" (Mal **3** 2); "Afflictions a. [await] me" (Acts **20** 23). The past tense **abode,** in frequent use, has the same meaning. "His bow a. [remained] in strength" (Gen **49** 24); "There he a." (dwelt) (Jn **10** 40).

Abode, as a noun (Gr *μονή*, *monḗ*) twice in NT: "make our a. with him" (Jn **14** 23); "mansions," RVm "*abiding*-places" (Jn **14** 2). The soul of the true disciple and heaven are dwelling-places of the Father, Son and Holy Spirit. DWIGHT M. PRATT

ABIEL, ā′bi-el, ab′yel, a-bī′el (אֲבִיאֵל, *'ăbhī'ēl*, "my father is God," or "God is father"):

(1) A descendant of Benjamin the son of Jacob. Father of Kish the father of King Saul, and also, apparently, the father of Ner the father of Saul's general, Abner (1 S **9** 1; **14** 51).

(2) One of David's mighty men (1 Ch **11** 32), called ABI-ALBON, which see, in 2 S **23** 31.

ABIEZER, ab-i-ē′zer, ā-bi-ē′-zer (אֲבִיעֶזֶר, *'ăbhī-'ezer*, "father of help," or "my father is help." Iezer, Iezerite [in AV **Jeezer, Jeezerite**], is Abiezer with the letter *bēth* omitted):

(1) A descendant of Joseph the son of Jacob, and head of one of the families of Manasseh that settled W. of the Jordan (Nu **26** 30; Josh **17** 1–6; 1 Ch **7** 14–19). As he was great uncle to Zelophehad's daughters, who brought a case before Moses (Nu **36**), he must have been an old man at the time of the conquest. He was the son of Gilead the son of Machir, in the sense of being a more remote descendant, for Machir had sons before the death of Joseph (Gen **50** 23). The Machir that possessed Gilead and Bashan because he was "a man of war" was the Manassite family of Machir, with Jair as its great general (Josh **17** 1; **13** 30.31; Nu **32** 39–41; Dt **3** 12–15). To Abiezer and other sons of Gilead territory was assigned W. of the Jordan.

In later generations the name survived as that of the family to which Gideon belonged, and perhaps also of the region which they occupied (Jgs **6** 34; **8** 2). They are also called Abiezrites (Jgs **6** 11.24; **8** 32). The region was W. of Shechem, with Ophrah for its principal city.

(2) One of David's mighty men, "the Anathothite" (2 S **23** 27; 1 Ch **11** 28), who was also one of David's month-by-month captains, his month being the ninth (1 Ch **27** 12). WILLIS J. BEECHER

ABIEZRITE, ab-i-ez′-rīt, ā-bi-ez′rīt: The Gentile adj. of ABIEZER, which see.

ABIGAIL, ab′i-gāl, **ABIGAL,** ab′i-gal (אֲבִיגַיִל, *'ăbhīghayil*, or אֲבִיגַל, *'ăbhīghal*, three times, or אֲבוּגַיִל, *'ăbhūghayil*, once, or אֲבִגַיִל, *'ăbhighayil*, once; "father," or "cause of joy"):

(1) The wife of Nabal, a rich shepherd of southern Judaea, whose home was Maon (1 S **25** 2.3); shortly after Nabal's death she became the wife of David. Nabal grazed his flocks in or along the Southern Wilderness, where David and his men protected them from marauding tribes, so that not a sheep was lost. When Nabal was sheep-shearing and feasting at Carmel (in Judaea), David sent messengers requesting provisions for himself and men. But Nabal, who was a churlish fellow, answered the messengers insultingly and sent them away empty-handed. David, angered by such mean ingratitude, gathered his 400 warriors and set out to destroy Nabal and all he had (1 S **25** 22). Meanwhile Abigail, a woman "of good understanding, and of a beautiful countenance" (ver 3), heard of the rebuff given the men of David by her husband; and fearing what vengeance David in his wrath might work, she gathered a considerable present of food (ver 18), and hastened to meet the approaching soldiers. Her beautiful and prudent words, as also her fair face, so won David that he desisted from his vengeful purpose and accepted her gift (vs 32–35). When Abigail told Nabal of his narrow escape, he was stricken with fear, and died ten days afterward. Shortly after this David took Abigail to be his wife, although about the same time, probably a little before, he had also taken Ahinoam (ver 43); and these two were with him in Gath (1 S **27** 3). After David became king in Hebron, Abigail bore him his second son, Chileab (2 S **3** 3) or Daniel, as he is called in 1 Ch **3** 1.

(2) Sister of David and mother of Amasa, at one time commander of David's army (1 Ch **2** 16.17; Abigal 2 S **17** 25). In the first passage she is called David's sister, along with Zeruiah; while in the second she is called the "daughter of Nahash." Several explanations of this connection with Nahash have been suggested, any one of which would be sufficient to remove contradiction: (1) That Nahash was another name of Jesse, as in Isa **14** 29, *mish-shōresh nāḥāsh yēçē'* (Kim); (2) That Nahash was the wife of Jesse and by him mother of Abigail, which is least probable; (3) That Nahash, the father of Abigail and Zeruiah, having died, his widow became the wife of Jesse, and bore sons to

him; (4) That the text of 2 S **17** 25 has been corrupted, "daughter of Nahash" having crept into the text. At all events she was the sister of David by the same mother. EDWARD MACK

ABIHAIL, ab'i-hāl (אֲבִיחַיִל *'ăbhīḥayil;* in some MSS אֲבִיהַיִל *'ăbhīhayil,* when feminine, but best reading is the former: "father, or cause, of strength"): Five persons in the OT are called by this name: (1) A Levite and the father of Zuriel, who in the Wilderness was head of the house of Merari, Levi's youngest son (Nu **3** 35); (2) The wife of Abishur, a man of the tribe of Judah, in the line of Hazron and Jerahmeel (1 Ch **2** 29); (3) One of the heads of the tribe of Gad, who dwelt in Gilead of Bashan (1 Ch **5** 14); (4) Either a wife of Rehoboam, king of Judah, or mother of his wife Mahalath, according to the interpretation of the text (2 Ch **11** 18); probably the latter view is correct, since there is no conjunction in the text, and since the following ver (19) contemplates only one wife as already mentioned. This being true, she was the wife of Jerimath, a son of David, and daughter of Eliab, David's eldest brother. It is interesting to note this frequent intermarriage in the Davidic house; (5) Father of Queen Esther, who became wife of Xerxes (Biblical Ahasuerus) king of Persia, after the removal of the former queen, Vashti (Est **2** 15; **9** 29). He was uncle of Mordecai.

EDWARD MACK

ABIHU, a-bī'hū (אֲבִיהוּא, *'ăbhīhū',* "father he is," or "my father he is"): Second son of Aaron, the high priest (Ex **6** 23). With his older brother Nadab he "died before Jehovah," when the two "offered strange fire" (Lev **10** 1.2). It may be inferred from the emphatic prohibition of wine or strong drink, laid upon the priests immediately after this tragedy, that the two brothers were going to their priestly functions in an intoxicated condition (Lev **10** 8–11). Their death is mentioned three times in subsequent records (Nu **3** 4; **26** 61; 1 Ch **24** 2).

ABIHUD, a-bī'hud (אֲבִיהוּד, *'ăbhīhūdh,* "father of majesty," or "my father is majesty," though some regard the second part as the proper name Judah): The son of Bela the oldest son of Benjamin (1 Ch **8** 3).

ABIJAH, a-bī'jä (אֲבִיָּה or אֲבִיָּהוּ [2 Ch **13** 20.21], *'ăbhīyāh* or *'ăbhīyāhū,* "my father is Jehovah," or "Jehovah is father"): The name of six or more men and two women in the OT.

(1) The seventh son of Becher the son of Benjamin (1 Ch **7** 8).

(2) The second son of the prophet Samuel (1 S **8** 2; 1 Ch **6** 28 [**6** 13]).

(3) The eighth among "the holy captains and captains of God" appointed by lot by David in connection with the priestly courses (1 Ch **24** 10). Compare "Zacharias of the course of Abijah" (Lk **1** 5).

(4) A son of Jeroboam I of Israel (1 K **14** 1–18). The narrative describes his sickness and his mother's visit to the prophet Ahijah. He is spoken of as the one member of the house of Jeroboam in whom there was "found some good thing toward Jehovah." With his death the hope of the dynasty perished.

(5) The son and successor of Rehoboam king of Judah (1 Ch **3** 10; 2 Ch **11** 20—**14** 1). As to the variant name Abijam (1 K **14** 31; **15** 1.7.8) see ABIJAM.

The statements concerning Abijah's mother afford great opportunity for a person who is interested in finding discrepancies in the Bible narrative. She is said to have been Maacah the daughter of Absalom (1 K **15** 2; 2 Ch **11** 20.21.22). As more than 50 years elapsed between the adolescence of Absalom and the accession of Rehoboam, the suggestion at once emerges that she may have been Absalom's daughter in the sense of being his granddaughter. But Maacah the daughter of Absalom was the mother of Asa, Abijam's son and successor (1 K **15** 10.13; 2 Ch **15** 16). Further we are explicitly told that Absalom had three sons and one daughter (2 S **14** 27). It is inferred that the three sons died young, inasmuch as Absalom before his death built him a monument because he had no son (2 S **18** 18). The daughter was distinguished for her beauty, but her name was Tamar, not Maacah. Finally, the narrative tells us that the name of Abijah's mother was "Micaiah the daughter of Uriel of Gibeah" (2 Ch **13** 2).

It is less difficult to combine all these statements into a consistent account than it would be to combine some pairs of them if taken by themselves. When all put together they make a luminous narrative, needing no help from conjectural theories of discrepant sources or textual errors. It is natural to understand that Tamar the daughter of Absalom married Uriel of Gibeah; that their daughter was Maacah, named for her great-grandmother (2 S **3** 3; 1 Ch **3** 2); that Micaiah is a variant of Maacah, as Abijah is of Abijam. Maacah married Rehoboam, the parties being second cousins on the father's side; if they had been first cousins perhaps they would not have married. Very likely Solomon, through the marriage, hoped to conciliate an influential party in Israel which still held the name of Absalom in esteem; perhaps also he hoped to supplement the moderate abilities of Rehoboam by the great abilities of his wife. She was a brilliant woman, and Rehoboam's favorite (2 Ch **11** 21). On Abijah's accession she held at court the influential position of king's mother; and she was so strong that she continued to hold it, when, after a brief reign, Abijah was succeeded by Asa; though it was a position from which Asa had the authority to depose her (1 K **15** 13; 2 Ch **15** 16).

The account in Ch deals mainly with a decisive victory which, it says, Abijah gained over northern Israel (2 Ch **13**), he having 400,000 men and Jeroboam 800,000, of whom 500,000 were slain. It is clear that these numbers are artificial, and were so intended, whatever may be the key to their meaning. Abijah's speech before the battle presents the same view of the religious situation which is presented in Kings and Amos and Hosea, though with fuller priestly details. The orthodoxy of Abijah on this one occasion is not in conflict with the representation in Kings that he followed mainly the evil ways of his father Rehoboam. In Chronicles coarse luxury and the multiplying of wives are attributed to both father and son.

(6) A priest of Nehemiah's time, who sealed the covenant (Neh **10** 7). Conjecturally the same with the one mentioned in Neh **12** 4.17.

(7) The wife of Judah's grandson Hezron, to whom was traced the origin of Tekoa (1 Ch **2** 24).

(8) The mother of King Hezekiah (2 Ch **29** 1), called Abi in 2 K. See ABI.

WILLIS J. BEECHER

ABIJAM, a-bī'jam (אֲבִיָּם, *'ăbhīyām,* "father of sea," or, "father of west"): The name given in Kings (1 K **14** 31; **15** 1.7.8) to the son of Rehoboam who succeeded him as king of Judah. See ABIJAH.

The name has puzzled scholars. Some have proposed, by adding one letter, to change it into "father of his people." Others have observed that the Gr rendering in Kings is *Abeioú.* Either the Heb copy used by the Gr translator read *'ăbhīyāhū,*

Abijah, or else the translator substituted the form of the name which was to him more familiar. A few existing copies of the Heb have the reading Abijah, and Mt **1** 7 presupposes that as the OT reading. So they infer that Abijam in K is an erroneous reading for Abijah. This seems at present to be the prevailing view, and it is plausible. It would be more convincing, however, if the name occurred but once in the passage in Kings, instead of occurring five times. It is improbable that a scribe would repeat the same error five times within a few sentences, while a translator, if he changed the name once, would of course change it the other four times.

Exploration has revealed the fact that the whole region near the eastern end of the Mediterranean was known as "the west." "Father of the west" is not an inapt name for Rehoboam to give to the boy who, he expects, will inherit the kingdom of Solomon and David. The effect of the secession of the ten tribes was to make that name a burlesque, and one does not wonder that it was superseded by Abijah, "My father is Jehovah."

WILLIS J. BEECHER

ABILA, ab'i-la. See ABILENE.

ABILENE, a-bi-lē'nē (**Ἀβειληνή**, *Abeilēnē*, BA; **Ἀβιληνή**, *Abilēnē*, ℵ[a]): Mentioned in Lk **3** 1 as the tetrarchy of Lysanias at the time when John the Baptist began his ministry. The district derived its name from Abila, its chief town, which was situated, according to the Itinerarium Antonini, 18 Roman miles from Damascus on the way to Heliopolis (Baalbec). This places it in the neighborhood of the village of *Suk Wady Barada* (see ABANA), near which there are considerable ancient remains, with an inscription in Gr stating that a "freedman of Lysanias the tetrarch" made a wall and built a temple, and another in Lat recording the repair of the road "at the expense of the Abilenians." The memory of the ancient name probably survives in the Moslem legend which places the tomb of Abel in a neighboring height where there are ruins of a temple. Jos calls this Abila, *hē Lusaníou*, lit. "the A. of Lysanius," thus distinguishing it from other towns of the same name, and as late as the time of Ptolemy (cir 170 AD) the name of Lysanias was associated with it.

The territory of Abilene was part of the Ituraean Kingdom, which was broken up when its king, Lysanias, was put to death by M. Antonius, c 35 BC. The circumstances in which A. became a distinct tetrarchy are altogether obscure, and nothing further is known of the tetrarch Lysanias (*Ant*, XIX, v, 1; XX, ii, 1). In 37 AD the tetrarchy, along with other territories, was granted to Agrippa I, after whose death in 44 AD it was administered by procurators until 53 AD, when Claudius conferred it again, along with neighboring territories, upon Agrippa II. On Agrippa's death, toward the close of the 1st cent., his kingdom was incorporated in the province of Syria. See LYSANIAS.

C. H. THOMSON

ABILITY, a-bil'i-ti (**δύναμις**, *dúnamis*, or **ἰσχύς**, *ischús*): Variously used of resources, material, mental and spiritual; e.g. of wealth, "gave after their a." (Ezr **2** 69); of mental endowment, "a. to stand in the king's palace" (Dnl **1** 4); of talents and character, "several a." (Mt **25** 15); of spiritual strength, "minister, as of the a. which God giveth" (AV 1 Pet **4** 11). It thus may signify either possessions, native capacity, or gifts of the Holy Spirit.

ABIMAEL, a-bim'a-el, ab-i-mā'el (אֲבִימָאֵל, *'ăbhīmā'ēl*, "my father is God," or "God is father"): The ninth of the thirteen sons of Joktan, who was descendant of Shem, and son of Eber, and brother of Peleg in whose days the earth was divided (Gen **10** 25–29; 1 Ch **1** 19–23). Like some of the other names in this list, the name is linguistically south Arabian, and the tribes indicated are south Arabians. On the Arab. elements in Heb proper names see Halévy, *Mélanges d'épigraphie et d'archéologie sémitiques; ZDMG*, esp. early in 1883; D. H. Müller, *Epigraphie Denkmäler aus Arabien;* Glaser, *Skizze der Gesch. und Geog. Arabiens;* and by index Hommel, *Ancient Hebrew Tradition;* and Gray, *Hebrew Proper Names;* and F. Giesebrecht, *Die alttestamentliche Schätzung des Gottesnamens.*

WILLIS J. BEECHER

ABIMELECH, a-bim'e-lek (אֲבִימֶלֶךְ, *'ăbhīmelekh*, "father of a king"): A name borne by five OT persons.

(1) The name of two kings of Philistia; the first was a contemporary of Abraham, the second, probably son of the former, was king in the days of Isaac. It is quite possible that Abimelech was the royal title rather than the personal name, since in the title of Ps **34** we find it applied to the king of Gath, elsewhere known by his personal name, Achish (1 S **27** 2.3). Shortly after the destruction of Sodom Abraham journeyed with his herds and flocks into the extreme S.E. country of Pal (Gen **20**). While sojourning at Gerar, the city of Abimelech, king of the Phili country, he made believe that Sarah was his sister (ver 2), and Abimelech took her, intending to make her one of his wives. But God rebuked him in a dream, besides sending barrenness on the women of his household (vs 3.17). After Abimelech had reproved Abraham most justly for the deception, he dealt generously with him, loading him with presents and granting him the liberty of the land (vs 14.15). When contention had arisen between the servants of the two men over the wells of water the two men made a covenant at a well, which took its name, Beersheba, from this fact of covenant-making (Gen **21** 31.32).

(2) Nearly a cent. later than the events connected with the first Abimelech, as outlined above, a second Abimelech, king of the Philistines, is mentioned in relations with Isaac (Gen **26**), who in time of grievous famine went down from his home, probably at Hebron, to Gerar. Fearing for his life because of his beautiful wife, Rebekah, he called her his sister, just as Abraham had done with reference to Sarah. Neither Abimelech nor any of his people took Rebekah to wife—quite a variation from the Abrahamic incident; but when the falsehood was detected, he upbraided Isaac for what might have happened, continuing nevertheless to treat him most graciously. Isaac continued to dwell in the vicinity of Gerar, until contention between his herdsmen and those of Abimelech became too violent; then he moved away by stages, reopening the wells digged by his father (vs 18–22). Finally, a covenant was made between Abimelech and Isaac at Beersheba, just as had been made between Abraham and the first Abimelech (Gen **26** 26–33). The two kings of Philistia were probably father and son.

(3) The title of Ps **34** mentions another Abimelech, who in all probability is the same as Achish king of Gath (1 S **21** 10—**22** 1); with whom David sought refuge when fleeing from Saul, and with whom he was dwelling at the time of the Phili invasion of Israel, which cost Saul his kingdom and his life (1 S **27**). It appears from this that Abimelech was the royal title, and not the personal name of the Phili kings.

(4) A son of Gideon (Jgs **9**) who aspired to be king after the death of his father, and did rule three

years (ver 22). He first won the support of the members of his mother's family and their recommendation of himself to all Israel (vs 3.4). He then murdered all the sons of his father, seventy in number, at Ophrah, the family home in the tribe of Manasseh, Jotham the youngest son alone escaping (ver 5). After this Abimelech was made ruler by an assembly of the people at Shechem. An insurrection led by Gaal the son of Ebed having broken out in Shechem, Abimelech, although he succeeded in capturing that city, was wounded to death by a mill-stone, which a woman dropped from the wall upon his head, while he was storming the citadel of Thebez, into which the defeated rebels had retreated, after that city also had been taken (vs 50–53). Finding that he was mortally wounded and in order to avoid the shame of death at a woman's hand, he required his armor-bearer to kill him with his sword (ver 54). His cruel treatment of the Shechemites (vs 46–49), when they took refuge from him in their strong tower, was a just judgment for their acquiescence in his crimes (vs 20.57); while his own miserable death was retribution for his bloody deeds (ver 56).

(5) A priest in the days of David; a descendant of Ithamar and Eli, and son of Abiathar (1 Ch **18** 16). In the LXX and in 1 Ch **24** he is called A*h*imelech; but is not to be confused with Ahimelech, the father of Abiathar, and therefore his grandfather. He shared with Zadok, of the line of Ithamar, the priestly office in the reign of David (1 Ch **24** 31). EDWARD MACK

ABINADAB, a-bin′a-dab (אֲבִינָדָב, *ʼăbhīnādhābh,* "father of willingness," or, "my father is willing." This is according to the ordinary usage of the second word in the name—"willing" rather than "munificent" or "noble"):

(1) The man in whose house the men of Kiriath-jearim placed the ark, after its return from the land of the Philis, his house being either in Gibeah of Benjamin or "in the hill" (1 S **7** 1; 2 S **6** 3.4). To account for the ambiguity note that *gibhʽāh* means hill, and that the place-name Gibeah ordinarily has the definite article. It is natural to think that Abinadab was himself a man of Kiriath-jearim, though the account does not explicitly say so. The record is that the men of Kiriath-jearim were summoned to take charge of the ark at a time when no one else dared to have it (1 S **6** 20.21); and the implication seems to be that they had no option to refuse. Possibly this was due to their being Gibeonites, and hereditary "bondmen" of "the house of my God" (Josh **9** 17.23). However this may be, they "sanctified" Abinadab's son Eleazar to have charge of the ark. According to the Heb and some of the Gr copies, the ark was in Gibeah in the middle of the reign of King Saul (1 S **14** 18).

About a century later, according to the Bible numbers, David went with great pomp to Kiriath-jearim, otherwise known as Baalah or Baale-judah, to bring the ark from Kiriath-jearim, out of the house of Abinadab in the hill (or, in Gibeah), and place it in Jerus (1 Ch **13**; 2 S **6**). The new cart was driven by two descendants of Abinadab. There may or may not have been another Abinadab then living, the head of the house.

(2) The second of the eight sons of Jesse, one of the three who were in Saul's army when Goliath gave his challenge (1 S **16** 8; **17** 13; 1 Ch **2** 13).

(3) One of the sons of King Saul (1 Ch **8** 33; **9** 39; **10** 2; 1 S **31** 2). He died in the battle of Gilboa, along with his father and brothers.

(4) In 1 K **4** 11 AV has "the son of Abinadab," where RV has BEN-ABINADAB, which see.

WILLIS J. BEECHER

ABINOAM, a-bin′ō-am, ab-i-nō′am (אֲבִינֹעַם, *ʼăbhīnōʽam,* "father of pleasantness," or, "my father is pleasantness"): A man of Kedesh-naphtali, the father of Barak who defeated the army of Jabin and Sisera (Jgs **4** 6.12; **5** 1.12).

ABIRAM, a-bī′ram (אֲבִירָם, *ʼăbhīrām,* "exalted father," or, "my father is an exalted one"):

(1) The son of Eliab the son of Pallu the son of Reuben (Nu **26** 5 ff; Dt **11** 6). In company with his brother Dathan and Korah the Levite and others, he disputed the authority of Moses and Aaron in the wilderness (Nu **16–17**, **26**; Dt **11** 6; Ps **106** 17). Two hundred and fifty followers of Korah perished by fire at the doorway of the tent of meeting. Dathan and Abiram refused to come to the tent of meeting, at the summons of Moses; and the earth opened where their tents were, and swallowed them and their families and their goods. See KORAH.

(2) The firstborn son of Hiel the Bethelite, who rebuilt Jericho in the time of Ahab (1 K **16** 34; cf Josh **6** 26). This incident has recently acquired a new interest owing to discoveries made at Gezer and Megiddo concerning foundation sacrifices as anciently offered in Palestine. One should not be too positive in making statements concerning this, but the following is a possible interpretation of the record. The curse pronounced by Joshua on the man who should rebuild Jericho was of a piece with the other details, Jericho being treated exceptionally, as a city placed under the ban. The language of Joshua's curse is capable of being translated: 'Cursed be the man before Jehovah who shall . . . . build . . . . Jericho; [who] shall lay its foundation in his firstborn, and set up its gates in his youngest.' According to this interpretation the death of the builder's eldest and youngest sons is not spoken of as the penalty involved in the curse, but as an existing horrible custom, mentioned in order to give solemnity to the diction of the curse. The writer in Kings cites the language of the curse by Joshua. The context in which he mentions the affair suggests that he regards Hiel's conduct as exceptionally flagrant in its wickedness. Hiel, in defiance of Jehovah, not only built the city, but in building it revived the horrible old Canaanite custom, making his firstborn son a foundation sacrifice, and his youngest son a sacrifice at the completion of the work.

WILLIS J. BEECHER

ABIRON, a-bī′ron (**Ἀβειρών,** *Abeirōn*):

(1) The LXX form (Ecclus **45** 18 AV) of Abiram, one of the sons of Eliab, who, with his brother Dathan, and with one of the same tribe, joined the conspiracy against Moses and Aaron (Nu **16** 1.12.24.25.27; **26** 9; Dt **11** 6; Ps **106** 17).

(2) The eldest son of Hiel, the Bethelite, who died prematurely, thus fulfilling the doom pronounced on the posterity of him who should undertake to rebuild Jericho (1 K **16** 34). See ABIRAM.

ABISEI, ab-i-sē′ī. See ABISSEI.

ABISHAG, ab′i-shag, a-bī′shag (אֲבִישַׁג, *ʼăbhīshagh,* apparently, "father of wandering," that is, "cause of wandering," or "my father wanders"): The Shunammite woman who became nurse to King David (1 K **1** 1–4.15; **2** 17.21.22). She was chosen for the service with great care on account of her youth and beauty and physical vigor. She ministered to the king, that is, waited on him as personal attendant and nurse. She also "cherished" him in his feebleness—gave to him through physical contact the advantage of her superabundant vitality. This was a mode of medical treatment recommended by the servants of the king, and it appears to have been not wholly unsuccessful. She had an intimate knowledge of the condition of David, and was present at the interview of Bath-sheba with David which resulted in the placing of Solomon on the throne. If that act had been questioned she would have been a most important witness. By reason of this and of her personal charms, she might become a strong helper to any rival of Solomon who should intrigue to supplant him. Adonijah sought Abishag in marriage. On the basis of this and of such other evidence as may supposably have been in his possession, Solomon put Adonijah to death as an intriguer.

Willis J. Beecher

ABISHAI, ab′i-shī, a-bī′shī (אֲבִישַׁי, *'ăbhīshai,* in Ch אַבְשַׁי, *'abhshai;* meaning is doubtful, probably "my father is Jesse," *BDB*): Son of Zeruiah, David's sister, and one of the three famous brothers, of whom Joab and Asahel were the other two (2 S **2** 18). He was chief of the second group of three among David's "mighty men" (2 S **23** 18). He first appears with David, who was in the Wilderness of Ziph, to escape Saul. When David called for a volunteer to go down into Saul's camp by night, Abishai responded, and counseled the killing of Saul when they came upon the sleeping king (1 S **26** 6–9). In the skirmish between the men of Ishbosheth and the men of David at Gibeon, in which Asahel was killed by Abner, Abishai was present (2 S **2** 18.24). He was with and aided Joab in the cruel and indefensible murder of Abner, in revenge for their brother Asahel (2 S **3** 30). In David's campaign against the allied Ammonites and Syrians, Abishai led the attack upon the Ammonites, while Joab met the Syrians; the battle was a great victory for Israel (2 S **10** 10–14). He was always faithful to David, and remained with him, as he fled from Absalom. When Shimei, of the house of Saul, cursed the fleeing king, Abishai characteristically wished to kill him at once (2 S **16** 8.9); and when the king returned victorious Abishai advised the rejection of Shimei's penitence, and his immediate execution (2 S **19** 21). In the battle with Absalom's army at Mahanaim Abishai led one division of David's army, Joab and Ittai commanding the other two (2 S **18** 2). With Joab he put down the revolt against David of Sheba, a man of Benjamin (2 S **20** 6.10), at which Joab treacherously slew Amasa his cousin and rival, as he had likewise murdered Abner, Abishai no doubt being party to the crime. In a battle with the Philistines late in his life, David was faint, being now an old man, and was in danger of death at the hands of the Phili giant Ishbihenob when Abishai came to his rescue and killed the giant (2 S **21** 17). In the list of David's heroes (2 S **23**) Abishai's right to leadership of the "second three" is based upon his overthrowing three hundred men with his spear (ver 18). He does not appear in the struggle of Adonijah against Solomon, in which Joab was the leader, and therefore is supposed to have died before that time.

He was an impetuous, courageous man, but less cunning than his more famous brother Joab, although just as cruel and relentless toward rival or foe. David understood and feared their hardness and cruelty. Abishai's best trait was his unswerving loyalty to his kinsman, David.

Edward Mack

ABISHALOM, a-bish′a-lom: Variant of Absalom, which see.

ABISHUA, a-bish′ū-a, abi-shōō′a (אֲבִישׁוּעַ, *'ăbhīshūaʿ,* uncertain, perhaps "father of wealth," or "my father is wealth"):

(1) A son of Bela the son of Benjamin (1 Ch **8** 4).
(2) The son of Phinehas, who was grandson to Aaron (1 Ch **6** 4.5.50; Ezr **7** 5).

ABISHUR, a-bī′shur (אֲבִישׁוּר, *'ăbhīshūr,* "my father is a wall"): Great-grandson of Jerahmeel and Atarah, Jerahmeel being great-grandson of Judah. Abishur was son of Shammai, and was the husband of Abihail, and the father of sons (1 Ch **2** 28.29).

ABISSEI, a-bis′ē-ī (AV **Abisei**): An ancestor of Ezra (2 Esd **1** 2) = Abisue (1 Esd **8** 2) and Abishua (1 Ch **6** 4 ff; Ezr **7** 5).

ABISUE, a-bis′ū-ē (B, **'Αβισαί,** *Abisaí;* A, *Abisouaí;* AV **Abisum** = Abishua [1 Ch **6** 4 ff; Ezr **7** 5] and Abissei [2 Esd **1** 2]): An ancestor of Ezra (1 Esd **8** 2).

ABISUM, ab′i-sum. See Abisue (Apoc).

ABITAL, ab′i-tal, a-bī′tal (אֲבִיטַל, *'ăbhīṭāl,* "my father is dew"): One of the wives of King David. In the duplicated list (2 S **3** 4; 1 Ch **3** 3) in which the sons born to David in Hebron are mentioned and numbered, the fifth is said to be Shephatiah the son of Abital.

ABITUB, ab′i-tub, a-bī′tub (אביטוב, *'ăbhīṭūbh,* "father of goodness," or, "my father is goodness"): In AV **Ahitub.** A descendant of Benjamin and son of Shaharaim and Hushim, born in the field of Moab (1 Ch **8** 11).

ABIUD, a-bī′ud (**'Αβιούδ,** *Abioúd,* perhaps "my father is majesty"; see Abihud): Mentioned in the genealogy of Jesus (Mt **1** 13 and not elsewhere) as the son of Zerubbabel. See Genealogy.

ABJECT, ab′jekt: Only as a noun, and but once (Ps **35** 15) for נֵכֶה, *nēkheh,* lit. "smitten ones," i.e. "men of the lowest grade" (Hengstenberg, Delitzsch), "the rabble," defined by the succeeding clause as those of such inferior station that they were unknown.

ABLE, ā′b'l: The Gr δύναμαι, *dúnamai,* "to have power," may refer either to inherent strength, or to the absence of external obstacles, or to what may be allowable or permitted. The Gr ἰσχύω, *ischúō,* as in Lk **13** 24; Jn **21** 6, refers always to the first of the above meanings. The use of the word as an adj. in AV of 2 Cor **3** 6, is misleading, and has been properly changed in RV into "sufficient as ministers," i.e. "hath fitted us to be ministers."

ABLUTION, ab-lū′shun: The rite of ablution for religious purification seems to have been practised in some form in all lands and at all times. The priests of Egypt punctiliously practised it (Herodotus ii.37). The Greeks were warned "never with unwashed hands to pour out the black wine at morn to Zeus" (Hesiod, *Opera et Dies* v.722; cf Homer, *Iliad* vi.266; *Od.* iv.759). The Romans also observed it (Virgil, *Aeneid* ii.217); as did and do Orientals in general (cf Koran, Sura **5** 8, etc).

Ablutions for actual or ritual purification form quite a feature of the Jewish life and ceremonial. No one was allowed to enter a holy place or to approach God by prayer or sacrifice without having first performed the rite of ablution, or "sanctification," as it was sometimes called (Ex **19** 10; 1 S **16** 5; 2 Ch **29** 5; cf Jos, *Ant,* XIV, xi, 5).

Three kinds of washing are recognized in Biblical and rabbinical law: (1) washing of the hands,

(2) washing of the hands and feet, and (3) immersion of the whole body in water. (1 and 2 = Gr νίπτω, *niptō;* 3 = Gr λούω, *loúō*).

Something more than an echo of a universal practice is found in the Scriptures. The rabbis claimed to find support for ceremonial hand-washing in Lev **15** 11. David's words, "I will wash my hands in innocency: so will I compass thine altar, O Jeh" (Ps **26** 6; cf Ps **73** 13), are regarded by them as warranting the inference that ablution of the hands was prerequisite to any holy act. This is the form of ablution, accordingly, which is most universally and scrupulously practised by Jews. Before any meal of which bread forms a part, as before prayer, or any act of worship, the hands must be solemnly washed in pure water; as also after any unclean bodily function, or contact with any unclean thing. Such hand-washings probably arose naturally from the fact that the ancients ate with their fingers, and so were first for physical cleansing only; but they came to be ceremonial and singularly binding. The Talm abundantly shows that eating with unwashed hands came to be reckoned a matter of highest importance—"tantamount to committing an act of unchastity, or other gross crime." Akiba, when in prison, went without water given him to quench his thirst, rather than neglect the rite of ablution ('Er. 216). Only in extreme cases, according to the Mish, as on a battlefield, might people dispense with it. Simeon, the Essene, "the Saint" (Toseph. *Kēlīm* i.6), on entering the holy place without having washed his hands, claiming that he was holier than the high priest because of his ascetic life, was excommunicated, as undermining the authority of the Elders (cf *'Edūy.* **5** 6).

Washing of the hands and feet is prescribed by the Law only for those about to perform priestly functions (cf Koran, Sura **5** 8, in contrast: "When ye prepare yourselves for prayer, wash your faces and hands up to the elbows, and wipe your heads and your feet to the ankles"; Hughes, *Dict. of Islam*). For example, whenever Moses or Aaron or any subordinate priest desired to enter the sanctuary (Tabernacle) or approach the altar, he was required to wash his hands and feet from the laver which stood between the Tabernacle and the altar (Ex **30** 19; **40** 31). The same rule held in the Temple at Jerusalem. The washing of the whole body, however, is the form of ablution most specifically and exactingly required by the Law. The cases in which the immersion of the whole body is commanded, either for purification or consecration, are very numerous. For example, the Law prescribed that no leper or other unclean person of the seed of Aaron should eat of holy flesh until he had washed his whole body in water (Lev **22** 4–6); that anyone coming in contact with a person having an unclean issue, or with any article used by such a one, should wash his whole body (**15** 5–10); that a sufferer from an unclean issue (**15** 16.18); a menstruous woman (2 S **11** 2.4), and anyone who touched a menstruous woman, or anything used by her, should likewise immerse the whole person in water (Lev **15** 19–27): that the high priest who ministered on the Day of Atonement (**16** 24–28), the priest who tended the red heifer (Nu **19** 7.8.19), and every priest at his installation (Ex **29** 4; **40** 12) should wash his whole body in water. Cf 'divers baptisms' (immersions) in He **9** 10, and see Broadus on Mt **15** 2–20 with footnote. (For another view on bathing see Kennedy in *HDB*, I, 257 *v.*)

Bathing in the modern and non-religious sense is rarely mentioned in the Scriptures (Ex **2** 5 Pharaoh's daughter; 2 S **11** 2 RV Bathsheba, and the interesting case 1 K **22** 38). Public baths are first met with in the Gr period—included in the "place of exercise" (1 Macc **1** 14), and remains of such buildings from the Rom period are numerous. Recently a remarkable series of bath-chambers have been discovered at Gezer, in Pal, in connection with a building which is supposed to be the palace built by Simon Maccabaeus (Kennedy [illust. in *PEFS*, 1905, 294 f]).

The rite of ablution was observed among early Christians also. Eusebius (*HE*, X, 4.40) tells of Christian churches being supplied with fountains or basins of water, after the Jewish custom of providing the laver for the use of the priests. The Apos Const (VIII.32) have the rule: "Let all the faithful . . . . when they rise from sleep, before they go to work, pray, after having washed themselves" (*nipsámenoi*).

The attitude of Jesus toward the rabbinical law of ablution is significant. Mk (**7** 3) prepares the way for his record of it by explaining, 'The Pharisees and all the Jews eat not except they wash their hands to the wrist' (*pugmḗ*). (See *LTJM*, II, 11). According to Mt **15** 1–20 and Mk **7** 1–23 Pharisees and Scribes that had come from Jerusalem (i.e. the strictest) had seen some of Jesus' disciples eat bread with unwashed hands, and they asked Him: "Why do thy disciples transgress the tradition of the elders? for they wash not their hands when they eat bread." Jesus' answer was to the Jews, even to His own disciples, in the highest degree surprising, paradoxical, revolutionary (cf Mt **12** 8). They could not but see that it applied not merely to hand-washing, but to the whole matter of clean and unclean food; and this to them was one of the most vital parts of the Law (cf Acts **10** 14). Jesus saw that the masses of the Jews, no less than the Pharisees, while scrupulous about ceremonial purity, were careless of inward purity. So here, as in the Sermon on the Mount, and with reference to the Sabbath (Mt **12** 1 ff), He would lead them into the deeper and truer significance of the Law, and thus prepare the way for setting aside not only the traditions of the elders that made void the commandments of God, but even the prescribed ceremonies of the Law themselves, if need be, that the Law in its higher principles and meanings might be "fulfilled." Here He proclaims a principle that goes to the heart of the whole matter of true religion in saying: "Well did Isaiah prophesy of you hypocrites" (Mk **7** 6–13)—you who make great pretense of devotion to God, and insist strenuously on the externals of His service, while at heart you do not love Him, making the word of God of none effect for the sake of your tradition!

LITERATURE.—For list of older authorities see McClintock and Strong, *Cyclopedia;* Nowack, *Biblische Archaeologie*, II, 275–99; and Spitzer, *Ueber Baden und Bäder bei den alten Hebräern*, 1884.

GEO. B. EAGER

ABNER, ab'nẽr (אַבְנֵר, *'abhnēr;* in 1 S **14** 50 the Heb has the fuller form, אֲבִינֵר, *'ăbhīnēr, Abiner;* cf *Abiram* by the side of *Abram;* meaning, "my father is a lamp"): Captain of the host under Saul and Ishbosheth (Eshbaal). He was Saul's cousin; Ner the father of Abner and Kish the father of Saul being brothers, the sons of Abiel (1 S **14** 50 f). In 1 Ch **8** 33; **9** 39 the text appears to be faulty; read: "And Ner begat Abner, and Kish begat Saul." According to 1 Ch **27** 21 Abner had a son by the name of Jaasiel.

Abner was to Saul what Joab was to David. Despite the many wars waged by Saul, we hear little of Abner during Saul's lifetime. Not even in the account of the battle of Gilboa is mention made of him. Yet both his high office and his kinship to the king must have brought the two men in close contact. On festive occasions it was the custom of Abner to sit at table by the king's side (1 S **20** 25). It was Abner who introduced the young David fresh from his triumph over Goliath to the king's court (so according to the account in 1 S **17** 57). We find Abner accompanying the king in his pursuit of David (1 S **26** 5 ff). Abner is rebuked by David for his negligence in keeping watch over his master (ib, **15**).

Upon the death of Saul, Abner took up the cause of the young heir to the throne, Ishbosheth, whom he forthwith removed from the neighborhood of David to Mahanaim in the East-Jordanic country. There he proclaimed him king over all Israel. By the pool of Gibeon he and his men met Joab and the servants of David. Twelve men on each side engaged in combat which ended disastrously for Abner who fled. He was pursued by Asahel, Joab's brother, whom Abner slew. Though Joab and his brother Abishai sought to avenge their brother's death on the spot, a truce was effected; Abner was permitted to go his way after three hundred and threescore of his men had fallen. Joab naturally watched his opportunity. Abner and his master soon had a quarrel over Saul's concubine, Rizpah, with whom Abner was intimate. It was certainly an act of treason which Ishbosheth was bound to resent. The disgruntled general made overtures to David; he won over the tribe of Benjamin. With twenty men of them he came to Hebron and arranged with the king of Judah that he would bring over to his side all Israel. He was scarcely gone when Joab learned of the affair; without the knowledge of David he recalled him to Hebron where he slew him, "for the blood of Asahel his brother." David mourned sincerely the death of Abner. "Know ye not," he addressed his servants, "that there is a prince and a great man fallen this day in Israel?" He followed the bier in person. Of the royal lament over Abner a fragment is quoted:

"Should Abner die as a fool dieth?
Thy hands were not bound, nor thy feet put into fetters:
As a man falleth before the children of iniquity, so didst thou fall."

(See 2 S **3** 6–38.) The death of Abner, while it thus cannot in any wise be laid at the door of David, nevertheless served his purposes well. The backbone of the opposition to David was broken, and he was soon proclaimed as king by all Israel.

MAX L. MARGOLIS

ABODE, a-bōd′. See ABIDE.

ABOLISH, a-bol′ish (חָתַת, *ḥāthath,* "to be broken down," "made void," "My righteousness shall not be abolished" [Isa **51** 6], i.e. as shown in God's faithfulness to His promises; מָחָה *māḥāh,* "to erase," "blot out," "that your works may be abolished" [Ezk **6** 6]; **καταργέω,** *katargéō,* "to render inoperative," "bring to nought," "make of no effect," "when he shall have abolished all rule" [1 Cor **15** 24], every power opposed to God's kingdom; "having abolished in his flesh the enmity" [Eph **2** 15]): By His death, Christ did away with the race separation due to historic ordinances and ceremonial laws (as of circumcision and uncircumcision); through the cross He wrought the reconciliation, and secured that common access to the Father by which the union is maintained.

"Our Saviour Christ Jesus . . . . abolished death" (2 Tim **1** 10). Men still die, "it is appointed unto men" (He **9** 27), but the fear of death as having power to terminate or affect our personal existence and our union with God, as a dreadful stepping out into the unknown and unknowable (into Sheol of the impenetrable gloom), and as introducing us to a final and irreversible judgment, has been removed. Christ has taken out of it its sting (1 Cor **15** 55 f) and all its hurtful power (He **2** 14); has shown it to be under His control (Rev **1** 18), brought to light the incorruptible life beyond, and declared the ultimate destruction of death (1 Cor **15** 26; cf Rev **20** 14). The Gr (*katargeítai*) indicates that the process of destruction was then going on. M. O. EVANS

ABOMINATION, a-bom-i-nā′shun (פִּגּוּל, *piggūl,* תּוֹעֵבָה, *tō'ēbhāh,* שֶׁקֶץ, *sheḳeç* [שִׁקּוּץ, *shiḳḳūç*]): Three distinct Heb words are rendered in the English Bible by "abomination," or "abominable thing," referring (except in Gen **43** 32; **46** 34) to things or practices abhorrent to Jehovah, and opposed to the ritual or moral requirements of His religion. It would be well if these words could be distinguished in tr, as they denote different degrees of abhorrence or loathsomeness.

The word most used for this idea by the Hebrews and indicating the highest degree of abomination is תּוֹעֵבָה, *tō'ēbhāh,* meaning primarily that which offends the religious sense of a people. When it is said, for example, "The Egyptians might not eat bread with the Hebrews; for that is an abomination unto the Egyptians," this is the word used; the significance being that the Hebrews were repugnant to the Egyptians as foreigners, as of an inferior caste, and especially as shepherds (Gen **46** 34).

The feeling of the Egyptians for the Greeks was likewise one of repugnance. Herodotus (ii.41) says the Egyptians would not kiss a Greek on the mouth, or use his dish, or taste meat cut with the knife of a Greek.

Among the objects described in the OT as "abominations" in this sense are heathen gods, such as Ashtoreth (Astarte), Chemosh, Milcom, the "abominations" of the Zidonians (Phoenicians), Moabites, and Ammonites, respectively (2 K **23** 13), and everything connected with the worship of such gods. When Pharaoh, remonstrating against the departure of the children of Israel, exhorted them to offer sacrifices to their God in Egypt, Moses said: "Shall we sacrifice the abomination of the Egyptians [i.e. the animals worshipped by them which were *taboo, tō'ēbhāh,* to the Israelites] before their eyes, and will they not stone us?" (Ex **8** 26; Kyle, *Moses and the Monuments,* 26 ff).

It is to be noted that, not only the heathen idol itself, but anything offered to or associated with the idol, all the paraphernalia of the forbidden cult, was called an "abomination," for it "is an abomination to Jeh thy God" (Dt **7** 25.26). The Deuteronomic writer here adds, in terms quite significant of the point of view and the spirit of the whole law: 'Neither shalt thou bring an abomination into thy house and thus become a thing set apart [*ḥērem = tabooed*] like unto it; thou shalt utterly detest it and utterly abhor it, for it is a thing set apart' (*tabooed*). *Tō'ēbhāh* is even used as synonymous with "idol" or heathen deity, as in Isa **44** 19; Dt **32** 16; 2 K **23** 13; and esp. Ex **8** 22 ff.

Everything akin to magic or divination is likewise an abomination (*tō'ēbhāh*); as are sexual transgressions (Dt **22** 5; **23** 18; **24** 4), esp. incest and other unnatural offences: "For all these abominations have the men of the land done, that were before you" (Lev **18** 27; cf Ezk **8** 15). It is to be noted, however, that the word takes on in the later usage a higher ethical and spiritual meaning: as where "divers measures, a great and a small," are forbidden (Dt **25** 14–16); and in Prov where "lying lips" (**12** 22), "the proud in heart"

(**16** 5), "the way of the wicked" (**15** 9), "evil devices" (**15** 26), and "he that justifieth the wicked, and he that condemneth the righteous" (**17** 15), are said to be an abomination in God's sight. At last prophet and sage are found to unite in declaring that any sacrifice, however free from physical blemish, if offered without purity of motive, is an abomination: 'Bring no more an oblation of falsehood—an incense of abomination it is to me' (Isa **1** 13; cf Jer **7** 10). "The sacrifice of the wicked" and the prayer of him "that turneth away his ear from hearing the law," are equally an abomination (see Prov **15** 8; **21** 27; **28** 9).

Another word rendered "abomination" in the AV is שֶׁקֶץ, *sheḳeç* or שִׁקּוּץ, *shiḳḳuç*. It expresses generally a somewhat less degree of horror or religious aversion than *tō'ēbhāh,* but sometimes seems to stand about on a level with it in meaning. In Dt **14** 3, for example, we have the command, "Thou shalt not eat any abominable thing," as introductory to the laws prohibiting the use of the unclean animals (see Clean and Unclean Animals), and the word there used is *tō'ēbhāh*. But in Lev **11** 10–13. 20.23.41.42; Isa **66** 17; and in Ezk **8** 10 *sheḳeç* is the word used and likewise applied to the prohibited animals; as also in Lev **11** 43 *sheḳeç* is used when it is commanded, "Ye shall not make yourselves abominable." Then *sheḳeç* is often used parallel to or together with *tō'ēbhāh* of that which should be held as detestable, as for instance, of idols and idolatrous practices (see esp. Dt **29** 17; Hos **9** 10; Jer **4** 1; **13** 27; **16** 18; Ezk **11** 18–21; **20** 7.8). It is used exactly as *tō'ēbhāh* is used as applied to Milcom, the god of the Ammonites, which is spoken of as the detestable thing (*sheḳeç*) of the Ammonites (1 K **11** 5). Still even in such cases *tō'ēbhāh* seems to be the stronger word and to express that which is in the highest degree abhorrent.

The other word used to express a somewhat kindred idea of abhorrence and tr[d] "abomination" in AV is פִגּוּל, *piggūl;* but it is used in the Heb Bible only of sacrificial flesh that has become stale, putrid, tainted (see Lev **7** 18; **19** 7; Ezk **4** 14; Isa **65** 4). Driver maintains that it occurs only as a "technical term for such state sacrificial flesh as has not been eaten within the prescribed time," and, accordingly, he would everywhere render it specifically "refuse meat." Compare *leḥem m'ghō'āl,* "the loathsome bread" (from *gā'al,* "to loathe") Mal **1** 7. A chief interest in the subject for Christians grows out of the use of the term in the expression "abomination of desolation" (Mt **24** 15 and Mk **13** 14), which see. See also Abhor.

Literature.—Commentators ad loc. Rabbinical lit. in point. Driver; Weiss; Grätz, *Gesch. der Juden*, IV, n. 15.

Geo. B. Eager

ABOMINATION, BIRDS OF, Lev **11** 13–19: "And these ye shall have in abomination among the birds; they shall not be eaten, they are an abomination: the eagle, and the gier-eagle, and the ospray, and the kite, and the falcon after its kind, every raven after its kind, and the ostrich, and the night-hawk, and the sea-mew, and the hawk after its kind, and the little owl, and the cormorant, and the great owl, and the horned owl, and the pelican, and the vulture, and the stork, the heron after its kind, and the hoopoe, and the bat." Dt **14** 12–18 gives the glede in addition.

Each of these birds is treated in order in this work. There are two reasons why Moses pronounced them an abomination for food. Either they had rank, offensive, tough flesh, or they were connected with religious superstition. The eagle, gier-eagle, ospray, kite, glede, falcon, raven, night-hawk, sea-mew, hawk, little owl, cormorant, great owl, horned owl, pelican and vulture were offensive because they were birds of prey or ate carrion or fish until their flesh partook of the odor of their food. Young ostriches have sweet, tender flesh and the eggs are edible also. In putting these birds among the abominations Moses must have been thinking of grown specimens. (Ostriches live to a remarkable age and on account of the distances they cover, and their speed in locomotion, their muscles become almost as hard as bone.) There is a trace of his early Egyp training when he placed the stork and the heron on this list. These birds, and the crane as well, abounded in all countries known at that time and were used for food according to the superstitions of different nations. These three were closely related to the ibis which was sacred in Egypt and it is probable that they were protected by Moses for this reason, since they were eaten by other nations at that time and cranes are used for food today by natives of our southeastern coast states and are to be found in the markets of our western coast. The veneration for the stork that exists throughout the civilized world today had its origin in Pal. Noting the devotion of mated pairs and their tender care for the young the Hebrews named the bird *ḥăṣīdhāh,* which means kindness. Carried down the history of ages with additions by other nations, this undoubtedly accounts for the story now universal, that the stork delivers newly-born children to their homes; so the bird is loved and protected. One ancient Rom writer, Cornelius Nepos, recorded that in his time both crane and storks were eaten; storks were liked the better. Later, Pliny wrote that no one would touch a stork, but everyone was fond of crane. In Thessaly it was a capital crime to kill a stork. This change from regarding the stork as a delicacy to its protection by a death penalty merely indicates the hold the characteristics of the bird had taken on people as it became better known, and also the spread of the regard in which it was held throughout Pal. The hoopoe (q.v.) was offensive to Moses on account of extremely filthy nesting habits, but was considered a great delicacy when captured in migration by residents of southern Europe. See also Abomination; Birds, Unclean.

Gene Stratton-Porter

ABOMINATION OF DESOLATION, des-o-lā'shun: The Heb root for abomination is שָׁקַץ, *shāḳaç,* "to be filthy," "to loathe," "to abhor," from which is derived שֶׁקֶץ or שִׁקּוּץ, *shiḳḳuç,* or *shiḳḳūç,* "filthy," esp. "idolatrous." This word is used to describe specific forms of idolatrous worship that were specially abhorrent, as of the Ammonites (**1** K **11** 5.7); of the Moabites (1 K **11** 7; 2 K **23** 13). When Daniel undertook to specify an abomination so surpassingly disgusting to the sense of morality and decency, and so aggressive against everything that was godly as to drive all from its presence and leave its abode desolate, he chose this as the strongest among the several synonyms, adding the qualification "that maketh desolate" (Dnl **11** 31; **12** 11), LXX βδέλυγμα ἐρημώσεως, *bdél-ug-ma er-ē-mō-se-ōs*. The same noun, though in the plural, occurs in Dt **29** 17; 2 K **23** 24; Isa **66** 3; Jer **4** 1; **7** 30; **13** 27; **32** 34; Ezk **20** 7.8.30; Dnl **9** 27; Hos **9** 10; Zec **9** 7. The NT equivalent of the noun is βδέλυγμα, *bdél-ug-ma* = "detestable," i.e. (specially) "idolatrous." Alluding to Daniel, Christ spoke of the "abomination of desolation" (Mt **24** 15; Mk **13** 14).

Since the invasion of the Assyrians and Chaldaeans, the Jewish people, both of the Northern and of the Southern kingdom, had been without political independence. From the Chaldaeans the rulership of Judaea had been transferred to the Persians, and from the Persians, after an interval of 200 years, to Alexander the Great. From the beginning of the Pers sovereignty, the Jews had been permitted to organize anew their religious and political commonwealth, thus establishing a state under the rulership of priests, for the high priest was not only the highest functionary of the cult, but also the chief magistrate in so far as these prerogatives were not exercised by the king of the conquering nation. Ezra had given a new significance to the *tōrāh* by having it read to the whole congregation of Israel and by his vigorous enforcement of the law of separation from the Gentiles. His emphasis of the law introduced the period of legalism and finical interpretation of the letter which called forth some of the bitterest invectives of our Saviour. Specialists of the law known as "scribes" devoted themselves to its study and subtle interpretation, and the pious beheld the highest moral accomplishment in the extremely conscientious observance of every precept. But in opposition to this class, there were those who, influenced by the Hellenistic culture, introduced by the conquests of Alexander the Great, were inclined to a more "liberal" policy. Thus two opposing parties were developed: the Hellenistic, and the party of the Pious, or the Chasidim, *ḥăṣīdhīm* (Hasidaeans, 1 Macc **2** 42; **7** 13), who held fast to the strict ideal of the scribes. The former gradually came into ascendency. Judaea was rapidly becoming Hellenistic in all phases of its political, social and religious life, and the "Pious" were dwindling to a small minority sect. This was the situation when Antiochus Epiphanes set out to suppress the last vestige of the Jewish cult by the application of brute force.

1. The Historical Background

Antiochus IV, son of Antiochus the Great, became the successor of his brother, Seleucus IV, who had been murdered by his minister, Heliodorus, as king of Syria (175–164 BC). He was by nature a despot; eccentric and unreliable; sometimes a spendthrift in his liberality, fraternizing in an affected manner with those of lower station; sometimes cruel and tyrannical, as witness his aggressions against Judaea. Polybius (**26** 10) tells us that his eccentric ideas caused some to speak of him as a man of pure motive and humble character, while others hinted at insanity. The epithet Epiphanes is an abbreviation of *theós epiphanḗs*, which is the designation given himself by Antiochus on his coins, and means "the god who appears or reveals himself." Egyp writers translate the inscription, "God which comes forth," namely, like the burning sun, Horos, on the horizon, thus identifying the king with the triumphal, appearing god. When Antiochus Epiphanes arose to the throne, Onias III, as high priest, was the leader of the old orthodox party in Judaea; the head of the Hellenists was his own brother Jesus, or, as he preferred to designate himself, Jason, this being the Gr form of his name and indicating the trend of his mind. Jason promised the king large sums of money for the transfer of the office of high priest from his brother to himself and the privilege of erecting a gymnasium and a temple to Phallus, and for the granting of the privilege "to enroll the inhabitants of Jerusalem as citizens of Antioch." Antiochus gladly agreed to everything. Onias was removed, Jason became high priest, and henceforth the process of Hellenizing Judaea was pushed energetically. The Jewish cult was not attacked, but the "legal institutions were set aside, and illegal practices were introduced" (2 Macc **4** 11). A gymnasium was erected outside the castle; the youth of Jerusalem exercised themselves in the gymnastic art of the Greeks, and even priests left their services at the altar to take part in the contest of the palaestra. The disregard of Jewish custom went so far that many artificially removed the traces of circumcision from their bodies, and with characteristic liberality, Jason even sent a contribution to the sacrifices in honor of Heracles on the occasion of the quadrennial festivities in Tyre.

2. Antiochus Epiphanes

Under these conditions it is not surprising that Antiochus should have had both the inclination and the courage to undertake the total eradication of the Jewish religion and the establishment of Gr polytheism in its stead. The observance of all Jewish laws, especially those relating to the Sabbath and to circumcision, were forbidden under pain of death. The Jewish cult was set aside, and in all cities of Judaea, sacrifices must be brought to the pagan deities. Representatives of the crown everywhere enforced the edict. Once a month a search was instituted, and whoever had secreted a copy of the Law or had observed the rite of circumcision was condemned to death. In Jerusalem on the 15th of Chislev of the year 145 *aet Sel*, i.e. in December 168 BC, a pagan altar was built on the Great Altar of Burnt Sacrifices, and on the 25th of Chislev, sacrifice was brought on this altar for the first time (1 Macc **1** 54.59). This evidently was the "abomination of desolation." The sacrifice, according to 2 Macc was brought to the Olympian Zeus, to whom the temple of Jerusalem had been dedicated. At the feast of Dionysus, the Jews were obliged to march in the Bacchanalian procession, crowned with laurel leaves. Christ applies the phrase to what was to take place at the advance of the Romans against Jerusalem. They who would behold the "abomination of desolation" standing in the holy place, He bids flee to the mountains, which probably refers to the advance of the Rom army into the city and temple, carrying standards which bore images of the Rom gods and were the objects of pagan worship.

3. The Suppression of the Jewish Cult

Frank E. Hirsch

ABOUND, a-bound′, **ABUNDANCE,** a-bun′dans, **ABUNDANT,** a-bun′dant, **-LY,** a-bun′dant-li: These words represent in the EV a considerable variety of different words in the Heb and Gr original. In the OT they most frequently stand for some form of the stem *rābh*, signifying "to cast together," "to increase." In Prov **8** 24 the primary idea is "to be heavy" (root *kābhadh*); in Dt **33** 19 and Job **22** 11 it is "to overflow" (*shāpha'*); in Job **36** 31 it is "to plait together," "to augment," "to multiply" (*makhbīr* from *kābhar*); in Isa **47** 9 it is "strength" (*'oçmāh*); in 1 K **18** 41 it is "tumult," "crowd" (*hāmōn*); in Eccl **5** 12 it is "to fill to satiety" (RV "fulness"); in Isa **15** 7 it is "excellence" (*yithrāh*) and in **66** 11 "a full breast" (*zīz*); in Jer **33** 6 it is "copiousness" (*'ăthereth* from *'āthar*). In several passages (e.g. Ezk **16** 49; Ps **105** 30; Isa **56** 12) RV gives other and better renderings than AV. In the NT *perissós*, *perisseúō*, *perisseía*, etc, are the usual words for "abundant," "abound," "abundance," etc (the adj. signifies "exceeding some number or measure"). A slight formal difference of conception may be noted in *pleonázō*, which suggests that the abundance has resulted from augmentation. In Rom **5** 20 the two words stand in the closest connection: 'Where sin abounded [by its increase] grace abounded more exceedingly [was rich beyond measure].' In Mk **12** 44; Lk **21** 4; 2 Cor **8** 20; **12** 7; Rev **18** 3 RV gives improved renderings instead of "abundance," and in Titus **3** 6 and 2 Pet **1** 11 instead of "abundantly."

J. R. Van Pelt

ABOUT, a-bout′: The use of this word as prep., in the sense of "around," is confined to the OT. In the NT, generally an adverb, for Gr ὡς, *hōs* or "*hōsei.*" RV adopts it in several idiomatic tr^s of *méllō,* referring to what is about to be, i.e. on the point of occurring, or immediately impending, amending AV, in Acts **5** 35; **27** 2; Rev **12** 4, etc.

ABRAHAM, ā′bra-ham:

I. Name
  1. Various Forms
  2. Etymology
  3. Association
II. Kindred
III. Career
  1. Period of Wandering
  2. Period of Residence at Hebron
  3. Period of Residence in the Negeb
IV. Conditions of Life
  1. Economic Conditions
  2. Social Conditions
  3. Political Conditions
  4. Cultural Conditions
V. Character
  1. Religious Beliefs
  2. Morality
  3. Personal Traits
VI. Significance in the History of Religion
  1. In the OT
  2. In the NT
  3. In Jewish Tradition
  4. In the Koran
VII. Interpretations of the Story Other Than Historical
  1. The Allegorical Interpretation
  2. The Personification Theory
  3. The Mythical Theory
  4. The "Saga" Theory

I. Name.—In the OT, when applied to the patriarch, the name appears as אַבְרָם, *'abhrām,* up to Gen **17** 5; thereafter always as

1. Various Forms

אַבְרָהָם, *'abhrāhām.* Two other persons are named אֲבִירָם, *'ăbhīrām.* The identity of this name with *'abhrām* cannot be doubted in view of the variation between *'ăbhīnēr* and *'abhnēr, 'ăbhīshālōm* and *'abhshālōm,* etc. A. also appears in the list at Karnak of places conquered by Sheshonk I: *'ꜣbrm* (no. 72) represents אברם, with which Spiegelberg (*Aegypt. Randglossen zum AT,* 14) proposes to connect the preceding name (no. 71) *pꜣ ḥkrꜣ*, so that the whole would read "the field of Abram." Outside of Palestine this name (*Abirāmu*) has come to light just where from the Biblical tradition we should expect to find it, viz., in Babylonia (e.g. in a contract of the reign of Apil-Sin, second predecessor of Hammurabi; also for the aunt (!) of Esarhaddon 680–669 BC). Ungnad has recently found it, among documents from Dilbat dating from the Hammurabi dynasty, in the forms *A-ba-am-ra-ma, A-ba-am-ra-am,* as well as *A-ba-ra-ma.*

Until this latest discovery of the apparently full, historical form of the Bab equivalent, the best that could be done with the etymology

2. Etymology

was to make the first constituent "father of" (construct *-i* rather than suffix *-i*), and the second constituent "Ram," a proper name or an abbreviation of a name. (Yet observe above its use in Assyria for a woman; cf Abishag; Abigail). Some were inclined rather to concede that the second element was a mystery, like the second element in the majority of names beginning with *'ābh* and *'āḥ,* "father" and "brother." But the full cuneiform writing of the name, with the case-ending *am,* indicates that the noun "father" is in the accusative, governed by the verb which furnishes the second component, and that this verb therefore is probably *rāmu* (=Heb רָחַם, *rāḥam*) "to love," etc; so that the name would mean something like "he loves the [his] father." (So Ungnad, also Ranke in Gressmann's art. "Sage und Geschichte in den Patriarchenerzählungen," *ZATW* [1910], 3.) Analogy proves that this is in the Bab fashion of the period, and that judging from the various writings of this and similar names, its pronunciation was not far from *'abh-rām.*

While the name is thus not "Hebrew" in origin, it made itself thoroughly at home among the Hebrews, and to their ears conveyed

3. Association

associations quite different from its etymological signification. "Popular etymology" here as so often doubtless led the Hebrew to hear in *'abh-rām,* "exalted father," a designation consonant with the patriarch's national and religious significance. In the form *'abh-rāhām* his ear caught the echo of some root (perhaps *r-h-m;* cf Arab. *ruhām,* "multitude") still more suggestive of the patriarch's extensive progeny, the reason ("for") that accompanies the change of name Gen **17** 5 being intended only as a verbal echo of the sense in the sound. This longer and commoner form is possibly a dialectical variation of the shorter form, a variation for which there are analogies in comparative Sem grammar. It is, however, possible also that the two forms are different names, and that *'abh-rāhām* is etymologically, and not merely by association of sound, "father of a multitude" (as above). (Another theory, based on South-Arabic orthography, in Hommel, *Altisraelitische Ueberlieferung,* 177.)

II. Kindred.—Gen **11** 27, which introduces A., contains the heading, "These are the generations of Terah." All the story of A. is contained within the section of Gen so entitled. Through Terah A.'s ancestry is traced back to Shem, and he is thus related to Mesopotamian and Arabian families that belonged to the "Semitic" race. He is further connected with this race geographically by his birthplace, which is given as *'ūr-kasdīm* (see Ur), and by the place of his pre-Canaanitish residence, Haran in the Aramaean region. The purely Sem ancestry of his descendants through Isaac is indicated by his marriage with his own half-sister (Gen **20** 12), and still further emphasized by the choice for his daughter-in-law of Rebekah, descended from both of his brothers, Nahor and Haran (Gen **11** 29; **22** 22 f). Both the beginning and the end of the residence in Haran are left chronologically undetermined, for the new beginning of the narrative at Gen **12** 1 is not intended by the writer to indicate chronological sequence, though it has been so understood, e.g. by Stephen (Acts **7** 4). All that is definite in point of time is that an Aramaean period of residence intervened between the Bab origin and the Palestinian career of A. It is left to a comparison of the Bib. data with one another and with the data of archaeology, to fix the opening of A.'s career in Pal not far from the middle of the 20th cent. BC.

III. Career.—Briefly summed up, that career was as follows. A., endowed with Jeh's promise of limitless blessing, leaves Haran with

1. Period of Wandering

Lot his nephew and all their establishment, and enters Canaan. Successive stages of the slow journey southward are indicated by the mention of Shechem, Bethel and the Negeb (South-country). Driven by famine into Egypt, A. finds hospitable reception, though at the price of his wife's honor, whom the Pharaoh treats in a manner characteristic of an Egyp monarch. (Gressmann, op. cit., quotes from Meyer, *Geschichte des Alterthums,* I², 142, the passage from a magic formula in the pyramid of Unas, a Pharaoh of the Fifth Dynasty: "Then he [viz. the Pharaoh] takes away the wives from their husbands whither he will, if desire seize his heart.") Retracing

WELL OF ABRAHAM AT BEERSHEBA

the path to Canaan with an augmented train, at Bethel A. and Lot find it necessary to part company. Lot and his dependents choose for residence the great Jordan Depression; A. follows the backbone of the land southward to Hebron, where he settles, not in the city, but before its gates "by the great trees" (LXX sing., "oak") of Mamre.

2. Period of Residence at Hebron

Affiliation between A. and the local Amoritish chieftains is strengthened by a brief campaign, in which all unite their available forces for the rescue of Lot from an Elamite king and his confederates from Babylonia. The pursuit leads them as far as the Lebanon region. On the return they are met by Melchizedek, king of Salem, priest of *'ēl 'elyōn,* and blessed by him in his priestly capacity, which A. recognizes by presenting him with a tithe of the spoils. A.'s anxiety for a son to be the bearer of the divine promises conferred upon a "seed" yet unborn should have been relieved by the solemn renewal thereof in a formal covenant, with precise specifications of God's gracious purpose. But human desire cannot wait upon divine wisdom, and the Egyp woman Hagar bears to A. a son, Ishmael, whose existence from its inception proves a source of moral evil within the patriarchal household. The sign of circumcision and the change of names are given in confirmation of the covenant still unrealized, together with specification of the time and the person that should begin its realization. The theophany that symbolized outwardly this climax of the Divine favor serves also for an intercessory colloquy, in which A. is granted the deliverance of Lot in the impending overthrow of Sodom. Lot and his family, saved thus by human fidelity and Divine clemency, exhibit in the moral traits shown in their escape and subsequent life the degeneration naturally to be expected from their corrupt environment. Moabites and Ammonites are traced in their origin to these cousins of Jacob and Esau.

3. Period of Residence in the Negeb

Removal to the South-country did not mean permanent residence in a single spot, but rather a succession of more or less temporary resting-places. The first of these was in the district of Gerar, with whose king, Abimelech, A. and his wife had an experience similar to the earlier one with the Pharaoh. The birth of Isaac was followed by the expulsion of Ishmael and his mother, and the sealing of peaceful relations with the neighbors by covenant at Beersheba. Even the birth of Isaac, however, did not end the discipline of A.'s faith in the promise, for a Divine command to sacrifice the life of this son was accepted *bona fide,* and only the sudden interposition of a Divine prohibition prevented its obedient execution. The death of Sarah became the occasion for A.'s acquisition of the first permanent holding of Pal soil, the nucleus of his promised inheritance, and at the same time suggested the probable approach of his own death. This thought led to immediate provision for a future seed to inherit through Isaac, a provision realized in Isaac's marriage with Rebekah, granddaughter of A.'s brother Nahor and of Milcah the sister of Lot. But a numerous progeny unassociated with the promise grew up in A.'s household, children of Keturah, a woman who appears to have had the rank of wife after Sarah's death, and of other women unnamed, who were his concubines. Though this last period was passed in the Negeb, A. was interred at Hebron, in his purchased possession, the spot with which Sem tradition has continued to associate him to this day.

IV. Conditions of Life.—The life of A. in its outward features may be considered under the following topics: economic, social, political and cultural conditions.

1. Economic Conditions

A.'s manner of life may best be described by the adjective "semi-nomadic," and illustrated by the somewhat similar conditions prevailing today in those border-communities of the East that fringe the Syrian and Arabian deserts. Residence is in tents, wealth consists of flocks, herds and slaves, and there is no ownership of ground, only at most a proprietorship in well or tomb. All this in common with the nomad. But there is a relative, or rather, intermittent fixity of habitation, unlike the pure Bedawi, a limited amount of agriculture, and finally a sense of divergence from the Ishmael type—all of which tend to assimilate the semi-nomadic A. to the fixed Canaanitish population about him. As might naturally be expected, such a condition is an unstable equilibrium, which tends, in the family of A. as in the history of all border-tribes of the desert, to settle back one way or the other, now into the city-life of Lot, now into the desert-life of Ishmael.

2. Social Conditions

The head of a family, under these conditions, becomes at the same time the chief of a tribe, that live together under patriarchal rule though they by no means share without exception the tie of kinship. The family relations depicted in Gen conform to and are illuminated by the social features of CH. (See K. D. Macmillan, art. "Marriage among the Early Babylonians and Hebrews," *Princeton Theol. Review,* April, 1908.) There is one legal wife, Sarah, who, because persistently childless, obtains the coveted offspring by giving her own maid to A. for that purpose (cf CH, §§ 144, 146). The son thus borne, Ishmael, is A.'s legal son and heir. When Isaac is later borne by Sarah, the elder son is disinherited by divine command (Gen **21** 10–12) against A.'s wish which represented the prevailing law and custom (CH, §§ 168 f). The "maid-servants" mentioned in the inventories of A.'s wealth (Gen **12** 16; **24** 35) doubtless furnished the "concubines" mentioned in Gen **25** 6 as having borne sons to him. Both mothers and children were slaves, but had the right to freedom, though not to inheritance, on the death of the father (CH, § 171). After Sarah's death another woman seems to have succeeded to the position of legal wife, though if so the sons she bore were disinherited like Ishmael (Gen **25** 5). In addition to the children so begotten by A. the "men of his house" (Gen **17** 27) consisted of two classes, the "home-born" slaves (Gen **14** 14; **17** 12 f.23.27) and the "purchased" slaves (ib). The extent of the patriarchal tribe may be surmised from the number (318) of men among them capable of bearing arms, near the beginning of A.'s career, yet after his separation from Lot, and recruited seemingly from the "home-born" class exclusively (Gen **14** 14). Over this entire establishment A. ruled with a power more, rather than less, absolute than that exhibited in detail in the CH: more absolute, because A. was independent of any permanent superior authority, and so combined in his own person the powers of the Bab *paterfamilias* and of the Can city-king. Social relations outside of the family-tribe may best be considered under the next heading.

3. Political Conditions

It is natural that the chieftain of so considerable an organism should appear an attractive ally and a formidable foe to any of the smaller political units of his environment. That Canaan was at the time composed of just such inconsiderable units, viz. city-states with petty kings, and scattered fragments of older populations, is abundantly clear from the Biblical tradition and verified from other sources. Egypt was the only great power with which A. came into political contact after leaving the East. In the section of Gen which describes this contact with the Pharaoh A. is suitably represented as playing no political rôle, but as profiting by his stay in Egypt only through an incidental social relation: when this terminates he is promptly ejected. The rôle of conqueror of Chedorlaomer, the Elamite invader, would be quite out of keeping with A.'s political status elsewhere, if we were compelled by the narrative in Gen **14** to suppose a pitched battle between the forces of A. and those of the united Bab armies. What that chapter requires is in fact no more than a midnight surprise, by A.'s band (including the forces of confederate chieftains), of a rear-guard or baggage-train of the Babylonians inadequately manned and picketed. ("Slaughter" is quite too strong a rendering of the original *hakkōth*, "smiting," ver 17.) Respect shown A. by the kings of Salem (ver 18), of Sodom (ver 21) and of Gerar (Gen **20** 14–16) was no more than might be expected from their relative degrees of political importance, although a moral precedence, assumed in the tradition, may well have contributed to this respect.

4. Cultural Conditions

Recent archaeological research has revolutionized our conception of the degree of culture which A. could have possessed and therefore presumably did possess. The high plane which literature had attained in both Babylonia and Egypt by 2000 BC is sufficient witness to the opportunities open to the man of birth and wealth in that day for the interchange of lofty thought. And, without having recourse to A.'s youth in Babylonia, we may assert even for the scenes of A.'s maturer life the presence of the same culture, on the basis of a variety of facts, the testimony of which converges in this point, that Canaan in the second millennium BC was at the center of the intellectual life of the East and cannot have failed to afford, to such of its inhabitants as chose to avail themselves of it, every opportunity for enjoying the fruits of others' culture and for recording the substance of their own thoughts, emotions and activities.

V. Character.—A.'s inward life may be considered under the rubrics of religion, ethics and personal traits.

1. Religious Beliefs

The religion of A. centered in his faith in one God, who, because believed by him to be possessor of heaven and earth (Gen **14** 22; **24** 3), sovereign judge of the nations (**15** 14) of all the earth (**18** 25), disposer of the forces of Nature (**18** 14; **19** 24; **20** 17 f), exalted (**14** 22) and eternal (**21** 33), was for A. at least the only God. So far as the Biblical tradition goes, A.'s monotheism was not aggressive (otherwise in later Jewish tradition), and it is theoretically possible to attribute to him a merely "monarchical" or "henotheistic" type of monotheism, which would admit the coexistence with his deity, say, of the "gods which [his] fathers served" (Josh **24** 14), or the identity with his deity of the supreme god of some Canaanite neighbor (Gen **14** 18). Yet this distinction of types of monotheism does not really belong to the sphere of religion as such, but rather to that of speculative philosophical thought. As religion, monotheism is just monotheism, and it asserts itself in corollaries drawn by the intellect only so far as the scope of the monotheist's intellectual life applies it. For A. Jeh not only was alone God; He was also his personal God in a closeness of fellowship (Gen **24** 40; **48** 15) that has made him for three religions the type of the pious man (2 Ch **20** 7; Isa **41** 8; Jas **2** 23; note the Arab. name of Hebron is *El-Khalīl*, i.e. the friend [viz. of God]). To Jeh A. attributed the moral attributes of justice (Gen **18** 25), righteousness (**18** 19), faithfulness (**24** 27), wisdom (**20** 6), goodness (**19** 19), mercy (**20** 6). These qualities were expected of men, and their contraries in men were punished by Jeh (Gen **18** 19; **20** 11). He manifested Himself in dreams (Gen **20** 3), visions (**15** 1) and theophanies (**18** 1), including the voice or apparition of the Divine *mal'ākh* or messenger ("angel") (Gen **16** 7; **22** 11). On man's part, in addition to obedience to Jeh's moral requirements and special commands, the expression of his religious nature was expected in sacrifice. This bringing of offerings to the deity was diligently practiced by A., as indicated by the mention of his erection of an altar at each successive residence. Alongside of this act of sacrifice there is sometimes mention of a "calling upon the name" of Jeh (cf 1 K **18** 24; Ps **116** 13 f). This publication of his faith, doubtless in the presence of Canaanites, had its counterpart also in the public regard in which he was held as a "prophet" or spokesman for God (Gen **20** 7). His mediation showed itself also in intercessory prayer (Gen **17** 20 for Ishmael; **18** 23–32; cf **19** 29 for Lot; **20** 17 for Abimelech), which was but a phase of his general practice of prayer. The usual accompaniment of sacrifice, a professional priesthood, does not occur in A.'s family, yet he recognizes priestly prerogative in the person of Melchizedek, priest-king of Salem (Gen **14** 20). Religious sanction of course surrounds the taking of oaths (Gen **14** 22; **24** 3) and the sealing of covenants (**21** 23). Other customs associated with religion are circumcision (Gen **17** 10–14), given to A. as the sign of the perpetual covenant; tithing (**14** 20), recognized as the priest's due; and child-sacrifice (**22** 2.12), enjoined upon A. only to be expressly forbidden, approved for its spirit but interdicted in its practice.

2. Morality

As already indicated, the ethical attributes of God were regarded by A. as the ethical requirement of man. This in theory. In the sphere of applied ethics and casuistry A.'s practice, at least, fell short of this ideal, even in the few incidents of his life preserved to us. It is clear that these lapses from virtue were offensive to the moral sense of A.'s biographer, but we are left in the dark as to A.'s sense of moral obliquity. (The "dust and ashes" of Gen **18** 27 has no moral implication.) The demands of candor and honor are not satisfactorily met, certainly not in the matter of Sarah's relationship to him (Gen **12** 11–13; **20** 2; cf 11–13), perhaps not in the matter of Isaac's intended sacrifice (**22** 5.8). To impose our own monogamous standard of marriage upon the patriarch would be unfair, in view of the different standard of his age and land. It is to his credit that no such scandals are recorded in his life and family as blacken the record of Lot (Gen **19** 30–38), Reuben (**35** 22) and Judah (**38** 15–18). Similarly, A.'s story shows only regard for life and property, both in respecting the rights of others and in expecting the same from them—the antipodes of Ishmael's character (Gen **16** 12).

3. Personal Traits

Outside the bounds of strictly ethical requirement, A.'s personality displayed certain characteristics that not only mark him out distinctly among the figures of history, but do him great credit as a singularly symmetrical and attractive character. Of his trust and reverence enough has been said under the head of religion. But this love that is "the fulfilling of the law," manifested in such piety toward God, showed itself toward men in exceptional generosity (Gen **13** 9; **14** 23; **23** 9.13; **24** 10; **25** 6), fidelity (**14** 14.24; **17** 18; **18** 23–32; **19** 27; **21** 11; **23** 2), hospitality (**18** 2–8; **21** 8) and compassion (**16** 6 and **21** 14 when rightly understood; **18** 23–32). A solid self-respect (Gen **14** 23; **16** 6; **21** 25; **23** 9.13.16; **24** 4) and real courage (**14** 14–16) were, however, marred by the cowardice that sacrificed Sarah to purchase personal safety where he had reason to regard life as insecure (**20** 11).

VI. Significance in the History of Religion.—A. is a significant figure throughout the Bible, and plays an important rôle in extra-Biblical Jewish tradition and in the Mohammedan religion.

1. In the OT

It is naturally as progenitor of the people of Israel, "the seed of A.," as they are often termed, that A. stands out most prominently in the OT books. Sometimes the contrast between him as an individual and his numerous progeny serves to point a lesson (Isa **51** 2; Ezk **33** 24; perhaps Mal **2** 10; cf 15). "The God of A." serves as a designation of Jeh from the time of Isaac to the latest period; it is by this title that Moses identifies the God who has sent him with the ancestral deity of the children of Israel (Ex **3** 15). Men remembered in those later times that this God appeared to A. in theophany (Ex **6** 3), and, when he was still among his people who worshipped other gods (Josh **24** 3) chose him (Neh **9** 7), led him, redeemed him (Isa **29** 22) and made him the recipient of those special blessings (Mic **7** 20) which were pledged by covenant and oath (so every larger historical book, also the historical Ps **105** [ver 9]), notably the inheritance of the land of Canaan (Dt **6** 10). Nor was A.'s religious personality forgotten by his posterity: he was remembered by them as God's friend (2 Ch **20** 7; Isa **41** 8), His servant, the very recollection of whom by God would offset the horror with which the sins of his descendants inspired Jeh (Dt **9** 27).

2. In the NT

When we pass to the NT we are astonished at the wealth and variety of allusion to A. As in the OT, his position of ancestor lends him much of his significance, not only as ancestor of Israel (Acts **13** 26), but specifically as ancestor, now of the Levitical priesthood (He **7** 5), now of the Messiah (Mt **1** 1), now, by the peculiarly Christian doctrine of the unity of believers in Christ, of Christian believers (Gal **3** 16.29). All that A. the ancestor received through Divine election, by the covenant made with him, is inherited by his seed and passes under the collective names of the promise (Rom **4** 13), the blessing (Gal **3** 14), mercy (Lk **1** 54), the oath (Lk **1** 73), the covenant (Acts **3** 25). The way in which A. responded to this peculiar goodness of God makes him the type of the Christian believer. Though so far in the past that he was used as a measure of antiquity (Jn **8** 58), he is declared to have "seen" Messiah's "day" (Jn **8** 56). It is his faith in the Divine promise, which, just because it was for him peculiarly unsupported by any evidence of the senses, becomes the type of the faith that leads to justification (Rom **4** 3), and therefore in this sense again he is the "father" of Christians, as believers (Rom **4** 11). For that promise to A. was, after all, a "preaching beforehand" of the Christian gospel, in that it embraced "all the families of the earth" (Gal **3** 8). Of this exalted honor, James reminds us, A. proved himself worthy, not by an inoperative faith, but by "works" that evidenced his righteousness (Jas **2** 21; cf Jn **8** 39). The obedience that faith wrought in him is what is especially praised by the author of Hebrews (He **11** 8.17). In accordance with this high estimate of the patriarch's piety, we read of his eternal felicity, not only in the current conceptions of the Jews (parable, Lk **16**), but also in the express assertion of Our Lord (Mt **8** 11; Lk **13** 28). Incidental historical allusions to the events of A.'s life are frequent in the NT, but do not add anything to this estimate of his religious significance.

3. In Jewish Tradition

Outside the Scriptures we have abundant evidence of the way that A. was regarded by his posterity in the Jewish nation. The oldest of these witnesses, Ecclesiasticus, contains none of the accretions of the later A.-legends. Its praise of A. is confined to the same three great facts that appealed to the canonical writers, viz. his glory as Israel's ancestor, his election to be recipient of the covenant, and his piety (including perhaps a tinge of "nomism") even under severe testing (Ecclus **44** 19–21). The improbable and often unworthy and even grotesque features of A.'s career and character in the later rabbinical *midrashim* are of no religious significance, beyond the evidence they afford of the way A.'s unique position and piety were cherished by the Jews.

4. In the Koran

To Mohammed A. is of importance in several ways. He is mentioned in no less than 188 verses of the Koran, more than any other character except Moses. He is one of the series of prophets sent by God. He is the common ancestor of the Arab and the Jew. He plays the same rôle of religious reformer over against his idolatrous kinsmen as Mohammed himself played. He builds the first pure temple for God's worship (at Mecca!). As in the Bible so in the Koran A. is the recipient of the Divine covenant for himself and for his posterity, and exhibits in his character the appropriate virtues of one so highly favored: faith, righteousness, purity of heart, gratitude, fidelity, compassion. He receives marked tokens of the Divine favor in the shape of deliverance, guidance, visions, angelic messengers (no theophanies for Mohammed!), miracles, assurance of resurrection and entrance into paradise. He is called "Imam of the peoples" (**2** 118).

VII. Interpretations of the Story of A. Other than the Historical.—There are writers in both ancient and modern times who have, from various standpoints, interpreted the person and career of A. otherwise than as what it purports to be, viz. the real experiences of a human person named A. These various views may be classified according to the motive or impulse which they believe to have led to the creation of this story in the mind of its author or authors.

1. The Allegorical Interpretation

Philo's tract on A. bears as alternative titles, "On the Life of the Wise Man Made Perfect by Instruction, or, On the Unwritten Law." A.'s life is not for him a history that serves to illustrate these things, but an allegory by which these things are embodied. Paul's use of the Sarah-Hagar episode in Gal **4** 21–31 belongs to this type of exposition (cf *allēgoroúmena*, ver 24), of which there are also a few other instances in his epistles; yet to infer from this that Paul shared Philo's general attitude toward the patriarchal narrative would be unwarranted, since his use of this method is incidental, exceptional, and merely confirmatory of points already established by sound reason. "Luther compares it to a painting which decorates a house already built" (Schaff, "Galatians," *Excursus*).

As to Philo A. is the personification of a certain type of humanity, so to some modern writers he is the personification of the Heb nation or of a tribe belonging to the Heb group. This view, which is indeed very widely held with respect to the patriarchal figures in general, furnishes so many more difficulties in its specific application to A. than to the others, that it has been rejected in A.'s case even by some who have adopted it for figures like Isaac, Ishmael and Jacob. Thus Meyer (*Die Israeliten und ihre Nachbarstämme*, 250; cf also note on p. 251), speaking of his earlier opinion, acknowledges that, at the time when he "regarded the assertion of Stade as proved that Jacob and Isaac were tribes," even then he "still recognized A. as a mythical figure and originally a god." A similar differentiation of A. from the rest is true of most of the other adherents of the views about to be mentioned. Hence also Wellhausen says (*Prolegomena*[6], 317): "Only A. is certainly no name of a people, like Isaac and Lot; he is rather ambiguous anyway. We dare not of course on that account hold him in this connection as an historical personage; rather than that he might be a free creation of unconscious fiction. He is probably the youngest figure in this company and appears to have been only at a relatively late date put before his son Isaac."

2. The Personification Theory

3. The Mythical Theory

Urged popularly by Nöldeke (*Im neuen Reich* [1871], I, 508 ff) and taken up by other scholars, especially in the case of A., the view gained general currency among those who denied the historicity of Gen, that the patriarchs were old deities. From this relatively high estate, it was held, they had fallen to the plane of mere mortals (though with remnants of the hero or even demigod here and there visible) on which they appear in Gen. A new phase of this mythical theory has been developed in the elaboration by Winckler and others of their astral-theology of the Bab world, in which the worship of A. as the moon-god by the Semites of Pal plays a part. A.'s traditional origin connects him with Ur and Haran, leading centers of the moon-cult. Apart from this fact the arguments relied upon to establish this identification of A. with Sin may be judged by the following samples: "When further the consort of A. bears the name Sarah, and one of the women among his closest relations the name Milcah, this gives food for thought, since these names correspond precisely with the titles of the female deities worshipped at Haran alongside the moon-god Sin. Above all, however, the number 318, that appears in Gen **14** 14 in connection with the figure of A., is convincing; because this number, which surely has no historical value, can only be satisfactorily explained from the circle of ideas of the moon-religion, since in the lunar year of 354 days there are just 318 days on which the moon is visible—deducting 36 days, or three for each of the twelve months, on which the moon is invisible" (Baentsch, *Monotheismus*, 60 f). In spite of this assurance, however, nothing could exceed the scorn with which these combinations and conjectures of Winckler, A. Jeremias and others of this school are received by those who in fact differ from them with respect to A. in little save the answer to the question, *what* deity was A. (see e.g. Meyer, op. cit., 252 f, 256 f).

4. The "Saga" Theory

Gunkel (*Genesis*, Introduction), in insisting upon the resemblance of the patriarchal narrative to the "sagas" of other primitive peoples, draws attention both to the human traits of figures like A., and to the very early origin of the material embodied in our present book of Gen. First as stories orally circulated, then as stories committed to writing, and finally as a number of collections or groups of such stories formed into a cycle, the A.-narratives, like the Jacob- and the Joseph-narratives, grew through a long and complex literary history. Gressmann (op. cit., 9–34) amends Gunkel's results, in applying to them the principles of primitive literary development laid down by Professor Wundt in his *Völkerpsychologie*. He holds that the kernel of the A.-narratives is a series of fairy-stories, of international diffusion and unknown origin, which have been given "a local habitation and a name" by attaching to them the (*ex hypothesi*) then common name of A. (similarly Lot, etc) and associating them with the country nearest to the wilderness of Judaea, the home of their authors, viz. about Hebron and the Dead Sea. A high antiquity (1300–1100 BC) is asserted for these stories, their astonishing accuracy in details wherever they can be tested by extra-Biblical tradition is conceded, as also the probability that, "though many riddles still remain unsolved, yet many other traditions will be cleared up by new discoveries" of archaeology.

J. Oscar Boyd

ABRAHAM, BOOK OF. See Apocalyptic Literature.

ABRAHAM'S BOSOM, bŏŏz'um (**κόλπος 'Αβραάμ,** *kólpos Abraám;* **κόλποι 'Α**): **Figurative.** The expression occurs in Lk **16** 22.23, in the parable of the Rich Man and Lazarus, to denote the place of repose to which Lazarus was carried after his death. The fig. is suggested by the practice of the guest at a feast reclining on the breast of his neighbor. Thus John leaned on the breast of Jesus at supper (Jn **21** 20). The rabbis divided the state after death (Sheol) into a place for the righteous and a place for the wicked (see Eschatology of OT; Sheol); but it is doubtful whether the fig. of Jesus quite corresponds with this idea. "Abraham's bosom" is not spoken of as in "Hades," but rather as distinguished from it (Lk **16** 23)—a place of blessedness by itself. There Abraham receives, as at a feast, the truly faithful, and admits them to closest intimacy. It may be regarded as equivalent to the "Paradise" of Lk **23** 43. See Hades; Paradise.

James Orr

ABRAM, ā'bram. See Abraham.

ABRECH, ā'brek: Transliteration of the Heb אַבְרֵךְ, *'abhrēkh*, in Gen **41** 43 RVm, of which both the origin and meaning are uncertain. It was the salutation which the Egyptians addressed to Joseph, when he was made second to Pharaoh, and appeared in his official chariot.

(1) The explanations based upon Heb derivation are unsatisfactory, whether as AV "bow the knee," from בּרךְ, *bārakh* (hiph. imp.) or marginal "tender father," or "father of a king" of the Tg. The form as hiph. imp. instead of הַבְרֵךְ, *habhrēkh*, is indefensible, while the other two derivations are fanciful.

(2) The surmises of Egyptologists are almost without number, and none are conclusive. Skinner in *Comm. on Gen.* selects "attention!" after Spiegelberg, as best. *Speaker's Comm.* suggests "rejoice thou" from *ab-nek*. *BDB* gives preference to the Coptic *a-bor-k*, "prostrate thyself."

(3) The most satisfying || is the Assyr *abarakku*, meaning "grand vizier" or "friend of a king," as suggested by Fried. Delitzsch; for Bab laws and customs were dominant in western Asia, and the Hyksos, through whom such titles would have been carried, were ruling then (Kyle, *Moses and the Monuments*, 29).

Edward Mack

ABROAD, a-brôd: An idiomatic rendering of ἀφίκετο, *aphíketo* (lit. "arrived"), "come abroad" is used in Rom **16** 19 to indicate a report that has been most widely diffused (lit. "did reach unto all"). Similar idiomatic trs of AV have been replaced in RV by those more literal, as in Mk **4** 22; Lk **8** 17; Mk **6** 14; 1 Thess **1** 8. Used also in other idiomatic renderings, as "spread abroad" (*diaphēmízō*), Mk **1** 45; "noised abroad" (*dialaléō*), Lk **1** 65; "scattered abroad," Jn **11** 52; Acts **8** 1, etc; in all these cases for the pervasive meaning of the Gr preposition in composition. In Gen **15** 5, *ḥuç* means "outside." H. E. JACOBS

ABROAD, SCATTERED. See DISPERSION.

ABRONAH, a-brō'na, AV **Ebronah** (עַבְרֹנָה, *'abhrōnāh*): One of the stations of Israel in the wilderness on the march from Sinai to Kadesh—the station next before that at Ezion-geber on the eastern arm of the Red Sea (Nu **33** 34.35).

ABSALOM, ab'sa-lom (אַבְשָׁלוֹם, *'abhshālōm*, "father is peace," written also **Abishalom,** 1 K **15** 2.10):

1. A General Favorite

David's third son by Maacah, daughter of Talmai, king of Geshur, a small territory between Hermon and Bashan. Absalom was born at Hebron (2 S **3** 3), and moved at an early age, with the transfer of the capital, to Jerus, where he spent most of his life. He was a great favorite of his father and of the people as well. His charming manners, his personal beauty, his insinuating ways, together with his love of pomp and royal pretensions, captivated the hearts of the people from the beginning. He lived in great style, drove in a magnificent chariot and had fifty men run before him. Such magnificence produced the desired effect upon the hearts of the young aristocrats of the royal city (2 S **15** 1 ff).

2. In Exile

When Amnon, his half-brother, ravished his sister Tamar, and David shut his eyes to the grave crime and neglected to administer proper punishment, Absalom became justly enraged, and quietly nourished his anger, but after the lapse of two years carried out a successful plan to avenge his sister's wrongs. He made a great feast for the king's sons at Baal-hazor, to which, among others, Amnon came, only to meet his death at the hands of Absalom's servants (**13** 1 ff). To avoid punishment he now fled to the court of his maternal grandfather in Geshur, where he remained three years, or until David, his father, had relented and condoned the murderous act of his impetuous, plotting son. At the end of three years (**13** 38) we find Absalom once more in Jerus. It was, however, two years later before he was admitted to the royal presence (**14** 28).

3. Rebels against His Father

Absalom, again reinstated, lost no opportunity to regain lost prestige, and having his mind made up to succeed his father upon the throne, he forgot the son in the politician. Full of insinuations and rich in promises, especially to the disgruntled and to those having grievances, imaginary or real, it was but natural that he should have a following. His purpose was clear, namely, to alienate as many as possible from the king, and thus neutralize his influence in the selection of a successor, for he fully realized that the court party, under the influence of Bathsheba, was intent upon having Solomon as the next ruler. By much flattery Absalom stole the hearts of many men in Israel (**15** 6). How long a period elapsed between his return from Geshur and his open rebellion against his father David is a question which cannot be answered with any degree of certainty. Most authorities regard the forty years of **15** 7 as an error and following the Syr and some editions of the LXX, suggest four as the correct text. Whether forty or four, he obtained permission from the king to visit Hebron, the ancient capital, on pretence of paying a vow made by him while at Geshur in case of his safe return to Jerus. With two hundred men he repairs to Hebron. Previous to the feast spies had been sent throughout all the tribes of Israel to stir up the discontented and to assemble them under Absalom's flag at Hebron. Very large numbers obeyed the call, among them Ahithophel, one of David's shrewdest counselors (**15** 7 ff).

4. David's Flight

Reports of the conspiracy at Hebron soon reached the ears of David, who now became thoroughly frightened and lost no time in leaving Jerus. Under the protection of his most loyal bodyguard he fled to Gilead beyond Jordan. David was kindly received at Mahanaim, where he remained till after the death of his disloyal son. Zadok and Abiathar, two leading priests, were intent upon sharing the fortunes of David; they went so far as to carry the Ark of the Covenant with them out of Jerus (**15** 24). David, however, forced the priests and Levites to take it back to its place in the city and there remain as its guardians. This was a prudent stroke, for these two great priests in Jerus acted as intermediaries, and through their sons and some influential women kept up constant communications with David's army in Gilead (**15** 24 ff). Hushai, too, was sent back to Jerus, where he falsely professed allegiance to Absalom, who by this time had entered the royal city and had assumed control of the government (**15** 32 ff). Hushai, the priests and a few people less conspicuous performed their part well, for the counsel of Ahithophel, who advised immediate action and advance upon the king's forces, while everything was in a panic, was thwarted (**17** 1 ff); nay more, spies were constantly kept in contact with David's headquarters to inform the king of Absalom's plans (**17** 15 ff). This delay was fatal to the rebel son. Had he acted upon the shrewd counsel of Ahithophel, David's army might have been conquered at the outset.

5. Absalom's Death and Burial

When at length Absalom's forces under the generalship of Amasa (**17** 25) reached Gilead, ample time had been given to David to organize his army, which he divided into three divisions under the efficient command of three veteran generals: Joab, Abishai and Ittai (**18** 1 ff). A great battle was fought in the forests of Ephraim. Here the rebel army was utterly routed. No fewer than 20,000 were killed outright, and a still greater number becoming entangled in the thick forest, perished that day (**18** 7 f). Among the latter was Absalom himself, for while riding upon his mule, his head was caught in the boughs of a great oak or terebinth, probably in a forked branch. "He was taken up between heaven and earth; and the mule that was under him went on" (**18** 9). In this position he was found by a soldier who at once ran to inform Joab. The latter without a moment's hesitation, notwithstanding David's positive orders, thrust three darts into the heart of Absalom. To make his death certain and encouraged by the action of their general, ten of Joab's young men "compassed about and smote Absalom, and slew him" (**18** 15). He was buried in a great pit, close to the spot where he was killed. A great pile of stones was heaped over his body (**18** 17), in accordance with the custom of dishonoring rebels and great criminals by burying them under great piles of stone (Josh **7** 26; **8** 29). Thomson informs us that Syrian people to this day cast stones upon the graves of murderers and outlaws (*LB*, II, 61).

The death of Absalom was a source of great grief to the fond and aged father, who forgot the ruler and the king in the tender-hearted parent. His lament at the gate of Mahanaim, though very brief, is a classic, and expresses in tender language the feelings of parents for wayward children in all ages of the world (2 S **18** 33).

6. David's Lament

Little is known of Absalom's family life, but we read in **14** 27 that he had three sons and one daughter. From the language of **18** 18, it is inferred that the sons died at an early age.

Absalom's Tomb: As Absalom had no son to perpetuate his memory "he reared up for himself a pillar" or a monument in the King's dale, which according to Josephus was two furlongs from Jerusalem (*Ant*, VII, x, 3). Nothing is known

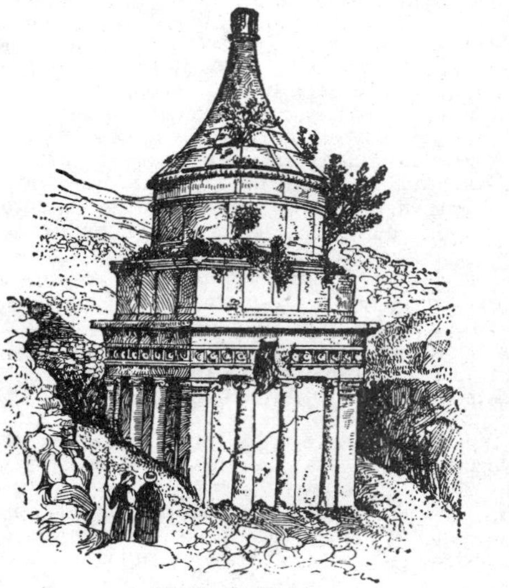

Absalom's Tomb.

with certainty about this monument. One of the several tombs on the east side of the Kidron passes under the name of Absalom's tomb. This fine piece of masonry with its graceful cupola and Ionic pillars must be of comparatively recent origin, probably not earlier than the Rom period.

W. W. Davies

ABSALOM (Apoc) (B, **'Αβεσσάλωμος,** *Abessálōmos* and *Abessalôm;* A, *Absálōmos;* AV **Absalon**):

(1) Father of Mattathias, a captain of the Jewish army (1 Macc **11** 70; *Ant*, XIII, v, 7).

(2) Father of Jonathan who was sent by Simon Maccabee to take possession of Joppa; perhaps identical with A (1) (1 Macc **13** 11; *Ant*, XIII, vi, 4).

(3) One of two envoys of the Jews, mentioned in a letter sent by Lysias to the Jewish nation (2 Macc **11** 17).

ABSALON, ab'sa-lon. See Absalom (Apoc).

ABSOLUTION, ab-so-lū'shun (tr of vbs. λύω, *lúō*, "loose," etc, and ἀφίημι, *aphíēmi*, "release," "give up," etc): Not a Bib., but an ecclesiastical term, used to designate the official act described in Mt **16** 19: "Whatsoever thou shalt loose on earth, shall be loosed in heaven," and Mt **18** 18: "What things soever ye shall loose," etc, and interpreted by Jn **20** 23: "Whose soever sins ye forgive, they are forgiven unto them" (see Keys, Power of). The Roman church regards this as the act of a properly ordained priest, by which, in the sacrament of Penance, he frees from sin one who has confessed and made promise of satisfaction. Protestants regard the promise as given not to any order within the church, but to the congregation of believers, exercising its prerogative through the Christian ministry, as its ordinary executive. They differ as to whether the act be only declarative or collative. Luther regarded it as both declarative and collative, since the Word always brings that which it offers. The absolution differs from the general promise of the gospel by individualizing the promise. What the gospel, as read and preached, declares in general, the absolution applies personally. See also Forgiveness.

H. E. Jacobs

ABSTINENCE, abs'ti-nens: Abstinence as a form of asceticism reaches back into remote antiquity, and is found among most ancient peoples. It may be defined as a self-discipline which consists in the habitual renunciation, in whole or in part, of the enjoyments of the flesh, with a view to the cultivation of the life of the spirit. In its extremest forms, it bids men to stifle and suppress their physical wants, rather than to subordinate them in the interest of a higher end or purpose, the underlying idea being that the body is the foe of the spirit, and that the progressive extirpation of the natural desires and inclinations by means of fasting, celibacy, voluntary poverty, etc, is "the way of perfection."

This article will be concerned chiefly with abstinence from food, as dealt with in the Bible. (For other aspects of the subject, see Temperance; Self-denial; Clean; Uncleanness; Meat, etc). Thus limited, abstinence may be either public or private, partial or entire.

Only one such fast is spoken of as having been instituted and commanded by the Law of Moses, that of the Day of Atonement. This is called "the Fast" in Acts **27** 9 (cf *Ant*, XIV, iv, 3; Philo, *Vit Mos*, II, 4; Schürer, *HJP*, I, i, 322).

1. Public Fasts

Four *annual* fasts were later observed by the Jews in commemoration of the dark days of Jerus—the day of the beginning of Nebuchadrezzar's siege in the tenth month, the day of the capture of the city in the fourth month, the day of its destruction in the fifth month and the day of Gedaliah's murder in the seventh month. These are all referred to in Zec **8** 19. See Fasts.

It might reasonably be thought that such solemn anniversaries, once instituted, would have been kept up with sincerity by the Jews, at least for many years. But Isaiah illustrates how soon even the most outraged feelings of piety or patriotism may grow cold and formal. 'Wherefore have we fasted and thou seest not?' the exiled Jews cry in their captivity. 'We have humbled our souls, and thou takest no notice.' Jeh's swift answer follows: 'Because your fasting is a mere form! Behold, in the day of your fast ye find your own pleasure and oppress all your laborers' (cf Isa **58** 3; *Expositor's Bible*, ad loc.). That is to say, so formal has your fasting grown that your ordinary selfish, cruel life goes on just the same. Then Jeh makes inquest: "Is such the fast that I have chosen? the day for a man to afflict his soul? Is not this the fast that I have chosen: to loose the bonds of wickedness, to undo the bands of the yoke, and to let the oppressed go free, and that ye break every yoke? Is it not to deal thy bread to the hungry, and that thou bring the poor that are cast out to thy house? Then shalt thou call, and Jeh will answer; thou shalt cry, and he will say, Here I am" (vs 5-9). The passage, as George Adam Smith says, fills the earliest, if not the highest place in the glorious succession of Scriptures exalting practical love, to which belong Isa **61**; Mt **25**; 1 Cor **13**. The high import is that in God's view character grows rich and life joyful, not by fasts or formal observances, but by acts of unselfish service inspired by a heart of love.

These fasts later fell into utter disuse, but they were revived after the destruction of Jerus by the Romans.

Occasional public fasts were proclaimed in Israel, as among other peoples, in seasons of drought or public calamity. It appears according to Jewish accounts, that it was customary to hold them on the second and fifth days of the week, for the reason that Moses was believed to have gone up to Mt. Sinai on the fifth day of the week (Thursday) and to have come down on the second (Monday) (cf *Did*, **8**; *Apos Const*, VIII, 23).

2. Private Fasts

In addition to these public solemnities, individuals were in the habit of imposing extra fasts upon themselves (e.g. Jth **8** 6; Lk **2** 37); and there were some among the Pharisees who fasted on the second and fifth days of the week all the year round (Lk **18** 12; see Lightfoot, ad loc.).

Tacitus alludes to the "frequent fasts" of the Jews (*History*, V, 4), and Jos tells of the spread of fasting among the Gentiles (*CAp*, II, 40; cf Tertullian, *ad Nat*, i.13). There is abundant evidence that many religious teachers laid down rules concerning fasting for their disciples (cf Mk **2** 18; Mt **9** 14; Lk **5** 33).

3. Degrees of Strictness in Abstinence

Individuals and sects differ greatly in the degrees of strictness with which they observe fasts. In some fasts among the Jews abstinence from food and drink was observed simply from sunrise to sunset, and washing and anointing were permitted. In others of a stricter sort, the fast lasted from one sunset till the stars appeared after the next, and, not only food and drink, but washing, anointing, and every kind of agreeable activity and even salutations, were prohibited (Schürer, II, ii, 119; Edersheim, *Life and Times*, I, 663). Such fasting was generally practised in the most austere and ostentatious manner, and, among the Pharisees, formed a part of their most pretentious externalism. On this point the testimony of Mt **6** 16 is confirmed by the Mish.

4. Abstinence among Different Kinds of Ascetics

There arose among the Jews various kinds of ascetics and they may be roughly divided into three classes.

(1) *The Essenes*.—These lived together in colonies, shared all things in common and practised voluntary poverty. The stricter among them also eschewed marriage. They were indifferent, Philo says, alike to money, pleasure, and worldly position. They ate no animal flesh, drank no wine, and used no oil for anointing. The objects of sense were to them "unholy," and to gratify the natural craving was "sin." They do not seem to come distinctly into view in the NT. See ESSENES.

(2) *The hermit ascetics*.—These fled away from human society with its temptations and allurements into the wilderness, and lived there a life of rigid self-discipline. Jos (*Vita*, 2) gives us a notable example of this class in Banus, who "lived in the desert, clothed himself with the leaves of trees, ate nothing save the natural produce of the soil, and bathed day and night in cold water for purity's sake." John the Baptist was a hermit of an entirely different type. He also dwelt in the desert, wore a rough garment of camel's hair and subsisted on "locusts and wild honey." But his asceticism was rather an incident of his environment and vocation than an end in itself (see "Asceticism," *DCG*). In the fragments of his sermons which are preserved in the Gospels there is no trace of any exhortation to ascetic exercises, though John's disciples practised fasting (Mk **2** 18).

(3) *The moderate ascetics*.—There were many pious Jews, men and women, who practised asceticism of a less formal kind. The asceticism of the Pharisees was of a kind which naturally resulted from their legal and ceremonial conception of religion. It expressed itself chiefly, as we have seen, in ostentatious fasting and externalism. But there were not a few humble, devout souls in Israel who, like Anna, the prophetess, served God "with fastings and supplications night and day" (Lk **2** 37), seeking by a true self-discipline to draw near unto God (cf Acts **13** 2.3; **14** 23; 1 Tim **5** 5).

5. Abstinence as Viewed in the Talmud

Some of the rabbis roundly condemned abstinence, or asceticism in any form, as a principle of life. "Why must the Nazirite bring a sin offering at the end of his term?" (Nu **6** 13.14) asks Eliezer ha-Kappār (*Siphrā'*, ad loc.); and gives answer, "Because he sinned against his own person by his vow of abstaining from wine"; and he concludes, "Whoever undergoes fasting or other penances for no special reason commits a wrong." "Man in the life to come will have to account for every enjoyment offered him that was refused without sufficient cause" (Rabh, in *Yer. Kid.*, **4**). In Maimonides (*Hā-Yādh ha-Ḥăzāḳāh*, *Dē'ōth* **3** 1) the monastic principle of abstinence in regard to marriage, eating meat, or drinking wine, or in regard to any other personal enjoyment or comfort, is condemned as "contrary to the spirit of Judaism," and "the golden middle-way of moderation" is advocated.

But, on the other hand, abstinence is often considered by the rabbis meritorious and praiseworthy as a voluntary means of self-discipline. "I partook of a Nazirite meal only once," says Simon the Just, "when I met with a handsome youth from the south who had taken a vow. When I asked the reason he said: 'I saw the Evil Spirit pursue me as I beheld my face reflected in water, and I swore that these long curls shall be cut off and offered as a sacrifice to Jeh'; whereupon I kissed him upon his forehead and blessed him, saying, May there be many Nazirites like thee in Israel!" (*Nāzīr*, **4***b*). "Be holy" was accordingly interpreted, "Exercise abstinence in order to arrive at purity and holiness" (*'Ab. Zārāh*, **20***b*; Ṣiphrā', *Ḳᵉdhōshīm*). "Abstain from everything evil and from whatever is like unto it" is a rule found in the Talm (*Ḥullin*, **44***b*), as also in the *Did* (**3** 1)—a saying evidently based on Job **31** 1, "Abstain from the lusts of the flesh and the world." The Mosaic laws concerning diet are all said by Rabh to be "for the purification of Israel" (Lev *R.* **13**)—"to train the Jew in self-discipline."

6. The Attitude of Jesus to Fasting

The question of crowning interest and significance to us is, What attitude did Jesus take toward fasting, or asceticism? The answer is to be sought in the light, first of His practice, and, secondly, of His teaching.

(1) *His practice*.—Jesus has even been accounted "the Founder and Example of the ascetic life" (Clem. Alex., *Strom*, III, 6). By questionable emphasis upon His "forty days' " fast, His abstinence from marriage and His voluntary poverty, some have reached the conclusion that complete renunciation of the things of the present was "the way of perfection according to the Saviour."

A fuller and more appreciative study of Jesus' life and spirit must bring us to a different conclusion. Certainly His mode of life is sharply differentiated in the Gospels, not only from that of the

Pharisees, but also from that of John the Baptist. Indeed, He exhibited nothing of the asceticism of those illustrious Christian saints, St. Bernard and St. John of the Cross, or even of St. Francis, who "of all ascetics approached most nearly to the spirit of the Master." Jesus did not flee from the world, or eschew the amenities of social life. He contributed to the joyousness of a marriage feast, accepted the hospitality of rich and poor, permitted a vase of very precious ointment to be broken and poured upon His feet, welcomed the society of women, showed tender love to children, and clearly enjoyed the domestic life of the home in Bethany. There is no evidence that He imposed upon Himself any unnecessary austerities. The "forty days'" fast (not mentioned in Mk, the oldest authority) is not an exception to this rule, as it was rather a necessity imposed by His situation in the wilderness than a self-imposed observance of a law of fasting (cf Christ's words concerning John the Baptist: "John came neither eating nor drinking"; see the article on "Asceticism," *DCG*). At any rate, He is not here an example of the traditional asceticism. He stands forth throughout the Gospels "as the living type and embodiment of self-denial," yet the marks of the ascetic are not found in Him. His mode of life was, indeed, so unascetic as to bring upon Him the reproach of being "a gluttonous man and a winebibber" (Mt **11** 19; Lk **7** 34).

(2) *His teaching.*—Beyond question, it was, from first to last, "instinct with the spirit of self-denial." "If any man will come after me, let him deny himself," is an ever-recurring refrain of His teaching. "Seek ye first the kingdom of God," is ever His categorical imperative (Mt **6** 33 AV; Lk **12** 31). This is to Him the *summum bonum*—all desires and strivings which have not this as their goal must be suppressed or sacrificed (cf Mt **13** 44–46; **19** 21; Mk **10** 21; Lk **9** 59.60; **14** 26 with Mt **5** 29.30; Mk **9** 43–47; Mt **16** 24 f; Mk **8** 34 f; Lk **9** 23 f; and **14** 33). In short, if any man find that the gratification of any desire of the higher or lower self will impede or distract him in the performance of his duties as a subject of the Kingdom, he must forego such gratification, if he would be a disciple of Christ. "If it cause thee to stumble," is always the condition, implied or expressed, which justifies abstinence from any particular good.

According to the record, Jesus alluded to fasting only twice in His teaching. In Mt **6** 16–18, where voluntary fasting is presupposed as a religious exercise of His disciples, He warns them against making it the occasion of a parade of piety: "Thou, when thou fastest, anoint thy head, and wash thy face; that thou be not seen of men to fast, but of thy Father who is in secret." In short, He sanctions fasting only as a genuine expression of a devout and contrite frame of mind.

In Mt **9** 14–17 (‖Mk **2** 18–22; Lk **5** 33–39) in reply to the question of the disciples of John and of the Pharisees, Jesus refuses to enjoin fasting. He says fasting, as a recognized sign of mourning, would be inconsistent with the joy which "the sons of the bridechamber" naturally feel while "the bridegroom is with them." But, he adds, suggesting the true reason for fasting, that the days of bereavement will come, and then the outward expression of sorrow will be appropriate. Here, as in the Sermon on the Mount, Jesus sanctions fasting, without enjoining it, as a form through which emotion may spontaneously seek expression. His teaching on the subject may be summarized in the one word, *subordination* (*DCG*).

To the *form* of fasting He attaches little importance, as is seen in the succeeding parables of the Old Garment and the Old Wine-skins. It will not do, He says, to graft the new liberty of the gospel on the body of old observances, and, yet more, to try to force the new system of life into the ancient molds. The new piety must manifest itself in new forms of its own making (Mt **9** 16.17; Mk **2** 21.22; Lk **5** 36.38). Yet Jesus shows sympathy with the prejudices of the conservatives who cling to the customs of their fathers: "No man having drunk old wine desireth new; for he saith, The old is good." But to the question, Was Jesus an ascetic? we are bound to reply, No.

"Asceticism," as Harnack says, "has no place in the gospel at all; what it asks is that we should struggle against Mammon, against care, against selfishness; what it demands and disengages is love—the love that serves and is self-sacrificing; and whoever encumbers Jesus' message with any other kind of asceticism fails to understand it" (*What is Christianity?* 88).

On the whole, unquestionably, the practice and teachings of the apostles and early Christians were in harmony with the example and teaching of the Master. But a tendency, partly innate, partly transmitted from Jewish legalism, and partly pagan, showed itself among their successors and gave rise to the *Vita Religiosa* and Dualism which found their fullest expression in Monasticism.

7. The Practice and Teaching of the Apostles

It is worthy of note that the alleged words of Jesus: 'But this kind goeth not out save by prayer and fasting' (Mk **9** 29; Mt **17** 21 AV), are corruptions of the text. (Cf Tob **12** 8; Sir **34** 26; Lk **2** 37). The Oxyrhynchus fragment (disc. 1897) contains a *logion* with the words *légei Iēsoús, eán mḗ nēsteúēte tón kósmon, ou mḗ heúrēte tḗn basileían toú theoú:* "Jesus saith, Except ye fast to the world, ye shall in no wise find the Kingdom of God," but the "fasting" here is clearly metaphorical.

Literature.—Bingham, *Antiquities;* W. Bright, *Some Aspects of Primitive Church Life* (1898); J. O. Hannay, *The Spirit and Origin of Christian Monasticism* (1902), and *The Wisdom of the Desert* (1904); Thomas à Kempis, *Imitation of Christ;* Migne, *Dictionnaire d' Ascétisme*, and *Enc Theol.*, XLV, XLVI, 45, 46; *Jew Enc*, and Bible Dictionaries ad loc.

Geo. B. Eager

ABUBUS, a-bū'bus (Ἄβουβος, *Áboubos*): The father of Ptolemy, who deceitfully slew Simon Maccabee and his sons at Dok near Jericho (1 Macc **16** 11.15).

ABUNDANCE, a-bun'dans, **ABUNDANT**, a-bun'dant. See Abound.

ABUSE, a-būz': "To dishonor," "to make mock of," "to insult," etc. (1) Tr[d] in the OT from עָלַל, *'ālal*, "to do harm," "to defile" (Jgs **19** 25), "to make mock of" (1 S **31** 4). (2) Tr[d] in the NT from ἀρσενοκοίτης, *arsenokoítēs*, lit. "one who lies with a male," "a sodomite" (1 Cor **6** 9; 1 Tim **1** 10; AV "for them that defile themselves with mankind"). (3) In AV 1 Cor **7** 31 "as not abusing it," from καταχράομαι, *katachráomai*, "to abuse," i.e. misuse; RV "using it to the full," also 1 Cor **9** 18. See Use.

ABYSS, a-bis', **THE** (ἡ ἄβυσσος, *hē ábussos*): In classical Gr the word is always an adj., and is used (1) lit. "very deep," "bottomless"; (2) fig. "unfathomable," "boundless." "Abyss" does not occur in the AV but the RV so transliterates ἄβυσσος in each case. The AV renders the Gr by "the deep" in two passages (Lk **8** 31; Rom **10** 7). In Rev the AV renders by "the bottomless pit" (**9** 1.2.11; **11** 7; **17** 8; **20** 1.3). In the LXX *abussos* is the rendering of the Heb word תְּהוֹם (*tehōm*). According to primitive Sem cosmogony the earth was supposed to rest on a vast body of water which was the source of all springs of water and rivers (Gen **1** 2; Dt **8** 7; Ps **24** 2; **136** 6). This subterranean ocean is sometimes described as "the water under the earth" (Ex **20** 4; Dt **5** 8). According to Job **41** 32 *tᵉhōm* is the home of the leviathan in which he ploughs his hoary path of foam. The LXX never uses *abussos* as a rendering of שְׁאוֹל, *shᵉ'ōl* (=*Sheol*= *Hades*) and probably *tᵉhōm* never meant the "abode of the dead" which was the ordinary meaning of *Sheol.* In Ps **71** 20 *tᵉhōm* is used **fig.**, and denotes "many and sore troubles" through which the psalmist has passed (cf Jon **2** 5). But in the NT the word *abussos* means the "abode of demons." In Lk **8** 31 the AV renders "into the deep" (Weymouth and *The Twentieth Century NT* ="into the bottomless pit"). The demons do not wish to be sent to their place of punishment before their destined time. Mk simply says "out of the country" (**5** 10). In Rom **10** 7 the word is equivalent to *Hades,* the abode of the dead. In Rev (where the AV renders invariably "the bottomless pit") *abussos* denotes the abode of evil spirits, but not the place of final punishment; it is therefore to be distinguished from the "lake of fire and brimstone" where the beast and the false prophet are, and into which the Devil is to be finally cast (**19** 20; **20** 10). See also Astronomy, III, 7. Thomas Lewis

ABYSSINIA, ab-i-sin'i-a. See Ethiopia.

ACACIA, a-kā'sha (שִׁטָּה, *shiṭṭāh,* the shittah tree of AV, Isa **41** 19, and עֲצֵי־שִׁטָּה, *'ăçē-shiṭṭāh,* acacia wood; shittah wood AV, Ex **25** 5.10.13; **26** 15.26; **27** 1.6; Dt **10** 3.): *Shiṭṭāh* (=*shinṭāh*) is equivalent to the Arab. *sant* which is now the name of the *Acacia Nilotica* (*NO, Leguminosae*), but no doubt the name once included other species of desert acacias. If one particular species is indicated in the OT it is probably the *Acacia Seyal*—the Arab. *Seyyāl*—which yields the well-known gum-arabic. This tree, which has finely bipinnate leaves and globular flowers, grows to a height of twenty feet or more, and its stem may sometimes reach two feet in thickness.

Shittim Wood—*Acacia Seyal.*

The tree often assumes a characteristic umbrella-like form. The wood is close-grained and is not readily attacked by insects. It would be well suited for such purposes as described, the construction of the ark of the covenant, the altar and boarding of the tabernacle. Even today these trees survive in considerable numbers around *'Ain Jidy* and in the valleys to the south. E. W. G. Masterman

ACATAN, ak'a-tan. See Akatan (Apoc).

ACCABA, ak'a-ba, ak-ā'ba (B, **'Ακκαβά,** *Akkabá;* A, **Γαβά,** *Gabá;* AV **Agaba**)=Hagab (Ezr **2** 46); see also Hagaba (Neh **7** 48): The descendants of A. (temple-servants) returned with Zerubbabel to Jerus (1 Esd **5** 30).

ACCAD, ak'ad, **ACCADIANS,** ak-ā'di-ans. See Babylonia.

ACCARON, ak'a-ron (**'Ακκαρών,** *Akkarōn*): Mentioned in 1 Macc **10** 89 AV; a town of the Philistines, known as Ekron (עֶקְרוֹן, *'ekrōn*) in OT, which King Alexander gave to Jonathan Maccabaeus as a reward for successful military service in western Pal. It is also mentioned in the days of the Crusades. See Ekron.

ACCEPT, ak-sept', **ACCEPTABLE,** ak-sep'ta-b'l, **ACCEPTATION,** ak-sep-tā'-shun: "To receive with favor," "to take pleasure in"; "well-pleasing"; "the act of receiving."

Accept, used (1) of sacrifice, "a. thy burnt-sacrifice" (דָּשֵׁן, *dāshēn,* "accept as fat," i.e. receive favorably; Ps **20** 3); (2) of persons, "Jeh a. Job" (Job **42** 9, נָשָׂא, *nāsā',* "to lift up," "take," "receive"); (3) of works, "a. the work of his hands" (Dt **33** 11 רָצָה, *rāçāh,* "to delight in"). In NT (1) of favors, "We a. . . . . with all thankfulness" (ἀποδέχομαι, *apodéchomai,* Acts **24** 3); (2) of personal appeal, "He a. our exhortation" (2 Cor **8** 17); (3) of God's impartiality (λαμβάνω, *lambánō,* "to take," "receive"); "accepteth not man's person" (Gal **2** 6).

Acceptable, used (1) of justice (בָּחַר, *bāḥar,* "choose, select"), "more a. . . . . than sacrifice" (Prov **21** 3); (2) of words (חֵפֶץ, *ḥēpheç,* "delight in," "sought . . . . a. words" (Eccl **12** 10); (3) of times (רָצוֹן, *rāçōn,* "delight," "approbation"; δεκτός, *dektós,* "receivable") "a. year of the Lord" (Isa **61** 2 [AV]; Lk **4** 19); (4) of spiritual sacrifice (εὐπρόσδεκτος, *euprósdektos,* "well received"), "a. to God" (1 Pet **2** 5); (5) of patient endurance (χάρις, *cháris,* "grace," "favor") "This is a. with God" (1 Pet **2** 20).

Acceptation, used twice to indicate the trustworthiness of the gospel of Christ's saving grace: "worthy of all a." (1 Tim **1** 15; **4** 9).

These words are full of the abundant grace of God and are rich in comfort to believers. That which makes man, in word, work and character, *acceptable* to God; and renders it possible for God to *accept* him, his service and sacrifice, is the fulness of the Divine mercy and grace and forgiveness. He "chose us" and made us, as adopted sons, the heirs of His grace "which he freely bestowed on us in the Beloved" (Eph **1** 6; cf AV). Dwight M. Pratt

ACCEPTANCE, ak-sep'-tans: A rendering of the Heb רְצוֹן, *rᵉçōn,* "delight," found only in Isa **60** 7. It pictures God's delight in His redeemed people in the Messianic era, when their gifts, in joyful and profuse abundance, "shall come up with acceptance on mine altar." With "accepted" and other kindred words it implies redeeming grace as the basis of Divine favor. It is the "living, holy sacrifice" that is "acceptable to God" (Rom **12** 1; cf Titus **3** 4-6).

ACCESS, ak'ses (**προσαγωγή,** *prosagōgḗ,* "a leading to or toward," "approach"): Thrice used in the NT to indicate the acceptable way of approach to God and of admission to His favor. Jesus said, "I am the way" (Jn **14** 6). His blood is the "new and living way" (He **10** 20). Only through Him have we "a. by faith into this grace wherein we stand" (Rom **5** 2); "Through him we both have a. by one Spirit unto the Father" (Eph **2** 18 AV); "in whom we have . . . . a. in confidence, through our faith in him" (Eph **3** 12).

The goal of redemption is life in God, "unto the Father." The means of redemption is the cross of Christ, "in whom we have our redemption through his blood" (Eph **1** 7). The agent in redemption is the Holy Spirit, "by one Spirit," "sealed with the Holy Spirit of promise" (Eph **1** 13). The human instrumentality, faith. The whole process of approach to, and abiding fellowship with, God is summed up in this brief sentence: Access to the Father, through Christ, by the Spirit, by faith.

DWIGHT M. PRATT

ACCO, ak'ō (עַכּוֹ, *'akkō;* **'Ακχώ,** *Akchō;* **"Ακη Πτολεμαΐς,** *Ákē Ptolemaïs;* Modern Arab. *'Akka,* Eng. Acre; AV **Accho**): A town on the Syrian coast a few miles north of Carmel, on a small promontory on the north side of a broad bay that lies between it and the modern town of Haifa. This bay furnishes the best anchorage for ships of any on this coast except that of St. George, at Beirût, and Alexandretta at the extreme north. As the situation commanded the approach from the sea to the rich plain of Esdraelon and also the coast route from the north, the city was regarded in ancient times of great importance and at various periods of history was the scene of severe struggles for its possession. It fell within the bounds assigned to the Israelites, particularly to the tribe of Asher, but they were never able to take it (Josh **19** 24-31; Jgs **1** 31). It was, like Tyre and Sidon, too strong for them to attack and it became indeed a fortress of unusual strength, so that it withstood many a siege, often baffling its assailants. In the period of the Crusades it was the most famous stronghold on the coast, and in very early times it was a place of importance and appears in the Am Tab as a possession of the Egyp kings. Its governor wrote to his suzerain professing loyalty when the northern towns were falling away (Am Tab 17 BM, 95 B). The Egyp suzerainty over the coast, which was established by Thothmes III about 1480 BC, was apparently lost in the 14th cent., as is indicated in Am Tab, but was regained under Seti I and his more famous son Rameses II in the 13th, to be again lost in the 12th when the Phoen towns seem to have established their independence. Sidon however surpassed her sisters in power and exercised a sort of hegemony over the Phoen towns, at least in the south, and A. was included in it (Rawl. *Phoenicia,* 407-8). But when Assyria came upon the scene it had to submit to this power, although it revolted whenever Assyria became weak, as appears from the mention of its subjugation by Sennacherib (ib 449), and by Asshur-bani-pal (ib 458). The latter "quieted" it by a wholesale massacre and then carried into captivity the remaining inhabitants. Upon the downfall of Assyria it passed, together with other Phoen towns, under the dominion of Babylon and then of Persia, but we have no records of its annals during that period; but it followed the fortunes of the more important cities, Tyre and Sidon. In the Seleucid period (BC 312-65) the town became of importance in the contests between the Seleucids and the Ptolemies. The latter occupied it during the struggles that succeeded the death of Alexander and made it their stronghold on the coast and changed the name to PTOLEMAIS, by which it was known in the Gr and Rom period as we see in the accounts of the Gr and Rom writers and in Jos, as well as in NT (1 Macc **5** 22; **10** 39; **12** 48; Acts **21** 7). The old name still continued locally and reasserted itself in later times. The Ptolemies held undisputed possession of the place for about 70 years but it was wrested from them by Antiochus III, of Syria, in 219 BC and went into the permanent possession of the Seleucids after the decisive victory of Antiochus over Scopas in that year, the result of which was the expulsion of the Ptolemies from Syria, Pal and Phoenicia (*Ant,* XII, iii, 3). In the dynastic struggles of the Seleucids it fell into the hands of Alexander Bala, who there received the hand of Cleopatra, the daughter of Ptolemy Philometor, as a pledge of alliance between them (ib XIII, iv, 1). Tigranes, king of Armenia, besieged it on his invasion of Syria, but was obliged to relinquish it on the approach of the Romans toward his own dominions (*BJ,* I, v, 3). Under the Romans Ptolemais became a colony and a metropolis, as is known from its coins, and was of importance, as is attested by Strabo. But the events that followed the conquests of the Saracens, leading to the Crusades, brought it into great prominence. It was captured by the Crusaders in 1110 AD, and remained in their hands until 1187, when it was taken from them by Saladin and its fortifications so strengthened as to render it almost impregnable. The importance of this fortress as a key to the Holy Land was considered so great by the Crusaders that they put forth every effort during two years to recapture it, but all in vain until the arrival of Richard Cœur de Lion and Philip Augustus with reinforcements, and it was only after the most strenuous efforts on their part that the place fell into their hands; but it cost them 100,000 men. The fortifications were repaired and it was afterward committed to the charge of the knights of St. John, by whom it was held for 100 years and received the name of St. Jean d'Acre. It was finally taken by the Saracens in 1291, being the last place held by the Crusaders in Pal.

It declined after this and fell into the hands of the Ottomans under Selim I in 1516, and remained mostly in ruins until the 18th cent., when it came into the possession of Jezzar Pasha, who usurped the authority over it and the neighboring district and became practically independent of the Sultan and defied his authority. In 1799 it was attacked by Napoleon but was bravely and successfully defended by the Turks with the help of the English fleet, and Napoleon had to abandon the siege after he had spent two months before it and gained a victory over the Turkish army at Tabor. It enjoyed a considerable degree of prosperity after this until 1831 when it was besieged by Ibrahim Pasha, of Egypt, and taken, but only after a siege of more than five months in which it suffered the destruction of its walls and many of its buildings. It continued in the hands of the Egyptians until 1840 when it was restored to the Ottomans by the English whose fleet nearly reduced it to ruins in the bombardment. It has recovered somewhat since then and is now a town of some 10,000 inhabitants and the seat of a Mutasarrifiyet, or subdivision of the Vilayet of Beirût. It contains one of the state prisons of the Vilayet, where long-term prisoners are incarcerated. Its former commerce has been almost wholly lost to the town of Haifa, on the south side of the bay, since the latter has a fairly good roadstead, while Acre has none, and the former being the terminus of the railway which connects with the interior and the Damascus-Mecca line, it has naturally supplanted Acre as a center of trade.

H. PORTER

ACCOMMODATION, a-kom-mo-dā'shun:

I. INTRODUCTORY
1. Three Uses of the Term
2. The Importance of the Subject

I. Introductory.—The term "accommodation" is used in three senses which demand careful discrimination and are worthy of separate treatment: (1) the use or application of a Scripture reference in a sense other than the obvious and literal one which lay in the mind and intent of the writer; (2) the theory that a passage, according to its original intent, may have more than one meaning or application; (3) the general principle of adaptation on the part of God in His self-revelation to man's mental and spiritual capacity.

1. Three Uses of the Term

Important issues are involved in the discussion of this subject in each of the three divisions thus naturally presented to us in the various uses of the term. These issues culminate in the supremely important principles which underlie the question of God's adaptation of His revelation to men.

2. The Importance of the Subject

II. Accommodated Application of Scripture Passages.—It is obvious that the nature of thought and of language is such as to constitute for all human writings, among which the Bible, as a document to be understood, must be placed, a science of interpretation with a definite body of laws which cannot be violated or set aside without confusion and error. This excludes the indeterminate and arbitrary exegesis of any passage. It must be interpreted with precision and in accordance with recognized laws of interpretation. The first and most fundamental of these laws is that a passage is to be interpreted in accordance with the intent of the writer in so far as that can be ascertained. The obvious, literal and original meaning always has the right of way. All arbitrary twisting of a passage in order to obtain from it new and remote meanings not justified by the context is unscientific and misleading.

1. Interpretation a Science

There is, however, a scientific and legitimate use of the principle of accommodation. For example, it is impossible to determine beforehand that a writer's specific application of a general principle is the only one of which it is capable. A bald and literal statement of fact may involve a general principle which is capable of broad and effective application in other spheres than that originally contemplated. It is perfectly legitimate to detach a writer's statement from its context of secondary and incidental detail and give it a harmonious setting of wider application. It will be seen from this that legitimate accommodation involves two things: (1) the acceptance of the author's primary and literal meaning; (2) the extension of that meaning through the establishment of a broader context identical in principle with the original one. In the article on Quotations in NT (q.v.) this use of the term accommodation, here treated in the most general terms, is dealt with in detail. See also Interpretation.

2. Scientific Accommodation

III. Double Reference in Scripture.—The second use of the term accommodation now emerges for discussion. Are we to infer the presence of double reference, or secondary meanings in Scripture? Here again we must distinguish between the legitimate and illegitimate application of a principle. While we wisely deprecate the tendency to look upon Scripture passages as cryptic utterances, we must also recognize that many Scripture references may have more than a single application.

We must recognize in the Scriptures the use of allegory, the peculiar quality of which, as a form of literature, is the double reference which it contains. To interpret the story of the Bramble-King (Jgs **9** 7–15) or the Parables of Our Lord without reference to the double meanings which they involve would be as false and arbitrary as any extreme of allegorizing. The double meaning is of the essence of the literary expression. This does not mean, of course, that the poetry of the Bible, even that of the Prophets and Apocalyptic writers, is to be looked upon as allegorical. On the contrary, only that writing, whether prose or poetry, is to be interpreted in any other than its natural and obvious sense, in connection with which we have definite indications of its allegorical character. Figures of speech and poetical expressions in general, though not intended to be taken literally because they belong to the poetical form, are not to be taken as having occult references and allegorical meanings. Dr. A. B. Davidson thus characterizes the prophetic style (*OT Prophecy*, 171; see whole chapter): "Prophecy is poetical, but it is not allegorical. The language of prophecy is real as opposed to allegorical, and poetical as opposed to real. When the prophets speak of natural objects or of lower creatures, they do not mean human things by them, or human beings, but these natural objects or creatures themselves. When Joel speaks of locusts, he means those creatures. When he speaks of the sun and moon and stars, he means those bodies." Allegory, therefore, which contains the double reference, in the sense of speaking of one thing while meaning another, is a definite and recognizable literary form with its own proper laws of interpretation. See Allegory.

1. Allegory in Scripture

There is progress in the understanding of Scripture. New reaches of truth are continually being brought to light. By legitimate and natural methods hidden meanings are being continually discovered.

2. Hidden Truths of Scripture

(1) It is a well-attested fact that apart from any supernatural factor a writer sometimes speaks more wisely than he knows. He is the partially unconscious agent for the expression of a great truth, not only for his own age, but for all time. It is not often given to such a really great writer or to his age to recognize all the implications of his thought. Depths of meaning hidden both from the original writer and from earlier interpreters may be disclosed by moving historical sidelights. The element of permanent value in great literature is due to the fact that the writer utters a greater truth than can exhaustively be known in any one era. It belongs to all time.

(2) The supernatural factor which has gone to the making of Scripture insures that no one man or group of men, that not all men together, can know it exhaustively. It partakes of the inexhaustibleness of God. It is certain, therefore, that it will keep pace with the general progress of man, exhibiting new phases of meaning as it moves along the stream of history. Improved exegetical apparatus and methods, enlarged apprehensions into widening vistas of thought and knowledge, increased insight under the tutelage of the Spirit in the growing Kingdom of God, will conspire to draw

up new meanings from the depths of Scripture. The thought of God in any given expression of truth can only be progressively and approximately known by human beings who begin in ignorance and must be taught what they know.

(3) The supernatural factor in revelation also implies a *twofold* thought in every important or fundamental statement of Scripture: the *thought of God* uttered through His Spirit to a man or his generation, and that *same thought* with reference to the coming ages and to the whole truth which is to be disclosed. Every separate item belonging to an organism of truth would naturally have a twofold reference: first, its significance alone and of itself; second, its significance with reference to the whole of which it is a part. As all great Scriptural truths are thus organically related, it follows that no one of them can be fully known apart from all the others. From which it follows also that in a process of gradual revelation where truths are given successively as men are able to receive them and where each successive truth prepares the way for others which are to follow, every earlier statement will have two ranges of meaning and application—that which is intrinsic and that which flows from its connection with the entire organism of unfolding truth which finally appears.

3. Prophecy and Its Fulfilment

(1) The principles thus far expressed carry us a certain way toward an answer to the most important question which arises under this division of the general topic: the relation between the OT and the NT through prophecy and its fulfilment. Four specific points of connection involving the principles of prophetic anticipation and historical realization in the career of Jesus are alleged by NT writers. They are of vital importance, inasmuch as these four groups of interpretations involve the most important elements of the OT and practically the entire NT interpretation of Jesus.

(2) (*a*) The promise made to Abraham (Gen **12** 1–3; cf **13** 14–18; **15** 1–6, etc) and repeated in substance at intervals during the history of Israel (see Ex **6** 7; Lev **26** 12; Dt **26** 17–19; **29** 12.13; 2 S **7**; 1 Ch **17**, etc) is interpreted as having reference to the distant future and as fulfilled in Christ (see Gal **3** for example of this interpretation, esp. ver 14; also QUOTATIONS IN NT).

(*b*) The OT system of sacrifices is looked upon as typical and symbolic, hence, predictive and realized in the death of Christ interpreted as atonement for sin (He **10**, etc).

(*c*) References in the OT to kings or a king of David's line whose advent and reign are spoken of are interpreted as definite predictions fulfilled in the advent and career of Jesus the Messiah (Ps **2, 16, 22, 110**; cf Lk **1** 69, etc).

(*d*) The prophetic conception of the servant of Jeh (Isa **42** 1 f; **44** 1 f; **52** 13—**53** 12; cf Acts **8** 32–35) is interpreted as being an anticipatory description of the character and work of Jesus centering in His vicarious sin-bearing death.

(3) With the details of interpretation as involved in the specific use of OT statements we are not concerned here (see "QUOTATIONS," etc) but only with the general principles which underlie all such uses of the OT. The problem is: Can we thus interpret any passage or group of passages in the OT without being guilty of what has been called "pedantic supernaturalism"; that is, of distorting Scripture by interpreting it without regard to its natural historical connections? Is the interpretation of the OT Messianically legitimate or illegitimate accommodation?

(*a*) It is a widely accepted canon of modern interpretation that the institutions of OT worship and the various messages of the prophets had an intrinsic contemporary significance.

(*b*) But this is not to say that its meaning and value are exhausted in that immediate contemporary application. Beyond question the prophet was a man with a message to his own age, but there is nothing incompatible, in that fact, with his having a message, the full significance of which reaches beyond his own age, even into the far distant future. It would serve to clear the air in this whole region if it were only understood that it is precisely upon its grasp of the future that the leverage of a great message for immediate moral uplift rests. The predictive element is a vital part of the contemporary value.

(*c*) The material given under the preceding analysis may be dealt with as a whole on the basis of a principle fundamental to the entire OT economy, namely: that each successive age in the history of Israel is dealt with on the basis of truth common to the entire movement of which the history of Israel is but a single phase. It is further to be remembered that relationship between the earlier and later parts of the Bible is one of organic and essential unity, both doctrinal and historical. By virtue of this fact the predictive element is an essential factor in the doctrines and institutions of the earlier dispensation *as originally constituted and delivered*, hence forming a part of its contemporary significance and value, both pointing to the future and preparing the way for it. In like manner, the element of fulfilment is an essential element of the later dispensation as the completed outcome of the movement begun long ages before. Prediction and fulfilment are essential factors in any unified movement begun, advanced and completed according to a single plan in successive periods of time. We have now but to apply this principle in general to the OT material already in hand to reach definite and satisfactory conclusions.

(4) (*a*) The promise made to Abraham was a living message addressed directly to him in the immediate circumstances of his life upon which the delivery and acceptance of the promise made a permanent impress; but it was of vaster proportions than could be realized within the compass of a single human life; for it included himself, his posterity, and all mankind in a single circle of promised blessing. So far as the patriarch was concerned the immediate, contemporary value of the promise lay in the fact that it concerned him not alone but in relationship to the future and to mankind. A prediction was thus imbedded in the very heart of the word of God which was the object of his faith—a prediction which served to ensphere his life in the plan of God for all mankind and to fasten his ambition to the service of that plan. The promise was predictive in its essence and in its contemporary meaning (see Beecher, *Prophets and Promise*, 213).

(*b*) So also it is with the Messianic King. The Kingdom as an institution in Israel is described from the beginning as the perpetual mediatorial reign of God upon earth (see Ex **19** 3–6; 2 S **7** 8–16, etc), and the King in whom the Kingdom centers is God's Son (2 S **7** 13.15) and earthly representative. In all this there is much that is immediately contemporaneous. The Kingdom and the Kingship are described in terms of the ideal and that ideal is used in every age as the ground of immediate appeal to loyalty and devotion on the part of the King. None the less the predictive element lies at the center of the representation. The very first recorded expression of the Messianic promise to David involves the prediction of unconditioned perpetuity to his house, and thus grasps the entire future. More than this, the characteristics, the functions, the dignities of the king are so described (Ps **102**; Isa **9** 6.7) as to make it clear that the conditions of the Kingship could be met only by an uniquely endowed person coming forth from God and exercising divine functions in a worldwide spiritual empire. Such a King being described and such a Kingdom being promised, the recipients of it, of necessity, were set to judge the present and scrutinize the future for its realization. The conception is, in its original meaning and expression, essentially predictive.

(*c*) Very closely allied with this conception of the Messianic King is the prophetic ideal of the Servant of Jeh. Looked at in its original context we at once discover that it is the ideal delineation of a mediatorial service to men in behalf of Jeh —which has a certain meaning of fulfilment in any person who exhibits the Divine character by teaching the truth and ministering to human need (for application of the term see Isa **49** 5.6.7; **50** 10; esp. **45** 1). But the service is described in such exalted terms, the devotion exacted by it is so high, that, in the application of the ideal as a test to the present and to the nation at large, the mind is inevitably thrown into the future and centered upon a supremely endowed individual to come, who is by preëminence the Servant of Jeh.

(*d*) The same principle may be applied with equal effectiveness to the matter of Israel's sacrificial system. In the last two instances this fact emerged: No truth and no institution can exhaustively be known until it has run a course in history. For example, the *ideas* embodied in the Messianic Kingship and the conception of the Servant of Jeh could be known only in the light of history. Only in view of the actual struggles and failures of successive kings and successive generations of the people to realize such ideals could their full significance be disclosed. Moreover, only by historic process of preparation could such ideals ultimately be realized. This is preeminently true of the OT sacrifices. It is clear that the NT conception of the significance of OT sacrifice in connection with the death of Christ is based upon the belief that the idea embodied in the original institution could be fulfilled only in the voluntary sacrifice of Christ (see He **10** 1–14). This view is justified by the facts. Dr. Davidson (op. cit., 239) holds that the predictive element in the OT sacrifices lay in their imperfection. This imperfection, while inherent, could be revealed only in experience. As they gradually deepened a sense of need which they could not satisfy, more and more clearly they pointed away from themselves to that transaction which alone could realize in fact what they express in symbol. A harmony such as obtained between OT sacrifice and the death of Christ could only be the result of design. It is all one movement, one fundamental operation; historically prefigured and prepared for by anticipation, and historically realized. OT sacrifice was instituted both to prefigure and to prepare the way for the sacrifice of Christ in the very process of fulfilling its natural historic function in the economy of Israel.

4. Conclusion

The total outcome of the discussion is this: the interpretation of these representative OT ideas and institutions as referring to Christ and anticipating His advent is no illegitimate use of the principle of accommodation. The future reference which takes in the entire historical process which culminates in Christ lies within the immediate and original application and constitutes an essential element of its contemporary value. The original statement is in its very nature predictive and is one in doctrinal principle and historic continuity with that which forms its fulfilment.

IV. Accommodation in Revelation.—(1) It is evident that God's revelation to men must be conveyed in comprehensible terms and adjusted to the nature of the human understanding. That is clearly not a revelation which does not reveal. A disclosure of God's character and ways to men involves the use and control of the human spirit in accordance with its constitution and laws. The doctrine of inspiration inseparable from that of revelation implies such a divine control of human faculties as to enable them, still freely working within their own normal sphere, to apprehend and interpret truth otherwise beyond their reach.

1. General Principles

(2) The Bible teaches that in the height and depth of His being God is unsearchable. His mind and the human mind are quantitatively incommensurable. Man cannot by searching find out God. His ways are not our ways and His thoughts are not our thoughts.

(3) But, on the other hand, the Bible affirms with equal emphasis the essential qualitative kinship of the divine and the human constitutions. God is spirit—man is spirit also. Man is made in the image of God and made to know God. These two principles together affirm the necessity and the possibility of revelation. Revelation, considered as an exceptional order of experience due to acts of God performed with the purpose of making Himself known in personal relationship with man, is necessary because man's finite nature needs guidance. Revelation is possible because man is capable of such guidance. The Bible affirms that God's thoughts are not our thoughts, but that they may become ours because God can utter them so that we can receive them.

(4) These two principles lead to a most important conclusion. In all discussions of the principle of accommodation it is to be remembered that the capacity of the human mind to *construct* does not measure its capacity to receive and appropriate. The human mind can be taught what it cannot independently discover. No teacher is limited by the capacity of his pupils to deal unaided with a subject of study. He is limited only by their capacity to follow him in his processes of thought and exposition. The determining factor in revelation, which is a true educative process, is the mind of God which stamps itself upon the kindred and plastic mind of man.

2. Accommodation a Feature of Progressive Revelation

(1) The beginnings of revelation. Since man's experience is organically conditioned he is under the law of growth. His entire mental and spiritual life is related to his part and lot in the kingdom of organisms. The very laws of his mind reveal themselves only upon occasion in experience. While it is true that his tendencies are innate, so that he is compelled to think and to feel in certain definite ways, yet it is true that he can neither think nor feel at all except as experience presents material for thought and applies stimulus to feeling. Man must live in order to learn. He must, therefore, learn gradually. This fact conditions all revelation. Since it must deal with men it must be progressive, and since it must be progressive it must necessarily involve, in its earlier stages, the principle of accommodation. In order to gain access to man's mind it must take him where he is and link itself with his natural aptitudes and native modes of thought. Since revelation involves the endeavor to form in the mind of man the idea of God in order that a right relationship with Him may be established, it enters both the

intellectual and moral life of the human race and must accommodate itself to the humble beginnings of early human experience. The chief problem of revelation seems to have been to bring these crude beginnings within the scope of a movement the aim and end of which is perfection. The application of the principle of accommodation to early human experience with a view to progress is accomplished by doing what at first thought seems to negate the very principle upon which the mental and moral life of man must permanently rest. (*a*) It involves the authoritative revelations of incomplete and merely tentative truths. (*b*) It involves also the positive enactment of rudimentary and imperfect morality.

In both these particulars Scripture has accommodated itself to crude early notions and placed the seal of authority upon principles which are outgrown and discarded within the limits of Scripture itself. But in so doing Scripture has saved the very interests it has seemed to imperil by virtue of two features of the human constitution which in themselves *lay hold upon perfection* and serve to bind together the crude beginnings and the mature achievements of the human race. These two principles are (*c*) the idea of truth; (*d*) the idea of obligation.

(2) It is mainly due to these two factors of human nature that any progress in truth and conduct is possible to men. What is true or right in matter of specific fact varies in the judgment of different individuals and of different ages. But the august and compelling twin convictions of truth and right, as absolute, eternal, authoritative, are present from the beginning of human history to the end of it. Scripture seizes upon the fact that these great ideas may be enforced through crude human conceptions and at very rudimentary stages of culture, and enforcing them by means of revelation and imperative law brings man to the test of truth and right and fosters his advance to larger conceptions and broader applications of both fundamental principles. Canon Mozley in discussing this principle of accommodation on its moral side, its necessity and its fruitfulness, says: "How can the law properly fulfil its object of correcting and improving the moral standard of men, unless it first maintains in obligation the standard which already exists? Those crudely delineated conceptions, which it tends ultimately to purify and raise, it must first impose" (*Ruling Ideas in Early Ages*, 183; cf Mt **5** 17 with 21.27.33).

3. The Limits of Revelation

Since the chief end of revelation is to form the mind of man with reference to the purpose and will of God to the end that man may enter into fellowship with God, the question arises as to how far revelation will be accommodated by the limitation of its sphere. How far does it seek to form the mind and how far does it leave the mind to its own laws and to historical educative forces? Four foundation principles seem to be sufficiently clear: (*a*) Revelation accepts and uses at every stage of its history such materials from the common stock of human ideas as are true and of permanent worth. The superstructure of revelation rests upon a foundation of universal and fundamental human convictions. It appeals continually to the rooted instincts and regulative ideas of the human soul deeply implanted as a preparation for revelation. (*b*) Regard is paid in Scripture to man's nature as free and responsible. He is a rational being who must be taught through persuasion; he is a moral being who must be controlled through his conscience and will. There must be, therefore, throughout the process of revelation an element of free, spontaneous, unforced life in and through which the supernatural factors work. (*c*) Revelation must have reference, even in its earliest phases of development, to the organism of truth as a whole. What is actually given at any time must contribute its quota to the ultimate summing up and completion of the entire process. (*d*) Revelation must guard against injurious errors which trench upon essential and vital matters. In short, the consistency and integrity of the movement through which truth is brought to disclosure must sacredly be guarded; while, at the same time, since it is God and man who are coming to know each other, revelation must be set in a broad environment of human life and entrusted to the processes of history. See REVELATION.

4. The Outcome of Revelation

It is now our task briefly to notice how in Scripture these interests are safeguarded. We must notice (*a*) the principle of accommodation in general. It has often been pointed out that in every book of the Bible the inimitable physiognomy of the writer and the age is preserved; that the Biblical language with reference to Nature is the language of phenomena; that its doctrines are stated vividly, tropically, concretely and in the forms of speech natural to the age in which they were uttered; that its historical documents are, for the most part, artless annals of the ancient oriental type; that it contains comparatively little information concerning Nature or man which anticipates scientific discovery or emancipates the religious man who accepts it as a guide from going to school to Nature and human experience for such information. All this, of course, without touching upon disputed points or debated questions of fact, involves, from the point of view of the Divine mind to which all things are known, and of the human mind to which certain facts of Nature hidden in antiquity have been disclosed, the principles of accommodation. Over against this we must set certain contrasting facts:

(*b*) The Scripture shows a constant tendency to transcend itself and to bring the teaching of the truth to a higher level. The simple, primitive ideas and rites of the patriarchal age are succeeded by the era of organized national life with its ideal of unity and the intensified sense of national calling and destiny under the leadership of God. The national idea of church and kingdom broadens out into the universal conception and world-wide mission of Christianity. The sacrificial symbolism of the OT gives way to the burning ethical realities of the Incarnate Life. The self-limitation of the Incarnation broadens out into the world-wide potencies of the era of the Spirit who uses the letter of Scripture as the instrument of His universal ministry. It is thus seen that by the progressive method through a cumulative process God has gradually transcended the limitation of His instruments while at the same time He has continuously broadened and deepened the Spirit of man to receive His self-disclosure.

(*c*) More than this, Scripture throughout is marked by a certain distinct and unmistakable quality of timelessness. It continually urges and suggests the infinite, the eternal, the unchangeable. It is part of the task of revelation to anticipate so as to guide progress. At every stage it keeps the minds of men on the stretch with a truth that they are not able at that stage easily to apprehend. The inexhaustible vastness and the hidden fulness of truth are everywhere implied. Prophets and Apostles are continually in travail with truths brought to their own ages from afar. The great fundamental verities of Scripture are stated with uncompromising fulness and finality. There is no accommodation to human weakness or error.

Its ideals, its standards, its conditions are absolute and inviolate.

Not only has Israel certain fundamental ideas which are peculiar to herself, but there has been an organizing spirit, an "unique spirit of inspiration" which has modified and transformed the materials held by her in common with her Sem kindred. Even her inherited ideas and institutions are transformed and infused with new meanings. We note the modification of Sem customs, as for example in blood revenge, by which savagery has been mitigated and evil associations eliminated. We note the paucity of mythological material. If the stories of Adam, Abraham, Isaac, Jacob, Samson were originally mythological they have ceased to be such in the Bible. They have been humanized and stripped of superhuman features. (See "Fable," *HGHL*, 220 ff.)

If we yield to the current hypothesis as to the Babylonian background of the narratives in Gen, we are still more profoundly impressed with that unique assimilative power, working in Israel, which has enabled the Biblical writers to eradicate the deep-seated polytheism of the Bab documents and to stamp upon them the inimitable features of their own high monotheism (see BABYLONIA). We note the reserve of Scripture, the constant restraint exercised upon the imagination, the chastened doctrinal sobriety in the Bible references to angels and demons, in its Apocalyptic imagery, in its Messianic promises, in its doctrines of rewards and punishments. In all these particulars the Bible stands unique by contrast, not merely with popular thought, but with the extra-canonical lit. of the Jewish people (see DEMONS, etc).

We come at this point upon a most central and difficult problem. It is, of course, alleged that Christ adopted the attitude of concurrence, which was also one of accommodation, in popular views concerning angels and demons, etc. It is disputed whether this goes back to the *essential accommodation* involved in the self-limiting of the Incarnation so that as man He should share the views of His contemporaries, or whether, with wider knowledge, He accommodated Himself for pedagogical purposes to erroneous views of the untaught people about Him (see *DCG*, art. "Accommodation"). The question is complicated by our ignorance of the facts. We cannot say that Jesus accommodated Himself to the ignorance of the populace unless we are ready to pronounce authoritatively upon the truth or falseness of the popular theory. It is not our province in this article to enter upon that discussion (see INCARNATION and KENOSIS). We can only point out that the reserve of the NT and the absence of all imaginative extravagance shows that if accommodation has been applied it is most strictly limited in its scope. In this it is in harmony with the entire method of Scripture, where the ignorance of men is regarded in the presentation of God's truth, while at the same time their growing minds are protected against the errors which would lead them astray from the direct path of progress into the whole truth reserved in the Divine counsel.

5. The Question as to Christ's Method

LITERATURE.—(*a*) For the first division of the subject consult standard works on Science of Interpretation and Homiletics sub loc.

(*b*) For second division, among others, Dr. A. B. Davidson, *OT Prophecy;* Dr. Willis J. Beecher, *Prophets and Promise.*

(*c*) For the third division, the most helpful single work is the one quoted: Mozley, *Ruling Ideas in Early Ages*, published by Longmans as "OT Lectures."

LOUIS MATTHEWS SWEET

ACCOMPLISH, a-kom′plish: Richly represented in the OT by seven Heb synonyms and in the NT by five Gr (AV); signifying in Heb (1) "to complete" (Lam **4** 11); (2) "to fulfil" (Dnl **9** 2); (3) "to execute" (1 K **5** 9); (4) "to set apart" i.e. "consecrate" (Lev **22** 21); (5) "to establish" (Jer **44** 25 AV); (6) "to have pleasure in" (Job **14** 6); (7) "to perfect" (Ps **64** 6); in Gr (1) "to finish" (Acts **21** 5); (2) "to bring to an end" (He **9** 6); (3) "to be fulfilled" (Lk **2** 6); (4) "to fill out" (Lk **9** 31); (5) "to complete" (Lk **12** 50).

ACCORD, a-kōrd′, **ACCORDING, ACCORDINGLY,** a-kōrd′ing-li: In OT פֶּה, *peh*, "mouth," "to fight with one accord" (Josh **9** 2). לְפִי, *l^ephī*, "according to the mouth of," "according to their families" (Gen **47** 12, "acc. to [the number of] their little ones" RVm). In Isa **59** 18 the same Heb word, כְּעַל, *k^eʿal*, is rendered "according to" and "accordingly." In NT ὁμοθυμαδόν, *homothumadón*, indicative of harmony of mind or action, (Acts **1** 14; **2** 46; **7** 57; **18** 12) and κατά, *katá*, "of the same mind . . . . acc. to Christ Jesus" (Rom **15** 5); αὐτόματος, *autómatos*, "of itself," "without constraint," "opened to them of its own accord" (Acts **12** 10), i.e. without human agency (cf Lev **25** 5 AV; Mk **4** 28); αὐθαίρετος, *authaíretos*, "of his own free choice" (2 Cor **8** 17). God "will render to every man according to his works" (Rom **2** 6), that is, agreeably to the nature of his works (1 Cor **3** 8), but salvation is not according to works (2 Tim **1** 9; Titus **3** 5). See DEED.

M. O. EVANS

ACCOS, ak′os (Ἀκχώς, *Hakchṓs*): The grandfather of Eupolemus, whom Judas Maccabaeus sent with others to Rome in 161 BC, to negotiate a "league of amity and confederacy" (1 Macc **8** 17). The name occurs in the OT as Hakkoz (הַקּוֹץ, *haḳḳōç*), who was a priest in the reign of David (1 Ch **24** 10).

ACCOUNT, a-kount′. See ACCOUNTABILITY.

ACCOUNTABILITY, a-koun-ta-bil′i-ti: The general teaching of Scripture on this subject is summarized in Rom **14** 12: "So then each one of us shall give account of himself to God." But this implies, on the one hand, the existence of a Moral Ruler of the universe, whose will is revealed, and, on the other, the possession by the creature of knowledge and free will. In Rom **4** 15 it is expressly laid down that, 'where no law is, neither is there transgression'; but, lest this might seem to exclude from accountability those to whom the law of Moses was not given, it is shown that even heathen had the law to some extent revealed in conscience; so that they are "without excuse" (Rom **1** 20). "For as many as have sinned without the law shall also perish without the law: and as many as have sinned under the law shall be judged by the law" (Rom **2** 12). So says Paul in a passage which is one of the profoundest discussions on the subject of accountability, and with his sentiment agrees exactly the word of Our Lord on the same subject, in Lk **12** 47.48: "And that servant, who knew his lord's will, and made not ready, nor did according to his will, shall be beaten with many stripes; but he that knew not, and did things worthy of stripes, shall be beaten with few stripes. And to whomsoever much is given, of him shall much be required: and to whom they commit much, of him will they ask the more." There is a gradual development of accountability accompanying the growth of a human being from infancy to maturity; and there is a similar development in

1. Scriptural Principles

the race, as knowledge grows from less to more. In the full light of the gospel human beings are far more responsible than they were in earlier stages of intellectual and spiritual development, and the doom to which they will be exposed on the day of account will be heavy in proportion to their privileges. This may seem to put too great a premium on ignorance; and a real difficulty arises when we say that, the more of moral sensitiveness there is, the greater is the guilt; because, as is well known, moral sensitiveness can be lost through persistent disregard of conscience; from which it might seem to follow that the way to diminish guilt was to silence the voice of conscience. There must, however, be a difference between the responsibility of a conscience that has never been enlightened and that of one which, having once been enlightened, has lost, through neglect or recklessness, the goodness once possessed. In the practice of the law, for example, it is often claimed that a crime committed under the influence of intoxication should be condoned; yet everyone must feel how different this is from innocence, and that, before a higher tribunal, the culprit will be held to be twice guilty—first, of the sin of drunkenness and then of the crime.

2. Connection with Immortality

Wherever civilization is so advanced that there exists a code of public law, with punishments attached to transgression, there goes on a constant education in the sense of accountability; and even the heathen mind, in classical times, had advanced so far as to believe in a judgment beyond the veil, when the shades had to appear before the tribunal of Rhadamanthus, Minos and Æacus, to have their station and degree in the underworld decided according to the deeds done in the body. How early the Hebrews had made as much progress has to be discussed in connection with the doctrine of immortality; but it is certain that, before the OT canon closed, they believed not only in a judgment after death but in resurrection, by which the sense of accountability was fastened far more firmly on the popular mind. Long before, however, there was awakened by the sacred literature the sense of a judgment of God going on during the present life and expressing itself in everyone's condition. The history of the world was the judgment of the world; prosperity attended the steps of the good man, but retribution sooner or later struck down the wicked. It was from the difficulty of reconciling with this belief the facts of life that the skepticism of Heb thought arose; but by the same constraint the pious mind was pushed forward in the direction of the full doctrine of immortality. This came with the advent of Him who brought life and immortality to light by His gospel (2 Tim **1** 10). In the mind of Jesus not only were resurrection, judgment and immortality unquestionable postulates; but He was brought into a special connection with accountability through His consciousness of being the Judge of mankind, and, in His numerous references to the Last Judgment, He developed the principles upon which the conscience will then be tried, and by which accordingly it ought now to try itself. In this connection the Parable of the Talents is of special significance; but it is by the grandiose picture of the scene itself, which follows in the same chapter of the First Gospel, that the mind of Christendom has been most powerfully influenced. Reference has already been made to the discussions at the commencement of the Epistle to the Romans in which our subject finds a place. By some the apostle John has been supposed to revert to the OT notion of a judgment proceeding now in place of coming at the Last Day; but Weiss (*Der johanneische Lehrbegriff*, II, 9) has proved that this is a mistake.

Up to this point we have spoken of individual accountability; but the subject becomes more complicated when we think of the joint responsibility of several or many persons.

3. Joint and Corporate Responsibility

From the first the human mind has been haunted by what is called the guilt of Adam's first sin. There is a solidarity in the human race, and the inheritance of evil is too obvious to be denied even by the most optimistic. There is far, however, from being agreement of opinion as to the relation of the individual to this evil legacy; some contending fiercely against the idea that the individual can have any personal responsibility for a sin hidden in a past so distant and shadowy, while others maintain that the misery which has certainly been inherited by all can only be justified in a world governed by a God of justice if the guilt of all precedes the misery. The question enters deeply into the Pauline scheme, although at the most critical point it is much disputed what the Apostle's real position is. While joint responsibility burdens the individual conscience, it may, at the same time, be said to lighten it. Thus, in Ezk **18** one of the most weighty ethical discussions to be found in Holy Writ is introduced with the popular proverb, "The fathers have eaten sour grapes, and the children's teeth are set on edge," which proves to be a way of saying that the responsibility of children is lightened, if not abolished, through their connection with their parents. In the same way, at the present time, the sense of responsibility is enfeebled in many minds through the control over character and destiny ascribed to heredity and environment. Even criminality is excused on the ground that many have never had a chance of virtue, and it is contended that to know everything is to forgive everything. There can be no doubt that, as the agents of trusts and partnerships, men will allow themselves to do what they would never have thought of in private business; and in a crowd the individual sustains psychological modifications by which he is made to act very differently from his ordinary self. In the actions of nations, such as war, there is a vast and solemn responsibility somewhere; but it is often extremely difficult to locate it—whether in the ruler, the ministry or the people. So interesting and perplexing are such problems often that a morality for bodies of people, as distinguished from individuals, is felt by many to be the great desideratum of ethics at the present time.

On this subject something will be found in most of the works on either philosophical or Christian ethics; see esp. Lemme's *Christliche Ethik*, 242 ff.

James Stalker

ACCOZ, ak′oz (**Ἀκβώς**, *Akbōs;* RV AKKOS, q.v.): 1 Esd **5** 38, head of one of the priestly families, which returned from the Exile, but was unable to prove its descent, when the register was searched. See also Ezr **2** 61.

ACCURSED, a-kûrs′ed, a-kûrst′: In the Book of Josh (**6** 17.18; **7** 1.11.12.13.15) and 1 Ch (**2** 7) "accursed" (or "accursed thing" or "thing accursed") is the AV rendering of the Heb word, חֵרֶם, *ḥērem*. The RV consistently uses "devoted" or "devoted thing," which the AV also adopts in Lev **27** 21.28.29 and in Nu **18** 14. "Cursed thing" is the rendering in two passages (Dt **7** 26; **13** 17); and in one passage (Ezk **44** 29 AV) "dedicated thing" is used. In four places the AV renders the word by "curse" (Josh **6** 18; Isa **34** 5; **43** 28; Mal **3** 24; [**4** 6]) whilst in another passage (Zec **14** 11) "utter destruction" is adopted in tr. These various renderings are due to the fact that the word *ḥērem* sometimes means the act of devoting or banning (or the condition or state resulting therefrom) and sometimes the object devoted or banned. We occasionally find periphrastic renderings, e.g. 1 S **15** 21: "the chief of the things which should have been utterly destroyed," AV (lit. "the chief part of the ban"); 1 K **20** 42: "a man whom I appointed to utter destruction," AV (lit. "a man of my ban" (or "banning"). The root-word meant "to separate," "shut off." The Arab. *ḥarīm* denoted the precincts of the temple at Mecca, and also the women's apartment (whence the word *harem*). In Heb the word always suggested "separating" or "devoting to God." Just as קָדֹשׁ, *ḳādhōsh*, meant "holy" or "consecrated to the service" of Jeh, and so not liable to be used for ordinary or secular purposes, so the stem of *ḥērem* meant "devoting" to Jeh anything which would, if spared, corrupt or contaminate the religious life of Israel, with the further idea of destroying (things) or exterminating (persons) as the surest way of avoiding such contamination. Everything that might paganize or affect the unique character of the religion of Israel was banned, e.g. idols (Dt **7** 26); idolatrous persons (Ex **22** 20); idolatrous cities (Dt **13** 13–18). All Can. towns—where the cult of Baal flourished—were to be banned (Dt **20** 16–18). The ban did not always apply to the gold and silver of looted cities (Josh **6** 24). Such valuable arts. were to be placed in the "treasury of the house of Yahweh." This probably indicates a slackening of the rigid custom which involved the total destruction of the spoil. According to Nu **18** 14, "everything devoted in Israel" belonged to Aaron, and Ezk **44** 29 AV ordained that "every dedicated thing" should belong to the priests (cf Ezr **10** 8). In the NT "accursed" is the AV rendering of Anathema (q.v.). Thomas Lewis

ACCUSER, a-kūz′ẽr: This word, not found in the OT, is the rendering of two Gr words: (1) Κατήγορος, *katēgoros*, that is, a prosecutor, or plaintiff in a lawsuit, or one who speaks in a derogatory way of another (Acts **23** 30.35; **25** 16.18; Rev **12** 10); (2) Διάβολος, *diábolos*, meaning adversary or enemy. This word is rendered "accuser" in the AV and "slanderer" in the RV and the ARV (2 Tim **3** 3; Titus **2** 3). According to the rabbinic teaching Satan, or the devil, was regarded as hostile to God and man, and that it was a part of his work to accuse the latter of disloyalty and sin before the tribunal of the former (see Job **1** 6 ff; Zec **3** 1 f; Rev **12** 10).

W. W. Davies

ACELDAMA, a-sel′da-ma. See Akeldama.

ACHAIA, a-kā′ya (Ἀχαιά, *Achaiá*): The smallest country in the Peloponnesus lying along the southern shore of the Corinthian Gulf, north of Arcadia and east of Elis. The original inhabitants were Ionians; but these were crowded out later by the Achaeans, who came from the East. According to Herodotus, the former founded twelve cities, many of which retain their original names to this day. These cities were on the coast and formed a confederation of smaller communities, which in the last century of the independent history of Greece attained to great importance (Achaean League). In Rom times the term Achaia was used to include the whole of Greece, exclusive of Thessaly. Today Achaia forms with Elis one district, and contains a population of nearly a quarter of a million. The old Achaean League was renewed in 280 BC, but became more important in 251, when Aratus of Sicyon was chosen commander-in-chief. This great man increased the power of the League and gave it an excellent constitution, which our own great practical politicians, Hamilton and Madison, consulted, adopting many of its prominent devices, when they set about framing the Constitution of the United States. In 146 BC Corinth was destroyed and the League broken up (see 1 Macc **15** 23); and the whole of Greece, under the name of Achaia, was transformed into a Rom province, which was divided into two separate provinces, Macedonia and Achaia, in 27 BC.

In Acts **18** 12 we are told that the Jews in Corinth made insurrection against Paul when Gallio was deputy of Achaia, and in **18** 27 that Apollos was making preparations to set out for Achaia. In Rom **16** 5, "Achaia" should read "Asia" as in RV. In Acts **20** 2 "Greece" means Achaia, but the oft-mentioned "Macedonia and Achaia" generally means the whole of Greece (Acts **19** 21; Rom **15** 26; 1 Thess **1** 8). Paul commends the churches of Achaia for their liberality (2 Cor **9** 13).

Literature.—See Gerhard, *Ueber den Volksstamm der A.* (Berlin, 1854); Klatt, *Forschungen zur Geschichte des achaischen Bundes* (Berlin, 1877); M. Dubois, *Les ligues étolienne et achéenne* (Paris, 1855); Capes, *History of the Achaean League* (London, 1888); Mahaffy, *Problems*, 177–86; Busolt, *Gr. Staatsalter*, 2d ed (1892), 347 ff; Toeppfer, in Pauly's *Realencyclopaedie*.

For Aratus see Hermann, *Staatsalter*, 1885; Krakauer, *Abhandlung ueber Aratus* (Breslau, 1874); Neumeyer, *Aratus aus Sikyon* (Leipzig, 1886); Holm, *History of Greece*.

J. E. Harry

ACHAICUS, a-kā′i-kus (Ἀχαικός, *Achaikós*, "belonging to Achaia"): A name honorably conferred upon L. Mummius, conqueror of Corinth and Achaia (cf Corinth). A. was one of the leaders of the Corinthian church (to be inferred from 1 Cor **16** 15 ff) who, visiting Paul at Ephesus with Stephanas and Fortunatus, greatly relieved the Apostle's anxiety for the Corinthian church (cf 1 Cor **5** 1 ff). Paul admonishes the members of the Cor church to submit to their authority (cf 1 Thess **5** 12) and to acknowledge their work (1 Cor **16** 15 ff).

ACHAN, ā′kan (עָכָן, *ʽākhān* [in 1 Ch **2** 7 Achar, עָכָר, *ʽākhār*], "troubler"): The descendant of Zerah the son of Judah who was put to death, in Joshua's time, for stealing some of the "devoted" spoil of the city of Jericho (Josh **7**). The stem *ʽākhan* is not used in Heb except in this name. The stem *ʽākhar* has sufficient use to define it. It denotes trouble of the most serious kind—Jacob's trouble when his sons had brought him into blood feud with his Can. neighbors, or Jephthah's trouble when his vow required him to sacrifice his daughter (Gen **34** 30; Jgs **11** 35). In Prov (**11** 17.29; **15** 6.27) the word is used with intensity to describe the results of cruelty, disloyalty, greed, wickedness. The record especially speaks of Achan's conduct as the troubling of Israel (1 Ch **2** 7; Josh **6** 18; **7** 24). In an outburst of temper Jonathan speaks of Saul as having troubled the land (1 S **14** 29). Elijah and Ahab accuse each the other of being the troubler of Israel (1 K **18** 17.18). The stem also appears in the two proper names Achor and Ochran (q.v.).

The crime of Achan was a serious one. Quite apart from all questions of supposable superstition, or even religion, the *ḥērem* concerning Jericho had been proclaimed, and to disobey the proclamation was disobedience to military orders in an army that was facing the enemy. It is commonly held that Achan's family were put to death with him, though they were innocent; but the record is not explicit on these points. One whose habits of thought lead him to expect features of primitive savagery in such a case as this will be sure to find what he expects; a person of different habits will not be sure that the record says that any greater cruelty was practised on the family of Achan than that of compelling them to be present at the execution. Those who hold that the Deuteronomic legislation comes in any sense from Moses should not be in haste to think that its precepts were violated by Joshua in the case of Achan (see Dt **24** 16).

The record says that the execution took place in the arable valley of Achor, up from the Jordan valley. See ACHOR. WILLIS J. BEECHER

ACHAR, ā'kar: Variant of ACHAN, which see.

ACHAZ, ā'kaz (**Ἄχαζ,** *Áchaz*), AV (Mt **1** 9): Gr form of *Ahaz* (thus RV). The name of a King of Israel.

ACHBOR, ak'bor (עַכְבּוֹר, *'akhbōr,* "mouse"): (1) The father of Baal-hanan, who was the seventh of the eight kings who reigned in Edom before there were kings in Israel (Gen **36** 38.39; 1 Ch **1** 49).

(2) The son of Micaiah (called in Ch Abdon the son of Micah) who went with Hilkiah the priest and other high officials, at the command of King Josiah, to consult Huldah the prophetess concerning the book that had been found (2 K **22** 12.14; 2 Ch **34** 20).

It may be presumed that this Achbor is also the man mentioned in Jer (**26** 22; **36** 12) as the father of Elnathan, who went to Egypt for King Jehoiakim in order to procure the extradition of Uriah the prophet, and who protested against the burning of Baruch's roll. WILLIS J. BEECHER

ACHIACHARUS, a-ki-ak'a-rus (B **'Αχιάχαρος,** *Achiácharos;* **'Αχείχαρος,** *Acheícharos*): Governor of Assyria. A. is the son of Anael, a brother of Tobit (Tob **1** 21). Sarchedonus (Esarhaddon), the king of Assyria, appointed him over all "accounts of his kingdom" and over all "his affairs" (Tob **1** 21 f; cf Dnl **2** 48). At his request Tobit comes to Nineveh (Tob **1** 22). A. nourishes Tobit, while the latter is afflicted with disease (Tob **2** 10). He attends the wedding-feast of Tobias (Tob **11** 18). Is persecuted by Aman, but saved (Tob **14** 10).

ACHIAS, a-kī'as: An ancestor of Ezra (2 Esd **1** 2). Omitted in other genealogies.

ACHIM, ā'kim (**'Αχείμ,** *Acheím*): A descendant of Zerubbabel and ancestor of Jesus, mentioned only in Mt **1** 14.

ACHIOR, ā'ki-or (**'Αχιώρ,** *Achiṓr*): General of the Ammonites, who spoke in behalf of Israel before Holofernes, the Assyr general (Jth **5** 5 ff). Holofernes ordered him bound and delivered at Bethulia to the Israelites (Jth **6**), who received him gladly and with honor. Afterward he became a proselyte, was circumcised, and joined to Israel (Jth **14**). In Nu **34** 27 it is the LXX reading for Ahihud, and in the Heb would be אֲחִיאוֹר, *'ăḥī'ōr,* "brother of light."

ACHIPHA, ak'i-fa; AV **Acipha,** as'i-fa (**'Αχιφά,** *Achiphá*), in the Apoc (1 Esd **5** 31) head of one of the families of the temple-servants, who returned with Zerubbabel; same as the OT HAKUPHA (Ezr **2** 51; Neh **7** 53), which see.

ACHISH, ā'kish (אָכִישׁ, *'ākhīsh*): King of the city of Gath in the days of David. His father's name is given as Maoch (1 S **27** 2), and Maacah (1 K **2** 39). David sought the protection of Achish when he first fled from Saul, and just after his visit to Nob (1 S **21** 10–15). Fearing rough treatment or betrayal by Achish, he feigned madness. But this made him unwelcome, whereupon he fled to the Cave of Adullam (1 S **22** 1). Later in his fugitive period David returned to Gath to be hospitably received by Achish (1 S **27** 1 ff), who gave him the town of Ziklag for his home. A year later, when the Philistines invaded the land of Israel, in the campaign which ended so disastrously for Saul (1 S **31**), Achish wished David to participate (1 S **28** 1–2), but the lords of the Philistines objected so strenuously, when they found him and his men with the forces of Achish, that Achish was compelled to send them back. Achish must have been a young man at this time, for he was still ruling forty years later at the beginning of Solomon's reign (1 K **2** 39). He is mentioned as Abimelech in the title of Ps **34**. See ABIMELECH 3. EDWARD MACK

ACHITOB, ak'i-tob: Same as Ahitob. Used in 1 Esd **8** 2; cf 2 Esd **1** 1 AV. See AHITUB 3.

ACHMETHA, ak'me-tha (Ezr **6** 2; אַחְמְתָא, *'aḥmethā';* LXX **'Αμαθά,** *Amathá;* Pesh ܐܚܡܬܢ, *aḥmāthān;* in Tiglath Pileser's inscr. cir 1100 BC Amadāna: in Darius' *Behistun Inscr.,* II, 76–78, *Hañgmatāna*="Place of Assembly"; 'Αγβάτανα, *Agbátana,* in Herodotus; 'Εκβάτανα, *Ekbátana,* Xenophon, etc; so 1 Esd **6** 23; Tob **3** 7; **6** 5; **7** 1; **14** 12.14; Jth **1** 1.2.14; 2 Macc **9** 3; Talm הַמְדָן, *hamdān;* now هَمَدان, *hamadān*): This, the ancient capital of Media, stood (lat. 34° 50′ N.—long. 48° 32′ E.) near the modern Hamadān, 160 miles W.S.W. of Ṭĕhrān, almost 6,000 feet above the sea, cir 1½ miles from the foot of Mt. Orontes (Alvand).

1. Location

It was founded or rebuilt by Dēïokēs (Dayaukku) about 700 BC on the site of Ellippi an ancient city of the Mandā, and captured by Cyrus 549 BC who brought Croesus there as captive (Herodotus i.153). It was the capital of the 10th Nome under Darius I. Cyrus and other Pers kings used to spend the two summer months there yearly, owing to the comparative coolness of the climate. Herodotus describes it as a magnificent city fortified with seven concentric walls (i.98). Its citadel (*bīrethā',* Ezr **6** 2, wrongly rendered "palace" in RV) is mentioned by Arrian, who says that, when Alexander took the city in 324 BC, he there stored his enormous booty. In it the royal archives were kept. It stood on a hill, where later was built a temple of Mithra. Polybius (x.27) speaks of the great strength of the citadel. Though the city was unwalled in his time, he can hardly find words to express his admiration for it, especially for the magnificent royal palace, nearly 7 stadia in circumference, built of precious kinds of wood sheathed in plates of gold and silver. In the city was the shrine of Aine (Nanæa, Anāhita?). Alexander is said to have destroyed a temple of Æsculapius (Mithra?) there. Diodorus tells us the city was 250 stadia in circumference. On Mt. Alvand (10,728 feet) there have been found inscriptions of Xerxes. Doubtless Ecbatana was one of the "cities of the Medes" to which Israel was carried captive (2 K **17** 6). It should be noted that Gr writers mention several other Ecbatanas. One of these, afterward called Gazaca (Takhti Sulaimān, a little S. of Lake Urmī, lat. 36° 28′ N., long. 47° 9′ E.) was capital of Atropatene. It was almost destroyed by the Mughuls in the 12th cent. Sir H. Rawlin-

2. History

son identifies the Ecbatana of Tobit and Herodotus with this northern city. The southern and far more important Ecbatana which we have described is certainly that of 2 Macc **9** 3. It was Cyrus' Median capital, and is doubtless that of Ezr **6** 2. Classical writers spoke erroneously of Ecbatăna (for Ecbatāna) as moderns too often do of *Hamadăn* for *Hamadān*.

3. Present Condition

Hamadān has perhaps never fully recovered from the fearful massacre made there in 1220 AD by the Mongols, but its population is about 50,000, including a considerable number of descendants of the Israelites of the Dispersion (tracing descent from Asher, Naphtali, etc). They point to the tombs of Esther and Mordecai in the neighborhood. It is a center for the caravan trade between Baghdād and Ṭĕhrān. There is an American Presbyterian mission at work.

Authorities (besides those quoted above): Ctesias, Curtius, Amm. Marcellinus, Pausanias, Strabo, Diod. Siculus; Ibnu'l Athīr, Yāqūt, Jahāngushā, Jâmi'u't Tawārīkh, and modern travelers.

W. St. Clair Tisdall

ACHO, ak'ō. See Acco.

ACHOR, ā'kor (עָכוֹר, *'ākhōr,* "trouble," the idea of the word being that of trouble which is serious and extreme. See Achan): The place where Achan was executed in the time of Joshua (Josh **7** 24.26). In all the five places where it is mentioned it is described as the *'ēmeḳ,* the arable valley of Achor. There is no ground in the record for the current idea that it must have been a locality with horrid and dismal physical features. It was on a higher level than the camp of Israel in the Jordan valley, and on a lower level than Debir—a different Debir from that of Josh **15** 15. In a general way, as indicated by the points mentioned in the border of Judah, it was north of Betharabah, and south of Debir (Josh **7** 24; **15** 7). Many identify it with the Wady Kelt which descends through a deep ravine from the Judaean hills and runs between steep banks south of the modern Jericho to Jordan, the stream after rains becoming a foaming torrent. Possibly the name may have been applied to a region of considerable extent. In Isa **65** 10 it is a region on the east side of the mountain ridge which is in some sense balanced with Sharon on the west side. By implication the thing depicted seems to be these rich agricultural localities so far recovered from desolation as to be good grounds for cattle and sheep. Hosea recognizes the comforting aspect of the dreadful affair in the valley of Achor; it was a doorway of hope to pardoned Israel (Hos **2** 15 [17]), and he hopes for like acceptance for the Israel of his own day.

Willis J. Beecher

ACHSA, ak'sa: Used in AV in **1** Ch **2** 49 for Achsah, which see.

ACHSAH, ak'sä (עַכְסָה, *'akhṣāh;* in some copies עַכְסָא, *'akhṣā'* in 1 Ch **2** 49), "anklet"): The daughter of Caleb whom he gave in marriage to his younger kinsman Othniel the son of Kenaz, as a reward for smiting Kiriath-sepher (Josh **15** 16 ff; Jgs **1** 12 ff). Caleb, the narrative says, established Achsah in the South-country, and in addition, at her asking, gave her certain important springs of water—the "upper basins" and the "nether basins." Professor G. F. Moore identifies these with the groups of springs in *Seit ed-Dilbeh* (notes on Jgs in Polychrome Bible).

Willis J. Beecher

ACHSHAPH, ak'shaf (אַכְשָׁף, *'akhshāph,* "sorcery," or "fascination"): A city in the northern part of the territory conquered by Joshua. The king of Achshaph was a member of the coalition against Israel under Jabin and Sisera. It is mentioned with Hazor, Megiddo, Taanach, etc, in the list of conquered kings. It is one of the cities marking the boundaries of the tribe of Asher (Josh **11** 1; **12** 20; **19** 25). Several attempts have been made to identify the site of it, but explorers are not agreed as to the identification.

ACHZIB, ak'zib (אַכְזִיב, *'akhzībh,* "lying" or "disappointing"): The name of two towns in Palestine: (1) A town in western Judah in the lowlands, mentioned in connection with Mareshah and Keilah as one of the cities allotted to Judah (Josh **15** 44), and in Mic (**1** 14), where it suggests play upon its meaning, "deceptive" or "failing," possibly the place having received its name from a winter spring or brook, which failed in summer. It is also called Chezib (כְּזִיב, *k^ezībh* [Gen **38** 5]), where Judah was at the time of the birth of his son Shelah. In 1 Ch **4** 22 it is called Cozeba, AV "Chozeba" (כֹּזֵבָא, *kōzēbhā'*), clearly seen to be the same as Achzib, from the places with which it is grouped. (2) It has been identified with the modern *'Ayin-Kezbeh* in the valley of Elah, and north of Adullam.

Edward Mack

(3) Mod. *Zib* LXX variously: Josh **19** 29, B, **Ἐχοζόβ,** *Echozób,* A, **Ἀχζείφ,** *Achzeiph;* Jgs **1** 31, B, **Ἀσχαζεί,** *Aschazei,* A, **Ἀσχενδεί,** *Aschendei;* Gr *Ecdippa:* A small town some miles north of Acre on the coast. It is mentioned in Josh **19** 29 as falling within the possessions of the tribe of Asher, but they never occupied it, as they did not the neighboring Acre (Acco). The Phoen inhabitants of the coast were too strongly entrenched to be driven out by a people who had no fleet. The cities on the coast doubtless aided one another, and Sidon had become rich and powerful before this and could succor such a small town in case of attack. Achzib was a coast town, nine miles north of Acco, now known as Ez-Zib. It appears in the Assyr inscriptions as Aksibi and Sennacherib enumerates it among the Phoen towns that he took at the same time as Acco (702 BC). It was never important and is now an insignificant village among the sand dunes of the coast. It was the bordertown of Galilee on the west, what lay beyond being unholy ground.

H. Porter

ACIPHA, as'i-fa. See Achiphah.

ACITHO, ACITHOH, as'i-thō (variant of **AHITUB**): The name in AV of an ancestor of Judith (Jth **8** 1).

ACKNOWLEDGE, ak-nol'ej (**γιγνώσκω,** *gignôskō*): To declare that one recognizes the claims of a person or thing fully established. Both in OT and NT expressed by various forms of the word "know" (Prov **3** 6; Isa **61** 9; Col **2** 2 AV). The Psalmist (Ps **32** 5) "acknowledged" his sin, when he told God that he knew the guilt of what he had done. The Corinthians (2 Cor **1** 14) "acknowledged" Paul and his companions when they formally recognized their claims and authority.

ACQUAINT, a-kwānt', **ACQUAINTANCE,** a-kwān'tans (**γνωστοί,** *gnōstoi*): Terms referring to various degrees of knowledge, but implying more or less detailed information; applied to God's omniscience (Ps **139** 3), to the grief of the Suffering Servant of Jehovah (Isa **53** 3), and to the knowledge which man should have of God. The noun in the concrete, unless limited by a qualifying term, means more than one who has been known simply in passing, and implies a degree of intimacy, as may be seen in Lk **2** 44; **23** 49; 2 K **12** 5. H. E. Jacobs

ACRA, ak'ra, ā'kra (1 Macc **1** 33 RV, "citadel"). See Jerusalem.

ACRABATTENE, ak-ra-ba-tē'nē. See Akrabattine (Apoc).

ACRABBIM, ak-rab'im: Incorrect transliteration of עַקְרַבִּים *'aḳrabbīm,* of Josh **15** 3 in AV. See Akrabbim.

ACRE, ā'kẽr, ä'kẽr. See Acco.

ACRE, ā'kẽr (צֶמֶד, *çemedh*): A term of land-measurement used twice in the English VSS of the Bible (Isa **5** 10; 1 S **14** 14), and said to be the only term in square measure found in the OT. The Eng. word "acre" originally signified field. Then it came to denote the measure of land that an ox team could plow in a day, and upon the basis of a maximum acre of this kind the standard acre of 160 square rods (with variations in different regions) was fixed. The Heb word trd acre denotes a yoke of animals, in the sense of a team, a span, a pair; it is never used to denote the yoke by which the team are coupled together. The phrase 'ten yokes of vineyard' (Isa **5** 10) may naturally mean vineyard covering as much land as a team would plow in ten days, though other plausible meanings can also be suggested. In 1 S **14** 14 the same word is used in describing the limits of space within which Jonathan and his armor-bearer slew twenty Philistines. The tr of RV, "within as it were half a furrow's length in an acre of land," means, strictly, that they were slain along a line from two to twenty rods in length. The word rendered "furrow," used only here and in Ps **129** 3, is in Brown's *Hebrew Lexicon* defined as "plowing-ground." This gives the rendering "as it were in half a plowing-stint, a yoke of ground," the last two phrases defining each the other, so that the meaning is substantially that of the paraphrase in AV. There is here an alleged obscurity and uncertainty in the text, but it is not such as to affect either the tr or the nature of the event.

Willis J. Beecher

ACROSTIC, a-kros'tik: The acrostic, understood as a short poem in which the first letters of the lines form a word, or name, or sentence, has not yet been proved to occur in ancient Heb literature. The supposed examples found by some scholars in Ps **2** 1–4 and **110** 1*b*–4 are not generally recognized. Still less can be said in favor of the suggestion that in Est **1** 20 four words read from left to right form by their initials an acrostic on the name Y H W H (cf König, *Einl* 293). In Byzantine hymn-poetry the term *acrostichis* with which our word "acrostic" is connected was also used of alphabetical poems, that is poems the lines or groups of lines in which have their initials arranged in the order of the alphabet. Acrostics of this kind are found in pre-Christian Heb literature as well as elsewhere in ancient oriental literature. There are twelve clear instances in the OT: Pss **25, 34, 37, 111** f, **119, 145;** Prov **31** 10–31, and Lam **1–4**. There is probably an example in Pss **9** and **10,** and possibly another in Nah **1** 2–10. Outside the Canon, Sir **51** 13–30 exhibits clear traces of alphabetic arrangement. Each of these fifteen poems must briefly be discussed.

Pss **9** and **10,** which are treated as one psalm in LXX and Vulg, give fairly clear indications of original alphabetic structure even in the MT. The initials of **9** 1.3.5 are respectively *'āleph, bēth, gīmel;* of vs 9.11.13.15.17 *vāv, zayin, ḥēth, ṭēth* and *yōdh.* The first ver of **10** begins with *lāmedh* and vs 12.14.15.17 with *ḳōph, rēsh, shīn* and *tāv.* Four lines seem to have been allotted to each letter in the original form of the poem. In Ps **25** all the letters are represented except *vāv* and *ḳōph.* In ver 18 we find *rēsh* instead of the latter as well as in its place in ver 19. In ver 2 the alphabetical letter is the initial of the second word. The last verse is a supernumerary. There are mostly two lines to a letter. In Ps **34** all the letters are represented except *vāv,* ver 6 beginning not with it, as was to be expected, but with *zayin.* The last verse is again a supernumerary. Since here and in **25** 22 the first word is a form of *pādhāh* it has been suggested that there may have been here a sort of acrostic on the writer's name Pedahel (*pedhah'ēl*), but there is no evidence that a psalmist so named ever existed. There are two lines to a letter. In Ps **37** all the letters are represented except *'ayin* which seems however from LXX to have been present in the earliest text. As a rule four lines are assigned to each letter. In Pss **111** f are found two quite regular examples with a line to each letter. Ps **119** offers another regular example, but with 16 lines to a letter, each alternate line beginning with its letter. Vs 1–8, for instance, each begin with *'āleph.* In Ps **145** are found all the letters but *nūn.* As we find in LXX between vs 13 and 14, that is where the *nūn* couplet ought to be:

> "Faithful is the Lord in his words
> And holy in his works,"

which may represent a Heb couplet beginning with *nūn,* it would seem that a ver has dropped out of the MT. Prov **31** 10–31 constitutes a regular alphabetical poem with (except in ver 15) two lines to a letter. Lam **1** is regular, with three lines to a letter. Lam **2, 3, 4,** are also regular with a curious exception. In each case *pē* precedes *'ayin,* a phenomenon which has not yet been explained. In **2** there are three or four lines to a letter except in ver 17, where there seem to be five. In **3** also there are three lines to a letter and each line begins with that letter. In **4** there are two lines to a letter except in ver 22 where there are probably four lines. Lam **5** has twice as many lines as the letters of the alphabet but no alphabetical arrangement. In Nah **1** 1–10 ff Delitzsch (following Frohnmeyer) in 1876, Bickell in 1880 and 1894, Gunkel in 1893 and 1895, G. B. Gray in 1898 (*Expos,* September) and others have pointed out possible traces of original alphabetical structure. In the Massoretic text, however, as generally arranged, it is not distinctly discernible. Sir **51** 13–30: As early as 1882 Bickell reconstructed this hymn on the basis of the Gr and Syr VSS as a Heb alphabetical poem. In 1897 Schechter (in the judgment of most scholars) discovered the original text in a collection of fragments from the Genizah of Cairo, and this proved the correctness of Bickell's idea and even the accuracy of some details of his reconstruction. The poem begins with *'āleph* and has *tāv* as the initial letter of the last line but one. In vs 21.22.24.25.26.27 the letters *mēm, nūn, 'ayin, pē, çādhē, ḳōph* and *rēsh* can be traced at the beginnings of lines in that order. *Ṣamekh* is absent (cf Schechter-Taylor, *The Wisdom of Ben Sira,* lxxvi–lxxxvii).

As this rapid survey will have shown, this form of acrostic as employed by Heb writers consisted in the use of letters of the alphabet as initials in their order, at regular intervals, the distance between two different letters ranging from one to sixteen lines. Once each letter is thus used three times, in another case eight times. The corruption of the text has in some cases led to considerable interference with the alphabetical arrangement, and textual criticism has endeavored to restore it with varying success.

These alphabetical poems have been unduly depreciated on account of their artificial structure and have also been regarded for the same reason as of comparatively late origin. This latter conclusion is premature with present evidence. The poems in Lam undoubtedly go back as far as the 6th cent. BC, and Assyr testimony takes us back farther still for acrostic poems of some kind. Strictly alphabetical poems are of course out of the question in Assyr because of the absence of an alphabet, but there are texts from the library of Ashur-bani-pal each verse-line in which begins with the same syllable, and others in which the initial syllables read together compose a word or sentence. Now these texts were written down in the 7th cent. BC, but may have been copied from far earlier Bab originals. There can be little doubt that oriental poets wrote acrostic at an early period, and therefore the use of some form of the acrostic is no clear indication of lateness of date. (For these Assyr acrostics cf Weber, *Die Literatur der Babylonier und Assyrer*, 37.)

LITERATURE.—In addition to authorities already cited: König, *Einl*, 58, 66, 74, 76, 399, 404, 419, and *Stilistik*, etc, 357 ff; Budde, *Geschichte der alt-hebräischen Litteratur*, 30, 90, 241, 291; art. "Acrostic" in *HDB* (larger and smaller) and Hastings, *Enc of Religion and Ethics*, and *Jew Enc*; commentaries on Ps, Nah, Prov and Lam; Driver, *Parallel Psalter;* King, *Early Religious Poetry of the Hebrews*, ch iv.

WILLIAM TAYLOR SMITH

ACTS, APOCRYPHAL, a-pok'ri-fal. See APOCRYPHAL ACTS.

ACTS OF THE APOSTLES, a-pos'ls:

I. TITLE
II. TEXT
III. UNITY OF THE BOOK
IV. THE AUTHOR
V. CANONICITY
VI. DATE
VII. SOURCES USED BY LUKE
VIII. THE SPEECHES IN THE ACTS
IX. RELATION OF THE ACTS TO THE EPISTLES
X. CHRONOLOGY OF ACTS
XI. HISTORICAL WORTH OF ACTS
XII. PURPOSE OF THE BOOK
XIII. ANALYSIS
LITERATURE

I. Title.—It is possible, indeed probable, that the book originally had no title. The manuscripts give the title in several forms. Aleph (in the inscription) has merely "Acts" (*Práxeis*). So Tischendorf, while Origen, Didymus, Eusebius quote from "The Acts." But BD Aleph (in subscription) have "Acts of Apostles" or "The Acts of the Apostles" (*Práxeis Apostólōn*). So Westcott and Hort, Nestle (cf Athanasius and Euthalius). Only slightly different is the title in 31.61, and many other cursives (*Praxeis tōn Apostolōn*, "Acts of the Apostles"). So Griesbach, Scholz. Several fathers (Clement of Alex, Origen, Dionysius of Alex, Cyril of Jerus, Chrysostom) quote it as "The Acts of the Apostles" (*Hai Praxeis tōn Apostolōn*). Finally A^2 EGH give it in the form "Acts of the Holy Apostles" (*Praxeis tōn Hagiōn Apostolōn*). The Memphitic VS has "The Acts of the Holy Apostles." Clearly, then, there was no single title that commanded general acceptance.

II. Text.—(1) The chief documents. These are the Primary Uncials (א ABCD), E which is a bilingual Uncial confined to Acts, later Uncials like HLP, the Cursives, the Vulgate, the Pesh and the Harclean Syriac and quotations from the Fathers. We miss the Curetonian and Syr Sin, and have only fragmentary testimony from the Old Latin.

(2) The modern editions of Acts present the types of text (TR; RV; the critical text like that of WH or Nestle or Weiss or von Soden). These three types do not correspond with the four classes of text (Syrian, Western, Alexandrian, Neutral) outlined by Hort in his *Introduction to the New Testament in Greek* (1882). These four classes are broadly represented in the documents which give us Acts. But no modern editor of the Gr NT has given us the Western or the Alex type of text, though Bornemann, as will presently be shown, argues for the originality of the Western type in Acts. But the *TR* (Stephanus' 3d ed in 1550) was the basis of the AV of 1611. This ed of the Gr NT made use of a very few MSS, and all of them late, except D, which was considered too eccentric to follow. Practically, then, the AV represents the Syr type of text which may have been edited in Antioch in the 4th cent. Various minor errors may have crept in since that date, but substantially the Syr recension is the text of the AV today. Where this text stands alone, it is held by nearly all modern scholars to be in error, though Dean Burgon fought hard for the originality of the Syr text (*The Revision Revised*, 1882). The text of WH is practically that of B, which is held to be the Neutral type of text. Nestle, von Soden, Weiss do not differ greatly from the text of WH, though von Soden and Weiss attack the problem on independent lines. The text of the RV is in a sense a compromise between that of the AV and the critical text, though coming pretty close to the critical text. Cf Whitney, *The Reviser's Greek Text*, 1892. For a present-day appreciation of this battle of the texts see J. Rendel Harris, *Side Lights on the New Testament*, 1908. For a detailed comparison between the AV and the RV Acts see Rackham, *The Acts of the Apostles*, xxii.

(3) In Acts the Western type of text has its chief significance. It is the merit of the late Friedrich Blass, the famous classicist of Germany, to have shown that in Luke's writings (Gospel and Acts) the Western class (especially D) has its most marked characteristics. This fact is entirely independent of the theory advanced by Blass which will be discussed directly. The chief modern revolt against the theories of WH is the new interest felt in the value of the Western type of text. In particular D has come to the front in the Book of Acts. The feeble support that D has in its peculiar readings in Acts (due to absence of Cur. Syr and of Old Lat) makes it difficult always to estimate the value of this document. But certainly these readings deserve careful consideration, and some of them may be correct, whatever view one holds of the D text. The chief variations are, as is usual with the Western text, additions and paraphrases. Some of the prejudice against D has disappeared as a result of modern discussion.

(4) Bornemann in 1848 argued that D in Acts represented the original text. But he has had very few followers.

(5) J. Rendel Harris (1891) sought to show that D (itself a bilingual MS) had been Latinized. He argued that already in 150 AD a bilingual MS existed. But this theory has not won a strong following.

(6) Chase (1893) sought to show that the peculiarities were due to tr from the Syr.

(7) Blass in 1895 created a sensation by arguing in his Commentary on Acts (*Acta Apostolorum*, 24 ff) that Luke had issued two editions of the Acts, as he later urged about the Gospel of Luke (*Philology of the Gospels*, 1898). In 1896 Blass published this Roman form of the text of Acts (*Acta Apostolorum, secundum Formam quae videtur Romanam*). Blass calls this first, rough, unabridged copy of Acts *β* and considers that it was issued at Rome. The later edition, abridged and revised, he calls *α*. Curiously enough, in Acts **11** 28, D has "when we had gathered together," making Luke present at Antioch. The idea of two edd is not wholly original with Blass. Leclerc, a Dutch philologist, had suggested the notion as early as the beginning of the 18th cent. Bishop Light-

foot had also mentioned it (*On a Fresh Revision of the NT*, 29). But Blass worked the matter out and challenged the world of scholarship with his array of arguments. He has not carried his point with all, though he has won a respectable following. Zahn (*Einl, II*, 338 ff, 1899) had already been working toward the same view (348). He accepts in the main Blass's theory, as do Belser, Nestle, Salmon, Zöckler. Blass acknowledges his debt to Corssen (*Der cyprianische Text der Acta Apostolorum*, 1892), but Corssen considers the α text as the earlier and the β text as a later revision.

(8) Hilgenfeld (*Acta Apostolorum*, etc, 1899) accepts the notion of two edd, but denies identity of authorship.

(9) Schmiedel (*EB*) vigorously and at much length attacks Blass's position, else "the conclusions reached in the foregoing sections would have to be withdrawn." He draws his conclusions and then demolishes Blass! He does find weak spots in Blass's armor as others have done (B. Weiss, *Der Codex D in der Apostelgeschichte*, 1897; Page, *Class. Rev.*, 1897; Harnack, *The Acts of the Apostles*, 1909, 45). See also Knowling, *The Acts of the Apostles*, 1900, 47, for a sharp indictment of Blass's theory as being too simple and lacking verification.

(10) Harnack (*The Acts of the Apostles*, 48) doubts if Luke himself formally published the book. He thinks that he probably did not give the book a final revision, and that friends issued two or more edd. He considers that the so-called β recension has a "series of interpolations" and so is later than the α text.

(11) Ramsay (*The Church in the Roman Empire*, 150; *St. Paul the Traveller*, 27; *Expos*, 1895) considers the β text to be a 2d-cent. revision by a copyist who has preserved some very valuable 2d-cent. testimony to the text.

(12) Headlam (*HDB*) does not believe that the problem has as yet been scientifically attacked, but that the solution lies in the textual license of scribes of the Western type (cf Hort, *Introduction*, 122 ff). But Headlam is still shy of "Western" readings. The fact is that the Western readings are sometimes correct as against the Neutral (cf Mt **27** 49). It is not necessary in Acts **11** 20 to say that *Hellenas* is in Western authorities (AD, etc) but is not a Western reading. It is at any rate too soon to say the final word about the text of Acts, though on the whole the α text still holds the field as against the β text. The Syr text is, of course, later, and out of court.

III. Unity of the Book.—It is not easy to discuss this question, apart from that of authorship. But they are not exactly the same. One may be convinced of the unity of the book and yet not credit it to Luke, or, indeed, to anyone in the 1st cent. Of course, if Luke is admitted to be the author of the book, the whole matter is simplified. His hand is in it all whatever sources he used. If Luke is not the author, there may still have been a competent historian at work, or the book may be a mere compilation. The first step, therefore, is to attack the problem of unity. Holtzmann (*Einl*, 383) holds Luke to be the author of the "we" sections only. Schmiedel denies that the Acts is written by a companion of Paul, though it is by the same author as the Gospel bearing Luke's name. In 1845 Schleiermacher credited the "we" sections to Timothy, not to Luke. For a good sketch of the theories of "sources," see Knowling on Acts, 25 ff. Van Manen (1890) resolved the book into two parts, *Acta Petri* and *Acta Pauli*, combined by a redactor. Sorof (1890) ascribes one source to Luke, one to Timothy. Spitta also has two sources (a Pauline-Lukan and a Jewish-Christian) worked over by a redactor. Clemen (1905) has four sources (History of the Hellenists, History of Peter, History of Paul, and a Journey of Paul), all worked over by a series of editors. Hilgenfeld (1895) has three sources (Acts of Peter, Acts of the Seven, Acts of Paul). Jungst (1895) has a Pauline source and a Petrine source. J. Weiss (1893) admits sources, but claims that the book has unity and a definite aim. B. Weiss (1902) conceives an early source for the first part of the book. Harnack (*The Acts of the Apostles*, 1909, 41 f) has small patience with all this blind criticism: "With them the book passes as a comparatively late patchwork compilation, in which the part taken by the editor is insignificant yet in all cases detrimental; the 'we' sections are not the property of the author, but an extract from a source, or even a literary fiction." He charges the critics with "airy conceit and lofty contempt." Harnack has done a very great service in carefully sifting the matter in his *Luke the Physician* (1907). He gives detailed proof that the "we" sections are in the same style and by the same author as the rest of the book (26–120). Harnack does not claim originality in this line of argument: "It has been often stated and often proved that the 'we' sections in vocabulary, in syntax, and in style are most intimately bound up with the whole work, and that this work itself (including the Gospel), in spite of all diversity in its parts, is distinguished by a grand unity of literary form" (*Luke the Physician*, 26). He refers to the "splendid demonstration of this unity" by Klostermann (*Vindiciae Lucanae*, 1866), to B. Weiss, who, in his commentary (1893, 2 Aufl, 1902) "has done the best work in demonstrating the literary unity of the whole work," to "the admirable contributions" of Vogel (*Zur Charakteristik des Lukas*, etc, 2 Aufl, 1899) to the "yet more careful and minute investigations" of Hawkins (*Horae Synopticae*, 1899, 2d ed, 1909), to the work of Hobart (*The Medical Language of St. Luke*, 1882), who "has proved only too much" (*Luke the Physician*, 175), but "the evidence is of overwhelming force" (198). Harnack only claims for himself that he has done the work in more detail and with more minute accuracy without claiming too much (27). But the conversion of Harnack to this view of Acts is extremely significant. It ought not to be necessary any more to refute the partition theories of the book, or to set forth in detail the proofs for the unity of the book. Perhaps the compilation theory of Acts is nowhere set forth more cogently than in McGiffert's *The Apostolic Age* (1897). See a powerful refutation of his argument by Ramsay in *Pauline and Other Studies* (1906, 302–21). "I think his clever argumentation is sophistical" (305). Harnack is fully aware that he has gone over to the side of "Ramsay, Weiss and Zahn": "The results at which I have arrived not only approach very nearly to, but are often coincident with, the results of their research" (*The Acts of the Apostles*, 302). He is afraid that if these scholars failed to get the ear of critics "there is little prospect of claiming the attention of critics and compelling them to reconsider their position." But he has the advantage of coming to this conclusion from the other side. Moreover, if Harnack was won by the force of the facts, others may be. This brief sketch of Harnack's experience may take the place of detailed presentation of the arguments for the unity of the book. Harnack sets forth in great wealth of detail the characteristic idioms of the "we" sections side by side with parallels in other parts of Acts and the Gospel of Luke. The same man wrote the rest of Acts who wrote the "we" sections. This fact should now be acknowledged as proven. This does not mean that the writer, a personal witness in the "we" sections, had no sources for the other parts of Acts. This aspect of the matter will be considered a little later.

IV. The Author.—Assuming the unity of the book, the argument runs as follows: The author was a companion of Paul. The "we" sections prove that (Acts **16** 10–17; **20** 6–16; **21**; **27**; **28**). These sections have the fulness of detail and vivid description natural to an eye-witness. This companion was with Paul in the second missionary journey at Troas and at Philippi, joined Paul's party again at Philippi on the return to Jerusalem during the third tour, and probably remained with Paul till he went to Rome. Some of Paul's companions came to him at Rome: others are so described in the book as to preclude authorship. Aristarchus, Aquila and Priscilla, Erastus, Gaius, Mark, Silas, Timothy, Trophimus, Tychicus and others more or less insignificant from the point of view of connection with Paul (like Crescens, Demas, Justus, Linus, Pudens, Sopater, etc) are easily eliminated. Curiously enough Luke and Titus are not mentioned in Acts by name at all. They are distinct persons as is stated in 2 Tim **4** 10 f. Titus was with Paul in Jerusalem at the conference (Gal **2** 1) and was his special envoy to Corinth during the time of trouble there. (2 Cor **2** 12 f; **12** 18.) He was later with Paul in Crete (Titus **1** 5). But the absence of mention of Titus in Acts may be due to the fact that he was a brother of Luke (cf 2 Cor **8** 18; **12** 18). So A. Souter in *DCG*, art. "Luke." If Luke is the author, it is easy to understand why his name does not appear. If Titus is his brother, the same explanation occurs. As between Luke and Titus the medical language of Acts argues for Luke. The writer was a physician. This fact Hobart (*The Medical Language of St. Luke*, 1882) has demonstrated. Cf Zahn, *Einl*, 2, 435 ff; Harnack's *Luke the Physician*, 177 ff. The arguments from the use of medical terms are not all of equal weight. But the style is colored at points by the language of a physician. The writer uses medical terms in a technical sense. This argument involves a minute comparison with the writings of physicians of the time. Thus in Acts **28** 3 f *katháptō*, according to Hobart (288), is used in the sense of poisonous matter invading the body, as in Dioscorides, *Animal. Ven. Proem.* So Galen, *De Typis* 4 (VII, 467), uses it "of fever fixing on parts of the body." Cf Harnack, *Luke the Physician*, 177 f. Harnack agrees also that the terms of the diagnosis in Acts **28** 8 "are medically exact and can be vouched for from medical literature" (ib, 176 f). Hobart has overdone his argument and adduced many examples that are not pertinent, but a real residuum remains, according to Harnack. Then *pímprasthai* is a technical term for swelling. Let these serve as examples. The interest of the writer in matters of disease is also another indication; cf Lk **8** 43. Now Luke was a companion of Paul during his later ministry and was a physician. (Col **4** 14). Hence he fulfils all the requirements of the case. The argument thus far is only probable, it is true; but there is to be added the undoubted fact that the same writer wrote both Gospel and Acts (Acts **1** 1). The direct allusion to the Gospel is reinforced by identity of style and method in the two books. The external evidence is clear on the matter. Both Gospel and Acts are credited to Luke the physician. The Muratorian canon ascribes Acts to Luke. By the end of the 2d cent. the authority of the Acts is as well established as that of the Gospel (Salmon, *Introduction to the NT*, 1885, 366). Irenaeus, Tertullian, Clement of Alexandria, all call Luke the author of the book. The argument is complete. It is still further strengthened by the fact that the point of view of the book is Pauline and by the absence of references to Paul's epistles. If one not Paul's companion had written Acts, he would certainly have made some use of them. Incidentally, also, this is an argument for the early date of the Acts. The proof that has won Harnack, the leader of the left in Germany, to the acknowledgment of the Lukan authorship of Acts ought to win all to this position.

V. Canonicity.—The use of the Acts does not appear so early or so frequently as is true of the gospels and the Pauline epistles. The reason is obvious. The epistles had a special field and the gospels appealed to all. Only gradually would Acts circulate. At first we find literary allusions without the name of book or author. But Holtzmann (*Einl*, 1892, 406) admits the use of Acts by Ignatius, Justin Martyr, Polycarp. The use of the Gospel according to Luke by Tatian and Marcion really involves knowledge of the Acts. But in Irenaeus frequently (*Adv. Haer.*, i. 23, 1, etc) the Acts is credited to Luke and regarded as Scripture. The Canon of Muratori lists it as Scripture. Tertullian and Clement of Alexandria attribute the book to Luke and treat it as Scripture. By the time of Eusebius the book is generally acknowledged as part of the canon. Certain of the heretical parties reject it (like the Ebionites, Marcionites, Manichaeans). But by this time the Christians had come to lay stress on history (Gregory, *Canon and Text of the NT*, 1907, 184), and the place of Acts is now secure in the canon.

VI. Date.—(1) Luke's relations to Josephus. The acceptance of the Lukan authorship settles the question of some of the dates presented by critics. Schmiedel places the date of Acts between 105 and 130 AD (*EB*). He assumes as proven that Luke made use of the writings of Jos. It has never been possible to take with much seriousness the claim that the Acts shows acquaintance with Jos. See Keim, *Geschichte Jesu*, III, 1872, 134, and Krenkel, *Josephus und Lucas*, 1894, for the arguments in favor of that position. The words quoted to prove it are in the main untechnical words of common use. The only serious matter is the mention of Theudas and Judas the Galilean in Acts **5** 36 f and Josephus (*Ant*, XX, v, 1 f). In Jos the names occur some twenty lines apart and the resemblance is only slight indeed. The use of *peíthō* in connection with Theudas and *apostḗsai* concerning Judas is all that requires notice. Surely, then, two common words for "persuade" and "revolt" are not enough to carry conviction of the writer's use of Josephus. The matter is more than offset by the differences in the two reports of the death of Herod Agrippa I (Acts **12** 19–23; Jos, *Ant*, XVIII, vi, 7; XIX, viii, 2). The argument about Jos may be definitely dismissed from the field. With that goes all the ground for a 2d-cent. date. Other arguments have been adduced (see Holtzmann, *Einl*, 1892, 405) such as the use of Paul's epistles, acquaintance with Plutarch, Arrian and Pausanias, because of imitation in method of work (i.e. ∥ lives of Peter and Paul, periods of history, etc), correction of Gal in Acts (for instance, Gal **1** 17–24 and Acts **9** 26–30; Gal **2** 1–10 and Acts **15** 1–33). The parallel with Plutarch is fanciful, while the use of Paul's epistles is by no means clear, the absence of such use, indeed, being one of the characteristics of the book. The variation from Gal is far better explained on the assumption that Luke had not seen the epistles.

(2) 80 AD is the limit if the book is to be credited to Luke. The majority of modern critics who accept the Lukan authorship place it between 70 and 80 AD. So Harnack, Lechler, Meyer, Ramsay, Sanday, Zahn. This opinion rests mainly on the idea that the Gospel according to Luke was written after the destruction of Jerusalem in 70 AD. It is claimed that Lk **21** 20 shows that this tragedy had already occurred, as compared with Mk **13** 14 and Mt **24** 15. But the mention of armies is very

general, to be sure. Attention is called also to the absence of the warning in Lk. Harnack (*The Acts of the Apostles*, 291 f) admits that the arguments in favor of the date 70–80 are by no means conclusive. He writes "to warn critics against a too hasty closing of the chronological question." In his new book (*Neue Untersuchungen zur Apostelgeschichte*, etc, 1911, S. 81) Harnack definitely accepts the date before the destruction of Jerus. Lightfoot would give no date to Acts because of the uncertainty about the date of the Gospel.

(3) Before 70 AD. This date is supported by Blass, Headlam, Maclean, Rackham, Salmon. Harnack, indeed, considers that "very weighty considerations" argue for the early date. He, as already stated, now takes his stand for the early date. It is obviously the simplest way to understand Luke's close of the Acts to be due to the fact that Paul was still in prison. Harnack contends that the efforts to explain away this situation are not "quite satisfactory or very illuminating." He does not mention Paul's death because he was still alive. The dramatic purpose to bring Paul to Rome is artificial. The supposition of a third book from the use of *prôton* in Acts **1** 1 is quite gratuitous, since in the *Koinē*, not to say the earlier Greek, "first" was often used when only two were mentioned (cf "our first story" and "second story," "first wife" and "second wife"). The whole tone of the book is that which one would naturally have before 64 AD. After the burning of Rome and the destruction of Jerusalem the attitude maintained in the book toward Romans and Jews would have been very difficult unless the date was a long time afterward. Harnack wishes "to help a doubt to its just dues." That "doubt" of Harnack is destined to become the certainty of the future. (Since this sentence was written Harnack has settled his own doubt.) The book will, I think, be finally credited to the time 63 AD in Rome. The Gospel of Luke will then naturally belong to the period of Paul's imprisonment in Caesarea. The judgment of Moffatt (*Historical NT*, 1901, 416) that "it cannot be earlier" than 80 AD is completely upset by the powerful attack of Harnack on his own previous position. See also Moffatt's *Introduction to the Lit. of the NT* (1911) and Koch's *Die Abfassungszeit des lukanischen Geschichtswerkes* (1911).

VII. Sources Used by Luke.—If we now assume that Luke is the author of the Acts, the question remains as to the character of the sources used by him. One is at liberty to appeal to Lk **1** 1–4 for the general method of the author. He used both oral and written sources. In the Acts the matter is somewhat simplified by the fact that Luke was the companion of Paul for a considerable part of the narrative (the "we" sections, **16** 11–17; **20** 5; **21** 18; **27** and **28**). It is more than probable that Luke was with Paul also during his last stay in Jerusalem and during the imprisonment at Caesarea. There is no reason to think that Luke suddenly left Paul in Jerusalem and returned to Caesarea only when he started to Rome (**27** 1). The absence of "we" is natural here, since it is not a narrative of travel, but a sketch of Paul's arrest and series of defences. The very abundance of material here, as in chs **20** and **21**, argues for the presence of Luke. But at any rate Luke has access to Paul himself for information concerning this period, as was true of the second, from ch **13** to the end of the book. Luke was either present or he could have learned from Paul the facts used. He may have kept a travel diary, which was drawn upon when necessary. Luke could have taken notes of Paul's addresses in Jerus (ch **22**) and Caesarea (chs **24–26**). From these, with Paul's help, he probably composed the account of Paul's conversion (**9** 1–30). **If, as I** think is true, the book was written during Paul's first Roman imprisonment, Luke had the benefit of appeal to Paul at all points. But, if so, he was thoroughly independent in style and assimilated his materials like a true historian. Paul (and also Philip for part of it) was a witness to the events about Stephen in **6** 8—**8** 1 and a participant of the work in Antioch (**11** 19–30). Philip, the host of Paul's company (**21** 8) on the last journey to Jerusalem, was probably in Caesarea still during Paul's confinement there. He could have told Luke the events in **6** 1–7 and **8** 4–40. In Caesarea also the story of Peter's work may have been derived, possibly even from Cornelius himself (**9** 32—**11** 18). Whether Luke ever went to Antioch or not we do not know (Codex Bezae has "we" in **11** 28), though he may have had access to the Antiochian traditions. But he did go to Jerus. However, the narrative in ch **12** probably rests on the authority of John Mark (**12** 12.25), in whose mother's house the disciples were assembled. Luke was apparently thrown with Mark in Rome (Col **4** 10), if not before. For Acts **1–5** the matter does not at first seem so clear, but these chapters are not necessarily discredited on that account. It is remarkable, as ancient historians made so little mention of their sources, that we can connect Luke in the Acts with so many probable fountains of evidence. Barnabas (**4** 36) was able to tell much about the origin of the work in Jerus. So could Mnason. Philip also was one of the seven (**6** 5; **21** 8). We do not know that Luke met Peter in Rome, though that is possible. But during the stay in Jerusalem and Caesarea (two years) Luke had abundant opportunity to learn the narrative of the great events told in Acts **1–5**. He perhaps used both oral and written sources for this section. One cannot, of course, prove by linguistic or historical arguments the precise nature of Luke's sources in Acts. Only in broad outlines the probable materials may be sketched.

VIII. The Speeches in Acts.—This matter is important enough to receive separate treatment. Are the numerous speeches reported in Acts free compositions of Luke made to order *à la* Thucydides? Are they verbatim reports from notes taken at the time and literally copied into the narrative? Are they substantial reports incorporated with more or less freedom with marks of Luke's own style? In the abstract either of these methods was possible. The example of Thucydides, Xenophon, Livy and Jos shows that ancient historians did not scruple to invent speeches of which no report was available. There are not wanting those who accuse Luke of this very thing in Acts. The matter can only be settled by an appeal to the facts so far as they can be determined. It cannot be denied that to a certain extent the hand of Luke is apparent in the addresses reported by him in Acts. But this fact must not be pressed too far. It is not true that the addresses are all alike in style. It is possible to distinguish very clearly the speeches of Peter from those of Paul. Not merely is this true, but we are able to compare the addresses of both Paul and Peter with their epistles. It is not probable that Luke had seen these epistles, as will presently be shown. It is crediting remarkable literary skill to Luke to suppose that he made up "Petrine" speeches and "Pauline" speeches with such success that they harmonize beautifully with the teachings and general style of each of these apostles. The address of Stephen differs also sharply from those of Peter and Paul, though we are not able to compare this report with any original work by Stephen himself. Another thing is true also, particularly of Paul's sermons. They are wonderfully suited to time, place and audience.

They all have a distinct Pauline flavor, and yet a difference in local color that corresponds, to some extent, with the variations in the style of Paul's epistles. Professor Percy Gardner (*The Speeches of St. Paul in Acts*, in Cambridge Biblical Essays, 1909) recognizes these differences, but seeks to explain them on the ground of varying accuracy in the sources used by Luke, counting the speech at Miletus as the most historic of all. But he admits the use of sources by Luke for these addresses. The theory of pure invention by Luke is quite discredited by appeal to the facts. On the other hand, in view of the apparent presence of Luke's style to some extent in the speeches, it can hardly be claimed that he has made verbatim reports. Besides, the report of the addresses of Jesus in Luke's Gospel (as in the other gospels) shows the same freedom in giving the substance without exact reproduction of the words that is found in Acts. Again, it seems clear that some, if not all, the reports in Acts are condensed, mere outlines in the case of some of Peter's addresses. The ancients knew how to make shorthand reports of such addresses. The oral tradition was probably active in preserving the early speeches of Peter and even of Stephen, though Paul himself heard Stephen. The speeches of Paul all show the marks of an eye-witness (Bethge, *Die paulinischen Reden*, etc, 174). For the speeches of Peter, Luke may have had documents, or he may have taken down the current oral tradition while he was in Jerusalem and Caesarea. Peter probably spoke in Greek on the day of Pentecost. His other addresses may have been in Aram. or in Gr. But the oral tradition would certainly carry them in Gr, if also in Aram. Luke heard Paul speak at Miletus (Acts **20**) and may have taken notes at the time. So also he almost certainly heard Paul's address on the steps of the Tower of Antonia (ch **22**) and that before Agrippa (ch **26**). There is no reason to think that he was absent when Paul made his defences before Felix and Festus (chs **24–25**). He was present on the ship when Paul spoke (ch **27**), and in Rome when he addressed the Jews (ch **28**). Luke was not on hand when Paul delivered his sermon at Antioch in Pisidia (ch **13**), or at Lystra (ch **14**), or at Athens (ch **17**). But these discourses differ so greatly in theme and treatment, and are so essentially Pauline that it is natural to think that Paul himself gave Luke the notes which he used. The sermon at Antioch in Pisidia is probably given as a sample of Paul's missionary discourses. It contains the heart of Paul's gospel as it appears in his epistles. He accentuates the death and resurrection of Jesus, remission of sins through Christ, justification by faith. It is sometimes objected that at Athens the address shows a breadth of view and sympathy unknown to Paul, and that there is a curious Attic tone to the Gr style. The sermon does go as far as Paul can (cf 1 Cor **9** 22) toward the standpoint of the Greeks (but compare Col and Eph). However, Paul does not sacrifice his principle of grace in Christ. He called the Athenians to repentance, preached the judgment for sin and announced the resurrection of Jesus from the dead. The fatherhood of God and the brotherhood of man here taught did not mean that God winked at sin and could save all men without repentance and forgiveness of sin. Chase (*The Credibility of Acts*) gives a collection of Paul's missionary addresses. The historical reality and value of the speeches in Acts may be said to be vindicated by modern scholarship. For a sympathetic and scholarly discussion of all of Paul's addresses see Jones, *St. Paul the Orator* (1910). The short speech of Tertullus (Acts **24**) was made in public, as was the public statement of Festus in ch **26**. The letter of Claudius Lysias to Felix in ch **23** was a public document. How Luke got hold of the conversation about Paul between Festus and Agrippa in ch **26** is more difficult to conjecture.

IX. Relation of Acts to the Epistles.—There is no real evidence that Luke made use of any of Paul's epistles. He was with Paul in Rome when Col was written (**4** 14), and may, indeed, have been Paul's amanuensis for this epistle (and for Eph and Philem). Some similarities to Luke's style have been pointed out. But Acts closes without any narrative of the events in Rome during the years there, so that these epistles exerted no influence on the composition of the book. As to the two preceding groups of Paul's epistles (1 and 2 Thess; 1 and 2 Cor, Gal, Rom) there is no proof that Luke saw any of them. The Epistle to the Romans was probably accessible to him while in Rome, but he does not seem to have used it. Luke evidently preferred to appeal to Paul directly for information rather than to his epistles. This is all simple enough if he wrote the book or made his data while Paul was alive. But if Acts was written very late, it would be strange for the author not to have made use of some of Paul's epistles. The book has, therefore, the great advantage of covering some of the same ground as that discussed in the earlier epistles, but from a thoroughly independent standpoint. The gaps in our knowledge from the one source are often supplied incidentally, but most satisfactorily, from the other. The coincidences between Acts and Paul's epistles have been well traced by Paley in his *Horae Paulinae*, still a book of much value. Knowling, in his *Witness of the Epistles* (1892), has made a more recent study of the same problem. But for the apparent conflict between Gal **2** 1–10 and Acts **15** the matter might be dropped at this point. It is argued by some that Acts, written long after Gal, brushes to one side the account of the Jerusalem conference given by Paul. It is held that Paul is correct in his personal record, and that Acts is therefore unhistorical. Others save the credit of Acts by arguing that Paul is referring to an earlier private conference some years before the public discussion recorded in Acts **15**. This is, of course, possible in itself, but it is by no means required by the variations between the two reports. The contention of Lightfoot has never been really overturned, that in Gal **2** 1–10 Paul gives the personal side of the conference, not a full report of the general meeting. What Paul is doing is to show the Galatians how he is on a par with the Jerusalem apostles, and how his authority and independence were acknowledged by them. This aspect of the matter came out in the private conference. Paul is not in Gal **2** 1–10 setting forth his victory over the Judaizers in behalf of Gentile freedom. But in Acts **15** it is precisely this struggle for Gentile freedom that is under discussion. Paul's relations with the Jerusalem apostles is not the point at all, though it is plain in Acts that they agree. In Gal also Paul's victory for Gentile freedom comes out. Indeed, in Acts **15** it is twice mentioned that the apostles and elders were gathered together (vs 4. 6), and twice we are told that Paul and Barnabas addressed them (vs 4. 12). It is therefore natural to suppose that this private conference narrated by Paul in Gal came in between vs 5 and 6. Luke may not, indeed, have seen the Epistle to the Galatians, and may not have heard from Paul the story of the private conference, though he knew of the two public meetings. If he did know of the private meeting, he thought it not pertinent to his narration. There is, of course, no contradiction between Paul's going up by revelation and by appointment of the church in Antioch. In Gal **2** 1 we have the second (Gal **1** 18) visit to

Jerusalem after his conversion mentioned by Paul, while that in Acts **15** is the third in Acts (**9** 28; **11** 29 f; **15** 2). But there was no particular reason for Paul to mention the visit in Acts **11** 30, which did not concern his relation to the apostles in Jerusalem. Indeed, only the "elders" are mentioned on this occasion. The same independence between Acts and Gal occurs in Gal **1** 17–24, and Acts **9** 26–30. In Acts there is no allusion to the visit to Arabia, just as there is no mention of the private conference in Acts **15**. So also in Acts **15** 35–39 there is no mention of the sharp disagreement between Paul and Peter at Antioch recorded in Gal **2** 11 ff. Paul mentions it merely to prove his own authority and independence as an apostle. Luke had no occasion to record the incident, if he was acquainted with the matter. These instances illustrate well how, when the Acts and the epistles vary, they really supplement each other.

X. Chronology of Acts.—Here we confront one of the most perplexing questions in New Testament criticism. In general, ancient writers were not so careful as modern writers are to give precise dates for historical events. Indeed, it was not easy to do so in view of the absence of a uniform method of reckoning time. Luke does, however, relate his narrative to outward events at various points. In his Gospel he had linked the birth of Jesus with the names of Augustus as emperor and of Quirinius as governor of Syria (Lk **2** 1 f), and the entrance of John the Baptist upon his ministry with the names of the chief Roman and Jewish rulers of the time (Lk **3** 1 f). So also in the Acts he does not leave us without various notes of time. He does not, indeed, give the date of the Ascension or of the Crucifixion, though he places the Ascension forty days after the Resurrection (Acts **1** 3), and the great Day of Pentecost would then come ten days later, "not many days hence" (**1** 5). But the other events in the opening chapters of Acts have no clear chronological arrangement. The career of Stephen is merely located "in these days" (**6** 1). The beginning of the general persecution under Saul is located on the very day of Stephen's death (**8** 1), but the year is not even hinted at. The conversion of Saul comes probably in its chronological order in **9**, but the year again is not given. We have no hint as to the age of Saul at his conversion. So again the relation of Peter's work in Caesarea (**10**) to the preaching to the Greeks in Antioch (**11**) is not made clear, though probably in this order. It is only when we come to **12** that we reach an event whose date is reasonably certain. This is the death of Herod Agrippa I in 44 AD. But even so, Luke does not correlate the life of Paul with that incident. Ramsay (*St. Paul the Traveller*, 49) places the persecution and death of James in 44, and the visit of Barnabas and Saul to Jerusalem in 46. About 44, then, we may consider that Saul came to Antioch from Tarsus. The "fourteen years" in Gal **2** 1, as already shown, probably point to the visit in Acts **15** some years later. But Saul had been in Tarsus some years and had spent some three years in Arabia and Damascus after his conversion (Gal **1** 18). Beyond this it is not possible to go. We do not know the age of Saul in 44 AD or the year of his conversion. He was probably born not far from 1 AD. But if we locate Paul at Antioch with Barnabas in 44 AD, we can make some headway. Here Paul spent a year (Acts **11** 26). The visit to Jerusalem in **11**, the first missionary tour in **13** and **14**, the conference at Jerusalem in **15**, the second missionary tour in **16–18**, the third missionary tour and return to Jerusalem in **18–21**, the arrest in Jerusalem and two years in Caesarea in **21–26**, all come between 44 AD and the recall of Felix and the coming of Festus. It used to be taken for granted that Festus came in 60 AD. Wieseler figured it out so from Josephus and was followed by Lightfoot. But Eusebius, in his "Chronicle," placed that event in the second year of Nero. That would be 56, unless Eusebius has a special way of counting those years. Mr. C. H. Turner (art. "Chronology" in *HDB*) finds that Eusebius counts an emperor's regnal year from the September following. If so, the date could be moved forward to 57 (cf Rackham on *Acts*, lxvi). But Ramsay (ch xiv, "Pauline Chronology," in *Pauline and Other Studies*) cuts the Gordian knot by showing an error in Eusebius due to his disregarding an interregnum with the reign of kings. Ramsay here follows Erbes (*Todestage Pauli und Petri*) in this discovery and is able to fix upon 59 as the date of the coming of Festus. Probably 59 will have to answer as a compromise date. Between 44 AD and 59 AD, therefore, we place the bulk of Paul's active missionary work. Luke has divided this period into minor divisions with relative dates. Thus a year and six months are mentioned at Corinth (Acts **18** 11), besides "yet many days" (**18** 18). In Ephesus we find mention of "three months" (**19** 8) and "two years" (**19** 10), the whole story summed up as "three years" (**20** 31). Then we have the "two years" of delay in Caesarea (**24** 27). We thus have about seven of these fifteen years itemized. Much of the remaining eight was spent in the journeys described by Luke. We are told also the time of year when the voyage to Rome was under way (**27** 9), the length of the voyage (**27** 27), the duration of the stay in Melita (**28** 11), and the time spent in Rome at the close of the book, "two whole years" (**28** 30). Thus it is possible to fix upon a relative schedule of dates, though not an absolute one. Harnack (*The Acts of the Apostles*, ch i, "Chronological Data") has worked out a very careful scheme for the whole of Acts. Knowling has a good critical résumé of the present state of our knowledge of the chronology of Acts in his *Commentary*, 38 ff; cf also Clemen, *Die Chronologie der paulinischen Briefe* (1893). It is clear, then, that a rational scheme for events of Paul's career so far as recorded in the Acts can be found. If 57 AD, for instance, should be taken as the year of Festus' coming rather than 59 or 60 AD, the other dates back to 44 AD would, of course, be affected on a sliding scale. Back of 44 AD the dates are largely conjectural.

XI. Historical Worth of Acts.—It was once fashionable to discredit Acts as a book of no real value as history. The Tübingen school regarded Acts as "a late controversial romance, the only historical value of which was to throw light on the thought of the period which produced it" (Chase, *The Credibility of Acts*, 9). There are not wanting a few writers who still regard Acts as a late *eirēnicon* between the Peter and Paul parties, or as a party pamphlet in the interest of Paul. Somewhat fanciful parallels are found between Luke's treatment of both Peter and Paul. "According to Holtzmann, the strongest argument for the critical position is the correspondence between the acts of St. Peter and the other apostles on the one side and those of St. Paul on the other" (Headlam in *HDB*). But this matter seems rather far fetched. Peter is the leading figure in the early chapters, as Paul is in the latter half of the book, but the correspondences are not remarkably striking. There exists in some minds a prejudice against the book on the ground of the miracles recorded as genuine events by Luke. But Paul himself claimed to have wrought miracles (2 Cor **12** 12). It is not scientific to rule a book out beforehand because it narrates miracles (Blass, *Acta Apostolorum*, 8). Ramsay (*St. Paul the Traveller*, 8) tells his experience in regard to the trustworthiness of Acts: "I began with a mind unfavorable to it, for the ingenuity and apparent completeness of the Tübingen theory had at one time quite convinced me." It was by actual verification of Acts in points where it could be tested by inscriptions, Paul's epistles, or current non-Christian writers, that "it was gradually borne in upon me that in various details the narrative showed marvelous truth." He concludes by "placing this great writer on the high pedestal that belongs to him" (10). McGiffert (*The Apostolic Age*) had been compelled by the geographical and historical evidence to abandon in part the older criticism. He also admitted that the Acts "is more trustworthy than previous critics allowed" (Ramsay, *Luke the Physician*, 5). Schmiedel (*EB*) still argues that the writer of Acts is inaccurate because he was not in possession of full information. But on the whole Acts has had a triumphant vindication in modern criticism. Jülicher (*Einl*, 355) admits "a genuine core overgrown with legendary accretions" (Chase, *Credibility*, 9). The moral honesty of Luke, his fidelity to truth (Rackham on *Acts*, 46), is clearly shown in both his Gospel and the Acts. This, after all, is the chief trait in the true historian (Ramsay, *St. Paul the Traveller*, 4). Luke writes as a man of serious purpose and is the one New Testament writer who mentions his careful use of his materials (Lk **1** 1–4). His attitude and spirit are those of the historian. He reveals artistic skill, it is true, but not to the discredit of his record. He does not give a bare chronicle, but he writes a real history, an interpretation of the events recorded. He had adequate resources in the way of materials and endowment and has made conscientious and skilful use of his opportunity. It is not necessary here to give in detail all the points in which Luke has been vindicated (see Knowling on *Acts*, Ramsay's books and Harnack's *Luke* and *Acts*). The most obvious are the following: The use of "proconsul" instead of "propraetor" in Acts **13** 7 is a striking instance. Curiously enough Cyprus was not a senatorial province very long. An inscription has been found in Cyprus "in the proconsulship of Paulus." The 'first men' of Antioch in Pisidia is like the (**13** 50) "First Ten," a title which "was only given (as here) to a board of magistrates in Gr cities of the East" (MacLean in one-vol. *HDB*). The "priest of Jupiter" at Lystra (**14** 13) is in accord with the known facts of the worship there. So we have Perga in Pamphylia (**13** 13), Antioch in Pisidia **13** 14), Lystra and Derbe in Lycaonia (**14** 6), but not Iconium (**14** 1). In Philippi Luke notes that the magistrates are called *strategoí* or praetors (**16** 20), and are accompanied by lictors or *rhabdoúchoi* (**16** 35). In Thessalonica the rulers are *politarchs* (**17** 6), a title found nowhere else, but now discovered on an inscription of Thessalonica. He rightly speaks of the Court of the Areopagus at Athens (**17** 19) and the proconsul in Achaia (**18** 12). Though Athens was a free city, the Court of the Areopagus at the time were the real rulers. Achaia was sometimes associated with Macedonia, though at this time it was a separate senatorial province. In Ephesus Luke knows of the Asiarchs (**19** 31), "the presidents of the 'Common Council' of the province in cities where there was a temple of Rome and the Emperor; they superintended the worship of the Emperor" (Maclean). Note also the fact that Ephesus is "temple-keeper of the great Diana" (**19** 35). Then observe the town clerk (**19** 35), and the assembly (**19** 39). Note also the title of Felix, "governor" or procurator (**24** 1), Agrippa the king (**25** 13), Julius the centurion and the Augustan band (**27** 1). Ch **27** is a marvel of interest and accuracy for all who wish to know details of ancient seafaring. The matter has been worked over in a masterful way by James Smith, *Voyage and Shipwreck of St. Paul.* The title "First Man of the Island" (**28** 7) is now found on a coin of Melita. These are by no means all the matters of interest, but they will suffice. In most of the items given above Luke's veracity was once challenged, but now he has been triumphantly vindicated. The force of this vindication is best appreciated when one recalls the incidental nature of the items mentioned. They come from widely scattered districts and are just the points where in strange regions it is so easy to make slips. If space allowed, the matter could be set forth in more detail and with more justice to Luke's worth as a historian. It is true that in the earlier portions of the Acts we are not able to find so many geographical and historical corroborations. But the nature of the material did not call for the mention of so many places and persons. In the latter part Luke does not hesitate to record miraculous events also. His character as a historian is firmly established by the passages where outside contact has been found. We cannot refuse him a good name in the rest of the book, though the value of the sources used certainly cuts a figure. It has been urged that Luke breaks down as a historian in the double mention of Quirinius in Lk **2** 2 and Acts **5** 37. But Ramsay (*Was Christ Born at Bethlehem?*) has shown how the new knowledge of the census system of Augustus derived from the Egyp papyri is about to clear up this difficulty. Luke's general accuracy at least calls for suspense of judgment, and in the matter of Theudas and Judas the Galilean (Acts **5**) Luke as compared with Josephus outclasses his rival. Harnack (*The Acts of the Apostles*, 203–29) gives in his usual painstaking way a number of examples of "inaccuracy and discrepancy." But the great bulk of them are merely examples of independence in narration (cf Acts **9** with **22** and **26**, where we have three reports of Paul's conversion). Harnack did not, indeed, once place as high a value on Luke as a historian as he now does. It is all the more significant, therefore, to read the following in Harnack's *The Acts of the Apostles* (298 f): "The book has now been restored to the position of credit which is its rightful due. It is not only, taken as a whole, a genuinely historical work, but even in the majority of its details it is trustworthy. . . . . Judged from almost every possible standpoint of historical criticism it is a solid, respectable, and in many respects an extraordinary work." That is, in my opinion, an understatement of the facts (see Ramsay), but it is a remarkable conclusion concerning the trustworthiness of Luke when one considers the distance that Harnack has come. At any rate the prejudice against Luke is rapidly disappearing. The judgment of the future is forecast by Ramsay, who ranks Luke as a historian of the first order.

XII. Purpose of the Book.—A great deal of discussion has been given to Luke's aim in the Acts. Baur's theory was that this book was written to give a conciliatory view of the conflict between Peter and Paul, and that a minute parallelism exists in the Acts between these two heroes. This tendency theory once held the critical field, but it does not take into view all the facts, and fails to explain the book as a whole. Peter and Paul are the heroes of the book as they undoubtedly were the two chief personalities in apostolic history (cf Wendt, *Apostelgeschichte*, 17). There is some parallelism between the careers of the two men (cf the worship offered Peter at Caesarea in Acts **10** 25, and that to Paul in **14** 11; see also the punishment of Ananias and Sapphira and that of Elymas). But Knowling (*Acts*, 16) well replies that curiously no use is made of the death of both Peter and Paul in Rome, possibly at the same time. If the Acts was written late, this matter would be open to the knowledge of the writer. There is in truth no real effort on Luke's part to paint Paul like Peter or Peter like Paul. The few similarities in incident are merely natural historical parallels. Others have seen in the Acts a strong purpose to conciliate gentile (pagan) opinion in the fact that the Rom governors and military officers are so uniformly presented as favorable to Paul, while the Jews are represented as the real aggressors against Christianity (cf Josephus' attitude toward Rome). Here again the fact is beyond dispute. But the other explanation is the more natural, viz. that Luke brings out this aspect of the matter because it was the truth. Cf B. Weiss, *Einl*, 569. Luke does have an eye on the world relations of Christianity and rightly reflects Paul's ambition to win the Roman Empire to Christ (see Rom **15**), but that is not to say that he has given the book a political bias or colored it so as to deprive it of its historical worth. It is probably true (cf Knowling, *Acts*, 15; J. Weiss, *Ueber die Absicht und den literarischen Charakter der Apostelgeschichte*) that Luke felt, as did Paul, that Judaism realized its world destiny in Christianity, that Christianity was the true Judaism, the spiritual and real Israel. If Luke wrote Acts in Rome, while Paul's case was still before Nero, it is easy to understand the somewhat long and minute account of the arrest and trials of Paul in Jerusalem, Caesarea and Rome. The point would be that the legal aspect of Christianity before Rom laws was involved. Hitherto Christianity had found shelter as a sect of Judaism, and so was passed by Gallio in Corinth as a *religio licita*. If Paul was condemned as a Christian, the whole aspect of the matter would be altered. Christianity would at once become *religio illicita*. The last word in the Acts comments on the fact that Paul, though still a prisoner, was permitted to preach unhindered. The importance of this point is clearly seen as one pushes on to the Neronian persecution in 64. After that date Christianity stood apart from Judaism in the eye of Rome. I have already stated my belief that Luke closed the Acts when he did and as he did because the events with Paul had only gone thus far. Numerous scholars hold that Luke had in mind a third book (Acts **1** 1), a possible though by no means necessary inference from "first treatise." It was a climax to carry the narrative on to Rome with Paul, but it is rather straining the point to find all this in Acts **1** 8. Rome was not "the nethermost part of the earth," Spain more nearly being that. Nor did Paul take the gospel to Rome. Besides, to make the arrival of Paul in Rome the goal in the mind of Christ is too narrowing a purpose. The purpose to go to Rome did dominate Paul's mind for several years (**19** 21), but Paul cuts no figure in the early part of the book. And Paul wished to push on from Rome to Spain (Rom **15** 24). It is probably true that Luke means to announce his purpose in Acts **1** 1–8. One needs to keep in mind also Lk **1** 1–4. There are various ways of writing history. Luke chooses the biographical method in Acts. Thus he conceives that he can best set forth the tremendous task of interpreting the first thirty years of the apostolic history. It is around persons (cf Harnack, *The Acts of the Apostles*, 117), two great figures (Peter and Paul), that the narrative is focused. Peter is most prominent in **1–12,** Paul in **13–28.** Still Paul's conversion is told in Acts **9** and Peter reappears in **15.** But these great personages do not stand alone. John the Apostle is certainly with Peter in the opening chapters. The other apostles are mentioned also by name (**1** 13) and a number of times in the first twelve chapters (and in **15**). But after **15** they drop out of the narrative, for Luke follows the fortunes of Paul. The other chief secondary figures in Acts are Stephen, Philip, Barnabas, James, Apollos, all Hellenists save James (Harnack, 120). The minor characters are numerous (John, Mark, Silas, Timothy, Aquila and Priscilla, Aristarchus, etc). In most cases Luke gives a distinct picture of these incidental personages. In particular he brings out sharply such men as Gallio, Claudius, Lysias, Felix, Festus, Herod, Agrippa I and II, Julius. Luke's conception of the apostolic history is that it is the work of Jesus still carried on by the Holy Spirit (**1** 1 f). Christ chose the apostles, commanded them to wait for power from on high, filled them with the Holy Spirit and then sent them on the mission of world conquest. In the Acts Luke records the waiting, the coming of the Holy Spirit, the planting of a powerful church in Jerus and the expansion of the gospel to Samaria and all over the Roman Empire. He addresses the book to Theophilus as his patron, a Gentile Christian plainly, as he had done with his gospel. The book is designed for the enlightenment of Christians generally concerning the historic origins of Christianity. It is in truth the first church history. It is in reality the Acts of the Holy Spirit as wrought through these men. It is an inspiring narration. Luke had no doubt whatever of the future of a gospel with such a history and with such heroes of faith as Peter and Paul.

XIII. Analysis.—

1. The connection between the work of the apostles and that of Jesus (**1** 1–11).
2. The equipment of the early disciples for their task (**1** 12—**2** 47).
   (*a*) The disciples obeying Christ's parting command (**1** 12–14).
   (*b*) The place of Judas filled (**1** 15–26).
   (*c*) Miraculous manifestations of the presence of the Holy Spirit (**2** 1–13).
   (*d*) Peter's interpretation of the situation (**2** 14–36).
   (*e*) The immediate effect of the sermon (**2** 37–41).
   (*f*) The new spirit in the Christian community (**2** 42–47).
3. The development of the work in Jerusalem (**3** 1—**8** 1*a*).
   (*a*) An incident in the work of Peter and John with Peter's apologetic (**3**).
   (*b*) Opposition of the Sadducees aroused by the preaching of the resurrection of Jesus (**4** 1–31).
   (*c*) An internal difficulty, the problem of poverty (**4** 32—**5** 11).
   (*d*) Great progress of the cause in the city (**5** 12–16).
   (*e*) Renewed hostility of the Sadducees and Gamaliel's retort to the Pharisees (**5** 17–42).
   (*f*) A crisis in church life and the choice of the seven Hellenists (**6** 1–7).
   (*g*) Stephen's spiritual interpretation of Christianity stirs the antagonism of the Pharisees and leads to his violent death (**6** 8—**8** 1*a*).
4. The compulsory extension of the gospel to Judaea, Samaria and the neighboring regions (**8** 1*b*–40).
   (*a*) The great persecution, with Saul as leader (**8** 1*b*–4).
   (*b*) Philip's work as a notable example of the work of the scattered disciples (**8** 5–40).
5. The conversion of Saul changes the whole situation for Christianity (**9** 1–31).
   (*a*) Saul's mission to Damascus (**9** 1–3).
   (*b*) Saul stopped in his hostile course and turns Christian himself (**9** 4–18).

(*c*) Saul becomes a powerful exponent of the gospel in Damascus and Jerusalem (**9** 19–30).
(*d*) The church has peace (**9** 31).

6. The door opened to the Gentiles, both Roman and Greek (**9** 32—**11** 30).
   (*a*) Peter's activity in this time of peace (**9** 32–43).
   (*b*) The appeal from Cornelius in Caesarea and Peter's response (**10**).
   (*c*) Peter's arraignment before the Pharisaic element in the church in Jerusalem (**11** 1–18).
   (*d*) Greeks in Antioch are converted and Barnabas brings Saul to this work (**11** 19–26).
   (*e*) The Greek Christians send relief to the Jewish Christians in Jerusalem (**11** 27–30).
7. Persecution from the civil government (**12**).
   (*a*) Herod Agrippa I kills James and imprisons Peter (**12** 1–19).
   (*b*) Herod pays the penalty for his crimes (**12** 20–23).
   (*c*) Christianity prospers (**12** 24 f).
8. The gentile propaganda from Antioch under the leadership of Barnabas and Saul (**13, 14**).
   (*a*) The specific call of the Holy Spirit to this work (**13** 1–3).
   (*b*) The province of Cyprus and the leadership of Paul (**13** 4–12).
   (*c*) The province of Pamphylia and the desertion of John Mark (**13** 13).
   (*d*) The province of Galatia (Pisidia and Lycaonia) and the stronghold of the gospel upon the native population (**13** 14—**14** 24).
   (*e*) The return and report to Antioch (**14** 25–28).
9. The gentile campaign challenged by the Judaizers (**15** 1–35).
   (*a*) They meet Paul and Barnabas at Antioch who decide to appeal to Jerusalem (**15** 1–3).
   (*b*) The first public meeting in Jerusalem (**15** 4 f).
   (*c*) The second and more extended discussion with the decision of the conference (**15** 6–29).
   (*d*) The joyful reception (in Antioch) of the victory of Paul and Barnabas (**15** 30–35).
10. The second great campaign extending to Europe (**15** 36—**18** 22).
   (*a*) The breach between Paul and Barnabas over John Mark (**15** 36–39).
   (*b*) From Antioch to Troas with the Macedonian Cry (**15** 40—**16** 10).
   (*c*) In Philippi in Macedonia the gospel gains a foothold in Europe, but meets opposition (**16** 11–40).
   (*d*) Paul is driven also from Thessalonica and Berea (cf Philippi), cities of Macedonia also (**17** 1–15).
   (*e*) Paul's experience in Athens (**17** 16–34).
   (*f*) In Corinth Paul spends nearly two years and the cause of Christ wins legal recognition from the Roman governor (**18** 1–17).
   (*g*) The return to Antioch by way of Ephesus, Caesarea and probably Jerusalem (**18** 18–22).
11. The third great tour, with Ephesus as headquarters (**18** 23—**20** 3).
   (*a*) Paul in Galatia and Phrygia again (**18** 23).
   (*b*) Apollos in Ephesus before Paul comes (**18** 24–28).
   (*c*) Paul's three years in Ephesus (**19** 1—**20** 1*a*).
   (*d*) The brief visit to Corinth because of the troubles there (**20** 1*b*–3).
12. Paul turns to Jerusalem again with plans for Rome (**20** 4—**21** 16).
   (*a*) His companions (**20** 4).
   (*b*) Rejoined by Luke at Philippi (**20** 5 f).
   (*c*) The story of Troas (**20** 7–12).
   (*d*) Coasting along Asia (**20** 13–16).
   (*e*) With the Ephesian elders at Miletus (**20** 17–38).
   (*f*) From Miletus to Tyre (**21** 1–6).
   (*g*) From Tyre to Caesarea (**21** 7–14).
   (*h*) From Caesarea to Jerusalem (**21** 15 f).
13. The outcome in Jerusalem (**21** 15—**23** 30).
   (*a*) Paul's reception by the brethren (**21** 15–17).
   (*b*) Their proposal of a plan by which Paul could undo the work of the Judaizers concerning him in Jerusalem (**21** 18–26).
   (*c*) The uproar in the temple courts raised by the Jews from Asia as Paul was carrying out the plan to disarm the Judaizers (**21** 27–30).
   (*d*) Paul's rescue by the Roman captain and Paul's defence to the Jewish mob (**21** 31—**22** 23).
   (*e*) Examination of the chief captain (**22** 24–29).
   (*f*) Brought before the Sanhedrin (**22** 30—**23** 10).
   (*g*) Cheered by the Lord Jesus (**23** 11).
   (*h*) Paul's escape from the plot of Jewish conspirators (**23** 12–30).
14. Paul a prisoner in Caesarea (**23** 31—**26**).
   (*a*) The flight to Caesarea and presentation to Felix (**23** 31–35).
   (*b*) Paul's appearance before Felix (**24**).
   (*c*) Paul before Festus (**25** 1–12).
   (*d*) Paul, as a matter of curiosity and courtesy, brought before Herod Agrippa II (**25** 13—**26** 32).
15. Paul going to Rome (**27** 1—**28** 15).
   (*a*) From Caesarea to Myra (**27** 1–5).
   (*b*) From Myra to Fair Havens (**27** 6–8).
   (*c*) From Fair Havens to Malta (**27** 9—**28** 10).
   (*d*) From Malta to Rome (**28** 11–15).
16. Paul in Rome at last (**28** 16–31).
   (*a*) His quarters (**28** 16).
   (*b*) His first interview with the Jews (**28** 17–22).
   (*c*) His second interview with the Jews (**28** 23–28).
   (*d*) Two years afterward still a prisoner, but with freedom to preach the gospel (**28** 30 f).

LITERATURE.—Besides the works referred to above see Wendt's edition of Meyer's *Kommentar* (1899); Headlam in *HDB;* Knowling on Acts in Expositor's Greek Testament (1900); Knowling, *Witness of the Epistles* (1892), *Testimony of St. Paul to Christ* (1905); Moffatt, *Historical NT* (1901).

Here is a selected list of important works:

1. Introduction: Bacon, *Intro to the NT* (1900); Bennett and Adeney, *Biblical Intro* (1899); Bleek, *Einl in das NT* (4 Aufl, 1900); S. Davidson, (3d ed, 1894); C. R. Gregory, *Canon and Text of the NT* (1907); H. J. Holtzmann, *Einl in das NT* (3 Aufl, 1892); Jacquies, *Histoire des livres du NT* (1905–8); Jülicher, *Intro to the NT* (tr, 1904); Peake, *Critical Intro to the NT* (1909); Reuss, *Canon of the Holy Scriptures* (tr, 1886); Salmon, *Hist Intro to the Study of the Books of the NT* (7th ed, 1896); von Soden, *The History of Early Christian Lit.* (tr, 1906); B. Weiss, *A Manual of Intro to the NT* (tr, 1889); Westcott, *History of the Canon of the NT* (1869); Zahn, *Intro to the NT* (tr, 1909); Moffatt, *Intro to the Lit. of the NT* (1911).

2. Text: See general works on textual criticism of the NT (Gregory, Kenyon, Nestle, Tischendorf, Scrivener, von Soden, B. Weiss, Westcott, etc). Of special treatises note Blass, *Philology of the Gospels* (1898). *Acta Apostolorum* (1895); Bornemann, *Acta Apostolorum* (1848); Chase, *Old Syriac Element in the Text of Codex Bezae* (1893); Corssen, *Der cyprianische Text der Acta Apostolorum* (1892); Klostermann, *Probleme im Apostel Texte* (1883); Klostermann, *Vindiciae Lucanae* (1866); Nestle, *Philologia* (1896); J. Rendel Harris, *Study of Codex Bezae* (1891).

3. Apostolic History: For literature on the life of Paul see Robertson, *Epochs in the Life of Paul* (1909), 321–27, and art. PAUL in this encyclopaedia. Important general works are the following: Bartlet, *The Apostolic Age* (1899); Baumgarten, *The Apostolic History* (tr, 1854); Blunt, *Studies in the Apostolic Age* (1909); Burton, *Records and Letters of the Apostolic Age* (1895); Doellinger, *The First Age of the Church* (tr, 1867); Dobschütz, *Christian Life in the Primitive Church* (tr,

1904); Ewald, *History of the Apostolic Times* (tr, Vol VI in History of Israel); Farrar, *Early Days of Christianity* (1887); Fisher, *The Beginnings of Christianity* (1877); Gilbert, *Christianity in the Apostolic Age* (1908); Harnack, *The Expansion of Christianity in the First Three Centuries* (tr, 1904–5); Hausrath, *Neut. Zeitgeschichte* (Bd. 2, 1872); Heinrici, *Das Urchristentum* (1902); Holtzmann, *Neut. Zeitgeschichte* (1895); Hort, *Judaistic Christianity* (1898); *Organization of the Early Christian Churches* (1895); Lechler, *The Apostolic and Post-Apostolic Times* (tr, 1886); Lightfoot, *Dissertations on the Apostolic Age* (1892); Lindsay, *The Church and the Ministry in the Early Centuries* (1902); McGiffert, *A History of Christianity in the Apostolic Age* (1897); Neander, *History of the Planting and Training of the Christian Church* (1889); Pfleiderer, *Christian Origins* (1906); Pressensé, *The Early Years of Christianity* (1870); Purves, *Christianity in the Apostolic Age* (1901); Ramsay, *The Church in the Roman Empire* (1893); Ritschl, *Die Entstehung der altkath. Kirche* (1857); Ropes, *The Apostolic Age in the Light of Modern Criticism* (1906); Weizsäcker, *The Apostolic Age of the Christian Church* (tr, 1894–95); *Pictures of the Apostolic Church* (1910).

4. Special Treatises on The Acts: Belser, *Beiträge zur Erklärung der Apostelgeschichte* (1897); Benson, *Addresses on the Acts of the Apostles* (1901); Bethge, *Die paulinischen Reden der Apostelgeschichte* (1887); Blass, *Acta Apostolorum secundum Formam quae videtur Romanam* (1896); Chase, *The Credibility of the Book of the Acts of the Apostles* (1902); Clemen, *Die Apostelgeschichte, im Lichte der neueren Forschungen* (1905); Fiene, *Eine vorkanonische Nebenlieferung des Lukas in Evangelium und Apostelgeschichte* (1891); Harnack, *Luke, the Physician* (tr, 1907); *The Acts of the Apostles* (1909); Hilgenfeld, *Acta Apostolorum Graece et Latine* (1899); Jüngst, *Die Quellen der Apostelgeschichte* (1895); Krenkel, *Josephus und Lucas* (1894); Luckok, *Footprints of the Apostles as Traced by St. Luke in the Acts* (1897); J. Lightfoot, *Hebrew and Talmudical Exercitations on the Acts of the Apostles* (1768); Paley, *Horae Paulinae* (Birks ed, 1850); Ramsay, *St. Paul the Traveller* (1896); *Pauline and Other Studies* (1906); *Cities of St. Paul* (1908), *Luke the Physician, and Other Studies* (1908); J. Smith, *Voyage and Shipwreck of St. Paul* (4th ed, 1880); Sorof, *Die Entstehung der Apostelgeschichte* (1890); Spitta, *Die Apostelgeschichte, ihre Quellen und deren geschichtlicher Werth* (1891); Stifler, *An Intro to the Book of Acts* (1892); Vogel, *Zur Characteristik des Lukas nach Sprache und Stil* (1897); J. Weiss, *Ueber die Absicht und die literarischen Charakter der Apostelgeschichte* (1897); Zeller, *The Contents and Origin of the Acts of the Apostles* (tr, 1875); Maurice Jones, *St. Paul the Orator* (1910).

5. Commentaries: There are the great standard works, like Bede, Bengel, Calvin, Chrysostom, Grotius. The chief modern commentaries are the following: Alexander (1857), Alford (6th ed, 1868), Bartlet (1901), Blass (*Acta Apostolorum*, 1895), Ewald (*Apostelgeschichte*, 1871), Felten (*Apostelgeschichte*, 1892), Hackett (1882), Holtzmann (*Hand-Commentar*, 3 Aufl, 1901), Knabenbauer (*Actus Apostol*, 1899), Knowling (*Expositor's Gr Text*, 1900), Luthardt und Zoeckler (*Apostelgeschichte*, 2d ed, 1894), McGarvey (1892), Meyer (tr by Gloag and Dickson, 1885), Meyer-Wendt (*Apostelgeschichte*, 1888). Noesgen (*Apostelgeschichte*, 1882), Olshausen (1832), Page (1897), Rackham (1901), Rendall, (1897), Stokes (1892), B. Weiss (*Apostelgeschichte*, 1892, 2d ed).

A. T. ROBERTSON

ACTS OF PILATE, pī′lat, pī′lȧt. See APOCRYPHAL GOSPELS.

ACTS OF SOLOMON: "The book of the acts of Solomon" (1 K **11** 41), probably a history based on the state documents kept by the official recorder. See **14** 19.29; **15** 23.31; **16** 5.14.20.27; **22** 39.45, etc.

ACUA, ak′u-a. See ACUD.

ACUB, ā′kub (B, **'Ακούφ,** *Akoúph;* A, **'Ακούμ,** *Akoúm*) = Bakbuk (Ezr **2** 51; Neh **7** 53): The descendants of A. (temple-servants) returned with Zerubbabel to Jerus (1 Esd **5** 31).

ACUD, ā′kud (**'Ακούδ,** *Akoúd;* AV Acua) = AKKUB (Ezr **2** 45) which see; omitted in Neh **7**: The descendants of A. (temple-servants) returned with Zerubbabel to Jerus (1 Esd **5** 30).

ADADAH, a-dā′da (עַדְעָדָה, *'adh'ādhāh*): A city in the southern part of Judah (Josh **15** 22). The older copies of the Gr text have *Arouēl,* but that is not a sufficient reason for identifying the name with the Aroer of 1 S **30** 28. Some scholars adopt the change of text, and identify the site with *Ararah,* about seven miles S.E. of Beer-sheba. Others identify it with *Adadah,* eight or nine miles S.E. of Arad.

ADADRIMMON, ā-dad-rim′on: Shorter and less accurate name of a place in the Valley of Megiddo, which tradition connected with the death of King Josiah (Zec **12** 11; 2 Ch **35** 22). See HADADRIMMON.

ADAH, ā′da (עָדָה, *'ādhāh,* "adornment"):

(1) One of the two wives of Lamech the descendant of Cain (Gen **4** 19.20.23). The narrative in Gen assigns to her two sons, Jabal the "father" of tent-dwelling people, and Jubal the "father of all such as handle the harp and pipe." Jos says that Lamech had 77 sons by Ada and Zillah (*Ant,* I, ii, 2).

(2) According to Gen **36** 2.4.10.12.16, the Hittite wife of Esau, daughter of Elon, and mother of Eliphaz. In this chapter Esau's other wives are Oholibamah, a Hivite, and Basemath the daughter of Ishmael. The names are differently given elsewhere (Gen **26** 34; **28** 9). Basemath is said to be the daughter of Elon. The daughter of Ishmael is called Mahalath. In place of Oholibamah the Hivite we find Judith the daughter of Beeri the Hittite. Data are lacking for the solution of the problem.

WILLIS J. BEECHER

ADAIAH, a-dā′ya, a-dī′a (עֲדָיָה, *'ădhāyāh,* "Jehovah hath adorned"):

(1) Apparently the seventh of the nine sons of Shimei, who is apparently the same with Shema, who is the fifth of the sons of Elpaal, who is the second of the two sons of Shaharaim and Hushim (1 Ch **8** 21). Shaharaim and his descendants are listed with the descendants of Benjamin, though his relations to Benjamin are not stated.

(2) A Levite; ancestor to David's singer Asaph, and a descendant of the fifth generation from Gershom (1 Ch **6** 41).

(3) The father of Maaseiah, who was one of the captains of hundreds associated with Jehoiada the priest in making Joash king (2 Ch **23** 1).

(4) A resident of Bozkath, and father of Jedidah the mother of King Josiah (2 K **22** 1).

(5) A descendant of Judah through Perez. His great-great-grandson Maaseiah resided in Jerus after Nehemiah had rehabilitated the city (Neh **11** 5).

(6) One of the men of Israel, not a priest or Levite, but "of the sons of Bani," who promised Ezra that he would part with his foreign wife (Ezr **10** 29).

(7) The same man or another, in a different group of the sons of Bani (Ezr **10** 39).

(8) One of the priests of the latest Bible times, mentioned with a partial genealogy (Neh **11** 12; 1 Ch **9** 12).

WILLIS J. BEECHER

ADALIA, a-da-lī′a (אֲדַלְיָא, *'ădhalyā',* probably a Pers name, meaning unknown): One of the ten sons of Haman who were put to death by the Jews (Est **9** 8).

ADAM, ad′am, **IN OT AND APOC** (אָדָם, *'ādhām;* LXX **'Αδάμ,** *Adám*): The Heb word occurs some 560 times in the OT with the meaning "man," "mankind." Outside Gen **1–5** the only case where it is unquestionably a proper name is 1 Ch **1** 1. Ambiguous are Dt **32** 8, AV "sons of Adam," RV "children of men"; Job **31** 33 AV "as" RV "like Adam," but margin "after the manner of men"; Hos **6** 7 AV "like men," RV "like Adam," and *vice versa* in the margin. In

1. Usage and Etymology

Gen **1** the word occurs only twice, vs 26.27. In Gen **2–4** it is found 26 times, and in **5** 1.3.4.5. In the last four cases and in **4** 25 it is obviously intended as a proper name; but the VSS show considerable uncertainty as to the rendering in the other cases. Most modern interpreters would restore a vowel point to the Heb text in **2** 20; **3** 17.21, thus introducing the definite article, and read uniformly "the man" up to **4** 25, where the absence of the art. may be taken as an indication that "the man" of the previous narrative is to be identified with "Adam," the head of the genealogy found in **5** 1 ff. Several conjectures have been put forth as to the root-meaning of the Heb word: (1) creature; (2) ruddy one; (3) earthborn. Less probable are (4) pleasant—to sight—and (5) social, gregarious.

2. Adam in the Narrative of Genesis

Many argue from the context that the language of Gen **1** 26.27 is general, that it is the creation of the human *species*, not of any particular individual or individuals, that is described. But (1) the context does not even descend to a *species*, but arranges created things according to the most general possible classification: light and darkness; firmament and waters; land and seas; plants; sun, moon, stars; swimming and flying creatures; land animals. No possible parallel to this classification remains in the case of mankind. (2) In the narrative of Gen **1** the recurrence of identical expressions is almost rigidly uniform, but in the case of man the unique statement occurs (ver 27), "Male and female created he them." Although Dillmann is here in the minority among interpreters, it would be difficult to show that he is wrong in interpreting this as referring to *one* male and *one* female, the first pair. In this case we have a point of contact and of agreement with the narrative of ch **2**. Man, created in God's image, is given dominion over every animal, is allowed every herb and fruit tree for his sustenance, and is bidden multiply and fill the earth. In Gen **2** 4—**5** 5 the first man is made of the dust, becomes a living creature by the breath of God, is placed in the garden of Eden to till it, gives names to the animals, receives as his counterpart and helper a woman formed from part of his own body, and at the woman's behest eats of the forbidden fruit of "the tree of the knowledge of good and evil." With her he is then driven from the garden, under the curse of brief life and heavy labor, since should he eat—or continue to eat?—of the fruit of the "tree of life," not previously forbidden, he might go on living forever. He becomes the father of Cain and of Abel, and of Seth at a time after the murder of Abel. According to **5** 3.5 Adam is aged 130 years at the birth of Seth and lives to the age of 930 years.

3. Teachings of the Narrative

That man was meant by the Creator to be in a peculiar sense His own "image"; that he is the divinely appointed ruler over all his fellow-creatures on earth; and that he enjoys, together with them, God's blessing upon a creature fit to serve the ends for which it was created—these things lie upon the surface of **1** 26–31. In like manner **2–4** tell us that the gift of a blessed immortality was within man's reach; that his Creator ordained that his moral development should come through an inward trial, not as a mere gift; and that the presence of suffering in the world is due to sin, the presence of sin to the machinations of a subtle tempter. The development of the doctrine of the fall belongs to the NT (see Adam in NT; Fall, The).

4. Adam in Apocrypha

Allusions to the narrative of the creation and the fall of man, covering most points of the narrative of Gen **1–4,** are found in 2 Esd **3** 4–7.10.21.26; **4** 30; **6** 54–56; **7** 11.46–48; Tob **8** 6; Wisd **2** 23 f; **9** 2 f; **10** 1 f; Ecclus **15** 14; **17** 1–4; **25** 24; **40** 1; **49** 16. In both 2 Esd and Wisd we read that death came upon all men through Adam's sin, while 2 Esd **4** 30 declares that "a grain of evil seed was sown in the heart of Adam from the beginning." Aside from this doctrinal development the Apoc offers no additions to the OT narrative. F. K. Farr

ADAM IN OT (Evolutionary[1] Interpretation): אָדָם, *'ādhām*, "man," Gen **1** 26, or "a man," Gen **2** 5; הָאָדָם, *hā-'ādhām*, "the man"; mostly with the article as a generic term, and not used as the proper name of a patriarch until **5** 3, after which the name first given to both man and woman [**5** 2] is used of the man alone): The being in whom is embodied the Scripture idea of the first created man and ancestor of mankind. The account, which belongs mostly to the oldest stratum of the Genesis narrative merits careful attention, because evolutionary science, history, and new theology have all quarreled with or rejected it on various grounds, without providing the smallest approach to a satisfactory substitute.

I. What the Writer Meant to Describe.—It is important first of all, if we can, to get at what the author meant to describe, and how it is related, if at all, to literal and factual statement.

1. Derivation and Use of the Name

(1) Scholars have exercised themselves much, but with little arrival at certainty, over the derivation of the name; a matter which, as it is concerned with one of the commonest words of the language, is of no great moment as compared with the writer's own understanding of it. The most plausible conjecture, perhaps, is that which connects it with the Assyr *adāmu*, "to make," or "produce," hence, "the produced one," "the creature." The author of Gen **2** 7 seems to associate it, rather by wordplay than derivation, with *hā-'ădhāmāh*, "the ground" or "soil," as the source from which man's body was taken (cf **3** 19.23). The name *'ădhāmāh* itself seems to be closely connected with the name Edom (אֱדוֹם, *'ĕdhōm*, Gen **25** 30), meaning "red"; but whether from the redness of the soil, or the ruddiness of the man, or merely the incident recorded in Gen **25** 30, is uncertain. Without doubt the writer of Gen **2, 3** had in mind man's earthly origin, and understood the name accordingly.

2. Outline of the Genesis Narrative

(2) The account of the creation is twice given, and from two very different points of view. In the first account, Gen **1** 26–31, man is represented as created on the sixth day along with the animals; a species in the animal world; but differing from them in bearing the image and likeness of God, in having dominion over all created things, and in having grains and fruits for food, while they have herbs. The writer's object in all this seems to be as much to identify man with the animal creation as to differentiate him from it. In the second account, **2** 4—**3** 24, man's identity with the animal is ignored or at least minimized (cf **2** 20), while the object is to determine his status in a spiritual individualized realm wherein he has the companionship of God. Jeh God "forms" or "shapes" him out of the dust of the ground, breathes into his nostrils the breath

[1] It ought to be superfluous to say that the unfolding or development of the human personality here identified with evolution is something far higher, deeper, and other than anything that can be fathered upon Darwin or Herbert Spencer. Evolution (unfolding) is the great process or movement; natural selection and survival of the fittest name only guesses at some of its methods.

of life, and with such special distinction he becomes, like other created things, a "living soul" (*nephesh ḥayyāh;* cf **2** 7 with **1** 30). He is placed in a garden situated somewhere among the rivers of Babylonia, his primitive occupation being to dress and keep it. In the midst of the garden are two mysterious trees, the tree of life, whose fruit seems to have the potency of conferring immortality (cf **3** 22), and the tree of the knowledge of good and evil, whose fruit is not to be eaten under penalty of death. Meanwhile, as in naming the animals the man finds no real companion, Jeh God "builds" one of the man's ribs into a woman, and the man recognizes her spiritual unity with him, naming her accordingly. The story goes on to relate, without note of time, how the serpent, the subtlest of beasts, urged on the woman the desirable qualities of the fruit of the forbidden tree, intimating that God had made the prohibition from envy, and roundly denying that death would be the consequence of eating. Accordingly the woman took and ate, and gave to her husband, who also ate; and the immediate consequence was a sense of shame, which caused them to cover their nakedness with girdles of fig leaves, and a sense of guilt (not differentiated by Adam from shame, **3** 10), which made the pair reluctant to meet Jeh God. He obtains the confession of their disobedience, however; and passes prophetic sentence: on the serpent, of perpetual antipathy between its species and the human; on the woman, of sorrows and pains and subservience to the man; and on the man, of hardship and severe labors, until he returns to the dust from which he was taken. As the pair have chosen to eat of the tree of knowledge, lest now they should eat of the tree of life they are expelled from the garden, and the gate is guarded by flaming sword and Cherubim.

3. History or Exposition?

(3) It is impossible to read this story with the entire detachment that we accord to an ancient myth, or even to a time- and space-conditioned historical tale. It continually suggests intimate relations with the permanent truths of human nature, as if there were a fiber in it truer than fact. And this provokes the inquiry whether the author himself intended the account of the Edenic state and the Fall to be taken as literal history or as exposition. He uniformly makes the name generic by the article (*the* adam or man), the only exceptions, which are not real exceptions in meaning, being **1** 26 and **2** 5, already noted. It is not until **5** 3, where the proper name Adam is as it were officially given, that such history as is conditioned by chronology and genealogy begins. What comes before this, except the somewhat vague location of the Eden region, **2** 10–14, reads rather like a description of the primordial manhood nature, not in philosophical but in narrative language. It is not fable; it is not a worked-over myth; it is not a didactic parable; it is (to speak technically) exposition by narration. By a descriptive story it traces the elemental movement of manhood in its first spiritual impact on this earthly life. In other words, instead of being concerned to relate a factual series of events from the remote past, the writer's penetrative intuition goes downward and inward to those spiritual movements of being which are germinal in all manhood. It is a spiritual analysis of man's intrinsic nature, and as such must be spiritually discerned. An analogous manner of exposition may be seen in the account of Our Lord's temptation in the wilderness, Mt **4** 1–11, which account, if authentic, must have come ultimately from Our Lord Himself.

II. How the Story Looks Today.—Scarcely any other Scripture story has so suffered from the changes wrought by modern thinking as has this story of Adam. On the one hand it is felt that to refer the fall and inherited guilt of mankind to this experience of Adam as a cause is to impose too great a burden, dogmatic and historic, on this primitive story. Yet on the other hand the story, including this implication of the primal fall, refuses to be dismissed as an outworn or fantastic myth. It lays hold so vitally on the roots of human nature that our only course is not to reject it but to re-read it with the best light our age affords. And whether best or not, the evolutionary light in which all modern thought is colored cannot be ignored.

1. In the Light of Evolution

(1) The divergent assumptions of the traditional and the evolutionary view may be roughly stated thus: of the traditional, that in consequence of this Eden lapse man is a ruined nature, needing redemption and reinstatement, and that therefore the subsequent spiritual dealing with him must be essentially pathological and remedial; of the evolutionary, that by the very terms of his creation, which the lapse from obedience did not annul, man is spiritually a child needing growth and education, and that therefore the subsequent dealing with him must foster the development within him of a nature essentially normal and true. It is evident that these two views, thus stated, merely regard two lines of potency in one nature. Without rejecting the traditional, or stopping to inquire how it and the evolutionary may coexist, we may here consider how the story before us responds to the evolutionary view. Only—it must be premised—the evolution whose beginning it describes is not the evolution of the human *species;* we can leave natural science and history to take care of that; but, beginning where this leaves off, the evolution of the *individual,* from the first forthputting of individual initiative and choice toward the far-off adult and complete personality. This, which in view of its culmination we may call the evolution of personality, is evolution distinctively spiritual, that stage and grade of upward moving being which succeeds to the material and psychical (cf 1 Cor **15** 45.46). On the material stage of evolution, which the human species shares with the beast and the plant, Scripture is silent. Nor is it greatly concerned with the psychical, or cultural development of the human species, except to reveal in a divinely ordered history and literature its essential inadequacy to the highest manhood potencies. Rather its field is the evolution of the spirit, in which alone the highest personal values are realized. In the delimitation of this field it has a consistent origin, course and culmination of its own, as it traces the line of spiritual uprise and growth from the first Adam, who as a "living soul" was subject to the determinism of the species, to the last Adam, who as a "life-giving spirit" is identified with the supreme Personality in whom Divine and human met and blended. Of this tremendous evolution the story of Adam, with a clearness which the quaint narrative style of exposition does not impair, reveals the primal and directive factors.

2. The Garden Habitat

(2) Just as the habitat and the nature of created things answer to each other, so the environment in which man is placed when he comes from his Creator's hand connotes the kind of life he is fitted to live. He is placed not in wild and refractory Nature but in a garden watered and planted with a view to his receiving care and nurture from above. Nature is kindly and responsive, furnishing fruits ready to his hand, and requiring only that he "dress and keep" the garden. Of all the trees he may freely eat, including the tree of life; save only the

most centrally located of all, the tree of "knowledge of good and evil." The being fitted to this habitat is a man adult in stature and intelligence, but still like a child; not yet individualized to determinate character, not yet exerting a will of his own apart from the will of his Creator; in other words, as spiritually considered, not yet detached from the spirit of his personal Source. All this reads like the description of a life essentially negative, or rather neutral, with free communication both downward and upward, but neither that of a domesticated animal nor of a captive god; a being balanced, as it were, between the earthly and the Divine, but not yet aware of the possession of that individual will and choice which alone can give spiritual significance to a committal to either.

3. The Organic Factor

(3) In the first story of man's creation, **1** 26–31, describing his creation as a species, the distinction of male and female is explicitly included (**1** 27). In the second story (**2**, **3**), wherein man is contemplated rather as an individual, the description of his nature begins before any distinction of sex exists. If the writer meant this latter to portray a condition of man in time or in natural fact, there is thus a discrepancy in accounts. If we regard it, however, as giving a factor in spiritual evolution, it not only becomes full of meaning but lays hold profoundly on the ultimate teleology of creation. The naïve story relates that the woman was "builded" out of the already shaped material of the man's body, in order to supply a fellowship which the animals could not; a help "answering to" him (*k^eneghdō;* cf **2** 18 margin). Then it makes the man recognize this conjugal relation, not at all with reference to sexual passion or the propagation of species but as furnishing man occasion, so to say, for loving and being loved, and making this capacity essential to the integrity of his nature. The value of this for the ultimate creative purpose and revelation is as marvelous as it is profound; it is the organic factor in realizing the far-reaching design of Him who is evolving a being bearing His image and deriving from Him the breath of life. That God is Spirit (Jn **4** 24), that God is love (1 Jn **4** 8.16) and love "creation's final law," may as an idea be later revelation; but meanwhile from the beginning, in the commonest relation of life, a pulsation of mutual love is implanted, by making man a dual nature, wherein love, which is the antithesis of self-seeking, has the equal and companionable object necessary to its existence. Thus in the conjugal relation the potency of the highest and broadest spiritual value is made intrinsic. In all the dubious course of his subsequent evolution, this capacity of love, though itself subject to the *corruptio optimi pessima,* is like a redeeming element at the heart alike of the individual and of society.

4. The Invasion of Subtlety

(4) Even in this neutral garden existence it is noteworthy that the man's nature evinces its superiority to the animal in the absence of determinism. He is not enslaved to an instinct of blind conformity to an external will. In other words, he can coöperate intelligently in his own spiritual evolution. He has the power of choice, ministered by the stimulus of an unmotived prohibition. He can abstain and live, or eat and die (**2** 16.17). No reasons are given, no train of spiritual consequences, to one whose spirit is not yet awake; in this pre-spiritual stage rather the beginnings of law and prescription must be arbitrary. Yet even in so rudimentary a relation we are aware of the essential contrast between animal and spiritual evolution, in that the latter is not a blind and instinctive imposition from without, but a free course submitted to man's intelligence and coöperation. And it is a supremely significant feature of the narrative to make the first self-interested impulse come by the way of subtlety. "The serpent," the writer premises, "was more subtle than any beast of the field which Jeh God had made." It points to a trait which he puts on the border-line between the species and the individual, the disposition, not indeed to rebel against a law of being, but to submit it to refinement and accommodation or perhaps from sheer curiosity to try conclusions with it. The suggestion came first from the lower creation, but not from what is animal in it; and it was eagerly responded to by the woman, the finer and more spiritually awake of the pair. Not to press this too far, it is significant that the first impulse toward individual initiative rises through the free play of intellect and reason. It seems to promise a subtler way of being "like God." To differentiate more minutely the respective parts of man and wife in the affair, which are portrayed in the light of sex distinction, would be beyond our present scope. See Eve.

5. The Fateful Venture

(5) Two trees "in the midst of the garden" (**2** 9) are mentioned at the outset; but the tree of life, the permitted one, seems no more to have been thought of until it was no longer accessible (**3** 22); indeed, when the woman speaks to the serpent of "the tree which is in the midst of the garden" (**3** 3) she has only one tree in mind, and that the prohibited one. The other, as it was counted in with their daily fare and opportunity, seems to have been put by them with those privileges of life which are ignored or postponed; besides, the life it symbolized was the perpetuation of the garden-life they were living, such life as man would live before his spirit was awake to the alternatives of living—a life innocent and blissful, but without the stimulus of spiritual reaction. And it was just this latter that the alternative of the two trees afforded; a reaction fateful for good or evil, needing only the impulse that should set the human spirit in motion. Consider the case. If manhood were ever to rise from a state of childhood, wherein everything was done and prescribed for him, into a life of free choice and self-moved wisdom, it is hard to see how this could have been brought about except by something involving inhibition and prohibition; something that he could not do without incurring a risk. This is what the "tree of the knowledge of good and evil" (**2** 17) means. The tree by its very name was alike a test and a lure. In a sense we may say the temptation began with God; but it was not a temptation to evil. Symbolized in the two trees, but actual in the opportunity of spiritual committal, two ways of life stood open before him. On the one hand, it was open to him to fortify his spirit in obedience and against the lure of perilous knowledge, thus deepening and seasoning his negative innocence into positive holiness. That such a course was feasible was shown centuries later in the Divine Son of Man, who in perfect loyalty of the child yet in perfect wisdom of adultness fulfilled the primal sinless ideal of the first Adam. On the other hand there was the lure of the forbidden knowledge, to which the serpent gave the false glamor of godlikeness, and which could be had by detaching his individual will from that of God, and incurring the experience of self-seeking, and taking the risk. It was the latter that was chosen; this however not in the spirit of rebellion or temptation, but in the desire for a good beyond what the childlike limitations of Eden afforded (**3** 6). This then was the first motived uprise of the spirit of manhood, taking the initiative and acting for itself. So far forth, as the self-

assertion of the individual, it was as truly a stage of spiritual evolution as if the man had maintained obedience; but there was in it the rupture of his spirit's union with its personal Source; and the hapless committal to self, which is rightly called a Fall. So strangely mingled were the spiritual elements in this primal manhood initiative. See FALL, THE.

6. The Fitted Sequel

(6) The Scripture does not say, or even imply, that by this forth-putting of initiative the man was committed to a life of sin and depravity. This was the idea of a later time. By the nature of the case, however, he was committed to the fallibility and unwisdom of his own untried nature; in other words, to the perils of self-reliance. Naturally, too, the gulf of detachment from his spiritual Support would tend to widen as he trusted himself more exclusively. It lay with him and his species to perfect the individual personality in the freedom which he had chosen. And in this the possibilities both upward toward godlikeness and downward toward the abysms of self were immensely enlarged. Life must henceforth be lived on a broader and profounder scale. But to this end Eden with its tender garden nurture can no longer be its habitat, nor can man's existence be fitly symbolized by a tree from which he has only to take and subsist indefinitely (**3** 22). It must encounter hardship and sweat and toil; it must labor to subdue a reluctant soil to its service (**3** 17–19); it must return at last to the dust from which man's body was formed (**3** 19). Yet there is vouchsafed a dim and distant presage of ultimate victory over the serpent-power, which henceforth is to be man's deadly enemy (**3** 15). At this point of the exposition it is that the inchoate manhood is transplanted from the garden to the unsubdued world, to work out its evolution under the conditions of the human species. The pair becomes the family, with its family interests and cares; the family becomes the unit of social and organized life; the members receive individual names (**3** 20; **5** 2); and chronologically measured history begins.

III. How Adam Is Recognized in the OT.—After the story of Adam is given as far as the birth of Cain and Abel (**4** 1.2) and Seth (**4** 25), the "book of the generations of Adam" begins at **5** 1, and five verses are taken up with a statistical outline of his life, his offspring, and his 930 years of earthly existence.

1. In the OT Canonical Books

(1) Here at Gen **5** 5, in the canonical books of the OT almost all allusion to him ceases, and nothing whatever is made of his fateful relation to the sin and guilt of the race. (See ADAM IN THE NT.) This latter idea seems to have come to consciousness only when men's sense of sin and a broken law was more ingrained than it seems to have been in canonical times. In the case of the few allusions that occur, moreover, the fact that the name "Adam" is identical with the word for "man" makes the reference more or less uncertain; one does not know whether the patriarch or the race is meant. In the Song of Moses (Dt **32**), in the clause ver 8, "when he separated the children of men" (or "Adam"), the reference, which is to the distribution of races as given in Gen **10,** may or may not have Adam in mind. In like manner Zophar's words (Job **20** 4), "Knowest thou not this of old time, since man [or Adam] was placed upon earth?" may or may not be recognition by name of the first created man. Job's words (**31** 33), "if like Adam I have covered my transgressions," sound rather more definite as an allusion to Adam's hiding himself after having taken the fruit. When Isaiah says (Isa **43** 27), "Thy first father sinned," it is uncertain whom he means; for in **51** 2 he says, "Look unto Abraham your father," and Ezekiel has told his people (Ezk **16** 3), "The Amorite was thy father, and thy mother was a Hittite." The historical consciousness of the prophets seems to have been confined to the history of the Israelitish race.

2. In the Apocrypha

(2) The references in the Apocryphal books (Sir, Tob, 2 Esd) deal with Adam's origin, his lordship over creation, and in the latest written book with the legacy of sin and misery that the race inherits from him. The passages in Sir (132 BC) where he is mentioned are **33** 10; **40** 1, and **49** 16. Of these the most striking, **40** 1, "Great travail is created for every man, and a heavy yoke is upon the sons of Adam," is hardly to be construed as a reference to our heritage of his sin. In Tob (BC 2d cent.) he is mentioned once (**8** 6), "Thou madest Adam, and gavest him Eve." 2 Esd, written supposedly some time after 70 AD, is of a somber and desponding tone throughout; and its references to Adam (2 Esd **3** 5.10.21.26; **4** 30; **6** 54; **7** 11.46.48) are almost all in lament over the evil he has implanted in the race of men by his transgression. The first reference (**3** 5) is rather remarkable for its theory of Adam's nature: "And [thou] commandedst the dust, and it gave thee Adam, a body without a soul, yet it was the workmanship of thine hands," etc. His indictment of Adam culminates (**7** 48) in the apostrophe: "O thou Adam, what hast thou done? for though it was thou that sinned, the evil is not fallen on thee alone, but upon all of us that come of thee."

JOHN FRANKLIN GENUNG

[EDITORIAL NOTE.—The promoters of the *Encyclopaedia* are not to be understood as endorsing all the views set forth in Dr. Genung's article. It was thought right, however, that a full and adequate presentation of so suggestive an interpretation should be given.]

ADAM IN THE NT (**'Αδάμ,** *Adám*): The name of Adam occurs nine times (in five different passages) in the NT, though several of these are purely incidental.

I. Gospels.—In Lk **3** 38 the ancestry of Jesus Christ is traced up to Adam, "Adam, the son of God," thereby testifying to the acceptance of the OT genealogies of Gen. This is the only place in the Gospels in which Adam is actually named, though there is an allusion to him in Mt **19** 4–6 (=Mk **10** 6–8), referring to Gen **1** 27 and **2** 24.

II. Epistles.—Adam is used by Paul as the founder of the race and the cause of the introduction of sin in order to point the comparison and contrast with Christ as the Head of the new race and the cause of righteousness.

1. Rom 5:12–21

The passage is the logical center of the ep., the central point to which everything that precedes has converged, and out of which everything which follows will flow. The great ideas of Sin, Death, and Judgment are here shown to be involved in the connection of the human race with Adam. But over against this there is the blessed fact of union with Christ, and in this union righteousness and life. The double headship of mankind in Adam and Christ shows the significance of the work of redemption for the entire race. Mankind is ranged under two heads, Adam and Christ. There are two men, two acts and two results. In this teaching we have the spiritual and theological illustration of the great modern principle of solidarity. There is a solidarity of evil and a solidarity of good, but the latter far surpasses the former in the quality of the obedience of Christ as compared with Adam, and the facts of the work of Christ for justification and life. The section is thus no mere episode, or illustration, but that which gives organic life to the entire ep. Although sin and death are ours in Adam righteousness and life are ours in Christ, and these latter two are infinitely the greater (ver 11); whatever we have lost in Adam we have more than gained in Christ. As all the evils of the race sprang from one man, so all the blessings of redemption come from One Person, and there is such a connection between the Person and the race that all men can possess what the One has done. In vs 12–19 Paul institutes a series of comparisons and contrasts between Adam and Christ; the two persons, the two works and the two consequences. The fulness of the apostle's meaning must be carefully observed. Not only does he teach that what we have derived from the first Adam is met by what is derived from Christ, but the transcendence of the work of the latter is regarded as almost infinite in extent. "The full meaning of Paul, however, is not grasped until we perceive that the benefits received from Christ, the Second Adam, are in *inverse ratio* to the disaster entailed by the first Adam. It is the *surplusage* of this grace that in Paul's presentation is commonly overlooked" (Mabie, *The Divine Reason of the Cross*, 116).

The contrast instituted here between Adam and Christ refers to death and life, but great difficulty turns on the interpretation of the two "alls." "As in Adam all die, so also in Christ shall all be made alive." Dods (*Expositor's Bible*, 366) interprets it of Adam as the source of physical life that ends in death, and of Christ as the source of spiritual life that never dies. "All who are by physical derivation truly united to Adam incur the death, which by sinning he introduced into human experience; and similarly, all who by spiritual affinity are in Christ enjoy the new life which triumphs over death, and which he won." So also Edwards, who does not consider that there is any real unfairness in interpreting the former "all" as more extensive than the latter, "if we bear in mind that the conditions of entrance into the one class and the other are totally different. They are not stated here. But we have them in Rom **5** 5–11, where the apostle seems as if he anticipated this objection to the analogy which he instituted between Adam and Christ. Both alike are heads of humanity, but they are unlike in this (as also in other things, Rom **5** 15), that men are in Adam by nature, in Christ by faith" (*Corinthians*, 412). Godet considers that "perhaps this interpretation is really that which corresponds best to the apostle's view," and he shows that *zōopoieîsthai*, "to be made alive," is a more limited idea than *egeîresthai*, "to be raised," the limitation of the subject thus naturally proceeding from the special meaning of the verb itself. "The two *pántes* (all) embrace those only to whom each of the two powers extends." But Godet favors the view of Meyer and Ellicott that "all" is to be given the same interpretation in each clause, and that the reference is to all who are to rise, whether for life or condemnation, and that this is to be "in Christ": "Christ will quicken all; all will hear His voice and will come forth from the grave, but not all to the true 'resurrection of life': see Jn **5** 29" (Ellicott, *Corinthians*, 301). Godet argues that "there is nothing to prevent the word 'quicken,' taken alone, from being used to denote restoration to the fulness of spiritual and bodily existence, with a view either to perdition or salvation" (*Corinthians*, 355). There are two serious difficulties to the latter interpretation: (1) The invariable meaning of "in Christ" is that of spiritual union; (2) the question whether the resurrection of the wicked really finds any place in the apostle's argument in the entire chapter.

2. 1 Cor 15:22

"The first man Adam became a living soul. The last Adam became a life-giving spirit." The reference to Adam is from Gen **2** 7; the reference to Christ is due to the fact of what He had done and was doing in His manifestation as Divine Redeemer. Behind results the apostle proceeds to nature. Adam was simply a living being; Christ a life-giving Being. Thus Christ is called Adam as expressive of His Headship of a race. In this ver He is called the "last" Adam, while in ver 47 the "second." In the former ver the apostle deals not so much with Christ's relation to the first Adam as to the part He takes in relation to humanity, and His work on its behalf. When precisely Christ became life-giving is a matter of difference of opinion. Rom **1** 4 associates power with the resurrection as the time when Christ was constituted Son of God for the purpose of bestowing the force of Divine grace. This gift of power was only made available for His church through the Ascension and the gift of the Holy Spirit at Pentecost. It is possible that the word "life-giving" may also include a reference to the resurrection of the body hereafter.

3. 1 Cor 15:45

Paul uses the creation of man and woman in his argument for the subordination of woman (Gen **2** 7–25). This is no mere Jewish reasoning, but an inspired statement of the *typical* meaning of the passage in Gen. The argument is a very similar one to that in 1 Cor **11** 8.9. When the apostle states that "Adam was not beguiled," we must apparently understand it as simply based on the text in Gen to which he refers (Gen **3** 13), in which Eve, not Adam, says, "The serpent beguiled me." In Gal **3** 16 he reasons similarly from "seed" in the singular number, just as He **7** reasons from the silence of Gen **14** in regard to the parentage of Melchizedek. Paul does not deny that Adam was deceived, but only that he was not directly deceived. His point is that Eve's facility in yielding warrants the rule as to women keeping silence.

4. 1 Tim 2:13.14

"And Enoch, the seventh from Adam" (Gen **5**). Bigg says that the quotation which follows is a combination of passages from Enoch, though the allusion to Enoch himself is evidently based on the story in Gen.

5. Jude ver 14

III. Conclusions.—As we review the use of "Adam" in the NT, we cannot fail to observe that Paul assumes that Adam was a historical personality, and that the record in Gen was a record of facts, that sin and death were introduced into the world and affected the entire race as the penalty of the disobedience of one ancestor. Paul evidently takes it for granted that Adam knew and was responsible for what he was doing. Again, sin and death are regarded as connected, that death obtains its moral quality from sin. Paul clearly believed that physical dissolution was due to sin, and that there is some causal connection between Adam and the human race in regard to physical death. While the reference to death in Rom **5** as coming through sin, is primarily to physical death, yet physical death is the expression and sign of the deeper idea of spiritual death; and even though physical death was in the world before Adam it was only in connection with sin that its moral meaning and estimate became clear. Whether we are to interpret, "for that all sinned," as sinning when Adam sinned, or sinning as the result of an inherited tendency from Adam, the entire passage implies some causal connection between him and them. The need of redemption is thus made by the apostle to rest on facts. We are bound to Adam by birth, and it is open to us to become bound to Christ by faith. If we refuse to exchange our position in Adam for that which is offered to us in Christ we become answerable to God; this is the ground of moral freedom. The NT assumption of our common ancestry in Adam is true to the facts of evolutionary science, and the universality of sin predicated is equally true to the facts of human experience. Thus redemption is grounded on the teaching of Scripture, and confirmed by the uncontradicted facts of history and experience. Whether, therefore, the references to Adam in the NT are purely incidental, or elaborated in theological discussion, everything is evidently based on the record in Gen. W. H. GRIFFITH THOMAS

ADAM, BOOKS OF: Books pretending to give the life and deeds of Adam and other OT worthies existed in abundance among the Jews and the early Christians. The Talm speaks of a Book of Adam, which is now lost, but which probably furnished some of the material which appears in early Christian writings. The *Vita Adami* was tr[d] from the Ethiopic by Dillmann (1853), and into English by Malan (*The Book of Adam and Eve*, London, 1882). The *Testament of Adam* is a portion of the *Vita Adami* (published by Renan in 1853) and so probably is the *Diathḗkē tôn Prōtoplástōn* (Fabricius, II, 83). See APOCALYPTIC LITERATURE; APOCRYPHA.

M. O. EVANS

ADAM, CITY OF (אָדָם, *'ādhām,* "red" or *BDB* "made"): A city in the middle of the Jordan valley near ZARETHAN (Josh **3** 16), which see. The name probably survives at the Damieh Ford, near the mouth of the Jabbok twenty miles above Jericho. An Arabian historian asserts that about 1265 AD the Jordan was here blocked by a land slide. The inner gorge of the Jordan is here narrow with high banks which would facilitate such an obstruction as permitted the waters to "pile up" above to Adam and run out below, permitting Joshua's host to cross on dry land (*SWP*, II, 15; Wright, *SCOTH*, 130–34).

GEORGE FREDERICK WRIGHT

ADAMAH, ad'a-mä (אֲדָמָה, *'ădhāmāh;* **'Αδαμί,** *Adamí*): A fortified city in the territory of Naphtali, named between Chinnereth and Ramah (Josh **19** 36). It is probably identical with the modern *'Admah,* a ruin on the plateau about 10 miles N. of *Beisān.*

ADAMANT, ad'a-mant (שָׁמִיר, *shāmīr* [Ezk **3** 9; Zec **7** 12]): In the passages cited and in Jer **17** 1, where it is rendered "diamond," the word *shāmīr* evidently refers to a hard stone. The word adamant ("unconquerable") is used in the early Gr writers for a hard metal, perhaps steel, later for a metal like gold and later for the diamond. The Heb *shāmīr,* the Gr *adamas* (from which word *diamond* as well as *adamant* is derived) and the Eng. adamant occur regularly in fig. expressions. All three are equally indefinite. Adamant may therefore be considered a good tr for *shāmīr,* though the LXX does not use *adamas* in the passages cited. There is a possible etymological identification of *shāmīr* with the Gr *smyris* (*smēris* or *smiris*), emery, a granular form of corundum well known to the ancients and used by them for polishing and engraving precious stones. Corundum in all its forms, including the sapphire and ruby, is in the scale of hardness next to the diamond. In EV Isa **5** 6; **7** 23–25; **9** 18; **10** 17; **27** 4; **32** 13, *shāmīr* is tr[d] *brier.* See also STONES, PRECIOUS.

ALFRED ELY DAY

ADAMI, ad'a-mī; a-dā'mī: Mentioned in AV as a separate name, where RV has ADAMI-NEKEB, which see (Josh **19** 33).

ADAMI-NEKEB, ad'a-mī nē'keb (אֲדָמִי הַנֶּקֶב, *'ădhāmī ha-neḳebh,* "the ground of the piercing," that is of the pass, or defile): A place mentioned in indicating the border of Naphtali (Josh **19** 33). In AV Adami and Nekeb are given as separate names, and it is an open question which view of the matter is correct. Most of the Gr texts give the names as two. The Vulg has "Adami quae est Neceb." The Jerusalem Talm gives two names, though instead of Hannekeb or Nekeb it has *Ṣīyadāthāh* (Meg **1** 1, or Neubauer's *Geog du Talm,* 225). In the list of places conquered by Thothmes III of Egypt occurs the name NḲBU (Tomkins, *Rec of Past,* new series, V, 47), which seems to be the same with Neḳeb.

The list of names for the border of Naphtali (Josh **19** 33.34) has no name in common with the list of cities (vs 35–38) unless Adami and Adamah are the same. The PE Survey maps locate Adamah at Damieh, about seven miles northwest of the exit of the Jordan from the Lake of Galilee, and Adami at Khurbet Adamah, five or six miles south of the exit. Conder, Tomkins and others place Adami at Damieh, and identify Nekeb by its Talmudic name in the neighboring ruin *Seiyâdeh.* Conder says (art. "Nekeb," *HDB*) that the "pass" implied in the name Nekeb "is probably one leading from the eastern precipices near Tiberias."

WILLIS J. BEECHER

ADAN, ā'dan. See ADDAN.

ADAR, ā'dar (אֲדָר, *'ădhār,* meaning uncertain): The Bab name of the twelfth month of the year. Used in the Bible only in Ezr **6** 15 and eight times in Est. At first the author in Est defines Adar as the twelfth month, but afterward omits the numeral. In order to maintain the relation of the year to the seasons it was customary to add a second Adar, as often as was needed, as an intercalary month.

ADAR, ā'dar: In AV (Josh **15** 3) for ADDAR, which see.

ADARSA, a-där'sa. See ADASA.

ADASA, ad'a-sa (**'Αδασά,** *Adasá;* AV **Adarsa**): A town less than four miles from Beth-horon (30 furlongs *Ant,* XII, x, 5; 1 Macc **7** 40) and a day's journey from Gazara (1 Macc **7** 45), where Judas Maccabee defeated and killed Nicanor, a general of Demetrius (1 Macc **7** 40 ff). The ruin of Adaseh near Gibeon (*SWP,* III, XVII).

ADBEEL, ad'bē-el (אַדְבְּאֵל, *'adhbe'ēl,* "God's discipline," possibly): The third of the twelve sons of Ishmael (Gen **25** 13; 1 Ch **1** 29). The name appears in the Assyr records as that of a north Arabian tribe residing somewhere S.W. of the Dead Sea.

ADD:

(1) **ἐπιδιατάσσομαι,** *epidiatássomai,* "to add to," "to arrange in addition": Found only in Gal **3** 15, which may thus be paraphrased: "To take a familiar illustration: even a man's will, when ratified, no third party may annul or supplement" (Dummelow, in loc.).

(2) **ἐπιτίθημι,** *epitíthēmi,* "to put upon," "If any man shall add unto them, God shall add unto him the plagues" (Rev **22** 18). The book is not to be falsified by addition or excision (see BOOK) by the interpolation of unauthorized doctrines or the neglect of essential ones (cf Dt **4** 2; **12** 32). See also IMPART; SUPPLY.

M. O. EVANS

ADDAN, ad'an (אַדָּן, *'addān;* in Neh אַדּוֹן, *'addōn;* connected in some way with the name of the god Addu): A name mentioned in the list of the returning exiles (Ezr **2** 59, duplicated in Neh **7** 61). It is one of several names of Bab localities from which came men who were unable to declare their genealogy as Israelites.

ADDAR, ad′är (אַדָּר, *'addār*, "glorious." See Ard):

(1) A grandson of Benjamin, sometimes counted as one of his sons (1 Ch **8** 3).

(2) A town on the southern border of Judah (Josh **15** 3, AV "Adar"). The same as Hazar-addar (Nu **34** 4).

ADDER, ad′ĕr (עַכְשׁוּב, *'akhshūbh* [Ps **140** 3]; פֶּתֶן, *pethen* [Ps **58** 4]; צִפְעֹנִי, *çiph'ōnī* [Prov **23** 32]; שְׁפִיפֹן, *shephīphōn* [Gen **49** 17]; צֶפַע, *çepha'* [AVm; Isa **14** 29]): This word is used for several Heb originals. In each case a poisonous serpent is clearly indicated by the context. It is

Hooded Snake. Length about 4 feet.

impossible to tell in any case just what species is meant, but it must be remembered that the Eng. word adder is used very ambiguously. It is from the Anglo-Saxon *nædre*, a snake or serpent, and is the common Eng. name for *Vipera berus*, L, the common viper, which is found throughout Europe and northern Asia, though not in Bible lands; but the word adder is also used for various snakes, both poisonous and non-poisonous, found in different parts of the world. In America, for instance, both the poisonous moccasin (*Ancistrodon*) and the harmless hog-nosed snakes (*Heterodon*) are called adders. See Serpent. Alfred Ely Day

ADDI, ad′ī (**Ἀδδί**, *Addí*; **Ἀδδεί**, *Addeí*): An ancestor of Joseph, the husband of Mary, mother of Jesus; fourth from Zerubbabel in the ascending genealogical series (Lk **3** 28).

ADDICT, a-dikt′: Found only in AV of 1 Cor **16** 15, for Gr *τάσσω*, *tássō*. The house of Stephanus is said to be "addicted to the ministry of the saints," i.e. they have so "arranged" their affairs as to make of this service a prime object; RV "set themselves to minister."

ADDO, ad′ō (A, **Ἀδδώ**, *Addṓ*; B, **Ἐδδείν**, *Eddeín*) = Iddo (Ezr **5** 1; **6** 14): The father (Zec **1** 1.7 grandfather) of Zechariah the prophet (1 Esd **6** 1).

ADDON, ad′on. See Addan.

ADDUS, ad′us (**Ἀδδούς**, *Addoús*): The descendants of A. (sons of Solomon's servants) returned with Zerubbabel to Jerusalem (1 Esd **5** 34). Omitted in Ezr **2** and Neh **7**.

ADER, ā′dẽr: Used in 1 Ch **8** 15 AV for Eder, which see.

ADIABENE, ā-di-a-bē′nē (**Ἀδιαβηνή**, *Adiabēnḗ*): A state lying on the east of the Tigris, on the greater and lesser rivers Zab, in the territory of ancient Assyria. For the half-century terminating with the destruction of Jerusalem by Titus, Adiabene is especially interesting by reason of the careers of its king, Izates, and his mother Helena, who became Jews. They had their part in the Jewish-Roman wars, and in various ways were typical of the existing situation. (See *Ant*, XX, 2–5; *BJ*, II, xvi, 4; xix. 2; V, iv, 2; vi. 1; xi. 5; VI, vi, 4.) Somewhat later Adiabene was absorbed into the Roman Empire and became one of the six provinces which formed the larger province of Assyria, though Pliny and Ammianus sometimes call the large province by the name Adiabene.

Willis J. Beecher

ADIDA, ad′i-da (**Ἀδιδά**, *Adidá*): A town of the Benjamin tribe near Lod and Ono located upon a hill facing the "plain country" of Judaea, rebuilt and fortified by Simon Maccabee (1 Macc **12** 38), who later encamped here to meet the army of Tryphon (1 Macc **13** 13; *Ant*, XIII, vi, 5). It was also here that Aretas, king of Arabia, met Alexander Janneus in battle and defeated him (*Ant*, XIII, xv, 2). Perhaps the *El-Hadītheh* of today located about three miles east of Lydda or Lod. See Hadid.

ADIEL, ad′i-el (עֲדִיאֵל, *'ădhī'ēl*, "ornament of God"):

(1) One of the "princes" of the tribe of Simeon, who, in the days of Hezekiah, smote the aborigines of Gedor and captured the valley (1 Ch **4** 36 ff).

(2) Father of Maasai, one of the priests who dwelt in Jerusalem after the return from the Exile (1 Ch **9** 12).

(3) Father of Azmaveth who was over David's treasures (1 Ch **27** 25).

ADIN, ā′din (עָדִין, *'ādhīn*, "adorned"): The name of a family, "the sons of Adin" (Ezr **2** 15; **8** 6; Neh **7** 20; **10** 16; 1 Esd **5** 14; **8** 32), mentioned among the returning exiles. The list in Ezr **2** is placed in the midst of the narrative concerning Zerubbabel, but its title and its contents show that it also includes the later Jewish immigrants into Pal. The list in Neh **7** is a duplicate of that in Ezr, but with variations; most of the variations are naturally accounted for by supposing that one copy was made later than the other and was brought up to date. In Ezr and 1 Esd the number of the sons of Adin is said to be 454; in Neh it is 655. The 50 males, led by Ebed the son of Jonathan, who came with Ezr, may or may not have been included in the numbers just mentioned. Among the names of those who sealed the covenant along with Neh are 44 that are placed under the caption "the chiefs of the people" (Neh **10** 14–26), and nearly half of these are the family names of the list in Ezr **2** and Neh **7**. It is natural to infer that in these cases a family sealed the covenant collectively through some representative. In that case the Adin here mentioned is the same that is mentioned in the other places. See also Adinu. Willis J. Beecher

ADINA, ad′i-na, a-dī′na (עֲדִינָא, *'ădhīnā'*, "adorned"): "Adina the son of Shiza the Reubenite, a chief of the Reubenites, and thirty with him" (1 Ch **11** 42). This is in that part of the list of David's mighty men in which the Chronicler supplements the list given in 2 S.

ADINO, ad′i-no, a-dī′no (עֲדִינוֹ, *'ădhīnō*, "his adorned one"): The senior of David's "mighty men." "Josheb-basshebeth a Tahchemonite, chief of the captains; the same was Adino the Eznite, against eight hundred slain at one time" (2 S **23** 8). This very exact rendering makes it evident even to an English reader that the text is imperfect. Ginsburg offers a corrected form taken substantially from the parallel passage in 1 Ch **11** 11: "Jashobeam a son of a Hachmonite, chief of the captains; he lifted up his spear." This is plausible, and is very generally accepted, and eliminates the names Adino and Eznite, which do not occur elsewhere in the Bible. Some of the facts are against this. The Sept has the names Adino and Eznite. The Lat finds no proper names in the passage, but so translates the words as to presuppose the Heb text as we have it. It may be a case for suspended judgment.

The texts concerning David's mighty men are fragmentary both in S and in Ch. If they were more complete they would perhaps make it clear that the three seniors were comrades of David at Pas-dammim, Ephes-dammim (1 Ch **11** 13; 1 S **17** 1); and that we have in them additional details concerning that battle. The record says that on the death of Goliath the Philistines fled and the Israelites pursued (1 S **17** 52 ff), but it is not improbable that during the retreat portions of the Phili force rallied, so that there was strenuous fighting. WILLIS J. BEECHER

ADINU, ad′i-nū, **ADIN** (**'Αδινού**, *Adinoú*, 1 Esd **5** 14; **'Αδίν**, *Adín*, 1 Esd **8** 32): Cf Adin (Ezr **2** 15; **8** 6; Neh **7** 20; **10** 16). The descendants of A. (leaders of the nation) returned with their families to Jerus: one party being with Zerubbabel (454 members 1 Esd **5** 14), a second party with Ezra (250 members 1 Esd **8** 32).

ADINUS, ad′i-nus. See IADINUS (Apoc).

ADITHAIM, ad-i-thā′im (עֲדִיתַיִם, *'ădhīthayim* "double ornament, passage, or prey"): A city in "the lowland" (Shephelah, not as AV **"valley"**) of Judah (Josh **15** 36). Site unknown, but possibly same as ADIDA (q.v.).

ADJURATION, ad-jū-rā′shun: The act of requiring or taking a solemn oath. In a time of military peril Saul adjured the people (אָלָה, *'ālāh*, "to take oath") and they took oath by saying "Amen" (1 S **14** 24). When Joshua pronounced a ban on Jericho (Josh **6** 26) he completed it with an oath (שָׁבַע, *shābha'*, "to cause to swear"). Often used in the sense of a solemn charge without the administration of an oath (1 K **22** 16; 2 Ch **18** 15; Cant **2** 7; **5** 8.9; 1 Thess **5** 27). With reference to the withholding of testimony, see Lev **5** 1 and Prov **29** 24. The high priest sought to put Jesus under oath (ἐξορκίζω, *exorkízō*, "to force to an oath," Mt **26** 63). *Adjure* also means to solemnly implore (ὁρκίζω, *horkízō*) as when the man with an unclean spirit appealed to Jesus: "I adjure thee by God, torment me not" (Mk **5** 7); or seven sons of Sceva, exorcists, sought in the name of Jesus to expel demons (Acts **19** 13).

(1) The exacting of an oath has, from time immemorial, been a customary procedure in conferring civil and ecclesiastical office and in taking legal testimony. Though often allowed to become painfully trivial and a travesty on its inherent solemnity, the taking of an official oath or the swearing of witnesses is still considered essential to the moral integrity of government, secular or spiritual. False swearing, under solemn oath, constitutes the guilt and heinousness of perjury. The universality of oath-taking is humanity's tribute, whether pagan or Christian, to the sacredness of truth.

(2) Civilized nations administer oaths under three heads: political, ecclesiastical, legal. The sovereign of England receives the crown only as he or she responds affirmatively to the solemn adjuration of the archbishop or bishop: "Will you solemnly promise and swear to govern," etc, closing with the affirmation, "So help me God." A fundamental conviction of civilized nations was expressed by Lycurgus: "An oath is the bond that keeps the state together." It is the most solemn appeal to the inviolability of the human conscience, and the sacredness of a vow as witnessed both by God and men. See also OATH. DWIGHT M. PRATT

ADLAI, ad′lā-ī, ad′lī (עַדְלַי, *'adhlay;* LXX **'Αδλί**, *Adlí* and **'Αδαί**, *Adaí*, "lax, weary"): The father of Shaphat, an overseer of David's herds in the lowlands (1 Ch **27** 29).

ADMAH, ad′mä (אַדְמָה, *'adhmāh*): From a root signifying red; one of the Cities of the Plain (Ciccar) (Gen **10** 19; **14** 2.8; Dt **29** 23; Hos **11** 8) upon which Abraham and Lot looked from the heights of Bethel; destroyed with Sodom and Gomorrah. Conder tentatively identifies it with the City of Adam referred to in Josh **3** 16, and thinks that perhaps the name may be preserved in that of Damieh Ford, near the mouth of the river Jabbok; but that point could not have been in view from Bethel. See VALE OF SIDDIM.

ADMATHA, ad′ma-tha, ad-mā′tha (אַדְמָתָא, *'adhmāthā'*): One of "the seven princes of Persia and Media, who saw the king's face, and sat first in the kingdom" (Est **1** 14); cf 2 K **25** 19; Ezr **7** 14. The LXX gives only three names.

ADMIN, ad′min. See ARNI.

ADMINISTER, ad-min′is-tẽr (**διακονέω**, *diakonéō*), **ADMINISTRATION,** ad-min-is-trā′shun (**διακονία**, *diakonía*): Terms used in AV in 1 Cor **12** 5; 2 Cor **8** 19.20; 2 Cor **9** 12 respectively, and replaced in RV by "minister" and "ministration." The root idea of both words is "service," hence to supply, or conduct or attend to anything; the performance of official duty, the conduct of affairs, the various forms of spiritual or social service. "Minister," used either of an act or of an office, is the term that best represents the apostolic thought and ideal. DWIGHT M. PRATT

ADMIRATION, ad-mi-rā′shun (**θαῦμα**, *thaúma*, "a marvel" or "wonder"; **θαυμάζω**, *thaumázō*, "to wonder"): A term thrice used in AV in the NT, to express a wonder that includes approval, high esteem; replaced in RV by three renderings better suited to convey the various kinds of surprise, wonder, admiration, expressed by this fertile word: viz. in 2 Thess **1** 10, "to be admired," reads in RV "to be marvelled at"; in Jude ver **16** "having men's persons in admiration" is rendered "showing respect of persons"; in Rev **17** 6 "wondered with great admiration" is replaced by "with a great wonder." The Gr original is used frequently in the NT, esp. in the Gospels, to express marvel and wonder at the supernatural works of Jesus. DWIGHT M. PRATT

ADNA, ad′na (עַדְנָא, *'adhnā'*, "pleasure"; **Αἰδαινέ**, *Aidainé*):

(1) An Israelite in Ezra's time who, having married a foreign wife, divorced her. He belonged to Pahath-moab (Ezr **10** 30).

(2) A priest of the family of Harum, during the high-priesthood of Joiakim son of Jethua (Neh **12** 12–15).

ADNAH, ad′nä (עַדְנָה, *'adhnāh*, "pleasure"; **'Εδνά,** *Edná*):

(1) A warrior of the tribe of Manasseh, who deserted Saul and joined David's forces at Ziklag (1 Ch **12** 20.21).

(2) An officer of high rank, perhaps the commander-in-chief of Jehoshaphat's army (2 Ch **17** 14). Here the spelling in Heb is עַדְנָה, *'adhnāh*.

ADO, a-dōō′: Found only in Mk **5** 39 AV: "Why make ye this *ado* and weep?" Here "make ado" is used to translate the Gr verb *θορυβέομαι*, *thorubéomai* (cf Mt **9** 23 AV, where it is likewise rendered "making a noise"). "Ado" as a subst. is OE for "trouble" or "fuss," used only in the sing.; and in the early Eng. VSS it combined well with the verb "make," as here, to translate the Gr word rendered elsewhere "causing an uproar," or "tumult," "making a noise," etc (see Acts **17** 5; **20** 10). Cf Shakespeare, *Romeo and Juliet*, III, 4, "We'll keep no great *ado;*—a friend or two." GEO. B. EAGER

ADONAI, a-dō′nī, ad-o-nā′ī (אֲדֹנָי, *'ădhōnāy*): A Divine name, trd "Lord," and signifying, from its derivation, "sovereignty." Its vowels are found in the MT with the unpronounceable tetragrammaton יהוה; and when the Heb reader came to these letters, he always substituted in pronunciation the word "*'ădhōnāy*." Its vowels combined with the tetragrammaton form the word "Jehovah." See GOD, NAMES OF.

ADONIBEZEK, a-dō-nī-bē′zek (אֲדֹנִי־בֶזֶק, *'ădhōnībhezek*, "lord of Bezek"): Lord of a town, Bezek, in southern Palestine, whom the tribes of Judah and Simeon overthrew. Adonibezek fled when his men were defeated, but was captured, and was punished for his cruelty in cutting off the thumbs and great toes of seventy kings by a similar mutilation. Being brought to Jerusalem, he died there (Jgs **1** 5–7). This not to be confused with Adonizedek, as in the LXX. This is quite another name.

ADONIJAH, ad-o-nī′jä (אֲדֹנִיָּהוּ or אֲדֹנִיָּה, *'ădhōnīyāhū* or *'ădhōnīyāh*, "my lord is Jehovah"):

(1) The son of David and Haggith, the fourth of David's sons, born in Hebron after David became king of Judah, principally known for his attempt to become king instead of Solomon (2 S **3** 4; 1 Ch **3** 2; 1 K **1** and **2**). The record gives no details concerning Chileab, the son of David and Abigail. Leaving him out, Adonijah was the oldest living son of David, after the death of Amnon and Absalom.

In treating the record it has been needlessly obscured by neglecting or distorting the time data. It says that the rebellion of Absalom broke out "at an end of forty years" (2 S **15** 7). The natural meaning is not forty years after the last-mentioned preceding date, but at the close of the fortieth calendar year of the reign of David. As David reigned 40½ years (2 S **5** 4.5), the close of his fortieth calendar year was the beginning of his last year. That the date intended was at the beginning of a vernal year is confirmed by the references to the season (2 S **17** 19.28). Instead of giving this number Jos says that 4 years had elapsed since the last preceding date, which is very likely correct.

Many considerations show that the outbreak cannot have occurred much earlier than the fortieth year of David; for Amnon and Absalom were born after David's reign began, and were men with establishments of their own before Amnon's offence against Tamar, and after that the record, if we accept the numeral of Jos, accounts for 2 plus 3 plus 2 plus 4, that is, for 11 years (2 S **13** 23.38; **14** 28; *Ant*, VII, ix, 1). In the year following David's fortieth year there was ample room for the rebellions of Absalom and of Sheba, the illness of David, the attempt of Adonijah, and the beginning of the reign of Solomon. All things confirm the number forty as giving the date of the outbreak. The common assumption that the forty is to be reduced to four, on the basis of the number in Jos, is contrary to the evidence.

On this view of the chronology all the events fall into line. David's idea of making Solomon king was connected with his temple-building idea. This is implied in K, and presented somewhat in full in Ch. The preparations described in Ch (1 Ch **22–29**) seem to have culminated in David's fortieth year (1 Ch **26** 31). David's policy was not altogether popular with the nation. His assembly (1 Ch **28** 1) is mostly made up of *sarim* and other appointed officials, the hereditary Israelitish "princes" and "elders" being conspicuous by their absence. The outbreak under Absalom was mainly a matter of skilful manipulation; the hearts of the people were really with David. And yet the party of Absalom was distinctly a legitimist party. It believed in the succession of the eldest son, and it objected to many things in the temple-building policy. Joab and Abiathar and others sympathized with this party, but they remained with David out of personal loyalty to him.

The Absalom campaign began early in the calendar year. There is no reason to think that it lasted more than a few weeks. Later in the year a few weeks are enough time to allow for the campaign against Sheba. Joab must have been more or less alienated from David by David's appointment of Amasa to supersede him. Then came David's serious illness. Abishag was brought in, not to "attend upon David during his declining years," but to put her vitality at his disposal during a few weeks. Joab and Abiathar did not believe that David would ever do business again. Their personal loyalty to him no longer restrained them from following their own ideas, even though these were contrary to his wishes.

The narrative does not represent that Nathan and Bathsheba influenced David to interfere in behalf of Solomon; it represents that they succeeded in arousing him from his torpor, so that he carried out his own wishes and intentions. Perhaps resting in bed had done something for him. The treatment by Abishag had not been unsuccessful. And now a supreme appeal to his mind proved sufficient to arouse him. He became himself again, and acted with his usual vigor and wisdom.

Adonijah is described as a handsome and showy man, but his conduct does not give us a high opinion of his capabilities. He had no real command of the respect of the guests who shouted "Live King Adonijah." When they heard that Solomon had been crowned, they "were afraid, and rose up, and went every man his way." Adonijah made his submission, but afterward attempted to engage in intrigues, and was put to death.

(2) One of the Levites sent out by Jehoshaphat, in his third year, with the Book of the Law, to give instruction in Judah (2 Ch **17** 8).

(3) One of the names given, under the heading "the chiefs of the people," of those who sealed the covenant along with Nehemiah (Neh **10** 16).

WILLIS J. BEECHER

ADONIKAM, ad-ō-nī′kam (אֲדֹנִיקָם, *'ădhōnīķām*, "my lord has risen up"): The name of a family of the returning exiles (Ezr **2** 13; Neh **7** 18). "The sons of Adonikam," men and women and children, numbered 666 according to the list as given in Ezr, but 667 according to the copy in Neh. Either included among these or in addition to them was the contingent that came with Ezr, "Eliphalet, Jeuel, and Shemaiah, and with them 60 males" (Ezr **8** 13).

ADONIRAM, ad-ō-nī′ram (אֲדֹנִירָם, *'ădhōnīrām*, "my lord is exalted"): An official of Solomon (1 K **4** 6; **5** 14). Near the close of the reign of David, and at the opening of the reign of Rehoboam, the same office was held by Adoram (2 S **20** 24; 1 K **12** 18). The name Adoram seems to be a contraction of Adoniram, and doubtless the same person held the office in all the three reigns. The name also appears as Hadoram (2 Ch **10** 18). In AV and RV the office is variantly described as "over the tribute," which is misleading, and "over the levy," which is correct, though obscure. In ARV it is uniformly "over the men subject to taskwork." Adoniram was at the head of the department of forced labor for the government. The record is to the effect that peoples conquered by Israel, excepting the Canaanites, were to be spared, subject to the obligation to forced labor on the public works (Dt **20** 11); that this law was actually extended to the Canaanites (Josh **16** 10; **17** 13; Jgs **1** 28 ff); that David, in his preparations for the temple, organized and handed over to Solomon a service of forced labor (1 Ch **22** 2.15, etc); that under Solomon this service was elaborately maintained (1 K **5** 13 ff; **9** 15 ff; 2 Ch **8** 7 ff). It was not for the temple only, but for all Solomon's numerous building enterprises. In theory men of Israelitish blood were free from this burden, but practically they found it a burden and a grievance. At the accession of Rehoboam they protested against it (1 K 12; 2 Ch **10**). Nothing in the account is more indicative of Rehoboam's utter lack of good judgment than his sending his veteran superintendent of the forced labor department to confer with the people. The murder of Adoniram, and the ignominious flight of Rehoboam, were natural consequences.

Willis J. Beecher

ADONIS, a-dō′nis: A name for the Bab god Tammuz, which see. The word occurs only in ERVm of Isa **17** 10, where for "pleasant plants" is read "plantings of Adonis." The ARV rightly omits this marginal suggestion.

ADONI-ZEDEK, a-dō-nī-zē′dek (אֲדֹנִי־צֶדֶק, *'ădhōnīçedheķ*, "lord of righteousness"): King of Jerus at the time of the conquest of Canaan (Josh **10** 1). When he heard of the fall of Ai and the submission of the Gibeonites, he entered into a league with four other kings to resist Joshua and Israel, and to punish Gibeon (Josh **10** 3.4), but was overthrown by Joshua in a memorable battle (vs 12–14). Adoni-zedek and his four allies were shut up in a cave, while the battle lasted, and afterward were taken out by Joshua's order, put to death and hanged on trees (Josh **10** 22–27). It is noticeable that the name is almost the equivalent of Melchizedek, מַלְכִּי־צֶדֶק, *malkīçedheķ*, "king of righteousness," who was ruler of Jerus in the time of Abraham.

Edward Mack

ADOPTION, a-dop′shun (**υἱοθεσία,** *huiothesía*, "placing as a son"):

I. The General Legal Idea
 1. In the OT
 2. Greek
 3. Roman
II. Paul's Doctrine
 1. In Gal as Liberty
 2. In Rom as Deliverance from Debt
III. The Christian Experience
 1. In Relation to Justification
 2. In Relation to Sanctification
 3. In Relation to Regeneration
IV. As God's Act
 1. Divine Fatherhood
 2. Its Cosmic Range

This term appears first in NT, and only in the epp. of Paul (Gal **4** 5; Rom **8** 15.23; **9** 4; Eph **1** 5) who may have coined it out of a familiar Gr phrase of identical meaning. It indicated generally the legal process by which a man might bring into his family, and endow with the status and privileges of a son, one who was not by nature his son or of his kindred.

I. The General Legal Idea.—The custom prevailed among Greeks, Romans and other ancient peoples, but it does not appear in Jewish law.

1. In the OT

Three cases of adoption are mentioned: of Moses (Ex **2** 10), Genubath (1 K **11** 20) and Esther (Est **2** 7.15), but it is remarkable that they all occur outside of Pal—in Egypt and Persia, where the practice of adoption prevailed. Likewise the idea appears in the NT only in the epistles of Paul, which were addressed to churches outside Pal. The motive and initiative of adoption always lay with the adoptive father, who thus supplied his lack of natural offspring and satisfied the claims of affection and religion, and the desire to exercise paternal authority or to perpetuate his family. The process and conditions of adoption varied with different peoples. Among oriental nations it was extended to slaves (as Moses) who thereby gained their freedom, but in Greece and Rome it was, with rare exceptions, limited to citizens.

2. Greek

In Greece a man might during his lifetime, or by will, to take effect after his death, adopt any male citizen into the privileges of his son, but with the invariable condition that the adopted son accepted the legal obligations and religious duties of a real son.

3. Roman

In Rome the unique nature of paternal authority (*patria potestas*), by which a son was held in his father's power, almost as a slave was owned by his master, gave a peculiar character to the process of adoption. For the adoption of a person free from paternal authority (*sui juris*), the process and effect were practically the same in Rome as in Greece (*adrogatio*). In a more specific sense, adoption proper (*adoptio*) was the process by which a person was transferred from his natural father's power into that of his adoptive father, and it consisted in a fictitious sale of the son, and his surrender by the natural to the adoptive father.

II. Paul's Doctrine.—As a Rom citizen the apostle would naturally know of the Rom custom, but in the cosmopolitan city of Tarsus, and again on his travels, he would become equally familiar with the corresponding customs of other nations. He employed the idea metaphorically much in the manner of Christ's parables, and, as in their case, there is danger of pressing the analogy too far in its details. It is not clear that he had any specific form of adoption in mind when illustrating his teaching by the general idea. Under this figure he teaches that God, by the manifestation of His grace in Christ, brings men into the relation of sons to Himself, and communicates to them the experience of sonship.

In Gal Paul emphasizes especially the *liberty* enjoyed by those who live by faith, in contrast to the bondage under which men are held, who guide their lives by legal ceremonies and ordinances, as the Galatians were prone to do (**5** 1).

The contrast between law and faith is first set forth on the field of history, as a contrast between both the pre-Christian and the Christian economies (**3** 23.24), although in another passage he carries the idea of adoption back into the covenant relation of God with Israel (Rom **9** 4). But here the historical antithesis is reproduced in the contrast between men who now choose to live under law and those who live by faith. Three figures seem to commingle in the description of man's condition under legal bondage—that of a slave, that of a minor under guardians appointed by his father's will, and that of a Rom son under the *patria potestas* (Gal **4** 1–3). The process of liberation is first of all one of redemption or buying out (Gr *exagorásēi*) (**4** 5). This term in itself applies equally well to the slave who is redeemed from bondage, and the Rom son whose adoptive father buys him out of the authority of his natural father. But in the latter case the condition of the son is not materially altered by the process: he only exchanges one paternal authority for another. If Paul for a moment thought of the process in terms of ordinary Rom adoption, the resulting condition of the son he conceives in terms of the more free and gracious Greek or Jewish family life. Or he may have thought of the rarer case of adoption from conditions of slavery into the status of sonship. The redemption is only a precondition of adoption, which follows upon faith, and is accompanied by the sending of "the Spirit of his Son into our hearts, crying, Abba, Father," and then all bondage is done away (**4** 5–7).

1. In Gal as Liberty

In Rom (**8** 12–17) the idea of obligation or debt is coupled with that of liberty. Man is thought of as at one time under the authority and power of the flesh (**8** 5), but when the Spirit of Christ comes to dwell in him, he is no longer a debtor to the flesh but to the Spirit (**8** 12.13), and debt or obligation to the Spirit is itself liberty. As in Gal, man thus passes from a state of bondage into a state of sonship which is also a state of liberty. "For as many as are led by the Spirit of God, these [and these only] are sons of God" (**8** 14). The spirit of adoption or sonship stands in diametrical opposition to the spirit of bondage (**8** 15). And the Spirit to which we are debtors and by which we are led, at once awakens and confirms the experience of sonship within us (**8** 16). In both places, Paul conveys under this figure, the idea of man as passing from a state of alienation from God and of bondage under law and sin, into that relation with God of mutual confidence and love, of unity of thought and will, which should characterize the ideal family, and in which all restraint, compulsion and fear have passed away.

2. In Rom as Deliverance from Debt

III. The Christian Experience.—As a fact of Christian experience, the adoption is the recognition and affirmation by man of his sonship toward God. It follows upon faith in Christ, by which man becomes so united with Christ that his filial spirit enters into him, and takes possession of his consciousness, so that he knows and greets God as Christ does (cf Mk **14** 36).

It is an aspect of the same experience that Paul describes elsewhere, under another legal metaphor, as justification by faith. According to the latter, God declares the sinner righteous and treats him as such, admits him to the experience of forgiveness, reconciliation and peace (Rom **5** 1). In all this the relation of father and son is undoubtedly involved, but in adoption it is emphatically expressed. It is not only that the prodigal son is welcomed home, glad to confess that he is not worthy to be called a son, and willing to be made as one of the hired servants, but he is embraced and restored to be a son as before. The point of each metaphor is, that justification is the act of a merciful judge setting the prisoner free, but adoption is the act of a generous father, taking a son to his bosom and endowing him with liberty, favor and a heritage.

1. In Relation to Justification

Besides, justification is the beginning of a process which needs for its completion a progressive course of sanctification by the aid of the Holy Spirit, but adoption is coextensive with sanctification. The sons of God are those led by the Spirit of God (Rom **8** 14); and the same spirit of God gives the experience of sonship. Sanctification describes the process of general cleansing and growth as an abstract process, but adoption includes it as a concrete relation to God, as loyalty, obedience, and fellowship with an ever-loving Father.

2. In Relation to Sanctification

Some have identified adoption with regeneration, and therefore many Fathers and Roman Catholic theologians have identified it with baptismal regeneration, thereby excluding the essential fact of conscious sonship. The new birth and adoption are certainly aspects of the same totality of experience, but they belong to different systems of thought, and to identify them is to invite confusion. The new birth defines especially the origin and moral quality of the Christian experience as an abstract fact, but adoption expresses a concrete relation of man to God. Nor does Paul here raise the question of man's natural and original condition. It is pressing the analogy too far to infer from this doctrine of adoption that man is by nature not God's son. It would contradict Paul's teaching elsewhere (e.g. Acts **17** 28), and he should not be convicted of inconsistency on the application of a metaphor. He conceives man outside Christ as morally an alien and a stranger from God, and the change wrought by faith in Christ makes him morally a son and conscious of his sonship; but naturally he is always a potential son because God is always a real father.

3. In Relation to Regeneration

IV. As God's Act.—Adoption as God's act is an eternal process of His gracious love, for He "foreordained us unto adoption as sons through Jesus Christ unto himself, according to the good pleasure of his will" (Eph **1** 5).

The motive and impulse of Fatherhood which result in adoption were eternally real and active in God. In some sense He had bestowed the adoption upon Israel (Rom **9** 4). "Israel is my son, my first-born" (Ex **4** 22; cf Dt **14** 1; **32** 6; Jer **31** 9; Hos **11** 1). God could not reveal Himself at all without revealing something of His Fatherhood, but the whole revelation was as yet partial and prophetic. When "God sent forth his Son" to "redeem them that were under the law," it became possible for men to receive the adoption; for to those who are willing to receive it, He sent the Spirit of the eternal Son to testify in their hearts that they are sons of God, and to give them confidence and utterance to enable them to call God their Father (Gal **4** 5.6; Rom **8** 15).

1. Divine Fatherhood

But this experience also is incomplete, and looks forward to a fuller adoption in the response, not only of man's spirit, but of the whole creation, including man's body, to the Fatherhood of God (Rom **8** 23). Every filial spirit now groans, because it finds itself imprisoned in a body subjected to

2. Its Cosmic Range

vanity, but it awaits a redemption of the body, perhaps in the resurrection, or in some final consummation, when the whole material creation shall be transformed into a fitting environment for the sons of God, the creation itself delivered from the bondage of corruption into the liberty of the glory of the children of God (Rom **8** 21). Then will adoption be complete, when man's whole personality shall be in harmony with the spirit of sonship, and the whole universe favorable to its perseverance in a state of blessedness. See CHILDREN OF GOD.

LITERATURE.—Lightfoot, *Galatians;* Sanday, *Romans;* Lidgett, *Fatherhood of God;* Ritschl, *Justification and Reconciliation.*

T. REES

ADOR, ā′dor, **ADORA,** a-dō′ra (**Ἀδωρά,** *Adōrá*): In Idumaea, mentioned in *Ant,* XIII, ix, 1 as one of the cities captured by Hyrcanus, and referred to in 1 Macc **13** 20. See ADORAIM.

ADORAIM, ad-o-rā′im (אֲדוֹרַיִם, *'ădhōrayim,* "a pair of knolls," perhaps): One of several cities in Judah that were fortified by Rehoboam (2 Ch **11** 9). The name appears in Jos and in 1 Macc as Adora or Dora or Dor. Its location is indicated in general by that of the other cities which the record in Ch groups with it. Common consent identifies it with Dûra, about five miles W. by S. of Hebron.

ADORAM, a-dō′ram. See ADONIRAM.

ADORATION, ad-o-rā′shun: Though this word never occurs in EV, it represents aspects of worship which are very prominent in the Bible.

I. Etymology.—The word is derived from Lat *adorare* = (1) "to speak to," (2) "to beseech," "entreat," (3) "to do homage," "to worship"; from *os* (*oris*), mouth. Some have supposed that the root *os* points to the Rom practice of applying the hand to the mouth, i.e. kissing the hand to (a person or thing), as a token of homage.

II. Meaning.—Adoration is intense admiration culminating in reverence and worship, together with the outward acts and attitudes which accompany such reverence. It thus includes both the subjective sentiments, or feelings of the soul, in the presence of some superior object or person, and the appropriate physical expressions of such sentiments in outward acts of homage or of worship. In its widest sense it includes reverence to beings other than God, esp. to monarchs, who in oriental countries were regarded with feelings of awe. But it finds its highest expression in religion. Adoration is perhaps the highest type of worship, involving the reverent and rapt contemplation of the Divine perfections and prerogatives, the acknowledgment of them in words of praise, together with the visible symbols and postures that express the adoring attitude of the creature in the presence of his Creator. It is the expression of the soul's mystical realization of God's presence in His transcendent greatness, holiness and lovingkindness. As a form of prayer, adoration is to be distinguished from other forms, such as petition, thanksgiving, confession and intercession.

III. Outward Postures.—In the OT and NT, these are similar to those which prevailed in all oriental countries, as amply illustrated by the monuments of Egypt and Assyria, and by the customs still in use among the nations of the East. The chief attitudes referred to in the Bible are the following:

1. Prostration

Among the Orientals, esp. Persians, prostration (i.e. falling upon the knees, then gradually inclining the body, until the forehead touched the ground) was common as an expression of profound reverence and humility before a superior or a benefactor. It was practised in the worship of Yahweh (Gen **17** 3; Nu **16** 45; Mt **26** 39, Jesus in Gethsemane; Rev **1** 17), and of idols (2 K **5** 18; Dnl **3** 5.6), but was by no means confined to religious exercises. It was the formal method of supplicating or doing obeisance to a superior (e.g. 1 S **25** 23 f; 2 K **4** 37; Est **8** 3; Mk **5** 22; Jn **11** 32).

2. Kneeling

A substitute for prostration was kneeling, a common attitude in worship, frequently mentioned in OT and NT (e.g. 1 K **8** 54; Ezr **9** 5; Ps **95** 6; Isa **45** 23; Lk **22** 41, Christ in Gethsemane; Acts **7** 60; Eph **3** 14). The same attitude was sometimes adopted in paying homage to a fellow-creature, as in 2 K **1** 13. "Sitting" as an attitude of prayer (only 2 S **7** 18 ‖ 1 Ch **17** 16) was probably a form of kneeling, as in Mahometan worship.

3. Standing

This was the most usual posture in prayer, like that of modern Jews in public worship. Abraham "*stood* before Jeh" when he interceded for Sodom (Gen **18** 22). Cf 1 S **1** 26. The Pharisee in the parable "*stood* and prayed" (Lk **18** 11), and the hypocrites are said to "pray *standing* in the synagogues, and in the corners of the streets" (Mt **6** 5 AV).

4. The Hands

The above postures were accompanied by various attitudes of the hands, which were either *lifted* up toward heaven (Ps **63** 4; 1 Tim **2** 8), or *outspread* (Ex **9** 29; Ezr **9** 5; Isa **1** 15), or both (1 K **8** 54).

5. Kiss of Adoration

The heathen practice of kissing hands to the heavenly bodies as a sign of adoration is referred to in Job **31** 27, and of kissing the idol in 1 K **19** 18; Hos **13** 2. The kiss of homage is mentioned in Ps **2** 12, if the text there be correct. Kissing hands to the object of adoration was customary among the Romans (Pliny xxviii.5). The NT word for "worship" (*proskunéō*) lit. means to kiss the hand to (one). See also ATTITUDES.

IV. Objects of Adoration.—The only adequate object of adoration is the Supreme Being. He only who is the sum of all perfections can fully satisfy man's instincts of reverence, and elicit the complete homage of his soul.

1. Fellow-Creatures

Yet, as already suggested, the crude beginnings of religious adoration are to be found in the respect paid to created beings regarded as possessing superior claims and powers, esp. to kings and rulers. As instances we may mention the woman of Tekoa falling on her face to do obeisance to King David (2 S **14** 4), and the king's servants bowing down to do reverence to Haman (Est **3** 2). Cf Ruth **2** 10; 1 S **20** 41; 2 S **1** 2; **14** 22.

2. Material Objects

On a higher plane, as involving some recognition of divinity, is the homage paid to august and mysterious objects in Nature, or to phenomena in the physical world which were supposed to have some divine significance. To give reverence to material objects themselves is condemned as idolatry throughout the OT. Such e.g. is the case with the worship of "the host of heaven" (the heavenly bodies) sometimes practised by the Hebrews (2 K **17** 16; **21** 3.5). So Job protests that he never proved false to God by kissing hands to the sun and moon in token of adoration (Job **31** 26–28). We have reference in the OT to acts of homage paid to an idol or an image, such as falling down before it (Isa **44** 15.17.19; Dnl **3** 7), or kissing it (1 K **19** 18; Hos **13** 2). All such practices are condemned in uncompromising terms. But when material things produce a reverential attitude, not to themselves, but to the Deity whose presence they symbolize, then they are regarded as legitimate aids to devotion; e.g. *fire* as a manifestation of the Divine presence is described as causing the spectator to perform acts of reverence (e.g. Ex **3** 2.5; Lev **9** 24; 1 K **18** 38 f). In these instances, it was Yahweh Himself that was worshipped, not the fire which revealed Him. The sacred writers are moved to religious adoration by the contemplation of the glories of Nature. To them, "the heavens declare the glory of God; and the firmament sheweth his handiwork." (Cf esp. the "nature-Pss" **8, 19, 29, 104.**)

3. Angels

On a still higher plane is the adoration practised in the presence of supernatural agents of the Divine will. When an angel of God appeared, men fell instinctively before him in reverence and awe (e.g. Gen **18** 2; **19** 1; Nu **22** 31; Jgs **13** 20; Lk **24** 4.5). This was not to worship the creature instead of the Creator, for the angel was regarded, not as a distinct individual having an existence and character of his own, but as a theophany, a self-manifestation of God.

4. The Deity

The highest form of adoration is that which is directed immediately to God Himself, His kingly attributes and spiritual excellencies being so apprehended by the soul that it is filled with rapture and praise, and is moved to do Him reverence. A classical instance is the vision that initiated Isaiah into the prophetic office, when he was so possessed with the sovereignty and sublimity of God that he was filled with wonder and self-abasement (Isa **6** 1–5). In the OT, the literature of adoration reaches its high-water mark in the Pss (cf esp. the group Pss **95–100**), where the ineffable majesty, power and holiness of God are set forth in lofty strains. In the NT, adoration of the Deity finds its most rapturous expression in Rev, where the vision of God calls forth a chorus of praise addressed to the thrice-holy God (**4** 8–11; **7** 11.12), with whom is associated the Redeemer-Lamb.

5. Jesus Christ

How far is Jesus regarded in the NT as an object of adoration, seeing that adoration is befitting only to God? During Our Lord's lifetime He was often the object of worship (Mt **2** 11; **8** 2; **9** 18; **14** 33; **15** 25; **20** 20; **28** 9.17; Mk **5** 6; Jn **9** 38). Some ambiguity, however, belongs to the Gr word *proskunein*, for while it is the usual word for "worshipping" God (e.g. Jn **4** 24), in some contexts it means no more than paying homage to a person of superior rank by kneeling or prostration, just as the unmerciful servant is said to have 'fallen down and worshipped' his master the king (Mt **18** 26), and as Jos speaks of the Jewish high priests as *proskunoúmenoi* (*BJ*, IV, v, 2). On the other hand, it certainly implies a consciousness, on the part of those who paid this respect to Jesus, and of Jesus Himself, of a very exceptional superiority in His person, for the same homage was refused by Peter, when offered to him by Cornelius, on the ground that he himself also was a man (Acts **10** 25 f), and even by the angel before whom John prostrated himself, on the ground that God alone was to be "worshipped" (Rev **22** 8.9). Yet Jesus never repudiated such tokens of respect. But whatever about the "days of His flesh," there is no doubt that after the ascension Christ became to the church the object of adoration as Divine, and the homage paid to Him was indistinguishable in character from that paid to God. This is proved not only by isolated passages, but still more by the whole tone of the Acts and epp. in relation to Him. This adoration reaches its highest expression in Rev **5** 9–14, where the Redeemer-Lamb who shares the throne of God is the subject of an outburst of adoring praise on the part of the angelic hosts. In **4** 8–11 the hymn of adoration is addressed to the Lord God Almighty, the Creator; here it is addressed to the Lamb on the ground of His redeeming work. In Rev the adoration of Him "who sitteth on the throne" and that of "the Lamb" flow together into one stream of ecstatic praise (cf **7** 9–11).

D. Miall Edwards

ADORN, a-dōrn′ (**κοσμέω**, *kosméō*): Has as its primary meaning "to arrange," "to put in order," "to decorate." It is used with reference to the manner in which Christian women were urged to dress. This was a vital question in the early church, and both Paul and Peter give advice on the subject (1 Tim **2** 9; 1 Pet **3** 3). See Dress.

Figurative: In Mt **12** 44 AV the word is tr[d] "garnish" and is used in a fig. sense. It describes accurately the condition of the Jewish nation. Even though they have swept out idolatry and have adorned the life with much ceremony and endless religious prescriptions yet the evil spirit can say, "I will return *to my house*." This same thing has repeatedly been done by individuals and nations when reforms have been instituted, but Christ was not enthroned and the heart or nation was still dominated by evil. It is used also in a fig. sense with reference to the graces of the Christian life. When we remember how very highly Orientals esteem the adornment of the body, its use here becomes very forceful. It is this that makes Ps **45** 13 of special significance as to the beauty and glory of the church as she is presented to God. See also Prov **1** 9; **4** 9; Isa **61** 10; 1 Pet **3** 4.5. Consecration to God, the indwelling of His Spirit, righteousness, a meek and quiet spirit—these are the true adornments of the life. All these passages carry with them the idea of joy, the satisfaction that should be ours in these possessions.

Jacob W. Kapp

ADRA, ā′dra. See Arad (city).

ADRAMMELECH, a-dram′el-ek, and **ANAMMELECH**, a-nam′el-ek (אַדְרַמֶּלֶךְ and עֲנַמֶּלֶךְ, *'adhrammelekh* and *'ănammelekh*, apparently, according to Assyrian usage, "Adar is prince," "Anu is prince." By Palestinian usage it would be "Adar is king," "Anu is king"):

(1) The names given by the Israelitish narrator to the god or gods imported into the Samaritan land by the men of Sepharvaim whom the king of Assyria had settled there (2 K **17** 31). In the Bab pantheon Anu, the god of heaven, is one of the three chief gods, and Adar, otherwise known as Ninib, is a solar god. Concerning the statements in this ver in K, archaeologists differ in some important points, and it is a case in which a suspended judgment may be becoming in one who is not an expert. But at least a portion of the alleged difficulties have arisen from failures to get the point of view of the Israelitish narrator. He is writing from a time considerably later than the establishment of the institutions of which he speaks—late enough to render the phrase "unto this day" suitable (2 K **17** 34), late enough so that words and usages may have undergone modification. He is describing a mixture of religions which he evidently regards as deserving of contempt and ridicule, even apart from the falsity of the religions included in it. This mixture he describes as containing ingredients of three kinds—first, the imported religions of the imported peoples; second, the local high-place religions (vs 32, etc), and third, the Jeh religion of Northern Israel (not that of Jerus). It is not likely that he thought that they practised any cult in its purity. They contaminated the religion of Jeh by introducing Canaanitish

usages into it, and they are likely to have done the same with the ancestral religions which they brought with them. The proper names may be correct as representing Pal usage, even if they differ somewhat from the proper Bab usage. The writer says that they "burnt their children in the fire to Adrammelech," but this does not necessarily prove that he thought that they brought this practice from Babylonia; his idea may be that they corrupted even their own false cult by introducing into it this horrible Canaanitish rite. In considering the bearings of the evidence of the monuments on the case, considerations of this kind should not be neglected.

(2) The name of a son of Sennacherib king of Assyria—one of the two who slew him and escaped, indirectly leading to the accession of Esar-haddon (2 K **19** 37; Isa **37** 38). Mention of the incident is found on the monuments, and traces of the name appear in the writings of Abydenus and Polyhistor. WILLIS J. BEECHER

ADRAMYTTIUM, ad-ra-mit'i-um (**Ἀδραμύττιον,** *Adramúttion;* for other forms see Thayer's lexicon): An ancient city of Mysia in the Rom Province of Asia. The only reference in the NT to it is in Acts **27** 2 which says that Paul, while being taken a prisoner from Caesarea to Rome, embarked upon a ship belonging to A.

The city, with a good harbor, stood at the head of the Gulf of Adramyttium facing the island of Lesbos, and at the base of Mt. Ida. Its early history is obscure. While some authors fancy that it was the Pedasus of Homer, others suppose that it was founded by Adramys, the brother of the wealthy Croesus; probably a small Athenian colony existed there long before the time of Adramys. When Pergamus became the capital of Asia, A. grew to be a city of considerable importance, and the metropolis of the N.W. part of the province. There the assizes were held. The coins which the peasants pick up in the surrounding fields, and which are frequently aids in determining the location and history of the cities of Asia Minor, were struck at A. as late as the 3d cent. AD, and sometimes in connection with Ephesus. Upon them the effigies of Castor and Pollux appear, showing that A. was the seat of worship of these deities.

The ancient city with its harbor has entirely disappeared, but on a hill, somewhat farther inland, is a village of about one thousand houses bearing the name Edremid, a corruption of the ancient name Adramys. The miserable wooden huts occupied by Gr fishermen and by Turks are surrounded by vineyards and olive trees, hence the chief trade is in olive oil, raisins and timber. In ancient times A. was noted for a special ointment which was prepared there (Pliny, *NH*, xiii.2.5).

E. J. BANKS

ADRIA, ā'dri-a (**ὁ Ἁδρίας,** [WH] *ho Hadrías* or *ho Adrías*): In Gr *Adrias* (Polybios i.2.4), *Adriatike Thalassa* (Strabo iv.204), and *Adriatikon Pelagos* (Ptolemy iii.15.2), and in Lat *Adriaticum mare* (Livy xl.57.7), *Adrianum mare* (Cicero *in Pisonem* 38), *Adriaticus sinus* (Livy x.2.4), and *Mare superum* (Cicero *ad Att.* 9.5.1). The Adriatic Sea is a name derived from the old Etruscan city Atria, situated near the mouth of the Po (Livy v. 33.7; Strabo v.214). At first the name Adria was only applied to the most northern part of the sea. But after the development of the Syracusan colonies on the Italian and Illyrian coasts the application of the term was gradually extended southward, so as to reach Mons Garganus (the Abruzzi), and later the Strait of Hydruntum (Ptolemy iii.1.1; Polybios vii.19.2). But finally the name embraced the Ionian Sea as well, and we find it employed to denote the Gulf of Tarentum (Servius Aen xi.540), the Sicilian Sea (Pausanias v. 25), and even the waters between Crete and Malta (Orosius i.2.90). Procopius considers Malta as lying at the western extremity of the Adriatic Sea (i.14). After leaving Crete the vessel in which the apostle Paul was sailing under military escort was "driven to and fro in the *sea of* Adria" fourteen days (Acts **27** 27) before it approached the shore of Malta. We may compare this with the shipwreck of Jos in "the middle of the Adria" where he was picked up by a ship sailing from Cyrene to Puteoli (Jos, *Vita*, 3). GEORGE H. ALLEN

ADRIEL, ā'dri-el (עַדְרִיאֵל, *'adhrī'ēl,* "my help is God"): The son of Barzillai the Meholathite, to whom Merab the daughter of King Saul was married when she should have been given to David (1 S **18** 19; 2 S **21** 8). "Michal" in **21** 8 is a textual error easily accounted for. Adriel and Merab had five sons, whom David handed over to the blood vengeance of the men of Gibeon. The name Adriel seems to be Aram., the equivalent of the Heb name Azriel.

ADUEL, a-dū'el (**Ἀδουήλ,** *Adouḗl*): An ancestor of Tobit (Tob **1** 1).

ADULLAM, a-dul'am (עֲדֻלָּם, *'ădhullām*):

(1) A city, with dependencies, and anciently having a king, mentioned five times in the OT, each time in a list with other cities (Josh **12** 15; **15** 35; 2 Ch **11** 7; Mic **1** 15; Neh **11** 30). In the list of 31 kings whom Joshua smote, Adullam follows Hormah, Arad, Libnah, and precedes Makkedah. Among the 14 Judahite cities of the first group in "the lowland" Adullam is mentioned between Jarmuth and Socoh. In the list of 15 cities fortified by Rehoboam it appears between Socoh and Gath. Micah gives what may be a list of cities concerned in some Assyr approach to Jerus; it begins with Gath, includes Lachish, and ends with Mareshah and Adullam. And Adullam is still in the same company in the list in Neh of the cities "and their villages" where the men of Judah then dwelt. In the time of the patriarchs it was a place to which men "went down" from the central mountain ridge (Gen **38** 1). Judas Maccabaeus found it still existing as a city (2 Macc **12** 38). Common opinion identifies Adullam with the ruin *'Aid-el-Ma,* 13 miles W.S.W. from Bethlehem (see *HGHL,* 229 ff). This is in spite of the testimony of the Onom, which, it is alleged, confuses Adullam with Eglon. Presumably the city gave its name to the cave of Adullam, the cave being near the city.

(2) The cave of Adullam, David's headquarters during a part of the time when he was a fugitive from Saul (1 S **22** 1; 2 S **23** 13; 1 Ch **11** 15). Sufficient care has not been exercised in reading the Bible statements on this subject. To begin with, Heb syntax permits of the use of the word "cave" collectively; it may denote a group or a region of caves; it is not shut up to the meaning that there was one immense cave in which David and his 400 men all found accommodations at once. All reasonings based on this notion are futile.

Further, by the most natural syntax of 2 S **23** 13–17 (duplicated with unimportant variations in 1 Ch **11** 15–19), that passage describes two different events, and does not connect the cave of Adullam with the second of these. "And three of the thirty chief men went down, and came to David in the harvest time unto the cave of Adullam; and the troop of the Philistines was encamped in the valley of Rephaim. And David was then in the stronghold; and the garrison of the Philistines was then in Beth-lehem. And David longed, and said,

Oh that one would give me water," etc. Concerning these three seniors among David's "mighty men" it is narrated, first, that they were David's comrades in a certain battle, a battle which the Chronicler identifies with Pas-dammim, where David slew Goliath; second, that they joined David at the cave of Adullam, presumably during the time when he was in hiding from Saul; third, that at a later time, when the Philistines were in the valley of Rephaim (cf 2 S **5** 18), and David was "in the stronghold" (Jos says "at Jerusalem," *Ant*, VII, xii, 4), these men broke through the Phili lines and brought him water from the home well of Bethlehem.

The cave of Adullam, like the city, was "down" from the central ridge (1 S **22** 1; 2 S **23** 13). The city was in Judah; and David and his men were in Judah (1 S **23** 3) at a time when, apparently, the cave was their headquarters. Gad's advice to David to return to Judah (1 S **22** 3.5) was given at a time when he had left the cave of Adullam. If the current identification of *'Aid-el-Ma.* as Adullam is correct, the cave of Adullam is probably the cave region which has been found in that vicinity.

It has been objected that this location is too far from Bethlehem for David's men to have brought the water from there. To this it is replied that thirteen or fourteen miles is not an excessive distance for three exceptionally vigorous men to go and return; and a yet stronger reply is found in the consideration just mentioned, that the place from which the men went for the water was not the cave of Adullam. The one argument for the tradition to the effect that St. Chariton's cave, a few miles S.E. of Bethlehem, is Adullam, is the larger size of this cave, as compared with those near *'Aid-el-Ma* We have already seen that this has no force.

In our current speech "cave of Adullam" suggests an aggregation of ill-assorted and disreputable men. This is not justified by the Bible record. David's men included his numerous and respectable kinsmen, and the representative of the priesthood, and some of David's military companions, and some men who afterward held high office in Israel. Even those who are described as being in distress and debt and bitter of soul were doubtless, many of them, persons who had suffered at the hands of Saul on account of their friendship for David. Doubtless they included mere adventurers in their number; but the Scriptural details and the circumstances alike indicate that they were mainly homogeneous, and that most of them were worthy citizens.

WILLIS J. BEECHER

ADULLAMITE, a-dul'am-īt: The gentilic adj. of ADULLAM, which see. It is used only of Judah's friend Hirah (Gen **38** 1.12.20).

ADULTERY, a-dul'tẽr-i: In Scripture designates sexual intercourse of a man, whether married or unmarried, with a married woman.

1. Its Punishment

It is categorically prohibited in the Decalogue (seventh commandment, Ex **20** 14; Dt **5** 18): "Thou shalt not commit adultery." In more specific language we read: "And thou shalt not lie carnally with thy neighbor's wife, to defile thyself with her" (Lev **18** 20). The penalty is death for both guilty parties: "And the man that committeth adultery with another man's wife, even he that committeth adultery with his neighbor's wife, the adulterer and the adulteress shall surely be put to death" (Lev **20** 10). The manner of death is not particularized; according to the rabbis (*Ṣiphrā'* ad loc.; *Ṣanhedhrīn* **52***b*) it is strangulation. It would seem that in the days of Jesus the manner of death was interpreted to mean stoning ("Now in the law Moses commanded us to stone such," Jn **8** 5, said of the woman taken in adultery). Nevertheless, it may be said that in the case in question the woman may have been a virgin betrothed unto a husband, the law (in Dt **22** 23 f) providing that such a person together with her paramour be stoned to death (contrast ver 22, where a woman married to a husband is spoken of and the manner of death is again left general). Ezk **16** 40 (cf **23** 47) equally mentions stoning as the penalty of the adulteress; but it couples to her sin also that of shedding blood; hence the rabbinic interpretation is not necessarily controverted by the prophet. Of course it may also be assumed that a difference of custom may have obtained at different times and that the progress was in the line of leniency, strangulation being regarded as a more humane form of execution than stoning.

2. Trial by Ordeal

The guilty persons become amenable to the death penalty only when taken "in the very act" (Jn **8** 4). The difficulty of obtaining direct legal evidence is adverted to by the rabbis (see *Makkōth* **7***a*). In the case of a mere suspicion on the part of the husband, not substantiated by legal evidence, the woman is compelled by the law (Nu **5** 11–30) to submit to an ordeal, or God's judgment, which consists in her drinking the water of bitterness, that is, water from the holy basin mingled with dust from the floor of the sanctuary and with the washed-off ink of a writing containing the oath which the woman has been made to repeat. The water is named bitter with reference to its effects in the case of the woman's guilt; on the other hand, when no ill effects follow, the woman is proved innocent and the husband's jealousy unsubstantiated. According to the Mish (*Ṣōṭāh* **9**) this ordeal of the woman suspected of adultery was abolished by Johanan ben Zaccai (after 70 AD), on the ground that the men of his generation were not above the suspicion of impurity. See article BITTER, BITTERNESS.

3. A Heinous Crime

Adultery was regarded as a heinous crime (Job **31** 11). The prophets and teachers in Israel repeatedly upbraid the men and women of their generations for their looseness in morals which did not shrink from adulterous connections. Naturally where luxurious habits of life were indulged in, particularly in the large cities, a tone of levity set in: in the dark of the evening, men, with their features masked, waited at their neighbors' doors (Job **24** 15; **31** 9; cf Prov **7**), and women forgetful of their God's covenant broke faith with the husbands of their youth (Prov **2** 17). The prophet Nathan confronted David after his sin with Bath-sheba, the wife of Uriah, with his stern rebuke ("Thou art the man," 2 S **12** 7); the penitential psalm (**51**) —"Miserere"—was sung by the royal bard as a prayer for divine pardon. Promiscuous intercourse with their neighbors' wives is laid by Jeremiah at the door of the false prophets of his day (Jer **23** 10.14; **29** 23).

4. Penal and Moral Distinctions

While penal law takes only cognizance of adulterous relations, it is needless to say that the moral law discountenances all manner of illicit intercourse and all manner of unchastity in man and woman. While the phrases "harlotry," "commit harlotry," in Scripture denote the breach of wedlock (on the part of a woman), in the rabbinic writings a clear distinction is made on the legal side between adultery and fornication. The latter is condemned morally in no uncertain terms; the seventh commandment is made to include all manner of fornication. The eye and the heart are the two intermediaries of sin (Palestinian Talm, *Bᵉrākhōth* **6***b*). A sinful thought is as wicked as a sinful act (*Niddāh* **13***b* and elsewhere). Job makes a covenant with his eyes lest he look upon a virgin (**31** 1). And so Jesus who came "not to destroy, but to fulfil" (Mt **5** 17), in full agreement with the ethical and religious teaching of Judaism, makes the intent of the seventh commandment explicit when he declares that "every one that looketh on a woman to lust after her hath committed adultery with her already in his heart" (Mt **5** 28). And in the spirit of Hosea (**4** 15) and Johanan ben Zaccai (see above) Jesus has but scorn for those that are ready judicially to condemn though they be themselves not free from sin! "He that is without sin among you, let him first cast a stone at her" (Jn **8** 7). Whereas society is in need of the death penalty to secure the inviolability of the home life, Jesus bids the erring woman go her way and sin no more. How readily His word might be taken by the unspiritual to imply the condoning of woman's peccability is evidenced by the fact that the whole section (Jn **7** 53—**8** 11) is omitted by "most ancient authorities" (see St. Augustine's remark).

5. A Ground of Divorce

Adultery as a ground of divorce.—The meaning of the expression "some unseemly thing" (Dt **24** 1) being unclear, there was great variety of opinion among the rabbis as to the grounds upon which a husband may divorce his wife. While the school of Hillel legally at least allowed any trivial reason as a ground for divorce, the stricter interpretation which limited it to adultery alone obtained in the school of Shammai. Jesus coincided with the stricter view (see Mt **5** 32; **19** 9, and commentaries). From a moral point of view, divorce was discountenanced by the rabbis likewise, save of course for that one ground which indeed makes the continued relations between husband and wife a moral impossibility. See also Crimes; Divorce. Max L. Margolis

ADUMMIM, a-dum′im (אֲדֻמִּים, *'ădhummīm*, perhaps "red spots"): "The ascent of Adummim" is one of the numerous landmarks mentioned in defining the northern border of Judah westward from the mouth of the Jordan to Jerusalem, and in defining the southern border of Benjamin eastward from Jerusalem to the mouth of the Jordan (Josh **15** 7; **18** 17). It is identified with the gorge part of the road from Jericho up to Jerusalem.

The Inn of the Good Samaritan.

Its present name is *Tala'at-ed-Dumm*, "ascent of blood." The stone is marked by "curious red streaks," a phenomenon which probably accounts for both the ancient and the modern names, and for other similar names which have been applied to the locality. It is the scene of our Saviour's story of the Good Samaritan, and tradition of course locates the inn to which the Sam brought the wounded man (see *HGHL*, 265). Willis J. Beecher

ADVANTAGE, ad-van′tāj (סָכַן, *ṣākhan*): In Job **35** 3 is interpreted in succeeding clause as "profit." In Rom **3** 1 περισσός, *perissós*, is likewise interpreted by a paraphrase in the next sentence. RV prefers to render *pleonektéō* by "take advantage," where AV has "defraud" (2 Cor **7** 2) or "make gain of" (2 Cor **12** 17; cf 2 Cor **2** 11). In Jude (ver 16), "advantage" (*ōphéleia*) means "profit."

ADVENT, ad′vent. See Incarnation; Millennium; Parousia.

ADVENTURE, ad-ven′ṭūr: "To risk," "to dare," referring always to an undertaking attended with some peril (Jgs **9** 17: "My father adventured his life"). Cf Dt **28** 56. So also Eccl **5** 14: "Riches perish by evil adventure." Only once in NT for δίδωμι, *dídōmi* (Acts **19** 31), where Paul's friends beg him "not to adventure himself [archaic for "venture"] into the theatre."

ADVERSARY, ad′vēr-sa-ri, ad′vēr-sā-ri: This word (in the sing. or pl.) is used in the OT to render different Heb words. In thirty-two cases the word corresponds to the noun צַר, *çār*, or the verb צָרַר, *çārar*. This noun is the ordinary word for "foe" or "adversary." In twelve passages the Heb word, of which "adversary" is the tr, is שָׂטָן, *sāṭān*=noun or שָׂטַן, *sāṭan*=verb. This stem means "to oppose," or "thwart" anyone in his purpose or claims.

The angel of Jeh was *sāṭān* to Balaam (Nu **22** 22). The word often denotes a political adversary (1 K **11** 14.23.25). In four cases (viz. Prologue to Job; Zec **3** 1.2; 1 Ch **21** 1; Ps **109** 6) the AV retains Satan as the rendering. But it is only in 1 Ch that the word is used without the art., that is, strictly as a proper name. The LXX gives διάβολος, *diábolos*, as the rendering, and both in Job and Zec, Satan is portrayed as the "false accuser." In two cases "adversary" represents two Heb expressions which mean the "opponent in a suit" or "controversy" (Job **31** 35; Isa **50** 8).

In the NT "adversary" represents: (1) ἀντικείμενοι, *antikeímenoi*, the participle of a verb which means "to be set over against," "to be opposed" (Lk **13** 17; Phil **1** 28). (2) ἀντίδικος, *antídikos*, "opponent in a lawsuit," "prosecutor" (Mt **5** 25; Lk **12** 58; **18** 3; 1 Pet **5** 8). According to the last passage the devil is the "accuser" or "prosecutor" of believers, but according to another writer they have an "advocate" or "counselor for the defense" with the Father (1 Jn **2** 1). In one passage (He **10** 27) "adversary" represents a Gr word, *hupenantíos*, which means "set over against," "contrary to"—a word used in classical Gr and in the LXX. Thomas Lewis

ADVERSITY, ad-vûr′si-ti: In RV exclusively an OT term, expressing the various forms of distress and evil conveyed by four Heb words: צֶלַע, *çela'*, "a halting" or "fall"; צָרָה, *çārāh*, "straits," "distress," "affliction"; צַר, *çar*, "straitness," "affliction"; רַע, *ra'*, "bad," "evil," "harmful." These words cover the whole range of misfortunes caused by enemies, poverty, sorrow and trouble. "Adversity," which occurs once in AV in NT (He **13** 3: κακουχούμενος, *kakouchoúmenos*, "ill-treated") is displaced in RV by the lit. rendering which illustrates or interprets a common phase of adversity.

Dwight M. Pratt

ADVERTISE, ad′vēr-tīz: This word is found twice in the OT: In Nu **24** 14 (from Heb יָעַץ, *yā'aç*, "to advise") Balaam advises Balak of the future of Israel and its influence upon his kingdom ("I will advertise thee"). In AV Ruth **4** 4 (from

גָּלָה אֹזֶן, *gālāh 'ōzen,* "to uncover the ear," "to reveal") Boaz in speaking to the nearer kinsman of Ruth: "I thought to advertise thee" (RVm "uncover thine ear").

ADVICE, ADVISE, ADVISEMENT, ad-vīs', ad-vīz', ad-vīz'ment: Aside from their regular meaning these words are peculiarly employed as follows: (1) *Advice:* In 2 S **19** 43 (from דָּבָר, *dābhār,* "word") the meaning is equal to "request" (RVm "were we not the first to speak of bringing back"). In 1 S **25** 33 AV (from טַעַם, *ṭa'am,* "taste," "reason") "advice" is equal to "sagacity" (RV "blessed be thy discretion"). In 2 Ch **25** 17 (from יָעַץ, *yā'aç,* "to give or take counsel") the meaning seems to be "to consult with oneself"; cf also Jgs **19** 30 AV (RV "take counsel"). (2) *Advise:* In 2 S **24** 13 AV (from יָדַע, *yādha',* "to know") "to advise" means "to advise oneself," i.e. "to consider" (RV "advise thee"). Cf also 1 Ch **21** 12 AV (RV "consider" from רָאָה, *rā'āh,* "to see") and Prov **13** 10 where "well-advised" is the same as "considerate" (from יָעַץ, *yā'aç;* see 2 Ch **25** 17). (3) *Advisement* (antiquated): Found once in the OT in 1 Ch **12** 19 (from עֵצָה, *'ēçāh,* "counsel"), where "upon advisement" means "upon deliberation." Cf 2 Macc **14** 20 AV (RV "when these proposals had been long considered"). A. L. Breslich

ADVOCATE, ad'vo-kāt (**παράκλητος,** *paráklētos*): Found in 1 Jn **2** 1, "If any man sin, we have an Advocate with the Father, Jesus Christ the righteous." The Gr word has several shades of meaning: (1) a legal advocate; (2) an intercessor; (3) a helper generally. In the passage before us the first and second meanings are included. Christ in heaven intercedes for Christians who sin upon earth. The next ver declares that He is the "propitiation for our sins" and it is His propitiatory work which lies at the basis of His intercession. The margins of RV and ARV give as alternative readings Comforter, Helper, Gr Paraclete. Beyond doubt however, "advocate" is the correct tr in the passage in the ep. The same Gr word also occurs in the Gospel of John (**14** 16.26; **15** 26; **16** 7) referring not to Christ but to the Holy Spirit, to whom Christ refers as "another comforter" whom He will send from the Father. In the Gospel various functions are ascribed to the Spirit in relation to believers and unbelievers. The word in the Gospel is inadequately trd "Comforter." The Spirit according to these passages, is more than Comforter and more than Advocate. See Paraclete; Comforter; Holy Spirit.

E. Y. Mullins

ADYTUM, ad'i-tum (Lat from Gr **ἄδυτον,** *áduton,* adj. *ádutos,* "not to be entered"): Applied to the innermost sanctuary or chambers in ancient temples, and to secret places which were open only to priests: hence also to the Holy of Holies in the Jewish temple. See Temple.

AEDIAS, ā-ē-dī'as (**'Αηδείας,** *Aēdeías*): Mentioned in 1 Esd **9** 27, being one of those who agreed to divorce their alien wives. This name is supposed to be a corruption of the Gr 'Ηλία, *Hēlía,* there being no Heb equivalent for it, and in Ezr **10** 26, the name occurs in the correct form as Elijah (אֵלִיָּה, *'ēlīyāh*="God is Jehovah").

AELIA, ē'li-a. See Jerusalem.

AENEAS, ē-nē'as (**'Αινέας,** *Ainéas*): A paralytic at Lydda, who, after he "had kept his bed eight years," was miraculously healed by Peter (Acts **9** 33.34).

AENON, ē'non (**Αἰνών,** *Ainṓn*): The place where John was baptizing "because there was much water there" (Jn **3** 23). It was on the west side of the Jordan, the place where John baptized at the first being on the east (Jn **1** 28; **3** 26; **10** 40). We may be sure it was not in Sam territory. *Onom* locates it 8 Rom miles S. of Scythopolis (*Beisān*), this stretch of land on the west of the Jordan being then, not under Samaria, but under Scythopolis. Its position is defined by nearness to Salim. Various identifications have been suggested, the most probable being the springs near *Umm el-'Amdān,* which exactly suit the position indicated by *Onom.* See discussion under Salim. W. Ewing

AEON, ē'on: This word originally meant "duration," "dispensation." In the philosophy of Plato and Aristotle the word is *αἰών, aiṓn,* from which this word is transliterated. In the gnostic philosophy it has a special meaning and is there used to solve the problem of the world order. In the infinite separation between God and the world, it was taught, there must of necessity be mediating powers. These powers are the aeons and are the successive emanations from God from eternity. They are spiritual, existing as distinct entities. They constituted the Divine fulness or the Divine Pleroma. The name was applied to these beings for two reasons: because they were thought to partake of the eternal existence of God and because they were supposed to govern the various ages. The idea of the aeons in various forms may be found in nearly all oriental philosophy that attempted to deal with the problem of the world order. It appears in the writings of Philo, in Shintoism, in the old Zoroastrian religion. See Gnosticism. Jacob W. Kapp

AESORA, ē'so-ra, AV **Esora,** ĕ-sō'ra (**Αἰσωρά,** *Aisōrá*): A town in the borders of Samaria, mentioned in connection with Beth-horon and Jericho (Jth **4** 4), and from this association we judge that it was in the eastern part of Samaria.

AFFECT, AFFECTION, a-fekt', a-fek'shun: The lit. meaning of "affect" is to act upon (Lat *ad,* "to," "upon," *facio,* "to do"). It has various shades of meaning, and occurs in the following senses in the Eng. Bible: (1) In its lit. sense: Lam **3** 51, "Mine eye affecteth my soul." (2) In the sense of "to endeavor after" "desire," "court": Gal **4** 17, "They zealously affect [RV "seek"] you . . . . that ye may affect [RV "seek"] them," i.e. they earnestly court your favor, that you may court theirs. Paul means that the proselytizing zeal of the Judaizers was rooted in personal ambition. The past part. "affected" (RV "sought") has the same meaning in ver 18. The same Gr word (*zēlóō*) is trd "desire earnestly" in RV (1 Cor **12** 31; **14** 1.39). "Affect" has a similar meaning in Ecclus **13** 11. (3) In the passive, it occurs in the sense of "to be disposed," in a neutral sense, with an advb. to characterize the nature of the disposition: Acts **14** 2, "evil affected against the brethren." So also 2 Macc **4** 21; **13** 26.

"Affection" occurs in the following senses: (1) In the lit. sense: the state of having one's feelings *acted upon* or affected in some way; bent or disposition of mind, in a neutral sense (the nature of the affection, whether good or bad, needing further description in the context). So Col **3** 2, "Set your affection [RV "mind"] on things above"; Col **3** 5, "inordinate affection" (here "affection" by itself is neutral; the addition of the adj. makes it equivalent to "passion" in an evil sense, as in RV). (2) In a good sense: tender feeling, warm attachment, good will; the word in itself carrying a good meaning apart from the context. 1 Ch **29**

3, "because I have set my affection on the house of my God"; Rom **1** 31; 2 Tim **3** 3, "without natural affection"; 2 Cor **6** 12 "Ye are straitened in your own affections" (lit. "bowels," regarded as the seat of kindly feelings; cf Eng. "heart"). So 2 Cor **7** 15. (3) In an evil sense in the plur. = passions: Gal **5** 24, "the flesh, with the affections [RV "passions"] and lusts"; Rom **1** 26, "God gave them unto vile affections" (RV "passions").

"Affectioned" occurs once, in a neutral sense: Rom **12** 10, "affectioned [i.e. "disposed"] one to another." In 1 Thess **2** 8, we have "affectionately," in a good sense. D. Miall Edwards

AFFINITY, a-fin'i-ti (חָתַן, *ḥāthan*, "to join oneself"): This term is used three times in the OT: (1) in 1 K **3** 1, where we read that "Solomon made affinity with Pharaoh king of Egypt"; (2) in 2 Ch **18** 1, where it is stated that Jehoshaphat "joined affinity with Ahab," and (3) in Ezr **9** 14, where it is asked: "Shall we . . . . join in affinity with the peoples that do these abominations?" The Heb word thus rendered in the above three passages refers in each case to marriage alliances rather than to family or political relationships. See Marriage; Family. W. W. Davies

AFFIRM, AFFIRMATIVES, a-fûr'ma-tivs (**διϊσχυρίζομαι**, *diischurízomai*): The verb "affirm" occurs in several passages of the NT in the sense of "assert" (Lk **22** 59; Acts **12** 15; **25** 19 [φάσκω, *phá-skō*]; Rom **3** 8 [φημί, *phēmí*]; 1 Tim **1** 7; Titus **3** 8 [διαβεβαιόομαι, *diabebaióomai*]. The Heb does not employ affirmative particles, but gives a positive reply by either repeating the word in question or by substituting the first person in the reply for the second person in the question, or by employing the formula: "Thou hast said" or "Thou hast rightly said." The Saviour used this idiom (σὺ εἶπας, *sù eípas*) when answering Judas and Caiaphas (Mt **26** 25.64). A peculiar elegance occasionally attaches to the interpretation of the Scriptures because of their use of an affirmative and a negative together, rendering the sense more emphatic; sometimes the negative occurs first, as in Ps **118** 17: "I shall not die, but live"; sometimes the affirmative precedes, as in Isa **38** 1: "Thou shalt die, and not live." Jn **1** 20 is made peculiarly emphatic because of the negative placed between two affirmatives: "And he confessed, and denied not; and he confessed, I am not the Christ." Frank E. Hirsch

AFFLICTION, a-flik'shun: Represents no fewer than 11 Heb words in the OT, and 3 Gr words in the NT, of which the most common are עֳנִי (*'ŏnī*), θλῖψις (*thlípsis*). It is used (1) actively = that which causes or tends to cause bodily pain or mental distress, as "the bread of *affliction*" (Dt **16** 3; 2 Ch **18** 26); often in pl., as "Many are the afflictions of the righteous" (Ps **34** 19); (2) passively = the state of being in pain or trouble, as "to visit the fatherless and widows in their *affliction*" (Jas **1** 27). The following are the chief forms of affliction referred to: (1) Individual affliction, esp. sickness, poverty, the oppression of the weak by the strong and rich, perverted justice. (2) National. A great place is given in the OT to affliction as a national experience, due to calamities, such as war, invasion, conquest by foreign peoples, exile. These form the background of much of the prophetic writings, and largely determine their tone and character. (3) In the NT the chief form of affliction is that due to the fierce antagonism manifested to the religion of Jesus, resulting in persecution.

I. The Source of Affliction.—The Heb mind did not dwell on secondary causes, but attributed everything, even afflictions, directly to the great First Cause and Author of all things: "Shall evil befall a city, and Jeh hath not done it?" (Am **3** 6);

1. God

"I form the light, and create darkness; I make peace, and create evil [i.e. calamity]; I am Jeh, that doeth all these things" (Isa **45** 7). Thus all things, including calamity, were referred to the Divine operation. The Heb when afflicted did not doubt the universal sovereignty of God; yet, while assuming this sovereignty, he was sometimes tempted to accuse Him of indifference, neglect or forgetfulness. Cf Job *passim;* Isa **40** 27; **49** 14; Ezk **8** 12; **9** 9.

2. Evil Agents

Yet there are traces of a dualism which assigns a certain vague limit to God's absolute sovereignty, by referring affliction to an evil agency acting in quasi-independence of God. There could, however, never be more than a tendency in this direction, for a strict dualism was incompatible with the standpoint of Jewish monotheism. Thus Saul's mental affliction is attributed to an "evil spirit," which is yet said to be "from Jeh" (1 S **16** 14; **18** 10; **19** 9); and the fall of Ahab is said by Micaiah to be due to the "lying spirit" which enticed him to his doom, in obedience to God's command (1 K **22** 20–22). In the prologue of Job, Job's calamities are ascribed to the Satan, but even he receives his word of command from God, and is responsible to Him, like the other "sons of God" who surround the heavenly throne. He is thus "included in the Divine will and in the circle of Divine providence" (Schultz). After the prologue, the Satan is left out of account, and Job's misfortunes are attributed directly to the Divine causality. In later Judaism, the tendency to trace the origin of evil, physical and moral, to wicked spirits became more marked, probably because of the influence of Pers dualism. In NT times, physical and mental maladies were thought to be due to the agency of evil spirits called demons, whose prince was Beelzebub or Satan (Mk **1** 23 ff; **3** 22 f; **5** 2 ff; Mt **9** 32 f, etc). Christ gave His assent to this belief (cf the woman under infirmity, "whom Satan hath bound," Lk **13** 16). Paul attributed his bodily affliction to an evil angel sent by Satan (2 Cor **12** 7), though he recognized that the evil agent was subordinate to God's purpose of grace, and was the means of moral discipline (vs 7.9). Thus, while the evil spirits were regarded as malicious authors of physical maladies, they were not, in a strictly dualistic fashion, thought to act in complete independence; rather, they had a certain place assigned to them in the Divine Providence.

II. Meaning and Purpose of Affliction.—Why did God afflict men? How is suffering to be explained consistently with the goodness and justice of God? This was an acute problem which weighed heavily upon the Heb mind, especially in the later, more reflective, period. We can only briefly indicate the chief factors which the Scriptures contribute to the solution of the problem. We begin with the OT.

1. Punitive or Retributive

The traditional view in early Heb theology was that afflictions were the result of the Divine law of retribution, by which sin was invariably followed by adequate punishment. Every misfortune was a proof of sin on the part of the sufferer. Thus Job's "friends" sought to convince him that his great sufferings were due to his sinfulness. This is generally the standpoint of the historians of Israel, who regarded national calamities as a mark of the Divine displeasure on account of the people's sins. But this naïve belief, though it contains an important element of truth, could not pass uncontested. The logic of facts would suffice to prove that it was inadequate to cover all cases;

e.g. Jeremiah's sufferings were due, not to sin, but to his faithfulness to his prophetic vocation. So the "suffering servant" in Isa. Job, too, in spite of his many woes, was firm in the conviction of his own integrity. To prove the inadequacy of the penal view is a main purpose of the Book of Job. A common modification of the traditional view was, that the sorrows of the pious and the prosperity of the wicked were only of brief duration; in the course of time, things would adjust themselves aright (e.g. Job **20** 5 ff; Ps **73** 3–20). But even granting time for the law of retribution to work itself out, experience contradicts the view that a man's fortune or misfortune is an infallible proof of his moral quality.

The thought is often expressed that afflictions are meant to test the character or faith of the sufferer.

2. Probational

This idea is especially prominent in Job. God allowed the Satan to test the reality of Job's piety by overwhelming him with disease and misfortunes (**2**). Throughout the poem Job maintains that he has stood the test (e.g. **23** 10–12). Cf Dt **8** 2.16; Ps **66** 10 f; **17** 3; Isa **48** 10; Jer **9** 7; Prov **17** 3.

For those who are able to stand the test, suffering has a purificatory or disciplinary value. (1) The

3. Disciplinary and Purificatory

thought of affliction as a discipline or form of Divine teaching is found in Job, especially in the speeches of Elihu, who insists that tribulation is intended as a method of instruction to save man from the pride and presumption that issue in destruction (Job **33** 14–30; **36** 8–10.15 RV). The same conception is found in Ps **94** 12; **119** 67.71. (2) The purificatory function of trials is taught in such passages as Isa **1** 25; Zec **13** 9; Mal **3** 2.3, where the process of refining metals in fire and smelting out the dross is the metaphor used.

The above are not fully adequate to explain the mystery of the afflictions of the godly. The pro-

4. Vicarious and Redemptive

foundest contribution in the OT to a solution of the problem is the idea of the vicarious and redemptive significance of pain and sorrow. The author of Job did not touch this rich vein of thought in dealing with the afflictions of his hero. This was done by the author of the Second-Isa. The classical passage is Isa **52** 13—**53**, which deals with the woes of the oppressed and afflicted Servant of God with profound spiritual insight. It makes no difference to the meaning of the afflictions whether we understand by the Servant the whole Heb nation, or the pious section of it, or an individual member of it, and whether the speakers in **53** are the Jewish nation or the heathen. The significant point here is the value and meaning ascribed to the Servant's sufferings. The speakers had once believed (in accordance with the traditional view) that the Servant suffered because God was angry with him and had stricken him. Now they confess that his sorrows were due, not to his own sin but to theirs (vs 4–6.8). His sufferings were not only vicarious (the punishment of their sin falling upon him), but redemptive in their effect (peace and health coming to them as a result of his chastisement). Moreover, it was not only redemptive, but expiatory ("his soul guilt-offering," ver 10)—a remarkable adumbration of the Christian doctrine of atonement.

So far we have dealt only with OT teaching on the meaning and purpose of affliction. The NT

5. The New Testament

makes no new contribution to the solution of the problem, but repeats and greatly deepens the points of view already found in the OT. (1) There is a recognition throughout the NT of the law of retribution (Gal **6** 7). Yet Jesus repudiates the popular view of the invariable connection between misfortune and moral evil (Jn **9** 2 f). It is clear that He had risen above the conception of God's relation to man as merely retributive (Mt **5** 45, sunshine and rain for evil men as well as for the good). His followers would suffer tribulation even more than unbelievers, owing to the hostile reaction of the evil world, similar to that which afflicted Christ Himself (Mt **5** 10 f; **10** 16–25; Jn **15** 18–20; **16** 33). Similarly the Acts and the epp. frequently refer to the sufferings of Christians (e.g. Acts **14** 22; 2 Cor **4** 8–11; Col **1** 24; He **10** 32; 1 Pet **4** 13; Rev **7** 14). Hence afflictions must have some other than a purely punitive purpose. (2) They are probational, affording a test by which the spurious may be separated from the genuine members of the Christian church (Jas **1** 3.12; 1 Pet **1** 7; **4** 17), and (3) a means of discipline, calculated to purify and train the character (Rom **5** 3; 2 Cor **12** 7.9; Jas **1** 3). (4) The idea of vicarious and redemptive suffering gets a far deeper significance in the NT than in the OT, and finds concrete realization in a historical person, Jesus Christ. That which is foreshadowed in Second-Isa becomes in the NT a central, pervasive and creative thought. A unique place in the Divine purpose is given to the passion of Christ. Yet in a sense, His followers partake of His vicarious sufferings, and "fill up . . . . that which is lacking of the afflictions of Christ" (Col **1** 24; cf Phil **3** 10; 1 Pet **4** 13). Here, surely, is a profound thought which may throw a flood of light on the deep mystery of human affliction. The cross of Christ furnishes the key to the meaning of sorrow as the greatest redemptive force in the universe.

III. Endurance of Affliction.—The Scriptures abound in words of consolation and exhortation adapted to encourage the afflicted. Two main considerations may be mentioned. (1) The thought of the beneficent sovereignty of God. "Jeh reigneth; let the earth rejoice," even though "clouds and darkness are round about him" (Ps **97** 1.2); "All things work together for good to them that love God" (Rom **8** 28 AV). Since love is on the throne of the universe, we may rest assured that all things are meant for our good. (2) The thought that tribulation is of brief duration, in comparison with the joy that shall follow (Ps **30** 5; Isa **54** 7 f; Jn **16** 22); a thought which culminates in the hope of immortality. This hope is in the OT only beginning to dawn, and gives but a faint and flickering light, except in moments of rare exaltation and insight, when the thought of a perfect future blessedness seemed to offer a solution of the enigmas of life (Job **19** 25–27; Pss **37, 49, 73**). But in the NT it is a postulate of faith, and by it the Christian is able to fortify himself in affliction, remembering that his affliction is light and momentary compared with the "far more exceeding and eternal weight of glory" which is to issue out of it (2 Cor **4** 17 AV; cf Mt **5** 12; Rom **8** 18). Akin to this is the comfort derived from the thought of the near approach of Christ's second coming (Jas **5** 7.8). In view of such truths as these, the Bible encourages the pious in trouble to show the spirit of patience (Ps **37** 7; Lk **21** 19; Rom **12** 12; Jas **1** 3.4; **5** 7–11; 1 Pet **2** 20), and even the spirit of positive joy in tribulation (Mt **5** 11 f; Rom **5** 3; 2 Cor **12** 10; Jas **1** 2.12; 1 Pet **4** 13). In the NT emphasis is laid on the example of Jesus in patient endurance in suffering (Jn **16** 33; Jas **5** 7–11; 1 Pet **2** 19–23; **3** 17 f). Above all, the Scriptures recommend the afflicted to take refuge in the supreme blessedness of fellowship with God, and of trust in His love, by which they may enter into a deep peace that is undisturbed by the trials and problems of life (Ps **73**, esp. 23–28; Isa **26** 3.4; Jn **14** 1.27; Phil **4** 7; *et passim*).

D. Miall Edwards

AFFRIGHT, a-frīt′: Designates a state of terror occasioned by some unexpected and startling occurrence; not as strong as "amazed," which refers more to the stupor resulting from fright. In the NT most frequently for ἔμφοβος, *émphobos* (Lk **24** 37; Acts **10** 4; Rev **11** 13). RV uses it also for *pturómenoi* of Phil **1** 28, a word "properly used of scared horses" (Ellicott).

AFOOT, a-fŏŏt′ (πεζεύω, *pezeúō*, "to go on foot"): By walking from Troas to Assos Paul avoided the tedious voyage round Cape Lectum (Acts **20** 13 AV; cf Mk **6** 33).

AFORE, a-fōr′: Archaic for "before" of time, or "formerly"; frequently occurs as compound, as in "aforetime," "aforehand," etc; in the NT most commonly for the Gr prefix πρό, *pró*, in compound words (Rom **1** 2; **15** 4); at other times, for Gr advb. ποτέ, *poté*, "at some time," "once" (Jn **9** 13; 1 Pet **3** 5; Col **3** 7).

AFRESH, a-fresh′: Only in He **6** 6, "seeing they crucify to themselves the Son of God afresh," where it stands for the prefix of the Gr *anastauroúntas*. It has been disputed whether in this word *ana* has the reiterative force ("again," "anew"). In classical Gr *anastauróō* has always the simple sense of "to crucify," (i.e. "to raise *up* on a cross," *ana* being merely "up"). So some would render it here (e.g. Cremer, *Lex. of NT Gr*). Against this it is argued (1) that the classical writers had no occasion for the idea of crucifying anew (cf Winer, *De verb. Comp.*, etc, Pt III, 9 ff, Leipzig, 1843); (2) that in many compounds *ana* signifies both "up" and "again," as in *anablépō*, which means "to recover sight" as well as "to look up"; (3) that the rendering "crucify afresh" suits the context; (4) that the Gr expositors (e.g. Chrys) take it so without questioning. (So also Bleek, Lünemann, Alford, Westcott; cf Vulg *rursum crucifigentes*.)

D. Miall Edwards

AFRICA, af′ri-ka: The name of this tract, as a continent, does not occur in the Bible, and it was only

1. Africa as Known to the Ancients

in later days known as one of the quarters of the world, under the name of Libya—that portion opposite the coast of Greece and W. of Egypt. Naturally the most considerable part of Africa known to the Hebrews was Egypt itself, but Libya is regarded as being referred to under the names of Lehabim and Lubim (Ludim) (Gen **10** 13; 2 Ch **12** 3)—words indicating, as often with the Semites, not the country itself, but its inhabitants. Other portions of Africa known to the Hebrews were Cush or Ethiopia, and Put, whose inhabitants they regarded as belonging to the Hamitic stock. Canaan, also Cushite and therefore Hamitic, naturally did not belong to the African continent, showing that the divisions of the then known world into "quarters" (Europe, Asia, Africa) had not taken place when the Table of the Nations (Gen **10** 1 ff) was drawn up—indeed, these divisions were not apparently thought of until many centuries later. The Casluhim and the Naphtuhim (Gen **10** 13.14) were in all probability African peoples, though their position is in general regarded as uncertain. For the Hebrews, to all appearance, the southernmost point of Africa was Cush or Ethiopia, called by the Assyrians and Babylonians Kusu and Meluḫḫa (Meroë), which included the district now known as the Soudan, or Black region. The sons of Cush, and also those of his firstborn, Sheba, were all Arabian tribes, nominally under the domain of Mizraim or Egypt, and on this account classed with the descendants of Ham.

2. The Cushites and the Negroes

It will thus be seen that the Negro districts were practically unknown to the ancient Hebrews, though men and women of Negro race must have come within their ken. It seems doubtful, therefore, whether there be, in the Bible, any reference to that race, either collectively or individually, the word Cushite standing, not for Negro, but for Ethiopian. This term is applied to Moses' (first) wife (Nu **12** 1); and it will probably be generally admitted, that the great Hebrew lawgiver is not likely to have espoused a Negro woman. The Ethiopian eunuch converted by Philip the Evangelist (Acts **8** 26 ff) was an official of Meroë, and an educated man, for he could read the OT in the Gr (Sept) version. Commerce must have revealed to the Hebrews the whereabouts of the various peoples of Africa with whom they came into contact, and they acquired a personal knowledge of Egypt when the 12 tribes were in bondage there. During this period, it may be supposed, they saw from time to time visitors from the South—people who are not mentioned in the sacred books of the OT because the Hebrews, as a nation, never came into contact with them. Apart from Egypt, the history of the portion of Africa known to the Hebrews was a chequered one, as it came successively under Egyp, Phoen, Gr and Rom civilization. That it was not overrun, or even influenced, by the barbarous tribes of the South, is due to the fact that the Mediterranean tract is isolated from the central (and southern) portion of that continent by the Sahara. In the Talm it is

3. Hebrew Tradition

related that Alexander penetrated Africa on Libyan asses to find a race of women, with whom he had conversation, and from whom, as he afterward confessed, being a fool, he learned wisdom—a legend suggesting some possible tradition of the Amazons of Dahomey. But even in the Talm it is mainly the nearer (N.E.) portion of Africa which is referred to, the Africans, who had the reputation of being flat-footed, being associated with the Canaanites. See also Cush; Ethiopia; Mizraim.

T. G. Pinches

AFTER, aft′ēr, **AFTERWARD**, aft′ēr-wērd: The fundamental thought, in which all shades of meaning unite, is that of succession either in time or place. This succession may be immediate or remote. A very common adaptation of this conception is the use of "after" to denote "according to," "after the manner of," or "in the order of," as in Gen **1** 26; Eph **4** 24; Lk **1** 59; Rom **5** 14; He **4** 11 (RVm "unto"), and in many passages where the Gr uses the preposition κατά, *katá*, as Mt **23** 3; Rom **8** 4; 1 Cor **1** 26, etc. "In proportion to": Ps **28** 4; cf **90** 15. It sometimes correctly translates a peculiar Gr idiom of the prep. διά, *diá*, with the gen, indicating time elapsed, as Mk **2** 1, lit. "through some days," "after some days had passed"; cf Acts **24** 17. While the Gr is expressed by a variety of words, the Heb uses *'aḥar* for both prep. and advb.

H. E. Jacobs

AFTERNOON, af-tēr-nōōn′ (נְטוֹת הַיּוֹם, *neṭōth ha-yōm*, "the declining of the day"; Jgs **19** 8 AV): The expression כְּחֹם הַיּוֹם, *keḥōm ha-yōm*, "in the heat of the day" (Gen **18** 1) refers to the early afternoon when the sun is a little past its zenith, its rays still being very strong. The phrase לְרוּחַ הַיּוֹם, *le-rūaḥ ha-yōm*, "in the cool of the day" (Gen **3** 8) is in contrast to the last phrase and points to the late afternoon; in the Orient a cooling breeze arises at this period of the day, and it is then that much of the day's business is transacted. See DAY.

AGABA, ag'a-ba: A fortress in Judaea. The first of 22 "strong places" which by its commander Galestus was given over to Aristobulus, the son of Alexander Janneus and Alexandra, when he (his mother, the queen, being dangerously ill) attempted to get control of the Judaean government (*Ant,* XIII, xvi, 5).

AGABUS, ag'a-bus (**Ἄγαβος,** *Ágabos*): A Christian prophet of Jerus, twice mentioned in Acts. (1) In Acts **11** 27 f, we find him at Antioch foretelling "a great famine over all the world," "which," adds the historian, "came to pass in the days of Claudius." This visit of Agabus to Antioch took place in the winter of 43–44 AD, and was the means of urging the Antiochian Christians to send relief to the brethren in Judaea by the hands of Barnabas and Saul. Two points should be noted. (*a*) The gift of prophecy here takes the form of prediction. The prophet's chief function was to reveal moral and spiritual truth, to "forth-tell" rather than to "foretell"; but the interpretation of God's message sometimes took the form of predicting events. (*b*) The phrase "over all the world" (practically synonymous with the Rom Empire) must be regarded as a rhetorical exaggeration if strictly interpreted as pointing to a general and simultaneous famine. But there is ample evidence of severe periodical famines in various localities in the reign of Claudius (e.g. Suet. *Claud.* 18; Tac. *Ann.* xii.43), and of a great dearth in Judaea under the procurators Cuspius Fadus and Tiberius Alexander, 44–48 AD (*Ant,* XX, ii, 6; v, 2), which probably reached its climax cir 46 AD. (2) In Acts **21** 10 f we find Agabus at Caesarea warning Paul, by a vivid symbolic action (after the manner of OT prophets; cf Jer **13** 1 ff; Ezk **3, 4**) of the imprisonment and suffering he would undergo if he proceeded to Jerus. (3) In late tradition Agabus is included in lists of the seventy disciples of Christ. D. MIALL EDWARDS

AGADE, ag'a-dē: Ancient name for Akkad (or ACCAD, q.v.), one of the chief cities of Babylonia (Gen **10** 10), and the capital city of Sargon, who lived and ruled in Babylonia cir 3500 BC. Together with Shunir it formed part of one of the royal titles: "kings of Shunir [Sumer] and Accad."

AGAG, ā'gag (**אֲגָג**, *'ăghāgh,* or **אֲגַג**, *'ăghagh,* meaning unknown, possibly "violent," *BDB*): A name, or title, applied to the king of the Amalekites, like Abimelech in Philistia and Pharaoh in Egypt. It is used of two of these kings: (1) A king of Amalek, mentioned by Balaam (Nu **24** 7) in his blessing of Israel; (2) A later king, in the days of King Saul (1 S **15**). Saul was sent with his army to destroy the Amalekites, who had so violently opposed Israel in the Wilderness. He disregarded the Divine command, sparing the best of the spoil, and saving Agag the king alive (1 S **15** 8.9). After rebuking Saul, Samuel had Agag put to death for all the atrocities committed by himself and his nation (1 S **15** 32.33). EDWARD MACK

AGAGITE, ā'gag-īt, (**אֲגָגִי**, *'ăghāghī,* from **אֲגַג**, *'ăghagh,* "a member of the house of Agag"): A title of opprobrium given to Haman (Est **3** 1.10; **8** 3.5; **9** 24). Jewish tradition always assigned the arch-enemies of Israel membership in the house of Amalek, the hereditary foe of the nation. Cf *Ant,* XI, vi, 5. The word Agag has properly been taken by Delitzsch as related to the Assyr *agagu,* "to be powerful," "vehement," "angry." In the Gr parts of Est, Haman is termed a Macedonian (**12** 6; **16** 10). The name Haman is probably of Elamitic origin. Oppert's attempt to connect the term "Agagite" with "Agaz," a Median tribe mentioned by Sargon, has found no supporters. See AGAG; BUGEAN. H. J. WOLF

AGAIN, a-gen': Advb. denoting repetition; in NT, generally for **πάλιν,** *pálin,* "back," "once more." Occasionally, it has the force of a connective, synonymous with "moreover," as in Rom **15** 10 ff; 1 Cor **3** 20, etc. The expression "born again" of AV, Jn **3** 3.7; 1 Pet **1** 23, translating the Gr *"ánōthen"* and *"aná"* in comp, becomes in RV *"anew,"* i.e. "over again." As these particles mean "from above" and "up," their use as indicating repetition is sometimes disputed, but without further foundation than that "again" does not exhaust the meaning.

AGAIN, BORN. See REGENERATION.

AGAINST, a-genst' (**κατά,** *katá;* **ἐναντίον,** *enantíon;* **πρός,** *prós*): Prep. expressing contrast. When used of direction, equivalent to "toward" (Mt **10** 35; **12** 14, etc); when of position, meaning "opposite," "facing," "in front of" (1 K **7** 5; Gen **15** 10; Rom **8** 31); when of action, "opposed to" (Mt **5** 11; **26** 59; 1 Cor **4** 6); "in resistance to" (He **12** 4); "provision for" (Gr *eis,* lit. "unto, toward" (1 Tim **6** 19). Sometimes also applied to what breaks an established order as "customs" (Acts **28** 17), "nature" (Rom **1** 26). Peculiar shades of meaning may be traced by careful examination of the variety of preps. in Heb and Gr employed in the Scriptures, that are translated into English by this one word. H. E. JACOBS

AGAPE, ag'a-pē (**ἀγάπη,** *agápē*): The name Agape or "love-feast," as an expression denoting the brotherly common meals of the early church, though of constant use in the post-canonical literature from the time of Ignatius onward, is found in the NT only in Jude ver 12 and in 2 Pet **2** 13 according to a very doubtful reading.

1. The Name and the Thing

For the existence of the Christian common meal, however, we have abundant NT evidence. The "breaking of bread" practised by the primitive community in Jerusalem according to Acts **2** 42.46 must certainly be interpreted in the light of Pauline usage (1 Cor **10** 16; **11** 24) as referring to the ceremonial act of the Lord's Supper. But the added clause in ver 46, "they took their food with gladness and singleness of heart," implies that a social meal was connected in some way with this ceremonial act. Paul's references to the abuses that had sprung up in the Corinthian church at the meetings for the observance of the Lord's Supper (1 Cor **11** 20–22.33.34) make it evident that in Corinth as in Jerusalem the celebration of the rite was associated with participation in a meal of a more general character. And in one of the "we" sections of Acts (**20** 11) where Luke is giving personal testimony as to the manner in which the Lord's Supper was observed by Paul in a church of his own founding, we find the breaking of bread associated with and yet distinguished from an eating of food, in a manner which makes it natural to conclude that in Troas, as in Jerusalem and Corinth, Christians when they met together on the first day of the week were accustomed to partake of a common meal. The fact that the name Agape or love-feast used in Jude ver 12 (RV) is found early in the 2d cent. and often afterward as a technical expression foı the religious common meals of the church puts the meaning of Jude's reference beyond doubt.

So far as the Jerusalem community was concerned, the common meal appears to have sprung out of the *koinōnía* or communion that characterized the first days of the Christian church (cf Acts **1** 14; **2** 1 etc). The religious meals familiar to Jews—the Passover being the great type—would make it natural in Jerusalem to give expression by means of table fellowship to the sense of brotherhood; and the community of goods practised by the infant church (**2** 44; **4** 32) would readily take the particular form of a common table at which the wants of the poor were supplied out of the abundance of the rich (**6** 1 ff). The presence of the Agape in the Gr church of Corinth was no doubt due to the initiative of Paul, who would hand on the observances associated with the Lord's Supper just as he had received them from the earlier disciples; but participation in a social meal would commend itself very easily to men familiar with the common meals that formed a regular part of the procedure at meetings of those religious clubs and associations which were so numerous at that time throughout the Gr-Rom world.

2. Origin of the Agape

In the opinion of the great majority of scholars the Agape was a meal at which not only bread and wine but all kinds of viands were used, a meal which had the double purpose of satisfying hunger and thirst and giving expression to the sense of Christian brotherhood. At the end of this feast, bread and wine were taken according to the Lord's command, and after thanksgiving to God were eaten and drunk in remembrance of Christ and as a special means of communion with the Lord Himself and through Him with one another. The Agape was thus related to the Eucharist as Christ's last Passover to the Christian rite which He grafted upon it. It preceded and led up to the Eucharist, and was quite distinct from it. In opposition to this view it has been strongly urged by some modern critical scholars that in the apostolic age the Lord's Supper was not distinguished from the Agape, but that the Agape itself from beginning to end was the Lord's Supper which was held in memory of Jesus. It seems fatal to such an idea, however, that while Paul makes it quite evident that bread and wine were the only elements of the memorial rite instituted by Jesus (1 Cor **11** 23–29), the abuses which had come to prevail at the social gatherings of the Corinthian church would have been impossible in the case of a meal consisting only of bread and wine (cf vs 21.33 f). Moreover, unless the Eucharist in the apostolic age had been discriminated from the common meal, it would be difficult to explain how at a later period the two could be found diverging from each other so completely.

3. Relation to the Eucharist

In the *Did* (cir 100 AD) there is no sign as yet of any separation. The direction that the second Eucharistic prayer should be offered "after being filled" (x.1) appears to imply that a regular meal had immediately preceded the observance of the sacrament. In the Ignatian Epistles (cir 110 AD) the Lord's Supper and the Agape are still found in combination (*Ad Smyrn* viii.2). It has sometimes been assumed that Pliny's letter to Trajan (cir 112 AD) proves that the separation had already taken place, for he speaks of two meetings of the Christians in Bithynia, one before the dawn at which they bound themselves by a "sacramentum" or oath to do no kind of crime, and another at a later hour when they partook of food of an ordinary and harmless character (*Ep* x.96). But as the word "sacramentum" cannot be taken here as necessarily or even probably referring to the Lord's Supper, the evidence of this passage is of little weight. When we come to Justin Martyr (cir 150 AD) we find that in his account of church worship he does not mention the Agape at all, but speaks of the Eucharist as following a service which consisted of the reading of Scripture, prayers and exhortation (*Apol*, lxvii); so that by his time the separation must have taken place. Tertullian (cir 200 AD) testifies to the continued existence of the Agape (*Apol*, 39), but shows clearly that in the church of the West the Eucharist was no longer associated with it (*De Corona*, 3). In the East the connection appears to have been longer maintained (see Bigg, *Christian Platonists of Alexandria*, 102 ff), but by and by the severance became universal; and though the Agape continued for long to maintain itself as a social function of the church, it gradually passed out of existence or was preserved only as a feast of charity for the poor.

4. Separation from the Eucharist

Various influences appear to have coöperated in this direction. Trajan's enforcement of the old law against clubs may have had something to do with it (cf Pliny as above), but a stronger influence probably came from the rise of a popular suspicion that the evening meals of the church were scenes of licentious revelry and even of crime. The actual abuses which already meet us in the apostolic age (1 Cor **11** 20 ff; Jude ver 12), and which would tend to multiply as the church grew in numbers and came into closer contact with the heathen world, might suggest the advisability of separating the two observances. But the strongest influence of all would come from the growth of the ceremonial and sacerdotal spirit by which Christ's simple institution was slowly turned into a mysterious priestly sacrifice. To Christ Himself it had seemed natural and fitting to institute the Supper at the close of a social meal. But when this memorial Supper had been transformed into a repetition of the sacrifice of Calvary by the action of the ministering priest, the ascetic idea became natural that the Eucharist ought to be received fasting, and that it would be sacrilegious to link it on to the observances of an ordinary social meal.

5. Reasons for the Separation

LITERATURE.—Zahn, art. "Agapen" in Hauck-Herzog, *Realencyklopädie;* Keating, *Agape and Eucharist;* Schaff, *The Oldest Church Manual,* ch xviii; Lambert, *Sacraments in the New Testament,* Lect viii; Weizsäcker, *The Apostolic Age,* etc, I, 52 ff.

J. C. LAMBERT

AGAR, ā'gar (Ἄγαρ, *Agar*): Found once in the Apoc in the Gr (Bar **3** 23) probably for the OT Hagar, mother of Ishmael, whose children are mentioned with the merchants of Meran (Midian) and Teman. In 1 Ch **5** 10 the "Hagarites" AV, are located E. of Gilead, and in the days of Saul were at war with the tribe of Reuben. See also vs 19.20 and 1 Ch **27** 31. In Ps **83** 6 the name of the same people is Hagarenes.

AGARENES, ag-a-rēnz': Bar **3** 23 AV. In the OT the word is HAGARENES (q.v.). See also AGAR above.

AGATE, ag'ăt. See STONES, PRECIOUS.

AGE, āj: A period of time or a dispensation. In the above sense the word occurs only once in AV, in the sing., as the tr of דּוֹר, *dōr,* which means, properly, a "revolution" or "round of time," "a period," "an age" or "generation of man's life"; almost invariably tr[d] "generation," "generations" (Job **8** 8, "Inquire, I pray thee, of the former age"); we have the plur. as the tr of *aiōn*, prop. "duration," "the course or flow of time," "an age or period of the world," "the world" (Eph **2** 7, "in the ages to come"; Col **1** 26, "the mystery which hath been hid from ages and from generations," ERV, "from all ages," etc, ARVm, of *geneai*, "generations" (Eph **3** 5 "generations," ver 21, "unto all generations for ever and ever," Gr m, "all the generations of the age of the ages"). "Ages" is given in m of AV (Ps **145** 13; Isa **26** 4, "the rock of ages").

We have "age" in the above sense (2 Esd **3** 18; Tob **14** 5; *aiōn*) "ages," *aiōn* (1 Esd **4** 40 [of Truth] "she is the strength," etc, "of all ages"), *genea*, RV, "generation" (Wisd **7** 27; 1 Macc **2** 61); Ecclus **24** 33, *eis geneás aiṓnōn*, "generations of ages"; Wisd **14** 6, "generations" (*genéseōs*).

RV has "age" for "world" (He **6** 5); "ages" for "worlds" (RVm He **1** 2; ARVm; cf 1 Tim **1** 17) (m, "unto the ages of the ages"); "ages" for "world" (1 Cor **10** 11; He **9** 26). ERV has "all ages" for "the beginning of the world" (Eph **3** 9, ARV "for ages"); "king of the ages" for "king of saints" (Rev **15** 3, corrected text; m, many ancient authorities read "nations"; Jer **10** 7). See EVERLASTING.

W. L. WALKER

AGE, OLD AGE, in individual lives (חֶלֶד, *ḥeledh*; **ἡλικία,** *hēlikía*): We have scarcely any word in the OT or NT which denotes "age" in the familiar modern sense; the nearest in the OT is perhaps *ḥeledh*, "life," "lifetime," and in the NT *hēlikia*, "full age," "manhood," but which is rendered "stature" in Mt **6** 27, etc, AV; *ḥeledh* occurs (Job **11** 17, "Thine age shall be clearer than the noonday," RV "[thy] life"; Ps **39** 5, "Mine age is as nothing before thee," ARV, "my life-time"); we have *hēlikia* (Jn **9** 21.23, "He is of age"; He **11** 11 "past age," Lk **2** 52, "Jesus increased in wisdom and age," so RVm, AVm, Eph **4** 13); *yōm*, day, (days), is used in the OT to express "age" (Gen **47** 28), "the whole age of Jacob," AV, "the days of the years of his life"; but it occurs mostly in connection with old age); *bēn*, "son" (Nu **8** 25; 1 Ch **23** 3.24); *kelaḥ*, "to be complete," is trd "full age" (Job **5** 26); *téleios*, "complete" (He **5** 14, RV, "fullgrown men," m, "perfect"), *dōr*, "a revolution," "a period" is trd "age" (Isa **38** 12, "Mine age is departed and removed from me as a shepherd's tent," ARV, "My dwelling is removed, and is carried away from me as a shepherd's tent," ERV, "mine age," m, "or habitation"; Delitzsch, "my home"; cf Ps **49** 19 [20]; 2 Cor **5** 8). In NT we have *étos*, "year" (Mk **5** 42, RV, "old"; Lk **2** 37; **3** 23, "Jesus . . . . about 30 years of age"). "Old age," "aged," are the tr of various words, *zāḳēn* (*zāḳān*, "the chin," "the beard"), perhaps to have the chin sharp or hanging down, often trd "elders," "old man," etc (2 S **19** 32; Job **12** 20; **32** 9; Jer **6** 11).

In NT we have *presbútēs*, "aged," "advanced in days" (Titus **2** 2; Philem 9); *presbútis*, "aged woman" (Titus **2** 3); *probebēkṓs en hēmérais*, "advanced in days" (Lk **2** 36); *gē̂ras*, "old age" (Lk **1** 36).

RV has "old" for "the age of" (1 Ch **23** 3), "own age" for "sort" (Dnl **1** 10); "aged" for "ancients" (Ps **119** 100); for "ancient" (Isa **47** 6); for "old" (He **8** 13); "aged men" for "the ancients" (Job **12** 12); for "aged" (Job **12** 20), "elders."

(1) Among the Hebrews (and Orientals generally) old age was held in honor, and respect was required for the aged (Lev **19** 32), "Thou shalt rise up before the hoary head, and honor the face of the old man"; a mark of the low estate of the nation was that "The faces of elders were not honored"; "The elders have ceased from the gate" (Lam **5** 12.14). Cf Job **29** 8 (as showing the exceptionally high regard for Job). See also Wisd **2** 10; Ecclus **8** 6.

Regard for Old Age

(2) Old age was greatly desired and its attainment regarded as a Divine blessing (Gen **15** 15; Ex **20** 12, "that thy days may be long in the land"; Job **5** 26; Ps **91** 16, "With long life will I satisfy him"; **92** 14; cf Isa **65** 20; Zec **8** 4; 1 S **2** 32).

(3) A Divine assurance is given, "Even to old age I am he, and even to hoar hairs will I carry you" (Isa **46** 4); hence it was looked forward to in faith and hope (Ps **71** 9.18).

(4) Superior wisdom was believed to belong to the aged (Job **12** 20; **15** 10; **32** 7.9; cf 1 K **12** 8); hence positions of guidance and authority were given to them, as the terms "elders," "presbyters" and (Arab.) "sheik" indicate.

W. L. WALKER

AGEE, ā'gē (אָגֵא, *'āghē'*, "fugitive"): A Hararite, father of Shammah, one of David's "three mighty men" (2 S **23** 11). In 1 Ch **11** 34 we read of one "Jonathan the son of Shagee the Hararite." The parallel in 2 S **23** 32.33 reads "Jonathan, Shammah the Hararite." If we read "Jonathan [son of] Shammah," then Agee is the grandfather of Jonathan. Some, however, think 1 Ch **11** 34 to be correct, and read "Shagee" for "Agee" in 2 S **23** 11, and for "Shammah" in 2 S **23** 33. This makes Jonathan and Shammah brothers.

AGES, ROCK OF: Applied to Jehovah as an encouragement for trust (Isa **26** 4 RVm; AV "everlasting strength").

AGGABA, a-gā'ba (**'Αγγαβά,** *Aggabá*, and **'Αγραβά,** *Agrabá*; AV **Graba**) = Hagabah (Ezr **2** 45) and Hagaba (Neh **7** 48): The descendants of A. (temple-servants) returned with Zerubbabel to Jerus (1 Esd **5** 29). See also ACCABA.

AGGAEUS, a-gē'us (**'Αγγαῖος,** *Aggaíos*; AV **Aggeus**): Haggai, one of the Minor Prophets. A. prophesied in the second year of the reign of Darius (cf Ezr **4** 24; **5** 1) with Zacharias in Jerus (1 Esd **6** 1; **7** 3). In 2 Esd **1** 40 he is mentioned as one who with others shall be given as "leader to the nation from the east."

AGIA, ā'gi-a (**'Αγιά,** *Agiá*; AV **Hagia**) = Hattil (Ezr **2** 57; Neh **7** 59): The descendants of A. (sons of the servants of Solomon) returned with Zerubbabel to Jerus (1 Esd **5** 34).

AGONE, a-gon': In AV of 1 S **30** 13. Old past part. of "to go." RV has "ago," viz. "three days ago," lit. "the third day."

AGONY, ag'o-ni (**ἀγωνία,** *agōnía*; Vulg *agonia*): A word occurring only once in the NT (Lk **22** 44), and used to describe the climax of the mysterious soul-conflict and unspeakable suffering of Our Lord in the garden at Gethsemane. The term is derived from the Gr *agṓn* "contest" and this in turn from the Gr *ágō* "to drive or lead," as in a chariot race. Its root idea is the struggle and pain of the severest athletic contest or conflict. The wrestling of the athlete has its counterpart in the wrestling of the suffering soul of the Saviour in the garden. At the beginning of this struggle He speaks of His soul being exceeding sorrowful even unto death, and this tumult of emotion culminated in the agony. All that can be suggested by the exhausting struggles and sufferings of charioteers, runners, wrestlers and gladiators, in Grecian and Roman amphitheaters, is summed up in the pain and death-struggle of this solitary word "agony." The word was rendered by Wyclif (1382) "maad in agonye"; Tindale (1534) and following translators use "an agony." The record of Jesus' suffering in Gethsemane, in the Synoptic Gospels (Mt **26** 36–46; Mk **14** 32–42; Lk **22** 39–46, and also in He **5** 7.8) indicates that it was threefold:

1. Physical

The agony of His soul wrought its pain on His body, until "his sweat became as it were great drops of blood falling down upon the ground" (Lk **22** 44, omitted by some ancient authorities). He offered His prayers and supplications "with strong crying and tears" (He **5** 7). The intensity of His struggle so distressed and weakened Him that Luke says "there appeared unto him an angel from heaven, strengthening him." The threefold record of the evangelists conveys the idea of the intensest physical pain. As the wire carries the electric current, so every nerve in Jesus' physical being felt the anguish of His sensitive soul as He took upon Himself the burden of the world's sin and moral evil.

2. Mental

The crisis of Jesus' career as Messiah and Redeemer came in Gethsemane. The moral issue of His atoning work was intelligently and voluntarily met here. The Gospels exhaust language in attempting to portray the stress and struggle of this conflict. "My soul is exceeding sorrowful even unto death." "Being in an agony he prayed more earnestly, saying, Father, if it be possible, let this cup pass away from me." The mental clearness of Christ's vision of humanity's moral guilt and the energy of will necessary to meet the issue and take "this cup" of being the world's sin-bearer, indicate the awful sorrow and anguish of His supernatural conflict. It is divinely significant that the word "agony" appears but once in all Scripture. This solitary word records a solitary experience. Only One ever compassed the whole range of the world's sorrow and pain, anguish and agony. The shame of criminal arrest in the garden and of subsequent condemnation and death as a malefactor had to His innocent soul the horror of humanity's entire and ageless guilt. The mental and moral anguish of Jesus in Gethsemane interprets the meaning of Paul's description of the atonement, "Him who knew no sin he made to be sin on our behalf" (2 Cor **5** 21).

3. Spiritual

The agony of Jesus was supremely within the realm of His spirit. The effect of sin in separating the human soul from God was fathomed by the suffering Saviour in the fathomless mystery of His supernatural sorrow. Undoubtedly the anguish of Gethsemane surpassed the physical torture of Calvary. The whole conflict was wrought out here. Jesus' filial spirit, under the burden of the world's guilt, felt isolated from the Father. This awful, momentary seclusion from His Father's face constituted the "cup" which He prayed might pass from Him, and the "agony" of soul, experienced again on the cross, when He felt that God had forsaken Him.

No theory of the atonement can do justice to the threefold anguish of Jesus in Gethsemane and on Calvary, or to the entire trend of Scripture, that does not include the substitutionary element in His voluntary sacrifice, as stated by the prophet: "Jeh hath laid on him the iniquity of us all," Isa **53** 6; and by His apostles: "who was delivered up for our trespasses," Rom **4** 25; "who his own self bare our sins," 1 Pet **2** 24.

The word "agony" also occurs in 2 Macc **3** 14.16.21 AV (RV "distress") in describing the distress of the people at the attempt of Heliodorus to despoil the treasury of the temple in the days of Onias.

Dwight M. Pratt

AGRAPHA, ag′ra-fa (**Ἄγραφα**, *ágrapha*): The word *ágraphos* of which *agrapha* is the neuter plur. is met with in classical Gr and in Gr papyri in its primary sense of "unwritten," "unrecorded."

1. The Term and Its History

In early Christian lit., esp. in the writings of Clement of Alexandria, it was used of oral tradition; and in this sense it was revived by Koerner in a Leipzig *Program* issued in 1776 under the title *De sermonibus Christi agraphois*. For some time it was restricted to sayings of Christ not recorded in the Gospels and believed to have reached the sources in which they are found by means of oral tradition. As however *graphē*, the noun with which *agrapha* is connected, can have not only the general meaning "writing," but the special meaning "Scripture," the adj. could signify not only "oral" but also "uncanonical" or "non-canonical"; and it was employed by Resch in the latter sense in the 1st ed of his great work on the subject which appeared in German in 1889 under the title, *Agrapha: Extra-canonical Gospel Fragments*. The term was now also extended so as to include narratives as well as sayings. In the second ed (also in German) it is further widened so as to embrace all extra-canonical sayings or passages connected with the Bible. The new title runs: *Agrapha: Extra-canonical Fragments of Scripture;* and the volume contains a first collection of OT *agrapha*. The term is still however used most frequently of non-canonical sayings ascribed to Jesus, and to the consideration of these this art. will mainly be devoted.

2. Extent of Material

Of the 361 *agrapha* and *apocrypha* given by Resch about 160 are directly ascribed to Christ. About 30 others can be added from Christian and Jewish sources and about 80 sayings found in Muhammadan literature (*Expos T*, V, 59, 107, 177 f, 503 f, 561, etc). The last-mentioned group, although not entirely without interest, may largely be disregarded as it is highly improbable that it represents early tradition. The others come from a variety of sources: the NT outside of the Gospels, Gospel MSS and VSS, Apocryphal Gospels and an early collection of sayings of Jesus, liturgical texts, patristic and mediaeval lit. and the Talm.

3. Sayings to Be Excluded

Many of these sayings have no claim to be regarded as independent *agrapha*. At least five classes come under this category. (1) Some are mere parallels or variants, for instance: "Pray and be not weary," which is evidently connected with Lk **18** 1; and the saying in the Talm: "I, the Gospel, did not come to take away from the law of Moses but to add to the law of Moses have I come" (*Shab* 116*b*) which is clearly a variant of Mt **5** 17. (2) Some sayings are made up of two or more canonical texts. "I chose you before the world was," for example, is a combination of Jn **15** 19 and Eph **1** 4; and "Abide in my love and I will give you eternal life" of Jn **8** 31 and **10** 28. (3) Misquotation or loose quotation accounts for a number of alleged *agrapha*. "Sodom is justified more than thou" seems to be really from Ezk **16** 53 and its context. "Let not the sun go down upon your wrath" is of apostolic not evangelic origin (Eph **4** 26). "Anger destroys even the prudent" comes from LXX of Prov **15** 1. (4) Some sayings must be rejected because they cannot be traced to an early source, for instance, the fine saying: "Be brave in war, and fight with the old serpent, and ye shall receive eternal life," which is first met with in a text of the 12th cent. (5) Several sayings are suspicious by reason of their source or their character. The reference to "my mother the Holy Spirit," in one of them, has no warrant in the acknowledged teaching of Christ and comes from a source of uncertain value, the

Gospel according to the He. Pantheistic sayings such as "I am thou and thou art I, and wherever thou art I am"; "You are I and I am you"; and perhaps the famous saying: "Raise the stone and thou wilt find me; cleave the wood and there am I," as well as the sayings reported by Epiphanius from the Gospel of the Ebionites seem to breathe an atmosphere different from that of the canonical Gospels.

When all the sayings belonging to these five classes, and a few others of liturgical origin, have been deducted there remain about thirty-five which are worthy of mention and in some cases of careful consideration. Some are dealt with in the art. LOGIA (q.v.). The others, which are given here, are numbered consecutively to facilitate reference. The best authenticated are of course those found in the NT outside of the Gospels. These are (1) the great saying cited by Paul at Miletus: "It is more blessed to give than to receive" (Acts **20** 35); (2) the words used in the institution of the Eucharist preserved only in 1 Cor **11** 24 f; (3) the promise of the baptism of the Spirit (Acts **1** 5 and **11** 16); and (4) the answer to the question: "Dost thou at this time restore the kingdom to Israel?" (Acts **1** 7 f). Less certain are (5) the description of the Second Advent, said to be "by the word of the Lord" (1 Thess **4** 15 ff); and (6) the promise of the crown of life to them that love God (Jas **1** 12).

4. Sayings in NT

Of considerable interest are some additions, in MSS of the Gospels and VSS. One of the most remarkable (7) is the comment of Jesus on a man's working on the Sabbath day inserted after Lk **6** 4 in Codex D and the Freer MS recently discovered in Egypt: "If thou knowest what thou doest, O man, blessed art thou, but if thou knowest not, thou art accursed and a transgressor of the law." Another (8) also found in D and in several other authorities is appended to Mt **20** 28: "But ye seek ye from little to increase and from greater to be less." In the Curetonian Syriac the latter clause runs: "and *not* from greater to be less." The new saying is noteworthy but obscure. A third passage (9) of less value but still of interest is an insertion in the longer ending of Mk, between ver 14 and ver 15, which was referred to by Jerome as present in codices in his day but has now been met with in Gr for the first time in the above-mentioned Freer MS. (For facsimile see *Am. Journal of Archaeology*, 1908.) In reply to a complaint of the disciples about the opposition of Satan and their request: "Therefore reveal thy righteousness even now," Jesus is reported to have said: "The limit of the years of the authority of Satan is fulfilled, but other dreadful things are approaching, and in behalf of those who had sinned was I delivered unto death in order that they might return to the truth and might sin no longer, that they might inherit the spiritual and incorruptible glory of righteousness in heaven." This alleged utterance of the risen Lord is most probably of secondary character (cf Gregory, *Das Freer Logion;* Swete, *Two New Gospel Fragments*).

5. Sayings in MSS and VSS

Apocryphal and patristic literature supplies some notable sayings. The first place must be given (10) to the great saying which in its shortest form consists of only three words: "Be ["become," "show yourselves to be"] approved money-changers." Resch (*Agrapha*², no. 87) gives 69 references, at least 19 of which date from the 2d and 3d cents., although they represent only a few authorities, all Egyptian. The saying seems to have circulated widely in the early church and may be genuine. Other early sayings of interest or value, from these sources, must be given without comment. (11) "The heavenly Father willeth the repentance of the sinner rather than his punishment" (Justin Martyr). (12) "That which is weak shall be saved by that which is strong" (cir 300 AD). (13) "Come out from bonds ye who will" (Clement of Alexandria). (14) "Be thou saved and thy soul" (Theodotus in id). (15) "Blessed are they who mourn for the perdition of unbelievers" (*Didaskalia*). (16) "He who is near me is near the fire; he who is far from me is far from the kingdom" (Origen). (17) "He who has not been tempted has not been approved" (*Didaskalia,* etc). (18) He who makes sad a brother's spirit is one of the greatest of criminals" (Ev Heb). (19) "Never be glad except when ye have seen your brother in love" (ib). (20) "Let not him who seeks cease . . . . until he find, and when he finds he shall be astonished; astonished he shall reach the kingdom, and when he has reached the kingdom he shall rest" (Clement of Alexandria and *Logia of Oxyrhynchus*). (21) In a fragment of a Gospel found by Grenfell and Hunt at Oxyrhynchus (*O Papyri* no. 655) is the following non-canonical passage in a canonical context: "He Himself will give you clothing. His disciples say unto Him: When wilt thou be manifest to us and when shall we see thee? He saith: When ye shall be stripped and not be ashamed." The saying or apocryphon exhibits considerable likeness to a saying cited by Clement of Alexandria from the Gospel according to the Egyptians, but the difference is great enough to make original identity doubtful. Another fragment found by the same explorers on the same site (*O Papyri* no. 840) preserves two *agrapha* or *apocrypha* which though clearly secondary are very curious. The first (22) is the concluding portion of a saying about the punishment of evil-doers: "Before a man does wrong he makes all manner of subtle excuses. But give heed lest you also suffer the same things as they for the evil-doers among men receive not their due among the living (Gr *zôis*) only but also await punishment and much torment." Professor Swete (*Two New Gospel Fragments*), accents *zōois* as the plural of *zōon* and thus finds a contrast between the fate of animals and that of human beings. The second saying (23) is a rather lengthy reply to the complaint of a Pharisaic stickler for outward purity. The most interesting part of it as edited by Swete runs as follows: "Woe to you blind who see not. . . . . But I and my disciples who thou sayest have not been dipped have dipped in the waters of eternal life which come down from God out of heaven." All these texts from Oxyrhynchus probably date from the 2d cent. Other Egypt sources, the so-called Coptic Apocryphal Gospels (*Texts and Studies* Camb. IV, 2, 1896), contain several sayings which are of interest as coming from the same religious environment. The following three are the most remarkable. (24) "Repent, for it is better that a man find a cup of water in the age that is coming than all the riches of this world" (130). (25) "Better is a single footstep in My Father's house than all the wealth of this world" (130 f). (26) "Now therefore have faith in the love of My Father; for faith is the end of all things" (176). As in the case of the *Logia* these sayings are found in association with canonical sayings and parallels. Since the *Logia* may well have numbered scores, if not hundreds, it is at least possible that these Coptic sayings may have been taken from the missing portions of this collection, or a recension of it, and therefore they are not unworthy of notice as conceivably early *agrapha*. To these sayings of Christian derivation may be added

6. Sayings from the Fathers, etc

(27) one Muhammadan saying, that inscribed in Arabic on the chief gateway of the city Futteypore Sikri built by Akbar: "The world is but a bridge, over which you must pass, but must not linger to build your dwelling" (*In the Himalayas* by Miss Gordon Cumming, cited by Griffenhoofe, *The Unwritten Sayings of Christ*, 128).

7. Result

Although the number of *agrapha* purporting to be sayings of Jesus which have been collected by scholars seems at first sight imposing, those which have anything like a strong claim to acceptance on the ground of early and reliable source and internal character are disappointingly few. Of those given above nos. 1–4, 7, 8, 10 which have mostly early attestation clearly take precedence of the rest. Nos. 11–20 are early enough and good enough to merit respectful consideration. Still the proportion of genuine, or possibly genuine, material is very small. Ropes is probably not far from the truth when he remarks that "the writers of the Synoptic Gospels did their work so well that only stray bits here and there, and these but of small value, were left for the gleaners." On the other hand it is not necessary to follow Wellhausen in rejecting the *agrapha in toto*. Recent discoveries have shown that they are the remains of a considerable body of extra-canonical sayings which circulated more or less in Christian circles, esp. in Egypt, in the early cents., and the possible presence in what we possess of a sentence or two actually spoken by Jesus fully justifies research.

8. Other Agrapha

The second edition of the work of Resch includes 17 *agrapha* from MSS of Acts and 1 Jn most of which are from Codex D, 31 apostolic *apocrypha*, and 66 *agrapha* and *apocrypha* connected with the OT. 19 of the latter are largely taken from pseudepigrapha, a pseudo-Ezekiel for instance. These *agrapha* some of which are really textual variants are of inferior interest and value.

LITERATURE.—The chief authorities are the German book of the American scholar J. H. Ropes, *Die Sprüche Jesu, die in den kanonischen Evangelien nicht überliefert sind*, and his art. "Agrapha" in *HDB* (extra vol); and the often-mentioned work of Resch. The former has great critical value, and the latter, especially in the 2d ed, is a veritable thesaurus of material. For a full survey of the literature up to 1905 see that work, pp. 14–17. There is much criticism in Bauer's *Das Leben Jesu im Zeitalter der neutestamentlichen Apokryphen*, ch vii. Among smaller works special mention may be made of Prebendary Blomfield's *Twenty-Five Agrapha* (1900); and the book of Griffenhoofe, the title of which is given above. There are recent arts. on the subject in *HDB* (1909), "Unwritten Sayings," and *DCG*, "Sayings (Unwritten)"; *Am. Journal of Archaeology*, XII (1908), 49–55; H. A. Sanders, *New MSS from Egypt;* also ib, XIII (1909), 130. See LOGIA.

WILLIAM TAYLOR SMITH

AGRARIAN LAWS, a-grā'ri-an lôz:

1. The Sabbath Year
2. The Jubilee
3. Its Object
4. The Legal Rules
5. Ideas and Circumstances of the Legislation
6. Form of the Legislation
7. Its Operation and Extension
8. Other Laws Affecting the Land

The Mosaic provisions on this subject form one of the most characteristic and interesting portions of the legislation. The main institutions are two, viz., the Sabbath year and the jubilee, and they are closely linked together.

1. The Sabbath Year

In every seventh year the land was to lie fallow "that the poor of thy people may eat: and what they leave the beast of the field shall eat" (Ex **23** 10 f; cf Lev **25** 2–7). 'And the Sabbath of the land shall be for food for you; for thee, and for thy servant, and for thy maid, and for thy hired servant and for thy stranger that sojourn with thee; *but* for thy cattle, and for the beasts that are in thy land, shall all the increase thereof be for food' (Lev **25** 6 f). This has been quoted at length because the rendering of EV is misleading. "The Sabbath of the land" does not mean that the natural increase thereof is to be eaten by the Israelitish peasant. That interpretation is excluded by vs 3–5.20–22. What is intended is clearly shown by the latter of these two passages, "I will command my blessing upon you in the sixth year." The principle on which the manna had been provided for Sabbaths was to apply to the harvest of the sixth year, and this is the import of the phrase.

2. The Jubilee

After "seven sabbaths of years, even forty and nine years" a trumpet was to be blown throughout the land on the tenth day of the seventh month (i.e. the Day of Atonement) and the fiftieth year was to be hallowed and celebrated as a "jubilee."

No agricultural work of any kind was to be performed, but "ye may [so correct EVV] eat the increase thereof out of the field" (Lev **25** 12). God would so bless the land in the sixth year that it would bring forth enough for the Sabbath year, the ensuing jubilee and the subsequent period to the harvest of the ninth year (vs 20–22).

3. Its Object

In addition to being a period in which the land was left fallow, the jubilee was intended to meet the economic evils that befell peasants in ancient societies. Wars or unfavorable seasons would soon reduce a farmer to a condition in which he would have to borrow. But money is rarely to be had without interest and security, and in early communities the rates of interest were very high indeed, while the only security the farmer could offer would consist of his land and the persons of himself and his children. Hence we find insolvency giving rise to the alienation of land and to slavery all over the world—sometimes with the retention of civil rights (as in Rome and Israel), at others in a more unalloyed form. The jubilee aims at both these evils. It is provided that in that year the peasants who had lost their full freedom through insolvency should be free (see *SBL*, 5 ff) and all lands that had been sold should return to the original owner or his family. "And the land shall not be sold in perpetuity; for the land is mine: for ye are strangers and sojourners with me" (ver 23). To this theory there are parallels elsewhere, e.g. in Togoland (Heinrici, *Zeitschrift für vergleichende Rechtswissenschaft*, XI, 138).

4. The Legal Rules

Lev **25** containing the land laws gives effect to this view by enacting that when an Israelite was compelled to part with his land there was to be a "redemption" of land, and that in default of redemption the land should return to its original owner in the jubilee year. This "redemption" covers two ideas—a right of preëmption by the next of kin in the first instance, and if that were not exercised, a right on the part of the original owner to buy back the land before the jubilee (vs 24–28). The theory did not apply to houses in walled cities. Those might be redeemed within a year of sale: in default the property passed for ever and was unaffected by the jubilee (vs 29 f). Villages were reckoned as country (ver 31). The Levitical cities were subject to the rules of land, not of walled cities (vs 32 f; read with the Vulg in ARVm, "if they have not been redeemed" in vs 32), and their fields were not to be sold (ver 34). All sales of lands to which the jubilee applied were to be made on the basis of the number of crops (vs 14 ff); in fact, what was sold was not the property itself but the usufruct (i.e. the right of using, reaping, etc) till the year of the jubilee. Similarly with the laws of Lev **27** 16–25, where the general principle is that if a field be sanctified the value shall be estimated according to the number of years to the jubilee. Unfortunately the text is corrupt and it is impossible to make out the exact circumstances in which no further redemption was allowed (ver 20).

5. Ideas and Circumstances of the Legislation

"The land laws are the product of many independent ideas and circumstances. . . . . First such a system as that expounded in the 25th chapter of Lev could only be put forward by one who had to work on what is so very rare in history—a clean slate. In other words, the system of land tenure here laid down could only be introduced in this way by men who had no preëxisting system to reckon with. Secondly, there is (*mutatis mutandis*) a marked resemblance between the provisions of Lev and the system introduced in Egypt by Joseph (Gen **47**). The land is the Lord's as it is Pharaoh's; but the towns which are built on that land are not subject to the same theory or the same rules. Perhaps the explanation is that Joseph's measures had affected only those who gained their living by agriculture, i.e. the dwellers in the country. Thirdly, the system shows the enormous power that the conception of family solidarity possessed in the Mosaic age. . . . . And fourthly, the enactment is inspired and illuminated by the humanitarian and religious convictions to which reference has already been made" (*Journal of Transactions of the Victoria Institute*, XLI, 160). Undoubtedly the most striking feature of the enactment is to be found in these religious convictions with the absolute reliance on constant Divine intervention to secure the working of the law (vs 20 ff).

6. Form of the Legislation

Lev **26** shows clearly that this legislation was conceived as the terms of a covenant made between God and the children of Israel, and it appears from vs 42–45 that this covenant was regarded as being connected with the covenants with the patriarchs though it is also a covenant made with the generation that came forth from Egypt. The land was originally promised to Abraham in a covenant (Gen **17**) and it would seem that these laws are regarded as attaching to that covenant which had been renewed with his descendants. Indeed the laws appear to be presented as terms of the sworn agreement (covenant) under which God was about to give Israel the possession of Canaan.

7. Its Operation and Extension

As respects the operation of these laws we have no information as to the observance of any fallow years before the Exile: 2 Ch **36** 21 is rather unfavorable, but so obviously echoes Lev **26** 43 that it scarcely seems to be meant as a historical statement. But traces are to be found of the operation of other parts of the system. Ruth **4** shows us the law of redemption working, but with two notable extensions. Widows have acquired a right of property in their husbands' estates, and when the next of kin refuses to redeem, the right passes to the kinsman who is nearest in succession. Neither of these cases is contemplated by the Pent: both appear to be fresh applications of the Levitical law which, like all other legislations, had to be adapted to meet new sets of facts as they arose. Similarly Jer **32** illustrates the law of preemption, but here a small difficulty arises, for Lev **25** 34 forbids the sale of the suburbs of the Levitical cities. Probably however this refers only to sale outside the family and not as here to the nearest kinsman and heir presumptive. Similarly Ezk twice refers to the jubilee (**7** 12 f and **46** 17) in terms that seem to show that he knew it as an existing institution (see *SBL*, 96; *Churchman*, May, 1906, 292). Historical traces of the Levitical cities are mentioned in the art. Levitical Cities. It should be added that under the monarchy a rule seems to have been introduced that derelict lands fell to the king (see 2 S **9** 9 f; 1 K **21** 16; 2 K **8** 3.6).

In later times there are several references to the fallow of the Sabbatical year (1 Macc **6** 49.53; *Ant*, XIII, viii, 1; XIV, x, 6, etc).

In addition to these laws Moses enacted provisions favoring gleaning, on which see Poor.

8. Other Laws Affecting the Land

He also prohibited sowing a field or vineyard with two kinds of seed (Lev **19** 19; Dt **22** 9) and prescribed that for three years the fruit of trees should not be eaten, while in the fourth it should be holy, and in the fifth it was to be available for ordinary purposes (Lev **19** 23 ff).

Harold M. Wiener

AGREE, a-grē′ (**συμφωνέω,** *sumphōnéō*, "to be of the same mind," "to come to a mutual understanding"): This is the sense of the word in Mt **20** 2; Jn **9** 22, and other passages. In Mk **14** 56 the word is *ísos* and has the thought not only that their words did not agree, but also that the testimony was not in agreement with or equal to what the law required in such a case. The thought of being equal occurs also in 1 Jn **5** 8.

The **fig.** use of the word in Mt **18** 19 makes it of special interest. The word there is *sumphōnéō*, from which comes our word symphony, meaning a harmonious blending. This agreement therefore is complete. Three persons are introduced: two human beings and the Father. They are in perfect agreement on the subject or purpose under consideration. It is therefore an inward unity produced by the Holy Spirit, leading the two into such an agreement with the Father. There will follow then, as a matter of course, what is promised in vs 19.20. In Acts **5** 9 it sets forth the justice of Peter in dealing in the same manner in both cases. Ananias and Sapphira were in perfect agreement and equally guilty (Lk **5** 36; Acts **15** 15).

Jacob W. Kapp

AGRICULTURE, ag′ri-kul-ṭūr, ag′ri-kul-chur:

I. Development of Agriculture
II. Climatic Conditions and Fertility
III. Agricultural Pursuits
   1. Growing of Grain
      (1) Plowing and Sowing
      (2) Reaping
      (3) Threshing
   2. Care of Vineyards
   3. Raising of Flocks

I. Development of Agriculture.—One may witness in Syria and Pal today the various stages of social progress through which the people of Bible times passed in which the development of their agriculture played an important part. To the E. the sons

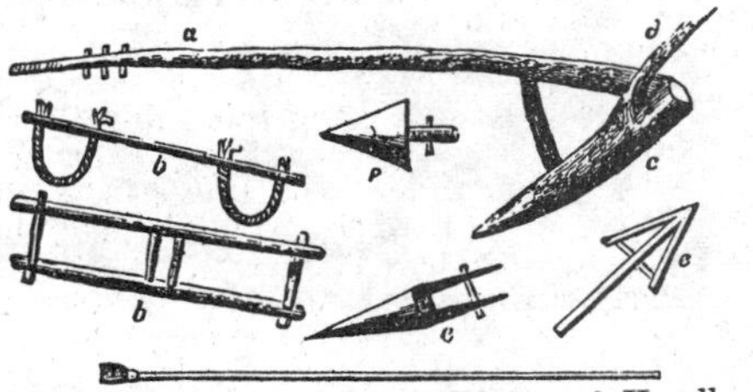

a, Pole or Beam. *b*, Yokes. *c*, Share. *d*, Handle. *e*, Points. Ox-goad (below).

of Ishmael still wander in tribes from place to place, depending upon their animals for food and raiment, unless by a raid they can secure the fruits of the soil from the peoples, mostly of their own blood, who have given up wandering and are supporting themselves by tilling the ground. It is only a short step from this frontier life to the more protected territory toward the Mediterranean, where in comparatively peaceful surroundings, the wanderers become stationary. If the land which they have come to possess is barren and waterless, they become impoverished physically and spiritually, but if they have chosen the rarer spots where underground streams burst forth into valleys covered with alluvial deposits (Ex **3** 8), they prosper and there springs up the more complicated community life with its servants, hirelings, gardeners, etc. A division of labor ensues. Some leave the soil for the crafts and professions but still depend upon their farmer neighbors for their sustenance. (1 K **5** 11.) Such was the variety of life of the people among whom Jesus lived, and of their ancestors, and of the inhabitants of the land long before the children of Israel came to take possession of it. Bible history deals with the Hebrews at a period when a large proportion of that people were engaged in agrarian pursuits, hence we find its pages filled with references to agricultural occupations.

II. Climatic Conditions and Fertility.—With climatic conditions and fertility so varied, the mode of cultivation, seedtime and harvest differed even in closely adjacent territory. On the coastal plains and in the low Jordan valley the soil was usually rich and the season was early, whereas in the mountainous regions and high interior plains the planting and reaping times were from two weeks to a month later. To make use of the soil on the hillsides, terracing was frequently necessary. Examples of these old terraces still exist. On the unwatered plains the crops could be grown only in the winter and spring, i.e. during the rainy season. These districts dried up in May or June and remained fallow during the rainless summer. The same was true of the hilly regions and valleys except where water from a stream could be diverted from its channel and spread over the fields. In such districts crops could be grown irrespective of the seasons. See IRRIGATION.

III. Agricultural Pursuits.—To appreciate the many references in the Bible to agricultural pursuits and the frequent allusions of Our Lord to the fields and their products, we must remember how

Primitive Plowing.

different were the surroundings of the farmers of that day from those among which most of us live or with which we are acquainted. What knowledge we have of these pursuits is drawn from such references as disclose methods bearing a close similarity to those of the present day. The strong tendency to resist change which is everywhere manifest throughout the country and the survival of ancient descriptive words in the language of today further confirm our belief that we now witness in this country the identical operations which were used two thousand or more years ago. It would be strange if there were not a variety of ways by which the same object was accomplished when we remember that the Heb people benefited by the experience of the Egyptians, of the Babylonians, of the inhabitants of the land of their adoption, as well as of its late European conquerors. For this reason the drawings found on the Egyp monuments, depicting agricultural scenes, help us to explain the probable methods used in Pal.

Three branches of agriculture were more prominent than the others; the growing of grain, the care of vineyards (Nu **18** 30), and the raising of flocks. Most households owned fields and vineyards and the richer added to these a wealth of flocks. The description of Job's wealth (in Job **1**) shows that he was engaged in all these pursuits.

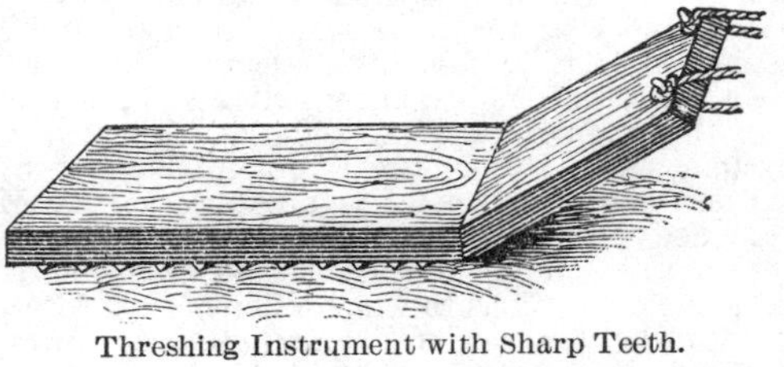

Threshing Instrument with Sharp Teeth.

Hezekiah's riches as enumerated in 2 Ch **32** 27.28 suggest activity in each of these branches.

In this and following descriptions, present-day methods as far as they correspond to ancient records will be dealt with.

1. Growing of Grain

(1) *Plowing and sowing.*—On the plains, little or no preparation for plowing is needed, but in the hilly regions, the larger stones, which the tilling of the previous season has loosened and which the winter's rains have washed bare, are picked out and piled into heaps on some ledge, or are thrown into the paths, which thus become elevated above the fields which they traverse. (See FIELD.) If grain is to be planted, the seed is scattered broadcast by the sower. If the land has not been used for some time the ground is first plowed, and when the seed has been scattered is plowed again. The sower may keep his supply of seed in a pocket made by pulling up his outer garment through his girdle to a sufficient extent for it to sag down outside his girdle in the form of a loose pouch. He may, on the other hand, carry it in a jar or basket as the sowers are pictured as doing on the Egyp monuments. As soon as the seed is scattered it is plowed in before the ever-present crows and ravens can gather it up. The path of the plow in the fields of the hilly regions is a tortuous one because of the boulders jutting out here and there (Mt **13** 3 ff) or because of the ledges which frequently lie hidden just beneath the surface (the rocky places of Christ's parable). When the plowman respects the footpaths which the sufferance of the owner has allowed to be trodden across his fields or which mark the boundaries between the lands of different owners, and leaves them unplowed, then the seed which has fallen on these portions becomes the food of the birds. Corners of the field where the plow cannot reach are hoed by hand. Harrowing-in as we know it is not practised today, except on some of the larger plains, and probably was not used in Pal in earlier times. (See HARROW.)

(2) *Reaping.*—After the plowing is over, the

fields are deserted until after the winter rains, unless an unusually severe storm of rain and hail (Ex 9 25) has destroyed the young shoots. Then a second sowing is made. In April, if the hot east winds have not blasted the grain (see BLASTING) the barley begins to ripen. The wheat follows from a week to six weeks later, depending upon the altitude. Toward the end of May or the first week in June, which marks the beginning of the dry season, reaping begins. Whole families move out from their village homes to spend the time in the fields until the harvest is over. Men and women join in the work of cutting the grain. A handful of grain is gathered together by means of a sickle held in the right hand. The stalks thus gathered in a bunch are then grasped by the left hand and at the same time a pull is given which cuts off some of the stalks a few inches above the ground (see STUBBLE) and pulls the rest up by the roots. These handfuls are laid behind the reapers and are gathered up by the helpers (see GLEANING), usually the children, and made into piles for transporting to the threshing-floor.

(3) *Threshing.*—The threshing-floors are constructed in the fields, preferably in an exposed position in order to get the full benefit of the winds. If there is danger of marauders they are clustered together close to the village. The floor is a level, circular area 25 to 40 ft. in diameter, prepared by first picking out the stones, and then wetting the ground, tamping or rolling it, and finally sweeping it. A border of stones usually surrounds the floor to keep in the grain. The sheaves of grain which have been brought on the backs of men, donkeys, camels, or oxen, are heaped on this area, and the process of tramping out begins. In some localities several animals, commonly oxen or donkeys, are tied abreast and driven round and round the floor. In other places two oxen are yoked together to a drag, the bottom of which is studded with pieces of basaltic stone. This drag, on which the driver, and perhaps his family, sits or stands, is driven in a circular path over the grain. In still other districts an instrument resembling a wheel harrow is used, the antiquity of which is confirmed by the Egyp records. The supply of unthreshed grain is kept in the center of the floor. Some of this is pulled down from time to time into the path of the animals. All the while the partly threshed grain is being turned over with a fork. The stalks gradually become broken into short pieces and the husks about the grain are torn off. This mixture of chaff and grain must now be winnowed. This is done by tossing it into the air so that the wind may blow away the chaff (see WINNOWING). When the chaff is gone then the grain is tossed in a wooden tray to separate from it the stones and lumps of soil which clung to the roots when the grain was reaped. The difference in weight between the stones and grain makes separation by this process possible (see SIFTED). The grain is now piled in heaps and in many localities is also sealed. This process consists in pressing a large wooden seal against the pile. When the instrument is removed it leaves an impression which would be destroyed should any of the grain be taken away. This allows the government officials to keep account of the tithes and enables the owner to detect any theft of grain. Until the wheat is transferred to bags some one sleeps by the piles on the threshing-floor. If the wheat is to be stored for home consumption it is often first washed with water and spread out on goats' hair mats to dry before it is stored in the wall compartments found in every house (see STOREHOUSE). Formerly the wheat was ground only as needed. This was then a household task which was accomplished with the hand-mill or mortar (see MILL).

THRESHING WITH OXEN.

No clearer picture to correspond with present-day practice in vine culture (see VINE) in Pal could be given than that mentioned in Isa 5 1.6. Grapes probably served an important part in the diet of Bible times as they do at present. In the season which begins in July and extends for at least three months, the humblest peasant as well as the richest landlord considers grapes as a necessary part of at least one meal each day. The grapes were not only eaten fresh but were made into wine (see WINEPRESS). No parallel however can be found in the Bible for the molasses which is made by boiling down the fresh grape juice. Some writers believe that this substance was meant in some passages tr[d] by wine or honey, but it is doubtful. The care of the vineyards fitted well into the farmer's routine, as most of the attention required could be given when the other crops demanded no time.

2. Care of Vineyards

The leaders of ancient Israel reckoned their flocks as a necessary part of their wealth (see SHEEP RAISING). When a man's flocks were his sole possession he often lived with them and led them in and out in search of pasturage (Ps **23**; Mt **18** 12), but a man with other interests delegated this task to his sons (1 S **16** 11) or to hirelings. Human nature has not changed since the time when Christ made the distinction between the true shepherd and the hireling (Jn **10** 12). Within a short time of the writing of these words the writer saw a hireling cursing and abusing the stray members of a flock which he was driving, not leading as do good shepherds.

3. Raising of Flocks

The flock furnished both food and raiment. The milk of camels, sheep and goats was eaten fresh or made into curdled milk, butter or cheese. More rarely was the flesh of these animals eaten (see FOOD). The peasant's outer coat is still made of a tawed sheepskin or woven of goats' hair or wool (see WEAVING). The various agricultural operations are treated more fully under their respective names, (q.v.). JAMES A. PATCH

AGRIPPA, a-grip′a. See HEROD.

AGUE, ā′gū (קַדַּחַת, *ḳaddaḥath*): In Lev **26** 16 AV is one of the diseases threatened as a penalty for disobedience to the law. The malady is said to "consume the eyes, and make the soul to pine away." The word means burning (Vulg "ardor") and was probably intended to denote the malarial fever so common now both in the Shephelah and in the Jordan valley. In LXX the word used (*ἴκτερος*, *íkteros*) means jaundice, which often accompanies this fever. RV translates it "fever." See FEVER.

AGUR, ā′gur (אָגוּר, *'āghūr*, seeming, from comparison with Arab. roots, to mean either "hireling," or "collector," "gatherer"): One of the contributors to Prov; his words being included in **30**. He takes an agnostic attitude toward God and transcendent things, and in general the range of his thought, as compared with that of other authors, is pedestrian. He shows, however, a tender reverence and awe. His most notable utterance, perhaps, is the celebrated Prayer of Agur (Prov **30** 7–9), which gives expression to a charming golden mean of practical ideal. His sayings are constructed on a rather artificial plan; having the form of the so-called numerical proverb. See under PROVERBS, BOOK OF, II, 6. JOHN FRANKLIN GENUNG

AH, ä, **AHA**, a-hä′: Interjections of frequent occurrence in the OT, representing different Heb words and different states of feeling. (1) אֲהָהּ, *'ăhāh*, expressing complaint and found in the phrase "Ah, Lord Jeh" (Jer **1** 6; **4** 10 etc; Ezk **4** 14 etc). Elsewhere the word is tr[d] "alas!" (Joel **1** 15). (2) אָח, *'aḥ*, occurs once (Ezk **21** 15), expressing grief in contemplating Israel's destruction. (3) הֶאָח, *he'āḥ*, usually expresses malicious joy over the reverses of an enemy, and is introduced by the verb "to say" (*BDB*); so in Ps **35** 21.25; Ezk **25** 3; **26** 2; **36** 2; in the repeated psalm **40** 15, **70** 3. It expresses satiety in Isa **44** 16; and represents the neighing of a horse in Job **39** 25. (4) הוֹי, *hōy*, expresses grief or pain, (Isa **1** 4; Jer **22** 18). In 1 K **13** 30 it is tr[d] "alas!" More frequently it is used to indicate that a threat of judgment is to follow (Isa **10** 5; **29** 1; or to direct attention to some important announcement (Isa **55** 1), where the Heb word is tr[d] "Ho." (5) Gr *οὐά*, *ouá*, in Mk **15** 29, used by those who mocked Jesus, as He hung upon the cross. All of these words are evidently imitative of the natural sounds, which spontaneously give expression to these emotions of complaint, grief, pain, exultation, etc. EDWARD MACK

AH in proper names. See AHI.

AHAB, ā′hab (אַחְאָב, *'aḥ'ābh; Assyr a-ḥa-ab-bu;* LXX **Ἀχαάβ**, *Achaáb*, but Jer **29** 21 f, **Ἀχιάβ**, *Achiáb*, which, in analogy with אחימלך, חיאל(א), etc, indicates an original אחיאב, *'ăḥī'ābh*, meaning "the father is my brother"): The compound probably signifies that "the father," referring to God, has been chosen as a brother.

Ahab, son of Omri, the seventh king of Israel, who reigned for twenty-two years, from 876 to 854 (1 K **16** 28 ff), was one of the strongest and at the same time one of the weakest kings of Israel. With his kingdom he inherited also the traditional enemies of the kingdom, who were no less ready to make trouble for him than for his predecessors. Occupying a critical position at the best, with foes ever ready to take advantage of any momentary weakness, the kingdom, during the reign of Ahab, was compelled to undergo the blighting effects of misfortune, drought and famine. But Ahab, equal to the occasion, was clever enough to win the admiration and respect of friend and foe, strengthening the kingdom without and within. Many of the evils of his reign, which a stronger nature might have overcome, were incident to the measures that he took for strengthening the kingdom.

1. Ahab's Reign

In the days of David and Solomon a beneficial commercial intercourse existed between the Hebrews and the Phoenicians. Ahab, recognizing the advantages that would accrue to his kingdom from an alliance with the foremost commercial nation of his time, renewed the old relations with the Phoenicians and cemented them by his marriage with Jezebel, daughter of Ethbaal, king of Tyre (the Ithobalos, priest of Astarte mentioned by Meander).

2. His Foreign Policy

He next turns his attention to the establishment of peaceful and friendly relations with the kindred and neighboring kingdom of Judah. For the first time since the division of the kingdoms the hereditary internecine quarrels are forgotten, "and Jehoshaphat," the good king of Judah, "made peace with the king of Israel." This alliance, too, was sealed by a marriage relationship, Jehoram, the crown-prince of Judah, being united in marriage with the princess Athaliah, daughter of Ahab.

Perhaps some additional light is thrown upon Ahab's foreign policy by his treatment of Benhadad, king of Damascus. An opportunity was given to crush to dust the threatening power of Syria. But when Benhadad in the garb of a suppliant was compelled to sue for his life, Ahab received him kindly as his brother, and although denounced by the prophets for his leniency, spared his enemy and allowed him to depart on the condition that he would restore the cities captured from Omri, and concede certain "streets" in Damascus as a quarter for Israelitish residents. No doubt Ahab thought that a king won as a friend by kindness might be of greater service to Israel than a hostile nation, made still more hostile by having its king put to death. Whatever Ahab's motives may have been, these hereditary foes really fought side by side against the common enemy, the king of Assyria, in the battle at Karkar on the Orontes in the year 854, as is proved by the inscription on the monolith of Shalmaneser II, king of Assyria.

Ahab's far-sighted foreign policy was the antithesis of his short-sighted religious policy. Through

3. His Religious Policy

his alliance with Phoenicia he not only set in motion the currents of commerce with Tyre, but invited Phoen religion as well. The worship of Jeh by means of the golden calves of Jeroboam appeared antiquated to him. Baal, the god of Tyre, the proud mistress of the seas and the possessor of dazzling wealth, was to have an equal place with Jeh, the God of Israel. Accordingly he built in Samaria a temple to Baal and in it erected an altar to that god, and at the side of the altar a pole to Asherah (1 K **16** 32.33). On the other hand he tried to serve Jeh by naming his children in his honor—Ahaziah ("Jeh holds"), Jehoram ("Jeh is high"), and Athaliah ("Jeh is strong"). However, Ahab failed to realize that while a coalition of nations might be advantageous, a syncretism of their religions would be disastrous. He failed to apprehend the full meaning of the principle, "Jeh alone is the God of Israel." In Jezebel, his Phoen wife, Ahab found a champion of the foreign culture, who was as imperious and able as she was vindictive and unscrupulous. She was the patron of the prophets of Baal and of the devotees of Asherah (1 K **18** 19.20; **19** 1.2). At her instigation the altars of Jeh were torn down. She inaugurated the first great religious persecution of the church, killing off the prophets of Jeh with the sword. In all this she aimed at more than a syncretism of the two religions; she planned to destroy the religion of Jeh root and branch and put that of Baal in its place. In this Ahab did not oppose her, but is guilty of conniving at the policy of his unprincipled wife, if not of heartily concurring in it.

Wrong religious principles have their counterpart in false ethical ideals and immoral civil acts. Ahab,

4. The Murder of Naboth

as a worshipper of Baal, not only introduced a false religion, but false social ideals as well. The royal residence was in Jezreel, which had probably risen in importance through his alliance with Phoenicia. Close to the royal palace was a vineyard (1 K **21** 1) owned by Naboth, a native of Jezreel. This piece of ground was coveted by Ahab for a vegetable garden. He demanded therefore that Naboth should sell it to him or exchange it for a better piece of land. Naboth declined the offer. Ahab, a Heb, knowing the laws of the land, was stung by the refusal and went home greatly displeased. Jezebel, however, had neither religious scruples nor any regard for the civil laws of the Hebrews. Accordingly she planned a high-handed crime to gratify the whim of Ahab. In the name and by the authority of the king she had Naboth falsely accused of blasphemy against God and the king, and had him stoned to death by the local authorities. The horror created by this judicial murder probably did as much to finally overthrow the house of Omri as did the favor shown to the Tyrian Baal.

Neither religious rights nor civil liberties can be trampled under foot without Divine retribution.

5. Ahab and Elijah

The attempt to do so calls forth an awakened and quickened conscience, imperatively demanding that the right be done. Like an accusing conscience, Elijah appeared before Ahab. His very name ("my God is Jeh") inspired awe. "As Jeh, the God of Israel, liveth, before whom I stand, there shall not be dew nor rain these years," was the conscience-troubling message left on the mind of Ahab for more than three years. On Elijah's reappearance, Ahab greets him as the troubler of Israel. Elijah calmly informs him that the king's religious policy has caused the trouble in Israel. The proof for it is to be furnished on Mount Carmel. Ahab does the bidding of Elijah. The people shall know whom to serve. Baal is silent. Jeh answers with fire. A torrent of rain ends the drought. The victory belongs to Jeh.

Once more Elijah's indignation flashes against the house of Ahab. The judicial murder of Naboth calls it forth. The civil rights of the nation must be protected. Ahab has sold himself to do evil in the sight of Jeh. Therefore Ahab's house shall fall. Jezebel's carcase shall be eaten by dogs; the king's posterity shall be cut off; the dogs of the city or the fowls of the air shall eat their bodies (1 K **21** 20–26). Like thunderbolts the words of Elijah strike home. Ahab "fasted, and lay in sackcloth, and went softly." But the die was cast. Jeh is vindicated. Never again, in the history of Israel can Baal, the inspirer of injustice, claim a place at the side of Jeh, the God of righteousness.

In common with oriental monarchs, Ahab displayed a taste for architecture, stimulated, no

6. Ahab's Building Operations

doubt, by Phoen influence. Large building operations were undertaken in Samaria (1 K **16** 32; 2 K **10** 21). Solomon had an ivory throne, but Ahab built for himself, in Jezreel, a palace adorned with woodwork and inlaid with ivory (1 K **21** 1; **22** 39). Perhaps Amos, one hundred years later, refers to the work of Ahab when he says, "The houses of ivory shall perish" (Am **3** 15). In his day Hiel of Bethel undertook to rebuild Jericho, notwithstanding the curse of Joshua (1 K **16** 33.34). Many cities were built during his reign (1 K **22** 39).

Ahab was not only a splendor-loving monarch, but a great military leader as well. He no doubt

7. Ahab's Military Career

began his military policy by fortifying the cities of Israel (1 K **16** 34; **22** 39). Benhadad (the Dadidri of the Assyr annals; Hadadezer and Barhadad are Heb, Aram. and Arab. forms of the same name), the king of Syria, whose vassals the kings of Israel had been (1 K **15** 19), promptly besieges Samaria, and sends Ahab an insulting message. Ahab replies, "Let not him that girdeth on his armor boast himself as he that putteth it off." At the advice of a prophet of Jeh, Ahab, with 7,000 men under 232 leaders, inflicts a crushing defeat upon Benhadad and his 32 feudal kings, who had resigned themselves to a drunken carousal (1 K **20–21**).

In the following year, the Syrian army, in spite of its overwhelming superiority, meets another defeat at the hands of Ahab in the valley, near Aphek. On condition that Benhadad restore all Israelitish territory and grant the Hebrews certain rights in Damascus, Ahab spares his life to the great indignation of the prophet (1 K **20** 22 f).

In the year 854, Ahab with 2,000 chariots and 10,000 men, fights shoulder to shoulder with Benhadad against Shalmaneser II, king of Assyria. At Karkar, on the Orontes, Benhadad, with his allied forces, suffered an overwhelming defeat (*COT*, II, i, 183 f).

Perhaps Benhadad blamed Ahab for the defeat. At any rate he fails to keep his promise to Ahab (1 K **22** 3; **20** 34). Lured by false prophets, but against the dramatic warning of Micaiah, Ahab is led to take up the gauntlet against Syria once more. His friend, Jehoshaphat, king of Judah, joins him in the conflict. For the first time since the days of David all Israel and Judah stand united against the common foe.

Possibly the warning of Micaiah gave Ahab a premonition that this would be his last fight.

8. Ahab's Death

He enters the battle in disguise, but in vain. An arrow, shot at random, inflicts a mortal wound. With the fortitude of a hero, in order to avoid a panic, Ahab remains in his chariot all day and dies at sunset. His body is taken to Samaria for burial. A great king had died, and the kingdom declined rapidly after his death. He had failed to comprehend the greatness of Jehovah; he failed to stand for the highest justice, and his sins are visited upon his posterity (1 K **22** 29 f).

9. Ahab and Archaeology

(1) *The Moabite Stone* (see MOABITE STONE) bears testimony (lines 7, 8) that Omri and his son (Ahab) ruled over the land of Mehdeba for forty years. When Ahab was occupied with the Syr wars, Moab rose in insurrection. Mesha informs us in an exaggerated manner that "Israel perished with an everlasting destruction." Mesha recognizes Jeh as the God of Israel.

(2) *The Monolith of Shalmaneser II* (Brit Mus; see ASSYRIA) informs us that in 854 Shalmaneser II came in conflict with the kingdom of Hamath, and that Benhadad II with Ahab of Israel and others formed a confederacy to resist the Assyrian advance. The forces of the coalition were defeated at Karkar.

(3) *Recent excavations.*—Under the direction of Harvard University, excavations have been carried on in Samaria since 1908. In 1909 remains of a Heb palace were found. In this palace two grades of construction have been detected. The explorers suggest that they have found the palace of Omri, enlarged and improved by Ahab. This may be the "ivory house" built by Ahab. In August, 1910, about 75 potsherds were found in a building adjacent to Ahab's palace containing writing. The script is the same as that of the Moabite Stone, the words being divided by ink spots. These *ostraca* seem to be labels attached to jars kept in a room adjoining Ahab's palace. One of them reads, "In the ninth year. From Shaphtan. For Ba'al-zamar. A jar of old wine." Another reads, "Wine of the vineyard of the Tell." These readings remind one of Naboth's vineyard. In another room not far from where the *ostraca* were found, "was found an alabaster vase inscribed with the name of Ahab's contemporary, Osorkon II of Egypt." Many proper names are found on the *ostraca*, which have their equivalent in the OT. It is claimed that the writing is far greater than all other ancient Hebrew writing yet known. Perhaps with the publication of all these writings we may expect much light upon Ahab's reign. (See OSTRACA; *Harvard Theological Review*, January, 1909, April, 1910, January, 1911; *Sunday School Times*, January 7, 1911; *The Jewish Chronicle*, January 27, 1911.) S. K. MOSIMAN

AHAB, ā'hab, **and ZEDEKIAH,** zed-e-kī'a (אַחְאָב, *'aḥ'ābh*, "uncle"; צִדְקִיָּהוּ, *çidhkīyāhū*, "Jeh is my righteousness"): Ahab, son of Kolaiah, and Zedekiah, son of Maaseiah, were two prophets against whom Jeremiah uttered an oracle for prophesying falsely in the name of Jeh, and for immoral conduct. They should be delivered over to Nebuchadrezzar and be slain, and the captives of Judah that were in Babylon should take up the curse concerning them. "Jeh make thee like Zedekiah and like Ahab, whom the King of Babylon roasted in the fire" (Jer **29** 21 ff). S. F. HUNTER

AHARAH, ä'har-a, a-här'a (אַחְרַח, *'aḥraḥ;* A, **'Αρά,** *Ará;* B, **'Ιαφαήλ,** *Iaphaḗl*, brother of Raḥ, or, a brother's follower, though some regard it as a textual corruption for Ahiram): A son of Benjamin (1 Ch **8** 1). See AHIRAM.

AHARHEL, a-här'hel (אֲחַרְחֵל, *'ăharḥēl*, "brother of Rachel"; LXX **ἀδελφοῦ Ρηχάβ,** *adelphoú Rēcháb*, "brother of Rechab"): A son of Harum of the tribe of Judah (1 Ch **4** 8).

AHASAI, ä'ha-sī, a-hā'sī. See AHZAI.

AHASBAI, a-has'bī (אֲחַסְבַּי, *'ăḥaṣbay*, "blooming"): The father of Eliphelet, a Maacathite, a soldier in David's army (2 S **23** 34). He was either a native of Abel-beth-maacah (**20** 14) or, more probably, of Maacah in Syria (**10** 6). The list in 1 Ch **11** 35.36 gives different names entirely. Here we have Ur and Hepher, which simply show that the text is corrupt in one or both places.

AHASUERUS, a-haz-ū-ē'rus, or **ASSEURUS** (LXX **'Ασσούηρος,** *Assoúēros*, but in Tob **14** 15 *Asúeros;* the Lat form of the Heb אֲחַשְׁוֵרוֹשׁ, *'ăḥashwērōsh*, a name better known in its ordinary Gr form of Xerxes): It was the name of two, or perhaps of three kings mentioned in the canonical, or apocryphal, books of the OT.

There seems to be little reasonable doubt, that we should identify the Ahasuerus of Est with the

1. In Esther

well-known Xerxes, who reigned over Persia from 485 to 465 BC, and who made the great expedition against Greece that culminated in the defeat of the Pers forces at Salamis and Plataea. If Est be taken as equivalent to Ishtar, it may well be the same as the Amestris of Herodotus, which in Bab would be Ammi-Ishtar, or Ummi-Ishtar. Amestris is said to have been the daughter of Otanes, a distinguished general of Xerxes, and the granddaughter of Sisamnes, a notorious judge, who was put to death with great cruelty by the king because of malfeasance in office. Sisamnes may be in Bab Shamash-ammanu-[shallim]. If he were the brother and Otanes the nephew of Mordecai, we can easily account for the ease with which the latter and his ward Est, were advanced and confirmed in their positions at the court of Xerxes.

An Ahasuerus is mentioned in Ezr **4** 6, as one to whom some persons unnamed wrote an accusation against Judah and Jerusalem.

2. In Ezra

Ewald and others have suggested that this Ahasuerus was Cambyses, the son and successor of Cyrus. It seems to be more probable that Xerxes, the son and successor of Darius Hystaspis, is meant: first, because in the following ver Artaxerxes, the son and successor of Xerxes, is mentioned; and secondly, because we have no evidence whatever that Cambyses was ever called Ahasuerus, whereas there is absolute certainty that the Pers Khshayarsha, the Heb *'ăḥashwērōsh*, the Gr Assoueros or Xerxes, and the Lat Ahasuerus, are the exact equivalents of one another.

3. In Tobit

In the apocryphal book of Tob (**14** 15 AV) it is said that before Tobias died he heard of the destruction of Nineveh, which was taken by Nabuchodonosor and Assuerus. This Assuerus can have been no other than Cyaxares, who according to Herod. (i.196) took Nineveh and reduced the Assyrians into subjection, with the exception of the Bab district. As we shall see below, he was probably the same as the Ahasuerus of Dnl (**9** 1). The phrase "which was taken by Nabuchodonosor and Assuerus" is not found in the Syr version of Tob.

4. In Daniel

An Ahasuerus is said in Dnl **9** 1 to have been the father of Darius the Mede, and to have been of the seed of the Medes. It is probable that this Ahasuerus is the same as the Uvakhshatara of the Pers recension of the Behistun inscription, which in the Bab is Umaku'ishtar, in the Susian Makishtarra, and in Herod Cyaxares. It will be noted that both the Gr Cyaxares and the Heb Akhashwerosh omit the preformative *uva* and the *t* of the Pers form Uvakhshatara. That this Median king had sons living in the time of Cyrus is shown by the fact that two rebel aspirants to the throne in the time of Darius Hystaspis claimed to be his sons, to wit: Fravartish, a Median, who lied saying, "I am Khshathrita of the family of Uvakhshatara" (Behistun Inscr, col. II, v); and Citrantakhma, who said, "I am king in Sagartia of the family of Uvakhshatara" (id, II, xiv). If we accept the identification of Gubaru with Darius the Mede, then the latter may well have been another of his sons, at first a sub-king to Astyages the Scythian, as he was later to Cyrus the Persian. R. Dick Wilson

AHAVA, a-hā'va (אַהֲוָא, *'ahăwā'*): The river in Babylonia on the banks of which Ezra gathered together the Jews who accompanied him to Jerusalem. At this rendezvous the company encamped for three days to make preparation for the difficult and dangerous journey (Ezr **8** 15 ff). On reviewing the people and the priests Ezra found no Levites among them; he therefore sent to Iddo, "the chief at the place Casiphia," a request for ministers for the temple. A number of Levites with 220 Nethinim returned to the rendezvous with the deputation. Ezra had expressed to the king his faith in the protection of God; being, therefore, ashamed to ask for a military escort he proclaimed a fast to seek of God "a straight way." To 12 priests Ezra assigned the care of the offering for the temple in Jerusalem. When all was ready the company "departed from the river Ahava," and journeyed in safety to Jerus.

This river, apparently called after a town or district toward which it flowed (**8** 15), remains unidentified, though many conjectures have been made. Rawlinson thinks it is the "Is" of Herod. (i.79), now called "Hit," which flowed past a town of the same name in the Euphrates basin, 8 days' journey from Babylon. Some identify the district with "Ivvah" (2 K **18** 34, etc). Most probably, however, this was one of the numerous canals which intersected Babylonia, flowing from the Euphrates toward a town or district "Ahava." If so, identification is impossible. S. F. Hunter

AHAZ, ā'haz (אָחָז, *'āḥāz*, "he has grasped," 2 K **16**; 2 Ch **28**; Isa **7** 10 ff; 'Αχάζ, *Acház*):

1. Name

The name is the same as Jehoahaz; hence appears on Tiglath-pileser's Assyr inscription of 732 BC as *Ia-u-ha-zi*. The sacred historians may have dropped the first part of the name in consequence of the character of the king.

2. The Accession

Ahaz was the son of Jotham, king of Judah. He succeeded to the throne at the age of 20 years (according to another reading 25). The chronology of his reign is difficult, as his son Hezekiah is stated to have been 25 years of age when he began to reign 16 years after (2 K **18** 2). If the accession of Ahaz be placed as early as 743 BC, his grandfather Uzziah, long unable to perform the functions of his office on account of his leprosy (2 Ch **26** 21), must still have been alive. (Others date Ahaz later, when Uzziah, for whom Jotham had acted as regent, was already dead.)

3. Early Idolatries

Although so young, Ahaz seems at once to have struck out an independent course wholly opposed to the religious traditions of his nation. His first steps in this direction were the causing to be made and circulated of molten images of the Baalim, and the revival in the valley of Hinnom, south of the city, of the abominations of the worship of Moloch (2 Ch **28** 2.3). He is declared to have made his own son "pass through the fire" (2 K **16** 3); the chronicler puts it even more strongly: he "burnt his children in the fire" (2 Ch **28** 3). Other acts of idolatry were to follow.

4. Peril from Syria and Israel

The kingdom of Judah was at this time in serious peril. Rezin, king of Damascus, and Pekah, king of Samaria, had already, in the days of Jotham, begun to harass Judah (2 K **15** 37); now a conspiracy was formed to dethrone the young Ahaz, and set upon the throne a certain "son of Tabeel" (Isa **7** 6). An advance of the two kings was made against Jerus, although without success (2 K **16** 5; Isa **7** 1); the Jews were expelled from Elath (2 K **16** 6), and the country was ravaged, and large numbers taken captive (2 Ch **28** 5 ff). Consternation was universal. The heart of Ahaz "trembled, and the heart of his people, as the trees of the forest tremble with the wind" (Isa **7** 2). In his extremity Ahaz appealed to the king of Assyria for help (2 K **16** 7; 2 Ch **28** 16).

5. Isaiah's Messages to the King

Amid the general alarm and perturbation, the one man untouched by it in Jerus was the prophet Isaiah. Undismayed, Isaiah set himself, apparently singlehanded, to turn the tide of public opinion from the channel in which it was running, the seeking of aid from Assyria. His appeal was to both king and people. By Divine direction, meeting Ahaz "at the end of the conduit of the upper pool, in the highway of the fuller's field," he bade him have no fear of "these two tails of smoking firebrands," Rezin and Pekah, for, like dying torches, they would speedily be extinguished (Isa **7** 3 ff). If he would not believe this he would not be established (ver 9). Failing to win the young king's confidence, Isaiah was sent a second time, with the offer from Jeh of any sign Ahaz chose to ask, "either in the depth, or in the height above," in attestation of the truth of the Divine word. The frivolous monarch refused the arbitrament on the hypocritical ground, "I will not ask, neither will I tempt Jeh" (vs 10–12). Possibly his ambassadors were already despatched to the Assyr king. Whenever they went, they took with them a large subsidy with which to buy that ruler's favor (2 K **16** 8). It was on this occasion that Isaiah, in reply to Ahaz, gave the reassuring prophecy of Immanuel (Isa **7** 13 ff).

6. Isaiah's Tablet

As respects the people, Isaiah was directed to exhibit on "a great tablet" the words "For Maher-shalal-hash-baz" ("swift the spoil, speedy the prey"). This was attested by two witnesses, one of whom was Urijah, the high priest. It was a solemn testimony that, without any action on the part of Judah, "the riches of Damascus and the spoil of Samaria shall be carried away before the king of Assyria" (Isa **8** 1–4).

7. Fall of Damascus and Its Results

It was as the prophet had foretold. Damascus fell, Rezin was killed (2 K **16** 9), and Israel was raided (**15** 29). The action brought temporary relief to Judah, but had the effect of placing her under the heel of Assyria. Everyone then living knew that there could be no equal alliance between Judah and Assyria, and that the request for help, accompanied by the message, "I am thy servant" (2 K **16** 7.8) and by "presents" of gold and silver, meant the submission of Judah and the annual payment of a heavy tribute. Had Isaiah's counsel been followed, Tiglath-pileser would probably, in his own interests, have been compelled to crush the coalition, and Judah would have retained her freedom.

8. Sun-Dial of Ahaz

The political storm having blown over for the present, with the final loss of the important port of Elath on the Red Sea (2 K **16** 6), Ahaz turned his attention to more congenial pursuits. The king was somewhat of a dilettante in matters of art, and he set up a sun-dial, which seems to have consisted of a series of steps arranged round a short pillar, the time being indicated by the position of the shadow on the steps (cf 2 K **20** 9–11; Isa **38** 8). As it is regarded as possible for the shadow to return 10 steps, it is clear that each step did not mark an hour of the day, but some smaller period.

9. The Lavers and Brazen Sea

Another act of the king was to remove from the elaborate ornamental bases on which they had stood (cf 1 K **7** 27–39), the ten lavers of Solomon, and also to remove Solomon's molten sea from the 12 brazen bulls which supported it (cf 1 K **7** 23–26), the sea being placed upon a raised platform or pavement (2 K **16** 17). From Jer **52** 20, where the prophet sees "the 12 brazen bulls that were under the bases," it has been conjectured that the object of the change may have been to transfer the lavers to the backs of the bulls.

10. The Damascus Altar

To this was added a yet more daring act of impiety. In 732 Ahaz was, with other vassal princes, summoned to Damascus to pay homage to Tiglath-pileser (2 K **16** 10; his name appears in the Assyr inscription). There he saw a heathen altar of fanciful pattern, which greatly pleased him. A model of this was sent to Urijah the high priest, with instructions to have an enlarged copy of it placed in the temple court. On the king's return to Jerus, he sacrificed at the new altar, but, not satisfied with its position, gave orders for a change. The altar had apparently been placed on the east side of the old altar; directions were now given for the brazen altar to be moved to the north, and the Damascus altar to be placed in line with it, in front of the temple, giving both equal honor. Orders were further given to Urijah that the customary sacrifices should be offered on the new altar, now called "the great altar," while the king reserved the brazen altar for himself "to inquire by" (2 K **16** 15).

11. Further Impieties

Even this did not exhaust the royal innovations. We learn from a later notice that the doors of the temple porch were shut, that the golden candlestick was not lighted, that the offering of incense was not made, and other solemnities were suspended (2 Ch **29** 7). It is not improbable that it was Ahaz who set up 'the horses of the sun' mentioned in 2 K **23** 11, and gave them accommodation in the precincts of the temple. He certainly built the "altars . . . . on the roof of the upper chamber of Ahaz," perhaps above the porch of the temple, for the adoration of the heavenly bodies (ver 12). Many other idolatries and acts of national apostasy are related regarding him (2 Ch **28** 22 ff).

12. Recurrence of Hostilities

In the later years of his unhappy reign there was a recurrence of hostilities with the inhabitants of Philistia and Edom, this time with disaster to Judah (see the list of places lost in 2 Ch **28** 18.19). New appeal was made to Tiglath-pileser, whose subject Ahaz now was, and costly presents were sent from the temple, the royal palace, and even the houses of the princes of Judah, but without avail (vs 19–21). The Assyr 'distressed' Ahaz, but rendered no assistance. In his trouble the wicked king only "trespassed yet more" (ver 22).

13. Death of Ahaz

Ahaz died in 728, after 16 years of misused power. The exultation with which the event was regarded is reflected in Isaiah's little prophecy written " in the year that King Ahaz died" (Isa **14** 28–32). The statement in 2 K **16** 20 that Ahaz "was buried with his fathers in the city of David" is to be understood in the light of 2 Ch **28** 27, that he was buried in Jerusalem, but that his body was not laid in the sepulchers of the kings of Israel. His name appears in the royal genealogies in 1 Ch **3** 13 and Mt **1** 9.

W. SHAW CALDECOTT

AHAZ, DIAL OF. See DIAL OF AHAZ.

AHAZIAH, ā-ha-zī'a (אֲחַזְיָה and אֲחַזְיָהוּ, *'ăhazyāh* and *'ăhazyāhū*, "Jeh holds, or sustains"):

I. Ahaziah.—Son of Ahab and Jezebel, eighth king of Israel (1 K **22** 51—2 K **1** 18).

1. His Reign

Ahaziah became king over Israel in the seventeenth year of Jehoshaphat, king of Judah, and he reigned two years, 854–853 BC. There is here an incongruity between the synchronism and the length of the reigns of the kings. Jehoshaphat began to reign in the fourth year of Ahab (1 K **22** 41), and he reigned 22 years (1 K **16** 29). Accordingly Ahaziah's first year, in the twenty-second year of Ahab, would fall in the nineteenth year of Jehoshaphat. The chronological statement in 2 K **1** 17 is probably taken from the Syr, and both are in harmony with a method of computation followed by certain Gr MSS.

2. His Character

A good name does not insure a good character. Ahaziah, the "God-sustained," served Baal and worshipped him, and provoked to anger Jehovah, the God of Israel, just as his father before him had done. He appears to have been weak and unfortunate, and calamities in quick succession pursued him.

3. The Revolt of Moab

Ahab had sought the good and became an enemy to the best. His house and the nation suffered the consequences. "Moab rebelled against Israel after the death of Ahab." Ahaziah appears to have been too weak to offer resistance. The Moabite Stone dates the revolt in the days of Ahab. No doubt it began at the time of Ahab's last campaign against Syria.

4. His Maritime Alliance

According to 1 K **22** 48 f Ahaziah attempted to form an alliance with Jehoshaphat of Judah to revive the ancient maritime traffic, but failed. According to 2 Ch **20** 35–37 the alliance was consummated, in consequence of which the enterprise came to nothing. See JEHOSHAPHAT.

Ahaziah suffered a severe accident by falling through the lattice in his upper apartment in

5. His Sickness and Death

Samaria, and lay sick. As a worthy son of Jezebel and Ahab, he sent messengers to consult Baal-zebub, the god of Ekron, regarding his recovery. But Israel belonged to Jehovah. Accordingly the messengers were met by the prophet Elijah who for the last time warns against the corrupting moral influences of the Baal religion. "Thus saith Jehovah, Is it because there is no God in Israel, that thou sendest to inquire of Baal-zebub, the god of Ekron? therefore thou shalt not come down from the bed whither thou art gone up, but shalt surely die" was the message which he sent back to the embassy, and the death of the king speedily followed.

II. Ahaziah.—Sixth king of Judah (2 K **8** 25–29; **9** 16 f = 2 Ch **22** 1–9); also written Jehoahaz (2 Ch **21** 17; **25** 23), which is merely a transposition of the component parts of the compound. The form "Azariah" (2 Ch **22** 6) is an error, fifteen Heb MSS and all the VSS reading Ahaziah.

1. His Brief Reign

Ahaziah, youngest son of Jehoram, began to reign in the twelfth year (2 K **8** 25) of Jehoram of Israel. In 2 K **9** 29 it is stated as the eleventh. The former is probably the Heb, the latter the Gr method of computation, the LXX Luc also reading eleventh in **8** 25. He was 22 years old when he began to reign and he reigned one year (2 K **8** 26). The reading "forty two" (2 Ch **22** 2) is a scribal error, since according to 2 Ch **21** 5.20 Jehoram the father was only 40 years old at the time of his death. Syr, Arab. and Luc read 22, LXX B 20. See Chronology of OT.

2. His Character

(Cf 2 K **8** 27; 2 Ch **22** 3.4.) In view of the disaster which befell the royal house (2 Ch **21** 16.17), the inhabitants of Jerusalem placed Ahaziah the youngest son upon the throne. That "he walked in the way of the house of Ahab" is exemplified by Ch to the effect that his mother, the daughter of Jezebel, counseled him in the ways of wickedness and that the house of Ahab led him to his destruction. The influence of Jezebel was at work in Judah. Ahaziah dedicated "hallowed things" to Jeh (2 K **12** 18), but he did evil in Jeh's eyes.

3. His Alliance with Jehoram of Israel

(Cf 2 K **8** 28.29; 2 Ch **22** 5.6.) Ahaziah cultivated the relations which had been established between the two kingdoms by Ahab. Accordingly he joined his uncle Jehoram of Israel in an expedition against Hazael, king of Syria. Ramoth-gilead was captured and held for Israel against the king of Syria (2 K **9** 14). However, Jehoram of Israel was wounded and returned to Jezreel to be healed of his wounds. It appears that the army was left in charge of Jehu at Ramoth-gilead. Ahaziah apparently went to Jerus and later went down to Jezreel to visit Jehoram. In the meantime Jehu formed a conspiracy against Jehoram.

4. His Death

The death of Ahaziah, as told in 2 K **9** 16 f, differs from the account in 2 Ch **22** 7–9. According to the account in K, Ahaziah who is visiting Jehoram, joins him in a separate chariot to meet Jehu. Jehoram suspecting treachery turns to flee, but an arrow from the bow of Jehu pierces his heart and he dies in his chariot. Ahaziah tries to escape, but is overtaken near Ibleam and mortally wounded by one of Jehu's men. He fled to the fortress of Megiddo, where he died. His servants conveyed his body in a chariot to Jerus, where he was buried. According to the Chronicler, this account is very much abbreviated (2 Ch **22** 7 f). His destruction is of God because of his alliance with Jehoram. Jehu, who was executing judgment on the house of Ahab, first slew the kinsmen of Ahaziah. He then sought Ahaziah who was hiding in Samaria. When he was found, he was brought to Jehu and put to death. He was buried, but where and by whom we are not told.

That there were other traditions respecting the death of Ahaziah, is proved by Jos, who says that when Ahaziah was wounded he left his chariot and fled on horseback to Megiddo, where he was well cared for by his servants until he died (*Ant*, IX, vi, 3).

S. K. Mosiman

AHBAN, ä'ban (אַחְבָּן, *'aḥbān*, "brother of an intelligent one"[?] **'Αχαβάρ**, *Achabár*): The son of Abishur of the tribe of Judah (1 Ch **2** 29).

AHER, ā'hēr (אַחֵר, *'aḥēr*, "another"; **'Αέρ**, *Aér*): A man of Benjamin (1 Ch **7** 12), apparently a contracted form, perhaps the same as **Ahiram** (AV) (Nu **26** 38) or Aharah (1 Ch **8** 1).

AHI or **AH** in proper names (אֲחִי or אַח, *'ăḥī* or *'aḥ* "brother"): The usage is practically the same with that of *'abh*, *'ăbhi*. See Abi; Names, Proper.

AHI, ā'hī (אֲחִי, *'ăḥī*, "my brother," or perhaps a contraction from Ahijah, which see): (1) A member of the tribe of Gad (1 Ch **5** 15). (2) A member of the tribe of Asher (1 Ch **7** 34).

AHIAH, a-hī'ä: A variant in AV (1 S **14** 3.18; 1 K **4** **3**; 1 Ch **8** 7) for Ahijah, which see. Also in the RV (Neh **10** 26).

AHIAM, a-hī'am (אֲחִיאָם, *'ăḥī'ām*, "mother's brother"): One of David's thirty heroes. He was the son of Sharar (2 S **23** 33) or according to 1 Ch **11** 35 of Sacar, the Hararite.

AHIAN, a-hī'an (אַחְיָן, *'aḥyān*, "brotherly"): A son of Shemida of the tribe of Manasseh (1 Ch **7** 19).

AHIEZER, ā-hī-ē'zer (אֲחִיעֶזֶר, *'ăḥī'ezer*, "brother is help"): (1) A son of Ammishaddai, a Danite prince, who acted as representative of his tribe on several occasions. (See Nu **1** 12; **2** 25; **7** 66.71; **10** 25.) (2) One of the mighty men or warriors, who joined David at Ziklag when a fugitive before Saul (1 Ch **12** 3).

AHIHUD, a-hī'hud (אֲחִיהוּד, *'ăḥīhūdh*, "brother is majesty"): (1) One of the chief men of the tribe of Asher. He was selected by Moses to help divide the land west of the Jordan (Nu **34** 27). (2) A son of Ehud of the tribe of Benjamin (1 Ch **8** 6.7). The text here is obscure and probably corrupt.

AHIJAH, a-hī'ja (אֲחִיָּה or אֲחִיָּהוּ, *'ăḥīyāh* or *'ăḥīyāhū*, "brother of Jeh," "my brother is Jeh," "Jeh is brother." In AV the name sometimes appears as **Ahiah**):

(1) One of the sons of Jerahmeel the great-grandson of Judah (1 Ch **2** 25).

(2) A descendant of Benjamin (1 Ch **8** 7).

(3) The son of Ahitub, priest in the time of King Saul (1 S **14** 3.18). Either he is the same with Ahimelech, who is mentioned later, or he is the father or brother of Ahimelech. He is introduced to us when Saul has been so long on the throne that his son Jonathan is a man grown and a warrior. He is in attendance upon Saul, evidently as an official priest, "wearing an ephod." When Saul wishes direction from God he asks the priest to bring hither the ark; but then, without waiting for the message, Saul counts the confusion in the Phili camp a sufficient indication of the will of Providence, and hurries off to the attack. Some copies of the Gr

here read "ephod" instead of "ark," but the documentary evidence in favor of that reading is far from decisive. If the Heb reading is correct, then the seclusion of the ark, from the time of its return from Philistia to the time of David, was not so absolute as many have supposed. See AHIMELECH I.

(4) One of David's mighty men, according to the list in 1 Ch **11** 36. The corresponding name in the list in 2 S **23** 34 is Eliam the son of Ahithophel the Gilonite.

(5) A Levite of David's time who had charge of certain treasures connected with the house of God (1 Ch **26** 20). The Gr copies presuppose the slightly different text which would give in Eng. "and their brethren," instead of Ahijah. This is accepted by many scholars, and it is at least more plausible than most of the proposed corrections of the Heb text by the Gr.

(6) Son of Shisha and brother of Elihoreph (1 K **4** 3). The two brothers were scribes of Solomon. Can the scribes Ahijah and Shemaiah (1 Ch **24** 6) be identified with the men of the same names who, later, were known as distinguished prophets? Shisha is probably the same with Shavsha (1 Ch **18** 16; cf 2 S **8** 17; **20** 25), who was scribe under David, the office in this case descending from father to son.

(7) The distinguished prophet of Shiloh, who was interested in Jeroboam I. In Solomon's lifetime Ahijah clothed himself with a new robe, met Jeroboam outside Jerusalem, tore the robe into twelve pieces, and gave him ten, in token that he should become king of the ten tribes (1 K **11** 29–39). Later, when Jeroboam had proved unfaithful to Jeh, he sent his wife to Ahijah to ask in regard to their sick son. The prophet received her harshly, foretold the death of the son, and threatened the extermination of the house of Jeroboam (1 K **14**). The narrative makes the impression that Ahijah was at this time a very old man (ver **4**). These incidents are differently narrated in the long addition at 1 K **12** 24 found in some of the Gr copies. In that addition the account of the sick boy precedes that of the rent garment, and both are placed between the account of Jeroboam's return from Egypt and that of the secession of the ten tribes, an order in which it is impossible to think that the events occurred. Further, this addition attributes the incident of the rent garment to Shemaiah and not to Ahijah, and says that Ahijah was 60 years old.

Other notices speak of the fulfilment of the threatening prophecies spoken by Ahijah (2 Ch **10** 15; 1 K **12** 15; **15** 29). In 2 Ch "the prophecy of Ahijah the Shilonite" is referred to as a source for the history of Solomon (**9** 29).

(8) The father of Baasha king of Israel (1 K **15** 27.33; **21** 22; 2 K **9** 9).

(9) A Levite of Nehemiah's time, who sealed the covenant (Neh **10** 26 AV). WILLIS J. BEECHER

AHIKAM, a-hī'kam (אֲחִיקָם, *'ăḥīḳām*, "my brother has risen up"): A prominent man of the time of King Josiah and the following decades (2 K **22** 12.14; **25** 22; 2 Ch **34** 20; Jer **26** 24; **39** 14; **40** 5 ff; **41** 1 ff; **43** 6). He was the son of Shaphan, who very likely is to be identified with Shaphan the scribe, who was at that time so prominent. Ahikam was the father of Gedaliah, whom, on the capture of Jerusalem, Nebuchadnezzar made governor of the land. Ahikam was a member of the deputation sent by Josiah to the prophetess Huldah to consult her concerning the contents of the Book of the Law which had been found. Under Jehoiakim he had sufficient influence to protect Jeremiah from being put to death. On the capture of Jerusalem Nebuchadnezzar committed Jeremiah into the care of Gedaliah. It is clear that both Shaphan and his son, like Jeremiah, belonged to the party which held that the men of Judah were under obligation to keep the oath which they had sworn to the king of Babylon. WILLIS J. BEECHER

AHILUD, a-hī'lud (אֲחִילוּד, *'ăḥīlūdh*, "child's brother," perhaps): The father of Jehoshaphat, who is mentioned as "recorder" in both the earlier and the later lists under David, and in the list under Solomon (2 S **8** 16 and 1 Ch **18** 15; 2 S **20** 24; 1 K **4** 3). In the absence of proof we may assume that the father of Baana, one of Solomon's district superintendents, was the same Ahilud (1 K **4** 12).

AHIMAAZ, a-hi-mā'az, a-him'ā-az (אֲחִימַעַץ, *'ăḥīma'aç*, perhaps "my brother is rage," or "brother of rage"):

(1) Father of Ahinoam the wife of King Saul (1 S **14** 50).

(2) The son of Zadok the high priest (1 Ch **6** 8.9.53). With his father he remained loyal to David in the rebellions both of Absalom and of Adonijah. With Jonathan the son of Abiathar he carried information to David when he fled from Absalom (2 S **15** 27.36; **17** 17.20). At his own urgent request he carried tidings to David after the death of Absalom (2 S **18** 19 ff). He told the king of the victory, and also, through his reluctance to speak, informed him of Absalom's death. By his reluctance and his sympathy he softened a little the message, which the Cushite presently repeated more harshly.

That Ahimaaz did not succeed his father as high priest has been inferred from the fact that in the Solomon list of heads of departments (1 K **4** 2) Azariah the son of Zadok is mentioned as priest. It is assumed that this Azariah is the one who appears in the genealogy as the son of Ahimaaz, and that for some reason Ahimaaz was left out of the succession. These inferences are not justified by the record, though possibly the record does not absolutely disprove them. As the list stands it makes Zadok and Abiathar the high priests. Azariah and Zabud, the son of Nathan (vs 2.5), are spoken of as holding priestly offices of a different kind. Ahimaaz may have died early, or may have followed some other career, but the simple fact is that we do not know.

(3) Ahimaaz, in Naphtali, was one of Solomon's twelve commissary officers (1 K **4** 15), who married Basemath the daughter of Solomon. It is not impossible that he was Ahimaaz the son of Zadok, though there is no proof to that effect.
WILLIS J. BEECHER

AHIMAN, a-hī'man (אֲחִימַן, *'ăḥīman*, perhaps, "brother of fortune," or, "my brother is fortune"):

(1) One of the names given as those of the three "children of the Anak" (Nu **13** 22; Josh **15** 14; cf Nu **13** 28; 2 S **21** 16.18), or the three "sons of the Anak" (Josh **15** 14; Jgs **1** 20). The three names (Ahiman, Sheshai, Talmai) also occur together in Jgs **1** 10. The word Anak in the Heb Bible has the definite article except in Nu **13** 33 and Dt **9** 2. Its use is that of a common noun denoting a certain type of man, rather than as the proper name of a person or a clan, though this need not prevent our thinking of the Anakim as a clan or group of clans, who regarded Arba as their founder. The question is raised whether Ahiman and Sheshai and Talmai are to be thought of as persons or as clans. The most natural understanding of the Bible statements is certainly to the effect that they were personal leaders among the Anakim of Kiriath-arba (Hebron). They were smitten and dispossessed by the tribe of Judah, with Caleb for leader.

(2) A Levite, one of the gatekeepers of the latest Bible times (1 Ch **9** 17). He is associated with Akkub and Talmon and their brethren: cf Neh **11** 19. WILLIS J. BEECHER

AHIMELECH, a-him'e-lek (אֲחִימֶלֶךְ, *'ăhīmelekh,* "brother of a king," or, "my brother is king," or, "king is brother"):

(1) The father of David's high priest Abiathar: son of Ahitub, the son of Phinehas, the son of Eli (1 S **21** 1.2.8; **22** 9–20; **23** 6; **30** 7). Ahijah the son of Ahitub (1 S **14** 3.18) was either the same person under another name, or was Ahimelech's father or brother. See AHIJAH, 3. Ahimelech is an interesting person, especially because he stands for whatever information we have concerning the priestly office in Israel during the period between Eli and David. Whether the Deuteronomic law for a central sanctuary originated with Moses or not, its provisions were very imperfectly carried out during the times of the Judges. This was particularly the case after the capture of the ark by the Philistines, and the deaths of Eli and his sons. From that time to the middle of the reign of David the ark was in the custody of the men of Kiriath-jearim "in the hill," or "in Gibeah" (1 S **7** 1; 2 S **6** 2.3). As a general proposition Israel "sought not unto it" (1 Ch **13** 3), though there is nothing to forbid the idea that it may, on occasion, have been brought out from its seclusion (1 S **14** 18). Before and after the accession of Saul some of the functions of the national sanctuary were transacted, of course very incompletely, at Gilgal (1 S **10** 8; **11** 14.15; **13** 7 ff; **15** 12.21.33). Whether there was a priesthood, with Ahitub the grandson of Eli as high priest, is a matter on which we have no information; but we may remind ourselves that the common assumption that such men as Samuel and Saul performed priestly offices is nothing but an assumption.

After Saul has been king for a good many years we find Ahijah in his retinue, acting as priest and wearing priestly vestments. A few years later Ahimelech is at the head of the very considerable priestly establishment at Nob. The scale on which it existed is indicated by the fact that 85 robed priests perished in the massacre (1 S **22** 18). They had families residing at Nob (ver 19). They were thought of as priests of Jehovah, and were held in reverence (ver 17). It was a hereditary priesthood (vs 11.15). Men deposited votive offerings there, the sword of Goliath, for example (**21** 9). There seems to have been some kind of police authority, whereby a person might be "detained" (**21** 7). It was customary to inquire of Jeh there (**22** 10.15). A distinction was made between the common and the holy (**21** 4–6). The custom of the shewbread was maintained (**21** 6). In fine, Jesus is critically correct in calling the place "the house of God" (Mk **2** 26). The account does not say that the ark was there, or that the burnt-offering of the morning and evening was offered, or that the great festivals were held. The priestly head of the establishment at Nob is represented to have been the man who had the right to the office through his descent from Aaron. It is gratuitous to assume that there were other similar sanctuaries in Israel, though the proposition that there were none might be, like other negative propositions, hard to establish by positive proof.

(2) A son of Abiathar (2 S **8** 17; 1 Ch **18** 16; **24** 6), and grandson of the above. In a list of the heads of departments under David, a list belonging later than the middle of David's 40 years, and in which David's sons appear, this Ahimelech, the son of David's friend, is mentioned as sharing with Zadok a high position in the priesthood. In this capacity, later, he shared with David and Zadok in the apportionment of the priests into 24 ancestral classes, 16 of the house of Eleazar, and 8 of the house of Ithamar (1 Ch **24**). In this account Ahimelech is mentioned three times, and with some detail. It is alleged as a difficulty that Abiathar was then living, and was high priest along with Zadok (1 Ch **15** 11; 2 S **15** 29; **19** 11; **20** 25; 1 K **2** 27.35; **4** 4, etc). But surely there is no improbability in the affirmation that Abiathar had a son named Ahimelech, or that this son performed prominent priestly functions in his father's lifetime.

Many regard "Ahimelech the son of Abiathar" (Mt gives *Ah*imelech) as an inadvertent transposition for "Abiathar the son of Ahimelech." This is rather plausible in the passage in 2 S **8** and the duplicate of it in 1 Ch **18** 16, but it has no application in the detailed account in 1 Ch **24**. One must accept Ahimelech the son of Abiathar as historical unless, indeed, one regards the testimony of Ch to a fact as evidence in disproof of that fact. See ABIATHAR.

(3) A Hittite, a companion and friend of David, when he was hiding from Saul in the wilderness (1 S **26** 6). WILLIS J. BEECHER

AHIMOTH, a-hī'moth (אֲחִימוֹת, *'ăhīmōth,* "brother of death," or, "my brother is death"): A descendant of Kohath the son of Levi (1 Ch **6** 25); ancestor of Elkanah the father of Samuel. The name Mahath holds a similar place in the list that follows (**6** 35).

AHINADAB, a-hin'a-dab (אֲחִינָדָב, *'ăhīnādhābh,* "brother of willingness," or, "my brother is willing"): Decidedly the ordinary use of the stem *nadhabh* is to denote willingness rather than liberality or nobleness. One of Solomon's twelve commissary officers (1 K **4** 14). He was the son of Iddo, and his district was Mahanaim.

AHINOAM, a-hi-nō'am, a-hin'o-am (אֲחִינֹעַם *'ăhīnō'am,* "my brother is pleasantness"):

(1) Daughter of Ahimaaz, and wife of King Saul (1 S **14** 50).

(2) The woman from Jezreel whom David married after Saul gave Michal to another husband. She and Abigail, the widow of Nabal, seem to have been David's only wives prior to the beginning of his reign in Hebron. His marriage to Abigail is mentioned first, with some details, followed by the statement, easily to be understood in the pluperfect, that he had previously married Ahinoam (1 S **25** 39–44). Three times they are mentioned together, Ahinoam always first (1 S **27** 3; **30** 5; 2 S **2** 2), and Ahinoam is the mother of David's first son, and Abigail of his second (2 S **3** 2; 1 Ch **3** 1). Ahinoam's son was Amnon. The record really represents David's polygamy as a series of bids for political influence; the names of Amnon, Absalom, Adonijah suggest that the method was not finally a success. WILLIS J. BEECHER

AHIO, a-hī'ō (אַחְיוֹ, *'aḥyō,* variously explained as "his brother," "brotherly," "brother of Jeh," "my brother is Jeh"): Proper names containing a similar form of the name of Jeh are found on the *ostraca* recently exhumed at Samaria. The word is always treated as a common noun in the ordinary Gr copies, being rendered either "brother" or "brothers," or "his brother" or "his brothers"; but this is probably to be taken as an instance of the relative inferiority of the Gr text as compared with the MT. See OSTRACA.

(1) One of the sons of Beriah, the son of Elpaal, the son of Shaharaim and Hushim, reckoned among the families of Benjamin (1 Ch **8** 14). Beriah

and Shema are described as 'ancestral heads' "of the inhabitants of Aijalon, who put to flight the inhabitants of Gath."

(2) A descendant of Jeiel ("the father of Gibeon") and his wife Maacah (1 Ch **8** 31; **9** 37). King Saul apparently came from the same family (**8** 30. 33; **9** 39).

(3) One of the men who drove the new cart when David first attempted to bring the ark from the house of Abinadab to Jerus (2 S **6** 3.4; 1 Ch **13** 7). In Samuel Uzza and Ahio are called sons of Abinadab. By the most natural understanding of the Biblical data about 100 years had elapsed since the ark was brought to the house; they were sons of that Abinadab in the sense of being his descendants. Whether he had a successor of the same name living in David's time is a matter of conjecture. WILLIS J. BEECHER

AHIRA, a-hī'ra (אֲחִירַע, *'ăḥīra'*, "brother of evil," or, "my brother is evil"): A man of Naphtali, contemporary with Moses. He is five times mentioned as the son of Enan. He was the representative of his tribe who assisted Moses in the census (Nu **1** 15). He was the hereditary "prince" of the tribe; he made the tribal offering (Nu **2** 29; **7** 78; cf ver 83), and was commander of the tribal host when on the march (Nu **10** 27).

AHIRAM, a-hī'ram (אֲחִירָם, *'ăḥīrām*, "exalted brother," or "my brother is exalted"): A son of Benjamin. Mentioned third of the five in Nu **26** 38.39. In 1 Ch **8** 1 five sons are likewise mentioned, being explicitly numbered; the third name, Aharah (*'aḥraḥ*), is conjectured to be either a corruption of Ahiram or a different name for the same person. In 1 Ch **7** 6 ff is a fuller list of Benjamite names, but it is fragmentary and not clear. In it occurs Aher (*'aḥēr*), which may be either Ahiram or Aharah with the end of the word lost. In Gen **46** 21 ten sons of Benjamin are mentioned, some being there counted as sons who, in the other lists, are spoken of as more remote descendants. In this list Ehi (*'ēḥī*) is perhaps Ahiram apocopated. See AHARAH; AHER; EHI.

WILLIS J. BEECHER

AHIRAMITE, a-hī'ram-īt (אֲחִירָמִי, *'ăḥīrāmī*, "of the family of Ahiram"; Nu **26** 38). See AHIRAM.

AHISAMACH, a-his'a-mak (אֲחִיסָמָךְ, *'ăḥīṣāmākh*, "my brother supports"): A man of the tribe of Dan, father of Oholiab, who was the assistant of Bezalel in the building of the tent of meeting and preparing its furniture (Ex **31** 6; **35** 34; **38** 23).

AHISHAHAR, a-hish'a-här (אֲחִישָׁחַר, *'ăḥīshaḥar*, "brother of dawn"): One of the sons of Bilhan, the son of Jediael, the son of Benjamin (1 Ch **7** 10).

AHISHAR, a-hish'är (אֲחִישָׁר, *'ăḥīshār*, "my brother has sung"): Mentioned in Solomon's list of heads of departments as "over the household" (1 K **4** 6).

AHITHOPHEL, a-hith'o-fel (אֲחִיתֹפֶל, *'ăḥīthōphel*, "brother of foolishness," perhaps): The real leader of the Absalom rebellion against David. He is described as "the king's counsellor," in a context connected with events some of which are dated in the fortieth year of David (1 Ch **27** 33. 34; cf **26** 31). Concerning him and his part in the rebellion we have rather full information (2 S **15** 12 ff).

Some hold that he was the grandfather of Bathsheba, and make much of this in forming their estimates of him. Does the evidence sustain this view? In the latter half of the list of David's mighty men, not among the older veterans with whom the list begins, appears "Eliam the son of Ahithophel the Gilonite" (2 S **23** 34), the corresponding name in the other copy of the list being "Ahijah the Pelonite" (1 Ch **11** 36). It is assumed that this is the same Eliam who was father to Bath-sheba (2 S **11** 3). Apparently the Chronicler testifies (1 Ch **3** 5) that the mother of Solomon was "Bath-shua the daughter of Ammiel." Bathshua may easily be a variant of Bathsheba, and the names Eliam and Ammiel are made up of the same parts, only in reversed order. It is not strange that men have inferred that the son of Ahithophel was the father of Bathsheba. But the inference is really not a probable one. The record does not make the impression that Ahithophel was an older man than David. The recorded events of David's life after his misconduct with Bathsheba cannot have occupied less than about twenty years; that is, he cannot have been at the time older than about fifty years. That Ahithophel had then a married granddaughter is less probable than that there were in Israel two Eliams. Further, Ahithophel was not the sort of man to conspire against the interests of his granddaughter and her son, however he may, earlier, have resented the conduct of David toward her. Ahithophel's motive in the rebellion was doubtless ambition for personal power, though he very likely shared with many of his countrymen in the conviction that it was unjust to push aside an older son by elevating a younger son to the throne.

Ahithophel has a reputation for marvelous practical sagacity (2 S **16** 23). He did not show this in joining the conspiracy but it is in evidence in his management of the affair. According to the record the hearts of the people, in spite of the much fault they had to find, were all the time with David. Absalom's only chance of success was by the method of surprise and stampede. There must be a crisis in which everybody would join Absalom because everybody thought that everybody else had done so. Such a state of public sentiment could last only a very few days; but if, in those few days, David could be put out of the way, Absalom might hold the throne in virtue of his personal popularity and in default of a rival. The first part of the program was carried out with wonderful success; when it came to the second part, Ahithophel's practical wisdom was blocked by Hushai's adroit appeal to Absalom's personal vanity. Ahithophel saw with absolute clearness that Absalom had sacrificed his one opportunity, and he committed suicide to avoid participation in the shameful defeat which he saw could not be averted. WILLIS J. BEECHER

AHITOB, a-hī'tob (Ἀχιτώβ, *Achitōb;* AV **Achitob**): One of the ancestors of Ezra (1 Esd **8** 2; 2 Esd **1** 1). Cf AHITUB, 3 (Ezr **7** 2 et al.).

AHITUB, a-hī'tub (אֲחִיטוּב, *'ăḥīṭūbh*, "brother of goodness," i.e. "good brother," or, "my brother is goodness"):

(1) The brother of Ichabod and son of Phinehas the son of Eli (1 S **14** 3; **22** 9.11.12.20). According to 1 Ch **24** he and his line were descended from Aaron through Ithamar. The record implies that he was born while his father and grandfather were priests at Shiloh, and it says that he was the father and grandfather of priests; but it is silent as to his own exercise of the priestly office. We have no information concerning the office from the time when the Philis captured the ark till Saul became king. See AHIJAH; AHIMELECH; ABIATHAR.

(2) A descendant of Aaron through Eleazar: by this fact distinguished from Ahitub, the descendant of Ithamar, though nearly contemporaneous with him. Esp. known as the father of Zadok

who, at Solomon's accession, became sole high priest (2 S **8** 17; 1 Ch **6** 8; **18** 16). His genealogical line, from Levi to the Exile, is given in 1 Ch **6** 1–15 (**5** 27–41). The three successive names, Ahitub and Zadok and Ahimaaz, appear in 2 S (**8** 17; **15** 27, etc). The line is paralleled by selected names in Ezr **7** 1–5, and relatively late parts of it are paralleled in 1 Ch **9** 11 and Neh **11** 11. The best explanation of certain phenomena in Ch is that the record was copied from originals that were more or less fragmentary. In some cases, also, a writer gives only such parts of a genealogy as are needed for his purpose. It is due to these causes that there are many omissions in the genealogical lists, and that they supplement one another. Allowing for these facts there is no reason why we should not regard the genealogies of Ahitub as having distinct historical value.

(3) In the genealogies, in the seventh generation from Ahitub, the descendant of Eleazar, appears another Ahitub, the son of another Amariah and the father (or grandfather) of another Zadok (1 Ch **6** 11 [**5** 37]; **9** 11; Neh **11** 11). The list in Ezr **7** omits a block of names, and the Ahitub there named may be either 2 or 3. He is mentioned in 1 Esd **8** 2 and 2 Esd **1** 1, and the name occurs in Jth **8** 1. In these places it appears in the Eng. versions in the various forms Ahitub, Ahitob, Achitob, Acitho. WILLIS J. BEECHER

AHLAB, ä′lab (אַחְלָב, *'aḥlābh,* "fat or fruitful"): A town of Asher. It is clear, however, that the Israelites failed to drive away the original inhabitants (Jgs **1** 31). Some have identified Ahlab with *Gush Halab* or Geschila, N.W. of the Sea of Galilee.

AHLAI, ä′lī (אַחְלַי, *'aḥlay* "O would that!"): (1) A Son of Sheshan (1 Ch **2** 31) or according to ver 34 a daughter of Sheshan, for here we read: "Now Sheshan had no sons, but daughters." (2) The father of Zabad, a soldier in David's army (1 Ch **11** 41).

AHOAH, a-hō′a (אֲחוֹחַ, *'ăḥōaḥ,* "brotherly"[?]): A son of Bela of the tribe of Benjamin (1 Ch **8** 4).

AHOHITE, a-hō′hīt (אֲחוֹחִי, *'ăḥōḥī*): A patronymic employed in connection with the descendants of AHOAH (q.v.) such as Dodai (2 S **23** 9) or Dodo 1 Ch **11** 12), Ilai (29) or Zalmon (2 S **23** 28), and also Eleazar, son of Dodo (1 Ch **11** 12). The family must have been fond of military affairs, for all the above were officers in David and Solomon's armies.

AHOLAH, a-hō′la. See OHOLAH.

AHOLIAB, a-ho-lī′ab. See OHOLIAB.

AHOLIAH, a-ho-lī′a. See OHOLIAH.

AHOLIBAH, a-hō′li-ba. See OHOLIBAH.

AHOLIBAMAH, a-ho-li-bä′ma. See OHOLIBAMAH.

AHUMAI, a-hū′mā-ī, a-hū′mī (אֲחוּמַי, *'ăḥūmay,* "brother of water"[?]): A descendant of Shobal of the tribe of Judah (1 Ch **4** 2).

AHUZZAM, a-huz′am, **AHUZAM,** a-hū′zam (אֲחֻזָּם, *'ăḥuzzām,* "possessor"): A son of Ashahur of the tribe of Judah; his mother's name was Naarah (1 Ch **4** 6); written **Ahuzam** in AV.

AHUZZATH, a-huz′ath (אֲחֻזַּת, *'ăḥuzzath,* "possession"): A "friend" perhaps a minister, of Abimelech, king of Gerar. He together with Phicol, commander of the army, accompanied their sovereign to Beersheba to make a covenant with Isaac (Gen **26** 26). The termination *-ath* reminds us of Phili proper names, such as Gath, Goliath, etc. Cf Genubath (1 K **11** 20).

AHZAI, ä′zī (אַחְזַי, *'aḥzay,* "my protector"): A priest who resided in Jerus (Neh **11** 13). The AV has **Ahasai** which is probably the same as Jahzevah of 1 Ch **9** 12.

AI, ā′ī (עַי, *'ay,* written always with the def. art., הָעַי, *hā-'ay,* probably meaning "the ruin," kindred root, עָוָה, *'āwāh*):

(1) A town of central Palestine, in the tribe of Benjamin, near and just east of Bethel (Gen **12** 8). It is identified with the modern *Haiyân,* just south of the village *Dêr Dîwân* (Conder in *HDB;* Delitzsch in *Comm. on Gen* **12** 8) or with a mound, *El-Tell,* to the north of the modern village (Davis, *Dict. Bib.*). The name first appears in the earliest journey of Abraham through Pal (Gen **12** 8), where its location is given as east of Bethel, and near the altar which Abraham built between the

Ascent to Ai: Path to Elijah's Translation.

two places. It is given similar mention as he returns from his sojourn in Egypt (Gen **13** 3). In both of these occurrences the AV has the form **Hai,** including the article in transliterating. The most conspicuous mention of Ai is in the narrative of the Conquest. As a consequence of the sin of Achan in appropriating articles from the devoted spoil of Jericho, the Israelites were routed in the attack upon the town; but after confession and expiation, a second assault was successful, the city was taken and burned, and left a heap of ruins, the inhabitants, in number twelve thousand, were put to death, the king captured, hanged and buried under a heap of stones at the gate of the ruined city, only the cattle being kept as spoil by the people (Josh **7, 8**). The town had not been rebuilt when Josh was written (Josh **8** 28). The fall of Ai gave the Israelites entrance to the heart of Canaan, where at once they became established, Bethel and other towns in the vicinity seeming to have yielded without a struggle. Ai was rebuilt at some later period, and is mentioned by Isa (**10** 28) in his vivid description of the approach of the Assyr army, the feminine form (עַיָּת, *'ayyāth*) being used. Its place in the order of march, as just beyond Michmash from Jerusalem, corresponds with the identification given above. It is mentioned also in post-exilic times by Ezr (**2** 28) and Neh (**7** 32, and in **11** 31 as עַיָּא, *'ayyā'*), identified in each case by the grouping with Bethel.

(2) The Ai of Jer **49** 3 is an Ammonite town, the text probably being a corruption of עָר, *'ār;* or הָעִיר, *hā-'īr,* "the city" (*BDB*). EDWARD MACK

AIAH, ā′ya (אַיָּה, *'ayyāh,* "falcon"; once in AV **Ajah,** Gen **36** 24): (1) A Horite, son of Zibeon, and brother of Anah, who was father of one of Esau's wives (Gen **36** 24; 1 Ch **1** 40). (2) Father of Rizpah, a concubine of Saul, about whom Ish-bosheth falsely accused Abner (2 S **3** 7), and whose sons were hanged to appease the Gibeonites, whom Saul had wronged (2 S **21** 8–11).

AIATH, ā′yath (עַיָּת, *'ayyāth*): Found in Isa **10** 28; feminine form of the city AI (q.v.).

AID, ād (חָזַק, *ḥāzaḳ,* "to strengthen," "to aid"): A military term used only once in OT in AV (Jgs **9** 24) and displaced in RV by the lit. rendering, "who strengthened his hands." The men of Shechem supported Abimelech in his fratricidal crime, with money, enabling him to hire men to murder his brethren. The fundamental idea in the word, as used in the OT, is abounding *strength.*

AIJA, ȧ-ī′ja (עַיָּא, *'ayyā'*): A form of name for city Ai, found in Neh **11** 31. See AI; AIATH.

AIJALON, ā′ja-lon (אַיָּלוֹן, *'ayyālōn,* "deerplace"; AV **Ajalon** [Josh **10** 12]):

(1) The name of a town allotted to the tribe of Dan (Josh **19** 42), which was also designated a Levitical city (Josh **21** 24), which fell to the Sons of Kohath (1 Ch **6** 69). The first mention of Aijalon is in the narrative of Joshua's defeat of the five Amorite kings: "thou, Moon, in the valley of Aijalon" (Josh **10** 12). The Danites failed to take it from the

Valley of Aijalon.

Amorites (Jgs **1** 35), although the men of Ephraim held it in vassalage. Here Saul and Jonathan won a great victory over the Philistines (1 S **14** 31). At one time it was held by the tribe of Benjamin (1 Ch **8** 13). Rehoboam fortified it against the kingdom of Israel (2 Ch **11** 10). In the days of King Ahaz it was captured by the Philis (2 Ch **28** 18). It has been identified with the modern Yalo; its antiquity goes back to Am Tab, in which it has mention. It is situated N.W. of Jerus in a valley of the same name, which leads down from the mountains to the sea.

(2) A town in the tribe of Zebulun, site unknown, where Elon the judge was buried (Jgs **12** 12).

EDWARD MACK

AIJELETH HASH-SHAHAR, ā′je-leth hash-shā′har. See PSALMS; SONG.

AIL, āl (AS *eglan,* "to pain"): As a verb trans, is "to trouble," "afflict" (obs); intrans, "to feel pain, trouble, uneasiness," etc; it represents Heb *mah l^ekhā* "what to thee" (Gen **21** 17, "What aileth thee, Hagar?"; Jgs **18** 23; 1 S **11** 5; 2 S **14** 5; 2 K **6** 28; Isa **22** 1); in Ps **114** 5, it is figuratively or poetically applied to the sea, the river Jordan, etc: "What ailed thee, O thou sea, that thou fleddest?" etc; RV, "What aileth thee, O thou sea that thou fleest?" etc; in 2 Esd **9** 42; **10** 31, "What aileth thee?"

AIM, ām: In Wisd **13** 9. Lit. tr by AV of Gr **στοχάσασθαι,** *stochásasthai,* which commonly means "to shoot at." This is interpreted and explained by RV as "explore," with a hint as to the nature of the process, and may be paraphrased: "If they be able to *conjecture* the mysteries of the universe."

AIN. See AYIN.

AIN, ā′in (עַיִן, *'ayin,* "eye or spring [of water]"):

(1) A town in the extreme N.W. corner of Canaan, so named, most probably, from a noted spring in the vicinity (Nu **34** 11). Thomson and after him Robinson make Ain the same as *'Ain el-'Asy,* the chief source of the Orontes, some fifteen miles S.W. of Riblah, which, in turn, is about twenty miles S.W. of Emesa (Hums). As Ain is named in connection with Lake Gennesaret, some claim that Riblah of Nu **34** 11 must be another place farther S. and closer to that lake.

(2) A Levitical city (Josh **21** 16) in the Negeb or southern part of Judah. It was first allotted to the tribe of Judah (**15** 32) but later to Simeon (**19** 7). The fact that it is several times named in immediate connection with Rimmon has lent plausibility to the view that we have here a compound word, and that we should read En-Rimmon, i.e. Ain-Rimmon (see Josh **15** 32; **19** 7; 1 Ch **4** 32). See also AYIN. W. W. DAVIES

AIR, âr (**ἀήρ,** *aēr*): In the OT "air" is used (with one exception) in the phrase "fowl" or "fowls (birds) of the air." The Heb word is usually rendered "heaven" or "heavens." According to ancient Heb cosmogony the sky was a solid dome (firmament) stretching over the earth as a covering. In the above phrase the air means the space between the earth and the firmament. In Job (**41** 16) "air" renders רוּחַ, *rū^aḥ,* "breath," "wind," "spirit." The scales of the leviathan are so closely joined together that no air can penetrate. In the NT the phrase "birds [or fowls] of the air," occurs ten times. This simply reproduces the Hebraism noticed above. Apart from this expression "air" in the AV represents *aēr,* which denotes the atmosphere which surrounds us. The expression "beating the air" (1 Cor **9** 26) means to "deal blows that do not get home"—that miss the mark. In his conflict with the lower life represented by the body, Paul compares himself to a boxer who aims with unerring accuracy at his opponent. No stroke is lost. Paul also uses the phrase "speaking into the air" (1 Cor **14** 9) in reference to the unintelligible utterances of those who "spake with tongues." In the expression, "prince of the powers of the air" (Eph **2** 2 AV) we find an echo of the current belief that the air was the dwelling place of spirits, especially of evil spirits.

THOMAS LEWIS

AIRUS, ȧ-ī′rus, âr′us (**'Ιαίρος,** *Iaíros*): AV, one of the heads of a family of temple servants (1 Esd **5** 31 RV JAIRUS), which returned from Babylon with Zerubbabel; in the OT called Reaiah (Ezr **2** 47; Neh **7** 50), and classed among the *Nethinim.*

AJAH, ā′ja. An Edomite tribe (Gen **36** 24 AV). See AIAH.

AJALON, aj′a-lon. See AIJALON.

AKAN, ā′kan (עֲקָן, *'ăḳān,* "twisted"): A son of Ezer, a descendant of Esau of Seir (Gen **36** 27). He is called Jaakan in 1 Ch **1** 42. The AVm has **Jakan.**

AKATAN, ak′a-tan (**'Ακατάν,** *Akatán;* AV **Acatan** = Hakkatan; Ezr **8** 12): The father of Joannes who returned with Ezra to Jerus (1 Esd **8** 38).

AKELDAMA, a-kel′da-ma (**Ἀκελδαμά,** *Akeldamá,* or, in many MSS, **Ἀκελδαμάχ,** *Akeldamách;* AV **Aceldama**): A field said in Acts **1** 19 to have been bought by Judas with the "thirty pieces of silver." In Mt **27** 6.7 it is narrated that the priests took the silver pieces which Judas had "cast down . . . . into the sanctuary" and "bought with them the potter's field, to bury strangers in. Wherefore that field was called, The field of blood, unto this day." Doubtless it was a supposed connection between this potter's field and the potter's house (Jer **18** 2) and the Valley of the Son of Hinnom (Jer **19** 2) which influenced the selection of the present site which, like the Aram. הקלדמא (Dalman), is today known as *hakk-ed-dumm,* "field of blood."

Tradition, which appears to go back to the 4th cent., points to a level platform on, and some distance up, the southern slope of the *Wady er Rababi* (Valley of Hinnom) just before it joins the Kidron Valley. Upon this spot there is a very remarkable ruin (78 ft.×57 ft.) which for many centuries was used as a charnel house. The earth here was reputed to have the property of quickly consuming dead bodies. So great was its reputation that vast quantities of it are said to have been transported in 1215 AD to the Campo Santo at Pisa. When this building was standing entire, the bodies were lowered into it through five openings in the roof and then left to disintegrate, so that a few years ago there were very many feet of bones all over the floor. These have now been removed. A little S.E. of this ruin is a new Greek monastery erected in recent years over the remains of a large number of cave tombs; many of the bones from "Akeldama" are now buried here. E. W. G. MASTERMAN

AKKAD, ak′ad, **AKKADIANS,** a-kā′di-ans. See BABYLONIA.

AKKOS, ak′os (**Ἀκβώς,** *Akbōs* in 1 Esd **5** 38; AV **Accos,** which see): The OT equivalent (1 Ch **24** 10; Ezr **2** 61; Neh **3** 4.21) is HAKKOZ (הַקּוֹץ, *hakkōç*), which also see.

AKKUB, ak′ub (עַקּוּב, *'akkūbh,* "pursuer"): (1) A son of Elioenai, a descendant of Zerubbabel (1 Ch **3** 24). (2) A Levite porter on duty at the east gate of the second Temple (1 Ch **9** 17).

AKRABATTINE, ak-ra-ba-tī′nē (**Ἀκραβαττίνη,** *Akrabattínē;* AV **Arabattine**): A place in Idumaea where Judas Maccabee defeated the children of Esau (1 Macc **5** 3).

AKRABBIM, ak-rab′im (once in AV **Acrabbim** [Josh **15** 3]; עַקְרַבִּים, *'akrabbīm,* "scorpions"): Three times found (Nu **34** 4; Josh **15** 3; Jgs **1** 36), and always with מַעֲלֵה, *ma'ăleh,* "ascent" or "pass"; and so "Ascent of the Scorpions," an ascent at the S.W. point of the Dead Sea and a part of the boundary line between Judah and Edom. At this pass Judas Maccabaeus won a victory over the Edomites (1 Macc **5** 3), called in the AV Arabattine.

ALABASTER, al′a-bas-tẽr (**ἀλάβαστρον,** *alábastron* [Mt **26** 7; Mk **14** 3; Lk **7** 37]): In modern mineralogy alabaster is crystalline gypsum or sulphate of lime. The Gr word *alabastron* or *alabastos* meant a stone casket or vase, and *alabastites* was used for the stone of which the casket was made. This stone was usually crystalline stalagmitic rock or carbonate of lime, now often called oriental alabaster, to distinguish it from gypsum. The word occurs in the Bible only in the three passages of the Synoptic Gospels cited above. See Box.

ALAMETH, al′a-meth (עָלָמֶת, *'ālāmeth,* "concealment"; 1 Ch **7** 8 AV): The name of a son of Becher and grandson of Benjamin. His name was preserved as the name of a town near Anathoth (ALLEMETH, 1 Ch **6** 60 RV). Except for the strong pausal accent in the Heb the form of the word would be the same as ALEMETH (q.v.).

ALAMMELECH, a-lam′e-lek: AV (Josh **19** 26) for ALLAMMELECH (q.v.).

ALAMOTH, al′a-mōth. See MUSIC.

ALARM, a-lärm′ (תְּרוּעָה, *t*^e^*rū'āh*): This expression is found six times in the OT. The Heb word so rendered is derived from a verb meaning "to shout" or "blow a horn," as a signal for breaking up camp, starting on a journey or into battle, or in triumphant shout over the defeat of enemies. In a few instances it is employed of a cry of despair or distress. The noun *t*^e^*rū'āh* translated "alarm" in Nu **10** 5 f refers to the signal given the people of Israel to start on their journey in the Wilderness. The passages in Jer (**4** 19; **49** 2) both refer to the summons for war. The same is true of Zeph **1** 16.

The law concerning the sounding of the alarm is fully stated in Nu **10** 1–10 Here we read that two silver trumpets of beaten work were sounded by the sons of Aaron in case of war and also "in the day of . . . . gladness" to gather the people together for the various feasts, new moons, sacrifices and offerings. W. W. DAVIES

ALBEIT, ôl-bē′it (**ἵνα μή,** *hína mḗ;* lit. "lest"): Occurs in a paraphrase rather than as a tr of a clause in Philem 19 AV. The thought is: "although" or "albeit" (synonym of "although") "I might say," etc. This RV translates with intense literalness: "that I say not."

ALCIMUS, al′si-mus (אֶלְיָקִים, *'elyāķūm,* "God will rise"; **Ἄλκιμος,** *Álkimos,* "valiant"): A high priest for three years, 163–161 BC, the record of whose career may be found in 1 Macc **7** 4–50; **9** 1–57; 2 Macc **14**; see also *Ant,* XII, 9–11; XX, 10. He was a descendant of Aaron, but not in the high-priestly line (1 Macc **7** 14; also *Ant,* XX, 10); and being ambitious for the office of high priest, he hastened to Antioch to secure the favor and help of the new king, Demetrius, who had just overthrown Antiochus Eupator and made himself king. Alcimus was of the Grecianizing party, and therefore bitterly opposed by the Maccabees. Demetrius sent a strong army under Bacchides to establish him in the high-priesthood at Jerus. The favor with which Alcimus was received by the Jews at Jerus on account of his Aaronic descent was soon turned to hate by his cruelties. When Bacchides and his army returned to Antioch, Simon Maccabaeus attacked and overcame Alcimus, and drove him also to Syria. There he secured from Demetrius another army, led by Nicanor, who, failing to secure Simon by treachery, joined battle with him, but was defeated and killed. A third and greater army, under Bacchides again, was dispatched to save the falling fortunes of Alcimus. Now Simon was overwhelmed and slain, Alcimus established as high priest and a strong force left in Jerus to uphold him. But he did not long enjoy his triumph, as he died soon after from a paralytic stroke. EDWARD MACK

ALCOVE, al′kōv (קֻבָּה, *kubbāh;* AV **tent;** ARV pavilion; ARVm alcove): Perhaps a large tent occupied by a prince (Nu **25** 8).

ALEMA, al′ē-ma (**Ἀλέμοις,** *Alémois*): A town in Gilead, mentioned once only (1 Macc **5** 26), besieged by the nations under Timotheus, together with Bosor and other cities; and probably relieved along with these cities by Judas Maccabaeus, although no mention is made of Alema's relief. The name occurs the one time as dative pl.

ALEMETH, al'ē-meth (עָלֶמֶת, *'ālemeth,* "concealment"): (1) RV for Alameth of the AV in 1 Ch **7** 8. (2) Descendant of Saul and Jonathan, and son of Jehoaddah, 1 Ch **8** 36, or of Jarah, 1 Ch **9** 42. The genealogies in the two chapters are identical, and he is the fifth generation after Jonathan. (3) In some Heb texts, Ginsburg and Baer, for ALLEMETH (q.v.); so in AV.

ALEPH, ä'lef (א, '): The first letter of the Heb alphabet. It is nearly soundless itself and best represented, as in this Enc, by the smooth breathing ('), but it is the direct ancestor of the Gr, Lat and Eng. *a* as in "father." In either case this beginning of the alphabet happens to be near the very basis of all speech—in one case the simple expiration of breath, in the other the simplest possible vocal action—the actual basis from which all other vowels are evolved. It became also the symbol for the number one (1) and, with the dieresis, 1,000. It is the symbol also for one of the most famous of Gr Biblical MSS, the Codex Sinaiticus. For name, written form, etc, see ALPHABET.

E. C. RICHARDSON

ALEPPO, a-lep'ō. See BEREA.

ALEXANDER, al-eg-zan'dẽr (Ἀλέξανδρος, *Aléxandros,* lit. meaning "defender of men." This word occurs five times in the NT, Mk **15** 21; Acts **4** 6; **19** 33; 1 Tim **1** 19.20; 2 Tim **4** 14): It is not certain whether the third, fourth and fifth of these passages refer to the same man.

1. A Son of Simon of Cyrene

(1) The first of these Alexanders is referred to in the passage in Mk, where he is said to have been one of the sons of Simon of Cyrene, the man who carried the cross of Christ. Alexander therefore may have been a North African by birth. Mt, Mk and Lk all record the fact, with varying detail, that Simon happened to be passing at the time when Christ was being led out of the city, to be crucified on Calvary. Mk alone tells that Simon was the father of Alexander and Rufus. From this statement of the evangelist, it is apparent that at the time the Second Gospel was written, Alexander and Rufus were Christians, and that they were well known in the Christian community. Mk takes it for granted that the first readers of his Gospel will at once understand whom he means.

There is no other mention of Alexander in the NT, but it is usually thought that his brother Rufus is the person mentioned by Paul in Rom **16** 13, "Salute Rufus the chosen in the Lord, and his mother and mine." If this identification is correct, then it follows, not only that the sons of Simon were Christians, but that his wife also was a Christian, and that they had all continued faithful to Christ for many years. It would also follow that the households were among the intimate friends of Paul, so much so that the mother of the family is affectionately addressed by him as "Rufus' mother and mine." The meaning of this is, that in time past this lady had treated Paul with the tender care which a mother feels and shows to her own son.

This mention of Rufus and his mother is in the list of names of Christians resident in Rome. Lightfoot (*Comm. on Phil,* 176) writes: "There seems no reason to doubt the tradition that Mk wrote especially for the Romans; and if so, it is worth remarking that he alone of the evangelists describes Simon of Cyrene, as 'the father of Alexander and Rufus.' A person of this name therefore (Rufus) seems to have held a prominent place among the Rom Christians; and thus there is at least fair ground for identifying the Rufus of St. Paul with the Rufus of St. Mark. The inscriptions exhibit several members of the household (of the emperor) bearing the names Rufus and Alexander, but this fact is of no value where both names are so common."

To sum up, Alexander was probably by birth a North African Jew; he became a Christian, and was a well-known member of the church, probably the church in Rome. His chief claim to recollection is that he was a son of the man who carried the cross of the Saviour of the world.

2. A Relative of Annas

(2) The second Alexander, referred to in Acts **4** 6, was a relative of Annas the Jewish high priest. He is mentioned by Lk, as having been present as a member of the Sanhedrin, before which Peter and Jn were brought to be examined, for what they had done in the cure of the lame man at the gate of the temple. Nothing more is known of this Alexander than is here given by Lk. It has been conjectured that he may have been the Alexander who was a brother of Philo, and who was also the alabarch or magistrate of the city of Alexandria. But this conjecture is unsupported by any evidence at all.

3. Alexander and the Riot at Ephesus

(3) The third Alexander is mentioned in Acts **19** 33: "And some of the multitude instructed Alexander, the Jews putting him forward. And Alexander beckoned with the hand, and would have made a defence unto the people. But when they perceived that he was a Jew, all with one voice," etc, RVm. In the matter of the riot in Ephesus the whole responsibility rested with Demetrius the silversmith. In his anger against the Christians generally, but specially against Paul, because of his successful preaching of the gospel, he called together a meeting of the craftsmen; the trade of the manufacture of idols was in jeopardy. From this meeting there arose the riot, in which the whole city was in commotion. The Jews were wholly innocent in the matter: they had done nothing to cause any disturbance. But the riot had taken place, and no one could tell what would happen. Modern anti-Semitism, in Russia and other European countries, gives an idea of an excited mob stirred on by hatred of the Jews. Instantly recognizing that the fury of the Ephesian people might expend itself in violence and bloodshed, and that in that fury they would be the sufferers, the Jews "put forward" Alexander, so that by his skill as a speaker he might clear them, either of having instigated the riot, or of being in complicity with Paul. "A certain Alexander was put forward by the Jews to address the mob; but this merely increased the clamor and confusion. There was no clear idea among the rioters what they wanted: an anti-Jewish and an anti-Christian demonstration were mixed up, and probably Alexander's intention was to turn the general feeling away from the Jews. It is possible that he was the worker in bronze, who afterward did Paul much harm" (Ramsay, *St. Paul the Traveller,* etc, 279).

4. Alexander an Ephesian Heretic

(4) The fourth of the NT Alexanders is one of two heretical teachers at Ephesus—the other being Hymenaeus: see art. s.v.—against whom Paul warns Timothy in 1 Tim **1** 19.20. The teaching of Hymenaeus and Alexander was to the effect that Christian morality was not required—antinomianism. They put away—"thrust from them," RV—faith and a good con-

science; they wilfully abandoned the great central facts regarding Christ, and so they made shipwreck concerning the faith.

5. His Heresy Incipient Gnosticism

In 2 Tim **2** 17.18, Hymenaeus is associated with Philetus, and further details are there given regarding their false teaching. What they taught is described by Paul as "profane babblings," as leading to more ungodliness, and as eating "as doth a gangrene." Their heresy consisted in saying that the resurrection was past already, and it had been so far successful, that it had overthrown the faith of some. The doctrine of these three heretical teachers, Hymenaeus, Alexander and Philetus, was accordingly one of the early forms of Gnosticism. It held that matter was originally and essentially evil; that for this reason the body was not an essential part of human nature; that the only resurrection was that of each man as he awoke from the death of sin to a righteous life; that thus in the case of everyone who has repented of sin, "the resurrection was past already," and that the body did not participate in the blessedness of the future life, but that salvation consisted in the soul's complete deliverance from all contact with a material world and a material body.

So pernicious were these teachings of incipient Gnosticism in the Christian church, that they quickly spread, eating like a gangrene. The denial of the future resurrection of the body involved also the denial of the bodily resurrection of Christ, and even the fact of the incarnation. The way in which therefore the apostle dealt with those who taught such deadly error, was that he resorted to the same extreme measures as he had employed in the case of the immoral person at Corinth; he delivered Hymenaeus and Alexander to Satan, that they might learn not to blaspheme. Cf 1 Cor **5** 5.

6. Alexander the Coppersmith

(5) The fifth and last occurrence of the name Alexander is in 2 Tim **4** 14.15, "Alexander the coppersmith did me much evil: the Lord will render to him according to his works: of whom do thou also beware [AV "of whom be thou ware also"]; for he greatly withstood our words." This Alexander was a worker in copper or iron, a smith. It is quite uncertain whether Alexander no. 5 should be identified with A. no. 4, and even with A. no. 3. In regard to this, it should be remembered that all three of these Alexanders were resident in Ephesus; and it is specially to be noticed that the fourth and the fifth of that name resided in that city at much the same time; the interval between Paul's references to these two being not more than a year or two, as not more than that time elapsed between his writing 1 Tim and 2 Tim. It is therefore quite possible these two Alexanders may be one and the same person.

In any case, what is said of this last A. is that he had shown the evil which was in him by doing many evil deeds to the apostle, evidently on the occasion of a recent visit paid by Paul to Ephesus. These evil deeds had taken the form of personally opposing the apostle's preaching. The personal antagonism of Alexander manifested itself by his greatly withstanding the proclamation of the gospel by Paul. As Timothy was now in Ephesus, in charge of the church there, he is strongly cautioned by the apostle to be on his guard against this opponent.

John Rutherfurd

ALEXANDER BALAS, A. bā'las (**'Αλέξανδρος ὁ Βάλας λεγόμενος,** *Aléxandros ho Bálas legómenos*): He contended against Demetrius I of Syria for the throne and succeeded in obtaining it. He was a youth of mean origin, but he was put forth by the enemies of Demetrius as being Alexander, the son and heir of Antiochus Epiphanes. He received the support of the Rom Senate and of Ptolemy VI of Egypt, and on account of the tyranny of Demetrius, was favored by many of the Syrians. The country was thrown into civil war and Demetrius was defeated by Alexander in 150 BC and was killed in battle. Demetrius II took up the cause of his father and in 147 BC, Alexander fled from his kingdom and was soon after assassinated.

Our chief interest in Alexander is his connection with the Maccabees. Jonathan was the leader of the Maccabean forces and both Alexander and Demetrius sought his aid. Demetrius granted Jonathan the right to raise and maintain an army. Alexander, not to be outdone, appointed Jonathan high priest, and as a token of his new office sent him a purple robe and a diadem (*Ant*, XIII, ii, 2). This was an important step in the rise of the Maccabean house, for it insured them the support of the Chasidim. In 153 BC, Jonathan officiated as high priest at the altar (1 Macc **10** 1–14; *Ant*, XIII, ii, 1). This made him the legal head of Judaea and thus the movement of the Maccabees became closely identified with Judaism. In 1 Macc **10** 1, he is called Alexander Epiphanes.

Tetradrachm (Ptolemaic talent) of Alexander Balas.

A. W. Fortune

ALEXANDER, THE GREAT (**'Αλέξανδρος,** *Aléxandros*):

1. Parentage and Early Life

Alexander, of Macedon, commonly called "the Great" (b. 356 BC), was the son of Philip, king of Macedon, and of Olympias, daughter of Neoptolemos, an Epeirote king. Although Alexander is not mentioned by name in the canonical Scriptures, in Dnl he is designated by a transparent symbol (**8** 5.21). In 1 Macc **1** 1 he is expressly named as the overthrower of the Pers empire, and the founder of that of the Greeks. As with Frederick the Great, the career of Alexander would have been impossible had his father been other than he was. Philip had been for some years a hostage in Thebes: while there he had learned to appreciate the changes introduced into military discipline and tactics by Epaminondas. Partly no doubt from the family claim to Heracleid descent, deepened by contact in earlier days with Athenians like Iphicrates, and the personal influence of Epaminondas, Philip seems to have united to his admiration for Gr tactics a tincture of Hel culture, and something like a reverence for Athens, the great center of this culture. In military matters his admiration led him to introduce the Theban discipline to the rough peasant levies of Macedon, and the Macedonian phalanx proved the most formidable military weapon that had yet been devised. The veneer of Gr culture which he had taken on led him, on the one hand, laying stress on his Hel descent, to claim admission to the comity of Hellas, and on the other, to appoint Aristotle to be a tutor to his son. By a combination of force and fraud, favored by circumstances, Philip got himself appointed generalissimo of the Hel states;

and further induced them to proclaim war against the "Great King." In all this he was preparing the way for his son, so soon to be his successor.

2. His Preparation for His Career

He was also preparing his son for his career. Alexander was, partly no doubt from being the pupil of Aristotle, yet more imbued with Gr feelings and ideas than was his father. He was early introduced into the cares of government and the practice of war. While Philip was engaged in the siege of Byzantium he sent his son to replace Antipater in the regency; during his occupancy of this post, Alexander, then only a youth of sixteen, had to undertake a campaign against the Illyrians, probably a punitive expedition. Two years later, at the decisive battle of Chaeroneia, which fixed the doom of the Gr autonomous city, Alexander commanded the feudal cavalry of Macedon, the "Companions." He not only saved his father's life, but by his timely and vehement charge materially contributed to the victory.

3. His Accession to the Hegemony of Greece

When all his plans for the invasion of Persia were complete, and a portion of his troops was already across the Hellespont, Philip was assassinated. Having secured his succession, Alexander proceeded to Corinth, where he was confirmed in his father's position of leader of Hellas against Darius. Before he could cross into Asia he had to secure his northern frontier against possible raids of barbarian tribes. He invaded Thrace with his army and overthrew the Triballi, then crossed the Danube and inflicted a defeat on the Getae. During his absence in these but slightly known regions, the rumor spread that he had been killed, and Thebes began a movement to throw off the Macedonian yoke. On his return to Greece he wreaked terrible vengeance on Thebes, not only as promoter of this revolt, but also as the most powerful of the Gr states.

4. Campaign in Asia Minor

Having thus secured his rear, Alexander collected his army at Pella to cross the Hellespont, that he might exact the vengeance of Greece on Persia for indignities suffered at the hands of Xerxes, who "by his strength through his riches" had stirred up "all against the realm of Grecia" (Dnl **11** 2 AV). Steeped as he was in the romance of the *Iliad*, Alexander, when he came to the site of Troy, honored Achilles, whom he claimed as his ancestor, with games and sacrifices. This may have been the outflow of his own romantic nature, but there was also wise policy in it; the Greeks were more readily reconciled to the loss of their freedom when it was yielded up to one who revived in his own person the heroes of the *Iliad*. It may be noted how exactly the point of Alexander's invasion is indicated in Daniel's prophecy (**8** 5). From Troy he advanced southward, and encountered the Pers forces at the Granicus. While in the conflict Alexander exhibited all the reckless bravery of a Homeric hero. He at the same time showed the skill of a consummate general. The Pers army was dispersed with great slaughter. Before proceeding farther into Persia, by rapid marches and vigorously pressed sieges, he completed the conquest of Asia Minor. Here, too, he showed his knowledge of the sensitiveness of Asiatic peoples to omens, by visiting Gordium, and cutting the knot on which, according to legend, depended the empire of Asia.

What he had done in symbol he had to make a reality; he had to settle the question of supremacy in Asia by the sword. He learned that Darius had collected an immense army and was coming to meet him. Although the Pers host was estimated at a half-million men, Alexander hastened to encounter it. Rapidity of motion, as symbolized

5. Battle of Issus and March through Syria to Egypt

in Dnl by the "he-goat" that "came from the west . . . . and touched not the ground" (Dnl **8** 5), was Alexander's great characteristic. The two armies met in the relatively narrow plain of Issus, where the Persians lost, to a great extent, the advantage of their numbers; they were defeated with tremendous slaughter, Darius himself setting the example of flight. Alexander only pursued the defeated army far enough to break it up utterly. He began his march southward along the seacoast of Syria toward Egypt, a country that had always impressed the Gr imagination. Though most of the cities, on his march, opened their gates to the conqueror, Tyre and Gaza only yielded after a prolonged siege. In the case of the latter of these, enraged at the delay occasioned by the resistance, and emulous of his ancestor, Alexander dragged its gallant defender Batis alive behind his chariot as Achilles had dragged the dead Hector. It ought to be noted that this episode does not appear in Arrian, usually regarded as the most authentic historian of Alexander. Josephus relates that after he had taken Gaza, Alexander went up to Jerus, and saw Jaddua the high priest, who showed him the prophecy of Daniel concerning him. The fact that none of the classic historians take any notice of such a détour renders the narrative doubtful: still it contains no element of improbability that the pupil of Aristotle, in the pursuit of knowledge, might, during the prosecution of the siege of Gaza, with a small company press into the hill country of Judaea, at once to secure the submission of Jerusalem which occupied a threatening position in regard to his communications, and to see something of that mysterious nation who worshipped one God and had no idols.

6. Founding of Alexandria and Visit to the Shrine of Jupiter Ammon

When he entered Egypt, the whole country submitted without a struggle. Moved at once by the fact that Pharos is mentioned in the *Odyssey*, and that he could best rule Egypt from the seacoast, he founded Alexandria on the strip of land opposite Pharos, which separated Lake Mareotis from the Mediterranean. The island Pharos formed a natural breakwater which made possible a spacious double harbor; the lake, communicating with the Nile, opened the way for inland navigation. As usual with Alexander, romance and policy went hand in hand. The city thus founded became the capital of the Ptolemies, and the largest city of the Hel world. He spent his time visiting shrines, in the intervals of arranging for the government of the country. The most memorable event of his stay in Egypt was his expedition to the oracle of Jupiter Ammon (Amen-Ra) where he was declared the son of the god. To the Egyptians this meant no more than that he was regarded a lawful monarch, but he pretended to take this declaration as assigning to him a Divine origin like so many Homeric heroes. Henceforward there appeared on coins Alexander's head adorned with the ram's horn of Amen-Ra. This impressed the eastern imagination so deeply that Mohammed, a thousand years after, calls him in the Quran *Iskander dhu al-qarnain*, "Alexander the lord of the two horns." It is impossible to believe that the writer of Dnl could, in the face of the universal attribution of the two ram's horns to Alexander, represent Persia, the power he overthrew, as a two-horned ram (Dnl **8** 3.20), unless he had written before the expedition into Egypt.

7. The Last Battle with Darius

Having arranged the affairs of Egypt, Alexander set out for his last encounter with Darius. In vain had Darius sent to Alexander offering to share the empire with him; the "king of Javan" (RVm) "was moved with anger against him" (Dnl **8** 7) and would have nothing but absolute submission. There was nothing left for Darius but to prepare for the final conflict. He collected a yet huger host than that he had had under him at Issus, and assembled it on the plain east of the Tigris. Alexander hastened to meet him. Although the plain around Gaugamela was much more suitable for the movements of the Pers troops, which consisted largely of cavalry, and gave them better opportunity of making use of their great numerical superiority to outflank the small Gr army, the result was the same as at Issus—overwhelming defeat and immense slaughter. The consequence of this victory was the submission of the greater portion of the Pers empire.

After making some arrangements for the government of the new provinces, Alexander set out in the pursuit of Darius, who had fled in the care or custody of Bessus, satrap of Bactria. Bessus, at last, to gain the favor of Alexander, or, failing that, to maintain a more successful resistance, murdered Darius. Alexander hurried on to the conquest of Bactria and Sogdiana, in the course of his expedition capturing Bessus and putting him to death. In imitation of Bacchus, he proceeded now to invade India. He conquered all before him till he reached the Sutlej; at this point his Macedonian veterans refused to follow him farther.

8. Close of His Life

Thus compelled to give up hopes of conquests in the farther East, he returned to Babylon, which he purposed to make the supreme capital of his empire, and set himself, with all his superabundant energy, to organize his dominions, and fit Babylon for its new destiny. While engaged in this work he was seized with malaria, which, aggravated by his recklessness in eating and drinking, carried him off in his 33d year.

9. His Influence

Alexander is not to be estimated merely as a military conqueror. If he had been only this, he would have left no deeper impress on the world than Tamerlane or Attila. While he conquered Asia, he endeavored also to Hellenize her. He everywhere founded Gr cities that enjoyed at all events a municipal autonomy. With these, Hel thought and the Hel language were spread all over southwestern Asia, so that philosophers from the banks of the Euphrates taught in the schools of Athens. It was through the conquests of Alexander that Gr became the language of literature and commerce from the shores of the Mediterranean to the banks of the Tigris. It is impossible to estimate the effect of this spread of Gr on the promulgation of the gospel. J. E. H. Thomson

ALEXANDRIA, al-eg-zan′dri-a (**ἡ Ἀλεξάνδρεια,** *hē Alexándreia*):

1. History

In 331 BC, Alexander the Great, on his way to visit the Oracle of Amon seeking divine honors, stopped at the W. extremity of the Delta at the isle of Pharos the landing-place of Odysseus (*Od.* iv.35) His keen eye noted the strategic possibilities of the site occupied by the little Egyptian village of Rhacotis, and his decision was immediate to erect here, where it would command the gateway to the richest domain of his empire, a glorious city to be called by his own name. Deinocrates, greatest living architect, already famous as builder of the Temple of Diana, was given free hand and like a dream the most beautiful city of the ancient or modern world (with the single exception of Rome) arose with straight, parallel streets—one at least 200 feet wide—with fortresses, monuments, palaces, government buildings and parks all erected according to a perfect artistic plan. The city was about fifteen miles in circumference (Pliny), and when looked at from above represented a Macedonian cloak, such as was worn by Alexander's heroic ancestors. A colossal mole joined the island to the main land and made a double harbor, the best in all Egypt. Before Alexander died (323 BC) the future of the city as the commercial metropolis of the world was assured and here the golden casket of the conqueror was placed in a fitting mausoleum. Under the protection of the first two Ptolemies and Euergetes A. reached its highest prosperity, receiving through Lake Mareotis the products of Upper Egypt, reaching by the Great Sea all the wealth of the West, while through the Red Sea its merchant vessels brought all the treasures of India and Arabia into the A. docks without once being unladen. The manufactories of A. were extensive, the greatest industry however being shipbuilding, the largest merchant ships of the world and battleships capable of carrying 1,000 men, which could hurl fire with fearful effect, being constructed here. This position of supremacy was maintained during the Rom domination up to the 5th cent. during which A. began to decline. Yet even when A. was captured by the Arabs (641) under the caliph Omar, the general could report: "I have taken a city containing 4,000 palaces and 4,000 baths and 400 theaters." They called it a "city of marble" and believed the colossal obelisks, standing on crabs of crystal, and the Pharos, that white stone tower 400 ft. high, "wonder of the world," to be the creation of *jinn*, not of men. With oriental exaggeration they declared that one amphitheater could easily hold a million spectators and that it was positively painful to go upon the streets at night because of the glare of light reflected from the white palaces. But with the coming of the Arabs A. began to decline. It sank lower when Cairo became the capital (cir 1000 AD), and received its death blow when a sea route to India was discovered by way of the Cape of Good Hope (cir 1500). Today the ancient A. lies entirely under the sea or beneath some later construction. Only one important relic remains visible, the so-called Pompey's Pillar which dates from the reign of Diocletian. Excavations by the English (1895) and Germans (1898–99) have yielded few results, though Dr. G. Botti discovered the Serapeum and some immense catacombs, and only recently (1907) some fine sphinxes. In its most flourishing period the population numbered from 600,000 to 800,000, half of whom were perhaps slaves. At the close of the 18th cent. it numbered no more than 7,000. Under the khedives it has recently gained something of its old importance and numbers now 320,000, of whom 46,000 are Europeans, chiefly Greeks (Baedeker, *Handbook*, 1902; Murray, *Handbook*, 1907).

2. The Jews in Alexandria

Among the private papers of Alexander it is said a sketch was found outlining his vast plan of making a Greek empire which should include all races as harmonious units. In accordance with this, Europeans, Asiatics and Africans found in A. a common citizenship. Indeed in several cities, under the Ptolemies, who accepted this policy, foreigners were even given superiority to natives. Egyptians and Greeks were conciliated by the introduction of a syncretic religion in which the greatest Gr god was worshipped as Osiris, Egyp god of the underworld, whose soul appeared visibly in the form of the Apis bull. This was the most popular and human form of the Egyp worship. This new religion obtained phenomenal success. It was in furtherance of this general policy that the Jews in A. were given special privileges, and though probably not possessing full civic rights, yet they "occupied in A. a more influential position than anywhere else in the ancient world" (*Jew Enc*). To avoid unnecessary friction a separate district was given to the Jews, another to the Greeks and another to the native Egyptians. In the Gr section were situated the palaces of the Ptolemies, the Library and Museum. In the Egyp district was the temple dedicated to Serapis (Osiris-Apis) which was only excelled in grandeur by the capitol at Rome. The Jews possessed many synagogues in their own district and in Philo's day these were not confined to any one section of the city. Some synagogues seem to have exercised the right of asylum, the same as heathen temples. One of these was so large that the *hazan* signaled by a flag when the congregation should give the Amen! Each district had a practically independent political government. The Jews were at first ruled by a Heb ethnarch. By the days of Augustus a Council of Elders (*gerusia*) had control, presided over by 71 archons. Because of their wealth, education and social position they reached high public office. Under Ptol. VI and Cleopatra the two generals-in-chief of the royal army were Jews. Ptol. I had 30,000 Jewish soldiers in his army, whose barracks have only recently been discovered. It may have been a good thing that the persecution of Antiochus Epiphanes (2d cent. BC) checked Jewish Hellenization. During the Rom supremacy the rights of the Jews were maintained, except during their persecution for a brief period by the insane Caligula, and the control of the most important industries, including the corn trade, came into their hands. When Christianity became the state religion of Egypt the Jews at once began to be persecuted. The victory of Heraclius over the Persians (629 AD) was followed by such a massacre of the Jews that the Copts of Egypt still denominate the first week in Lent as the "Fast of Heraclius." Wisd and many other influential writings of the Jews originated in A. Doubtless numbers of the recently discovered documents from the Cairo g^{e}nīzāh came originally from A. But the epochal importance of A. is found in the teaching which prepared the Heb people for the reception of a gospel for the whole world, which was soon to be preached by Hebrews from Hellenized Galilee.

3. Alexandria's Influence on the Bible

(1) In Dnl **11** the Ptolemies of A. and their wives are made a theme of prophecy. Apollos, the "orator," was born in A. (Acts **18** 24). Luke twice speaks of himself and Paul sailing in "a ship of A." (Acts **27** 6; **28** 11). Stephen 'disputed' in Jerusalem in the synagogue of the Alexandrians (Acts **6** 9). These direct references are few, but the influence of A. on the Bible was inestimable.

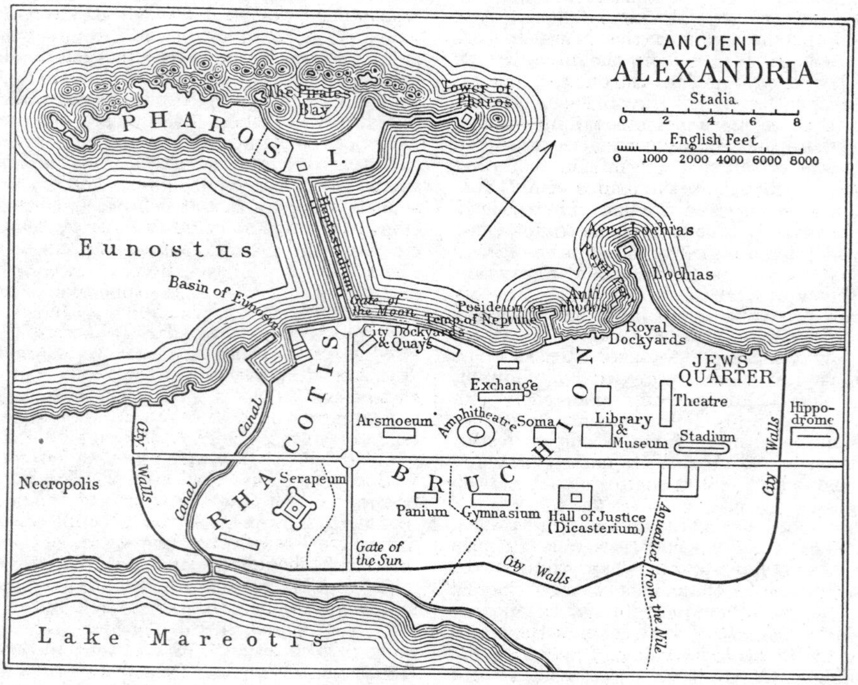

(2) The Sept, tr^{d} in A. (3d to 2d cent. BC), preserves a Heb text 1,000 years older than any now known. This tr if not used by Jesus was certainly used by Paul and other NT writers, as shown by their quotations. It is Egyp even in trifles. This Gr Bible not only opened for the first time the "Divine Oracles" to the Gentiles and thus gave to the OT an international influence, but it affected most vitally the Heb and Christian development.

(3) The Alex Codex (4th to 5th cent.) was the first of all the great uncials to come into the hands of modern scholars. It was obtained in A. and sent as a present to the king of England (1628) by Cyrellus Lucaris, the Patriarch of Constantinople. The Sin and Vatican uncials with many other most important Bible MSS—Heb, Gr, Coptic and Syr—came from A.

(4) Jn and several other NT writings have justly been regarded as showing the influence of this philosophic city. Neither the phraseology nor conceptions of the Fourth Gospel could have been grasped in a world which A. had not taught. Pfleiderer's statement that He "may be termed the most

finished treatise of the A. philosophy" may be doubted, but no one can doubt the fact of Alex influence on the NT.

4. Influence of Alexandria on Culture

With the founding of the University of A. began the "third great epoch in the history of civilization" (Max Müller). It was modeled after the great school of Athens, but excelled, being preëminently the "university of progress" (Mahaffy). Here for the first time is seen a school of science and literature, adequately endowed and offering large facilities for definite original research. The famous library which at different eras was reported as possessing from 400,000 to 900,000 books and rolls—the rolls being as precious as the books—was a magnificent edifice connected by marble colonnades with the Museum, the "Temple of the Muses." An observatory, an anatomical laboratory and large botanical and zoölogical gardens were available. Celebrated scholars, members of the various faculties, were domiciled within the halls of the Museum and received stipends or salaries from the government. The study of mathematics, astronomy, poetry and medicine was especially favored (even vivisection upon criminals being common); Alex architects were sought the world over; Alex inventors were almost equally famous; the influence of Alex art can still be marked in Pompeii and an Alex painter was a hated rival of Apelles. Here Euclid wrote his *Elements of Geometry;* here Archimedes, "that greatest mathematical and inventive genius of antiquity," made his spectacular discoveries in hydrostatics and hydraulics; here Eratosthenes calculated the size of the earth and made his other memorable discoveries; while Ptolemy studied here for 40 years and published an explanation of the stellar universe which was accepted by scientists for 14 cents., and established mathematical theories which are yet the basis of trigonometry. "Ever since this epoch the conceptions of the sphericity of the earth, its poles, axis, the equator, the arctic and antarctic circles, the equinoctial points, the solstices, the inequality of climate on the earth's surface, have been current notions among scientists. The mechanism of the lunar phases was perfectly understood, and careful though not wholly successful calculations were made of inter-sidereal distances. On the other hand literature and art flourished under the careful protection of the court. Literature and its history, philology and criticism became sciences" (A. Weber). It may be claimed that in literature no special originality was displayed though the earliest "love stories" and pastoral poetry date from this period (Mahaffy); yet the literature of the Augustan Age cannot be understood "without due appreciation of the character of the Alex school" (*EB*, 11th ed), while in editing texts and in copying and translating MSS inconceivable patience and erudition were displayed. Our authorized texts of Homer and other classic writers come from A. not from Athens. All famous books brought into Egypt were sent to the library to be copied. The statement of Jos that Ptolemy Philadelphus (285–247) requested the Jews to translate the OT into Gr is not incredible. It was in accordance with the custom of that era. Ptol. Euergetes is said to have sent to Athens for the works of Aeschylus, Sophocles, Euripides, etc, and when these were transcribed, sent back beautiful copies to Greece and kept the originals! No library in the world excepting the prophetic library in Jerusalem was ever as valuable as the two Alex libraries. The story that the Arabs burned it in the 7th cent. is discredited and seemingly disproved (Butler). At any rate after this period we hear of great private libraries in A., but the greatest literary wonder of the world has disappeared.

5. Influence on Philosophy

Though no department of philosophy was established in the Museum, nevertheless from the 3d cent. BC to the 6th cent. AD it was the center of gravity in the philosophic world. Here Neo-Pythagoreanism arose. Here Neo-Platonism, that contemplative and mystical reaction against the materialism of the Stoics, reached its full flower. It is difficult to overestimate the influence of the latter upon religious thought. In it the profoundest Aryan speculations were blended with the sublimest Sem concepts. Plato was numbered among the prophets. Greece here acknowledged the Divine Unity to which the OT was pledged. Here the Jew acknowledged that Athens as truly as Jerusalem had taught a vision of God. This was the first attempt to form a universal religion. The Alex philosophy was the Elijah to prepare the way for a Saviour of the world. The thought of both Sadducee and Pharisee was affected by it and much late pre-Christian Jewish lit. is saturated with it. Neo-Platonism drew attention to the true relation between matter and spirit, good and evil, finite and infinite; it showed the depth of antagonism between the natural and spiritual, the real and ideal; it proclaimed the necessity of some mystic union between the human and the Divine. It stated but could not solve the problem. Its last word was escape, not reconciliation (Ed. Caird). Neo-Platonism was the "germ out of which Christian theology sprang" (Caird) though later it became an adverse force. Notwithstanding its dangerous teaching concerning evil, it was on the whole favorable to piety, being the forerunner of mysticism and sympathetic with the deepest, purest elements of a spiritual religion.

6. Christian Church in Alexandria

According to all tradition St. Mark, the evangelist, carried the gospel to A., and his body rested here until removed to Venice, 828 AD. From this city Christianity reached all Egypt and entered Nubia, Ethiopia and Abyssinia. During the 4th cent. ten councils were held in A., it being the theological and ecclesiastical center of Christendom. The first serious persecution of Christians by heathen occurred here under Decius (251) and was followed by many others, the one under Diocletian (303–11) being so savage that the native Coptic church still dates its era from it. When the Christians reached political power they used the same methods of controversy, wrecking the Caesarion in 366 and the Serapeum twenty-five years later. Serapis (Osiris-Apis) was the best beloved of all the native deities. His temple was built of most precious marbles and filled with priceless sculptures, while in its cloisters was a library second only to the Great Library of the Museum. When Christianity became the state religion of Egypt the native philosophers, moved by patriotism, rallied to the support of Serapis. But Theodosius (391) prohibited idolatry, and led by the bishop, the Serapeum was seized, and smitten by a soldier's battle-axe, the image—which probably represented the old heathen religion at its best—was broken to pieces, and dragged through the streets. That day, as Steindorff well puts it, "Egyp paganism received its death blow; the Egyp religion fell to pieces" (*History of Egypt*). Thereafter heathen worship hid itself in the dens and caves of the earth. Even secret allegiance to Serapis brought persecution and sometimes death. The most appalling tragedy of this kind occurred in 415 when Hypatia, the virgin philosopher, celebrated equally for beauty, virtue and learning, was dragged by a mob to the cathedral, stripped, and torn to pieces before the altar. Some of the greatest Christian leaders used all their influence against such atrocities, but the Egyp Christians were always noted for their excitability. They killed heretics easily, but they would themselves be killed rather than renounce the very slightest and most intangible theological tenet. It only needed the change of a word e.g. in the customary version to raise a riot (*Expos*, VII, 75). Some curious relics of the early Egyp church have very recently come to light. The oldest autographic Christian letter known (3d cent.) proves that at that time the church was used as a bank, and its ecclesiastics (who, whether priests or bishops, were called "popes") were expected to help the country merchants in their dealings with the Rom markets. Some sixty letters of the 4th cent. written to a Christian cavalry officer in the Egyp army are also preserved, while papyri and ostraca from cir 600 AD show that at this time no deacon could be ordained without having first learned by heart as much as an entire Gospel or 25 Pss and two epistles of Paul, while a letter from a bishop of this period is filled with Scripture, as he anathematizes the "oppressor of the poor," who is likened unto him who spat in the face of Our Lord on the cross and smote Him on the head (Adolph Deissmann, *Light from the Ancient East*, etc, 1910). Oppression of Jews and heretics was not, however, forbidden and during the 5th and 6th cents. Egypt was a battle-field in which each sect persecuted every other. Even when the Arabs under the caliph Omar captured the city on Good Friday (641), Easter Day was spent by the orthodox in torturing supposed heretics! The next morning the city was evacuated and Jews and Copts received better treatment from the Arabs than they had from the Rom or Gr ecclesiastics. After the Arab conquest the Coptic church, being released from persecution, prospered and gained many converts even from the Mohammedans. But the Saracenic civilization and religion steadily displaced the old, and the native learning and native religion soon disappeared into the desert. By the 8th cent. Arab. had taken the place of Gr and Coptic, not only in public documents but in common speech. Then for 1,000 years the Egyp church remained without perceptible influence on culture or theology. But its early influence was immeasurable and can still be marked in Christian art, architecture and ritual as well as in philosophy and theology. Perhaps its most visible influence was in the encouragement of image-reverence and asceticism. It is suggestive that the first hermit (Anthony) was a native Egyp, and the first founder of a convent (Pachomius) was a converted Egyp (heathen) monk. Today A. has again become a Christian metropolis containing Copts, Romans, Greeks, Armenians, Maronites, Syrians, Chaldaeans and Protestants. The Protestants are represented by the Anglican church, the Scotch Free church, the evangelical church of Germany and the United Presbyterian church of the U.S. (For minute divisions see *Catholic Enc.*)

7. Catechetical School in Alexandria

The first theological school of Christendom was founded in A. It was probably modeled after earlier Gnostic schools established for the study of religious philosophy. It offered a three years' course. There were no fees, the lecturers being supported by gifts from rich students. Pantaenus, a converted Stoic philosopher, was its first head (180). He was followed by Clement (202) and by Origen (232) under whom the school reached its zenith. It always stood for the philosophical vindication of Christianity. Among its greatest writers were Julius Africanus (215), Dionysius (265), Gregory (270), Eusebius (315), Athanasius (373) and Didymus (347), but Origen (185–254) was its chief glory; to him belongs the honor of defeating paganism and Gnosticism with their own weapons; he gave to the church a "scientific consciousness," his threefold interpretation of Scripture affected Biblical exegesis clear down to the last century. Arius was a catechist in this institution, and Athanasius, the "father of orthodoxy" and "theological center of the Nicene age" (Schaff), though not officially connected with the catechetical school was greatly affected by it, having been bred and trained in A. The school was closed toward the end of the 4th cent. because of theological disturbances in Egypt, but its work was continued from Caesarea and other centers, affecting profoundly Western teachers like Jerome and Ambrose, and completely dominating Eastern thought. From the first there was a mystical and Docetic tendency visible, while its views of inspiration and methods of interpretation, including its constant assumption of a secret doctrine for the qualified initiate, came legitimately from Neo-Platonism. For several centuries after the school disbanded its tenets were combated by the "school of Antioch," but by the 8th cent. the Alex theology was accepted by the whole Christian world, east and west.

Literature.—Besides works mentioned in the text see especially: Petrie, *History of Egypt* (1899), V, VI; Mahaffy, *Empire of the Ptolemies* (1895); *Progress of Hellenism* (1905); Butler, *Arab Conquest of Egypt* (1902); Ernst Sieglin, *Ausgrabungen in Alexandrien* (1908); Harnack, *Lehrbuch der Dogmengeschichte* (1895–1900), and in *New Sch-Herz* (1910); Inge, Alexandrian Theology in *Enc of Religion and Ethics* (1908); Ed. Caird, *Evolution of Theology in the Greek Philosophers* (1904); Pfleiderer, *Philosophy and Development of Religion* (1894); Schaff, *History of Christian Church* (1884–1910); Zogheb, *Études sur l'ancienne Alexandrie* (1909).

Camden M. Cobern

ALEXANDRIANS, al-eg-zan′dri-ans (**Ἀλεξανδρεῖς**, *Alexandreís*): Jews of Alexandria, who had, with the Libertines and Cyrenians, a synagogue in Jerusalem. They were among those who disputed with Stephen (Acts **6** 9).

ALGUM, al′gum (אַלְגּוּמִּים, *'algūmmīm* [2 Ch **2** 8; **9** 10 f]; or **ALMUG** [אַלְמֻגִּים, *'almuggīm*, 1 K **10** 11 f]): It is generally supposed that these

Algum Tree—*Santalum album.*

two names refer to one kind of tree, the consonants being transposed as is not uncommon in Sem words. Solomon sent to Hiram, king of Tyre, saying, "Send me also cedar-trees, fir-trees, and algum-trees, out of Lebanon" (2 Ch **2** 8). In 1 K **10** 11 it is said that the navy of Hiram "that brought gold from Ophir, brought in from Ophir great plenty of almug-trees and precious stones." In the parallel passage in 2 Ch **9** 10 it is said that "algum-trees and precious stones" were brought. From this wood "the king made . . . . pillars for the house of Jeh, and for the king's house, harps also and psalteries for the singers: there came no such almug-trees, nor were seen, unto this day" (1 K **10** 12). The wood was evidently very precious and apparently came from E. Asia—unless we suppose from 2 Ch **2** 8 that it actually *grew* on Lebanon, which is highly improbable; it was evidently a fine, close-grained wood, suitable for carving. Tradition says that this was the famous sandal wood, which was in ancient times put to similar uses in India and was all through the ages highly prized for its color, fragrance, durability and texture. It is the wood of a tree, *Pterocar pussantalinus* (N.D. *Santalaceae*), which grows to a height of 25 to 30 feet; it is a native of the mountains of Malabar.

E. W. G. Masterman

ALIAH, a-lī'a (עַלְיָה, *'alyāh*): One of the dukes, or heads of thousands of Edom (1 Ch **1** 51). In Gen **36** 40 the name is Alvah (עַלְוָה, *'alwāh*), the only difference being the change of the weaker ו, *v*, of Gen to the somewhat stronger, י, *y*, of the later Ch, a change which is not infrequent in Heb. He is not to be confused, as in *HDB*, with the Alian of the same chapter.

ALIAN, a-lī'an (עַלְיָן, *'alyān*): A descendant of Esau, and son of Shobal (1 Ch **1** 40). In the corresponding earlier genealogy (Gen **36** 23) the same person is given as Alvan (עַלְוָן, *'alwān*), the change of the third consonant being a simple one, common to Heb, occurring similarly in Aliah (q.v.). Alian is not to be identified with Aliah, since the groups of names in which these occur are quite different, and the context in each case is not the same.

ALIEN, āl'yen: Found in the AV for גֵּר, *gēr*, (Ex **18** 3) = "guest," hence: "foreigner," "sojourner" RV; also for נֵכָר, *nēkhār* (Isa **61** 5) = "foreign," "a foreigner" RV (concrete), "heathendom" (abstract), "alien," "strange" (-er); and for נָכְרִי, *nokhrī* (Dt **14** 21 RV "foreigner"; cf Job **19** 15; Ps **69** 8; Lam **5** 2)—"strange," in a variety of degrees and meanings: "foreign," "non-relative," "adulterous," "different," "wonderful," "alien," "outlandish," "strange." In the NT we find ἀπηλλοτριωμένος, *apēllotriōménos* (Eph **4** 18; Col **1** 21) = "being alienated," and *allótrios* (He **11** 34) = "another's," "not one's own," hence: "foreign," "not akin," "hostile." In the OT the expression was taken in its lit. sense, referring to those who were not Israelites—the heathen; in the NT it is given a **fig.** meaning, as indicating those who have not become naturalized in the kingdom of God, hence are outside of Christ and the blessing of the gospel.

Frank E. Hirsch

ALIENATE, āl'yen-āt (עָבַר, *'ābhar;* **ἀπαλλοτριόω,** *apallotrióō*, "to estrange from"): In OT, for the break between husband and wife caused by unfaithfulness to the marriage vow (Jer **6** 8; Ezk **23** 17); also applied to the diversion of property (Ezk **48** 14). In NT, spiritually, for the turning of the soul from God (Eph **2** 12; Col **1** 21). The Gr *allótrios*, which is the root of the verb, is the opposite of *íd-i-os*, "one's own." The word implies a former state, whence the person or thing has departed, and that, generally, by deterioration.

ALIVE, a-līv' (חַי, *ḥai*, "living"; **ζάω,** *záō*, "to live," **ἀναζάω,** *anazáō*, "to live again"): These Heb and Gr originals are the chief terms for life in both Testaments. They cover all life, including soul and spirit, although primarily referring to physical vitality. Striking examples may be cited: "Is your father yet a.?" (Gen **43** 7); "To whom he also showed himself a." (Acts **1** 3). Often used of God: "the *living* God" (Josh **3** 10); also of the resurrection life: "In Christ shall all be made a." (1 Cor **15** 22); of the soul's regenerate life: "Reckon . . . . yourselves . . . . a. unto God," "as those that are a. from the dead" (Rom **6** 11.13 AV). The term is vital with the creative energy of God; the healing, redemptive, resurrection life of Christ; the renewing and recreative power of the Holy Spirit.

Dwight M. Pratt

ALL, ôl: Used in various combinations, and with different meanings.

(1) *All along*, "Weeping all along as he went" (Jer **41** 6), i.e. throughout the whole way he went, feigning equal concern with the men from Shiloh, etc, for the destruction of the Temple, so as to put them off their guard.

(2) *All in all*, "That God may be all in all" (1 Cor **15** 28, Gr *pánta en pásin*, "all things in all [persons and] things"). "The universe, with all it comprises, will wholly answer to God's will and reflect His mind" (Dummelow).

(3) *All one*, "It is all one" (Job **9** 22), "it makes no difference whether I live or die."

(4) *At all*, "If thy father miss me at all" (1 S **20** 6), "in any way," "in the least."

(5) *All to*, "All to brake his skull" (Jgs **9** 53 AV) an obsolete form signifying "altogether"; "broke his skull in pieces."

(6) Often used indefinitely of a large number or a great part, "All the cattle of Egypt died" (Ex **9** 6; cf vs 19.25); "all Judaea, and all the region round about" (Mt **3** 5); "that all the world should be enrolled" (Lk **2** 1); "all Asia and the world" (Acts **19** 27); "All [people] verily held John to be a prophet" (Mk **11** 32).

M. O. Evans

ALLAMMELECH, a-lam'ĕ-lek (אַלַּמֶּלֶךְ, *'allammelekh*, "oak of a king"): A town in the tribe of Asher, the location of which is not known (Josh **19** 26; AV **Alammelech**).

ALLAR, al'ar (AV **Aalar; 'Ααλάρ,** *Aalár*): Occurring once (1 Esd **5** 36) and used apparently to indicate a place from which certain Jews came on the return from captivity, who could not prove their lineage, and were excluded for this reason from the privileges of the priesthood. *HDB* identifies with Immer of Ezr **2** 59 and Neh **7** 61 (q.v.), but this is not at all certain.

ALLAY, a-lā' (הֵנִיחַ, *hēnīaḥ*, "to cause to rest," "soothe": "Gentleness allayeth [lit., "pacifieth"] great offences" [Eccl **10** 4]): The word is applied to what "excites, disturbs and makes uneasy" (Smith, *Synonyms Discriminated*, 106).

ALLEGE, a-lej' (**παρατίθημι,** "*paratíthēmi*," "to set forth," Acts **17** 3): It is not used in the Eng. Bible in its more modern and usual sense, "to assert," but is about equivalent to "to prove."

ALLEGIANCE, a-lē'jans (מִשְׁמֶרֶת, *mishmereth*, "a charge," from *shāmar*, "to keep," 1 Ch **12** 29): RVm gives as lit. meaning, "kept the charge of the house of Saul," which revisers consider **fig.** for "maintaining their loyalty and fidelity," i.e. "allegiance."

ALLEGORY, al'ĕ-go-ri: The term allegory, being derived from **ἄλλο ἀγορεύειν,** *állo agoreúein*, signifying to say something different from what the words themselves imply, can etymologically be applied to any fig. form of expression of thought. In actual usage in theology, the term is employed in a restricted sense, being used however in three ways, viz. rhetorically, hermeneutically and homiletically. In the first-mentioned sense it is the ordinary allegory of rhetoric, which is usually defined as an extended or continued metaphor, this extension expanding from two or more statements to a whole volume, like Bunyan's *Pilgrim's Progress.* Allegories of this character abound in the Scriptures, both in OT and in NT. Instructive examples of this kind are found in Ps **80** 8–19; Eccl **12** 3–7; Jn **10** 1–16; Eph **6** 11–17. According to traditional interpretation of both the Jewish exegesis and of the Catholic and Protestant churches the entire book of Cant is such an allegory. The subject is discussed in full in Terry's *Biblical Hermeneutics*, etc, ch vii, 214–38.

In the history of Biblical exegesis allegory represents a distinct type of interpretation, dating back to pre-Christian times, practised particularly by the Alex Jews, and adopted by the early Church Fathers and still practised and defended by the Roman Catholic church. This method insists that the literal sense, particularly of historical passages, does not exhaust the divinely purposed meaning of such passages, but that these latter also include a deeper and higher spiritual and mystical sense. The fourfold sense ascribed to the Scriptures finds its expression in the well-known saying: *Littera gesta docet; quid credas, allegorica; moralis, quid agas; quid speres, anagogica* ("The letter shows things done; what you are to believe, the allegoric; what you are to do, the moral; what you are to hope, the anagogic"), according to which the allegorical is the hidden dogmatical meaning to be found in every passage. Cremer, in his *Biblico-Theological New Testament Lexicon,* shows that this method of finding a hidden thought behind the simple statement of a passage, although practised so extensively on the Jewish side by Aristobulus and especially Philo, is not of Jewish origin, but was, particularly by the latter, taken from the Alex Greeks (who before this had interpreted Gr mythology as the expression of higher religious conceptions) and applied to a deeper explanation of OT historical data, together with its theophanies, anthropomorphisms, anthropopathies, and the like, which in their plain meaning were regarded as unworthy of a place in the Divine revelation of the Scriptures. Such allegorizing became the common custom of the early Christian church, although not practised to the same extent in all sections, the Syrian church exhibiting the greatest degree of sobriety in this respect. In this only Jewish precedent was followed; the paraphrases commonly known as the Tg, the Midr, and later in its extremest form in the Kabbalah, all showed this mark of eisegesis instead of exegesis. This whole false hermeneutical principle and its application originated doubtless in an unhistorical conception of what the Scriptures are and how they originated. It is characteristic of the NT, and one of the evidences of its inspiration, that in the entire Biblical literature of that age, both Jewish and Christian, it is the only book that does not practise allegorizing but abides by the principle of the lit. interpretation. Nor is Paul's exegesis in Gal **4** 21–31 an application of false allegorical methods. Here in ver 24 the term *allēgoroúmena* need not be taken in the technical sense as expressive of a method of interpretation, but merely as a paraphrase of the preceding thought; or, if taken technically, the whole can be regarded as an *argumentum ad hominem,* a way of demonstration found also elsewhere in Paul's writings. The Protestant church, beginning with Luther, has at all times rejected this allegorizing and adhered to the safe and sane principle, practised by Christ and the entire NT, viz. *Sensum ne inferas, sed efferas* ("Do not carry a meaning into [the Scriptures] but draw it out of [the Scriptures]"). It is true that the older Protestant theology still adheres to a *sensus mysticus* in the Scriptures, but by this it means those passages in which the sense is conveyed not *per verba* (through words), but *per res verbis descriptas* ("through things described by means of words"), as e.g. in the parable and the type.

In homiletics allegorizing is applied to the method which draws spiritual truths from common historical statements, as e.g. when the healing of a leper by Christ is made the basis of an exposition of the healing of the soul by the Saviour. Naturally this is not interpretation in the exegetical sense.

G. H. Schodde

ALLELUIA, al-ē-lōō′ya. See Hallelujah.

ALLEMETH, al′ē-meth (עַלֶּמֶת, *'allemeth,* "concealment"; AV **Alemeth,** 1 Ch **6** 60): Name of a town in tribe of Benjamin, near Anathoth, one of the cities given to the sons of Aaron, the same as Almon of Josh **21** 18. The AV Alemeth (q.v.) is based upon the Heb reading עָלֶמֶת, *'ālemeth.* Its site is the modern Almît, a village a short distance N.E. of Anathoth.

ALLIANCE, a-lī′ans: Frequent references are made to alliances between the patriarchs and foreigners. Abraham is reported to have had "confederates" among the chiefs of the Canaanites (Gen **14** 13). He also allied with Abimelech, king of Gerar (**21** 22–34). Isaac's alliance with Abimelech (**26** 26–34), which is offered as an explanation of the name Beer-sheba (ver 33), appears to be a variant of the record of alliance between Abraham and Abimelech. Jacob formed an alliance with Laban, the Syrian (**31** 44–54), by which Gilead was established as a boundary line between Israel and Aram. These treaties refer, in all probability, to the early period of Israel's history, and throw a good deal of light upon the relation between Israel and the Philis and the Syrians immediately after the conquest of Canaan.

1. In the Patriarchal Stories

The only reference to an alliance between Israel and foreign people prior to the conquest of Canaan, that might be regarded as historical, is that made between Israel and the Kenite tribes at the foot of Sinai, the precise nature of which, however, is not very clearly indicated. Such alliances led to intermarriages between the members of the allied tribes. Thus Moses married a Kenite woman (Jgs **1** 16; **4** 11). The patriarchal marriages refer to the existing conditions after the conquest. Possibly one more alliance belonging to that period is that between Israel and Moab (Nu **25** 1–3). According to the narrative, Israel became attached to the daughters of Moab, at Shittim, and was led astray after Baal-peor. Its historicity is proven from the prophetic allusions to this event (cf Hos **9** 10; Mic **6** 5).

2. In Pre-Canaanitic History

The invading hordes of Israel met with strong opposition on the part of the natives of Pal (Jgs **1** 21.27–36). In time, alliances were formed with some of them, which generally led, as might be expected, to considerable trouble. One concrete illustration is preserved in the story of the Gibeonites (Josh **9**). Intermarriages were frequent. The tribe of Judah thus became consolidated through the alliance and the amalgamation with the Kenites and Calebites (Jgs **1** 10–16). These

3. During the Conquest

relations between Israel and the Canaanites threatened the preservation of Yahwism.

Prohibitory measures were adopted in the legal codes with a view to Jewish separateness and purity (Ex **23** 32; **34** 12.15; Dt **7** 2; cf Jgs **2** 2.3; Lev **18** 3.4; **20** 22 f).

4. The Monarchy

But at a very early date in the history of the Jewish kingdom the official heads of the people formed such alliances and intermarried. David became an ally to Achish of Gath (1 S **27** 2–12) and later on with Abner, which led to the consolidation of Judah and Israel into one kingdom (2 S **3** 17–21; **5** 1–3). It appears likewise that Toi, king of Hamath, formed an alliance with David (2 S **9** 10) and that Hiram of Tyre was his ally (1 K **5** 12*a*). Alliances with foreign nations became essential to the progress of trade and commerce during the reign of Solomon. Two of his treaties are recorded: one with Hiram of Tyre (1 K **5** 12–18; **9** 11–14) and one with Pharaoh, king of Egypt (1 K **9** 16).

5. The Divided Kingdom

After the disruption, Shishak of Egypt invaded Judaea, and probably also Israel. This meant an abrogation of the treaty existing between Israel and Egypt during the reign of Solomon. In consequence of the war between the two kingdoms, Asa formed an alliance with Ben-hadad of Syria (1 K **15** 18–20). Later on Ahab sought an alliance with Ben-hadad (1 K **20** 31–34). Friendly relations ensued between Israel and Judah, during the reign of Jehoshaphat, which continued to the close of the dynasty of Omri (1 K **22** 2–4.50; 2 K **3** 7). With the accession of Jehu, hostilities were resumed. In the Syro-Ephraimitic war, Israel was allied with Syria, and Judah with Assyria (2 K **16** 6–9; Isa **7**). This opened the way to the Assyr power into both kingdoms. Relief against Assyria was sought in Egypt; Hoshea rebelled against Shalmaneser, and allied with So (Sevechus, the Shabaka of the 25th Dynasty) and thus brought about the fall of Samaria.

6. The Kingdom of Judah

Hezekiah likewise sought an alliance with So, but derived no assistance from him. He is recorded to have formed friendly relations with Berodach-baladan of Babylon (2 K **20** 12–18). These alliances resulted in the introduction of foreign cults into Jerus (2 K **16** 10.11). During the reign of Manasseh, Yahwism was seriously threatened by foreign religious practices (2 K **21** 2–9). The protesting spirit against the prevailing conditions found expression in the Dt code, which emphasizes the national policy. Josiah fought against Pharaoh-necoh as an ally of Assyria (2 K **23** 29). Jehoahaz continued the Assyr alliance and was dethroned in consequence by Pharaoh-necoh (ver 33). Jehoiakin was disposed to be friendly with Egypt, and even after his subjection to Nebuchadnezzar, he remained loyal to the Pharaoh (ver 35). Zedekiah came to the throne as an ally of Babylon. When he broke this alliance, the destruction of Jerus resulted (**25**).

7. In Post-exilic Times

Judas Maccabaeus sought an alliance with the Romans (1 Macc **8**; Jos, *Ant*, XII, x, 6) which was renewed by Jonathan (1 Macc **12** 1; *Ant*, XIII, v, 8) and by Simon (1 Macc **15** 17; *Ant*, XIII, vii, 3). Treaties were concluded with the Spartans (1 Macc **12** 2; **14** 20; *Ant*, XII, iv, 10; XIII, v, 8). The Rom alliance was again renewed by Hyrcanus about 128 BC (*Ant*, XIII, ix, 2). This alliance proved to be of fatal consequence to the independence of the Jews (*Ant*, XIV, iv, 4; and xiv, 5). For the rites connected with the formation of the earlier alliances, see Covenant. Samuel Cohon

ALLIED, a-līd′ (קָרֹב, *ḳārōbh,* "near," as in Gen **45** 10; Ex **13** 17, etc): Neh **13** 4 refers either to family ties, as in Ruth **2** 20, or to intimate association.

ALLOM, al′om (**Ἀλλών,** *Allōn*): RV Allon (q.v.): One of the families of the "servants of Solomon," whose descendants returned with Zerubbabel from Babylon in the First Return, 537 BC (1 Esd **5** 34). The name is not found in the parallel lists of Ezra and Nehemiah, although some have tried to identify with the last name of each list, Ami of Ezr **2** 57, and Amon of Neh **7** 59. This is not probable.

ALLON, al′on (אַלּוֹן, *'allōn,* "oak"):

(1) A town in the tribe of Naphtali in northern Palestine (Josh **19** 33), according to AV, which follows some Heb texts. It is better however to read with the RV, "oak" (אֵלוֹן, *'ēlōn*), rather than as proper noun.

(2) A prominent descendant of the tribe of Simeon (1 Ch **4** 37).

(3) RV for **Allom** of the AV in 1 Esd **5** 34 (q.v.).

ALLON-BACUTH, al′on-bā′kuth (אַלּוֹן בָּכוּת, *'allōn bākhūth;* AV transliterates **Allon-bachuth,** al-on-bak′uth, "oak of weeping"): The burial place of Deborah, the nurse of Rebekah (Gen **35** 8); it appears from the narrative that she made her home with Jacob, who had returned from Paddan-aram, and was sojourning at the time at Bethel, in the vicinity of which was the "oak of weeping," under which she was buried.

ALLOW, a-lou′, **ALLOWANCE,** a-lou′ans: The vb. "to allow" is used in AV to tr four different Gr words: (1) *suneudokéō,* "to approve together" (with others) (RV "consent unto"), Lk **11** 48. (2) *prosdéchomai,* "to receive to oneself," "admit" (RV "look for," m "accept"); Acts **24** 15. (3) *ginōskō,* "to know," "recognize": "That which I do, I allow not" (RV "I know not"), i.e. "I do not understand what I am doing, my conduct is inexplicable to me" (Grimm-Thayer); Rom **7** 15. (4) *dokimázō,* "to prove," "approve." "Happy is he that condemneth not himself in the thing which he alloweth" (RV "approveth," i.e. in practice), i.e. who is not troubled with scruples; Rom **14** 22. Thus RV has removed the vb. "allow" in each case in which it occurs in AV, it being somewhat ambiguous in meaning (its original sense, as derived from Lat *allocare,* "to place," "assign," "grant," being influenced by another word, Lat *allaudare,* "to praise"). The noun "allowance" occurs in the sense of quantity of food allowed, in 2 K **25** 30 (AV, RV) and the ‖ passage Jer **52** 34 (RV; "diet" in AV).

D. Miall Edwards

ALLOY, a-loi′ (בְּדִיל, *b^edhīl*): In Isa **1** 25 RVm; tr^d "tin" in the text. Elsewhere in both VSS *b^edhīl* is tr^d Tin (q.v.).

ALLURE, a-lūr′ (פָּתָה, *pāthāh,* "to persuade," "woo," "entice"; **δελεάζω,** *deleázō,* "to entrap," "lay a bait"):

(1) "I will allure her, and bring her into the wilderness" (Hos **2** 14), with evident reference to the Assyr invasion and the devastation of the land, followed up by the Exile. Thus would Jeh entice Israel to repent by gentle punishment; then would follow her restoration and the outpouring of His love (vs 14 ff).

(2) "They allure through the lusts of the flesh" (2 Pet **2** 18, RV "entice"). Wicked men allure to destruction; God (as above) allures to punishment, repentance and restoration. M. O. Evans

ALMIGHTY, ôl-mīt'i: (1) (שַׁדַּי, *shaddai* [Gen **17** 1]): Found in the OT forty-eight times, most of these in the Book of Job; it occurs either alone or in combination with אֵל, *'ēl,* "God"). The root meaning is uncertain. (2) (παντοκράτωρ, *pantokrátōr*), the exclusive tr of this Gr word in the NT, found principally in Rev (nine times); once besides (2 Cor **6** 18). Its occurrence in the Apoc is frequent. See God, Names of.

ALMODAD, al-mō'dad (אַלְמוֹדָד, *'almōdhādh,* "the beloved," or, "God is beloved"): The first mentioned of the thirteen sons of Joktan (Gen **10** 25–29; 1 Ch **1** 19–23). A south Arabian name, and pointing to a south Arabian tribe. See Abimael.

ALMON, al'mon (עַלְמוֹן, *'almōn,* "hidden"): A Levitical city in the tribe of Benjamin (Josh **21** 18), the same as "Allemeth" RV, "Alemeth" AV, of 1 Ch **6** 60 (q.v.).

ALMON-DIBLATHAIM, al'mon-dib-la-thā'im (עַלְמֹן דִּבְלָתַיִם, *'almōn dibhlāthayim,* "Almon of the double cake of figs"): A station in the wilderness journeyings of the Israelites, located in Moab between Dibon-gad and the mountains of Abarim (Nu **33** 46.47). It was near the end of the forty years' wanderings. The name was probably given because the location was like two lumps of pressed figs. In both occurrences the word has the accusative ending of direction, and should properly be read: "Almon toward Diblathaim." It was probably the same place as Beth-diblathaim of Jer **48** 22, mentioned in the prophet's oracle against Moab.

ALMOND, ä'mund:

(1) שָׁקֵד, *shāḳēdh,* Gen **43** 11; Nu **17** 8, etc. The word *shaked* comes from a Heb root meaning to "watch" or "wait." In Jer **1** 11.12 there is a play on the word, "And I said, I see a rod of an

Almond—*Amygdalus communis.*

almond-tree [*shāḳēdh*]. Then said Jehovah unto me, Thou hast well seen: for I will watch [*shōḳēdh*] over my word to perform it."

(2) לוּז, *lūz;* AV **hazel,** Gen **30** 37; *lauz* is the mod Arab. name for "almond"—Luz was the old name of Bethel (q.v.).

1. Almond Tree

The almond tree is mentioned in Eccl **12** 5, where in the description of old age it says "the almond-tree shall blossom." The reference is probably to the white hair of age. An almond tree in full bloom upon a distant hillside has a certain likeness to a head of white hair.

2. A Rod of Almond

A rod of almond is referred to Gen **30** 37, where "Jacob took him rods of fresh poplar, and of the almond [*lūz*] and of the plane-tree; and peeled white streaks in them" as a means of securing "ring-streaked, speckled, and spotted" lambs and goats—a proceeding founded doubtless upon some ancient folklore. Aaron's rod that budded (Nu **17** 2.3) was an almond rod. Also see Jer **1** 11 referred to above.

3. The Blossoms

The blossoms of the almond are mentioned Ex **25** 33 f; **37** 19 f, etc. "Cups made like almond-blossoms in one branch, a knop (i.e. knob) and a flower," is the description given of parts of the sacred candlesticks. It is doubtful exactly what was intended—the most probable is, as Dillmann has suggested, that the cup was modeled after the calyx of the almond flower. See Candlestick.

4. The Fruit

Israel directed his sons (Gen **43** 11) to carry almonds as part of their present to Joseph in Egypt. Palestine is a land where the almond flourishes, whereas in Egypt it would appear to have been uncommon. Almonds are today esteemed a delicacy; they are eaten salted or beaten into a pulp with sugar like the familiar German *Marzipan.*

The almond is *Amygdalus communis* (N.O. *Rosaceae*), a tree very similar to the peach. The common variety grows to the height of 25 feet and produces an abundant blossom which appears before the leaves; in Pal this is fully out at the end of January or beginning of February; it is the harbinger of spring. This early blossoming is supposed to be the origin of the name *shāḳēdh* which contains the idea of "early." The masses of almond trees in full bloom in some parts of Pal make a very beautiful and striking sight. The bloom of some varieties is almost pure white, from a little distance, in other parts the delicate pink, always present at the inner part of the petals, is diffused enough to give a pink blush to the whole blossom. The fruit is a drupe with a dry fibrous or woody husk which splits into two halves as the fruit ripens. The common wild variety grows a kernel which is bitter from the presence of a substance called amygdalon, which yields in its turn prussic (hydrocyanic) acid. Young trees are grafted with cuttings from the sweet variety or are budded with apricot, peach or plum. E. W. G. Masterman

ALMOST, ôl'most (ἐν ὀλίγῳ): In Acts **26** 28 the Gr *en oligō* does not mean "almost," although scholars have for centuries trd the clause "Almost thou persuadest me to become a Christian." The revisers saw clearly the errors of their predecessors, so far as the signification of the first two words is concerned; but their explanation of the sentence is also erroneous; for the Gr cannot mean "With but little persuasion thou wouldst fain make me a Christian." Paul's reply proves that *en oligō* must be taken with the last word *poiēsai,* not with *peítheis,* since he takes up Agrippa's *en oligō,* couples it with *en megálō* and continues with *genésthai* which is the regular passive of *poiēsai* (cf Lysias xii.71 with 72). And the idea of "Christian" is also taken up and repeated in *hopoíos kaí egō eimi.*

An investigation of the usage of *en oligō* shows that it was never used in the sense of "almost."

The phrase occurs first in the *Hymn to Hermes*, 240, and here it is evidently an abbreviated expression for the Homeric ὀλίγῳ ἐνὶ χώρῳ, *olígō ení chōrō* (M 423). Cf K 161, P 394. But it was used for both time and place, with the substantive expressed or understood (Thuc. i.93.1; iii.66.3; iv. 26.3; iv.55.3; ii.84.3; ii.86.5; iv.96.3; v.112; vii. 67.3; vii.87.1; Pind. Pyth. viii.131; Eur. Suppl. 1126; Hel. 771; Isoc. iv.83; Dem. lviii.60; iii.18). These uses persist from Homer far down into the post-classical literature (Plut. Per. 159 F; Coriol. 217 F; Mar. 427 A; Crass. 547 C; Polyb. x.18; Appian, Mithrad. 330; Themistius xi.143 C; Eustath. II.B, p.339.18). In the NT the phrase occurs also in Eph **3** 3. Here too the common versions are incorrect. The clause in which the phrase occurs means simply, "as I said a little while ago"—the addition of *en olígō* merely indicates that the interval indicated by *pro* is short, an idea which would have been expressed in classical Gr by the simple dative, *olígō* and the adverb *próteron* (Ar. Thesm. 578; Aeschin. i. 2, 26, 72, 165; ii. 77, 147). Only a short while before Paul had expressed practically the same thought (Eph **3** 3) and in almost identical language.

Consequently, *en olígō*, in the NT, means "a little," and is equivalent to *olígōs* which occurs in 2 Pet **2** 18. In classical writers the idea would have been expressed by *olígon*, or *kat' olígon*. So *en olígō*, which originally signified "in a little space" (or time), comes to mean simply "a little" (bit), *ein bischen*, but is never equivalent to *olígou* ("within a little") in any period of the language. The King James translators disregarded the real significance of *poiēsai*, or adopted the reading of the inferior MSS (*genesthai*), so as to make the rest of the sentence harmonize with their tr of the first two words; and the revisers force the last two words into an impossible service, since the object of *poiēsai* of which *christianón* is the factitive predicate, must be a third person, but certainly not Agrippa. Some scholars are of the opinion that the thought is: "You are trying to persuade me so as to make me a Christian." This is, indeed, the Spanish version; but examples show that the infinitive after πείθειν was used in a different sense. The best MS reads ΠΙΘΕΙC. This might, of course, stand for πείθεις. But μεπιθεις may point to an original μεπιποθεις. Cf Jas **4** 5 and 2 Cor **5** 2, Plato *Leg.* 855 E. If these contentions be correct, the verb means simply "earnestly desire," and not "persuade." Cf Herod. v.93; Plato *Protag.* 329 D; Aesch. *Pers.* 542; Soph. *Phil.* 534; Eur. *H.F.* 1408; *I.T.* 542; *Cycl.* 68; *Ion* 1432; *Ar. Lys.* 605, *toū deī; tí potheīs;* Agrippa is asking, "What do you want, Paul? What are you trying to do? Make me a Christian?" The implication in Paul's reply is that he is very desirous indeed of making him a Christian. And this interpretation harmonizes with the scene. The apostle's business at this juncture is not to convert heathen to Christianity; for he is in chains before Agrippa, Berenice, Festus and prominent men of Caesarea, *metá pollēs phantasías* (ver 23), to answer the charges brought against him by the Jews. But he holds forth at length and with such ardor that the Roman king says (though not necessarily in irony): "You seem to be anxious to make me a Christian in small measure." And Paul responds: "both small and great." All the MSS, except Sinaiticus, have πείθεις (Alexandr. ΠΕΙΘΗ·). Several read *genesthai* (instead of *poiēsai*). Wetstenius (Amsterdam 1752) and Knapp (Halle 1829) follow these MSS. So most of the old trs: Coverdale (1535), "Thou persuadest me in a parte to become a Christen"; *Biblia Sacra* (Paris 1745) "In modico·suades me C. fieri"; a Latin MS, 14th cent., now in Lane Sem., Cincinnati; Rosenmueller's *Scholia* (1829), "Parum abest quin mihi persuadeas ut fiam"; Stier und Theile's *Polyglotten Bibel* (1849); Tregelles (1857–79, with Jerome's version); Edouard Reuss, *Histoire apostolique* (Paris 1876), "Tu vas me persuader bientôt de devenir Chrétien." The tr of Queen Elizabeth's Bible is "Somewhat thou bryngeste me in minde for to become Chryste." Wycliffe renders "In litil thing thou councelist me for to be maad a Christen man." Erasmus takes *en olígō* in the sense of "a little." Calvin's rendering, "Thou wilt make me a Christian in a moment," has been adopted in various countries (Wetstenius, Kuinoel, Neander, de Wette, Lange, Robinson, Hackett, Conybeare). The older scholars generally hold to "almost" (Valla, Luther, Beza, Grotius, Castalio, Du Veil, Bengel, Stier). Some interpret the phrase "with little labor" (Oecumenius, Olshausen, Baumgarten, Meyer, Lechler). Neander maintains that if we adopt the readings *en megalō* in Paul's answer, Agrippa's words must be explained "with a few reasons" ("which will not cost you much trouble"). Meyer-Wendt (*Kritisch-exegetisches Handbuch über die Apostelgeschichte*) translates "mit Wenigem ueberredest du mich Christ zu werden." Meyer himself conceives the words to have been spoken sarcastically. See *Classical Review*, XXII, 238–41.

J. E. Harry

ALMS, äms, **ALMSGIVING**, äms-giv′ing: The Eng. word "alms" is an abridged form of the Gr word, ἐλεημοσύνη, *eleēmosúnē* (cf "eleemosynary"), appearing in gradually reduced forms in German *Almosen*, Wyclif's *Almesse*, Scotch *Aw'mons*, and our alms.

The later Jews often used "righteousness" *ç*ᵉ*dhākāh* as meaning alms, that being in their view the foremost righteousness. (Cf our modern use of "charity" to denote almsgiving.) This use is seen in the Talm and in the frequent translations of the Hebrew word for "righteousness" (*ç*ᵉ*dhākāh*) by "alms" (*eleēmosunē*) in the LXX, though nothing warranting this is found in the Heb OT, or in the true text of the NT. This notion of righteousness as alms being well-nigh universal among Jews in Jesus' day, and spreading even among Christians, accounts for "alms" in Mt **6** 1, where the true text has "righteousness": "Take heed that ye do not your righteousness before men, to be seen of them" (RV with *B*ℵ*D*, the Lat versions, etc). The oriental versions which generally read "alms" may be accounted for on the supposition that "alms" was first written on the margin as explaining the supposed meaning of "righteousness," and then, as according with this accepted oriental idea, was substituted for it in the text by the copyists.

Dikaiosúnē and *eleēmosunē* are both used in the LXX to tr *ḥesedh*, "kindness," and are also both used to tr *ç*ᵉ*dhākāh*, "justice." Almsgiving was regarded not merely as a plain evidence of righteousness in general but also as an act of justice, a just debt owing to the needy. "No one refuses directly," Mackie says, hence, possibly, Christ's teaching in Lk **11** 41, "Let your righteousness [charity] be from within," "Give your hearts to almsgiving."

In the course of time the impulse and command to give alms in a true human way, out of pity, such as is found expressed in Dt **15** 11 AV, "Thou shalt open thine hand wide unto thy brother, to thy poor, and to thy needy, in thy land," gave place to a formal, "meritorious" practice, possessing, like sacrifice, as men came to think, the power of atoning for man's sins, and redeeming him from calamity and death. For instance, Prov **11** 4 (cf **16** 6;

21 3) was expounded: "Water will quench blazing fire; so doth almsgiving make atonement for sins" (Ecclus 3 30). "Lay up alms in thy storehouse; it shall deliver thee from affliction" (Ecclus 29 12). The story of Tob is especially in point: it is simply a lesson on almsgiving and its redeeming powers: "Alms delivers from death and will purge away all sin" (Tob 1 3.16; 2 14; 4 7–11; 12 8.9. Cf Sir 29 11 ff). Kindred teaching abounds in the Talm: "Alms-giving is more excellent than all offerings," is "equal to the whole law," will "deliver from the condemnation of hell," will "make one perfectly righteous," etc. According to Rabbi Assi, "Almsgiving is a powerful paraclete between the Israelites and their Father in heaven; it brings the time of redemption nigh" (*Bābhā' Bathrā'* Talm 10*a*).

The Roman Catholics, holding the books of Tob and Sir to be canonical, find in them proof-texts for their doctrine of almsgiving, and likewise attach great value to the gifts to the poor as atoning for sins. Protestants, by a natural reaction, have failed to hold always at its true value what was and is an important Christian duty (see Lk 12 33 AV, and cf Mt 6 19–24: "Sell that ye have and give alms," etc). It seems to have been so regarded and kept up in the Christian communities until the beginning of the 4th cent. (Apos Const II 36; Cyprian, *De Opera* and *Eleemos.* xiv).

The teaching of Jesus on the subject is important, first, as bearing upon Jewish ideas and practices, and second, as bearing upon present-day Christian ideas and practices.

This teaching appears most conspicuously in the Sermon on the Mount. While showing what is required of the subjects of the Messianic reign, He avowedly sets forth a higher and more spiritual morality than that which was taught and practised by the scribes and Pharisees: "Except your righteousness shall exceed the righteousness of the scribes and Pharisees, ye shall in no wise enter into the kingdom of heaven" (Mt 5 20). There, too, He lays down the general principle embodied in the words of Mt 6 1: "Take heed that ye do not your righteousness before men, to be seen of them," and illustrates it by applying it to the three exercises most valued among the Jews (commended together in Tob 12 8), viz. almsgiving (Mt 6 2.4), prayer (vs 5–15), and fasting (vs 16–18). Jewish writers claim that these are "the three cardinal disciplines which the synagogue transmitted to the Christian church and the Mohammedan mosque" (cf Koran, Sura 2 40, 104; 9 54).

Clearly what Jesus here forbids in general is not publicity in performing good deeds, which is often necessary and proper, but ostentatious publicity, *for the purpose* of attracting attention. (The Gr conveys distinctly this idea of purpose, and the verb for "to be seen" is the one from which comes our word "theater.")

Jewish writers, as also Gr and Rom philosophers, have many notable maxims upon the beauty and importance of being unostentatious in virtue, especially in deeds of benevolence. The Essenes had their treasury in a chamber of their own in the temple that both the giving and the taking should be unobserved (Mish, *Sh^eḳ*, v.6). Rabbi Eleazer said, "Alms-giving should be done in secret and not before men, for he who gives before men is a sinner, and God shall bring also the good deed before his judgment" (*B.B.* 9*a;* cf Eccl 12 14).

In applying this principle to almsgiving Jesus teaches His disciple: "When . . . thou doest alms, sound not a trumpet before thee, as the hypocrites do" (Mt 6 2). The conjecture of Calvin, followed by Stier and others, and mentioned as early as Euthymius, that it was a practice among Jews for an ostentatious almsgiver literally to sound a trumpet, or cause a trumpet to be sounded before him, in public places to summon the needy, is without foundation (Lightfoot); as is also the notion, made current by the rabbis and accepted by Edersheim (*The Temple*, etc, 26), that by "sounding a trumpet" Jesus was alluding to the trumpet-like receptacles of brass in the temple treasury. There is no proof that these were found "in the synagogues," or "in the streets." "Sound a trumpet," according to the Gr commentators, and the best modern authorities, is merely a fig. expression common to many languages, for self-parade—efforts to attract notice and win applause (cf our vulgar Eng. saying about "blowing your own horn"). The contrast with the common practice instituted by Jesus is the significant thing: "But when *thou* doest alms"—"thou" is emphatic by position in the Gr—"let not thy left hand know what thy right hand doeth," etc, i.e. "So far from trumpeting your almsgiving before the public, do not even let it be known to yourself." Jesus here, Calvin well says, "silently glances at a kind of folly which prevails everywhere among men, that they think they have lost their pains if there have not been many spectators of their virtues." (The traditional saying of Mohammed, "In almsgiving, the left hand should not know what the right has given," is evidently borrowed from this saying of Jesus.) It is worthy of note that, despite popular practice, to give alms with right motives, and only to those who were worthy to receive, was a matter of special solicitude and instruction with the best among Jews as well as among Christians. The words of the Psalmist, "Blessed is he that considereth the poor," are construed to be an admonition to "take personal interest in him and not simply give him alms" (*Lev. R.* xxxiv). "When thou wilt do good, know to whom thou doest it. Give unto the good and help not the sinner" (Ecclus 12 1–6; cf *Did* 1 5.6). "He that gives a free offering should give with a well-meaning eye" (*Yer. B.D.* 4 11). Jesus' words concerning the "single" and the "evil" eye (cf Lk 11 34–36), and Paul's teaching, "God loveth a cheerful giver" (2 Cor 9 7–9) have their counterparts in Jewish teaching. Rabbi Eleazer, referring to Hos 10 12, taught this high doctrine: "The kindness displayed in the giving of alms decides the final reward" (*Ṣuk.* 49*b*). Other kindred teaching in a way anticipated Jesus' supreme lesson, "that thine alms may be in secret: and thy Father who seeth in secret shall recompense thee" (Mt 6 4).

LITERATURE.—Commentaries ad loc. Rabbinical literature in point. D. Cassel, *Die Armenverwaltung des alten Israel*, 1887.

GEO. B. EAGER

ALMUG, al′mug. See ALGUM.

ALNATHAN, al′na-than (Ἀλναθάν, *Alnathán*, "God has given," RV ELNATHAN): Apocryphal name of a person (1 Esd 8 44) corresponding to Elnathan of Ezr 8 16. He was one of the learned men summoned by Ezra, as he was beginning his journey to Jerus, and sent to Iddo to ask for ministers for the house of Jeh.

ALOES, LIGNALOES, līn-al′ōz, lig-nal′ōz (אֲהָלִים, *'ăhālīm*, Nu 24 6, tr "lign-aloes" [=*lignum aloes*, "wood of aloes"], Prov 7 17; אֲהָלוֹת, *'ăhālōth*, Ps 45 8; Cant 4 14; ἀλόη, *alóē*, Jn 19 39): Mentioned as a substance for perfuming garments (Ps 45 8) and beds (Prov 7 17). In Cant 4 14, it occurs in a list of the most precious spices. The most memorable use of aloes as a spice is in Jn 19 39: "There came also Nicodemus, he who at the first came to him at night, bringing a mixture of myrrh and aloes, about a hundred pounds." This was an immense quantity and if the aloes bore any large proportion to the myrrh the mixture must have been purchased at a very high cost. The most difficult mention of aloes is the earliest where (Nu **24** 5.6) Balaam in his blessing on Israel exclaims—

"How goodly are thy tents, O Jacob,
Thy tabernacles, O Israel!
As valleys are they spread forth,
As gardens by the river-side,
As lign-aloes which Jehovah hath planted,
As cedar-trees beside the waters."

As the aloes in question grow in E. Asia it is difficult to see how Balaam could have come to speak of them as living trees. Post (*HDB*, I, 69) suggests that they may possibly have been growing at that time in the Jordan valley; this is both improbable and unnecessary. Balaam need have had no actual tree in his mind's eye but may have mentioned the

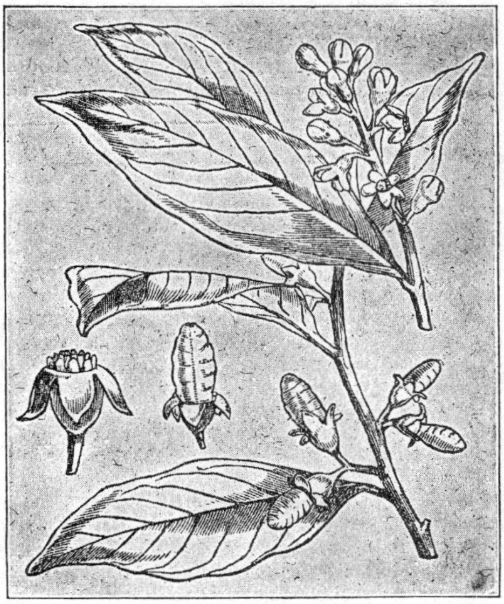

Aloes—*Aquilaria agallocha.*

aloe as a tree famous over the Orient for its preciousness. That the reference is poetical rather than literal may be supposed by the expression in the next ver "cedar-trees beside the waters"—a situation very unnatural for the high-mountain-loving cedar. Yet another explanation is that the Heb has been altered and that אֵילִים, *'ēlīm*, "terebinths" instead of אהלים, *'ăhālīm*, "aloes" stood in the original text.

The aloe wood of the Bible is eaglewood—so misnamed by the Portuguese who confused the Malay name for it (*agila*) with the Lat *aquila*, "eagle"—a product of certain trees of the N.O. *Aquilariaceae*, growing in S.E. Asia. The two most valued varieties are *Aquilaria malaccensis* and *A. agallocha*—both fine spreading trees. The resin, which gives the fragrant quality to the wood, is formed almost entirely in the heart wood; logs are buried, the outer part decays while the inner part, saturated with the resin, forms the "eagle wood" or "aloe wood" of commerce; "aloes" being the same wood in a finely powdered condition. To the Arabs this wood is known as *'ud*. It shows a beautiful graining and takes a high polish.

These aloes must be clearly distinguished from the well-known medicinal aloes, of ancient fame. This is a resin from *Aloes socatrina*, and allied species, of the N.O. *Liliaceae*, originally from the island of Socotra, but now from Barbadoes, the Cape of Good Hope and other places. The "American aloe" (*Agave americana*) which today is cultivated in many parts of Palestine, is also quite distinct from the Biblical plant. E. W. G. MASTERMAN

ALOFT, a-loft' (ἐπάνω, *epánō*): Only in 1 Esd **8** 92. Meaning obscure. The statement following a confession of sin means probably that Israel in penitence returning to the Lord, is exultant in the assurance of His forgiveness, and encouraged in efforts at reformation.

ALONG, a-long': Corresponding to two different Heb words, Jgs **9** 25; 1 S **6** 12; Jer **41** 6, joined with "come" and "go," vividly describes a course that is taken—it emphasizes its directness and immediateness. In Jgs **7** 12, "lay *along* in the valley," probably means "all the length" or "at length."

ALOTH, ā'loth (עָלוֹת, *'ālōth*): So found in AV and RVm in 1 K **4** 16, where the RV has BEALOTH (בְּעָלוֹת, *b^e'ālōth*). A town, or district in northern Pal, together with Asher under Baana, one of Solomon's twelve civil officers. Conder identifies with the ruin 'Alia, near Achzib. There was another Bealoth in southern Pal (Josh **15** 24). The difference in the form of the word in AV and RV is due to interpretation of the initial *b* as preposition "in" in the former, and as part of the word itself in the latter.

ALPHA, al'fa, **AND OMEGA**, ō'me-ga, o-mē'ga, o-meg'a (**A** and **Ω**=A and O): The first and last letters of the Gr alphabet, hence symbolically, "beginning and end"; in Rev "The Eternal One" in **1** 8 of the Father, in **21** 6 and **22** 13 of the Son. Cf Theodoret, *HE*, iv.8: "We used alpha down to omega, i.e. *all*." A similar expression is found in Lat (Martial, v.26). Cf Aretas (Cramer's *Catenae Graecae in NT*) on Rev **1** 8 and Tertullian (*Monog*, 5): "So also two Gr letters, the first and last, did the Lord put on Himself, symbols of the beginning and the end meeting in Him, in order that just as A rolls on to Ω and Ω returns again to A, so He might show that both the evolution of the beginning to the end is in Him and again the return of the end to the beginning." Cyprian, *Testim*, ii.1; vi. 22; iii.100, Paulinus of Nola *Carm.* xix.645; xxx. 89; Prudentius, *Cathem.*, ix.10–12. In Patristic and later literature the phrase is regularly applied to the Son. God blesses Israel from *'ālēph* to *taw* (Lev **26** 3–13), but curses from *waw* to *mem* (Lev **26** 14–43). So Abraham observed the whole law from *'ālēph* to *taw*. Consequently, "Alpha and Omega" may be a Gr rendering of the Heb phrase, which expressed among the later Jews the whole extent of a thing. J. E. HARRY

ALPHABET, al'fa-bet: An alphabet is a list of the elementary sounds used in any language. More strictly speaking it is that particular series, commonly known as the Phoen or Can alphabet, which was in use in the region of Pal about 1000 BC, and which is the ancestor of nearly all modern written alphabets whether Sem or European. It is the alphabet therefore of OT Heb and Aram. and NT Gr, of the superscription of Caesar and the Lat inscription on the cross, as well as of Eng. through the Gr and Lat. It is an interesting fact, with many practical bearings on text and exegesis, that three sets of letters so very unlike in appearance as Heb, Gr and modern Eng. should be the same in origin and alike in nature. Although the earliest surviving inscriptions must be a good deal later than the separation between the Gr and Heb, the records in each are more like one another than either is like its own modern printed form.

1. Definition

The characteristics of an alphabet are (1) the analysis of sounds into single letters rather than syllables or images, (2) the fixed order of succession in the letters, (3) the signs for the sounds, whether names or written symbols.

Of these the analysis into single letters, instead of whole words or syllables, is the characteristic element. The order of the letters may vary, as that of the Sanskrit does from the European, and yet the list remain not only alphabetic but the "same" alphabet, i.e. each sound represented by a similar name or written character. On the face of it, therefore, it might be imagined that the Egyp and Bab, the Cypriote, the Minoan and other forms earlier than the Can which are known or suspected to have had phonetic systems, may have had lists of these forms arranged in a fixed order, but these lists were not alphabetic until the final analysis into individual letters.

2. Name

The name alphabet comes from the first two letters of the Gr, *alpha beta*, just as the old Eng. name for the alphabet, *abc* or *abece*, is simply the first three letters of the Eng. alphabet, and thus is merely an abbreviation for the whole alphabet. It appears that the Greeks also used the first and last letters of the alphabet (*alpha* and *omega*) as the Jews did the first and last, or the first, middle and last letters of their alphabet, as abbreviation for the whole and in the same sense that in Eng. one says "a to izzard." *Alpha* and *beta* are themselves derived from the Sem names for the same letters (*'ālēph*, *bēth*) and have no meaning in the Gr.

3. Invention

The question of the invention of this alphabet differs from the question of the origin of the written forms of the letters with which it is often confused, and relates to the recognition of the individual letters. Alphabetical language whether written or spoken, inward or outward, is distinguished from the pictographic, hieroglyphic, and syllabic stages by this analysis into individual sounds or letters. It begins with the picture, passes to the ideogram and syllable, and from the syllable to the letter. This is best seen in writing, but it is equally true in speech. At the letter stage the alphabet begins. It is alleged by some that another stage, a consonantal writing, between syllabic and alphabetic writing, should be recognized. This would deny to the Phoen the character of a true alphabet since, as in all Sem languages, the vowels were anciently not written at all. Some go so far as to speak of it as syllabic in character, but on the other hand it may be said with equal pertinence that various syllabaries are nearly alphabetic. When a syllabic writing is reduced, as was the case with the Egyp, the Cypriote and others, to a point where a character represents uniformly a certain consonant and a certain vowel, the vocal analysis has been made and the essential alphabet begun, although it was only later that men discovered that the consonant common to several syllables might be expressed to advantage in writing by one unvarying sign, and later still that the vowels too might be distinguished to advantage.

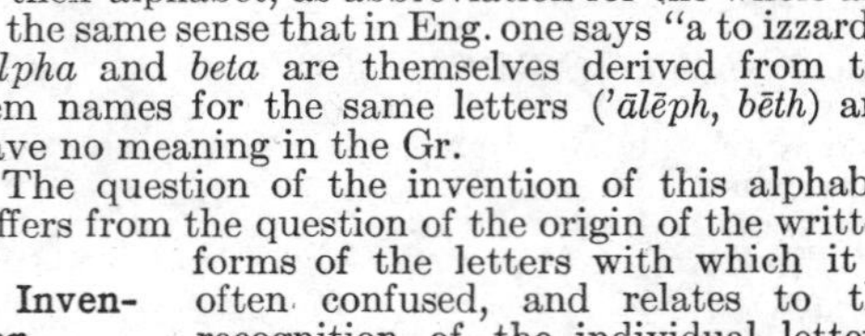

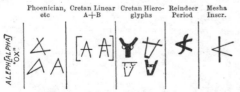

Primitive Signs like A. (Chiefly from Evans, *Scripta minoa.*)

4. Origin of the Letters

Few modern questions are changing shape so rapidly as that of the historical predecessor of the Can or Phoen alphabet. For a long time it was thought that De Rougé had solved the problem by tracing the letters to the Egyp hieratic. This is the view of most of the popular literature of the present time, but is wholly surrendered by most workers in the field now, in spite of the fact that the latest studies in hieratic show a still greater resemblance in forms (Möller, *Hierat. Paläographie*, 1909). Winckler and others have claimed derivation from the Cuneiform, Praetorius from the Cypriote, Sayce gets at least three letters from the Hittite, while Evans and others incline to believe that the Minoan was the direct source of the alphabet, introduced from Crete into Pal by the Philis who were Cretans, or at least that the two are from a common ancestor, which is also the ancestor of many other of the Mediterranean alphabets.

The Paestos Disk, Face A.

Some, like Evans and Mosso, even suggest that, perhaps through the Minoan, the letter forms may be traced to the pictographs of the neolithic era in the caves of Europe. There is, in fact, an extraordinary resemblance between some of the letters of the Phoen alphabet and some of the conventionalized signs of the neolithic age, and it may not be too fantastic to imagine that these early signs are the historic ancestors of the written alphabetical characters, but that they were in any sense alphabetical themselves is impossible if the invention of the alphabet was historical as here supposed, and is unlikely from any point of view.

If in fact the Paestos disk dates from before 1600 BC, and if Dr. Hempl's resolution of it into Ionic Gr is sound, we have another possible source or stock of characters from which the inventor of the alphabet may have chosen (*Harper's Magazine*, January, 1911).

5. Number of Letters

The ideal written alphabet contains a separate character for each sound used in any or every language. Practically in most languages the alphabet falls a good deal short of the number of recognized sounds to be expressed in that language and in pronouncing dictionaries they have to be analyzed into say *a* broad, *a* short, *a* open, etc, by adding diacritical marks. "In educated English without regarding finer distinctions" (Edmonds, *Comparative Philology*, 45) about 50 sounds are commonly used, but Murray distinguishes at least 96, and the number sometimes used or which may be used is much greater,

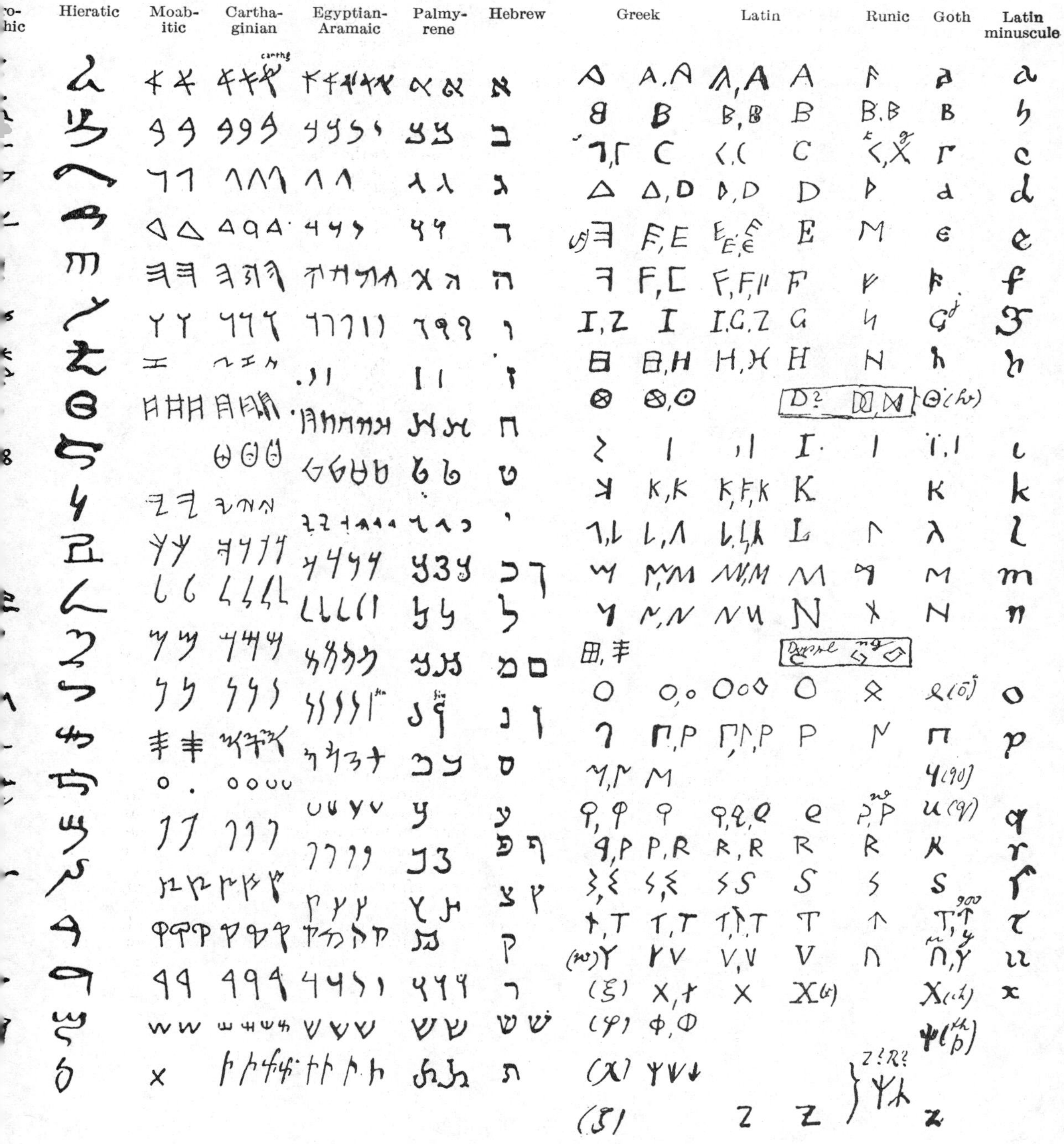

PRIMITIVE ALPHABETS

the possible number of vowel sounds alone being as many as 72.

Moreover the individual letters differ in sound in different individuals, and even in the same individual in successive utterances of what would be called the same letter or the same sound. It is alleged that the average sound of the *a* for example, is never the same in any two languages; the *a* in "father," even, is never the same in any two individuals, and that the same individual, even, never pronounces it twice so exactly in the same fashion that the difference may not be detected by sound photography.

The written alphabet is always thus less than the number of sounds used. The Phoen and the Sem alphabets generally had 22 letters, but they omitted the vowels. English has 26, of which many have two or more sounds.

6. Names of the Letters

The names of the Gr alphabet are derived from the Sem names and are meaningless in the Gr, while in the Sem it has been pretty clearly shown that they signify for the most part some object or idea of which the earliest form of the written letter was a picture, as e.g. *'ālēph*, the ox. The forms of the letters are apparently derived from pictures of the ox, house, etc, made linear and finally reduced to a purely conventional sign which was itself reduced to the simplest writing motion. All this has been boldly denied by Mr. Pilcher (*PSBA*, XXVI [1904], 168–73; XXVII [1905], 65–68), and the original forms declared to be geometric; but he does not seem to have made many converts, although he has started up rival claimants to his invention.

The names of the letters at least seem to indicate the Sem origin of the alphabet, since the majority of them are the Sem names for the objects which gave name to the letter, and the picture of which gives form to the written letter.

Following is Sayce's list (*PSBA*, XXXII [1910], 215–22) with some variants: (1) *'ālēph*=ox; (2) *bēth* =house (tent); (3) *gīmel*=camel; (4) *dāleth*=door; (5) *hê*=house; (6) *waw*=nail (Evans, tent peg); (7) *zâyin*=weapon; (8) *ḥêth*=fence; (9) *ṭêth*=cake of bread (Lidzbarski, a package); (10) *yôdh*=hand; (11) *kaph*=palm of hand; (12) *lamedh*=ox-goad; (13) *mêm*=water flowing; (14) *nûn*=fish; (15) *ṣamekh*=?; (16) *'ayin*=eye; (17) *pê*=mouth; (18) *çadhē*=trap (others, hook or nose or steps); (19) *ḳoph*=cage (Evans says picture is an outline head and Lidzbarski, a helmet); (20) *rêsh*=head; (21) *shîn*=tooth (not teeth); (22) *taw*=mark. Not all of these meanings are, however, generally accepted (cf also Nöldeke, *Beiträge Strassb.* [1904], 124–36; Lidzbarski, *Ephemeris*, II, 125–39).

7. Order of Letters

The order of the letters differs more or less in different languages, but it is in the main the same in all the Sem and Western alphabets derived from the Phoen alphabet and this is roughly the order of the Eng. alphabet. This order is, however, full of minor variations even among the Western alphabets and in the Indian languages the letters are entirely regrouped on a different principle.

The conventional order of the Semitic alphabet may be traced with some certainty in the Biblical books to as early as the 6th cent. BC, even accepting the dates of a radical higher criticism, for there are more than a dozen passages in the OT composed on the principle of the alphabetical acrostic (Pss **111, 112, 119**; Prov **31** 10–31; Lam **1, 2, 3, 4,** etc) and the oldest of these are of this period (see Acrostic). The Formello abecedarium, if it is in fact from the 7th cent. BC, carries the known order back a century farther still and shows it prevailing in Italy as well as Pal. Moreover there are those who still consider some of the alphabetical psalms older even than this.

It must be noted, however, that while the order is in general fixed, there are local and temporary differences. In several cases e.g. the order of the sixteenth and seventeenth letters of the alphabet is inverted in the alphabetical acrostics, and this would seem to point to a time or place where *pē*, *'ayin*, was the accepted order. It happens that the inversion occurs in both the passages which are counted earliest by the modern critics (G. B. Gray in *HDB*², 8). Mr. Sayce too has recently altered or restored the order by relegating the original *ṣamekh* to a place after *shîn*, while Mr. Pilcher has quite reconstructed the original order on a geometrical basis, to his own taste at least, as ***brd; hvg; mnl; szt.***

Hebrew Inscribed Tablet from Gezer.

A certain grouping together of signs according to the relationship of the objects which they represent has often been noticed, and Sayce (*PSBA*, XXXII [1910], 215–22) thinks that he has (after having put *ṣamekh* in its right place) reduced the whole matter to a sequence of pairs of things which belong together: ox-house, camel-tent door, house-nail, weapon-fence (city wall), bread-hand, open hand-arm with goad, water-fish, eye-mouth, trap-cage, head-tooth, *ṣamekh*, *taw*. This arranging he thinks was done by someone who knew that *'alûph* was the West Sem for "leader" and *taw* was the Cretan sign for ending—an Amorite therefore in touch with the Phili. The final word on order seems not yet to have been spoken.

8. The Earliest Texts

The chief North Sem texts are (1) Moabite stone (cir 850 BC); (2) inscriptions of Zkr, Zenjirli, etc (cir 800); (3) Baal-Lebanon inscription (cir 750); (4) Siloam inscription (cir 700 BC); (5) Harvard Samaritan ostraca (time of Ahab?); (6) Gezer tablet; (7) various weights and seals before 600 BC. The striking fact about the earliest inscriptions is that however remote geographically, there is on the whole so little difference in the forms of the letters. This is particularly true of the North Sem inscriptions and tends to the inference that the invention was after all not so long before the surviving inscriptions. While the total amount of the earliest Pal inscriptions is not even yet very large, the recent discovery of the Sam ostraca, the Gezer tablet, and various minor inscriptions, is at least pointing to a general use of Sem writing in Pal at least as early as the 9th cent. BC.

9. Changes in Letter Forms

The tendency of letters to change form in consequence of changed environment is not peculiar to alphabetical writing but is characteristic of the transmission of all sorts of writing. The morphology of alphabetical writing has however its own history. The best source for studying this on the Sem side is Lidzbarski's *Handbuch* (see below), and on the Gr side the best first source is E. S. Roberts, *Intro to Gr Epigraphy* (Cambr.). The best synoptical statement of the Sem is found in the admirable tables in the *Jew Enc*, V, i, 449–53.

For the later evolution of both Gr and Lat alphabets, E. M. Thompson's *Introduction to Greek and Latin Palaeography*, Oxford, 1912, is far the best introduction. In this he takes account of the great finds of papyri which have so revolutionized the study of the forms of Greek letters around the beginning of the Christian era, since his first Handbook was published. (See arts. on the text of OT and NT.)

In the Heb, the old Phoen alphabet of the early inscriptions had in the NT times given way to the square Aram. characters of the modern Heb which possibly came into use as early as the time of Ezra.

The most comprehensive modern brief conspectus covering both Heb and Gr is that reproduced in this art. from the little manual of Specht. See also WRITING.

LITERATURE.—Isaac Taylor's *Alphabet* (2d ed, 1899) is still useful for orientation, and his article in the *HDB* likewise, but Edward Clodd's little *Story of the Alphabet* (New York, 1907), taken with Faulmann's *Geschichte der Schrift* and *Buch der Schrift*, is better for general purposes. For scientific purposes see the bibliography prefixed to Lidzbarski's *Handbuch der nordsemitischen Epigraphik* (1898, 2 vols) and his *Ephemeris* passim to date, Evans' *Scripta minoa*, Oxf., 1909, and the lit. of the art. WRITING in this Encyclopaedia. See also C. G. Ball, "Origin of the Phoen Alphabet," *PSBA*, XV, 392–408; E. J. Pilcher, "The Origin of the Alphabet," *PSBA*, XXVI (1904), 168–73; Franz Praetorius, "The Origin of the Canaanite Alphabet," *Smithsonian Rep.* (1907), 595–604; S. A. Cook, "The Old Hebrew Alphabet and the Gezer Tablet," *PEFS* (1909), 284–309. For Bible class work, H. N. Skinner's *Story of the Letters and Figures* (Chicago, 1905) is very admirably adapted to the purpose.

E. C. RICHARDSON

ALPHAEUS, al-fē'us (**'Αλφαῖος**, *Alphaíos;* WH, **Ἁλφαῖος**, *Halphaíos*):

(1) The father of the second James in the list of the apostles (Mt **10** 3; Mk **3** 18; Lk **6** 15; Acts **1** 13).

(2) The father of Levi, the publican (Mk **2** 14). Levi is designated as Matthew in the Gospel of Mt (**9** 9). There is no other reference to this Alphaeus.

Some writers, notably Weiss, identify the father of Levi with the father of the second James. He says that James and Levi were undoubtedly brothers; but that seems improbable. If they were brothers they would quite likely be associated as are James and John, Andrew and Peter. Chrysostom says James and Levi had both been taxgatherers before they became followers of Jesus. This tradition would not lend much weight as proof that they were brothers, for it might arise through identifying the two names, and the western MSS do identify them and read James instead of Levi in Mk **2** 14. This, however, is undoubtedly a corruption of the text. If it had been the original it would be difficult to explain the substitution of an unknown Levi for James who is well known.

Many writers identify Alphaeus, the father of the second James, with Clopas of Jn **19** 25. This had early become a tradition, and Chrysostom believed they were the same person. This identity rests on four suppositions, all of which are doubtful:

(*a*) That the Mary of Clopas was the same as the Mary who was the mother of the second James. There is a difference of opinion as to whether "Mary of Clopas" should be understood to be the wife of Clopas or the daughter of Clopas, but the former is more probable. We know from Mt **27** 56 and Mk **15** 40 that there was a James who was the son of Mary, and that this Mary belonged to that little group of women that was near Jesus at the time of the crucifixion. It is quite likely that this Mary is the one referred to in Jn **19** 25. That would make James, the son of Mary of Mt **27** 56, the son of Mary of Clopas. But Mary was such a common name in the NT that this supposition cannot be proven.

(*b*) That the James, who was the son of Mary, was the same person as the James, the son of Alphaeus. Granting the supposition under (*a*), this would not prove the identity of Clopas and Alphaeus unless this supposition can also be proven, but it seems impossible to either prove it or disprove it.

(*c*) That Alphaeus and Clopas are different variations of a common original, and that the variation has arisen from different pronunciations of the first letter ח (*ḥ*) of the Aram. original. There are good scholars who both support and deny this theory.

(*d*) That Clopas had two names as was common at that time; but there is nothing to either substantiate or disprove this theory. See CLOPAS.

It seems impossible to determine absolutely whether or not Alphaeus, the father of the second James, and Clopas of Jn **19** 25 are the same person, but it is quite probable that they are.

A. W. FORTUNE

ALSO, ôl'sō: In the Gr **καί**, *kaí*, when it is equivalent to "also" or "even," is always placed before the word or phrase which it is intended to emphasize (e.g. Acts **12** 3; 1 Jn **4** 21). Mt **6** 14 should therefore read, "Your heavenly Father will forgive *you* also"; Lk **6** 13, "Whom also he named apostles"; He **8** 6, "The mediator of a better covenant also"; and 1 Thess **4** 14, 'If we believe that Jesus died and rose again, so also [we believe that] those who are fallen asleep in Jesus, God will bring with Him.'

ALTANEUS, al-ta-nē'us. See MALTANNEUS (Apoc).

ALTAR, ôl'tẽr (מִזְבֵּחַ, *mizbēaḥ*, lit. "place of slaughter or sacrifice," from זָבַח, *zābhaḥ*, which is found in both senses; **βωμός**, *bōmós* [only in Acts **17** 23], **θυσιαστήριον**, *thusiastḗrion*):

I. CLASSIFICATION OF HEBREW ALTARS
Importance of the Distinction
II. LAY ALTARS
1. Pre-Mosaic
2. In the Mosaic Age
3. Dangers of the Custom
4. The Mosaic Provisions
III. HORNED ALTARS OF BURNT OFFERING
1. The Tabernacle Altar
2. The Altar of Josh **22**
3. The Altar till Solomon
4. The Horned Altar in Use
5. The Temple of Solomon
6. The Altar of Ahaz
7. Ezekiel
8. The Post-exilic Altar
9. Idolatrous and Unlawful Altars
10. The Horns
IV. ALTARS OF INCENSE

V. Recent Archaeological Materials
1. A Gezer Altar
2. The Taanach Altar of Incense
Literature

A. Critical

I. Classification of Hebrew Altars.—Before considering the Biblical texts attention must be drawn to the fact that these texts know of at least two

Fig. 1.—Cairn Altar.

kinds of altars which were so different in appearance that no contemporary could possibly confuse them. The first was an altar consisting of earth or unhewn stones. It had no fixed shape, but varied with the materials. It might consist of a rock (Jgs **13** 19) or a single large stone (1 S **14** 33–35) or again a number of stones (1 K **18** 31 f). It could have no horns, for it would be impossible to give the stone horns without hewing it, nor would a heap of earth lend itself to the formation of horns. It could have no regular pattern for the same reason. On the other hand we meet with a group of passages that refer to altars of quite a different type. We read of horns, of fixed measurements, of a particular pattern, of bronze as the material. To bring home the difference more rapidly illustrations of the two types are given side by side. The first figure represents a cairn altar such as was in use in some other ancient religions. The second is a conjectural restoration of Heb altars of burnt offering and incense of the second kind.

Importance of the Distinction

Both these might be and were called altars, but it is so evident that this common designation could not have caused any eye-witness to confuse the two that in reading the Bible we must carefully examine each text in turn and see to which kind the author is referring. Endless confusion has been caused, even in our own time, by the failure to note this distinction, and the reader can hope to make sense of the Biblical laws and narratives only if he be very careful to picture to himself in every case the exact object to which his text refers. For the sake of clearness different terms will be adopted in this article to denote the two kinds of altars. The first will be termed "lay altars" since, as will be seen, the Law permitted any layman to offer certain sacrifices at an altar of earth or unhewn stone without the assistance of a priest, while the second will be styled "horned altars," owing to their possession of horns which, as already pointed out, could not exist in a lay altar that conformed with the provisions of the law.

II. Lay Altars.—In Gen we often read of the erection of altars, e.g. **8** 20; **12** 7; **13** 4. Though

1. Pre-Mosaic

no details are given we are able to infer their general character with considerable precision. In reading the accounts it is sometimes evident that we are dealing with some rough improvised structure. For example, when Abraham builds the altar for the sacrifice of Isaac in Gen **22** it cannot be supposed that he used metal or wrought stone. When Jacob makes a covenant with Laban a heap of stones is thrown up "and they did eat there by the heap" (**31** 46). This heap is not expressly termed an altar, but if this covenant be compared with later covenants it will be seen that in these its place is taken by an altar of the lay type (*SBL*, ch 2), and it is reasonable to suppose that this heap was in fact used as an altar (cf ver 54). A further consideration is provided by the fact that the Arabs had a custom of using any stone as an altar for the nonce, and certainly such altars are found in the Mosaic and post-Mosaic history. We may therefore feel sure that the altars of Gen were of the general type represented by Fig. 1 and were totally unlike the altars of Fig. 2.

2. In the Mosaic Age

Thus Moses found a custom by which the Israelite threw up rude altars of the materials most easily obtained in the field and offered sacrificial worship to God on sundry occasions. That the custom was not peculiar to the Israelites is shown by such instances as that of Balaam (Nu **23** 1, etc). Probably we may take the narrative

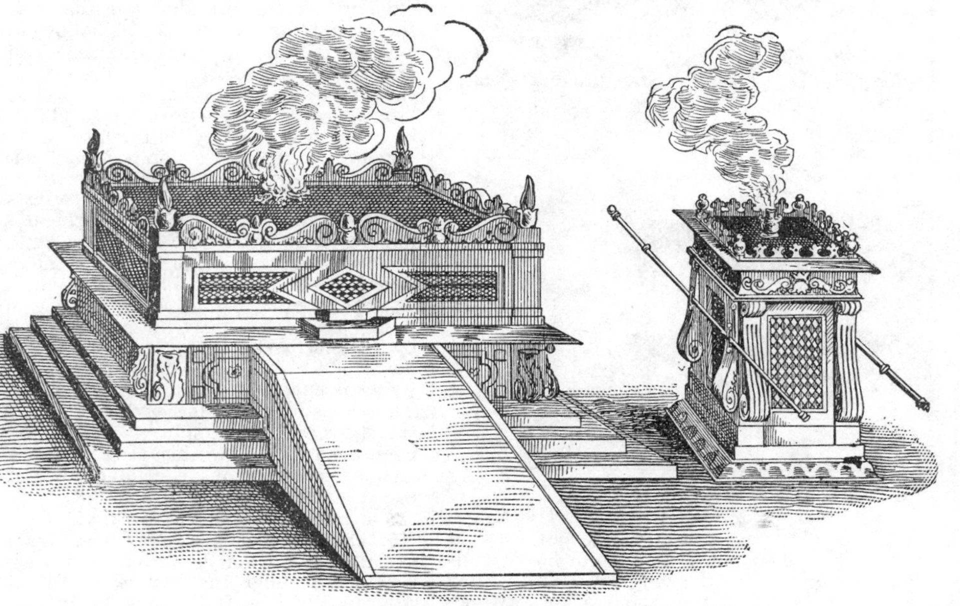

Fig. 2.—Altar of Burnt Offering and Altar of Incense.

of Jethro's sacrifice as a fair example of the occasions on which such altars were used, for it cannot be supposed that Aaron and all the elders of Israel were openly committing an unlawful act when they ate bread with Moses' father-in-law before God (Ex **18** 12). Again, the narrative in which we see Moses building an altar for the purposes of a covenant probably exemplifies a custom that was in use for other covenants that did not fall to be narrated (Ex **24** 4 ff).

3. Dangers of the Custom

But a custom of erecting altars might easily lend itself to abuses. Thus archaeology has shown us one altar—though of a much later date—which is adorned with faces (Fig. 4), a practice that was quite contrary to the Mosaic ideas of preserving a perfectly imageless worship. Other possible abuses were suggested by the current practices of the Canaanites or are explained by the terms of the laws. See HIGH PLACE.

FIG. 3.—Stone Altar of Gezer.

4. The Mosaic Provisions

Accordingly Moses regulated these lay altars. Leaving the occasion of their erection and use to be determined by custom he promulgated the following laws: "An altar of earth mayest thou make unto me, and mayest sacrifice thereon thy burnt offerings and thy peace offerings, thy sheep, and thine oxen; in all the place where I record my name I will come unto thee and I will bless thee. And if thou make me an altar of stone, thou shalt not build it of hewn stones; for if thou lift thy tool upon it, thou hast polluted it. Neither mayest thou go up by steps unto mine altar," etc (Ex **20** 24–26; so correct EV). Several remarks must be made on this law. It is a law for laymen, not priests. This is proved by the second person singular and also by the reason given for the prohibition of steps—since the priests were differently garbed. It applies "in *all the* place where I record my name," not, as the ordinary rendering has it, "in *every* place." This latter is quite unintelligible: it is usually explained as meaning places hallowed by theophanies, but there are plenty of instances in the history of lay sacrifices where no theophany can be postulated; see e.g. Gen **31** 54; 1 S **20** 6.29 (*EPC*, 185 f). "All the place" refers to the territory of Israel for the time being. When Naaman desired to cease sacrificing to any deity save the God of Israel he was confronted by the problem of deciding how he could sacrifice to Him outside this "place." He solved it by asking for two mules' burden of the earth of the "place" (2 K **5** 17). Lastly, as already noticed, this law excludes the possibility of giving the altars horns or causing them to conform to any given pattern, since the stone could not be wrought. One other law must be noticed in this connection: Dt **16** 21 f: 'Thou shalt not plant thee an *'ăshērāh* of any kind of tree beside the altar of the Lord thy God, which thou shalt make thee. Neither shalt thou set thee up a pillar, which the Lord thy God hateth.' Here again the reference is probably to the lay altars, not to the religious capital which was under the control of the priests.

III. Horned Altars of Burnt Offering.—In Ex **27** 1–8 (cf **38** 1–7) a command is given to construct for the Tabernacle an altar of shittim wood covered with bronze. It was to be five cubits long by five broad and three high. The four corners were to have horns of one piece with it. A network of bronze was to reach halfway up the altar to a ledge. In some way that is defined only by reference to what was shown to Moses in the Mount the altar was to be hollow with planks, and it was to be equipped with rings and staves for facility of transport. The precise construction cannot be determined, and it is useless to speculate where the instructions are so plainly governed by what was seen by Moses in the Mount; but certain features that are important for the elucidation of the Bible texts emerge clearly. The altar is rectangular, presenting at the top a square surface with horns at the four corners. The more important material used is bronze, and the whole construction was as unlike that of the ordinary lay altar as possible. The use of this altar in the ritual of the Tabernacle falls under the heading SACRIFICES. Here we must notice that it was served by priests. Whenever we find references to the horns of an altar or to its pattern we see that the writer is speaking of an altar of this general type. Thus a criminal seeking asylum fled to an altar of this type, as appears from the horns which are mentioned in the two historical instances and also from such expressions as coming down or going up. See ASYLUM.

1. The Tabernacle Altar

2. The Altar of Josh 22

We read in Josh **22** 9 ff that the children of Reuben and the children of Gad built an altar. In ver 28 we find them saying, "Behold the *pattern* of the altar," etc. This is decisive as to the meaning, for the lay altar had no pattern. Accordingly in its general shape this altar must have conformed to the type of the Tabernacle altar. It was probably not made of the same materials, for the word "build" is continually used in connection with it, and this word would scarcely be appropriate for working metal: nor again was it necessarily of the same size, but it was of the same pattern: and it was designed to serve as a witness that the descendants of the men who built it had a portion in the Lord. It seems to follow that the pattern of the Tabernacle altar was distinctive and unlike the heathen altars in general use in Palestine and this appears to be confirmed by modern excavations which have revealed high places with altars quite unlike those contemplated by the Pent. See HIGH PLACE.

3. The Altar till Solomon

In the subsequent history till the erection of Solomon's Temple attention need only be directed to the fact that a horned altar existed while the Ark was still housed in a tent. This is important for two reasons. It shows a historical period in which a horned altar existed at the religious capital side by side with a number of lay altars all over the country, and it negatives the suggestion of G. A. Smith (*Jerusalem*, II, 64) that the bare rock eṣ-Ṣakhra was used by Solomon as the altar, since the unhewn rock obviously could not provide a horned altar such as we find as early as 1 K **1** 50–53. Note too that we read here of *bringing down* from the altar, and this expression implies elevation. Further in **9** 25 we hear that Solomon was in the habit of

4. The Horned Altar in Use

Fig. 4.—Rock Altar from Taanach.

offering on the altar which he had built, and this again proves that he had built an altar and did not merely use the temple rock. (See also Watson in *PEFS* [January, 1910], 15 ff, in reply to Smith.)

5. The Temple of Solomon

For the reasons just given it is certain that Solomon used an altar of the horned type, but we have no account of the construction in K. According to a note preserved in the LXX but not in the Heb, Solomon enlarged the altar erected by David on Araunah's threshing-floor (2 S **24** 25), but this notice is of very doubtful historical value and may be merely a glossator's guess. According to 2 Ch **4** 1 the altar was made of bronze and was twenty cubits by twenty by ten. The Chronicler's dimensions are doubted by many, but the statement of the material is confirmed by 1 K **8** 64; 2 K **16** 10–15. From the latter passage it appears that an altar of bronze had been in use till the time of Ahaz. This king saw an

6. The Altar of Ahaz

altar in Damascus of a different pattern and had a great altar made for the temple on its model. As the text contrasts the great altar with the altar of bronze, we may infer that the altar of Ahaz was not made of bronze. Whether either or both of these altars had steps (cf Ezk **43** 17) or were approached by a slope as in Fig. 2 cannot be determined with certainty. It may be noted that in Isa **27** 9 we read of the stones of the altar in a passage the reference of which is uncertain.

7. Ezekiel

Ezekiel also gives a description of an altar (**43** 13–17), but there is nothing to show whether it is purely ideal or represents the altar of Solomon or that of Ahaz, and modern writers take different views. In the vision it stood before the house (**40** 47). In addition he describes an altar or table of wood (**41** 22). This of course could only be a table, not in any sense an altar. See Table.

8. The Post-exilic Altar

Ezr **3** 2 f tells of the setting up of the altar by Zerubbabel and his contemporaries. No information as to its shape, etc, can be extracted from this notice. We read of a defilement of the temple altar in 1 Macc **1** 54. This was made of stones (Ex **20** 24–26 having at this date been applied to the temple altar contrary to its original intent) and a fresh altar of whole stones was constructed (1 Macc **4** 44–49). Presumably this altar had no horns.

9. Idolatrous Altars

It is clear from the historical and prophetical books that in both kingdoms a number of unlawful altars were in use. The distinction which has been drawn between lay altars and horned altars helps to make these passages easy to understand. Thus when Amos in speaking of Bethel writes, "The horns of the altar shall be cut off," we see that he is not thinking of lay altars which could have no horns (**3** 14). Again Hosea's "Because Ephraim hath multiplied altars 'to sin,' altars have been to him 'for sin'" (**8** 11; cf **10** 1–8; **12** 11 [12]), is not in contradiction to Ex **20** 24–26 because the prophet is not speaking of lay altars. The high places of Jeroboam (1 K **12** 28–33) were clearly unlawful and their altars were unlawful altars of the horned type. Such cases must be clearly distinguished from the lay altars of Saul and others.

10. The Horns

The origin of the horns is unknown, though there are many theories. Fugitives caught hold of them (1 K **1** 50.51), and victims could be tied to them (Ps **118** 27).

IV. Altars of Incense.—Ex **30** 1–10 contains the commands for the construction and use of an altar of incense. The material was shittim wood, the dimensions one cubit by one by two, and it also had horns. Its top and sides were overlaid with gold and it was surrounded by a crown or rim of gold. For facility of transport it had golden rings and staves. It stood before the veil in front of the ark.

Solomon also constructed an altar of incense (1 K **6** 20; **7** 48; 1 Ch **28** 18), cedar replacing shittim wood. The altar of incense reappears in 1 Macc **1** 21; **4** 49.

Fig. 5.—Incense Altars of Sandstone Found in the Rock Shrine at Sinai.

V. Recent Archaeological Materials.—Recently several altars have been revealed by excavations. They throw light on the Bible chiefly by showing what is forbidden. See esp. High Place. Fig. 3

1. A Gezer Altar

represents an altar found at Gezer built into the foundation of a wall dating about 600 BC. Mr. Macalister describes it in the following words: "It is a four-sided block of limestone, 1 ft. 3 in. high. The top and bottom are approximately 10½ and 9 in. square respectively; but these are only the average dimensions of the sides, which are not regularly cut. The angles are prolonged upward for an additional 1½ in. as rounded knobs—no doubt the 'horns' of the altar. The top is very slightly concave so as to hold perhaps an eighth of a pint of liquid" (*PEFS* [July, 1907], 196 f). The size suggests an altar of incense rather than an altar of burnt offering, but in view of the general resemblance between the Tabernacle altars of burnt offering and incense, this is a fact of minor importance. On the other hand, the shape, pattern and material are of great interest. That the altar violates in principle the law of Ex **20** 25 forbidding the dressing of the stones is obvious, though that passage does not apply in terms to altars of incense, but certainly the appearance of the block does recall in a general way the altars of the other type—the horned altars. Like them it is four-sided with a square top, and like them it has knobs or horns at each corner. Possibly it was formed in general imitation of the Temple altars.

Other altars in Can high places exemplify by their appearance the practices prohibited by the Pent. See for illustrations H. Vincent, *Canaan d'après l'exploration récente;* R. Kittel, *Studien zur hebräischen Archäologie und Religions-Geschichte;* S. R. Driver, *Modern Research as Illustrating the Bible.*

2. The Taanach Altar of Incense

Importance attaches to a terra cotta altar of incense found by Sellin at Taanach, because its height and dimensions at the base recall the altar of Ex. "It was just 3 ft. high, and in shape roughly like a truncated pyramid, the four sides at the bottom being each 18 in. long, and the whole ending at the top in a bowl a foot in diameter. . . . . The altar is hollow. . . . . Professor Sellin places the date of the altar at about 700 BC. . . . . An incense-altar of exactly the same shape . . . . but of much smaller size . . . . has been found quite recently at Gezer in débris of about 1000–600 BC" (Driver, *Modern Research,* etc, 85). These discoveries supply a grim comment on the theories of those critics who maintain that incense was not used by the Hebrews before the time of Jer. The form of the altar itself is as contrary to the principles of the Pent law as any thing could be.

On altar furniture see POTS; SHOVELS; BASINS; FLESH-HOOKS; FIREPANS. On the site, TEMPLE, and generally, ARIEL; SACRIFICE; SANCTUARY; TABERNACLE; HIGH PLACE.

LITERATURE.—R. Kittel, *Studien zur hebräischen Archäologie und Religions-Geschichte,* I and II; Hastings, *Encyclopedia of Religion and Ethics;* Murray, *Illustrated Bible Dictionary; EB,* s.v. "Altar"; *EPC,* ch 6. The discussions in the ordinary works of reference must be used with caution for the reason given in *I* above.

HAROLD M. WIENER

B. IN WORSHIP

I. In Worship: Tabernacle and Temples.—In the literature of the Bible, sacrifices are prior to altars, and altars prior to sacred buildings.

1. Patriarchal Altars

Their first mention is in the case of the altar built by Noah after the Flood (Gen **8** 20). The next is the altar built at the place of Shechem, by which Abraham formally took possession, on behalf of his descendants, of the whole land of Canaan (Gen **12** 7). A second altar was built between Bethel and Ai (ver 8). To this the patriarch returned on his way from Egypt (Gen **13** 4). His next place of sacrifice was Hebron (ver 18); and tradition still professes to show the place where his altar stood. A subsequent altar was built on the top of a mountain in the land of Moriah for the sacrifice of Isaac (Gen **22** 9).

2. Sacred Sites

Each of these four spots was the scene of some special revelation of Jehovah; possibly to the third of them (Hebron) we may attribute the memorable vision and covenant of Gen **15**. These sites became, in after years, the most venerated and coveted perquisites of the nation, and fights for their possession largely determined its history. To them Isaac added an altar at Beersheba (Gen **26** 25), probably a reërection, on the same site, of an altar built by Abraham, whose home for many years was at Beersheba. Jacob built no new altars, but again and again repaired those at Shechem and Bethel. On one occasion he offered a sacrifice on one of the mountains of Gilead, but without mention of an altar (Gen **31** 54). There were thus four or five spots in Canaan associated at once with the worship of Jehovah, and the name of their great ancestor, which to Hebrews did not lose their sanctity by the passage of time, viz. Shechem, Bethel, Hebron, Moriah and Beersheba.

3. Pre-Tabernacle Altars

The earliest provision for an altar as a portion of a fixed establishment of religion is found in Ex **20** 24–26, immediately after the promulgation of the Decalogue. Altars are commanded to be made of earth or of unhewn stone, yet so as to have, not steps, but only slopes for ascent to the same—the injunction implying that they stood on some elevation (see ALTAR, A, above). Before the arrival at Sinai, during the war with Amalek, Moses had built an emergency altar, to which he gave the name Jehovah-Nissi (Ex **17** 15). This was probably only a memorial altar (cf the altar Ed in Josh **22** 21 ff). At Sinai took place the great crisis in Israel's national history. It was required that the covenant about to be made with Jehovah should be ratified with sacrificial blood; but before Moses could sprinkle the Book of the Covenant and the people who covenanted (Ex **24** 6.7; cf He **9** 19), it was necessary that an altar should be built for the sacrificial act. This was done "under the mount," where, beside the altar, were reared twelve pillars, emblematic of the twelve tribes of Israel (ver 4).

In connection with the tabernacle and the successive temples there were two altars—the Altar of Burnt Offering (*the* altar by preëminence, Ezk **43** 13), and the Altar of Incense. Of these it is now necessary to speak more particularly.

II. The Altar of Burnt Offering (מִזְבַּח הָעֹלָה, *mizbaḥ hā-'ōlāh*), ***The Brazen Altar*** (מִזְבַּח הַנְּחֹשֶׁת, *mizbaḥ ha-neḥōsheth*).—

1. Altar before the Tabernacle

(By "brass" throughout understand "bronze.") The altar which stood before the tabernacle was a portable box constructed of acacia wood and covered on the outside with plates of brass (Ex **27** 1 ff). "Hollow with planks," is its definition (ver 8). It was five cubits long, five cubits broad, and three cubits high; on the ordinary reckoning, about $7\frac{1}{2}$ ft. on the horizontal square, and $4\frac{1}{2}$ ft. in height (possibly less; see CUBIT). On the "grating of network of brass" described as around and half-way up the altar (vs 4.5), see GRATING. Into the corners of this grating, on two sides, rings were riveted, into which the staves were inserted by which the Ark was borne (see STAVES). For its corner projections, see HORNS OF THE ALTAR. The prohibition of steps in Ex **20** 26 and the analogy of later altars suggest that this small altar before the tabernacle was made to stand on a base or platform, led up to by a slope of earth. The right of sanctuary is mentioned in Ex **21** 14. For the utensils connected with the altar, see PANS; SHOVELS; BASINS; FLESH-HOOKS; CENSERS. All these utensils were made of brass.

The history of the altar before the tabernacle was that of the tabernacle itself, as the two were not parted during its continuance (see TABERNACLE). Their abolition did not take place till Solomon's temple was ready for use, when the great high place at Gibeon (1 K **3** 4) was dismantled, and the tabernacle and its holy vessels were brought to the new temple (**8** 4). Another altar had meanwhile been raised by David before the tabernacle he had made on Zion, into which the Ark of the Covenant was moved (1 Ch **15** 1; **16** 1). This would be a duplicate of that at Gibeon, and would share its supersession at the erection of the first temple.

2. Its History

In Solomon's temple the altar was considerably enlarged, as was to be expected from the greater size of the building before which it stood. We are indebted to the Chronicler for its exact dimensions (2 Ch **4** 1). It formed a square of twenty cubits, with an elevation of ten cubits (30×30×15 ft.; or somewhat less). It is described as "an altar of brass" (2 Ch **4** 1), or "brazen altar" (1 K **8** 64; 2 Ch **7** 7; cf 2 K **16** 14), either as being, like its predecessors, encased in brass, or, as others think, made wholly of brass. It was not meant to be portable, but that the altar itself was movable is shown by the fact of Ahaz having it removed (2 K **16** 14). Further details of its structure are not given. The altar stood in "the middle of the court that was before the house," but proved too small to receive the gifts on the day of the temple's dedication (1 K **8** 64; 2 Ch **7** 7). It remained, however, the center of Israelitish worship for $2\frac{1}{2}$ centuries, till Ahaz removed it from the forefront of the house, and placed it on the northern side of his Damascene altar (2 K **16** 14). This indignity was repaired by Hezekiah (cf 2 K **18** 22), and the altar assumed its old place in the temple service till its destruction by Nebuchadnezzar in 586 BC.

3. Altar of Solomon's Temple

The altar of Ezekiel's ideal temple was, as planned, a most elaborate structure, the cubit used for this purpose being that of "a cubit and an handbreadth" (Ezk **43** 13), or the large cubit of history (see CUBIT). The paragraph describing it (**43** 13–17) is very specific, though uncertainty rests on the meaning of some of the details. The altar consisted of four stages lying one above another, gradually diminishing in size till the hearth was reached upon which the fire was lit. This was a square of twelve cubits (18 ft.), from the corners of which 4 horns projected upward (ver 15). The base or lowest stage was one cubit in height, and had a border round about, half a cubit high (ver 13); the remaining stages were two, four, and four cubits high respectively (vs 14.15); the horns may have measured another cubit (thus LXX). Each stage was marked by the inlet of one cubit (vs 13.14). The basement was thus, apparently, a square of eighteen cubits or 27 ft. The word "bottom" (lit. "bosom") in Ezekiel's description is variously interpreted, some regarding it as a "drain" for carrying off the sacrificial blood, others identifying it with the "basement." On its eastern face the altar had steps looking toward the east (ver 17)—a departure from the earlier practice (for the reason of this, cf Perowne's art. "Altar" in *DB*).

4. Altar of Ezekiel's Temple

Of the altar of the second temple no measurements are given. It is told only that it was built prior to the temple, and was set upon its base (Ezr **3** 3), presumably on the Ṣakhra stone—the ancient site.

5. Altar of Second Temple

In Herod's temple a difficulty is found in harmonizing the accounts of the Mish and Jos as to the size of the altar. The latter gives it as a square of fifty cubits (*BJ*, V, v, 6). The key to the solution probably lies in distinguishing between the structure of the altar proper (thirty-two cubits square), and a platform of larger area (fifty cubits square=75 ft.) on which it stood. When it is remembered that the Ṣakhra stone is 56 ft. in length and 42 ft. in width, it is easy to see that it might form a portion of a platform built up above and around it to a level of this size. The altar, like that of Ezekiel's plan, was built in diminishing stages; in the Mish, one of one cubit, and three of five cubits in height, the topmost stage measuring twenty-six cubits square, or, with deduction of a cubit for the officiating priests, twenty-four cubits. Jos, on the other hand, gives the height at fifteen cubits. The altar, as before, had 4 horns. Both Jos and the Mish state that the altar was built of unhewn stones. The ascent, thirty-two cubits long and sixteen broad, likewise of unhewn stone, was on the south side. See further, TEMPLE, HEROD'S. It is of this altar that the words were spoken, "Leave there thy gift before the altar, and go thy way, first be reconciled to thy brother, and then come and offer thy gift" (Mt **5** 24).

6. Altar of Herod's Temple

III. The Altar of Incense (מִזְבַּח הַקְּטֹרֶת, *mizbaḥ ha-ḳṭōreth*), ***Golden Altar*** (מִזְבַּח הַזָּהָב, *mizbaḥ ha-zāhābh*).—This was a diminutive table of acacia overlaid with gold, the upper surface of which was a square of one cubit, and its height two cubits, with an elevated cornice or crown around its top (Ex **30** 2 ff). Like the great altar of burnt offering, it was in the category of "most holy" things (Ex **30** 10); a distinction which gave it a right to a place in the inner room of the cella or holy of holies. Hence, in 1 K **6** 22, it is said to "belong to the oracle," and in He **9** 4 that chamber is said to have the "altar of incense." It did not, however, actually stand there, but in the outer chamber, "before the veil" (Ex **40** 26). The reason for this departure from the strict rule of temple ritual was that sweet incense was to be burnt daily upon it at the offering of every daily sacrifice, the lamps being then lit and extinguished (cf Nu **28** 3 f; Ex **30** 7.8), so that a cloud of smoke might fill the inner chamber at the moment when the sacrificial blood was sprinkled (see MERCY-SEAT). To have burnt this incense within the veil would have required repeated entries into the holy of holies, which entries were forbidden (Lev **16** 2). The altar thus stood immediately without the veil, and the smoke of the incense burnt upon it entered the inner chamber by the openings above the veil.

1. In the Tabernacle

For the material construction which admitted of this, see Holy Place.

For other uses of the altar of incense see Horns of the Altar, where it is shown that at the time of the offerings of special sin offerings and on the day of the annual fast its horns were sprinkled with blood. This, with the offering of incense upon it, were its only uses, as neither meal offerings might be laid upon it, nor libations of drink offerings poured thereon (Ex **30** 9). The Tāmīd, or standing sacrifice for Israel, was a whole burnt offering of a lamb offered twice daily with its meal offering, accompanied with a service of incense.

It is probable that the censers in use at the time of the construction of this altar and after were in shape like a spoon or ladle (see Table of Shewbread), which, when filled with live coals from the great altar, were carried within the sanctuary and laid upon the altar of incense (Lev **16** 12). The incense-sticks, broken small, were then placed upon the coals. The narrative of the deaths of Aaron's sons, Nadab and Abihu, is thus made intelligible, the fire in their censers not having been taken from the great altar.

2. Mode of Burning Incense

The original small altar made by Moses was superseded by one made by Solomon. This was made of cedar wood, overlaid with gold (1 K **6** 20.22; **7** 48; **9** 25; 2 Ch **4** 19); hence was called the "golden altar." This was among "all the vessels of the house of God, great and small," which Nebuchadnezzar took to Babylon (2 Ch **36** 18). As a consequence, when Ezekiel drew plans for a new temple, he gave it an incense altar made wholly of wood and of larger dimensions than before (Ezk **41** 22). It had a height of three cubits and a top of two cubits square. There was an incense altar likewise in the second temple. It was this altar, probably plated with gold, which Antiochus Epiphanes removed (1 Macc **1** 21), and which was restored by Judas Maccabaeus (1 Macc **4** 49). (On critical doubts as to the existence of the golden altar in the first and second temples, cf *POT*, 323.)

3. In Solomon's Temple and Later

That the Herodian temple also had its altar of incense we know from the incident of Zacharias having a vision there of "an angel .... standing on the right side of the altar of incense" when he went into the temple of the Lord to burn incense (Lk **1** 11). No representation of such an altar appears on the arch of Titus, though it is mentioned by Jos (*BJ*, V, v, 5). It was probably melted down by John during the course of the siege (V, xiii, 6).

4. In Herod's Temple

In the apocalypse of John, no temple was in the restored heaven and earth (Rev **21** 22), but in the earlier part of the vision was a temple (Rev **14** 17; **15** 6) with an altar and a censer (**8** 3). It is described as "the golden altar which was before the throne," and, with the smoke of its incense, there went up before God the prayers of the saints. This imagery is in harmony with the statement of Lk that as the priests burnt incense, "the whole multitude of the people were praying without at the hour of incense" (**1** 10). Both history and prophecy thus attest the abiding truth that salvation is by sacrificial blood, and is made available to men through the prayers of saints and sinners offered by a great High Priest.

5. Symbolism of Incense Burning

W. Shaw Caldecott

AL-TASHHETH, al-tash′heth, **AL-TASCHITH**, al-tas′ kith. See Psalms; Song.

ALTOGETHER, ôl-to͝o-geth′ẽr: Representing five Heb and three Gr originals, which variously signify (1) "together"; i.e. all, e.g. 'all men, high and low, weighed *together* in God's balance are lighter than vanity' (Ps **62** 9); so also **53** 3; Jer **10** 8. (2) "all": so RV, Isa **10** 8: "Are not my princes all of them kings?" (3) "*with one accord* have broken the yoke"; so RV, Jer **5** 5. (4) "completely," "entirely," "fully": "so as not to destroy him altogether" (2 Ch **12** 12; cf Gen **18** 21; Ex **11** 1; Ps **39** 5; Jer **30** 11 AV; cf RV). (5) "wholly": "altogether born in sins," Jn **9** 34. (6) In 1 Cor **5** 10 RV rendered "at all"; 1 Cor **9** 10 "assuredly." (7) A passage of classic difficulty to translators is Acts **26** 29, where "altogether" in RV is rendered "with much," Gr *en megálō* (*en pollō*). See Almost. Many of the instances where "altogether" occurs in AV become "together" in RV. Used as an adj. in Ps **39** 5 ("altogether vanity"). Dwight M. Pratt

ALUSH, ā′lush (אָלוּשׁ, *'ālūsh*): A desert camp of the Israelites between Dophkah and Rephidim (Nu **33** 13.14). The situation is not certainly known. See Wanderings of Israel.

ALVAH, al′va (עַלְוָה, *'alwāh*): A chief (AV **duke**) of Edom (Gen **36** 40), called "Aliah" in 1 Ch **1** 51. Probably the same as Alvan, or Alian, son of Shobal son of Seir (Gen **36** 23; 1 Ch **1** 40).

ALVAN, al′van (עַלְוָן, *'alwān*, "tall"?): A son of Shobal, the Horite (Gen **36** 23). In 1 Ch **1** 40 the name is written Alian, LXX 'Ωλάμ. It is probably the same as Alvah of Gen **36** 23, which appears in 1 Ch **1** 51 as Aliah.

ALWAY, ôl′wā (archaic and poetic); **ALWAYS**, ôl′wāz: Properly applied to acts or states perpetually occurring, but not necessarily continuous. In Heb, most frequently, תָּמִיד, *tāmīdh*. In Gr **διὰ παντός**, *diá pantós*, ordinarily expresses continuity. In Mt **28** 20 "alway" AV, RV "always," tr Gr *pásas tás hēméras*, "all the days," corresponding to the Heb idiom similarly rendered in Dt **5** 29; **6** 24; **11** 1; **28** 33; 1 K **11** 36, etc. Gr *aeí* in Acts **7** 51; 2 Cor **6** 10; 1 Pet **3** 15, means "at every and any time."

AMAD, ā′mad (עַמְעָד, *'am'ādh*): A town in northern Pal, which fell to the tribe of Asher in the division of the land (Josh **19** 26). The modern ruin 'Amūd near Accho may be the site.

AMADATHA, a-mad′a-tha, **AMADATHUS**, a-mad′a-thus (Ad Est **12** 6). See Aman; Hammedatha.

AMAIN, a-mān′ (tr[d] from the Gr **εἰς φυγὴν ὥρμησαν**, *eis phugḗn hṓrmēsan*, "they rushed to flight"): The word is composed of the prefix "a" and the word "main," meaning "force." The expression is used by Milton, Parker, et al., but in Bib. lit. found only in 2 Macc **12** 22 where it is used to describe the flight of Timotheus and his army after he suffered defeat at the hands of Judas Maccabee ("They fled amain," i.e. violently and suddenly).

AMAL, ā′mal (עָמָל, *'āmāl*, "toiler"): A son of Helem of the tribe of Asher (1 Ch **7** 35).

AMALEK, am′a-lek (עֲמָלֵק, *'ămālēḳ*): The son, by his concubine Timna, of Eliphaz, the eldest son of Esau. He was one of the chiefs (AV **dukes**) of Edom (Gen **36** 12.16). See Amalekite.

AMALEK, am′a-lek, **AMALEKITE**, a-mal′e-kīt, am′a-lek-īt (עֲמָלֵק, *'ămālēḳ*, עֲמָלֵקִי, *'ămālēḳī*): A tribe dwelling originally in the region south of

Judah, the wilderness of et-Tih where the Israelites came into conflict with them. They were nomads as a people dwelling in that tract would naturally be. When they joined the Midianites to invade Israel they came "with their cattle and their tents" (Jgs **6** 3–5). They are not to be identified with the descendants of Esau (Gen **36** 12.16) because they are mentioned earlier, in the account of the invasion of Chedorlaomer (Gen **14** 7) and in Balaam's prophecy (Nu **24** 20) A. is called "the first of the nations," which seems to refer to an early existence. We are uncertain of their origin, for they do not appear in the list of nations found in Gen **10**. They do not seem to have had any relationship with the tribes of Israel, save as, we may surmise, some of the descendants of Esau were incorporated into the tribe. It is probable that they were of Sem stock though we have no proof of it.

The first contact with Israel was at Rephidim, in the wilderness of Sinai, where they made an unprovoked attack and were defeated after a desperate conflict (Ex **17** 8–13; Dt **25** 17.18). On account of this they were placed under the ban and Israel was commanded to exterminate them (Dt **25** 19; 1 S **15** 2.3). The next encounter of the two peoples was when the Israelites attempted to enter Canaan from the west of the Dead Sea. The spies had reported that the Amalekites were to be found in the south, in connection with the Hittites, Jebusites and Amorites (Nu **13** 29). The Israelites at first refused to advance, but later determined to do so contrary to the will of God and the command of Moses. They were met by A. and the Canaanites and completely defeated (Nu **14** 39–45). A. is next found among the allies of Moab in their attack upon Israel in the days of Eglon (Jgs **3** 13). They were also associated with the Midianites in their raids upon Israel (Jgs **6** 3), and they seemed to have gained a foothold in Ephraim, or at least a branch of them, in the hill country (Jgs **5** 14; **12** 15), but it is evident that the great body of them still remained in their old habitat, for when Saul made war upon them he drove them toward Shur in the wilderness toward Egypt (1 S **15** 1–9). David also found them in the same region (1 S **27** 8; **30** 1). After this they seem to have declined, and we find, in the days of Hezekiah, only a remnant of them who were smitten by the Simeonites at Mount Seir (1 Ch **4** 41–43). They are once mentioned in Pss in connection with other inveterate enemies of Israel (Ps **83** 7). The hatred inspired by the Amalekites is reflected in the passages already mentioned which required their utter destruction. Their attack upon them when they were just escaped from Egypt and while they were struggling through the wilderness made a deep impression upon the Israelites which they never forgot, and the wrath of David upon the messenger who brought him news of the death of Saul and Jonathan, declaring himself to be the slayer of Saul, was no doubt accentuated by his being an Amalekite (2 S **1** 1–16). H. PORTER

AMAM, ā′mam (אֲמָם, *'ămām*): An unidentified town in southern Pal, which fell to Judah in the allotment of the land; occurs only in Josh **15** 26.

AMAN, ā′man (**'Αμάν**, *Amán;* B reads **'Αδάμ**, *Adám*): Tob **14** 10; Ad Est **12** 6; **16** 10.17, probably in each case for Haman, the arch-enemy of the Jews in the canonical Book of Est (cf Est **3** 1 with Ad Est **12** 6). In Ad Est (**16** 10) Aman is represented as a Macedonian, in all other points corresponding to the Haman of Est.

AMANA, a-mā′na, a-mä′na (אֲמָנָה, *'ămānāh*): A mountain mentioned in Cant **4** 8 along with Lebanon, Senir and Hermon. The name probably means the "firm," or "constant." "From the top of Amana" is mistrd by the LXX ἀπὸ ἀρχῆς πίστεως, *apó archês písteōs*. The Amana is most naturally sought in the Anti-Lebanon, near the course of the river Abana, or Amana (see ABANAH). Another possible identification is with Mt. Amanus in the extreme north of Syria.

AMARIAH, am-a-rī′a (אֲמַרְיָה, *'ămaryāh*, and אֲמַרְיָהוּ, *'ămaryāhū*, "the Lord has said"; cf *HPN*, 180, 285): (1) A Levite in the line of Aaron-Eleazar; a son of Meraioth and grandfather of Zadok (1 Ch **6** 7.52) who lived in David's time. Cf Zadok (2 S **15** 27, etc) also *Ant*, VIII, i, 3 and X, viii, 6. (2) A Levite in the line of Kohath-Hebron referred to in 1 Ch **23** 19 and **24** 23 at the time when David divided the Levites into courses. (3) A Levite in the line of Aaron-Eleazar; a son of Azariah who "executed the priest's office in the house that Solomon built" (1 Ch **6** 10 f). Cf Ezr **7** 3 where in the abbreviated list this Am. is mentioned as an ancestor of Ezra. See AMARIAS (1 Esd **8** 2; 2 Esd **1** 2) and no. (4) of this art. (4) Chief priest and judge "in all matters of Jehovah" appointed by Jehoshaphat (2 Ch **19** 11). Possibly identical with Am. no. (3). (5) A descendant of Judah in the line of Perez and an ancestor of Ataiah who lived in Jerus after the Bab exile (Neh **11** 4). Cf Imri (1 Ch **9** 4) and no. (7) of this art., which Am. seems to be of the same family, (6) A Levite and an assistant of Kore who was appointed by Hezekiah to distribute the "oblations of Jehovah" to their brethren (2 Ch **31** 15). (7) A son of Bani who had married a foreign woman (Ezr **10** 42). See no. (5) of this art. (8) A priest who with Nehemiah sealed the covenant (Neh **10** 3); he had returned to Jerusalem with Zerubbabel (Neh **12** 2) and was the father of Jehohanan (cf Hanani, Ezr **10** 20), priest at the time of Joiakim (Neh **12** 13). Cf Immer (Ezr **2** 37; **10** 20; Neh **7** 40) and also Emmeruth (AV "Meruth," 1 Esd **5** 24). (9) An ancestor of Zephaniah, the prophet (Zeph **1** 1). A. L. BRESLICH

AMARIAS, am-a-rī′as (A, **'Αμαρίας**, *Amarías;* B, **'Αμαρθείας**, *Amartheías*) = Amariah no. 3: An ancestor of Ezra (1 Esd **8** 2; 2 Esd **1** 2).

AMARNA, TELL EL-, tel-el-ä-mär′nä. See TELL EL-AMARNA TABLETS.

AMASA, a-mā′sa (עֲמָשָׂא, *'ămāsā'*, or read עַמִּשַׁי, *'ammishai*, i.e. עַם יִשַׁי, *'am yishai*, "people of Jesse"): The form עמשא, is based upon a mistaken etymology (from = עמס [*'āmaṣ*] "to burden").

(1) According to 2 S **17** 25, Amasa is the son of Abigail, the sister of Zeruiah and David, and Ithra, an Israelite; but another source, 1 Ch **2** 17, calls his father Jether the Ishmaelite. He was a nephew of David and a cousin of Absalom, who made him commander of the army of rebellion. When the uprising had been quelled, David, in order to conciliate Amasa, promised him the position held by Joab; the latter had fallen from favor (2 S **19** 13 ff). When a new revolt broke out under Sheba, the son of Bichri (2 S **20**), Amasa was intrusted with the task of assembling the men of Judah. But Joab was eager for revenge upon the man who had obtained the office of command that he coveted. When Amasa met Joab at Gibeon, the latter murdered him while pretending to salute him (2 S **20** 8–10; 1 K **2** 5).

(2) Son of Hadlai, of the *Bᵉnē 'Ephrayim* ("Children of Ephraim"), who, obeying the words of the prophet Oded, refused to consider as captives the

Judaeans who had been taken from Ahaz, king of Judah, by the victorious Israelites under the leadership of Pekah (2 Ch **28** 12). H. J. Wolf

AMASAI, a-mā'sī (עֲמָשַׂי, *'ămāsay,* perhaps rather to be read עַמִּשַׁי, *'ammishay;* so Wellhausen, *IJG,* II, 24, n.2):

(1) A name in the genealogy of Kohath, son of Elkanah, a Levite of the Kohathite family (cf 1 Ch **6** 25; 2 Ch **29** 12).

(2) Chief of the captains who met David at Ziklag and tendered him their allegiance. Some have identified him with Amasa and others with Abishai, who is called Abshai in 1 Ch **11** 20m (cf 1 Ch **18** 12). The difficulty is that neither Amasa nor Abishai occupied the rank of the chief of thirty according to the lists in 2 S **23** and 1 Ch **11,** the rank to which David is supposed to have appointed him (cf 1 Ch **12** 18).

(3) One of the trumpet-blowing priests who greeted David when he brought back the Ark of the Covenant (cf 1 Ch **15** 24).

AMASHSAI, a-mash'sī (עֲמַשְׁסַי, *'ămashṣay,* probably a textual error for עֲמָשַׁי, *'ămāshay;* the ס [s] implies a reading עמסי, based on a mistaken derivation from עמס. The original reading may have been עַמִּשַׁי, *'ămmishay;* cf Amasai): Amashsai is a priestly name in the post-exilic list of inhabitants of Jerus (Neh **11** 13; **Maasai,** 1 Ch **9** 12); the reading in Ch is מַעֲשַׂי, *ma'ăsay,* AV "Maasiai," RV "Maasai."

AMASIAH, am-a-sī'a (עֲמַסְיָה, *'ămaṣyāh,* "Yahwe bears"): One of the captains of Jehoshaphat (cf 2 Ch **17** 16).

AMATH, ā'math, **AMATHIS,** am'a-this (1 Macc **12** 25). See Hamath.

AMATHEIS, am-a-thē'is. See Ematheis.

AMAZED, a-māzd': A term which illustrates the difficulty of expressing in one Eng. word the wide range of startled emotion, wonder, astonishment, awe, covered, in the OT, by four Heb words and in the NT by as many Gr words. Its Scripture originals range in meaning from amazement accompanied with terror and trembling to an astonishment full of perplexity, wonder, awe and joyous surprise. It is the word esp. used to show the effect of Christ's miracles, teaching, character and Divine personality on those who saw and heard Him, and were made conscious of His supernatural power (Mt **12** 23: "All the multitudes were *amazed*"). The miracles of Pentecost and the Holy Spirit's bestowal of the gift of tongues produced the same universal wonder (Acts **2** 7: "They were all *amazed* and marvelled"). Dwight M. Pratt

AMAZIAH, am-a-zī'a (אֲמַצְיָה, אֲמַצְיָהוּ, *'ămaçyāh, 'ămaçyāhū,* "Jehovah is mighty"; 2 K **14** 1–20; 2 Ch **25**): Son of Jehoash, and tenth king of Judah. Amaziah had a peaceable accession at the age of 25. A depleted treasury, a despoiled palace and temple, and a discouraged people were among the consequences of his father's war with Hazael, king of Syria. When settled on the throne, Amaziah brought to justice the men who had assassinated his father. A verbal citation of Dt **24** 16 in 2 K **14** 6, forbidding the punishment of children for a father's offence, shows that the laws of this book were then known, and were recognized as authoritative, and, in theory, as governing the nation. His accession may be dated cir 812 (some put later).

The young king's plan for the rehabilitation of his people was the restoration of the kingdom's military prestige, so severely lowered in his father's reign. A militia army, composed of all the young men above 20 years of age, was first organized and placed upon a war footing (2 Ch **25** 5; the number given, 300,000, is not a reliable one). Even this not being considered a large enough force to effect the project, 100 talents of silver were sent to engage mercenary troops for the expedition from Israel. When these came, a man of God strongly dissuaded the king from relying on them (2 Ch **25** 7 ff). When this was communicated to the soldiers, and they were sent back unemployed, it roused them to "fierce anger" (ver 10).

1. The Edomite War

Amaziah's purpose in making these extensive preparations for war, in a time of profound peace, is clear. To the S.E. of Judah lay the Edomite state, with its capital at Petra. For many years Edom had been subject to Jehoshaphat, and a Heb "deputy" had governed it (1 K **22** 47). In the reign of his son and successor, Jehoram, a confederacy of Philistines, Arabians and Edomites took Libnah and made a raid on Jerusalem. A band of these penetrated the palace, which they plundered, abducted some women, and murdered all the young princes but the youngest (2 Ch **21** 17; **22** 1). The public commotion and distress caused by such an event may be seen reflected in the short oracle of the prophet Obadiah, uttered against Edom, if, with some, Obadiah's date is put thus early.

2. Its Occasion

From that time "Edom . . . . made a king over themselves" (2 Ch **21** 8), and for fifty years following were practically independent. It was this blot on Jerusalem and the good name of Judah that Amaziah determined to wipe out. The army of retaliation went forward, and after a battle in the Valley of Salt, south of the Dead Sea, in which they were the victors, moved on to Petra. This city lies in a hollow, shut in by mountains, and approached only by a narrow ravine, through which a stream of water flows. Amaziah took it "by storm" (such is Ewald's rendering of "by war," in 2 K **14** 7). Great execution was done, many of the captives being thrown from the rock, the face of which is now covered with rock-cut tombs of the Gr-Rom age.

3. The Victory in the Valley of Salt

The campaign was thus entirely successful, but had evil results. Flushed with victory, Amaziah brought back the gods of Edom, and paid them worship. For this act of apostasy, he was warned of approaching destruction (2 Ch **25** 14–17). Disquieting news soon came relating to the conduct of the troops sent back to Samaria. From Beth-horon in the south to the border of the northern state they had looted the villages and killed some of the country people who had attempted to defend their property (2 Ch **25** 13). To Amaziah's demand for reparation, Jehoash's answer was the contemptuous one of the well-known parable of the Thistle and the Cedar.

4. Apostasy and Its Punishment

War was now inevitable. The kings "looked one another in the face," in the valley of Beth-shemesh, where there is a level space, suitable to the movements of infantry. Judah was utterly routed, and the king himself taken prisoner. There being no treasures in the lately despoiled capital, Jehoash contented himself with taking hostages for future good behavior, and with breaking down 400 cubits of the wall of Jerus at the N.W. corner of the defence (2 K **14** 13.14; 2 Ch **25** 22–24).

5. Battle of Beth-shemesh

Amaziah's career as a soldier was now closed. He outlived Jehoash of Israel "fifteen years" (2 K **14** 17). His later years were spent in seclusion and dread, and had a tragical ending. The reason for his unpopularity is not far to seek. The responsibility for the war with Jehoash is by the inspired writer placed upon the shoulders of Amaziah (2 K **14** 9–11). It was he who "would not hear." The quarrel between the kings was one which it was not beyond the power of diplomacy to remedy, but no brotherly attempt to heal the breach was made by either king. When the results of the war appeared, it could not be but that the author of the war should be called upon to answer for them. So deep was his disgrace and so profound the sense of national humiliation, that a party in the state determined on Amaziah's removal, so soon as there was another to take his place. The age of majority among the Heb kings was 16, and when Amaziah's son was of this age, the conspiracy against his life grew so strong and open that he fled to Lachish. Here he was followed and killed; his body being insultingly carried to Jerusalem on horses, and not conveyed in a litter or coffin (2 K **14** 19.20; 2 Ch **25** 27.28). He was 54 years old and had reigned for 29 years. The Chronicler (2 Ch **26** 1) hardly conceals the popular rejoicings at the exchange of sovereigns, when Uzziah became king.

6. Closing Years and Tragical End

In the last ver of 2 Ch **25** is a copyist's error by which we read "in the city of Judah," instead of "in the city of David," as in the corresponding passage in Kings. The singular postscript to the record of Amaziah in 2 K **14** 22 is intended to mark the fact that while the port of Elath on the Red Sea fell before the arms, in turn, of Amaziah and of his son Uzziah, it was the latter who restored it to Judah, as a part of its territory. Amaziah is mentioned in the royal genealogy of 1 Ch **3** 12, but not in that of Mt **1**. There is a leap here from Jehoram to Uzziah, Ahaziah, Jehoash and Amaziah being omitted. W. Shaw Caldecott

AMBASSADOR, am-bas'a-dor (מַלְאָךְ, *mal'ākh*, "messenger"; לוּץ, *lūç*, "interpreter"; צִיר, *çīr*, "to go"; hence a messenger; **πρεσβεύω,** *presbeúō*, "to act as an ambassador," lit. to be older): An ambassador is an official representative of a king or government, as of Pharaoh (Isa **30** 4); of the princes of Babylon (2 Ch **32** 31); of Neco, king of Egypt (2 Ch **35** 21); of the messengers of peace sent by Hezekiah, king of Judah, to Sennacherib, king of Assyria (Isa **33** 7). The same Heb term is used of the messengers sent by Jacob to Esau (Gen **32** 3); by Moses to the king of Edom (Nu **20** 14). For abundant illustration consult "Messenger" (מַלְאָךְ, *mal'ākh*) in any concordance. See Concordance. The inhabitants of Gibeon made themselves pretended ambassadors to Joshua in order to secure by deceit the protection of a treaty ("covenant") (Josh **9** 4).

In the NT the term is used in a **fig.** sense. As the imprisoned representative of Christ at Rome Paul calls himself "an ambassador in chains" (Eph **6** 20); and in 2 Cor **5** 20 includes, with himself, all ministers of the gospel, as "ambassadors . . . . on behalf of Christ," commissioned by Him, as their sovereign Lord, with the ministry of reconciling the world to God. The Bible contains no finer characterization of the exalted and spiritual nature of the minister's vocation as the representative of Jesus Christ, the King of kings, and Saviour of the world. Dwight M. Pratt

AMBASSAGE, am'ba-sāj (**πρεσβεία,** *presbeía*, "an embassy," a body of ambassadors on the message entrusted to them): Twice used by Christ (1) in the parable of the Pounds, of the citizens who hated the nobleman and sent an ambassage, refusing to have him reign over them, thus illustrating those who wilfully rejected His own spiritual sovereignty and kingdom (Lk **19** 14); (2) of a weak king who sends to a stronger an ambassage to ask conditions of peace (Lk **14** 32). Not used elsewhere in the Bible.

AMBER, am'bēr. See Stones, Precious.

AMBITIOUS, am-bish'us (**φιλοτιμέομαι,** *philotiméomai*, "to be strongly desirous," "strive earnestly," "make it one's aim"): Given as a marginal reading in Rom **15** 20 ("being ambitious to bring good tidings"), 2 Cor **5** 9 ("We are ambitious, whether at home or absent, to be well-pleasing unto him"), and 1 Thess **4** 11 ("that ye be ambitious to be quiet").

AMBUSH, am'bo͝osh (אָרַב, *'ārabh*, "to set an ambush"; מַאֲרָב, *ma'ărābh*, "an ambush"): A military stratagem in which a body of men are placed in concealment to surprise an enemy unawares, or to attack a point when temporarily undefended. This stratagem was employed successfully by Joshua at Ai (Josh **8**). Jeremiah calls upon the Medes to "set up a standard against the walls of Babylon, make the watch strong, set the watchmen, prepare the ambushes" (Jer **51** 12).

AMBUSHMENT, am'bo͝osh-ment (as above) has now disappeared in 2 Ch **20** 22, where RV gives for "ambushment" "liers-in-wait." It still remains in 2 Ch **13** 13 where both AV and RV render the Hebrew noun "ambushment."

AMEN, ā-men' (in ritual speech and in singing ä-men', ä'men) (אָמֵן, *'āmēn;* **ἀμήν,** *amḗn*, = "truly," "verily"): Is derived from the reflexive form of a vb. meaning "to be firm," or "to prop." It occurs twice as a noun in Isa **65** 16, where we have (AV, RV) "God of truth." This rendering implies the pointing *'ōmēn* or *'ēmūn* i.e. "truth," or "faithfulness," a reading actually suggested by Cheyne and adopted by others. Amen is generally used as an advb. of assent or confirmation—*fiat*, "so let it be." In Jer **28** 6 the prophet indorses with it the words of Hananiah. Amen is employed when an individual or the whole nation confirms a covenant or oath recited in their presence (Nu **5** 22; Dt **27** 15 ff; Neh **5** 13, etc). It also occurs at the close of a ps or book of pss, or of a prayer.

That Amen was appended to the doxology in the early church is evident both from St. Paul and Rev, and here again it took the form of a response by the hearers. The ritual of the installation of the Lamb (Rev **5** 6–14) concludes with the Amen of the four beasts, and the four and twenty elders. It is also spoken after "Yea: I come quickly" (**22** 20). And that Rev reflects the practice of the church on earth, and not merely of an ideal, ascended community in heaven, may be concluded from 1 Cor **14** 16, whence we gather that the lay brethren were expected to say Amen to the address. (See Weizsäcker's *The Apostolic Age of the Christian Church*, Eng. tr, II, 289.) James Millar

AMERCE, a-mûrs': Found in AV only in Dt **22** 19, "And they shall amerce him in an hundred shekels of silver." Amerce is a legal term derived from the French (*à* = "at"; *merci* = "mercy," i.e. lit. "at the mercy" [of the court]). Here it is used of the imposing of a fine, according to the Law of Moses, upon the man who has been proven by the Elders to have brought a false charge against the virginity of the maid he has married by saying to the father, "I found not thy daughter a maid."

AMERICAN REVISED VERSION, a-mer'i-kan rē-vīzd' vûr'shun: On July 7, 1870, it was moved in the Lower House of the Convocation of Canterbury that in the work of revision the coöperation of American divines be invited. This resolution was assented to, and on December 7, 1871, the arrangements were completed. Under the general presidency of Dr. Philip Schaff, an OT Company of fifteen scholars was formed, with Dr. W. H. Green as chairman, and a NT Company of sixteen members (including Dr. Schaff), with Dr. T. D. Woolsey as chairman. Work was begun on October 4, 1872, and took the form of offering criticisms on the successive portions of the English revision as they were received. These criticisms of the American Companies were duly considered by the English Companies during the second revision and the decisions were again sent to America for criticism. The replies received were once more given consideration and, finally, the unadopted readings for which the American Companies professed deliberate preference were printed as appendices to the two Testaments as published in 1881 and 1885. These lists, however, were not regarded by the American Companies as satisfactory. In the first place, it became evident that the English Companies, on account of their instructions and for other reasons, were not willing to make changes of a certain class. Consequently the American Companies insisted on only such readings as seemed to have a real chance of being accepted. And, in the second place, the English presses hurried the last part of the work and were unwilling to allow enough time for adequate thoroughness in the preparation of the lists. But it was hoped that the first published edition of the ERV would not be considered definitive and that in the future such American proposals as had stood the test of public discussion might be incorporated into the text. This hope was disappointed —the English Companies disbanded as soon as their revision was finished and their work stood as final. As a result the American Companies resolved to continue their organization. They were pledged not to issue or indorse any new revision within fourteen years after the publication of the ERV, and so it was not until 1900 that the ARV NT was published. The whole Bible was issued in the following year.

1. History

As the complete editions of the ARV give a full list of the changes made, only the more prominent need be mentioned here. A few of the readings printed in the appendices to the ERV were abandoned, but many new ones were introduced, including some that had been adopted while the English work was in progress but which had not been pressed. (See above.) Still, in general appearance, the ARV differs but slightly from the English. The most important addition is found in the page-headings. Some changes have been made in shortening the titles of the NT books. The printing of poetical passages in poetical form has been carried through more consistently. The paragraphs have been altered in some cases and (especially in the OT) shortened. The punctuation has been simplified, especially by the more frequent use of the semicolon. The removal of obsolete words ("magnifical," "neesings," etc) has been effected fairly thoroughly, obsolete constructions ("jealous over," etc) have been modernized, particularly by the use of "who" or "that" (instead of "which") for persons and "its" (instead of "his") for things. In the OT "Jehovah" has been introduced systematically for the proper Heb word, as has "Sheol" ("Hades" in the NT). Certain passages too literally rendered in the ERV ("reins," "by the hand of," etc) are given in modern terms. In the NT, the substitution of "Holy Spirit" for "Holy Ghost" was completed throughout (in the ERV it is made in some twenty places), "demons" substituted for "devils," "Teacher" for "Master," and "try" for "tempt" when there is no direct reference to wrongdoing. And so on.

2. Differences from ERV

It may be questioned whether the differences between the two Revisions are great enough to counterbalance the annoyance and confusion resulting from the existence of two standard versions in the same language. But, accepting the ARV as an accomplished fact, and acknowledging a few demerits that it has or may be thought to have in comparison with the ERV (a bit of pedantry in Ps **148** 12 or renderings of disputed passages such as Ps **24** 6), these demerits are altogether outweighed by the superiorities—with one exception. In the Psalter, when used liturgically, the repetition of the word "Jehovah" becomes wearisome and the ERV which retains "The Lord" is much preferable. Most to be regretted in the ARV is its extreme conservatism in the readings of the original texts. In the OT the number of marginal variants was actually *reduced*. In the NT, only trivial changes are made from the so-called Revisers' Greek Text, although this text did not represent the best scholarly opinion even in 1881, while in 1900 it was almost universally abandoned. (Today—in 1914—it is obsolete.) It is very unfortunate that the American Revisers did not improve on the example of their English brethren and continue their sessions *after* the publication of their version, for it is only by the successive revisions of *published* work that a really satisfactory result can be attained.

3. Criticism

No ARV Apoc was attempted, a particularly unfortunate fact, as the necessity for the study of the Apoc has become imperative and the ERV Apoc is not a particularly good piece of work. However, copies of the ARV can now be obtained with the ERV Apoc included. See English Versions.

4. Apocrypha

Burton Scott Easton

AMETHYST, am'e-thist. See Stones, Precious.

AMI, ā'mī, ä'mē (אָמִי, *'āmī*): Ancestor of a family among "Solomon's servants" in the Return (Ezr **2** 57); the same as Amon in Neh **7** 59.

AMIABLE, ā'mi-a-b'l (יָדִיד, *ydhīdh*, "beloved"): Applied to the tabernacle or tent of meeting. "How a. ["lovely" RVm] are thy tabernacles" (Ps **84** 1), the pl. having reference to the subdivisions and appurtenances of the sanctuary (cf **68** 35). The adj. is rendered "amiable" in the sense of the French *aimable*, lovely; but the usage of the Heb word requires it to be understood as meaning "dear," "beloved." Cf "so amiable a prospect" (Sir T. Herbert), "They keep their churches so cleanly and amiable" (Howell, 1644). "What made the tabernacle of Moses lovely was not the outside, which was very mean, but what was within" (John Gill). See Tabernacle.

M. O. Evans

AMINADAB a-min'a-dab (**Ἀμιναδάβ**, *Aminadáb*): AV: Gr form of **Amminadab** (q.v.). Thus RV (Mt **1** 4; Lk **3** 33).

AMISS, a-mis': There are two words tr[d] "amiss" in the NT, ἄτοπος, *átopos*, referring to that which is improper or harmful (Lk **23** 41; Acts **28** 6), while κακῶς, *kakṓs*, refers to that which is evil in the sense of a disaster, then to that which is wicked, morally wrong. This latter is the use of it in Jas **4** 3. The purpose of the prayer is evil, it is therefore amiss and cannot be granted (cf 2 Ch **6** 37 ff).

AMITTAI, a-mit'ī (אֲמִתַּי, *'ămittay*, "faithful"): The father of the prophet Jonah. He was from Gath-hepher in Zebulun (2 K **14** 25; Jon **1** 1).

AMMAH, am'a (אַמָּה, *'ammāh*, "mother" or "beginning"): A hill in the territory of Benjamin (2 S **2** 24), where Joab and Abishai halted at nightfall in their pursuit of Abner and his forces after their victory over him in the battle of Gibeon. It "lieth before Giah by the way of the wilderness of Gibeon"; but the exact location has not been identified. The same Heb word appears as the second part of Metheg-ammah in 2 S **8** 1 AV, but rendered "mother city" in RV, probably however not the same place as in 2 S **2** 24.

AMMI, am'ī (עַמִּי, *'ammī*, "my people"): A symbolic name given to Israel by Hosea (**2** 1; **2** 3 in Heb text), descriptive of Israel in the state of restoration, and in contrast to sinful and rejected Israel, represented by Hosea's son, who was called Lo-ammi, "not my people," when born to the prophet (Hos **1** 9.10). This restoration to the Divine favor is more fully described in Hos **2** 21.23 in words quoted by Paul (Rom **9** 25.26). The use of such fig. and descriptive names is frequent in the OT; cf Isa **62** 4.12.

AMMIDIOI, a-mid'i-oi (AV **Ammidoi**, am'i-doi; **'Αμμίδιοι**, *Ammídioi* [also with aspirate]; occurring only in 1 Esd **5** 20): One of the families returning from the Bab Captivity in the First Return, under Zerubbabel, in 537 BC. This name is not found in the corresponding lists of the canonical books, Ezr **2** and Neh **7**. Their identity is uncertain.

AMMIEL, am'i-el (עַמִּיאֵל, *'ammī'ēl*, "my kinsman is God"; **'Αμειήλ**, *Ameiḗl*]): A name borne by four men in the OT.

(1) One of the twelve spies sent into Canaan by Moses; son of Gemalli, of the tribe of Dan (Nu **13** 12).

(2) A Benjamite, the father of Machir, a friend of David, living at Lodebar in Gilead (2 S **9** 4.5; **17** 27).

(3) Father of Bathshua (or Bathsheba), one of David's wives, who was mother of Solomon (1 Ch **3** 5). In the ‖ passage, 2 S **11** 3, by transposition of the two parts of the name, he is called Eliam, meaning "my God is a kinsman."

(4) The sixth son of Obed-edom, a Levite, one of the doorkeepers of the tabernacle of God in David's life-time (1 Ch **26** 5). EDWARD MACK

AMMIHUD, a-mī'hud (עַמִּיהוּד, *'ammīhūdh*, "my kinsman is glorious"; variously in LXX, **'Εμιούδ**, *Emioúd* or **Σεμιούδ**, *Semioúd* or **'Αμιούδ**, *Amioúd*): The name of several OT persons.

(1) Father of Elishama, who in the Wilderness was head of the tribe of Ephraim (Nu **1** 10; **2** 18; **7** 48.53; **10** 22; 1 Ch **7** 26).

(2) Father of Shemuel, who was appointed by Moses from the tribe of Simeon to divide the land among the tribes after they should have entered Canaan (Nu **34** 20).

(3) Father of Pedahel, who was appointed from the tribe of Naphtali for the same purpose as the Ammihud of (2) (Nu **34** 28).

(4) In the AV and RVm for the **Ammihur** (עַמִּיחוּר, *'ammīḥūr*, "my kinsman is noble"), who was father of Talmai of Geshur, a little Aram. kingdom E. of the Lebanon mountains, to whom Absalom fled after the murder of his brother Amnon. The weight of evidence seems to favor the reading Ammiḥur (2 S **13** 37).

(5) A descendant of Judah through the line of Perez (1 Ch **9** 4). EDWARD MACK

AMMIHUR, a-mī'hur (AV and RVm; עַמִּיחוּר, *'ammīḥūr*, "my kinsman is noble"; **'Εμιούδ**, *Emioúd*). See AMMIHUD (4).

AMMINADAB, a-min'a-dab (עַמִּינָדָב, *'ammīnādhābh*="my people [or my kinsman] is generous or noble"): Three persons bearing this name are mentioned in the OT.

(1) In Ruth **4** 19.20 and 1 Ch **2** 10 Amminadab is referred to as one of David's ancestors. He was the great-grandson of Perez, a son of Judah (Gen **38** 29; **46** 12) and the great-grandfather of Boaz, who again was the great-grandfather of David. Aaron's wife, Elisheba, was a daughter of Amminadab (Ex **6** 23), while one of the sons, viz. Nahshon, occupied an important position in the Judah-clan (Nu **1** 7; **2** 3; **7** 12; **10** 14).

(2) In the first Book of Ch (**6** 22) Amminadab is mentioned as a son of Kohath (and therefore a grandson of Levi) and the father of Korah. But in other genealogical passages (Ex **6** 18; Nu **3** 19; 1 Ch **6** 2) the sons of Kohath are Amram, Izhar, Hebron and Uzziel, and in two places (Ex **6** 21; 1 Ch **6** 38) Izhar is mentioned as the father of Korah.

(3) According to 1 Ch (**15** 10.11) Amminadab was the name of a priest who took part in the removal of the ark to Jerusalem. He was the son of Uzziel, and therefore a nephew of Amminadab, son of Kohath (=Izhar). THOMAS LEWIS

AMMINADIB, a-min'a-dib (עַמִּי נָדִיב, *'ammī nādhībh*): The name occurs in AV and RVm only in one passage (Cant **6** 12, "the chariots of Amminadib"). In AVm and RV text, however, it is not regarded as a proper name, and the clause is rendered, "among the chariots of my princely people." Interpretations widely vary (see COMMENTARIES).

AMMISHADDAI, am-i-shad'ī, am-i-shad-ā'ī (עַמִּישַׁדַּי, *'ammīshadday*, "Shaddai is my kinsman"): The father of Ahiezer, a Danite captain or "head of his fathers' house," during the Wilderness journey (Nu **1** 12; **2** 25, etc).

AMMIZABAD, a-miz'a-bad (עַמִּיזָבָד, *'ammīzābhādh*, "my kinsman has made a present"): The son of Benaiah, one of David's captains for the third month (1 Ch **27** 6).

AMMON, am'on; **AMMONITES**, am'on-īts (עַמּוֹן, *'ammōn*; עַמּוֹנִים, *'ammōnīm*): The Heb tradition makes this tribe descendants of Lot and hence related to the Israelites (Gen **19** 38). This is reflected in the name usually employed in OT to designate them, *Ben 'Ammī*, *B*[e]*nē 'Ammōn*, "son of my people," "children of my people," i.e. relatives. Hence we find that the Israelites are commanded to avoid conflict with them on their march to the Promised Land (Dt **2** 19). Their dwelling-place was on the east of the Dead Sea and the Jordan, between the Arnon and the Jabbok, but, before the advance of the Hebrews, they had been dispossessed of a portion of their land by the Amorites, who founded, along the east side of the Jordan and the Dead Sea, the kingdom of Sihon (Nu **21** 21–31). We know from the records of Egypt, esp. Am Tab, the approximate date of the Amorite invasion (14th and 13th cents., BC). They were pressed on the north by the Hittites who forced them upon the tribes of the south, and some of them settled east of the Jordan. Thus Israel helped A. by destroying their old enemies, and this makes their conduct at a later period the more reprehensible. In the days of Jephthah they oppressed the Israelites east of the Jordan, claiming that the latter had deprived them of their territory when they came from Egypt, whereas it was the possessions of the Amorites they took (Jgs **11** 1–28). They were defeated, but their hostility did not cease, and their conduct toward the Israelites was particularly shameful, as in the days of Saul (1 S **11**) and of David (2 S **10**). This may account for the cruel treatment meted out to them in the war that followed (2 S **12** 26–31). They seem to have been completely subdued by David and their capital was taken, and we find a better spirit manifested afterward, for Nahash of Rabbah showed kindness to him when a fugitive (2 S **17** 27–29). Their country came into the possession of Jeroboam, on the division of the kingdom, and when the Syrians of Damascus deprived the kingdom of Israel of their possessions east of the Jordan, the A. became subjects of Benhadad, and we find a contingent of 1,000 of them serving as allies of that king in the great battle of the Syrians with the Assyrians at Qarqar (854 BC) in the reign of Shalmaneser II. They may have regained their old territory when Tiglath-pileser carried off the Israelites E. of the Jordan into captivity (2 K **15** 29; 1 Ch **5** 26). Their hostility to both kingdoms, Judah and Israel, was often manifested. In the days of Jehoshaphat they joined with the Moabites in an attack upon him, but met with disaster (2 Ch **20**). They paid tribute to Jotham (2 Ch **27** 5). After submitting to Tiglath-pileser they were generally tributary to Assyria, but we have mention of their joining in the general uprising that took place under Sennacherib; but they submitted and we find them tributary in the reign of Esarhaddon. Their hostility to Judah is shown in their joining the Chaldaeans to destroy it (2 K **24** 2). Their cruelty is denounced by the prophet Amos (**1** 13); and their destruction by Jer (**49** 1–6), Ezk (**21** 28–32), Zeph (**2** 8.9). Their murder of Gedaliah (2 K **25** 22–26; Jer **40** 14) was a dastardly act. Tobiah the A. united with Sanballat to oppose Neh (Neh **4**), and their opposition to the Jews did not cease with the establishment of the latter in Judaea.

They joined the Syrians in their wars with the Maccabees and were defeated by Judas (1 Mac **5** 6).

Their religion was a degrading and cruel superstition. Their chief god was Molech, or Moloch, to whom they offered human sacrifices (1 K **11** 7) against which Israel was especially warned (Lev **20** 2–5). This worship was common to other tribes for we find it mentioned among the Phoenicians.

H. Porter

AMMONITESS, am-on-ī′tes, a-mon′i-tes (עַמֹּנִית, *ʿammōnīth*): A woman of the Ammonites, Naamah, the mother of Rehoboam (1 K **14** 21.31; 2 Ch **12** 13; **24** 26).

AMNON, am′non (אַמְנוֹן, *'amnōn*, "faithful"; cf אֲמִינוֹן, *'ămīnōn*, 2 S **13** 20, which is probably a diminutive. Wellhausen [*IJG*, II, 24, n.2] resolves אֲמִינוֹן into אִמִּי, *'immī*, and נוּן, *nūn*, "my mother is the serpent"; cf Nun):

(1) The eldest son of David and Ahinoam, the Jezreelites (cf 2 S **3** 2). As the crown prince and heir presumptive to the throne, he was intensely hated by Absalom, who was, therefore, doubly eager to revenge the outrage committed by Amnon upon his sister Tamar (2 S **3** 2; **13** 1 ff; 1 Ch **3** 1).

(2) A name in the genealogy of Judah (1 Ch **4** 20).

AMOK, ā′mok (עָמוֹק, *ʿāmōḳ*, "deep"): A chief priest who came to Jerus with Zerubbabel (Neh **12** 7) and the forefather of Eber, who was priest in the days of Joiakim (Neh **12** 20).

AMON, ā′mon (אָמוֹן, *'āmōn*): A name identical with that of the Egyp local deity of Thebes (No); cf Jer **46** 25. The foreign name given to a Heb prince is remarkable, as is also the fact that it is one of the two or three royal names of Judah not compounded with the name of Jehovah. See Manasseh. It seems to reflect the sentiment which his fanatical father sought to make prevail that Jeh had no longer any more claim to identification with the realm than had other deities.

(1) A king of Judah, son and successor of Manasseh; reigned two years and was assassinated in his own palace by the officials of his household. The story of his reign is told briefly in 2 K **21** 19–26, and still more briefly, though in identical terms, so far as they go, in 2 Ch **33** 21–25. His short reign was merely incidental in the history of Judah; just long enough to reveal the traits and tendencies which directly or indirectly led to his death. It was merely a weaker continuation of the régime of his idolatrous father, though without the fanaticism which gave the father positive character, and without the touch of piety which, if the Chronicler's account is correct, tempered the father's later years.

If the assassination was the initial act of a revolution, the latter was immediately suppressed by "the people of the land," who put to death the conspirators and placed Amon's eight-year-old son Josiah on the throne. In the view of the present writer the motive of the affair was probably connected with the perpetuity of the Davidic dynasty, which, having survived so long according to prophetic prediction (cf 2 S **7** 16; Ps **89** 36.37), was an essential guarantee of Jeh's favor. Manasseh's foreign sympathies, however, had loosened the hold of Jeh on the officials of his court; so that, instead of being the loyal center of devotion to Israel's religious and national idea, the royal household was but a hotbed of worldly ambitions, and all the more for Manasseh's prosperous reign, so long immune from any stroke of Divine judgment. It is natural that, seeing the insignificance of Amon's administration, some ambitious clique, imitating the policy that had frequently succeeded in the Northern Kingdom, should strike for the throne. They had reckoned, however, without estimating the inbred Davidic loyalty of the body of the people. It was a blow at one of their most cherished tenets, committing the nation both politically and religiously to utter uncertainty. That this impulsive act of the people was in the line of the purer religious movement which was ripening in Israel does not prove that the spiritually-minded "remnant" was minded to violence and conspiracy; it merely shows what a stern and sterling fiber of loyalty still existed, seasoned and confirmed by trial, below the corrupting cults and fashions of the ruling classes. In the tragedy of Amon's reign, in short, we get a glimpse of the basis of sound principle that lay at the common heart of Israel.

(2) A governor of Samaria (1 K **22** 26); the one to whom the prophet Micaiah was committed as a prisoner by King Ahab, after the prophet had disputed the predictions of the court prophets and foretold the king's death in battle.

(3) The head of the "children of Solomon's servants" (Neh **7** 59) who returned from captivity; reckoned along with the Nethinim, or temple slaves. Called also Ami (Ezr **2** 57).

John Franklin Genung

AMORITES, am′o-rīts; **Amorites** (אֱמֹרִי, *'ĕmōrī*, always in the singular like the Bab *Amurrū* from which it is taken; **'Αμορραῖοι,** *Amorraîoi*):

1. Varying Use of the Name Explained
2. The Amorite Kingdom
3. Sihon's Conquest
4. Disappearance of the Amorite Kingdom
5 Physical Characteristics of the Amorites

The name Amorite is used in the OT to denote (1) the inhabitants of Pal generally, (2) the population of the hills as opposed to the plain, and (3) a specific people under a king of their own. Thus (1) we hear of them on the west shore of the Dead Sea (Gen **14** 7), at Hebron (Gen **14** 13), and Shechem (Gen **48** 22), in Gilead and Bashan (Dt **3** 10) and under Hermon (Dt **3** 8; **4** 48). They are named instead of the Canaanites as the inhabitants of Pal whom the Israelites were required tó exterminate (Gen **15** 16; Dt **20** 17; Jgs **6** 10; 1 S **7** 14; 1 K **21** 26; 2 K **21** 11); the older population of Judah is called Amorite in Josh **10** 5.6, in conformity with which Ezk (**16** 3) states that Jerus had an Amorite father; and the Gibeonites are said to have been "of the remnant of the Amorites" (2 S **21** 2). On the other hand (2), in Nu **13** 29 the Amorites are described as dwelling in the mountains like the Hittites and Jebusites of Jerus, while the Amalekites or Bedouins lived in the south and the Canaanites on the seacoast and in the valley of the Jordan. Lastly (3) we hear of Sihon, "king of the Amorites," who had conquered the northern half of Moab (Nu **21** 21–31; Dt **2** 26–35).

Assyriological discovery has explained the varying use of the name. The Heb form of it is a transliteration of the Bab *Amurrū*, which was both sing. and pl. In the age of Abraham the Amurru were the dominant people in western Asia; hence Syria and Pal were called by the Babylonians "the land of the Amorites." In the Assyr period this was replaced by "land of the Hittites," the Hittites in the Mosaic age having made themselves masters of Syria and Canaan. The use of the name "Amorite" in its general sense belongs to the Bab period of oriental history.

1. Varying Use of the Name Explained

The Amorite kingdom was of great antiquity. About 2500 BC it embraced the larger part of Mesopotamia and Syria, with its capital probably at Harran, and a few centuries later northern Babylonia was occupied by an "Amorite" dynasty of kings who traced their descent from Samu or Sumu (the Biblical Shem), and made Babylon their capital. To this dynasty belonged Khammu-rabi, the Amraphel of Gen **14** 1. In the astrological documents of the period frequent reference is made to "the king of the Amorites." This king of the Amorites was subject to Babylonia in the age of the dynasty of Ur, two or three centuries before the birth of Abraham. He claimed suzerainty over a number of "Amorite" kinglets, among whom those of Khana on the Euphrates, near the mouth of the Khabur, may be named, since in the Abrahamic age one of them was called Khammu-rapikh and another Isarlim or Israel. A payment of a cadastral survey made at this time by a Bab governor with the Can name of Urimelech is now in the Louvre. Numerous Amorites were settled in Ur and other Bab cities, chiefly for the purpose of trade. They seem to have enjoyed the same rights and privileges as the native Babylonians. Some of them were commercial travelers, but we hear also of the heads of the great firms making journeys to the Mediterranean coast.

2. The Amorite Kingdom

In an inscription found near Diarbekir and dedicated to Khammu-rabi by Ibirum (=Eber), the governor of the district, the only title given to the Bab monarch is "king of the Amorites," where instead of *Amurrū* the Sumerian *Martu* (Heb *mōreh*) is used. The great-grandson of Khammu-rabi still calls himself "king of the widespread land of the Amorites," but two generations later Babylonia was invaded by the Hittites, the Amorite dynasty came to an end, and there was once more a "king of the Amorites" who was not also king of Babylonia.

Heads of Amorites, akin to North Africans.

The Amorite kingdom continued to exist down to the time of the Israelitish invasion of Pal, and mention is made of it in the Egyp records as well as in the cuneiform Am Tab, and the Hittite archives recently discovered at Boghaz-keui, the site of the Hittite capital in Cappadocia. The Egyp conquest of Canaan by the kings of the XVIIIth Dynasty had put an end to the effective government of that country by the Amorite princes, but their rule still extended eastward to the borders of Babylonia, while its southern limits coincided approximately with what was afterward the northern frontier of Naphtali. The Amorite kings, however, became, at all events in name, the vassals of the Egyp Pharaoh. When the Egyp empire began to break up, under the "heretic king" Amenhotep IV, at the end of the XVIIIth Dynasty (1400 BC), the Amorite princes naturally turned to their more powerful neighbors in the north. One of the letters in the Tell el-Amarna correspondence is from the Pharaoh to his Amorite vassal Aziru the son of Ebed-Asherah, accusing him of rebellion and threatening him with punishment. Eventually Aziru found it advisable to go over openly to the Hittites, and pay the Hittite government an annual tribute of 300 shekels of gold. From that time forward the Amorite kingdom was a dependency of the Hittite empire, which, on the strength of this, claimed dominion over Pal as far as the Egyp frontier.

The second successor of Aziru was Abi-Amurru (or Abi-Hadad), whose successor bore, in addition to a Sem name, the Mitannian name of Bente-sinas. Bente-sinas was dethroned by the Hittite King Muttallis and imprisoned in Cappadocia, where he seems to have met the Hittite prince Khattu-sil, who on the death of his brother Muttallis seized the crown and restored Bente-sinas to his kingdom. Bente-sinas married the daughter of Khattu-sil, while his own daughter was wedded to the son of his Hittite suzerain, and an agreement was made that the succession to the Amorite throne should be confined to her descendants. Two or three generations later the Hittite empire was destroyed by an invasion of "northern barbarians," the Phrygians, probably, of Gr history, who marched southward, through Pal, against Egypt, carrying with them "the king of the Amorites." The invaders, however, were defeated and practically exterminated by Ramses III of the XXth Egyp Dynasty (1200 BC). The Amorite king, captured on this occasion by the Egyptians, was probably the immediate predecessor of the Sihon of the OT.

Egyp influence in Canaan had finally ceased with the invasion of Egypt by the Libyans and peoples of the Aegean in the fifth year of Meneptah, the successor of Ramses II, at the time of the Israelitish Exodus. Though the invaders were repulsed, the Egyp garrisons had to be withdrawn from the cities of southern Pal, where their place was taken by the Philis who thus blocked the way from Egypt to the north. The Amorites, in the name of their distant Hittite suzerains, were accordingly able to overrun the old Egyp provinces on the east side of the Jordan; the Amorite chieftain Og possessed himself of Bashan (Dt **3** 8), and Sihon, "king of the Amorites," conquered the northern part of Moab.

3. Sihon's Conquest

The conquest must have been recent at the time of the Israelitish invasion, as the Amorite song of triumph is quoted in Nu **21** 27–29, and adapted to the overthrow of Sihon himself by the Israelites. 'Woe unto thee,' it reads, 'O Moab; thou art undone, O people of Chemosh! [Chemosh] hath given thy sons who escaped [the battle] and thy daughters into captivity to Sihon king of the Amorites.' The flame that had thus consumed Heshbon, it is further declared, shall spread southward through Moab, while Heshbon itself is rebuilt and made the capital of the conqueror: "Come to Heshbon, that the city of Sihon [like the city of David, 2 S **5** 9] may be rebuilt and restored. For the fire has spread from Heshbon, the flame from the capital of Sihon, devouring as far as Moab [reading *'adh* with the LXX instead of *'ār*], and swallowing up [reading *bāle'āh* with the LXX] the high places of Arnon." The Israelitish invasion, however, prevented the expected conquest of southern Moab from taking place.

4. Disappearance of the Amorite Kingdom

After the fall of Sihon the Amorite kingdom disappears. The Syrians of Zobah, of Hamath and of Damascus take its place, while with the rise of Assyria the "Amorites" cease to be the representatives in contemporary lit. of the inhabitants of western Asia. At one time their power had extended to the Bab frontier, and Bente-sinas was summoned to Cappadocia by his Hittite overlord to answer a charge made by the Bab ambassadors of his having raided northern Babylonia. The Amorite king urged, however, that the raid was merely an attempt to recover a debt of 30 talents of silver.

5. Physical Characteristics of the Amorites

In Nu **13** 29 the Amorites are described as mountaineers, and in harmony with this, according to Professor Petrie's notes, the Egyp artists represent them with fair complexions, blue eyes and light hair. It would, therefore, seem that they belonged to the Libyan race of northern Africa rather than to the Sem stock. In western Asia, however, they were mixed with other racial elements derived from the subject populations, and as they spoke a Sem language one of the most important of these elements would have been the Semites. In its general sense, moreover, the name "Amorite" included in the Bab period all the settled and civilized peoples west of the Euphrates to whatever race they might belong.

Literature.—Hugo Winckler, *Mitteilungen der deutschen Orient-Gesellschaft* (1907), No. 35, Berlin; Sayce, *The Races of the OT*, Religious Tract Soc., 1890; Clay, *Amurru* and *Empire of Amorites*.

A. H. Sayce

AMOS, ā'mos (עָמוֹס, *'āmōṣ*, "burdensome" or "burden-bearer"; Ἀμώς, *Amṓs*):

I. The Prophet
  1. Name
  2. Native Place
  3. Personal History
  4. His Preparation
    (1) Knowledge of God
    (2) Acquaintance with History of His People
    (3) Personal Travel
    (4) Scenery of His Home
  5. His Mission
  6. Date
II. The Book
  1. Its Divisions
  2. Its Outlook
  3. Value of the Book
    (1) As a Picture of the Social Condition
    (2) As Picture of the Religious Condition
    (3) Testimony to History
    (4) Testimony to the Law
      (a) The Ritual
      (b) Ethical Teaching
    (5) The Prophetic Order
    (6) The Prophetic Religion
Literature

I. The Prophet.—Amos is the prophet whose book stands third among the "Twelve" in the Hebrew canon. No other person bearing the same name is mentioned in the OT, the name of the father of the prophet Isaiah being written differently (*'āmōç*). There is an Amos mentioned in the genealogical series Lk **3** 25, but he is otherwise unknown, and we do not know how his name would have been written in Hebrew. Of the signification of the prophet's name all that can be said is that a verb with the same stem letters, in the sense of to load or to carry a load, is not uncommon in the language.

1. Name

2. Native Place

Tekoa, the native place of Amos, was situated at a distance of 5 miles S. from Bethlehem, from which it is visible, and 10 miles from Jerusalem, on a hill 2,700 ft. high, overlooking the wilderness of Judah. It was made a "city for defence" by Rehoboam (2 Ch **11** 6), and may have in fact received its name from its remote and exposed position; for the stem of which the word is a derivative is of frequent occurrence in the sense of sounding an alarm with the trumpet: e.g. "Blow the trumpet in Tekoa, and set up a sign of fire in Beth-haccerem" (Jer **6** 1 AV). The same word is also used to signify the setting up of a tent by striking in the tent-pegs; and Jerome states that there was no village beyond Tekoa in his time. The name has survived, and the neighborhood is at the present day the pasture-ground for large flocks of sheep and goats. From the high ground on which the modern village stands one looks down on the bare undulating hills of one of the bleakest districts of Palestine, "the waste howling wilderness," which must have suggested some of the startling imagery of the prophet's addresses. The place may have had—as is not seldom the case with towns or villages—a reputation for a special quality of its inhabitants; for it was from Tekoa that Joab fetched the "wise woman" who by a feigned story effected the reconciliation of David with his banished son Absalom (2 S **14**). There are traces in the Book of Am of a shrewdness and mother-wit which are not so conspicuous in other prophetical books.

3. Personal History

The particulars of a personal kind which are noted in the book are few but suggestive. Amos was not a prophet or the son of a prophet, he tells us (**7** 14), i.e. he did not belong to the professional class which frequented the so-called schools of the prophets. He was "among the herdmen of Tekoa" (**1** 1), the word here used being found only once in another place (2 K **3** 4) and applied to Mesha, king of Moab. It seems to refer to a special breed of sheep, somewhat ungainly in appearance but producing an abundant fleece. In **7** 14 the word rendered "herdman" is different, and denotes an owner of cattle, though some, from the LXX rendering, think that the word should be the same as in **1** 1. He was also "a dresser of sycomore-trees" (**7** 14). The word rendered "dresser" (RV) or "gatherer" (AV) occurs only here, and from the rendering of the LXX (κνίζων) it is conjectured that there is reference to a squeezing or nipping of the sycamore fig to make it more palatable or to accelerate its ripening, though such a usage is not known in Pal at the present day.

4. His Preparation

Nothing is said as to any special preparation of the prophet for his work: "The Lord took me from following the flock, and the Lord said unto me, Go, prophesy unto my people Israel" (**7** 15 ERV). In these words he puts himself in line with all the prophets who, in various modes of expression, claim a direct revelation from God. But the mention of the prophetic call in association with the mention of his worldly calling is significant. There was no period interposed between the one and the other, no cessation of husbandry to prepare for the work of prophesying. The husbandman was prepared for this task, and when God's time came he took it up. What was that preparation? Even if we suppose that the call was a momentary event, the man must have been ready to receive it, equipped for its performance. And, looking at the way in which he accomplished it, as exhibited in his book, we can see that there was a preparation, both internal and external, of a very thorough and effective character.

(1) *Knowledge of God.*—First of all, he has no doubt or uncertainty as to the character of the God in whose name he is called to speak. The God of Amos is one whose sway is boundless (**9** 2 ff), whose power is infinite (**8** 9 f), not only controlling the forces of Nature (**4**; **5** 8 f) but guiding the movements and destinies of nations (**6** 1 ff.14; **9** 7 ff). Moreover, He is righteous in all His ways, dealing with nations on moral principles (**1** 3 ff; **2** 1 ff); and, though particularly favorable to Israel, yet making that very choice of them as a people a ground for visiting them with sterner retribution for their sins (**3** 2). In common with all the prophets, Amos gives no explanation of how he came to know God and to form this conception of His character. It was not by searching that they found out God. It is assumed that God is and that He is such a Being; and this knowledge, as it could come only from God, is regarded as undisputed and undisputable. The call to speak in God's name may have come suddenly, but the prophet's conception of the character of the God who called him is no new or sudden revelation but a firm and well-established conviction.

(2) *Acquaintance with history of his people.*—Then his book shows not only that he was well acquainted with the history and traditions of his nation, which he takes for granted as well known to his hearers, but that he had reflected upon these things and realized their significance. We infer that he had breathed an atmosphere of religion, as there is nothing to indicate that, in his acquaintance with the religious facts of his nation, he differed from those among whom he dwelt, although the call to go forth and enforce them came to him in a special way.

(3) *Personal travel.*—It has been conjectured that Amos had acquired by personal travel the accurate acquaintance which he shows in his graphic delineations of contemporary life and conditions; and it may have been the case that, as a wool-merchant or flock-master, he had visited the towns mentioned and frequented the various markets to which the people were attracted.

(4) *Scenery of his home.*—Nor must we overlook another factor in his preparation: the scenery in which he had his home and the occupations of his daily life. The landscape was one to make a solemn impression on a reflective mind: the wide-spreading desert, the shimmering waters of the Dead Sea, the high wall of the distant hills of Moab, over all which were thrown the varying light and shade. The silent life of the desert, as with such scenes ever before him, he tended his flock or defended them from the ravages of wild beasts, would to one whose thoughts were full of God nourish that exalted view of the Divine Majesty which we find in his book, and furnish the imagery in which his thoughts are set (**1** 2; **3** 4 f; **4** 13; **5** 8; **9** 5 f). As he is taken from following the flock, he comes before us using the language and figures of his daily life (**3** 12), but there runs through all the note of one who has seen God's working in all Nature and His presence in every phenomenon. Rustic he may be, but there is no rudeness or rusticity in his style, which is one of natural and impassioned eloquence, ordered and regular as coming from a mind which was responsive to the orderly working of God in Nature around him. There is an aroma of the free air of the desert about his words; but the prophet lives in an ampler ether and breathes a purer air; all things in Nature and on the field of history are seen in a Divine light and measured by a Divine standard.

5. His Mission

Thus prepared in the solitudes of the extreme south of Judah, he was called to go and prophesy unto the people of Israel, and appears at Bethel the capital of the Northern Kingdom. It may be that, in the prosecution of his worldly calling, he had seen and been impressed by the conditions of life and religion in those parts. No reason is given for his mission to the northern capital, but the reason is not far to seek. It is the manner of the prophets to appear where they are most needed; and the Northern Kingdom about that time had come victorious out of war, and had reached its culmination of wealth and power, with the attendant results of luxury and excess, while the Southern Kingdom had been enjoying a period of outward tranquillity and domestic content.

6. Date

The date of the prophet Amos can approximately be fixed from the statement in the first ver that his activity fell "in the days of Uzziah king of Judah, and in the days of Jeroboam the son of Joash king of Israel, two years before the earthquake." Both these monarchs had long reigns, that of Uzziah extending from 779 to 740 BC and that of Jeroboam II from 783 to 743 BC. If we look at the years when they were concurrently reigning, and bear in mind that, toward the end of Uzziah's reign, Jotham acted as co-regent, we may safely place the date of Amos at about the year 760 BC. In a country in which earthquakes are not uncommon the one here mentioned must have been of unusual severity, for the memory of it was long preserved (Zec **14** 5). How long he exercised his ministry we are not told. In all probability the book is the deposit of a series of addresses delivered from time to time till his plain speaking drew upon him the resentment of the authorities, and he was ordered to leave the country (Am **7** 10 ff). We can only conjecture that, some time afterward, he withdrew to his native place and put down in writing a condensed record of the discourses he had delivered.

II. The Book.—We can distinguish with more than ordinary certainty the outlines of the individual addresses, and the arrangement of the book is clear and simple. The text, also, has been on the whole faithfully preserved; and though in a few places critics profess to find the traces of later editorial hands, these conclusions rest mainly on subjective grounds, and will be estimated differently by different minds.

The book falls naturally into three parts, recognizable by certain recurring formulas and general literary features.

1. Its Divisions

(1) The first section, which is clearly recognizable, embraces chs **1** and **2.** Here, after the title and designation of the prophet in ver 1, there is a solemn proclamation of Divine authority for the prophet's words: "Jeh will roar from Zion, and utter his voice from Jerusalem" (ver 2). This is notable in one who throughout the book recognizes God's power as world-wide and His operation as extensive as creation; and it should be a caution in view, on the one hand, of the assertion that the temple at Jerusalem was not more sacred than any of the numerous "high places" throughout the land, and, on the other hand, the superficial manner in which some writers speak of the Heb notion of a Deity whose dwelling-place was restricted to one locality beyond which His influence was not felt. For this God, who has His dwelling-place in Zion, now through the mouth of the prophet denounces in succession the surrounding nations, and this mainly not for offences committed against the chosen people but for moral offences against one another and for breaches of a law binding on humanity. It will be observed that the nations denounced are not named in geographical order, and the prophet exhibits remarkable rhetorical skill in the order of selection. The interest and sympathy of the hearers is secured by the fixing of the attention on the enormities of guilt in their neighbors, and curiosity is kept awake by the uncertainty as to where the next stroke of the prophetic whip will fall. Beginning with the more distant and alien peoples of Damascus, Gaza and Tyre, he wheels round to the nearer and kindred peoples of Edom, Ammon and Moab, till he rests for a moment on the brother tribe of Judah, and thus, having relentlessly drawn the net around Israel by the enumeration of seven peoples, he swoops down upon the Northern Kingdom to which his message is to be particularly addressed.

(2) The second section embraces chs **3** to **6,** and consists apparently of a series of discourses, each introduced by the formula: "Hear this word" (**3** 1; **4** 1; **5** 1), and another introduced by a comprehensive: "Woe to them that are at ease in Zion, and to them that are secure in the mountain of Samaria" (**6** 1). The divisions here are not so clearly marked. It will be observed e.g. that there is another "Woe" at **5** 18; and in ch **4,** though the address at the outset is directed to the luxurious women of Samaria, from ver 4 onward the words have a wider reference. Accordingly some would divide this section into a larger number of subsections; and some, indeed, have described the whole book as a collection of ill-arranged fragments. But, while it is not necessary to suppose that the written book is an exact reproduction of the spoken addresses, and while the division into chs has no authority, yet we must allow for some latitude in the details which an impassioned speaker would introduce into his discourses, and for transitions and connections of thought which may not be apparent on the surface.

(3) The third section has some well-marked characteristics, although it is even less uniform than the preceding. The outstanding feature is the phrase, "Thus the Lord Jeh showed me" (**7** 1.4.7; **8** 1) varied at **9** 1 by the words, "I saw the Lord standing beside the altar." We have thus a series of "visions" bearing upon, and interpreted as applying to, the condition of Israel. It is in the course of one of these, when the prophet comes to the words, "I will rise against the house of Jeroboam with the sword" (**7** 9) that the interposition of Amaziah, the priest of Bethel, is recorded, with the prophet's noble reply as to his Divine call, and his rebuke and denunciation of the priest, ending with a prophetic announcement of the downfall and captivity of Israel (**7** 14–17).

2. Its Outlook

If the discourses are put down in chronological order of their delivery, it would appear that Amos did not immediately take his departure, since more visions follow this episode; and there is a special appropriateness in the intervention of Amaziah just at the point where it is recorded. As to the closing passage of this section (**9** 11–15) which gives a bright prospect of the future, there is a class of critics who are inclined to reject it just on this account as inconsistent with the severe denunciatory tone of the rest of the book. It is quite possible, however, that the prophet himself (and no succeeding later editor) may have added the passage when he came to write down his addresses. There is no reason to believe that any of the prophets—harsh though their words were—believed that the God of Israel would make a full end of His people in captivity: on the contrary, their assurance of God's faithfulness to His promise, and the deep-seated conviction that right would ultimately prevail, lead us to expect even in the sternest or earliest of the prophets the hope of a future glory—that hope which grew brighter and brighter as the nation's outlook grew darker, and attained intensity and clearness in the Messianic hope which sustained them in the darkest days of exile. It is difficult to believe that any of the prophets were prophets of despair, or to conceive how they could have prophesied at all unless they had a firm faith in the ultimate triumph of the good.

3. Value of the Book

The Book of Am is particularly valuable from the fact that he is certainly one of the earliest prophets whose writings have come down to us. It is, like the Book of Hosea which belongs to about the same time, a contemporaneous document of a period of great significance in the history of Israel; and not only gives graphic sketches or illuminating hints of the life and religious condition of the people, but furnishes a trustworthy standard for estimating the value of some other books whose dates are not so precisely determined, a definite starting-point for tracing the course of Israel's history.

(1) *As a picture of the social condition.*—The book is valuable as embodying a contemporary picture of society and the condition of religion. From the abuses which the prophet denounces and the life-like sketches he draws of the scenes amid which he moved, taken along with what we know otherwise of the historical movements of the period, we are able to form a fairly adequate estimate of the condition of the age and the country. During the reign of Jeroboam II the kingdom of Israel, after having been greatly reduced during preceding reigns, rose to a degree of extent and influence unexampled since the days of Solomon (2 K **14** 25); and we are not astonished to read in the Book of Am the haughty words which he puts into the mouth of the people of his time when they spoke of Israel as the "chief of the nations," a *first-class power* in modern language, and boasted of the "horns" by which they had attained that eminence (**6** 1.13). But success in war, if it encouraged this boastful spirit, brought also inevitable evils in its train. Victory, as we know from the Assyr monuments, meant plunder; for king after king recounts how much spoil he had taken, how many prisoners he had carried away; and we must assume that wars among smaller states would be conducted on the same methods. In such wars, success meant an

extension of territory and increase of wealth, while defeat entailed the reverse. But it is to be remembered that, in an agricultural country and in a society constituted as that of Israel was, the result of war to one class of the population was to a great extent disastrous, whatever was the issue, and success, when it was achieved, brought evils in its train which even aggravated their condition. The peasant, required to take up arms for offence or defence, was taken away from the labors of the field which, in the best event, were for a time neglected, and, in the worst, were wasted and rendered unproductive. And then, when victory was secured, the spoils were liable to fall into the hands of the nobles and leaders, those "called with a name" (**6** 1), while the peasant returned to his wasted or neglected fields without much substantial resource with which to begin life again. The wealth secured by the men of strong hand led to the increase of luxury in its possessors, and became actually the means of still further adding to the embarrassment of the poor, who were dependent on the rich for the means of earning their livelihood. The situation would be aggravated under a feeble or corrupt government, such as was certainly that of Jeroboam's successors. The condition prevails in modern eastern countries, even under comparatively wise and just administration; and that it was the state of matters prevailing in the time of Amos is abundantly clear from his book. The opening denunciation of Israel for oppression of the poor and for earth-hunger (**2** 6.7) is reëchoed and amplified in the succeeding chs (**3** 9.10; **4** 1; **5** 11.12; **8** 4–6); and the luxury of the rich, who battened on the misfortune of their poorer brethren, is castigated in biting irony in such passages as **6** 3–6. Specially noticeable in this connection is the contemptuous reference to the luxurious women, the "kine of Bashan" (**4** 1), whose extravagances are maintained by the oppression of the poor. The situation, in short, was one that has found striking parallels in modern despotic countries in the East, where the people are divided into two classes, the powerful rich, rich because powerful and powerful because rich, and the poor oppressed, men who have no helper, no "back" in the common eastern phrase, dependent on the rich and influential and tending to greater poverty under greedy patrons.

(2) *As a picture of the religious condition.*—In such a social atmosphere, which poisoned the elementary virtues, religion of a vital kind could not flourish; and there are plain indications in the words of Amos of the low condition to which it had sunk. There was, indeed, as we gather from his addresses, no lack of outward attention to the forms of worship; but these forms were of so corrupted a character and associated with so much practical godlessness and even immorality, that instead of raising the national character it tended to its greater degradation. The people prided themselves in what they regarded the worship of the national God, thinking that so long as they honored Him with costly offerings and a gorgeous ritual, they were pleasing Him and secure in His protection. Bethel, Dan, Gilgal, Beersheba, and we know not how many other places were resorted to in pilgrimage by crowds of worshippers. With all the accompaniments of ceremonious ritual which the newly found wealth put in their power, with offerings more than the legally prescribed or customary (**4** 4.5) the service of these sanctuaries was maintained; but even these offerings were made at the expense of the poor (**5** 11), the prevailing luxury forced its way even to the precincts of the altars (**2** 8), and justice and mercy were conspicuously absent from the religious life. The people seemed to have settled down to a complacent optimism, nourished no doubt by national prosperity, and, though there had not been wanting reminders of the sovereignty of a righteous God, in convulsions of Nature—drought, famine, pestilence and earthquake (**4** 6–11)—these had been of no avail to awaken the sleeping conscience. They put the evil day far from them (**6** 3), for Jeh was their national God and "the day of the Lord," the good time coming (**5** 18), when God would come to their help, was more in their mind than the imperative duty of returning to Him (**4** 6.8, etc).

(3) *Testimony to history.*—The book is valuable for the confirmation it gives of the historical statements of other books, particularly for the references it contains to the earlier history contained in the Pentateuch. And here we must distinguish between references to, or quotations from, books, and statements or hints or indications of historical events which may or may not have been written in books or accessible to the prophet and his hearers. Opinions differ as to the date of composition of the books which record the earlier history, and the oldest Biblical writers are not in the habit of saying from what sources they drew their information or whether they are quoting from books. We can hardly believe that in the time of Amos copies of existing books or writings would be in the hands of the mass of the people, even if the power to read them was general. In such circumstances, if we find a prophet like Amos in the compass of a small book referring to outstanding events and stages of the past history as matters known to all his hearers and unquestionable, our confidence in the veracity of the books in which these facts are recorded is greatly increased, and it becomes a matter of comparatively less importance at what date these books were composed. Now it is remarkable how many allusions, more or less precise, to antecedent history are found in the compass of this small book; and the significance of them lies not in the actual number of references, but in the kind of reference and the implications involved in the individual references. That is to say, each reference is not to be taken as an isolated testimony to some single event in question, but involves a great deal more than is expressed, and is intelligible only when other facts or incidents are taken into consideration. Thus e.g. the reference to the overthrow of Sodom and Gomorrah (**4** 11) is only intelligible on the supposition that the story of that catastrophe was a matter of common knowledge; and it would be a carping criticism to argue that the destruction of other cities of the plain at the same time and the whole story of Lot were unknown in the days of Amos because they are not mentioned here in detail. So, when we have in one passage a reference to the house of Isaac (**7** 16), in another to the house of Jacob (**3** 13), in another to the house of Joseph (**5** 6) and in another to the enmity between Jacob and Esau (**1** 11), we cannot take these as detached notices, but must supply the links which the prophet's words would suggest to his hearers. In other words, such slight notices, just because they are incidental and brief, imply a familiarity with a connected patriarchal history such as is found in the Book of Gen. Again, the prophet's references to the "whole family" of the "children of Israel" whom the Lord "brought up out of the land of Egypt" (**3** 1), to the Divine leading of the people "forty years in the wilderness, to possess the land of the Amorite" (**2** 10) are not odds and ends of popular story but links in a chain of national history. It seems to be on the strength of these and similar references in the books of Am and Hos, whose dates are known, that critics have agreed to fix the date of the earliest historical por-

tions of the Pent as they understand them, viz. the parts designated as J and E, in the 8th and 9th cents. BC, i.e. at or shortly before the time of these prophets. It may be left to the unbiased judgment of the reader to say whether the references look like references to a newly composed document, or whether it is not more probable that, in an age when written documents were necessarily few and not accessible to the multitude, these references are appeals to things well fixed in the national memory, a memory extending back to the things themselves. Or, if the prophet's words are to be taken as sufficient proof of the existence of *written* sources, the fact that the matters are assumed as well known would rather encourage the conclusion that the written sources in question go back to a much earlier period, since the matters contained in them had by this time become matters of universal knowledge.

(4) *Testimony to the Law.*—And what about those other elements of the Pent of a legal and ritual character which bulk so prominently in those books? The question whether the Book of Am indicates an acquaintance with these or not is important because it is to a great extent on the silence of prophetical and historical writers that critics of a certain school relegate these legalistic portions of the Pent to a late date. Now at the outset it is obvious to ask what we have a reasonable right to expect. We have to bear in mind what was the condition of the people whom Amos addressed, and the purpose and aim of his mission to the Northern Kingdom. It is to be remembered that, as we are told in the Book of K (1 K **12** 25 ff), Jeroboam I deliberately sought to make a breach between the worship of Jerusalem and that of his own kingdom, while persuading his people that the worship of Jeh was being maintained. The schism occurred some 170 years before the time of Amos and it is not probable that the worship and ritual of the Northern Kingdom tended in that interval to greater purity or greater conformity to what had been the authoritative practice of the undivided kingdom at the temple of Jerus. When, therefore, Amos, in face of the corrupt worship combined with elaborate ritual which prevailed around him, declares that God hates and despises their feasts and takes no delight in their solemn assemblies (**5** 21), we are not justified in pressing his words, as is sometimes done, into a sweeping condemnation of all ritual. On the contrary, seeing that, in the very same connection (**5** 22), he specifies burnt offerings and meal offerings and peace offerings, and, in another passage (**4** 4.5), daily sacrifices and tithes, sacrifices of thanksgiving and free-will offerings, it is natural to infer that by these terms which are familiar in the Pent he is referring to those statutory observances which were part of the national worship of united Israel, but had been overlaid with corruption and become destitute of spiritual value as practised in the Northern Kingdom. So we may take his allusions to the new moon and the Sabbath (**8** 5) as seasons of special sacredness and universally sanctioned. Having condemned in such scornful and sweeping terms the worship that he saw going on around him, what was Amos to gain by entering into minute ritual prescriptions or defining the precise duties and perquisites of priests and Levites; and having condemned the pilgrimages to the shrines of Bethel, Gilgal, Beersheba, Samaria and Dan (**4** 4; **5** 5; **8** 14), what was he to gain by quoting the law of Deut as to a central sanctuary? And had one of his hearers, like the woman of Samaria of a later day, attempted to draw him into a discussion of the relative merits of the two temples, we can conceive him answering in the spirit of the great Teacher: "Ye worship ye know not what: we know what we worship" (Jn **4** 22 AV). A regulation of the form was of no avail while the whole spirit of the observance was corrupt; the soul of religion was dead, and the prophet had a higher duty than to dress out the carcase.

At the root of the corruption of the religion lay a rottenness of moral sense; and from beginning to end Amos insists on the necessity of a pure and righteous life. In this connection his appeals are in striking agreement with the specially ethical demands of the law books, and in phraseology so much resemble them as to warrant the conclusion that the requirements of the law on these subjects were known and acknowledged. Thus his denunciations of those who oppress the poor (**2** 7; **4** 1; **8** 4) are quite in the spirit and style of Ex **22** 21.22; **23** 9; his references to the perversion of justice and taking bribes (**2** 6; **5** 7.10 ff; **6** 12) are rhetorical enforcements of the prohibitions of the law in Ex **23** 6–8; when he reproves those that "lay themselves down beside every altar upon clothes taken in pledge" (**2** 8) we hear an echo of the command: "If thou at all take thy neighbor's garment to pledge, thou shalt restore it unto him before the sun goeth down" (Ex **22** 26); and when he denounces those making "the ephah small, and the shekel great, and dealing falsely with balances of deceit" (**8** 5) his words are in close agreement with the law, "Ye shall do no unrighteousness in judgment, in mete-yard, in weights, or in measure. Just balances, just weight, a just ephah, and a just hin, shall ye have" (Lev **19** 35.36 AV).

Ethical teaching. As a preacher of righteousness, Amos affirms and insists upon those ethical parts of the law which are its vital elements, and which lie at the foundation of all prophecy; and it is remarkable how even in phraseology he agrees with the most ethical book of the Pent, Dt. He does not, indeed, like his contemporary Hosea, dwell on the *love* of God as Dt does; but, of sterner mould, in almost the very words of Dt, emphasizes the keeping of God's commandments, and denounces those who despise the law (cf **2** 4 with Dt **17** 19). Among verbal coincidences have been noticed the combinations "oppress" and "crush" (**4** 1; Dt **28** 33), "blasting" and "mildew" (**4** 9; Dt **28** 22), and "gall" and "wormwood" (**6** 12; Dt **29** 18). Cf also **9** 8 with Dt **6** 15, and note the predilection for the same word to "destroy" common to both books (cf **2** 9 with Dt **2** 22). In view of all of which it seems an extraordinary statement to make that "the silence of Amos with reference to the centralization of worship, on which Dt is so explicit, alone seems sufficient to outweigh any linguistic similarity that can be discovered" (H. G. Mitchell, *Amos, an Essay in Exegesis*, 185).

(5) *The prophetic order.*—As Amos is without doubt one of the earliest writing prophets, his book is invaluable as an example of what prophecy was in ancient Israel. And one thing cannot fail to impress the reader at the very outset: viz. that he makes no claim to be the first or among the first of the line, or that he is exercising some new and hitherto unheard-of function. He begins by boldly speaking in God's name, assuming that even the people of the Northern Kingdom were familiar with that kind of address. Nay, he goes farther and states in unequivocal terms that "the Lord God will do nothing, but he revealeth his secret unto his servants the prophets" (**3** 7 AV). We need not search farther for a definition of the prophet as understood by him and other OT writers: the prophet is one to whom God reveals His will, and who comes forward to declare that will and purpose to man. A great deal has been made of the words of Amaziah the priest of Bethel (**7** 12), as if they proved that the prophet in those times was

regarded as a wandering rhetorician, earning his bread by reciting his speeches; and it has been inferred from the words of Amos himself that the prophets of his day were so disreputable a class that he disdained to be named along with them (**7** 14). But all this is fanciful. Even if we admit that there were men calling themselves prophets who prophesied for hire (Mic **3** 5.11), it cannot be assumed that the expression here to "eat bread" has that meaning; for in other passages it seems simply to signify to lead a quiet or ordinary life, to go about one's daily business (see Ex **24** 11; Jer **22** 15). In any case we are not to take the estimate of a man like Amaziah or a godless populace in preference to the conception of Amos himself and his account of his call. It was not by man or by any college of prophets but by Jeh Himself that he was appointed, and by whatever name he might be called, the summons was "Go, *prophesy* unto my people Israel" (**7** 15). There is no trace here of the "prophets becoming conscious of a distinction between themselves and the professional *n^{e}bhī'īm*, who were apt simply to echo the patriotic and nationalistic sentiments of the people, and in reality differed but little from the soothsayers and diviners of Sem heathenism" (Ottley, *The Religion of Israel*, 90). Whoever the "professional *n^{e}bhī'īm*" may have been in his day, or whatever he thought of them if they existed, Amos tells us nothing; but he ranges himself with men to whom Jeh has spoken in truth (**3** 7.8), and indicates that there had been a succession of such men (**2** 11), faithful amid the prevailing corruption though tempted to be unfaithful (**2** 12); in short he gives us to understand that the "prophetic order" goes back to a period long before his day and has its roots in the true and original religion of Israel.

(6) *The prophetic religion.*—Finally, from the Book of Am we may learn what the prophetic religion was. Here again there is no indication of rudimentary crudeness of conception, or of painful struggling upward from the plane of naturalism or belief in a merely tribal God. The God in whose name Amos speaks has control over all the forces of Nature (**4** 6 ff; **5** 8.9), rules the destinies of nations (**6** 2.14; **9** 2–6), searches the thoughts of the heart (**4** 13), is inflexible in righteousness and deals with nations and with men on equal justice (**1** and **2**; **9** 7), and is most severe to the people who have received the highest privileges (**3** 2). And this is the God by whose name his hearers call themselves, whose claims they cannot deny, whose dealings with them from old time are well known and acknowledged (**2** 11), whose laws they have broken (**2** 4; **3** 10) and for whose just judgment they are warned to prepare (**4** 12). All this the prophet enforces faithfully and sternly; not a voice is raised in the circle of his hearers to controvert his words; all that Amaziah the priest can do is to urge the prophet to abstain from unwelcome words in Bethel, because it is the king's sanctuary and a royal house; the only inference is that the people felt the truth and justice of the prophet's words. The "prophetic religion" does not begin with Amos.

LITERATURE.—W. R. Harper, "Amos and Hosea," in the *ICC;* S. R. Driver, "Joel and Amos" in *Cambridge Bible for Schools and Colleges;* H. G. Mitchell, *Amos, an Essay in Exegesis* (Boston); A. B. Davidson, two arts. in *Expos*, 3d ser, V, VI (1887); W. R. Smith, *The Prophets of Israel;* G. A. Smith, "The Book of the Twelve Prophets," in *Expositor's Bible;* J. J. P. Valeton, *Amos und Hosea* (1894); C. von Orelli, *Die zwölf kleinen Propheten*, 3. Aufl. (1908) and ET; Nowack, "Die kleinen Propheten," in *Hand-Commentar zum AT;* Marti, "Das Dodekapropheton erklärt," in *Kurzer Hand-Commentar zum AT.*

JAS. ROBERTSON

AMOS, ā'mos (Ἀμώς, *Amṓs*): An ancestor of Jesus in Lk's genealogy, the eighth before Joseph, the husband of Mary (Lk **3** 25).

AMOZ, ā'moz (אָמוֹץ, *'āmōç*, "strong"): The father of Isa the prophet (2 K **19** 2.20; **20** 1; 2 Ch **26** 22; **32** 20.32; Isa **1** 1; **2** 1; **13** 1; **20** 2; **37** 2.21; **38** 1).

AMPHIPOLIS, am-fip'o-lis (Ἀμφίπολις, *Amphípolis*): A town in Macedonia, situated on the eastern bank of the Strymon (mod. *Struma* or *Karasu*) some three miles from its mouth, near the point where it flows out of Lake Prasias or Cercinitis. It lay on a terraced hill, protected on the N., W. and S. by the river, on the E. by a wall (Thuc. iv.102), while its harbor-town of Eïon lay on the coast close to the river's mouth. The name is derived either from its being nearly surrounded by the stream or from its being conspicuous on every side, a fact to which Thucydides draws attention (l.c.). It was at first called *Ennea Hodoi*, Nine Ways, a name which suggests its importance both strategically and commercially. It guarded the main route from Thrace into Macedonia and later became an important station on the Via Egnatia, the great Rom road from Dyrrhachium on the Adriatic to the Hebrus (*Maritza*), and it was the center of a fertile district producing wine, oil, figs and timber in abundance and enriched by gold and silver mines and considerable manufactures, especially of woolen stuffs. In 497 BC Aristagoras, ex-despot of Miletus, tried to settle there, and a second vain attempt was made in 465–464 by the Athenians, who succeeded in founding a colony there in 437 under the leadership of Hagnon. The population, however, was too mixed to allow of strong Athenian sympathies, and in 424 the town fell away to the Spartan leader Brasidas and defied all the subsequent attempts of the Athenians to recover it. It passed under the protectorate of Perdiccas and Philip of Macedon, and the latter finally made himself master of it in 358. On the Rom partition of Macedonia after the battle of Pydna (168 BC) Amphipolis was made a free city and capital of Macedonia Prima. Paul and Silas passed through it on their way from Philippi to Thessalonica, but the narrative seems to preclude a long stay (Acts **17** 1). The place was called *Popolia* in the Middle Ages, while in modern times the village of *Neochori* (Turkish, *Yenikeui*) marks the site (Leake, *Northern Greece*, III, 181 ff; Cousinéry, *Macédoine*, I, 100 ff, 122 ff; Heuzey et Daumet, *Mission archéol. de Macédoine*, 165 ff).

MARCUS N. TOD

AMPLIAS, am'pli-as (*TR* Ἀμπλιᾶς, *Ampliâs*). AV form: a contraction of AMPLIATUS (thus RV; q.v.).

AMPLIATUS, am-pli-ā'tus (Ἀμπλιᾶτος, א ABF, *Ampliâtos;* Ἀμπλιᾶς, DELP, RV form; AV **Amplias**): The name of a member of the Christian community at Rome, to whom Paul sent greetings (Rom **16** 8). He is designated "my beloved in the Lord." It is a common name and is found in inscriptions connected with the imperial household. The name is found twice in the cemetery of Domitilla. The earlier inscription is over a cell which belongs to the end of the 1st or the beginning of the 2d cent. The bearer of this name was probably a member of her household and conspicuous in the early Christian church in Rome.

AMRAM, am'ram (עַמְרָם, *'amrām*, "people exalted"):

(1) Father of Aaron, Moses and Miriam (Ex **6** 20; Nu **26** 59; 1 Ch **6** 3; **23** 13); and a son of Kohath, the son of Levi (Ex **6** 18; Nu **3** 19, etc). It is not certain that he was *literally* the son of Kohath, but rather his descendant, since there were ten generations from Joseph to Joshua

(1 Ch **7** 20–27), while only four are actually mentioned from Levi to Moses for the corresponding period. Moreover the Kohathites at the time of the Exodus numbered 8,600 (Nu **3** 28), which would therefore have been an impossibility if only two generations had lived. It seems best to regard Amram as a descendant of Kohath, and his wife Jochebed as a "daughter of Levi" in a general sense.

(2) One of the Bani, who in the days of Ezra had taken a foreign wife (Ezr **10** 34).

(3) In 1 Ch **1** 41 (AV) for the properly read HAMRAN of the RV (חַמְרָן, *ḥamrān*), a Horite, who in Gen **36** 26 is called HEMDAN (q.v.).

EDWARD MACK

AMRAMITES, am′ram-īts (עַמְרָמִי, *'amrāmī*): The descendants of Amram, one of the Levitical families mentioned in Nu **3** 27 and 1 Ch **26** 23, who had the charge of the tabernacle proper, guarding the ark, table, candlestick, etc, called in 1 Ch **26** 22 "the treasures of the house of Jeh."

AMRAPHEL, am′ra-fel, am-rā′fel (אַמְרָפֶל, *'amrāphel,* or, perhaps better, *'ameraphel*): This name, which is identified with that of the renowned Bab king Ḫammurabi (q.v.), is only found in Gen **14** 1.9, where he is mentioned as the king of Shinar (Babylonia), who fought against the cities of the plain, in alliance with Arioch king of Ellasar, Chedorlaomer king of Elam, and Tidal king of Nations (RV GOIIM). The narrative which follows is very circumstantial.

1. The Expedition Against Sodom and Gomorrah

From it we learn, that Bera king of Sodom, Birsha king of Gomorrah, Shinab king of Admah, Shemeber king of Zeboiim, and the king of Bela or Zoar, had served Chedorlaomer for 12 years, rebelled in the 13th, and in the 14th year Chedorlaomer, with the kings enumerated, fought with and defeated them in the vale of Siddim, which is described as being the Salt Sea. Previous to this engagement, however, the Elamites and their allies had attacked the Rephaim (*Onkelos:* "giants") in Ashtaroth-karnaim, the Zuzim (O: "mighty ones," "heroes") in Ham (O: *Ḥamtā'*), the Emim (O: "terrible ones") in Shaveh-kiriathaim, and the Horites in their Mount Seir, by the Desert. These having been rendered powerless to aid the revolted vassals, they returned and came to En-mishpat, or Kadesh, attacked the country of the Amalekites, and the Amorites dwelling in Hazazon-tamar (vs 2–7).

2. The Preparation and the Attack

At this juncture the kings of the cities of the plain came out against them, and opposed them with their battle-array in the vale of Siddim. The result of the fight was, that the kings of Sodom and Gomorrah, with their allies, fled, and fell among the bitumen-pits of which the place was full, whilst those who got away took refuge in the mountain. All the goods and food (the camp-equipment and supplies) of the kings of the plain were captured by Chedorlaomer and his allies, who then continued their march (to their own lands) (vs 8–11).

3. Abraham's Rescue of Lot

Among the captives, however, was Lot, Abram's nephew, who dwelt in Sodom. A fugitive, having escaped, went and announced the result of the engagement to Abram, who was at that time living by Mamre's oak plantation. The patriarch immediately marched forth with his trained men, and pursued them to Dan, where he divided his forces, attacked the Elamite-Bab army by night, and having put them to flight, pursued them again to Hobah, on the left (or N.) of Damascus. The result of this sudden onslaught was that he rescued Lot, with the women and people, and recaptured Lot's goods, which the allies of Amraphel had carried off (vs 12–16).

4. Difficulties of the Identification of Amraphel

There is no doubt that the identification of Amraphel with the Ḫammurabi of the Bab inscriptions is the best that has yet been proposed, and though there are certain difficulties therein, these may turn out to be apparent rather than real, when we know more of Bab history. The *l* at the end of Amraphel (which has also *ph* instead of *p* or *b*) as well as the fact that the expedition itself has not yet been recognized among the campaigns of Ḫammurabi, must be acknowledged as two points hard to explain, though they may ultimately be solved by further research.

5. Historical Agreements

It is noteworthy, however, that in the first ver of Gen **14** Amraphel is mentioned first, which, if he be really the Bab Ḫammurabi, is easily comprehensible, for his renown to all appearance exceeded that of Chedorlaomer, his suzerain. In vs 4 and 5, however, it is Chedorlaomer alone who is referred to, and he heads the list of eastern kings in ver 9, where Tidal comes next (a quite natural order, if Goiim be the Bab Gutê, i.e. the Medes). Next in order comes Amraphel, king of Babylonia and suzerain of Arioch of Ellasar (*Eri-Aku* of *Larsa*), whose name closes the list. It may also be suggested, that Amraphel led a Bab force against Sodom, as the ally of Chedorlaomer, before he became king, and was simply crown prince. In that case, like Belshazzar, he was called "king" by anticipation. For further details see ARIOCH and CHEDORLAOMER, and cf ERI-AKU and ḪAMMURABI; for the history of Babylonia during Ḫammurabi's period, see that article.

T. G. PINCHES

AMULET, am′ū-let (קְמִיעַ, *ḳemīa'*, לְחָשִׁים, *leḥāshīm*, מְזוּזָה, *mezūzāh*, תְּפִלִּין, *tephillīn*, צִיצִת, *çīçith;* **φυλακτήριον,** *phulaktērion*): Modern scholars are of opinion that our Eng. word amulet comes from the Lat *amuletum*, used by Pliny (*Naturalis Historia*, xxviii, 28; xxx, 2, etc), and other Lat writers; but no etymology for the Lat word has been discovered. The present writer thinks the root exists in the Arab. *himlat*, "something carried" (see Dozy, *Supplément aux Dictionnaires Arabes*, I, 327), though there is no known example of the use of the Arab. word in a magical sense. Originally "amulet" denoted any object supposed to have the power of removing or warding noxious influences believed to be due to evil spirits, etc, such as the evil eye, etc. But in the common usage it stands for an object worn on the body, generally hung from the neck, as a remedy or preservative against evil influences of a mystic kind. The word "amulet" occurs once in the RV (Isa **3** 20) but not at all in the AV.

The substances out of which amulets have been made and the forms which they have taken have been various.

1. Classes of Amulets

(1) The commonest have consisted of pieces of stone or metal, strips of parchment with or without inscriptions from sacred writings (Bible, Koran, etc). The earliest Egyp amulets known are pieces of green schist of various shapes—animal, etc. These were placed on the breast of a deceased person in order to secure a safe passage to the under-world. When a piece of stone is selected as an amulet it is always portable and generally of some striking fig. or shape (the human face, etc). The use of such a stone for this purpose is really a survival of animism.

(2) Gems, rings, etc. It has been largely held that all ornaments worn on the person were originally amulets. (3) Certain herbs and animal prepa-

rations; the roots of certain plants have been considered very potent as remedies and preservatives.

The practice of wearing amulets existed in the ancient world among all peoples, but esp. among Orientals; and it can be traced among most modern nations, esp. among peoples of backward civilization. Nor is it wholly absent from peoples of the most advanced civilization of today, the English, Americans, etc. Though the word charm (see CHARM) has a distinct meaning, it is often inseparably connected with amulets, for it is in many cases the incantation or charm inscribed on the amulet that gives the latter its significance. As distinguished from talisman (see TALISMAN) an amulet is believed to have negative results, as a means of protection: a talisman is thought to be the means of securing for the wearer some positive boon.

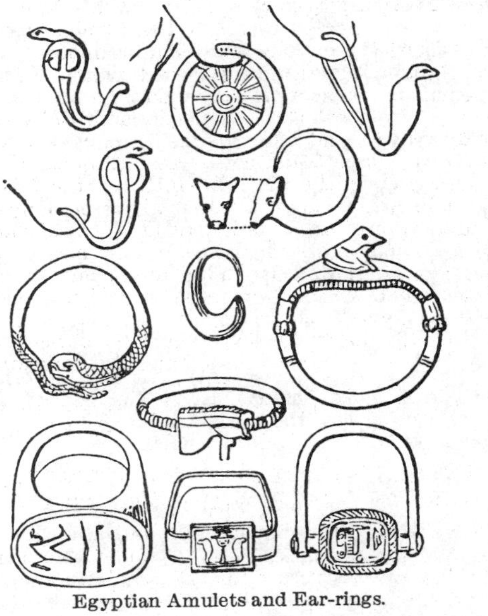

Egyptian Amulets and Ear-rings.

2. Amulets in the Bible

Though there is no word in the Heb or Gr Scriptures denoting "amulet," the thing itself is manifestly implied in many parts of the Bible. But it is remarkable that the general teaching of the Bible and esp. that of the OT prophets and of the NT writers is wholly and strongly opposed to such things.

(1) *The Old Testament.*—The golden ear-rings, worn by the wives and sons and daughters of the Israelites, out of which the molten calf was made (Ex **32** 2 f), were undoubtedly amulets. What other function could they be made to serve in the simple life of the desert? That the women's ornaments condemned in Isa **3** 16–26 were of the same character is made exceedingly likely by an examination of some of the terms employed. We read of moonlets and sunlets (ver 18), i.e. moon and sun-shaped amulets. The former in the shape of crescents are worn by Arab girls of our own time. The "ear-drops," "nose-rings," "arm chains" and "foot chains" were all used as a protection to the part of the body implied, and the strong words with which their employment is condemned are only intelligible if their function as counter charms is borne in mind. In Isa **3** 20 we read of *leḥāshīm* rendered "ear-rings" (AV) and "amulets" (RV). The Heb word seems to be cognate with the word for "serpent" (*neḥāshīm*; *l* and *r* often interchange), and meant probably in the first instance an amulet against a serpent bite (see *Magic, Divination, and Demonology among the Hebrews and Their Neighbours*, by the present writer, 50 f, 81; cf Jer **8** 7; Eccl **10** 11; Ps **58** 5). Crescent-shaped amulets were worn by animals as well as human beings, as Jgs **8** 21.26 shows.

At Bethel, Jacob burned not only the idols ("strange gods") but also the ear-rings, the latter being as much opposed to Yahwism as the former, on account of their heathen origin and import.

In Prov **17** 8 the Heb words rendered "a precious stone" (Heb "a stone conferring favor") mean without question a stone amulet treasured on account of its supposed magical efficacy. It is said in Prov **1** 9 that wisdom will be such a defence to the one who has it as the head amulet is to the head and that of the neck to the neck. The words rendered in the RV "a chaplet of grace unto thy head" mean lit. "something bound to the head conferring favor," the one word for the latter clause being identical with that so rendered above (*ḥēn*). The Talm word for an amulet (*ḳemīaʿ*) denotes something tied or bound (to the person).

We have reference to the custom of wearing amulets in Prov **6** 21 where the reader is urged to "bind *them* [i.e. the admonitions of father and mother] . . . . upon thy heart" and to "tie them about thy neck"—words implying a condemnation of the practice of trusting to the defence of mere material objects.

Underneath the garments of warriors slain in the Maccabean wars amulets were found in the shape apparently of idols worshipped by their neighbors (2 Macc **12** 40). It is strange but true that like other nations of antiquity the Jews attached more importance to amulets obtained from other nations than to those of native growth. It is probable that the signet ring referred to in Cant **8** 6; Jer **22** 24; Hag **2** 23 was an amulet. It was worn on the heart or on the arm.

(2) *The phylacteries and the mezūzāh.*—There is no distinct reference to these in the OT. The Heb technical term for the former (*tephillīn*) does not occur in Bib. Heb, and although the Heb word *mezūzāh* does occur over a dozen times its sense is invariably "door-[or "gate-"] post" and not the amulet put on the door-post which in later Heb the word denotes.

It is quite certain that the practice of wearing phylacteries has no Bib. support, for a correct exegesis and a proper understanding of the context put it beyond dispute that the words in Ex **13** 9.16; Dt **6** 8 f; **11** 18–20 have reference to the exhortations in the foregoing verses: "Thou shalt bind them [the commands previously mentioned] for a sign upon thy hand, and they shall be for frontlets between thy eyes. And thou shalt write them upon the door-posts of thy house, and upon thy gates" (Dt **6** 8 f). The only possible sense of these words is that they were to hold the precepts referred to before their minds constantly as if they were inscribed on their arms, held in front of their eyes, and written on the door- or gate-posts which they daily passed. That the language in Ex **13** 9.16 does not command the use of phylacteries is obvious; and that the same is true of Prov **3** 3; **6** 21; **7** 3 where similar words are used is still more certain. Yet, though none of the passages enjoin the use of phylacteries or of the *mezūzāh*, they may all contain allusions to both practices as if the sense were, "Thou shalt keep constantly before thee my words and look to them for safety and not to the phylacteries worn on head and arm by the heathen." If, however, phylacteries were in use among the Jews thus early, it is strange that there is not in the OT a single instance in which the practice of wearing phylacteries is mentioned. Jos, however, seems to refer to this practice (*Ant*, IV, viii, 13), and it is frequently spoken of in the Mish (*Berākhōth*, i, etc).

It is a striking and significant fact that the Apoc is wholly silent as to the three signs of Judaism, phylacteries, the *m^ezūzāh* and the *çîçith* (or tassel attached to the corner of the prayer garment called *ṭallith;* cf Mt **9** 20; **14** 36 AV where "hem of the garment" is inaccurate and misleading).

It is quite evident that phylacteries have a magical origin. This is suggested by the Gr name *phulaktērion* (whence the Eng. name) which in the 1st cent. of our era denoted a counter charm or defence (*phulassō*, "to protect") against evil influences. No scholar now explains the Gr word as denoting a means of leading people to keep (*phulassō*) the law. The Heb name *t^ephillīn* (="prayers") meets us first in post-Bib. Heb, and carries with it the later view that phylacteries are used during prayer in harmony with the prayers or other formulae over the amulet to make it effective (see Budge, *Egyptian Magic*, 27). See more fully under CHARM.

LITERATURE.—In addition to the lit. given in the course of the foregoing art., the following may be mentioned. On the general subject see the great works of Tyler (*Early History of Mankind, Primitive Culture*) and Frazer, *Golden Bough;* also the series of arts. under "Charms and Amulets" in Hastings' *Enc of Religion and Ethics* and the excellent article "Amulet" in the corresponding German work, *Die Religion in Geschichte und Gegenwart.* See further the art. "Amulet" in *Jew Enc*, and on Egyp amulets, Budge, *Egyptian Magic*, 25 ff.

T. WITTON DAVIES

AMZI, am'zī (עַמְצִי, *'amçī*, "my strength"): (1) A Levite of the family of Merari (1 Ch **6** 46). (2) A priest of the family of Adaiah in the second temple. His father's name was Zechariah (Neh **11** 12).

ANAB, ā'nab (עֲנָב, *'ănābh*, "grapes"; B, **'Ανών**, *Anōn* or **'Ανώβ**, *Anōb*): Mentioned in the list of cities which fell to Judah (Josh **15** 50). In the list it follows Debir, from which it was a short distance to the S.W. It lay about twelve miles to the S.W. of Hebron. It was a city of the Anakim, from whom Joshua took it (Josh **11** 21). Its site is now known as the ruin *'Anab.*

ANAEL, an'a-el (**'Αναήλ**, *Anaēl*): A brother of Tobit mentioned once only (Tob **1** 21) as the father of Achiacharus, who was an official in Nineveh under Esar-haddon.

ANAH, ā'na (עֲנָה, *'ănāh*, meaning uncertain; a Horite clan-name [Gen **36**]):

(1) Mother of Aholibamah, one of the wives of Esau and daughter of Zibeon (cf Gen **36** 2.14.18. 25). The LXX, the Sam Pent, and the Pesh read "son," identifying this Anah with no. 3 (see below); Gen **36** 2, read הַחֹרִי (*ha-ḥōrī*), for הַחִוִּי (*ha-ḥiwwī*.

(2) Son of Seir, the Horite, and brother of Zibeon; one of the chiefs of the land of Edom (cf Gen **36** 20.21 = 1 Ch **1** 38). Seir is elsewhere the name of the land (cf Gen **14** 6; Isa **21** 11); but here the country is personified and becomes the mythical ancestor of the tribes inhabiting it.

(3) Son of Zibeon, "This is Anah who found the hot springs in the wilderness" (cf Gen **36** 24 = 1 Ch **1** 40.41). The word הַיֵּמִם, *ha-yēmīm*, occurs only in this passage and is probably corrupt. Ball (*SBOT*, Gen, crit. note 93) suggests that it is a corruption of וְהֵימָם, *w^e-hēmām* (cf Gen **36** 22) in an earlier ver. Jerome, in his commentary on Gen **36** 24, assembles the following definitions of the word gathered from Jewish sources: (1) "seas" as though יַמִּים, *yammīm;* (2) "hot springs" as though חַמִּים, *ḥammīm;* (3) a species of ass, יְמִין, *y^emīn;* (4) "mules." This last explanation was the one most frequently met with in Jewish lit.; the tradition ran that Anah was the first to breed the mule, thus bringing into existence an unnatural species. As a punishment, God created the deadly water-snake, through the union of the common viper with the Libyan lizard (cf Gen Rabbah **82** 15; Yer. Ber **1** 12*b;* Bab Pes **54***a;* Ginzberg, *Monatschrift*, XLII, 538–39).

The descent of Anah is thus represented in the three ways pointed out above as the text stands. If, however, we accept the reading בֵּן, *ben*, for בַּת, *bath*, in the first case, Aholibamah will then be an unnamed daughter of the Anah of ver 24, not the Aholibamah, daughter of Anah of ver 25 (for the Anah of this verse is evidently the one of ver 20, not the Anah of ver 24). Another view is that the words, "the daughter of Zibeon," are a gloss, inserted by one who mistakenly identified the Anah of ver 25 with the Anah of ver 24; in this event, Aholibamah, the daughter of Anah, will be the one mentioned in ver 25.

The difference between (2) and (3) is to be explained on the basis of a twofold tradition. Anah was originally a sub-clan of the clan known as Zibeon, and both were "sons of Seir"—i.e. Horites.

H. J. WOLF

ANAHARATH, a-nā'ha-rath (אֲנָחֲרָת, *'ănāḥărāth*, meaning unknown): A place which fell to the tribe of Issachar in the division of the land (Josh **19** 19). Located in the valley of Jezreel toward the E., the name and site being preserved as the modern *en-Na'ūra*. *BDB* is wrong in assigning it to the tribe of Naphtali.

ANAIAH, an-a-ī'a, a-nī'a (עֲנָיָה, *'ănāyāh*, "Jah has answered"): (1) a Levite who assisted Ezr in reading the law to the people (Neh **8** 4), perhaps the person called Ananias in Esd **9** 43. (2) One of those who sealed the covenant (Neh **10** 22). He may have been the same as Anaiah (1).

ANAK, ā'nak. See ANAKIM.

ANAKIM, an'a-kim (עֲנָקִים, *'ănāḳīm;* **'Ενακίμ**, *Enakím*, or **'Ενακείμ**, *Enakeím;* also called "sons of Anak" [Nu **13** 33], and "sons of the Anakim" [Dt **1** 28]): The spies (Nu **13** 33) compared them to the Nephilim or "giants" of Gen **6** 4, and according to Dt **2** 11 they were reckoned among the REPHAIM (q.v.). In Nu **13** 22 the chiefs of Hebron are said to be descendants of Anak, while "the father of Anak" is stated in Josh (**15** 13; **21** 11) to be Arba after whom Hebron was called "the city of Arba." Josh "cut off the Anakim . . . . from Hebron, from Debir, from Anab, ... and from all the hill-country of Israel," remnants of them being left in the Phili cities of Gaza, Gath and Ashdod (Josh **11** 21.22). As compared with the Israelites, they were tall like giants (Nu **13** 33), and it would therefore seem that the "giant" Goliath and his family were of their race. At Hebron, at the time of the Israelitish conquest, we may gather that they formed the body-guard of the Amorite king (see Josh **10** 5) under their three leaders Sheshai, Ahiman and Talmai (Nu **13** 22; Josh **15** 14; Jgs **1** 20). Am Tab show that the Can princes were accustomed to surround themselves with body-guards of foreign mercenaries. It appears probable that the Anakim came from the Ægean like the Philistines, to whom they may have been related. The name Anak is a masculine corresponding with a feminine which we meet with in the name of the goddess Onka, who according to the Gr writers, Stephanus of Byzantium and Hesychius, was the "Phoen," i.e. Syrian equivalent of Athena. Anket or Anukit was also the name of the goddess worshipped by the Egyptians at the First Cataract. In the name Ahi-man it is possible that *-man* denotes a non-Sem deity.

A. H. SAYCE

ANAMIM, an'a-mim (עֲנָמִים, *'ănāmīm*): Descendants of Mizraim (Gen **10** 13; 1 Ch **1** 11). See Table of Nations.

ANAMMELECH, a-nam'e-lek (עֲנַמֶּלֶךְ, *'ănammelekh*=Assyr *Anu-malik,* "Anu is the prince"): A Bab (?) deity worshipped by the Sepharvites in Samaria, after being transported there by Sargon. The worship of Adrammelech (who is mentioned with Anammelech) and Anammelech is accompanied by the sacrifice of children by fire: "The Sepharvites burnt their children in the fire to Adrammelech and Anammelech, the gods of Sepharvaim" (2 K **17** 31). This passage presents two grave difficulties. First, there is no evidence in cuneiform lit. that would point to the presence of human sacrifice, by fire or otherwise, as part of the ritual; nor has it been shown that the sculptures or bas-reliefs deny this thesis. Much depends upon the identification of "Sepharvaim"; if, as some scholars hold, Sepharvaim and Sippar are one and the same cities, the two deities referred to are Bab. But there are several strong objections to this theory. It has been suggested that Sepharvaim (LXX, *seppharín, seppharеími*) is rather identical with "Shabara'in," a city mentioned in the Bab Chronicle as having been destroyed by Shalmaneser IV. As Sepharvaim and Arpad and Hamath are grouped together (2 K **17** 24; **18** 34) in two passages, it is probable that Sepharvaim is a Syr city. Sepharvaim may then be another form of "Shabara'in," which, in turn, is the Assyr form of Sibraim (Ezk **47** 16), a city in the neighborhood of Damascus (cf Halévy, *ZA*, II, 401 ff). One objection to this last is the necessity for representing ס (ṣ) by *sh;* this is not necessarily insurmountable, however. Then, the attempt to find an Assyr etymology for the two god-names falls to the ground. Besides, the custom of sacrifice by fire was prevalent in Syria. Secondly, the god that was worshipped at Sippar was neither Adrammelech nor Anammelech but Šamaš. It is improbable, as some would urge, that Adrammelech is a secondary title of the tutelary god of Sippar; then it would have to be shown that Anu enjoyed special reverence in this city which was especially consecrated to the worship of the Sun-god. (For "Anu" see Assyria.) It may be that the text is corrupt. See also Adrammelech.

H. J. Wolf

ANAN, ā'nan (עָנָן, *'ānān,* "cloud"): (1) One of those who, with Neh, sealed the covenant (Neh **10** 26). (2) A returned exile (1 Esd **5** 30). He is called Hanan in Ezr **2** 46 and Neh **7** 49.

ANANI, a-nā'nī (עֲנָנִי, *'ănānī,* perhaps a shortened form of Ananiah, "Jehovah has covered"): A son of Elioenai of the house of David, who lived after the captivity (1 Ch **3** 24).

ANANIAH, an-a-nī'a (עֲנָנְיָה, *'ănanyāh,* "Jehovah has covered"): (1) Grandfather of Azariah. He assisted in repairing the walls of Jerus after his return from the exile (Neh **3** 23). (2) A town of Benjamin mentioned in connection with Nob and Hazor (Neh **11** 32). It is commonly identified with Beit Hanina, between three and four miles N.N.W. from Jerus.

ANANIAS, an-a-nī'as (Ἀνανίας; WH, Ἁνανίας, *Hananías;* חֲנַנְיָה, *ḥănanyāh,* "Jeh has been gracious"): The name was common among the Jews. In its Heb form it is frequently found in the OT (e.g. 1 Ch **25** 4; Jer **28** 1; Dnl **1** 6). See Hananiah.

1. A Disciple at Jerusalem

Husband of Sapphira (Acts **5** 1–10). He and his wife sold their property, and gave to the common fund of the church part of the purchase money, pretending it was the whole. When his hypocrisy was denounced by Peter, Ananias fell down dead; and three hours later his wife met the same doom. The following points are of interest. (1) The narrative immediately follows the account of the intense brotherliness of the believers resulting in a common fund, to which Barnabas had made a generous contribution (Acts **4** 32–37). The sincerity and spontaneity of the gifts of Barnabas and the others set forth in dark relief the calculated deceit of Ananias. The brighter the light, the darker the shadow. (2) The crime of Ananias consisted, not in his retaining a part, but in his pretending to give the whole. He was under no compulsion to give all, for the communism of the early church was not absolute, but purely voluntary (see esp. **5** 4). Falsehood and hypocrisy ("lie to the Holy Spirit" ver 3), rather than greed, were the sins for which he was so severely punished. (3) The severity of the judgment can be justified by the consideration that the act was "the first open venture of deliberate wickedness" (Meyer) within the church. The punishment was an "awe-inspiring act of Divine church-discipline." The narrative does not, however, imply that Peter consciously willed their death. His words were the occasion of it, but he was not the deliberate agent. Even the words in ver 9*b* are a prediction rather than a judicial sentence.

2. A Disciple at Damascus

A disciple in Damascus, to whom the conversion of Saul of Tarsus was made known in a vision, and who was the instrument of his physical and spiritual restoration, and the means of introducing him to the other Christians in Damascus (Acts **9** 10–19). Paul makes honorable mention of him in his account of his conversion spoken at Jerus (Acts **22** 12–16), where we are told that Ananias was held in high respect by all the Jews in Damascus, on account of his strict legal piety. No mention is made of him in Paul's address before Agrippa in Caesarea (Acts **26**). In late tradition, he is placed in the list of the seventy disciples of Jesus, and represented as bishop of Damascus, and as having died a martyr's death.

3. A High Priest at Jerusalem

A high priest in Jerus from 47–59 AD. From Jos (*Ant*, XX, v, 2; vi, 2; ix, 2; *BJ*, II, xvii, 9) we glean the following facts: He was the son of Nedebaeus (or Nebedaeus) and was nominated to the high-priestly office by Herod of Chalcis. In 52 AD he was sent to Rome by Quadratus, legate of Syria, to answer a charge of oppression brought by the Samaritans, but the emperor Claudius acquitted him. On his return to Jerus, he resumed the office of high priest. He was deposed shortly before Felix left the province, but continued to wield great influence, which he used in a lawless and violent way. He was a typical Sadducee, wealthy, haughty, unscrupulous, filling his sacred office for purely selfish and political ends, anti-nationalist in his relation to the Jews, friendly to the Romans. He died an ignominious death, being assassinated by the popular zealots (*sicarii*) at the beginning of the last Jewish war. In the NT he figures in two passages. (1) Acts **23** 1–5, where Paul defends himself before the Sanhedrin. The overbearing conduct of Ananias in commanding Paul to be struck on the mouth was characteristic of the man. Paul's ire was for the moment aroused, and he hurled back the scornful epithet of "whited wall." On being called to account for "reviling God's high priest," he quickly recovered the control of his feelings, and said "I knew not, brethren, that he was high priest:

for it is written, Thou shalt not speak evil of a ruler of thy people." This remark has greatly puzzled the commentators. The high priest could have been easily identified by his position and official seat as president of the Sanhedrin. Some have wrongly supposed that Ananias had lost his office during his trial at Rome, but had afterward usurped it during a vacancy (John Lightfoot, Michaelis, etc). Others take the words as ironical, "How could I know as high priest one who acts so unworthily of his sacred office?" (so Calvin). Others (e.g. Alford, Plumptre) take it that owing to defective eyesight Paul knew not from whom the insolent words had come. Perhaps the simplest explanation is that Paul meant, "I did not for the moment bear in mind that I was addressing the high priest" (so Bengel, Neander, etc). (2) In Acts **24** 1 we find Ananias coming down to Caesarea in person, with a deputation from the Sanhedrin, to accuse Paul before Felix. D. Miall Edwards

ANANIAS (Apoc), an-a-nī'as: (1) **'Ανανίας,** RV ANNIS, RVm Annias (1 Esd **5** 16). See Annis. (2) A son of Emmer (1 Esd **9** 21) = Hanani, son of Immer in Ezr **10** 20. (3) A son of Bebai (1 Esd **9** 29) = Hananiah in Ezr **10** 28. The two last are mentioned in the list of priests who were found to have strange wives. (4) One of those who stood by Esdras while he read the law to the people (1 Esd **9** 43) = Anaiah in Neh **8** 4. (5) One of the Levites who explained the law to the people (1 Esd **9** 48) = Hanan in Neh **8** 7. (6) Ananias the Great, son of Shemaiah the Great; a kinsman of Tobit, whom Raphael the angel, disguised as a man, gave out to be his father (Tob **5** 12 f). (7) Son of Gideon, mentioned as an ancestor of Judith (Jth **8** 1). (8) Another Ananias is mentioned in Three (ver 66). D. Miall Edwards

ANANIEL, a-nan'i-el (**'Ανανιήλ,** *Ananiēl,* "God is gracious"): An ancestor of Tobit (Tob **1** 1).

ANATH, ā'nath (עֲנָת, *'ănāth*): Father of Shamgar (Jgs **3** 31; **5** 6). This name is connected with the Phoen and Can goddess 'Anât, which was also worshipped in Egypt. She is mentioned in monuments of the 18th Dynasty, coupled with the wargoddess Astart (Moore, *Judges*, 105–896; *DB*; *EB*).

ANATHEMA, a-nath'ē-ma (**ἀνάθεμα,** *anáthema*): This word occurs only once in the AV, viz. in the phrase "Let him be anathema. Maranatha" (1 Cor **16** 22); elsewhere the AV renders *anathema* by "accursed" (Rom **9** 3; 1 Cor **12** 3; Gal **1** 8.9), once by "curse" (Acts **23** 12). Both words—*anathēma* and *anathema*—were originally dialectical variations and had the same connotation, viz. offering to the gods. The non-Attic form—*anathema*—was adopted in the LXX as a rendering of the Heb *ḥērem* (see Accursed), and gradually came to have the significance of the Heb word—"anything devoted to destruction." Whereas in the Gr Fathers *anathema*—as *ḥērem* in rabbinic Heb—came to denote excommunication from society, in the NT the word has its full force. In common speech it evidently became a strong expression of execration, and the term connoted more than physical destruction; it invariably implied *moral worthlessness*. In Rom **9** 3 Paul does not simply mean that, for the sake of his fellow-countrymen, he is prepared to face death, but to endure the moral degradation of an outcast from the kingdom of Christ. In 1 Cor **12** 3 the expression, "Jesus is anathema"—with its suggestion of moral unfitness—reaches the lowest depths of depreciation, as the expression, "Jesus is Lord," reaches the summit of appreciation. Thomas Lewis

ANATHOTH, an'a-thoth (עֲנָתוֹת, *'ănāthōth;* **'Αναθώθ,** *Anathōth*): A town which lay between Michmash and Jerus (Isa **10** 30), in the territory of Benjamin, assigned to the Levites (Josh **21** 18). It was the native place of Abiathar (1 K **2** 26), and of the prophet Jer (Jer **1** 1; **11** 21 ff, etc). Here lay the field which, under remarkable circumstances, the prophet purchased (Jer **32** 7 ff). Two of David's distinguished soldiers, Abiezer (2 S **23** 27) and Jehu (1 Ch **12** 3), also hailed from Anathoth. It was again occupied by the Benjamites after the return from the Exile (Neh **11** 32, etc). It is identified with *'Anātā,* two and a quarter miles N.E. of Jerus, a small village of some fifteen houses with remains of ancient walls. There are quarries in the neighborhood from which stones are still carried to Jerus. It commands a spacious outlook over the uplands to the N., and especially to the S.E., over the Jordan valley toward the Dead Sea and the mountains of Moab. There is nothing to shelter it from the withering power of the winds from the eastern deserts (Jer **4** 11; **18** 17, etc). W. Ewing

ANATHOTHITE, an'a-thoth-īt (הָעַנְּתֹתִי, *hā-'anneᵉthōthī*): RV form of AV **Anethothite, Anetothite, Antothite.** An inhabitant of Anathoth, a town of Benjamin assigned to the Levites. The Anathothites are (1) Abiezer, one of David's thirty heroes (2 S **23** 27; 1 Ch **11** 28; **27** 12), and (2) Jehu who came to David at Ziklag (1 Ch **12** 3).

ANCESTORS, an'ses-tẽrs (רִאשֹׁנִים, *rī'shōnīm,* "first ones"): The word ancestor appears in the Eng. Bible only once (Lev **26** 45). The Heb word, the ordinary adj. "first," occurs more than 200 times, and in a few places might fairly be rendered ancestors (e.g. Dt **19** 14; Jer **11** 10). In speaking of ancestors the OT ordinarily uses the word for "fathers" (*'ābhōth*).

ANCHOR, aṇ'kẽr. See Ships.

ANCIENT, ān'shent: This word renders several Heb words: (1) קֶדֶם, *ḳedhem,* which denotes "beforetime," "yore"; generally the remote past (cf Dt **33** 15, "ancient mountains"; Jgs **5** 21, Kishon, the "ancient river"; Isa **19** 11 "ancient kings"). (2) זָקֵן, *zāḳēn,* "old" in years. Whereas the AV generally renders the word by "old" (or "elders" when the pl. form is found) in six cases "ancient" is used and "ancients" in nine cases. See Ancients. (3) עוֹלָם, *'ōlām,* which denotes "long duration"—past or future. In regard to the past it suggests remote antiquity. The connotation may be discovered in such expressions as: "the years of a. times" (Ps **77** 5); "a. land-mark" or "paths" (Prov **22** 28; Jer **18** 15); "a. people" or "nation" (Isa **44** 7; Jer **5** 15); "a. high places" (Ezk **36** 2). (4) עַתִּיק, *'attīḳ.* This word—really Aram.—comes from a stem which means "to advance," i.e. in age; hence old, aged (1 Ch **3** 22). (5) יָשִׁישׁ, *yāshīsh,* lit. "weak," "impotent," hence decrepit, aged; a rare and poetical word, and found only in Job. It is rendered "ancient" only in one instance (Job **12** 12 AV). Thomas Lewis

ANCIENT OF DAYS (עַתִּיק יוֹמִין, *'attīḳ yōmīn,* = Aram.): On עַתִּיק, *'attīḳ,* see Ancient (4). The expression is used in reference to God in Dnl (**7** 9.13.22) and is not intended to suggest the existence of God from eternity. It was the venerable appearance of old age that was uppermost in the writer's mind. "What Daniel sees is not the eternal God Himself, but an aged man, in whose dignified and impressive form God reveals Himself (cf Ezk **1** 26)" (Keil).

ANCIENTS, ān-shents: This word (except in one instance) renders the Heb word זְקֵנִים, *zeḳēnīm*, (pl. of זָקֵן, *zāḳēn*), which should always be tr[d] "old men" or "elders." The Heb word never has the connotation which "ancients" has in modern Eng. The words "I understand more than the ancients" (Ps **119** 100 AV) do not mean that the Psalmist claims greater wisdom than his distant forbears but than his contemporaries with all their age and experience. In the parallel clause "teachers" is the corresponding word. In such phrases as "ancients of the people" (Jer **19** 1 AV), "ancients of the house of Israel" (Ezk **8** 12), "elders" would obviously be the correct rendering, as in RV. Even in Isa **24** 23 ("before his *ancients* gloriously" ERV) "elders" is the right tr (ARV). The writer probably alludes to the Sin. theophany witnessed by the "seventy . . . . elders" (Ex **24** 9–18). Generally speaking the word suggests the experience, insight and practical acquaintance with life which age ought to bring with it (Ps **119** 100; Ezk **7** 26). In one instance (1 S **24** 13) "ancients" is the right rendering for the Heb word קַדְמוֹנִים, *ḳadhmōnīm*, which means "men of former times."

THOMAS LEWIS

ANCLE, aŋ'k'l. See ANKLE.

ANDREW, an'drōō (Ἀνδρέας, *Andréas*, i.e. "manly." The name has also been interpreted as "the mighty one, or conqueror"): Andrew was the first called of the Twelve Apostles.

I. In New Testament.—Andrew belonged to Bethsaida of Galilee (cf Jn **1** 44). He was the brother of Simon Peter and his father's name was John (cf Jn **1** 42; **21** 15.16.17). He occupies a more prominent place in the Gospel of Jn than in the synoptical writings, and this is explicable at least in part from the fact that Andrew was Gr both in language and sympathies (cf *infra*), and that his subsequent labors were intimately connected with the people for whom Jn was immediately writing. There are three stages in the call of Andrew to the apostleship. The first is described in Jn **1** 35–40. Andrew had spent his earlier years as a fisherman on the Sea of Galilee, but on learning of the fame of John the Baptist, he departed along with a band of his countrymen to Bethabara (RV "Bethany") beyond Jordan, where John was baptizing (Jn **1** 28). Possibly Jesus was of their number, or had preceded them in their pilgrimage. There Andrew learned for the first time of the greatness of the "Lamb of God" and "followed him" (Jn **1** 40). He was the means at this time of bringing his brother Simon Peter also to Christ (Jn **1** 41). Andrew was probably a companion of Jesus on his return journey to Galilee, and was thus present at the marriage in Cana of Galilee (Jn **2** 2), in Capernaum (Jn **2** 12), at the Passover in Jerus (Jn **2** 13), at the baptizing in Judaea (Jn **3** 22), where he himself may have taken part (cf Jn **4** 2), and in Samaria (Jn **4** 5).

1. Early History and First Call

On his return to Galilee, Andrew resumed for a time his old vocation as fisherman, till he received his second call. This happened after John the Baptist was cast into prison (cf Mk **1** 14; Mt **4** 12) and is described in Mk **1** 16–18; Mt **4** 18.19. The two accounts are practically identical, and tell how Andrew and his brother were now called on definitely to forsake their mundane occupations and become fishers of men (Mk **1** 17). The corresponding narrative of Lk varies in part; it does not mention Andrew by name, and gives the additional detail of the miraculous draught of fishes. By some it has been regarded as an amalgamation of Mk's account with Jn **21** 1–8 (see JAMES, SON OF ZEBEDEE). After a period of companionship with Jesus, during which, in the house of Simon and Andrew, Simon's wife's mother was healed of a fever (Mk **1** 29–31; cf Mt **8** 14.15; Lk **4** 38.39), the call of Andrew was finally consecrated by his election as one of the Twelve Apostles (Mt **10** 2; Mk **3** 18; Lk **6** 14; Acts **1** 13).

2. Second Call and Final Ordination

Further incidents recorded of Andrew are: At the feeding of the five thousand by the Sea of Galilee, the attention of Jesus was drawn by Andrew to the lad with five barley loaves and two fishes (Jn **6** 8.9). At the feast of the Passover, the Greeks who wished to "see Jesus" inquired of Philip, who turned for advice to Andrew, and the two then told Jesus (Jn **12** 20–36). On the Mount of Olives, Andrew along with Peter, James and John, questioned Jesus regarding the destruction of Jerus and the end of the world (Mk **13** 3–23; cf also Mt **24** 3–28; Lk **21** 5–24).

3. Subsequent History

II. In Apocryphal Literature.—The name of Andrew's mother was traditionally Joanna, and according to the "Genealogies of the Twelve Apostles" (Budge, *Contendings of the Apostles*, II, 49) he belonged to the tribe of Reuben, the tribe of his father. A fragment of a Coptic gospel of the 4th or 5th cent. tells how not only Thomas (Jn **20** 27), but also Andrew was compelled, by touching the feet of the risen Saviour, to believe in the bodily resurrection (Hennecke, *Neutestamentlichen Apokryphen*, etc, 38, 39). Various places were assigned as the scene of his subsequent missionary labors. The Syr *Teaching of the Apostles* (ed Cureton, 34) mentions Bithynia, Eusebius gives Scythia (*HE*, III, i, 1), and others Greece (Lipsius, *Apokryphen Apostelgeschichten*, I, 63). The Muratorian Fragment relates that John wrote his gospel in consequence of a revelation given to Andrew, and this would point to Ephesus (cf Hennecke id, 459). The *Contendings of the Twelve Apostles* (for historicity, authorship, etc, of this work, cf Budge, *Contendings of the Apostles*, Intro; Hennecke, *Handbuch zu den neutestamentlichen Apokryphen*, 351–58; *RE*, 664–66) contains several parts dealing with Andrew: (1) "The Preaching of St. Andrew and St. Philemon among the Kurds" (Budge, II, 163 ff) narrates the appearance of the risen Christ to His disciples, the sending of St. Andrew to Lydia and his conversion of the people there. (2) The "Preaching of St. Matthias in the City of the Cannibals" (Budge, II, 267 ff; *REH*, 666) tells of how St. Matthias, on being imprisoned and blinded by the Cannibals, was released by St. Andrew, who had been brought to his assistance in a ship by Christ, but the two were afterward again imprisoned. St. Matthias then caused the city to be inundated, the disciples were set free, and the people converted. (3) "The Acts of St. Andrew and St. Bartholomew" (Budge, II, 183 ff) gives an account of their mission among the Parthians. (4) According to the "Martyrdom of St Andrew" (Budge, II, 215) he was stoned and crucified in Scythia.

According to the surviving fragments of "The Acts of St. Andrew," a heretical work dating probably from the 2d cent., and referred to by Eusebius (*HE*, III, ii, 5), the scene of St. Andrew's death was laid in Achaia. There he was imprisoned and crucified by order of the proconsul Eges (or Aegeates), whose wife had been estranged from him by the preaching of St. Andrew (cf Hennecke, 459–73; Pick, *Apocryphal Acts*, 201–21; Lipsius, I, 543–622). A so-called "Gospel of St. Andrew" is mentioned by Innocent I (Ep, I, iii, 7) and Augustine (*Contra Advers. Leg. et Prophet.*, I, 20), but this is probably due to a confusion with the above-mentioned "Acts of St. Andrew."

The relics of St. Andrew were discovered in Constantinople in the time of Justinian, and part of his cross is now in St. Peter's, Rome. St. Andrew is the patron saint of Scotland, whither his arm is said to have been transferred by St. Regulus. The ascription to him of the decussate cross is of late origin.

III. Character.—There is something significant in Andrew's being the first called of the apostles. The choice was an important one; for upon the lead given by Andrew depended the action of the others. Christ perceived that the soul's unrest, the straining after higher things and a deeper knowledge of God, which had induced Andrew to make the pilgrimage to Bethany, gave promise of a rich spiritual growth, which no doubt influenced Him in His decision. His wisdom and insight were justified of the after event. Along with a keenness of perception regarding spiritual truths was coupled in Andrew a strong sense of personal conviction which enabled him not only to accept Jesus as the Messiah, but to win Peter also as a disciple of Christ. The incident of the Feeding of the Five Thousand displayed Andrew in a fresh aspect: there the practical part which he played formed a striking contrast to the feeble-mindedness of Philip. Both these traits—his missionary spirit, and his decision of character which made others appeal to him when in difficulties—were evinced at the time when the Greeks sought to interview Jesus. Andrew was not one of the greatest of the apostles, yet he is typical of those men of broad sympathies and sound common sense, without whom the success of any great movement cannot be assured.

C. M. Kerr

ANDRONICUS, an-dro-nī'kus (**Ἀνδρόνικος,** *Andrónikos*):

(1) A deputy of Antiochus Epiphanes, who, while ruling at Antioch, excited the Jews by the murder of Onias, and, upon their formal complaint, was executed by his superior (2 Macc **4** 32–38); generally distinguished from another officer of the same name, also under Antiochus (2 Macc **5** 23).

(2) A kinsman of Paul, residing at Rome (Rom **16** 7). He had been converted to Christianity before Paul, and, like Paul, had suffered imprisonment, although when and where can only be surmised. When he and Junias, another kinsman of Paul, are referred to as "of note among the apostles," this may be interpreted as either designating the high esteem in which they were held by the Twelve, or as reckoning them in the number of apostles. The latter is the sense, if "apostle" be understood here in the more general meaning, used in Acts **14** 14 of Barnabas, in 2 Cor **8** 23 of Titus, in Phil **2** 25 of Epaphroditus, and in the *Did* of "the traveling evangelists or missionaries who preached the gospel from place to place" (Schaff, *The Teaching of the Twelve Apostles*, 67; see also Lightfoot on *Philippians*, 196). On this assumption, Andronicus was one of the most prominent and successful of the traveling missionaries of the early church.

H. E. Jacobs

ANEM, ā'nem (עָנֵם, *'ānēm*, "two springs"; **Ἀνάμ,** *Anám*): Anem is mentioned with Ramoth among the cities of Issachar assigned to the priests, the sons of Gershom (1 Ch **6** 73). In the parallel list (Josh **21** 29), there are mentioned Jarmuth and En-gannim, corresponding to Ramoth and Anim, therefore Anim and En-gannim (Jenīn) are identical. As the name denotes (Anem="two springs"; En-gannim="the spring of gardens"), it was well watered. Anem is identified by Eusebius with Aner, but Conder suggests the village of "Anim," on the hills W. of the plain of Esdraelon which represents the Anea of the **4**th cent. AD (*Onom* s.v. "Aniel" and "Bethara"), a city lying 15 Rom miles from Caesarea, which had good baths.

M. O. Evans

ANER, ā'nẽr (עָנֵר, *'ānēr;* LXX **Αὐνάν,** *Aunán;* Sam, עַנְרָם, *'anrām*, "sprout," "waterfall"): One of the three "confederates" of Abraham in his pursuit after the four kings (Gen **14** 13.14). Judging from the meanings of the two other names, Mamre being the name of the sacred grove or tree (J) and synonymous with Hebron (P); and Eschol—a name of a valley (lit. "grape cluster") from which the personal names are derived—it may be expected to explain the name **Aner** in a similar way. Dillmann suggested the name of a range of mountains in that vicinity (*Comm.* ad loc. and Rosen in *ZDMG*, XII, 479; Skinner, *Genesis*, 365).

S. Cohon

ANER, ā'nẽr (עָנֵר, *'ānēr*, meaning doubtful): A Levitical town in Manasseh, W. of the Jordan (1 Ch **6** 70). Gesenius and others identified it with Taanach of Josh **21** 25. There is, however, no agreement as to its location.

ANETHOTHITE, an'e-thoth-īt: AV form of Anathothite (thus RV 2 S **23** 27).

ANETOTHITE, an'e-toth-īt: AV form of Anathothite (thus RV 1 Ch **27** 12).

ANGEL, ān'jel (מַלְאָךְ, *mal'ākh;* LXX and NT, **ἄγγελος,** *ággelos*):

I. Definition and Scripture Terms
II. Angels in OT
1. Nature, Appearances and Functions
2. The Angelic Host
3. The Angel of the Theophany
III. Angels in NT
1. Appearances
2. The Teaching of Jesus about Angels
3. Other NT References
IV. Development of the Doctrine
V. The Reality of Angels
Literature

I. Definition and Scripture Terms.—The word angel is applied in Scripture to an order of supernatural or heavenly beings whose business it is to act as God's messengers to men, and as agents who carry out His will. Both in Heb and Gr the word is applied to human messengers (1 K **19** 2; Lk **7** 24); in Heb it is used in the singular to denote a Divine messenger, and in the plural for human messengers, although there are exceptions to both usages. It is applied to the prophet Haggai (Hag **1** 13), to the priest (Mal **2** 7), and to the messenger who is to prepare the way of the Lord (Mal **3** 1). Other Heb words and phrases applied to angels are *b^enē hā-'ĕlōhīm* (Gen **6** 2.4; Job **1** 6; **2** 1) and *b^enē 'ēlīm* (Ps **29** 1; **89** 6), i.e. sons of the *'ĕlōhīm* or *'ēlīm;* this means, according to a common Heb usage, members of the class called *'ĕlōhīm* or *'ēlīm*, the heavenly powers. It seems doubtful whether the word *'ĕlōhīm*, standing by itself, is ever used to describe angels, although LXX so translates it in a few passages. The most notable instance is Ps **8** 5; where RV gives, "Thou hast made him but little lower than God," with ERVm reading of "the angels" for "God" (cf He **2** 7.9); *ḳ^edhōshīm* "holy ones" (Ps **89** 5.7), a name suggesting the fact that they belong to God; *'īr, 'īrīm*, "watcher," "watchers" (Dnl **4** 13.17.23). Other expressions are used to designate angels collectively: *ṣōdh*, "council" (Ps **89** 7), where the reference may be to an inner group of exalted angels; *'ēdhāh* and *ḳāhāl*, "congregation" (Ps **82** 1; **89** 5); and finally *çābhā', ç^ebhā'ōth*, "host," "hosts," as in the familiar phrase "the God of hosts."

In NT the word *ággelos*, when it refers to a Divine messenger, is frequently accompanied by some phrase which makes this meaning clear, e.g. "the angels of heaven" (Mt **24** 36). Angels belong to the "heavenly host" (Lk **2** 13). In reference to their nature they are called "spirits" (He **1** 14). Paul evidently referred to the ordered ranks of supra-mundane beings in a group of words that are found in various combinations, viz. *archaí*, "principalities," *exousíai*, "powers," *thrónoi*, "thrones," *kuriótētes*, "dominions," and *dunámeis*, also translated "powers." The first four are apparently used in a good sense in Col **1** 16, where it is said that all these beings were created through Christ and unto Him; in most of the other passages in which words from this group occur, they seem to represent *evil* powers. We are told that our wrestling is against them (Eph **6** 12), and that Christ triumphs over the principalities and powers (Col **2** 15; cf Rom **8** 38; 1 Cor **15** 24). In two passages the word *archággelos*, "archangel" or chief angel, occurs: "the voice of the archangel" (1 Thess **4** 16), and "Michael the archangel" (Jude ver 9).

II. Angels in OT.—Everywhere in the OT the existence of angels is assumed. The creation of angels is referred to in Ps **148** 2.5 (cf Col **1** 16). They were present at the creation of the world, and were so filled with wonder and gladness that they "shouted for joy" (Job **38** 7). Of their nature we are told nothing. In general they are simply regarded as embodiments of their mission. Though presumably the holiest of created beings, they are charged by God with folly (Job **4** 18), and we are told that "he putteth no trust in his holy ones" (Job **15** 15). References to the fall of the angels are only found in the obscure and probably corrupt passage Gen **6** 1–4, and in the interdependent passages 2 Pet **2** 4 and Jude ver 6, which draw their inspiration from the Apocryphal book of *Enoch*. Demons are mentioned (see DEMONS); and although Satan appears among the sons of God (Job **1** 6; **2** 1), there is a growing tendency in later writers to attribute to him a malignity that is all his own (see SATAN).

1. Nature, Appearances and Functions

As to their outward appearance, it is evident that they bore the human form, and could at times be mistaken for men (Ezk **9** 2; Gen **18** 2.16). There is no hint that they ever appeared in female form. The conception of angels as winged beings, so familiar in Christian art, finds no support in Scripture (except, perhaps Dnl **9** 21; Rev **14** 6, where angels are represented as "flying"). The cherubim and seraphim (see CHERUB; SERAPH) are represented as winged (Ex **25** 20; Isa **6** 2); winged also are the symbolic living creatures of Ezk (Ezk **1** 6; cf Rev **4** 8).

As above stated, angels are messengers and instruments of the Divine will. As a rule they exercise no influence in the physical sphere. In several instances, however, they are represented as destroying angels: two angels are commissioned to destroy Sodom (Gen **19** 13); when David numbers the people, an angel destroys them by pestilence (2 S **24** 16); it is by an angel that the Assyr army is destroyed (2 K **19** 35); and Ezekiel hears six angels receiving the command to destroy those who were sinful in Jerus (Ezk **9** 1.5.7). In this connection should be noted the expression "angels of evil," i.e. angels that bring evil upon men from God and execute His judgments (Ps **78** 49; cf 1 S **16** 14). Angels appear to Jacob in dreams (Gen **28** 12; **31** 11). The angel who meets Balaam is visible first to the ass, and not to the rider (Nu **22** 22 ff). Angels interpret God's will, showing man what is right for him (Job **33** 23). The idea of angels as caring for men also appears (Ps **91** 11 f), although the modern conception of the possession by each man of a special guardian angel is not found in OT.

2. The Angelic Host

The phrase "the host of heaven" is applied to the stars, which were sometimes worshipped by idolatrous Jews (Jer **33** 22; 2 K **21** 3; Zeph **1** 5); the name is applied to the company of angels because of their countless numbers (cf Dnl **7** 10) and their glory. They are represented as standing on the right and left hand of Jeh (1 K **22** 19). Hence God, who is over them all, is continually called throughout OT "the God of hosts," "Jeh of hosts," "Jeh God of hosts"; and once "the prince of the host" (Dnl **8** 11). One of the principal functions of the heavenly host is to be ever praising the name of the Lord (Ps **103** 21; **148** 1 f). In this host there are certain figures that stand out prominently, and some of them are named. The angel who appears to Joshua calls himself "prince of the host of Jeh" (Josh **5** 14 f). The glorious angel who interprets to Daniel the vision which he saw in the third year of Cyrus (Dnl **10** 5), like the angel who interprets the vision in the first year of Belshazzar (Dnl **7** 16), is not named; but other visions of the same prophet were explained to him by the angel Gabriel, who is called "the man Gabriel," and is described as speaking with "a man's voice" (Dnl **9** 21; **8** 15 f). In Daniel we find occasional reference made to "princes": "the prince of Persia," "the prince of Greece" (**10** 20). These are angels to whom is intrusted the charge of, and possibly the rule over, certain peoples. Most notable among them is Michael, described as "one of the chief princes," "the great prince who standeth for the children of thy people," and, more briefly, "your prince" (Dnl **10** 13; **12** 1; **10** 21); Michael is therefore regarded as the patron-angel of the Jews. In Apoc Raphael, Uriel and Jeremiel are also named. Of Raphael it is said (Tob **12** 15) that he is "one of the seven holy angels who present the prayers of the saints" to God (cf Rev **8** 2, "the seven angels that stand before God"). It is possible that this group of seven is referred to in the above-quoted phrase, "one of the chief princes." Some (notably Kosters) have maintained that the expressions "the sons of the *'ĕlōhīm*," God's "council" and "congregation," refer to the ancient gods of the heathen, now degraded and wholly subordinated to Jeh. This rather daring speculation has little support in Scripture; but we find traces of a belief that the patron-angels of the nations have failed in establishing righteousness within their allotted sphere on earth, and that they will accordingly be punished by Jeh their over-Lord (Isa **24** 21 f; Ps **82**; cf Ps **58** 1 f RVm; cf Jude ver 6).

3. The Angel of the Theophany

This angel is spoken of as "the angel of Jeh," and "the angel of the presence (or face) of Jeh." The following passages contain references to this angel: Gen **16** 7 ff—the angel and Hagar; Gen **18**—Abraham intercedes with the angel for Sodom; Gen **22** 11 ff—the angel interposes to prevent the sacrifice of Isaac; Gen **24** 7.40—Abraham sends Eliezer and promises him the angel's protection; Gen **31** 11 ff—the angel who appears to Jacob says "I am the God of Beth-el"; Gen **32** 24 ff—Jacob wrestles with the angel and says, "I have seen God face to face"; Gen **48** 15 f—Jacob speaks of God and the angel as identical; Ex **3** (cf Acts **7** 30 ff)—the angel appears to Moses in the burning bush; Ex **13** 21; **14** 19 (cf Nu **20** 16)—God or the angel leads Israel out of Egypt; Ex **23** 20 ff—the people are commanded to obey the angel; Ex **32** 34—**33** 17 (cf Isa **63** 9)—Moses pleads for the presence of God with His people; Josh **5** 13—**6** 2—the angel appears to Joshua; Jgs **2** 1–5—the angel speaks to the people; Jgs **6** 11 ff—the angel appears to Gideon.

A study of these passages shows that while the

angel and Jeh are at times distinguished from each other, they are with equal frequency, and in the same passages, merged into each other. How is this to be explained? It is obvious that these apparitions cannot be the Almighty Himself, whom no man hath seen, or can see. In seeking the explanation, special attention should be paid to two of the passages above cited. In Ex **23** 20 ff God promises to send an angel before His people to lead them to the promised land; they are commanded to obey him and not to provoke him "for he will not pardon your transgression: for my name is in him." Thus the angel can forgive sin, which only God can do, because God's name, i.e. His character and thus His authority, are in the angel. Further, in the passage Ex **32** 34—**33** 17 Moses intercedes for the people after their first breach of the covenant; God responds by promising, "Behold, mine angel shall go before thee"; and immediately after God says, "I will not go up in the midst of thee." In answer to further pleading, God says, "My presence shall go with thee, and I will give thee rest." Here a clear distinction is made between an ordinary angel, and the angel who carries with him God's presence. The conclusion may be summed up in the words of Davidson in his *OT Theology*: "In particular providences one may trace the presence of Jeh in influence and operation; in ordinary angelic appearances one may discover Jeh present on some side of His being, in some attribute of His character; in the angel of the Lord He is fully present as the covenant God of His people, to redeem them." The question still remains, Who is the theophanic angel? To this many answers have been given, of which the following may be mentioned: (1) This angel is simply an angel with a special commission; (2) He may be a momentary descent of God into visibility; (3) He may be the Logos, a kind of temporary preincarnation of the second person of the Trinity. Each has its difficulties, but the last is certainly the most tempting to the mind. Yet it must be remembered that at best these are only conjectures that touch on a great mystery. It is certain that from the beginning God used angels in human form, with human voices, in order to communicate with man; and the appearances of the angel of the Lord, with his special redemptive relation to God's people, show the working of that Divine mode of self-revelation which culminated in the coming of the Saviour, and are thus a foreshadowing of, and a preparation for, the full revelation of God in Jesus Christ. Further than this it is not safe to go.

III. Angels in NT.—Nothing is related of angels in NT which is inconsistent with the teaching of OT on the subject.

1. Appearances

Just as they are specially active in the beginning of OT history, when God's people is being born, so they appear frequently in connection with the birth of Jesus, and again when a new order of things begins with the resurrection. An angel appears three times in dreams to Joseph (Mt **1** 20; **2** 13.19). The angel Gabriel appears to Zacharias, and then to Mary in the annunciation (Lk **1**). An angel announces to the shepherds the birth of Jesus, and is joined by a "multitude of the heavenly host," praising God in celestial song (Lk **2** 8 ff). When Jesus is tempted, and again during the agony at Gethsemane, angels appear to Him to strengthen His soul (Mt **4** 11; Lk **22** 43). The verse which tells how an angel came down to trouble the pool (Jn **5** 4) is now omitted from the text as not being genuine. An angel descends to roll away the stone from the tomb of Jesus (Mt **28** 2); angels are seen there by certain women (Lk **24** 23) and (two) by Mary Magdalene (Jn **20** 12). An angel releases the apostles from prison, directs Philip, appears to Peter in a dream, frees him from prison, smites Herod with sickness, appears to Paul in a dream (Acts **5** 19; **8** 26; **10** 3; **12** 7 ff; **12** 23; **27** 23). Once they appear clothed in white; they are so dazzling in appearance as to terrify beholders; hence they begin their message with the words "Fear not" (Mt **28** 2–5).

It is quite certain that Our Lord accepted the main teachings of OT about angels, as well as the later Jewish belief in good and bad angels.

2. The Teaching of Jesus about Angels

He speaks of the "angels in heaven" (Mt **22** 30), and of "the devil and his angels" (Mt **25** 41). According to Our Lord the angels of God are holy (Mk **8** 38); they have no sex or sensuous desires (Mt **22** 30); they have high intelligence, but they know not the time of the Second Coming (Mt **24** 36); they carry (in a parable) the soul of Lazarus to Abraham's bosom (Lk **16** 22); they could have been summoned to the aid of Our Lord, had He so desired (Mt **26** 53); they will accompany Him at the Second Coming (Mt **25** 31) and separate the righteous from the wicked (Mt **13** 41.49). They watch with sympathetic eyes the fortunes of men, rejoicing in the repentance of a sinner (Lk **15** 10; cf 1 Pet **1** 12; Eph **3** 10; 1 Cor **4** 9); and they will hear the Son of Man confessing or denying those who have confessed or denied Him before men (Lk **12** 8 f). The angels of the presence of God, who do not appear to correspond to our conception of guardian angels, are specially interested in God's little ones (Mt **18** 10). Finally, the existence of angels is implied in the Lord's Prayer in the petition, "Thy will be done, as in heaven, so on earth" (Mt **6** 10).

Paul refers to the ranks of angels ("principalities, powers," etc) only in order to emphasize the complete supremacy of Jesus Christ.

3. Other NT References

He teaches that angels will be judged by the saints (1 Cor **6** 3). He attacks the incipient Gnosticism of Asia Minor by forbidding the worship of angels (Col **2** 18). He speaks of God's angels as "elect," because they are included in the counsels of Divine love (1 Tim **5** 21). When Paul commands the women to keep their heads covered in church because of the angels (1 Cor **11** 10) he probably means that the angels, who watch all human affairs with deep interest, would be pained to see any infraction of the laws of modesty. In He (**1** 14) angels are described as ministering spirits engaged in the service of the saints. Peter also emphasizes the supremacy of Our Lord over all angelic beings (1 Pet **3** 22). The references to angels in 2 Pet and Jude are colored by contact with Apoc lit. In Rev, where the references are obviously symbolic, there is very frequent mention of angels. The angels of the seven churches (**1** 20) are the guardian angels or the personifications of these churches. The worship of angels is also forbidden (**22** 8 f). Specially interesting is the mention of elemental angels—"the angel of the waters" (**16** 5), and the angel "that hath power over fire" (**14** 18; cf **7** 1; **19** 17). Reference is also made to the "angel of the bottomless pit," who is called Abaddon or Apollyon (q.v.), evidently an evil angel (**9** 11 AV, RV "abyss"). In **12** 7 ff we are told that there was war between Michael with his angels and the dragon with his angels.

IV. Development of the Doctrine.—In the childhood of the race it was easy to believe in God, and He was very near to the soul. In Paradise there is no thought of angels; it is God Himself who walks in the garden. A little later the thought of angels appears, but God has not gone away, and as "the angel of Jeh" He appears to His people and redeems them. In these early times the Jews believed that there were multitudes of angels, not yet divided in thought into good and bad; these had no names or personal characteristics, but were simply embodied messages. Till the time of the captivity the Jewish angelology shows little development. During that dark period they came into close contact with a polytheistic people, only to be more deeply confirmed in their monotheism thereby. They also became acquainted with the purer faith of the Persians, and in all probability viewed the tenets of Zoroastrianism with a more favorable eye, because of the great kindness of Cyrus to their nation. There are few direct traces of Zoroastrianism in the later angelology of the OT. It is not even certain that the number seven as applied to the highest group of angels is Pers in its origin; the number seven was not wholly disregarded by the Jews. One result of the contact was that the idea of a hierarchy of the angels was more fully developed. The conception in Dnl of angels as "watchers," and the idea of patron-princes or angel-guardians of nations may be set down to Pers influence. It is probable that contact with the Persians helped the Jews to develop ideas already latent in their minds. According to Jewish tradition, the names of the angels came from Babylon. By this time the consciousness of sin had grown more intense in the Jewish mind, and God had receded to an immeasurable distance; the angels helped to fill the gap between God and man.

The more elaborate conceptions of Daniel and Zechariah are further developed in Apoc, especially in 2 Esd, Tob and 2 Macc.

In the NT we find that there is little further development; and by the Spirit of God its writers were saved from the absurdly puerile teachings of contemporary Rabbinism. We find that the Sadducees, as contrasted with the Pharisees, did not believe in angels or spirits (Acts **23** 8). We may conclude that the Sadducees, with their materialistic standpoint, and denial of the resurrection, regarded angels merely as symbolical expressions of God's actions. It is noteworthy in this connection that the great priestly document P makes no mention of angels. The Book of Revelation naturally shows a close kinship to the books of Ezk and Dnl.

Regarding the rabbinical developments of angelology, some beautiful, some extravagant, some grotesque, but all fanciful, it is not necessary here to speak. The Essenes held an esoteric doctrine of angels, in which most scholars find the germ of the gnostic æons.

V. The Reality of Angels.—A belief in angels, if not indispensable to the faith of a Christian, has its place there. In such a belief there is nothing unnatural or contrary to reason. Indeed, the warm welcome which human nature has always given to this thought, is an argument in its favor. Why should there not be such an order of beings, if God so willed it? For the Christian the whole question turns on the weight to be attached to the words of Our Lord. All are agreed that He teaches the existence, reality, and activity of angelic beings. Was He in error because of His human limitations? That is a conclusion which it is very hard for the Christian to draw, and we may set it aside. Did He then adjust His teaching to popular belief, knowing that what He said was not true? This explanation would seem to impute deliberate untruth to Our Lord, and must equally be set aside. So we find ourselves restricted to the conclusion that we have the guaranty of Christ's word for the existence of angels; for most Christians that will settle the question.

The visible activity of angels has come to an end, because their mediating work is done; Christ has founded the kingdom of the Spirit, and God's Spirit speaks directly to the spirit of man. This new and living way has been opened up to us by Jesus Christ, upon whom faith can yet behold the angels of God ascending and descending. Still they watch the lot of man, and rejoice in his salvation; still they join in the praise and adoration of God, the Lord of hosts; still can they be regarded as "ministering spirits sent forth to do service for the sake of them that shall inherit salvation."

LITERATURE.—All OT and NT theologies contain discussions. Among the older books Oehler's *OT Theology* and Hengstenberg's *Christology of OT* (for "angel of Jeh") and among modern ones Davidson's *OT Theology* are specially valuable. The ablest supporter of the theory that the "sons of the Elohim" are degraded gods is Kosters, "Het onstaan der Angelologie onder Israel," *TT* 1876. See also arts. on "Angel" in *HDB* (by Davidson), *EB*, *DCG*, *Jew Enc*, *RE* (by Cremer). Cremer's *Biblico-Theological NT Lexicon* should be consulted s.v. "aggelos." For Jewish beliefs see also Edersheim's *Life and Times of Jesus*, II, Appendix xiii. On the Pauline angelology see Everling, *Die paulinische Angelologie*. On the general subject see Godet, *Biblical Studies;* Mozley, *The Word*, ch lix, and Latham, *A Service of Angels*.

JOHN MACARTNEY WILSON

ANGEL OF GOD. See ANGEL.

ANGEL OF JEHOVAH. See ANGEL (II, 3).

ANGELS OF THE SEVEN CHURCHES: It is evident from the contexts of the various Biblical passages in which the word "angel" appears, that the word does not always represent the same idea. In such passages as Dnl **12** 1 and Acts **12** 15 it would seem that the angel was generally regarded as a superhuman being whose duty it was to guard a nation or an individual, not unlike the *jenei* of the Arabs. However, in Mal **2** 7 and **3** 1 (Heb) the word is clearly used to represent men. In the NT also, there are passages, such as Jas **2** 25 (Gr), in which the word seems to be applied to men. The seven angels of the seven churches (Rev **1** 20) received seven letters, **fig.** letters, and therefore it would seem that the seven angels are also **fig.** and may refer to the seven bishops who presided over the seven churches of Asia. Or the angels may be regarded as the personifications of the churches.

E. J. BANKS

ANGER, aŋ'gẽr: In the OT, the tr of several Heb words, esp. of אַף, *'aph* (lit. "nostril," "countenance"), which is used some 45 times of human, 177 times of Divine, anger (*OHL*). The word occurs rarely in the NT (Mk **3** 5; Eph **4** 31; Col **3** 8; Rev **14** 10), its place being taken by the word "wrath" (see WRATH). As a tr of words denoting God's "anger," the Eng. word is unfortunate so far as it may seem to imply selfish, malicious or vindictive personal feeling. The anger of God is the response of His holiness to outbreaking sin. Particularly when it culminates in action is it rightly called His "wrath." The OT doctrine of God's anger is contained in many passages in the Pent, Pss and the prophets. In Prov men are dissuaded from anger (**15** 1; **27** 4), and the "slow to anger" is commended (**15** 18; **16** 32; **19** 11). Christians are enjoined to put away the feeling of self-regarding, vindictive anger (Eph **4** 31; Col **3** 8), and to cherish no desire of personal revenge (Eph **4** 26). F. K. FARR

ANGLE, aŋ'g'l: Used in Isa **19** 8 for a Heb noun that is rendered "hook" in Job **41** 1: "The fishers shall lament, and all they that cast *angle* [hook] into the Nile shall mourn." For a striking **fig.** use of it see Hab **1** 15 where, speaking of the wicked devouring the righteous, "making men as the fishes of the sea," the prophet says: "They take up all of them with the *angle*, they catch them in their net" (RV uses singular).

ANGLING, an̦'gling: *Angling,* i.e. fishing with a hook or angle, was little known among the ancients. The fish were chiefly taken by casting nets, etc (see Mt **13** 47). Cf e.g. "Then did Deucalion first the art invent of *angling*" (Davors, *Secret of Angling,* I). See NET.

ANGLO-SAXON VERSIONS, an̦-glo-sax'on vûr'-shuns. See ENGLISH VERSIONS.

ANGUISH, an̦'gwish: Extreme distress of body, mind or spirit; excruciating pain or suffering of soul, e.g. excessive grief, remorse, despair. Chiefly expressed in OT, by four derivatives of צוּק, *çûḳ,* "straitened," "pressed," and צַר, *çar,* and two derivatives signifying "straitness," "narrowness," hence distress; also שָׁבָץ, *shābhāç,* "giddiness," "confusion of mind"; חוּל, *ḥûl,* "to twist" with pain, "writhe." So in the NT, θλῖψις, *thlīpsis,* "a pressing together," hence affliction, tribulation; στενοχωρία, *stenochōría,* "narrowness of place," hence extreme affliction; συνοχή, *sunochḗ,* "a holding together," hence distress. The fundamental idea in these various terms is pressure—being straitened, compressed into a narrow place, or pain through physical or mental torture. Used of the physical agony of child-birth (Jer **4** 31; **6** 24; **49** 24; **50** 43; Jn **16** 21); of distress of soul as the result of sin and wickedness (Job **15** 24; Prov **1** 27; Rom **2** 9); of anguish of spirit through the cruel bondage of slavery (Ex **6** 9) and Assyr oppression (Isa **8** 22); of the anxiety and pain of Christian love because of the sins of fellow-disciples (2 Cor **2** 4). DWIGHT M. PRATT

ANIAM, a-nī'am (עֲנִיעָם, *'ănī'ām,* "lament of the people"): A son of Shemidah of Manasseh (1 Ch **7** 19).

ANIM, ā'nim (עָנִים, *'ānīm,* "springs"): One of the cities of the hill country of Judah mentioned immediately after Eshtemoa (Josh **15** 50). It is probably represented by the double ruin of *el Ghuwein* situated S. of *es Semu'a.* The surface remains are Byzantine—a Christian town called Anem was here in the 4th cent., but it is clearly an ancient site of importance (*PEF,* III, 408; *Sh,* XXV).

ANIMAL, an'i-mal: See under the various names and also general art. on ZOÖLOGY.

ANISE, an'is, or **DILL,** dil; (RVm, ἄνηθον, *ánēthon*): Not the true anise, *Pimpinella anisum,* as was supposed by AV translators, but Dill, *Anethum graveolens.* This is an annual or biennial herb of NO Umbelliferae, growing from one to three feet high, with small yellow flowers and brownish, flattened, oval fruits ⅕ in. long. It grows wild in lands bordering on the Mediterranean. The seeds have an aromatic flavor and are used as condiment in cooking, as carminative in medicine. "Dill water" is a favorite domestic remedy. Jesus said (Mt **23** 23): "Woe unto you scribes and Pharisees, hypocrites! for ye tithe mint and anise and cummin, and have left undone the weightier matters of the law," etc. In the tract, *Ma'asĕrōth* (**4** 5) it is mentioned that this plant (Heb *shābhath*), its stem, leaves and seed, was subject to tithe. (See cut.)

E. W. G. MASTERMAN

ANKLE, an̦'k'l (in older edd of AV **ancle**): From Heb מֵי אָפְסַיִם, *mē 'āphᵉṣayim,* lit. "water of ankles," *i.e.* shallow water (Ezk **47** 3); "ankle-bones" (Acts **3** 7) from σφυδρόν, *sphudrón;* "ankle chains" (AV "chains"), from a Heb root meaning "to walk about proudly" (Nu **31** 50). The same Heb word is trᵈ "bracelet" (2 S **1** 10), but in Isa **3** 20 another word from the same root "ankle chains" (AV "ornaments of the legs"). Cf ANKLET (Isa **3** 18).

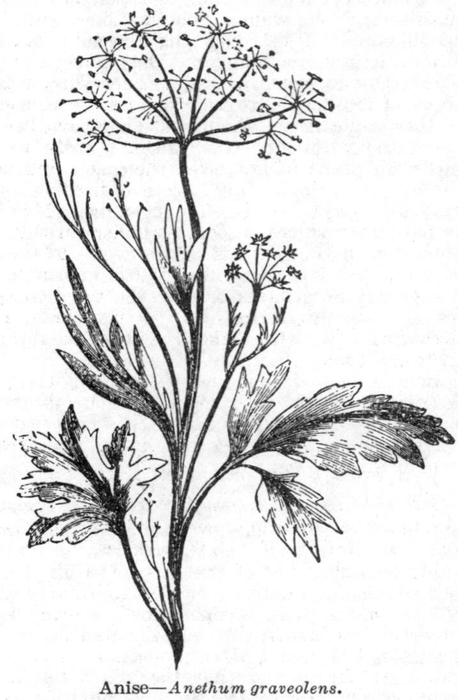

Anise—*Anethum graveolens.*

ANKLET, ANKLE-CHAIN, an̦'klet, an̦'k'l-chān: "Anklets" is rightly found in Isa **3** 18 RV, and "ankle-chains" in Nu **31** 50 RV. A cognate word of essentially the same meaning is used in Isa **3** 20, and is rendered by AV "ornaments of the legs." It was these "anklets" that Isaiah represented the ladies of Jerusalem as "rattling" as they walked (Isa **3** 16 to end), "making a tinkling with their feet"; and a part of the punishment threatened is, "The Lord will take away the bravery of their *tinkling ornaments* about their feet" (Isa **3** 16 AV).

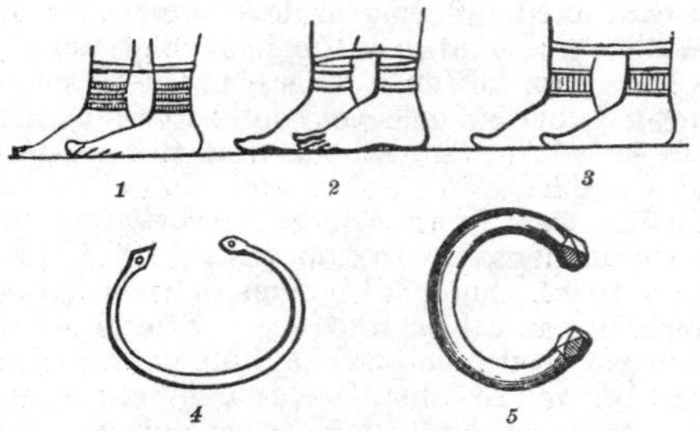

Egyptian Anklets. 1–4, Ancient; 5, Modern.

ANNA, an'a (Ἄννα, *Ánna* [WH, *Hánna;* see Intro, 408]; Heb equivalent חַנָּה, *ḥannāh,* signifying "grace" 1 S **1** 2):

(1) The wife of Tobit (Tob **1** 9).

(2) A "prophetess," daughter of Phanuel, of the tribe of Asher, and thus a Galilean, living in Jerus at the time of Jesus' birth (Lk **2** 36–38). "Of a great age," she must have been considerably over 100 years, having been a widow 84 years after a short married life of seven (see RV). Exceptionally devout and gifted in spirit, she worshipped so constantly "with fastings and supplications night and day," that she is said to have "departed not from the temple." Some have mistakenly supposed

that this signified permanent residence in the temple. The fact that her lineage is recorded indicates the distinction of her family. Tradition says that the tribe of Asher was noted for the beauty and talent of its women, who, for these gifts, were qualified for royal and high-priestly marriage. While the tribe of Asher was not among the tribes that returned from the Bab exile to Pal, many of its chief families must have done so as in the case of the prophetess. The period of war and national oppression, through which Anna's early life was passed, created in her, as in the aged Simeon, an intense longing for the "redemption" promised through the Messiah. See SIMEON. This hope of national deliverance sustained her through more than four decades of patient waiting. In the birth of Jesus her faith was abundantly rewarded, and she became a grateful and ceaseless witness "to all them that were looking for the redemption of Jerusalem," that the day of their spiritual deliverance had come.

LITERATURE.—See Edersheim, *Life and Times of Jesus*, I, 200–201; Geikie, *Life and Words of Christ*, I, 133–34.

DWIGHT M. PRATT

ANNAAS, an'a-as (**Σανάας**, *Sanáas*, 1 Esd **5** 23, RV SANAAS): The Senaah of Ezr **2** 35.

ANNAS, an'as (**Ἄννας**, *Ánnas*; WH *Hannas*; Jos *Ananos*, the Gr form of Heb חָנָן, *ḥānān*; "merciful," "gracious"; cf Neh **8** 7, etc):

(1) A high priest of the Jews, the virtual head of the priestly party in Jerus in the time of Christ, a man of commanding influence. He was the son of Seth (Jos, Sethi), and was elevated to the high-priesthood by Quirinius, governor of Syria, 7 AD. At this period the office was filled and vacated at the caprice of the Rom procurators, and Annas was deposed by Valerius Gratus, 15 AD. But though deprived of official status, he continued to wield great power as the dominant member of the hierarchy, using members of his family as his willing instruments. That he was an adroit diplomatist is shown by the fact that five of his sons (*Ant*, XX, ix, 1) and his son-in-law Caiaphas (Jn **18** 13) held the high-priesthood in almost unbroken succession, though he did not survive to see the office filled by his fifth son Annas or Ananus II, who caused Jas the Lord's brother to be stoned to death (cir 62 AD). Another mark of his continued influence is, that long after he had lost his office he was still called "high priest," and his name appears first wherever the names of the chief members of the sacerdotal faction are given. Acts **4** 6, "And Annas the high priest was there, and Caiaphas, and John, and Alexander, and as many as were of the kindred of the high priest." Annas is almost certainly called high priest in Jn **18** 19.22, though in vs 13.24 Caiaphas is mentioned as the high priest. Note especially the remarkable phrase in Lk **3** 2, "in the high-priesthood of Annas and Caiaphas," as if they were joint holders of the office. The cases in which Jos gives the title "high-priest" to persons who no longer held the office afford no real parallel to this. The explanation seems to be that owing to age, ability and force of character Annas was the virtual, though Caiaphas the titular, high priest. He belonged to the Sadducean aristocracy, and, like others of that class, he seems to have been arrogant, astute, ambitious and enormously wealthy. He and his family were proverbial for their rapacity and greed. The chief source of their wealth seems to have been the sale of requisites for the temple sacrifices, such as sheep, doves, wine and oil, which they carried on in the four famous "booths of the sons of Annas" on the Mount of Olives, with a branch within the precincts of the temple itself. During the great feasts, they were able to extort high monopoly prices for their goods. Hence our Lord's strong denunciation of those who made the house of prayer "a den of robbers" (Mk **11** 15–19), and the curse in the Talm, "Woe to the family of Annas! woe to the serpent-like hisses" (Pes 57*a*). As to the part he played in the trial and death of our Lord, although he does not figure very prominently in the gospel narratives, he seems to have been mainly responsible for the course of events. Renan's emphatic statement is substantially correct, "Annas was the principal actor in the terrible drama, and far more than Caiaphas, far more than Pilate, ought to bear the weight of the maledictions of mankind" (*Life of Jesus*). Caiaphas, indeed, as actual high priest, was the nominal head of the Sanhedrin which condemned Jesus, but the aged Annas was the ruling spirit. According to Jn **18** 12.13, it was to him that the officers who arrested Jesus led Him first. "The reason given for that proceeding [*"for* he was father-in-law of Caiaphas"] lays open alike the character of the man and the character of the trial" (Westcott, in loc.). Annas (if he is the high priest of Jn **18** 19–23, as seems most likely) questioned Him concerning His disciples and teaching. This trial is not mentioned by the synoptists, probably because it was merely informal and preliminary and of a private nature, meant to gather material for the subsequent trial. Failing to elicit anything to his purpose from Jesus, "Annas therefore sent him bound unto Caiaphas the high priest" (Jn **18** 24 AV is incorrect and misleading) for formal trial before the Sanhedrin, "but as one already stamped with a sign of condemnation" (Westcott). Doubtless Annas was present at the subsequent proceedings, but no further mention is made of him in NT, except that he was present at the meeting of the Sanhedrin after Pentecost when Peter and John defended themselves for preaching the gospel of the resurrection (Acts **4** 6).

(2) Head of a family who returned with Ezra (1 Esd **9** 32), called "Harim" in Ezr **10** 31.

D. MIALL EDWARDS

ANNIS, an'is (AV **Ananias**; RVm Annias; **'Αννεῖς**, *Anneís* B, **'Αννιάς**, *Anniás* A): The name of a family in the list of the returning exiles (1 Esd **5** 16). The name is not given in the || list in Ezr and Neh.

ANNUL, DISANNUL, a-nul', dis-a-nul': God, as the Supreme Ruler, can disannul His covenant for cause (Isa **28** 18); man, through wilfulness and transgression, as party of the second part, may break the contract and thus release Jeh, as party of the first part (Job **40** 8; Isa **14** 27), though there are some purposes and laws which the Almighty will carry out in spite of ungodly rage and ravings (Gal **3** 15 AV); or an old law or covenant might be conceived as disannulled by a new one (Gal **3** 17), or because of its becoming obsolete and ineffective (He **7** 18). For the first idea, the Heb employs כָּפַר, *kāphar*="to cover," "to expiate," "condone," "placate," "cancel," "cleanse," "disannul," "purge," "put off" (Isa **28** 18); and the Gr (Gal **3** 15), *athetéō* = "to set aside," "disesteem," "neutralize," "violate," "frustrate." One covenant disannulling another by "conflict of laws" is expressed by *akuróō*, "to invalidate," "disannul," "make of no effect." *Athetéō* is employed to express also the disannulling through age and disuse (He **7** 18).

FRANK E. HIRSCH

ANNUS, an'us (A, **Ἄννους**, *Ánnous*, B, *Anniouth;* AV **Anus**=Bani, Neh **8** 7): One of the Levites who interpreted the law to the people (1 Esd **9** 48).

ANNUUS, an'ū-us (Ἄννουνος, *Ánnounos*): Returned with Ezra from Babylon to perform the functions of a priest in Jerus (1 Esd **8** 48). Omitted in Ezr **8** 19.

ANOINT, a-noint', **ANOINTED,** a-noint'ed (ἀλείφω, *aleíphō*, χρίω, *chríō*): Refers to a very general practice in the East. It originated from the relief from the effect of the sun that was experienced in rubbing the body with oil or grease. Among rude people the common vegetable or animal fat was used. As society advanced and refinement became a part of civilization, delicately perfumed ointments were used for this purpose. Other reasons soon obtained for this practice than that stated above. Persons were anointed for health (Mk **6** 13), because of the widespread belief in the healing power of oil. It was often employed as a mark of hospitality (Lk **7** 46); as a mark of special honor (Jn **11** 2); in preparation for social occasions (Ruth **3** 3; 2 Sam **14** 2; Isa **61** 3). The **fig.** use of this word (*chriō*) has reference strictly to the coming of the Holy Spirit upon the individual (Lk **4** 18; Acts **4** 27; **10** 38). In this sense it is God who anoints (He **1** 9; 2 Cor **1** 21). The thought is to appoint, or qualify for a special dignity, function or privilege. It is in this sense that the word is applied to Christ (Jn **1** 41m; Acts **4** 27; **10** 38; He **1** 9; cf Ps **2** 2; Dnl **9** 25). See also ANOINTING.

JACOB W. KAPP

ANOINTING, a-noint'ing: A distinction was made by the ancient Hebrews between anointing with oil in private use, as in making one's toilet (סוּךְ, *ṣūkh*), and anointing as a religious rite (מָשַׁח, *māshaḥ*).

1. Ordinary Use

(1) As regards its secular or ordinary use, the native olive oil, alone or mixed with perfumes, was commonly used for toilet purposes, the very poor naturally reserving it for special occasions only (Ruth **3** 3). The fierce protracted heat and biting lime dust of Palestine made the oil very soothing to the skin, and it was applied freely to exposed parts of the body, especially to the face (Ps **104** 15).

(2) The practice was in vogue before David's time, and traces of it may be found throughout the OT (see Dt **28** 40; Ruth **3** 3; 2 S **12** 20; **14** 2; 2 Chron **28** 15; Ezk **16** 9; Mic **6** 15; Dnl **10** 3) and in the NT (Mt **6** 17, etc). Indeed it seems to have been a part of the daily toilet throughout the East.

(3) To abstain from it was one token of mourning (2 S **14** 2; cf Mt **6** 17), and to resume it a sign that the mourning was ended (2 S **12** 20; **14** 2; Dnl **10** 3; Jth **10** 3). It often accompanied the bath (Ruth **3** 3; 2 S **12** 20; Ezk **16** 9; Sus 17), and was a customary part of the preparation for a feast (Eccl **9** 8; Ps **23** 5). One way of showing honor to a guest was to anoint his head with oil (Ps **23** 5; Lk **7** 46); a rarer and more striking way was to anoint his feet (Lk **7** 38). In Jas **5** 14, we have an instance of anointing with oil for medicinal purposes, for which see OIL.

2. Religious Use

Anointing as a religious rite was practised throughout the ancient East in application both to persons and to things.

(1) It was observed in Canaan long before the Heb conquest, and, accordingly, Weinel (Stade's *Zeitschrift*, XVIII, 50 ff) holds that, as the use of oil for general purposes in Israel was an agricultural custom borrowed from the Canaanites, so the anointing with sacred oil was an outgrowth from its regular use for toilet purposes. It seems more in accordance with the known facts of the case and the terms used in description to accept the view set forth by Robertson Smith (*Religion of the Semites*, 2d ed, 233, 383 ff; cf Wellhausen, *Reste des arabischen Heidenthums*, 2d ed, 125 ff) and to believe that the *ṣūkh* or use of oil for toilet purposes, was of agricultural and secular origin, and that the use of oil for sacred purposes, *māshaḥ*, was in origin nomadic and sacrificial. Robertson Smith finds the origin of the sacred anointing in the very ancient custom of smearing the sacred fat on the altar (*maççēbhāh*), and claims, rightly it would seem, that from the first there was a distinct and consistent usage, distinguishing the two terms as above.

(2) The primary meaning of *māshaḥ* in Heb, which is borne out by the Arab., seems to have been "to daub" or "smear." It is used of painting a ceiling in Jer (**22** 14), of anointing a shield in Isa (**21** 5), and is, accordingly, consistently applied to sacred furniture, like the altar, in Ex **29** 36 and Dnl **9** 24, and to the sacred pillar in Gen **31** 13: "where thou *anointedst* a pillar."

(3) The most significant uses of *māshaḥ*, however, are found in its application, not to sacred *things*, but to certain sacred *persons*. The oldest and most sacred of these, it would seem, was the anointing of the *king*, by pouring oil upon his head at his coronation, a ceremony regarded as sacred from the earliest times, and observed religiously, not in Israel only, but in Egypt and elsewhere (see Jgs **9** 8.15; 1 S **9** 16; **10** 1; 2 S **19** 10; 1 K **1** 39. 45; 2 K **9** 3.6; **11** 12). Indeed such anointing appears to have been reserved exclusively for the king in the earliest times, which accounts for the fact that "the Lord's anointed" became a synonym for "king" (see 1 S **12** 3.5; **26** 11; 2 S **1** 14; Ps **20** 6). It is thought by some that the practice originated in Egypt, and it is known to have been observed as a rite in Canaan at a very early day. Am Tab 37 records the anointing of a king.

(4) Among the Hebrews it was believed not only that it effected a transference to the anointed one of something of the holiness and virtue of the deity in whose name and by whose representative the rite was performed, but also that it imparted a special endowment of the spirit of Jeh (cf 1 S **16** 13; Isa **61** 1). Hence the profound reverence for the king as a sacred personage, "the anointed" (Heb, *m*[e]*shīaḥ YHWH*), which passed over into our language through the Gr *Christos*, and appears as "Christ."

(5) In what is known today as the PC, the high priest is spoken of as "anointed" (Ex **29** 7; Lev **4** 3; **8** 12), and, in passages regarded by some as later additions to the PC, other priests also are thus spoken of (Ex **30** 30; **40** 13–15). Elijah was told to anoint Elisha as a prophet (1 K **19** 16), but seems never to have done so. 1 K **19** 16 gives us the only recorded instance of such a thing as the anointing of a prophet. Isa **61** 1 is purely metaphorical (cf Dillmann on Lev **8** 12–14 with *ICC* on Nu **3** 3; see also Nowack, *Lehrbuch der hebräischen Archäologie*, II, 124).

LITERATURE.—*Jew Enc*, art. "Anointing"; *BJ*, IV, ix, 10; *DB*, art. "Anointing," etc.

GEO. B. EAGER

ANON, a-non' (εὐθέως, *euthéōs*, εὐθύς, *euthús*): In AV of Mk **1** 30; Mt **13** 20, for "straightway" of RV, i.e. "without delay," "immediately."

ANOS, ā'nos (Ἄνως, *Ánōs*=Vaniah (Ezr **10** 36): A son of Bani who put away his "strange wife" (1 Esd **9** 34).

ANSWER, an'sẽr: In our Eng. Bible the word "answer" does not always mean a simple reply to a question.

Six different words are tr[d] by answer. (1) It is frequently used where no question has been asked and in such cases it means a word, a statement. (2) It also means a response (Job **21** 34; **34** 36). (3) It often means a declaration or proclamation from God where no question has been asked. See the many passages that read: "The Lord answered and said." (4) The other words tr[d] "answer" or "answered" in the OT are unimportant shadings and variations.

1. In the OT

The words tr[d] "answer" are not so varied. (1) It sometimes means an apology, a defence (1 Pet **3** 15; Acts **24** 10.25). (2) It may mean simply "to say" (Mk **9** 6). (3) It may mean a revelation from God (Rom **11** 4). (4) It is also used to apply to unspoken thoughts of the heart, esp. in the sayings of Jesus; also by Peter to Sapphira (Acts **5** 8).

2. In the NT

G. H. Gerberding

ANSWERABLE, an'sẽr-a-b'l: This word is found in the OT only. Moses and Ezekiel alone use it (Ex **38** 18; Ezk **40** 18; **45** 7; **48** 13.18). It is used in the OE sense of "corresponding to," "in harmony with." Bunyan uses it in the same sense (*Holy War*, Clar. Press ed, 92).

ANT (נְמָלָה, *n[e]mālāh*=Arab. *namalah*): The word occurs only twice in the Bible, in the familiar passages in Prov (**6** 6; **30** 25) in both of which this insect is made an example of the wisdom of providing in the summer for the wants of the winter. Not all ants store up seeds for winter

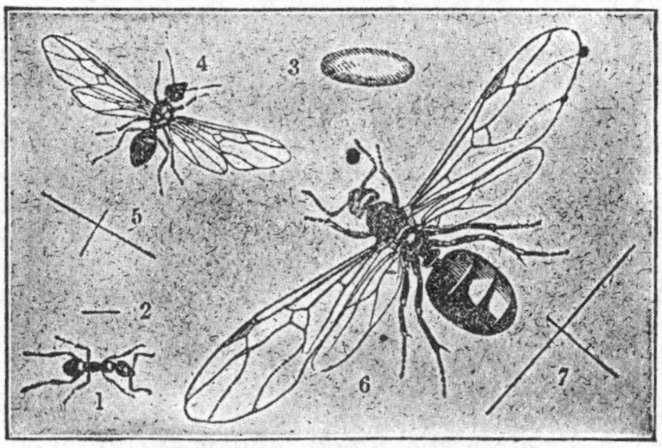

Brown Ant—*Formica brunnea.*
1. Worker or neuter. 2. Its natural size. 3. Cocoon. 4. Male. 6. Female. 5, 7. Natural sizes of 4 and 6.

use, but among the ants of Pal there are several species that do so, and their well-marked paths are often seen about Palestinian threshing-floors and in other places where seeds are to be obtained. The path sometimes extends for a great distance from the nest.

Alfred Ely Day

ANTEDILUVIAN PATRIARCHS, an-tē-di-lū'vi-an pā'tri-ärks: Ten patriarchs who lived before the Flood are listed in the genealogical table of Gen **5**, together with a statement of the age of each at the birth of his son, the number of years that remained to him till death, and the sum of both periods or the entire length of his life.

1. The Ten Antediluvian Patriarchs

The first half of the list, from Adam to Mahalalel inclusive, together with Enoch and Noah is the same in the three texts, except that the Sept has 100 years more in the first column in each case save that of Noah, and 100 years less in the second column. See Chronology of OT.

Divergence exists in the case of Jared, Methuselah and Lamech only. Even here the longevity of Jared and Methuselah is given similarly in the Heb and the Sept; and probably represents the reading of the source, especially since the different data in the Sam text bear evidence of adjustment to a theory. The customary excess of 100 years in the Sept over the other texts for the age of the patriarch at the birth of the son, and the variously divergent data for the total age of Jared, Methuselah and Lamech are, therefore, the matters that await explanation.

2. Divergences between the Three Texts

The general superiority of the Heb text of the Pent as a whole to the Sam text and the Sept is no longer questioned by Bib. scholars. But whether the superiority obtains in this particular passage has given rise to long and earnest discussion. Keil and Delitzsch in their commentaries on Genesis, Preuss (*Zeitrechnung der Septuaginta*, 1859, 30ff), Nöldeke (*Untersuchung zur Kritik des AT*, 1869, 112), and Eduard König (*ZKW*, 1883, 281 ff), hold to the originality of the Heb data. Bertheau (*Jahrbücher für deutsche Theologie*, XXIII, 657 ff) and Dillmann ascribe prior authority to the Sam numbers in Gen **5**, but to the Heb numbers in Gen **11**. Klostermann argues for the originality of the Sept (*Pentateuch*, Neue Folge, 1907, 37–39).

Ten Patriarchs from Adam to Noah	Hebrew Text			Samaritan Text			Septuagint*		
	Age at Son's Birth	Remaining Years	Length of Life	Age at Son's Birth	Remaining Years	Length of Life	Age at Son's Birth	Remaining Years	Length of Life
Adam......	130	800	930	130	800	930	230	700	930
Seth.......	105	807	912	105	807	912	205	707	912
Enosh.....	90	815	905	90	815	905	190	715	905
Kenan.....	70	840	910	70	840	910	170	740	910
Mahalalel..	65	830	895	65	830	895	165	730	895
Jared......	162	800	962	62	785	847	162	800	962
Enoch.....	65	300	365	65	300	365	165	200	365
Methuselah	187	782	969	67	653	720	167†	802†	969
Lamech....	182	595	777	53	600	653	188	565	753
Noah......	500	...	...	500	...	...	500	....	...
To the Flood..	100	...	...	100	...	...	100	....	...
Creation of man to the Flood.	1,656 years			1,307 years			2,242 years		

* Jos (*Ant*, I, iii, 4) states only the age at son's birth and the total length of life; and in texts O and E (see Niese) agrees with the Sept as tabulated, except that the longevity of Jared is given as 969 (but texts S, P and L as 962) and of Lamech as 707, and the age of Methuselah at son's birth as 187 (texts S and P 177).

† So Lucian; but A reads 187 and 782, and compare Jos.

It is agreed by all that the divergences between the texts are mainly due, not to accidental corruption, but to systematic alteration. Accordingly two tasks devolve upon the investigator, namely (1) the removal of accidental corruptions from the numerical data in the several texts and (2) the discovery of a principle that underlies and explains the peculiarities in each one or in two of the three sets of data.

3. Divergences not Accidental

On the interpretation that the names denote individuals and that no links have been omitted in the genealogy, readers of the Sept noticed that according to its data Methuselah survived the flood, and in order to avoid this incongruity a scribe changed the 167 years, ascribed to his age at the birth of his son, to 187 years. This reading was early in existence, and was followed by Jos. Holding the same theory regarding the genealogy, the Samaritans noticed that by their data three men, Jared, Methuselah, and Lamech, survived the Flood. To correct the

4. Different Explanations

apparent mistake, without tampering with the age of these three men at parenthood, their longevity was reduced sufficiently to enable them to die in the year of the Deluge. If the Heb text in its present form is not original, and is to be emended from the Sam and Sept, the same difficulty inhered in it. To overcome this difficulty, perhaps, 100 years were borrowed from the years that elapsed between parenthood and death and were added to the age of the three men at the time of begetting a son. This relieved the matter as far as Jared was concerned and perhaps in the case of Lamech also, and the borrowing of an additional 20 years set Methuselah right also. If the original number for Lamech was 53 in the Heb, as in the Sam, then it was necessary to increase the time between Methuselah's birth and the Flood not 20, but 49 years. These 49 years could not be added directly to either Methuselah's or Lamech's age at begetting a son without making this age exceed 200 years, and thus be out of proportion; and accordingly the 49 years were distributed.

The difference of a cent. in the age assigned to the patriarchs at the son's birth which distinguishes the data of the Heb in most cases from the Sept, and likewise from the Sam in several instances, in Gen **5** and regularly until Nahor in **11** 10–26, is commonly explained in the following manner or in a similar way: namely, when any of these long-lived patriarchs was found recorded as having begotten a son at a more youthful age than 150 years, the translators of the Sept added 100 years; on the other hand the Sam struck off 100 years when necessary in order that no one save Noah might be recorded as reaching 150 years of age before entering upon parenthood, and added 100 years when the record made a patriarch become father of a son before attaining even 50 years. A different explanation is, however, attempted, and the reason for the constant variant is sought in the purpose to construct an artificial chronology; for on interpreting the names as denoting individual persons and the genealogy as proceeding from father to son without break, a method employed as early as the 1st cent. of the Christian era (*Ant*, I, iii, 3), the time that elapsed between the creation of man and the Deluge was 1,656 years according to the Heb text, 1,307 according to the Sam text, and 2,242 according to the Sept; and numerous attempts have been made to bring one or other of these totals into arithmetical relation with some conceivable larger chronological scheme. A conspectus of these studies is furnished by Delitzsch (*Neuer Commentar über die Genesis*, 136–39), Dillmann (*Genesis*, 6te Aufl, 111–13), and most recently by Skinner (*Critical and Exegetical Comm. on Genesis*, 135, 136, 234). The different explanations that are offered naturally vary in plausibility; but all possess the common fault of lacking cogency at critical points and somewhere doing violence to the data.

5. The Relation of the Cainite and Sethite Genealogies

In Gen **4** there are two distinct genealogies, one proceeding through Cain and the other through Seth. Since Hupfeld, the representative critics who partition Genesis have generally reached the conclusion that both of these genealogies were found in the primary document of J or in an ancient recension of it (Wellhausen, *Composition des Hexateuchs*³, 8–14; Delitzsch, *Neuer Commentar*, etc, 126; Kautzsch und Socin; Dillmann, *Genesis*⁶, 104, 116; Budde, *Urgeschichte*, 182, 527–31; Driver, *Introduction*¹⁰, 14, 21; Strack, *Genesis*², 23; Gunkel, *Genesis*, 49; Skinner, *Genesis*, 2, 14, 99 [4]; Stade on the other hand regards **4** 25.26; **5** 29 as the compilation of a redactor, *ZATW*, XIV, 281). In Gen **5** there is also a genealogy through Seth to Noah.

Portions assigned to J (see above)		P
Gen **4** 17–24	**4** 25.26; **5** 29; **9** 20–27	**5** 3–32 (except 28*c*.29)
	Adam	Adam
Cain [Kain]	Cain and Seth	Seth
Enoch	Enosh	Enosh
ʿIrad		Kenan
Mehujael		Mahalalel
Methushael		Jared
Lamech		Enoch
Jabal and Jubal, Tubal-Cain and Naamah		Methuselah
		Lamech
	Noah	Noah
	Shem, Ham and Japheth	Shem, Ham and Japheth

6. Resemblances and Differences in the Two Lists

By removing vs 25 and 26 of ch **4** from their present position and placing them before ver 1 or, as Guthe does, before ver 17; and by exscinding the word "Eve" from ver 1 and understanding "the man" (*hā-'ādhām*) to be Enosh; and by exscinding from ver 25 the words "again," "another," and "instead of Abel, for Cain slew him"; and by introducing the words "and Lamech begat" before "a son" in **5** 28.29 and inserting this material in ch **4** between vs 18 and 19 or after ver 24: then the two genealogies of ch **4** are reduced to one and, so far as the names are concerned, have become almost identical with the Sethite genealogy contained in ch **5**. In fact the resemblances between the six names in **4** 17.18 with six in ch **5** have from the first been the basis of every attempt to identify the two genealogies (Buttmann, *Mythologus*, 170–72). The procedure is violent (see strictures, Skinner, *Genesis*, 99). It is a serious objection also that the work of reconstruction has been conducted without thought of the possible bearing of the tribal theory of the genealogies on this problem.

It is important to note that the number of links in the two genealogies may indicate that Jabal, Jubal, and Tubal-Cain, who mark stages of developing culture, lived several generations before Noah. It was ancient Sem belief that civilization was far advanced before the Flood, and was continued in its various forms by the survivors (Berosus; and inscription 13, col. i. 18 in Lehmann's *Shamash-shumukin*). However, for the sake of comparison, the six links in the genealogical chain of the Cainites are placed side by side with those of the Sethites so as the better to reveal the resemblances and differences.

Cainites	Sethites
Ḳain	Ḳenan [= Ḳainan]
Enoch	Mahalalel [praise of God]
ʿIrad	Jared
Mehujael [smitten of God]	Enoch
Methushael	Methuselah [correctly, Methushelaḥ]
Lamech	Lamech
Jabal and Jubal, Tubal-Cain and Naamah	Shem, Ham and Japheth

Of these names two, Enoch and Lamech, occur in each genealogy, though Enoch does not occupy the same place in both lists. Kenan is readily derived from the same root as Kain. Instead of ʿIrad the original Hebrew text may have been ʿIdad, as was read by the LXX, A and Lucian. But, accepting ʿIrad as original, ʿIrad and Jared may conceivably have been distorted in the oral tradition; yet as they stand they are radically different, and one might as well compare Prussia and Russia, Swede and Swiss, Austria and Australia. Methushael is written in the Sept exactly as is Methuselah; but both names are fully established by textual evidence and are fine Semitic names. Methushael particularly is of good Bab form, meaning "man of God"; archaic in Heb or smacking of the northern dialect, but quite intelligible to the Israelite.

The resemblance between the six consecutive names in the two lists is indeed striking, but the differences are also great; and the wisdom of caution in pronouncing judgment is suggested and emphasized by a comparison of two lists from the later history of the people of Israel. The twelve kings of Judah compared with their nineteen contemporaries in northern Israel show almost as many resemblances as the ten Cainites to the twelve Sethites, Adam as the common ancestor not being reckoned. The two series begin with Rehoboam and Jeroboam, names as similar externally as ʽIrad and Jared. Ahaziah of Israel was almost contemporary with Ahaziah of Judah; Jehoram was on the throne of Judah while Jehoram ruled over Israel, the reign of Jehoash of Judah overlapped that of Jehoash of Israel, and Jehoahaz of Israel preceded about half a century Ahaz, or, as his name appears in Assyr inscriptions, Jehoahaz of Judah. If there can be two contemporary dynasties with these coincidences, surely there could be two antediluvian races with an equal similarity in the names. Then, too, the material differences between the Cainite and Sethite lines are great. Cain is the son of Adam; whereas Kenan is the third remove, being descended through Seth and Enosh. The two Enochs seeem to have nothing in common save the name (**4** 17.18; **5** 22.23). The character of the two Lamechs is quite different, as appears from their speeches (**4** 19.23; **5** 28.29). The line of Cain terminated in Lamech and his four children, of whom the three sons became of note in the annals of civilization; whereas the line of Seth continued through Noah, the hero of the Flood, and his three sons who were known only as the ancestors of peoples. Moreover, even excluding the section of Genesis assigned to P, the two lines were distinguished from each other, and most of the characteristic differences between them were clearly set forth, in the most ancient form of the Heb tradition, as it is actually known (Green, *Unity of Genesis*, 43–49; Delitzsch, *Neuer Commentar*, etc, 126, 127, 132, 140; Strack, *Genesis*², 22, 23, § III).

7. The Need of Caution

The order of narration in the Book of Genesis is also significant. It indicates the writer's perception of a profound difference between the two races. The narrative regarding Cain and his descendants is completed, according to invariable custom in the Book of Genesis, before the line of Seth, in which eventually Abraham appeared, is taken up and its history recorded (Green, *Unity of Genesis*, 49; Delitzsch, *Neuer Commentar*, etc, 126). Thus at each stage of the history the story of the branch line is told before the fortunes are recited of the direct line of promise.

8. The Register of Gen 5 and Berosus' List of Antediluvian Kings

Berosus, a priest of Marduk's temple at Babylon about 300 BC, in the second book of his history tells of the ten kings of the Chaldaeans who reigned before the Deluge. He says[2] that

> The first king was ALOROS of [the city of[5]] Babylon, a Chaldaean. [He gave out a report about himself that God had appointed him to be shepherd of the people.[3]] He reigned ten sars. [A sar is thirty-six hundred years.[3]]
>
> And afterwards ALAPAROS [his son reigned three sars[3, 5]].
>
> And [after him[3]] AMELON [a Chaldaean[5]], who was of [the city of[3, 5]] Pautibibla [reigned thirteen sars[3]].
>
> Then AMMENON the Chaldaean [of Pautibibla reigned twelve sars[3, 5]].
>
> Then MEGALAROS of the city of Pautibibla, and he reigned eighteen sars.
>
> And after him DAONOS the shepherd of Pautibibla reigned ten sars.
>
> Then EUEDORACHOS of Pautibibla reigned eighteen sars.
>
> Then AMEMPSINOS, a Chaldaean of Laraucha, reigned; and he, the eighth, was king ten sars. Next OTIARTES a Chaldaean of Laraucha, reigned; and he [the ninth[1]] was king eight sars.
>
> And [last of all[3]], upon the death of Otiartes, his son Xisouthros reigned eighteen sars. In his time the great deluge occurred. Thus, when summed up, the kings are ten; and the sars are one hundred and twenty [or four hundred and thirty-two thousand years, reaching to the Flood[1]].

The original Bab form of seven of these ten names has been determined with a fair degree of certainty. Alaparos is in all probability a misreading by a copyist of the Gr Adaparos (Hommel, *PSBA*, XV, 243 ff; Zimmern, *KAT*³, 530 ff), and accordingly represents Adapa, followed perhaps by another element beginning with the letter *r;* Amelon and Ammenon are equivalent to the Bab nouns *amêlu* (Delitzsch, *Wo lag das Paradies?* *S* 149; Hommel, *PSBA*, XV, 243 ff; Zimmern, *KAT*³, 530 ff), man, and *ummanu* (Hommel, *PSBA*, XV, 243 ff; Zimmern, *KAT*³, 530 ff), workman; Euedorachos is Enmeduranki (pronounced Evveduranki) (Zimmern, *KAT*³, 530 ff); Amempsinos is probably Amelu-Sin (Delitzsch, *Wo lag das Paradies?* 149; Hommel, *PSBA*, XV, 243 ff; Zimmern, *KAT*³, 530 ff), servant of the moon-god; Otiartes, a misreading of the Greek Opartes, is Ubara-Tutu (Delitzsch, *Wo lag das Paradies?* 149; Hommel, *PSBA*, XV, 243 ff; Zimmern, *KAT*³, 530 ff), meaning servant of Marduk; and Xisouthros is Ḥasîs-atra (Haupt, *KAT*², 503; Zimmern, *KAT*³, 530 ff), equivalent to Atra-ḥasîs, an epithet given to the hero of the Flood.

Several of these names are well known in Babylonian literature: Adapa was a human being, a wise man, a wizard, who failed to obtain immortality. He was an attendant at the temple of Ea in the town of Eridu, prepared bread and water for the sanctuary and provided it with fish. Perhaps it was his connection with the temple that led to his being called son of Ea, and described as created or built by Ea (Schrader, *Keilinschriftliche Bibliothek*, VI, 91–101). Similarly King Esarhaddon calls himself the faithful son, child of Beltis; and Ashurbanipal claims to have been created or built by the gods Ashur and Sin in the womb of his mother (cf Adam, the son of God, Lk **3** 38). Enmeduranki, whose name has been interpreted as possibly meaning chief priest of Duranki, the meeting place of sky and earth, was a king of Sippar, a city whose patron deity was the sun-god Shamash. He was a notable wise man who, it seems, was reputed to have been taken by the gods Shamash and Ramman into their fellowship and made acquainted with the secrets of heaven and earth (*KAT*³, 530 f). As among the Hebrews the priests were descended from Aaron, so among the Babylonians Enmeduranki was regarded as the ancestor of the wizards and soothsayers or the founder of their guild. Amel-Sin is elsewhere mentioned as the wise one of Ur (*KAT*³, 537). In the Babylonian account of the Flood the hero is addressed as son of Ubara-Tutu. It is worth mention that legends grew up about the hero of the Flood, as they have about other historical personages since; and he even appears like some

[1] Syncellus quoting Alexander Polyhistor. [2] Syncellus quoting Apollodorus. [3] Syncellus quoting Abydenus. [4] Syncellus quoting Abydenus concerning the deluge. [5] Eusebius, Armenian Chronicle, quoting Alexander Polyhistor. [6] Eusebius, Armenian Chronicle, quoting Abydenus. The royal names have been transmitted with substantial uniformity, except the third, fifth, seventh and ninth. Amelon (2) is given as Amillaros (3) and Almelon (5, 6); Megalaros (2, 3) appears also as Amegalarus (5, 6); Euedorachos (2) as Eudoreschos (3), Edoranchus (5), and Edoreschus (6); and Ardates (1) as Otiartes (2, 5). For texts and readings see Richter, *Berosi Chaldaeorum Historiae*, 52–56; Migne, *Patrologia Græca*, XIX, "Eusebii Chronicorum," Lib. I, cap. i et vi, pp. 106, 121; Schoene, *Eusebii Chronicorum*, Lib. I, pp. 7, 31.

ancient kings, with the determinative for god before his name. Adapa also, who was classed with the wizards, early came to have a place in story.

The first name in the list of Berosus is Aloros. Professor Hommel would understand the original

9. Corre- spondences

Bab form to have been Aruru, a goddess. The identification is precarious, to say the least; and evidently it was not the conception of the Bab priest, for it makes his line of kings begin with a goddess. He should have called Aloros a queen. Professor Hommel regards Adapa also as a deity, contrary to the statements of the tale itself; thus holding that the second Bab king like the first was a Divine being. On such an interpretation the Bab and Heb lists are not identical, for the Heb genealogy commences in Adam, human being. With the third name, however, certain remarkable correspondences begin to appear. The third Bab king is Amelu, man, and the third patriarch is Enosh, also meaning man; the fourth king is Ummanu, artificer, and the fourth patriarch is Kenan, a name derived from a root meaning to form or fabricate. The seventh king is Enmeduranki, who apparently was reputed to have been summoned by the gods Shamash and Ramman into their fellowship and made acquainted with the secrets of heaven and earth; and the seventh patriarch was Enoch who walked with God (like Noah, Gen **6** 9; see *KAT*[3], 540). The tenth king, like the tenth patriarch, was the hero of the Flood. These facts are capable of two interpretations: either the two catalogues are fundamentally different, having been constructed for different purposes, yet as they deal with prominent persons belonging to the same period of history and to the same country, cross each other at various points and culminate in the same individual (as do the genealogies of Mt **1** and Lk **3**); or else when the unexplained names of both lists shall have been finally interpreted, the two catalogues will be found to represent the same tradition.

Differences between the catalogues exist, which in some instances may be more apparent than real.

10. Differ- ences

(1) In the Babylonian list the descent of the government from father to son is asserted in two instances only, namely, from the first king to the second and from the ninth to the tenth. The Heb asserts kinship, however remote, between the successive links. Yet the two records are quite compatible with each other in this respect on the theory (see below) that the Heb genealogy was shortened by omissions in order to name but ten generations. (2) Each of the ten patriarchs is assigned a long life; each of the ten kings has a greatly longer reign. The contrast is twofold: between the number of years in corresponding cases, and between length of life and length of reign. But instead of this difference indicating non-identity of the two lines, it may be found, when the Sem tradition is fully known, to afford the explanation for the duration of life which is assigned to the patriarchs. (3) There is no arithmetical ratio between the years connected with the corresponding names of the two lists. And the symmetry of the numbers in the Bab transmission is open to the suspicion of being artificial. The number of kings is ten; the sum of their united reigns is one hundred and twenty sars, a multiple of ten and of the basal number of the Bab duodecimal system. There are three reigns of ten sars each, and three successive reigns which taken together, 3+13+12, make ten and eighteen sars. Taking the reigns in the order in which they occur, we have as their duration the series 10, 18+10, 18, 10, 18, 10, 8,

and 18 (Davis, *Genesis and Semitic Tradition*, 96–100; Strack, *Genesis*[2], 24).

Three explanations of the genealogy in Gen **5** may be mentioned. (1) An interpretation, current

11. The In- terpretation of the Genealogy in Gen 5

at the time of Jos (*Ant*, I, iii, 4) and adopted by Archbishop Usher in 1650 in his attempt to fix the dates of the events recorded in the Scriptures, assumes an unbroken descent from father to son, during ten generations, from Adam to Noah. On this theory the time from the creation of man to the Flood is measured by the sum of the years assigned to the patriarchs at the birth of the son and successor, together with Noah's age when he entered the Ark; so that all the years from the creation of Adam to the Flood were 1,656 years. The extraordinary longevity of these patriarchs is accounted for by the known physical effects of sin. Sin works disease and death. Man was not as yet far removed from his state of sinlessness. The physical balance between man sinless and man the sinner had not been attained (cf Delitzsch, *Genesis*[3], 139; see *Ant*, I, iii, 9). But after all are we really justified in supposing that the Heb author of these genealogies designed to construct a chronology of the period? He never puts them to such a use himself. He nowhere sums these numbers. No chronological statement is deduced from them. There is no computation anywhere in Scripture of the time that elapsed from the Creation or from the Deluge, as there is from the descent into Egypt to the Exodus (Ex **12** 40), or from the Exodus to the building of the temple (1 K **6** 1; Green, *Bibliotheca Sacra*, 1890, 296). (2) A second method of interpretation assumes that links of the genealogy have been intentionally omitted in order that exactly ten may be named. It is based on the phenomena presented by other Heb genealogical registers. Matthew, for example, has outlined the lineage of Christ from Abraham. The history naturally divides into three sections, and to give the tabulation symmetry Matthew names twice seven generations in each division, in one instance omitting three famous kings of Judah and saying "Joram begat Uzziah." As Joram is said to have begotten Uzziah, his grandson's grandson, so Enoch may be said to have begotten Methuselah, although the latter may have been Enoch's greatgrandson or remoter descendant. The book of Genesis is divided by its author into ten sections, each introduced by the same formula (**2** 4; **5** 1; **6** 9, etc). In the period from the creation of man to the birth of Abraham the crisis of the history was the Flood. Twice ten generations are named in the symmetrical register, ten before the Flood, Adam to Noah, and ten after the Flood, Shem to Abraham; and the latter period in its turn is divided into two equal parts, and five generations are named for the time to, and five for the time after, the birth of Peleg, in whose days 'the earth was divided' (**11** 10–26; **10** 25; cf perhaps **11** 1–9). On this conception of the tables, which is fully justified, there is no basis in the genealogy from Adam to Noah for the calculation of chronology. The table was constructed for a different purpose, and the years are noted for another reason than chronology (Green, *Bibliotheca Sacra*, 1890, 285–303; Warfield, *Princeton Theological Review*, 1911, 2–11; cf Dillmann, *Genesis*[6], 106 "dritte Absicht"). The longevity is explained as it is on Usher's interpretation of the data (see above). (3) A third method of interpretation understands the patriarchal name to denote the individual and his family spoken of collectively. The person and tribe form one conception. This method also agrees with the phenomena presented by Heb genealogical registers. Thus, Keturah bears to Abraham Jokshan, and Jokshan begat Sheba and Dedan, tribes and the countries they inhabited (Gen **25** 1–5). Mizraim, as Egypt was called by the Hebrews, begat the Lydians and other ancient peoples (**10** 13); and Canaan begat the town of Sidon and such famous tribes as the Jebusite and the Amorite (vs 15–18). Similarly, countries like Media, Ionia (Javan), Tubal and Meshech, and peoples named by gentile adjectives in the plural number, like Kittim and Dodanim, are listed as sons of Japheth; and Ethiopia, Egypt, Punt and Canaan, and districts in Arabia like Sheba and Havilah are recorded as descendants of Ham (2–7). Moreover, outside of genealogies, in common parlance Israel denotes a man and the tribe that sprang from him; David, the king of that name and the dynasty he founded (1 K **12** 16; cf Jer **30** 9); Nebaioth, a people and its prince (Gen **25** 13.16; **28** 9). Sometimes the family takes its name from its progenitor or later leading member; sometimes the name of the tribe or of the country it inhabits is given to its chief representative, as today men are constantly addressed by their family name, and nobles are called by the name of their duchy or county. It is quite in accordance with usage, therefore, that Noah, for example, should denote the hero of the Flood and the family to which he belonged. The longevity is the period during which the family had prominence and leadership; the age at the son's birth is the date in the family history at which a new family originated that ultimately succeeded to the dominant position. If no links have been omitted in constructing the register, the period from the creation of man to the Flood is measured by the sum of the ages of Adam and his successors to Noah and 600 years of the life of Noah, amounting to 8,225 years. Thus, the family of Seth originated when Adam was 130 years old (Gen **5** 3). Adam and his direct line were at the head of affairs for 930 years (5), when they were superseded by the family of Seth. In Seth, 105 years after it attained headship, the family of Enosh took its rise (6). Seth, after being at the head of affairs for 912 years (8) was succeeded by the family of Enosh, in the year of the world 1842. And so on. JOHN D. DAVIS

ANTEDILUVIANS, an-tē-di-lū′vi-ans:

1. Chronology Uncertain

According to the ordinary interpretation of the genealogical tables in Gen **5** the lives of the antediluvians were prolonged to an extreme old age, Methuselah attaining that of 969 years. But before accepting these figures as a basis of interpretation it is important to observe that the Heb, the Sam and the Sept texts differ so radically in their sums that probably little confidence can be placed in any of them. The Sept adds 100 years to the age of six of the antediluvian patriarchs at the birth of their eldest sons. This, taken with the great uncertainty connected with the transmission of numbers by the Heb method of notation, makes it unwise to base important conclusions upon the data accessible. The most probable interpretation of the genealogical table in Gen **5** is that given by the late Professor William Henry Green, who maintains that it is not intended to give chronology, and does not give it, but only indicates the line of descent, as where (1 Ch **26** 24) we read that "Shebuel the son of Gershom, the son of Moses, was ruler over the treasures"; whereas, while Gershom was the immediate son of Moses, Shebuel was separated from Gershom by several generations. According to the interpretation of Professor Green all that we can certainly infer from the statement in Heb that Adam was 130 years old when he begat Seth, is that at that age the line branched off which culminated in Seth, it being permitted, according to Heb usage, to interpolate as many intermediate generations as other evidence may compel. As in the genealogies of Christ in the Gospels, the object of the tables in Genesis is evidently not to give chronology, but the line of descent.

2. Meaning of Genealogies

This conclusion is supported by the fact that no use is made afterward of the chronology, whereas the line of descent is repeatedly emphasized. This method of interpretation allows all the elasticity to prehistoric chronology that any archaeologist may require. Some will get further relief from the apparent incredibility of the figures by the interpretation of Professor A. Winchell, and Rev. T. P. Crawford (Winchell, *Preadamites*, 449 ff) that the first number gives the age of actual life of the individual while the second gives that of the ascendancy of his family, the name being that of dynasties, like Caesar or Pharaoh.

3. The Nephilim

The *n^ephīlīm* (giants) and the mighty men born of "the sons of God" and the "daughters of men" (Gen **6** 4.5) are according to the best interpretation "giants in wickedness," being the fruit of intermarriage between the descendants of Seth ("sons of God" who called on the name of Jeh, Gen **4** 26), and the "daughters of men." The idea that "sons of God" refers to angels or demigods has no support in Scripture. On this familiar designation of the worshippers of the true God see Ex **4** 22; Dt **14** 1; **32**, repeatedly; Isa **1** 2; **43** 6; **45** 11; Hos **1** 10; **11** 1. Intermarriage with depraved races such as is here intimated produced the results which were guarded against in the Mosaic law prohibiting marriages with the surrounding idolatrous nations. The word Nephilim in Gen **6** 4 occurs again only in Nu **13** 33 (AV "giants"). But the word is more probably a descriptive term than the name of a race. In the older Gr VSS it is tr[d] "violent men."

4. The Ice Age

The antediluvians are, with great probability, identified by some geologists (Sir William Dawson, e.g.) with glacial or paleolithic man, whose implements and remains are found buried beneath the deposits of glacial floods in northern France, southern England, southern Russia, and in the valleys of the Delaware, Ohio and Missouri rivers in America. The remains of "paleolithic" men reveal only conditions of extreme degradation and savagery, in which violence reigned. The sparse population which was spread over the northern hemisphere during the closing floods of the Glacial period lived in caves of the earth, and contended with a strange variety of gigantic animals which became extinct at the same time with their human contemporaries. See DELUGE.

LITERATURE.—Green, "Primeval Chronology," *Bibliotheca Sacra*, April, 1890; Dawson, *Modern Science in Bible Lands;* B. B. Warfield, "On the Antiquity and the Unity of the Human Race," *Princeton Theol. Review*, January, 1911; Winchell, *Pre-adamites;* Wright, *Ice Age in North America*, 5th ed; *Man and the Glacial Period*, and *Scientific Confirmations of Old Testament History*.

GEORGE FREDERICK WRIGHT

ANTELOPE, an′tē-lōp (RV; AV "wild ox," תְּאוֹ, *t^e'ō* [Dt **14** 5], and "wild bull," תּוֹא, *tō'* [Isa **51** 20]; **ὄρυξ,** *órux* [LXX in B has **ὡς σευτλίον ἡμίεφθον,** *hōs seutlíon hēmíephthon*, lit. "like a half-cooked beet-root"): The dorcas gazelle (*Gazella dorcas*) is widely distributed in Syria, Pal and Arabia. The recently discovered Merrill's gazelle (*Gazella Merrilli*) inhabits the hilly country near Jerus and is not commonly distinguished from the dorcas gazelle. Probably the only other antelope within this range is the Arabian oryx (*Oryx* *beatrix*). Tristram cites two African species (the bubaline antelope, *Bubalis mauretanica*, and the addax, *Addax nasomaculatus*) as existing in the Sin peninsula, southern Pal and Arabia, but he did not collect specimens of either and was probably misled by statements of the Arabs which in both cases really referred to the oryx. The only naturalist who has ever penetrated into N.W. Arabia is Mr. Douglas Carruthers, who went in 1909 on a collecting expedition for the Syrian Protestant College at Beirût, his object being to obtain the oryx and any other large antelopes which might be found there. Through observation and repeated inquiry he became convinced that neither the addax nor the bubaline antelope is found in Arabia. Tristram says the addax is called *maha'* and the bubaline antelope *baḳar-ul-waḥsh*, both of which names are in fact used by the Arabs for the oryx, which is also according to Doughty called *waḍîḥah*.

Antelope—*Oryx beatrix*.

Ç^{e}bhī in the list of clean animals in Dt **14** 5 (AV "roebuck"; RV "gazelle") is quite certainly gazelle, Arab. *ẓabī* (q.v.), so it is quite possible that *t^e'ō* may be the oryx. It is noteworthy that it is rendered oryx (ὄρυξ) in the LXX. It must be borne in mind that *rē'm* or *r^e'ēm*, rendered "unicorn" (q.v.) in AV and "wild ox" in RV, may perhaps also be the oryx. That the oryx should be called by two names in the Bible need not be considered strange, in view of the indefiniteness of Sem ideas of natural history, which is directly evidenced by the three names now used for this animal by the Arabs.

The slightly different form *tō'* (AV "wild bull"; RV "antelope") found in Isa **51** 20 ("Thy sons have fainted, they lie at the head of all the streets, as an antelope in a net") may quite as well refer to the oryx as to any other animal. According to Gesenius the word is derived from the verb *tā'āh*, "to outrun," which would be appropriate for this or any antelope.

The accompanying illustration is from a photograph of a well-grown female oryx in the zoölogical gardens at Cairo, which is 35 in. high at the shoulder and whose horns are 21 in. long. An adult male measures 40 in. at the shoulders, 59 in. from tip of nose to root of tail, and the longest horns known measure $27\frac{1}{4}$ in. The color is pure white with dark brown or black markings. It is a powerful animal and its horns may inflict dangerous wounds. It inhabits the deserts of Arabia and its remarkably large hoofs seem well adapted to traversing the sands. It feeds upon grasses and upon certain succulent roots, and the Bedawin declare that it never drinks. Under its name of *maha'* it is celebrated in Arab. poetry for the beauty of its eyes. Cf the Homeric "ox-eyed goddess Hera" (βοῶπις πότνια Ἥρη). *Baḳar-ul-waḥsh*, the name most commonly used by the Bedawin, means "wild cow" or "wild ox," which is identical with the tr of *t^e'ō* in the AV.

ALFRED ELY DAY

ANTHEDON, an-thē'don: A city of Pal, rebuilt along with Samaria, Ashdod, Gaza, and other cities, at Gabinius' command (Jos, *Ant*, XIV, v, 3).

ANTHOTHIJAH, an-tho-thī'ja (עַנְתֹתִיָּה, *'anthōthīyāh*, "belonging to Anathoth"[?]): A son of Shasak of Benjamin (1 Ch **8** 24), written in AV **Antothijah.**

ANTHROPOLOGY, an-thrō-pol'o-ji:

I. TERMS EMPLOYED
II. NATURE OF MAN: BIBLICAL CONCEPTION
III. ORIGIN OF MAN FROM SCRIPTURE ACCOUNT: NARRATIVES OF CREATION
IV. UNITY OF THE RACE: VARIOUS THEORIES
V. EVOLUTIONARY THEORY AS TO ORIGIN OF MAN
  1. Darwinism
  2. Difficulties
  3. Objections
  4. The New Evolutionism
  5. Evolution and Genesis
VI. PRIMITIVE AND PRESENT CONDITIONS OF MAN: ANTIQUITY OF MAN
LITERATURE

Under this heading is grouped whatever the Bible has to say regarding man's origin, nature, destiny and kindred topics. No systematized doctrine concerning man is found in Scripture; but the great facts about human nature and its elements are presented in the Bible in popular language and not in that of the schools. Delitzsch has well said: "There is a clearly defined psychology essentially proper to Holy Scripture, which underlies all the Biblical writers, and intrinsically differs from that many-formed psychology which lies outside the circle of revelation. . . . We do not need first of all to force the Biblical teaching: it is one in itself" (*Biblical Psychology*, 17, 18). What is said of the psychology of Scripture may with good reason be applied to its anthropology.

I. Terms Employed.—Several words are used in the OT for our word *Man*.

1. 'Ādhām

אָדָם, *'ādhām*, either as the name of the first man, (cf Lk **3** 38; Rom **5** 14; 1 Cor **15** 45); or as an appellative—*the man;* or, as the generic name of the human race (LXX *ánthrōpos;* Vulg *homo*). The origin of the name is obscure. In Gen **2** 7 Adam is connected with *'ădhāmāh*, from the earthly part of man's nature (dust out of the *'ădhāmāh*), as the earth-born one. The derivation of Adam from *'ădhāmāh,* however, is disputed—among others by Dillmann: "Sprachlich lässt sich die Ableitung aus *Adamah* nicht *vertheidigen*" (*Genesis*, 53). Delitzsch refers to Jos (*Ant*, I, i, 2), who maintained that Adam really meant *purrhós* ("red as fire"), in reference to the redness of the earth, out of which man was formed. "He means," adds Del., "the wonderfully fruitful and aromatic red earth of the Hauran chain of mountains, which is esteemed of marvelously strong and healing power, and which is believed to be self-rejuvenescent" (*N. Comm. on Gen*, 118). The connection with *Edom* in Gen **25** 30 may perhaps point in the same direction. A connection has also been sought with the Assyr *admu* ("child"), especially the young of the bird, in the sense of *making* or *producing* (Delitzsch; *Oxford Dictionary*); while Dillmann draws attention to an Ethiopic root *adma*, "pleasant," "agreeable," "charming"—a derivation, however, which he rejects. Suffice it to say, that no certain derivation has yet been found for the term (thus Dillmann, "ein sicheres Etymon für Adam ist noch nicht gefunden," *Gen*, 53). Evidently in the word the earthly side of man's origin is indicated.

2. Son of Man

The phrase בֶּן־אָדָם, *ben-'ādhām*, "son of man" (Nu **23** 19; Job **25** 6; Ezk **2** 3) is frequently found to denote man's frailty and unworthiness in the sight of God. So in the much-disputed passage in Gen **6** 2, where the "sons of God" are contrasted with the degenerate "daughters of men" (*b^enōth hā-ādhām*). See also Ps **11** 4; **12** 1.8; **14** 2. On the other hand the dignity of man is sometimes indicated in the word *Adam*. Thus in Eccl **7** 28, "One man (*'ādhām*) among a thousand have I found: but a woman among all those have I not found."

3. 'Ĕnōsh

אֱנוֹשׁ, *'ĕnōsh* (Ps **8** 4; **10** 18; **90** 3; **103** 15; frequently in Job and Ps), man in his impotence, frailty, mortality (like the Gr *brotós*) as against *'īsh*, man in his strength and vigor. In Gen **4** 26 the word becomes a proper name, applied to the son of Seth. Delitzsch derives it from a root *'ānash* (related to the Arab. and Assyr), signifying "to be or become frail." To intensify this frailty, we have the phrase in Ps **10** 18, "*'ĕnōsh* [man] who is of the earth."

4. 'Īsh

אִישׁ (*'īsh*), LXX *anḗr;* Vulg, *vir*, male as against female, even among lower animals (Gen **7** 2); husband as contrasted with wife (*'ishshāh*, Gen **2** 23.24); man in his dignity and excellence (Jer **5** 1: "seek, ... if ye can find *a man*"); persons of standing (Prov **8** 4, where *'īsh* is contrasted with *b^enē 'ādhām*, "Unto you, O men, I call; and my voice is to the sons of men")—"like the Attic *ándres* and *anthrōpoi*, wisdom turning her discourse to high and low, to persons of standing and to the proletariat" (Delitzsch on *Prov*). Delitzsch maintains, that *'īsh* points to a root *'ōsh* "to be strong," and *'ishshāh* to *'ānash*, as designating woman in her weakness (cf 1 Pet **3** 7: "the weaker vessel"). "Thus *'ishshāh* and *'ĕnōsh* come from a like verbal stem and fundamental notion" (Delitzsch, *A New Comm. on Gen*, 145). The term *'īsh* is sometimes used generally, as the Gr *tis*, the French *on*, to express "anyone," as in Ex **21** 14; **16** 29.

5. Gebher

גֶּבֶר, *gebher*, גִּבּוֹר, *gibbōr*, man in his strength. The term is applied to men as contrasted with women and children (Job **3** 3), "a male child," in opposition to a female (LXX *ársēn*); also in contrast to noncombatants (Ex **10** 11) and in NT, see Mt **8** 9; Jn **1** 6, where *anthrōpos* is used. Thus we read: "Neither shall a man [*gebher*] put on a woman's garment" (Dt **22** 5). Heroes and warriors are specially indicated by the term in such phrases as "mighty man of valor" (Jgs **6** 12). Sometimes animals are denoted by the term, as in Prov **30** 30 ("mightiest among beasts"); sometimes it is applied to God (Isa **10** 21) and to the Messiah (Isa **9** 6). In combination with *'īsh* it gives intensity to the meaning, as in 1 S **14** 52 "any mighty man."

6. Anthrōpos

Of the Gr terms *anthrōpos* stands for man generally—a human being (Mt **12** 12; Mk **10** 27); though it is sometimes used to indicate man in his imperfection and weakness (1 Cor **3** 3.4), in such expressions as "to speak as a man" (Rom **3** 5 AV), gospel "after man" (Gal **1** 11), "after the manner of men" (1 Cor **15** 32) etc; or as showing the contrast between the perishable and the imperishable (2 Cor **4** 16, where the "outward man" is represented as slowly dying, while the "inward man" is being renewed from day to day). Thus Paul contrasts the "natural man" (1 Cor **2** 14), the "old man," with the "new" (Rom **6** 6; Col **3** 9.10).

7. Anēr

Anēr, Lat *vir*—man in his vigor as contrasted with woman in her weakness (1 Cor **11** 3; 1 Pet **3** 7): sometimes, however, standing for "men in general" (Mk **6** 44: "They that ate the loaves were five thousand men"—*andres*).

II. The Nature of Man.—The Biblical idea of man's nature may be summed up in the words of St. Paul, "of the earth, earthy" (1 Cor **15** 47), as compared and contrasted with the statement in Gen **1** 27: "God created man in his own image."

1. Biblical Terms

This act of creation is described as the result of special deliberation on the part of God—the Divine Being taking counsel with Himself in the matter (ver 26). Man therefore is a creature, formed, fashioned, shaped out of "earth" and made after the "image of God." More than one word is employed in the OT to express His idea: (1) *bārā'*, "create," a word of uncertain derivation, occurring five times in Gen **1**, to indicate the origin of the *universe* (ver 1), the origin of *life* in the waters (ver 24), the origin of *man* (ver 27), and always in connection with God's *creative* work, never where "second causes" are introduced. (2) *yāçar*, "fashion," "form," "knead" (Gen **2** 7), "of the dust of the ground." (3) *bānāh*, "build," in special reference to the creation of woman, "built out of the rib" (Gen **2** 22).

By God's special interposition man becomes a *nephesh ḥayyāh* ("a living soul"), where evidently there is a reference to the breath of life, which man shares with the animal world (Gen **1** 20.21.24); yet with this distinction, that "God Himself breathed into man's nostrils the breath of life" (lit. "breath of lives," *nishmath ḥayyīm*). With a single exception, that of Gen **7** 22, the word *n^eshāmāh*, "breath," is confined to man. In Job reference is made to his creative act, where Elihu says: "There is a spirit in man, and the breath [*nishmath*] of the Almighty [*shaddai*] giveth them understanding" (Job **32** 8); cf also Isa **42** 5: "He . . . . giveth breath (*n^eshāmāh*) unto the people." Man therefore is a being separated from the rest of creation and yet one with it.

2. Image and Likeness

This distinction becomes more clear in the declaration that man was made in the "image" (*çelem*, *eikōn*, *imago*), and after the *likeness* (*d^emūth*, *homoiōsis*, *similitudo*) of God. The question has been asked whether the two terms differ essentially in meaning; some maintaining that "image" refers to the physical, "likeness" to the ethical side of man's nature; others holding that "image" is that which is natural to man, was created with him, was therefore as it were stamped upon him (*concreata*), and "likeness" that which was acquired by him (*acquisita*); while others again declare that "image" is the concrete and "likeness" the abstract for the same idea. There is very little scriptural ground for these assertions. Nor can we accept the interpretation of the older Socinians and some of the Remonstrants, that God's image consisted in dominion over all creatures, a reference to which is made in Gen **1** 28.

3. Meaning of Terms

Turning to the narrative itself, it would appear that the two terms do not denote any real distinction. In ver 27 *çelem* ("image") alone is used to express all that separates man from the brute and links him to his Creator. Hence the expression "*in* our image." In ver 26, however, the word *d^emûth* ("similitude") is introduced, and we have the phrase "*after* our likeness," as though to indicate that the creature bearing the impress of God's "image" truly corresponded in "likeness" to the original, the ectype resembling the archetype. Luther has translated the clause: "An image which is like unto us"—*ein Bild das uns gleich sei*—and in the new Dutch (Leyden) of the OT by Kuenen, Hooijkaas and others, it is rendered: "as our image, like unto us"—*als ons evenbeeld ons gelijkende.* The two words may therefore be taken as standing to each other in the same relation in which copy or model stands to the original image. "The idea in *çelem*—says Delitzsch—is more rigid, that of *d^emûth* more fluctuating and so to speak more spiritual: in the former the notion of the original image, in the latter that of the ideal predominates." At any rate we have scriptural warrant (see especially Gen **9** 6; Jas **3** 9) for the statement, that the "image is the inalienable property of the race" (Laidlaw), so that offence against a fellow-man is a desecration of the Divine image impressed upon man. Calvin has put it very clearly: *Imago Dei est integra naturae humanae praestantia*("The image of God is the complete excellence of human nature").

4. Subsidiary Questions

Other questions have been asked by early Church Fathers and by Schoolmen of later days, which may here be left out of the discussion. Some, like Tertullian, considered the "image" to be that of the coming Christ (*Christi futuri*); others have maintained that Adam was created after the image of the Logos (the Word, the second person in the Trinity), which was impressed upon man at his creation. Of all this Scripture knows nothing. There man is represented as made after the image of "Elohim," of the Godhead and not of one person of the Trinity. Paul calls man "the image and glory (*eikôn kaí dóxa*) of God" (1 Cor **11** 7). We may safely let the matter rest there. The strange theory, that the image of God indicates the sphere or element into which man was created, may be mentioned without further discussion (on this see Bohl, *Dogmatik*, 154 and Kuijper, *De vleeschwording des Woords*).

5. Constituents of Image

In what then does this image or likeness consist? Certainly in what is inalienably human—a *body* as the temple of the Holy Ghost (the "earthly house" of 2 Cor **5** 1), and the rational, inspiring, inbreathed *spirit.* Hence man's personality, linking him to what is above, separating him from what is beneath, constitutes him a being apart—a rational, self-conscious, self-determining creature, intended by his Creator for fellowship with Himself. "The animal feels the Cosmos and adapts himself to it. Man feels the Cosmos, but also thinks it" (G. H. Lewes, *Problems of Life and Mind*). Light is thrown on the subject by the NT, and esp. by the two classical texts: Eph **4** 24 and Col **3** 10, where the "new man" is referred to as "after God hath been created in righteousness and holiness of truth" and "renewed unto knowledge after the image of him that created him." Knowledge, righteousness and holiness may fitly be considered elements in the character of man as originally designed by God. Likeness to God therefore is man's privilege above all created beings. What was said of the Son of God absolutely, "He is the express image [character] of God," is applied to man relatively: the created son is not the only-begotten Son. The *created* son was "like unto God" (*homoíōsis;* 1 Jn **3** 2), and even in his degradation there is the promise of renewal after that image: the *eternal, only-begotten* Son is God's *equal* (Phil **2** 6.7), though he became a servant and was made in the *likeness* (*homoiṓmati*) of men.

This likeness of man with God is not merely a Scriptural idea. Many ancient nations seem to have grasped this thought. Man's golden age was placed by them in a far-off past, not in a distant future. St. Paul quotes a pagan poet in Acts **17** 28, "We are also his offspring" (Aratus of Soli, in Cilicia, a countryman of the apostle). This statement also occurs in the beautiful hymn to Jupiter, ascribed to Cleanthes, a Stoic native of Assos in the Troad, and contemporary of Aratus. Psychologically and historically therefore the Bible view is justified.

III. The Origin of Man.—The Divine origin of man is clearly taught in the early chapters of Gen, as has just been seen.

1. Scriptural Account

Two narratives from different sources are supposed to have been combined by an unknown R to form a not very harmonious whole. It is the purpose of criticism to determine the relationship in which they stand to each other and the dates of their composition. In both accounts man is the crowning glory of creation. The first account (Gen **1** 1—**2** 3) is general, the second particular (Gen **2** 4–25); in the first we have an account of man's appearance on a prepared platform—a gradual rise in the scale of organized existence from chaos upward to the climax, which is reached in man. There is recognized order in the whole procedure, represented by the writer as a process which occupied six days, or periods, measured by the appearance and dissipation of darkness. In the first period, chaotic disturbance is succeeded by the separation of light from darkness, which in its turn is followed by the separation of water from dry land, and to this a second period is assigned. Then gradually in the next four periods we have in orderly sequence the rise of vegetable life, the formation of the creatures of the deep, of the air, of the dry land. When all is prepared man is called into being by a special fiat of the Almighty. Moreover, while other creatures were produced "after their kind," man alone as a unique conception of the Divine Intelligence is made to appear upon the scene, called into existence by direct Divine interposition, after a Divine type, and in distinction of sex; for both man and wife, in a later chapter, are called by the same name: Adam (Gen **5** 2). Such is the scope of the first narrative. No wonder, then, that Scripture elsewhere calls the first man "the son of God" (Lk **3** 38). It need not be determined here, whether the account is strictly chronological, whether the "days" are interludes between successive periods of darkness and not periods of twenty-four hours regulated by the rising and setting of the sun, or whether the whole narrative is but a prose poem of creation, not strictly accurate, or strictly scientific.

2. The Two Narratives

In the second narrative (Gen **2** 2–25) the order of procedure is different. Man here is not the climax, but the center. He is a creature of the dust, but with the breath of God in his nostrils (Gen **2** 7), holding sway over all things, as God's vice-gerent upon earth, creation circling around him and submitting to his authority. To this is added a description of man's early home and of his home-relationships. The second narrative therefore seems on the face of it to be supplementary to the first, not contradictory of it: the agreements indeed are far greater than the differences. "The first may be called typical, the second, physiological. The former is the generic account of man's creation—of man the race, the ideal; the latter is the production of the actual man, of the historic Adam" (Laidlaw).

The differences between the two narratives have been magnified by supporters of the various documentary hypotheses. They are supposed to differ in *style*—the first "displaying clear marks of study and deliberation," the second being "fresh, spontaneous, primitive" (Driver, *Genesis*). They differ also in *representation*, i.e. in detail and order of events—the earth, in the second narrative not emerging from the waters as in the first, but dry and not fitted for the support of vegetation, and man appearing not last but first on the scene, followed by beasts and birds and lastly by woman. The documents are further supposed to differ in their *conception of Divine interposition* and a consequent choice of words, the first employing words, like "creating," "dividing," "making," "setting," which imply nothing local, or sensible in the Divine nature, the second being strongly anthropomorphic —Jeh represented as "moulding," "placing," "taking," "building," etc—and moreover locally determined within limits, confined apparently to a garden as His accustomed abode. Without foreclosing the critical question, it may be replied that the first narrative is as anthropomorphic as the second, for God is there represented as "speaking," "setting" (**1** 17; **2** 17), "delighting in" the work of His hands (**1** 31), "addressing" the living creatures (ver 22), and "resting" at the close (**2** 2). As to the home of Jeh in a limited garden, we are expressly told, not that man was admitted to the home of his Maker, but that Jeh specially "planted a garden" for the abode of man. The order of events may be different; but certainly the scope and the aim are not.

3. Contrasts

More serious have been the objections raised on scientific grounds. The cosmogony of Gen has been disputed, and elaborate comparisons have been made between geological theories as to the origin of the world and the Mosaic account. The points at issue are supposed to be the following: geology knows of no "periods" corresponding to the "days" of Gen; "vegetation" in Gen appears before animal life, geology maintains that they appear simultaneously; "fishes and birds" in Gen preceded all land animals; in the geological record "birds" succeed "fishes" and are preceded by numerous species of land animals (so Driver, *Genesis*). To this a twofold reply has been given: (1) The account in Gen is not scientific, or intended to be so: it is a prelude to the history of human sin and of Divine redemption, and gives a sketch of the world's origin and the earth's preparation for man as his abode, with that one object in view. The starting-point of the narrative is the creation of the *universe* by God; the culminating point is the creation of *man* in the image of God. Between these two great events certain other acts of creation in orderly sequence are presented to our view, in so far as they bear upon the great theme of sin and redemption discussed in the record. The aim is practical, not speculative; theological, not scientific. The whole creation-narrative must be judged from that point of view. See COSMOGONY. (2) What has struck many scientists is not so much the difference or disharmony between the Mosaic and the geological record, as the wonderful agreements in general outline apart from discrepancies in detail. Geologists like Dana and Dawson have expressed this as clearly as Haeckel. The latter, e.g., has openly given utterance to his "just and sincere admiration of the Jewish lawgiver's grand insight into nature and his simple and natural hypothesis of creation . . . . which contrasts favorably with the confused mythology of creation current among most of the ancient nations" (*History of Creation*, I, 37, 38). He draws attention to the agreement between the Mosaic account, which accepts "the direct action of a constructive Creator," and the non-miraculous theory of development, inasmuch as "the idea of separation and differentiation of the originally simple matter and of a progressive development" is to be found in "the Jewish lawgiver's" record.

4. Objections

Latterly it has been maintained that Israel was dependent upon Babylon for its creation-narrative; but even the most serious supporters of this view have had to concede that the first introduction of Bab myth into the sacred narrative "must remain a matter of conjecture," and that "it is incredible, that the monotheistic author of Gen **1**, at whatever date he lived, could have borrowed any detail, however slight, from the polytheistic epic of Marduk and Tiamat" (Driver, *Gen*, 31). The statement of Bauer in his *Hebräische Mythologie*, 1802: "Es ist heut zu Tage ausser allen Zweifel gesetzt, dass die ganze Erzählung ein Mythus ist" (It is beyond all doubt, that the whole narrative is a myth), can no longer be satisfactorily maintained; much less the assertion that we have here an introduction of post-exilic Bab or Pers myth into the Heb narrative (cf Van Leeuwen, *Anthropologie*).

5. Babylonian Origin

Whether the division of the narrative into Elohistic and Jehovistic documents will stand the test of time is a question which exercises a great many minds. Professor Eerdmans of Leyden, the present occupant of Kuenen's chair, has lately maintained that a "thorough application of the critical theories of the school of Graf-Kuenen-Wellhausen leads to highly improbable results," and that "the present OT criticism has to reform itself" (*HJ*, July, 1909). His own theory is worked out in his *Alttestamentliche Studien*, to which the reader is referred.

6. Later Critical Views

IV. The Unity of the Race.—The solidarity of the race may be said to be as distinctly a doctrine of science as it is of Scripture. It is implied in the account of the Creation and of the Deluge. It is strongly affirmed by St. Paul in his address to the Athenians (Acts **17** 26), and is the foundation of the Bib. scheme of redemption (Jn **3** 16). The human race in the OT is described as "sons of Adam" (Dt **32** 8 AV), as derived from one pair (Gen **1** 27; **3** 20), as having its origin in one individual (Gen **2** 18; cf 1 Cor **11** 8, where woman is described as derived 'from man'). Hence the term "Adam" is applied to the race as well as to the individual (Gen **1** 26; **2** 5.7; **3** 22.24; **5** 2); while in the NT this doctrine is applied to the history of redemption—Christ as the "second Adam" restoring what was lost in the "first Adam" (1 Cor **15** 21.22.47–49).

1. Its Solidarity

Outside of Holy Scripture various theories have been held as to the origin, antiquity and primeval condition of the human race. That of *polygenism* (plurality of origin) has found special favor, partly as *co-adamitism*, or descent of different races from different progenitors (Paracelsus and others), partly as *pre-adamitism*, or descent of dark-colored races from an ancestor who lived before Adam—the progenitor of the Jews and the light-colored races (Zanini and esp. de la Peyrère). But no serious attempts have yet been made to divide the human race among a number of separately originated ancestors.

2. Various Theories

The Bib. account, however, has been brought into discredit by modern theories of evolution. Darwinism in itself does not favor polygenism; though many interpreters of the evolutionary hypothesis have given it that application. Darwin distinctly repudiates polygenism. He says: "Those naturalists who admit the principle

3. Evolutionary View

of evolution will feel no doubt, that all the races of man are descended from a single primitive stock" (*Descent of Man*, 2d ed, 176); and on a previous page we read: "Man has been studied more carefully than any other animal, and yet there is the greatest possible diversity amongst capable judges, whether he should be classed as a single species, or race, or as two (Verey), as three (Jacquinot), as four (Kant), five (Blumenbach), six (Buffon), seven (Hunter), eight (Agassiz), eleven (Pickering), fifteen (Bory St. Vincent), sixteen (Desmoulins), twenty-two (Morton), sixty (Crawford), or as sixty-three, according to Burke" (p. 174).

V. Evolutionary Theory as to the Origin of Man.—Modern science generally accepts the theory of evolution. Darwin gave to the hypothesis a character it never had before; but since his day its application has been unlimited. "From the organic it is extended to the inorganic world; from our planet and the solar system to the cosmos, from nature to the creations of man's mind—arts, laws, institutions, religion. We speak in the same breath of the evolution of organic beings and of the steam engine, of the printing-press, of the newspaper, now even of the atom" (Orr, *God's Image in Man*, 84). And yet, in spite of this very wide and far-reaching application of the theory, the factors that enter into the process, the method or methods by which the great results in this process are obtained, may still be considered as under debate. Its application to the Bible doctrine of man presents serious difficulties.

1. Darwinism

Darwin's argument may be presented in the following form. In Nature around us there is to be observed a *struggle for existence*, to which every organism is exposed, whereby the weaker ones are eliminated and the stronger or best-fitted ones made to survive. Those so surviving may be said metaphorically to be chosen by Nature for that purpose—hence the term "natural selection," assisted in the higher forms of life by "sexual selection," under the influence of which the best-organized males are preferred by the females, and thus as it were selected for propagation of the species. The properties or characteristics of the organisms so chosen are transmitted to their descendants, so that with indefinite *variability* "from a few forms or from one, into which life has been originally breathed, endless forms most beautiful and most wonderful have been, or are being evolved" (*Origin of Species*, 6th ed, 429). Applying this mode of procedure to the origin of man, the strength of the argument is found to lie in the analogies between man and the brute, which may be summed up as follows: (1) *morphological* peculiarities in the structure of the bodily organs, in their liability to the same diseases, in their close similarity as regards tissues, blood, etc; (2) *embryological* characteristics, in the development of the human being, like the brute, from an ovule, which does not differ from and passes through the same evolutionary process as that of any other animal; (3) the existence of *rudimentary organs*, which are considered to be either absolutely useless, in some cases harmful, often productive of disease, or in any case of very slight service to the human being, pointing back therefore—so it is maintained—to an animal ancestry, in which these organs may have been necessary; (4) *mental peculiarities* of the same character, but perhaps not of the same range, in the brute as in man though the differences between the two may be as great as between "a terrier and a Hegel, a Sir William Hamilton, or a Kant"; (5) *paleontological agreements*, to show that a comparison of fossil remains brings modern civilized man and his primeval, anthropoid ancestor into close correspondence. Latterly Friedenthal's experiments, in regard to blood-transfusion between man and the ape, have been introduced into the argument by evolutionists.

2. Difficulties

The difficulties which beset the theory are so great that naturalists of repute have subjected it to very severe criticism, which cannot be disregarded. Some, like Du Bois-Reymond, have openly declared that supernaturalism has gained the day ("es scheint keine andere Ausnahme übrig zu sein, als sich dem Supranaturalismus in die Arme zu werfen" (cf Bavinck, *Gereformeerde Dogmatik*, II, 548). Others, like Virchow, have to the last pronounced against Darwinism as an established hypothesis, and a simian ancestry as an accepted fact ("auf dem Wege der Speculation ist man zu der Affen-Theorie gekommen: man hätte eben so gut zu anderen theromorphischen Theorien kommen können, z. B. zu einer Elefanten-Theorie, oder zu einer Schaf-Theorie"—i.e. one might as well speak of an elephant- or a sheep- or any other animal-theory as of an ape-theory). This was in 1892. When two years later the discovery of the so-called *pithecanthropus erectus*, supposed to be the "missing link" between man and the lower animals, came under discussion, Virchow held as strongly, that "neither the *pithecanthropus* nor any other anthropoid ape showed any of the characteristics of primeval man." This was in 1896.

The difference of opinion among scientists on this point seems to be great. While Darwin himself uncompromisingly held to the simian ancestry of man, several of his followers reject that line of descent altogether. This may be seen in the Cambridge volume, dedicated to the memory of the British naturalist. Schwalbe, while instancing Cope, Adloff, Klaatsch and others as advocating a different ancestry for man, acknowledges, though reluctantly, that "the line of descent disappears in the darkness of the ancestry of the mammals," and is inclined to admit that "man has arisen independently" (*Darwinism and Modern Science*, 134). Two things therefore are clear, viz. that modern science does not indorse the favorite maxim of Darwin, *Natura non facit saltum*, "Nature does not make a jump," with which according to Huxley he "has unnecessarily hampered himself" (*Lay Sermons*, 342), and that "man probably arose by a *mutation*, that is, by a discontinuous variation of considerable magnitude" (J. A. Thomson, *Darwinism and Human Life*, 123). Granted therefore an ascent in the scale of evolution by "leaps" or "lifts," the words of Otto (*Naturalism and Religion*, 133) receive a new meaning for those who accept as historic the tradition recorded in the early chapters of Gen: "There is nothing against the assumption, and there is much to be said in its favor, that the last step, or leap, was such an immense one, that it brought with it a freedom and richness of psychical life incomparable with anything that had gone before."

3. Objections Summarized

The objections raised against the Darwinian theory are in the main threefold: (1) its denial of teleology, for which it substitutes natural selection; (2) its assumption, that the evolutionary process is by slow and insensible gradations; (3) its assertion, that organic advance has been absolutely continuous from the lowest form to the highest (Orr, *God's Image in Man*, 108). This may be illustrated a little more fully:

(1) *Chance versus creation.*—The denial of teleology is clear and distinct, though Professor Huxley has spoken of a "wider teleology," by which however he simply meant (*Critiques and Addresses*, 305)

that the teleologist can defy his opponent to prove that certain changes in structure were not intended to be produced. In Darwinism the choice seems to lie between *chance* and *creation*. Mind, purpose, forethought, intention, Divine guidance and superintendence are banished from the evolutionary process. Darwin himself, though originally inclined to call in the aid of a creator (*Origin of Species*, 6th ed, 429), regretted afterward, that he "had truckled to public opinion and used the pentateuchal term, by which he really meant *appearance by some wholly unknown process*" (*Life and Letters*, III, 18).

Admittedly Darwin attributed too great a power to natural selection. He himself in the *Descent of Man* considered it "one of the greatest oversights" in his work, that "he had not sufficiently considered the existence of many structures which are neither beneficial nor injurious," and that he had "probably attributed too much to the action of natural selection on the survival of the fittest" (*Descent of Man* [2d ed], 61). Dr. A. R. Wallace, though like Darwin acknowledging the potency of natural selection, considers its operations to be largely negative. Writing to his friend he says: "Nature does not so much select special varieties, as exterminate unfavorable ones" (Darwin's *Life and Letters*, III, 46). It is this very insistence on a method of advance by slow and imperceptible gradations that has met with strong opposition from the very beginning. "Natural selection" Darwin writes, "acts solely by accumulating slight, successive, favorable variations; it can produce no great or sudden modifications; it can only act by short and slow steps" (*Origin of Species* [6th ed], ch 15). The process therefore according to Darwin is wholly fortuitous. This non-teleological aspect of Darwinism is characteristic of many treatises on evolution. Weismann states with great clearness and force, that the philosophical significance of the theory lies in the fact that "mechanical forces" are substituted for "directive force" to explain the origin of useful structures. Otto speaks of its radical opposition to teleology. And yet an ardent supporter of Darwinism, Professor J. A. Thomson, admits that "there is no logical proof of the doctrine of descent" (*Darwinism and Human Life*, 22)—a statement which finds its counterpart in Darwin's letters: "We cannot prove that a single species has changed" (*Life and Letters*, III, 25). Still more clearly, almost epigrammatically this is indorsed by Professor J. A. Thomson: "The *fact* of evolution forces itself upon us: the *factors* elude us" (*Bible of Nature*, 153), and again: "Natural selection explains the survival of the fittest, not the arrival of the fit" (ib 162). Still more extraordinary is the view expressed by Korchinsky that struggle "prevents the establishment of new variations and in reality stands in the way of new development. It is rather an unfavorable than advantageous factor" (Otto, *Nature and Rel*, 182). We are in fact being slowly led back to the teleology which by Darwin was considered fatal to his theory. Scientists of some repute are fond of speaking of directive purpose. "Wherever we tap organic nature," says Professor J. A. Thomson, "it seems to flow with purpose" (*Bible of Nature*, 25); and again, "If there is Logos at the end [of the long evolutionary process ending in man] we may be sure it was also at the beginning" (ib 86). Where there is purpose there must be mind working with purpose and for a definite end; where there is mind there may be creation at the beginning; where creation is granted, an overruling Providence may be accepted. If natural selection "prunes the growing tree"; if it be "a directive, not an originative factor" (J. A. Thomson, *Darwinism and Human Life*, 193); if it produces nothing, and the evolutionary process is dependent upon forces which work from within and not from without, then surely the Duke of Argyll was right in maintaining (*Unity of Nature*, 272) that "creation and evolution, when these terms have been cleared from intellectual confusion, are not antagonistic conceptions mutually exclusive. They are harmonious and complementary." The ancient narrative, therefore, which posits God at the beginning, and ascribes the universe to His creative act, is after all not so unscientific as some evolutionists are inclined to make out.

(2) *Variability indefinite*.—Indefinite variability, assumed by the theory, is not supported by fact. Development there doubtless is, but always within carefully defined limits: at every stage the animal or plant is a complete and symmetrical organism, without any indication of an everlasting progression from the less to the more complex. Reversion to type seems ever to have a development proceeding indefinitely, and the sterility of hybrids seems to be Nature's protest against raising variability into a law of progression. It has been repeatedly pointed out, that variations as they arise in any organ are not of advantage to its possessor: "A very slight enlarged sebaceous follicle, a minute pimple on the nose of a fish, a microscopic point of ossification or consolidation amongst the muscles of any animal could (hardly) give its possessor any superiority over its fellows" (Elam, *Winds of Doctrine*, 128).

(3) *Existing gaps*.—Nor can it be denied that no theory of evolution has been able to bridge the chasms which seem to exist between the various kingdoms in Nature. A gradual transition from the inorganic to the organic, from the vegetable to the animal kingdom, from one species of plant or animal to another species, from the animal to man, is not found in Nature. This is acknowledged by scientists of repute. Du Bois-Reymond has maintained that there are seven great enigmas, indicating a sevenfold limit to investigation, viz. (*a*) the existence of matter and force; (*b*) the origin of motion; (*c*) the origin of life; (*d*) the appearance of design in Nature; (*e*) the existence of consciousness; (*f*) intelligent thought and the origin of speech; (*g*) the question of freewill. Others have found equally serious difficulties in a theory of descent which ignores the existence of such gaps. Thus Dr. A. R. Wallace—a strong upholder of the theory of natural selection—allows that "there are at least three stages in the development of the organic world, when some new cause or power must necessarily have come into action," viz. at the introduction of life, at the introduction of sensation and consciousness and at the introduction of man" (*Darwinism*, 474–75).

(4) *Applied to man*.—When the theory is applied to the human species the difficulties are enormously increased. Psychically man is akin to, yet vastly different from, the brute. Consciousness, thought, language (called by Max Müller "the Rubicon" between the human and the animal world), morality, religion cannot easily be explained under any theory of evolution. The recognition of moral obligations, the freedom of choice between moral alternatives, the categorical imperative of conscience, the feeling of responsibility and the pain of remorse are unaccounted for by the doctrine of descent. Man stands apart, forming psychologically a kingdom by himself, "infinitely divergent from the simian stirps" (Huxley, *Man's Place in Nature*, 103)—*the* riddle of the universe, apart from the Biblical narrative. In the very nature of things the conscious and the unconscious lie far apart. "The assertion of the difference between them does not rest on our ignorance, but on our knowledge of the perceived distinction between material particles in motion and internal consciousness related to a

self" (Orr, *Homiletic Review*, August, 1907). There can be no transition from the one to the other. The "gulf" remains in spite of all attempts to bridge it. Strong supporters of Darwinism have acknowledged this. Thus Dr. A. R. Wallace, though vigorously maintaining the "essential identity of man's bodily structure with that of the higher mammals and his descent from some ancestral form common to man and the anthropoid apes," discards the theory that "man's entire nature and all his faculties, moral, intellectual, spiritual, have been derived from their rudiments in lower animals"—a theory which he considers unsupported by adequate evidence and directly opposed to many well-ascertained facts (*Darwinism*, 461; *Natural Selection*, 322 ff).

(5) *Transitional forms absent.*—The absence of transitional forms is another difficulty which strikes at the very root of Darwinism. Zittel, a paleontologist of repute, indorsed the general opinion, when in 1895 at Zurich he declared, that the extinct transitional links are slowly not forthcoming, except in "a small and ever-diminishing number." The derivation of the modern horse from the "Eohippus," on which great stress is sometimes laid, can hardly be accepted as proved, when it is maintained by scientists of equal repute, that no "Eohippus," but "Palaeotherium" was the progenitor of the animal whose ancestry is in dispute. And as for man, the discovery by Dr. E. Du Bois, in the island of Java, of the top of a skull, the head of a leg bone, a few teeth of an animal supposed to be a man-like mammal, does not convey the absolute proof demanded. From the very first, opinion was strangely divided among naturalists. Virchow doubted whether the parts belonged to the same individual, and considered Du Bois' drawings of the curves of a skull-outline to prove the gradual transition from the skull of a monkey to that of a man as imaginary. Of twenty-four scientists, who examined the remains when originally presented, ten thought they belonged to an ape, seven to a man, seven to some intermediate form (Otto, *Naturalism and Religion*, 110). At the Anthropological Congress held at Lindau in September, 1899, "Dr. Bumiller read a paper in which he declared that the supposed 'pithecanthropus erectus' is nothing but a gibbon, as Virchow surmised from the first" (Orr, in *Expos*, July, 1910).

4. The New Evolutionism

Evolutionism apparently is undergoing a great change. Among others Fleischmann, and Dennert in Germany have submitted Darwinism to a keen and searching criticism. The latter especially, as a scientist, raises a strong protest against the acceptance of the Darwinian theory. He closes his researches with the remarkable words: "The theory of descent is accepted by nearly all naturalists. But in spite of assertions to the contrary, the theory has not yet been fully [*ganz unzweifelhaft*] proved. . . . . Darwinism on the other hand, i.e. the doctrine of natural selection through struggle for existence, has been forced back all along the line" (*vom Sterbelager des Darwinismus*, 120). With equal vigor Professor Hugo de Vries, of Amsterdam, has recently taught a "theory of mutation," a term applied by him to "express the process of origination of a new species, or of a new specific character, when this takes place by the discontinuous method at a single step" (Lock, *Recent Progress in the Study of Variation*, 113). New species, according to De Vries, may arise from old ones by leaps, and this not in long-past geological times, but in the course of a human life and under our very eyes. This theory of "halmatogenesis," or evolution by leaps and not by insensible gradations, was not unknown to scientists. Lyell, who was a slow convert to Darwinism, in his *Antiquity of Man*, admitted the possibility of "occasional strides, breaks in an otherwise continuous series of psychical changes, mankind clearing at one bound the space which separated the highest stage of the unprogressive intelligence of inferior animals from the first and lowest form of improvable reason of man." Even Professor Huxley, one of the staunchest supporters of Darwinism, acknowledged that "Nature does *make jumps* now and then," and that "a recognition of the fact is of no small importance in disposing of many minor objections to the doctrine of transmutation" (Orr, *God's Image in Man*, 116). Less conciliatory than either De Vries or Huxley is Eimer, who, while repudiating the "chance" theory of Darwinism, sets against it "definitely directed evolution," and holds that "natural selection is insufficient in the formation of species" (Otto, *Naturalism and Religion*, 174). Evidently the evolution theory is undergoing modifications, which may have important bearing on the interpretation of the Mosaic narrative of creation and especially on the descent of man. Man may therefore, from a purely scientific point of view, be an entirely new being, not brought about by slow and gradual ascent from a simian ancestry. He may have been introduced at a bound, not as a semi-animal with brute impulses, but as a rational and moral being, "internally harmonious, with possibilities of sinless development, which only his free act annulled." If the new theory of "mutational" evolution be accepted, the scriptural view of man's origin will certainly not be discredited.

5. Evolution and Genesis

This much may fairly be granted, that within certain limits Scripture accepts an evolutionary process. In regard to the lower animals the *creating* (Gen **1** 21), or *making* (ver 28), is not described as an immediate act of Almighty Power, but as a creative impulse given to water and earth, which does not exclude, but rather calls into operation the powers that are in the sea and dry land (vs 11.20.24 AV): "And God said, Let the earth bring forth grass . . . . Let the waters bring forth abundantly the moving creature." It is only in the creation of man that God works immediately: "And God said, Let us make man in our image . . . . And God created man" (vs 26.27). The *stride* or *jump* of Lyell and Huxley, the "halmatogenesis" of De Vries are names which in the simple narrative disappear before the pregnant sentence: "And God said." Theologians of repute have given a theistic coloring to the evolution theory (cf Flint, *Theism*, 195 ff), inasmuch as development cannot be purposeless or causeless, and because "Nature is but effect whose cause is God." The deathblow which, according to Professor Huxley, the teleological argument has received from Darwin, may after all not be so serious. At any rate Lord Kelvin (Sir William Thomson) in 1871 before the British Association openly pleaded for "the solid and irrefragable argument so well put forward by Paley . . . . teaching us, that all living things depended upon an everacting Creator and Ruler." See EVOLUTION.

VI. Primitive and Present Conditions of Man.—

1. The Time-Distance of Man's Origin

The newer anthropology has carried the human race back to a remote antiquity. Ordinary estimates range between 100,000 and 500,000 years. Extraordinary computations go far beyond these numbers. Haeckel, e.g. speaks of "Sirius distances" for the whole evolutionary process; and what this means may easily be conjectured. The sun is 92,700,000 miles away from the earth, and Sirius is a million times as far from us as we are from the sun, so that the time-distance of man from the very lowest organisms, from the first germ or seed or ovule, is according to Haeckel almost incalculable. The human race is thus carried back by evolutionists into an immeasurable distance from the present inhabitants of the earth. Several primeval races are by some declared to have existed, and fossil remains of man are supposed to have been found, bringing him into touch with extinct animals. The time-computations of evolutionists, however, are not shared by scientists in general. "These millionaires in time have received a rude blow, when another Darwin, Sir G. H. Darwin of Cambridge, demonstrated that the physical conditions were such that geology must limit itself to a period of time inside of 100,000 years" (Orr, *God's Image*, etc, 176). Professor Tait of Edinburgh limited the range to no more than 10,000,000 years and he strongly advised geologists to "hurry up their calculations." "I dare say," he says, "many of you are acquainted with the speculations of Lyell and others, especially of Darwin, who tells us, that even for a comparatively brief portion of recent geological history, three hundred millions of years will not suffice! We say, so much the worse for geology as at present understood by its chief authorities" (*Recent Advances in Phys. Science*, 168). Recently, however, attention has been drawn to new sources of energy in the universe as the result of radio-activity. Duncan, in *The New Knowledge*, contrasts the old conception, according to which God made the universe and started it at a definite time to run its course, with the need, which though it does not distinctly teach, at least is inclined to maintain, that the universe is immortal or eternal, both in the future and the past (p. 245). If this view be correct the Darwinian "eons" of time may be considered restored to the evolutionist. On the other hand it appears that Lord Kelvin seriously doubted the validity of these speculations. Professor Orr writes: "In a personal communication Lord Kelvin states to me that he thinks it 'almost infinitely improbable' that radium had any appreciable effects on the heat and light of the earth or sun, and suggests it as 'more probable that the energy of radium may have come originally in connection with the excessively high temperatures' produced by gravitational action" (*Homiletic Review*, Aug., 1906).

2. Antiquity of Primeval Man

In regard to primeval man there is no agreement among scientists. Some, like Delaunay, de Mortillet, Quatrefages, believed that man existed in the Tertiary; while others, such as Virchow, Zittel, Prestwich, Dawson, maintain that man appeared on the scene only in the Quaternary. As the limits between these periods are not well defined a decision is by no means easy. Even if man be found to have been a contemporary of extinct animals, such as the mammoth, the inference from this fact would be equally just, not that man is as old as the extinct animal, but that the animal is as young as man and that the period assigned to these fossil remains must be brought considerably nearer to present-day life.

3. Various Calculations

Calculations based on the gravels of the Somme, on the cone of the Tinière, on the peat-bogs of France and Denmark, on fossil bones discovered in caves of Germany and France, on delta-formations of great rivers like the Nile and the Mississippi, on the "kitchen middings" of Denmark, and the lake-dwellings of Switzerland, must be carefully scrutinized. Sir J. W. Dawson, a geologist of great repute, has made the deliberate statement, that "possibly none of these reach farther back than six or seven thousand years, which according to Dr. Andrews have elapsed since the close of the boulder-clay in America," and that "the scientific pendulum must swing backward in this direction" (*Story of the Earth and Man*, 293). The "ice-age," formerly hypothetically calculated, has latterly been brought within calculable distance. G. F. Wright, Winchell and others have arrived at the conclusion that the glacial period in America, and consequently in Europe, does not lie more than some eight or ten thousand years behind us. If such be the case, the antiquity of man is brought within reasonable limits, and may consequently not be in contradiction to the Biblical statements on this point. If the careful and precise calculations of Dr. Andrews on the raised beaches of Lake Michigan are accepted, then N. America must have risen out of the waters of the Glacial period some 5,500 or 7,500 years ago; and if so, the duration of the human period in that continent is fixed and must be considerably reduced (Dawson, *Story*, etc, 295). One of the latest deliverances on this subject is that of Professor Russell of the University of Michigan (1904), who maintains that "we find no authentic and well-attested evidence of the presence of man in America either previous to or during the Glacial period." He is confident, that "all the geological evidence thus far gathered bearing on the antiquity of man in America points to the conclusion that he came after the Glacial epoch." Where all is vague and experts differ great caution is necessary in the arrangement of dates and periods of time. If moreover a comparatively rapid post-glacial submergence and reëlevation is accepted, as some naturalists hold, and man were then on the earth, the question may fairly be asked, whether this subsidence did not "constitute the deluge recorded in that remarkable 'log-book' of Noah preserved to us in Gen" (Dawson, op. cit., 290).

4. Chronology

The chronology of ancient nations—China, Babylon, Egypt—has been considered as subversive of the scriptural view as to the age of the human race. But it is a well-known fact, that experts differ very seriously upon the point. Their calculations range, for Egypt—starting from the reign of King Menes—from 5,867 (Champollion) to 4,455 (Brugsch), and from 3,892 (Lepsius) to 2,320 (Wilkinson). As to Babylon Bunsen places the starting-point for the historic period in 3,784, Brandis in 2,458, Oppert in 3,540—a difference of thousands of years (cf Bavinck, *Geref. Dogmatik*, II, 557). Perhaps here, too, future research will bring the scientific and the Biblical view into fuller harmony. At any rate Hommel's words on all these calculations require careful study: "The chronology for the first thousand years before Christ is fairly fixed: in the second thousand BC some points seem to be fixed: in the third thousand, i.e. before 2000 BC, all is uncertain." In this connection it may be mentioned, that attempts have frequently been made to cast discredit on the chronology of the early chapters of Gen. Suffice it to say that the calculations are based on the genealogies of the patriarchs and their descendants, and that the generally accepted dates assigned to them by Archbishop Ussher and introduced into the margins of some editions of the Bible are not to be trusted. The LXX differs in this respect from the Heb text by more than 1,500 years: precise chronological data are not and cannot be given. The basis of calculation is not known. Perhaps we are not far wrong in saying that, "if we allow, say, from 12,000 to 15,000 years since the time of man's first appearance on the earth, we do ample justice to all the available facts" (Orr, *God's Image*, etc, 180). See CHRONOLOGY.

That all these discussions have a bearing upon our view of man's primitive conditions can easily be understood. According to Scripture man's destiny was to 'replenish the earth, and subdue it; and have dominion over fish, fowl and every living thing' (Gen **1** 28), as God's steward (*oikónomos*, Titus **1** 7), as fellow-laborer with God (*sunergós*, 1 Cor **3** 9). Hence he was placed by God in the garden of Eden (*gan bᵉʿēdhen;* LXX *parádeisos tḗs trophḗs;* Vulg *paradisus voluptatis,* "paradise of delight"). The situation of that garden is carefully described, though the proper site remains unknown (Gen **2** 14.15). Some, like Driver, consider this an *ideal* locality (*Genesis*, 57); others take a very wide range in fixing upon the true site. Every continent has been chosen as the cradle of the race—Africa, among others, as the home of the gorilla and the chimpanzee—the supposed progenitors of humanity. In America, Greenland and the regions around the North Pole have had their supporters. Certain parts of Europe have found favor in some quarters. An imaginary island—Lemuria—situated between the African and Australian continents—has been accepted by others. All this, however, lies beyond the scope of science, and beyond the range of Scripture. Somewhere to the east of Pal, and in or near Babylonia, we must seek for the cradle of humanity. No trace of primeval man has been found, nor has the existence of primeval races been proved. The skulls which have been found (Neanderthal, Engis, Lansing) are of a high type, even Professor Huxley declaring of the first, that "it can in no sense be regarded as the intermediate between Man and the Apes," of the second, that it is "a fair, average skull, which might have belonged to a philosopher, or might have contained the thoughtless brains of a savage" (*Man's Place in Nature*, 156, 157). Of the Lansing skeleton found in Kansas, in 1902, this may at least be said—apart from the question as to its antiquity—that the skull bears close resemblance to that of the modern Indian. Even the skull of the Cro-Magnon man, supposed to belong to the paleolithic age, Sir J. W. Dawson considers to have carried a brain of greater size than that of the average modern man (*Meeting-Place of Geology and History*, 54). Primeval man can hardly be compared to the modern savage; for the savage is a deteriorated representative of a better type, which has slowly degenerated. History does not know of an *unaided* emergence from barbarism on the part of any savage tribe; it does know of degradation from a better type. Whatever view we take of the original state of man, the following points must be borne in mind: we need not suppose him to have been a humanized ape, rising into true manhood by a slow and gradual process; nor need we picture him either as a savage of pronounced type, or as in every sense the equal of modern man, "the heir of all the ages." Scripture represents him to us as a moral being, "with possibilities of sinless development, which his own free act annulled." There the matter may rest, and the words of a non-canonical Scripture may fitly be applied to him: "God created man to be immortal, and made him to be an image of His own eternity" (Wisd **2** 23 AV). See also PSYCHOLOGY.

5. Man's Primitive Condition

LITERATURE.—Darwin, *Origin of Species, Descent of Man;* Lock, *Recent Progress in the Study of Variation,* etc; A. R. Wallace, *Darwinism, Natural Selection;* Sir J. W. Dawson, *Story of the Earth and Man, Origin of World acc. to Revelation and Science, Meeting-Place of Geology and History;* R. Otto, *Naturalism and Religion;* Cambridge Memorial vol, *Darwin and Modern Science;* J. H. Stirling, *Darwinianism;* J. Young, *Evolution and Design;* J. Orr, *God's Image in Man;* J. A. Thomson, *Bible of Nature, Darwinism and Human Life;* Weismann, *Essays on Heredity;* Bavinck, *Gereformeerde Dogmatik;* Van Leeuwen. *Bijbelsche Anthropologie;* Laidlaw, *Bible Doctrines of Man;* O. Zöckler, *Vom Urstand des Menschen;* A. Fleischmann, *Die Darwin'sche Theorie;* E. Dennert, *Vom Sterbelager des Darwinismus, Bibel und Naturwissenschaft;* Huxley, *Man's Place in Nature;* Herzog, *RE*, arts. "Geist" and "Seele"; Driver, *Genesis;* Delitzsch, *Genesis;* Dillmann, *Die Genesis*, etc, etc.

J. I. MARAIS

ANTHROPOMORPHISM, an-thro-po-mor'fiz'm:

1. Definition of the Term
2. OT Anthropomorphisms
3. In What Senses an Anthropomorphic Element Is Necessary
4. Anthropomorphism and the Exigencies of Human Thinking
5. Anthropomorphism and Theism
6. Symbolic Forms of Thought
7. Philosophic Pantheism
8. Anthropomorphism and Personalized or Mediated Knowledge
9. From Greek Polytheism to Modern Ethical Monotheism
10. Greek Thought
11. Anthropomorphism of Israel
12. Twofold Nature of the Anthropomorphic Difficulty
13. Need of Rising Higher
14. God in Christ the True Solution

1. Definition

By this term is meant, conformably with its etymological signification, i.e. as being in the form or likeness of man, the attribution to God of human form, parts or passions, and the taking of Scripture passages which speak of God as having hands, or eyes, or ears, in a literal sense. This anthropomorphic procedure called forth Divine rebuke so early as Ps **50** 21: "Thou thoughtest that I was altogether such a one as thyself." Fear of the charge of anthropomorphism has had a strangely deterrent effect upon many minds, but very needlessly so. Even that rich storehouse of apparently crude anthropomorphisms, the OT, when it ascribes to Deity physical characters, mental and moral attributes, like those of man, merely means to make the Divine nature and operations intelligible, not to transfer to Him the defects and limitations of human character and life.

2. OT Anthropomorphisms

3. Anthropomorphic Element a Necessity

In all really theistic forms of religion, there is an anthropomorphic element present, for they all presuppose the psychological truth of a certain essential likeness between God and man. Nor, perfect as we may our theistic idea or conception of Deity, can we, in the realm of spirit, ever wholly eliminate the anthropomorphic element involved in this assumption, without which religion itself were not. It is of the essence of the religious consciousness to recognize the analogy subsisting between God's relations to man, and man's relations to his fellow. We are warned off from speaking of "the Divine will" or "the Divine purpose," as too anthropomorphic—savoring too much of simple humanity and human psychology—and are bidden speak only of "the Divine immanence" or "the Divine ground of our being." But these speculative objections really spring from a shallow interpretation of the primary facts of human consciousness, which, in the deepest realm of inner experience, claims the indefeasible right to speak of the Divine nature in human terms, as may best be possible to our being. The proper duty or function of philosophy is to take due account of such direct and primary facts of our nature: the basal facts of our being cannot be altered to suit her convenience.

4. Anthropomorphism and Human Thinking

If we were to interpret the impalpable and omnipresent Energy, from which all things proceed, in terms of force, then, as Fiske said, "there is scarcely less anthropomorphism lurking in the phrase 'Infinite Power,' than in the phrase 'Infinite Person.'" Besides which, the soul of man could never be content with the former phrase, for the soul wants more than dynamics. But if we have ascribed to God certain attributes in keeping with the properties of the one Protean force behind all nature-manifestations, it has been to help purge our conception of God of objectionable anthropomorphic elements. The exigencies of human thinking require us to symbolize the nature of Deity in some psychical way whereby He shall have for us some real meaning; hence those quasi-personal or anthropomorphic forms of expression, which inhere in the most perfected conceptions of Deity, as well as in the crude ideas of unreflective spiritism. And if all anthropomorphism could be dissipated by us, we should in the process have demolished theism—a serious enough issue for religion.

5. Anthropomorphism and Theism

Even speech has been declared to be a sensuous symbol, which makes knowledge of God impossible. To such an extent have the hyper-critical objections to anthropomorphism been pressed. Symbol of the Divine, speech may, in this sense, be; but it is a symbol whereby we can mark, distinguish or discern the super-sensible. Thus our abstract conceptions are by no means sensuous, however the language may originally have set out from a sensuous significance. Hence it would be a mistake to suppose that our knowledge of God must remain anthropomorphic in content, and cannot think the Absolute Being or Essence save in symbolic form. It is a developmental law of religion—as of spirit in general—that the spiritual grows always more clearly differentiated from the symbolic and sensuous. The fact that our knowledge of God is susceptible of advance does not make the idea of God a merely relative one. God's likeness to man, in respect of the attributes and elements essential to personal spirit, must be presupposed as a fundamental reality of the universe. In this way or sense, therefore, any true idea of God must necessarily be anthropomorphic.

6. Symbolic Thought

We cannot prove in any direct manner—either psychological or historical—that man was really made in God's image. But there is no manner of doubt that, on the other hand, man has always made God in his (man's) own image. Man can do no otherwise. Because he has purged his conceptions of Deity after human pattern, and no longer cares much to speak of God as a jealous or repentant or punitive Deity, as the case may be, it yet by no means follows that "the will of God" and "the love of God" have ceased to be of vital interest or primary importance for the religious consciousness. All man's constructive powers—intellectual, aesthetical, ethical, and spiritual—combine in evolving such an ideal, and believing in it as the personal Absolute, the Ideal-Real in the world of reality. Even in the forms of philosophic pantheism, the factors which play in man's personal life have not ceased to project themselves into the pantheistic conceptions of the cosmic processes or the being of the world.

7. In Pantheism

But man's making of God in his (man's) own image takes place just because God has made man in His own image. For the God, whom man makes for himself, is, before all things, real—no mere construction of his intellect, no figure or figment of his imagination, but the *prius* of all things, the Primal, Originative Reality. Thus we see that any inadequacy springing out of the anthropomorphic character of our religious knowledge or conceptions is not at all so serious as might at first sight be supposed, since it is due merely to the necessarily personalized or mediated character of all our knowledge whatsoever. For all our experience is human experience, and, in that sense, anthropomorphic. Only the most pitiful timidity will be scared by the word "anthropomorphism," which need not have the least deterrent effect upon our minds, since, in the territory of spirit, our conceptions are purged of anthropomorphic taint or hue, the purer our human consciousness becomes.

8. Personalized or Mediated Knowledge

To say, as we have done, that all knowledge is anthropomorphic, is but to recognize its partial, fallible, progressive or developmental character. It is precisely because this is true of our knowledge of God that our improved and perfected conceptions of God are the most significant feature in the religious progress of humanity. Only in course of the long religious march, wherein thought has shot up through the superincumbent weight of Greek polytheism into monotheism, and emerged at last into the severely ethical monotheism of our time, has religion been gradually stripped of its more crude anthropomorphic vestments. It cannot too clearly be understood that the religious ideal, which man has formed in the conception of the Absolute Personality, is one which is rooted in the realm of actuality. Not otherwise than as a metaphysical unity can God be known by us—intelligible only in the light of our own self-conscious experience.

9. Religious Progress

It is a mere modern—and rather unillumined—abuse of the term anthropomorphic which tries to affix it, as a term of reproach, to every hypothetical endeavor to frame a conception of God. In the days of the Greeks, it was only the ascription to the gods of human or bodily form that led Xenophanes to complain of anthropomorphism. This Xenophanes naturally took to be an illegitimate endeavor to raise one particular kind of being—one form of the finite—into the place of the Infinite. Hence he declared, "There is one God, greatest of all gods and men, who is like to mortal creatures neither in form nor in mind."

10. Greek Thought

But the progressive anthropomorphism of Greece is seen less in the humanizing of the gods than in the claim that "men are mortal gods," the idea being, as Aristotle said, that men become gods by transcendent merit. In this exaltation of the nature of man, the anthropomorphism of Greece is in complete contrast with the anthropomorphism of Israel, which was prone to fashion its Deity, not after the likeness of anything in the heavens above, but after something in the earth beneath. Certain professors of science have been mainly responsible for the recent and reprehensible use of the term, so familiar to us, for which we owe them no particular gratitude.

11. Anthropomorphism of Israel

The anthropomorphic difficulty is a twofold one. Religion, as we have just shown, must remain anthropomorphic in the sense that we cannot get rid of imputing to the universe the forms of our own mind or life, since religion is rooted in our human experience. As we have already hinted, however, religion is in no worse case in that respect than science. For nothing is more idle than the pretension that science is less anthropomorphic than religion—or philosophy either—as if science were not, equally with these, an outcome and manifestation of human thinking! It is surely most obvious that the scientist, in any knowledge of reality he may gain, can, no more than the religionist—or the metaphysician—jump off his own shadow,

12. Difficulty of Anthropomorphism Twofold

or make escape from the toils of his own nature and powers. For knowledge of any sort—whether religious or scientific or philosophical—a certain true anthropomorphism is necessary, for it is of the essence of rationality. Nature, of which science professes a knowledge, is really a man-made image, like unto its human maker. Say what science will, this is the objectively real of science—a cognition which, critically viewed, is only subjectively valid. There is no other way by which science can know the being of the world than after the human pattern. It is, however, a serious issue that this human element or factor has often unduly penetrated the realm of the Divine, subordinating it and dragging it down to human aims and conceptions.

Hence arises the second aspect of the anthropomorphic difficulty, which is, the need of freeing religion from anthropomorphic tendency, since it can be no satisfactory revealer of truth, so long as its more or less unrefined anthropomorphism contracts or subjugates reality to the conditions of a particular kind of being. It is perfectly clear that religion, whose every aim is to raise man beyond the limitations of his natural being, can never realize its end, so long as it remains wholly within the human sphere, instead of being something universal, transcendent, and independent. This is precisely why religion comes to give man's life the spiritual uplift whereby it rises to a new center of gravity—a true center of immediacy—in the universe, rises, indeed, beyond time and its own finitude to a participation in the universal and transcendent life of the Eternal. It does so without feeling need to yield to the anthropomorphic tendency in our time to attribute a necessity in God for an object to love, as if His egoistic perfection were not capable of realizing love's infinite ideal in itself, and without dependence upon such object.

13. Need of Rising Higher

We affirm that God in Christ, in revealing the fact of the likeness of man being eternal in God, disclosed the true anthropomorphism of our knowledge of God—it is with respect to the essential attributes and elements of personal spirit. It is easy to see how the early ascriptions to God of the form and members of the human body, and other non-essential accompaniments of personality, arose. The scriptural representations as to God's hand, eye, and ear, were declared by Calvin to be but adaptations to the slow spiritual progress of men—an infantile mode of talk, as Calvin puts it, like that of nurses to children. But we have got finely clear of essential anthropomorphism, if, with Isa **55** 8, we fully recognize that God's "thoughts are not" our "thoughts," nor God's "ways" our "ways."

14. God in Christ

LITERATURE.—E. Caird, *Evolution of Religion*, 1893; J. Martineau, *A Study of Religion*, 1889; J. Fiske, *The Idea of God*, 1901; J. Orr, *God's Image in Man*, 1905; D. B. Purinton, *Christian Theism*, 1889; J. Lindsay, *Recent Advances in Theistic Philosophy of Religion*, 1897; *Studies in European Philosophy*, 1909.

JAMES LINDSAY

ANTICHRIST, an'ti-krīst (ἀντίχριστος, *antichristos*):

The word "antichrist" occurs only in 1 Jn **2** 18.22; **4** 3; 2 Jn ver 7, but the idea which the word conveys appears frequently in Scripture.

I. In the OT.—As in the OT the doctrine concerning Christ was only suggested, not developed, so is it with the doctrine of the Antichrist. That the Messiah should be the divine Logos, the only adequate expression of God, was merely hinted at, not stated: so Antichrist was exhibited as the opponent of God rather than of His anointed. In the historical books of the OT we find "Belial" used as if a personal opponent of Jeh; thus the flagitiously wicked are called in AV "sons of Belial" (Jgs **19** 22; **20** 13), "daughter of Belial" (1 S **1** 16), etc. The RV translates the expression in an abstract sense, "base fellows," "wicked woman." In Dnl **7** 7.8 there is the description of a great heathen empire, represented by a beast with ten horns: its full antagonism to God is expressed in a little eleventh horn which had "a mouth speaking great things" and "made war with the saints" (vs 8.21). Him the 'Ancient of Days' was to destroy, and his kingdom was to be given to a 'Son of Man' (vs 9–14). Similar but yet differing in many points is the description of Antiochus Epiphanes in **8** 9–12.23–25.

Antichrist in the OT

II. In the NT.—In the Gospels the activity of Satan is regarded as specially directed against Christ. In the Temptation (Mt **4** 1–10; Lk **4** 1–13) the Devil claims the right to dispose of "all the kingdoms of the world," and has his claim admitted. The temptation is a struggle between the Christ and the Antichrist. In the parable of the Tares and the Wheat, while He that sowed the good seed is the Son of Man, he that sowed the tares is the Devil, who is thus Antichrist (Mt **13** 37–39). Our Lord felt it the keenest of insults that His miracles should be attributed to Satanic assistance (Mt **12** 24–32). In Jn **14** 30 there is reference to the "Prince of the World" who "hath nothing" in Christ.

1. Antichrist in the Gospels

The Pauline epistles present a more developed form of the doctrine. In the spiritual sphere Paul identifies Antichrist with Belial. "What concord hath Christ with Belial?" (2 Cor **6** 15). 2 Thess, written early, affords evidence of a considerably developed doctrine being commonly accepted among believers. The exposition of 2 Thess **2** 3–9, in which Paul exhibits his teaching on the 'Man of Sin,' is very difficult, as may be seen from the number of conflicting attempts at its interpretation. See MAN OF SIN. Here we would only indicate what seems to us the most plausible view of the Pauline doctrine. It had been revealed to the apostle by the Spirit that the church was to be exposed to a more tremendous assault than any it had yet witnessed. Some twelve years before the epistle was penned, the Rom world had seen in Caligula the portent of a mad emperor. Caligula had claimed to be worshipped as a god, and had a temple erected to him in Rome. He went farther, and demanded that his own statue should be set up in the temple at Jerus to be worshipped. As similar causes might be expected to produce similar effects, Paul, interpreting "what the Spirit that was in him did signify," may have thought of a youth, one reared in the purple, who, raised to the awful, isolating dignity of emperor, might, like Caligula, be struck with madness, might, like him, demand Divine honors, and might be possessed with a thirst for blood as insatiable as his. The fury of such an enthroned maniac would, with too great probability, be directed against those who, like the Christians, would refuse as obstinately as the Jews to give him Divine honor, but were not numerous enough to make Rom officials pause before proceeding to extremities. So long as Claudius lived, the

2. Antichrist in the Pauline Epistles

manifestation of this "lawless one" was restrained; when, however, the aged emperor should pass away, or God's time should appoint, that "lawless one" would be revealed, whom the Lord would "slay with the breath of his mouth" (ver 8).

Although many of the features of the "Man of Sin" were exhibited by Nero, yet the Messianic kingdom did not come, nor did Christ return to His people at Nero's death. Writing after Nero had fallen, the apostle John, who, as above remarked, alone of the NT writers uses the term, presents us with another view of Antichrist (1 Jn **2** 18.22; **4** 3; 2 Jn ver 7). From the first of these passages ("as ye have heard that antichrist cometh"), it is evident that the coming of Antichrist was an event generally anticipated by the Christian community, but it is also clear that the apostle shared to but a limited extent in this popular expectation. He thought the attention of believers needed rather to be directed to the antichristian forces that were at work among and around them ("even now have .... arisen many antichrists"). From 1 Jn **2** 22; **4** 3; 2 Jn ver 7 we see that the apostle regards erroneous views of the person of Christ as the real Antichrist. To him the Docetism (i.e. the doctrine that Christ's body was only a *seeming* one) which portended Gnosticism, and the elements of Ebionism (Christ was only a man), were more seriously to be dreaded than persecution.

3. Antichrist in the Johannine Epistles

In the Book of Revelation the doctrine of Antichrist receives a further development. If the traditional date of the Apocalypse is to be accepted, it was written when the lull which followed the Neronian persecution had given place to that under Domitian—"the bald Nero." The apostle now feels the whole imperial system to be an incarnation of the spirit of Satan; indeed from the identity of the symbols, seven heads and ten horns, applied both to the dragon (**12** 3) and to the Beast (**13** 1), he appears to have regarded the *raison d'être* of the Rom Empire to be found in its incarnation of Satan. The ten horns are borrowed from Dnl **7**, but the seven heads point, as seen from Rev **17** 9, to the "seven hills" on which Rome sat. There is, however, not only the Beast, but also the "image of the beast" to be considered (**13** 14.15). Possibly this symbolizes the cult of Rome, the city being regarded as a goddess, and worshipped with temples and statues all over the empire. From the fact that the seer endows the Beast that comes out of the earth with "two horns like unto a lamb" (**13** 11), the apostle must have had in his mind some system of teaching that resembled Christianity; its relationship to Satan is shown by its speaking "as a dragon" (ver 11). The number 666 given to the Beast (ver 18), though presumably readily understood by the writer's immediate public, has proved a riddle capable of too many solutions to be now readily soluble at all. The favorite explanation *Nerōn Ḳēṣar* (Nero Caesar), which suits numerically, becomes absurd when it implies the attribution of seven heads and ten horns. There is no necessity to make the calculation in Heb; the corresponding arithmogram in the Sib Or, **1** 328–30, in which 888 stands for *Iesous,* is interpreted in Gr. On this hypothesis *Lateinos,* a suggestion preserved by Irenaeus (V, 30) would suit. If we follow the analogy of Daniel, which has influenced the Apocalyptist so much, the Johannine Antichrist must be regarded as not a person but a kingdom. In this case it must be the Rom Empire that is meant.

4. Antichrist in the Book of Revelation

III. In Apocalyptic Writings.—Although from their eschatological bias one would expect that the Jewish Apocalytic Writings would be full of the subject, mention of the Antichrist occurs only in a few of the apocalypses. The earliest certain notice is found in the Sibylline books (**1** 167). We are there told that "Beliar shall come and work wonders," and "that he shall spring from the Sebasteni (Augusti)" a statement which, taken with other indications, inclines one to the belief that the mad demands of Caligula, were, when this was written, threatening the Jews. There are references to Beliar in the XII P, which, if the date ascribed to them by Dr. Charles, i.e. the reign of John Hyrcanus I, be assumed as correct, are earlier. Personally we doubt the accuracy of this conclusion. Further, as Dr. Charles admits the presence of many interpolations, even though one might assent to his opinions as to the nucleus of the XII P, yet these Beliar passages might be due to the interpolator. Only in one passage is "Beliar" *antichristos* as distinguished from *antítheos;* Dnl **5** 10.11 (Charles' tr), "And there shall rise unto you from the tribe of Judah and of Levi the salvation of the Lord, and he shall make war against Beliar, and execute everlasting vengeance on our enemies, and the captivity shall he take from Beliar and turn disobedient hearts unto the Lord." Dr. Charles thinks he finds an echo of this last clause in Lk **1** 17; but may the case not be the converse?

Antichrist in the Apocalyptic Writings

The fullest exposition of the ideas associated with the antichrist in the early decades of Christian history is to be found in the Asc Isa. In this we are told that "Beliar" (Belial) would enter into "the matricide king" (Nero), who would work great wonders, and do much evil. After the expiry of 1,332 days during which he has persecuted the plant which the twelve apostles of the Beloved have planted, "the Lord will come with his angels and with armies of his holy ones from the seventh heaven, with the glory of the seventh heaven, and he will drag Beliar into Gehenna and also his armies" (**4** 3.13, Charles' tr). If the date at which Beliar was supposed to enter into Nero was the night on which the great fire in Rome began, then the space of power given to him is too short by 89 days. From the burning of Rome till Nero's death was 1,421 days. It is to be noted that there are no signs of the writer having been influenced either by Paul or the Apocalypse. As he expected the coming of the Lord to be the immediate cause of the death of Nero, we date the writing some months before that event. It seems thus to afford contemporary and independent evidence of the views entertained by the Christian community as to Antichrist.

IV. In Patristic Writings.—Of the patristic writers, Polycarp is the only one of the Apostolic Fathers who refers directly to Antichrist. He quotes John's words, "Whosoever doth not confess that Jesus Christ has come in the flesh is Antichrist" (**7**), and regards Docetism as Antichrist in the only practical sense. Barnabas, although not using the term, implies that the fourth empire of Daniel is Antichrist; this he seems to identify with the Rom Empire (**4** 5). Irenaeus is the first-known writer to occupy himself with the number of the Beast. While looking with some favor on *Lateinos,* he himself prefers *Teitan* as the name intended (**5** 30). His view is interesting as showing the belief that the arithmogram was to be interpreted by the Gr values of the letters. More particulars as to the views prevailing can be gleaned from Hippolytus,

Patristic References to Antichrist

who has a special work on the subject, in which he exhibits the points of resemblance between Christ and Antichrist (*On Christ and Antichrist*, 4.14.15. 19.25). In this work we find the assertion that Antichrist springs from the terms of Jacob's blessing to Dan. Among other references, the idea of Commodian (250 AD) that Nero risen from the dead was to be Antichrist has to be noticed. In the commentary on Revelation attributed to Victorinus of Petau there is, inserted by a later hand, an identification of Genseric with the "Beast" of that book. It is evident that little light is to be gained on the subject from patristic sources.

V. Mediaeval Views.—Much time need not be spent on the *mediaeval* views of Antichrist in either of the two streams in which it flowed, Christian and Jewish.

1. Christian Views

The Christian was mainly occupied in finding methods of transforming the names of those whom monkish writers abhorred into a shape that would admit of their being reckoned 666. The favorite name for this species of torture was naturally *Maometis* (Mohammed). Gregory IX found no difficulty in accommodating the name of Frederic II so as to enable him to identify his great antagonist with "the beast coming up out of the sea": this identification the emperor retorted on the pope. Rabanus Maurus gives a full account of what Antichrist was to do, but without any attempt to label any contemporary with the title. He was to work miracles and to rebuild the temple at Jerusalem. The view afterward so generally held by Protestants that the papacy was Antichrist had its representatives among the sects denounced by the hierarchy as heretical, as the *Kathari*. In various periods the rumor was spread that Antichrist had been already born. Sometimes his birthplace was said to be Babylon, sometimes this distinction was accorded to the mystical Babylon, Rome.

2. Jewish Views

The Jewish views had little effect on Christian speculation. With the Talmudists Antichrist was named Armilus, a variation of Romulus. Rome is evidently primarily intended, but Antichrist became endowed with personal attributes. He makes war on Messiah, son of Joseph, and slays him, but is in turn destroyed by Messiah, Son of David.

VI. Post-Reformation Views.—In immediately post-Reformation times the divines of the Romish church saw in Luther and the Reformed churches the Antichrist and Beast of Revelation. On the other hand the Protestants identified the papacy and the Roman church with these, and with the Pauline Man of Sin. The latter view had a certain plausibility, not only from the many undeniably antichristian features in the developed Rom system, but from the relation in which the Romish church stood to the city of Rome and to the imperial idea. The fact that the Beast which came out of the earth (Rev **13** 11) had the horns of a lamb points to some relation to the lamb which had been slain (**5** 6). Futurist interpreters have sought the Antichrist in historical persons, as Napoleon III. These persons, however, did not live to realize the expectations formed of them. The consensus of critical opinion is that Nero is intended by the Beast of the Apocalypse, but this, on many grounds, as seen before, is not satisfactory. Some future development of evil may more exactly fulfil the conditions of the problem.

Post-Reformation Theories of Antichrist

LITERATURE.—Bousset, *Der Antichrist;* "The Antichrist Legend," *Expos T*, contains an admirable vidimus of ancient authorities in the subject. See arts. on subject in Schenkel's *Bib. Lex.* (Hausrath); Herzog's *RE*, 2d ed (Kähler), 3d ed (Sieffert); *EB* (Bousset); with Commentaries on 2 Thess and Rev. A full account of the interpretations of the "Man of Sin" may be seen in Dr. John Eadie's essay on that subject in his *Comm. on Thess.*

J. E. H. THOMSON

ANTILEGOMENA, an-ti-le-gom'e-na. See BIBLE; CANON OF NT; DEUTERO-CANONICAL BOOKS.

ANTI-LIBANUS, an-ti-lib'a-nus. See LEBANON.

ANTIMONY, an'ti-mō-ni. See COLOR.

ANTIOCH, an'ti-ok, **OF PISIDIA,** pi-sid'i-a (**'Αντιόχεια πρὸς Πισιδίᾳ,** *Antiócheia prós Pisidía*, or **'Αντιόχεια ἡ Πισιδία,** *Antiócheia hē Pisidía*= "Pisidian"):

1. History

(1) **Antioch of Pisidia** was so called to distinguish it from the many other cities of the same name founded by Seleucus Nicator (301–280 BC) and called after his father Antiochus. It was situated in a strong position, on a plateau close to the western bank of the river Anthios, which flows down from the Sultan Dagh to the double lake called Limnai (Egerdir Göl). It was planted on the territory of a great estate belonging to the priests of the native religion; the remaining portions of this estate belonged later to the Rom emperors, and many inscriptions connected with the cult of the emperors, who succeeded to the Divine as well as to the temporal rights of the god, have survived. (See Sir W. M. Ramsay's paper on "The Tekmoreian Guest-Friends" in *Studies in the History and Art of the Eastern Rom Provinces*, 1906.) The plateau on which Antioch stood commands one of the roads leading from the East to the Maeander and Ephesus; the Seleucid kings regularly founded their cities in Asia Minor at important strategical points, to strengthen their hold on the native tribes. There is no evidence that a Gr city existed on the site of Antioch before the foundation of Seleucus. Ramsay must be right in connecting Strabo's statement that Antioch was colonized by Greeks from Magnesia on the Maeander with the foundation by Seleucus; for it is extremely unlikely that Greeks could have built and held a city in such a dangerous position so far inland before the conquest of Alexander. Pre-Alexandrian Gr cities are seldom to be found in the interior of Asia Minor, and then only in the open river valleys of the west. But there must have been a Phrygian fortress at or near Antioch when the Phrygian kings were at the height of their power. The natural boundary of Phrygian territory in this district is the Pisidian Mts., and the Phrygians could only have held the rich valley between the Sultan Dagh and Egerdir Lake against the warlike tribes of the Pisidian mountains on condition that they had a strong settlement in the neighborhood. We shall see below that the Phrygians did occupy this side of the Sultan Dagh, controlling the road at a critical point.

The Seleucid colonists were Greeks, Jews and Phrygians, if we may judge by the analogy of similar Seleucid foundations. That there were Jews in Antioch is proved by Acts **13** 14.50, and by an inscription of Apollonia, a neighboring city, mentioning a Jewess Deborah, whose ancestors had held office in Antioch (if Ramsay's interpretation of the inscription, *The Cities of St. Paul*, 256, is correct). In 189 BC, after the peace with Antiochus the Great, the Romans made Antioch a "free city"; this does not mean that any change was made in its constitution but only that it ceased to pay tribute to the Seleucid kings. Antony gave Antioch to Amyntas of Galatia in 39 BC, and hence it was included in the province Galatia (see GALATIA) formed in 25 BC out of Amyntas' kingdom. Not much before 6 BC, Antioch was made a Rom colony, with the title *Caesareia Antiocheia;* it was now the capital of southern Galatia and the chief of a series of military colonies founded by Augustus, and connected by a system of roads as yet insufficiently explored, to hold down the wild tribes of Pisidia, Isauria and Pamphylia.

2. Pisidian Antioch

Much controversy has raged round the question whether Antioch was in Phrygia or in Pisidia at the time of St. Paul. Strabo defines Antioch as a city of Phrygia toward Pisidia, and the same description is implied in Acts **16** 6, and **18** 23. Other authorities assign Antioch to Pisidia, and it admittedly belonged to Pisidia after the province of that name was formed in 295 AD. In the Pauline period it was a city of Galatia, in the district of Galatia called Phrygia (to distinguish it from other ethnical divisions of Galatia, e.g. Lycaonia). This view is certain on a study of the historical conditions (see Ramsay, *The Church in the Roman Empire,* 25 f), and is supported by the fact that Phrygian inscriptions (the surest sign of the presence of a Phrygian population, for only Phrygians used the Phrygian language) have been found around Antioch. See PISIDIA. This corner of Phrygia owed its incorporation in the province Galatia to the military situation in 39 BC, when Amyntas was entrusted with the task of quelling the disorderly Pisidian tribes. No scheme of military conquest in the Pisidian mountains could omit this important strategical point on the N.W. This fact was recognized by Seleucus when he founded Antioch, by Antony when he gave Antioch to Amyntas, and by Augustus when he made Antioch the chief of his military colonies in Pisidia. A military road, built by Augustus, and called the Royal Road, led from Antioch to the sister colony of Lystra. According to the story preserved in the legend of "Paul and Thekla," it was along this road that Paul and Barnabas passed on their way from Antioch to Iconium (Acts **13** 51; cf 2 Tim **3** 11; see Ramsay, *The Church in the Roman Empire,* 27–36).

3. Language and Religion

Latin continued to be the official language of Antioch, from its foundation as a Rom colony until the later part of the 2d cent. AD. It was more thoroughly Romanized than any other city in the district; but the Gr spirit revived in the 3d cent., and the inscriptions from that date are in Gr. The principal pagan deities were Men and Cybele. Strabo mentions a great temple with large estates and many *hieródouloi* devoted to the service of the god.

4. Paul at Antioch

Antioch, as has been shown above, was the military and administrative center for that part of Galatia which comprised the Isaurian, Pisidian and Pamphylian mountains, and the southern part of Lycaonia. It was hence that Rom soldiers, officials, and couriers were despatched over the whole area, and it was hence, according to Acts **13** 49, that Paul's mission radiated over the whole region. (On the technical meaning of "region" here, see PISIDIA.) The "devout and honorable women" (AV) and the "chief men" of the city, to whom the Jews addressed their complaint, were perhaps the Rom colonists. The publicity here given to the action of the women is in accord with all that is known of their social position in Asia Minor, where they were often priestesses and magistrates. The Jews of Antioch continued their persecution of Paul when he was in Lystra (Acts **14** 19). Paul passed through Antioch a second time on his way to Perga and Attalia (Acts **14** 21). He must have visited Antioch on his second journey (Acts **16** 6; Ramsay, *The Church in the Roman Empire,* 74 ff), and on his third (Acts **18** 23; ib 96).

LITERATURE.—Antioch was identified by Arundel, *Discoveries in Asia Minor,* I, 281 f, with the ruins north of Yalovadj. A full account of the city in the Gr and Rom periods is given in Ramsay, *The Cities of St. Paul,* 247–314. The inscriptions are published in *CIG,* 3979–81; LeBas, III, 1189 ff, 1815–25; *CIL,* III, 289 ff; Sterrett, *Epigraphical Journey in A.M.,* 121 ff; *Wolfe Expedition in A.M.,* 218 ff; *Ephem. Epigr.,* V, 575; *Athen. Mitth.,* XIV, 114. Add to this list (borrowed from Pauly-Wissowa) the inscriptions published in Ramsay's article on "The Tekmoreian Guest-Friends," referred to above. For the Phrygian inscriptions of the Antioch district, see Ramsay's paper in *Jahresh. Oest. Arch. Inst.,* VIII, 85.

W. M. CALDER

ANTIOCH, an'ti-ok, **IN SYRIA** (**Ἀντιόχεια,** *Antiócheia*):

(2) **Antioch in Syria.**—In 301 BC, shortly after the battle of Ipsus, which made him master of Syria, Seleucus Nicator founded the city of Antioch, naming it after his father Antiochus. Guided, it was said, by the flight of an eagle, he fixed its site on the left bank of the Orontes (the El-ʿAsi) about 15 miles from the sea. He also founded and fortified Seleucia to be the port of his new capital. The city was enlarged and embellished by successive kings of the Seleucid Dynasty, notably by Seleucus Callinicus (246–226 BC), and Antiochus Epiphanes (175–164 BC). In 83 BC, on the collapse of the Seleucid monarchy, Antioch fell into the hands of Tigranes, king of Armenia, who held Syria until his defeat by the Romans fourteen years later. In 64 BC the country was definitely annexed to Rome by Pompey, who granted considerable privileges to Antioch, which now became the capital of the Rom province of Syria. In the civil wars which terminated in the establishment of the Rom principate, Antioch succeeded in attaching itself constantly to the winning side, declaring for Caesar after the fall of Pompey, and for Augustus after the battle of Actium. A Rom element was added to its population, and several of the emperors contributed to its adornment. Already a splendid city under the Seleucidae, Antioch was made still more splendid by its Rom patrons and masters. It was the "queen of the East," the third city, after Rome and Alexandria, of the Rom world. About five miles distant from the city was the suburb of Daphne, a spot sacred to Apollo and Artemis. This suburb, beautified by groves and fountains, and embellished by the Seleucidae and the Romans with temples and baths, was the pleasure resort of the city, and "Daphnic morals" became a by-word. From its foundation Antioch was a cosmopolitan city. Though not a seaport, its situation was favorable to commercial development, and it absorbed much of the trade of the Levant. Seleucus Nicator had settled numbers of Jews in it, granting them equal rights with the Greeks (*Ant,* XII, iii, 1). Syrians, Greeks, Jews, and in later days, Romans, constituted the main elements of the population. The citizens were a vigorous, turbulent and pushing race, notorious for their commercial aptitude, the licentiousness of their pleasures, and the scurrility of their wit. Literature and the arts, however, were not neglected.

In the early history of Christianity, Antioch occupies a distinguished place. The large and flourishing Jewish colony offered an immediate field for Christian teaching, and the cosmopolitanism of the city tended to widen the outlook of the Christian community, which refused to be confined within the narrow limits of Judaism. Nicolas, a proselyte of Antioch, was one of the first deacons (Acts **6** 5). Antioch was the cradle of gentile Christianity and of Christian missionary enterprise. It was at the instance of the church at Antioch that the council at Jerus decided to relieve gentile Christians of the burden of the Jewish law (Acts **15**). Antioch was Paul's starting-point in his three missionary journeys (Acts **13** 1 ff; **15**

36 ff; **18** 23), and thither he returned from the first two as to his headquarters (Acts **14** 26 ff; **18** 22). Here also the term "Christian," doubtless originally a nickname, was first applied to the followers of Jesus (Acts **11** 26). The honorable record of the church at Antioch as the mother-church of gentile Christianity gave her a preëminence which she long enjoyed. The most distinguished of her later sons was St. John Chrysostom. The Antioch chalice, supposed to contain the Holy Grail, is still an uncertainty. Most exhaustive research on the subject (Eisen, *The Great Antioch Chalice;* Bacon, *Annual of American Schools,* V) reaches the conclusion that the chalice belongs about the 4th cent.

C. H. Thomson

ANTIOCHIANS, an-ti-ō′ki-ans (**'Αντιοχεῖς,** *Antiocheís,* peculiar to the Apoc, 2 Macc **4** 9.19): Antiochus Epiphanes was on the throne of Syria from 175 to 164 BC. His determined policy was to Hellenize his entire kingdom. The greatest obstacle to his ambition was the fidelity of the Jews to their historic religion. Many worldly Hebrews, however, for material advantage were willing to apostatize, among them, Jason, the brother of the faithful high priest Onias III. With a large sum of money (2 Macc **4** 7–10) he bribed Antiochus to appoint him high priest in his brother's stead. This office, being, since Ezra's time, political as well as religious, made him virtually the head of the nation. He promised, on condition the king would permit him to build a Gr gymnasium at Jerus, "to train up the youth of his race in the fashions of the heathen," and to enrol the Hellenized people as Antiochians, i.e. to give all Jews who would adopt Gr customs and the Gr religion the rights and privileges of citizens of Antioch. The granting of this request made Jason the head of the Gr party at Jerus. "Such was the height of Gr fashions, and the increase of heathenish manners" under his perverted high-priesthood, that the priests under him lost courage to "serve any more at the altar, but despising the temple and neglecting the sacrifices, hastened" to ally themselves with the Grecians. When the sacrifice of Hercules was observed in connection with the Grecian games at Tyre "Jason sent special messengers from Jerus, who were Antiochians" (2 Macc **4** 19) with a large contribution of money. This Hellenizing program was supported by a decree of Antiochus which enjoined uniformity of worship throughout his dominions. He forbade the further observance of Jewish festivals, Sabbath, sacrifices in the temple and the rite of circumcision. His ambition included the like subjugation of Egypt, but being thwarted in his expedition thither by Rom envoys, he returned to Jerus to vent his anger on the Jews who refused to deny the faith of their fathers. The persecutions inflicted by the king upon these devout Jews abounded in every atrocity. All sacred books of the law that could be found were burned. This attempt to Hellenize the Jews was pushed to every remote rural village of Pal. The universal peril led the Samaritans, eager for safety, to repudiate all connection and kinship with the Jews. They sent ambassadors and an epistle asking to be recognized as belonging to the Gr party, and to have their temple on Mt. Gerizim named "The Temple of Jupiter Hellenius." The request was granted. This was evidently the final breach between the two races indicated in Jn **4** 9, "For Jews have no dealings with Samaritans."

Among those who refused to be enrolled as Antiochians was Mattathias, an aged priest of the order of Joarib. Mourning the terrible profanation of the holy city and temple he retired with his five sons to his ancestral estates among the mountains N.W. of Jerus. The emissaries of Antiochus followed him thither and commanded him to offer sacrifices upon a heathen altar. He was promised special royal favor in case of obedience. The indignant priest not only "had no ear for the temptations of an abhorred Hellenism," but in his fury instantly slew the apostate priest who attempted to comply with the command. He killed also the king's commissioner and tore down the detested altar.

This act of heroism became the dawn of a new era. The people rallied to Mattathias' support. The rebellion grew in power. After a year of inspiring leadership "the venerable priest-captain" died, having first committed "the cause of the law" to his sons, henceforth called Maccabees, from Judas Maccabaeus, the son to whom he committed his work. Their victorious career brought to an end the Hellenizing process and the Gr party to which the Antiochians belonged. See also Antiochus IV.

Literature.—*Ant,* XII, v; Stanley, *History of the Jewish Church,* III, § 48; Riggs, *History of the Jewish People,* ch ii, §§ 15–26 (Kent's Hist. Series, IV).

Dwight M. Pratt

ANTIOCHIS, an-tī′o-kis (**'Αντιοχίς,** *Antiochís*): A concubine of Antiochus Epiphanes who had presented her with the two Cilician cities, Tarsus and Mallus. Dissatisfied with this the cities made insurrection (2 Macc **4** 30).

ANTIOCHUS, an-tī′o-kus (**'Αντίοχος,** *Antíochos;* A, **'Αντίμαχος,** *Antímachos* [1 Macc **12** 16]): The father of Numenius, who in company with Antipater, son of Jason, was sent by Jonathan on an embassy to the Romans and Spartans to renew "the friendship" and "former confederacy" made by Judas (1 Macc **12** 16; **14** 22; *Ant,* XIII, vi, 8).

ANTIOCHUS I, an-tī′o-kus (**'Αντίοχος Σωτήρ,** *Antíochos Sōtḗr,* "savior"): B. 323 BC; d. 261, son of Seleucus Nicator. He fell in love with his stepmother, Stratonike, and became very ill. His father, when he discovered the cause of his son's illness, gave her to him in 293, and yielded to him the sovereignty over all the countries beyond the Euphrates, as well as the title of king. When Seleucus returned to Macedonia in 281, he was murdered by Ptolemaeus Ceraunus. Antiochus thus became ruler of the whole Syrian kingdom. He waged war on Eumenes of Pergamum, but without success. For the victories of his elephant corps over the Gauls, who had settled in Asia Minor, he received the surname of Soter ("Deliverer"). It was in a battle with these inveterate foes of his country that he met his death (261 BC). See also Seleucidae.

J. E. Harry

ANTIOCHUS II, surnamed Theos (**Θεός,** *Theós,* "god"): Son and successor of Antiochus I (261–246 BC). He made a successful war on Ptolemy Philadelphus of Egypt, but was obliged to buy peace in 250 by divorcing his wife, Laodice, and by marrying Ptolemy's daughter, Berenice. After the death of Ptolemy, "the king of the south" (Dnl **11** 6) 248 BC, he recalled Laodice and named her eldest son (Seleucus Kallinikos) as his successor to the throne; but Laodice (probably because she feared a second repudiation) had Berenice, her child, and Antiochus all murdered (246 BC). The Milesians gave him the surname of Theos in gratitude for his liberating them from the tyranny of Timarchus. (See Arrian, I, 17, 10, and 18, 2; Jos, *Ant,* XII, iii, 2; Dittenberger, *Sylloge Inscr. Graec,* 166–71.)

J. E. Harry

ANTIOCHUS III (**Μέγας,** *Mégas,* "The Great," mentioned in 1 Macc **1** 10; **8** 6–8): Son of Seleucus Kallinikos; succeeded to the throne of Syria in

WATER WHEEL ON RIVER ORONTES AT ANTIOCH

222 BC; put to death his general, Hermeas, and then led an army against Egypt. Theodotus surrendered to him Tyre, Ptolemais and his naval fleet. Rhodes and Cyzicus, as well as Byzantium and Aetolia, desired peace, but Antiochus declined to accept their terms. He renewed the war, but was defeated at Raphia in 217, and was obliged to give up Phoenicia and Coelesyria; Seleucia, however, he retained. He undertook to bring under his sway again all the territory of the Far East. His expedition against Bactria and Parthia gained for him the surname of "The Great." In 209 he carried away the treasure of the goddess Aine in Ecbatana, defeated the Parthians, and in 208 marched against the Bactrians. Later he made a treaty with an Indian rajah, and then returned to

Tetradrachm (Attic talent) of Antiochus III.

the West by way of Arachosia and Carmania, forcing the Gerraean Arabs to furnish him with frankincense, myrrh and silver. Then he took Ephesus, which he made his headquarters. In 196 he had crossed the Hellespont and rebuilt Lysimachia. Hannibal visited Antiochus in Ephesus the next year and became one of the king's advisers. He sought the friendship also of Eumenes of Pergamum, but without success. Rome now requested the king not to interfere in Europe, or to recognize the right of the Romans to protect the Greeks in Asia. A war broke out in 192, and Antiochus was persuaded to come to Greece. The Aetolians elected him their general, who asked the Achaeans to remain neutral. But the patriotic Philopoemen decided that an alliance with Rome was to be preferred. Antiochus first captured Calchis; then succeeded in gaining a footing in Boeotia, and later made an effort to get possession of Thessaly, but retired on the approach of the Macedonian army. In 191 the Romans made a formal declaration of war on Antiochus, who, being at that time in Acarnania, returned to Calchis, and finally sailed back to Ephesus. The Romans regained possession of Boeotia, Euboea and Sestus; but Polyxenidas defeated the Rom fleet near Samos, which island, together with Cyme and Phocaea, fell into the hands of Antiochus. The victorious Polyxenidas, however, soon sustained a crushing defeat at the hands of the Romans, and Antiochus abandoned Lysimachia, leaving an open road to Asia to the Romans. He was finally defeated at Magnesia and sent word to Scipio, who was at Sardis, that he was willing to make peace; but Scipio ordered him to send envoys to Rome. A decision was reached in 189; the Asiatic monarch was obliged to renounce everything on the Rom side of the Taurus; give up all his ships of war but ten and pay 15,000 talents to Rome, and 500 to Eumenes. Antiochus marched against the revolted Armenians in 187. In order to replenish his exhausted treasury, he attempted to plunder a temple and both he and his soldiers were slain by the Elymaeans.

LITERATURE.—Polyb. v.40.21; Livy xxxi.14; xxxiii. 19 ff; Jos, *Ant*, XII; Heyden, *Res ab Ant;* Babelon, *Rois de Syrie*, 77–86; Dnl **11** 10–19; Tetzlaff, *De Antiochi III Magni rebus gestis* (Münster, 1874).

J. E. HARRY

ANTIOCHUS IV (**Ἐπιφανής**, *Epiphanḗs*, ē-pif′-a-nēz, "Illustrious"): Son of Antiochus III who became king after his brother, Seleucus IV, had been murdered by Heliodorus. As a boy Antiochus lived at Rome as a hostage. The Pergamene monarchs, Eumenes and Attalus, succeeded in placing upon the throne the brother of Seleucus, although Heliodorus had wished to ascend the throne himself. The young king was even more enterprising than his father. He was called in to settle a quarrel between Onias III and his brother, Jason, the leader of the Hellenizing faction in Jerus, and Onias was driven out (2 Macc **4** 4–6). Jason became high priest in his stead (2 Macc **4** 9–16; 1 Macc **1** 10–15; *Ant*, XII, v, 1). Antiochus himself afterward visited Jerus and was signally honored (2 Macc **4** 22). On the death of Ptolemy VI in 173, Antiochus laid claim to Coelesyria, Pal and Phoenicia; whereupon war broke out between Syria and Egypt. In this war Antiochus was victorious. Ptolemy Philometor was taken prisoner, and Antiochus had himself crowned king of Egypt (171–167) at Memphis; whereupon Alexandria revolted and chose Ptolemy's brother as their king. The Rom ambassador, Popilius Laenas, demanded the surrender of Egypt and the immediate withdrawal of its self-constituted king. Antiochus yielded; gave up Pelusium and withdrew his fleet from Cyprus, but retained Coelesyria, Pal and Phoenicia.

While Antiochus was on a second campaign in Egypt, he heard of the siege of Jerusalem. He returned immediately, slew many thousands of the inhabitants and robbed the temple of its treasures (1 Macc **1** 20–24; 2 Macc **5** 11–21). By his prohibition of the Jewish worship and his introduction or substitution of the worship of the Olympian Zeus (1 Macc **1** 54; 2 Macc **6** 2; *Ant*, XII, v, 4) he brought about the insurrection of the Jews, under the Maccabees, upon whom he made an unsuccessful war in 167–164 BC. After this war Antiochus retired to the eastern provinces and died, after having failed in an attack on the temple of the Sun in Elymais, in Persia. See also ABOMINATION OF DESOLATION; ANTIOCHIANS.

J. E. HARRY

ANTIOCHUS V (**Εὐπάτωρ**, *Eupátōr*, "Noble-born"): Son and successor to Antiochus Epiphanes, ascended the throne as a mere boy (163–161 BC) under the guardianship of Lysias, who led an expedition to the relief of Jerusalem, which had been besieged by Judas Maccabaeus (1 Macc **6** 18–30; *Ant*, XII, ix, 4), who was defeated (1 Macc **6** 42). Antiochus then besieged Jerusalem. Peace was finally concluded on the condition that the Jews should not be compelled to change any of their national customs (1 Macc **6** 55–60; *Ant*, XII, ix, 7). Philip, the king's foster-brother (2 Macc **9** 29), was defeated at Antioch, but soon afterward Lysias and Antiochus were themselves defeated by Demetrius Soter, son of Seleucus Philopator (1 Macc **7** 4; 2 Macc **14** 2; *Ant*, XII, x, 1; Polyb. xxxi.19; Livy *Epit*. 46).

J. E. HARRY

ANTIOCHUS VI (surnamed Theos [**θεός**], or, according to coins, Dionysus Epiphanes): Was the son of Alexander Balas, who claimed to be the son of Antiochus Epiphanes. Alexander left the throne to his son in 146 BC. The young king retired to Arabia—perhaps through compulsion. The shrewd diplomatist and skilful general, Tryphon, succeeded first in winning over to his side the two leaders of the Jews, Jonathan and Simon, and then, by force of arms, in making the Syrians recognize his protégé. As soon as the monarchy had been firmly established, Tryphon unmasked his projects: he had been ambitious only for himself; Antiochus had been only an instrument in his hands.

In 143, after a reign of a little more than three years, Antiochus was assassinated by Tryphon, who ascended the throne himself (1 Macc **13** 31; *Ant*, XIII, vii, 1; Livy *Epit.* 55). J. E. Harry

ANTIOCHUS VII (surnamed Sidetes, **Σιδήτης**, *Sidḗtēs*, after Sida in Pamphylia, where he was educated): Younger son of Demetrius Soter and brother of Demetrius Nicator, whose wife, Cleopatra, he married when Demetrius was taken prisoner by the Parthians. Antiochus overthrew the usurper, Tryphon, and ascended the throne himself and reigned from 139 to 130 BC. He defeated John Maccabaeus and besieged Jerus (*Ant*, XIII, viii, 2), but concluded a favorable peace (*Ant*, XIII, viii, 3) from fear of Rome. Later he waged war with the Parthians and was slain in battle (1 Macc **15** 2–9.28–31). J. E. Harry

ANTIPAS, an'ti-pas (**'Αντίπας**): The name is an abbreviation of Antipater: (1) A name of Herod "the tetrarch" (in Jos), son of Herod the Great, the brother of Archelaus (Mt **14** 1; Lk **3** 1; **9** 7; Acts **13** 1). See Herod. (2) A martyr of the church of Pergamum, described as "my witness, my faithful one" (Rev **2** 13).

ANTIPATER, an-tip'a-tẽr (**'Αντίπατρος**, *Antípatros*): One of two envoys sent by the senate of the Jews to the Romans and Spartans (1 Macc **12** 16; **14** 22).

ANTIPATRIS, an-tip'a-tris (**'Αντίπατρις**, *Antípatris*): Is mentioned in Scripture only once, in connection with the descent of Paul from Jerus to Caesarea (Acts **23** 31). References will be found in *Ant*, XIII, xv, 1; XVI, v, 2; *BJ*, I, xxi, 9. It was a town built by Herod the Great, and called after his father Antipater. It is probably identical with the modern *Rās el-'Ain*, "fountain head," a large mound with ruins at the source of *Nahr el-'Aujeh*, in the plain to the N.E. of Jaffa. There are remains of a crusading castle which may be the Mirabel of those times. W. Ewing

ANTIQUITY, an-tik'wi-ti (קַדְמָה, *ḳadhmāh*, from קָדַם, *kādham*, "to precede in time," "to be old"): In Ezk **16** 55; **36** 11, rendered "former"; in Ps **129** 6, "before." Trd "antiquity" only in Isa **23** 7 to indicate the primeval age of Tyre, which Strabo terms, "after Sidon," the oldest Phoen city. Delitzsch renders it "whose origin is from the days of the olden time."

ANTONIA, an-tō'ni-a. See Jerusalem.

ANTOTHIJAH, an-to-thī'ja. See Anthothijah.

ANTOTHITE, an'toth-īt: AV form of Anathothite (q.v.) (thus RV) (1 Ch **11** 28; **12** 3).

ANUB, ā'nub (עָנוּב, *'ānūbh*, "ripe"): A descendant of Judah and son of Hakkoz (AV **Coz**) 1 Ch **4** 8.

ANUS, ā'nus. See Annus (Apoc).

ANVIL, an'vil (פַּעַם, *pa'am*): The word is used only once to mean anvil. The passage (Isa **41** 7) refers to the custom still very common of workmen encouraging each other at their work. See Crafts. Just how pretentious the anvil of the ancients was we do not know. Most work requiring striking or beating, from the finest wrought jewelry to the largest copper vessels, is now done on an anvil shaped like an inverted letter L which is driven into a block of wood, or into the ground, or into a crack between two of the stone slabs of the workman's floor. The only massive anvils seen in the country today are modern and of foreign make.
James A. Patch

APACE, a-pās' ("at a pace"): With "come," 2 S **18** 25; "flee," Jer **46** 5, for "rapidly," "hastily," "fast," corresponding to a Heb idiom that adds emphasis or intensity to an idea by repetition of the word or its equivalent.

APAME, a-pā'mē, ap'a-mē (**'Απάμη**, *Apámē*): A concubine of Darius and a daughter of Bartacus the Illustrious, whose behavior to the king is referred to in a speech of Zerubbabel before the king to prove to him the great power of women (1 Esd **4** 29). See Bartacus; Illustrious.

APART, a-pärt' (בַּד, *badh*, "separation," i.e. alone, by oneself; נִדָּה, *niddāh*, "uncleanness," i.e. something put away: "an abomination"): In Zec **12** 12–14 the former word is used eleven times with powerful effect to indicate the separation of families and the isolation of wives through excessive grief in Jerus on account of the slain Messiah. The latter word signifies removal from ceremonial uncleanness (Lev **15** 19; **18** 19; Ezk **22** 10). In Gr, κατ' ἰδίαν, *kat' idian*, "by themselves," of marked significance as expressing Christ's desire for privacy in prayer, alone or with His disciples; either in a desert (Mt **14** 13); a mountain (ver 23); or a high mountain, at the time of the transfiguration (**17** 1.19), thus suggestive of the secrecy of prayer and communion with God. Used with reference also to Christ's disclosures of His purpose and of the purport of His teaching in private to His disciples (Mt **20** 17). Dwight M. Pratt

APE, āp (קוֹף, *ḳōph*): The word occurs only in the two ‖ passages (1 K **10** 22; 2 Ch **9** 21) in which the magnificence of Solomon is illustrated by the things which are brought to him from foreign countries. Apes are mentioned with gold, silver, ivory and peacocks. Peacocks are natives of India and Ceylon. Apes and ivory may have been brought from India or Africa. Gold and silver may have come from these or other quarters. An Indian origin may be inferred from the fact that the Heb *ḳōph*, the Gr *kēbos*

Monkey from the Praenestine Mosaic.

(κῆβος) and the Eng. ape are akin to the Sanskrit *kapi*, which is referred to the root *kap, kamp*, "to tremble"; but the question of the source of these imports depends upon what is understood by Tarshish and Ophir (q.v.). Canon Cheyne in *EB* (s.v. "Peacock") proposes a reading which would give "gold, silver, ivory and precious stones" instead of "gold, silver, ivory, apes and peacocks." Assuming, however, that animals are here referred to, the word ape should be understood to mean some kind of monkey. The word ape is sometimes used for the tailless apes or anthropoids such as the gorilla, the chimpanzee and the orang-outang, as opposed to the tailed kinds, but this distinction is not strictly held to, and the usage seems formerly to have been freer than now. Alfred Ely Day

APELLES, a-pel'ēz (**'Απελλῆς**, *Apellḗs*): A Christian at Rome to whom Paul sends greetings

(Rom **16** 10). He is described by Paul as "the approved in Christ," i.e. "that approved Christian" (Denney). In some way unknown to us Apelles had been tested and he had proved faithful (cf Jas **1** 12; 2 Tim **2** 15). It is a common name. Many commentators refer to Horace (*Satires*, i.5.100): "Credat Judaeus Apella, non ego."

APHAEREMA, a-fēr'ē-ma (**'Αφαίρεμα,** *Aphaírema* and *Aphérema;* AV **Apherema**). One of three districts taken from Samaria and added to Judaea by Demetrius Nicator (1 Macc **11** 34). Cf *Ant*, XIII, iv, 9.

APHARSATHCHITES, af-ar-sath'kīts, **APHARSACHITES,** a-fär'sak-īts (אֲפַרְסַתְכָיֵא, *'ăpharṣath-khāyē'*): A tribe living in Samaria that protested against the rebuilding of the Temple, and brought their complaint to Darius (Ezr **4** 9; **5** 6; **6** 6). The tribe has not yet been recognized with any certainty in the inscriptions. Rawlinson identifies them with the Persians; other scholars deny that any Assyr king was ever so situated as to have been able to obtain colonists from Persia. Some maintain with Marquardt that the term is not the name of a tribe, but the title of certain officers under Darius. Fred. Delitzsch suggests the inhabitants of one of the two great Medean towns "Partakka" and "Partukka" mentioned in Esarhaddon's inscriptions. Andreas plausibly connects it with the Assyr *šuparšak* (Muss-Arnolt, *Assyr Dict.*, 1098), *šaqu* (3) "general"; Scheft takes it from an old Iranian word *aparasarka*, "lesser ruler." H. J. WOLF

APHARSITES, a-fär'sīts (אֲפָרְסָיֵא, *'ăphārṣāyē'*): A tribe transferred to Samaria by Asnappar of Assyria (Ezr **4** 9). Rawlinson identifies them with the APHARSACHITES (q.v.), taking Apharsites to be an accidental repetition of the same word. He understands "the Persians" to be meant in both cases. Others identify them with a Median tribe mentioned in the inscriptions of Sennacherib as dwellers in the district of Parsua.

APHEK, ā'fek (אֲפֵק, *'ăphēḳ*, "fortress"; **'Αφέκ,** *Aphék*):

(1) In Josh **12** 18 we should probably read with the LXX "the king of Aphek in Sharon." This may correspond to Aphek in 1 S **4** 1. It was a royal city of the Canaanites whose king was slain by Josh. Probably it is the Aphek mentioned by Jos as being near to Antipatris (*BJ*, II, xix, 1). *Kakon*, a strong position commanding the main entrance to Samaria might suit; but the name has perished.

(2) (Gr *Taphék* or *Aphekά*): A city in the lot of Asher (Josh **13** 4). The inhabitants were not ejected by Asher, nor is it said that they became tributary (Jgs **1** 31). In this passage it is written *'ăphīḳ* (Heb). It may be represented by *'Afḳa* on *Nahr Ibrahīm*, although this is probably farther north than we should expect.

(3) To this place the Philis gathered their hosts, while the Israelites pitched by the fountain which is in Jezreel (1 S **29** 1). It has been generally supposed that these two positions were over against each other, and that therefore Aphek must be sought in the plain of Esdraelon. No place answering this description has been found here. *Fuḳū'ah* on Mount Gilboa is plainly impossible. If, however, this was only the rallying point of the Philis from which they went up to Jezreel (ver 11), it may be identical with the Aphek in the plain of Sharon (cf 1 above).

(4) A city on the plateau east of the Jordan, where disaster befell Benhadad (1 K **20** 26.30). The same place may be intended in **2** K **13** 17. The modern *Fīḳ* or *Afīḳ* (for both forms are heard) on the brow of the hill beyond *Ḳal'at el-Ḥuṣn*, east of the Sea of Galilee, probably represents this ancient city. W. EWING

APHEKAH, a-fē'ka (אֲפֵקָה, *'ăphēḳāh*, "force" or "strength"): An unidentified city in the hill country of Judah (Josh **15** 53).

APHEREMA, a-fer'ē-ma. See APHAEREMA (Apoc).

APHERRA, a-fer'a (**'Αφερρά,** *Apherrá*): Head of a family of children of Solomon's servants in the post-exilic list, one of eight listed in **1** Esd **5** 34 after Pochereth-hazzebaim of Ezr **2** 57 = Neh **7** 59.

APHIAH, a-fī'a (אֲפִיחַ, *'ăphīaḥ*): A Benjaminite and an ancestor of King Saul (1 S **9** 1).

APHIK, ā'fik: Variant of APHEK (q.v.).

APHRAH, af'ra: AV form for RV BETH-LE-APHRAH (Mic **1** 10).

APHSES, af'sēz: AV form for RV HAPPIZZEZ (1 Ch **24** 15).

APOCALYPSE, a-pok'a-lips. See APOCALYPTIC LITERATURE; REVELATION OF JOHN.

APOCALYPSE OF BARUCH, bā'ruk. See APOCALYPTIC LITERATURE.

APOCALYPTIC LITERATURE, a-pok-a-lip'tik lit'ēr-a-ṭūr:

A series of pseudepigraphic works, mainly of Jewish origin, appeared during the period between 210 BC and 200 AD. They have many features in common. The most striking is the resemblance they all bear to the Book of Daniel. Following this model, most of them use "vision" as a literary device by which to introduce their conceptions of the remote future. A side product of this same movement was the composition, mainly in Alexandria, of the Sibylline books. The literary device of "vision" was one used in the *Aeneid* by Virgil, the classical contemporary of a large number of these works. One peculiarity in regard to the majority of these documents is the fact that while popular among the Christian writers of the first Christian cents., they disappeared with the advent of the Middle Ages, and remained unknown until the first half of the 19th cent. was well on in its course.

INTRODUCTORY

I. Background of Apocalyptic.—When the Jews came back from Babylon to Palestine, though surrounded by heathen of various creeds, they were strongly monotheistic. The hold the Persians had of the empire of S.W. Asia, and their religion—Zoroastrianism—so closely akin to monotheism, prevented any violent attempts at perverting the Jews. With the advent of the Gr power a new state of things emerged. Certainly at first there does not seem to have been any direct attempt to force them to abandon their religion, but the calm contempt of the Hellene who looked down from the superior height of his artistic culture on all barbarians, and the influence that culture had in the ruling classes tended to seduce the Jews into idolatry. While the governing orders, the priests and the leaders of the Council, those who came in contact with the generals and governors of the Lagids of Egypt, or the Seleucids of Syria, were thus inclined to be seduced into idolatry, there was a large class utterly uninfluenced by Hellenic culture, and no small portion of this class hated fanatically all tampering with idolatry. When the dominion over Pal passed out of the hands of the Ptolemies into that of the house of Seleucus, this feeling was intensified, as the Syrian house regarded with less tolerance the religion of Israel. The opposition to Hellenism and the apprehension of it naturally tended to draw together those who shared the feeling. On the one side was the scribist legal party, who developed into the Pharisaic sect; on the other were the mystics, who felt the personal power of Deity. These afterward became first the Chasidim, then later the Essenes. These latter gradually retired from active participation in national life. As is natural with mystics their feelings led them to see visions and to dream dreams. Others more intellectual, while they welcomed the enlightenment of the Greeks, retained their faith in the one God. To them it seemed obvious that as their God was the true God, all real enlightenment must have proceeded from Him alone. In such thinkers as Plato and Aristotle they saw many things in harmony with the Mosaic law. They were sure that there must have been links which united these thinkers to the current of Divine revelation, and were led to imagine of what sort these links necessarily were. The names of poets such as Orpheus and Linus, who survived only in their names, suggested the source of these links—these resemblances. Hence the wholesale forgeries, mainly by Jews, of Gr poems. On the other hand, there was the desire to harmonize Moses and his law with the philosophical ideas of the time. Philo the Alexandrian, the most conspicuous example of this effort, could not have been an isolated phenomenon; he must have had many precursors. This latter movement, although most evident in Egypt, and probably in Asia Minor, had a considerable influence in Judaea also.

1. Judaism and Hellenism

Political events aided in the advance of both these tendencies. The distinct favor that Antiochus the Great showed to the Greeks and to those barbarians who Hellenized, became with his son Antiochus Epiphanes a direct religious persecution. This emphasized the protest of the Chasidim on the one hand, and excited the imagination of the visionaries to greater vivacity on the other. While the Maccabees and their followers were stirred to deeds of valor, the meditative visionaries saw in God their refuge, and hoped for deliverance at the hand of the Messiah. They pictured to themselves the tyrant smitten down by the direct judgment of Jehovah. After the death of Epiphanes, the Maccabeans had become a power to be reckoned with, and the visionaries had less excitement from external events till the Herodian family found their way into supreme power. At first the Herodians favored the Pharisaic party as that which supported John Hyrcanus II, the friend of Antipater, the father of Herod the Great, and the Essenes seem to have taken Herod at first into their special favor. However, there was soon a change. In consequence of the compliance with heathen practices, into which their connection with the Romans forced the Herodians, the more religious among the Jews felt themselves compelled to withdraw all favor from the Idumean usurper, and to give up all hope in him. This naturally excited the visionaries to new expectation of Divine intervention. Behind the Herodians was the terrible iron power of Rome. The Romans had intervened in the quarrel between John Hyrcanus II and his brother Aristobulus. Pompey had desecrated the temple by intruding into the Holy of Holies. The disastrous overthrow that he suffered at the hands of Caesar and his miserable end on the shores of Egypt seemed to be a judgment on him for his impiety. Later, Nero was the especial mark for the Apocalyptists, who by this time had become mainly Christian. Later Rom emperors impressed the imagination of the Apocalyptists, as the Flavians.

2. Political Influences

II. General Characteristics of Apocalyptic.—Both in matter and form apocalyptic lit. and the writings associated with it differ from the prophetic writings of the preceding periods. As already mentioned, while the predictive element is present in Apocalypses, as in Prophecy, it is more prominent and relates to longer periods and involves a wider grasp of the state of the world at large. Apocalypse could only have been possible under the domination of the great empires. Alike in Prophecy and in Apocalypse there is reference to the coming of the Messiah, but in the latter not only is the Messianic hope more defined, it has a wider reference. In the Prophets and Psalmists the Messiah had mainly to do with Israel. "He will save his people"; "He will die for them"; "His people shall be all righteous." All this applies to Israel; there is no imperial outlook. In the Apocalypses the imperial outlook is prominent, beginning with Daniel in which we find the Messianic kingdom represented by a "son of man" over against the bestial empires that had preceded (Dnl **7** 13) and reaching the acme of Apocalypse, if not its conclusion, in the Rev of St. John: "The kingdom of the world is become the kingdom of our Lord, and of his Christ" (Rev **11** 15). While the prophet was primarily a preacher of righteousness, and used prediction either as a

1. Differences from Prophecy in Content

guarantee, by its fulfilment, of his Divine mission, or as an exhibition of the natural result of rebellion against God's righteous laws, to the Apocalyptist prediction was the thing of most importance, and in the more typical Apocalypse there is no moral exhortation whatever.

2. Differences from Prophecy in Literary Form

In the literary form employed there are marked differences between Apocalyptic and Prophecy. Both make use of vision, but in Prophecy, in the more restricted sense of the word, these visions are as a rule implied, rather than being described. Although Isaiah calls the greater part of his Prophecy "vision," yet in only one instance does he describe what he sees; as a rule he assumes throughout that his audience knows what is visible to him. The only instance (ch **6**) in which he does describe his vision is not at all predictive; the object is exhortation. In the case of the Apocalypses the vision is the vehicle by which the prediction is conveyed. In Ezekiel there are visions, but only one of these—"the valley of dry bones"—is predictive. In it the symbols used are natural, not, as always in Apocalypses, arbitrary. Cf in Daniel's vision of the Ram and the He-goat (ch **8**). In Ezekiel the dry bones naturally suggest death, and the process by which they are revivified the reader feels is the natural course such an event would take did it come within the sphere of ordinary experience; while in what is told of the horns on the head of the Gr goat there is no natural reason for the changes that take place, only a symbolical one. This is still more marked in the vision of the Eagle in 4 Esd **11**. What may be regarded as yet more related to the form is the fact that while the Prophets wrote in a style of so elevated prose that it always hovered on the border of poetry—indeed, frequently passed into it and employed the form of verse, as Isa **26** 1—the apocalyptists always used pure prose, without the elaborate parallelism or cadenced diction of Heb poetry. The weird, the gorgeous, or the terrible features of the vision described are thrown into all the higher relief by the baldness of the narrative.

III. Authorship of Jewish Apocalyptic Works.—In most cases the question of authorship is one that has to be discussed in regard to each work individually.

1. Pseudepigraphic Authors not Known Individually

A number of the characteristics of these works render such a procedure impossible in regard to them. If we put to the one side the two Apocalypses that form part of the canon, they are all pseudonymous, as En and Bar, or anonymous, as the Book of Jub. Many of them in addition show traces of interpolation and modification by later hands. If we had a full and clear history of the period during which they were written, and if its literature had to a great extent been preserved to us we might have been in a position to fix on the individual; but as matters stand, this is impossible. At the same time, however, from internal evidence, we may form some idea of the surroundings of those who have written these works. From the striking resemblance in general style which they exhibit, and from the way in which some of them are related to the others, many of these works seem to have been the product of similar circumstances.

2. Products of One Sect

Even those most removed from the rest in type and general attitude are nearer them than they are to any other class of work. All affirmative evidence thus points to these works having been composed by authors that were closely associated with each other. The negative evidence for this is the very small traceable influence these works had on later Jewish thought. Many of them are quoted by the Christian Fathers, some of them by NT writers. The whole of these works have been preserved to us through Christian means. A large number have been preserved by being adopted into the OT canon of the Ethiopic church; a considerable number have been unearthed from Ambrosian Library in Milan; most of them have been written in Pal by Jewish writers; yet no clear indubitable sign of the knowledge of these books can be found in the Talm.

3. Jewish Sects

The phenomenon here noted is a striking one. Works, the majority of which are written in Heb by Jews, are forgotten by the descendants of these Jews, and are retained by gentile Christians, by nations who were ignorant of Heb and preserved them in Gr, Lat or Ethiopic translations. A characteristic of the Judaism during the period in which these books were appearing was the power exercised by certain recognized sects. If one takes the most nearly contemporary historian of the Jews, Jos, as one's authority, it is found how prominent the three sects, Pharisees, Sadducees and Essenes, were. To a certain extent this is confirmed by the Gospels and the Acts, with this noticeable exception—the Essenes are never mentioned by name.

4. Not from Sadducees

The scribes, the literary class among the Jews, all belonged to one or other of these ruling sects. Consequently these works must have proceeded from members of one of those sects. Their mutual resemblance precludes their authors from belonging some to one sect and some to another. We know pretty exactly from Jos and the NT what the character and tenets of the Sadducees were. They were the priestly sacerdotal class, and were above all, political schemers. They received only the Pent as authoritative, and had no share in the Messianic hopes of which the Prophets were full. They believed neither in angel nor spirit, and had no hope of immortality (Acts **23** 8). Jos compares them with the followers of Epicurus among the Greeks. Nothing could be farther removed from the spirit and doctrines of the Apocalypses than all this. The Messianic hopes bulk largely; angels are prominent, their hierarchies are described and their names given. The doctrine of immortality is implied, and the places of reward and punishment are described. The Apocalypses cannot therefore be attributed to the Sadducees. There is greater plausibility in attributing them to the Pharisees. So far as doctrines are concerned, there is no doubt that the agreement is relatively close. There are, however, difficulties in accepting this view of their origin.

5. Nor from the Pharisees

With the fall of the Jewish state, the Sadducees disappeared when there was no field for political activity, and when with the destruction of the temple there were no more sacrifices to require the services of Aaronic priests. Nearly contemporaneously the Essenes disappeared in Christianity. The Pharisees alone remained to carry on the traditions of Judaism. We have in the Talm the result of Pharisaic literary activity. The Mish is the only part of this miscellaneous conglomeration which is at all nearly contemporary with the works before us. It has none of the characteristics of the apocalyptic writings. The later Hagadic Midr have more resemblance to some of these, noticeably to the Book of Jub. Still, the almost total want of any references to any of the Apocalypses in the recognized Pharisaic writings, and the fact that no Jewish version of any of these books has been preserved, seems conclusive against the idea that the Apocalypses owed their origin to the Pharisaic schools. The books that form the ordinary Apoc are in a different position. The majority, if not the whole of them, were received into the Jewish canon of Alexandria. Some of them are found in Heb or Aram., as Ecclus, Tob and Jth. None of the Apocalypses have been so found. This leads necessarily to the conclusion that the Pharisees did not write these books.

By the method of exclusions, we are led thus to adopt the conclusion of Hilgenfeld, that they are the work of the Essenes. We have, however, positive evidence. We know from Jos that the Essenes had many secret sacred books. Those books before us would suit this description. Further, in one of these books (4 Esd) we find a story which affords an explanation of the existence of these books. 2 (4) Esd **14** 40–48 tells how to Ezra there was given a cup of water as it were fire to drink, and then he dictated to five men. These men wrote in characters which they did not understand "for forty days," until they had written "four score and fourteen books" (RV). He is commanded, "The first that thou hast written publish openly, and let the worthy and unworthy read it: but keep the seventy last that thou mayest deliver them to such as be wise among thy people." While the twenty-four books of the ordinary canon would be open to all, these other seventy books would only be known by the wise—presumably, the Essenes. This story proceeds on the assumption that all the Biblical books had been lost during the Bab captivity, but that after he had his memory quickened, Ezra was able to dictate the whole of them; but of these only twenty-four were to be published to all; there were seventy which were to be kept by a society of wise men. This would explain how the Books of En and Noah, and the account of the Asm M could appear upon the scene at proper times, and yet not be known before. In the last-named book there is another device. Moses tells Joshua to embalm (*hedriare*) the writing which gives an account of what is coming upon Israel. Books so embalmed would be liable to be found when Divine providence saw the occasion ripe. These works are products of a school of associates which could guard sacred books and had prepared hypotheses to explain at once how they had remained unknown, and how at certain crises they became known. All this suits the Essenes, and especially that branch of them that dwelt as Coenobites beside the Dead Sea. We are thus driven to adopt Hilgenfeld's hypothesis that the Essenes were the authors of these books. Those of them that formed the Community of Engedi by their very dreamy seclusion would be especially ready to see visions and dream dreams. To them it would seem no impossible thing for one of the brotherhood to be so possessed by the spirit of Enoch or of Noah that what he wrote were really the words of the patriarch. It would not be inconceivable, or even improbable, that Moses or Josh might in a dream open to them books written long before and quicken their memories so that what they had read in the night they could recite in the day-time. As all the Essenes were not dwellers by the shores of the Dead Sea, or "associates with the palms of Engedi," some of the writings of this class, as we might expect, betray a greater knowledge of the world, and show more the influence of events than those which proceeded from the Coenobites. As to some extent confirmatory of this view, there is the slight importance given to sacrifice in most of these works.

6. Probably from Essenes

Works Entitled Apocalyptic

In the classification of plants and animals in natural science the various orders and genera present the observer with some classes that have all the features that characterize the general class prominent and easily observable, while in others these features are so far from prominent that to the casual observer they are invisible. This may be seen in the apocalyptic writings: there are some that present all the marks of *Apocalypses*, such as the Book of Enoch, the Asm M and the Apoc Bar. They all claim to be revelations of the future—a future which begins, however, from the days of some ancient saint—and then, passing over the time of its actual composition, ends with the coming of the Messiah, the setting up of the Messianic kingdom and the end of the world. There are others, like the Book of Jub, in which the revelation avowedly looks back, and which thus contain an amount of legendary matter. One of the books which are usually reckoned in this class, has, unlike most of the Apocalypses, which are in prose, taken the Book of Psalms as its model—the Ps Sol. A very considerable number of the works before us take the form of farewell counsels on the part of this or that patriarch. The most famous of these is the XII P. Although the great majority have been written in Heb or Aram by Jews resident in Pal, the Sibylline books, composed to a great extent by Jews of Alexandria, present an exception to this.

Classes of Books

We shall in the remainder of the art. consider these sub-classes in the order now mentioned: (1) Typical Apocalypses; (2) Legendary Testaments; (3) Psalmic; (4) Testaments; (5) Sibylline Oracles.

I. Apocalypses Proper.—As above indicated, all these take the Book of Daniel as their model, and imitate it more or less closely. One peculiarity in this connection must be referred to. While we have already said these later Apocalypses were practically unknown by the Jews of a couple of cents. after the Christian era, the Book of Dnl was universally regarded as authoritative alike by Jews and Christians. In considering these works, we shall restrict ourselves to those Apocalypses that, whether Jewish or Christian by religion, are the production of those who were Jews by nation.

The most important of these is the Book, or rather, Books of Enoch. After having been quoted in Jude and noticed by several of the Fathers, this work disappeared from the knowledge of the Christian church.

1. Books of Enoch

(1) *History of the books.*—Fairly copious extracts from this collection of books had been made by George Syncellus, the 8th cent. chronographer. With the exception of those fragments, all the writings attributed to Enoch had disappeared from the ken of European scholars. In the last quarter of the 18th cent. Bruce, the Abyssinian traveler, brought to Europe three copies of the Book of En in Ethiopic, which had been regarded as canonical by the Abyssinian church, and had consequently been preserved by them. Of these three copies, one he retained in Kinnaird House, another he presented to the Bodleian Library in Oxford, the third he gave to the Royal Library in Paris. For more than a quarter of a cent. these manuscripts remained as unknown as if they had still been in Abyssinia. In the year 1800 Sylvestre de Sacy published an art. on Enoch in which he gave a tr of the first sixteen chs. This was drawn from the Parisian copy. Twenty-one years after Archbishop Laurence published a tr of the whole work from the MS in the Bodleian. Seventeen years after he published the text from the same MS. The expedition to Magdala under Lord Napier brought a number of fresh MSS to Europe; the German missionaries, for whose release the advance had been undertaken, brought a number to Germany, while a number came to the British

Museum. Some other travelers had brought from the East MSS of this precious book. Flemming, the latest R of the text, claims to have used 26 MSS. It needs but a cursory study of the Ethiopic text to see that it is a tr from a Gr original. The quotations in George Syncellus confirmed this, with the exception of a small fragment published by Mai. Until the last decade of last cent. Syncellus' fragments formed the only remains of the Gr text known. In 1892 M. Bouriant published from MSS found in Gizeh, Cairo, the Gr of the first 32 chs. More of the Gr may be discovered in Egypt. Meantime we have the Gr of chs **1–32,** and from the Vatican fragment a portion of ch **89**. A study of the Gr shows it also to have been a tr from a Heb original. Of this Heb original, however, no part has come down to us.

As we have it, it is very much a conglomeration of fragments of various authorship. It is impossible to say whether the Gr translator was the collector of these fragments or whether, when the mass of material came into his hands, the interpolations had already taken place. However, the probability, judging from the usual practice of translators, is that as he got the book, so he translated it.

(2) *Summary of the book.*—The first chapter gives an account of the purpose of the book, chs **2–5** an account of his survey of the heavens. With **6** begins the book proper. Chs **6–19** give an account of the fallen angels and Enoch's relation to them. Chs **20–36** narrate Enoch's wanderings through the universe, and give an account of the place of punishment, and the secrets of the West and of the center of the earth. This may be regarded as the First Book of Enoch, the Book of the Angels. With ch **37** begins the Book of Similitudes. The first Similitude (chs **37–44**) represents the future kingdom of God, the dwelling of the righteous and of the angels; and finally all the secrets of the heavens. This last portion is interesting as revealing the succession of the parts of this conglomeration—the more elaborate the astronomy, the later; the simpler, the earlier. The second Similitude (chs **45–57**) brings in the Son of Man as a superhuman if not also superangelic being, who is to come to earth as the Messiah. The third Similitude occupies chs **58–71,** and gives an account of the glory of the Messiah and of the subjugation of the kings of the earth under Him. There is interpolated a long account of Leviathan and Behemoth. There are also Noachian fragments inserted. The Book of the Courses of the Luminaries occupies the next eleven chs, and subjoined to these are two visions (chs **83–90**), in the latter of which is an account of the history of the world to the Maccabean Struggle. Fourteen chs which follow may be called "The Exhortations of Enoch." The exhortations are emphasized by an exposition of the history of the world in 10 successive weeks. It may be noted here that there is a dislocation. The passage **91** 12 contains the 8, 9, and 10 weeks, while ch **93** gives an account of the previous 7. After ch **104** there are series of sections of varying origin which may be regarded as appendices. There are throughout these books many interpolations. The most observable of these are what are known as "Noachian Fragments," portions in which Noah and not Enoch is the hero and spokesman. There are, besides, a number of universally acknowledged interpolations, and some that are held by some to be interpolated, are regarded by others as intimately related to the immediate context. The literary merit of the different portions is various: of none of them can it be called high. The Book of Similitudes, with its revelations of heaven and hell, is probably the finest.

(3) *The language.*—We have the complete books only in Ethiopic. The Ethiopic, however, is not, as already observed, the original language of the writings. The numerous portions of it which still survive in Gr, prove that at all events our Ethiopic is a tr from the Gr. The question of how far it is the original is easily settled. The angels assemble on Mt. Hermon, we are told (ch **6**), and bind themselves by an oath or curse: "and they called it Mount Hermon because they had sworn and bound themselves by mutual imprecation upon it." This has a meaning only in Heb or Aram., not in Gr. A very interesting piece of evidence of the original language is got from a blunder. In **90** 38 we are told that "they all became white bullocks, and the first was the Word" (*nagara*). As for the appearance of this term, from its connection it is obvious that some sort of bullocks is intended. In Heb the wild ox is called *rᵉʼēm* (Aram. *rîma*). The Gr translators, having no Gr equivalent available, transliterated as *rēm* or *rēma*. This the translators confused with *Tēma*, "a word." It is impossible to decide with anything like certainty which of the two languages, Heb or Aram., was the original, though from the sacred character ascribed to Enoch the probability is in favor of its being Heb.

(4) *The date.*—The question of date is twofold. Since Enoch is really made up of a collection of books and fragments of books, the question of the temporal relation of these to each other is the primary one. The common view is that chs **1–36** and **72–91** are by the same author, and form the nucleus of the whole. Although the weighty authority of Dr. Charles is against assigning these portions to one author, the resemblances are numerous and seem to us by no means so superficial as he would regard them. He, with most critics, would regard the Book of Similitudes as later. Nevertheless, we venture to differ from this view, for reasons which we shall assign.

(5) *The Book of Noah.*—The fragments of the Book of Noah above alluded to present an intrusive element in the Book of En. These, though fairly numerous, are not so numerous as Dr. Charles would claim. Those that show clear traces not only of being interpolations, but also of being interpolations from this Book of Noah, are found only in those portions of the Book that appear to be written by the author of chs **37–71.** In them and in the Noachian fragments there are astronomical portions, as there are also in the portion that seems to proceed from another hand, chs **1–36, 72–91.** When these are compared, the simplest account of the phenomena of the heavens is found in the non-Noachian portions, the first noted chs **37–71, 92–107;** the next in complexity is that found in the Noachian interpolations; the most complex is that contained in chs **72–91.** This would seem to indicate that the earliest written portion was chs **37–71, 92–107.** Our view of the date of this middle portion of En, the Book of Similitudes, is opposed by Dr. Stanton (*Jewish and Christian Messiah*, 60–63, 241–44), who maintains that it is post-Christian. For this decision he rests mainly on the use of the title "Son of Man." This title, he says, as applied to the Messiah, is unknown in rabbinic lit. Rabbinic lit. is all so late as to be of no value. The Mish has few traces of Messianic belief, and was not committed to writing till the end of the 2d cent., when the difference between church and synagogue was accentuated. He further states that it was not understood by the Jews who heard our Lord, and brings as proof Jn **12** 34, "The Son of Man must be lifted up. Who is this—the Son of Man?" Dr. Stanton (*Jewish and Christian Messiah*, 241) so translates the passage. To us, the last clause is a mistr. The Gr usage in regard to *hoútos ho* would lead

us to translate: "Who is this peculiar kind of Son of Man?" This is the meaning which suits the context. Our Lord had not in all the preceding speech used the title "Son of Man" of Himself. This sentence really proves that the multitude regarded the title as equivalent to Messiah or Christ. It might be paraphrased, "The Christ abideth ever; how sayest thou then, the Christ must be lifted up? Who is this Christ?" In fact, Our Lord's adoption of the title is unintelligible unless it were understood by His audience as a claim to being Messiah. It had the advantage that it could not be reported to the Romans as treasonable. There are supplementary portions of En which may be neglected. At first sight **10** 1-3 appear to declare themselves as Noachian, but close inspection shows this to be a misapprehension. If we take the Gr text of Syncellus, Uriel is the angel sent to Noah. The Ethiopic and Gizeh Gr are at this point clearly corrupt. Then the introduction of Raphael implies that the first portion of this ch and this Raphael section are by the same author. But the Raphael section has to do with the binding of Azazel, a person intimately connected with the earlier history of the Jews. Should it be objected that according to the Massoretic reckoning, as according to that of the LXX, Noah and Enoch were not living together, it may be answered that according to the Sam they were for 180 years contemporaries. In ch **68** Noah speaks of Enoch as his grandfather, and assumes him to be a contemporary of himself. Moreover, we must not expect precise accuracy from Apocalyptists.

(6) *Relation of external chronology.*—When the internal chronology of the book is fixed, the way is open for considering the relation of external chronology. Dr. Charles has proved that the Book of Jub implies the Noachian portion in the Enoch Books. There are notices of the existence of a Book of Noah (**10** 13). There is reference also to a Book of En (**21** 10). Dr. Charles would date the Book of Jub between 135 and 105 BC. If, then, the Book of Noah was already known, and, as we have seen, the Book of En was yet older, it would be impossible to date En earlier than 160 BC. Personally we are not quite convinced of the correctness of Dr. Charles's reasonings as to the date of the Book of Jub, as will be shown at more length later. There appears to us a reference in En **66** 5 to the campaign of Antiochus the Great against the Parthians and the Medes. Early in his reign (220 BC) he had made an expedition to the East against the revolted provinces of Media and Persia, which he subdued. This was followed (217 BC) by a campaign in Pal, which at first successful, ended in the defeat of Raphia. In the year 212 BC he made a second expedition to the East, in which he invaded India, and subdued into alliance the formidable Parthian and Bactrian kingdoms. The expectation was natural that now, having gained such an access of power and reputation, Antiochus would desire to wipe out the dishonor of Raphia. It was to be anticipated that along with the nationalities from which ordinarily the Syr armies were recruited, the Parthians would be found, and the earlier subdued Medes. The description of the treading down of the land of the Elect is too mild for a description of the desecration wrought by Epiphanes. If we are right, we may fix on 205 BC, as the probable date of the nucleus. The Book of the Luminaries of the Heavens which we feel inclined to attribute to the same hand as chs **1-36** contains a history of Israel that terminates with the Maccabean Struggle still proceeding. Dr. Charles would date this portion 161 BC. Personally, we should be inclined to place it a few years earlier. He would place chs **1-36** before the Maccabean Struggle. According to our thinking the genuine Noachian fragments fall between these. The Book of Noah seems to have existed as a separate book in the time when the Book of Jub was written. It is dependent on Enoch, and therefore after it. The use of portions taken from it to interpolate in the En Books must have taken place before the Maccabean Struggle. There are other passages that have every appearance of being interpolations, the date of which it is impossible to fix with any definiteness.

(7) *The Slavonic Enoch.*—In the year 1892 the attention of Dr. Charles was directed to the fact that a Book of En was extant in Slavonic. Perusal proved it not to be a version of the book before us, but another and later pseudepigraphic book, taking, as the earlier had done, the name of Enoch. It is totally independent of the Ethiopic En Book, as is seen by the most cursory consideration. It begins by giving an account of En's instruction to his descendants how he had been taken up to the seventh heaven. Another manuscript adds other three heavens. In the third (?) heaven Enoch is shown the place of the punishment of the wicked. In the description of the fourth heaven there is an account of the physical conditions of the universe, in which the year is said to be $365\frac{1}{4}$ days; but the course of the sun is stated as a course of 227 days; which appears to be all that is accounted for. Here the independence of the Slavonic En is clear, as the Ethiopic En makes the year 364 days. There are many points of resemblance which show that the writer of the Slavonic En had before him the book which has come down to us in Ethiopic, but the relationship is not by any means so close as to be called dependence. The definite numbering of the heavens into seven or ten is a proof of its later date. It is related to the XII P, and also to the Asc Isa. We cannot quite acknowledge the cogency of the proofs that any portion of this Book has been composed in Gr: hence we cannot agree with Dr. Charles that it was composed in Alexandria. The resemblances to Philo are too few and slight to be convincing. That some of it was originally Heb Dr. Charles admits. The date Dr. Charles assigns to it—1-50 AD—seems reasonable, with this qualification, that it seems nearer the later than the earlier of these dates. A double tr, with the certainty of some interpolations and the probability of many more, makes any decided judgment as to date hazardous, so much has to depend on resemblances between books in cases where it is impossible to decide which is dependent on which. It is at once an interesting and a valuable addition to our knowledge of the mind of the age preceding the publication of the gospel.

(8) *Secrets of Enoch.*—In imitation of this Book and in some sense in dependence on it was written a rabbinic Book of the Secrets of En. It is attributed to Rabbi Ishmael, who was a prominent figure in the rebellion of Barcochba. En is there noted as Metatron. It follows to some extent the course of the Slavonic Book of En. It is this book that is referred to in the Talm, not the more important book quoted by Jude.

Though not without its value in estimating the trend of pre-Christian speculation, the Apocalypse of Bar did not influence thought in the way that the Books of En have done. It is neither quoted nor referred to by any of the Christian Fathers. Irenaeus (V, 33) quotes a saying which he attributes to Our Lord on the authority of Papias, who claims to have in this attribution the authority of John behind him. This saying we find in the Apocalypse before us, though considerably expanded. In regard to this,

2. Apocalypse of Baruch

in the first place we have only the Lat VS of Irenaeus, not the Gr original. In the next place, even though the Lat may be a faithful tr of the Gr, still it is only a quotation from a lost book, which itself records traditions. The fact that it is in the shortest form in the book before us would seem to indicate that it is the original. If that is so, we may regard it as having a certain vogue among the Essenian school and their sympathizers. In the Syr Apocrypha published by Lagarde there is a small book entitled "The Epistle of Baruch the Scribe." This occurs at the end of our Apocalypse of Bar. In Cyprian's *Test. contra Jud.*, III, 29, we have a passage of considerable length attributed to Bar, a few words of which agree with a passage in this Apocalypse. Hippolytus quotes an oath used by certain Gnostics which he says is found in the Book of Bar. There are features in the passage thus quoted which seem to be echoes of the book before us. This was all that was known of the Apocalypse of Bar until the last half-cent., when Ceriani discovered a Syr version of it in the Ambrosian Library in Milan, nearly complete.

(1) *Summary of the book.*—It begins after the model of a prophecy: "The word of the Lord came to Baruch, the son of Neriah, saying." In this he follows the phraseology of Jeremiah. He and Jeremiah are commanded to leave Jerus as God is about to pour forth His judgment upon it. Baruch entreats God for his city, and God shows him that the punishment will be temporary. Then the Chaldaeans come to fulfil what God has threatened, but Baruch is shown the angel ministers of Divine vengeance saving the sacred vessels by calling upon the earth to swallow them up. Then the angels helped the Chaldaeans to overthrow the walls of Jerus. Notwithstanding that in the canonical Book of Jer (**43** 6.7) and in 2 K the prophet goes down to Egypt, Baruch declares that Jeremiah is sent to comfort the captives in Babylon, while he, Baruch, is to remain in Judaea. He mourns over Jerus and denounces woes in Babylon (chs **1–12**). While he is standing upon Mt. Zion he is called into colloquy with God as to the method of Divine dealing with Judah, and a revelation is promised him (chs **13–20**). This revelation is introduced by a prayer of Baruch followed by a colloquy with the Almighty. Baruch asks, "Will that tribulation continue a long time?" He is answered that there will be twelve successive different forms of judgment which shall come. Then follows an enigmatic sentence, "Two parts weeks of seven weeks" are "the measure and reckoning of the time" which probably means that each of the parts is a jubilee or half a cent. At the expiry of this period the Messiah is to appear. Here a description is given of the glories of the Messianic kingdom in the course of which occurs the passage already referred to as quoted by Papias (chs **21–30**). The writer, forgetting what he has already said of the desolation of Jerus, makes Bar assemble the Elders of Jerus and announce that he is going to retire into solitude. In his retirement he has a vision of a wooded hill, and at the foot of it is a vine growing and beside the vine a spring of water. This fountain swelled and became tempestuous, sweeping away all the forest on the hill but one great cedar. It, too, falls at length. The interpretation is given. The forest is the fourth Empire of Daniel—the Rom—the many magistracies being symbolized by the numerous trees of the forest. The Messiah is the vine and the fountain. It is probable that Pompey is the leader referred to (chs **31–40**). Then follows a colloquy of Baruch first with God, then with his son and the Elders of the people. A long prayer with God's answer which includes a description of the punishment of the wicked and the reward of the righteous—the latter is next given with greater fulness (chs **41–52**). Another vision is given to Baruch of twelve showers of rain alternately bright and dark and a final torrent blacker than anything else and closed by a bright light. The angel Ramiel comes to Baruch to interpret the vision. It represents the history of Israel to the return to Judaea under the decree of Cyrus. The last dark waters represent the Maccabean Struggle. It would seem as if the vision carried the conflict on to the fratricidal conflict between John Hyrcanus II and Aristobulus (chs **53–77**). Then follows the epistle to the nine and a half tribes (chs **78–87**).

(2) *Structure.*—Preliminary to anything further is the discussion of the state of the book—how far it is one, how far it is composite or interpolated. That it contains different portions is obvious on the slightest careful study. The first portion that the reader marks off is the "epistle to the nine tribes and a half." As has already been mentioned this portion appears independently and is preserved by Lagarde in his *Libri Vet. Test. Apocryphi*, in which collection it precedes the ordinary apocryphal Book of Bar. The last section, which relates how this epistle was sent to the nine tribes and a half by an eagle, is omitted. The last section (ch **79**) has been added, and has been modified in order to introduce this epistle. It is not at all in the spirit of the rest of this Apocalypse that the tribes carried away captive by "Salmanasser, king of Assyria" have any share in the blessings revealed in the vision. The epistle itself merely narrates the capture of the city, and the help of the angels who hid the sacred vessels. It is to be noted that in the earlier portion of this Apocalypse it is the earth that opens her mouth and swallows down the sacred vessels. Another division reveals itself on further scrutiny. From the beginning to the end of ch **30** the course of the narrative is fairly continuous. A revelation is promised, and in the end we have a picture of the glory and plenty of the times of the Messiah. The next section begins with an exhortation which has little bearing on what has preceded. Then follows the vision of the forest and the surviving tree. The colloquy and the prayers that follow, to ch **52**, are all connected, though not closely. But close connection is not to be expected from an oriental and an Apocalyptist. Then follow the sections connected with the vision of the twelve showers of rain, and its interpretation. There are thus five independent sections exclusive of interpolations which may be due to different writers.

(3) *Language.*—In the first place it is clear that the Syr in which the work has come down to us is itself a tr from Gr. The MS of Ceriani states this in its title. This is confirmed by Graecisms filtering through, as *ho Manasseh* in **65** 1, where *ho* represents the Gr article. In some cases the readings that are unintelligible can be explained by tr back into Gr, as shown by Dr. Charles. The most convincing is the use made of this book by the writer of the "Rest of the Words of Bar," who wrote in Gr. Although not a few scholars have followed Langen in maintaining that Gr was the original tongue, careful investigation proves that behind the Gr was Heb. The strongest of these proofs is that the echoes of Scriptural texts are almost invariably from the Heb as against the LXX. Thus in **6** 8 Jer three times addresses the earth and calls upon it to hear the word of the Lord. So it is in the MT and in the Vulg, but not in the LXX, where the word "earth" is only given twice. There are several other instances. Dr. Charles has carefully compared the idiomatic phrases and sees proof that usages of the MT have been preserved in the Gr, and thence conveyed to the Syr. The most interesting of these is the peculiar Heb idiom of infinitive with finite verb to emphasize the action

narrated. This is rendered in LXX sometimes by cognate noun and verb, and sometimes by participle and verb. The examples chosen by Dr. Charles have the disadvantage that none of them show the effect on this idiom of passing through the two languages, Gr and Syr. In Paulus Tellensis there are examples—e.g. 2 K **18** 33. He is scarcely accurate in saying that this idiom never occurs in the Pesh unless it is in the Gr. See Lk **1** 22; Jn **13** 29, etc, as examples to the contrary. The proof seems conclusive that Heb was the original language of this Apocalypse, and that it was first tr[d] into Gr, and from that into Syr. From this it follows almost necessarily that its place of origin was Pal. That it has had practically no effect on Jewish lit., and was potent enough among the Christians to lead a Christian about the middle of the 2d Christian cent. to compose an addition to it, proves to our thinking its Essenian origin.

(4) *Date.*—Although the writer assumes the destruction of Jerus by the army of the Chaldaeans, he evidently has no conception of what such a catastrophe would really mean. He has no conception of the length of time occupied by a siege, the terrors of famine, or the desolation that follows the capture of a city. Jos tells us (*BJ*, VII, i, 1) that save a portion of the west wall and three towers, the city was utterly razed to the ground—"there was nothing left to make those who came there believe that ever it had been inhabited." Yet, when endeavoring to realize the similar destruction which had befallen the city under Nebuchadnezzar, he speaks of himself sitting "before the gates of the temple" (**10** 5), when the gates had wholly disappeared. Again, he assembles the people and their elders "after these things" "in the valley of the Kedron." The Apocalypse must be dated at all events considerably before 70 AD. On the other hand, it is subsequent to the first part of En; it assumes it as known (**56** 10–13). But a closer discrimination may be reached. In the vision of the wood and the one tree that survives we have Pompey pointed out clearly. The multitude of trees points to the numerous magistracies of Rome. (Cf description of Senate of Rome in 1 Macc **8** 15.) The seer in his vision sees all these swept away and one remaining. It could not be an emperor, as that title was regarded as equivalent to "king," as Nero in the Asc Isa is called "the matricide king." The only other besides Pompey likely to be pointed to would be Julius Caesar. But the fall of the great desecrator of the temple, which the seer foresaw, would not have failed to be noted as succeeded by that of Caesar who had conquered him. It is difficult for us to realize the position Pompey occupied in the eyes especially of the eastern world before the outbreak of the civil war. Cicero's letters and his oration *Pro lege Manilia* show the way Pompey filled the horizon even in republican Rome, in a society most of the prominent members of which claimed a descent that would have enabled them to look down on Pompey. But in the East he had enjoyed dictatorial powers. His intervention in the contest between the brothers John Hyrcanus II and Aristobulus could not fail to impress the Jews, and his desecration of the temple would mark him off for a very special destruction. The date is so far before the death of Pompey (48 BC)—though after the desecration of the temple—that the possibility of anyone entering into conflict with him is not dreamed of. When we turn to the twelve showers, we are led to the time of this struggle also as that which shall immediately precede the coming of the Messiah. Another note of time is to be found in ch **28**—"The measure and reckoning of the time are two parts, weeks of seven weeks." This we regard as two jubilees—i.e. approximately a cent. The point to be fixed is the time from which this cent. is to be reckoned. To our idea it must be from some event connected with the temple. Such an event was the dedication of the temple by Judas Maccabaeus in the 148th year of the Seleucid era—that is, 163 BC. A cent. brings us exactly to the year of Pompey's capture of Jerus and desecration of the temple. Thus three different lines converge in pointing to 60 or 59 BC as the date at which this book was written.

(5) *Relation to other books.*—The strange mingling of knowledge of Scripture and ignorance of it is a phenomenon to be observed. The very first clause contains a gross anachronism, whatever explanation may be given of the statement. Taken with what follows, the statement is that Jerus was taken by Nebuchadnezzar, "in the 25th year of Jeconiah, king of Judah." This naturally ought to mean the 25th year of the reign of Jeconiah, but he only reigned three months. Whether the date is reckoned from his life or his captivity, it will not suit the date of the capture of Jerus by the Chaldaeans. Another strange blunder appears in the subjoined "Epistle of Bar"; the number of northern tribes who rebelled against Rehoboam is confused, with that of the tribes settled on the west of Jordan, and that of the tribes following the House of David with that of those on the east of Jordan. Yet the general course of Biblical history is quite understood. The author seems fairly well acquainted with Jer and Ps, as there are frequent echoes of these books. Most marked is the connection between this Apocalypse and the other books of the same class. This connection is not so obvious in quotable sentences as in the general atmosphere. This is very marked in regard to the En books, Ethiopic and Slavonic. In the case of the latter, of course, the resemblance is not imitation on the part of the writer of this Apocalypse. One marked distinction, one that precludes any thought of direct imitation, is the elaborate angelology of the En books as compared with the one name which appears in the Apocalypse of Bar. The book with which the present Apocalypse has closest relation is 2 (4) Esd. Dr. Charles has given at the end of his tr of the work before us (*Apoc of Baruch*, 171) a long list of resemblances, not always of equal value. Sometimes the references are inaccurate. The main thing to be observed is that while 2 Esd as we have it has on the one hand a markedly Christian coloring, which it seems impossible to attribute to interpolation, and on the other, to have seen the desolation of Jerus under the Romans, there is no Christian element in the genuine Baruch, and the desolation is more sentimental as proved by the inability to realize the conditions consequent on the capture of the city by victorious enemies.

(6) *The words of Baruch.*—One of the evidences of the influence our Apocalypse had in the Christian community is the composition by a Christian of "The Rest of the Words of Bar" (or Jer). This was found, like so many other treasures, by Ceriani in the Ambrosian Library, Milan. Jer is the principal spokesman in the book. It is revealed to him that Jerus is to be given into the hands of the Chaldaeans, and he announces this to Baruch. He is desirous to save Abimelech (Ebedmelech), and prays God for him, and Abimelech is sent away out of the city while the angels are overturning it. He goes to the vineyard of Agrippa and falls asleep. His sleep continues sixty years. When, arising from sleep, he enters Jerus again he does not recognize it. An angel leads him to Baruch who had made his abode in a tank. Baruch writes to Jeremiah, who has departed to Babylon. His letter is conveyed by an eagle. Jer on receipt of this epistle collects all

the captives and leads them back to Jerus. Certain of them would not submit to the law in all its strictness, but, turning aside, founded Samaria. After some time Jeremiah dies, rises again on the third day and preaches Christ as the Son of God, and is stoned by the Jews. A noticeable thing is the relatively accurate account of the date of Christ's appearance after the return from the captivity, 477 years, only it must be calculated from the reign of Artaxerxes and to the resurrection. This, however, would make Jeremiah nearly two hundred years old. Such a thing, however, is not a matter that would disturb a Jewish chronologer. "The Rest of the Words of Baruch" seems to have been written by a Christian Jew in Pal before the rebellion of Barcochba.

3. The Assumption of Moses

In the Epistle of Jude is a reference to a conflict between the archangel Michael and Satan, when they "disputed about the body of Moses." Origen (*de Princip,* iii.2) attributes this to a book he calls *Ascensio Mosis.* Clement Alexandrinus gives an account of the burial of Moses quoted from the same book. There are several references to the book up to the 6th cent., but thereafter it disappeared till Ceriani found the fragment of it which is published in the *Acta Sacra et Profana* (Vol I). This fragment is in Lat. It is full of blunders, some due to transcription, proving that the last scribe had but an imperfect knowledge of the tongue in which he wrote. Some of the blunders go farther back and seem to have been due to the scribe who trd it from Gr. Even such a common word as *thlī́psis* ("affliction") he did not know, but attempted, by no means with conspicuous success, to transliterate it as *clipsis.* So with *allóphuloi* "foreigners," the common LXX equivalent of "Philistine," and yet commoner *skēnḗ* ("a tent") and several others. It probably was dictated, as some of the blunders of the copyist may be better explained as mistakes in hearing, as *fynicis* for *Phoenices,* and *venient* for *veniet.* Some, however, are due to blunders of sight on the part of the translator, as *monses* for *moyses.* From this we may deduce that he read from a MS in cursive characters, in which ν and υ were alike. This Milan MS has been frequently edited. Dr. Charles has suggested with great plausibility that there were two works, a Testament of Moses, and an Assumption, and that these have been combined; and, while Jude ver 9 is derived from the Assumption, as also the quotation in Clement of Alexandria, he thinks that Jude ver 16 is derived from separate clauses of the Testament. It may be observed that in the fragment which has been preserved to us, neither the passages in Clement nor that referred to in Jude ver 16 are to be found.

(1) *Summary of the book.*—Moses, now in the plain of Moab, calls Joshua to him and gives him commands for the people. He had already blessed them tribe by tribe. Now he calls his successor to him and urges him to be of good courage. He tells him that the world has been created for Israel, and that he, Moses, had been ordained from before the foundation of the world to be the mediator of this covenant. These commands are to be written down and preserved in clay jars full of cedar oil. This sentence is added to explain the discovery and publication. A rapid summary of the history of Israel to the fall of the Northern Kingdom follows. The successive reigns are called years—eighteen years before the division of the kingdom, 15 Judges and Saul, David and Solomon, and nineteen after, the kings from Jeroboam to Hoshea. The Southern Kingdom has twenty years or reigns. The Southern Kingdom was to fall before Nebuchadnezzar, the king from the East who would cover the land with his cavalry. When they are in captivity one prays for them. Here follows a prayer modeled on Dnl **9** 4–19—almost a version of it. In this connection it may be noted that of the ten tribes it is asserted they will multiply among the Gentiles. There is a sudden leap forward to the time of the Gr domination. Singularly, the period of the Maccabees does not appear in this sketch of history. The times of Judas Maccabaeus are not mentioned, but the kings of his house, the descendants of Simon, are referred to as "Kings ruling shall rise from them, who shall be called priests of the Most High God." To them follows Herod, *rex petulans,* "who will not be of the race of the priests." He will execute judgment on the people like those of Egypt. Herod is to leave children who will reign after him for a short period. The Rom emperor is to put an end to their rule and to burn up Jerus. Then comes a mutilated chapter, which, while following in the narrative, may yet be only another aspect of the oppression. The Roman officials figure duly as the source of this, and the Sadducean high-priestly party as their instruments. The resemblance to the terms in which Our Lord denounces the Pharisees leads one to think that they, too, are meant by the Essene authors. We have noted above that the Maccabean period is completely omitted. The persecution under Antiochus appears in chs **8** and **9**. With Dr. Charles we are inclined to think they have been displaced. In ch **9** occurs the reference to the mysterious *Taxo* with his seven sons. Dr. Charles is quite sure the reference is to the seven sons of the widow who suffered before Antiochus Epiphanes as related in 2 Macc **7** (4 Macc **8–17**), but the "mother" is the prominent person in all the forms of the story, while in no form of it is their father mentioned. It is to be noted that if T of this mysterious name, represents ת in the Heb (=400), and Ξ represents the letter ס (=60) which occupies the same place in the Heb alphabet, and if the O represents ו (= 6), adding those numbers together we have the number 466, which is the sum of the letters of Shimeon. But nothing in the history of the second son of Mattathias resembles the history of the mysterious Taxo. On this subject the reader is recommended to study Charles, *Assumption of Moses,* 32–34. Taxo recommends his sons, having fasted to retire into a cave, and rather to die than to transgress the commands of God. In this conduct there is a suggestion of the action of several of the pious in the beginning of the Antiochus persecutions. Taxo then breaks into a song of praise to God, in the course of which he describes the final discomfiture of the enemies of God and of His people. The establishment of the Messianic kingdom is to be 250 times after the Assumption of Moses. The interpretation of this is one of the difficulties in regard to this Apocalypse. Langen takes the times as equivalent to decades, and Dr. Charles as year-weeks. The latter seems a more probable meaning of "time," as more in the line of Jewish thought. It should be noted that Dr. Charles thinks *illius adventum* refers not to the Messiah's coming, but to the last judgment. In answer to the declaration of Moses as to his approaching death, Joshua rends his garments and breaks forth into lamentations, wondering who will lead on the people when his master has departed. There is one phrase that seems to imply a tincture of classical culture. Joshua says of Moses, "All the world is thy Sepulchre," which seems to be a reminiscence of Pericles' funeral oration (Thucyd. ii.4), "The whole earth is the monument of men of renown." He then casts himself at the feet of Moses. His master encourages

him and promises him success. At this point the fragment ends. It is to be expected that shortly after this would occur the passage quoted by Clement of Alexandria, and still later that quoted in Jude.

(2) *Structure.*—It seems to have been united with one, if not two other books, a "Testament of Moses" and our Book of Jub. It would seem that in the present work we have mostly the "Testament." The insertion of the word *receptione* after *morte* in **10** 12 indicates that when this copy was made the two writings were united. As above remarked, there appears to have been a displacement of chs **8** and **9**; they ought to have been placed between chs **4** and **5**.

(3) *Language.*—As already mentioned, the MS found by Ceriani in the Ambrosian Library is in Lat. No one, however, has maintained that this was the language in which it was originally written. It is evidently a tr from the Gr. A number of Gr words are transliterated, some of them common enough. So clearly does the Gr shine through, that Hilgenfeld has reproduced what he imagines the Gr text to have been. That having been settled, a further question rises, Is the Gr the original tongue, or was it, too, a tr from a Sem original? The first alternative is that adopted by Hilgenfeld. His arguments from the alleged impossibility of certain grammatical constructions being found in Heb are due to mistake. The presence of such words as *Allofile* and *Deuteronomion* simply prove that in translating a book which claimed to be written about Moses, the writer followed the diction used by the LXX, just as Archbishop Laurence in translating En used the diction of the AV of the Bible. These questions have been ably investigated by Dr. Charles in his edition of the Asm M (**42–45**). He shows a number of Sem idioms which have persisted through the Gr—some cases in which the meaning can only be got by reconstructing the Heb text. Again, corruption can only be explained by means of a Sem text. It might be suggested that a *falsarius* writing in Gr would naturally employ the diction of the LXX as has been done frequently in English; the diction of the AV is used to cover the imitation of a sacred book. The fact that style was so little regarded as a means of settling dates and authorship renders this unlikely. The more delicate question of which of the two Sem tongues—Aram. or Heb—is employed, is more difficult to settle. There are, however, one or two cases in which we seem to see traces of the *vav* (*waw*) conversive—a construction peculiar to Heb—e.g. **8** 2, "Those who conceal [their circumcision] he *will* torture and *has* delivered up to be led to prison." The ignorance of the scribe may, however, be invoked to explain this. On the other hand, the change of tense is so violent that even an ignorant scribe would not be likely to make it by mistake. Over and above, a narrative attributed to Joshua and asserted to be written down by him at the dictation of Moses, would necessarily be in Heb. From this we would deduce that Heb rather than Aram. has been the Sem original.

(4) *Date.*—The identification of the *rex petulans* with Herod and the statement that he should be succeeded by his sons who should reign a short time, fix the date of the composition of the work before us within narrow limits. It must have been written after the death of Herod and also after the deposition of Archelaus, 6 AD, and before it was seen that Antipas and Philip were secure on their thrones. Thus we cannot date it later than 7 or 8 AD. The intense hatred of the Herodians was a characteristic of this time. Later they came to be admired by the patriotic party.

(5) *Relation to other books.*—The most striking phrase is the name given to Moses—*arbiter testamenti*, "the mediator of the covenant," which we find repeatedly used in the Epistle to the He: *mesítēs* is the Gr tr of *mōkhīaḥ* in Job **9** 33, but in translating the Epistle to the He into Heb Delitzsch uses *ṣarṣōr*, a purely rabbinic word. Another rendering is *m^e^naçē^a^ḥ*. There are several echoes in this book of passages in the OT, as the address to Josh (**1** 1 ff) is parallel with Dt **31** 7 f. The prayer in ch **4**, as before observed, is modeled on Dnl **9** 4–19. There are traces of acquaintance with the Psalter of Solomon in ch **5** as compared with Ps **4**. In these there appear to be echoes of the present work in Our Lord's description of the Pharisees, when we compare Mt 23 with ch **5**.

There is a fragment published by Ceriani entitled "History and Life [*diḗgēsis kaí politeía*] of Adam, Which Was Revealed by God to Moses, His Servant." It is an account of the life of our first parents after the death of Abel to their own death. It has been composed to all appearance in Gr, and really belongs not to Mosaic lit., but to that connected with Adam. It is to be noted that to Cain and Abel other names are given besides those so well known. They are called *Adiaphotos* and *Amilabes*, names of no assignable origin. There are no evidences of Christian influence; from this one would be led to regard it as a Jewish writing; as the middle of it has been lost, any decision is to be made with caution.

4. The Ascension of Isaiah

The Ascension of Isaiah was often referred to by name in the works of early Christian Fathers, especially by Origen. It is called by him "The Apocryphon of Isaiah." Epiphanes gives it the title by which it is more commonly known. Now that we have the book, we find numerous echoes of it. Indeed, Origen claims that He **11** 37 contains a reference to it in speaking of saints who were sawn asunder. Justin Martyr speaks of the death of Isaiah in terms that imply an acquaintance with this book. It had disappeared till Archbishop Laurence found a copy of it in Ethiopic on a London book-stall. The capture of Magdala brought home more manuscripts. A portion of it had been printed in Venice from a Lat version.

(6) *Summary.*—In the 26th year of his reign Hezekiah calls Isaiah before him to deliver certain writings into his hand. Isaiah informs him that the devil Sammael Malkira would take possession of his son Manasseh, and that he, Isaiah, will be sawn asunder by his hand. On hearing this, Hezekiah would order his son to be killed, but Isaiah tells him that the Chosen One will render his counsel vain. On the death of his father, Manasseh turned his hand to serve Berial Matanbukes. Isaiah retired to Bethlehem, and thence, with certain prophets—Mic, Joel and Hab—and also Hananiah and his own son Joab, he removed to a desert mountain. Balkira, a Sam, discovered their hiding-place. They are brought before Manasseh, and Isaiah is accused of impiety because he has said that he has seen God, yet God had declared to Moses, "There shall no flesh see my face." He had also called Jerus, Sodom, and its rulers, those of Gomorrah. For Berial (Belial) had great wrath against Isaiah because he had revealed the coming of Christ and the mission of the apostles. At this point there appears to be a confusion between the first coming of Christ and His second. Lawless elders and shepherds are referred to as appearing, and it is assumed the elders of the church and the pastors are intended, though this is not necessarily so. There certainly was much contention in the churches, as we know, concerning the question of circumcision. The reference, however, may be to the rulers and elders of Israel who crucified Our Lord. Then

follows the account of the incarnation of Beliar in Nero, "the matricide monarch," and the persecution of the twelve apostles, of whom one will be delivered into his hand—the reference here being probably to the martyrdom of Peter. If it is Paul, then it is a denial of Peter's martyrdom at Rome altogether; if it is Peter, it means the denial of Paul's apostleship. The reign of the Antichrist is to be "three years, seven months and twenty-seven days," that is, on the Rom reckoning, 1,335 days. This would seem to be calculated from Nero's persecution of the Christians. He makes a singular statement: "The greater number of those who have been associated together in order to receive the Beloved he will turn aside after him"—a statement that implies a vastly greater apostasy under the stress of persecution than we have any record of from other sources. A good deal is to be said for the insertion of 1,000 in the number 332 in **4** 14, so as to make it read 1,332. At the end of this period "the Lord will come with His angels and will drag Beliar into Gehenna with his armies." Then follows a reference to the descent of the Beloved into Sheol. The following chapter gives an account of the martyrdom of Isaiah, how he was "sawn in sunder with a wooden saw," and how Balkira mocked him, and strove to get Isaiah to recant. With ch **6** begins the Ascension proper. This ch, however, is merely the introduction. It is in ch **7** that the account is given of how the prophet is carried up through the firmament and then through heaven after heaven to the seventh. A great angel leads him upward. In the firmament he found the angels of the devil envying one another. Above this is the first heaven where he found a throne in the midst, and angels on the right and the left, the former of whom were the more excellent. So it was in the second, third, fourth and fifth heavens. Each heaven was more glorious than that beneath. In the sixth heaven there was no throne in the midst nor was there any distinction between angels on the right and left; all were equal. He is then raised to the seventh heaven—the most glorious of all—where he sees not only God the Father, but also the Son and the Holy Spirit. As to the Son we are told that he should descend, and having assumed human form should be crucified through the influence of the Prince of this World. Having descended into Sheol, he spoiled it, and ascended up on high. In ch **10** there is a more detailed account of the descent of the Son through the successive heavens, how in each He assumed the aspect of the angels that dwelt therein, so that they did not know Him. In the Firmament, the quarreling and envying appeared at first to hinder Him. In ch **11** we have a semi-docetic account of the miraculous birth. With the declaration that it was on account of these revelations that he, Isaiah, was sawn in sunder, the Apocalypse ends.

(2) *Structure.*—Dr. Charles has maintained that three works are incorporated—the Testament of Hezekiah, the Martyrdom of Isaiah and the Vision of Isaiah. The names have been taken from those given to this work in patristic literature, and are not strictly descriptive of the contents, at least of the first. The confused chronology of the work as we have it may to some extent be due to transcription and translation. From the opening paragraph, there appears to have been an Apocryphon attributed to Hezekiah. Manasseh is called into his father's presence in order that here may be delivered to him words of righteousness "which the king himself had seen" "of eternal judgment, the torments of Gehenna and the Prince of this World and his angels and of his principalities and powers"—a phrase which implies a knowledge of the Epistle to the Eph on the part of the writer. The contents given thus summarily are not further detailed. The Vision of Isa does not give any account of the powers and principalities of Satan's kingdom. It would seem better to regard the present work as composed of two—the Martyrdom of Isaiah and the Vision or Ascension proper. The references backward and forward seem to imply a similarity of authorship in both parts. This would seem to suggest that the editor and author were one and the same person. There is a knowledge of Rom affairs at the time of Nero's fall so much beyond what anyone living in Pal could attain that Rome would seem to be the place of composition.

(3) *Language.*—The immediate original from which the tr, Ethiopic, Lat and Sclavonic were made appears to have been Gr. It is clear in regard to the Ethiopic where the proper names which end in Heb in *h* and in the Gr transcription end in *s*, as Hezekias, Isaias, the latter is followed, but Manasseh is Manassa. An interesting case is to be found in **2** 12: Mikayas is called "son of Amida," where "Amida" stands for Imlah. In the Ethiopic transliteration *'ālēph* is generally used for the initial *yōdh* as a vowel, as it is in "Israel" (Ethiopic *Asreal*); hence "Imida" might as correctly represent the name. Then as Δ (*d*) and Λ (*l*) are like each other the change is explained. Although certainly as said above, Gr has been the immediate original, it is possible if not even probable that behind the Gr there was Heb. The structure of the sentences suggests the same thing (see **2** 5 Gr). The mysterious name given to Berial, Mattanbûkus—which, unfortunately, we have not in Gr—seems to be intelligible only in the idea that it has a Heb etymology, *mattan būḳāh*, "the gift of emptiness," the latter word being equivalent to "the void," "the abyss." The title given to Sammael, *Malkira*, seems naturally to mean king of "the watchers"—*'īrim*, the angels who, as related in En (**10** 5), did not continue in their first estate, but defiled themselves with women. So *Belkira* is "Lord of the fort"—*ba'al ḳīr*. There thus seems to be a probability that like so many others of this class, the "Ascension" was originally written in Heb.

(4) *Date.*—No one reading the "Ascension" can fail to feel that he has to do with a Christian document, and one belonging to the very beginning of Christian history. There may have been an earlier Jewish Apocalypse behind, though to our thinking that does not seem necessary. It is made up of two documents, but the Christian element appears to be woven into the structure of both portions. That it is to be dated early in the history of the church may be seen from the expectation of Christ's speedy reappearance in the world in His parousia. The conflict in the church between elders and shepherds gives a picture of the struggle between Judaizers and the Pauline Christians on the other side. The emphasis laid on the *twelve*, the omission of all reference to Paul, indicates that it was Judaizing. The docetic account of the birth of Jesus, its independence of the canonical Gospels, all speak of an early date. The date, however, it seems to us, can be fixed with great certainty. The reign of Berial, who has come down upon Nero and incarnated himself in him is to be three years, seven months and twenty-seven days, in all 1,335 days (**4** 12), the number in the end of Dnl (**12** 12). This number, it may be noted, is reached by reckoning the years and months according to the Julian Calendar, proving this Apocalypse to have been written in Rome. But the number is singularly near the actual duration of Nero's reign after the persecution had begun. From the burning of Rome (July 19, 64) to the death of Nero (June 9, 68) was 1,421 days—that is, 86 days more. It was at least a month after the confla-

gration that the persecution began, and longer till the mad orgy of cruelty when Christians wrapt in pitch and set on fire illuminated Nero's gardens. If a Christian in Rome saw the persecution, he might hope for the end of this reign of terror, and fix on the number he found in Daniel. It would seem that already the 1,290 days had been overpassed, so he hopes that the 1,335 days will see the end of the tyrant. There is a difficulty in the 332 days of **4** 14. The temptation is great to hold with Lücke, Dillmann and Charles that 1,000 has dropped out, and that the last figure ought to be 5; then we have the same number. In that case, this Apocalypse must have been written after the news of the rebellion of Vindex had reached Rome, but before the death of Nero. If we may adopt this—though the fact that the shorter no. is found in all three Ethiopic MSS makes this method of adding a figure necessary to an explanation one to be avoided—this would point to the time immediately preceding Nero's death. The difficulty is, where did the author get the number? If it is correct, it is probably the arithmogram of some name of Satan. Berial gives 322 by *gematria*. It would seem that another mark of time is given in the martyrdom of Peter, which may be dated 64 AD. Another negative note is the absence of any reference to the fall of Jerus. Had it happened, Jew though the writer was, his love for his crucified Master would have led him to see the vengeance of heaven on the city which had put Him to death, and exult in it. It must have been written in the course of the year 68.

5. The 4th Book of Esdras

Unlike the books we have been discussing hitherto 4 Esd has never disappeared from the knowledge of the church. It has, however, come down to us primarily in a Lat translation of a Gr original. Archbishop Laurence discovered an Ethiopic version of it. Later an Armenian version with Lat translation was published in Venice. An Arab. version is also in existence. It was received into the Apocrypha of the Anglican church, though excluded from that of Germany; by the Council of Trent 1 Esd and 2 Esd of our Apocrypha were excluded from the Roman Catholic canon, and placed after Rev, along with Pr Man.

(1) *Summary*.—The first two chs contain a prophecy after the model of Isa. Not a few passages show the influence of the NT on it. Cf 2(4) Esd **1** 30 with Mt **23** 37, and 2(4) Esd **2** 45 with Rev **7** 13. With ch **3** there is a new beginning. This opens with a prayer which occupies the whole ch. In answer, Uriel is sent from God and reveals to Ezra by various symbols the plan of God in regard to Israel. This goes on to the middle of ch **5**, and forms the first vision. After fasting seven days, a new communication is made by Uriel to Ezr. It begins as the former did with a prayer. Then follows a series of questions intended to bring out the limited understanding of man. When these are finished, Uriel gives an account of the history of the world from the creation. This vision ends with **6** 35. The third vision is very interesting, as a large section of 70 vs had been lost, and were recovered only comparatively recently. This vision contains an account of Creation as it is in Gen, only rhetorical expansions occur, and a full description is given of Leviathan and Behemoth. Ezra is shown the heavenly Zion in vision as difficult of access. The portion recently discovered contains an account of the place of punishment, and there is mention of Paradise. The end of this is a prayer of Ezra, which seems an independent composition (**8** 20). The fourth vision begins with **9** 26. In it Ezra is shown a woman weeping, who is interpreted to be Zion. She is transformed into a city (**10** 27). The fifth vision is the most important. It begins with an eagle appearing, which has three heads and twelve wings. This is interpreted as referring to the Rom empire. It would seem that this had been added to, as in addition to the twelve wings, eight other wings are spoken of. A lion appears who rebukes and destroys the eagle with the twelve wings. This lion is the Messiah and his kingdom. The sixth vision begins with ch **13** and contains an account of the coming of Christ. In the seventh we have an account of the re-writing of the books at the dictation of Ezra, and the retention of the seventy secret sacred books. In what has preceded we have followed the scheme of Fritzsche. The last ch proceeds from the same pen as do the opening chs, and is combined with them by Fritzsche and called the Fifth Book of Esd.

(2) *Structure*.—As has been indicated above, 4 Esd is marked off into several distinct portions, preceded by Ezra fasting, and introduced by a prayer on the part of the prophet. Kabisch has a more elaborate scheme than Fritzsche. Like him, he recognizes seven visions, and like him he separates off the first ch and the last **17, 15, 16,** as by a different hand from the rest of the book. But in addition, he recognizes additions made by a R throughout the book. To us the scheme appears too elaborate.

(3) *Language*.—As above mentioned, the immediate source of the Lat text appears to have been Gr. There is very little to enable us to settle the question whether Gr was the language in which this book was composed, or whether even the Gr is a tr from Heb or Aram. There are many echoes of the other Scriptures, but no direct quotations, so there is nothing to show whether the author used the Heb text or the LXX. The proper names do not supply any clue. Although there are so many versions of the Gr, they are all so paraphrastic that the Gr in most cases is not by any means certain. The few vs quoted in Gr by Clemens Alexandrinus do not afford space enough to discover through them if there is any other language behind. It possibly was written in Heb, as it seems to have been written in Pal.

(4) *Date*.—From the tone of the book there is no doubt that it was written after the capture of Jerus by Titus. Had it been due to the later cataclysm, when the rebellion of Barcochba was overthrown, a Christian Jew would not have manifested such sorrow. The break between the church and the synagogue was complete by that time. Further, had this book been written under Hadrian, the previous disaster would have been referred to. Over and above the distinctly and avowedly Christian passages, there are numerous echoes of the NT Scriptures. The fifth vision affords notes of time which would be more unambiguous if there had not been additions made. The eagle with the three heads and twelve wings is declared to be the fourth monarchy of Daniel, and by the context this is shown to be imperial Rome. The question that has exercised critics is the portion of the Rom history referred to. Lücke regarded the reference to be to rulers prominent in the time of Sulla, and the three heads to be the first triumvirate. This view implies a knowledge of Rom politics not possessed by any Jew of the pre-Christian period. Further, the echoes of NT language which occur (cf 2[4] Esd **5** 1 with Lk **18** 8; 2[4] Esd **6** 5 with Rev **7** 3, etc) determine the decision against any idea that it was pre-Christian. The realization of the horrors of the overthrow of Jerus is too vivid to be the result merely of imagination. Another theory would see in the three heads the three Septimians, Severus and his sons Caracalla and Geta. This

would find a place for the eight under-wings, as that is exactly the number of emperors between Domitian and Severus, if one neglects the short reign of Didius Julianus. The destruction of "the two under wings that thought to have reigned" (2[4] Esd **11** 31) would be fulfilled in the defeat and death of Pescennius Niger and Clodius Albinus. The fact that it is the right-hand head that devours the head to the left fits the murder of Geta the younger son, by Caracalla, the elder. Against this view is the fact that the book is quoted by Clemens Alexandrinus. Further, the eight under-wings are said to be kings "whose times shall be small, and their years swift" (2[4] Esd **12** 20). Though this might be said of Nerva, it could not be affirmed of Trajan, Hadrian, Antoninus Pius or Marcus Aurelius. We are thus restricted to the view which maintains that the three heads are the three Flavians. The twelve wings are the first emperors, beginning with Julius Caesar. The reign of Augustus is longer than any of the monarchs that succeeded him, and it is noted that the second wing was to have that distinction (2[4] Esd **12** 15). The date then may be placed between the death of Titus and that of Domitian—that is, from 81 to 96. The Lion who rebukes the Eagle for his unrighteousness is the Messiah—the Christ—in His second coming, when He shall come in the glory of His kingdom. The Christians had begun to doubt the speedy coming of the Master; hence He is spoken of as "kept unto the end of days" (2 Esd **12** 32). Such are the Apocalypses, strictly speaking.

II. Legendary Works.—The Book of Jub is the only one which survives of this class of composition.

Book of Jubilees

The portion of Asc Isa which contains the account of his martyrdom has much of this character. It, however, has been conjoined to the Apocalyptic "Ascension." It would seem that in some copies the Asm M was added to this work as a supplement. It is frequently cited as *lepto Genesis*—sometimes *leptogenesis*, and again *microgenesis*, "the little Genesis." This title cannot be meant to refer to its actual size, for it is considerably longer than the canonical book. It may either mean that this book is to be less regarded than the canonical Genesis, or that it is taken up with *leptá*—"minutiae." Another, and possibly more plausible explanation is to be found in the Heb or Aram. There is a rabbinic book known as *B*[e]*rē'shīth Rabbā'*, in which the whole of Gen is expanded by Midrashic additions, amplifications and explanations, to many times the size of the work before us, which, in comparison, would be *B*[e]*rē'shīth Zūṭā'*—"the small Genesis." The main difficulty is that the Jewish work, B. Rabbah, cannot well be dated earlier than 300 AD. We owe the work before us mainly—in its complete form—like so many others, to its inclusion in the canon of the Ethiopic church. Portions of it in Lat and Syr have been found in the second main source of apocalyptic lit. in recent times, the Ambrosian Library of Milan. There have been several editions of the Ethiopic text.

(1) *Summary.*—It is difficult to give anything like a summary of the Book of Jub in the ordinary sense of the word. Roughly speaking, the canonical Book of Gen is the summary. The writer has omitted many features and incidents, but these have been more than compensated for by additions and expansions. Most of these omissions have an apologetic aim. The acts of deception of which Abraham was guilty in Egypt and toward Abimelech in regard to Sarah, the similar act of Isaac, would involve matters difficult to palliate. The way Simeon and Levi entrapped the Shechemites into being circumcised and then took advantage of their condition to murder them, is omitted also. Jacob's devices to increase his flocks at Laban's expense are also passed over in silence. The most marked omission is the blessing of Jacob in Gen **49**. This is to be explained by the way the writer has praised Simeon and Levi earlier, which Jacob's denunciation of them flatly contradicts. Many of the additions have a similar apologetic intention, as the statement that Dinah was twelve years old at the time of the rape, the presents Jacob gave to his parents four times a year, etc. When Jacob deceives his father, he does not say he is Esau, but only "I am thy son." There are longer additions, chiefly ceremonial. Two incidents narrated at length are the warfare of the Amorites against Jacob (**34** 1–9), and the war of Esau (**37** and **38**).

(2) *Structure.*—The most marked characteristic of the book is that from which it has its most common name, "The Book of Jub," the dating of events by successive Jubilees. The whole history of the world is set in a framework of Jubilees and every event is dated by the Jubilee of the world's history in which it had occurred, and the year-week of that Jubilee and the year of that week. The writer has carried his septenary principle into the year and made the days in it, as did the writer of one of the En books, a multiple of seven, $364 = 7 \times 52$ days. It does not seem to have been interpolated.

(3) *Language.*—Like so many more of the pseudepigrapha, the Ethiopic, from which our modern tr[s] have been made, has been tr[d] from a Gr original, which in turn has had a Sem source. It is somewhat difficult to form a decision as to which of the two Sem languages in use in Pal was that in which it was composed. Certainly some, as Frankel, have maintained that it was written in Gr first of all. This is contrary to ancient evidence, as Jerome refers to the use of *rissah*, "a stadium," as used in the Book of Jub. More can be said for an Aram. original. The use of *Mastēma* for Satan, and the plurals in *in*, point in that direction. Dr. Charles's arguments seem to us to settle the matter in favor of Heb. Cf the case of **47** 9, in which *bath*, "a daughter," is confused with *bayith*, "a house." One of his arguments is not so conclusive: **2** 9 *wahaba*, "gave," appears where "appointed" is the meaning—a confusion of meanings only possible from the double meaning of *nathan*, as the Aram. *yahabh* has the same double force: "See I have made thee [*yeh*[e]*bhēthākh*] a God to Pharaoh" (cf Pesh Ex **7** 1). These indications are few, but they seem sufficient.

(4) *Date.*—The formidable authority of Dr. Charles and that of Littmann are in favor of an early date—before the quarrel of John Hyrcanus with the Pharisees. Our reading of the history is different from that of either of these scholars. The Ḥassidh party had been lukewarm to the Maccabeans from the latter portion of the pontificate of Judas Maccabaeus; the insult offered to Hyrcanus at his own table was the enmity reaching its height. If with Dr. Charles we assume the author to be a Pharisee, then the date is impossible. The Pharisaic party were never enthusiastic supporters of the Maccabeans, except when Alexandra threw herself into their arms. Two characteristics of this book strike the reader—its apologetic tone, and its hatred of Edom. During the time of John Hyrcanus the nation did not assume an apologetic attitude. It had thrown off the Syrian-Gr domination and repelled the attempt to Hellenize its religion. It would be only Greeks, or those under Gr influences, that would necessitate the apologetic attitude. We are driven to the Herodian period when Romans abounded in the court and Greeks and Graeculi were frequent, when those who, being Jews and knowing Heb, yet had imbibed Hellenic culture, and readily saw the points where assault might be made on their faith and its sacred literature.

This date would explain the hatred of Edom. We therefore would place it about the death of Herod—from 5 BC to 6 AD.

Unlike the other books of this class, much of it has been found in the Talm; hence, though we still think the author to have been an Essene, we think that he had much sympathy with the Pharisaic school in its latest development.

III. Psalmic Pseudepigrapha.—The Ps Sol is the one of all the pseudepigrapha which seems to have hovered most nearly on the border of deutero-canonicity. Even 4 Esd, as not being found in Gr, scarcely can be counted an exception, as it was never admitted into the canon of Alexandria. The famous Codex Alexandrinus, as its table of contents proves, originally contained the book before us. In several catalogues of books that were acknowledged, by some at least, to be authoritative, it is named — sometimes to be declared uncanonical. Like so many other books — Jewish and Christian—during the Middle Ages, it sank into oblivion. A MS of it was first noticed by Hoeschel the librarian in the Library at Augsburg, in the beginning of the 17th cent., and published by de la Cerda in 1626. This MS has since been lost. More recently, four other Gr MSS have been brought to light. From these, with the assistance of de la Cerda's text, it has repeatedly been published. The name given to it, "The Psalter of Solomon," seems purely gratuitous; the writer makes no claim, direct or indirect, to be the Son of David.

1. Psalter of Solomon

(1) *Summary.*—The present collection consists of 18 pss closely modeled as to line of thought and diction on the canonical Pss. The first ps announces the declaration of war, but is occupied with the denunciation of hypocrites. The second describes a siege of Jerus and acknowledges that the distresses of the siege have been deserved, but ends by the description of the death of the besieger on the coast of Egypt. The third ps is one of thanksgiving on the part of the righteous. In the fourth we have the description and denunciation of a hypocrite in terms which suggest strongly Our Lord's words against the Pharisees. It is evidently directed against a prominent individual member of the Sanhedrin. On the generally received date, Antipater may be the person denounced. The fifth ps is a prayer for mercy from God and an appeal to His loving-kindness. The sixth is occupied with a description of the blessedness of the righteous. The short ps which follows is a prayer of Israel under chastisement, intreating God not to remove His tabernacle from their midst. The eighth ps describes the siege of the temple and denounces the sins of the inhabitants of Jerus, which had brought the Smiter from afar against them, and a prayer for restoration to favor. Israel, a captive, prays to God for forgiveness in the ninth ps. In the tenth we have the blessedness of the man who submits to the chastening of the Lord. The theme of the eleventh is the return of the captives. The idea of the following ps is not unlike the middle stanza of Ps **120** of the canonical Psalter. The next has as its theme the blessedness of the righteous and the evil estate of the wicked. The fourteenth has a similar subject. The next begins with the sentiment so frequent in the canonical Pss: "When I was in trouble I called upon the Lord." The ps which follows is experimental in the sense of the old Puritans. The seventeenth ps is the most important, as it is Messianic, and exhibits the hopes prevalent among the Jews at the time when it was written. The eighteenth gives a description of the blessedness of the return of the Jews to Divine favor. Messrs. Ryle and James would divide this ps into two, as there seems to be a conclusion at the tenth ver with the sign *diapsalma*. Moreover, a slightly different theme is introduced at this point, but there is a reference in the *Pistis Sophia* to the 19th ps, and this is not the one implied. There seems to be some probability that a Lat tr once existed from references, though few, in the Lat Fathers; but no MS of it has yet been discovered. A Syr tr has been discovered by Dr. Rendel Harris, along with a number of other pss also attributed to Solomon, which he has called "Odes." Of these more will be said below.

(2) *Language.*—That the Gr of these pss is a tr from the Heb may be proved by what seem to have been errors in translation, as *toû eipeîn*, "to say," where the sense implies "to destroy," from the double meaning of *dābhar*, "to say," and later "to destroy"; *hḗōs eníkēse*, "till he conquered," where the meaning must be "forever" or "continuously," equivalent to *ʽadh, lā-neçaḥ*, which might be taken as in Aram., and tr[d] as in the Gr. Further, the general character, the frequent occurrence of *en* in senses strained in Gr but suiting thoroughly the Heb preposition ב, the omission of the substantive verb, the general simplicity in the structure of the sentences, serve to confirm this. For fuller elucidation the reader is directed to Ryle and James ed of this book (lxxviii–lxxxiv). Hilgenfeld has urged some arguments in favor of Gr being the original language. These really prove that the translator was very much influenced in making his translation by the LXX version of the canonical Psalter.

(3) *Date.*—While Ewald would place it back in the time of Epiphanes, if not even earlier, and Movers and Delitzsch would place it about the time of Herod, the description of the siege does not suit any siege but that of Pompey. Still more the death of the proud oppressor who besieged the Temple suits down to the minutest detail the death of Pompey, and suits that of no other. This is the opinion of Langen, Hilgenfeld, Drummond, Stanton, Schürer, Ryle and James. The pss, however, were written at various dates between 64 BC, the year preceding the Pompeian siege, and the death of Pompey 46 BC. The common critical idea is that it is the Psalter of the Pharisees. The singular thing is that though the writer reverences the Temple, he speaks nothing of the sacrifices, and shows no horror at the dishonor of the high priests—the attitude one would expect, not from a Pharisee, but from an Essene.

(4) *Christology.*—The main interest of this pseudepigraphon is its Christology, which is principally to be seen in the 17th ps. The Messiah is to be of the seed of David: He is to come on the downfall of the Asmoneans, to overthrow the Romans in turn. He is to gather the dispersed of Israel, and is to subject the Gentiles to His rule. The character of this rule is to be spiritual, holy, wise and just. All these features indicate a preparation for the coming of Him who fulfilled the expectation of the Jews in a way which they had so little dreamed of.

2. The Odes of Solomon

The students of Gnosticism in perusing the *Pistis Sophia*, one of the few literary remains left us by those bizarre heresies, found repeated quotations from the Ps Sol, not one of which was to be found in the received collection. There was one numbered reference, but it was to the 19th psalm, whereas only eighteen were known to exist. Lactantius has a quotation from the Ps Sol which, like those in *Pistis Sophia*, has no place in the "eighteen." It was obvious that there were more Solomonic writings that were called Psalms than those ordinarily known. In the beginning of 1909 the learned world was startled by the information that Dr. Rendel Harris had found on his shelves the missing Ps Sol in a Syr tr. The MS was defective both at the beginning and end, but there was, after all, little missing of the whole book. The title and the colophon were of course wanting. It begins with the new Psalms, or, to give them Dr. Harris' title, "Odes," which are followed by those till now known.

(1) *Relation to "Pistis Sophia."*—This cannot have been the order of the time when *Pistis Sophia* was published, as the first of these odes is quoted as the 19th. There are forty-two of them. They are the work of a Christian. The doctrine of the Trinity is present; very prominent is the miraculous birth of the Saviour; the descent upon Mary of the Holy Ghost in the form of a dove; the crucifixion, and the descent into Hades; and, though less clearly, the resurrection. One striking thing is the resemblance of the account of the virgin birth to that we find in the Asc Isa.

(2) *Date.*—Dr. Rendel Harris dates these Christian odes in the last quarter of the 1st cent., and there seems every reason to agree with this. The relation the 19th ps (Ode 37) bears to the Asc Isa is not discussed by him, but to our thinking, the Asc Isa seems the more primitive.

IV. Testaments.—Although, strictly speaking, Jewish law had no place for "testamentary dispositions" by those about to die—"the portion of goods" that fell to each being prescribed—yet the dying exhortations of Jacob addressed to his sons, the farewell song of Moses, David's deathbed counsels to Solomon, were of the nature of spiritual legacies. Under Gr and Rom law testaments were the regularly understood means of arranging heritages; with the thing the name was transferred, as in the Mish, *Bābhā' Bathrā'* **15** 26 f, דייתיקי, *dayytikē*, so also in Syr. The idea of these pseudepigrapha is clearly not drawn from the "Last Will and Testament," but the dying exhortations above referred to.

Gen **49** in which Jacob addresses his sons gathered round his dying bed furnished the model for a number of pseudepigraphic writings. Of these the longest known is XII P. In it the writer imagines each of the sons of Jacob following his father's example and assembling his descendants in order that he might give his dying charge. While Jacob addressed each of his sons separately, the sons of none of his sons, save those of Joseph, became at all prominent; so in the case of the sons of Jacob they each address their descendants as a whole. These Testaments are occupied with moral advices mainly. The sin most warned against is incontinence.

1. The Testament of the Twelve Patriarchs

(1) *Summary.*—(*a*) Reuben: The first Patriarch whose Testament is given is Reuben. While he bewails the sin that deprived him of his birthright, he gives an account of the various propensities that tend to sin, and accommodates each of these with an evil spirit—spirits of deceit. He gives details of his sin, which, resembling those given in the Book of Jub, differs in an apologetic direction. This apologetic effort is carried farther in the Targ of the pseudo-Jonathan. In it Reuben is declared to have disordered the bed of Bilhah because it was put beside his mother's, and he was accused of impurity with her; but the Spirit revealed to Jacob that he was not guilty.

(*b*) Simeon: The next Testament is that of Simeon. The crime that seems to have most affected Jacob, if we may judge by Gen **49** 5–7, was the murder of the Shechemites by Simeon and Levi. That, however, is not touched upon in the Testament; his envy of Joseph is what he most repents of. A stanza, however, is inserted, warning against fornication (ver 3).

(*c*) Levi: The Testament of Levi follows. It is mainly apocalyptic. The murder of the Shechemites is regarded as a wholly estimable action, and is commended by God. The treachery of the circumcision is not mentioned at all. He tells how he was admitted in dream to the third heaven. In another vision he is clothed with the garments of the priesthood. After a piece of autobiography followed by general admonitions Levi tells what he had learned from the writing of Enoch. He tells how his descendants will fall away and become corrupt. It is to be noted that fornication becomes very prominent in the picture of the future. The destruction of Jerus is foretold, and the captivity of Judah among all nations. This cannot refer to the setting up of the "Abomination of Desolation" by Epiphanes. The Temple was not laid waste, although it was desecrated; and there did not follow on the desecration by Epiphanes the scattering of the Jews unto all nations. It seems necessary to understand by this wasting the capture of Jerus by Titus. Consequently, the "new priest" of ch **18** seems to us the priest "after the order of Melchizedek" according to the NT interpretation.

(*d*) Judah: Judah is the next whose Testament is given. He first declares his own great personal prowess, slaying a lion, a bear, a boar, a leopard and a wild bull. When the Canaanite kings assailed Jacob as related in the Book of Jub, he showed his courage. Several warlike exploits, of which we only learn here, he relates. The assault made by the descendants of Esau upon the sons of Jacob and Jacob's victory is related in the manner and nearly in the terms of the account in the Book of Jub. He mentions with a number of explanatory and excusatory details his sin in the matter of Tamar. He denounces covetousness, drunkenness and fornication. Then he commands his descendants to look to Levi and reverence him. Then follows a Messianic passage which seems most naturally to bear a Christian interpretation.

(*e*) Issachar: The Testament of Issachar is much shorter than either of the two preceding ones. After telling the story of the mandrakes, he dwells on husbandry. As is noted by Dr. Charles, this is at variance with the rabbinic representation of the characteristics of the tribe. He, too, denounces impurity and drunkenness.

(*f*) Zebulun: Zebulun's Testament is little longer than that of Issachar. This Testament is greatly occupied with the history of the sale of Joseph in which Zebulun protests he took only the smallest share and got none of the price.

(*g*) Dan: The Testament of Dan also is short. He confesses his rage against Joseph, and so warns against anger. Here also are warnings against whoredom. The Messiah is to spring from Judah and Levi. Dr. Charles thinks the first of these was not in the original, because it would naturally have been "tribes," not "tribe," as it is. This is somewhat hasty, as in 1 K **12** 23 (LXX) we have the precisely similar construction *prós pánta oíkon Ioúda kaí Beniamín*, a sentence which represents the construction of the Heb. In this there is a Messianic passage which describes the Messiah as delivering the captives of Beliar.

(*h*) Naphtali: The Testament that follows, that of Naphtali, has apocalyptic elements in it. It opens with the genealogy of Bilhah, his mother, whose father is said to be Rotheus. His vision represents Levi seizing the sun and Judah the moon. The young man with the twelve palm branches seems to be a reference to the Apostles. Joseph seizes a bull and rides on it. He has a further dream in which he sees a storm at sea and the brethren being separated. Again there is a reference to the recurrent theme of sexual relation (ch **8**).

(*i*) Gad: The subject of the Testament of Gad is hatred. Gad is associated with Simeon as being most filled with wrath against Joseph.

(*j*) Asher: Asher urges whole-hearted obedience to righteousness, as the apostle James does in his epistle.

(*k*) Joseph: One of the most important of these Testaments is that of Joseph. The opening is occupied with a prolonged description of the temptation of Joseph by Potiphar's wife. There is in that connection the unhealthy dwelling on sexual matters which is found in monkish writers. There are not a few resemblances to the language of the Gospels (cf **1** 6 and Mt **25** 36). There is a more important passage (**19** 8): "And I saw that from Judah was born a virgin wearing a linen garment, and from her was born a lamb, and on his left hand there was, as it were, a lion: and all the beasts rushed against him, and the lamb overcame them, and destroyed them, and trod them under foot." This to us is clearly Christian. Dr. Charles, without apocalyptic evidence to support him, would amend it and change the reading.

(*l*) Benjamin: The Testament of Benjamin is very much an appendix to that of Joseph. It opens with the account Joseph gave Benjamin of how he was sold to the Ishmaelites. He exhorts his descendants against deceit, but, as all his brethren, he warns them against fornication. There is a long Christian passage which certainly seems an interpolation, as it is not found in some of the texts, though others have all vs. The text concerning Paul (**11** 1.2) appears in varying forms in all VSS.

(2) *Structure.*—That these "Testaments" have been interpolated is proved by the variations in the different texts. Dr. Charles has, however, gone much farther, and wherever there is a Christian clause has declared it an obvious interpolation. For our part, we would admit as a rule those passages to be genuine that are present in all the forms of the text. The Gr text was first in, so to say, recent times edited by Grosseteste, bishop of Lincoln, in the 13th cent. Since then other MSS have been found, and a Slavonic and an Aram. version. We are thus able to check the interpolations. In essence the Christian passage in T Jos is found in all versions.

(3) *Language.*—Dr. Charles makes a very strong case for Heb being the original language. His numerous arguments are not all of equal value. While some of the alleged Hebraistic constructions may be actually so, not a few may be explained by imitation of the language of the LXX. As an example of the first, cf T Jud (**7**): *óchlos barús*= *ḥēl kābhēdh*, "a numerous host." On the other hand T Reub **3** 8: "understanding in the Law," is a turn of expression that might quite well be common among Gr-speaking Jews. Of passages that are only explicable by retranslation, as in T Jos **11** 7, "God . . . . increased him in gold and silver and in *work*," this last turn is evidently due to the translator's rendering *'ăbhuddāh*, "servant," as if it were *'ăbhōdhāh*, "work." On the whole, we are prepared to amend the decision elsewhere, and admit that the probability is that this book, like so many more of the same class, has been translated from Heb.

(4) *Date and authorship.*—Dr. Charles declares the author to have been a Pharisee who wrote in the early part of the reign of John Hyrcanus I. The initial difficulty with this, as with the other pseudepigrapha in attributing a Pharisaic authorship, is the preservation of the book among the Christian communities, and the ignorance or the ignoring of it among the Jews. The only sect of the Jews that survived the destruction of Jerus was that of the Pharisees. The Sadducees, who were more a political than a religious party, disappeared with the cessation of the Jewish state. When Judaism became merely a religion—a church—not a nation, their function was gone. The third sect, the Essenes, disappeared, but did so into the Christian church. If the writer had been an Essene, as we suppose he was, the preservation of this writing by the Christians is easily explicable. If it were the work of a Pharisee, its disappearance from the literature of the synagogue is as inexplicable as its preservation by the Christians. The constant harping on the sin of fornication—in T Naph **8** 8 even marital intercourse is looked at askance—indicates a state of mind suitable to the tenets of the Essenes. The date preferred by Dr. Charles, if the author is a Pharisee, appears to us impossible. The Pharisees had, long before the final break, been out of sympathy with the Maccabeans. The Chasidim deserted Judas Maccabaeus at Elasa, not improbably in consequence of the alliance he had made with the heathen Romans, and perhaps also his assumption of the high-priesthood. Further, the temple is laid waste and the people driven into captivity unto all nations (T Levi **15** 1). This does not suit the desecration of the temple under Epiphanes. During that time the temple was not laid waste. The orgies of the worship of Bacchus and of Jupiter Olympius dishonored it, but that is a different thing from its being laid waste. The scattering unto all nations did not take place then. Some were taken captive and enslaved, but this was not general. The description would only apply to destruction of the temple by Titus and the enslaving and captivity of the mass of the inhabitants of Jerus. The "New Priest" cannot refer to the Maccabeans, for they were Aaronites as much as Alcimus or Onias, though not of the high-priestly family. This change of the priesthood only has point if it refers to the priesthood of Christ as in He **7** 12. If Dr. Charles is right in maintaining that 2 Macc in its account of Menelaus is to be preferred to Jos, the change of the priesthood was not unprecedented, for Menelaus was a Benjamite, not a Levite. Yet 1 Macc takes no notice of this enormity. Further, there are the numerous passages that are directly and indirectly Christian. Dr. Charles certainly marks them all as interpolations, but he gives no reason in most of the cases for doing so. That the omission of such passages does not dislocate the narrative arises from the simpler construction of Sem narrative, and is therefore not to be regarded as conclusive evidence of interpolation. The reference to Paul in T Ben **11**, occurring in all the sources, although with variations, also points to a post-Christian origin. For these reasons, we would venture to differ from Dr. Charles and regard the XII P as post-Christian, and to be dated in the first quarter of the 2d cent. AD.

(5) *Relation to other books.*—From the decision we have reached in regard to the date of these Testaments, it follows that all the many resemblances which have been noted between them and the books of the NT are due to imitation on the part of the Testaments, not the reverse. A case in point is T Jos **1** 6 where the resemblance to Mt **25** 31–36 is close; only, whereas in the Gospel the judge approves of the righteous on account of their visiting the sick and the imprisoned, and condemns the wicked because they did not do so, in T Jos God ministers to His servants. The Testament is really an imitation of the passage in the Gospel. The direct visiting of the afflicted, whatever the form of the affliction, was a thing of everyday occurrence. To think of the Almighty doing so is the result of a bold metaphor. One familiar with the Gospel narrative might not unnaturally think of God's dealings with the saints in terms drawn from

Our Lord's description of the Last Judgment. In T Naph **2** 2 the figure of the potter and the clay is, as in Rom **9** 21, applied to God's power over His creatures. The passage in the T Naph is expanded, and has not the close intimate connection with the argument that the Pauline passage has. While none of the other resemblances give one any ground to decide, these instances really carry the others with them. We may thus regard the resemblances to the NT in XII P as due to the latter's copying of the former.

2. The Testament of Adam

The Testament of Adam survives merely in a group of fragments published first by Renan in the *Journal Asiatique* (1853). A Gr fragment was published by M. R. James. A portion of it is apocalyptic, and gives an account of the adoration offered by all the different classes of God's creatures. More strictly of the nature of a Testament is a Syr fragment entitled "More of Adam Our Father." It contains a prophecy of the incarnation, and appears to be of late date. It was used by the Sethites.

3. The Testament of Abraham

The Testament of Abraham is a late document. It opens with representing Abraham at his tent-door. One recension declares his age then to be 995 years. Michael comes to him. The purpose for which Michael has been sent is to reveal to Abraham that he must die. He hesitates to do this. When, however, the fatal message is revealed, Abraham will not yield up his spirit at first. He is after a while persuaded, and as a reward, before his death he has a revelation: there is given to him a vision of the whole world in the widest sense—the world of spirits as well. Seeing a soul, which, weighed in the balance, is nearly being found wanting, by his intercession the soul is admitted to Paradise. There are several traces of Christian influence; many of the thoughts and phrases are similar to those to be found in the Gospels. At the same time, although to one who had read John's Gospel the statement of Our Lord that Abraham had seen His day "and was glad" (Jn **8** 55.56) would inevitably have led a Christian writer to have exhibited Abraham as seeing in vision the day of Christ. The writer's failure to do so seems to show that he was not a Christian. The echoes of the Gospel in the language and the want of that distinctive Christian mark is to be explained if we regard the translator as a Christian, while the original Midr was the work of a Jew. The language was probably Aram. There are two Gr recensions, one longer than the other. There is an Arab. version which appears to be a tr direct from Aram. As there is no reference to the coming of Christ, this Testament is probably pre-Christian. The tr may be dated early in the 2d cent., as Origen knew it.

In Arab. there is a MS of the Testaments of Isaac and Jacob. They are late and Christian. The latter is founded on the last ch of Gen.

4. Testament of Job

More interesting is the Testament of Job published in *Anecdota Apocrypha* by M. R. James in 1897. It purports to be an account of his sufferings related by Job himself. It appears to be the work of a Jew, tr[d] by a Christian. The position of Satan in the Midr is not so subordinate as in the drama. Elihu, when not confused with Eliphaz, is regarded as inspired by Satan.

(1) *Summary.*—It begins with Job, "who is called Jobab," summoning his seven sons and three daughters. The list of the sons forms a singular assemblage of names, most probably of Sem origin. Most of them are certainly Gr words, though not Gr proper names—*Chorós* and *Níkē*, "dance" and "victory," *Huṓn*, "of pigs," *Phóros*, "tribute." The other names are *Tersi*, *Phiphi*, *Phrouōn*. He tells his descendants how he had been called in the night and had had it revealed to him that the sacrifices that had been offered previously in the great temple near him were not offered to God, but to Satan. He was ordered to destroy the temple thus devoted to false worship. He did so, but knew that Satan would seek him, to take his revenge. Satan came disguised as a beggar, and Job, recognizing him, ordered his porteress to give him a burned cake of bread, all ashes. Satan reveals himself and threatens Job. With ch **9** begins an account of Job's wealth and lordly beneficence founded on the canonical book. It continues to ch **16.** This portion is an expansion of the canonical Job. In some portions there are marked variations. Job is a king, and since this is so, the power of Persia is invoked to overthrow him. After twenty years his friends come to condole with him. They also are kings. Sitis his wife is bemoaning her children. Job declares he sees them crowned with heavenly beauty. On learning this, Sitis dies, and so rejoins her children. The speeches of the friends are much condensed, and scarcely of the same character as those in the canonical book. Lyric passages are introduced. The most singular difference from the canonical book is the rôle assigned to Elihu. Job says, "Elihu inspired by Satan addressed to me rash words" (ch **42**). God then speaks to Job in the whirlwind and blames Elihu. Job sacrifices for the three friends, and Eliphaz in a lyric piece congratulates himself and his friends, and declares that the lamp and glory of Elihu will be quenched (ch **43**). By a second wife we are told Job had the seven sons and three daughters who are summoned to his bedside. Closing his narrative (ch **44**) Job exhorts kindness to the poor. In the end of the book his successive daughters speak. He had divided his property, now double what it had originally been, among his seven sons and had left the daughters unprovided for. He, however, bestows upon them other gifts. Three golden vessels are brought him and given them, three cords besides, and each one has a several endowment. The first daughter, called, as in LXX, Hemera, (Jemima in the canonical Job), had another heart given her, and she spoke in the tongue of the angels. Casia (Keziah), the second daughter, also had a changed heart, and it was given to her to speak in the dialect of the principalities (*árchōn*). Then the third daughter girded herself, and with the changed heart it was given her to speak in the language of the Cherubim. This daughter is called *Amaltheías Kéras*, the rather strange tr of *Ḳeren Hāphukh* adopted by the LXX. All the names are transferred from that source. A brother of Job named *Nereus* (or Nereias) is introduced, who records further gifts to these daughters—a lyre to the first, a censer to the second and a drum to the third. This brother is a relative of whose existence we have no hint elsewhere. He is introduced to supply the conclusion to the narrative.

(2) *Structure.*—It would appear that from chs **1** to **45** is the original Testament in which Job is the speaker. In chs **46–51** a new state of matters comes into prominence, in which Nereus is the speaker. The last two chs seem decidedly to be additions: the new gifts to the daughters seem unexplained. Of course, oriental authors do not look so strictly to the unity of parts as do Occidentals.

(3) *Language.*—The dependence on the LXX would suggest that Gr was the original tongue. One or two phenomena point to a Sem tongue being behind the Gr. The names of Job's daughters are taken from the LXX; those of the seven sons

have been invented. As we have seen, they are not Gr names, but are probably really Hellenized VSS of some Sem appellations. At the same time, they do not seem to be Heb, but rather Aram. It would seem to have been tr[d] by one familiar with the NT.

(4) *Date and authorship.*—It has no direct references to Christian doctrines or the facts of Christian history. This seems conclusive against its having a Christian origin. The reason that would lead a Christian to compose such a document would be to give a further prophetic evidence for the mission of his Master. He would have no object in making Job out to be a connection of Israel, unless he were so himself. Dr. James thinks the writer to have been a Jewish Christian of the 2d cent. resident in Egypt. By the 2d cent. few Jews passed from Judaism to the faith of Jesus: the break between church and synagogue had become complete. That Job is made king of all Egypt (ch **28**) may indicate some relationship to that country, as if the writer had identified Job with Psammeticus, the Egyp king overthrown by Cambyses. This, however, may have been due to the translator. If the original language were Sem—Aram. or Heb—the probability is that the author wrote in Pal. There are no direct signs to indicate the date. There is no appearance of knowledge of Rome. The fire of the opposition to the Seleucids had died down. It may have been written in the reign of Alexander.

V. The Sibylline Oracles.—The burning of the Capitol (83 BC) and the destruction of the famous Sibylline books led Sulla to search in Italy and Greece for any Oracles that might replace the contents of the vols which had been burnt. About half a cent. later Augustus revived the search for Oracles. Such a demand would naturally produce a supply. It would seem that certain Jews of Alexandria, eager to propagate the faith of their fathers, invented vs in the shape in which these Oracles had been preserved, as we learn from Herodotus—i.e. in hexameter lines and in the epic dialect in which Homer and Hesiod had written. Those in Herodotus are mainly from the Oracle of Delphi. From Pausanias, who quotes several of them, we learn that the Oracles attributed to the various Sibyls were delivered in a similar style. Hence these Jewish forgeries were written in epic hexameters. Later, this industry was pursued with even greater zeal by Christians. These have been collected into several books—some 15 are named—of which some have been lost. The books are made up of fragments of different ages. The first book begins with the creation, and narrates the history of the race to the flood and the going out of Noah from the ark. Then the history of Our Lord is given succinctly, the miracle of the loaves, the crucifixion, and the destruction of Jerus. In it *Hades* is derived from "Adam." Reference is made to the sin of the watchers, as in En, and an arithmograph is given which seems to be fulfilled in *Theós Sōtḗr*. The second book is modeled largely on Our Lord's eschatological discourses, many passages bearing a distinct echo of it. It may be noted that the four archangels of the Book of En—Michael, Gabriel, Raphael and Uriel—are introduced. The third is by much the longest, but it is a confused mass of fragments. There is early reference to the conquest of Egypt by Rome; the building of the tower of Babel, the siege of Troy, the conquest of Alexander and many other events appear. The fourth book is Christian throughout. After praise to the Christians, there is a sketch of the history of the great empires, beginning with the Assyrians and ending with Alexander; then an account of Nero appearing from the East and doing evil fills the end of all things. The fifth book begins with an account of the successive emperors from Julius Caesar to the Antonines. Then a new song begins with Egypt, and wanders off indefinitely, referring to Xerxes crossing the Hellespont, the impurities of Rome, and ending with Egypt and the burning up of all things. The sixth is short—28 lines in praise of the Cross; and the seventh is fragmentary. In the eighth is the arithmogram and acrostic: ΙΗϹΟΥϹ ΧΡΙϹΤΟϹ ΘΕΟΥ ΥΙΟϹ ϹѠΤΗΡ ϹΤΑΥΡΟϹ, *Iēsous christós theoû huiós sōtḗr staurós.* The remaining books have similar characteristics. The place of composition is evidently Egypt, as, whatever the immediate context may be, the writer gravitates to Egypt; and the authors are Jews or Jewish Christians. The dates of the various fragments of which this collection is composed fall between the first triumvirate and the age of Diocletian.

VI. Conclusion.—There are many points in which the theology of the Apocalyptic prepared the way for that of Christianity. These, however, are more naturally taken up under their special headings. Angelology is much more developed in certain apocalyptic writings than it is in Christianity, if we except the writings published under the name of Dionysius the Areopagite. Most of them are occupied with the coming Messiah. The Christology of these writings is decidedly in advance of that of the OT. That question, however, is discussed under its appropriate heading. Closely connected with this is the doctrine of God, or theology proper. In this, too, there is an approximation to the Christian doctrine of the Trinity. With these writers the doctrine of the Last Things is always brought into close relationship to that of the Messiah. His coming is the signal for the end of the world, the last judgment, the punishment of the wicked and the reward of the righteous. What we have just said applies mainly to the strictly Jewish and pre-Christian Apocalypses. In the Christian Jewish Apocalypses the place the incarnation and the miraculous birth hold is worthy of special note. The representation in regard to the latter of these subjects is independent of the gospel narrative. Connected with this independence of the written Scriptures are the variations these writings introduce into history. Many of these are due to apologetic reasons, not a few to the desire to enhance the national glory. The reverence for the letter of Scripture, so markedly characteristic of the rabbinic teachings found in the Talm, is not found in the apocalyptic writings. Apocalyptic thus presents a stage in the doctrine of Scripture.

Literature.—On Apocalyptic generally: Deane, *Pseudepigrapha;* Derembourg, *Histoire de la Palestine;* Drummond, *Jewish Messiah;* Ewald, *History of Israel,* tr V; Grätz, *Geschichte der Juden,* III; Hilgenfeld, *Messias Judaeorum; Jüdische Apocalyptik;* Kautzsch, *Die Apocryphen und Pseudepigraphen des Alten Testaments;* Langen, *Palästina zur Zeit Christi;* Renan, *Histoire du Peuple d'Israel;* Schürer, *Jewish People,* tr V; Stanton, *Jewish and Christian Messiah;* Thomson, *Books Which Influenced Our Lord.* On special books: Enoch (Text, Ethiopic): Laurence, Dillmann, Flemming; (English): Laurence, Schodde, Charles. Slavonic Book of Enoch: Morfill. Baruch (Text, Syriac): Ceriani; (English): Charles, *The Assumption of Moses* (Text, Latin): Ceriani; (English): Charles, *The Ascension of Isaiah* (Text, Ethiopic): Laurence, Dillmann; (English): Charles, *Fourth Book of Esdras* (Text, Latin): Vulg; (English): *Apoc RV Book of Jubilees* (Text, Ethiopic): Dillmann, Charles; (English): Schodde, Charles, *Psalter of Solomon* (Text, Greek): Pick, Ryle and James; (English): Whiston, Pick, Ryle and James, Rendel Harris (from Syriac). *Odes of Solomon* (English): Rendel Harris, *Testaments of the XII Patriarchs* (Text, Greek): Sinker, Charles; (English): Sinker, Charles, *Testaments of Abraham and Job; Texts and Studies; Sibylline Oracles* (Text): Alexandre, Rzach.

J. E. H. Thomson

APOCRYPHA, a-pok'ri-fa:

I. Definition
II. The Name Apocrypha

I. Definition.—The word Apocrypha, as usually understood, denotes the collection of religious writings which the LXX and Vulg (with trivial differences) contain in addition to the writings constituting the Jewish and Protestant canon. This is not the original or the correct sense of the word, as will be shown, but it is that which it bears almost exclusively in modern speech. In critical works of the present day it is customary to speak of the collection of writings now in view as "the Old Testament Apocrypha," because many of the books at least were written in Heb, the language of the OT, and because all of them are much more closely allied to the OT than to the NT. But there is a "New" as well as an "Old" Testament Apoc consisting of gospels, epistles, etc. Moreover the adj. "Apocryphal" is also often applied in modern times to what are now generally called "Pseudepigraphical writings," so designated because ascribed in the titles to authors who did not and could not have written them (e.g. Enoch, Abraham, Moses, etc). The persons thus connected with these books are among the most distinguished in the traditions and history of Israel, and there can be no doubt that the object for which such names have been thus used is to add weight and authority to these writings.

The late Professor E. Kautzsch of Halle edited a German tr of the Old and New Testament Apocrypha, and of the Pseudepigraphical writings, with excellent introductions and valuable notes by the best German scholars. Dr. Edgar Hennecke has edited a similar work on the New Testament Apocrypha. Nothing in the Eng. language can be compared with the works edited by Kautzsch and Hennecke in either scholarship or usefulness. [A similar Eng. work to that edited by Kautzsch is now passing through the (Oxford) press, Dr. R. H. Charles being the editor, the writer of this art. being one of the contributors.]

II. The Name Apocrypha.—The investigation which follows will show that when the word "Apocryphal" was first used in ecclesiastical writings it bore a sense virtually identical with "esoteric": so that "apocryphal writings" were such as appealed to an inner circle and could not be understood by outsiders. The present connotation of the term did not get fixed until the Protestant Reformation had set in, limiting the Bib. canon to its present dimensions among Protestant churches.

1. Original Meanings

(1) *Classical.*—The Gr adjective ἀπόκρυφος, *apókruphos*, denotes strictly "hidden," "concealed," of a material object (Eurip. *Herc. Fur.* 1070). Then it came to signify what is obscure, recondite, hard to understand (Xen. *Mem.* 3.5, 14). But it never has in classical Gr any other sense.

(2) *Hellenistic.*—In Hellenistic Gr as represented by the LXX and the NT there is no essential departure from classical usage. In the LXX (or rather Theodotion's version) of Dnl **11** 43 it stands for "hidden" as applied to gold and silver stores. But the word has also in the same text the meaning "what is hidden away from human knowledge and understanding." So Dnl **2** 20 (Theod.) where the *apokrupha* or hidden things are the meanings of Nebuchadnezzar's dream revealed to Daniel though "hidden" from the wise men of Babylon. The word has the same sense in Sir **14** 21; **39** 3.7; **42** 19; **48** 25; **43** 32.

(3) *In the NT.*—In the NT the word occurs but thrice, viz. Mk **4** 22 and the ‖ Lk **8** 17; Col **2** 3. In the last passage Bishop Lightfoot thought we have in the word *apokruphoi* (treasures of Christ *hidden*) an allusion to the vaunted esoteric knowledge of the false teachers, as if Paul meant to say that it is in Christ alone we have true wisdom and knowledge and not in the secret books of these teachers. Assuming this, we have in this verse the first example of *apokruphos* in the sense "esoteric." But the evidence is against so early a use of the term in this—soon to be its prevailing—sense. Nor does exegesis demand such a meaning here, for no writings of any kind seem intended.

(4) *Patristic.*—In patristic writings of an early period the adj. *apokruphos* came to be applied to Jewish and Christian writings containing secret knowledge about the future, etc, intelligible only to the small number of disciples who read them and for whom they were believed to be specially provided. To this class of writings belong in particular those designated Apocalyptic (see Apocalyptic Literature), and it will be seen as thus employed that *apokruphos* has virtually the meaning of the Gr *esoterikos*.

A brief statement as to the doctrine in early Gr philosophy will be found helpful at this point.

2. "Esoteric" in Gr Philosophy, etc

From quite early times the philosophers of ancient Greece distinguished between the doctrines and rites which could be taught to *all* their pupils, and those which could profitably be communicated only to a select circle called the initiated. The two classes of doctrines and rites—they were mainly the latter—were designated respectively "exoteric" and "esoteric." Lucian (d. 312; see *Vit. Auct.* 26) followed by many others referred the distinction to Aristotle, but as modern scholars agree, wrongly, for the ἐξωτερικοὶ λόγοι, *exōterikoí lógoi*, of that philosopher denote popular treatises. The Pythagoreans recognized and observed these two kinds of doctrines and duties and there is good reason for believing that they created a corresponding double lit. though unfortunately no explicit examples of such lit. have come down to us. In the Gr mysteries (Orphic, Dionysiac, Eleusinian, etc) two classes of hearers and readers are implied all through, though it is a pity that more of the lit. bearing on the question has not been preserved. Among the Buddhists the *Samga* forms a close society open originally to monks or *bhikhus* admitted only after a most rigid examination; but in later years nuns (*bhikshunis*) also have been allowed admission, though in their case too after careful testing. The *Vinaya Pitaka* or "Basket of Discipline" contains the rules for entrance and the regulations to be observed after entrance. But this and kindred lit. was and is still held to be caviare to outsiders. See tr in the *Sacred Books of the East*, XI (Rhys Davids and Oldenberg).

III. Usage as to Apocrypha.—It must be borne in mind that the word *apocrypha* is really a Gr adj. in the neuter pl., denoting strictly "things hidden."

But almost certainly the noun *biblia* is understood, so that the real implication of the word is "apocryphal books" or "writings." In this article *apocrypha* will be employed in the sense of this last, and *apocryphal* as the equivalent of the Gr *apokruphos*.

Apocalyptic literature.—The word *apocrypha* was first used technically by early Christian writers for the Jewish and Christian writings usually classed under "Apocalyptic" (see APOCALYPTIC LITERATURE). In this sense it takes the place of the classical Gr word *esoterika* and bears the same general meaning, viz. writings intended for an inner circle and capable of being understood by no others. These writings give intimations regarding the future, the ultimate triumph of the kingdom of God, etc, beyond, it was thought, human discovery and also beyond the intelligence of the uninitiated. In this sense Gregory of Nyssa (d. 395; *De Ordin.*, II, 44) and Epiphanius (d. 403; *Haeres*, **51** 3) speak of the Apocalypse of John as "apocryphal."

1. Early Christian Usage

Christianity itself has nothing corresponding to the idea of a doctrine for the initiated or a lit. for a select few. The gospel was preached in its first days to the poor and ignorant, and the reading and studying of the sacred Scriptures have been urged by the churches (with some exceptions) upon the public at large.

2. The Eastern Church

(1) *Esoteric literature.*—The rise of this conception in the eastern church is easily understood. When devotees of Gr philosophy accepted the Christian faith it was natural for them to look at the new religion through the medium of the old philosophy. Many of them read into the canonical writings mystic meanings, and embodied those meanings in special books, these last becoming esoteric lit. in themselves: and as in the case of apocalyptic writings, this esoteric lit. was more revered than the Bible itself. In a similar way there grew up among the Jews side by side with the written law an oral law containing the teaching of the rabbis and regarded as more sacred and authoritative than the writings they profess to expound. One may find some analogy in the fact that among many Christians the official lit. of the denomination to which they belong has more commanding force than the Bible itself. This movement among Gr Christians was greatly aided by gnostic sects and the esoteric lit. to which they gave rise. These Gnostics had been themselves influenced deeply by Bab and Pers mysticism and the corresponding lit. Clement of Alexandria (d. 220) distinctly mentions esoteric books belonging to the Zoroastrian (Mazdean) religion.

Oriental and esp. Gr Christianity tended to give to philosophy the place which the NT and western Christianity assign the OT. The preparation for the religion of Jesus was said to be in philosophy much more than in the religion of the OT. It will be remembered that Marcian (d. end of 2d cent. AD), Thomas Morgan, the Welsh 18th-cent. deist (d. 1743) and Friedrich Schleiermacher (d. 1834) taught this very same thing.

Clement of Alexandria (see above) recognized 4(2) Esd (to be hereafter called the Apocalypse of Ezra), the Asm M, etc, as fully canonical. In addition to this he upheld the authority and value of esoterical books, Jewish, Christian, and even heathen. But he is of most importance for our present purpose because he is probably the earliest Gr writer to use the word *apocrypha* as the equivalent of *esoterika*, for he describes the esoteric books of Zoroastrianism as *apocryphal*.

But the idea of esoteric religious lit. existed at an earlier time among the Jews, and was borrowed from them by Christians. It is clearly taught in the Apocalyptic Esdras (2 or 4 Esd) ch **14**, where it is said that Ezra aided by five amanuenses produced under Divine inspiration 94 sacred books, the writings of Moses and the prophets having been lost when Jerus and the temple were destroyed. Of this large number of sacred books 24 were to be published openly, for the unworthy as well as the worthy, these 24 books representing undoubtedly the books of the Heb OT. The remaining 70 were to be kept for the exclusive use of the "wise among the people": i.e. they were of an esoteric character. Perhaps if the Gr original of this book had been preserved the word "apocrypha" would have been found as an epithetic attached to the 70 books. Our Eng. VSS are made from a Lat original (see 2(4) EZRA or the APOCALYPTIC ESD. Modern scholars agree that in its present form this book arose in the reign of Domitian 81–96 AD. So that the conception of esoteric lit. existed among the Jews in the 1st cent. of our era, and probably still earlier.

It is significant of the original character of the religion of Israel that no one has been able to point to a Heb word corresponding to esoteric (see below). When among the Jews there arose a lit. of oral tradition it was natural to apply to this last the Gr notion of esoteric, esp. as this class of lit. was more highly esteemed in many Jewish circles than the OT Scriptures themselves.

(2) *Non-canonical religious books.*—The next step in the history of the word "apocrypha" is that by which it came to denote religious books inferior in authority and worth to the Scriptures of the OT and NT. This change of attitude toward non-canonical writings took place under the influence of two principles: (1) that no writer could be inspired who lived subsequent to the apostolic age; (2) that no writing could be recognized as canonical unless it was accepted as such by the churches in general (in Lat the principle was—*quod ubique, quod semper, quod ab omnibus*). Now it was felt that many if not most of the religious writings which came in the end of the 2d cent. to be called "apocryphal" in a disparaging sense had their origin among heretical sects like the Gnostics, and that they had never commanded the approval of the great bulk of the churches. Origen (d. 253) held that we ought to discriminate between books called "apocryphal," some such having to be firmly rejected as teaching what is contrary to the Scriptures. More and more from the end of the 2d cent., the word "apocrypha" came to stand for what is spurious and untrustworthy, and esp. for writings ascribed to authors who did not write them: i.e. the so-called "Pseudepigraphical books."

Irenaeus (d. 202) in opposition to Clement of Alexandria denies that esoteric writings have any claims to credence or even respect, and he uses the Gr word for "apocryphal" to describe all Jewish and Christian canons. To him, as later to Jerome (d. 420), "canonical" and "apocryphal" were antithetic terms.

Tertullian (d. 230) took the same view: "apocryphal" to him denoted non-canonical. But both Irenaeus and Tertullian meant by *apocrypha* in particular the apocalyptic writings. During the Nicene period, and even earlier, sacred books were divided by Christian teachers into three classes: (1) books that could be read in church; (2) books that could be read privately, but not in public; (3) books that were not to be read at all. This classification is implied in the writings of Origen, Clement of Alexandria, Athanasius (d. 373), and in the Muratorian Fragments (about 200 AD).

(3) *"Spurious" books.*—Athanasius, however, restricted the word *apocrypha* to the third class, thus making the corresponding adj. synonymous with

"spurious." Nicephorus, patriarch of Constantinople (806–15 AD) in his chronography (belonging essentially to 500 AD according to Zahn) divides sacred books thus: (1) the canonical books of the OT and NT; (2) the Antilegomena of both Testaments; (3) the Apocrypha of both Testaments.

The details of the Apoc of the NT are thus enumerated: (1) Enoch; (2) The 12 Patriarchs; (3) The Prayer of Joseph; (4) The Testament of Moses; (5) The Assumption of Moses; (6) Abram; (7) Eldad and Modad; (8) Elijah the Prophet; (9) Zephaniah the Prophet; (10) Zechariah, father of John; (11) The Pseudepigrapha of Baruch, Habakkuk, Ezekiel and Daniel.

The books of the NT Apoc are thus given: (1) The Itinerary of Paul; (2) The Itinerary of Peter; (3) The Itinerary of John; (4) The Itinerary of Thomas; (5) The Gospel according to Thomas; (6) The Teaching of the Apostles (the *Didache*); (7) and (8) The Two Epistles of Clement; (9) Epistles of Ignatius, Polycarp and Hermas.

The above lists are repeated in the so-called *Synopsis of Athanasius*. The authors of these so-called apocryphal books being unknown, it was sought to gain respect for these writers by tacking onto them well-known names, so that, particularly in the western church, "apocryphal" came to be almost synonymous with "pseudepigraphical."

Of the OT lists given above nos. 1, 2, 4, 5 are extant wholly or in part. Nos. 3, 7, 8 and 9 are lost though quoted as genuine by Origen and other eastern Fathers. They are all of them apocalypses designated apocrypha in accordance with early usage.

(4) *"List of Sixty."*—In the anonymous "List of Sixty," which hails from the 7th cent., we have represented probably the attitude of the eastern church. It divides sacred books into three classes: (1) The sixty canonical books. Since the Protestant canon consists of but 57 books it will be seen that in this list books outside our canon are included. (2) Books excluded from the 60, yet of superior authority to those mentioned as apocryphal in the next class. (3) Apocryphal books, the names of which are as follows: (*a*) Adam; (*b*) Enoch; (*c*) Lamech; (*d*) The 12 Patriarchs; (*e*) The Prayer of Joseph; (*f*) Eldad and Modad; (*g*) The Testament of Moses; (*h*) The Assumption of Moses; (*i*) The Psalms of Solomon; (*j*) The Apocalypse of Elijah; (*k*) The Ascension of Isaiah; (*l*) The Apocalypse of Zephaniah (see no. 9 of the OT Apoc books mentioned in the Chronography of Nicephorus); (*m*) The Apocalypse of Zechariah; (*n*) The Apocalyptic Ezra; (*o*) The History of James; (*p*) The Apocalypse of Peter; (*q*) The Itinerary and Teaching of the Apostles; (*r*) The Epistles of Barnabas; (*s*) The Acts of Paul; (*t*) Apocalypse of Paul; (*u*) Didascalia of Clement; (*v*) Didascalia of Ignatius; (*w*) Didascalia of Polycarp; (*x*) Gospel according to Barnabas; (*y*) Gospel according to Matthew.

The greater number of these books come under the designation "apocryphal" in the early sense of "apocalyptic," but by this time the word had taken on a lower meaning, viz. books not good for even private reading. Yet the fact that these books are mentioned at all show that they were more highly esteemed than heathen and than even heretical Christian writings. The eastern churches down to the present day reject the meaning of "apocrypha" current among Protestants (see definition above), and their Bible includes the OT Apoc, making no distinction between it and the rest of the Bible.

(1) *The "Decretum Gelasii."*—In the western church the word apocrypha and the corresponding adj. had a somewhat different history. In general it may be said that the western church did not adopt the triple division of sacred books prevalent in the eastern church. Yet the *Decretum Gelasii* (6th cent. in its present form) has a triple list which is almost certainly that of the Rom synod of 382 under Damasus, bishop of Rome, 366 to 384. It is as follows: (1) the canonical books of both Testaments; (2) writings of the Fathers approved by the church; (3) apocryphal books rejected by the church. Then there is added a list of miscellaneous books condemned as heretical, including even the works of Clement of Alexandria, Tertullian, and Eusebius, these works being all branded as "apocryphal." On the other hand Gregory of Nyssa and Epiphanius, both writing in the 4th cent., use the word "apocrypha" in the old sense of apocalyptic, i.e. esoteric.

3. Western Church

(2) *Non-canonical books.*—Jerome (d. 420) in the *Prologus Galeatus* (so called because it was a defence and so resembled a helmeted warrior) or preface to his Lat version of the Bible uses the word "Apoc" in the sense of non-canonical books. His words are: *Quidquid extra hos* (i.e. the 22 canonical books) *inter Apocrypha ponendum:* "Anything outside of these must be placed within the Apocrypha" (when among the Fathers and rabbis the OT is made to contain 22 [not 24] books, Ruth and Lam are joined respectively to Jgs and Jer). He was followed in this by Rufinus (d. cir 410), in turns Jerome's friend and adversary, as he had been anticipated by Irenaeus. The western church as a whole departed from Jerome's theory by including the antilegomena of both Testaments among the canonical writings: but the general custom of western Christians about this time was to make apocryphal mean non-canonical. Yet Augustine (d. 430; *De Civitate Dei*, XV, 23) explained the "apocrypha" as denoting obscurity of origin or authorship, and this sense of the word became the prevailing one in the West.

Separation from canonical books.—But it is to the Reformers that we are indebted for the habit of using Apoc for a collection of books appended to the OT and generally up to 1827 appended to every printed English Bible. Bodenstein of Carlstadt, usually called Carlstadt (d. 1541), an early Reformer, though Luther's bitter personal opponent, was the first modern scholar to define "Apoc" quite clearly as writings excluded from the canon, whether or not the true authors of the books are known, in this, going back to Jerome's position. The adj. "apocryphal" came to have among Protestants more and more a disparaging sense. Protestantism was in its very essence the religion of a book, and Protestants would be sure to see to it that the sacred volume on which they based their religion, including the reforms they introduced, contained no book but those which in their opinion had the strongest claims to be regarded as authoritative. In the eastern and western churches under the influence of the Gr (LXX) and Lat (Vulg) VSS the books of the Apoc formed an integral part of the canon and were scattered throughout the OT, they being placed generally near books with which they have affinity. Even Protestant Bibles up to 1827 included the Apoc, but as one collection of distinct writings at the end of the OT. It will be seen from what has been said that notwithstanding the favorable attitude toward it of the eastern and western churches, from the earliest times, our Apoc was regarded with more or less suspicion, and the suspicion would be strengthened by the general antagonism toward it. In the Middle Ages, under the influence of Reuchlin (d. 1532)—great scholar and Reformer—Heb came to be studied and the OT read in its original language. The fact that

4. The Reformers

the Apoc is absent from the Heb canon must have had some influence on the minds of the Reformers. Moreover in the Apoc there are parts inconsistent with Protestant principles, as for example the doctrines of prayers for the dead, the intercession of the saints, etc. The Jews in the early Christian cents. had really two Bibles: (1) There was the Heb Bible which does not include the Apoc, and which circulated in Pal and Babylon; (2) there was the Gr version (LXX) used by Gr-speaking Jews everywhere. Until in quite early times, instigated by the use made of it by Christians against themselves, the Jews condemned this version and made the Heb canon their Bible, thus rejecting the books of the Apoc from their list of canonical writings, and departing from the custom of Christian churches which continued with isolated remonstrances to make the Gr OT canon, with which the Vulg agrees almost completely, their standard. It is known that the Reformers were careful students of the Bible, and that in OT matters they were the pupils of Jewish scholars—there were no other competent teachers of Heb. It might therefore have been expected that the OT canon of the Reformers would agree in extent with that of the Jews and not with that of the Gr and Lat Christians. Notwithstanding the doubt which Ryle (*Canon of the OT*², 156) casts on the matter, all the evidence goes to show that the LXX and therefore the other great Gr VSS included the Apoc from the first onward.

But how comes it to be that the Gr OT is more extensive than the Heb OT? Up to the final destruction of Jerus in 71 AD the temple with its priesthood and ritual was the center of the religious thought and life of the nation. But with the destruction of the sanctuary and the disbanding of its officials it was needful to find some fresh binding and directing agency and this was found in the collection of sacred writings known by us as the OT. By a national synod held at Jamnia, near Jaffa, in 90 AD, the OT canon was practically though not finally closed, and from that date one may say that the limits of the OT were once and for all fixed, no writings being included except those written in Heb, the latest of these being as old as 100 BC. Now the Jews of the Dispersion spoke and wrote Gr, and they continued to think and write long after their fellow-countrymen of the homeland had ceased to produce any fresh original lit. What they did produce was explanatory of what had been written and practical.

The Gr Bible—the Sept—is that of the Jews in Egypt and of those found in other Gr-speaking countries. John Wycliffe (d. 1384) puts the Apoc together at the end of the OT and the same course was taken by Luther (1546) in his great German and by Miles Coverdale (d. 1568) in his Eng. tr.

5. Hebrew Words for Apocrypha

Is it quite certain that there is no Heb word or expression corresponding exactly to the word "apocrypha" as first used by Christian writers, i.e. in the sense "esoteric"? One may answer this by a decisive negative as regards the OT and the Talm. But in the Middle Ages *ḳabbālāh* (lit. "tradition") came to have a closely allied meaning (cf our "*kabbalistic*").

(1) *Do such exist?*—Is there in Heb a word or expression denoting "non-canonical," i.e. having the secondary sense acquired by "apocrypha"? This question does not allow of so decided an answer, and as matter of fact it has been answered in different ways.

(2) *Views of Zahn, et al.*—Zahn (*Gesch. des neutest. Kanons*, I, i, 123 ff); Schürer (*RE*³, I, 623); Porter (*HDB*, I) and others maintain that the Gr word "*Apocrypha* (*Biblia*)" is a tr of the Heb *Ṣᵉphārīm gᵉnūzīm*, lit. "books stored away." If this view is the correct one it follows that the distinction of canonical and non-canonical books originated among the Jews, and that the Fathers in using the word *apocrypha* in this sense were simply copying the Jews substituting Gr words for the Heb equivalent. But there are decisive reasons for rejecting this view.

(3) *Reasons for rejection.*—(*a*) The verb *gānaz* of which the passive part. occurs in the above phrase means "to store away," "to remove from view"—of things in themselves sacred or precious. It never means to exclude as from the canon.

(*b*) When employed in reference to sacred books it is only of those recognized as canonical. Thus after copies of the Pent or of other parts of the Heb Bible had, by age and use, become unfit to be read in the home or in the synagogue they were "buried" in the ground as being too sacred to be burnt or cut up; and the verb denoting this burying is *gānaz*. But those buried books are without exception canonical.

(*c*) The Heb phrase in question does not once occur in either the Bab or the Jerus Talm, but only in rabbinical writings of a much later date. The Gr *apocrypha* cannot therefore be a rendering of the Heb expression. The Heb for books definitely excluded from the canon is *Ṣᵉphārīm ḥīçōnīm*="outside" or "extraneous books." The Mish (the text of the Gemara, both making up what we call Talm) or oral law with its additions came to be divided analogously into (1) The Mish proper; (2) the external (*ḥīçōnāh*) Mish: in Aram. called *Bāraiythā'*.

What has been said may be summarized:

6. Summary

(1) Among the Protestant churches the word Apoc is used for the books included in the LXX and Vulg, but absent from the Heb Bible. This restricted sense of the word cannot be traced farther back than the beginning of the Reformation.

(2) In classical and Hellenistic Gr the adj. *apokruphos* denotes "hidden" of visible objects, or obscure, hard to understand (of certain kinds of knowledge).

(3) In early patristic Gr this adj. came into use as a synonym of the classical Gr *esoterikos*.

(4) In later patristic Gr (Irenaeus, etc) and in Lat works beginning with Jerome, Gr *apokruphos* meant non-canonical, implying inferiority in subject-matter to the books in the canon.

(4) By the Protestant Reformers the term "apocrypha" ("apocryphal" "books" being understood) came to stand for what is now called the "OT Apoc." But this usage is confined to Protestants, since in the eastern church and in the Rom branch of the western church the OT Apoc is as much an integral part of the canon as Genesis or Kings or Psalms or Isaiah.

(5) There are no equivalents in Heb for *apokruphos* in the sense of either "esoteric" or in that of "non-canonical."

IV. Contents of the Apocrypha.—The following is a list of the books in the Apoc in the order in which

1. List of Books

they occur in the Eng. VSS (AV and RV): (1) 1 Esdras; (2) 2 Esdras (to be hereafter called "The Apocalyptic Esdras"); (3) Tobit; (4) Judith; (5) The Rest of Esther; (6) The Wisdom of Solomon; (7) Ecclesiasticus (to be hereafter called "Sirach"); (8) Baruch, with the Epistle of Jeremiah; (9) The Song of the Three Holy Children; (10) The History of Susanna; (11) Bel and the Dragon; (12) The Prayer of Manasses; (13) 1 Maccabees; (14) 2 Maccabees.

No. 5 in the above, "Addition to Esther," as it may be called, consists of the surplusage (107 out of 270 verses) of the Book of Esther as it occurs in the best MSS of the LXX and in the Vulg over the text in the Heb Bible. These additions are in the LXX scattered throughout the book and are intelligible in the context thus given them, but not when brought together as they are in the collected Apoc of our Eng. VSS and as they are to some extent in Jerome's Lat version and the Vulg (see *Century Bible*, Ezra, Neh and Esther, 294 f). Nos. 9–11 in the above enumeration are additions made in the Gr LXX and Vulg VSS of Daniel to the book as found in the MT. It will be well to name them "Additions to Daniel." The bringing together of the writings of the Apoc into an apart collection was due in a large measure to Jerome, who separated many of the apocryphal additions from their original context because he suspected their genuineness. His version influenced the Vulg, which follows Jerome's version closely.

Though it is generally true that the Apoc is the excess of the Gr (LXX) and Lat (Jer, *Vulg*) over the Heb (MT) Bibles, the statement needs qualification. 2 (4) Ezra, i.e. the Apocalyptic Ezra (Esdras), is absent from the LXX, from Jerome's version, and also from Luther's Bible, but it occurs in the Vulg and in the Eng. and other modern VSS of the Apoc. On the other hand 3 and 4 Macc occur in the best MSS of the LXX, but the Vulg, following Jerome's version, rejects both as do modern VSS (Eng. etc) of the Apoc. Moreover it has to be pointed out that in the Vulg proper the Prayer of Manasses and 1 (3) Esdras and the Apocalyptic Esdras are appended to the NT as apocryphal.

2. Classification of Books

(1) *Historical.*—The books of the Apoc proper may be thus classified: (*a*) 1 and 2 (i.e. 3) Esdras; (*b*) 1 and 2 Maccabees; (*c*) Additions to Daniel (nos. 9–11 in the above list); (*d*) Additions to Esther; (*e*) The Epistle of Jeremy (usually appended to Baruch); (*f*) Prayer of Manasses.

(2) *Legendary.*—(*a*) Book of Baruch (sometimes classed with prophetic books, sometimes with Apocalypses); (*b*) Tobit; (*c*) Judith.

(3) *Apocalyptic.*—The Apocalyptic Esdras or 2 (4) Esdras.

(4) *Didactic.*—(*a*) The Wisdom of Solomon; (*b*) Sirach (Ecclesiasticus).

R. H. Charles, our greatest living authority on the Apocalyptic and Apocryphal writings, embraces the following under the heading "Hellenistic Jewish Literature," the rest coming under the heading "Palestinian Jewish Literature" (*Enc Brit*, 11th ed, II, 177): (1) The Additions to Daniel and Esther (2) The Epistle of Jeremy; (3) 2 Macc; (4) The Wisdom of Solomon.

V. Original Languages of the Apocrypha.—The bulk of the Apoc was written originally in the Gr language and existed at the first in that language alone. The following books were however written in Heb: Tobit, Judith, Sirach, Baruch (part probably in Gr), and 1 Macc. In these cases some prefer regarding Aram. as the original language in at least parts of the above books. For detailed information see under the several books.

VI. Date of the Apocryphal Writings.—The question of date as it applies to the separate books of the Apoc will be discussed in connection with the arts. dealing with the several books. But a general statement regarding the extreme limits between which all the books were completed may safely be made. The oldest apocryphal book is Sirach, which in its original Heb form belongs to between 190–170 BC. In its Gr form the best modern scholars agree in fixing it at between 130–120 BC. None of the books can well belong to a date later than 100 AD, though some (2 Esd, etc) may be as late as that. The whole of the Apoc may with more than average certainty be said to have been written some time between 200 BC and 100 AD. It will be seen that it is an inaccurate assumption that the Apoc was in all its parts of later date than the latest parts of the OT. The canonical Book of Daniel and many of the Psalms are of later date than Sirach and 1 Esdras, and there are cogent reasons for giving the canonical Esther a later date than any of the books named and perhaps than Judith as well (see, however, DANIEL; ESTHER). But it is quite certain that by far the greater part of the Apoc is of later date than the OT; it is therefore of the utmost importance as reflecting the state of the Jews and the character of their intellectual and religious life at the various periods represented. And in later years much use has been made of it.

LITERATURE.—The Gr text of the Apoc is given in the various editions of the LXX (except the Apocalyptic Esdras, not extant in Gr). The best editions of the LXX are those by Tischendorf revised by E. Nestle (1887); and Swete (1895–99 and later editions). Critical editions of the Apoc have been issued by A. Fabricius (Hamburg, 1722–23); Apel (ib 1804) and a very valuable edition by O. T. Fritzsche (Leipzig, 1871) which includes the Lat version of the Apocalyptic Esdras—without the missing fragment. There are several modern translations, far the best being that in German edited by E. Kautzsch, containing Introductions, general and special, and valuable notes by the best German scholars. In English besides the RV there is the useful Variorum ed, edited by C. J. Ball. An Eng. critical edition of the Apoc edited by R. H. Charles, with introd. notes, is now being printed at Oxford and will be very valuable.

The best commentary is that by O. F. Fritsche and C. L. W. Grimm, *Kurzgef. Exeg. Handbuch*, 1851–60; but the commentary by Bissell in Lange's Series of Commentaries and that edited by Wace, in the Speaker's Bible Series, are meritorious.

Introductory matter will be found in the various Bible Dictionaries s.v.: see esp. H. E. Ryle in *DB* (1893), Schürer (*RE*[3]), but esp. in the valuable *Intro to the OT in Gr*, by H. B. Swete (1900), *HDB* (C. F. Porter), and R. H. Charles (*Enc Brit*[11]). See also the *Einleitungen* by König, Budde (A. Bertholet has written the part dealing with the Apoc), and Schürer, *Geschichte*, III, 1898 (Eng. tr, II, iii), where much lit. is specified. For monographs on the several books of the Apoc or discussing special points, see the special articles.

THOMAS WITTON DAVIES

APOCRYPHAL ACTS, a-pok′ri-fal akts:

A. GENERAL INTRODUCTION
- I. *The Meaning of "Apocryphal"*
  1. Secret
  2. False and Heretical
  3. Extra-canonical
- II. *General Characteristics*
  1. Romance
  2. The Supernatural
  3. Sexual Asceticism
  4. Heretical Teaching
  5. Religious Feeling
- III. *Origin*
  1. Reverence for Apostles
  2. Pious Curiosity
  3. Apostolic Authority Desired
  4. Interests of Local Churches
- IV. *Sources*
  1. Canonical Acts
  2. Traditions
  3. Romances of Travel
- V. *Ecclesiastical Testimony*
  1. Eastern
  2. Western
  3. Photius
  4. Ecclesiastical Condemnation
- VI. *Authorship*
- VII. *Relationship of Different Acts*
- VIII. *Value*
  1. As History
  2. As Records of Early Christianity
- IX. *Influence*

Literature

B. THE SEPARATE ACTS
- I. *Acts of Paul*
- II. *Acts of Peter*
- III. *Acts of John*
- IV. *Acts of Andrew*
- V. *Acts of Thomas*

A. GENERAL INTRODUCTION

I. The Meaning of "Apocryphal."—As applied to early-Christian writings the term "apocryphal" has the secondary and conventional sense of "extra-canonical."

Originally, as the etymology of the word shows (Gr *apokrúpto*="hide"), it denoted what was "hidden" or "secret." In this sense "apocryphal" was, to begin with, a title of honor, being applied to writings used by the initiated in esoteric circles and highly valued by them as containing truths miraculously revealed and kept secret from the outside world. Just as there were writings of this kind among the Jews, so there were in Christian circles, among gnostic sects, *apocrypha,* which claimed to embody the deeper truths of Christianity, committed as a secret tradition by the risen Christ to His apostles.

1. Secret

When the conception of a catholic church began to take shape, it was inevitable that these secret writings should have been regarded with suspicion and have been ultimately forbidden, not only because they fostered the spirit of division in the church, but because they were favorable to the spread of heretical teaching. By a gradual and intelligible transference of ideas "apocryphal," as applied to secret writings thus discredited by the church, came to have the bad sense of *spurious* and *heretical.* In this sense the word is used both by Irenaeus and Tertullian.

2. False and Heretical

Short of being stigmatized as false and heretical many books were regarded as unsuitable for reading in public worship, although they might be used for purposes of private edification. Chiefly under the influence of Jerome the term "apocryphal" received an extension of meaning so as to include writings of this kind, stress now being laid on their non-acceptance as authoritative Scriptures by the church, without any suggestion that the ground of non-acceptance lay in heretical teaching. It is in this wide sense that the word is used when we speak of "Apocryphal Acts." Although the Acts which bear this name had their origin for the most part in circles of heretical tendency, the description of them as "apocryphal" involves no judgment as to the character of their contents, but simply denotes that they are Acts which were excluded from the NT canon because their title or claims to recognition as authoritative and normative writings were not admitted by the church. This definition limits the scope of our investigation to those Acts which belong to the 2d cent., the Biblical Acts having secured their place as an authoritative scripture by the end of that cent. See further, APOCRYPHA.

3. Extra-Canonical

II. General Characteristics.—The Apocryphal Acts purport to give the history of the activity of the apostles in fuller detail than the canonical Acts. The additions to the NT narrative found in them are highly flavored with romance and reveal an extravagant and unhealthy taste for the miraculous. Wonderful tales, the product of an exuberant fancy, often devoid of delicacy of feeling and always out of touch with reality, are freely heaped one upon the other. The apostles are no longer conceived as living on the ordinary levels of humanity; their human frailties, to which the canonical writers are not blind, have almost entirely disappeared; they walk through the world as men conversant with the mysteries of heaven and earth and possessed of powers to which no limit can be set. They have the power to heal, to exorcise demons, to raise the dead; and while marvelous deeds of that nature constantly recur, there are other miracles wrought by the apostles which remind one of the bizarre and non-moral prodigies of the Childhood Gospel of Thomas. A smoked fish is made to swim; a broken statue is made whole by the use of consecrated water; a child of seven months is enabled to talk with a man's voice; animals receive the power of human speech.

1. Romance

The romantic character of the Apocryphal Acts is intensified by the frequent introduction of the supernatural. Angelic messengers appear in vision and in dream; heavenly voices are heard; clouds descend to hide the faithful in the hour of danger and lightnings smite their foes; the terrifying forces of Nature, earthquake, wind and fire, strike dismay into the hearts of the ungodly; and martyrs die transfigured in a blaze of unearthly glory. Especially characteristic of these Acts are the appearances of Christ in many forms; now as an old man, now as a comely youth, now as a child; but most frequently in the likeness of this or that apostle. (It is interesting to observe that Origen is familiar with a tradition that Jesus during His earthly life could change His appearance when and how He pleased, and gives that as a reason for the necessity of the traitor's kiss. Cf also Mk **16** 9.12.)

2. The Supernatural

One must not suppose from the foregoing that the Apocryphal Acts with their profusion of romantic and supernatural details were designed merely to exalt the personality of the apostles and to satisfy the prevalent desire for the marvelous. They had a definite practical end in view. They were intended to confirm and popularize a type of Christianity in strong reaction against the world, in which emphasis was laid on the rigid abstinence from sexual relations as the chief moral requirement. This sexual asceticism is the dominant *motif* in all the Acts. The "contendings" of the apostles, their trials and their eventual martyrdom are in almost every case due to their preaching the sinfulness of conjugal life and to their success in persuading women to reject the society of their husbands. The Acts are penetrated throughout by the conviction that abstinence from marriage is the supreme condition of entering upon the highest life and of winning heaven. The gospel on its practical side is (to use the succinct expression of the Acts of Paul) "the word of God regarding abstinence and the resurrection."

3. Sexual Asceticism

Besides inculcating an ascetic morality the Apocryphal Acts show traces more or less pronounced of dogmatic heresy. All of them with the exception of the Acts of Paul represent a docetic view of Christ; that is to say, the earthly life of Jesus is regarded merely as an appearance, phantasmal and unreal. This docetic Christology is most prominent in the Acts of John, where we read that when Jesus walked no footprints were discernible; that sometimes when the apostle attempted to lay hold of the body of Jesus his hand passed through it without resistance; that when the crowd gathered round the cross on which to all appearance Jesus hung, the Master Himself had an interview with His disciple John on the Mount of Olives. The crucifixion was simply a symbolical spectacle; it was only in appearance that Christ suffered and died. Allied with the docetic Christology is a naïve Modalism, according to which there is no clear distinction between the Father and the Son.

4. Heretical Teaching

In spite of the unfavorable impression created by the flood of miraculous and supernatural details, the pervading atmosphere of sexual asceticism and the presence of dogmatic misconception, it is impossible not to feel in many sections of the Apocryphal Acts the rapture of a great spiritual enthusiasm. Particularly in the Acts of John, Andrew and Thomas there are passages (songs, prayers, homilies), sometimes of genuine poetic

5. Religious Feeling

beauty, which are characterized by religious warmth, mystic fervor and moral earnestness. The mystical love to Christ, expressed though it frequently is in the strange language of gnostic thought, served to bring the Saviour near to men as the satisfaction of the deepest yearnings of the soul for deliverance from the dark power of death. The rank superstition and the traces of unconquered heathenism should not blind us to the fact that in the Apocryphal Acts we have an authentic if greatly distorted expression of the Christian faith, and that through them great masses of people were confirmed in their conviction of the spiritual presence and power of Christ the Saviour.

III. Origin.—The Apocryphal Acts had their origin at a time when the canonical Acts of the Apostles were not yet recognized as alone authoritative. Various motives contributed to the appearance of books dealing with the life and activity of the different apostles.

1. Reverence for Apostles

Behind every variety of motive lay the profound reverence for the apostles as the authoritative depositaries of Christian truth. In apostolic times the sole authority in Christian communities, outside OT Scripture, was "the Lord." But as the creative period of Christianity faded into the past, "the apostles" (in the sense of the college of the Twelve, including Paul) were raised to a preeminent position alongside of Christ with the object of securing continuity in the credentials of the faith. The commandments of the Lord had been received through them (2 Pet **3** 2). In the Ignatian epistles they have a place of acknowledged supremacy by the side of Christ. Only that which had apostolic authority was normative for the church. The authority of the apostles was universal. They had gone into all the world to preach the gospel. They had, according to the legend referred to at the beginning of the Acts of Thomas, divided among themselves the different regions of the earth as the spheres of their activity. It was an inevitable consequence of the peculiar reverence in which the apostles were held as the securities for Christian truth that a lively interest should everywhere be shown in traditional stories about their work and that writings should be multiplied which purported to give their teaching with fulness of detail.

2. Pious Curiosity

The canonical Acts were not calculated to satisfy the prevailing desire for a knowledge of the life and teaching of the apostles. For one thing many of the apostles are there ignored, and for another the information given about the chief apostles Peter and Paul is little more than a meager outline of the events of their life. In these circumstances traditions not preserved in the canonical Acts were eagerly accepted, and as the actual history of the individual apostles was largely shrouded in obscurity, legends were freely invented to gratify the insatiable curiosity. The marvelous character of these inventions is a testimony to the supernatural level to which the apostles had been raised in popular esteem.

3. Apostolic Authority Desired

As in the case of the apocryphal Gospels, the chief motive in the multiplication of apostolic romances was the desire to set forth with the full weight of apostolic authority conceptions of Christian life and doctrine which prevailed in certain circles. (1) Alongside the saner and catholic type of Christianity there existed, especially in Asia Minor, a popular Christianity with perverted ideals of life. On its practical side the Christian religion was viewed as an ascetic discipline, involving not only abstinence from animal food and wine but also (and chiefly) abstinence from marriage. Virginity was the Christian ideal. Poverty and fastings were obligatory on all. The Apocryphal Acts are permeated by this spirit, and their evident design is to confirm and spread confidence in this ascetic ideal by representing the apostles as the zealous advocates of it. (2) The Apocryphal Acts were also intended to serve a dogmatic interest. Heretical sects used them as a means of propagating their peculiar doctrinal views and sought to supplement or supplant the tradition of the growing catholic church by another tradition which claimed to be equally apostolic.

4. Interests of Local Churches

A subsidiary cause in the fabrication of apostolic legends was the desire of churches to find support for the claims which they put forward for an apostolic foundation or for some connection with apostles. In some cases the tradition of the sphere of an apostle's activity may have been well based, but in others there is a probability that stories of an apostolic connection were freely invented for the purpose of enhancing the prestige of some local church.

IV. Sources.—In general it may be said that the Apocryphal Acts are full of legendary details. In

1. Canonical Acts

the invention of these everything was done to inspire confidence in them as historically true. The narratives accordingly abound in clear reminiscences of the canonical Acts. The apostles are cast into prison and are marvelously set at liberty. Converts receive the apostles into their houses. The description of the Lord's Supper as "the breaking of bread" (Acts **2** 42.46) is repeated in the Apocryphal Acts and is strictly apposite to the ritual there set forth in which there is frequently no mention of wine in the celebration of the sacrament. In the Acts of Paul the author evidently used the canonical Acts as the framework of his narrative. This dependence on the canonical Acts and the variety of allusions to details in them served to give an appearance of historical truthfulness to the later inventions and to secure for them a readier acceptance. The fact that the canonical Acts were so used clearly shows that they had a position of exceptional authority at the time when the Apocryphal Acts were written.

2. Traditions

The legendary character of the Apocryphal Acts does not preclude the possibility of authentic details in the additions made to the canonical history. There must have been many traditions regarding the apostles preserved in Christian communities which had a foundation in actual fact. Some of these would naturally find a place in writings which were designed in part at least to satisfy the popular curiosity for a fuller knowledge of the apostles. It is certain that there is some substratum of historical fact in the episode of Paul's association with Thecla (Acts of Paul). The description of Paul's appearance given in the same connection is in all likelihood due to trustworthy historical reminiscence. But it must be confessed that the signs of the presence of reliable traditions are very scanty. The few grains of historical fact are hidden in an overwhelming mass of material whose legendary character is unmistakable.

3. Romances of Travel

Although a formal connection with the canonical Acts is recognizable and reliable traditions are to a slight extent incorporated in the Apocryphal Acts, it is unquestionable that as a whole they are the creation of the Hellenic spirit which reveled in the miraculous. A noteworthy type of popular literature whose influence is apparent on almost every page of the Apocryphal Acts was that of the travel-romance. The most famous example of this romantic literature is the Life of the neo-Pythagorean preacher, the great wonder-worker Apollonios of Tyana, who died about the end of the 1st cent. AD. The marvelous deeds reported to have been wrought by him on his travels were freely transferred in a somewhat less striking form to other teachers. It is in the atmosphere of these romances that the Apocryphal Acts had their birth. In particular the Acts of Thomas recall the history of Apollonios. For just as Thomas was a missionary in India, so "Apollonios as a disciple of Pythagoras had traveled, a peaceful Alexander, to the Indian wonderland and there preached his master's wisdom" (Geffcken, *Christliche Apokryphen*, 36).

V. Ecclesiastical Testimony.—From the nature of his reference to the canonical Acts it is probable that the writer of the Muratorian Canon (cir 190 AD) had the existence of other Acts in mind. "The Acts of all the apostles," he says, "are written in a single book. Luke relates them admirably to Theophilus, confining himself to such as fell under his own notice, as he plainly shows by the omission of all reference either to the martyrdom of Peter or to the journey of Paul from Rome to Spain." During the 3d cent. there are slight allusions to certain of the Apocryphal Acts, but it is only in the 4th cent. that distinct references are frequent in writers both of the East and of the West. A few of the more important references may be given here. (For a full account of the ecclesiastical testimony see Harnack, *Gesch. der altchr. Lit.*, I, 116 ff.)

1. Eastern Testimony

Among eastern writers Eusebius (d. 340) is the first to make any clear reference to Apocryphal Acts. He speaks of "Acts of Andrew, of John and of the other apostles," which were of such a character that no ecclesiastical writer thought it proper to invoke their testimony. Their style and their teaching showed them to be so plainly of heretical origin that he would not put them even among spurious Scriptures, but absolutely rejected them as absurd and impious (*HE*, III, 25.6.7). Ephraem (d. 373) declares that Acts were written by the Bardesanites to propagate in the name of the apostles the unbelief which the apostles had destroyed. Epiphanius (cir 375) repeatedly refers to individual Acts which were in use among heretical sects. Amphilochius of Iconium, a contemporary of Epiphanius, declares that certain writings emanating from heretical circles were "not Acts of the apostles but accounts of demons." The Second Synod of Nicaea (787 AD), in the records of which those words of Amphilochius are preserved, dealt with apocryphal literature and had under special consideration the Acts of John to which the Iconoclasts appealed. In the synod's finding these Acts were characterized as "this abominable book," and on it the judgment was passed: "Let no one read it; and not only so, but we judge it worthy of being committed to the flames."

2. Western Testimony

In the West from the 4th cent. onward references are frequent. Philastrius of Brescia (cir 387) testifies to the use of Apocryphal Acts among the Manichaeans, and declares that although they are not suitable for general reading they may be read with profit by mature Christians (*De Haeres*, 88). The reason for this favorable judgment is to be found in the pronounced ascetic tendency of the Acts, which was in line with the moral ideal prevalent at that time in the West. Augustine refers repeatedly to apocryphal Acts in use among the Manichaeans and characterizes them as the work of "cobblers of fables" (*sutoribus fabularum*). The Manichaeans accepted them as true and genuine; and in respect of this claim Augustine says: "They would in the time of their authors have been counted worthy of being welcomed to the authority of the Holy Church, if saintly and learned men who were then alive and could examine such things had acknowledged them as speaking the truth" (*Contra Faustum*, XXII, 79). The Acts of John and the Acts of Thomas are mentioned by Augustine by name. He also refers to Leucius as the author of Apocryphal Acts. Turribius of Astorga (cir 450) speaks of Acts of Andrew, of John, of Thomas, and attributes them to the Manichaeans. Of the heretical teaching in the Acts of Thomas, Turribius singles out for special condemnation baptism by oil instead of by water. Leucius is mentioned as the author of the Acts of John. The Acts of Andrew, Thomas, Peter, and Philip are condemned as apocryphal in the Gelasian Decree (496 AD) and in the same condemnation are included "all books written by Leucius, a disciple of the devil."

3. Photius

The fullest and most important reference to the Apocryphal Acts is found in Photius, the Patriarch of Constantinople in the second half of the 9th cent. In his *Bibliotheca*, which contains an account of 280 different books which he had read during his absence on a mission to Bagdad, we learn that among these was a volume, "the so-called Wanderings of the Apostles, in which were included Acts of Peter, John, Andrew, Thomas, Paul. The author of these Acts, as the book itself makes plain, was Leucius Charinus." The language had none of the grace which characterized the evangelic and apostolic writings. The book teemed with follies and contradictions. Its teaching was heretical. In particular it was taught that Christ had never really become man. Not Christ but another in His place had been crucified. After referring to the ascetic doctrine and the absurd miracles of the Acts and to the part which the Acts of John had played in the Iconoclastic Controversy, Photius concludes: "In short this book contains ten thousand things which are childish, incredible, ill-conceived, false, foolish, inconsistent, impious and godless. If anyone were to call it the fountain and mother of all heresy, he would not be far from the truth."

4. Ecclesiastical Condemnation

There is thus a consensus of ecclesiastical testimony as to the general character of the Apocryphal Acts. They were writings used by a number of heretical sects but regarded by the church as unreliable and harmful. It is probable that the corpus of the Acts in five parts referred to by Photius was formed by the Manichaeans of North Africa, who attempted to have them accepted by the church in place of the canonical Acts which they had rejected. These Acts in consequence were stamped by the church with a heretical character. The sharpest condemnation is that pronounced by Leo I (cir 450) who declares that "they should not only be forbidden but should be utterly swept away and burned. For although there are certain things in them which seem to have the appearance of piety, yet they are never free of poison and secretly work through the allurements of fables so that they involve in the snares of every possible error those who are seduced by the narration of marvelous things." The Acts of Paul, which show no trace of dogmatic heresy, were included in the ecclesiastical censure owing to the fact that they had received a place at the end of the corpus. Many teachers in the church, however, made a distinction between the miraculous details and the heretical doctrines of the Acts, and while they rejected the latter they retained the former. Witness the words of an orthodox reviser in regard to his heretical predecessor: "Quaedam de virtutibus quidem et miraculis quae per eos Dominus fecit, vera dixit; de doctrina vero multa mentitus est."

VI. Authorship.—In the notice of Photius (*Bibliotheca* cod. 114) all the five Acts are ascribed to one author, Leucius Charinus. Earlier writers had associated the name of Leucius with certain Acts. In particular he is, on the witness of several writers, declared to be the author of the Acts of John. As these Acts show, the author professes to be a follower and companion of the apostle, and Epiphanius (*Haeres*, **51** 6) mentions one named Leucius as being in the *entourage* of John. This notice of Epiphanius, however, is of doubtful value, as it probably rested on the association in his mind of the name of Leucius with the Acts of John. Whether or not there is any truth in the ascription of these Acts to a disciple of John must be left undecided, but the probabilities are against there being any. Be that as it may, when the different Acts were collected, the name of the reputed author of the Acts of John was transferred to the whole collection. This probably happened not later than the 4th cent. Although all the Acts are certainly not from one hand (the difference of style is sufficient proof of this), there are so many striking similarities between some of them as to suggest a possible common authorship in those cases or at least a relation of literary dependence.

VII. Relationship of Different Acts.—That some connection existed between the different Acts was clearly recognized in early times, and it was doubtless due to this recognition that they were gathered together in a corpus under the name of one author. It is acknowledged that there is a close relationship between the Acts of Peter and the Acts of John, some holding that they are the work of the same author (James, Zahn), others that the former are dependent on the latter (Schmidt, Hennecke), while others again believe that their origin in the same theological school and in the same ecclesiastical atmosphere sufficiently explains all similarities (Ficker). The Acts of Andrew, too, reveal a near kinship to the Acts of Peter. But however the matter may stand in regard to literary dependence, the affinity between the different Acts in a material sense is manifest. All are pervaded by the ascetic spirit; in all Christ appears in the form of the apostle; in all women visit the apostle in prison. In respect of theological doctrine the Acts of Paul stand by themselves as anti-gnostic in tendency, but the others agree in their docetic view of Christ's person; while in the Acts of John, Peter and Thomas, there is a similar mystical doctrine of the cross.

VIII. Value.—As a source for information about the life and work of the apostles the Apocryphal Acts are almost entirely worthless. A possible exception in this respect is the section of the Acts of Paul dealing with Paul and Thecla, although even there any historical elements are almost lost in the legendary overgrowth. The spheres of the apostles' work, so far as they are mentioned only in these Acts, cannot be accepted without question, although they may be derived from reliable tradition. Taken as a whole the picture given in the Apocryphal Acts of the missionary labors of the apostles is a grotesque caricature.

1. As History

The Apocryphal Acts, however, though worthless as history, are of extreme value as throwing light on the period in which they were written. They belong to the 2d cent. and are a rich quarry for information about the popular Christianity of that time. They give us a vivid picture of the form which Christianity assumed in contact with the enthusiastic mystery-cults and gnostic sects which then flourished on the soil of Asia Minor. We see in them the Christian faith deeply tinged with the spirit of contemporary paganism; the faith in Christ the Saviour–God, which satisfied the widespread yearning for redemption from the powers of evil, in association with the as yet unconquered elements of its heathen environment. (1) The Acts show us *popular Christianity under the influence of gnostic ideas* as contrasted with the Gnosticism of the schools which moves in a region of mythological conceptions, cold abstractions and speculative subtleties. At the basis of Gnosticism lay a contempt for material existence; and in the Christianity of the Apocryphal Acts we see the practical working up of the two chief ideas which followed from this fundamental position, a docetic conception of Christ's person and an ascetic view of life. In this popular religion Christ had few of the features of the historic Jesus; He was the Saviour–God, exalted above principalities and powers, through union with whom the soul was delivered from the dread powers of evil and entered into the true life. The manhood of Christ was sublimated into mere appearance; and in particular the sufferings of Christ were conceived mystically and symbolically, "sometimes in the form that in the story of His sufferings we see only the symbol of human sufferings in general; sometimes in the form that Christ who is present in His church shares in the martyr-sufferings of Christians; sometimes, again, in the form that the sin, weakness and unfaithfulness of His people inflict upon Him ever-renewed sufferings" (Pfleiderer, *Prim. Christianity*, III, 181). The ethical influence of Gnosticism is apparent in the spirit of strict asceticism which is the most characteristic feature of these Acts. It is true that the ascetic ideal obtained not only in gnostic but also in orthodox church circles, as we gather from the Acts of Paul as well as from other sources. The prominence of the strict ascetic ideal in early Christianity is intelligible. The chief battle which the Christian faith had to fight with Hellenic heathenism was for sexual purity, and in view of the coarseness and laxity which prevailed in sexual relations it is not surprising that the Christian protest was exaggerated in many cases into a demand for complete continence. This ascetic note in primitive Christianity was emphasized by the spirit of Gnosticism and finds clear expression in the Acts which arose either in gnostic circles or in an environment tinged with gnostic ideas. It goes without saying that the influence of these romances which are so largely concerned with sexual morality and occasionally are unspeakably coarse, was to preoccupy the mind with unhealthy thoughts and to sully that purity of spirit which it was their intention to secure. There are, however, other ethical elements in these Acts which are in complete harmony with a true Christian morality. (2) The Apocryphal Acts are an invaluable source for information about *early-Christian forms of worship*. The ritual of the sacraments is fully described in the Acts of Thomas. Some of the prayers found in the Acts are pervaded by a warm religious spirit and are rich in liturgical expression. (3) The beginnings of *Christian hymnology* may be traced in the Acts of Thomas, in which occur gnostic hymns breathing the fantastic oriental spirit. (4) Apparent in the Acts throughout is the excessive *love for the supernatural* and the *religious enthusiasm* which flourished in Asia Minor in the 2d cent. (cf especially the dance of the disciples round Jesus in the Acts of John: ch **94** ff).

2. As Records of Early Christianity

IX. Influence.—The Apocryphal Acts had a remarkable influence in the later history of the church. After the establishment of Christianity under Constantine men turned their eyes to the earlier years of struggle and persecution. A deep interest was awakened in the events of the heroic age of the faith—the age of martyrs and apostles. Acts of martyrs were eagerly read, and in particular the Apocryphal Acts were drawn upon to satisfy the desire for a fuller knowledge of the apostles than was afforded by the canonical books. The heretical teaching with which the apostolic legends were associated in these Acts led to their condemnation by ecclesiastical authority, but the ban of the church was unavailing to eradicate the taste for the vivid colors of apostolic romance. In these circumstances church writers set themselves the task of rewriting the earlier Acts, omitting what was clearly heretical and retaining the miraculous and supernatural elements. And not only so, but the material of the Acts was freely used in the fabrication of lives of other apostles, as we find in the collection of the so-called Abdias in the 6th cent. The result was that from the 4th to the 11th cent. literature of this kind, dealing with the apostles, grew apace and "formed the favorite reading of Christians, from Ireland to the Abyssinian mountains and from Persia to Spain" (Harnack). Apostolic legends were reproduced in religious poems; they appeared in martyrologies and calendars; they formed the subject of homilies on the feast-days of the apostles, and incidents from them were depicted in Christian art. New cycles of legends arose in the Syrian and Coptic churches; and the Coptic legends were translated into Arab. and from Arab. into Ethiopic (Gadla Ḥawâryât—The Contendings of the Apostles). Literature of this kind was the fruitful mother of every kind of superstition. "Whole generations of Christians [as Harnack says], yes, whole Christian nations were intellectually blinded by the dazzling appearance of these tales. They lost the eye not only for the true light of history but also for the light of truth itself" (*Gesch. der altchr. Lit.*, I, xxvi). It is noteworthy that the apocryphal correspondence with the Corinthians in the Acts of Paul was received as canonical in the Syrian and Armenian churches.

LITERATURE.—The Apocryphal Acts form the subject of a voluminous literature. The earlier editions of the available texts by Fabricius (1703) and Tischendorf (1851) have been completely superseded by Lipsius-Bonnet, *Acta Apostolorum apocrypha* (1891–1903), which contains texts not only of the earlier but also of many of the later Acts. Translations of earlier Acts with valuable introductions are to be found in Hennecke, *NT Apokryphen* (1904), while critical discussions and elucidation of the text are given in Hennecke, *Handbuch zu den NT Apokryphen* (1904). These two works are indispensable to the student. English trs of earlier Acts with short introductions in Pick, *Apocryphal Acts* (1909). The critical work of Lipsius on these Acts was epoch-making: *Die apokryphen Apostelgeschichten und Apostellegenden* (1883–90). Full lists of literature may be found in Hennecke and Pick. The following may be mentioned here: Zahn, *Geschichte des NT Kanons*, II, 832 ff (1892); *Forschungen zur Gesch. des NT Kanons*, VI, 14 ff, 194 ff (1900); Harnack, *Geschichte der altchristlichen Literatur*, I, 116 ff (1893); II, 493 ff, 541 ff (1897); James, *Apocrypha Anecdota* (Texts and Studies, V, 1, 1897); Ehrhard, *Die altchristliche Litteratur u. i. Erforsch.* (1900); C. Schmidt, "Die Alten Petrusakten" (*TU*, IX, 1, 1903). Useful as setting forth the religious significance of the Acts are Pfleiderer, *Primitive Christianity*, III, 170 ff (tr 1910); Liechtenhahn, *Die Offenbarung im Gnosticismus* (1901). The chapter in Salmon's *Intro to the NT* (325 ff) may be consulted. A short account of the Acts written with full knowledge is given in Geffcken, *Christliche Apokryphen* (Religionsgeschichtliche Volksbücher, 1908).

B. The Separate Acts

The Apocryphal Acts dealt with in this article are the Leucian Acts mentioned by Photius in his *Bibliotheca*. As we now have them they have undergone revision in the interest of ecclesiastical orthodoxy, but in their original form they belonged to the 2d cent. It is impossible to say how much the Acts in their present form differ from that in which they originally appeared, but it is evident at many points that the orthodox revision which was meant to eliminate heretical elements was not by any means thorough. Passages which are distinctly gnostic were preserved probably because the reviser did not understand their true meaning.

I. Acts of Paul.—Origen in two passages of his extant writings quotes the Acts of Paul with approval, and it was possibly due to his influence that these Acts were held in high regard in the East. In the Codex Claromontanus (3d cent.), which is of eastern origin, the Acts of Paul are treated as a catholic writing and take rank with the Shepherd of Hermas and the Apocalypse of Peter. Eusebius, who utterly rejects "The Acts of Andrew, John and the rest of the apostles," puts the Acts of Paul in the lower class of debated writings alongside Hermas, Epistle of Barnabas, Did, the Apocalypse of John, etc (*HE*, III, 25.4). In the West, where Origen was viewed with suspicion, the Acts of Paul were apparently discredited, the only use of them as a reliable source being found in Hippolytus, the friend of Origen, who however does not mention them by name. (The reference by Hippolytus is found in his commentary on Daniel. He argues from Paul's conflict with the wild beasts to the credibility of the story of Daniel in the lions' den.)

1. Ecclesiastical Testimony

Of the Acts of Paul only fragments remain. Little was known of them until in 1904 a translation from a badly preserved Coptic version was published by C. Schmidt, and the discovery was made that the well-known Acts of Paul and Thecla were in reality a part of the Acts of Paul. From the notes regarding the extent of the Acts given in the Cod. Claromontanus and in the Stichometry of Nicephorus we gather that the fragments amount to about one-fourth of the whole.

2. Contents

(1) Of these fragments the longest and the most important is the section which came to have a separate existence under the name The Acts of Paul and Thecla. When these were separated from the Acts of Paul we cannot tell, but this had happened before the time of the Gelasian Decree (496 AD), which without making mention of the Acts of Paul condemns as apocryphal the Acts of Paul and Thecla. (*a*) An outline of the narrative is as follows: At Iconium, Thecla, a betrothed maiden, listened to the preaching of Paul on virginity and was so fascinated that she refused to have anything further to do with her lover. On account of his influence over her, Paul was brought before the proconsul and was cast into prison. There Thecla visited him with the result that both were brought to judgment. Paul was banished from the city and Thecla was condemned to be burned. Having been miraculously delivered at the pile, Thecla went in search of Paul and when she had found him she accompanied him to Antioch. (There is confusion in the narrative of Antioch of Pisidia and Syrian Antioch.) In Antioch an influential citizen, Alexander by name, became enamored of her and openly embraced her on the street. Thecla, resenting the familiarity, pulled off the crown which Alexander wore and in consequence was condemned to fight with the wild beasts at the games. Until the day of the games Thecla was placed under the care of Queen Tryphaena, then living in Antioch. When Thecla was exposed in the amphitheater a lioness died in defending her against attack. In her peril Thecla cast herself into a tank containing seals and declared: "In the name of Jesus Christ I baptize myself on my last day." (It was with reference partly to this act of self-baptism that Tertullian gave the information about the authorship of these Acts: *infra* 3.) When it was proposed to have Thecla

torn asunder by maddened bulls Queen Tryphaena fainted, and through fear of what might happen the authorities released Thecla and handed her over to Tryphaena. Thecla once again sought Paul and having found him was commissioned by him to preach the Word of God. This she did first at Iconium and then in Seleucia where she died. Various later additions described Thecla's end, and in one of them it is narrated that she went underground from Seleucia to Rome that she might be near Paul. Finding that Paul was dead she remained in Rome until her death. (*b*) Although the Thecla story is a romance designed to secure apostolic authority for the ideal of virginity, it is probable that it had at least a slight foundation in actual fact. The existence of an influential Thecla-cult at Seleucia favors the view that Thecla was a historical person. Traditions regarding her association with Paul which clustered round the temple in Seleucia built in her honor may have provided the materials for the romance. In the story there are clear historical reminiscences. Tryphaena is a historical character whose existence is established by coins. She was the mother of King Polemon II of Pontus and a relative of the emperor Claudius. There are no grounds for doubting the information given us in the Acts that she was living at Antioch at the time of Paul's first visit. The Acts further reveal striking geographical accuracy in the mention of "the royal road" by which Paul is stated to have traveled from Lystra on his way to Iconium —a statement which is all the more remarkable because, while the road was in use in Paul's time for military reasons, it was given up as a regular route in the last quarter of the 1st cent. In the Acts Paul is described as "a man small in stature, bald-headed, bow-legged, of noble demeanor, with meeting eyebrows and a somewhat prominent nose, full of grace. He appeared sometimes like a man, and at other times he had the face of an angel." This description may quite well rest on reliable tradition. On the ground of the historical features in the story, Ramsay (*The Church in the Roman Empire*, 375 ff) argued for the existence of a shorter version going back to the 1st cent., but this view has not been generally accepted. (*c*) The Acts of Paul and Thecla were very widely read and had a remarkable influence owing to the widespread reverence for Thecla, who had a high place among the saints as "the first female martyr." References to the Acts in the Church Fathers are comparatively few, but the romance had an extraordinary vogue among Christians both of the East and of the West. In particular, veneration for Thecla reached its highest point in Gaul, and in a poem entitled "The Banquet" (Caena) written by Cyprian, a poet of South-Gaul in the 5th cent., Thecla stands on the same level as the great characters of Biblical history. The later Acts of Xanthippe and Polyxena are entirely derived from the Acts of Paul and Thecla.

(2) Another important fragment of the Acts of Paul is that containing the so-called Third Epistle to the Corinthians. Paul is represented as being in prison at Philippi (not at the time of Acts **16** 23 ff, but at some later time). His incarceration was due to his influence over Stratonice, the wife of Apollophanes. The Corinthians who had been disturbed by two teachers of heresy sent a letter to Paul describing their pernicious doctrines, which were to the effect that the prophets had no authority, that God was not almighty, that there was no resurrection of the body, that man had not been made by God, that Christ had not come in the flesh or been born of Mary, and that the world was not the work of God but of angels. Paul was sorely distressed on receipt of this epistle and, "under much affliction," wrote an answer in which the popular gnostic views of the false teachers are vehemently opposed. This letter which abounds in allusions to several of the Pauline epistles is chiefly remarkable from the fact that it found a place, along with the letter which called it forth, among canonical writings in the Syrian and Armenian churches after the 2d cent. The correspondence was strangely enough believed to be genuine by Rinck who edited it in 1823. The original Gr version has not been preserved, but it exists in Coptic (not quite complete), in Armenian and in two Lat tr^s (both mutilated), besides being incorporated in Ephraem's commentary (in Armenian tr). The Syr version has been lost.

(3) Besides the two portions of the Acts of Paul mentioned above there are others of less value, the Healing of a Dropsical Man at Myra by the apostle (a continuation of the Thecla-narrative), Paul's conflict with wild beasts at Ephesus (based on the misunderstanding of 1 Cor **15** 32), two short citations by Origen, and a concluding section describing the apostle's martyrdom under Nero, to whom Paul appeared after his death. Clement of Alexandria quotes a passage (*Strom.*, VI, 5, 42 f) —a fragment from the mission-preaching of Paul—which may have belonged to the Acts of Paul; and the same origin is possible for the account of Paul's speech in Athens given by John of Salisbury (cir 1156) in the *Policraticus*, IV, 3.

3. Authorship and Date

From a passage in Tertullian (*De Baptismo*, ch 17) we learn that the author of the Acts of Paul was "a presbyter of Asia, who wrote the book with the intention of increasing the dignity of Paul by additions of his own," and that "he was removed from office when, having been convicted, he confessed that he had done it out of love to Paul." This testimony of Tertullian is supported by the evidence of the writing itself which, as we have seen, shows in several details exact knowledge of the topography and local history of Asia Minor. A large number of the names occurring in these Acts are found in inscriptions of Smyrna, although it would be precarious on that ground to infer that the author belonged to that city. It is possible that he was a native of a town where Thecla enjoyed peculiar reverence and that the tradition of her association with Paul, the preacher of virginity, was the chief motive for his writing the book. Along with this was linked the motive to oppose the views of some Gnostics (the Bardesanites). The date of the Acts of Paul is the latter half of the 2d cent., probably between 160 and 180 AD.

4. Character and Tendency

The Acts of Paul, though written to enhance the dignity of the apostle, clearly show that both in respect of intellectual equipment and in breadth of moral vision the author, with all his love for Paul, was no kindred spirit. The intellectual level of the Acts is low. There is throughout great poverty in conception; the same *motif* occurs without variation; and the defects of the author's imagination have their counterpart in a bare and inartistic diction. NT passages are frequently and freely quoted. The view which the author presents of Christianity is narrow and one-sided. Within its limits it is orthodox in sentiment; there is nothing to support the opinion of Lipsius that the work is a revision of a gnostic writing. The frequent occurrence of supernatural events and the strict asceticism which characterize the Acts are no proof of gnostic influence. The dogmatic is indeed anti-gnostic, as we see in the correspondence with the Corinthians. "The Lord Jesus Christ was born of Mary, of the Seed of David, the Father having sent the Spirit from heaven into her." The resurrection of the body is assured by Christ's resurrection from the dead. Resurrection, however, is only for those who believe in it—in this we have the one thought which betrays any originality on the part of the author: "they who say that there is no resurrection shall have no resurrection." With faith in the resurrection is associated the demand for strict sexual abstinence. Only they who are pure (i.e. who live in chastity) shall see God: "Ye have no part in the resurrection unless ye remain chaste and defile not the flesh." The gospel which the apostle preached was "the word regarding self-control and the resurrection." In the author's desire to secure authority for a prevalent form of Christianity, which demanded sexual abstinence as a condition of eternal life, we recognize the chief aim of the book. Paul is represented as the apostle of this popular conception, and his teaching is rendered attractive by the miraculous and supernatural elements which satisfied the crude taste of the time.

LITERATURE.—Books mentioned under "Literature" (p. 188); C. Schmidt, "Die Paulusakten" (*Neue Jahrbücher*, 217 ff, 1897), *Acta Pauli* (1904); dealing with Acts of Paul and Thecla: Ramsay, *The Church in the Roman Empire* (4th ed, 1895); Conybeare, *The Apology and Acts of Apollonius* . . . . (1894); Cabrol, *La légende de sainte Thècle* (1895); Orr, *The NT Apoc Writings* (introd. tr, and notes, 1903). For further lit. see Hennecke, *Handbuch*, etc, 358 ff; Pick, *Apoc Acts*, 1, 8 f.

II. Acts of Peter.—A large portion (almost two-thirds) of the Acts of Peter is preserved in a Lat translation—the *Actus Vercellenses*, so named from the town of Vercelli in Piedmont, where the MS containing them lies in the chapter-library. A Coptic fragment discovered and published (1903) by C. Schmidt contains a narrative with the subscription *Praxis Petrou* (Act of Peter). Schmidt is of opinion that this fragment formed part of the work to which the Actus Vercellenses also belonged, but this is somewhat doubtful. The fragment deals with an incident in Peter's ministry at Jerus, while the Act. Vercell., which probably were meant to be a continuation of the canonical Acts, give an account of Peter's conflict with Simon Magus and of his martyrdom at Rome. References in ecclesiastical writers (Philastrius of Brescia, Isidore of Pelusium and Photius) make it practically certain that the Act. Vercell. belong to the writing known as the Acts of Peter, which was condemned in the rescript of Innocent I (405 AD) and in the Gelasian Decree (496 AD).

1. Contents

(1) The Coptic Fragment contains the story of Peter's paralytic daughter. One Sunday while Peter was engaged in healing the sick a bystander asked him why he did not make his own daughter whole. To show that God was able to effect the cure through him, Peter made his daughter sound for a short time and then bade her return to her place and become as before. He explained that the affliction had been laid upon her to save her from defilement, as a rich man Ptolemy had been enamored of her and had desired to make her his wife. Ptolemy's grief at not receiving her had been such that he became blind. As the result of a vision he had come to Peter, had received his sight and had been converted, and when he died he had left a piece of land to Peter's daughter. This land Peter had sold and had given the proceeds to the poor. Augustine (*Contra Adimantum*, 17.5) makes a reference to this story but does not mention Acts of Peter. There are also two references to the incident in the Acts of Philip. In the later Acts of Nereus and Achilleus the story is given with considerable changes, the name of Peter's daughter, which is not mentioned in the fragment, being given as Petronilla.

(2) The contents of the Actus Vercellenses fall into three parts: (*a*) The first three chapters which clearly are a continuation of some other narrative and would fitly join on to the canonical Acts tell of Paul's departure to Spain. (*b*) The longest section of the Acts (**4–32**) gives an account of the conflict between Peter and Simon Magus at Rome. Paul had not been gone many days when Simon, who "claimed to be the great power of God," came to Rome and perverted many of the Christians. Christ appeared in a vision to Peter at Jerus and bade him sail at once for Italy. Arrived at Rome Peter confirmed the congregation, declaring that he came to establish faith in Christ not by words merely but by miraculous deeds and powers (allusion to 1 Cor **4** 20; 1 Thess **1** 5). On the entreaty of the brethren Peter went to seek out Simon in the house of one named Marcellus, whom the magician had seduced; and when Simon refused to see him, Peter unloosed a dog and bade it go and deliver his challenge. The result of this marvel was the repentance of Marcellus. A section follows describing the mending of a broken statue by sprinkling the pieces with water in the name of Jesus. Meantime the dog had given Simon a lecture and had pronounced on him the doom of unquenchable fire. After reporting on its errand and speaking words of encouragement to Peter, the dog expired at the apostle's feet. A smoked fish is next made to swim. The faith of Marcellus waxed strong at the sight of the wonders which Peter wrought, and Simon was driven out of his house with every mark of contempt. Simon, enraged at this treatment, came to challenge Peter. An infant of seven months speaking in a manly voice denounced Simon and made him speechless until the next Sabbath day. Christ appeared in a vision of the night encouraging Peter, who when morning was come narrated to the congregation his triumph over Simon, "the angel of Satan," in Judaea. Shortly afterward, in the house of Marcellus which had been "cleansed from every vestige of Simon," Peter unfolded the true understanding of the gospel. The adequacy of Christ to meet every kind of need is shown in a characteristic passage which reveals docetic traits: "He will comfort you that you may love Him, this Great and Small One, this Beautiful and Ugly One, this Youth and Old Man, appearing in time yet utterly invisible in eternity, whom a human hand has not grasped, who yet is now grasped by His servants, whom flesh had not seen and now sees," etc. Next in a wonderful blaze of heavenly light blind widows received their sight and declared the different forms in which Christ had appeared to them. A vision of Marcellus is described in which the Lord appearing in the likeness of Peter struck down with a sword "the whole power of Simon," which had come in the form of an ugly Ethiopian woman, very black and clad in filthy rags. Then follows the conflict with Simon in the forum in presence of the senators and prefects. Words were first exchanged between the combatants; then from words it came to deeds, in which the power of Peter was signally exhibited as greater than Simon's in the raising of the dead. Simon was now discredited in Rome, and in a last attempt to recover his influence he declared that he would ascend to God. Before the assembled crowd he flew up over the city, but in answer to Peter's prayer to Christ he fell down and broke his leg in three places. He was removed from Rome and after having his limb amputated died. (*c*) The Actus Vercellenses close with an account of Peter's martyrdom (**33–41**). Peter had incurred the enmity of several influential citizens by persuading their wives to separate from them. Then follows the well-known "Quo vadis?" story. Peter being warned of the danger he was in fled from Rome; but meeting Christ and learning that He was

going to the city to be crucified again, Peter returned and was condemned to death. At the place of execution Peter expounded the mystery of the cross. He asked to be crucified head downward, and when this was done he explained in words betraying gnostic influence why he had so desired it. After a prayer of a mystical nature Peter gave up the ghost. Nero was enraged that Peter should have been put to death without his knowledge, because he had meant to heap punishments upon him. Owing to a vision he was deterred from a rigorous persecution of the Christians. (The account of Peter's martyrdom is also found in the Gr original.)

2. Historical Value

It is plain from the account given of these Acts that they are entirely legendary in character. They have not the slightest value as records of the activity of Peter. They are in reality the creation of the ancient spirit which delighted in the marvelous and which conceived that the authority of Christianity rested on the ability of its representatives to surpass all others in their possession of supernatural power. The tradition that Simon Magus exercised a great influence in Rome and that a statue was erected to him (**10**) may have had some basis in fact. Justin Martyr (*Apol*, I, 26, 56) states that Simon on account of the wonderful deeds which he wrought in Rome was regarded as a god and had a statue set up in his honor. But grave doubts are thrown on the whole story by the inscription SEMONI SANCO DEO FIDIO SACRUM which was found on a stone pedestal at Rome in 1574. This refers to a Sabine deity Semo Sancus, and the misunderstanding of it may have led to Justin's statement and possibly was the origin of the whole legend of Simon's activity at Rome. The tradition that Peter died a martyr's death at Rome is early, but no reliance can be placed on the account of it given in the Acts of Peter.

3. Authorship and Date

Nothing can be said with any certainty as to the authorship of the Acts of Peter. James (*Apocrypha Anecdota*, II) believes them to be from the same hand as the Acts of John, and in this he is supported by Zahn (*Gesch. des NT Kanons*, II, 861). But all that can definitely be said is that both these Acts had their origin in the same religious atmosphere. Both are at home on the soil of Asia Minor. Opinion is not unanimous on the question where the Acts of Peter were written, but a number of small details as well as the general character of the book point to an origin in Asia Minor rather than at Rome. There is no knowledge of Rom conditions, while on the other hand there are probable reminiscences of historical persons who lived in Asia Minor. The date is about the close of the 2d cent.

4. General Character

The Acts of Peter were used by heretical sects and were subjected to ecclesiastical censure. That however does not necessarily imply a heretical origin. There are traces in them of a spirit which in later times was regarded as heretical, but they probably originated within the church in an environment strongly tinged by gnostic ideas. We find the principle of gnosticism in the stress that is laid on *understanding* the Lord (**22**). The gnostic view that the Scripture required to be supplemented by a secret tradition committed to the apostles is reflected in several passages (**20** in particular). At the time of their earthly fellowship with Christ the apostles were not able to understand the full revelation of God. Each saw only so far as he was able to see. Peter professes to communicate what he had received from the Lord "in a mystery." There are slight traces of the docetic heresy. The mystical words of Peter as he hung on the cross are suggestive of gnostic influence (**33** f). In these Acts we find the same negative attitude to creation and the same pronounced ascetic spirit as in the others. "The virgins of the Lord" are held in special honor (**22**). Water is used instead of wine at the Eucharist. Very characteristic of the Acts of Peter is the emphasis laid on the boundless mercy of God in Christ toward the backsliding (especially **7**). This note frequently recurring is a welcome revelation of the presence of the true gospel-message in communities whose faith was allied with the grossest superstition.

Literature.—Books mentioned under "Literature" (p. 188). In addition, Ficker, *Die Petrusakten, Beiträge zu ihrem Verständnis* (1903); Harnack, "Patristische Miscellen" (*TU*, V, 3, 1900).

III. Acts of John.—According to the Stichometry of Nicephorus the Acts of John in their complete state formed a book about the same length as the Gospel of Matthew.

1. Contents

A number of sections which show links of connection with one another are extant—about two-thirds of the whole. The beginning of the Acts is wanting, the existing narrative commencing at **18**. What the contents of the earlier chapters were we cannot surmise. In Bonnet's reconstruction the first fourteen chapters deal with John's journey from Ephesus to Rome and his banishment to Patmos, while **15–17** describe John's return to Ephesus from Patmos. The sections given by Bonnet may contain material which belonged to the original Acts, but it is improbable that they stood at the beginning of the work, as it seems clear that the narrative commencing at **18** describes John's *first* visit to Ephesus. The first extant portion of the Acts (**18–25**) narrates that Lycomedes "the commander-in-chief of the Ephesians" met John as he drew near the city and besought him on behalf of his beautiful wife Cleopatra, who had become paralyzed. When they came to the house the grief of Lycomedes was so great that he fell down lifeless. After prayer to Christ John made Cleopatra whole and afterward raised Lycomedes to life again. Prevailed upon by their entreaties John took up his abode with them. In **26–29** we have the incident of the picture of John which played so prominent a part in the discussion at the Second Council of Nicaea. Lycomedes commissioned a friend to paint a picture of John and when it was completed he put it in his bedroom with an altar before it and candlesticks beside it. John discovering why Lycomedes repaired so frequently to his room, taxed him with worshipping a heathen god and learned that the picture was one of himself. This he believed only when a mirror was brought that he might see himself. John charged Lycomedes to paint a picture of his soul and to use as colors faith in God, meekness, love, chastity, etc. As for the picture of his body it was the dead picture of a dead man. Chs **30–36** narrate the healing of infirm old women, and in the theater where the miracles were wrought John gave an address on the vanity of all earthly things and on the destroying nature of fleshly passion. In **37–45** we read that in answer to the prayer of John the temple of Artemis fell to the ground, with the result that many people were won to the worship of Christ. The priest of Artemis who had been killed through the fall of the temple was raised to life again and became a Christian (**46** f). After the narration of further wonders (one of them the driving of bugs out of a house) follows the longest incident of the Acts, the inexpressibly repulsive story of Drusiana (**62–86**), which was used as the theme of a poem by the nun Hroswitha of Gandersheim (10th cent.). The following section gives a discourse of John on the life, death and ascension of Jesus (**87–105**) which is characterized by distinct docetic traits, a long passage dealing with Christ's appearance in many forms and with the peculiar nature of His body. In this section occurs the strange hymn used by the Priscillianists, which purports to be that which Jesus sang after supper in the upper room (Mt **26** 30), the disciples dancing round Him in a ring and responding with Amen. Here too we find the mystic doctrine of the Cross revealed to John by Christ. Chs **106–15** narrate the end of John. After addressing the brethren and dispensing the sacrament of the Lord's Supper with bread alone, John ordered a grave to be dug; and when this was done, he prayed, giving thanks that he had been delivered from "the filthy madness of the flesh" and asking a safe passage through the darkness and dangers of death. Whereupon he lay down quietly in the grave and gave up the ghost.

2. Historical Value

The Acts of John, it need hardly be said, have not the slightest historical value. They are a tissue of legendary incidents which by their miraculous character served to insinuate into the popular mind the dogmatic conceptions and the ideal of life which the author entertained. The Acts however are in harmony with the well-founded tradition that Ephesus was the scene of John's later activity. Very remarkable is the account of the destruction of the Artemis-temple by John—a clear proof that the Acts were not written in Ephesus. The Ephesian temple of Artemis was destroyed by the Goths in 262 AD.

3. General Character

The Acts of John are the most clearly heretical of all the Acts. The docetic traits have already been referred to. The unreality of Christ's bodily existence is shown by the changing forms in which He appeared (**88–90**), by His ability to do without food (**93**) and without sleep ("I never at any time saw His eyes closing but only open," **89**), by His leaving no footprint when He walked (**93**), by the varying character of His body when touched, now hard, now soft, now completely immaterial (**89, 93**). The crucifixion of Jesus, too, was entirely phantasmal (**97, 99**). The ascension followed immediately on the apparent crucifixion; there was no place for the resurrection of One who had never actually died. Gnostic features are further discernible in the disparagement of the Jewish Law (**94**), in the view which lays emphasis on a secret tradition committed by Christ to the apostles (**96**) and in the contempt for those who were not enlightened ("Care not for the many, and them that are outside the mystery despise," **100**). The historical incidents of Christ's sufferings are sublimated into something altogether mystical (**101**); they are simply a symbol of human suffering, and the object of Christ's coming is represented as being to enable men to understand the true meaning of suffering and thus to be delivered from it (**96**). The real sufferings of Christ are those caused by His grief at the sins of His followers (**106** f). He is also a partaker in the sufferings of His faithful people, and indeed is present with them to be their support in every trial (**103**). The Acts of John also reveal a strong encratite tendency, although that is not so pronounced as in the Acts of Andrew and of Thomas. Nowhere however do we get a more horrifying glimpse into the depths of corrupt sexualism than in these Acts. The writing and circulation of the story of Drusiana cast a lurid light on the gross sensual elements which survived in early Hellenic Christianity. Apart from this there are passages which reveal a warm and true religious feeling and some of the prayers are marked by glow and unction (**112** ff). The Acts show that the author was a man of considerable literary ability; in this respect they form a striking contrast to the Acts of Paul.

4. Authorship and Date

The author of the Acts of John represents himself as a companion of the apostle. He has participated in the events which he describes, and in consequence the narrative possesses a certain lively quality which gives it the appearance of actual history. The author according to testimony which goes back to the 4th cent. was Leucius, but nothing can with any certainty be said of him (see above A, *VI*). It is possible that in some part of the Acts which is lost the author mentioned his name. The early date of the Acts is proved by a reference in Clement of Alexandria (cir 200) to the immaterial nature of Christ's body, the passage plainly indicating that Clement was acquainted with the Acts or had heard another speak of them (Hypotyposeis on 1 Jn **1** 1). The probable date is between 150 and 180 and Asia Minor is the place of origin.

5. Influence

The Acts of John exerted a wide influence. They are in all probability the earliest of the Apocryphal Acts and those written later owe much to them. The Acts of Peter and of Andrew show so close affinities with the Acts of John that some have regarded them as being from the same hand; but if that be not so, there is much to be said for the literary dependence of the former on the latter. We are probably right in stating that the author of the Acts of John was the pioneer in this sphere of apostolic romance and that others eagerly followed in the way which he had opened up. That the Acts of John were read in orthodox circles is clear from the reference in Clement of Alexandria. In later days however they were regarded with suspicion. Augustine quotes part of the hymn (**95**) which he read in a Priscillianist work sent him by a bishop Ceretius and makes severe animadversions on it and on the claim advanced regarding it that it had been revealed in secret to the apostles. The second Synod of Nicaea (787 AD) passed judgment on the Acts of John in words of great severity (see above A, *V*, 1). The stories found in the Acts had, however, before this time passed into orthodox tradition and had been used by Prochorus (5th cent.), a supposed disciple of John, in the composition of his travel-romance dealing with the apostle, as well as by Abdias (6th cent.) whose work contains material from the older Acts which is not otherwise preserved.

Literature.—See under "Literature" (p. 188); also Zahn, *Acta Joannis* (1880).

IV. Acts of Andrew.—The first mention of these Acts which are referred to frequently by ecclesiastical writers is in Eusebius (*HE*, III, 25, 6). They are there, along with other Acts, rejected as absurd and impious. Epiphanius refers to them in several passages (*Haeres*, **47, 61, 68**) as being in use among various heretical sects which practised a strict ascetic morality. Early writers attribute them to Leucius, the author of the Acts of John.

1. Contents

Of the Acts of Andrew only small portions remain. A fragment is preserved by Euodius of Uzala (d. 424), a contemporary of Augustine, and a longer piece, found in a MS of the 10th or 11th cent., containing lives of saints for November, was identified by Bonnet as belonging to the Acts of Andrew. The account of the death of Andrew is preserved in many forms; that which has the most appearance of retaining the form of the original Acts being found in a letter of the presbyters and deacons of the churches of Achaia. (1) The fragment of Euodius gives two short passages describing the relations of Maximilla with her husband Egetes, whose claims she resisted. (2) The longest section of the Acts deals with Andrew's imprisonment because he had induced Maximilla to separate from her husband "Aegeates" and to live a life of chastity. ("Aegeates," which occurs as the name of Maximilla's husband, denotes in reality "a native of Aegae," Aegae being a town in the vicinity of Patrae, where Andrew was described as carrying on his work.) The section opens in the middle of an address spoken to the brethren by Andrew in prison, in which they were enjoined to glory in their fellowship with Christ and in their deliverance from the baser things of earth. Maximilla with her companions frequently visited the apostle in prison. Aegeates expostulated with her and declared that if she did not resume relations with him he would subject Andrew to torture. Andrew counseled her to resist the importunity of Aegeates, and delivered an address on the true nature of man and stated that torture had no terrors for him. If Maximilla should yield, the apostle would suffer on her account. Through her fellowship with his sufferings she would know her true nature and thus escape from affliction. Andrew next comforted Stratocles, the brother of Aegeates, who declared his need of Andrew, the sower in him of the "seed of the word of salvation." Andrew thereafter announced his crucifixion on the following day. Maximilla again visited the apostle in prison, "the Lord going before her in the form of Andrew." To a company of the brethren the apostle delivered an address, in which he discoursed on the deceitfulness of the devil, who first had dealt with men as a friend but now was manifest as an enemy. (3) When brought to the place of crucifixion Andrew addressed the cross which he joyfully welcomed. After being bound to the cross he hung smiling at the miscarriage of the vengeance of Aegeates, for (as he explained) "a man who belongs to Jesus because he is known of Him is armed against every vengeance." For three days and nights Andrew addressed the people from the cross, and they, moved by his nobility and eloquence, went to Aegeates, demanding that he should be delivered from death. Aegeates, fearing the wrath of the people, went to take Andrew down from the cross, but the apostle refused deliverance and prayed to Christ to prevent his release. After this he gave up the ghost. He was buried by Maximilla, and Aegeates soon afterward cast himself down from a great height and died.

2. General Character

The encratite ideal in its most pronounced form is exhibited in the Acts of Andrew. (In view of this, and of Andrew's association elsewhere in ecclesiastical tradition with a strict asceticism, there is a curious irony in the fact that in some parts of Germany Andrew is the patron saint of maidens seeking husbands. In the Harz and in Thüringen St. Andrew's Night [November 30] is considered by maidens the most favorable time for the vision of their future husbands.) The gnostic spirit is revealed in the feeling for the preëminent worth of the spiritual man (**6**). The true nature of man is pure; the weakness and sin are the work of the "evil enemy who is averse to peace." In seducing men he did not come out openly as an enemy but pretended friendship. When the light of the world appeared the adversary of man was seen in his true colors. Deliverance from sin comes through enlightenment. The mystical view of sufferings (**9**) reminds us of the similar view in the Acts of John. The addresses of the apostle are characterized by religious earnestness and warmth (words flow from his lips "like a stream of fire" **12**), and by a profound sense of the Divine pity for sinful and tempted men.

3. Historical Value

The only detail in the Acts of Andrew which has a claim to be considered historical is his activity at Patrae on the Corinthian Gulf. (Patrae is not actually mentioned in the fragmentary Acts, but that the scene of the imprisonment and martyrdom of Andrew is laid in that city may be inferred from the name "Aegeates"—see above **1** [2].) Ecclesiastical tradition speaks with great uncertainty of the sphere of Andrew's missionary labors, Scythia, Bithynia and Greece being all mentioned. It may be regarded as probable that Andrew came to Greece and suffered martyrdom at Patrae, although one must reckon with the possibility that the account of his work and crucifixion there was invented for the purpose of representing the church at Patrae as an apostolic foundation. The crucifixion of the apostle on the so-called St. Andrew's cross is a later tradition.

V. Acts of Thomas.—These Acts exist in a complete state and their great popularity in church circles is shown by the large number of MSS which contain them. It is probable that they were written originally in Syr and that they were later freely translated into Gr and worked over from the Catholic point of view.

1. Contents

In the Stichometry of Nicephorus the Acts of Thomas are mentioned as containing 1,600 *stichoi* (lines of about sixteen syllables), one-fifth fewer than the Gospel of Mark. If this notice is correct, the form in which we have the Acts is very much more extended. In the Gr versions the Acts are divided into thirteen "deeds" followed by the martyrdom of Thomas. Some idea of the contents may be given as follows: (1) At a meeting of the apostles in Jerus, Thomas had India allotted to him as his sphere of service. He was unwilling to go, but at last consented when the Lord sold him to a messenger from King Gundaforus in India. On the journey to India, Thomas came to the city of Andrapolis where the nuptials of the king's daughter were being celebrated. In these the apostle took part and sang a hymn in praise of the heavenly wedding. The king asked Thomas to pray for his daughter and after he had done so the Lord appeared in the form of Thomas and won the newly married pair to a life of sexual abstinence. The king incensed at this sought Thomas, but the apostle had departed. (2) Arrived in India Thomas undertook to build a palace for King Gundaforus. He received money for this purpose but gave it away in alms. The king discovering this cast Thomas into prison, but afterward released him when he learned from his brother who came back from the dead that Thomas had built a heavenly palace for him. Gundaforus and his brother became Christians. (3) Traveling farther east Thomas found a youth who had been slain by a dragon because of a woman whom both desired. The dragon at the command of Thomas sucked the poison from the youth's body and itself died. The young man, restored to life, embraced the ideal of sexual abstinence and was counseled to set his affections on Christ. (4) The story of a speaking colt. (5) Thomas delivered a woman from the power of a filthy demon. An account is given of the celebration of the Eucharist (with bread alone) which includes a gnostic prayer. (6) A youth partaking of the Eucharist was convicted of sin and confessed that he had killed a maiden who refused to live with him in unchaste intercourse. The maiden was raised to life and gave an account of her experience in hell. (7) Thomas was besought by a commander named Sifor to deliver his wife and daughter from a demon of uncleanness. (8) While they were on their way to the commander's house the beast which drew the carriage became exhausted and four wild asses allowed themselves to be quietly yoked. One of the wild asses was instructed by Thomas to exorcise the demons which dwelt in the women. (9) A woman, Mygdonia, married to Charis, a near relative of King Misdai, listened to a discourse of the apostle and was led to reject the society of her husband. Charis complained to the king about the magician who had put a spell upon his wife and Thomas was cast into prison. At the request of his fellow-prisoners Thomas prayed for them and recited a hymn (known as "the hymn of the soul") which is entirely gnostic in character. (10) Mygdonia received the seal of Jesus Christ, being first anointed with oil, then being baptized, then receiving the Eucharist in bread and water. Thomas was released from prison, and Sifor, his wife and his daughter all received the seal. (11) Tertia the queen was sent by Misdai to reason with Mygdonia and as a result she herself was won to the new life. Thomas was then brought to the place of judgment. (12) There Vazan, the king's son, talked with the apostle and was converted. The king gave orders that Thomas should be tortured with hot plates of iron, but when these were brought water gushed forth from the earth and submerged them. Then follow an address and prayer of Thomas in prison. (13) The apostle was visited in prison by the women and by Vazan and thereafter Vazan along with others was baptized and received the Eucharist, Thomas coming from prison to Vazan's house for this purpose. (14) Thomas was put to death by the command of the king, being pierced with lances, but afterward he showed himself to his followers. Later a son of Misdai was cured of an unclean spirit by dust taken from the apostle's grave and Misdai himself became a Christian.

2. Character and Tendency

The Acts of Thomas are in reality a treatise in the form of a travel-romance whose main design was to set forth abstinence from sexual intercourse as the indispensable condition of salvation. In the addresses of Thomas, however, positive Christian virtues are emphasized; and in particular the duty and the recompense of compassion are strikingly exhibited in the story of the building of the heavenly palace. The Acts clearly had their origin in gnostic circles and were held in high estimation by various encratite sects. The original Acts underwent revision in the interest of orthodoxy. The hymns and dedication-prayers which showed marked gnostic features were probably retained because their meaning was not understood. As Lipsius says, speaking of "the hymn of the soul": "The preservation of this precious relic of gnostic poetry we owe to the happy ignorance of the Catholic reviser, who had no idea what heretical serpent lurked beneath the beautiful flowers of this poem." The hymn, probably written by Bardesanes, the founder of a gnostic sect, narrates in the form of an allegory the descent of the soul into the world of sense, its forgetfulness of its heavenly origin, its deliverance by the Divine revelation which awoke it to a consciousness of its true dignity, and its return to the heavenly home from which it came. In the opinion of some, however, the hymn is falsely called "the hymn of the soul." As Preuschen says: "It describes rather the descent of the Saviour to the earth, His deliverance of the soul which languishes there in the bondage of evil, and His return to the heavenly kingdom of light. One may characterize the whole as a gnostic embellishment and extension of Phil **2** 5–11" (Hennecke, *Handbuch*, etc, 587). In whichever way the hymn is to be interpreted, it is a poem of great beauty and rich in oriental imagery. The ascriptions of praise to Christ in the addresses of the apostle are sometimes couched in noble language and always suffused by great warmth of feeling. Throughout the Acts we have miraculous and supernatural elements in abundance. Christ frequently appears in the likeness of Thomas who is represented as his twin-brother. The full name of the apostle is Judas Thomas—Judas the Twin. In **55** ff there is a graphic account of the tortures of the damned, which remind one of the Apocalypse of Peter.

3. Historical Value

It goes without saying that the Acts of Thomas, which are a romance with a purpose, are in no sense a historical source for information about the apostle. The author however has made use of the names of historical persons. King Gundaforus (Viñdafra) is known from other sources as an Indo-Parthian ruler in the 1st cent. AD. It is very doubtful whether the tradition preserved in the Acts as to the activity of Thomas in India is trustworthy. The earliest tradition with which we are acquainted places the sphere of his missionary labors in Parthia. Syrian tradition states that he died at Edessa, where in the 4th cent. there was a church dedicated to him. Thomas is also indirectly associated with Edessa in the Abgar Legend, in which we read that Thaddaeus who founded the church at Edessa was sent by Thomas. In the existing form of the Acts of Thomas we have a combination of the traditions regarding India and Edessa; we read (**170**) that some time after the apostle's death his bones were carried "into the regions of the West." Early tradition knows nothing of Thomas as a martyr; according to a statement of the Valentinian Heracleon (cir 170) quoted by Clement of Alexandria (*Strom*, IV, 9) the apostle died quietly in his bed. The name of the apostle is given in the Acts as Judas Thomas, and this we also find in the Doctrine of Addai and elsewhere. The statement in the Acts that the apostle was a twin-brother of Jesus was no doubt suggested by the meaning of the name Thomas (="twin") and by the desire to enhance the dignity of the apostle. In **110** (in the Hymn of the Soul) there is a reference to the still existing Parthian kingdom, and as that kingdom came to an end in 227 AD, the poem must have been written before that date. The hymn, however, does not seem to have belonged to the original Acts, which probably were in existence before the end of the 2d cent.

Literature.—Besides books mentioned under "Literature" (p. 188) Thilo, *Acta Sancti Thomae apostoli* (1823); Hoffman, *ZNTW* (1903, 273–309); Preuschen, *Zwei gnostische Hymnen* (1904); Hilgenfeld, *ZWT* (1904, 229–41). The Syrian Acts of Thomas were ed and trd by W. Wright, *Apocryphal Acts of the Apostles* (1871); also Bevan, in *Texts and Studies*, V, 3 (1897). The later Ethiopic version is found in Malan, *The Conflicts of the Holy Apostles* (1871), and in Budge, *The Contendings of the Apostles* (2 vols containing Ethiopic text and tr, 1899–1901).

A. F. Findlay

APOCRYPHAL EPISTLES, a-pok′ri-fal ē-pis′l's: A few epistles have been attributed to the Virgin Mary, but these are very late and without value. The following epistles fall to be noted as apocryphal:

1. Letter Attributed to Our Lord

The letter attributed to Our Lord is given in Eusebius (*HE*, I, 13) who records that in his day a copy of the letter was to be found among the archives of Edessa. Abgarus, king of Osroene, which was a small country in Mesopotamia, writes from Edessa, the capital, to Our Lord, asking for healing and offering Him protection. Our Lord sends back a short letter saying that He cannot leave Palestine, but that, after His ascension, a messenger will come and heal Abgarus. The letters are obviously spurious. Osroene was actually Christianized about the beginning of the 3d cent., and the legend took shape and received official sanction in order to show that the country had received the Gospel at a much earlier date. See ABGAR.

The *Clementine Homilies* is a work of fiction attributed to Clement of Rome; it was actually written about the end of the 2d cent. or the beginning of the 3d. At the beginning of it there is set a letter of Peter to James. In it Peter counsels James not to show the book containing Peter's preaching except to a limited circle, and makes a violent attack upon the apostle Paul. It is thus evidently Ebionitic in tendency, and is, like the homilies to which it is prefixed, spurious.

2. Letter Attributed to Peter

(1) *The Epistle from Laodicea.*—The mention of such an ep in Col **4** 16 evidently tempted someone to forge a letter. It is written in Latin, and consists of 20 vs; it is a mere cento of Pauline phrases strung together. It is mentioned in the Muratorian Fragment (170 AD); and by the end of the 4th cent. it had a wide circulation. It is now almost universally rejected as spurious. See COLOSSIANS; EPHESIANS; EPISTLE TO LAODICEANS.

3. Letters Attributed to Paul

(2) *Lost Epistle to the Corinthians.*—In 1 Cor **5** 9 a letter to the Corinthians is mentioned which appears to have been lost. In a 5th cent. Armenian VS of the Scriptures there is inserted after 2 Cor a short letter from the Corinthians to Paul, and one from Paul to the Corinthians. These are also found in Syr, and were evidently accepted in many quarters as genuine at the end of the 4th cent. They formed a part of the Apocryphal Acts of St. Paul, and date from about 200 AD. See CORINTHIANS.

(3) *An Epistle to the Alexandrines.*—This is mentioned only in the Muratorian Fragment, and has not come down to us.

(4) *Letters of Paul to Seneca.*—This is a correspondence in Latin, six of the letters being attributed to Paul and eight to Seneca. Regarding this correspondence Lightfoot says: "This correspondence was probably forged in the 4th cent., either to recommend Seneca to Christian readers, or to recommend Christianity to students of Seneca." It had a wide circulation in the Middle Ages.

LITERATURE.—See art. "Apocrypha" in *EB* and *RE*. For text of Peter's letter to James, see Roberts' and Donaldson's *Ante-Nicene Christian Library*, XVII. For the Pauline letters consult Zahn, *Geschichte des NT Kanons*, II. For Paul's Laodicean letter, see Lightfoot's *Comm. on Col* (where the text of the letter is given); and for the letters to Seneca, Lightfoot's *Comm. on Phil*, Dissertation II, with Appendix.

JOHN MACARTNEY WILSON

APOCRYPHAL GOSPELS, a-pok'ri-fal gos'pels:

The apocryphal gospels form a branch of the apocryphal literature that attended the formation of the NT canon of Scripture. Apocryphal here means non-canonical. Besides gospels, this literature included acts, epistles and apocalypses.

I. Introductory.—The introduction to the third canonical Gospel shows that in the days of the writer, when the apostles of the Lord were still living, it was a common practice to write and publish accounts of the acts and words of Jesus. It has even been maintained (S. Baring-Gould, *Lost and Hostile Gospels*, xxiii, London, 1874) that at the close of the 1st cent., almost every church had its own gospel with which alone it was acquainted. These were probably derived, or professed to be derived, from the oral reports of those who had seen, heard, and, it may be, conversed with Our Lord. It was dissatisfaction with these compositions that moved Luke to write his Gospel. Whether any of these ante-Lukan documents are among those still known to us is hardly longer doubtful. Scholars of repute—Grotius, Grabe, Mill—were in earlier times disposed to place the Gospel of the Hebrews, the Gospel of the Ebionites, and the Gospel of the Egyptians among those alluded to by Luke, some holding the Gospel of the Hebrews to be as early as just after the middle of the 1st cent. More recent criticism does not allow so early an appearance for those gospels, though a fairly early date is still postulated for the Gospel of the Hebrews. The Protevangelium of James (noticed below) is still held by some as possibly falling within the 1st cent. (*EB*, I, 259).

1. Early Gospels

However this may be, there can be no doubt that by the close of the 1st cent. and the early part of 2d, opinion was practically unanimous in recognition of the authority of the four Gospels of the canonical Scriptures. Irenaeus, bishop of Lyons (180 AD), recognizes four, and only four Gospels, as "pillars" of the church. The Harmonies of Theophilus, bishop of Antioch (168–80 AD), and of Tatian, and the Apology of Justin Martyr carry back the tradition to a much earlier period of the cent., and, as Liddon proves at considerable length (*Bampton Lectures*, 2d ed, 210–19), "it is scarcely too much to assert that every decade of the 2d cent. furnishes its share of proof that the four Gospels as a whole, and St. John's in particular, were to the church of that age what they are to the church of the present." The recent attempt of Professor Bacon of Yale to get rid of the important authority of Irenaeus (*The Fourth Gospel in Research and Debate*, New York, 1910) will not succeed; it has been shown to be merely assertive where there is no evidence and agnostic where evidence is apparently demonstrative. During the last cent. the Gospels, as regards their composition, credibility and historicity, were subjected to the most searching and unsparing criticism which, though intimations of it were previously not wanting, may be said to have begun when Strauss, to use Liddon's words, "shocked the conscience of all that was Christian in Europe" by the publication of his first *Life of Jesus*. The methods pursued in this work consisted largely in the application to the sacred books, and especially to the Gospels, of the principles of criticism that had for forty years previously been used in estimating the structure and composition of some of the literary products of antiquity; and the controversy excited by this criticism can hardly yet be said to have subsided. This is not the place for entering upon an account of the controversy; it may be sufficient here to say that the traditional positions of the church have been ably defended,

2. Canonical Gospels

and in particular, that the claims of the canonical Gospels have been abundantly maintained.

Whatever was the fate of the ante-Lukan and other possible 1st-cent. gospels, it is with the 2d cent. and the formation of an authoritative canon that the apocryphal gospels, such as we now have, for the most part begin to appear. In the days of the reproduction of documents by manuscript, of restricted communications between different localities, and when the church was only as yet forming and completing its organization, the formation and spread of such gospels would be much easier than now. The number of such gospels is very considerable, amounting to about fifty. These exist mainly in fragments and scattered notices; though some, as pointed out below, are either entire or nearly so. The apparent number has probably been increased by the use of different names for the same document. Thirty are named by Hofmann with more or less explanation in *RE*, I, 511; a complete list is given in Fabricius (*Cod. Apoc NT*, I, 355 ff). Ebionistic and gnostic circles were specially prolific of such gospels. "It would be easy," says Salmon (*Intro*, 1st ed, 239) "to make a long list of names of gospels said to have been in use in different gnostic sects; but very little is known as to their contents, and that little is not such as to lead us to attribute to them the very slightest historical value." Of many indeed no more is known than the names of the authors, such as the gospels of Basilides, of Cerinthus, of Apelles, of Matthias, of Barnabas, of Bartholomew, of Eve, of Philemon and many others. The scholars and authorities of the early church were quite well aware of the existence and aims of these productions. It is noteworthy also that they had no hesitation in characterizing them as they deserved. The Marcosians, according to Irenaeus, adduced "an unspeakable number of apocryphal and spurious writings, which they themselves had forged, to bewilder the minds of the foolish"; and Eusebius (*HE*, III, 25) gives the following list of spurious and disputed books: "That we have it in our power to know both these books [the canonical] and those that are adduced by the heretics under the name of the apostles such, viz., as compose the gospels of Peter, of Thomas, and of Matthew, and certain others beside these or such as contain the Acts of Andrew and John, and of the other apostles, of which no one of those writers in the ecclesiastical succession has condescended to make any mention in his works: and, indeed, the character of the style itself is very different from that of the apostles, and the sentiments, and the purport of these things that are advanced in them, deviating as far as possible from sound orthodoxy, evidently prove they are the fictions of heretical men: whence they are not only to be ranked among the spurious writings but are to be rejected as altogether absurd and impious." In the appendix to Westcott's *Intro to the Study of the Gospels* will be found, with the exception of those recently discovered in Egypt, a complete list of the non-canonical sayings and deeds ascribed to Our Lord as recorded in the patristic writings; and also a list of the quotations from the non-canonical gospels where these are only known by quotations.

3. Apocryphal Gospels

The aim of the apocryphal gospels may be regarded as (1) heretical or (2) supplemental or legendary: that is to say, such as either were framed in support of some heresy or such as assume the canonical gospels and try to make additions—largely legendary—to them. Before considering these it may be well to take separate account of the Gospel according to the Hebrews.

4. The Gospel According to the Hebrews

The undoubted early date of this gospel, the character of most of its not very numerous quotations, the respect with which it is uniformly mentioned by early writers, and the esteem in which it is at present held by scholars in general, entitle the Gospel according to the Hebrews to special notice. Apart from the tradition, to which it is not necessary to attach too great importance, that represented Our Lord as commanding His disciples to remain for twelve years in Jerus, it is reasonable to suppose that for the Christian communities resident in Jerus and Pal a written gospel in their own language (Western Aram.) would soon be a necessity, and such a gospel would naturally be used by Jewish Christians of the Diaspora. Jewish Christians, for example, settled in Alexandria, might use this gospel, while native Christians, as suggested by Harnack, might use the Gospel of the Egyptians, till of course both were superseded by the four Gospels sanctioned by the church. There is no proof however that the gospel was earlier than the Synoptics, much less that it was among the ante-Lukan gospels. Harnack, indeed, by a filiation of documents for which there seems hardly sufficient warrant, placed it as early as between 65 and 100 AD. Salmon, on the other hand (*Intro*, Lect X) concludes that "the Nazarene gospel, so far from being the mother, or even the sister of one of our canonical four, can only claim to be a granddaughter or grand-niece." Jerome (400 AD) knew of the existence of this gospel and says that he translated it into Gr and Lat; quotations from it are found in his works and in those of Clement of Alexandria. Its relation to the Gospel of Matthew, which by almost universal consent is declared to have been originally written in Heb (i.e. Aram.), has given rise to much controversy. The prevalent view among scholars is that it was not the original of which Matthew's Gospel was a Gr tr, but still that it was a fairly early composition. Some, like Salmon and Harnack, are disposed to regard Jerome's Heb Gospel as to all intents a fifth gospel originally composed for Palestinian Christians, but which became of comparatively insignificant value with the development of Christianity into a world-religion. Besides two references to the baptism of Jesus and a few of his sayings, such as—"Never be joyful except when ye shall look upon your brother in love"; "Just now my Mother, the Holy Spirit, took me by one of my hairs and bore me away to the great mountain Thabor"—it records the appearance of Our Lord to James after the resurrection, adduced by Paul (1 Cor **15** 7) as one of the proofs of that event; but of course Paul might have learned this from the lips of James himself as well as from ordinary tradition, and not necessarily from this gospel. This indeed is the principal detail of importance which the quotations from this gospel add to what we know from the Synoptics. In other divergences from the Synoptics where the same facts are recorded, it is possible that the Gospel according to the Hebrews may relate an earlier and more reliable tradition. On the other hand, the longest quotation, which gives a version of Christ's interview with the Rich Young Ruler, would seem to show, as Westcott suggests, that the Synoptics give the simpler and therefore the earlier form of the common narrative. Many scholars, however, allow that the few surviving quotations of this gospel should be taken into account in constructing the life of Christ. The Ebionites gave the name of Gospel of the Hebrews to a mutilated gospel of Matthew. This brings us to the heretical gospels.

II. Heretical Gospels.—The Ebionites may be described generally as Jewish Christians who aimed at maintaining as far as possible the doctrines and practices of the OT and may be taken as representing originally the extreme conservative section of the Council of Jerusalem mentioned in Acts **15** 1–29. They are frequently mentioned in patristic literature from the 2d to the 4th cents., and the prolonged gnostic controversies of those times may well have founded among them different sects or at least parties. Accordingly Jerome, a writer of the 4th cent., states (*Ep ad August.* **122** 13) that he found in Pal Jewish Christians known as Nazarenes and Ebionites. Whether these were separate sects or simply supporters of more liberal or narrower views of the same sect cannot well be determined. Some, such as Harnack and Uhlhorn, have held that the two names are general designations for Jewish Christians; others regard the Ebionites as the most retrograde and the narrowest of Jewish Christians, while the Nazarenes were more tolerant of difference of belief and practice. The Gospel of the Ebionites or the Gospel of the Twelve Apostles, as it was also called, represented along with the Gospel of the Hebrews (noticed above) this Judaeo-Christian spirit. Some fragments of the Gospel of the Ebionites are preserved in Epiphanius (d. 376). He speaks of the Nazarenes as "having the Gospel according to Matthew in a most complete form, in Heb" (i.e. Aram.), though he immediately adds that he does not know whether "they removed the genealogies from Abraham to Christ," that is to say, whether they accepted or rejected the virgin birth of Christ. In contrast with this statement he says that the Ebionites had a gospel "called the Gospel according to Matthew, not entire and perfectly complete, but falsified and mutilated, which they call the Hebrew gospel." The extant fragments from the gospel are given in Westcott (*Intro*, 437 f). They "show that its value is quite secondary and that the author has simply compiled it from the canonical, and especially from the Synoptic Gospels, adapting it at the same time to the views and practices of gnostic Ebionism" (*DCG*, I, 505).

1. Gospel of the Ebionites

Three short and somewhat mystic verses are all that are left of what is known as the Gospel of the Egyptians. They occur in Book III of the *Stromateis* of Clement of Alexandria, who devoted that book to a refutation of Encratism, that is, the rejection, as absolutely unlawful, of the use of marriage, of flesh meat and of wine. Already in the Pauline Epistles are met parties with the cry (Col **2** 21) "Handle not, nor taste, nor touch," and (1 Tim **4** 3) "forbidding to marry, and commanding to abstain from meats." The vs in Clement read as follows: "When Salome asked how long will death prevail? The Lord said, As long as ye women bear children: for I have come to destroy the function of women. And Salome said to him: Did I not well then in not bearing children? And the Lord answered and said, Eat of every herb, but do not eat of that which is bitter. And when Salome asked when the things would be known about which she had enquired, the Lord said, When ye trample on the garment of shame, and when the two shall be one, and the male with the female neither male nor female." The words assuredly vary much from the usual character of those of Our Lord. Modern writers vary as to their encratite tendency and as to how far the Gospel of the Egyptians was practical. With so little to go upon, it is not easy to form a conclusion. It may have contained other passages on account of which Origen deemed it heretical. It was used by the Naassenes and Sabellians. The date of the Gospel is between 130 and 150.

2. Gospel of the Egyptians

The Gospel of Marcion would seem to have been intended as a direct counteractive to the Aram. gospels. A native of Pontus and the son of a bishop, Marcion settled at Rome in the first half of the 2d cent. and became the founder of the anti-Jewish sect that acknowledged no authoritative writings but those of Paul. This work forms a striking example of what liberties, in days before the final formation of the canon, could be taken with the most authoritative and the most revered documents of the faith, and also as showing the free and practically unlimited nature of the controversy, of which the canon as finally adopted was the result. He rejected the OT entirely, and of the NT retained only the Gospel of Lk, as being of Pauline origin, with the omission of sections depending on the OT and ten epistles of Paul, the pastoral epistles being omitted. The principal Church Fathers agree upon this corruption of Lk's Gospel by Marcion; and the main importance of his gospel is that in modern controversy it was for some time assumed to be the original gospel of which Lk's Gospel was regarded as merely an expansion. The theory was shown first in Germany and afterward independently in England to be quite untenable. It was lately revived by the author of *Supernatural Religion;* but Dr. Sanday's work on *The Gospels in the Second Century* (ch viii) may be said to have closed the controversy. (Cf also Salmon's *Intro*, Lect XI.)

3. Gospel of Marcion

Until about a quarter of a cent. ago no more was known of the Gospel of Peter than of the crowd of heretical gospels referred to above. From Eusebius (*HE*, VI, 12, 2) it was known that a Gospel of Peter was in use in the church of Rhossus, a town in the diocese of Antioch at the end of the 2d cent., that controversy had arisen as to its character, and that after a careful examination of it Serapion, bishop of Antioch (190–203), had condemned it as docetic. Origen (d. 253 AD), in his commentary on Mt **10** 17, refers to the gospel as saying that "there are certain brothers of Jesus, the sons of Joseph by a former wife, who lived with him before Mary." Eusebius further in *HE*, III, 3, 2 knows nothing of the Gospel according to Peter being handed down as a catholic writing, and in *HE*, III, 25, 6 he includes the Gospel of Peter among the forged heretical gospels. Theodoret, one of the Gr ecclesiastical historians (390–459), says that the Nazarenes used a gospel called "according to Peter." The gospel is also referred to in Jerome (*De Viris Illustr.*, ch 1) and it is condemned by the Decretum Gelasianum (496?). Salmon (*Intro*, 231) remarks: "Of the book no extracts have been preserved, and apparently it never had a wide range of circulation." These words were written in 1885. In the following year the French Archaeological Mission, working in upper Egypt, found in a tomb, supposed to be a monk's, at Akhmim (Panopolis), a parchment containing portions of no less than three lost Christian works, the Book of Enoch, the Gospel of Peter and the Apocalypse of Peter. These were published in 1892 and have given rise to much discussion. The gospel has been carefully reproduced in facsimile and edited by competent scholars. The fragment is estimated to contain about half of the original gospel. It begins in the middle of the history of the Passion, just after Pilate has washed his hands from all responsibility and ends in the middle of a sentence when the disciples at the end of the Feast of Unleavened Bread were betaking themselves to their homes. "But I [Simon Peter,

4. Gospel of Peter

the ostensible writer] and Andrew my brother took our nets and went to the sea; and there was with us Levi the son of Alphaeus whom the Lord. . . . . " Harnack (*Texte und Untersuchungen*, IX, 2, 2d ed, 76) exhibits about thirty new traits contained in the Petrine account of the Passion and burial. These are given in detail in an additional volume of the Ante-Nicene Library: *Recently Discovered MSS*, etc, Edinburgh, 1897. But Dr. Swete (*Gospel of Peter*, xv, London, 1893) shows that "even details which seem to be entirely new or which directly contradict the canonical narrative, may have been suggested by it"; and he concludes that notwithstanding the large amount of new matter which it contains, "there is nothing in this portion of the Petrine Gospel which compels us to assume the use of sources other than the canonical gospels." To Professor Orr (*NT Apocryphal Writings*, xix f) the gnostic origin of the gospel seems clear in the story given of the Resurrection; and its docetic character—that is, that it proceeded from those who held that Christ had only the semblance of a body—from the statement that on the cross Jesus was silent as one who felt no pain, and from the dying cry from the cross, "My power, my power, thou hast forsaken me," the really Divine Christ having departed before the crucifixion. The date of the gospel has been placed by some in the first quarter, and by others in the third quarter, of the 2d cent. For the other newly discovered "Sayings of Jesus," see LOGIA.

A Gospel of the Twelve is mentioned by Origen (Hom. I, *in Luc*), and a few fragments of it are preserved by Epiphanius (*Haeres*, **30** 13–16, 22). It commenced with the baptism, and was used by the Ebionites. It was written, Zahn thinks, about 170 AD. A Gospel of Barnabas and Gospel of Bartholomew are condemned in the decree of Pope Gelasius. The latter is mentioned by Jerome (*Prooem ad Matt*).

III. Supplemental or Legendary Gospels.—In all of the gospels of this class it is noteworthy that considering the desire of the writers of non-canonical gospels to multiply miracles, no notice is taken of the period in the life of Christ that intervened between his twelfth year and his thirtieth. The main reason for the omission probably is that no special dogmatic end was to be served by the narrative of this period of the Saviour's life. Where access cannot be had to these documents in their original languages, it may be useful to point out that a good and full translation of them may be found in Vol XVI of Clark's *Ante-Nicene Library*, Edinburgh, 1870.

1. The Protevangelium of James

1. Gospels of the Nativity: (*a*) The earliest of these documents is the Protevangelium of James. James is supposed to be the Lord's brother. The title "Protevangelium" or First Gospel—a catching title which assumes much and suggests more—was given to this document by Postellus, a Frenchman, who first published it in Latin in the year 1552. In the Gr and Syr MSS, it is known by various other titles, such as, *The History of James concerning the Birth of the All-Holy and Ever-Virgin Mother of God and of Her Son Jesus Christ.* Tischendorf in the notes to ch i of his *Evang. Apoc* gives a long list of the names descriptive of it in the various MSS. In the Gelasian Decree depriving it of canonical authority it is simply styled *Evangelium nomine Jacobi minoris apocryphum.* In this document the birth of Mary is foretold by angelic announcement to her parents, Joachim and Anna, as was that of Jesus to Mary. It contains in twenty-five chs the period from this announcement to the Massacre of the Innocents, including accounts of the early training of Mary in the temple, the Lukan narrative of the birth of Christ with some legendary additions, and the death of Zacharias by order of Herod for refusing to give information regarding the place of concealment of Elisabeth and the child John who, in their flight during the massacre, are miraculously saved by the opening of a mountain. At ch **18** a change takes place in the narrative from the third to the first person, which has been taken (*NT Apoc Writings* by Professor Orr, D.D., London, 1903) to suggest an Essenian-Ebionitic origin for the document, and at least to argue for it a composite character, which again may account for the great variety of view taken of its date. It has been assigned (*EB*, I, 259) to the 1st cent. Zahn and Krüger place it in the first decade, many scholars in the second half of the 2d cent.; while others (e.g. Harnack) place it in its present form as late as the middle of the 4th cent. Good scholars (Sanday, *The Gospels in the Second Cent.*) admit references to it in Justin Martyr which would imply that possibly in some older form it was known in the first half of the 2d cent. In its latest forms the document indicates the obvious aim of the writer to promote the sanctity and veneration of the Virgin. It has been shown to contain a number of unhistorical statements. It was condemned in the western church by Popes Damasus (382), Innocent I (405) and by the Decretum Gelasianum (496?). It would seem as if the age thus deprived of the Protevangelium demanded some document of the same character to take its place.

2. Gospel of Pseudo-Matthew

(*b*) A forged correspondence between Jerome and two Italian bishops supplied a substitute in the Gospel of the Pseudo-Matthew, which Jerome was falsely represented to have rendered in Lat from the original Heb of Mt. The gospel is known only in Latin and, as already indicated, is not earlier than the 5th cent. The Protevangelium is freely used and supplemented from some unknown (probably gnostic) source, and further miracles especially connected with the sojourn in Egypt have been wrought into it with others added from the Childhood Gospel of Thomas. Some of the miracles recorded of Egypt are represented as fulfilments of OT prophecy, as when (ch **18**) the adoration of the infant Jesus by dragons recalls the fulfilment of what was said by David the prophet: "Praise the Lord from the earth, ye dragons: ye dragons and all ye deeps"; or as when (ch **19**) lions and panthers adored them, showing the company the way in the desert, "bowing their heads and wagging their tails and adoring Him with great reverence," which was regarded as a fulfilment of the prophecy: "Wolves shall feed with lambs and the lions and the ox shall eat straw together." In this gospel, too, appears for the first time the notice of the ox and the ass adoring the child Jesus in the manger, of which much was made in Christian art. The gospel is further eked out by the relation of several of the miracles connected with the Gospel of the Childhood.

3. Nativity of Mary

(*c*) The Gospel of the Nativity of Mary was written in Lat. It goes over much the same ground as the earlier portion of the Pseudo-Matthew, but so differs from it as to indicate a later date and a different author. It includes more of the miraculous element and daily angelic visits to Mary during her residence in the temple. This gospel makes Mary leave the temple in her 14th year; according to the gospel next described, where the narrator is represented as the Son of Mary Himself, she left the temple in her 12th year, having lived in it nine years. It was for long held to be the work of Jerome, and from this gospel was almost entirely formed the "Golden Legend" which largely took the place of the Scriptures in the 13th cent. throughout Europe before the invention of printing. It was among the books early printed in some countries where (as in England) it might not be safe to print the Scriptures. Its services to mediaeval literature and art should not blind us to the fact that it was a forgery deliberately introduced into the service of the church about the 6th cent., when the worship of Mary was specially promoted in the church.

4. The Gospel of Joseph the Carpenter

(*d*) To the same class of compositions belongs the Gospel of Joseph the Carpenter. Originally written in Coptic, it was translated into Arab., in which language with a Lat VS it was published in 1722. The composition is devoted to the glorification of Joseph, a cult which was specially favored by the monophysite Copts. It dates from the 4th cent. It contains in 22 chs the whole history of Joseph and relates in the last part the circumstances of his death at the age of 111 years. These are of some importance for the history of dogma.

5. The Passing of Mary

(*e*) *Transitus Mariae:* although not strictly a gospel of the Nativity notice may here be taken of the account of St. John the Theologian of the Falling Asleep (*koimēsis*) of the Holy Mother of God or as it is more commonly called "the Passing of Mary" (*transitus Mariae*). It was originally written in Gr, but appears also in Lat and several other languages. Two years, it seems, after the ascension of Jesus, Mary, who paid frequent visits to the "Holy tomb of our Lord to burn incense and pray" was persecuted by the Jews and prayed her Son that He would take her from the earth. The archangel Gabriel brings an answer to her prayers and announces that after three days she shall go to the heavenly places to her Son, into true and everlasting life. Apostles from their graves or from their dioceses are summoned to her bedside at Bethlehem and relate how they were occupied when the summons reached them. Miracles of healing are wrought round the dying bed; and after the instantaneous transportation of Mary and the attendant apostles to Jerus, on the Lord's Day, amidst visions of angels Christ Himself appears and receives her soul to Himself. Her body is buried in Gethsemane and thereafter translated to Paradise. Judged by its contents which reveal an advanced stage of the worship of the Virgin and also of church ritual, the document cannot have been produced earlier than the end of the 4th or the beginning of the 5th cent., and it has a place among the apocryphal documents condemned by the Gelasian Decree. By this time indeed it appears as if the writers of such documents assumed the most unrestricted license in imagining and embellishing the facts and situations regarding the gospel narrative.

1. The Gospel of Thomas

2. The Gospels of the Childhood: (*a*) Next to the Protevangelium the oldest and the most widely spread of the apocryphal gospels is the Gospel of Thomas. It is mentioned by Origen and Irenaeus and seems to have been used by a gnostic sect of the Nachashenes in the middle of the 2d cent. It was docetic as regards the miracles recorded in it and on this account was also acceptable to the Manichees. The author was one of the Marcosians referred to by Irenaeus. Great variations exist in the text, of which there are only late catholic recasts, two in Gr, one in Lat and one in Syr. One of the Gr versions is considerably longer than the other, while the Lat is somewhat larger than either. They are very largely concerned with a record of miracles wrought by Jesus before He was 12 years of age. They depict Jesus as an extraordinary but by no means a lovable child. Unlike the miracles of the canonical Gospels those recorded in this gospel are mainly of a destructive nature and are whimsical and puerile in character. It rather shocks one to read them as recorded of the Lord Jesus Christ. The wonder-worker is described by Renan as "un gamin omnipotent et omniscient," wielding the power of the Godhead with a child's waywardness and petulance. Instead of being subject to His parents He is a serious trouble to them; and instead of growing in wisdom He is represented as forward and eager to teach His instructors, and to be omniscient from the beginning. The parents of one of the children whose death He had caused entreat Joseph, "Take away that Jesus of thine from this place for he cannot dwell with us in this town; or at least teach him to bless and not to curse." Three or four miracles of a beneficent nature are mentioned; and in the Lat gospel when Jesus was in Egypt and in his third year, it is written (ch **1**), "And seeing boys playing he began to play with them, and he took a dried fish and put it into a basin and ordered it to move about. And it began to move about. And he said again to the fish: 'Throw out the salt which thou hast, and walk into the water.' And it so came to pass, and the neighbors seeing what had been done, told it to the widowed woman in whose house Mary his mother lived. And as soon as she heard it she thrust them out of her house with great haste." As Westcott points out in his *Intro to the Study of the Gospels*, 444, "In the apocryphal miracles we find no worthy conception of the laws of providential interference; they are wrought to supply present wants or to gratify present feelings, and often are positively immoral; they are arbitrary displays of power, and without any spontaneity on our Lord's part or on that of the recipient." Possibly the compilers of the 1st-cent. narratives above mentioned had in many cases deemed it expedient to make the miraculous an essential—even a too prominent—part of their story; and this may be the reason why John in the opening of the Fourth Gospel declared all the reported miracles of the Childhood to be unauthorized by the statement that the first miracle was that performed, after the beginning of the public ministry, at the marriage at Cana of Galilee. "This beginning of his signs did Jesus in Cana of Galilee, and manifested his glory; and his disciples believed on him" (Jn **2** 11).

2. Arabic Gospel of the Childhood

(*b*) The Arab. Gospel of the Childhood is a composite production. Though first published in Arab. with a Latin translation in 1697, its Syr origin may be inferred from the use of the era of Alexander the Great in ch **2**, from the acquaintance of the writer with oriental learning, and from that of the child Jesus, when in Egypt, with astronomy and physics. The popularity of the book among the Arabs and Copts in Egypt may also be explained by the fact that the most important of its miracles take place during the Sojourn in Egypt. It is noteworthy also that according to this gospel (ch **7**) it was on the ground of a prophecy of Zoroaster regarding the birth of the Messiah that the Magi undertook their journey to Bethlehem. Some of its stories also appear in the Koran and in other Mohammedan writings. Chs **1**-**9** are based on the canonical Gospels of Matthew and Luke and on the Protevangelium of James, while chs **26** to the end are derived from the Gospel of Thomas. The intermediate portion of the work is thoroughly oriental in character and reads like extracts from the *Arabian Nights*. It is not easy to treat seriously the proposal to set productions like these on anything approaching equality with the canonical Gospels. The gospel also has much to do with the growth of the veneration of the Virgin.

3. Gospels of the Passion and Resurrection: The principal documents in this connection are the Gospel of Nicodemus and to some extent, as above shown, the Gospel of Peter. The Gospel of Nicodemus is a name given not earlier than the 13th cent. to a duplicate composition the two parts of which were (1) the *Acta Pilati* or Acts of Pilate and (2) the Descent of Christ to the Lower World. The document professes to be a translation into Gr from the Heb, and to have been made in the 17th year of the emperor Theodosius and the 6th of Valentinian. It exists in six forms, two Gr and one Lat of the Acts of Pilate, and two Lat and one Gr of the Descent to the Lower World. The general consensus of scholars places the composition in the 5th cent., though Tischendorf, relying upon references in Justin and Tertullian, places it in the 2d, a date by which it is quite possible for the legend to have arisen. Possibly there has been some confusion between the report on the proceedings connected with the trial and crucifixion of Jesus that had to be furnished to the emperor, as required by the rules of the Rom civil service, and the extended record of the proceedings contained in the Gospel of Nicodemus. The writer was obviously a Jewish Christian. He wrote for this class and was anxious to establish his record by evidence from the mouths of the enemies of Jesus and especially of the officials connected with the events before and after the death of Jesus. Pilate in particular is shown to be favorable to Jesus and—a gap that must have struck many readers of the canonical narratives—several of those on whom miracles of healing had been wrought come forward to give evidence in favor of Jesus—a most natural step for a late narrator to suppose as having taken place in a regular and formal trial, but one which, as may be gathered from the silence of the canonical writers, was omitted in the turbulent proceedings of the priestly conspiracy that ended with the crucifixion. With all the writer's acquaintance with Jewish institutions "he shows himself in many points ignorant of the topography of Pal; thinks, e.g. that Jesus was crucified in the garden in which he was seized (ch **9**) and places Mt. Mamilch or Malek (S. of Jerus) in Galilee, and confounds it with the Mount of Ascension" (Orr, op. cit., xix). The second part of the gospel—The Descent of Christ to the Lower World—is an account of an early and widely accepted tradition not mentioned in any canonical Gospel but based upon 1 Pet **3** 19: "He went and preached unto the spirits in prison." Two saints who were raised at His resurrection relate how they had been confined in Hades when the Conqueror appeared at its entrance, how the gates of brass were broken and the prisoners released, Jesus taking with Him to Paradise the souls of Adam, Isaiah, John the Baptist and other holy men who had died before Him. The document is purely imaginary: its only importance is in showing how this article of the creed was regarded in the 4th cent.

1. Gospel of Nicodemus

Of even less importance are some late fabrications referring to Pilate sometimes in the MSS attached to the Gospel of Nicodemus, such as Pilate's Letter to the emperor Tiberius; Pilate's Official Report, above referred to; the Paradoses of Pilate and the Death of Pilate, who, after condemnation to the most disgraceful death, is represented as dying by his own hand. In the Narrative of Joseph of Arimathea the writer gives a loose rein to his imagination.

The study of the documents above described fully justifies the observation of the editors of the Ante-Nicene Library that while they afford us "curious glimpses of the state of the Christian conscience, and of modes of thought in the first centuries of our era, the predominant impression which they leave on our minds is a profound sense of the immeasurable superiority, the unapproachable simplicity and majesty, of the Canonical Writings."

Literature.—In addition to the books quoted above may be mentioned the following: Fabricius, *Codex Apocryphus*, 1719; the collections and prolegomena of Thilo (1832); Tischendorf, *Gospels*, 1853; Ellicott, "On the Apocryphal Gospels" in *Cambridge Essays*, 1856; Lipsius, art. "Gospels (Apoc)" in *Dict. of Christ. Biog.*; Dr. W. Wright in *Journal of Sacred Lit.* (January and April, 1865) on the Syr VSS of the Protevangelium, The Gospel of Thomas, and the Transitus Mariae: Studia Sinaitica (No. XI, 1902) giving new Syr texts of the Protevangelium and Transitus Mariae. A. F. Findlay, art. "Acts (Apoc)," where will be found a very copious body of references to works, British and foreign, dealing with all branches of the subject.

J. Hutchison

APOLLONIA, ap-o-lō′ni-a (**Ἀπολλωνία**, *Apollōnía*): A town in Mygdonia, a district in Macedonia. It was situated a little to the south of Lake Bolbe, on the Via Egnatia, the great Rom road leading from the coast of the Adriatic to the river Hebrus (*Maritza*), one of the main military and commercial highways of the empire: it lay between Amphipolis and Thessalonica, a day's journey (Livy xlv.28) or about 30 Rom miles from the former and 38 from the latter. The foundation of the town may perhaps be attributed to about 432 BC; in any case, coins are extant which attest its existence in the 4th cent. BC (Head, *Historia Numorum*, 181). Paul and Silas passed through the town on their journey from Philippi to Thessalonica, but do not appear to have stayed there (Acts **17** 1). The name seems to have survived in the modern *Pollina* (Leake, *Northern Greece*, III, 458; Cousinéry, *Voyage dans la Macédoine*, I, 115).

Marcus N. Tod

APOLLONIUS, ap-o-lō′ni-us (**Ἀπολλώνιος**, *Apollōnios*): A common name among the Syro-Macedonians. Prideaux (*Connexion*) interrupts his narrative of the year 148 BC to give an account of the different persons who bore this name. (1) Son of Thrasaeus (2 Macc **3** 5) who was governor of Coele-Syria (Pal and Phoenicia) under Seleucus Philopator, when Heliodorus came to Jerus to rob the temple, and afterward, by his authority in that province, supported Simon the governor of the temple at Jerus against Onias the high priest. He was also chief minister of state to King Seleucus. But on the accession of Antiochus Epiphanes, Apollonius, in some way becoming obnoxious to the new king, left Syria and retired to Miletus. (2) A son of (1) who, while his father resided at Miletus, was brought up at Rome along with Demetrius, son of Seleucus Philopator, and at that time held as a hostage by the Romans. This Apollonius lived in great intimacy with Demetrius, who, on recovering the crown of Syria, made him governor of Coele-Syria and Phoenicia, the same government which his father held under Seleucus Philopator. He seems to have been continued in the same government by Alexander (1 Macc **10** 69) but he revolted from him to embrace the interest of Demetrius. (3) Son of Menestheus, and favorite and chief minister of Antiochus Epiphanes (2 Macc **4** 21). He went as ambassador from Antiochus, first to Rome (Livy xlii.6) and afterward to Ptolemy Philometor, king of Egypt (2 Macc **4** 21). This is generally held to be the same who is said to have been over the tribute (1 Macc **1** 29; 2 Macc **5** 24) and who, on the return of Antiochus from his last expedition into Egypt, was sent with a detachment of 22,000 men to destroy Jerusalem. He attacked the Jews while keeping the Sabbath day holy and slew great multitudes of them (2 Macc **5** 24–27). (4) Governor of Samaria in the time of Antiochus Epiphanes. He was slain in battle by Judas Maccabaeus (1 Macc **3** 10.11; *Ant*, XII, vii, 10). (5) Son of Gennaeus (2 Macc **12** 2); as governor of a toparchy in Pal under Antiochus Eupator he proved a bitter enemy of the Jews.

J. Hutchison

APOLLOPHANES, ap-o-lof'a-nēz, a-pol-ō-fā'nēz (**Ἀπολλοφάνης**, *Apollophánēs*): A Syrian killed by Judas Maccabaeus (2 Macc **10** 37).

APOLLOS, a-pol'os (**Ἀπολλῶς**, *Apollôs*, the short form of Apollonius): Apollos was a Jew of Alexandrian race (Acts **18** 24) who reached Ephesus in the summer of 54 AD, while St. Paul was on his third missionary journey, and there he "spake and taught accurately the things concerning Jesus" (Acts **18** 25). That he was eminently fitted for the task is indicated by the fact of his being a "learned man," "mighty in the scriptures," "fervent in spirit," "instructed in the way of the Lord" (vs 24.25). His teaching was however incomplete in that he knew "only the baptism of John" (ver 25), and this has given rise to some controversy. According to Blass, his information was derived from a written gospel which reached Alexandria, but it was more probably the fruits of what Apollos had heard, either directly or from others, of the preaching of John the Baptist at Bethany beyond Jordan (cf Jn **1** 28). Upon receiving further instruction from Priscilla and Aquila (Acts **18** 26), Apollos extended his mission to Achaia, being encouraged thereto by the brethren of Ephesus (ver 27). In Achaia "he helped them much that had believed through grace; for he powerfully confuted the Jews, and that publicly, showing by the scriptures that Jesus was the Christ" (vs 27.28). During Apollos' absences in Achaia, St. Paul had reached Ephesus and learned of what had been taught by Apollos there (**19** 1). As St. Paul was informed that the Ephesians still knew nothing of the baptism of the Spirit (vs 2–4), it is probable that Apollos had not imparted to his hearers the further instruction he had received from Priscilla and Aquila, but had departed for Achaia shortly after receiving it. St. Paul remained upward of two years among the Ephesians (vs 8.10), and in the spring of 57 AD he wrote the First Epistle to the Corinthians. By this time Apollos was once more in Ephesus (cf 1 Cor **16** 12). It is incredible that this epistle of St. Paul could have been prompted by any feelings of jealousy or animosity on his part against Apollos. It was rather the outcome of discussion between the two regarding the critical situation then existing in Corinth. The mission of Apollos had met with a certain success, but the breeding of faction, which that very success, through the slight discrepancies in his teaching (cf 1 Cor **1** 12; **3** 4) with that of Paul or of Cephas, had engendered, was utterly alien to his intentions. The party spirit was as distasteful to Apollos as it was to St. Paul, and made him reluctant to return to the scene of his former labors even at the desire of St. Paul himself (**16** 12). The epistle voiced the indignation of both. St. Paul welcomed the coöperation of Apollos (**3** 6: "I planted, Apollos watered"). It was not against his fellow-evangelist that he fulminated, but against the petty spirit of those who loved faction more than truth, who saw not that both he and Apollos came among them as "God's fellow-workers" (**3** 9), the common servants of the one Lord and Saviour Jesus Christ. This view is also borne out by the tenor of Clement's Ep. to the Cor (cf Hennecke, *Neutestamentliche Apokryphen*, 84–112, esp. 105): nor does it conflict with the passages 1 Cor **12** 1–7; 2 Cor **3** 1; **11** 16, where St. Paul seems to allude to Apollos' eloquence, wisdom, and letter of commendation. St. Paul wrote thus not in order to disparage Apollos, but to affirm that, even without these incidental advantages, he would yield to none in the preaching of Christ crucified.

The last mention of Apollos is in the Ep. to Titus, where he is recommended along with Zenas to Titus (Titus **3** 13). He was then on a journey through Crete (**1** 5), and was probably the bearer of the epistle. The time of this is uncertain, as the writing of the Ep. to Titus, though generally admitted to have been after the release of St. Paul from imprisonment at Rome, has been variously placed at 64–67 AD. See Titus, Ep. to.

C. M. Kerr

APOLLYON, a-pol'i-on (**Ἀπολλύων**, *Apollúōn*; אֲבַדּוֹן, *'ăbhaddōn*, "destroyer"): Present part. of the vb. ἀπολλύω, "to destroy."

I. Definition.—A proper name, original with the author of the Apocalypse and used by him once (Rev **9** 11) as a tr of the Heb word "Abaddon" (see Abaddon) to designate an angel or prince of the lower world.

II. OT Background.—The term Abaddon ("destruction") appears solely in the Wisd lit. of the OT and in the following narrow range of instances: Job **26** 6; **28** 22; **31** 12; Ps **88** 11; Prov **15** 11. In all these passages save one (Job **31** 12) the word is combined either with Sheol, "death," or "the grave," in such a way as to indicate a purely eschatological term based upon the advanced idea of moral distinctions in the realm of the dead. In the one exceptional passage (Est **8** 6 is incorrectly referred to—the word here is different, viz. אָבְדָן, *'ābhedhān*) where the combination does not occur, the emphasis upon the moral element in the "destruction" mentioned is so definite as practically to preclude the possibility of interpreting the term in any general sense (as Charles, *HDB*, art. "Abaddon"; per con., Briggs, *ICC*, "Psalms" in loc.; *BDB*, sub loc.). The meaning of the word, therefore, is: the place or condition of utter ruin reserved for the wicked in the realm of the dead.

1. Fundamental Meaning

One other feature of OT usage is worthy of consideration as throwing light upon Rev **9** 11. Abaddon and the accompanying terms "Death" and Sheol are personified (as in Job **28** 22) and represented as living beings who speak and act (cf Rev **6** 8).

2. Personification

III. NT Usage.—The starting-point of the Apocalyptist's use of "Apollyon" is to be found in the fundamental meaning of "Abaddon" as moral destruction in the underworld, together with the occasional personification of kindred terms in the OT. The imagery was in general terms familiar while the NT writer felt perfectly free to vary the usage to suit his own particular purposes.

1. The Starting-Point

(1) Since Apollyon is a personification he is not to be identified with Satan (cf Rev **9** 1 where Satan seems to be clearly indicated) or with any other being to whom historical existence and definite characteristics are ascribed. He is the central figure in an ideal picture of evil forces represented as originating in the world of lost spirits and allowed to operate destructively in human life. They are pictured as locusts, but on an enlarged scale and with the addition of many features inconsistent with the strict application of the figure (see vs 7–10). The intention is, by the multiplication of images which the author does not attempt to harmonize,

2. Apollyon not Satan but Part of an Ideal Description

to convey the impression of great power and far-reaching destructiveness. (2) This interpretation finds additional support in the writer's significant departure from the familiar usage. In the OT the *place* of destruction is personified—in Rev **9** 11, personal forces *issue* from the Abyss, of which the presiding genius is Destruction in person. The seer's picture is equally independent of the tradition represented by the Talm (Shab f. 55) where Abaddon is personified as jointly with Death president over six destroying angels. These modifications are evidently due to the exigencies of the pictorial form. It is clearly impossible to portray forces proceeding from the place of ruin in the charge of the place itself.

3. Apollyon Necessary to the Picture

The importance of the conception of Apollyon to the completeness of the picture should not be overlooked. It is intended to represent these forces as having a certain principle of internal unity and as possessors of the power of effective leadership.

As to the specific significance of the vision of the locusts as a whole it is not easy to reach a conclusion.

4. General Significance of the Description

Professor Swete suggests (*Comm. on Apocalypse* in loc.) that "the locusts of the abyss may be the memories of the past brought home at times of divine visitation; they hurt by recalling forgotten sins." It seems to us more probable that it represents an actual historical movement, past or to come, demoniacal in origin and character, human in the mode of its operation and the sphere of its influence, used by God for a scourge upon mankind and kept in restraint by His grace and power. See ABADDON.

LOUIS MATTHEWS SWEET

APOSTASY, a-pos'ta-si, **APOSTATE,** a-pos'-tāt (ἡ ἀποστασία, *hē apostasía,* "a standing away from"): I.e. a falling away, a withdrawal, a defection. Not found in the EV, but used twice in the NT, in the Gr original, to express abandonment of the faith. Paul was falsely accused of teaching the Jews apostasy from Moses (Acts **21** 21); he predicted the great apostasy from Christianity, foretold by Jesus (Mt **24** 10–12) which would precede "the day of the Lord" (2 Thess **2** 2). Apostasy, not in name but in fact, meets scathing rebuke in the Epistle of Jude, e.g. the apostasy of angels (ver 6). Foretold, with warnings, as sure to abound in the latter days (1 Tim **4** 1–3; 2 Thess **2** 3; 2 Pet **3** 17). Causes of: persecution (Mt **24** 9.10); false teachers (Mt **24** 11); temptation (Lk **8** 13); worldliness (2 Tim **4** 4); defective knowledge of Christ (1 Jn **2** 19); moral lapse (He **6** 4–6); forsaking worship and spiritual living (**10** 25–31); unbelief (**3** 12). Biblical examples: Saul (1 S **15** 11); Amaziah (2 Ch **25** 14.27); many disciples (Jn **6** 66); Hymenaeus and Alexander (1 Tim **1** 19.20); Demas (2 Tim **4** 10). For further illustration see Dt **13** 13; Zeph **1** 4–6; Gal **5** 4; 2 Pet **2** 20.21.

"Forsaking Jehovah" was the characteristic and oft-recurring sin of the chosen people, esp. in their contact with idolatrous nations. It constituted their supreme national peril. The tendency appeared in their earliest history, as abundantly seen in the warnings and prohibitions of the laws of Moses (Ex **20** 3.4.23; Dt **6** 14; **11** 16). The fearful consequences of religious and moral apostasy appear in the curses pronounced against this sin, on Mount Ebal, by the representatives of six of the tribes of Israel, elected by Moses (Dt **27** 13–26; **28** 15–68). So wayward was the heart of Israel, even in the years immediately following the national emancipation, in the wilderness, that Joshua found it necessary to re-pledge the entire nation to a new fidelity to Jeh and to their original covenant before they were permitted to enter the Promised Land (Josh **24** 1–28). Infidelity to this covenant blighted the nation's prospects and growth during the time of the Judges (Jgs **2** 11–15; **10** 6.10.13; 1 S **12** 10). It was the cause of prolific and ever-increasing evil, civic and moral, from Solomon's day to the Assyr and Bab captivities. Many of the kings of the divided kingdom apostatized, leading the people, as in the case of Rehoboam, into the grossest forms of idolatry and immorality (1 K **14** 22–24; 2 Ch **12** 1). Conspicuous examples of such royal apostasy are Jeroboam (1 K **12** 28–32); Ahab (1 K **16** 30–33); Ahaziah (1 K **22** 51–53); Jehoram (2 Ch **21** 6.10.12–15); Ahaz (2 Ch **28** 1–4); Manasseh (2 Ch **33** 1–9); Amon (2 Ch **33** 22). See IDOLATRY. Prophecy originated as a Divine and imperative protest against this historic tendency to defection from the religion of Jeh.

In classical Gr, apostasy signified revolt from a military commander. In the Roman Catholic church it denotes abandonment of religious orders; renunciation of ecclesiastical authority; defection from the faith. The persecutions of the early Christian cents. forced many to deny Christian discipleship and to signify their apostasy by offering incense to a heathen deity or blaspheming the name of Christ. The emperor Julian, who probably never vitally embraced the Christian faith, is known in history as "the Apostate," having renounced Christianity for paganism soon after his accession to the throne.

An apostate's defection from the faith may be *intellectual,* as in the case of Ernst Haeckel, who, because of his materialistic philosophy, publicly and formally renounced Christianity and the church; or it may be *moral and spiritual,* as with Judas, who for filthy lucre's sake basely betrayed his Lord. See exhaustive art. on "Apostasy" in *Jew Enc.*

DWIGHT M. PRATT

APOSTLE, a-pos''l (ἀπόστολος, *apóstolos,* lit. "one sent forth," an envoy, missionary): For the meaning of this name as it meets us in the NT, reference is sometimes made to classical and Jewish parallels. In earlier classical Gr there was a distinction between an *ággelos* or messenger and an *apostolos,* who was not a mere messenger, but a delegate or representative of the person who sent him. In the later Judaism, again, *apostoloi* were envoys sent out by the patriarchate in Jerus to collect the sacred tribute from the Jews of the Dispersion. It seems unlikely, however, that either of these uses bears upon the Christian origin of a term which, in any case, came to have its own distinctive Christian meaning. To understand the word as we find it in the NT it is not necessary to go beyond the NT itself. To discover the source of its Christian use it is sufficient to refer to its immediate and natural signification. The term used by Jesus, it must be remembered, would be Aram., not Gr, and *apostolos* would be its literal equivalent.

In the NT history we first hear of the term as applied by Jesus to the Twelve in connection with

1. The Twelve

that evangelical mission among the villages on which He dispatched them at an early stage of His public ministry (Mt **10** 1 ff; Mk **3** 14; **6** 30; Lk **6** 13; **9** 1 ff). From a comparison of the Synoptics it would seem that the name as thus used was not a general designation for the Twelve, but had reference only to this particular mission, which was typical and prophetic, however, of the wider mission that was to come (cf Hort, *Christian Ecclesia,* 23–29). Luke, it is true, uses the word as a title for the Twelve apart from reference to the mission among the villages. But the explanation probably is, as Dr. Hort suggests, that since the Third Gospel and the Book of Acts formed two sections of what was really one work, the author in the Gospel employs the term in that wider sense which it came to have after the Ascension.

When we pass to Acts, "apostles" has become an ordinary name for the Eleven (Acts **1** 2.26), and after the election of Matthias in place of Judas, for the Twelve (**2** 37.42.43, etc). But even so it does not denote a particular and restricted office, but rather that function of a world-wide missionary service to which the Twelve were especially called. In His last charge, just before He ascended, Jesus had commissioned them to go forth into all the world and preach the gospel to every creature (Mt **28** 19.20; Mk **16** 15). He had said that they were to be His witnesses not only in Jerus and Judaea, but in Samaria (contrast Mt **10** 5), and unto the uttermost part of the earth (Acts **1** 8). They were apostles, therefore, *qua* missionaries—not merely because they were the Twelve, but because they were now sent forth by their Lord on a universal mission for the propagation of the gospel.

2. Paul

The very fact that the name "apostle" means what it does would point to the impossibility of confining it within the limits of the Twelve. (The "twelve apostles" of Rev **21** 14 is evidently symbolic; cf in **7** 3 ff the restriction of God's sealed servants to the twelve tribes.) Yet there might be a tendency at first to do so, and to restrict it as a badge of honor and privilege peculiar to that inner circle (cf Acts **1** 25). If any such tendency existed, Paul effectually broke it down by vindicating for himself the right to the name. His claim appears in his assumption of the apostolic title in the opening words of most of his epistles. And when his right to it was challenged, he defended that right with passion, and especially on these grounds: that he had seen Jesus, and so was qualified to bear witness to His resurrection (1 Cor **9** 1; cf Acts **22** 6 ff); that he had received a call to the work of an apostle (Rom **1** 1; 1 Cor **1** 1, etc; Gal **2** 7; cf Acts **13** 2 ff; **22** 21); but, above all, that he could point to the signs and seals of his apostleship furnished by his missionary labors and their fruits (1 Cor **9** 2; 2 Cor **12** 12; Gal **2** 8). It was by this last ground of appeal that Paul convinced the original apostles of the justice of his claim. He had not been a disciple of Jesus in the days of His flesh; his claim to have seen the risen Lord and from Him to have received a personal commission was not one that could be proved to others; but there could be no possibility of doubt as to the seals of his apostleship. It was abundantly clear that "he that wrought for Peter unto the apostleship of the circumcision wrought for [Paul] also unto the Gentiles" (Gal **2** 8). And so perceiving the grace that was given unto him, Peter and John, together with James of Jerus, recognized Paul as apostle to the Gentiles and gave him the right hand of fellowship (ver 9).

3. The Wider Circle

It is sometimes said by those who recognize that there were other apostles besides the Twelve and Paul that the latter (to whom some, on the ground of 1 Cor **15** 7; Gal **1** 19, would add James the Lord's brother) were the apostles *par excellence*, while the other apostles mentioned in the NT were apostles in some inferior sense. It is hardly possible, however, to make out such a distinction on the ground of NT usage. There were great differences, no doubt, among the apostles of the primitive church, as there were among the Twelve themselves—differences due to natural talents, to personal acquirements and experience, to spiritual gifts. Paul was greater than Barnabas or Silvanus, just as Peter and John were greater than Thaddaeus or Simon the Cananaean. But Thaddaeus and Simon were disciples of Jesus in the very same sense as Peter and John; and the Twelve and Paul were not more truly apostles than others who are mentioned in the NT. If apostleship denotes missionary service, and if its reality, as Paul suggests, is to be measured by its seals, it would be difficult to maintain that Matthias was an apostle *par excellence*, while Barnabas was not. Paul sets Barnabas as an apostle side by side with himself (1 Cor **9** 5 f; Gal **2** 9; cf Acts **13** 2 f; **14** 4.14); he speaks of Andronicus and Junias as "of note among the apostles" (Rom **16** 7); he appears to include Apollos along with himself among the apostles who are made a spectacle unto the world and to angels and to men (1 Cor **4** 6.9); the natural inference from a comparison of 1 Thess **1** 1 with **2** 6 is that he describes Silvanus and Timothy as "apostles of Christ"; to the Philippians he mentions Epaphroditus as "your apostle" (Phil **2** 25 RVm), and to the Corinthians commends certain unknown brethren as "the apostles of the churches" and "the glory of Christ" (2 Cor **8** 23 RVm). And the very fact that he found it necessary to denounce certain persons as "false apostles, deceitful workers, fashioning themselves into apostles of Christ" (**11** 13) shows that there was no thought in the primitive church of restricting the apostleship to a body of 12 or 13 men. "Had the number been definitely restricted, the claims of these interlopers would have been self-condemned" (Lightfoot, *Galatians*, 97).

4. Apostles in Didache

When we come to the *Did*, which probably lies beyond the boundary-line of NT history, we find the name "apostles" applied to a whole class of nameless missionaries—men who settled in no church, but moved about from place to place as messengers of the gospel (ch **11**). This makes it difficult to accept the view, urged by Lightfoot (op. cit., 98) and Gwatkin (*HDB*, I, 126) on the ground of Lk **24** 48; Acts **1** 8.22; 1 Cor **9** 1, that to have seen the Lord was always the primary qualification of an apostle—a view on the strength of which they reject the apostleship of Apollos and Timothy, as being late converts to Christianity who lived far from the scenes of Our Lord's ministry. Gwatkin remarks that we have no reason to suppose that this condition was ever waived unless we throw forward the *Did* into the 2d cent. But it seems very unlikely that even toward the end of the 1st cent. there would be a whole class of men, not only still alive, but still braving in the exercise of their missionary functions all the hardships of a wandering and homeless existence (cf *Did* **11** 4–6), who were yet able to bear the personal testimony of eye-witnesses to the ministry and resurrection of Jesus. In Lk **24** 48 and Acts **1** 8.22 it is the chosen company of the Twelve who are in view. In 1 Cor **9** 1 Paul is meeting his Judaizing opponents on their own ground, and answering their insistence upon personal intercourse with Jesus by a claim to have seen the Lord. But apart from these passages there is no evidence that the apostles of the early church were necessarily men who had known Jesus in the flesh or had been witnesses of His resurrection—much less that this was the primary qualification on which their apostleship was made to rest.

5. The Apostleship

We are led then to the conclusion that the true differentia of the NT apostleship lay in the missionary calling implied in the name, and that all whose lives were devoted to this vocation, and who could prove by the issues of their labors that God's Spirit was working through them for the conversion of Jew or Gentile, were regarded and described as apostles. The apostolate was not a limited circle of officials holding a well-defined position of authority in the church, but a large class of men who discharged one—and that the highest—of the functions of the prophetic ministry (1 Cor **12** 28; Eph **4** 11). It was on the foundation of the apostles and prophets that the Christian church was built, with Jesus Christ Himself as the chief corner-stone (Eph **2** 20). The distinction between the two classes was that while the prophet was God's spokesman to the believing church (1 Cor **14** 4.22.25.30.31), the apostle was His envoy to the unbelieving world (Gal **2** 7.9).

The *call* of the apostle to his task might come in a variety of ways. The Twelve were called personally by Jesus to an apostolic task at the commencement of His earthly ministry (Mt **10** 1 ff ||), and after His resurrection this call was repeated, made permanent, and given a universal scope (Mt **28** 19.20; Acts **1** 8). Matthias was called first by the voice of the general body of the brethren and thereafter by the decision of the lot (Acts **1** 15.23.26). Paul's call came to him in a heavenly vision (Acts **26** 17–19); and though this call was subsequently ratified by the church at Antioch, which sent him forth at the bidding of the Holy Ghost (**13** 1 ff), he firmly maintained that he was an apostle not from men neither through man, but through Jesus Christ and God the Father who raised Him from the dead (Gal **1** 1). Barnabas was sent forth (*exapostéllō* is the vb. used) by the church at Jerus (Acts **11** 22) and later, along with Paul, by the church at Antioch (**13** 1); and soon after this we find the two men described as apostles (**14** 4). It was the mission on which they were sent that explains the title. And when this particular mission was completed and they returned to Antioch to rehearse before the assembled church "all things that God had done with them, and that he had opened a door of faith unto the Gentiles" (ver 27), they thereby justified their claim to be the apostles not only of the church, but of the Holy Spirit.

The *authority* of the apostolate was of a spiritual, ethical and personal kind. It was not official, and in the nature of the case could not be transmitted to others. Paul claimed for himself complete independence of the opinion of the whole body of the earlier apostles (Gal **2** 6.11), and in seeking to influence his own converts endeavored by manifestation of the truth to commend himself to every man's conscience in the sight of God (2 Cor **4** 2). There is no sign that the apostles collectively exercised a separate and autocratic authority. When the question of the observance of the Mosaic ritual by gentile Christians arose at Antioch and was referred to Jerus, it was "the apostles and elders" who met to discuss it (Acts **15** 2.6.22), and the letter returned to Antioch was written in the name of "the apostles and the elders, brethren" (ver 23). In founding a church Paul naturally appointed the first local officials (Acts **14** 23), but he does not seem to have interfered with the ordinary administration of affairs in the churches he had planted. In those cases in which he was appealed to or was compelled by some grave scandal to interpose, he rested an authoritative command on some express word of the Lord (1 Cor **7** 10), and when he had no such word to rest on, was careful to distinguish his own judgment and counsel from a Divine commandment (vs 12.25.40). His appeals in the latter case are grounded upon fundamental principles of morality common to heathen and Christian alike (1 Cor **5** 1), or are addressed to the spiritual judgment (**10** 15), or are reinforced by the weight of a personal influence gained by unselfish service and by the fact that he was the spiritual father of his converts as having begotten them in Christ Jesus through the gospel (**4** 15 f).

It may be added here that the expressly missionary character of the apostleship seems to debar James, the Lord's brother, from any claim to the title. James was a prophet and teacher, but not an apostle. As the head of the church at Jerus, he exercised a ministry of a purely local nature. The passages on which it has been sought to establish his right to be included in the apostolate do not furnish any satisfactory evidence. In 1 Cor **15** 7 James is contrasted with "all the apostles" rather than included in their number (cf **9** 5). And in Gal **1** 19 the meaning may quite well be that with the exception of Peter, none of the apostles was seen by Paul in Jerus, but only James the Lord's brother (cf RVm).

LITERATURE.—Lightfoot, *Galatians*, 92–101; Hort, *Christian Ecclesia*, Lect II; Weizsäcker, *The Apostolic Age*, II, 291–99; Lindsay, *The Church and the Ministry*, 73–90.

J. C. LAMBERT

APOSTLES' CREED, krēd, **THE:** The Apostles' Creed is the oldest creed, and lies at the basis of most others. Though not, as the long-current legend of its origin affirmed, the direct work of the Apostles, it has its roots in apostolic times, and embodies, with much fidelity, apostolic teaching. It will be seen immediately that it had an important place in the early church, when as yet no creed but itself existed. The oldest usage of the term "Rule of Faith" (*regula fidei*), now commonly given to the Scriptures, has reference to this creed. It was the creed that could be appealed to as held by the church in all its great branches, and so as forming the test of catholicity. It was as resting on this creed that the church could be called "catholic and apostolic." Of late the creed has been the subject of great controversy, and violent attempts have been made to thrust out some of its chief articles from the Christian faith. This is a special reason for considering the foundations on which these articles of faith rest.

The Oldest Creed

I. Form of the Creed.—In the first place, what *is* the creed? Here, first of all, it is to be pointed out that the received form of the creed is not its oldest or original form. The creed exists in two forms—a shorter and a longer; the former, known as the Old Rom Form, going back certainly as early as the middle of the 2d cent. (about 140 AD), the latter, the enlarged form, in its present shape, of much later date. Its final form was probably given to it in S. Gaul not before the middle of the 5th cent. (in one or two clauses, as late as the 7th). It is desirable, at the outset, to put these two forms of the creed (in translation) clearly before the reader.

1. Old Roman Form

First, the Old Rom Form is given from the Gr of Marcellus, of Ancyra, 341 AD. It runs thus: "I believe in God the Father Almighty. And in Jesus Christ His only (begotten) Son our Lord, who was born of the Holy Ghost and the Virgin Mary; crucified under Pontius Pilate, and buried; the third day He rose from the dead; He ascended into heaven, and sitteth at the right hand of the Father, from thence He shall come to judge the quick and the dead. And in the Holy Ghost; the holy Church; the forgiveness of sins; the resurrection of the body; (the life everlasting)."

The last clause is omitted in the Latin form preserved by Rufinus, 390 AD.

2. The Received Form

The Received Form of the creed reads thus: "I believe in God the Father Almighty; Maker of Heaven and Earth; and in Jesus Christ His only (begotten) Son our Lord; who was conceived by the Holy Ghost, born of the Virgin Mary; suffered under Pontius Pilate, was crucified, dead, and buried; He descended into hell; the third day He rose from the dead; He ascended into heaven; and sitteth at the right hand of God the Father Almighty; from thence He shall come to judge the quick and the dead. I believe in the Holy Ghost; the holy catholic Church; the communion of saints; the forgiveness of sins; the resurrection of the body; and the life everlasting. Amen."

Such is the form of the creed. Something must now be said of its origin and history.

II. Origin of the Creed.—The legend was that the creed took shape at the dictation of the Twelve Apostles, each of whom contributed a special article. Thus Peter, it was alleged, under the inspiration of the Holy Ghost, commenced, "I believe in God the Father Almighty"; Andrew (or according to others, John) continued, "And in Jesus Christ, His only Son, our Lord"; James the elder went on, "Who was conceived by the Holy Ghost," etc. This legend is not older than the 5th or 6th cent., and is absurd on the face of it.

The real origin of the creed has now been traced with great exactness. The original germ of it is to be sought for in the baptismal confession made by converts in the reception of that rite. The primitive confession may have contained no more than "I believe that Jesus is the Son of God," but we have evidence within the NT itself that it soon became enlarged. Paul speaks of the "form of teaching" delivered to converts (Rom **6** 17), and reminds Timothy of "the good [beautiful] confession" he had made in sight of many witnesses (1 Tim **6** 12). Similar language is used of Christ's confession before Pilate (ver 13). We may perhaps conjecture from the epistles that Timothy's confession contained references to God as the author of life, to Jesus Christ and His descent from David, to His witness before Pontius Pilate, to His being raised from the dead, to His coming again to judge the quick and the dead (1 Tim **6** 13; 2 Tim **2** 8; **4** 1). Early Christian writers, as Ignatius (110 AD), and Aristides the apologist (cir 125 AD), show traces of other clauses.

1. Baptismal Confession

In any case, the fact is certain that before the middle of the 2d cent. the confession at baptism had crystallized into tolerably settled shape in all the greater churches. We have accounts given us of its contents (besides the Old Rom Form) in Irenaeus, Tertullian, Novatian, Origen, etc; and they show substantial unity with a certain freedom of form in expression. But the form in the Rom church came gradually to be the recognized type. After the middle of the cent., the confession rose to new importance as the result of the gnostic controversies, and assumed more of the character of a formal creed. It came to be known as the "Rule of Truth," or "Rule of Faith," and was employed to check the license of interpretation of Scripture of these fantastic heretical speculators. The creed had originated independently of Scripture—in the early oral teaching and preaching of the apostles; hence its value as a witness to the common faith. But it was not used to supersede Scripture; it was held to corroborate Scripture, where men by their allegorical and other perversions sought to wrest Scripture from its real sense. It was employed as a check on those who sought to allegorize away the Christian faith.

2. "Rule of Faith"

III. History of the Creed.—The Old Rom Form of the creed was, as said above, certainly in use by the middle of the 2d cent., in Rome; probably a considerable time before. We have it in both its Gr and Lat forms (the Gr being probably the original). The Lat form is given by Rufinus about 390 AD who compares it with the creed of his own church of Aquileia—a very old church. The Gr form is preserved by Marcellus, of Ancyra, in the 4th cent. The old shorter form of the creed long maintained itself. We find it in England, e.g. up to nearly the time of the Norman Conquest (in 8th or 9th cent. MSS in British Museum).

1. The Roman Creed

The Received Form of the creed has a much more obscure history. The additional clauses came in at different times, though in themselves some of them are very old. The addition to the first art., e.g. "Maker of heaven and earth," first appears in in this form in Gaul about 650 AD, though similar forms are found in much older creeds. Another addition, "He descended into hell," meets us first in Rufinus as part of the creed of Aquileia, but is probably also old in that church. It is known that the creed had assumed nearly its present shape (perhaps without the above clauses, and that on the communion of saints) by the time of Faustus of Reiz, about 460 AD. Thence it spread, and had reached Ireland apparently before the end of the 7th cent. In England it appears a cent. later, about 850 AD (from the court of Charlemagne?), and from the beginning of the 10th cent. it largely superseded the older form. The same applies to other countries, so that the Gallican form is now the one in common use. Two significant changes may be noted in the form given to it. In England, whose form we follow, the Reformers substituted for "the resurrection of the flesh" the words, "the resurrection of the body," and in Germany the Lutherans change the word "catholic" to "Christian," in "the holy catholic Church."

2. The Received Creed

IV. Structure of the Creed.—The Apostles' Creed, it will be perceived, has no theological or metaphysical character. It is not only the oldest, but the simplest and least developed of all creeds. It is a simple enumeration, in order, of the great verities which the church was known to have held, and to have handed down from the beginning—which Scripture also taught. Originating from the baptismal confession, it naturally follows the Trinitarian order suggested by the customary formula for baptism. The first art. declares belief in God the Father Almighty, Maker of heaven and earth. The second to the seventh arts. declare belief in Jesus Christ, His only Son, our Lord, and in the great facts embraced in the gospel testimony regarding Him. The eighth art. affirms belief in the Holy Ghost, to which are appended the additional clauses, declaring belief in the holy catholic church, the communion of saints, the forgiveness of sins, the resurrection of the flesh (body), and the life everlasting.

1. Its Trinitarian Form

It will help to show the kind of heresies the church of that age had to contend with, and what the earnest struggles of the Fathers of the time (using the Apostles' Creed as a bulwark), if we append here the Creed of Apelles, a 2d-cent. Gnostic, as reconstructed by Principal Lindsay (*The Church and the Ministry*, 222) from Hippolytus:

"We believe, that Christ descended from the Power above, from the Good, and that He is the Son of the Good; that He was not born of a virgin, and that when He did appear He was not devoid of flesh. That He formed His Body by taking portions of it from the substance of the universe, i.e. hot and cold, moist and dry; That He received cosmical powers in the Body, and lived for the time He did in the world; That He was crucified by the Jews and died; That being raised again after three days He appeared to His disciples; That He showed them the prints of the nails and (the wound) in His

2. Creed of Apelles

side, being desirous of persuading them that He was no phantom, but was present in the flesh; That after He had shown them His flesh He restored it to the earth; That after He had once more loosed the chains of His Body He gave back heat to what is hot, cold to what is cold, moisture to what is moist, and dryness to what is dry; That in this condition He departed to the Good Father, leaving the Seed of Life in the world for those who through His disciples should believe in Him."

V. Modern Controversies.—It was mentioned that of late the Apostles' Creed has been the subject of many attacks and of keen controversies. In Germany, particularly, quite a fierce controversy broke out in 1892 over the refusal of a Lutheran pastor, named Schrempf, to use the creed in the administration of baptism. He did not believe in its arts. about the virgin-birth of Christ, the resurrection of the flesh, etc. The offender was deposed, but a great battle ensued, giving rise to an enormous literature. The conflict has been overruled for good in leading to a more thorough examination than ever before of the history and meaning of the creed, but it has given precision also to the attacks made upon it. A leading part in this controversy was taken by Professor Harnack, of Berlin, whose objections may be regarded as representative. Professor Harnack, and those who think with him, criticize the creed from a twofold point of view: (1) They deny that in all respects it represents true apostolical doctrine—this not only in its later arts., but even in such an art. as that affirming the virgin-birth of Christ: (2) They deny that the meaning we now put on many of the clauses of the creed is its true original meaning, i.e. we use the words, but with a different sense from the original framers.

Harnack's Criticism

In considering these objections, it is always to be remembered that those who urge them do so from the standpoint of rejection of most that is usually considered essential to Christianity. There is in their view no incarnation, no real Godhead of Christ, no real miracle in His life (only faith-cures), no resurrection from Joseph's tomb. This no doubt takes the bottom from the Apostles' Creed, but it takes the bottom also out of apostolic Christianity. Where Harnack, for instance, objects that "Father" and "Son" in the first and second arts. of the creed have no Trinitarian reference, but relate only, the former to God's relation to creation, the latter, to Christ's historical appearance, the reply can only be the whole evidence in the NT for a Trinitarian distinction and for the essential Divinity of Christ. When it is declared that the virgin-birth is no part of the early Christian tradition, one can only appeal to the evidence of the fact in the Gospels, and recall that no section of the Christian church, except a heretical branch of the Ebionites, and some of the gnostic sects, is known to have rejected it. (See VIRGIN-BIRTH.) For detailed replies to Harnack's criticisms, Dr. Swete's book on the *Apostles' Creed* may be consulted.

LITERATURE.—A list of the voluminous pamphlet literature produced by the German controversy on the Apostles' Creed may be seen in Nippold's *Die theologische Einzelschule*, II, 232–33. The most important contributions are those of Harnack (*Das apostolische Glaubensbekenntniss*, also *ET*); Kattenbusch, and Cremer. Cf also Schaff, *Creeds of Christendom*, I, 14–23; II, 45–55. Special works are: Pearson, *Exposition of the Creed* (1659); Kattenbusch, *Das apostolische Symbolum*, 2 vols (1894–1900); Zahn, *Das apostolische Symbolum* (1893); *ET* (1899); H. B. Swete, *The Apostles' Creed and Primitive Christianity* (1894); A. C. McGiffert, *The Apostles' Creed, Its Origin, Its Purpose, and Its Historical Interpretation* (1902).

JAMES ORR

APOSTLES, GOSPEL OF THE TWELVE. See APOCRYPHAL GOSPELS.

APOSTOLIC AGE, ap-os-tol'ik āj:

1. The Mission

(1) When the disciples realized that they had seen the risen Christ for the last time and that it had now become their duty to spread His message, they gathered themselves together and restored the number of "witnesses" to the appointed Twelve. Immediately afterward the outpouring of the Holy Spirit gave them the signal to begin work. At first this work was rigidly centered in Jerus, and the first journeyings were the result of forcible dispersion and not of planned effort (Acts **11** 19). But pilgrims to the feasts had carried away the gospel with them, and in this way Christianity had been spread at least as far as Damascus (**9** 2.19). The dispersion itself widened the circle to Cyprus and to Antioch and marked the beginning of the gentile work (**11** 19–20). Here the extreme prominence of St. Paul's ministry in the NT should not obscure the success of the other missionaries. When the apostles began their journeys we do not know but at the time of Gal **1** 19 only St. Peter represented the Twelve in Jerus. St. Paul mentions their extended work in 1 Cor **9** 5.6 and it seems certain that St. Peter was in Rome shortly before his death. The troubles caused St. Paul by the Judaizers at least give evidence of the missionary zeal of the latter. Barnabas and Mark worked after their separation from St. Paul (Acts **15** 39) and gentile Christianity existed in Rome long before the latter's arrival there (Rom **1** 13). By the year 100 it appears that Christianity extended around the Mediterranean from Alexandria to Rome (and doubtless farther, although data are scanty), while Asia Minor was especially pervaded by it. (2) Many factors coöperated to help the work: Peace was universal and communication was easy. Gr was spoken everywhere. The protection given Judaism sheltered from civil interference. The presence of Judaism insured hospitality and hearers for at least the first efforts to convert. The Jews' own proselytizing zeal (Mt **23** 15) had prepared Gentiles to receive Christianity. And not the least element was the break-up of the old religions and the general looking to the East for religious satisfaction. (3) For the methods, St. Paul's procedure is probably typical. Avoiding the smaller places, he devoted himself to the cities as the strategic points and traveled in a direct route, without side-journeys. In this way a "line of fire" (Harnack) was traced, and the flame could be trusted to spread of its own accord to each side of the road. So as fruits of St. Paul's work at Ephesus there appear churches at Colossae and Laodicea some hundred and twenty miles away (Col **2** 1; **4** 16). The churches founded needed revisiting and confirming, but when the apostle felt that they could shift for themselves, he felt also that his work in the East was over (Rom **15** 23).

2. Jerusalem Church

The members of the earliest Jerus church thought of themselves simply as Jews who had a true understanding of the Messiah and so constituting a new "way" or "party" (hardly "sect") in Judaism (Acts **22** 4, esp.). At first they were suffered to grow unmolested and their right to exist was apparently unquestioned, for the Sadducean actions of Acts **4** 1; **5** 17 were in the nature of police precautions. And it is significant that the first attack was made on a foreigner, St. Stephen. He seems to have angered the crowds by preaching the impending destruction of the Temple, although he was martyred for ascribing (practically) Divine honors to Jesus (**7** 56). Yet the apostles were not driven from the city (**8** 1) and the church was able to continue its development. In 41, the Rom representatives gave way to the Pharisaically inclined Agrippa I and (for reasons that are not clear) persecution broke out in which St. James was martyred and St. Peter delivered only by a miracle (Acts **12**). With the resumption of Rom rule in 44 the persecution ceased. Some peaceable mode of living was devised, as appears from the absence of further allusions to troubles (cf Acts **21** 17–26) and from the accounts of Josephus and Hegesippus of the esteem in which James the Lord's brother was held. His martyrdom (in 62?) was due to the tension that preceded the final revolt against Rome, in which the Christians of Jerus took no part. Instead, they retired across the Jordan to Pella (Rev **12** 13–17), where they formed a close, intensely Jewish body under the rule of the descendants of Christ's brethren according to the flesh. Some mission work was done farther to the east but in the 2d cent. they either were absorbed in normal Christianity or became one of the factors that produced Ebionism.

Many members of this body (and, doubtless, other Jewish Christians outside it) showed various degrees of inability to understand the gentile work. The acceptance of an uncircumcised Christian as "saved" offered fairly slight difficulty (Gal **2** 3; Acts **15**). But to eat with him was another thing and one that was an offence to many who accepted his salvation (Gal **2** 12.13). The rigorous conclusion that the Law bound *no* Christian was still another thing and one that even St. James could not accept (Acts **21** 21). At the time of Gal **2** 9, the "pillars" were as yet not thinking of doing gentile work. St. Paul's controversies are familiar and probably the last friction did not end until the fall of Jerus. But the difficulties grew gradually less and 1 Pet is evidence that St. Peter himself finally accepted the full status of Gentiles.

3. Judaists

From the Rom power Christianity was safe at first, as the distinctions from Judaism were thought too slight to notice (Acts **18** 14–16; **25** 19). (Troubles such as those of Acts **17** 9 were due to disturbance of the peace.) So the government was thought of as a protector (2 Thess **2** 7) and spoken of in the highest terms (Rom **13** 1; 1 Pet **2** 13.14). But, while absolute isolation was not observed (1 Cor **10** 27), yet the Christians tended more and more to draw themselves into bodies with little contact with the world around them (1 Pet **4** 3–5), so provoking suspicion and hostility from their neighbors. Hence they were a convenient scapegoat for Nero after the burning of Rome. It is uncertain how far his persecution spread or how far persecutions occurred from his time until the end of the reign of Domitian (see PETER, FIRST EPISTLE OF), but in Rev Rome has become the symbol for all that is hostile to Christ.

4. Relations with Rome

Influence of the "pagan" religions on Christianity is not very perceptible in the 1st cent. But syncretism was the fashion of the day and many converts must have attempted to combine the new religion with views that they held already (or that they learned still later). Apparently little attention was paid to this attempt, if restricted to entirely minor details (1 Cor **15** 29?), but in Col **2** 8–23 a vital matter is touched. The danger is more acute in the Pastorals (1 Tim **1** 4; **4** 3; Titus **3** 9) and in Rev **2** great harm is being done. And Jude, 2 Pet, and 1 Jn contain direct polemics against the systems so arising, the beginnings of what in the 2d cent. appeared as Gnosticism.

5. "Hellenism"

For further details see the separate articles, esp. MINISTRY; NEW TESTAMENT CANON; and (for life in the Apostolic Age) SPIRITUAL GIFTS.

LITERATURE.—See the separate articles. Works with the title *Apostolic Age* are by Gilbert (brief), Bartlet (useful), Purves (very conservative), Ropes, McGiffert, and Weizsäcker. The last three are for critical study.

BURTON SCOTT EASTON

APOSTOLIC CONSTITUTIONS. A Syrian ecclesiastical collection based largely on the Didache. See LITERATURE, SUB-APOSTOLIC, II.

APOSTOLIC COUNCIL, ap-os-tol'ik koun'sil: The assembly of the apostles and elders held in Jerus (49 AD), an account of which is given in Acts 15.

APOSTOLIC FATHERS: An appellation usually given to the writers of the 1st cent. who employed their pens in the cause of Christianity. See LITERATURE, SUB-APOSTOLIC.

APOSTOLIC FATHERS, EPISTLES OF. See LITERATURE, SUB-APOSTOLIC.

APOTHECARY, a-poth'ē-kā-ri: Found in EV eight times in the OT and Apoc for Heb word rendered more accurately "perfumer" by RV in Ex **30** 25.35; **37** 29; Eccl **10** 1; though inconsistently retained elsewhere (2 Ch **16** 14 ERV; Neh **3** 8 ERV [cf m]); Sir **38** 8; **49** 1). See PERFUMER.

APPAIM, ap'a-im, ap'-ā-im (אַפַּיִם, *'appayim*, "nostrils"): A son of Nadab of the house of Jerahmeel, of Judah (1 Ch **2** 30 f).

APPAREL, a-par'el: The Eng. equivalent of six Heb and three Gr words, variously signifying all kinds of raiment, chiefly garments costly and beautiful: *ornamental* (2 S **1** 24); *royal*, as of Ahasuerus (Est **6** 8), of Herod (Acts **12** 21, ἐσθής, *esthḗs*); of *kings' daughters* (2 S **13** 18); *priestly* (Ezr **3** 10); also *mourning* (2 S **14** 2). In 1 S **17** 38.39 "apparel" replaces "armor" of AV: "Saul clad David with his apparel," probably some close-fitting garment worn under the armor, or sometimes without it. Severe judgment was pronounced on Jewish princes who clothed themselves with "strange" (AV), i.e. "with foreign apparel" (Zeph **1** 8; cf Isa **2** 6–8). "Modest apparel" as against "costly raiment" is commended as suited to Christians (1 Tim **2** 9; ἱματισμός, *himatismós*, and καταστολή, *katastolḗ*). Angels are robed in *white* apparel (Acts **1** 10; cf Lk **24** 4, "dazzling"). **Fig.** of the *glorious* and *red* (suggestive of the wine-press) *apparel* of the Messiah (Isa **63** 1.2), and of "a meek and quiet spirit" (1 Pet **3** 4).

DWIGHT M. PRATT

APPARENTLY, a-pâr'ent-li (מַרְאֶה, *mar'eh*, RV "manifestly," signifying in the only place so trd [Nu **12** 8] "in the form of seeing" [Keil and Delitzsch], i.e. "an appearance," "a similitude," a manifestation of the invisible God in human form): This is the OT manner of Divine revelation "in the person and form of the angel of Jeh": "In the bush I did manifestly reveal myself, and talked with Moses" (2 Esd **14** 3). God talked with Moses openly, without figure, in a direct manner revealing to him His will in the clear distinctness of a spiritual communication: "With him will I speak mouth to mouth, even manifestly, and not in dark speeches; and the form of Jeh shall he behold."

M. O. EVANS

APPARITION, ap-a-rish'un (ἴνδαλμα, *índalma*, ἐπιφάνεια, *epipháneia*; φάντασμα, *phántasma*): This word is not found in the OT or NT canon, AV or ARV, but occurs twice in RV and thrice in Apoc AV as follows: Wisd **17** 3, Gr *indalma*, RV "spectral form"; 2 Macc **3** 24, Gr *epiphaneia*, RV "apparition," RVm "manifestation"; 2 Macc **5** 4, Gr *epiphaneia*, RV "vision," RVm "manifestation." NT, RV: Mt **14** 26; Mk **6** 49: Gr *phantasma*, ARV "ghost," AV "Spirit."

APPEAL, a-pēl′: If an appeal be, as it properly is, a petition for the removal of a case that has been decided for rehearing and review and final decision by a higher court, we find no such instance either in the OT or the NT.

In the institution of judges by Moses (Ex **18** 26), the reference: "The hard cases they brought unto Moses, but every small matter they judged themselves," indicates simply a distribution of cases between two courts, but gives no trace of any provision for the rehearing of any case, by a higher court, that has already been decided by a lower. In Dt **17** 8–13, directions are given that a lower court, under certain conditions, shall ask a higher for instructions as to procedure, and shall strictly follow the order prescribed: nevertheless, the decision itself belongs to the lower court. When its sentence was once given, there was no appeal.

In the NT, the provision of the Rom law, for an appeal from a lower to a higher court, is clearly recognized, although the case of Paul in Acts **25** does not strictly fall within its scope. The Rom law originally gave a citizen the right of appeal to the tribune of the people, but, with the establishment of the Empire, the emperor himself assumed this function of the tribune, and became the court of last resort. The case of Paul, however, had not been tried before Festus, nor any verdict rendered, when (Acts **25** 10.11) he utters the proper legal formula: "I appeal unto Caesar" (Καίσαρα ἐπικαλοῦμαι, *Kaísara epikaloúmai*). That Rom citizens could insist upon such procedure, as right, is not perfectly certain (*HJP*, II, 2:279). Paul evidently acted upon the suggestion of the governor himself (ver 9), who seems to have been desirous of avoiding the responsibility of a case involving questions most remote from his ordinary attention. At first sight, Paul's decision to appeal seems premature. He throws away his chance of acquittal by Festus, and acts upon the assumption that he has been already condemned. Acts **26** 32 shows that the possibility of his acquittal had amounted almost to a certainty. His course is explicable only by regarding his appeal the master stroke of a great leader, who was ready to take risks. In the proposition of Festus, he grasps at what had been an object of hope long deferred. For many years, he had been desiring and praying to get to Rome (Acts **19** 21; Rom **1** 11.15; **15** 23.24). The Lord had just assured him (Acts **23** 11), that as he had testified at Jerus, "so must thou bear witness also at Rome." With this promise and direction in view, he hastens toward the world's capital and the center of the world's influence, in the seemingly precipitate words, "I appeal," which a lower order of prudence would have deferred until he had first been condemned. H. E. Jacobs

APPEAR, a-pēr′: Of eight Heb originals the chief is רָאָה, *rā'āh*, "to be seen." Used mainly of God's self-revelations in person and in dreams and visions: "Jehovah appeared unto Abram" (Gen **12** 7); to Moses (Ex **3** 2); to Solomon (1 K **3** 5). All originals used of Nature's processes, of the appearing, i.e. coming of the morning (Ex **14** 27); stars (Neh **4** 21); flowers, flocks of goats, tender grapes (Cant **2** 12; **4** 1m; **7** 12m). So NT ὤφθην, *ōphthēn*, passive of *hōráō*, "I see," "to be seen" used esp. of angelic revelations and visions: as on the Mount of Transfiguration (Mt **17** 3); an angel (Lk **1** 11); the risen Lord (Lk **24** 34); cloven tongues at Pentecost (Acts **2** 3); vision to Paul (Acts **16** 9); a great wonder in heaven (Rev **12** 1 AV).

ὀπτάνω, *optánō*, in Acts **1** 3, of Christ appearing after his suffering; φαίνομαι, *phaínomai*, "to shine," like the above with the added thought of a resplendent, luminous revelation, as of the Bethlehem star (Mt **2** 7); the bringing to light of sin (Rom **7** 13 AV). Also φανερόω, *phaneróō*, "to make manifest," used exclusively of the post-resurrection appearances and second coming of Christ and of the disclosures of the great judgment day. See Col **3** 4; 2 Cor **5** 10; Rev **3** 18 and seven other passages AV. Dwight M. Pratt

APPEARANCE, a-pēr′ans (מַרְאֶה, *mar'eh;* chiefly used of the mystic and supernatural visions of Ezekiel and Daniel): A semblance, as of lightning, wheels, sapphire stone (Ezk **1** 14.16.26); Gabriel's overpowering revelation (Dnl **8** 15; see also **10** 6.18). In the NT refers exclusively, through three Gr words, πρόσωπον, *prósōpon*, "sight," "countenance," to "outward appearance" (2 Cor **10** 7 AV); and its possibly deceptive nature: ὄψις, *ópsis*, "Judge not according to a." (Jn **7** 24); "them that glory in a." (2 Cor **5** 12; cf 1 S **16** 7). See also 1 Thess **5** 22 ERVm (*eídos* = "sight").

APPEARING, a-pēr′ing (**ἀποκάλυψις,** *apokálupsis*, "an unveiling"; **ἐπιφάνεια,** *epipháneia*, "a manifestation"): Exclusively technical, referring in the six passages where found to the return, the millennial advent of Christ (e.g. 1 Pet **1** 7 AV; 2 Tim **1** 10; Titus **2** 13).

APPEASE, a-pēz′: "To make one at peace." Esau is appeased, i.e. placated, won over by means of presents (Gen **32** 20). One "slow to anger appeaseth strife," i.e. puts an end to it (Prov **15** 18). RV changes "appeased" of AV in Acts **19** 35 into "quieted" (Gr *katastéllō*, "put down," "suppress," "restrain," referring to a popular commotion).

APPERTAIN, ap-ẽr-tān′: Only once in EV, viz. in Jer **10** 7, for יָאָה, *yā'āh*, "it becometh," "it is seemly," Vulg "*Tuum est enim decus*," "it is Thy honor." Generally in the sense of "to belong to" (Lev **6** 5, "to whom it appertaineth"); Neh **2** 8, "the castle which appertained to the house" (Tob **6** 12; 1 Esd **8** 95; 1 Macc **10** 42).

APPETITE, ap′ē-tīt (חַי, *ḥai*, נֶפֶשׁ, *nephesh*): This word occurs four times in OT text and once in AVm. Once (Job **38** 39) it is a tr of *ḥai*, "life"; "Canst thou . . . . satisfy *the appetite* (*life*) of the young lions?" Twice (Prov **23** 2; Eccl **6** 7; also Isa **56** 11, AVm) it is a tr of *nephesh:* Prov **23** 2, *ba'al nephesh* "a man given to appetite"; Eccl **6** 7, "the *nephesh* is not filled." In Isa **56** 11, "strong of *nephesh*" is trd "greedy." *Nephesh* means originally "breath," hence "the soul," *psuchḗ*, "the vital principle," "life"; therefore in certain expressions referring to the sustaining of life the *nephesh* hungers (Prov **10** 3), thirsts (Prov **25** 25), fasts (Ps **69** 10). *Nephesh* then comes to mean the seat of the senses, affections, emotions, and to it is ascribed love, joy, desire (cf Dt **12** 20; Prov **6** 30 RVm; Mic **7** 1, where the *nephesh* "desires"). The idea of desire or appetite of the *nephesh* may include all forms of longing; e.g. lust (Jer **2** 24; "her desire" is lit. "the desire of her *nephesh*"), the appetite for revenge (Ps **41** 2, "*the will* of his enemies" is lit. "the *nephesh*," etc). The next step is to identify the *nephesh* with its desire, hence in the cases above *nephesh* is trd "appetite." In the 4th case (Isa **29** 8) "His soul hath appetite" is a free tr of *naphshō shōḳēḳāh*, lit. "His soul runneth to and fro." S. F. Hunter

APPHIA, af′i-a, ap′fi-a (**'Απφίᾳ,** *Apphía*, dative case of *Apphía;* in Philem 2, though *Apphía*, *Amphía*, and *Appía*, also occur): A Christian of Colossae, probably the wife of Philemon; certainly **a**

member of his household, greeted as "the sister" RVm. In the Greek church, November 22 is sacred to her memory. It has been supposed, since this epistle concerns one household exclusively, that Apphia was Philemon's wife and the mother or sister of Archippus (q.v.). She was stoned to death with Philemon, Onesimus, and Archippus in the reign of Nero. (See Lightfoot, *Col.*, 372.)

APPHUS, af′us, ap′fus: A name borne by Jonathan, the fifth son of Mattathias (**'Απφούς**, *Apphoús*, 1 Macc **2** 5). All the brothers, according to this passage, had double names; John is said to have been called Gaddis; Simon, Thassi; Judas, Maccabaeus; Eleazar, Avaran; Jonathan, Apphus (1 Macc **2** 2–5). The latter were probably the names which Mattathias gave his sons, while the former were received later when they became "leaders of the people." The common explanation of the word "Apphus" relates it to the Syr חַפּוּשׁ, *ḥoppūs*, "the dissembler"; but Torrey (art. "Maccabees," *EB*) points out that we have no means of ascertaining with what guttural consonant the word began, or what Sem consonant the Gr ς (s) represents. Both the form and meaning of the name are, therefore, still to be explained. H. J. Wolf

APPII FORUM, ap′i-ī fō′rum, transliteration of Lat; APPIUS, ap′i-us, MARKET OF (RV) (**'Αππίου φόρον,** *Appíou phóron*): Appi Forum (*Cicero ad Att.* 2.10; Suetonius *Tib.* 2: Appii Forum; Vulg RV: Forum Appi; Horace *Satires* i.5; Pliny, *Nat. Hist.*, iii.64; xiv.61; *CIL*, X, 6824), or Market of Appius, was a town situated at the forty-third milestone on the Appian Road (39½ English miles from Rome, a single day's journey for energetic travelers) according to the imperial itineraries (*Ant*, 108; *Hierosol.* 611; *Geog. Rav.* 4.34). Its existence probably dates from the time of Appius Claudius Caecus (Suet. *Tib.* 2; cf Mommsen, *Röm. Forsch.*, I, 308), who laid out the famous highway from Rome to Capua in 312 BC. In the 1st cent. it had the rank of a municipality (Pliny, iii.64). Its importance as a highway station is due chiefly to the canal which ran by the side of the road from there to within a short distance of Tarracina (at the sixty-second milestone), affording an alternative means of conveyance (Strabo v.3.6). It was customary to cover this section of the journey, passing through the Pontine Marshes, by night in canal boats drawn by mules. Horace (*Sat.* i.5) offers a lively picture of the discomforts of the trip, mentioning the importunate inn-keepers and intolerable drinking water at Appii Forum, the gnats and frogs which were enemies to repose, and the exasperating procrastination of the muleteer.

The Christian brethren in Rome went out along the Appian Road to welcome the apostle Paul upon hearing of his arrival at Puteoli. One party awaited him at Three Taverns while another proceeded as far as Appii Forum (Acts **28** 15). George H. Allen

APPLE, ap′'l, **APPLE-TREE** (תַּפּוּחַ, *tappūaḥ*): A fruit tree and fruit mentioned chiefly in Cant, concerning the true nature of which there has been much dispute.

Cant **2** 3 says: "As the apple-tree among the trees of the wood, so is my beloved among the sons. I sat down under his shadow with great delight"; Cant **8** 5: "Under the apple-tree I awakened thee: there thy mother was in travail with thee, there was she in travail that brought thee forth." Of the fruit it is said, Cant **2** 3: "His fruit was sweet to my taste"; Cant **2** 5: "Stay ye me with raisins, refresh me with apples"; Cant **7** 8: "the smell of thy breath [Heb "nose"] like apples."

In all the above references the true apple, *Pyrus malus*, suits the conditions satisfactorily. The apple tree affords good shade, the fruit is sweet, the perfume is a very special favorite with the people of the East. Sick persons in Pal delight to hold an apple in their hands, simply for the smell. (Cf *Arabian Nights*, "Prince Hassan and the Paribanou.") Further the Arab. for apple *tuffāh* is without doubt identical with the Heb *tappūaḥ*. The apple was well known, too, in ancient times; it was, for example, extensively cultivated by the Romans.

The one serious objection is that apples do not easily reach perfection in Pal; the climate is too dry and hot; farther north in the Lebanon they flourish. At the same time it is possible to exaggerate this objection, for with careful grafting and cultivation exceedingly good apples may be produced in the mountain regions. **Apple trees** there need special care and renewal of the grafts, but there is no impossibility that at the time of the writing of Cant skilled gardeners should have been able to produce sweet and perfumed apples in Pal. Small but very sweet and fragrant apples are now grown at Gaza. Good apples are now plentiful in the market at Jerus, but they are chiefly importations from the North.

On account of the above difficulty three other fruits have been suggested by various writers. Two doubtless have been brought forward with a view to Prov **25** 11: "A word fitly spoken is like apples of gold in network of silver," but the reference would certainly seem to be to some silver filigree work ornamented with gold modeled to look like fruit rather than to any actual fruit. The citron and the apricot (Tristram) have both been suggested as the true *tappūaḥ*. The former, which is a native of Persia, does not appear to have been introduced into Pal until well into the Christian era and the apricot, though an attractive substitute for the apple and today one of the most beautiful and productive of fruit trees, can hardly have been established in Pal at the time of the scriptural references. It is a native of China and is said to have first begun to find its way westward at the time of Alexander the Great.

The third of the fruits is the quince, *Cydonia vulgaris* (N.O. *Rosaceae*), and this had more serious claims. It flourishes in Pal and has been long indigenous there. Indeed it is probable that even if *tappūaḥ* was a name for apple, it originally included also the closely allied quince. The greatest difficulty is its harsh and bitter taste. Further the Mish distinguishes the *tappūaḥ* from the quince, which is called *pārīsh*, and from the crab apple or *ḥāzōr* (Kohler in *Jew Enc*, II, 23). The quince along with the apple was sacred to Aphrodite, the goddess of love.

On the whole there does not appear to be any sufficient reason for rejecting the tr of the AV and RV; the Biblical references suit it; the identity of the Heb and Arab. words favor it and there is no insuperable objection on scientific grounds.

The word *tappūaḥ* appears in two place names, Beth-tappuah and Tappuah (q.v.). E. W. G. Masterman

APPLE, ap′'l, **OF THE EYE:** The eyeball, or globe of the eye, with pupil in center, called "apple" from its round shape. Its great value and careful protection by the eyelids automatically closing when there is the least possibility of danger made it the emblem of that which was most precious and jealously protected. The Heb terms for it were, *'īshōn*, dimin. of *'īsh*, "man," *little man* or *mannikin*, referring perhaps specially to the *pupil*, probably from "the little image one sees of himself when looking into another's pupil" (Davies' *Lexicon*). "He kept him (Israel) as the apple of his eye"

(Dt **32** 10); "Keep me as the apple of the eye," lit., "as the apple, the daughter of the eye" (Ps **17** 8). "Keep my law [RVm "teaching"] as the apple of thine eye" (Prov **7** 2). Cf Prov **7** 9 where it is used to denote what is the *center* (ARV, "in the middle of the night"; ERV "in the blackness of night"; m "Heb pupil [of the eye]"); *bābhāh* perhaps an "opening," "gate"; others regard it as a mimetic word akin to Lat *pupa, pupilla* ("He that toucheth you toucheth the apple of his eye," i.e. Jeh's; Zec **2** 8); *bath-'ayin*, "daughter of the eye"; "Give thyself no respite, let not the apple of thine eye cease" (Lam **2** 18), which means, either "sleep not," or "cease not to weep." κόρη, *kórē*, "young girl," "pupil of the eye": "He (the Lord) will keep the good deeds [RV "bounty"] of a man as the apple of the eye" (Ecclus **17** 22); the LXX also has *korē* in all instances except Lam **2** 18, where it has θυγάτηρ, *thugátēr*, "daughter." W. L. Walker

APPLES OF SODOM, sod'um: Jos (*BJ*, IV, viii, 4) says that "the traces [or shadows] of the five cities [of the plain] are still to be seen, as well as the ashes growing in their fruits, which fruits have a color as if they were fit to be eaten; but if you pluck them with your hands they dissolve into smoke and ashes." What this "Dead Sea fruit" is, is uncertain. The name "Dead Sea apples" is often given to the fruit of the *Solanum Sodomaean*, "a prickly shrub with fruit not unlike a small yellow tomato." Cheyne thinks that the fruits referred to by Jos (cf Tacitus *Hist.* v.37) may be either (1) those of the *'osher*-tree (*'ŭsar*, *Calotropis procera*, described by Hasselquist [*Travels*, 1766]), found in abundance about Jericho and near the Dead Sea, which are filled with dust when they have been attacked by an insect, leaving the skin only entire, and of a beautiful color. Tristram describes the fruit as being "as large as an apple of average size, of a bright yellow colour, hanging three or four together close to the stem"; or as suggested by Tristram (2) those of the wild colocynth; the fruit is fair of aspect with a pulp which dries up into a bitter powder (*EB*, art. "Sodom," col. 4669, n. 2). This colocynth is supposed to be the "wild vine" mentioned 2 K **4** 39. The "vine of Sodom" of Dt **32** 32 has been supposed to bear the "Dead Sea fruit"; but most modern writers regard the passage as **figurative.** W. L. Walker

APPLY, a-plī': Purely an OT term representing five Heb originals which signify respectively, "to enter," "to incline," "to give," "to go about," "to put or place," in each instance spoken of the heart in its attitude to wisdom (Ps **90** 12 AV); instruction (Prov **23** 12); understanding (**2** 2); knowledge (**22** 17).

APPOINT, a-point': This word is used for the expression of a large variety of ideas and the tr of almost as many words.

נָקַב, *nāḳabh*="stipulate" (Gen **30** 28). פָּקַד, *pāḳadh*="put into office" (Gen **41** 34; Nu **1** 50; Est **2** 3); "select" (Jer **51** 27); "put in charge" (Jer **49** 19; **50** 44); "assign" (Nu **4** 27; Jer **15** 3); "send" (Lev **26** 16); "designate," "select" (Ex **21** 13; Nu **4** 19; 2 S **7** 10; Isa **61** 3); "single out" (1 S **8** 11.12; Hos **1** 11). נָתַן, *nāthan*="designate," "select" (Nu **35** 6 AV; Josh **20** 2 AV; Ezk **45** 6); "set aside" (Ex **30** 16). שִׁית, *shīth*="designate," "select" (Job **14** 13; Isa **26** 1). So also עָמַד, *'āmadh* (1 Ch **15** 16; Neh **7** 3); so שָׁלַח, *shālaḥ* (1 K **5** 9); קָרָה, *ḳārāh* (Nu **35** 11). צָוָה, *çāwāh*="choose" (2 S **6** 21). בָּחַר, *bāḥar*="select" (2 S **15** 15 AV). אָמַר, *'āmar*="command" (1 K **5** 6 AV). τίθημι, *títhēmi*="designate," "select" (Mt **24** 51; Lk **12** 46). A careful reading of the above passages will bring to mind the doctrine that with reference to the world's work, God Himself calls men into office, selecting them from among the multitude and setting them aside for His special purposes; and that He calls to His assistance not only men but also events and forces of Nature (Lev **26** 16). Frank E. Hirsch

APPREHEND, ap-rē-hend': Occurs in the NT in two meanings: "to arrest" (πιάζω, *piázō;* Acts **12** 4; 2 Cor **11** 32 RV, "take"); and "to seize," "grasp," "take into one's possession," "attain," "inquire eagerly" (καταλαμβάνω, *katalambánō*, ARV "laid hold on," "laid fast hold of," Phil **3** 12.13; Eph **3** 18). In Jn **1** 5, "The darkness apprehended it not," RVm gives "overcame not." See Comprehend.

APPROVE, a-prōōv': This word, as ordinarily used, means "to entertain a favorable opinion concerning" (Ps **49** 13; Lam **3** 36). Its Biblical and archaic use conveys a much stronger meaning and is equivalent to its use in legal formalities of today, "to approve a bill," i.e. by some act, generally a signature, to express approval. In NT, a number of times, for Gr *dokimázō*, "to test, try, make proof of," and its derivative, *dókimos*, "tested," "tried." The word will, in almost every case, imply that the proof is victoriously demonstrated, the proved is also approved, just as in English we speak of "tried men" (Trench, *Gr Synonyms of NT*). It is the word most frequently used for the testing of ores. That which does not stand the test is *adókimos*, "reprobate." Cf Jer **6** 30 AV: "reprobate silver." That which stands the test is *dokimos*, "approved." "Salute Apelles the approved in Christ" (Rom **16** 10); "they that are approved" (1 Cor **11** 19); "Present thyself approved unto God" (2 Tim **2** 15); when he hath been "approved" (Jas **1** 12). See also Rom **14** 18.22; 1 Thess **2** 4. H. E. Jacobs

APRON, ā'prun: Appears only in Gen **3** 7 and Acts **19** 12 EV. (Eng. na-prun, N. of England nap-peon, from Low Lat, through Fr. *nape, nappe*, "napkin." The *n* was dropped owing to false division of the art. *a* from the noun; thus "a napron" became "an apron:" In Gen **3** 7 it is used to translate a Heb word rendered "girdles" in RVm: "And they sewed fig-leaves together and made themselves aprons." In Acts **19** 12 σιμικίνθια, *simikínthia*, stands for *semicinctia*, which is really a Lat word meaning "half-girdle," i.e. girdles going only half round the body and covering the front of the person: "Unto the sick were carried away from his [Paul's] body handkerchiefs [*soudária*, rendered "napkins" Lk **19** 20; Jn **11** 44; **20** 7] or aprons." The word denotes here, probably, a workman's apron, perhaps those of Paul himself; though it seems more natural to suppose that the people brought their own "handkerchiefs" or "aprons" to Paul to secure the miraculous effect desired. The garments, at any rate, were such as could be easily removed and carried back and forth. (See Rich, *Dict. of Rom and Gr Ant*, s.v., for illust.; also Pope's *Lexicon*, s.v.). Geo. B. Eager

APT (lit. "fitted"): Applied to one distinguished for readiness in meeting demands of some special situation, or emergency. For this, there is no specific Biblical word in either OT or NT. It occurs always in the English trs in paraphrases, as "apt for war" (2 K **24** 16), "apt to teach," Gr "*didaktikós*" (1 Tim **3** 2; 2 Tim **2** 24).

AQUEDUCT, ak'wē-dukt. See Cistern.

AQUILA, ak′wi-la (**Ἀκύλας**, *Akúlas*, "an eagle"): Aquila and his wife Priscilla, the diminutive form of Prisca, are introduced into the narrative of the Acts by their relation to Paul. He meets them first in Corinth (Acts **18** 2). Aquila was a native of Pontus, doubtless one of the colony of Jews mentioned in Acts **2** 9; 1 Pet **1** 1. They were refugees from the cruel and unjust edict of Claudius which expelled all Jews from Rome in 52 AD. The decree, it is said by Suetonius, was issued on account of tumults raised by the Jews, and he especially mentions one Chrestus (Suetonius *Claud.* 25). Since the word Christus could easily be confounded by him to refer to some individual whose name was Chrestus and who was an agitator, resulting in these disorders, it has been concluded that the fanatical Jews were then persecuting their Christian brethren and disturbances resulted. The cause of the trouble did not concern Claudius, and so without making inquiry, all Jews were expelled. The conjecture that Aquila was a freedman and that his master had been Aquila Pontius, the Rom senator, and that from him he received his name is without foundation. He doubtless had a Heb name, but it is not known. It was a common custom for Jews outside of Pal to take Rom names, and it is just that that this man does, and it is by that name we know him. Driven from Rome, Aquila sought refuge in Corinth, where Paul, on his second missionary journey, meets him because they have the same trade: that of making tents of Cilician cloth (Acts **18** 3). The account given of him does not justify the conclusion that he and his wife were already Christians when Paul met them. Had that been the case Lk would almost certainly have said so, esp. if it was true that Paul sought them out on that account. Judging from their well-known activity in Christian work they would have gathered a little band of inquirers or possibly converts, even though they had been there for but a short time. It is more in harmony with the account to conclude that Paul met them as fellow-tradespeople, and that he took the opportunity of preaching Christ to them as they toiled. There can be no doubt that Paul would use these days to lead them into the kingdom and instruct them therein, so that afterward they would be capable of being teachers themselves (Acts **18** 26). Not only did they become Christians, but they also became fast and devoted friends of Paul, and he fully reciprocated their affection for him (Rom **16** 3.4). They accompanied him when he left Corinth to go to Ephesus and remained there while he went on his journey into Syria. When he wrote the first letter to the church at Corinth they were still at Ephesus, and their house there was used as a Christian assembly-place (1 Cor **16** 19). The decree of Claudius excluded the Jews from Rome only temporarily, and so afterward Paul is found there, and his need of friends and their affection for him doubtless led them also to go to that city (Rom **16** 3). At the time of the writing of Paul's second letter to Tim they have again removed to Ephesus, possibly sent there by Paul to give aid to, and further the work in that city (2 Tim **4** 19). While nothing more is known of them there can be no doubt that they remained the devoted friends of Paul to the end.

The fact that Priscilla's name is mentioned several times before that of her husband has called forth a number of conjectures. The best explanation seems to be that she was the stronger character.

JACOB W. KAPP

AR, är, **AR OF MOAB**, mō′ab (עָר־מוֹאָב, עָר, *ʿār*, *ʿār-mō'ābh;* **"Ηρ**, *Ē′r;* **'Αροήρ**, *Aroḗr* or **Σηείρ**, *Sēeír*): The city of Ar is named in a snatch of ancient song (Nu **21** 15), lit. "the site of Ar." It is identical with "Ar of Moab" (ver 28; Isa **15** 1). This is probably the place called the City of Moab in Nu **22** 36, where the Heb is *ʿīr mō'ābh.* It is probably also intended by "the city that is in the middle of the valley" (Dt **2** 36; Josh **13** 9.16; 2 S **24** 5). It lay "on the border of the Arnon, which is in the utmost part of the border" (Nu **22** 36). A possible identification might be the ruin noted by Burckhardt, in the floor of the valley, on a piece of pasture-land below the confluence of the *Lejjun* and the *Mōjib.* Buhl however thinks that not a city but a Moabite district somewhere in the region south of the Arnon may be intended (*GAP*, 269).

W. EWING

ARA, ā′ra (אֲרָא, *'ărā'*, meaning unknown): A son of Jether of the tribe of Asher (1 Ch **7** 38).

ARAB, ā′rab (אֲרָב, *'ărābh*, "ambush"): A city in the hill country of Judah, probably the site of the ruins Er-Rabiyeh S. of Hebron (Josh **15** 52).

ARAB, ar′ab, **ARABIANS**, a-rā′bi-ans. See ARABIA.

ARABAH, ar′a-ba, a-rā′ba (הָעֲרָבָה, *hā-ʿărābhāh*, "the Arabah"): This word indicates in general a barren district, but is specifically applied in whole or in part to the depression of the Jordan valley, extending from Mount Hermon to the Gulf of Akabah. In the AV it is transliterated only once (Josh **18** 18) describing the border of Benjamin. Elsewhere it is rendered "plain." But in the RV it is everywhere transliterated. South of the Dead Sea the name is still retained in Wady el-Arabah. In Dt **1** 1; **2** 8 (AV "plain") the southern portion is referred to; in Dt **3** 17; **4** 49; Josh **3** 16; **11** 2; **12** 3 and 2 K **14** 25 the name is closely connected with the Dead Sea and the Sea of Chinnereth (Gennesaret). The allusions to the Arabah in Dt **11** 30; Josh **8** 14; **12** 1; **18** 18; 2 S **2** 29; **4** 7; 2 K **25** 4; Jer **39** 4; **52** 7 indicate that the word was generally used in its most extended sense, while in Josh **11** 16, and **12** 8 it is represented as one of the great natural divisions of the country.

The southern portion, which still retains the name of Arabah, is included in the wilderness of Zin (Nu **34** 3). According to the survey of Lord Kitchener and George Armstrong made in 1883, under the auspices of the Pal Exploration Fund, its length from the head of the Gulf of Akabah to the Dead Sea is 112 miles. The lowest point of the watershed is 45 miles from Akabah, and 660 feet above tide (1,952 above the Dead Sea). The average width of the valley up to this point is about 6 miles, but here a series of low limestone ridges (called Er Risheh) rising 150 feet above the plain runs obliquely across it for a distance of 10 miles, narrowing it up to a breadth of about one-half mile. North of this point, opposite Mount Hor, the valley widens out to 13 miles and then gradually narrows to 6 miles at the south end of the Dead Sea. At Ain Abu Werideh, 29 miles north of the watershed, the valley is at the sea-level—1,292 feet above that of the Dead Sea. North of the watershed, the main line of drainage is the Wady el-Jeib, which everywhere keeps pretty close to the west side of the valley. At Ain Abu Werideh it is joined by numerous wadies descending from the Edomite mountains on the east, which altogether water an oasis of considerable extent, covered with a thicket of young palms, tamarisks, willows and reeds. Twenty-four miles farther north the Arabah breaks down suddenly into the valley of the Dead Sea, or the Ghôr, as it is technically called. Lord Kitchener's report is here so vivid as to be worthy of literal reproduction. "The descent to the Ghôr was down a sandy slope of 300 feet, and the change of climate was most marked, from the sandy desert to masses of tangled vegetation with streams of water running in all directions, birds fluttering from every tree, the whole country alive with life; nowhere have I seen so great and sudden a contrast" (*Mount Seir*, 214). The descent here described was on the eastern side of the semicircular line of cliffs formed of sand, gravel, and marl which inclose the Ghôr at the south end, and which are probably what are referred to in Josh **15** 3 as the "ascent of Akrabbim." The ordinary route, however, leading to the plain of the Arabah from the Dead Sea is up the trough worn by the Wady el-Jeib along the west side of the valley. But this route would be impracticable during the rainy season after the cloudbursts which occasionally visit this region, when torrents of water pour down it, sufficient to roll bowlders of considerable size and to transport an immense amount of coarse sediment.

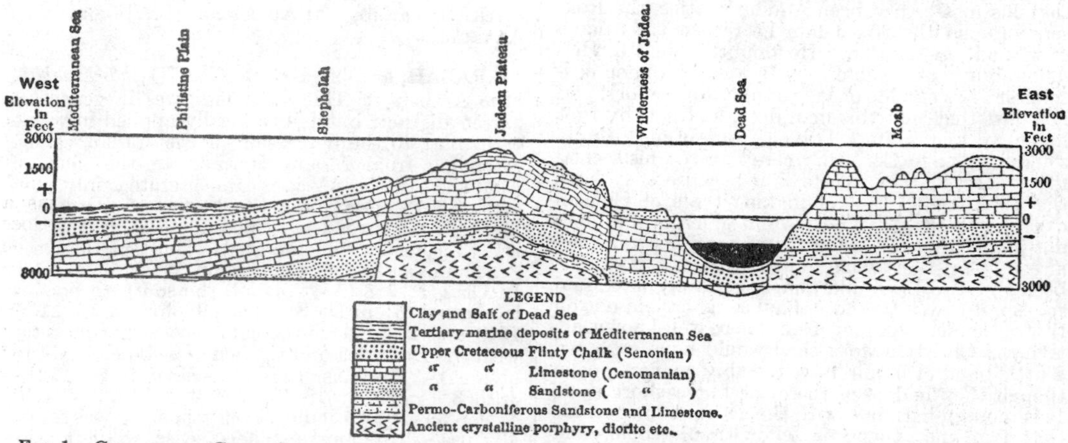

FIG. 1.—GEOLOGICAL CROSS-SECTION OF SOUTHERN PALESTINE, THROUGH BETHLEHEM. AFTER BLANCKENHORN.

South of the Dead Sea a muddy plain, known as the Sebkah, extends 6 miles, filling about one-half of the width of the Ghôr. During most of the year the mud over this area is so thin and deep that it is impossible to cross it near its northern end. This whole area between the "ascent of Akrabbim" and the Dead Sea has evidently been greatly transformed by the sedimentary deposits which have been brought in by the numerous tributary wadies during the last 4,000 years, the coarser material having encroached upon it from either side, and the fine material having been deposited over the middle portion, furnishing the clay which is so embarrassing to travelers. (For further considerations upon this point see DEAD SEA; CITIES OF THE PLAIN.)

1. Geology of the Region

The Arabah in its whole extent occupies a portion of the great geological fault or crevasse in the earth's crust which extends from Antioch near the mouth of the Orontes southward between the Lebanon and the Anti-Lebanon Mountains to the valley of the Jordan and the Dead Sea, and onward to the Gulf of Akabah, whence it can be traced with considerable probability through the Red Sea and the interior lakes of Africa. The most remarkable portion of this phenomenal crevasse is that which extends from the Waters of Merom to the springs of Ain Abu Werideh; for through this entire distance the Arabah is below sea-level, the depression at the Dead Sea being approximately 1,292 feet. See DEAD SEA. Throughout the entire distance from the Waters of Merom to the watershed, 45 miles from Akabah, the western side of the Arabah is bordered by strata of Cretaceous (chalk) limestone rising pretty continuously to a height of from 2,000 to 3,000 feet above sea-level, no older rocks appearing upon that side. But upon the eastern side older sandstones (Nubian and lower Carboniferous) and granitic rocks border the plain, supporting, however, at a height of 2,000 or 3,000 feet Cretaceous limestones corresponding to those which descend to the level of the gorge on the western side (Fig. 1). Throughout this entire distance, therefore, the strata have either slipped down upon the western side or risen upon the eastern side, or there has been a movement in both directions. The origin of this crevasse dates from the latter part of the Cretaceous or the early part of the Tertiary period.

But in post-Tertiary times an expanded lake filled the region, extending from the Waters of Merom to Ain Abu Werideh, a distance of about 200 miles, rising to an elevation of about 1,400 feet above the present level of the Dead Sea, but not sufficiently high to secure connection with the ocean either through the Arabah proper or across the valley of Esdraelon. This body of water was, on the average, 30 miles wide and over the northern part of the Dead Sea had an extreme depth of 2,700 feet. The most distinct evidence of the existence of this enlargement of the lake is to be found at Ain Abu Werideh, where Hull reports "banks of horizontally stratified materials . . . . sometimes of coarse material, such as gravel; at other times consisting of fine sand, loam, or white marl, with very even stratification, and containing blanched semi-fossil shells of at least two kinds of univalves, which Professor Haddon has determined to be *Melania tuberculata* Müll, and *Melanopsis Saulcyi*, Bourg" (*Mount Seir*, 99, 100). These are shells which are now found, according to Tristram, in great numbers in semi-fossil condition in the marl deposits of the Dead Sea, and both of these genera are found in the fluvio-marine beds formed in the brackish or salt water of the Isle of Wight. The existence of the shells indicates the extent to which the saline waters of the Dead Sea were diluted at that time (Figs. 2, 3). It should be added, however, that species somewhat similar still exist around the borders of the Dead Sea in lagoons where fresh water is mingled in large quantities with that of the Dead Sea. This is especially true in eddies near the mouth of the Jordan. (See Merrill, *East of the Jordan*.) Huntington in 1909 confirms the fact that these high-level shore lines are found on both sides of the Dead

Sea, though for some reason they have not been traced farther north.

At lower levels, especially at that which is 650 feet above the Dead Sea, there is, however, a very persistent terrace of gravel, sand and clay marking a shore line all the way from the south end of the Dead Sea to Lake Galilee. This can be seen running up into all the wadies on either side, being very prominent opposite their mouths, but much eroded since its deposition. On the shores of the lake between the wadies the line is marked by a slight accumulation of coarse material. Below the 650-foot line there are several other minor strands marking periods when the subsiding waters were for a short time stationary.

This period of enlargement of the waters in the Arabah is now, with abundant reason, correlated with the Glacial epoch whose influence was so generally distributed over the northern hemisphere in early post-Tertiary times. There were, however, no living glaciers within the limits of the Arabah Valley — Mount Hermon not being sufficiently large to support any extensive ice-sheet. The nearest glacier of any extent was on the west side of the Lebanon Mountains, 40 to 50 miles north of Beirût, where according to my own observations one descended from the summit of the mountains (10,000 feet high) 12 miles down the valley of the Kadesha River to a level 5,500 feet above the sea, where it built up an immense terminal moraine several miles across the valley, and 5 miles up it from its front, upon which is now growing the celebrated grove of the Cedars of Lebanon. (See *Records of the Past*, Am. ser., V, 195–204.) The existence of the moraine, however, had been noted by Sir Joseph Hooker forty years before. (See *Nat. Hist. Rev.*, January, 1862.)

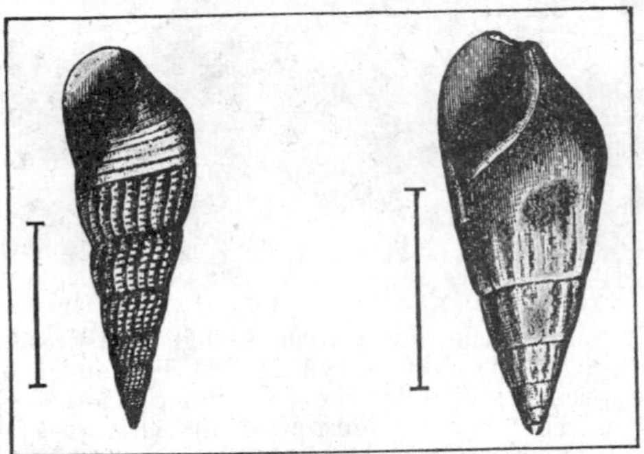

Fig. 2.—Shells from Ancient Bed of the Salt Sea.

But while there were no glaciers in the Arabah Valley itself, there, as elsewhere, semi-glacial conditions extended beyond the glacial limits a considerable distance into the lower latitudes, securing the increased precipitation and the diminished evaporation which would account for the enlargement of the bodies of water occupying inclosed basins within reach of these influences. The basin of Great Salt Lake in Utah presents conditions almost precisely like those of the Arabah, as do the Caspian and Aral seas, and lakes Urumiah, Van, and various others in central Asia. During the Glacial epoch the water level of Great Salt Lake rose more than 1,000 feet higher than now and covered ten times its present area. At the same time the Aral Sea discharged into the Caspian Sea through an outlet as large as Niagara. When the conditions of the Glacial epoch passed away the evaporation again prevailed, until the water areas of these inclosed basins were reduced to the existing dimensions and the present equilibrium was established between the precipitation and the evaporation.

While it is susceptible of proof that the close of this epoch was geologically recent, probably not more than 10,000 years ago (see Wright, *Ice Age in North America*, 5th ed, ch xx), the present conditions had become established approximately long before the time of Abraham and the development of civilization in Babylonia and Egypt.

Fig. 3.—White Marl and Silt near the Dead Sea.

East of the Arabah between the Dead Sea and Akabah numerous mountain peaks rise to the height of more than 4,000 feet above tide level, the highest being Mount Hor, though back of it there is a limestone range reaching 5,000 feet. This mountainous region contains numerous fertile areas and furnishes through its numerous wadies a considerable amount of water to favor vegetation. The limestone floor of the Arabah south of the Dead Sea is deeply covered with sand and gravel, washed in from the granitic areas from the east. This greatly favors the accumulation of sediment at the mouths of the wadies emptying into the south end of the Ghôr.

At present the Egyp government maintains a fort and harbor at Akabah, but its authority does not extend into the interior. The Arabah has, however, from time immemorial furnished a caravan route between northern Arabia and the Sinaitic Peninsula. It was this which supported the great emporium of Petra. The Israelites traversed its southern portion both on their way from Horeb to Kadesh-barnea and on their return, when the king of Edom refused passage through his land (Nu **20** 21; Dt **2** 3). This opposition compelled them to turn up the forbidding Wady el-Ithem, which opens into the Arabah a few miles north of Akabah and leads to the Pilgrim route between Damascus and Mecca. The terrors of this passage are referred to in Nu **21** 4, where it is said "the soul of the people was much discouraged because of the way." Around Akabah itself there are still groves of palms, the existence of which, at the time of the Exodus, is indicated by the name Elath (Dt **2** 8), "a grove of trees."

2. History

Literature.—Burckhardt, *Travels in Syria and the Holy Land*, 1822; De Laborde, *Voyage en Orient*, 1828; Hull, *Mount Seir, Sinai, and Western Pal*, 1889; "The Physical Geol. and Geog. of Arabia Petræa," etc, in *PEF*, 1886; Lartet, *Voyage d'exploration de la Mer Morte*, t. 3me, 1880; Robinson, *BR*, 1855; Stanley, *Sinai and Pal*[5], 1860; Blankenkorn, "Entstehung u. Gesch. des Todten Meeres," in *ZDPV*, 1896; Ritter, "*Comp. Geog. of Pal and the Sinaitic Peninsula*," 1866, tr by Wm. L. Gage; Huntington, *Pal and Its Transformation*, 1911.

George Frederick Wright

ARABATTINE, ar-a-ba-tī'nē. See Akrabattine (Apoc).

ARABIA, a-rā'bi-a (עֲרָב, *'ărābh*, **'Αραβία**, *Arabía*):

I. Name and Situation
1. Name
2. Situation and Configuration
II. Physical Features
1. The Desert
2. Climate
3. Mountains
4. Rivers
5. Oases and Wells
III. Political Divisions
1. Ancient Divisions
2. Modern Divisions
3. Political Situation
4. Chief Towns

I. Name and Situation.—The Heb word *'ărābh* always denotes, strictly speaking, not the country, but the people of Arabia taken collectively, and especially the nomadic Arabs. The name of the country does not occur in the OT, but in the NT it is used to denote the Syrian desert or the peninsula of Sinai.

1. Name

Modern Arabs Encamped in the Valley of Achor.

2. Situation and Configuration

Surrounded as it is on three sides by the sea—by the Indian Ocean on the south, and its two branches, the Red Sea on the west and the Persian Gulf on the east—and on the fourth side by the desert of Syria, the country of Arabia is to all intents and purposes an island; and it is named by its inhabitants and by those who speak their language "the Island of the Arabs." In configuration the country is roughly of the form of a parallelogram, about 1,000 miles in length by 500 or 600 miles broad. This parallelogram is not of uniform altitude, but the generally even surface is tilted to one corner in such a way that the most southerly point contains mountains rising to 10,000 feet in height, whilst the N.E. corner is almost on a level with the sea. The altitudes of the intervening portions are in proportion to their situation with respect to these extremes. Thus the mountains of the S.E. corner have an altitude of from 5,000 to 6,000 feet, those of the N.W. of 4,000 or 5,000, whereas those which are situated near the middle of the W. coast rise to 8,000 feet, and the plateau which forms the northern half of the interior of the peninsula is between 3,000 and 4,000 feet above sea-level. In consequence of this configuration the main watershed of the country runs parallel to the W. coast at a distance of between 50 and 100 miles from the sea, with a subsidiary watershed running along the south; and the principal outlets for the drainage run in a N.E. direction. The whole of Arabia stretches from about 13° to about 36° north of the equator, and it lies between 33° and 60° east of Greenwich. Its area is about eight times that of the British Isles, or nearly 1,000,000 square miles.

II. Physical Features.—Although Arabia is considered by geographers as part of the continent of Asia, it belongs in almost every respect to Africa. The great bulk of the country is desert, of fine sand in the southern part, but consisting of coarse sand (the *nefūd*), gravel and flints in the northern. It is in fact an offshoot from the great African Sahara. Of the southern half little is known, and it has never been crossed by the foot of European. The northern has been traversed in many directions; it has numerous caravan routes, and some important towns are situated in the heart of it. Arabian fancy has peopled the desert with strange creatures not of human kind (cf Isa **13** 21; **34** 14), and fancy has been justified by the common phenomena of the mirage and the Fata Morgana (Isa **35** 7; **49** 10). To the keen sight of the nomad the glowing desert heat is visible as a fine gossamer (Isa **18** 4). Perhaps this is the meaning of *shārābh* in **35** 7; **49** 10 also. It is quite certain, however, that the whole of Arabia and especially the northern borders in the neighborhood of the Sinai peninsula and eastward to the south of Pal and the country of Edom, were at one time very much better watered than they are at the present day. For centuries a constant process of desiccation has been going on. Indeed, persons now living can remember the existence of wells one or two generations ago, where now there are none. It follows that this district must formerly have supported a very much larger population that it does at present.

1. The Desert

2. Climate

It will be obvious that the climate of Arabia must vary greatly in its different parts, the temperature and rainfall depending not so much upon latitude as upon altitude, so that within a few miles the greatest extremes co-exist. In the southern angle where the mountains are highest there are two rainy seasons, one in spring the other in autumn, so that this province well deserves its Grecian name of

Arabia Felix. In the higher reaches of this province, for example, at its capital San'a, snow falls in December; while on the coast of the Red Sea at Loheia, scarcely 100 miles distant, the thermometer rarely falls below 80°. In the Red Sea 93° is a common reading in the shade in summer, while the heat of the Persian Gulf, owing to its steep shores and great evaporation, is hardly endurable by a European. In the N.W. province, in which are situated the two sacred cities of Mecca and Medina, the rainfall is unreliable and takes the form of heavy thunder showers which occasion frequent floods in the former town, and are, owing to the arborial denudation of the country, of little use for the purpose of agriculture or irrigation. These winter rains may commence as early as September, and by December at latest the new pasture will have covered the ground. Hence the true spring in northern Arabia, or in Syria, falls in our autumn, but there is not the distinction of former and latter rain (cf Hos **6** 3) which obtains in Pal. The climate of the northern central plateau is described by Palgrave as one of the most salubrious in the world.

3. Mountains

As has been indicated above, the backbone of the peninsula is the mountain range which runs down its western side. In its northern parts this is said to be an extension of the limestone ranges of the Lebanon and Anti-Libanus. In its midmost reaches it attains an elevation of between 8,000 and 9,000 feet, and at its southern extremity it spreads out into the plateau of Arabia Felix, where its highest peaks have an altitude of as much as 11,000 feet. In the S.E. corner of the peninsula the range of Jebel Akhdar runs parallel to that on the W., and is connected with it along the S. coast by a range of less elevation. In the interior the northern plateau is intersected by numerous irregular mountain ranges of moderate length, of which the most frequently mentioned are Jebel Aja and Jebel Selma, which face one another in the Shammar country.

4. Rivers

The course of the rivers is determined by the direction of the mountain ranges. As has been said the drainage is mainly from W. to E., but the fact is that Arabia is a land almost without rivers. The only quarter in which perennial streams are found is Arabia Felix, and to some extent they occur along the S. coast. The rest of the peninsula is destitute of rivers and lakes. The scour (*seyl*) from the winter thunder showers cuts out for itself a torrent bed (*wādī*), which, however, may be filled only once or twice in a generation, and even so dries up as soon as the rain ceases. The most important of these *wadis* is the W. Sirhan, which runs from the Hauran in a S.E. direction to the Jauf (see DUMAH), the W. el-Kora to the N. of Medina, the W. el-Hamth between Medina and Mecca, and the W. Duweisir to the S. of Mecca. Larger than any of these however is the W. er-Rumma, which extends from the neighborhood of Medina to the head of the Persian Gulf. It has never been explored, and is filled with water only at long intervals.

5. Oases and Wells

In these circumstances the Arabs have to seek their water supply elsewhere than in their rivers. In many places the surface of the country sinks into a depression down to the level of permanent water, thus forming an oasis, which word is probably none other than the Arab. *wādī*. The best known of these occur at Kheibar and Teima (see TEMA) to the N. of Medina, and also at Tabuk to the N.W. The W. Duweisir is itself practically an oasis of a length of three days' journey. In addition to these natural depressions there are also dotted over all the inhabited parts of Arabia and along the caravan routes numerous wells, these routes following naturally the course of the *wādīs*. These wells are plentiful in the W. Sirhan, and a number were sunk by command of Zubeida the wife of Harun al-Rashīd, along the Pilgrim way from Persia to Mecca; but the most famous of all is the well of Zemzem in the Holy City itself. It is said that the water in it flows, so that it is probably one of those subterranean rivers which are not uncommon in Arabia. Its water, however, is

Modern Arabs.

heavy and brackish and causes indigestion, and the sweetest water obtainable in Mecca for drinking purposes was originally brought by Zubeida from a source some 15 miles distant. The purest water of all is that which collects after rain in the hollows of the numerous outcrops of lava which occur at frequent intervals and in great masses along the western mountain ranges. A spot where lava predominates is called a *harrah* (from the Arabic verb "to be hot"), and several of these volcanic regions still show signs of activity.

III. Political Divisions.—The peninsula of Arabia was divided by the ancient geographers into three parts: A. Petraea, A. Deserta and A. Felix.

1. Ancient Divisions

The first of these names, which is found in Ptolemy, means, not A. the Rocky, but that part of A. in which is situated the city of Petra (see SELA), and it also includes the peninsula of Sinai. It is identical with the desert of the Wanderings. A. Deserta is a translation from the Gr *A. érēmos* of Strabo (cir 24 AD). It denotes the extreme north of the continent of A. which is thrust in like a wedge between the fertile lands which drain into the Euphrates on the E. and into the Jordan valley on the W. It is thus equivalent to the Syrian Desert. The third term, A. Felix, is also a tr from the Gr—*A. eudaímōn*—which is again a tr, or rather a mistranslation of the Arab. El-Yemen. This last name denotes the country to the right hand, i.e. the S, just as the Arab. Es-Shem (Syria) means the country to the left hand, or to the N. El-Yemen, however, was interpreted as equivalent to El-Eyman, the Fortunate or Happy, a name which the district truly deserves.

2. Modern Divisions

Since before the time of Mohammed (6th cent.) A. has been divided into seven or eight tribal or political states, the boundaries of which are for the most part clearly defined by intervening deserts or uninhabited tracts. The most important of these from a religious point of view is the *Hijāz*, which may be described as the northern half of the western coast, stretching from the Red Sea to a distance of between 100 and 200 miles inland. The whole of the coast line, indeed, where the land is low lying is called the *Tihāma*. This may, however, be considered as belonging to the adjacent high land beneath which it lies. Hijāz means "Barrier," and the district is so called because it consists mainly of the mountain ranges which separate the great northern central plateau from the Tihāma. This last name is connected with a root meaning "to be unwholesome." Whether the district gave its origin to the verb, or the verb gave its denomination to the district, the name is equally appropriate. The chief importance of the Hijāz arises from the fact that in it are situated the two holy cities of Mecca and Medina—the cradle and the grave of the Prophet. It is thus the religious center of the Islamic world. The *Yemen* forms the southern corner of the peninsula. It is identical with A. Felix, and its physical characteristics have been described above. The Hijāz often fell to the sovereign of Egypt, but for the last four centuries it has, like Egypt, been subject to the Turk. It is only within the last fifty years, on the other hand, that the sultan has attempted to enforce his sovereign rights in the Yemen. The southern coast of A. is generally designated as *Hadramaut*, although in strictness that appellation is properly applicable to a section of it only. The eastern corner of A. is taken up by *Omān*, a state which has generally claimed and secured a position of independence. Both it and the southern states are now under the protection of the Indian government. The country adjacent to Omān toward the N. formed the province of *El-Bahrein* ("the Two Seas"), but this name is now restricted to a large island at the western end of it and some smaller islands famous for their pearl fishery. The remaining province of *El-Hasa* is occupied by practically independent tribes. From many points of view the most interesting province of A. is the great northern central plateau called *Nejd*, that is, "high land." From its situation it is least susceptible to foreign influence. It contains some fairly large towns, but the bulk of its population live, as their fathers have done from time immemorial, the life of the Bedawi. Two small provinces remain to be noticed. Between the Yemen and the Hijāz lies the district of *'Asīr*, which largely resembles the first-named province in its physical features. To the E. of Nejd lies the district of *Yemāma*, which used to be the territory of an important tribe.

3. Political Situation

On the whole the political situation in A. today bears a considerable resemblance to that which obtained immediately before the mission of Mohammad. At that time (about 600 AD) the N.W. parts of the peninsula were more or less subject to the Byzantine emperor, while the whole E. and S. coasts were under the sway of Persia. Today the W. coast of A. is again subject to Constantinople, and the E. and S. coasts are under the protection of an eastern power—in this case the government of India.

4. Chief Towns

The principal towns of A. and the other centers of population owe their existence to the natural features of the country and have probably remained the same in all ages, just as those of Pal have, and even their population does not seem to have altered much. Thus Mecca owes its existence to the presence of the famous well Zemzem; Teima, Kheibar and Tabuk to their oases; Mascat, the capital of Omān, to its natural harbor; and so on. An exception is the ancient town of Saba (see SHEBA) or Marib, which probably sprang up as the result of the building in prehistoric times of a gigantic dam for the purposes of irrigation. When the dam burst in the 2d or 3d Christian cent., the population dispersed. Owing to the absence of a census it is not possible to make accurate statements regarding the population of an eastern town, and estimates by European travelers always vary greatly. Speaking generally, the cities of A. of the first magnitude appear to have some 35,000 inhabitants, though Mascat is said to have as many as 60,000.

IV. Flora and Fauna.—The peninsula of A. belongs, as has been said, in its physical features to Africa, and its flora and fauna are those of that continent. Of all the products of the soil by far the most important is the date palm. It flourishes in every oasis. In the Wādī Duweisir alone it is said one may ride straight on for three days without leaving the shelter of the palm groves. The dates, which are the staff of life of the Arab, differ in quality in each locality, each district producing a variety of its own. In the Yemen, with its varied altitudes, almost every kind of fruit and vegetable known in temperate latitudes is cultivated on the terraced mountain sides. Vines are grown, as Ibn Khaldūn remarks, for the sake of the berry, not for the purposes of wine making. The vine is common to Arabia and Pal, whereas the date palm has almost gone out of cultivation in the latter country. On the other land the olive, which is so important in the northern country is almost unknown in the southern. The olive is constantly referred to in the Bible (Jgs **9** 8 and often), the date never. From the S. coast especially are exported frankincense, balsam, myrrh and other aromatic plants; and cotton is cultivated in the province of Omān. Cereals flourish in the Yemen and tobacco is grown wherever possible in A. The coffee of the Yemen is famous; it is exported to Constantinople and named from the port of export Mokha coffee; but the bulk of it is consumed within A. itself. Coffee and tobacco are the only two articles of consumption which are used in A. today, and which have not been used from time immemorial. Coffee was probably introduced into A. from Gallaland on the African mainland two or three cents. ago. The Arabs are most inveterate coffee drinkers. Tobacco was probably first brought from English ships at Constantinople in the reign of James I. It is cultivated in every oasis, unless in the interior in Nejd, where its use is discouraged on religious grounds. There is only one other point in regard to which the Arabs of today differ from the Arabs of Mohammed's time—the use of gunpowder. Except in respect of the three commodities just mentioned, everyday life in the desert today goes on exactly as it did 1,600 years ago. Forest trees are extremely rare in A., but a species of tamarisk called *ghada* which grows in the northern *nefūd* is proverbial for the quality of charcoal it affords and is a favorite food of the camel. An acacia called *katād* is likewise a by-word on account of its long spines. The wood is used for making camels' saddles; it grows in the Tihāma. As in Pal and in most countries which have been inhabited for many thousands of years, the larger trees have long been cut down for fuel or for building purposes.

1. Flora

2. Fauna

Among beasts of prey panthers, wolves, hyaenas, jackals and (it is said) even lions are found in A. Many of the tribes are named after these and other animals. The wild ox or oryx (see UNICORN) is rarely seen, but gazelles are plentiful. Apes abound in the Yemen, as they do all along the N. of Africa, and are kept as pets (cf 1 K **10** 22). By far the most important domestic animal is the camel. Without it many parts of the country would be uninhabited. It is commonly supposed that the best breed of horses comes from Nejd, but this appears to be an error. In Nejd the camel is the indispensable beast of burden and mount; horses are comparatively useless there. The best Arabian horses are reared in Mesopotamia. Studs are, indeed, kept by the emirs of Nejd, but the horses are small and of little use. The pedigrees of the best horses go back, according to tradition, to the time of Solomon (1 K **10** 28). Dogs are trained to hunt the wild ox, to tend sheep and to watch the camp. All domestic animals—dogs, horses, mules, asses—receive names as with us. The ostrich is rarely met with, but is found as far north as the Jauf; it no doubt found its way into A. from Africa. A common bird is the *kata* or sand grouse. It is noted for going straight to its watering place. "Better guided than a *kata*" is a common proverb. Hawks and falcons are found, and falconry among the Arabs was a favorite sport. In A. the locust, so far from being a scourge wherever it appears, is a valuable article of food. It is eaten not only by human beings (Mt **3** 4), but also by dogs, horses and even beasts of prey. As might be expected in a rocky and sun-scorched land like A., scorpions and various sorts of serpents abound. The chameleon (Lev **11** 30) is common here. It is used as a simile for fickle people and those who do not fulfil their promises. It may be regarded as a substitute for the thermometer, as on very hot days it ascends trees or any high places. Another sign of extreme heat is that the vipers writhe on the ground.

The Persian Gulf, especially the Bahrein archipelago, is famous for its pearls, while the Red Sea is noted for its coral reefs, which have caused many a shipwreck. It is believed that in the interior of Hadramaut there are many mineral deposits including gold.

V. Inhabitants.—The inhabitants of A. are divided into three classes. There are in the first place a number of tribes which became extinct, and which are not connected genealogically with those which survived. The latter are divided into two great stems, the south Arabian and indigenous branch descended from Kahtan, and the north Arabian or immigrant tribes descended from Ishmael, the son of Abraham. There is naturally a good deal of inconsistency in the various traditions of the origins of these tribes and their subsequent history.

1. Classification

Of the extinct tribes the most familiar name is that of Amlāk or Amlīk (*Amalek*). By the Arabian genealogists he is variously described as a grandson of Shem and as a son of Ham. In Gen **36** 12 he is a son of Esau's son, Eliphaz, by Timna. They are said to be first met with in Chaldaea, from which they were expelled on the rise of the Assyr power under Nimrod. They migrated into Ar, occupying in turn the Bahrein, Omān, the Yemen, and finally the Hijāz, where they are said to have been the first settlers at Yathrib (Medina) and also to have occupied land round Mecca and Kheibar. In the time of Abraham they were expelled from Mecca on the arrival of two new tribes from the S., those of Jurhum and Katūra (Gen **25** 1). Later, it is said, David, during the rebellion of Absalom, took up his quarters in Kheibar and ruled over the surrounding districts. According to another tradition Moses sent an expedition against the Amalekites in the Hijāz, on which occasion the Israelites, disobeying his orders, spared their king Arkam (cf Rekem, Nu **31** 8; Josh **13** 21)—a reminiscence of the incident in the life of Saul (1 S **15**). In any case the Amalekites were supplanted in the northern Hijāz by Jewish tribes, who continued there until the time of Mohammad. The Amalekites migrated into Egypt and southern Pal. The Pharaohs of the time of Abraham, Joseph and Moses are represented to have been Amalekites. Finally, broken up by Josh, they fled into northern Africa, where they are said to have grown into the Berber races. The rest of the tribes which became extinct like the Amalekites are of less interest for the present purpose, being unconnected with the Bible narrative. They are mentioned in the Koran, in which book their destruction is attributed to their idolatrous proclivities and to their rejection of the monotheistic prophets. The best known and most important are ʽAd and Thamūd. *ʽAd* is variously named the son of Amalek and the son of Uz (Gen **10** 23). The tribe dwelt in the deserts behind the Yemen. They became polytheists; the prophet Hūd was sent to them; they rejected him, and were destroyed by a hurricane. The remnant grew into a new tribe, whose chief, Lokmān, built the great dam at Marib. In the end they were conquered by a tribe of Kahtan. *Thamūd* was closely related to ʽAd, being a son of Aram the father of Uz. They were driven out of the Yemen and settled in the northern Hijāz; they rejected their prophet Salih and were destroyed by an earthquake accompanied by a loud noise. The rock-cut sepulchral monuments of Medaīn Salih in the Wādī el-Kora are still pointed out as their dwellings. They were, therefore, considered to have been troglodites like the Horites of the Bible. A second pair were the brother tribes of *Tasm* and *Jadīs*, grandsons of Aram. Tasm oppressing Jadīs, the latter rose and almost exterminated the former, only to be in turn destroyed by a king of the Yemen. Their home was Yemāma.

2. Extinct Tribes

The southern Arabs claim to be descended from an ancestor called Kahtan son of ʽAbir, son of Shalikh, son of Arfakhshad, son of Shem, son of Noah. Kahtan is undoubtedly the Biblical Joktan (Gen **10** 26), and the names of his descendants reappear as Arab. place names. Indeed the tenth chapter of Gen throws much light on the earliest history of A. and the movements of the tribes. Thus the fact that Sheba and Dedan appear as grandsons of Cush, that is, as Abyssinian tribes descended from Ham, in Gen **10** 7 and again as descendants of Keturah and Abraham in **25** 3 points to the fact that parts of these tribes migrated from the one country to the other. Havilah in Gen **10** 7 may similarly be connected with Havilah in **10** 29, the intercourse between S.W. Arabia and the opposite coast of Africa being always very close. Among the sons of Joktan are mentioned Almodad, Hazarmaveth, Uzal (Izal), Sheba, Ophir, Havilah. In Almodad we have probably the Arab. El-Mudād, a name which occurs among the descendants of Jurhum, son of Yaktan (Joktan). Hazarmaveth is obviously Hadramaut. Uzal is the ancient name of Sanʽa, the capital of the Yemen. Sheba is the Arab. Saba or Marib. Ophir and Havilah were probably in S. or E. Arabia. In Gen **10** 30 it is said that the camping grounds of these tribes stretched from Mesha as you go toward Sephar, the mountain of the East, that is, probably from the N. of the Persian Gulf to the center of S. Arabia, Sephar being Zafār, the capital of the S. Arab kingdom near to the present Mirbat.

3. South Arabian Tribes

Many of the most illustrious tribes are descended from Kahtan, and some of them still survive. A constant stream of migration went on toward the N. Thus the tribe of Jurhum left the Yemen on account of drought and settled in the Hijāz and the Tihāma, from which they drove out the Amalekites, and were in turn driven out by Kodaʽa, another Kahtanite tribe. After that they disappear from history and are reckoned among the

4. Migration of Tribes

extinct tribes. Koda'a was a descendant of Himyar. The Himyarites founded, about the 1st cent. BC, a kingdom which lasted for five centuries. The king bore the title of Tubba', and the capital was successively Marib (Saba), Zafār and San'a. One of their monarchs was the queen Bilkīs whom the Arabian historians identify with the queen of Sheba who visited Solomon, though she must have lived much later. The story of the meeting is given in the Korān, ch 38. A chief occasion on which many of the tribes left the district N.E. of the Yemen was the bursting of the great dam, built by Lokman at Marib, about the 2d cent. AD. A section of these grew into the Arabian kingdom of Ghassan, whose capital was Damascus and many of whose kings bore the name Al-Harith (Aretas, 2 Cor **11** 32). This kingdom lasted till the time of Mohammad (7th cent.) and was in alliance with the Rom and Gr empires. On the opposite side of the Syrian desert the Lakhmid kingdom of Al-Hira on the Euphrates (also of Kahtanite origin) was allied to Persia. The two Arabian "buffer-states" were almost constantly at war with one another.

5. North Arabian Tribes

Among the Arabs Ishmael holds the place occupied by Isaac in the Heb tradition. It was to the valley, afterward the site of the town of Mecca, that Abraham conducted Hagar and her son, and that Ishmael grew up and became the father of a great nation. The locality is full of spots connected by tradition with his life history, the ground where Hagar searched for water, the well Zemzem of which Gabriel showed her the place, the mount Thabīr where Abraham would have sacrificed his son (Ishmael), and the graves of Hagar and Ishmael. The Jurhum, among whom Ishmael grew up, gave him seven goats: these were the capital with which he began life. He married a woman of Jurhum. He had twelve sons (Gen **25** 16) of whom Kaidar and Nabat are the best known, perhaps the Cedrei and Nabataei of Pliny; other sons were Dumah and Tema (q.v.). The subsequent history of the Ishmaelites is lost for several generations until we come to 'Adnān, who is said to have been defeated by Nebuchadnezzar, when the latter invaded Arabia. All the Ishmaelite tribes are descended from 'Adnān. They are the north Arabian tribes, as opposed to the Kahtanite or south Arabian. One of them, Koreish, under their chief, Kosay, became master of Mecca, driving out Koda'a. Later, as the tribe of the Prophet, they became the rulers of Arabia and the aristocracy of the Muslim empire; and the descendants of Mohammad remain to this day the only hierarchy known to Islām.

6. Other Tribes

There are one or two other branches which are not included in the above classification: such are the Nabateans (see Nebaioth), and the descendants of Esau and Keturah. The Nabateans are not generally reckoned among the Arabian tribes. They were an Aramaean stock, the indigenous inhabitants of Mesopotamia, and spoke not Arabic but Aramaic. They founded a kingdom in A. of which the capital was Petra (see Sela). This was the most famous of their colonies, and it endured, at first in alliance with the Romans and later in subjection to them, for 500 years—from the 2d cent. BC to the 3d cent. AD. Petra was an important trading emporium, but, when the trade left the overland routes and was carried by way of the Red Sea, it quickly fell into poverty and oblivion. The descendants of Esau are named in Gen **36** 1 ff; they were allied to the Hittites and Ishmaelites. Among the tribes descended from Keturah are Jokshan and Midian, Sheba and Dedan (Gen **25** 2 ff).

7. Foreign Elements

In Arabia there was and still, in spite of religious disabilities, is a large Jewish population. Before the age of Mohammad they lived chiefly in the N.W., the two best known tribes—An-Nadīr and Koreiza—occupying Yathrib (Medina). After the rise of Islām they were expelled from A.; but at the present time there are probably some 60,000 Jews in the Yemen alone. There has always been a close connection between the S. and W. of A. and the opposite African coast. Especially in the 6th cent. there was a large influx of Abyssinians into the Yemen, as there still is into the western districts. A like intermixture of population went on between Zanzibar and Omān.

VI. Religion.—The religion of the greater part of the Arabs before the time of Mohammad consisted of a vague deism combined with a primitive form of stone-worship. This is chiefly true of the Ishmaelite tribes descended from Modan, a great-grandson of 'Adnān, and among them it is especially true of Koreish. The origin of this stone worship may have been that as each family was forced to hive off from the main stock and quit the sacred territory around Mecca, it carried with it a stone as a monument of the homeland. This stone soon became a fetich. It was worshipped by stroking it with the hand. Before setting out on a journey a man would perform this religious duty, and also immediately on his return, before even visiting his wife and family. The best known idols of the pagan Arabs, from the mention of them in the Korān, are Al-Lāt, Al-Ozza and Al-Manāt (Kor **53** 19.20), worshipped by the Thakīf at Taïf, by the two tribes of Medina, the Aus and the Khazraj, and by Koreish, in a shrine near Mecca, respectively. Koreish had also a great idol named Hubal in the "house of God" at Mecca, which contained other idols besides. The deity in each case was probably at first a large bowlder of stone, then a portable image was made, apparently in human form. They were regarded as feminine and called the daughters of God. Indeed, Al-Lāt is apparently merely the feminine of Allah (God). The deities mentioned in the Korān (**71** 23), Yaghūth, Ya'ūk and Nesr, were worshipped in the Yemen. It is certain, however, that the idolatry of the Arabs of "the Ignorance" (Jāhilīyah, "roughness," "ignorance"; cf Acts **17** 30)—so native writers name the ages before Mohammad (Korān **3** 148, etc)—has been greatly exaggerated by Mohammadan historians. It is remarkable that the words denoting an idol, *sanam* and *wethen*, are not Arab. roots, and the practice of idolatry seems also to have been an importation from without. Even the idolatrous Arabs believed in a supreme deity, whose daughters the idol deities were, and with whom they had powers of intercession. They therefore were rather images of saints than of gods. As Renan has said, the desert is monotheistic; it is too empty to give birth to a pantheon, as the fruitful plains of India could do. At the present day the desert Arabs are more strictly monotheistic than the Muslims themselves. Their religion consists in nothing save a vague belief in God.

2. The Ka'ba, Pilgrimages and Fairs

Though there were many houses of God in the country, the chief religious resort even before the time of Mohammad was Mecca. The House of God (see Bethel) here was called the Ka'ba, which is the English word "cube," the building being so called from its shape. It was believed to have been built by Abraham and Ishmael. The honor of acting as guardians of the House was a subject of rivalry among the tribes. The office was held consecutively by the tribes of

Jurhum, Koda'a and Koreish, and last by the grandfather and uncles of Mohammad. These, therefore, correspond to the tribe of Levi in Israel. It is said to have contained a large number of images, but it is remarkable that the nearer our authorities get to the time of Mohammad the smaller is the number of images mentioned. The chief of these, Hubal, is not named in the Korān. The worship took the form of circumambulation (*tawāf*), running or marching round the sanctuary (cf Ps **26** 6). An annual visitation was and still is made by those living at a distance, and sacrifices are offered. This is the *hajj* or pilgrimage; the same name is used for the corresponding rite among the Hebrews (Ex **10** 9 and often). These religious assemblies were combined with fairs, at which markets were held and a considerable trade carried on. Before the time of Mohammad the great annual fair was held at Okāz, a place still pointed out about three days' journey E. of Mecca and one day W. of Taïf. Here were not only all kinds of commercial transactions carried on—auctions, sales, settling of accounts and payment of blood-wit, but an academy was held at which poets recited their odes, and received judgment upon their merits. These fairs were generally held in the sacred months, that is, the first, seventh, eleventh and twelfth months, in which fighting was forbidden. They had therefore a great civilizing and pacifying influence.

3. Judaism

Before the time of Mohammad Judaism prevailed extensively in Arabia, especially in the Hijāz. It began no doubt with the migration of families due to disturbed political conditions at home. The conquest of Pal by Nebuchadnezzar, by the Seleucids, by the Romans under Pompey, Vespasian and finally Hadrian, drove many Jews to seek peace and safety in the deserts out of which their forefathers had come. Thither St. Paul also withdrew after his conversion (Gal **1** 17). Two of these emigrant tribes, the Nadīr and Koreiza, settled at Medina, first in independence, then as clients of the Aus and Khazraj. In the end they were harried and destroyed by Mohammad. The Jewish colony at Kheibar met the same fate. Several free Arab tribes also professed the Jewish faith, especially certain branches of Himyar and Kinda, both descendants of Kahtan, the former in southern, the latter in central Arabia. Judaism was introduced into the Yemen by one of the Tubbas, probably in the 3d cent. AD, but it was not until the beginning of the 6th cent. that it made much headway. At that epoch the Tubba Dhu Nuwās became a fierce protagonist of this creed. He seems to have attacked the Aus and Khazraj to whom the Jews of Yathrib (Medina) were subject. He instituted against the Christians of Nejran, a territory lying to the N.E. of the Yemen, a persecution which brought upon him the vengeance of the Byzantine emperor and of the Negus of Abyssinia and involved his kingdom and dynasty in ruin.

4. Christianity

Judaism did not hold such a large place in Arabia as did Christianity. The apostle Bartholomew is said to have carried the gospel thither. One of the Jurhum kings who may have lived about the beginning of the 2d cent. AD is named Abd el-Masīh ("Christ's slave"). There is said to have been a representation of the Virgin Mary and her Son in the Ka'ba. The Christian emperor Constans (337–50) sent the Bishop Theophilus into S. Arabia in order to obtain toleration for the Christians. The mission was successful. Churches were built at Zafār, at Aden, and on the shore of the Persian Gulf. The emperor's real object was doubtless political—to counteract the influence of Persia in these regions. Most of the Yemenite tribes were at this time pagan: they worshipped the idols mentioned above (Korān **71** 23). Some time after we find the Abyssinian sovereign describing himself in the inscriptions at Axum as king of the Himyarites. This supremacy would be favorable to the spread of Christianity. One of the chief seats, however, of the Christian religion, was at the above-mentioned Nejran, the territory of the tribe Harith ibn Ka'b, whom ecclesiastical writers seem to denote by Arethas son of Caleb. It was this tribe that Dhu Nuwās, Tubba of the Yemen, on his conversion to Judaism, attacked. He threw all the Christians who held by their faith into a trench of fire in which they were burned (Korān **85** 4). News of this atrocity was either carried by those who escaped or sent by the Lakhmid, king of Al-Hira, to the emperor Justin I, who, in turn, either directly or through the patriarch of Alexandria, invoked the coöperation of the Axumite king. The result was that the Abyssinians invaded the Yemen and overthrew the Himyarite dynasty. Christianity then became the prevailing religion of S. Arabia. The Abyssinians were in their turn, however, expelled by the Persians, under whom all religions—Christianity, Judaism and paganism—were tolerated, until they all disappeared before Islām. Several of the Lakhmid kings of Al-Hira, although they were from circumstances under the influence of the Persian Zoroastrianism, professed Christianity. Nu'mān I who reigned at the end of the 4th and beginning of the 5th cent., perhaps under the influence of Simon Stylites, retired from the world and became an ascetic. Mundhir II, in the middle of the 6th cent., seems to have come temporarily under the influence of the Eutychian heresy. Nu'mān V, one of his successors, was also converted to Christianity. But the kingdom in which Christianity flourished most was naturally that in closest contact with the Byzantine empire—the kingdom of the Ghassanids, although it seems not to have been until after the conversion of Constantine that this was the case. From his reign date the monasteries of which the ruins are still visible in the Ghassanid country. The powerful Ishmaelite tribe of Taghlib, whose settlements were in Mesopotamia was also converted to Christianity through similar influences, but not until the end of the 6th cent. Some members of the Kahtanite Koda'a professed the same religion, as did the Kelb in the Jauf.

5. The Sabians

In the Korān a third creed is bracketed with those of the Jews and Christians as entitled to toleration—that of the Sabians. These are monotheists who also worshipped the stars or the angels. The name Sabian has no connection with Sabaean which is derived from the name of the town of Saba. An account of their religion, taken from Abu'l Faraj (Bar Hebraeus), the Jacobite bishop, who wrote about the middle of the 13th cent., will be found in Sale's *Korān*, Preliminary Discourse, sec. I. Sale, however, identified Sabianism with the primitive religion of the Arabs, which Mohammad sought to supplant. This is impossible, however, in view of the fact that Mohammad tolerated the one and proscribed the other. Since the publication of Chwolson's *Ssabier und Ssabismus* it has been recognized that under the term Sabians are included two very different groups of people. In the first place the devotees of the old Sem idolatry which flourished at Harran assumed the name Sabian to enable them to claim the protection afforded by the Korān. It is the tenets of these Harranians of which Chwolson's work contains an exposition. The true Sabians, however, were a survival of primitive Christian Gnosticism; whence they were also called Mandaeans. From their frequent ablutions they received their name derived from the Aram. *ç^ebha'*, to "baptize," the *'ayin* being softened to *'ālēph*, and connected with St. John the Baptist.

The Jews, Christians and Sabians are called in the Korān "the people of the book," that is, those to whom a revelation had been vouchsafed, and who were in consequence of this tolerated. In one passage of the Korān (**22** 17) a fourth religion is added to these—the Magian, or Zoroastrian, introduced from Persia.

6. Seekers after Truth

Shortly before the appearance of Mohammad a number of thinking persons had become dissatisfied with the old Arabian religion of their ancestors, and yet had not joined the Christian or Jewish faith. They gave up the worship of idols, studied the various sacred books, and sought to find out the true way. They are considered in the Korān as having been of the true faith even before Mohammad had appeared. About a dozen are mentioned by the historians, of whom the most important are four—Waraka the cousin of Mohammad's wife Khadīja; Othmān who became a Christian; Obeidallah who became a Christian and then a Muslim; Zeid who traveled in pursuit of Truth, but did not attach himself to any one faith. The Heb prophets and those who accepted their doctrines are regarded as belonging to the same class. A person who is a monotheist, and who yet does not attach himself to any particular creed is called in the Korān a Hanīf. This pure religion is called the religion of Abraham. Mohammad claimed to restore this primeval religion in Islām. By John of Damascus Mohammad was regarded as the founder of a Christian sect. It is probable that but for his appearance Christianity would have spread over the whole of Arabia.

LITERATURE.—Caussin de Perceval, *Essai sur l'histoire des Arabes;* Sprenger, *Die alte Geographie Arabiens;* Hamdāni, ed, Müller, *Geographie der arabischen Halbinsel;* Niebuhr, *Travels through Arabia;* Burckhardt, *Travels in Arabia;* Wellsted, *Travels in Arabia;* Burton, *Personal Narrative of a Pilgrimage to El-Medinah and Meccah;* Palgrave, *Journey through Central and Eastern Arabia;* Blunt, *A Pilgrimage to Nejd;* Hurgronje, *Mecca;* Doughty, *Travels in Arabia Deserta;* Harris, *A Journey through the Yemen;* Brünnow and Domazewski, *Die Provincia Arabia;* Musil, *Arabia Deserta;* Glaser, *Skizze der Geschichte und Geographie Arabiens.*

THOMAS HUNTER WEIR

ARABIAN. See ARABIA.

ARABIC GOSPEL OF THE INFANCY. See APOCRYPHAL GOSPELS.

ARABIC HISTORY OF JOSEPH THE CARPENTER. See APOCRYPHAL GOSPELS.

ARABIC LANGUAGE, ar'a-bik laŋ'gwāj: For the student of the Bible the Arab. language is of interest, first, as one of the members of the Sem group of languages, to which belong the Heb and Aram. tongues of the Bible; secondly, as one of the languages into which the Bible and other church literature were early tr[d] and in which a Christian lit. was produced; and thirdly, as the vernacular of Mohammed and his followers, the classical tongue of that religious system which is the offspring of a degenerate Judaism and Christianity.

1. Philological Characterization

Scholars are generally agreed in grouping the Arabic and Ethiopic together as a South-Sem branch of the Sem stock. For the geographical and ethnological background of the Arab. language, see ARABIA. A general characteristic of this tongue of the desert is its remarkable retention into a late historical period, of grammatical features obliterated or in process of obliteration in the other Sem tongues at their earliest emergence in lit.; so that in the period since the golden age of its lit., the Arab. has been undergoing changes in some respects analogous to those which its sister-dialects underwent in their pre-literary or earliest literary stage. Thus, for example, the case-endings of nouns, lost in Aram. and Canaanitish (including Heb), all but lost in the Abyssinian dialects, beginning to be disregarded in even the early (popular) Bab, lost also in the dialects of modern Arab. are in full vitality throughout the classical period of Arab. literature.

The Arab. language itself, ancient and modern, divides into a vast number of dialects, many of which have attained the distinction of producing a lit. greater or less. But the dialect of the tribe of Koreish, to which Mohammed belonged, is the one that, naturally, by the circumstance of the Korān's composition and diffusion, has become the norm of pure Arabic. Old Arab. poems, some of them produced in "the Ignorance," that is, before the days of Mohammed, are in substantially the same dialect as that of the Korān, for it appears that Bedouin tribes ranging within the limits of the Arabian desert spoke an Arabic little differentiated by tribal or geographical peculiarities. On the other hand the inhabitants of the coast of the Indian Ocean from Yemen to Oman, and of the island of Socotra off that coast, spoke an Arabic differing widely from that of the northern tribes. The various dialects of this "South-Arabic," known partly through their daughter-dialects of today (Mehri, Socotri, etc), partly from the numerous and important inscriptions ("Minaean" and "Sabaean") found in Yemen by recent travelers, notably Halévy and Glaser, show a closer affinity than do the "North-Arabic" with the Abyssinian dialects (Ge'ez, i.e. "Ethiopic," Tigre, Tigriña, Amharic, etc), as might indeed be expected from the admitted S. Arabian origin of the Habesh-tribes or Abyssinians.

For the interpretation of the OT the Arab. language has been of service in a variety of ways. In the department of lexicography it has thrown light not only on many a word used but once in the Bible or too seldom for usage alone to determine its meaning, but also on words which had seemed clear enough in their Biblical setting, but which have received illustration or correction from their usage in the immense bulk and range of Arab. lit. with its enormous vocabulary. For the modern scientific study of Heb grammar, with its genetic method, Arab. has been of the greatest value, through the comparison of its cognate forms, where, in the main, the Arab. has the simpler, fuller and more regular morphology, and through the comparison of similar constructions, for which the highly developed Arab. syntax furnishes useful rubrics. In addition to this the Arab. language plays a prominent part, perhaps the foremost part, in the determination of those laws of the mutation of sounds, which once governed the development and now reveal the mutual relationships of the various Sem languages.

The script which we know as Arab. script, with its numerous varieties, developed out of the vulgar Aram. alphabet in N. Arabia; diacritical points were added to many of those letters, either to distinguish Arab. sounds for which no letter existed, or to differentiate letters the forms of which had become so similar as to create confusion. In Yemen another script arose early, that of the inscriptions above mentioned, admirably clear and adapted to express probably all the chief varieties of consonantal sounds in actual use, though quite without vowels.

For Arab. VSS of the Bible, see ARABIC VERSIONS. Outside of the Scriptures themselves there was most felt by Christian communities living in the Arab.-speaking world (primarily, though not exclusively, in Egypt and Syria) the need of a

2. Christian Arabic Literature

Christian lit. suited to the tastes of the time and region. Apocryphal and legendary material makes up a large part, therefore, of the list of Christian Arab. lit. See Apocryphal Gospels. But this material was not original. With the small degree of intellectual activity in those circles it is not surprising that most of such material, and indeed of the entire literary output, consists of translations from Syr, Gr or Coptic, and that original productions are few in number.

Of these last the most noteworthy are the following: theological and apologetic tracts by Theodore, bishop of Haran, the same who held the famous disputation with Mohammedan scholars at the court of Caliph Al-Mamun early in the 9th cent.; apologetic and polemic writings of Yahya ibn Adi of Tekrit, and of his pupil Abu Ali Isa ibn Ishaq, both in the 10th cent.; the Arab. works of Bar Hebraeus, better known for his numerous Syr compositions, but productive also of both historical and theological works in Arab. (13th cent.); in Egypt, but belonging to the same Jacobite or Monophysite communion as the above, the polemic and homiletic productions of Bishop Severus of Eshmunain (10th cent.), and, a generation earlier than Severus and belonging to the opposing or Melkite Egyp church, the chronicle of Eutychius, patriarch of Alexandria, continued a cent. later by Yahya ibn Said of Antioch; large compilations of church history, church law and theological miscellany by the Coptic Christians Al-Makin, Abu Ishaq ibn Al-Assal, Abu'l-Barakat and others, the leaders in a general revival of Egyp Christianity in the 13th cent.; on the soil of Nestorianism, finally, the ecclesiastical, dogmatic and exegetical writings of Abulfaraj Abdallah ibn At-Tayyib, (11 cent.), the apologetic compositions of his contemporary, Elias ben Shinaya, the historian, and the Nestorian church chronicle begun in the 12th cent. by Mari ibn Suleiman and continued two cents. later by Amr ibn Mattai and Saliba bar Johannan. After this date there is no original literature produced by Arab.-speaking Christians until the modern intellectual revival brought about by contact with European Christianity.

3. The Literary Vehicle of Islām

What Aram., Gr and Lat have been successively in the history of Christianity, all this, and more, Arab. has been in the history of Islam. The language of its founder and his "helpers," the language of the Korān "sent down" from God to Mohammed by the angel Gabriel, the language therefore in which it has always been preserved by the faithful, untranslated, whithersoever it has spread in the wide world of Islam, Arab. is identified with Islam in its origin, its history, its lit. and its propaganda. All the points of contact between the religion of the Bible and the religion of the Korān, literary, historical, apologetic and missionary, are alike in this, that they demand of the intelligent student of Christianity a sympathetic acquaintance with the genius and the masterpieces of the great Arab. tongue.

J. Oscar Boyd

ARABIC VERSIONS, ar'a-bik vûr'shuns: Arab. trs of the Bible must have been made at a very early date, for Christianity and Judaism had penetrated far into Arabia by the 6th cent. of our era, but the oldest of which a copy has come down to our time is that of Saadiah the Gaon (942 AD). This version was made directly from the MT and is said to have covered the whole of the OT, but much of it is no longer extant. It is characterized by an avoidance of anthropomorphisms (e.g. Gen **6** 2, "sons of nobles" and "daughters of common people") and by giving modern equivalents, e.g. Turks, Franks, Chinese, for the Heb names. Saadiah's Pent was first printed at Constantinople in 1546 and was incorporated into the Paris (1629–45) and London (1657) Polyglots. When, after the rise of Islam, Arab. became the common language of Syria, Egypt and N. Africa, trs were made from the LXX, from the Pesh and from Coptic. In the Polyglots the tr of Joshua is, like the Pent, made from the MT, as also portions of Kings and Nehemiah, with interpolations from the Pesh. Judges, Ruth, 1 and 2 Samuel, 1 and 2 Kings (in parts), 1 and 2 Chronicles (?), Nehemiah (in parts) and Job have been trd into Arab. from Syr. The remaining books (Prophets, Psalms, Proverbs, etc) are from the LXX, and that according to Codex A. In the NT the Gospels have been trd from the Vulg, and the remaining books, although from the Gr, are late. A revised edition of the versions in Walton's Polyglot was published by J. D. Carlyle, professor of Arab. in Cambridge, and printed at Newcastle by Sarah Hodgson in 1811. A very fine tr of the entire Bible in classical Arab. has been issued by the Jesuit Fathers in Beirût, and a simpler version in Arab. which can be understood by the common people, educated and uneducated alike, was made by the late Dr. Cornelius Van Dyck of the Syrian Protestant College and published by the American Press in Beirût. Dr. Van Dyck had the benefit of the help and advice of the Sheikh Nāṣîf al-Yāziji.

A large number of MSS of the Bible in Arab., in whole or in part, are to be found in the British Museum, the Bibliothèque Nationale and the great libraries of the Continent, but none of them are of sufficient age to make them of value for the criticism of the text.

Thomas Hunter Weir

ARABOTH, ar'a-both. See Arubboth.

ARAD, ā'rad (עֲרָד, *'ărādh;* **'Αράδ,** *Arád*):

(1) A city mentioned four times in the OT. In AV it is twice mistakenly rendered as the name of a king (Nu **21** 1; **33** 40). Three times it is spoken of as in the South Country, one mention using the phrase 'the wilderness of Judah which is in the South Country of Arad' (Jgs **1** 16), that is, the part of the wilderness of Judah which is in the South Country near Arad. It was situated near the frontier of Judah and Simeon, being grouped with Debir, Hormah, Makkedah, etc (Josh **12** 14). Arad and other cities joined in attacking Israel in the fortieth year of the sojourn in the wilderness (Nu **21** 1–3), and Israel vowed to "make their cities a devoted thing." In the case of Zephath, one of the cities, this vow was fulfilled after the death of Joshua (Jgs **1** 17). The Kenite relatives of Moses had their inheritance near Arad (Jgs **1** 16). In the form *a-ru-dâ* the city is mentioned by Shishak of Egypt as among the places which he conquered in Pal. The identification of the site with *Tel Arad,* about 17 miles S. of Hebron, seems to be generally accepted.

(2) One of the descendants of Elpaal the son of Shaharaim, mentioned among the descendants of Benjamin (1 Ch **8** 15).

Willis J. Beecher

ARADUS, ar'a-dus (**"Αραδος,** *Árados,* 1 Macc **15** 23): Gr name of the OT Arvad (q.v.), a city on the coast of Phoenicia.

ARAH, ā'ra (אָרַח, *'ārah,* "traveler"?): (1) The son of Ulla, an Asherite (1 Ch **7** 39). (2) The head of a family that returned from the exile with Zerubbabel (Ezr **2** 5; Neh **7** 10). He is sometimes identified with Arah of Neh **6** 18 whose granddaughter became the wife of Tobiah, the Ammonite who tried to thwart Nehemiah in rebuilding Jerus.

ARAM, ā′ram (אֲרָם, *'ărām*): (1) A son of Shem (Gen **10** 22; 1 Ch **1** 17). See Arameans; Syria. (2) A grandson of Nahor (Gen **22** 21). (3) A descendant of Asher (1 Ch **7** 34). (4) Ἀράμ, *Arám*, AV: Gr form of *Ram* (thus RV Mt **1** 3.4; *Arní* Lk **3** 33), grandson of Perez.

ARAMAEANS, ARAMEANS, ar-a-mē′ans: Often in AV and RV **Syrians**. See Syria.

ARAMAIC LANGUAGE, ar-a-mā′ik lan̦′gwāj (אֲרָמִית, *'ărāmīth;* AV **Syrian, Syriac; SYRIAN** in RV):

1. Early Notices in Scripture
2. Extra-Biblical Evidences of Aramaic
3. The Script of Aramaic
4. Dialects of Aramaic
5. Grammatical Peculiarities
6. Comparison of Aramaic of Sinjirli with That of Bible
7. Comparison of Aramaic of Assouan with That of Daniel
8. Elephantine Papyri
9. Comparison with Aramaic of Targums
10. Chief Differences in Latter

Literature

The name is given to a form of Sem speech, most nearly related to Heb and Phoen, but exhibiting marked peculiarities, and subsisting in different dialects. Its original home may have been in Mesopotamia (Aram), but it spread N. and W., and, as below shown, became the principal tongue throughout extensive regions. After the return from the Captivity, it displaced Heb as the spoken language of the Jews in Pal. In its eastern form it is known as Syr. In its occurrence in the OT, it formerly, though incorrectly, generally bore the name Chaldee. The present article deals with it chiefly in its OT relations.

1. Early Notices of Aramaic in Scripture

If we neglect two words which occur in Gen **31** 47, the earliest notice of the use of this language in Scripture is in the request which the representatives of Hezekiah make to Rabshakeh: "Speak, I pray thee, to thy servants in the Syr language" (*'ărāmīth*, 2 K **18** 26; Isa **36** 11). The narrative from which we have made this excerpt, even if it stood alone, would prove that Aram., "the Syr language," was so different from Heb, "the Jews' language," that it was not understood by the inhabitants of Jerus. Further, it shows that Aram. was the ordinary language of Assyr diplomacy. We next meet with Aram. in a ver in Jer **10** 11 which appears to be an answer put into the mouths of the Jews as a reply to any attempt to seduce them to the worship of idols. If we assume the traditional date of Daniel to be correct, the six chs in that book (Dnl **2** 4—**7** 28), forming the greater part of the whole, are the next and most important occurrence of Aram. in Scripture. There are, further, passages in Ezr **4** 8—**6** 18; **7** 12–26, amounting approximately to three chs, in which Aram. is used. In the NT several Aram. words and phrases occur, modified by having passed through Gr.

2. Extra-Biblical Evidences of Aramaic

Formerly our knowledge of Aram. earlier than the Tgs and the Pesh was restricted to the above-noticed passages of Scripture. Now, however, discoveries, still comparatively recent, have put us in a different position. In the closing decade of last cent. extensive inscriptions were discovered in Sinjirli, in the neighborhood of Aleppo, dated in the reigns of Tiglath-pileser and the Sargonid monarchs, and one that seems earlier. More recent has been the discovery of the Assouan papyri; these bear dates which synchronize with Ezra and Nehemiah. Earlier than these in discovery, but between them in date of origin, are weights of the reign of Sargon, with two inscriptions, one, official, in cuneiform, which not only gives the designation of the weight, but relates the name and titles of the king; the other, popular, in Aram., which only tells the weight. More striking is the fact that frequently, in regard to contract tablets, while the binding document is in cuneiform character and the Assyr language, the inscription on the clay envelope which served as a docquet is in Aram., language and letter. This affords proof that at all events before the reign of Tiglath-pileser Aram. was the general speech for commerce and diplomacy all over S.W. Asia.

3. The Script of Aramaic Inscriptions

When we come in contact with it, Aram. is a fully formed alphabetical language, and has attained a further stage of development than the Assyr with its cumbrous cuneiform. To the end, Assyr was largely ideographic and hieroglyphic. The same group of symbols represented very different sounds according to circumstances, and widely differing meanings were connected with the same sound, with the consequent necessity for determinatives. The alphabet employed in Aram. is practically that found on the Moabite Stone. It evidently stands at the end of a long process of evolution. It is probable that a hieroglyphic stood behind it; whether it is derived from the Hittite (Conder), or from Egyp (Rougé), or Assyr (Delitzsch), or is of independent origin (Gesenius), cannot be determined. Aram. is, like Heb and Assyr, a North Sem tongue, standing in a manner between them. It is more regular in its formation than either of the others, a character that may to some extent be due to its use as a *lingua franca* over so wide a territory. Aram. was the official language of the extensive Pers empire, as it had been to some extent that of its predecessor, the empire of Assyria. It may be regarded as having been generally understood from Asia Minor on the N., to the Cataracts of the Nile on the S., and from the mountains of Media on the E., to the Mediterranean on the W. Its history has been long; spoken, as we learn by inscriptions, from before the days of Tiglath-pileser, it is still spoken on the banks of the Tigris and the Euphrates.

4. Dialects of Aramaic

These extensive limits, geographical and chronological, imply dialectic differences. Means of communication were so ineffective that the distance between the eastern and western limits would require greater time to traverse, than does that which separates America from Europe, or New York from Brazil. The primary dialectic distinction was between eastern Aram. (Syr) and western (formerly called Chaldee). The peculiarity which most prominently distinguishes these is the preformative of the imperfect; in the western, as in Heb and Arab., it is *yodh*, while in the eastern it is *nun* or *lāmedh*. Each of these has sub-dialects. In Pal, besides the Chaldee of the Jewish Tgs, there was Sam; in it, besides many foreign elements in the vocabulary, the use of *'ayin* instead of *vav* in the preterite of *'ayin-vav* verbs is the most striking feature. The sub-dialect of eastern Aram. is Mandaean; it is characterized by the use of the *matres lectionis* instead of vowel signs. From the inscriptions and the papyri it would seem to follow that the eastern peculiarities are the more recent—changes introduced through passage of time. In eastern Aram. the script became more cursive than in western, which retained the square character we associate with Heb: except the Sam, which used a still earlier script, less removed from the angular style of the inscriptions. The script of the Assouan papyri indicated a tendency toward the later square character.

Although an article like the present is not the place to give a full grammar of Aram., yet we may advert to some of the more prominent peculiarities, common to all branches of the language, which distinguish it from Heb, the best-known of north Sem tongues. The peculiarity that most strikes the beginner in Aram. is the want of the article, and the presence instead of the *status emphaticus*, which follows the syntactic rules of the Heb article. The next thing likely to attract attention is the use of the relative pronoun *zī* or *dī* as if it were a preposition meaning "of." While in Heb the passive voice is generally indicated in the derived conjugations by internal vocalic changes, as the *pu'al* from the *pi'el;* in Aram. the syllable *'eth* (E) or *'ith* (W) is prefixed (earlier *hith*). Instead of the Heb causative *hiph'īl* there is the *'aph'ēl* (earlier *haph'ēl* with its passive *'ethtaph'al* or *'ittaph'al* (earlier *hoph'al*). The causative had also *shaph'ēl* and *taph'ēl* forms, which occasionally are found. While in the Tgs and the OT Pesh the syllable *yath* is the sign of the accusative (earlier *vath*, as in the Sinjirli inscriptions), the letter *lāmedh* serves that purpose in Aram. which is not a tr from Heb. A characteristic of later Aram. prominent in the Pesh of the NT is the facility with which it adopted words and phrases from Gr which had already largely displaced it as the common language. New Syr shows a similar facility in regard to Arab. and Pers.

5. Grammatical Peculiarities of Aramaic

A question of very considerable importance to the Biblical student is the relation in which the Aram. of Daniel and Ezra stands to that of the Sinjirli inscriptions and that of the more nearly contemporary Assouan papyri. In making the comparison we must bear in mind that the Heb MT is the result of transcriptions extending over 1,500 or 1,200 years, according as we take the traditional or the critical dates for the books in question. This implies probably a score or more of transcriptions each with its quota of variations from the original. While the variations introduced by any one transcription might be few and unimportant, they would all be in the direction of lateness, and cumulatively might easily become very great. The late Heb of Ecclesiastes, notwithstanding its ascription to Solomon, shows how little the idea of the chronology of style entered into the thoughts of the scribes of those days, to check this tendency to modernization. It follows that while the presence of late peculiarities proves nothing but the inaccuracy of the copyist, early grammatical forms and modes of spelling are nearly indisputable evidences of antiquity.

6. Comparison of the Aramaic of Sinjirli with That of the Bible

The Sinjirli inscriptions, if we neglect the less important, are three, the Panammu inscription, the Hadad inscription and the Barrekab inscription (*Bauenschrift*, Sachau). The first and last of these are dated in the reign of Tiglath-pileser, the middle one is placed by Sachau in the preceding cent. It ought to be noted that, when first discovered, it was a matter of doubt whether the inscriptions should not be reckoned as Heb, rather than Aram. The close affinity between them and Heb is shown in various ways. By a relation among the north Sem tongues similar to that among the Aryan languages expressed by Grimm's law, where letters with the *s*-sound appear in Heb, in later Aram. we find corresponding letters with the *t*-sound. But in the Sinjirli inscriptions we do not find this mark of the later language; thus we have *shᵉḳēl*, not *thᵉkēl*, *shᵉlāthīn* instead of *tᵉlāthīn*, *zᵉhābh* for *dhᵉhābh*, etc. That this is not due to the proximity of Heb is proved by the fact that on the weights in Sargon's palace we find *sheḳel*. Thus the Sinjirli inscriptions date from a period when Heb and Aram. had not been completely differentiated. There are other points of likeness. Instead of the *'aph'ēl* and *'ethtaph'al* or *'ittaph'al* of later Aramaic, there is *haph'ēl* and *hoph'al;* instead of the *'eth* or *'ith* as the sign of the passive, there is *hith*. The vocabularies also are nearly identical. In both, the syllable *yath* or *vath*, sign of the accusative, is present, as if a survival, only as the support of the oblique case of a pronoun (Dnl **3** 12; Sinjirli, Had 28). The pronouns exhibit a similar resemblance to Heb and also to Biblical Aramaic. The 1st per. pronoun is *'anōkh* (once *'anōkhī* in Pan. l. 19), as in the Phoen and Moabite dialects of Heb; *'ănāh* occurs occasionally as in Daniel. The most marked differences from later Aram. is *z* instead of *dh* in the demonstrative pronoun; here there is relation to the Heb *zeh*. Another case in frequent evidence is *'arḳā'* instead of *'ar'ā*.

7. Comparison of Aramaic of Assouan with That of Daniel

More nearly contemporary with the Aram. of Daniel and Ezra is that of the Assouan papyri. These are carefully dated, and extend from 471 BC to 411 BC; these two dates include the whole reign of Artaxerxes I, the king whose cupbearer Nehemiah was, and who sent him as governor to Jerus, and a few years of his predecessor's and successor's reigns. These documents, as written with a reed pen on papyrus, and not cut with a chisel on stone, manifest a very different style of letter; as already said, there is some approximation to the later square character. The resemblance between the grammar and vocabulary of these papyri and those of Biblical Aram. is closer than that of the latter to the Sinjirli grammar and diction. Where, in the more ancient Aram., we have *z*, in these papyri we occasionally find the later *dh*. It is not improbable that, as in Spain, a lisping pronunciation became prevalent; the *dh* pronounced as *th* in "then" would in that case represent more accurately the sound actually uttered than would *z*. The word already noticed, *'arḳā'* which generally appears in Biblical Aram. as *'ar'ā*, is a similar case. In northern Palestine the Arab. *ḳaf* is pronounced much as if it were *'ain*, if not even the related sound *hemzeh;* instances of this spelling also are found in the Assouan papyri. Both of these differences are due to frequent transcription assimilating the spelling to the pronunciation. Another peculiarity is probably due to a different cause. In Biblical Aram. the preformative of the 3d per. sing. and plur. of the impf. of the substantive verb is *lāmedh*. Of this peculiarity Dr. Bevan gives an ingenious explanation. If the *yodh* preformative were used, the resulting word would have a resemblance to the sacred name: to avoid this, he thinks, the *yodh* was changed into a *lāmedh*. Unfortunately this explains too much, therefore explains nothing. Had this been the explanation, the name "Jehu," which consonantally is nearly the same as the 3d per. sing. and plur. of the substantive verb, would never have been written as it is. Further, if Jewish reverence for the Divine name expressed itself in this way, we should expect to find this preformative in the Tgs, which, however, we do not. Hundreds of cases in proof may be found in Onkelos alone. The truth is, it is a Mandaean form, which proves that the Aram. of Daniel and Ezra is eastern. A further peculiarity is the *nun* compensative; as *tinda'* (Dnl **4** 23), which regularly would be *tidda'*. This also is found in the Mandaean; it is, however, also found in papyri of Assouan, an evidence that the Mandaean characteristic was a survival from an earlier time.

Another interesting point of contact between the Aram. of this period and that of Daniel is exhibited in the Elephantine papyri published by Sachau. These papyri, discovered in the island of Elephantine (opposite Assouan) in 1907, are three in number, and are dated in the 14th year of Darius II (407 BC). In the first, ll. 2, 27, 28, the second, l. 26, and the third ll. 3, 4, we have God called "the God of heaven," the title given to God throughout Dnl 2. This is also the appellation used in the Aram. of Ezra (**5** 11.12; **6** 9 etc.) From the passages where it occurs it would seem that during the Bab and Pers rule this was the recognized governmental title of the God of the Hebrews.

8. Elephantine Papyri

As it is frequently asserted that the Aram. of Daniel and Ezra is that of the Tgs, it is necessary to examine the truth of this statement. In considering this question we must have regard to the history of these paraphrases, as only in this way can we estimate truly the chronological value of this "great" resemblance, should it be found to exist. According to Talmudic tradition the Tgs were delivered orally, and were not committed to writing till late in the 2d cent. of our era. A traditional rendering was handed on from *m^e^turg^e^mān* (interpreter) to *m^e^turg^e^mān*. In such circumstances archaic forms, words and idioms, are perpetuated. The sacred always tends to preserve the antique; in illustration we need only refer to the song of the *Fratres Arvales*, a college of priests dating from primitive Lat times and continuing to the days of the Gordians. This sacred song of theirs preserves to us the most ancient form of the Lat tongue, though the inscriptions, from which we learn of it, date from the classic period. Hence the Aram. of the Tgs may represent the form of the language a couple of cents. before the Christian era.

9. Comparison with Aramaic of the Targums

We cannot attempt to give an exhaustive summary of the differences between Biblical and Targumic Aram., but indicate only some of the more obvious. Account need not be taken of *yath*, the sign of the accusative, as it appears only as representing the Heb *'eth*. In verbs, reference has already been made to the *l* preformative in the substantive verb, a peculiarity which Biblical Aram. shares with Mandaean in distinction from other forms of the language: also to the fact that the *hith* of the earlier verbal forms is replaced by *'ith* in the more recent *'ithp^e^'ēl* and *'ithpa'al*. This also is the case with *'aph'ēl* (in earlier and Biblical Aram. *haph'ēl*), the passive of which is *hoph'al*, not *'ittaph'al*, as in Targumic. The importance of verbal forms in determining age is readily recognized; thus in English, if the 3d per. sing. of the verbs in an English writing is in *eth* we decide that writing to belong, in fact or feigning, to a period not later than the 17th cent. In regard to pronouns, while in Biblical Aram., as in Sinjirli and Assouan, the 1st per. sing. is *'an'ā*, in Targumic it is *'ănāh:* the plur. in Biblical Aram. is *'ănaḥnā'* akin to *'ănaḥnāh* in Assouan, whereas in the Tgs it is usually *'ănān*, though sometimes the Biblical form appears. The 2d per. sing. in Biblical Aram. is *'ant* as in Assouan, with the plur. *'antūm* (Assouan, *'antem*): in Targumic it is *'att* and *'attūn*. To compare our own language, when we find "thou" and "ye" in a writing, we date it as not later than the 17th cent. The ordinary vocabulary, though not without value in this respect, is not very important chronologically. Connective particles, however, are. Everyone acquainted with Heb knows how frequently *yēsh*, "is," occurs; as frequent is *'īth* in Targumic. In the Bible, as in the papyri, the form found is *'īthi*. In the Tgs *'ī* stands for "if"; in the Bible and papyri it is *hēn*. Cognate with this, the Bible and the papyri have *lāhēn*, "therefore": this is not found in the Tgs, which have instead *'al-kēn*. In our own language the presence of "eke" in serious prose or poetry as a conjunction would prove the antiquity of the composition. The fact that the distinction between ס and שׂ has disappeared in the Tgs, but is still preserved in the Bible, is a note of age that cannot be passed over. Other examples might be given, but these will suffice. Professor Bevan lightly dismisses many of these differences as mere matters of orthography; yet in French the presence of *l* for *u* or as strengthening the *u* in such words as *alx, eulx, aultres* is regarded as a note of old as distinct from modern French; yet probably the pronunciation was not different.

10. Chief Differences

In pursuing this part of the subject the latter portion of Pusey's first Lecture (*Daniel the Prophet*) is worthy of study. Pusey had not the advantage of contemporary documents with which to compare Biblical Aram.; he could only emphasize the nature and amount of the differences which separated the language of Daniel from that of the Tgs. The argument can now be supplemented by a yet stronger argument from the resemblance between the former and the contemporary papyri of Assouan, and yet the earlier Sinjirli inscriptions.

See further, SYRIAC; LANGUAGES OF THE OT; and cf art. "Aramaic" in *EB*.

LITERATURE.—Numerous grammars and dictionaries of the two principal dialects of Aram., eastern (Syr) and western (Chaldee) may be seen in any catalogues. There is an excellent compendium of the grammar of Biblical Aram. in Delitzsch's intro to Baer's Text of Dnl and Ezr. For Sam there is a small grammar by Nicholls, also one in the series "Porta Linguarum Orientalium." Nöldeke has published grammars for Mandaean and New Syr.

J. E. H. THOMSON

ARAMAIC VERSIONS. See TARGUMS.

ARAM-DAMMESEK, ā-ram-dam'es-ek: Syria of Damascus, conquered by David (2 S **8** 5.6). See SYRIA.

ARAMITESS, ar-am-īt'es, ar'am-īt-es, ar'am-it-es (אֲרַמִּיָּה, *'ărammīyāh*): The term applied to the concubine-mother of Machir, the father of Gilead (1 Ch **7** 14); the inhabitants of Gilead were thus in part Aramaeans (Syrians) by descent.

ARAM-MAACAH, ā-ram-mā'a-ka. See SYRIA.

ARAM-NAHARAIM, ā-ram-nā-ha-rā'im. See SYRIA.

ARAM-REHOB, ā-ram-rē'hob. See SYRIA.

ARAM-ZOBAH, ā-ram-zō'ba. See SYRIA.

ARAN, ā'ran (אֲרָן, *'ărān*, "wild goat"): A son of Dishan, the Horite (Gen **36** 28; 1 Ch **1** 42). It may possibly be connected with the Yerahmelite Oren (אֹרֶן) (1 Ch **2** 25; cf Curtis, *Chron.* ad loc.; Dillmann, *Gen* ad loc.; *ZDMG*, L, 168); Robertson Smith claims that this name is equivalent to the Sam ארן, "wild goat" (*Jour. Phil.*, IX, 90). J. Jacobs translates it by "ass" (*Stud. Bib. Arch.*, 71). This is one of the many totem names in the Bible. More than one-third of the Horites, the descendants of Seir, bear animal names, and those clans of the Edomites connected with the Horites also have animal names. The very name "Seir" means a "he-goat," and Dishan, "a gazelle" (*Stud. Bib. Arch.*, 70–72). Gray, however, remarks that "the instance [Aran] is most uncertain" (*HPN*, 108).

SAMUEL COHON

ARARAH. Same as ARARAT (Tob **1** 21).

ARARAT, ar'a-rat (אֲרָרָט, *'ărārāṭ*): A mountainous plateau in western Asia from which flow in different directions the Euphrates, the Tigris, the Aras and the Choruk rivers. Its general elevation is 6,000 feet above the sea. Lake Van, which like the Dead Sea has no outlet, is nearly in its center. The Bab name was Urartu, the consonants being the same in both words. In 2 K **19** 37 and Isa **37** 38 the word is tr[d] in AV **Armenia,** which correctly represents the region designated. It was to Armenia that the sons of Sennacherib fled. In Jer **51** 27 Ararat is associated with Minni and Ashkenaz, which according to the Assyr monuments lay just to the east of Armenia. In Gen **8** 4 the ark is said to have rested "upon the mountains of Ararat," i.e. in the mountainous region of Armenia, the plur. showing that the mountain peak known as Ararat was not referred to. This peak is of volcanic origin and lies outside the general region, rising from the lowlands of the Araxes (Aras) River to a height of 17,000 feet, supported by another peak seven miles distant, 13,000 feet high. It is only in comparatively modern times that the present name has been given to it. The Armenians still call it Massis, but believe, however, that Noah was buried at Nachitchevan near its base.

The original name of the kingdom occupying Armenia was Bianias, which Ptolemy transliterated Byana. Later the B was modified into V and we have the modern Van, the present capital of the province. The "mountains of Ararat" on which the ark rested were probably those of the Kurdish range which separates Armenia from Mesopotamia and Kurdistan. In the Bab account the place is called "the mountain of Nizir" which is east of Assyria. Likewise Berosus locates the place "in the mountain of the Kordyaeans" or Kurds (*Ant*, I, iii, 6), while the Syr version has Hardu in Gen **8** 4 instead of Ararat. The Kurds still regard Jebel Judi, a mountain on the boundary between Armenia and Kurdistan, as the place where the ark rested.

This elevated plateau of Armenia has still many attractions, and is eminently suited to have been the center from which the human race spread in all directions. Notwithstanding its high elevation the region is fertile, furnishing abundant pasture, and producing good crops of wheat and barley, while the vine is indigenous. Moreover there are unmistakable indications that in early historic times there was a much more abundant rainfall in all that region than there is now, so that the climate was then better adapted to the wants of primitive man. This is shown by the elevated beaches surrounding lakes Van, Urumiah, and, indeed, all the lakes of central Asia. Great quantities of mammoth bones have been found in these bordering lacustrine deposits corresponding to those found in the glacial and postglacial deposits of Europe and America. It should, also, be remembered that the drying up of the waters of the flood is represented to have been very gradual—it being 170 days from the time the waters began to subside before Noah could disembark. It may have been many cents. before the present conditions were established, the climate, meanwhile, being modified to a corresponding degree by the proximity of vast surrounding bodies of water.

Armenia abounds in inscriptions carved on the rocks, altar stones and columns, but they have been only imperfectly translated. The script is cuneiform and each letter has only a single phonetic character attached to it. But there are introduced a good many borrowed ideographs which have assisted in the decipherment. According to Sayce this cuneiform syllabary was introduced from Assyria after the conquest of Shalmaneser II in the 9th cent. BC.

George Frederick Wright

ARARATH, ar'a-rath: Same as Ararat (q.v.).

ARATHES, a-rā'thēz (AV **Araiarthes;** **'Αράθης,** *Aráthēs;* **'Αριαράθης,** *Ariaráthēs*): King of Cappadocia, 163–130 BC. Educated in Rome, he imbibed Rom ideas and became a faithful ally of the Romans, in conformity with whose wishes he declined a proposal of marriage with the sister of Demetrius Soter. The latter declared war, drove Arathes from his kingdom and set up Holophernes in his stead. He fled to Rome about 158, and through the good offices of the Romans succeeded in obtaining for himself a participation in the government of Cappadocia. Later he again became sole king. In 139 BC, as a result of an embassy sent by Simon Maccabaeus, the Romans wrote letters to Arathes (1 Macc **15** 22) and other eastern kings in behalf of the Jews. (See Diodor. XXXI, 19, 28, 32; Justin, XXXV, 1; Polyb. III, 5; XXXII, 20–30; XXXIII, 12).

J. E. Harry

ARAUNAH, a-rô'na (אֲרַוְנָה, *'ărawnāh*, 2 S **24** 16.20 ff; אֲרַנְיָה, *'ăranyāh*, 2 S **24** 18, and אָרְנָן, *'ornān*, 1 Ch **21** 15 ff; 2 Ch **3** 1, all from a Heb root meaning "to be strong"): A Jebusite from whom David at the request of the prophet Gad bought a threshing-floor located upon Mt. Moriah, as a site for an altar of the Lord at the time of the great plague (2 S **24** 15 ff; 1 Ch **21** 15 ff), upon which Solomon later erected the temple (2 Ch **3** 1).

ARBA, CITY OF. See Kiriath-arba.

ARBA, ar'ba (אַרְבַּע, *'arba'*, "four"): Variously described as "the greatest man among the Anakim" (Josh **14** 15), "the father of Anak" (**15** 13), "the father of Anok" (**21** 11m). Thus he seems to have been regarded as the ancestor of the Anakim, and as the most famous hero of that race. He was the reputed founder of the city called after him, on the site of which Hebron was built (**21** 11).

ARBATHITE, är'bath-īt (הָעַרְבָתִי, *hā-'arbhāthī*): Perhaps "a native of the Arabah." Klostermann suggests "a native of Beth-arabah." The Arbathite is Abi-albon (2 S **23** 31), also named Abiel (1 Ch **11** 32), one of David's heroes.

ARBATTA, är-bat'a, AV **Arbattis,** är-bat'is (**ἐν 'Αρβάττοις** [plur.], *en Arbáttois*): Apparently a district in the neighborhood of Galilee, from which the Jews who were in danger of attack by the heathen were carried by Simon Maccabaeus to Jerus (1 Macc **5** 21 ff). It cannot be identified with certainty. Ewald (*Hist*, V, 314, Eng. tr) favors *el-Baṭeiḥa*, the plain through which the Jordan flows into the Lake of Galilee. *EB* (s.v.) suggests "the Arabah, or Araboth of Jordan." Possibly however we should look for it in the toparchy of Akrabattis, to the S.E. of Shechem (*BJ*, III, iii, 4 f).

W. Ewing

ARBELA, är-bē'la (**ἐν 'Αρβήλοις,** *en Arbēlois*): This place is mentioned in 1 Macc **9** 1 ff, and in *Ant*, XII, xi, 1, describing the march and encampment of Bacchides. The former says that "Demetrius sent Bacchides and Alcimus into the land of Judaea . . . . who went forth by the way that leadeth to Galgala, and pitched their tents before Masaloth, which is in Arbela, and after they had won it they slew much people." Jos says that Bacchides "marched out of Antioch and came into Judaea and pitched his camp at Arbela, a city of Galilee, and having besieged and taken those that were there in caves (for many people fled into such places), he removed and made all the haste he could to Jerusalem." It was from the caves near the village of Arbela in Galilee that Herod dislodged the robbers (*Ant*, XIV, xv, 4 f; *BJ*, I, xvi, 2 ff). Jos fortified the caves of Arbela in lower Galilee (*Vita*, 37), "near the lake of Gennesar" (*BJ*, II, xx, 6).

The references in Jos point plainly to the caves in the cliff forming the south wall of the tremendous gorge of *Wādy el-Ḥamām* which opens on the plain of Gennesaret, west of the village *el-Mejdel*. A series of these caves, skilfully adapted to purposes of refuge and defence, is still known as *Qal'at ibn Ma'ān*, "fortress of the son of Ma'ān." On the height above stand the ruins of *Irbid* or *Irbil* (both forms are heard today), which unquestionably represent the Arbela of Jos. The army from Antioch may quite well have come this way. No name however in the least resembling Masaloth has been recovered in this district. We may mention Robinson's suggestion (*BR*, II, 398, n.), that it may stand for the Heb *m^eṣillōth*, "steps, stories, terraces," and may apply to the fortress in the rocks.

On the other hand the writer of 1 Macc is an earlier authority than Jos. If we accept his guidance, Bacchides must have crossed the plain of Esdraelon and followed the main highway southward through Samaria. Galgala may then be identified with *Jiljilia*, about 8 miles N. of Bethel, and Masaloth with *Meselieh*, about 3 miles S.E. of Dothan. *Onom* mentions an Arbela in the great plain, 9 miles from Legio (*Lejjūn*), but it is now unknown. The phrase *en arbēlois* might mean that Masaloth was in the district of Arbela; but there is no trace of this name as attaching to any tract in this neighborhood.

One or other of these routes must have been taken. While no certain decision can be reached, special weight attaches to the statement of Jos, on account of his acquaintance with the localities in the region, and his unquestionable familiarity with the history. See also BETH-ARBEL. W. EWING

ARBITE, är'bīt (הָאַרְבִּי, *hā-'arbī*): The Arbite or perhaps an inhabitant of Arabia in southern Judah (Josh **15** 52). The epithet is used in connection with one of David's mighty men in 2 S **23** 35; where Paarai the Arbite occurs. In the ‖ list (1 Ch **11** 37) we have Naarai the son of Ezbai.

ARBONAI, ar-bō'nai, ar-bō'nā-ī (**'Αβρωνᾶ**, *Abrōná*): A torrent mentioned in Jth **2** 24. Beyond what is indicated in this passage, it is not possible to determine the location; but from this it appears to have been near Cilicia. Identification with the modern Nahr Ibrahim is rejected on the ground (1) that the ancient name of this river was Adonis, and (2) that this does not answer to the term "torrent" applied by Judith. A possible misreading of "the high cities that were בעבר הנהר," *b^e'ēbher ha-nāhār* ("beyond the river"; *EB* s.v.).

ARCH, ärch (אַיִל, *'ayil;* LXX **τὰ αἰλάμ**, *tá ailám*, in sense of "posts" or "colonnade"): Referred to repeatedly in Ezk **40** 16 ff, but tr is an error for "porch" or "portico." RV gives in marg, "or, *colonnade.* The meaning of the Heb word is uncertain." The principle of arch construction was known to the Jews and examples of early Jewish rude arches have been found in Pal. An arched form need not necessarily be constructed with radiating joints; it can be corbelled as at Mycenae (Treasury of Atreus). This type of construction has been found also in Pal.

ARCHAEOLOGY, är-kē-ol'o-ji, **AND CRITICISM**, krit'i-siz'm: Archaeology, the science of antiquities, is in this article limited to the Biblical field, a field which has been variously delimited (De Wette, 1814, Gesenius), but which properly includes not only all ancient facts bearing upon the Bible which had been lost and have been recovered, but all literary remains of antiquity bearing upon the Bible and, also, as of the first importance, the Bible itself (Hogarth, *Authority and Archaeology*, vi).

Scope of Article

Criticism, the art of scrutiny, is here limited mainly, though not exclusively, to the literary criticism of the Bible, now, following Eichhorn, commonly called the Higher Criticism. Thus "Archaeology and Criticism," the title of this art., is meant to designate the bearing of the archaeology of Bible lands upon the criticism, esp. the Higher Criticism, of the Bible. The subject as thus defined calls for the discussion of, I. What archaeology can do in the case—the powers, rights and authority, that is to say, the **Function** of archaeology in criticism; and II. What archaeology has done in the case, the resulting effects of such archaeological evidence, that is to say, the **History** of the bearing of archaeology upon the criticism of the Bible.

I. Function.—The function of archaeology in criticism has only recently been given much attention and the opinions thereon have varied greatly.

1. Ignored by Encyclopaedists

(*a*) Biblical encyclopaedists generally, until the most recent, have not given this subject a place at all (*HDB*, *EB*, *DB*, Kitto, *Enc Bib. Lit.*, Hamburger, *RE*, Eadie, *Bib. Enc*). McClintock and Strong's *Enc Bib. and Eccles Lit.* has an art. on "Bib. Arch." consisting entirely of bibliography, also an art. of a general character under "Sac. Ant." The *Sch-Herz Enc* has an art., *The Catholic Enc*, 1907, has an art. under the title "Biblical Antiquities," and the *Jew Enc*, 1902, has an art. of five pages on "Bib. Arch." But on the function of archaeology in criticism there is almost nothing anywhere.

2. Variously Estimated by Critics

(*b*) Critics have varied much in their estimate of the value of archaeology in criticism, according to their individual predilections and their critical theories, but until very recently archaeology has not generally been given a commanding, or even a prominent, place in criticism. Wellhausen seems to declare for the dominancy of archaeology in criticism in the beginning of his *History of Israel*, though he very much ignores it in the pages that follow (*Hist of Israel*, 12). Driver (*Authority and Archaeology*, 143–50), thinks "testimony of archaeology sometimes determines the question decisively," but is "often strangely misunderstood," and the defeats of criticism at the hands of archaeology are often "purely imaginary" (*LOT*, 1897, 4). Orr thinks "archaeology bids fair before long to control both criticism and history" (*POT*, 305–435). Eerdmans, successor to Kuenen at Leyden, definitely and absolutely breaks with the Wellhausen school of criticism, chiefly on the ground that archaeology has discredited their viewpoint and the historical atmosphere with which they have surrounded the OT. Wiener, the most prominent of recent Jewish critics, also believes that a proper apprehension of the nature of ancient institutions, customs, documents and codes, i.e. archaeology, and esp. the archaeology of the Bible itself, is clearly decisive in its influence on the issue raised by the Wellhausen school (*BS*, 1908–10).

3. Urged by Archaeologists

(*c*) Archaeologists generally for a long time have been putting forward the superior claims of their science in the critical controversy (Brugsch, *Egypt under the Pharaohs;* Naville, *Recueil de Travaux*, IV, N.S.; Petrie, *Hyksos and Israelite Cities*, chs i–iv; *Researches in Sinai*, 188–223; Spiegelberg, *Aufenthalt Israels in Aegypten;* Steindorf, *Explorations in Bible Lands* [Hilprecht], 623–90; Sayce, *Higher Criticism and the Monuments;* Hommel, *Ancient Heb Tradition*, xi; Jeremias, *Das alte Testament im Lichte des alten Orients*).

The function of archaeology in criticism, as fully brought to light by recent discussion, is as follows:

1. *Historical setting.*—Archaeology furnishes the true historical setting of Scripture. In the criticism of a painting, it is of the utmost importance to hang the picture aright before criticism begins. It is not greatly different in the criticism of lit., and esp. Bib. lit. The patriarchs and prophets and psalmists are the "old masters" of spirituality and of religious lit.; their productions were brought forth under certain social, political, moral and religious conditions, and within certain surroundings of influences, enemies, opportunities, temptations and spiritual privileges. It is only archaeology that can hang their pictures aright, and it is only when thus hung that true criticism is ready to begin. The critic is only then a critic when he has seen how archaeology has hung the picture (*BST*, 1906, 366).

2. *Guidance to methods.*—Archaeology gives guidance to the *methods* of criticism. This it does; (*a*) With regard to *presuppositions*. Presuppositions are inevitable from our mental constitutions, and necessary to the consideration of any subject, since all subjects cannot be considered at once. But our presuppositions are naturally, to a large extent, those induced by our own experience and environment, until we are otherwise instructed. As it is only archaeology that is able to instruct us concerning the exact circumstances of certain portions of the Bible it is evident that, in those portions, without the instruction which archaeology can give, we cannot be assured of correct presuppositions in the critic.

4. Presuppositions

(*b*) Archaeology gives guidance concerning the *canons* of criticism. It is of the utmost importance that a literature should be judged only by the canons followed by its own literati. The innumerable literary remains of Egypt and Babylonia reveal methods and standards very different from each other, and still more different from those of modern western lit., but exhibiting to a marked degree the literary peculiarities of the OT. In Bab lit., much attention is paid to epochal chronology. In Egyp lit., comparatively little attention is given to chronology, and what chronology there is, is seldom epochal, but either synchronistic or merely annalistic. In the OT there is a mixture of all these kinds of chronology. Again, in Bab lit., there is carefulness and some degree of accuracy; in Egyp lit., carelessness, slovenliness and inaccuracy are provokingly frequent. The Scriptures of the OT are, in this respect, in striking contrast to these other literatures, yet nowhere in ancient oriental lit. is there the mathematical rigidity of statement demanded in occidental lit. today; on the other hand there is frequently a brevity and abruptness of literary method which, to western minds, appears to be fragmentariness of documents. The attempt to elucidate oriental lit. in the Bible and out of it by applying thereto the tests and standards of western lit. is not less disastrous than would be the attempt to judge western lit. by these oriental peculiarities.

5. Canons

(*c*) Archaeology gives guidance concerning *literary form.* Much of the definiteness and unity of modern lit. is due to the arts of printing and book-binding. All archaeological lit. of Bible lands, lacking, as it does, the influence of these arts, is, in form, indefinite, or fragmentary, or both. These peculiarities in form and the causes of the same, archaeology makes very plain by abundant illustration. It makes clear, also, that fragmentariness and indefiniteness in oriental lit., in so far as it arises from the literary form and not from partial destruction of documents, in no wise militates against integrity.

6. Literary Form

(*d*) Archaeology gives guidance concerning *interpretation.* Archaeology admonishes us of the truism, too often overlooked, that a language or lit. means only what it is understood to mean by those from whom it comes, so that the etymological, syntactical and speculative methods of interpretation employed in criticism, in order to be reliable, must have the support of the historical method. In the absence of this support, more especially if contemporary history as revealed by archaeology be antagonistic, interpretation, though supported by all the other methods of criticism, is very precarious. The interpretation of a rubric by the etymological and analytical methods may be partly or completely overthrown by a single picture or a brief description of the priest at the altar. For instance, it is very disquieting to compare the remarks of commentators on Bible references to the worship at high places with the facts revealed by the recent discovery of high places and the worship there conducted (Macalister, *PEFS*, 1903, 23–31; Robinson, *BW*, January, 1901; January, 1908, 219–25, 317–18; Vincent, *Canaan*, 144). Archaeology must guide in the interpretation of ancient lit., whether that which has just been dug up, as the recent finds of MSS and monuments, or that which has never been lost, as in the Bible itself.

7. Interpretation

3. *Facts to test theories.*—Archaeology supplies facts wherewith to test theories. There can be no real antagonism between the facts of archaeology and a correct literary criticism of trustworthy documents. But who or what is to determine when the criticism is correct? If there is conflict between the facts of archaeology and the conclusions of criticism, which must give way? To ask the question is to answer it. Theory must always give way to facts. "Where the testimony of archaeology is direct, it is of the highest possible value, and, as a rule, determines a question decisively; even where it is indirect, if it is sufficiently circumstantial and precise, it may make a settlement highly probable" (Driver, *Authority and Archaeology*, 143).

8. Facts and Correct Criticism Agree

This prerogative of archaeological facts in the testing of critical theories must, then, of necessity be given wide and positive recognition.

(*a*) No theory is to be finally accepted and made applicable to faith and life until *tested* and *attested* by facts; if it be a theory in the field of Nature, by the facts of Nature; if in the field of experience, by facts of experience; if in the field of history, by facts of history. The Master brings even revelation to this test when He says, "If any man willeth to do his will, he shall know of the teaching, whether it is of God, or whether I speak from myself" (Jn **7** 17). Anything in the Bible may be discredited by theory; as everything in heaven and earth may be—indeed, has been—discredited by theory. One might as safely abandon the beaten track for the most alluring but unconfirmed appearance of an eastern desert, as turn one's life aside to a theory unattested by fact. However perfect the appearance, it may, after all, be only the mirage, and the disappointed pilgrim may never get back to the safe road. Let theory first be confirmed by fact; then it may be received into the life.

9. Theories Need Attestation

(*b*) Even a theory which meets all the known conditions of the case in hand is not by that fact proved to be true, and therefore to be received into the life. The most alluring danger to which criticism is subject is the contrary assumption that a theory which meets all the known conditions of the case in hand is thereby proved to be true. This is not the case. Such a theory must, in addition, be corroborated by facts independently brought to light, or by mysteries unlocked; and even if mysteries be unlocked, the theory is not necessarily an entirely correct theory—the key that turns the lock must be something like the key that belongs to it, but may after all, be a false key. There must, in any case, whether of mysteries unlocked or of facts otherwise brought to light, be independent, genuine evidence in addition to the adaptability of the theory to all the known conditions of the case in hand. And furthermore, a theory must not only be able to meet the test of some additional facts, but the test of all the conditions imposed by any additional facts brought to light, and be able, also, to incorporate these new facts as naturally as those upon which the theory was originally constructed.

10. Success not Attestation

The *problem* is not to determine one or several of the ways in which an event might have taken place, but the one way in which it did take place. A theory which meets all the conditions of the case in hand may be one of the several ways in which the event might have taken place, but only by independent, genuine, corroborative evidence is any theory to be attested as the way in which the event actually did take place. That this statement of the case is correct in *the experiences of life*, we have abundant evidence in the proceedings of courts of law. The most careful procedure does not wholly prevent false convictions. The prosecutor presents a theory of the commission of a crime which meets all the conditions of the case as made out by the evidence, convinces twelve jurymen, and secures a conviction. Yet sometimes afterward it is found out that another person committed the crime in an entirely different way. That the dictum under discussion is inapplicable to *literature* is equally well established.

11. Theory in Life

Sir Peter LePage Renouf argued with great acuteness and force that it is possible to assign significations to an unknown script, give meanings to the words thus formed, construct a grammar and translate inscriptions as historical statements and make good sense, though not a single sign, or word, or construction, or thought be correct (*Life-work*, I, 6, 7). He says of such a method: "It is not difficult to make out the Ten Commandments, the Psalms of David, the Homeric Poems, or the Irish Melodies, on any ancient or modern monument whatever, and in any language you please."

Actual examples in fulfilment of Renouf's warning thesis are not wanting. The grotesque, yet confident, efforts at the decipherment of the Egyp hieroglyphs before the discovery of the Rosetta Stone are not forgotten. Dr. Budge says (*The Mummy*, 124): "In more modern times the first writer at any length on hieroglyphics was Athanasius Kircher, the author of some ponderous works in which he pretended to have found the key to the hieroglyphic inscriptions, and to translate them. Though a man of great learning, it must be plainly said that, judged by scholars of today, he would be considered an impostor." Joseph de Guignes (1770) maintained that China was settled by Egyptians, and the Chinese characters only degenerate Egyp hieroglyphs. Similar failures in the attempt to decipher the Hittite hieroglyphs and translate the Hittite inscriptions must form painful recollections to distinguished scholars yet living, whose efforts, extending in some cases not only to lists of signs but to syllabaries, vocabularies, grammars and translations, are now, in part, and in some cases, *in toto*, rejected by the whole learned world. However successful present or future efforts of these scholars may prove to be, they have, in part at least, themselves repudiated their former work. The most plausible theory of a lit., though it seem to embrace every detail, may, after all, be found to be, as in one or two of the instances referred to above, wholly false when tested by the principles of philology and the facts of contemporary history.

12. Theory in Literature

The dangers of unconfirmed theory in life and literature are even greater in *history*, which, in its present-day form, is but life written down, human experiences given over to all the accidents and conventionalities of lit. The warnings here from Egyp and classical history and lit. are not to be disregarded. Menes and other early kings of Egypt were declared by critics to be mere mythological characters; likewise Minos of Crete; and the stories of Troy and her heroes were said to belong to "cloudland." But the spades of Petrie at Abydos (*Royal Tombs*), of Evans at Knossos (*Quarterly Review*, October, 1904, 374–95), and of Schliemann at Troy (*Ilios: City and Country of the Trojans*), have shown the "cloudland" as solid earth, and the ghostly heroes to be substantial men of flesh and blood. If we are to learn anything from experience, certainly no theory of either sacred or profane history is to be accepted as final until tested and attested by facts.

13. Theory in History

(*c*) Only archaeology is bringing forth any new facts on the questions raised by criticism. Criticism produces only theories; it combines facts, but produces none. Exegetes and commentators rarely, if ever, now bring to light new facts any more than present-day philosophers give the world new thoughts. A flood of light is, indeed, pouring across the page of the exegete and the commentator in these latter days which makes their work inestimably more helpful for interpretation, but the source of that light is neither criticism nor exegesis, but archaeology. Archaeology it is which sets alongside the Bible history the facts of contemporary life and thus illustrates Biblical lit. and literary methods by contemporary lit. and the methods of contemporary literati, and which makes the purity, sanctity and divinity of the things of revelation stand out in their own glorious light by setting round about them the shadows of contemporary ritual and morality and superstition.

14. Source of the Needed Facts

Hence no critical theory of the Bible is to be finally accepted and made a part of our faith until tested and attested by archaeological facts. Even Wellhausen, however far he departs from this principle in the course of his criticism, seems to lay it down as fundamental in the beginning of his *History of Israel*, when he says: "From the place where the conflagration was first kindled the firemen keep away; I mean the domain of religious antiquities and dominant religious ideas—that whole region as Vatke in his *Biblical Theology* has marked it out. But only here, where the conflict was kindled, can it be brought to a definite conclusion" (*Hist of Israel*, 12). G. A. Smith quotes also with approval these words from Napoleon (*Campagnes d'Egypte et de Syrie dictées par Napoléon lui-même*, II): "When camping upon the ruins of the ancient cities, someone read the Bible aloud every evening in the tent of the General-in-Chief.

15. Scope of Function

The verisimilitude and the truthfulness of the descriptions were striking. They are still suited to the land after all the ages and the vicissitudes." But Dr. Smith adds, "This is not more than true, yet it does not carry us very far. . . . . All that geography can do is to show whether or not the situations are possible at the time to which they are assigned; even this is a task often beyond our resources" (*HGHL*, 108). Thus critics, while here and there acknowledging the proper function of archaeology in criticism, have not heretofore allowed it much scope in the exercise of that function.

II. History.—The history of archaeology in criticism to be set forth here has mainly to do with the testing of critical theories by archaeological facts. The contributions of archaeology to the furnishing of the historical setting of the Biblical narratives make up a large part of this and every dictionary of the Bible. The history of the guidance of critical methods by archaeological information is in the making. There can hardly as yet be said to be any to record.

1. Limitations of Discussion

The field opened up for the testing of critical theories by the results of archaeological research is so varied and so extended that only an outline can be given here. Extravagant claims concerning the outcome of this testing have been made both by some critics and by some of their opponents; as when Dr. Driver says, after excepting the points upon which the evidence of archaeology is neutral, "On all other points the facts of archaeology, so far as they are at present known, harmonize entirely with the position generally adopted by the critics" (*Authority and Archaeology*, 145); or as when the astronomer, C. Piazzi Smyth, thought that the great pyramid proved the "wisdom of the Egyptians" to have included some of the abstruse problems of higher mathematics; and Dr. Seiss, in his *Miracle in Stone*, was confident that the same colossal monument of Egypt definitely portrayed some of the extreme positions of the premillennial theology.

2. A Wide Field

Some of the instances of the testing of critical theories concerning the Scriptures by the facts of archaeology, for which unquestionable historical proofs can be offered, are here presented.

1. *Theories not affecting historicity or integrity.*—Many critical theories, notably those not affecting the historicity or the integrity of the Scriptures, i.e. accordant with the face value of Scripture, have been corroborated and others discredited.

(*a*) Theories corroborated: (1) The theory of the *geographical* and *topographical* trustworthiness of Scripture, i.e. that the peoples, places and events of Scripture are to be found just where the Bible places them. Attempts to belittle the importance of this geographical and topographical corroboration of the trustworthiness of the Scriptures have been made (Driver, *Authority and Archaeology*, 148; also *LOT*, xi; Smith, *HGHL*, 108), but such attempts are not satisfying. The theory of the correctness of the Biblical statements has been of well-nigh universal acceptance; archaeologists have fitted out expensive expeditions in accordance with it, exegesis has allowed it to enter into its conclusions, discussion has proceeded upon the assumption of its correctness, the whole body of identifications which make up Biblical geography and topography attest it, and the whole list of sacred geographies, uniform in every essential particular, are in evidence in support of this theory, even the works of those writers who have spoken disparagingly of it.

3. Geography and Topography

(2) The theory of the *ethnographical* correctness of Scripture. That the relation between peoples as indicated in Scripture is correct, has been a working theory for all general purposes and only departed from for special ends. Kautzsch says (*Die bleibende Bedeutung des Alttestaments*, 17): "The so-called Table of Nations remains, according to all the results of monumental exploration, an ethnographic original document of the first rank, which nothing can replace." The progress of archaeological research has confirmed this general working theory and every year adds new confirmation with regard to particular items which, for some special end, have been represented as against the theory. That the general theory of the correctness of the tribal relationships in Scripture has been, and is being, sustained, is indisputable (Hommel, *Ancient Heb Tradition;* Gunkel, *Israel und Babylonien*, ch vi; Sayce, *Patriarchal Palestine*, ch ii; Winckler, *OLZ*, December 15, 1906; Budge, *Hist of Egypt*, I; Orr, *POT*, 400–401, 529–30). See TABLE OF NATIONS.

4. Story of the Nations

(3) The theory of the *accuracy of Scripture* in both the originals and the copies. Every theory of inspiration postulates this in greater or less degree, and the most prevalent analytical theory put forth by criticism, with its lists of words indicating, as it is asserted, authorship, demands, for its very life, a degree of accuracy and invariableness in the use of words in both the writing of originals and the transmission of them by copyists greater than that demanded by any the most exacting theory of inspiration. Wherever it has been possible to test the statements of Scripture in its multitudinous historical notices and references, archaeology has found it correct to a remarkable degree, and that in its present form and even in minute peculiarities of statement (Brugsch, Broderick ed, *Egypt under the Pharaohs*, chs v–vi; Sayce, *Patriarchal Palestine;* Naville, *Recueil de Travaux*, IV, N.S.; Petrie, *Tahpanhes;* Tompkins, *The Age of Abraham;* Clay, *Light on the OT from Babel*).

5. Accuracy of Scripture

(4) The theory of the *correctness of the imagery* of the Bible. This is another of the fundamental and universal working theories of criticism which is, however, sometimes forgotten. Whatever the theory of the authorship and the origin of the various books of the Bible, there is always, with only a few special exceptions, the underlying assumption on the part of the critics of the correctness of the imagery reflecting the topography, the flora and the fauna, the seasons and the customs. Indeed, upon the trustworthiness of the imagery, as upon the exactness in the use of words, criticism depends. And this underlying assumption of criticism of every hue has been confirmed indisputably in its general features, and is being corroborated year by year in its minutest details, and even in those very special instances where it has been disputed. To this end testify the whole company of oriental residents, intelligent travelers and scientific investigators (Thomson; Van Lennap; Robinson; Stanley; Palmer, *Desert of the Exodus;* Trumbull, *Kadesh Barnea;* Clermont-Ganneau, *Archaeological Researches;* Van Dyke, *Out of Doors in the Holy Land*).

6. Bible Imagery

Besides these theories of a general character, some concerning particulars may be noticed:

(5) The theory of the *location of the Garden of Eden* somewhere in the Euphrates Valley. This theory has been all but universally held and, while it is not yet definitely substantiated, is receiving cumulative corroboration along ethnological lines. Wherever it is possible to trace back the lines of emigration of the early nations mentioned in the

7. Garden of Eden

Bible, it is always found that the ultimate direction is toward a certain comparatively small area in western Asia.

8. The Flood

(6) The geological theory concerning the *flood of Noah* as the last great change in land levels is being most exactly confirmed, not only by investigations into glacial history, but by examination of the records of the cataclysm left upon the mountains and valleys of central and western Asia (Wright, *The Ice Age in North America;* and *Scientific Confirmations of OT History*, chs vii–xi). See DELUGE.

9. Sodom and Gomorrah

(7) The geological theory of the *destruction of the Cities of the Plain* has been exactly confirmed by the examination of the strata; a bituminous region, a great stratum of rock-salt capped by sulphur-bearing marls and conglomerates cemented by bitumen, an explosion of pent-up gases, which collect in such geological formations, blowing the burning brimstone high in the air, and the waters of the Jordan coming down to dissolve the salt of the ruptured rock-salt stratum—all this provides for exactly what the Bible describes and for the conditions found there today; the pillar of smoke rising up to heaven, the rain of fire and brimstone falling back from the blowing-off crater, the catching of Lot's wife in the edge of the cataclysm and her incrustation with salt (Wright, *Scientific Confirmations of OT History*, 144; Blankenkorn, *ZDPV*, XIX, 1).

10. Hyksos and Patriarchs

(8) It has long been thought that there might be some relationship between the mysterious *Hyksos kings* of Egypt and the *Patriarchs* to account for the favorable reception, even royal distinction, given the latter. This theory of relationship has been very fully established by the discoveries of Petrie at Tell el-Yehudiyeh (Petrie, *Hyksos and Israelite Cities*, 1–16). He has not shown to what race the Hyksos belonged, but he has shown their tribal character, that they were, as their name indicates, "Bedouin princes," leaders of the nomadic or semi-nomadic tribes of Upper and Lower Ruthen, i.e. Syria and Pal, and northern and western Arabia, as were the Patriarchs, so that the latter were shown by the former the consideration of one "Bedouin prince" for another.

11. Uncivilized Canaan

(*b*) Theories discredited: (1) The interesting picture which was wont to be drawn of Abraham leaving all his friends and civilization behind him to become a pioneer in a barbarous land has become dim and dimmer and at last faded out completely in the ever-increasing light of contemporary history revealed by Bab and Palestinian discoveries (Vincent, *Canaan*, chs i–ii).

12. Concerning Melchizedek

(2) Concerning Melchizedek, "without father and without mother" (He **7** 3), Am Tab, while not wholly affording the needed information, have put to flight a host of imaginings of old commentators, and pointed toward Melchizedek's place in a line of kings at Jerus of unique title disclaiming any hereditary rights in the crown. "It was not my father and it was not my mother who established me in this position, but it was the mighty arm of the king himself who made me master of the lands and possessions of my father." This title, over the correct translation of which there has been much controversy, occurs not once only, but seems to have been required at every formal mention of the sovereignty of the king (Budge, *History of Egypt*, IV, 231–35).

13. Oriental Chronology

(3) The theory of the *chronology* of the early portions of the OT, which made it to be so exactly on the principle of the system of chronology in vogue in our western world today, which, indeed, assumed that there could be no other system of chronology, and which was universally held as a working hypothesis by all classes of critics and commentators until very recently, has been greatly modified, if not utterly discredited, by both archaeological and ethnological research. Whatever may have been the system and method of chronology in use in early Biblical history, it certainly was not the same as our epochal chronology based upon exact astronomical time. The early chronologies of the Orient were usually annalistic, ofttimes synchronistic, but very seldom epochal. The first, and usually the only, intent of present-day chronology is to chronicle the flight of time; the ancient systems of the East often introduced a moral element; events, rather than time, were chronicled, and the time in which nothing took place and the man who accomplished nothing were apt to be passed over in silence. Sometimes chronicles were arranged symmetrically, and again the visional conception of time found in all prophecy seems sometimes to have prevailed in the writing of history. Certain it is that ancient oriental thought regarded man's relation to life as of far greater importance than his relation to time—a more deeply moral conception of chronology than our own (Green, *BS*, April, 1890, 285–303).

2. *Theories affecting the integrity or historicity of Scripture.*—Many critical theories attacking the integrity or historicity of Scripture, i.e. reconstructive theories, have been utterly discredited by archaeological evidence, and, in some cases, abandoned by those who held them (cf Driver, *Genesis*, addenda, 7th ed, xx).

14. Ignorance of Patriarchal Age

(*a*) The *ignorance of the patriarchal age* was once a frontier fortress which threatened away all literary pretensions beyond that limit. This ignorance, though never held by all advocates of a reconstructing criticism, was held by some. Von Bohlen scoffed at the idea of the "undisciplined horde" possessing knowledge of laws (*Gen*, 29–41; cf Reuss, *Gesch des AT*, 96; Dillmann, *Nu and Josh*, 594). Dr. Driver says, indeed, "It is not denied that the patriarchs possessed the art of writing," but thinks the possession of a lit. by them a mere hypothesis, for the truth of which no positive ground can be alleged (*Gen*, xlii–xliii; also Orr, *POT*, 375). That this theory is absolutely abandoned by everyone hardly needs to be stated. The discovery of evidence of a postal system in Canaan in the days of Naram Sin (Sayce, *Archaeology of the Cuneiform Inscriptions*, 143; Heuzey, *Revue d'Assyriologie*, 1897, 1–12), the strict conformity of many of the patriarchal customs and events to written law, as revealed by DeMorgan's discovery of the CH, Dr. Murch's discovery of the Am Tab, revealing as they do the wide diffusion of the art of writing about one hundred and thirty years before the Exodus, together with the gradual pushing back by epigraphic evidence of the date of the origin of the Hebrew script (Clay, *Amurru*, 30–32), and the overwhelming evidence, from recent excavations, of the general culture and refinement of patriarchal Pal, while not yet making known fully the exact state of the patriarchal civilization, has made any theory of the ignorance of that age impossible.

15. Religious Ideas in Canaan

(*b*) The theory of the *nomadic, semi-barbarous condition of Pal* and of the impossibility of high religious ideas among the patriarchs before the Exodus (Kuenen, *Rel of Israel*, I, 108–9), though most closely connected with the preceding, demands separate notice. This theory is essential to the current evolutionary view of Israel's history and has been definitely espoused by nearly all holding that view (G. A. Smith, *Expos*, 1908, 254–72; cf *POT*, 60). This theory, though less important to other schools of critics, has in fact been held by nearly all commentators. But the discovery of the earliest wall- and cistern-work at Taanach (Sellin), and the engineering feats on the defences and the water-works at Gezer (Macalister and Vincent, *PEFS*), and the 40-ft. city wall pictured in Egyp illustration of Can war (Petrie, *Deshasha*, pl IV), as well as the list of richest booty taken by Thothmes III (Sayce, *Archaeology of the Cuneiform Inscriptions*, 156–57; Birch, *RP*, 1st ser, II, 35–52; Lepsius, *Denkmäler*, Abth. III, bl. 32, 32A, 30A, 30B; *Auswahl*, III, L. 42–45), which could scarcely be duplicated by all the museums of the world today, testify equally to the luxurious culture and refinement of the times. All this, in addition to the mass of evidence against the ignorance of the patriarchal age (see [*a*] above), overwhelmingly sustains the opinion of W. Max Müller that "the civilization of Pal in the patriarchal age was fully equal to that of Egypt."

16. Evolutionary History

(*c*) The theory of the *evolution of Israel's history* chiefly from a Palestinian origin and environment (Budde, *Hist of Israel before the Exile*, esp. 77; Kuenen, *Hist of Israel*, 225; Wellhausen, *Hist of Israel*, 462). Palestinian discoveries show a contrast between the unique religion of the Hebrews and the religion of the surrounding peoples of Canaan as marked as it may well be. The evidence is not at all of a purer religion growing up out of the vile culture of Pal, but of a purer religion coming down and overwhelming it (*PEFS*, 1902–9; G. A. Smith, *Mod. Crit. and the Preaching of the OT*, ch iv, esp. 142; *PEFS*, 1905, 287–88).

Descending now to a few of the great mass of particulars, we may mention:

17. Mythology and the Bible

(*d*) The theory of the legendary character of the *four kings of Gen* **14**, and of the *Hittites;* and the theory of the generally *mythological character* of the early portions of the Bible. The four kings have been called "petty sheiks of the desert," and their names "etymological inventions." The historical character of the account of these kings has been utterly discredited by many. Nöldeke in his *Untersuchungen* arrives at the result that the history (Gen **14**) is throughout a "free creation," and the person of Melchizedek a "poetical figure." And Wellhausen thinks Nöldeke gave the "death-blow" to the historicity of the story (Wellhausen, *Comp. of the Hex*, 311–12). Ed. Meyer is of the same opinion as Nöldeke, but expresses himself in a still more unfavorable manner (*Gesch*, 136). Hitzig, however, goes to the extreme of depreciation when he sees in the expedition of Chedorlaomer only an adumbration of the invasion by Sennacherib (2 K **19** 13). Delitzsch gives a very comprehensive review of those critics who have regarded this narrative of the kings as legend of small or no historical basis (*Gen*, I, 396–99; cf Dillmann, *Gen*, II, 32–33). In addition, the mythological character of the early portions of the Bible generally has had ardent advocates (Stade, *Gesch*, 129–30; Schultz, *OT Theology*, I, 31; Wellhausen, *Gesch Israels*, 317–20).

18. Chedorlaomer and Allies

But the four kings have appeared in archaeological discoveries. While there is still some dispute about the identification of certain of them, the confederacy has appeared in Babylonia and also the Bab suzerainty over Pal in the age called for by the narrative, and, indeed, the whole historical setting into which the narrative fits with perfect naturalness (Jeremias, *Das alte Testament im Lichte des alten Orients;* Hommel, *Hebrew Tradition*, ch v; Clay, *Light on the OT from Babel*, ch vi). But myths do not receive archaeological confirmation such as has not only been given to the narrative of the confederacy of the four kings, but which is rapidly bringing out the features of the whole early OT history (Gunkel, *Gen*, 263; Ladd, *Doct of Sac Scrip*, I, 737).

19. The Hittites

Then grave doubts in the past have been raised concerning the *Hittites*. Occasionally it has been boldly said that "no such people ever existed" (cf Newman, *Heb Monarchy*, 184–85; Budge, *Hist of Egypt*, IV, 136). But in addition to the treaty of Rameses II with the "Kheta," long generally believed to have been the Hittites (*RP*, 2d ser, IV, 25–32), and the references to the "Hatti" in the Am Tab, also thought to be the same people, we now have Winckler's great discovery of the Hittite capital at Boghaz-Köi, and the Hittite copy of the treaty with Rameses II in the cuneiform script. The Hittites are seen to be a great nation, a third with Egypt and Babylonia (*OLZ*, December 15, 1906). See HITTITES.

(*e*) The theory of *anachronisms*. Aside from the general application of this theory by many critics to the traditional view of Scripture and the assertion of the systematic representation of earlier events in the light of much later times (Robertson, *Early Religion*, 30; Frip, *Comp. of Gen*), many special instances of anachronisms have been alleged. Edom has been said to be mentioned too early in the narrative (De Wette, *Int*, II, 71, Parker's note; also Gunkel, *Gen*, 61). But an officer of Seti Meremptah II, about the time of the Exodus, in an official report, mentions the people of Edom as desiring to pasture their flocks in Goshen. They had thus early found their way clear across the Sinai peninsula (Müller, *Asien und Europa*, 135; cf Papyrus Anastasia). Then Moab, long unidentified, has had doubt cast on its existence at so early a time as its first mention; but it also occurs in an inscription of Rameses II near the time of the Exodus, and the land of Moab is placed in "Ruthen," the Egyp name for Syria and Pal and northern and western Arabia (Kyle, "Geographical and Ethnic Lists of Rameses II," *Recueil de Travaux*, XXX).

3. *Theories now challenged.*—Several critical theories are just now challenged in the name of archaeological discovery; whether or not the challenges will ultimately be sustained remains to be determined. A few only are mentioned here, but they are of such a character as, if ultimately sustained, will have a far-reaching effect upon criticism.

20. Semitic Origins

(*a*) The theory, long established and almost universally held, of the Bab origin and westward course of *early Sem culture*, esp. of religious traditions (Barton, *Semitic Origins*, ch i; also "Tiamat," *JAOS*, XVI, 1–27; Paton, *Early Hist of Pal and Syria*, chs iii–viii; Driver, *Gen*, 30–31; Orr, *POT*, 397). This theory has been mildly questioned for some time and is now boldly challenged. A complete "right-about-face" is proposed by reason of many archaeological considerations, which, it is claimed, make Amurru, Syria and Pal, the home of the northern Semite, to be, if not the original source of Sem culture, at least an earlier source than Babylonia, and the course of religious culture among Semites in that early age to be not westward but eastward, as apparently in Gen **11** 2 RV (Clay, *Amurru, the Home of the Northern Semites*).

(*b*) The theory of the *gradual invasion of Palestine* instead of the conquest is now for the first time challenged by evidence other than the record in Joshua. Such Palestinian researches and the collection of such evidence have but begun within a few years, and from the very breadth of the question the process is necessarily slow. So far, however, as the excavations have gone, the evidence is of a decided change in the culture even at such towns as Gezer, without, however, the Can culture coming fully under Israelite influence and succumbing to it; exactly, in fact, as is represented in the Biblical narrative (*PEFS*, 1903, 49, Macalister; ib, 1908, Macalister, 17; Vincent, 228).

21. Invasion of Canaan

(*c*) The post-Christian view of the *Hermetic Writings*. These Egyp documents in the Gr tongue have been thought to reflect early Christian thought in Egypt, chiefly because of a certain "unholy resemblance" to gospel language found in them. A recent critical examination of these writings has established, it is claimed, by archaeological evidence gathered from the writings themselves, that the "unholy resemblance" to gospel expressions arose not from the reflection of Christian teaching, but from the appropriation by the evangelists of current expressions of Alex Gr in use in pre-Christian theological language. This view of the Hermetic Writings, if finally established, cannot but have a far-reaching effect upon NT study (Petrie, *Personal Religion in Egypt before Christianity*).

22. AD Date of Hermetic Writings

4. *Reconstructive criticism not confirmed.*—Not a single critical theory still maintained, either generally or by prominent individual critics, which proposes to take Scripture at other than its face value, has been sustained by archaeology. The assertion that it is otherwise, that "on all other (controverted) points, the facts of archaeology, so far as they are at present known, harmonize entirely with the positions generally advocated by the critics" (Driver, *Authority and Archaeology*, 145; *LOT* (1897), Pref, xviii; *Gen*, addenda to 7th ed, XXXIV–XXXVI), means either that such unsustained theories are not advocated by the person making the assertion and not by him regarded as generally advocated by critics, or, more commonly, that the theories in question have not been positively and definitely contradicted by archaeological evidence. But it is not enough that theories are not definitely contradicted by archaeological evidence; we have seen (cf above) that they must be definitely corroborated before being accepted and allowed to affect one's faith. An instance of the claims of criticism concerning the harmony between its theories and the facts of archaeology, a claim whose importance merits presentation at length, is found in the Addenda to the 7th ed of Driver's Introduction to *Gen*, the latest and most positive utterance of criticism on this subject. Driver says (xxxiv):

23. The Claims of Some Critics

It is stated by Professor Sayce expressly, and by Dr. Orr and Professor A. T. Clay, by implication, that Nöldeke's arguments against the historical character of the narrative of Gen **14** have been refuted by archaeology. The statement supplies such an object-lesson of the methods on which the opponents of criticism not unfrequently rely, that it may be worth while to explain here the grounds upon which it rests. Here are Professor Sayce's words (*Monumental Facts*, 1904, 54; cf, though without Nöldeke's name, *Monuments*, 161 f): "In 1869 the great Semitic scholar, Professor Nöldeke, published a treatise on the *Unhistorical Character of Gen* **14**. He declared that 'criticism' had forever disproved its claim to be historical. The political situation presupposed by it was incredible and impossible; at so distant a date Bab armies could not have marched to Canaan, much less could Canaan have been a subject province of Babylonia. The whole story, in fact, was a fiction based upon the Assyr conquest of Pal in later days. The names of the princes commemorated in it were etymological inventions: eminent Sem scholars had already explained those of Chedorlaomer and his allies from Sanskrit, and those of the Can princes were derived from the events in which they were supposed to have borne a part." And then he goes on to declare triumphantly (55) how the progress of archaeology has refuted all these statements. . . . .

It will probably surprise the reader to be told that, of the series of arguments thus attributed to Professor Nöldeke, while the one about the names is attributed to him with partial correctness (though in so far as it is stated correctly, it has not been refuted by archaeology), the other arguments were never used by him at all . . . . (xxxv). The one grain of truth in Professor Sayce's long indictment is that of the names of the five Can kings, which are given, Bera and Birsha (suggesting the idea of "evil" and "wickedness"), and perhaps Shinab and Shemeber as well, are formed artificially; but this (NB) is not asserted of the name of any of the four kings from the East. . . . . The fact is, Nöldeke's arguments on Gen **14** have not been refuted, or even touched, by archaeology. . . . . Professor Sayce has simply not mentioned Nöldeke's real arguments at all. Nor are they mentioned by Dr. Orr or Professor Clay. . . . . Archaeology has met the arguments which Nöldeke did not use; it has not met the arguments which he did use. Nöldeke never questioned, as Professor Sayce declares that he did, the general possibility at this time of an expedition being sent from the far East into Palestine: his argument consisted in pointing out various historical improbabilities attaching to the details of a particular expedition; and archaeology can overthrow this argument only by producing evidence that this expedition, with the details as stated in Gen **14**, actually took place. And this up to the present time (June, 1909) archaeology has not done.

Compare with these declarations of Driver, one by one, though in somewhat different order, Nöldeke's own words. He says (*Untersuchungen*, 157–60):

24. Nöldeke's Assertions

"The chapter begins with an imposing enumeration of kings, in whose time the narrated event is alleged to have occurred. . . . . Of what use is the dating according to kings, the time of whose reign is perfectly unknown to us? . . . . so that the dating is wholly superfluous and tells us nothing."

Bera and Birsha are said to be

"quite decidedly unhistorical. . . . . The alliterative pairing also of these names speaks more for their fictitious than for their historical origin. It is striking that for the single historical city of Zoar, no name of the king is given. . . . . Besides, we are bound to no time, for the event recounted could quite as well have taken place in the year 4000 as 2000; the artificial chronology of Gen is for us no rule. . . . . Whence the narrator got the names of the hostile kings we cannot say. They may really have been handed down to him, perhaps quite in another connection. However that may be, the utmost we can admit is that he has employed a few correct names intermingled with false or invented ones, and the appearance of historicity thus produced can as little permanently deceive us as the proper names and dates in the book of Esther. . . . . Concede provisionally the correctness of the names of the kings and test the narrative further."

Here in a long paragraph, Nöldeke follows the *reductio ad absurdum*, arguing that, from a historical standpoint, the provisional supposition is incredible and impossible, and concludes (163), "Now this whole expedition is historically improbable to the same extent that it is adapted to the production of a striking effect; the usual sign that it is fictitious. . . . . Does not the manifest improbability of the narrative lie precisely in the details which give it the appearance of historicity?"

Concerning the story of Abram's pursuit of the kings and the rescue of Lot, he says (165): "If that is possible, then is nothing impossible. It may be replied that the number of Abram's servants was in reality much greater; but everything depends upon it, and the number belongs again to the very things which spread over the narrative the deceptive shimmer of historicity."

Of Melchizedek and the Amorite allies of Abram, he says (168): "So do the proofs pile up, that our narrative has no historical worth. . . . . Even if the rest of the chapter were historical we would still hold Melchizedek a poetical figure." He sums up the argument in the following words

(170–71): "In accordance with what has been said, it is very improbable that the composer in the chief matters rested upon a real tradition of the people, but we must accept as a fact that it is a free creation throughout."

On the same subject, in reply to some of his critics (*Zeitschrift für W. Theol*, 1870, 218–19), he says:

"I sum up once more the general points: (1) Of the names mentioned in Gen **14**, several are unhistorical (the name of Sodom and Gomorrah, the three Amorites, Melchizedek; in my view, also, Abram and Lot, and probably the four overwhelmed cities). (2) The expedition of the kings cannot have taken place as narrated . . . . even through the very clearness of the narrative are we made to know that we have here to do with a romantic expedition, the course of which is determined by aim at sharper effect, and which has for itself no historical probability. (3) The small number of the host, in whose complete victory over the army of the four kings the story at last comes to a climax, is contrary to sense, while yet it designates about the utmost number which, as his own fighting men, a private citizen could put in the field.

"Whoever now throughout all of this will hold to an historical kernel may do so; he must then admit that at some perfectly uncertain time in great antiquity a king of Elam ruled over the Jordan land and made a warlike expedition thither. But that would be the utmost concession I could make. Everything more precise, as numbers, names, etc, and also exactly that which produces the appearance of careful tradition and trustworthiness is partly false, partly quite unreliable . . . . more especially, beyond the conquest itself nothing whatever could be known. But to me it still seems much more probable, in view of the consistent, and for the aim of the narrator, exceedingly well ordered, but still, in reality, impossible course of the narrative, out from which there cannot be separated any single things as bare exaggeration of the tradition, that we have here a conscious fiction in which only a few historical names have been used."

Now, recalling to mind the facts of archaeology in this case (cf above) it becomes evident that they are very far from "harmonizing entirely" with the opinion advanced by Nöldeke and reiterated by Driver, and the method of advocating such "harmonizing" appears very clearly. Moreover, what is true of this particular theory of Nöldeke and Driver is equally true of other radical critical theories at present held. Of the current reconstructive theories of criticism—the patriarchs not individuals but personifications; the rude, nomadic, semi-barbarous condition of Pal in the patriarchal age; the desert; Egypt; the comparative unimportance of Moses as a lawgiver; the gradual invasion of Pal; the naturalistic origin of Israel's religion from astral myths; and the late authorship of the Pent—not one is being sustained. In fact, however much archaeological evidence there may be that is negative in character or that is not definitely against the reconstructive theories of criticism, no one can point to a single definite particular of archaeological evidence whereby any one of these theories is positively sustained and corroborated.

25. The Facts of Archaeology

5. *The present state of the discussion.*—The present stage of progress of the testing of critical theories by archaeological evidence may briefly be stated. The Bible at its face value is being corroborated wherever archaeology immediately and definitely touches it. To illustrate this statement fully would be to cite every definite piece of archaeological evidence in the Biblical field of scientific research during the last one hundred years.

But views of Scripture must finally square with the results of archaeology, i.e. with contemporaneous history, and, just as archaeological research makes that contemporaneous history to appear, critical theories at variance therewith are of necessity giving way; so that, as far as the process has been carried to the present time, archaeology is bringing criticism into harmony with the face value of Scripture, and is not definitely and unequivocally encouraging attempts at literary reconstruction of any portion of the Bible, although sometimes asked to render such service.

Literature.—The bibliography of the discussion has appeared in the references fully given throughout this article. The bibliography on the subject of this art., "Archaeology and Criticism," is, as indicated above, exceedingly meager, since the importance of the subject has but recently come to the front and been generally recognized. The following may be cited: Driver, in *Authority and Archaeology* (Hogarth), ch i; Eerdmans, *Hibbert Journal*, July, 1909; also *Alttestamentliche Studien;* Orr, *The Problem of the OT*, ch xi; Bennett, *Contemporary Review*, 1906, 518.

M. G. Kyle

ARCHAEOLOGY OF ASIA MINOR. See Asia Minor, Archaeology of.

ARCHANGEL, ärk-ān′jel. See Angel.

ARCHELAUS, är-kē-lā′us (Ἀρχέλαος, *Archélaos*, Mt **2** 22): Son of Herod the Great by his wife Malthacē. He succeeded on his father's death to the government of Judaea, Samaria and Idumaea, but was deposed by the Romans for misgovernment in 6 AD. See Herod.

ARCHERY, är′chēr-i:

(1) The art of using the *arcus*, or bow and arrow for hunting and in battle is of great antiquity. It is mentioned in Gen **21** 20, as well as in the *Iliad* and the *Odyssey*, and depicted on Egyp monuments and in Assyr sculptures. The Philis excelled in the art, which led David to order that special training in it be given to the Hebrews (2 S **1** 18). It was an important art throughout the world in Biblical times (see Gen **27** 3; Isa **22** 6; **49** 2; Ps **127** 4). The Benjamites among the Hebs were noted as archers (Jgs **20**), and archers constituted much of the fighting strength, and played no mean part in the victories, of the world-famed Gr and Rom armies.

(2) *The bow* was common to civil (Gen **21** 20) and military life (Zec **9** 10), and vies with the spear in importance and antiquity. It was usually made of tough, elastic, seasoned wood, and often mounted with bronze (see Ps **18** 34 RV; cf Job **20** 24). But horn, too, was used for bows by the ancients, some with double curves being evidently modeled after the horns of oxen. The bow-string was commonly ox-gut and the arrows were of reed, or light wood tipped with flint, bronze, or iron.

(3) *The battle bows*, such as are mentioned in Zec **9** 10; **10** 4, must have been of great size, since they required to be strung by pressing the foot on the lower end, while the upper end was bent down to receive the string into a notch; hence the expression "to tread [=string] the bow," and "bow-treaders," for archers (Jer **50** 14.29 Heb). *The arrows*, "the sons of his quiver" (Lam **3** 13m, RV "shafts"), were ordinarily, of course, carried in the quiver, which was either placed on the back or slung on the left side, secured by a belt over the right shoulder (*HDB*). The day of gunpowder and firearms, of course, was not yet.

Geo. B. Eager

ARCHEVITE, är′ke-vīt (Kethībh, אַרְכְּוֵי, *'arkāwēy;* Ḳerē, אַרְכְּוָיֵא, *'arkewāyē'*): One of the tribes which Osnappar transplanted to swell the mixed multitudes in the cities of Samaria (Ezr **4** 9). The Archevites were the inhabitants of Erech, one of the four cities originally founded by Nimrod in Babylonia. (For its modern site cf Loftus, *Travels in Chaldea and Susiana*, 162 ff). Marquardt (*Fund*, 64 ff) emends the text to read דִּ[י] כוּ[תָ]יֵא, *dī kūthāyē'*, "who are Cuthaeans" (2 K **17** 24).

ARCHI, är′kī. See Archites.

ARCHIPPUS, är-kip′us (Ἄρχιππος, *Archíppos*): Addressed by Paul in his letter to Philem, as "our fellow-soldier"; probably a member of Philem's family circle, holding some official position in the church (Col **4** 17; Philem 2). See Apphia. The tradition that he was one of the seventy disciples, became bishop of Laodicea and later became a martyr, seems to have little historical foundation.

ARCHITECTURE, är′ki-tek-tūr:

I. Historical.—The words "architect" and "architecture" do not occur in the OT or the NT.

As the greatness of a nation and its social elevation are reflected in the course of architectural development, so is a nation's failure to rise to firm establishment, after victory in war, reflected in the absence of such development. The latter condition was that of the Jews in Pal; they failed so to establish themselves that their character and aims could find true expression in architecture. The country by reason of its geographical position and its broken territorial character, which exaggerated the tribal nature of its inhabitants, did not favor political empire (see *HGHL*, 10). The great difficulty of the Jews was the preservation of their own integrity. There could be no victorious expeditions to foreign lands to inspire monumental evidence of achievement in arms, nor had they the inspiration of various gods or saints, to whose glory great and separate buildings might be raised. Their dwellings were, by force of circumstances, unpretentious, and their tombs were of the same character.

Fig. 1.—Streets of a Jewish City.

1. Plans, Estimates and Measuring

Although in the smaller buildings there is very little evidence of the builder having been governed by a previously drawn plan, there seems no doubt that in larger works a plan was prepared. The Tabernacle was made according to a "pattern" (Ex **25** 9) and Solomon's Temple was also designed and submitted for approval (1 Ch **28** 11). Estimated cost was also considered (Lk **14** 28). The equivalents to a tape line and foot rule can be identified (Ezk **40** 3.5; **47** 3; Rev **11** 1; **21** 15).

The Israelites arrived in tents, and the walled cities, "great and walled up to heaven" (Dt **1** 28 AV) which they took and occupied were well fortified, unlovely shelters, covering areas of anything from 12 acres, as at Taanach and Megiddo, to about 23 acres as at Gezer (*Canaan d'après l'exploration récente*). The habitations within the walls were poor structures of mud bricks or rude stone; in many cases they were rock-cut caves. True,

Fig. 2.—Modern City of Es Salt.

the Jews attempted, at the outset of their full possession, to build in beauty, and made efforts toward greater substantiality, using the best available help; the attempt, however, was doomed to failure. Their most important buildings were their fortifications. The engineering skill displayed in the construction of aqueducts and other water systems was forced out of them by sheer necessity, and proved the existence of a latent constructive power, which they never had sustained opportunity to apply to architecture. In striking contrast is the architecture of the Crusaders. In a comparatively short time of less than 200 years, during the half of which practice in the arts of peace was well-nigh impossible, they stamped their occupation by the erection of an enormous number of great and beautiful buildings, the ruins of which are among the most imposing landmarks in the country.

2. OT References

The often-repeated references to building greatness in the OT, indicate a pride out of all scale with actuality. They tell the story of a long desert pilgrimage during which the Jews, as dwellers in tents, were impressed with the walled cities which, with extraordinary fortitude, they stormed and occupied, and which, with pardonable enthusiasm, they consequently exaggerated, to the glory of God. Although references to buildings in the OT are frequent, they are seldom sufficiently detailed to convey an idea of their character.

Cain built a city and named it Enoch (Gen **4** 17); his descendant Tubal Cain was "an instructor of every artificer in brass and iron" (ver 22 RVm). The description of the plan of the ark (Gen **6** 14 ff) is the first detailed architectural description in the OT. Asshur, a descendant of Ham, built Nineveh and other cities (Gen **10** 11). The tower of Babel was built of "brick for stone and slime for mortar" (Gen **11** 3). In Ex **27** 9–21 plan, dimensions and construction of the Tabernacle are given.

II. Temple and Palace of Solomon.—The most complete architectural reference is the description of the Temple and Palace of Solomon (1 K **6, 7**) and (Ezk **40, 41**). These buildings are fully dealt with under Temple, but a brief note is here necessary, as they are by far the greatest buildings of which there is mention in the OT. It is clear that Solomon had ambition for architectural greatness, and, following the example of David (2 S **5** 11)

Russian Church Built on Site of Garden of Gethsemane

Latin Church Built over Spot Where Jesus Taught the Lord's Prayer

Tomb of St. James

Tomb of Zacharias, Father of John the Baptist

Absalom's Pillar

ABSALOM'S PILLAR AND TOMBS OF ST. JAMES AND ZACHARIAS

he employed Phoen designers and craftsmen to carry out the work.

Fig. 3.—Doorway with Voluted Slabs at Lachish.

It is known that the buildings were of stone, that the chambers surrounding the Temple were three stories high, that the Temple was roofed (presumably flat) with cedar. Fergusson's restoration shows a sloping roof, following the precedent of the sloping roof of the Tabernacle (*Temples of the Jews*, 26). The walls and ceilings were lined with cedar, so that "there was no stone seen" (1 K **6** 18) within the house. The interior was enriched with carved foliage and cherubim, and in the decorative scheme, gold was freely applied. The description of the exterior is less minutely detailed. Stones were large and, as in the buildings of Egypt, were "sawed with saws" "from foundation to coping" (1 K **7** 9), "foundation to the top of walls" (3 K **7** 9, Douay VS). The inference therefore is that the masonry was smooth-faced: "no sign of any hammer" (*Ant*, VIII, iii, 2). Windows were "narrow" (1 K **6** 4 AV), repeatedly referred to (Ezk **40** 16.26). In the interior of the palace, cedar beams were carried on rows of cedar columns, and there were three rows of windows, one row to each story, directly opposite each other. Doors and posts were "square in prospect" (1 K **7** 5 ERV), i.e. square-headed. In Ezk **40** 21 ff EV arches are repeatedly mentioned but this is an error of translation. See Arch.

1. Construction and Materials

In the description, there is very little indication of the style of architecture. The rich nature of the pillars of brass and their "chapiters" (1 K **7** 15 ff EV) point to some hankering after an ornate trabeated style. There is no indication, however, of such a style in constructive stone. No mention is made of a crowning feature of a distinctive kind, not even an eave, simply a "coping." The use of a coping suggests that the walls were topped by parapets, "battlement" (Dt **22** 8 EV), according to the law. Fergusson's restoration shows both cornice and battlements (*Temples of the Jews*, Frontispiece).

2. Style

One can only vaguely conjecture the sources of influence which guided the builders. The description clearly shows that the great columnar architecture of Egypt was not taken as a model, although certain Egyp characteristics in detail are evident in contemporary work. Probably Phoen intercourse with the Mediterranean, generally, showed its influence, in which case a comparatively poor result might be inferred.

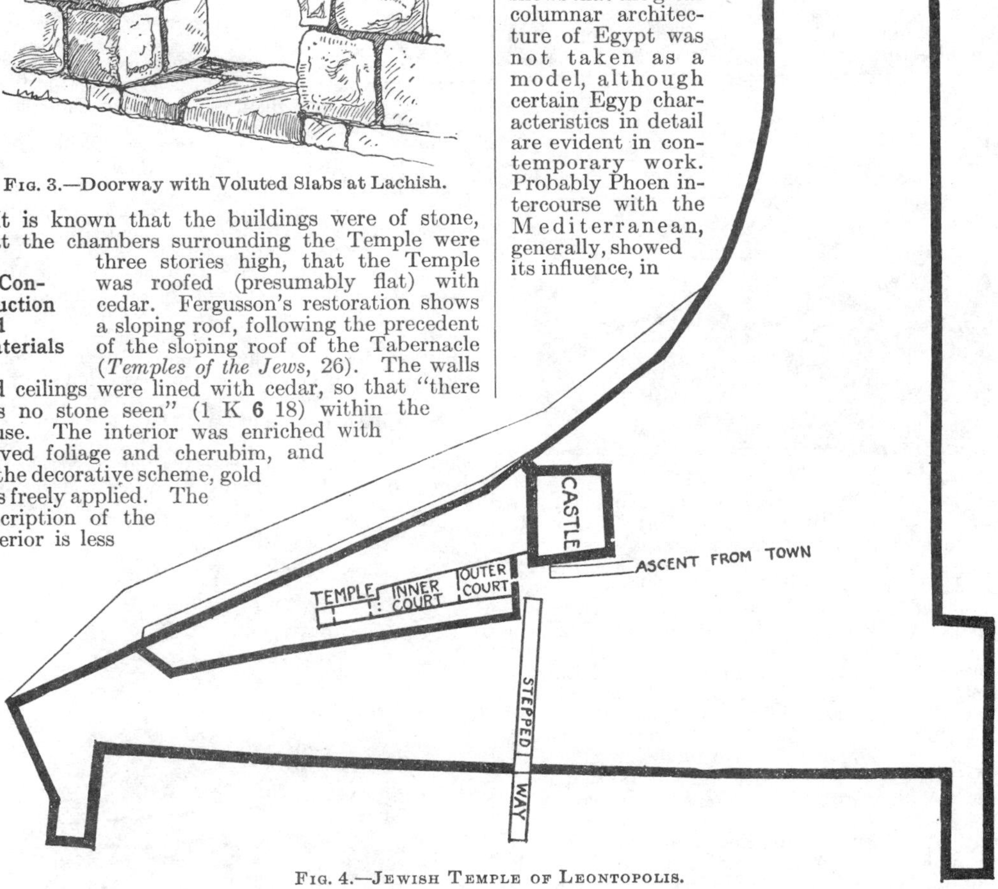

Fig. 4.—Jewish Temple of Leontopolis.

There remain these facts, viz. that here is described a group of buildings, of comparatively great scale; internally, at least, richly detailed and disposed in a way which shows considerable appreciation of architectural fitness, inspired by ambition for monumental greatness and dedicated, as was all that is great and spontaneous in architecture, to the glory of God. The one great flaw lay in the complete lack of a national constructive ability to respond to the call.

3. Facts

The Phoenicians who were employed seem to have been indifferent builders. They took 13 years to build Solomon's house (1 K **7** 1) and 7½ years to build the Temple (1 K **6** 38), and they, in all probability, found such a great work beyond their powers of adequate conception, more especially as the housement of a strange God was uninspiring. "Shalt thou build me an house for me to dwell in?" (2 S **7** 5 EV) was a command which they were only hired to fulfil.

4. Phoenician Designers

III. Conclusions from Actual Remains.—There are only a very few known examples from which a knowledge of Jewish architecture can be obtained. There are none now standing, and what the spade has uncovered proves little more than a mere building craft of an inferior order. Remains of the period of the monarchy have been uncovered on several sites, notably Jerus, Lachish, Tel es Safi (Gath?), Gezer, Taanach, Tel es Mutesellim (Megiddo), Jericho, and these give a general idea of the building craft of the period, but give no evidence of an architectural style. It may, with good reason, be argued that there was no style, but it is too much to conclude that the Jews had no architectural instinct. Ideals were not lacking:

FIG. 5.—Painted Tombs of Marissa.

"Behold, I will set thy stones in fair colors, and lay thy foundations with sapphires. And I will make thy pinnacles of rubies, and thy gates of carbuncles, and all thy border of precious stones" (Isa **54** 11. 12). Had history been different, Solomon's great example might have laid a foundation from which a national style would have been developed. The arts of peace, however, did not even bud, and the bane of internal and external conflict forced building energy to concentrate itself on fortifications.

Indeed in the great defence walls lies the building history of the Jews. They were hurriedly built and frequently destroyed. Destruction and reparation alternated so consistently, that each successive city within was little more than a temporary housement, at all times subservient to the more important work of defence. Under such conditions nothing flourished, least of all architecture. Building art became a thing of bare temporary utility.

1. Defence Walls

Streets (Fig. 1) were laid out without method; narrow, tortuous alleys broken into by projections, founded at the will of each individual builder, served as main thoroughfares (*Bible Sidelights*, 95; *Excavation of Gezer*, Vol I, p. 167 ff); cf similarity of conditions with streets of Mediterranean city of Philakopi (Journal *RIBA*, XI, 531). See CITY. Masonry was usually of rough unhewn stones, unskilfully laid without mortar, and buildings were rarely on the square. Under these conditions the enthusiasm displayed in the description of Solomon's work can be understood.

2. Streets

FIG. 6.—Lintel Stones.

In Jerus the Temple area was the center of architectural grandeur, and it is possible that it may have inspired building endeavor of another nature in other cities. Pal has as yet yielded no such parallel. Free areas, where they are found to have existed, seem to have happened so, and do not always coincide in position in successive superincumbent cities. They lay claim to no particular "lay out" and, in all probability, they served as space for the dump heaps of the town refuse or for the penning-up of cattle and sheep (Isa **58** 12, "waste places"). Fig. 2 shows the modern city of Es Salt, and gives a fairly good idea of the general appearance of an ancient Jewish city. The use of wooden shafts for porticos and roofs of large covered areas appears to have been prevalent, and these were frequently set in stone sockets which served as bases. Stone columns seem to have been sparingly used; in fact, there is no evidence whatever that a stone columnar

3. Absence of the "Grand Manner"

FIG. 7.—Tomb of Zechariah.

style of architecture prevailed in the more important buildings.

4. Solomonic Detail

At Lachish (*Lachish,* 23 ff) a number of voluted low-relief slabs were discovered which were originally built into the left reveals of the doorways of a building of considerable importance. These slabs were found in conjunction with a molded lintel of Egyp character. The discovery disclosed the only authentic examples of the architectural detail of the Solomonic period, and is particularly interesting as furnishing, perhaps, the earliest prototype of the Ionic volute. Fig. 3 is a sketch reconstruction of the doorway after Petrie's restoration. At its best it is a shoddy unconstructive adaptation of exotic features, and if it is to be taken as a key to the work of the period throughout Pal, there can be nothing great to record.

5. Temple of Onias

When Onias fled to Egypt from the persecution of Antiochus Epiphanes, cir 154 BC, he gained permission from Ptolemy and Cleopatra to build a temple at Leontopolis like to that at Jerus (*Ant,* XIII, iii, 3). The temple was built in fulfilment of the prophecy of Isa and modeled after the temple of Zerubbabel, but "smaller and poorer" and "resembled a tower." Petrie recovered this temple (*Hyksos,* 19 ff) on an artificial mound resembling the Temple hill at Jerus, raised alongside the Hyksos camp, where an influential Jewish community had established itself. It is the most complete plan of a Jewish building of monumental character yet discovered (Fig. 4). A sort of rude Corinthian detail was used, and certain fragments point to a battlemented treatment, suggestive of Bab origin, and to some extent confirming the inference drawn from the description of Solomon's Temple.

6. Maccabean Work

Fragments of contemporary architecture of the Maccabean dynasty throughout Pal show a Greco-Syrian style of considerable dignity and interest, illustrating a readiness to respond to the Hellenizing influence in the arts, which at that time was characterized, in architecture, by a decadent Gr provincialism. The battlemented details, found at Hyksos, seem to indicate the use of a style antedating the Maccabean work, preserving, to some extent, Bab traditions.

Fig. 8.—Synagogue at Kefr Berim.

7. Painted Tombs at Marissa

From the 3d cent. BC up to the Christian era architecture shows a consistent Gr origin with local character in detail (see *Expl. in Pal,* 18, 19) at Tel Sandahannah and Mareshah (*Painted Tombs of Marissa*). These Marissa tombs show most interesting decorated elevations, with painted architectural detail (see Fig. 5). The work is Phoen (93) and the date probably 194 to 119 BC (79). Gr Ionic capitals are used, with wreath enrichments painted on the architrave over the capital, and a deep frieze of painted animals, surmounted by a representation of a "battlement" "coping" (Dt **22** 8; 1 K **7** 9) remarkably like the details found by Petrie at Hyksos. An interesting detail is the pointed head to the intercolumnar opening, a form which seems to have suggested itself universally to the primitive builder, where the handling of large lintel stones presented a difficulty (see Fig. 6). They call to mind the heads of Anglo-Saxon openings.

A liking for mural decoration existed throughout the whole Jewish period, as is seen from the small fragments of painted plaster discovered in the various excavated cities, but the decoration on the Marissa tombs is the most complete example, and resembles in many ways the mural decoration at Knossos and Phylakopi.

8. A Characteristic Feature

The tomb of Zechariah in the Kedron valley (Fig. 7) probably belongs to the same date as its neighbor, the tomb of St. James, which De Vogüé, from the inscription upon it, ascribes to the time of Herod (*Le Temple de Jérusalem*, 46). The detail of the crowning part of the entablature is an often-recurring feature in Pal architecture, appearing as early as the Solomonic era at Lachish (see Fig. 3). It is characteristically Egyp, and is also seen at Persepolis (Gwilt's *Enc*, 22), and although neither might have been borrowed from the other, they are not many removes from the common parent. (A curious eastern tradition mentioned [*BD*, "Cities," 610] ascribes the building of Persepolis to Solomon.) It was a feature commonly used by the Phoenicians (Rawlinson, *Hist. of Phoen*, 142), and was probably introduced by them from Egypt. It seems to have been in favor up to the time of Herod and was abandoned after the wholesale introduction of the classic entablature which in Hellenistic times was only partially incorporated into the prevailing style. The successive variations of the crowning feature of their design is an important factor in tracing the development of Jewish architecture.

IV. Herodian Work.—The Temple of Siah (described by De Vogüé in *Recovery of Jerus*, 419 ff, and *Temples of the Jews*, 140 ff) is an interesting example of the work of the Herodian period and is more Gr in character than one would expect. Here, local character in carving is strongly marked, foliage and figures being freely used with a certain Assyr manner which, in spite of loose handling, betrays its origin. In fact this chord of architectural enrichment can be traced through the work of India, Assyria, Persia and Syria on to the Byzantine period, when the great cathedral church of St. Sophia in Constantinople displayed it in the most perfect harmony of all time.

The great building period of Herod need not be detailed. Herod was an Edomite and his architecture partook of the more robust Rom style which dominated Jewish art at a time when the opportunity of national incorporation had passed.

V. Synagogues.—This Rom influence, however, remained in Pal as can be seen by the important remains of synagogues in Galilee of the 3d cent. AD (see Fig. 8 from Kefr Berim; *Studies in Galilee*, ch vi; *SWP*, special papers, 294 ff). The many remains investigated shed light upon the plan of these post-exilic places of worship, of which there is little or no mention in the OT. See SYNAGOGUE. The plans vary considerably in proportion. The example at Meiron measures 90 ft.×44 ft. 8 in., while that at Irbid measures 57 ft. 3 in.×53 ft. (*SWP*, special papers, 299). In general arrangement the plans vary very little, consisting usually of five aisles with a triple entrance, most often facing south. The details are richly carved and "a surprising feature common to all is the use of animal figures, especially lions, or lambs and eagles. . . . In some examples human figures, usually intentionally mutilated, are found" (*Studies in Galilee*, 110).

VI. Final.—It is probable that future researches may add to our knowledge of early Jewish architecture, but it is doubtful whether there is more to discover than is constituted in the crude and unskilled use of building materials, influenced by limited knowledge of exotic features, which the Jews had neither the time nor the knowledge properly to apply. See CITY; BUILDING; FORTIFICATIONS; HOUSE; TEMPLE.

LITERATURE.—Conder, *Survey of Western Pal;* Warren, *Recovery of Jerus;* Bliss and Dickie, *Excavations in Jerus, 1894–97;* Fergusson, *Temple of Jerus;* Masterman, *Studies in Galilee;* Bliss and Macalister, *Excavations in Pal;* Macalister, *Excavations at Gezer;* Petrie, *Excavations at Hyksos;* Rawlinson, *History of Phoen;* Petrie, *Lachish;* Sellin, *Excavations at Taanach;* Schumacher, *Excavations at Tell Mutesellim;* Macalister, *Bible Sidelights;* Peters and Thierch, *Painted Tombs of Marissa.*

ARCH. C. DICKIE

ARCHITES, är′kīts (הָאַרְכִּי, *hā-'arkī;* AV **Archi**): A clan mentioned in connection with the marking of the southern boundary of Joseph (Josh **16** 2). The phrase גְּבוּל הָאַרְכִּי עֲטָרוֹת (*gebhūl hā-'arkī 'ăṭārōth*) offers difficulties, and it has been suggested that the order of the last two words be changed to read "the border of Ataroth-of-the-Archites." See ATAROTH. G. A. Smith identifies Ataroth with the present Atara on the high road from Jerus to Bethel, three and one-half miles S. of Bethel and six E. of the upper Beth-horon. Hushai, the "friend" of David, was an Archite (2 S **16** 16).

H. J. WOLF

ARCHIVES, är′kīvs (the more correct RV rendition of בֵּית סִפְרַיָּא, *bēth ṣiphrayyā'*, in Ezr **6** 1, "house of the archives" instead of "house of rolls" as in the AV): A part of the royal treasure-house (**5** 17), in which important state documents were kept.

ARCTURUS, ärk-tū′rus: The "Plough" or "Charles's Wain" is intended. See ASTRONOMY, II, 13.

ARD, ärd (אַרְדְּ, *'ard,* meaning unknown): Either directly or more remotely a son of Benjamin. Nu **26** 38–40 mentions five sons of Benjamin, together with Ard and Naaman, the sons of Bela, Benjamin's oldest son, counting all seven as ancestors of Benjamite families. In 1 Ch **8** 1–3 Addar and Naaman are mentioned, with others, as sons of Bela, Addar and Ard being apparently the same name with the consonants transposed. In Gen **46** 21 ten sons of Benjamin are counted, including at least the three grandsons, Ard and Naaman and Gera.

ARDAT, ärd′at (AV **Ardath;** Syr and Ethiopic have Arphad): A certain field where Ezr communed with God (2 Esd **9** 26).

ARDITES, är′dīts: Patronymic of ARD, which see.

ARDON, är′don (אַרְדּוֹן, *'ardōn,* meaning unknown): One of the three sons of Caleb and Azubah, of the tribe of Judah (1 Ch **2** 18).

ARELI, a-rē′lī (אַרְאֵלִי, *'ar'ēlī,* apparently the gentilic form of a compound that would mean "God's lioness," or "God's hearth"): One of the sons of Gad the son of Jacob (Gen **46** 16; Nu **26** 17). "Arelites" (q.v.) is exactly the same word.

ARELITES, a-rē′līts: In Nu **26** 17. See ARELI.

AREOPAGITE, ar-ē-op′a-jīt. See DIONYSIUS.

AREOPAGUS, ar-ē-op′a-gus (Ἄρειος πάγος, *Áreios págos;* Acts **17** 19.22. **Mars' Hill, 17** 22 AV): A sort of spur jutting out from the western end of the Acropolis and separated from it by a very short saddle. Traces of old steps cut in the rock are still to be seen. Underneath are deep grottoes, once the home of the Eumenides (Furies). On the flat surface of the summit are signs still visible of a smoothing of the stone for seats. Directly below to the N. was the old Athenian agora, or market-place. To the E., on the descent from the Acropolis, could be seen in antiquity a small semicircular platform—the orchestra—from which rose the precipitous rock of the citadel. Here the booksellers kept their stalls; here the work of Anaxagoras could be bought for a drachma; from here his physical philosophy was disseminated, then, through Euripides, the poetic associate of Socrates and the sophists, leavened the drama, and finally reached the people of Athens. Then came the Stoics and Epicureans who taught philosophy and religion as a system, not as a faith, and spent their time in searching out some new thing in creed and dogma and opinion. Five cents. earlier Socrates was brought to this very Areopagus to face the charges of his accusers. To this same spot the

Areopagus at Athens.

apostle Paul came almost five hundred years after 399 BC, when the Attic martyr was executed, with the same earnestness, the same deep-rooted convictions, and with even greater ardor, to meet the philosophers of fashion. The Athenian guides will show you the exact place where the apostle stood, and in what direction he faced when he addressed his audience. No city has ever seen such a forest of statues as studded the market-place, the streets and the sides and summit of the Acropolis of Athens. A large part of this wealth of art was in full view of the speaker, and the apostle naturally made this extraordinary display of votive statues and offerings the starting-point of his address. He finds the Athenians extremely religious. He had found an altar to a god unknown. Then he develops the theme of the great and only God, not from the Heb, but from the Gr, the Stoic point of view. His audiences consisted, on the one hand, of the advocates of prudence as the means, and pleasure as the end (the Epicureans); on the other, of the advocates of duty, of living in harmony with the intelligence which rules the world for good. He frankly expresses his sympathy with the nobler principles of the Stoic doctrine. But neither Stoic nor Epicurean could believe the declarations of the apostle: the latter believed death to be the end of all things, the former thought that the soul at death was absorbed again into that from which it sprang. Both understood Paul as proclaiming to them in Jesus and *Anástasis* ("resurrection") some new deities. When they finally ascertained that Jesus was ordained by God to judge the world, and that *Anastasis* was merely the resurrection of the dead, they were disappointed. Some scoffed, others departed, doubtless with the feeling that they had already given audience too long to such a fanatic.

The Areopagus, or Hill of Ares, was the ancient seat of the court of the same name, the establishment of which leads us far back into the mythical period long before the dawn of history. This court exercised the right of capital punishment. In 594 BC the jurisdiction in criminal cases was given to the archons who had discharged the duties of their office well and honorably, consequently to the noblest, richest and most distinguished citizens of Athens. The Areopagus saw that the laws in force were observed and executed by the properly constituted authorities; it could bring officials to trial for their acts while in office, even raise objections to all resolutions of the Council and of the General Assembly, if the court perceived a danger to the state, or subversion of the constitution. The Areopagus also protected the worship of the gods, the sanctuaries and sacred festivals, and the olive trees of Athens; and it supervised the religious sentiments of the people, the moral conduct of the citizens, as well as the education of the youth. Without waiting for a formal accusation the Areopagus could summon any citizen to court, examine, convict and punish him. Under unusual circumstances full powers could be granted by the people to this body for the conduct of various affairs of state; when the safety of the city was menaced, the court acted even without waiting for full power to be conferred upon it. The tenure of office was for life, and the number of members without restriction. The court sat at night at the end of each month and for three nights in succession. The place of meeting was a simple house, built of clay, which was still to be seen in the time of Vitruvius. The Areopagus, hallowed by the sacred traditions of the past, a dignified and august body, was independent of and uninfluenced by the wavering discordant multitude, and was not affected by the ever-changing public opinion. Conservative almost to a fault, it did the state good service by holding in check the too rash and radical younger spirits. When the democratic party came to power, after Cimon's banishment, one of its first acts was to limit the powers of the Areopagus. By the law of Ephialtes in 460 the court lost practically all jurisdiction. The supervision of the government was transferred to the *nomophulakes* (law-guardians). At the end of the Peloponnesian war, however, in 403 its old rights were restored. The court remained in existence down to the time of the emperors. From Acts **17** 19 and 22 we learn that it existed in the time of Claudius. One of its members was converted to the Christian faith (**17** 34). It was probably abolished by Vespasian.

As to whether Paul was "forcibly apprehended and formally tried," see Conybeare and Howson, *The Life and Epistles of St. Paul*, ch x, and *Expos*, 5th ser, II, 209 f, 261 f (Ramsay).

Literature.—P. W. Forchhammer, *De Areopago* (Kiel, 1828); Philippi, *Der A. und die Epheten* (Leipzig, 1874); Lange, *Die Epheten und der A. vor Solon* (Leipzig, 1874).

J. E. Harry

AREOPOLIS, ar-ē-op′o-lis. The Gr name of Ar (q.v.).

ARES, ā′rēs, är′es (Ἄρες, *Áres*=Arah [Ezr **2** 5; Neh **7** 10]): 756 of the sons of A. returned to Jerus with Zerubbabel (1 Esd **5** 10).

ARETAS, ar'ē-tas (**'Αρέτας,** *Arétas*): The name is a common one among Arabian princes and signifies "virtuous or pleasing." It is mentioned several times in Biblical lit. and in Jos. Here it refers to an Arabian king, who was a contemporary of Antiochus Epiphanes (cir 170 BC), before whom Jason the high priest was accused.

1. 2 Macc 5:8

Another Arabian prince of this name, surnamed Obodas (*Ant*, XIII, xv, 2; xvi, 2; XVI, ix, 4) defeated Antiochus Dionysius and reigned over Coele-Syria and Damascus. He participated with Hyrcanus in the war for the Jewish throne against his brother Aristobulus, but the allies were completely defeated at Papyron, by Aristobulus and Scaurus, the Rom general. The latter carried the war into Arabia and forced Aretas to make an ignominious peace, at the price of three hundred talents of silver. Of that event a memorial denarius still exists, with a Rom chariot in full charge on the one side and a camel on the other, by the side of which an Arab is kneeling, who holds out a branch of frankincense.

2. Obodas

The successor of Obodas was apparently surnamed Aeneas and this is the Arabian king who figures in the NT (2 Cor **11** 32; cf Acts **9** 24). The Aretas, here mentioned, is the father-in-law of Herod Antipas, who divorced his wife to marry Herodias, the wife of his brother Philip (Mt **14** 3; Mk **6** 17; Lk **3** 19). Jos (*Ant*, XVIII, v, 1.3) gives us a circumstantial narration of the events leading up to and following the conduct of Antipas. Coupled with a boundary dispute, it occasioned a bitter war between the two princes, in which Antipas was completely overwhelmed, who thereupon invoked the aid of the Romans. Tiberius ordered Vitellius, proconsul of Syria, to make war on Aretas and to deliver him dead or alive into the hands of the emperor. On the way, at Jerus, Vitellius received intelligence of the death of Tiberius, March 16, 37 AD, and stopped all warlike proceedings (*Ant*, XVIII, v, 1.3). According to 2 Cor **11** 32, Damascus, which had formerly belonged to the Arabian princes, was again in the hands of Aretas, when Paul escaped from it, not immediately after his conversion, but on a subsequent visit, after his Arabian exile (Gal **1** 16.17). It is inconceivable that Aretas should have taken Damascus by force, in the face of the almost omnipotent power of Rome. The picture moreover, which Jos draws of the Herodian events, points to a passive rather than an active attitude on the part of Aretas. The probability is that Cajus Caligula, the new emperor, wishing to settle the affairs of Syria, freely gave Damascus to Aretas, inasmuch as it had formerly belonged to his territory. As Tiberius died in 37 AD, and as the Arabian affair was completely settled in 39 AD, it is evident that the date of Paul's conversion must lie somewhere between 34 and 36 AD. This date is further fixed by a Damascus coin, with the image of King Aretas and the date 101. If that date points to the Pompeian era, it equals 37 AD, making the date of Paul's conversion 34 AD (Mionnet, *Descript. des médailles antiques*, V, 284–85). HENRY E. DOSKER

3. Aeneas

ARGOB, är'gob (אַרְגֹּב, *'argōbh*, "story"): A locality or a person mentioned in the obscure passage 2 K **15** 25. The context deals with Pekah's conspiracy against Pekahiah; but it is not clear, owing to the state of the text, whether Argob and his associate Arieh (if these are the names of men) were officers of Pekahiah who were slain with him, or fellow-conspirators with Pekah. The Vulg takes them as names of places; they may then be considered glosses that have crept into the text. Rashi holds that Argob was the royal palace. Argob is more likely the name of a place than a person. See ARIEH. H. J. WOLF

ARGOB, är'gob (הָאַרְגֹּב or אַרְגֹּב, *'argōbh* or *hā-'argōbh;* **'Αργόβ,** *Argób*): A region E. of the Jordan which in Dt **3** 4.5 is equivalent to the kingdom of Og in Bashan, and in ver 13 is referred to as "all the region of Argob, even all Bashan." Ver 14 is evidently corrupt. Havvoth-jair lay not in Bashan but in Gilead (Jgs **10** 4; Nu **32** 40 f; 1 K **4** 13). It contained threescore cities. "All these were cities fortified with high walls, gates and bars; besides the unwalled towns a great many." Dt **3** 14 seems to say that it marched with Geshur and Maacah; but we cannot lay stress on this. We may take it that Argob lay in the land of Bashan; beyond this, on available data, we cannot certainly go.

The word *ḥebhel*, tr[d] "region," means primarily a line or cord, then "a measuring line," then "the portion measured," e.g. "the part of the children of Judah" (Josh **19** 9), the "lot" or "portion" of an inheritance (Dt **32** 9; Josh **17** 14, etc). *Ḥebhel* precedes Argob in each of the four cases where it is named. This has led many to think that a district with very clearly marked borders is intended. No region so well meets this condition as *el-Lejā'*, a volcanic tract lying about 20 miles S. of Damascus, and 30 miles E. of the Sea of Galilee. It is roughly triangular in form, with the apex to the N., and is about 25 miles long, with a base of some 20 miles. The lava which has hardened into this confused wilderness of black rock, rent and torn by countless fissures, flowed from the craters whose dark forms are seen on the E. It rises to an average height of about 20 ft. above the plain, on which it lies like an island on a sea of emerald, the edges being sharply defined. At all points it is difficult of entrance, and might be defended by a few resolute men against an army. To this fact doubtless it owes its name *el-Lejā'*, "the refuge." There are many traces of considerable cities in the interior. The present writer collected there the names of no fewer than seventy-one ruined sites. See further TRACHONITIS. This identification is supported by taking *'argōbh* as the Heb equivalent of the Gr *trachōn*, "stony." This is possible only if, as Gesenius assumes, the root *rāghabh* is cognate with *rāgham*, an extremely precarious assumption. "Clod" is the tr of the word *reghebh* in Job **21** 33; **38** 38; probably therefore *'argōbh* should be tendered "a region of clods," i.e. "arable land." This practically rules out *el-Lejā'*. We have seen above that the term *ḥebhel* need have no reference to the clearly marked rocky boundaries. As regards the great cities, all Bashan is studded with the ruins of such. The splendid remains that everywhere meet the traveler's eye were thought by Porter (*Giant Cities of Bashan*) and others, to be the wreck of the great cities that struck the invading Israelites with wonder. It is now clear that the ruins above ground are not older than the beginning of our era. The Gr and Rom architecture is easily recognized. Probably, however, excavation will prove that in very many cases the sites have been occupied from very ancient times. Cave dwellings, chambers cut in the rock and covered with stone vaults, and what may be described as subterranean cities, have been found in different parts, the antiquity of which it is impossible to estimate. There is nothing which enables us to identify the region of Argob. The whole country of Bashan, with the exception of *el-Lejā'*, is "arable land." The soil is very fertile, composed of lava detritus. In almost every district might have been found the threescore cities. Guthe suggests the western part of *el-Haurān*, stretching from Edrei (*Ḍer'ah*) to *Nawā*. Buhl would locate it in the district of *eṣ-Ṣuweit*, to the S.E. of the low range of *ez-Zumleh*. This however seems too far to the S. The S.W. slopes of *Jebel ed-Druze* seem to meet the conditions as well as any. They form quite a well-marked district; they are very fertile, and the strong cities in the region must have been numerous.

W. Ewing

ARGUE, är'gū: Only in RV in Job **40** 2. יָכַח, *yākhah*, which it translates, lit. means "to be right," and in the causative form "reason with," "answer back," and is found in AV rendered **"reproach."**

ARIARATHES, ā-ri-a-rā'thēz. See Arathes.

ARIDAI, ar'i-dī, a-rid'ā-ī (אֲרִידַי, *'ărīdhay:* a son of Haman [Est **9** 9]): The name may be related to the Pers *Hari-dayas*, "delight of Hari"; the text is very uncertain.

ARIDATHA, ar-i-dā'tha, a-rid'a-tha (אֲרִידָתָא, *'ărīdhāthā'*): A son of Haman (Est **9** 8). It may be related to the Pers *Hari-dâta*, "given by Hari." The LXX reads *Pharadátha*.

ARIEH, ā'ri-e: "(the) Lion." See Argob.

ARIEL, ā'ri-el (אֲרִאֵל or אֲרִיאֵל, *'ărī'ēl*, "lioness of God"): But the word occurs in Ezk **43** 15.16, and is there tr[d] in RV "ALTAR HEARTH."

(1) According to RV a man of Moab whose two sons were slain by David's warrior Benaiah the son of Jehoiada (2 S **23** 20; 1 Ch **11** 22). Here AV translates "two lionlike men of Moab."

(2) A name applied to Jerus (Isa **29** 1.2.7). The many explanations of the name are interesting, but mainly conjectural.

(3) One of the members of the delegation sent by Ezra to the place Casiphia, to secure temple ministers for his expedition to Jerus (Ezr **8** 16).

Willis J. Beecher

ARIGHT, a-rīt': "In a right way," "correctly," "going straight to the point," without error or deviation. "Set aright" (Job **11** 13; Ps **78** 8). Its use in Ps **50** 23 is without authority in the Heb text; hence in italics.

ARIMATHAEA, ar-i-ma-thē'a (**'Αριμαθαία,** *Arimathaía*): "A city of the Jews," the home of Joseph in whose sepulchre the body of Jesus was laid. Its identity is the subject of much conjecture. The *Onomasticon* of Eusebius and Jerome identifies it with Ramathaim-Zophim in the hill-country of Ephraim (1 S **1** 1), which is Ramah the birthplace and burial-place of Samuel (1 S **1** 19; **25** 1), and places it near Timnah on the borders of Judah and Dan. G. A. Smith thinks it may be the modern Beit Rima, a village on an eminence 2 miles N. of Timnah. Others incline to Rāmallah, 8 miles N. of Jerus and 3 miles from Bethel (Mt **27** 57; Mk **15** 43; Lk **23** 51; Jn **19** 38).

S. F. Hunter

ARIOCH, ar'i-ok: (אַרְיוֹךְ, *'aryōkh*):

(1) The name of the vassal king of Ellasar, under Chedorlaomer, king of Elam, and Amraphel, king of Shinar (Babylonia), who took part in the expedition against Sodom, Gomorrah and other states (Gen **14** 1.9). Assyriologists generally, and probably rightly, identify A. with Êri-Aku (q.v.), king of Larsa, Ellasar being for Al-Larsa (now *Sinqāra* in central Babylonia).

For an account of the expedition see Amraphel, and for the Babylonian texts bearing upon the reign, see Êri-Aku. In Gen **14** 1.9, where the names of the allied kings who marched against the Cities of the Plain are given, that of Arioch follows his more immediate suzerain, Amraphel, and not Chedorlaomer, who, however, appears to have been the real overlord (ver 4), which agrees with the indications of the Bab records. No details of the expedition are available from Bab sources. Besides Larsa, Êri-Aku's inscriptions inform us that Ur (*Muqayyar, Mugheir*) was in the principality of which Larsa was the capital.

Texts Referring to the Reign of Arioch

(2) The Arioch of Dnl **2** 14.25 was captain of the bodyguard of King Nebuchadnezzar. Nothing else is known about him except that it was he who was commanded to slay the "wise men" who failed to repeat to the king his dream and its interpretation; and who communicated to his royal master that Daniel had undertaken the task. T. G. Pinches

ARISAI, ar'i-sai, a-ris'ā-ī (אֲרִיסַי, *'ărīṣai*): Probably a Pers word of unknown meaning. One of Haman's sons, slain by the Jews (Est **9** 9).

ARISTARCHUS, ar-is-tär'kus (**'Αρίσταρχος,** *Arístarchos*, "best ruler"): He was one of those faithful companions of the apostle Paul who shared with him his labors and sufferings. He is suddenly mentioned along with Gaius as having been seized by the excited Ephesians during the riot stirred up by the silversmiths (Acts **19** 29). They are designated "men of Macedonia, Paul's companions in travel." We learn later that he was a native of Thessalonica (**20** 4; **27** 2). They were probably seized to extract from them information about their leader Paul, but when they could tell nothing, and since they were Greeks, nothing further was done to them.

When Aristarchus attached himself to Paul we do not know, but he seems ever after the Ephesian uproar to have remained in Paul's company. He was one of those who accompanied Paul from Greece via Macedonia (**20** 4). Having preceded Paul to Troas, where they waited for him, they traveled with him to Pal. He is next mentioned as accompanying Paul to Rome (**27** 2). There he attended Paul and shared his imprisonment. He is mentioned in two of the letters of the Rom captivity, in the Epistle to the church at Col (**4** 10), and in the Epistle to Philem (ver 24), in both of which he sends greetings. In the former Paul calls him "my fellow-prisoner." According to tradition he was martyred during the persecution of Nero.

S. F. Hunter

ARISTOBULUS, ar-is-to-bū'lus (**'Αριστόβουλος,** *Aristóboulos*, "best counselor"):

(1) Son of the Maccabean, John Hyrcanus, who assumed the power and also the title of king after his father's death (105 BC) and associated with him, as co-regent, his brother Antigonus (*Ant*, XIII, xi), though by the will of his father the government was intrusted to his mother. Three other brothers and his mother he cast into prison, where they died of starvation. He murdered Antigonus, and died conscience-stricken himself in 104 BC. See Maccabees.

(2) Aristobulus, nephew of the former, dethroned his mother, Alexandra (69 BC), and forced his brother Hyrcanus to renounce the crown and mitre in his favor. In 64 Pompey came to Pal and supported the cause of Hyrcanus. See Hyrcanus. Aristobulus was defeated and taken prisoner, and Hyrcanus was appointed ethnarch in 63 BC. Aristobulus and his two daughters were taken to Rome, where he graced the triumph of Pompey. The father escaped later (56 BC) and appeared in Pal again as a claimant to the throne. Many

followers flocked to his standard, but he was finally defeated, severely wounded and taken prisoner a second time and with his son, Antigonus, again taken to Rome. Julius Caesar not only restored him to freedom (49 BC), but also gave him two legions to recover Judaea, and to work in his interest against Pompey. But Quintus Metellus Scipio, who had just received Syria as a province, had Aristobulus poisoned as he was on his way to Pal.

(3) Grandson of the preceding, and the last of the Maccabean family. See ASMONEANS.

(4) The Jewish teacher of Ptol. VII (2 Macc **1** 10).

(5) An inhabitant of Rome, certain of whose household are saluted by Paul (Rom **16** 10). He was probably a grandson of Herod and brother of Herod Agrippa, a man of great wealth, and intimate with the emperor Claudius. Lightfoot (*Philippians*, 172) suggests that "the household of A." were his slaves, and that upon his death they had kept together and had become the property of the emperor either by purchase or as a legacy, in which event, however, they might still retain the name of their former master. Among these were Christians to whom Paul sends greeting.

M. O. EVANS

ARITHMETIC, a-rith′me-tik. See NUMBER.

ARIUS, a-rī′us, ā′ri-us (**Ἄρης**, *Árēs*): The reading of the Vulg adopted in RV for the former reading *Areus* and *Areios* of Jos. A king of Sparta (309–265 BC) who wrote the letter to Onias, the high priest, given in 1 Macc **12** 7.20–23. There were two Spartan kings named Arius, and three high priests named Onias. Chronology requires the letter mentioned to have been written by Arius I to Onias I, most probably in the interval between 309 and 300 BC. See LACEDAEMONIANS.

ARK, ärk, **OF BULRUSHES**, bŏŏl′rush-iz (תֵּבָה, *tēbhāh;* Egyp *tĕbt;* LXX **θῖβις**, *thībis*, "a chest," "a vessel to float"):

1. Definitions

The Heb word here tr^d "ark" is used in the OT only of the ark of Noah (Gen **6** 14 ff) and of the ark of bulrushes (Ex **2** 3), and always in the secondary meaning, a vessel to float. The LXX translates it of Noah's ark by *κιβωτός*, *kibōtós*, "a casket," and of the ark of bulrushes by *thībis*, a little basket made of osiers or flags. For the Ark of the Covenant, the Heb employed a different word (אָרוֹן, *'ārōn*, "a chest"). *Bulrushes* (גֹּמֶא, *gōme'*, "papyrus"): This species of reed was used by the Egyptians for many different vessels, some of which were intended to float or even to be used as a skiff. *Slime* (חֵמָר, *ḥēmār*, "bitumen"), *pitch* (זֶפֶת, *zepheth*, "pitch") was probably the sticky mud of the Nile with which to this day so many things in Egypt are plastered. In this case it was mixed with bitumen. *Flags* (סוּף, *ṣūph*, "sedge") were reeds of every kind and tall grass growing in the shallow water at the edge of the river.

Thus the ark of bulrushes was a vessel made of papyrus stalks and rendered fit to float by being

2. History

covered with a mixture of bitumen and mud. Into this floating vessel the mother of Moses placed the boy when he was three months old, and put the vessel in the water among the sedge along the banks of the Nile at the place where the ladies from the palace were likely to come to bathe. The act was a pathetic imitation of obedience to the king's command to throw boy babies into the river, a command which she had for three months braved and which now she so obeyed as probably to bring the cruelty of the king to the notice of the royal ladies in such way as to arouse a womanly sympathy.

A similar story is related of Sargon I of Babylonia (*Records of the Past,* 1st ser., V, 1–4; Rogers, *Hist. Bab and Assyr,* I, 362).

The one story in no wise discredits the other. That method of abandoning children, either willingly or by necessity, is as natural along the Nile and the Euphrates, where the river is the great artery of the land and where the floating basket had been used from time immemorial, as is the custom in our modern cities of placing abandoned infants in the streets or on door-steps where they are likely to be found, and such events probably occurred then as often as now.

M. G. KYLE

ARK OF THE COVENANT, kuv′e-nant (אֲרוֹן הַבְּרִית, *'ărōn ha-b^erīth*):

I. The Statements of the OT Concerning the Ark of the Covenant.—In Ex **25** 10 ff, Moses receives

1. Pentateuch

the command to build an ark of acacia wood. Within this ark were to be placed the tables of the law which God was about to give to Moses. Upon the top of the ark, probably not as a lid but above the lid, the כַּפֹּרֶת, *kappōreth*, in the NT *τὸ ἱλαστήριον*, *tó hilastḗrion* (He **9** 5), is to be placed, which was a golden plate upon which two cherubim, with raised wings and facing each other, covered the ark. From the place between the two cherubim God promises to speak to Moses, as often as He shall give him commands in reference to the Israelites.

The portion of the Pent in which this is recorded belongs to the so-called Priest Code, the name given by some critics who hold to the correctness of the documentary theory for such portions of the Pentateuchal books as record the directions for the making and use of the ark of the covenant and the statutes concerning the ceremonial law. Having thus included all the portions of the Pent which speak of these things it results, as a matter of course, that the other portions of the Pent assigned to other supposed authors do not contain similar accounts, although they do contain allusions which imply the correctness of the statement concerning the ark of the covenant. Thus Ex **33** 6 states that the Israelites, in order to demonstrate their repentance on account of the golden calf, had, at God's command, laid aside their ornaments. In vs 7–9 there follows a statement concerning the erection of the sacred tent; but this is explained only by the fact that between vs 6–7 a record concerning the ark of the covenant must be assumed. In Dt the ark was built on this occasion. We further conclude that it was not so much the tabernacle which could serve as a guide to the people, something which at that time they needed, but rather the ark which symbolized to them that God was on the march with them. Again in Ex **33** 4 it is a justifiable assumption that some use was made of the ornaments discarded, and Dt **10** 1–5 clearly states the case, the construction of the ark. In Nu **10** 33 ff we read that the ark preceded the people as they broke camp and marched from Sinai. At this place the words are found which Moses was accustomed to speak when the ark began to move out and when it arrived at a halting-place. The intricately involved discussion of the supposed documents of the Pent in which the actualities of the ark of the covenant come up for consideration is a most cogent objection to the whole documentary theory. That the story of the ark of the covenant, and with it the whole Pentateuchal account, could have been made in such fashion as the documentary theory requires is evident enough. Children do so with scissors and paste; literati gather fragments from many sources to make scrapbooks. But that anyone would make a law book so, gathering paragraphs and scraps, even portions of phrases, from different sources and distributing them throughout a historical narrative which might be lifted out and read consecutively by itself is a very different matter. The great elaborateness of the method by which the actuality of the ark of the covenant is made to appear by critics is in itself a presumptive refutation of the theory; elaborate explanations are nearly always wrong; the truth has simplicity as one of its characteristic marks (Kyle, *The Problem of the Pentateuch*, Investigation IV). For the intricateness of the documentary theory, see Haupt, *The Polychrome Bible*.

According to the narrative in Josh **3** the ark coöperated at the crossing of the Jordan in such a way that the waters of the river ceased to continue flowing as soon as the feet of the priests who were carrying the ark entered the water, and that it stood still above until these priests, after the people had crossed over, again left the bed of the river with the ark. In the account of the solemn march around Jericho, which according to ch **6** caused the walls of the city to fall, the carrying of the ark around the city is regarded as an essential feature in vs 4.7.11. In ch **7** it is narrated that Joshua, after the defeat of the army before Ai, lamented and prayed before the ark. In ch **8** this is mentioned in connection with Mount Ebal.

2. Joshua

At the time of Eli the ark stood in the sanctuary at Shiloh (1 S **3** 3). From this place it was taken after Israel had been defeated by the Philis at Ebenezer, in order to assure the help of Jeh to the people; but, instead of this, the ark fell into the hands of the Philis (1 S **4**). But the various misfortunes that now afflicted the Philis induced these to regard the possession of the ark as a calamity (1 S **5**) and they sent it back to Israel (1 S **6**). It was brought first to Bethshemesh in the tribe of Judah, near the borders of the Philis, and soon after to Kiriath-jearim, about 7.5 miles N.W. of Jerus. There the ark remained for years in the house of a man by the name of Abinadab, whose son was its guardian (1 S **7** 1), until David brought it to Mount Zion, after he had established his camp and court there. He there placed it in a tent prepared for it (2 S **6**; 1 Ch **13**, **15**). In David's time again the ark was taken along into battle (2 S **11** 11). When David fled from the presence of Absalom, the priests wanted to accompany him with the ark, but he sent it back (2 S **15** 24 f). David had also intended to build a temple, in which the ark was to find its place, since before this it had always found its resting-place in a tent. But God forbade this through Nathan, because He was willing to build a house for David, but was not willing that David should build one for Him (2 S **7**). Solomon then built the temple and placed the ark of the covenant in the Holy of Holies of this temple, where it was placed under the wings of two mighty cherubim images (1 K **8**; 2 Ch **5**).

3. Other Historical Books

Jeremiah in the passage **3** 16, which certainly was written after the destruction of Jerus, states that in the future new Jerus nobody will any more concern himself about the ark of the covenant of Jeh, and no one will again build such a one. In the post-exilic Ps **132** (ver 8), Jeh is petitioned to occupy together with the ark, the symbol of His omnipotent presence, also the sanctuary that has been erected for Him, the poet describing himself and those who sing this psalm as participants in the home-bringing of the ark by David. No further mention is made of the ark of the covenant in the Psalter or the prophetical books. In the NT the ark of the covenant is mentioned only in He **9** 4 in the description of the Solomonic temple.

4. Prophetical and Poetical Books

5. The NT

II. The Form of the Ark of the Covenant.—According to the statement in Scripture, the ark was a chest made out of acacia wood, $2\frac{1}{2}$ cubits (about 3 ft.) long, and $1\frac{1}{2}$ cubits wide, and $1\frac{1}{2}$ cubits high. The statement that it was made of acacia wood is repeated in Dt **10** 3. According to the account in Ex it was covered with gold within and without and was ornamented with a molding of gold running all around it. At its four feet rings were added through which the gold-covered carrying staves were put. These staves were also mentioned in 1 K **8** 7–8; and 2 Ch **5** 8–9; and mention is often made of those who carried the ark (2 S **6** 13; **15** 24). There is no reason whatever to doubt the correctness of this simple statement of fact thus repeated in different places. Questions raised about the reality of the gold *Kappōreth* seem almost frivolous; were not the Israelite craftsmen trained in Egypt? The correct interpretation of the tabernacle narrative is thus to be found rather in the facts of the life of the people and their historical antecedents than by microscopic literary study of the documents in which they are recorded (Kyle, *Moses and the Monuments*, 162 ff).

The statement that Solomon placed the ark in the Holy of Holies between two massive cherubim figures (1 K **6** 19.23 ff; **8** 6) does not prove that there were no cherubim figures on the ark itself, or even that those cherubim figures, which according to Ex **25** 19 were found on the ark, were nothing else than those of Solomon's days in imagination transferred back to an earlier period (Vatke, *Biblische Theologie*, 1835, 333; Popper, *Der biblische Bericht über die Stiftshütte*, 1862). In recent times the view has been maintained that the ark in reality was no ark at all but an empty throne. It was Reichel, in his work *Vorhellenische Götterkulte*, who first expressed this view, and then Meinhold, *Die Lade Jahwes*, Tübingen, 1910, and *Theologische Studien und Kritiken*, 1901, 593–617, who developed this view in the following manner. It is claimed that in the days of Moses a throne-like rock at Mount Sinai was regarded as the seat of Jeh, and when the Israelites departed from Sinai they made for themselves a portable throne, and Jeh was regarded as sitting visibly enthroned upon this and accompanying His people. In the main the same view was maintained by Martin Dibellius (*Die Lade Jahwes*, Göttingen, 1906; Hermann Gunkel, *Die Lade Jahwes ein Thronsitz*, reprinted from the *Zeitschrift für Missionskunde und Religionswissenschaft*, Heidelberg, 1906). The occasion for this view was given by the fact that among the Persians and other people there were empty thrones of the gods, which were carried or hauled around in processions. The reasons for finding in the ark of the covenant such an empty throne are found chiefly in this, that the passages in the OT, in which it seems that the presence of God is made conditional on the presence of the ark (cf Nu **14** 42–44), can be explained if the ark is regarded as a throne of Jeh. However, empty thrones of the gods are found only among the Aryan people, and all of the passages of the OT which refer to the ark can be easily explained without such a supposition. This view is to be rejected particularly for this reason, that in the OT the ark is always described as an ark, and never as a throne or a seat; and because it is absolutely impossible to see what reason would have existed at a later period to state that it was an ark if it had originally been a throne. Dibelius and Gunkel appeal also particularly to this, that in several passages, of which 1 S **4** 4; 2 S **6** 2 are the oldest, Jeh is declared to be enthroned on the cherubim. But this proves nothing, because He is not called "He who is enthroned on the ark," and the cherubim and the ark are two different things, even if there were cherubim on the lid of the ark. Cf the refutation of Meinhold and Dibelius by Budde (*ZATW*, 1901, 193–200, and *Theol. Studien und Kritiken*, 1906, 489–507).

III. The Contents of the Ark of the Covenant.—According to the Pent the two tables of the law constituted the contents of the ark. In Ex **25** 16; **40** 20, as also Dt **10** 5, and, too, in 1 K **8** 9, we have the same testimony. The majority of the modern critics regard this as an unhistorical statement first concocted by the so-called "Deuteronomistic school." Their reasons for this are the following: (1) The critics deny that the existence of the Mosaic tables of the law is a historical fact; (2) The critics declare that if these tables had really been in possession of the Israelites, they would not have been so foolish as to put them into a box which it was forbidden to open; (3) The critics declare that the views entertained in olden times on the importance of the ark cannot be reconciled with the presence of the tables in the ark. But we reply: (1) that the actual existence of the two tables of the law is denied without sufficient reasons; that the ten principal formulas of the Decalogue, as these are given in Ex **20** and Dt **5**, come from Moses, must be insisted upon, and that according to Ex **34** other ten commandments had been written on these tables is incorrect. The laws in Ex **34** 17–26 are not at all declared there to be the ten words which God intended to write upon the tables. But if Moses had prepared the tables for the commandments, then it is (2) only probable that he caused to be made a suitable chest for their preservation and their transportation through the desert. Now it might be thought that the view that the ark was so holy that it dared not be opened had originated only after the time of Moses. However, it is just as easily possible, that that importance had already been assigned by Moses to the tables in the ark which the sealed and carefully preserved copy of a business agreement would have and which is to be opened only in case of necessity (Jer **32** 11–14). Such a case of necessity never afterward materialized, because the Israelites were never in doubt as to what was written on these tables. On a verbatim reading no stress was laid in olden times. (3) With regard to the importance of the ark according to the estimate placed upon it in the earlier period of Israel, we shall see later that the traditions in reference to the tables harmonize fully with this importance.

Of the modern critics who have rejected this tradition, some have thought that the ark was empty, and that the Israelites thought that Jeh dwelt in it (Guthe, *Geschichte des Volkes Israel*, 39), or that the empty chest was a kind of fetish (Schwally, *Semitische Kriegsaltertümer*, 1901, I, 10). As a rule they believe that a stone image of Jeh or two stones had been placed in the ark, these being possibly meteor stones, in which it was thought that some divine power was dwelling (Stade, *Geschichte Israels*, I, 458); or possibly stones that in some battle or other had been hurled and through which a victory had been won (Couard, *ZATW*, XII, 76); or possibly they were the stones which at the alliance of the tribes that dwelt about Mount Sinai were first set up as testimonials of this covenant (Kraetzschmar, *Die Bundesvorstellung im Alten Testament*, 216). Of these views only the one which declares that the ark contained meteor stones deserves any notice, because it could indeed be thought possible that Israel would have taken with them on their journey through the desert such stones which they could have regarded as pledges of the Divine Presence fallen from heaven and could have preserved these in a sacred ark. But it is impossible to show that this view is probable, not to speak of proving it to be correct. The only extant tradition says that the ark contained the tables of the law, and this is the only view that is in harmony with what we must think of the whole work of Moses. Finally it must be remembered that all the supposed documents either state explicitly that the "tables of the law" were placed in the ark or used language which makes it highly important to assume this as a fact (Ex **33** 4–6; 7–10; Dt **10** 1–5).

IV. The Names of the Ark of the Covenant.—The name "ark of the covenant of Jeh" was not originally found everywhere where it now stands, but in many places the words "of the covenant" were added later. However, the expression "ark of the covenant" is found in the oldest source of the Book of S (2 S **15** 24), and in 1 K **3** 15 in the old source for the history of Solomon, of which the Deuteronomistic author of the Book of Kings made use; in 1 K **8** 1, a very old account of the building of the temple; and the genuineness of the expression "ark of the covenant" in these passages is not with any good reasons to be called into question. Further the expression is found in the books of Numbers and Joshua, in a number of passages (Nu **10** 33; **14** 44; Josh **3** 3.6.8; **4** 9.18; **6** 6.8), which in all probability belong to the document E. It appears that E designates the ark as the "ark of the covenant of God," or more briefly, as the "ark of the covenant," unless in a connected narrative he writes only "the ark," while in J the principal appellation was "ark of Jeh, the Lord of the whole earth" (cf Lotz, *Die Bundeslade*, 1901, 30–36). From this we must conclude that the appellation "ark of the covenant of Jeh" must go back to very ancient times, and we must reject the view that this term took the place of the term "ark of Jeh" in consequence of a change of views with reference to the ark, brought about through Deuteronomy. Indeed, assuming the truth of the documentary theory, the expression, "ark of the covenant", was nowhere more used than in Ephraim where they did not possess the ark and so would have had the least occasion to introduce a new name for it, it can be accepted that the name originated in the oldest times, namely those of Moses. The other expression "ark of Jeh" may be just as old and need not be an abbreviation of the other. It was possible to designate the ark as "ark of Jeh" because it was a sanctuary belonging to Jeh; and it was possible to call it also "the ark of the covenant of Jeh," because it was a monument and evidence of the covenant which Jeh had made with Israel. It is for this reason not correct to translate the expression *'arōn b^erīth Yahweh* by "the ark of the law of Jeh," as equivalent to "the ark which served as a place for preserving the law of the covenant." For *b^erīth* does not signify "law," even if it was possible under certain circumstances to call a covenant "law" figuratively and synecdochically the "covenant"; and when 1 K **8** 21 speaks of "the ark wherein is the covenant of Jeh," the next words, "which he made with our fathers," show that covenant does not here mean "law," but rather the covenant relationship which in a certain sense is embodied in the tables.

Again assuming the correctness of the documentary theory, in P the ark is called "the ark of testimony," not signifying "the ark of the law." For only in later documents did the word *ʿēdhūth* receive the meaning "law" (Lotz, *Die Bundeslade*, 40). The supposition required by P uses "testimony" to mean "The Ten Words" through which God has given evidence of His nature. But where this testimony is found engraved in the handwriting of God on the tables of stone, just there also is the place where He too is to be regarded as locally present.

V. The History of the Ark of the Covenant.—According to the tradition contained in the Pent the sacred ark was built at Mount Sinai and was taken by the Israelites along with them to Canaan. This must be accepted as absolutely correct. The supposition is groundless, that it was a shrine that the Israelites had taken over from the Canaanites. This view is refuted by the high estimate in which in Eli's time the ark was held by all Israel (1 S **1** ff; **2** 22); and especially by the fact that the ark was at that time regarded as the property of that God who had brought Israel out of Egypt, and accordingly had through this ark caused the Canaanites to be conquered (1 S **4 8; 6** 6; 2 S **7** 6; 1 K **12** 28). The opinion also that the ark was an ancient palladium of the tribe of Ephraim or of the descendants of Joseph and was only at a later period recognized by all Israel (Stade, *Geschichte des Volkes Israel*, I, 458) is not tenable, for we hear nothing to the effect that the descendants of Joseph concerned themselves more for the ark than the other tribes did. In the time of Eli the ark stood in the sanctuary at Shiloh. When Israel had been conquered by the Philis, the ark was taken from Shiloh in order that Jeh should aid His people. But notwithstanding this the Philis yet conquered and captured the ark (1 S **5**). But the many misfortunes that overtook them made them think that the possession of the ark was destructive to them and they sent it back (1 S **6**). The ark first came to Bethshemesh, in the tribe of Judah, and then to Kiriath-jearim (or Baale-judah, 2 S **6** 2), about 7.5 miles N.W. of Jerus. There the ark remained for many years until David, after he had taken possession of Mount Zion, took it there (2 S **6**) and deposited it in a tent. Solomon brought it into the Holy of Holies in the temple (1 K **8** 3–8), where in all probability it remained until the destruction of Jerus by Nebuchadnezzar; for Jer **3** 16 proves that the Israelites felt that they were in possession of the ark up to this time.

VI. The Significance of the Ark.—According to many investigators the ark was originally a war sanctuary. In favor of this it can be urged that Israel took it into their camp, in order that they might receive the help of Jeh in the battle with the Philis (1 S **4**); and further that also in the time of David the ark was again taken along into battle (2 S **11** 11; cf Ps **24**); note also the word of Moses, which he spoke when the ark was taken up to be carried: "Rise up, O Jeh, and let thine enemies be scattered" (Nu **10** 35). However, nothing of what we know or presuppose concerning the form and the contents of the ark points to an original military purpose of the same; and in the other statements that are found elsewhere concerning the ark, a much more general significance is assigned to it. The significance which the ark had for the Israelites in connection with their wars is only the outcome of its signification as the symbol of the presence of Jeh, who was not at all a God of war, but when His people were compelled to fight was their helper in the struggle.

A Symbol of the Divine Presence

That the ark was designed to be a symbol of the presence of God in the midst of His people is the common teaching of the OT. According to Ex the ark was made to serve as a comfort to the people for this, that they were to leave the mountain where God had caused them to realize His presence (Ex **30** 6). In Ex **25** 21–22, God purposed to speak with Moses from the place between the cherubim upon the ark. According to Jgs **2** 1 ff, the angel of Jeh spoke in Bethel (Bochim) in reproof and exhortation to the people, after the ark of the covenant had been brought to that place; for the comparison of Nu **10** 33 ff and Ex **23** 20 ff shows that Jgs **2** 1 is to be understood as speaking of the transfer of the ark to Bethel. When Israel in the time of Eli was overpowered by the Philis, the Israelites sent for the ark, in order that Jeh should come into the camp of Israel, and this was also believed to be the case by the Philis (1 S **4** 3 ff). After the ark had come to Bethshemesh and a pestilence had broken out there, the people did not want to keep the ark, because no one could live in the presence of Jeh, this holy God (1 S **6** 20); and Jeremiah says (**3** 16.17) that an ark of the covenant would not be again made after the restoration of Israel, but then Jerus would be called the "throne of Jeh," i.e. it would so manifestly be the city of God that it would guarantee the presence of God at least just as much as the ark formerly did.

In olden times these things appeared more realistic to the people than they do to us; and when the ark was considered the visible representation of the presence of Jeh, and as guaranteeing His presence, a close material connection was thought to exist between the ark and Jeh, by virtue of which Divine powers were also thought to be present in the ark. The people at Bethshemesh were not willing to keep the ark any longer in their midst, because they could not live in its near presence. David's dancing before the ark is regarded by him and by the narrator of the event as a dancing before the Lord (2 S **6** 5.14.21), and in 2 S **7** 5 ff God says, through Nathan, that He had wandered around in a tent since He had led the Israelites out of Egypt.

But the view advocated by some of the modern critics, that the Israelites had thought that the ark was the dwelling-place or the throne-seat of Jehovah, is nevertheless not correct. This opinion cannot be harmonized with this fact, that in the sources, dating from the same olden times, mention is made of His dwelling in many places in Canaan and outside of Canaan, so that the idea that His presence or even He Himself is confined to the ark is impossible. The statement of Moses, "Rise up, O Jeh, and let thine enemies be scattered" (Nu **10** 35), is not the command addressed to those who carry the ark to lift it up and thereby to lift Jeh up for the journey, but is a demand made upon Jeh, in accordance with His promise, to go ahead of Israel as the ark does. According to 1 S **4** 3 the Israelites did not say "We want to go and get Jeh," but "We want to go and get the ark of Jeh, so that He may come into our midst." They accordingly only wanted to induce Him to come by getting the ark. This, too, the priests and the soothsayers of the Philis say: "Do not permit the ark of the God of the Israelites to depart without sending a gift along," but they do not speak thus of Jeh. That Samuel, who slept near the ark, when he was addressed by Jeh, did not at all at first think that Jeh was addressing him, proves that at that time the view did not prevail that He was in the ark or had His seat upon it. Ancient Israel was accordingly evidently of the conviction that the ark was closely connected with Jeh, that something of His power was inherent in the ark; consequently the feeling prevailed that when near the ark they were in a special way in the presence of and near to the Lord. But this is something altogether different from the opinion that the ark was the seat or the dwelling-place of Jeh. Even if the old Israelites, on account of the crudeness of antique methods of thought, were not conscious of the greatness of this difference, the fact that this difference was felt is not a matter of doubt. That the ark was built to embody the presence of God among His people seems equally clear from each one of the suppositional documents of the documentary theory, and if these have accordingly regarded the tables of the law as constituting the contents of the ark, then this is in perfect harmony with their views of this purpose, and we too must cling to these same views. For what would have been better adapted to make the instrument which represents the presence of God more suitable for this than the stone tables with the Ten Words, through which Jeh had made known to His people His ethical character? For this very purpose it had to be an ark. The words on these tables were a kind of a spiritual portrait of the God of Israel, who could not be pictured in a bodily form. In this shape nobody in ancient Israel has formulated this thought, but that this thought was present is certain.

REVISED BY M. G. K. WILHELM LOTZ

ARK, ärk, OF NOAH, nō'a: A structure built by Noah at the command of God to preserve from the Flood a remnant of the human race and of the animals associated with man. It was constructed of "gopher wood" (Gen **6** 14)—very likely the cypress used extensively by the Phoenicians for ship-building. It was divided into rooms or nests, and was three stories high, pitched within and without with bitumen or "asphalt," of which there are extensive deposits at Hit, in the Euphrates valley, a little above Babylon. It was 300 cubits long, 50 cubits broad, 30 cubits high, which according to Petrie's estimate of a cubit as 22.5 inches would make it to be 562½ ft. long, 93⅔ ft. wide, 56¼ ft. deep, which are natural proportions of a ship of that size. The dimensions of the "Great Eastern," built in 1858, were 692 ft. long, 83 ft. broad, 58 ft. deep; those of the "Celtic" built in 1901 are 700 ft. long, 75 ft. wide, 49⅓ ft. deep. It is extremely improbable that such reasonable dimensions should have been assigned to the Ark except they were based on fact. Unrestrained tradition would have been sure to distort the proportions, as is shown by what actually occurred in other accounts of the Ark. The cuneiform tablets represent it as six stories high, with the length, width, and depth, each as 140 cubits (262 ft.), and having a mast on top of all, and a pilot to guide the impossible craft (see *Deluge Tablet*, ll. 22, 23, 38-41). Berosus, the Gr historian, represents it to have been five stadia (3,000 ft.) long and two stadia (1,200 ft.) broad, while Origen, in order to confound Celsus (*Against Celsus* 4.41) gave the figures an interpretation which made the Ark 25 miles long and ¾ of a mile wide.

It is needless to speculate upon the capacity of the Ark for holding absolutely all the species of animals found in the world, together with the food necessary for them, since we are only required to provide for such animals as were native to the area to which the remnants of the human race living at that time were limited, and which (see DELUGE) may not have been large. But calculations show that the structure described contained a space of about 3,500,000 cubic feet, and that after storing food enough to support several thousand pairs of animals, of the average size, on an ocean voyage of a year, there would remain more than 50 cubic feet of space for each pair.

No mention is made in the Bible of a pilot for the Ark, but it seems to have been left to float as a derelict upon the waters. For that purpose its form and dimensions were perfect, as was long ago demonstrated by the celebrated navigator, Sir Walter Raleigh, who notes it had "a flat bottom, and was not raised in form of a ship, with a sharpness forward, to cut the waves for the better speed" —a construction which secured the maximum of storage capacity and made a vessel which would ride steadily upon the water. Numerous vessels after the pattern of the Ark, but of smaller dimensions, have been made in Holland and Denmark and proved admirably adapted for freightage where speed was not of the first importance. They would hold one-third more lading than other vessels, and would require no more hands to work them. The gradual rise and subsidence of the water, each continuing for six months, and their movement inland, render the survival of such a structure by no means unreasonable. According to Gen **6** 3; 1 Pet **3** 20; 2 Pet **2** 5, warning of the Flood was given 120 years beforehand, and during that time Noah, while preparing the Ark, became a preacher of righteousness. For evidence that there was a gradual destruction of the race previous to the Flood, see DELUGE.

GEORGE FREDERICK WRIGHT

ARK OF TESTIMONY, test'i-mo-ni. See ARK OF COVENANT.

ARKITE, ark'īt (עַרְקִי, *'arḳī*): An inhabitant of the town of Arka, situated some ten or twelve miles N.E. of Tripolis, Syria, and about four miles from the shore of the sea. The Arkites are mentioned in Gen **10** 17 and 1 Ch **1** 15 as being the descendants of Canaan, and they were undoubtedly of Phoen stock. The place was not of much importance, but it is mentioned in the Assyr inscriptions, under the name Irkatah and taken by Tiglath-pileser III in 738 BC. Not being on the sea its trade was small and it probably belonged to Tripoli or Botrys originally. It was the birthplace of Alexander Severus, hence its Rom name, Caesarea Libani. Its site is marked by a high mound near the foothills of Lebanon.

H. PORTER

ARM, ärm (זְרוֹעַ, *z^erō^a'*, אֶזְרוֹעַ, *'ezrō^a'*, דְּרָע, *d^erā'*; **βραχίων,** *brachíōn;* חֹצֶן, *ḥōçen*, כָּתֵף, *kāthēph*): The usual form is *z^erō^a'* from the root *zāra'*, "to spread." The arm may be "stretched out." *'Ezrō^a'* is this form with prosthetic *'ālēph* (Job **31** 22; Jer **32** 21), and *d^erā'* is the Aram. form. *Ḥōçen* is really "bosom," thus RV (Isa **49** 22); and *kāthēph* is "shoulder," thus RV (Job **31** 22). Cf χείρ, *cheír*, also, in Acts **11** 21.

Figurative: The arm denotes influence, power, means of support or conquest. The arms of Moab (Jer **48** 25) and of Pharaoh (Ezk **30** 21 ff) are broken. The arm of Eli and the arm of his father's house are to be cut off (1 S **2** 31). Because the arm wielded the sword it signified "oppression" (Job **35** 9). The arms are the means of support, therefore to refuse to aid the fatherless is to break their arms (Job **22** 9).

Applied anthropomorphically to God the arm denotes also His power, power to deliver, support, conquer. His "outstretched arm" delivered Israel from Egypt (Ex **6** 6; Dt **4** 34, etc). They support: "Underneath are the everlasting arms" (Dt **33** 27). His arm protects (Isa **40** 11). Jeh is sometimes likened to a warrior and smites with His arm (Ps **89** 10; Isa **63** 5; Jer **21** 5). The arm of Jeh is holy (Ps **98** 1; Isa **52** 10). Many other passages of Scripture might be quoted showing how the power of God to redeem, judge, protect, punish is expressed by the idea of "the arm of Jeh."

S. F. HUNTER

ARMAGEDDON, är-ma-ged'on (**'Αρμαγεδδών,** *Armageddōn:* Rev **16** 16; RV "HAR-MAGEDON") (q.v.).

ARMENIA, är-mē'ni-a:

I. GEOGRAPHY
II. HISTORY (ANCIENT)
1. Turanian Armenians
Their Religion
2. Aryan Armenians: History to 114 AD
LITERATURE

I. Geography.—אֲרָרָט, *'ărārāṭ* (Šumerian *Ar*, "region," +*ar* "high," +*ṭu*, "mountain," = "high mountainous region"): in Assyr, *Urṭu*, *Urarṭu*, *Uraštu*: in Ægyp, *Ermenen* (= "Region of the Minni") *OP*, *Armina*, *Armaniya* (Ἀρμενία, *Armenía*): in Hecatæus of Miletus, cir 520 BC, the people are Ἀρμένιοι (Gen **8** 4; 2 K **19** 37; Isa **37** 38; Jer **51** 27). Throughout the Bible, this is a *country*, not a mountain. Armenia Major was bounded on the N. by the River Cyrus (Kour), Iberia, Colchis, and the Moschici Mts.; on the W. by Asia Minor and the Euphrates; on the S. by Mesopotamia and Assyria; on the E. by the Caspian and Media. (Armenia Minor lay between the Euphrates and the Halys.) Ararat was originally the name of the central district. Most of Armenia is between 8,000 and 3,000 feet above sea-level, and slopes toward Euphrates, Cyrus, and the Caspian. Mt. Massis (generally called Greater Ararat) is 16,969 ft. and Lesser Ararat, 12,840 ft. Both are of igneous origin, as is Aṛagds (A'lā Göz), 13,436 ft. Sulphur springs and earthquakes still attest volcanic activity. The largest rivers are the Euphrates, Tigris and Araxes. The latter, swift and famed for violent floods, joins the Cyrus, which falls into the Caspian. The lakes Van, Urmi and Sevan are veritable inland seas. The many mountain chains, impassable torrents and large streams divide the country into districts far less accessible from one another than from foreign lands. Hence invasions are easy and national union difficult. This has sadly affected the history of Armenia. Xenophon (*Anab.* iv.5) describes the people as living in houses partly underground, such as are still found. Each village was ruled by its chief according to ancient customary laws. He well describes the severity of the winters. In summer the climate in some places is like that of Italy or Spain. Much of Armenia is extremely fertile, producing large herds of horses and cattle, abundant crops of cereals, olives and fruit. It is rich in minerals, and is probably the home of the rose and the vine.

LITERATURE.—Minas Gaphamatzean; Garagashean; Palasanean; *Entir Ḥatouadsner*, I; Rawlinson, *Seven Anc. Monarchies;* Strabo; Xenophon; Petermann, *Mittheilungen* for 1871; Bryce, *Transcaucasia and Ararat.*

ARARAT.

II. Ancient History.—The country is first mentioned in Gen **8** 4 as the *land* upon (some one of) the mountains of which Noah's Ark rested. (According to Jewish tradition this was one of the Kurdish mountains.) It is next spoken of by Sargon I of Agadē, cir 3800 BC, as among his conquests. In early Babylonian legends Armenia figures as an almost unknown land far to the N., full of high mountains and dense forests, containing the entrance to the Lower World (*Mād Nū-gā*, "Land of No Return"). On its borders stood Mt. Niṣir where the gods dwelt and *Ṣit-napištim's* "ship" stopped. This "Mountain of the World" was the present Jabal Jūdī, S. of Lake Van. Next came Egyp influence. Thothmes III, in his twenty-third year (cir 1458 BC), after a great victory over the Rutennu or Ludennu (Mesopotamians and Lydians), received the submission of the "chiefs of *Ermenen*" and others. It is remarkable that the name by which the land is still known to foreigners (Armenians call it *Ḥaiāstān*) should occur so early. In his thirty-third year, Thothmes III mentions the people of Ermenen as paying tribute when he held his court at Nineveh, and says that in their land "heaven rests upon its four pillars." In Seti I's Hall of Columns at Karnak we see the people of Ermenen felling trees in order to open a way through their forests for that king's armies. Rameses II in his twenty-first year, in war with Kheta-sira, king of the Hittites, probably subdued Armenia (cf Taci-

1. Turanian Armenians

tus *Ann.* ii.60). Many places conquered by Rameses III, and mentioned in the Medînet Habū lists, were probably in Armenia. The Assyr king Uras-Pal-aṣur (cir 1190–1170 BC) made a raid into Armenia, and mentions the central district (Urarṭu proper, near Lake Van), the land of the Mannā (Minni, Jer **51** 27), Nahri ("the Rivers"), Ashguza (Ashkenaz, ib), etc. Another invader was Tiglath-pileser I (cir 1110–1090 BC). Asshur-naṣir-pal in 883 BC advanced to Urarṭu. A little later he mentions as articles of Armenian tribute chariots, horses, mules, silver, gold, plates of copper, oxen, sheep, wine, variegated cloths, linen garments. Again and again he carried fire and sword through the country, but it constantly revolted. Under Shalmaneser II (860–825 BC) and afterward for centuries wars continued. By uniting and forming powerful kingdoms (of which the principal was Biainash around Lake Van) the Armenians resisted. Finally in 606 BC they took part in the destruction of Nineveh, and in that of Babylon later. Shalmaneser II tells of the wicker-work coracles on Lake Van. The Balawāt bronzes depict Armenians dressed like the Hittites (to whom they were sometimes subject) in tunics and snow-shoes with turned-up and pointed ends, wearing helmets, swords, spears and small round shields. Sayce compares their faces in form to the Negro type. Possibly they were Mongolians.

The founder of the kingdom of Biainash was Sardurish I, about 840 BC, who built as his capital Tushpash, now Van. He ruled most of Armenia, defending it against the Assyrians, and apparently, inflicting a check on Shalmaneser II in 833 BC. He introduced the cuneiform characters, and his inscriptions are in Assyr. His son Ishpuinish adapted the Assyr syllabary to his own tongue, which bears a slight resemblance to Georgian in some points. The next king, Menuash, has left inscriptions almost all over Armenia, telling of his victories over the Hittites, etc. The kingdom of Biainash reached its acme under the great monarch Argishtish I, who succeeded in defending his country against Shalmaneser III (783–772 BC). But in his son's reign Tiglath-pileser IV (748–727 BC: Pul) crushed the Armenians to the dust in a great battle near Commagene in 743. Pul failed to capture Van in 737, but he ravaged the country far and wide. Rusash I, at the head of an Armenian confederacy, began a great struggle in 716 with Sargon (722–705), who in 714 captured Van with Rusash's family. After 5 months' wandering Rusash committed suicide. His brother Argishtish II to some degree recovered independence. His successor Erimenash gave an asylum to Adrammelech and Sharezer (Aššur-šar-uṣur) in 680 (2 K **19** 37; Isa **37** 38) after the murder of their father Sennacherib. Invading Assyria in the same year, they were defeated by Esar-haddon I. Armenia from the Cyrus River to the S. of Lake Van was ravaged by the Kimmerians (679–677). Rusash II (cir 660–645) and his son Sandurish III (the latter cir 640 or soon after) submitted to Asshur-bani-pal (668–626). Nebuchadnezzar (604–561) boasts of reaching Van in his conquests, though the Armenians had probably their share in the destruction of Nineveh in 606. Jer (**51** 27) mentioned the kingdoms of Ararat, Minni and Ashkenaz about 595, and said they would help in the overthrow of Babylon (in 538). Cyrus had therefore probably subdued or won them over after capturing Ekbatana (549). After this the Turanians gradually gave place in Armenia to the Âryan Armenians of later times.

(*a*) *Their religion.*—The supreme god of the Turanian Armenians was Ḥaldish, who was father of all the rest. They were styled "children of mighty Ḥaldish." He, with Teishbash, god of the atmosphere, and Ardinish, the Sun-god, formed "the company of the mighty gods." Auish, god of water; Ayash, god of the earth; Shelardish, the Moon-god; Sardish, the Year-god; and 42 other gods are mentioned. Sari was a goddess, probably corresponding to Ishtar. Adoration was offered to the spirits of the dead also. Somewhat strangely, some of the divine names we have mentioned remind one of certain Âryan (Gr and Old Pers) words, however this may be accounted for.

LITERATURE.—Valdemar Schmidt, *Assyriens og Ægyptens Gamle Historie;* Masp; Rawlinson, *West. Asiat. Inscrs; KB; Airarat,* 1883; Sayce in *JRAS,* new ser., XIV; *RP;* Hastings, *Enc of Religion and Ethics,* I.

2. Âryan Armenians

The ancestors of the present Armenians (who call themselves *Ḥaik'h,* i.e. *Pati-s,* "Lords") may have settled in the country in the 8th cent. BC, when Sargon mentions a king of part of Armenia who bore the Âryan name Bagadatti (=Theodore). They came from Phrygia (Herod. vii.73), used the Phrygian dress and armor (Dion. of Halicarnassus; Eudoxius; Herod.) and spoke the same language (Herod. i.171). In the Bible they are called the "House of Togarmah" (Gen **10** 3; 1 Ch **1** 6; Ezk **27** 14; **38** 6) and "Ashkenaz" (Gen **10** 3; 1 Ch **1** 6; Jer **51** 27; the Assyr Ashguza), as by their own writers of later times. Xenophon in the *Cyropaedia* mentions a Median conquest of Armenia, Strabo their Median attire; yet Armenian girls could not understand Xenophon's Pers interpreter (*Anab.* iv.5). Three of the four Armenians mentioned by Darius have Âryan names. The Armenians joined the Median noble Fravartish in his revolt against Darius I (519 BC). Much of the consequent fighting took place in Armenia, which was with difficulty subdued (517). It formed part of Darius' thirteenth Nome, and afterward two satrapies (apparently Armenia Major and Minor). The government (of Armenia Major) was made hereditary in the family of Vidarna (Hydarnês) for helping to put down Fravartish. Xenophon's interesting description of the country and people and the severity of its winters is well known. Herodotus tells of Armenians in skin and wicker-work coracles bringing wine, etc, to Babylon. Xenophon says they and the Chaldaeans traded with India. Strabo mentions their caravan trade across central Asia. The satrap of Armenia had to present 20,000 young horses annually to the king of Persia at the great annual festival of Mithra. A large body of Armenian soldiers served in Xerxes' invasion of Greece. At the battle of Arbela (331 BC), 40,000 of their infantry and 7,000 cavalry took part. Armenia then became a portion of Alexander's empire, and later of that of Seleucus (301 BC), under a native satrap, Artavasdēs. Armenia revolted after Antiochus' defeat at Magnesia (190 BC), and the Romans encouraged the two satraps to declare themselves kings. Artaxias, king of Armenia Major, used Hannibal's aid in fortifying his capital Artaxata (189 BC). Artaxias was overthrown by Antiochus Epiphanes in 165, but was restored on swearing allegiance. Civil confusion ensued. The nobles called in the Parthians under Mithridates I (150 BC), who became master of the whole Pers empire. He made his brother Valarsacēs king of Armenia. Thus the Arsacide dynasty was established in that country and lasted till the fall of the Parthian empire (226 AD), the Armenian kings very generally recognizing the Parthian monarchs as their suzerains. The greatest Armenian king was Tigranes I (96–55 BC), a warrior who raised Armenia for a time to the foremost position in Asia. He humbled the Parthians, joined Mithridates VI in war with

Rome, ruled Syria for over 14 years, built near Mārdīn as his capital Tigranocerta, and assumed the Assyrio-Persian title of "King of Kings." Lucullus defeated Tigranes and destroyed Tigranocerta in 69 BC. Tigranes surrendered to Pompey near Artaxata (66 BC), paid 6,000 talents, and retained only Armenia. Under him Gr art and lit. flourished in the country. Armenia as a subject-ally of Rome became a "buffer state" between the Rom and Parthian empires. Tigranes' son and successor Artevasdēs joined in the Parthian invasion of Syria after Crassus' overthrow at Sinnaca 53 BC. He treacherously caused great loss to Antony's army in 36 BC. Antony carried him in chains to Egypt, where Cleopatra put him to death in 32 BC. After this, Armenia long remained subject to the Romans whenever not strong enough to join the Parthians, suffering much from intrigues and the jealousy of both powers. There is no proof of the later Armenian story that Armenia was subject to Abgarus, king of Edessa, in Our Lord's time, and that the gospel was preached there by Thaddaeus, though the latter point is possible. In 66 AD, Tiridates, elder brother of the Parthian king Vologēsēs, having defeated the Romans under Paetus and established himself on the throne of Armenia, went by land to Rome and received investiture from Nero. Peace between Rome and Parthia ensued, and Armenia remained closely united to Parthia till Trajan's expedition in 114 AD.

Literature.—Spiegel, *Altpers. Keilinschriften;* Herodotus; Xenophon; Arrian; Tacitus; Velleius Paterculus; Livy; Polybius; Ammianus Marcellinus.

W. St. Clair Tisdall

ARMENIAN, är-mē'ni-an (**ARYAN,** är'i-an, ar'i-an) **RELIGION.** This greatly resembled that of Persia, though Zoroastrianism and its dualistic system were not professed. We are thus enabled to judge how far the religion of the Avesta is due to Zoroaster's reformation. Aṛamazd (Ahura Mazdā), creator of heaven and earth, was father of all the chief deities. His spouse was probably Spandaṛamet (Speñta Ārmaiti), goddess of the earth, who was later held to preside over the underworld (cf Persephone; Hel). Among her assistants as genii of fertility were Hoṛot and Moṛot (Haurvatāṭ and Ameretāṭ), tutelary deities of Mt. Massis (now styled Ararat). Aṛamazd's worship seems to have fallen very much into the background in favor of that of inferior deities, among the chief of whom was his daughter Anaḥit (Anāhita), who had temples in many places. Her statues were often of the precious metals, and among her many names were "Golden Mother" and "Goddess of the Golden Image." Hence to the present day the word "Golden" enters into many Armenian names. White heifers and green boughs were offered her as goddess of fruitfulness, nor was religious prostitution in her honor uncommon. Next in popularity came her sister Astghik ("the little star"), i.e. the planet Venus, goddess of beauty, wife of the deified hero Vaḥagn (Verethraghna). He sprang from heaven, earth, and sea, and overthrew dragons and other evil beings. Another of Anaḥit's sisters was Nanē (cf Assyr Nanā, Nannaea), afterward identified with Athēnē. Her brother Miḥṛ (Mithra) had the sun as his symbol in the sky and the sacred fire on earth, both being objects of worship. In his temples a sacred fire was rekindled once a year. Aṛamazd's messenger and scribe was Tiuṛ or Tiṛ, who entered men's deeds in the "Book of Life." He led men after death to Aṛamazd for judgment. Before birth he wrote men's fates on their foreheads. The place of punishment was Dzho*kh*k'h (=Pers Dūza*kh*). To the sun and moon sacrifices were offered on the mountain-tops. Rivers and sacred springs and other natural objects were also adored. Prayer was offered facing eastward. Omens were taken from the rustling of the leaves of the sacred Sōnean forest. Aṛmaviṛ was the religious capital.

Among inferior spiritual existences were the Aṛlezk'h, who licked the wounds of those slain in battle and restored them to life. The Parikk'h were evidently the Pairakas (Peris) of Persia. The Armenian mythology told of huge dragons which sometimes appeared as men, sometimes as worms, or basilisks, elves, sea-bulls, dragon-lions, etc. As in Persia, the demons made darts out of the parings of a man's nails to injure him with. Therefore these parings, together with teeth and trimmings of hair, must be hidden in some sacred place.

Literature.—Eznik Goghbatzi; Agathangelos; Moses of Khorēnē; Eghishē; Palasanean; Faustus Byzantinus; Chhamchheantz; Plutarch; Strabo; Tacitus. See my "Conversion of Armenia," *R.T.S.; Expos T*, II, 202 ff.

W. St. Clair Tisdall

ARMENIAN VERSIONS, är-mē'ni-an vûr'shuns, **OF THE BIBLE,** bī'b'l.

I. Ancient Armenian.—Armenia was in large measure Christianized by Gregory Lousavorich ("the Illuminator": consecrated 302 AD; died 332), but, as Armenian had not been reduced to writing, the Scriptures used to be read in some places in Gr, in others in Syr, and tr[d] orally to the people. A knowledge of these tongues and the training of teachers were kept up by the schools which Gregory and King Tiridates had established at the capital Vagharṣhapat and elsewhere. As far as there was any Christianity in Armenia before Gregory's time, it had been almost exclusively under Syrian influence, from Edessa and Samosata. Gregory introduced Gr influence and culture, though maintaining bonds of union with Syria also. When King Sapor of Persia became master of Armenia (378 AD), he not only persecuted the Christians most cruelly, but also, for political reasons, endeavored to prevent Armenia from all contact with the Byzantine world. Hence his viceroy, the renegade Armenian Meṛouzhan, closed the schools, proscribed Gr learning, and burnt all Gr books, especially the Scriptures. Syr books were spared, just as in Persia itself; but in many cases the clergy were unable to interpret them to their people. Persecution had not crushed out Christianity, but there was danger lest it should perish through want of the Word of God. Hence several attempts were made to translate the Bible into Armenian. It is said that Chrysostom, during his exile at Cucusus (404–7 AD), invented an Armenian alphabet and tr[d] the Psalter, but this is doubtful. But when Arcadius ceded almost all Armenia to Sapor about 396 AD, something had to be done. Hence in 397 the celebrated Mesṛob Mashtots and Isaac (Saḥak) the Catholicos resolved to translate the Bible.

1. Circumstances

Mesṛob had been a court secretary, and as such was well acquainted with Pahlavī, Syr and Gr, in which three languages the royal edicts were then published. Isaac had been born at Constantinople and educated there and at Caesarea. Hence he too was a good Gr scholar, besides being versed in Syr and Pahlavī, which latter was then the court language in Armenia. But none of these three alphabets was suited to express the sounds of the Armenian tongue, and hence an alphabet had to be devised for it.

A council of the nobility, bishops and leading clergy was held at Vagharshapat in 402, King Vramshapouh being present, and this council requested Isaac to translate the Scriptures into the vernacular. By 406, Mesrob had succeeded in inventing an alphabet—practically the one still in use—principally by modifying the Gr and the Pahlavī characters, though some think the Palmyrene alphabet had influence. He and two of his pupils at Samosata began by translating the Book of Prov, and then the NT, from the Gr. Meanwhile, being unable to find a single Gr MS in the country, Isaac tr[d] the church lessons from the Pesh Syr, and published this VS in 411. He sent two of his pupils to Constantinople for copies of the Gr Bible. These men were present at the Council of Ephesus, 431 AD. Probably Theodoret (*De Cura Graec. Affect.*, I, 5) learned from them what he says about the existence of the Bible in Armenian. Isaac's messengers brought him copies of the Gr Bible from the Imperial Library at Constantinople —doubtless some of those prepared by Eusebius at Constantine's command. Mesrob Mashtots and Isaac, with their assistants, finished and published the Armenian (ancient) VS of the whole Bible in 436. La Croze is justified in styling it Queen of VSS. Unfortunately the OT was rendered (as we have said) from the LXX, not from the Heb. But the Apoc was not tr[d], only "the 22 Books" of the OT, as Moses of Khorene informs us. This was due to the influence of the Pesh OT.

2. The Translators

(*a*) *Apocrypha omitted.*—Not till the 8th cent. was the Apoc rendered into Armenian: it was not read in Armenian churches until the 12th. Theodotion's VS of Dnl was tr[d], instead of the very inaccurate LXX. The Alexandrine text was generally followed but not always.

In the 6th cent. the Armenian VS is said to have been revised so as to agree with the Pesh. Hence probably in Mt **28** 18 AV, the passage, "As my Father hath sent me, even so send I you," is inserted as in the Pesh, though it occurs also in its proper place (Jn **20** 21). It reads "Jesus Barabbas" in Mt **27** 16.17—a reading which Origen found "in very ancient MSS." It contains Lk **22** 43.44. As is well known, in the Etschmiadzin MS of 986 AD, over Mk **16** 9–20, are inserted the words, "of Ariston the presbyter"; but Nestle (*Text. Criticism of the Gr NT*, Plate IX, etc) and others omit to notice that these words are *by a different and a later hand*, and are merely an unauthorized remark of no great value.

3. Revision

Mesrob's VS was soon widely circulated and became the one great national book. Lazarus Pharpetsi, a contemporary Armenian historian, says he is justified in describing the spiritual results by quoting Isaiah and saying that the whole land of Armenia was thereby "filled with the knowledge of the Lord as the waters cover the sea." But for it, both church and nation would have perished in the terrible persecutions which have now lasted, with intervals, for more than a millennium and a half.

4. Results of Circulation

This VS was first printed somewhat late: the Psalter at Rome in 1565, the Bible by Bishop Oskan of Erivan at Amsterdam in 1666, from a very defective MS; other edd at Constantinople in 1705, Venice in 1733. Dr. Zohrab's ed of the NT in 1789 was far better. A critical ed was printed at Venice in 1805, another at Serampore in 1817. The OT (with the readings of the Heb text at the foot of the page) appeared at Constantinople in 1892 ff.

5. Printed Editions

II. Modern Armenian Versions.—There are two great literary dialects of modern Armenian, in which it was necessary to publish the Bible, since the ancient Armenian (called *Grapar*, or "written") is no longer generally understood. The American missionaries have taken the lead in translating Holy Scripture into both.

The first VS of the NT into Ararat Armenian, by Dittrich, was published by the British and Foreign Bible Society at Moscow in 1835; the Psalter in 1844; the rest of the OT much later. There is an excellent ed, published at Constantinople in 1896.

1. Ararat-Armenian

A VS of the NT into Constantinopolitan Armenian, by Dr. Zohrab, was published at Paris in 1825 by the British and Foreign Bible Society. This VS was made from the Ancient Armenian. A revised ed, by Adger, appeared at Smyrna in 1842. In 1846 the American missionaries there published a VS of the OT. The American Bible Society have since published revised edd of this version.

2. Constantinopolitan-Armenian

III. Armenian Language.—The Armenian language is now recognized by philologists to be, not a dialect or subdivision of ancient Persian or Iranian, but a distinct branch of the Âryan or Indo-European family, standing almost midway between the Iranian and the European groups. In some respects, especially in weakening and ultimately dropping *t* and *d* between vowels, it resembles the Keltic tongues (cf Gaelic *A(th)air*, Arm. *Hair = Pater, Father*). As early as the 5th cent. it had lost gender in nouns, though retaining inflections (cf Brugmann, *Elements of Comp. Gr. of Indo-Ger. Languages*).

Literature.—Koriun; Agathangelos; Lazarus Pharpetsi; Moses Khorenatsi (=of Chorene); Faustus Byzantinus; Chhamchheants; Haikakan Hin Dprouthian Patm; Haikakan Thargmanouthiunk'h Nak'hneants; *The Bible of Every Land*; Tisdall, *Conversion of Armenia*; Nestle, *Textual Criticism of the Gr NT*; *HDB*; *N.Y. Cyclopaedia of Bib. and Theol. Lit.*; Hauck, *Realencyklopädie für protest. Theol. und Kirche*.

W. St. Clair Tisdall

ARMHOLE, ärm'hōl: The Heb word אַצִּיל, *'aççîl*, is used in Jer **38** 12 in the sense of armpits. When the prophet was pulled up out of the pit by ropes, the armpits were protected with rags and old garments. The meaning in Ezk **13** 18 AV (RV "elbows," RVm "joints of the hands") is far from clear. The phrase is used, without doubt, of some ornament or article of dress worn by the false prophetesses and priestesses of Ashtaroth in order to allure the unwary and tempt the simple. The "pillows" were probably "amulets" supposed to have magical virtues, and worn on the arms or wrists.

W. W. Davies

ARMLET, ärm'let: The word tr[d] "bracelet" in 2 S **1** 10 AV, probably denotes an "armlet," or "arm-band," worn on the upper arm. But it is the same word which with a different context is rendered "ankle-chains" (in Nu **31** 50 RV). The "bracelet" of Sir **21** 21 AV, worn upon the right arm, was an "armlet," as is seen from the list given of Judith's ornaments: who "decked herself bravely with her *armlets* [RV 'chains'] and her bracelets, and her rings, and her ear-rings, and all her ornaments" (Jth **10** 4). The nature of the ornaments given in RV as "armlets," Ex **35** 22; Nu **31** 50, and in the AV as "tablets," is uncertain. For full and distinguishing descriptions of "armlets," "anklets," "bracelets," etc, found in ancient graves, see *PEFS*, 1905, 318 ff. See also Ornaments.

Geo. B. Eager

ARMONI, ar-mō′nī (אַרְמֹנִי, *'armōnī*, "belonging to the palace"): One of the two sons of Saul by Rizpah, the daughter of Aiah (2 S **21** 8). David delivered them over to the blood vengeance of the Gibeonites.

ARMOR, ARMS, är′mẽr, ärms.

I. Armor in General—OT
II. In the NT; Polybius
III. Offensive Weapons
1. Rod
2. Sling
3. Bow and Arrows
4. Spear—Javelin
5. Sword
IV. Defensive Weapons
1. Shield
2. Helmet
3. Coat of Mail
4. Greaves
5. Girdle
Literature

I. Armor in General—OT.—(מַדִּים, *maddīm;* 1 S **17** 38; 1 S **14** 1 RV APPAREL; נֶשֶׁק, *nēshek,* 1 K **10** 25; Job **39** 21; כֵּלִים, *kēlīm;* **τὰ ὅπλα,** *tá hópla*): Under this head it may be convenient to notice the weapons of attack and defence in use among the Hebrews, mentioned in Scripture. There are no such descriptions given by the sacred writers as are to be found in Homer, who sets forth in detail the various pieces of armor worn by an Achilles or a Patroclus, and the order of putting them on. There is an account of the armor offensive and defensive of the Phili Goliath (1 S **17** 5–7); and from a much later time we read of shields and spears and helmets and habergeons, or coats of mail, and bows and slings with which Uzziah provided his soldiers (2 Ch **26** 14). In Jeremiah's ode of triumph over the defeat of Pharaoh-neco, there is mention of the arms of the Egyptians: "Prepare ye the buckler and shield, and draw near to battle. Harness the horses, and get up, ye horsemen, and stand forth with your helmets; furbish the spears, put on the coats of mail" (Jer **46** 3.4). Of the arms of Assyr, Chaldean, Egyp and Hittite soldiery there have come down to us sculptured representations from their ancient monuments, which throw light upon the battle-pieces of the Heb annalists and prophets.

Group of Ancient Arms.

II. In the NT; Polybius.—In the NT, St. Paul describes the panoply of the Christian soldier, naming the essential pieces of the Rom soldier's armor—the girdle, the breastplate, the footgear, the shield, the helmet, the sword—although it is to be noticed that his most characteristic weapon, the *pilum* or spear, is omitted (Eph **6** 10–17). In a similar context the same apostle speaks of "the armor" of light (Rom **13** 12), "of righteousness on the right hand and on the left" (2 Cor **6** 7). Of the equipment of the Rom soldier in detail, the most useful illustration is the account given by Polybius (vi.23): "The Roman panoply consists in the first place of a shield [*thureós*]. . . . . Along with the shield is a sword [*máchaira*]. . . . . Next

Heavy-armed Greek Soldier.

come two javelins [*hussoí*] and a helmet [*perikephalaía*], and a greave [*knēmís*]. . . . . Now the majority, when they have further put on a bronze plate, measuring a span every way, which they wear on their breasts and call a heart-guard [*kardiophúlax*], are completely armed, but those citizens who are assessed at more than 10,000 drachmae wear instead, together with the other arms, cuirasses made of chain mail [*halusidōtoús thōrakas*]."

III. Offensive Weapons.—The commonest weapon in the hands of the shepherd youth of Pal today is the *rod* (*shēbheṭ; ῥάβδος, rhábdos*), a stick loaded at one end, which he carries in his hand, or wears attached to his wrist by a loop of string, ready for use. It is of considerable weight and is a formidable weapon whether used in self-defence or in attacking a foe. With such a weapon David may well have overcome the lion and the bear that invaded the fold. This shepherd's rod, while used for guidance, or comfort, or for numbering the flock (Ps **23** 4; Lev **27** 32), was also a weapon with which to strike and punish (Ps **2** 9; Isa **10** 5.15). In this sense it has for a synonym *maṭṭeh* (Isa **9** 4; Ezk **7** 11), and both came to have the derived meaning of spearheads (*shēbheṭ,* 2 S **18** 14; *maṭṭeh,* 1 S **14** 27). They may have been the original of the *maul* or hammer (*mēphīç,* Prov **25** 18; Jer **51** 20, where Cyrus, as God's battle-axe, is to shatter Babylon and its inhabitants for the wrongs they have done to His people Israel).

1. Rod

Scarcely less common and equally homely is the *sling* (*ḳelaʽ; σφενδόνη, sphendónē*) (1 S **17** 40). It consists of plaited thongs, or of one strip of leather, made broad at the middle to form a hollow or pocket for the stone or other contents, the ends being held firmly in the hand as it is whirled loaded round the

2. Sling

head, and one of them being at length let go, so that the stone may take its flight. It is used by the shepherd still to turn the straying sheep, and it can also be used with deadly effect as a weapon of war. The slingers (*ha-ḳallā'īm*, 2 K **3** 25) belonged to the light infantry, like the archers. The Benjamites were specially skilled in the use of the sling, which they could use as well with their left hand as the right (Jgs **20** 16). The sling was a weapon in use in the armies of Egypt and Babylonia, and Jeremiah in a powerful **figure** makes the Lord say to Jerus in a time of impending calamity: "Behold, I will sling out the inhabitants of the land at this time" (Jer **10** 18; cf 1 S **25** 29).

Egyptian Slinger.

3. Bow and Arrows

A very important offensive weapon in the wars of Israel was the *bow* (*ḳesheth*) and *arrows* (*ḥiççīm*), and the archers whether mounted or on foot formed a powerful element of the fighting forces of the Philis, Egyptians and Assyrians (s.v. Archer; Bow and Arrows).

4. Spear—Javelin

The *spear* has various words to represent it. (1) The *ḥănīth* had a wooden staff or shaft of varying size and length with a head, or blade, of bronze, or, at a later time, of iron (1 S **17** 7). In AV it is sometimes trd "javelin," but in RV "spear" (see 1 S **13** 22; **18** 11). Saul's spear, stuck in the ground, betokened the abode of the king for the time, just as today the spear in front of his tent marks the halting-place of the Bedouin Sheikh (1 S **22** 6; **26** 7). Nahum, describing the arms of the Assyrians, joins together the flashing sword and the glittering spear (Nah **3** 3). The bearers of the *ḥănīth* belonged to the heavy-armed troops. (2) The *rōmaḥ*, also trd in AV "javelin," was of the character of a lance. It does not appear to have differed much from the *ḥănīth*—they appear as synonyms in Joel **3** 10, where *rōmaḥ* is used, and in Isa **2** 4 where *ḥănīth* is used, of spears beaten into pruning hooks. It describes the Egyp spear in Jer **46** 4.

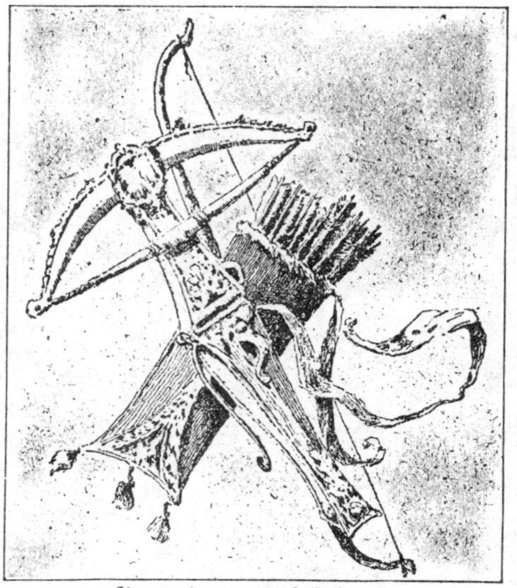

Bows, Arrows and Quiver.

The bearers of the *rōmaḥ* also belonged to the heavy-armed troops. (3) The *kīdhōn* was lighter than either of the preceding and more of the nature of a javelin (*gaison* in LXX, Josh **8** 18 and Polybius vi.39, 3; Job **41** 29; Jer **6** 23). (4) In the NT the word "spear" occurs only once and is represented by the Gr *lógchē*, the equivalent no doubt of *ḥănīth* as above (Jn **19** 34).

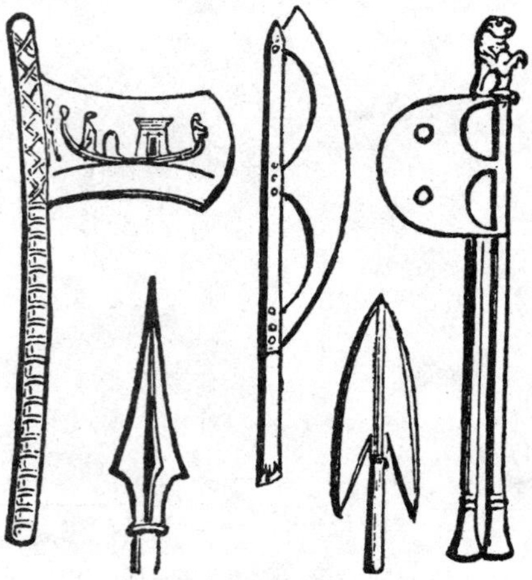

Battle-Axes and Spears.

5. Sword

The *sword* (*ḥerebh*) is by far the most frequently mentioned weapon in Scripture, whether offensive or defensive. The blade was of iron (1 S **13** 19; Joel **3** 10). It was hung from the girdle on the left side, and was used both to cut and to thrust. Ehud's sword (Jgs **3** 16) was double-edged and a cubit in length, and, as he was left-handed, was worn on his right thigh under his clothes. The sword was kept in a sheath (1 S **17** 51); to draw the sword was the signal for war (Ezk **21** 3). Soldiers are "men who draw the sword." It is the flashing sword (Nah **3** 3); the oppressing sword (Jer **46** 16); the devouring sword (2 S **18** 8; Jer **12** 12); the sword which drinks its fill of blood (Isa **34** 5.6). The sword of the Lord executes God's judgments (Jer **47** 6; Ezk **21** 9.10 ff).

Figurative: In the highly metaphorical language of the prophets it stands for war and its attendant calamities (Jer **50** 35–37; Ezk **21** 28).

In the NT *machaira* is employed for sword in its natural meaning (Mt **26** 47.51; Acts **12** 2; He **11** 34.37). St. Paul calls the Word of God the sword of the Spirit (Eph **6** 17); and in the Epistle to He the Word of God is said to be sharper than any two-edged sword (He **4** 12). As a synonym the word *rhomphaía* is used in the Apoc alone of the NT books, save for Lk **2** 35. It was the Thracian sword with large blade, and is classed by the ancients rather as a spear. The word is used frequently in the LXX like *machaira* to translate *ḥerebh*. In Rev **1** 16 the sharp two-edged sword of judgment, *rhomphaia* is seen in vision proceeding out of the mouth of the glorified Lord (cf Rev **19** 15). *Xiphos* is still another word for sword, but it is found only in the LXX, and not in the NT.

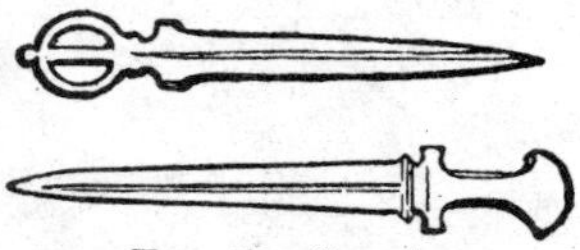

Egyptian Swords.

IV. Defensive Weapons.—The most ancient and universal weapon of defence is the shield. The two chief varieties are (1) the *çinnāh*, Lat *scutum*, the large shield, worn by heavy-armed infantry, adapted to the form of the human body, being made oval or in the shape of a door; hence its Gr name, *thureos*, from *thúra*, a door; and (2) the *māghēn*, Lat *clypeus*, the light, round hand-buckler, to which

1. Shield

péltē is the Gr equivalent. The two are often mentioned together (Ezk **23** 24; **38** 4; Ps **35** 2).

Shield, Sword and Girdle.

The *çinnāh* was the shield of the heavy-armed (1 Ch **12** 24); and of Goliath we read that his shield was borne by a man who went before him (1 S **17** 7.41) The *māghēn* could be borne by bowmen, for we read of men of Benjamin in Asa's army that bare shields and drew bows (2 Ch **14** 8). The ordinary material of which shields were made was wood, or wicker-work overlaid with leather. The wood-work of the shields and other weapons of Gog's army were to serve Israel for fuel for seven years (Ezk **39** 9). The anointing of the shield (2 S **1** 21; Isa **21** 5) was either to protect it from the weather, or, more probably, was part of the consecration of the warrior and his weapons for the

Helmet.

campaign. Solomon in his pride of wealth had 200 shields (*çinnōth*) of beaten gold, and 300 targets (*māghinnīm*) of beaten gold made for himself, and hung in the house of the forest of Lebanon (1 K **10** 16.17). They were only for show, and when Shishak of Egypt came up against Rehoboam and carried them off, Rehoboam replaced them with others of bronze (1 K **14** 27). On the march, the shield was strapped over the shoulder and kept in a cover, which was removed before the battle (Isa **22** 6). Both words are used of the mechanical device known to the Romans as the *testudo* employed by the besiegers of a city against the darts and stones and blazing torches thrown out by the besieged (Isa **37** 33; Ezk **26** 8).

Figurative: Jeh is spoken of as the shield and protector of His people—of Abraham (Gen **15** 1); of Israel (Dt **33** 29); of the Psalmist (Ps **18** 30; **35** 2, and many other passages). In his description of the panoply of the Christian soldier, St. Paul introduces faith as the *thureos*, the large Gr-Rom shield, a defence by which he may quench all the fiery darts of the evil one.

Breastplate.

2. Helmet

The helmet, *ḳōbha'* or *kōbha'*, seems to have been originally in the form of a skull-cap, and it is thus figured in representations of Hittites on the walls of Karnak in Egypt. In the earliest times it is found worn only by outstanding personages like kings and commanders. When King Saul armed David with his own armor he put a helmet of brass upon his head (1 S **17** 38). Uzziah at a later time provided his soldiers with helmets, as part of their equipment (2 Ch **26** 14). The men of Pharaoh-neco's army also wore helmets (Jer **46** 4), and the mercenaries in the armies of Tyre had both shield and helmet to hang up within her (Ezk **27** 10). The materials of the helmet were at first of wood, linen, felt, or even of rushes; leather was in use until the Seleucid period when it was supplanted by bronze (1 Macc **6** 35); the Gr and Rom helmets both of leather and brass were well known in the Herodian period.

Figurative: St. Paul has the helmet, *perikephalaía*, for his Christian soldier (Eph **6** 17; 1 Thess **5** 8). In the LXX *perikephalaia* occurs eleven times as the equivalent of the Heb term.

3. Coat of Mail

Body armor for the protection of the person in battle is mentioned in the OT and is well known in representations of Egyp, Pers and Parthian warriors. The *shiryōn*, tr[d] "habergeon" in AV, rendered in RV "coat of mail," is part of the armor of Nehemiah's workers (Neh **4** 16), and one of the pieces of armor supplied by King Uzziah to his soldiers (2 Ch **26** 14). Goliath was armed with a *shiryōn*, and when Saul clad David in his own armor to meet the Phili champion he put on him a coat of mail, his *shiryōn* (1 S **17** 5.38). Such a piece of body armor Ahab wore in the fatal battle of Ramoth-gilead (1 K **22** 34). In the battle of Bethsura in the Maccabean struggle the Syrian war-elephants were protected with breastplates, the word for which, *thōrax*, represents the *shiryōn* in the LXX (1 Macc **6** 43).

Figurative: Isaiah in a striking figure describes Jeh as putting on righteousness for a coat of mail and salvation as a helmet, where *thōrax* and *perikephalaia* are the Gr words of the LXX to render *shiryōn* and *kōbha'*. It is from this passage (Isa **59** 17) that St. Paul obtains his "breastplate of righteousness" (Eph **6** 14).

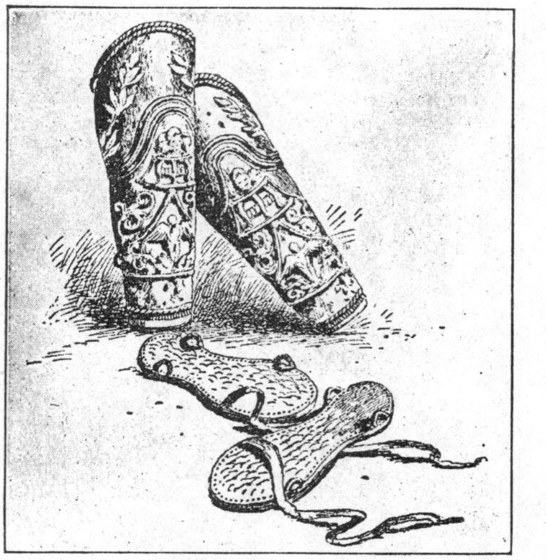

Greaves and Sandals.

4. Greaves Greaves (*miçhāh;* κνημῖδες, *knēmídes*) are mentioned once in Scripture as part of the armor of Goliath (1 S **17** 6). They were of brass or leather, fastened by thongs round the leg and above the ankles.

5. Girdle The girdle (*ḥăghōrāh;* Gr *zṓnē*) was of leather studded with nails, and was used for supporting the sword (1 S **18** 4; 2 S **20** 8). See GIRDLE.

Figurative: For fig. uses see under the separate weapons.

LITERATURE.—Nowack, *Hebräische Archaeologie*, I, 359–67; Benzinger, Herzog, *RE*, art. "Kriegswesen bei den Hebräern"; McCurdy, *HPM*, I, II; Woods and Powell, *The Heb Prophets for Eng. Readers*, I, II; G. M. Mackie, *Bible Manners and Customs;* Browne, *Heb Antiquities*, 40–46; corresponding arts. in Kitto, Hastings, and other Bible dictionaries.

T. NICOL

ARMOR-BEARER, är'mẽr-bâr'ẽr (נֹשֵׂא כֵלִי, *nōsē' kelī;* Gr uses a phrase, ὁ αἴρων τὰ σκεύη, *ho aírōn tá skeúē*, lit. "the one carrying the armor"): One who carried the large shield and perhaps other weapons for a king (1 S **31** 4), commander-in-chief (2 S **23** 37), captain (1 S **14** 7) or champion (1 S **17** 7). All warriors of distinction had such an attendant. Rather than perish by the hand of a woman, Abimelech called upon his armor-bearer to give him the finishing stroke (Jgs **9** 54), and when King Saul's armor-bearer refused to do this office for him that he might not become the prisoner of the Philis, he took a sword himself and fell upon it (1 S **31** 4). David became Saul's armor-bearer for a time, and Jonathan's armor-bearer was a man of resource and courage (1 S **14** 7). The shield-bearer was a figure well known in the chariots of Egypt and Assyria and the Hittites, his business being to protect his fighting companion during the engagement.

T. NICOL

ARMORY, är'mẽr-i: (1) (אוֹצָר, *'ōçār;* θησαυρός, *thēsaurós*): A storehouse (1 K **7** 51; Neh **10** 38), but employed fig. of the stored-up anger of Jeh which breaks forth in judgments (Jer **50** 25). (2) (נֵשֶׁק, *nēshek*): Identical with Solomon's "house of the forest of Lebanon," the arsenal close to the temple (1 K **10** 17; Neh **3** 19; Isa **22** 8), in which were stored the shields and targets of beaten gold. (3) (תַּלְפִּיּוֹת, *talpīyōth*): A puzzling word rendered "armory" in our VSS (Cant **4** 4)—"the tower of David builded for an *armory*, whereon there hang a thousand bucklers, all shields of mighty men." RVm renders "builded with turrets."

T. NICOL

ARMY, är'mi (חַיִל, *ḥayil*, "army," צָבָא, *çābhā'*, "host," מַעֲרָכָה, *ma'ărākhāh*, "army in battle array," גְּדוּד, *gedhūdh*, "troop"):

1. The First Campaign of History
2. In the Wilderness
3. The Times after the Conquest
4. In the Early Monarchy
5. From the Time of Solomon Onward
6. Organization of the Hebrew Army
7. The Army in the Field
8. The Supplies of the Army
9. In the NT

The Israelites were not a distinctively warlike people and their glory has been won on other fields than those of war. But Canaan, between the Mediterranean and the desert, was the highway of the East and the battle-ground of nations. The Israelites were, by the necessity of their geographical position, often involved in wars not of their own seeking, and their bravery and endurance even when worsted in their conflicts won for them the admiration and respect of their conquerors.

1. The First Campaign of History The first conflict of armed forces recorded in Holy Scripture is that in Gen **14**. The kings of the Jordan valley had rebelled against Chedorlaomer, king of Elam—not the first of the kings of the East to reach the Mediterranean with his armies—and joined battle with him and other kings in the Vale of Siddim. In this campaign Abraham distinguished himself by the rescue of his nephew Lot, who had fallen with all that he possessed into the hands of the Elamite king. The force with which Abraham effected the defeat of Chedorlaomer and the kings that were with him was his own retainers, 318 in number, whom he had armed and led forth in person in his successful pursuit.

2. In the Wilderness When we first make the acquaintance of the Israelites as a nation, they are a horde of fugitives who have escaped from the bitter oppression and hard bondage of Pharaoh. Although there could have been but little of the martial spirit in a people so long and grievously oppressed, their journeyings through the wilderness toward Canaan are from the first described as the marching of a great host. It was according to their "armies" ("hosts" RV) that Aaron and Moses were to bring the Children of Israel from the land of Egypt (Ex **6** 26). When they had entered upon the wilderness they went up "harnessed" ("armed" RV) for the journeyings that lay before them—where "harnessed" or "armed" may point not to the weapons they bore but to the order and arrangements of a body of troops marching five deep (*hămushshīm*) or divided into five army corps (Ex **13** 18). On the way through the wilderness they *encamped* (Ex **13** 20; and *passim*) at their successive halting-places, and the whole army of 600,000 was, after Sinai, marked off into divisions or army corps, each with its own camp and the ensigns of their fathers' houses (Nu **2** 2). "From twenty years old and upward, all that are able to go forth to war in Israel," the males of the tribes were numbered and assigned to their place in the camp (Nu **1** 3). Naturally, in the wilderness they are footmen (Nu **11** 21), and it was not till the period of the monarchy that other arms were added. Bow and sling and spear and sword for attack, and shield and helmet for defence, would be the full equipment of the men called upon to fight in the desert. Although we hear little of gradations of military rank, we do read of captains of thousands and captains of hundreds in the wilderness (Nu **31** 14), and Joshua commands the fighting men in the battle against the Amalekites at Rephidim (Ex **17** 9 ff). That the Israelites acquired in their journeyings in the wilderness the discipline and martial spirit which would make them a warlike people, may be gathered from their successes against the Midianites, against Og, king of Bashan, toward the close of the forty years, and from the military organization with which they proceeded to the conquest of Canaan.

3. The Times after the Conquest

In more than one campaign the Israelites under Joshua's leadership established themselves in Canaan. But it was largely through the enterprise of the several tribes that the conquest was achieved. The progress of the invaders was stubbornly contested, but Joshua encouraged his kinsmen of Ephraim and Manasseh to press on the conquest even against the invincible war-chariots of the Canaanites—"for thou shalt drive out the Canaanites, though they have iron chariots, and though they are strong" (Josh **17** 18). As it was in the early history of Rome, where the defence of the state was an obligation resting upon every individual according to his stake in the public welfare, so it was at first in Israel. Tribal jealousies, however, impaired the sentiment of nationality and hindered united action when once the people had been settled in Canaan. The tribes had to defend their own, and it was only a great emergency that united them in common action. The first notable approach to national unity was seen in the army which Barak assembled to meet the host of Jabin, king of Hazor, under the command of Sisera (Jgs **4** 5). In Deborah's war-song in commemoration of the notable victory achieved by Barak and herself, the men of the northern tribes, Zebulun, Naphtali, Issachar, along with warriors of Manasseh, Ephraim and Benjamin, are praised for the valor with which they withstood and routed the host—foot, horse and chariots—of Sisera. Once again the tribes of Israel assembled in force from "Dan even to Beersheba, with the land of Gilead" (Jgs **20** 1) to punish the tribe of Benjamin for condoning a gross outrage. The single tribe was defeated in the battle that ensued, but they were able to put into the field "26,000 men that drew sword," and they had also "700 chosen men left-handed; every one could sling stones at a hair-breadth, and not miss" (Jgs **20** 15.16).

4. In the Early Monarchy

Up to this time the fighting forces of the Israelites were more of the character of a militia. The men of the tribes more immediately harassed by enemies were summoned for action by the leader raised up by God, and disbanded when the emergency was past. The monarchy brought changes in military affairs. It was the plea of the leaders of Israel, when they desired to have a king, that he would go out before them and fight their battles (1 S **8** 20). Samuel had warned them that with a monarchy a professional soldiery would be required. "He will take your sons, and appoint them unto him, for his chariots, and to be his horsemen; and they shall run before his chariots; and he will appoint them unto him for captains of thousands, and captains of fifties; and he will set some to plow his ground, and reap his harvest, and to make his instruments of war, and the instruments of his chariots" (1 S **8** 11.12). That this was the course which military reform took in the period following the establishment of the monarchy may well be. It fell to Saul when he ascended the throne to withstand the invading Philis and to relieve his people from the yoke which they had already laid heavily upon some parts of the country. The Philis were a military people, well disciplined and armed, with 30,000 chariots and 6,000 horsemen at their service when they came up to Michmash (1 S **13** 5). What chance had raw levies of vine-dressers and herdsmen from Judah and Benjamin against such a foe? No wonder that the Israelites hid themselves in caves and thickets, and in rocks, and in holes, and in pits (1 S **13** 6). And it is quoted by the historian as the lowest depth of national degradation that the Israelites had to go down to the Philis "to sharpen every man his share, and his coulter, and his axe, and his mattock" (1 S **13** 20) because the Philis had carried off their smiths to prevent them from making swords or spears.

It was in this desperate condition that King Saul was called to begin the struggle for freedom and national unity in Israel. The victories at Michmash and Elah and the hotly contested but unsuccessful and fatal struggle at Gilboa evince the growth of the martial spirit and advance alike in discipline and in strategy. After the relief of Jabesh-gilead, instead of disbanding the whole of his levies, Saul retained 3,000 men under arms, and this in all probability became the nucleus of the standing army of Israel (1 S **13** 2). From this time onward "when Saul saw any mighty man, or any valiant man, he took him unto him" (1 S **14** 52). Of the valiant men whom Saul kept round his person, the most notable were Jonathan and David. Jonathan had command of one division of 1,000 men at Gibeah (1 S **13** 2), and David was captain of the king's bodyguard (1 S **18** 5; cf **18** 13). When David fell under Saul's jealousy and betook himself to an outlaw life in the mountain fastnesses of Judah, he gathered round him in the cave of Adullam 400 men (1 S **22** 1.2) who were ere long increased to 600 (1 S **23** 13). From the story of Nabal (1 S **25**) we learn how a band like that of David could be maintained in service, and we gather that landholders who benefited by the presence of an armed force were expected to provide the necessary supplies. On David's accession to the throne this band of warriors remained attached to his person and became the backbone of his army. We can identify them with the *gibbōrīm*—the mighty men of whom Benaiah at a later time became captain (2 S **23** 22.23; 1 K **1** 8) and who are also known by the name of Cherethites and Pelethites (2 S **8** 18). These may have received their name from their foreign origin, the former, in Heb *k^{e}rēthī* being originally from Crete but akin to the Philis; and the latter, in Heb *p^{e}lēthī* being Philis by birth. That there were foreign soldiers in David's service we know from the examples of Uriah the Hittite and Ittai of Gath. David's *gibbōrīm* have been compared to the Praetorian Cohort of the Rom emperors, the Janissaries of the sultans, and the Swiss Guards of the French kings. Of David's army Joab was the commander-in-chief, and to the military genius of this rough and unscrupulous warrior, the king's near kinsman, the dynasty of David was deeply indebted.

In the reign of Solomon, although peace was its prevailing characteristic, there can have been no diminution of the armed forces of the kingdom, for we read of military expeditions against Edom and Syria and Hamath, and also of fortresses built in every part of the land, which would require troops to garrison them. Hazor, the old Can capital, at the foot of Lebanon; Megiddo commanding the rich plain of Jezreel; Gezer overlooking the Phili plain; the Bethhorons (Upper and Nether); and Tadmor in the wilderness; not to speak of Jerus with Millo and the fortified wall, were fortresses requiring strong garrisons (1 K **9** 15). It is probable that "the levy," which was such a burden upon the people at large, included forced military service as well as forced labor, and helped to create the dissatisfaction which culminated in the revolt of Jeroboam, and eventually in the disruption of the kingdom. Although David had reserved from the spoils of war in his victorious campaign against Hadadezer, king of Zobah, horses for 100 chariots (2 S **8** 4), cavalry and chariots were not an effective branch of the service in his reign. Solomon, however, disregarding the scruples of the stricter Israelites, and the ordinances of the ancient law (Dt **17** 16), added horses and chariots on a large scale to the military equipment of the nation (1 K **10** 26–29). It is believed that it was from Musri, a country of northern Syria occupied by the Hittites, and Kue in Cilicia, that Solomon obtained horses for his cavalry and chariotry (1 K **10** 29; 2 Ch **1** 16, where the best text gives *Muçrī*, and not the Heb word for Egypt). This branch of the service was not only looked upon with distrust by the stricter Israelites, but was expressly denounced in later times by the prophets (Isa **2** 7; Hos **1** 7; Mic **5** 10). In the prophets, too, more than in the historical books, we are made acquainted with the cavalry and chariotry of Assyria and Babylon which in the days of Sargon, Sennacherib, and Nebuchadnezzar had become so formidable. Their lancers and mounted archers, together with their chariots, gave them a sure ascendancy in the field of war (Nah **3** 2.3; Hab **1** 8; Jer **46** 4). In comparison with these, the cavalry of the kings of Israel and Judah was insignificant, and to this Rabshakeh contemptuously referred (2 K **18** 23) when he promised to the chiefs of Judah from the king of Assyria 2,000 horses if Hezekiah could put riders upon them.

5. From the Time of Solomon Onward

As we have seen, every male in Israel at the age of twenty, according to the ancient law, became liable for military service (Nu **1** 3; **26** 2; 2 Ch **25** 5), just as at a later time every male of that age became liable for the half-shekel of Temple dues. Jos is our authority for believing that no one was called upon to serve after the age of fifty (*Ant*, III, xii, 4). From military service the Levites were exempt (Nu **2** 33). In Deuteronomic law exemption was allowed to persons betrothed but not married, to persons who had built a house but had not dedicated it, or who had planted a vineyard but had not eaten of the fruit of it, and to persons faint-hearted and fearful whose timidity might spread throughout the ranks (Dt **20** 1–9). These exemptions no doubt reach back to a high antiquity and in the Maccabean period they still held good (1 Macc **3** 56). The army was divided into bodies of 1,000, 100, 50, and in Maccabean times, 10, each under its own captain (*Sar*) (Nu **31** 14; 1 S **8** 12; 2 K **1** 9; 2 Ch **25** 5; 1 Macc **3** 55). In the army of Uzziah we read of "heads of fathers' houses," mighty men of valor who numbered 2,600 and had under their hand a trained army of 307,500 men (2 Ch **26** 12.13), where, however, the figures have an appearance of exaggeration.

6. Organization of the Hebrew Army

Over the whole host of Israel, according to the fundamental principle of the theocracy, was Jeh Himself, the Supreme Leader of her armies (1 S **8** 7 ff); it was "the Captain of the Lord's host," to whom Joshua and all serving under him owned allegiance, that appeared before the walls of Jericho to help the gallant leader in his enterprise. In the times of the Judges the chiefs themselves, Barak, Gideon, Jephthah, led their forces in person to battle. Under the monarchy the captain of the host was an office distinct from that of the king, and we have Joab, Abner, Benaiah, named as commanders-in-chief. An armor-bearer attended the captain of the host as well as the king (1 S **14** 6; **31** 4.5; 2 S **23** 37). Mention is made of officers who had to do the numbering of the people, the *ṣōphēr*, scribe, attached to the captain of the host (2 K **25** 19; cf 2 S **24** 2; 1 Macc **5** 42), and the *shōṭēr*, muster-master, who kept the register of those who were in military service and knew the men who had received authorized leave of absence (Dt **20** 5, Driver's n.).

7. The Army in the Field

Before the army set forth, religious services were held (Joel **3** 9), and sacrifices were offered at the opening of a campaign to consecrate the war (Mic **3** 5; Jer **6** 4; **22** 7). Recourse was had in earlier times to the oracle (Jgs **1** 1; **20** 27; 1 S **14** 37; **23** 2; **28** 6; **30** 8), in later times to a prophet (1 K **22** 5 ff; 2 K **3** 13; **19** 2; Jer **38** 14). Cases are mentioned in which the Ark accompanied the army to the field (1 S **4** 4; **14** 18), and before the engagement sacrifices also were offered (1 S **7** 9; **13** 9), ordinarily necessitating the presence of a priest (Dt **20** 2). Councils of war were held to settle questions of policy in the course of siege or a campaign (Jer **38** 7; **39** 3). The signal for the charge or retreat was given by sound of a trumpet (Nu **10** 9; 2 S **2** 28; **18** 16; 1 Macc **16** 8). The order of battle was simple, the heavy-armed spearmen forming the van, slingers and archers bringing up the rear, supported by horses and chariots, which moved to the front as need required (1 S **31** 3; 1 K **22** 31; 2 Ch **14** 9). Strategy was called into play according to the disposition of the opposing forces or the nature of the ground (Josh **8** 3; **11** 7; Jgs **7** 16; 1 S **15** 5; 2 S **5** 23; 2 K **3** 11 ff).

Although David had in his service foreign soldiers like Uriah the Hittite and Ittai of Gath, and although later kings hired aliens for their campaigns, it was not till the Maccabean struggle for independence that mercenaries came to be largely employed in the Jewish army. Mercenaries are spoken of in the prophets as a source of weakness to the nation that employs them (to Egypt, Jer **46** 16.21; to Babylon, Jer **50** 16). From the Maccabean time onward the princes of the Hasmonaean family employed them, sometimes to hold the troublesome Jews in check, and sometimes to support the arms of Rome. Herod the Great had in his army mercenaries of various nations. When Jewish soldiers, however, took service with Rome, they were prohibited by their law from performing duty on the Sabbath. Early in the Maccabean fight for freedom, a band of Hasidaeans or Jewish Puritans, allowed themselves to be cut down to the last man rather than take up the sword on the Sabbath (1 Macc **2** 34 ff). Cases are even on record where their gentile adversaries took advantage of their scruples to inflict upon them loss and defeat (*Ant*, XIII, xii, 4; XIV, iv, 2).

8. Supplies

Before the army had become a profession in Israel, and while the levies were still volunteers like the sons of Jesse, the soldiers not only received no pay, but had to provide their own supplies, or depend upon rich landholders like Nabal and Barzillai (1 S **25**; 2 S **19** 31). In that period and still later, the chief reward of the soldier was his share of the booty gotten in war (Jgs **5** 30 f; 1 S **30** 22 ff). By the Maccabean period we learn that an army like that of Simon, consisting of professional soldiers, could only be maintained at great expense (1 Macc **14** 32).

9. In the NT

Although the first soldiers that we read of in the NT were Jewish and not Rom (Lk **3** 14; Mk **6** 27), and although we read that Herod with his "men of war" joined in mocking Jesus (Lk **23** 11), it is for the most part the Rom army that comes before us. The Rom legion, consisting roughly of 6,000 men, was familiar to the Jewish people, and the word had become a term to express a large number (Mt **26** 53; Mk **5** 9). Centurions figure most honorably alike in the Gospels and the Acts (*kenturiōn*, Mk **15** 39; *hekatontárchēs, -os*, Mt **8** 5; Lk **23** 47; Acts **10** 1; **22** 25.27). "The Praetorium" is the residence of the Rom procurator at Jerus, and in Caesarea (Mt **27** 27; Acts **23** 35), or the praetorian guard at Rome (Phil **1** 13). The Augustan band and the Italian band (Acts **10** 1; Acts **27** 1) are cohorts of Rom soldiers engaged on military duty at Caesarea. In Jerus there was one cohort stationed in the time of St. Paul under the command of a *chilíarchos*, or military tribune (Acts **22** 24). It was out of this regiment that the *dexiolúboi* (Acts **23** 23) were selected, who formed a guard for St. Paul to Caesarea, spearmen, or rather javelin-throwers.

Figurative: Among the military metaphors employed by St. Paul, who spent so much of his time in the later years of his life among Rom soldiers, some are taken from the weapons of the Rom soldier (see Arms), and some also from the discipline and the marching and fighting of an army. Thus, "campaigning" is referred to (2 Tim **2** 3.4; 2 Cor **10** 3–6); the "order and solid formation of soldiers" drawn up in battle array or on the march (Col **2** 5); the "triumphal procession" to the capitol with its train of captives and the smoke of incense (2 Cor **2** 14–16); and "the sounding of the trumpet," when the faithful Christian warriors shall take their place every man in his own order or "division" of the resurrection army of the Lord of Hosts (1 Cor **15** 52.53). (See Dean Howson, *Metaphors of St. Paul*—"Roman Soldiers.")

The armies which are in heaven (Rev **19** 14.19) are the angelic hosts who were at the service of their Incarnate Lord in the days of His flesh and in His exaltation follow Him upon white horses clothed in fine linen white and pure (see Swete's n.). See further Armor, Arms.

T. Nicol

ARMY, är′mi, **ROMAN,** rō′man; The treatment of this subject will be confined to (I) a brief description of the organization of the army, and (II) a consideration of the allusions to the Rom military establishment in the NT.

I. Organization.—There were originally no standing forces, but the citizens performed military service like any other civic duty when summoned by the magistrates. The gradual development of a military profession and standing army culminated in the admission of the poorest class to the ranks by Marius (about 107 BC). Henceforth the Rom army was made up of a body of men whose character was essentially that of mercenaries, and whose term of continuous service varied in different divisions from 16 to 26 years.

The forces which composed the Rom army under the Empire may be divided into the following five groups: (1) the imperial guard and garrison of the capital, (2) the legions, (3) the *auxilia*, (4) the *numeri*, (5) the fleet. We shall discuss their organization in the order mentioned.

1. The Imperial Guard

The imperial guard consisted of the *cohortes praetoriae*, which together with the *cohortes urbanae* and *vigiles* made up the garrison of Rome. In the military system as established by Augustus there were nine cohorts of the praetorian guard, three of the urban troops, and seven of the vigiles. Each cohort numbered 1,000 men, and was commanded by a tribune of equestrian rank. The praetorian prefects (*praefecti praetorii*), of whom there were usually two, were commanders of the entire garrison of the capital, and stood at the highest point of distinction and authority in the equestrian career.

2. The Legions

There were 25 legions in 23 AD (Tacitus *Annals* 4, 5), which had been increased to 30 at the time of the reign of Marcus Aurelius, 160–180 AD (*CIL*, VI, 3492 *a–b*) and to 33 under Septimius Severus (*Dio Cassius*, iv. 23–24). Each legion was made up, ordinarily, of 6,000 men, who were divided into 10 cohorts, each cohort containing 3 maniples, and each maniple in turn 2 centuries.

The *legatus Augustus pro praetore*, or governor of each imperial province, was chief commander of all the troops within the province. An officer of senatorial rank known as *legatus Augusti legionis* was intrusted with the command of each legion, together with the bodies of *auxilia* which were associated with it. Besides, there were six *tribuni militum*, officers of equestrian rank (usually sons of senators who had not yet held the quaestorship) in each legion. The centurions who commanded the centuries belonged to the plebeian class. Between the rank of common soldier and centurion there were a large number of subalterns, called *principales*, who correspond roughly to the non-commissioned officers and men detailed from the ranks for special duties in modern armies.

3. The "Auxilia"

The *auxilia* were organized as infantry in *cohortes*, as cavalry in *alae*, or as mixed bodies, *cohortes equitatae*. Some of these divisions contained approximately 1,000 men (*cohortes* or *alae miliariae*), but the greater number about 500 (*cohortes* or *alae quingenariae*). They were commanded by *tribuni* and *praefecti* of equestrian rank. The importance of the *auxilia* consisted originally in the diversity of their equipment and manner of fighting, since each group adhered to the customs of the nation in whose midst it had been recruited. But with the gradual Romanization of the Empire they were assimilated more and more to the character of the legionaries.

4. The "Numeri"

The *numeri* developed out of the provincial militia and began to appear in the 2d cent. AD. They maintained their local manner of warfare. Some were bodies of infantry, others of cavalry, and they varied in strength from 300 to 90 (Mommsen, *Hermes*, XIX, 219 f, and XXII, 547 f). Their commanders were *praepositi*, *praefecti* or *tribuni*, all men of equestrian rank.

5. The Fleet

The fleet was under the command of prefects (*praefecti classis*), who took rank among the highest officials of the equestrian class. The principal naval stations were at Misenum and Ravenna.

Augustus established the northern boundary of the Empire at the Rhine and at the Danube, throughout the greater part of its course, and bequeathed to his successors the advice that they should not extend their sovereignty beyond the limits which he had set (Tacitus *Annals* i.11; *Agricola* 13); and although this policy

6. Defensive Arrangements

was departed from in many instances, such as the annexation of Thrace, Cappadocia, Mauretania, Britain, and Dacia, not to mention the more ephemeral acquisitions of Trajan, yet the military system of the Empire was arranged primarily with the view of providing for the defence of the provinces and not for carrying on aggressive warfare on a large scale. Nearly all the forces, with the exception of the imperial guard, were distributed among the provinces on the border of the Empire, and the essential feature of the disposition of the troops in these provinces was the permanent fortress in which each unit was stationed. The combination of large camps for the legions with a series of smaller forts for the *alae*, cohorts, and *numeri* is the characteristic arrangement on all the frontiers. The immediate protection of the frontier was regularly instrusted to the auxiliary troops, while the legions were usually stationed some distance to the rear of the actual boundary. Thus the army as a whole was so scattered that it was a difficult undertaking to assemble sufficient forces for carrying out any considerable project of foreign conquest, or even to cope at once with a serious invasion, yet the system was generally satisfactory in view of the conditions which prevailed, and secured for the millions of subjects of the Rom Empire the longest period of undisturbed tranquillity known to European history.

7. Recruiting System

In accordance with the arrangements of Augustus, the *cohortes praetoriae* and *cohortes urbanae* were recruited from Latium, Etruria, Umbria, and the older Rom colonies (Tacitus *Annals* 4, 5), the legions from the remaining portions of Italy, and the *auxilia* from the subject communities of the Empire (Seeck, *Rheinisches Museum*, XLVIII, 616).

But in course of time the natives of Italy disappeared, first from the legions, and later from the garrison of the capital. Antoninus Pius established the rule that each body of troops should draw its recruits from the district where it was stationed. Henceforth the previous possession of Rom citizenship was no longer required for enlistment in the legions. The legionary was granted the privilege of citizenship upon entering the service, the auxiliary soldier upon being discharged (Seeck, *Untergang der antiken Welt*, I, 250).

II. Allusions in the NT to the Rom Military Establishment.—Such references relate chiefly to the bodies of troops which were stationed in Judaea. Agrippa I left a military establishment of one *ala* and five cohorts at his death in 44 AD (Jos, *Ant*, XIX, ix, 2; *BJ*, III, iv, 2), which he had doubtless received from the earlier Rom administration. These divisions were composed of local recruits, chiefly Samaritans (Hirschfeld, *Verwaltungsbeamte*, 395; Mommsen, *Hermes*, XIX, 217, n. 1).

The *Ala I gemina Sebastenorum* was stationed at Caesarea (Jos, *Ant*, XX, 122; *BJ*, II, xii, 5; *CIL*, VIII, 9359).

1. Augustan Band

Julius, the centurion to whom Paul and other prisoners were delivered to be escorted to Rome (Acts **27** 1), belonged to one of the five cohorts which was stationed at or near Caesarea. This *Speira Sebastē* (*WH*), "Augustus' Band" (RV "Augustan band"; RVm "cohort"), was probably the same body of troops which is mentioned in inscriptions as *Cohors I Augusta* (*CIL*, Supp, 6687) and *Speira Augoustē* (Lebas-Waddington 2112). Its official title may have been *Cohors Augusta Sebastenorum* (*GVN*). It will be observed that all divisions of the Rom army were divided into companies of about 100 men, each of which, in the infantry, was commanded by a centurion, in the cavalry, by a decurion.

2. Italian Band

There was another cohort in Caesarea, the "Italian band" (*Cohors Italica*, Vulg) of which Cornelius was centurion (Acts **10** 1: *ek speírēs tḗs kalouménēs Italikḗs*). The *cohortes Italicae* (*civium Romanorum*) were made up of Rom citizens (Marquardt, *Römische Staatsverwaltung*, II, 467).

3. Praetorian Guard

One of the five cohorts was stationed in Jerus (Mt **27** 27; Mk **15** 16), the "chief captain" of which was Claudius Lysias. His title, *chiliarchos* in the Gr (Acts **23** 10.15.17.19.22.26; **24** 7 AV), meaning "leader of a thousand men" (*tribunus*, Vulg), indicates that this body of soldiers was a *cohors miliaria*. Claudius Lysias sent Paul to Felix at Caesarea under escort of 200 soldiers, 70 horsemen, and 200 spearmen (Acts **23** 23). The latter (*dexiolaboi*, WH) are thought to have been a party of provincial militia. Several centurions of the cohort at Jerus appear during the riot and subsequent rescue and arrest of Paul (Acts **21** 32; **22** 25.26; **23** 17.23). The *cohortes miliariae* (of 1,000 men) contained ten centurions. A centurion, doubtless of the same cohort, was in charge of the execution of the Saviour (Mt **27** 54; Mk **15** 39.44.45; Lk **23** 47). It was customary for centurions to be intrusted with the execution of capital penalties (Tacitus *Ann.* i.6; xvi.9; xvi.15; *Hist.* ii.85).

The AV contains the passage in Acts **28** 16: "The centurion delivered the prisoners to the captain of the guard" (*stratopedárchēs*), which the RV omits. It has commonly been held that the expression *stratopedarchēs* was equivalent to praetorian prefect (*praefectus praetorius*), and that the employment of the word in the singular was proof that Paul arrived in Rome within the period 51–62 AD when Sex. Afranius Burrus was sole praetorian prefect. Mommsen (*Sitzungsberichte der Berliner Akademie* [1895], 491–503) believes that the sentence in question embodies an ancient tradition, but that the term *stratopedarchēs* could not mean *praefectus praetorius*, which is never rendered in this way in Gr. He suggests that it stands for *princeps castrorum peregrinorum*, who was a centurion in command of the *frumentarii* at Rome. These were detachments of legionary soldiers who took rank as *principales*. They served as military couriers between the capital and provinces, political spies, and an imperial police. It was probably customary, at least when the tradition under discussion arose, for the *frumentarii* to take charge of persons who were sent to Rome for trial (Marquardt, *Römische Staatsverwaltung*, II, 491–94).

Literature.—Comprehensive discussions of the Rom military system will be found in Marquardt, *Römische Staatsverwaltung*, II, 319–612, and in Pauly-Wissowa, *Realencyclopädie*, art. "Exercitus."

George H. Allen

ARNA, är′na (Lat Arna): One of the ancestors of Ezra given in 2 Esd **1** 2, evidently identical with Zerahiah of Ezr **7** 4 and Zaraias of 1 Esd **8** 2.

ARNAN, är′nan (עַרְנָן, *'arnān*, "joyous"): A descendant of David and founder of a family (1 Ch **3** 21). The LXX has *Orna*.

ARNI, är′nī (Ἀρνεί, *Arneí*, found only in Lk **3** 33 RV, following WH): The name of an ancestor of Jesus Christ. But in AV, following TR, and in the genealogical list of Mt **1** 3.4 the same person is called Aram (Gr Ἀράμ, *Arám*) in both AV and RVm. In Mt RV, however, the form is Ram, which is nearest to the OT name Ram (רָם, *rām*, "high").

Ram was great-grandson of Judah and ancestor of David (Ruth **4** 19; 1 Ch **2** 9.10).

ARNON, är′non (אַרְנוֹן, *'arnōn;* **'Αρνῶν,** *Arnôn*): Is first mentioned in Nu **21** 24 as the border between Moab and the Amorites. "The valleys of Arnon" in the next ver undoubtedly indicate the numerous wadies contributary to the main stream. It formed the southern boundary of the land assigned to Reuben (Dt **3** 12). The city of Aroer stood on the northern edge of the valley (Dt **2** 36; Jgs **12** 2, etc). Arnon was claimed by the Ammonites as having marked the southern limit of their territory when Israel invaded the land (Jgs **11** 13). They, however, had already been driven out by the Amorites, and the region north of Arnon was held by Sihon. From the inscription of Mesha on the Moabite Stone we gather that Moab had established herself on the north of the Arnon before the time of Omri. Under Omri and Ahab she was confined to the south of the river. A rebellion under Mesha was put down by Jehoram son of Ahab (2 K **3**), and the expedition of Hazael against Israel reached the valley of the Arnon (2 K **10** 33). But according to Mesha he regained for Moab the lost land; and this agrees with Isa **15, 16,** where cities north of Arnon are located in Moab, e.g. Heshbon.

The modern name of Arnon is *Wādy el-Mōjib,* which enters the Dead Sea from the E. about 11 miles N. of *el-Lisān.* Some 13 miles E. of the Dead Sea two streams, *Seil es-Sa'ideh* from the S., and *Wādy Enkeileh* from the E., unite their waters and flow westward in the bottom of an enormous trench. The waters of *Wādy Weleh* come in from the N.E. A wide stretch of country thus drains into the valley by means of a great network of smaller wadies—the "valleys of Arnon." The "fords of the Arnon" (Isa **16** 2) were doubtless crossed by Mesha's highway which he claims to have built in Arnon; and may be marked by the traces of the old Rom road and bridge immediately to the W. of where, on the northern edge of the *Wādy,* stands *'Arā'ir,* the ancient Aroer. W. Ewing

AROD, ā′rod, ar′od (אֲרוֹד, *'ărōdh*): The sixth son of Gad (Nu **26** 17). His descendants are called Arodi or Arodites (Gen **46** 16; Nu **26** 17).

ARODI, âr′o-dī. See Arod.

ARODITES, ā′rod-īts. See Arod.

AROER, a-rō′ēr (עֲרוֹעֵר, *'ărō'ēr;* **'Αροήρ,** *Aroḗr*): (1) A city of the Amorites which stood on the northern edge of the Arnon (Dt **2** 36, etc). Taken by Israel, it shared the vicissitudes of the country north of the river, and when last named (Jer **48** 19) is again in the hands of Moab. It is one of the cities which Mesha claims to have built, i.e. fortified. It was within the territory allotted to Reuben, yet its building (fortification) is attributed to Gad (Nu **32** 34). Thus far came the Syrian, Hazael, in his raid upon Israel (2 K **10** 33). The Rom road across the valley lay about an hour to the W. of *Khirbet 'Arā'ir.*

(2) A city in Gilead described as "before Rabbah," on the boundary between Gad and the Ammonites (Josh **13** 25). No name resembling this has yet been recovered in the district indicated.

(3) A city in the territory of Judah named only in 1 S **30** 28. Probably however in Josh **15** 22 we should read *'ar'ārāh* instead of *'adh'ādhāh,* which may be the same city, and may be identical with *'Ar'āra,* a site with cisterns and some remains of ancient buildings about 14 miles S.E. of Beersheba. W. Ewing

AROERITE, a-rō′ēr-īt (הָעֲרֹעֵרִי, *hā-'ărō'ērī*): A native of Aroer. The Aroerite was Hotham, father of two of David's heroes (1 Ch **11** 44).

AROM, ā′rom (**'Αρόμ,** *Arôm*): The sons of A. returned to Jerus with Zerubbabel (1 Esd **5** 16). Omitted in Ezr and Neh. Hashum is found in place of A. in Ezr **2** 19.

ARPACHSHAD, är-pak′shad. See Arphaxad.

ARPAD, är′pad; **ARPHAD,** är′fad (אַרְפָּד, *'arpādh,* "support"): A city of Syria, captured frequently by the Assyrians, and finally subjugated by Tiglath-pileser III in 740 BC, after a siege of two years. It is now the ruin Tell Erfād, 13 miles N.W. of Aleppo. Arpad is one of the conquered cities mentioned by Rabshakeh, the officer of Sennacherib, in his boast before Jerus (2 K **18** 34; **19** 13; Isa **36** 19; **37** 13; AV **Arphad**). Isaiah puts a boast about its capture in the mouth of the Assyr king (Isa **10** 9), and Jeremiah mentions it as "confounded" because of evil tidings, in the oracle concerning Damascus (Jer **49** 23). On every occasion Arpad is mentioned with Hamath. S. F. Hunter

ARPHAXAD, ar-fak′sad: (1) AV form (Gen **10** 22.24; **11** 12.13; 1 Ch **1** 17) of RV "ARPACHSHAD," which see. See also Table of Nations. (2) In Apoc (Jth **1**) a king of the Medes, who reigned in Ecbatana. He was defeated and slain by Nebuchadrezzar.

ARRAY, a-rā′ ([1] לָבֵשׁ, *lābhēsh,* עָטָה, *'āṭāh;* **περιβάλλω,** *peribállō,* **ἐνδύομαι,** *endúomai,* **ἱματισμός,** *himatismós.* [2] עָרַךְ, *'ārakh,* שִׁית, *shīth*): "Array," composed of prefix *ar* and *rai,* "order," is used in two senses, (1) in reference to clothing and (2) in reference to the disposition of an army.

(1) (*a*) *Lābhēsh* is the most common Heb word meaning "to clothe," and is used in all cases but one in the OT for "array" (cf Gen **41** 42: Pharaoh "arrayed him [Joseph] in vestures of fine linen"; see also 2 Ch **28** 15; Est **6** 9.11; Job **40** 10; 2 Ch **5** 12). (*b*) *'Āṭāh,* meaning "to veil," "to cover," is once used. Nebuchadrezzar "shall array himself with the land of Egypt" (Jer **43** 12). (*c*) *Periballō,* "to throw around," is used 6 times in the NT. It is the word used of Herod's "arraying" Jesus "in gorgeous apparel" (Lk **23** 11; the other references are Mt **6** 29; Lk **12** 27; Rev **7** 13; **17** 4; **19** 8). (*d*) *Enduomai,* mid. or pass. of *endúō,* "to enter," means, therefore, "to be entered into" clothing. Once it is used in reference to Herod (Acts **12** 21). (*e*) *Himatismos,* "clothing," is tr[d] once "array" = raiment (from same root). This is the only occurrence of "array" in this sense (1 Tim **2** 9).

(2) (*a*) *'Ārakh* is the common word in the OT, used in reference to the disposition of an army, and is tr[d] "to put in array," "to set in array," the object being "the battle" or the army. The root meaning is that of orderly arrangement, and the verb is used in other senses than the military, e.g. arranging the table of shewbread. In 1 Ch **12** 33 RV has "order the battle array" for AV "keep rank," tr of Heb *'ādhār.* (*b*) *Shīth,* "to set, to place," used once for battle array: "and the horsemen set themselves in array at the gate" (Isa **22** 7). S. F. Hunter

ARREST, a-rest′, **AND TRIAL OF JESUS.** See Jesus Christ, Arrest and Trial of.

ARRIVE, a-rīv′: Originally a nautical term (Lat *ad ripam*) for reaching shore, is used in lit. sense in Lk **8** 26, and, fig. for Gr *phthánō,* instead of "attain to," RV in Rom **9** 31.

ARROGANCY, ar′o-gan-si: Excessive pride, leading to boastfulness and insolence (1 S **2** 3; Prov **8** 13; Isa **13** 11; Jer **48** 29).

ARROW, ar′ō. See ARCHERY; ARMOR.

ARROWS, DIVINATION BY. See AUGURY, IV, 1.

ARROWSNAKE, är′o-snāk: In Isa **34** 15 the Heb word קִפּוֹז, *ḳippōz,* which in AV is rendered "great owl," is in ERV rendered "arrowsnake," and in ARV "dart-snake." Gesenius, who translates "arrowsnake," says, "so called from the spring with which it propels itself." Others, from the mention of "make her nest, lay, and hatch," think some kind of bird is meant. See OWL; SERPENT.

ARSACES, är-sā′sēz, är′sa-sēz (**'Αρσάκης,** *Arsákēs*): The common name assumed by all the Parthian kings, is mentioned in 1 Macc **14** 1–3, and in **15** 22 in connection with the history of Demetrius, one of the Gr, or Seleucid, kings of Syria, and successor to Antiochus Epiphanes, the oppressor of the Jews, who caused the uprising against the Syrian domination under the leadership of the Maccabees. This particular Arsaces was the sixth of the line of independent Parthian rulers which had been founded in 250 BC by Arsaces I, who revolted from Antiochus Theos, killed the Syrian satraps, and with his successor Tiridates I firmly established the independence of the Parthian kingdom. About 243 BC, Tiridates added Hyrcania to his dominions; but it was not till the reign of Arsaces VI, whose pre-regnal name was Mithridates, that Parthia through the conquest of Bactria, Media, Persia, Armenia, Elymais and Babylonia, threatened the very existence of the kingdom of the Seleucids and became a dangerous competitor of Rome itself. It was this king who about 141 BC was attacked by Demetrius Nicator, king of Syria. According to the account preserved in 1 Macc **14** 1–3, Arsaces sent one of his captains, who went and smote the host of Demetrius, and took him alive, and brought him to Arsaces, by whom he was put in ward. At first, the captive king was treated with great severity, being carried in triumph from city to city and exhibited to his enemies. Later, however, Arsaces gave him his daughter in marriage and assigned him a residence in Hyrcania. Some time after the death of Arsaces, Demetrius was sent back to Syria by Phraates, the son of Mithridates, and reigned from 128 to 125 BC. Arsaces VI is mentioned, also, in 1 Macc **15** 22, as one of the kings whom the Romans forbade to make war on their Jewish allies.

LITERATURE.—See 1 Macc **14** 1–3, and **15** 22; *Ant*, XIII, v, 11; XIV, viii, 5; Appian, *Syria*, 67; Strabo, XI, 515; XV, 702; Justin, XLI, 5, 6; XXXVI, 1; Orosius, V, 4; Rawlinson's *Parthia*, in the Story of the Nations ser. and *Die Herrschaft der Parther* in Justi's *Geschichte des alten Persiens* in Oncken's *Allgemeine Geschichte*, I, 4.

R. DICK WILSON

ARSARETH, är′sa-reth. See ARZARETH.

ARSIPHURITH, är-si-fū′rith (**'Αρσιφουρίθ,** *Arsiphouríth*; AV **Azephurith**): 112 of the sons of A. returned to Jerus with Zerubbabel (1 Esd **5** 16). The name is omitted in Ezra and Nehemiah, but the number corresponds to those mentioned with Jorah (Ezr **2** 18) and Hariph (Neh **7** 24).

ARTAXERXES, är-taks-ûrk′sēz (**'Αρταξέρξης,** *Artaxérxēs*): Is the Gr and Lat form of one, and perhaps of two or three kings of Persia mentioned in the OT.

(1) All are agreed that the Artaxerxes at whose court Ezra and Nehemiah were officials is Artaxerxes I, the son of Xerxes, commonly called Longimanus, who reigned from 465 to 424 BC. This Artaxerxes was the third son of Xerxes and was raised to the throne by Artabanus, the murderer of Xerxes. Shortly after his accession, Artaxerxes put his older brother Darius to death; and a little later, Artabanus, who perhaps aimed to make himself king, was killed. Hystaspes, the second brother, who seems to have been satrap of Bactria at the time of his father's death, rebelled, and after two battles was deprived of his power and probably of his life. The reign of Artaxerxes was further disturbed by the revolt of Egypt in 460 BC, and by that of Syria about 448 BC. The Egyptians were assisted by the Athenians, and their rebellion, led by Inarus and Amyrtaeus, was suppressed only after five years of strenuous exertions on the part of the Persians under the command of the great general Megabyzus. After the re-conquest of Egypt, Artaxerxes, fearing that the Athenians would make a permanent subjugation of Cyprus, concluded with them the peace of Callias, by which he retained the island of Cyprus; but agreed to grant freedom to all Gr cities of Asia Minor. Shortly after this Megabyzus led a revolt in Syria and compelled his sovereign to make peace with him on his own terms, and afterward lived and died in high favor with his humiliated king. Zopyrus, the son of Megabyzus, at a later time, while satrap of Lycia and Caria, led a rebellion in which he was assisted by the Greeks. It is thought by some that the destruction of Jerus which is lamented by Nehemiah occurred during the rebellion of Syria under Megabyzus. Artaxerxes I died in 424 BC, and was succeeded by his son Xerxes II, and later by two other sons, Sogdianus and Ochus, the last of whom assumed the regnal name of Darius, whom the Greeks surnamed Nothus.

(2) Ewald and others have thought that the Artaxerxes of Ezr **4** 7 was the pseudo-Smerdis. The principal objection against this view is that we have no evidence that either the pseudo-Smerdis, or the real Smerdis, was ever called Artaxerxes. The real Smerdis is said to have been called Tanyoxares, or according to others Oropastes. Ewald would change the latter to Ortosastes, which closely resembles Artaxerxes, and it must be admitted that many of the Pers kings had two or more names. It seems more probable, however, that Artaxerxes I is the king referred to; and there is little doubt that the identification of the Artaxerxes of Ezr **4** 7 with the pseudo-Smerdis would never have been thought of had it not been for the difficulty of explaining the reference to him in this place.

(3) The Gr tr of the LXX renders the Ahasuerus of the Book of Est by Artaxerxes, and is followed in this rendering by Jos. There is no doubt that by this Artaxerxes Jos meant the first of that name; for in the *Antiquities*, XI, vi, 1 he says that "after the death of Xerxes, the kingdom came to be transferred to his son Cyrus, whom the Greeks called Artaxerxes." He then proceeds to show how he married a Jewish wife, who was herself of the royal family and who is related to have saved the nation of the Jews. In a long chapter, he then gives his account of the story of Vashti, Esther and Mordecai. In spite of this rendering of the LXX and Jos, there is no doubt that the Heb *ăḥashwērōsh* is the same as the Gr Xerxes; and there is no evidence that Artaxerxes I was ever called Xerxes by any of his contemporaries. The reason of the confusion of the names by the LXX and Jos will probably remain forever a mystery.

R. DICK WILSON

ARTEMAS, är′tē-mas (**'Αρτεμᾶς,** *Artemás*): One of the seventy disciples and bishop of Lystra, according to Dorotheus (*Bibl. Maxima* [Lugd.

1677], III, 429). He is mentioned in Titus **3** 12 as one of the faithful companions of Paul. The name is probably Gr, a masc. form of *Artemis*, or, as has been suggested, a short form of Artemidorus, a common name in Asia Minor. These contracted forms were by no means rare in the Gr world. The Athenian orator, Lysias, was doubtless named after his grandfather, Lysanias, and at first may even have been called Lysanias himself.

ARTEMIS, är′te-mis. See DIANA.

ARTIFICER, är-tif′i-sẽr. See CRAFTS.

ARTILLERY, är-til′ẽr-i (כְּלִי, *kelī*): In 1 S **20** 40 (AV) of Jonathan's bow and arrows, replaced in RV by WEAPONS; and in 1 Macc **6** 51 (AV) where the Gr words are trd in RV "instruments for casting fire and stones."

ARTISAN, är′ti-zan. See CRAFTS.

ARTS. See CRAFTS.

ARUBBOTH, a-rub′oth, **ARUBOTH,** ar′ū-both (הָאֲרֻבּוֹת, *hā-'ărubbōth;* AV **Aruboth**): One of the 12 districts from which victuals for Solomon's household were obtained (1 K **4** 10). With Arubboth are mentioned "Socoh, and all the land of Hepher," and as Socoh lay in the Shephelah (Josh **15** 35), Arubboth probably lay in the southern part of the Shephelah.

ARUMAH, a-rōō′ma (אֲרוּמָה, *'ărūmāh,* "lofty"): The town in which Abimelech, the son of Jerubbaal (Gideon), dwelt when driven from Shechem (Jgs **9** 41). The ruins El-Ormeh, 6 miles S.E. of Shechem, may be on the site, though its position is not known with certainty.

ARVAD, är′vad, **ARVADITES,** är′vad-īts (אַרְוַד, *'arwadh;* Ἄραδος, *Árados;* mod. *Ruad*): An island city off the coast of Syria some 30 miles N. of Tripolis, and the race inhabiting it. It was a barren rock covered with fortifications and houses several stories in height. The island was about 800 ft. long by 500 wide, surrounded by a massive wall, and an artificial harbor was constructed on the E. toward the main land. It developed into a trading city in early times, as did most of the Phoen cities on this coast. It had a powerful navy, and its ships are mentioned in the monuments of Egypt and Assyria. It seems to have had a sort of hegemony over the northern Phoen cities, from Mt. Cassius to the northern limits of Lebanon, something like that of Sidon in the S. It had its own local dynasty and coinage, and some of the names of its kings have been recovered. Its inhabitants are mentioned in the early lists of Gen (**10** 18), and Ezk (**27** 8.11) refers to its seamen and soldiers in the service of Tyre. It brought under its authority some of the neighboring cities on the main land, such as Marathus and Simyra, the former nearly opposite the island and the latter some miles to the S. Thothmes III, of Egypt, took it in his campaign in north Syria (1472 BC) and it is noticed in the campaigns of Rameses II in the early part of the 13th cent. BC (Breasted, *Ancient Records*). It is also mentioned in the Am Tab as being in league with the Amorites in their attacks upon the Egyp possessions in Syria (44 and 28, B.M. Am Tab). About the year 1200, or later, it was sacked by invaders from Asia Minor or the islands, as were most of the cities on the coast (Paton, *Syria and Pal,* 145) but it recovered when they were driven back. Its maritime importance is indicated by the inscriptions of the Assyr kings. Tiglath-pileser I (cir 1020) boasts that he sailed in the ships of Arvad. Asshur-nazir-pal (cir 876) made it tributary, but it revolted and we find 200 men of Arvad mentioned among the allies of Ben-hadad, of Damascus, at the great battle of Quarqar, when all Syria seems to have been in league against Shalmaneser II (cir 854). At this time the king of Arvad was Mattan Baal. It was afterward tributary to Tiglath-pileser III and Sennacherib, the king who paid it to the latter being Abd-ilihit (cir 701). Asshur-bani-pal (cir 664) compelled its king Yakinlu to submit and send one of his daughters to become a member of the royal harem (Rawlinson, *Phoenicia,* 456–57). Under the Persians Arvad was allowed to unite in a confederation with Sidon and Tyre, with a common council at Tripolis (ib 484). When Alexander the Great invaded Syria in 332 BC Arvad submitted without a struggle under her king Strato, who sent his navy to aid Alexander in the reduction of Tyre. It seems to have received the favor of the Seleucid kings of Syria and enjoyed the right of asylum for political refugees. It is mentioned in a rescript from Rome about 138 BC, in connection with other cities and rulers of the East, to show favor to the Jews. It was after Rome had begun to interfere in the affairs of Judaea and Syria, and indicates that A. was of considerable importance at that time (see 1 Macc **15** 16–23). The town is not mentioned in the NT, and in modern times has sunk to a small village, chiefly inhabited by fishermen. See ARADUS. H. PORTER

ARZA, är′za (אַרְצָא, *'arçā'*): A steward of King Elah, in whose house at Tirzah Zimri murdered the king at a drinking debauch. The text is not quite clear, and Arza might have been a servant of Zimri (1 K **16** 9).

ARZARETH, är′za-reth (AV **Arsareth,** är′sa-reth): This is the land to which the ten tribes were deported (2 Esd **13** 45). It is described as "another land" lying a year and a half's journey beyond the river, i.e. the Euphrates. It probably answers to the Heb אֶרֶץ אַחֶרֶת, *'ereç 'aḥereth* (Dt **29** 28). In Jos' time the people were still believed to be there in countless numbers (*Ant,* XI, v, 2).

AS, az: Conj. and adv. (usually Gr ὡς, *hōs,* ὥσπερ, *hōsper,* καθώς, *kathōs*), designating: (1) Likeness: (*a*) between nouns (Gen **3** 5; Jgs **6** 5; Phil **2** 8; He **11** 27.29); (*b*) between verbs (Lk **6** 36; Jn **5** 30; 1 Cor **10** 7); (*c*) between adjectives (1 Cor **15** 48). (2) Limitation (with respect to a particular aspect or relation) (1 Pet **4** 15.16). (3) Time (Lk **8** 5; **15** 25; Acts **8** 36). (4) Cause (1 Cor **4** 1). (5) Concession (Jn **7** 10; 2 Cor **11** 21). (6) Illustration, in numerous passages, beginning "as it is written," "as it is said," etc.

ASA, ā′sa (אָסָא, *'āsā',* "healer"; Ἀσά, *Asá*):

(1) A king of Judah, the third one after the separation of Judah and Israel. He was the son of Abijah and grandson of Rehoboam. Maacah, his mother, or rather grandmother, was daughter of Abishalom (Absalom) (1 K **15** 1 ff). The first ten years of his reign were prosperous and peaceful (2 Ch **14** 1). He introduced many reforms, such as putting away the sodomites or male prostitutes, removing idols from holy places, breaking down altars, pillars and Asherim. He even deposed the "queen mother" because of her idolatrous practices, and of the image which she had made for Asherah (1 K **15** 12 ff; 2 Ch **14** 3). Though the king himself, in the main, was a zealous reformer, his subjects did not always keep pace with him (**15** 17). With an army of 580,000 he repelled an attack of Zerah, the Ethiopian, and

routed him completely at Mareshah in the lowlands of Judah (**14** 6 ff). Directed and encouraged by Azariah the prophet, he carried on a great revival. Having restored the great altar of burnt offering in the temple, he assembled the people for a renewal of their covenant with Jeh. On this occasion 700 oxen and 7,000 sheep were offered in sacrifice. For the next twenty years there was apparently great prosperity and peace throughout his kingdom, but in the thirty-sixth year of his reign, Judah was attacked by Baasha, king of Israel, at all times hostile to Judah (1 K **15** 32). Baasha continued to encroach and finally fortified Ramah as a frontier fortress. Asa, faint-hearted, instead of putting his entire trust in Jeh, made an alliance with Ben-hadad, of Damascus. The Syrian king, in consideration of a large sum of money and much treasure from the temple at Jerus, consented to attack the northern portion of Baasha's territory. It was at this favorable moment that Asa captured Ramah, and with the vast building material collected there by Baasha, he built Geba of Benjamin and Mizpah (1 K **15** 16–22). This lack of faith in Jeh was severely criticized by Hanani the prophet. Asa, instead of listening patiently to this prophet of God, was greatly offended and enraged and Hanani was put in prison (2 Ch **16** 1–10). Three years later, Asa was attacked by gout or some disease of the feet. Here again he is accused of lack of faith, for "he sought not to Jeh, but to the physicians" (2 Ch **16** 12). Having ruled forty-one years, he died and was buried with great pomp in a tomb erected by himself in the city of David, i.e. Jerus. On the whole his reign was very successful, but it is sad to chronicle that as the years rolled on he became less and less faithful to Jeh and His law.

(2) A son of Elkanah, a Levite, who dwelt in one of the villages of the Netophathites (1 Ch **9** 16).

W. W. Davies

ASADIAS, as-a-dī'as (Ἀσαδίας, *Asadías*): An ancestor of Baruch (Bar **1** 1).

ASAEL, ā'sa-el, as'a-el. See Asiel (Apoc).

ASAHEL, as'a-hel (עֲשָׂהאֵל, *'ăsāh'ēl*, "God hath made"; Ἀσαήλ, *Asaēl*):

(1) The brother of Joab and Abishai. The three were sons of Zeruiah, one of David's sisters (1 Ch **2** 15.16; 2 S **2** 18, etc). The three brothers seem to have been from the beginning members of David's troop of strangely respectable brigands. Asahel was distinguished for his swift running, and this fact brought misfortune upon him and upon Israel. When Abner and the forces of Ish-bosheth were defeated near Gibeon, Asahel pursued Abner. Abner knew that he could outfight Asahel, though he could not outrun him. He also knew that the time had come for making David king, and that a blood feud among the leaders would be a calamity. He expostulated with Asahel, but in vain. It came to a fight, and Abner slew Asahel (2 S **2, 3**). As a result the coming of David to the throne of all Israel was delayed; and when at last Abner brought it about, he himself was treacherously killed by Joab in alleged blood revenge for Asahel. Asahel is mentioned as sixth in the list of David's "mighty men" (2 S **23** 24; 1 Ch **11** 26). The earlier of the names in this list are evidently arranged in the order of seniority. If it be assumed that the list was not made till after the death of Asahel, still there is no difficulty in the idea that some of the names in the list were placed there posthumously. Asahel is also mentioned as the fourth of David's month-by-month captains (1 Ch **27** 7). Superficial criticism describes this position as that of "commander of a division of David's army," and regards the statement, "and Zebadiah his son after him," as a note added to explain the otherwise incredible assertion of the text. This criticism is correct in its implication that the fourth captain was, as the text stands, the dead Asahel, in the person of his son Zebadiah. Coming from an annotator, the criticism regards this meaning as intelligible; is it any the less so if we regard it as coming from the author? In fact, the statement is both intelligible and credible. The second of David's month-by-month captains is Dodai, the father of the second of David's "mighty men"; and the fourth is Asahel, with his son Zebadiah. With these two variations the twelve month-by-month captains are twelve out of the nineteen seniors in the list of mighty men, and are mentioned in practically the same order of seniority. The 24,000 men each month were not a fighting army mobilized for war. The position of general for a month, whatever else it may have involved, was an honor held by a distinguished veteran. There is no absurdity in the idea that the honor may in some cases have been posthumous, the deceased being represented by his father or his son or by someone else.

(2) A Levite member of the commission of captains and Levites and priests which Jehoshaphat, in his third year, sent among the cities of Judah, with the book of the law, to spread information among the people (2 Ch **17** 7–9).

(3) One of the keepers of the storechambers in the temple in the time of Hezekiah (2 Ch **31** 13).

(4) The father of Jonathan who was one of the two men who "stood upon this," at the time when Ezra and the people appointed a court to consider the cases of those who had married foreign wives (Ezr **10** 15). The text of RV translates "stood up against this," while the margin has "were appointed over this."

Willis J. Beecher

ASAHIAH, as-a-hī'a (עֲשָׂיָה, *'ăsāyāh*, "Jeh hath made"; AV form; RV ASAIAH): "The king's servant" sent by Josiah with Hilkiah, the priest, and others to inquire of Jeh concerning the words of the book found in the temple (2 K **22** 12.14; 2 Ch **34** 20).

ASAIAH, a-sā'ya (עֲשָׂיָה, *'ăsāyāh*, "Jehovah has made," written **Asahiah** twice in AV [2 K **22** 12.14]):

(1) A Levite of the family of Merari, and one of those who helped bring the ark from the house of Obed-edom to Jerus (1 Ch **6** 30; **15** 6.11).

(2) A leading man of the tribe of Simeon. He was in the incursion which attacked and dispossessed the Meunim (q.v.), or the shepherd people, in the valley of Gedor (1 Ch **4** 36).

(3) An officer of Josiah sent to Huldah the prophetess for advice regarding the law book found by Hilkiah (2 K **22** 12.14; see Asahiah).

(4) A Shilonite resident of Jerus (1 Ch **9** 5). He is called Maaseiah in Neh **11** 5.

W. W. Davies

ASANA, as'a-na (Ἀσανά, *Asaná, Assaná*) = Asnah (Ezr **2** 50); omitted in Neh. The sons of A. (temple-servants) returned with Zerubbabel to Jerus (1 Esd **5** 31).

ASAPH, ā'saf (אָסָף, *'āṣāph*): Is the name of three men in the OT, of whom one is the reputed author of Pss **50** and **73–83**. He was one of David's three chief musicians, the other two being Heman, and Ethan or Jeduthun, and we first hear of him when the ark was taken to Jerus (1 Ch **15** 16–19). He conducted with cymbals the music performed in the tent where the ark was housed (1 Ch **16** 4.5.7.37), while his two coadjutors discharged the same office at Gibeon (**16** 41.42). In 1 Ch **25** 1 ff we are told that four of his sons were appointed to conduct under him detachments of the great chorus, the families of Heman and Jeduthun also furnishing leaders, and all took part at the dedication of the temple (2 Ch **5** 12). A., H., and J. were called the king's seers (1 Ch **25**; 2 Ch **35** 15), no doubt an official title of rank or dignity. The "Sons of Asaph" are mentioned in later times. They formed a guild, and played a prominent part at each revival of the national religion. See MUSIC; PSALMS.

JAMES MILLAR

ASARA, as'a-ra (**'Ασαρά,** *Asará;* AV **Azara**): The sons of A. (temple-servants) returned to Jerus with Zerubbabel (1 Esd **5** 31). Omitted in Ezr and Neh.

ASARAMEL, a-sar'a-mel (**'Ασαραμέλ,** *Asaramél* or *Saramél*): A name of uncertain origin occurring in 1 Macc **14** 28, in the inscription set up in memory of Simon and the Maccabean family. "On the eighteenth day of Elul, in the hundred and seventy and second year, and this is the third year of Simon the high priest, in Asaramel, in a great congregation of priests and people and princes of the nation, and of the elders of the country," etc. The phrase "in Asaramel" has been taken as referring to a place, and as the name of a title of Simon. Ewald and others take it to be the equivalent of בחצר עם אל, *ba-ḥăçar ‛am ’ēl,* "in the court of the people of God." Another reading is "in Saramel." The majority prefer to take the phrase as a title of Simon; the original phrase is then taken to have been ושר עם אל, *w*[e]*sar ‛am ’ēl,* "and prince of the people of God," i.e. ethnarch. If the translator mistook ו (*w*) for ב (*bh*) and read *’en,* he might have left the phrase untr[d] because he supposed it to be the name of a place. Schürer disposes of the *ἐν* by taking it as a corruption of *σεγεν, segen* = סגן, *ṣeghen,* which is equivalent to the Gr *στρατηγός, stratēgós* (*GVI,* I, 197, n. 17).

H. J. WOLF

ASAREEL, a-sā'rē-el, a-sär'ē-el. See ASAREL.

ASAREL, as'ar-el (אֲשַׂרְאֵל, *’ăsar’ēl,* "God is ruler"; AV **Asareel**): A descendant of Judah and a son of Jehallelel (1 Ch **4** 16).

ASARELAH, as-a-rē'la. See ASHARELAH.

ASBACAPHATH, as-bak'a-fath. See ASBASARETH.

ASBASARETH, as-bas'a-reth (LXX **'Ασβακαφάθ,** *Asbakapháth,* or **'Ασβασαρέθ,** *Asbasaréth*): The Gr rendering of the Assyr *Asshur-ah-iddina* ("Esarhaddon") (1 Esd **5** 69; cf also Ezr **4** 2.10). See OSNAPPAR.

ASCALON, as'ka-lon (**'Ασκάλων,** *Askálōn*): In Apoc, both AV and RV (Jth **2** 28; 1 Macc **10** 86; **11** 60; **12** 33). See ASHKELON.

ASCEND, a-send': By derivation the Eng. word implies motion from a lower place to (not merely toward) a higher one; and usage tends to restrict it to cases where the beholder is in the lower, not the higher, position. AV uses it 39 times in all: (1) of the going up of vapor (Ps **135** 7), flame (Jgs **20** 40), or smoke (Rev **8** 4); (2) of travel from one place to another (Acts **25** 1) or of the course of a boundary (Josh **15** 3); (3) of coming up from the underworld (1 S **28** 13; Rev **11** 7; **17** 8); and (4) of the going up (of men, angels, Our Lord) from earth to the skies or to heaven (Gen **28** 12; Jn **3** 13). RV uses the appropriate form of "to go up" in all cases falling under (2) and (3); in those under (4) it retains "ascend" with an occasional change in tense; under (1) it retains "ascend" everywhere in OT (Ex **19** 18; Josh **8** 20.21; Ps **135** 7 ‖ Jer **10** 13 ‖ **51** 16) except Jgs **20** 40, but substitutes "went up," "goeth up," in NT (Rev **8** 4; **14** 11). The like change in the OT passages would make the usage of RV uniform.

F. K. FARR

ASCENSION, a-sen'shun: Most modern Lives of Christ commence at Bethlehem and end with the Ascension, but Christ's life began earlier and continued later. The Ascension is not only a great fact of the NT, but a great factor in the life of Christ and Christians, and no complete view of Jesus Christ is possible unless the Ascension and its consequences are included. It is the consummation of His redemptive work. The Christ of the Gospels is the Christ of history, the Christ of the past, but the full NT picture of Christ is that of a living Christ, the Christ of heaven, the Christ of experience, the Christ of the present and the future. The NT passages referring to the Ascension need close study and their teaching careful observation.

I. In the Gospels.—The Ascension is alluded to in several passages in the Gospels in the course of Our Lord's earthly ministry (Lk **9** 31.51; Jn **6** 62; **7** 33; **12** 32; **14** 12.28; **16** 5.10.17.28; **20** 17). These passages show that the event was constantly in view, and anticipated by Our Lord. The Ascension is also clearly implied in the allusions to His coming to earth on clouds of heaven (Mt **24** 30; **26** 64).

1. Anticipations

If with most modern scholars we regard Mark's Gospel as ending with ver 8 of the last ch, it will be seen to stop short at the resurrection, though the present ending speaks of Christ being received up into heaven, of His sitting at the right hand of God, and of His working with the disciples as they went preaching the word (Mk **16** 19.20). In any case this is a bare summary only. The close of the Third Gospel includes an evident reference to the fact of the Ascension (Lk **24** 28–53), even if the last six words of ver 51, "and was carried up into heaven" are not authentic. No difficulty need be felt at the omission of the Fourth Gospel to refer to the fact of the Ascension, though it was universally accepted at the time the apostle wrote (Jn **20** 17). As Dr. Hort has pointed out, "The Ascension did not lie within the proper scope of the Gospels . . . . its true place was at the head of the Acts of the Apostles" (quoted, Swete, *The Ascended Christ,* 2).

2. Records

II. In the Acts.—The story in **1** 6–12 is clear. Jesus Christ was on the Mount of Olives. There had been conversation between Him and His disciples, and in the course of it He was taken up; and a cloud received Him out of their sight (ver 9). His body was uplifted till it disappeared, and while they continued to gaze up they saw two men who assured them that He would come back exactly as He had gone up. The three Gr words rendered "taken up" (*ἐπήρθη, epérthē*) (ver 9); "went" (*πορευομένου, poreuoménou*) (ver 10); "received up" (*αναλημφθεὶς, analēmphtheís*) (ver 11); deserve careful notice. This account must either be attributed to invention, or to the testimony of an eye-witness. But Luke's historicity now seems abundantly proved.

1. Record

The Ascension is mentioned or implied in several passages in Acts (**2** 33 ff; **3** 21; **7** 55 f; **9** 3–5; **22** 6–8; **26** 13–15). All these passages assert the present life and activity of Jesus Christ in heaven.

2. References

III. In the Pauline Epistles.—In **8** 34 the apostle states four facts connected with Christ Jesus: His death; His resurrection; His session at God's right hand; His intercession. The last two are clearly the culminating points of a series of redemptive acts.

1. Romans

While for its purpose Rom necessarily lays stress on the Resurrection, Eph has as part of its special aim an emphasis on the Ascension. In **1** 20 God's work wrought in Christ is shown to have gone much farther than the Resurrection, and to have "made him to sit at his right hand in the heavenly places," thereby constituting Him the supreme authority over all things, and especially Head of the church (**1** 20–23). This idea concerning Christ is followed in **2** 6 by the association of believers with Christ "in the heavenly places," and the teaching finds its completest expression in **4** 8–11, where the Ascension is connected with the gift of the heavenly Christ as the crowning feature of His work. Nothing is more striking than the complementary teaching of Rom and Eph respectively in their emphasis on the Resurrection and Ascension.

2. Ephesians

In **2** 6–11 the exaltation of Christ is shown to follow His deep humiliation. He who humbled Himself is exalted to the place of supreme authority. In **3** 20 Christians are taught that their commonwealth is in heaven, "whence also we wait for a Saviour."

3. Philippians

The emphasis placed on the second advent of Christ in 1 Thess is an assumption of the fact of the Ascension. Christians are waiting for God's Son from heaven (**1** 10) who is to "descend from heaven, with a shout, with the voice of the archangel, and with the trump of God" (**4** 16).

4. Thessalonians

The only allusion to the Ascension in the Pastoral Epistles is found in the closing statement of what seems to be an early Christian song in 1 Tim **3** 16. He who was "manifested in the flesh .... received up in glory."

5. Timothy

IV. In Hebrews.—In this epistle there is more recorded about the Ascension and its consequences than in any other part of the NT. The facts of the Ascension and Session are first of all stated (**1** 3) with all that this implies of definite position and authority (**1** 4–13). Christians are regarded as contemplating Jesus as the Divine Man in heaven (**2** 9), though the meaning of the phrase, "crowned with glory and honor" is variously interpreted, some thinking that it refers to the result and outcome of His death, others thinking that He was "crowned for death" in the event of the Transfiguration (Matheson in Bruce, *Hebrews*, 83). Jesus Christ is described as "a great High Priest, who hath passed through the heavens" (**4** 14), as a Forerunner who is entered within the veil for us, and as a High Priest for ever after the order of Melchizedek (**6** 20). As such He "abideth for ever," and "ever liveth to make intercession" (**7** 24.25). The chief point of the epistle itself is said to be "such a high priest, who sat down on the right hand of the throne of the Majesty in the heavens" (**8** 1), and His position there implies that He has obtained eternal redemption for His people and is appearing before God on their behalf (**9** 12.24). This session at God's right hand is also said to be with a view to His return to earth when His enemies will have become His footstool (**10** 12.13), and one of the last exhortations bids believers to look unto Jesus as the Author and Perfecter of faith who has "sat down at the right hand of the throne of God" (**12** 2).

V. In the Petrine Epistles.—The only reference to the Ascension is in 1 Pet **3** 22, where Christ's exaltation after His sufferings is set forth as the pattern and guarantee of Christian glorification after endurance of persecution.

VI. In the Johannine Writings.—Nothing is recorded of the actual Ascension, but 1 Jn **2** 1 says that "we have an Advocate with the Father." The word "Advocate" is the same as "Comforter" in Jn **14** 16, where it is used of the Holy Spirit. Christ is the Comforter "in relation to the Father," and the Holy Spirit is the Comforter dwelling in the soul.

1. Epistles

All the references in the Apocalypse either teach or imply the living Christ who is in heaven, as active in His church and as coming again (Rev **1** 7.13; **5** 5–13; **6** 9–17; **14** 1–5).

2. Apocalypse

VII. Summary of NT Teaching.—The NT calls attention to the fact of Ascension and the fact of the Session at God's right hand. Three words are used in the Gr in connection with the Ascension: *anabaínein* (*ascendere*), "to go up"; *analambánesthai* (*adsumi*), "to be taken up"; *poreúesthai*, "to go." The Session is connected with Ps **110**, and this OT passage finds frequent reference or allusion in all parts of the NT. But it is used especially in He in connection with Christ's priesthood, and with His position of authority and honor at God's right hand (Swete, *The Ascended Christ*, 10–15). But the NT emphasizes the fact of Christ's exaltation rather than the mode, the latter being quite secondary. Yet the acceptance of the fact must be carefully noticed, for it is impossible to question that this is the belief of all the NT writers. They base their teaching on the fact and do not rest content with the moral or theological aspects of the Ascension apart from the historic reality. The Ascension is regarded as the point of contact between the Christ of the gospels and of the epistles. The gift of the Spirit is said to have come from the ascended Christ. The Ascension is the culminating point of Christ's glorification after His Resurrection, and is regarded as necessary for His heavenly exaltation. The Ascension was proved and demanded by the Resurrection, though there was no need to preach it as part of the evangelistic message. Like the Virgin birth, the Ascension involves doctrine for Christians rather than non-Christians. It is the culmination of the Incarnation, the reward of Christ's redemptive work, and the entrance upon a wider sphere of work in His glorified condition, as the Lord and Priest of His church (Jn **7** 39; **16** 7).

1. The Fact

We may summarize what the NT tells us of Our Lord's present life in heaven by observing carefully what is recorded in the various passages of the NT. He ascended into heaven (Mk **16** 19; Lk **24** 51; Acts **1** 9); He is seated on the right hand of God (Col **3** 1; He **1** 3; **8** 1; **10** 12); He bestowed the gift of the Holy Spirit on the Day of Pentecost (Acts **4** 9.33); He added disciples to the church (Acts **2** 47); He worked with the disciples as they went forth preaching the gospel (Mk **16** 20); He healed the impotent man (Acts **3** 16); He stood to receive the first martyr (Acts **7** 56); He appeared to Saul of Tarsus (Acts **9** 5); He makes intercession for His people (Rom **8** 26; He **7** 25); He is able to succor the tempted (He **2** 18); He is able to sympathize (He **4** 15); He is able to save to the uttermost (He **7** 25); He lives forever (He **7** 24; Rev **1** 18); He is our Great High Priest (He **7** 26; **8** 1; **10** 21); He possesses an intransmissible or inviolable priesthood (He **7** 24); He appears in the presence of God for us (He **9** 24); He is our Advocate with the Father (1 Jn **2** 1); He is waiting until all oppo-

2. The Message

sition to Him is overcome (He **10** 13). This includes all the teaching of the NT concerning our Lord's present life in heaven.

VIII. Problems.—There are two questions usually associated with the Ascension which need our attention.

1. Relation to the Laws of Nature

There is no greater difficulty in connection with the Ascension than with the Resurrection, or the Incarnation. Of Our Lord's resurrection body we know nothing. All we can say is that it was different from the body laid in the tomb and yet essentially the same; the same and yet essentially different. The Ascension was the natural close of Our Lord's earthly life, and as such, is inseparable from the Resurrection. Whatever, therefore, may be said of the Resurrection in regard to the laws of nature applies equally to the Ascension.

2. Localization of the Spiritual World

The record in Acts is sometimes objected to because it seems to imply the localization of heaven above the earth. But is not this taking the narrative in too absolutely bald and literal a sense? Heaven is at once a place and a state, and as personality necessarily implies locality, some place for Our Lord's Divine, yet human person is essential. To speak of heaven as "above" may be only symbolical, but the ideas of fact and locality must be carefully adhered to. And yet it is not merely local, and "we have to think less of a transition from one locality than of a transition from one condition to another. . . . . the real meaning of the ascension is that . . . . Our Lord withdrew from a world of limitations" to that higher existence where God is (Milligan, *Ascension and Heavenly Priesthood*, 26). It matters not that our conception today of the physical universe is different from that of NT times. We still speak of the sun setting and rising, though strictly these are not true. The details of the Ascension are really unimportant. Christ disappeared from view, and no question need be raised either of distance or direction. We accept the fact without any scientific explanation. It was a change of conditions and mode of existence; the essential fact is that He departed and disappeared. Even Keim admits that "the ascension of Jesus follows from all the facts of His career" (quoted, Milligan, 13), and Weiss is equally clear that the Ascension is as certain as the Resurrection, and stands and falls therewith (Milligan, 14).

IX. Its Relation to Christ Himself.—The Ascension was the exaltation and glory of Jesus Christ after His work was accomplished (Phil **2** 9). He had a threefold glory: (1) as the Son of God before the Incarnation (Jn **17** 5); (2) as God manifest in the flesh (Jn **1** 14); (3) as the exalted Son of God after the Resurrection and Ascension (Lk **24** 26; 1 Pet **1** 21). The Ascension meant very much to Christ Himself, and no study of the subject must overlook this aspect of NT teaching. His exaltation to the right hand of God meant (1) the proof of victory (Eph **4** 8); (2) the position of honor (Ps **110** 1); (3) the place of power (Acts **2** 33); (4) the place of happiness (Ps **26** 11); (5) the place of rest ("seated"); (6) the place of permanence ("for ever").

X. Its Teaching for Christians.—The importance of the Ascension for Christians lies mainly in the fact that it was the introduction to Our Lord's present life in heaven which means so much in the believer's life. The spiritual value of the Ascension lies, not in Christ's physical remoteness, but in His spiritual nearness. He is free from earthly limitations, and His life above is the promise and guarantee of ours. "Because I live ye shall live also."

1. Redemption Accomplished

The Ascension and Session are regarded as the culminating point of Christ's redemptive work (He **8** 1), and at the same time the demonstration of the sufficiency of His righteousness on man's behalf. For sinful humanity to reach heaven two essential features were necessary: (*a*) the removal of sin (negative); and (*b*) the presence of righteousness (positive). The Resurrection demonstrated the sufficiency of the atonement for the former, and the Ascension demonstrated the sufficiency of righteousness for the latter. The Spirit of God was to convict the world of "righteousness" "because I go to the Father" (Jn **16** 10). In accord with this we find that in the Epistle to the He every reference to Our Lord's atonement is in the past, implying completeness and perfection, "once for all."

2. High Priesthood

This is the peculiar and special message of He. Priesthood finds its essential features in the representation of man to God, involving access into the Divine presence (He **5** 1). It means drawing near and dwelling near to God. In He, Aaron is used as typical of the work, and Melchizedek as typical of the person of the priest; and the two acts mainly emphasized are the offering in death and the entrance into heaven. Christ is both priest and priestly victim. He offered propitiation and then entered into heaven, not "with," but "through" His own blood (He **9** 12), and as High Priest, at once human and Divine, He is able to sympathize (He **4** 15); able to succor (He **2** 18); and able to save (He **7** 25). See CHRIST AS PRIEST.

3. Lordship

The Ascension constituted Christ as Head of the church (Eph **1** 22; **4** 10.15; Col **2** 19). This Headship teaches that He is the Lord and Life of the church. He is never spoken of as King in relation to His Body, the Church, only as Head and Lord. The fact that He is at the right hand of God suggests in the symbolical statement that He is not yet properly King on His own throne, as He will be hereafter as "King of the Jews," and "King of Kings."

4. Intercession

In several NT passages this is regarded as the crowning point of Our Lord's work in heaven (Rom **8** 33.34). He is the perfect Mediator between God and man (1 Tim **2** 5; He **8** 6); our Advocate with the Father (1 Jn **2** 1). His very presence at God's right hand pleads on behalf of His people. There is no presentation, or representation, or pleading, of Himself, for His intercession is never associated with any such relation to the sacrifice of Calvary. Nor is there any hint in the NT of a relation between the Eucharist and His life and work in heaven. This view popularized by the late Dr. William Milligan (*The Ascension*, etc, 266), and indorsed from other standpoints in certain aspects of Anglican teaching (Swete, *The Ascended Christ*, 46), does not find any support in the NT. As Westcott says, "The modern conception of Christ pleading in heaven His passion, 'offering His blood,' on behalf of man, has no foundation in this epistle" (*Hebrews*, 230). And Hort similarly remarks, "The words, 'Still . . . . His prevailing death He pleads' have no apostolic warrant, and cannot even be reconciled with apostolic doctrine" (*Life and Letters*, II, 213). Our Lord's intercession is not so much in what He says as in what He is. He pleads by His presence on His Father's throne, and he is able to save to the uttermost through His intercession, because of His perpetual life and His inviolable, undelegated, intransmissible priesthood (He **7** 24.25).

There is an intimate and essential connection between the Ascension of Christ and the descent of the Holy Spirit. The Holy Spirit was given to Christ as the acknowledgment and reward of His work done, and having received this "Promise of the Father" He bestowed Him upon His people (Acts **2** 33). By means of the Spirit the twofold work is done, of convincing sinners (Jn **16** 9), and of edifying believers (Jn **14** 12; see also Jn **14** 25.26; **16** 14.15).

5. The Gift of the Spirit

It is in connection with the Ascension and Our Lord's life in heaven that we understand the force of such a passage as "Lo, I am with you always" (Mt **28** 20). "He ever liveth" is the supreme inspiration of the individual Christian and of the whole church. All through the NT from the time of the Ascension onward, the one assurance is that Christ is living; and in His life we live, hold fellowship with God, receive grace for daily living and rejoice in victory over sin, sorrow and death.

6. Presence

Our Lord's life in heaven looks forward to a consummation. He is "expecting till his enemies be made his footstool" (He **10** 13 AV). He is described as our Forerunner (He **6** 18 ff), and His presence above is the assurance that His people will share His life hereafter. But His Ascension is also associated with His coming again (Phil **3** 20.21; 1 Thess **4** 16; He **9** 28). At this coming there will be the resurrection of dead saints, and the transformation of living ones (1 Thess **4** 16.17), to be followed by the Divine tribunal with Christ as Judge (Rom **2** 16; 2 Tim **4** 1.8). To His own people this coming will bring joy, satisfaction and glory (Acts **3** 21; Rom **8** 19); to His enemies defeat and condemnation (1 Cor **15** 25; He **2** 8; **10** 13).

7. Expectation

Reviewing all the teaching of Our Lord's present life in heaven, appearing on our behalf, interceding by His presence, bestowing the Holy Spirit, governing and guiding the church, sympathizing, helping and saving His people, we are called upon to "lift up our hearts," for it is in occupation with the living Christ that we find the secret of peace, the assurance of access, and the guaranty of our permanent relation to God. Indeed, we are clearly taught in He that it is in fellowship with the present life of Christ in heaven that Christians realize the difference between spiritual immaturity and maturity (He **6** 1; **10** 1), and it is the purpose of this epistle to emphasize this truth above all others. Christianity is "the religion of free access to God," and in proportion as we realize, in union with Christ in heaven, this privilege of drawing near and keeping near, we shall find in the attitude of "lift up your hearts" the essential features of a strong, vigorous, growing, joyous Christian life.

LITERATURE.—Milligan, *Ascension and Heavenly Priesthood of Our Lord;* Swete, *The Appearances of the Risen Lord; The Ascended Christ;* Lacey, *The Historic Christ;* Lives of Christ, by Neander, B. Weiss, Edersheim, Farrar, Geikie, Gilbert; Fairbairn, *Studies in the Life of Christ;* Knowling, *Witness of the Epistles;* Bernard in *Expos T,* 1900–1901, 152–55; Bruce in *Expos. Gr Test,* I; Swete, *Apostles' Creed;* Westcott, *Historic Faith,* ch vi; *Revelation of the Risen Lord,* chs x, xi; *Ep. to He;* art. "Ascension" in *HDB;* Paget, *Studies in the Christian Character,* sermons xxi, xxii; Findlay, *Things Above;* art. "Priest" in *HDB* (in NT), "Hebrews"; Davidson, *Hebrews,* special note on "Priesthood of Christ"; Dimock, *Our One Priest on High; The Christian Doctrine of Sacerdotium;* Perowne, *Our High Priest in Heaven;* Rotherham, *Studies in He;* Soames, *The Priesthood of the New Covenant;* Hubert Brooke, *The Great High Priest;* H. W. Williams, *The Priesthood of Christ;* J. S. Candlish, *The Christian Salvation* (1899), 6; G. Milligan, *The Theol. of Ep. to He* (1899), 111; R. C. Moberly, *Ministerial Priesthood* (1897); A. S. Peake, "Hebrews" in *Cent. Bible;* Beyschlag, *NT Theol.,* II, 315; art. "Ascension" in *DCG;* art. "Assumption and Ascension" in *HDRE;* art. "Ascension" in *JE;* Charles, *The Book of En; The Slavonic Secrets of En; The Book of Jub; The Apocalypse of Bar; The Ascension of Isaiah; Assumption of Moses;* M. R. James, "Testament of Abraham" *TS,* II, 2, 1892; Martensen, *Christian Dogmatics.*

W. H. GRIFFITH THOMAS

ASCENSION OF ISAIAH. See APOCALYPTIC LITERATURE.

ASCENT, a-sent′:

(1) The rendering in AV twice, RV 14 times correctly, of Heb *ma'ălеh,* "ascent," "pass," as a geographical term (AV Nu **34** 4; 2 S **15** 30; RV Josh **10** 10; Jgs **8** 13, etc).

(2) The rendering in AV and RV of *'ōlāh* in 1 K **10** 5, "his ascent by which he went up unto the house of Jeh"; but *'ōlāh* everywhere else means "burnt-offering," and all ancient VSS support RVm, "his burnt-offering which he offered" (caused to go up), etc.

(3) In 2 Ch **9** 4 (‖ 1 K **10** 5) a very slight textual correction (supported by LXX) gives us the same words as in 1 K instead of the difficult *'ălīyāh,* "upper chamber," not "ascent" as AV and RV render it against all usage elsewhere.

(4) In RV Ezk **40** 31.34.37; Neh **12** 37, of a flight of steps, stairs.

(5) In RV (Heb *'ălīyāh*), Neh **3** 31.32, m "upper chamber" is to be preferred to text "ascent."

F. K. FARR

ASCHENAZ, ash′ē-naz. See ASHKENAZ.

ASEAS, a-sē′as (**'Ασαίας,** *Asaías*=Isshijah [Ezr **10** 31]): A son of Annas, who put away his "strange wife" (1 Esd **9** 32).

ASEBEBIAS, a-seb-ē-bī′as (**'Ασεβηβίας,** *Asebēbías;* AV **Asebebia,** a-seb-e-bī′a): A., his sons and brethren returned with Ezra to perform the functions of priesthood in Jerus (1 Esd **8** 47). Cf Sherebiah (Ezr **8** 18).

ASEBIAS, as-ē-bī′as (**'Ασεβίας,** *Asebías;* AV **Asebia,** as-ē-bī′a): A. returned with Ezra to perform the function of a priest in Jerus (1 Esd **8** 48). Cf Hashabiah (Ezr **8** 19).

ASENATH, as′ē-nath (**'Ασενέθ,** *Asenéth*): The wife of Joseph, daughter of Poti-phera, mother of Manasseh and Ephraim (Gen **41** 45.50; **46** 20). She was evidently an Egyp woman and bore an Egyp name. אסנת, pointed by the Massoretes as אָסְנַת, *'āṣᵉnath,* appears in the LXX as *āseneth* or *asenneth.* The last two consonants appear to represent the name of the Egyp goddess Neith. The first part of the name will then represent either *ns*="belonging to" (so Brugsch and generally), or *'ws-n* (note the doubled *n* in the LXX transcription)="she belongs to" (so Spiegelberg). It is possible that these four letters represent the Egyp name *Sn-t* (so Lieblein and others), though the א must then be explained as *'ālēph prostheticum* and the ת would be less regular than a ה to stand for the Egyp feminine *t.* J. OSCAR BOYD

ASER, ā′sẽr (**'Ασήρ,** *Asḗr*): AV: Gr form of **Asher** (thus RV) (Lk **2** 36; Rev **7** 6).

ASERER, as′ē-rẽr. See SERAR.

ASH, ash (אֹרֶן, *'ōren;* RV FIR TREE; RVm Ash): A maker of idols "planteth a fir-tree [m, "ash"], and the rain doth nourish it" (Isa **44** 14). It is a suggestion as old as Luther that the final letter ן, *n,* was originally a ז, *z,* and that the word should be *'erez,* "cedar"; the chief objection is that cedar occurs just before in the same ver. The word *'ōren* seems to be connected with the Assyr *irin,* meaning fir or cedar or allied tree. "Fir" has support from the LXX and from the rabbis. Post (*HDB*) suggests as probable the stone pine, *Pinus pinea,* which has been extensively planted round Beirût and unlike most planted trees flourishes without artificial watering—"the rain doth nourish it."

The tr "ash" was probably suggested by the

fanciful resemblance of the Heb *'ōren* and the Lat *ornus,* the manna ash of Europe. Three varieties of ash flourish in Syria, *Fraxinus ornus, F. excelsior* and *F. oxycarpa.* The last mentioned, which is common in parts of N. Pal, being a large tree some 30 to 40 ft. high, might suit the context were there anything philological to support the idea.

E. W. G. Masterman

ASH (Bear). See Astronomy.

ASHAMED, a-shāmd′: Almost exclusively moral in significance; confusion or abashment through consciousness of guilt or of its exposure. Often including also a sense of terror or fear because of the disgrace connected with the performance of some action. Capacity for shame indicates that moral sense (conscience) is not extinct. "Ashamed" occurs 96 out of 118 times in the OT. Heb בּוֹשׁ, *bōsh,* "to feel shame" (Lat *pudere*), with derivatives occurs 80 times; כָּלַם, *kālam,* "to shame," including the thought of "disgrace," "reproach"; חָפֵר, *ḥāphēr,* "to blush": hence shame because of frustrated plans (uniformly in RV "confounded"); Gr αἰσχύνομαι, *aischúnomai,* "suffused with shame," passive only and its compounds. Uses: (1) A few times, of actual *embarrassment,* as of Hazael before the steadfast look of Elisha (2 K **8** 11; see also 2 S **10** 5; 2 K **2** 17; Ezr **8** 22). (2) Innocence not capable of shame: "both naked .... and .... not a." (Gen **2** 25; see Shame); the redeemed no occasion for (Ps **34** 5 AV; 1 Jn **2** 28); Christ not of "brethren" (He **2** 11); nor Christian of gospel (Rom **1** 16); nor God of men of faith (He **11** 16); nor they who trust in God (Isa **50** 7; **54** 4; Joel **2** 26). (3) Sense of guilt: "I am a. . . . . for our iniquities" (Ezr **9** 6); "of thy lewd way" (Ezk **16** 27.61); ascribed to idolaters chagrined at worthlessness of idols (Isa **1** 29; **44** 9.11; **45** 16; Jer **2** 26); to enemies (Ps **6** 10); to wicked (Ps **31** 17); to all who forsake God (Jer **17** 13); to those who trust in human help, as Israel of Egypt and Assyria, and Moab of Chemosh (Jer **2** 36; **48** 13); to a mother of wicked children (Jer **50** 12). (4) Repentance causes shame for sin (Jer **31** 19; Rom **6** 21). (5) Calamities also, and judgments (Jer **14** 3.4; **15** 9; **20** 11). (6) Capacity for shame may be lost through long-continued sin (Jer **6** 15; **8** 12; cf **3** 3), exceptionally striking passages on the deadening power of immorality, suggestive of 1 Tim **4** 2; Titus **1** 15. (7) The grace of Christ delivers from the shame of moral timidity (Rom **1** 16; 2 Tim **1** 8.12.16; 1 Pet **4** 16). (8) At Christ's second coming His followers will "not be a. before him" (1 Jn **2** 28); at the final judgment He will be a. of all who have been a. of Him (Mk **8** 38; Lk **9** 26; cf Mt **10** 33; He **11** 16). (9) The word lends itself to rich poetic use, e.g. Lebanon, with faded and falling foliage, "is a." (RV "confounded") at the desolations of the land under Sennacherib (Isa **33** 9); so great is God's glory in the new Jerus that "the sun [is] a." in His presence (Isa **24** 23), explaining the glorious fig. in Rev **21** 23; **22** 5. (The references in this art. are from AV; RV frequently replaces 'ashamed' by 'put to shame.') See Shame.

Dwight M. Pratt

ASHAN, ā′shan (עָשָׁן, *'āshān*): An unknown site in the domain of Judah (Josh **15** 42), possessed by Simeon (Josh **19** 7), and mentioned among the priests' cities in 1 Ch **6** 59 (44) = Josh **21** 16 (עַיִן, *'ayin,* is a corruption of עָשָׁן, *'āshān*). Chorashan (or Borashan), which was probably the site of some reservoir in the S.W. part of Judah (1 S **30** 30), is the same as Ashan.

ASHARELAH, ash-a-rē′la, **ASARELAH** (אֲשַׂרְאֵלָה, *'ăsar'ēlāh*): One of the Asaphites appointed by David to the temple service (1 Ch **25** 2); in ver 14 he is called Jesharelah. The latter element in both forms may be (*'ēl*) "God," but the meaning of the former part in the first form is doubtful. Thes. compares אסר, *'āṣar,* "to bind," "whom God has bound [by a vow]."

ASHBEA, ash′bē-a, ash-bē′a (אַשְׁבֵּעַ, *'ashbēa'*): "The house of Ashbea," a family of linen-workers mentioned in 1 Ch **4** 21. We might render *bēth 'ashbēa'* as their dwelling-place; nothing is known of such a place nor is this house of weavers referred to in any other place.

ASHBEL, ash′bel, **ASHBELITE**, ash′bel-īt (אַשְׁבֵּל, *'ashbēl*): The gentilic name "Ashbelite" is found in Nu **26** 38, second son of Benjamin (Gen **46** 21). In 1 Ch **7** 6–11 (6) "Jediael" ("known to God") is substituted for the heathen-sounding "Ashbel" ("Ishbaal," "man of Baal"). The chronicler, in this case, conforms literally to the principle laid down in Hos **2** 17; the title "Baal" ("lord") was applied in early days (e.g. in the days of Saul) to the national God of Israel, but in later days the prophets objected to it because it was freely applied to heathen gods (cf Ishbosheth). In 1 Ch **8** 1 the three names Bela, Ashbel, Aharah (= Ahiram) are taken from Nu **26** 38, however, without change.

H. J. Wolf

ASHDŌD, ash′dod (אַשְׁדּוֹד, *'ashdōdh;* **Ἄζωτος,** *Azōtós;* mod. *Esdūd*): One of the five chief cities of the Philis. The name means stronghold or fortress, and its strength may be inferred by the fact that Psammetik I, of Egypt, besieged it for many years (Herodotus says 29). Some of the Anakim were found there in the days of Joshua (Josh **11** 22), and the inhabitants were too strong for the Israelites at that time. It was among the towns assigned to Judah, but was not occupied by her (Josh **13** 3; **15** 46.47). It was still independent in the days of Samuel, when, after the defeat of the Israelites, the ark was taken to the house of Dagon in Ashdod (1 S **5** 1.2). We have no account of its being occupied even by David, although he defeated the Philis many times, and we have no definite knowledge of its coming into the hands of Judah until the time of Uzziah (2 Ch **26** 6). Ashdod, like the other Phili towns, came under the authority of the Assyr monarchs, and we have mention of it in their records. It revolted against Sargon in 711 BC, and deposed the Assyr governor, Akhimiti, who had been appointed by him in 720. Sargon at once dispatched a force to subdue the rebels and the city was severely punished. This is referred to by Isaiah (Isa **20** 1). Amos had prophesied such a calamity some years before (**1** 8), and Jeremiah refers to "the remnant of Ashdod" as though it had continued weak until his day (Jer **25** 20). Zephaniah (Zeph **2** 4) refers to the desolation of Ashdod and Zechariah to its degraded condition (Zec **9** 6). It continued to be inhabited, however, for we find the Jews intermarried with them after the return from Babylon (Neh **13** 23.24). In the Maccabean period we are told that Judas and Jonathan both took it and purified it of idolatry (1 Macc **5** 68; **10** 84). In these passages it is called **Azotus,** as it is also in the NT (Acts **8** 40). In the 4th cent. AD it became the seat of a bishopric. It had been restored in the time of Herod, by the Rom general Gabinius, and was presented to Salome, the sister of Herod, by the emperor Augustus. It is now a small village about 18 miles N.E. of Gaza.

H. Porter

ASHDODITES, ash′dod-īts: Inhabitants of Ashdod (q.v.) (Josh **13** 3; AV **Ashdothites,** ash′-doth-īts; Neh **4** 7).

ASHDOTH PISGAH, ash'doth piz'ga (אַשְׁדּוֹת הַפִּסְגָּה, *'ashdōth ha-piṣgāh*): Thus AV for RV "The slopes [RVm springs] of Pisgah." The spurs and ravines, or the "shoulders" of Pisgah are meant. *'Ashēdāh* is "a pouring out," and *'ăshēdōth* are the slopes of a mountain from which springs gush forth. In Josh **10** 40; **12** 8, 'Ăshēdōth, trd "springs" in AV, is "slopes" in RV (Dt **3** 17; Josh **12** 3; **13** 20). See Pisgah.

ASHER, ash'ẽr (אָשֵׁר, *'āshēr*; **'Ασήρ**, *Asḗr*): According to the Bib. account Asher was the eighth of Jacob's sons, the second borne to him by Zilpah the handmaid of Leah. His uterine brother was Gad (Gen **35** 26). With four sons and one daughter he went down into Egypt (Gen **46** 17). At his birth Leah exclaimed, "Happy am I! for the daughters will call me happy: and she called his name Asher," i.e. *Happy* (Gen **30** 13). This foreshadowing of good fortune for him is repeated in the blessing of Jacob: "His bread shall be fat, and he shall yield royal dainties" (Gen **49** 20); and again in that of Moses: "Blessed be Asher with children; let him be acceptable unto his brethren, and let him dip his foot in oil" (Dt **33** 24). His family prospered in Egypt, and at the Exodus the tribe of Asher is numbered at 41,500 adult males (Nu **1** 41). At the second census the number is given 53,400 (Nu **26** 47). The place of Asher in the desert march was with the standard of the camp of Dan, on the north of the tabernacle, along with Dan and Naphtali; the prince of the tribe being Pagiel the son of Ochran (Nu **2** 27 ff). Among the spies Asher was represented by Sethur (Nu **13** 13). The tribe seems to have taken no important part in the subsequent history. It raised no hero, and gave no deliverer to the nation. In the time of David it was of so little consequence that the name is not found in the list of chief rulers (1 Ch **27** 16 ff). The rich land assigned to Asher sloped to the Phoen seaboard, and brought him into touch with the Phoenicians who were already world-famous in trade and commerce. He probably soon became a partner in their profitable enterprises, and lost any desire he may ever have had to eject them from their cities (Jgs **1** 31). He cared not who ruled over him if he were free to pursue the ends of commerce. Zebulun might jeopard their lives unto the death, and Naphtali upon the high places of the field, to break the power of the foreign oppressor, but Asher "sat still at the haven of the sea, and abode by his creeks" (Jgs **5** 17 ff). He was probably soon largely absorbed by the people with whose interests his were so closely identified: nevertheless "divers of Asher," moved by the appeal of Hezekiah, "humbled themselves, and came to Jerus" (2 Ch **30** 11 AV). To this tribe belonged the prophetess Anna (Lk **2** 36 ff).

1. Biblical Account

According to a modern theory, the mention of the slave girl Zilpah as the mother of Asher is meant to indicate that the tribe was of mixed blood, and arose through the mingling of Israelites with the Canaanites. It is suggested that the name may have been taken from that of the Can. clan found in the Am Tab, *Mārī abd-Ashirti*, "sons of the servant of Asherah." A similar name occurs in the inscriptions of the Egyp Seti I (14th cent. BC), *'Aseru*, a state in western Galilee (W. Max Müller, *As. und Eur.*, 236–39). This people it is thought may have associated themselves with the invaders from the wilderness. But while the speculations are interesting, it is impossible to establish any relationship between these ancient tribes and Asher.

2. Modern Theory

The boundaries of the territory are given in considerable detail in Josh **19** 25 ff (cf Jgs **1** 31 f; Josh **17** 10 f). Only a few of the places named can be identified with certainty. Dor, the modern Ṭanṭūrah, although occupied by Manasseh belonged to Asher. Wādy ez-Zerqā, possibly identical with Shihor-libnath, which enters the sea to the S. of Dor, would form the southern boundary. The lot of Asher formed a strip of land from 8 to 10 miles wide running northward along the shore to the neighborhood of Sidon, touching Issachar, Zebulun and Naphtali on the E. Asher seems to have taken possession of the territory by a process of peaceful penetration, not by conquest, and as we have seen, he never drove out the Phoenicians from their cities. The rich plain of Acre, and the fertile flats between the mountain and the sea near Tyre and Sidon therefore remained in Phoen hands. But the valleys breaking down westward and opening on the plains have always yielded fine crops of grain. Remains of an ancient oak forest still stand to the N. of Carmel. The vine, the fig, the lemon and the orange flourish. Olive trees abound, and the supplies of olive oil which to this day are exported from the district recall the word of the old-time blessing, "Let him dip his foot in oil." W. Ewing

3. Territory of Asher

ASHER, ash'ẽr (אָשֵׁר, *'āshēr*):

(1) See preceding article.

(2) A town on the southern border of Manasseh (Josh **17** 7). The site is unknown.

(3) A place of this name is mentioned in Apoc (Tob **1** 2), identified with Hazor, in Naphtali. See Hazor.

ASHERAH, a-shē'ra (אֲשֵׁרָה, *'ăshērāh*; **ἄλσος**, *álsos*, mistranslated "grove" in the AV, after the LXX and Vulg):

1. References to the Goddess
2. Assyrian Origin of the Goddess
3. Her Symbol
4. The Attributes of the Goddess

Was the name of a goddess whose worship was widely spread throughout Syria and Canaan; plur. **Asherim,** ash'er-im.

1. References to the Goddess

Her "image" is mentioned in the OT (1 K **15** 13; 2 K **21** 7; 2 Ch **15** 16), as well as her "prophets" (1 K **18** 19) and the vessels used in her service (2 K **23** 4). In Assyria the name appears under the two forms of Asratu and Asirtu; it was to Asratu that a monument found near Diarbekir was dedicated on behalf of Khammu-rabi (Amraphel) "king of the Amorites," and the Amorite king of whom we hear so much in Am Tab bears the name indifferently of Ebed-Asrati and Ebed-Asirti.

2. Assyrian Origin of the Goddess

Like so much else in Can. religion, the name and worship of Asherah were borrowed from Assyria. She was the wife of the war-god Asir whose name was identified with that of the city of Assur with the result that he became the national god of Assyria. Since Asirtu was merely the feminine form of Asir, "the superintendent" or "leader," it is probable that it was originally an epithet of Istar (Ashtoreth) of Nineveh. In the W., however, Asherah and Ashtoreth came to be distinguished from one another, Asherah being exclusively the goddess of fertility, whereas Ashtoreth passed into a moon-goddess.

3. Her Symbol

In Assyr *asirtu*, which appears also under the forms *asrātu*, *esrēti* (plur.) and *asru*, had the further signification of "sanctuary." Originally Asirtu, the wife of Asir, and *asirtu*, "sanctuary," seem to have had no connection with one another, but the identity in the pronunciation of the two words caused them to be identified in signification, and as the tree-trunk or cone of stone which symbolized Asherah was regarded as a Beth-el or "house of the deity," wherein the goddess was immanent, the word Asirtu, Asherah, came to denote the symbol of the goddess. The trunk of the tree was often provided with branches, and assumed the form of the tree of life. It was as a trunk, however, that it was forbidden to be erected by the side of "the altar of Jehovah" (Dt **16** 21; see Jgs **6** 25.28.30; 2 K **23** 6). Accordingly the symbol made for Asherah by his mother was "cut down" by Asa (1 K **15** 13). So, too, we hear of Asherim or symbols of the goddess being set up on the high places under the shade of a green tree (Jer **17** 2; see 2 K **17** 10). Manasseh introduced one into the temple at Jerus (2 K **21** 3.7).

4. The Attributes of the Goddess

Asherah was the goddess of fertility, and thus represented the Bab Istar in her character as goddess of love and not of war. In one of the cuneiform tablets found at Taanach by Dr. Sellin, and written by one Can. sheikh to another shortly before the Israelitish invasion of Pal, reference is made to "the finger of Asherah" from which oracles were derived. The "finger "seems to signify the symbol of the goddess; at any rate it revealed the future by means of a "sign and oracle." The practice is probably alluded to in Hos **4** 12. The existence of numerous symbols in each of which the goddess was believed to be immanent led to the creation of numerous forms of the goddess herself, which, after the analogy of the Ashtaroth, were described collectively as the Asherim. A. H. SAYCE

ASHERITES, ash'ēr-īts (הָאָשֵׁרִי, *hā-'āshērī*): The descendants of Asher, Jacob's eighth son (Jgs **1** 32).

ASHES, ash'iz: Among the ancient Hebrews and other Orientals, to sprinkle with or sit in ashes was a mark or token of grief, humiliation, or penitence. *Ashes on the head* was one of the ordinary signs of mourning for the dead, as when "Tamar put ashes on her head . . . . and went on crying" (2 S **13** 19 AV), and of national humiliation, as when the children of Israel were assembled under Nehemiah "with fasting, and with sackcloth, and earth [ashes] upon them" (Neh **9** 1), and when the people of Nineveh repented in sackcloth and ashes at the preaching of Jonah (Jon **3** 5.6; cf 1 Macc **3** 47). The afflicted or penitent often *sat in ashes* (cf Job **2** 8; **42** 6: "I abhor myself, and repent in dust and ashes"), or even *wallowed in ashes,* as Jeremiah exhorted sinning Israel to do: "O daughter of my people . . . . wallow thyself in ashes" (Jer **6** 26), or as Ezekiel in his lamentation for Tyre pictures her mariners as doing, crying bitterly and 'casting up dust upon their heads' and 'wallowing themselves in the ashes' (in their weeping for her whose head was lifted up and become corrupted because of her beauty), "in bitterness of soul with bitter mourning" (Ezk **27** 30.31).

However, these and various other modes of expressing grief, repentance, and humiliation among the Hebrews, such as rending the garments, tearing the hair and the like, were not of Divine appointment, but were simply the natural outbursts of the impassioned oriental temperament, and are still customary among eastern peoples.

Figurative: The term "ashes" is often used to signify worthlessness, insignificance or evanescence (Gen **18** 27; Job **30** 19). "Proverbs of ashes," for instance, in Job **13** 12, is Job's equivalent, says one writer, for our modern "rot." For the ritual use of the ashes of the Red Heifer by the priests, see RED HEIFER. GEO. B. EAGER

ASHHUR, ash'ur (אַשְׁחוּר, *ashḥūr,* AV **Ashur**): The "father of Tekoa" (1 Ch **2** 24; **4** 5), probably the founder of the village. The original meaning of the name is the "man of Horus," **Ashurites** (הָאֲשׁוּרִי, *hā-'ashūrī*). This name occurs in the list of Ish-bosheth's subjects (2 S **2** 9). The Syr, Arab. and Vulg versions read הַגְּשׁוּרִי, *ha-geshūrī,* "the Geshurites," designating the small kingdom to the S. or S.E. of Damascus. This reading, though adopted by Ewald, Thenius and Wellhausen, is untenable, for during the reign of Ish-bosheth Geshur was ruled by its own king Talmai, whose daughter was married to David (2 S **3** 3; **13** 37). Furthermore Geshur was too far away from the rest of Ish-bosheth's territory. A more consistent reading is הָאָשֵׁרִי, *hā-'āshērī,* as given in the Tg of Jonathan and accepted by Köhler, Klost, Kirkpatrick and Budde, "those of the house of Asher" (cf Jgs **1** 32). The term would, then, denote the country to the W. of Jordan above Jezreel. SAMUEL COHON

ASHIMA, a-shī'ma, ash'i-ma (אֲשִׁימָא, *'ăshīmā'; 'Ασιμάθ, Asimáth*): A deity worshipped at Hamath (2 K **17** 30) of whom nothing further is known. It has been suggested that the name is the same as that of the goddess Simi, the daughter of the supreme god Hadad, who was worshipped at Membij, but there is nothing to support the suggestion.

ASHKELON, ash'ke-lon (AV **Eshkalon,** esh'-ka-lon [Eshkalonites; Josh **13** 3]; **Askelon,** as'-kĕ-lon [Jgs **1** 18; 1 S **6** 17; 2 S **1** 20]; אַשְׁקְלוֹן, *'ashkelōn;* mod. *Askelan*): A maritime town between Jaffa and Gaza, one of the five chief cities of the Philis. The Ashkelonites are mentioned by Joshua (Josh **13** 3), and the city was taken by the tribe of Judah (Jgs **1** 18). One of the golden tumors (AV "emerods") sent back with the ark by the Philis was from A. (1 S **6** 17). David couples A. with Gath in his lament over Saul and Jonathan (2 S **1** 20) indicating its importance, and it is joined with Gaza, Ashdod and Ekron in the denunciations of Amos (**1** 7.8). It is referred to in a similar way by Jeremiah (Jer **25** 20; **47** 5.7). Zephaniah (**2** 4.7) speaks of the desolation of A. and Zechariah announces the fear of A. on the destruction of Tyre (**9** 5). The city is mentioned in the Am Tab, and a certain Yitia is referred to as king. It revolted against Rameses II and was subdued, and we have mention of it as being under the rule of Assyria. Tiglath-pileser III names it among his tributaries, and its king, Mitinti, is said to have lost his reason when he heard of the fall of Damascus in 732 BC. It revolted in the reign of Sennacherib and was punished, and remained tributary to Assyria until the decay of that power. In Maccabean times we learn of its capture by Jonathan (1 Macc **10** 86; **11** 60, RV "Ascalon"). Herod the Great was born there (*BJ,* III, ii, 1 ff). In the 4th cent. AD it was the seat of a bishopric. It became subject to the Moslems in the 7th cent. and was taken by the Crusaders. It was taken in 1187 by Saladin, who dismantled it in 1191 to make it useless to Richard of England, into whose hands it was expected to fall. Richard restored it the next year but it was again destroyed by Saladin. It was an important fortress because of its vicinity to the trade route between Syria and Egypt. H. PORTER

ASHKELONITES, ash'ke-lon-īts (Josh **13** 3): The people of Ashkelon, who were Philistines.

ASHKENAZ, ash'kĕ-naz (אַשְׁכְּנַז, *'ashkenaz*): The name occurs in Gen **10** 3; 1 Ch **1** 6, in the list of the sons of Japheth as a son of Gomer. See

TABLE OF NATIONS. It occurs also in Jer **51** 27 (AV "Ashchenaz") in connection with the kingdoms of Ararat and Minni, which suggests a location about Armenia.

ASHNAH, ash'na (אַשְׁנָה, *'ashnāh*): Two sites, (1) Josh **15** 33, a site in the lowlands of Judah, probably near Estaol and Zorah. The small ruin *Aslîn* between those two places may retain an echo of the old name; (2) Josh **15** 43, an unknown site farther south.

ASHPENAZ, ash'pē-naz (אַשְׁפְּנַז, *'ashp^e naz*): The master of the eunuchs of Nebuchadnezzar was an officer into whose hands the king intrusted those of the children of Israel, and of the princes, and of the seed of the king of Judah, whom he had carried captive to Babylon, that they might be taught the learning and tongue of the Chaldaeans in order to serve in the king's palace. He is mentioned by name in Dnl **1** 3 only. It used to be supposed that the name was Pers; but it now seems more probable that it is Bab. We would suggest Ashipu-Anu-Izzu, "the Aship-priest of Anu is mighty," as a possible form of the original. R. DICK WILSON

ASHRIEL, ash'rē-el. See ASRIEL.

ASHTAROTH, ash'ta-roth (עַשְׁתָּרוֹת, *'ashtārōth;* AV **Astaroth,** as'ta-roth; **'Ασταρώθ,** *Astarōth*, the city of Og, king of Bashan [Dt **1** 4, etc]; **ASHTEROTH-KARNAIM** [עַשְׁתְּרוֹת קַרְנַיִם, *'asht^e rōth karnayim*], the scene of the defeat of the Rephaim by Chedorlaomer [Gen **14** 5]; **BEESHTERAH** [בְּעֶשְׁתְּרָה, *b^e-'esht^e rāh*] a Levitical city in Manasseh E. of the Jordan [Josh **21** 27]): The name probably means "house" or "temple of Ashtoreth." It is identical with Ashtaroth of 1 Ch **6** 71. Ashtaroth is the plur. of ASHTORETH (q.v.). The name denotes a place associated with the worship of this goddess. Ashteroth-karnaim is mentioned only once in canonical Scripture unless we accept Grätz's restoration, when Karnaim appears as a city taken by Israel: "Have we not taken to us horns [*karnayim*] by our own strength?" (Am **6** 13). It is identical with Carnion or Carnaim of 1 and 2 Macc, a city of Gilead with a temple of Atar-gatis. The name Ashtaroth has been identified with *Âstertu* in the lists of Tahutmes III of the XVIIIth Egyp Dynasty; and with *Ashtarti* of the Am Tab. Its claim to antiquity is therefore well established.

As far as the Bib. record is concerned, the names at the head of this art. might stand for one and the same city, Ashtaroth being a contraction from Ashteroth-karnaim. But in the days of Eusebius and Jerome, we learn from the *Onom*, there were two forts of this name 9 miles apart, lying between Adara (*Der'ah*) and Abila (*Abīl*), while Ashtaroth, the ancient city of Og, king of Bashan, lay 6 miles from Adara. Carnaim Ashtaroth, which is evidently identical with Ashteroth-karnaim, they describe as a large village in the angle of Bashan where tradition places the home of Job. This seems to point to *Tell 'Ashtarā*, a hill which rises about 80 ft. above the plain, 2 miles S. of *el-Merkez*, the seat of the governor of the *Ḥaurān*. Three-quarters of a mile N. of *el-Merkez*, at the south end of a ridge on which the village of *Sheikh Ṣa'ad* is built, stands the weley of the stone of Job, *Weley Sakhret 'Ayyūb*. By the large stone under the dome Job was said to have sat to receive his friends during his affliction. An Egyp inscription, found by Schumacher, proves the stone to be a monument of the time of Rameses II. At the foot of the hill is pointed out the bath of Job. In *el-Merkez* the building known as *Deir 'Ayyūb*, "Monastery of Job," is now part of the barracks. There is also shown the tomb of Job. The stream which flows southward past *Tell 'Ashtarā*, is called *Moyet en-Neby 'Ayyūb*, "stream of the prophet Job," and is said to have risen where the patriarch stamped his foot on his recovery. It is to be noted also that the district lying in the angle formed by *Nahr er-Raḳḳād* and the *Yarmūk* is called to this day *ez-Zāwiyet esh-sharḳīyeh*, "the eastern angle" (i.e. of the *Jaulān*). The term may in Jerome's time have covered the land east of the *'Allān*, although this is now part of the *Ḥaurān*. At *Tell 'Ashtarā* there are remains pointing to a high antiquity. The site was also occupied during the Middle Ages. Perhaps here we should locate Carnaim Ashtaroth of the *Onom*. It does not, however, agree with the description of Carnaim in 1 and 2 Macc. The Ashtaroth of the *Onom* may have been at *el-Muzērīb*, on the great pilgrimage road, about 6 Rom miles from *Ḍer'ah*—the distance indicated by Eusebius. The old fortress here was situated on an island in the middle of the lake, *Baḥeiret el-Bajjeh*. A full description of the place is given in Schumacher's *Across the Jordan*, 137 ff. It must have been a position of great strength in antiquity; but the ancient name has not been recovered.

Some would place Ashteroth-karnaim, the Carnaim of the Maccabees, at *Tell 'Ash'arī*, a site 10 Rom miles N. of *Ḍer'ah*, and 4½ Rom miles S. of *Tell 'Ashtarā*. This clearly was "a place hard to besiege, and difficult of access by reason of the narrowness of the approaches on all sides "(2 Macc **12** 21). It crowns a promontory which stands out between the deep gorge of the *Yarmūk* and a great chasm, at the head of which is a waterfall. It could be approached only by the neck connecting it with the mainland; and here it was guarded by a triple wall, the ruins of which are seen today. The remains of a temple close by the bridge over the *Yarmūk* may mark the scene of the slaughter by Judas.

The whole question however is obscure. Eusebius is clearly guilty of confusion, with his two Ashtaroth-karnaims and his Carnaim Ashtaroth. All the places we have named lie considerably N. of a line drawn from *Tell Abīl* to *Ḍer'ah*. For light upon the problem of identification we must wait the results of excavation. W. EWING

ASHTAROTH, plur. of Ashtoreth. See ASHTORETH.

ASHTERATHITE, ash'tē-rath-īt, ash-ter'ath-īt (הָעַשְׁתְּרָתִי, *hā-'asht^e rāthī*): A native of Ashtaroth: Uzzia, one of David's heroes (1 Ch **11** 44).

ASHTEROTH-KARNAIM, ash'tē-roth kar-nā'-im: I.e. "Ashteroth of the two horns," mentioned in Gen **14** 5 as the place of Chedorlaomer's defeat of the Rephaim. See ASHTAROTH. A Carnaim or Carnion in Gilead, with a temple of Atar-gatis attached, was captured by Judas Maccabaeus (1 Macc **5** 43.44; 2 Macc **12** 26).

ASHTORETH, ash'to-reth, ash-tō reth (עַשְׁתֹּרֶת, *'ashtōreth;* plur. עַשְׁתָּרוֹת, *'ashtārōth;* **'Ασταρτή,** *Astartē*):

1. Name and Origin
2. Attributes of the Goddess
3. Ashtoreth as a Moon-goddess
4. The Local Ashtaroth

The name of the supreme goddess of Canaan and the female counterpart of Baal.

The name and cult of the goddess were derived from Babylonia, where Istar represented the evening and morning stars and was accordingly androgynous in origin. Under Sem influence, however, she became solely female, but retained a memory of her primitive character by standing, alone among the Assyro-Bab goddesses, on a footing of equality with the male divinities. From Babylonia the worship of the goddess was carried to the Semites of the West, and in most instances the feminine suffix was attached to her name; where this was not the case the deity was regarded as a male. On the Moabite Stone, for example, ʽAshtar is identified with Chemosh, and in the inscriptions of southern Arabia ʽAthtar is a god. On the other hand, in Atar-gatis or Derketo (2 Macc **12** 26), Atar, without the feminine suffix, is identified with the goddess ʽAthah or ʽAthi (Gr *Gatis*). The cult of the Gr *Aphrodítē* in Cyprus was borrowed from that of Ashtoreth; whether the Gr name also is a modification of Ashtoreth, as has often been maintained, is doubtful.

1. Name and Origin

2. Attributes of the Goddess

In Babylonia and Assyria Istar was the goddess of love and war. An old Bab legend related how the descent of Istar into Hades in search of her dead husband, Tammuz, was followed by the cessation of marriage and birth in both earth and heaven, while the temples of the goddess at Nineveh and Arbela, around which the two cities afterward grew up, were dedicated to her as the goddess of war. As such she appeared to one of Assur-bani-pal's seers and encouraged the Assyr king to march against Elam. The other goddesses of Babylonia, who were little more than reflections of the god, tended to merge into Istar who thus became a type of the female divinity, a personification of the productive principle in nature, and more especially the mother and creatress of mankind.

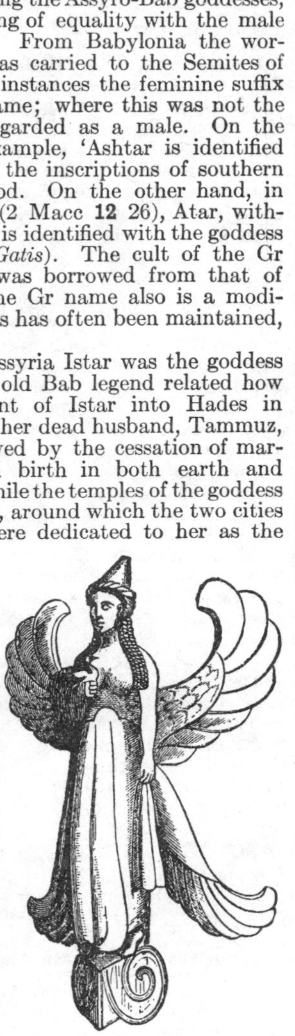

Ashtoreth.

The chief seat of the worship of Istar in Babylonia was Erech, where prostitution was practised in her name, and she was served with immoral rites by bands of men and women. In Assyria, where the warlike side of the goddess was predominant, no such rites seem to have been practised, and, instead, prophetesses were attached to her temples to whom she delivered oracles.

3. Ashtoreth as a Moon-Goddess

In Canaan, Ashtoreth, as distinguished from the male ʽAshtar, dropped her warlike attributes, but in contradistinction to Ashērāh, whose name and cult had also been imported from Assyria, became, on the one hand, the colorless consort of Baal, and on the other hand, a moon-goddess. In Babylonia the moon was a god, but after the rise of the solar theology, when the larger number of the Bab gods were resolved into forms of the sun-god, their wives also became solar, Istar, "the daughter of Sin" the moon-god, remaining identified with the evening-star. In Canaan, however, when the solar theology had absorbed the older beliefs, Baal, passing into a sun-god and the goddess who stood at his side becoming a representative of the moon—the pale reflection, as it were, of the sun—Ashtoreth came to be regarded as the consort of Baal and took the place of the solar goddesses of Babylonia.

4. The Local Ashtaroth

Hence there were as "many Ashtoreths" or Ashtaroth as Baals. They represented the various forms under which the goddess was worshipped in different localities (Jgs **10** 6; 1 S **7** 4; **12** 10, etc). Sometimes she was addressed as Naamah, "the delightful one," Gr *Astro-noē*, the mother of Eshmun and the Cabeiri. The Philis seem to have adopted her under her warlike form (1 S **31** 10 AV reading "Ashtoreth," as LXX), but she was more usually the moon-goddess (Lucian, *De Dea Syr.*, 4; Herodian, v.6, 10), and was accordingly symbolized by the horns of a cow. See Ashtaroth-karnaim. At Ashkelon, where Herodotus (i.105) places her most ancient temple, she was worshipped under the name of *Atar-gatis*, as a woman with the tail of a fish, and fish were accordingly sacred to her. Elsewhere the dove was her sacred symbol. The immoral rites with which the worship of Istar in Babylonia was accompanied were transferred to Canaan (Dt **23** 18) and formed part of the idolatrous practices which the Israelites were called upon to extirpate. A. H. Sayce

ASHUR, ash′ur. See Ashhur.

ASHURBANIPAL, ā-shōōr-bä′nē-pal (*Ashur-bâni-apal*, "Ashur creates a son"): Before setting out on his last campaign to Egypt, Esarhaddon king of Assyria doubtless having had some premonition that his days were numbered, caused his son Ashurbanipal to be acknowledged the crown prince of Assyria (668 BC). At the same time he proclaimed his son Shamash-shum-ukin as the crown prince of Babylonia. At the father's death the latter, however, was only permitted to become viceroy of Babylonia.

Ashurbanipal is generally believed to be the great and noble Osnappar (Ezr **4** 10). See Osnappar. If this identification should not prove correct, the king is not mentioned by name in the OT. In the annals of Ashurbanipal there is a list of twenty tributary kings in which Manasseh (written Minsê) of the land of Judah is mentioned. With a few exceptions the list is the same as that given by Esarhaddon, his father. In 2 Ch **33** 11 ff we learn that the captains of the host of the king of Assyria took Manasseh with hooks and bound him with fetters, and carried him to Babylon. The king to whom reference is made in this passage was either Esarhaddon or Ashurbanipal. If the latter, his restoration of Manasseh was paralleled in the instance of Necho, the vassal king of Memphis and Sais, who also had revolted from Assyria; for he was accorded similar treatment, being sent back to Egypt with special marks of favor, and reinstated upon his throne.

Another reference in the OT, at least to one of the acts of Ashurbanipal, is the prophecy of Nahum, who in predicting the downfall of Nineveh, said, "Art thou [Nineveh] better than No-amon?" This passage is illustrated by the annals of the king, in which he recounts the destruction of the city. No (meaning "city") is the name of Thebes, while Amon (or Amen) was the chief deity of that city.

Esarhaddon died on his way to Egypt, which he had previously conquered, an insurrection having taken place. Tirhakah, whom Esarhaddon had vanquished, and who had fled to Ethiopia, had returned, and had advanced against the rulers appointed by Assyria. He formed a coalition with Necho and others. Not long after Ashurbanipal came to the throne, he set out for Egypt and defeated the forces. The leaders of the insurrection were carried to Nineveh in fetters. Necho, like

Manasseh, as mentioned above, was restored to his rule at Sais. Tirhakah died shortly after. His sister's son Tanut-Amon (Tandami) then took up the cause, and after the departure of the Assyr army he advanced against the Assyr vassal governors. The Assyr army returned and relieved the besieged. Tanut-Amon returned to Thebes, which was conquered and which was spoiled by the rapacious Assyrians, 663 BC. This is what the prophet Nahum referred to (**3** 8). A few years later Psammetik, the son of Necho, who had remained faithful after his restoration, declared his independence. As the Assyr army was required elsewhere, Egypt was henceforth free from the yoke of the Assyrian.

Ba'al of Tyre, after a long siege, finally submitted. Yakinlu, king of Arvad, paid tribute and sent hostages. Other rebellious subjects, who had become emboldened by the attitude of Tirhakah, were brought into submission. Under Urlaki, the old enemy Elam, which had been at peace with Assyria since the preceding reign, now became aggressive and made inroads into Babylonia. Ashurbanipal marched through the Zagros mountains, and suddenly appeared before Susa. This move brought Teumman, who had in the meanwhile succeeded Urlaki, back to his capital. Elam was humiliated.

In 652 BC the insurrection of Shamash-shum-ukin, the king's brother, who had been made viceroy of Babylon, broke out. He desired to establish his independence from Assyria. After Ashurbanipal had overcome Babylon, Shamash-shum-ukin took refuge in a palace, set it on fire, and destroyed himself in the flames.

There is much obscurity about the last years of Ashurbanipal's reign. The decadence of Assyria had begun, which resulted not only in the loss to the title of the surrounding countries, but also in its complete annihilation before the cent. was over. Nineveh was finally razed to the ground by the Umman-Manda hordes, and was never rebuilt.

Ashurbanipal is also distinguished for his building operations, which show remarkable architectural ingenuity. In many of the cities of Assyria and Babylonia he restored, enlarged or embellished the temples or shrines. In Nineveh he reared a beautiful palace, which excelled all other Assyr structures in the richness of its ornamentations.

During his reign the study of art was greatly encouraged. Some of his exquisite sculptures represent not only the height of Assyr art, but also belong to the most important aesthetic treasures of the ancient world. The themes of many of the chief sculptures depict the hunt, in which the king took special delight.

Above all else Ashurbanipal is famous for the library he created, because of which he is perhaps to be considered the greatest known patron of literature in the pre-Christian centuries.

For Bibliography see ASSYRIA. A. T. CLAY

ASHURITES, ash'ur-īts (הָאֲשׁוּרִי, *hā-'ăshūrī*): According to the MT of 2 S **2** 9, a tribe included in the short-lived kingdom of Ish-bosheth, Saul's son. A slight textual correction gives "Asherites," that is, the tribe of Asher; with this the Tg of Jonathan agrees. The tribe of Asher lay where it would naturally fall to Ish-bosheth's kingdom. The reading "Geshurites" (Vulg and Syr) is excluded by the known independence of Geshur at this time (2 S **3** 3; **13** 37). For similar reasons we cannot think of Assyria (Heb *Asshur*) nor of the Arab. Asshurim of Gen **25** 3.

ASHVATH, ash'vath (עַשְׁוָת, *'ashwāth*): A man of Asher, of the house of Japhlet (1 Ch **7** 33).

ASIA, ā'shi-a (**'Ασία**, *Asía*): A Rom province embracing the greater part of western Asia Minor, including the older countries of Mysia, Lydia, Caria, and a part of Phrygia, also several of the independent coast cities, the Troad, and apparently the islands of Lesbos, Samos, Patmos, Cos and others near the Asia Minor coast (Acts **16** 6; **19** 10. 27). It is exceedingly difficult to determine the exact boundaries of the several countries which later constituted the Rom province, for they seem to have been somewhat vague to the ancients themselves, and were constantly shifting; it is therefore impossible to trace the exact borders of the province of Asia. Its history previous to 133 BC coincides with that of Asia Minor of which it was a part. However, in that year, Attalus III (Philometer), king of Pergamos, bequeathed his kingdom to the Rom Empire. It was not until 129 BC that the province of Asia was really formed by Rome. Its first capital was Pergamos, the old capital of Mysia, but in the time of Augustus, when Asia had become the most wealthy province of the Empire, the seat of the government was transferred to Ephesus. Smyrna was also an important rival of Ephesus. The governor of Asia was a pro-consul, chosen by lot by the Rom senate from among the former consuls who had been out of office for at least five years, and he seldom continued in office for more than a single year. The diet of the province, composed of representatives from its various districts, met each year in the different cities. Over it presided the asiarch, whose duty it was, among other things, to offer sacrifices for the welfare of the emperor and his family.

In 285 AD the province was reduced in size, as Caria, Lydia, Mysia and Phrygia were separated from it, and apart from the cities of the coast little remained. The history of Asia consists almost entirely of the history of its important cities, which were Adramyttium, Assos, Cnidus, Ephesus, Laodicea, Miletus, Pergamos, Philadelphia, Sardis, Smyrna, Thyatira, Troas, etc. E. J. BANKS

ASIA MINOR, ā'shi-a mī'nẽr:

Introductory

Technically, it is only on sufferance that an account of "Asia Minor" can find a place in a Biblical encyclopaedia, for the country to which this name applies in modern times was never so called in OT or NT times. The term first appears in Orosius, a writer of the 5th cent. AD, and it is now applied in most European languages to the peninsula forming the western part of Asiatic Turkey.

The justification for the inclusion in this work of a summary account of A.M. as a whole, its geography, history, and the social and political condition of its people in NT times, is to be found in the following sentence of Gibbon: "The rich provinces that extend from the Euphrates to the Ionian Sea were the principal theatre on which the Apostle to the Gentiles displayed his zeal and piety"; and no region outside the city of Rome has preserved to modern times so many records of the growth and character of its primitive Christianity.

I. The Country.—Asia Minor (as the country was called to distinguish it from the continent of Asia), or Anatolia, is the name given to the peninsula which reaches out between the Black Sea (Pontus Euxinus) on the N. and the Mediterranean on the S., forming an elevated land-bridge between central Asia and southeastern Europe. On the N.W. corner, the peninsula is separated from Europe by the Bosporus, the Sea of Marmora and the Hellespont. On the W. the peninsula borders on the Aegean Sea, whose numerous islands tempted the timid mariner of ancient times on toward Greece. The W. coast, with its alternation of mountain and river-valley, is deeply indented: there is a total coast line of four times the length of a line drawn from N. to S. The numerous land-locked bays and harbors of this coast have made it the happy hunting-ground of Mediterranean traders in all ages. On the E. it is usual to delimit A.M. by a line drawn from Alexandretta to Samsun, but for the purposes of NT history it must be remembered that part of Cilicia, Cappadocia and Pontus (Galatia) lie to the E. of this line (Long. 26° to 36° E.; lat. 36° to 42° N.).

1. Position and Boundaries

There are two distinct countries, implying distinct historical development, in the Anatolian peninsula, the country of the coast, and the country of the central plateau. The latter takes its shape from that of the great mountain ranges which bound it on the W., E. and N. The high central tableland is tilted down toward the N. and W.; the mountain ranges on these sides are not so lofty as the Taurus chain on the S. and S.E. This chain, except at its S.E. corner, rises sharply from the S. coast, whose undulations it determines. On the N., the mountains of Pontus (no distinctive name), a continuation of the Armenian range, give the coast-line a similar character. On the inhospitable N. coast, there is only one good harbor, that of Sinope, and no plain of any extent. The S. coast can boast of the plains of Pamphylia and Cilicia, both highly fertile, the harbors of Makri and Marmariki, and the sheltered bays of Adalia and Alexandretta. On the W., the ascent from the littoral to the plateau is more gradual. A distance of over 100 miles separates the Phrygian mountains, where the oriental plateau begins, from the W. seaboard with its inlets and trading cities. These hundred miles are composed of river valleys, divided off by mountain ranges, and forming the channels of communication between the interior and the coast. While these two regions form part of a single country it is obvious that—in all that gives individuality to a country, their flora, fauna, climate, conditions of life and history—the one region is sharply marked off from the other. For the plateau naturally connects itself with the E. In its vegetation and climate, its contrasts of temperature, its dry soil and air, it forms part of the region extending eastward to central Asia. The coast land recalls the scenery and general character of the Gr mainland and islands. It naturally looked to, it influenced and was influenced by, the populations on the other side of the Aegean Sea. At Smyrna, the traveler in all ages recognizes the bright, active life of southern Europe; at Iconium he feels the immobile and lethargic calm of the East. A.M. in its geographical structure as well as in its population, has been throughout history the meeting-place, whether for peaceful intermixture or for the clash in war, of the eternally contrasted systems of East and West.

2. General Description

The Armenian mountains reach westward, and fork, close to the line we have chosen as the E. boundary of A.M., into two ranges, the Taurus Mountains on the S., and the mountains of Pontus on the N. Mount Argaeus (over 12,000 ft.) stands in the angle formed by these ranges, nearer to Taurus than to the northern system. Taurus is pierced on the northern side of the Cilician plain by the pass, easy to traverse and still more easy to defend, of the Cilician Gates, while another natural route leads from central Cappadocia to Amisus on the Black Sea. These mountain ranges (average height of Taurus 7,000 to 10,000 ft.; the N. range is much lower) enfold the central Galatian and Lycaonian plains, which are bounded on the W. by the Sultan Dagh and the Phrygian mountains. From the latter to the west coast extend three mountain ranges, delimiting the valleys of the Caicus, Hermus and Maeander. These valleys lie E. and W., naturally conducting traffic in those directions.

3. Mountains

The great plains of the interior, covering parts of Galatia, Lycaonia and Cappadocia, lie at an altitude of from 3,000 to 4,000 ft. Rivers enter them from the adjoining mountains, to be swallowed up in modern times in salt lakes and swamps. In ancient times much of this water was used for irrigation. Regions which now support only a few wretched villages were covered in the Rom period by numerous large cities, implying a high degree of cultivation of the naturally fertile soil. The remaining rivers cut their way through rocky gorges in the fringe of mountains around the plateau; on the W. side of the peninsula their courses open into broad valleys, among which those of the Caicus, Hermus and Maeander are among the most fertile in the world. Down those western valleys, and that of the Sangarius on the N.W., ran the great highways from the interior to the seaboard. In those valleys sprang up the greatest and most prosperous of the Hellenistic and Gr-Rom cities, from which Gr education and Christianity radiated over the whole country. The longest river in A.M. is the Halys, which rises in Pontus, and after an enormous bend south-westward flows into the Black Sea. This, and the Iris, E. of Amisus, are the only rivers of note on the N. coast. The rivers on the S. coast, with the exception of the Sarus and the Pyramus which rise in Cappadocia and water the Cilician plain, are mere mountain torrents, flowing immediately into the sea. A remarkable feature of A.M. is its *duden*, rivers disappearing underground in the limestone rock, to reappear as springs and heads of rivers many miles away. Mineral and thermal springs abound all over the country, and are especially numerous in the Maeander valley. There are several salt lakes, the largest being Lake Tatta in Lycaonia. Fresh-water lakes, such as Karalis and the Limuae, abound in the mountains in the S.W.

4. Rivers, Lakes and Plains

The road-system of A.M. is marked out by Nature, and traffic has followed the same lines since the dawn of history. The traveler from the Euphrates or from Syria enters by way of Melitene and Caesarea, or by the Cilician Gates. From Caesarea he can reach the Black Sea by Zela and Amisus. If he continues westward, he must enter the Aegean area by one of the routes marked out, as indicated above, by the valleys of the Maeander, Hermus or Caicus. If his destination is the Bosporus, he travels down the valley of the Sangarius. Other roads lead from the bay of Adalia to Antioch in

5. Roads

Pisidia or to Apameia, or to Laodicea on the Lycus and thence down the Maeander to Ephesus. The position of the Hittite capital at Pteria fixed the route N. of the central plain in general usage for travelers from E. to W., and this was the route followed by the Pers Royal Road. Later, traffic from the E. took the route passing along the S. side of the Axylon, N. of Iconium, and Pisidian Antioch to the Lycus, Maeander and Ephesus. This route coincides with that from the Cilician Gates, from a point N.E. of Iconium. The need to control the Pisidian tribes in the reign of Augustus led to the building of a series of roads in Pisidia, radiating from Antioch; one of these roads led from Antioch to Lystra, and it was the one traversed by Paul on his journey from Antioch to Iconium (Acts **13** 51).

6. Climate and Products

The winter on the central plateau is long and severe, the summer is short and hot: but a cool breeze from the N. (the *inbat*) tempers the hot afternoons. The south coast in summer is hot and malarious; in winter its climate is mild. Much snow falls in the regions adjacent to the Black Sea. The climate of the west coast resembles that of southern Europe. The country contains vast mineral wealth; many of the mines were worked by the ancients. There are forests of pine, oak and fir in the mountains of the N. and S. The central plateau has always been famous for its vast flocks of sheep. King Amyntas of Galatia owned enormous flocks which pastured on the Lycaonian plain. Carpets and rugs and other textile products have always been characteristic of A.M. The wealth of the cities in the province of Asia depended largely on textile and dyeing industries (Rev **1–3**).

II. History.—It follows from what has been said above that the clue to the history of A.M. more almost than in the case of any other country, lies in its geographical position and structure. "Planted like a bridge between Asia and Europe," it has been throughout human history the meeting-place and the battle ground of the peoples of the East and those of the West. From the earliest period to which our records reach, we find it inhabited by an amalgam of races, religions and social systems, none of which has ever quite died out. And throughout history new races, religions and social systems, alike imperishable in many of their features, have poured into the peninsula to find a home there.

1. The Hittites

At the dawn of history, A.M. was ruled by a non-Aryan people, the Hatti or Hittites about which knowledge is at present accumulating so fast that no final account of them can be given. See HITTITES. A.M. is now recognized to have been the center of their civilization, as against the older view that they were a Mesopotamian people. Sculptures and hieroglyphs belonging to this people have long been known over the whole country from Smyrna to the Euphrates, and it is almost unanimously assumed that their capital was at Boghaz Keui (across the Halys from Ancyra). This site has been identified with much probability with the *Pteria* of Herodotus, which Croesus captured when he marched against the Persians, the inference being that the portion of the Hittite land which lay E. of the Halys was at that time a satrapy of the Pers Empire. Excavations in the extensive ancient city at Boghaz Keui have recently been carried out by Winckler and Puchstein, who have discovered remains of the royal archives. These records are written on clay tablets in cuneiform script; they are couched partly in Bab, partly (presumably) in the still undeciphered native language. The documents in the Bab tongue prove that close political relations existed between the Hatti and the eastern monarchy. In the 14th cent. BC the Hittites appear to have conquered a large part of Syria, and to have established themselves at Carchemish. Thenceforth, they were in close touch with Mesopotamia. From about the beginning of the first millennium, the Hittites "were in constant relations, hostile or neutral, with the Ninevites, and thenceforward their art shows such marked Assyr characteristics that it hardly retains its individuality."

2. Phrygian and Bithynian Immigrations

The date of the Phrygian and Bithynian immigrations from southeastern Europe cannot be fixed with certainty, but they had taken place by the beginning of the first millennium BC. These immigrations coincide in time with the decline of the Hittite power. After many wanderings, the Phrygians found a home at the western side of the plateau, and no power exercised such an influence on the early development of A.M. as the Phrygian, principally in the sphere of religion. The kings of Phrygia "bulked more impressively in the Gr mind than any other non-Gr monarchy; their language was the original language and the speech of the goddess herself; their country was the land of great fortified cities, and their kings were the associates of the gods themselves." The material remains of the "Phrygian country"—the tomb of Midas with the fortified acropolis above it, and the many other rock-tombs around—are the most impressive in A.M. Inscriptions in a script like the early Ionian are cut on some of the tombs. The Phrygian language, an Indo-Germanic speech with resemblances to both Gr and the Italian languages, is proved by some seventy inscriptions (a score of them still unpublished) to have been in common use well into the Christian period. Two recently found inscriptions show that it was spoken even in Iconium, "the furthermost city of Phrygia," on the Lycaonian side, until the 3d cent. of our era. Those inscriptions mention the names of Ma (Cybele) and Attis, whose cult exercised a profound influence on the religions of Greece and Rome.

3. Lydians, Greeks and Persians

The next monarchy to rise in A.M. is that of Lydia, whose origin is obscure. The Phrygian empire had fallen before an invasion of the Cimmerii in the 9th or 8th cent. BC; Alyattes of Lydia, which lay between Phrygia and the Aegean, repelled a second invasion of the Cimmerii in 617 BC. Croesus, king of Lydia (both names afterward proverbial for wealth), was lord of all the country to the Halys, as well as of the Gr colonies on the coast. Those colonies—founded from Hellas—had reached their zenith by the 8th cent., and studded all three coasts of A.M. Their inability to combine in a common cause placed them at the mercy of Croesus, and later of his conquerors, the Persians (546 BC). The Persians divided A.M. into satrapies, but the Gr towns were placed under Gr dynasts, who owned the suzerainty of Persia, and several of the inland races continued under the rule of their native princes. The defeat of Xerxes by Hellas set the Gr cities in A.M. free, and they continued free during the period of Athenian greatness. In 386 BC they were restored to the king of Persia by the selfish diplomacy of Sparta.

4. Alexander and His Successors

When Alexander the Great crossed the Hellespont in 334 BC, a new era opened for the Asiatic Greeks. Hitherto the Gr cities in A.M., apart from spasmodic efforts at combination, had been mere trading communities, independent of each other, in competition with each other, and anxious for reasons of self-interest to bring each other to ruin. These colonies had moreover been confined to the coast, and to the open river valleys of the west. The idea of a Gr empire in A.M. was originated by Alexander, and materialized by his successors. Henceforward the city rivalries certainly lasted on, and at a later period excited the scorn of the stolid Romans; but henceforward the Gr cities were members of a Gr empire, and were conscious of an imperial mission. It is to this period that the Hellenization or, as Mommsen would tr the term, the civilization of the interior of A.M. belongs. The foundations of Alexander's successors, the Attalids and Seleucids, covered the peninsula; their object was to consolidate the Gr rule over the native races, and, most important of all, to raise those races to the Gr level of civilization and education. The experiment succeeded only partially and temporarily; but such success as it and the later Rom effort in the same direction had, exercised a profound influence on the early growth of Christianity in the country (see below).

5. The Galatians

In their manner of entering and settling in the country, in the way in which they both came under the influence of the Asiatic environment, and impressed the stamp of their vigorous individuality on the culture and the history of the land, the Galatae, a Celtic nation who crossed from Europe in 278–277 BC, to establish themselves ultimately on the E. of ancient Phrygia and on both sides of the Halys, recall the essential features of the Phrygian immigration of a thousand years earlier. "The region of Galatia, at a remote period the chief seat of the oriental rule over anterior Asia, and preserving in the famed rock-sculptures of the modern Boghaz Keui, formerly the royal town of Pteria, reminiscences of an almost forgotten glory, had in the course of cents. become in language and manners a Celtic island amidst the waves of eastern peoples, and remained so in internal organization even under the [Rom] empire." But these Gauls came under strong oriental influence; they modified to some extent the organization of the local religion, which they adopted; but they adopted it so completely that only one deity with a Celtic name has so far appeared on the numerous cult-inscriptions of Galatia (Anderson in *Jour. of Hell. Studies*, 1910, 163 ff). Nor has a single inscription in the Galatian language been found in the country, although we know that that language was spoken by the lower classes at least as late as the 4th cent. AD. The Galatian appears to have superseded the Phrygian tongue in the part of Galatia which was formerly Phrygian; no Phrygian inscriptions have been found in Galatia, although they are common in the district bordering on its southern and western boundaries. But Galatian was unable to compete with Gr as the language of the educated classes, and even such among the humbler orders as could write, wrote in Gr, and Gr-Rom city-organization replaced the Celtic tribal system much earlier and much more completely in Galatia than Rom municipal organization did in Gaul. Still, the Galatians stood out in strong contrast both to the Greeks and to the Orientals. Rom diplomacy recognized and encouraged this sense of isolation, and in her struggle against the Orientals and the Greeks under Mithridates, Rome found trusty allies in the Galatians. In the Imperial period, the Galatians were considered the best soldiers in A.M. See GALATIA.

6. The Romans in A.M.

The Romans exercised an effective control over the affairs of A.M. after their defeat of Antiochus the Great in 189 BC, but it was only in 133 BC, when Attalus of Pergamus bequeathed his kingdom of "Asia" to the Rom state, that the Rom occupation began. This kingdom formed the province Asia; a second inheritance which fell to Rome at the death of Nicomedes III in 74 BC became the province Bithynia, to which Pontus was afterward added. Cilicia, the province which gave St. Paul to the empire and the church, was annexed in 100 BC, and reorganized by Pompey in 66 BC. These provinces had already been organized; in other words the Rom form of government had been definitely established in them at the foundation of the empire, and, in accordance with the principle that all territory which had been thoroughly "pacified" should remain under the administration of the senate, while the emperor directly governed regions in which soldiers in numbers were still required, the above-mentioned provinces, with the exception of Cilicia, fell to the senate. But all territory subsequently annexed in A.M. remained in the emperor's hands. Several territories over which Rome had exercised a protectorate were now organized into provinces, under direct imperial rule. Such were: Galatia, to which under its last king Amyntas, part of Phrygia, Lycaonia, Pisidia and Pamphylia had been added, and which was made a Rom province at his death in 25 BC (the extension of Galatia under Amyntas to include Antioch, Iconium, Lystra and Derbe and the consequent incorporation of these cities in the province Galatia, forms the ultimate historical basis of the "South Galatian Theory"); Paphlagonia, annexed in 7 BC; Cappadocia, in 17 AD; Lycia, in 43 AD, and in 63 AD the part of Pontus lying between the Iris and Armenia. This formed the Roman A.M. of Paul's time. See ASIA; BITHYNIA, etc.

III. A.M. in the First Century AD.—The partition of A.M. into Rom provinces did not correspond to its ethnological divisions, and even those divisions were not always clearly marked. As is clear from the brief historical sketch given above, the population of A.M. was composed of many overlying strata of races, which tended in part to lose their individuality and sink into the original Anatolian type. Answering roughly to the above-mentioned separation of A.M. into two countries, and to its characterization as the meeting-place of East and West, we can detach from among a medley of races and institutions two main coexistent social systems, which we may call the native system, and the Hellenistic system. These systems (esp. as the result of Rom government) overlap and blend with each other, but they correspond in a general way to the distinction (observed in the country by Strabo) between city-organization and life on the village system. A deep gulf separated these forms of society.

1. The Population

2. The Native Social System

Under the Rom Empire, there was a continuous tendency to raise and absorb the Anatolian natives into Gr cities and Rom citizenship. But in the Apostolic Age, this process had not gone far in the interior of the country, and the native social system was still that under which a large section of the population lived. It combined the theocratic form of government with institutions derived from a preëxistent matriarchal society. The center of the native community was the temple of the god, with its great corporation of priests living on the temple revenues, and its people, who were the servants of the god (*hierodouloi;* cf St. Paul's expression, "servant of God"), and worked on the temple estates. The villages in which these workers lived were an inseparable adjunct of the temple, and the priests (or a single priest-dynast) were the absolute rulers of the people. A special class called *hieroi* performed special functions (probably for a period only) in the temple service. This included, in the case of women, sometimes a service of chastity, sometimes one of ceremonial prostitution. A woman of Lydia, of good social position (as implied in her Rom name) boasts in an inscription that she comes of ancestors who had served before the god in this manner, and that she has done so herself. Such women afterward married in their own rank, and incurred no disgrace. Many inscriptions prove that the god (through his priests) exercised a close supervision over the whole moral life and over the whole daily routine of his people; he was their Ruler, Judge, Helper and Healer.

3. Emperor Worship

Theocratic government received a new direction and a new meaning from the institution of emperor-worship; obedience to the god now coincided with loyalty to the emperor. The Seleucid kings and later the Rom emperors, according to a highly probable view, became heirs to the property of the dispossessed priests (a case is attested at Pisidian Antioch); and it was out of the territory originally belonging to the temples that grants of land to the new Seleucid and Rom foundations were made. On those portions of an estate not gifted to a *polis* or *colonia*, the theocratic government lasted on; but alongside of the Anatolian god there now appeared the figure of the god-emperor. In many places the cult of the emperor was established in the most important shrine of the neighborhood; the god-emperor succeeded to or shared the sanctity of the older god, grecized as Zeus, Apollo, etc; inscriptions record dedications made to the god and to the emperor jointly. Elsewhere, and esp. in the cities, new temples were founded for the worship of the emperor. A.M. was the home of emperor-worship, and nowhere did the new institution fit so well into the existing religious system. Inscriptions have recently thrown much light on a society of *Xenoi Tekmoreioi* ("Guest-Friends of the Secret Sign") who lived on an estate which had belonged to Men Askaenos beside Antioch of Pisidia, and was now in the hands of the Rom emperor. A *procurator* (who was probably the chief priest of the local temple) managed the estate as the emperor's representative. This society is typical of many others whose existence in inner A.M. has come to light in recent years; it was those societies which fostered the cult of the emperor on its local as distinct from its provincial side (see ASIARCH), and it was chiefly those societies that set the machinery of the Rom law in operation against the Christians in the great persecutions. In the course of time the people on the imperial estates tended to pass into a condition of serfdom; but occasionally an emperor raised the whole or part of an estate to the rank of a city.

4. The Hellenistic System

Much of inner A.M. must originally have been governed on the theocratic system, but the Gr city-state gradually encroached on the territory and privileges of the ancient temple. Several of these cities were "founded" by the Seleucids and Attalids; this sometimes meant a new foundation, more often the establishment of Gr city-government in an older city, with an addition of new inhabitants. These inhabitants were often Jews whom the Seleucids found trusty colonists: the Jews of Antioch in Pisidia (Acts **13** 14 ff) probably belong to this class. The conscious aim of those foundations was the Hellenization of the country, and their example influenced the neighboring cities. With the oriental absolutism of the native system, the organization of the Gr and Rom cities was in sharp contrast. In the earlier cents. of the Rom Empire these cities enjoyed a liberal measure of self-government. Magistracies were elective; rich men in the same city vied with each other, and city vied with city, in erecting magnificent public buildings, in founding schools and promoting education, in furthering all that western nations mean by civilization. With the Gr cities came the Gr Pantheon, but the gods of Hellas did little more than add their names to those of the gods of the country. Wherever we have any detailed information concerning a cult in inner Anatolia, we recognize under a Gr (or Rom) disguise the essential features of the old Anatolian god.

The Greeks had always despised the excesses of the Asiatic religion, and the more advanced education of the Anatolian Greeks could not reconcile itself to a degraded cult, which sought to perpetuate the social institutions under which it had arisen, only under their ugliest and most degraded aspects. "In the country generally a higher type of society was maintained; whereas at the great temples the primitive social system was kept up as a religious duty incumbent on the class called *Hieroi* during their regular periods of service at the temple. . . . . The chasm that divided the religion from the educated life of the country became steadily wider and deeper. In this state of things St. Paul entered the country; and wherever education had already been diffused, he found converts ready and eager." This accounts for "the marvellous and electrical effect that is attributed in Acts to the preaching of the Apostle in Galatia" (Ramsay, *Cities and Bishoprics of Phrygia*, 96).

5. Roman "Coloniae"

Under the Rom Empire, we can trace a gradual evolution in the organization of the Gr cities toward the Rom municipal type. One of the main factors in this process was the foundation over inner A.M. of Rom colonies, which were "bits of Rome" set down in the provinces. These *coloniae* were organized entirely on the Rom model, and were usually garrisons of veterans, who kept unruly parts of the country in order. Such in NT time were Antioch and Lystra (Iconium, which used to be regarded as a *colonia* of Claudius, is now recognized to have been raised to that rank by Hadrian). In the 1st cent. Lat was the official language in the *coloniae;* it never ousted Gr in general usage, and Gr soon replaced it in official documents. Education was at its highest level in the Gr towns and in the Rom colonies, and it was to those exclusively that St. Paul addressed the gospel.

IV. Christianity in A.M.—Already in St. Paul's lifetime, Christianity had established itself firmly in many of the greater centers of Gr-Rom culture in Asia and Galatia. The evangelization of Ephesus, the capital of the province Asia, and the terminus of one of the great routes leading along the peninsula, contributed largely to the spread of Christianity in the inland parts of the province, and esp. in Phrygia. Christianity, in accordance with the program of St. Paul, first took root in the cities, from which it spread over the country districts.

Christian Inscriptions, etc

The Christian inscriptions begin earliest in Phrygia, where we find many documents dating from the end of the 2d and beginning of the 3d cents. AD. The main characteristic of those early inscriptions — a feature which makes them difficult to recognize — is their suppression as a rule of anything that looked overtly Christian, with the object of avoiding the notice of persons who might induce the Rom officials to take measures against their dedicators. The Lycaonian inscriptions begin almost a cent. later, not, we must suppose, because Christianity spread less rapidly from Iconium, Lystra, etc, than it did from the Asian cities, but because Gr education took longer to permeate the sparsely populated plains of the central plateau than the rich townships of Asia. The new religion is proved by Pliny's correspondence with Trajan (111–13 AD) to have been firmly established in Bithynia early in the 2d cent. Farther east, where the great temples still had much influence, the expansion of Christianity was slower, but in the 4th cent. Cappadocia produced such men as Basil and the Gregories. The great persecutions, as is proved by literary evidence and by many inscriptions, raged with especial severity in A.M. The influence of the church on A.M. in the early cents. of the Empire may be judged from the fact that scarcely a trace of the Mithraic religion, the principal competitor of Christianity, has been found in the whole country. From the date of the Nicene Council (325 AD) the history of Christianity in A.M. was that of the Byzantine Empire. Ruins of churches belonging to the Byzantine period are found all over the peninsula; they are especially numerous in the central and eastern districts. A detailed study of a Byzantine Christian town of Lycaonia, containing an exceptionally large number of churches, has been published by Sir W. M. Ramsay and Miss G. L. Bell: *The Thousand and One Churches*. Gr-speaking Christian villages in many parts of A.M. continue an unbroken connection with the Rom Empire till the present day.

Literature.—Ramsay's numerous works on A.M., especially *St. Paul the Traveller*, etc, *The Church in the Rom Empire*, *The Cities of St. Paul*, *The Letters to the Seven Churches*, and *Cities and Bishoprics of Phrygia* have been freely drawn upon in this account. For a fuller bibliography, see *EB* (11th ed), art. "Asia Minor" (Hogarth and Wilson).

W. M. Calder

ASIA MINOR, ā'shi-a mī'nēr, **THE ARCHAEOLOGY OF**, är'kē-ol'o-ji ov: At the present stage of our information it is difficult to write with acceptance on the archaeology of Asia Minor. Views unquestioned only a few years ago are already passing out of date, while the modern archaeologist, enthusiastically excavating old sites, laboriously deciphering worn inscriptions, and patiently collating documentary evidence, has by no means completed his task. But it is now clear that an archaeological field, worthy to be compared with those in the valleys of the Euphrates and the Nile, invites development in Asia Minor.

1. Earliest Influences from Mesopotamia

In the *Contemporary Review* for August, 1907, Professor Sayce reminded his readers that the Gr geographers called Cappadox the son of Ninyas, thereby tracing the origin of Cappadocian culture to Nineveh, and similarly they derived the Mermnad Dynasty of Lydia from Ninos the son of Belos, or from Babylonia through Assyria. Actual history is probably at the back of these legends, and the Table of Nations supports this (Gen **10** 22), when it calls Lud, or Lydia, a son of Shem and brother of Asshur. This is not to assert, however, that any great number of Sem people ever made A.M. their home. But Professor Winckler and others have shown us that the language, script, ideas and institutions characteristic of the Bab civilization were widespread among the nations of western Asia, and from very early times A.M. came within their sphere of influence. Strabo records the tradition that Zile, as well as Tyana, was founded upon "the mound of Semiramis," thus connecting these ancient sites with the Mesopotamian culture. Dr. David Robinson in his *Ancient Sinope* (145 ff), argues that "the early foundations of Sinope are probably Assyr," though established history cannot describe in detail what lay back of the Milesian settlement of this the northern point and the best harbor of the peninsula. Neither could Strabo go back of the Milesian colonists for the foundation of Samsoun, the ancient Amisus, an important commercial city east of Sinope, but the accompanying illustration (Fig. 1) seems clearly to show the influence

Fig. 1.—Head from Old Samsoun (Showing Assyrian Influence).

of Assyria. The original is a terra cotta figure of gray clay found recently in Old Samsoun. Mesopotamian religious and cultural influences thus appear to have tinged A.M., at least at certain points, as far as the coast of the Black Sea, and indeed the great peninsula has been what its shape suggests, a friendly hand stretching out from the continent of Asia toward the continent of Europe.

Fig. 2.—Excavating for Cuneiform Tablets at Boghazkeuy.

2. Third Millennium BC

Professor Sayce's article referred to above was based upon the evidence furnished by cuneiform tablets from Kara Eyuk, the "Black Mound," an ancient site just within the ox-bows of the Halys River near Caesarea Mazaca. These tablets, as deciphered by himself and Professor Pinches, were of the period of Abraham, or of

Hammurabi, about 2250 BC, and were written in a dialect of Assyrian. The settlers were soldier colonists from the Assyr section of the Bab empire, engaged in mining and in trade. Silver, copper

FIG. 3.—Hittite Lion, Boghaz-keuy; at the "Lion Gate."

and perhaps iron were the metals sought. "Time was reckoned as in Assyria by means of officials called *limmi*, who gave their name to the year." The colonists had a temple with its priests, where financial transactions were carried on under the sanctity of religion. There were roads, mail carriers whose pouches were filled with cuneiform bricks, and commercial travelers who made a speciality of fine clothing. This makes quite natural the finding of a goodly Bab mantle by Achan at the pillage of Ai (Josh **7** 21). Slavery is a recognized institution; a boy is sent to a barber for circumcision; a house, wife and children are pledged as security for a debt. An oath is taken "on the top of a staff," an interesting fact that sheds its light on the vs describing the oath and blessing of dying Jacob (Gen **47** 31; He **11** 21). Early A.M. is thus lighted up at various points by the culture of Mesopotamia, and transmits some of the scattered rays to the Gr world.

The earliest native inhabitants to be distinguished in A.M. are the Hittites (see HITTITES). Ever since 1872, when Dr. Wright suggested that the strange hieroglyphics on four black basalt stones which he had discovered at Hamath were perhaps the work of Hittite art, there has been an ever-growing volume of material for scholars to work upon. There are sculptures of the same general style, representing figures of men, women, gods, lions and other animals, eagles with double heads, sphinxes, musical instruments, winged discs and other symbols, all of which can be understood only in part. These are accompanied by hieroglyphic writing, undeciphered as yet, and the inscriptions read "boustrophedon," that is from right to left and back again, as the oxen go in plowing an oriental field. There have also been discovered great castles with connecting walls

3. Second Millennium BC

and ramparts, gates, tunnels, moats, palaces, temples and other sanctuaries and buildings. More than this, occasional fragments of cuneiform tablets picked up on the surface of the ground led to the belief that written documents of value might be found buried in the soil. Malatia, Marash, Sinjirli, Sakje Geuzi, Gurun, Boghaz-keuy, Eyuk, Karabel, not to mention perhaps a hundred other sites, have offered important Hittite remains. Carchemish and Kedesh on the Orontes were capital cities in northern Syria. The Hittites of the Holy Land, whether in the days of Abraham or in those of David and Solomon, were an offshoot from the main stem of the nation. A.M. was the true home of the Hittites.

Boghaz-keuy has become within the last decade the best known Hittite site in A.M., and may be described as typical. It lies in northern Cappadocia, fifty muleteer hours S. of Sinope. Yasili-kaya, the "written" or "sculptured" rocks, is a suburb, and Eyuk with its sphinx-guarded temple is but 15 miles to the N. It was the good fortune of Professor Hugo Winckler of the University of Berlin to secure the funds, obtain permission from the Turkish government, and, in the summer of 1906 to unearth over 3,000 more or less fragmentary tablets written in the cuneiform character and the Hittite language. This is the first considerable store of the yet undeciphered Hittite literature for scholars to work upon. These tablets are of clay, written on both sides, and baked hard and red. Often the writing is in ruled columns. The cuneiform character, like the Lat alphabet in modern times, was used far from its original home, and that for thousands of years. The language of a few Boghaz-keuy tablets is Bab, notably a copy of the treaty between Rameses II of Egypt and Khita-sar, king of the Hittites in central A.M. The scribes adopted not only the Bab characters but certain *ideographs,* and it is these ideographs which have furnished the key to provisional vocabularies of several hundred words which have

FIG. 4.—Hittite Warrior, Boghaz-keuy.

been published by Professors Pinches and Sayce. When Professor Winckler and his German collaborators publish the tablets they have deposited in the Constantinople museum, we may listen to the voice of some Hittite Homer speaking from amid the dusty bricks written in the period of Moses. Beside Boghaz-keuy the beetling towers of lofty Troy sink to the proportions of a fortified hamlet.

Hittite sculptures show a very marked type of men, with squat figures, slant eyes, prominent noses and Mongoloid features. We suppose they were of Turanian or Mongolian blood; certainly not Sem and probably not Aryan. As they occupied various important inland centers in A.M. before, during and after the whole of the second millennium BC, it is probable that they occupied much or most of the intervening territory (see *Records of the Past* for December, 1908). A great capital like Boghaz-keuy, with its heavy fortifications, would require extensive provinces to support it, and would extend its sway so as to leave no enemy within striking distance. The "Amazons" are now generally regarded as the armed Hittite priestesses of a goddess whose cult spread throughout A.M. The "Amazon Mountains," still known locally by the old name, run parallel with the coast of the Black Sea near the Iris River, and tradition current there now holds that the women are stronger than the men, work harder, live longer and are better at a quarrel! A comparative study of the decorated pottery, so abundant on the old sites of the country, makes it more than possible that the artificial mounds, which are so common a feature of the Anatolian landscape, and the many rock-hewn tombs, of which the most famous are probably those at Amasia, were the work of Hittite hands.

The Hittite sculptures are strikingly suggestive of religious rather than political or military themes. The people were pagans with many gods and goddesses, of whom one, or one couple, received recognition as at the head of the pantheon. Such titles as Sutekh of Carchemish, Sutekh of Kadesh, Sutekh of the land of the Hittites, show that the

Fig. 5.—Hittite Sculptures, Yasili-kaya.

chief god was localized in various places, perhaps with varying attributes. A companion goddess was named Antarata. She was the great Mother Goddess of A.M., who came to outrank her male counterpart. She is represented in the sculptures with a youthful male figure, as a consort, probably illustrating the legend of Tammuz for whom the erring Heb women wept (Ezk **8** 14). He was called

Fig. 6.—Hittite Sculptures, Yasili-kaya.

Attys in later days. He stands for life after death, spring after winter, one generation after another. The chief god worshipped at Boghaz-keuy was Teshub. Another was named Khiba, and the same name appears in the Tell el-Amarna correspondence from Jerus. This affords a remarkable illustration of the prophet's address to Jerus, "Your mother was a Hittite" (Ezk **16** 45).

The worship of the Hittites of the era of the Exodus is still seen pictured on the rocks at Yasili-kaya. This spot was the sanctuary of the metropolis. There are two hypaethral rock galleries, the larger of which has a double procession of about 80 figures carved on the natural rock walls, which have been smoothed for the purpose, and meeting at the inmost recess of the gallery. The figures nearest the entrance are about half life-size. As the processions advance the height of the figures increases, until the two persons at the head, the chief priest and priestess or the king and queen, are quite above life-size. These persons advance curious symbols toward each other, each is followed by a retinue of his or her own sex, and each is supported—the priest-king upon the heads of two subjects or captives, and the priestess-queen upon a leopard. The latter figure is followed by her consort son.

The ruins at Eyuk are compact, and consist of a small temple, its sphinx-guarded door, and a double procession of approaching worshippers to the number of about 40. The main room of the sanctuary is only 7 yds. by 8 in measurement. This may be compared with the Holy Place in the tabernacle of the Israelites, which was approximately contemporary. Neither could contain a worshipping congregation, but only the ministering priests. The solemn sphinxes at the door suggest the cherubim that adorned the Israelite temple, and winged eagles with double heads decorate the inner walls of the doorway. Amid the sculptured processions moving on the basalt rocks toward the sanctuary is an altar before which stands a bull on a pedestal, and behind which is a priest who wears a large earring. Close behind the priest a flock of three sheep and a goat approach the sacrificial altar. Compare the description in Ex **32**. The Israelites said to Aaron, "Up, make us gods"; he required their golden earrings, made a calf, "and built an altar before it"; they offered burnt offerings and brought peace offerings; they sat down to eat and drink and rose up to play. Israelite worship was in certain forms similar to the worship of the Hittites, but its spiritual content was wholly different. For musical instruments the Eyuk procession exhibits a lituus, a (silver?) trumpet and a shapely guitar. The animal kingdom is represented by another bull with a chest or ark on its back, a well-executed lion and two hares held in the two talons of an eagle. A spring close by furnished all the water required by the worshippers and for ritual purposes.

Professor Garstang in *The Land of the Hittites* shows that the power which had been waning after about 1200 BC enjoyed a period of recrudescence in the 10th and 9th cents. He ascribes to this period the monuments of Sakje Geuzi, which the professor himself excavated, together with other Hittite remains in A.M. The Vannic power known as Urartu, akin to the Hittites but separate, arose in the N.E.; the Phrygians began to dominate in the W.; the Assyrians pressed upon the S.E. The overthrow of the Hittites was completed by the bursting in of the desolating Cimmerian hordes, and after 717, when Carchemish was taken by the Assyrians, the Hittites fade from the archaeological records of their home land. See ASIA MINOR, II, 1.

4. First Millennium BC

Before the Hittites disappeared from the interior of A.M., sundry Aryan peoples, more or less closely related to the Greeks, were established at various points around the coast. Schliemann, of Trojan fame, was the pioneer archaeologist in this field, and his boundless enthusiasm, optimism and resourcefulness recovered the treasures of Priam's city, and made real again the story of days when the world was young. Among the most valuable collections in the wonderful Constantinople Museum is that from Troy, which contains bronze axes and lance heads, implements in copper, talents of silver, diadems, earrings and bracelets of gold, bone bodkins and needles, spindle whorls done in baked clay, numbers of idols or votive offerings, and other objects found in the Troad, at the modern Hissarlik. Phrygian, Thracian

FIG. 7.—Artificial Mound, Marsovan Plain; Possibly Hittite.

and subsequently Galatian immigrants from the N.W. had been filtering across the Hellespont, and wedging themselves in among the earlier inhabitants. There were some points in common between the Cretan or Aegean civilization and that of A.M., but Professor Hogarth in his *Ionia and the East* urges that these resemblances were few. It was otherwise with the Greeks proper. Herodotus gave the names of twelve Aeolian, twelve Ionian and six Dorian cities on the west coast, founded by colonists who came across the Aegean Sea, and who leavened, led and intermarried with the native population they found settled there. One of these Asiatic Gr colonies, Miletus, was sufficiently populous and vigorous to send out from 60 to 80 colonies of its own, the successive

FIG. 8.—Modern Traffic on the Halys River.

swarms of adventurers moving N. and E., up the coast of the Aegean, through the Bosphorus and along the south shore of the Black Sea. In due season Xenophon and the Ten Thousand, and then Alexander with his Macedonians, scattered yet more widely the seeds of Hellenic culture upon a soil already prepared for its reception. The inscriptions, sculptures, temples, tombs, palaces, castles, theaters, jewelry, figurines in bronze or terra cotta, coins of silver or copper and other objects remaining from this period exhibit a style of art, culture and religion which may best be named Anatolian, but which are akin to those of Greece proper. The excavations at Ephesus, Pergamus, Sardis and other important sites show the same grafting of Gr scions upon the local stock.

One marked feature survived as a legacy from Hittite days in the worship of a great Mother Goddess. Whether known as Ma, or Cybele, or Anaitis, or Diana, or designated by some other title, it was the female not the male that headed the pantheon of gods. With the Gr culture came also the city-state organization of government. The ruder and earlier native communities were organized on the village plan. Usually each village had its shrine, in charge of priests or perhaps more often priestesses; the land belonged to the god, or goddess; it paid tithes to the shrine; sacrifices and gifts were offered at the sacred center; this was often on a high hill, under a sacred tree, and beside a holy fountain; there was little of education, law or government except as guiding oracles were proclaimed from the temple.

In the early part of this millennium the Phrygians became a power of commanding importance in the western part of the peninsula, and Professor

Hogarth says of the region of the Midas Tomb, "There is no region of ancient monuments which would be better worth examination" by excavators. Then came Lydia, whose capital, Sardis, is now in process of excavation by Professor Butler and his American associates. Sardis was taken and Croesus dethroned by the Persians about 546 BC, and for two cents., until Alexander, Pers authority overshadowed A.M., but permanent influences were scanty.

5. The Romans in A.M.

By about the year 200 BC the Romans began to become entangled in the politics of the four principal kingdoms that then occupied A.M., namely Bithynia, Pergamus, Pontus and Cappadocia. By slow degrees their influence and their arms advanced under such leaders civil and military as Sulla, Lucullus, Pompey, Cicero and Julius Caesar, while Attalus of Pergamus and Prusias of Bithynia bequeathed their uneasy do-

Fig. 9.—Cuneiform Tablet from Boghaz-keuy, Containing the Name of Khibu.

mains to the steady power arising from the W. In 133 BC the Romans proceeded to organize the province of Asia, taking the name from a Lydian district included in the province. Step by step the Rom frontiers were pushed farther to the E. Mithridates VI, king of Pontus, was called "the most formidable enemy the republic ever had to contend with," but he went down before the conquering arms of Rome. See PONTUS. Caesar chastised the unfortunate Pharnaces at Zile in central A.M., and coolly announced his success in the memorable message of three words, *"veni, vidi, vici."* Ultimately all of this fair peninsula passed under the iron sway, and the Rom rule lasted more than 500 years, until in 395 AD Theodosius divided the empire between his sons, giving the E. to Arcadius and the W. to Honorius, and the Rom Empire was cleft in twain.

True to their customs elsewhere the Romans built roads well paved with stone between the chief cities of their eastern provinces. The archaeologist or common traveler often comes upon sections of these roads, sometimes in the thickest forests, as sound and as rough as when Rom chariots rumbled over them. Milestones were erected to mark the distances, usually inscribed in both Lat and Gr, and the decipherment of these milestone records

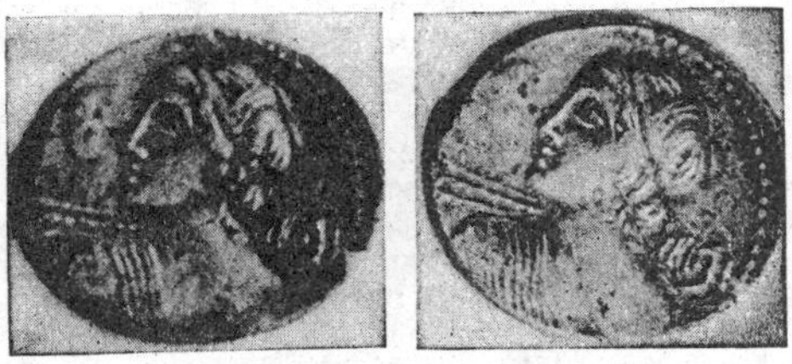

Fig. 10.—Coin of Licinius, Roman Emperor in the East, 313 AD.

contributes to the recovery of the lost history. Bridges over the important streams have been rebuilt and repaired by successive generations of men, but in certain cases the Rom character of the original stands clearly forth. The Romans were a building people, and government houses, aqueducts, baths, theaters, temples and other structures confront the archaeologist or await the labor of the spade. Epigraphical studies such as those of Professor Sterrett indicate what a wealth of inscriptions is yet to be recovered, in Lat as well as in Gr.

It was during the Rom period that Christianity made its advent in the peninsula. Christian disciples as well as Rom legions and governors used the roads, bridges and public buildings. Old church buildings and other religious foundations have their stories to tell. It is very interesting to read on Gr tombstones of the 1st or 2d cent. AD such inscriptions as, "Here lies the servant of God, Daniel," "Here lies the handmaid of God, Maria." Our great authority for this period is Sir William M. Ramsay, whose *Historical Geography of A.M.* and other works must be read by anyone who would familiarize himself with this rich field.

6. The Byzantine Period

By almost imperceptible degrees the Rom era was merged into the Byzantine. We are passing so rapidly now from the sphere of archaeology to that of history proper that we must be brief. For a thousand years after the fall of Rome the Eastern Empire lived on, a Gr body pervaded with lingering Rom influences and with Constantinople as the pulsating heart. The character of the times was nothing if not religious, yet the prevailing Christianity was a syncretistic compound including much from the nature worship of earlier Anatolia. The first great councils of the Christian church convened upon the soil of A.M.,

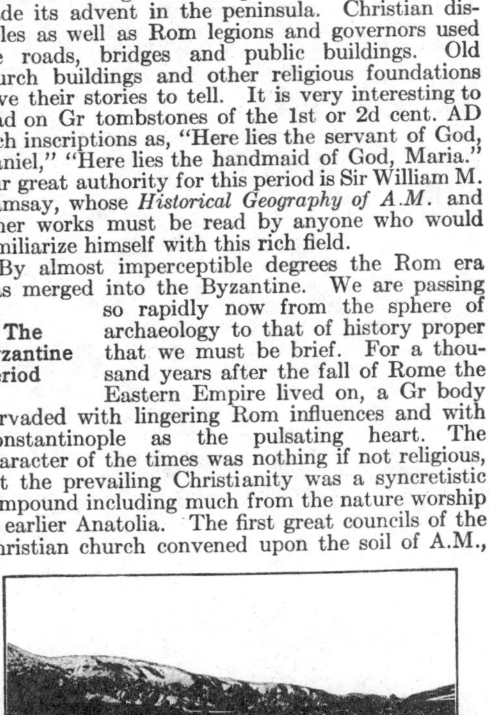

Fig. 11.—Roman Bridge over the Halys.

the fourth being held at Ephesus in 431, and at this council the phrase "Mother of God" was adopted. We have seen that for fifty generations or more the people of A.M. had worshipped a great mother goddess, often with her consort son. It was at Ephesus, the center of the worship of Diana, that ecclesiastics, many of whom had but a slight training in Christianity, adopted this article into their statement of religious faith.

Again the government of the country, the dominant race, the religion, language and culture, all are changed—this time with the invasions of the Seljukian Turks. This tribe was the precursor of the Ottoman Turks and later became absorbed among them. These Seljukians entered A.M., coming up out of the recesses of central Asia, about the time that the Normans were settling along the coasts of western Europe. Their place in history is measurably clear, but they deserve mention in archaeology by reason of their remarkable architecture. Theirs was a branch of the Saracenic or Moorish architecture, and many examples remain in A.M. Mosques, schools, government buildings, khans, fortifications, fountains and other structures remain in great numbers and in a state of more or less satisfactory preservation, and they are buildings remarkably massive, yet ornate in delicacy and variety of tracery.

7. The Seljukian Turks

The Ottoman Turks, cousins of the Seljukians, came up out of the central Asian hive later, and took Constantinople by a memorable siege in 1453. With this event the archaeology of A.M. may be said to close, and history to cover the field instead.

George E. White

ASIARCH, ā'shi-ärk (**'Ἀσιάρχης,** *Asiárchēs;* ERV "the chief officers of Asia," AV **"the chief of Asia"**): The title given to certain men of high honorary rank in the Rom province of Asia. What their exact functions were is not altogether clear. They derived their appellation from the name of the province over which they presided (cf Bithyniarch; Cariarch; Syriarch). Brandis has shown that they were not "high priests of Asia," as some have thought, but delegates of individual cities to the provincial Council (*Commune Asiæ;* see Asia Minor) which regulated the worship of Rome and of the emperor. They were probably assembled at Ephesus, among other places, to preside over the public games and the religious rites at the festival, in honor of the gods and the emperor, when they sent word to Paul and gave him a bit of friendly advice, not to present himself at the theater (*mḗ doúnai heautón eis tó théatron,* Acts **19** 31). The title could be held along with any civil office and with the high-priesthood of a particular city. They served for one year, but reelection was possible (the tenure of office, according to Ramsay, was four years). The municipalities must have shown the Asiarchs high honor, as we find the names of many perpetuated on coins and inscriptions. The office could only be held by men of wealth, as the expenses of the provincial games were for the greater part defrayed by the Asiarchs.

Literature.—*CI,* 2511, 2912; *CIL,* 296, 297; Brandis, Pauly-Wissowa's *Real-Encyclopaedia,* arts. "Archiereus" and "Asiarches"; Strabo, XIV, 649; Eusebius, *HE,* IV, 15; Hicks, *Ancient Gr Inscrs in the British Museum;* Ramsay, *Classical Review,* III, 174 ff; *Cities and Bishoprics of Phrygia,* I, 55–58, and II, ch xi; Guiraud, *Les assemblées provinciales de l'Empire Romain;* Lightfoot, *St. Ignatius and St. Polycarp,* II, 987 ff.

M. O. Evans

ASIBIAS, as-i-bī'as (**'Ἀσιβίας,** *Asibías* and *Asebías*): A. put away his "strange wife" (1 Esd **9** 26). Cf Malchijah (Ezr **10** 25).

ASIDE, a-sīd': "Distinct from others," "privately," such is the sense of the word in 2 K **4** 4; Mk **7** 33. Also "to withdraw" (Lk **9** 10 AV; Acts **23** 19: *ὑποχωρέω, hupochōréō,* also *anachoréō*). One is said to have turned aside when he departs from the path of rectitude (Ps **14** 3; Sir **2** 7; 1 Tim **1** 6). In a **fig.** sense it is used to express the thought of putting aside, to renounce, every hindrance or impediment to a consecrated earnest Christian life (He **12** 1: *ἀποτίθημι, apotíthēmi*).

ASIEL, ā'si-el, as'i-el (**'Ἀσιήλ,** *Asiḗl;* AV **Asael** [Tob **1** 1]):

(1) Grandfather of Jehu, one of the Simeonite "princes" mentioned in 1 Ch **4** 35 as sharing Judah's inheritance (see Josh **19** 9).

(2) A swift writer engaged by Ezra to transcribe the law (2 Esd **14** 24).

(3) An ancestor of Tobit (Tob **1** 1). Cf Jahzeel or Jahziel (Gen **46** 24).

ASIPHA, as'i-fa (A, **'Ἀσειφά,** *Aseiphá;* B, *Taseiphá*)=Hasupha (Ezr **2** 43; Neh **7** 46). The sons of A. (temple-servants) returned with Zerubbabel to Jerus (1 Esd **5** 29).

ASK, ask (שָׁאַל, *shā'al* "to inquire," "to seek for counsel," "to demand"): It is the word commonly used in the OT and is equivalent to *ἐπερωτάω, eperōtáō,* "to request," used in the NT. It does not imply any inferiority on the part of the person asking (Ps **2** 8). It is the Son who is bidden to ask, and therefore the word expresses the request of an equal. It has also the meaning "to inquire": "Wherefore . . . . ask after my name?" (Gen **32** 29) signifying, "Surely you must know who I am." "Ye shall ask me no question" (Jn **16** 23), i.e. "about the true meaning of My words, for all will then be clear to you" (Dummelow). *αἰτέω, aitéō,* is the word commonly used with reference to prayer. It means "to ask," "to implore," and presents the petitioner as an inferior asking from a superior (Mt **6** 8; **7** 7.8; Mk **10** 35; Jn **14** 13, and in many other places). It is not, however, asking in the sense of the word beg, but rather that of a child making request of its father. The petitioner asks both because of his need and of the assurance that he is welcome. He is assured before he asks that the petition will be granted, if he asks in accordance with God's will (1 Jn **3** 22; **5** 15). Moreover the Spirit leads us to such asking in that He reveals our need and the goodness of God to us. See Amiss; Prayer.

Jacob W. Kapp

ASKELON, as'ke-lon: AV form in Jgs **1** 18; 1 S **6** 17; 2 S **1** 20, for Ashkelon (q.v.).

ASLEEP, a-slēp' (יָשֵׁן, *yāshēn,* "sleeping," רָדַם, *rādham,* "deep sleep"; **καθεύδω,** *katheúdō,* "to fall asleep," **ἀφυπνόω,** *aphupnóō,* "to fall asleep"): A state of repose in sleep, Nature's release from weariness of body and mind, as of Jonah on shipboard (Jon **1** 5); of Christ in the tempest-tossed boat (Mt **8** 24); of the exhausted disciples in Gethsemane (Mt **26** 43 AV). Used with beautiful and comforting significance of death (*κοιμάομαι, koimáomai,* "to put to sleep"). Sleep implies a subsequent waking, and as a symbol of death implies continued and conscious life beyond the grave. In the presence of death no truth has been so sustaining to Christian faith as this. It is the distinct product of Christ's resurrection. Paul speaks of departed believers as having "fallen asleep in Christ" (1 Cor **15** 6.18); as proof of the soul's immortality he terms the risen Christ "the first-fruits of them that are asleep." Lazarus and Stephen, at death, are said to have "fallen asleep" (Jn **11** 11; Acts **7** 60); so of David and the ancient patriarchs (Acts **13** 36; 2 Pet **3** 4). The most beautiful description of death in human language and lit. is Paul's characterization of the dead as "them also which sleep in Jesus" (1 Thess **4** 14 AV). This blessed hope has wrought itself permanently into the life and creed and hymnology of the Christian church, as in the hymn often used with such comforting effect at the burial service of believers: "Asleep in Jesus! blessed sleep!" DWIGHT M. PRATT

ASMODAEUS, az-mo-dē'us (אַשְׁמְדַי, *'ashmᵉdhai;* **'Ασμοδαῖος,** *Asmodaíos*): An evil spirit first mentioned in Tob **3** 8. Older etymologists derived the name from the Heb verb *shāmadh,* "destroy"; but it is now generally held to be associated with Zoroastrianism, with which the Jews became acquainted during the exile, and by which later Jewish views on the spirit-world were greatly influenced. It is now held to be the equivalent of the Pers Aeshma-Deva, the spirit of concupiscence. The spirit is at times reckoned as the equal in power of "Abaddon" (Job **31** 12) and of "Apollyon" (Rev **9** 11), and in Tobit is represented as loving Sara, only daughter of Raguel of Ecbatana, and as causing the death on the bridal night of seven husbands who had in succession married her. His power was broken by the young Tobias acting on the advice of the angel Raphael (Tob **6** 15). He burnt on the "ashes of incense" the heart and liver of a fish which he caught in the Tigris. "But when the devil smelled the smell, he fled into the uppermost parts of Egypt, and the angel bound him" (Tob **8** 3). Milton refers to the incident in *Paradise Lost,* 4, 168–71, founding on Jewish demonology and the "loves of the angels" (Gen **6** 2).

J. HUTCHISON

ASMONEANS, as-mo-nē'ans: A remarkable priestly family of Modin, in Judaea, also called Hasmonaeans or Maccabees. They belonged to that portion of the Jewish nation which under all trials and temptations remained loyal to Jeh, even when the national life and religion seemed at their lowest ebb, and they succeeded, for a while at least, in restoring the name and fame of Israel. All in all they were an extremely warlike family. But the entire Asmonean history affords abundant proof of the bitter partisanships which, even more than the persecutions of their enemies, sapped the national strength and divided the nation into bitterly hostile factions. The Asmoneans never, in all their history, or at any given period in it, had a united people behind their backs. They had to fight disloyalty at home, as well as deadly enmity abroad. A considerable portion of the people was unable to withstand the paganizing influence of the Macedonian and Syrian periods, and in this direction the thousands of Heb soldiers, who fought under the Gr banners, must have exerted an inestimable influence. The Asmonean struggle is therefore, in all its phases, a three-sided one, and it makes the ascendancy of the family all the more remarkable. The sources of our knowledge of this period are mainly found in the Books of the Macc, in the *Ant* and *BJ* of Jos, and in occasional references of Strabo, Livy and other classic historians. The contents of *Ant* plainly prove that Jos used the Books of the Macc as far as possible, but that besides he was possessed of sources of information now wholly lost. The name "Asmonean" is derived from the Heb *Ḥashmān,* "wealthy." Hashman was a priest of the family Joarib (*Ant,* XII, vi, 1; 1 Macc **2** 1; 1 Ch **24** 7). The name "Maccabee," from the surname of Judas, the son of Mattathias, may be derived from the Heb *maḳḳābhāh,* "a hammer"; *makhbī,* "an extinguisher"; or from the first letters of the Heb sentence, *Mī Khāmōkhāh Bā-'ēlīm YHWH?* "Who among the gods, O Lord, can be likened unto thee," inscribed on the Maccabaean banner in the word *MaKHBiY.*

1. The Asmonean Revolt

Antiochus Epiphanes returned in 169 BC from the Egyp wars, the fruits of which had been wrested from him by the Rom power, which a year later, in his fourth war, in the person of Pompilius Laenas, was to order him peremptorily to leave Egypt once and for all time. Thus his four campaigns against his hereditary foe were made utterly barren. Grave suspicions had been aroused in the king's heart against the Jews, and when their wrangling about the high-priesthood afforded him an opportunity, he resolved forever to crush the power of Judaism and to wipe out its detested religion. Thus Apollonius (Jos tells us, the king himself, *BJ,* V, ix, 4) in 168 BC appeared before Jerus, devastated the city, defiled the temple by the sacrifice of swine on the altar of burnt offering, destroyed all the holy writings that could be obtained, sold numberless Jews and their families into slavery, forbade circumcision on pain of death and inaugurated the dark period spoken of by Dnl (**9** 27; **11** 31). Thus Antiochus marked his name in blood and tears on the pages of Jewish history. Against this cruel tyranny and this attempt to root out the religion of Israel and their ancient faith, the Maccabaean family revolted and thus became the leaders in a desperate struggle for Jewish independence. How far they succeeded in these efforts the following sketch will show.

2. Mattathias

Mattathias was a priest of the house of Joarib, at the time of the breaking out of the revolt most likely a refugee from Jerus, living at Modin, W. of the city, in the highlands of Judaea, where he may have owned an estate. When compulsion was tried by the Syrians to make him sacrifice to idols, he not only refused to obey, but slew a Jew, who came forward to the altar, as well as Apelles, the Syrian commander and a portion of his guard (*Ant,* XII, vi, 2). Overthrowing heathen altars as he went, he was followed into the wilderness by large bands of loyal Jews. And when the refusal to fight on the Sabbath day had led to the slaughter of a thousand of his followers, he gave liberty to the Jews to give battle on that day. In 167 BC, soon after the beginning of the conflict, he sank under the unequal task, leaving the completion of the work to his five sons, John (Gaddis), Simon (Matthes), Judas (Maccabaeus), Eleazar (Auran) and Jonathan (Apphes). On his deathbed he appointed Simon as the counselor and Judas as the military leader of the movement (*Ant,* XII, vi, 1). These two with Jonathan were to carry the work to completion.

3. Judas Maccabaeus, 166–160 BC

Judas proved himself full worthy of his father's foresight and trust. His military talent was marvelous, his cunning baffling, his courage leonine, his swiftness that of the eagle. He reminds one strongly of Joshua, the ancient military genius of Israel. Nearly all his battles were fought against impossible odds and his victories inspired the Syrians with awe. In sudden night attacks he surprised the Syrian generals, Apollonius and Seron (1 Macc **3** 10.13), and scattered their armies. Antiochus, ready to chastise the countries eastward, who appeared on the point of rebellion, intrusted the conduct of the Judaean war to Lysias, his kinsman and favorite, who was charged to wipe Israel and its hated religion off the face of the earth. The latter intrusted the actual conduct of hostilities to a great and well-equipped army, under Ptolemaeus, Nicanor and Gorgias. This army was encamped at Emmaus, S. of Modin, while Judas lay with his small force a little to the S.E. When Gorgias attempted to surprise him by night, Judas himself fell like an avalanche on the rest of the Syrian army and crushed it, then met and defeated the returning Gorgias and gained an immense booty. Equally successful in the campaign of 165 BC Judas captured Jerus and purified and rededicated the temple, just five years after its defilement. Thus the Jewish "Festival of Lights" came into existence. The next year was spent in the reduction of Idumaea, the Jordan territory, the Ammonites, and several important strongholds of the enemy, whilst Simon marched northward and brought back the Jewish captives from Galilee and the sources of the Jordan.

Meanwhile Antiochus had died in the eastern campaign and his death inaugurated the collapse of the Syrian empire. Philip was appointed guardian of the infant king, while his uncle Demetrius sought to dethrone him by the aid of the Romans. The siege of the stronghold of Jerus, still in the hands of the Syrians, by the Maccabees, led Philip to make a heroic effort to crush Judas and his growing power, and he swiftly marched upon Judaea with a large and well-equipped army. The odds were too strong for Judas, his band was frightened by the Syrian war-elephants and in the battle of Beth-zacharias the Maccabees were defeated and Eleazar, the youngest brother, was killed. Jerus was taken by the Syrians, the temple wall broken down and only the threatening danger of an attack from the king's southern foes saved the Maccabaean cause. Lysias retreated but left a strong garrison in Jerus. All seemed lost. Alcimus, leader of the disloyal Jews and a mortal enemy of Judas, was made high priest and he prayed Demetrius, who had captured the Syrian throne, to come to his aid against the Maccabees in 162 BC. Bacchides was sent with a strong force and sought in vain to obtain possession of the person of Judas by treachery. He made havoc of the Jews, by killing friend and foe alike, and returned to the East to be succeeded by Nicanor, who also failed to dispose of Judas by treachery. In the ensuing battle at Capharsalama he was defeated and compelled to fall back on Jerus and thence on Beth-horon, where Judas attacked, again defeated and killed him. In this hour of hope and fear Judas was led to seek a Rom alliance whose consummation he never saw. From that day his fortune changed. A new Syrian army under Bacchides and the false priest Alcimus approached Jerus. Judas gave them battle at Elasa, in April, 161 BC. With only 3,000 men he engaged the Syrian forces. He succeeded in defeating the left wing of the Syrians under Bacchides, but was in turn surrounded and defeated by the right wing. All hope of escape being cut off, Judas surrounded himself with his best warriors and fell at last surrounded by heaps of slain foes. Strange to say the Syrians surrendered his body to Simon and Jonathan his brother, who buried him by his father's side at Modin.

The death of Judas for the moment paralyzed the revolutionary movement, while it increased the determination of the Syrians. All previous privileges were revoked, and the Maccabaean sympathizers were rigorously persecuted. But all this served only to bind the party closer together, and the chief command was conferred on Jonathan, the youngest brother, as daring as, and perhaps more crafty than, Judas. He plunged into the wilderness, relieved himself of the burden of the women and children, and when the latter under the care of John, his brother, were exterminated by the Amri, he took bloody vengeance on them. Surprised by Bacchides, the Syrian general, he inflicted great losses on the latter and escaped across the Jordan. The death of the traitor Alcimus, in 160 BC, for a while relieved the situation and the strength of the Maccabaeans rapidly grew. A second campaign of Bacchides proved fruitless against the daring and cunning of Jonathan and Simon, and they succeeded in making peace with the Syrians (*Ant*, XIII, i, 5, 6), but the citadel of Jerus and other strongholds remained in the hands of the enemy. The events of the year 153 BC however changed the entire aspect of affairs. Demetrius saw his throne menaced by Alexander Balas, a Rom favorite. Trying to secure the aid of the Maccabees, he greatly extended the former concessions, and when Balas outstripped him in generosity and appointed Jonathan high priest with practically royal powers, the Maccabees craftily played out the one against the other. Since the death of Alcimus the high-priesthood had now been vacant for seven years (*Ant*, XIII, ii, 3); for which reason the appointment was exceedingly gratifying to the Jews. In his extremity, Deme-

4. Jonathan, 160–143 BC

THE ASMONEAN FAMILY-TREE

- Asamonaeus (Hashmon)
  - Simeon
    - John
      - MATTATHIAS
        - John
        - SIMON 143–135
          - Judas
          - JOHN HYRCANUS 135–105
            - ARISTOBULUS 104
            - Antigonus
            - ALEXANDER JANNAEUS 104–78 = wife ALEXANDRA 78–69
              - HYRCANUS II 63–40
                - Alexandra, wife of Alexander
              - ARISTOBULUS II 69–63
                - Alexander
                  - Mariamne, wife of Herod
                  - Aristobulus
                - ANTIGONUS 40–37
            - Two sons
          - Mattathias
          - Daughter, wife of Ptolemaeus, governor of Jericho (1 Macc **16** 11)
        - JUDAS (MACCABAEUS) 166–160
        - Eleazar
        - Jonathan 160–143

trius offered the practical equivalent of independence, but the Maccabees had learned the value of these promises by bitter experience. The shrewdness of Jonathan led him to turn a cold shoulder to all the fine promises of Demetrius and to intrust his fortunes to Balas, and not in vain, for the former died in battle with the latter (*Ant*, XIII, ii, 4). Jonathan excelled all his brothers in craft and ever embraced the most promising side, as is evident from his relations with Ptolemy Philometer, Balas and Demetrius. When the latter's cause was embraced in 148 BC by Apollonius, governor of Syria, Jonathan revealed the true Maccabaean military genius, by gaining a signal victory over him. Balas now gave the long-coveted permission to break down the old Syrian tower at Jerus, which for so long had been a thorn in the sides of the Maccabaeans. Alas, during the siege both Balas and Philometer died and Demetrius breathed vengeance against Jonathan. But the latter dexterously won over the king by large presents (*Ant*, XIII, iv, 9) and accepted the restricted liberties offered. Profiting however by the endless cabals of the Syrian court, he soon sided with Tryphon, the new claimant, and with the aid of his brother Simon extended the Maccabaean power over nearly all Pal. In the next Syrian war he gained an almost miraculous victory over the enemy (*Ant*, XIII, v, 7; 1 Macc **11** 67 ff). Tired of the endless struggle and longing for a strong arm to lean on, like Judas, he sought a renewal of the Rom alliance, but never saw its realization. Tryphon, who feared him, treacherously made him prisoner at Ptolemais; all his followers were immediately killed and he himself subsequently executed at Basca in Coele-Syria (*Ant*, XIII, vi, 2, 6).

5. Simon, 143–135 BC

Thus again the Maccabees faced a great crisis. But Simon, the sole survivor of the sons of Mattathias, now stepped in the breach, foiled all the treacherous plans of Tryphon, met strategy with strategy, renewed the alliance with Demetrius and obtained from him the high-priesthood. All the old privileges were renewed, the alliance with Tryphon was condoned by the king, and the Maccabees resolved to count this era as the beginning of their true freedom (1 Macc **13** 41). The hated stronghold of Gazara fell and last of all the citadel of Jerus was reduced, and even the hill, on which it had stood, was completely leveled in the following three years (*Ant*, XIII, vi, 7). Simon, favored by the decadence of the Syrian power, brought the rule of the Maccabaeans to the zenith of its glory. The only considerable architectural work undertaken in the whole period was the magnificent tomb of the Asmoneans at Modin, built by Simon, which was visible even from the Mediterranean. He was the first of the Maccabees to strike his own coinage, maintained himself, with the aid of his sons, John and Judas, against the new Syrian pretender, Antiochus Sidetes, 139 BC, but fell at last a victim to the treachery of his own son-in-law, Ptolemaeus (Ptolemy, 1 Macc **16** 11) at a banquet prepared for him (135 BC). His wife and sons, Mattathias and Judas, were made captives at the same time (*Ant*, XIII, vii, 4; *BJ*, I, ii, 3).

6. John Hyrcanus, 135–105 BC

John succeeded his father both as prince and high priest, and his long reign displayed all the characteristics of the true Maccabees. The older sources here are lost sight of, and nearly all we know is derived from Jos. The reign of John Hyrcanus started amid great difficulties. Hardly was Ptolemaeus disposed of before Antiochus appeared before Jerus with a strong army and closely invested it. In a truce with the king, Hyrcanus obtained as favorable conditions as possible, paid a ransom and had to permit the razing of the city wall. To obtain money he opened and spoiled the tomb of David (*Ant*, XIII, viii, 4) and thus obtained a standing army for the defence of the country. With this army he accompanied the king to the Parthian war, in which Antiochus was killed. Hyrcanus now threw off the Syrian yoke and began a war of conquest. In a quick campaign he conquered the trans-Jordanic territory, destroyed Samaria and its temple and devastated the land of Idumaea, whose people were now embodied in the Jewish commonwealth by an enforced circumcision (*Ant*, XIII, ix, 1). By an embassy, the third in the Asmonean history, he made an alliance with Rome. Meanwhile a strong partisan spirit had been aroused against him at home, on account of his leaving the party of the Pharisees, to affiliate himself with that of the Sadducees, their bitter enemies. Thus the men who had been the very core of the Maccabaean revolt from the beginning now raised a sedition against him. The hagiocratic view of Jewish life, from the start, had been the essence of the Asmonean movement and, as the years rolled on, the chasm between the two great parties in Israel grew ever wider. The break with the Pharisees seemed like a break with all Asmonean antecedents. The core of the trouble lay in the double power of Hyrcanus, who, against the Pharisaic doctrine, combined in one person both the royal and priestly dignities. And as the Pharisees grew in strength they also grew in reverence for the traditions of the fathers, whilst the Sadducees paid attention only to the written testimony, and besides were very liberal in their views in general. Only the immense popularity of Hyrcanus enabled him to weather this storm. After a reign of nearly three decades he died in peace, envied for three things—the possession of the supreme power in Israel, the possession of the high-priesthood and the gift of prophecy (*Ant*, XIII, x, 7).

7. A Dying House, 105–37 BC

With John Hyrcanus the glory of the Maccabaean house passed away. What remains is only the sad tale of outward and inward decay. The period covered is only six or seven decades. Knowing his family, Hyrcanus had nominated his wife to the supreme power, while Aristobulus, his oldest son, was to take the high-priesthood. But the latter was no sooner installed in this office than he threw off the mask, assumed the royal title, imprisoned and starved to death his mother and incarcerated his three youngest brothers, leaving at liberty only Antigonus, whom he soon after caused to be murdered in a frenzy of jealousy of power (*Ant*, XIII, xi, 1,2,3). Shortly after this he died of an intestinal disease, little lamented by his people. His childless widow elevated the oldest of the surviving sons of Hyrcanus, Jannaeus Alexander, to the throne and married him. This man began his reign with the murder of one of his remaining brothers and, following the example of his father, affiliated himself with the party of the Sadducees. Involved in bitter wars, which arose on every hand, he proved that the old military genius of the Maccabees had not wholly perished. When the Pharisees aroused a widespread sedition against him, he crushed the movement in a torrent of blood (*Ant*, XIII, xiv, 2). In the internecine war that followed, he killed some 50,000 of his own people and was practically an exile from his own city and government. Ruling only by brute force, he made the last years of his reign dark and gloomy. Jos touches but lightly on the bitter events of this sedition, on both sides marked with great barbarity (*Ant*, XIII, xiv, 2).

Though suffering from an incurable form of quartan fever, he waged war to the last and died during the siege of Ragaba. On his deathbed he advised his queen to cast herself upon the mercy of the Pharisees: a wise counsel as the event proved, for she was permitted to retain the crown and to place her son Hyrcanus in the high-priestly office. Thus she ruled for nine years (78–69 BC). On her death, her son Aristobulus, whom she had kept from public affairs and who espoused the cause of the Sadducees, aspired to the crown. Another internecine war resulted, in which Aristobulus was victorious. Hyrcanus agreed, for a large financial consideration, to leave public affairs entirely alone. The Herodian family, which owed everything to the Maccabees (*Ant*, XIV, i, 3), now appears on the scene. Antipater, a friend of Hyrcanus, induced him to escape to Aretas, king of Arabia, at Petra, with whom he made an alliance. In the ensuing war, Aristobulus was conquered, shut up in Jerus and compelled to invoke the aid of the Romans, with whose assistance the Arabs were repelled (*Ant*, XIV, ii, 3). In this same year Pompey came to Damascus, where he found himself between three fires, for not only the two brothers, but a large hagiocratic party of Pharisees as well clamored for a hearing. This last party refused both Aristobulus and Hyrcanus as rulers. Through the machinations of Antipater, Pompey sided with Hyrcanus, upon which Aristobulus prepared for war. Pompey promptly marched on Jerus and the irresolute Aristobulus met him with promises of subjection and presents. When his followers however refused to carry out these promises, Aristobulus was imprisoned and Pompey at once invested Jerus, which was taken by assault on the passover of 63 BC, after a siege of three months. Pompey entered the holiest place of the temple, thus forever estranging the Pharisaic party from Rome. But he did not spoil the temple, and appointed Hyrcanus high priest. This event marks the collapse of the Maccabaean power. What follows are only the throes of death. Aristobulus, and his two sons, Alexander and Antigonus, were taken to Rome as prisoners. On the way Alexander escaped and renewed the fruitless struggle in Judaea, only to be at once crushed by the Rom general Gabinius. A little later both Aristobulus and Antigonus also escaped. Returning to the homeland, the former, like his son, fought a brief and valiant but fruitless campaign and was returned captive to Rome, where he died by poison, on the eve of beginning service under the Rom standards, 49 BC. Alexander was executed at Antioch by Pompey. Of all the Maccabaean princes thus only Antigonus and Hyrcanus remained. The Idumaean power was now about to supplant the Maccabaean. Herod the son of Antipater sided, as his father had done, with Hyrcanus against Antigonus. The factional disturbances at Rome and throughout the empire permitted of the enactment of the last stage of the Asmonean drama, in the final contest of Hyrcanus and Antigonus. Herod was in Judaea with Hyrcanus, when Antigonus with the Parthian hordes overran the country, caused Herod precipitately to evacuate Pal, and after capturing Jerus in 40 BC, sent his uncle Hyrcanus as a captive to the East, after having cropped off his ears, to incapacitate him forever for the high-priestly office (*Ant*, XIV, xiii, 10). Herod now obtained the aid of the Romans and permission to reconquer Judaea. In a furious campaign, marked by the most shocking barbarities, he occupied the greater part of the country, and finally in 37 BC succeeded in taking Jerus. Antigonus surrendered but was executed at Antioch by Antony, at the instigation of Herod (*Ant*, XIV, xvi, 4). The fate of the remnants of the Maccabaean stem, at the hands of Herod, may be found by consulting the article under MACCABEES.

HENRY E. DOSKER

ASNAH, as′na (אַסְנָה, *'aṣnāh,* "thornbush"): One of the Nethinim, who returned with Zerubbabel from the exile (Ezr **2** 50).

ASNAPPER, as-nap′ẽr. See OSNAPPAR.

ASOCHIS, a-sō′kis, **PLAIN OF.** See CANA OF GALILEE.

ASOM, ā′som (**Ἀσόμ,** H, *Asóm*) = Hashum (Ezr **10** 33): The sons of A. put away their "strange wives" (1 Esd **9** 33).

ASP (פֶּתֶן, *pethen* [Dt **32** 33; Job **20** 14.16; Isa **11** 8]; **ἀσπίς,** *aspís* [Rom **3** 13]): Any poisonous snake, or even poisonous snakes in general, would satisfy the context in all the passages cited. *Pethen* is also tr[d] ADDER (q.v.) in Ps **58** 4; **91** 13. Most authors have supposed the Egyp cobra (*Naia haje,* L.) to be the snake meant, but while this is widely distributed throughout Africa, its occurrence in Southern Pal seems to rest solely on the authority of Canon Tristram, who did not collect it. There are other poisonous snakes in Pal, any one of which would satisfy the requirements of these passages. See SERPENT. While the *aspis* of classical Gr lit. may well have been the Egyp cobra, it is to be noted that *Vipera aspis,* L., is confined to central and western Europe.

Asp.

ALFRED ELY DAY

ASPALATHUS, as-pal′a-thus (**ἀσπάλαθος,** *aspálathos*): An aromatic plant mentioned in Ecclus **24** 15 AV, where "wisdom" says, "I gave a sweet smell like cinnamon and aspalathus," etc. It would appear, from a reference in Pliny, to have been a prickly shrub, the wood of which was scented, but nothing certain is known about it.

ASPATHA, as-pā′tha (אַסְפָּתָא, *'aṣpāthā'*): One of the ten sons of Haman (Est **9** 7) (Pers *aspadâta,* "given by a sacred horse," acc. to *Thesaurus,* Add. 71, after Pott and Benfey).

ASPHALT, as′falt. See SLIME.

ASPHAR, as′fär, **THE POOL** (**λάκκος Ἀσφάρ,** *lákkos Asphár*): When Jonathan and Simon fled from Bacchides they encamped by this pool in the wilderness of Tekoa (1 Macc **9** 33; *Ant,* XIII, i, 2). It is probably identical with *Ez-Za'ferāneh,* a ruined site with an ancient cistern, to the S. of Tekoa, and E. of *Ḥalḥūl*. *Bîr Selhub* about 6 miles S.W. of *'Ain Jidy* is favored by some (*EB,* s.v.), the hills around it being known as *Ṣafrā,* in which there may be a survival of the old name.

ASPHARASUS, as-far′a-sus (**Ἀσφάρασος,** *Aspháraso*s = Mispar [Ezr **2** 2; Mispereth, Neh **7** 7]): A leader of the captives, who returned with Zerubbabel to Jerus (1 Esd **5** 8).

ASRIEL, as'ri-el (אַשְׂרִיאֵל, *'asrī'ēl,* "Vow of God"?): A man of Manasseh (Nu **26** 31; Josh **17** 2). The form Asrielites, i.e. family of Asriel, occurs in Nu **26** 31. According to 1 Ch **7** 14, Asriel was born to Manasseh by an Aramitess concubine. AV has "Ashnel."

ASS, as (חֲמוֹר or חֲמֹר, *ḥămōr,* cf Arab. *ḥamār,* apparently connected with Arab. root *'aḥmar,* "red," but referred by some to root *hamal,* "to carry"; also, but less commonly, both in Heb and in Arab., אָתוֹן, *'āthōn,* Arab. *'atan,* used in Arab. only of the females; פֶּרֶה, *pereh,* or פֶּרֶא, *pere',* and עֲרָד, *'ărādh,* or עָרוֹד *'ārōdh,* Arab. *'ard,* "wild ass," and also עַיִר, *'ayir,* Arab. *'aīr,* "a young" or "wild ass"): The name *'ārōdh* (Job **39** 5) is rare; ὄνος, *ónos* (Mt **21** 2).

1. Names

(1) *Ḥămōr* is derived from the root which means, in all probability, "to carry a burden" (see Fürst, *Handwörterbuch,* חמר ii), or "heap up." While no analogies are contained in the OT this root occurs in New Heb. The Aram. חֲמַר, *ḥamēr,* means "to make a ruin-heap" (from which the noun *ḥămōr,* "a heap," used in Jgs **15** 16 in a play of words:

2. Meaning

Asses at a Mill.

"With the jawbone of an ass, heaps upon heaps, with the jawbone of an ass have I smitten a thousand men"). The root may also mean "to be red." In this case the nominal form *ḥămōr* may have been derived from the reddish-brown skin of a certain type of the ass.

(2) *'Āthōn,* Assyr *'atânu* and Aram. אֲתָנָא, *'atānā',* is derived from אֲתָא, *'āthā',* "to come," "go," etc (Fürst suggests that it may be derived from אֲתַן, *'āthan,* Aram. עֲדַן, *'ādhan,* "to be slender," "docile," etc); אֲתֹנוֹת צְחוֹרוֹת, *'ăthōnōth çᵉḥōrōth,* "red-white asses" (Jgs **5** 10) designates a better breed.

(3) *'Ayir,* Arab. *'airu* ("male ass") used of the young and vigorous animal, is derived from the root עִיר, "to go away," "escape through swiftness" (Hommel, *Namen der Säugethiere,* 121–23). This name is used as a parallel to בְּנֵי אֲתֹנוֹ, *bᵉnī 'ăthōnō* (Gen **49** 11) and as a compound of עַיִר פֶּרֶא, *'ayir pere'* (Job **11** 12), "a wild ass's colt."

(4) *Pere',* "wild ass," is derived from the root which means "to run," suggestive of the animal's swiftness.

(5) *'Ārōdh,* is, in all probability, an Aram. loan-word for the Heb *pere'.* The Tg uses עֲרוֹדָא, *'ărōdhā'* and עֲרָדָא, *'ărādhā'.*

3. Uses

From the references to these various names in the OT it is clear that (1) *ḥămōr* was used for riding purposes: (*a*) by men (2 S **16** 2; **17** 23; **19** 26; 1 K **2** 40; **13** 13.23.24.27); (*b*) by women (Ex **4** 20; Josh **15** 18; Jgs **1** 14; 1 S **25** 20.23.42; cf 2 Ch **28** 15). צֶמֶד חֲמֹרִים, *çemedh ḥămōrīm,* "a pair of asses" was used for riding as well as for burdens (Jgs **19** 3.10.19.21, etc). (2) It was also used in tillage (Isa **32** 20). In this connection the law prohibits the use of an ass in plowing with an ox (Dt **22** 10). The she-ass (*'āthōn*) was used as a beast of burden (Gen **45** 23) and for riding (Jgs **5** 10; Nu **22** 21.22; 2 K **4** 24). The *'ayir* is also referred to as used in riding (Jgs **10** 4), carrying (Isa **30** 6) and tilling (ver 24).

4. As a Domestic Animal

Besides the use of the ass in agriculture and riding it was employed in the caravans of commerce, and sent even upon long expeditions through the desert. The ass is and always has been one of the most common domestic animals. It is a much more important animal in Bible lands than in England and America. The humblest peasant owned his own ass. It is associated throughout the Bible with peaceful pursuits (Gen **42** 26 f; **22** 3; 1 S **16** 20; 2 S **19** 26; Neh **13** 15), whereas the horse is referred to in connection with war and armies. Reference is also made to the use of the flesh of the ass in time of famine (2 K **6** 25). The origin of the ass like that of most domestic animals is lost in antiquity and it cannot be confidently stated from what species of wild ass it was derived. There are three races of wild asses in Asia, one of which is found in Syria, but they may all be referred to one species, *Equus hemionus.* The African species is *E. asinus,* and good authorities consider our domestic asses to have descended from this, and to have been introduced at an early period into the entire Orient. The *Ṣulaib* Arabs of the Syrian desert, who have no horses, have a famous breed of swift and hardy grey asses which they assert they cross at intervals with the wild asses of the desert. It is not unlikely that domestic asses like dogs are the result of crosses with more than one wild species.

As a domestic animal it preceded the horse, which was first introduced into Egypt by the Hyksos about 1800 BC. See HORSE.

5. Figurative Uses in the OT

(1) חֲמוֹר גָּרֶם, *ḥămōr gārem,* "an ass of strong bones," is used metaphorically of Issachar (Gen **49** 14); בְּשַׂר חֲמוֹר, *bᵉsar ḥămōr,* "the genital organ of an ass," is used in contempt (Ezk **23** 20); קְבוּרַת חֲמוֹר, *ḳᵉbhūrath ḥămōr,* "the burial of an ass," is applied to ignominious treatment of a corpse (Jer **22** 19); *ḥămōr* is used as a symbol of peace and humility (2 S **19** 26). Zechariah speaks of the future Messiah as "lowly, and riding upon an ass, even upon a colt the foal of an ass" (Zec **9** 9; cf Mt **21** 5.7).

(2) *Pere'* is used as a symbol of wildness (Hos **8** 9), and פֶּרֶא אָדָם, *pere' 'ādhām,* 'a wild ass of a man' (Gen **16** 12), referring to Ishmael, designates a free nomad. In Job the name *pere'* is applied to the desert dwellers (Job **24** 5). Jeremiah employs this name as a symbol of lust. He compares Israel's love of idolatry to the lust of the wild ass (Jer **2** 24).

6. Wider Use in Literature

The ass (*'āthōn*) figures prominently in the Balaam story (Nu **22**; 2 Pet **2** 16. See Gray, *ICC,* "Numbers," ad loc.). It is interesting to note that Apion charged the Jews that they "placed an ass's head in their holy place," affirming that "this was discovered when Antiochus Epiphanes spoiled our temple, and found that ass's head there made of gold, and worth a great deal of money." Jos, refuting this absurdity, states that the Rom conquerors of Judaea found nothing in the temple "but what was agreeable to the strictest piety." He goes on to say: "Apion ought to have had a regard to these facts. . . . . As for us Jews, we ascribe no honor or power to asses, as do the Egyptians to crocodiles and asps. . . . . Asses are the same with us which they are with other wise men; viz. creatures that bear the burdens that we lay upon them" (*CAp*, II, 7).

LITERATURE.—G. A. Smith, *Jerusalem*, I, 307 ff; Gesenius' and Fürst's Lexicons to the OT; arts. in *EB* and *HDB*.

SAMUEL COHON

ASSALIMOTH, a-sal'i-moth. See SALIMOTH (Apoc).

ASSAMIAS, a-sa-mī'as (B, **'Ασσαμίας,** *Assamías;* A, **'Ασαμίας,** *Asamías;* AV **Assanias**; cf Hashabiah [Ezr **8** 24]): A. (chief priest) returned with Ezra to Jerus. He was one of twelve who had charge of the silver, gold and the temple-vessels (1 Esd **8** 54).

ASSAPHIOTH, a-sā'fi-oth (A, **'Ασαφφιώθ,** *Asaphphiōth;* B, **'Ασσαφειώθ,** *Assapheiōth;* AV **Azaphion**): The head of a family, which returned with Zerubbabel from captivity, called also the servants of Solomon (1 Esd **5** 33). Probably the same as Hassophereth of Ezr **2** 55 and Sophereth of Neh **7** 57.

ASSARION, as-ā'ri-on. See FARTHING.

ASSASSINATION, a-sas-i-nā'shun: The language of Scripture distinguishes less clearly than the modern juridical between assassination and murder. "Murderer" = רֹצֵחַ, *rōçē^aḥ* (Nu **35** 16–19.21.30.31; 2 K **6** 32; Job **24** 14); הֹרֵג, *hōrēgh*, from הָרַג, *hāragh* = "to slay," "kill," AV tr "murderer" in Hos **9** 13; but "slayer" in Ezk **21** 11. Where the RV renders "slayers," we find רָצַח, *rāçaḥ*, in Nu **35** 11.25–28; Dt **4** 42; **19** 3.4.6; Josh **20** 3.5.6; **21** 13.21.27.32.38, irrespective of whether wilful, deliberate killing is spoken of, or hasty or merely accidental; and נָכָה, *nākhāh* = "to strike," "wound," "kill," "slay," in Nu **35** 24. The prohibition against killing is all-inclusive, even to suicide, placing the ban not only on deliberate, purposeful slaying (Ex **21** 12.14.18), but on all endangering of life through negligence (Dt **22** 8) or recklessness (Lev **19** 14) or hatred, anger and revengefulness (Lev **19** 17 ff).

1. Meaning of the Term

The Mosaic law presupposes the punishment of all killing of human beings on the ground of Gen **9** 6, and repeatedly reiterates it (Ex **21** 12.14 ff; Lev **24** 17.21; Nu **35** 33; Dt **19** 11 ff), the reason assigned being that man is made in the image of God; hence to slay a man is paramount to lifting the hand against the Creator. And while the degrees of guilt are not indicated by the language, they are closely distinguished by the punishments prescribed. Not only notorious enmity against the slain and deliberate lying-in-wait on the part of the murderer (Ex **21** 13; Nu **35** 20 ff; Dt **19** 4.11), but also the nature of the instrument was taken into account to determine the nature of the crime (Nu **35** 16 ff). See CRIMES.

2. Punishment of the Act

FRANK E. HIRSCH

ASSASSINS, a-sas'inz (**σικάριοι,** *sicárioi;* AV **murderers**): Jos (*BJ*, II, xiii, 3, xvii) relates that "there sprang up in Jerus a class of robbers called Sicarii, who slew men in the daytime, and in the midst of the city. This they did chiefly when they mingled with the populace at the festivals, and, hiding short daggers in their garments, stabbed with them those that were their enemies. The first to be assassinated by them was Jonathan the high priest, and after him many were slain daily" (see also *Ant*, XX, viii, 6, ix). The name is derived from Lat *sīca*, "a dagger." The *sicarioi* were implacable in their hatred to Rome and to those Jews who were suspected of leaning toward Rome. They took a leading part in the Jewish rebellion and in the disturbance previous to it, and also in the faction quarrels during the war. After the war they continued their nefarious practices in Egypt and Cyrene whither they had fled.

Lysias mistook Paul for 'the Egyptian who . . . . led out into the wilderness the 4,000 men of the *sicarioi*' (Acts **21** 38). S. F. HUNTER

ASSAULT, a-sôlt' (צוּר, *çūr;* **ὁρμή,** *hormḗ*): The Heb verbal form is used of pressing forward a siege (see SIEGE), but also of a hostile attack upon a person then tr[d] "assault" (Est **8** 11). The Gr word *hormḗ* used of an attack upon persons in Acts **14** 5 (AV) is rendered "onset" in RV. The word "assault" remains in Acts **17** 5, of attacking the house of Jason in Thessalonica, where the verb is *ephistánai*, "to come suddenly upon."

ASSAY, a-sā' (יָאַל, *yā'al;* נָסָה, *nāṣāh;* **πειράζειν,** *peirázein;* **πειρᾶσθαι,** *peirásthai;* **πεῖραν λαμβάνειν,** *peîran lambánein*): The Heb and Gr words which are rendered in AV "assay" are so rendered in RV, and the use of it is extended in RV in two additional cases. The Heb word *yā'al* (1 S **17** 39) is used of David clad in Saul's armor, who "assayed," that is, "tried unsuccessfully," to go and attack Goliath in it, for "he had not proved it," where *nāṣāh* is the vb. In Dt **4** 34 and Job **4** 2 *nāṣāh* is rendered "assay," in the sense of "attempt," "venture." In Acts **16** 7 St. Paul is said to have "assayed," that is, "attempted" (but was hindered), to go into Bithynia, and now in Acts **24** 6 St. Paul is charged with having "assayed," that is, "having had the audacity," to profane the temple, where *peirazein* is the vb. used in both cases. In Acts **9** 26, and now in RV Acts **26** 21, "assay," renders the vb. *peirasthai*, "to attempt," in both cases unsuccessfully. In He **11** 29 it translates two Gr words *peiran lambanein* "to make an attempt unsuccessfully." T. NICOL

ASSEMBLIES, a-sem'bliz, **MASTERS OF** (בַּעֲלֵי אֲסֻפּוֹת, *ba'ălē 'ăṣuppōth*, Eccl **12** 11): ARVm "collectors of sentences," thus *Kimḥi*, Grotius and others. This has been variously interpreted. Tyler translates "editors of collections." Kleinert renders "protectors of the treasure-chambers," *'ăṣuppōth* being considered equivalent to the *'ăṣuppīm* of 1 Ch **26** 15.17; Neh **12** 25 (see ASUPPIM). The proverbs are like nails guarding the sacred storehouse, the book closing with this warning against touching the collection (cf Rev **22** 18.19). Delitzsch translates "like fastened nails which are put together in collections." "As *ba'ălē b^erīth* (Gen **14** 13) signifies 'the confederates,' *ba'ălē sh^ebhū'āh* (Neh **6** 18) 'the sworn,' and the frequently occurring *ba'ălē hā-'īr* 'the citizens': so *ba'ălē 'ăṣuppōth* means, the possessors of assemblies and of the assembled themselves, or the possessors of collections and of things collected. Thus *ba'ălē 'ăṣuppōth* will be a designation of the 'words of the wise' (as in *shālīshīm*, "choice men" = choice proverbs, Prov **22** 20, in a certain measure personified), as of those which form or constitute collections and which stand together in order and rank" ("Eccl," *ET*, 434).

The Jerus Talm takes *'ăṣuppōth* as the Sanhedrin.

On the whole it is better to interpret the phrase "persons skilled in collections" of wise sayings, grouped in a compact whole (cf Wright, *Eccl*, 102).

S. F. Hunter

ASSEMBLY, a-sem′bli (קָהָל, *ḳāhāl;* **ἐκκλησία,** *ekklēsía*): The common term for a meeting of the people called together by a crier. It has reference therefore to any gathering of the people called for any purpose whatsoever (Ex **12** 6; Ps **22** 16 AV; **89** 7 AV; Acts **19** 32.41). The solemn assemblies of the Jews were their feasts or religious gatherings of any kind (Isa **1** 13). The word *panḗguris*, "a general festal assembly" (Heb **12** 23), is transferred from the congregation of the people of Israel to the Christian church of which the congregation of Israel was a figure. In the same passage, *ekklēsia* has the sense of calling, summoning. In classical Gr *ekklēsia* was the name for the body of free citizens summoned by a herald. In this sense the church calls all the world to become identified with it. It denotes the whole body of believers, all who are called. Or it may refer to a particular congregation or local church (*sunagōgḗ*, "synagogue" Jas **2** 2 RVm). See Called; Church; Congregation.

Jacob W. Kapp

ASSEMBLY, SOLEMN. See Congregation; Feasts.

ASSENT, a-sent′: Twice used in AV as equivalent to "voice," and to "consent," and displaced in both instances in the RV by the lit. rendering of the Heb *peh*, "mouth" (2 Ch **18** 12); and the Gr *suntithēmi*, "agree to," i.e. "affirm" (Acts **24** 9).

ASSESSOR, a-ses′ẽr: Lit. one who sits by another, an assistant; among the ancients esp. an assistant to the king (cf "The assessor of his throne," Dryden, Milton's *P.L.*, Bk vi), or to the judge (see Dryden, Virgil's *Aeneid*, vi.583). Later it came to mean one who assesses people or property for purposes of taxation.

(1) Royal officials in Israel have the general title *sārīm*, "princes," and this general title included the officer who was "over the tribute," who seems to have had charge of the assessment, as well as the collection of taxes. In the days of the later monarchy "the governor of the royal household," "the royal steward and high chamberlain," seems to have held some such important position (Isa **22** 15; **36** 3.22).

(2) The early kings do not seem to have subjected the people to heavy taxes, but we find much in the prophets about the injustice and extortion practised by these officials on the poor of the land (cf Am **2** 6.7; Isa **5** 8; Jer **5** 28; Mic **3** 11). Special taxes seem to have been imposed to meet emergencies (cf 2 K **23** 35), but it is not clear that anything of the nature of a regular land tax, or property tax, existed in early times; though something of the kind may be referred to in the reward promised by Saul to the slayer of Goliath (1 S **17** 25) and the tenth mentioned in 1 S **8** 15–17. The kings of Judah, it would seem, made free use of the temple treasures.

(3) Later the Rom government "farmed out" the taxes of the provinces. The publicans, or tax-gatherers of the Gospels, seem to have been agents of the imperial procurator of Judaea, instead of direct agents of the great Rom financial companies, who ordinarily let out the business of the collection of the taxes to officers of their own.

During the Empire there was ample imperial machinery provided for the regular collection of the taxes, and the emperor appointed a procurator in each province whose business it was to supervise the collection of revenue. Some Jews found the business profitable, but these were objects of detestation to their countrymen. See Publican.

Geo. B. Eager

ASSHUR, ash′o͞or, **ASSUR,** as′o͞or. See Assyria.

ASSHURIM, a-sho͞o′rim (אַשּׁוּרִים, *'ashshūrīm*): Mentioned among the sons of Dedan, son of Jokshan, son of Abraham by Keturah (Gen **25** 3).

ASSIDAEANS, as-i-dē′ans. See Hasidaeans (Apoc).

ASSIDUOUS, a-sid′ū-us: Occurs only in Wisd **8** 18 RV, "In assiduous communing with her is understanding," i.e. "in continued exercise of fellowship." The idea expressed in the adj. is contained in the prepositional prefix, *sūn* of the original *suggumnasía*, giving the vb. intensive force.

ASSIGN, a-sīn′ (נָתַן, *nāthan*, "to give," or "grant," i.e. apportion): Used (Josh **20** 8) of Moses setting apart Bezer as one of the three cities of refuge on the E. of the Jordan (cf Dt **4** 41–43); also of Joab's stationing Uriah in a place of mortal peril in battle (2 S **11** 16).

ASSIR, as′ẽr (אַסִּיר, *'aṣṣīr*, "captive"):

(1) A Levite of the family of Korah (Ex **6** 24; 1 Ch **6** 22).

(2) A son of Ebiasaph and grandson of Assir. Samuel was descended from him (1 Ch **6** 23).

(3) A son of Jeconiah, king of Judah, according to AV and RVm and ARVm. It is a question whether the Assir of this passage (1 Ch **3** 17) is not a common adj. modifying Jeconiah. The ARV and RV render it "the captive." It is to be noticed, however, that there is no definite art. in the Heb.

ASSOCIATE, a-sō′shi-āt: Only in Isa **8** 9 AV, where the Heb רֹעוּ, *rō'ū*, is variously interpreted, according to differences of opinion as to the vb. whence it comes. RV "make an uproar"; RVm "break"; Vulg "*Congregamini*"; LXX γνῶτε, *gnōte* ("know ye"); Luther: *seid boese* ("be wicked").

ASSOS, as′os (**Ἄσσος,** *Ássos*): An ancient city of Mysia in the Rom province of Asia, at which, according to Acts **20** 13, Paul and Luke rested while on their way from Troas to Mitylene. Standing upon a conical-shaped rock on the southern coast of the Troad, it occupied one of the finest sites in Asia. The rock is about 700 ft. high; its sides are covered with terraces, both natural and artificial, and so steep is it that Stratoricus wrote of it: "If you wish to hasten your death, try and climb Assos." The view from the summit is extensive and magnificent.

The city, which is very ancient, is said to have been founded by the Aeolians, and to have always been singularly Gr. As early as the 5th cent. BC it struck its own coins, and its coinage system continued until 235 AD. One of its early rulers or tyrants was Hermeas, a eunuch, once a slave, who gave his niece in marriage to Aristotle. There the great Gr philosopher lived three years, from 348 to 345 BC. During the time of the kings of Pergamus, the city bore the name of Apollonia. To the Byzantines it was known as Machramion, and at present the town, which has dwindled in importance under Turkish rule, is called Bekhram, a Turkish corruption of the Byzantine name.

The ruins of Assos are among the most imposing in Asia Minor, and yet they have long served as a quarry; from its public buildings the stones for the Constantinople docks were taken. The Turkish sultan Murad II presented the many beautiful bas-reliefs of the Doric temple of Athene to the French government, which are now preserved in the Louvre. The ruins were carefully explored and partially excavated in 1882–83 by Mr. Clarke for the Archaeological Institute of America, and the entire plan of the ancient city is clear. Upon the very summit of the hill stood the temple of Athene which is said to have been erected about 470 BC. Among its ruins Clarke found eight other bas-reliefs which are now in the Boston Museum and which possess a special interest because of their connection between the art of the Orient and of Greece. Upon the several natural terraces of the hill which have been enlarged by artificial means, stood the many public buildings, as the gymnasium, the public treasury, the baths, the market place and the theater, of which but little now remains. The city was surrounded by a double wall which in places is still well preserved. The inner wall of dressed stones laid without mortar, and filled with loose stones, is 8 ft. thick, and the larger outer wall was protected with towers at intervals of 60 ft. The ancient road leading to Troas was well paved. The harbor from which Paul sailed has now been filled up and is covered with gardens, but at its side is the modern harbor protected by an artificial mole, about which are clustered the few houses bearing the name of Bekhram. Upon the summit of the hill, by the ruins of the temple, are cisterns, a Turkish fortress and a Byzantine church which has been converted into a mosque. Without the city walls is a necropolis. Its many sarcophagi of all ages and sizes and shapes are made of the native trachyte stone which, so the ancients believed, possessed the quality of consuming the bodies buried in it. The stone is the famous "Lapis Assius," or the flesh-eating, hence the word sarcophagus. In former times wheat was raised extensively in the fields about Assos, but now valonia, or acorn cups, form the chief article for export. E. J. Banks

ASSUAGE, a-swāj′ (AV **Asswage**): Lit. "sweeten," "soften down"; then, "mitigate," "abate"; used of "flood," Gen **8** 1 ("subside"); of grief, Job **16** 5.6 ("restrain"); also applied to any strong emotion; not used in the NT.

ASSUMPTION, a-sump′shun, **OF MOSES.** See Apocalyptic Literature.

ASSUR, as′ur. See Asur.

ASSURANCE, a-shōōr′ans: A term exceptionally rich in spiritual meaning. It signifies the joyous, unwavering confidence of an intelligent faith; the security of a fearless trust. The original words have to do with the heart of vital religion. בָּטַח, *bāṭaḥ*, "trust"; אָמַן, *'āman*, "to prop," "to support," hence to confide in, to trust. Jesus repeatedly used this word "amen" to express the trustworthiness and abiding certainty of his sayings. πίστις, *pistis*, "faith"; πληροφορία, *plērophoría*, "full assurance." The confidence of faith is based, not on "works of righteousness which we have done" (cf Titus **3** 4.5 AV) but on the high-priesthood and atoning sacrifice of Christ (He **10** 21.22; cf ver 19, "boldness to enter . . . . by the blood of Jesus," AV). Assurance is the soul's apprehension of its complete emancipation from the power of evil and from consequent judgment, through the atoning grace of Christ. It is the exact opposite of self-confidence, being a joyous appropriation and experience of the fulness of Christ—a glad sense of security, freedom and eternal life in Him. This doctrine is of immeasurable importance to the life of the church and of the individual believer, as a life of spiritual doubt and uncertainty contradicts the ideal of liberty in Christ Jesus which is the natural and necessary fruitage of "the washing of regeneration and renewing of the Holy Spirit . . . shed on us abundantly, through Jesus Christ our Saviour." Paul unhesitatingly said, "I know" (2 Tim **1** 12) —a word which, oft-repeated in 1 Jn, furnishes the groundwork of glad assurance that runs through the entire epistle. For the classic passage on "full assurance" see Col **2** 1–10.

Dwight M. Pratt

ASSURBANIPAL, as-ur-bä′ni-pal. See Ashur-bani-pal.

ASSYRIA, a-sir′i-a:

I. Geography
II. Early History
III. Climate and Productions
IV. Population
V. Trade and Law
VI. Art
VII. Mechanics
VIII. Furniture, Pottery and Embroidery
IX. Language, Literature and Science
X. Government and Army
XI. Religion
XII. Excavations
XIII. Chronology
XIV. History
 1. Early Period
 2. The Older Empire
 3. The Second Empire
 4. Last Period and Fall of Empire
Literature

Assyria, a Gr name formed from **Asshur** (אַשּׁוּר, *'ashshūr;* **Ἀσσούρ,** *Assoúr;* Assyr *Assur*): The primitive capital of the country.

I. Geography.—The origin of the city (now *Kala'at Shergat*), which was built on the western bank of the Tigris between the Upper and Lower Zab, went back to pre-Sem times, and the meaning of the name was forgotten (see Gen **2** 14, where the *Hiddekel* or Tigris is said to flow on the eastern side of Asshur). To the N. of the junction of the Tigris and Upper Zab, and opposite the modern *Mossul*, was a shrine of the goddess Istar, around which grew up the town of Nina, Ninua or Nineveh (now *Kouyunjik* and *Nebi Yunus*). Another early sanctuary of Istar was at Urbillu, Arbailu or Arbela, E. of the Upper Zab. N. of Nineveh was Dur-Sargina (now *Khorsabad*) where Sargon built his palace (720 BC). All this district was embraced in the kingdom of Assyria which extended from Babylonia northward to the Kurdish mountains and at times included the country westward to the Euphrates and the Khabur.

II. Early History.—The whole region was known to the early Babylonians as Subartu. Its possession was disputed between Sem *Amurrû* or Amorites (q.v.) and a non-Sem people from the N. called Mitannians. The earlier high priests of Assur known to us bear Mitannian names. About 2500 BC the country was occupied by Bab Semites, who brought with them the religion, law, customs, script and Sem language of Babylonia (Gen **10** 11.12, where we should read "He went forth to Asshur"; see Mic **5** 6). The foundation of Nineveh, Rehoboth-'Ir (Assyr *Rebît-Ali*, "the suburbs of the city"), Calah and Resen (Assyr *Res-eni*, "head of the spring") is ascribed to them. The triangle formed by the Tigris and Zab, which inclosed these cities, was in later times included within the fortifications of the "great city" (Gen **10** 12; Jon **3** 3). Assyria is always distinguished from Babylonia in the OT, and not confounded with it as by Herodotus and other classical writers.

III. Climate and Productions.—Assyria, speaking generally, was a limestone plateau with a temperate climate, cold and wet in winter, but warm during the summer months. On the banks of the rivers there was abundant cultivation, besides pasture-land. The apple of the North grew by the side of the palm-tree of the South. Figs, olives, pomegranates, almonds, mulberries and vines were also cultivated as well as all kinds of grain. Cotton is mentioned by Sennacherib (King, *PSBA*, December, 1909). The forests were tenanted by lions, and the plains by wild bulls (*rîmi*, Heb *re'ēmīm*), wild asses, wild goats and gazelles. Horses were imported from Cappadocia; ducks were kept, and mastiffs were employed in hunting.

IV. Population.—The dominant type was Sem, with full lips, somewhat hooked nose, high forehead, black hair and eyes, fresh complexion and abundance of beard. In character the Assyrians were cruel and ferocious in war, keen traders, stern disciplinarians, and where religion was concerned, intense and intolerant. Like the Ottoman Turks they formed a military state, at the head of which was the king, who was both leader in war and chief priest, and which offered a striking contrast to the theocratic state of the Babylonians. It seems probable that every male was liable to conscription, and under the Second Empire, if not earlier, there was a large standing army, part of which consisted of mercenaries and recruits from the subject races. One result of this was the necessity for constant war in order to occupy the soldiery and satisfy their demands with captured booty; and the result, as in the Northern Kingdom of Israel, was military revolution, with the seizure of the throne by the successful general. As might be expected, education was confined to the upper classes, more especially to the priests and scribes.

V. Trade and Law.—As far back as the age of Abraham, when Assyria was still a dependency of Babylonia, trade was carried on with Cappadocia and an Assyr colony of merchants settled at Kara Eyuk near Kaisariyeh. Down the Euphrates came the silver, copper and bronze of Asia Minor, together with horses. Cedar wood was brought from Mount Amanus, and there was already trade, through Syria, with the Mediterranean. Nineveh itself was probably founded in the interests of the trade with the North. In later days commercial reasons had much to do with the efforts of the Assyr kings to conquer eastern Asia Minor and the Mediterranean coast of Syria and Pal: under the

Bronze Panel from Palace Gate at Balawât.

Second Empire no pains were spared to obtain possession of the Phoen cities and divert their commerce into Assyr hands. Hence the importance of the capture of the Hittite stronghold, Carchemish, by Sargon in 717 BC, as it commanded the road to Syria and the passage across the Euphrates. Nineveh had at that time already become a great resort of merchants, among whom the Sem Aramaeans were the most numerous. Aram., accordingly, became the language of trade, and then of diplomacy (cf 2 K **18** 26), and commercial documents written in cuneiform were provided with Aram. dockets. As in Babylonia, land and houses were leased and sold, money was lent at interest, and the leading firms employed numerous *damgari* or commercial agents.

Assyr law was, in general, derived from Babylonia and much of it was connected with trade. The code of Khammu-rabi (CH) or AMRAPHEL (q.v.) underlay it, and the same system of judicial procedure, with pleading before judges, the hearing of witnesses, and an appeal to the king, prevailed in both countries.

Impression of a Seal Cylinder.

VI. Art.—Unlike Babylonia, Assyria abounded in stone; the brick buildings of Babylonia, accordingly, were replaced by stone, and the painted or tiled walls by sculptured slabs. In the bas-reliefs discovered at Nineveh three periods of artistic progress may be traced. Under Assur-nazir-pal the sculpture is bold and vigorous, but the work is immature and the perspective faulty. From the beginning of the Second Empire to the reign of Esar-haddon the bas-reliefs often remind us of embroidery in stone. Attempts are made to imitate the rich detail and delicate finish of the ivory carvings; the background is filled in with a profusion of subjects, and there is a marked realism in the delineation of them. The third period is that of Assur-bani-pal, when the overcrowding is avoided by once more leaving the background bare, while the animal and vegetable forms are distinguished by a certain softness, if not effeminacy of tone. Sculpture in the round, however, lagged far behind that in relief, and the statuary of Assyria is very inferior to that of Babylonia. It is only the human-headed bulls and winged lions that can be called successful: they were set on either side of a gate to prevent the entrance of evil spirits, and their majestic proportions were calculated to strike the observer with awe (cf the description of the four cherubim in Ezk **1**).

In bronze work the Assyrians excelled, much of the work being cast. But in general it was hammered, and the scenes hammered in relief on the bronze gates discovered by Mr. Rassam at Balawât near Nineveh are among the best examples of ancient oriental metallurgy at present known. Gold and silver were also worked into artistic forms; iron was reserved for more utilitarian purposes. The beautiful ivory carvings found at Nineveh were probably the work of foreign artificers, but gems and seal cylinders were engraved by native artists in imitation of those of Babylonia, and the Bab art of painting and glazing tiles was also practised. The terra-cotta figures which can be assigned to the Assyr period are poor. Glass was also manufactured.

VII. Mechanics.—The Assyrians were skilled in the transport of large blocks of stone, whether sculptured or otherwise. They understood the use of the lever, the pulley and the roller, and they had invented various engines of war for demolishing or undermining the walls of a city or for protecting the assailants. A crystal lens, turned on the lathe, has been found at Kouyunjik: it must have been useful to the scribes, the cuneiform characters inscribed on the tablets being frequently very minute. Water was raised from the river by means of a *shaduf*.

VIII. Furniture, Pottery and Embroidery.—The furniture even of the palace was scanty, consisting mainly of couches, chairs, stools, tables, rugs and curtains. The chairs and couches were frequently of an artistic shape, and were provided with feet in the form of the legs of an ox. All kinds of vases, bowls and dishes were made of earthenware, but they were rarely decorated. Clothes, curtains and rugs, on the other hand, were richly dyed and embroidered, and were manufactured from wool and flax, and (in the age of the Second Empire) from cotton. The rug, of which the Pers rug is the modern representative, was a Bab invention.

IX. Language, Literature and Science.—The Assyr language was Sem, and differed only dialectically from Sem Bab. In course of time, however, differences grew up between the spoken language and the language of lit., which had incorporated many Sumerian words, and retained grammatical terminations that the vernacular had lost, though these differences were never very great. Assyr lit., moreover, was mainly derived from Babylonia. Assur-bani-pal employed agents to ransack the libraries of Babylonia and send their contents to Nineveh, where his library was filled with scribes who busied themselves in copying and editing ancient texts. Commentaries were often written upon these, and grammars, vocabularies and interlinear translations were compiled to enable the student to understand the extinct Sumerian, which had long been the Lat of Sem Babylonia. The writing material was clay, upon which the cuneiform characters were impressed with a stylus while it was still moist: the tablet was afterward baked in the sun or (in Assyria) in a kiln. The contents of the library of Nineveh were very various; religion, mythology, law, history, geography, zoology, philology, mathematics, astronomy, astrology and the pseudo-science of omens were all represented in it, as well as poetry and legendary romance. See NINEVEH, LIBRARY OF.

Assyrian King in His Chariot.

X. Government and Army.—Assyria was a military kingdom which, like the Northern Kingdom of Israel, had established itself by a successful revolt from Babylonia. In contradistinction to Babylonia, which was a theocratic state, the king being subordinate to the priest, the Assyr king was supreme. Whereas in Babylonia the temple was the chief public building, in Assyria the royal palace dominated everything, the temple being merely a royal chapel attached to the palace. The king, in fact, was the commander of an army, and this army was the Assyr people. How far the whole male population was liable to conscription is still uncertain; but the fact that the wars of Assur-bani-pal so exhausted the fighting strength of the nation as to render it unable to resist the invaders from the North shows that the majority of the males must have been soldiers. Hence the constant wars partly to occupy the army and prevent revolts, partly for the sake of booty with which to pay it. Hence too, the military revolutions, which, as in the kingdom of Israel, resulted in changes of dynasty and the seizure of the throne by successful generals. The *turtannu* or commander-in-chief, who took the place of the king when the latter was unable or unwilling to lead his forces, ranked next to the sovereign. From the reign of Tiglath-pileser IV onward, however, the autocracy was tempered by a centralized bureaucracy, and in the provinces a civil governor was appointed by the side of the military commander. Among the high officials at court were the *rab-saki* or "vizier," and the *rab-sa-risi* or "controller," the *rabhṣārīṣ* (RAB SARIS [q.v.]) of the OT.

The army consisted of cavalry, infantry, bowmen and slingers, as well as of a corps of charioteers. After the rise of the Second Empire the cavalry were increased at the expense of the chariotry, and were provided with saddles and boots, while the unarmed groom who had run by the side of the horse became a mounted archer. Sennacherib further clothed the horseman in a coat of mail. The infantry were about ten times as numerous as the cavalry, and under Sargon were divided into bowmen and spearmen, the bowmen again being subdivided into heavy-armed and light-armed, the latter being apparently of foreign origin. Sennacherib introduced a corps of slingers, clad in helmet and cuirass, leather drawers and boots. He also deprived the heavy-armed bowmen of the long robes they used to wear, and established a body of pioneers with double-headed axes, helmets and buskins. Shields were also worn by all classes of soldiers, and the army carried with it standards, tents, battering-rams and baggage-carts. The royal sleeping-tent was accompanied by tents for cooking and dining. No pains, in fact, were spared to make the army both in equipment and discipline an irresistible engine of war. The terror it excited in western Asia is therefore easily intelligible (Isa **10** 5–14; Nah **2** 11–13; **3** 1–4).

XI. Religion.—The state religion of Assyria was derived from BABYLONIA (q.v.) and in its main outlines is Bab. But it differed from the religion of Babylonia in two important respects: (1) the king, and not the high priest, was supreme, and (2) at the head of it was the national god Asur or Assur, whose high priest and representative was the king. Asur was originally Asir, "the leader" in war, who is accordingly depicted as a warrior-god armed with a bow and who in the age when solar worship became general in Babylonia was identified with the sun-god. But the similarity of the name caused him to be also identified with the city of Asur, where he was worshipped, at a time when the cities of northern Babylonia came to be deified, probably under Hittite influence. Later still, the scribes explained his name as a corruption of that of the primeval cosmogonic deity An-sar, the upper firmament, which in the neo-Bab age was pronounced Assōr. The combination of the attributes of the warrior-god, who was the peculiar god of the commander of the army, with the deified city to which the army belonged, caused Assur to become the national deity of a military nation in a way of which no Bab divinity was capable. The army were "the troops of Assur," the enemies were "the enemies of Assur" who required that they should acknowledge his supremacy or be destroyed. Assur was not only supreme over the other gods, he was also, in fact, unlike them, without father or wife. Originally, it is true, his feminine counterpart, Asirtu, the ASHERAH (q.v.) of the OT, had stood at his side, and later literary pedants endeavored to find a wife for him in Belit, "the Lady," or Istar, or some other Bab goddess, but the attempts remained purely literary. When Nineveh took the place of Assur as the capital of the kingdom, Istar, around whose sanctuary Nineveh had grown up, began to share with him some of the honor of worship, though her position continued to be secondary to the end. This was also the case with the war-god Nin-ip, called Mas in Assyria, whose cult was specially patronized by the Assyr kings. See BABYLONIA AND ASSYRIA, RELIGION OF.

XII. Excavations.—Rich, who had first visited Mossul in 1811, examined the mounds opposite in 1820 and concluded that they represented the site of Nineveh. The few antiquities he discovered were contained in a single case in the British Museum, but the results of his researches were not published until 1836. In 1843–45 the Frenchman Botta disinterred the palace of Sargon at Khorsabad, 15 miles N. of Nineveh, while at Nimrud (*Calah*) and Kouyunjik (*Nineveh*) Layard (1845–51) brought to light the ruins of the great Assyr palaces and the library of Assur-bani-pal. His work was continued by Rassam (1851–54). Nothing more was done until 1873–75 when George Smith resumed excavations on the site of Assur-bani-pal's library; this was followed in 1877–79 by the excavations of Rassam, who discovered among other things the bronze gates of Balawât. At present a German expedition under Andrae is working at Kala'at Shergat (Assur) where the English excavators had already found the cylinder-inscription of Tiglath-pileser I (see SHERGAT).

XIII. Chronology.—The Assyrians reckoned time by means of *limmi*, certain officials appointed every New Year's day, after whom their year of office was named. The lists of *limmi* or "Eponyms" which have come down to us form the basis of Assyr chronology. Portions of a "synchronous" history of Assyria and Babylonia have also been discovered, as well as fragments of two "Babylonian Chronicles" written from a Bab point of view. The "Eponym" lists carry back an exact dating of time to the beginning of the 10th cent. BC. Before that period Sennacherib states that Tiglath-pileser I reigned 418 years before himself. Tiglath-pileser, moreover, tells us that Samas-Ramman son of Isme-Dagon had built a temple at Assur 641 years earlier, while Shalmaneser I places Samas-Ramman 580 years before his own reign and Erisu 159 years before Samas-Ramman, though Esar-haddon gives the dates differently. Apart from the native documents, the only trustworthy sources for the chronology (as for the history) of Assyria are the OT records. In return the "Eponym" lists have enabled us to correct the chronology of the BOOKS OF KINGS (q.v.).

XIV. History.—Assyrian history begins with the high priests (*patesis*) of Assur. The earliest known to us are Auspia and Kikia, who bear Mitannian names. The early Sem rulers, however, were subject to Babylonia, and under Khammurabi (AMRAPHEL) Assyria was still a Bab province.

1. Early Period

According to Esar-haddon the kingdom was founded by Bel-bani son of Adasi, who first made himself independent; Hadad-nirari, however, ascribes its foundation to Zulili. Assyr merchants and soldiers had already made their way as far as Cappadocia, from whence copper and silver were brought to Assyria, and an Assyr colony was established at Kara Eyuk near Kaisariyeh, where the Assyr mode of reckoning time by means of *limmi* was in use. In the age of Am Tab (1400 BC) Assur-uballid was king of Assyria. He corresponded with the Egyp Pharaoh and married his daughter to the Bab king, thereby providing for himself a pretext for interfering in the affairs of Babylonia. The result was that his son-in-law was murdered, and Assur-uballid sent troops to Babylonia who put the murderers to death and placed the grandson of the Assyr king on the Bab throne. Babylonia had fallen into decay and been forced to protect herself from the rising power of Assyria by forming an alliance with Mitanni (Mesopotamia) and Egypt, and subsequently, when Mitanni had been absorbed by the Hittites, by practically becoming dependent on the Hittite king. Shalmaneser I (1300 BC), accordingly, devoted himself to crippling the Hittite power and cutting it off from communication with Babylonia. Campaign after campaign was undertaken against the Syrian and more eastern provinces of the Hittite empire, Malatiyeh was destroyed, and Carchemish threatened. Shalmaneser's son and successor Tukulti-Mas entered into the fruits of his father's labors. The Hittites had been rendered powerless by an invasion of the northern barbarians, and the Assyr king was thus left free to crush Babylonia. Babylon was taken by storm, and for seven years Tukulti-Mas was master of all the lands watered by the Tigris and Euphrates. The image of Merodach was carried to Assur as a sign that the scepter had passed from Babylon to the *parvenu* Assyria. A successful revolt, however, finally drove the Assyr conqueror back to his own country, and when he was murdered soon afterward by his own son, the Babylonians saw in the deed a punishment inflicted by the god of Babylon.

A few years later the Assyr king Bel-kudur-uzur lost his life in battle against the Babylonians, and a new dynasty appears to have mounted the Assyr throne. About 1120 BC the Assyr king was Tiglath-pileser I, whose successful wars extended the Assyr empire as far westward as

2. The Older Empire

Cappadocia. In one of his campaigns he made his way to the Mediterranean, and received presents from the king of Egypt, which included a crocodile. At Assur he planted a botanical garden stocked with trees from the conquered provinces. After his death the Assyr power declined; Pitru (Pethor, Nu **22** 5) fell into the hands of the Aramaeans and the road to the Mediterranean was blocked. A revival came under Assur-nazir-pal III (884–860 BC) who rebuilt CALAH (q.v.) and established the seat of the government at Nineveh, where he erected a palace. Various campaigns were carried on in the direction of Armenia and Comagene, the brutalities executed upon the enemy being described in detail by their conqueror. He then turned westward, and after receiving homage from the Hittite king of Carchemish, laid the Phoenicians under tribute. The road to the West was thus again secured for the merchants of Assyria. Assur-nazir-pal was succeeded by his son Shalmaneser II (859–825 BC), who, instead of contenting himself, like his father, with mere raids for the sake of booty, endeavored to organize and administer the countries which his armies had subdued. The famous bronze gates of Balawât were erected by him in commemoration of his victories. In his reign the Israelites and Syrians of Damascus first came into direct relation with the Assyrians. In 854 BC

Assur-bani-pal Hunting.

he attacked Hamath and at Qarqar defeated an army which included 1,200 chariots, 1,200 cavalry and 20,000 infantry from Ben-hadad of Damascus, 2,000 chariots, and 10,000 infantry from "Ahab of Israel," besides considerable contingents from Ammon, Arvad, Arabia and elsewhere. In 842 BC Shalmaneser penetrated to Damascus where Hazael, the successor of Ben-hadad, who had already been defeated in the open field, was closely besieged. The surrounding country was ravaged, and "Jehu son of Omri" hastened to offer tribute to the conqueror. The scene is represented on the Black Obelisk found at Nimrud and now in the British Museum. Shalmaneser's campaigns were not confined to the West. He overran Armenia, where the kingdom of Van had just been established, made his way to Tarsus in Cilicia, took possession of the mines of silver, salt and alabaster in the Taurus mountains among the Tabal or Tubal, and obliged the Bab king to acknowledge his supremacy. In his later days, when too old to take the field himself, his armies were led by the *turtannu* or commander-in-chief, and a rebellion, headed by his son Assur-danin-pal (Sardanapalus) broke out at home, where Nineveh and Assur were jealous of the preference shown for Calah. Nineveh, however, was captured and the revolt suppressed after two years' duration by another son, Samas-Ramman IV, who shortly afterward, on his father's death, succeeded to the throne (824–812 BC). His chief campaigns were directed against Media. His son Hadad-nirari III (811–783 BC) was the next king, whose mother was Sammu-ramat (Semiramis). He claims to have reduced to subjection the whole of Syria, including Phoenicia, Edom and Philistia, and to have taken Mari'a, king of Damascus, prisoner in his capital city. After this, however, Assyria once more fell into a state of decay, from which it was delivered by the successful revolt of a military officer Pulu (Pul), who put an end to the old line of kings and took the name of Tiglath-pileser IV (745–727 BC).

3. The Second Empire

Tiglath-pileser founded the second Assyr empire, and made Assyria the dominant power in western Asia. The army was reorganized and made irresistible, and a new administrative system was introduced, the empire being centralized at Nineveh and governed by a bureaucracy at the head of which was the king. Tiglath-pileser's policy was twofold: to weld western Asia into a single empire, held together by military force and fiscal laws, and to secure the trade of the world for the merchants of Nineveh. These objects were steadily kept in view throughout the reigns of Tiglath-pileser and his successors. For the history of his reign, see TIGLATH-PILESER. In 738 BC Tiglath-pileser put an end to the independent existence of the kingdom of Hamath, Menahem of Samaria becoming his tributary, and in 733 BC he commenced a campaign against Rezin of Damascus which ended in the fall of Damascus, the city being placed under an Assyr governor. At the same time the land of Naphtali was annexed to Assyria, and Yahu-khazi (Ahaz) of Judah became an Assyr vassal, while in 731 BC, after the murder of Pekah, Hoshea was appointed king of Israel (cf 2 K **15-17**). In 728 BC Tiglath-pileser was solemnly crowned at Babylon and the following year he died. His successor was another military adventurer, Shalmaneser IV (727–722 BC), whose original name was Ululā. While engaged in the siege of Samaria Shalmaneser died or was murdered, and the throne was seized by another general who took the name of Sargon (722–705 BC). Sargon, for whose history see SARGON, captured Samaria in 722 BC, carrying 27,290 of its inhabitants into captivity. A large part of his reign was spent in combating a great confederation of the northern nations (Armenia, Mannâ, etc) against Assyria. Carchemish, the Hittite capital, was captured in 717 BC, a revolt of the states in southern Pal was suppressed in 711 BC and Merodach-Baladan, the Chaldaean, who had possessed himself of Babylonia in 722 BC, was driven back to the marshlands at the head of the Pers Gulf. In 705 BC Sargon was murdered, and succeeded by his son SENNACHERIB (q.v.). Sennacherib (705–681 BC) had neither the military skill nor the administrative abilities of his father. His campaign against Hezekiah of Judah in 701 BC was a failure; so, also, was his policy in Babylonia which was in a constant state of revolt against his rule, and which ended in his razing the sacred city of Babylon to the ground in 689 BC. Nine years previously his troops had been called upon to suppress a revolt in Cilicia, where a battle was fought with the Greeks.

4. Last Period and Fall of the Empire

His son Esar-haddon, who succeeded him (681–669 BC) after his murder by two other sons on the 20th Tebet (cf 2 K **19** 37), was as distinguished a general and administrator as his father had been the reverse. For his history see ESAR-HADDON. Under him the Second Empire reached the acme of its power and prosperity. Babylon was rebuilt and made the second capital of the empire, Pal became an obedient province, and Egypt was conquered (674 and

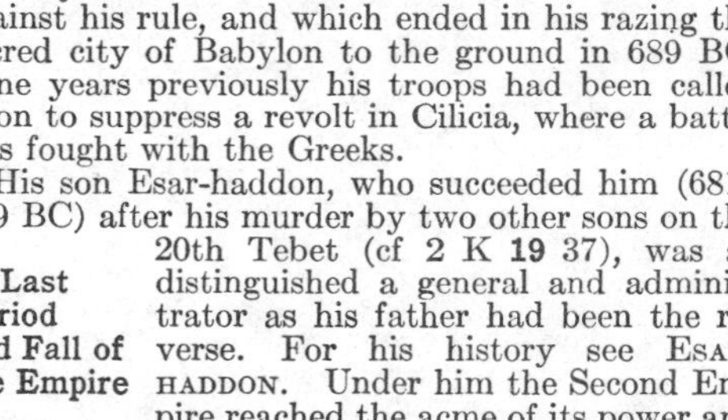

Assur-bani-pal's Account of His Restoration of the Stage-Tower at Nippur.

671 BC), while an invasion of the Cimmerians (Gomer) was repelled, and campaigns were made into the heart of both Media and Arabia. Esar-haddon died while on his way to repress a revolt in Egypt, and his son Assur-bani-pal succeeded him in the empire (669–626 BC), while another son Samas-sum-ukin was appointed viceroy of Babylonia. Assur-bani-pal was a munificent patron of learning, and the library of Nineveh owed most of its treasures to him, but extravagant luxury

had now invaded the court, and the king conducted his wars through his generals, while he himself remained at home. The great palace at Kouyunjik (Nineveh) was built by him. Egypt demanded his first attention. Tirhakah the Ethiopian who had headed its revolt was driven back to his own country, and for a time there was peace. Then under Tandamane, Tirhakah's successor, Egypt revolted again. This time the Assyr punishment was merciless. Thebes—"No-amon" (Nah **3** 8)—was destroyed, its booty carried away and two obelisks transported to Nineveh as trophies of victory. Meanwhile Tyre, which had rebelled, was forced to sue for peace, and ambassadors arrived from Gyges of Lydia asking for help against the Cimmerians. Elam still remained independent and endeavored to stir up disaffection in Babylonia. Against his will, therefore, Assur-bani-pal was obliged to interfere in the internal affairs of that country, with the result that the Elamites were finally overthrown in a battle on the Eulaeus beneath the walls of Susa, and the conquered land divided between two vassal kings. Then suddenly a revolt broke out throughout the greater part of the Assyr empire, headed by Assur-bani-pal's brother, the viceroy of Babylonia. For a time the issue was doubtful. Egypt recovered its independence under Psammetichus, the founder of the XXVIth Dynasty (660 BC) who had received help from Lydia, but Babylonia was reconquered and Babylon after a long siege was starved out, Samas-sum-ukin burning himself in the ruins of his palace. Elam remained to be dealt with, and an Assyr army made its way to Susa, which was leveled to the ground, the shrines of its gods profaned and the bones of its ancient kings torn from their graves. Then came the turn of northern Arabia, where the rebel sheikhs were compelled to submit. But the struggle had exhausted Assyria; its exchequer was empty, and its fighting population killed. When the Cimmerians descended upon the empire shortly afterward, it was no longer in a condition to resist them. Under Assur-etil-ilāni, the son and successor of Assur-bani-pal, Calah was taken and sacked, and two reigns later, Sin-sar-iskun, the last king of Assyria, fell fighting against the Scythians (606 BC). Nineveh was utterly destroyed, never again to be inhabited, and northern Babylonia passed into the hands of Nabopolassar, the viceroy of Babylon, who had joined the northern invaders. Assur, the old capital of the country, was still standing in the age of Cyrus, but it had become a small provincial town; as for Nineveh and Calah, their very sites were forgotten.

LITERATURE.—See G. Rawlinson, *Five Great Monarchies of the Eastern World*, 1862–67; Perrot and Chipiez, *Histoire de l'art dans l'antiquité*, II, 1884; Maspero, *Struggle of the Nations*, and *Passing of the Empires*, 3 vols, 1894–1900; Rogers, *A History of Babylonia and Assyria*, 1900; Johns, *Assyr Deeds and Documents*, 1898; Schrader, *KAT*, English tr by Whitehouse, 1885; Pinches, *The OT in the Light of the Historical Records of Assyria and Babylonia*, 1902.

A. H. SAYCE

ASSYRIA AND BABYLONIA, RELIGION OF. See BABYLONIA AND ASSYRIA, RELIGION OF.

ASSYRIAN AND BABYLONIAN LIBRARIES. See NINEVEH, LIBRARY OF.

ASSYRIANS, a-sir'i-ans (אַשּׁוּר, *'ashshūr*): The inhabitants of Assyria. In Heb the name of the people is the same as that of the country. See ASSYRIA.

ASTAD, as'tad: The reading of the Eng. versions of 1 Esd **5** 13 for the name which appears as Azgad in Ezr **2** 12 and Neh **7** 17. In the different Gr copies of 1 Esd the name varies. See AZGAD; ASTATH.

ASTAROTH, as'ta-roth. See ASHTAROTH.

ASTARTE, as-tär'tē, **ASTORETH.** See ASHTAROTH.

ASTATH, as'tath (**'Ασтάθ**, *Astáth*): The form given in 1 Esd **8** 38 to the name which in Ezr **8** 12 appears as Azgad. See AZGAD.

ASTONISHED, as-ton'isht, **ASTONIED,** as-ton'id (שָׁמֵם, *shāmēm*, "astonished," the root idea being "silent," i.e. struck dumb with amazement; **ἐκπλήσσομαι**, *ekplēssomai*, "to be struck with astonishment," as if by a blow or a shock; **ἐξίστημι**, *existēmi*, "to amaze," "to throw into wonderment"; **θαμβέομαι**, *thambéomai*, "to astonish" to the point of fright): The state of being surprised, startled, stunned by some exceptional wonder, some overwhelming event or miracle, as e.g. Nebuchadnezzar's amazement at the miracle in the burning fiery furnace (Dnl **3** 24) (תְּוַהּ, *tᵉwah*, "astonished"); of the passer-by at the desolation of Babylon (Jer **50** 13). The personality, teaching and works of Jesus were so wonderful, Divine, supernatural, as to awaken emotions of surprise and awe never before known in the presence of man. The people "were astonished out of measure" at His doctrine (Mk **10** 26 AV); "astonished with a great astonishment" at His raising the dead (Mk **5** 42 AV). The gift of the Holy Ghost to the Gentiles was in like manner a source of astonishment to those Jews who believed through the power of Peter's preaching (Acts **10** 45 AV). The miracle of regeneration today, which renews and transforms debased and fallen men into saints, makes the same impression on an observing world.

DWIGHT M. PRATT

ASTONISHMENT, as-ton'ish-ment: Amazement; mental surprise, excitement, wonder; often the cause of the startled emotion, as in Dt **28** 37: "Thou shalt become an astonishment." The chosen people, visited with calamities for idolatry would become a source of amazement to all nations (Jer **25** 9.11.18); Solomon's lofty and beautiful temple would be "an astonishment" (2 Ch **7** 21 AV). For original terms and fuller study see ASTONISHED.

ASTRAY, a-strā' (תָּעָה, *tā'āh*, "to wander," "to err"; **πλανάομαι**, *planáomai*, "to go astray," each carrying the idea of being lost): With one exception (Ex **23** 4 "his ass going astray") used **metaphorically** of moral wandering, going astray in paths of error and sin, like "sheep going astray" (1 Pet **2** 25 AV; Isa **53** 6; Ps **119** 176). This wandering may be due (1) to inherent evil (Ps **58** 3); (2) to false shepherds (Jer **50** 6); contrast the beautiful and classic passage, Mt **18** 12.13, the Son of man (ver 12) seeketh that which is gone astray. No word more vividly portrays sin as a straying, a separation from God. To be morally "astray" is to be "lost."

DWIGHT M. PRATT

ASTROLOGY, as-trol'o-ji:

I. THE DESIRE TO FORECAST THE FUTURE
1. Methods of Soothsaying
2. Divination
3. Looking in the Liver
4. The Astrologers, or Dividers of the Heavens
5. The Stargazers, or Seers of the Constellations
6. The Monthly Prognosticators, or Men Who Knew the Omens of the New Moon

II. THE WORSHIP OF THE HEAVENLY BODIES THE FORM OF IDOLATRY TO WHICH THE ISRAELITES WERE MOST PRONE
1. Chiún, Certainly the Planet Saturn
2. Saturn or Moloch Worship
3. Mazzālōth, or Planet Worship
4. Gadh and Menī or Star Worship
5. Lucifer, the Shining Star

III. Systems of Astrology
1. Names of the Week-Days, Due to an Astrological System
2. Origin of Modern Astrology
3. "Curious Arts" of Ephesus
Literature

I. The Desire to Forecast the Future.—The desire to penetrate the future and influence its events has shown itself in all lands and ages. But it is clear that a knowledge of the future does not lie within the scope of man's natural powers; "divination" therefore has always been an attempt to gain the help of beings possessing knowledge and power transcending those of man. The answer of the Chaldaeans to King Nebuchadnezzar when he demanded that they should tell his dream was a reasonable one: "There is not a man upon the earth that can show the king's matter: . . . . there is no other that can show it before the king, except the gods, whose dwelling is not with flesh" (Dnl **2** 10.11). "Divination," therefore, in all its forms is but an aspect of polytheism.

It was for the twofold reason that the arts of divination were abominable in themselves, and gave to their votaries no knowledge of the will of God, that such arts were forbidden in the Law (Dt **18** 9–15). Israel was to be perfect with God and He would reveal to them His will perfectly through that prophet like unto Moses whom He would send. Keil and Delitzsch in commenting on this passage well remark: "Moses groups together all the words which the language contained for the different modes of exploring the future and discovering the will of God, for the purpose of forbidding every description of soothsaying, and places the prohibition of Moloch-worship at the head, to show the inward connection between soothsaying and idolatry, possibly because februation, or passing children through the fire in the worship of Moloch, was more intimately connected with soothsaying and magic than any other description of idolatry" (*Commentary on the Pentateuch*, III, 393).

1. Methods of Soothsaying

The forms of soothsaying mentioned in this catalogue are as follows: "One that practiseth augury" (*m*[e]*'ōnēn*) is of uncertain etymology, but the rabbins connect it with *'ayin*, "an eye"; literally therefore one who ogles, or who bewitches with the evil eye. "An enchanter" (*m*[e]*naḥēsh*), sometimes supposed to be a snake-charmer, is probably one who fascinates like a snake; in other words a mesmerist or hypnotist. The word occurs in connection with Joseph's divining-cup, and such cups were employed both in Babylon and Egypt, and their use was akin to the more modern crystal-gazing, the hypnotic state being induced by prolonged staring, as in the fascination ascribed to serpents. On this account, snakes were sometimes figured upon such cups. Thus in Talm we read: "If one finds vessels with delineations of the sun, the moon, or of a serpent upon them, let him cast them into the salt sea" (*'Abhōdhāh-Zārāh*, fol 42, col. 2). "A sorcerer" (*m*[e]*khashshēph*) is one who mutters incantations or speaks in ventriloquial whispers, as if under the influence of the spirits of the dead. "A charmer" (*ḥōbhēr ḥebher*), is one who inflicts a spell by weaving magical knots. "A consulter with a familiar spirit" (*'ōbh*), denotes one who is possessed of a python or soothsaying demon. Such were the woman of Endor whom Saul consulted on the eve of the battle of Gilboa (1 S **28**) and the pythoness of Philippi out of whom St. Paul cast the spirit (Acts **16** 16–18). The word (*'ōbh*) means "bottle" and either indicates that the medium was the receptacle of the spirit or is a relic of the old tradition that genii (*jinns*) might be enslaved and imprisoned in bottles by means of magical incantations. "A wizard" (*yidh'ōnī*) means a wise man, "a knowing one." The word in OT is always used in connection with *'ōbh*, and denotes a man who could interpret the ravings of the medium. "A necromancer" (*dōrēsh 'el ha-mēthīm*) is one who calls up the spirits of the dead and has intercourse with them. "Consulting the teraphim" (Ezk **21** 21) may have been a form of consulting the dead, if, as is probable, the teraphim were ancestral images, raised by superstition to the rank of household gods. The manner of consultation we do not know; but as an illustration of the use of the image of a dead person, we may remember that a modern medium will often ask for a portrait of a deceased relative for the alleged purpose of entering into communication with the departed spirit.

It will be seen that these forms of soothsaying are allied to the arts which in modern times bear the names of hypnotism and mediumship. They are more briefly referred to in Isa **8** 19, "When they shall say unto you, Seek unto them that have familiar spirits and unto the wizards, that chirp and that mutter: should not a people seek unto their God? on behalf of the living should they seek unto the dead?" Here again mediumship and spiritism are connected with the ventriloquial whispers and mutterings, which are supposed to be characteristic of the utterances of the dead.

2. Divination

But the first term in the catalogue, "one that useth divination" (*ḳeṣem*) is of wider application. It signifies a "divider" and refers to the practice which men have followed in an infinite variety of ways for trying to get light upon the future by resorting to what seems to them the arbitrament of chance. The results of a battle and of the fall of dice are alike unknown beforehand. But the second can be tested, and men assume that the result of the first will correspond to the second. Any chance will serve; the shuffling of a pack of cards; the flight of birds; the arrangement of dregs in a cup; nothing is too trivial for the purpose. The allotment of a particular interpretation to a particular sign was of course purely arbitrary, but the method could be applied in an infinite number of ways, every one of which could be worked out to an extent only limited by the limits of the misdirected ingenuity of man. Two such forms of "divination," that is of "dividing," are mentioned by Ezekiel in his description of the king of Babylon: "The king of Babylon stood at the parting of the way, at the head of the two ways, to use divination [*ḳeṣem*]: he shook the arrows to and fro, he consulted the teraphim, he looked in the liver" (Ezk **21** 21). The arrows were either marked to represent certain courses of action, and one was drawn out or shaken out, or else they were thrown promiscuously up into the air, and the augury was deduced from the way in which they fell.

3. "Looking in the Liver"

"Looking in the liver" is one of the most venerable forms of divination. Here again it was a question of "division." Each of the various parts of the liver, its lobes, the gall bladder, the ducts and so forth, had a special significance allotted to it, the theory, apparently, being that the god to whom the animal was sacrificed revealed his will by the way in which he molded the organ which was supposed to be the seat of the victim's life.

It will be noted that no explicit mention is made of astrology in this catalogue of the modes of soothsaying. But astrology was, as will be shown, closely connected with Moloch-worship, and was most directly a form of "divination," that is of division. Morris Jastrow the Younger indeed considers that astrology rose from hepatoscopy, and points out that the common designation for "planet" amongst the Babylonians is a compound ideograph, the two elements of which signify "sheep" and "dead." He considers that the sacrificial sheep was offered to the deity specially for the purpose of securing an omen. Hence when the planets were used as omens, this name of "slain sheep" was naturally applied to them, even as "augury," divination by the flight of birds, came to represent amongst the Romans all kinds of divination. "On the famous bronze model of a liver found near Piacenza and which dating from about the 3d cent. BC was used as an object-lesson for instruction in hepatoscopy, precisely as the clay model of a liver dating from the Hammurabi period was used in a Bab temple school, we find the edge of the liver divided into sixteen regions with names of the deities inhabiting them corresponding to divisions of the heavens in which the gods have their seats, while on the reverse side there is a line dividing the liver into 'day' and 'night.' Professor Korte, in a study of this remarkable object, summing up the results of many years of research, explains this by showing that the liver was regarded as a microcosm reflecting the macrocosm, or, in other words, the liver of the sacrificial animal from being originally a reflection of the soul or mind of the god to whom the animal was offered, was brought into connection with the observation of the heavenly bodies revealing the intention of the gods acting in concert" (Morris Jastrow, Jr., "Hepatoscopy and Astrology in Babylonia and Assyria," in *Proc. Amer. Phil. Soc.*, 665–66).

Three well-marked classes of astrology, that is to say of divination by the heavenly bodies, are mentioned in Isa **47** 13, as being practised in Babylon. "Let now the astrologers, the star-gazers, the monthly prognosticators, stand up, and save thee."

4. Astrologers

The astrologers are the "dividers of the heavens" (*hōbh^erē shāmayīm*); that is to say the significance of any stellar conjunction was made to depend upon the division of the heavens in which it occurred. The earliest of such divisions appears to have been into the four quarters, N., S., E., W., and astrological tablets of this character have been discovered in considerable numbers. Thus tablet *W.A.I.* III, 56, 1, gives a table of eclipses for each day of the month Tammuz up to the middle of the month, and the significance of the eclipse is connected with the quarter in which it was seen. On the first day the eclipse is associated with the S., on the second with the N., on the third with the E., and on the fourth with the W. (Sayce, *Astronomy and Astrology of the Babylonians*, 222). Tablets of this description are very instructive since they prove that those who drew up such lists of omens had not even a rudimentary knowledge of astronomy. For the Bab months were intended to be natural months, yet at this time it was not realized that an eclipse of the sun could only take place when the moon was invisible, that is to say about the 28th or 29th day of the month, if the calendar was correct. Further, it was not realized that neither sun nor moon can ever be in the N. in the latitude of Babylon. Such tables of omens then were not derived, as has sometimes been supposed, from a striking event having occurred near the time of an observed eclipse, but they must have been drawn up on an entirely arbitrary plan.

The same principle of "division" was applied to the moon itself for the purpose of drawing omens from its eclipses. Thus in R. C. Thompson's *Reports of the Magicians and Astrologers of Nineveh and Babylon* we read in No. 268, "The omens of all lands. The right of the moon is Akkad, the left Elam, the top Aharru, the bottom Subartu." The constellations of the zodiac also had omens allotted to them in a similar manner.

5. Star-gazers

The astrologers mentioned in the Book of Dnl (*'ashshāphīm*) were not "dividers of the heavens," but mutterers of incantations. The star-gazers or seers of the stars or constellations (*ḥōzīm ba-kōkhābhīm*) may be illustrated from two of Thompson's *Reports*. No. 216, "Saturn has appeared in *Leo*. When Leo is obscured, for three years lions and jackals . . . . and kill men"; and No. 239, "When Mars (*apin*) approaches *Scorpio* the prince will die by a scorpion's sting and his son after him will take the throne." It may be remarked that as the planet Saturn takes three years to pass through the constellation *Leo*, the ravages of lions are predicted to last for that time.

At a later date we find a complete system of astrology based upon the constellations of the zodiac which happen to be rising at the moment when the stars were consulted. Examples of this form of divination are found in the works of Zeuchros of Babylon, who flourished about the beginning of our era. By his day the system had received a considerable development. Twelve signs did not give much scope for prediction, so each sign had been divided into three equal portions or "decans"; each decan therefore corresponding nearly to the part of the ecliptic which the sun would pass through in a decade or "week" of 10 days of the Egyptians. A yet further complexity was brought about by associating each one of the 36 decans with one of the 36 extra-zodiacal constellations, and a further variety was obtained by associating each zodiacal constellation with its *sunanatéllon*, or constellation rising with it; that is, at the same time; or with its *paranatéllon*, or constellation rising beside it; that is, a constellation on the same meridian. At what time these particular forms of augury by the constellations came into use we do not know, but the division into the decans is distinctly alluded to in the 5th tablet of the Bab Creation Epic: "4. For the twelve months he [Marduk] fixed three stars."

6. Monthly Prognosticators

The monthly prognosticators were the men who knew the omens of the new moon (*mōdhī'īm l^e-ḥŏdhāshīm*). At one time the error of the calendar was made the basis of prediction. This is seen in the great astrological work based on the omens drawn up for Sargon of Agadé, and entitled from its opening phrase *Enuma anu Bel*, "When the heaven god Bel" (the "Illumination of Bel"), as, for instance, "The moon as on the 1st day is seen in its appearance on the 27th day; evil is fixed for the land of Elam"; and "The moon as on the 1st day is seen on the 28th day: evil is fixed for the land of the Ahurru." Other omens were drawn from the position of the horns of the new moon when first seen; the right horn being assigned to the king and the left to his enemies, as in Thompson's *Reports*, No. 25: "When at the moon's appearance its right horn is high [lit. "long"] and its left horn is low [lit. "short"] the king's hand will conquer land other than this." The "monthly prognosticators" had not learned that the right-hand horn is always the higher and that the amount of its elevation depends on the time of the year, or they kept the knowledge to themselves.

II. Worship of the Heavenly Bodies.— As we should naturally expect, the earliest astrological tablets relate chiefly to omens dependent upon the two great lights, the sun and moon. There is no evidence at present available to fix the date when the planets were first recognized as distinct from the fixed stars. Probably this discovery was intimately connected with the formation of the constellations; it cannot have been long delayed after it. Certainly planet-worship, and as connected with it, planetary divination, prevailed in the Euphrates valley at a very early period.

1. Chiun

One planet is certainly mentioned in OT, and we may safely infer that the other four were known, since this particular planet is the least conspicuous both in brightness and in motion, and was therefore probably the last to be discovered. The reference to Saturn occurs in Am **5** 25.26: "Did ye bring unto me sacrifices and offerings in the wilderness forty years, O house of Israel? Yea, ye have borne the tabernacle of your king [AV Moloch] and the shrine of [AV Chiun] your images, the star of your god, which ye made to yourselves." This passage was quoted from LXX by St. Stephen in his defence, "And they made a calf in those days, and brought a sacrifice unto the idol, and rejoiced in the works of their hands. But God turned, and gave them up to serve the host of heaven; as it is written in the book of the prophets,

"Did ye offer unto me slain beasts and sacrifices
Forty years in the wilderness, O house of Israel?
And ye took up the tabernacle of Moloch,
And the star of the god Rephan,
The figures which ye made to worship them"
(Acts **7** 41–43).

The difference between the names *Chiun* and *Rephan*, is due either to *Rephan* being a local Egyp name for the planet Saturn, and therefore used by the LXX as its equivalent, or to an actual error of transcription in the text from which they were translating: the initial of the word being taken as *rēsh* when it should have been *kāph*, *r* instead of *k*. The word should therefore be transliterated *Kaivan*, which was the name of the planet Saturn amongst the ancient Arabs and Syrians, while *kaimanu*, "constant" or "regular," was its name with the Assyrians. The ERV in Am **5** 26 adopts the reading of the AVm, "Siccuth your king," Moloch meaning king; but the authority of the LXX and the parallelism of the text and its general line of thought support the reading given by some of the ancient versions and followed by the AV.

2. Saturn or Moloch Worship

The difficulty of the passage is that both Amos and St. Stephen appear to represent the worship of the golden calf as identical with the worship of Moloch and of the planet Saturn; yet though *Kaivan* is only mentioned here, the nature of the reference would imply that this deity was one familiar both to speaker and hearers. The difficulty vanishes at once, if the plain statement of St. Stephen be accepted, that when God permitted Israel to "go after the stubbornness of their heart, that they might walk in their own counsels" (Ps **81** 12) He "gave them up to serve the host of heaven." The worship of the golden calf was star worship; it was the solar bull, the constellation Taurus, in which the sun was at the time of the spring equinox, that was thus represented. The golden calf was therefore analogous to the familiar symbol of the Mithraic cult, the bull slain by Mithra, *Sol Invictus*, if indeed the latter did not take its origin from this apostasy of Israel. See CALF, GOLDEN.

And Moloch the king, the idol of the Ammonites and Phoenicians, was intimately connected both with the solar bull and the planet Saturn. According to the rabbins, his statue was of brass, with a human body but the head of an ox. On the Carthaginian worship of Moloch or Saturn, Diodorus (book xx, ch i) writes: "Among the Carthaginians there was a brazen statue of Saturn putting forth the palms of his hands bending in such a manner toward the earth, as that the boy who was laid upon them, in order to be sacrificed, should slip off, and so fall down headlong into a deep fiery furnace. Hence it is probable that Euripides took what he fabulously relates concerning the sacrifice in Taurus, where he introduces Iphigenia asking Orestes this question: 'But what sepulchre will me dead receive, shall the gulf of sacred fire me have?' The ancient fable likewise that is common among all the Grecians, that Saturn devoured his own children, seems to be confirmed by this law among the Carthaginians." The parallelism of the text therefore is very complete. The Israelites professed to be carrying the tabernacle of Jeh upon which rested the Shekinah glory; but in spirit they were carrying the tabernacle of the cruelest and most malignant of all the deities of the heathen, and the light in which they were rejoicing was the star of the planet assigned to that deity.

Moloch then was the sun as king, and especially the sun as he entered upon what might be considered his peculiar kingdom, the zodiac from *Taurus* to *Serpens* and *Scorpio*, the period of the six summer months. The connection of the sun with Saturn may seem to us somewhat forced, but we have the most direct testimony that such a connection was believed in by the Babylonians. In Thompson's *Reports*, obv. of No. 176 reads: "When the sun stands in the place of the moon, the king of the land will be secure on his throne. When the sun stands above or below the moon, the foundation of the throne will be secure." The "sun" in this inscription clearly cannot be the actual sun, and it is explained on the reverse as being "the star of the sun," the planet Saturn. No. 176 rev. reads: "Last night Saturn drew near to the moon. Saturn is the star of the sun. This is the interpretation: it is lucky for the king. The sun is the king's star." The connection between the sun and Saturn probably arose from both being taken as symbols of Time. The return of the sun to the beginning of the zodiac marked the completion of the year. Saturn, the slowest moving of all the heavenly bodies, accomplished its revolution through the signs of the zodiac in about 30 years, a complete generation of men. Saturn therefore was in a peculiar sense the symbol of Time, and because of Time, of Destiny.

3. Mazzālōth

The connection between the worship of the golden calves, of the heavenly host and of Moloch, and of these with divination and enchantments, is brought out very clearly in the judgment which the writer of the Book of K pronounces upon the apostate ten tribes: "They forsook all the commandments of Jehovah their God, and made them molten images, even two calves, and made an Asherah, and worshipped all the host of heaven, and served Baal. And they caused their sons and their daughters to pass through the fire, and used divination and enchantments" (2 K **17** 16.17). The sin of apostate Judah was akin to the sin of apostate Israel. In the reformation of Josiah, he put down the idolatrous priests that "burned incense unto Baal, to the sun, and to the moon, and to the planets [*mazzālōth*], and to all the host of heaven" (2 K **23** 5). He also destroyed the *'ăshērāh* and he "defiled Topheth . . . . that no man might make his son or his daughter to pass through the fire to Molech" (ver 10). "Moreover them that had familiar spirits, and the wizards, and the teraphim, and the idols, and all the abominations that were seen in the land of Judah and in Jerus, did Josiah put away" (ver 24). The idolatries to which the Israelites of both kingdoms were especially prone were those of the heavenly bodies, and inextricably woven with them was the passion for employing those heavenly bodies as omens, and in consequence for every kind of divination and witchcraft.

The word tr[d] "planets" in 2 K **23** 5 is *mazzālōth*,

closely akin to the *mazzārōth* of Job **38** 32. This rendering probably reproduces correctly the meaning of the original. R. C. Thompson in his introduction to the *Reports* writes (xxvii): "The places where the gods stood in the zodiac were called *manzalti*, a word which means literally 'stations,' and we are probably right in assuming that it is the equivalent of the *mazzālōth* mentioned in 2 K **23** 5. The use of the word in late Heb is, however, somewhat more vague, for *mazzāl*, though literally meaning a constellation of the zodiac, is also applied to any or every star, and in the *B*ᵉ*rē'shīth Rabbā'*, cx, it is said 'One *mazzāl* completeth its circuit in thirty days, another completeth it in thirty years.'" The two bodies referred to are evidently the moon with its lunation of about 30 days, and Saturn with its revolution of about 30 years; these being the two planets with the shortest and longest periods respectively. By a natural metonymy, *mazzālōth*, the complete circuit of the zodiac, came also to mean *mazzālōth*, the bodies that performed that circuit, just as in the present day we speak of a railway, which means literally the "permanent way," when we really mean the trains that travel upon it.

4. Gadh and Mᵉnī

The references in OT to the planets other than Saturn are not so clear. In Isa **65** 11 two deities are apparently referred to: "Ye that forsake Jehovah, that forget my holy mountain, that prepare a table for Fortune [Gad], and that fill up mingled wine unto Destiny [Meni]; I will destine you to the sword, and ye shall all bow down to the slaughter." It is clear that Gad and Meni are the titles of two closely associated deities, and Gesenius identifies them with Jupiter and Venus, the Greater and Lesser Good Fortunes of the astrologers. But as I have suggested in the *Astronomy of the Bible* (133, 217), if any of the heavenly bodies are here intended (which cannot as yet be considered certain), it is more probable that they are the two beautiful star-clusters that stand on the head and the shoulder of the Bull at the old commencement of the zodiac, as if they marked the gateway of the year—the Hyades and Pleiades. Both groups were considered traditionally as composed of seven stars; and the two names *Gadh* (the Hyades) and *M*ᵉ*nī* (the Pleiades) taken together give the meaning of the "Fortunate Number," i.e. seven. The *lectisternia*—the spreading the table and mingling the wine to *Gadh* and *M*ᵉ*nī*—at the beginning of the year to secure good fortune throughout its course, were therefore held about the time of the Passover, as if in parody, if indeed they were not a desecration of it: heathen rites added to one of the most solemn services of Jeh.

5. Venus

The planet Venus is more distinctly referred to in Isa **14** 12: "How art thou fallen from heaven, O Lucifer, son of the morning!" (AV). The word here rendered Lucifer, that is, "light-bearer," is the word *hēlēl* corresponding to the Assyr *mustelil*, "the shining star," an epithet to which the planet Venus has a preëminent claim.

Mars and Mercury, the two remaining planets, are not mentioned as such in OT, but the deities connected with them, Nergal = Mars (2 K **17** 30) and Nebo = Mercury (Isa **46** 1), both occur.

III. Systems of Astrology.—In astrology the planets were regarded as being 7 in number, but

1. Names of the Week-Days

the idea that the number 7 derived its sacredness from this fact is an inversion of the true state of the case. It was that 7 being regarded as a sacred number, the number of the planets was artificially made to correspond by including in the same class as the five wandering stars, bodies that differed so widely from them in appearance as the sun and moon. So artificial a classification cannot have been primitive, and it is significant that in Gen **1** 14 the sun and moon are presented as being (as indeed they appear to be) of an altogether different order from the rest of the heavenly bodies. Yet there is one feature that they have in common with the five planets: all move among the stars within the band of the zodiac; each of the seven makes the circuit of the *mazzālōth*.

We owe the names of the days of the week to this astrological conception of the planets as being 7 in number, and some writers (e.g. R. A. Proctor in his *Myths and Marvels of Astronomy*, 43–47) have supposed that the week of 7 days owed its origin to this astrological conception and that the 7th day—Saturn's Day—became the Sabbath, the Day of Rest, because Saturn was the planet of ill-omen and it was then unlucky to undertake any work. The way in which the allotment of the planets to the days of the week was arrived at was the following. The Gr astronomers and mathematicians concluded that the planet Saturn was the most distant from the earth and that the others followed in the descending order of Jupiter, Mars, Sun, Venus, Mercury, Moon. In the progress of astrology there came a time when it was found necessary to assign a planet to every hour so as to increase the number of omens it could afford. Starting then with Saturn as presiding over the first hour of the first day, each planet was used three times over on that day, and three planets were used a fourth time. The sun, the fourth planet, took therefore the first hour of the second day, and gave it its name, so that Sunday followed Saturday. In like manner the third day became the moon's day, and so on with the other planets which followed in the order Mars, Mercury, Jupiter, Venus, and again Saturn. This idea of the relative distances of the planets was that arrived at by the astronomers of Alexandria, and was necessarily subsequent to the reduction of the planetary motions to a mathematical system by Eudoxus and his successors. The division of the day implied was one of 24 hours, not of 12; the Egyp division, not the Bab. But the Egyp week was one of 10 days, the 7-day week was Sem, and the week implied in the system is the free week, running on continuously, the Jewish week, not the Bab. For the Babylonians, though they paid some attention to the 7th day, began their reckoning afresh at the beginning of each month. This particular astrological system therefore owed its origin to four distinct nationalities. The conception of the influence of the planets was Bab; the mathematical working out of the order of the planets was exclusively Gr; the division of the day into 24 hours was Egyp; the free continuous 7-day week was particularly Jewish. These four influences were brought together in Alexandria not very long before the Christian era. Here therefore and at this time, this particular system of astrology took its origin.

This form of astrology was readily adopted by the Jews in their degenerate days, as we find from references in Talm. Thus Rabbi Chanena said to his disciples, "Go and tell Ben Laive, the planetary influence does not depend upon days but hours. He that is born under the influence of the sun (no matter on what day) will have a beaming face"; and so the rabbi went through the whole list of the planets (*Shabbāth*, fol 156, col. 1). The above was spoken as a criticism of Rabbi Shimon Ben Laive who had written, "Whoever is born on the first day of the week will be either a thoroughly good or a thoroughly bad man; because light and darkness was created on that day"; and the rabbi spoke similarly for the other days. We get a relic of this superstition in our nursery rhyme, "Monday's child is full of grace; Tuesday's child is fair of face," etc; and some present-day astrologers still use the system for their forecasts. It will of course be noted that the system takes no account of the actual positions of the heavenly bodies; the moon does not shine more or less on Monday than on any other day.

2. Origin of Modern Astrology

It was from Alexandrian astrology that modern astrology immediately derived its form; but the original source of all astrology in the ancient world lay in the system of planetary idolatry prevalent in the Euphrates valley, and in the fact that this idolatry was practised chiefly for the purpose of divination. At one time it was supposed that a real astronomy was cultivated at an early time in Babylonia, but Jastrow, Kugler and others have shown that this idea is without basis. The former writes, "The fact however is significant that, with perhaps some exceptions, we have in the library of Ashurbanipal representing to a large extent copies from older originals, no text that can properly be called astronomical. . . . . It is certainly significant that the astronomical tablets so far found belong to the latest period, and in fact to the age following on the fall of the Bab empire. According to Kugler the oldest dated genuinely astronomical tablet belongs to the 7th year of Cambyses, i.e. 522 BC" ("Hepatoscopy and Astrology in Babylonia and Assyria," in *Proc. Amer. Phil. Soc.*, 667).

The conquests of Alexander the Great brought into close connection with each other the Bab and Gr systems of thought, and Bab astrology was introduced to the Greeks by Berosus the Chaldaean priest. In Gr hands, astrology was changed from its character of an oriental religion into the appearance of a science. In Babylonia the stars had been consulted for the benefit of the king as representing the state; amongst the Greeks, with their strong individualistic tendency, the fortunes of the individual became the most frequent subject of inquiry, and the idea was originated of determining the character and fortune of a man from the position of the stars at his birth—genethlialogy—a phase of astrology which never existed in the Euphrates valley. This extension rendered it necessary to increase greatly the complexities of the omens, and the progress which the Greeks had made in mathematics supplied them with the means of doing so. Thus came into existence that complex and symmetrical system of divination of which we have the earliest complete exposition in the writings of Claudius Ptolemy about 130 AD; a system which, though modified in details, is in effect that in use today.

3. Curious Arts

Since this mathematical astrology did not come into existence until about the commencement of the Christian era, it is clear that there could not be any reference to its particular form in the OT. We may probably see one reference in the NT (Acts **19** 19). Of the converts at Ephesus it is written, "Not a few of them that practised magical arts brought their books together and burned them in the sight of all; and they counted the price of them, and found it 50,000 pieces of silver." Books of magical incantations and prescriptions were certainly included, but it is also likely that the almanacs, tables and formulae, essential to the astrologer for the exercise of his art, were also in the number. It was of course impossible then, as now, for the convert to Christianity to consult astrologers or to practise astrological divination. Partly because it was an absurdity, for the divisions of the heavens upon which the predictions are based, are purely imaginary; the "signs" of the zodiac, and the "houses" have nothing whatsoever corresponding to them in Nature; such division is exactly that denounced by the prophets of old as *ḳeṣem*, "divination." Next, and of more importance, it ascribes to mere creatures, the planets or the spirits supposed to preside over them, the powers that belong to God alone; it was and is essentially idolatrous. As one of the chief living astrologers puts it, "The TRUE astrologer believes that the sun is the body of the Logos of this solar system, 'in Him we live and move and have our being.' The planets are his angels, being modifications in the consciousness of the Logos" (*Knowledge*, XXIII, 228). Astrology is indeed referred to in the OT, with other forms of divination, and the idolatry inherent in them, but they are only mentioned in terms of the most utter reprobation. The Jews alone of all the nations of antiquity were taught by their religion neither to resort to such arts nor to be afraid of the omens deduced from them. Isaiah knew the Lord to be He that "frustrateth the signs of the liars, and maketh diviners mad" (Isa **44** 25), and Jeremiah declared, "Thus saith Jehovah, Learn not the way of the nations, and be not dismayed at the signs of heaven; for the nations are dismayed at them" (Jer **10** 2). And what held good for the Jews of old holds good for us today. Above all, astrology is an attempt to ascertain the will of God by other means than those which He has appointed—His Son, who is the Way and the Truth and the Life, and His Holy Scriptures in which we learn of Him, and which are able to make us "wise unto salvation through faith which is in Christ Jesus" (2 Tim **3** 15).

LITERATURE.—Franz Boll, *Sphaera: Neue griechische Texte und Untersuchungen zur Geschichte der Sternbilder*, 1903; Kugler, *Kulturhistorische Bedeutung der babylonischen Astronomie*, 1907; *Sternkunde und Sterndienst in Babel*; E. W. Maunder, *Astronomy of the Bible*, 1908; *The Bible and Astronomy*, Annual Address before the Victoria Institute, 1908; E. W. Maunder and A. S. D. Maunder, "Note on the Date of the Passage of the Vernal Equinox from Taurus into Aries," in *Monthly Notices of the Royal Astronomical Society*, LXIV, 488–507; also three papers on "The Oldest Astronomy" in *Journal of the British Astronomical Association*, VIII, 373; IX, 317; XIV, 241; R. A. Proctor, *Myths and Marvels of Astronomy*; R. C. Thompson, *Reports of the Magicians and Astrologers of Nineveh and Babylon*; G. V. Schiaparelli, *Astronomy in the OT*; also two papers, "I Primordi" and "I Progressi dell' Astronomia presso i Babilonesi," in *Rivista di Scienzia*, 1908; C. Virolleaud, *L'astrologie chaldéenne. Le livre intitulé "Enuma Anu Bel,"* 1908, 1909.

E. W. MAUNDER

ASTRONOMY, as-tron′o-mi:

I. THE HEAVENLY BODIES
1. The Ordinances of Heaven
2. The Sun
(1) The Names for the Sun
(2) The "City of the Sun"
(3) The Greater Light-Giver
(4) The Purpose of the Sun
(5) The Sun as a Type
3. The Moon
(1) The Names for the Moon
(2) The Lesser Light-Giver
(3) Phases of the Moon
4. Signs
(1) Solar and Lunar Eclipses
(2) The Wings of the Morning
5. Seasons
(1) The Meaning of the Word
(2) Natural Seasons for Worship
(3) The Hallowing of the Seventh
(4) The Jubilee a Luni-solar Cycle
(5) The 19-Year Luni-solar Cycle
(6) The Jewish Ritual Preëxilic
(7) The Luni-solar Cycles of Daniel
6. The Stars
(1) Their Number
(2) Their Distance
(3) Their Brightness
7. Morning Stars
The Stars as a Dial
8. Falling Stars
(1) Meteorites
(2) The Star "Wormwood"
9. Wandering Stars
(1) Comets as a Spiritual Type
(2) Comets Referred to in Scripture?

The keynote of the Heb writers respecting the heavenly bodies is sounded in Ps **8**:

"When I consider thy heavens, the work of thy fingers,
The moon and the stars, which thou hast ordained;
What is man, that thou art mindful of him?
And the son of man, that thou visitest him?
For thou hast made him but little lower than God,
And crownest him with glory and honor.
Thou makest him to have dominion over the works of thy hands;
Thou hast put all things under his feet" (Ps **8** 3–6).

The heavenly bodies were inexpressibly glorious, and they were all the handiwork of Jeh—without power or vitality of their own—and man, not by any inherent virtue, but by the will and grace of God, was superior to them in importance. Thus there was a great gulf fixed between the superstitions of the heathen who worshipped the sun, moon and stars as gods, and the faith of the pious Hebrew who regarded them as things made and moved by the will of one only God. And it followed from this difference that the Hebrew, beyond all nations of like antiquity, was filled with a keen delight in natural objects and phenomena, and was attentively observant of them.

I. The Heavenly Bodies.—To the sacred writers, the ordinances of heaven taught the lesson of Order—great, magnificent and immutable. Day by day, the sun rose in the east, "as a bridegroom coming out of his chamber" (Ps **19** 5), and pursued unswervingly his appointed path across the sky, to his going down. Night by night, the stars, the "host of heaven," moved in their "highways" or "courses" (*m^eṣillāh*), and the words of Joel (**2** 7) respecting the Assyr army might be applied to them. "They march every one on his ways, and they break not their ranks. Neither doth one thrust another; they march every one in his path." Some wheeled in northern circuits that were wholly seen; some swept in long courses from their rising in the E. to their setting in the W.; some scarcely lifted themselves above the southern horizon. Little wonder that this celestial army on the march, "the host of heaven," suggested to the Hebrews a comparison with the "angels," the unseen messengers of God who in their "thousands of thousands ministered unto him" (Dnl **7** 10).

1. The Ordinances of Heaven

But, as the year revolved, the dial of stars in the N. shifted round; whilst of the other stars, those in the W. disappeared into the light of the setting sun, and new stars seemed to spring out of the dawning light. There was thus a yearly procession of the stars as well as a nightly one.

And to this "ordinance of the heaven" the Hebrews noted that there was an answer from the earth, for in unfailing correspondence came the succession of seasons, the revival of vegetation, the ripening of harvest and of fruits, the return of winter's cold. Of them God asked the question: "Knowest thou the ordinances of the heavens? Canst thou establish the dominion thereof in the earth?" (Job **38** 33), and they recognized that to this question no answer could be given, for these ordinances of heaven were the sign and evidence of Almighty wisdom, power and unchangeableness. "Thus saith Jehovah, who giveth the sun for a light by day, and the ordinances of the moon and of the stars for a light by night . . . . Jehovah of hosts is his name" (Jer **31** 35).

We have no writings of the early Hebrews other than the books of the OT, and in them there is no record of any research into the mechanical explanation of the movements of the heavenly bodies. Nor should we expect to find in them a record of the research if such were made, since the purpose of Holy Scripture was, not to work out the relation of thing to thing—the inquiry to which modern science is devoted—but to reveal God to man. Therefore the lesson which is drawn from the observed ordinances of heaven is, not that the earth rotates on its axis or revolves round the sun, but that God is faithful to His purpose for mankind. "Thus saith Jehovah: If my covenant of day and night stand not, if I have not appointed the ordinances of heaven and earth; then will I also cast away the seed of Jacob, and of David my servant" (Jer **33** 25.26). And "the glory of God" which "the heavens declare" is not only His almighty power, but the image which the order and perfection of the heavenly movements supply of the law which He has revealed unto man. The "speech" that they "utter," the "knowledge" that they "show" is: "The law of Jehovah is perfect, restoring the soul" (Ps **19** 7).

2. The Sun

(1) *The names for the sun.*—Four words are tr[d] "sun" in the OT:

(*a*) *'Ōr* simply means "light" and is usually rendered thus, but in one instance (Job **31** 26), being in antithesis to "moon," it is given as "sun," the great light-giver.

(*b*) *Ḥammāh* means "heat" and is used for the sun when this is in association with *l^ebhānāh* or "snow-white" for the moon, as in Isa **24** 23, 'Then the *snow-white* [moon] shall be confounded, and the *heat* [sun] ashamed,' the antithesis being drawn between the cold light of the silver moon and the fiery radiance of the glowing sun.

(*c*) *Shemesh*, the Šamaš of the Babylonians, is a primitive word, probably with the root meaning of "ministrant." This is the word most frequently used for the sun, and we find it used topographically as, for instance, in Beth-shemesh, "the house of the sun." Four places of this name are mentioned in the OT: one in Judah, a Levitical city, to which the two milch kine bearing the ark took their straight way from the country of the Philis; one on the border of Issachar; one in Naphtali, a fenced city; and one in Egypt, supposed to be the same as Heliopolis or On, the city of Asenath, wife of Joseph.

(*d*) *Ḥereṣ* means "blister" or "burning heat," from a root "to scratch" or "be rough," and is an unusual term for the sun, and its precise rendering is sometimes in doubt. Once it is tr[d] as "itch," when it occurs amongst the evils threatened in the "cursings" that the six tribes uttered from Mount Ebal (Dt **28** 27). Once it is certainly used of the sun itself when Job (**9** 7) said of God, He "commandeth the sun [*ḥereṣ* or *ḥeres*], and it riseth not." Once it is certainly the name of a hill, for Mount Heres was near Aijalon, on the borders of Judah and Dan. In another passage, authorities differ in their rendering, for when Gideon overcame Zebah and Zalmunna (Jgs **8** 13), he "returned from the battle," according to AV, "before the sun was up," but according to RV, "from the ascent of Heres." In yet another passage (Jgs **14** 18), when the Philis answered Samson's riddle, both AV and RV tr *ḥereṣ* as sun—"before the sun went down." We moreover get slight variants of the same word, joined with *ḳīr* ("wall" or "fortress"), in *Ḳīr-Hăreseth* (2 K **3** 25; Isa **16** 7) and *Ḳir-Ḥeres* (Isa **16** 11; Jer **48** 31.36). These are probably to be identified with the modern Kerak of Moab.

(2) *City of the sun.*—But the most interesting reference is found in Isa **19** 18: "In that day there shall be five cities in the land of Egypt that speak the language of Canaan, and swear to Jehovah of hosts; one shall be called The city of destruction." The word here rendered "destruction" is in Heb *hereṣ*, which has that meaning, but Gesenius and other authorities would substitute for the initial letter, *he*, the letter, *ḥeth*, which it so closely resembles, and so read it "The city of the sun." With this reading it was identified with On, that is, Heliopolis (the city of the sun), and on this belief Onias, the son of Onias the high priest, persuaded Ptolemy Philometor to allow him to build a temple to Jeh in that prefecture, 149 BC (*Ant*, XIII, iii, 1).

(3) *The greater light-giver.*—(*e*) Yet a fifth expression is used to denote the sun, and in one respect it is the most important and significant of all. In the creation narrative it is called the greater light or rather light-giver (*mā'ōr*): 'And God made the two great light-givers; the greater light-giver to rule the day, and the lesser light-giver to rule the night: He made the stars also' (Gen **1** 16). The extreme simplicity of this passage is most significant. In marked contrast to the Bab creation poem, which by its more complex astronomy reveals its later origin (see *post*, sec. II, 12, Mazzārōth), the sun and moon have no distinctive names assigned to them; there is no recognition of the grouping of the stars into constellations, none of any of the planets. The celestial bodies could not be referred to in a more simple manner. And this simplicity is marred by no myth; there is not the faintest trace of the deification of sun or moon or stars; there is no anthropomorphic treatment, no suggestion that they formed the vehicles for spirits. They are described as they were observed when they were first noticed by men, simply as "light-givers" of different brightness. It is the expression of man's earliest observation of the heavenly bodies, but it is real observation, free from any taint of savage phantasies; it marks the very first step in astronomy. No record, oral or written, has been preserved to us of a character more markedly primitive than this.

(4) *Purpose of the sun.*—Two purposes for the great heavenly bodies are indicated in Gen **1** 14.15. The sun and moon are appointed to give light and to measure time. These, from the human and practical point of view, are the two main services which they render to us.

Their purpose for measuring time by their movements will be taken up under another heading; but here it may be pointed out that when it is stated in the Book of Wisd (**7** 18) that King Solomon knew "the alternations of the solstices and the changes of seasons," the reference is to the whole cycle of changes from winter through summer back to winter again. From winter onward the places of sunrise and sunset move northward along the horizon until midsummer when for some days they show no change—the "solstice" is reached; then from midsummer onward the movement "turns" southward until midwinter, when again a "solstice" is reached, after which the places of sunrise and sunset again move northward. This changing place of sunrise is also referred to when God asked Job (**38** 12-14): Hast thou "caused the dayspring to know its place," and the passage goes on, "It [the earth] is changed as clay under the seal; and all things stand forth as a garment." As the shapeless clay takes form under the pressure of the seal, as the garment, shapeless while folded up, takes form when the wearer puts it on, so the earth, shapeless during the darkness, takes form and relief and color with the impress upon it of the dawning light. In the NT when St. James (**1** 17) speaks of "the Father of lights, with whom can be no variation [*parallagē*], neither shadow that is cast by turning [*tropē*]" he is using astronomical technical terms for these same apparent movements of the sun.

(5) *The sun as a type.*—But the apparent unchangeability of the sun makes it, as it were, a just measure of eternal duration (Ps **72** 5.17). The penetration of its rays renders "under the sun" (Eccl **1** 9) a fit expression for universality of place, and on the other hand the fierceness of its heat as experienced in Pal makes it equally suitable as a type of oppression and disaster, so the sun is said, in Scripture, to "smite" those oppressed by its heat (Ps **121** 6).

But it was in its light-giving and ministering power that the Heb writers used the sun as a type to set forth the power and beneficence of God. Words are the symbols of ideas and it was only by this double symbolism that it was possible to express in intelligible human speech, and to make men partly apprehend some of the attributes of God. So we find in the Ps of pilgrimage (Ps **84** 11) "Jehovah God is a sun and a shield"; Malachi (**4** 2) foretells that "the sun of righteousness shall arise with healing in its wings." But the old Heb writers were very guarded and careful in the symbolism they used, whether of word or illustration. Men in those days terribly perverted the benefits which they received through the sun, and made them the occasion and excuse for plunging into all kinds of nature worship and of abominable idolatries. It was not only clear thinking on the part of the sacred writers that made them refer all the benefits that came to them in the natural world direct to the action of God; it was a necessity for clean living. There is no bottom to the abyss in which men plunged when they "worshipped and served the creature rather than the Creator, who is blessed for ever" (Rom **1** 25).

In NT times, though men were no less prone to evil, the fashion of that evil was changing. "The pillars of Beth-shemesh" were broken down (Jer **43** 13), idolatry was beginning to fall into disrepute and men were led away rather by "the knowledge [*gnōsis*] which is falsely so called" (1 Tim **6** 20). The apostles could therefore use symbolism from the natural world more freely, and so we find St. John speaking of Our Lord as "There was the true light, even the light which lighteth every man, coming into the world" (Jn **1** 9), and again, "God is light, and in him is no darkness at all" (1 Jn **1** 5); and again, that the glory of the New Jerus shall be that "the city hath no need of the sun, neither of the moon, to shine upon it: for the glory of God did lighten it, and the lamp thereof is the Lamb" (Rev **21** 23); while the great modern discovery that nearly every form of terrestrial energy is derived ultimately from the energy of the sun's rays, gives a most striking appropriateness to the imagery of St. James that 'Every good gift and perfect boon is from above, coming down from the Father of lights, with whom can be no variation, neither shadow that is cast by turning' (Jas **1** 17 ERV).

3. The Moon

(1) *The names for the moon.*—Three words are trd "moon" in the OT, not including cases where "month" has been rendered "moon" for the sake of a more flowing sentence: (*a*) *Lebhānāh*, "white"; a poetic expression, used in connection with *ḥammāh*, "heat," for the sun.

(*b*) *Ḥōdhesh*, "new moon," meaning "new," "fresh." As the Hebrews reckoned their months from the actual first appearance of the young crescent, *ḥōdhesh* is most frequently trd "month." Thus "In the six hundredth year of Noah's life, in the second month, on the seventeenth day of the month" (Gen **7** 11), and in the great majority of cases, the word for month is *ḥōdhesh*, "new moon." In Isa **66** 23, "from one new moon to another," should be lit. "from new moon to new moon." Once it is rendered "monthly" (Isa **47** 13), when it is used to denote the astrologers who fixed the omens of the opening month. *Ḥōdhesh*, therefore, when trd "new moon" is not a designation of the actual heavenly body, but denotes the first day of the month. It is a term directly or indirectly connected with the calendar.

(*c*) *Yārēaḥ*, probably "wandering," a very appropriate primitive term for the moon, since her motion among the stars from night to night is sufficiently rapid to have caught the attention of very early observers. Its use therefore as the proper name for the "lesser light" indicates that the systematic observation of the heavenly bodies had commenced, and that the motion of the moon, relative to the stars, had been recognized.

Yeraḥ, "month," is twice trd "moon" (Dt **33** 14; Isa **60** 20), but without any great reason for the variation in either case.

(2) *The lesser light-giver.*—The direct references in Scripture to the moon as a light-giver are not numerous, but those that occur are significant of the great importance of moonlight in ancient times, when artificial lights were few, expensive and dim, and the lighting of streets and roads was unthought of. To shepherds, the moon was of especial assistance, and many of the people of Israel maintained the habits of their forefathers and led the shepherd's life long after the settlement of the nation in Pal. The return of the moonlit portion of the month was therefore an occasion for rejoicing and for solemn thanks to God, and the "new moon" as well as the Sabbath was a day of special offerings. On the other hand one of the judgments threatened against the enemies of God was that the light of the moon should be withheld. The threat made against Pharaoh is "I will cover the sun with a cloud, and the moon shall not give its light" (Ezk **32** 7); and in the day of the Lord denounced against Babylon, "The sun shall be darkened in its going forth, and the moon shall not cause its light to shine" (Isa **13** 10). But among the glories of the restoration of Israel it is promised that "the light of the moon [*lebhānāh*] shall be as the light of the sun [*ḥammāh*]" (Isa **30** 26).

(3) *Phases of the moon.*—There is no direct mention of the phases of the moon in Scripture; a remarkable fact, and one that illustrates the foolishness of attempting to prove the ignorance of the sacred writers by the argument from silence, since it is not conceivable that men at any time were ignorant of the fact that the moon changes her apparent shape and size. So far from the Hebrews being plunged in such a depth of more than savage ignorance, they based their whole calendar on the actual observation of the first appearance of the young crescent. In two passages in RV we find the expression "at the full moon," *keṣeh* (Ps **81** 3; Prov **7** 20), but though this is what is intended, the literal meaning of the word is doubtful, and may be that given in AV, "at the day appointed." In another passage already quoted, there is a reference to the dark part of the month. "Thy sun shall no more go down, neither shall thy moon [*yeraḥ*, "month"] withdraw itself"—the "withdrawn" part of the month being the time near new moon when the moon is nearly in conjunction with the sun and therefore invisible.

The periodical changes of the moon are its ordinances (Jer **31** 35). It was also appointed for "seasons" (Ps **104** 19), that is, for religious assemblies or feasts (*mō'ădhīm*). Two of these were held at the full of the moon, the Passover and the Feast of Tabernacles; one at the new moon, the Feast of Trumpets; but the ordinary new moon did not rank among the great "appointed feasts" (*mō'ădhīm*). As light-giver, assisting men in their labors with the flock and in the field and helping them on their journeys; as time-measurer, indicating the progress of the months and the seasons for the great religious festivals, the moon was to the pious Hebrew an evidence of the goodness and wisdom of God.

The "round tires like the moon," worn by the daughters of Zion (Isa **3** 18 AV), and those on the camels of Zeba and Zalmunna (Jgs **8** 21 AVm), were designated by the same Heb word, *sahărōnīm*, trd in the Vulg as *lunulae*, and were little round ornaments, probably round like crescents, not discs like the full moon.

Jericho possibly means "the city of the moon," and Jerah, "moon," was the name of one of the sons of Joktan.

4. Signs

(1) *Solar and lunar eclipses.*—The sun and moon were not only given "for days and years" (Gen **1** 14), but also "for signs," and in no way do they better fulfil what was in the old time understood by this word than in their eclipses. Nothing in Nature is more impressive than a total eclipse of the sun; the mysterious darkness, the sudden cold, the shining forth of the weird corona, seen at no other time,

Corona of Minimum Type.

affect even those who know its cause, and strike unspeakable terror in those who cannot foresee or understand it. In bygone ages an eclipse of the sun was counted an omen of disaster, indeed as itself the worst of disasters, by all nations except that one to whom the word of the prophet came: "Learn not the way of the nations, and be not dismayed at the signs of heaven; for the nations are dismayed at them" (Jer **10** 2). To the Heb prophets, eclipses were "signs" of the power and authority of God who forbade them to be alarmed at portents which distressed the heathen.

The phenomena of both solar and lunar eclipses are briefly but unmistakably described by several of the prophets. Joel refers to them twice (**2** 10 and 31), the second time very definitely: "The sun shall be turned into darkness, and the moon into blood," and this was quoted by St. Peter on the Day of Pentecost (Acts **2** 19.20). St. John also says that when the sixth seal was opened "the sun became black as sackcloth of hair, and the whole moon became as blood" (Rev **6** 12). When the new moon in its revolution or turning comes exactly between the earth and the sun, and its shadow—the "shadow that is cast by turning" of Jas **1** 17—falls on the earth, the sun is completely hidden and its glowing disc is replaced by the dark body of the moon; "the sun is turned into darkness." When the shadow of the earth falls upon the full moon, and the only rays from the sun that reach it have passed through an immense thickness of our atmosphere and are therefore of a dull copper-red color like clotted blood, "the moon is turned into blood."

(2) *The wings of the morning.*—But a solar eclipse is not solely darkness and terror. Scarcely has the dark moon hidden the last thread of sunlight than a beautiful pearly halo, the corona, is seen surrounding the blackness. This corona changes its shape from one eclipse to another, but the simplest form is that of a bright ring with outstretched wings,

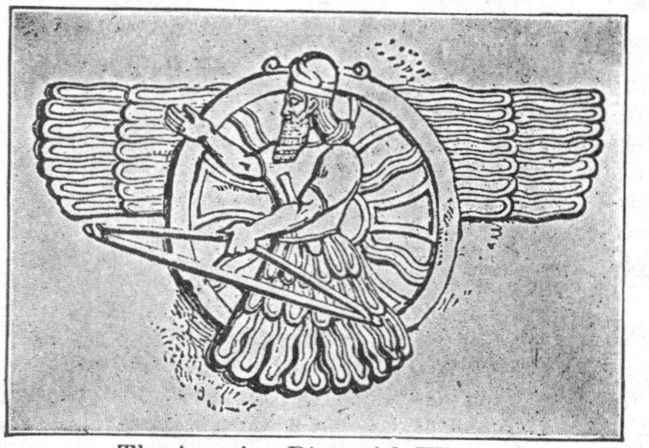

The Assyrian Ring with Wings.

and is characteristic of times when the sun has but few spots upon it. This form appears to have been the origin of the sacred symbol of the ring or disc with wings, so frequently figured on Egyp, Bab and Pers monuments. It is possible that these coronal "wings of the sun" may have been in the mind of the prophet Malachi when he wrote, "Unto you that fear my name shall the sun of righteousness arise with healing in its wings" (Mal **4** 2). The metaphor "wings of the morning" of Ps **139** 9 is however more probably due to the long streamers, the crepuscular rays, seen at dawn when the sun rises behind a low bank of clouds.

Total eclipses of the moon must frequently have been visible in Pal as in other countries, but only two or three total eclipses of the sun were visible there during OT history; that of 831 BC, August 15, was total in Judaea, and that of 824 BC, April 2, very nearly total. It has been suggested that two eclipses of the sun were predicted in the OT—that of Nineveh, 763 BC, June 15, in Am **8** 9, and that of Thales, 585 BC, May 28, in Isa **13** 10, but the suggestion has little to support it.

5. Seasons

(1) *The meaning of the word.*—The sun and moon were appointed "to give light upon the earth," and "for signs," and "for days and years." They were also appointed "for seasons" (*mō‘ădhīm*), i.e. "appointed assemblies." These seasons were not primarily such seasons as the progress of the year brings forth in the form of changes of weather or of the condition of vegetation; they were seasons for worship. The word *mō‘ēdh* occurs some 219 times; in 149, it is trd "congregation," and in about 50 other instances by "solemn assembly" or some equivalent expression. Thus before ever man was created, God had provided for him times to worship and had appointed two great lights of heaven to serve as signals to call to it.

The appointed sacred seasons of the Jews form a most complete and symmetrical series, developing from times indicated by the sun alone to times indicated by the sun and moon together, and completed in times indicated by luni-solar cycles.

(2) *Natural seasons for worship.*—The sun alone indicated the hours for daily worship; at sunrise, when the day began, there was the morning sacrifice; at sunset, when the day closed, there was the evening sacrifice.

The moon indicated the time for monthly worship; when the slender crescent of the new moon was first seen in the western sky, special sacrifices were ordained with the blowing of trumpets over them.

The sun and moon together marked the times for the two great religious festivals of the year. At the beginning of the bright part of the year, when the moon was full in the first month of spring, the Passover, followed by the Feast of Unleavened Bread, was held. At the end of the bright part of the year, when the moon was full in the first month of autumn, the Feast of Tabernacles was held. These may all be termed natural seasons for worship, obviously marked out as appropriate. The beginning and close of the bright part of the day, and of the bright part of the year, and the beginning of the bright part of the month, have been observed by many nations.

(3) *Hallowing of the seventh.*—But that which was distinctive in the system of the Jewish festivals was the hallowing of the seventh: the seventh day, the seventh week, the seventh month, the seventh year were all specially marked out. The sun alone indicated the Sabbath by the application of the sacred number seven to the unit of time given by the day. For the period of seven days, the week was not dependent upon any phase of the moon's relation to the sun; it was not a quarter month, but a free week, running on independently of the month. The Jewish Sabbath therefore differed from the Bab, which was tied to the lunar month. The same principle was applied also to the year; every seventh year was set apart as a period of rest, the Sabbatic year.

Every seventh day, every seventh year, was thus observed. But for the week and month, the principle of hallowing the seventh came into operation only once in each year. The Feast of Pentecost, or as it was also called, the Feast of Weeks, was held at the close of the seventh week from the morrow after the Sabbath of Unleavened Bread; and the new moon of the seventh month was held as a special feast, the Feast of Trumpets, "a holy convocation. Ye shall do no servile work" (Lev **23** 24.25). The other new moons of the year were not thus distinguished.

The weekly Sabbath, the Passover, Pentecost, and the Feasts of Trumpets and of Tabernacles, with one other day of solemnity, were in an especial sense, the *mō‘ădhīm* of the Lord.

The seventh day was especially the day of worship, and to correspond, the seventh month was especially the month of worship; and this, not only because it was ushered in with peculiar solemnity, and included one of the chief great feasts of the year, but because it furnished the culminating ceremony of the entire Jewish system, the great Day of Atonement, held on the tenth day of the month, and therefore on a day not marked directly by any phase of the moon. The Day of Atonement purged away the offences of the past year, and restored Israel to the full enjoyment of the Divine favor.

(4) *The Jubilee a luni-solar cycle.*—The Jewish month was a natural month, based upon the actual observation of the young crescent. The Jewish year was a natural year, that is, a solar tropical year, based upon actual observation of the ripening of the grain. But there is not an exact number of days in a lunar month, nor is there an exact number of months in a solar year; twelve lunar months falling short of the year, by eleven days; so that in three years the error would amount to more than a complete month, and to restore the balance a thirteenth month would have to be intercalated. As the months were determined from actual observation, and as observation would be interrupted from time to time by unfavorable weather, it was necessary to have some means for determining when intercalation would take place, irrespective of it. And this was provided by carrying the principle of hallowing the seventh, one stage farther. Not only was the seventh of the day, week, month and year distinguished, but the seventh week of years was marked by the blowing of the trumpet of Jubilee on the Day of Atonement. The Day of Atonement meant the restitution of Israel to the Divine favor; the blowing of the trumpet of Jubilee every forty-ninth year meant "the restitution of all things"; every Hebrew in servitude returned to freedom, all land, mortgaged or sold, returned to its original owner.

And this period of 49 solar years was astronomically a period of restitution, for the sun and moon returned nearly to their original positions relative to each other, since 49 solar years are 606 lunar months with an error of only 32 hours. So that though the Jubilee period is not a perfect lunar cycle, it was quite exact enough to guide the Jewish priests in drawing up their calendar in cases where the failure of observation had given rise to some doubt.

The beginning of each month was marked by the blowing of the two silver trumpets (*ḥăçōçerāh:* Nu **10** 2.10). The beginning of the civil, that is to say, of the agricultural year, was marked by a special blowing of trumpets (*terū'āh*), giving the name "Feast of Trumpets" to that new moon (Lev **23** 24; Nu **29** 1). And the beginning of a new cycle of 49 years was marked by the Jubilee, the loud trumpet (*shōphār:* Lev **25** 9). Thus the cycle of the Jubilee made symmetrical, completed, and welded together all the *mō'ădhīm* of the Lord —the two great lights were set "for seasons."

(5) *The 19-year luni-solar cycle.*—The cycle of the Jubilee was sufficient for the purposes of the religious calendar so long as the nation inhabited its own land, since from its small extent there would be no conflict of time reckoning and it would be easy to notify the appearance of the new moon from one end of the country to the other. But after the captivities, when the people were scattered from Gozan of the Medes to Syene on the Nile, it was necessary to devise some method by which the Jews, however far they had been dispersed, would be able to reckon for themselves as to when the moon was new for Jerus. We have lately learned from the discovery of a number of Aram. papyri at Syene that there was a colony of Jews there who used a calendar constructed, not from observation, but from calculation based upon a very exact luni-solar cycle (E. B. Knobel, "Ancient Jewish Calendar Dates in Aramaic Papyri," *Monthly Notices of the Royal Astronomical Society*, LXVIII, 334). This cycle, known to us by the name of its supposed discoverer, Meton, is one of 19 years, which is only two hours short of 235 complete months. As this Jewish colony appears to have been founded after Nebuchadnezzar's destruction of Jerus by some of the refugees who fled into Egypt with Johanan the son of Kareah (Jer **40–44**), this acquaintance with the Metonic cycle cannot have been due to Bab influence. Nor can it have been due to Egyp, since the Egyptians did not use or require any such cycle, their year being a solar one of 365 days. Indeed no other nation appears to have been aware of it until, a generation later, Meton, the Athenian, won immortal fame by announcing it. The evidence of these Syene papyri renders it probable that Meton did not himself discover the cycle but learned it from Jewish sources. Many of the Sem nations used, like the Jews, a natural month in conjunction with the natural year, but the Jews were the most likely to have discovered this cycle, since they alone had their worship centralized at a single shrine which became, in consequence, their standard observatory for their observation of the new moon. These observations, therefore, would all be comparable, and during the 400 years that the Temple stood, it must have been quite clear to them that the 19-year cycle not only gave them seven, the sacred number, of intercalated months, but brought the setting places of the new moons to the same points of the western horizon and in the same order.

It is clear from the evidence of these Syene papyri that the Jews, there, used the 19-year cycle both for fixing the day of the new moon, and in order to determine when a thirteenth month had to be intercalated, an illustration of the futility of "the argument from silence," for so far from there being any notice in Scripture of the use of a cycle for determining intercalation, there is no mention of intercalation at all.

(6) *The Jewish ritual preëxilic.*—Ever since this date of the Captivity, the 19-year cycle has been used by the Jews, and it gives to us the "Golden Number" which is employed in fixing the date of Easter in our own ecclesiastical calendar. Since the 19-year cycle has been in use ever since the Captivity, the 49-year cycle, the Jubilee, cannot have been an exilic or post-exilic innovation. In this fact we find the decision of the controversy which has so long divided critics as to whether the ritual legislation of the Jews dated from before or from after their captivity. We may take Kuenen as representing the more recent school: "Even the later prophets and historians, but more especially and emphatically those that lived before the Exile, were unacquainted with any ritual legislation, and specifically with that which has come down to us" (*The Hexateuch*, 273–74). "In determining its antiquity we must begin by considering its relation to Deuteronomy, to which it is evidently subsequent. . . . . This comes out most clearly in the legislation concerning the feasts. Other indications though less unequivocal, plead for the same relationship. In the next place the legislation itself gives evidence of the date of its origin, and those data which justify a positive inference point to the Babylonian captivity. . . . . It would follow that the 'legislation of sanctity' arose in the second half of the Bab captivity, presumably shortly before its close; and there is not a single valid objection to this date" (ib, 276). Kuenen was evidently unaware of the astronomical relations concerned in the ritual legislation, and was unable to anticipate the striking discoveries made from the Syene papyri. More recent knowledge has reversed the verdict which he pronounced so confidently. The traditional view, that the Heb ritual preceded the Captivity, was correct. For the Jubilee, with which the Day of Atonement was bound up, was both the culmination and the completion of the entire ritual, and, since the period of the Jubilee, as a luni-solar cycle, was preëxilic, the ritual, as a system, must have been preëxilic likewise.

(7) *The luni-solar cycles of Daniel.*—The seasons for which the sun and moon were appointed are mentioned in yet another connection. In the last vision given to Daniel the question was asked, "How long shall it be to the end of these wonders?" and it was answered, "It shall be for a time, times [dual], and a half; and when they have made an end of breaking in pieces the power of the holy people, all these things shall be finished" (Dnl **12** 6.7). From the parallel passage in Dnl **7** 25, where it is said of the fourth beast, "He shall think to change the times and the law; and they shall be given into his hand until a time [*'iddān*] and times [dual] and half a time," it is inferred that *mō'ēdh* in the first instance stands, like *'iddān* in the second, for a year; or the period is equivalent to half a week nomical significance is clear: 840,057 days are precisely 2,300 solar years, or 28,447 lunar months, or 30,487 anomalistic months, the anomalistic month being the period in which the moon travels from perigee to perigee. It is the most perfect luni-solar cycle known, and restores the two great lights exactly to their former relationship. This fullest "season" indicated by the sun and moon is given as that for the cleansing of the sanctuary, for the bringing in, as it were, of the full and perfect Jubilee.

It is not possible at present to decide as to whether the Jews had learnt of this cycle and its significance from their astronomical observations. If so, they must have been far in advance in mathematical science of all other nations of antiquity.

West

North

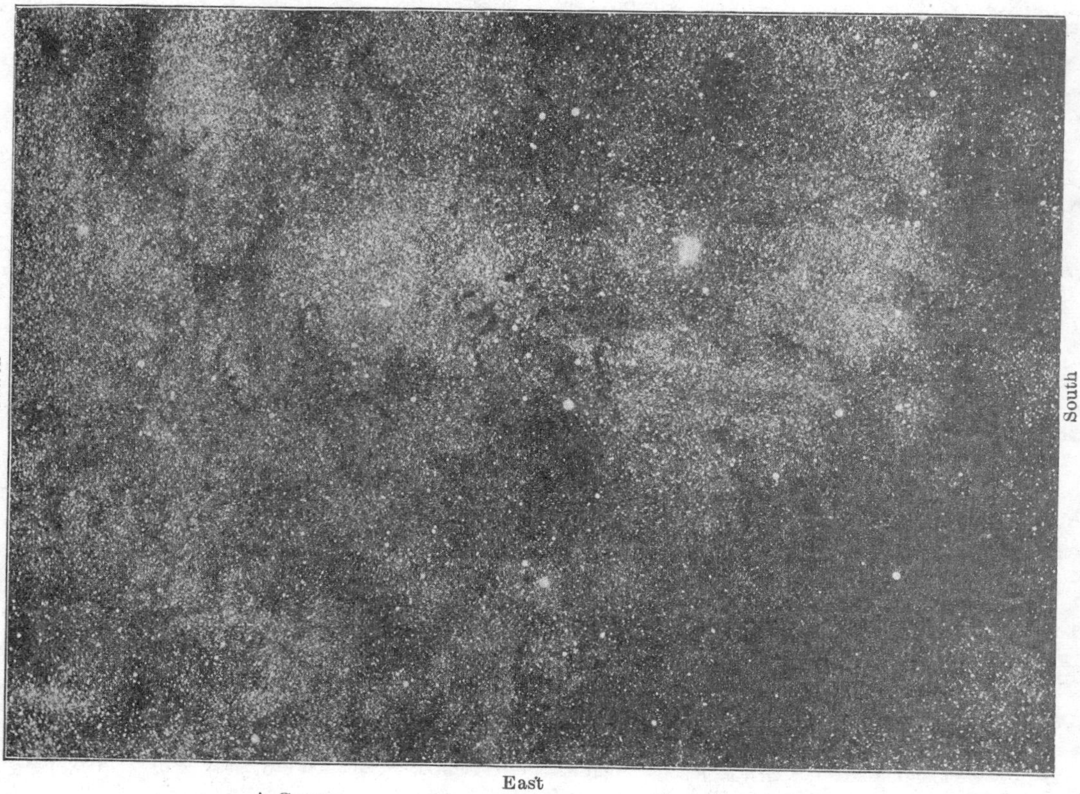

South

East

A Corner of the Milky Way (Region of *Theta Ophiuchi*).
(Photograph by Prof. E. E. Barnard, taken June 5, 1905.)

of years. The parallel passages in Rev **11** 2.3; **12** 6.14; **13** 5 have caused these years to be taken as conventional years of 360 days, each year being made up of 12 conventional months of 30 days, and on the year-day principle of interpretation, the entire period indicated would be one of 1,260 tropical years. This again is a luni-solar cycle, since 1,260 years contain 15,584 months correct to the nearest day. To the same prophet Daniel a further chronological vision was given, and a yet more perfect cycle indicated. In answer to the question, "How long shall be the vision concerning the continual burnt-offering, and the transgression that maketh desolate, to give both the sanctuary and the host to be trodden under foot?" the answer was returned, "Unto two thousand and three hundred evenings and mornings; then shall the sanctuary be cleansed" (Dnl **8** 13.14). Whatever may be the prophetic significance of the passage its astro-

If not, then it must have been given to them by Divine revelation, and its astronomical significance has been left for modern science to reveal.

As with the sun and moon, the stars are regarded under the two aspects of light-givers and time-measurers; or, in other words, as marking the seasons.

6. The Stars

(1) *Their number.*—But two other ideas are also strongly dwelt upon; the stars and the heaven of which they form the "host" are used to express the superlatives of number and of height. "Look now toward heaven, and number the stars, if thou be able to number them" (Gen **15** 5); "As the host of heaven cannot be numbered" (Jer **33** 22) are a few of the passages in which the stars are used for limitless number. Those separately visible to the naked eye at any one time do not exceed 2,000 in number, but it was just as evident to the Hebrews of old, as it was to

Ptolemy, the astronomer of Alexandria, that beside the stars separately visible, there is a background, a patterned curtain of light, which indicates by its granular and mottled appearance that it is made up of countless myriads of stars, too faint to be individually detected, too close to be individually defined. The most striking feature of this curtain is the grand stellar stream that we call the Milky Way, but the mind easily recognizes that the minute points of light, composing its pattern, are as really stars as the great leaders of the constellations. Later astronomy has confirmed the testimony of the prophets that the stars are without number. The earliest star catalogue, that of Hipparchus, contained a little over one thousand stars; the great International Photographic Chart will show the images of more than fifty millions, and there are photographs which show more than a hundred thousand stars on a single plate. The limit that has been reached is due only to the limited power of our telescopes or the limited time of exposure of the photographs, not to any limitation in the number of stars. To us today, as to the Psalmist of old, it is a token of the infinite power and knowledge of God that "He telleth the number of the stars; He giveth them all their names" (Ps **147** 4 AV).

(2) *Their distance.*—As regards the height, that is to say, the distance of the stars, this is immeasurable except in a very few cases. By using as a base line the enormous diameter of the earth's orbit—186,000,000 miles—astronomers have been able to get a hint as to the distance of some 40 or 50 stars. Of these the nearest, Alpha Centauri, is distant about twenty-five millions of millions of miles; the brighter stars are on the average quite ten times as far; whilst of the distances of the untold millions of stars beyond, we have no gauge. For us, as for King Solomon, the "heaven" of the stars is "for height" (Prov **25** 3), for a height that is beyond measure, giving us therefore the only fitting image for the immensity of God. So Zophar the Naamathite asked, "Canst thou find out the Almighty unto perfection? It is high as heaven; what canst thou do?" And Eliphaz the Temanite reiterated the same thought, "Is not God in the height of heaven? And behold the height of the stars, how high they are!" (Job **11** 7.8; **22** 12). And the height of the heaven, that is to say, the distance of the stars, stands as a symbol, not only of God's infinitude, but of His faithfulness and of His mercy: "Thus saith Jehovah: If heaven above can be measured, and the foundations of the earth searched out beneath, then will I also cast off all the seed of Israel for all that they have done, saith Jehovah" (Jer **31** 37). And the Psalmist sings, "For as the heaven is high above the earth, so great is his mercy toward them that fear him" (Ps **103** 11 AV).

(3) *Their brightness.*—The stars are not all of equal brightness; a fact alluded to by St. Paul when he wrote that "one star differeth from another star in glory" (1 Cor **15** 41). The ancient Gr astronomers divided the stars according to their brightness into six classes or magnitudes, to use the modern technical term, the average star in any particular magnitude giving about two and a half times as much light as the average star of the next magnitude.

Just as the number of the stars and their ordered

West

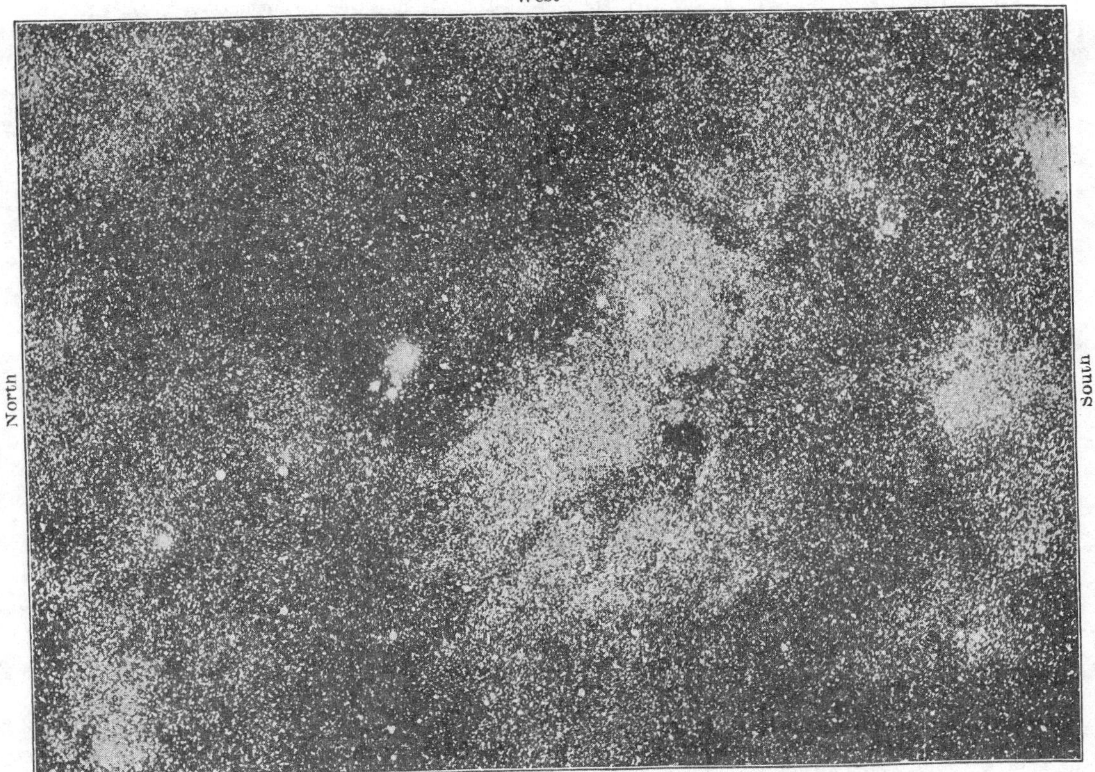

East

STAR SWARMS. SMALL STAR CLOUD IN *Sagittarius.*
(Photograph by Prof. E. E. Barnard, taken July 31, 1905.)

movement led them to be considered as a mighty army, "the host of heaven," and as a type of that other celestial host, the holy angels, so the individual stars are taken as fitly setting forth, by their brightness and exalted position, spiritual powers and intelligences, whether these are the angels of God, as in Job **38** 7, or rulers of churches, as in Rev **1** 20. The same image is naturally applied in a yet higher sense to Christ Himself, who is the "star out of Jacob" (Nu **24** 17), and "the bright, the morning star" (Rev **22** 16; 2 Pet **1** 19).

7. Morning Stars

In ancient times there were two methods by which the progress of the year could be learned from observation of the heavens. The sun was "for seasons," and the change in its place of rising or of setting supplied the first method. The second method was supplied by the stars. For as the Heb shepherds, such as Jacob, Moses, David and Amos, kept watch over their flocks by night, they saw the silent procession of the stars through the hours of darkness, and knew without clock or timepiece how they were progressing. They noticed what stars were rising in the E., what stars were culminating in the S., what were setting in the W., and how the northern stars, always visible, like a great dial, were turning. But as the eastern horizon began to brighten toward the dawn, they would specially note what stars were the last to rise before their shining was drowned in the growing light of day. These, the last stars to appear in the E. before sunrise, were the "morning stars," the heralds of the sun. As morning followed morning, these morning stars would be seen earlier and earlier, and therefore for a longer time before they disappeared in the dawn, until some morning, other stars, unseen before, would shine out for a few moments, and thus supplant the stars seen earlier as the actual heralds of the sun. Such a first appearance of a star was termed by the Gr astronomers its "heliacal" rising, and the mention in Scripture of "morning stars," or "stars of the twilight" (Job **38** 7; **3** 9), shows that the Hebrews like the Greeks were familiar with this feature of the ordinances of heaven, and noted the progress of the year by observation of the apparent changes of the celestial host. One star would herald the beginning of spring, another the coming of winter; the time to plow, the time to sow, the time of the rains would all be indicated by successive "morning stars" as they appeared.

8. Falling Stars

(1) *Meteorites.*—Meteors are not stars at all in the popular sense of the word, but are quite small bodies drawn into our atmosphere, and rendered luminous for a few moments by the friction of their rush through it. But as they have been shown not to be mere distempers of the air, as they were considered at one time, but bodies of a truly planetary nature, traveling round the sun in orbits as defined as that of the earth itself, the epithet is quite appropriate to them. They are astronomical and not merely terrestrial bodies. Meteors are most striking either when they are seen as solitary aerolites or when they fall in some great shower. The most celebrated shower which seemed to radiate from the constellation Leo—and hence called the Leonid—gave for centuries a magnificent spectacle every thirty-three years; the last great occasion having been on November 14, 1866. Those who saw that shower could appreciate the vivid description given by St. John when he wrote, "The stars of the heaven fell unto the earth, as a fig tree casteth her unripe figs when she is shaken of a great wind" (Rev **6** 13), for the meteors fell like autumn leaves, driven by a great storm, as numerous and as fast. The prophet Isaiah also used a very similar figure (Isa **34** 4).

(2) *The star "Wormwood."*—Such great meteoric showers are most impressive spectacles, but solitary meteors are sometimes hardly less striking. Bolides or aerolites, as such great solitary meteors are termed, are apparently of great size, and are sometimes so brilliant as to light up the sky even in broad daylight. Such a phenomenon is referred to by St. John in his description of the star Wormwood: "There fell from heaven a great star, burning as a torch" (Rev **8** 10). Such aerolites are not entirely consumed in their passage through our atmosphere, but portions of them reach the ground, and in some cases large masses have been found intact. These are generally of a stony nature, but others are either almost pure iron or contain much of that metal. Such a meteoric stone was used as the pedestal of the image of the goddess Diana at Ephesus, and the "townclerk" of the city referred to this circumstance when he reminded the Ephesians that their city was "temple-keeper of the great Diana, and of the image which fell down from Jupiter" (Acts **19** 35).

9. Wandering Stars

It has already been noted that the moon may perhaps have received its Heb name from the fact of its being a "wanderer" among the stars, but there is no direct and explicit reference in Scripture to other celestial "wanderers" except in Jude ver 13: "Wandering stars, for whom the blackness of darkness hath been reserved for ever." These *astéres planḗtai* are not our "planets," but either meteors or comets, more probably the latter, as meteors are more appropriately described as "falling stars."

(1) *Comets as a spiritual type.*—But as comets and meteors are intimately connected with each other—meteors being in many cases the débris of comets—the simile applies to either. False professors of religion, unstable or apostate teachers, are utterly unlike the stars which shine forth in heaven for ever, but are fitly represented by comets, which are seen only for a few weeks or days, and then are entirely lost to sight, or by meteors, which flash out for a few moments, and are then totally extinguished.

All the great comets, all the comets that have been conspicuous to the naked eye, with the single exception of that named after Halley, have appeared but once within the period of human records and Halley's Comet only takes 80 days to traverse that part of its orbit which lies within the orbit of the earth; the rest of its period of revolution—76 years—is passed outside that boundary, and for 38 years at a time it remains outside the orbit of Neptune, more than 2,800,000,000 miles from the sun. The other great comets have only visited our neighborhood once within our experience.

(2) *Comets referred to in Scripture?*—The question has been raised whether the appearance of comets is ever referred to in Scripture. Jos, speaking of the signs which preceded the destruction of Jerus by Titus, says, "Thus there was a star resembling a sword which stood over the city, and a comet that continued a whole year" (*BJ*, VI, v, 3). The "star resembling a sword" was doubtless the return of Halley's Comet in 66 AD, and the phrase used by Jos has suggested that it was a stellar phenomenon that is referred to in 1 Ch **21** 16: "The angel of Jehovah . . . . between earth and heaven, having a drawn sword in his hand stretched out over Jerus." But this, and the corresponding suggestion as to the nature of the flaming sword that kept the way of the tree of life (Gen **3** 24), are unsupported conjectures not worthy of attention. The astronomer Pingré thought that the first vision of Jeremiah of the "rod of an almond tree" and of a "boiling caldron" (Jer **1** 11.13) had its physical

basis in a return of Halley's Comet, and other commentators have thought that cometary appearances were described in the "pillars of smoke" of Joel **2** 30; but none of these suggestions appear to have plausibility.

II. The Constellations.—The principal achievement of the science of astronomy in the cents. during which the books of the OT were written was the arrangement and naming of the constellations, and there can be no reasonable doubt that the same system was known to the Hebrews as that which has been handed down to us through the Gr astronomers. St. Paul certainly knew the Gr constellations, for in his sermon on Mars' Hill (Acts **17** 28) he quoted from that poetical description of them which Aratus the great poet of Cilicia had written about 270 BC. But these constellations have a much greater antiquity than this, and it is probable that they were well known to Abraham before he left Ur of the Chaldees. It has been frequently shown (*The Astronomy of the Bible*, 158; *Astronomy without a Telescope*, 5) that these constellations themselves supply evidence that they were designed about 2700 BC. They thus antedated the time of Abraham by some cents., and since some of their most characteristic forms are found upon old Bab "boundary stones," it is clear that they were known in the country from whence he came out.

The direct references to these old constellation-forms in Scripture are not numerous. One of the clearest is in Job **26** 13, where "formed the crooked serpent" (AV) is used as the correlative of "garnished the heavens"; the great constellation of the writhing Dragon, placed at the crown of the heavens, being used, metaphorically, as an expression for all the constellations of the sky. For by its folds it encircles both the poles, that of the equator and that of the ecliptic.

1. Nāḥāsh, the "Crooked Serpent"

The term *bārīaḥ*, rendered "crooked" but better as in RVm as "fleeing," is applied by Isaiah to "Leviathan" (*liwyāthān:* Isa **27** 1), properly a "wreathed" or writhing animal, twisted in folds, and hence also called by the prophet *'ăḳallāthōn*, "crooked," "twisted," or "winding"; a very appropriate designation for *Draco*, the great polar Dragon. But the latter was not the only "crooked serpent" in the constellations; there were three others, two of which were placed with an astronomical significance not less precise than the coiling of *Draco* round the poles. *Hydra*, the Watersnake, marked out the original celestial equator for about one-third of its circumference, and *Serpens*, the Adder, lay partly along the celestial equator and then was twisted up the autumnal colure, and reached the zenith with its head.

2. Leviathan

The arrangement of the twelve signs of the zodiac to mark out the apparent yearly path of the sun, and of these three serpent-forms to hold their respective and significant positions in the heavens, shows that a real progress in astronomy had been made before the constellations were designed, and that their places were allotted to these figures on a definite astronomical plan.

A further purpose is shown by the relation of the three serpents to the neighboring figures, and it is clear that the history preserved in Gen **3** was known to the designers of the constellations, and that they wished to perpetuate its memory by means of the stellar frescoes. For the constellations, *Scorpio*, *Ophiuchus* and *Serpens*, show us a man strangling a snake and standing on a scorpion; the head of the latter he crushes with one foot, but his other foot is wounded by its reverted sting. When these three constellations were due S., that is to say, at midnight in spring-time, *Hercules* and *Draco* were due north, and presented the picture of a man kneeling on one knee, and pressing down with his other foot the head of the great northern serpent or dragon. During the winter midnight the zodiacal constellation on the meridian was the Virgin, figured as a woman holding an ear of corn in her hand, while

3. The Seed of the Woman

Hercules and *Draco*.

beneath her the immense length of *Hydra* was stretched out upon its belly in the attitude of a snake when fleeing at full speed. These figures are evidently meant to set forth in picture that which is expressed in word in Gen **3** 14.15, "And Jehovah God said unto the serpent, Because thou hast done this, cursed art thou above all cattle, and above every beast of the field; upon thy belly shalt thou go, and dust shalt thou eat all the days of thy life: and I will put enmity between thee and the woman, and between thy seed and her seed: he shall bruise thy head, and thou shalt bruise his heel."

Nor is this the only narrative in Genesis which finds a parallel in the constellations. Among the southern groups we find a ship *Argo* that has grounded on a rock; and close to it stands a figure, *Centaurus*, who is apparently slaying an animal, *Lupus*, beside an Altar. The cloud of smoke arising from the Altar is represented by the Milky Way, and in the midst of the cloud there is set the Bow of the Archer, *Sagittarius*. Here there seems to be pictured the covenant made with Noah after he offered his sacrifice when he left the ark: "I do set my bow in the cloud, and it shall be for a token of a covenant between me and the earth" (Gen **9** 13). Thus the constellations, designed several cents. before the time of Abraham,

4. The Bow Set in the Cloud

clearly express a knowledge, and appear designed to preserve a remembrance of the two first promises made by God to mankind as recorded in the early chapters of Gen.

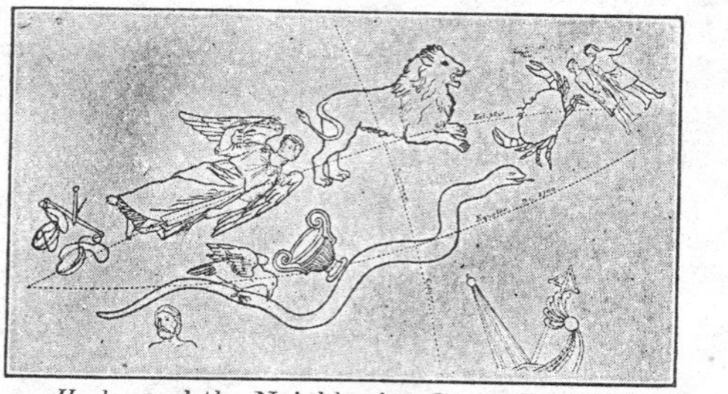

Hydra and the Neighboring Constellations.

There is no need to assume, as some writers have done, that all the 48 primitive constellations were of Divine origin, or even that any of them were. If some of the early astronomers possessed in one form or another the histories that we have in Gen **3**, **8** and **9**, it would not be unnatural for them to attempt to preserve a memorial of them in the heavens by associating these figures with the stars.

It does not follow that all the old constellations have an analogous significance, or that if they have, we should now be able to detect it, and a great deal of ingenuity has been wasted in the attempt to convert the old 48 constellations into a sort of gospel in hieroglyphic. Interpretations of this order were current quite early in Christian times, for they are denounced at considerable length and in detail by St. Hippolytus in his *Refutation of All the Heresies*, cir 210 AD. Their revival in recent years is chiefly due to *Mazzārōth*, a series of papers by the late Miss Frances Rolleston in which fanciful etymologies were given to the Arab. names by which the principal stars are known. These names, for the most part, simply indicate the places which the stars were severally supposed to hold in the figures to which they were assigned, and Miss Rolleston's derivations for them are quite misleading and unfounded. Nevertheless her results have been blindly accepted by a number of writers.

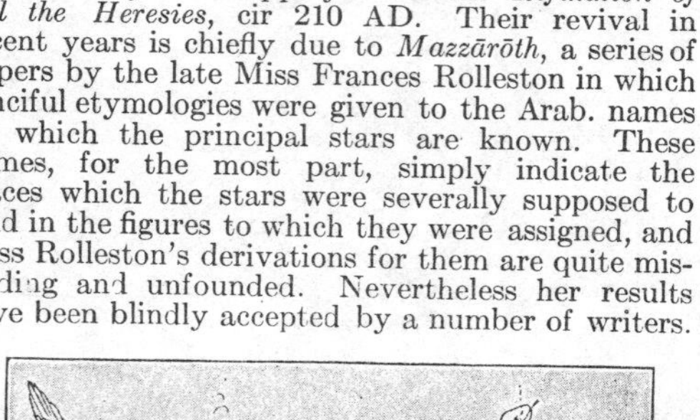

Ophiuchus and the Neighboring Constellations.

5. The Dragon of Eclipse

The peculiar arrangement of the serpent forms in the constellations, and especially the position allotted to *Hydra*, extended along the equator with its head near the spring equinox and its tail near that of autumn, appears to have given rise to the terms "Dragon's Head" ☊, and "Dragon's Tail" ☋, for the nodes or points of intersection of the ecliptic (the apparent path of the sun) with the celestial equator, and hence for nodes in general. As eclipses of the sun and moon can only occur when those bodies are near the nodes of the moon's orbit, that is, near the Dragon's Head or Tail, the myth seems to have arisen that such eclipses were due to one or other of the two great lights being swallowed by a dragon, and a reference to this myth is found in Job **3** 8: "Let them curse it that curse the day, who are ready [RVm skilful] to rouse up leviathan." The persons referred to are the magicians who pretended to be able by their incantations to cause an eclipse of the sun by bringing up the mythical dragon that was supposed to devour it. Astronomical nomenclature still retains a trace of these old expressions, for the time taken by the moon to pass from one node to the same node again is still called a "draconic month," a "month of the dragon."

6. Joseph's Dream

If we realize that the Hebrews were quite familiar with the same constellation figures that we have inherited through the Greeks, several indirect allusions to them gain an added meaning. Thus Joseph dreamed that "the sun and the moon and eleven stars made obeisance" to him (Gen **37** 9). The twelve constellations of the zodiac are the twelve among which the sun and moon move, and thus constitute, as it were, their family. Eleven of them therefore represented eleven sons of Jacob, Joseph himself being of course the twelfth. There is some evidence that the time came when the suggestion of this dream was acted upon to the extent that some of the tribes adopted certain of the constellation figures by way of crest or armorial bearing. In Nu **2** it is stated that each of the four camps into which the host of Israel was divided had its own standard: "Neither the Mosaic law nor the OT generally gives us any intimation as to the form or character of the standard (*deghel*). According to rabbinical tradition, the standard of Judah bore the figure of a lion, that of Reuben the likeness of a man, or of a man's head, that of Ephraim the figure of an ox, and that of Dan the figure of an eagle; so that the four living creatures united in the cherubic forms described by Ezekiel were represented upon these four standards" (Keil and Delitzsch, *Commentary on the Pentateuch*, III, 17). A variant of this tradition gives as the standard of Reuben, "unstable as water" (Gen **49** 4 AV), a Man and a River, and of Dan, "Dan shall be a serpent in the way" (Gen **49** 17), an Eagle and a Serpent. These four forms are also found in the constellations in the four quarters of the heavens. *Aquarius*, the man with a stream of water, and *Leo* were the original zodiacal constellations of the two solstices, *Taurus* was that of the spring equinox, and *Aquila* and *Serpens* were close to the autumnal equinox, the latter being actually upon the colure.

7. The Standards of the Tribes

8. The Cherubim

This distribution of the four cherubic forms in the four quarters of heaven gives a special significance to the invocation used by Hezekiah and the Psalmist, "Thou that dwellest between the cherubims" (Isa **37** 16 AV; Ps **80** 1 AV). The Shekinah glory rested indeed between the golden cherubim over the ark in the Holy of Holies, but "the Most High dwelleth not in houses made with hands" (Acts **7** 48), and the same cherubic forms were pictured on the curtains of the heavens. "Behold, heaven and the heaven of heavens cannot contain thee" (1 K **8** 27); 'Thou dwellest between the cherubim,' filling the infinite expanse of the stellar universe.

When Balaam saw "Israel dwelling according to their tribes; and the Spirit of God came upon him" (Nu **24** 2), it was not unnatural that he should allude in his prophecy to the great standards which he would see floating above the camps, and three of the four appear to be indicated:

9. Balaam's Prophecy

the bull of Joseph—"He hath as it were the strength of the wild-ox"; the lion of Judah—"He lay down as a lion and as a great lion," AV; and *Aquarius*, the man pouring out a stream of water from a pitcher, the cognizance of Reuben—"Water shall flow from his buckets" (Nu **24** 7.8.9).

In a similar way when the prophets refer to the enemies of Israel under the figure of dragons or reptiles, there seems occasionally an indirect reference to the serpents that represent the powers of evil in the pictures that have been associated with

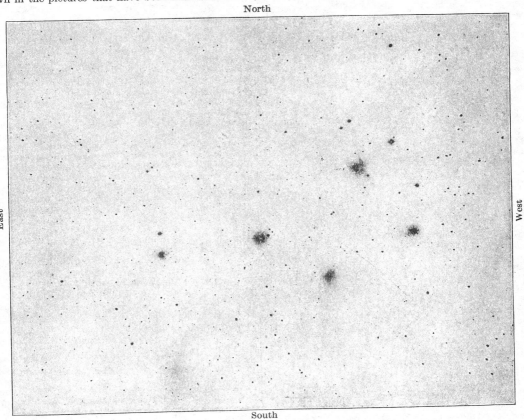

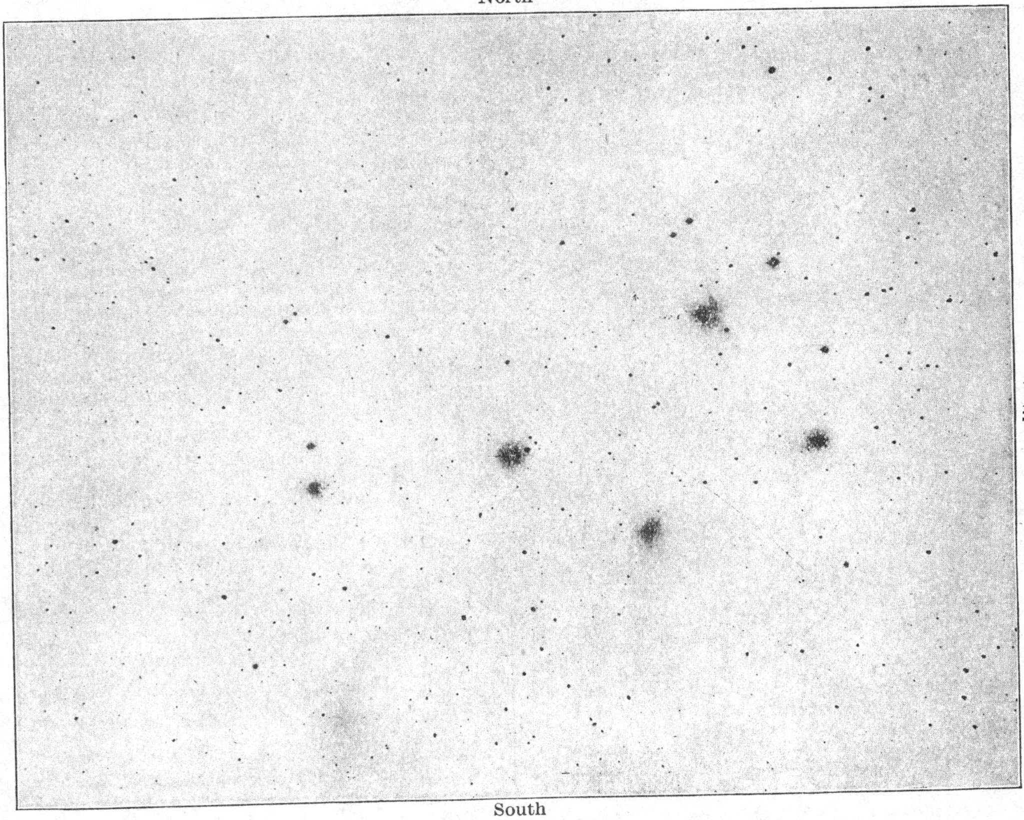

THE PLEIADES.

the star groups. Thus in Isa **27** 1, ERV, it is prophesied that the Lord "shall punish leviathan the swift serpent, and leviathan the crooked serpent; and He shall slay the dragon that is in the sea"; the first allusion being appropriate to the attitude of *Hydra*, the second to *Draco*, the third to *Cetus*. Whilst the group of constellations, *Andromeda*, *Cetus* and *Eridanus*, the woman persecuted by a dragon that casts a river out of its mouth, a river which flowing down below the horizon appears to be swallowed up by the earth, would seem to have furnished St. John with some of the material for the imagery of Rev **12** in his great vision.

Besides references direct or indirect to the familiar constellation figures, four special astronomical terms occur in the Heb of the OT which have given rise to much discussion. These are *Kīmāh*, *Keṣīl*, *Mazzārōth* and *'Ayish*. The tradition of their significance had been lost before the LXX tr was made, but it may be taken as practically certain that the renderings given in RV are substantially correct.

The word *Kīmāh* occurs in three passages, in each case in conjunction with *Keṣīl* (Am **5** 8; Job **9** 9; **38** 31). It apparently means a "heap"

10. Pleiades

or "cluster," and is hence especially applicable to the beautiful little group of the Pleiades, the most conspicuous star cluster visible to the naked eye. There is the less uncertainty about this identification since "*kima*" is the term generally used in Syr lit. to denote the Pleiades.

Six stars can now easily be seen by any good sight, but very keen-sighted persons can detect more; thus Maestlin, the tutor of Kepler, mapped 11 before the invention of the telescope, and in recent times Carrington and Denning have counted 14 with the naked eye. Still, 6 is the number visible to most persons, though there is a curiously widespread and uniform tradition that they once "were seven who now are six," and seven is the number almost always assigned to them in literature. Hesiod calls them "the seven sisters, the Virgin stars," and Milton, "the seven Atlantic sisters," as representing the daughters of Atlas. Many of the Gr poets, however, regarded them as *Peleiádes*, "rock pigeons," doves, flying from the hunter Orion; but whether they have been considered as representing doves or maidens, seven has still been their traditional number. Possibly one of the group has declined in brightness in the course of the cents.; Alcyone would seem to have increased in brightness, for though now the brightest, it is not one of the four that figure in Ptolemy's Catalogue, and if one has increased in brightness, others may have diminished. In the telescope many hundreds of stars are visible. The photographic plate has registered thousands and shows the principal stars as enveloped and threaded together by delicate streams of nebulous matter, the stars shining on these filamentous lines of light like pearls upon a string. This, the appearance of the Pleiades on the best modern photographs, would be strikingly appropriate to the rendering of Job **38** 31, which has been adopted in the RV, "Canst thou bind the cluster [m "chain"] of the Pleiades?" and the question put to Job would be equivalent to asking him if it were his power that had brought together the Pleiades and bound them in so compact a cluster. This rendering which involves the reading "*ma'ănaddōth*" is supported by the LXX, and all the early versions, and hence by nearly all Orientalists. The reading in MT, "*ma'ădhannōth*," that is to say, "dainties" or "delights," and adopted in AV, where the word is paraphrased as "sweet influences," is however correct, as will be shown below.

The designation of the group as that of the seven stars gives a special significance to one of the details of the vision of St. John: "I saw seven golden candlesticks; and in the midst of the candlesticks one like unto a son of man, ... And He had in his right hand seven stars: . . . . The seven stars are the angels of the seven churches: and the seven candlesticks are seven churches" (Rev **1** 12.13.16.20). The seven stars in a single compact cluster shining as one, furnish an image of the church in its many diversities and its essential unity.

It may be well to correct here a certain widely diffused error. When it was discovered that the sun itself with all its attendant planets was traveling rapidly through space, the German astronomer Mädler hazarded the suggestion that the center of the sun's motion, the attracting body that governed it, might lie in the group of the Pleiades, and this suggestion has been quoted in many popular writings as if it were a demonstrated fact. It soon became evident that there was no sufficient ground for the suggestion, and the idea has been entirely abandoned by astronomers.

11. Orion

The word *K*^{e}*ṣīl* as denominating a constellation occurs in the singular number in three passages, and in each it is placed in antithesis to *Kīmāh*. In a fourth passage (Isa **13** 10) it occurs by itself and is in the plural. There is no doubt as to the significance of the word in its common use. In 70 cases it is tr^d either "fool" or "foolish." It does not signify a weak-minded person, so much as a violent, impious, self-confident one. As a star name, it is probably rightly considered to refer to the glorious constellation of Orion. According to an old tradition, the name of Nimrod, mentioned in Gen **10** 10, as the founder of Babel, Erech, Accad and Calneh, was given by his courtiers to this most brilliant of all the constellations, one that by its form somewhat suggests a gigantic warrior armed for the fight. Until recently it was not found possible to identify the Nimrod of Scripture with any Bab monarch until Dr. T. G. Pinches suggested that "Nimrod" was a deliberate Heb transmutation of "Marduk," the name of the great Bab national hero, and chief deity of their pantheon. "The change was brought about by making the root triliteral, and the ending *uk* (*ak*) in Merodach-Baladan disappearing first, Marduk appeared as Marad. This was connected with the root *māradh*, 'to be rebellious,' and the word was still further mutilated, or rather deformed, by having a *ni* attached, assimilating it to a certain extent to the *niph'al* forms of the Heb vbs., and making a change altogether in conformity with the genius of the Heb language" (*The Old Testament in the Light of the Historical Records of Assyria and Babylonia*, 129–30). In the very brief reference to Nimrod in Gen **10** 8.9, he is three times overemphatically termed *gibbōr*, "a mighty (one)" and this has been the name of this constellation among Syrians, Arabs and Jews for many centuries. Indeed the brightest star of the constellation, the one in the left knee, now generally known as Rigel, is still occasionally called Algebar, a corruption of *Al Jabbar*, though now one of the fainter stars near it more generally bears that name. The word *K*^{e}*ṣīl* as applied to this constellation would parallel closely the etymology suggested for the name "Merodach," by its transformation into "Nimrod" as if it were derived from *māradh*, "to rebel." He who was to the Babylonians a deified hero, was to the Hebrews a rebel Titan, bound in chains among the stars that all might behold his punishment, and in this aspect the question, "Canst thou . . . . loose the bands of Orion?" (Job **38** 31) would be equivalent to asking "Canst thou bring down out of their places the stars that make up this figure and so, as it were, set the Titan free?"

In Isa **13** 10, *k*^{e}*ṣīl* occurs in the plur. *k*^{e}*ṣīlīm*, "for the stars of heaven and the constellations thereof shall not give their light"; *k*^{e}*ṣīlīm* being tr^d as "constellations" under the impression that Orion, the brightest of all the constellations, is here put for the constellations in general. This is no doubt correct, but the context shows that the meaning goes farther than this, and that the *k*^{e}*ṣīlīm* who were to be darkened were the proud and arrogant tyrants like Nimrod or Merodach who would, if possible, climb up into heaven itself, even as Orion is represented in our star atlases as if trying to climb up into the zodiac—the home of the sun.

12. Mazzāroth

A further astronomical term which occurs in Job **38** 32 is left untr^d in both AV and the RV, viz. the word *Mazzārōth*. It occurs only once in the OT, but the similar word *mazzālōth*, tr^d "planets" in AV and RV, occurs in 2 K **23** 5. For the latter see Astrology. In the fifth tablet of the Bab Epic of Creation, we read:

1. He [Marduk] made the station for the great gods;
2. The stars, their images, as the stars of the zodiac he fixed.
3. He ordained the year, and into sections [*mizrāta*] he divided it.
4. For the twelve months he fixed three stars.

Here in the third line, *mizrāta*, cognate with the Heb *mazzārōth*, means the sections or divisions of the year, corresponding to the signs of the zodiac mentioned in the second line.

Yet again when Job **9** 9 is compared with Job **38** 31.32, it is seen that the place of the word *mazzārōth* in the latter passage is held by the expression "the chambers of the south" (*ḥadhrē thēmān*) in the earlier. *Mazzārōth* therefore is equivalent to "the chambers of the south," and clearly signifies the twelve constellations of the zodiac through which the sun appears to pass in the course of the year, poetically likened to the "inns," the "chambers" or "tabernacles" in which the sun successively rests during the several monthly stages of his annual journey. The same idea was employed by the Arabs in their "mansions of the moon," its "lodging-houses" (*menazil*), which are 28 in number, since the moon takes 28 days to make the circuit of the heavens, just as the sun takes 12 months.

The word *Mazzārōth* therefore represents the twelve "signs" or, to speak more correctly, the twelve "constellations" of the zodiac. These two terms are often used indiscriminately, but there is a real difference between their significations. The constellations of the zodiac are the actual groupings of the stars, lying along the ecliptic, and are quite irregular in form and length. The signs have no connection with the actual stars but are imaginary divisions of the ecliptic, all exactly equal in length, and they are reckoned from that point in the heavens where the sun is at the moment that it is crossing the celestial equator in its northward motion in springtime. As this point, known to astronomers as "the first point of Aries," moves slowly amongst the stars, taking 25,800 years to complete a revolution of the heavens, the signs of the zodiac also move among the stars, and hence, though at one time each sign bore a rough and general correspondence to the constellation of the same name, the signs have gradually drawn away from them. The constellations of the zodiac were designed about 2700 BC, but the signs—the equal divisions of the zodiac named from them—cannot have been adopted earlier than 700 BC, and were probably even later. For since *Aries* is the first of the signs, it is clear that it was the first of the constellations at the time when the equal division of the zodiac was effected, and 700 BC is the very earliest date that the constellation *Aries* can have been so regarded. Incidentally it may be remarked that the mention in the Bab story of creation of the allotment of three stars to each of the sections (*Mizrata*) of the year, shows that not only had the division of the zodiac into 12 equal signs been effected, but that a further step had been taken, namely, the division of each sign into 3 equal parts, later known amongst the Greeks as its "decans," corresponding roughly to the 36 decades of the Egyp calendar. Whatever, therefore, may have been the antiquity of the traditions embodied in it, the actual Bab poem quoted above, so far from being an early document, as it was at one time supposed to be, is probably almost as late as the destruction of Jerus by Nebuchadnezzar.

13. "Arcturus"

There are three constellations, natural groupings of the stars, the Pleiades and Orion and "Charles's Wain," which have always attracted men's attention, and we accordingly find them referred to in the earliest poems extant. Thus they are the three groups of the stars most frequently mentioned by Homer and Hesiod. The two first groups, the Pleiades and Orion, are, as we have seen, indicated by *Kīmāh* and *K^{e}ṣīl*. We should therefore naturally expect that the third constellation which we find associated with these in the Book of Job should be none other than the seven bright stars in the N., the principal part of the Great Bear. The Heb name for this third constellation appears in two slightly different forms. It is *ʿash* in Job **9** 9, and *ʿayish* in Job **38** 32, and in the latter case it is connected with its "sons." The last star of Charles's Wain or the Plough, as the group is often called among ourselves, still bears the name *Benetnasch*, derived from the Arab. name *Benet Naʿsh*, "the daughters of the Bier," by which the Arabs designated the three stars in the Plough-handle, while they called the four stars in the body of the Plough, *Naʿsh*, "the bier" or "litter." *Naʿsh* and its daughters so closely correspond to "*ʿayish* and its sons," that there can be no reasonable doubt that the same seven bright stars are intended; so that the rendering of RV, "Canst thou guide the Bear with her train?" correctly reproduces the original meaning. The *Arcturus* of the AV is derived from Vulg, where it is probably a mistake for *Arctos*, that is to say, *Ursa Major*, the Great Bear.

The antithesis which is presented in Job **38** 32 now reveals itself. The *Mazzārōth* are the twelve constellations of the zodiac, and of these each one rules the night for about a month in its turn; they are each "led forth" in its "season." Each, in its turn, is the "chamber," "tabernacle" or "resting-place" of the sun, and they are appropriately called "chambers of the south," since it is especially in the southern sky that each is seen. In contrast to these are the northern constellations, those round the pole, of which the Great Bear or Charles's Wain is the brightest and best known At the time of the origin of the constellations, this group was much nearer the pole of the heavens than at present, but now as then these stars are not "led forth," for they are visible at all hours and during every night; but they are "guided"; they move round the pole of the heavens in an unending circle, as if the wain or chariot were being guided by a skilful driver.

(1) *The "Scatterers."*—There is some probability that in Job **37** 9 the same two regions of the heavens are alluded to: "Out of the chamber *of the south* cometh the storm, and cold out of the north." It will be observed that the complete expression, "chamber of the south," is not in the original, the translators having supplied "of the south" from analogy with Job **9** 9. The sirocco comes then from the region held by the *mazzāl*, the "chamber," or constellation of the zodiac, then on the meridian. But the cold, the blizzard, comes

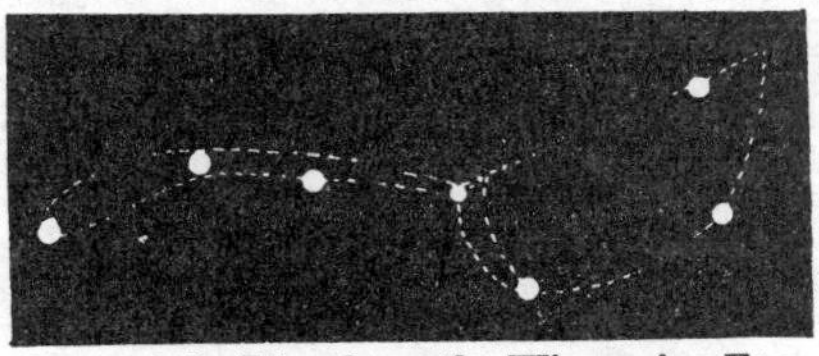

Stars of the Plough, as the Winnowing Fan.

from "the scatterers" (*M^{e}zārīm*). Who or what are the scatterers, and why do they represent the north? The late Professor Schiaparelli suggested that by a slight difference in the pointing, the word might be read as *mizrayim*, "the two winnowing fans," and that this may well have been a native term for the stars which we now know as the two Bears, *Ursa Major* and *Minor*, emphatically the northern constellations; the names being given them from the natural grouping of their chief stars, just as they are known as the two "Dippers" in the United States, or the two "Ladles" in China (*Astronomy in the Old Testament*," 67–72).

(2) *The ordinances of heaven.*—The astronomical antithesis between *Mazzārōth*, the constellations of the zodiac ("led forth" each "in its season"), and *ʿAyish*, "the Bear with her train" ("guided" in its unceasing revolution round the pole), is so complete and astronomically appropriate, that there is reason to expect an antithesis as clear and as astronomically significant between the two clauses of the preceding verse. But the rendering of RV does not afford anything of the kind: "Canst thou bind the cluster of the Pleiades, or loose the bands of Orion?" is simply equivalent to the question as to whether Job could fix these stars in their places in the sky; and for an inquiry so perfectly general, one constellation would be no more appropriate than another. The true rendering must certainly bring out some difference or at least distinction between the two constellations or the use that was made of them.

And in the third passage in which *Kīmāh* and *K^{e}ṣīl* are mentioned together an important distinction is hinted at. The order in Am **5** 8 suggests that the Pleiades corresponded in some way to daybreak, Orion to nightfall: "That maketh the Pleiades and Orion, and turneth the shadow of death into the morning, and maketh the day dark with night." Sunrise turns "the shadow of death into the morning," and in the progress of the seasons the analogous change on the higher scale is effected when Nature revives from the death of winter in the morning of the year, that is to say, at the return of spring. And at the time of the origin of the constellations the Pleiades were the harbingers of this change at their "cosmical" rising, that is to say, when they rose with the sun at daybreak they brought back the "delights" of springtime.

Similarly sunset makes "the day dark with night," and in the progress of the seasons the analogous change on the higher scale is effected when the long nights and short days of winter set in the evening of the year, and all nature is bound as by iron bands, in cold and frost. And at the time of the origin of the constellations, the "acronychal" rising of Orion, i.e. its rising at nightfall, was the harbinger of this change; the rigor of winter formed "the bands of Orion."

These regular changes in the appearings and positions of the constellations constitute the ordinances of the heavens, ordinances which Job could neither alter for the worse by holding back the delights of springtime, or for the better by breaking the bonds of winter cold. But these ordinances were not confined in their effects to the heavens; their dominion was established on the earth, which answered by the revival of vegetation when the Pleiades, then nearly in conjunction with the sun, appeared for a short time before sunrise; and by the return of the constraints of cold and frost when Orion, in opposition to the sun, rode the sky the whole night long.

The completeness and beauty of the imagery will now be apparent.

The Pleiades stood for the East, since by their rising just before daybreak, they heralded the morning of the year and the "delights" of springtime.

Orion stood for the West, since his appearing just after nightfall heralded the evening of the year, and the bands of winter cold.

Mazzārōth, the twelve constellations of the zodiac, the "chambers of the south," each "led forth" from the underworld in its own "season," stood for the South.

And the "Bear with her train," "guided" in their unceasing course round the pole, stood for the circumpolar constellations in the North.

And the movements of them all in a perfect obedience to the law of God were the ordinances of heaven; whilst the dominion of them was seen to be established upon the earth in the constant succession of the seasons there in unfailing answer to the changes in the stars above.

These three verses give us a vivid picture of the work of primitive astronomy. The science was then in an early stage of development, but it was a real science, a science of observation, thoroughly sound so far as it had progressed, and showing high intelligence on the part of those who pursued it. We now know that the movement of "the Bear with her train," that is, the apparent rotation of the heavens round the pole, is due to the real rotation of the earth upon its axis; that the bringing out of "the *Mazzārōth* in their season," apparently due to the revolution of the sun round the earth, is due to the real revolution of the earth round the sun. But this knowledge which has enabled us to see where the actual movements lie has not brought us any nearer penetrating the mystery of those movements. What is the ultimate cause of the rotation of this vast globe, we know no more than the ancients knew what caused the heavens to rotate; what causes it to fly through pace 18 miles in every second of time, we know no more than the ancients knew why the sun appeared to move among the stars. To us, as to them, it is the power of God, and the will of God.

14. The Date of the Book of Job

It has been supposed by some scholars that the Book of Job was written during the Captivity in Babylon, but this supposition is untenable in view of the statement in Job's Apology that the worship of the heavenly bodies was "an iniquity to be punished by the judges" (Job **31** 26–28). This could not have been written by Jews in exile amongst the worshippers of *Šamaš* and *Sin*. But neither can this book have been written after the Return. The meaning of the three terms, *'Ayish, Kīmāh* and *K^{e}ṣīl*, had been lost before the LXX made the rendering of the Heb Scriptures into Gr, for in Am **5** 8 they left *Kīmāh* and *K^{e}ṣīl* untr^d, and they rendered *'Ayish* and *K^{e}ṣīl* differently in Job **9** 9, and **38** 31.32. Before the Captivity, *Kīmāh* and *K^{e}ṣīl* were plainly in common use, since Amos uses them as if they were familiar to his hearers, and as he himself points out, he was not a man of learning but a simple herdsman. The obvious and sufficient explanation of the later ignorance respecting these three terms lies in the catastrophes of the Assyr and Bab conquests. Not less significant of their complete loss of the old Heb astronomy is the alteration which the LXX made in the Heb text. The "delights of the Pleiades" had evidently no more meaning for them than they have had for the majority of modern Orientalists, and no doubt it seemed a plausible and legitimate emendation to write *ma'ănaddōth*, "chains," instead of *ma'ădhannōth*, "delights," so as to bring about a fancied parallelism with *mōsh^{e}khōth*, the "bands" of Orion. But the alteration transforms a complete, beautiful and symmetrical figure, an epitome of the astronomical observation of the time, into a bald tautology. Those critics are therefore right who assign the Book of Job and the Isa **13** to the period before the Captivities, and the three names come to us as indications, not of a Bab science of astronomy, learned by the Jews during their exile, but of a Heb astronomy destroyed by the unspeakable disaster of the conquest.

III. Physiography.—It has generally been assumed that the Hebrews considered the earth to be a vast circular plain, arched over by a solid vault—"the firmament"—above which were stored, as if in cisterns, the "treasuries" (Job **38** 22) of the rain, snow and hail, and some writers have even attempted to express this supposed conception in diagrammatic form. One of the best of these attempts, reproduced below, is given by Schiaparelli, in his *Astronomy in the OT*.

1. The Circle of the Earth

But this assumption is in reality based more upon the ideas prevalent in Europe during the Dark Ages than upon any actual statements in the OT. The same word (*ḥūgh*) used in the OT to express the roundness of the heavens (Job **22** 14) is also used when the circle of the earth is spoken of (Isa **40** 22), and it is likewise applied to the deep (Prov **8** 27). Now it is obvious that the heavens are spherical in appearance, and to an attentive observer it is clear that the surface of the sea is also rounded. There is therefore no sufficient warrant for the assumption that the Hebrews must have regarded the earth as flat.

(1) *The earth a sphere.*—Certain astronomical relations were recognized very early. The stars appear as if attached to a globe rotating round the earth once in 24 hours, and this appearance was clearly familiar to the author of the Book of Job, and indeed long before the time of Abraham, since the formation of the constellations could not have been effected without such recognition. But the spherical form of the heavens almost involves a

similar form for the earth, and their apparent diurnal rotation certainly means that they are not rigidly connected with the earth, but surround it on all sides at some distance from it. The earth therefore must be freely suspended in space, and so the Book of Job describes it: "He stretcheth out the north over empty space, and hangeth the earth upon nothing" (Job **26** 7).

SCHIAPARELLI'S HEBREW WORLD

The author's cut representing **the Hebrew** universe, with his accompanying **explanations,** is here reproduced.

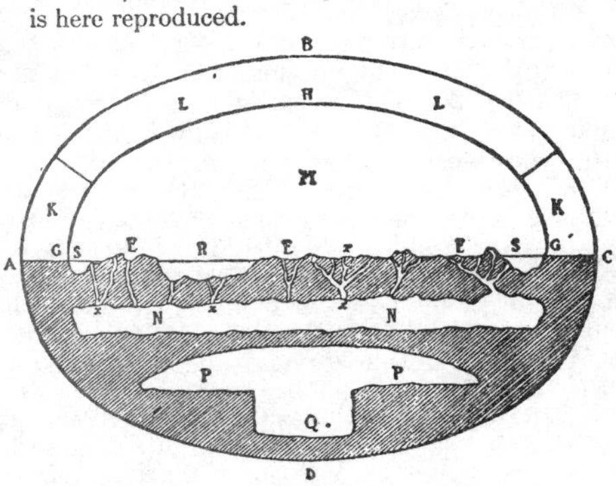

HEAVEN, THE EARTH, AND THE ABYSSES
According to the writers of the Old Testament.—**Schiaparelli**

Explanatory Key:
ABC = the upper heaven; ADC = the curve of the abyss; AEC = the plane of the earth and seas; SRS = various parts of the sea, EEE = various parts of the earth; GHG = the profile of the firmament or lower heaven; KK = the storehouses of the winds; LL = the storehouses of the upper waters, of snow, and of hail, M = the space occupied by the air, within which the clouds move; NN = the waters of the great abyss; xxx = the fountains of the great abyss; PP = Sheol or limbo; Q = the lower part of the same, the inferno properly so called.

From "The Earliest Cosmologies." By W. F. Warren.

(2) *The north stretched over empty space.*—Here the "north" signifies the northern circumpolar constellations and the writer recognized that they stretch out beyond the utmost confines of the earth; so that he was not under any impression that the heavens rested upon the earth, or were borne up by mountains. The celestial sphere surrounded the earth entirely, but at a distance from it; between the two there was "empty space." Some commentators have indeed claimed that Job **26** 10, "He hath described a boundary upon the face of the waters, unto the confines of light and darkness," is equivalent to a statement that the circumference of the terrestrial plain extended to the place where sea and sky met. But no man of intelligence can, at any time, have supposed that the sea horizon marked the dividing line between day and night, and the meaning of the passage is correctly given in AV, "until the day and night come to an end"; in other words, the waters of the sea will be confined to their appointed place never again to overflow the earth so long as the succession of day and night shall continue (cf Gen **8** 22; **9** 15).

(3) *The corners of the earth.*—See EARTH, CORNERS OF.

2. The Pillars of the Earth

'ereç, "the earth," is in general the surface of the earth, the dry land inhabited by man and beast. Hence "the pillars" of the earth (Job **9** 6) are the rocks that bear up that surface, for as has been shown, it was quite clear to the author of the Book of Job, and to the primitive astronomers, that our world was unsupported in space. For "Vault of the Earth" see EARTH, VAULT OF.

(1) *The Hebrew conception.*—Above the spherical earth was stretched out the "firmament" (*rāḳīaʿ*) made on the second day of creation to "divide the waters from the waters" (Gen 1 6). To the Hebrews the "firmament" was the apparent void

3. The Firmament

above, in which clouds float and the lights of heaven pursue their appointed paths. The word *rāḳīaʿ*, by its etymology, suggests an expanse, something stretched, spread or beaten out, as when Isaiah (**40** 22) says that the Lord "stretcheth out the heavens as a curtain, and spreadeth them out as a tent to dwell in." But the Gr word *sterĕōma*, by which the LXX rendered *rāḳīaʿ*, gives the meaning of a firm and solid structure, and our translators have carried out this same idea in their Eng. rendering of "firmament."

(2) *The Alexandrian conception.*—In this however the LXX simply expressed the astronomical science of their day as accepted in Alexandria, where the doctrine of a succession of solid crystalline spheres, each carrying a planet, held currency. But in order to express the Heb idea, *rāḳīaʿ* should be rendered "expanse" or "space"; it corresponds to the "empty space" of Job **26** 7. This "expanse" was appointed to divide "the waters which were under the expanse, from the waters which were above the expanse"; and it has been argued from this that the upper waters must have been regarded as being inclosed in a watertight reservoir, furnished with sluices or floodgates, which could be opened to allow the rain to fall.

Thus in the account of the Flood, "the windows of heaven" are said to have been opened. But,

4. The Windows of Heaven

'ărubbāh, "window," means a network, or lattice, a form which can never have been ascribed to a literal floodgate; and in the other passages where "the windows of heaven" are mentioned the expression is obviously metaphorical (2 K **7** 2.19; Isa **24** 18; Mal **3** 10).

Further the numerous other references to rain connect it with the clouds, as "I will also command

5. Rain

the clouds that they rain no rain" (Isa **5** 6), or in the Song of Deborah, "The clouds dropped water" (Jgs **5** 4; see also Ps **77** 17; **147** 8; Prov **16** 15; Eccl **12** 2). The fantastic idea of solidly built cisterns in the sky furnished with sluices has no warrant in Scripture. So far from any such crude conception, there is a very clear and complete account of the atmospheric circulation. Elihu describes the process of evaporation, "For he draweth up the drops of water, which distil in rain from his vapor, which the skies pour down and drop upon man abundantly" (Job **36** 27.28).

Jeremiah and the Psalmist repeat the description, "He causeth the vapors to ascend from the

6. Clouds

ends of the earth; he maketh lightnings for the rain, and bringeth forth the wind out of his treasuries" (Jer **10** 13). By the foreshortening that clouds undergo in the distance they inevitably appear to form chiefly on the horizon, "at the ends of the earth," whence they move upward toward the zenith. Thus God "calleth for the waters of the sea, and poureth them out upon the face of the earth" (Am **9** 6); and thus "All the rivers run into the sea, yet the sea is not full; unto the place whither the rivers go, thither they go again" (Eccl **1** 7). Other references to the clouds in the Book of Job reveal not merely observation but acute reflection. "Dost thou know the balancings of the clouds, the wondrous works of him who is perfect in knowledge?" (Job **37** 16) indicates a perception that the clouds float, each in its own place, at its own level, each perfectly balanced in the thin air.

(1) *Meaning of the word.*—*T^{e}hōm*, "the deep," means moving water, and hence the ocean, which is represented as being essentially one, exactly as we

now know it to be by actual exploration—"Let the waters under the heavens be gathered together unto one place" (Gen **1** 9). And the earth is stretched out "above the waters" (Ps **136** 6; Ps **24** 2). That is to say that the water surface lies lower than the land surface; and not only so, but, within the substance of the earth itself, there are subterranean waters which form a kind of ocean underground. This also is called in Ezk **31** 4 the "deep," *t*ᵉ*hōm;* "The waters nourished it, the deep made it to grow." But in general *t*ᵉ*hōm* denotes the sea, as when Pharaoh's chosen captains were drowned in the Red Sea, "The deeps cover them" (Ex **15** 5). Indeed the word appears to be onomatopoetic derived from the "moaning" or "humming" of the sea; whilst *'ereç*, the "earth," seems intended to represent the "rattle" of shingle, "the scream of a madden'd beach dragged down by the wave."

7. The Deep

(2) *The Bab dragon of Chaos.*—In Gen **1**, *t*ᵉ*hōm* denotes the primeval waters, and the resemblance of the word to *Tiamat*, the name of the Bab she-dragon of Chaos, has led some commentators to ascribe a Bab origin to this ch. It need hardly be pointed out that if this resemblance proves any connection between the Heb and Bab accounts of creation, it proves the Heb to be the original. The natural object, *t*ᵉ*hōm*, the sea, must have preceded the mythological personification of it.

LITERATURE.—Maunder, *Astronomy of the Bible; Astronomy without a Telescope;* Schiaparelli, *Astronomy in the OT;* Warren, *The Earliest Cosmologies*, 1909.

E. W. MAUNDER

ASTYAGES, as-tī'a-jēs (**'Ἀστυάγης**; *Astuágēs;* or Astyigas [in Ktesias], or Istuvigu, son of Cyaxares I, king of the Medes 585–550 BC, and predecessor of Cyrus [Bel ver 1]): His wife was the daughter of Alyattes, king of Lydia. The daughter of Astyages (Mandane) married a Persian, Cambyses, and a son was born to them who later became Cyrus the Great. Astyages had given orders to expose the babe; but Harpagus, on whom the task had been imposed, gave the child to a herdsman, with instructions to kill him. When the boy, who had been brought up as his own by the herdsman, arrived at the age of twelve, Astyages discovered that he was the son of Mandane. The king in wrath then had the son of Harpagus killed and served to his father as food. The latter concealed his feelings of hatred and resentment, and bided his time; and when the young Cyrus had grown to manhood, he stirred up the grandson in insurrection against Astyages, who was defeated and taken prisoner (*Herodotus* i.127–30). When Astyages marched against the Persians, the Medes, under the command of Harpagus, deserted their king, and sided with the disappointed Persians; and Cyrus was crowned king. This account of Herodotus is confirmed by the Annalistic Tablet of Cyrus (*RP*, ser. ii, 159). The dethroned monarch was treated with kindness by his conqueror. According to Ktesias, a home was provided for him by Cyrus in Hyrcania.

Astyages was the last of the kings of the Manda (Media). An exceedingly shrewd man, Deioces by name, had founded the kingdom 150 years before (699–646). Phraortes was the second in line (646–624), and Cyaxares the third (624–584).

J. E. HARRY

ASUNDER, a-sun'dēr: This word occurs 22 times in AV, 13 in OT and 9 in the NT. It is found in combination with break (twice), burst, cleave (twice), depart, cut (six times), divide (three times), drive, part, pluck, put (twice), rend, saw. These are the tr of 9 Heb, and 4 Gr words.

Break asunder (1) (פַּרְפַּר, *parpar*): Job, in reply to Eliphaz, complains about God, "I was at ease, and he brake me asunder" (Job **16** 12). (2) (נִתֵּק, *nittēḳ*): In Ps **2** the kings and rulers, meditating rebellion against Jeh and His anointed, say, "Let us break their bonds asunder" (Ps **2** 3).

Burst asunder (**λάσκω**, *láskō*): This was the fate of Judas (Acts **1** 18).

Cleave asunder (1) (נִבְקַע, *nibhḳa'*): The same root as of *biḳ'āh*, "a valley." "The ground clave asunder" and swallowed up Dathan and Abiram with their households (Nu **16** 31). (2) (פָּלַח, *pillaḥ*): Job complains of God, "He cleaveth my reins asunder" (Job **16** 13).

Cut asunder (1) (קִצֵּץ, *ḳiççēç*): The Lord "cut asunder the cords of the wicked" (Ps **129** 4). The Heb word is used of cutting into wires or strips (Ex **39** 3). (2) (גָּדַע, *gādha'*): "to cut off a branch or cut down a tree." "How is the hammer of the whole earth [Babylon] cut asunder!" (Jer **50** 23). Zechariah "cut asunder" the staff "Beauty," signifying the breach of the covenant between Jeh and His people, and also the staff "Bands," signifying the breach of the brotherhood between Judah and Israel (Zec **11** 10.14). (3) (**διχοτομέω**, *dichotoméō*): The fate of the Unfaithful Steward, lit. "cut in two"; RVm "severely scourge him" (Mt **24** 51; Lk **12** 46). See PUNISHMENTS.

Depart asunder (**ἀποχωρίζομαι**, *apochōrízomai*): Paul and Barnabas "departed asunder from one another" (Acts **15** 39 AV); RV "parted asunder."

Divide asunder (1) (הִבְדִּיל, *hibhdīl*): Usually to separate, to make a division between. Here the reference is to the offering of pigeons or turtledoves (Lev **1** 17; **5** 8). (2) (**μερισμός**, *merismós*): From *merízō*, "to divide." The noun is abstract, "the act of dividing." The word of God pierces "even to the dividing of soul and spirit" (He **4** 12).

Drive asunder (הִתִּיר, *hittīr*): Lit. "to cause to tremble," then "to loosen." God "drove asunder the nations" (Hab **3** 6).

Part asunder (הִפְרִיד, *hiphrīdh*): With prep. *bēn*, "between," "to separate." The chariot and horses of fire "parted asunder" Elijah and Elisha (2 K **2** 11).

Pluck asunder (**διασπάω**, *diaspáō*): To bear asunder, to part forcibly. "Chains had been plucked asunder" by the demoniac of the Gerasenes (Mk **5** 4 AV); RV "rent asunder."

Put asunder (**χωρίζω**, *chōrízō*): To sever one from another. See the words of Jesus on divorce (Mt **19** 6; Mk **10** 9).

Rend asunder (נִבְקַע, *nibhḳa'*): The same Heb word as "cleave asunder." (1) "And No shall be rent asunder" (Ezk **30** 16 AV): RV "broken up." (2) RV for AV "plucked asunder" (Mk **5** 4).

Saw asunder (**πρίζω**, *prízō* or **πρίω**, *príō*): The fate of some on the roll of faith, "They were sawn asunder" (He **11** 37). See also PUNISHMENTS.

S. F. HUNTER

ASUPPIM, a-sup'im, **HOUSE OF ASUPPIM** (בֵּית הָאֲסֻפִּים, *bēth hā-'ăṣuppīm*): AVm "gatherings"; RV "the storehouses." In Neh **12** 25, AV renders the same word **thresholds** (AVm "treasuries, assemblies"). A storehouse most probably at the southern gate of the temple (1 Ch **26** 15.17; Neh **12** 25).

ASUR, as'ur (**'Ἀσούρ**, *Asoúr*): RV for Assur in 1 Esd **5** 31. Same as Harhur of Ezr **2** 51.

ASYLUM, a-sī'lum: The custom of fleeing to specially sacred places to obtain the protection of a deity is found all over the world (Post, *Grundriss*, II, 252 ff). In ancient Israel we meet with it in two forms—the asylum of the altar and the asylum of the cities of refuge. The altar at the House of

God was a place to which persons in danger fled for protection (1 K **1** 50; **2** 28). It had horns and must not be confused with the altars of earth or stone that were used for lay sacrifices. See ALTAR; SANCTUARY. Ex **21** 14 provides that a murderer is to be taken from the altar to be put to death. The law of the cities of refuge proceeds upon a somewhat different principle. Its objects are (1) to shield a homicide from the avenger of blood until trial, and (2) to provide a refuge for the manslayer who has not been guilty of murder. There is one reference to the institution in the history of the kingdom (2 S **14** 14). For the legal and geographical information, see CITIES OF REFUGE; HOMICIDE. HAROLD M. WIENER

ASYNCRITUS, a-sin′kri-tus (**Ἀσύνκριτος**, *Asúnkritos*, "incomparable"): An unknown Christian at Rome to whom St. Paul sent an affectionate salutation (Rom **16** 14).

ATAD, ā′tad (אָטָד, *'āṭādh*, "a thorn"). See ABEL-MIZRAIM.

ATAR, at′ar (**Ἀτάρ**, *Atár;* AV **Jatal**=Ater [Ezr **2** 42; Neh **7** 45]): The sons of A. (porters) returned with Zerubbabel to Jerus (1 Esd **5** 28).

ATARAH, at′a-rä, a-tā′ra (עֲטָרָה, *'ăṭārāh*, "crown"): One of Jerahmeel's wives and mother of Onam (1 Ch **2** 26).

ATARGATIS, a-tär′ga-tis (**Ἀταργάτις**, *Atargátis;* RV wrongly ATERGATIS): Is stated in 2 Macc **12** 26 to have been worshipped at Karnion, the Ashtaroth-Karnaim of the OT (cf *Ant*, XII, viii, 4). The name is found on coins of Membij as עתר־עתה, *'atar-'atah*, where 'Atar (i.e. Ashtoreth) is identified with the goddess 'Atah, whose name is sometimes written עתי, *'Atī*. 'Atah or 'Ati was also worshipped at Palmyra, and (according to Melito) in Adiabene. The compound Atargatis, often corrupted by the Greeks into Derketo, had her chief temples at Membij (Hierapolis) and Ashkelon where she was represented with the body of a woman and the tail of a fish, fish being sacred to her. Herodotus made her the Aphroditē Urania of the Greeks. 'Ati may have been originally a Hittite goddess with whom the Assyr Istar ('Atar) came afterward to be identified. A. H. SAYCE

ATAROTH, at′a-roth, a-tā′roth (עֲטָרוֹת, *'ăṭārōth*, "crowns," or "wreaths"; **Ἀταρώθ**, *Atarōth*):

(1) A city E. of the Jordan, apparently in the territory given to Reuben, but built, or fortified, by the children of Gad (Nu **32** 3.34). It is named along with Dibon, which is identified with *Dhībān*. Eight miles N.E. by N. of Dibon, on the S. of Wādy *Zerḳā Ma'īn*, stands *Jebel 'Attārūs*, in which the ancient name is preserved. The city is doubtless represented by *Khirbet 'Attārūs*, about 4 miles W. of the mountain.

(2) A place on the boundary between Ephraim and Benjamin, toward the W. (Josh **16** 2). It seems to be the same as Ataroth-addar of ver 5 and **18** 13. It is probably to be identified with the modern *ed-Dāriyeh* S. of nether Bethhoron, and about 12½ miles W. of Jerus.

(3) A place on the eastern frontier of Ephraim (Josh **16** 7). This town has not been identified. Conder thinks it may be identified with *et-Trūneh* in the Jordan valley, or with *Khirbet et-Taiyereh*. W. EWING

ATAROTH-ADDAR, at′a-roth-ad′är (עַטְרוֹת אַדָּר, *'aṭrōth 'addār*, "crowns of Addar"). See ATAROTH (2).

ATER, ā′tēr (אָטֵר, *'āṭēr*, "bound" [?]): (1) The ancestor of a family of 98 persons who returned from Bab captivity with Zerubbabel (Ezr **2** 16; Neh **7** 21). AV has "Ater of Hezekiah"; RV of 1 Esd **5** 15 has "Ater of Ezekias," m, "Ater of Hezekiah." AV has "Aterezias."

(2) The head of a family of porters who returned from Babylon to Jerus (Ezr **2** 42; Neh **7** 45).

ATEREZAIAS, a-tēr-ē-zī′as (**Ἀτὴρ τῷ Ἐζεκίᾳ**, *Atḗr tō Hezekíą*): Usually found in the abbreviated form Ater. Head of a Jewish family, which returned with Zerubbabel, under the decree of Cyrus. Mentioned (Ezr **2** 16) as sprung from Hezekiah. Their number is given as 98. Mentioned again as found in the register of the genealogies of the first returned exiles by Nehemiah (**7** 21). Again among those who sealed "the sure covenant" (Neh **10** 17). Also found in 1 Esd **5** 15, where the name is given variously as Ater or Aterezaias. The number of the family, given by Esdras, is 92.

ATERGATIS, a-tēr′ga-tis. See ATARGATIS.

ATETA, a-tē′ta (AV **Teta**; A, **Ἀτητά**, *Atētá*, B, om.): Head of a family of Levites; gate keepers who returned from the captivity with Zerubbabel (1 Esd **5** 28); called Hatita in Ezr **2** 42; Neh **7** 45.

ATHACH, ā′thak (עֲתָךְ, *'ăthākh*, "lodging-place"): One of the cities of Judah to which David sent from Ziklag the spoil of the Amalekites (1 S **30** 30). Its site is unknown. Driver, Budde, and Wellhausen identify it with Ether (Josh **15** 42).

ATHAIAH, a-thā′ya (עֲתָיָה, *'ăthāyāh*="Jeh is helper"; **Ἀθεά**, *Atheá*, or **Ἀθεαί**, *Atheaí*): He is designated (Neh **11** 4) as a descendant of Judah and the son of Uzziah. After the return from Babylon, he dwelt in Jerus. In 1 Ch **9** 4 his name is given as Uthai.

ATHALIAH, ath-a-lī′a (עֲתַלְיָה, *'ăthalyāh;* meaning uncertain, perhaps, "whom Jeh has afflicted"; 2 K **8** 26; **11**; 2 Ch **22**, **23**):

(1) Daughter of Ahab and Jezebel, granddaughter of Omri, 6th king of Israel.

1. Relationship

In her childhood the political relations of the two kingdoms of Judah and Israel had, after many years of strife, become friendly, and she was married to Jehoram, eldest son of Jehoshaphat, king of Judah (2 K **8** 18). The marriage was one of political expediency, and is a blot on the memory of Jehoshaphat.

When Jehoram was 32 years of age, he succeeded to the throne, and Athaliah became queen of Judah.

2. Athaliah as Queen

She inherited her mother's strength of will, and like her developed a fanatical devotion to the cultus of the Zidonian Baal. Elijah's blow at the worship of Baal in Samaria shortly before her accession to power did nothing to mitigate her zeal. It probably intensified it. The first recorded act of Jehoram's reign is the murder of his six younger brothers; some princes of the realm, who were known to be favorable to the ancient faith of the nation, were also destroyed (2 Ch **21** 4). There can be little doubt that these deeds of blood were supported, and perhaps instigated, by Athaliah, who was a much stronger character than her husband.

After eight years of royal life, Athaliah became a widow, and her son, Ahaziah, then 22 years of age (2 K **8** 26; not 42 as in 2 Ch **22** 2), ascended his father's throne. As queen-mother, Athaliah was now supreme in the councils of the nation, as well as in the royal palace. Within a single year, the young king fell (see Jehu), and the only persons who stood between Athaliah and the throne were her grandchildren. It is in such moments that ambition, fired by fanaticism, sees its opportunity, and the massacre of the royal seed was determined on. This was carried out: but one of them, Jehoash, a babe, escaped by the intervention of his aunt, Jehosheba (1 K **11** 2; 2 Ch **22** 11).

3. Murder of Her Grandchildren

The palace being cleared of its royal occupants, Athaliah had herself proclaimed sovereign. No other woman, before or since, sat upon the throne of David, and it is a proof of her energy and ability that, in spite of her sex, she was able to keep it for six years. From 2 Ch **24** 7 we gather that a portion of the temple of Jeh was pulled down, and the material used in the structure of a temple of Baal.

4. Her Usurpation

The high priest at this time was Jehoiada, who had married the daughter of Athaliah, Jehosheba (2 Ch **22** 11). His promotion to the primacy led to the undoing of the usurper, as Jehoiada proved staunchly, if secretly, true to the religion of Jeh. For six years he and his wife concealed in their apartments, near the temple, the young child of Ahaziah. In the seventh year a counter-revolution was planned. The details are given with unusual fulness in K and Ch, the writings of which supplement one another. Thus, when the Chronicler wrote, it had become safe to give the names of five captains who led the military rising (2 Ch **23** 1). With the Book of K before him, it was not necessary to do more than extract from the ancient records such particulars as had not hitherto appeared. This it is which has chiefly given rise to the charge of variations in the two narratives. See Jehoash.

5. The Counter-Revolution

At the time of her deposition, Athaliah was resident in the royal palace. When roused to a sense of danger by the acclamations which greeted the coronation ceremony, she made an attempt to stay the revolt by rushing into the temple court, alone; her guards, according to Jos, having been prevented from following her (*Ant*, IX, vii, 3). A glance sufficed. It showed her the lad standing on a raised platform before the temple, holding the Book of the Law in his hand, and with the crown upon his brow. Rending her robe and shouting, "Treason! Treason!" she fled. Some were for cutting her down as she did so, but this was objected to as defiling the temple with human blood. She was, therefore, allowed to reach the door of the palace in flight. Here she fell, smitten by the avenging guards.

6. Her Death

Athaliah's usurpation lasted for six years (2 K **11** 3; **12** 1; 2 Ch **22** 12). Her 1st year synchronizes with the 1st of Jehu in Israel, and may be placed 846 BC (some put later). See Chronology of OT. The statement of 2 K **12** 1 is here understood in the sense that Jehoash began his *public* reign in the 7th year of Jehu, and that he reigned 40 years counting from the time of his father's death. A modern parallel is the dating of all official records and legal documents of the time of Charles II of England from the death of Charles I.

The only other reference to Athaliah is that above alluded to in 2 Ch **24** 7, where she is spoken of as "that wicked woman."

(2) A Benjamite who dwelt in Jerus (1 Ch **8** 26.28).

(3) Father of Jeshaiah, who returned with Ezra (**8** 7); called Gotholias in Apoc (1 Esd **8** 33).

W. Shaw Caldecott

ATHANASIAN, ath-a-nā'zhan, **CREED.** See Creed.

ATHARIAS, ath-a-rī'as. See Attharias.

ATHARIM, ath'a-rim (אֲתָרִים, *'ăthārīm*): RV "The way of Atharim"; AV "The way of the spies." RV regards Atharim as a place (so LXX). AV follows Syr and Tg, rendering Atharim as if Tarim = spies. Dillmann translates "the caravan path," connecting it with Arab. *athar*, "a track or foot-print." Here the king of Arad fought against Israel, taking some captives (Nu **21** 1). See Hormah.

ATHEISM, ā'thē-iz'm (ἄθεος, *átheos*, "without God" [Eph **2** 12]): Ordinarily this word is interpreted to mean a denial of the existence of God, a disbelief in God, the opposite of theism. But it seems better that we should consider it under four heads, in order to obtain a clear idea of the different meanings in which it has been used.

(1) *The classical.*—In this sense it does not mean a denial of the existence of a Divine Being, but the denial of the existence or reality of the god of a particular nation. Thus the Christians were repeatedly charged with atheism, because of their disbelief in the gods of heathenism. It was not charged that they did not believe in any god, but that they denied the existence and reality of the gods worshipped, and before whom the nation hitherto had bowed. This was considered so great a crime, so dangerous a thing to the nation, that it was felt to be a just cause for most cruel and determined persecutions. Socrates' teaching cast a shadow on the reality of the existence of the gods, and this charge was brought against him by his contemporaries. Cicero also uses the word in this sense in his charge against Diagoras of Athens. Indeed, such use of it is common in all classical literature.

(2) *Philosophic.*—It is not meant that the various philosophic systems to which this term is applied actually deny the existence of a Divine Being or of a First Cause, but that they are atheistic in their teaching, and tend to unsettle the faith of mankind in the existence of God. There is indeed a belief in a first cause, in force, in motion, in a certain aggregation of materials producing life, but the Divine Being as taught by theism is absolutely denied. This is true of the Idealism of Fichte, of the Ideal Pantheism of Spinoza, the Natural Pantheism of Schelling, and similar forms of thought. In applying the word atheism to the teaching here given, theism does not intend to assail them as wholly without a belief in a Divine Being; but it affirms that God is a person, a self-conscious Being, not merely a first cause or force. To deny this fundamental affirmation of theism is to make the teaching atheistic, a denial of that which is essential to theism (He **11** 3).

(3) *Dogmatic.*—It absolutely denies the existence of God. It has often been held that this is, in fact, impossible. Cousin has said, "It is impossible, because the existence of God is implied in every assertion." It is true, however, that in all ages there have been persons who declared themselves absolute atheists. Esp. is this true of the 18th cent.—a period of widespread skepticism—when not a few, particularly in France, professed themselves atheists. In many cases, however, it resulted from a loose use of the word, careless definition, and sometimes from the spirit of boastfulness.

(4) *Practical atheism.*—It has nothing at all to do with belief. Indeed it accepts the affirmations of theism. It has reference wholly to the mode of life. It is to live as though there was no God.

It takes the form often of complete indifference to the claims of the Divine Being or again of outbroken and defiant wickedness (Ps **14** 1). That this form of atheism is widely prevalent is well known. It is accompanied in many cases with some form of unbelief or prejudice or false opinion of the church or Christianity. Dogmatic atheism is no longer a menace or even a hindrance to the progress of Christianity, but practical atheism is widespread in its influence and a dangerous element in our modern life (cf Isa **31** 1; Jer **2** 13.17.18; **18** 13–15). Whatever the form, whether it be that of religious agnosticism, denying that we can know that God exists, or critical atheism, denying that the evidence to prove His existence is sufficient, or dogmatic, or practical atheism, it is always a system of negation and as such tears down and destroys. It destroys the faith upon which all human relations are built. Since there is no God there is no right nor wrong, and human action is neither good nor bad, but convenient or inconvenient. It leaves human society without a basis for order and human government without foundation (Rom **1** 10–32). All is hopeless, all is wretchedness, all is tending to the grave and the grave ends all.

Arguments against atheism may be summarized as follows: (1) It is contrary to reason. History has shown again and again how impossible it is to bring the mind to rest in this doctrine. Although Buddhism is atheistic in its teaching, idolatry is widespread in the lands where it prevails. While the Positive Philosophy of Auguste Comte was based on a denial of the existence of God, his attempt to found the new religion of humanity with rites and ceremonies of worship reveals how the longing for worship cannot be suppressed. It is a revelation of the fact so often seen in the history of human thought, that the mind cannot rest in the tenets of atheism.

(2) It is contrary to human experience. All history testifies that there are deep religious instincts within the human breast. To regard these as deceptive and unreasonable would itself be utterly unreasonable and unscientific. But the fact of such spiritual longing implies also that there is a Being who is responsive to and can satisfy the cry of the heart (He **11** 6). In his Bampton Lectures Reville has said on this subject: "It would be irrational in the last degree to lay down the existence of such a need and such a tendency, and yet believe that the need corresponds to nothing, that the tendency has no goal."

(3) It fails to account for the evidence of design in the universe. See COSMOLOGY.

(4) It fails to account for the existence of man and the world in general. Here is the universe: how did it come to be? Here is man: how is he to be accounted for? To these and like questions, atheism and atheistic philosophy have no adequate answer to give. See also COSMOLOGY; CREATION; GOD.

JACOB W. KAPP

ATHENIANS, a-thē′ni-ans (**Ἀθηναῖοι,** *Athēnaíoi*): Inhabitants of Athens. Luke has a remark on their curiosity and their delight in novelty (Acts **17** 21). See ATHENS.

ACROPOLIS AND AREOPAGUS, ATHENS.

ATHENOBIUS, ath-e-nō′bi-us (**Ἀθηνόβιος,** *Athēnóbios*): A "friend" of Antiochus VII (Sidetes), who was sent to Jerus by the king to protest against the occupation of Joppa and Gazara, and the citadel Jerus. A demand was made on Simon Maccabaeus to give up all the places he had taken or pay 1,000 talents in silver. Simon declined to pay more than 100 talents, and Athenobius returned to Antiochus from his fruitless mission (1 Macc **15** 28–36).

ATHENS, ath′enz (**Ἀθῆναι,** *Athḗnai*): In antiquity the celebrated metropolis of Attica, now the capital of Greece. Two long walls, 250 ft. apart, connected the city with the harbor (Peiraeus). In Acts **17** we are told what Paul did during his single sojourn in this famous city. He came up from the sea by the new road (N. of the ancient) along which were altars of unknown gods, entered the city from the W., and passed by the Ceramicus (burial-ground), which can be seen to this day, the "Theseum," the best preserved of all Gr temples, and on to the Agora (Market-Place), just N. of the Acropolis, a steep hill, 200 ft. high, in the center of the city. Cimon began and Pericles completed the work of transforming this citadel into a sanctuary for the patron goddess of the city. The magnificent gateway (Propylaea), of which the Athenians were justly proud, was built by Mnesicles (437–432 BC). A monumental bronze statue by Phidias stood on the left, as one emerged on the plateau, and the mighty Parthenon a little farther on, to the right. In this temple was the famous gold and ivory statue of Athena. The eastern pediment contained sculptures representing the birth of the goddess (Elgin Marbles, now in the British Museum), the western depicting her contest with Poseidon for supremacy over Attica. This, the most celebrated edifice, architecturally, in all history, was partially destroyed by the Venetians in 1687. Other temples on the Acropolis are the Erechtheum and the "Wingless Victory." In the city the streets were exceedingly narrow and crooked. The wider

Temple of Jupiter at Athens.

avenues were called *plateiai* (πλατεῖαι), whence Eng. "place," Spanish "plaza." The roofs of the houses were flat. In and around the Agora were many porticoes (*stoai*). In the *Stoa Poecile* ("Painted Portico"), whose walls were covered with historical paintings, Paul met with the successors of Zeno, the Stoics, with whom he disputed daily. In this vicinity also was the Senate Chamber for the Council of Five Hundred, and the Court of the Areopagus, whither Socrates came in 399 BC to face his accusers, and where Paul, five cents. later, preached to the Athenians the unknown God. In this neighborhood also were the Tower of the Winds and the water-clock, which must have attracted Paul's attention, as they attract our attention today.

The apostle disputed in the synagogue with the Jews (Acts **17** 17), and a slab found at the foot of Mount Hymettus (a range to the E. of the city, 3,000 ft. high), with the inscription *αὔτη ἡ πύλη τοῦ κυρίου, δίκαιοι εἰσελεύσονται ἐν ἀυτῇ* (Ps **118** 20), was once thought to indicate the site, but is now believed to date from the 3d or 4th cent. Slabs bearing Jewish inscriptions have been found in the city itself.

The population of Athens was at least a quarter of a million. The oldest inhabitants were Pelasgians. Cecrops, the first traditional king, came from Egypt in 1556 BC, and by marrying the daughter of Actaeon, obtained the sovereignty. The first king was Erechtheus. Theseus united the twelve communities of Attica and made Athens the capital. After the death of Codrus in 1068 BC, the governing power was intrusted to an archon who held office for life. In 753 the term of office was limited to ten years. In 683 nine archons were chosen for a term of one year. Draco's laws, "written in blood," were made in 620. Solon was chosen archon in 594 and gave the state a constitution. The tyrant Pisistratus was in control permanently from 541 to 527; his son Hipparchus was assassinated in 514. Clisthenes changed the constitution and introduced the practice of ostracism. In 490 the Athenians defeated the Persians at Marathon, and again in 480 at Salamis. In 476 Aristides organized the great Athenian Confederacy. After his death Conon became the leader of the conservative party; and when the general Cimon was killed, Pericles became the leader of the people. In 431 the Peloponnesian War broke out and continued till 404, when Athens succumbed to Sparta. An oligarchical government was set up with Critias and Theramenes at the head. War broke out again but peace was restored by the pact of Antalcidas (387 BC). In the Sacred War (357–355) Athens exhausted her strength. When Philip of Macedon began to interfere in Gr affairs, Athens could neither resolve on war measures (to which the oratory of Demosthenes incited her), nor make terms with Philip. Finally, she joined Thebes in making armed resistance, but in spite of her heroic efforts at Chaeronea, she suffered defeat (338). Philip was murdered in 336, and Alexander the Great became master. After the subjugation of Greece by the Romans, Athens was placed under the supervision of the governor of Macedonia, but was granted local independence in recognition of her great history. As the seat of Gr art and science, Athens played an important rôle even under Rom sway—she became the university city of the Rom world, and from her radiated spiritual light and intellectual energy to Tarsus, Antioch and Alexandria. Philo, the Jew, declares that the Athenians were Ἑλλήνων ὀξυδερκέστατοι διάνοιαν ("keenest in intellect") and adds that Athens was to Greece what the pupil is to the eye, or reason to the soul. Although the city had lost her real independence, the people retained their old characteristics: they were still interested in art, literature and philosophy. Paul may possibly have attended the theater of Dionysus (under the S.E. cliff of the Acropolis) and witnessed a play of the Gr poets, such as Euripides or Menander. Many gifts were received from foreign monarchs by Athens. Attalus I of Pergamum endowed the Academy, Eumenes added a splendid Stoa to the theater and Antiochus Epiphanes began the Olympeium (15 columns of which are still standing), the massive sub-basement of which had been constructed by Pisistratus. Athens became a favorite residence for foreign writers who cultivated history, geography and literature. Horace, Brutus and Cassius sojourned in the city for some time. Jos declares that the Athenians were the most god-fearing of the Greeks (*εὐσεβεστάτους τῶν* Ἑλλή*νων*). Cf Livy xlv.27.

LITERATURE.—See Wordsworth, *Athens and Attica;* Butler, *Story of Athens;* Ernest Gardner, *Ancient Athens;* Tucker, *Life in Ancient Athens;* A. Mommsen, *Athenae Christianae;* Conybeare and Howson, *Life and Epistles of St. Paul*, ch x; Gregorovius, *Stadt Athen im Mittelalter;* Leake, Grote, Thirlwall, Curtius, Wachsmuth, Holm, and Pausanias' *Attica*, recently edited by Carroll (Ginn & Co.), or in the large work of Frazer.

J. E. HARRY

ATHLAI, ath'lā̇-ī (עַתְלַי, *'athlay*, "afflicted"[?]): A Jew, the son of Bebai, who was influenced by Ezra to put away his wife (Ezr **10** 28).

ATIPHA, at'i-fa. See HATIPHA.

AT ONE (**εἰς εἰρήνην,** *eis eirēnēn,* "at one," "at peace"): "Set them at one again" (Acts **7** 26), the reconciliation of persons at variance. From this adv. we have the words "atone" and "atonement."

ATONEMENT, a-tōn'ment: Translates כָּפַר, *kāphar;* חָטָא, *ḥāṭā';* רָצָה, *rāçāh,* the last employed only of human relations (1 S **29** 4); translates the following Gr stems *hilas-*, simple and compounded with various preps.; *allag-* in composition only, but with numerous preps. and even two at a time, e.g. Mt **5** 24; *lip-* rarely (Dnl **9** 24).

I. Terms Employed.—The root meanings of the Heb words, taking them in the order cited above,

1. Heb and Gr Words

are, to "cover," hence expiate, condone, cancel, placate; to "offer," or "receive a sin offering," hence make atonement, appease, propitiate; "effect reconciliation," i.e. by some conduct, or course of action. Of the Gr words the meanings, in order, are "to be," or "cause to be, friendly"; "to render other," hence to restore; "to leave" and with prep. to leave off, i.e. enmity, or evil, etc; "to render holy," "to set apart for"; hence of the Deity, to appropriate or accept for Himself.

It is obvious that the Eng. word, Atonement, does not correspond etymologically with any Heb

2. The Eng. Word

or Gr word which it translates. Furthermore, the Gr words in both LXX and NT do not correspond exactly to the Heb words; especially is it true that the root idea of the most frequently employed Heb word, *"cover,"* is not found in any of the Gr words employed. These remarks apply to both vbs. and substs. The Eng. word is derived from the phrase "at one," and signifies, etymologically, harmony of relationship or unity of life, etc. It is a rare instance of an AS theological term; and like all purely Eng. terms employed in theology, takes its meaning, not from its origin, but from the theological content of the thinking of the Continental and Lat-speaking Schoolmen who employed such Eng. terms as seemed most nearly to convey to the hearers and readers their ideas. Not only was no effort made to convey the original Heb and Gr meanings by means of Eng. words, but no effort was made toward uniformity in tr of Heb and Gr words by their Eng. equivalents.

It is at once clear that no mere word-study can determine the Bible teaching concerning atonement.

3. Not to Be Settled by Lexicon Merely

Even when first employed for expressing Heb and Christian thought, these terms, like all other religious terms, already had a content that had grown up with their use, and it is by no means easy to tell how far heathen conceptions might be imported into our theology by a rigidly etymological study of terms employed. In any case such a study could only yield a dictionary of terms, whereas what we seek is a body of teaching, a circle of ideas, whatever words and phrases, or combinations of words and phrases, have been employed to express the teaching.

There is even greater danger of making the study of the Atonement a study in dogmatic theology.

4. Not Chiefly a Study in Theology

The frequent employment of the expression *"the* Atonement" shows this tendency. The work of Christ in reconciling the world to God has occupied so central a place in Christian dogmatics that the very term atonement has come to have a theological rather than a practical atmosphere, and it is by no means easy for the student, or even for the seeker after the saving relation with God, to pass beyond the accumulated interpretation of *the* Atonement and learn of atonement.

The history of the explanation of the Atonement and the terms of preaching atonement cannot, of

5. Notes on Use of Terms

course, be ignored. Nor can the original meaning of the terms employed and the manner of their use be neglected. There are significant features in the use of terms, and we have to take account of the history of interpretation. Only we must not bind ourselves nor the word of God in such forms.

(1) The most frequently employed Heb word, *kāphar*, is found in the Prophets only in the priestly section (Ezk **45** 15.20; Dnl **9** 24) where EV has "make reconciliation," m, "purge away." Furthermore it is not found in Dt, which is the prophetic book of the Pent (Hex). This indicates that it is an essentially priestly conception. The same term is frequently trd by "reconcile," construed as equivalent to "make atonement" (Lev **6** 30; **8** 15; **16** 20; 1 S **29** 4; Ezk **45** 15.20; Dnl **9** 24). In this latter sense it connects itself with *ḥāṭā'*. In 2 Ch **29** 24 both words are used: the priests make a sin offering (*ḥāṭā'*) to effect an atonement (*kāphar*). But the first word is frequently used by metonymy to include, at least suggestively, the end in view, the reconciliation; and, on the other hand, the latter word is so used as to involve, also, doing that by which atonement is realized.

(2) Of the Gr words employed *hiláskesthai* means "to make propitious" (He **2** 17; Lev **6** 30; **16** 20; Ezk **45** 20); *allāttein*, used however only in composition with preps., means "to render other," "to restore" to another (former?) condition of harmony (cf Mt **5** 24 = "to be reconciled" to a fellow-man as a condition of making an acceptable sacrifice to God).

(3) In the Eng. NT the word "atonement" is found only at Rom **5** 11 and the ARV changes this to "reconciliation." While in strict etymology this word need signify only the active or conscious exercise of unity of life or harmony of relations, the causative idea probably belongs to the original use of the term, as it certainly is present in all current Christian use of the term. As employed in Christian theology, both practical and technical, the term includes with more or less distinctness: (*a*) the fact of union with God, and this always looked upon as (*b*) a broken union to be restored or an ideal union to be realized, (*c*) the procuring cause of atonement, variously defined, (*d*) the crucial act wherein the union is effected, the work of God and the response of the soul in which the union becomes actual. Inasmuch as the reconciliation between man and God is always conceived of as effected through Jesus Christ (2 Cor **5** 18–21) the expression, "the Atonement of Christ," is one of the most frequent in Christian theology. Questions and controversies have turned mainly on the procuring cause of atonement, (*c*) above, and at this point have arisen the various "theories of the Atonement."

II. Bible Teaching concerning Atonement in General.—The Atonement of Christ must be interpreted in connection with the conception of atonement in general in the Scriptures. This idea of atonement is, moreover, part of the general circle of fundamental ideas of the religion of Jeh and Jesus. Theories of the Atonement root themselves in conceptions of the nature and character of God, His holiness, love, grace, mercy, etc; of man, his nature, disposition and capacities; of sin and guilt.

The basal conception for the Bible doctrine of atonement is the assumption that God and man are ideally one in life and interests, so far as man's true life and interest may be conceived as corresponding with those of God. Hence it is everywhere assumed that God and man should be in all respects in harmonious relations, at-one. Such is the ideal picture of Adam and Eve in Eden. Such is the assumption in the parable of the Prodigal Son; man ought to be at home with God, at peace in the Father's house (Lk **15**). Such also is the ideal of Jesus as seen esp. in Jn **14–17**; cf particularly **17** 21 ff; cf also Eph **2** 11–22; 1 Cor **15** 28. This is quite possibly the underlying idea of all those offerings in which the priests—God's representatives—and the people joined in eating at a common meal parts of what had been presented to God. The prohibition of the use of blood in food or drink is grounded on the statement that the life is in the blood (Lev **17** 10 f) or is the blood (Gen **9** 4; Dt **12** 23). Blood was used in the consecration of tabernacle, temple, vessels, altars, priests; all things and persons set apart for Jeh. Then blood was required in offerings made to atone for sin and uncleanness. The reason for all this is not easy to see; but if we seek an explanation that will account for all the facts on a single principle, shall we not find it in the idea that in the life-principle of the blood God's own life was present? Through this life from God all living beings shared God's life. The blood passing out of any living being must therefore return to God and not be consumed. In sprinkling blood, the life-element, or certainly the life-symbol, over persons and things set apart for God they were, so to say, visibly taken up into the life of God, and His life extending over them made them essentially of His own person. Finally the blood of sacrifices was the returning to God of the life of the man for whom the beasts stood. And this blood was not burned with the dead sacrifice but poured out beside the holy altar. The now dead sin offering was burned, but the blood, the life, returned to God. In peace-offerings of various sorts there was the common meal in which the common life was typified.

1. Primary Assumption of Unity of God and Man

In the claim of the first-fruits of all crops, of all flocks and of all increase, God emphasized the common life in production; asserted His claim to the total life of His people and their products. God claimed the lives of all as belonging essentially to Himself and a man must recognize this by paying a ransom price (Ex **30** 12). This did not purchase for the man a right to his own life in separation from God, for it was in no sense an equivalent in value to the man's time. It the rather committed the man to living the common life with God, without which recognition the man was not fit to live at all. And the use of this recognition-money by the priests in the temple was regarded as placing the man who paid his money in a sort of continuous worshipful service in the tabernacle (or temple) itself (Ex **30** 11–16).

2. The Breach in the Unity

In both OT and NT the assumption of unity between God and man stands over against the contrasted fact that there is a radical breach in this unity. This breach is recognized in all God's relations to men; and even when healed it is always subject to new failures which must be provided for, by the daily oblations in the OT, by the continuous intercession of the Christ (He **7** 25; **9** 24) in the NT. Even when there is no conscious breach, man is taught to recognize that it may exist and he must avail himself of the appointed means for its healing, e.g. daily sacrifices. This breach is universally attributed to some behavior on man's part. This may be moral or ceremonial uncleanness on man's part. He may have broken with God fundamentally in character or conduct and so by committing sin have incurred guilt; or he may have neglected the fitting recognition that his life is in common with God and so by his disregard have incurred uncleanness. After the first breach between God and man it is always necessary that man shall approach God on the assumption that this breach needs healing, and so always come with an offering. In human nature the sin breach is rooted and universal (Rom **3** 9–19; **5** 12–14).

3. Means for Expressing, Restoring and Maintaining

Numerous and various means were employed for expressing this essential unity of life, for restoring it since it was broken off in sin, and for maintaining it. These means were primarily spiritual and ethical but made extensive use of material substances, physical acts and symbolical ceremonials; and these tended always to obscure and supplant the spiritual and ethical qualities which it was their function to exhibit. The prophet came to the rescue of the spiritual and ethical and reached his highest insight and function in the doctrine of the Suffering Servant of Jeh through whom God was to be united with a redeemed race (cf among many passages, Isa **49** 1–7; **66** 18 ff; Ps **22** 27 ff).

Atonement is conceived in both OT and NT as partly personal and partly social, extending to the universal conception. The acts and attitudes by which it is procured, restored and maintained are partly those of the individual alone (Ps **51**), partly those in which the individual secures the assistance of the priest or the priestly body, and partly such as the priest performs for the whole people on his own account. This involves the distinction that in Israel atonement was both personal and social, as also were both sin and uncleanness. Atonement was made for the group by the priest without specific participation by the people although they were, originally at least, to take cognizance of the fact and at the time. At all the great feasts, especially upon the DAY OF ATONEMENT (q.v.) the whole group was receptively to take conscious part in the work of atonement (Nu **29** 7–11).

The various sacrifices and offerings by means of which atonement was effected in the life and worship of Israel will be found to be discussed under the proper words and are to be spoken of here only summarily. The series of offerings, *guilt-*, *burnt-*, *sin-*, *peace-offerings*, reveal a sense of the breach with God, a conviction of the sin making the breach and an ethical appreciation of the holiness of God entirely unique among religions of ancient or modern times, and this fact must never be overlooked in interpreting the NT Christian doctrine of the Atonement. In the OT there are sins and sinful circumstances for which no atonement is possible. Many passages, indeed, almost seem to provide against atonement for any voluntary wrongdoing (e.g. Lev **4** 2.13.22.27; **5** 14 ff). This is, no doubt, an extreme interpretation, out of harmony with the general spirit of the OT, but it does show how seriously sin ought to be taken under the OT régime. No atonement for murder could make possible the residence of the murderer again in that section of the land where the murder was done (Nu **35** 33), although the land was not by the murder rendered unfit for occupation by others. When Israel sinned in making the golden calf, God refused to accept any atonement (Ex **32** 20 ff) until there had been a great loss of life from among the sinners. No repentance could find atonement for the refusal to follow Jeh's lead at Kadesh-barnea (Nu **14** 20–25), and complete atonement was effected only when all the unbelieving generation had died in the wilderness (Nu **26** 65; **32** 10 ff); i.e. no atonement was possible, but the people died in that sin, outside the Land of Promise, although the sin was not allowed to cut off finally from Jeh (Nu **14** 29 f).

Permanent uncleanness or confirmed disease of an unclean sort caused permanent separation from the temple and the people of Jeh (e.g. Lev **7** 20 f), and every uncleanness must be properly removed (Lev **5** 2*b;* **17** 15; **22** 2–8; Dt **23** 10 f). A house in which an unclean disease was found must be cleansed—have atonement made for it (Lev **14** 53), and in extreme cases must be utterly destroyed (Lev **14** 43 ff).

After childbirth (Lev **12** 7 f) and in all cases of hemorrhage (cf Lev **15** 30) atonement must be effected by prescribed offerings, a loss, diminution, or pollution of blood, wherein is the life, having been suffered. All this elaborate application of the principle of atonement shows the comprehensiveness with which it was sought by the religious teachers to impress the people with the unity of all life in the perfectly holy and majestic God whom they were called upon to serve. Not only must the priests be clean who bear the vessels of the Lord (Isa **52** 11), but all the people must be clean also from all defilement of flesh and spirit, seeking perfect holiness in the fear of their God (cf 2 Cor **7** 1).

III. The Atonement of Jesus Christ.—All the symbols, doctrine and examples of atonement in the OT among the Hebrews find their counterpart, fulfilment and complete explanation in the new covenant in the blood of Jesus Christ (Mt **26** 28; He **12** 24). By interpreting the inner spirit of the sacrificial system, by insisting on the unity and holiness of God, by passionate pleas for purity in the people, and especially by teaching the principle of vicarious suffering for sin, the Prophets laid the foundation in thought-forms and in religious atmosphere for such a doctrine of atonement as is presented in the life and teaching of Jesus and as is unfolded in the teaching of His apostles.

1. Preparation for NT Doctrine

The personal, parabolic sufferings of Hosea, the remarkable elaboration of the redemption of a spiritual Israel through a Suffering Servant of Jeh and the extension of that redemption to all mankind as presented in Isa **40–66,** and the same element in such psalms as Ps **22,** constitute a key to the understanding of the work of the Christ that unifies the entire revelation of God's righteousness in passing over human sins (Rom **3** 24 f). Yet it is remarkable that such a conception of the way of atonement was as far as possible from the general and average Jewish mind when Jesus came. In no sense can the NT doctrine of the Atonement be said to be the product of the thought and spirit of the times.

2. The One Clear Fact

However much theologians may disagree as to the rationale of the Atonement, there is, as there can be, no question that Jesus and all His interpreters in the NT represent the Atonement between God and men as somehow accomplished through Jesus Christ. It is also an agreed fact in exegesis that Jesus and His apostles understood His death to be radically connected with this Atonement.

(1) *Jesus Himself* teaches that He has come to reveal the Father (Jn **14** 9), to recover the lost (Lk **19** 10), to give life to men (Jn **6** 33; **10** 10), to disclose and establish the kingdom of heaven (or of God), gathering a few faithful followers through whom His work will be perpetuated (Jn **17** 2 ff; Mt **16** 13 ff); that salvation, personal and social, is dependent upon His person (Jn **6** 53 ff; **14** 6). He cannot give full teaching concerning His death but He does clearly connect His sufferings with the salvation He seeks to give. He shows in Lk **4** 16 ff and **22** 37 that He understands Isa **52–53** as realized in Himself; He is giving Himself (and His blood) a ransom for men (Mt **20** 28; **26** 26 ff; cf 1 Cor **11** 23 ff). He was not a mere martyr but gave Himself up willingly, and voluntarily (Jn **10** 17 f; Gal **2** 20), in accordance with the purpose of God (Acts **2** 23), as the Redeemer of the world, and expected that by His lifting up all men would be drawn to Him (Jn **12** 31–33). It is possible to explain the attention which the Evangelists give to the death of Jesus only by supposing that they are reflecting the importance which they recall Jesus Himself to have attached to His death.

(2) *All the NT writers agree* in making Jesus the center of their idea of the way of salvation and that His death is an essential element in His saving power. This they do by combining OT teaching with the facts of the life and death of the Lord, confirming their conclusion by appeal to the Resurrection. Paul represents himself as holding the common doctrine of Christianity at the time, and from the beginning, when in 1 Cor **15** 3 f he sums up his teaching that salvation is secured through the death and resurrection of Jesus according to the Scriptures. Elsewhere (Eph **2** 16.18; 1 Tim **2** 5; cf Acts **4** 12) in all his writings he emphasizes his belief that Jesus Christ is the one Mediator between God and man, by the blood of His cross (Col **1** 20; 1 Cor **2** 2), removing the sin barrier between God and men. Peter, during the life of Jesus so full of the current Jewish notion that God accepted the Jews *de facto,* in his later ministry makes Jesus in His death the one way to God (Acts **4** 12; 1 Pet **1** 2.18.19; **2** 21.24; **3** 18).

John has this element so prominent in his Gospel that radical critical opinion questions its authorship partly on that account, while the epistles of Jn and the Revelation are, on the same ground, attributed to later Gr thought (cf 1 Jn **1** 7; **2** 2; **3** 5; **4** 10; Rev **1** 5; **5** 9). The Epistle to the He finds in Jesus the fulfilment and extension of all the sacrificial system of Judaism and holds that the shedding of blood seems essential to the very idea of remission of sins (**9** 22; cf **2** 17; **7** 26 f; **9** 24–28).

3. How Shall We Understand the Atonement?

When we come to systematize the teaching concerning the Atonement we find, as in all doctrine, that definite system is not offered us in the NT, but all system, if it is to have any value for Christianity, must find its materials and principles in the NT. Proceeding in this way some features may be stated positively and finally, while others must be presented interrogatively, recognizing that interpretations may differ.

(1) *An initial consideration* is that *the Atonement originates with God* who "was in Christ reconciling the world unto himself" (2 Cor **5** 19), and whose love gave Jesus to redeem sinful men (Jn **3** 16; Rom **5** 8, etc). In all atonement in OT and NT the initiative is of God who not only devises and reveals the way to reconciliation, but by means of angels, prophets, priests and ultimately His only begotten Son applies the means of atonement and persuades men to accept the proffered reconciliation. Nothing in the speculation concerning the Atonement can be more false to its true nature than making a breach between God and His Christ in their attitude toward sinful men.

(2) It follows that *atonement is fundamental in the nature of God* in His relations to men, and that redemption is in the heart of God's dealing in history. The "Lamb slain from the foundation of the world" (Rev **13** 8 AV and ERV; cf **5** 5–7) is the interpreter of the seven-sealed book of God's providence in history. In Jesus we behold the Lamb of God taking away the sin of the world (Jn **1** 29).

(3) The question will arise in the analysis of the doctrine: *How does the death of Christ save us?* No specific answer has ever been generally satisfactory. We have numerous *theories of the Atonement*. We have already intimated that the answer to this question will depend upon our idea of the nature of God, the nature of sin, the content of salvation, the nature of man, and our idea of Satan and evil spirits. We ought to dismiss all *exclusively* quantitative and commercial conceptions of exchange of merit. There is no longer any question that the doctrines of imputation, both of Adam's sin and of Christ's righteousness, were overwrought and applied by the early theologians with a fatal exclusiveness, without warrant in the Word of God. On the other hand no theory can hold much weight that presupposes that sin is a thing of light consequence in the nature of man and in the economy of God. Unless one is prepared to resist unto blood striving against sin (He **12** 2–4), he cannot know the meaning of the Christ. Again, it may be said that the notion that the death of Christ is to be considered apart from His life, eternal and incarnate life, as the atoning work, is far too narrow to express the teaching of the Bible and far too shallow to meet the demands of an ethical conscience.

It would serve clearness if we reminded ourselves that the question of *how* in the Atonement may involve various elements. We may inquire: (*a*) for the ground on which God may righteously receive the sinner; (*b*) for the means by which God places the restoration within the reach of the sinner; (*c*) for the influence by which the sinner is persuaded to accept the reconciliation; (*d*) for the attitude or exercise of the sinner toward God in Christ wherein he actually enters the state of restored union with God. The various theories have seemed to be exclusive, or at least mutually antagonistic, largely because they have taken partial views of the whole subject and have emphasized some one feature of the whole content. All serious theories partly express the truth and all together are inadequate fully to declare how the Daystar from on high doth guide our feet into the way of peace (Lk **1** 79).

(4) Another question over which the theologians have sorely vexed themselves and each other concerns the *extent of the Atonement*, whether it is available for all men or only for certain particular, elect ones. That controversy may now be passed by. It is no longer possible to read the Bible and suppose that God relates himself sympathetically with only a part of the race. All segregated passages of Scripture formerly employed in support of such a view have now taken their place in the progressive self-interpretation of God to men through Christ who is the propitiation for the sins of the whole world (1 Jn **2** 2). No man cometh unto the Father but by Him (Jn **14** 6): but whosoever does thus call upon the name of the Lord shall be saved (Joel **2** 32; Acts **2** 21). See also ATONEMENT, DAY OF; PROPITIATION; RECONCILIATION; SACRIFICE.

LITERATURE.—In the vast literature on this subject the following is suggested: Articles by Orr in *HDB*; by Mackenzie in *Standard BD*; in *Cath. Enc*; in *Jewish Enc*; by Simpson in *DCG*; J. McLeod Campbell, *The Nature of the Atonement*; John Champion, *The Living Atonement*; W. M. Clow, *The Cross in Christian Experience*; T. J. Crawford, *The Doctrine of Holy Scripture Respecting the Atonement*; R. W. Dale, *The Atonement*; J. Denney, *The Death of Christ: Its Place and Interpretation in the NT*, and *The Atonement and the Modern Mind*; W. P. DuBose, *The Soteriology of the NT*; P. T. Forsyth, *The Cruciality of the Cross*; J. Scott Lidgett, *The Spiritual Principle of the Atonement*; Oxenham, *The Catholic Doctrine of the Atonement*; A. Ritschl, *The Christian Doctrine of Justification and Reconciliation*, I, II; Rivière, *Le dogme de la rédemption*; D. W. Simon, *Reconciliation by Incarnation*; W. L. Walker, *The Cross and the Kingdom*; various writers, *The Atonement and Modern Religious Thought*.

WILLIAM OWEN CARVER

ATONEMENT, a-tōn′ment, DAY OF:

I. The Legal Enactments.—In addition to the chief passage, Lev **16**, which is treated under a separate head, we have the following:

1. Named In Ex **30** 10 it is mentioned in the directions that are given for the construction of the altar of incense that Aaron, once a year, is to make an atonement on the horns of the altar, with the blood of the sin offering, which is used for the purpose of an atonement for sin.

In Lev **23** 26–32 mention is made in the list of festivals of the Day of Atonement, on the 10th day of the 7th month. It is ordered that for this day there shall be a holy convocation at the sanctuary, a fast, an offering by fire, and rest from labor from the 9th day of the 7th month in the evening.

According to Lev **25** 9 the year of jubilee begins with the Day of Atonement.

Nu **18** speaks of the duties and the rights of the priests and the Levites. In contrast with the latter, according to ver 7, Aaron and his sons are to perform the duties of the priesthood in all matters pertaining to the altar and of the service within the veil and shall render this service. We have here doubtless a comprehensive law for the entire priestly order, so that from this alone it cannot be determined that the service within the veil, by which reference is made to the ceremony of the Day of Atonement, has been reserved for the high priest alone, just as in Dt **10** 8; **33** 8 ff, everything that pertains to the whole tribe of Levi is found combined, without thereby the division into high priest, priests and Levites, being regarded as excluded (cf EZEKIEL, II, 2, (1), *c*).

Nu **29** 7–11 contains in connection with the laws treating of sacrifices also the enactment, that on the 10th day of the 7th month there shall take place a holy convocation at the sanctuary, fasting and rest from labor. In addition to the sin offering, which is brought for the purpose of atonement for sin, and in addition to the regular burnt offerings and the accompanying meal offerings and drink offerings, burnt offerings also are to be brought, viz. one young bullock, one young ram, seven lambs of the first year (all without blemish); then meal offerings, viz. three-tenths (cf **28** 12–14) of fine flour mingled with oil for each bullock; two-tenths for each ram; one-tenth for each lamb; then a sin offering, viz. one he-goat.

Ezekiel in his vision of the new temple, of the holy city and the holy country (chs **40–48**), in **45** 18 ff, gives a series of enactments for the festivals and the sacrifices. According to these, on the 1st day of the 1st month and on the 7th day of the 1st month (on the 1st day of the 7th month according to the LXX), the sanctuary is to be cleansed through a young bullock without blemish, the priest taking some of the blood of the sin offering and putting it on the posts of the temple, on the four corners of the altar and on the posts of the gate of the inner court; and this is to be done for the sake of those who perhaps have sinned through error or ignorance. Further, that sacrifice which is to be brought on the Passover by the princes for themselves and all the people of the land (cf **45** 22) appears to present a clear analogy to Lev **16**. As for the rest, Ezk **40–48** cannot without further consideration be put on the same level with the other legal enactments, but are to be regarded as an ideal scheme, the realization of which is conditioned on the entrance of the wonderful future (cf EZEKIEL).

2. Lev Ch 16

(1) *Contents, structure and position.*—Lev **16** 1–28 contains instructions given by Jeh to Moses for his brother Aaron (vs 1.2). (*a*) Vs 1–10 contain presuppositions, preparations and summary statements of the ceremonies on the Day of Atonement. According to vs 1.2 Aaron is not allowed to enter the holy place at any time whatever, lest he may die as did his sons with their unseemly fire offering (cf Lev **10** 1 ff); vs 3–5 tell what is necessary for the ceremony: For himself four things: a young bullock as a sin offering (cf vs 6.11.14.15.27); a ram for burnt offering (cf ver 24); sacred garments, viz. a linen coat, linen breeches, linen girdle, linen mitre (cf vs 23.32); a bath. For the congregation: two he-goats as a sin offering (cf vs 7 ff.15–22.25.27.28.32.33), a ram as a burnt offering (cf ver 24). The passages in parentheses show how closely the succeeding parts of this account are connected with this introductory part, vs 1–10. In other parts of Lev also it is often found that the materials used for the sacrifices are mentioned first, before anything is said in detail of what is to be done with this material. Cf **8** 1.2 with vs 6.7 ff.10.14.18.22.26 and **9** 2–4 with vs 7.8 ff.12 ff.15–18. In ver 6 Aaron's sin-offering bullock is to be used as an atonement for himself; vs 7–10 refer to the two goats: they are to be placed at the door of the tent of meeting (ver 7); lots are to be cast upon them for Jeh and Azazel (ver 8); the first to be prepared as a sin offering for Jeh (ver 9); the second, in accordance with the law, to be sent into the desert (ver 10).

(*b*) Vs 11–24 describe the ceremony itself and give fuller directions as to how the different sacrificial materials mentioned under (*a*) are to be used by Aaron: vs 11–14 speak of the atonement for Aaron and his house; ver 11, of his sin-offering bullock to be killed; ver 12, of burning coal from the altar and two handfuls of sweet incense beaten small to be placed behind the veil; ver 13, of the cloud of incense to be made in the Holy of Holies, so that the top covering is hidden and Aaron is protected from the danger of death; ver 14, of some of the blood to be sprinkled once on the front of the top covering and seven times in front of it. Vs 15–19 prescribe the ceremony with the first sin-offering goat for the congregation: in vs 15.16*a*, the ceremony described in ver 14 is directed also to be carried out with the goat, as an atonement for the inner sanctuary, cleansing it from blemishes; in ver 16*b* the same thing is directed to be done in regard to the tabernacle of revelation, i.e. the holy place; in ver 17, no one is permitted to be present even in the holy place when these ceremonies take place; in vs 18.19, the altar too is directed to be cleansed by an atonement, some of the blood of both sin-offering animals being smeared on the horns and sprinkled seven times on the ground. Vs 20–22 prescribe the ceremony with the second sin-offering goat for the congregation: ver 20 directs it to be brought there; in ver 21 there takes place the transfer of guilt; Aaron shall lay both his hands upon the goat; shall confess all guilt over him; shall lay them upon the head of the goat; shall through a man send him into the desert; in ver 22*a*, the goat carries the guilt into an uninhabited land; in ver 22*b*, he is not to be let go until he is in the desert. Vs 23.24, the concluding act: in ver 23*a*, Aaron takes off his linen garments in the tent of meeting, and in ver 23*b* puts them down there; in ver 24*a*, he bathes in the holy place and again puts on his usual clothing; in ver 24*b* he brings the burnt offering for himself and his people. (The statement 'for himself and his people' at this place concludes the ritual as such.)

(*c*) Vs 25–28 are explanatory, with three additional directions. In ver 25, the fat of the sin offering is directed to be consumed into smoke on the altar; ver 26, he who has taken away the second goat must wash his clothes and bathe himself, and only then is he permitted to enter the camp; ver 27, the fat, flesh and dung of the sin-offering animal, and then the blood that was brought into the (inner) sanctuary, are to be burned outside of the camp; ver 28, he who has burned these must wash his clothes, and must bathe, and only after this can he enter the camp. (In this case vs 25 and 27 correspond, and also vs 26 and 28; and in addition vs 26, 27 and 28 are united by their reference to the camp.)

(*d*) Vs 29–34: Over against these sections (*a*)–(*c*) (vs 1–28), which contain the instructions for the high priest, we have a fourth (vs 29–34), which already through the address in the second person plur. and also by its contents is intended for the congregation. In vs 29–31, the demand is made of the congregation. As in Lev **23** 26 ff; Nu **29** 7 ff, a fast and absolute rest are prescribed for the 10th day of the 7th month as the Day of Atonement; in vs 32–34, a number of directions are given in a summary to the congregation on the basis of **16** 1 ff, viz. ver 32, how the atonement is to take place: the priest who is anointed; he shall be consecrated; that he perform the service in his father's place; in his linen garments; ver 33 prescribes when and for whom the atonement is to take place: for the holy of holies; for the holy place; for the altar; for the order of priests and all the people; in ver 34, the one Day of Atonement in the year for all sins is declared to be an everlasting statute. The statement that Aaron (ver 2), according to Jeh's command, did as Moses directed aptly closes the whole chapter.

The number four appears to occupy a predominating place in this chapter, as the bird's-eye view above already shows, and as this can be traced still further in the details of the accounts. But even if this significance of the number four in the division of the chapter is accidental, although this number appears almost as a matter of course, and in Ex **35** 4—**40** 38, in Gen **12–25**, in the story of Abraham, Lev **11–15**, and Dt **12–26** naturally fall into four pericopes with four subdivisions, yet this chapter is, as far as contents are concerned, so closely connected, and so well organized as a whole, that all attempts to ascribe it to different sources, concerning which we shall speak immediately, must come to naught in view of this fact.

At this point we first of all draw attention to the fact that ch **16** has its well-established place in the whole of the Book of Lev (cf LEVITICUS). The whole book has as its purpose to regulate the dealings of the Israelites with their God, and it does this in such a way that the first part (chs **1–17**) removes the hindrances that have been caused by sin. In this the ordinances with reference to the Day of Atonement (Lev **16**), and with reference to the significance of the blood (Lev **17**), constitute a natural acme and excellent conclusion, while this prepares for the positive sanctification, which is discussed in chs **18** ff. In **15** 31 we find in addition a clear transition to the thoughts of Lev **16**, for in this passage mention is made of the uncleanness of the Israelites, which contaminates the dwelling-place of Jeh that is in their midst.

(2) *Modern attempts to disprove unity of chapter.*—A large number of attempts have been made to destroy the unity of this chapter, which has been demonstrated in division (1) above. Thus Stade separates vs 3–10 as the original kernel from the explanatory and changing details that were added in vs 11–28. But we have already seen that vs 3–10 are the preparation for all that follows, so that these verses demand vs 11 ff as a necessary complement. Again Oort separates vs 1–4, 11*b*–14.16.18*a*.19.23.24*a*.25*a*.29*a* from the rest, by using the purification of the sanctuary and the atonement of the people as the measure for this separation; but above all it is proved by Ezk **45** 18–20 that just these two thoughts are inseparably united. In recent times it has become the custom, following the leadership of Benzinger, to divide the text into three parts. Baentsch divides as follows: (*a*) **16** 1–4.6.12 f.34*b* contain a single pericope, which on the basis of the fate of the sons of Aaron, described in ch **10**, determines under what circumstances Aaron alone is permitted to enter the Holy of Holies; (*b*) vs 29–34*a* contain "an older, relatively simpler law in reference to the yearly day of penitence and atonement"; (*c*) vs 5.7–10.11.14–28 are a "later enlargement of this ritual, with a more complicated blood rite," and above all with "the rite of the sin goat." Of these three pieces only (*a*) is thought to belong to the original Priest Codex, as proved esp. by its reference back to ch **10**; (*b*) is regarded as belonging to the secondary parts, because the day of repentance is not yet mentioned in Neh **8** ff; cf III, 1; at any rate the anointing of all the priests is there not yet presupposed (cf LEVITICUS); (*c*), however, is declared to be very late and its separate parts are regarded as having originated only after the others (thus recently also Bertholet). It is impossible here to enter into all the minor parts eliminated by the exegetes; and in the same way we do not intend in our examination to enter into all the incorrect views found in these criticisms. We confine ourselves to the chief matter. The very foundation of the criticism is wrong. What Aaron's sons experienced according to Lev **10** could very easily have furnished a connecting link for that ritual which is introduced in vs 2 ff, but could never have furnished the occasion for the composition of the pericope described above (*a*); for Nadab and Abihu had not entered into the Holy of Holies at all. Just as little justifiable is the conclusion drawn from ch **10**, that ch **16** originally followed immediately on ch **10**. For who could possibly have conceived the thought of inserting chs **11–15** in an altogether unsuitable place between chs **10** and **16** and thus have split asunder a connection so transparent? In general, the different attempts to break the unity of this chapter show how subjective and arbitrary these attempts are. They are a characteristic example of the manner in which the Priest Codex is now being further divided (cf LEVITICUS). In general, sufficient material for the positive refutation of such attempts has been given above.

II. The Significance of the Day of Atonement.—The significance of the day is expressed in the name "Day of Atonement" (*Yōm ha-kippurīm:* Lev **23** 27 f; **25** 9) in the same manner as it is in the fast which was enjoined on the congregation as a sign of sorrow for their sins (this fasting being the only one enjoined by the law: Lev **16** 29.31; **23** 26 ff; Nu **29** 7 ff), as also finally and chiefly in the entire ritual (Ex **30** 10; Lev **23** 28; Nu **29** 11; Lev **16**; cf also Ezk **45** 18–20.22). Then, too, the atonement takes place for the sanctuary which has been defiled by the contamination of the Israelites (Ex **30** 10; Lev **16** 16–20.33; cf also Ezk **45** 18–20). In particular, mention is made of the Holy of Holies (Lev **16** 33, called *Miḳdash ha-ḳōdhesh;* otherwise in Lev regularly *ha-ḳōdhesh*), then of the holy place (**16** 16*b*.20.33), and then of the altar (**16** 18.20.33). In the last-mentioned case it is a matter of discussion whether the altar of incense is meant, as is claimed by Jewish tradition, on the basis of Ex **30** 10, or the altar of burnt offerings, for which reference could be made to the additional statements in Lev **16** 18, to those of ver 16, and to the conclusion in ver **17**. The altar of incense (Ex **30** 10) would then be included in the atonement of the tent of meeting. The somewhat remarkable position of ver 17*b* would then at the same time find its motive in this, that, while vs 6 and 11*b* mention an atonement only for Aaron and his house, the atonement of the Holy of Holies and of the holy place in ver 17 is for Aaron, his house, and the whole congregation, while the atonement of the burnt-offering altar in the forecourt (vs 18) would be intended only for the sins of the congregation. The atonement, however, takes place for all the transgressions of the congregation since the last Day of Atonement (cf vs 21 f.30.34). In reference to the significance of what is done with the second goat of sin offering, cf vs 8 ff.20 ff, and AZAZEL, II, 1. In this way Delitzsch has correctly called the Day of Atonement "the Good Friday of the Old Testament." How deeply the consciousness of sin must have been awakened, if the many otherwise commanded private and congregational sacrifices did not make such an institution superfluous, and if even the high priest himself stood before God as a sinner (vs 6.11 ff). On this day, with the exception of the mitre, he does not wear the insignia of his high-priestly office, but wears white garments, which in their simplicity correspond to the earnestness of the situation. The repetition of the bath, both in his case and in that of the other persons engaged in the ceremony (vs 4.24.26.28), was necessary, because the mere washing of the hands and feet (Ex **30** 19 f) would not suffice on this occasion (cf Nu **19** 7 ff.19.21). The flesh of the sin-offering animals was not permitted to be eaten but had to be burned (ver 27) because it was sacrificed also for Aaron's sin, and its blood was carried not only into the holy place but also into the Holy of Holies (cf **16** 27 with Lev **6** 23; **4** 11 f.21; Ex **29** 14; Lev **8** 17; **9** 11; **10** 19). And in comparison with the consciousness of sin that had been aroused, how great must on the other hand God's grace appear, when once in each year a general remission of all the sins that had been forgiven was guaranteed.

1. The Significance for Israel

"The Day of Atonement, the good Friday of the Old Testament"—these words express not only the highest significance of the day but also its limitations. As the tabernacle, the sacrificial system, the entire law, thus too the Day of Atonement in particular contained only the shadow of future good things, but not these things themselves (He **10** 1), and is "like in pattern to the true" (He **9** 24). Christ Himself entered into the holy place, which was not made with hands, namely, into heaven itself, and has now appeared before God, by once for all giving Himself as a sacrifice for the removal of sin (He **9** 23 ff). By this act the purpose of the OT sacrificial cultus and its highest development, viz. the Day of Atonement, understood in its typical significance, has been fulfilled, and at the same time surpassed and thereby abrogated (cf LEVITICUS). Accordingly, our hope, too, like an anchor (He **6** 19), penetrates to the inner part of the veil in the higher sense of the term, i.e. to heaven.

2. Significance from a Christian Standpoint

III. On the History of the Day of Atonement.—(1) *The facts and the false conclusions.*—The Day of Atonement is stated to have been instituted in the times of Moses (Lev **16** 1); the ceremony takes place in the tabernacle (tent of meeting); the people are presupposed to be in the camp (vs 26 ff); Aaron is still the high priest.

1. The Long Silence of History

Very remarkably there is but little evidence of the observance of this prominent day in the later history of Israel. Down to the time of the Exile there is found a deep silence on this subject. The days of atonement in Ezk **45** 18 ff (cf under I, 1) differ in number and observance from that in Lev **16.** According to Zec **3** 9, God in the Messianic future will take away the guilt of the land in a single day; but this too presents no more than an analogy to the results of the Day of Atonement. On the other hand, there is no reference made to the day where we could expect it. Not only 2 Ch **7** 7–9 in connection with the consecration of Solomon's temple, and Ezr **3** 1–6, in the account of the reintroduction of the sacrificial services after the return from the Exile, are silent on the subject, which fact could possibly be explained in an easy manner; but also Neh **8** f. According to **8** 2 f, Ezra begins on the 1st day of the 7th month in the year 444 BC to read from the law; on the 2d day of the 7th month remembrance is made of the ordinance treating of the feast of tabernacles, and on the 22d day of the 7th month (**8** 13 ff), this festival is observed; on the 24th day of the 7th month a day of penance is observed (**9** 1); but of the Day of Atonement coming in between ch **8** 1 and ch **9** 1, viz. on the 10th day of the 7th month, which would seem to make the day of penance superfluous, nothing is said. From these facts the Wellhausen school has drawn the conclusion, in accordance with its principles elsewhere observed, that all those legal enactments that have not in the history a sufficient evidence of having been observed, did not exist until the time when they have such historical evidence; that therefore the Day of Atonement did not originate until after the year 444 BC. It is claimed that the day originated in the two days of atonement mentioned in Ezk **45** 18–20 (cf under I, 1); in the four national fast days of Zec **7** 5, and **8** 19, and in the day of penance of 444 BC, just mentioned, on the 24th day of the 7th month, which is said to have been repeated on the following New Year's day, the 10th day of the 7th month; and that by the sacred character of its observance it soon crowded the New Year day upon the 1st day of the 7th month (cf Lev **23** 23 ff; Nu **29** 1 ff; contrary to Lev **25** 9 and Ezk **40** 1). In this way it is thought that Lev **16** 29 ff first originated, and that at a still later time the complicated blood ritual had been added (cf under I, 1, 2). But it is to be observed that in still later times there is found no more frequent mention of the Day of Atonement than in the earlier, although it is the custom of modern criticism to place a much larger bulk of Biblical lit. into this later period. It is only when we come to Jesus Sirach (Ecclus **50** 5 ff) that the high priest Simon is praised, when he came forth from behind the veil; and this is certainly a reference to the Day of Atonement, although no further mention is made at this place of the ceremony as such. Then there is a further silence on the subject down to Philo and the Epistle to the He (**6** 19; **9** 7.13 ff; **10** 1 ff; cf under II, 2). It is probable too that the fasting mentioned in Acts **27** 9 is based on the Day of Atonement. We have in this manner a characteristic example to show how carefully we must handle the argument from silence, if we do not want to arrive at uncomfortable results.

(2) *The historicity of the Day of Atonement.*—Since Lev **16** constitutes only one part of the Levitical legislation, the question as to the original and historical character of the day cannot be fully discussed at this place (see Leviticus). At so late a period, naturally all the data that would lead to an explanation of the origin of such a fundamental institution as the Day of Atonement are lacking. It is all the more impossible to separate Lev **16** from the other priestly ordinances, because the name of the lid of the ark of covenant (*ha-kappōreth:* Ex **25** 17 ff; **26** 34) stands in the clearest relation to the ceremony that takes place with this ark on the Day of Atonement. The impossibility of splitting up Lev **16** as is the manner of critics, or even as much as separating it from Lev **11–15,** has been sufficiently demonstrated above (cf under I). Against the view which forces the Priest Codex down at least to the Exile and to claim the tabernacle as the product of imagination and as a copy of the temple of Solomon (see Exodus), we have still the following to add: If the ark of the covenant was no longer in existence after the Exile and if, according to Jer **3** 16, the Israelites no longer expected its restoration, then it would have been absolutely impossible in the ritual of the Day of Atonement to connect the most important ceremony of this ritual with this ark and on this to base the atonement. In the second temple, as is well known, the incense pan was placed on the "foundation stone" in the Holy of Holies, because there was no tabernacle. Against these facts the counter-arguments mentioned above cannot stand. Even those who deny the existence of the Day of Atonement do not lay much stress on 2 Ch **7** 1–9 and Ezr **3** 1–6; but Neh **8** ff also does not deserve mention, since in this place the emphasis lies on the purpose of showing how the congregation was to declare its adherence to the law, and how the Day of Repentance, which had been observed since the beginning of the history of Israel, was instituted to be observed on the 24th day of the 7th month for all sins (**9** 1 ff), and was not made superfluous by the celebration of the Day of Atonement on the 10th day of the 7th month, on which day only the sins of the last year were taken into consideration. But Ezekiel changed or ignored also other preëxilic arrangements (cf Ezekiel), so that he is no authority in deciding the question as to the earlier existence of the Day of Atonement. Finally, attention must be drawn to the fact that the Passover festival is mentioned in prophetic literature, in addition to the mere reference in Isa **30** 29, only in Ezk **45** 21; the ark of the covenant only in Jer **3** 16; the Feast of Tabernacles only in Hos **12** 9; Ezk **45** 25; and that in its historical connection the Feast of Weeks is mentioned incidentally only in 2 Ch **8** 13, and possibly in 1 K **9** 25, and is not at all found in Ezk (cf **45** 18 ff), although the existence of these institutions has for a very long time been called into question.

The Day of Atonement, in accordance with its purpose in later times, came more and more into the foreground and was called "the great fast" or "the great day," or merely "the day." Its ritual was further enlarged and the special parts mentioned in the law were fully explained, fixed and specialized. Cf esp. the tract "Yoma" in the Mish; and for the further elaborations and stories in poetry and prose on the basis of the Talm, see, e.g. Delitzsch's translation from Maim, *Ha-yādh ha-ḥăzāḳāh*, in the supplement to his *Commentary on the Epistle to the Hebrews*, 1857. According to these accounts, e.g. the high priest had to be a married man. Already seven days before the beginning

2. Further Development

of the Day of Atonement he was ordered to leave his house and had to submit to a series of purifications and had to practise for the performance of the different purification ceremonies, some of which were difficult. The last night he was not allowed to sleep and had to spend his time in studying the sacred writings. On the Day of Atonement he took five baths and ten washings. Four times he enters the Holy of Holies (with the incense), with the blood of both sin offerings, and when he brings out the utensils used with the incense he makes three confessions of sins (for himself, for himself and his house, for Israel); 10 times in all he utters the name of Jeh; 43 times he sprinkles; in addition he must read certain sections of the Scriptures or repeat them from memory (cf also AZAZEL). When he returns home he celebrates a festival of rejoicing, because he has without harm been able to leave the sanctuary. In addition, he had performed severe physical work, and especially difficult was the manipulation of the incense. The modern estimate put on the Day of Atonement appears from the following citation of Wellhausen: "The rite and the sacrifice through the unfavorable circumstances of the times have disappeared; but it has retained the same sacred character. He who has not yet entirely broken with Judaism observes this day, no matter how indifferent he may be otherwise to old customs and festivals."

WILHELM MÖLLER

ATROTH-BETH-JOAB, at-roth-beth-jō'ab (עַטְרוֹת בֵּית יוֹאָב, *'aṭrōth bēth yō'ābh*, "crowns of the house of Joab"): AV "Ataroth," the house of Joab. Probably a family in Judah (1 Ch **2** 54).

ATROTH-SHOPHAN, at'roth-shō'fan (עַטְרוֹת שׁוֹפָן, *'aṭrōth shōphān;* LXX γῆν σωφάν, *gḗn sōphán*): A town built or fortified by the children of Gad E. of the Jordan (Nu **32** 35), named next to Aroer. If it had been at *Khirbet 'Attārūs* or *Jebel 'Attārūs* (*HDB* and *EB* s.v.) Aroer would hardly have been named between them. AV reads **Atroth, Shophan**, understanding that two places are named. No identification is yet possible.

ATTAI, at'ā-ī, at'ī (עַתַּי, *'attay*, "timely"[?]):

(1) A son of Jarha, the Egyptian, by a daughter of Sheshan (1 Ch **2** 35 f).

(2) A Gadite soldier who joined David's army at Ziklag (1 Ch **12** 11).

(3) A son of Rehoboam and grandson of Solomon (2 Ch **11** 20).

ATTAIN, a-tān': The rendering of קָנָה, *ķānāh*= "buy," "get" (Prov **1** 5); נָשַׂג, *nāsagh*="reach," "a meal-offering . . . . according as he is able" (Ezk **46** 7m), "not attained unto the days" (Gen **47** 9); יָכֹל or יָכוֹל, *yākhōl*="be able," "overcome," "attain to innocency" (Hos **8** 5); בּוֹא, *bō'*="come," "follow" (2 S **23** 19.23; 1 Ch **11** 21.25); καταντάω, *katantáō*="arrive at" (Acts **27** 12 AV; Phil **3** 11); καταλαμβάνω, *katalambánō*="take eagerly," "seize," "apprehend," "attained to righteousness" (Rom **9** 30); φθάνω, *phthánō*="have arrived at" (Rom **9** 31 AV; Phil **3** 16); λαμβάνω, *lambánō*= "take," "get a hold of," "catch," RV "already obtained" (Phil **3** 12); παρακολουθέω, *parakolouthéō*= "follow," "trace out," "conform to" (1 Tim **4** 6). Here RV corrects AV.

FRANK E. HIRSCH

ATTALIA, at-a-lī'a (Ἀτταλία, *Attalía*): A city on the southern coast of Asia Minor in ancient Pamphylia which, according to Acts **14** 25, was visited by Paul and Barnabas on the way to Antioch during their first missionary journey. The city was founded by Attalus II Philadelphus (159–138 BC), hence its name Attalia, which during the Middle Ages was corrupted to Satalia; its modern name is Adalia. Attalia stood on a flat terrace of limestone, about 120 ft. high, near the point where the Catarrhactes River flowed into the sea. The river now, however, has practically disappeared, for the greater part of its water is turned into the fields for irrigation purposes. The early city did not enjoy the ecclesiastical importance of the neighboring city of Perga; but in 1084 when Perga declined, Attalia became a metropolis. In 1148 the troops of Louis IV sailed from there to Syria; in 1214 the Seljuks restored the city walls, and erected several public buildings. The city continued to be the chief port for ships from Syria and Egypt, and the point of entry to the interior until modern times, when the harbor at Mersine was reopened; it has now become a place of little importance.

The town possesses considerable which is of archaeological interest. The outer harbor was protected by ancient walls and towers now in ruins; its entrance was closed with a chain. The inner harbor was but a recess in the cliff. The city was surrounded by two walls which were constructed at various times from material taken from the ruins of the ancient city; the outer wall was protected by a moat. The modern town, lying partly within and partly without the walls is thus divided into quarters. In the southern quarter live the Christians; in the northern the Moslems. Among other objects of archaeological interest still to be seen may be mentioned the inscribed arched gateway of Hadrian and the aqueduct. Rich gardens now surround the town; the chief exports are grain, cotton, licorice root and valonia or acorn-cups.

E. J. BANKS

ATTALUS, at'a-lus: King of Pergamum, mentioned in 1 Macc **15** 22 among the kings to whom was sent an edict (*Ant*, XIV, viii, 5) from Rome forbidding the persecution of the Jews. See ATTALIA.

ATTEND, a-tend', **ATTENDANCE**, a-tend'ans: (1) "To incline," "listen," "regard" (קָשַׁב, *ķāshabh;* Ps **17** 1 etc); then, in AV, "observe," but in RV, more frequently, "give heed" (προσέχειν νοῦν, *proséchein noún*), as in 1 Tim **4** 13. (2) "To be with," "take care of," "wait upon" (Est **4** 5; He **7** 13; Rom **13** 6); lit. "give unremitting care to," as in 1 Cor **7** 35 (Luther: "serve the Lord constantly and without hindrance").

ATTENT, a-tent' (archaic; 2 Ch **6** 40), **ATTENTIVE**, a-tent'iv: Expresses the direction of thought and interest toward some one point. Same Heb word as "attend," and is used particularly in prayers (Ps **130** 2; Neh **1** 6). "Very attentive" (Lk **19** 48) is a paraphrase for what is lit. rendered in RV, "the people all hung upon him, listening" (ἐξεκρέμετο, *exekrémeto*).

ATTHARATES, a-thar'a-tēz: A title assigned to Nehemiah, probably by a later editor (Neh **8** 9). The LXX omits the title; the Vulg gives "Athersatha"; AV reads "Nehemiah, which is the Tirshatha." Tirshatha is the Pers title for a local or provincial governor (Neh **8** 9=1 Esd **9** 49). See TIRSHATHA.

ATTHARIAS, a-tha-rī'as, **ATHARIAS:** 1 Esd **5** 40=Ezr **2** 63. See TIRSHATHA.

ATTIRE, a-tīr', **DYED ATTIRE:** "Can a virgin forget her ornaments, or a bride her attire?" asks the prophet Jeremiah in hot remonstrance against Israel's unfaithfulness. "Yet," saith Jeh, "my people have forgotten me" (**2** 32). "And I saw that she was defiled," cries Ezekiel against Jerus; "she saw men . . . girded with girdles upon their loins, with flowing turbans [AV exceeding in dyed attire] upon their heads, ... after the likeness of the Babylonians in Chaldea, ... and . . . . she doted upon them . . . ." (Ezk **23** 13–16). "And, behold, there met him," says the author of Prov (**7** 10) in his description of the "strange woman," that "lieth in wait at every street corner," "a woman with the attire of a harlot, and wily of heart," whose "house is the way to Sheol" (ver 27). These passages show how diversely and elastically the term "attire" was used among the Hebrews. The numerous synonyms for "dress," "attire," "apparel," "clothes," "raiment," "garment," etc, found in EVV, reflect a similar wealth of nomenclature in the original Heb and Gr; but the lack of exactness and consistency in the renderings of translators makes the identification of the various articles of dress referred to very difficult, sometimes impossible. See DRESS.

GEO. B. EAGER

ATTITUDES, at′i-tūds: Customs change slowly in Bible lands. This becomes clear by a comparison of the many references found in the Bible and other literatures of the Orient with existing circumstances and conditions. The same fact is attested by the pictures illustrating daily life upon the monuments of Assyria, Babylonia and Egypt in the countries between the Nile and the Tigris. Many of these, dating back to the second or third millennium before our era, prove conclusively that the same practices and usages as are now common among the inhabitants of those lands were in vogue in the days of Hammurabi and the early rulers of Egypt. This is esp. true of matters pertaining to the worship of the gods, and of the attitudes or positions assumed in homage and respect to monarchs and those in authority.

The many references found in the Bible to these same usages prove that the Hebrews too had much in common with the nations around them, not only in creed, but also in the mode of worship, as well as in general everyday etiquette. This is not strange, at least among the Sem peoples, for there is more or less agreement, even among all nations, ancient and modern, in the attitude of the worshipper in temple and high place.

Kissing the Hand.

The outward tokens of respect and honor shown by Orientals to their superiors, above all to monarchs, may seem exaggerated. But when we consider that the king was God's vicegerent upon the earth or over a certain country, and in some sense Divine, worthy even of adoration, it is not strange that almost equal homage should be paid him as the gods themselves. The higher the person was in power, the greater the honor and respect shown him. It is natural, therefore, that God, the Lord of Lords, and the King of Kings should be the recipient of the highest reverence and adoration.

There are several Heb words used to describe the various attitudes assumed by those who worshipped Jeh and heathen gods; these same words are constantly employed in speaking of the homage or respect paid to rulers and persons in authority. The most common terms are those rendered "to stand," "to bow," "to kneel" and "prostrate oneself" or "fall on the face." It is not always easy to differentiate between them, for often one passes imperceptibly into the other. No doubt several attitudes were assumed by the worshipper or suppliant while offering a prayer or petition. The

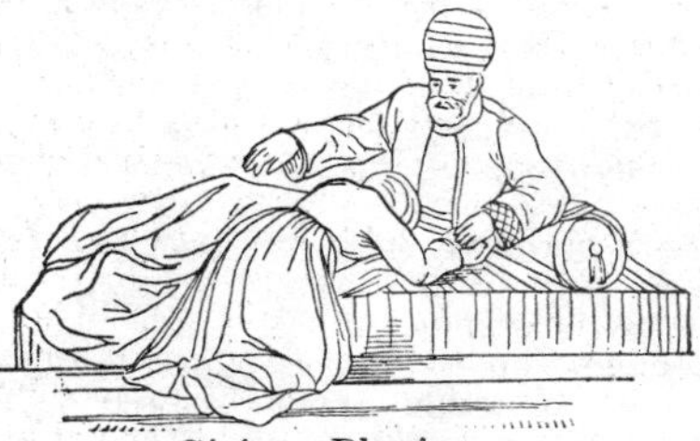

Giving a Blessing.

intensity, the ardor or earnestness with which such a petition or prayer was presented would naturally have much to do with the words and posture of the petitioner, though the same expression might be employed to designate his posture or attitude. Thus "to fall on the face" might be done in many different ways. The Moslems observe a regular course of nine or more different postures in their worship. These are more or less faithfully observed by the faithful everywhere. It is almost certain that the Hebrews in common with other Orientals observed and went through almost every one of these attitudes as they presented themselves in prayer to Jeh. We shall call attention to just four postures: (1) standing, (2) bowing, (3) kneeling, and (4) falling on the face or prostration.

1. Standing

This was one of the very common postures in prayer to God, esp. in public worship. It is still customary to stand either erect or with slightly bowed head while offering the public prayers in the synagogue. This is likewise the common practice of a large number of Christians in this and other lands, and no doubt such a posture is sanctioned by the example of the early church and primitive Christians, who, in turn, adopted the usages of the Jewish church. The same practice was in vogue among the Persians, Egyptians and Babylonians and other ancient people as is evidenced by their sculptures and paintings. The famous stela of Hammurabi shows this great king in a standing position as he receives the famous Code from the sun-god. There are numerous Bab and Assyr seals on which are pictured a priest in a standing position before the throne of Sin or Shamash. In this attitude with uplifted hands, he is sometimes accompanied by the person in whose behalf prayers are made. A beautiful rock sculpture at Ibriz, S.E. of Eregli in Lycaonia, shows us a king or satrap in a standing position, worshipping a local Baal. Rev. E. J. Davies, the discoverer of this Hittite monument, in describing it, makes this remark, which we cannot refrain from inserting, inasmuch as it gives another proof of the unchangeable East. He says: "He [the god] wears boots turned up in front, and bound round the leg above the ankle by thongs and a piece of leather reaching half-way up the shin, *exactly as it is worn to this day by the peasants of the plain of Cilicia round Adana.*" King Solomon, during at least a portion of his prayer at the dedication of the temple, stood before the altar with his hands stretched out toward heaven (1 K **8** 22). Numerous allusions to prayer in the NT prove that standing was the common posture (Mt **6** 5; Mk **11** 25; Lk **18** 11).

What has been said about standing while praying to God is true also of the attitude of the petitioner when paying homage or making an entreaty to man. The Assyr and Bab monuments are full of evidence on this point; we shall give only one illustration: One of the sculptures describing the siege of Lachish by Sennacherib represents the monarch as seated upon his throne while the conquered stand or kneel before him. Joseph stood before Pharaoh (Gen **41** 46). Solomon's advisers stood before him (2 Ch **10** 6) and so did those of Rehoboam (ver 8). The same attitude was assumed by suppliants in the Pers court (Est **5** 2; **8** 4). The same is true of Babylonia (Dnl **1** 19; **2** 2).

Though standing seems to have been the usual attitude, it is quite certain that kneeling was common at all times.

2. Kneeling

The monuments afford abundant proof for this statement; so too the many references in the Bible. Solomon not only stood before the altar on the occasion of dedicating his famous temple, but he also knelt (1 K **8** 54; 2 Ch **6** 13). Jos, describing this ceremony, says that the king at the conclusion of his prayer prostrated himself on the ground and in this posture continued worshipping for a long time. Ezra fell upon his knees as he addressed Jeh in prayer (Ezr **9** 5). Daniel, too, knelt upon his knees and prayed three times a day (Dnl **6** 10). The same practice was observed by the apostles and the early church; for we read that Stephen (Acts **7** 60), Peter (**9** 40), Paul (**20** 36) and others (**21** 5) assumed this posture as they prayed.

Kneeling.

As already stated, it is not always easy to determine the exact posture of those described as kneeling or bowing, for this varied with the temperament of the suppliant and the intensity of his prayer or supplication.

3. Bowing

Eleazer when sent to select a wife for his master, Isaac, bowed before Jeh (Gen **24** 26). The Hebrews on leaving Egypt were commanded to bow to Jeh (Ex **11** 8; **12** 27.28). The injunction of the Psalmist shows the prevalence of this posture in prayer: "O come, let us worship and bow down" (Ps **95** 6). Isaiah refers to the same when he says: "Every knee shall bow" to God

Bowing.
Touching the Forehead, Touching the Breast; Folding the Arms; Placing Hands on Knees.

(Isa **45** 23). St. Paul too bowed his knees to the Father (Eph **3** 14). The same practice obtained among the heathen nations as they worshipped their gods or idols. Naaman bowed before Rimmon, his god. The numerous prohibitions in the Heb Scriptures against bowing down at the shrines of the nations around Israel prove the prevalence of this method of adoration. Indeed, one of the ten commandments is directed explicitly against bowing to or worshipping idols (Ex **20** 5). The same prohibition was often repeated, as by Joshua (**23** 7) and the author of 2 K (**17** 35). Unfortunately Israel did transgress in this very thing, for while still in the Wilderness they bowed down to the gods of Moab (Nu **25** 2) and again after their settlement in Canaan (Jgs **2** 12). Amaziah bowed down to the gods of Edom (2 Ch **25** 14).

Like deference was also shown to angels or supernatural beings. Thus Abraham bows to the three angels as they appear to him at Mamre

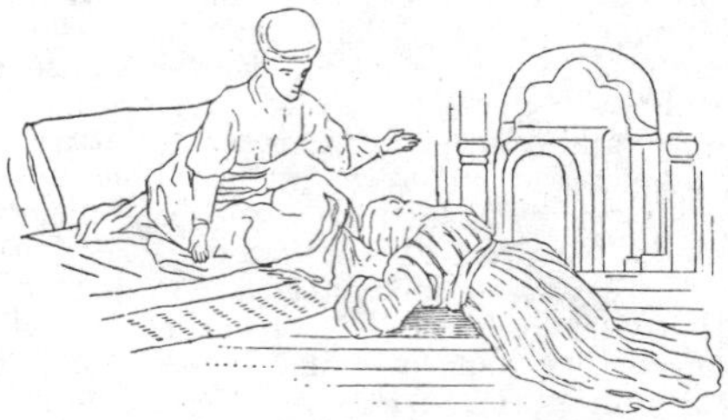

Supplication: "Falling at the Feet."

(Gen **18** 2). And so did Lot at Sodom (**19** 1). Joshua fell on his face before the prince of the host of Jeh (Josh **5** 14). This attitude was a common one to Ezekiel as he saw his wonderful visions (Ezk **1** 28; **3** 23, and often). Daniel when he saw Gabriel in a vision was affrighted and fell upon his face (Dnl **8** 17). The three disciples had the same experience on the Mount of Transfiguration (Mt **17** 6).

Monarchs and persons of superior rank were the recipients of like honors and marks of respect. Joseph's brothers bowed as they came into his presence, thinking that he was an Egyptian of high rank (Gen **43** 28). Bathsheba bowed to King David when she entered his presence in the interest of their son Solomon (1 K **1** 16.31). But such deference was not shown to monarchs only, for Jacob and his household bowed down seven times to the irate Esau (Gen **33** 3 ff). Abigail fell on her face before David as he was marching to avenge himself upon Nabal, her husband (1 S **25** 23). David too when he went to meet Jonathan fell on his face to the ground and bowed himself three times (1 S **20** 41). The Shunammite woman, as she came to entreat Elisha for the life of her boy, bowed before the prophet (2 K **4** 37). The same custom prevailed not only among the Persians, as is evident from the Book of Esther and the monuments at Persepolis, but also in Babylonia, Assyria and other countries.

This was but an intenser way of showing one's regard or of emphasizing a petition. It was the token of abject subjection or the deepest reverence.

4. Prostration

Abraham, when Jeh appeared to him and promised him a son, with profoundest gratitude and greatest joy fell prostrate on his face (Gen **17** 3). Moses and Aaron were often found in this posture (Nu **14** 5; **16** 4.45; **20** 6). Elijah, eccentric in many ways, cast himself upon the earth and placed his face between his knees (cf 1 K **18** 42). Job fell on the ground and worshipped Jeh (Job **1** 20). Such homage was often shown to our Saviour (Mk **5** 22; Jn **11** 32), not because men realized that He was God in the flesh, but simply as a mark of respect for a great teacher and miracle-worker. It is to be noticed that our Saviour never refused such homage, but accepted it as pertinent and proper. Did He not realize that honor and worship Divine belonged to Him, He would have refused them just as Peter did when Cornelius fell down at his feet and worshipped him (Acts **10** 25) or as the angel in Rev **19** 10, who said to John, prostrate at his feet, "See thou do it not: I am a fellow servant," etc. See ADORATION, III. W. W. DAVIES

ATTUS, at'us (1 Esd 8 29=Ezr 8 2). See HATTUSH.

AUDIENCE, ô'di-ens: Tr[d] from the Heb אֹזֶן, *'ōzen,* "ear." In Gen **23** 10 f "in the audience of" is equal to "in the presence of," or "while they listened." Cf Ex **24** 7; 1 S **25** 24 (RV "in thine ears"); 1 Ch **28** 8; Neh **13** 1. In the NT the expression "to give audience" (Acts **22** 22; **13** 16, RV "hearken"; **15** 12, RV "they hearkened") is tr[d] from the Gr ἀκούω, *akoúō,* "to hear" or derivatives, and means "to listen," "to pay attention." In AV Lk **7** 1 (RV "in the ears of") and AV **20** 45 (RV "in the hearing of") the usage is similar to that of the OT.

AUGIA, ô'ji-a (Αὐγία, *Augía*): The wife of Jaddus, whose sons were removed from priesthood because their names were not found in the register, their ancestors having "usurped the office of the priesthood" (1 Esd **5** 38). Omitted in Ezr **2** and Neh **7.**

AUGURS' OAK, ô'gurs' ōk: If we tr the Heb vb. *'ōnēn,* "to practise augury" (see AUGURY) we should in Jgs **9** 37 for "the oak of Meonenim" render "the augurs' oak" as in RVm, for the last word is simply the part. of the same vb. and means "one who practises augury," though there is some doubt as to the exact connotation of the word. See under DIVINATION. Both the EVV make this noun the name of a place; but no such place is known and the derivation and form of the word are clear and certain. We have a similar phrase similarly misunderstood by our translators in Gen **12** 6 where the "oak of Moreh" should be "the oak" (or "terebinth"[?]) "of the diviner" or "augur," for *mōreh* is also a part.="one who teaches" or "directs." Probably the same tree is meant, since in each case the neighborhood is that of Shechem. The worship of trees, or rather the deity supposed to make them his home, has prevailed very widely. See W. R. Smith, *Rel. Sem.*[2], 195; cf Jgs **4** 5; 2 S **5** 24 and "the oak of Zeus at Dodona." In Jgs **9** 6 we read of a "*maççēbhāh,* oak tree": the tree with an altar on which sacrifices were offered. The oak trees of Gen **12** 6 and of Jgs **9** 37, if two distinct trees are meant, would be trees which the Canaanites had been in the habit of consulting: hence the name.

T. WITTON DAVIES

AUGURY, ô'gū-ri, ô'gur-i: This word occurs in the RV in Lev **19** 26; Dt **18** 10.14; 2 K **21** 6, and the ∥ 2 Ch **33** 6. In all these cases the vb. "practise augury" is in the AV "to observe times." The vb. thus tr[d] is עוֹנֵן, *'ōnēn,* which means probably to utter a low croaking sound as was done in divining. See DIVINATION.

I. Definition.—The derivation of "augur" is doubtful, but that it means strictly to divine from the flight of birds is suggested by its likeliest etymology (*avis, gur*) and esp. from the fact that in early Lat the augur was called *auspex* (=*avi spex*). But both words came to be applied to all forms of divining from omens.

II. Augury among the Romans.—The Rom augur was a government official, paid to guide the councils of the nation in times of peace and of war. The principal signs from which these augurs deduced their omens were these: (1) celestial signs, chiefly lightning and thunder, the direction of the former (right to left a good sign, and vice versa); (2) signs from the flight, cries and feeding of birds; (3) signs from the movements and audible sounds of animals, including serpents; (4) signs from the examination of the entrails of animals; (5) belomancy, or divination by arrows; (6) sortilege, or divination by lot. Among the Romans as among other nations (Babylonians, etc), a sacrifice was offered before omens were taken, so as to propitiate the gods.

III. Augury among the Greeks.—Almost the only kind of divination practised or even known among the Romans was that by signs or omens, though Cicero (*de Div.* i.1 f) notices another kind which may be called divining by direct inspiration from the gods. It is this higher and more spiritual mode of divining that obtained most largely among the Greeks, whose chief word for diviner (*mántis*) implies this. Yet the lower kind of divination known as augury was to some extent practised among the Greeks.

IV. Augury among the Hebrews.—In general it may be said that the religion of Israel set itself steadfastly and consistently against augury; a very remarkable fact when one remembers how rife it was among the surrounding peoples—Arabs, Assyrians, Babylonians, Egyptians, etc. Surely there is in this evidence of special Divine guidance, for those ancient Hebrews are not fit to be compared with the Babylonians or Egyptians or Romans for achievements in art and general secular literature. For the attitude of the OT toward augury see the passages enumerated in the opening of this article. Several kinds of augury are mentioned in the OT, and in some cases without explicit condemnation.

1. Belomancy

Belomancy was a method of divination by arrows, a number of which were marked in certain ways, then mixed and drawn at random. We have a reference to this in Hos **4** 12: 'My people ask counsel from their wood [lit. "tree"] and their staff [i.e. "arrow"] tells them [their oracles]'; and also in Ezk **21** 21: 'For the king of Babylon . . . . used divination, shaking the arrows to and fro.' The first passage shows that belomancy was practised by Israelites though the prophet condemned it. The second is interesting as showing how the Babylonian used his arrows. It is to be noticed that the prophet Ezekiel records the incident without making any comment on it, favorable or otherwise. He would, however, had he spoken, almost certainly have condemned it. Mohammed forbade this use of arrows as "an abomination of Satan's work" (Koran, Sur. **5** 92).

2. Hydromancy

Hydromancy, or divination by water, was practised by Joseph (Gen **44** 3–5) without any censure on the part of the writer. There were among the Romans and other ancient nations, as among modern Arabs, etc, many modes of divining by means of water. Generally a piece of silver or gold or a precious stone was thrown into a vessel containing water: the resulting movements of the water and the figures formed were interpreted according to certain fixed signs. See August., *de Civ. Dei,* vii.31; Strabo xvi.11.39; Iamblichus, *de Myst.,* iii.4.

3. Sortilege

Of sortilege, or divination by lot, we have instances in Lev **16** 8; Mt **27** 35; 1 Ch **25** 8; Jon **1** 2 ff; Acts **1** 26, etc. The Urim and Thummim was simply a case of sortilege, though in this case, as in the cases enumerated above, God was supposed to control the result. A proper tr of 1 S **14** 41 f, based on a text corrected according to the LXX of Lucian, is the following: "And Saul said, O Lord the God of Israel, why hast thou not answered thy servant this day? If the iniquity be in me or in Jonathan my son, give Urim; and if thou sayest thus, The iniquity is in the people, give Thummim." It seems almost certain that these words refer to two balls put into the high priest's ephod and drawn by him at random, the one divining one answer, and the other the contrary.

We meet with several other signs. The prophet Elisha directs King Joash to throw two arrows through the window in order to find out whether the king will be victorious or not (2 K **13** 14–19). If Gideon's fleece were wet and the ground dry this was to be a sign of coming victory over the Midianites. There is nothing in the narrative disapproving of the course taken (Jgs **6** 36–40). In 1 S **14** 8 ff Jonathan is represented as deciding whether or not he is to attack the Philis by the words he will hear them speak. See further Gen **24** 12–19; 2 K **20** 9.

4. Other Methods

Dreams are very commonly mentioned in the Bible as a means of forecasting the future. See Gen **20** 3.6 f (Abimelech); **31** 10–13 (Jacob); **37** 5; **40** 3 ff (Joseph), and also Jgs **7** 13; 1 K **3** 5 f; Mt **1** 20; **2** 12 ff; **27** 19, etc. The part of the Pent ascribed by Wellhausen, etc, to E abounds with accounts of such significant dreams.

5. Dreams

That omens were taken from the heavenly bodies by the Babylonians, and other ancient nations is matter of definite knowledge, but it is never countenanced in the OT. Indeed the only explicit reference to it in the Heb Scriptures occurs in Isa **47** 13 where the Exilic author mockingly urges Babylon to turn to her astrologers that they may save her from her threatened doom.

6. Astrology

Several cuneiform inscriptions give lists of celestial omens by which Bab augurs prognosticated the future. In Mt **2** the wise men received their first intimation of the birth of the child Jesus from a bright star which they saw in the East.

V. Higher Character of Heb Prophecy.—Though OT prophecy in its lowest forms has features in common with heathen divination, it stands on an infinitely higher level. The prophet speaks under a strong impulse and from a sense of duty. The heathen diviner plied his calling for money. The Gr *mántis* worked himself into a state of frenzy, thought to imply inspiration, by music and certain drugs. The prophet believed himself directly guided by God. See ASTROLOGY, 1; DIVINATION.

LITERATURE.—T. Witton Davies, *Magic, Divination and Demonology among the Hebrews*, 1898, 72 ff; arts. on "Divination" in *HDB* (Jevons); *EB* (T. Witton Davies), and on "Augury" in *Jew Enc* (Blau), valuable as giving the rabbinical side as well.

T. WITTON DAVIES

AUGUSTAN, ô-gus′tan **(AUGUSTUS') BAND.** See ARMY, ROMAN.

AUGUSTUS, ô-gus′tus (**Αὔγουστος,** *Aúgoustos*): (1) The first Rom emperor, and noteworthy in Bible history as the emperor in whose reign the Incarnation took place (Lk **2** 1). His original name was Caius Octavius Caepias and he was born in 63 BC, the year of Cicero's consulship. He was the grand-nephew of Julius Caesar, his mother Atia having been the daughter of Julia, Caesar's younger sister. He was only 19 years of age when Caesar was murdered in the Senate house (44 BC), but with a true instinct of statesmanship he steered his course through the intrigues and dangers of the closing years of the republic, and after the battle of Actium was left without a rival. Some difficulty was experienced in finding a name that would exactly define the position of the new ruler of the state. He himself declined the names of *rex* and *dictator*, and in 27 BC he was by the decree of the Senate styled Augustus. The epithet implied respect and veneration beyond what is bestowed on human things:

"Sancta vocant augusta patres: augusta vocantur
Templa sacerdotum rite dicata manu."
—Ovid *Fasti* i. 609; cf Dion Cass., 5316

The Greeks rendered the word by Σεβαστός, *Sebastós*, lit. "reverend" (Acts **25** 21.25). The name was connected by the Romans with *augur*—"one consecrated by religion"—and also with the vb. *augere*. In this way it came to form one of the German imperial titles "Mehrer des Reichs" (extender of the empire). The length of the reign of A., extending as it did over 44 years from the battle of Actium (31 BC) to his death (14 AD), doubtless contributed much to the settlement and consolidation of the new régime after the troublous times of the civil wars.

Coin of Augustus.

It is chiefly through the connection of Judaea and Palestine with the Rom Empire that Augustus comes in contact with early Christianity, or rather with the political and religious life of the Jewish people at the time of the birth of Christ: "Now it came to pass in those days, there went out a decree from Caesar Augustus, that all the world should be enrolled" (Lk **2** 1). During the reign of Herod the Great the government of Palestine was conducted practically without interference from Rome except, of course, as regarded the exaction of the tribute; but on the death of that astute and capable ruler (4 BC) none of his three sons among whom his kingdom was divided showed the capacity of their father. In the year 6 AD the intervention of Augustus was invited by the Jews themselves to provide a remedy for the incapacity of their ruler, Archelaus, who was deposed by the emperor from the rule of Judaea; at the same time, while Caesarea was still the center of the Rom administration, a small Rom garrison was stationed permanently in Jerus. The city, however, was left to the control of the Jewish Sanhedrin with complete judicial and executive authority except that the death sentence required confirmation by the Rom procurator. There is no reason to believe that Augustus entertained any specially favorable appreciation of Judaism, but from policy he showed himself favorable to the Jews in Pal and did everything to keep them from feeling the pressure of the Rom yoke. To the Jews of the eastern Diaspora he allowed great privileges. It has even been held that his aim was to render them pro-Rom, as a counterpoise in some degree to the pronounced Hellenism of the East; but in the West autonomous bodies of Jews were never allowed (see Mommsen, *Provinces of the Rom Empire*, ch 11).

(2) For Augustus in Acts **25** 21.25 AV, see EMPEROR. J. HUTCHISON

AUL, ôl. See AWL.

AUNT, änt (דּוֹדָה, *dōdhāh*, "loving"): A father's sister (Ex **6** 20); an uncle's wife (Lev **18** 14; **20** 20). See RELATIONSHIPS, FAMILY.

AURANITIS, ô-ran-ī′tis: Used by Jos for HAURAN (q.v.).

AUSTERE, ôs-tēr′ (**αὐστηρός,** *austērós*, "harsh," "rough"): Twice used by Christ in the parable of the Pounds (Lk **19** 21.22), and of special significance as illustrating the false conception of God cherished by the sinful and disobedient. The fear resident in a guilty conscience sees only sternness and severity in God's perfect righteousness. The word may be made an eminent study in the psychology of an evil heart. Wrongdoing eclipses the soul's vision of God's love and pictures His righteousness as harsh, unfeeling, partial, unjust, forbidding. The awfulness of sin may thus be seen in its power so to pervert the soul as to make goodness seem evil, justice unjust, and even love unlovely. Cf "hard" (σκληρός, *sklērós*, "dried up," "harsh") in the parable of the Talents (Mt **25** 24). DWIGHT M. PRATT

AUTHOR, ô'thēr: This word is used to translate two Gr words: (1) αἴτιος, *aítios*, lit. "cause," hence "author." He **5** 9, He "became the author of eternal salvation." (2) ἀρχηγός, *archēgós* = lit. "chief leader," "prince," "captain"; then author, originator. It is rendered "author" in the following passages: (*a*) He **12** 2, "looking unto Jesus, the author [AV, RV] and finisher [RV "perfecter"] of our faith." But here it seems better to take *archēgos* in its primary sense, "leader" (RVm "captain"), rather than in its secondary sense "author." The meaning is, not that He is the originator of faith in us, but that He Himself is the pioneer in the life of faith. He is first in the company of the faithful (cf references to His "faithfulness," **2** 17; **3** 2.5.6), far surpassing in His fidelity even the OT saints mentioned in ch **11**; and therefore we are to look to Him as our perfect pattern of faith. Faith has not only Christ for its object, but Christ for its supreme example. So Bengel, Bleek, B. Weiss, Alford, A. B. Davidson, Grimm-Thayer. Others, however, take the word in the sense of "author." (*b*) He **2** 10, "to make the author [AV "captain"] of their salvation perfect through sufferings." Here the idea of Christ as originator or author of our salvation is present (cf the passage He **5** 9, where however a different word is used; see above). But here again the original meaning of "leader" is not to be lost sight of. He, being the first possessor of salvation, becomes the author of it for others. "The idea that the Son goes before the saved in the same path ought perhaps to be retained" (Davidson). Cf He **6** 20, where Jesus is said to be our "forerunner." (*c*) Acts **3** 15, AVm and RVm have "author," where text has "prince." Here again it is possible that the two ideas are present. D. MIALL EDWARDS

AUTHORITY, ô-thor'i-ti (**IN GENERAL**). See AUTHORITY (IN RELIGION), I.

AUTHORITY, ô-thor'i-ti (**IN RELIGION**) (רָבָה, *rābhāh*, תֹּקֶף, *tōḳeph;* **ἐξουσία,** *exousía*, **ἐξουσιάζω,** *exousiázō*, **κατεξουσιάζω,** *katexousiázō*, **ἐπιταγή,** *epitagḗ*, **ὑπεροχή,** *huperochḗ*, **αὐθεντέω,** *authentéō*, **δυνάστης,** *dunástēs*):

I. GENERAL IDEA
 1. Of Two Kinds
  (1) External
  (2) Internal
 2. Universal Need of Authority
 3. Necessity for Infallible Criterion of Truth
 4. Ultimate Nature of Authority
 5. It Is God
 6. Different Ideas of God and Different Views of Authority
 7. A Problem of Knowledge for Christians
II. THE BIBLICAL REFERENCES
 1. In OT
 2. In NT
 3. Common Elements in their Meaning
III. BIBLICAL TEACHING
 1. OT Teaching
  (1) Earliest Form Patriarchal
  (2) Tribal and Personal Authority
  (3) Seers and Priests
  (4) Kings and Established Religion
  (5) The Great Prophets
  (6) The Canon and Rabbinical Tradition
 2. NT Teaching
  (1) Jesus Christ's Authority
   (*a*) His Teaching
   (*b*) His Works
   (*c*) Forgiving and Judging
   (*d*) Life and Salvation
   (*e*) Derived from His Sonship
   (*f*) In His Ascended State
   (*g*) Christ and the Paraclete
  (2) The Disciples' Authority
   (*a*) Derived from Christ
   (*b*) Paul's Authority
   (*c*) Authority of All Believers
   (*d*) Authority over the Nations
  (3) Church's Authority Moral and Personal
  (4) Authority of the Bible
IV. OUTLINE HISTORY OF ECCLESIASTICAL DOCTRINE OF AUTHORITY
 1. Appeal to Reason as Logos
 2. Orthodox Dogma
 3. Scholasticism
 4. Ecclesiastical Absolutism
 5. Reformation Principles
 6. New Scholasticism
 7. The Inner Light
 8. Back to Experience
 9. Distrust of Reason
 10. Christian Skepticism
V. CLASSIFICATION OF THEORIES
 1. External
  (1) Incipient Catholicism
  (2) General Councils
  (3) Romanism
  (4) Papal Infallibility
  (5) Inerrancy of Scripture
  (6) Anglican Appeal to Antiquity
  (7) Limitations of External Authority
   (*a*) Not Infallible
   (*b*) Rests on Personal Authority
   (*c*) No Apostolical Tradition Extant
   (*d*) No Consensus of Fathers
   (*e*) Bible Needs Interpretation
   (*f*) Authority Necessarily Spiritual
 2. Internal Authority
LITERATURE

I. General Idea.—The term is of manifold and ambiguous meaning. The various ideas of authority fall into two main classes: as external or public tribunal or standard, which therefore in the nature of the case can only apply to the outward expressions of religion; and as immanent principle which governs the most secret movements of the soul's life.

1. Of Two Kinds

(1) *External.*—A characteristic instance of the former idea of authority is found in A. J. Balfour's *Foundations of Belief:* "Authority as I have been using the term is in all cases contrasted with reason, and stands for that group of non-rational causes, moral, social and educational, which produces its results by psychic processes other than reasoning" (p. 232, 8th ed). The bulk of men's important beliefs are produced and authorized by "custom, education, public opinion, the contagious convictions of countrymen, family, party or church" (p. 226). Authority and reason are "rival claimants" (p. 243). "Authority as such is, from the nature of the case, dumb in the presence of argument" (p. 234). Newman makes a kindred distinction between authority in revealed religion and conscience in natural religion, although he does not assign as wide a sphere to authority, and he allows to conscience a kind of authority. "The supremacy of conscience is the essence of natural religion, the supremacy of apostle or pope or church or bishop is the essence of revealed; and when such external authority is taken away, the mind falls back again of necessity upon that inward guide which it possessed even before revelation was vouchsafed" (*Development of Doctrine,* 86, ed 1878). From a very different standpoint the same antithesis appears in the very title of Sabatier's book, *The Religions of Authority and the Religion of the Spirit.* He knows both kinds of authority. "The authority of material force, of custom, tradition, the code, more and more yields place to the inward authority of conscience and reason, and in the same measure becomes transformed for the subject into a true autonomy" (p. xxxiii, ET).

(2) *Internal.*—Martineau distinguishes the two types of authority to reject the former and accept the latter. "The mere resort to testimony for information beyond our province does not fill the meaning of 'authority'; which we never acknowledge till that which speaks to us from another and a higher strikes home and wakes the echoes in ourselves, and is thereby instantly transferred from external attestation to self-evidence. And this response it is which makes the moral intuitions, started by outward appeal, reflected back by inward veneration, more than egoistic phenomena, and turning them into correspondency between the universal and the individual mind, invests them with true authority" (*Seat of Authority*, Preface, ed 1890).

Confusion would disappear if the fact were recognized that for different persons, and even for the same persons at different times, authority means different things. For a child his father's or his teacher's word is a decree of absolute authority. He accepts its truth and recognizes his obligation to allow it to determine his conduct. But when reason awakes in him, he may doubt their knowledge or wisdom, and he will seek other guides or authorities. So it is in religious development. Some repudiate authorities that others acknowledge. But no one has a monopoly of the term or concept, and no one may justly say to Dr. Martineau or anybody else that "he has no right to speak of 'authority' at all."

2. Universal Need of Authority

All religion involves a certain attitude of thought and will toward God and the Universe. The feeling element is also present, but that is ignored in the theories of external authority. All religion then involves certain ideas or beliefs about God, and conduct corresponding to them, but ideas may be true or false, and conduct right or wrong. Men need to know what is true, that they may do that which is right. They need some test or standard or court of appeal which distinguishes and enforces the truth; forbids the wrong and commands the right. As in all government there is a legislative and an executive function, the one issuing out of the other, so in every kind of religious authority recognized as such, men require that it should tell them what ideas they ought to believe and what deeds to perform.

In this general sense authority is recognized in every realm of life, even beyond that which is usually called religious life. Science builds up its system in conformity with natural phenomena. Art has its ideals of beauty. Politics seeks to realize some idea of the state. Metaphysics reconstructs the universe in conformity with some principle of truth or reality.

3. There Must Be an Infallible Criterion of Truth

"If we are . . . . to attach any definite intelligible meaning to the distinction between things as they really are, and things as they merely appear to be, we must clearly have some universal criterion or test by which the distinction may be made. This criterion must be in the first place infallible; that is, must be such that we cannot doubt its validity without falling into a contradiction in our thought. . . . . Freedom from contradiction is a characteristic that belongs to everything that is real . . . . and we may therefore use it as a test or criterion of reality "(Taylor, *Elements of Metaphysics*, 18–19). A more skeptical philosopher writes: "That the truth itself is one and whole and complete, and that all thinking and all experience moves within its recognition, and subject to its manifest authority, this I have never doubted" (Joachim, *The Nature of Truth*, 178). It is only a thoroughgoing skeptic that could dispense with authority, a "Pyrrho," who holds suspense of judgment to be the only right attitude of mind, and he, to be logical, must also suspend all action and cease to be. There can be no question, therefore, except in total nescience, as to the fact of authority in general; and the problem to decide is, "What is *the* authority in religion?" It is a problem involved in the difficulties of all ultimate problems, and all argument about it is apt to move in a circle. For the ultimate must bear

4. Ultimate Nature of Authority

witness of its own ultimacy, the absolute of its own absoluteness, and authority of its own sovereignty. If there were a court of appeal or a standard of reference to which anything called ultimate, absolute and supreme, could apply for its credentials, it would therefore become relative and subordinate to that other criterion. There is a sense in which Mr. Balfour's saying is true, "that authority is dumb in the presence of argument." No process of mediate reasoning can establish it, for no premise can be found from which it issues as a conclusion. It judges all things, but is judged of none. It is its own witness and judge. All that reason can say about it is the dictum of Parmenides: "it is."

5. It Is God

In this sense, there can be no question again among religious people, that the authority is God. The one idea involves the other. He alone is self-existent and supreme, who is what He is of His own right. If God exists, He is the ultimate criterion and power of truth and reality. All truth inheres in Him and issues from Him. The problem of authority thus becomes one with the proof and definition of God. These questions lie beyond the purpose of the present article (see art. God). Their solution is assumed in this discussion of authority, although different theories of authority no doubt involve

6. Different Ideas of God Involve Different Views of Authority

different ideas of God. External theories generally involve what is called a deistic conception of God. Spiritualistic theories of authority correspond to theistic views of God. If He is immanent as well as transcendent, He speaks directly to men, and has no need of intermediaries. Pantheism results in a naturalistic theory of truth. The mind of God is the law of Nature. But pantheism in practice tends to become polytheism, and then to issue in a crude anarchy which is the denial of all authority and truth. But within Christendom the problem of authority lies between those who agree in believing in one God, who is personal, transcendent and to some extent immanent. The differences on these points are really consequences of differences of views as to His mode of self-communication. It is, therefore,

7. For Christians a Problem of Knowledge

a problem of epistemology rather than of ontology. The question is, in what way does God make known Himself, His mind and His authority to men generally? The purpose of this article is the exposition of the Biblical teaching of authority, with some attempt to place it in its true position in the life of the church.

II. The Biblical References.—Only for (1) *rābhāh* (Prov **29** 2): "to be great" or "many."

1. In the OT

"When the righteous are in authority, the people rejoice." So AV and RVm, but RV "When the righteous are increased" (so *BDB*). Toy in loc. remarks, "The Heb has: 'When the righteous increase,' the suggestion being that they then have control of affairs; the change of a letter gives the reading 'rule' which is required by the 'govern' of the second line." (2) *tōḳeph* (Est **9** 29): "Esther the queen . . . . wrote with all authority to confirm this second letter of Purim" (RVm "strength" [so *BDB*]).

2. In the NT

(1) Most frequently for *exousia, exousiazō* and *katexousiazō:* (*a*) of God's authority (Acts **1** 7): as the potter's over clay (Rom **9** 21, "a right"; Jude ver 25, "power"; Rev **16** 9, "power"); (*b*) of Christ's teaching and works (Mt **7** 29; **21** 23.24.27 = Mk **1** 22.27; Mk **11** 28.29.33 = Lk **4** 36; **20** 2.8; Jn **5** 27, authority to execute judgment. The same Gr word, tr[d] "power" in AV but generally "authority" in RV or RVm, appears also in Mt **9** 6.8, to forgive sins: **28** 18; Mk **2** 10; Lk **4** 32; **5** 24; Jn **10** 18; **17** 2; Rev **12** 10); (*c*) of the disciples, as Christ's representatives and witnesses (Lk **9** 1, the twelve; 2 Cor **10** 8, Paul); also of their rights and privileges; (the same Gr word in Mt **10** 1; Mk **3** 15; **6** 7; Lk **10** 19 = RV "authority"; Jn **1** 12; Acts **8** 19; 2 Cor **13** 10; 2 Thess **3** 9; He **13** 10; Rev **2** 26; **22** 14 = RV "right"); (*d*) of subordinate heavenly authorities or powers (1 Cor **15** 24; 1 Pet **3** 22; and the same Gr word in Eph **1** 21; **3** 10; **6** 12; Col **1** 16; **2** 10.15; Rev **11** 6; **14** 18; **18** 1); (*e*) of civil authority, as of king, magistrate or steward (Lk **7** 8 = Mt **8** 9 [centurion]; Mk **13** 34; Lk **19** 17; **20** 20; **22** 25 = Mt **20** 25 = Mk **10** 42; and Acts **9** 14; **26** 10. 12 [of Saul]; and the same Gr word in Lk **12** 11; **23** 7; Jn **19** 10.11; Acts **5** 4; Rom **13** 1.2.3; Tit **3** 1; Rev **17** 12.13); (*f*) of the powers of evil (Rev **13** 2, "the beast that came out of the sea"; and the same Gr word in Lk **4** 6; **12** 5; **22** 53; Acts **26** 18; Eph **2** 2; Col **1** 13; Rev **6** 8; **9** 3.10.19; **13** 4.5.7.12; **20** 6). (*g*) of man's inward power of self-control (the same Gr word in 1 Cor **7** 37; **8** 9, "liberty"; **6** 12; **7** 4; **9** 4.5.6.12.18, RV "right"; **11** 10).

(2) For *epitagē:* commandment, authority to exhort and reprove the church (Tit **2** 15).

(3) For *huperochē:* "for kings and all that are in high place" (RV 1 Tim **2** 2).

(4) For *authenteō:* "I permit not a woman . . . . to have dominion over a man" (RV 1 Tim **2** 12).

(5) For *dunastēs:* "A eunuch of great authority" (Acts **8** 27).

3. Common Elements in Their Meaning

Of the words tr[d] "authority," *exousia* alone expresses the idea of religious authority, whether of God, of Christ or of man. The other uses of this word are here instructive as bringing out the common element in secular and religious authority. The control of the state over its subjects, whether as supreme in the person of emperor or king, or as delegated to and exercised by proconsul, magistrate or soldier, and the control of a householder over his family and servants and property, exercised directly or indirectly through stewards, have some characteristics which also pertain to religious authority; and the differences, essential though they are, must be derived from the context and the circumstances of the case. In one passage indeed the civil type of authority is mentioned to be repudiated as something that should not obtain within the religious community (Mt **20** 25–27 = Mk **10** 42–44 = Lk **22** 25.26). But although its principle and power are so entirely different in different realms, the fact of authority as determining religious thought, conduct and relations permeates the whole Bible, and is expressed by many terms and phrases besides those tr[d] "authority."

III. Biblical Teaching.—A summary of the Biblical account of authority is given in He **1** 1; "God, having of old time spoken unto the fathers in the prophets by divers portions and in divers manners, hath at the end of these days spoken unto us in a Son [RVm]." Behind all persons and institutions stands God, who reveals His mind and exercises His sovereignty in many ways, through many persons and institutions, piecemeal and progressively, until His final revelation of His mind and will culminates in Jesus Christ.

1. OT Teaching

(1) The earliest form of authority is patriarchal. The father of the family is at once its prophet, priest and king. The consciousness of individuality was as yet weak. The unit of life was the family, and the father sums up the family in himself before God and stands to it as God. Such is the earliest picture of religious life found in the Bible. For whatever view may be taken of the historicity of Gen, there can be little doubt that the stories of the patriarchs represent an early stage of religious life, before the national or even the tribal consciousness had developed.

(2) When the tribal consciousness emerges, it is clad in a network of customs and traditions which had grown with it, and which governed the greater part of the life of the tribe. The father had now become the elder and judge who exercised authority over the larger family, the tribe. But also, men of commanding personality and influence appear, who change and refashion the tribal customs. They may be men of practical wisdom like Jethro, great warriors like Joshua, or emergency men like the judges. Moses stands apart, a prophet and reformer who knew that he bore a message from God to reform his people's religion, and gave Israel a knowledge of God and a covenant with God which set them forever apart from all other peoples. Other tribes might have a Jethro, a Joshua and a Jephtha, but Israel alone had its Moses. His authority has remained a large factor in the life of Israel to the present day and should hereafter be assumed as existing side by side with other authorities mentioned.

(3) In our earliest glimpses of Heb life in Canaan we find bands of seers or prophets associated with religion in Israel, as well as a disorganized priesthood which conducted the public worship of Jeh. These features were probably common to Israel and neighboring Sem tribes. Here again the individual person emerges who rises above custom and tradition, and exercises an individual authority direct from God over the lives of the people. Samuel, too, was a prophet, priest and king, but he regarded his function as so entirely ministerial, that God might be said to govern His people directly and personally, though He made known His will through the prophet.

(4) In the period of the kingship, religious authority became more organized, institutional and external. The occasional coöperation of the tribes developed into nationality, and the sporadic leadership of emergency chieftains gave way to the permanent rule of the king. Priests and prophets became organized and recognized guilds which acted together under the protection and influence of the king, along the lines of traditional morality and religion. The Heb church in its middle ages was an established church and thoroughly "Erastian." We know very little of the details of its organization, but it is clear that the religious orders as a rule offered little resistance to the corrupting influences of the court and of the surrounding heathenism.

(5) Opposition to corruption and advance to higher levels of religious life invariably originated outside the recognized religious authorities. God raised for Himself prophets such as Elijah, Amos, Isaiah and Jeremiah, who spoke out of the consciousness of an immediate vision or message or command from God. In turn they influenced the established religious authorities, as may be seen

in the reformations of Hezekiah and Josiah. All that is distinctive in the religion of Israel, all revelation of God in the OT, proceeded from the inner experiences of the irregular prophets.

(6) In the Judaism of the post-exilic period, the disappearance of the kingship, and the cessation of prophecy produced new conditions which demanded a readaptation of religious authorities. The relative position of the priesthood was greatly enhanced. Its chiefs became princes of Jerus, and exercised all the powers of the theocracy that remained under foreign rule. And new developments emerged. The formation of the canon of the OT set up a body of writings which stood as a permanent and external standard of doctrine and worship. But the necessity was felt to interpret the Scriptures and to apply them to existing conditions. The place of the old prophetic guilds was taken by the new order of rabbis and scribes. Gradually they secured a share with the priests in the administration of the law. "In the last two pre-Christian cents. and throughout the Talmudic times, the scribes (*ṣōph*ᵉ*rīm*), also called the wise (*ḥăkhāmīm*), who claimed to have received the true interpretation of the Law as 'the tradition of the Elders and Fathers' in direct line from Moses, the prophets, and the men of the great synagogue, ... included people from all classes. They formed the court of justice in every town as well as the high court of justice, the Sanhedrin in Jerus" (Köhler in *Jew Enc*, II, 337). In the time of Christ, these courts were the recognized authorities in all matters of religion.

2. NT Teaching

(1) *Of Jesus Christ.*—When He began to teach in Pal, all knowledge of God, and all exercise of His authority were mediated through the priests and scribes, who however claimed the OT as their source. Christ was neither the destroyer nor the creator of institutions. He never discussed the abstract right or capacity of the Jewish orders to be religious teachers. He enjoined obedience to their teaching (Mt **23** 2.3). Still less did He question the authority of the OT. He came not to destroy, but to fulfil the law and the prophets (Mt **5** 17). But He did two things which involved the assertion of a new and superior authority in Himself. He repudiated the scribes' interpretation of the law (Mt **23** 13–16), and He declared that certain of the provisions of the Mosaic law itself were temporary and tentative, and to be replaced or supplemented by His own more adequate teaching (Mt **5** 32.34.39.44; **19** 8.9). In doing this, He was really fulfilling a line of thought which permeates the entire OT. All its writers disclaim finality and look forward to a fuller revelation of the mind of God in a day of Jeh or a new covenant or a Messiah. Jesus Christ regarded these expectations as being realized in Himself, and claimed to complete and fulfil the development which had run through the OT. As such, He claims finality in His teaching of the will of God, and absolute authority in the realm of religion and morals. (*a*) His *teaching* is with authority. His hearers contrast it with that of the scribes, who, with all the prestige of tradition and establishment, in comparison with Him, entirely lacked authority (Mt **7** 29; Mk **1** 22; Lk **4** 32; Jn **7** 46). (*b*) His authority as a teacher is closely associated with His *works*, especially as these revealed His authority over that world of evil spirits whose influence was felt in the mental disorders that afflicted people (Mk **1** 27; Lk **4** 36). (*c*) In His claim to *forgive sins*, sanctioned by works of healing, He seemed to exercise a Divine prerogative (Mt **9** 6.8; Mk **2** 10; Lk **5** 24). It implied an infallible moral judgment, a power to dispense with the recognized laws of retribution and to remove guilt, which could only inhere in God. All these powers are asserted in another form in the statement that He is the final judge (Jn **5** 27). (*d*) He therefore possesses authority over *life and salvation*. The Father gave Him authority over all flesh, "that whatsoever thou hast given him, to them he should give eternal life" (Jn **17** 2 ARVm). This authority begins in His power over His own life to give it in sacrifice for men (Jn **10** 18). By faith in Him and obedience to Him, men obtain salvation (Mt **10** 32; **11** 28–30). Their relation to Him determines their relation to God and to the kingdom of heaven (Mt **10** 40; Lk **12** 8). (*e*) When challenged by the chief priests and elders, the established religious authorities, to state by what authority He taught, He gives no categorical reply, but tells them the parable of the Vineyard. All the prophets and teachers that had come from God before Him were servants, but He is the Son (Mt **21** 23–27.37; Mk **11** 28–33; **12** 6; Lk **20** 2.8.13). The Fourth Gospel definitely founds His authority upon His *sonship* (**5** 19–27). Paul deduces it from His self-sacrifice (Phil **2** 5–11). (*f*) In His *ascended state*, all authority in heaven and on earth is given unto Him (Mt **28** 18). It is not only authority in the church, and in the moral kingdom, but in the universe. God has set Him "far above all rule, and authority, and power, and dominion, and every name that is named, not only in this world, but also in that which is to come" (Eph **1** 21; cf Col **2** 10; 1 Pet **3** 22; 1 Cor **15** 24; Rev **12** 10). (*g*) His authority in the church as revealer of truth and Lord of spirits is not limited or completed within His earthly life. By His resurrection and exaltation He lives on in the church. "Where two or three are gathered . . . . in my name, there am I in the midst of them" (Mt **18** 20). "Lo, I am with you always, even unto the end of the world" (Mt **28** 20). Greater works than He did in the flesh will be done in the church, because of His exaltation: (Jn **14** 12); and by His sending the *Paraclete*, "Comforter" (ARV) (Jn **14** 16). The Paraclete, which is the Holy Spirit, will teach the disciples all things, and bring to their remembrance all that He said unto them (**14** 26). He has many things to tell them which in the days of His flesh they cannot receive, but the Spirit of truth shall guide them into all truth (**16** 12.13). And the Paraclete is neither separated nor distinct from Him in His exalted and permanent life (**14** 18.28). Herein is the authority of Christ made complete and permanent. His teaching, works and character, as facts outside of men, even while He lived, and still more when He was dead, could only partially and imperfectly rule their spirits. "Have I been so long time with you, and dost thou not know me, Philip?" In the day of the Spirit's revelation "ye shall know that I am in my Father" (Jn **14** 9.20). Nor, again, did or could He define the truth as it applied to every contingency throughout all time, while He lived under the limitations of time and place. Such a revelation, if it could have been given, would have been quite useless, for men can only apprehend the truth progressively and in relation to the position they occupy in time and place. But by His permanent spiritual presence in the church, He enters into, inhabits and governs its whole life and determines for it what is true and right at every stage of its development. (See Forrest, *Authority of Christ*, 202–3.) To ask whence Christ derives or how He possesses the authority above described, is to raise the whole question of His metaphysical existence. Empirically, we see it issuing from two facts, which are essentially one—His filial consciousness and His moral perfection. These chiefly are the empirical facts which the church has sought to interpret and express in the metaphysical doctrine of the Incarnation. (See Forrest, op. cit.)

(2) *Of the disciples.*—The first disciples acknowledged Christ in all things as their Lord and Master; not the teaching they had heard, nor the example they had witnessed, but Christ in His permanent, living presence. They pray to Him to fill Judas' place among the Twelve (Acts **1** 24.25). He gave the Spirit at Pentecost (**2** 33). In His name they perform their miracles (**3** 6; **9** 34). With Him Saul meets on the way to Damascus (**9** 5; Gal **1** 12). From Him they receive the teaching and commands which they deliver to the churches (1 Cor **11** 23).

But they too exercised an authority which is derivative, secondary, and dependent upon Him. (*a*) While Jesus Christ yet lived He gave the Twelve, and again the Seventy, authority to cast out unclean spirits and to heal all manner of diseases, while they went about preaching (Mt **10** 1; Mk **3** 15; **6** 7; Lk **9** 1; **10** 19). After His resurrection He gave them commission to bear witness for Him, to baptize and to teach all nations (Mt **28** 18–20; Lk **24** 48.49). Paul also traced his authority to preach directly to Jesus Christ (Gal **1** 1. 12). From Him they received their endowment with the Holy Spirit for the work (Acts **1** 5; **2** 33). (*b*) Paul claimed for himself, and by inference, for the other apostles, authority to exercise discipline in the churches, "which the Lord gave for building you up" (2 Cor **10** 8; **13** 10). All the church's ministers exercise oversight and admonition over the churches (1 Thess **5** 12; 2 Tim **4** 2; **2** 2). (*c*) The authority of sonship, and of participation in the tree of life belongs to all believers (Jn **1** 12; Rev **22** 14). (*d*) And in virtue of their faith they have authority over the nations (Rev **2** 26; **20** 4). Christ makes them to be kings (RV a kingdom) and priests (Rev **1** 6), a royal priesthood (1 Pet **2** 9).

In all this we are to see the authority of faith, of character, of men who are messengers of Christ because they are in living union with Him. It pertains to no office or institution, and exists only where Christ reigns in men, and therefore, through them.

(3) *Of the church.*—It is moral and personal and more concerned with life than with doctrine. Paul was the greatest teacher of the early church, but he claims no infallibility, promulgates no dogma, imposes no standard of orthodoxy beyond faith in Christ. He reasons, argues and persuades men to accept the gospel he had received of the Lord, but he knows no other authority than the truth as it is a living fact in Jesus Christ.

In the Pastoral Epistles we certainly read of a "sound doctrine" which should be taught and believed, but it has not crystallized into a creed, and the only condition of salvation laid down is living faith in Jesus Christ. See DOCTRINE.

The authority of the apostolic church, then, is in the first place that of individual men in whom Jesus Christ lives, a direct personal and individual authority. It is true that the individual can only live the Christian life, and therefore know the Christian truth, in a society, but that does not impair the individual and personal character of his witness. Yet as the church lives a collective life, there is a sense in which it may be said to bear a collective witness. Men are naturally more readily impressed by an idea held by the many. That is right in so far as the probability of the truth of a doctrine increases with the number of minds which approve it. That is the element of truth in the Catholic dictum *quod ubique, quod semper, quod ab omnibus creditum est* ("what is believed everywhere, always, and by all"). But the assent of the many does not constitute the truth of an idea or fact, nor enhance its authority. And there are levels of truth to which only few minds can attain, so that the assent of the many may be a presumption against the truth of an idea. And in the last resort, men do not accept ideas with mind and heart, because many believe them, but because of their inherent truth, their power to govern their minds. And the essential truth of a doctrine is no greater, whether one or a million accept it.

The apostolic church recognized this principle, for it never claimed for itself greater authority than that of a tutor to bring men to Christ, the one Lord. Peter, Paul, John, each knew Christ in a degree, and each spoke of Him as well as he could, but none of them claims to say all, or demands that his own teaching should absolutely rule men's minds; and the collective authority of the church can never rise higher than that of its best spirits.

(4) *Of the Bible.*—And the authority of the Bible as a whole is of the same nature as that of the church. It is a record of the experiences of men who knew God in various ways and degrees, but among them all there is only one Master. 'No one knows the Father save the Son, and he to whomsoever the Son willeth to reveal Him.' In varying degrees obedience should be rendered to many men in the church and outside of it, as they satisfy the demands of reason and conscience, but in the last resort every soul by itself must find, choose and obey its own King. For Christians Christ alone is King, as He revealed Himself in His human personality, in the experience and history of the church, and ultimately in the personal experience of every believer. (For a different view see J. H. Leckie, *Authority in Religion.*)

IV. Outline History of Ecclesiastical Doctrine of Authority.—Different ideas, drawn from many sources, soon replaced NT principles of authority in the life and thought of the church.

1. Appeal to Reason as Logos

The Gr apologists and Fathers were generally dominated by the Platonic doctrine of the Logos, and thought of God as dwelling in man and communicating His mind to him by giving him a share of His own mind and reason. While they accepted the Scriptures and the traditions of the church as Divine teaching, they did not regard them as external and sovereign authorities, but rather as copies of the Divine reason which dwelt in every man, but in complete and perfect manner only in Jesus Christ.

Neo-Platonism followed, and it underlies much of the church teaching from Origen to Augustine. God as pure being could not make known His essence to men, and His Logos in all the forms of its manifestation tended to become a spoken word which God had sent forth from Himself, rather than the living indwelling of God with men. When the Logos ceased to be living, it tended to become external and stereotyped, and upon this basis grew up Gr orthodoxy. Men who knew but little of the living personal Word felt the need of defining and establishing the central truths of Christianity in fixed and permanent forms which should become the standard of all thinking.

2. Developed into Orthodox Dogma

The inward witness of the Logos disappears, and the external authority of tradition and dogma as defined by the councils took its place. The bishops preserved the tradition and constituted the councils and thus became the organs of authority. The Scriptures were still venerated in words, but in fact subordinated to the episcopacy.

Aristotle's philosophy dominated the Middle Ages, or rather the pale ghost of Aristotle's system, the formal logic only.

3. Scholastic System

The forms of thought were mistaken for its essence. Truth consisted in logical consistency and systematic coherence. The dogmas of earlier ages were assumed as premises from which to deduce, by syllogistic inference, the whole structure of the church and its organs and sacraments, as the infallible representatives of God on earth.

4. Ecclesiastical Absolutism

Nominalism emptied the forms of thought of all reality and reared the ecclesiastical system upon negation. All the more necessary was it to affirm the absolute and unquestioned authority of the church, since it rested upon no reason or reality to which appeal could be made to justify its position and teaching. Thus the growth of absolutism in the church went *pari passu* with the disappearance of idealism, of any contact of the mind with reality, truth and God. Another way of saying this truth is that the doctrine of the Holy Spirit and of the living Christ suffered a total eclipse during the Middle Ages, while the authority of the church as the organ of revelation became absolute.

5. Reformation Principles

The Reformation was not consciously based upon any philosophic principles. It was the product of practical necessities. Men's spiritual needs drove them back to God, and they found Him in two sources, in the Bible, which was the record of His self-revelation through prophet, psalmist, apostle and preëminently through Jesus Christ, and in the accordant testimony of the Holy Spirit in their own hearts. But the underlying principles of this teaching were not articulated in a philosophy of knowledge and revelation for two centuries.

6. New Scholasticism

Therefore the second and third generations of Reformers, no longer possessed by the visions and convictions of Luther and Calvin, were thrown back upon the old scholastic philosophy which recognized no kinship of mind between God and man, and knew no direct communication between them. Hence it was necessary to find a new external authority, and this they discovered in the Bible which they made into a law of truth, as defined anew by ecclesiastical councils.

7. Inner Light

But the mystical side of the Reformers' teaching was not altogether lost, and a few obscure bodies of Christians continued to hold the doctrine of the inner light. Yet as the scholastic Protestants took only half—the objective half of the Reformers' teaching—the mystics only took the subjective half, and every man's imagination tended to become a law unto himself.

8. Back to Experience

Kant did for philosophy what Luther had done for religion. He rejected its dogmas and external authorities in order to come back to its realities. He was the first philosopher of the Protestant principle. He sought to discover a direct relation between man's mind and reality. He did not fully succeed. The old dogma of the *noumenon* as something that lay completely beyond man's ken clung to him, and vitiated his system. But through man's moral nature, he found a way to the heart of reality and to God. His idealistic principles were developed by his successors into the modern idealism, upon which it has been possible to erect a theory of knowledge that brings man's mind into direct contact with God, and therefore, a theory of authority which represents God as directly the sovereign of the soul.

9. Distrust of Reason

But the other side of Kant's philosophy, too, was developed into a theory of religious skepticism and external authority. Man's reason, he had taught, could not come into contact with reality, with the thing-in-itself, and therefore it could know nothing of God. This distrust of reason was made the basis of two different systems of external authority by Dean Mansel and Cardinal Newman. The skeptical element really descended from Locke and Hume, but men who would have disdained to learn their theology from Hume accepted Hume's principles from Kant, and built upon them, as a house upon sand, one, the authority of Anglicanism, and the other, the authority of Romanism.

10. Christian Skepticism

Kant's skepticism also allied itself with elements of Luther's teaching and traveled a middle course in the school of Ritschl. While holding that man may have knowledge and experience of Divine things in Jesus Christ, who is of the practical value of God for religious experience, the Ritschlians scruple to affirm that it is a direct and actual knowledge of God as He is essentially. This they will neither deny nor affirm, but the refusal to affirm has for many minds the effect of denial, and it leads to a subjectivism which is not far removed from skepticism and the denial of all authority.

V. Classification of Theories.—The various theories of authority may be now classed as follows:

1. External Theories

(1) *Incipient Catholicism in the 2d and 3d centuries.*—All ideas of a living and present revelation were suppressed as in the case of Montanism. Three more or less coördinate authorities were set up which determined for individual Christians what was Christian truth and conduct. The canon of the NT was gradually formed to define what writings, in addition to the OT taken over from the Jewish church, were inspired by the Holy Spirit and of Divine authority. The outline of a common creed or rule of faith grew up as the standard interpretation of Scripture. Above all was the episcopacy, which was supposed to preserve in unbroken tradition the unwritten teaching of the apostles. As the only living factor in this system of authority the last easily secured the predominant place. (See Harnack, *History of Dogma*, II, ch ii, ET.)

(2) *General councils.*—The authority of the episcopacy was organized into a permanent and general form in the councils, to whose decision obedience was demanded on pain of excommunication. The councils professed and believed that they were only defining the teaching that had always obtained in the church, and therefore invested themselves and their decisions with the authority of Christ.

(3) *Romanism.*—During the Middle Ages, the church of Rome concentrated in itself, that is, in its episcopacy, all the authority of tradition, bishops, councils and whatever else had held sway over the mind of the church. Scripture was ignored and the Bishop of Rome exercised the plenary authority of God over men's minds and lives. "Boniface VIII accepted in the Bull *Unam sanctam* (*ecclesiam*) of November 18, 1302, the Thomist doctrine of the papacy: 'We declare, say, define and pronounce that it is essential to salvation that every human creature should subject himself to the Roman Pontiff'" (Loofs, *Dogmengeschichte*, 307).

(4) *Papal infallibility.*—This theory culminated in 1870 in the formal declaration of the infallibility of the pope. "The Roman Pontiff, when he speaks *ex cathedra* . . . . has that infallibility, with which the Divine Redeemer endowed His church, in defining a doctrine of faith or morals" (Vatican Council, 1870, Session 4, cap. 4). This authority of the pope extends over all questions of knowledge and conduct, of discipline and government in the whole church. The theory is based upon the doctrine of tradition, as laid down in the Council of Chalcedon. "The doctrine of Catholic teaching is, that the body of publicly revealed doctrine has received no ob-

jective increase since the days of the apostles," and "it is no change of doctrine when that which has always been held implicitly becomes the subject of an explicit declaration" (Hunter, *Outlines of Dogmatic Theology*, I, 159, 164). Newman and recent modernists, however, concede a development in the doctrines of the church, but on the basis of the traditional teaching derived from the apostles. But once a development is conceded, questions arise as to its principles and conditions, and the whole authority that rests upon them falls to the ground by the mere fact of an appeal from it to the principles that govern its development. The attempt to evade criticism by positing the miraculous preservation of the tradition from error involves a further appeal from the supposed authority to a hypothetical miracle for which there is no tittle of evidence. All the evidence is against it. The history of the church shows that it has been as liable to error, and as readily influenced by natural conditions, as any other human institution.

(5) *Inerrancy of Scripture.*—When Protestants sought an external authority, they posited the inerrancy and infallibility of the Bible, and the whole Christian faith was founded upon that dogma. "Holy Scripture is the judge, or rather the voice of the supreme and infallible judge, the Holy Spirit, and the norm to which an inferior judge should refer in deciding controversies of faith, and according to which alone he should give sentence" (Quenstedt, quoted in *Hutterus Redivivus*, 119, 10th ed). Protestants found it necessary to interpret Scripture, and to define doctrines in synods and councils, but their decisions had authority only because they were supposed to be expositions of Scripture, and in that sense, the expression of God's mind. They differed from the "Catholic" councils in that they claimed no authority of their own and repudiated any authority that might be derived from tradition or the ministerial office.

(6) *Anglican appeal to antiquity.*—In the Anglican church too, the Scriptures as infallible were the ultimate authority, but some kind of a coördinate authority was claimed for the priesthood as standing in the succession of the apostles, and for the church Fathers and councils of the first six cents. And the tendency has been to lay increasing emphasis on the latter factors, as criticism has undermined the literal and external authority of Scripture.

(7) *Limitations of external authority.*—All the above-mentioned theories contain an element of truth, and the authorities they posit have in their turns ruled the minds and lives of men; but none of them can be regarded as adequate and final expressions of the mind of God to man. (*a*) It is superfluous to demonstrate that they are not infallible; in spite of that they might still be all the authority that man can have or need. (*b*) They all rest on the assumption that God's self-revelation came to an end with the apostolic age. The Biblical theory admittedly does, and the tradition theories strictly interpreted are in exactly the same case. An authority resting upon a traditional teaching handed down faithfully from the apostles would differ in no essential respect from one resting upon the written words of the apostles. They would be equally limited, literal, external and mechanical. But problems of mind and conduct have arisen, which the apostles never contemplated, and which their teaching (whether preserved in written or oral tradition matters nothing) could not solve. (*c*) As a matter of fact no traditional teaching of the apostles supplementing their writings has ever been discovered or can be discovered. What has been put forward as such is in manifest contradiction to their writings. (*d*) The idea that there is a consensus of opinion among church Fathers is equally illusory. If there were, it would need to be proved that such opinion could have any binding authority in religion. (*e*) The Bible is not one body of truth all standing at the same level, and whatever view of its inspiration may be held, some further authority will be needed to discriminate between the lower and the higher in its teaching. (*f*) Above all, an authority which is merely external and objective is no authority at all to the mature religious life. Blind submission to any external authority, creed, church or book, is the condition of a slave, and in such case "our spiritual intelligence is not quickened and developed by communion with the infinite wisdom, but arrested and quelled. Only then, on the other hand, are we spiritually enfranchised when we receive a revelation as from God, not because we are awed or terrified or allured by our selfish interests into reception of it, but because our own minds and hearts respond to it, because we see and know it to be true" (J. Caird, *University Sermons* [1898], 204–5).

2. Internal Authority

Theories of internal authority are in the nature of the case not so easily classified or defined as those of external; nor have they as yet filled so large a place in the public life of the church. But it would be a serious error to suppose that all the men who gave their adherence to systems of external authority lived in mere subjection to them. The history of mysticism in the church is the history of independent thought resting in a direct knowledge of God that transcended all external authority. Montanism and Gnosticism each in its own way appealed to an inner criterion of truth. All heresies involved some independent judgment, and appealed to authorities that were neither objective nor established. The Protestant Reformation was an open revolt against external authority, and although it resulted for a time in the substitution of another external authority, neither its original motive, nor its permanent force had any kinship with it. Luther's free criticism of the Bible, and Calvin's appeal to the testimony of the Holy Spirit as the final principle of its interpretation, are well known. No body of Protestants at present founds its faith on the mere letter of Scripture or creed. Inward authority has been conceived in many ways and expressed by many terms, such as the Logos (Gr apologists); the Paraclete (Montanus); ecstasy (Mystics); knowledge as opposed to faith or creed (Gnostics); the personal experience of faith (Luther); the testimony of the Holy Spirit (Calvin); the inner light (Quakers); individual experience (Pietists); practical reason (Kant); religious feeling (Schleiermacher); the historical Christ (Ritschl); conscience (Martineau); the living Christ (R. W. Dale); the consciousness of Christ (A. M. Fairbairn); the Christ of history and of experience (D. W. Forest) and many more. The variety suggests at first the denial rather than the affirmation of authority, but it is only in such a variety that the principles of an adequate authority can be recognized.

The ultimate authority in religion is God as He reigns in men's hearts. But both the experience itself and the expression and interpretation of it vary with each individual. A religious authority to be real and effective must win the response of the human spirit, and in that personal relation of Spirit with spirit lie the conditions of variation. Yet human reason and conscience everywhere tend to acknowledge one standard, to recognize one ideal and to obey one Lord. Nothing can force such a uniformity but the inward fitness of one supreme revelation to the common demands of humanity. No agreement yet exists as to the possibility or reality of such a revelation. But wherever men lend themselves to the spiritual contact of Jesus Christ with their souls, without the intervention of human creeds or institutions, their conscience and reason approve His moral supremacy and their spirits recognize His intimate knowledge of the Father.

Literature.—Besides books already mentioned, Bruce, *Chief End of Revelation;* Sanday, *Inspiration*, and *Oracles of God;* Oman, *Vision and Authority*, and *The Problem of Faith and Freedom;* A. M. Fairbairn, *Catholicism, Roman and Anglican;* Sabatier, *The Religions of Authority;* Watson, *The Philosophical Basis of Religion;* Kaftan, *The Truth of the Christian Religion;* Gwatkin, *The Knowledge of God;* Iverach, art. "Authority" in Hastings, *Enc of Theol. and Ethics;* E. O. Davies, *Prolegomena to Systematic Theology*, esp. for Bibliography.

T. Rees

AUTHORIZED, ô′-thor-īz′d, **VERSION.** See English Versions.

AVA, ā′va. See Avva.

AVAIL, a-vāl′ (שָׁוָה, *shāwāh*, "to be equal," hence "to be enough," "to avail"): Used in the sense of "satisfy" (Est **5** 13). Queen Esther's exceptional favor availed not to satisfy Haman, because of his insane jealousy of his rival Mordecai. Ἰσχύω, *ischúō*, "to be strong," tr^d^ also "prevail" (Rev **12** 8); with a negative signifies incompetence, e.g. the impossibility of redemptive merit or power in an outward ceremony or act (Gal **5** 6; **6** 15 AV): "neither circumcision availeth anything," contrasted with the efficacy of faith "in Christ Jesus." Used also to express the efficacy of prayer (Jas **5** 16).

AVARAN, av′a-ran: A surname of Eleazar, the third son of Mattathias (1 Macc **2** 5). It is doubtfully conjectured that Eleazar received this surname from the episode related in 1 Macc **6** 43–46; the word may mean "the piercer," referring to his stabbing of the elephant. Some connect it with חוּר, *ḥūr*, "to be white," and connect it with Eleazar's white complexion. The Syr reads "Chavran" and the Vulg "Abaron"; the LXX in **6** 43 gives *Sauarán* which is an error for *Eleázaros aúran;* LXX V corrects to *aúran*.

AVEN, ā′ven (אָוֶן, *'āwen*, "emptiness," "vanity"): Used in Ezk **30** 17 for On or Heliopolis, in Egypt. See On. As a term of contempt Hosea calls Beth-el "Beth-aven" (**4** 15; **10** 5). So Amos speaks of some valley near Damascus as "the valley of Aven" (i.e. of the idol, **1** 5), in which Baalbek (Heliopolis) was situated. The word is rendered "idol" in Isa **66** 3.

AVENGE, a-venj′, **AVENGER,** a-venj′ẽr:

Avenge.—The general idea connected with this word is that of inflicting punishment upon the wrongdoer. Since emphasis may be placed upon the deed itself, the wrongdoer, or the injured party, the vb. is found as intransitive (only Lev **19** 18; see below), transitive (2 S **4** 8 et al.); and also active (Dt **32** 43), passive (Jer **5** 9) and reflexive (Est **8** 13). In 1 S **25** 26 ff avenge is tr^d^ from יָשַׁע, *yāsha'*, "to save" (RVm "thine own hand saving thee"), in Hos **1** 4 from פָּקַד, *pāḳadh*, "to visit," and in 2 S **18** 19 ff from שָׁפַט, *shāphaṭ*, "to judge," but the usual Heb word is נָקַם, *nāḳam*, or derivatives, "to avenge." The tr in RV differs in some places from AV: Nu **31** 3 (RV "execute Jeh's vengeance"; cf 2 S **22** 48; Ps **18** 47; Lev **26** 25); Lev **19** 18 (RV "take vengeance"); Jgs **5** 2 (RV "for that the leaders took the lead in Israel" from פָּרַע, *pāra'*, "to be free, to lead"). In the NT avenge is tr^d^ from the Gr ἐκδικέω, *ekdikéō*, "to do justice," "to protect" (Lk **18** 3 ff et al.) and AV Rev **18** 20, κρίνω, *krínō*, "to judge" (RV "God hath judged your judgment").

Avenger.—I.e. the person who inflicts punishment upon the evil-doer for a wrong experienced by himself (from נָקַם, *nāḳam*, "to avenge"; Ps **8** 2 et al.) or by someone else from גָּאַל, *gā'al*, "to redeem"; Nu **35** 12 ff et al.). In the NT avenger occurs only once; "the Lord is an avenger in all things" (1 Thess **4** 6). It was the duty of the nearest relative to execute vengeance upon the murderer of his kin: he became the *gō'ēl*. With reference to the protective legislation and custom, see Goel. Cf Blood; Revenge, Revenger.

A. L. Breslich

AVERSE, a-vûrs′ (שׁוּב, *shūbh*, "to turn back," "retreat"): Quiet, peaceful wanderers (Mic **2** 8).

AVIM, av′im. See Avvim.

AVIMS, av′imz (Dt **2** 23). See Avvim.

AVITES, ā′vīts. See Avvim.

AVITH, ā′vith (עֲוִית, *'ăwīth*): The royal city of Hadad king of Edom (Gen **36** 35; 1 Ch **1** 46). The LXX reads Γετθαίμ, *Getthaím*. There is no clue to its identification.

AVOID, a-void′: Archaic use in 1 S **18** 11 for "escaped." In RV of NT only in 2 Cor **8** 20 (στελλόμενοι, *stellómenoi* with negative), lit. "arranging that not," etc, i.e. by anticipation providing that something should not occur. In AV for "turn away from," ἐκκλίνετε, *ekklínete:* Rom **16** 17; 1 Tim **6** 20; "refuse," παραιτοῦ, *paraitoú*, 2 Tim **2** 23; περιίστασο, *periístaso*, Tit **3** 9.

AVOUCH, a-vouch′: In EV only in Dt **26** 17. 18, in the sense of "to confess," "avow," "publicly and solemnly declare." The Heb form is likewise unique (Hiph. of *'āmar*).

AVVA, av′a (עַוָּא, *'awwā';* AV **Ava,** ā′va): A province, the people of which Shalmaneser king of Assyria placed in the cities of Samaria in the room of the children of Israel taken into exile by him (2 K **17** 24). It is probably the same as Ivva (2 K **18** 34; **19** 13; Isa **37** 13), a province conquered by Assyria.

AVVIM, av′im, **AVITES,** ā′vīts (עַוִּים, *'awwīm;* **Εὐαῖοι**, *Heuaíoi*, also unaspirated; also used to represent the name of the Hivites): The early inhabitants of the southern extremity of Canaan afterward occupied by the Philis (Dt **2** 23; cf Josh **13** 3.4, AV "Avim," ā′vim). The Avvim of Josh **18** 23 was a town of Benjamin, not a people. Gesenius supposes the name to mean "dwellers in the desert," but it was more probably the name of some pre-Sem tribe. The Avvim are described as living in *Ḥăçērīm* or "encampments" and extending as far as the outskirts of Gaza.

AWAIT, a-wāt′: Only in Acts **9** 24 AV, in its now obsolete sense as a noun, "ambush": "their laying await was known of Saul." RV "their plot."

AWAKE, a-wāk′ (יָקַץ, *yāḳaç*, "to waken"; עוּר, *'ūr*, "to rouse up" from sleep; ἐγείρω, *egeírō*, "to arouse from sleep"): The ordinary terms for awaking from natural slumber: as of Jacob at Bethel (Gen **28** 16); of Solomon at Gibeon (1 K **3** 15); of Jesus in the storm-tossed boat (Lk **8** 24). Used **fig.** with striking effect of awaking from mental, moral and spiritual sleep: as when Deborah calls upon herself to awake to the fervor and eloquence of poetry (Jgs **5** 12); of Zion's awaking to moral vigor and beauty (Isa **52** 1); of waking from spiritual death (Eph **5** 14); from the grave in resurrection (Dnl **12** 2). Poetically used of the rising north wind (Cant **4** 16); of music (Ps **108** 2); of the sword in battle (Zec **13** 7); of a lover's affection (Cant **2** 7); of God Himself responding to prayer (Ps **59** 4). Also used of moral awaking, as from drunkenness: ἐκνήφω, *eknḗphō*, "to become sober" (cf Joel **1** 5). DWIGHT M. PRATT

AWAY WITH: (1) "To endure," "to bear with" (Isa **1** 13), "I cannot away with iniquity and the solemn meeting," i e. endure the combination of wickedness and worship. In the Heb merely, "I am unable iniquity and the solemn meeting." (2) To destroy (αἴρω, *aírō*). Found in such expressions as Acts **22** 22, "Away with such a fellow from the earth."

AWE, ô: Fear mingled with reverence and wonder, a state of mind inspired by something terrible or sublime. In AV and RV it occurs in Ps **4** 4: "Stand in awe, and sin not" (where RVm has, "Be ye angry," so LXX; cf Eph **4** 26); Ps **33** 8; **119** 161. In the following passages RV substitutes "stand in awe of" for AV "fear": Ps **22** 23 (Gr *phoboúmenoi*); Isa **29** 23; 1 S **18** 15; Mal **2** 5; and in He **12** 28 it substitutes "awe" for AV "reverence" (Gr *déos*, here only in NT). In all these passages, except 1 S **18** 15 (Gr *eulabeíto*, where it describes Saul's feeling toward David), the word stands for man's attitude of reverential fear toward God. This is the characteristic attitude of the pious soul toward God in the Scriptures, esp. in the OT. It arises from a consciousness of the infinite power, sublimity and holiness of God, which fills the mind with the "fear of the Lord," and a dread of violating His law. See FEAR.

D. MIALL EDWARDS

AWL, ôl (מַרְצֵעַ, *marçēaʿ*): "Bore his ear through with an awl" (Ex **21** 6; Dt **15** 17). The ear was pierced as being the organ of hearing, thus signifying the servant's promise of obedience. See BORE.

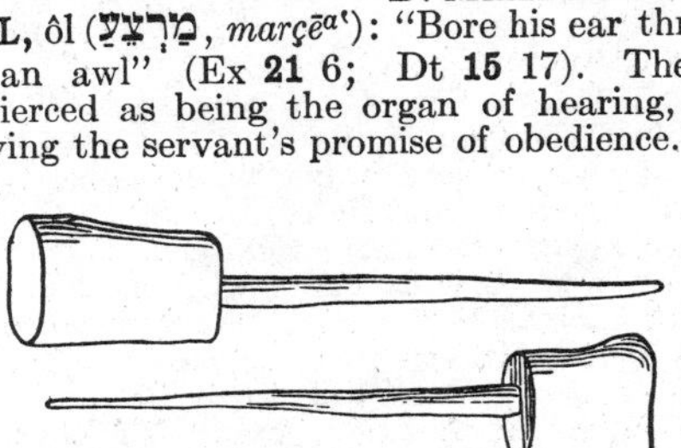

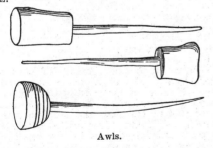

Awls.

AX (AXE), AX-HEAD, aks'hed: Nine different Heb words have been rendered "ax":

(1) גַּרְזֶן, *garzen*. This unquestionably was one of the larger chopping instruments, as the uses to which it was put would imply (Dt **19** 5; **20** 19; 1 K **6** 7; Isa **10** 15). The modern ax used by the woodchoppers in Syria has a shape much like the ancient stone and bronze axes, with the exception that it is fastened to the handle by passing the latter through a hole in the ax-head, whereas the Egyp sculptures show that their ax-heads were held to the handles by means of thongs. The so-called battle-ax found at *Tell el-Ḥesy* was probably fastened in this way. Syrian peasants are frequently seen carrying in their belts small hatchets the heads of which are shaped like a battle-ax and which are bound to the handles by thongs.

(2) מַעֲצָר, *maʿăçār*, is used in Isa **44** 12 (AV renders "tongs") and in Jer **10** 3.

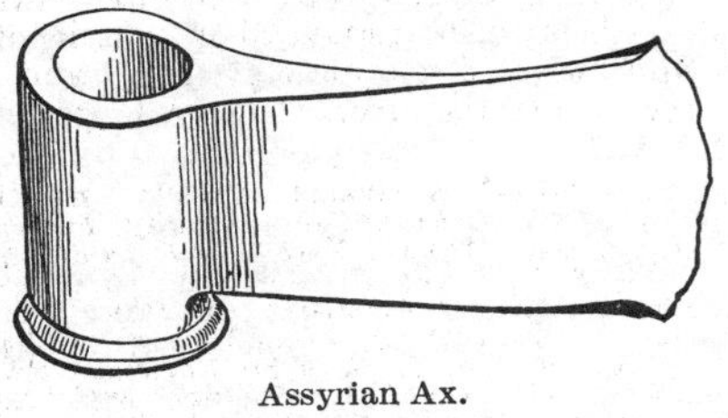

Assyrian Ax.

(3) קַרְדֹּם, *ḳardōm*, is used in Jgs **9** 48; 1 S **13** 20.21; Ps **74** 5; Jer **46** 22. The present Arab. word, *ḳudûm*, which is the name for the native adze, is from the same origin. Ancient forms of the adze are shown in Figs. 4 and 7. The adze is the only chopping instrument of the Syrian carpenter. He uses it for many purposes, where a foreigner would use a saw or chisel or plane, and with a skill which the foreigner envies. Many students of Syrian life believe that the adze is a tool which has survived from the early Heb times.

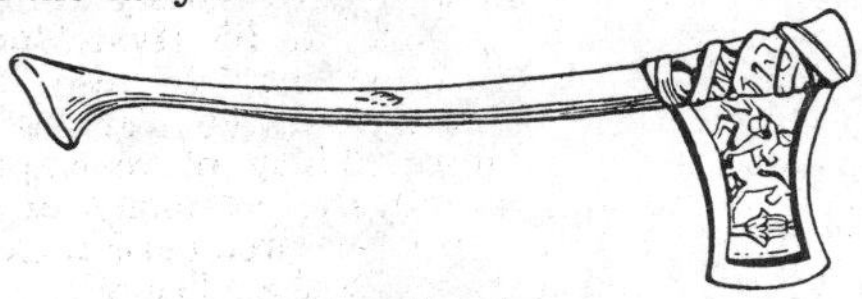

Egyptian Ax.

(4) בַּרְזֶל, *barzel* (Dt **19** 5; 2 K **6** 5): The interest associated with this word is that it literally means "iron," although the context indicates that it means "ax." If the word iron was not used here to mean "metal," then iron axes were used by the children of Israel. If iron axes existed, however, they have long since disappeared as the result of corrosion, since the only ones discovered have been of stone, copper or bronze. See BRONZE.

(5) מַגְזֵרָה, *maghzērāh* (2 S **12** 31) is lit. "a cutting instrument," and might be rendered, "a blade" or sickle.

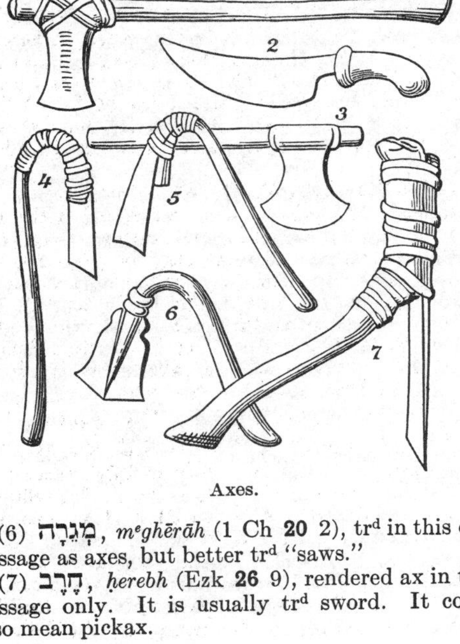

Axes.

(6) מְגֵרָה, *meghērāh* (1 Ch **20** 2), tr^d in this one passage as axes, but better tr^d "saws."

(7) חֶרֶב, *ḥerebh* (Ezk **26** 9), rendered ax in this passage only. It is usually tr^d sword. It could also mean pickax.

(8) כַּשִּׁיל, *kashshīl* (Ps **74** 6 AV), lit. "a feller," hence an ax.

(9) מַפֵּץ, *mappēç* (Jer **51** 20), lit. "a smiter," hence a war club or battle-ax. The Gr word used in the NT is ἀξίνη, *axínē* (Mt **3** 10; Lk **3** 9).

JAMES A. PATCH

AXLE-TREE, ak′s′l-trē. See SEA, THE MOLTEN.

AYIN, ä′yēn (עַיִן, *'ayin*, "eye" or "fountain"): The 16th letter of the Heb alphabet, so named, probably, because the original form resembled the eye. *'Ayin* (ع) is usually neglected in pronunciation, and the inverted comma (') is the sign most commonly employed to represent it in transliteration. The same sound is found in the Arab. and other Sem languages. The Arabs have two pronunciations, one a very strong guttural formed at the back of the palate, something like a rattled *r* or *rg*, the other similar in quality, only less harsh and guttural. The LXX reproduced *'ayin* in some cases by *gamma, g*. The numerical value of this letter is 70. *'Ayin* begins each verse of the 16th section of Ps **119** in the Heb. W. W. DAVIES

AZAEL, az′a-el (Ἀζάηλος, *Azáēlos;* cf Asahel [Ezr **10** 15]): Father of Jonathan, one of two chief investigators of foreign marriages (1 Esd **9** 14).

AZAELUS, az-a-ē′lus (B, Ἀζάηλος, *Azáēlos;* A, Ἀζαήλ, *Azaēl;* omitted in Ezr **10**): A., son of Ezora, put away his "strange wife" (1 Esd **9** 34).

AZAL, ā′zal. See AZEL.

AZALIAH, az-a-lī′a (אֲצַלְיָהוּ, *'ăçalyāhū*, "Jeh has set aside"): A son of Meshullam and father of Shaphan the scribe, famous in connection with the discovery of the law in the reign of King Josiah (2 K **22** 3).

AZANIAH, az-a-nī′a (אֲזַנְיָה, *'ăzanyāh*, "Jeh has given ear"): A son of Jeshua, a Levite who signed the covenant (Neh **10** 9).

AZAPHION, a-zā′fi-on. See ASSAPHIOTH.

AZARA, az′a-ra. See ASARA.

AZARAEL, a-zä′ra-el. See AZAREL.

AZARAIAS, az-a-rā′yas (B, Ἀζαραίας, *Azaraías;* A, Σαραίας, *Saraías;* AV **Saraias**); cf Seraiah [Ezr **7** 1]): An ancestor of Ezra (1 Esd **8** 1).

AZAREEL, a-zär′ē-el. See AZAREL.

AZAREL, az′a-rel (עֲזַרְאֵל, *'ăzar'ēl*, "God is helper"; AV reads **Azareel** in nos. 1–5, **Azarael** in no. 6):

(1) A Korahite who entered the army of David at Ziklag (1 Ch **12** 6).

(2) A musician in the temple appointed by lot; son of Heman (1 Ch **25** 18; cf Uzziel, ver 4).

(3) A captain of the tribe of Dan in the service of David (1 Ch **27** 22).

(4) One of those who had "strange wives," a son of Bani (Ezr **10** 41).

(5) The father of Amashai, a priest who dwelt in Jerus after the Exile (Neh **11** 13).

(6) A priest's son who played the trumpet in the procession when the wall was dedicated (Neh **12** 36). A. L. BRESLICH

AZARIAH, az-a-rī′a (עֲזַרְיָהוּ and עֲזַרְיָה, *'ăzaryāhū* and *'ăzaryāh*, "Jeh has helped"):

(1) King of Judah. See UZZIAH.

(2) A Judahite of the house of Ethan the Wise (1 Ch **2** 8).

(3) The son of Jehu, descended from an Egyp through the daughter of Sheshan (1 Ch **2** 38).

(4) A son of Ahimaaz and grandson of Zadok (1 Ch **6** 9).

(5) A son of Zadok the high priest and an official of Solomon (1 K **4** 2).

(6) A high priest and son of Johanan (1 Ch **6** 10).

(7) A Levite, ancestor of Samuel, and Heman the singer (1 Ch **6** 36).

(8) A son of Nathan and captain of Solomon's tax collectors (1 K **4** 5).

(9) A prophet in the reign of King Asa; his father's name was Oded (2 Ch **15** 1–8).

(10 and 11) Two sons of Jehoshaphat, king of Judah (2 Ch **21** 2).

(12) King of Judah (2 Ch **22** 6, called Ahaziah in ver 1).

(13) A son of Jeroham, who helped to overthrow Athaliah, and place Joash on the throne (2 Ch **23** 1).

(14) A son of Johanan and a leading man of Ephraim, mentioned in connection with the emancipated captives taken by Pekah (2 Ch **28** 12).

(15) A Levite of the family of Merari, who took part in cleansing the temple in the days of Hezekiah (2 Ch **29** 12).

(16) A high priest who rebuked King Uzziah for arrogating to himself priestly functions (2 Ch **26** 16–20).

(17) The father of Seraiah and son of Hilkiah (1 Ch **6** 13 f).

(18) A son of Hoshaiah, and a bitter enemy of Jeremiah (Jer **43** 2 ff).

(19) One of the royal captives taken to Babylon, whose name was changed to Abed-nego (Dnl **1** 7).

(20) The son of Maaseiah, who helped repair the walls of Jerus (Neh **3** 23 f).

(21) A Levite who assisted Ezra to expound the Law (Neh **8** 7).

(22) A priest who sealed the covenant (Neh **10** 2).

(23) A prince of Judah mentioned in connection with the dedication of the walls of Jerus (Neh **12** 32 f). W. W. DAVIES

AZARIAS, az-a-rī′as (Ἀζαρίας, *Azarías*, and Ἀζαρείας, *Azareías*):

(1) A., who put away his "strange wife" (1 Esd **9** 21); cf Uzziah (Ezr **10** 21).

(2) A., who stood at the right side of Ezra when the law was read to the people (1 Esd **9** 43); omitted in Ezr **8** 4.

(3) A., who interpreted the law to the people (1 Esd **9** 48); cf Azariah (Neh **8** 7).

(4) A., a name assumed by the angel Raphael (Tob **5** 12; **6** 6.13; **7** 8; **9** 2). See RAPHAEL.

(5) A., a general in the service of Judas Maccabee (1 Macc **5** 18.56.60).

(6) A., one of the three men thrown into the fiery furnace (Three vs 2.66); cf Azariah (Dnl **1** 6 ff; **2** 17), Abed-nego (Dnl **1** 7; **2** 49; **3** 12 ff). A. L. BRESLICH

AZARU, az′a-rū̂ (B, Ἀζαρού, *Azaroú;* A, Ἀζουρού, *Azouroú;* AV **Azuran**): The descendants of A. returned with Zerubbabel to Jerus (1 Esd **5** 15); omitted in Ezr and Neh; cf however Azzur (Neh **10** 17).

AZAZ, a′zaz (עָזָז, *'āzāz*, "powerful"): A descendant of Reuben (1 Ch **5** 8).

AZAZEL, a-zā′zel (עֲזָאזֵל, *'ăzā'zēl;* ἀποπομπαῖος, *apopompaíos;* AV **Scapegoat**, RVm "removal"):

I. THE MEANING OF THE WORD
 1. The Passages to Be Considered
 2. The Proposed Interpretations
  (1) The Etymology
  (2) The Explanation
II. WHAT IS DONE IN CONNECTION WITH AZAZEL
 1. The Significance of This Action
 2. The Jewish Liturgy

I. The Meaning of the Word.—This word is found in connection with the ceremony of the Day of Atonement (q.v.). According to Lev **16** 8, Aaron is to cast lots upon the two goats which on the part of the congregation are to serve as a sin offering (ver 5), "one lot for Jeh, and the other lot for Azazel." In ver 10, after the first goat has been set apart as a sin offering for Jeh, we read: "But the goat, on which the lot fell for Azazel, shall be set alive before Jeh, to make atonement for him, to send him away for Azazel into the wilderness." In ver 26 we read: "And he that letteth go the goat for Azazel shall wash his clothes, and bathe his flesh in water." Before this, in vs 21 f mention had been made of what should be done with the goat. After the purification of the (inner) sanctuary, of the tent of meeting, and of the altar, the living goat is to be brought, "and Aaron shall lay both his hands upon the head of the live goat, and confess over him all . . . their sins; and he shall put them upon the head of the goat, and shall send him away by the hand of a man that is in readiness into the wilderness: and the goat shall bear upon him all their iniquities unto a solitary land: and he shall let go the goat in the wilderness." But in this last mentioned and most important passage the term under consideration is not found.

1. The Passages to Be Considered

(1) *The etymology.*—Some have derived the word from *'az+'azal* (*fortis abiens*, "passing away in his strength" or from an intentional alteration of *'el+'azaz, robur Dei*, "strength of God"; cf below the angel of the Book of Enoch); while others have regarded the word as a broken plur. of a subst. in the Arab. *'azālā*, and tr it as "lonesomeness," "desert." Now there is an inclination to regard it as a reduplication from *'ăzalzēl*, derived from the root *'āzal*. If we accept this view, although it is without certainty and an exact analogue cannot be found, we could conclude from the way in which this noun has been formed that we have before us not an abstract term (*remotio*, "removal," or *abitus*, "departure"), but a concrete noun, or an adj., *longe remotus* ("far removed") or *porro abiens* ("going far away").

2. The Proposed Interpretations

(2) *The explanation.*—In vs 10.22.26, we would have an acceptable sense, if we regarded this word as expressive of a distinct locality in the wilderness (cf JEWISH TRADITION, II, 2). But this interpretation is impossible, since the law in Lev **16** was given during the wanderings in the wilderness and accordingly presupposed a constant change in the encampment, even if this should be regarded only as the historical background. By the use of the same preposition *l^e* in connection with Jeh and Azazel, it seems natural to regard the expressions as entirely ‖ and to think of some personal being. Some interpret this word as referring to a demon of the wilderness (cf Ps **106** 37; Dt **32** 17; Lev **17** 7; 2 Ch **11** 15; Isa **13** 21; **34** 14; Mt **12** 43 ff; Lk **11** 24 ff; Rev **18** 2) and explain the term as "one who has separated himself from God," or "he who has separated himself," or "he who misleads others." But a demon of this kind could not possibly be placed in contrast to Jeh in this way; and as in the Book of En **6** 6; **8** 1 ff; **9** 6; **10** 4 ff; **13** 1 ff; **69** 2 one of the most prominent of the fallen angels who taught mankind the arts of war and luxury, revealed secrets to them, and is now bound in the wilderness, and is there preserved for the final judgment, because he was mainly responsible for the presence of evil in the world, is called Azael (also Azazel, or Azalzel), it is highly probable that this name was taken from Lev **16**. In later times the word Azazel was by many Jews and also by Christian theologians, such as Origen, regarded as that Satan himself who had fallen away from God. In this interpretation the contrast found in ver 8, in case it is to be regarded as a full parallelism, would be perfectly correct. But it must be acknowledged that in Holy Scripture, Satan is nowhere called by the name of Azazel, and just as little is the wilderness regarded as his permanent place of abode. Against these last two interpretations we must also recall that in the most significant passage, viz. vs 20 ff, the term Azazel is not found at all. The same is true in the case of the ceremony in connection with the purification of leprous people and houses (Lev **14** 7 ff. 49 ff), which throughout suggests Lev **16.** In this place we have also the sevenfold sprinkling (cf **14** 16 with Lev **16** 14 f); and in addition two animals, in this case birds, are used, of which the one is to be slain for the purpose of sprinkling the blood, but the other, after it has been dipped into the blood of the one that has been slain, is to be allowed to fly away. In this way the essential thought in Lev **16** as also in Lev **14** seems to be the *removal* of the animal in either case, and it is accordingly advisable to interpret Azazel adjectively, i.e. to forego finding a complete parallelism in ver 8, and to regard the preposition in connection with Jeh as used differently from its use with Azazel, and to translate as follows: "And Aaron shall cast lots over both goats, the one lot [i.e. for the one goat] for Jeh, and one lot for the goat that is destined to go far away." On the preposition *l^e* used with the second Azazel in ver 10 cf Ex **21** 2. With this interpretation a certain hardness yet remains for our linguistic sense, because we cannot find a good tr for the adj. But in favor of this interpretation and against the personal interpretation we can appeal also to the feeling of the LXX translators who translate *apopompaíos, diestalménos*, and also to that of Aquilos, who translates *trágos apoluómenos, apoleluménos, kekrataiōménos*, and of Symmachus who translates *aperchómenos, aphieménos*. (The general idea expressed by all these words is "removal," "sending away," "releasing" or "dismissal.") It is true that the LXX in one place translates *eis tḗn apopómpēn*, which however could be also an abstract circumlocution for a conception that, though used elsewhere, is yet awkward. In the Vulg we have *caper emissarius* and Luther says "der ledige Bock," which are probably based on a wrong etymology, since *'ēz* signifies only a goat or perhaps this word "Bock" is here only supplied from the connection, and that quite correctly, so that Luther and the Vulg can also be cited in favor of our interpretation.

II. What Is Done in Connection with Azazel.—Both goats, according to ver 5, are to be regarded as a single sin-sacrifice, even should we interpret Azazel as demon or Satan, and we are accordingly not at all to understand that a sacrifice was brought to these beings. This too is made impossible by the whole tenor of the OT in general, as of Lev **16** in particular, so that in ver 8 the two members introduced by the preposition *l^e* would not at all be beings of exactly the same importance. Both goats, so to say, represent two sides of the same thing. The second is necessary to make clear what the first one, which has been slain, can no longer represent, namely, the removal of the sin, and accordingly has quite often aptly been called the *hircus redivivus*. But what is to be represented finds its expression in the ceremony described in vs 20 f. Whatever may be the significance of the laying on of hands in other connections, whether the emphasis is placed more on the disposal or on the appropriation of the property,

1. The Significance of This Action

at this place it certainly is only a symbol of the transfer of guilt, which is confessed over the goat and is then carried into the wilderness by the goat upon which it has been laid. In order to make this transfer all the more impressive, both the hands are here brought into action, while e.g. in Lev **1** 4 only one hand is used. The fact that the goat is accompanied by somebody and that it is to be taken to an uninhabited place is to indicate the absolute impossibility of its return, i.e. the guilt has been absolutely forgiven and erased, a deep thought made objectively evident in a transparent manner and independently of the explanation of Azazel, which is even yet not altogether certain. In the personal interpretation, we could have, in addition to the idea of the removal of the guilt, also a second idea, namely, that Azazel can do no harm to Israel, but must be content with his claim to a goat which takes Israel's place.

2. The Jewish Liturgy

The actions in connection with Azazel, as was also the case with the Day of Atonement, were interpreted more fully by the Talm and the traditions based on it (cf Atonement, Day of, III, 2). The lots could be made of different materials; in later times they were made of gold. The manner of casting the lots was described in full. The goat that was to be sent into the wilderness was designated by a black mark on the head, the other by one on the neck. On the way from Jerus to the wilderness, huts were erected. From a distance it was possible to see how the goat was hurled backward from a certain cliff, called Bēth-Hadûdû (*Bēth-ḥudêdûn*, 12 miles E. of Jerus). By means of signals made with garments, news was at once sent to Jerus when the wilderness had been reached.

Wilhelm Möller

AZAZIAH, az-a-zī'a (עֲזַזְיָהוּ, *'ăzazyāhū*, "Yahwe is strong," or "strengthens"):

(1) A Levite musician who participated in the services held on the return of the ark to Jerus (1 Ch **15** 21). His name is omitted from the list in ver 18.

(2) Father of Hoshea, who was the leader of Ephraim at the time that David enumerated the people (1 Ch **27** 20).

(3) A Levite who had charge of the offerings brought to the temple in the days of Hezekiah (2 Ch **31** 13).

AZBASARETH, az-bas'a-reth: The name of an Assyr king. AV form "Azbasareth" comes from the Vulg. See Asbasareth.

AZBUK, az'buk (עַזְבּוּק, *'azbūḳ*): The father of a certain Nehemiah—not the great governor of the same name, though a contemporary (Neh **3** 16).

AZEKAH, a-zē'ka (עֲזֵקָה, *'ăzēḳāh*): A town of some importance in the Shephelah of Judah mentioned (Josh **15** 35) next to Socoh. In Josh **10** 10 the defeated kings of the Amorites are described as flying before Joshua "by the way of the ascent of Beth-horon . . . . to Azekah, and unto Makkedah" and (ver 11) as the host fled "Jeh cast down great stones from heaven upon them unto Azekah, and they died." In 1 S **17** 1 it is recorded that before David's combat with Goliath, the Philis "gathered together at Socoh, which belongeth to Judah, and encamped between Socoh and Azekah, in Ephesdammin." In 2 Ch **11** 9 it is mentioned as one of the frontier cities which Rehoboam fortified and in Jer **34** 7 it is one of the two fortified cities remaining to Judah in the Shephelah which Nebuchadnezzar was besieging. "Azekah and the towns [m, "daughters"] thereof" is mentioned among the cities reoccupied by Jews returning after the Exile (Neh **11** 30). In all the three last references the place is mentioned along with Lachish.

All the data suit *Tell Zaḳarēyeh* on the N. side of the Vale of Elah (*Wâdy es-Sunṭ*) and some 3 miles N.W. of Socoh (*Kh. Shuweikeh*). This site, which was partially excavated by the Palestine Exploration Fund, is one of great natural strength. "The hill stands almost isolated, rising abruptly for almost 350 ft. above the Vale of Elah; . . . . to the W. the fall is also very great, while to the S. the *tell* is joined by a neck of land (about 100 ft. below the summit) to a hill behind." The summit is about 350 yds. by 150 yds., and is much larger than *Tell el-Ḥesy* (Lachish) (Bliss). Excavations showed that it was a very ancient site which had been powerfully fortified, and the rock under the city was excavated in a series of very extraordinary underground chambers which could be used as places of refuge. The site suits the narrative of Joshua's battle very well, as there is a long-used high route running N. to S. from the neighborhood of Ajalon. Its position as a frontier fortress is comparable with that of Lachish: the name Zaḳarēyeh, seems to be a survival of Azekah.

See *PEFS*, 1899, 10 ff; *PEF*, III, 441.

E. W. G. Masterman

AZEL, ā'zel (אָצֵל, *'āçēl*, "noble"):

(1) A descendant of King Saul, through Jonathan (1 Ch **8** 37 f; **9** 43 f).

(2) **Azel**, ā'zel, AV **Azal** (אָצַל, *'āçēl;* **'Ασαήλ**, *Asaēl;* Zec **14** 5): A place not far from Jerus. There may be an echo of the name in that of *Wādy Yasūl*, to the right of *'Ain el-Lōz*, in *Wādy en-Nār*.

AZEM, ā'zem: AV form for Ezem (thus RV) (Josh **15** 29; **19** 3).

AZEPHURITH, az-ē-fū'rith. See Arsiphurith.

AZETAS, a-zē'tas (**'Αζητάς**, *Azētás*): The head of a family accompanying Zerubbabel out of captivity (1 Esd **5** 15). Neither Ezra nor Nehemiah gives this name in his list.

AZGAD, az'gad (עַזְגָּד, *'azgādh*, "strong is Gad"): In the list of those who returned from Babylon with Zerubbabel are mentioned "the children of Azgad" (1,222, Ezr **2** 12; 2,322, Neh **7** 17). 110 males with their chief returned with Ezra (Ezr **8** 12). Azgad was among the leaders who signed the Covenant after Nehemiah (Neh **10** 15).

AZIEI, a-zī'ē-ī: An ancestor of Ezra (2 Esd **1** 2). Cf Azariah (Ezr **7** 3) and Ozias (1 Esd **8** 2; AV Ezias).

AZIEL, ā'zi-el (עֲזִיאֵל, *'ăzī'ēl*, "God is power"; cf *HPN*, 210, 309): A Levite singer who played the psalteries (1 Ch **15** 20); cf Jaaziel (1 Ch **15** 18).

AZIZA, a-zī'za (עֲזִיזָא, *'ăzīzā'*, "the powerful"): A. had taken a foreign wife (Ezr **10** 27): cf Zardeus (1 Esd **9** 28 RV).

AZMAVETH, az-mā'veth (עַזְמָוֶת, *'azmāweth*):

(1) One of David's 30 mighty men (2 S **23** 31; 1 Ch **11** 33).

(2) A descendant of Jonathan, the son of Saul (1 Ch **8** 36; **9** 42).

(3) Father of two warriors who joined David at Ziklag (1 Ch **12** 3).

(4) The name of one set over David's treasures (1 Ch **27** 25). Some identify him with (1) and (3).

AZMAVETH, az-mā'veth (עַזְמָוֶת, *'azmāweth;* Ἀσμώθ or Ἀζμώθ, *Asmôth* or *Azmôth,* "strong one of death"; Ezk **2** 24): Is probably identical with *el-Ḥizmā,* a village a little to the N. of *'Anātā* (Anathoth). It corresponds to Beth-azmaveth (Neh **7** 28).

AZMON, az'mon (עַצְמוֹן, *'açmōn;* Ἀσεμώνα, *Asemōna,* "strong"): On the S.W. border of Israel (Nu **34** 4.5; Josh **15** 4). Trumbull identifies it with *'Ain el-Qaseimeh,* N.W. of Kadesh Barnea (*Kad. Bar.,* 117, 289 f).

AZNOTH-TABOR, az'noth-tā'bor (אַזְנוֹת תָּבֹר, *'aznôth tābhōr,* "peaks of Tabor"): A place in western Naphtali, evidently in the vicinity of Mt. Tabor (Josh **19** 34). The exact locality is not known.

AZOR, ā'zor (Ἀζώρ, *Azôr,* "help"[?]): An ancestor of Jesus Christ (Mt **1** 13 f).

AZOTUS, a-zō'tus. See Ashdod (1 Macc **9** 15; Acts **8** 40).

AZRIEL, az'ri-el (עַזְרִיאֵל, *azrī'ēl,* "God's help"):
(1) One of the leading men of the half-tribe of Manasseh, E. of the Jordan, who with others of his tribe was carried captive by the king of Assyria (1 Ch **5** 24 ff).
(2) The father of Jerimoth of the tribe of Naphtali in the reign of King David (1 Ch **27** 19).
(3) The father of Seraiah, one of the officers sent by Jehoiakim to arrest Jeremiah and Baruch (Jer **36** 26).

AZRIKAM, az-rī'kam (עַזְרִיקָם, *'azrīḳām,* "my help has arisen"):

(1) A descendant of King David through Zerubbabel (1 Ch **3** 23).
(2) A prince of Judah in the time of Ahaz. He was slain by Zichri, an Ephraimite soldier (2 Ch **28** 7).
(3) One of Azel's sons, a Benjamite, descended from King Saul (1 Ch **8** 38; **9** 44).
(4) A Levite of the house of Merari and a resident of Jerus (1 Ch **9** 14; Neh **11** 15).

AZUBAH, a-zū'ba (עֲזוּבָה, *'ăzūbhāh,* "desolation"):
(1) A wife of Caleb, by whom she had three sons (1 Ch **2** 18 f).
(2) The daughter of Shilhi and mother of King Jehoshaphat (1 K **22** 42; 2 Ch **20** 31).

AZUR, ā'zur. See Azzur.

AZURAN, az'ū-ran, a-zū'ran. See Azaru.

AZZAH, az'a (עַזָּה, *'azzāh,* "strong"): AV form (Dt **2** 23; 1 K **4** 24; Jer **25** 20) for RV "Gaza."

AZZAN, az'an (עַזָּן, *'azzān,* "strong" or "thorn"): Father of Paltiel of the tribe of Issachar. One of the commissioners selected to divide the land between the tribes (Nu **34** 26).

AZZUR, az'ur (עַזּוּר, *'azzūr,* "helpful"):
(1) The father of Hananiah, a false prophet of Gibeon in the days of Zedekiah (Jer **28** 1 ff).
(2) One of those who, with Nehemiah, sealed the covenant on the return from Babylon (Neh **10** 17).
(3) The father of Jaazaniah, "one of" the princes of the people who gave wicked counsel to the city of Jerus (Ezk **11** 1 f). AV has "Azur" for (1) and (3), but the Heb form of (3) is עָזֻר, *'azur.*

B

BAAL, bā'al:
I. Name and Character of Baal
II. Attributes of Baal
III. Baal-Worship
IV. Temples, etc
V. Use of the Name
VI. Forms of Baal
　1. Baal-berith
　2. Baal-gad
　3. Baal-hamon
　4. Baal-hermon
　5. Baal-peor
　6. Baal-zebub

Baal (בַּעַל, *ba'al;* Βάαλ, *Báal,* or Βαάλ, *Baál*): The Bab Belu or Bel, "Lord," was the title of the supreme god among the Canaanites.

I. Name and Character of Baal.—In Babylonia it was the title specially applied to Merodach of Babylon, which in time came to be used in place of his actual name. As the word in Heb also means "possessor," it has been supposed to have originally signified, when used in a religious sense, the god of a particular piece of land or soil. Of this, however, there is no proof, and the sense of "possessor" is derived from that of "lord." The Bab Bel-Merodach was a Sun-god, and so too was the Can Baal whose full title was Baal-Shemaim, "lord of heaven." The Phoen writer Sanchuniathon (*Philo Byblius,* Fragmenta II) accordingly says that the children of the first generation of mankind "in time of drought stretched forth their hands to heaven toward the sun; for they regarded him as the sole Lord of heaven, and called him Beel-samēn, which means 'Lord of Heaven' in the Phoen language and is equivalent to Zeus in Gr." Baal-Shemaim had a temple at Umm el-Awāmid between Acre and Tyre,

and his name is found in inscriptions from the Phoen colonies of Sardinia and Carthage.

II. Attributes of Baal.—As the Sun-god, Baal was worshipped under two aspects, beneficent and destructive. On the one hand he gave light and warmth to his worshippers; on the other hand the fierce heats of summer destroyed the vegetation he had himself brought into being. Hence human victims were sacrificed to him in order to appease his anger in time of plague or other trouble, the victim being usually the first-born of the sacrificer and being burnt alive. In the OT this is euphemistically termed "passing" the victim "through the fire" (2 K **16** 3; **21** 6).

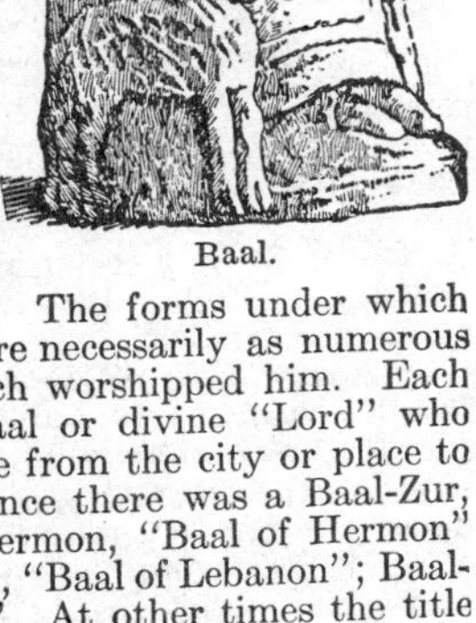

Baal.

The forms under which Baal was worshipped were necessarily as numerous as the communities which worshipped him. Each locality had its own Baal or divine "Lord" who frequently took his name from the city or place to which he belonged. Hence there was a Baal-Zur, "Baal of Tyre"; Baal-hermon, "Baal of Hermon" (Jgs **3** 3); Baal-Lebanon, "Baal of Lebanon"; Baal-Tarz, "Baal of Tarsus." At other times the title was attached to the name of an individual god; thus we have Bel-Merodach, "the Lord Merodach" (or "Bel is Merodach") at Babylon, Baal-Melkarth at Tyre, Baal-gad (Josh **11** 17) in the north of Palestine. Occasionally the second element was a noun as in Baal-Shemaim, "lord of heaven," Baal-zebub (2 K **1** 2), "Lord of flies," Baal-Hammān, usually interpreted "Lord of heat," but more probably "Lord of the sunpillar," the tutelary deity of Carthage. All these various forms of the Sun-god were collectively known as the Baalim or "Baals" who took their place by the side of the female Ashtaroth and Asherim. At Carthage the female consort of Baal was termed Penē-Baal, "the face" or "reflection of Baal."

III. Baal-Worship.—In the earlier days of Heb history the title Baal, or "Lord," was applied to the national God of Israel, a usage which was revived in later times, and is familiar to us in the AV. Hence both Jonathan and David had sons called Merib-baal (1 Ch **8** 34; **9** 40) and Beeliada (1 Ch **14** 7). After the time of Ahab, however, the name became associated with the worship and rites of the Phoen deity introduced into Samaria by Jezebel, and its idolatrous associations accordingly caused it to fall into disrepute. Ḥosea (**2** 16) declares that henceforth the God of Israel should no longer be called Baali, "my Baal," and personal names like Esh-baal (1 Ch **8** 33; **9** 39), and Beeliada into which it entered were changed in form, Baal being turned into *bōsheth* which in Heb at any rate conveyed the sense of "shame."

IV. Temples, etc.—Temples of Baal at Samaria and Jerus are mentioned in 1 K **16** 32; 2 K **11** 18; where they had been erected at the time when the Ahab dynasty endeavored to fuse Israelites and Jews and Phoenicians into a single people under the same national Phoen god. Altars on which incense was burned to Baal were set up in all the streets of Jerus according to Jeremiah (**11** 13), apparently on the flat roofs of the houses (Jer **32** 29); and the temple of Baal contained an image of the god in the shape of a pillar or Bethel (2 K **10** 26.27). In the reign of Ahab, Baal was served in Israel by 450 priests (1 K **18** 19), as well as by prophets (2 K **10** 19), and his worshippers wore special vestments when his ritual was performed (2 K **10** 22). The ordinary offering made to the god consisted of incense (Jer **7** 9) and burnt sacrifices; on extraordinary occasions the victim was human (Jer **19** 5). At times the priests worked themselves into a state of ecstasy, and dancing round the altar slashed themselves with knives (1 K **18** 26.28), like certain dervish orders in modern Islam.

V. Use of the Name.—In accordance with its signification the name of Baal is generally used with the definite art.; in the LXX this often takes the feminine form, αἰσχύνη (*aischúnē*) "shame" being intended to be read. We find the same usage in Rom **11** 4. The feminine counterpart of Baal was Baalah or Baalath which is found in a good many of the local names (see Baethgen, *Beiträge zur semitischen Religionsgeschichte*, 1888).

VI. Forms of Baal.—Baal-berith (בַּעַל בְּרִית, *ba'al b^erīth;* **Βααλβερίθ**, *Baalberíth*), "Covenant-Baal," was worshipped at Shechem after the death of Gideon (Jgs **8** 33; **9** 4). In Jgs **9** 46 the name is replaced by El-berith, "Covenant-god." The covenant was that made by the god with his worshippers, less probably between the Israelites and the native Canaanites.

1. Baal-berith

Baal-gad (בַּעַל גָּד, *ba'al gādh;* **Βαλαγάδα**, *Balagáda*), "Baal [lord] of good luck" (or "Baal is Gad") was the god of a town called after his name in the north of Pal, which has often been identified with Baalbek. The god is termed simply Gad in Isa **65** 11 RVm; where he is associated with Meni, the Assyr Manu (AV "troop" and "number").

2. Baal-gad

Baal-hamon (בַּעַל הָמוֹן, *ba'al hāmōn;* **Βεελαμών**, *Beelamṓn*) is known only from the fact that Solomon had a garden at a place of that name (Cant **8** 11). The name is usually explained to mean "Baal of the multitude," but the cuneiform tablets of the Tell el-Amarna age found in Pal show that the Egyp god Amon was worshipped in Canaan and identified there with the native Baal. We are therefore justified in reading the name Baal-Amon, a parallel to the Bab Bel-Merodach. The name has no connection with that of the Carthaginian deity Baal-hammān.

3. Baal-hamon

Baal-hermon (בַּעַל חֶרְמוֹן, *ba'al ḥermōn;* **Βαλαερμών**, *Balaermṓn*) is found in the name of "the mountain of Baal-hermon" (Jgs **3** 3; cf 1 Ch **5** 23), which also bore the names of Hermon, Sirion and Shenir (Saniru in the Assyr inscriptions), the second name being applied to it by the Phoenicians and the third by the Amorites (Dt **3** 9). Baal-hermon will consequently be a formation similar to Baal-Lebanon in an inscription from Cyprus; according to the Phoen writer Sanchuniathon (*Philo Byblius*, Fragmenta II) the third generation of men "begat sons of surprising size and stature, whose names were given to the mountains of which they had obtained possession."

4. Baal-hermon

Baal-peor (בַּעַל פְּעוֹר, *ba'al p^e'ōr;* **Βεελφεγώρ**, *Beelphegṓr*) was god of the Moabite mountains, who took his name from Mount Peor (Nu **23** 28), the modern Fa'ūr, and was probably a form of Chemosh (Jerome, *Comm.*, Isa **15**). The sensual rites with which he was worshipped (Nu **25** 1–3) indicate his connection with the Phoen Baal.

5. Baal-peor

Baal-zebub (בַּעַל זְבוּב, *ba'al z^ebhūbh;* **Βααλμυία Θεός**, *Baalmuía Theós* ("Baal the fly god") was worshipped at Ekron where he had a famous oracle (2 K **1** 2.3.16). The name is generally tr^d "the Lord of flies," the Sun-god being associated with the flies which swarm in Pal during the earlier summer months. It is met with in Assyr inscriptions. In the NT the name assumes the form of Beelzebul (βεελζεβούλ), in AV BEELZEBUB (q.v.).

6. Baal-zebub

A. H. SAYCE

BAAL, bā'al (בַּעַל, *ba'al*, "lord," "master," "possessor"):

(1) A descendant of Reuben, Jacob's first-born son, and the father of Beerah, prince of the Reubenites, "whom Tiglath-pileser (1 Ch **5** 5.6) king of Assyria carried away captive."

(2) The fourth of ten sons of Jeiel (AV "Jehiel"), father and founder of Gibeon. His mother was Maacah; his brother Kish father of Saul (1 Ch **8** 29 f; **9** 35.36.39; cf 1 S **14** 50 f). These passages identify Jeiel and Abiel as the father of Kish and thus of Baal. For study of confusions in the genealogical record, in 1 Ch **9** 36.39, see NER; KISH; ABIEL; JEIEL.

(3) In composition often the name of a man and not of the heathen god, e.g. Baal-hanan, a king of Edom (Gen **36** 38; 1 Ch **1** 49); also a royal prefect of the same name (1 Ch **27** 28). Gesenius thinks that Baal in compound words rarely refers to the god by that name. See BAAL (deity).

(4) A city of the tribe of Simeon (1 Ch **4** 33). See BAALATH-BEER.

DWIGHT M. PRATT

BAAL (בַּעַל, *ba'al;* **Βάαλ**, *Báal*): 1 Ch **4** 33. See BAALATH-BEER.

BAALAH, bā'a-la (בַּעֲלָה, *ba'ălāh;* "possessor," "mistress"): Three occurrences of this name:

(1) = KIRIATH-JEARIM (q.v.) (Josh **15** 9.10; 1 Ch **13** 6).

(2) A city in the Negeb of Judah (Josh **15** 29). In Josh **19** 3 Balah and in 1 Ch **4** 29 Bilhah; perhaps also Bealoth of Josh **15** 24. The site is unknown; but see *PEF*, III, 26.

(3) Mount Baalah (Josh **15** 11), a mountain ridge between Shikkeron (Ekron) and Jabneel unless, as seems probable, the suggestion of M. Clermont-Ganneau (*Rev. Crit*, 1897, 902) is correct that for הר, *har* (="mount"), we should read נהר, *nāhār* ("river"). In this case the border in question would be the *Nahr rubîn.* Here there is an annual feast held—attended by all classes and famous all over Syria—which appears to be a real survival of "Baal worship."

E. W. G. MASTERMAN

BAALATH, bā'a-lath (בַּעֲלָת, *ba'ălāth;* A, **Βααλών**, *Baalṓn*):

(1) A town on the border of Dan (Josh **19** 44) associated with Eltekeh and Gibbethon—possibly *Bela'în.*

(2) ("Mistress-ship"): A store city of Solomon, mentioned with Beth-horon (1 K **9** 18; 2 Ch **8** 6) and possibly the same as (1).

BAALATH-BEER, bā'a-lath-bē'ēr (בַּעֲלַת בְּאֵר, *ba'ălath b^e'ēr*, "lady [mistress] of the well"; Josh **19** 8 [in 1 Ch **4** 33, Baal]): In Josh this place is designated "Ramah of the South," i.e. of the Negeb, while in 1 S **30** 27 it is described as Ramoth of the Negeb. It must have been a prominent hill (*rāmāh*="height") in the far south of the Negeb and near a well (*b^e'ēr*). The site is unknown though Conder suggests that the shrine *Kubbet el Baul* may retain the old name.

BAALBEK, bäl'bek, bäl-bek'. See AVEN; ON.

BAAL-BERITH, bā-al-bē'rith (בַּעַל בְּרִית, *ba'al b^erīth* ="Baal of the Covenant"): An idol worshipped by the Shechemites after Gideon's death (Jgs **8** 33), as protector and guardian of engagements. His temple is also referred to in Jgs **9** 4. See BAAL (1).

BAALE-JUDAH, bā'al-ē-jōō'da. See KIRIATH-JEARIM.

BAAL-GAD, bā'al-gad (בַּעַל גָּד, *ba'al gādh;* **Βαλαγαδά**, *Balagadá*, **Βαλγάδ**, *Balgád*): Joshua in his conquest reached as far north as Baal-gad in the valley of Lebanon, under Mount Hermon (Josh **11** 17). This definitely locates it in the valley between the Lebanons, to the W. or N.W. of Hermon. It must not be confused with Baal-hermon. Conder thinks it may be represented by *'Ain Jedeideh.*

BAAL-HAMON, bā-al-hā'mon. See BAAL (1).

BAAL-HANAN, bā-al-hā'nan (בַּעַל חָנָן, *ba'al ḥānān*, "the Lord is gracious"):

(1) A king of Edom (Gen **36** 38 f; 1 Ch **1** 49 f).

(2) A gardener in the service of David (1 Ch **27** 28).

BAAL-HAZOR, bā-al-hā'zor (בַּעַל חָצוֹר, *ba'al ḥāçōr;* **Βαιλασώρ**, *Bailasṓr*, **Βελλασώρ**, *Bel-la-sṓr*): A place on the property of Absalom where his sheep-shearers were gathered, beside Ephraim (2 S **13** 23). The sheep-shearing was evidently the occasion of a festival which was attended by Absalom's brethren. Here he compassed the death of Amnon in revenge for the outrage upon his sister. The place may be identified with *Tell 'Aṣūr*, a mountain which rises 3,318 ft. above the sea, 4 miles N.E. of Bethel.

BAAL-HERMON, bā'al-hûr'mon (בַּעַל חֶרְמוֹן, *ba'al ḥermōn;* **Βαὰλ Ἑρμών**, *Baál Ermṓn*): Baal-gad under Mount Hermon is described as "toward the sunrising" in Josh **13** 5. If Mount Lebanon proper is here intended the reading may be taken as correct. But in Jgs **3** 3 Baal-gad is replaced by Baal-hermon. One or the other must be due to a scribal error. The Baal-hermon of 1 Ch **5** 23 lay somewhere E. of the Jordan, near to Mount Hermon. It may possibly be identical with *Bāniās.*

BAALI, bā'a-lī (בַּעֲלִי, *ba'ălī*, "my master"): Baal, a common name for all heathen gods, had in common practice been used also of Jeh. Hosea (**2** 16.17) demands that Jeh be no longer called *Ba'ălī* ("my Baal"="my lord") but *'Ishī* ("my husband"), and we find that later the Israelites abandoned the use of *Ba'al* for Jeh.

BAALIM, bā'a-lim (הַבְּעָלִים, *ha-b^e'ālīm*): Plur. of BAAL (q.v.).

BAALIS, bā'a-liṣ (בַּעֲלִיס, *ba'līṣ*, perhaps for Baalim, "gods"; LXX **Βελεισά**, *Beleisá*, **Βελισά**, *Belisá*, **Βααλίς**, *Baalís; Ant*, X, ix, 3, **Βαάλιμος**, *Baálimos*): King of the children of Ammon, the instigator of the murder of Gedaliah (Jer **40** 14). Cf *Ant*, X, ix, 3.

BAAL-MEON, bā'al-mē'on (בַּעַל מְעוֹן, *ba'al m^e'ōn;* **Βεελμεών**, *Beelmeṓn*): A town built by the children of Reuben along with Nebo, "their names being changed" (Nu **32** 38), identical with Beon of ver 3. As Beth-baal-meon it was given by Moses to the tribe of Reuben (Josh **13** 17). Mesha names it as fortified by him (MS, l. 9). It appears in Jer **48** 23 as Beth-meon, one of the cities of Moab. *Onom* speaks of it as a large village near the hot springs, i.e. Callirrhoe, in *Wādy Zerḳā Ma'in*, 9 miles from Heshbon. This points to the ruined site of *Ma'în*, about 4 miles S.W. of *Madeba.* The ruins now visible however are not older than Rom times.

W. EWING

BAAL-PEOR, bā-al-pē'or. See BAAL (1).

BAAL-PERAZIM, bā-al-pē-rā'zim, bā-al-per'a-zim (בַּעַל־פְּרָצִים, *ba'al p^erāçīm;* **Βααλ'φαρασεῖν**, *Baal'pharaseín*, "the lord of breakings through"): The spot in or near the Valley of Rephaim where David obtained a signal victory over the Philis; it was higher than Jerus for David asked, "Shall I go up against the Philis?" (2 S **5** 20; 1 Ch **14** 11). The exact site is unknown, but if the Vale of Rephaim is *el Beka'a*, the open valley between Jerus and Mar Elias, then Baal-perazim would probably be the mountains to the E. near what is called the "Mount of Evil Counsel" (see JERUSALEM). The Mount Perazim of Isa **28** 21 would appear to be the same spot.

E. W. G. MASTERMAN

BAALSAMUS, bā-al'sa-mus (**Βαάλσαμος**, *Baálsamos;* AV **Balasamus**): B. stood at the right side of Ezra, when the law was read to the people (1 Esd **9** 43). Cf Maaseiah (Neh **8** 7).

BAAL-SHALISHAH, bā-al-shal'i-sha, ba-al-sha-lē'sha (בַּעַל שָׁלִשָׁה, *ba'al shālīshāh;* **Βαιθσαρισά**, *Baithsarisá*): Whence a man came to Gilgal with first-fruits (2 K **4** 42) was probably not far from the latter place. According to the Talm (*Ṣanh.* 12*a*) the fruits of the earth nowhere ripened so quickly.

It is called by Eusebius Baithsarith (Jerome "Bethsalisa"), and located 15 miles N. of Diospolis (Lydda). *Khirbet Sirīsiā* almost exactly fits this description. Gilgal (*Jiljūlieh*) lies in the plain about 4½ miles to the N.W. *Khirbet Kefr Thilth*, 3½ miles farther north, has also been suggested. The Arab. *Thilth* exactly corresponds to the Heb *Shālī-shāh.* W. Ewing

BAAL-TAMAR, bā-al-tā'mar (בַּעַל תָּמָר, *ba'al tāmār;* **Βαὰλ Θαμάρ,** *Baál Thamár,* "Baal of the palm tree"): Evidently a seat of heathen worship (Jgs **20** 33) between Bethel and Gibeah (cf vs 18.31). The place was known to Eusebius (*Onom* s.v.), but all trace of the name is now lost. Conder suggests that it may be connected with the palm tree of Deborah (Jgs **4** 5) which was between Bethel and Ramah (*HDB*, s.v.).

BAALZEBUB, bā-al-zē'bub (בַּעַל זְבוּב, *ba'al zebhūbh* = "Lord of flies"; **Βάαλ-μυῖαν,** *Báal-muian*): A deity worshipped by the Philis at Ekron (2 K **1** 2. 3.6.16). All that can be gathered from this one reference to him in ancient lit. is that he had some fame as a god that gave oracles. Ahaziah, son of Ahab, and king of Israel, went to consult him whether he should recover of his sickness, and was therefore rebuked by Elijah, who declared that his death would be the result of this insult to Jeh. Why he was called "lord of flies," or whether his real name has not been corrupted and lost are matters of conjecture. See Baal (1).

BAAL-ZEPHON, bā-al-zē'fon (בַּעַל צְפוֹן, *ba'al çephōn;* **Βεελσεπφῶν,** *Beelsepphôn;* Ex **14** 2. 9; Nu **33** 7): The name means "Lord of the North," and the place was opposite the Heb camp, which was between Migdol and the sea. It may have been the shrine of a Sem deity, but the position is unknown (see Exodus). Goodwin (see Brugsch, *Hist. Egt.*, II, 363) found the name *Baali-Zapuna* as that of a god mentioned in an Egyp papyrus in the British Museum.

BAANA, bā'a-na (OT and Apoc; **Βαανά,** *Baaná;* בַּעֲנָא, *ba'ănā',* "son of oppression"):

(1, 2) Two commissariat-officers in the service of Solomon (1 K **4** 12; **4** 16; AV "Baanah").

(3) Father of Zadok, the builder (Neh **3** 4).

(4) A leader who returned with Zerubbabel to Jerus (1 Esd **5** 8). Cf Baanah (Ezr **2** 2; Neh **7** 7; **10** 27).

BAANAH, bā'a-na (בַּעֲנָה, *ba'ănāh,* "son of oppression"):

(1) Captain in the army of Ish-bosheth (2 S **4** 2 ff).

(2) Father of Heleb, one of David's mighty men (2 S **23** 29; 1 Ch **11** 30).

(3) Returned with Zerubbabel to Jerus; a leader and one who sealed the covenant (Ezr **2** 2; Neh **7** 7; **10** 27). See Baana (4).

BAANI, bā'a-nī (A, **Βαανί,** *Baaní;* B, **Βαανεί,** *Baaneí;* AV **Maani** = Bani [Ezr **10** 34]): The descendants of B. put away their "strange wives" (1 Esd **9** 34).

BAANIAS, bā-a-nī'as. See Banneas (Apoc).

BAARA, bā'a-ra (בַּעֲרָא, *ba'ărā',* "the burning one"): A wife of the Benjamite Shaharaim (1 Ch **8** 8).

BAASEIAH, bā-a-sī'a, bā-a-sē'ya (בַּעֲשֵׂיָה, *ba'ăsēyāh,* "the Lord is bold"): Perhaps for מַעֲשֵׂיָה, *ma'ăsēyāh,* after the Gr **Μαασαί,** B, *Maasaí,* "the work of the Lord." Cf *HPN*, 293. An ancestor of Asaph, the musician (1 Ch **6** 40).

BAASHA, bā'a-sha (בַּעְשָׁא, *ba'shā',* "boldness"): King of Israel. B., son of Ahijah, and of common birth (1 K **16** 2), usurped the throne of Nadab, the son of Jeroboam, killed Nadab and exterminated the house of Jeroboam. He carried on a long warfare with Asa, the king of Judah (cf Jer **41** 9), began to build Ramah, but was prevented from completing this work by Ben-hadad, the king of Syria. He is told by the prophet Jehu that because of his sinful reign the fate of his house would be like that of Jeroboam. B. reigned 24 years. His son Elah who succeeded him and all the members of his family were murdered by the usurper Zimri (1 K **15** 16 ff; **16** 1 ff; 2 Ch **16** 1 ff). The fate of his house is referred to in 1 K **21** 22; 2 K **9** 9. Cf Asa; Elah; Zimri. A. L. Breslich

BABBLER, bab'lẽr (בַּעַל הַלָּשׁוֹן, *ba'al ha-lāshōn;* AV of Eccl **10** 11 lit. "master of the tongue"; RV CHARMER; **λαπιστής,** *lapistḗs,* AV of Ecclus **20** 7; RV BRAGGART; **σπερμολόγος,** *spermológos;* AV and RV of Acts **17** 18): The latter Gr word is used of birds, such as the crow, that live by picking up small seeds (*spérma,* "a seed," *légein,* "to gather"), and of men, for "hangers on" and "parasites" who obtained their living by picking up odds and ends off merchants' carts in harbors and markets. It carries the "suggestion of picking up refuse and scraps, and in lit. of plagiarism without the capacity to use correctly" (Ramsay). The Athenian philosophers in calling Paul a *spermologos,* or "ignorant plagiarist," meant that he retailed odds and ends of knowledge which he had picked up from others, without possessing himself any system of thought or skill of language—without culture. In fact it was a fairly correct description of the Athenian philosophers themselves in Paul's day.

Ramsay, *St. Paul the Traveller and Roman Citizen,* 141 ff. T. Rees

BABBLING, bab'ling (שִׂיחַ, *sī^ah;* RV COMPLAINING): The consequence of tarrying long at the wine (Prov **23** 29 AV); λαλία, *lalía,* RV "talk" (Ecclus **19** 6; **20** 5 AV); κενοφωνία, *kenophōnía,* lit. "making an empty sound" (1 Tim **6** 20; 2 Tim **2** 16 AV and RV).

BABE, bāb:

(1) (נַעַר, *na'ar;* **παῖς,** *país*) of a male infant 3 months old (Ex **2** 6) tr^d elsewhere "boy" or "lad."

(2) (עוֹלֵל, *'ōlēl,* תַּעֲלוּלִים, *ta'ălūlīm*) in the general sense of "child" (Ps **8** 2; **17** 14; Isa **3** 4).

(3) (**βρέφος,** *bréphos*) an unborn or newborn child (AV and RV of Lk **1** 41.44; **2** 12.16; 1 Pet **2** 2 and RV of Lk **18** 15 [AV "infants"]; Acts **7** 19 [AV "young children"] and 2 Tim **3** 15 [AV "child"]).

(4) (**νήπιος,** *nēpios* = Lat *infans*) "a child that cannot speak." (AV and RV of Mt **11** 25; **21** 16; Lk **10** 21; Rom **2** 20; 1 Cor **3** 1; He **5** 13) the same word is tr^d "child," plur. "children" (in AV and RV of 1 Cor **13** 11; Gal **4** 1.3; Eph **4** 14) the vb. *nēpiázete* is tr^d in AV "be ye children" and in RV "be ye babes" (1 Cor **14** 20). *Nēpios* is used **metaphorically** of those who are like children, of simple and single minds, as opposed to the "wise and understanding" (Mt **11** 25 = Lk **10** 21; cf 1 Cor **14** 20). "Babes in Christ" are men of little spiritual growth, carnal as opposed to spiritual (1 Cor **3** 1; cf He **5** 13; Eph **4** 14). *Nēpios* is also used of a child as a *minor* or *infant* in the eye of the law (Gal **4** 1.3). T. Rees

BABEL, bā'bel, **BABYLON,** bab'i-lon (Topographical): Babylon was the Gr name of the city written in the cuneiform script of the Babylonians, *bab-ili,* which means in Sem, "the gate of god." The Hebrews called the country, as well as the city, *Bābhel.* This name they considered came from the root, *bālal,* "to confound" (Gen **11** 9). The name in Sumerian ideographs was written *Din-tir,* which means "life of the forest," and yet ancient etymologists explained it as meaning "place of the seat of life" (*shubat balâṭe*). *Ka-dingirra,* which also means "gate of god," was another form of the name in Sumerian. It was also called *Su-anna* (which is of uncertain meaning) and *Uru-azagga,* "the holy city."

Mound Covering Nippur Tower.

Herodotus, the Gr historian, has given us a picture of Babylon in his day. He says that the city was a great square, 42 miles in circuit. Ctesias makes it 56 miles. This, he writes, was surrounded by a moat or rampart 300 ft. high, and 75 ft. broad. The earliest mention of Babylon is in the time of Sargon I, about 2700 BC. That monarch laid the foundations of the temple of Anunit, and also those of the temple of Amal. In the time of Dungi we learn that the place was sacked. The city evidently played a very unimportant part in the political history of Babylonia of the early period, for besides these references it is almost unknown until the time of Ḥammurabi, when its rise brought about a new epoch in the history of Babylonia. The seat of power was then transferred permanently from the southern states. This resulted in the closing of the political history of the Sumerians. The organization of the empire by Ḥammurabi, with Babylon as its capital, placed it in a position from which it was never dislodged during the remaining history of Babylonia.

The mounds covering the ancient city have frequently been explored, but systematic excavations of the city were not undertaken until 1899, when Koldewey, the German excavator, began to uncover its ancient ruins in a methodical manner. In spite of what ancient writers say, certain scholars maintain that they grossly exaggerated the size of the city, which was comparatively small, especially when considered in connection with large cities of the present era.

In the northern part of the city there was situated what is called the North Palace on the east side of the Euphrates, which passed through the city. A little distance below this point the Arakhtu canal left the Euphrates, and passing through the southern wall rejoined the river. There was also a Middle and Southern Palace. Near the latter was located the Ishtar gate. The temple E-makh was close to the east side of the gate. Other canals in the city were called Merodach and Libilkhegala. In the southern portion of the city was located the famous temple E-sag-ila. This fane was called by the Gr historian, "the temple of Belus." Marduk or Merodach (as written in the OT), the patron deity of the city, received from Enlil, as Ḥammurabi informs us, after he had driven the Elamites out of Babylonia, the title *bêl matâte,* "lord of lands," not the name which Enlil of Nippur had possessed. In the past there has been a confusion. The ideogram Enlil or Ellil had been incorrectly read *Bel.* This necessitated speaking of the old Bel and the young Bel. Beyond being called *bêl,* "lord," as all other gods were called, Enlil's name was not Bel. Marduk is the Bel of the OT, as well as the god called Bel in the Assyr and Bab inscriptions.

The temple area included an outer, central and inner court. The shrine of Ishtar and Zamama occupied the central court, and the ziggurrat the inner court. In the temple proper, the shrine Ekua was located, in which stood the golden image of Marduk. This, the ancient writers say, was 40 ft. high. On the topmost stage there was a shrine dedicated to Marduk. It is assumed that it was 50 ft. long by 70 ft. broad and 50 ft. in height.

Nabopolassar rebuilt the temple and its tower. Nebuchadrezzar enlarged and embellished the sanctuary. He raised the tower so that "its head was in the heavens," an expression found in the story of the Tower of Babel in Gen, as well as in many of the building inscriptions. See *LOTB,* 121 ff, and the art. on Babel, Tower of.

One of the chief works of Nebuchadrezzar was the building of Aiburshabu, the famous procession street of the city, which extended from the Ishtar gate to E-sag-ila. It was a great and magnificent causeway, built higher than the houses. Walls lined it on either side, which were decorated with

Building Inscription of Nebuchadrezzar II.

glazed tiles, portraying lions, life size in relief. The pavement was laid with blocks of stone brought from the mountains. This procession street figured prominently on the New Year's festal day, when the procession of the gods took place.

A knowledge of the work Nebuchadrezzar did serves as a fitting commentary to the passage in

Dnl **4** 30: "Is not this great Babylon, which I have built?" He had made the city one of the wonders of the world.

The two sieges by Darius Hystaspes and the one by Xerxes destroyed much of the beauty of the city. Alexander desired to make it again a great center and to build an immense fortress in the city; but in the midst of this undertaking he was murdered, while living in the palace of Nebuchadrezzar. The temple, though frequently destroyed, was in existence in the time of the Seleucids, but the city had long since ceased to be of any importance. See also BABYLONIA.

A. T. CLAY

BABEL, BABYLON (בָּבֶל, *bābhēl;* Assyro-Bab *Bâb-îli, Bâb-îlâni,* "gate of god," or "of the gods," rendered in Sumerian as *Ka-dingira,* "gate of god," regarded as a folk-etymology): (See BABEL, TOWER OF, sec. 14.)

1. Names by Which the City Was Known
2. Probable Date of Its Foundation
3. Its Walls and Gates from Herodotus
4. Its Position, Divisions, Streets and Temple
5. The Works of Semiramis and Nitocris
6. Ctesias' Description—the Palaces and Their Decorated Walls
7. The Temple of Belus and the Hanging Gardens
8. Other Descriptions
9. Nebuchadrezzar's Account
10. Nebuchadrezzar's Architectural Work at Babylon
11. The Royal Palaces
12. Quick Building
13. The Temples Restored by Nebuchadrezzar
14. The Extent of Nebuchadrezzar's Architectural Work
15. Details Concerning the City from Contract-Tablets
16. Details Concerning Babylon from Other Sources
17. Modern Exploration
18. Description of the Ruins—the Eastern Walls
19. The Western Walls
20. The Palaces
21. The Site of Babylon's Great Tower
22. The Central and Southern Ruins
23. A Walk through Babylon
24. The Ištar-Gate and the Middle Palace
25. The Festival-Street
26. The Chamber of the Fates
27. The Northern Palace and the Gardens
28. Historical References to Babylonian Buildings

LITERATURE

1. Names by Which the City Was Known

The name of the great capital of ancient Babylonia, the Shinar of Gen **10** 10; **14** 1, other names of the city being *Tin-dir,* "seat of life," *Ê* (*ki*), probably an abbreviation of *Êridu* (*ki*) "the good city" (=Paradise), Babylonia having seemingly been regarded as the Garden of Eden (*PSBA,* June 1911, p. 161); and *Šu-anna,* "the high-handed" (meaning, apparently, "high-walled," "hand" and "defense" being interchangeable terms). It is possible that these various names are due to the incorporation of outlying districts as Babylon grew in size.

2. Probable Date of Its Foundation

According to Gen **10** 9, the founder of Babylon was Nimrod, but among the Babylonians, it was Merodach who built the city, together with Erech and Niffer (Calneh) and their renowned temples. The date of its foundation is unknown, but it certainly went back to primitive times, and Babylon may even have equaled Niffer in antiquity (the American explorers of that site have estimated that its lowest strata of habitations go back to 8,000 years BC). Babylon's late assumption of the position of capital of the country would therefore be due to its rulers not having attained power and influence at an earlier period. Having once acquired that position, however, it retained it to the end, and its great god, Merodach, became the head of the Bab pantheon—partly through the influence of Babylon as capital, partly because the city was the center of his worship, and the place of the great Tower of Babel, concerning which many wonderful things were said. See BABEL, TOWER OF; CONFUSION OF TONGUES.

3. Its Walls and Gates from Herodotus

According to Herodotus, the city, which lay in a great plain, was square in its plan and measured 120 furlongs (*stadia*) each way—480 in all. Each side was therefore about 14 miles long, making a circuit of nearly 56 miles, and an area of nearly 196 sq. miles. As the space inclosed is so great, and traces of the walls would seem to be wanting, these figures may be regarded as open to question. Around the city, Herodotus says, there was a deep and broad moat full of water, and then came a wall 50 royal cubits thick and 200 cubits high, pierced by 100 gateways with brazen gates and lintels. Reckoning the cubit at 18⅔ in., this would mean that Babylon's walls were no less than 311 ft. high; and regarding the royal cubit as being equal to 21 in., their thickness would be something like 87 ft. Notwithstanding that Babylon has been the quarry of the neighboring builders for two millenniums, it is surprising that such extensive masses of brickwork should have disappeared without leaving at least a few recognizable traces.

4. Its Position, Divisions, Streets and Temple

The city was built on both sides of the Euphrates, and at the point where the wall met the river there was a return-wall running along its banks, forming a rampart. The houses of Babylon were of 3 and 4 stories. The roads which ran through the city were straight, and apparently intersected each other at right angles, like the great cities of America. The river-end of each of the streets leading to the river was guarded by a brazen gate. Within the great outer wall was another, not much weaker, but inclosing a smaller space. Each division of the city contained a great building, the one being the king's palace, strongly fortified around, and the other the temple of Zeus Belos—an erection with brazen gates measuring two furlongs each way. Within this sacred precinct was a solid tower measuring a furlong each way, and surmounted by other towers to the number of eight. An ascent ran around these towers, with a stopping-place about the middle where the visitor might rest. Upon the topmost tower a large cell was built, wherein was a couch and a golden table. No image was placed in the cell, and no one passed the night there, except a woman of the people, chosen by the god. In another cell below was a golden image of Zeus sitting, his seat and footstool being likewise of gold, with, near by, a large golden table. The total weight of the precious metal here was 800 talents. Upon a small golden altar outside the cell young sucklings only were sacrificed, and upon another (not of gold) full-grown animals were offered.

5. The Works of Semiramis and Nitocris

The hydraulic works of Babylon are attributed by Herodotus to two queens, Semiramis and Nitocris. The former made banks of earth on the plain which were worth seeing, preventing the river from flooding the plain like a sea. The second, Nitocris, altered the channel of the river in such a way that it flowed three times in its course to the village Andericca, and the traveler by water therefore took three days to pass this spot. She also raised the banks of the river, and dug a great lake above Babylon. The place which was dug out she made into a swamp, the object being to retard the course of the river. The many bends and the swamp were on the shortest route to Media, to prevent the Medes from having dealings with her kingdom and learning of her affairs. Other works were a bridge across the Euphrates, and a tomb for herself over the most frequented gate of the city.

Both Herodotus and Ctesias were eyewitnesses

of the glory of Babylon, though only at the period when it had begun to wane. It is exceedingly probable, however, that their accounts will be superseded in the end, by those of the people who best knew the city, namely, the inhabitants of Babylon itself.

6. Ctesias' Description—the Palaces and Their Decorated Walls

According to Ctesias, the circuit of the city was not 480, but 360 furlongs—the number of the days in the Bab year—and somewhat under 42 miles. The E. and W. districts were joined by a bridge 5 furlongs or 1,080 yards long, and 30 ft. broad. At each end of the bridge was a royal palace, that on the eastern bank being the more magnificent of the two. This palace was defended by three walls, the outermost being 60 furlongs or 7 miles in circuit; the second, a circular wall, 40 furlongs (4½ miles), and the third 20 furlongs (2½ miles). The height of the middle wall was 300 ft., and that of its towers 420 ft., but this was exceeded by the height of the inmost wall. Ctesias states that the walls of the second and third inclosures were of colored brick, showing hunting-scenes—the chase of the leopard and the lion, with male and female figures, which he regarded as Ninus and Semiramis. The other palace (that on the W. bank) was smaller and less ornate, and was inclosed only by a single wall 30 furlongs (3½ miles) in circuit. This also had representations of hunting-scenes and bronze statues of Ninus, Semiramis and Jupiter-Belus (Bel-Merodach). Besides the bridge, he states that there was also a tunnel under the river. He seems to speak of the temple of Belus (see BABEL, TOWER OF) as being surmounted by three statues—Bel (Bel-Merodach), 40 ft. high, his mother Rhea (Dawkina, the Dauké of Damascius), and Bel-Merodach's spouse Juno or Beltis (Zēr-panîtu^{m}). The celebrated Hanging Gardens he seems to describe as a square of which each side measured 400 ft., rising in terraces, the topmost of which was planted with trees of various kinds. If this was the case, it must have resembled a temple-tower covered with verdure. The Assyr sculptures, however, indicate something different (see sec. 27).

7. The Temple of Belus and the Hanging Gardens

8. Other Descriptions

With regard to the size of the city as given by other authorities, Pliny copies Herodotus, and makes its circuit 480 furlongs (*Nat. Hist.* vi.26); Strabo (xvi.i. sec. 5), 385; Q. Curtius (v.i. sec. 26), 368; Clitarchus (*apud Diod. Sic.* ii.7), 365. Though the difference between the highest and the lowest is considerable, it is only what might be expected from independent estimates, for it is doubtful whether any of them are based on actual measurements. Diodorus (ii.9, end) states that but a small part of the inclosure was inhabited in his time (he was a contemporary of Caesar and Augustus), but the abandonment of the city must then have been practically completed, and the greater part given over, as he states, to cultivation—even, perhaps, within the space inclosed by the remains of walls today. It is noteworthy that Q. Curtius says (v.i. sec. 27) that as much as nine-tenths consisted, even during Babylon's most prosperous period, of gardens, parks, paradises, fields and orchards; and this the later contract-tablets confirm. Though there is no confirmation of the height of the walls as given by these different authorities, the name given to the city, *Šu-anna*, "the high walled" (see above), indicated that it was renowned for the height of its defensive structures.

9. Nebuchadrezzar's Account

Among the native accounts of the city, that of Nebuchadrezzar is the best and most instructive. From this record it would seem that there were two principal defensive structures, *Imgur-Enlil* and *Nêmitti-Enlil*—"Enlil has been gracious" and "Enlil's foundation" respectively. The construction of these, which protected the inner city only, on the eastern and western sides of the Euphrates, he attributes to his father Nabonidus, as well as the digging of the moat, with the two "strong walls" on its banks, and the embankment of the Araḫtu canal. He had also lined the Euphrates with quays or embankments—probably the structures to which the Gr writers refer—but he had not finished the work. Within Babylon itself he made a roadway from Du-azaga, the place where the fates were declared, to Aa-ibur-šabû, Babylon's festival-street, which lay by the gate of Beltis or Maḫ, for the great New-Year's festival of Merodach and the gods.

10. Nebuchadrezzar's Architectural Work at Babylon

Nebuchadrezzar, after his accession, completed the two great walls, lined the ditches with brick, and increased the thickness of the two walls which his father had built. He also built a wall, traces of which are apparently extant, on the W. side of Babylon (he apparently refers to what may be called the "city," in contradistinction to "greater Babylon"), and raised the level of Aa-ibur-šabû from the "holy gate" to the gate of Nanâ; together with the gateways (in consequence of the higher level of the pathway) through which it passed. The gates themselves were constructed of cedar overlaid with copper (bronze), most likely in the same manner as the gates of Imgur-Bêl (Balawat) in Assyria (reign of Shalmaneser II, cir 850 BC). Probably none of Babylon's gates were of solid bronze, notwithstanding the statements of Herodotus; but the thresholds were wholly of that metal, stone being very rare, and perhaps less durable. These gates were guarded by images of bulls and giant serpents or composite dragons of the same metal. Nebuchadrezzar also built a wall on the E. bank of the river, 4,000 cubits distant, "high like a mountain," to prevent the approach of an enemy. This wall also had cedar gates covered with copper. An additional defense made by him was an enormous lake, "like unto the broad sea to cross," which was kept in by embankments.

11. The Royal Palaces

The royal palaces next claimed the great king's attention. The palace in which Nabopolassar had lived, and wherein, in all probability, Nebuchadrezzar had passed his younger days, had suffered from the floods when the river was high. The foundations of this extensive edifice, which extended from the wall called Imgur-Enlil to Lîbil-ḫêgala, the eastern canal, and from the banks of the Euphrates to Aa-ibur-šabû, the festival-street, were thoroughly repaired with burnt brick and bitumen, and the doorways, which had become too low in consequence of the raising of that street, were raised to a suitable height. He caused the whole to tower aloft, as he has it, "mountainlike" (suggesting a building more than one story high). The roof of this palace was built of cedar, and the doors were of the same wood covered with bronze. Their thresholds, as in other cases, were bronze, and the interior of the palace was decorated with gold, silver, precious stones and other costly material.

Four hundred and ninety cubits from Nêmitti-Enlil lay, as the king says, the principal wall, Imgur-Enlil, and in order to guarantee the former against attack, he built two strong embankments, and an outer wall "like a mountain," with a great building between which served both as a fortress and a palace, and attached to the old palace built by his father. According to Nebuchadrezzar's account, which is confirmed by Berosus (as quoted by Jos and Eusebius), all this work was completed in 15 days. The decorations were like those of the other palace, and blocks of alabaster, brought, apparently, from Assyria, strengthened the battlements. Other defences surrounded this stronghold.

12. Quick Building

Among the temples which Nebuchadrezzar restored or rebuilt may be mentioned Ê-kua, the shrine of Merodach within Ê-sagila (the temple of Belus); the sanctuary called Du-azaga, the place of fate, where, on every New-Year's festival, on the 8th and 9th of Nisan, "the king of the gods of heaven and earth" was placed, and the future of the Bab monarch and his people declared. Every whit as important as Ê-sagila, however, was the restoration of Ê-temen-an-ki, called "the Tower of Babylon" (see Babel, Tower of), within the city; and connected, as will be seen from the plan, with that structure. Among the numerous temples of Babylon which he rebuilt or restored were Ê-maḫ, for the goddess Nin-maḫ, near the Ištar-gate; the white limestone temple for Sin, the Moon-god; Ê-ditur-kalama, "the house of the judge of the land," for Šamaš, the Sun-god; Ê-sa-tila for Gula, the goddess of healing; Ê-ḫursag-ella, "the house of the holy mountain," etc.

13. The Temples Restored by Nebuchadrezzar

The amount of work accomplished by this king, who, when walking on the roof of his palace, lifted up with pride, exclaimed "Is not this great Babylon, which I have built?" (Dnl **4** 30), was, according to his own records and the Gr writers, enormous, and the claim he made fully justified. But if he boasts of the work he did, he is just in attributing much to his father Nabopolassar; though in connection with this it is to be noted that his ascribing the building of the walls of Babylon to his father is not to be taken literally—in all probability he only restored them, though he may have added supplementary defences, as Nebuchadrezzar himself did.

14. The Extent of Nebuchadrezzar's Architectural Work

Besides Nebuchadrezzar's inscriptions, various other texts give details concerning the topography of Babylon, among them being the contract-tablets, which mention various districts or quarters of the city, such as Tê which is within Babylon; the city of Sula which is within Babylon; the new city which is within Babylon, upon the new canal. Within the city were also several *Ḫuṣṣêtu*—perhaps "farms," such as *Ḫuṣṣêtu ša Iddina-Marduk*, "Iddina-Marduk's farm," etc. The various gates are also referred to, such as the gate of Šamaš, the city-gate of Uraš, and the gate of Zagaga, which seems to have lain in "the province of Babylon," and had a field in front of it, as had also the gate of Enlil. According to an Assyr and a Bab list of gates, the streets bore names connected with those of the gates to which they led. Thus the street of the gate of Zagaga, one of the gods of war, was called "the street of Zagaga, who expels his enemies"; that of the gate of Merodach was "the street of Merodach, shepherd of his land"; while the street of Ištar's gate was "the street of Ištar, patron of her people." The city-gates named after Enlil, Addu (Hadad or Rimmon), Šamaš the Sun-god, Sin the Moon-god, etc, had streets similarly indicated. Certain of the streets of Babylon are also referred to on the contract-tablets, and such descriptive indications as "the broad street which is at the southern gate of the temple Ê-tur-kalama", seem to show that they were not in all cases systematically named. If the streets of Babylon were really, as Herodotus states, straight, and arranged at right angles, this was probably outside the walls of the ancient (inner) city, and most likely due to some wise Bab king or ruler. Details of the streets have been obtained at the point called Merkes (sec. 22) and elsewhere, and seem to show that the Babylonians liked the rooms of their houses to be square. Such streets as slanted were therefore full of rectangles, and must have presented a quite peculiar appearance.

15. Details Concerning the City

16. Details Concerning Babylon from Other Sources

It is this inner city which has most attracted the attention of explorers, both English and German, and it is on its site that the latter have carried on their systematic excavations. Indeed, it is probable that the houses of the most numerous class of the people —artisans, merchants, workmen, etc— lay outside the walls to which the Bab royal inscriptions refer. It may be supposed that the

17. Modern Exploration

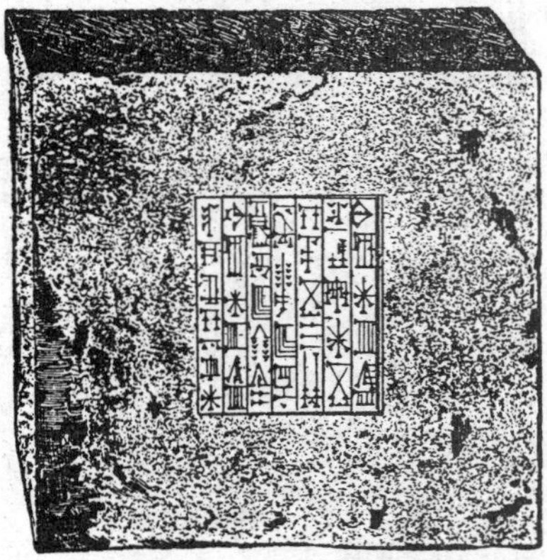

Brick Bearing the Name of Nebuchadrezzar.

houses in this district were mainly low buildings of unbaked clay (of which, indeed, portions of the temples and palaces were built), and these would naturally disappear more easily than if they had been built of baked brick. Even when baked, however, the brick-built ruins of Babylonia and Assyria have a tendency to disappear, owing to the value which bricks, both baked and unbaked, have for the erection of new houses in the neighborhood. Concerning the extent of the exterior city much doubt naturally exists, but it may well have covered the tract attributed to it (see sec. 3, above). Nineveh, at the time of its prosperity, also had enormous suburbs (see Nineveh).

The ruins of Babylon lie between 80 and 90 kilometers (50 miles or less) from Bagdad. The first thing seen on approaching them is the broad high ridge of Babil, which marks the site of the ruins of the Northern Palace. After some time, the ruins of the ancient walls are reached. They are still several yards high, and slope down gently to the plain. Starting to the N. of Babil, the wall stretches for about 875 yds. due E., and then runs southwards for another 930 yds., taking at that point a course to the S.E. for about 2 miles 160 yds. (3,300 meters). A wide gap occurs here, after which it runs to the S.W., and is lost in the open fields at the end of about $1\frac{1}{4}$ miles (2 kilometers). "That this is the old city-wall," says Weissbach, "there can be no doubt, and the name *Sur*, 'city-wall,' given it by the

18. Description of the Ruins—The Eastern Walls

Arabs, proves that they have fully recognized its nature." At the northern end it exists in its original extent, the plain out of which it rises being the old bed of the Euphrates, which, in the course of the cents., has become filled up by the desert-sand. At the period of Babylon's glory, the river had a much straighter course than at present, but

Stone Object Containing an Inscription of Nebuchadrezzar I.

it reoccupies its old bed about 600 meters (656 yds.) S. of Babil, leaving it afterward to make a sharp bend to the W. From the point where the city wall first becomes recognizable on the N. to its apparent southernmost extremity is about 3 miles.

19. The Western Walls

On the W. side of the river the traces of the wall are much less, the two angles, with the parts adjoining them, being all that is recognizable. Beginning on the N. where the Euphrates has reached its midpoint in its course through the city, it runs westward about 547 yds. (500 meters) W.S.W., and then, bending almost at a right angle S.S.E., turns E. again toward the Euphrates, but is lost in the plain before reaching the river. The distance of the two angles from each other is about 1 mile, 208 yds. (1,800 meters), and its distance from the Euphrates is at most $\frac{5}{8}$ of a mile (1 kilometer). The western portion of the city therefore formed a rectangle with an area of about 1.8 miles, and the eastern quarter, with the projection on the N., $6\frac{1}{4}$ square miles. According to Fried. Delitzsch, the size of Babylon was about the same as Munich or Dresden. This, of course, is an estimate from the extant remains—as has been indicated above, there was probably a large suburban extension beyond the walls, which would account for the enormous size attributed to the city by the ancients.

20. The Palaces

Among the Arabs, the northern ruin is called Babil, though it is only the remains of a palace. Its present height is 30 meters (98 ft., 5 in.), and its rectangular outline is still easily recognizable. Its sides face the cardinal points, the longest being those of the N. and S. This building, which measures 100 meters (109 yds.), was well protected by the city wall on the N. and E., the Euphrates protecting it on the W. Continuing to the S., the path at present leads through orchards and palm-groves, beyond which is a rugged tract evidently containing the remains of ancient structures, probably of inconsiderable height. After further palm-groves, an enormous ruin is encountered, steep on the E. and S., sloping on the N. and W. This is the *Gasr* (*Qasr*), also called *Emjellibeh* (*Mujellibah*), "the overturned," identical with the great palace of Nabopolassar and his son Nebuchadrezzar, referred to so prominently by the latter king in his records. Its longest side skirts the old Euphrates bed, and measures 300 meters (328 yds.). Its surface is very uneven, projections of 15 meters (over 49 ft.) alternating with deep depressions. On the N.W. side enormous walls of exceedingly hard yellow brick still tower to a considerable height. S. of this the plain, broken only by a few inconsiderable mounds, extends for a distance of half a kilometer ($\frac{5}{16}$ mile), and terminates on the S. with another enormous ruin-mound, called *Ishan Amran ibn 'Ali.* It measures 600 meters (656 yds.) from N. to S., and 400 (437 yds.) from E. to W., its average height being 25 meters (82 ft.). About the middle, and close to each other, are two Moslem domed tombs, the first called *Ibrahim al-Khalil* ("Abraham the Friend" [of God]—probably a late addition to the name of another Abraham than the Patriarch), and the other *Amran ibn 'Ali,* from which the ruin receives its modern name.

21. The Site of Babylon's Great Tower

Near the S. termination of the plain on which the village of Jim-jimeh lies, there is a square depression several yards deep, measuring nearly 100 meters (over 100 yds.) each way. In the middle of this depression, the sides of which do not quite face the cardinal points, there rises, to a height of about 13 ft., a platform of sun-dried brick about 60 meters (197 ft.) each way, its sides being parallel with the outer boundary of the depression. This depression, at present called *Sahan,* "the dish," is partly filled with foundation-water. Centered in its southern side is a rectangular hollowing-out similarly formed, about 50 meters (164 ft.) long, extending toward the ruin called *Amran.*

22. The Central and Southern Ruins

E. of the *Qasr* and *Emjellibeh* are several mounds bearing the name of *Ehmereh,* so called from the principal mound on the S.E., named *Ishan al-Oheimar,* "the red ruin," from the color of its bricks. Close to the S.E. corner of the Qasr lies the ruin called *Merkes,* "the central-point," and to the S. of that again is a long and irregularly shaped mound bearing the name of

Ishan al-Aswad, "the black ruin." From this enumeration of the principal remains on the site of Babylon, it will be easily seen that public buildings in this, the most ancient quarter of the city, were exceedingly numerous. Indeed, the district was regarded as being of such importance that the surrounding walls were not thought altogether sufficient to protect it, so another seemingly isolated rampart, on the E., was built, running N. and S., as an additional protection.

The remains on the western side of the river are insignificant, the changed course of the river being in all probability responsible for the destruction of at least some of the buildings.

23. A Walk through Babylon

There is much work to be done before a really complete reconstruction of the oldest quarter of Babylon can be attempted; but something may be said about the sights to be seen when taking a walk through the more interesting portion, which, as we know from Herodotus' narrative, could be visited by strangers, though it is possible that permission had to be obtained beforehand. Entering by the Uraš-gate, some distance to the E. of the Euphrates, one found oneself in *Aa-ibur-šabû,* the Festival-street, which was a continuation of the royal roadway without the inner wall, coming from the S. This street ran alongside the Araḫtu canal, on its western bank. After a time, one had the small temple of Ninip on the right (on the other side of the canal), and Ê-sagila, the great temple of Belus, on the left. This celebrated shrine was dedicated to Merodach and other deities associated with him, notably his spouse Zēr-panîtu^{m} (= Juno), and Nebo, "the teacher," probably as the one who inculcated Merodach's faith. The shrine of Merodach therein, which was called *Ê-kua,* is said by Nebuchadrezzar to have been magnificently decorated, and into the temple itself that king had caused to be brought many costly gifts, acquired by him in the lands over which he had dominion. Connected with Ê-sagila on the N.W. by a causeway and probably a staircase, was the great temple-tower *Ê-temen-an-ki,* which, as is indicated above, is not now represented by a tower, but by a depression, the bricks having been employed, it is said, to repair the Hindiyeh canal. This great building was a striking monument of the city, and must have been visible for a considerable distance, its height being something over 300 ft. The stages of which it was composed are thought to have been colored like those of the similar tower laid bare by the French excavations at Khorsabad (*Dûr-Šarru-ukîn*) in Assyria. Causeways or streets united this building with Aa-ibur-šabû, the festival-street along which the traveler is supposed to be proceeding. Continuing to the N., the visitor crossed a canal at right angles, named *Lîbil-ḫêgalli,* "may he [the god] bring fertility," and found himself immediately opposite the royal palace—the extensive building now known as the *Qasr.* According to Weissbach, its area occupied no less than 4½ hectares (rather more than 11 acres) and it was divided, as we know from the inscriptions of Nebuchadrezzar, into two parts, connected by a corridor. The building was richly decorated, as the Babylonians understood such things, the interior walls being lined with enameled brick and other material.

Passing along the eastern side of the palace, the visitor came to the Ištar-gate—a massive doorway faced with enameled brick in Nebuchadrezzar's time, and decorated with colored enameled reliefs of the lion, the bull and the dragon of Babylon. On the right of this gateway was to be seen the temple of the goddess Nin-maḫ, Merodach's spouse—a temple of sun-dried brick with traces of white coloring. It was a celebrated shrine of the Babylonians, in the usual architectural style with recessed buttresses, but modest from our modern point of view. Nin-maḫ was the goddess of reproduction, who, under the name of Aruru, had aided Merodach to create mankind, hence the honor in which she was held by the Babylonians.

24. The Ištar-Gate and the "Middle-Palace"

The Ištar-gate was apparently a part of the more ancient fortifications of Babylon, but which portion of the primitive city it enclosed is doubtful. In the time of Nebuchadrezzar it pierced the continuation, as it were, of the wall on the western bank of the river. Passing through this gateway, the visitor saw, on the W., the "middle-palace," an enormous structure, built by Nebuchadrezzar, as he boasts, in 15 days—a statement which seems somewhat of an exaggeration, when we come to consider the massiveness of the walls, some of which have a thickness of several yards. He describes this as having been "a fortress" (*dûru*), "mountainlike" (*šadaniš*), and on its summit he built an abode for himself—a "great palace," which was joined with his father's palace on the S. of the intervening wall. It is possibly this latter which was built in 15 days—not the whole structure, including the fortress. It was raised "high as the forests," and decorated with cedar and all kinds of costly woods, its doors being of palm, cedar, cypress, ebony(?) and ivory, framed in silver and gold, and plated with copper. The thresholds and hinges of its gates were bronze, and the cornice round its top was in (an imitation of) lapis-lazuli. It was a house for men to admire; and it is not improbable that this was the palace upon which he was regarded as having been walking when he referred to "great Babylon," which he had built.

25. The Festival-Street

But the street Aa-ibur-šabû, along which the visitor is conceived to be walking, was also a highly decorated causeway, fitted for the pathway of the great gods. Its width varied from 11 to 22 yds., and it was paved with regularly hewn and fitted natural stones—limestone and a brownish-red stone with white veins—while its walls were provided with a covering of brick enameled in various colors with representations of lions, some of them in relief. The inscriptions which it bore were white on a rich dark-blue ground, also enameled. There were various other streets in Babylon, but these have still to be identified.

26. The Chamber of the Fates

At the end of the Procession-street, and at right angle to it, was the Merodach canal, which communicated directly with the Euphrates. At this point also, and forming its end-portion, was the Chamber of Fates (*Parak šîmāte*), where, yearly, the oracles were asked and declared. In close connection with this was the Temple of Offerings (*Bît nikê*) or festival-house (*Bît âkiti*). Concerning these places more information is needed, but it would seem that, before Nebuchadrezzar's time, the Chamber of Fates was simply decorated with silver—he, however, made it glorious with pure gold. It is at this point that the Procession-street is at its widest. The position of the Temple of Offerings is at present uncertain.

27. The Northern Palace and the Gardens

What may have lain on the other side of the Araḫtu-canal, which here made a bend to the N.W., and flowed out of the Euphrates somewhat higher up, is uncertain; but in the extreme N. of the city was the palace now represented by the ruin called Babil. This was likewise built by Nebuchadrezzar, but it may be doubted whether it was really founded by him.

The presence of traces of wells here made Hormuzd Rassam think that this was probably the site of the Hanging Gardens, but further exploration is needed to decide the point, though it may be regarded as not unlikely that this identification is correct. In that case it would represent the palace shown in the Assyr saloon at the British Museum—a building apparently protected by three walls, and adorned with columns resting on the backs of lions in an attitude of walking. On the adjoining slab is a representation of a small building—also with columns—on a hill. A figure of a king sculptured on a stele is seen on the left, with an altar in front of it, showing that divine honors were paid to him. The hill is thickly wooded with trees which may be olives, poplars, etc, and on the right is a series of arches on which other trees are planted. Irrigation channels stretch in a long stream to the left and in shorter streams to the right. As this belongs to the time of Aššur-bani-âpli, about 650 BC, and refers to that king's operations against his brother Šamaš-šum-ukîn, the king of Babylon, it is clear that something similar to the Hanging Gardens existed before the time of Nebuchadrezzar, and therefore, if it was his queen who had them made, before the time of their reputed founder. This would be the point first reached by the Assyr army when advancing to the attack. Such a park as is represented here with its hills and streams, and thickly planted trees, must have made the palace in the vicinity the pleasantest, in all probability, in all Babylonia, and excited the admiration of every one who visited the sights of the city.

28. Historical References to Babylonian Buildings

The architectural history of the city of Babylon has still to be written, but something is already known about it, especially its central point of interest, the great temple Ê-sagila, wherein Merodach was worshipped. The 5th year of Sumu-la-ila was known as that in which the great fortress of Babylon was built; and his 22d was that in which a throne of gold and silver was completed and made for Merodach's supreme abode (*paramaḫa*). Later on Abil-Sin, in his 17th year, made a throne(?) for Šamaš of Babylon; and Ḫammu-rabi, in his 3rd, 12th and 14th years, also made thrones for the gods—Nannar of Babylon (the Moon-god), Zēr-panîtu^{m}, Merodach's consort, and Ištar of Babylon. Samsu-iluna, his son, in his 6th year, placed a "praying statue" in Ê-sagila before Merodach, followed, in his 8th, by the dedication of some bright-shining object (mace?) of gold and silver, to the god; and on that occasion it is stated that he made Ê-sagila to shine like the stars of heaven. Passing over many other references to kings who adorned the temples of the city, the work done there by Agukakrime (cir 1480 BC) may be mentioned. This ruler, who belonged to the Kassite dynasty, not only brought back the images of Merodach and Zēr-panîtu^{m} to their temple, but also restored the building and its shrine, and made rich offerings thereto. Later on, after the destruction of the city by Sennacherib, his son Esarhaddon, and his grandsons Šamaš-šum-ukîn, king of Babylon, and Aššur-bani-âpli, king of Assyria, all took part in the restoration of Babylon's temples and palaces. The work of Nabopolassar and Nebuchadrezzar has already been referred to. In 330 BC (reign of Alexander the Great), an attempt was made, by the tithes of the pious, to clear away the rubbish around Ê-sangil (Ê-sagila), but to all appearance no real restorations were made—or, at least, the stage at which they could have been put in hand was not reached. In the year 269 BC Antiochus Soter claims, like Nebuchadrezzar and other Bab kings, to have restored the temples Ê-sagila and Ê-zida (the latter at Borsippa). Though in late times the temples were more or less dilapidated, the services to all appearance continued to be performed, and may even have gone on until well in the Christian era, Bab religion and philosophy being still held in honor as late as the 4th cent. The downfall of Babylon as a city began with the founding of Seleucia on the Tigris, in the reign of Seleucus Nicator (after 312 BC). The inhabitants of Babylon soon began to migrate to this new site, and the ruined houses and walls of the old capital ultimately became the haunts of robbers and outlaws. It is said that the walls were demolished by later (Seleucid) kings on that account, and it is not improbable that, with the walls, any houses which may have remained habitable were cleared away. Fortunately, the palaces restored by Nebuchadrezzar were too firmly built to be easily demolished, hence their preservation to the present day.

Literature.—Fried. Delitzsch, *Babel and Bible*, 1903; Fr. H. Weissbach, *Das Stadtbild von Babylon*, 1904; R. Koldeway, *Die Tempel von Babylon und Borsippa*, 1911.

T. G. Pinches

BABEL, TOWER OF: This expression does not occur in the OT, but is used popularly for the tower (מִגְדֹּל, *mighdōl*) built by the inhabitants of the world who, traveling in the East, built a city on the Plain of Shinar, with a tower "whose top may reach unto heaven"—an expression which is regarded as meaning "a very high tower."

1. General Form of Babylonian Temple-Towers

There was a great difference, however, between a Can *mighdōl* or watchtower, and the great Tower at Babylon. The watchtower was simply a high structure, probably without any special shape or form, which depended upon the will of the architect and the nature of the ground upon which it was erected. The Tower of Babel or Babylon, however, was a structure peculiar to Babylonia and Assyria. According to all accounts, and judging from the ruins of the various erections extant in those countries, Bab towers were always rectangular, built in stages, and provided with an inclined ascent continued along each side to the top. As religious ceremonies were performed thereon, they were generally surmounted by a chapel in which sacred objects or images were kept.

2. Their Babylonian Name

These erections had, with the Babylonians, a special name: *ziqqurātu*, meaning, apparently, "peak," or the highest point of a mountain, this word being applied to the mountain-height upon which Ut-napištim, the Bab Noah, offered sacrifices on coming forth from the ark (or ship) when the waters of the great Flood had sufficiently subsided. It has also been thought that they were used as observatories when the Babylonians studied the starry heavens. This is probable, but as these structures were of no great height, it is possible that, in the clear atmosphere of the Bab plains, there was no real necessity to go above the surface of the earth when making their observations.

3. Whereabouts of the Tower of Babel

There has been much difference of opinion as to the geographical position of the Tower of Babel. Most writers upon the subject, following the tradition handed down by the Jews and Arabs, have identified it with the great Temple of Nebo in the city of Borsippa, now called the *Birs-Nimroud* (explained as a corruption of *Birj Nimroud*, "Tower of Nimrod"). This building, however, notwithstanding its importance, was to all appearance never regarded by the Babylonians as the Tower of Babel, for the very good reason that it was not situated in Babylon, but in Borsippa, which, though called, in later times, "the second Babylon," was naturally not the original city of that name. The erection regarded by the Babylonians as the great Tower of their ancient city was *Ê-temen-ana-ki*, "the Temple of the foundation of heaven and earth," called by Nabopolassar and Nebuchadrezzar *ziqqurat Bâbîli*, "the Tower of Babylon"—the world-renowned fane dedicated to Merodach and his consort *Z*ēr-panîtu^{m}, Babylon's chief deities.

4. Its Position at Babylon

This structure was situated in the southern portion of the city, not far from the right bank of the Euphrates, and according to Weissbach, is now represented by a depression within which is the original rectangular core of unbaked brick. From its shape, the Arabs have made this site *Sahan*, "the dish." These remains of the great temple-tower of Babylon, within the memory of men not so very old, towered, even in its ruined state, high above the surrounding plain. The burnt bricks of the ancient Babylonians, however, who "had brick for stone, and slime [bitumen] for mortar" (11 3 m), are still good and have a commercial value, so they were all cleared out, with whatever precious material in the way of antiquities they may have contained, to repair, it is said, the banks of the Hindiyeh Canal. Certain records in the shape of conical "cylinders," however, came into the market, and were acquired by the museums of Europe and America. As these refer to the restoration of the building by Nabopolassar, and the part taken by his sons Nebuchadrezzar and Nabû-šum-lîšir in the ceremonies attending the rebuilding, it is very probable that they formed part of the spoils acquired.

5. A Babylonian Description of the Tower

Ê-temen-ana-ki, to give the Bab (Sumerian) name, consisted of six stages built upon a platform, and provided with a sanctuary at the top. A tablet seemingly giving a detailed description of this building was for a time in the hands of the late George Smith in the year 1876. Unfortunately he had not time to give a tr of the document, or to publish the text, but his detailed account of it (*Athenaeum*, February 12, 1876) is exceedingly interesting.

First there was the outer court called the "grand court," measuring, according to G. Smith's estimate, 1,156 ft. by 900 ft., and a smaller one, called "the court of Ištar and Zagaga," 1,056 ft. by 450 ft. Round the court were six gates admitting to the temples: (1) the grand gate; (2) the gate of the rising sun (east); (3) the great gate; (4) the gate of the colossi; (5) the gate of the canal; and (6) the gate of the tower-view.

6. The Platform

After this came a space or platform apparently walled—a *ki-gallu* square in form, and measuring 3 *ku* each way. Its size is doubtful, as the value of the *ku* is unknown. The sides of this inclosure faced the cardinal points. In its walls were four gates, one on each side, and named from the points toward which they looked. Within this inclosure stood a large building measuring 10 *gar* (Smith: 200 ft.) each way. Unfortunately, the name of this erection was damaged, so that its nature and use are uncertain.

7. The Chapels and Shrines

Round the base of the Tower were small temples or chapels dedicated to the various gods of the Babylonians. On the E. were 16 shrines, the principal of them being dedicated to Nebo and Tašmêtu, his spouse; on the N. were two temples dedicated to Êa (Aê) and Nusku respectively; on the S. was a single temple to the two great gods, Anu and Bel (Enlil?). It was on the W., however, that the principal buildings lay—a double house with a court between the wings 35 cubits (Smith: 58 ft.) wide. These two wings were not alike in dimensions, the erection on one side being 100 cubits by 20 (166 ft. by 34 ft.) and on the other 100 cubits by 65 (166 ft. by 108 ft.). In these western chambers stood the couch of the god, and the golden throne mentioned by Herodotus, with other objects of great value. The couch was stated to have measured 9 cubits by 4 (15 ft. by 6 ft. 8 in.).

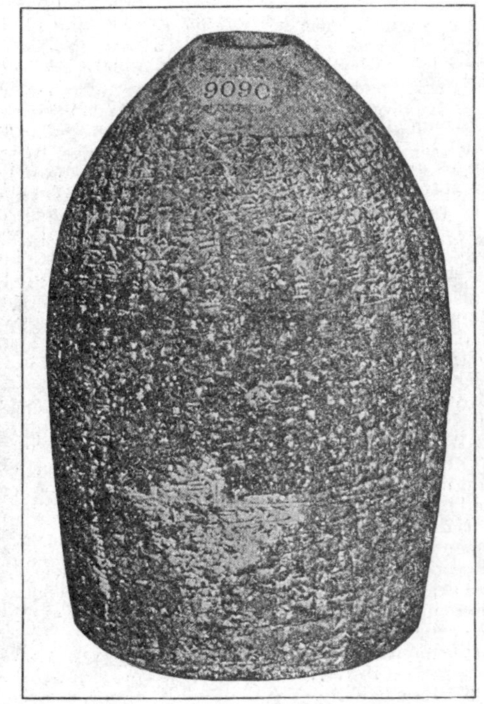

Building Inscription of Nabopolassar.
(Giving an account of his restoration of the Tower of Babel.)

8. The Tower in Its First Stage

In the center of these groups of buildings stood the great Tower in stages, called by the Babylonians "the Tower of Babel" (*ziqqurat Bâbîli*). The stages decreased from the lowest upward, but each was square in plan. The first or foundation-stage was 15 *gar* each way by $5\frac{1}{2}$ *gar* high (300 ft. by 110 ft. high), and seems to have been decorated with the usual double recesses which are a characteristic of Assyr-Bab architecture.

9. The Remaining Stages

The second stage was 13 *gar* square and 3 *gar* high (260 ft. by 60 ft.). A term was applied to it which G. Smith did not understand, but he notes that it probably had sloping sides. The stages from the 3d to the 5th were all of equal height, namely, 1 *gar* (20 ft.), and were respectively 10 *gar* (200 ft.), $8\frac{1}{3}$ *gar* (170 ft.) and 7 *gar* (140 ft.) square. The dimensions of the 6th stage were omitted, but may be restored in accordance with the others, namely, $5\frac{1}{2}$ *gar* sq. (110 ft.) by 1 *gar* (20 ft.) high.

10. The Chapel at the Top

On this was raised what Smith calls the 7th stage, namely, the upper temple or sanctuary of the god Bel-Merodach, 4 *gar* long, $3\frac{1}{2}$ *gar* broad and $2\frac{1}{2}$ *gar* high (80, 60 and 50 ft. respectively). He does not mention the statue of the god, but it may be supposed that it was set up in this topmost erection. The total height of the tower above its foundation was therefore 15 *gar* (300 ft.), the same as the breadth of its base. It cannot be said that it was by any means a beautiful erection, but there was probably some symbolism in its measurements, and in appearance it probably resembled (except the decoration) the temple-tower of Calah as restored in the frontispiece to Layard's *Monuments of Nineveh*, 1st series, in which a step-pyramid with a similarly high basement-stage is shown.

With this detailed description, which is quite what would be expected in a Bab account of such a celebrated fane, the description in Herodotus (i.181 ff) agrees. He states that it was a temple square in form, two furlongs (1,213 ft.) each way, in the midst of which was built a solid tower a furlong square (nearly 607 ft.). This, however, must have been the platform, which, with the six stages and the chapel on the top, would make up the total of eight stages of which Herodotus speaks. The ascent by which the top was reached he describes as running "outside round about all the towers"—wording which suggests, though not necessarily, that it was spiral—i.e. one had to walk round the structure 7 times to reach the top. Representations on Bab boundary-stones suggest that this view would be correct, though a symmetrical arrangement of inclined paths might have been constructed which would have greatly improved the design. At the middle of the ascent, Herodotus says, there was a stopping-place with seats to rest upon, which rather favors this idea. At the top of the last tower there was a large cell, and in the cell a large couch was laid, well covered; and by it a golden table. There was no image there, nor did any human being spend the night there, except only a woman of the natives of the place chosen by the god, "as say the Chaldeans who are the priests of this god." These men told Herodotus that the god often came to the cell, and rested upon the couch, "but," he adds, "I do not believe them." After mentioning parallels to this at Egyp Thebes and Patara in Lycia, he goes on to speak of another cell below (that referred to in G. Smith's tablet) wherein was a great image of Zeus (Bel-Merodach) sitting, with a footstool and a large table, all of gold, and weighing no less than 800 talents. Outside of this cell was an altar to the god, made of gold; and also another altar, whereon full-grown animals were sacrificed, the golden altar being for sucklings only. The Chaldaeans also told him that there was, in the precincts of the building, a statue 12 cubits high, and of solid gold. Darius Hystaspis desired to take possession of this valuable object, but did not venture. His son Xerxes, however, was not so considerate of the feelings of the people and the priesthood, for he also killed the priest when he forbade him to meddle with it.

11. Herodotus' Description

The Bible record does not state who the people were who journeyed in the East and built the city and the Tower. The indefinite "they" might be taken to mean whatever people were there at the time the record was written, and probably presupposes that the reader would certainly know. As the Tower of Babel bears, in the native inscriptions, a Sumero-Akkadian name, it may be supposed that the builders referred to belonged to that race. It is noteworthy that nothing is said in Gen concerning the stoppage of the erection, though they ceased to build the city. Bochart records a Jewish tradition which makes the tower to have been split through to its foundation by fire which fell from heaven —suggested probably by the condition of the tower at "the second Babylon," i.e. the Birs Nimroud. Another tradition, recorded by Eusebius (*Prep. Evang.*, ix; *Chronicon*, 13; *Syncel. Chron.*, 44) makes it to have been blown down by the winds; "but when it approached the heavens, the winds assisted the gods, and overturned the work upon its contrivers: and the gods introduced a diversity of tongues among men, who, until that time, had all spoken the same language." The place where they built the Tower was called Babylon, on account of the confusion of languages.

12. The Builders of the Tower

13. Traditions Concerning Its Destruction

Here we have again the statement as in Gen that the meaning of Babel is "confusion." This, as is well known, is based upon the purely Heb etymological law, which makes *bālal*, "to confuse," or "mingle," assume a reduplicate form; but as far as the cuneiform inscriptions, which are now very numerous, give us information, Babel, from *balālu*, "to mingle" (the root in question), was an impossibility. But on the Bab side, that the rendering of the name as *Bâb-îli* (*-îlāni*), "gate of god" ("of the gods") was a folk-etymology, is undoubted, notwithstanding that the Sumero-Akkadian form *Ka-dingira*, with the same meaning, is far from rare. It is noteworthy, however, that one of the forms used by Nebuchadrezzar is *Bab-ilam*, with the mimmation or "emming," which is a characteristic of the Bab language; moreover, a place-name *Babalam* also occurs, which may be a still earlier, and perhaps the original, form. Notwithstanding that one would like to see in *Babalam*, "the place of bringing together," and in *Babilam*, "the bringer together," the termination *-am* would seem to be an insurmountable difficulty.

14. The Meaning of "Babel"

That the building of the city would have been stopped when the confusion of tongues took place is natural—the departure of the greater part of the inhabitants made this inevitable. When the population increased again, the building of the city was continued, with the result that Babylon ultimately became the greatest city of the then known world. The Tower, notwithstanding what had been said as to its destruction, remained, and when, as happened from time to time, its condition became ruinous, some energetic Bab king would restore it. Alexander and Philip of Macedon began clearing away the rubbish to rebuild the great temple of Belus (Bel-Merodach) connected with it and there is hardly any doubt that the Tower would have been restored likewise, but the untimely death of the former, and the deficient mental caliber of the latter for the ruling of a great empire, put an end to the work. The Tower therefore remained unrepaired—"The tower was exceedingly tall. The third part of it sank down into the ground, a second third was burned down, and the remaining third was standing until the time of the destruction of Babylon" (Rabbi Yēḥānān, *Sanhedhrīn*, 109, 1).

15. The Ultimate Destruction of the Tower

Concerning the reputed intention of the builders of the Tower, to carry it as high as the heavens, that, notwithstanding the Talm and other writings, may be dismissed at once. The intention was to build a very high tower, and that is all that is implied by the words employed. That the Babylonians would have liked their tower to reach heaven may be conceded, and the idea may be taken as symbolical of Babylon's pride, the more especially as they regarded it as "the house of the foundation of heaven and earth." Though at present brought lower than the other temple-towers of Babylonia, its renown remains as one of the great glories of that renowned capital. Dedicated as it was to the gods whom they worshipped, and chiefly to the glory of Merodach, the

16. No Idea of Reaching Heaven

representative of Bab monotheism, the Babylonians' descendants, the native Christians, have no reason to remember this erection of their forefathers with shame, but rather with pride. The rallying-point of nations, Babylon, while it existed, was always a great commercial center, and many are the languages which have resounded in the Tower's vicinity. The confusion of tongues led to the Jewish fiction that the air of Babylon and Borsippa caused forgetfulness, and was therefore injurious to students of the Law, causing them to forget it as the builders of the Tower had of old forgotten their speech (Rashi, *Ṣanhedhrīn,* 109, 1). This, however, did not prevent the rabbis of Babylon from being more celebrated than those of the Holy Land, and even of Jerus itself. See also ASTRONOMY.

T. G. PINCHES

BABI, bā'bī (A, **Βαβί,** *Babí;* B, **Βαιήρ,** *Baiēr*) = Bebai (Ezr **8** 11). The descendants of B. returned with Ezra to Jerus (1 Esd **8** 37).

BABYLON IN THE NT: Babylon (**Βαβυλών,** *Babulṓn*), is used in NT in at least two different senses:

1. Mesopotamian Babylon

In Mt **1** 11.12.17; Acts **7** 43 the old Mesop city is plainly meant. These all refer to the captivity in Babylon and do not demand any further discussion.

2. Symbolic Sense

All the references to Babylon in Rev are evidently symbolic. Some of the most important passages are **14** 8; **16** 19; **17** 5; **18** 2.10.21. In **17** 5 Babylon is designated as *mustērion.* This undoubtedly indicates that the name is to be understood **fig.** A few interpreters have believed that Jerus was the city that was designated as Babylon, but most scholars hold that Rome was the city that was meant. That interpretation goes back at least to the time of Tertullian (*Adv. Marc.,* iii.13). This interpretation was adopted by Jerome and Augustine and has been commonly accepted by the church. There are some striking facts which point to Rome as the city that is designated as Babylon.

(1) The characteristics ascribed to this Babylon apply to Rome rather than to any other city of that age: (*a*) as ruling over the kings of the earth (**17** 18); (*b*) as sitting on seven mountains (**17** 9); (*c*) as the center of the world's merchandise (**18** 3.11–13); (*d*) as the corrupter of the nations (**17** 2; **18** 3; **19** 2); (*e*) as the persecutor of the saints (**17** 6).

(2) Rome is designated as Babylon in the Sibylline Oracles (**5** 143), and this is perhaps an early Jewish portion of the book. The comparison of Rome to Babylon is common in Jewish apocalyptic literature (see 2 Esd and the Apoc Bar).

(3) Rome was regarded by both Jews and Christians as being antagonistic to the kingdom of God, and its downfall was confidently expected. This conception is in accord with the predicted downfall of Babylon (Rev **14** 8; **18** 2.10–21). As Babylon had been the oppressor of Israel, it was natural that this new power, which was oppressing the people of God, should be designated as Babylon.

3. In 1 Peter

In **5** 13 Babylon is designated as the place from which 1 Pet was written. Down to the time of the Reformation this was generally understood to mean Rome, and two cursives added "en Roma." Since the Reformation, many scholars have followed Erasmus and Calvin and have urged that the Mesop Babylon is meant. Three theories should be noted:

(1) That the Egyp Babylon, or Old Cairo, is meant. Strabo (XVII, 807) who wrote as late as 18 AD, says the Egyp Babylon was a strong fortress, founded by certain refugees from the Mesop Babylon. But during the 1st cent. this was not much more than a military station, and it is quite improbable that Peter would have gone there. There is no tradition that connects Peter in any way with Egypt.

(2) That the statement is to be taken lit. and that the Mesop Babylon is meant. Many good scholars hold to this view, and among these are Weiss and Thayer, but there is no evidence that Peter was ever in Babylon, or that there was even a church there during the 1st cent. Mark and Silvanus are associated with Peter in the letter and there is no tradition that connects either of them with Babylon. According to Jos (*Ant,* XVIII, ix, 5–9), the Jews at this time had largely been driven out of Babylon and were confined to neighboring towns, and it seems improbable that Peter would have made that his missionary field.

(3) That Rome was the city that was designated as Babylon. The Apocalypse would indicate that the churches would understand the symbolic reference, and it seems to have been so understood until the time of the Reformation. The denial of this position was in line with the effort to refute Peter's supposed connection with the Rom church. Ancient tradition, however, makes it seem quite probable that Peter did make a visit to Rome (see Lightfoot, *Clement,* II, 493 ff).

Internal evidence helps to substantiate the theory that Rome was the place from which the letter was written. Mark sends greetings (1 Pet **5** 13), and we know he had been summoned to Rome by the apostle Paul (2 Tim **4** 11). The whole passage, "She that is in Babylon, elect together with you, saluteth you," seems to be **fig.,** and that being true, it is natural that Babylon should have been used instead of Rome. The character of the letter as a whole would point to Rome as the place of writing. Ramsay thinks this book is impregnated with Rom thought beyond any other book in the Bible (see *The Church in the Rom Empire,* 286).

A. W. FORTUNE

BABYLON IN OT. See BABEL, BABYLON.

BABYLONIA, bab-i-lō'ni-a:

1. Mounds
2. Explorations
3. Names
4. Semites
5. Sumerians
6. Home of the Semites
7. Immigration
8. Language
9. Script
10. Architecture
11. Art
12. Literature
13. Libraries
14. Personal Names
15. History of Kingdoms
16. Kish
17. Lagash
18. Adab
19. Nippur
20. Erech
21. Larsa
22. Shuruppak
23. Kisurra
24. Umma
25. Accad
26. Opis
27. Basime
28. Drehem
29. Urumma
30. First Dynasty of Babylon
31. Sealand Dynasty
32. Cassite Dynasty
33. Cassite Rule
34. Isin Dynasty
35. Nebuchadrezzar I
36. Sealand Dynasty
37. Bit-Bazi Dynasty
38. Other Rulers
39. Babylonian Dynasty
40. Neo-Babylonian Rulers
41. Persian Rulers of Bab

LITERATURE

Babylonia is a plain which is made up of the alluvial deposits of the mountainous regions in the North, where the Tigris and Euphrates have their source. The land is bounded on the N. by Assyria and Mesopotamia; on the E. by Elam, separated by the mountains of Elam; on the S. by the sea marshes, and the country Kaldu (Chaldaea); and on the W. by the Syrian desert. Some of the cities of the lower country were seaport towns in the early period, but now are far inland. This land-making process continues even at the present time at the rate of about 70 ft. a year.

This plain, in the days when Babylonia flourished, sustained a dense population. It was covered with a network of canals, skilfully planned and regulated, which brought prosperity to the land, because of the wonderful fertility of the soil. The neglect of these canals and doubtless, also, the change of climate, have resulted in altered conditions in the country. It has become a cheerless waste. During some months of the year, when the inundations take place, large portions of the land are partially covered with swamps and marshes. At other times it looks like a desolate plain.

1. Mounds

Throughout the land there are seen, at the present time, ruin-hills or mounds of accumulation of débris, which mark the site of ancient cities. Some of these cities were destroyed in a very early era, and were never rebuilt. Others were occupied for millenniums, and their history extends far into the Christian era. The antiquities generally found in the upper stratum of the mounds which were occupied up to so late a period, show that they were generally inhabited by the Jews, who lived there after the Babylonians had disappeared.

2. Explorations

The excavations conducted at various sites have resulted in the discovery, besides antiquities of almost every character, of hundreds of thousands of inscriptions on clay and stone, but principally on the former material. At Tello more than 60,000 tablets were found, belonging largely to the administrative archives of the temple of the 3d millennium BC. At Nippur about 50,000 inscriptions were found, many of these also belonging to temple archives. But about 20,000 tablets and fragments found in that city came from the library of the school of the priests, which had been written in the 3d millennium BC. At Sippar, fully 30,000 tablets were found, many being of the same general character, also representing a library. At Delehem and Djokha, temple archives of the same period as those found at Tello have come to light in great numbers, through the illicit diggings of Arabs. Babylon, Borsippa, Kish, Erech and many other cities have yielded to the explorer and the Arab diggers inscribed documents of every period of Bab history, and embracing almost every kind of lit., so that the museums and libraries of America and Europe have stored up unread inscriptions numbering hundreds of thousands. Many also

Bronze Goat Head from Tello.

are in the possession of private individuals. After the work of excavating Babylonia has been completed and the inscriptions deciphered, many of the pre-Christian cents. in Bab history will be better known than some of those of our Christian era. The ancient history of the Babylonians will be reconstructed by the help of these original sources. Lengthy family genealogies will be known, as indeed in some instances is now the case, as well as the Bab contemporaries of Ezekiel, Abraham and all the other Bib. characters.

Silver Vase of Entemena, 3d Millennium BC.

3. Names

The Gr name of Babylonia which is in use at the present time is derived from the name of the city of Babylon, the capital and chief city of the land from the time of the First Dynasty of Babylon, about 2000 BC (see BABYLON). The name of the land in the very earliest period which is represented by antiquities, and even inscribed objects, is not known. But in a comparatively early age the northern part is called Uri, and the southern part, Engi or En-gira. The second part of the latter name is perhaps the same as in Su-gir, which is thought to be the origin of the OT Shinar. Su-gir and Su-mer are names of the same country. And inasmuch as Mer and Gir were names of the same west Sem deity, who played an important rôle in the early history of Babylonia, it is not improbable that the element Su is also to be identified with the ancient name of Mesopotamia. Su is also in Su-bartu, the name of the country to the N. This name is also written Su-Gir.

Subsequent to 2000 BC the ideograms read in Sumerian, Uri and Engi, were pronounced in Sem-Bab, Accad and Sumer. The former received its name from the capital of the kingdom Accad, one of the cities mentioned in Gen **10** 10. The title, "king of Accad and Sumer" was used by rulers as late as the 1st millennium BC.

The name by which the land is known in the 2d millennium BC is Kar-Duniash, the exact derivation of which is in doubt. Kar means "garden, land" in Sem and Sumerian; and Duniash being preceded by the determinative for deity, has been regarded as a name of a Cassite god. A more recently advanced explanation is that Duniash is equivalent to *Bêl-matâti*, which means "lord of lands." The meaning of the name, as stated, must be regarded as undetermined.

In the time of the late Assyr empire a nation in the extreme southern part of the land, called by the Greeks Chaldaea, which is derived from the name Kaldu, came into existence. In the Assyr historical inscriptions the land is usually called Bit-Yakin. This people seems to have issued from Aram. Under Bib. Merodach-baladan they ruled Babylonia for a time. The Neo-Bab Dynasty, founded by Nabopolassar, is supposed to be Chaldaean in origin, in consequence of which the whole land in the Gr period was called Chaldaea.

6. Home of the Semites

The home of the Semites has been placed in different parts of the ancient world. A number of scholars look to Arabia and others to Africa for their original habitation, although their theories generally are not based upon much archaeological evidence. Unquestionably, the previous, if not the original home of the Sem Babylonians, is to be found in the land of the Amorites, that is in Syria. In the earliest known period of Bab history, which apparently belongs to the age not very far removed from the time when the Semites entered Babylonia, Amurru was an important factor in the affairs of the nations, and it was a land which the world conquerors of Babylonia, both Sumerian and Sem, endeavored to subjugate. This points to the fact that the culture of Amurru was then already old. Egyp inscriptions fully substantiate this. We look to the land of the Amorites as the home of the Sem Babylonians, because of the important part played by the chief god of that land Amurru or Uru, in the Bab religion and nomenclature. In fact nearly all of the original names of the Sem Bab sun-deities are derived from the names and epithets of the great Sun-god of the Amorites and Aramaeans (see *Amurru*, 108 ff). These and many other considerations point to Amurru, or the land of the Amorites, as the previous home of the Semites who migrated into Babylonia and who eventually became masters of the land.

FRAGMENTS OF INSCRIBED VASES OF THE EARLY SUMERIAN PERIOD.

4. Semites

Two distinct races are found occupying the land when we obtain the first glimpses of its history. The northern part is occupied by the Semites, who are closely allied to the Amorites, Aramaeans and Arabs; and the southern part by a non-Sem people called Sumerians. Their cultures had been originally distinct, but when they first become known to us there has taken place such an amalgamation that it is only by the knowledge of other Sem cultures that it is possible to make even a partial differentiation of what was Sem-Bab and what was Sumerian. The Semites, it would almost seem, entered the land after the Sumerians had established themselves, but this can only be regarded as a conjecture.

5. Sumerians

Although the earliest Sumerian settlement belongs to a remote period, few traces of the pre-historic Sumerian have been found. The archaeological remains indicate that this non-Sem race is not indigenous to the land, and that when they came into the country they had already attained to a fair degree of culture. But there is no evidence, as yet, in what part of the ancient world the elements of their culture were evolved, although various attempts have been made by scholars to locate their original home.

7. Immigrations

The original settlements in Babylonia, as stated above, belong to a prehistoric time, but throughout the history of the land fresh Sem migrations have been recognized. In the Isin and First Dynasty of Babylonia, Amorites or Canaanites seem to flood the country. In the 2d millennium a foreign people known as Cassites ruled Babylonia for nearly six centuries. The nomenclature of the period shows that many Hittites and Mittanaeans as well as Cassites lived in Babylonia. In the 1st millennium the thousands of names that appear in the contract lit. indicate a veritable Babel of races: Egyptians, Elamites, Persians, Medes, Tabalites, Hittites, Cassites, Ammorites, Edomites, notably Hebrews, are among the peoples that occupied the land. The deportation of the Israelites by the Assyr kings and of the Jews by the Bab kings, find confirmation besides the historical inscriptions in the names of Hebrews living in Babylonia in the corresponding periods.

8. Language

The languages of Babylonia are Sem and Sumerian. The latter is an agglutinative tongue like the Turkish, and belongs to that great unclassifiable group of languages, called for the sake of convenience, Turanian. It has not been shown, as yet, to be allied to any other known language.

The Sem language known as the Bab, with which the Assyr is practically identical, is of the common Sem stock. After the Semites entered the land, their language was greatly influenced by the Sumerian tongue. The Semites being originally dependent upon the Sumerian scribes, with whom the script had originated, considered in connection with the fact that the highly developed culture of the Sumerians greatly influenced that of the Semites, brought about the peculiar amalgamation known as Bab. The language is, however, distinctively Sem, but it has a very large percentage of Sumerian loan-words. Not knowing the cognate tongues of the Sumerian, and having a poor understanding of the pronunciation of that language, it is impossible to ascertain, on the other hand, how much the Sumerian language was influenced by the Sem.

In the late period another Sem tongue was used extensively in the land. It was not because of the position occupied by the Aramaeans in the political history of western Asia, that their language became the *lingua franca* of the 1st millennium BC. It must have been on account of the widespread migrations of the people. In the time of Sennacherib it seems to have been used as the diplomatic language in Assyria as well as among the Hebrews, as the episode in 2 K **18** 26 would show. Then we recall the story of Belshazzar, and the edicts of the late period referred to in the OT, which were in Aram. (Ezr **4** 7, etc). In Assyria and Babylonia, many contract tablets have been found with Aram. reference notes written upon them, showing that this was the language of those who held the documents. The Hebrews after the exile used Aramaic. This would seem to point to Babylonia as the place where they learned the language. The Bab language and the cuneiform script continued to be used until the 3d or 2d cent. BC, and perhaps even later, but it seems that the Aram. had generally supplanted it, except as the literary and legal language. In short the tongue of the common people or the spoken language in all probability in the late period was Aramaic.

9. Script

The cuneiform writing upon clay was used both by the Sumerians and the Semites. Whether this script had its origin in the land, or in the earlier home of the Sumerians, remains a question. It is now known that the Elamites had their own system of writing as early as that of the earliest found in Babylonia; and perhaps it will be found that other ancient peoples, who are at the present unknown to us, also used the cuneiform script. A writing similar to the Bab was in use at an early time in Cappadocia. The Hittites and other peoples of that region also employed it. The origin of the use of clay as a writing material, therefore, is shrouded in mystery, but as stated above, the system used by the Semites in Babylonia was developed from the Sumerian.

The script is not alphabetic, but ideographic and phonetic, in that respect similar to the Chinese. There are over 500 characters, each one of which has from one to many values. The combination of two or more characters also has many values. The compilation of the values of the different signs used in various periods by both the Sumerians and Assyrians numbers at the present about 25,000, and the number will probably reach 30,000.

10. Architecture

The architecture of Babylonia is influenced by the fact that the building material, in this alluvial plain, had to be of brick, which was largely sun-dried, although in certain prosperous eras there is much evidence of kiln-dried bricks having been used. The baked brick used in the earliest period was the smallest ever employed, being about the size of the

Brick Stamp of Sargon I.

ordinary brick used at the present time. The size of the bricks in the era prior to the 3d millennium varied from this to about 6×10×3 in. At Nippur, Sargon and his son Naram-Sin used a brick, the largest found, about 20 in. square, and about 4 in. in thickness. Following the operations of these kings at Nippur is the work of Ur-Engur, who used a brick about 14 in. square and nearly 4 in. in thickness. This size had been used at Tello prior to Sargon's time, and was thereafter generally employed. It remained the standard size of brick throughout the succeeding cents. of Bab history. Adobes, of which the greater portion of the buildings were constructed, were usually double the thickness of kiln-dried bricks. The pillar made of bricks, as well as the pilaster constructed of the same material, seems to have come into use at a very early age, as is shown by the excavations at Tello.

A large number of Bab builders had the brick makers employ brick stamps which gave their names and frequently their titles, besides the name of the temple for which the bricks were intended. These enable the excavator to determine who the builders or restorers were of the buildings uncovered. Naturally, in a building like the temple of Enlil at Nippur, inscribed bricks of many builders covering a period of over 2,000 years were found. These by the help of building inscriptions, which have been found, enable scholars to rewrite considerable of the history of certain Bab temples. The walls of the city were also built of clay bricks, principally adobes. The walls usually were of very great thickness.

Clay was also employed extensively in the manufacture of images, weights, drains, playthings, such as animals, baby rattles, etc, and of inscriptions of every kind. Pottery, with the exception of the blue glaze employed in the late period, was usually plain, although some traces of painted pottery have been found. Although every particle of stone found in Babylonia was carried into the country, either by man or by inundations, still in certain periods it was used freely for statues, steles, votive objects, and in all periods for door sockets, weights and seal cylinders. Building operations in stone are scarcely known in Babylonia until perhaps the time of the greatest of all ancient builders, Nebuchadrezzar II, who laid a pavement in the causeway of Babylon, Aa-ibur-sabu, with blocks of stone from a mountain quarry. See Babylon.

11. Art

The sculpture of the Sumerians, although in most instances the hardest of materials was used, is one of the great achievements of their civilization. Enough examples have been found to trace the development of their art from comparatively rude reliefs of the archaic period to the finished sculpture of Gudea's time, 3d millennium BC, when it reached a high degree of excellence. The work of the sculpture of this age shows spirit and originality in many respects unique. In the earliest period the Babylonians attempted the round, giving frequently the main figures in full face. The perfection of detail, in their efforts to render true to life, makes their modeling very superior in the history of art. The Sumerian seems to have been able to overcome difficulties of technique which later sculptors systematically avoided.

Practically every Babylonian had his own personal seal. He used it as the signature is used at the present time or rather as the little stamp upon which is engraved the name of the individual at the present time, in the Orient, to make an impression upon the letter which was written for him by a public scribe. Thousands of these ancient seals have been found. They were cut out of all kinds of stone and metal. The style in the early period was usually cylindrical, with a hole passing lengthwise through them. In the late period the signet was commonly used. Many of these gems were exquisitely cut by lapidists of rare ability. Some of the very best work of this art belongs to the 3d millennium BC. The boldness in outline, and the action displayed are often remarkable. The most delicate saws, drills and other tools must have been employed by the early lapidist. Some of his early work is scarcely surpassed in the present age.

The gold and silver smiths of the early age have left us some beautiful examples of their art and skill. A notable one is the silver vase of Entemena of Lagash, mounted on a bronze pedestal, which stands on four feet. There is a votive inscription engraved about its neck. The bowl is divided into two compartments. On the upper are engraved seven heifers, and on the lower four eagles with extended wings, in some respects related to the totem or the coat of arms of Lagash. While attention to detail is too pronounced, yet the whole is well rendered and indicates remarkable skill, no less striking than the well-known work of their Egyp contemporaries. Bronze was also used extensively for works of art and utensils. Some remarkable specimens of this craft have been found at Tello.

In studying the magnificent remains of their art, one is thoroughly impressed with the skill displayed, and with the fact that there must have been a long period of development prior to the age to which these works belong, before such creations could have been possible. Although much of the craftsman's work is crude, there is considerable in the sculpture and engraving that is well worthy of study. And in studying these remains one is also impressed with the fact that they were produced in an alluvial plain.

Statue of Gudea from Tello.

12. Literature

The literature in a narrow sense is almost entirely confined to the epics, which are of a religious character, and the psalms, hymns, incantations, omens, etc. These are the chief remains of their culture. See Babylonia and Assyria, Religion of.

In a general sense almost every kind of lit. is found among the hundreds of thousands of clay tablets unearthed in Babylonia. The inscribed votive objects are of all kinds and descriptions. The stone vase taken in booty was dedicated to the deity of the conqueror. The beautiful piece of lapis lazuli, agate, cornelian, etc, obtained, was inscribed and devoted in the same way. Slabs, tablets and cones of all shapes and sizes, were inscribed with the king's name and titles, giving the different cities over which he ruled and referring esp. to the work that he had accomplished for his deity. From the decipherment of these votive objects much valuable data are gathered for the reconstruction of the ancient history of the land.

The same is true of what are known as building inscriptions, in which accounts of the operations of the kings in restoring and enlarging temples, shrines, walls and other city works are given. Canal digging and dredging, and such works by which the people benefited, are frequently mentioned in these inscriptions.

Epistolary literature, for example, the royal letters of Ḥammurabi, the diplomatic correspondence found in Egypt (see Tell el-Amarna) or the royal letters from the Library of Ashurbanipal (see Ashurbanipal), as well as the private correspondence of the people, furnishes valuable historical and philological data.

The thousands of tablets found in the school libraries of Sippar and Nippur, as well as of the library of Ashurbanipal, among which are all kinds of inscriptions used in the schools of the priests and scribes, have furnished a great deal of material for the Assyr dictionary, and have thrown much light upon the grammar of the language. The legal lit. is of the greatest importance for an understanding of the social conditions of the people. It is also valuable for comparative purposes in studying the codes of other peoples. See CODE OF ḤAMMURABI.

The commercial or legal transactions, dated in all periods, from the earliest times until the latest, also throw important light upon the social conditions of the people. Many thousands of these documents have been found, by the help of which the very life that pulsated in the streets of Bab cities is restored.

The administrative documents from the temple archives also have their value, in that they furnish important data as regards the maintenance of the temples and other institutions; and incidentally much light on the nationality and religion of the people, whose names appear in great numbers upon them. The records are receipts of taxes or rents from districts close by the temples, and of commercial transactions conducted with this revenue. A large portion of these archives consists of the salary payments of storehouse officials and priests. There seems to have been a host of tradesmen and functionaries in connection with the temple. Besides the priest, elder, seer, seeress, sorcerer, sorceress, singer, etc, there were the farmer, weaver, miller, carpenter, smith, butcher, baker, porter, overseer, scribe, measurer, watchman, etc. These documents give us an insight into Bab system of bookkeeping, and show how carefully the administrative affairs of the temple were conducted. In fact the temple was provided for and maintained along lines quite similar to many of our modern institutions.

13. Libraries

The discovery of the Library of Ashurbanipal at Nineveh speaks volumes for the culture of Assyria, but that culture was largely borrowed from the Babylonians. Much that this library contained had been secured from Bab libraries by the scribes employed by Ashurbanipal. In every important center there doubtless existed schools and libraries in connection with the temples. At Nippur, in 1890, Dr. J. P. Peters found such a library, but unfortunately, although he termed it such, his Assyriologists did not recognize that one of the greatest discoveries of antiquity had been made. It remained for Dr. J. H. Haynes, a decade later, to discover another portion of this library, which he regarded as such, because of the large number of tablets which he uncovered. Père Scheil, prior to Dr. Haynes's discovery, had the good fortune while at Sippar to discover a part of the school and library of that important center. Since Professor Scheil's excavations, Arabs have unearthed many inscriptions of this library, which have found their way to museums and into the hands of private individuals.

The plan of the Nippur Library, unearthed by Dr. Haynes, has been published by Mr. C. S. Fisher, the architect of the Nippur expedition (see *LOTB*, 183). Professor Scheil, in publishing his results, has also given a plan of the school he discovered, and a full description of its arrangements, as well as the pedagogical methods that had been employed in that institution of learning. This has also been attempted by others, but in a less scientific manner. One of the striking features of these libraries is the use of the large reference cylinders, quadrangular, pentagonal and hexagonal in shape. There was a hole cut lengthwise through them for the purpose of mounting them like revolving stands. These libraries, doubtless, contained all the works the Babylonians possessed on law, science, literature and religion. There are lexical lists, paradigm tablets, lists of names, of places, countries, temples, rivers, officers, stones, gods, etc. Sufficient tablets have been deciphered to determine their general character. Also hundreds of exercise tablets have been found, showing the progress made by pupils in writing, in mathematics, in grammar, and in other branches of learning. Some tablets appear to have been written after dictation. Doubtless, the excavators found the waste heaps of the school, where these tablets had been thrown for the purpose of working them over again as raw material, for new exercises. The school libraries must have been large. Considering for instance that the ideographic and phonetic values of the cuneiform signs in use numbered perhaps 30,000, even the syllabaries which were required to contain these different values must have been many in number, and esp. as tablets, unlike books made of paper, have only two sides to them. And when we take into consideration all the different kinds of lit. which have been found, we must realize that these libraries were immense, and numbered many thousands of tablets.

SEAL CYLINDERS.

14. Personal Names

In modern times the meaning of names given children is rarely considered; in fact, in many instances the name has suffered so much through changes that it is difficult to ascertain its original meaning. Then also, at present, in order to avoid confusion the child is given two or more names. It was not so with the ancient Babylonian. Originally the giving of a name was connected with some special circumstance, and though this was not always the case throughout the history of Babylonia, the correct form of the name was always preserved.

The name may have been an expression of their religious faith. It may have told of the joy experienced at the birth of an heir. It may even betray the suffering that was involved at the birth of the child, or the life that the parents had lived. In short, the names afford us an intimate glimpse into the everyday life of the people.

The average Bab name is theophorous, and indicates one of the deities worshipped by the family, and often the city. For example, it is suggestive that persons with names compounded with Enlil and Ninib hailed from Nippur. Knowing the deities of the surrounding people we have also important evidence in determining the origin of peoples in Babylonia having foreign names. For example, if a name is composed of the Hittite deity Teshup, or the Amorite deity Amurru, or the Aramaean god Dagan, or the Egyp god Esi (Isis), foreign influence is naturally looked for from the countries represented. Quite frequently the names of foreign deities are compounded with Bab elements, often resulting from mixed marriages.

Clay Tablet with Seal Impression.

Theophorous names are composed of two, three, four and even five elements. Those having two or three elements predominate. Two-element names have a diety plus a verbal form or a subst.; or vice versa: for example, *Nabu-na'id* (Nabonidus), "Nebo is exalted," or *Shulman-asharedu* (Shalmaneser), "Shalman is foremost." Many different combinations are found in three-element names which are composed of the name of the deity, a subst., a verbal form, a pronominal suffix, or some other form of speech, in any of the three positions. Explanations of a few of the familiar Bib. names follow: *Sin-akhe-erba* (Sennacherib), "Sin has increased the brothers"; *Marduk-apal-iddin* (Merodach-baladan), "Marduk has given a son"; *Ashur-akh-iddin* (Esarhaddon), "Ashur has given a brother"; *Ashur-bani-apal*, "Ashur is creating a son"; *Nabu-kudurri-usur* (Nebuchadrezzar), "O Nebo, protect the boundary"; *Amel-Marduk* (Evil-Merodach), "Man of Marduk"; *Bel-shar-uṣur* (Belshazzar), "O Bel, protect the king." Some Bab names mentioned in the Bible are really of foreign origin, for example, Amraphel and Sargon. Amraphel originally is west Semitic and is written *Ḥammurabi* (pronounced *Ḥammu-rabi*, the first letter being the Semitic *ḥeth*). Sargon was perhaps originally Aramaean, and is composed of the elements *shar* and the god *Gan*. When written in cuneiform it was written *Shargani*, and later *Sharrukin*, being tr[d] "the true king." Many names in use were not theophorous; for example, such personal names as *Ululâ*, "the month Ulul"; names of animals, as *Kalbâ*, "dog," gentilic names, as *Akkadai*, "the Akkadian," names of crafts, as *Paḥâru*, "potter," etc.

The lit. abounds in hypochoristica. One element of a name was used for the sake of shortness, to which usually a hypochoristica suffix was added, like *Mardukâ* (Mordecai). That is, the ending *a* or *ai* was added to one of the elements of a longer name.

15. History of City-Kingdoms

The written history of Babylonia at the present begins from about 4200 BC. But instead of finding things crude and aboriginal in this, the earliest period, the remains discovered show that the people had attained to a high level of culture. Back of that which is known there must lie a long period of development. This is attested in many ways; for instance, the earliest writing found is so far removed from the original hieroglyphs that it is only possible to ascertain what the original pictures were by knowing the values which the signs possessed. The same conclusion is ascertained by a study of the art and literature. Naturally, as mentioned above, it is not impossible that this development took place in a previous home of the inhabitants.

The history of early Babylonia is at present a conflict of the kings and patesis (priest-kings) of the different city-kingdoms, for supremacy over each other, as well as over the surrounding peoples. The principal states that figure in the early history are: Kish, Lagash, Nippur, Akkad, Umma, Erech, Ur and Opis. At the present time more is known of Lagash, because the excavations conducted at that site were more extensive than at others. This makes much of our knowledge of the history of the land center about that city. And yet it should be stated that the hegemony of Lagash lasted for a long period, and the kingdom will ultimately occupy a prominent position when the final history of the land is written. Nippur, where considerable work was also done, was not the seat of rulers, but the sacred city of the god Enlil, to whom the kings of other cities generally did obeisance. Following is a list of known rulers of the different city-kingdoms.

16. Kish

El-Ohemir, identified as the ancient city of Kish, not far from Babylon, is one of the oldest Sem centers of the land. No systematic excavations have been conducted at this site, but besides the inscriptions which the Arabs have unearthed, several of the rulers are known to us through votive inscriptions discovered at Nippur and elsewhere. The rulers of Kish are: Utug p. (patesi), cir 4200 BC; Mesilim k. (king), cir 4000 BC; Lugal-tarsi k.; Enbi-Ishtar k.; Manishtusu k., cir 2650 BC; Urumush k., cir 2600; Manana k.; Sumu-ditana k. and Tanium k.

17. Lagash

The excavations by the French under De Sarsez and Cross at *Tello*, the ancient city Lagash, have yielded more inscriptions of ancient Bab rulers than those at any other site. Lagash was destroyed about 2000 BC, and only partially rebuilt in the post-Bab period. The known rulers are: Lugal-shag-Engur patesi, cir 4000 BC, contemporary with Mesilim k. of Kish; *Badu k.; *En-khegal k.; Ur-Nina k.; Akurgal p.; Eannatum p. and k.; Enannatum I p.; Entemena p.; Enannatum II p.; Enetarzi p.; Enlitarzi p.; Lugal-anda p.; Uru-kagina k., contemporary with Lugal-zaggisi, k. of Uruk; Engilsa p., contemporary with Manishtusu k. of Kish; Lugul-ushumgal p., contemporary with Sargon of Accad; Ur-Babbar p., contemporary with Naram-Sin of Accad; Ur-E p.; Lugal-bur p.; Basha-Kama p.; Ur-Mama p.; Ug-me p.; Ur-Bau p.; Gudea p.; Nammakhini p.; Ur-gar p.; Ka-azag p.; Galu-Bau p.; Galu-Gula p.; Ur-Ninsun p.; Ur-Ningirsu p.; contemporary with Ur-Engur k. of Ur-abba p.; *Galu-kazal p.; *Galu-andul p.; *Ut-Lama I p.; *Alla, *Ur-Lama II p.; contemporary with Dungi k. of Ur; Arad-Nannar p. Unfortunately, with the exception of about one-third of these rulers, the exact order is yet to be ascertained. (Asterisk denotes unidentified forms.)

18. Adab

The mounds of Bismaya which have been identified as Adab were partially excavated by Dr. Edgar J. Banks, for the University of Chicago. Its remains indicate that it is one of the oldest cities discovered. A ruler named Esar, cir 4200 BC, is known from a number of inscriptions, as well as a magnificent statue of the king, discovered by Dr. Banks.

The large group of mounds covering an area, the circumference of which is three miles, called in ancient times Nippur, but now Noufar, was excavated as mentioned above by Drs. Peters and Haynes for the University of Pennsylvania. While a great number of Bab kings and patesis are represented by inscriptions discovered at Nippur, practically all had their seats of government at other places, it being the sacred city.

19. Nippur

The mounds at the present called Warka, but representing ancient Erech (Gen **10** 10), covering an area whose circumference is 6 miles, have been tentatively examined by Loftus and other explorers. Many inscriptions have also been unearthed by the Arabs at this site. The rulers of this city known to us are: Ilu-(m)a-ilu, Lugal-zaggisi k., contemporary with Uru-kagina of Lagash; Lugal-kigubnidudu k.; Lugal-kisalsi k.; Sin-gashid k., cir 2200 BC, and Sin-gamil k.

20. Erech

Senkereh known in the OT as Ellasar (Gen **14** 1), and in the inscriptions as Larsa, has been explored by Loftus and others. The known rulers of the city are: Gungunu k., contemporary of Ur-Ninib k. of Isin; Sumu-ilu; Nur-Adad; Sin-iddinam; Eri-Aku (Bib. Arioch) cir 2000 BC, son of Kudur-Mabug k. of Elam, and Rim-Sin (or Rim-Aku), his brother.

21. Larsa

The present Fara, which in ancient times was called Shuruppak, was partially excavated by the Germans under Koldewey, Andraea, and Noeldeke. It is also a very ancient city. It yielded little to the spade of the excavator. It is close by Abu-Hatab, and known as the place where the scenes of the Bab Deluge story occurred. Two rulers known from the inscriptions found there are Dada and Haladda, belonging to a comparatively early period.

22. Shuruppak

The site now known as Abu-Hatab is the ancient Kisurra. It was partially excavated by the Germans. It flourished as a city in the 3d millennium BC. The two rulers of this city that are known are Idinilu p., and Itur-Shamash p. (?).

23. Kisurra

The site now called Jokha lying to the N.W. of Lagash is an ancient Sumerian city known as Umma. The site has been explored by Dr. Peters and others, but more recently surveyed by Andraea and Noeldeke. It proved to be a city destroyed in the early period. Arabs have lately found thousands of documents belonging to the ancient archives of the city. Some of the rulers known are: Ush p., Enakalli and Urlumma p., contemporaries of Enannatum I of Lagash; Ili p., appointed by Entemena p., of Lagash; Kur-Shesh p., time of Manishtusu; *Galu-Babbar p.; Ur-nesu p., contemporary of Dungi k., of Ur.

24. Umma

The city mentioned in Gen **10** 10 as Accad, one of Nimrod's cities, has not been explored, but is well known by the inscriptions of Sargon and his son Naram-Sin as well as omen-texts of later eras. Sargon was a usurper. He was born in concealment, and sent adrift in an ark of bulrushes like Moses. He was rescued and brought up by Akki, a farmer. He assumed the title "king of the city" (*Shar-ali*), or "king of Uri" (*Shar Uri*). Later he conquered the entire country, and became the "king of Accad and Sumer." In his latter years he extended his conquests to Elam, Amurru and Subartu, and earned for himself the title "king of the Four Quarters," which his son Naram-Sin inherited. The latter followed up the successes of his father and marched into Magan, in the Sinaitic peninsula. Naram-Sin, as well as his father, was a great builder. Evidences of their operations are seen in many cities. Naram-Sin was succeeded by Bingani, who apparently lost the title "king of the Four Quarters," being only called "king of the City, or Uri."

25. Accad

The exact site of the city of Opis is still in doubt, but the city is represented by the ruler Zuzu k., who was defeated by Eannatum p., of Lagash.

26. Opis

The city Basime also remains unidentified, but is represented by Ibalum p., a contemporary of Manishtusu k., of Kish, and son of Ilsu-rabi, apparently another patesi of that city.

27. Basime

A site not far from Nippur, called Delehem or Drehem, which was explored by Dr. Peters, has recently yielded thousands of tablets from the Temple archives dated in the reigns of kings in the Ur Dynasty.

28. Drehem

The extensive group of mounds lying on the west side of the Euphrates, called Mugayyar, and generally known as Ur of the Chaldees, is the ancient Urumma. It was explored by Taylor and others, and proved to have been an important capital from the middle of the 3d millennium BC. The dynasty which had made the city its capital is known through inscriptions discovered there and at Tello, Nippur, Drehem and Djokha. Thousands of inscriptions dated in what is commonly called the Ur Dynasty have been published. The dynasty was founded by Ur-Engur, who is conspicuous for his building operations at Nippur and other cities. A dynastic tablet of a much later period, the provenience of which is in doubt, gives the rulers of this dynasty founded about 2400 BC, and the number of years that they reigned.

29. Urumma

Urumma Dynasty

Ur-Engur, 18 years
Dungi (son), 58 years
Bur-Sin (son), 9 years
Gimil-Sin (son), 7 years
Ibi-Sin (son), 25 years
Five kings, 117 years

The same tablet gives also the following list of the rulers of Isin. Ishbi-Urra, the founder, lived about 2283 BC.

Isin Dynasty

Ishbi-Urra, 32 years
Gimil-ilishu (son), 10 years
Idin-Dagan (son), 21 years
Ishme-Dagan (son), 20 years
Libit-Ishtar (son), 11 years
Ur-Ninib, 28 years
Bur-Sin II (son), 28 years
Iter-iqisha (son), 5 years
Urra-imitti (brother), 7 years
Sin-iqisha, 6 months
Enlil-bani, 24 years
Zambia, 3 years
———, 5 years
Ea———, 4 years
Sin-magir, 11 years
Damiq-ilishu (son), 23 years
Sixteen kings, 225 years and 6 months

About the time the Nisin Dynasty came to a close, and while the Larsa Dynasty was ruling, the First Dynasty of Babylon was established. Following is a list of 11 rulers of this dynasty who ruled 300 years:

30. First Dynasty of Babylon

I. First Dynasty of Babylon

Sumu-abum, 14 years
Sumu-la-el, 36 years

Sabium (son), 14 years
Abil-Sin (son), 18 years
Sin-muballit (son), 20 years
Ḥammu-rabi (son), 43 years
Samsu-iluna (son), 38 years
Abi-eshuh (son), 28 years
Ammi-Ditana (son), 37 years
Ammi-Zaduga (son), 21 years
Samsu-Ditana (son), 32 years

The First Dynasty of Babylon came into prominence in the reign of Sin-muballit who captured Nisin. Eri-Aku of the Larsa Dynasty shortly afterward took the city. When Ḥammurabi came to the throne he was subject to Eri-Aku (Bib. Arioch) of Larsa, the son of the Elamite king, Kudur-Mabug. The latter informs us that he was suzerain of Amurru (Pal and Syria), which makes intelligible the statement in Gen **14**, that the kings of Canaan were subject to the king of Elam, whose name was Chedorlaomer (Kudur-Lagamar). In his 31st year, Ḥammurabi, who is the Amraphel of Gen **14** 1, succeeded in throwing off the Elamite yoke, and not only established his independence but also became the complete master of Babylonia by driving out the Elamites.

31. Sealand Dynasty

In the region of the Pers Gulf, south of Babylonia, ruled a dynasty partly contemporaneously with the First Dynasty, extending over the reigns of about five of the last kings, and over several of the Cassite Dynasty, known as the Sealand Dynasty. The annalist records for the latter the following list of 11 kings who ruled 368 years:

II. Sealand Dynasty

Ilima-ilu, 60 years
Itti-ili-nibi, 55 years
Damqi-ilishu, 36 years
Ishkibal, 15 years
Shushshi (brother), 27 years
Gulkishar, 55 years
Pesh-gal-daramash (son), 50 years
Adara-kalama (son), 28 years
Ekur-ul-anna, 26 years
Melamma-kurkura, 7 years
Ea-gamil, 9 years

32. Cassite Dynasty

The First Dynasty of Babylon came to an end through an invasion of the Hittites. They plundered Babylon and perhaps ruled that city for a number of years. A new dynasty was then established about 1750 BC by a foreign people known as Cassites. There were 36 kings in this dynasty ruling 576 years and 9 months. Unfortunately the tablet containing the list is fragmentary.

III. Cassite Dynasty

Gandash, 16 years
Agum I (s), 22 years
Kashtiliash I, usurper, 22 years; b. of Ulamburiash and s. of Burna-buriash
Du(?) shi (s), 8 years
Abirattash (b?)
Tazzigurmash (s)
Agum II (s)
———; ——— Long gap
———
*Kara-indash I, contemporary with Ashur-rim-nisheshu, k. of Assyria
*Kadashman-Enlil I (s?)
*Kuri-Galzu I
Burna-buriash II, contemporary of Buzur-Ashur, k. of Assyria
*Kara-Indash II, son-in-law of Ashur-uballit, k. of Assyria
*Nazi-Bugash (usurper)
Kuri-Galzu II (s. of Burna-buriash), 23 years; contemporary of Ashur-uballit, and Enlil-nirari, kings of Assyria
Nazi-Maruttash (s), 26 years; contemporary of Adad-nirari I, p. of Assyria.
Kadashman-Turgu (s), 17 years
Kadashman-Enlil II, 7 years
Kudur-Enlil (s), 9 years
Shagarakti-Shuriash (s), 13 years
Kashtiliash II (s), 8 years
Enlil-nadin-shum, 1½ years
Kadashman-Kharbe II, 1½ years
Adad-shum-iddin, 6 years
Adad-shum-usur, 30 years
Meli-Shipak (s?), 15 years
Marduk-apil-iddin (s), 13 years
Zamama-shum-iddin, 1 year
Bel-mu—, 3 years

33. Cassite Rule

The region from which these Cassites came has not yet been determined, although it seems to be the district N.E. of Assyria. Gandash, the first king, seems to have enjoyed the all-embracing title, "King of the Four Quarters of the World." Little is known of the other rulers until Agum II, who claims the rule of the Cassites, Accad, Babel, Padan, Alman and Guti. In his inscriptions he records the conquest of Khani in Asia Minor, and the fact that he brought back to Babylon the statues of Marduk and Zarpanit, which had been carried off by the Hittites. The Cassite rule, while extending over many cents., was not very prosperous. At Nippur the excavations showed active operations on the part of a few kings in restoring the temple and doing obeisance to Enlil. The rulers seemed to have conformed to the religion of the land, for few foreign elements have been recognized as having been introduced into it during this era. The many Cassite names found in the inscriptions would indicate an influx from a Cassite quarter of no small proportion. And yet it should be noted that, in the same era, Hittite and Mittanean influence, as is shown by the nomenclature, is as great as the Cassite. It was during this period that Assyria rose to power and influence, and was soon to become the master of the Mesopotamian region.

IV. Isin or Pashe Dynasty

11 Kings; began to rule about 1172 BC

34. Isin Dynasty

Marduk . . . . 17 years
Wanting, 6 years
Nebuchadrezzar I, contemporary of Ashur-resh-ishi, k. of Assyria
Enlil-nadin-apal
Marduk-nadin-akhi, contemporary of Tiglath-pileser I, k. of Assyria
Marduk-shapik-zer-mati, contemporary of Ashur-bel-kala, k. of Assyria
Adad-apal-iddin, 22 years
Marduk-akh-erba, 11/2
Marduk-zer . . . . , 12 years
Nabu-shum-libur, 8(?) years

35. Nebuchadrezzar I

The most famous king of this dynasty, in fact of this era, was Nebuchadrezzar I, who reëstablished firmly the rule of Babylon. He carried on a successful expedition into Elam as well as into Amurru where he fought against the Hittite. He also conquered the Lulubites. But in contest for supremacy with Assyria Ashur-resh-ishi triumphed, and he was forced to retreat ingloriously to Babylon. His successors failed to withstand the Assyrians, esp. under Tiglath-pileser I, and were allowed to rule only by sufferance. The Babylonians had lost their prestige; the Assyrians had become the dominant people of the land. Few rulers of the dynasty which followed are known except by name. The dynasties with one exception were of short duration.

V. Sealand Dynasty

3 Kings

36. Sealand Dynasty

Simmash-Shipak, 18 years; about 1042 BC
Ea-mukin-shum, 6 months
Kashshu-nadin-akhi, 3 years

VI. Bit-Bazi Dynasty

3 Kings

37. Bit-Bazi Dynasty

Eulmash-shakin-shum, 17 years; about 1020 BC
Ninib-kudur-usur, 3 years
Shilanim-Shuqamuna, 3 months

38. Other Rulers

VII. An Elamitic King, whose name is not known
VIII. 13(?) kings who ruled 36 years
IX. A dynasty of 5(?) kings

X. Babylonian Dynasty

39. Babylonian Dynasty

Following is a partial list of the 22 kings who ruled until the destruction of Babylon by Sennacherib, when the Assyr kings assumed direct control. Ashurbanipal, however, introduced a new policy and viceroys were appointed.

Shamash-mudammiq
Nabu-shar-ishkun I
Nabu-apal-iddin
Marduk-nadin-shum
Marduk-balatsu-iqbi
Bau-akh-iddin
Nabu-shum-ishkun II
Nabonassar
Nabu-nadin-zer; 747–734 BC
Nabu-shum-ishkun III; 733–732 BC
Nabu-mukin-zer; 731–729 BC
Pul (Tiglath-pileser III); 729–727 BC
Ulula (Shalmanesar V); 727–722 BC
Merodach-baladan I; 722–710 BC
Sargon; 710–705 BC
Sennacherib; 704–702 BC
Marduk-zakir-shum (1 month)
Merodach-baladan II (9 months)
Bel-ibni; 702–700 BC
Ashur-nadin-shum; 700–694 BC
Nergal-ushezib; 694–693 BC
Mushezib-Marduk; 692–689 BC
Sennacherib; 689–681 BC
Esarhaddon; 681–668 BC
Ashurbanipal; 668–626 BC
Shamash-shum-ukin; 668-648 BC
Kandalanu; 648–626 BC
Ashur-etil-ilani-ukin; 626–
Nabopolassar; 626–

During the time of Sennacherib, Merodach-baladan the Chaldaean became a great obstacle to Assyria's maintaining its supremacy over Babylonia. Three times he gained possession of Babylon, and twice had himself proclaimed king. For thirty years he plotted against Assyria. What is learned from the inscriptions concerning him furnishes an interesting commentary on the sending of the embassy, in 704 BC, to Hezekiah (2 K **20** 12; Isa **39** 1) in order to induce him to revolt against Assyria, which he knew would help his own cause. Finally Sennacherib, in 690, after he had experienced much trouble by the repeated uprisings of the Babylonians, and the aspirations of Merodach-baladan, endeavored to obliterate Babylon from the map. His son and successor Esarhaddon, however, tried to make Babylon again happy and prosperous. One of his first acts was to send back to Babylon the statue of Bel-Merodach. He rebuilt the city, and also restored other Bab temples, for instance, that of Enlil at Nippur. The Babylonians solemnly declared him king. Ashurbanipal, his son and successor, followed his policy. The evidence of his operations at Nippur is everywhere seen in the shape of stamped, kiln-dried bricks.

Before Esarhaddon died, he had planned that Babylonia should become independent and be ruled by his son, Shamash-shum-ukin, while Assyria he handed down to Ashurbanipal. But when the latter came to the throne, Assyria permitted the former only to be appointed viceroy of Babylon. It seems also that even some portions of Babylonia were ruled directly by Ashurbanipal.

After fifteen years Shamash-shum-ukin rebelled and attempted to establish his independence, but Sennacherib besieged Babylon and took it, when Shamash-shum-ukin destroyed himself. Kadalanu was then appointed viceroy, and ruled over part of the country. Nabopolassar was the last viceroy appointed by Assyria. At last the time had arrived for the Babylonians to come again unto their own. Nabopolassar who perhaps was a Chaldaean by origin, made an alliance with the Umman Manda. This he strengthened by the marriage of his son Nebuchadrezzar to the daughter of Astyages, the king. Nineveh finally fell before the Umman Manda hordes, and was razed to the ground. This people took possession of Northern Assyria. The Armenian vassal states, and Southern Assyria, as well as the title to Pal, Syria and Egypt, fell to Babylonia.

Rulers of Neo-Babylonian Empire

40. Neo-Babylonian Rulers

Nabopolassar; 625–604 BC
Nebuchadrezzar II (s); 604–568 BC
Evil-Merodach (s); 561–560 BC
Neriglissar (brother-in-law); 559–556 BC
Labosoarchad (s); 556 BC
Nabonidus; 555–539 BC
Cyrus conquered Babylonia in 539 BC

Nabopolassar having established himself king of Babylon became the founder of the neo-Babylonian empire. He was succeeded by his son, Nebuchadrezzar II, who like Ḥammurabi and Sargon is among the greatest known characters in Bab history. He is the Bib. Nebuchadrezzar who carried the Jews into captivity. There are a number of lengthy records of Nebuchadrezzar concerning the buildings he erected, as well as of other public acts, but unfortunately only a fragment of a historical inscription referring to him has been found. The building inscriptions portray him as the great builder he is represented to be in the OT (see Babylon). He made Babylon the mistress of the civilized world.

Evil-Merodach, his son and successor, is also mentioned in the OT. Two short reigns followed when the ruling dynasty was overthrown and Nabonidus was placed upon the throne. The king, who delighted in exploring and restoring ancient temples, placed his son at the head of the army. Nabonidus desiring to centralize the religion of Babylonia, brought to Babylon many of the images of deities from other cities. This greatly displeased the people, and excited a strong feeling against him. The priesthood was alienated, and the military party was displeased with him, for in his antiquarian pursuits he left the defence of the empire to others. So when Cyrus, king of Anshan and ruler of Persia, entered the country, he had little difficulty in defeating the Babylonians in a battle at Opis. Sippar immediately surrendered to the invader, and the gates of Babylon were thrown open to his army under Gobryas, his general. Nabonidus was imprisoned. Three months later Cyrus entered Babylon; Belshazzar, who doubtless had set up his throne after his father had been deposed, was slain a week later on the night of the eleventh of Marchesvan. This scene may have occurred in the palace built by Nebuchadrezzar. This event, told by the chronicler, is a remarkable verification of the interesting story related of Belshazzar in Dnl. The title used by the kings who follow the Bab Dynasty is "King of Babylon and King of Countries."

41. Persian Rulers of Babylonia

PERSIAN RULERS OF BABYLONIA

Cyrus; 538–529 BC
Cambyses; 529–522 BC
Barzia
Nebuchadrezzar III
Darius I; 521–485 BC
Xerxes; 485–464 BC
Artaxerxes I; 464–424 BC
Xerxes II; 424–423 BC
Darius II; 423–404 BC
Artaxerxes II; 405–358 BC
Artaxerxes III (Ochos); 358–338 BC
Arses; 338–335 BC
Darius III; 335–331 BC

Alexander the Great conquered Babylonia 331 BC.

Several of the Pers rulers figured prominently in the OT narratives. Cyrus in a cylinder inscription, which is preserved in a fragmentary form, endeavors to justify himself in the eyes of the people. He claims that the god Marduk raised him up to take the place of Nabonidus, and to defend the religion of the people. He tries to show how considerate he was by returning to their respective cities the gods that had been removed from their shrines; and esp. by liberating foreign peoples held in bondage. While he does not mention what exiles were allowed to return to their native homes, the OT informs us that the Jews were among those delivered. And the returning of the images to their respective places is also an interesting commentary on Ezr **1** 7, in which we are told that the Jews were allowed to take with them their sacred vessels. The spirit manifested in the proclamation for the rebuilding of the temple (Ezr **1** 1.4) seems also to have been in accordance with his policy on ascending the Bab throne. A year before his death he associated with himself Cambyses his son, another character mentioned in the OT. He gave him the title "King of Babylon," but retained for himself "King of Countries." A usurper Smerdis, the Magian, called Barzia in the inscriptions, assumed the throne of Babylonia, but Darius Hystaspes, who was an Aryan and Zoroastrian in religion, finally killed Smerdis and made himself king of Babylon. But before he was acknowledged king he had to reconquer the Babylonians. By so doing the ancient tradition that Bel of Babylon conferred the legitimate right to rule that part of the world ceased to be acknowledged. Under Nidinta-Bel, who assumed the name Nebuchadrezzar III, the Babylonians regained their independence, but it was of short duration, lasting less than a year.

LITERATURE.—History: Rogers, *History of Bab and Assyr*, 1902; Winckler, *History of Bab and Assyr*, 1907; King, *Sumer and Accad*, 1910. Religion: Jastrow, *Religion of Bab and Assyr*, 1898; Rogers, *Religion of Bab and Assyr, Esp. in Its Relation to Israel*, 1908; Sayce, *The Religions of Ancient Egypt and Bab*, 1903. Literature: *Assyr and Bab Lit.*, in "The World's Great Books"; edited by R. F. Harper. Relation to OT: Price, *The Monuments and the OT*, 1907; Pinches, *The OT in the Light of the Records of Assyr and Bab*, 1902; Clay, *Light on the OT from Babel*, 1908; Clay, *Amurru, the Home of the Northern Semites*, 1909. See also "Literature" in ASSYRIA.

A. T. CLAY

BABYLONIA AND ASSYRIA, THE RELIGION OF:

I. Definition.—The religion of Babylonia and Assyria is that system of belief in higher things with which the peoples of the Tigris and Euphrates valley strove to put themselves into relations, in order to live their lives. The discoveries of the past cent. have supplied us with a mass of information concerning this faith from which we have been able to secure a greater knowledge of it than of any other ancient oriental religion, except that of Israel. Yet the information which is thus come into our hands is embarrassing because of its very richness, and it will doubtless be a long time before it is possible to speak with certainty concerning many of the problems which now confront us. Progress in the interpretation of the literature is however so rapid that we may now give a much more intelligible account of this religion than could have been secured even so recently as five years ago.

For purposes of convenience, the religion of Babylonia and Assyria may be grouped into three great periods.

(1) The first of these periods extends from the earliest times, about 3500 BC, down to the union of the Bab states under Ḥammurabi, about 2000 BC.

(2) The second period extends to the rise of the Chaldaean empire under Nabopolassar, 625 BC, and

(3) The third period embraces the brief history of this Chaldaean or neo-Bab empire under Cyrus, 538 BC.

The Assyr religion belongs to the second period, though it extends even into the third period, for Nineveh did not fall until 607 BC.

II. The Sources.—The primary sources of our knowledge of this religion are to be found in the distinctively religious texts, such as hymns, prayers, priestly rituals and liturgies, and in the vast mass of magical and incantation literature. The major part of this religious lit. which has come down to us dates from the reign of Ashurbanipal (668–625 BC) though much of it is quite clearly either copied from or based upon much older material. If, however, we relied for our picture of the Bab and Assyr religion exclusively upon these religious texts, we should secure a distorted and in some places an indefinite view. We must add to these in order to perfect the picture practically the whole of the lit. of these two peoples.

The inscriptions upon which the kings handed down to posterity an account of their great deeds contain lists of gods whom they invoked, and these must be taken into consideration. The laws also have in large measure a religious basis, and the business inscriptions frequently invoke deities at the end. The records of the astronomers, the state despatches of kings, the reports of general officers from the field, the handbooks of medicine, all these and many other divisions of a vast lit. contribute each its share of religious material. Furthermore, as the religion was not only the faith of the king, but also the faith of the state itself, the progress of the commonwealth to greater power oftentimes carried some local god into a new relationship to other gods, or the decadence of the commonwealth deprived a god of some of his powers or attributes, so that even the distinctively political inscriptions have importance in helping us to reconstruct the ancient literature.

III. The History.—The origin of the Bab religion is hid from our eyes in those ancient days of which we know little and can never hope to know much.

Babylonian Idols.

In the earliest documents which have come down to us written in the Sumerian language, there are found Sem words or constructions or both. It seems now to be definitely determined that a Sumerian people whose origin is unknown inhabited Babylonia before the coming of the Semites, whose original home was in Arabia. Of the Sumerian faith before a union was formed with the Semites, we know very little indeed. But we may perhaps safely say that among that ancient people, beneath the belief in gods there lay deep in their consciousness the belief in animism. They thought that every object, animate or inanimate, had a *zi* or spirit. The word seems originally to have meant life. Life manifests itself to us as motion; everything which moves has life. The power of motion separates the animate from the inanimate. All that moves possesses life, the motionless is lifeless or dead.

Besides this belief in animism, the early Sumerians seem to have believed in ghosts that were related to the world of the dead as the *zi* was related to the world of the living. The *lil* or ghost was a night demon of baleful influence upon men, and only to be cast out by many incantations. The *lil* was attended by a serving-maid (*ardat lili*, "maid of night") which in the later Sem development was transformed into the feminine *lilitu*. It is most curious and interesting that this ghost demon of the Sumerians lived on through all the history of the Bab religion, and is mentioned even in one of the OT prophets (Isa **34** 14; Heb *Lillīth*, tr[d] "night monster"). The origin of the Sem religion brought by the ancient Sem people and united with this Sumerian faith is also lost in the past.

It seems to be quite clear that the gods and the religious ideas which these Semites brought with them from the desert had very little if any importance for the religion which they afterward professed in Babylonia. Some of the names of their gods and images of these they very probably brought with them, but the important thing, it must always be remembered, about the gods is not the names but the attributes which were ascribed to them, and these must have been completely changed during the long history which follows their first contact with the Sumerians. From the Sumerians there flowed a great stream of religious ideas, subject indeed to modifications from time to time down the succeeding cents. In our study of the pantheon we shall see from time to time how the gods changed their places and how the ideas concerning them were modified by political and other movements. In the very earliest times, besides these ideas of spirits and ghosts, we find also numbers of local gods. Every center of human habitation had its special patron deity and this deity is always associated with some great natural phenomenon. It was natural that the sun and moon should be made prominent among these gods, but other natural objects and forces were personified and deified, streams, stones and many others.

Our chief source of information concerning the gods of the first period of religious development before the days of Ḥammurabi is found in the historical inscriptions of the early kings and rulers. Many of these describe offerings of temples and treasures made to the gods, and all of them are religious in tone and filled with ascriptions of praise to the gods. From these early texts Professor Jastrow has extricated the names of the following deities, gods and goddesses. I reproduce his list as the best yet made, but keep in mind that some of the readings are doubtful and some were certainly otherwise read by the Babylonians or Sumerians, though we do not now know how they ought to be read. The progress of Assyr research is continually providing corrected readings for words hitherto known to us only in ideograms. It is quite to be expected that many of these strange, not to say grotesque, names will some day prove to be quite simple, and easy to utter: En-lil (Ellil, Bel) Belit, Nin-khar-sag, Nin-gir-su, who also appears as Dun-gur, Bau, Ga-tum-dug, Nin-din-dug, Ea, Nin-a-gal, Gal-dim-zu-ab, Nin-ki, Dam-gal-nun-na, Nergal, Shamash, A or Malkatu, the wife of Shamash, Nannar, or Sin, Nin-Urum, Innanna, Nana, Anunit, Nina, Ishtar, Anu, Nin-dar-a, Gal-alim, Nin-shakh, Dun-shagga, Lugal-banda, with a consort Nin-sun, Dumu-zi-zu-ab, Dumu-zi, Lugal-Erim, Nin-e-gal and Ningal, Nin-gish-zi-da, Dun-pa-uddu, Nin-mar, Pa-sag, Nidaba, Ku(?)-anna, Shid, Nin-agid-kha-du, Nin-shul-li, En-gubarra, Im-mi-khu(?), Ur-du-zi, Kadi, Nu-ku-sir-da, Ma-ma, Za-ma-ma, Za-za-ru, Im-pa-ud-du, Ur-e-nun-ta-ud-du-a, Khi-gir-nunna, Khi-shagga, Gur-mu, Zar-mu, Dagan, Damu, Lama, Nesu, Nun-gal, An-makh, Nin-si-na, Nin-asu. In this list great gods and goddesses and all kinds of minor deities are gathered together, and the list looks and sounds hopeless. But these are local deities, and some of them are mere duplications. Nearly every place in early times would have a sun-god or a moon-god or both, and in the political development of the country the moon-god of the conquering city displaced or absorbed the moon-god of the conquered. When we have eliminated these gods, who have practically disappeared, there remains a comparatively small number of gods who outrank all the others.

In the room of some of these gods that disappeared, others, esp. in Assyria, found places. There was, however, a strong tendency to diminish the number of the gods. They are in early days mentioned by the score, but as time goes on many of these vanish away and only the few remain. As Jastrow has pointed out, Shalmaneser II (859-825 BC) had only eleven gods in his pantheon: Ashur, Anu, Bel, Ea, Sin, Shamash, Ninib, Nergal,

Worshipping Heavenly Bodies (from a Cylinder of White Agate).

Nusku, Belit and Ishtar. Sennacherib (704–681 BC) usually mentions only eight, namely, Ashur, Sin, Shamash, Bel (that is, Marduk), Nabu, Nergal, Ishtar of Nineveh and Ishtar of Arbela. But we must not lay much emphasis upon the smallness of this number, for in his building inscriptions at the end he invokes twenty-five deities, and even though some of these are duplicates of other gods, as Jastrow correctly explains, nevertheless the entire list is considerably increased over the eight above mentioned. In the late Bab period the worship seems chiefly devoted to Marduk, Nabu, Sin, Shamash and Ishtar. Often there seem little faint indications of a further step forward. Some of the hymns addressed to Shamash seem almost upon the verge of exalting him in such a way as to exclude the other deities, but the step is never taken. The Babylonians, with all their wonderful gifts, were never able to conceive of one god, of one god alone, of one god whose very existence makes logically impossible the existence of any other deity. Monotheism transcends the spiritual grasp of the Bab mind.

Amid all this company of gods, amid all these speculations and combinations, we must keep our minds clear, and fasten our eyes upon the one significant fact that stands out above all others. It is that the Babylonians were not able to rise above polytheism; that beyond them, far beyond them, lay that great series of thoughts about God that ascribe to him aloneness, to which we may add the great spiritual ideas which today may roughly be grouped under ethical monotheism. Here and there great thinkers in Babylonia grasped after higher ideas, and were able only to attain to a sort of pantheism of a speculative kind. A personal god, righteous and holy, who loved righteousness and hated sin, this was not given to them to conceive.

The character of the gods changed indeed as the people who revered them changed. The Babylonians who built vast temples and composed many inscriptions emphasizing the works of peace rather than of war, naturally conceived their deities in a manner different from the Assyrians whose powers were chiefly devoted to conquests in war, but neither the Babylonians nor the Assyrians arose to any such heights as distinguish the Heb book of Psalms. As the influence of the Babylonians and Assyrians waned, their gods declined in power, and none of them survived the onrush of Gr civilization in the period of Alexander.

IV. The Pantheon.—The chief gods of the Bab and Assyr pantheon may now be characterized in turn.

1. Enlil, Ellil

In the earliest times known to us the greatest of the gods is the god of Nippur whose name in the Sumerian texts is *Enlil* or *Ellil*. In the Sem pantheon of later times he was identified with the god *Bel*, and it is as Bel he has been chiefly known. During the whole of the first epoch of Bab history up to the period of Ḥammurabi, he is the Lord of the World and the King of the Land. He was originally the hero of the Flood story, but in the form in which it has come down to us Marduk of Babylon has deprived him of these honors. In Nippur was his chief temple, called *E-kur* or "mountain house." It was built and rebuilt by the kings of Babylonia again and again from the days of Sargon I (3800 BC) onward, and no less than twenty kings are known to us who pride themselves on their work of rebuilding this one temple. He is saluted as "the Great Lord, the command of whose mouth cannot be altered and whose grace is steadfast." He would seem, judging from the name of his temple and from some of his attributes, to have been originally a god of the mountains where he must have had his original dwelling-place.

2. Anu

The name of the god *Anu* was interpreted as meaning heaven, corresponding to the Sumerian word *ana*, "heaven," and he came thus to be regarded as the god of heaven as over against Enlil who was the god of earth, and Ea who was the god of the waters. Anu appears first among the great gods in an inscription of Lugalsaggi, and in somewhat later times he made his way to the top of the earliest triad which consists of Anu, Enlil and Ea. His chief seat of worship was Uruk, but in the Assyr period he was associated with the god Adad in a temple in the city of Asshur. In the myths and epics he fills an important rôle as the disposer of all events, but he cannot be thought of as quite equal in rank with Enlil in spite of his position in the heavens. Antu or Anatu is mentioned as the wife of Anu, but hers is a colorless figure, and she may probably be regarded as little else than a grammatical invention owing to the desire of the Semites to associate the feminine with the masculine in their languages.

Ea.

3. Ea

The reading of the name of the god *Ea* still remains uncertain. It may perhaps have been *Ae*, as the Gr *Aos* would seem to indicate. His chief city of worship was Eridu, which in the earliest period was situated on the Pers Gulf, near the mouths of the Euphrates and the Tigris. His temple was there called *E-absu*, which means "house of the deeps," interpreted also as "house of wisdom." He must have been a god of great importance in early times, but was left behind by the growing influence of Ellil and in a later period retained honor chiefly because he was assumed to be the father of the god Marduk, and so was reverenced by the people of the city of Babylon. As the lord of wisdom he filled a great rôle in exorcisms down to the very last, and was believed to be the god who was most ready to respond to human need in direful circumstances. Ea's wife is called Damkina.

4. Sin

Sin was the city god of Uru (Ur of the Chaldaeans in the OT). He was originally a local god who came early to a lofty position in the canon because he seems always to have been identified with the moon, and in Babylon the moon was always of more importance than the sun because of its use in the calendar. His

Worshipping the Lunar Deity.

temple was called E-kishshirgal, i.e. "house of light." His worship was widespread, for at a very early date he had a shrine at Harran in Mesopotamia. His wife is called Ningal, the Great Lady, the Queen, and his name probably appears in Mt. Sinai. He is addressed in hymns of great beauty and was regarded as a most kindly god.

5. Shamash

The Sun-god, *Shamash*, ranks next after Sin in the second or later triad, and there can be no doubt that he was from the beginning associated with the sun in the heavens. His seats of worship were Larsa in southern Babylonia and Sippar in northern Babylonia, in both of which his temple was called E-bab-

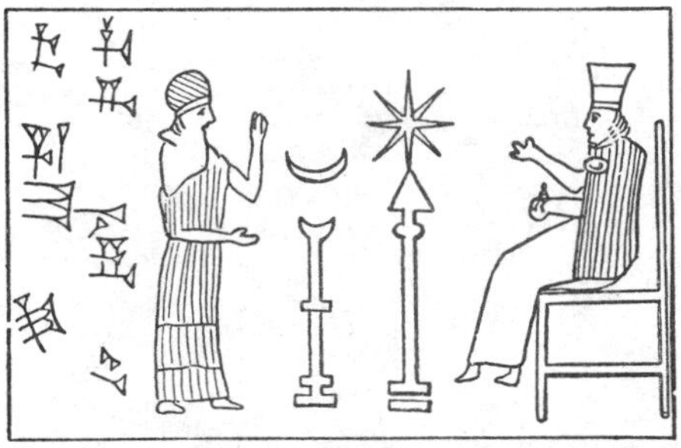

From an Engraving on a Babylonian Cylinder, Representing the Sun-God and One of His Priests.

bar, "shining house." He also is honored in magnificent hymns in which he is saluted as the enemy and the avenger of evil, but as the benignant furtherer of all good, esp. of that which concerns the races of men. All legislation is ascribed to him as the supreme judge in heaven. To him the Babylonians also ascribe similar powers in war to those which the Egyptians accorded to Re. From some of the texts one might have supposed that he would have come to the top of the triad, but this appears not to have been the case, and his influence extended rather in the direction of influencing minor local deities who were judged to be characterized by attributes similar to those ascribed to him in the greater hymns.

6. Ishtar

The origin and the meaning of the name of the goddess *Ishtar* are still disputed, but of her rank there can be no doubt. In the very earliest inscriptions known to us she does not seem to have been associated with the planet Venus as she is in later times. She seems rather to have been a goddess of fruitfulness and of love, and in her temple at Uruk temple-prostitution was a feature. In the mythological lit. she occupies a high place as the goddess of war and of the chase. Because of this later identification she became the chief goddess of the warlike Assyrians. Little by little she absorbed all the other goddesses and her name became the general word for goddess. Her chief seats of worhip were Uruk in southern Babylonia, where she was worshipped in earliest times under the name of Nana, and Akkad in northern Babylonia, where she was called Anunitu, and Nineveh and Arbela in Assyria. Some of the hymns addressed to her are among the noblest products of Bab and Assyr religion and reach a considerable ethical position. This development of a sexual goddess into a goddess who severely judged the sins of men is one of the strangest phenomena in the history of this religion.

7. Marduk

Marduk (in the OT Merodach) is the city-god of Babylon where his temple was called *E-sagila* ("lofty house") and its tower *E-temenanki* ("house of the foundation of heaven and earth"). His wife is Sarpanitu, and, as we have already seen, his father was Ea, and in later days Nabu was considered his son. The city of Babylon in the earliest period was insignificant in importance compared with Nippur and Eridu, and this city-god could not therefore lay claim to a position comparable with the gods of these cities, but after Ḥammurabi had made Babylon the chief city of all Babylonia its god rapidly increased in importance until he absorbed the attributes of the earlier gods and displaced them in the great myths. The speculative philosophers of the neo-Bab period went so far as to identify all the earlier gods with him, elevating his worship into a sort of henotheism. His proper name in the later periods was gradually displaced by the appellative *Belu* "lord," so that finally he was commonly spoken of as Bel, and his consort was called Belit. He shares with Ishtar and Shamash the honor of having some of the finest hymns, which have come down to us, sung to his name.

Nebo.

8. Nabu

Nabu (in the OT Nebo) was the city-god of Borsippa. His name is clearly Sem, and means "speaker" or "announcer." In earlier times he seems to have been a more important god than Marduk and was worshipped as the god of vegetation. His temple in Borsippa bore the name *E-zida* ("perpetual house") with the tower *E-uriminanki* ("house of the seven rulers of heaven and earth"). In later times he was identified with the planet Mercury.

9. Nergal

Nergal, the city-god of Kutu (in the OT Cuthah), was the god of the under-world and his wife Eresh-kigal was the sovereign lady of the under-world. He was also the god of plague and of fever, and in later days was associated with the planet Mars, though scholars who are attached to the astral theory (see below) think that he was identified at an earlier date with Saturn. For this view no certain proof has yet been produced.

Unfortunately the correct pronunciation of the name of the god *Ninib* has not yet been secured.

10. Ninib

He seems originally to have been a god of vegetation, but in the later philosophical period was associated with the planet Saturn, called Kaimanu (Kewan, Chiun, Am 5 26 AV, ERV). As a god of vegetation he becomes also a god of healing and his wife Gula was the chief patroness of physicians. He comes also to be regarded as a mighty hero in war, and, in this capacity generally, he fills a great rôle in the Assyr religion.

Ramman is the god of storms and thunder among the Babylonians and in the Assyr pantheon he is

11. Ramman

usually called Adad. This form of the name is doubtless connected with the Aram. god Hadad. In the Sumerian period his name seems to have been Ishkur. His wife is called Shala.

The name *Tammuz* is derived from the Sumerian *Dumuzi-zuab* ("real child of the water depths").

12. Tammuz

He is a god of vegetation which is revived by the rains of the spring. Tammuz never became one of the great gods of the pantheon, but his popularity far exceeded that of the many gods who were regarded as greater than he. His worship is associated with that of Ishtar whose paramour he was, and the beautiful story of the descent of Ishtar to Hades was written to describe Ishtar's pursuit of him to the depths of the under-world seeking to bring him up again. His disappearance in the under-world is associated with the disappearance of vegetation under the midsummer heat which revives again when the rain comes and the god appears once more on the earth. The cult of Tammuz survived the decay of Bab and Assyr civilization and made its way into the western world. It was similar in some respects to that of Osiris in Egypt, but was not so beautiful or so humane.

The supreme god of Assyria, *Asshur*, was originally the local god of the city which bears the same

13. Asshur

name. During the whole of Assyr history his chief rôle is as the god of war, but the speculative philosophers of Assyria absorbed into him many of the characteristics of Ellil and Marduk, going even so far as to ascribe to him the chief place in the conflict with the sea monster Tiamat in the creation epoch.

V. Hymns and Prayers.—The religious lit. of the Babylonians and Assyrians culminated in a great series of hymns to the gods. These have come down to us from almost all periods of the religious history of the people. Some of them go back to the days of the old city-kingdoms and others were composed during the reign of Nabonidus when the fall of Babylon at the hands of Cyrus was imminent. The greatest number of those that have come down to us are dedicated to Shamash, the Sun-god, but many of the finest, as we have already seen, were composed in honor of Sin, the Moon-god. None of these reached monotheism. All are polytheistic, with perhaps tendencies in the direction of pantheism or henotheism. This incapacity to reach monotheism may have been partially due to the influence of the local city whose tendency was always to hold tightly to the honor of the local god. Babylonia might struggle never so hard to lift Marduk to high and still higher position, but in spite of all its efforts he remains to the very end of the days only one god among many. And even the greatest of the Bab kings, Nebuchadrezzar and Nabonidus, continued to pay honor to Shamash in Sippar, whose temple they continually rebuilt and adorned with ever greater magnificence. Better than any description of the hymns is a specimen adequately to show their quality. Here are some lines taken from an ancient Sumerian hymn to the Moon-god which had been copied and preserved with an Assyr tr in the library of Ashurbanipal:

O Lord, chief of the gods, who alone art exalted on earth and in heaven,
Father Nannar, Lord, Anshar, chief of the gods,
Father Nannar, Lord, great Anu, chief of the gods,
Father Nannar, Lord, Sin, chief of the gods,
Father Nannar, Lord of Ur, chief of the gods,
Father Nannar, Lord of E-gish-shir-gal, chief of the gods,
Father Nannar, Lord of the veil, brilliant one, chief of the gods,
Father Nannar, whose rule is perfect, chief of the gods,
Father Nannar, who does march in great majesty, chief of the gods,
O strong, young bull, with strong horns, perfect in muscles, with beard of lapis lazuli color, full of glory and perfection,
Self-created, full of developed fruit, beautiful to look upon, in whose being one cannot sufficiently sate himself;
Mother womb, begetter of all things, who has taken up his exalted habitation among living creatures;
O merciful, gracious father, in whose hand rests the life of the whole world,
O Lord, thy divinity is full of awe, like the far-off heaven and the broad ocean.
O creator of the land, founder of sanctuaries, proclaimer of their names,
O father, begetter of gods and men, who dost build dwellings and establish offerings,
Who dost call to lordship, dost bestow the scepter, determinest destinies for far-off days.

Much of this is full of fine religious feeling, and the exaltation of Sin sounds as though the poet could scarcely acknowledge any other god, but the proof that other gods were invoked in the same terms and by the same kings is plentiful.

Some of these hymns are connected with magical and incantation lit., for they serve to introduce passages which are intended to drive away evil demons. A very few of them on the other hand rise to very lofty conceptions in which the god is praised as a judge of righteousness. A few lines from the greatest of all the hymns addressed to Shamash, the Sun-god, will make this plain:

Column II

Who plans evil—his horn thou dost destroy,
Whoever in fixing boundaries annuls rights.
The unjust judge thou restrainest with force.
Whoever accepts a bribe, who does not judge justly—on him thou imposest sin.
But he who does not accept a bribe, who has a care for the oppressed,
To him Shamash is gracious, his life he prolongs.
The judge who renders a just decision
Shall end in a palace, the place of princes shall be his dwelling.
. . . .

Column III

The seed of those who act unjustly shall not flourish.
What their mouth declares in thy presence
Thou shalt burn it up, what they purpose wilt thou annul.
Thou knowest their transgressions: the declaration of the wicked thou dost cast aside.
Everyone, wherever he may be, is in thy care.
Thou directest their judgments, the imprisoned dost thou liberate.
Thou hearest, O Shamash, petition, prayer, and appeal.
Humility, prostration, petitioning, and reverence.
With loud voice the unfortunate one cries to thee.
The weak, the exhausted, the oppressed, the lowly,
Mother, wife, maid appeal to thee.
He who is removed from his family, he that dwelleth far from his city.

There is in this hymn no suggestion of magic or sorcery. We cannot but feel how close this poet came to an appreciation of the Sun-god as a judge of men on an ethical basis. How near he was to passing through the vale into a larger religious life!

The prayers are on the whole upon a lower plane, though some of them, notably those of Nebuchadrezzar, reach lofty conceptions. The following may serve as a sufficient example:

O eternal ruler, lord of all being, grant that the name of the king that thou lovest, whose name thou hast proclaimed, may flourish as seems pleasing to thee. Lead him in the right way. I am the prince that obeys thee, the creature of thy hand. Thou hast created me, and hast intrusted to me dominion over mankind. According to thy mercy, O Lord, which thou bestowest upon all, may thy supreme rule be merciful! The worship of thy divinity implant in my heart! Grant me what seems good to thee, for thou art he that hast fashioned my life.

VI. Magic.—Next in importance to the gods in the Bab religion are the demons who had the power to afflict men with manifold diseases of body or mind. A large part of the religion seems to have been given up to an agonized struggle against these demons, and the gods were everywhere approached by prayer to assist men against these demons. An immense mass of incantations, supposed to have the power of driving the demons out, has come down to us. The use of these incantations lay chiefly in the hands of the priests who attached great importance to specific words or sets of words. The test of time was supposed to have shown that certain words were efficacious in certain instances. If in any case the result was not secured, it could only be ascribed to the use of the wrong formula; hence there grew up a great desire to preserve exactly the words which in some cases had brought healing. Later these incantations were gathered into groups or rituals classified according to purpose or use. Of the rituals which have come down to us, the following are the most important:

1. Maqlu

Maqlu, i.e. "burning," so called because there are in it many symbolic burnings of images or witches. This series is used in the delivering of sufferers from witches or sorcerers.

2. Shurpu

Shurpu is another word for burning, and this series also deals much in symbolic burnings and for the same purposes as the former. In these incantations we make the acquaintance of a large number of strange demons such as the *rabisu*, a demon that springs unawares on its victims; the *labartu*, which attacks women and children; and the *lilu* and the *lilitu*, to which reference has been made before, and the *utuku*, a strong demon.

These incantations are for the most part a wretched jargon without meaning, and a sad commentary on the low position occupied by the religion which has attained such noble heights as that represented in the hymns and prayers. It is strange that the higher forms of religion were not able to drive out the lower, but these incantations continued to be carefully copied and used down to the very end of the Bab commonwealth.

VII. The Last Things.—In Babylonia, the great question of all the ages—"If a man die shall he live again?"—was asked and an attempt made to answer it. The answer was usually sad and depressing. After death the souls of men were supposed to continue in existence. It can hardly be called life. The place to which they have gone is called the "land of no return." There they lived in dark rooms amid the dust and the bats covered with a garment of feathers, and under the dominion of Nergal and Ereshkigal. When the soul arrived among the dead he had to pass judgment before the judges of the dead, the Annunaki, but little has been preserved for us concerning the manner of this judgment. There seems to have been at times an idea that it might be possible for the dead to return again to life, for in this underworld there was the water of life, which was used when the god Tammuz returned again to earth. The Babylonians seem not to have attached so much importance to this after-existence as did the Egyptians, but they did practice burial and not cremation, and placed often with the dead articles which might be used in his future existence. In earlier times the dead were buried in their own houses, and among the rich this custom seems to have prevailed until the very latest times. For others the custom of burying in an acropolis was adopted, and near the city of Kutha was an acropolis which was especially famous. In the future world there seem to have been distinctions made among the dead. Those who fell in battle seem to have had special favor. They received fresh water to drink, while those who had no posterity to put offerings at their graves suffered sore and many deprivations. It is to be hoped that later discoveries of religious texts may shed more light upon this phase of the religion which is still obscure.

VIII. Myths and Epics.—In ancient religions the myth fills a very important place, serving many of the functions of dogma in modern religions. These myths have come down to us associated usually with epics, or made a part of ancient stories which belong to the library of Ashurbanipal. Most of them have been copied from earlier Bab originals, which go back in origin to the wonderful period of intellectual and political development which began with Ḥammurabi. The most interesting of those which have been preserved for us are the story of Adapa and the story of Gilgames. This same divine being Adapa, son of Ea, was employed in Ea's temple at Eridu supplying the ritual bread and water. One day, while fishing in the sea, the south wind swept sharply upon him, overturned his boat, and he fell into the sea, the "house of the fishes." Angered by his misfortune, he broke the wings of the south wind, and for seven days it was unable to bring the comfort of the sea coolness over the hot land. And Anu said:

"Why has the south wind for seven days not blown
over the land?"
His messenger Ilabrat answered him:
"My Lord,
Adapa, the son of Ea, hath broken the wing of
The south wind."

Then Anu ordered the culprit brought before him, and before he departed to this ordeal Ea gave him instructions. He is to go up to the gatekeepers of heaven, Tammuz and Gish-zida, clad in mourning garb to excite their sympathy. When they ask why he is thus attired he is to tell them that his mourning is for two gods of earth who have disappeared (that is, themselves), and then they will intercede for him. Furthermore, he is cautioned not to eat the food or drink the water that will be set before him, for Ea fears that food and water of death will be set before him to destroy him. But exactly the opposite happened. Tammuz and Gish-zida prevailed in pleading, and Anu said: "Bring for him food of life that he may eat it." They brought him food of life, but he did not eat. They brought him water of life, but he did not drink. They brought him a garment; he put it on. They brought him oil; he anointed himself with it.

Adapa had obeyed Ea literally, and by so doing had missed the priceless boon of immortality. Some of the motives in this beautiful myth are similar to those found in Gen. Food of life seems to belong to the same category as the tree of life in Gen. The Bab doctrine was that man, though of Divine origin, did not share in the Divine attribute of immortality. In the Gen story Adam lost immortality because he desired to become like God. Adapa, on the other hand, was already endowed with knowledge and wisdom and failed of immortality, not because he was disobedient like Adam, but because he was obedient to Ea his creator. The legend would seem to be the Bab attempt to explain death.

The greatest of all the Bab epics is the story of Gilgames, for in it the greatest of the myths seem to pour into one great stream of epic. It was written upon twelve big tablets in the library of Ashurbanipal, some of which have been badly broken. It was, however, copied from earlier tablets which go back to the First Dynasty of Babylon. The whole story is interesting and important, but its greatest significance lies in the eleventh tablet which contains a description of the great flood and is curiously parallel to the Flood story in the Book of Gen.

The Deluge Tablet.

IX. The Astral Theory of the Universe.—We have now passed in review the main features of the Bab and Assyr religion. We have come all the way from a primitive animism to a higher organized polytheism with much theological speculation ending in a hope for existence after death, and we must now ask whether there is any great organizing idea which will bring all this religion and speculation into one great comprehensive system. A theory has been propounded which owes its exposition generally to Professor Hugo Winckler of the University of Berlin, who in a series of volumes and pamphlets has attempted to prove that the whole of the serious thinking and writing in the realm of religion among both the Babylonians and Assyrians rests down upon a *Weltanschauung*, a theory of the universe. This theory of Winckler's has found acceptance and propagation at the hands of Dr. Alfred Jeremias, and portions of it have been accepted by other scholars. The doctrine is extremely complicated and even those who accept it in part decline it in other parts and the exposition of it is difficult. In the form which it takes in the writings of Winckler and Jeremias, it has been still further complicated quite recently by sundry alterations which make it still more difficult. Most of these can only be regarded as efforts to shield the theory from criticisms which have been successful in pointing out its weakness.

According to Winckler and Jeremias, the Babylonians conceived of the cosmos as divided primarily into a heavenly and an earthly world, each of which is further subdivided into three parts. The heavenly world consists of (1) the northern ocean; (2) the zodiac; (3) the heavenly ocean; while the earthly world consists of (1) the heaven, i.e. the air above the earth; (2) the earth itself; (3) the waters beneath the earth. These great subdivisions were ruled by the gods Anu in the heaven above, Bel in the earth and air, and Ea in the waters beneath. More important than these is the zodiac, the twelve heavenly figures which span the heavens and through which the moon passes every month, the sun once a year, and the five great planets which are visible to the naked eye have their courses. These moving stars serve as the interpreters of the Divine will while the fixed stars, so says Jeremias, are related thereto as the commentary written on the margin of the Book of Rev. The rulers of the zodiac are Sin, Shamash and Ishtar, and according to the law of correspondence, the Divine power manifested in them is identical with the power of Anu, Bel and Ea. The zodiac represents the world-cycle in the year, and also in the world-year, one of these gods may represent the total Divine power which reveals itself in the cycle. By the side of these three, Sin, Shamash and Ishtar, which represent respectively the moon, sun and Venus, there are arranged Marduk which is Jupiter, Nabu which is Mercury, Ninib which is Mars, and Nergal which is Saturn, these being the planets known to the ancients. Now upon these foundations, according to Winckler, and his school, the ancient priests of Babylonia built a closely knit and carefully thought-out world-system of an astral character, and this world-system forms the kernel of the ancient and oriental conception of the universe. This conception of the universe as a double-sided principle is of tremendous importance. First, the heavenly world with its three divisions corresponds exactly to the earthly world with its three divisions. Everything on earth corresponds to its counterpart in heaven. The heavens are a mirror of earth, and in them the gods reveal their will and purpose. Everything which has happened is only an earthly copy of the heavenly original. It is still written in the heavens above and still to be read there. All the myths and all the legends, not only of Babylonia, but of all the rest of the ancient world, are to be interpreted in accordance with this theory; nothing even in history is to be understood otherwise. "An oriental history without consideration of the world era is unthinkable. The stars rule the changes of the times" (Jeremias). The consequences of this theory are so overpowering that it is difficult to deal with it in fairness to its authors and in justice to the enormous labor and knowledge which they have put upon it.

It is impossible within the reasonable limits which are here imposed to discuss the theory in detail, and for our purpose it will be sufficient to say that to the great majority of modern scholars who have carefully considered it in its details it seems to lack evidence sufficient to support so enormous a structure. That an astrological structure similar at least to this actually did arise in the Hellenistic period is not here disputed. The sole dispute is as to the antiquity of it. Now it does not appear that Winckler and Jeremias have been able to produce proof, first, that the Babylonians had enough knowledge of astronomy before the 7th cent. BC to have constructed such a system; and in the second place, there is no evidence that all the Bab gods had an astral character in the earlier period. On the contrary, there seems, as we have already attempted to show in the discussion of the pantheon, to be good reason to believe that many of the deities had no relation whatever to the stars in early times, but were rather gods of vegetation or of water or of other natural forces visible in earthly manifestations. The theory indeed may be said to have broken down by its own weight, for Winckler and Jeremias attempted to show that this theory of the universe spread to Israel, to the Greeks and to the Romans, and that it affords the only satisfactory explanation of the religion and of the history of the entire ancient world. An attempt has been made similar to previous abortive efforts to unlock all the doors of the ancient past with one key (see an interesting example cited in Rogers, *Religion of Babylonia and Assyria*, 224–25). Instead of gaining adherence in recent times, the theory would appear to have lost, and even those who have given a tentative adherence to its claims, cautiously qualify the extent of their submission.

X. The Relations with the Religion of Israel.—No question concerning the religion of Babylonia and Assyria is of so great interest and importance to students of the Bible as the question of the relation between this religion and the faith of Jeh, as professed by Israel. It seems now to be clearly demonstrated that the religion of Israel has borrowed various literary materials from its more ancient neighbor. The stories of creation and of the flood, both of them, as far as the literary contents are concerned, certainly rest upon Bab originals. This dependence has, however, been exaggerated by some scholars into an attempt to demonstrate that Israel took these materials bodily, whereas the close shifting and comparison to which they have been subjected in the past few years would seem to demonstrate beyond peradventure that Israel stamped whatever she borrowed with her own genius and wove an entirely new fabric. Israel used these ancient narratives as a vehicle for a higher and purer religious faith. The material was borrowed, the spirit belonged to Israel, and the spirit was Divine. Words and literary materials were secured from Babylonia, but the religious and spiritual came from Israel and from Israel's God. The word Sabbath is Bab indeed, but the great social and religious institution which it represents in Israel is not Bab but distinctively Heb. The Divine name Yahweh appears among other peoples, passes over into Babylonia and afterward is used by Israel, but the spiritual God who bears the name in Israel is no Bab or Kenite deity. The Babylonians, during all their history and in all their speculations, never conceived a god like unto Him. He belongs to the Hebrews alone.

The gods of Babylonia are connected, as we have seen, with primitive animism or they are merely local deities. The God of Israel, on the other hand, is a God revealed in history. He brought Israel out of Egypt. He is continually made known to His people through the prophets as a God revealed in history. His religion is not developed out of Bab polytheism which existed as polytheism in the earliest periods and endured as polytheism unto the end. The religion of Israel, on the other hand, though some of its material origins are humble, moved steadily onward and upward until the great monotheistic idea found universal acceptance in Israel. The religions of Philistia and Phoenicia, Moab, and of Edom, were subject to the same play of influences from Babylonia and Egypt, but no larger faith developed out of them. In Israel alone ethical monotheism arose, and ethical monotheism has no roots in Babylonia. The study of the religion of Babylonia is indeed of the highest importance for the understanding of Israel's faith, but it is of less importance than some modern scholars have attempted to demonstrate.

LITERATURE.—L. W. King, *Bab Religion and Mythology*, London, 1899; M. Jastrow, Jr., *The Religion of Babylonia and Assyria*, Boston, 1898 (completely revised by the author and trd into German under the title *Die Religion Babyloniens und Assyriens*, Giessen, appearing in parts, and soon to be completed. This is the standard book on the subject); Rogers, *The Religion of Babylonia and Assyria, Esp. in Its Relation to Israel*, New York, 1908; Hermann Schneider, *Kultur und Denken der Babylonier und Juden*, Leipzig, 1910; R. P. Dhorme, *La religion assyrio-babylonienne*, Paris, 1910. Detailed lit. on the separate phases of the religion will be found in these books.

ROBERT W. ROGERS

BABYLONIAN CAPTIVITY. See CAPTIVITY.

BABYLONIANS, bab-i-lō'ni-anz: The inhabitants of BABYLONIA (q.v.). They were among the colonists planted in Samaria by the Assyrians (Ezr **4** 9). "The likeness of the Babylonians in Chaldea" (Ezk **23** 15) refers to the pictures which were common on the walls of Bab palaces, and the reports of them being heard in Jerus, or copies of them seen there, awakened the nation's desire for these unknown lovers, which Judah had ample occasion to repent of (vs 17.23; cf 2 K **24**).

BABYLONISH GARMENT, bab-i-lō'nish gär'-ment: In AV, Josh **7** 21, for BABYLONISH MANTLE, which see.

BABYLONISH MANTLE, man't'l (AV **Babylonish Garment**): One of the articles taken by Achan from the spoil of Jericho (Josh **7** 21). In the Heb "a mantle of Shinar." Entirely gratuitous is the suggested correction of Shinar to *sē'ār*, making "a hairy mantle." The Gr has *psilēn poikílēn*, which Jos apparently understood to mean "a royal garment all woven out of gold" (*Ant*, V, i, 10). The Vulg calls it a "scarlet pallium," and some of the rabbinical traditions make it a purple robe. Such classical writers as Pliny and Martial speak of the weaving of embroidered stuffs as a famous industry of Babylonia. Many tablets that have been deciphered indicate that the industry was indeed widely extended, that its costly products were of great variety and that some of them were exported to distant markets; in fine, that the account in Joshua is characterized by great verisimilitude.

WILLIS J. BEECHER

BACA, bā'ka (בָּכָא, *bākhā'*): In AV in Ps **84** 6, where RV has "the valley of Weeping," with a marginal variant which is best put in the form, "the valley of the balsam-trees." The word is elsewhere used only in the duplicated account of one of David's battles (2 S **5** 23.24; 1 Ch **14** 14.15). There the tr is "the mulberry trees," with "the balsam-trees" in the margin in RV. Conjecturally the word is, by variant spelling, of the stem which denotes weeping; the tree is called "weeper" from some habit of the trickling of its gum or of the moisture on it; the valley of weeping is not a geographical locality, but a picturesque expression for the experiences of those whose strength is in Jeh, and who through His grace find their sorrows changed into blessings. WILLIS J. BEECHER

BACCHIDES, bak'i-dēz (**Βακχίδης**, *Bakchídēs*): B., ruler over Mesopotamia and a faithful friend of both Antiochus Epiphanes and Demetrius Soter, established at the request of the latter the rulership over Judaea for Alcimus, who, desiring to become high priest, had made false accusations against Judas Maccabee (1 Macc **7** 8 ff; *Ant*, XII, x, 2). B. is sent the second time to Judaea after the Syrian general Nicanor was killed near Adasa and Judas Maccabee had gained control of the government (1 Macc **9** 1 ff; *Ant*, XII, x). B. after an unsuccessful battle near Bethbasi was forced to make peace with Jonathan, the brother of Judas Maccabee (1 Macc **9** 58 ff; *Ant*, XIII, i). In 1 Macc **10** 12 and 2 Macc **8** 30 reference is made to the strongholds B. built during his 2d campaign against Jerus (1 Macc **9** 50). Cf ALCIMUS; BETHBASI; JONATHAN MACCABEE; JUDAS MACCABEE; ADASA; NICANOR. A. L. BRESLICH

BACCHURUS, ba-kū'rus (**Βακχοῦρος,** *Bakchoúros*): One of the "holy singers" who put away his "strange wife" (1 Esd **9** 24). Omitted in Ezr **10.**

BACCHUS, bak'us (**Διόνυσος,** *Diónusos;* later **Βάκχος,** the Feast of Bacchus; **Διονύσια,** *Dionúsia*): The god of wine. His worship had extended over the whole Gr and Rom world cents. before the Christian era, and had degenerated into an orgy of drunkenness and unnamable immoralities, possibly under the influence of oriental Baal worship, such as the Heb prophets condemned. It has been surmised that Dionysus was originally not a Gr, but an oriental deity. His worship had been introduced into Egypt, perhaps by the Ptolemies, and Ptolemy Philopator (222–204 BC) had branded the Jews there with his emblem, the sign of the ivy. When Antiochus Epiphanes made his assault upon Jerus in the year 168 BC, he determined to extirpate the worship of Jeh, which he recognized as the strength of the Jewish resistance, and to replace it by Gr religion. All worship of Jeh and the observance of Jewish rites, such as the Sabbath and circumcision, were prohibited. Heathen worship was set up all over Judaea, and in the temple at Jerus on the altar of burnt offering an altar to Jupiter was erected, "the abomination that maketh desolate" (Dnl **11** 31), and a swine was sacrificed upon it (see ABOMINATION OF DESOLATION). The immoral practices associated with heathen worship in those days established themselves in the temple. When this feast of Bacchus (Dionysus) with all its revelry came round, the Jews were compelled to go in procession in honor of Bacchus (Dionysus), wearing wreaths of ivy, the emblem of the god (2 Macc **6** 7). Some years later, when the worship of Jeh had been restored, Nicanor the general of Demetrius I, in conducting the war against Judas Maccabaeus, threatened the priests that, unless they delivered Judas up as a prisoner, "he would raze the temple of God even with the ground, break down the altar, and erect there a temple unto Bacchus (Dionysus) for all to see" (2 Macc **14** 33). See DIONYSIA.

LITERATURE.—Cheyne, art. "Bacchus," *EB;* Kent, *Hist of the Jewish People,* I, 328–29; Jos, *Ant,* XII, v, 4.
T. REES

BACENOR, ba-sē'nor (**Βακήνωρ,** *Bakḗnōr*): An officer in the army of Judas Maccabee engaged in war against Gorgias, governor of Idumaea (2 Macc **12** 35). Cf *Ant,* XII, viii, 6.

BACHRITE, bak'rīt. See BECHER.

BACK, BACK PARTS:

(1) (אַחַר, *'aḥar,* "back side" as in AV): "He led the flock to the back of the wilderness" (Ex **3** 1), i.e. "to the pasture-lands on the other side of the desert from the Midianite encampments."

(2) (אָחוֹר, *'āḥōr,* "hinder part," "the West"): Used of God in an anthropomorphic sense ("Thou shalt see my back," Ex **33** 23) to signify "the afterglow of the Divine radiance," the faint reflection of God's essential glory. See also Isa **38** 17 and cf 1 K **14** 9 and Neh **9** 26.

(3) (ὄπισθεν, *ópisthen,* "back side"): "A book written within and on the back" (Rev **5** 1), "but the back of a book is not the same as the reverse side of a roll. St. John was struck, not only with the fact that the roll was sealed, but also with the amount of writing it contained" (*HDB,* I, 231). Cf Ezk **2** 10. M. O. EVANS

BACKBITE, bak'bīt (רָגַל, *rāghal;* **δολόω,** *dolóō*): To slander the absent, like a dog biting behind the back, where one cannot see; to go about as a talebearer. "He that backbiteth [RV slandereth] not with his tongue" (Ps **15** 3).

Backbiters, bak'bīt-ẽrz (Gr **κατάλαλοι,** *katálaloi*): Men who speak against. Vulg "detractors" (Rom **1** 30).

Backbiting, bak'bīt-ing (סֵתֶר, *ṣether*): Adj. "a backbiting tongue"; lit. "a tongue of secrecy" (Prov **25** 23). καταλαλιά, *katalaliá:* subst. "a speaking against" (2 Cor **12** 20; Wisd **1** 11); "evil speaking" (1 Pet **2** 1). γλῶσσα τρίτη, *glōssa trítē:* "a backbiting tongue" (AV of Ecclus **28** 14.15); more lit. tr[d] in RV "a third person's tongue."
T. REES

BACKSIDE, bak'sīd'. See BACK.

BACKSLIDE, bak'slīd' (מְשׁוּבָה, *m[e]shūbhāh;* Hos **11** 7; **14** 4 and often in Hos and Jer, שׁוֹבָב, *shōbhābh;* שׁוֹבֵב, *shōbhēbh,* in Jer, 4 times: all meaning "turning back or away," "apostate," "rebellious." סָרַר, *ṣārar,* in Hos **4** 16 = "stubborn," "rebellious"; RV "stubborn"): In all places the word is used of Israel forsaking Jeh, and with a reference to the covenant relation between Jeh and the nation, conceived as a marriage tie which Israel had violated. Jeh was Israel's husband, and by her idolatries with other gods she had proved unfaithful (Jer **3** 8.14; **14** 7; Hos **14** 4). It may be questioned whether Israel was guilty so much of apostasy and defection, as of failure to grow with the growing revelation of God. The prophets saw that their contemporaries fell far short of their own ideal, but they did not realize how far their predecessors also had fallen short of the rising prophetic standard in ideal and action. See APOSTASY.

Backslider, bak'slīd'ẽr (סוּג לֵב, *ṣūgh lēbh*): "The backslider in heart shall be filled with his own ways" (Prov **14** 14). But RV "backslider" conveys the wrong impression of an apostate. The Heb expression here implies simply non-adherence to the right, "The bad man reaps the fruits of his act" (Toy, *Prov,* in loc.). T. REES

BADGER, baj'ẽr (תַּחַשׁ or תָּחַשׁ, *taḥash* or *tāḥash*): The word *taḥash* occurs in the descriptions of the tabernacle in Ex **25, 26, 35, 36** and **39,** in the directions for moving the tabernacle as given in Nu **4,** and in only one other passage, Ezk **16** 10, where Jerus is spoken of as a maiden clothed and adorned by her Lord. In nearly all these passages the word *taḥash* occurs with *'ōr,* "skin," rendered: AV "badgers' skins," RV "sealskin," RVm "porpoise-skin," LXX *dérmata huakínthina.* In all the passages cited in Ex and Nu these skins are mentioned as being used for coverings of the tabernacle; in Ezk **16** 10, for shoes or sandals. The LXX rendering would mean purple or blue skins, which however is not favored by Talmudic writers or by modern grammarians, who incline to believe that *taḥash* is the name of an animal. The rendering, "badger," is favored by the Talmudic writers and by the possible etymological connection of the word with the Lat *taxus* and the German *Dachs.* The main objection seems to be that badgers' skins would probably not have been easily available to the Israelites. The badger, *Meles taxus,* while fairly abundant in Lebanon and Anti-Lebanon, does not seem to occur in Sinai or Egypt.

A seal, *Monachus albiventer* (Arab. *fukmeh*), the porpoise, *Phocoena communis,* and the common dolphin, *Delphinus delphis,* are all found in the Mediterranean. The dugong, *Halicore dugong,* inhabits the Indian Ocean and adjoining waters from the Red Sea to Australia. The Arab. *tukhas* or *dukhas* is near to *taḥash* and is applied to the dolphin, which is also called *delfîn*. It may be used also for the porpoise or even the seal, and is said by Tristram and others to be applied to the dugong. The statement of Gesenius (Boston, 1850, s.v. "taḥash") that the Arabs of Sinai wear sandals of dugong skin is confirmed by recent travelers, and is of interest with reference to Ezk **16** 10, "I . . . . shod thee with badgers' skin" (AV). The dugong is a marine animal from 5 to 9 ft. in length, frequenting the shore and feeding upon seaweed. It belongs to the order *Sirenia*. While outwardly resembling *Cetacea* (whales and porpoises), the *Sirenia* are really more allied to the *Ungulata*, or hoofed animals. The dugong of the Indian Ocean and the manatee of the Atlantic and of certain rivers of Africa and South America, are the only living representatives of the *Sirenia*. A third species, the sea-cow of Behring Sea, became extinct in the 18th cent. The seal and porpoise of the RV, the dolphin, and the dugong are all of about the same size and all inhabit the seas bordering on Egypt and Sinai, so that all are possible candidates for identification with the *taḥash*. Of the four, recent opinion seems most to favor the dugong.

Mr. S. M. Perlmann has suggested (*Zoölogist*, ser. 4, XII, 256, 1908) that the okapi is the animal indicated by *taḥash*.

Gesenius (Leipzig, 1905) cites Bondi (*Aegyptiaca*, i. ff) who adduces the Egyp root *tḥs* and makes the expression *'ōr taḥash* mean "soft-dressed skin." This suits the context in every passage and is a very promising explanation. ALFRED ELY DAY

BAEAN, bē'an (**υἱοὶ Βαιαν**, *huioí Baían;* AV **Bean**; 1 Macc **5** 4): A tribe mentioned only because of its malignant hatred of the Jews. Its aggressive hostility against their religion and the rebuilding of their sanctuary duplicated the conspiracy of Sanballat and his confederates against the restoration of Jerus and the temple in the days of Nehemiah (cf Neh **4** 7.8). Utterly exterminated by Judas Maccabaeus who burned alive, in towers, many of the imprisoned people. See MAON.

BAG: Bags of various kinds are mentioned in the Eng. Bible, but often in a way to obscure rather than tr the original.

(1) "Bag" is used for a Heb word which means a shepherd's "bag," rendered "wallet" in RV. This "bag" of the shepherd or "haversack" of the traveler was of a size sufficient for one or more days' provisions. It was made of the skin of animals, ordinarily undressed, as most of the other "bags" of ancient times were, and was carried slung across the shoulder. This is the "scrip for the journey" (πήρα, *pḗra*) mentioned in Mt **10** 10 and ∥ (AV). ("Scrip" is OE, now obsolete.) A unique word appears in 1 S **17** 40.49 which had to be explained even to Heb readers by the gloss, "the shepherd's bag," but which is likewise rendered "wallet" by the ARV.

(2) "Bag" translates also a word (*βαλλάντιον*, *ballántion*) which stands for the more finished leather pouch, or satchel which served as a "purse" (see Christ's words, Lk **10** 4 AV: "Carry neither *purse*, nor scrip," and **12** 33 AV: "Provide yourselves *bags* which wax not old"). The word rendered "purse" in Mt **10** 9: "Get you no gold, nor silver, nor brass in your *purses*"; Mk **6** 8: "No money in their *purse*," is a different word entirely (*ζώνη*, *zṓnē*), the true rendering of which is "girdle" (RVm). The oriental "girdle," though sometimes of crude leather, or woven camel's hair (see GIRDLE), was often of fine material and elegant workmanship, and was either made hollow so as to carry money, or when of silk or cloth, worn in folds, when the money was carried in the folds.

(3) The small "merchant's bag" often knotted in a handkerchief for carrying the weights, such as is mentioned in Dt **25** 13: "Thou shalt not have in thy bag divers weights, a great and a small," was another variety. This too was used as a "purse," as in the case of the proposed common purse of the wicked mentioned in Prov **1** 14: "We will all have one *purse*," and sometimes carried in the girdle (cf Isa **46** 6).

Bag: Scrip.

(4) Then there was the "bag" (צְרוֹר, *ççerōr*, rendered "bundle" in Gen **42** 35) which was the favorite receptacle for valuables, *jewels*, as well as money, used **fig.** with fine effect in 1 S **25** 29: "The soul of my lord shall be bound in *the bundle* of life" = "life's *jewel-case*" (see 2 K **12** 10 where the money of the temple was said to be put up "tied up" in *bags*). This was a "bag" that could be tied with a string: "Behold, every man's *bundle* of money was in his sack," and (cf Prov **7** 20) "He hath taken a *bag* of money with him" (cf Hag **1** 6: "earneth wages to put it into a *bag* with holes").

A *seal* was sometimes put on the knot, which occasions the **figure** of speech used in Job (**14** 16.17), "Dost thou not watch over my sin? My transgression is *sealed up in a bag*," i.e. it is securely kept and reckoned against me (cf also 1 S **9** 7; **21** 5 where the Heb כְּלִי, *kelī*, is rendered by "vessels" and stands for receptacles for carrying food, not necessarily bags).

(5) Another Heb word חָרִט, *ḥārīṭ;* Arab. *ḥariṭat*, is used, on the one hand, for a "bag" large enough to hold a talent of silver (see 2 K **5** 23, "bound two talents of silver in two *bags*"), and on the other, for a dainty lady's *satchel*, such as is found in Isa **3** 22 (wrongly rendered "crisping pins" in AV). This is the most adequate Heb word for a large bag.

(6) The "bag" which Judas carried (see Jn **12** 6 AV, "He was a thief and had *the bag*"; cf **13** 29) was in reality the small "*box*" (RVm) originally used for holding the mouthpieces of wind instruments (Kennedy, in 1-vol *HDB*). The Heb (אַרְגָּז, *'argāz*, found only here) of 1 S **6** 8, rendered "coffer" in EV and trd *γλωσσόκομον*, *glossókomon*, by Jos, appears to stand for a small "chest" used to hold the gold figures sent by the Philis as a guilt offering. It is from a word that means "to wag," "to move to and fro"; cf the similar word in Arab. meaning a bag filled with stones hung at the side of the camel to "preserve" equilibrium (Gesenius). But the same word Jos uses is found in modern Gr and means "purse" or "bag" (Hatch). Later to "carry the bag" came to mean to be treasurer. GEO. B. EAGER

BAGGAGE, bag'āj:

(1) (כְּלִי, *kelī*, "the *impedimenta* of an army"): "David left his b. in the hand of the keeper of the b." (1 S **17** 22); "at Michmash he layeth up his b." (Isa **10** 28). ARV gives b. for "stuff" at 1 S **10** 22; **25** 13; **30** 24.

(2) (*ἀποσκευή*, *aposkeuḗ:* "Beside the b." (Jth **7** 2), "a great ado and much b." (1 Macc **9** 35.39),

"the women and the children and also the b." (AV "and other b."; 2 Macc **12** 21).

(3) (ἀποσκευάζομαι, *aposkeuázomai*, "to make ready for leaving," "to pack up baggage"): "We took up [made ready RVm] our b." (Acts **21** 15, AV "carriages"), i.e. what they could carry = Eng. "luggage"; but others understand the term of the loading of the baggage animals. M. O. EVANS

BAGO, bā'gō (A, **Βαγό,** *Bagó;* B, **Βαναί,** *Banaí* = Bigvai [Ezr **8** 14]): The descendants of B. returned with Ezra to Jerus (1 Esd **8** 40).

BAGOAS, ba-gō'as (**Βαγώας,** *Bagṓas*): The eunuch in charge of the household of Holofernes whom the latter engaged to bring Judith to his palace (Jth **12** 11 ff; **13** 1.3; **14** 14). Cf JUDITH.

BAGOI, bag'ō-ī (A, **Βαγοΐ,** *Bagoí;* B, **Βοσαί,** *Bosaí* = Bigvai [Ezr **2** 14; Neh **7** 19]): The descendants of B. returned with Zerubbabel to Jerus (1 Esd **5** 14).

BAHARUMITE, ba-hā'rum-īt, **BARHUMITE,** bär-hū'mīt (1 Ch **11** 33; 2 S **23** 31): A native of BAHURIM (q.v.).

BAHURIM, ba-hū'rim (בַּחֻרִים, *bahurīm;* **Βαουρείμ,** *Baoureím*, usually, but there are variants): A place in the territory of Benjamin which lay on an old road from Jerus to Jericho followed by David in his flight from Absalom (2 S **15** 32—**16** 5 ff). It ran over the Mount of Olives and down the slopes to the E. The Talm identifies it with Alemath, the modern *Almīt*, about a mile beyond *'Anātā*, going from Jerus. If this identification is correct, *Wādy Fārah* may be the brook of water (2 S **17** 20). Here Paltiel was parted from his wife Michal by Abner (2 S **3** 16). It was the home of Shimei, who ran along a ridge of the hill cursing and throwing stones at the fugitive king (2 S **16** 5; 1 K **2** 8). In Bahurim Jonathan and Ahimaaz, the messengers of David, were concealed in a well by a loyal woman (2 S **17** 18 ff). Azmaveth, one of David's heroes, was a native of Bahurim. In 2 S **23** 31 we should read, as in 1 Ch **11** 33, Barahumite. W. EWING

BAITERUS, bā-ī'tēr-us (**Βαιτηρούς,** *Baitēroús;* AV **Meterus**): The descendants of B. returned with Zerubbabel to Jerus (1 Esd **5** 17). Omitted in Ezr **2** and Neh **7.**

BAJITH, bā'jith. See BAYITH.

BAKBAKKAR, bak-bak'ar (בַּקְבַּקַּר, *bakbakkar*, "investigator"): A Levite (1 Ch **9** 15).

BAKBUK, bak'buk (בַּקְבּוּק, *bakbūk*, "bottle" perhaps onomatopoetical, referring to the clucking noise created by the pouring out of the contents of a bottle = **Acub** [1 Esd **5** 31]): The descendants of B. returned with Zerubbabel to Jerus (Ezr **2** 51; Neh **7** 53).

BAKBUKIAH, bak-bū-kī'a (בַּקְבֻּקְיָה, *bakbukyāh*, "the Lord pours out"):

(1) A Levite who "dwelt in Jerus" after the return from Babylon (Neh **11** 17).

(2) A Levite who returned with Zerubbabel to Jerus (Neh **12** 9).

(3) A Levite and porter keeping "the watch at the store-houses of the gates" (Neh **12** 25).

BAKEMEATS, bāk'mēts: Only in Gen **40** 17 AV and ERV. "All manner of baked food for Pharaoh" ARV. Any kind of meat baked or cooked. See BREAD; FOOD.

BAKING, bāk'ing. See BREAD.

BAKING PAN. See BREAD; PAN.

BALAAM, bā'lam (בִּלְעָם, *bil'ām*, "devourer"): The son of Beor, from a city in Mesopotamia called Pethor, a man possessing the gift of prophecy, whose remarkable history may be found in Nu **22** 2—**24** 25; cf **31** 8.16; Dt **23** 4; Josh **13** 22; **24** 9; Neh **13** 2; Mic **6** 5; 2 Pet **2** 15; Jude ver **11**; Rev **2** 14.

1. History

When the children of Israel pitched their tents in the plains of Moab, the Moabites entered into some sort of an alliance with the Midianites. At the instigation of Balak, at that time king of the Moabites, the elders of the two nations were sent to Balaam to induce him, by means of a bribe, to pronounce a curse on the advancing hosts of the Israelites. But in compliance with God's command B. refused to go with the elders. Quite different was the result of a second request enhanced by the higher rank of the messengers and by the more alluring promises on the part of Balak. Not only did God permit B. to go with the men, but he actually commanded him to do so, cautioning him, however, to act according to further instructions. While on his way to Balak, this injunction was strongly impressed on the mind of B. by the strange behavior of his ass and by his encounter with the Angel of the Lord.

Accompanied by Balak who had gone out to meet the prophet, B. came to Kiriath-huzoth. On the next morning he was brought up "into the high places of Baal" commanding a partial view of the camp of the Israelites. But instead of a curse he pronounced a blessing. From there he was taken to the top of Peor, yet this change of places and external views did not alter the tendency of B.'s parables; in fact, his spirit even soared to greater heights and from his lips fell glowing words of praise and admiration, of benediction and glorious prophecy. This, of course, fully convinced Balak that all further endeavors to persuade the seer to comply with his wishes would be in vain, and the two parted.

Nothing else is said of B., until we reach Nu **31.** Here in ver 8 we are told of his violent death at the hands of the Israelites, and in ver 16 we learn of his shameful counsel which brought disgrace and disaster into the ranks of the chosen people.

Now, there are a number of interesting problems connected with this remarkable story. We shall try to solve at least some of the more important ones.

2. Problems

(1) Was B. a prophet of Jeh? For an answer we must look to Nu **22–24.** Nowhere is he called a prophet. He is introduced as the son of Beor and as a man reputed to be of great personal power (cf Nu **22** 6*b*). The cause of this is to be found in the fact that he had intercourse of some kind with God (cf Nu **22** 9.20; **22** 22–35; **23** 4; **23** 16). Furthermore, it is interesting to note how B. was enabled to deliver his parables. First it is said: "And Jeh put a word in B.'s mouth" (Nu **23** 5; cf ver 16), a procedure seemingly rather mechanical, while nothing of the kind is mentioned in Nu **24.** Instead we meet with the remarkable sentence: "And when B. saw that it pleased Jeh to bless Israel, he went not, as at the other times, to meet with enchantments . . . . " (Nu **24** 1), and then: "the Spirit of God came upon him" (ver 2*b*). All this is very noteworthy and highly instructive, esp. if we compare with it vs 3 RVm and 4: "The man whose eye is opened saith; he saith, who heareth the words of God, who seeth the vision of the

Almighty," etc. The inference is plain enough: B. knew the Lord, the Jeh of the Israelites, but his knowledge was dimmed and corrupted by heathen conceptions. He knew enough of God to obey Him, yet for a long time he hoped to win Him over to his own selfish plan (cf **23** 4). Through liberal sacrifices he expected to influence God's actions. Bearing this in mind, we see the import of Nu **24** 1. After fruitless efforts to cajole God into an attitude favorable to his hidden purpose, he for a time became a prophet of the Lord, yielding to the ennobling influences of His spirit. Here was a chance for his better nature to assert itself permanently and to triumph over the dark forces of paganism. Did he improve this opportunity? He did not (cf Nu **31** 8.16).

(2) Is the B. of Nu **22–24** identical with the person of the same name mentioned in Nu **31**? Quite a number of scholars deny it, or, to be more accurate, there are according to their theory two accounts of B.: the one in Nu **22–24** being favorable to his character, and the other in Nu **31** being quite the reverse. It is claimed the two accounts could only be made to agree by modifying or eliminating Nu **24** 25. Now, we believe that Nu **31** 16 actually does modify the report of B.'s return contained in Nu **24** 25. The children of Israel slew B. with the sword (Nu **31** 8). Why? Because of his counsel of ver 16. We maintain that the author of **24** 25 had this fact in mind when he wrote the 1st ver of Nu **25**: "And . . . . the people began to play the harlot," etc. Thus, he closely connects the report of B.'s return with the narrative contained in Nu **25**. Therefore we regard Nu **31** 8.16 as supplementary to Nu **22–24**. But here is another question:

(3) Is the narrative in Nu **22–24** the result of combining different traditions? In a general way, we may answer this question in the affirmative, and only in a general way we can distinguish between two main sources of tradition. But we maintain that they are not contradictory to each other, but supplementary.

(4) What about the talking of the ass and the marvelous prophecies of B.? We would suggest the following explanation. By influencing the soul of B., God caused him to interpret correctly the inarticulate sounds of the animal. God's acting on the soul and through it on the intellect and on the hearts of men—this truth must be also applied to B.'s wonderful prophetic words. They are called *m^eshālīm* or sayings of a prophet, a diviner.

In the 1st of these "parables" (Nu **23** 7–10) he briefly states his reasons for pronouncing a blessing; in the 2d (vs 18–24) he again emphasizes the fact that he cannot do otherwise than bless the Israelites, and then he proceeds to pronounce the blessing at some greater length. In the 3d (Nu **24** 3–9) he describes the glorious state of the people, its development and irresistible power. In the last four parables (vs 15–24) he partly reveals the future of Israel and other nations: they are all to be destroyed, Israel's fate being included in the allusion to Eber. Now, at last, B. is back again in his own sphere denouncing others and predicting awful disasters. (On the "star out of Jacob," ver 17, see ASTRONOMY, ii, 9; STAR OF THE MAGI.)

This may furnish us a clue to his character. It, indeed, remains "instructively composite." A

3. B.'s Character

soothsayer who might have become a prophet of the Lord; a man who loved the wages of unrighteousness, and yet a man who in one supreme moment of his life surrendered himself to God's holy Spirit; a person cumbered with superstition, covetousness and even wickedness, and yet capable of performing the highest service in the kingdom of God: such is the character of B., the remarkable OT type and, in a sense, the prototype of Judas Iscariot.

In 2 Pet **2** 15 B.'s example is used as a means to illustrate the pernicious influence of insincere

4. B. as a Type

Christian teachers. The author might have alluded to B. in the passage immediately preceding 2 Pet **2** 15 because of his abominable counsel. This is done in Rev **2** 14. Here, of course, B. is the type of a teacher of the church who attempts to advance the cause of God by advocating an unholy alliance with the ungodly and worldly, and so conforming the life of the church to the spirit of the flesh.

LITERATURE.—Bishop Butler's *Sermons*, "Balaam"; *ICC*, "Numbers."

WILLIAM BAUR

BALAC, bā′lak. See BALAK.

BALADAN, bal′a-dan (בַּלְאֲדָן, *bal′ădhān*, "He [i.e. Merodach] has given a son"): Baladan is said in 2 K **20** 12 and Isa **39** 1 to have been the father of Berodach (Merodach)-Baladan, king of Babylon. Some have thought that the Bib. writer was wrong here, inasmuch as it is said in the inscriptions of Sargon (*Annals*, 228, 315; *Pr.*, 122), that Merodach-Baladan was the son of Yakin. It is evident, however, from the analogy of Jehu, who is called by the Assyr kings the son of Omri, that Yakin is to be looked upon as the founder of the dynasty or kingdom, rather than as the father of Merodach-Baladan. The *Bith Yakin*, over which Merodach-Baladan is said to have been king, corresponds exactly to the phrase *Bith Khumria*, or House of Omri, over which Jehu is said to have ruled. There is no reason, then, for supposing that there is an error in either case. There is, however, good reason for believing that the Merodach-Baladan of the Book of Kings was the son of another king of the same name. That only the latter part of the father's name is here mentioned may be compared with the Shalman of Hos **10** 14 for the more fully written Shalmaneser of 2 K **17** 3; and with the Jareb of Hos **5** 13 and **10** 6, probably for Sennacherib. Such abbreviation of proper names was usual among the Assyrians and Babylonians. See Tallquist, *Namenbuch*, xiv–xix.

R. DICK WILSON

BALAH, bā′la (בָּלָה, *bālāh;* **Βωλά**, *Bōlá*): A place, unidentified, in the territory of Simeon (Josh **19** 3), called Bilhah in 1 Ch **4** 29. It may be identical with Baalah in Judah (Josh **15** 29).

BALAK, bā′lak (בָּלָק, *bālāḳ*, "devastator" or "one who lays waste"): Mentioned in connection with the story of Balaam (Nu **22–24**; cf Josh **24** 9; Jgs **11** 25; Mic **6** 5; Rev **2** 14). He was the king of Moab who hired Balaam to pronounce a curse on the Israelites. See BALAAM.

BALAMON, bal′a-mon (**Βαλαμών**, *Balamṓn;* AV **Balamo**): In the field between Balamon and Dothaim Manasses, the husband of Judith, was buried (Jth **8** 3). Cf Baal-hamon (Cant **8** 11).

BALANCE, bal′ans: The Eng. word "balance" is from the Lat *bilanx*="having two scales" (*bi*="two" and *lanx*="plate," or "scale"). It is used to render three Heb words: (1) מֹאזְנַיִם, *mō′znayim* (Lev **19** 36; Job **6** 2; Ps **62** 9; Prov **11** 1; Isa **40** 12.15; Jer **32** 10, etc); (2) קָנֶה, *ḳāneh* (Isa **46** 6), and (3) פֶּלֶס, *peleṣ* (Prov **16** 11). It is found in the sing., e.g. "a just *balance*" (Prov **16** 11); "a pair of *balances*" (Rev **6** 5, etc), as well as in the plur., e.g. "just *balances*" (Lev **19** 36), "weighed in the *balances*" (Dnl **5** 27, etc).

Balance (from Egyptian Tomb).

1. Balances among the Ancient Hebrews; the Parts, etc

(1) The "balances" of the ancient Hebrews differed little, if at all, from those used by the Egyptians (Wilkinson, *Anc. Egypt* [1878], II, 246 f). They consisted, probably, of a horizontal bar, either pivoted on a perpendicular rod (see Erman, *Aegypten*, I, 615 for similar Egyp balances), or suspended from a cord and held in the hand, the more primitive form. At the ends of the bar were pans, or hooks, from which the things to be weighed were suspended, sometimes in bags.

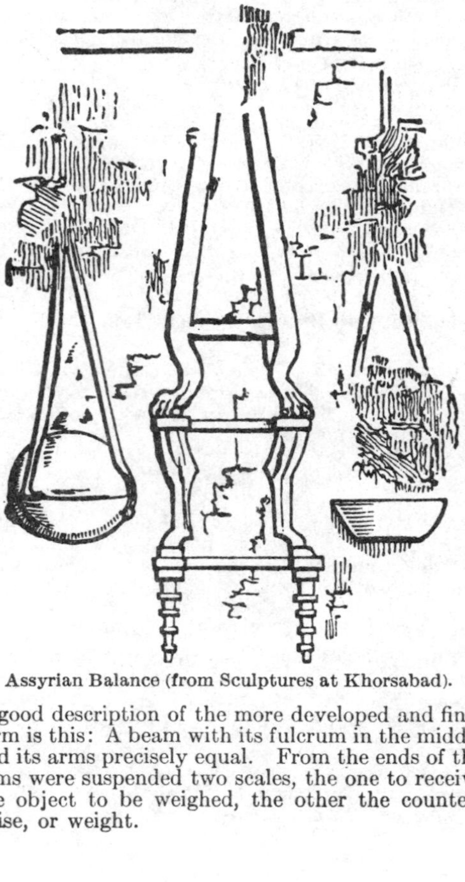

Assyrian Balance (from Sculptures at Khorsabad).

A good description of the more developed and final form is this: A beam with its fulcrum in the middle and its arms precisely equal. From the ends of the arms were suspended two scales, the one to receive the object to be weighed, the other the counterpoise, or weight.

(2) The weights were of stone at first and are so named in Dt **25** 13 AVm. A pair of scales (AV "a pair of balances") is used in Rev **6** 5 by a figure of speech for the balance as a whole; only once is the beam so used, in Isa **46** 6, lit. "weigh silver in the beam." Abraham, we are told (Gen **23** 16), "weighed the silver."

2. Probably of Bab Origin

The basis and fountain-head of all systems of weights and measurements is to be traced, it is now thought, to Babylonia; but the primitive instruments and systems were subject to many modifications as they entered other regions and passed into the derivative systems. The Rom "balance" is the same as our *steelyard* (vulgarly called "stillyards"). Cf the Chinese, Danish, etc.

3. The System of Weighing Liable to Fraud

Though the "balances" in ancient times were rudely constructed, the weighing could be done quite accurately, as may be seen in the use of equally primitive balances in the East today. But the system was liable to fraud. A "false balance" might be lit. one so constructed that the arms were of unequal length, when the longer arm would be intended, of course, for the article to be weighed. The system was liable, however, to various other subtle abuses then as now; hence the importance in God's sight of "true weights" and a "just balance" is enforced again and again (see Lev **19** 36; Prov **11** 1; **16** 11; **20** 23; Am **8** 5; Mic **6** 11, etc).

4. "Wicked Balances" Condemned

"A false balance is an abomination to Jehovah" (Prov **11** 1; cf **20** 23), and "a just balance and scales are Jehovah's" (Prov **16** 11). Hos (**12** 7) condemns "the balances of deceit" in the hand of the wicked; Am (**8** 5 AV) cries out upon "falsifying the balances by deceit," and Mic (**6** 11) denounces "wicked balances." Indeed, the righteousness of a just balance and true weights, and the iniquity of false ones are everywhere emphasized by the lawmakers, prophets and moral teachers of Israel, and the preacher or teacher who would expose and denounce such things in God's name today need be at no loss for texts and precedents. See WEIGHTS AND MEASURES.

LITERATURE.—Wilkinson, *Ancient Egypt;* Erman, *Egypt;* Lepsius, *Denkmäler;* and arts. on "Balance," etc, in *DB*, *EB*, *Jew Enc*, *HDB*, *EB*, etc.

GEO. B. EAGER

BALANCINGS, bal'ans-ins: "The balancings of the clouds" (Job **37** 16), the manner in which they are poised and supported in the air, alike with their mysterious spreadings and motions, challenge the strongest intellect to explain.

BALASAMUS, ba-las'a-mus. See BAALSAMUS.

BALD LOCUST, bôld lō'kust. See LOCUST.

BALDNESS, bôld'ness (קָרְחָה, *ḳorḥāh*): The reference in the Bible to baldness is not to the natural loss of hair, but to baldness produced by shaving the head. This was practised as a mark of mourning for the dead (Lev **21** 5; Isa **15** 2; **22** 12); as the result of any disaster (Am **8** 10; Mic **1** 16). The custom arose from the fact that the hair was regarded as a special ornament. It was the custom of the people of the land, and the Israelites were strictly forbidden to practise it (Lev **21** 5; Deut **14** 1). These are striking passages with reference to the knowledge the Israelites had concerning the future life. This is saying to them what Paul said to the Thessalonians (1 Thess **4** 13). To call one a "bald head" was an epithet of contempt, and was sometimes applied to persons who were not naturally bald. It was the epithet applied by certain infidel young men to Elisha

(2 K **2** 23.24). In a **fig.** sense it is used to express the barrenness of the country (Jer **47** 5). See HAIR; SHAVE. JACOB W. KAPP

BALL, bôl (דּוּר, *dūr*): A rare Heb word used in this sense only in Isa **22** 18, and correctly rendered in ARV "He will surely wind thee round and round, *and toss thee* like a ball into a large country." De Or, Böttcher, Jastrow, following Talm, regard the noun as *kaddūr*, but perhaps incorrectly. See also GAMES.

BALM, bäm (צְרִי, *çerī*, צֳרִי, *çŏrī;* LXX **ῥητίνη**, *rhētínē*): The name of an odoriferous resin said to be brought from Gilead by Ishmaelite Arabs on their way to Egypt (Gen **37** 25). It is trd "balm" in AV and RV, but is called "mastic," RVm. In Gen **43** 11 it is one of the gifts sent by Jacob to Joseph, and in Ezk **27** 17 it is named as one of the exports from Judaea to Tyre. The prophet Jeremiah refers **fig.** to its medicinal properties as an application to wounds and as a sedative (**8** 22; **46** 11; **51** 8). The name is derived from a root signifying "to leak," and is applied to it as being an exudation. There is a sticky, honey-like gum resin prepared at the present day at Jericho, extracted from the *Balanites Aegyptiaca* grown in the Ghōr, and sold to travelers in small tin boxes as **"Balm of Gilead,"** but it is improbable that this is the real *çŏrī* and it has no medicinal value. The material to which the classic authors applied the name is that known as Mecca balsam, which is still imported into Egypt from Arabia, as it was in early times. This is the exudation from the *Balsamodendron opobalsamum,* a native of southern Arabia and Abyssinia. The tree is small, ragged-looking and with a yellowish bark like that of a plane tree, and the exudation is said to be gathered from its smaller branches. At the present day it grows nowhere in Pal. Dr. Post and other botanists have sought for it on the Ghōr and in Gilead, and have not found it, and there is no trace of it in the neighborhood of Jericho, which Pliny says is its only habitat. Strabo describes it as growing by the Sea of Galilee, as well as at Jericho, but both these and other ancient writers give inconsistent and incorrect descriptions of the tree evidently at second hand. We learn from Theophrastus that many of the spices of the farther East reached the Mediterranean shore through Pal, being brought by Arab caravans which would traverse the indefinitely bounded tract E. of Jordan to which the name Gilead is given, and it was probably thus that the balm received its local name. *Mecca balsam* is an orange-yellow, treacly fluid, mildly irritating to the skin, possibly a weak local stimulant and antiseptic, but of very little remedial value.

ALEX. MACALISTER

BALM OF GILEAD: The people of Jericho today prepare for the benefit of pilgrims a "Balm of Gilead" from the *zakkūm* (*Balanites Aegyptiaca*), but this has no serious claims to be the balm of antiquity. If we are to look beyond the borders of modern Pal we may credit the tradition which claims that Mecca balsam, a product of *Balsamodendron Gileadense* and *B. opobalsamum,* was the true "balm," and Post (*HDB*, I, 236) produces evidence to show that these plants were once grown in the Jordan valley. Yet another suggestion, made by Lagarde, is that the *çŏrī* = *στύραξ*, and if so then "balm" would be the inspissated juice of the Storax-tree (*Styrax officinalis*), a common inhabitant of Gilead. See also BALM.

E. W. G. MASTERMAN

BALNUUS, bal-nū'us (A, **Βαλνοῦος**, *Balnoúos;* B, **Βαλνοῦς**, *Balnoús* = Binnui [Ezr **10** 30]): B. put away his "strange wife" (1 Esd **9** 31).

BALSAM, bôl'sam (בָּשָׂם, *bāsām,* בֶּשֶׂם, *besem;* **ἡδύσματα**, *hēdúsmata;* **θυμιάματα**, *thumiámata*): Is usually "spices" but in RVm (Cant **5** 1.13; **6** 2) is rendered as "balsam." It was an ingredient in the anointing oil of the priests (Ex **25** 6; **35** 28). The Queen of Sheba brought it as a present to Solomon (1 K **10** 2) in large quantity (ver 10) and of a finer quality (2 Ch **9** 9) than that brought as a regular tribute by other visitors (1 K **10** 25). In the later monarchy Hezekiah had a treasure of this perfume (2 Ch **32** 27) which he displayed to his Bab visitors (Isa **39** 2); and after the captivity the priests kept a store of it in the temple (1 Ch **9** 30). According to Ezekiel the Syrians imported it from Sheba (**27** 22). There is a tradition preserved in Jos (*Ant*, VIII, vi, 6) that the Queen of Sheba brought roots of the plant to Solomon, who grew them in a garden of spices at Jericho, probably derived from the references to such a garden in Cant **5** 1.13; **6** 2. This may be the source of the statements of Strabo, Trogus and Pliny quoted above (see BALM). It was probably the same substance as the BALM described above, but from the reference in Ex **30** 7; **35** 8, it may have been used as a generic name for fragrant resins. The root from which the word is derived signifies "to be fragrant," and fragrant balsams or resins are known in modern Arab. as *bahasân*. The trees called in 2 S **5** 23.24 (RVm) "balsam-trees" were certainly not those which yielded this substance, for there are none in the *Shephēlāh*, but there are both mulberry trees and terebinths in the district between Rephaim and Gezer. When used as a perfume the name *bāsām* seems to have been adopted, but as a medicinal remedy it is called *çŏrī*.

ALEX. MACALISTER

BALTASAR, bal-tā'sar (**Βαλτασάρ**, *Baltasár;* AV **Balthasar**):

(1) The Gr of Heb, בֵּלְטְשַׁאצַּר, *bēlṭesha'çcar,* or בֵּלְטְאשַׁצַּר, *bēlṭe'shaççar,* perhaps corresponding to *Balâṭ-šar-uṣur,* "protect the life of the king," the Bab cognomen of Daniel. Cf Belteshazzar (Dnl **1** 7; **2** 26; **4** 8 ff, et al.).

(2) B. is also the Gr of the Heb בֵּלְשַׁאצַּר, *bēlsha'çcar,* or בֵּלְאשַׁצַּר, *bēl'shaççar,* the name of the last king of Babylon (corresponding to the Bab *Bêl-šar-uṣur; KAT*, III, 396; Syr Blitshazzar; Vulg Baltassar). Cf Bar **1** 11 and Belshazzar (Dnl **5** 1 ff; **7** 1; **8** 1).

(3) The name of one of the Magi who according to the legend visited Jesus at Bethlehem: Melchior from Nubia, Balthasar from Godolia, Caspar from Tharsis. A. L. BRESLICH

BAMAH, bä'mä, bā'mä (בָּמָה, *bāmāh,* "high place"): The word appears in Ezk **20** 29 where reference is made to former "high-place worship," the prophet speaking with contempt of such manner of worship. Ewald suggests a play of words, בָּא, *bā',* "come," and מָה, *māh,* "what," "what [*māh*] is the high place [*bā-māh*] whereunto *ye* come [*bā'*]?" It is possible that reference is made to a prominent high place like the one at Gibeon (cf 1 K **3** 4; 1 Ch **16** 39; **21** 29; 2 Ch **1** 3) for which the name "Bamah" was retained after the reform mentioned by the prophet.

BAMOTH, bā'moth, **BAMOTH-BAAL,** bā'moth-bā'al (בָּמוֹת בַּעַל, *bāmōth-ba'al,* "high places of Baal"): Bamoth is referred to in Nu **21** 19.20, as a station in the journeyings of Israel N. of the Arnon. It is probably the same place as the Bamoth-baal of Nu **22** 41 (RVm), whither Balak, king of Moab, conducted Balaam to view and to curse Israel. Bamoth-baal is named in Josh **13** 17 as one of the cities given to Reuben. Mesha, on the M S, speaks of having "rebuilt" Beth-bamoth.

BAN (A, **Βάν**, *Bán;* B, **Βαινάν**, *Bainán;* 1 Esd **5** 37 = Tobiah [Ezr **2** 60; Neh **7** 62]; some MSS of the LXX read **Βουά**, *Bouá*): The descendants of B. were not able to trace their ancestry to show "how they were of Israel."

BANAIAS, ban-ā-ī'as (**Βαναίας**, *Banaías;* 1 Esd **9** 35 = Benaiah [Ezr **10** 43]): B. put away his "strange wife."

BAND: The Eng. word has two generic meanings, each shading off into several specific meanings: (1) that which holds together, binds or encircles: a bond; (2) a company of men. The second sense may philologically and logically have been derived from the first, men being held together by social ties. Both meanings appear in OT and NT representing various Heb and Gr words.

(1) A band (*a*) (אֵסוּר, *'ēṣūr*): a flaxen rope (Jgs **15** 14); a band of iron and brass (Dnl **4** 15.23); **metaphorically** of a false woman's hands (Eccl **7** 26). (*b*) (חֶבֶל, *ḥebhel*): "The bands of the wicked have robbed me" (AV of Ps **119** 61), where "bands" = "troops" by mistr; RV "The cords of the wicked have wrapped me round"; plur. *ḥobhlīm* = "bands" = the name of the prophet's symbolic staff representing the brotherhood between Judah and Israel (Zec **11** 7.14). (*c*) (עֲבֹת, *'ăbhōth*): "I drew them with cords of a man, with bands of love" (Hos **11** 4; cf Ezk **3** 25; **4** 8; Job **39** 10). (*d*) (שָׂפָה, *sāphāh*): the edge of the round opening in the robe of the ephod with a band (RV "binding") round about the hole of it (only in Ex **39** 23). (*e*) (חַרְצֻבּוֹת, *ḥarçūbbōth*): bands (RV "bonds") of wickedness (Isa **58** 6); bands (= pains) in death (Ps **73** 4); RVm ("pangs," Cheyne, "torments"). (*f*) (מוֹטָה, *mōṭāh*): the cross bar of oxen's yoke, holding them together (Lev **26** 13; Ezk **34** 27 AV; RV "bars"). (*g*) (מוֹסֵר, *mōṣēr*): a fetter: "Who hath loosed the bonds of the swift ass?" (Job **39** 5; Ps **2** 3; **107** 14; Isa **28** 22; **52** 2; Jer **2** 20; all in AV and RV). The same Heb word (in Ps **116** 16; Jer **5** 5; **27** 2; **30** 8; Nah **1** 13) is tr^d^ "bonds" in AV, and in ERV of Ps **116** 16, and Nah **1** 13, but "bands" in ERV of Jer **5** 5; **27** 2; **30** 8; ARV has "bonds" throughout. See BOND. (*h*) (מוֹשְׁכוֹת, *mōshᵉkhōth*): "Canst thou . . . . loose the bands of Orion?" (only in Job **38** 31). (*i*) (δεσμός, *desmós*, σύνδεσμος, *súndesmos*): a fetter: that which binds together: of the chains of a lunatic or prisoner (Lk **8** 29; Acts **16** 26; **22** 30 AV), **metaphorically** of the mystic union of Christ and the church (Col **2** 19). These words are often tr^d^ by "bond" in AV and RV. (*j*) (ζευκτηρία, *zeuktēría*): the rudder's bands (only in Acts **27** 40).

(2) A company of men (*a*) (גְּדוּד, *gᵉdhūdh*): a band of soldiers (2 S **4** 2; 1 K **11** 24 AV; 2 K **6** 23; **13** 20.21; **24** 2; 1 Ch **7** 4; **12** 18.21; 2 Ch **22** 1). So RV (except in 1 K **11** 24, "troop"). (*b*) (רֹאשׁ, *rō'sh*): "head" = "division": "The Chaldeans made three bands" (Job **1** 17); 1 Ch **12** 23 RV translates "heads." (*c*) (חַיִל, *ḥayil*): "a band of men" RV the "host" (only in 1 S **10** 26). (*d*) (אֲגַפִּים, *'ăghappīm*): "the wings of an army," only in Ezk armies of the King of Judah (**12** 14; **17** 21); of Gomer and of Togarmah (**38** 6); of Gog (RV "hordes") (**38** 9.22; **39** 4). (*e*) (מַחֲנֶה, *maḥăneh*): "camp": only in Gen **32** 7.10; RV "companies." (*f*) (חֹצֵץ, *ḥōçēç*): of locusts dividing into companies or swarms (Prov **30** 27). (*g*) (σπεῖρα, *speíra*): usually a "cohort" (see RVm) of Rom soldiers; the tenth part of a legion, about 600 men: (Mt **27** 27; Mk **15** 16; Acts **10** 1; **21** 31; **27** 1). A smaller detachment of soldiers (Jn **18** 3.12; cf 2 Macc **8** 23; Jth **14** 11). (*h*) (ποιεῖν συστροφήν, *poieín sustrophḗn*): "to make a conspiracy": "The Jews banded together" (Acts **23** 12). T. REES

(3) **The Augustan Band** (**σπεῖρα Σεβαστή**, *speíra Sebastḗ*) to which Julius, the Rom centurion who had charge of St. Paul as a prisoner on his voyage to Rome, belonged, was a cohort apparently stationed at Caesarea at the time (Acts **27** 1). Schürer (*GJV*, I³, 461 f) is of opinion that it was one of five cohorts mentioned by Jos, recruited in Samaria and called Sebastenes from the Gr name of the city of Samaria (Sebaste). This particular cohort had in all likelihood for its full name *Cohors Augusta Sebastenorum*, Augusta being an honorific title of which examples are found in the case of auxiliary troops. Sir William Ramsay, following Mommsen (*St. Paul the Traveller*, 315, 348), thinks it denotes a body of legionary centurions, selected from legions serving abroad, who were employed by the emperor on confidential business between the provinces and Rome, the title Augustan being conferred upon them as a mark of favor and distinction. The grounds on which the views of Mommsen and Ramsay rest are questioned by Professor Zahn (*Introduction to the NT*, I, 551 ff), and more evidence is needed to establish them. See ARMY (ROMAN).

(4) **The Italian Band** (**σπεῖρα Ἰταλική**, *speíra Italikḗ*) was a cohort composed of volunteer Rom citizens born in Italy and stationed at Caesarea at this time (Acts **10** 1). Schürer maintains that there could have been no Rom cohort there at this time, although he accepts the testimony of inscriptions to the presence of an Italian cohort at a later time. He accordingly rejects the story of Cornelius, holding that the author of the Acts has given in this narrative conditions belonging to a later time (*GJV*, I³, 462 f). In reply to Schürer, Blass asks why one of the five cohorts mentioned by Jos may not have been composed of Rom citizens living at Caesarea or Sebaste, and bearing this name (Blass, *Acta Apostolorum*, 124). From a recently discovered inscription, Sir W. M. Ramsay has ascertained that there was an Italian cohort stationed in Syria in 69 AD, which heightens the probability of one actually being found in Caesarea at 41–44 AD, and he shows that even if his cohort was at the time on duty elsewhere a centurion like Cornelius might well have been at Caesarea at the time mentioned (*Expositor*, 5th ser., IV, V, with Schürer's rejoinder). The subject of detached service in the provinces of the Rom Empire is admittedly obscure, but nothing emerges in this discussion to cast doubt upon the historical character of St. Luke's narrative. See ARMY (ROMAN).

T. NICOL

BANDS, BEAUTY AND. See BEAUTY AND BANDS.

BANDS OF RUDDER. See RUDDER.

BANI, bā'nī (בָּנִי, *bānī*, "posterity"):

(1) A Gadite, one of David's mighty men (2 S **23** 36).

(2) A Levite whose son was appointed for service in the tabernacle at David's time (1 Ch **6** 46).

(3) A Judahite whose son lived in Jerus after the captivity (1 Ch **9** 4).

(4) The descendants of B. (called Binnui, Neh **7** 15) returned with Zerubbabel (Ezr **2** 10) and had taken "strange wives" (Ezr **10** 29).

(5) B. who had taken a "strange wife" (Ezr **10** 38) mentioned with his brothers, the sons of B. who also had taken "strange wives" (Ezr **10** 34).

(6) Son of B., a Levite and builder (Neh **3** 17).

(7) B., who instructed the people at Ezra's time (Neh **8** 7).

(8) Three Levites mentioned in connection with the temple worship at Ezra's time (Neh **9** 4.5).

(9) A Levite who sealed the covenant with Neh (Neh **10** 13).

(10) A leader of the people who also signed the covenant (Neh **10** 14).

(11) One whose son Uzzi was overseer of the Levites at Jerus (Neh **11** 22). See Binnui.

A. L. Breslich

BANIAS, ba-nī'as (B, **Βανίας**, *Banías;* A, **Βανί**, *Baní;* AV **Banid** [1 Esd **8** 36]): An ancestor of Salimoth. The descendants of B. returned with Ezra to Jerus. The name is omitted (Ezr **8** 10), perhaps due to the oversight of a copyist or a mistaken reading of בְּנֵי, *b*ᵉ*nē*, "sons of," for בָּנִי, *bānī*.

BANIAS. See Caesarea Philippi.

BANID, bā'nid (1 Esd **8** 36): In RV Banias, which see.

BANISHMENT, ban'ish-ment. See Punishments.

BANK, baṇk:

(1) (שָׂפָה, *sāphāh*, "lip," "edge"): "By the b. of the Jordan" (2 K **2** 13); "Upon the b. of the river were very many trees" (Ezk **47** 7.12).

(2) (גָּדָה, *gādhāh*, "cuttings"): Always of banks overflowed (Josh **3** 15; **4** 18; Isa **8** 7), as also

(3) (גִּדְיָה, *gidhyāh*, 1 Ch **12** 15).

(4) (סֹלְלָה, *sōl*ᵉ*lāh*, "mound," "rampart"): "Cast up a b. against the city" (2 S **20** 15, ERV "mount," ARV "mound"; cf 2 K **19** 32; Isa **37** 33). "Banks of sweet herbs" (Cant **5** 13); "the marginal rendering is the right one, 'towers of perfumes,' i.e. plants with fragrant leaves and flowers trained on trellis-work" (*Speaker's Comm.* in loc.).

(5) (χάραξ, *chárax*, "a stake," "entrenchment"): "Thine enemies shall cast up a bank about thee" (Lk **19** 43 AV "trench"). It is probably a military term and stands for a "palisade" (so RVm), i.e. probably an embankment of stakes strengthened with branches and earth, with a ditch behind it, used by the besiegers as a protection against arrows or attacking parties (Lat *vallum*), such, no doubt, as was employed by Titus in the siege of Jerus, 70 AD (Jos, *BJ*, V, vi, 2).

(6) Bank, Banking (q.v.).

M. O. Evans

BANK, BANKING: "Banking" in the full modern sense, of taking money on deposit and lending it out on interest, is of comparatively recent origin. A few "banks of deposit" were founded in Italy in the Middle Ages, but the earliest "banks of issue," of the modern sort, were those of Amsterdam (1609) and Hamburg (1619), beginning in the 17th cent. The law of Moses forbade Israelites to charge each other interest (Ex **22** 25; Lev **25** 35.37; Dt **23** 19), but let them lend on interest to Gentiles (Dt **23** 20), though this law was often evaded or disregarded (Neh **5** 10.12). Banks and banking, however, are found in operation in the Gr cities; "money-changers," sitting at their tables (*trápezai*) in the market place, both changed coins and took money on deposit, giving high interest; and banking of a sort, in its incipient stages, existed among the ancient Hebrews. But the Phoenicians are now thought to have been the inventors of the money-changing, money-lending system which is found in more or less modified and developed forms among ancient peoples and in full development and operation in the palmy days of the Rom Empire. In the Gr-Rom period, without doubt, bankers both received money on deposit, paying interest, and let it out at a higher rate, or employed it in trade, as the *publicani* at Rome did, in farming the revenues of a province (Plumptre).

1. Introductory

2. Banking among the Ancient Hebrews

(1) The Heb money-changer, like his modern Syrian counterpart, the *sarāf* (see *PEFS*, 1904, 49 ff, where the complexity of exchange in Pal today is graphically described), changed the large coins current into those of smaller denominations, e.g. giving *denarii* for *tetradrachms*, or silver for gold, or copper for silver.

(2) But no mean part of his business was the exchanging of foreign money, and even the money of the country of a non-Phoen standard, for shekels and half-shekels on this standard, the latter being accepted only in payment of the temple dues (see Money). The "money-changers" of Mt **21** 12, as the Gr signifies, were men who made small change. Such men may be seen in Jerus now with various coins piled in slender pillars on a table (cf *epí trápezan*, Lk **19** 23), ready to be used in changing money for a premium into such forms, or denominations, as would be more current or more convenient for immediate use.

(3) "Usury" in EV is simply OE for what we today call "interest," i.e. the sum paid for the use of money, Lat *usura;* and "interest" should take the place of it in all passages in the OT and NT, where it has such significance.

The Gr word rendered (*tókos*), "usury" in the NT (see Lk **19** 23 f) means lit. "what is born of money," "what money brings forth or produces." "Usury" has come to mean "exorbitant interest," but did not mean this at the time of AV, 1611.

3. Banking in NT Times

(1) In Christ's time, and immediately following, there was great need for money-changers and money-changing, esp. on the part of foreign Jews whom custom forbade to put any but Jewish coins into the temple treasury (see Mk **12** 41). It was mainly for the convenience of these Jews of the Dispersion, and because it was in order to a sacred use, that the people thought it proper to allow the money-changers to set up their tables in the outer court of the temple (see Mt **21** 12 ff).

Bank: Money Changer.

(2) The language of Mt **25** 27, 'Thou oughtest to have put my money to the *bankers*,' etc, would seem to indicate the recognition by Christ of the custom and propriety of lending out money on interest (cf **19** 23). The "exchangers" here are "bankers" (cf Mt **25** 27). The Gr (*trapezítai*) is from a word for "bank" or "bench" (*trápeza*), i.e. the "table" or "counter" on which the money used to be received and paid out. These "bankers" were clearly of a higher class than the "small-change men" of Mt **21** 12, etc (cf "changers of

money," Jn **2** 14, and "changers," Jn **2** 15 EV). Christ upbraids the "slothful servant" because he had not given his pound to "the bank" (or "banker," *epi trapezan*, lit. "on a banker's table"), who, it is implied, would have kept it safe and paid interest for it (Lk **19** 23 f). It is noteworthy that the "ten minae" of ver 24 are those acquired by "the good servant" from the "one" which was first lent him. So these wealthier bankers even then in a way received money on deposit for investment and paid interest on it, after the fashion of the Greeks.

4. Interpretations, Figurative Uses, etc

(1) In Christ's parable (Lk **19** 23 ff) "the *bank*" (lit. "a bank," "table") is taken by some to mean "the *synagogue*," by others to mean "the *church*" (Lange, *LJ*, II, 1, 414); i.e. it is thought that Christ meant to teach that the organized body, "synagogue" or "church," might use the gifts or powers of an adherent or disciple, when he himself could not exercise them (cf *DCG*, art. "Bank").

(2) Then some have thought that Christ was here pointing to prayer as a substitute for good works, when the disciple was unable to do such. Such views seem far-fetched and unnecessary (cf Bruce, *Parabolic Teaching of Christ*, 209 f).

(3) The "money-changers," then as now, had ever to be on guard against false money, which gives point to the oft-quoted extra-scriptural saying (*agraphon*) of Jesus to His disciples: "Be ye expert money-changers" (Gr *ginésthai trapezítai dókimoi;* see Origen, *in Joam*, XIX), which was taken (Clem., *Hom.*, III, 61) to mean, "Be skilful in distinguishing true doctrine from false" (*HDB*, 1-vol).

Geo. B. Eager

BANNAIA, ba-nā'ya. See Sabanneus.

BANNAS, ban'as (**Bάννος,** *Bánnos;* AV **Banuas**): A name occurring in the list of those who returned from the captivity with Zerubbabel (1 Esd **5** 26). Bannas and Sudias are represented by Hoodaviah in the lists of Ezra and Nehemiah.

BANNEAS, ban-ē'as (**Βανναίας,** *Bannaías;* AV Baanias [1 Esd **9** 26] = Benaiah [Ezr **10** 25]): B. put away his "strange wife."

BANNER, ban'ẽr (Ensign, Standard): The Eng. word "banner" is from *banderia*, Low Lat, meaning a banner (cf *bandum*, Lat, which meant first a "band," an organized military troop, and then a "flag"). It has come to mean a *flag*, or standard, carried at the head of a military band or body, to indicate the line of march, or the rallying point,

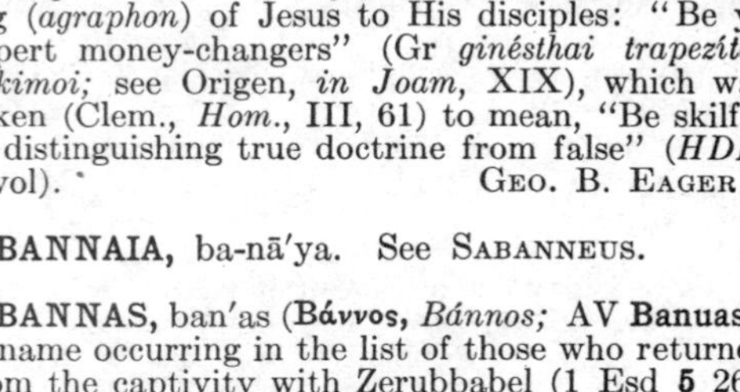

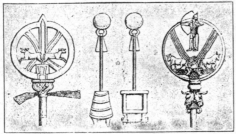

Assyrian Standards and Banners.

and it is now applied, in its more extended significance, to royal, national, or ecclesiastical "banners" also. We find it applied sometimes to a streamer on the end of a lance, such as is used by the Arab *sheik* today. "B." occurs in the following significant OT passages: (1) in the sing., "Lift ye up a b. upon the high mountain" (Isa **13** 2 AV); "a b. to them that fear thee" (Ps **60** 4); and (2) in the plur., "In the name of our God we will set up our b." (Ps **20** 5); "terrible as an army with b." (Cant **6** 4).

1. Military Ensigns among the Hebrews

The Hebrews, it would seem, like the Assyrians, the Egyptians, and other ancient nations, had military ensigns. As bearing upon this question, a very significant passage is that found in Nu **2** 2: "The children of Israel shall encamp every man by his own standard, with the *ensigns* of their fathers' houses." "Standard-bearer" in Isa **10** 18 AV, "They shall be as when a *standard-bearer* fainteth," is not a case in point, but is to be rendered as in RVm, "as when a sick man pineth away."

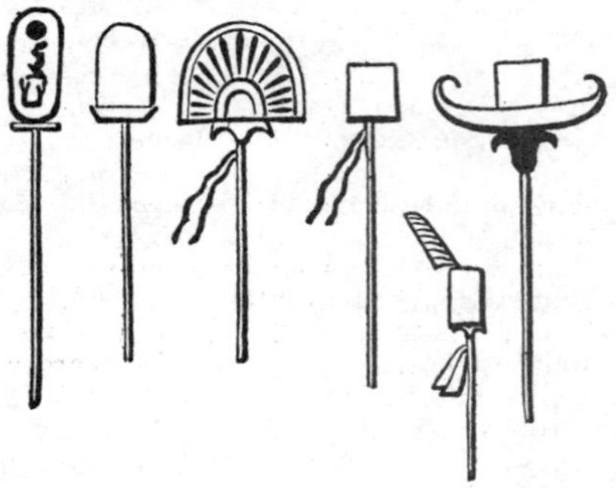

Egyptian Standards.

2. A Distinction with a Difference

In this noted passage a distinction seems intentionally made (another view is held by some) between "the *ensigns* of their fathers' houses" (lit. "signs"; cf Ps **74** 4, where the reference is thought by some today to be to the standards of Antiochus' army), and "the *standards*" of the four great divisions of the Heb tribes in the wilderness (cf the "banner" of Cant **2** 4 and **6** 4. 10). The relation of these to the "standard" of Nu **21** 8 f (Heb *nēṣ*, AV and RV "standard") is by no means clear. The word *nēṣ*, here tr[d] "standard," seems to have meant at first a pole set up on an eminence as a signal for mustering troops (cf "mast" Isa **30** 17 ERVm). But it occurs frequently in the prophets both in this lit. and original sense, and in the **fig.** or derived sense of a rallying point for God's people (see Isa **5** 26; **11** 10; Jer **4** 21 and elsewhere). Here the rendering in EV alternates between "ensign" and "banner" (see *HDB*, 1-vol, art. "Banner").

Geo. B. Eager

BANNUS, ban'us (**Βαννούς,** *Bannoús* [1 Esd **9** 34] = Bani or Binnui [Ezr **10** 29.30]): The sons of B. put away their "strange wives."

BANQUET, baṇ'kwet:

1. The Ancient Hebrew Customs

(1) "Banquet" and "banqueting" in AV always include and stand for wine-drinking, not simply "feast" or "feasting" in our sense. Thus (Cant **2** 4), "He brought me to the banqueting-house" is lit. "the house of wine," and Est **7** 2 has in the Heb "a banquet of wine." In the NT we see a reflection of the same fact in 1 Pet **4** 3 AV, "We walked in . . . . excess of wine, *banquetings*" (Gr "drinkings"; RV "carousings"). Cf Amos **6** 7 AV, "The banquet of them that stretched themselves," where the reference seems to be to reclining at wine-drinkings. See Meals.

The Heb of Job **1** 4 (עשו משתה), AV tr "make a banquet," may refer to a social feast of a less objectionable sort (cf **41** 6 AV), though the Heb משתה = "to drink" יין = "wine," was used as synonymous with "banquet." See Symposium.

Music, dancing and merriment usually attended all such festivities. Certainly the ancient Hebrews, like other peoples of the ancient East, were very fond of social feasting, and in Christ's day had acquired, from contact with Greeks and Romans, luxurious and bibulous habits, that often carried them to excess in their social feasts.

Among the Greeks the word for "feast" (*dochḗ*) is from *déchomai* "to receive" (cf our Eng. usage, "to receive" and "reception"). This word *dochē* is used with *poieín* "to make," to signify "to make" or "give a feast." Cf Lk **5** 29 where Levi "made a feast."

2. In Christ's Teaching and Practice

(1) In view of existing customs and abuses, Christ taught His followers when they gave a banquet to invite the poor, etc (Lk **14** 13), rather than, as the fashion of the day called for, to bid the rich and influential. Much in the NT that has to do with banquets and banquetings will be obscure to us of the West if we do not keep in mind the many marked differences of custom between the East and the West.

(2) "Banquets" were usually given in the house of the host to specially invited guests (Lk **14** 15; Jn **2** 2), but much more freedom was accorded to the uninvited than we of the West are accustomed to, as one finds to be true everywhere in the East today. The custom of reclining at meals (see MEALS; TRICLINIUM, etc) was everywhere in vogue among the well-to-do in Christ's day, even in the case of the ordinary meals, the guest leaning upon the left arm and eating with the aid of the right (cf Mt **26** 20m "reclining," and 1 Cor **11** 20, "the Lord's supper").

(3) "Banquets" were considered normal parts of weddings as they are now throughout the East. Jesus and His disciples were bidden to one at Cana in Galilee, and accepted the invitation (Jn **2** 2 ff), and wine-drinking was a part of the feast. The "banquet" Levi gave was in Christ's honor (Lk **5** 29). There were numbers present and marked gradations in the places at table (Mt **23** 6; Mk **12** 39; Lk **14** 7; **20** 46). Guests were invited in advance, and then, as time-pieces were scarce, specially notified when the feast was ready, which helps to explain Christ's words (Mt **22** 4), "All things are ready: come to the marriage" (cf Lk **14** 17; Est **5** 8; **6** 14).

(4) Matthew tells us (**23** 6) that the Pharisees "love the chief place ["uppermost rooms" AV] at feasts."

In Mt **22** 3.4 "made a marriage feast," is rendered by some simply "a feast," because Gr *gámos*, "marriage," was used by LXX to translate the Heb for "feast" in Est **1** 5. But, as this is the only known example of such a use of *gamos*, it is better to take it here in the lit. sense of "marriage feast," as would seem to be required by the words "for his son" (Messiah). The Gr is plur. (*gamous*) to indicate the several parts or stages of the feast (Button, 23; cf Eng. "nuptials").

The "ruler of the feast" (*architríklinos*, Jn **2** 8.9), was usually one of the guests, and his business was to see that wine was provided, superintend the drinking, etc (cf Lk **22** 27).

3. A Distinction Giving Rise to a Question

(1) In Mt **22** 4, "I have made ready my *dinner*," "dinner" in Gr is *ariston* (cf Lk **11** 38). "Supper" (Gr *deipnon*) is found in Mt **23** 6 and often in the NT. Both words are found in Lk **14** 12. The question arises, What was the distinction? Thus much may be said in answer: The *ariston* (EV "dinner") was a meal usually taken about the middle of the forenoon, with variations of earlier or later; the *deipnon* (EV "supper"), the one taken at the close of the day, often after dark. In *Ant*, V, iv, 2 Jos supposes Eglon's guards (Jgs **3** 24) were negligent about noon, "both because of the heat and because their attention was turned to dinner" (*ariston*). So the "dinner" (*ariston*) was sometimes as late as noon. Yet Jn (**21** 12.15) shows, on the other hand, that the *ariston* was on some occasions taken shortly after dawn.

(2) Another question raised is this, Were the ancient Jews accustomed to have two or three meals a day? Vambery, quoted by Morison, gives a saying of the Turks that is in point: "There are only two meals a day, the smaller at 10 or 11 o'clock in the morning, the second and larger after sunset." There seems no evidence to sustain the view, maintained by Grimm and entertained by others, that the Jews of Christ's day were accustomed to take a separate and slight meal on rising, as the later Greeks and some of the later Romans did. There is certainly no clear evidence that the Jews of that day had more than two meals a day (see *DB*, art. "Meals").

(3) The marriage feast of Mt **22** 3 f was an *ariston*, somewhat like an Eng. "wedding-breakfast"; but that in Lk **14** 16 f was a *deipnon*, which was as usual delayed till after dark (ver 17). Perhaps the *ariston* in this case was preliminary, while the marriage with its accompanying *deipnon* was after dark; such things are not unheard of today (cf Mt **26** 20 and 1 Cor **11** 20, "the Lord's *deipnon*").

GEO. B. EAGER

BANUAS, ban'ū-as (1 Esd **5** 26): A misprint for BANNAS (RV), which see.

BAPTISM, bap'tiz'm (THE BAPTIST INTERPRETATION):

I. MEANING OF BAPTISM
1. Terminology
2. Proselyte Baptism
3. Greek Usage
4. NT Usage
5. The *Didache*
6. Baptismal Regeneration
II. THE SUBJECTS OF BAPTISM
III. THE PRESENT OBLIGATION
LITERATURE

This art. is not a discussion of the whole subject, but is merely a presentation of the Baptist interpretation of the ordinance. The origin and history of the ordinance, as a whole, do not come within the range of the present treatment.

I. Meaning of Baptism.—The vb. used in the NT is βαπτίζω (*baptízō*). The subst. *báptisma* and *baptismós* occur, though the

1. Terminology

latter is not used in the NT of the ordinance of baptism except by implication (He **6** 2, "the teaching of baptisms") where the reference is to the distinction between the Christian ordinance and the Jewish ceremonial ablutions. Some documents have it also in Col **2** 12 (cf He **9** 10, "divers washings") for a reference purely to the Jewish purifications (cf the dispute about purifying in Jn **3** 25). The verb *baptizō* appears in this sense in Lk **11** 38m where the Pharisee marveled that Jesus "had not first bathed himself before breakfast" (noon-day meal). The Mosaic regulations required the bath of the whole body (Lev **15** 16) for certain uncleannesses. Tertullian (*de Baptismo*, XV) says that the Jew required almost daily washing. Herodotus (ii.47) says that if an Egyptian "touches a swine in passing with his clothes, he goes to the river and dips himself [*báptō*] from it" (quoted by Broadus in *Comm. on Matthew*, 333). See also the Jewish scrupulosity illustrated in Sir **34** 25 and Jth **12** 7 where *baptizō* occurs. The same thing appears in the correct text in Mk **7** 4, "And when they come from the market-place, except they bathe themselves, they eat not." Here *baptizō* is the true text. The use of *rhantízō* ("sprinkle") is due to the difficulty felt by copyists not familiar with Jewish customs.

See also the omission of "couches" in the same verse. The couches were "pallets" and could easily be dipped into water. It is noteworthy that here *rhantizō* is used in contrast with *baptizō*, showing that *baptizō* did not mean sprinkle. The term *baptismós* occurs in Jos (*Ant*, XVIII, v, 2) in connection with John's baptism (cf also Irenaeus 686 B about Christ's baptism). In general, however, *baptisma* is the subst. found for the ordinance. The vb. *baptizō* is in reality a frequentative or intensive of *baptō* ("dip"). Examples occur where that idea is still appropriate, as in 2 K **5** 14 (LXX) where Naaman is said to have "dipped himself seven times in the Jordan" (*ebaptísato*). The notion of repetition may occur also in Jos (*Ant*, XV, iii, 3) in connection with the death of Aristobulus, brother of Mariamne, for Herod's friends "dipped him as he was swimming, and plunged him under water, in the dark of the evening." But in general the term *baptizō*, as is common with such forms in the late Gr, is simply equivalent to *baptō* (cf Lk **16** 24) and means "dip," "immerse," just as *rhantizō*, like *rhainō*, means simply "sprinkle."

If *baptizō* never occurred in connection with a disputed ordinance, there would be no controversy on the meaning of the word. There are, indeed, **fig.** or **metaphorical** uses of the word as of other words, but the **fig.** is that of immersion, like our "immersed in cares," "plunged in grief," etc. It remains to consider whether the use of the word for a ceremony or ordinance has changed its significance in the NT as compared with ancient Gr.

It may be remarked that no Baptist has written a lexicon of the Gr language, and yet the standard lexicons, like that of Liddell and Scott, uniformly give the meaning of *baptizō* as "dip," "immerse." They do not give "pour" or "sprinkle," nor has anyone ever adduced an instance where this verb means "pour" or "sprinkle." The presumption is therefore in favor of "dip" in the NT.

Before we turn directly to the discussion of the ceremonial usage, a word is called for in regard to Jewish proselyte baptism.

2. Proselyte Baptism

It is still a matter of dispute whether this initiatory rite was in existence at the time of John the Baptist or not. Schürer argues ably, if not conclusively, for the idea that this proselyte baptism was in use long before the first mention of it in the 2d cent. (cf *The Jewish People in the Time of Jesus Christ*, Div ii, II, 319 ff; also Edersheim, *Life and Times of Jesus*, Appendix, xii, Baptism of Proselytes). It matters nothing at all to the Baptist contention what is true in this regard. It would not be strange if a bath was required for a Gentile who became a Jew, when the Jews themselves required such frequent ceremonial ablutions. But what was the Jewish initiatory rite called proselyte baptism? Lightfoot (*Horae Hebraicae*, Mt **3** 7) gives the law for the baptism of proselytes: "As soon as he grows whole of the wound of circumcision, they bring him to Baptism, and being placed in the water they again instruct him in some weightier and in some lighter commands of the Law. Which being heard, he plunges himself and comes up, and, behold, he is an Israelite in all things." To this quotation Marcus Dods (Presbyterian) *HDB* adds: "To use Pauline language, his old man is dead and buried in the water, and he rises from this cleansing grave a new man. The full significance of the rite would have been lost had immersion not been practised." Lightfoot says further: "Every person baptized must dip his whole body, now stripped and made naked, at one dipping. And wheresoever in the Law washing of the body or garments is mentioned, it means nothing else than the washing of the whole body." Edersheim (op. cit.) says: "Women were attended by those of their own sex, the rabbis standing at the door outside." Jewish proselyte baptism, an initiatory ceremonial rite, harmonizes exactly with the current meaning of *baptizō* already seen. There was no peculiar "sacred" sense that changed "dip" to "sprinkle."

The Gr language has had a continuous history, and *baptizō* is used today in Greece for baptism. As is well known, not only in Greece, but

3. Greek Usage

all over Russia, wherever the Gr church prevails, immersion is the unbroken and universal practice. The Greeks may surely be credited with knowledge of the meaning of their own language. The substitution of pouring or sprinkling for immersion, as the Christian ordinance of baptism, was late and gradual and finally triumphed in the West because of the decree of the Council of Trent. But the Baptist position is that this substitution was unwarranted and subverts the real significance of the ordinance. The Gr church does practice trine immersion, one immersion for each person of the Trinity, an old practice (cf *ter mergitamur*, Tertullian ii.79 A), but not the Scriptural usage. A word will be needed later concerning the method by which pouring crept in beside immersion in the 2d and later cents. Before we turn directly to the NT use of *baptizō* it is well to quote from the *Greek Lexicon of the Roman and Byzantine Periods* by Professor E. A. Sophocles, himself a native Greek. He says (p. 297): "There is no evidence that Luke and Paul and the other writers of the NT put upon this verb meanings not recognized by the Greeks." We expect therefore to find in the NT "dip," as the meaning of this word in the ceremonial sense of an initiatory Christian rite. Thayer's *Lexicon* likewise defines the word in this ceremonial Christian use to mean "an immersion in water, performed as a sign of the removal of sin."

Baptists could very well afford to rest the matter right here. There is no need to call for the testimony of a single Baptist scholar on this subject. The world of scholarship has rendered its decision with impartiality and force on the side of the Baptists in this matter. A few recent deliverances will suffice. Dr. Alfred Plummer (Church of England) in his new *Commentary on Matthew* (p. 28) says that the office of John the Baptist was "to bind them to a new life, symbolized by immersion in water." Swete (Church of England) in his *Commentary on Mark* (p. 7) speaks of "the added thought of immersion, which gives vividness to the scene." The early Gr ecclesiastical writers show that immersion was employed (cf *Barnabas*, XI, 11): "We go down into the water full of sins and filth, and we come up bearing fruit in the heart." For numerous ecclesiastical examples see Sophocles' *Lexicon*.

But the NT itself makes the whole matter perfectly plain. The uniform meaning of "dip" for *baptizō* and the use of the river Jordan

4. NT Usage

as the place for baptizing by John the Baptist makes inevitable the notion of immersion unless there is some direct contradictory testimony. It is a matter that should be lifted above verbal quibbling or any effort to disprove the obvious facts. The simple narrative in Mt **3** 6 is that "they were baptized of him in the river Jordan." In Mk **1** 9.10 the baptism is sharpened a bit in the use of *eis* and *ek*. Jesus "was baptized of John in [*eis*] the Jordan. And straightway coming up out of [*ek*] the water, he saw." So in Acts **8** 38 we read: "They both went down into [*eis*] the water, both Philip and the eunuch; and he baptized him. And when they came up out of [*ek*] the water, the Spirit . . . . caught away Philip." If one could still be in doubt about the matter, Paul sets it at rest by the symbolism used in Rom **6** 4, "We were buried therefore with him through baptism into death: that like as Christ was raised from the dead through the glory of the Father, so we also might walk in newness of life." The submergence and emergence of immersion thus, according to Paul, symbolize the death and burial to sin on the one hand and the resurrection to the new life in Christ on the other. Sanday and Headlam (Church of England) put it thus in their *Comm. on Romans* (p. 153): "It expresses **symbolically** a series of acts corresponding to the redeeming acts of Christ. Immersion= Death. Submersion=Burial (the ratification of death). Emergence=Resurrection." In Col **2** 12 Paul again says: "having been buried with him in baptism, wherein ye were also raised with him through faith in the working of God, who raised him from the dead." The same image is here presented. Lightfoot (Church of England) on *Colossians* (p. 182) says: "Baptism is the grave of the old man, and the birth of the new. As he sinks beneath the baptismal waters, the believer buries there all his corrupt affections and past sins; as he emerges thence, he rises regenerate, quickened to new hopes and new life."

There is nothing in the NT to offset this obvious and inevitable interpretation. There are some things which are brought up, but they vanish on examination. The use of "with" after baptize in the English tr is appealed to as disproving immersion. It is enough to reply that the Committee of the American Standard Revision, which had no Baptist member at the final revision, substituted "in" for "with." Thus: "I indeed baptize you in water unto repentance" (Mt **3** 11; cf also Mk **1** 8). The use of both "with" and "in" in Lk **3** 16 is a needless stickling for the use of the Gr *en* with the locative case. In Mk **1** 8 *en* is absent in the best MSS, and yet the American Revisers correctly render "in." In Acts **1** 5 they seek to draw the distinction between the mere locative and *en* and the locative. As a matter of fact the locative case alone is amply sufficient in Gr without *en* for the notion of "in." Thus in Jn **21** 8 the tr is: "But the other disciples came in the little boat." There is no *en* in the Gr, but "the boat" is simply in the locative case. If it be argued that we have the instrumental case (cf the instrumental case of *en* as in Rev **6** 8, "kill with sword"), the answer is that the way to use water as an instrument in dipping is to put the subject in the water, as the natural way to use the boat (Jn **21** 8) as an instrument is to get into it. The presence or absence of *en* with *baptizō* is wholly immaterial. In either case "dip" is the meaning of the vb. The objection that three thousand people could not have been immersed in Jerus on the day of Pentecost is superficial. Jerus was abundantly supplied with pools. There were 120 disciples on hand, most of whom were probably men (cf the 70 sent out before by Jesus). It is not at all necessary to suppose that the 12 (Matthias was now one of them) apostles did all the baptizing. But even so, that would be only 250 apiece. I myself have baptized 42 candidates in a half-hour in a creek where there would be no delay. It would at most be only a matter of four or five hours for each of the twelve. Among the Telugus this record has been far exceeded. It is sometimes objected that Paul could not have immersed the jailer in the prison; but the answer is that Luke does not say so. Indeed Luke implies just the opposite: "And he took [took *along* in the Gr, *para*] them the same hour of the night, and washed their stripes; and was baptized." He took Paul and Silas along with him and found a place for the baptism, probably, somewhere on the prison grounds. There is absolutely nothing in the NT to controvert the unvarying significance of *baptizō*.

5. The "Didache"

Appeal has been made to the *Teaching of the Twelve Apostles*, which may belong to the first half of the 2d cent. Here for the first time pouring is distinctly admitted as an ordinance in place of immersion. Because of this remarkable passage it is argued by some that, though immersion was the normal and regular baptism, yet alongside of it, pouring was allowed, and that in reality it was a matter of indifference which was used even in the 1st cent. But that is not the true interpretation of the facts in the case. The passage deserves to be quoted in full and is here given in the tr of Philip Schaff (Presbyterian) in his edition of the *Did* (pp. 184 ff): "Now concerning baptism, baptize thus: Having first taught all these things, baptize ye into [*eis*] the name of the Father, and of the Son, and of the Holy Ghost, in living water. And if thou hast not living water, baptize into other water; and if thou canst not in cold, then in warm [water]. But if thou hast neither, pour water thrice upon the head in [*eis*] the name of the Father, and of the Son, and of the Holy Ghost." There is thus no doubt that early in the 2d cent. some Christians felt that baptism was so important that, when the real baptism (immersion) could not be performed because of lack of water, pouring might be used in its place. This is absolutely all that can be deduced from this passage. It is to be noted that for pouring another word (*ekcheō*) is used, clearly showing that *baptizō* does not mean "to pour." The very exception filed proves the Baptist contention concerning *baptizō*. Now in the NT *baptizō* is the word used for baptism. *Ekcheō* is never so used. Harnack in a letter to Rev. C. E. W. Dobbs, Madison, Ind. (published in *The Independent* for February 9, 1885), under date of January 16, 1885 says: "(1) *Baptizein* undoubtedly signifies immersion (*eintauchen*). (2) No proof can be found that it signifies anything else in the NT and in the most ancient Christian literature. The suggestion regarding 'a sacred sense' is out of the question." This is the whole point of the Baptists admirably stated by Adolph Harnack. There is no thought of denying that pouring early in the 2d cent. came to be used in place of immersion in certain extreme cases. The meaning of *baptizō* is not affected a particle by this fact. The question remains as to why this use of pouring in extreme cases grew up. The answer is that it was due to a mistaken and exaggerated estimate put upon the value of baptism as essential to salvation. Those who died without baptism were felt by some to be lost. Thus arose "clinic" baptisms.

6. Baptismal Regeneration

(For the doctrine of baptismal regeneration see Justin Martyr, *First Apology*, 61.) Out of this perversion of the symbolism of baptism grew both pouring as an ordinance and infant baptism. If baptism is necessary to salvation or the means of regeneration, then the sick, the dying, infants, must be baptized, or at any rate something must be done for them if the real baptism (immersion) cannot be performed because of extreme illness or want of water. The Baptist contention is to protest against the perversion of the significance of baptism as the ruin of the symbol. Baptism, as taught in the NT, is the picture of death and burial to sin and resurrection to new life, a picture of what has already taken place in the heart, not the means by which spiritual change is wrought. It is a privilege and duty, not a necessity. It is a picture that is lost when something else is substituted in its place. See BAPTISMAL REGENERATION.

II. The Subjects of Baptism.—It is significant that even the *Teaching of the Twelve Apostles* with its exaggerated notion of the importance of baptism does not allow baptism of infants. It says: "Having first taught all these things." Instruction precedes baptism. That is a distinct denial of infant baptism. The uniform practice in the NT is that baptism follows confession. The people "confessing their sins" were baptized by John (Mt **3** 6). It is frankly admitted by Paedobaptist scholars that the NT gives no warrant for infant baptism. Thus Jacobus (Congregationalist) in the *Standard BD* says: "We have no record in the NT of the baptism of infants." Scott (Presbyterian) in the 1-vol *HDB* says: "The NT contains no explicit reference to the baptism of infants or young children." Plummer (Church of England), *HDB*, says: "The *recipients* of Christian baptism were required to repent and believe." Marcus Dods (Presbyterian), *DCG*, says: "A rite wherein by immersion in water the participant symbolizes and signalizes his transition from an impure to a pure life, his death to a past he abandons, and his new birth to a future he desires." It would be hard to state the Baptist interpretation in better terms. Thus no room is found in the NT for infant baptism which would symbolize what the infant did not experience or would be understood to cause the regeneration in the child, a form of sacramentalism repugnant to the NT teaching as understood by Baptists. The dominant Baptist note is the soul's personal relation to God apart from ordinance, church or priest. The infant who dies unbaptized is saved without baptism. The baptized individual, child (for children are often baptized by Baptists, children who show signs of conversion) or man, is converted before his baptism. The baptism is the symbol of the change already wrought. So clear is this to the Baptist that he bears continual protest against that perversion of this beautiful ordinance by those who treat it as a means of salvation or who make it meaningless when performed before conversion. Baptism is a preacher of the spiritual life. The Baptist contention is for a regenerated church membership, placing the kingdom before the local church. Membership in the kingdom precedes membership in the church. The passages quoted from the NT in support of the notion of infant baptism are wholly irrelevant, as, for instance, in Acts **2** 39 where there is no such idea as baptism of infants. So in 1 Cor **7** 14, where note husband and wife. The point is that the marriage relation is sanctified and the children are legitimate, though husband or wife be heathen. The marriage relation is to be maintained. It is begging the question to assume the presence of infants in the various household baptisms in Acts. In the case of the family of Cornelius they all spake with tongues and magnified God (Acts **10** 46). The jailer's household "rejoiced greatly" (Acts **16** 34). We do not even know that Lydia was married. Her household may have been merely her employés in her business. The NT presents no exceptions in this matter.

III. The Present Obligation.—The Baptists make one more point concerning baptism. It is that, since Jesus himself submitted to it and enjoined it upon His disciples, the ordinance is of perpetual obligation. The arguments for the late ecclesiastical origin of Mt **28** 19 are not convincing. If it seem strange that Jesus should mention the three persons of the Trinity in connection with the command to baptize, one should remember that the Father and the Spirit were both manifested to Him at His baptism. It was not a mere ceremonial ablution like the Jewish rites. It was the public and formal avowal of fealty to God, and the names of the Trinity properly occur. The new heart is wrought by the Holy Spirit. Reconciliation with the Father is wrought on the basis of the work of the Son, who has manifested the Father's love in His life and death for sin. The fact that in the Acts in the examples of baptism only the name of Jesus occurs does not show that this was the exact formula used. It may be a mere historical summary of the essential fact. The name of Jesus stood for the other two persons of the Trinity. On the other hand the command of Jesus may not have been regarded as a formula for baptism; while in no sense sacramental or redemptive, it is yet obligatory and of perpetual significance. It is not to be dropped as one of the Jewish excrescences on Christianity. The form itself is necessary to the significance of the rite. Hence Baptists hold that immersion alone is to be practised, since immersion alone was commanded by Jesus and practised in the NT times. Immersion alone sets forth the death to sin, and burial in the grave the resurrection to new life in Christ. Baptism as taught in the NT is "a mould of doctrine," a preacher of the heart of the gospel. Baptists deny the right of disciples of Jesus to break that mould. The point of a symbol is the form in which it is cast. To change the form radically is to destroy the symbolism. Baptists insist on the maintenance of primitive NT baptism because it alone is baptism, it alone proclaims the death and resurrection of Jesus, the spiritual death and resurrection of the believer, the ultimate resurrection of the believer from the grave. The disciple is not above his Lord, and has no right to destroy this rich and powerful picture for the sake of personal convenience, nor because he is willing to do something else which Jesus did not enjoin and which has no association with Him. The long years of perversion do not justify this wrong to the memory of Jesus, but all the more call upon modern disciples to follow the example of Jesus who himself fulfilled righteousness by going into the waters of the Jordan and receiving immersion at the hands of John the Baptist.

Literature.—The Greek Lexicons, like Suicer, Liddell and Scott, Sophocles, Thayer, Preuschen; the Bib. Dictionaries; the Critical Commentaries on the NT; books of antiquities like Smith's *Dictionary of Christian Antiquities;* the new *Sch-Herz;* Bingham's *Antiquities of the Christian Church;* Schaff's *Creeds of Christendom;* Neale's *History of the Holy Eastern Church;* Lives of Christ, like Edersheim's *LTJM*, or a survey of the customs of the Jews like Schürer's *HJP;* books on John the Baptist like Reynolds' *John the Baptist*, Feather's *Last of the Prophets*, Robertson's *John the Loyal;* special treatises on Baptism like Wall's *History of Infant Baptism*, Stanley's *Christian Institutions*, Dargan's *Ecclesiology*, Conant's *Baptizein*, Mozley's *Review of the Baptismal Controversy*, Christian's *Immersion*, Broadus' *Immersion*, Frost's *The Moral Dignity of Baptism*, Whitsitt's *A Question in Baptist History*, Lofton's *The Baptist Reformation*, Lambert's *The Sacraments of the New Testament*, Dale's *Classic Baptism* and *Christian and Patristic Baptism*, Kirtley's *Design of Baptism*, Forester's *The Baptist Position*, Frost's *Baptist Why and Why Not*, Ford's *Studies in Baptism*.

A. T. Robertson

BAPTISM (Non-Immersionist View):

Baptism (**Βάπτισμα**, *báptisma*, **Βαπτισμός**, *baptismós*, **Βαπτίζειν**, *baptízein*) has been from the earliest times the initiatory rite signifying the recognition of entrance into or of presence within the Christian church. We find the earliest mention of the ceremony in the Epistle to the Gal (**3** 27), written about 20 years after the death of Jesus. There and in 1 Cor (**1** 13; **12** 13) St. Paul takes for granted that everyone who becomes a Christian (himself included) must be baptized. The rite seems also to have existed among the discipleship of Jesus before His death. We are told (Jn **4** 1.2) that, although Jesus Himself did not baptize, His disciples did, and that their baptisms were more numerous than those of John.

I. Scriptural Names for the Rite.—The words commonly used in the NT to denote the rite are the verb *baptízō*, and the nouns *baptisma* and *baptismos;* but none are employed in this sense alone. The vb. is used to denote the ceremonial purification of the Jews before eating, by pouring water on the hands (Lk **11** 38; Mk **7** 4); to signify the sufferings of Christ (Mk **10** 38.39; Lk **12** 50); and to indicate the sacrament of baptism. It is the intensive form of *báptein*, "to dip," and takes a wider meaning. The passages Lk **11** 38 and Mk **7** 4 show conclusively that the word does not invariably signify to immerse the whole body. Some have held that *baptismos* invariably means ceremonial purification, and that *baptisma* is reserved for the Christian rite; but the distinction can hardly be maintained. The former certainly means ceremonial purification in Mk **7** 4, and in **7** 8 (AV); but it probably means the rite of baptism in He **6** 2. Exegetes find other terms applied to Christian baptism. It is called 'the Water' in Acts **10** 47: "Can any man forbid 'the Water,' that these should not be baptized?"; the laver of the water in Eph **5** 26 RVm (where baptism is compared to the bridal bath taken by the bride before she was handed over to the bridegroom); and perhaps the laver of regeneration in Tit **3** 5 RVm (cf 1 Cor **6** 11), and illumination in He **6** 4; **10** 32.

II. Pre-Christian Baptism.—Converts in the early cents., whether Jews or Gentiles, could not have found this initiatory rite, in which they expressed their new-born faith, utterly unfamiliar. Water is the element naturally used for cleansing the body and its symbolical use entered into almost every cult; and into none more completely than the Jewish, whose ceremonial washings were proverbial. Besides those the Jew had what would seem to the convert a counterpart of the Christian rite in the baptism of proselytes by which Gentiles entered the circle of Judaism. For the Jews required three things of strangers who declared themselves to be converts to the Law of Moses: circumcision, baptism, and to offer sacrifice if they were men: the two latter if they were women. It is somewhat singular that no baptism of proselytes is forthcoming until about the beginning of the 3d cent.; and yet no competent scholar doubts its existence. Schürer is full of contempt for those who insist on the argument from silence. Its presence enables us to see both how Jews accepted readily the baptism of John and to understand the point of objectors who questioned his right to insist that all Jews had to be purified ere they could be ready for the Messianic kingdom, although he was neither the Messiah nor a special prophet (Jn **1** 19–23).

1. The Baptism of Proselytes

The baptism of John stood midway between the Jewish baptism of proselytes and Christian baptism. It differed from the former because it was more than a symbol of ceremonial purification; it was a baptism of repentance, a confession of sin, and of the need of *moral* cleansing, and was a symbol of forgiveness and of moral purity. All men, Jews who were ceremonially pure and Gentiles who were not, had to submit to this baptism of repentance and pardon. It differed from the latter because it only symbolized preparation to receive the salvation, the kingdom of God which John heralded, and did not imply entrance into that kingdom itself. Those who had received it, as well as those who had not, had to enter the Christian community by the door of Christian baptism (Acts **19** 3–6). The Jewish custom of baptizing, whether displayed in their frequent ceremonial washings, in the baptism of proselytes or in the baptism of John, made Christian baptism a familiar and even expected rite to Jewish converts in the 1st cent.

2. The Baptism of John

Baptism, as an initiatory rite, was no less familiar to gentile converts who had no acquaintance with the Jewish religion. The ceremonial washings of the priests of pagan religions have been often adduced as something which might familiarize gentile converts with the rite which introduced them into the Christian community, but they were not initiations. A more exact parallel is easily found. It is often forgotten that in the earlier cents. when Christianity was slowly making its way in the pagan world pagan piety had deserted the official religions and taken refuge within the Mysteries, and that these Mysteries represented the popular pagan religions of the times. They were all private cults into which men and women were received one by one, and that by rites of initiation which each had to pass through personally. When admitted the converts became members of coteries, large or small, of like-minded persons, who had become initiated because their souls craved something which they believed they would receive in and through the rites of the cult. These initiations were secret, jealously guarded from the knowledge of all outsiders; still enough is known about them for us to be sure that among them baptism took an important place (Apuleius *Metamorphoses* xi). The rite was therefore as familiar to pagan as to Jewish converts, and it was no unexpected requirement for the convert to know that baptism was the doorway into the church of Christ. These heathen baptisms, like the baptism of proselytes, were for the most part simply ceremonial purifications; for while it is true that both in the cult of the Mysteries and beyond it a mode of purifying after great crimes was baptizing in flowing water (Eurip. *Iph. in Tauri* 167) or in the sea, yet it would appear that only ceremonial purification was thought of. Nor were ceremonial rites involving the use of water confined to the paganism of the early cents. Such a ceremony denoted the reception of the newly born child into pagan Scandinavian households. The father decided whether the infant was to be reared or exposed to perish. If he resolved to preserve the babe, water was poured over it and a name was given to it.

3. Baptism in the Pagan Mysteries

III. Christian Baptism.—In the administration of the rite of Christian baptism three things have to be looked at: the act of baptizing; those who are entitled to perform it; and the recipients or those entitled to receive it. A complete act of baptizing involves three things: what has been called the *materia sacramenti;* the method of its use; and the *forma sacramenti*, the baptismal formula or form of words accompanying the use of the water. The *materia sacramenti* is water and for this reason baptism is called the Water Sacrament. The oldest ecclesiastical manual of discipline which has descended to us, the *Didache*, says that the water to be preferred is "living," i.e. running

1. The Administration of the Rite

water, water in a stream or river, or fresh flowing from a fountain; "But if thou hast not living water, baptize in other water; and if thou canst not in cold, then in warm" (c. 7). In those directions the prescriptions of the ceremonial for the Jewish baptism of proselytes are closely followed. The earlier canons of the church permit any kind of water, fresh or salt, provided only it be true and natural water (*aqua vera et naturalis*).

2. The Mode of Using the Water

(1) *Immersion.*—The use of the water is called *ablutio.* According to the rules of by far the largest portion of the Christian church the water may be used in any one of three ways: *immersion,* where the recipient enters bodily into the water, and where, during the action, the head is plunged either once or three times beneath the surface; *affusion,* where water was poured upon the head of the recipient who stood either in water or on dry ground; and *aspersion* where water was sprinkled on the head or on the face. It has frequently been argued that the word *baptizein* invariably means "to dip" or immerse, and that therefore Christian baptism must have been performed originally by *immersion* only, and that the two other forms of *affusion* and *aspersion* or sprinkling are invalid—that there can be no real baptism unless the method of *immersion* be used. But the word which invariably means "to dip" is not *baptizein* but *baptein. Baptizein* has a wider signification; and its use to denote the Jewish ceremonial of pouring water on the hands (Lk **11** 38; Mk **7** 4), as has already been said, proves conclusively that it is impossible to conclude from the word itself that *immersion* is the only valid method of performing the rite. It may be admitted at once that *immersion,* where the whole body including the head is plunged into a pool of pure water, gives a more vivid picture of the cleansing of the soul from sin; and that complete surrounding with water suits better the metaphors of burial in Rom **6** 4 and Col **2** 12, and of being surrounded by cloud in 1 Cor **10** 2.

(2) *Affusion.*—On the other hand *affusion* is certainly a more vivid picture of the bestowal of the Holy Spirit which is equally symbolized in baptism. No definite information is given of the mode in which baptism was administered in apostolic times. Such phrases as "coming up out of the water," "went down into the water" (Mk **1** 10; Acts **8** 38) are as applicable to *affusion* as to *immersion.* The earliest account of the mode of baptizing occurs in the *Didache* (c. 7), where it is said: "Now concerning Baptism, thus baptize ye: having first uttered all these things, baptize in the name of the Father, and of the Son and of the Holy Ghost, in living water. But if thou hast not living water, baptize in other water; and if thou canst not in cold, then in warm. But if thou hast neither, pour water upon the head thrice in the name of Father, and Son, and Holy Ghost." This seems to say that to baptize by immersion was the practice recommended for general use, but that the mode of affusion was also valid and enjoined on occasions. What is here prescribed in the *Didache* seems to have been the practice usually followed in the early cents. of the Christian church. Immersion was in common use: but affusion was also widely practised: and both were esteemed usual and valid forms of baptizing. When immersion was used then the head of the recipient was plunged thrice beneath the surface at the mention of each name of the Trinity; when the mode was by affusion the same reference to the Trinity was kept by pouring water thrice upon the head. The two usages which were recognized and prescribed by the beginning of the 2d cent. may have been in use throughout the apostolic period although definite information is lacking. When we remember the various pools in Jerus, and their use for ceremonial washings it is not impossible to suppose that the 3,000 who were baptized on the day of Pentecost may have been immersed, but, when the furnishing and conditions of Palestinian houses and of oriental jails are taken into account, it is difficult to conceive that at the baptisms of Cornelius and of the jailer, the ceremony was performed otherwise than by affusion. It is a somewhat curious fact that if the evidence from written texts, whether ancient canons or writings of the earlier Fathers, be studied by themselves, the natural conclusion would seem to be that immersion was the almost universal form of administering the rite; but if the witness of the earliest pictorial representation be collected, then we must infer that affusion was the usual method and that immersion was exceptional; for the pictorial representations, almost without exception, display baptism performed by affusion, i.e. the recipient is seen standing in water while the minister pours water on the head. It may therefore be inferred that evidence for the almost universal practice of immersion, drawn from the fact that baptisms took place in river pools (it is more than probable that when we find the names of local saints given to pools in rivers, those places were their favorite places of administering the rite), or from the large size of almost all early mediaeval baptisteries, is by no means so conclusive as many have supposed, such places being equally applicable to affusion. It is also interesting to remember that when most of the Anabaptists of the 16th cent. insisted on adult baptism (re-baptism was their name for it) immersion was not the method practised by them. During the great baptismal scene in the market-place of the city of Münster the ordinance was performed by the ministers pouring three cans of water on the heads of the recipients. They baptized by affusion and not by immersion. This was also the practice among the Mennonites or earliest Baptists. This double mode of administering the sacrament—by immersion or by affusion—prevailed in the churches of the first twelve cents., and it was not until the 13th that the practice of *aspersio* or sprinkling was almost universally employed.

(3) *Aspersion.*—The third method of administering baptism, viz. by *aspersio* or sprinkling, has a different history from the other two. It was in the early cents. exclusively reserved for sick and infirm persons too weak to be submitted to *immersion* or *affusion.* There is evidence to show that those who received the rite in this form were somewhat despised; for the nicknames *clinici* and *grabatorii* were, unworthily Cyprian declares, bestowed on them by neighbors. The question was even raised in the middle of the 3d cent., whether baptism by *aspersio* was a valid baptism and Cyprian was asked for his opinion on the matter. His answer is contained in his lxxvth epistle (lxix Hartel's ed). There he contends that the ordinance administered this way is perfectly valid, and quotes in support of his opinion various OT texts which assert the purifying effects of water sprinkled (Ezk **36** 25.26; Nu **8** 5–7; **19** 8.9.12.13). It is not the amount of the water or the method of its application which can cleanse from sin: "Whence it appears that the sprinkling also of water prevails equally with the washing of salvation . . . . and that where the faith of the giver and receiver is sound, all things hold and may be consummated and perfected by the majesty of God and by the truth of faith." His opinion prevailed. *Aspersio* was recognized as a valid, though exceptional, form of baptism. But it was long of commending itself to ministers and people, and did not attain to almost general use until the 13th cent.

The idea that baptism is valid when practised in the one method only of immersion can scarcely be looked on as anything else than a ritualistic idea.

3. Who May Perform Baptism

The Scripture nowhere describes or limits the qualifications of those who are entitled to perform the rite of baptism. We find apostles, wandering preachers (Acts **8** 38), a private member of a small and persecuted community (Acts **9** 18) performing the rite. So in the subapostolic church we find the same liberty of practice. Clement of Alexandria tells us that the services of Christian women were necessary for the work of Christian missions, for they alone could have access to the *gynaeceum* and carry the message of the gospel there (*Strom.*, III, 6). Such women missionaries did not hesitate to baptize. Whatever credit may be given to the Acts of Paul and Theckla, it is at least historical that Theckla did exist, that she was converted by Paul, that she worked as a missionary and that she baptized her converts. Speaking generally it may be said that as a sacrament has always been looked upon as the recognition of presence within the Christian church, it is an act of the church and not of the individual believer; and therefore no one is entitled to perform the act who is not in some way a representative of the Christian community—the representative character ought to be maintained somehow. As soon as the community had taken regular and organized form the act of baptism was suitably performed by those who, as office-bearers, naturally represented the community. It was recognized that the pastor or bishop (for these terms were synonymous until the 4th cent. at least) ought to preside at the administration of the sacrament; but in the early church the power of delegation was recognized and practised, and elders and deacons presided at this and even at the Eucharist. What has been called lay-baptism is not forbidden in the NT and has the sanction of the early church. When superstitious views of baptism entered largely into the church and it was held that no unbaptized child could be saved, the practice arose of encouraging the baptism of all weakling infants by nurses. The Reformed church protested against this and was at pains to repudiate the superstitious thought of any mechanical efficacy in the rite by deprecating its exercise by any save approved and ordained ministers of the church. Still, while condemning lay-baptism as irregular, it may be questioned whether they would assert any administration of the rite to be invalid, provided only it had been performed with devout faith on the part of giver and receiver.

4. Who May Receive Baptism

The recipients of Christian baptism are all those who make a presumably sincere profession of repentance of sin and of faith in the Lord Jesus Christ, the Saviour; together with the children of such believing parents. The requirements are set forth in the accounts given us of the performance of the rite in the NT, in which we see how the apostles obeyed the commands of their Master. Jesus had ordered them to "make disciples of all the nations, baptizing them into the name of the Father and of the Son and of the Holy Spirit" (Mt **28** 19)—to "preach the gospel to the whole creation. He that believeth and is baptized shall be saved; but he that disbelieveth shall be condemned" (Mk **16** 15.16). The apostle Peter said to the inquirers on the Day of Pentecost, "Repent ye, and be baptized every one of you in the name of Jesus Christ unto the remission of your sins; and ye shall receive the gift of the Holy Spirit"; and 3,000 were added to the church through the initiatory rite of baptism. The Samaritans, who believed on Jesus through the preaching of Philip, were admitted to the Christian community through baptism; though in this case one of the baptized, Simon Magus, after his reception, was found to be still in "the bond of iniquity" (Acts **8** 12.23). The jailer *and all his,* Lydia *and her household,* at Philippi, were baptized by St. Paul on his and her profession of faith on Jesus, the Saviour. There is no evidence in any of the accounts we have of apostolic baptisms that any prolonged course of instruction was thought to be necessary; nothing of classes for catechumens such as we find in the early church by the close of the 2d cent., or in modern missionary enterprise. We find no mention of baptismal creeds, declarative or interrogative, in the NT accounts of baptisms. The profession of faith in the Lord Jesus, the Saviour, made by the head of the family appears, so far as the NT records afford us information, to have been sufficient to secure the baptism of the "household"—a word which in these days included both servants and children.

(1) *Baptism of infants.*—This brings us to the much-debated question whether infants are to be recognized as lawful recipients of Christian baptism. The NT Scriptures do not in so many words either forbid or command the baptism of children. The question is in this respect on all fours with the change of the holy day from the seventh to the first day of the week. No positive command authorizes the universal usage with regard to the Christian Sabbath day; that the change is authorized must be settled by a weighing of evidence. So it is with the case of infant baptism. It is neither commanded nor forbidden in so many words; and the question cannot be decided on such a basis. The strongest argument against the baptizing of infants lies in the thought that the conditions of the rite are repentance and faith; that these must be exercised by individuals, each one for himself and for herself; and that infants are incapable either of repentance or of faith of this kind. The argument seems weak in its second statement; it is more dogmatic than historical; and will be referred to later when the doctrine lying at the basis of the rite is examined. On the other hand a great deal of evidence supports the view that the baptism of infants, if not commanded, was at least permitted and practised within the apostolic church. St. Paul connects baptism with circumcision and implies that under the gospel the former takes the place of the latter (Col **2** 12); and as children were circumcised on the 8th day after birth, the inference follows naturally that children were also to be baptized. In the OT, promises to parents included their children. In his sermon on the Day of Pentecost St. Peter declares to his hearers that the gospel promise is "to you and to your children" and connects this with the invitation to baptism (Acts **2** 38.39). It is also noteworthy that children shared in the Jewish baptism of proselytes. Then we find in the NT narratives of baptisms that "households" were baptized—of Lydia (Acts **16** 15), of the jailer at Philippi (Acts **16** 32), of Stephanas (1 Cor **1** 16). It is never said that the children of the household were exempted from the sacred rite. One has only to remember the position of the head of the household in that ancient world, to recollect how the household was thought to be embodied in its head, to see how the repentance and faith of the head of the household was looked upon as including those of all the members, not merely children but servants, to feel that had the children been excluded from sharing in the rite the exclusion would have seemed such an unusual thing that it would have at least been mentioned and explained. Our Lord expressly made very

young children the types of those who entered into His kingdom (Mk **10** 14–16); and St. Paul so unites parents with children in the faith of Christ that he does not hesitate to call the children of the believing husband or wife "holy," and to imply that the children had passed from a state of "uncleanness" to a state of "holiness" through the faith of a parent. All these things seem to point to the fact that the rite which was the door of entance into the visible community of the followers of Jesus was shared in by the children of believing parents. Besides evidence for the baptism of children goes back to the earliest times of the subapostolic church. Irenaeus was the disciple of Polycarp, who had been the disciple of St. John, and it is difficult to draw any other conclusion from his statements than that he believed that the baptism of infants had been an established practice in the church long before his days (*Adv. Haer.*, II, 22; cf 39). The witness of Tertullian is specially interesting; for he himself plainly thinks that adult baptism is to be preferred to the baptism of infants. He makes it plain that the custom of baptizing infants existed in his days, and we may be sure from the character and the learning of the man, that had he been able to affirm that infant-baptism had been a recent innovation and had not been a long-established usage descending from apostolic times, he would certainly have had no hesitation in using what would have seemed to him a very convincing way of dealing with his opponents. Tertullian's testimony comes from the end of the 2d cent. or the beginning of the 3d. Origen, the most learned Christian writer during the first three cents. and who comes a little later than Tertullian, in his 14th Homily on St. Luke bears witness to the fact that the baptism of infants was usual. He argues that original sin belongs to children because the church baptizes them. At the same time it is plain from a variety of evidence too long to cite that the baptism of infants was not a universal practice in the early church. The church of the early cents. was a mission church. It drew large numbers of its members from heathendom. In every mission church the baptism of adults will naturally take the foremost place and be most in evidence. But is is clear that many Christians were of the opinion of Tertullian and believed that baptism ought not to be administered to children but should be confined to adults. Nor was this a theory only; it was a continuous practice handed down from one generation to another in some Christian families. In the 4th cent. few Christian leaders took a more important place than Basil the Great and his brother Gregory of Nyssa. They belonged to a family who had been Christians for some generations; yet neither of the brothers was baptized until after his personal conversion, which does not appear to have come until they had attained the years of manhood. The whole evidence seems to show that in the early church, down to the end of the 4th cent. at least, infant and adult baptism were open questions and that the two practices existed side by side with each other without disturbing the unity of the churches. In the later Pelagian controversy it became evident that the theory and practice of infant baptism had been able to assert itself and that the ordinance was always administered to children of members of the church.

(2) *Baptism for the dead.*—St. Paul refers to a custom of "baptizing for the dead" (1 Cor **15** 29). What this "vicarious baptism" or "baptism for the dead" was it is impossible to say, even whether it was practised within the primitive Christian church. The passage is a very difficult one and has called forth a very large number of explanations, which are mere guesses. Paul neither commends it nor disapproves of it; he simply mentions its existence and uses the fact as an argument for the resurrection. See BAPTISM FOR THE DEAD.

IV. The Formula of Baptism.—The Formula of Christian baptism, in the mode which prevailed, is given in Mt **28** 19: "I baptize thee in the name of the Father, of the Son, and of the Holy Ghost." But it is curious that the words are not given in any description of Christian baptism until the time of Justin Martyr: and there they are not repeated exactly but in a slightly extended and explanatory form. He says that Christians "receive the washing with water in the name of God, the Ruler and Father of the universe, and of our Saviour, Jesus Christ, and of the Holy Spirit" (*1 Apol.*, 61). In every account of the performance of the rite in apostolic times a much shorter formula is in use. The 3,000 believers were baptized on the Day of Pentecost "in the name of Jesus" (Acts **2** 38); and the same formula was used at the baptism of Cornelius and those that were with him (Acts **10** 48). Indeed it would appear to have been the usual one, from St. Paul's question to the Corinthians: "Were ye baptized into the name of Paul?" (1 Cor **1** 13). The Samaritans were baptized "into the name of the Lord Jesus" (Acts **8** 16); and the same formula (a common one in acts of devotion) was used in the case of the disciples at Ephesus. In some instances it is recorded that before baptism the converts were asked to make some confession of their faith, which took the form of declaring that Jesus was the Lord or that Jesus Christ was the Son of God. It may be inferred from a phrase in 1 Pet **3** 21 that a formal interrogation was made, and that the answer was an acknowledgment that Jesus Christ was Lord. Scholars have exercised a great deal of ingenuity in trying to explain how, with what appear to be the very words of Jesus given in the Gospel of Mt, another and much shorter formula seems to have been used throughout the apostolic church. Some have imagined that the shorter formula was that used in baptizing disciples during the lifetime of Our Lord (Jn **4** 1.2), and that the apostles having become accustomed to it continued to use it during their lives. Others declare that the phrases "in the name of Jesus Christ" or "of the Lord Jesus" are not meant to give the formula of baptism, but simply to denote that the rite was Christian. Others think that the full formula was always used and that the narratives in the Book of Acts and in the Pauline Epistles are merely brief summaries of what took place—an idea rather difficult to believe in the absence of any single reference to the longer formula. Others, again, insist that baptism in the name of one of the persons of the Trinity implies baptism in the name of the Three. While others declare that St. Matthew does not give the very words of Jesus but puts in His mouth what was the common formula used at the date and in the district where the First Gospel was written. Whatever explanation be given it is plain that the longer formula became universal or almost universal in the sub-apostolic church. Justin Martyr has been already quoted. Tertullian, nearly half a century later, declares expressly that the "law of baptism has been imposed and the formula prescribed" in Mt **28** 19 (*De Bapt.*, 13); and he adds in his *Adversus Praxean* (c. 26): "And it is not once only, but thrice, that we are immersed into the Three Persons, at each several mention of Their names." The evidence to show that the formula given by St. Matthew became the established usage is overwhelming; but it is more than likely that the use of the shorter formula did not altogether die out, or, if it did, that it was revived. The historian Socrates informs us that some of the more extreme Arians "corrupted" baptism by using the name of Christ only in the formula; while injunctions to use the longer formula and punishments, including deposition, threatened to those who presumed to employ the shorter which meet us in collections of ecclesiastical canons (*Apos. Canons*, 43, 50), prove that the practice of using the shorter formula existed in the 5th and 6th cents., at all events in the East.

V. The Doctrine of Baptism.—The sacraments, and baptism as one of them, are always described to be (1) signs representing as in a picture or figure spiritual benefits (1 Pet **3** 21), and also (2) as seals or personal tokens and attestations confirmatory of solemn promises of spiritual benefits. Hence the sacrament is said to have two parts: "the one an outward and sensible sign, used according to Christ's appointment; the other an inward and spiritual grace thereby signified." It is held, moreover, that when the rite of baptism has been duly and devoutly performed with faith on the part of both giver and receiver, the spiritual benefits do follow the performance of the rite. The question therefore arises: What are the spiritual and evangelical blessings portrayed and solemnly promised in baptism? In the New Testament we find that baptism is intimately connected with the following: with remission of sins, as in Acts **22** 16 ("Arise, and be baptized, and wash away thy sins"), and in He **10** 22; with regeneration or the new birth, as in Tit **3** 6 and Jn **3** 5 (this idea also entered into the baptism of proselytes and even into the thought of baptism in the Mysteries; neophytes were taught that in the water they died to their old life and began a new one [Apuleius *Meta.* xi]); with ingrafting into Christ, with union with Him, as in Gal **3** 27—and union in definite ways, in His death, His burial and His resurrection, as in Rom **6** 3–6; with entering into a new relationship with God, that of sonship, as in Gal **3** 26.27; with the bestowal of the Holy Spirit, as in 1 Cor **12** 13; with belonging to the church, as in Acts **2** 41; with the gift of salvation, as in Mk (?) **16** 16; Jn **3** 5. From these and similar passages theologians conclude that baptism is a sign and seal of our ingrafting into Christ and of our union with Him, of remission of sins, regeneration, adoption and life eternal; that the water in baptism represents and signifies both the blood of Christ, which takes away all our sins, and also the sanctifying influence of the Holy Spirit against the dominion of sin and the corruption of our human nature; and that baptizing with water signifies the cleansing from sin by the blood and for the merit of Christ, together with the mortification of sin and rising from sin to newness of life by virtue of the death and resurrection of Christ. Or to put it more simply: Baptism teaches that all who are out of Christ are unclean by reason of sin and need to be cleansed. It signifies that just as washing with water cleanses the body so God in Christ cleanses the soul from sin by the Holy Spirit and that we are to see in this cleansing not merely pardon but also an actual freeing of the soul from the pollution and power of sin and therefore the beginnings of a new life. The sacrament also shows us that the cleansing is reached only through connection with the death of Christ, and further that through the new life begun in us we become in a special way united to Christ and enter into a new and filial relationship with God. Probably all Christians, reformed and unreformed, will agree in the above statement of the doctrinal meaning in the rite of baptism; and also that when the sacrament is *rightly used* the inward and spiritual grace promised is present along with the outward and visible signs. But Romanists and Protestants differ about what is meant by the *right use* of the sacrament. They separate on the question of its efficacy. The former understand by the *right use* simply the correct performance of the rite and the placing no obstacle in the way of the flow of efficacy. The latter insist that there can be no *right use* of the sacrament unless the recipient exercises faith, that without faith the sacrament is not efficacious and the inward and spiritual blessings do not accompany the external and visible signs. Whatever minor differences divide Protestant evangelical churches on this sacrament they are all agreed upon this, that where there is no faith there can be no regeneration. Here emerges doctrinally the difference between those who give and who refuse to give the sacrament to infants.

The Doctrine of Infant Baptism

The latter taking their stand on the fundamental doctrine of all evangelical Christians that faith is necessary to make any sacrament efficacious, and assuming that the effect of an ordinance is always tied to the precise time of its administration, insist that only adults can perform such a conscious, intelligent, and individually independent act of faith, as they believe all Protestants insist on scriptural grounds to be necessary in the *right use* of a sacrament. Therefore they refuse to baptize infants and young children.

The great majority of evangelical Protestants practise infant baptism and do not think, due explanations being given, that it in any way conflicts with the idea that faith is necessary to the efficacy of the sacrament. The Baptist position appears to them to conflict with much of the teaching of the NT. It implies that all who are brought up in the faith of Christ and within the Christian family still lack, when they come to years of discretion, that great change of heart and life which is symbolized in baptism, and can only receive it by a conscious, intelligent and thoroughly independent act of faith. This seems in accordance neither with Scripture nor with human nature. We are told that a child may be full of the Holy Ghost from his mother's womb (Lk **1** 15); that little children *are* in the kingdom of Christ (Mt **19** 14); that children of believing parents are holy (1 Cor **7** 14). Is there nothing in the fact that in the NT as in the OT the promise is "to you and your children"? Besides, the argument of those who oppose the baptism of infants, if logically carried out, leads to consequences which few of them would accept. Faith is as essential to salvation, on all evangelical theology, as it is for the *right use* of the sacrament; and every one of the arguments brought against the baptism of infants is equally applicable to the denial of their salvation. Nor can the Baptist position be said to be true to the facts of ordinary human nature. Faith, in its evangelical sense of *fiducia* or trust, is not such an abrupt thing as they make it. Their demand for such a conscious, intelligent, strictly individualist act of faith sets aside some of the deepest facts of human nature. No one, young or old, is entirely self-dependent; nor are our thoughts and trust always or even frequently entirely independent and free from the unconscious influences of others. We are interwoven together in society; and what is true generally reveals itself still more strongly in the intimate relations of the family. Is it possible in all cases to trace the creative effects of the subtle imperceptible influences which surround children, or to say when the slowly dawning intelligence is first able to apprehend enough to trust in half-conscious ways? It is but a shallow view of human nature which sets all such considerations on the one side and insists on regarding nothing but isolated acts of knowledge or of faith. With all those thoughts in their minds, the great majority of evangelical churches admit and enjoin the baptism of infants. They believe that the children of believing parents are "born *within* the church and have interest in the covenant of grace and a right to its seal." They explain that the efficacy of a sacrament is not rigidly tied to the exact time of administration, and can be appropriated whenever faith is kindled and is able to rest on the external sign, and that the spiritual blessings signified in the rite can be appropriated again and again with each fresh kindling of faith. They declare that no one can tell how soon the dawning intelligence may awaken to the act of appropriation. Therefore these churches instruct their ministers in dispensing the sacrament to lay vows on parents that they will train up the infants baptized "in the knowledge and fear of the Lord," and will teach them the great blessings promised to them in and through the sacrament and teach them to appropriate these blessings for themselves. They further enjoin their ministers to admonish all who may witness a baptismal service to look back on their own baptism in order that their faith may be stirred afresh to appropriate for themselves the blessings which accompany the proper use of the rite.

LITERATURE.—The literature on the subject of baptism is very extensive. It may be sufficient to select the following: J. S. Candlish, *The Sacraments*, 10th thousand, 1900; J. C. W. Augusti, *Denkwürdigkeiten aus d. christ. Archäologie*, V, 1820; Höfling, *Das Sakrament der Taufe*, 1846–48; J. B. Mozley, *Review of the Baptismal Controversy*, 2d ed, 1895; W. Goode, *The Doctrine of the Church of England as to the Effects of Baptism in the Case of Infants*, 1849; W. Wall, *History of Infant Baptism*, 1705; E. B. Underhill, *Confessions of Faith . . . . of Baptist Churches of England* (Hanserd Knollys Soc., IX), 1854.

T. M. LINDSAY

BAPTISM (LUTHERAN DOCTRINE):

I. THE TERM
  1. The Derivation
  2. The Meaning
  3. The Application
  4. Equivalent Terms
II. THE ORDINANCE
  1. The Teaching of Scripture
    (1) An Authoritative Command
    (2) A Clear Declaration of the Object in View
    (3) A Definite Promise
    (4) A Plain Indication of the Scope
  2. The Biblical History of the Ordinance
  3. Types of Baptism
III. DIFFICULTIES
  1. Are Mt 28 18–20 and Mk 16 15.16 Genuine?
  2. Was the Trinitarian Formula Used in NT Times?
  3. Was Christian Baptism Really a New Ordinance?
  4. Should Infants Be Baptized?
  5. Why Did Paul not Baptize?
  6. What Is the Baptism for the Dead?

I. The Term.—The word "baptism" is the Anglicized form of the Gr *báptisma*, or *baptismós*.

1. The Derivation

These Gr words are verbal nouns derived from *baptízō*, which, again, is the intensive form of the vb. *báptō*. "*Baptismos* denotes the action of *baptízein* (the baptizing), *baptisma* the result of the action (the baptism)" (Cremer). This distinction differs from, but is not necessarily contrary to, that of Plummer, who infers from Mk **7** 4 and He **9** 10 that *baptismos* usually means lustrations or ceremonial washings, and from Rom **6** 4; Eph **4** 5; 1 Pet **3** 21 that *baptisma* denotes baptism proper (*HDB*).

The Gr words from which our Eng. "baptism" has been formed are used by Gr writers, in classical

2. The Meaning

antiquity, in the LXX and in the NT, with a great latitude of meaning. It is not possible to exhaust their meaning by any single Eng. term. The action which the Gr words express may be performed by plunging, drenching, staining, dipping, sprinkling. The nouns *baptisma* and *baptismos* do not occur in the LXX; the verb *baptizō* occurs only in four places, and in two of them in a fig. sense (2 K **5** 14; Jth **12** 7; Isa **21** 4; Ecclus **31** (**34**) 25). Wherever these words occur in the NT, the context or, in the case of quotations, a comparison with the OT will in many instances suggest which of the various renderings noted above should be adopted (cf Mk **7** 4; He **9** 10 with Nu **19** 18.19; **8** 7; Ex **24** 4–6; Acts **2** 16.17.41 with Joel **2** 28). But there are passages in which the particular form of the act of baptizing remains in doubt. "The assertion that the command to baptize is a command to immerse is utterly unauthorized" (Hodge).

In the majority of Bib. instances the vbs. and nouns denoting baptism are used in a lit. sense, and

3. The Application

signify the application of water to an object or a person for a certain purpose. The ceremonial washings of the Jews, the baptism of proselytes to the Jewish faith, common in the days of Christ, the baptism of John and of the disciples of Christ prior to the Day of Pentecost, and the Christian sacrament of baptism, are literal baptisms (*baptismus fluminis*, "baptism of the river," i.e. water). But Scripture speaks also of fig. baptisms, without water (Mt **20** 22; Mk **10** 38; Lk **12** 50=the sufferings which overwhelmed Christ and His followers, especially the martyrs—*baptismus sanguinis*, "baptism of blood"; Mt **3** 11; Mk **1** 8; Lk **3** 16; Acts **1** 5; **11** 16=the outpouring of the miraculous gifts of the Holy Ghost, which was a characteristic phenomenon of primitive Christianity —*baptismus flaminis*, "baptism of wind, breeze," i.e. "spirit"). Some even take Mt **21** 25; Mk **11** 30; Acts **18** 25; 1 Cor **10** 2 in a synecdochical sense, for doctrine of faith, baptism being a prominent feature of that doctrine (*baptismus luminis*, "baptism of light").

Scripture occasionally alludes to Christian baptism without employing the regular term. Thus

4. Equivalent Terms

in Tit **3** 5, and Eph **5** 26 we have the term *loutrón*, "washing," instead of *baptisma*. From this term the Lat church derived its *lavacrum* (Eng. "laver") as a designation of baptism. In He **10** 22 we have the verbs *rhantízō* and *loúō*, "sprinkle" and "wash"; in Eph **5** 26 the verb *katharízō*, "cleanse"; in 1 Cor **6** 11 the verb *apoloúō*, "wash," are evidently synonyms of *baptizō*, and the act has been so denominated from its prime effect.

II. The Ordinance.—Christian baptism, as now practised, is a sacred ordinance of evangelical

1. The Teaching of Scripture

grace, solemnly appointed by the risen Christ, prior to His entering into the state of glory by His ascension, and designed to be a means, until His second coming, for admitting men to discipleship with Him. Mt **28** 18–20 and its parallel Mk **16** 15.16 are the principal texts of Scripture on which the church in all ages has based every essential point of her teaching regarding this ordinance. The host of other baptismal texts of Scripture expand and illustrate the contents of these two texts. We have in these texts:

(1) *An authoritative* (Mt **28** 19) *command*, issued in plain terms: "Make disciples . . . . baptizing." This command declares (*a*) *speciem actus*, i.e. it indicates with sufficient clearness, by the use of the term "baptize," the external element to be employed, viz. water, and the form of the action to be performed by means of water, viz. any dipping, or pouring, or sprinkling, since the word "baptize" signifies any of these modes. On the strength of this command Luther held: "Baptism is not simple water only, but it is the water comprehended in God's command"; and the Westminster Shorter Catechism (Ques. 94) calls baptism "a washing with water." Water is dis-

tinctly mentioned as the baptismal element in Acts **8** 38; **10** 47; Eph **5** 26; He **10** 22. "There is no mention of any other element" (Plummer). The phraseology of Eph **5** 26, "the washing of water with the word," shows that not the external element alone, nor the physical action of applying the water, constitutes baptism; but "the word" must be added to the element and the action, in order that there may be a baptism. (*Detrahe verbum, et quid est aqua nisi aqua? Accedit verbum ad elementum, et fit sacramentum,* "Remove the word and what is water but water? The word is added to the element and it becomes a sacrament" Augustine). "Without the Word of God the water is simple water, and no baptism" (Luther). The command prescribes (*b*) *exercitium actus,* i.e. it enjoins a continued exercise of this function of the messengers of Christ for all time.

(2) *A clear declaration of the object in view.*—The participle "baptizing" qualifies the imperative "make disciples," and expresses that, what the imperative states as the end, is to be attained by what the participle names as a means to that end. The participle "baptizing," again, is qualified by "teaching" (ver 20). The second participle is not connected by "and" with the first, hence, is subordinate to the first (Meyer). Discipleship is to be obtained by baptizing-teaching. There is no rigid law regarding the order and sequence of these actions laid down in these words; they merely state that Christ desires His disciples to be both baptized and fully informed as to His teaching.

(3) *A definite promise:* salvation (Mk **16** 16), i.e. complete and final deliverance from all evil, the securing of "the end of faith" (1 Pet **1** 9). This is a comprehensive statement, as in 1 Pet **3** 21, of the blessing of baptism. Scripture also states, in detail, particular baptismal blessings: (*a*) *Regeneration,* Tit **3** 5; Jn **3** 3.5. Despite Calvin and others, the overwhelming consensus of interpreters still agrees with the ancient church and with Luther in explaining both these texts of baptism. (*b*) *Remission of sins,* or justification (Acts **2** 38; **22** 16; 1 Cor **6** 11; Eph **5** 26; He **10** 22). This blessing, no doubt, is also intended in 1 Pet **3** 21, where *eperṓtēma* has been rendered "answer" by the AV while the RV renders "interrogation." The word denotes a legal claim, which a person has a right to set up (see Cremer s.v. and Rom **8** 1). (*c*) *The establishment of a spiritual union with Christ,* and a new relationship with God (Gal **3** 26.27; Rom **6** 3.4; Col **2** 12). In this connection the prepositions with which *baptizein* in the NT connects may be noted. *Baptizein eis,* "to baptize into," always denotes the relation into which the party baptized is placed. The only exception is Mk **1** 9. *Baptizein en,* or *epí,* "to baptize in" (Acts **10** 48; **2** 38), denotes the basis on which the new relation into which the baptized enters, is made to rest (Cremer). (*d*) *The sanctifying gifts of the Holy Spirit* (1 Cor **12** 13; Tit **3** 5). All these blessings Scripture declares to be effects of baptism (*Wirkung der Taufe,* Riehm, *Handwörterb.*). "Baptism is called 'washing of regeneration,' not merely because it symbolizes it, or pledges a man to it, but also, and chiefly, because it effects it" (Holtzmann, Huther, Pfleiderer, Weiss). "Regeneration, or being begotten of God, does not mean merely a new capacity for change in the direction of goodness, but an actual change. The legal washings were actual external purifications. Baptism is actual internal purification" (Plummer). To these modern authorities Luther can be added. He says: "Baptism worketh forgiveness of sin, delivers from death and the devil, and gives eternal salvation to all who believe, as the words and promises of God declare" (Smaller Catech.). In Tit **3** 5 AV the force of the preposition *diá,* "by," deserves to be noted: it declares baptism to be the regenerating, renewing, justifying, glorying medium to the heirs of eternal life. The baptismal promise is supported, not only in a general way, by the veracity and sincerity of the Speaker, who is the Divine Truth incarnate, but also in a special way, by the Author's appeal to His sovereign majesty (Mt **28** 18), and by the significant assurance of His personal ("I" =*egṓ,* is emphatic: Meyer) presence with the disciples in their afore-mentioned activity (Mt **28** 20; cf Mk **16** 20).

(4) *A plain indication of the scope:* "all nations," "the whole creation" (*pásē tē ktísei* to be understood as in Col **1** 23="all men"). Baptism is of universal application; it is a cosmopolitan ordinance before which differences such as of nationality, race, age, sex, social or civil status, are leveled (cf Col **3** 11 with 1 Cor **12** 13). Accordingly, Christ orders baptism to be practised "alway" (lit. "all days"), "even unto the end of the world," i.e. unto the consummation of the present age, until the Second Advent of the Lord. For, throughout this period Christ promises His coöperative presence with the efforts of His disciples to make disciples.

(5) *A prescribed formula for administering the ordinance:* "into the name of the Father and of the Son and of the Holy Spirit." The belief in the Trinity is fundamental to Christianity; accordingly, the sacred rite by which men are initiated into the Christian religion justly emphasizes this belief. The three Persons are mentioned as distinct from one another, but the baptismal command is issued upon their joint and coequal authority ("in the name," not "names"), thus indicating the Unity in Trinity. This ancient baptismal formula represents "the Father as the Originator, the Son as the Mediator, the Holy Ghost as the Realization, and the vital and vitalizing blessing of the promise and fulfilment," which is extended to men in this ordinance (Cremer).

2. The Biblical History of the Ordinance

After the Lord had entered into His glory, we find that in the era of the apostles and in the primitive Christian church baptism is the established and universally acknowledged rite by which persons are admitted to communion with the church (Acts **2** 38.41; **8** 12 f.36.38; **9** 18; **10** 47 f; **16** 15.33; **18** 8; **22** 16; Rom **6** 3; 1 Cor **12** 13; Gal **3** 27). Even in cases where an outpouring of the special gifts of the Holy Spirit had already taken place, baptism is still administered (Acts **10** 44 ff; **11** 15 f). "Thus, baptism occupied among the Gentile converts to Christianity, and later among all Christians, the same position as circumcision in the Old Covenant (Col **2** 11 f; Gal **5** 2). It is, essentially, part of the foundation on which the unity of the Christian society rested from the beginning (Eph **4** 5; 1 Cor **12** 13; Gal **3** 27 f)" (Riehm, *Handwörterb.*).

3. Types of Baptism

In 1 Cor **10** 1.2 the apostle states that the Israelites "were all baptized unto Moses in the cloud and in the sea." Farrar attempts the following solution of this type: "The passing under the cloud (Ex **14** 19) and through the sea, constituting as it did their deliverance from bondage into freedom, their death to Egypt, and their birth to a new covenant, was a general type or dim shadow of Christian baptism (compare our collect, 'figuring thereby Thy holy baptism'). But the typology is quite incidental; it is the moral lesson which is paramount. 'Unto Moses'; rather, into. By this 'baptism' they accepted Moses as their Heaven-sent guide and teacher" (*Pulpit Comm.*). In 1 Pet **3** 21 the apostle calls baptism the *antítupon* of the

Deluge. Delitzsch (on He **9** 24) suggests that *túpos* and *antitupon* in Gr represent the original figure and a copy made therefrom, or a prophetic foretype and its later accomplishment. The point of comparison is the saving power of water in either instance. Water saved Noah and his family by floating the ark which sheltered them, and by removing from them the disobedient generation which had sorely tried their faith, as it had tried God's patience. In like manner the water of baptism bears up the ark of the Christian church and saves its believing members, by separating them from their filthy and doomed fellow-men.

III. Difficulties.—Feine (*PER*³, XIX, 396 f) and Kattenbusch (*Sch-Herz*, I, 435 f) argue that the Trinitarian formula in Mt **28** 19 is spurious, and that the text in Mk belongs to a section which was added to this Gospel at a later time. The former claim had first been advanced by Conybeare, but later research by Riggenbach has established the genuineness of the Trinitarian formula in Mt. Feine still maintains his doubts, however, on subjective grounds. As to the concluding section in Mk (**16** 9–20), Jerome is the first to call attention to its omission in most Gr MSS to which he had access. But Jerome himself acknowledged ver 14 as genuine. Gregory of Nyssa reports that, while this section is missing in some MSS, in the more accurate ones many MSS contain it. No doctrinal scruple can arise on account of this section; for it contains nothing that is contrary to the doctrine of Scripture in other places on the same subject; and it has always been treated as genuine by the Christian church. The question is a purely historical one (see Bengel, *Apparatus Criticus*, 170 f).

1. Are Mt 28 vs 18–20 and Mk 16 vs 15.16 Genuine?

No record of such use can be discovered in the Acts or the epistles of the apostles. The baptisms recorded in the NT after the Day of Pentecost are administered "in the name of Jesus Christ" (Acts **2** 38), "into the name of the Lord Jesus" (**8** 16), "into Christ" (Rom **6** 3; Gal **3** 27). This difficulty was considered by the Fathers; Ambrose says: *Quod verbo tacitum fuerat, expressum est fide*, "What had not been expressed in word, was expressed by faith." On close inspection the difficulty is found to rest on the assumption that the above are records of baptismal formulas used on those occasions. The fact is that these records contain no baptismal formula at all, but "merely state that such persons were baptized as acknowledged Jesus to be the Lord and the Christ" (Plummer). The same can be said of any person baptized in our day with the Trinitarian formula. That this formula was the established usage in the Christian church is proven by records of baptisms in Justin (*Apol.*, I, 61) and Tertullian (*Adv. Prax.*, XXVI).

2. Was the Trinitarian Formula Used in NT Times?

Baptism was practised among the Jews prior to the solemn inauguration of this ordinance by the risen Christ. The ceremonial washings of the Jews are classed with the transient forms of the Levitical worship (He **9** 9.10), which had not been intended to endure except "until a time of reformation." They were removed when Christian baptism was erected into an abiding ordinance of the church of God (Col **2** 11–13). It is erroneous to say that those ancient washings developed into Christian baptism. A shadow does not develop into a substance. Nor do we find the origin of Christian baptism in the baptism of proselytes, which seems to have been a Jewish church custom in the days of Christ. Though the rite of baptism was not unknown to the Jews, still the baptism of John startled them (Jn **1** 25). Such passages as Isa **4** 4 (**1** 16); Ezk **36** 25; **37** 23; Zec **13** 1 had, no doubt, led them to expect a rite of purification in the days of the Messiah, which would supersede their Levitical purification. The delegation which they sent to John was to determine the Messianic character of John and his preaching and baptizing. Johannic baptism has been a fruitful theme of debate. The question does not affect the personal faith of any Christian at the present time; for there is no person living who has received Johannic baptism (Chemnitz). The entire subject and certain features of it, as the incident recorded Acts **19** 1–7, will continue to be debated. It is best to fix in our minds a few essential facts, which will enable us to put the Scriptural estimate on the baptism of John. John had received a Divine commission to preach and baptize (Lk **3** 2; Jn **1** 33; Mt **21** 25). He baptized with water (Jn **3** 23). His baptism was honored by a wonderful manifestation of the holy Trinity (Mt **3** 16.17), and by the Redeemer, in His capacity as the Representative of sinful mankind, the sin-bearing Lamb of God, accepting baptism at John's hand (Mt **3** 13 ff; Jn **1** 29 ff). It was of the necessity of receiving John's baptism that Christ spoke to Nicodemus (Jn **3** 3 ff). The Pharisees invited their eternal ruin by refusing John's baptism (Lk **7** 30); for John's baptism was to shield them from the wrath to come (Mt **3** 7); it was for the remission of sin (Mk **1** 4); it was a washing of regeneration (Jn **3** 5). When Jesus began His public ministry, He took up the preaching and baptism of John, and His disciples practised it with such success that John rejoiced (Jn **3** 22.25–36; **4** 1.2). All this evidence fairly compels the belief that there was no essential difference between the baptism of John and the baptism instituted by Christ; that what the risen Christ did in Mt **28** 18–20 was merely to elevate a rite that had previously been adopted by an order "from above" to a permanent institution of His church, and to proclaim its universal application. The contrast which John himself declares between his baptism and that of Christ is not a contrast between two baptisms with water. The baptism of Christ, which John foretells, is a baptism with the Holy Ghost and with fire, the Pentecostal baptism. But for the general purpose of begetting men unto a new life, sanctifying and saving them, the Spirit was also bestowed through John's baptism (Jn **3** 5).

3. Was Christian Baptism Really a New Ordinance?

The command in Mt **28** 19; Mk **16** 16 is all-embracing; so is the statement concerning the necessity of baptism in Jn **3** 5. After reading these statements, one feels inclined, not to ask, Should infants be baptized? but Why should they *not* be baptized? The *onus probandi* rests on those who reject infant baptism. The desire to have their infants baptized must have been manifested on the day when the first three thousand were baptized at Jerus, assuming that they were all adults. The old covenant had provided for their children; was the new to be inferior to the old in this respect? (See Plummer in *HDB*.) The baptism of entire households is presumptive evidence that children and infants were baptized in apostolic times (Acts **16** 15.33; **18** 8; 1 Cor **1** 16). The arguments against infant baptism imply defective views on the subject of original sin and the efficacy of baptism. Infant faith—for, faith is as necessary to the infant as to the adult—may baffle our attempts at explanation and definition; but God who extends His promises also to children (Acts **2** 39), who established His covenant even with beasts (Gen **9** 16.17); Christ who blessed also little children (Mk

4. Should Infants Be Baptized?

10 13 ff), and spoke of them as believers (Mt **18** 6), certainly does not consider the regeneration of a child or infant a greater task than that of an adult (cf Mt **18** 3.4).

5. Why Did Paul not Baptize?

Paul did baptize Crispus, Gaius and Stephanas with his household. These baptisms he performed at Corinth alone; we have no record of his baptisms at other places. What Paul declares in 1 Cor **1** 14–17 is, that by his baptizing he could not have become the cause of the divisions in the Corinthian congregation, because he had baptized only a few persons at Corinth, and, moreover, he had not baptized in his own name, hence had attached no one to his person. The statement, "Christ sent me not to baptize," is made after the Sem idiom, and means: "not so much to baptize as to preach" (Farrar in *Pulpit Comm.*). If they are taken in any other sense, it is impossible to protect Paul against the charge that he did something that he was not authorized to do, when he baptized Crispus, etc.

6. What Is the Baptism for the Dead?

1 Cor **15** 29 is sometimes taken to mean that the early Christians practised baptism by proxy. After they had been converted to Christianity, it is held, they desired to convey the benefits of their faith to their departed friends who had died in paganism, by having themselves baptized "in their behalf," perhaps on their graves. We have no evidence from history that such a practice prevailed in the early Christian churches. Nor does the text suggest it. The Gr preposition *hupér* expresses also the motive that may prompt a person to a certain action. In this case the motive was suggested by the dead, viz. by the dead in so far as they shall rise. The context shows this to be the meaning: If a person has sought baptism in view of the fact that the dead are to rise to be judged, his baptism is valueless, if the dead do not rise. See BAPTISM FOR THE DEAD.

W. H. T. DAU

BAPTISMAL REGENERATION, bap-tiz′mal rē-jen-ĕr-ā′shun: As indicated in the general arts. on BAPTISM and SACRAMENT, the doctrine ordinarily held by Presbyterians, Congregationalists, Baptists, Methodists, and also by Low-Church Episcopalians, differs from that of the Roman and Greek churches, and of High-Church Anglicans, in its rejection of the idea that baptism is the instrumental cause of regeneration, and that the grace of regeneration is effectually conveyed through the administration of that rite wherever duly performed. The teaching of Scripture on this subject is held to be that salvation is immediately dependent on faith, which, as a fruit of the operation of the Spirit of God in the soul, already, in its reception of Christ, implies the regenerating action of that Spirit, and is itself one evidence of it. To faith in Christ is attached the promise of forgiveness, and of all other blessings. Baptism is administered to those who already possess (at least profess) this faith, and symbolizes the dying to sin and rising to righteousness implicit in the act of faith (Rom **6**). It is the symbol of a cleansing from sin and renewal by God's Spirit, but not the agency effecting that renewal, even instrumentally. Baptism is not, indeed, to be regarded as a *bare* symbol. It may be expected that its believing reception will be accompanied by fresh measures of grace, strengthening and fitting for the new life. This, however, as the life is already there, has nothing to do with the idea of baptism as an *opus operatum*, working a spiritual change in virtue of its mere administration. In Scripture the agency with which regeneration is specially connected is the Divine "word" (cf 1 Pet **1** 23). Without living faith, in those capable of its exercise, the outward rite can avail nothing. The supposed "regeneration" may be received—in multitudes of instances is received—without the least apparent change in heart or life.

The above, naturally, applies to adults; the case of children, born and growing up within the Christian community, is on a different footing. Those who recognize the right of such to baptism hold that in the normal Christian development children of believing parents should be the subjects of Divine grace from the commencement (Eph **6** 4); they therefore properly receive the initiatory rite of the Christian church. The faith of the parent, in presenting his child for baptism, lays hold on God's promise to be a God to him and to his children; and he is entitled to hope for that which baptism pledges to him. But this, again, has no relation to the idea of regeneration *through* baptism.

JAMES ORR

ANGLICAN (HIGH-CHURCH) DOCTRINE

Regeneration, the initial gift of life in Christ, is, in the church's normal system, associated with the sacrament of baptism. The basis for this teaching and practice of the church is found primarily in Our Lord's discourse to Nicodemus (Jn **3** 1–8) wherein the new birth is associated not only with the quickening Spirit but with the element of water. The Saviour's words, lit. tr[d], are as follows: "Except one be born [out] of water and Spirit (*ex húdatos kaí pneúmatos gennáomai*), he cannot enter into the kingdom of God." (That it is the impersonal aspect of the Divine Spirit, i.e. as equivalent to "spiritual life" which is here presented, is indicated by the absence of the art. in the Gr of ver 5.) Entrance into the kingdom of God implies entrance into the church as the outward and visible embodiment of that kingdom. Our Lord, in the passage above cited, does not limit the possibility or the need of "new birth" to those who have arrived at adult age, or "years of discretion," but uses the general pronoun τὶς, *tís*, "anyone." The Anglican church does not, however, teach that baptism is unconditionally necessary, but only that it is "generally" necessary to salvation (cf the language of the Church Catechism with the qualification mentioned in the Prayer-Book "Office for the Baptism of Those of Riper Years," "Whereby ye may perceive the great necessity of this Sacrament, where it may be had"). It is not taught that the grace of God is absolutely or unconditionally bound to the external means, but only that these sacramental agencies are the ordinary and normal channels of Divine grace.

The typical form of baptism is that appropriate to the initiation of adults into the Christian body. Justin Martyr in his First Apology (ch lxi) no doubt testifies to what was the general view of Christians in the 2d cent. (cir 150 AD): "As many as are persuaded and believe that the things taught and said by us are true, and, moreover, take upon them to live accordingly, are taught to pray and ask of God with fasting for forgiveness of their former sins; . . . . and then they are brought to a place of water, and there regenerated after the same manner with ourselves; for they are washed in the name of God, the Father and Lord of the universe, and of our Saviour Jesus Christ, and of the Holy Spirit." For the due administration of this sacrament, personal faith and repentance on the part of the candidate are prerequisite conditions. However, "the baptism of young children" (i.e. of infants) "is in any wise to be retained in the Church, as most agreeable to the institution of Christ" (XXXIX Articles, Art. XXVII, sub fin.). In the service "For the Baptism of Infants," repentance and faith are promised for the children by their "sureties" (ordinarily known as "sponsors" or "godparents"), "which promise, when they come to age [the children] themselves are bound to perform."

The person, whether adult or infant, receives in his baptism a real forgiveness; a washing away of all sins, whether original or actual. He also receives, at least in germ, the beginnings of new life in Christ; which life, however, must be developed and brought to perfection through his personal coöperation with the grace of God. But regeneration, as such, is not conversion; it is not even faith or love, strictly speaking. These latter, while they are *conditions*, or *effects*, or *evidences* of regeneration, are not regeneration itself, which is purely the work of God, operating by His creative power, through the Holy Ghost. The moral test of the existence of spiritual life is the presence in heart and conduct of the love of God and of obedience to His commandments (see 1 Jn *passim*).

It may be added that the bestowment of the gifts of spiritual strength—of the manifold graces and of the fulness of the Holy Spirit—is primarily associated with the laying on of hands (confirmation) rather than with baptism proper; the rite of confirmation was, however, originally connected with the baptismal service, as an adjunct to it. The newly-made Christian is not to rest content with the initial gift of life; he is bound to strive forward unto perfection. Confirmation is, in a sense, the completion of baptism. "The doctrine of laying on of hands" is accordingly connected with "the doctrine of baptisms," and both are reckoned by the author of the Epistle to the He as among "the first principles of Christ" (He **6** 1.2 AV).

LITERATURE.—For the Anglican doctrine on the subject of regeneration in baptism the following authorities may be consulted: Hooker, *Ecclesiastical Polity*, V, lix, lx; Waterland, *The Doct. Use of Christian Sacraments; Regeneration;* Wall, *Infant Baptism;* R. I. Wilberforce, *The Doctrine of Holy Baptism;* Darwell Stone, *Holy Baptism*, in "The Oxford Library of Practical Theology"; A. J. Mason, *The Faith of the Gospel*. For patristic teaching on this subject, cf Tertullian, *De Baptismo*.

WILLIAM SAMUEL BISHOP

LUTHERAN DOCTRINE

1. Definition of Terms

Regeneration is here taken in its strict meaning to denote that internal spiritual change, not of the substance, but of the qualities, of the intellect and will of natural man, by which blindness, darkness in regard to spiritual matters, esp. the gospel, is removed from the former, and spiritual bondage, impotency, death from the latter (2 Cor **3** 5; Acts **26** 18; Phil **2** 13), and the heart of the sinner is made to savingly know and appropriate the Lord Jesus Christ and the merits of His atoning sacrifice, as its only hope for a God-pleasing life here in time and a life in glory hereafter. Regeneration in the strict sense signifies the first spiritual movements and impulses in man, the beginning of his thinking Divine thoughts, cherishing holy desires and willing God-like volitions. But it does not signify the radical extinction of sin in man; for evil concupiscence remains also in the regenerate as a hostile element to the new life (Rom **7** 23–25; Gal **5** 16.17). *Peccatum tollitur in baptismo, non ut non sit, sed ut non obsit*—Augustine. "Sin is removed in baptism, not that it may not be, but that it may not hurt." Reduced to its lowest terms, regeneration in the strict sense may be defined as the kindling of saving faith in the heart of the sinner; for according to 1 Jn **5** 1, "whosoever believeth that Jesus is the Christ is begotten of God." Such terms as new creation (2 Cor **5** 17; Gal **6** 15 m), spiritual quickening, or vivification (Eph **2** 5; Rom **6** 11), spiritual resurrection (Eph **2** 6; Col **3** 1), are true synonyms of regeneration in the strict sense. In the point of time justification coincides with regeneration in the strict sense; for it is by faith, too, that the sinner is justified. But these two spiritual events must not be confounded; for justification affects, not the internal conditions of the sinner's heart, but his legal standing with God the righteous Judge. Regeneration is called baptismal regeneration in so far as it occurs in the event and as an effect of the application of the Christian baptism. See BAPTISM (1), I, 6.

2. Scriptural Basis of This Doctrine

The two leading texts of Scripture which declare in plain terms that baptism is a means for effecting regeneration in the strict sense are Jn **3** 5 and Tit **3** 5. But this doctrine is implied in Acts **2** 38; Eph **5** 26; Gal **3** 27; 1 Pet **3** 21. In Jn **3** 7 it is immaterial whether *ánōthen gennēthēnai* is rendered "to be born from above" or "to be born a second time." For the second birth is never of the flesh (Jn **1** 13; **3** 4.5); hence, is always of divine origin, "from above." It is ascribed to the agency of the entire Trinity: the Father (Jas **1** 18; 1 Pet **1** 3); the Son (Jn **1** 12); and the Spirit (Tit **3** 5). But by appropriation it is generally attributed to the Spirit alone, whose particular function is that of Quickener (see Cremer, *Bibl.-theol. Wörterb.*, 9th ed, s.v. "*pneuma*," 894 f). Baptism is an instrument by which the Holy Spirit effects regeneration. "Water and the Spirit" (Jn **3** 5) is a paraphrastic description of baptism: "water," inasmuch as the man is baptized therewith (1 Jn **5** 7.8; Eph **5** 26) for the forgiveness of sin (Acts **2** 33; **22** 16; 1 Cor **6** 11), and "*Spirit*," inasmuch as the Holy Ghost is given to the person baptized in order to his spiritual renewal and sanctification; "both together—the former as *causa medians*, the latter as *causa efficiens*—constitute the objective and causative *element out of which* (cf **1** 13) the birth from above is produced [*ek*]" (Meyer). In Tit **3** 5 "the expression *tó loutroú palingenesías*, lit. 'bath of regeneration,' has been very arbitrarily interpreted by some expositors, some taking *loutron* as a fig. name for the *regeneration* itself, or for the *praedicatio evangelii*, 'preaching of the gospel' or for the Holy Spirit, or for the abundant imparting of the Spirit. From Eph **5** 26 it is clear that it can mean nothing else than baptism; cf too, He **10** 22; 1 Cor **6** 11; Acts **22** 16." Of this laver of regeneration Paul says that through it (*diá*), i.e. by its instrumentality, men are saved. Meyer is right when, correcting a former view of his, he states: "According to the context, Paul calls baptism the bath of the new birth, not meaning that it pledges us to the new birth ('to complete the process of moral purification, of expiation and sanctification,' Matthies), nor that it is a visible image of the new birth (De Wette), for neither in the one sense nor in the other could it be regarded as a means of saving. Paul uses that name for it as the bath by means of which God *actually* brings about the new birth." The application of baptism and the operation of the Spirit must be viewed as one undivided action. Thus the offense of Spurgeon, Weiss and others at "regeneration by water-baptism" can be removed.

3. Faith in Baptism

Baptism does not produce salutary effects *ex opere operato*, i.e. by the mere external performance of the baptismal action. No instrument with which Divine grace works does. Even the preaching of the gospel is void of saving results if not "mixed with faith" (He **4** 2 AV). Luther correctly describes the working of baptism thus: "How can water do such great things? It is not the water indeed that does them, but the Word of God which is in and with the water (God's giving hand), and faith which trusts such word of God in the water (man's receiving hand)." But this faith, which is required for a salutary use of the gospel and baptism, is wrought by these as instruments which the Holy Spirit employs to produce faith; not by imparting to them a magical power but by uniting His Divine power with them (Rom **10** 17; 2 Cor **4** 6; Eph **5** 26).

4. Infants and Adults

The comprehensive statements in Jn **3** 6; Eph **2** 3 ("by nature") show that infants are in need of being regenerated, and Mt **18** 3.6, that they are capable of faith. It is not more difficult for the Holy Spirit to work faith in infants by baptism, than in adults by the preaching of the gospel. And infant faith, though it may baffle our attempts at exact definition, is nevertheless honored in Scripture with the word which denotes genuine faith, *pisteúein*, i.e. trustfully relying on Christ (Mt **18** 6; cf 2 Tim **3** 15; **1** 5). In the case of adults who have received faith through hearing and reading the gospel (Jas **1** 18; 1 Pet **1** 23; 1 Cor **4** 15), baptism is still "the washing of regeneration," because it is a seal to them of the righteousness which these people have previously obtained by believing the gospel (Rom **4** 11–13; Gal **3** 7); and it reminds them of, and enables them to discharge, their daily duty of putting away the old and putting on the new man (Eph **4** 22.24), just as the Word is still the regenerating word of truth (Jas **1** 18) though it be preached to persons who are regenerated a long time ago. Accordingly, Luther rightly extends the regenerating and renewing influences of baptism throughout the life of a Christian, when he says "Baptizing with water signifies that the old Adam in us should, by daily contrition and repentance, be drowned and die, with all sins and evil lusts; and, again, a new man should come forth and arise, who shall live before God in righteousness and purity forever" (Smaller Catech.).

W. H. T. Dau

BAPTISM FOR THE DEAD (**βαπτίζομαι ὑπὲρ τῶν νεκρῶν**, *baptízomai hupér tôn nekrôn*): Some of the Corinthian Christians denied the resurrection of the dead, and Paul advances three arguments to convince them that the dead will be raised: (1) "If there is no resurrection of the dead, neither hath Christ been raised," but Christ is raised (1 Cor **15** 13.20). (2) If the dead are not raised, why are men being baptized for the dead (ib **15** 29)? (3) Why should the apostle himself wage his spiritual warfare (ib **15** 30)? The first argument rests upon the central fact of Christianity, and the other two are appeals to the consistency of the Corinthians, and of Paul himself. Whatever "baptism for the dead" meant, it was, in Paul's opinion, as real, valid and legitimate a premise from which to conclude that the dead would rise as his own sufferings. The natural meaning of the words is obvious. Men in Corinth, and possibly elsewhere, were being continually baptized on behalf of others who were at the time dead, with a view to benefiting them in the resurrection, but if there be no resurrection, what shall they thus accomplish, and why do they do it? "The only legitimate reference is to a practice . . . . of survivors allowing themselves to be baptized on behalf of (believing?) friends who had died without baptism" (Alford in loc.).

1. Paul's Argument

2. Patristic Evidence

Tertullian believed that Paul referred to a custom of vicarious baptism (*Res.*, 48*c*; *Adv. Marc.*, 5.10). There is evidence that the early church knew such a practice. Epiphanius mentions a tradition that the custom obtained among the Cerinthians (*Haer.*, **28** 6). And Chrysostom states that it prevailed among the Marcionites.

3. Modern Views

But commentators have offered between thirty and forty other interpretations, more or less strained, of the passage. (For a summary of different views see T. C. Edwards and Stanley, *Comms.*, ad loc.) Two of the most reasonable views from recent commentators are: "What shall they do who receive baptism on account of the dead? i.e. with a view to the resurrection of the dead?" and therefore to sharing in it themselves (Canon Evans, *Speaker's Comm.*, ad loc.); "that the death of Christians led to the conversion of survivors, who in the first instance 'for the sake of the dead' (their beloved dead), and in the hope of reunion, turn to Christ" (Findlay, *Expositor's Greek Test.*, ad loc.). Both ideas may be true, but they are simply imported into this passage, and the latter also is quite irrelevant to the argument and makes Paul identify conversion with baptism.

4. The Difficulty

But why is all this ingenuity expended to evade the natural meaning? Because (1) such a custom would be a superstition involving the principle of *opus operatum;* and (2) Paul could not share or even tolerate a contemporary idea which is now regarded as superstition. To reply (with Alford) that Paul does not approve the custom will not serve the purpose, for he would scarcely base so great an argument, even as an *argumentum ad hominem*, on a practice which he regarded as wholly false and superstitious. The retort of those who denied the resurrection would be too obvious. But why should it be necessary to suppose that Paul rose above all the limitations of his age? The idea that symbolic acts had a vicarious significance had sunk deeply into the Jewish mind, and it would not be surprising if it took more than twenty years for the leaven of the gospel to work all the Jew out of Paul. At least it serves the apostle's credit ill to make his argument meaningless or absurd in order to save him from sharing at all in the inadequate conceptions of his age. He made for himself no claim of infallibility.

T. Rees

BAPTISM OF FIRE (**ἐν πνεύματι ἁγίῳ καὶ πυρί**, *en pneúmati hagíō kaí purí*): This expression is used in Mt **3** 11. The copulative *καὶ* requires that the baptism "in the Holy Ghost and in fire," should be regarded as one and the same thing. It does violence to the construction, therefore, to make this statement refer to the fire of judgment. The difficulty has always been in associating fire with the person of the Holy Ghost. But in the connection of fire with the work or influence of the Holy Ghost the difficulty disappears. The thought of John is that the Saviour would give them the Divine Sanctifier as purifying water to wash away their sins and as a refining fire to consume their dross; to kindle in their hearts the holy flame of Divine love and zeal; to illuminate their souls with heavenly wisdom. The statement, therefore, in this verse indicates the manner in which Christ will admit them to discipleship and prepare them for His service. See Baptism; Fire.

Jacob W. Kapp

BAPTISM OF THE HOLY SPIRIT: The expression "baptism of the Holy Spirit" is based on a number of predictions found in our four Gospels and in connection with these the record of their fulfilment in the Book of Acts. The passages in the Gospels are as follows: Mt **3** 11: "I indeed baptize you in water unto repentance: but he that cometh after me is mightier than I, whose shoes I am not worthy to bear: he shall baptize you in the Holy Spirit and in fire." The last clause is *αὐτός ὑμᾶς βαπτίσει ἐν πνεύματι ἁγίῳ*

1. The Biblical Material

καὶ πυρί = *autós humás baptísei en pneúmati hagíō kaí purí*. In Mk 1 8 and Lk 3 16 we have the declaration in a slightly modified form; and in Jn 1 33 John the Baptist declares that the descent of the Spirit upon Jesus at the baptism of the latter marked out Jesus as "he that baptizeth in the Holy Spirit." Again in Jn 7 37.38 we read: "Now on the last day, the great day of the feast, Jesus stood and cried, saying, If any man thirst, let him come unto me and drink. He that believeth on me, as the scripture hath said, from within him shall flow rivers of living water." Then the evangelist adds in ver 39: "But this spake he of the Spirit, which they that believed on him were to receive: for the Spirit was not yet given; because Jesus was not yet glorified." These are the specific references in the four Gospels to the baptisms of the Holy Spirit. In Acts we find direct reference by Luke to the promised baptism in the Holy Spirit. In 1 5 Jesus, just before the ascension, contrasts John's baptism in water with the baptism in the Holy Spirit which the disciples are to receive "not many days hence," and in ver 8 power in witnessing for Jesus is predicted as the result of the baptism in the Holy Spirit. On the evening of the resurrection day Jesus appeared to the disciples and "he breathed on them, and saith unto them, Receive ye the Holy Spirit" (Jn 20 22). This was probably not a wholly symbolic act but an actual communication to the disciples, in some measure, of the gift of the Spirit, preliminary to the later complete bestowal.

We observe next the fulfilment of these predictions as recorded in Acts. The gift of the Holy Spirit on the Day of Pentecost and the miraculous manifestations which followed are clearly the chief historical fulfilment of the prediction of the baptism of the Holy Spirit. Among the manifestations of the coming of the Spirit at Pentecost were first those which were physical, such as "a sound as of the rushing of a mighty wind, and it filled all the house where they were sitting" (Acts 2 2), and the appearance of "tongues parting asunder, like as of fire; and it sat upon each one of them" (Acts 2 3). Secondly, there were spiritual results: "And they were all filled with the Holy Spirit, and began to speak with other tongues, as the Spirit gave them utterance" (Acts 2 4). In vs 16 ff Peter declares that this bestowment of the Holy Spirit is in fulfilment of the prediction made by the prophet Joel and he cites the words in 2 28 ff of Joel's prophecy.

There is one other important passage in Acts in which reference is made to the baptism of the Holy Spirit. While Peter was speaking to Cornelius (Acts 10 44) the Holy Spirit fell on all that heard the word and they of the circumcision who were with Peter "were amazed" "because that on the Gentiles also was poured out the gift of the Holy Spirit." When giving the brethren at Jerus an account of his visit to Cornelius, Peter declares that this event which he had witnessed was a baptism of the Holy Spirit (Acts 11 16): "And I remembered the word of the Lord, how he said, John indeed baptized with water; but ye shall be baptized in the Holy Spirit."

We consider next the significance of the baptism of the Holy Spirit from various points of view.

2. Significance of Baptism of the Holy Spirit

(1) *From the point of view of OT teaching as to the gift of the Spirit.*—The prophecy of Joel quoted by Peter indicates something extraordinary in the gift of the Spirit at Pentecost. The Spirit now comes in new forms of manifestation and with new power. The various classes mentioned as receiving the Spirit indicate the wide diffusion of the new power. In the OT usually the Spirit was bestowed upon individuals; here the gift is to the group of disciples, the church. Here the gift is permanently bestowed, while in the OT it was usually transient and for a special purpose. Here again the Spirit comes in fulness as contrasted with the partial bestowment in OT times.

(2) *From the point of view of the ascended Christ.*—In Lk 24 49 Jesus commands the disciples to tarry in the city "until ye be clothed with power from on high," and in Jn 15 26 He speaks of the Comforter "whom I will send unto you from the Father," "he shall bear witness of me"; and in Jn 16 13 Jesus declares that the Spirit when He comes shall guide the disciples into all truth, and He shall show them things to come. In this verse the Spirit is called the Spirit of truth. It was fitting that the Spirit who was to interpret truth and guide into all truth should come in fulness after, rather than before, the completion of the life-task of the Messiah. The historical manifestation of Divine truth as thus completed made necessary the gift of the Spirit in fulness. Christ Himself was the giver of the Spirit. The Spirit now takes the place of the ascended Christ, or rather takes the things of Christ and shows them to the disciples. The baptism of the Spirit at Pentecost thus becomes the great historic event signalizing the beginning of a new era in the kingdom of God in which the whole movement is lifted to the spiritual plane, and the task of evangelizing the world is formally begun.

(3) *The significance of the baptism of the Spirit from the point of view of the disciples.*—It can scarcely be said with truth that Pentecost was the birthday of the church. Jesus had spoken of His church during His earthly ministry. The spiritual relation to Christ which constitutes the basis of the church existed prior to the baptism of the Holy Spirit. But that baptism established the church in several ways. First in unity. The external bond of unity now gives place to an inner spiritual bond of profound significance. Secondly, the church now becomes conscious of a spiritual mission, and theocratic ideals of the kingdom disappear. Thirdly, the church is now endued with power for its work. Among the gifts bestowed were the gift of prophecy in the large sense of speaking for God, and the gift of tongues which enabled disciples to speak in foreign tongues. The account in the second ch of Acts admits of no other construction. There was also bestowed power in witnessing for Christ. This was indeed one of the most prominent blessings named in connection with the promise of the baptism of the Spirit. The power of working miracles was also bestowed (Acts 3 4 ff; 5 12 ff). Later in the epistles of Paul much emphasis is given to the Spirit as the sanctifying agency in the hearts of believers. In Acts the word of the Spirit is chiefly Messianic, that is, the Spirit's activity is all seen in relation to the extension of the Messianic kingdom. The occasion for the outpouring of the Spirit is Pentecost when men from all nations are assembled in Jerus. The symbolic representation of tongues of fire is suggestive of preaching, and the glossolalia, or speaking with tongues which followed, so that men of various nations heard the gospel in their own languages, indicates that the baptism of the Spirit had a very special relation to the task of world-wide evangelization for the bringing in of the kingdom of God.

3. Finality of the Baptism of the Holy Spirit

The question is often raised whether or not the baptism of the Holy Spirit occurred once for all or is repeated in subsequent baptisms. The evidence seems to point to the former view to the extent at least of being limited to outpourings which took place in connection with events recorded in the early chapters of the Book of Acts. The following considerations favor this view:

(1) In the first ch of Acts Jesus predicts, according to Luke's account, that the baptism of the Holy Spirit would take place, "not many days hence" (Acts **1** 5). This would seem to point to a definite and specific event rather than to a continuous process.

(2) Again, Peter's citation in Acts **2** 17–21 of Joel's prophecy shows that in Peter's mind the event which his hearers were then witnessing was the definite fulfilment of the words of Joel.

(3) Notice in the third place that only one other event in the NT is described as the baptism of the Holy Spirit, and for special reasons this may be regarded as the completion of the Pentecostal baptism. The passage is that contained in Acts **10** 1—**11** 18 in which the record is given of the following events: (*a*) miraculous vision given to Peter on the housetop (**10** 11–16) indicating that the things about to occur are of unique importance; (*b*) the speaking with tongues (**10** 45.46); (*c*) Peter declares to the brethren at Jerus that the Holy Ghost fell on the Gentiles in this instance of Cornelius and his household "as on us at the beginning" (**11** 15); (*d*) Peter also declares that this was a fulfilment of the promise of the baptism of the Holy Spirit (**11** 16.17); (*e*) the Jewish Christians who heard Peter's account of the matter acknowledged this as proof that God had also extended the privileges of the gospel to the Gentiles (**11** 18). The baptism of the Holy Spirit bestowed upon Cornelius and his household is thus directly linked with the first outpouring at Pentecost, and as the event which signalized the opening of the door of the gospel formally to Gentiles it is in complete harmony with the missionary significance of the first great Pentecostal outpouring. It was a turning point or crisis in the Messianic kingdom and seems designed to complete the Pentecostal gift by showing that Gentiles as well as Jews are to be embraced in all the privileges of the new dispensation.

(4) We observe again that nowhere in the epistles do we find a repetition of the baptism of the Spirit. This would be remarkable if it had been understood by the writers of the epistles that the baptism of the Spirit was frequently to be repeated. There is no evidence outside the Book of Acts that the baptism of the Spirit ever occurred in the later NT times. In 1 Cor **12** 13 Paul says, "For in one Spirit were we all baptized into one body . . . . and were all made to drink of one Spirit." But here the reference is not to the baptism of the Spirit, but rather to a baptism into the church which is the body of Christ. We conclude, therefore, that the Pentecostal baptism taken in conjunction with the baptism of the Spirit in the case of Cornelius completes the baptism of the Holy Spirit according to the NT teaching. The baptism of the Spirit as thus bestowed was, however, the definite gift of the Spirit in His fulness for every form of spiritual blessing necessary in the progress of the kingdom and as the permanent and abiding gift of God to His people. In all subsequent NT writings there is the assumption of this presence of the Spirit and of His availability for all believers. The various commands and exhortations of the epistles are based on the assumption that the baptism of the Spirit has already taken place, and that, according to the prediction of Jesus to the disciples, the Spirit was to abide with them forever (Jn **14** 16). We should not therefore confound other forms of expression found in the NT with the baptism of the Holy Spirit. When Christians are enjoined to "walk by the Spirit" (Gal **5** 16) and "be filled with the Spirit" (Eph **5** 18), or when the Spirit is described as an anointing (χρίσμα= *chrísma*) as in 1 Jn **2** 20–27, and as the "earnest of our inheritance" (ἀρραβών=*arrabṓn*). as in Eph **1** 14, and when various other similar expressions are employed in the epistles of the NT, we are not to understand the baptism of the Holy Spirit. These expressions indicate aspects of the Spirit's work in believers or of the believer's appropriation of the gifts and blessings of the Spirit rather than the historical baptism of the Spirit.

Three final points require brief attention, viz. the relation of the baptism of the Spirit to the baptism in water, and to the baptism in fire, and to the laying on of hands.

4. Relation of Baptism of the Spirit to Other Baptisms

(1) We note that the baptism in fire is coupled with the baptism in the Spirit in Mt **3** 11 and in Lk **3** 16. These passages give the word of John the Baptist. John speaks of the coming One who "shall baptize you in the Holy Spirit and in fire" (Lk **3** 16). This baptism in fire is often taken as being parallel and synonymous with the baptism in the Spirit. The context however in both Mt and Lk seems to favor another meaning. Jesus' Messianic work will be both cleansing and destructive. The "you" addressed by John included the people generally and might naturally embrace both classes, those whose attitude to Jesus would be believing and those who would refuse to believe. His action as Messiah would affect all men. Some He would regenerate and purify through the Holy Ghost. Others He would destroy through the fire of punishment. This view is favored by the context in both gospels. In both the destructive energy of Christ is coupled with His saving power in other terms which admit of no doubt. The wheat He gathers into the garner and the chaff He burns with unquenchable fire.

(2) The baptism of the Holy Spirit was not meant to supersede water baptism. This is clear from the whole of the history in the Book of Acts, where water baptism is uniformly administered to converts after the Pentecostal baptism of the Spirit, as well as from the numerous references to water baptisms in the epistles. The evidence here is so abundant that it is unnecessary to develop it in detail. See Rom **6** 3; 1 Cor **1** 14–17; **10** 2; **12** 13; **15** 29; Gal **3** 27; Eph **4** 5; Col **2** 12; 1 Pet **3** 21.

(3) In Acts **8** 17 and **19** 6 the Holy Spirit is bestowed in connection with the laying on of the hands of apostles, but these are not to be regarded as instances of the baptism of the Spirit in the strict sense, but rather as instances of the reception by believers of the Spirit which had already been bestowed in fulness at Pentecost.

LITERATURE.—Arts. on Holy Spirit in *HDB* and *DCG;* art. on "Spiritual Gifts" in *EB;* Moule, *Veni Creator;* Smeaton, *The Doctrine of the Holy Spirit;* Kuyper, *The Work of the Holy Spirit.* See also HOLY SPIRIT.

E. Y. MULLINS

BAPTISM, INFANT. See BAPTISM (I), II; (II), III, 3, v; (III), III, 3.

BAPTIST, bap′tist. See JOHN THE BAPTIST.

BAR, bär (prefix): Aram. for the Heb בֵּן, *bēn*, "son." Cf Aram. sections of Ezr and Dnl. In the OT the word is found three times in Prov **31** 2 and once in Syr Ps **2** 12 (Hier. translates "pure"). In the NT "Bar" is frequently employed as prefix to names of persons. Cf Barabbas; Bar-Jesus; Bar-Jonah; Barnabas; Barsabbas; Bartholomew; Bartimaeus. See BEN.

BAR, bär (subst.):

(1) בְּרִיחַ, *b*e*rī*a*ḥ*="a bolt" (Ex **26** 26–29; **35** 11; **36** 31–34; **39** 33; **40** 18; Nu **3** 36; **4** 31; Dt **3** 5; Jgs **16** 3; 1 S **23** 7; 1 K **4** 13; 2 Ch **8** 5; **14** 7; Neh **3** 3.6.13–15; Job **38** 10 "bars and doors"

for the sea (the bank or shore of the sea); Ps **107** 16; **147** 13 "the bars of thy gates": the walls of the city were now rebuilt and its gates only closed and barred by night [see Neh **7** 3]; Prov **18** 19, "bars of a castle"; Isa **45** 2; Jer **49** 31; **51** 30; Lam **2** 9; Ezk **38** 11): meaning "a rock in the sea" (Jon **2** 6).

(2) מוֹט, *mōṭ*="a staff," "stick," "pole" (Nu **4** 10.12m); "strong fortification and great impediment" (Isa **45** 2; Am **1** 5, "the bolt of Damascus": no need here to render *prince*, as some do [G. A. Smith in loc.]).

(3) בַּד, *badh*="staff," "part of body," "strength" (Job **17** 16, "bars of Sheol": the gates of the world of the dead; cf Isa **38** 10; some read, "Will the bars of Sheol fall?").

(4) מְטִיל, *m*ᵉ*ṭīl*="something hammered out, a (forged) bar" (Job **40** 18). See DOOR; GATE; HOUSE. FRANK E. HIRSCH

BARABBAS, ba-rab'as (Βαραββᾶς, *Barabbâs*): For Aram. Bar-abba=lit. "son of the father," i.e. of the master or teacher. Abba in the time of Jesus was perhaps a title of honor (Mt **23** 9), but became later a proper name. The variant Barrabban found in the Harclean Syr would mean "son of the rabbi or teacher." Origen knew and does not absolutely condemn a reading of Mt **27** 16.17, which gave the name "Jesus Barabbas," but although it is also found in a few cursives and in the Aram. and the Jerus Syr VSS in this place only, it is probably due to a scribe's error in transcription (*WH*, App., 19–20). If the name was simply Barabbas or Barrabban, it may still have meant that the man was a rabbi's son, or it may have been a purely conventional proper name, signifying nothing. He was the criminal chosen by the Jerus mob, at the instigation of the priests, in preference to Jesus Christ, for Pilate to release on the feast of Passover (Mk **15** 15; Mt **27** 20.21; Lk **23** 18; Jn **18** 40). Mt calls him "a notable [i.e. notorious] prisoner" (**27** 16). Mk says that he was "bound with them that had made insurrection, men who in the insurrection had committed murder" (**15** 7). Luke states that he was cast into prison "for a certain insurrection made in the city, and for murder" (**23** 19; cf Acts **3** 14). John calls him a "robber" or "brigand" (**18** 40). Nothing further is known of him, nor of the insurrection in which he took part. Luke's statement that he was a murderer is probably a deduction from Mark's more circumstantial statement, that he was only one of a gang, who in a rising had committed murder. Whether robbery was the motive of his crime, as Jn suggests, or whether he was "a man who had raised a revolt against the Rom power" (Gould) cannot be decided. But it seems equally improbable that the priests (the pro-Rom party) would urge the release of a political prisoner and that Pilate would grant it, esp. when the former were urging, and the latter could not resist, the execution of Jesus on a political charge (Lk **23** 2). The insurrection may have been a notorious case of brigandage. To say that the Jews would not be interested in the release of such a prisoner, is to forget the history of mobs. The custom referred to of releasing a prisoner on the Passover is otherwise unknown. "What Mt [and Jn] represents as brought about by Pilate, Mk makes to appear as if it were suggested by the people themselves. An unessential variation" (Meyer). For a view of the incident as semi-legendary growth, see Schmiedel in *EB*. See also Allen, *Matthew*, and Gould, *Mark*, ad loc., and art. "Barabbas" by Plummer in *HDB*.
T. REES

BARACHEL, bar'a-kel (בָּרַכְאֵל, *bārakh'ēl*, "God blesses"): B., the Buzite, of the family of Ram, was the father of Elihu, who was the last one to reason with Job (Job **32** 2.6). Cf BUZ; RAM.

BARACHIAH, bar-a-kī'a (Βαραχίας, *Barachías*; AV **Barachias**; Mt **23** 35): Father of Zachariah who was murdered between the sanctuary and the altar. It is possible that reference is made to Zechariah, the son of Jehoiada (2 Ch **24** 20 ff), whom Matthew by mistake calls "Z., the son of B." Lk **11** 51 omits the name of the father of Z. (cf Zahn's *Kommentar*, 649, note).

BARACHIAS, bar-a-kī'as. See BARACHIAH.

BARAK, bā'rak (בָּרָק, *bārāḳ*, "lightning flash"): The name occurs in Sabaean ברקם, in Palmyrene ברק, and in Punic *Barcas*, as surname of Hamilcar; and as Divine name in Assyr *Ramman-Birḳu* and *Gibil-Birḳu* (Del. Assyr, *HWB*, 187). Barak was the son of Abinoam of Kedesh, a refuge city in Mt. Naphtali. He was summoned by the prophetess Deborah to lead his countrymen to war against the Canaanites under the leadership of Sisera. From the celebrated ode of Deborah we gather that Israel suffered at the hand of the enemy; the caravan roads were in danger, traffic almost ceased; the cultivated country was plundered (Jgs **5** 6.7). The fighting men in Israel were disarmed, a shield was not to be seen nor a spear among forty thousand men (ver 8). The prophetess raised the signal of struggle for independence. Soon Barak came to her aid. With an army of 10,000 men—according to Jgs **4** 10 they were all drawn from Zebulun and Naphtali, whereas Jgs **5** 13–18 adds Benjamin, Machir and Issachar to the list of faithful tribes—Barak, accompanied by Deborah, rushed to the summit of Mt. Tabor. This location was very favorable to the rudely armed Israelites in warding off the danger of the well-armed enemy. The wooded slopes protected them against the chariots of the Canaanites. In addition they were within striking distance should the enemy expose himself on the march. Under the heavy rainfall the alluvial plain became a morass, in which the heavy-armed troops found it impossible to move. Soon the little stream Kishon was filled with chariots, horses and Canaanites. Sisera abandoned his chariot and fled on foot. Barak pursued him and found him murdered by Jael in her tent. This completed the victory. See BEDAN; Moore, "Judges," ad loc.
SAMUEL COHON

BARBARIAN, bär-bā'ri-an, **BARBAROUS,** bär-ba-rus (βάρβαρος, *bárbaros*): A word probably formed by imitation of the unintelligible sounds of foreign speech, and hence in the mouth of a Greek it meant anything that was not Gr, language, people or customs. With the spread of Gr language and culture, it came to be used generally for all that was non-Gr. Philo and Jos sometimes called their own nation "barbarians," and so did Rom writers up to the Augustan age, when they adopted Gr culture, and reckoned themselves with the Greeks as the only cultured people in the world. Therefore Greek and barbarian meant the whole human race (Rom **1** 14).

In Col **3** 11, "barbarian, Scythian" is not a classification or antithesis but a "climax" (Abbott) ="barbarians, even Scythians, the lowest type of barbarians." In Christ, all racial distinctions, even the most pronounced, disappear.

In 1 Cor **14** 11 Paul uses the term in its more primitive sense of one speaking a foreign, and therefore, an unintelligible language: "If then I know not the meaning of the voice, I shall be to him that speaketh a barbarian, and he that speaketh will be a barbarian unto me." The speaking with tongues would not be a means of communication. The excited inarticulate ejaculations of the Corinthian revivalists were worse than useless unless someone had the gift of articulating in intelligible language the force of feeling that produced them (*dúnamis tḗs phōnḗs*, lit. "the power of the sound").

In Acts **28** 2.4 (in AV of ver 2 "barbarous people"=barbarians) the writer, perhaps from the Gr-Rom standpoint, calls the inhabitants of Melita barbarians, as being descendants of the old Phoen settlers, or possibly in the more general sense of "strangers." For the later sense of "brutal," "cruel," "savage," see 2 Macc **2** 21; **4** 25; **15** 2.

T. REES

BARBER, bär'bẽr:

(1) The Eng. word "barber" is from Lat *barba*, "beard"=a man who shaves the beard. Dressing and trimming the hair came to be added to his work. "Barber" is found only once EV, in Ezk **5** 1, "Take thee a sharp sword; as a *barber's* razor shalt thou take it unto thee, and shalt cause it to pass upon thy head and upon thy beard" (cf *Ḥăghīgha'* 4*b*, *Shab*, § 6).

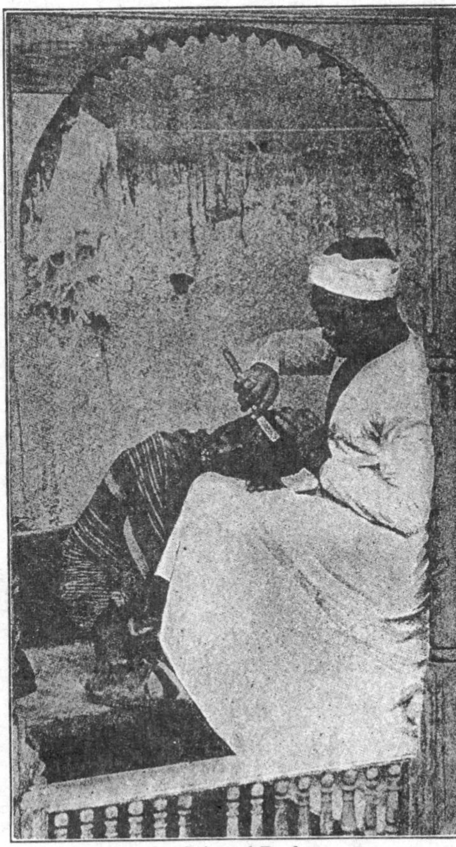

An Oriental Barber.

(2) In Gen **41** 14 we probably have a case of conformity to Egyp, rather than Palestinian custom, where Joseph "*shaved himself*, and changed his raiment, and came in unto Pharaoh." It is known that Egyptians of the higher classes shaved the beard regularly and completely (as the Hittites, Elamites and early Babylonians seem to have done), except that fashion allowed, as an exception to the rule, a small tuft, or "goatee," under the chin.

(3) We learn from various Scriptural allusions, as well as from other sources (cf W. Max Müller, *Asien und Europa*, 296 ff), that the business of the oriental barber included, besides ceremonial shaving, the trimming and polling of the hair and the beard. Cf 2 S **19** 24 where it appears that the moustache (Heb *sāphām;* AV "beard") received regular *trimming;* and 1 S **21** 14, where the neglect of the beard is set down as a sign of madness.

That men wore wigs and false beards in ancient days, the latter showing the rank of the wearer, appears from Herod. ii.36; iii.12; and Wilkinson, *Anc. Egypt*, II, 324, etc. Jos, *Vita*, II, gives one case where false hair appears to have been used as an intentional disguise. See also Polyb. iii.78.

(4) The business of the barber (see Ezk **5** 1, "as *a barber's razor* shalt thou take it unto thee, and shalt cause it to pass upon thy head and upon thy beard"), outside of ceremonial shaving, may have consisted in trimming and polling the beard and the hair of the head. Of other nations with whom Israel of old came in contact, the Hittites and Elamites, it is now known, shaved the beard completely, as the earliest Babylonians also seem to have done.

(5) The prohibition enjoined in the Mosaic law upon "the priests the Levites, the sons of Zadok" (Ezk **44** 15.20) forbidding either "shaving the head," or "suffering their locks to grow long," or shaving off the corners of their beard (Lev **21** 5), was clearly, in a sense peculiar to the priests, etc: "They [the priests] shall only cut off," i.e. trim, not shave, "the hair of their heads" (Ezk **44** 20*b*). But in the Apos Const, I, 3, insistence is laid upon the Bib. prohibition as applicable to all as regards the removal of the beard (cf Clement of Alex., *Paed.*, III, ed Migne, I, 580 f). Jerome on Ezk **44** 20 and some of the Jewish sages find the basis of this prohibition in the fact that God gave a beard to man to distinguish him from the woman—so, they reasoned, it is wrong thus to go against Nature (cf Bahya, on Lev **19** 27).

(6) In the Pal of the Gr period, say in the 3d cent. BC, when there was a large infusion of Hellenic population and influence, clipping of the beard prevailed in some circles, being omitted only in times of mourning, etc. The common people, however, seem to have seen little distinction between clipping the beard and shaving. But see pictures of captive Jews with clipped beard in the British Museum.

LITERATURE.—Benzinger, *heb. Arch.*, 110; Nowack, *Lehrbuch der Heb. Arch.*, 134; W. Max Müller, *Asien und Europa*, 296 ff.

GEO. B. EAGER

BARCHUS, bär'kus (B, **Βαχούς,** *Bachoús;* A, **Βαρχουέ,** *Barchoué;* AV **Charchus,** from Aldine ed, *Charkoús;* 1 Esd **5** 32 = Barkos [Ezr **2** 53; Neh **7** 55]): The descendants of B. (temple-servants) returned with Zerubbabel to Jerus.

BAREFOOT, bâr'fo͝ot: The word is found in the following passages: EV, "He went *barefoot*" (2 S **15** 30); "[Isaiah] did so, walking

1. Introductory

.... *barefoot*" (Isa **20** 2); and like the Egyptians, "naked and *barefoot*" (Isa **20** 3.4). It seems that David in his flight before Absalom "went barefoot," not to facilitate his flight, but to show his grief (2 S **15** 30), and that Micah (**1** 8) makes "going barefoot" a sign of mourning (LXX "to be barefoot"; AV "stripped"). The nakedness and bare feet of the prophet Isaiah (**20** 2) may have been intended to symbolize and express sympathy for the forlorn condition of captives (cf Job **12** 17.19, where AV and RV have "spoiled," but some authorities give as the true tr "barefoot").

Jastrow, in art. on "Tearing the Garments" (*Jour. of the Am. Oriental Soc.*, XXI, 23–39) presents a view worth considering of going barefoot as a sign of mourning and then of grief in general (cf also *Jew Enc*, art. "Barefoot"). All these passages seem to imply the discomfort of going barefoot on long journeys, over stony roads or hot sands; but then, as now, in the Orient sandals seem to have been little worn ordinarily in and around the house. See SHOES.

2. An Ancient Oriental Custom

The "shoes" of the ancients, as we know from many sources, were "sandals," i.e. simply soles, for the most part of rawhide, tied to the feet to protect them against the gravel, stones or thorns of the road. Shoes of the modern sort, as well as socks and stockings, were unknown. In ancient times it was certainly a common custom in Bible lands to go about in and around one's house without sandals. The peasantry, indeed, like the *fellaheen* of today, being hardened to it, often went afield barefoot. But for a king, or a prophet, a priest or a worshipper, to go barefoot, was another matter, as it was also for a mourner, for one in great distress, to be found walking the streets of a city, or going any distance in bare feet. Here we come again to customs peculiar to the Orient, and of various significance. For instance, it was considered then, as it is now in the Moslem world, profane and shocking, nothing short of a desecration, to enter a sanctuary, or walk on "holy ground," with dust-covered shoes, or unwashed feet. Moses and Joshua were commanded to take off their shoes when on "holy ground" (Ex **3** 5; Josh **5** 15). "No one was allowed to walk on the temple ground with shoes on, or with dust on his feet" (*Ber.*, IX, 5; cf Jamblichus, *Pythagoras*, § 105). No one in the East today is allowed to enter any mosque with shoes on, or without first putting slippers furnished for the purpose over his shoes. As a rule, too, the feet must be cleansed by ablution in every such case, as well as hands and feet before each meal.

3. Priests on Duty Went Barefoot

The priests of Israel, as would seem true of the priests in general among the ancients, wore no shoes when ministering (see *Silius Italicus*, III, 28; cf Theodoret on Ex **3**, *questio* 7; and *Yer. Shet.*, **5**, 48*d*). Anciently, certainly the priests of Israel, when going upon the platform to serve before the ark, in Tabernacle or temple, as later in the synagogue to bless the congregation, went barefoot; though today, strange to say, such ministering priests among the Jews wear stockings, and are not supposed to be barefoot (*Ṣōṭāh*, 40*a;* RH, 316; *Shulḥān 'Ārūkh*, *'Ōraḥ Ḥayyīm*, 128, 5; see *Jew Enc*, art. "Barefoot").

4. Reasons for the Ancient Custom

The reason or reasons for the removal of the shoes in such cases as the above, we are not at a loss to divine; but when it comes to the removal of the shoes in times of mourning, etc, opinions differ. Some see in such customs a trace of ancestor-worship; others find simply a reversion or return to primitive modes of life; while others still, in agreement with a widely prevalent Jewish view, suggest that it was adopted as a perfectly natural symbol of humility and simplicity of life, appropriate to occasions of grief, distress and deep solemnity of feeling.

The shoes are set aside now by many modern Jews on the Day of Atonement and on the Ninth of Ab.

LITERATURE.—Winer, *BR*, s.v. "Priester und Schuhe"; Riehm, *Handwörterbuch des bib. Alt.*, s.v. "Schuhe."

GEO. B. EAGER

BARHUMITE, bär-hū'mīt. See BAHARUMITE.

BARIAH, ba-rī'ah (בָּרִיחַ, *bārīaḥ*, "fugitive"): B. was a descendant of David in the line of Solomon (1 Ch **3** 22).

BAR-JESUS, bär-jē'zus (Βαριησοῦς, *Barīēsoús*): "A certain sorcerer [Gr *mágos*], a false prophet, a Jew" whom Paul and Silas found at Paphos in Cyprus in the train of Sergius Paulus, the Rom proconsul (Acts **13** 6 ff). The proconsul was "a man of understanding" (lit. a prudent or sagacious man), of an inquiring mind, interested in the thought and magic of his times. This characteristic explains the presence of a *magos* among his staff and his desire to hear Barnabas and Saul. Bar-Jesus was the magician's Jewish name. Elymas is said to be the interpretation of his name (ver 8). It is the Gr transliteration of an Aram. or Arab. word equivalent to Gr *magos*. From Arab. *'alama*, "to know" is derived *'alīm*, "a wise" or "learned man." In Ḳorān, Sur n. 106, Moses is called *Sāḥir 'alīm*, "wise magician." Elymas therefore means "sorcerer" (cf Simon "Magus").

The East was flooding the Rom Empire with its new and wonderful religious systems, which, culminating in neo-Platonism, were the great rivals of Christianity both in their cruder and in their more strictly religious forms. Superstition was extremely prevalent, and wonder-workers of all kinds, whether imposters or honest exponents of some new faith, found their task easy through the credulity of the public. Babylonia was the home of magic, for charms are found on the oldest tablets. "Magos" was originally applied to the priests of the Persians who overran Babylonia, but the title degenerated when it was assumed by baser persons for baser arts. Juvenal (vi.562, etc), Horace (*Sat.* i.2.1) and other Lat authors mention Chaldaean astrologers and impostors, probably Bab Jews. Many of the Magians, however, were the scientists of their day, the heirs of the science of Babylon and the lore of Persia, and not merely pretenders or conjurers (see MAGIC). It may have been as the representative of some oriental system, a compound of "science" and religion, that Bar-Jesus was attached to the train of Sergius Paulus.

Both Sergius and Elymas had heard about the teaching of the apostles, and this aroused the curiosity of Sergius and the fear of Elymas. When the apostles came, obedient to the command of the proconsul, their doctrine visibly produced on him a considerable impression. Fearing lest his position of influence and gain would be taken by the new teachers, Elymas "withstood them, seeking to turn aside the proconsul from the faith" (ver 8). Paul, inspired by the Holy Spirit, worked a wonder on the wonder-worker by striking him blind with his word, thus revealing to the proconsul that behind him was Divine power. Sergius Paulus believed, "being astonished at the teaching of the Lord" (ver 12).

S. F. HUNTER

BAR-JONAH, bär-jō'na (Βαρ-ιωνᾶς, *Bar-iōnás*): Simon Peter's patronymic (Mt **16** 17). Bar is Aram. for "son" (cf Bar-timaeus, Bartholomew, etc), and corresponds to Heb *bēn*. Thus we are to understand that Peter's father's name was Jonah. But in Jn **1** 42; **21** 15–17, according to the best reading, his name is given as John (so RV, instead of AV Jona, Jonas). There are two hypotheses to account for this difference: (1) *Iōnas* (Jonah) in Mt **16** 17 may be simply a contraction of *Iōanēs* (John); (2) Peter's father may have been known by two names, Jonah and John.

D. MIALL EDWARDS

BARKOS, bär'kos (בַּרְקוֹס, *barḳōş*, "party-colored" [?]; cf *HPN*, 68, n. 2): The descendants of B. returned with Zerubbabel to Jerus (Ezr **2** 53; Neh **7** 55). Cf Barchus (1 Esd **5** 32).

BARLEY, bär'li (שְׂעֹרָה, *seʽōrāh*):

(1) In the Bible, as in modern times, barley was a characteristic product of Pal—"a land of wheat and barley, and vines and fig-trees," etc (Dt **8** 8), the failure of whose crop was a national disaster (Joel **1** 11). It was, and is, grown chiefly as provender for horses and asses (1 K **4** 28), oats being practically unknown, but it was, as it now is, to some extent, the food of the poor in country districts (Ruth **2** 17; 2 K **4** 42; Jn **6** 9.13). Probably this is the meaning of the dream of the Midianite concerning Gideon: "Behold, I dreamed a dream; and, lo, a cake of barley bread tumbled into the camp of Midian, and came unto the tent, and smote it so that it fell, and turned it upside down, so that the tent lay flat. And his fellow answered and said, This is nothing else save the sword of Gideon, the son of Joash, a man of Israel" (Jgs **7** 13 f). Here the barley loaf is type of the peasant origin of Gideon's army and perhaps, too, of his own lowly condition.

Bringing Home the Barley Harvest.

Barley was (Ezk **4** 9) one of the ingredients from which the prophet was to make bread and "eat it as barley cakes" after having baked it under repulsive conditions (ver 12), as a sign to the people. The false prophetesses (Ezk **13** 19) are said to have profaned God among the people for "handfuls of barley and for pieces of bread."

Barley was also used in the Ordeal of Jealousy (s.v.). It was with five barley loaves and two fishes that Our Lord fed the five thousand (Jn **6** 9.10).

(2) Several varieties of barley are grown in Pal. The *Hordeum distichum* or two-rowed barley is probably the nearest to the original stock, but *Hordeum tetrastichum,* with grains in four rows, and *Hordeum hexastichum,* with six rows, are also common and ancient; the last is found depicted upon Egyp monuments.

Barley is always sown in the autumn, after the "early rains," and the barley harvest, which for any given locality precedes the wheat harvest (Ex **9** 31 f), begins near Jericho in April—or even March—but in the hill country of Pal is not concluded until the end of May or beginning of June.

The barley harvest was a well-marked season of the year (see Time) and the **barley-corn** was a well-known measure of length. See Weights and Measures. E. W. G. Masterman

BARN, bärn (מְגוּרָה, *meghūrāh,* "a granary," "fear," Hag **2** 19; אָסָם, *'āsām,* "a storehouse," Prov **3** 10; מַמְּגֻרָה, *mammeghūrāh,* "a repository," Joel **1** 17; ἀποθήκη, *apothḗkē,* Mt **6** 26; **13** 30; Lk **12** 18.24): A place for the storing of grain, usually a dry cistern in the ground, covered over with a thick layer of earth. "Grain is not stored in the East until it is threshed and winnowed. The *apothēkē* in Rom times was probably a building of some kind. But the immemorial usage of the East has been to conceal the grain, in carefully prepared pits or caves, which, being perfectly dry, will preserve it for years. It thus escaped, as far as possible, the attentions of the tax-gatherer as well as of the robber—not always easily distinguished in the East; cf Jer **41** 8" (*Temple Dictionary,* 215).

Figurative of heaven (Mt **13** 30). See Agriculture; Garner. M. O. Evans

BARNABAS, bär'na-bas (Βαρνάβας, *Barnábas,* "son of exhortation," or possibly "son of Nebo"): This name was applied to the associate of Paul, who was originally called Joses or Joseph (Acts **4** 36), as a testimony to his eloquence. Its lit. meaning is "son of prophecy" (*bar,* "son"; *nebhū'āh,* "prophecy"). Cf word for prophet in Gen **20** 7; Dt **18** 15.18, etc. This is interpreted in Acts **4** 36 as "son of exhortation" RV, or "son of consolation" AV, expressing two sides of the Gr *paráklēsis,* that are not exclusive. The office of a prophet being more than to foretell, all these interpretations are admissible in estimating Barnabas as a preacher. "Deismann (*Bibelstudien,* 175–78) considers Barnabas the Jewish Grecized form of Barnebous, a personal Sem name recently discovered in Asia Minor inscriptions, and meaning "son of Nebo" (*Standard BD* in loc.).

He was a Levite from the island of Cyprus, and cousin, not "nephew" (AV), of the evangelist Mark, the word *anépsios* (Col **4** 10), being used in Nu **36** 11, for "father's brothers' sons." When we first learn of him, he had removed to Jerus, and acquired property there. He sold "a field," and contributed its price to the support of the poorer members of the church (Acts **4** 36 ff). In Acts **11** 24 he is described as "a good man and full of the Holy Spirit" (cf Isa **11** 2; 1 Cor **12** 8.11) "and of faith," traits that gave him influence and leadership. Possibly on the ground of former acquaintanceship, interceding as Paul's sponsor and surety, he removed the distrust of the disciples at Jerus and secured the admission of the former persecutor into their fellowship. When the preaching of some of the countrymen of Barnabas had begun a movement toward Christianity among the Greeks at Antioch, Barnabas was sent from Jerus to give it encouragement and direction, and, after a personal visit, recognizing its importance and needs, sought out Paul at Tarsus, and brought him back as his associate. At the close of a year's successful work, Barnabas and Paul were sent to Jerus with contributions from the infant church for the famine sufferers in the older congregation (**11** 30). Ordained as missionaries on their return (**13** 3), and accompanied by John Mark, they proceeded upon what is ordinarily known as the "First Missionary Journey" of Paul (Acts **13** 4.5). Its history belongs to Paul's life. Barnabas as well as Paul is designated "an apostle" (Acts **14** 14). Up to Acts **13** 43, the precedency is constantly ascribed to Barnabas; from that point, except in **14** 14 and **15** 12.25, we read "Paul and Barnabas," instead of "Barnabas and Saul." The latter becomes the chief spokesman. The people at Lystra named Paul, because of his fervid oratory, Mercurius, while the quiet dignity and reserved strength of Barnabas gave him the title of Jupiter (Acts **14** 12). Barnabas escaped the violence which Paul suffered at Iconium (**14** 19).

Upon their return from this first missionary tour, they were sent, with other representatives of the church at Antioch, to confer with the apostles and elders of the church at Jerus concerning the obligation of circumcision and the ceremonial law in general under the NT—the synod of Jerus. A separation from Paul seems to begin with a temporary yielding of Barnabas in favor of the inconsistent course of Peter (Gal **2** 13). This was followed by a more serious rupture concerning Mark. On the second journey, Paul proceeded alone, while Barnabas and Mark went to Cyprus. Luther and Calvin regard 2 Cor **8** 18.19 as meaning Barnabas by "the brother whose praise is spread through all the churches," and indicating, therefore, subsequent joint work. The incidental allusions in 1 Cor **9** 6 and Gal **2** 13 ("even Barnabas") show at any rate Paul's continued appreciation of his former associate. Like Paul, he accepted no support from those to whom he ministered.

Tertullian, followed in recent years by Grau and Zahn, regard him as the author of the Epistle to the He. The document published among patristic writings as the Epistle of Barnabas, and found in full in the Codex Sinaiticus, is universally assigned today to a later period. "The writer nowhere claims to be the apostle Barnabas; possibly its author was some unknown namesake of 'the son of consolation'" (Lightfoot, *Apostolic Fathers*, 239 f). H. E. JACOBS

BARNABAS, EPISTLE OF. See APOCRYPHAL EPISTLES.

BARNABAS, GOSPEL OF. See APOCRYPHAL GOSPELS.

BARODIS, ba-rō′dis (**Βαρωδεΐς**, *Barōdeis*, 1 Esd **5** 34): The descendants of B. (sons of the servants of Solomon) returned with Zerubbabel to Jerus. Omitted in Ezr **2** and Neh **7**.

BARREL, bar′el: The word "barrel" in AV (see 1 K **17** 12.14.16; **18** 33: "The barrel of meal," "fill four barrels with water," etc) stands for the large earthenware jar (so ARV) used in the East for carrying water from the spring or well, and for storing grain, etc, according to a custom that still persists. It is elsewhere (EV) more fitly rendered "pitcher." See HOUSE; PITCHER, etc.

BARREN, bar′en, **BARRENNESS**, bar′en-nes (צִיָּה, *çīyāh;* מְלֵחָה, *m^elēḥāh;* שָׁכֹל, *shākhōl;* עָקָר, *'āḳār;* **στεῖρος**, *steíros;* **ἀργός**, *argós*):

(1) Of land that bears no crop, either (*a*) because it is naturally poor and sterile: *çīyāh* "dry" (Joel **2** 20), *m^elēḥāh*, "salt" (Job **39** 6 AV), *shākhōl*, "miscarrying" (2 K **2** 19.21), or (*b*) because it is, under God's curse, turned into a *m^elēḥāh* or salt desert, for the wickedness of the people that dwell therein (Ps **107** 34 AV; cf Gen **3** 17.18).

(2) Of females that bear no issue: *'āḳār:* Sarah (Gen **11** 30); Rebekah (**25** 21); Rachel (**29** 31); Manoah's wife (Jgs **13** 2.3); Hannah (1 S **2** 5); *steiros:* Elisabeth (Lk **1** 7.36).

In Israel and among oriental peoples generally barrenness was a woman's and a family's greatest misfortune. The highest sanctions of religion and patriotism blessed the fruitful woman, because children were necessary for the perpetuation of the tribe and its religion. It is significant that the mothers of the Heb race, Sarah, Rebekah and Rachel, were by nature sterile, and therefore God's special intervention shows His particular favor to Israel. Fruitfulness was God's special blessing to His people (Ex **23** 26; Dt **7** 14; Ps **113** 9). A complete family is an emblem of beauty (Cant **4** 2; **6** 6). Metaphorically, Israel, in her days of adversity, when her children were exiled, was barren, but in her restoration she shall rejoice in many children (Isa **54** 1; Gal **4** 27). The utter despair and terror of the destruction of Jerus could go no farther than that the barren should be called blessed (Lk **23** 29).

(3) *Argós* is tr^d in AV "barren," but in RV more accurately "idle" (2 Pet **1** 8). T. REES

BARSABAS, bär′sa-bas, **BARSABBAS**, bär-sab′-as. See JOSEPH BARSABBAS; JUDAS BARSABBAS.

BARTACUS, bär′ta-kus (**Βάρτακος**, *Bártakos;* Jos **'Ραβεζάκης**, *Rhabezákēs;* Vulg Bezazes [1 Esd **4** 29]): The father of Apame. He is called "the illustrious," probably because of rank and merits. The family seems to be of Pers origin since the name Bartacus (Syr ארטק) in the form of Artachaeas is mentioned by Herod. (vii.22.117) as a person of rank in the Pers army of Xerxes and the name of his daughter Apame is identical with that of a Pers princess who married Seleucus I, Nicator, and became the mother of Antiochus I. Apamea, a city in Asia Minor founded by Seleucus I, is named in honor of his wife Apame. Cf APAME; ILLUSTRIOUS.

BARTHOLOMEW, bär-thol′ō-mū (**Βαρθολομαῖος**, *Bartholomaíos*, i.e. "son of Tolmai or Talmai"): One of the Twelve Apostles (Mt **10** 3; Mk **3** 18; Lk **6** 14; Acts **1** 13). There is no further reference to him in the NT. According to the "Genealogies of the Twelve Apostles" (Budge, *Contendings of the Apostles*, II, 50) "Bartholomew was of the house of Naphtali. Now his name was formerly John, but Our Lord changed it because of John the son of Zebedee, His beloved." A "Gospel of Bartholomew" is mentioned by Hieronymus (*Comm. Proem ad Matth.*), and Gelasius gives the tradition that Bartholomew brought the Heb gospel of St. Matthew to India. In the "Preaching of St. Bartholomew in the Oasis" (cf Budge, II, 90) he is referred to as preaching probably in the oasis of Al Bahnâsâ, and according to the "Preaching of St. Andrew and St. Bartholomew" he labored among the Parthians (Budge, II, 183). The "Martyrdom of St. Bartholomew" states that he was placed in a sack and cast into the sea.

From the 9th cent. onward, Bartholomew has generally been identified with Nathanael, but this view has not been conclusively established. See NATHANAEL. C. M. KERR

BARTHOLOMEW, GOSPEL OF. See APOCRYPHAL GOSPELS; BARTHOLOMEW.

BARTIMAEUS, bär-ti-mē′us (**Βαρτίμαιος**, *Bartimaios*): A hybrid word from Aram. *bar* = "son," and Gr *timaios* = "honorable." For the improbability of the derivation from *bar-tim'ai* = "son of the unclean," and of the allegorical meaning = the Gentiles or spiritually blind, see Schmiedel in *EB*. In Mk (**10** 46–52) Bartimaeus is given as the name of a blind beggar, whose eyes Jesus Christ opened as He went out from Jericho on His last journey to Jerus. An almost identical account is given by Lk (**18** 35–43), except that the incident occurred "as he drew nigh unto Jericho," and the name of the blind man is not given. Again, according to Mt (**20** 29–34), "as they went out from Jericho" (like Mk) *two* blind men (unlike Mk and Lk) receive their sight. It is not absolutely impossible that two or even three events are recorded, but so close is the similarity of the three accounts that it is highly improbable. Regarding them as referring to the same event, it is easy to understand how the discrepancies arose in the passage of the story from mouth to mouth. The main incident is clear enough, and on purely historical grounds, the miracle cannot be denied. The discrepancies themselves are evidence of the wide currency of the story before our Gospels assumed their present form. It is only a most mechanical theory of inspiration that would demand their harmonization.

T. Rees

BARUCH, bā'ruk, bâr'uk (בָּרוּךְ, *bārūk;* **Βαρούχ,** *Baroúch,* "blessed"):

(1) Son of Neriah and brother of Seraiah, King Zedekiah's chamberlain (Jer **51** 59). He was the devoted friend (Jer **32** 12), the amanuensis (**36** 4 ff.32) and faithful attendant (**36** 10 ff; Jos, *Ant,* X, vi, 2) of the prophet Jeremiah. He seems to have been of noble family (see *Ant,* X, ix, 1; cf Jer **51** 59; Bar **1** 1). He was also according to Jos a man of unusual acquirements (*Ant,* X, ix, 1). He might have risen to a high position and seemed conscious of this, but under Jeremiah's influence (see Jer **45** 5) he repressed his ambition, being content to throw in his lot with the great prophet whose secretary and companion he became. Jeremiah dictated his prophecies to Baruch, who read them to the people (Jer **36**). The king (Jehoiakim) was greatly angered at these prophecies and had Baruch arrested and the roll burnt. Baruch however rewrote the prophet's oracles. In the final siege of Jerus Baruch stood by his master, witnessing the purchase by the latter of his ancestral estate in Anathoth (Jer **32**). According to Jos (*Ant,* X, ix, 1) he continued to reside with Jeremiah at Mizpah after the fall of Jerus. Subsequent to the murder of Gedaliah, he was accused of having unduly influenced Jeremiah when the latter urged the people to remain in Judah—a fact which shows how great was the influence which Baruch was believed to have had over his master (Jer **43** 3). He was carried with Jeremiah to Egypt (Jer **43** 6; *Ant,* X, ix, 6), and thereafter our knowledge of him is merely legendary. According to a tradition preserved by Jerome (on Isa **30** 6 f) he died in Egypt soon after reaching that country. Two other traditions say that he went, or by Nebuchadnezzar was carried, to Babylon after this king conquered Egypt. The high character of Baruch and the important part he played in the life and work of Jeremiah induced later generations still further to enhance his reputation, and a large number of spurious writings passed under his name, among them the following: (*a*) The Apocalypse of Baruch (q.v.); (*b*) the Book of Baruch; (*c*) the Rest of the Words of Baruch; (*d*) the gnostic Book of Baruch; (*e*) the Lat Book of Baruch, composed originally in Lat; (*f*) a Gr Apocalypse of Baruch belonging to the 2d cent. of our era; (*g*) another Book of Baruch belonging to the 4th or 5th cent.

(2) A son of Zabbai who aided Nehemiah in rebuilding the walls of Jerus (Neh **3** 20).

(3) One of the priests who signed the covenant with Nehemiah (**10** 6).

(4) The son of Colhozeh, a descendant of Perez, the son of Judah (Neh **11** 5).

T. Witton Davies

BARUCH, APOCALYPSE OF. See Apocalyptic Literature.

BARUCH, BOOK OF: One of the Apocryphal or Deutero-canonical books, standing between Jer and Lam in the LXX, but in the Vulg after these two books.

I. Name.—See under Baruch for the meaning of the word and for the history of the best-known Bib. personage bearing the name. Though Jewish traditions link this book with Jeremiah's amanuensis and loyal friend as author, it is quite certain that it was not written or compiled for hundreds of years after the death of this Baruch. According to Jer **45** 1 it was in the 4th year (604 BC) of the reign of Jehoiakim (608–597 BC) that Baruch wrote down Jeremiah's words in a book and read them in the ears of the nobles (EV "princes," but king's sons are not necessarily meant; Jer **36**). The Book of Baruch belongs in its present form to the latter half of the 1st cent. of our era; yet some modern Roman Catholic scholars vigorously maintain that it is the work of Jeremiah's friend and secretary.

II. Contents.—This book and also the Epistle of Jeremy have closer affinities with the canonical Book of Jer than any other part of the Apoc. It is probably to this fact that they owe their name and also their position in the LXX and in the Vulg. The book is apparently made up of four separate parts by independent writers, brought together by an R, owing it is very likely to a mere accident —each being too small to occupy the space on one roll they were all four written on one and the same roll. The following is a brief analysis of the four portions of the book:

1. Historical Introduction

Historical Introduction, giving an account of the origin and purpose of the book (**1** 1–14). Vs 1 f tell us that Baruch wrote this book at Babylon "in the fifth month [not "year" as LXX], in the seventh day of the month, what time as the Chaldeans took Jerus, and burnt it with fire" (see 2 K **25** 8 ff). Fritzsche and others read: "In the fifth year, in the month Sivan [see ver 8], in the seventh day of the month," etc. Um gives the date of the feast Pentecost, and the supposition is that the party who made a pilgrimage to Jerus did so in order to observe that feast. According to vs 3–14, Baruch read his book to King Jehoiachin and his court by the (unidentified) river Sud. King and people on hearing the book fell to weeping, fasting and praying. As a result money was collected and sent, together with Baruch's book, to the high priest Jehoiakim,[1] to the priests and to the people at Jerus. The money is to be used in order to make it possible to carry on the services of the temple, and in particular that prayers may be offered in the temple for the king and his family and also for the superior lord King Nebuchadnezzar and his son Baltasar (= the Belshazzar of Dnl **5**).

2. Confession and Prayer

Confession and prayer (**1** 15—**3** 8) (1) of the Palestinian remnant (**1** 15—**2** 15). The speakers are resident in Judah not in Babylon (ver 15; cf **2** 4), as J. T. Marshall and R. H. Charles rightly hold. This section follows throughout the arrangement and phraseology of a prayer contained in Dnl **9** 7–15. It is quite impossible to think of Dnl as being based on Bar, for the writer of the former is far more original than the author or authors of Bar. But in the present section the original passage in Dnl is altered in a very significant way. Thus in Dnl (**9** 7) the writer describes those for whom he wrote as 'the men of Judah and the inhabitants of Jerus *and all Israel*[*ites*]*: those near and those far off, in all the lands* [*countries*] *whither thou hast driven them on account of their unfaithfulness toward thee.*' The italicized words are omitted from Bar **1** 15, though the remaining part of Dnl **9** 7 is added. Why this difference? It is evident, as Marshall has ably pointed out, that the R of the section intends to put the confession and prayer of **1** 15—**2** 5 into the mouths of Jews who had not been removed into exile. Ewald (*History,* V, 208, 6) holds that Dnl **9** 7–9 is dependent on Bar **1** 15—**2** 17. The section may thus be analyzed:

(*a*) **1** 15–22: Confession of the sins of the nation from the days of Moses down to the exile. The

[1] So spelt in the canonical books; but it is Joacim or Joachim in Apoc AV, and in the Apoc RV it is invariably Joakim.

principle of solidarity (see *Century Bible*, "Psalms," II, **21**, **195**, **215**) so governed the thoughts of the ancient Israelites that the iniquities of their forefathers were in effect their own.

(*b*) **2** 1–5: God's righteous judgment on the nation in humbling and scattering them.

Confession and prayer (2) of the exiles in Babylon **2** 16—**3** 8. That the words in this section are supposed to be uttered by Bab exiles appears from **2** 13 f; **3** 7 f and from the general character of the whole. This portion of the book is almost as dependent on older Scriptures as the foregoing. Three sources seem in particular to have been used.

(*a*) The Book of Jer has been freely drawn upon.

(*b*) Deuteronomic phrases occur frequently, esp. in the beginning and end. These are perhaps taken second-hand from Jer, a book well known to the author of these verses and deeply loved by him.

(*c*) Solomon's prayer as recorded in 1 K **8** is another quarry from which our author appears to have dug.

This section may be thus divided:

(*α*) **2** 6–12: Confession, opening as the former (see **1** 15) with words extracted from Dnl **9** **7**.

(*β*) **2** 13—**3** 8: Prayer for restoration.

3 1–8 shows more independence than the rest, for the author at this point makes use of language not borrowed from any original known to us. As such these verses are important as a clue to the writer's position, views and character.

In **3** 4 we have the petition: "Hear now the prayer of the dead Israelites," etc, words which as they stand involve the doctrine that the dead (Solomon, Daniel, etc) are still alive and make intercession to God on behalf of the living. But this teaching is in opposition to **2** 17 which occurs in the same context. Without making any change in the Heb consonants we can and should read for "dead [*mēthē*] Israelites" "the men of [*m*ᵉ*thē*] Israel." The LXX confuses the same words in Isa **5** 13.

3. The Praise of Wisdom

The praise of "Wisdom," for neglecting which Israel is now in a strange land. God alone is the author of wisdom, and He bestows it not upon the great and mighty of this world, but upon His own chosen people, who however have spurned the Divine gift and therefore lost it (**3** 9—**4** 4).

The passage, **3** 10–13 (Israel's rejection of "Wisdom" the cause of her exile), goes badly with the context and looks much like an interpolation. The dominant idea in the section is that God has made Israel superior to all other nations by the gift of "wisdom," which is highly extolled. Besides standing apart from the context these four verses lack the rhythm which characterize the other verses. What is so cordially commended is described in three ways, each showing up a different facet, as do the eight synonyms for the Divine word in each of the 22 strophes in Ps **119** (see *Century Bible*, "Psalms," **II**, **254**).

(1) It is called most frequently "Wisdom."

(2) In **4** 1 it is described as the Commandments of God and as the Law or more correctly as authoritative instruction. The Heb word for this last (*tōrāh*) bears in this connection, it is probable, the technical meaning of the Pent, a sense which it never has in the OT. Cf Dt **4** 6, where the keeping of the commandments is said to be "wisdom" and understanding.

4. The Dependence of This Wisdom Section

(1) The line of thought here resembles closely that pursued in Job **28**, which modern scholars rightly regard as a later interpolation. Wisdom, the most valuable of possessions, is beyond the unaided reach of man. God only can give it—that is what is taught in these parts of both Bar and Job with the question "Where shall wisdom be found?" (Job **28** 12; cf Bar **3** 14 f, where a similar question forms the basis of the greater portion of the section of Job **38** f). Wisdom is not here as in Prov hypostatized, and the same is true of Job **28**. This in itself is a sign of early date, for the personifying of "wisdom" is a later development (cf Philo, John **1**).

(2) The language in this section is modeled largely on that of Dt, perhaps however through Jer, which is also esp. after ch **10** Deuteronomic in thought and phraseology. See ante II, 2 (**2** 1*b*).

The most original part of this division of the book is where the writer enumerates the various classes of the world's great ones to whom God had not given "wisdom": princes of the heathen, wealthy men, silversmiths, merchants, theologians, philosophers, etc (**3** 16 ff). See WISDOM.

5. Words of Cheer to Israel

The general thought that pervades the section, **4** 5—**5** 9, is words of cheer to Israel (i.e. Judah) in exile, but we have here really, according to Rothstein, a compilation edited so skilfully as to give it the appearance of a unity which is not real. Earlier Bib. writings have throughout been largely drawn upon. Rothstein (Kautzsch, *Die Apokryphen*, etc, 213–15) divides the section in the following manner:

(1) **4** 5–9*a*: Introductory section, giving the whole its keynote—"Be of good cheer," etc; **4** 7 f follows Dt **32** 15–18.

(2) **4** 9*b*–29: A song, divisible into two parts.

(*a*) Personified Jerus deplores the calamities of Israel in exile (vs 9*b*–16).

(*b*) She urges her unfortunate children to give themselves to hope and prayer, amending their ways so that God may bring about their deliverance (vs 17–29).

(*c*) **4** 30—**5** 9: A second song, beginning as the first with the words, "Be of good cheer," and having the same general aim, to comfort exiled and oppressed Israel.

In all three parts earlier Scriptures have been largely used, and in particular Deutero-Isaiah has had much influence upon the author. But there do not seem to the present writer reasons cogent enough for concluding, with Rothstein, that these three portions are by as many different writers. There is throughout the same recurring thought "Be of good cheer," and there is nothing in the style to suggest divergent authorship.

(3) The relation between **4** 36—**5** 9 and Ps Sol **11**. It was perhaps Ewald (*Geschichte*, IV, 498) who first pointed out the similarity of language and viewpoint between Bar **4** 36—**5** 9 and Ps Sol **11**, esp. **11** 3–8. The only possible explanation is that which makes Bar **4** 36 ff an imitation of Ps Sol **11**. So Ewald (op. cit.); Ryle and James (Ps Sol, lxx, ii ff).

Ps Sol were written originally in Heb, and references to Pompey (d. 48 BC) and to the capture of Jerus (63 BC) show that this pseudepigraphical Psalter must have been written in the first half of the 1st cent. BC. Bar, as will be shown, is of much later date than this. Besides it is now almost certain that the part of Bar under discussion was written in Gr (see below, IV) and that it never had a Heb original. Now it is exceedingly unlikely that a writer of a Heb psalm would copy a Gr original, though the contrary supposition is a very likely one.

On the other hand A. Geiger (*Psalt. Sol.*, XI, 137–39, 1811), followed by W. B. Stevenson (*Temple Bible*), and many others argue for the priority of Bar, using this as a reason for giving Bar an earlier date than is usually done. It is possible, of course, that the Pseudo-Solomon and the Pseudo-Baruch have been digging in the same quarry; and that the real original used by both is lost.

III. Language.—For our present purpose the book must be divided into two principal parts: (1) **1**—**3** 8; (2) **3** 9—**5** 9. There is general agreement among the best recent scholars from Ewald downward that the first portion of the book at least was written originally in Heb. (1) In the Syro-Hex. text there are margin notes to **1** 17 and **2** 3 to the effect that these verses are lacking in the Heb, i.e. in the original Heb text.

(2) There are many linguistic features in this first part which are best explained on the supposition that the Gr text is from a Heb original. In **2** 25 the LXX EV *apostolē* at the end of the verse means "a sending of." The EV ("pestilence") renders a Heb word which, without the vowel signs (introduced late) is written alike for both meanings (*dbr*). The mistake can be explained only on the assumption of a Heb original. Similarly the reading "dead Israelites" for "men of Israel" (=Israelites) in **3** 4 arose through reading wrong vowels with the same consonants, which last were alone written until the 7th and 8th cents. of our era.

Frequently, as in Heb, sentences begin with Gr *kaí* (="and") which, without somewhat slavish copying of the Heb, would not be found. The construction called *parataxis* characterizes Heb; in good Gr we meet with *hypotaxis*.

The Heb way of expressing "where" is put lit. into the Gr of this book (**2** 4.13.29; **3** 8). Many other Heb idioms, due, it is probable, to the translator's imitations of his original, occur: in "to speak in the ears of" (**1** 3); the word "man" (*anthrōpos*) in the sense "everyone" (**2** 3); "spoken by thy servants the prophets" is in Gr by "the hand of the servants," which is good Heb but bad Gr. Many other such examples could be added.

There is much less agreement among scholars as to the original language or languages of the second part of the book (**3** 9—**5** 9). That this part too was written in Heb, so that in that case the whole book appeared first in that language, is the position held and defended by Ewald (op. cit.), Kneucker (op. cit.), König (*Ein*), Rothstein (op. cit.) and Bissell (Lange). It is said by these writers that this second part of Bar equally with the first carries with it marks of being a tr from the Heb. But one may safely deny this statement. It must be admitted by anyone who has examined the text of the book that the most striking Hebraisms and the largest number of them occur in the first part of the book. Bissell writes quite fully and warmly in defense of the view that the whole book was at first written in Heb, but the Hebraisms which he cites are all with one solitary exception taken from the first part of the book. This one exception is in **4** 15 where the Gr conjunction *hóti* is used for the relative *hó*, the Heb *'ăsher* having the meaning of both. There seems to be a Hebraism in **4** 21: "He shall deliver thee from . . . . *the hand of your* enemies," and there are probably others. But there are Hebraisms in Hellenistic Gr always—the present writer designates them "Hebraisms" or "Semiticisms" notwithstanding what Deismann, Thumb and Moulton say. In the first part of this book it is their overwhelming number and their striking character that tell so powerfully in favor of a Heb original.

(3) The following writers maintain that the second part of the book was written first of all in Gr: Fritzsche, Hilgenfeld, Reuss, Schürer, Gifford, Cornill and R. H. Charles, though they agree that the first part had a Heb original. This is probably the likeliest view, though much may be written in favor of a Heb original for the whole book and there is nothing quite decisively against it. J. Turner Marshall (*HDB*, I, 253) tries to prove that **3** 9—**4** 4 was written first in Aram., the rest of the book (**4** 5—**5** 9) in Gr. But though he defends his case with great ability he does not appear to the present writer to have proved his thesis. Ewald (op. cit.), Hitzig (*Psalmen*², II, 119), Dillmann, Ruetschi, Fritzsche and Bissell were so greatly impressed by the close likeness between the Gr of Bar and that of the LXX of Jer, that they came to the conclusion that both books were trᵈ by the same person. Subsequently Hitzig decided that Bar was not written until after 70 AD, and therefore abandoned his earlier opinion in favor of this one—that the translator of Bar was well acquainted with the LXX of Jer and was strongly influenced by it.

IV. Date or Dates.—It is important to distinguish between the date of the completion of the entire book in its present form and the dates of the several parts which in some or all cases may be much older than that of the whole as such.

1. The Historical Introduction

1 1-14 was written after the completion of the book expressly to form a prologue or historical explanation of the circumstances under which the rest of the book came to be written. To superficial readers it could easily appear that the whole book was written by one man, but a careful examination shows that the book is a compilation. One may conclude that the introduction was the last part of the book to be composed and that therefore its date is that of the completion of the book. Reasons will be given (see below) for believing that **4** 5—**5** 9 belongs to a time subsequent to the destruction of Jerus and its temple in 70 AD. This is still more true of this introduction intended as a foreword to the whole book.

2. Confession and Prayer

The following points bear on the date of the section **1** 15—**3** 8, assuming it to have one date:

(1) The generation of Israelites to which the writer belonged were suffering for the sins of their ancestors; see esp. **3** 1-8.

(2) The second temple was in existence in the writer's day. **2** 26 must (with the best scholars) be trᵈ as follows: "And thou hast made the house over which thy name is called as it is this day," i.e. the temple—still in being—is shorn of its former glory. Moreover though Dnl **9** 7-14 is largely quoted in **1** 15—**2** 12, the prayer for the sanctuary and for Jerus in Dnl **9** 16 is omitted, because the temple is not now in ruins.

(3) Though it is implied (see above II, 2, [1]) that there are Jews in Judah who have never left their land there are a large number in foreign lands, and nothing is said that they were servants of the Bab king.

(4) The dependence of **2** 13—**3** 8 on Dt, Jer and 1 K **8** (Solomon's prayer) shows that this part of the book is later than these writings, i.e. later than say 550 BC. Cf **2** 13 with Dt **28** 62 and Jer **42** 2.

(5) The fact that Dnl **9** 7-14 has influenced Bar **1** 15—**2** 12 proves that a date later than Dnl must be assumed for at least this portion of Bar. The temple is still standing, so that the book belongs somewhere between 165 BC, when Dnl was written, and 71 AD, when the temple was finally destroyed.

Ewald, Gifford and Marshall think that this section belongs to the period following the conquest of Jerus by Ptolemy I (320 BC). According to Ewald the author of **1** 1—**3** 8 (regarded as by one hand) was a Jew living in Babylon or Persia. But Dnl had not in 320 BC been written. Fritzsche, Schrader, Keil, Toy and Charles assign the section to the Maccabean age—a quite likely date. On the other hand Hitzig, Kneucker and Schürer prefer a date subsequent to 70 AD. The last writer argues for the unity of this section, though he admits that the middle of ch **1** comports ill with its context.

It has been pointed out (see above, II, 3) that **3** 10–13 does not belong to this section, being manifestly a later interpolation.

3. The Wisdom Section 3:9—4:4

The dependence of this Wisdom portion on Job **28** and on Dt implies a post-exilic date. The identification of Wisdom with the Torah which is evidently a synonym for the Pent, argues a date at any rate not earlier than 300 BC. But how much later we have no means of ascertaining. The reasons adduced by Kneucker and Marshall for a date immediately before or soon after the fall of Jerus in 70 AD have not convinced the present writer.

The situation implied in these words may be thus set forth:

4. Words of Cheer 4:5—5:9

(1) A great calamity has happened to Jerus (**4** 9 f). Nothing is said proving that the whole land has shared the calamity, unless indeed this is implied in **4** 5 f.

(2) A large number of Jerusalemites have been transported (**4** 10).

(3) The nation that has sacked Jerus and carried away many of its inhabitants is "shameless," having "a strange language, neither reverencing old men nor pitying children" (**4** 15).

(4) The present home of the Jerusalemites is a great city (**4** 32–35), not the country.

Now the above details do not answer to any dates in the history of the nation except these two: (*a*) 586 BC, when the temple was destroyed by the Babylonians; (*b*) 71 AD, when the temple was finally destroyed by the Romans. But the date 586 BC is out of the question, and no modern scholar pleads for it. We must therefore assume for this portion of the book a date soon after 70 AD. In the time of Pompey, to which Graetz assigns the book, neither Jerus nor the temple was destroyed. Nor was there any destruction of either during the Maccabean war. In favor of this date is the dependence of **4** 36 ff on Ps Sol **11** (see above, II, 5, [3]).

Rothstein (in Kautzsch) says that in this section there are at least three parts by as many different writers. Marshall argues for four independent parts. But if either of these views is correct the R has done his work exceedingly well, for the whole harmonizes well together.

Kneucker, author of the fullest Commentary, endeavors to prove that the original book consisted of **1** 1 f+3*a* (the heading) +**3** 9—**5** 9, and that it belongs to the reign of Domitian (81–96 AD). The confession and prayer in **1** 15—**3** 8 were written, he says, somewhat earlier and certainly before 71 AD, and as a separate work, being inserted in the book by the scribe who wrote **1** 4–14.

V. Versions.—The most important VSS are the following. It is assumed in the article that the Gr text of the book up to **3** 8 is itself a tr from a Heb text now lost. The same remark may be true of the rest of the book or of a portion of it (see above, III).

There are two versions in this language: (1) The Vulg which is really the Old Lat, since Jerome's

1. Latin

revision was confined to the Heb Scriptures, the Apoc being therefore omitted in this revision. This version is a very lit. one based on the Gr. It is therefore for that reason the more valuable as a witness to the Gr text. (2) There is a later Lat tr, apparently a revision of the former, for its Latinity is better; in some cases it adopts different readings and in a general way it has been edited so as to bring it into harmony with the Vatican uncial (B). This Lat version was published in Rome by J. Maria Caro (a. cir 1688) and was reprinted by Sabatier in parallel columns with the pre-Jeromian version noticed above (see *Bibliotheca Casinensis*, I, 1873).

There are also in this language two extant versions: (1) The Pesh, a very lit. tr, can be seen in

2. Syriac

the London (Walton's) *Polyglot* and most conveniently in Lagarde's *Libr. Apoc. Syr.*, the last being a more accurate reproduction. (2) The Hexap. Syr tr made by Paul, bishop of Telle, near the beginning of the 7th cent. AD. It has been published by Ceriani with critical apparatus in his beautiful photograph-lithographed edition of the Hexap. Syr Bible.

3. Arabic

There is a very literal tr to be found in the London *Polyglot*, referred to above.

Literature.—For editions of the Gr text see under Apocrypha. Of commentaries the fullest and best is that by Kneucker, *Das Buch Baruch* (1879), who gives an original German rendering based on a restored Heb original. Other valuable commentaries are those by Fritzsche (1851); Ewald, *Die Propheten²*, etc (1868), III, 251–82 (Eng. tr); *The Prophets of the OT*, V, 108–37, by Reusch (1855); Zöckler (1891) and Rothstein (op. cit.); and in Eng., Bissell (in Lange's series edited by D. S. Schaff, 1880); and Gifford (*Speaker's Comm.*, 1888). The S.P.C.K. has a handy and serviceable volume published in the series of popular commentaries on the OT. But this commentary, though published quite recently (my copy belongs to 1894, "nineteenth thousand"), needs strengthening on the side of its scholarship.

Arts. dealing with introduction occur in the various Bible Dictionaries (*DB*, Westcott and Ryle; *HDB*, J. T. Marshall, able and original; *EB*, Bevan, rather slight). To these must be added excellent arts. in *Jew Enc* (G. F. Moore), and *EB* (R. H. Charles).

T. Witton Davies

BARZILLAI, bär-zil'ā-ī, bär-zil'ī (בַּרְזִלַּי, *bārzillay;* **Βερζελλί,** *Berzelli*, "man of iron" [*BDB*, but cf Cheyne, *EB*]):

(1) A Gileadite of Rogelim who brought provisions to David and his army to Mahanaim, in their flight from Absalom (2 S **17** 27–29). When David was returning to Jerus after Absalom's defeat, B. conducted him over Jordan, but being an old man of 80 years of age, he declined David's invitation to come to live in the capital, and sent instead his son Chimham (2 S **19** 31–39). David before his death charged Solomon to "show kindness unto the sons of B." (1 K **2** 7). Cheyne in *EB*, without giving any reason, differentiates this B. from B. the Gileadite (Ezr **2** 61=Neh **7** 63). See (2) below.

(2) The father of a family of priests who in Ezra's time, after the return of the exiles, could not trace their genealogy. "Therefore were they deemed polluted and put from the priesthood." This B. had taken "a wife of the daughters of B. the Gileadite," and had adopted his wife's family name (Ezr **2** 61.62=Neh **7** 63.64). His original name is given as Jaddus (AV Addus) (1 Esd **5** 38). (See Zorzelleus; RVm "Phaezeldaeus.")

(3) B. the Meholathite, whose son Adriel was married to Saul's daughter, either Michal (2 S **21** 8) or Merab (1 S **18** 19). T. Rees

BASALOTH, bas'a-loth (A, **Βααλώθ,** *Baalōth;* B, **Βασαλέμ,** *Basalém;* 1 Esd **5** 31=Bazluth [Ezr **2** 52] and Bazlith [Neh **7** 54]): The descendants of B. (temple-servants) returned with Zerubbabel to Jerus.

BASCAMA, bas'ka-ma (**Βασκαμά,** *Baskamá* [1 Macc **13** 23]): A town located in the country of Gilead, where Tryphon slew Jonathan, the son of Absalom. Cf Jonathan (Apoc).

BASE, bās:

(1) Subst. from Lat *basis*, Gr **βάσις,** *básis*, a foundation. (*a*) (מְכוֹנָה, *mekhōnāh*): the fixed resting-place on which the lavers in Solomon's temple were set (1 K **7** 27–43; 2 K **16** 17; **25** 13. 16; 2 Ch **4** 14; Jer **27** 19; **52** 17.20; cf Ezr **3** 3; Zec **5** 11 ARVm). (*b*) (כֵּן, *kēn*): pedestal in AV and RV (1 K **7** 29.31) and in RV only (Ex **30** 18. 28; **31** 9; **35** 16; **38** 8; **39** 39; **40** 11; Lev **8** 11) of

the base of the laver of the tabernacle (AV "foot").
(c) (יָרֵךְ, yārēkh): "base of candlestick" (RV of Ex
25 31; 37 17) AV "shaft." (d) (יְסוֹד, yᵉṣōdh):
RV "base of altar"; AV "bottom" (Ex 29 12; 38
8; Lev 4 7.18.25.30.34; 5 9; 8 15; 9 9). (e) (גַּב,
gabh): RV "elevation," i.e. basement of altar; AV
"higher place" (Ezk 43 13).

(2) Adj. from Fr. bas—low, or Welsh bâs—
"shallow": of lowly birth or station, of voluntary
humility and of moral depravity. (a) (שָׁפָל,
shāphāl, שָׁפֵל, shᵉphal): of David's self-humiliation
(2 S 6 22): "a modest unambitious kingdom"
(Ezk 17 14; 29 14.15 [BDB]; Dnl 4 17 [ARV
"lowest"]): cf shᵉphēlāh = "lowland." (b) (קָלָה,
ḳālāh): men of humble birth and station as opposed
to the nobles (Isa 3 5). (c) (בְּלִי־שֵׁם, bᵉlī-shēm):
"nameless," "of no account": "children of fools,
yea, children of base men" (Job 30 8). (d) AV men,
sons, daughters, children of Belial; lit. "worthless
persons"; in ARV "base," except 1 S 1 16 "wicked
woman"; also ERV of Dt 13 13, "base," which
elsewhere retains AV rendering. (e) (ταπεινός, ta-
peinós): "lowly," "humble or abject" (2 Cor 10 1);
RV, "lowly"; so Paul's enemies said he appeared
when present in the church at Corinth. (f) (ἀγενής,
agenḗs): "of low birth," "of no account" (1 Cor
1 28): "base things of the world." (g) (ἀγοραῖος,
agoraíos): "belonging to the market-place," loafers,
worthless characters (Acts 17 5): "certain lewd
fellows of the baser sort"; RV "certain vile fellows
of the rabble."   T. Rees

BASEMATH, bas'ĕ-math, BASHEMATH, bash'-
ĕ-math, BASMATH, bas'math (בָּשְׂמַת, bāsᵉmath,
"fragrant"):
(1) Basemath, one of the wives of Esau, a
daughter of Elon, the Hittite (Gen 26 34; AV
Bashemath), probably identical with or a sister
of Adah whom he also married (Gen 36 2). Cf
Adah.
(2) Basemath (AV Bashemath), another wife
of Esau, a daughter of Ishmael and a sister of Nebaioth (Gen 36 3.4.10.13.17). This wife is also
called Mahalath (Gen 28 9), and is of the house
of Abraham. Esau married her because his father
was not pleased with his other wives who were
daughters of Canaan. Cf Mahalath.
(2) Basemath (AV Basmath), the daughter of
Solomon, and wife of Ahimaaz, a commissariat-
officer in the service of Solomon (1 K 4 15).
                                         A. L. Breslich

BASHAN, bā'shan (הַבָּשָׁן, ha-bāshān, "the
Bashan"; Βασάν, Basán): This name is probably
                      the same in meaning as the cognate
1. Bound-   Arab. bathneh, "soft, fertile land,"
aries   or bathaniyeh (batanaea), "this land
                      sown with wheat" ("wheatland").
It often occurs with the art., "the Bashan," to
describe the kingdom of Og, the most northerly
part of the land E. of the Jordan. It stretched
from the border of Gilead in the S. to the slopes of
Hermon in the N. Hermon itself is never definitely
included in Bashan, although Og is said to have
ruled in that mountain (Josh 12 5; 13 11). In
Dt 3 10 Salecah and Edrei seem to indicate the E.
and W. limits respectively. This would agree with
Josh 12 5; 13 11, which seem to make Geshur
and Maacath the western boundary of Bashan.
If this were so, then these unconquered peoples
literally "dwelt in the midst of Israel." On the
other hand Dt 4 47 may mean that the Jordan
formed the western boundary; while Dt 33 22
makes Bashan extend to the springs of the Jordan.
If Golan lay in the district in which its name is
still preserved (el Jaulān), this also brings it to the lip

of the Jordan valley (Dt 4 43). "A mountain of
summits," or "protuberances" (Ps 68 15.16: Heb),
might describe the highlands of the Jaulan, with
its many volcanic hills as seen from the W. "A
mountain of God" however does not so well apply
to this region. Perhaps we should, with Wetz-
stein (Das batanäische Giebelgebirge) take these
phrases as descriptive of Jebel Ḥaurān, now usually
called Jebel ed-Druze, with its many striking summits. This range protected the province from en-
croachment by the sands of the wilderness from the
E. On the S. Bashan marched with the desert
steppe, el-Ḥamād, and Gilead. Of the western
boundary as we have seen there can be no certainty.
It is equally impossible to draw any definite line
in the N.
Bashan thus included the fertile, wooded slopes
of Jebel ed-Druze, the extraordinarily rich plain of
                      el-Ḥaurān (en-Nuḳrah—see Hauran),
2. Charac- the rocky tract of el-Leja', the region
teristics   now known as el-Jēdūr, resembling the
Ḥaurān in character, but less cultivated; and, perhaps, the breezy uplands of el-
Jaulān, with its splendid reaches of pasture land.
It was a land rich in great cities, as existing ruins
sufficiently testify. It can hardly be doubted that
many of these occupy sites of great antiquity. We
may specially note Ashtaroth and Edrei, the cities
of Og; Golan, the city of refuge, the site of which
is still in doubt; and Salecah (Ṣalkhad), the fortress
on the ridge of the mountain, marking the extreme
eastern limit of Israel's possessions.
The famous oaks of Bashan (Isa 2 13; Ezk
27 6) have their modern representatives on the
mountain slopes. It seems strange that in Scripture there is no notice of the wheat crops for which
the country is in such repute today. Along with
Carmel it stood for the fruitfulness of the land
(Isa 33 9 etc); and their languishing was an evident mark of God's displeasure (Nah 1 4). The
"bulls of Bashan" represent blatant and brutal
strength (Ps 22 12, etc). It is long since the lion
deserted the plateau (Dt 33 22); but the leopard
is still not unknown among the mountains (Cant
4 8).
In pre-Israelite days Bashan was ruled by Og
the Amorite. His defeat at Edrei marked the end
                      of his kingdom (Nu 21 33 ff; Josh
3. History 13 11), and the land was given to the
                      half tribe of Manasseh (Josh 13 30,
etc). In the Syrian wars Bashan was lost to Israel
(1 K 22 3 ff; 2 K 8 28; 10 32 f), but it was regained by Jeroboam II (2 K 14 25). It was incorporated in the Assyr empire by Tiglath-pileser
III (2 K 15 29). In the 2d cent. BC it was in
the hands of the Nabataeans. It formed part of
the kingdom of Herod the Great, and then belonged
to that of Philip and Agrippa II.   W. Ewing

BASHAN-HAVVOTH-JAIR, bā'shan-hav'oth-
jā'ir (בָּשָׁן חַוֹּת יָאִיר, bāshān ḥawwōth yā'īr). See
Havvoth-Jair.

BASHEMATH, bash'ĕ-math. See Basemath.

BASILISK, baz'i-lisk (צֶפַע, çepha', צִפְעוֹנִי,
çiph'ōnī, from obs root צָפַע, çāpha', "to hiss": Isa
11 8; 14 29; 59 5; Jer 8 17; Prov 23 32m. In
Prov 23 32, AV has "adder," m "cockatrice"; in
the other passages cited AV has "cockatrice," m
"adder" [except Jer 8 17, no m]): The word is
from βασιλίσκος, basilískos, "kinglet," from basi-
leús, "king," and signifies a mythical reptile hatched
by a serpent from a cock's egg. Its hissing drove
away other serpents. Its look, and esp. its breath,
was fatal. According to Pliny, it was named from
a crown-like spot on its head. It has been identified

with the equally mythical COCKATRICE (q.v.). In all the passages cited, it denotes a venomous serpent (see ADDER; SERPENTS), but it is impossible to tell what, if any, particular species is referred to. It must be borne in mind that while there are poisonous snakes in Pal, there are more which are not poisonous, and most of the latter, as well as some harmless lizards, are commonly regarded as deadly. Several of the harmless snakes have crown-like markings on their heads, and it is quite conceivable that the basilisk myth may have been founded upon one of these. ALFRED ELY DAY

BASIN, bā′s'n, **BASON:** The ARV has "basin," the AV and RV "bason," the preferred spelling of the Eng. revisers. In the Appendix to the Revised OT the American Revisers (§ viii) say, "The modern spelling is preferred for the following words"; then follow among others "basin" for "bason"; but no similar statement appears in the Appendix to the Revised NT. The Heb word so rendered in EV is chiefly used for the large bowl of bronze (AV "brass") employed by the priests to receive the blood of the sacrificial victims (Ex **27** 3; cf **29** 16; 1 K **7** 45, etc). It is found only once in secular use (Am **6** 6, "drink wine in bowls"), if the text there is correct; the LXX has it otherwise. See BOWL. The "basins" of Ex **12** 22; 2 S **17** 28 were probably of earthenware.

1. The Terms Used and Their Meaning

Washing before Eating.

While the priests' bowls were of bronze, similar bowls or basins of silver were presented by the princes of the congregation, according to Nu **7** 13 ff; and those spoken of in 1 K **7** 50 as destined for Solomon's temple were of gold (cf 1 Ch **28** 17).

2. Of Various Materials and Forms

(1) The well-known eastern mode of washing the hands was and is by pouring water on the hands, not by dipping them in water, an act, of course, calling for the aid of an attendant. Elisha "poured water on the hands of Elijah" (2 K **3** 11; see Kitto's note in *Pictorial Bible*², II, 330). A disciple came to be known as "one who poured water on the hands of another." Such was beyond question the prevailing custom among the ancient Hebrews, as it was, and is, among eastern peoples in general. They incline to look with disgust, if not with horror, upon our western practice of washing face and hands in water retained in a basin.

3. The Typical Ewer of the East

(2) The typical vessel of the East used in such ablutions has a long spout, not unlike our large coffee-pot (see Kitto, *Pict. Bib.*, II, 331, note). While the EV unfortunately often suggests nothing like such *pouring*, the Heb expresses it, e.g. in 1 S **25** 41, where we have the Qal of *rāḥaç* (רחץ); cf Kennedy in 1-vol *HDB*, and *HDB*, arts. "Bath," "Bathing." Kennedy shows that "affusion," "pouring on" of water, was meant in many cases where we read "bathe" or "wash" in EV. Lane (*Mod. Egypt*, ch v) says: "A servant brings him a *basin and ewer* (called *ṭisht* and *ibreek*) of tinned copper or brass. The first has a cover with holes, with a raised receptacle for the soap; and the water is poured upon the hands and passes through the ewer into the space below; so that when the basin is brought to a second person the water with which the former has washed is not seen."

4. A Basin of a Unique Sort

(1) A wash-basin of a special sort was used by Jesus for washing the disciples' feet (see Jn **13** 5). The Gr is *niptḗr* (νιπτήρ), *eíta bállei húdōr eis tón niptēra*, tr^d RV, "then he poureth water into *the basin*." This word *niptēr* is not found elsewhere in the NT, nor in the LXX, nor, indeed, in Gk profane lit. But fortunately the general sense is here made plain by the context and by comparison of the cognate verbs *níptein* and *nízein*. It evidently denotes an article, not necessarily a vessel, specifically suited to the use of washing a part of the body, e.g. the hands or the feet, and hence is used with the art., "the basin," RV. It is doubtful, therefore, if "basin," or "bason," conveys a true idea of either the oriental article here meant or the scene portrayed. The fact that, according to the custom of the day, the position of the disciples here was reclining, precludes the possibility of the use of a "basin" of our sort, in the way we are accustomed to, i.e. for immersing the feet in the water, in whole or in part.

(2) So it is likely that the *niptēr* was a *jug*, or *ewer*, with a dish, saucer, or *basin* placed under it and combined with it to catch the dripping water. We know from other sources that such a vessel was kept in the Jewish house regularly for ordinary handwashings, etc (see Mt **15** 2; Mk **7** 3), and for ceremonial ablutions. Hence it would naturally be ready here in the upper room as a normal part of the preparation of the "goodman of the house" for his guests (AV Mk **14** 14; Lk **22** 12), and so it is distinguished by the Gr art. *tón*. Jesus Himself used the *niptēr*, standing, doubtless, to impress upon His disciples the lessons of humility, self-abasement and loving service which He ever sought to impart and illustrate.

(3) Our conclusion, we may say with George Farmer in *DCG*, art. "Bason," is that *niptēr* was not simply one large basin, but the set of ewer and basin combined, such a set as was commonly kept in the Jewish house for the purpose of cleansing either the hands or the feet by means of affusion. The Arab. *ṭisht*, authorities tell us, is the exact rendering of *niptēr*, and it comes from a root which means "to pour," or "rain slightly." (See Anton Tien, reviser of the Arab. prayer-book, author of *Arab. and Mod. Gr Grammars*, etc, quoted in *DCG*, art. "Bason.") See LAVER. GEO. B. EAGER

BASKET, bas′ket: Four kinds of "baskets" come to view in the OT under the Heb names, *dūdh*, *ṭene'*, *ṣal* and *kᵉlūbh*. There is little, however, in these names, or in the narratives where they are found, to indicate definitely what the differences of size and shape and use were. The Mish renders us some help in our uncertainty, giving numerous names and descriptions of "baskets" in use among the ancient Hebrews (see Kreugel, *Das Hausgerät in der Mishnah*, 39–45). They were variously made of willow, rush, palm-leaf, etc, and were used for various purposes, domestic and agricultural, for instance, in gathering and serving fruit, collecting alms in kind for the poor, etc. Some had handles, others lids, some both, others neither.

1. Meaning of OT Terms

(1) *Dūdh* was probably a generic term for various kinds of baskets. It was probably the "basket" in which the Israelites in Egypt carried the clay for bricks (cf Ps **81** 6, where it is used as a symbol of Egyp bondage), and such as the Egyptians themselves used for that purpose (Wilk., *Anc. Egypt*, I, 379), probably a large, shallow basket, made of wicker-work. It stood for a basket that was used in fruit-gathering (see Jer **24** 1), but how it differed from Amos' "basket of summer fruit" (Am **8** 1) we do not know. *Dūdh* is used for the "pot" in which meat was boiled (1 S **2** 14), showing probably that a pot-shaped "basket" was known by this name. Then it seems to have stood for a basket tapering toward the bottom like the *calathus* of the Romans. So we seem forced to conclude that the term was generic, not specific.

(2) The commonest basket in use in OT times was the *ṣal*. It was the "basket" in which the court-baker of Egypt carried about his confectionery on his head (Gen **40** 16). It was made in later times at least of peeled willows, or palm-leaves, and was sometimes at least large and flat like the *canistrum* of the Romans, and, like it, was used for carrying bread and other articles of food (Gen **40** 16; Jgs **6** 19). Meat for the meat offerings and the unleavened bread, were placed in it (Ex **29** 3; Lev **8** 2; Nu **6** 15). It is expressly required that the unleavened cakes be placed and offered in such a "basket." While a "basket," it was dish-shaped, larger or smaller in size, it would seem, according to demand, and perhaps of finer texture than the *dūdh*.

(3) The *ṭenc'* was a large, deep basket, in which grain and other products of garden or field were carried home and kept (Dt **28** 5.17), in which the first-fruits were preserved (Dt **26** 2), and the tithes transported to the sanctuary (Dt **26** 2 f). It has been thought probable that the *ḥabya*, the basket of clay and straw of the Pal peasantry of today, is a sort of survival or counterpart of it. It has the general shape of a jar, and is used for storing and keeping wheat, barley, oats, etc. At the top is the mouth into which the grain is poured, and at the bottom is an orifice through which it

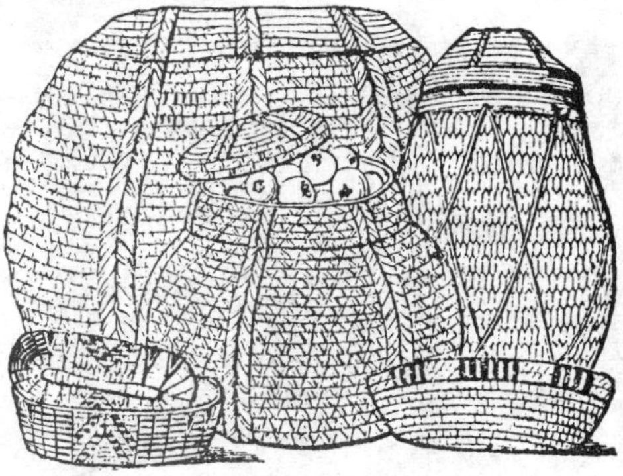

Ancient Egyptian Baskets.

can be taken out as needed, when the opening is again closed with a rag. The LXX translates *ṭene'* by *kártallos*, which denotes a basket of the shape of an inverted cone.

(4) The term *kᵉlubh*, found in Am **8** 1 for a "fruit-basket," is used in Jer **5** 27 (AV and RV "cage") for a bird-cage. But it is not at all unreasonable to suppose that a coarsely woven basket with a cover would be used by a fowler to carry home his feathered captives.

2. Meaning of NT Terms

In the NT interest centers in two kinds of "basket," distinguished by the evangelists in their accounts of the feeding of the 5,000 and of the 4,000, called in Gr *kóphinos* and *spurís* (WH *sphurís*).

(1) The *kophinos* (Mt **14** 20; Mk **6** 43; Lk **9** 17; Jn **6** 13) may be confidently identified with the *kūphtā'* of the Mish, which was provided with a cord for a handle by

Modern Oriental Baskets.

means of which it could be carried on the back with such provisions as the disciples on the occasions under consideration would naturally have with them (cf Kreugel, and Broadus, *Comm.* in loc.). The Jews of Juvenal's day carried such a specific "provision-basket" with them on their journeys regularly, and the Lat for it is a transliteration of this Gr word, *cophinus* (cf Juvenal iii.14, and Jastrow, *Dict.*, art. "Basket"). Some idea of its size may be drawn from the fact that in *CIG*, 1625, 46, the word denotes a Boeotian measure of about two gallons.

(2) The *sphuris* or *spuris* (Mt **15** 37; Mk **8** 8) we may be sure, from its being used in letting Paul down from the wall at Damascus (Acts **9** 25, etc), was considerably larger than the *kophinos* and quite different in shape and uses. It might for distinction fitly be rendered "hamper," as Professor Kennedy suggests. Certainly neither the Gr nor ancient usage justifies any confusion.

(3) The *sargánē* (2 Cor **11** 33) means anything plaited, or sometimes more specifically a fish-basket.

GEO. B. EAGER

BASMATH, bas′math. See BASEMATH.

BASON, bā′s'n. See BASIN.

BASSA, bas′a. See BASSAI.

BASSAI, bas′å-ī, bas′ī (**Βασσαί**, *Bassaí*, *Bassá*; AV **Bassa**; 1 Esd **5** 16; Bezai [Ezr **2** 17; Neh **7** 23]): The sons of B. returned with Zerubbabel to Jerus.

BASTAI, bas′tå-ī. See BASTHAI.

BASTARD, bas′tard (מַמְזֵר, *mamzēr*; **νόθος**, *nóthos*): In Dt **23** 2 probably the offspring of an incestuous union, or of a marriage within the prohibited degrees of affinity (Lev **18** 6–20; **20** 10–21). He and his descendants to the tenth generation are excluded from the assembly of the Lord. (See Driver, ad loc.). Zechariah (**9** 6), after prophesying the overthrow of three Phili cities, declares of the fourth: "And a bastard [RVm "a bastard race"] shall dwell in Ashdod," meaning probably that a "mixed population" (*BDB*) of aliens shall invade and settle in the capital of the Philis. In He (**12** 8) in its proper sense of "born out of wedlock," and therefore not admitted to the privileges of paternal care and responsibility as a legitimate son.

T. REES

BASTHAI, bas′thā-ī, bas′thī (**Βασθαί,** *Basthai;* AV Bastai; 1 Esd **5** 31 = Besai [Ezr **2** 49; Neh **7** 52]): The descendants of B. (temple-servants) returned with Zerubbabel to Jerus.

BAT (עֲטַלֵּף, *'ăṭalēph;* Lev **11** 19; Dt **14** 18; Isa **2** 20): Bats are the most widely distributed of mammals, reaching even the oceanic islands, and modern science has revealed the existence of an astonishing number of species, nearly twenty being recorded from Pal. These include both fruit-eating and insect-eating bats, the latter being the smaller.

Bats' Ears.

It has not always been realized that they are mammals, and so it is not surprising that they should be mentioned at the end of the list of unclean birds in Lev **11** 19 and Dt **14** 18. It may, however, be significant that they are at the end of the list and not in the middle of it. The fruit bats are a pest to horticulturists and often strip apricot and other trees before the fruit has ripened enough to be picked. On this account the fruit is often inclosed in bags, or the whole tree may be surrounded with a great sheet or net. They commonly pick the fruit and eat it on some distant perch beneath which the seeds and the ordure of these animals are scattered. The insect bats, as in other countries, flit about at dusk and through the night catching mosquitoes and larger insects, and so are distinctly beneficial.

The reference in Isa **2** 20, "cast . . . . idols . . . . to the moles and to the bats" refers of course to these animals as inhabitants of dark and deserted places. As in the case of many animal names the etymology of *'ăṭalēph* is doubtful. Various derivations have been proposed but none can be regarded as satisfactory. The Arab. name, *waṭwāṭ,* throws no light on the question. ALFRED ELY DAY

BATANAEA, bat-a-nē′a: The name used in Gr times for BASHAN (q.v.), Jos, *Life,* II; *Ant,* XV, x, 1; XVII, ii, 1, "toparchy of Batanaea."

BATH (בַּת, *bath*): A liquid measure equal to about 9 gallons, Eng. measure. It seems to have been regarded as a standard for liquid measures (Ezk **45** 10), as in the case of the molten sea and the lavers in Solomon's temple (1 K **7** 26.38), and for measuring oil and wine (2 Ch **2** 10; Ezr **7** 22; Isa **5** 10; Ezk **45** 14). Its relation to the homer is given in Ezk **45** 11.14). See WEIGHTS AND MEASURES.

BATH, BATHING, bāth′ing: Bathing in the ordinary, non-religious sense, public or private, is rarely met with in the Scriptures.

1. Ordinary Bathing

We find, however, three exceptional and interesting cases: (1) that of Pharaoh's daughter, resorting to the Nile (Ex **2** 5); (2) that of Bath-sheba, bathing on the house-top (2 S **11** 2 RV); (3) the curious case mentioned in 1 K **22** 38. (To wash with royal blood was supposed to be beneficial to the complexion.)

The dusty, limestone soil of Pal and the open foot-gear of the Orient on stockingless feet, called for frequent washing of the feet (Gen **24** 32; **43** 24; Jgs **19** 24; 1 S **25** 41; 2 S **11** 8; Cant **5** 3, etc), and bathing of the body for refreshment; but the chief concern of the writers of Scripture was with bathing of another sort. Indeed, something of the religious sense and aspect of bathing, in addition to that of bodily refreshment, seems to have entered into the ordinary use of water, as in the washing of the hands before meals, etc (see Gen **18** 4; **19** 2; Lk **7** 44).

The streams and ponds, when available, were the usual resorts for bathing (Ex **2** 5; 2 K **5** 10, etc),

2. Bathing Resorts

but the water-supply of large cities, stored up in great pools or large cisterns, was certainly available at times to some degree for bathing (2 S **11** 2); though, as Benzinger says, no traces of bathrooms have been found in old Heb houses, even in royal palaces. In Babylon, it would seem from Sus 15, there were bathing pools in gardens, though this passage may refer simply to bathing in the open air. Certainly *public baths* as now known, or plunge-baths of the Gr type, were unknown among the Hebrews until they were brought in contact with the Gr civilization. Such baths first come into view during the Gr-Rom period, when they are found to be regularly included in the *gymnasia,* or "places of exercise" (1 Macc **1** 14). Remains of them, of varying degrees of richness and architectural completeness, may be seen today in various parts of the East, those left of the cities of the Decapolis, esp. at Gerash and Amman, being excellent examples (cf also those at Pompeii). A remarkable series of bath-chambers has recently been discovered

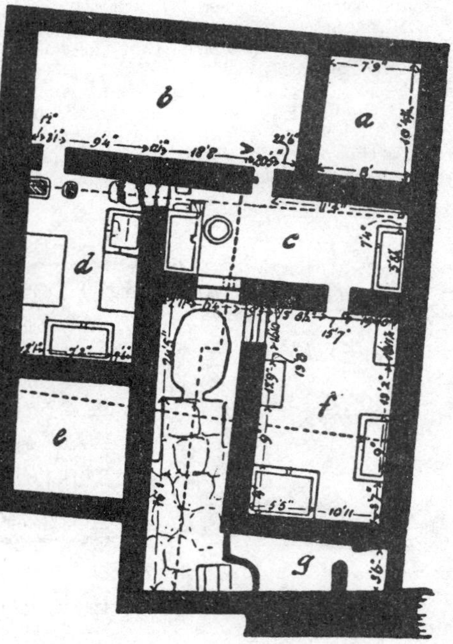

Plan of the Baths in the Castle at Gezer (*PEF*).

by Mr. R. A. S. Macalister at Gezer in Pal, in connection with a building supposed to be the palace built by Simon Maccabaeus. For an interesting account of it see *PEFS,* 1905, 294 f.

When we consider that in Pal six months of the year are rainless, and how scarce and pricelessly valuable water is during most of the year, and in many places all the year round; and when we recall how the Bedouin of today looks on the use of water for cleansing in such times and places of scarcity, viewing it as a wanton waste (see Benzinger, *Heb. Arch.*, 108, note), the rigid requirement of it for so many ritual purposes by the Mosaic law is, to say the least, remarkable (see ABLUTION; CLEAN AND UNCLEAN, etc). Certainly there was a marked contrast between the Gr idea of bathing and that of the Hebrews and Asiatics in general, when they came in contact. But when Gr culture invaded Pal under Antiochus Epiphanes (cir 168 BC), it brought Gr ideas and Gr bathing establishments with it; and under Herod (40–44 BC) it was given the right of way and prevailed to no mean degree (see Anecdote of Gamaliel II in Schürer, *HJP*, II, i, 18, 53).

3. Gr versus Sem Ideas

VIEW (FROM THE NORTH) OF THE SERIES OF BATHS IN THE CASTLE AT GEZER (*PEF*).

But "bathing" in the Bible stands chiefly for ritual acts—purification from ceremonial uncleanness, from contact with the dead, with defiled persons or things, with "holy things," i.e. things "devoted," or "under the ban," etc (see CLEAN AND UNCLEAN, etc). The Heb of the OT does not sharply distinguish between bathing and partial washing—both are expressed by *rāḥaç*, and the RV rightly renders "wash" instead of "bathe" in some cases. Talmudic usage simply codified custom which had been long in vogue, according to Schürer. But Kennedy grants that the "bath" at last became, even for the laity, "an important factor in the religious life of Israel." We read of daily bathing by the Essenes (Jos, *BJ*, II, viii, 5). Then later we find John, the Baptizer, immersing, as the record clearly shows the apostles of Christ did also (Acts **8** 38; Rom **6** 3 f); cf Lk **11** 38 where βαπτίζω, *baptízō*, in passive = "washed."

4. Ceremonial Purification

In Jn **5** 2–7 we have an example of bathing for health. There are remains of ancient baths at Gadara and at Callirrhoe, E. of the Jordan, baths which were once celebrated as resorts for health-seekers. There are hot baths in full operation today, near Tiberias, on the southwestern shore of the Lake of Galilee, which have been a health resort from time immemorial. It is probably true, however, as some one has said, that in OT times and in NT times, the masses of the people had neither privacy nor inclination for bathing. GEO. B. EAGER

5. Bathing for Health

BATH KOL, bath'kol, bath kōl (בַּת קוֹל, *bath ḳōl*, "the daughter of the voice"): Originally signifying no more than "sound," "tone," "call" (e.g. water in pouring gives forth a "sound," *bath ḳōl*, while oil does not), sometimes also "echo." The expression acquired among the rabbis a special use, signifying *the Divine voice*, audible to man and unaccompanied by a visible Divine manifestation. Thus conceived, *bath ḳōl* is to be distinguished from God's speaking to Moses and the prophets; for at Sinai the voice of God was part of a larger theophany, while for the prophets it was the resultant inward demonstration of the Divine will, by whatever means effected, given to them to declare (see VOICE). It is further to be distinguished from all natural sounds and voices, even where these were interpreted as conveying Divine instruction. The conception appears for the first time in Dnl **4** 28 (EV 31)—it is in the Aram. portion—where, however, *ḳal* = *ḳōl*, "voice" stands without *berath* = *bath*, "daughter": "A voice fell from heaven." Jos (*Ant*, XIII, x, 3) relates that John Hyrcanus (135–104 BC) heard a voice while offering a burnt sacrifice in the temple, which Jos expressly interprets as the voice of God (cf Bab *Ṣōṭāh* 33*a* and Jerus *Ṣōṭāh* 24*b*, where it is called *bath ḳōl*). In the NT mention of "a voice from heaven" occurs in the following passages: Mt **3** 17; Mk **1** 11; Lk **3** 22 (at the baptism of Jesus); Mt **17** 5; Mk **9** 7; Lk **9** 35 (at His transfiguration); Jn **12** 28 (shortly before His passion); Acts **9** 4; **22** 7; **26** 14 (conversion of Paul), and **10** 13.15 (instruction of Peter concerning clean and unclean). In the period of the Tannaim (cir 100 BC–200 AD) the term *bath ḳōl* was in very frequent use and was understood to signify not the direct voice of God, which was held to be supersensible, but the echo of the voice (the *bath* being somewhat arbitrarily taken to express the distinction). The rabbis held that *bath ḳōl* had been an occasional means of Divine communication throughout the whole history of Israel and that since the cessation of the prophetic gift it was the sole means of Divine revelation. It is noteworthy that the rabbinical conception of *bath ḳōl* sprang up in the period of the decline of OT prophecy and flourished in the period of extreme traditionalism. Where the gift of prophecy was clearly lacking—perhaps even because of this lack—there grew up an inordinate desire for special Divine manifestations. Often a voice from heaven was looked for to clear up matters of doubt and even to decide between conflicting interpretations of the law. So strong had this tendency become that Rabbi Joshua (cir 100 AD) felt it to be necessary to oppose it and to insist upon the supremacy and the sufficiency of the written law. It is clear that we have here to do with a conception of the nature and means of Divine revelation that is distinctly inferior to the Bib. view. For even in the Bib. passages where mention is made of the voice from heaven, all that is really essential to the revelation is already present, at least in principle, without the audible voice.

LITERATURE.—F. Weber, *System der altsynagogalen palästinischen Theologie*, 2d ed, 1897, 194 ff; J. Hamburger, *Real-Enc des Judentums*, II, 1896; W. Bacher, *Agada der Tannaiten* and *Agada der paläst. Amoräer* (see Index); *Jew Enc*, II, 588 ff; "*Bath Kol*" in *TSBA*, IX, 18; P. Fiebig, *Rel. in Gesch. und Gegenwart*, I, s.v.

J. R. VAN PELT

BATH-RABBIM, bath-rab′im, **THE GATE OF** (שַׁעַר בַּת־רַבִּים, *sha'ar bath-rabbīm;* LXX **ἐν πύλαις θυγατρὸς πολλῶν,** *en púlais thugatrós pollōn*, lit. "in the gates of the daughter of the many." The gate of Heshbon near which were the pools compared to the Shulammite's eyes (Cant **7** 4). Guthe would translate "by the gate of the populous city." Cheyne would amend the passage and read

"Thine eyes are like Solomon's pools,
By the wood of Beth-cerem,"

and transfer the scene to the pools of Solomon, S. of Bethlehem (*EB*, s.v.). But this is surely very violent. One of the pools of Heshbon still survives, measuring 191 ft.×139 ft., and is 10 ft. deep. The walls however have been rent by earthquakes, and now no longer retain the water. W. EWING

BATH-SHEBA, bath-shē′ba, bath′shē̆-ba (בַּת־שֶׁבַע, *bath-shebha'*, "the seventh daughter," or "the daughter of an oath," also called Bathshua [בַּת־שׁוּעַ, *bath-shūa'*], "the daughter of opulence" [1 Ch **3** 5]; the LXX however reads *Bērsabeé* everywhere; cf BATHSHUA; *HPN*, 65, 67, 77, 206 for Bath-sheba, and 67, 69, n. 3, for Bathshua): Bath-sheba was the daughter of Eliam (2 S **11** 3) or Ammiel (1 Ch **3** 5); both names have the same meaning. She was the beautiful wife of Uriah the Hittite, and because of her beauty was forced by David to commit adultery (2 S **11** 2 ff; Ps **51**). Her husband Uriah was treacherously killed by the order of David (2 S **11** 6 ff). After the death of her husband David made her his wife and she lived with him in the palace (2 S **11** 27). Four sons sprang from this marriage (2 S **5** 14; 1 Ch **3** 5), after the first child, the adulterine, had died (2 S **12** 14 ff). With the help of the prophet Nathan she renders futile the usurpation of Adonijah and craftily secures the throne for her son Solomon (1 K **1** 11 ff). Later Adonijah succeeds in deceiving Bath-sheba, but his plan is frustrated by the king (1 K **2** 13 ff). According to Jewish tradition, Prov **31** is written by Solomon in memory of his mother. In the genealogy of Jesus (Mt **1** 6) Bath-sheba is mentioned as the former wife of Uriah and the mother of Solomon by David. See ADONIJAH; AMMIEL; BATHSHUA DAVID; ELIAM; NATHAN; SOLOMON.

A. L. BRESLICH

BATHSHUA, bath′shū-a (בַּת־שׁוּעַ, *bath-shūa'*, "the daughter of opulence" or "the daughter of Shua"; cf BATH-SHEBA; for derivation see *HPN*, 67, 69, n. 3):

(1) In Gen **38** 2 and 1 Ch **2** 3, where the name is tr[d] "Shua's daughter," the wife of Judah.

(2) In 1 Ch **3** 5, the daughter of Ammiel and wife of David. See BATH-SHEBA.

BATH-ZACHARIAS, bath-zak-a-rī′as. See BETH-ZACHARIAS.

BATTERING-RAM, bat′ẽr-ing-ram. See SIEGE.

BATTLE. See WAR.

BATTLE-AXE, bat′′l-ax. See ARMOR, ARMS, III, 1; Ax (AXE).

BATTLE-BOW, bat′′l-bō: Found in the striking Messianic prophecy: "The battle bow shall be cut off" (Zec **9** 10). The prophet is predicting the peace that shall prevail when Zion's king cometh, "just, and having salvation; lowly, and riding upon an ass, even upon a colt the foal of an ass." The words convey their full significance only when read in the light of the context: "I will cut off the chariot from Ephraim, and the horse from Jerus; and the battle bow shall be cut off; and he shall speak peace unto the nations" (cf **10** 4). The battle-bow was sometimes made of tough wood, sometimes of two straight horns joined together (Hom. *Il.* iv.105–11), and sometimes of bronze. In Ps **18** 34 RV we find "bow of *brass*," but it probably should be of "bronze" (נְחֹשֶׁת, *n^eḥōsheth*), a metal very different from our brass, which is a mixture of copper and zinc. The point of the passage in this connection ("He teacheth my hands to war; so that mine arms do bend a bow of bronze"), as well as of that in 2 K **9** 24 ("And Jehu drew his bow with his full strength") is that it required great strength to bend the battle-bow. See ARCHERY; ARMOR. GEO. B. EAGER

BATTLEMENT, bat′′l-ment. See FORTIFICATION; HOUSE.

BAVAI, bav′ā-ī. See BAVVAI.

BAVVAI, bav′ā-ī (בַּוַּי, *bawway;* LXX A, **Βενεί,** *Beneí;* B, **Βεδεί,** *Bedeí;* AV **Bavai,** "wisher" [?] [Neh **3** 18]): Perhaps identical with or a brother of Binnui (Neh **3** 24). See BINNUI. B., "the son of Henadad, the ruler of half the district of Keilah," was of a Levitical family. He is mentioned as one of those who repaired the wall of Jerus after the return from Babylon (Neh **3** 17 f).

BAY, bā. See COLORS.

BAY, bā (לָשׁוֹן, *lāshōn*, lit. "tongue"; **κόλπος,** *kólpos*): The word occurs in the sense of inlet of the sea in the OT only in Josh **15** 2.5; **18** 19, and in NT only in Acts **27** 39 (of Malta, AV "creek").

BAYITH, bā′yith (בַּיִת, *bayith;* AV **Bajith,** "house" [Isa **15** 2]): A town in the country of Moab. The reading of RVm, "Bayith and Dibon are gone up to the high places to weep," seems to be the proper rendering of this passage. Duhm et al., by changing the text, read either "house of" or "daughter of." The construct of this word *beth* is frequently used in compound words. See BETH.

BAY TREE, bā'trē' (AV only; Ps **37** 35; אֶזְרָח, *'ezrāh*): The word means "native," "indigenous," and RV trs "a green tree in its native soil."

BAZLITH, baz'lith, **BAZLUTH,** baz'luth (בַּצְלִית, *baçlīth*, Neh **7** 54; בַּצְלוּת, *baçlūth*, Ezr **2** 52; Basaloth, 1 Esd **5** 31, "asking"): The descendants of B. (temple-servants) returned with Zerubbabel to Jerus.

BDELLIUM, del'i-um (בְּדֹלַח, *b^e dhōlah*): The word occurs twice in the Pent: (1) in Gen **2** 12, in conjunction with gold and onyx, as a product of the land of Havilah (q.v.), and (2) in Nu **11** 7, where the manna is likened to this substance in appearance: "The appearance thereof as the appearance of bdellium." The latter comparison excludes the idea of *b^e dhōlah* being a precious stone, and points to the identification of it with the fragrant resinous gum known to the Greeks as *bdellion*, several kinds being mentioned by Dioscorides and Pliny. It was a product of Arabia, India, Afghanistan, etc. James Orr

BEACH, bēch (αἰγιαλός, *aigialós*): The part of the shore washed by the tide on which the *waves dash* (Mt **13** 2.48; Jn **21** 4; Acts **21** 5; **27** 39.40).

BEACON, bē'k'n. The tr of the Heb תֹּרֶן, *tōren*, which usually means "mast" (cf Isa **33** 23; Ezk **27** 5), but in Isa **30** 17 being used in parallelism with "ensign" the meaning may be "signal-staff" (Isa **30** 17 ARVm "pole").

BEALIAH, bē-a-lī'a (בְּעַלְיָה, *b^e'alyāh*, "Jehovah is Lord," cf *HPN*, 144, 287): B., formerly a friend of Saul, joined David at Ziklag (1 Ch **12** 5).

BEALOTH, bē'a-loth (בְּעָלוֹת, *b^e'ālōth;* Βαλώθ, *Balōth*): An unidentified city of Judah in the Negeb (Josh **15** 24).

BEAM, bēm: The word is used to translate various OT terms:

(1) גֵּב, *gēbh* (1 K **6** 9), צֵלָע, *çēlā'*, "a rib" (1 K **7** 3), קוֹרָה, *ķūrāh* (2 Ch **3** 7; **34** 11; Cant **1** 17), all refer to constructional beams used in buildings for roofing and upper floors, main beams being carried on pillars generally of wood. The last term is used in 2 K **6** 2.5 ("as one was felling a beam") of trees which were being cut into logs. A related form is קָרָה, *ķārāh* (used of the Creator, Ps **104** 3; of building, Neh **2** 8; **3** 3.6). Yet another term, כָּפִים, *kāphīm*, is used in Hab **2** 11: "The stone shall cry out of the wall, and the beam out of the timber shall answer it"—a protest against sin made by inanimate things. The Douay version, in translating, "the timber that is between the joints of the building," suggests the use of bond timbers in buildings, similar to that used at one time in Eng. brickwork It probably refers to its use in mud brick buildings, although bond timbers might also be used in badly built stone walls. The Arabs of the present day use steel joints to strengthen angles of buildings.

(2) Beam, in weaving, represents two words, אֶרֶג, *'eregh* (Jgs **16** 14, the beam of a loom to which Samson's hair was fastened; used in Job **7** 6 of a weaver's shuttle), and מָנוֹר, *mānōr* (1 S **17** 7; 2 S **21** 19; 1 Ch **11** 23; **20** 5), of a spear-staff.

(3) In the NT Jesus uses the word δοκός, *dokós*, "a rafter," in bidding the censorious person first cast the "beam" out of his own eye before attempting to remove the "mote" from another's eye (Mt **7** 3; Lk **6** 41.42). See Architecture; House.
Arch. C. Dickie

BEAN, bē'an. See Baean.

BEANS, bēnz (פּוֹל, *pōl;* Arab. *fūl*): A very common product of Pal; a valuable and very ancient article of diet. The Bible references are probably to the *Faba vulgaris* (N.D. *Leguminosae*) or horsebean. This is sown in the autumn; is in full flower—filling the air with sweet perfume—in the early spring; and is harvested just after the barley and wheat. The bundles of black bean stalks, plucked up by the roots and piled up beside the newly winnowed barley, form a characteristic feature on many village threshing-floors. Beans are threshed and winnowed like the cereals. Beans are eaten entire, with the pod, in the unripe state, but to a greater extent the hard beans are cooked with oil and meat.

In Ezk **4** 9, beans are mentioned with other articles as an unusual source of bread and in 2 S **17** 28 David receives from certain staunch friends of his at Mahanaim a present, which included "beans, and lentils, and parched pulse."
E. W. G. Masterman

BEAR, bâr (דֹּב or דּוֹב, *dōbh;* cf Arab. *dubb*): In 1 S **17** 34–37, David tells Saul how as a shepherd boy he had overcome a lion and a bear. In 2 K **2** 24 it is related that two she bears came out of the wood and tore forty-two of the children who had been mocking Elisha. All the other references to bears are **fig.**; cf 2 S **17** 8; Prov **17** 12; **28** 15; Isa **11** 7; **59** 11; Lam **3** 10; Dnl **7** 5; Hos **13** 8; Am **5** 19; Rev **13** 2. The Syrian bear, sometimes named

Syrian Bear—*Ursus Syriacus.*

as a distinct species, *Ursus Syriacus*, is better to be regarded as merely a local variety of the European and Asiatic brown bear, *Ursus arctos.* It still exists in small numbers in Lebanon and is fairly common in Anti-Lebanon and Hermon. It does not seem to occur now in Pal proper, but may well have done so in Bible times. It inhabits caves in the high and rugged mountains and issues mainly at night to feed on roots and vegetables. It is fond of the *ḥummuṣ* or chick-pea which is sometimes planted in the upland meadows, and the fields have to be well guarded. The **fig.** references to the bear take account of its ferocious nature, esp. in the case of the she bear robbed of her whelps (2 S **17** 8; Prov **17** 12; Hos **13** 8). It is with this character of the bear in mind that Isaiah says (**11** 7), "And the cow and the bear shall feed; their young ones shall lie down together." Alfred Ely Day

BEAR, bâr, **THE (ARCTURUS).** A great northern constellation. See Astronomy, II, 13.

BEAR, bâr (vb.), **BORN,** bôrn (יָלַד, *yāladh*): Occurs frequently in its lit. sense, alluding to motherhood (Gen **16** 11; **17** 17.19.21; **18** 13; **22** 23; **30** 3; Lev **12** 5; Jgs **13** 3; **5** 7; Ruth **1** 12; 1 K **3** 21; Jer **29** 6); in the NT γεννάω, *gennáō*, in the same sense (Lk **1** 13).

Figurative: It is often used with reference to the beginning of the spiritual life or regeneration (Jn **1** 13; **3** 3–8; 1 Jn **2** 29; **3** 9; **4** 7; **5** 1.4.18 AV). See REGENERATION.

BEAR, bâr, **BORNE,** bōrn (נָשָׂא, *nāsā'*; **λαμβάνω,** *lambánō*, **ἀναφέρω,** *anaphérō*, **βαστάζω,** *bastázō*): In EV the physical sense is familiar, of supporting or carrying any weight or burden. The tr of RV is to be preferred in Ps **75** 3 ("have set up"); Lam **3** 28 ("hath laid it upon him"); Zeph **1** 11 ("were laden with silver"); Lk **18** 7 ("he is longsuffering over them"); Jn **12** 6 ("took away what was put therein"); Acts **27** 15 ("could not face the wind").

Figurative: The words are used in the **fig.** sense of enduring or taking the consequences of, be it for oneself or as representative for others: one's own iniquity (Lev **5** 17 and often); chastisement (Job **34** 31); reproach (Ps **69** 7; **89** 50); or the sins of others (Isa **53** 4.11.12; Mt **8** 17; He **9** 28; 1 Pet **2** 24). In Isa **46** 1–7 a striking contrast is presented between the idols of Babylon whom their worshippers had carried (borne) about and which would be borne away by the conquerors, and Jeh who had carried (borne) Israel from the beginning. "Jacob and Israel . . . . borne by me from their birth . . . . and I will bear; yea, I will carry." "They bear it upon the shoulder," etc.

M. O. EVANS

BEARD, bērd:

(1) Western Semites in general, according to the monuments, wore full round beards, to which they evidently devoted great care. The nomads of the desert, in distinction from the settled Semites, wore a clipped and pointed beard (see Jer **9** 26: "all that have the corners of their hair cut off, that dwell in the wilderness"; and cf **25** 23; **49** 32, etc).

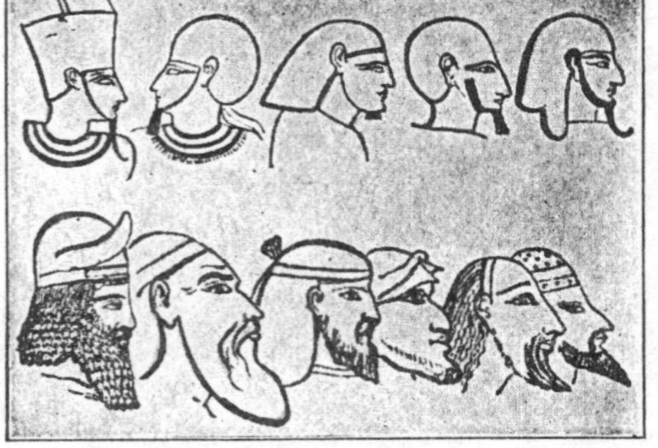

Beards (Egyptian in Top Row; Other Nationalities in Bottom Row).

(2) Long beards are found on Assyr and Bab monuments and sculptures as a mark of the highest aristocracy (cf Egyp monuments, esp. representations by W. Max Müller, *Asien und Europa*, 140). It is not clear that it was ever so with the Jews. Yet it is significant that the Heb "elder" (*zāḳēn*) seems to have received his name from his long beard (cf *bene barbatus*).

(3) The view of some that it was customary among the Hebrews to shave the upper lip is considered by the best authorities as without foundation. The mustache (Heb *sāphām*, "beard"), according to 2 S **19** 24, received regular "trimming" (thus EV after the Vulg, but the Heb is generic, not specific: "He had neither dressed his feet, nor trimmed his beard").

(4) In one case (1 S **21** 13.14) the neglect of the beard is set down as a sign of madness: "[He] let his spittle fall down upon his beard. Then said Achish, ... Lo, ye see the man is mad."

(5) It was common Sem custom to cut both hair and beard as a token of grief or distress. Isaiah (**15** 2), describing the heathen who have "gone up to the high places to weep," says "Moab waileth over Nebo, and over Medeba; on all their heads is baldness, every beard is cut off." Jeremiah (**41** 5), describing the grief of the men of Samaria for their slain governor, Gedaliah, says, "There came men from . . . . Samaria [his sorrowing subjects] even four score men, having their beards shaven and their clothes rent," etc. And Amos, in his prophecy of the vision of the "basket of summer fruit" (**8** 1 ff), makes Jeh say to His people: "I will turn your feasts into mourning; . . . . I will bring sackcloth upon all loins, and baldness upon every head" (**8** 10). On the other hand it was even more significant of great distress or fear to leave the beard untrimmed, as did Mephibosheth, the son of Saul, when he went to meet King David, in the crisis of his guilty failure to go up with the king according to his expectation: "He had neither dressed his feet, nor trimmed his beard, nor washed his clothes, from the day the king departed until the day he came home in peace." (Cf 1 S **21** 13.14; 2 S **19** 24.)

(6) Absalom's hair was cut only once a year, it would seem (2 S **14** 26; cf rules for priests, Levites, etc, Ezk **44** 20). But men then generally wore their hair longer than is customary or seemly with us (cf Cant **5** 2.11, "His locks are bushy, and black as a raven"). Later, in NT times, it was a disgrace for a man to wear long hair (1 Cor **11** 6–15). To mutilate the beard of another was considered a great indignity (see 2 S **10** 4; cf Isa **50** 6, "plucked off the hair"). The shaving of the head of a captive slave-girl who was to be married to her captor marked her change of condition and prospects (Dt **21** 12; W. R. Smith, *Kinship*, 209).

LITERATURE.—Wilkinson, *Ancient Egyptians*, II, 324, 349; Herod. i.195; ii.36; iii.12; Jos, *Ant*, VIII, viii, 3; XVI, viii, 1; W. R. Smith, *Kinship*, 209; *RS*, 324; Wellhausen, *Skizzen*, III, 167.

GEO. B. EAGER

BEAST, bēst: This word occurs often in both Old and New Testaments and denotes generally a mammal (though sometimes a reptile) in distinction to a man, a bird or a fish. In this distinction the Eng. is fairly in accord with the Heb and Gr originals. The commonest Heb words *b^ehēmāh* and *ḥai* have their counterpart in the Arab. as do three others less often used, *b^e'īr* (Gen **45** 17; Ex **22** 5; Nu **20** 8 AV), *nephesh* (Lev **24** 18), and *ṭebhaḥ* (Prov **9** 2). *B^ehēmāh* and Arab. *bahīmah* are from a root signifying vagueness or dumbness and so denote primarily a dumb beast. *Ḥai* and Arab. *ḥaiwān* are from the root *ḥāyāh* (Arab. *ḥaya*), "to live," and denote primarily living creatures. *B^e'īr*, "cattle," and its root-verb, *bā'ar*, "to graze," are identical with the Arab. *ba'īr* and *ba'ara*, but with a curious difference in meaning. *Ba'īr* is a common word for camel among the Bedawin and the root-verb, *ba'ara*, means "to drop dung," *ba'rah* being a common word for the dung of camels, goats, and sheep. *Nephesh* corresponds in every way with the Arab. *nephs*, "breath," "soul" or "self" *Ṭebhaḥ* from *ṭābhaḥ*, "to slaughter," is equivalent to the Arab. *dhibḥ* from *dhabaḥa*, with the same meaning. Both θηρίον, *thērion* ("wild beast"), and ζῷον, *zōon* ("living thing"), occur often in the Apocalypse. They are found also in a few other places, as mammals (He **13** 11) or **fig.** (Tit **1** 12). *Thērion* is used also of the viper which fastened on Paul's hand, and this has parallels in classical Gr. Beasts of burden and beasts used for food were and are an important form of property, hence κτῆνος, *ktēnos* ("possession"), the word used for the good Samaritan's beast (Lk **10** 34) and for the beasts with which Lysias provided Paul for his journey to Caesarea (Acts **23** 24).

For "swift beast," *kirkārōth*, "dromedary" (Isa **66** 20 AV), see CAMEL. For "swift beast," *rekhesh*, see HORSE (Mic **1** 13 AV; 1 K **4** 28 AVm; cf Est **8** 10.14). See also WILD BEAST.

ALFRED ELY DAY

BEAST-FIGHT, bēst'fīt. See GAMES.

BEATEN GOLD. See GOLD (BEATEN).

BEATEN OIL. See OIL (BEATEN).

BEATING, bēt'ing. See PUNISHMENTS.

BEATITUDES, bē̇-at'i-tūds: The word "beatitude" is not found in the Eng. Bible, but the Lat *beatitudo*, from which it is derived, occurs in the Vulg version of Rom **4** 6 where, with reference to Ps **32** 1.2, David is said to pronounce the "beatitude" of the man whose transgressions are forgiven. In the Lat church *beatitudo* was used not only as an abstract term denoting blessedness, but in the secondary, concrete sense of a particular declaration of blessedness and esp. of such a declaration coming from the lips of Jesus Christ. Beatitudes in this derivative meaning of the word occur frequently in the OT, particularly in the Pss (**32** 1.2; **41** 1; **65** 4, etc), and Jesus on various occasions threw His utterances into this form (Mt **11** 6; **13** 16; **16** 17; **24** 46, with the Lukan parallels; Jn **13** 17; **20** 29). But apart from individual sayings of this type the name Beatitudes, ever since the days of Ambrose, has been attached specifically to those words of blessing with which, according to both Mt and Lk, Jesus began that great discourse which is known as the Sermon on the Mount.

1. The Name

When we compare these Beatitudes as we find them in Mt **5** 3–12 and Lk **6** 20–23 (24–26), we are immediately struck by the resemblances and differences between them. To the ordinary reader, most familiar with Mt's version, it is the differences that first present themselves; and he will be apt to account for the discrepancy of the two reports, as Augustine did, by assigning them to two distinct occasions in the Lord's ministry. A careful comparative study of the two narratives, however, with some attention to the introductory circumstances in each case, to the whole progress of the discourses themselves, and to the parabolic sayings with which they conclude, makes this view improbable, and points rather to the conclusion that what we have to do with is two varying versions given by the Evangelists of the material drawn from an underlying source consisting of Logia of Jesus. The differences, it must be admitted, are very marked. (*a*) Mt has 8 Beatitudes; Lk has 4, with 4 following Woes. (*b*) In Mt the sayings, except the last, are in the 3d per.; in Lk they are in the 2d. (*c*) In Mt the blessings, except the last, are attached to spiritual qualities; in Lk to external conditions of poverty and suffering. Assuming that both Evangelists derived their reports from some common Logian source, the question arises as to which of them has adhered more closely to the original. The question is difficult, and still gives rise to quite contrary opinions. One set of scholars decides in favor of Mt, and accounts for Lk's deviation from the Matthaean version by ascribing to him, on very insufficient grounds, an ascetic bias by which he was led to impart a materialistic tone to the utterances of Jesus. Another set inclines to the theory that Lk's version is the more literal of the two, while Mt's partakes of the nature of a paraphrase. In support of this second view it may be pointed out that Lk is usually more careful than Mt to place the sayings of Jesus in their original setting and to preserve them in their primitive form, and further that owing to the natural tendency of the sacred writers to expand and interpret rather than to abbreviate an inspired utterance, the shorter form of a saying is more likely to be the original one. It may be noted, further, that in Mt **5** 11.12 the Beatitude takes the direct form, which suggests that this may have been the form Mt found in his source in the case of the others also. On the whole, then, probabilities appear to favor the view that Lk's version is the more literal one. It does not follow, however, that the difference between the two reports amounts to any real inconsistency. In Lk emphasis is laid on the fact that Jesus is addressing His disciples (**6** 20), so that it was not the poor as such whom He blessed, but His own disciples although they were poor. It was not poverty, hunger, sorrow or suffering in themselves to which He promised great rewards, but those experiences as coming to spiritual men and thus transformed into springs of spiritual blessing. And so when Mt, setting down the Lord's words with a view to their universal application rather than with reference to the particular circumstances in which they were uttered, changes "the poor" into "the poor in spirit," and those that "hunger" into those that "hunger and thirst after righteousness," he is giving the real purport of the words of Jesus and recording them in the form in which by all men and through all coming time they may be read without any chance of misunderstanding.

2. The Two Groups

As regards the Beatitudes of the meek, the merciful, the pure in heart, the peacemakers, which are given by Mt only, they may have been spoken by Jesus at the same time as the rest and have been intended by Him in their association with the other four to fill out a conception of the ideal character of the members of the Kingdom of God. In view, however, of their omission from Luke's list, it is impossible to affirm this with certainty. That they are all authentic utterances of Jesus Himself there is no reason to doubt. But they may have been originally scattered through the discourse itself, each in its own proper place. Thus the Beatitude of the meek would go fitly with vs 38 ff, that of the merciful with 43 ff, that of the pure in heart with 27 ff, that of the peacemakers with 23 ff. Or they may even have been uttered on other occasions than that of the Sermon on the Mount and have been gathered together by Matthew and placed at the head of the Sermon as forming along with the other four a suitable introduction to Our Lord's great discourse on the laws and principles of the Kingdom of God.

With regard to the number of the Beatitudes in Matthew's fuller version, some have counted 7 only, making the list end with ver 9. But though the blessing pronounced on the persecuted in vs 10–12 differs from the preceding Beatitudes, both in departing from the aphoristic form and in attaching the blessing to an outward condition and not to a disposition of the heart, the ∥ in Lk (**6** 22 f) justifies the view that this also is to be added to the list, thus making 8 Beatitudes in all. On the arrangement of the group much has been written, most of it fanciful and unconvincing. The first four have been described as negative and passive, the second four as positive

3. Number, Arrangement, Structure

and active. The first four, again, have been represented as pertaining to the desire for salvation, the second four as relating to its actual possession. Some writers have endeavored to trace in the group as a whole the steadily ascending stages in the development of the Christian character. The truth in this last suggestion lies in the reminder it brings that the Beatitudes are not to be thought of as setting forth separate types of Christian character, but as enumerating qualities and experiences that are combined in the ideal character as conceived by Christ—and as exemplified, it may be added, in His own life and person.

In respect of their structure, the Beatitudes are all alike in associating the blessing with a promise —a promise which is sometimes represented as having an immediate realization (vs 3.10), but in most cases has a future or even (cf ver 12) an eschatological outlook. The declaration of blessedness, therefore, is based not only on the possession of the quality or experience described, but on the present or future rewards in which it issues. The poor in spirit are called blessed not merely because they are poor in spirit, but because the kingdom of heaven is theirs; the mourners because they shall be comforted; those that hunger and thirst after righteousness because they shall be filled; those who are persecuted because a great reward is laid up for them in heaven. The Beatitudes have often been criticized as holding up an ideal of which limitation, privation and self-renunciation are the essence, and which lacks those positive elements that are indispensable to any complete conception of blessedness. But when it is recognized that the blessing in every case rests on the associated promise, the criticism falls to the ground. Christ does demand of His followers a renunciation of many things that seem desirable to the natural heart, and a readiness to endure many other things from which men naturally shrink. But just as in His own case the great self-emptying was followed by the glorious exaltation (Phil **2** 6 ff), so in the case of His disciples spiritual poverty and the bearing of the cross carry with them the inheritance of the earth and a great reward in heaven.

LITERATURE.—Votaw in *HDB*, V, 14 ff; Adeney in *Expositor*, 5th ser., II, 365 ff; Stanton, *The Gospels as Historical Documents*, II, 106 ff, 327 f; Gore, *Sermon on the Mount*, 15 ff; Dykes, *Manifesto of the King*, 25–200.

J. C. LAMBERT

BEAUTIFUL, bū'ti-fo͝ol, **GATE,** gāt. See TEMPLE.

BEAUTY, bū'ti: The space allotted to this topic allows liberty only for the statement of two problems to students of the Bible. They should give distinct attention to the interblending of aesthetics with ethics in the Scripture. They should observe the extent and meaning of aesthetics in Nature.

That the Bible is an ethical book is evident. Righteousness in all the relations of man as a moral being is the key to its inspiration, the guiding light to correct understanding of its utterance. But it is everywhere inspired and writ in an atmosphere of aesthetics. Study will bring out this fact from Gen to Rev. The first pair make their appearance in a garden where grew "every tree that is pleasant to the sight" (Gen **2** 9), and the last vision for the race is an abode in a city whose gates are of pearl and streets of gold (Rev **21** 21). Such is the imagery that from beginning to end is pictured as the home of ethics—at first in its untried innocence and at last in its stalwart righteousness. The problem will be to observe the intermingling of these two elements—the beautiful and the good—in the whole Scripture range. A few texts will set before us this kinship and then the Bible student can detect it as he reads.

1. Aesthetics in Scripture

"One thing have I asked of Jeh, that will I seek after:
That I may dwell in the house of Jeh all the days of my life,
To behold the beauty of Jeh,
And to inquire in his temple" (Ps **27** 4).

"For all the gods of the peoples are idols;
But Jeh made the heavens.
Honor and majesty are before him:
Strength and beauty are in his sanctuary" (Ps **96** 5.6).

If we catch the spirit set forth in such and similar Psalms, we can use it as a magnetic needle to detect its like wherever we shall read: and we shall find that like in abundance. It is only necessary to turn to the directions given for making the Ark of the Covenant and its encircling tabernacle, and the decorations of the priests that were to minister in the worship of Jeh in the ceremonies described, as given in Ex **25** ff, to see that every resource of Israel was brought to bear to render ark and tabernacle and their service beautiful. One will find in a concordance half a column of references under the word "Ark" and a column and a half under the word "Tabernacle." By looking up these references one can realize how much care was spent to give and preserve to these aids to worship the attractiveness of beauty.

In 1 Ch **15** and **16** we have an account of David's bringing in the Ark of the Covenant into his own city to rest in a tent he had provided for it. On this occasion a demonstration was made with all the aesthetics of which the music of that day was capable. "And David spake to the chief of the Levites to appoint their brethren the singers, with instruments of music, psalteries and harps and cymbals, sounding aloud and lifting up the voice with joy." And David himself gave to the celebration the aesthetics of one of the noblest of his psalms (1 Ch **16** 8–36).

It is almost idle to refer to Solomon and his temple (1 K **6** ff; 2 Ch **3** ff). It is a common understanding that the civilization of Solomon's day was drawn upon to its utmost in every department of aesthetics, in the building of that house for Jeh and in the appointments for the worship there to be conducted. Beauty of form and color and harmony of sound were then and there integrated—made one—with worship in holiness. The propriety of that association has been seen and felt through the ages.

There is beauty in speech. It is a fact that the supreme classics in the lit. of the tongues of two of the dominant nations of the earth, the Eng. and the German, are tr^s of the Bible. There is no explanation of such fact except that the original justified the tr^s. You can read indifferently from one tr to the other and catch the same aesthetic gleam. Nobility and poetry of thought lay in what was to be tr^d. Here is proof that cannot be gainsaid that the Scripture authors sought the aid of aesthetics as garb for the ethics they taught. So they wrote in poetry. So they used allegory, illustration, figure, metaphor that would charm and hold. The parables of Jesus are examples of this method of clothing thought. They do their ethical work because they have swept into it figure and imagery from familiar aesthetic perceptions. "The sower went forth to sow" (Mt **13** 3). That is a glad sight—always has been and always will be. That is why a picture of "The Sower" hangs on the walls of a Christian home. Just the painting—and every beholder remembers the parable and cannot forget its ethics. The intensity of thought concentrated upon ethics in the NT has drawn away attention from the partnership between these two principles in religion. But it is there, and we shall see it when once we look for it.

It is something to which we do not wake up till late in life—to wit, the illimitableness of the provision in Nature for beauty. Common consent awards beauty to the rainbow. Reflect that every

2. Aesthetics in Nature

drop of water in the ocean, or in the hydrated rocks, or in the vapor floating over Saturn, has in it the possibility of rainbow coloring. In fact all matter has color of which the rainbow is only specimen. Any element incandescent has a spectrum partially coincident with that of water and ranging above and below it in the infinite capacity it has to start ether undulations. As apparently the larger part of the matter of the universe is incandescent, we can see that the field for expression in color is infinite. No one but the Infinite God can see it all.

If we come down to this plain, plodding earth, cultivation of aesthetic sense will bring out beauty everywhere, from the grandeur of mountain scenery to aesthetic curves and colors revealed only by the microscope. We say the butterfly is beautiful. But the larva from which it is derived often carries as much beauty in mottling of color and of the fineness of finish of spine and mandible. Looking across the scale in this way the evidence of theism from beauty itself becomes convincing. Beauty becomes a messenger of and from God—as Iris was to the Greek and the rainbow to the Hebrew (Eccl **3** 11).

This from Amiel's *Journal Intime*, I, 233, sets forth the radical, inexpugnable position of beauty in Nature and in philosophy thereof correctly interpretative: "To the materialist philosopher the beautiful is a mere accident, and therefore rare. To the spiritualist philosopher the beautiful is the rule, the law, the universal foundation of things, to which every form returns as soon as the force of accident is withdrawn."

As we accustom ourselves to make larger and larger synthesis in the department of aesthetics, what diapason of theistic message may we not hear? Beauty wherever and however expressed is a medium of revelation. It is a bush ever burning, never consumed. Before it "put off thy shoes from off thy feet, for the place whereon thou standest is holy ground." That beauty should be—to *that* intent, for *that* end, from everlasting hath wrought the Ancient of Days. C. Caverno

BEAUTY, bū'ti, **AND BANDS,** bandz (נֹעַם, *nō'am*, and חֹבְלִים, *ḥōbhᵉlīm*): The names given in Zec **11** 7.14 to two symbolical staves, the first signifying Jeh's covenant of grace with the peoples, and the second representing the brotherhood of Judah and Israel. The breaking of the two staves is symbolic of the breaking of Jeh's covenant and of the union between Judah and Israel.

BEBAI, bē'bā-ī, beb'a-ī (בֵּבָי, *bēbhay;* LXX **Βηβαί,** *Bēbaí*, "fatherly"):

(1) Descendants of B. returned with Ezra to Jerus (Ezr **8** 11 called Babi; 1 Esd **8** 37); one of these is Zechariah, the son of Bebai (Ezr **8** 11, Zacharias; 1 Esd **8** 37). 623 returned with Zerubbabel to Jerus (Ezr **2** 11; 1 Esd **5** 13; Neh **7** 16 gives the number 628); some of these had married "strange wives" (Ezr **10** 28; 1 Esd **9** 29).

(2) A chief of the people who sealed the covenant with Nehemiah (Neh **10** 15).

(3) An unknown town (Jth **15** 4). Omitted in B and Vulg.

BECAUSE, bē-kôs' (**ἵνα,** *hína*, "in order that"): "The multitude rebuked them, b. [AV; RV "that"] they should hold their peace" (Mt **20** 31).

BECHER, bē'kēr (בֶּכֶר, *bekher*, "the firstborn"; cf *HPN*, 88):

(1) Son of Benjamin (Gen **46** 21; 1 Ch **7** 6.8).

(2) Son of Ephraim whose family is called Becherites (AV "Bachrites"), Nu **26** 35 (1 Ch **7** 20 called Bered). Cf Bered.

BECHORATH, bē-kor'ath. See Becorath.

BECK, bek, **BECKON,** bek''n (**νεῦμα,** *neúma*): This word from *neúō*, "to nod," "beckon," "make a sign" by moving the head or eyes (Lk **5** 7; Jn **13** 24; Acts **21** 40; **24** 10), occurs only in 2 Macc **8** 18, "Almighty God who at a beck can cast down both them that come against us, and also all the world," RV, "able at a beck." So Shak, "troops of soldiers at their beck"; "nod" is now generally used.

BECOME, bē-kum':

(1) Gr *gínomai*, used in NT for a change of state, corresponding to Heb *hāyāh* of OT. Cf Mt **18** 3 with Dt **27** 9.

(2) For what is fitting, suitable, proper, in NT: "*prépei*" (Mt **3** 15; Eph **5** 3; 1 Tim **2** 10); in OT, נָאוָה, *nā'āwāh*, נָאָה, *nā'āh*, Ps **93** 5: "Holiness becometh thy house." In this sense, the adv. "becomingly" must be interpreted: "Walk becomingly toward them that are without" (1 Thess **4** 12), i.e. in a way that is consistent with your profession.

BECORATH, bē-kō'rath (בְּכוֹרַת, *bᵉkhōrath*, "the first birth"; AV **Bechorath**): A forefather of Saul of the tribe of Benjamin (1 S **9** 1).

BECTILETH, bek'ti-leth (**τὸ πεδίον Βαικτειλαίθ,** *tó pedíon Baikteilaíth*): A plain which is defined as "near the mountain which is at the left hand of the upper Cilicia" (Jth **2** 21). The name in Syr is *Beth Ḳᵉṭilath*, "house of slaughter." So far there is no clue to its identification.

BED, BEDCHAMBER, BEDSTEAD: For the very poor of the East, in ancient times as now, the "bed" was and is, as a rule, the bare ground; and the bedclothes, the gown, *simlāh*, or "outer garment," worn during the day ("For that is his only covering, it is his garment for his skin: wherein shall he sleep?" [Ex **22** 27]; cf Dt **24** 13, "Thou shalt surely restore to him the pledge when the sun goeth down, that he may sleep in his garment").

When one was on a journey, or watching his flock by night as a shepherd, such a "bed" was the most natural, and often a stone would serve as a pillow. (See Gen **28** 11, where Jacob "took one of the stones of the place, and put it under his head, and lay down in that place to sleep.")

Mat.

An advance on this custom, which came in due course of time, or under change of circumstances, was the use of a mat on the floor as a bed, with or without covering. At first it was lit. laid on the floor, which was generally of one common level, in some convenient place near the wall; but later it was put on an elevation, either a raised part of the floor on one side, or a bedstead, which gave rise to the expression "going up to the bed" (cf Gen **49** 33 EV, "He gathered up his feet into the bed," and Ps **132** 3, "go up into my bed").

With a later development and civilization, "beds" came to be built upon supports and constructed in different forms, which fact is reflected in the variety of names given the "bed" in the Heb and related languages.

Mattress with Pillow.

1. OT Terms for Bed, and Sleeping Customs of the Hebrews

(1) The following Heb words are used in the Bible for "bed," and, though it is impossible at this remove of time and place and custom to differentiate them sharply, they will repay study: מִטָּה, *miṭṭāh* (Gen **48** 2, "And Israel strengthened himself, and sat upon the bed"; Ex **8** 3, "frogs . . . . shall come into thy bedchamber, and upon thy bed"); מִשְׁכָּב, *mishkābh*, cf (Gen **49** 4, Jacob to Reuben: "Because thou wentest up to thy father's bed; then defiledst thou it"); עֶרֶשׂ, *'eres* (Prov **7** 16, the "strange woman" says: "I have spread my couch with carpets of tapestry"; cf Ps **41** 3, "Thou makest all his bed in his sickness"); מַצָּע, *maççā'* (once only, Isa **28** 20, "For the bed is shorter than that a man can stretch himself on it; and the covering narrower than that he can wrap himself in it"); and יָצוּעַ, *y^eçūa'* (Job **17** 13, "I have spread my couch in the darkness"; 1 Ch **5** 1, "He defiled his father's couch"; cf Gen **49** 4 where the same "father's bed" is *mishkābh;* Ps **63** 6, "when I remember thee upon my bed"; Ps **132** 3, "nor go up into my bed").

(2) It is a far cry from the simple sleeping customs of Dt **24** 13 to the luxurious arts and customs of the post-exilic days, when beds of fine wood and ivory are found in use among the Hebrews, as well as pillows of the most costly materials elaborately embroidered (see Jth **10** 21; Est **1** 6; cf Cant **3** 10); but it all came about as a natural, as well as artificial development, with changed conditions and contacts and increasing civilization

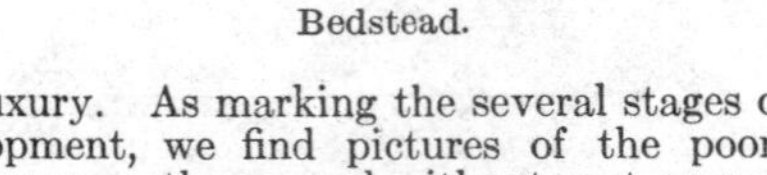

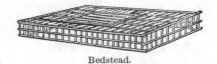

Bedstead.

and luxury. As marking the several stages of that development, we find pictures of the poor, first sleeping upon the ground without mat or mattress, then in a single sleeping-room for the whole family, often without a separate bed, then with "beds" that were simply wadded quilts, or thin mattresses, and mats for keeping them off the ground; then with still better "beds" laid upon light portable, wooden frames, or upon more elevated bedsteads (cf Ps **132** 3 and Mk **4** 21 RV "under the bed"). The degree of richness depended, of course, upon time and place, in a measure, but more upon the wealth and station of the family and the style of the house or tent in which they lived, as it does even with the Bedouin of today. The prophet Amos gives a vivid and significant picture of the luxury of certain children of Israel, "that sit in Samaria in the corner of a couch, and on the silken cushions of a bed" (**3** 12); and of certain children of luxury "that lie upon beds of ivory, and stretch themselves upon their couches, and eat the lambs out of the flock . . . . that drink wine in bowls, and anoint themselves with the chief oils; but they are not grieved for the affliction of Joseph" (Am **6** 4–6; cf Rev **18** 10–13).

(3) We find that the poor, while sleeping for the most part in their ordinary clothing, often, in cold weather, made their beds of the skins of animals, old cloaks, or rugs, as they do still in the East. The "beds" and "bedding" now in ordinary use among Orientals are much the same, we may be sure, as they were in olden times. "Bedsteads" of any pretention were and are rare among the common people; but the richness of "beds" and "bedsteads" among Asiatics of wealth and rank was quite equal to that of the Greeks and Romans (cf Prov **7** 16.17, "I have spread my couch with carpets of tapestry, with striped cloths of the yarn of Egypt. I have perfumed my bed with myrrh, aloes, and cinnamon"); Cant **1** 16.17: "The beams of our house are cedars, and our rafters are firs . . . .

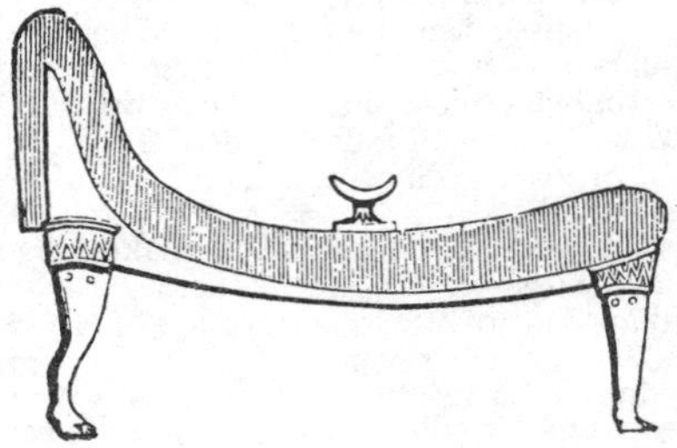

Couch Bed with Head Rest.

also our couch is green." Cf the "*palanquin*" of Solomon, "of the wood of Lebanon," "the pillars thereof of silver," "the bottom of gold," and "the seat of purple" (**3** 9.10).

(4) As soon as any family could afford it, a special bedroom would be set apart, and the whole family would sleep in it (see Lk **11** 5–8, "My children are with me in bed"). When the house had two stories the upper story was used for sleeping, or, during very hot weather, preferably the roof, or the room on the roof. See HOUSE. When morning came the "bed," a wadded quilt or mattress, used with or without covering according to the season, was rolled up, aired and sunned, and then put aside on the raised platform, or packed away in a chest or closet.

The words *mishkābh* and *miṭṭāh* came to have a fig. meaning signifying the final resting-place; and *'eres* used of the "bedstead" of the King of Og (Dt **3** 11) is thought by some to mean his sarcophagus (Benzinger, *Heb Arch.*, 123; Nowack, I, 143). Gen **47** 31, "And Israel bowed himself upon the bed's head" is not rightly rendered (see STAFF, and *Crit. Comm.* in loc.).

2. NT Terms for Bed, Their Meaning, etc

(1) We find several Gr words, κλίνη, *klínē*, κράββατος, *krábbatos*, and κοίτη, *koítē*, used in the NT somewhat indiscriminately and rendered EV by "bed," "couch," etc; but, as with the Heb words noted, there is little to indicate just exactly what they severally stand for, or how they are related to the Heb terms rendered "bed" or "couch" in the OT. Of one thing we can be sure, reasoning from

what we know of "the unchanging East," the "beds" and sleeping customs of the Hebrews in Christ's time were in the main about what they were in later OT times.

(2) An interesting case for study is that of the man "sick of the palsy" whom they brought to Jesus "lying on a bed," and who when healed "took up the bed, and went forth before them all" (Mt **9** 2.6; Mk **2** 4.12; Lk **5** 18.19; cf Jn **5** 8–12). Here the "bed" on which the sick of the palsy lay was let down from the housetop "through the tiles with his couch into the midst before Jesus" (Lk **5** 18.19); and when the man was healed Jesus commanded him, as Luke says, to "take up [his] couch and go unto [his] house," and he "took up that whereon he lay, and departed to his house, glorifying God" (**5** 24.25). It seems, therefore, that this "bed" was a "pallet" and "couch" combined, a thin mattress upon a light portable frame, such as we have already seen was in use among the ancients. Another kindred case was that of the sick man at the pool of Bethesda (Jn **5** 2 ff) whom Jesus healed and commanded to "take up his bed and walk," and he "took up his bed and walked"; only in this case the "bed" is a "pallet" without the frame, it would seem.

(3) Jesus in His teaching (Mk **4** 21; cf Lk **8** 16) asks, in language which is significant in this connection: "Is the lamp brought to be put under .... the bed?" (Lk **8** 16: "No man, when he hath lighted a lamp, covereth it with a vessel, or putteth it under a bed"). Here, clearly, "the bed" is the "bedstead," bedclothes, draperies and all, under which "the lamp" would be obscured and hindered in its function of "giving light to all in the room." Again (Lk **17** 34) Jesus says, "In that night there shall be two men on one bed," which is incidental evidence that the "beds" of that day were not all "pallets" or "couches" for one only (cf Lk **11** 7, "My children are with me in bed"; Cant **1** 16; **3** 10; Prov **7** 16.18).

(4) For **fig.** use in the prophets (e.g. Ezk **23** 17) and in the NT (e.g. "Let the bed be undefiled," He **13** 4), see commentaries in loc.

Geo. B. Eager

BEDAD, bē′dad (בְּדַד, *b^edhadh*, "alone"): Father of Hadad, king of Edom "before there reigned any king over the children of Israel" (Gen **36** 35; 1 Ch **1** 46).

BEDAN, bē′dan (בְּדָן, *b^edhān*, "son of judgment" [?]):

(1) One of the leaders in Israel who with Jerubbaal, Jephthah and Samuel is mentioned as a deliverer of the nation (1 S **12** 11). The text is questioned because LXX, Syr and Arab. read Barak instead.

(2) A son of Ulam of the house of Manasseh (1 Ch **7** 17).

BEDCHAMBER, bed′cham-bẽr. See Bed.

BEDEIAH, be-dē′ya (בֵּדְיָה, *bēdh^eyāh*, "servant of Jeh"): A son of Bani who had married a "strange wife" (Ezr **10** 35).

BEDSTEAD, bed′sted. See Bed.

BEE, bē (דְּבוֹרָה, *d^ebhōrāh;* cf Arab. *dabr*, "a swarm of bees," also Arab. *debbūr*, "a wasp," said to be a corruption of *zunbūr*, "a wasp"; all are apparently from the Heb *dābhar*, "to speak," "arrange," "lead," "follow," or from Arab. *dabara*, "follow" [cf Arab. *dabbara*, "arrange"], though the connection in meaning is not apparent): Honey is mentioned many times in the Bible, esp. in the OT, but the word "bee" occurs only four times, and only one of the four times in connection with honey, in the story of Samson (Jgs **14** 8). Both wild and domesticated bees are found today in Pal, but it is not clear that bees were kept in Bible times, although it would seem very probable. The frequently recurring phrase, "a land flowing with milk and honey," certainly suggests that the honey as well as the milk is a domestic product. The hives now in use are very primitive and wasteful as compared with hives that are made in Europe and America. Sometimes a large water jar is used. More frequently a cylinder about 3 or 4 ft. long and 6 in. in diameter is constructed of mulberry withes plaited together and plastered with mud or cow dung. A number of these cylinders are placed horizontally, being piled up together under some rude structure which serves as a protection from the direct rays of the sun. In the passage already cited it is related that Samson found a swarm of bees and honey in the carcase of the lion which he had killed on his previous visit. We are not told how much time had intervened, but it does not take long in the dry climate of Pal for scavenging beasts and insects to strip the flesh from the bones and make the skeleton a possible home for a swarm of bees. The other three passages refer to the offensive power of bees. In Dt **1** 44, in the speech of Moses he says, "The Amorites .... chased you, as bees do"; in Ps **118** 12, the psalmist says, "They compassed me about like bees"; in Isa **7** 18, the bee is the type of the chastisement that the Lord will bring from the land of Assyria.

Alfred Ely Day

BEEF, bēf. See Cattle.

BEELIADA, bē-ē-lī′a-da (בְּעֶלְיָדָע, *b^e'elyādhā'*, "the Lord knows"; Eliada, which see; cf *HPN*, 144, 192, n. 1, 202): A son of David (1 Ch **14** 7).

BEELSARUS, bē-el′sa-rus, bē-el-sā′rus (**Βεελσάρος,** *Beelsáros*): One who accompanied Zerubbabel in the return from the captivity (1 Esd **5** 8), called Bilshan in Ezr **2** 2 and Neh **7** 7.

BEELTETHMUS, bē-el-teth′mus (**Βεέλτεθμος,** *Beéltethmos;* Balthemus): One of the officers of King Artaxerxes in Pal (1 Esd **2** 16.25). According to Professor Sayce, the name by etymology means "lord of official intelligence" or "postmaster." Rendered "chancellor" in Ezr **4** 8 and "story-writer" in 1 Esd **2** 17.

BEELZEBUB, bē-el′zē-bub (in AV and RV is an error [after Vulg] for Beelzebul [RVm], **Βεελζεβούλ,** *Beelzeboúl;* WH, **Βεεζεβούλ,** *Beezeboúl*): In the time of Christ this was the current name for the chief or prince of demons, and was identified with Satan (q.v.) and the Devil (q.v.). The Jews committed the unpardonable sin of ascribing Christ's work of casting out demons to Beelzebul, thus ascribing to the worst source the supreme manifestation of goodness (Mt **10** 25; **12** 24.27; Mk **3** 22; Lk **11** 15.18.19). There can be little doubt that it is the same name as Baalzebub (q.v.). It is a well-known phenomenon in the history of religions that the gods of one nation become the devils of its neighbors and enemies. When the Aryans divided into Indians and Iranians, the Devas remained gods for the Indians, but became devils (*daevas*) for the Iranians, while the Ahuras remained gods for the Iranians and became devils (*asuras*) for the Indians. Why Baalzebub became Beelzebul, why the *b* changed into *l*, is a matter of conjecture. It may have been an accident of popular pronunciation, or a conscious perversion (Beelzebul in Syr = "lord of dung"), or OT *z^ebhūbh* may have been a perversion, accidental or intentional of *z^ebhūl*

(="house"), so that Baalzebul meant "lord of the house." These are the chief theories offered (Cheyne in *EB;* Barton in Hastings, *ERE*).

T. Rees

BEER, bē'ēr (בְּאֵר, *b*ᵉ*'ēr;* φρέαρ, *phréar;* Lat *puteus*="well"):

(1) A station on the march of the Israelites to the N. of the Arnon (Nu **21** 16). Here it was that they sang round the well this song:

'Spring up O well; greet it with song,
Well, that the princes have dug,
The nobles of the people have bored,
With the sceptre—with their staves' (Nu **21** 16ff).

The place is not identified.

(2) The town to which Jotham fled from his brother Abimelech after declaring his parable from Mt. Gerizim (Jgs **9** 21). This may be identical with Beeroth, which see.

BEERA, bē̆-ē'ra, bē'ēr-a (בְּאֵרָא, *b*ᵉ*'ērā',* "expounder"): A descendant of Asher (1 Ch **7** 37).

BEERAH, bē̆-ē'ra, bē'ēr-a (בְּאֵרָה, *b*ᵉ*'ērāh;* "expounder"): A prince of the house of Reuben whom Tiglath-pileser carried away captive (1 Ch **5** 6). Cf 2 K **15** 29; **16** 7.

BEER-ELIM, bē-ēr-ē'lim (בְּאֵר אֵלִים, *b*ᵉ*'ēr 'ēlīm;* φρέαρ τοῦ 'Αιλείμ, *phréar toú Aileim,* lit. "well of E."): Probably lay to the N. of Moab, answering to Eglaim in the S. (Isa **15** 8). It may possibly be identical with Beer (1); but there is no certainty.

BEERI, bē̆-ē'rī (בְּאֵרִי, *b*ᵉ*'ērī,* "expounder"):

(1) Father of Judith, one of Esau's wives (Gen **26** 34).

(2) The father of the prophet Hosea (Hos **1** 1).

BEER-LAHAI-ROI, bē-ēr-la-hī'roi, bē-ēr-lā-hī-rō'i (בְּאֵר לַחַי רֹאִי, *b*ᵉ*'ēr laḥai rō'ī,* "well of the Living One that seeth me"): "A fountain of water in the wilderness," "the fountain in the way to Shur" (Gen **16** 7–14). It was the scene of Hagar's theophany, and here Isaac dwelt for some time (Gen **16** 7 f; **24** 62; **25** 11). The site is in The Negeb between Kadesh and Bered (**16** 14). Rowland identifies the well with the modern *'Ain Moilâhhi,* cir 50 miles S. of Beersheba and 12 miles W. of *'Ain Kadis.* Cheyne thinks that Hagar's native country, to which she was fleeing and from which she took a wife for Ishmael, was not Egypt (*miçrayim*), but a north Arabian district called by the Assyrians *Muṣri* (*EB*).

S. F. Hunter

BEEROTH, bē̆-ē'roth, bē'ēr-oth (בְּאֵרוֹת, *b*ᵉ*'ērōth;* Βηρώθ, *Bērōth*): One of the cities of the Canaanites whose inhabitants succeeded in deceiving Israel, and in making a covenant with them (Josh **9** 3 ff). Apparently they were Hivites (ver 7). The occasion on which the Beerothites fled to Gittaim where they preserved their communal identity is not indicated. The town was reckoned to Benjamin (2 S **4** 2 f). *Onom* places it under Gibeon, 7 Rom miles from Jerus on the way to Nicopolis (*Amwās*). If we follow the old road by way of Gibeon (*el-Jīb*) and Bethhoron, Beeroth would lie probably to the N.W. of *el-Jīb.* The traditional identification is with *el-Bīreh,* about 8 miles from Jerus on the great north road. If the order in which the towns are mentioned (Josh **9** 17; **18** 25) is any guide as to position, *el-Bīreh* is too far to the N.W. The identification is precarious. To Beeroth belonged the murderers of Ish-bosheth (2 S **4** 2), and Naharai, Joab's armor-bearer (2 S **23** 37; 1 Ch **11** 39). It was reoccupied after the Exile (Ezr **2** 25; Neh **7** 29).

W. Ewing

BEEROTH BENE-JAAKAN, ben'ē-jā'a-kan (בְּאֵרֹת בְּנֵי־יַעֲקָן, *b*ᵉ*'ērōth b*ᵉ*nē ya'ăḳān;* RVm "the wells of the children of Jaakan"): A desert camp of the Israelites mentioned before Moserah (Dt **10** 6). In Nu **33** 31.32 the name is given simply "Bene-jaakan," and the situation after Moseroth. See Wanderings of Israel.

BEEROTHITE, bē̆-ē'roth-īt, bē'ēr-oth-īt, **BEROTHITE** (בְּאֵרֹתִי, *b*ᵉ*'ērōthī;* 2 S **4** 5.9; 2 S **23** 37; shortened form, 1 Ch **11** 39). See Beeroth.

BEERSHEBA, bē-ēr-shē'ba (בְּאֵר שֶׁבַע, *b*ᵉ*'ēr shebha';* Βηρσαβέε, *Bērsabée*): Allotted originally to Simeon (Josh **19** 2), one of "the uttermost cities of the tribe of the children of Judah" (Josh **15** 28).

1. The Meaning of the Name

(1) The most probable meaning of Beersheba is the "well of seven." "Seven wells" is improbable on etymological grounds; the numeral should in that case be first. In Gen **21** 31 Abraham and Abimelech took an oath of witness that the former had dug the well and seven ewe lambs were offered in sacrifice, "Wherefore he called that place Beer-sheba; because there they sware both of them." Here the name is ascribed to the Heb root שָׁבַע, *shābha',* "to swear," but this same root is connected with the idea of seven, seven victims being offered and to take an oath, meaning "to come under the influence of seven."

Another account is given (Gen **26** 23–33), where Isaac takes an oath and just afterward, "the same day Isaac's servants came, and told him concerning the well which they had digged, and said unto him, We have found water. And he called it Shibah: therefore the name of the city is Beer-sheba unto this day."

2. A Sacred Shrine

(2) Beersheba was a sacred shrine. "Abraham planted a tamarisk tree in Beer-sheba, and called there on the name of Jeh, the Everlasting God" (Gen **21** 33). Theophanies occurred there to Hagar (Gen **21** 17), to Isaac (**26** 24), to Jacob (**46** 2), and to Elijah (1 K **19** 5). By Amos (**5** 5) it is classed with Bethel and Gilgal as one of the rival shrines to the pure worship of Jeh, and in another place (**8** 14) he writes "They shall fall, and never rise up again," who sware, "As the way [i.e. *cultus*] of Beer-sheba liveth." The two unworthy sons of Samuel were judges in Beersheba (1 S **8** 2) and Zibiah, mother of King Jehoash, was born there (2 K **12** 1; 2 Ch **24** 1).

3. Its Position

(3) Geographically Beersheba marked the southern limit of Judah, though theoretically this extended to the "river of Egypt" (Gen **15** 18)—the modern *Wady el'Avīsh*—60 miles farther south. It was the extreme border of the cultivated land. From Dan to Beersheba (2 S **17** 11, etc) or from Beersheba to Dan (1 Ch **21** 2; 2 Ch **30** 5) were the proverbial expressions, though necessarily altered through the changed conditions in later years to "from Geba to Beer-sheba" (2 K **23** 8) or "from Beer-sheba to the hill-country of Ephraim" (2 Ch **19** 4).

4. Modern Beersheba

(4) Today Beersheba is *Bîr es-Seba'* in the *Wady es Seba',* 28 miles S.W. of Hebron on "the southern border of a vast rolling plain broken by the torrent beds of Wady Khalîl and Wady Seba" (Robinson). The plain is treeless but is covered by verdure in the spring; it is dry and monotonous most of the year. Within the last few years this long-deserted spot—a wide stretch of shapeless ruins, the haunt of the lawless Bedouin—has been re-occupied; the Turks, and later the English,

BEERSHEBA OVERLOOKING THE DESERT

established stable, intelligent government; government offices and shops have been built; wells have been cleared, and there is now an abundant water supply pumped even to the separate houses. Robinson (*BW*, XVII, 247 ff) has described how he found seven ancient wells there—probably still more will yet be found. The whole neighborhood is strewn with the ruins of the Byzantine city which once flourished there; it was an episcopal see. It is probable that the city of OT times stood where *Tell es Seba'* now is, some 2½ miles to the E.; from the summit a commanding view can be obtained (*PEF*, III, 394, Sheet XXIV).

E. W. G. MASTERMAN

BEESHTERAH, bē-esh'tē-ra (Josh **21** 27). See ASHTAROTH.

BEETLE, bē't'l (RV CRICKET; חַרְגֹּל, *ḥargōl;* see LOCUST): This name occurs only in Lev **11** 22 as one of four winged jumping insects (*shereç hā-'ōph*) which may be eaten. It certainly is not a beetle and is probably not a cricket. Probably all four are names of locusts, of which more than 30 species have been described from Syria and Pal, and for which there are at least 8 Arab. names in use, though with little distinction of species. Closely allied to *ḥargōl* are the Arab. *ḥarjalet,* a troop of horses or a flight of locusts, from *ḥarjal,* "to gallop," and *harjawān,* "a wingless locust."

ALFRED ELY DAY

BEEVES, bēvs (Lev **22** 21 AV). See CATTLE.

BEFORE, bē-fōr': The tr of a great variety of Heb and Gr words. "Haran died b. [ERV "in the presence of," lit. "before the face of"] his father Terah" (Gen **11** 28). To be "before" God is to enjoy His favor (Ps **31** 22). "The Syrians before" (Isa **9** 12 RVm "on the east," as "behind," owing to the position of Canaan, relative to Syria, implies the west).

BEG, BEGGAR, BEGGING: It is significant that the Mosaic law contains no enactment concerning beggars, or begging, though it makes ample provision for the relief and care of "the poor in the land." Bib. Heb seems to have no term for professional begging, the nearest approach to it being the expressions "to ask [or seek] bread" and "to wander." This omission certainly is not accidental; it comports with the very nature of the Mosaic law, the spirit of which is breathed in this, among other kindred provisions, that a poor Hebrew who even sold himself for debt to his wealthy brother was allowed to serve him only until the Jubilee (see JUBILEE), and his master was forbidden to treat him as a slave (Lev **25** 39). These laws, as far as actually practised, have always virtually done away with beggars and begging among the Jews.

1. No Law Concerning Beggars or Begging in Israel

Begging, however, came to be known to the Jews in the course of time with the development of the larger cities, either as occurring among themselves, or among neighboring or intermingling peoples, as may be inferred from Ps **59** 15; cf **109** 10, where Jeh is besought that the children of the wicked may be cursed with beggary, in contra-distinction to the children of the righteous, who have never had to ask bread (Ps **37** 25, "I have been young, and now am old; yet have I not seen the righteous forsaken, nor his seed asking [EV "begging"] bread." For the Heb expression corresponding to "begging" see Ps **59** 15, "They shall wander up and down for food"; and cf Ps **119** 10, "Let me not wander," etc.

2. Begging Not Unknown to the Ancient Jews

The first clear denunciation of beggary and almstaking in Jewish lit. is found in Ecclus (Sirach) **40** 28–30, where the Heb for "begging" is to "wander," etc, as in Ps **59** 15, according to the ed of Cowley and Neubauer, Oxford, 1897. There as well as in Tobit, and in the NT, where beggars are specifically mentioned, the word *eleēmosúnē* has assumed the special sense of alms given to the begging poor (cf Tob **4** 7.16.17; **12** 8–11; Ecclus [Sir] **3** 14.30; **7** 10; **16** 14; Mt **6** 2–4; **20** 30–34; Mk **10** 46–52; Lk **11** 41; **12** 33; Jn **9** 1–41; Acts **9** 36; **10** 2.4.31; **24** 17).

3. Begging and Almstaking Denounced in Jewish Literature

Jerusalem Beggars.

As to professional beggars, originally, certainly, and for a long time, they were a despised class among the Hebrews; and the Jewish communities are forbidden to support them from the general charity fund (*BB*, 9*a*; *Yōreh Dē'āh*, 250, 3). But the spirit of the law is evinced again in that it is likewise forbidden to drive a beggar away without an alms (*ha-Yādh ha-Ḥăzāḳāh*, l.c. **7** 7).

4. Professional Beggars a Despised Class

Begging was well known and beggars formed a considerable class in the gospel age. Proof of this is found in the references to almsgiving in the Sermon on the Mount (Mt **5–7** and parallels), and in the accounts of beggars in connection with public places, e.g. the entrance to Jericho (Mt **20** 30 and parallels), which was a gateway to pilgrims going up to Jerus to the great festivals and in the neighborhood of rich men's houses (Lk **16** 20), and esp. the gates of the Temple at Jerus (Acts **3** 2). This prevalence of begging was due largely to the want of any adequate system of ministering relief, to the lack of any true medical science and the resulting ignorance of remedies for common diseases like ophthalmia, for instance, and to the impoverishment of the land under the excessive taxation of the Rom government (Hausrath, *Hist of NT Times*, I, 188 [Eng. tr Williams and Norgate], cf Edersheim, *L and T of Jesus*, II, 178). That begging was looked down upon is incidentally evidenced by the remark of the unjust steward, "To beg I am ashamed" (Lk **16** 3); and that, when associated with indolence, it was strongly condemned by public opinion appears from Sir (**40** 28–30).

5. In the Gospel Age

The words used for "beg," "beggar" of EV in the NT differ radically in idea: in those formed from *aitéō* (Mk **10** 46; Lk **16** 3; **18** 35; Jn **9** 8 RV) the root idea is that of "asking," while *ptōchós* (Lk **16** 20.22) suggests the cringing or crouching of a beggar. But see Mt **5** 3 where the word for "humble" is *ptōchos.*

A marked change has come over Jewish life in modern times, in this as well as in other respects.

6. A Change in Modern Times

Since the 17th cent. the Jewish poor in many parts of the world have made it a practice, esp. on Fridays and on the eves of certain festivals, to go systematically from house to house asking alms. In parts of Europe today it is a full-grown abuse: crowds of Jewish beggars push their way and ply their trade about the synagogue doors (Abrahams, *EB*, art. "Alms," 310). So the Jewish beggar, in spite of the spirit of the law and ancient Jewish custom, has, under modern conditions too well known to require explanation here, become a troublesome figure and problem in modern Jewish society. For such beggars and begging, see *Jew Enc*, arts. "Schnorrers," "Alms," etc, and for another kind of begging among modern Jews, and collections for poverty-stricken Jewish settlers in Pal, see arts. "Ḥalukah," "Charity," etc.

Literature.—Saalschütz, *Arch. der Hebräer*, II, ch xviii (Königsberg, 1855–56); Riehm, *Handwörterbuch zu den Büchern des AT*, s.v. "Almosen"; cf *Jew Enc, HDB*, and *Enc B*, arts. "Alms"; and Abrahams, *Jewish Life in the Middle Ages*, chs xvii, xviii (Philadelphia, 1896); Mackie, *Bible Manners and Customs;* Day, *The Social Life of the Hebrews.*

Geo. B. Eager

BEGGARLY, beg′ẽr-li (**πτωχός**, *ptōchós*): The word has the thought of "to crouch" or "cringe," such as is common with professional beggars. It is used in Mt **5** 3 and Gal **4** 9, and in both cases means complete spiritual destitution. As used in Gal it expresses the contrast between their present condition and the former estate, toward which he says they are again tending. Paul has in mind both the Jewish and heathen systems of religion with all their outward show. He therefore here emphasizes the immeasurable superiority of the riches and liberty in Christ. He further expresses this same thought of the law in Rom **8** 3 and He **7** 18. In view of the wretchedness of the condition indicated by the word "beggarly," he states his astonishment that they should so little appreciate the liberty and riches which they now enjoy as even to think of going back to the former condition.

Jacob W. Kapp

BEGIN, bē̆-gin′: To make the first movement toward a given end (חָלַל, *ḥālal;* **ἄρχομαι**, *árchomai*). Those who interpret it in many passages pleonastically mean by this, that in such passages as "began to teach" or "began to speak," nothing more is intended than to express vividly and graphically the thought of the dependent infinitive. Mt **4** 17; Lk **3** 23; Acts **1** 1 are so understood. For contrary opinion, see Thayer's *Lexicon* and Winer's *Grammar of NT Greek.*

The noun, ἀρχή, *archḗ*, "beginning," in the writings of John, is used sometimes in an abstract sense, to designate a previous stage (Jn **1** 1.2; **8** 25; 1 Jn **1** 1; **3** 8) and, sometimes, the Source or First Cause (Rev **3** 14; **21** 6; **22** 13). Often used also, not for the absolute beginning, but, relatively, for the starting-point of some important movement (1 Jn **2** 7.24; Acts **11** 15; Phil **4** 15).

H. E. Jacobs

BEGINNING, bē̆-gin′ing (רֵאשִׁית, *rē'shīth;* **ἀρχή**, *archḗ*): The natural meaning of the word is with reference to time. The primitive Gr root means "to be long," "to draw out." Thus it is used to refer to some point of time long drawn out, or long past (Gen **1** 1). It is used also to express the inauguration of a particular event (Ex **12** 2). The principal interest in the word centers in the use of it in Jn **1** 1. It must be interpreted here by that which follows in the statement as to the relation of the Logos to the Eternal God and the use of the word "was." It is true that the word *archē* cannot be separated from the idea of time, but when time began He already was, and therefore He was from eternity. See Time; Eternity.

Figurative: In a **fig.** sense it is used of that which is most excellent, the chief part (Prov **1** 7); of the most eminent person (Col **1** 18); the author (Rev **3** 14).

Jacob W. Kapp

BEGOTTEN, bē̆-got′'n (יָלַד, *yāladh;* "to bear," "bring forth," "beget"; denotes the physical relation of either parent to a child, Gen **3** 16; **4** 18): Used **metaphorically** of God's relation to Israel (Dt **32** 18) and to the Messianic king (Ps **2** 7); (γεννάω, *gennáō*, "to beget," or "bear"): generally used of a father (Mt **1** 1–16); more rarely of a mother (Lk **1** 13.57); used **metaphorically** of causing or engendering moral and spiritual relations and states (1 Cor **4** 15; Philem **10**); of the new birth of the Holy Spirit (Jn **3** 3 ff). Men who obey and love God as sons are begotten of Him (Jn **1** 13; 1 Jn **2** 29; **3** 9; **4** 7; **5** 1.4.18; cf 1 Pet **1** 23). Used esp. of God's act in making Christ His Son: "Thou art my Son; this day have I begotten thee" (Ps **2** 7) quoted in Acts (**13** 33) in reference to His resurrection (cf Rom **1** 4). The same passage is cited (He **1** 5) as proving Christ's filial dignity, transcending the angels in that "he hath inherited a more excellent name than they," i.e. the name of son; and again (He **5** 5) of God conferring upon Christ the glory of the priestly office.

Commentators differ as to whether the act of begetting the Son in these two passages is (*a*) the eternal generation, or (*b*) the incarnation in time, or (*c*) the resurrection and ascension. The immediate context of **1** 5 (see **1** 3) seems to favor the last view (Westcott). The first view would not be foreign to the author's thought: with **5** 5 cf **6** 20, "a high priest forever" (Alford). The author of He thinks of the eternal and essential sonship of Christ as realized in history in His ascension to the "right hand of the Majesty" (**1** 3). And what is emphatic is the fact and status of sonship, rather than the time of begetting.

T. Rees

BEGUILE, bē̆-gīl′: In 2 Pet **2** 14 AV (cf Jas **1** 14) the word δελεάζω, *deleázō*, is tr[d] "beguile," and means particularly to "entice," "catch by bait." Doubtless Peter got this idea from his old business of fishing, baiting the hook to beguile the fish. In Rom **7** 11; **16** 18; 1 Cor **3** 18 the word is ἐξαπατάω, *exapatáō*, and means "to cheat" or "to thoroughly deceive." The thought is to be so completely deceived as to accept falsehood for the truth, believing it to be the truth. In Col **2** 4.18 AV; Jas **1** 22 the word is παραλογίζομαι, *paralogízomai*, and means "to miscalculate," "to be imposed upon." It refers particularly to being beguiled by mere probability. See Deceit; Delusion.

Jacob W. Kapp

BEHALF, bē̆-häf′: "On the part of" (Ex **27** 21, i.e. so far as it affects them); "on the side of" (Job **36** 2). For *hupér*, "over," in the sense of furnishing assistance, as in 2 Cor **5** 20, "in the interest of Christ" (ver 21); "for our good," "in his cause" (Phil **1** 29); also, often in 2 Cor, in general sense of "concerning" (**5** 12; **7** 4; **8** 24; **9** 2; **12** 5). *Huper* does not of itself indicate substitution, although one who shelters ["is over"] another, suffers "in his stead" (AV 2 Cor **5** 20), as well as "in his behalf."

BEHAVIOR, bē̆-hāv′yẽr (טַעַם, *ṭa'am*, "taste," "flavor," hence "intellectual taste," i.e. judgment, reason, understanding): Of significance as referring to David's feigning madness before Achish, king of Gath, being "sore afraid." Gesenius renders it "changed his understanding," i.e. his mental behavior and outward manner (1 S **21** 13, and title to Ps **34**).

Twice used in the NT (AV) of the well-ordered life of the Christian (κόσμιος, *kósmios*, "well-arranged," "modest," i.e. living with decorum: 1 Tim **3** 2), defining the blameless life expected of a minister (overseer), "A bishop must be . . . . of good behavior," RV "orderly" (κατάστημα, *katástēma*, "demeanor," "deportment"), including, according to Dean Alford, "gesture and habit" as the outward expression of a reverent spirit (1 Pet **3** 1.2). "Aged women . . . . in behavior as becometh holiness" (Tit **2** 3; RV "reverent in demeanor"). DWIGHT M. PRATT

BEHEADING, bē̆-hed′ing. See PUNISHMENTS.

BEHEMOTH, bē′hē̆-moth, bē̆-hē′moth (בְּהֵמוֹת, *beh*ē*mōth:* Job **40** 15): Apparently the pl. of *beh*ē*māh*, "a beast," used of domestic or wild animals. The same form, *behēmōth*, occurs in other passages, e.g. Dt **28** 26; **32** 24; Isa **18** 6; Hab **2** 17, where it is not rendered "behemoth" but "beasts." According to some, the word *behēmōth*, occurring in Job **40** 15, is not a Heb word, the pl. of *behēmāh*, but a word of Egyp origin signifying "water ox." This etymology is denied by Cheyne and others. The word has by various writers been understood to mean rhinoceros and elephant, but the description (Job **40** 15–24) applies on the whole very well to the hippopotamus (*Hippopotamus amphibius*) which inhabits the Nile and other rivers of Africa. Esp. applicable are the references to its great size, its eating grass, the difficulty with which weapons penetrate its hide, and its frequenting of streams.

The behemoth of Job is best interpreted not as a zoölogical, but as a mythological animal, the greatest enemy of immortality according to Egypt mythology. Assertion of divine control over him is a dramatic assertion of immortality (Cobern, *Methodist Review*, May, 1913).

The remains of a fossil hippopotamus of apparently the same species are found over most of Europe, so that it may have inhabited Pal in early historical times, although we have no record of it. There is a smaller living species in west Africa, and there are several other fossil species in Europe and India. The remains of *Hippopotamus minutus* have been found in enormous quantities in caves in Malta and Sicily.

For an elaborate explanation of behemoth and leviathan (q.v.) as mythical creatures, see Cheyne, *EB*, s.v. REVISED BY M. G. K. ALFRED ELY DAY

BEHOLDING, bē̆-hōld′ing: Many Heb and Gr words are so rendered in EV, but ἐποπτεύσαντες, *epopteúsantes*, "your good works, which they behold" (1 Pet **2** 12); "beholding your chaste behavior" (**3** 2), and ἐπόπται, *epóptai*, "We were eyewitnesses of his majesty" (2 Pet **1** 16) are peculiar to Peter. The fact that this word is used only by Peter and is used in both epistles is an argument for identity of authorship. The word *epóptēs* denotes one who had been initiated into the innermost secrets of his faith and who enjoyed the highest religious privileges; but now in contradiction to the secrecy of all pagan "mysteries" (Eleusinian, etc) the apostles would share with all the faithful every spiritual vision which they enjoyed ("we made known unto you").

In 2 Cor **3** 18, for κατοπτριζόμενοι, *katoptrizómenoi*, the ERV gives "reflecting (as a mirror) the glory of the Lord," ARV "beholding (as in a mirror," etc). *Kátoptron* was a mirror of polished metal. We cannot clearly and fully behold the outshining of spiritual grandeur in Christ Jesus, but in the gospel God accommodates and adjusts the vision as we are able to bear it, and the glory beheld becomes glory imparted to (and reflected by) the beholder.

John's Gospel gives us θεάομαι, *theáomai* ("to look closely at"), and θεωρέω, *theōréō* ("to discern"). "We beheld [*etheasámetha*] his glory" (Jn **1** 14), "that they may behold [*theōrôsin*] my glory" (**17** 24). In classic lit., the former word is closely associated with theatrical spectacles, and the latter with athletic games, and they both convey the idea of unceasing interest, deepening in this connection into love and joy. M. O. EVANS

BEHOOVE, bē̆-hōōv′: Used in the NT for two Gr words *deí* (Lk **24** 26; Acts **17** 3) and *opheílō* (He **2** 17); the former referring to a physical, and the latter to a moral, necessity (Bengelon, 1 Cor **11** 10). The former means "must," that is, it is required by the order which God has ordained; the latter, "ought," that is, it is required as a debt.

BEIRUT, bā′rōōt′. See BERYTUS.

BEKA, bē′kä (בֶּקַע, *beḳa'*, "half"): Half a shekel, the amount contributed by each male of the Israelites for the use of the Sanctuary (Ex **38** 26). Its value varied according to the standard used, but on the ordinary, or Phoen, standard it would represent about 122 grains. See WEIGHTS AND MEASURES.

BEL, bel, bāl (בֵּל, *bēl*): Appellative name of a Bab god (cf BAAL), in the OT and Apoc identified with Marduk or Merodach, the tutelary deity of Babylon (cf Isa **46** 1; Jer **51** 44; Bar **6** 41). See BABYLONIA AND ASSYRIA, THE RELIGION OF.

BEL AND THE DRAGON. See DANIEL, BOOK OF, X.

BEL, bel, bāl, **AND THE DRAGON,** drag′un (Gr words: **δράκων**, *drákōn*, "dragon," "serpent"; **ἐκτός**, *ektós*, "except"; **ὅρασις**, *hórasis*, "vision," "prophecy"; **ὄφις**, *óphis*, "serpent"; **σφραγισάμενος**, *sphragisámenos*, "having sealed"; **χωρίς**, *chōrís*, "except." Heb or Aram. words: חָתַם, *ḥātham*, "to seal"; זִיפָא, *zēphā'*, "pitch"; זַעְפָּא, *za'ăphā'*, "storm," "wind"; נָחָשׁ, *nāḥāsh*, "snake"; תַּנִּין, *tannīn*, "serpent," "sea monster"):

I. INTRODUCTORY
II. NAME OF BEL AND THE DRAGON (in the Various Recensions, Versions and Codices)
III. CONTENTS
  1. The Bel Story: the God of Bel
  2. The Dragon Story; Meaning of "Dragon"; Serpent-Worship in Babylon
IV. TEXTUAL AUTHORITIES
  1. Manuscripts
  2. Recensions or Versions
    (1) Greek
    (2) Syriac
    (3) Latin
    (4) Aramaic
V. ORIGINAL LANGUAGE: PRINCIPAL OPINIONS
  1. Greek
  2. Hebrew
  3. Aramaic
  4. Reasons for Regarding Hebrew as Likeliest
VI. TEACHING
  Little in this work that is distinctly Jewish. God is great, absolute and ever-living; angels intervene for special ends; the absurdity of idol-worship
VII. AUTHOR, PLACE AND DATE OF COMPOSITION
  Probably not in Babylon; perhaps the Heb text originated in Pal about 146 BC or later. The LXX version produced in Egypt about 100 BC, which may be the date and language of the Book. Θ (Theodotion's version) was produced probably at Ephesus about 180 AD

VIII. CANONICITY AND AUTHENTICITY
Accepted as canonical by the Jews of Egypt but rejected by the Jews of Pal. Accepted as part of the Bible by Gr and Lat church Fathers, by the Council of Trent and therefore by the Rom church; denied by Protestants to be canonical
LITERATURE

I. Introductory.—Bel and the Dragon is the third of the three Apocryphal additions to Daniel, The SONG OF THE THREE CHILDREN and SUSANNA (q.v.) being the other two. In the Gr and Lat VSS (see below, "IV. Textual Authorities") these "additions" form an integral part of the canonical Book of Dnl, and they are recognized as such and therefore as themselves canonical by the Council of Trent. But the Song of the Three Children is the only piece having a necessary connection with the Heb canonical Book of Dnl; in the Gr and Lat texts it follows Dnl **3** 24. The other two are appended and appear to have an origin independent of the book to which they are appended and also of each other, though in all three as also in the Heb Book of Dnl the name and fame of Daniel stand out prominently.

II. Name.—Since in the Gr and Lat recensions or VSS Bel forms a portion of the Book of Dnl it does not bear a special name. But in the only two known MSS of the LXX in Syro-Hexaplar (see below, "IV. Textual Authorities") these words stand at the head of the "addition" now under consideration: "From [or "a part of"] the prophecy of Habakkuk son of Joshua of the tribe of Levi." That the Bib. writing prophet of that name is meant is beyond question. In Θ this fact is distinctly stated (see ver 33); and it is equally beyond question that these tales could never have come from the prophet so called (see below "VIII. Canonicity and Authenticity").

In codd. A and B of Θ the title is: *Horasis* 12, i.e. ch **12** of Dnl, canonical Dnl being comprised in 11 chs. In the Vulg, Bel forms ch **14,** but, as in the case of the earlier chs, it has no heading.

In the Syr Pesh (W) the story of Bel is preceded by "Bel the idol," and that of the Dragon by "Then follows the Dragon." Bel and the Dragon is the title in all Protestant VSS of the Apocrypha, which rigidly keep the latter separate from the books of the Heb canon.

III. Contents.—The stories of Bel and of the Dragon have a separate origin and existed apart: they are brought together because they both agree in holding up idolatry to ridicule and in encouraging Jewish believers to be true to their religion. The glorification of Daniel is also another point in which both agree, though while the Daniel of the Bel story appears as a shrewd judge corresponding to the etymology of that name, he of the Dragon story is but a fearless puritan who will die rather than be faithless to his religion.

It is evident however that the editor of the "additions" has fused both stories into one, making the Dragon story depend on that which precedes (see vs 23 f). It seems very likely that, in a Nestorian list mentioned by Churton (*Uncanonical and Apocryphal Scriptures*, 391), Bel and the Dragon is comprised under the title, *The Little Daniel.*

The two stories as told in common by LXX and Θ may be thus summarized:

1. The Story of Bel

There is in Babylon an image of Bel which Daniel refuses to worship, though no form of worship is mentioned except that of supplying the god with food. The king (Cyrus according to Θ) remonstrates with the delinquent Hebrew, pointing out to him the immense amount of food consumed daily by Bel, who thus proves himself to be a living god. Daniel, doubting the king's statement as to the food, asks to be allowed to test the alleged fact. His request being granted, he is shown by expressed desire the *lectisternia*, the sacred tables being covered by food which the god is to consume during the night. The doors are all sealed by arrangement, and after the priests have departed Daniel has the temple floor strewn with light ashes. When the morning breaks it is found that the doors are still sealed, but the food has disappeared. Upon examination the tracks of bare feet are found on the ash-strewn floor, showing that the priests have entered the temple by a secret way and removed the food. Angered by the trick played on him the king has the priests put to death and the image destroyed.

The word Bel, a short form of Baal, occurs in the OT in Isa **46** 1; Jer **50** 2; **51** 44, where it stands for Merodach or Marduk, chief of the Bab deities. Originally however it denotes any one of the Bab local deities, and esp. the principal deity worshipped at Nippur (for similar use of the Heb "Baal" see art. on this word). In Θ Cyrus appears as an abettor of Bel-worship, which is quite in accordance with the practice of the early Pers kings to show favor to the worship of the countries they conquered. See *Century Bible*, "Ezr, Neh and Est," 40.

2. The Dragon Story

There is in Babylon a great live dragon worshipped by a large number of the inhabitants, who lavishly feed it. In the present case the god is or is represented by a living creature which can be fed, and, indeed, needs feeding. Daniel refuses to bow down before the dragon and makes an offer to the king to kill it. Believing the god well able to care for himself, the king accepts Daniel's challenge. Daniel makes a mixture of which pitch forms the principal ingredient and thrusts it down the dragon's throat, so that "it bursts asunder and dies." The people are infuriated at the death of their god and demand that the king shall have the god-murderer put to death, a demand to which the royal master yields by having Daniel cast into a den of lions, as was done to other culprits found guilty of capital charges. But though the prophet remained in the company of 7 lions for 6 days he suffered no injury. On the last day when Daniel, without food, was naturally hungry, a miracle was performed by way of supplying him with food. Habakkuk (see above, "II. Name"), when cooking food for his reapers, heard an angel's voice commanding him to carry the food he had prepared to Daniel in the lions' den in Babylon. Upon his replying that he did not know where the den, or even Babylon, was, the angel laid hold of his hair and by it carried the prophet to the very part of the den where Daniel was. Having handed the latter the meal intended for the reapers, he was safely brought back by the angel to his own home. It would seem that Habakkuk was protected from the lions as well as Daniel. Seeing all this the king worshipped God, set Daniel free, and in his stead cast his accusers into the lions' den, where they were instantly devoured.

Zöckler in his commentary (p. 215) speaks of the "fluidity" of the Dragon myth, and he has been followed by Marshall and Daubney. But what in reality does the Gr word *drakōn*, rendered "dragon," mean? In the LXX the word is used generally (15 times) to translate the Heb *tannīn* which denotes a serpent or sea monster. It is this word (*tannīn*) which in the Aram. version of the Dragon story translates the Gr *drakōn*. Now in Ex **4** 3 and **7** 9 the Heb *tannīn* and *nāḥāsh* ("serpent") seem identified as are the Gr *drakōn* and *ophis* in Rev **12** 9. We may therefore take *drakōn* in the present story to stand for a serpent. We know that in Babylon the god Nina was worshipped in the form of a serpent (see Sayce, *Hibbert Lectures*, 281 f), and it is more probable that it is the worship of this god or of some other serpent deity that is here meant, than that there is any allusion to the Bab story according to which Marduk the supreme deity of Babylon engaged in a conflict with Tiamat the monster—foe to light and order. (1) The dragon of the present story is a god and not as Tiamat, a kind of devil, and a male, not a female. (2) The dragon in the present story is a serpent, which is not true of Tiamat. (3) Apsu (male) and Tiamat (female) are Bab deities who give birth to the gods of heaven; these gods subsequently led by their mother Tiamat engaged in a fierce contest with Marduk.

Since Gunkel published his book, *Schöpfung und Chaos* (1895), it has been the fashion to see reflections of the Marduk-Tiamat conflict throughout the OT. But recent investigations tend to show that Bab mythology has not dominated Heb thought to the extent that was formerly thought, and with this statement Gunkel himself now agrees, as the last ed of his commentary on Genesis proves.

IV. Textual Authorities.—

1. Manuscripts

(1) *Greek.*—There exist in Gr two forms of the text (see below). (*a*) The LXX text has been preserved in but one original MS, the cod. Christianus (from the Chigi family who owned it, published in Rome in 1772). This belongs to about the 9th cent. This text has been printed also in Cozza's *Sacrorum Bibliorum vestustissima fragmenta Graeca et Latina*, part iii, Romae, 1877, and in Swete's ed of the LXX side by side with Θ. In Tischendorf's LXX it occurs at the close of the ordinary text of the LXX. (*b*) Of Θ (the text of Theodotion) we have the following important MSS: B, A, Q (cod Marchalianus), Γ (vs 1.2–4 only) and Δ (from ver 21 to ver 41).

(2) *Syriac.*—There exists in the Ambrosian Library at Milan, a MS of the 8th cent. of the Syro-Hexaplar version made by Paul of Tella in 617 AD at Alexandria from col vi (LXX) of Origen's Hexapla. This most valuable MS has been edited and published by Ceriani.

2. Recensions or Versions

(1) *Greek.*—(*a*) The LXX: Of this we have but one MS (see above under "Manuscripts") and until its publication at Rome in 1772 what is now known as Θ was believed to be the real LXX version, notwithstanding hints to the contrary by early Christian writers. (*b*) Θ, or the version of Theodotion: This version appears to be a revision of the LXX, with the help, perhaps, as in the case of the canonical Daniel, of a Heb (or Aram.) original, now lost. It is much less pedantic than Aquila's Gr tr which preceded it, and its Gr is better. It is also a better tr than the LXX; yet it has many transliterations of Heb words instead of trs. This version of Daniel displaced that of the LXX at a very early time, for though Origen gave place to the LXX in his Hexapla, in his writings he almost always cites from Θ. In his preface to Daniel Jerome points to the fact that in his own time the church had rejected the LXX in favor of Θ, mentioning the defectiveness of the former as the ground. Even Irenaeus (d. 202) and Porphyry (d. 305) preferred Θ to the LXX. Field was the first to point out that it is the work of Theodotion (not the LXX) that we have in 1 Esd, etc.

(2) *Syriac.*—In addition to the Syro-Hexaplar version (see above, under "Manuscripts") the Pesh version must be noted. It follows Θ closely, and is printed in Walton's *Polyglot* (in one recension only of Bel and the Dragon) and in a revised text edited by Lagarde in 1861; not as R. H. Charles (*Enc Brit*, VII, 807) erroneously says in *The Book of Tobit* by Neubauer.

(3) *Latin.*—(*a*) The old Lat version, which rests on Θ, fragments of which occur in Sabatier's work, *Bibliorum sacrorum Latinae versiones antiquae* (1743, etc, II). (*b*) The Vulg, which follows Jerome's tr, is also based on Θ, and follows it closely.

(4) *Aramaic.*—For the Aram. version published by M. Gaster and claimed to be the text of the book as first written, see below, "V. Original Language."

V. Original Language.—It has been until recent years most generally maintained that Bel and the Dragon was composed and first edited in the Gr language. So Eichhorn, de Wette, Schrader, Fritzsche, Schürer and König. In favor of this the following reasons have been given: (1) No Sem original with reasonable claims has been discovered. Origen, Eusebius and Jerome distinctly say that no Heb (or Aram.) form of this tract existed or was known in their time. (2) The Hebraisms with which this work undoubtedly abounds are no more numerous or more crucial than can be found in works by Jewish authors which are known to have been composed in the Gr language, such as the continual recurrence of *kaí* (="and"), *kai eípe* ("and he said"), etc.

On the other hand, the opinion has been growing among recent scholars that this work was written first of all either in Heb or Aram. Some of the grounds are the following: (1) It is known that Theodotion in making his tr of other parts of the OT (Dnl) endeavored to correct the LXX with the aid of the MT. A comparison of the LXX and of Θ of Bel and the Dragon reveal differences of a similar character. How can we account for them unless we assume that Theodotion had before him a Sem original? A very weak argument, however, for the translator might have corrected on a priori principles, using his own judgment; or there might well have been in his time different recensions of the LXX. Westcott (*DB*, I, 397*a;* 2d ed, 714*a*) holds that some of Θ's changes are due to a desire to give consistency to the facts. (2) Much has been made of the Semiticisms in the work, and it must be admitted that they are numerous and striking. But are these Hebraisms or Aramaisms? The commonest and most undoubted Semiticism is the repeated use of *kai* and *kai egéneto* with the force of the *waw*-consecutive and only to be explained and understood in the light of that construction. But the *waw*-consecutive exists only in classical Heb; Aram. and post-Bib. Heb, including late parts of the OT (parts of Eccl, etc), know nothing of it. It must be assumed then that if the Semiticisms of this work imply a Sem original, that original was Heb, not Aram.

The following Hebraisms found in the LXX and in Θ may briefly be noted: (1) The use of the Gr *kai* with all the varied meanings of the *waw*-consecutive (see below, under "VI. Teaching"). The beginning of a sentence with *kai ēn* ("and there was") (vs 1.3 in LXX; 2 f, etc, in Θ) agrees with the Heb *waw*-consecutive construction, but makes poor Gr. In ver 15 *kai egeneto* can be understood only in the light of the Heb for which it stands. (2) The syntactical feature called parataxy (coördination) presents itself throughout the Gr of this piece, and it has been reproduced in the Eng. trs (AV, RV) as any Eng. reader can see. In the classical languages it is hypotaxy that prevails. If, as seems likely, those responsible for LXX and Θ followed a Heb original, they failed to make sufficient allowance for the peculiar force of the *waw*-consecutive idiom, for this does not involve hypotaxy to any considerable extent. (3) The constant occurrence of *Kúrios* ("Lord") without the art. implies the Heb Yahwe; and the phrase the "Lord God" is also Heb. (4) There are difficulties and differences best explained by assuming a Heb origin. The Gr word *sphragisamenos* has no sense in ver 14 (LXX) for, retaining it, we should read of a sealing of the temple (of Bel) and also of a sealing with signet rings of the doors. The Heb word "shut" (*ṣāṭham*) is written much like that for "seal" (*ḥātham*), and was probably, as Marshal suggests, mistaken for the latter. The temple was "shut" and the doors "sealed." In ver 10 the LXX (*chorís*) and Θ (*ektós*) have 2 words of similar sense, which are best explained as independent renderings of one Heb word.

Marshall, identifying this dragon story with the Bab creation-myth of Marduk and Tiamat, thinks that instead of "pitch" used in making the obolus with which Daniel destroyed the dragon, the original Aram. document has "storm wind," the two words being in Aram. written much alike (*za'ăphā'* = "storm wind," and *zēphā'* = pitch). But the fact is quite overlooked that the obolus contained not only pitch, but also "fat" and "hair" (see ver 27). Besides, in the Aram. version, published by Gaster, to which Marshall attaches great importance as at least a real source, we have four ingredients, viz. pitch (*zĕpᵉthā'*), fat, flax (*kittān*) and hair. Dr. Marshall's suggestion involves therefore not only the confusion of two words spelled differently in Aram., but the substitution of 3 or 4 terms for one in the original draft. Moreover in Bel and the Dragon the several ingredients are made up into a cake with which the dragon was gorged. Dr. Marshall's view assumes also an Aram. original which is against the evidence. But the suggestion would not have been made but for a desire to assimilate the dragon story to the Bab creation-myth, though in motive and details both differ so essentially.

In favor of a Sem original many writers have cited the fact that forms of the story have been found in Heb and Aram. In the 13th cent. Raymund Martini in his *Pugio Fidei* (written against the Jews) quotes Bel and the Dragon from a Heb Midr on Gen which Neubauer discovered and which is almost *verbaṭim* identical with the unique MS containing Midr Rabba de Rabba (see Neubauer, *Tobit*, viii, and Franz Delitzsch, *de Habacuci*, 82). Still other Heb forms of these stories have been found. All the "additions" to Dnl "occur in Heb in the remains of Yosippon," the "Heb Josephus," as he has been called. He wrote in the 10th cent.

But most important of all is the discovery by Dr. M. Gaster of the dragon story in Aram., imbedded in the Chronicles of Yerahmeel, a work of the 10th cent. Dr. Gaster maintains that in this Aram. fragment we have a portion of the original Bel and the Dragon (see *PSBA*, 1894, 280 ff [Introd.], 312 [Text] and 1895 [for notes and tr]). The present writer does not think Dr. Gaster has made out his case. (1) If such an Aram. original did really exist at any time we should have learned something definite about it from early writers, Jewish and Christian. (2) Dr. Gaster has discovered an Aram. form of only two of the three "additions," those of the Song of the Three Children and of the dragon story. What of the rest of the Aram. document? (3) It has already been pointed out that the *waw*-consecutive constructions implied in the Gr texts go back to a Heb, not an Aram. original. (4) The Aram. text of the Dragon story not seldom differs both from the LXX and Θ as in the following and many other cases: The two Gr VSS have in ver 24 "The king [said]," which the Aram. omits: in ver 35 the Aram. after "And Habakkuk said" adds "to the angel," which the LXX and Θ are without. (5) The compiler of the Yerahmeel Chronicle says distinctly that he had taken the Song of the Three Children and the dragon story from the writings of Theodotion (see *PSBA*, 1895, 283), he having, it is quite evident, himself put them into Aram. Dr. Gaster lays stress on the words of the compiler, that what he gives in Aram. is that which "Theodotion found" (loc. cit.). But the reference can be only to the LXX which this translator made the basis of his own version; it is far too much to assume that the Chronicler means an Aram. form of the stories.

VI. Teaching.—The two stories teach the doctrine of the oneness and absoluteness of Yahwe, called throughout *Kúrios* ("Lord"), a lit. rendering of the Heb word *'ădhōnāi* ("Lord") which the Jews substituted for Yahwe in reading the Heb as do now-a-day Jews. In the Gr and Lat VSS it is the word read (the Ḳᵉrē *perpetuum*), not that written Kᵉthībh), which is trᵈ. It would have been more consonant with universal practice if the proper name Yahwe had been transliterated as proper names usually are.

But very little is said of the character of Yahwe. He is great and the only (true) God (ver 41), the living God in contrast with Bel (ver 57). Of the nature of His demands on His worshippers, ritualistic and ethical, nothing is said. There is no reference to any distinctly Jewish beliefs or practices; nothing about the *tōrāh* or about any Divine revelation to men, about sacrifice or the temple or even a priesthood, except that in the LXX (not in Θ) Daniel the prophet is spoken of as a priest—strong evidence of the low place assigned by the writer to the external side of the religion he professed. We do however find mention of an angel, a sort of *deus ex machina* in the Dragon story (vs 34 ff); cf Dnl **6** 22.

The incident of the transportation of Habakkuk to Babylon shows that the writer had strong faith in supernatural intervention on behalf of the pious. Apart from this incident the two stories steer fairly clear of anything that is supernatural. But vs 33–39 are a late interpolation.

VII. Author, Place and Date of Composition.—Nothing whatever is known of the author of the book and nothing definite or certain of the place or date of composition. It has been commonly felt, as by Bissell, etc, that it reflects a Bab origin. Clay (see ver 7) abounded in Babylon (but surely not only in Babylon); bronze (ver 7) was often used in that country for the manufacturing of images, and the lion, it is known, was native to the country (but that was the case also in Pal in Bib. and even post-Bib. times). None of the arguments for a Bab origin have much weight, and there are contrary arguments of considerable force.

The anachronisms and inconsistencies are more easily explained on the assumption of a non-Bab origin. Besides, the Judaism of Babylon was of a very strict and regulation kind, great attention being given to the law and to matters of ritual. There is nothing in Bel and the Dragon regarding these points (see above under "Teaching").

If we assume a Heb original, as there are good grounds for doing, it is quite possible that these legends were written in Pal at a time when the Jewish religion was severely persecuted: perhaps when Antiochus VII (Sidetes, 139–128 BC) reconquered Judah for Syria and sorely oppressed the subject people. Yet nothing very dogmatic can be said as to this. We cannot infer much from the style of the Heb (or Aram.?), since no Sem original has come down to us. It is quite clear that these "additions" imply the existence of the canonical Book of Dnl and belong to a subsequent date, for they contain later developments of traditions respecting Daniel. The canonical Book of Dnl is dated by modern scholars about 160 BC, so that a date about 133 BC (see above) could not be far amiss.

If, on the other hand, we take for granted that

the LXX is the original text of the book, the date of that recension is the date of the work itself. It seems probable that this recension of Dnl was made in Egypt about 150 BC (see 1 Macc **1** 54; **2** 59), and we have evidence that up to that date the "three additions" formed no part of the book, though they exist in all Gr and Syr MSS of Dnl, which have come down to us. Probably the "additions" existed as separate compositions for some time before they were joined to Dnl proper, but it is hardly too much to assume that they were united no later than 100 BC. Yet the data for reaching a conclusion are very slight. It may be added that the Gr of the LXX is distinctly Alex in its character, as Westcott, Bissell and others have pointed out. Theodotion's version is supposed to have been made at Ephesus toward the end of the 2d cent. AD.

VIII. Canonicity and Authenticity.—The Alex Jews, recognizing the LXX as their Bible, accepted the whole of the Apoc as canonical. The Pal Jews, on the other hand, limited their canonical Scriptures to the Heb OT. There is, of course, some uncertainty (largely no doubt because it was originally a tr from the Heb) as to whether the LXX at the first included the Apoc in its whole extent or not, but all the evidence points to the fact that it did, though individual books like Dnl existed apart before they formed a portion of the Gr or Egyp canon.

In the early Christian church all the three "additions" are quoted as integral parts of Dnl by Gr and by Lat Fathers, as e.g. by Irenaeus (IV, 5, 2 f); Tertullian (*De idololatria*, c.18); Cyprian (*Ad fortunatum*, c.11).

By a decree of the Council of Trent these "additions" were for the Rom church made as much a part of the Bible canon as the Heb Book of Dnl. Protestant churches have as a rule excluded the whole of the Apoc from their Bibles, regarding its books as either "Deutero-canonical" or "non-canonical." In consequence of this attitude among Protestants the Apoc has until lately been greatly neglected by Protestant writers. But a great change is setting in, and some of the best commentaries by Protestant scholars produced in recent years deal with the Apoc and its teaching.

Julius Africanus (fl. first half of 3d cent. AD) was the first to impugn the truth of the stories embodied in the "additions" to Daniel. This he did in a letter to Origen to which the recipient vigorously replied.

The improbabilities and contradictions of these three pieces have often been pointed out from the time of Julius Africanus down to the present day. The following points may be set down as specimens: (1) Daniel is called a priest in the LXX (ver 1), and yet he is identified with the prophet of that name. (2) Habakkuk the prophet (he is so called in Θ [see ver 33], and no other can be intended) is made to be a contemporary of Daniel and also of the Pers king Cyrus (see vs 1 and 33 in the Eng. Bible). Now Cyrus conquered Babylon in 538 BC, the principal Jews in Babylon returning to Pal the following year. The events narrated in Bel and the Dragon could not have occurred during the time Cyrus was king of Babylon, but the LXX speaks of "the king" without naming him. (3) It was not Cyrus but Xerxes who destroyed the image of Bel, this being in 475 BC (see Herod. i.183; Strabo xvi.1; Arrian, *Exped. Alex.*, vii.1). (4) It is further objected that dragon-worship in Babylon, such as is implied in the dragon story, is contrary to fact. Star-worship, it has been said, did exist, but not animal-worship. So Eichhorn and Fritzsche. But there is every reason for believing that the worship of living animals as representing deity, and esp. of the living serpent, existed in Babylon as among other nations of antiquity, including the Greeks and Romans (see Herzog, 1st ed, art. "Drache zu Babylon," by J. G. Müller). It has already been pointed out (see list of meanings) that the word "dragon" denotes a serpent.

LITERATURE.—Eichhorn, *Einleitung in die apoc. Schriften des Alten Testaments* (1795), 431 ff (remarkable for its time: compares the LXX and Θ); W. H. Daubney, *The Three Additions to Daniel* (Cambridge, 1906; contains much matter though rather uncritically treated); the commentaries of Fritzsche (Vol I: still very rich in material; it forms part of the *Kurzgefasstes exegetisches Handbuch*); Bissell (in Lange's series, but not a tr); Ball, *Speaker's Commentary* (this is the best Eng. commentary on the Apoc. See also Schürer, *Geschichte*³, III, 333, and his art. in *RE*³, I, 639; and the articles by Kamphausen in *EB*, I, 1014; Toy, in *Jew Enc*, II, 650; R. H. Charles, *Enc Brit*¹¹, VII, 807, and esp. that by J. Turner Marshall in *HDB*, I, 267. Fritzsche, *Libri Veteris Testamenti Graece* (1871), and Swete, *The Old Testament in Greek*, III, 1894, and later editions, give the LXX and Θ on parallel pages. In the ed of the LXX edited by Tischendorf, the LXX is given in the text and Θ in an appendix.

T. WITTON DAVIES

BELA, bē'la. See ZOAR.

BELA, BELAH, bē'la (בֶּלַע, *bela'*, "destruction"; AV **Belah**, Gen **46** 21):

(1) B., the son of Beor, was the first king of Edom previous to the kingdom of Israel and reigned in the city of Dinhabah (Gen **36** 32 f; 1 Ch **1** 43 f). LXX A, Βαλάκ, *Balák*.

(2) B., the firstborn son of Benjamin (Gen **46** 21; 1 Ch **7** 6 f; 1 Ch **8** 1). He was the head of the family of the Belaites (Nu **26** 38), the father of Addar (called Ard, Nu **26** 40), Gera, Abihud, Abishua, Naaman, Ahoah, Gera, Shephuphan (cf Shephupham, Nu **26** 39), Huram (1 Ch **8** 3–5; Nu **26** 40).

(3) B., a son of Azaz, of the tribe of Reuben, was a man of great power and wealth. His possessions reached from Nebo to the Euphrates (1 Ch **5** 8 ff).

A. L. BRESLICH

BELAITES, bē'la-īts (בַּלְעִי, *bal'ī*, "belonging to Bela"): The descendants of Bela (Nu **26** 38). Cf BELA (2).

BELCH, belsh: The primary idea of this word is "to gush forth" as a fountain. As used in Ps **59** 7 the thought is that these enemies had so cherished these evil thoughts and bitter wrath that now the heart is a very fountain of evil, and has taught the tongue how to give utterance thereto. But the previous verse shows that the Psalmist also had in mind the howling and barking of the dogs about the city. The imprecations of his enemies are like the snarling, howling, barking of dogs which in an eastern city makes the night hideous with the noise, and is continued until the daybreak.

JACOB W. KAPP

BELEMUS, bel'ē-mus (**Βήλεμος**, *Bēlemos;* Balsamus): An officer of King Artaxerxes in Pal associated with Beeltethmus in hindering the rebuilding of the temple (1 Esd **2** 16): called Bishlam in Ezr **4** 7.

BELIAL, bē'li-al, bēl'yal (בְּלִיַּעַל, *beliya'al*; **Βελίαρ**, *Belíar*): This name, occurring very frequently in the OT, has the sense of "worthlessness" (cf 2 S **23** 6m); accordingly in such phrases as "sons of Belial" (Jgs **20** 13; 1 S **10** 27, etc), "men of Belial" (1 S **30** 22; 1 K **21** 13, etc), which the ERV usually retains, the ARV more correctly renders, "base fellows" (so "daughter of Belial" 1 S **1** 16, "wicked woman"). There is here no suggestion of a proper name. Afterward, however, "Belial" became a proper name for Satan, or for Antichrist (thus frequently in the Jewish Apocalyptic writings, e.g. in XII P, Bk Jub, Asc Isa, Sib Or). In this sense Paul used the word in 2 Cor **6** 15, "What concord hath Christ with Belial?" (*Beliar*). Bousset thinks that Paul's "man of sin" in 2 Thess **2** 3, where some authorities read "man of lawlessness," is a tr of this term. The sense at least is similar. See ANTICHRIST; MAN OF SIN. JAMES ORR

BELIE, bē-lī′: Is the tr of כָּחַשׁ, *kāḥash*, "to be untrue" (Jer **5** 12). "They have belied the Lord" (ARV "denied Jeh"), here used as synonym of "give the lie to."

In Wisd **1** 11 "belie" tr^s καταψεύδομαι, *katapseúdomai* (the *kata* prefix referring to the *kata* in *katalaliá* in the same verse), "A mouth that belieth destroyeth a soul."

BELIEF, bē-lēf′. See FAITH.

BELIEVERS, bē-lēv′ẽrs (in AV and RV of Acts **5** 14, for **πιστεύοντες,** *pisteúontes*, RVm "believing"; in AV of 1 Tim **4** 12 for **οἱ πιστοί,** *hoi pistoí*, RV "them that believe"): Equivalent phrases, they (he, she) that believe (for οἱ πεπιστευκότες, *hoi pepisteukótes;* οἱ πιστεύοντες, *hoi pisteúontes;* πιστός [adj.], *pistós*, etc) occur frequently as a regular description of those who professed their faith in Christ, and attached themselves to the Christian church. The one essential condition of admission into the Christian community was, that men should believe in Jesus Christ (Acts **16** 31). The actual experiences of the men thus denoted varied with all the possible degrees and modifications of FAITH (q.v.). Believers are nowhere in the NT distinguished as a subordinate class from the "Christians who know" as in the gnostic antithesis of *pistikoí* and *gnōstikoí*, "believers" and "knowers." T. REES

BELL (מְצִלּוֹת, *m^eçillōth*, פַּעֲמוֹן, *pa'ămōn*): The former of these terms occurs only once (Zec **14** 20) where it is thus tr^d. It is derived from a verb meaning "to tingle" or "dirl" (1 S **3** 11), and there is, therefore, no objection etymologically to rendering the noun by "bells." But the little bell attached to the harness of horses would hardly be a suitable place for a fairly long inscription, and as buckles shaped exactly like cymbals (see MUSIC) were used as ornaments for horses, "cymbals" is probably a better rendering.

The other Heb word for bell is found only in Ex **28** 33 f; **39** 25.26, where "bells of gold" are directed to be attached to the hem of Aaron's official robe, that the people may hear him when he enters and quits the sanctuary. Bells were not employed by the Hebrews to summon the congregation to worship, nor do Mohammedans so use them at the present day. The church bell is a peculiarly Christian institution, said to have been introduced by Bishop Paulinus of Nola in Campania, who lived about the end of the 4th cent. Little bells, however, like those attached to the hem of Aaron's robe, frequently form part of the harness of horses, or are fastened to the necks of the he-goats or wethers that lead the flock in eastern lands. JAMES MILLAR

BELLOWS, bel′ōz, bel′us: The word occurs once only in EV, in Jer **6** 29, where the prophet is predicting the coming of the destroyer (ver 26), "a great nation" from "the north country" (ver 22), down upon Israel, because "all of them deal corruptly" (ver 28). "The bellows blow fiercely; the lead is consumed of the fire." Here the imagery is drawn from the refiner's art, and the "bellows" are those used to make the refiner's fires burn fiercely. See CRAFTS, II, 10.

BELLY, bel′i: גָּחוֹן, *gāḥōn*="the external abdomen" (Gen **3** 14; Lev **11** 42). קֵבָה, *ḳēbhāh* ="the abdominal cavity" (Nu **25** 8 ARV "body"). בֶּטֶן, *beṭen*="the internal abdomen," "the womb" (1 K **7** 20; Job **15** 2.35 AV; **20** 15.23; **40** 16; Ps **17** 14; Prov **13** 25; **18** 20; Jer **1** 5; Ezk **3** 3); also fig. "the internal regions," "the body of anything" (Jon **2** 2). מֵעֶה, *mē'eh*="intestines," "abdomen" (Dnl **2** 32; Jon **1** 17; **2** 1.2). In the NT κοιλία, *koilía*="a cavity," esp. the abdominal (Mt **12** 40; **15** 17; Mk **7** 19); the seat of appetite and of the carnal affections (Rom **16** 18; 1 Cor **6** 13; Phil **3** 19; Rev **10** 9.10); the innermost of the soul (ARVm Jn **7** 38). FRANK E. HIRSCH

Egyptian Bellows.

BELMAIM, bel′mā-im, AV Belmen (**Βελμαίμ,** *Belmaím*, Jth **7** 3; **Βαιλμαίν,** *Bailmaín*, **4** 4): A place in the neighborhood of Dothan (**7** 3), to which warning was sent to prepare for the invasion of Holofernes (**4** 4). It probably answers to the modern *Bīr Bil'āmeh* (Ibleam), a ruined site about half a mile S. of *Jenīn*.

BELMEN, bel′men, **BELMON,** bel′mon. See BELMAIM.

BELOMANCY, bel′ō-man-si. See AUGURY, IV, 2.

BELOVED, bē-luv′ed, bē-luv′d′ (**ἀγαπητός,** *agapētós*): A term of affectionate endearment common to both Testaments; in the OT found, 26 out of 42 times, in Solomon's Song of Love. Limited chiefly to two Heb words and their derivatives: אָהֵב, *'āhēbh*, "to breathe" or "long for," hence to love, corresponding to the NT, ἀγαπάω, *agapáō*, "to prefer," i.e. a love based on respect and benevolent regard; דּוֹד, *dōdh*, "love," chiefly love between the sexes, based on sense and emotion, akin to φιλέω, *philéō* (Lat *amare*). Used occasionally, in their nobler sense, interchangeably, e.g. the former of a husband's love for his wife (Dt **21** 15.16); twice of a lover (Cant **1** 14.16), thus lifting the affection of the Song of Sol out of mere amorousness into the realm of the spiritual and possibly Messianic. Both words used of God's love for His chosen: e.g. Solomon, "b. of his God" (Neh **13** 26); Benjamin "b. of Jehovah" (Dt **33** 12); so even of wayward Israel (Jer **11** 15).

In the NT "beloved" used exclusively of Divine and Christian love, an affection begotten in the community of the new spiritual life in Christ, e.g. "b. in the Lord" (Rom **16** 8). The beauty, unity, endearment of this love is historically unique, being peculiarly Christian. "Brethren" in Christ are "beloved" (1 Thess **1** 4; 1 Cor **15** 58; Jas **1** 16; **2** 5). Many individuals are specified by name: Timothy (2 Tim **1** 2); Philemon (Philem ver 1); Amplias, Urbane, Stachys, Persis (Rom **16** 8.9.12), etc. The aged John is the conspicuous NT illustration of the depth and tenderness of Christian love. In his epistles alone he addresses his disciples 12 times as "beloved." Paul terms "God's elect" "holy and beloved" (Col **3** 12).

The term rises to still Diviner significance as an epithet of Christ, whom Paul, grateful for His "freely bestowed" grace, terms "the Beloved." This is the word used repeatedly to express God the Father's infinite affection for Jesus His "beloved Son" (Mt **3** 17; **12** 18; **17** 5; Mk **1** 11; **9** 7; Lk **3** 22; **20** 13).

Agapētos rendered as above 47 times is 9 times "dearly beloved" (RV uniformly omits "dearly") and 3 times "well beloved" (RV omits "well"). The former rendering found only once in the OT (יְדִידוּת, *yᵉdhīdhūth*, "something beloved"), portraying God's tender love for His people: "dearly beloved of my soul" (Jer **12** 7). Thrice is Daniel spoken of as "greatly beloved" of Gabriel and of God (חֲמוּדוֹת, *ḥămūdhōth*, "precious," i.e. delight = beloved; Dnl **9** 23; **10** 11.19). Through the apostles the word has become familiar in pastoral and sermonic address. Few NT words better illustrate the power and impress of the Christian spirit on succeeding centuries than this.

DWIGHT M. PRATT

BELSHAZZAR, bel-shaz′ar (בֵּלְשַׁאצַּר, *bēlsha′ççar;* **Βαλτασάρ,** *Baltasár*, Bab Bel-shar-usur): According to Dnl **5** 30, he was the Chaldaean king under whom Babylon was taken by Darius the Mede. The Bab monuments speak a number of times of a Bel-shar-uṣur who was the "firstborn son, the offspring of the heart of" Nabunaid, the last king of the Bab empire, that had been founded by Nabopolassar, the father of Nebuchadnezzar, at the time of the death of Ashurbanipal, king of Assyria, in 626 BC. There is no doubt that this Belshazzar is the same as the Belshazzar of Dnl. It is not necessary to suppose that Belshazzar was at any time king of the Bab empire in the sense that Nebuchadnezzar and Nabunaid were. It is probable, as M. Pognon argues, that a son of Nabunaid, called Nabunaid after his father, was king of Babylon, or Bab king, in Harran (Haran), while his father was overlord in Babylon. This second Nabunaid is called "the son of the offspring of the heart" of Nabunaid his father. It is possible that this second Nabunaid was the king who was killed by Cyrus, when he crossed the Tigris above Arbela in the 9th year of Nabunaid his father, and put to death the king of the country (see the Nabunaid-Cyrus Chronicle, col. ii, 17); since according to the Eshki-Harran inscription, Nabunaid the Second died in the 9th year of Nabunaid the First. Belshazzar may have been the son of the king who is said in the same chronicle to have commanded the Bab army in Accad from the 6th to the 11th year of Nabunaid I; or, possibly longer, for the annals before the 6th and after the 11th year are broken and for the most part illegible. This same son of the king is most probably mentioned again in the same chronicle as having died in the night in which Babylon was captured by Gobryas of Gutium. As Nabunaid II, though reigning at Harran under the overlordship of his father, is called king of Babylon on the same inscription on which his father is called by the same title; so Belshazzar may have been called king of Babylon, although he was only crown prince. It is probable, also, that as Nabunaid I had made one of his sons king of Harran, so he had made another king of Chaldaea. This would account for Belshazzar's being called in Dnl **5** 30 the Chaldaean king, although, to be sure, this word Chaldaean may describe his race rather than his kingdom. The 3d year of Belshazzar, spoken of in Dnl **8** 1, would then refer to his 3d year as sub-king of the Chaldaeans under his father Nabunaid, king of Babylon, just as Cambyses was later sub-king of Babylon, while his father Cyrus was king of the lands. From the Book of Dnl we might infer that this subkingdom embraced Chaldaea and Susiana, and possibly the province of Babylon; and from the Nabunaid-Cyrus Chronicle that it extended over Accad as well. That the city of Babylon alone was sometimes at least governed by an official called king is highly probable, since the father of Nergal-shar-uṣur is certainly, and the father of Nabunaid I is probably, called king of Babylon, in both of which cases, the city, or at most the province, of Babylon must have been meant, since we know to a certainty all of the kings who had been ruling over the empire of Babylon since 626 BC, when Nabopolassar became king, and the names of neither of these fathers of kings is found among them.

In addition to Nabunaid II, Belshazzar seems to have had another brother named Nebuchadnezzar, since the two Bab rebels against Darius Hystaspis both assumed the name of Nebuchadnezzar the son of Nabunaid (see the Behistun Inscription, I, 85, 89, 95). He had a sister also named Ina-esagila-remat, and a second named probably Ukabu′-shai′-na.

Belshazzar had his own house in Babylon, where he seems to have been engaged in the woolen or clothing trade. He owned also estates from which he made large gifts to the gods. His father joins his name with his own in some of his prayers to the gods, and apparently appointed him commander of the army of Accad, whose especial duty it was to defend the city of Babylon against the attacks of the armies of Media and Persia.

It would appear from the Nabunaid-Cyrus Chronicle, that Belshazzar was *de facto* king of the Bab empire, all that was left of it, from the 4th to the 8th month of the 17th year of the reign of his father Nabunaid, and that he died on the night in which Babylon was taken by Gobryas of Gutium (that is, probably, DARIUS THE MEDE [q.v.]).

The objection to the historical character of the narrative of Dnl, based upon the fact that Belshazzar in **5** 11.18 is said to have been the son of Nebuchadnezzar, whereas the monuments state that he was the son of Nabunaid, is fully met by supposing that one of them was his real and the other his adoptive father; or by supposing that the queen-mother and Daniel referred to the greatest of his predecessors as his father, just as Omri is called by the Assyrians the father of Jehu, and as the claimants to the Medo-Pers throne are called on the Behistun Inscription the sons of Cyaxares, and as at present the reigning sheikhs of northern Arabia are all called the sons of Rashid, although in reality they are not his sons.

LITERATURE.—The best sources of information as to the life and times of Belshazzar for English readers are: *The Records of the Past;* Pinches, *The Old Testament in the Light of the Historical Records of Assyria and Babylonia;* Sayce, *The Higher Criticism and the Monuments;* and W. W. Wright's two great works, *Daniel and His Prophecies* and *Daniel and His Critics.*

R. DICK WILSON

BELT. See ARMOR; DRESS.

BELTESHAZZAR, bel-tē-shaz′ar (בֵּלְטְשַׁאצַּר, *bēltsha′ççar;* Bab *Balaṭ-sharuṣur*, "protect his life"; Dnl **4** 8): The Bab name given to Daniel (Dnl **1** 7; **2** 26; **5** 12). Not to be confounded with Belshazzar.

BELUS, bē′lus, **TEMPLE OF.** See BABEL.

BEN-, ben (prefix) (sing. בֵּן, *ben*, "son of"; pl. בְּנֵי, *bᵉnē*, "sons of" = Aram. בַּר, *bar*): This word is used in sing. or pl. to express relationship of almost any kind: (1) to a person; as such it is found as part of many compound names like Benjamin, Ben-hur, etc (cf Bar); (2) to a clan; in this connection it is found in the pl. only: "children of Israel," "children of Ammon," etc; (3) to a town; perhaps as place of birth ("son of Jabesh"; 2 K **15** 10 ff); (4) to occupation, state of life, age, character, quality even of things; (5) peculiarly employed in the sense of "scholar," "disciple" ("son of prophet"), or in phrases like "son of death," etc; (6) in poetry, "sons of flame" for "sparks" (Job **5** 7m), etc. The frequent metaphorical use of the word indicates that it was rarely used to express the relation of father to son like the Arab. *Ibn*. Cf *HPN*, 64 ff.

A. L. Breslich

BEN, ben (בֵּן, *bēn*, "son"): A Levite appointed to assist as musician in the temple service (1 Ch **15** 18). The text seems to be doubtful, since the name is omitted in ver 20 and not mentioned at all in the LXX.

BEN-ABINADAB, ben-a-bin′a-dab, ben-ab-i-nā′dab (בֶּן־אֲבִינָדָב, *ben 'ăbhīnādhābh*, "son of Abinadab"): One of the "captains" of Solomon who provided for the king and his household, each for a month in the year (1 K **4** 11). His district was the region of Dor. In AV he is called "the son of Abinadab." His wife was Tappath, the daughter of Solomon.

BENAIAH, bē-nā′ya, bē-nī′a (בְּנָיָה, *b^e nāyāh*, בְּנָיָהוּ, *b^e nāyāhū*, "Jeh has built." Cf *HPN*, 182, 265, 268):

(1) B., the son of Jehoiada of Kabzeel (cf Josh **15** 21), was a man of "mighty deeds" and was more honorable than any of the mighty men of David except the three chiefs. Therefore David made him his chief counselor (2 S **23** 23m; cf 1 Ch **27** 34 where the order of names seems to be reversed) and set him over the Cherethites (cf Carites, 2 K **11** 4 ff and m) and Pelethites and he was made the 3d captain of the host and chief over the course of the 3d month (1 Ch **27** 5 f; 2 S **8** 18; **20** 23; 1 Ch **18** 17; 2 S **23** 20 ff; **11** 22 ff). Being a true friend of David (cf 2 S **15** 18) he did not take part in the usurpation of Adonijah (1 K **1** 8.10. 26), and was therefore with others chosen by the king to proclaim Solomon king over Israel (1 K **1** 32 ff) and later by Solomon to execute Adonijah (1 K **2** 25), Joab (1 K **2** 29 ff), and Shimei (1 K **2** 46). In recognition of his services Solomon appointed him over the host in Joab's place (1 K **2** 35; **4** 4).

(2) B., a Pirathonite (cf Jgs **12** 13.15), was one of David's 30 mighty men (2 S **23** 30; 1 Ch **11** 31). He was captain over the course of the 11th month numbering 24,000 (1 Ch **27** 14).

(3) A ruler of the house of Simeon (1 Ch **4** 36).

(4) A Levite of second degree appointed as singer (1 Ch **15** 18) with "psalteries set to Alamoth" (1 Ch **15** 20; **16** 5).

(5) A priest appointed "to blow the trumpet before the ark of God" (1 Ch **15** 24; **16** 6).

(6) The father of Jehoiada (1 Ch **27** 34), but see (1) above.

(7) An ancestor of Jahaziel of the house of Asaph (2 Ch **20** 14).

(8) An overseer in the service of Hezekiah (2 Ch **31** 13).

(9, 10, 11, 12) Four different men of Israel who had taken "strange wives" (Ezr **10** 25.30.35.43).

(13) The father of Pelatiah who was seen by Ezekiel in his vision (Ezk **11** 1.13).

A. L. Breslich

BEN-AMMI, ben-am′ī (בֶּן־עַמִּי, *ben 'ammī*, "son of my kinsman," Gen **19** 38): The progenitor of the Ammonites was a son of Lot's younger daughter, born after the destruction of Sodom. The account of his birth as well as that of Moab was commonly regarded as an expression of Israel's intense hatred and contempt toward these two nations. However, this idea is rather unwarranted, in view of the fact that the origin of the tribe of Judah (which is held in especial honor by J) is accounted for in a similar way (Gen **38**). Gunkel (*Schöpfung und Chaos*, 190) suggests that the narrative (**19** 30–38) was originally a Moabitic account tracing the common origin of Moab and Ammon to Lot. It presupposes a universal catastrophe—such as the conflagration of Sodom and Gomorrah, Admah and Zeboim suggests—in which all the human race, save Lot and his two daughters, perished. In order to avert the extinction of the race, his daughters resorted to incestuous practices. In this case we have here a Moabite parallel to the Deluge story (Skinner, *Genesis*, 313–14). While the common origin of the two brother tribes is undoubtedly a fact (Jgs **10** 6; **11** 15.18.25; Dt **2** 19; 2 Ch **20**, etc), the folk-etymology of their names is rather suspicious. The name Ben-Ammi is probably derived from the deity "Emu," which is the name for Nergal among the Shuḥites on the W. of the Euphrates, a land which corresponds to the position of the *B^e nē-'Ammō*, "children of his people" (Nu **22** 5). The chief god of the Ḳataban Arabs was called Ammi (*Hom.*, *ZDMG*, V, 95, 525, n. 1). In cuneiform inscriptions this name appears as part of the title of the Ammonite rulers (*HDB*). Neubauer (*Studia Biblica*, 1–26) suggests that the name Balaam is a compound of Bel + Am, that is, "Am is Lord." For other compounds with Ammi see Gray, *HPN*, 41–60.

S. Cohon

BENCH (קֶרֶשׁ, *ḳeresh*): Found only in EV in Ezk **27** 6, in the prophet's "lamentation over Tyre": "They have made thy benches of ivory inlaid in boxwood, from the isles of Kittim," where the word evidently stands for the "benches" of the boat whose "mast" (ver 5) and "oars" (ver 6) have just been described, in the vivid figs. of speech in which the city itself is pictured as a merchant-ship. Cf ver 8, "Thy wise men, O Tyre, were in thee, they were thy pilots." See Seat.

BEN-DEKER, ben-dē′kẽr (בֶּן־דֶּקֶר, *ben-deḳer*, "son of Deker," AV **"son of Dekar"**): The word is derived from a Heb root meaning "to pierce." Cf *HPN*, 69. One of the 12 officers who provided victuals for King Solomon and his household (1 K **4** 9).

BENEATH, bē-nēth′: The adv. for "under" (*kátō*). In Jn **8** 23, the words "ye are from beneath," suggest hell in contrast to heaven. But the succeeding clause, "ye are of this world," gives the key for the interpretation. Earth, not hell, is expressed, although "that more awful meaning surely is not excluded" (Alford).

BENE-BERAK, ben-ē-bē′rak (בְּנֵי בְרַק, *b^e nē b^e raḳ*; **Βανηβαράκ**, *Banēbarák*): A town in the territory of Dan (Josh **19** 45), represented by the modern village *Ibn Ibraḳ*, about an hour S.E. of Jaffa.

BENEDICTION, ben-ē-dik′shun: From the earliest times the records bear testimony that pronouncing the benediction or giving the blessing was a common practice. In the temple service, this duty was assigned to the Aaronites and was made an impressive part of the service. The form of the benediction used is given in Nu **6** 22–27. References to this practice may be found in Lev **9** 22; Dt **10** 8; 2 Ch **30** 27. After a time, minute directions were given concerning it and careful preparation was made for this part of the service. All Aaronites, of proper age, were entitled to perform this service, except those who by previous conduct or on account of physical defect were disqualified. One who had killed another, whether intentionally or otherwise, or who had violated the marriage vows, had given himself excessively to wine drinking or other excesses, or indeed had been guilty of unrighteous conduct or life, was not only prohibited from pronouncing the blessing, but was required to withdraw before this part of the service was performed. If one was blind even of one eye, or had a defect in his hands or speech, or was a hunchback, he was also excluded. Before the priest could engage in this service he was required to wash his hands. Then, with uplifted hands, while the people stood, he uttered the words of blessing. The main idea was that thus the name of Jeh was put on the people. Later it came to be regarded as having some special blessing in and of itself, a result against which the more spiritual of the priests protested.

It was common not only to pronounce the benediction in the public worship but also in the family. We have such instances in Gen **9** 26.27; **27** 27–30. This practice prevailed also on many other occasions not only in Israel, but among the heathen as well. We may readily see, therefore, that from the very beginning of the Christian church the use of the benediction was common. In the course of time an extensive lit. developed on this subject and it may be said that there are now three distinct ideas in the church as to the benediction. That section of the church which regards the minister as clothed with sacerdotal powers, holds that the blessings pronounced are actually conferred in the act of the utterance of the words, because of the powers conferred upon him when he was set aside for the sacred office. On the other hand it is held that it is merely a prayer that God may bestow certain blessings on the people. From this position others dissent, and teach that it is the declaration of the special privileges and relations in which those stand who have entered into covenant fellowship with Christ; that the blessings now declared are theirs by right of that relation, and are conferred upon them by the Holy Spirit. The Gr and Rom Catholic churches take the first position, and therefore we find among them much of detail and minutiae as to the manner in which it should be pronounced. In the Gr church the priest raises his hand with the thumb touching the third finger, signifying the procession of the Holy Ghost from the Father alone; or according to others to form the sacred name IHS. In the Rom church the form is, the thumb, first and second fingers are to be open, to symbolize the Trinity. In this church too, the benediction is pronounced in a multitude of cases and in each case the thing so blessed by the priest is made sacred. Crosses, church vessels, houses, paschal eggs, churchyards, are thus blessed. Every parish has a collection of these forms of blessing in what is known as the "Benedictionale." The authority for this is based on some documents claiming to reach back to early church history, but as they belong to the forged decretal class, the position of the Rom church on this subject is untenable.

Apostolic benedictions, as we find them in the epistles, present considerable variety. One of the striking features is that in a number of cases there is the omission of the Holy Ghost. The best explanation seems to be that the Father and the Son effect the redemption of the world and the Holy Ghost applies the blessing so wrought out. "Grace, mercy and peace" may then be said to be sent from the Father and the Son through the Holy Ghost to be the possession of all who have come into the kingdom. The third person of the Trinity, being thus in the act of applying the blessing, is not mentioned. The fact that in other cases Father, Son and Holy Ghost are mentioned, proves that the writers knew the character and office of the Holy Ghost. The most common form used today is that in 2 Cor **13** 14. Occasionally some changes are introduced by ministers, but it would seem best to adhere strictly to the Scriptural forms. See Blessing; Salutation.

Jacob W. Kapp

BENEFACTOR, ben-ḗ-fak′tẽr (Gr *euergétēs*, Lk **22** 25): There is here a probable allusion to two kings of Egypt (Ptolemy III and VII), who had the surname "Euergetes," of whom the period of the first was 247–242 BC, and of the second, 147–117 BC. Jesus draws the contrast between worldly kingdoms, in which the title "benefactor" is given those who rule with all the splendor of earthly display and luxury, and His kingdom, in which it belongs only to those whose work is that of humble, obscure and often menial service.

BENEFIT, ben′ḗ-fit (גְּמוּל, *g*ᵉ*mūl*="a deed," 2 Ch **32** 25); יָטַב, *yāṭabh*=(causat.) "to make well," "to do good" (Jer **18** 10). The pl. of גְּמוּל, *g*ᵉ*mūl*, is found in Ps **103** 2. Ps **68** 19 (AV) should be tr[d] "Blessed be the Lord. Day by day he sustains us; God is our salvation." χάρις, *cháris*= "gift"; "grace" (2 Cor **1** 15, "a second benefit": that is, two visits in the same journey). εὐεργεσία, *euergesía*="good deed done" (1 Tim **6** 2: "because they that partake of the benefit [of their service] are believing and beloved"); ἀγαθός, *agathós*="good" (Philem ver 14 AV; RV "goodness").

Frank E. Hirsch

BENE-JAAKAN, ben-ḗ-jā′a-kan, bē-nḗ-jā′a-kan (בְּנֵי יַעֲקָן, *b*ᵉ*nē ya‛ăḳān:* Nu **33** 31.32). See Beeroth Bene-jaakan.

BENEVOLENCE, bḗ-nev′ṓ-lens: AV tr of phrase in *TR* of 1 Cor **7** 3, rejected by RV which following WH translates Gr *opheilḗ*, "due." This reference to the marriage relation is explained in ver 4. Cf Ex **21** 10.

BEN-GEBER, ben-gē′bẽr (בֶּן־גֶּבֶר, *ben-gebher*, "son of Geber"; AV **son of Geber;** the word is derived from a Heb root meaning "to be strong." Cf *HPN*, 66, 69): One of the twelve commissariat officers in the service of Solomon (1 K **4** 13).

BENHADAD, ben-hā′dad (בֶּן־הֲדַד, *ben-hădhadh;* LXX υἱὸς Ἁδέρ, *huiós Hadér*):

The Name
I. Benhadad I
1. The Kingdom of Syria Founded
2. Syria and Judah
3. Shortsightedness of Asa
II. Benhadad II
1. Hadad-'idri of the Monuments
2. Expeditions against Israel
3. Alliance with Ahab
4. Biblical History Confirmed by the Monuments
5. Alliance Broken Off
6. Benhadad and Elisha
7. Panic of Syrians at Samaria
8. Murder of Benhadad
III. Benhadad III
1. His Contemporaries
2. The Assyrians in the West
3. Downfall of Damascus before Ramman-Nirari III
4. Breathing Space for Israel

The name of three kings of Syria mentioned in the historical books. Hadad is the Syrian god of storms, and is apparently identical with Rimmon (2 K **5** 18), the Assyr Rammânu, "the Thunderer," whose temple was in Damascus.

The Name The name Benhadad, "son of Hadad," accords with the custom which obtained in Sem mythology of calling a king or a nation the son of the national god, as we have Mesha', son of Chemosh, and the Moabites, children of Chemosh. Benhadad seems to have become a general designation for the kings of Syria (Am **1** 4; Jer **49** 27).

I. Benhadad I was the son of Tabrimmon, who is called (1 K **15** 18) "the son of Hezion, king of Syria, that dwelt at Damascus."

1. The Kingdom of Syria Founded

Hezion has been with some plausibility identified with Rezon (1 K **11** 23.25) who founded the kingdom of Damascus and imparted to Syria that temper of hostility to Israel which became hereditary. Meanwhile the Aramaeans had shaken themselves free from the rule of the Hittites, and with Damascus for a center had planted strong settlements in the plains westward from the Euphrates. By the time that Benhadad entered into this succession, Syria was the strongest power in this region of Western Asia, and ready to take advantage of every opportunity of increasing her dominions.

Such an opportunity presented itself in the appeal of Asa, king of Judah, for help against Baasha, king of Israel. The two Heb kingdoms had been at feud ever since their disruption.

2. Syria and Judah

Baasha had pushed his frontier southward to Ramah, within 5 miles of Jerus, and this commanding eminence he proceeded to fortify. The danger of a hostile fortress overlooking his capital, and the humiliation of his rival's presence so near, were more than Asa could bear. It was at this juncture that he bethought him of Benhadad. Taking all the silver and the gold that were left in the treasury of the house of the Lord, and the treasury of the king's house, he sent them to Benhadad with a request for an alliance, begging him at the same time to break off the league he had with Baasha and thus enable Asa to dislodge his enemy. Benhadad saw an opening for the aggrandizement of his kingdom and broke off the alliance he had had with Jeroboam and Baasha. By an invasion of Northern Israel he obliged Baasha to withdraw from Ramah and confine himself to the neighborhood of his own capital (1 K **15** 16 ff). Judah obtained relief, but the price paid for it was too great. Asa had surrendered his treasures, and very likely some of his independence.

For his shortsightedness in laying himself under obligation to Benhadad and relying upon the help of Syria rather than upon the Lord his God, Asa was rebuked by the prophet Hanani (2 Ch **16** 1 ff).

3. Shortsightedness of Asa

Benhadad had extended his territories by the transaction and seems to have exercised henceforward some sort of sovereignty over both the Heb kingdoms.

Literature.—McCurdy, *HPM*, I, 256; H. P. Smith, *OT History*, 186.

II. Benhadad II was in all probability the son of Benhadad I. He is the Hadad-ezer, or Hadad-'idri, of the monuments.

1. Hadad-'idri of the Monuments

He comes first upon the scene of the Bib. history invading the land of Israel with a large host, in which were 32 tributary kings, and horses and chariots. He had penetrated as far as Samaria, the newly built city of Omri, now the capital of his son Ahab. Benhadad and his Syrian host had laid siege to Samaria and Ahab had been summoned to surrender. Ahab was disposed to come to terms, but the intolerable proposals made by Benhadad drove him to resistance. Encouraged by the elders of the people, and acting on the counsel of a prophet, Ahab made a sortie and falling upon the carousing Syrians put them so completely to rout that Benhadad himself only escaped on a horse with the horsemen.

Monolith of Shalmaneser II.

Next year the Syrians resolved to retrieve their defeat saying of the Israelites, "Their God is a god of the hills; therefore they were stronger than we: but let us fight against them in the plain, and surely we shall be stronger than they."

2. Expeditions against Israel

Ahab had been warned to expect the return of the Syrians and was prepared for the fresh attack. For seven days the two armies faced each other, the Israelites "like two little flocks of kids" before a host that filled the country. On the seventh day they joined battle near to Aphek, and the Syrians met again an overwhelming defeat. Jeh was proved to be God both of the plains and of the hills. Benhadad was taken prisoner, and appealing to the clemency of the victor, he persuaded

Ahab to spare his life. A treaty was agreed upon between the two monarchs under which Ahab's people were to have bazaars of their own in Damascus, as it would appear Benhadad I had had for his subjects before in Samaria (1 K **20** 1–34). The treaty was denounced by a prophet, and Ahab was warned that this man whom God had devoted to destruction would be the destruction of himself and his people. Under the treaty, however, there were three years without war between Syria and Israel.

3. Alliance with Ahab

The treaty and the resulting period of peace receive striking confirmation from the monuments. From the monolith inscription of Shalmaneser II we learn that this Assyr king in the 6th year of his reign (854 BC) had crossed the Tigris and made his way across the Euphrates on boats of sheepskin into Syria to Ḥalman (Aleppo). At Karkar he encountered the combined forces of Damascus, Hamath, Israel and the states which had united to oppose his progress westward. Aḥabbu Sir-'lai, Ahab of Israel and Dad'idri, Hadadezer (Benhadad II) of Damascus are named in the inscription with chariots, horsemen and infantry, making common cause against Shalmaneser and fighting on the same side. It was Benhadad, as we gather, that bore the brunt of the assault, but the result of the battle was the complete rout of the allies with the loss of 14,000 men. That the assistance of Israel on the occasion was the outcome of the treaty between Ahab and Benhadad, and that the combination against Shalmaneser took place during the three years of peace, are in the highest degree probable.

4. Biblical History Confirmed by the Monuments

The disaster to the allies, however, seems to have broken up the confederacy. When the king of Syria is next mentioned in Bib. history, it is defending the city of Ramoth-Gilead against the attack made upon it by Ahab, who is found now in alliance with Jehoshaphat, the king of Judah, attempting unsuccessfully and with fatal results to himself, to recover this city of Israel from the weakened power of Damascus. At Ramoth-Gilead Benhadad is not said to have 32 tributary kings in his train, but 32 military commanders who have taken their place (1 K **22** 2.29–31).

5. Alliance Broken Off

The peace between Israel and Syria having been broken, there was frequent, if not continuous, war between the kingdoms, in which the prophet Elisha is a prominent figure. He healed of his leprosy Naaman, Benhadad's commander-in-chief. He disclosed to the king of Israel the places wherever Benhadad pitched his camp. He smote with blindness a great host whom Benhadad had sent with horses and chariots to seize him at Dothan, and led them into Samaria where he saw them treated kindly and sent back to their master (2 K **6** 8–23).

6. Benhadad and Elisha

Some time after Benhadad again assembled all his host and laid siege to Samaria. So great was the famine that women ate their own children. The king of Israel sent one of his men to put Elisha to death, but Elisha closed his house against him and announced that on the morrow there would be great plenty in the city. And so it happened. Certain lepers, despairing of relief, had gone into the Syrian camp and learned that the Syrians had abandoned their camp in a panic, believing that the king of Israel had hired the kings of the Muṣri and the northern Hittites to raise the siege (2 K **6** 24—**7** 20; cf Burney's note, **7** 6).

7. Panic of Syrians at Samaria

Still another notice of Benhadad II is found in the Annals of Shalmaneser, who records that in the 11th year of his reign he defeated a combination of 12 kings of the Hittites with Benhadad at their head, and slew 10,000 men. Of this there is no record in Bib. history, but it must have been shortly before the tragedy which ended the career of the Syrian king. Benhadad had fallen sick and sent his commander-in-chief, Hazael, to inquire as to the issue of his sickness of the prophet Elisha, who was visiting Damascus. Elisha foretold the king's death, and wept as he read to Hazael the cruel purpose which the Syrian commander was even then maturing. Hazael professed to be incredulous, but he departed from Elisha and the very next day in cold blood put his master to death and ascended the throne (2 K **8** 7–15). Thus ingloriously ended the reign of one of the most powerful of the Syrian kings.

8. Murder of Benhadad

LITERATURE.—McCurdy, *HPM*, I, 267 ff; Schrader, *COT*, I, 179 ff; Winckler, *Geschichte Israels*, Theil I, 133–55.

III. Benhadad III was the son of the usurper Hazael, and though not in the dynastic succession, assumed on the death of his father the dynastic name. He was contemporary with Amaziah, king of Judah; Jehoahaz, the son of Jehu, king of Israel; and Ramman-Nirari III, king of Assyria. The fortunes of Israel had fallen low in the days of Jehoahaz, and Hazael and Benhadad III were the instruments of Jeh's displeasure with the nation. At this time Jehoahaz had no more than 53 horsemen and 10 chariots and 10,000 footmen; for the king of Syria had destroyed them and made them like the dust in threshing (2 K **13** 7). It was when the fortunes of Israel were at the lowest ebb by reason of the oppression of the king of Syria—by this time Benhadad—that help came to them and Jeh gave Israel a savior, so that Israel went out from under the hands of the Syrians, "and the children of Israel dwelt in their tents [in their homes] as beforetime" (2 K **13** 5). The "saviour" of the Bib. narrative is the one allusion in Scripture to the king of Assyria of that day, Ramman-Nirari III, whose inscriptions record his victorious expedition to the West. "From the Euphrates to the land of the Hittites," runs an inscription, "the west country in its entire compass, Tyre, Zidon, the land Omri, Edom, Philistia as far as the Great Sea of the sunsetting, I subjected to my yoke; payment of tribute I imposed upon them. Against Syria of Damascus I marched; Mari, the king of Syria, in Damascus his royal city I besieged." He then proceeds to tell of the subjugation of the monarch and of the spoils obtained from his capital. That Mari, which means in Aramaic "lord," is Benhadad III, the son of Hazael, is now generally believed.

1. His Contemporaries

2. The Assyrians in the West

With the capture of Damascus and the collapse of the Syrian power under Mari (Benhadad III), an era of recuperation and prosperity became possible to Israel and Judah. So it came to pass that "Jehoash the son of Jehoahaz took again out of the hand of Benhadad the son of Hazael the cities which he had taken out of the hand of Jehoahaz by war. Three times did Joash smite him, and recovered the cities of Israel" (2 K **13** 25). Israel was able to breathe freely for a time and Jeroboam II restored the Northern Kingdom to its former extent and glory. But the flame of war which had been sent into the house of Hazael and which devoured the palaces of Benhadad (Am **1** 4 ff) was only

3. Downfall of Damascus before Ramman-Nirari III

4. Breathing Space for Israel

waiting the time when the Assyrians would be free to renew their expeditions to the West and carry Samaria and Israel "into captivity beyond Damascus" (Am **5** 27).

LITERATURE.—McCurdy, *HPM*, I, 291 ff; Schrader, *COT*, I, 202 ff.

T. NICOL

BEN-HAIL, ben-hā'il (בֶּן־חַיִל, *ben-ḥayil*, "son of strength"; cf *HPN*, 65, 231): One of the princes who was sent by Jehoshaphat "to teach in the cities of Judah" (2 Ch **17** 7).

BEN-HANAN, ben-hā'nan (בֶּן־חָנָן, *ben-ḥānān*, "son of grace"): A son of Shimon of the house of Judah (1 Ch **4** 20).

BEN-HESED, ben-hē'sed (בֶּן־חֶסֶד, *ben-ḥeṣedh*, "son of Hesed"; AV **son of Hesed;** the word is derived from a Heb root meaning "to be kind"): A commissariat officer in the service of Solomon (1 K **4** 10).

BEN-HUR, ben-hûr' (בֶּן־חוּר, *ben-ḥūr*, "son of Hur"; AV **son of Hur;** from a Heb root meaning "to be white." Cf *HPN*, 69, n. 3): One of the twelve commissariat officers in the service of Solomon (1 K **4** 8).

BENINU, bē-nī'nū (בְּנִינוּ, *b*ᵉ*nīnū*, "our son"): A Levite who with Nehemiah sealed the covenant (Neh **10** 13).

BEN-JAAKAN, ben-jā'a-kan. See BENE-JAAKAN.

BENJAMIN, ben'ja-min (בִּנְיָמִין, *binyāmīn*, or בִּנְיָמִן, *binyāmin;* **Βενιαείν**, *Beniaeín*, **Βενιαμίν**, *Beniamín*):

(1) The youngest of Jacob's sons. His mother Rachel died in giving him birth. As she felt death

1. The Patriarch

approaching she called him Benoni, "son of my sorrow." Fearing, probably, that this might bode evil for the child—for names have always preserved a peculiar significance in the East—Jacob called him Benjamin, "son of the right hand" (Gen **35** 17 ff). He alone of Jacob's sons was born in Pal, between Bethel and Ephrath. Later in the ch, in the general enumeration of the children born in Paddan-aram, the writer fails to except Benjamin (ver 24). Joseph was his full brother. In the history where Benjamin appears as an object of solicitude to his father and brothers, we must not forget that he was already a grown man. At the time of the descent of Israel to Egypt Joseph was about 40 years of age. Benjamin was not much younger, and was himself the father of a family. The phrase in Gen **44** 20, "a little one," only describes in oriental fashion one much younger than the speaker. And as the youngest of the family no doubt he was made much of. Remorse over their heartless treatment of his brother Joseph may have made the other brothers especially tender toward Benjamin. The conduct of his brethren all through the trying experiences in Egypt places them in a more attractive light than we should have expected; and it must have been a gratification to their father (Gen **42** ff). Ten sons of Benjamin are named at the time of their settlement in Egypt (Gen **46** 21).

(2) At the Exodus the number of men of war in the tribe is given as 35,400. At the second

2. The Tribe

census it is 45,600 (Nu **1** 37; **26** 41). Their place in the host was with the standard of the camp of Ephraim on the west of the tabernacle, their prince being Abidan the son of Gideoni (Nu **2** 22 f). Benjamin was represented among the spies by Palti the son of Raphu; and at the division of the land the prince of Benjamin was Elidad the son of Chislon (Nu **13** 9; **34** 21).

(3) The boundaries of the lot that fell to Benjamin are pretty clearly indicated (Josh **18** 11 ff).

3. Territory

It lay between Ephraim on the N. and Judah on the S. The northern frontier started from the Jordan over against Jericho, and ran to the north of that town up through the mountain westward past Beth-aven, taking in Bethel. It then went down by Ataroth-addar to Beth-horon the nether. From this point the western frontier ran southward to Kiriath-jearim. The southern boundary ran from Kiriath-jearim eastward to the fountain of the waters of Netophah, swept round by the south of Jerus, and passed down through the wilderness by Geliloth and the stone of Bohan, to the northern shore of the Dead Sea at the mouth of the Jordan. The river formed the eastern boundary. The lot was comparatively small. This, according to Jos, was owing to "the goodness of the land" (*Ant*, V, i, 22); a description that would apply mainly to the plains of Jericho. The uplands are stony, mountainous, and poor in water; but there is much good land on the western slopes.

It will be seen from the above that Benjamin held the main avenues of approach to the high-

4. Importance of Position

lands from both E. and W.: that by which Joshua led Israel past Ai from Gilgal, and the longer and easier ascents from the W., notably that along which the tides of battle so often rolled, the Valley of Aijalon, by way of the Beth-horons. Benjamin also sat astride the great highway connecting N. and S., which ran along the ridge of the western range, in the district where it was easiest of defense. It was a position calling for occupation by a brave and warlike tribe such as Benjamin proved to be. His warriors were skilful archers and slingers, and they seem to have cultivated the use of both hands, which gave them a great advantage in battle (Jgs **20** 16; 1 Ch **8** 40; **12** 2, etc). These characteristics are reflected in the Blessing of Jacob (Gen **49** 27). The second deliverer of Israel in the period of the Judges was Ehud, the left-handed Benjamite (Jgs **3** 15).

The Benjamites fought against Sisera under Deborah and Barak (Jgs **5** 14). The story told

5. History

in Jgs **20** 21 presents many difficulties which cannot be discussed here. It is valuable as preserving certain features of life in these lawless times when there was no king in Israel. Whatever may be said of the details, it certainly reflects the memory of some atrocity in which the Benjamites were involved and for which they suffered terrible punishment. The election of Saul as first king over united Israel naturally lent a certain prestige to the tribe. After the death of Saul they formed the backbone of Ish-bosheth's party, and most unwillingly conceded precedence to Judah in the person of David (2 S **2** 15.25; **3** 17 ff). It was a Benjamite who heaped curses upon David in the hour of his deep humiliation (2 S **16** 5); and the jealousy of Benjamin led to the revolt on David's return, which was so effectually stamped out by Joab (2 S **19** f). Part of the tribe, probably the larger part, went against Judah at the disruption of the kingdom, taking Bethel with them. 1 K **12** 20 says that none followed the house of David but the house of Judah only. But the next verse tells us that Rehoboam gathered the men of Judah and Benjamin to fight against Jeroboam. It seems probable that as Jerus had now become the royal city of the house of David, the adjoining parts of Benjamin proved loyal, while the more distant joined the Northern

Kingdom. After the downfall of Samaria Judah assumed control of practically the whole territory of Benjamin (2 K **23** 15.19, etc). Nehemiah gives the Valley of Hinnom as the south boundary of Benjamin in his time (Neh **11** 30), while westward it extended to include Lod and Ono. Saul of Tarsus was a member of this tribe (Phil **3** 5).

(4) A great-grandson of Benjamin, son of Jacob (1 Ch **7** 10).

(5) One of those who had married a foreign wife (Ezr **10** 32, and probably also Neh **3** 23; **12** 34).

W. Ewing

BENJAMIN, GATE OF. See Jerusalem.

BENJAMITE, ben'ja-mīt: One belonging to the tribe of Benjamin, such as Ehud (Jgs **3** 15), Saul (1 S **9** 1.2), Sheba (2 S **20** 1), Shimei (1 K **2** 8), etc.

BENO, bē'no (בְּנוֹ, *b^enō*, "his son"): The son of Jaaziah of the house of Levi (1 Ch **24** 26.27).

BEN-ONI, ben-ō'nī (בֶּן־אוֹנִי, *ben-'ōnī;* **υἱὸς ὀδύνης μου,** *huiós odúnēs mou,* "son of my sorrow"): The name given by the dying Rachel to her new-born son; changed by his father Jacob to Benjamin (Gen **35** 18) q.v.

BEN-ZOHETH, ben-zō'heth (בֶּן־זוֹחֵת, *ben-zōḥēth,* "son of Zoheth," from a Heb root meaning "to be strong[?]"): A son of Ishi of the house of Judah (1 Ch **4** 20).

BEON, bē'on (Nu **32** 3). See Baal-meon.

BEOR, bē'or (בְּעוֹר, *b^e'ōr,* "destroyer"[?]):

(1) Father of Bela, the first king of Edom (Gen **36** 32; 1 Ch **1** 43).

(2) The father of the seer Balaam (Nu **22** 5; **24** 3.15; **31** 8; Dt **23** 4; Josh **13** 22; **24** 9, omitted in LXX; Mic **6** 5; 2 Pet **2** 15, AV and RVm "Bosor").

BERA, bē'ra (בֶּרַע, *bera',* "gift"[?]; cf *HPN*, 74 n.): King of Sodom (Gen **14** 2) who in the battle of Siddim was subdued by Chedorlaomer.

BERACAH, bē-rā'ka (בְּרָכָה, *b^erākhāh,* "blessing," AV **Berachah**): A Benjamite who joined David at Ziklag (1 Ch **12** 3).

BERACAH, bē-rā'ka, ber'a-ka, **VALLEY OF** (AV **Berachah;** עֵמֶק בְּרָכָה, *'ēmeḳ b^erākhāh;* **κοιλὰς εὐλογίας,** *koilás eulogías*): After the victory of Jehoshaphat and his people over Moab and Ammon, "On the fourth day they assembled themselves in the valley of Beracah; for there they blessed Jeh: therefore the name of that place was called The valley of Beracah [i.e. of blessing] unto this day" (2 Ch **20** 26). In the *Wady 'Arrûb* there is a ruin called *Breikût* and the valley in its proximity receives the same name. This is on the main road from Hebron to Jerus and not far from Tekoa; it suits the narrative well (see *PEF*, III, 352).

E. W. G. Masterman

BERACHIAH, ber-a-kī'a. See Berechiah.

BERAIAH, bē-rī'a (בְּרָאיָה, *b^erā'yāh,* "Jeh hath created"): A son of Shimei of the house of Benjamin (1 Ch **8** 21).

BEREA, be-rē'a. See Berœa.

BEREAVE, bē-rēv', **BEREAVER,** bē-rēv'ēr, **BEREFT,** bē-reft': Bereave is frequently used in the OT in the (now almost obsolete) meaning of "to deprive," "to take away," esp. with reference to loss of children. The Heb word used here is שָׁכֹל, *shākhōl,* "to be childless," or in the Piel "to make childless" (cf Gen **42** 36 et al.). In AV Eccl **4** 8 (from the Heb חָסֵר, *ḥāṣēr,* "to lack") we read "and bereave my soul of good" (RV "deprive"), and in Ezk **36** 14 (from Heb כָּשַׁל, *kāshal,* "to stumble"), "neither bereave thy nations any more" (RVm "cause to stumble").

Bereaver, otherwise very rare, is found RV Ezk **36** 13 (from Heb שָׁכֹל, *shākhōl,* "to be childless"), "a bereaver of thy nation" (AV "hast bereaved").

Bereft is found in 1 Tim **6** 5 (from the Gr *aposteréō,* "to rob") "bereft of the truth" (AV "destitute"). The expression *bereavement* (RV Isa **49** 20) in the phrase "the children of thy b." means "the children born to thee in the time when God had afflicted thee."

A. L. Breslich

BERECHIAH, ber-ē-kī'a (בֶּרֶכְיָה, בֶּרֶכְיָהוּ, *berekhyāh, berekhyāhū,* "Jeh blesses," *HPN*, 216, 287):

(1) A descendant of David (1 Ch **3** 20).

(2) The father of Asaph, the singer (1 Ch **6** 39 AV "Berachiah"; **15** 17).

(3) A former inhabitant of Jerus, a Levite (1 Ch **9** 16).

(4) A doorkeeper for the ark at David's time (1 Ch **15** 23).

(5) One of the heads of the children of Ephraim (2 Ch **28** 12).

(6) The father of Meshullam the builder (Neh **3** 4.30; **6** 18).

(7) The father of the prophet Zechariah (Zec **1** 1.7).

A. L. Breslich

BERED, bē'red (בֶּרֶד, *beredh,* "hail," from a Heb root meaning "to be cold"): The son of Shuthelah of the house of Ephraim (1 Ch **7** 20). Cf Becher.

BERED, bē'red (בֶּרֶד, *beredh;* **Βαράδ,** *Barád*): A place in the Negeb mentioned in the story of Hagar (Gen **16** 14). The well Beer-lahai-roi was "between Kadesh and Bered." The Onkelos Tg renders it *Ḥaghrā',* which is the usual equivalent of Shur, while the Jerus Tg renders it *Ḥălūçāh* which is also Shur (Ex **15** 22). *Ḥălūçāh* is clearly the city of Elusu mentioned by Ptolemy and from the 4th to the 7th cents. by various ecclesiastical writers. It was an important town on the road from Pal to Kadesh and Mt. Sinai. This is without doubt the very large and important ruin *Kh. Khalaṣa,* some 70 miles S. of Jerus on the road from Beersheba and Rehoboth. "These ruins cover an area of 15 to 20 acres, throughout which the foundations and inclosures of houses are distinctly to be traced. . . . We judged that here there must have been a city with room enough for a population of 15,000 to 20,000 souls" (Robinson, *BR*, I, 201).

E. W. G. Masterman

BERENICE, ber'e-nēs. See Bernice.

BERI, bē'rī (בֵּרִי, *bērī,* "wisdom"): A descendant of Asher (1 Ch **7** 36).

BERIAH, bē-rī'a, **BERIITES,** bē-rī'īts (בְּרִיעָה, *b^erī'āh,* "in shouting," prob. derived from a Heb root meaning "to make noise," or "in evil," from another Heb root):

(1) A son of Asher and father of Heber and Malchiel (Gen **46** 17; 1 Ch **7** 30.31; the head of the family of the Beriites, Nu **26** 44 ff).

(2) A son of Ephraim, called B. by his father because "it went evil with his house" (1 Ch **7** 23).

(3) A descendant of Benjamin (1 Ch **8** 13.16).

(4) A Levite in the line of Gershon (1 Ch **23** 10 f).

BERITES, bē′rīts (בֵּרִים, *bērīm;* according to Klostermann and others, בִּכְרִים, *bikhrīm*): The word is found only once in the OT (2 S **20** 14). The passage seems to be doubtful. The suggestion of Klostermann does not improve matters any; the other proposed reading, בַּחֻרִים, *baḥūrīm* (Vulg *viri electi*), "choice young men," is to be preferred.

BERITH, bē′rith (בְּרִית, *berīth,* "covenant"). See BAAL-BERITH.

BERNICE, bẽr-nī′sē (Βερνίκη, *Berníkē,* "victorious"): One of the shameless women of the Bible, mentioned in Acts **25** 13.23; **26** 30. She was the eldest daughter of Herod Agrippa I (Acts **12** 1.6.11.21) who ruled from 38–45 AD. Her whole life from the Jewish standpoint was incestuous. Its story is told by Jos (*Ant,* XIX, v, 1; XX, vii, 1–3), also by Juvenal (6, 156). Her first husband was her own uncle, Herod of Calchis. After his death she consorted with her own brother Agrippa II, with whom she listened to the impassioned defense of Paul at Caesarea before Felix. For a while she was married to King Ptolemy or Polemo of Sicily, who for her sake embraced Judaism, by the rite of circumcision. But she left him soon to return to Agrippa. Later on she figures shamefully in the lives of Vespasian and Titus, father and son. If heredity stands for anything, its lessons are forcibly taught in the history of the Herodian family. HENRY E. DOSKER

BERODACH-BALADAN, bē-rō′dak-bal′a-dan. See MERODACH-BALADAN.

BERŒA, be-rē′a (Βέροια or Βέῤῥοια, *Béroia*):

(1) A town of southwestern Macedonia, in the district of Emathia. It lay at the foot of Mt. Bermius, on a tributary of the Haliacmon, and seems to have been an ancient town, though the date of its foundation is uncertain. A passage in Thucydides (i.61) relating to the year 432 BC probably refers to another place of the same name, but an inscription (*Inscr Graec,* II, 5, 296*i*) proves its existence at the end of the 4th cent. BC, and it is twice mentioned by Polybius (xxvii.8; xxviii.8). After the battle of Pydna in 168 BC Berœa was the first city to surrender to Rome and fell in the third of the four regions into which Macedonia was divided (Livy xliv.45; xlv.29). Paul and Silas came to Berœa from Thessalonica, which they had been forced by an uproar to leave, and preached in the synagogue to the Jews, many of whom believed after a candid examination of the apostolic message in the light of their Scriptures (Acts **17** 10.11). A number of "Gr women of honorable estate and of men" also believed, but the advent of a body of hostile Jews from Thessalonica created a disturbance in consequence of which Paul had to leave the city, though Silas and Timothy stayed there for a few days longer (Acts **17** 12–15). Perhaps the Sopater of Berœa who accompanied Paul to Asia on his last journey to Jerus was one of his converts on this visit (Acts **20** 4). Berœa, which was one of the most populous cities of Macedonia, early became a bishopric under the metropolitan of Thessalonica and was itself made a metropolis by Andronicus II (1283–1328): there is a tradition that the first bishop of the church was Onesimus. It played a prominent part in the struggles between the Greeks and the Bulgarians and Serbs, and was finally conquered by the Turks in 1373–74. The town, which still bears among the Greeks its ancient name (pronounced *Verria*) though called by the Turks *Karaferia,* possesses but few remains of antiquity with the exception of numerous inscriptions (Leake, *Travels in Northern Greece,* III, 290 ff; Cousinéry, *Voyage dans la Macédoine,* I, 57 ff; Dimitsas, *Makedonia,* in Greek, 57 ff). MARCUS N. TOD

(2) The place where Menelaus the ex-high priest was executed by order of Antiochus Eupator, the victim, according to local custom, being cast from a tower 50 cubits high into a bed of ashes (2 Macc **13** 3 ff). It was the ancient city of *Ḥalab,* lying about midway between Antioch and Hierapolis. Seleucus Nicator gave it the name Berœa. It was a city of importance under the Moslems in the Middle Ages, when the old name again asserted itself, and remains to the present time.

The name "Aleppo" came to us through the Venetian traders in the days before the great overland route to India via Aleppo lost its importance through the discovery of the passage round the Cape. Aleppo is now a city of nearly 130,000 inhabitants. The governor exercises authority over a wide district extending from the Euphrates to the Mediterranean.

(3) (Βερέα, *Beréa*): A place mentioned in 1 Macc **9** 4. It may be identical with BEEROTH (q.v.) in Benjamin, a Hivite town, 8 miles N. of Jerus, or with the modern *Bīrez-Zait,* 1½ miles N.W. of *Jifneh.* W. EWING

BEROTH, bē′roth (1 Esd **5** 19). See BEEROTH.

BEROTHAH, bē-rō′tha (Ezk **47** 16: בֵּרוֹתָה, *bērōthāh;* LXX B, Ἀβθηρά, *Abthērá;* or BEROTHAI, 2 S **8** 8; בֵּרֹתַי, *bērōthai,* where for מִבֵּרֹתַי, *mibbērōthai,* LXX reads *ek tōn eklektōn póleōn,* "from the select cities"): Probably two forms of the same name. Ezk **47** 16 places it on the ideal northern frontier of Israel, between Damascus and Hamath. According to 2 S **8** 8 it was a city of Hadadezer, king of Zobah. In the ‖ passage (1 Ch **18** 8) Cun is given in place of Berothai. Its site is unknown. Ewald connected it with Beirût (so also apparently H. P. Smith, *ICC,* "Samuel," 307), but Ezekiel's description excludes this view. Others have sought it in the Wady Brissa, in the E. slope of Lebanon, N. of Baalbec. A more plausible conjecture identifies it with Bereitān (Brithēn), a village somewhat S. of Baalbec (Baedeker, *Pal*[3], 369). Possibly, however, the ideal northern frontier line should be drawn farther south. See HETHLON; ZEDAD; ZOBAH. C. H. THOMSON

BEROTHITE, bē′roth-īt. See BEEROTHITE.

BERRIES, ber′is: Occurs in Jas **3** 12 (AV) in the phrase "olive berries" (ἐλαῖαι, *elaíai*). The RV reads simply "olives."

BERYL, ber′il. See STONES, PRECIOUS.

BERYTUS, ber′i-tus, bē-rī′tus (Βηρυτός, *Bērutós;* Arab. بيروت; mod. Beirût, Beyrout, Beyrouth): An ancient Phoen city situated on the N. side of a promontory jutting out from the base of Lebanon to the W. into the Mediterranean and forming a bay on the N. connected with the fable of St. George and the Dragon, and hence called St. George's Bay. The city is about 25 miles N. of Sidon and about 12 S. of the famous Lycus, or Dog River, at the mouth of which are found the sculptured rocks bearing the monuments of the ancient kings of Egypt, Babylonia and Assyria.

The city has been thought by some to be the Berothai of 2 S **8** 8 or the Berothah of Ezk **47** 16, but the connection in which these cities are mentioned seems to preclude the identification. The town is, however, an ancient one, for it occurs in Am Tab as *Beruti* where it is closely connected with Gebal of which it may have been a dependency.

Though not mentioned in OT or NT it appears in the history of Herod the Great as an important town where was assembled a court of 150 judges, presided over by Saturninus, a former Rom consul, to try the case which Herod brought against his two sons, Alexander and Aristobulus, who were condemned there by the Rom court (*Ant*, XVI, xi, 2). Beirût was a Rom colony at this time where many veterans settled and it afterward became the seat of a great Rom law school which was attended, in the days of Justinian, by thousands of students. It was utterly destroyed by an earthquake in 551 AD, and for a time was abandoned. Many remains of temples and public buildings of the Rom period remain. It rose to some importance during the Crusades and is at present the chief seaport of Syria, and has the only harbor on the coast. It is a town of about 125,000 inhabitants.

H. Porter

BERZELUS, bẽr-zē'lus. See Zorzelleus.

BESAI, bē'sī (בֵּסַי, *bēṣay*, "downtrodden"): The descendants of B. (Nethinim) returned with Zerubbabel to Jerus (Ezr **2** 49; Neh **7** 52=Basthai, 1 Esd **5** 31).

BESET, bḗ-set' (**εὐπερίστατος,** *euperístatos*): The most common sense of this word is "to surround." This is the thought in Ps **139** 5, and teaches the omnipresence of God. Often wicked men find that the things which they have done so envelope them that they cannot escape ruin (Hos **7** 2). The reference in He **12** 1 is first of all against the sin of apostasy against which repeated warning is given in this book. But the warning is also against any sin that is esp. dangerous to us. It, again and again, surrounds us like a besieging army. To surrender would be traitorous and disgraceful, since the Captain of the Lord's host is with us.

Jacob W. Kapp

BESIDE, bḗ-sīd': Near to, or close to (Ps **23** 2). It is often used to refer to the mental state, to the derangement of the mind (*ἐξίστημι, existēmi*, Mk **3** 21; Acts **26** 24 AV). Or it may refer to the condition of being out of the ordinary course of the life. A life consecrated to God and spent in the interest of humanity is so designated (2 Cor **5** 13). It has the sense also of a state of being out of one's usual mind, but not of mental derangement, occasioned by something that causes amazement or astonishment (Mk **5** 42). Or it may refer to a state in which one is not conscious of present conditions, but is rapt in vision (Acts **10** 10).

Besides is used in the sense of in addition to or that which is over and above what has been said or is possessed (Lk **16** 26; see ARVm "in"; Philem ver 19).

Jacob W. Kapp

BESIEGE, bḗ-sēj'. See Siege.

BESODEIAH, bes-ō-dē'ya, bes-ō-dī'a (בְּסוֹדְיָה, *beṣōdheyāh*, "in the confidence or counsel of Jeh"; cf Jer **23** 18.22; and *HPN*, 207, 221, 286): Father of Meshullam, the builder (Neh **3** 6).

BESOM, bē'zum: Occurs only once in Scripture: "I will sweep it with the besom of destruction" (Isa **14** 23). Refers to what was in store for Babylon. The Heb word *maṭ'ăṭē'*, rendered "besom," is close of kin to the one (*ṭī'ṭē'thīhā*) rendered "sweep." In early Eng. "besom" was synonymous with "broom," and is still so used in some parts of England.

BESOR, bē'sor, **THE BROOK** (נַחַל בְּשׂוֹר, *nahal beṣōr;* A, **Βεχώρ,** *Bechōr*, B, **Βεανά,** *Beaná;* **1** S **30** 9.10.21; Jos, *Ant*, VI, xiv, 6): A torrent-bed (*naḥal*) mentioned in the account of David's pursuit of the Amalekites. Thought to be *Wady Ghazza*, which enters the sea S.W. of Gaza.

BEST: Of five Heb originals the chief is טוֹב, *ṭōbh*, "good," expressing quality, character. Variously used of objects pleasing to the senses, feelings, mind, moral sense, e.g. "best of the land" (Gen **47** 6); "of sheep" (1 S **15** 9); of persons "married to whom they think best" (Nu **36** 6); of abode, "where it liketh [RV "pleaseth"] him best" (Dt **23** 16).

In Nu **18** 12 the revenues of the priests were to be "holy gifts," e.g. the "best of the oil," etc (חֵלֶב, *ḥēlebh*, "fat"); also vs 29.30.32, the gifts of the heave-offering were to be "of all the best," indicating that the richest elements of life were to go into the support and service of the sanctuary. So "the choice [best] fruits" (זִמְרָה, *zimrāh*, lit. "the song of the land"), a beautifully poetic expression for the most celebrated fruits (Gen **43** 11); equally choice is פָּזַז, *pāzaz*, "separate," "the finest [best] gold," hence "purified" (1 K **10** 18).

Used but twice in the NT: (1) of spiritual gifts (*κρεῖττον, kreítton*, "better" [RV "greater"]; 1 Cor **12** 31); (2) of raiment (*πρῶτος, prṓtos*, "first"), "best robe" (Lk **15** 22), of special significance as expressing the Father's lavish love for the repentant and returning sinner.

Dwight M. Pratt

BESTEAD, bḗ-sted' (נִקְשֶׁה, *niḳsheh*, "caught in a snare," "entrapped"; as Judah hard pressed in their own land by the Assyrians [Isa **8** 21 AV]): Found only here. OE word *steden* meaning "place," hence "set," "beset"; usually with "ill," "sorely bested." In RV rendered "sore distressed."

BESTIALITY, bes-ti-al'i-ti. See Crimes.

BESTOW, bḗ-stō': The seven Heb words rendered by this term variously mean "to put" or "place," "to give"; "do," "deposit," as e.g. to locate chariots and horsemen in cities (1 K **10** 26); or give a blessing (Ex **32** 29). Four Gr words so tr[d] signify "to give," "to labor," "to feed," "to place around"; as *συνάγω, sunágō*, "to stow away goods" (Lk **12** 17); or *ψωμίζω, psōmízō*, "give away" (1 Cor **13** 3). The term has richest significance in expressing God's abundant gift of grace and love, *δίδωμι, dídōmi* (2 Cor **8** 1 AV; 1 Jn **3** 1).

BETAH, bē'ta (2 S **8** 8). See Tibhath.

BETANE, bet'a-nḗ (**Βαιτάνη,** *Baitánē*): A place named in Jth **1** 9, among those to which the messengers of Nebuchadnezzar were sent. From the order in which they are named we should seek for it S. of Jerus. It may be identical with *Beit 'Ainūn*, about 3 miles N. of Hebron.

BETEN, bē'ten (בֶּטֶן, *beṭen;* **Βατνέ,** *Batné*): A city of Asher mentioned between Hali and Achshaph (Josh **19** 25). *Onom* places it 8 Rom miles E. of Ptolemais, giving it the name Bethseten. It may be identical with the modern village *el-B'aneh*, but no certainty is possible.

BETH, bāth (ב): The second letter of the Heb alphabet. With the *daghesh* it is transliterated in this dictionary as *b*, and, without, as *bh* (=*v*). It came also to be used for the number two (2) and with the dieresis for 2,000. For name, etc, see Alphabet; Bayith.

BETH, beth (in proper names; Gr transliteration in LXX, **βηθ,** *bēth, baith,* or *beth*): This is the Eng.

transliteration for the Heb בֵּית, *bēth*, meaning "house," "tent," "place." It occurs in many compound proper names formed similarly to the method of compounding words in the German language, as shown in the arts. immediately following. Thus we have *bēth ʿănāth* or *ʿănoth*="house of replies" (Josh **19** 38; Jgs **1** 33); *bēth'ēl*="house of God" (Gen **12** 8; **13** 3), etc. We also find the word in hybrid formations, e.g. Βηθφαγή, *Bēthphagē*=Bethphage="fig house" (Mt **21** 1).

FRANK E. HIRSCH

BETHABARA, beth-ab'a-ra (בֵּית עֲבָרָה, *bēth ʿăbhārāh;* **Βηθαβαρά,** *Bēthabará,* "house of the ford"): According to AV (following *TR*) the place where John baptized (Jn **1** 28). RV (with Tisch, WH following א*BAC*) reads BETHANY. It is distinguished from the Bethany of Lazarus and his sisters as being "beyond the Jordan." The reading "Bethabara" became current owing to the advocacy of Origen. Various suggestions have been made to explain the readings. G. A. Smith (*HGHL*) suggests that Bethany ("house of the ship") and Bethabara ("house of the ford") are names for the same place. Bethabara has also been identified with Bethbarah, which, however, was probably not on the Jordan but among the streams flowing into it (Jgs **7** 24). It is interesting to note that LXX[B] reads *Baithabara* for MT *Bēth-ʿărābhāh*, one of the cities of Benjamin (Josh **18** 22). If this be correct, the site is in Judaea.

Another solution is sought in the idea of a corruption of the original name into Bethany and Bethabara, the name having the consonants *n*, *b* and *r* after Beth. In Josh **13** 27 (LXX[B]) we find *Baithanabra* for Bēthnimrāh (MT), and Sir George Grove in *DB* (arts. "Bethabara" and "Bethnimrah") identifies Bethabara and Beth-nimrah. The site of the latter was a few miles above Jericho (see BETH-NIMRAH), "immediately accessible to Jerus and all Judaea" (cf Mt **3** 5; Mk **1** 5, and see art. "Bethany" in *EB*). This view has much in its favor.

Then, again, as Dr. G. Frederick Wright observes: "The traditional site is at the ford east of Jericho; but as according to Jn **1** 29.35.43 it was only one day's journey from Cana of Galilee, while according to Jn **10** 40; **11** 3.6.17 it was two or three days from Bethany, it must have been well up the river toward Galilee. Conder discovered a well-known ford near Beisan called Abarah, near the mouth of the valley of Jezreel. This is 20 miles from Cana and 60 miles from Bethany, and all the conditions of the place fit in with the history." See also BETHANY (2).

S. F. HUNTER

BETH-ANATH, beth-ā'nath (בֵּית עֲנָת, *bēth ʿănāth;* **Βαιναθάθ,** *Bainatháth*): A city in the territory of Naphtali, named with Horem and Beth-shemesh (Josh **19** 38; Jgs **1** 33). It is represented by the modern village *Ainatha*, about 12 miles N.W. of *Ṣafed*. The name signifies the "house" or "temple" of Anath, a goddess of the Canaanites.

BETH-ANOTH, beth-ā'noth (בֵּית עֲנוֹת, *bēth ʿănōth;* **Βαιθανάμ,** *Baithanám*, probably "House of Anath"—a god; Josh **15** 59): The ruin of *Beit ʿAinûn*, 1½ miles S.E. of *Halhûl*, in the neighborhood also of Bethzur and Gedor—places mentioned in association with it as towns in the hill country of Judah—appears to be a probable site. The present surface ruins belong to later ages.

BETHANY.

BETHANY, beth'a-ni (**Βηθανία,** *Bēthanía*):

(1) A village, 15 furlongs from Jerus (Jn **11** 18), on the road to Jericho, at the Mount of Olives (Mk **11** 1; Lk **19** 29), where lived "Simon the leper" (Mk **14** 3) and Mary, Martha and Lazarus (Jn **11** 18 f). This village may justifiably be called the Judaean home of Jesus, as He appears to have preferred to lodge there rather than in Jerus itself (Mt **21** 17; Mk **11** 11). Here occurred the incident of the raising of Lazarus (Jn **11**) and the feast at the house of Simon (Mt **26** 1–13; Mk **14** 3–9; Lk **7** 36–50; Jn **12** 1–8). The Ascension as recorded in Lk **24** 50–51 is thus described: "He led them out until they were over against Bethany: and he lifted up his hands, and blessed them. And it came to pass, while he blessed them, he parted from them, and was carried up into heaven."

Bethany is today *el'Azarēyeh* ("the place of Lazarus"—the L being displaced to form the art.). It is a miserably untidy and tumble-down village facing E. on the S.E. slope of the Mount of Olives, upon the carriage road to Jericho. A fair number of fig, almond and olive trees surround the houses. The traditional tomb of Lazarus is shown and there are some remains of mediaeval buildings, besides rock-cut tombs of much earlier date (*PEF*, III, 27, Sheet XVII).

(2) "Bethany beyond the Jordan" (Jn **1** 28; AV **Bethabara; Βηθαβαρά,** *Bēthabará,* a reading against the majority of the MSS, supported by Origen on geographical grounds): No such place is known. Grove suggested that the place intended is BETH-NIMRAH (which see), the modern *Tell nimrîn,* a singularly suitable place, but hard to fit in with Jn **1** 28; cf **2** 1. The traditional site is the ford E. of Jericho. E. W. G. MASTERMAN

BETH-ARABAH, beth-ar′a-ba (בֵּית הָעֲרָבָה, *bēth hā-ʽărābhāh;* **Βαιθαραβά,** *Baitharabá,* "place of the Arabah"):

(1) One of the 6 cities of Judah "in the wilderness" (Josh **15** 61), on the borders of Benjamin and Judah (Josh **15** 6; **18** 18 LXX). "The wilderness of Judah" is the barren land W. of the Dead Sea. Beth-arabah is not yet identified.

(2) One of the cities of Benjamin (Josh **18** 22). LXX^B reads *Baithabara,* and this may be correct. The names are easily confounded. See BETHABARA.

BETHARAM, beth-ā′ram (בֵּית הָרָם, *bēth hā-rām*). See BETH-HARAM.

BETH-ARBEL, beth-är′bel (בֵּית אַרְבֵּאל, *bēth ʼarbēʼl*): The scene of a terrific disaster inflicted on the inhabitants by Shalman (Hos **10** 14). If the place intended was in Pal, and was not the famous city of that name on the Euphrates, then probably it should be identified either with *Irbid* (or *Irbil*) in Galilee, or with *Irbid,* which corresponds to Arbela of the *Onom,* E. of the Jordan, about 12 miles S.E. of Gadara. If, as Schrader thinks (*COT,* II, 140), Shalman stands for the Moabite king, Shalamanu, a tributary of Tiglath-pileser, the eastern town would be the more natural identification. Possibly however the reference is to Shalmaneser III or IV. For the Galilean site, see ARBEL; see also *DB,* s.v. W. EWING

BETHASMOTH, beth-az′moth (AV **Bethsamos; Βαιθασμώθ,** *Baithasmōth* [1 Esd **5** 18]; corresponds to Beth-azmaveth in Neh **7** 28): A town in the territory of Benjamin, and may be identified with the modern *el-Hizmeh.* See AZMAVETH.

BETH-AVEN, beth-ā′ven (בֵּית אָוֶן, *bēth ʼāwen;* **Βαιθών,** *Baithōn,* **Βαιθαύν,** *Baithaún*): A place on the northern boundary of the territory of Benjamin (Josh **18** 12) E. of Bethel, near Ai (Josh **7** 2), W. of Michmash (1 S **13** 5; **14** 23). Beth-aven, "house of vanity," i.e. "idolatry," may possibly represent an original *bēth-ʼōn,* "house of wealth." Wilson (*PEFS,* 1869, 126) suggests *Khirbet An,* W. of Michmash. The name is used in mockery for Bethel by Hosea (**4** 15; **10** 5.8, etc; cf Am **5** 5).

BETH-AZMAVETH, beth-az-mā′veth (Neh **7** 28). See AZMAVETH.

BETH-BAAL-MEON, beth-bā-al-mē′on (Josh **13** 17). See BAAL-MEON.

BETH-BARAH, beth-bā′ra (בֵּית בָּרָה, *bēth bārāh;* **Βαιθηρά,** *Baithērá*): Perhaps *Bēth-ʽăbhāra,* the guttural being lost in copying. It is a ford which the Midianites were expected to pass in fleeing from Gideon. Messengers were therefore sent by Gideon to the Ephraimites bidding them "take before them the waters, as far as Beth-barah, even [RVm "and also"] the Jordan" (Jgs **7** 24). "The waters" were the streams emptying themselves into the Jordan: "even the Jordan" is a gloss on "the waters." Between the Jordan and the modern *Wady Fariʽah* an enemy could be entrapped; it is therefore probable that Beth-barah was on that stream near its entrance into the Jordan. See BETHABARA. S. F. HUNTER

BETHBASI, beth-bā′sī (**Βαιθβασί,** *Baithbasí*): The name may mean "place of marshes" = Heb *bēth-beçī.* According to G. A. Smith there is a *Wādy el-Bassah* E. of Tekoa in the wilderness of Judaea. The name means "marsh," which Dr. Smith thinks impossible, and really "an echo of an ancient name." Jonathan and Simon repaired the ruins of the fortified place "in the desert" (1 Macc **9** 62.64). Jos reads *Bethalaga,* i.e. Beth-hoglah (*Ant,* XIII, i, 5). Pesh VS reads *Beth-Yashan* (see JESHANAH), which Dr. Cheyne thinks is probably correct. Thus the origin of the name and the site of the town are merely conjectural. S. F. HUNTER

BETH-BIRI, beth-bir′ī (AV **Beth-birei,** beth-bir′ē-ī) בֵּית־בִּרְאִי, *bēth birʼī;* **οἶκος Βραουμσεωρείμ,** *oíkos Braoumseōreím;* 1 Ch **4** 31 [called in Josh **19** 6, Beth-lebaoth, "abode of lions"]): A site belonging to Simeon in the Negeb—unidentified.

BETH-CAR, beth′kär (בֵּית־כָּר, *bēth-kār;* **Βαιθχόρ,** *Baithchór,* **Βελχόρ,** *Belchór*): "And the men of Israel went out of Mizpah, and pursued the Philis, and smote them, until they came under Beth-car" (1 S **7** 11). *ʽAin Kārem* has been suggested; if Mizpah is *nebi Samwîl* then this identification is probable, as the pursuit would be along the deep *Wady beit Hannîneh*—a natural line of retreat for the Philis to take. See BETH-HACCHEREM.

BETH-DAGON, beth-dā′gon (בֵּית־דָּגוֹן, *bēth-dāghōn;* **Βηθδαγών,** *Bēthdagôn*):

(1) A town in the Shephelah of Judah named with Gederoth, Naamah, and Makkedah (Josh **15** 41). It may be represented by the modern *Beit Dijan,* about 6 miles S.E. of Jaffa. This however is a modern site, and not in the Shephelah. Nearly 2 miles to the south is *Khirbet Dājūn,* a Rom site. The connection in which it occurs leads us to expect a position farther S.E.

(2) A city on the border of Asher (Josh **19** 27) which Conder would identify with *Tell D'auk,* near the mouth of the Belus, in the plain of Acre.

The name seems to have been of frequent occurrence. There is a *Beit Dejan* about 6 miles E. of *Nāblus,* and Jos speaks of a fortress called Dagon above Jericho (*Ant,* XII, viii, 1; *BJ,* I, ii, 3). This would seem to indicate a widespread worship of Dagon. But the name may mean "house of corn." W. EWING

BETH-DIBLATHAIM, beth-dib-la-thā′im (בֵּית דִּבְלָתַיִם, *bēth dibhlāthayim;* **οἶκος Δεβλαιθαίμ,** *oíkos Deblaithaím,* lit. "house of D."): A town in Moab mentioned with Dibon and Nebo (Jer **48** 22). It is probably identical with Almon-diblathaim (Nu **33** 46 f). Mesha claims to have fortified it along with Mehedeba and *Baʽal-meʽon* (see MOABITE STONE). The place is not yet identified.

BETH-EDEN, beth-ē′den (Am **1** 5 AVm; EV "house of Eden"). See CHILDREN OF EDEN.

BETHEL, beth′el (בֵּית־אֵל, *bēth-ʼēl;* **Βαιθήλ,** *Baithēl* and **οἶκος θεοῦ,** *oíkos theoú,* lit. "house of God"):

(1) A town near the place where Abraham halted and offered sacrifice on his way south from Shechem.

1. Identification and Description

It lay W. of Ai (Gen **12** 8). It is named as on the northern border of Benjamin (the southern of Ephraim, Josh **16** 2), at the top of the ascent from the Jordan valley by way of Ai (Josh **18** 13). It lay S. of Shiloh (Jgs **21** 19). *Onom* places it 12 Rom miles from Jerus, on the road to Neapolis. It is represented by the modern *Beitīn*, a village of some 400 inhabitants, which stands on a knoll E. of the road to *Nāblus*. There are four springs which yield supplies of good water. In ancient times these were supplemented by a reservoir hewn in the rock S. of the town. The surrounding country is bleak and barren, the hills being marked by a succession of stony terraces, which may have suggested the form of the ladder in Jacob's famous dream.

Bethel.

2. The Sanctuary

The town was originally called Luz (Gen **28** 19, etc). When Jacob came hither on his way to Paddan-aram we are told that he lighted upon "the place" (Gen **28** 11, Heb). The Heb *māḳōm*, like the cognate Arab. *maḳām*, denotes a sacred place or sanctuary. The *māḳōm* was doubtless that at which Abraham had sacrificed, E. of the town. In the morning Jacob set up "for a pillar" the stone which had served as his pillow (Gen **28** 18; see PILLAR—*maççēbhāh*), poured oil upon it and called the name of the place Bethel, "house of God"; that is, of God whose epiphany was for him associated with the pillar. This spot became a center of great interest, lending growing importance to the town. In process of time the name Luz disappeared, giving place to that of the adjoining sanctuary, town and sanctuary being identified. Jacob revisited the place on his return from Paddan-aram; here Deborah, Rebekah's nurse, died and was buried under "the oak" (Gen **35** 6 f). Probably on rising ground E. of Bethel Abraham and Lot stood to view the uninviting highlands and the rich lands of the Jordan valley (Gen **13** 9 ff).

3. History

Bethel was a royal city of the Canaanites (Josh **12** 16). It appears to have been captured by Joshua (**8** 7), and it was allotted to Benjamin (Josh **18** 22). In Jgs **1** 22 ff it is represented as held by Canaanites, from whom the house of Joseph took it by treachery (cf 1 Ch **7** 28). Hither the ark was brought from Gilgal (Jgs **2** 1 LXX). Israel came to Bethel to consult the Divine oracle (**20** 18), and it became an important center of worship (1 S **10** 3). The home of the prophetess Deborah was not far off (Jgs **4** 5). Samuel visited Bethel on circuit, judging Israel (1 S **7** 16).

With the disruption of the kingdom came Bethel's greatest period of splendor and significance. To counteract the influence of Jerus as the national religious center Jeroboam embarked on the policy which won for him the unenviable reputation of having "made Israel to sin." Here he erected a temple, set up an image, the golden calf, and established an imposing ritual. It became the royal sanctuary and the religious center of his kingdom (1 K **12** 29 ff; Am **7** 13). He placed in Bethel the priests of the high places which he had made (1 K **12** 32). To Bethel came the man of God from Judah who pronounced doom against Jeroboam (1 K **13**), and who, having been seduced from duty by an aged prophet in Bethel, was slain by a lion. According to the prophets Amos and Hosea the splendid idolatries of Bethel were accompanied by terrible moral and religious degradation. Against the place they launched the most scathing denunciations, declaring the vengeance such things must entail (Am **3** 14; **4** 4; **5** 11m; **9** 1; Hos **4** 15; **5** 8; **10** 5.8.13). With the latter the name Bethel gives place in mockery to Beth-aven. Bethel shared in the downfall of Samaria wrought by the Assyrians; and according to an old tradition, Shalmaneser possessed himself of the golden calf (cf Jer **48** 13). The priest, sent by the Assyrians to teach the people whom they had settled in the land how to serve Jeh, dwelt in Bethel (2 K **17** 28). King Josiah completed the demolition of the sanctuary at Bethel, destroying all the instruments of idolatry, and harrying the tombs of the idolaters. The monument of the man of God from Judah he allowed to stand (2 K **23** 4.15). The men of Bethel were among those who returned from Babylon with Zerubbabel (Ezr **2** 28; Neh **7** 32), and it is mentioned as reoccupied by the Benjamites (Neh **11** 31). Zechariah (**7** 2) records the sending of certain men from Jerus in the 4th year of King Darius to inquire regarding particular religious practices. Bethel was one of the towns fortified by Bacchides in the time of the Maccabees (1 Macc **9** 50; *Ant*, XIII, i, 3). It is named again as a small town which, along with Ephraim, was taken by Vespasian as he approached Jerus (*BJ*, IV, ix, 9).

(2) A city in Judah which in 1 S **30** 27 is called Bethel; in Josh **19** 4 Bethul; and in 1 Ch **4** 30 Bethuel. The site has not been identified. In Josh **15** 30 LXX gives Baithel in Judah, where the Heb has *K^{e}sīl*—probably a scribal error.

W. EWING

BETHELITE, beth'el-īt: The term applied to a man who in the days of Ahab rebuilt Jericho (1 K **16** 34). See HIEL.

BETHEL, MOUNT (הַר בֵּית־אֵל, *har bēth-'ēl;* **Βαιθήλ λοῦζα**, *Baithēl loúza* [1 S **13** 2, RV "the mount of Bethel"; Josh **16** 1]): The hill which stretches from the N. of the town to *Tell 'Aṣūr*. The road to Shechem lies along the ridge. An army in possession of these heights easily commanded the route from north to south.

BETH-EMEK, beth-ē'mek (בֵּית הָעֵמֶק, *bēth hā-'ēmeḳ;* **Βηθαεμέκ**, *Bēthaemék*, "house of the valley"): A town in the territory of Zebulun (Josh **19** 27). It has not been identified, but must be sought somewhere E. of Acre, not far from *Kābūl*, the ancient Cabul.

BETHER, bē'thẽr (בֶּתֶר, *bether*): In Cant **2** 17 mention is made of "the mountains of Bether." It is doubtful if a proper name is intended. The RVm has, "perhaps, the spice *malobathron*." A Bether is prominent in late Jewish history as the place where the Jews resisted Hadrian under Bar Cochba in 135 AD. Its identity with *Bittīr*, 7 miles S.W. of Jerus, is attested by an inscription.

BETHESDA, bĕ-thez'da (**Βηθεσδά**, *Bēthesdá; TR*, Jn **5** 2 [probably בֵּית חִסְדָּא, *bēth ḥiṣdā'*, "house of mercy"]; other forms occur as *Bēthzathá* and *Bēthsaidá*):

(1) The only data we have is the statement in Jn **5** 2–4: "Now there is in Jerus by the sheep

gate a pool, which is called in Hebrew Bethesda, having five porches. In these lay a multitude of them that were sick, blind, halt, withered." Many ancient authorities add (as in RVm) "waiting for the moving of the water: for an angel of the Lord went down at certain seasons into the pool, and troubled the water," etc.

Pool of Bethesda.

The name does not help as to the site, no such name occurs elsewhere in Jerus; the mention of the sheep gate is of little assistance because the word "gate" is supplied, and even were it there, its site is uncertain. Sheep "pool" or "place" is at least as probable; the tradition about the "troubling of the water" (which may be true even if the angelic visitant may be of the nature of folk-lore) can receive no rational explanation except by the well-known phenomenon, by no means uncommon in Syria and always considered the work of a supernatural being, of an intermittent spring. The arrangement of the five porches is similar to that demonstrated by Dr. F. Bliss as having existed in Rom times as the "Pool of Siloam"; the story implies that the incident occurred outside the city walls, as to carry a bed on the Sabbath would not have been forbidden by Jewish traditional law.

1. The Conditions of the Narrative: Jn 5:2

(2) Tradition has varied concerning the site. In the 4th cent., and probably down to the Crusades, a pool was pointed out as the true site, a little to the N.W. of the present St. Stephen's Gate; it was part of a twin pool and over it were erected at two successive periods two Christian churches. Later on this site was entirely lost and from the 13th cent. the great *Birket Israel*, just N. of the Temple area, was pointed out as the site.

Within the last quarter of a cent., however, the older traditional site, now close to the Church of St. Anne, has been rediscovered, excavated and popularly accepted. This pool is a rock-cut, rain-filled cistern, 55 ft. long × 12 ft. broad, and is approached by a steep and winding flight of steps. The floor of the rediscovered early Christian church roofs over the pool, being supported upon five arches in commemoration of the five porches. At the western end of the church, where probably the font was situated, there was a fresco, now much defaced and fast fading, representing the angel troubling the waters.

2. The Traditional Site

(3) Although public opinion supports this site, there is much to be said for the proposal, promulgated by Robinson and supported by Conder and other good authorities, that the pool was at the "Virgin's Fount" (see GIHON), which is today an intermittent spring whose "troubled" waters are still visited by Jews for purposes of cure. As the only source of "living water" near Jerus, it is a likely spot for there to have been a "sheep pool" or "sheep place" for the vast flocks of sheep coming to Jerus in connection with the temple ritual. See *BW*, XXV, 80 ff. E. W. G. MASTERMAN

3. A More Probable Site

BETH-EZEL, beth-ē′zel (בֵּית הָאֵצֶל, *bēth hā-'ēçel;* **οἶκος ἐχόμενος αὐτῆς,** *oíkos echómenos autḗs;* lit. "adjoining house"): A place named along with other cities in the Phili plain (Mic **1** 11). The site has not been identified. By some it is thought to be the same as Azel of Zec **14** 5; but see AZEL.

BETH-GADER, beth-gā′dēr (בֵּית־גָּדֵר, *bēth-gādhēr;* **Βαιθγεδώρ,** *Baithgedṓr,* or **Βαιθγαιδών** (B), *Baithgaidṓn*): The name occurs between those of Bethlehem and Kiriath-jearim in 1 Ch **2** 51. It is possibly identical with Geder of Josh **12** 13.

BETH-GAMUL, beth-gā′mul (בֵּית גָּמוּל, *bēth gāmūl;* **οἶκος Γαιμώλ,** *oíkos Gaimṓl;* ℵ, **Γαμωλά,** *Gamōlá*): A city in Moab named with Dibon, Kiriathaim and Beth-meon (Jer **48** 23). Conder places it at *Umm el-Jamāl*, toward E. of the plateau, S. of Medeba (*HDB*, s.v.). Others (Guthe, *Kurz. bib. Wörterbuch,* s.v.; Buhl, *GAP*, 268, etc) favor *Jemeil*, a site 6 miles E. of *Dhībān*. Since the town is not mentioned among the cities of Israel Buhl doubts if it should be sought N. of the Arnon.

BETH-GILGAL, beth-gil′gal (בֵּית הַגִּלְגָּל, *bēth ha-gilgāl;* **Βηθαγγαλγάλ,** *Bēthaggalgál;* AV **house of Gilgal**): The Gilgal which lay in the plain E. of Jericho (Neh **12** 29). See GILGAL.

BETH-HACCHEREM, beth-ha-kē′rem, beth-hak′e-rem (AV **Beth-haccerem;** בֵּית הַכֶּרֶם, *bēth ha-kerem;* **Βηθαχχαρμά,** *Bēthachcharmá* [see *DB*], "place of the vineyard"): A district (in Neh **3** 14) ruled over by one, Malchijah; mentioned in Jer **6** 1 as a suitable signal station. From its association with Tekoa (Jer **6** 1) and from the statement by Jerome that it was a village which he could see daily from Bethlehem, the Frank mountain (Herodium) has been suggested. It certainly would be a unique place for a beacon. More suitable is the fertile vineyard country around *'Ain Kārem* (the "spring of the vineyard"). On the top of *Jebel 'Ali,* above this village, are some remarkable cairns which, whatever their other uses, would appear to have been once beacons. *'Ain Kārem* appears as *Carem* in the LXX (Josh **15** 59). See BETH-CAR.
E. W. G. MASTERMAN

BETH-HAGGAN, beth-hag′an (בֵּית הַגָּן, *bēth-ha-gān,* "house of the garden"). The place where Ahaziah was slain by Jehu (2 K **9** 27). The words are rendered in EV "the garden house," but some take them to be a proper name. The location is doubtful.

BETH-HANAN, beth-hā′nan (1 K **4** 9), **ELON-BETH-HANAN.** See ELON.

BETH-HARAM, beth-hā′ram (בֵּית הָרָם, *bēth hārām;* **Βαιθαράν**, *Baitharán;* A, **Βαιθαρρά**, *Baitharrá;* AV wrongly, **Beth-Aram**): An Amorite city taken and fortified by the Gadites (Josh **13** 27; Nu **32** 36; in the latter passage the name appears as Beth-haran, probably the original form). It corresponds to *Bēthramphtha* of Jos (*Ant*, XVIII, ii, 1), which, according to Eusebius, was the name used by the Syrians. Here was a palace of Herod (*Ant*, XVII, x, 6; *BJ*, II, iv, 2). *Onom* says it was called Livias. Jos says it was fortified by Herod Antipas, who called it Julias for the wife of Augustus (*Ant*, XVIII, ii, 1; *BJ*, II, ix, 1). The name would be changed to Julias when Livia, by the will of the emperor, was received into the Gens Julia. It is represented by *Tell er-Rāmeh* in *Wādy Ḥesbān*, about 6 miles E. of Jordan. W. EWING

BETH-HARAN, beth-hā′ran (בֵּית הָרָן, *bēth hārān*): A fenced city E. of the Jordan (Nu **32** 36) identical with BETH-HARAM, which see.

BETH-HOGLAH, beth-hog′la (בֵּית חָגְלָה, *bēth-ḥoghlāh;* LXX **Βαιθαγλαάμ**, *Baithaglaám*, "house of partridge"): Mentioned in Josh **15** 6; **18** 19, identified with *Ain Hajlah* ("partridge spring") lying between Jericho and the Jordan, where in 1874 there was still a ruined Gr monastery called *Kasr Hajlah*, dating from the 12th cent. The ruins are now destroyed. In Josh **15** 5; **18** 19 it is said to be at the mouth of the Jordan on a Tongue (*Lisân*) of the Salt Sea. But it is now several miles inland, probably because the Jordan has silted up a delta to that extent. See DEAD SEA.
GEORGE FREDERICK WRIGHT

BETH-HORON, beth-hō′ron (בֵּית־חוֹרֹן, *bēth-ḥōrōn* [other Heb forms occur]; **Βηθωρών**, *Bēthōrōn*, probably the "place of the hollow"; cf *Hauran*, "the hollow"):

1. The Ancient Towns

(1) The name of two towns, Beth-horon the Upper (Josh **16** 5) and Beth-horon the Lower (Josh **16** 3), said to have been built (1 Ch **7** 24) by Sheeraḥ, the daughter of Beriah. The border line between Benjamin and Ephraim passed by the Beth-horons (Josh **16** 5; **21** 22), the cities belonging to the latter tribe and therefore, later on, to the Northern Kingdom. Solomon "built Beth-horon the upper, and Beth-horon the nether, fortified cities, with walls, gates, and bars" (2 Ch **8** 5; 1 K **9** 17).

From Egyp sources (Müller, *As. und Europa*, etc) it appears that Beth-horon was one of the places conquered by Shishak of Egypt from Rehoboam. Again, many cents. later, Bacchides repaired Beth-horon, "with high walls, with gates and with bars and in them he set a garrison, that they might work malice upon ["vex"] Israel" (1 Macc **9** 50.51), and at another time the Jews fortified it against Holofernes (Jth **4** 4.5).

2. The Modern Beit Ur el foḳa and el taḥta

(2) These two towns are now known as *Beit Ur el foḳa* (i.e. "the upper") and *Beit Ur el taḥta* (i.e. "the lower"), two villages crowning hill tops, less than 2 miles apart; the former is some 800 ft. higher than the latter. Today these villages are sunk into insignificance and are off any important lines of communication, but for many cents. the towns occupying their sites dominated one of the most historic roads in history.

3. The Pass of the Beth-horons

(3) When (Josh **10** 10) Joshua discomfited the kings of the Amorites "he slew them with a great slaughter at Gibeon, and chased them by the way of the 'Ascent of Beth-horon.'" When the Philis were opposing King Saul at Michmash they sent a company of their men to hold "the way of Beth-horon." This pass ascends from the plain of Ajalon (now *Yālo*) and climbs in about ¾ hr. to *Beit Ur el taḥta* (1,210 ft.); it then ascends along the ridge, with valleys lying to north and south, and reaches *Beit Ur el foḳa* (2,022 ft.), and pursuing the same ridge arrives in another 4½ miles at the plateau to the N. of *el Jîb* (Gibeon). At intervals along this historic route traces of the ancient Rom paving are visible. It was the great highroad into the heart of the land from the earliest times until about three or four cents. ago. Along this route came Canaanites, Israelites, Philis, Egyptians, Syrians, Romans, Saracens and Crusaders. Since the days of Joshua (Josh **10** 10) it has frequently been the scene of a rout. Here the Syrian general Seron was defeated by Judas Maccabaeus (1 Macc **3** 13–24), and six years later Nicanor, retreating from Jerus, was here defeated and slain (1 Macc **7** 39 ff; Jos, *Ant*, XII, x, 5). Along this pass in 66 AD the Rom general Cestius Gallus was driven in headlong flight before the Jews.

Now the changed direction of the highroad to Jerus has left the route forsaken and almost forgotten. See *PEF*, III, 86, Sh XVII.
E. W. G. MASTERMAN

BETH-HORON, THE BATTLE OF:

1. The Political Situation
2. Joshua's Strategy
3. Joshua's Command to the Sun and Moon
4. The Astronomical Relations of the Sun and Moon to Each Other and to the Neighborhood of the Field of Battle
5. The "Silence" of the Sun
6. "Jehovah Fought for Israel"
7. The Afternoon's March
8. The Chronicle and the Poem Independent Witnesses
9. Date of the Events
10. The Records Are Contemporaneous with the Events

1. The Political Situation

The battle which gave to the Israelites under Joshua the command of southern Pal has always excited interest because of the astronomical marvel which is recorded to have then taken place.

In invading Pal the Israelites were not attacking a single coherent state, but a country occupied by different races and divided, like Greece at a later period, into a number of communities, each consisting practically of but a single city and the cultivated country around it. Thus Joshua destroyed the two cities of Jericho and Ai without any interference from the other Amorites. The destruction of Jericho gave him full possession of the fertile valley of the Jordan; the taking of Ai opened his way up to the ridge which forms the backbone of the country, and he was able to lead the people unopposed to the mountains of Ebal and Gerizim for the solemn reading of the Law. But when the Israelites returned from this ceremony a significant division showed itself amongst their enemies. Close to Ai, Joshua's most recent conquest, was Beeroth, a small town inhabited by Hivites; and no doubt because in the natural order of events Beeroth might look to be next attacked, the Hivites determined to make terms with Israel. An embassy was therefore sent from Gibeon, their chief city, and Joshua and the Israelites, believing that it came from a distant land not under the Ban, entered into the proposed alliance.

The effect on the political situation was immediate. The Hivites formed a considerable state, relatively speaking; their cities were well placed on the southern highland, and Gibeon, their capital, was one of the most important fortresses of that district, and only 6 miles distant from Jerus, the chief Amorite stronghold. The Amorites recognized at once that, in view of this important defection, it was imperative for them to crush the Gibeonites before the Israelites could unite with them, and this they endeavored to do. The Gibeonites, seeing themselves attacked, sent an urgent message to Joshua, and he at the head of his picked men made a night march up from Gilgal and fell upon the Amorites at Gibeon the next day and put them to flight.

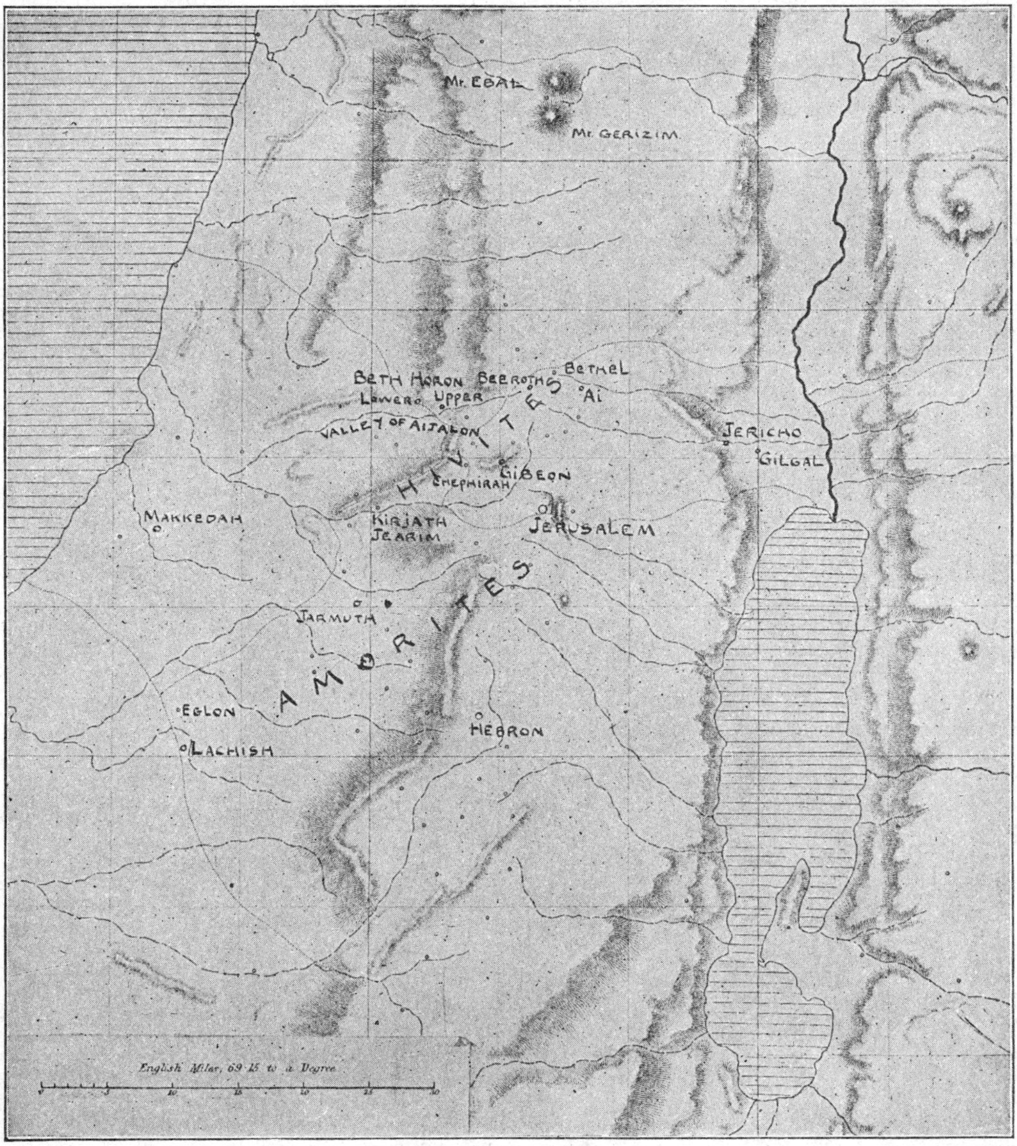

Battle of Beth-horon.

2. Joshua's Strategy

We are not told by which route he marched, but it is significant that the Amorites fled by the way of Beth-horon; that is to say, not toward their own cities, but away from them. A glance at the map shows that this means that Joshua had succeeded in cutting their line of retreat to Jerus. He had probably therefore advanced upon Gibeon from the south, instead of by the obvious route past Ai which he had destroyed and Beeroth with which he was in alliance. But, coming up from Gilgal by the ravines in the neighborhood of Jerus, he was exposed to a great danger, for the Amorites might have caught him before he had gained a footing on the plateau, and have taken him at a complete disadvantage. It was thus that the eleven tribes suffered such terrible loss at the hands of the Benjamites in this very region during the first inter-tribal war, and probably the military significance of the first repulse from Ai was of the same character; the forces holding the high ground being able to overwhelm their opponents without any fear of reprisals.

It would seem possible, therefore, that Joshua may have repeated, on a larger scale, the tactics he employed in his successful attack upon Ai. He may have sent one force to draw the Amorites away from Gibeon, and when this was safely done, may have led the rest of his army to seize the road to Jerus, and to break up the forces besieging Gibeon. If so, his strategy was successful up to a certain point. He evidently led the Israelites without loss up to Gibeon, crushed the Amorites there, and cut off their retreat toward Jerus. He failed in one thing. In spite of the prodigious efforts which he and his men had made, the greater part of the Amorite army succeeded in escaping him and gained a long start in their flight, toward the northwest, through the two Beth-horons.

It was at this point that the incident occurred upon which attention has been chiefly fixed. The Book of Jashar (which seems to have been a collection of war songs and other ballads) ascribes to Joshua the command:

3. Joshua's Command

'Sun, be thou silent upon (*be*) Gibeon [cf RVm];
And thou, Moon, in (*be*) the valley of Aijalon.
And the Sun was silent,
And the Moon stayed,
Until the nation had avenged themselves of their enemies' (Josh **10** 12.13).

And the prose narrative continues, "The sun stayed in the midst of heaven, and hasted not to go down about a whole day."

In these two, the ballad and the prose chronicle, we have several distinct astronomical relations indicated. The sun to Joshua was associated with Gibeon, and the sun can naturally be associated with a locality in either of two positions: it may be overhead to the observer, in which case he would consider it as being above the place where he himself was standing; or on the other hand, he might see the locality on the skyline and the sun rising or setting just behind it. In the present instance there is no ambiguity, for the chronicle distinctly states that the sun was in "the midst of heaven"; lit. in the halving of the heaven, that is to say overhead. This is very important because it assures us that Joshua must have been at Gibeon when he spoke, and that it must have been noonday of summer when the sun in southern Pal is only about 8° or 12° from the exact zenith. Next, the moon appeared to be associated with the valley of Aijalon; that is, it must have been low down on the horizon in that direction, and since Aijalon is N.W. of Gibeon it must have been about to set, which would imply that it was about half full, in its "third quarter," the sun being, as we have seen, on the meridian. Thirdly, "the sun hasted not to go down," that is to say, it had already attained the meridian, its culmination; and henceforward its motion was downward. The statement that it was noonday is here implicitly repeated, but a further detail is added. The going down of the sun appeared to be slow. This is the work of the afternoon, that is of half the day, but on this occasion the half-day appeared equal in length to an ordinary whole day. There is therefore no question at all of the sun becoming stationary in the sky: the statement does not admit of that, but only of its slower progress.

4. The Astronomical Relations

The idea that the sun was fixed in the sky, in other words, that the earth ceased for a time to rotate on its axis, has arisen from the unfortunate rendering of the Heb vb. *dūm*, "be silent," by "stand thou still." It is our own word "dumb," both being onomatopoetic words from the sound made when a man firmly closes his lips upon his speech. The primary meaning of the word therefore is "to be silent," but its secondary meaning is "to desist," "to cease," and therefore in some cases "to stand still."

5. The "Silence" of the Sun

From what was it then that Joshua wished the sun to cease: from its moving or from its shining? It is not possible to suppose that, engaged as he was in a desperate battle, he was even so much as thinking of the sun's motion at all. But its shining, its scorching heat, must have been most seriously felt by him. At noon, in high summer, the highland of southern Pal is one of the hottest countries of the world. It is impossible to suppose that Joshua wished the sun to be fixed overhead, where it must have been distressing his men who had already been 17 hours on foot. A very arduous pursuit lay before them and the enemy not only had a long start but must have been fresher than the Israelites. The sun's heat therefore must have been a serious hindrance, and Joshua must have desired it to be tempered. And the Lord hearkened to his voice and gave him this and much more. A great hailstorm swept up from the west, bringing with it a sudden lowering of temperature, and no doubt hiding the sun and putting it to "silence." And "Jehovah fought for Israel," for the storm burst with such violence upon the Amorites as they fled down the steep descent between the Beth-horons, that "they were more who died with the hailstones than they whom the children of Israel slew with the sword" (ver 11). This was the culminating incident of the day, the one which so greatly impressed the sacred historian. "There was no day like that before it or after it, that Jehovah hearkened unto the voice of a man" (ver 14). It was not the hailstorm in itself nor the veiling of the sun that made the day so remarkable. It was that Joshua had spoken, not in prayer or supplication, but in command, as if all Nature was at his disposal; and the Lord had hearkened and had, as it were, obeyed a human voice: an anticipation of the time when a greater Joshua should command even the winds and the sea, and they should obey Him (Mt **8** 23-27).

6. "Jehovah Fought for Israel"

The explanation of the statement that the sun "hasted not to go down about a whole day" is found in ver 10, in which it is stated that the Lord discomfited the Amorites before Israel, "and he slew them with a great slaughter at Gibeon, and chased them by the way of the ascent of Beth-horon, and smote them to Azekah, and unto Makkedah." The Israelites had of course no time-keepers, no clocks or watches, and the only mode of measuring time available to them was the number of miles they marched. Now from Gibeon to Makkedah by the route indicated is some 30 miles, a full day's march for an army. It is possible that, at the end of the campaign, the Israelites on their return found the march from Makkedah to Gibeon heavy work for an entire day. Measured by the only means available to them, that afternoon seemed to be double the ordinary length. The sun had "hasted not to go down about a whole day."

7. The Afternoon's March

Joshua's reference to the moon in connection with the Valley of Aijalon appears at first sight irrelevant, and has frequently been assumed to be merely inserted to complete the parallelism of the poem. But when examined astronomically it becomes clear that it cannot have been inserted haphazard. Joshua must have mentioned the moon because he actually saw it at the moment of speaking. Given that the sun was "in the midst of heaven," above Gibeon, there was only a very restricted arc of the horizon in which the moon could appear as associated with some terrestrial object; and from Gibeon, the Valley of Aijalon does lie within that narrow arc. It follows therefore that unless the position assigned to the moon had been obtained from actual observation at the moment, it would in all probability have been an

8. The Chronicle and the Poem Independent Witnesses

impossible one. The next point is esp. interesting. The ballad does not expressly state whether the sun was upon Gibeon in the sense of being upon it low down on the distant horizon, or upon it, in the sense of being overhead both to Joshua and to that city. But the moon being above the Valley of Aijalon, it becomes clear that the latter is the only possible solution. The sun and moon cannot both have been setting—though this is the idea that has been generally held, it being supposed that the day was far spent and that Joshua desired it to be prolonged—for then sun and moon would have been close together, and the moon would be invisible. The sun cannot have been setting, and the moon rising; for Aijalon is W. of Gibeon. Nor can the sun have been rising, and the moon setting, since this would imply that the time of year was either about October 30 of our present calendar, or about February 12. The month of February was already past, since the Israelites had kept the Feast of the Passover. October cannot have come; for, since Beeroth, Gibeon and Jerus were so close together, it is certain that the events between the return of the Israelites to Gilgal and the battle of Beth-horon cannot have been spread over several months, but must have occupied only a few days. The poem therefore contains implicitly the same fact that is explicitly stated in the prose narrative—that the sun was overhead—but the one statement cannot, in those days, have been inferred from the other.

A third point of interest is that the position of the moon gives an indication of the time of the year.

9. Date of the Events

The Valley of Aijalon is 17° N. of W. from Gibeon, of which the latitude is 31° 51′′ N. With these details, and assuming the time to be nearly noon, the date must have been about the 21st day of the 4th month of the Jewish calendar, corresponding to July 22 of our present calendar, with a possible uncertainty of one or two days on either side. The sun's declination would then be about 21° N., so that at noon it was within 11° of the zenith. It had risen almost exactly at 5 AM and would set almost exactly at 7 PM. The moon was now about her third quarter, and in N. lat. about 5°. It had risen about 11 o'clock the previous night, and was now at an altitude of under 7°, and within about half an hour of setting. The conditions are not sufficient to fix the year, since from the nature of the luni-solar cycle there will always be one or two years in each cycle of 19 that will satisfy the conditions of the case, and the date of the Heb invasion of Pal is not known with sufficient certainty to limit the inquiry to any particular cycle.

It will be seen however that the astronomical conditions introduced by the mention of the moon

10. The Records Contemporaneous with the Events

are much more stringent than might have been expected. They supply therefore proof of a high order that the astronomical details, both of the poem and prose chronicle, were derived from actual observation at the time and have been preserved to us unaltered. Each, therefore, supplies a strictly contemporaneous and independent record.

This great occurrence appears to be referred to in one other passsage of Scripture—the Prayer of Habakkuk. Here again the rendering of the Eng. VSS is unfortunate, and the passage should stand:

'The sun and moon ceased [to shine] in their habitation;
At the light of Thine arrows they vanished,
And at the shining of Thy glittering spear.
Thou didst march through the land in indignation,
Thou didst thresh the nations in anger' (Hab **3** 11.12).

E. W. Maunder

BETHINK, bē-think′ (הֵשִׁיב אֶל לֵב, *hēshībh 'el lēbh,* "to lay to heart," hence "recall to mind"): Anglo-Saxon word used only in seventh petition of Solomon's prayer at the dedication of the Temple. If the people, carried into captivity, because of sin, should "take it to heart," then God (he prayed) would hear and forgive (1 K **8** 47; 2 Ch **6** 37). A choice illustration of the mental and heart process in reflection, repentance and conversion.

BETH-JESHIMOTH, beth-jesh′i-moth (בֵּית הַיְשִׁמוֹת, *bēth ha-yeshīmōth;* B, **Αἰσιμώθ,** *Haisimṓth;* A, **Ἀσιμώθ,** *Asimṓth,* and other variants [see *DB,* s.v.]): Mentioned as the point in the south from which the camp of Israel stretched to Abel-shittim in the plains of Moab (Nu **33** 49). In Josh **12** 3 the way to Beth-jeshimoth is described as S. of the Arabah, near the Dead Sea. It was in the lot assigned to Reuben (Josh **13** 20), At what times and how long it was actually held by Israel we do not know; but it appears in Ezk **25** 9 as belonging to Moab. It may be indentical with *Khirbet es-Suweimeh,* where there are some ruins and a well, about 3 miles E. of the mouth of the Jordan.

W. Ewing

BETH-LE-'APHRAH, beth-lē-af′ra (בֵּית לְעַפְרָה, *bēth le'aphrāh;* LXX **ἐξ οἴκου κατὰ γέλωτα,** *ex oíkou katá gélōta,* "house of dust"): The name of a place found only in Mic **1** 10. From the connection in which it is used it was probably in the Phili plain. There seems to be a play upon the name in the sentence, "at *Beth le-'aphrāh* have I rolled myself in the *dust,*" *'aphrāh* meaning "dust," and possibly another on *Philistine* in *rolled,* הִתְפַּלָּשְׁתִּי, *hithpallāshithī* (see G. A. Smith, *The Book of the Twelve Prophets, called Minor,* in loc.).

BETH-LEBAOTH, beth-lē-bā′oth, beth-leb′a-oth (בֵּית לְבָאוֹת, *bēth lebhā'ōth;* **Βαιθαλβάθ,** *Baithalbáth,* "house of lionesses"): A town in the territory of Simeon (Josh **19** 6). In 1 Ch **4** 31 the name is given as Beth-birei: RV Beth-biri (q.v.).

BETHLEHEM, beth′lē-hem (בֵּית־לֶחֶם, *bēth-leḥem;* **Βαιθλεέμ,** *Baithleém,* or **Βηθλεέμ,** *Bēthleém,* "house of David," or possibly "the house of Lakhmu," an Assyr deity):

I. Bethlehem Judah, or Ephrath or Ephrathah (q.v.) is now *Beit Lahm* (Arab. = "house of meat"), a town of upward of 10,000 inhabitants, 5 miles S. of Jerus and 2,350 ft. above sea level. It occupies an outstanding position upon a spur running E. from the watershed with deep valleys to the N.E. and S. It is just off the main road to Hebron and the south, but upon the highroad to Tekoa and En-gedi. The position is one of natural strength; it was occupied by a garrison of the Philis in the days of David (2 S **23** 14; 1 Ch **11** 16) and was fortified by Rehoboam (2 Ch **11** 6). The surrounding country is fertile, cornfields, fig and olive yards and vineyards abound. Bethlehem is not naturally well supplied with water, the nearest spring is 800 yds. to the S.E., but for many cents. the "low level aqueduct" from "Solomon's Pools" in the *Arṭās* valley, which has here been tunneled through the hill, has been tapped by the inhabitants; there are also many rock-cut cisterns.

In 1 Ch **2** 51 Salma, the son of Caleb, is described as the "father of Bethlehem." In Gen **35** 19;

1. Early History

48 7 it is recorded that Rachel "was buried in the way to Ephrath (the same is Beth-lehem)." Tradition points out the site of Rachel's tomb near where the road to Bethlehem leaves the main road. The Levites of the events of Jgs **17, 19** were Bethlehemites. In the list of the towns of Judah the name Bethlehem occurs, in the LXX version only in Josh **15** 57.

2. David the Bethlehemite

Ruth, famous chiefly as the ancestress of David, and of the Messiah, settled in Bethlehem with her second husband Boaz, and it is noticeable that from her new home she could view the mountains of Moab, her native land. David himself "was the son of that Ephrathite of Bethlehem-judah, whose name was Jesse" (1 S **17** 12). To Bethlehem came Samuel to anoint a successor to unworthy Saul (1 S **16** 4): "David went to and fro from Saul to feed his father's sheep at Bethlehem" (1 S **17** 15). David's "three mighty men"

The Shepherd's Field and Field of Boaz.

"brake through the host of the Philis, and drew water out of the well of Beth-lehem, that was by the gate, and took it, and brought it to David" (2 S **23** 14.16). Tradition still points out the well. From this town came those famous "sons of Zeruiah," David's nephews, whose loyalty and whose ruthless cruelty became at once a protection and a menace to their royal relative: in 2 S **2** 32 it is mentioned that one of them, Asahel, was buried "in the sepulchre of his father, which was in Bethlehem."

3. Later Bible History

After the time of David, Bethlehem would appear to have sunk into insignificance. But its future fame is pointed at by Micah (**5** 2): "But thou, Beth-lehem Ephrathah, which art little to be among the thousands of Judah, out of thee shall one come forth unto me that is to be ruler in Israel; whose goings forth are from of old, from everlasting."

In the return of the Jews captive Bethlehemites re-inhabited the place (Ezr **2** 21; Neh **7** 26 "men"; 1 Esd **5** 17 "sons").

4. The Christian Era

In the NT Bethlehem is mentioned as the birthplace of the Messiah Jesus (Mt **2** 1.5; Lk **2** 4.15) in consequence of which event occurred Herod's "massacre of the innocents" (Mt **2** 8.16). Inasmuch as Hadrian devastated Bethlehem and set up there a sacred grove to Adonis (Jerome, *Ep. ad Paul*, lviii.3) it is clear that veneration of this spot as the site of the Nativity must go back before 132 AD. Constantine (cir 330) founded a basilica over the cave-stable which tradition pointed out as the scene of the birth, and his church, unchanged in general structure though enlarged by Justinian and frequently adorned, repaired and damaged, remains today the chief attraction of the town. During the Crusades, Bethlehem became of great importance and prosperity; it remained in Christian hands after the overthrow of the Lat kingdom, and at the present day it is in material things one of the most prosperous Christian centers in the Holy Land.

II. Bethlehem of Zebulun (Josh **19** 15) was probably the home of Ibzan (Jgs **12** 8.10) though Jewish tradition is in support of (1). See Jos, *Ant*, V, vii, 13. This is now the small village of *Beit Lahm*, some 7 miles N.W. of Nazareth on the edge of the oak forest. Some antiquities have been found here recently, showing that in earlier days it was a place of some importance. It is now the site of a small German colony. See *PEF*, I, 270, Sh V.

E. W. G. MASTERMAN

BETH-LEHEMITE, beth'lē-hem-īt (בֵּית הַלַּחְמִי, *bēth ha-laḥmī*): An inhabitant of Bethlehem, a town in Judah, 5 miles S. of Jerus. Jesse is so named in 1 S **16** 18; **17** 58, and Elhanan in 2 S **21** 19. The children of Bethlehem are referred to in Ezr **2** 21; Neh **7** 26; 1 Esd **5** 17.

BETHLEHEM, STAR OF. See STAR OF THE MAGI.

BETH-LOMON, beth-lō'mon (**Βαιθλωμών,** *Baithlōmōn;* B, **Ῥαγεθλωμών,** *Rhagethlōmōn*): The inhabitants of this city are mentioned as returning with Zerubbabel from Babylon (1 Esd **5** 17). It is the city of Bethlehem in Judah, the modern *Beit Laḥm* (Ezr **2** 21).

BETH-MAACAH, beth-mā'a-ka. See ABEL-BETH-MAACAH.

BETH-MARCABOTH, beth-mär'ka-both (בֵּית הַמַּרְכָּבֹת, *bēth ha-markābhōth;* **Βαιθμαχερέβ,** *Baithmacheréb,* "the house of chariots"): Mentioned along with Hazar-susah, "the station of horses" (Josh **19** 5; 1 Ch **4** 31) as cities in the Negeb near Ziklag. It is tempting to connect these stations with "the cities for his chariots, and the cities for his horsemen" which Solomon built (1 K **9** 19; cf 1 K **10** 26). The site of Beth-marcaboth has not been identified, but Guérin (*La Terre Sainte. Jerus et le Nord de la Judée*, II, 230) suggests *Khan Yunas*, S.W. of Gaza, as a suitable chariot city.

E. W. G. MASTERMAN

BETH-MEON, beth-mē'on: A city of Moab (Jer **48** 23), identical with BAAL-MEON (q.v.).

BETH-MERHAK, beth-mer'hak (בֵּית הַמֶּרְחָק, *bēth ha-merḥāḳ;* **ἐν οἴκῳ τῷ μακράν,** *en oíkō tō̂ makrán,* lit. "a place [house] that was far off" [2 S **15** 17 RVm "the Far House"]): A place mentioned in the account of David's flight from Absalom. No town of this name is known on the route which he followed. Some scholars think the name denotes simply the outermost of the houses of the city.

BETH-MILLO, beth-mil'ō. See JERUSALEM.

BETH-NIMRAH, beth-nim'ra (בֵּית נִמְרָה, *bēth nimrāh,* "house of leopard," Nu **32** 36, but in ver 3 it is simply Nimrah): In Josh **13** 27 the full name appears. In Isa **15** 6 the name appears as Nimrim, identified as Tell Nimrim, between Jericho and the mountains on the east, where there is a fountain of large size. The city was assigned to Gad. In the 4th cent. AD it was located as five Rom miles N. of Livias. Eusebius calls it Bethamnaram (*SEP*, I, Tell Nimrin).

BETH-PALET, beth-pā'let. See BETH-PELET.

BETH-PAZZEZ, beth-paz'ez (בֵּית פַּצֵּץ, *bēth paççēç;* **Βηρσαφής,** *Bērsaphḗs,* **Βαιθφρασῆς,** *Baithphrasē̂*): A town in the territory of Issachar, named with En-gannim and En-haddah (Josh **19** 21). The site has not been discovered; it probably lay near the modern *Jenīn.*

BETH-PELET, beth-pē'let (בֵּית־פֶּלֶט, *bēth-peleṭ;* **Βαιθφαλέθ,** *Baithphaléth,* "house of escape"; AV **Beth-pàlet;** Josh **15** 27, Beth-phelet, AV

Neh **11** 26): One of "the uttermost cities of the tribe of the children of Judah toward the border of Edom in the [Negeb] South" (Josh **15** 21.27). Site unknown.

BETH-PEOR, beth-pē'or (בֵּית פְּעוֹר, *bēth* p^e*'ōr;* **οἶκος Φογώρ,** *oíkos Phogṓr;* in Josh (B), **Βαιθφογώρ,** *Baithphogṓr,* or **βεθ-,** *beth-*): "Over against Beth-peor" the Israelites were encamped, "beyond the Jordan, in the valley," when Moses uttered the speeches recorded in Dt (Dt **3** 29; **4** 46). "In the valley in the land of Moab over against Beth-peor" Moses was buried (Dt **34** 6). Beth-peor and the slopes of Pisgah (AV "Ashdoth-pisgah") are mentioned in close connection in Josh **13** 20. According to *Onom*, Beth-peor was situated near Mt. Peor (Fogor) opposite Jericho, 6 miles above Livias. Mt. Peor is the "top" or "head" of Peor (Nu **23** 28). Some height commanding a view of the plain E. of the river in the lower Jordan valley is clearly intended, but thus far no identification is possible. "The slopes of Pisgah" are probably the lower slopes of the mountain toward *Wādy 'Ayūn Mūsa.* Somewhere N. of this the summit we are in search of may be found. Conder suggested the cliff at *Minyeh,* S. of *Wādy Jedeideh,* and of Pisgah; and would locate Beth-peor at *el-Mareighāt,* "the smeared things," evidently an ancient place of worship, with a stone circle and standing stones, about 4 miles E., on the same ridge. This seems, however, too far S., and more difficult to reach from Shittim than we should gather from Nu **25** 1 ff.

W. EWING

BETHPHAGE, beth'fa-jē, beth'fāj (from בֵּית פַּגָה, *bēth paghāh;* **Βεθφαγή,** *Bethphagḗ,* or **Βηθφαγή,** *Bēthphagḗ;* in Aram. "place of young figs"): Near the Mount of Olives and to the road from Jerus to Jericho; mentioned together with Bethany (Mt **21** 1; Mk **11** 1; Lk **19** 29). The place occurs in several Talmudic passages where it may be inferred

Bethphage.

that it was near but outside Jerus; it was at the Sabbatical distance limit E. of Jerus, and was surrounded by some kind of wall. The mediaeval Bethphage was between the summit and Bethany. The site is now inclosed by the Roman Catholics. As regards the Bethphage of the NT, the most probable suggestion was that it occupied the summit itself where *Kefr et Tûr* stands today. This village certainly occupies an ancient site and no other name is known. This is much more probable than the suggestion that the modern *Abu Dîs* is on the site of Bethphage.

E. W. G. MASTERMAN

BETH-PHELET, beth-fē'let. See BETH-PELET.

BETH-RAPHA, beth-rā'fa (בֵּית רָפָא, *bēth rāphā';* B, **ὁ Βαθραία,** *ho Bathraía,* **Βαθρεφά,** *Bathrephá*): The name occurs only in the genealogical list in 1 Ch **4** 12. It does not seem possible now to associate it with any particular place or clan.

BETH-REHOB, beth-rē'hob (בֵּית־רְחוֹב, *bēth-*r^e*ḥōbh;* **ὁ οἶκος 'Ραάβ,** *ho oíkos Rhaáb*): An Aramaean town and district which, along with Zobah and Maacah, assisted Ammon against David (2 S **10** 6.8, Rehob). It is probably identical with Rehob (Nu **13** 21), the northern limit of the spies' journey. Laish-Dan (probably *Tell el-Kadi*) was situated near it (Jgs **18** 28). The site of the town is unknown. It has been conjecturally identified with Hunin, W. of Banias, and, more plausibly, with Banias itself (Thomson, *The Land and the Book*[2], 218; Buhl, *Geog.*, 240; Moore, *ICC*, Jgs, 399).

C. H. THOMSON

BETHSAIDA, beth-sā'i-da (**Βηθσαϊδά,** *Bēthsaïdá,* "house of fishing"):

(1) A city E. of the Jordan, in a "desert place" (that is, uncultivated ground used for grazing) at which Jesus miraculously fed the multitude with five loaves and two fishes (Mk **6** 32 ff; Lk **9** 10). This is doubtless to be identified with the village of Bethsaida in Lower Gaulonitis which the Tetrarch Philip raised to the rank of a city, and called Julias, in honor of Julia, the daughter of Augustus. It lay near the place where the Jordan enters the Sea of Gennesaret (*Ant,* XVIII, ii, 1; *BJ,* II, ix, 1; III, x, 7; *Vita,* 72). This city may be located at *et-Tell,* a ruined site on the E. side of the Jordan on rising ground, fully a mile from the sea. As this is too far from the sea for a fishing village, Schumacher (*The Jaulān,* 246) suggests that *el-'Araj,* "a large, completely destroyed site close to the lake," connected in ancient times with *et-Tell* "by the beautiful roads still visible," may have been the fishing village, and *et-Tell* the princely residence. He is however inclined to favor *el-Mes'adīyeh,* a ruin and winter village of *Arab et-Tellawīyeh,* which stands on an artificial mound, about a mile and a half from the mouth of the Jordan. Bethsaida Julias cannot be identified with *et-Tell,* for the reason that the mound yields only Bronze Age pottery and so cannot have been occupied in the time of our Lord. The site is still uncertain, but most probably near the southeast corner of that wide plain (Jn **6**; *Bull. American Schools of Oriental Research,* Feb. 1928).

To this neighborhood Jesus retired by boat with His disciples to rest awhile. The multitude following on foot along the northern shore of the lake would cross the Jordan by the ford at its mouth which is used by foot travelers to this day. The "desert" of the narrative is just the *barrīyeh* of the Arabs where the animals are driven out for pasture. The "green grass" of Mk **6** 39, and the "much grass" of Jn **6** 10, point to some place in the plain of *el-Baṭeiḥah,* on the rich soil of which the grass is green and plentiful compared with the scanty herbage on the higher slopes.

(2) Bethsaida of Galilee, where dwelt Philip, Andrew, Peter (Jn **1** 44; **12** 21), and perhaps also James and John. The house of Andrew and Peter seems to have been not far from the synagogue in Capernaum (Mt **8** 14; Mk **1** 29, etc). Unless they had moved their residence from Bethsaida to Capernaum, of which there is no record, and which for fishermen was unlikely, Bethsaida must have lain close to Capernaum. It may have been the fishing town adjoining the larger city. As in the case of the other Bethsaida, no name has been recovered to guide us to the site. On the rocky promontory, however, E. of *Khān Minyeh* we find *Sheikh 'Aly eṣ-Ṣaiyādīn,* "Sheikh Aly of the Fishermen," as the name of a ruined *weley,* in which the second element in the name Bethsaida is represented. Near by is the site at *'Ain et-Ṭābigha,* which many have identified with Bethsaida of Galilee. The warm water from copious springs runs into a little

bay of the sea in which fishes congregate in great numbers. This has therefore always been a favorite haunt of fishermen. If Capernaum were at *Khān Minyeh*, then the two lay close together. The names of many ancient places have been lost, and others have strayed from their original localities. The absence of any name resembling Bethsaida need not concern us.

Were There Two Bethsaidas?

Many scholars maintain that all the NT references to Bethsaida apply to one place, viz. Bethsaida Julias. The arguments for and against this view may be summarized as follows:

(*a*) Galilee ran right round the lake, including most of the level coastland on the E. Thus Gamala, on the eastern shore, was within the jurisdiction of Jos, who commanded in Galilee (*BJ*, II, xx, 4). Judas of Gamala (*Ant*, XVIII, i, 1) is also called Judas of Galilee (ib, i, 6). If Gamala, far down the eastern shore of the sea, were in Galilee, *a fortiori* Bethsaida, a town which lay on the very edge of the Jordan, may be described as in Galilee.

But Jos makes it plain that Gamala, while added to his jurisdiction, was not in Galilee, but in Gaulonitis (*BJ*, II, xx, 6). Even if Judas were born in Gamala, and so might properly be called a Gaulonite, he may, like others, have come to be known as belonging to the province in which his active life was spent. "Jesus of Nazareth" was born in Bethlehem. Then Jos explicitly says that Bethsaida was in Lower Gaulonitis (*BJ*, II, ix, 1). Further, Luke places the country of the Gerasenes on the other side of the sea from Galilee (**8** 26)—*antípera tḗs Galilaías* ("over against Galilee").

(*b*) To go to the other side—*eis tó péran* (Mk **6** 45)—does not of necessity imply passing from the E. to the W. coast of the lake, since Jos uses the vb. *diaperaióō* of a passage from Tiberias to Tarichaea (*Vita*, 59). But (α) this involved a passage from a point on the W. to a point on the S. shore, "crossing over" two considerable bays; whereas if the boat started from any point in *el-Baṭeiḥah*, to which we seem to be limited by the "much grass," and by the definition of the district as belonging to Bethsaida, to sail to *et-Tell*, it was a matter of coasting not more than a couple of miles, with no bay to cross. (β) No case can be cited where the phrase *eis to peran* certainly means anything else than "to the other side." (γ) Mark says that the boat started to go unto the other side to Bethsaida, while John gives the direction "over the sea unto Capernaum" (6 17). The two towns were therefore practically in the same line. Now there is no quesion that Capernaum was on "the other side," nor is there any suggestion that the boat was driven out of its course; and it is quite obvious that, sailing toward Capernaum, whether at *Tell Ḥūm* or at *Khān Minyeh*, it would never reach Bethsaida Julias. (δ) The present writer is familiar with these waters in both storm and calm. If the boat was taken from any point in *el-Baṭeiḥah* towards *et-Tell*, no east wind would have distressed the rowers, protected as that part is by the mountains. Therefore it was no contrary wind that carried them toward Capernaum and the "land of Gennesaret." On the other hand, with a wind from the W., such as is often experienced, eight or nine hours might easily be occupied in covering the four or five miles from *el-Baṭeiḥah* to the neighborhood of Capernaum.

(*c*) The words of Mark (**6** 45), it is suggested (Sanday, *Sacred Sites of the Gospels*, 42), have been too strictly interpreted: as the Gospel was written probably at Rome, its author being a native, not of Galilee, but of Jerus. Want of precision on topographical points, therefore, need not surprise us. But as we have seen above, the "want of precision" must also be attributed to the writer of Jn **6** 17. The agreement of these two favors the strict interpretation. Further, if the Gospel of Mark embodies the recollections of Peter, it would be difficult to find a more reliable authority for topographical details connected with the sea on which his fisher life was spent.

(*d*) In support of the single-city theory it is further argued that (α) Jesus withdrew to Bethsaida as being in the jurisdiction of Philip, when he heard of the murder of John by Antipas, and would not have sought again the territories of the latter so soon after leaving them. (β) Mediaeval works of travel notice only one Bethsaida. (γ) The E. coast of the sea was definitely attached to Galilee in AD 84, and Ptolemy (cir 140) places Julias in Galilee. It is therefore significant that only the Fourth Gospel speaks of "Bethsaida of Galilee." (δ) There could hardly have been two Bethsaidas so close together.

But: (α) It is not said that Jesus came hither that he might leave the territory of Antipas for that of Philip; and in view of Mk **6** 30 ff, and Lk **9** 10 ff, the inference from Mt **14** 13 that he did so, is not warranted. (β) The Bethsaida of mediaeval writers was evidently on the W. of the Jordan. If it lay on the E. it is inconceivable that none of them should have mentioned the river in this connection. (γ) If the 4th Gospel was not written until well into the 2d cent., then the apostle was not the author; but this is a very precarious assumption. John, writing after 84 AD, would hardly have used the phrase "Bethsaida of Galilee" of a place only recently attached to that province, writing, as he was, at a distance from the scene, and recalling the former familiar conditions. (δ) In view of the frequent repetition of names in Pal the nearness of the two Bethsaidas raises no difficulty. The abundance of fish at each place furnished a good reason for the recurrence of the name.

W. Ewing

BETHSAMOS, beth-sā′mos. See Bethasmos.

BETH-SHEAN, beth-shē̩′an, **BETH-SHAN,** beth′shan (בֵּית־שַׁן or בֵּית־שְׁאָן, *bēth-shan*, or *bēth-sheʼān*; in Apoc **Βαιθσάν** or **Βεθσά,** *Baithsán* or *Bethsá*): A city in the territory of Issachar assigned to Manasseh, out of which the Canaanites were not driven (Josh **17** 11; Jgs **1** 27); in the days of Israel's strength they were put to taskwork (Jgs **1** 28). Beth-shean is represented by the modern *Beisān*. Here the bodies of Saul and Jonathan were exposed by the Philistines after the battle of Gilboa (1 S **31** 7 ff) and later rescued by the men of Jabesh (1 S **31** 7 ff; 2 S **21** 12). The name was applied also to the district (1 K **4** 12) and later was called Scythopolis by the Greeks, so called probably from the results of the Scythian invasion (George Syncellus; cf. Herod. I 104–6; 1 Macc **12** 40; *Ant*, XIV, v, 3; *BJ*, III, ix, 7), and later it was the seat of a bishop.

Recent excavations here, begun Jan 1921 by the University of Pennsylvania, are among the most important in Bible lands since the Great War. The work included both the *Tell* and the cemetery. The height of the mound varies from 134 ft. to 213 ft. and it is 899 ft. long at the base. Eight levels have been examined totaling only 37 ft. from the top of the mound. Arabic, Crusader, Byzantine, Hellenistic, late Rameside times, Rameses II, Seti I, and Amenophis III strata are represented. The multiplicity of important finds already make consideration of the work an embarrassment of riches. Still below lies the early Canaanite remains of the Bronze Age. It is already clear that Palestine remained in alien hands of the Egypt suzerain down to the time of

David, as indicated in the Biblical record. The temple of Ashtaroth (I S **31** 10) in which were hung up the trophies of Saul and Jonathan has been examined. A stele of Seti and a historical tablet of Rameses II are found. The latter tells of the building of the store city of Rameses and that Asiatic Semitic slaves did the work. The small finds have been most numerous: nearly fifty Hittite cylinder seals, gold rosettes, variegated Egyptian glass vases, scarabs, gold pendants, and beads and amulets; a bronze Syrian dagger, a magnificent bronze Hittite ax, a mass of silver ingots, and a gold armlet 3½ in. in diameter (*Mus Jour*, Univ of Pennsylvania, 1922). The temple of Dagon, a Philistine god, has been found (*Mus Jour*, Sept, 1926) also a 4th-cent. Christian church of Scythopolis (*Mus Jour*, Sept, 1924).

REVISED BY M. G. K. W. EWING

BETH-SHEMESH, beth-shē′mesh, beth′shē-mesh (בֵּית־שֶׁמֶשׁ, *bēth-shemesh;* **Βαιθσάμυς,** *Baithsámus,* "house of the sun"):

The first mention of a place by this name is in the description of the border of the territory of Judah (Josh **15** 10) which "went down to B." This topographical indication "down" puts the place toward the lowlands on the E. or W. side of Pal, but does not indicate which. This point is clearly determined by the account of the return of the ark by the Phili lords from Ekron (1 S **6** 9–19). They returned the ark to Beth-shemesh, the location of which they indicated by the remark that if their affliction was from Jeh, the kine would bear the ark "by the way of its own border." The Philis lay along the western border of Judah and the location of B. of Judah is thus clearly fixed near the western lowland, close to the border between the territory of Judah and that claimed by the Philis. This is confirmed by the account of the twelve officers of the commissariat of King Solomon. One of these, the son of Dekar, had a Beth-shemesh in his territory. By excluding the territory assigned to the other eleven officers, the territory of this son of Dekar is found to be in Judah and to lie along the Phili border (1 K **4** 9). A Phili attack upon the border-land of Judah testifies to the same effect (2 Ch **28** 18). Finally, the battle between Amaziah of Judah and Jehoash of Israel, who "looked one another in the face" at Beth-shemesh, puts B. most probably near the border between Judah and Israel, which would locate it near the northern part of the western border of Judah's territory. In the assignment of cities to the Levites, Judah gave Beth-shemesh with its suburbs (Josh **21** 16). It has been identified with a good degree of certainty with the modern *'Ain Shems.*

1. Beth-shemesh of Judah

It may be that Ir-shemesh, "city of the sun," and *Har-ḥereṣ,* "mount of the sun," refer to Beth-shemesh of Judah (Josh **15** 10; **19** 41–43; 1 K **4** 9; Jgs **1** 33.35). But the worship of the sun was so common and cities of this name so many in number that it would be hazardous to conclude with any assurance that because these three names refer to the same region they therefore refer to the same place.

In the description of the tribal limits, it is said of Issachar (Josh **19** 22), "And the border reached to Tabor, and Shahazumah, and Beth-shemesh; and the goings out of their border were at the Jordan." The description indicates that Beth-shemesh was in the eastern part of Issachar's territory. The exact location of the city is not known.

2. Beth-shemesh of Issachar

A Beth-shemesh is mentioned together with Beth-anath as cities of Naphtali (Josh **19** 38). There is no clear indication of the location of this city. Its association with Beth-anath may indicate that they were near each other in the central part of the tribal allotment. As at Gezer, another of the cities of the Levites, the Canaanites were not driven out from Beth-shemesh.

3. Beth-shemesh of Naphtali

A doom is pronounced upon "Beth-shemesh, that is in the land of Egypt" (Jer **43** 13). The Seventy identify it with Heliopolis. There is some uncertainty about this identification. If Beth-shemesh, "house of the sun," is here a description of Heliopolis, why does it not have the art.? If it is a proper name, how does it come that a sanctuary in Egypt is called by a Heb name? It may be that the large number of Jews in Egypt with Jeremiah gave this Heb name to Heliopolis for use among themselves, B. being a tr of Egyp *Perra* as suggested by Griffith. Otherwise, B. cannot have been Heliopolis, but must have been some other, at present unknown, place of Sem worship. This latter view seems to be favored by Jeremiah's double threat: "He shall also break the pillars of Beth-shemesh, that is in the land of Egypt; and the houses of the gods of Egypt shall he burn with fire" (ib). If B. were the "house of the sun," then the balancing of the statement would be only between "pillars" and "houses," but it seems more naturally to be between Beth-shemesh, a Sem place of worship "that is in the land of Egypt" on the one hand, and the Egyp place of worship, "the houses of the gods of Egypt," on the other.

4. Beth-shemesh "that is in the Land of Egypt"

But the Seventy lived in Egypt and in their interpretation of this passage were probably guided by accurate knowledge of facts unknown now, such as surviving names, tradition and even written history. Until there is further light on the subject, it is better to accept their interpretation and identify this Beth-shemesh with Heliopolis. See ON.

M. G. KYLE

BETH-SHEMITE, beth-shē′mīt (בֵּית־שִׁמְשִׁי, *bēth-shimshī* [1 S **6** 14.18]): An inhabitant of Beth-shemesh in Judah (cf BETH-SHEMESH 1).

BETH-SHITTAH, beth-shit′a (בֵּית הַשִּׁטָּה, *bēth ha-shiṭṭāh,* "house of the acacia"): A place on the route followed by the Midianites in their flight before Gideon (Jgs **7** 22). It is probably identical with the modern *Shuṭṭa,* a village in the Vale of Jezreel, about 6 miles N.W. of *Beisān.*

BETHSURA, beth-sū′ra (**Βαιθσούρα,** *Baithsoúra* [1 Macc **4** 29, etc]), **BETHSURON** (2 Macc **11** 5 RV): The Gr form of the name BETH-ZUR (q.v.).

BETH-TAPPUAH, beth-tap′ū-a (בֵּית־תַּפּוּחַ, *bēth-tappūaḥ;* **Βεθθαπφουέ,** *Beththapphoué,* "place of apples" [see however APPLE]): A town in the hill country of Judah (Josh **15** 53), probably near Hebron (cf Tappuah, 1 Ch **2** 43), possibly the same as Tephon (1 Macc **9** 50). The village of *Tuffūḥ,* 3½ miles N.W. of Hebron, is the probable site; it stands on the edge of a high ridge, surrounded by very fruitful gardens; an ancient highroad runs through the village, and there are many old cisterns and caves. (See *PEF,* III, 310, 379, Sh XXI.) E. W. G. MASTERMAN

BETHUEL, be-thū′el (בְּתוּאֵל, *bethū′ēl;* "dweller in God"): A son of Nahor and Milcah, Abraham's nephew, father of Laban and Rebekah (Gen **22** 23; **24** 15.24.47.50; **25** 20; **28** 2.5). In the last-named passage, he is surnamed "the Syrian." The only place where he appears as a leading character in the narrative is in connection with Rebekah's betrothal to Isaac; and even here, his son Laban stands out more prominently than he —a fact explainable on the ground of the custom which recognized the right of the brother to take a special interest in the welfare of the sister (cf Gen **34** 5.11.25; 2 S **13** 20.22). *Ant*, I, xvi, 2 states that Bethuel was dead at this time.

FRANK E. HIRSCH

BETHUEL, be-thū'el, beth'ū-el (בְּתוּאֵל, *b^ethū'ēl*, "destroyed of God"): A town of Simeon (1 Ch **4** 30), the same as Bethul (Josh **19** 4), and, probably, as the Beth-el of 1 S **30** 27.

BETHUL, beth'ul, bē'thul (בְּתוּל, *b^ethūl*): See BETHUEL; CHESIL.

BETHULIA, bē-thū'li-a (**Βαιθουλουά,** *Baithouloúa*): A town named only in the Book of Jth (**4** 6; **6** 10 ff; **7** 1 ff; **8** 3; **10** 6; **12** 7; **15** 3.6; **16** 21 ff). From these references we gather that it stood beside a valley, on a rock, at the foot of which was a spring, not far from *Jenīn;* and that it guarded the passes by which an army might march to the S. The site most fully meeting these conditions is that of *Sānūr*. The rock on the summit of which it stands rises sheer from the edge of *Merj el-Gharik*, on the main highway, some 7 miles S. of *Jenīn*. Other identifications are suggested: Conder favoring *Mithilīyeh*, a little farther north; while the writer of the article "Bethulia" in *EB* argues for identification with Jerus. W. EWING

BETH-ZACHARIAS, beth-zak-a-rī'as (**Βαιθζαχαριά,** *Baith-zachariá*): Here Judas Maccabaeus failed in battle with Antiochus Eupator, and his brother Eleazar fell in conflict with an elephant (1 Macc **6** 32 ff; AV "Bathzacharias"). It was a position of great strength, crowning a promontory which juts out between two deep valleys. It still bears the ancient name with little change, *Beit Zakārīā*. It lies about 4 miles S.W. of Bethlehem (*BR*, III, 283 ff; *Ant*, XII, ix, 4).

BETH-ZUR, beth'zûr (בֵּית־צוּר, *bēth-çūr;* **Βαιθσούρ,** *Baith-soúr*, "house of rock"; less probably "house of the god Zur"):

(1) Mentioned (Josh **15** 58) as near Halhul and Gedor in the hill country of Judah; fortified by Rehoboam (2 Ch **11** 7). In Neh **3** 16 mention is made of "Nehemiah the son of Azbuk, the ruler of half the district of Beth-zur." During the Maccabean wars it (Bethsura) came into great importance (1 Macc **4** 29.61; **6** 7.26.31.49.50; **9** 52; **10** 14; **11** 65; **14** 7.33). Jos describes it as the strongest place in all Judaea (*Ant*, XIII, v, 6). It was inhabited in the days of Eusebius and Jerome.

(2) It is the ruined site *Beit Ṣûr*, near the main road from Jerus to Hebron, and some 4 miles N. of the latter. Its importance lay in its natural strength, on a hilltop dominating the highroad, and also in its guarding the one southerly approach for a hostile army by the Vale of Elah to the Judaean plateau. The site today is conspicuous from a distance through the presence of a ruined mediaeval tower. (See *PEF*, III, 311, Sh XXI).

E. W. G. MASTERMAN

BETIMES, bē-tīmz': In the sense of "early" is the tr of two Heb words: (1) שָׁכַם, *shākham*, a root meaning "to incline the shoulder to a load," hence "to load up," "start early": in Gen **26** 31 "they rose up betimes in the morning," also in 2 Ch **36** 15 (ARV "early"); (2) of שָׁחַר, *shāḥar*, a root meaning "to dawn" in Job **8** 5; **24** 5, ARV "diligently," and in Ps **13** 24, "chasteneth him betimes."

In the Apoc (Sir **6** 36) "betimes" is the tr of ὀρθίζω, *orthízō*, lit. "to rise early in the morning," while in Bel ver 16 the same word is tr^d "betime."

In other cases the AV "betimes" appears as "before the time" (Sir **51** 30); "early" (1 Macc **4** 52; **11** 67); "the morning" (1 Macc **5** 30).

ARTHUR J. KINSELLA

BETOLION, bē-tō'li-on (**Βετολιώ** [A], **Βητολιώ** [B], *Betoliṓ* or *Bētoliṓ;* AV **Betolius,** bē-tō'-li-us): A town the people of which to the number of 52 returned from Babylon with Zerubbabel (1 Esd **5** 21). It corresponds to Bethel in Ezr **2** 28.

BETOMESTHAIM, bē-tō-mes'thā-im, AV **Betomestham,** bē-tō-mes'tham (**Βετομεσθάιμ,** *Betomestháim* [Jth **4** 6]): **BETOMASTHAIM,** AV **Betomasthem** (**Βαιτομασθάϊμ,** *Baitomastháïm* [Jth **15** 4]): The place is said to have been "over against Jezreel, in the face of [i.e. eastward of] the plain that is near Dothan." It can hardly be *Deir Massīn*, which lies W. of the plain. The district is clearly indicated, but no identification is yet possible.

BETONIM, bet'ō-nim, bē-tō'nim (בְּטֹנִים, *b^eṭōnīm;* **Βοτανεί,** *Botaneí* or *Botanín*): A town E. of the Jordan in the territory of Gad (Josh **13** 26). It may be identical with *Baṭneh*, about 3 miles S.W. of *es-Salṭ*.

BETRAY, bē-trā' (רָמָה, *rāmāh;* **παραδίδωμι,** *paradídōmi*): In the OT only once (1 Ch **12** 17). David warns those who had deserted to him from Saul: "If ye be come to betray me to mine adversaries . . . . the God of our fathers look thereon." The same Heb word is elsewhere tr^d "beguile" (Gen **29** 25; Josh **9** 22), "deceive" (1 S **19** 17; **28** 12; 2 S **19** 26; Prov **26** 19; Lam **1** 19).

In the NT, for *paradidōmi:* 36 times, of the betrayal of Jesus Christ, and only 3 times besides (Mt **24** 10; Mk **13** 12; Lk **21** 16) of kinsmen delivering up one another to prosecution. In these three places RV translates according to the more general meaning, "to deliver up," and also (in Mt **17** 22; **20** 18; **26** 16; Mk **14** 10.11; Lk **22** 4.6) where it refers to the delivering up of Jesus. The Revisers' idea was perhaps to retain "betray" only in direct references to Judas' act, but they have not strictly followed that rule. Judas' act was more than that of giving a person up to the authorities; he did it under circumstances of treachery which modified its character: (*a*) he took advantage of his intimate relation with Jesus Christ as a disciple to put Him in the hands of His enemies; (*b*) he did it stealthily by night, and (*c*) by a kiss, an act which professed affection and friendliness; (*d*) he did it for money, and (*e*) he knew that Jesus Christ was innocent of any crime (Mt **27** 4).

T. REES

BETRAYERS, bē-trā'ērs (**προδόται,** *prodótai*, "betrayers," "traitors"): Stephen charged the Jews with being betrayers of the Righteous One (Acts **7** 52) i.e. as having made Judas' act their own; cf Lk **6** 16: "Judas Iscariot, who became a traitor"; 2 Tim **3** 4, "traitors."

BETROTH, bē-troth', bē-trōth' (אָרַשׂ, *'āras*): On betrothal as a social custom see MARRIAGE. Hosea, in his great parable of the prodigal wife, surpassed only by a greater Teacher's parable of the Prodigal Son, uses betrothal as the symbol of Jeh's pledge of His love and favor to penitent Israel (Hos **2** 19.20). In Ex **21** 8.9 the RV renders "espouse" for the "betroth" of AV, the context implying the actual marriage relation.

BETWEEN THE TESTAMENTS:

As the title indicates, the historical period in the life of Israel extends from the cessation of OT prophecy to the beginning of the Christian era.

I. The Period in General.—The Exile left its ineffaceable stamp on Judaism as well as on the Jews. Their return to the land of their fathers was marked by the last rays of the declining sun of prophecy. With Malachi it set. Modern historical criticism has projected some of the canonical books of the Bible far into this post-exilic period. Thus Kent (*HJP*, 1899), following the lead of the Wellhausen-Kuenen hypothesis, with all its later leaders, has charted the period between 600 BC, the date of the first captivity, to 160 BC, the beginning of the Hasmonean period of Jewish history, in comparative contemporaneous blocks of double decades. Following the path of Koster, the historical position of Ezr and Neh is inverted, and the former is placed in the period 400–380 BC, contemporaneously with Artaxerxes II; Joel is assigned to the same period; portions of Isa (chs **63–66, 24–27**) are placed about 350 BC; Zec is assigned to the period 260–240, and Dnl is shot way down the line into the reign of the Seleucidae, between 200 and 160 BC. Now all this is very striking and no doubt very critical, but the ground of this historical readjustment is wholly subjective, and has the weight only of a hypothetical conjecture. Whatever may be our attitude to the critical hypothesis of the late origin of some of the OT lit., it seems improbable that any portion of it could have reached far into the post-exilic period. The interval between the Old and the New Testaments is the dark period in the history of Israel. It stretches itself out over about four cents., during which there was neither prophet nor inspired writer in Israel. All we know of it we owe to Jos, to some of the apocryphal books, and to scattered references in Gr and Lat historians. The seat of empire passed over from the East to the West, from Asia to Europe. The Pers Empire collapsed, under the fierce attacks of the Macedonians, and the Gr Empire in turn gave way to the Rom rule.

II. A Glance at Contemporaneous History.—For the better understanding of this period in the history of Israel, it may be well to pause for a moment to glance at the wider field of the history of the world in the cents. under contemplation, for the words "fulness of time" deal with the all-embracing history of mankind, for whose salvation Christ appeared, and whose every movement led to its realization.

1. The Egyptian Empire

(1) In the four cents. preceding Christ, the Egyp empire, the oldest and in many respects the most perfectly developed civilization of antiquity, was tottering to its ruins. The 29th or Mendesian Dynasty, made place, in 384 BC, for the 30th or Sebennitic Dynasty, which was swallowed up, half a century later, by the Pers Dynasty. The Macedonian or 32d replaced this in 332 BC, only to give way, a decade later, to the last or 33d, the Ptolemaic Dynasty. The whole history of Egypt in this period was therefore one of endless and swiftly succeeding changes. In the Ptolemaic Dynasty there was a faint revival of the old glory of the past, but the star of empire had set for Egypt, and the mailed hand of Rome finally smote down a civilization whose beginnings are lost in the dim twilight of history. The Caesarian conquest of 47 BC was followed, 17 years later, by the annexation of Egypt to the new world-power, as a Rom province. Manetho's history is the one great literary monument of Egyp history in this period. Her priests had been famous for their wisdom, to which Lycurgus and Solon, the Gr legislators, had been attracted, as well as Pythagoras and Plato, the world's greatest philosophers.

2. Greece

(2) In Greece also the old glory was passing away. Endless wars sapped the strength of the national life. The strength of Athens and Sparta, of Corinth and Thebes had departed, and when about the beginning of our period, in 337 BC, the congress of Gr states had elected Philip of Macedon to the hegemony of united Greece, the knell of doom sounded for all Gr liberty. First Philip and after him Alexander wiped out the last remnants of this liberty, and Greece became a fighting machine for the conquest of the world in the meteoric career of Alexander the Great. But what a galaxy of illustrious names adorn the pages of Gr history, in this period, so dark for Israel! Think of Aristophanes and Hippocrates, of Xenophon and Democritus, of Plato and Apelles, of Aeschines and Demosthenes, of Aristotle and Praxiteles and Archimedes, all figuring, amid the decay of Gr liberty, in the 4th and 3d cents. before Christ! Surely if the political glory of Greece had left its mark on the ages, its intellectual brilliancy is their pride.

3. Rome

(3) Rome meanwhile was strengthening herself, by interminable wars, for the great task of world-conquest that lay before her. By the Lat and Samnite and Punic wars she trained her sons in the art of war, extended her territorial power and made her name dreaded everywhere. Italy and north Africa, Greece and Asia Minor and the northern barbarians were conquered in turn. Her intellectual brilliancy was developed only when the lust of conquest was sated after a fashion, but in the cent. immediately preceding the Christian era we find such names as Lucretius and Hortentius, Cato and Cicero, Sallust and Diodorus Siculus, Virgil and Horace. At the close of the period between the Testaments, Rome had become the mistress of the world and every road led to her capital.

4. Asia

(4) In Asia the Pers empire, heir to the civilization and traditions of the great Assyr-Bab world-power, was fast collapsing and was ultimately utterly wiped out by the younger Gr empire and civilization. In far-away India the old ethnic religion of Brahma a cent. or more before the beginning of our period passed through the reformatory crisis inaugurated by Gatama Buddha or Sakya Mouni, and thus Buddhism, one of the great ethnic religions, was born. Another reformer of the Tauistic faith was Confucius, the sage of China, a contemporary of Buddha, while Zoroaster in Persia laid the foundations of his dualistic world-view. In every sense and in every direction, the period between the Testaments was therefore one of political and intellectual ferment.

III. Historical Developments.—As regards Jewish history, the period between the Testaments may be divided as follows: (1) the Pers period;

(2) the Alexandrian period; (3) the Egyp period; (4) the Syrian period; (5) the Maccabean period; (6) the Rom period.

(1) The Pers period extends from the cessation of prophecy to 334 BC. It was in the main uneventful in the history of the Jews, a breathing spell between great national crises, and comparatively little is known of it. The land of Pal was a portion of the Syrian satrapy, while the true government of the Jewish people was semi-theocratic, or rather sacerdotal, under the rule of the high priests, who were responsible to the satrap. As a matter of course, the high-priestly office became the object of all Jewish ambition and it aroused the darkest passions. Thus John, the son of Judas, son of Eliashib, through the lust of power, killed his brother Jesus, who was a favorite of Bagoses, a general of Artaxerxes in command of the district. The guilt of the fratricide was enhanced, because the crime was committed in the temple itself, and before the very altar. A storm of wrath, the only notable one of this period, thereupon swept over Judaea. The Persians occupied Jerus, the temple was defiled, the city laid waste in part, a heavy fine was imposed on the people and a general persecution followed, which lasted for many years (*Ant*, XI, 7; Kent, *HJP*, 231). Then as later on, in the many persecutions which followed, the Samaritans, ever pliable and willing to obey the tyrant of the day, went practically scot free.

1. The Persian Period

(2) The Alexandrian period was very brief, 334–323 BC. It simply covers the period of the Asiatic rule of Alexander the Great. In Greece things had been moving swiftly. The Spartan hegemony, which had been unbroken since the fall of Athens, was now destroyed by the Thebans under Epaminondas, in the great battles of Leuctra and Mantinea. But the new power was soon crushed by Philip of Macedon, who was thereupon chosen general leader by the unwilling Greeks. Persia was the object of Philip's ambition and vengeance, but the dagger of Pausanias (*Ant*, XI, viii, 1) forestalled the execution of his plans. His son Alexander, a youth of 20 years, succeeded him, and thus the "great he-goat," of which Daniel had spoken (Dnl **8** 8; **10** 20), appeared on the scene. In the twelve years of his reign (335–323 BC) he revolutionized the world. Swift as an eagle he moved. All Greece was laid at his feet. Thence he moved to Asia, where he defeated Darius in the memorable battles of Granicus and Issus. Passing southward, he conquered the Mediterranean coast and Egypt and then moved eastward again, for the complete subjugation of Asia, when he was struck down in the height of his power, at Babylon, in the 33d year of his age. In the Syrian campaign he had come in contact with the Jews. Unwilling to leave any stronghold at his back, he reduced Tyre after a siege of several months, and advancing southward demanded the surrender of Jerus. But the Jews, taught by bitter experience, desired to remain loyal to Persia. As Alexander approached the city, Jaddua the high priest, with a train of priests in their official dress, went out to meet him, to supplicate mercy. A previous dream of this occurrence is said to have foreshadowed this event, and Alexander spared the city, sacrificed to Jeh, had the prophecies of Daniel concerning him rehearsed in his hearing, and showed the Jews many favors (*Ant*, XI, viii, 5) From that day on they became his favorites; he employed them in his army and gave them equal rights with the Greeks, as first citizens of Alexandria, and other cities, which he founded. Thus the strong Hellenistic spirit of the Jews was created, which marked so large a portion of the nation, in the subsequent periods of their history.

2. The Alexandrian Period

(3) The Egyptian period (324–264 BC). The death of Alexander temporarily turned everything into chaos. The empire, welded together by his towering genius, fell apart under four of his generals—Ptolemy, Lysimachus, Cassander, and Selenus (Dnl **8** 21.22). Egypt fell to the share of Ptolemy Soter and Judaea was made part of it. At first Ptolemy was harsh in his treatment of the Jews, but later on he learned to respect them and became their patron as Alexander had been. Hecataeus of Thrace is at this time said to have studied the Jews, through information received from Hezekiah, an Egyp Jewish immigrant, and to have written a Jewish history from the time of Abraham till his own day. This book, quoted by Jos and Origen, is totally lost. Soter was succeeded by Ptolemy Philadelphus, an enlightened ruler, famous through the erection of the lighthouse of Pharos, and esp. through the founding of the celebrated Alexandrian library. Like his father he was very friendly to the Jews, and in his reign the celebrated Gr tr of the OT Scriptures, the LXX, was made, according to tradition (*Ant*, XII, ii). As however the power of the Syrian princes, the Seleucidae, grew, Pal increasingly became the battle ground between them and the Ptolemies. In the decisive battle between Ptolemy Philopator and Antiochus the Great, at Raphia near Gaza, the latter was crushed and during Philopator's reign Judaea remained an Egyp province. And yet this battle formed the turning-point of the history of the Jews in their relation to Egypt. For when Ptolemy, drunk with victory, came to Jerus, he endeavored to enter the holy of holies of the temple, although he retreated, in confusion, from the holy place. But he wreaked his vengeance on the Jews, for opposing his plan, by a cruel persecution. He was succeeded by his son Ptolemy Epiphanes, a child of 5 years. The long-planned vengeance of Antiochus now took form in an invasion of Egypt. Coele-Syria and Judaea were occupied by the Syrians and passed over into the possession of the Seleucidae.

3. The Egyptian Period

(4) The Syrian period (204–165 BC). Israel now entered into the valley of the shadow of death. This entire period was an almost uninterrupted martyrdom. Antiochus was succeeded by Seleucis Philopator. But harsh as was their attitude to the Jews, neither of these two was notorious for his cruelty to them. Their high priests, as in former periods, were still their nominal rulers. But the aspect of everything changed when Antiochus Epiphanes (175–164 BC) came to the throne. He may fitly be called the Nero of Jewish history. The nationalists among the Jews were at that time wrangling with the Hellenists for the control of affairs. Onias III, a faithful high priest, was expelled from office through the machinations of his brother Jesus or Jason (2 Macc **4** 7–10). Onias went to Egypt, where at Heliopolis he built a temple and officiated as high priest. Meanwhile Jason in turn was turned out of the holy office by the bribes of still another brother, Menelaus, worse by far than Jason, a Jew-hater and an avowed defender of Gr life and morals. The wrangle between the brothers gave Antiochus the opportunity he craved to wreak his bitter hatred on the Jews, in the spoliation of Jerus, in the wanton and total defilement of the temple, and in a most horrible persecution of the Jews (1 Macc **1** 16–28; 2 Macc **5** 11–23; Dnl **11** 28; *Ant*, XII, v, 3.4). Thousands were slain, women and children were sold into captivity, the city wall was torn down, all

4. The Syrian Period

sacrifices ceased, and in the temple on the altar of burnt offering a statue was erected to Jupiter Olympius (1 Macc **1** 43; 2 Macc **6** 1–2). Circumcision was forbidden, on pain of death, and all the people of Israel were to be forcibly paganized. As in the Pers persecution, the Samaritans again played into the hands of the Syrians and implicitly obeyed the will of the Seleucidae. But the very rigor of the persecution caused it to fail of its purpose and Israel proved to be made of sterner stuff than Antiochus imagined. A priestly family dwelling at Modin, west of Jerus, named Hasmonean, after one of its ancestors, consisting of Mattathias and his five sons, raised the standard of revolt, which proved successful after a severe struggle. See ASMONAEAN.

5. The Maccabean Period

(5) The Maccabean period (165–63 BC). The slaying of an idolatrous Jew at the very altar was the signal of revolt. The land of Judaea is specially adapted to guerilla tactics, and Judas Maccabaeus, who succeeded his father, as leader of the Jewish patriots, was a past master in this kind of warfare. All efforts of Antiochus to quell the rebellion failed most miserably, in three Syrian campaigns. The king died of a loathsome disease and peace was at last concluded with the Jews. Though still nominally under Syrian control, Judas became governor of Pal. His first act was the purification and rededication of the temple, from which the Jews date their festival of purification (see PURIFICATION). When the Syrians renewed the war, Judas applied for aid to the Romans, whose power began to be felt in Asia, but he died in battle before the promised aid could reach him (*Ant*, XII, xi, 2). He was buried by his father's side at Modin and was succeeded by his brother Jonathan. From that time the Maccabean history becomes one of endless cabals. Jonathan was acknowledged by the Syrians as meridarch of Judaea, but was assassinated soon afterward. Simon succeeded him, and by the help of the Romans was made hereditary ruler of Pal. He in turn was followed by John Hyrcanus. The people were torn by bitter partisan controversies and a civil war was waged, a generation later, by two grandsons of John Hyrcanus, Hyrcanus and Aristobulus. In this internecine struggle the Rom general Pompey participated by siding with Hyrcanus, while Aristobulus defied Rome and defended Jerus. Pompey took the city, after a siege of three months, and entered the holy of holies, thereby forever estranging from Rome every loyal Jewish heart.

6. The Roman Period

(6) The Roman period (63–4 BC). Judaea now became a Rom province. Hyrcanus, stripped of the hereditary royal power, retained only the high-priestly office. Rome exacted an annual tribute, and Aristobulus was sent as a captive to the capital. He contrived however to escape and renewed the unequal struggle, in which he was succeeded by his sons Alexander and Antigonus. In the war between Pompey and Caesar, Judaea was temporarily forgotten, but after Caesar's death, under the triumvirate of Octavius, Antony and Lepidus, Antony, the eastern triumvir, favored Herod the Great, whose intrigues secured for him at last the crown of Judaea and enabled him completely to extinguish the old Maccabean line of Judaean princes.

IV. Internal Developments in This Period.—One thing remains, and that is a review of the developments within the bosom of Judaism itself in the period under consideration. It is self-evident that the core of the Jewish people, which remained loyal to the national traditions and to the national faith, must have been radically affected by the terrible cataclysms which mark their history, during the four cents. before Christ. What, if any, was the literary activity of the Jews in this period? What was their spiritual condition? What was the result of the manifest difference of opinion within the Jewish economy? What preparation does this period afford for the "fulness of time"? These and other questions present themselves, as we study this period of the history of the Jews.

1. Literary Activity

(1) The voice of prophecy was utterly hushed in this period, but the old literary instinct of the nation asserted itself; it was part and parcel of the Jewish traditions and would not be denied. Thus in this period many writings were produced, which although they lack canonical authority, among Protestants at least, still are extremely helpful for a correct understanding of the life of Israel in the dark ages before Christ.

(*a*) *The Apocrypha.*—First of all among the fruits of this literary activity stand the apocryphal books of the OT. It is enough here to mention them. They are fourteen in number: 1 and 2 Esdras, Tobit, Judith, 2 Esther, Wisdom of Solomon, Ecclesiasticus, Baruch, Song of the Three Holy Children, History of Susannah, Bel and the Dragon, Prayer of Manasses, 1 and 2 Maccabees. As 3 and 4 Maccabees fall presumably within the Christian era, they are not here enumerated. All these apocryphal writings are of the utmost importance for a correct understanding of the Jewish problem in the day in which they were written. For fuller information, see APOCRYPHA.

(*b*) *Pseudepigrapha.*—Thus named from the spurious character of the authors' names they bear. Two of these writings very probably belong to our period, while a host of them evidently belong to a later date. In this class of writings there is a mute confession of the conscious poverty of the day. First of all, we have the Psalter of Solomon, originally written in Heb and tr[d] into Gr—a collection of songs for worship, touching in their spirit, and evincing the fact that true faith never died in the heart of the true believer. The second is the Book of Enoch, a production of an apocalyptic nature, named after Enoch the patriarch, and widely known about the beginning of the Christian era. This book is quoted in the NT (Jude ver 14). It was originally written in Heb or Aram. and tr[d] into Gr. As there is no trace of a Christian influence in the book, the presumption is that the greater part of it was written at an earlier period. Both Jude and the author of Revelation must have known it, as a comparative study of both books will show. The question of these quotations or allusions is a veritable *crux interpretum:* how to reconcile the inspiration of these books with these quotations?

(*c*) *The Septuagint.*—The tradition of the LXX is told by Jos (*Ant*, XII, ii, 13). Aristeas and Aristobulus, a Jewish priest in the reign of Ptolemy Philometor (2 Macc **1** 10), are also quoted in support of it by Clement of Alexandria and by Eusebius. See SEPTUAGINT. The truth of the matter is most probably that this great tr of the OT Scriptures was begun at the instance of Ptolemy Philadelphus 285–247 BC, under the direction of Demetrius Phalereus, and was completed somewhere about the middle of the 2d cent. BC. Internal evidence abounds that the tr was made by different hands and at different times. If the tr was in any way literal, the text of the LXX raises various interesting questions in regard to the Heb text that was used in the tr, as compared with the one we now possess. The LXX was of the utmost missionary value and contributed perhaps more than any other thing to prepare the world for the "fulness of time."

2. Spiritual Conditions

The return from Babylon marked a turning-point in the spiritual history of the Jews. From that time onward, the lust of idolatry, which had marked their whole previous history, utterly disappears. In the place of it came an almost intolerable spirit of exclusiveness, a striving after legal holiness, these two in combination forming the very heart and core of the later Pharisaism. The holy books, but especially the law, became an object of almost idolatrous reverence; the spirit was utterly lost in the form. And as their own tongue, the classic Heb, gradually gave way to the common Aram., the rabbis and their schools strove ever more earnestly to keep the ancient tongue pure, worship and life each demanding a separate language. Thus the Jews became in a sense bilingual, the Heb tongue being used in their synagogues, the Aram. in their daily life, and later on, in part at least, the Gr tongue of the conqueror, the *lingua franca* of the period. A spiritual aristocracy very largely replaced the former rule of their princes and nobles. As the core of their religion died, the bark of the tree flourished. Thus tithes were zealously paid by the believer (cf Mt **23** 23), the Sabbath became a positive burden of sanctity, the simple laws of God were replaced by cumbersome human inventions, which in later times were to form the bulk of the Talm, and which crushed down all spiritual liberty in the days of Christ (Mt **11** 28; **23** 4.23). The substitution of the names "Elohim" and "Adonai" for the old glorious historic name "Jahveh" is an eloquent commentary on all that has been said before and on the spiritual condition of Israel in this period (Ewald, *H of I*, V, 198), in which the change was inaugurated. The old centripetal force, the old ideal of centralization, gave way to an almost haughty indifference to the land of promise. The Jews became, as they are today, a nation without a country. For, for every Jew that came back to the old national home, a thousand remained in the land of their adoption. And yet scattered far and wide, in all sorts of environments, they remained Jews, and the national consciousness was never extinguished. It was God's mark on them now as then. And thus they became world-wide missionaries of the knowledge of the true God, of a gospel of hope for a world that was hopeless, a gospel which wholly against their own will directed the eyes of the world to the fulness of time and which prepared the fallow soil of human hearts for the rapid spread of Christianity when it ultimately appeared.

3. Parties

During the Gr period the more conservative and zealous of the Jews were all the time confronted with a tendency of a very considerable portion of the people, especially the younger and wealthier set, to adopt the manners of life and thought and speech of their masters, the Greeks. Thus the Hellenistic party was born, which was bitterly hated by all true-blooded Jews, but which left its mark on their history, till the date of the final dispersion 70 AD. From the day of Mattathias, the Chasids or Hasideans (1 Macc **2** 42) were the true Jewish patriots. Thus the party of the Pharisees came into existence (*Ant*, XIII, x, 5; XVIII, i, 2; *BJ*, I, v, 2). See Pharisees. They were opposed by the more secular-minded Sadducees (*Ant*, XIII, x, 6; XVIII, i, 3; *BJ*, II, viii, 14), wealthy, of fine social standing, wholly free from the restraints of tradition, utterly oblivious of the future life and closely akin to the Gr Epicureans. See Sadducees. These parties bitterly opposed each other till the very end of the national existence of the Jews in Pal, and incessantly fought for the mastery, through the high-priestly office. Common hatred for Christ, for a while, afforded them a community of interests.

4. Preparation for Christianity

Throughout this entire dark period of Israel's history, God was working out His own Divine plan with them. Their Scriptures were trd into Gr, after the conquest of Alexander the Great the common language in the East. Thus the world was prepared for the word of God, even as the latter in turn prepared the world for the reception of the gift of God, in the gospel of His Son. The LXX thus is a distinct forward movement in the fulfilment of the Abrahamic promise (Gen **12** 3; **18** 18). As the sacrificial part of Jewish worship declined, through their wide separation from the temple, the eyes of Israel were more firmly fixed on their Scriptures, read every Sabbath in their synagogues, and, as we have seen, these Scriptures, through the rendering of the LXX, had become the property of the entire world. Thus the synagogue everywhere became the great missionary institute, imparting to the world Israel's exalted Messianic hopes. On the other hand, the Jews themselves, embittered by long-continued martyrdoms and suffering, utterly carnalized this Messianic expectation in an increasing ratio as the yoke of the oppressor grew heavier and the hope of deliverance grew fainter. And thus when their Messiah came, Israel recognized Him not, while the heart-hungry heathen, who through the LXX had become familiar with the promise, humbly received Him (Jn **1** 9–14). The eyes of Israel were blinded for a season, 'till the fulness of the Gentiles shall be gathered in' (Rom **9** 32; **11** 25).

Henry E. Dosker

BEULAH, bū'la (בְּעוּלָה, *beʻūlāh*, "married"): A name symbolically applied to Israel: "Thy land [shall be called] B. . . . . thy land shall be married. . . . . so shall thy sons marry thee" (Isa **62** 4 f). In this figure, frequently used since Hosea, the prophet wishes to express the future prosperity of Israel. The land once desolate shall again be populated.

BEWAIL, bē-wāl' (**κόπτω,** *kóptō*): In the middle voice, this word has the thought of striking on the breast and of loud lamentation, so common among oriental people in time of great sorrow. It is used to express the most intense grief, a sorrow that compels outward demonstration (Lk **8** 52; **23** 27). A striking instance of this grief is that of the daughter of Jephthah (Jgs **11** 37; Lev **10** 6). See Burial, IV, 4, 5, 6; Grief.

BEWITCH, bē-wich' (**ἐξίστημι,** *existēmi*): There are two Gr words in the NT trd "bewitch." The one given above (Acts **8** 9.11 AV "bewitched," RV "amazed") has reference to the work of Simon Magus. It means "to be out of one's mind," "to astonish," "to overwhelm with wonder." The other word, *βασκαινω*, *baskainō* (Gal **3** 1), means "to fascinate by false representation." It is by this means the apostle complains they have been led to accept a teaching wholly contrary to the gospel of Christ. Both these words reveal to us something of the difficulty the early teachers had to eradicate the idea so widely held by the Jews and Egyptians especially, that there were certain powers, dark and mysterious, which by certain occult forces they could control. For a long time this had to be contended with as one of the corrupt practices brought into the church by the converts, both from Judaism and heathenism. These words have a reference to the evil eye which for cents. was, and even today is, an important factor in the life of the people of the East. 1 Tim **6** 20 is a reference to this thought and explains the word "science" (AV) as there used. See Divination; Evil Eye; Sorcery; Superstition.

Jacob W. Kapp

BEWRAY, bḗ-rā′, **BEWRAYER,** bḗ-rā′ẽr: In its derivation is entirely different from betray (Lat *tradere*), and meant originally "to disclose," "reveal" (cf Shakspere, *Titus Andronicus*, II, iv, 3: "Write down thy mind, bewray thy meaning so"); but has been affected by the former word and is used almost synonymously. It is the tr of three Heb words: (1) קָרָא, *ḳārā′*, meaning "to call out" (Prov **27** 16), "the ointment of his right hand which bewrayeth itself" (ARV "his right hand encountereth oil," ARVm "the oil of his right hand betrayeth itself"); (2) נָגַד, *nāghadh*, meaning "to front," "to announce" (by word of mouth): Prov **29** 24, "heareth cursing and bewrayeth it not" (ARV "heareth the adjuration and uttereth nothing"); (3) גָּלָה, *gālāh*, "to denude," **fig.** "to reveal" (Isa **16** 3), "bewray not him that wandereth" (ARV "betray not the fugitive").

In Sir **27** 17 "bewray [RV "reveal"] his secrets" is the tr of ἀποκαλύπτω, *apokalúptō*, lit. "to uncover"; so also in Sir **27** 21 (RV "revealeth"). Bewrayer of 2 Macc **4** 1 ("bewrayer of the money and of his country," RV "had given information of the money and had betrayed his country") is the tr of ἐνδείκτης, *endeíktēs*, lit. "one who shows."

In the NT "bewrayeth" is the AV of Mt **26** 73; "thy speech bewrayeth thee" is the tr of the phrase δῆλον ποιεῖν, *dḗlon poieín*, which the ARV renders "maketh thee known." ARTHUR J. KINSELLA

BEYOND, bḗ-yond′: Found in the Heb only in its application to space and time, and for these ideas three words are employed: הָלְאָה, *hāleʼāh* (Gen **35** 21) = "to the distance"; עָבַר, *ʽābhar* = "to go beyond," "to cross," derivative עֵבֶר, *ʽēbher* (Chald. עֲבַר, *ʽăbhar*) = "across," "beyond" (Dt **30** 13; Josh **18** 7; Jgs **3** 26; 1 S **20** 36; 2 Ch **20** 2; Ezr **4** 17.20; Jer **25** 22); and עַל, *ʽal* (Lev **15** 25) = "beyond the time." In the NT πέραν, *péran*, is used to express "beyond" in the spatial sense (Mt **4** 15), while other words and phrases are employed for adverbial ideas of degree: ὑπερπερισσῶς, *huperperissôs* (Mk **7** 37); ὑπέρ, *hupér* (2 Cor **8** 3; **10** 16); καθυπερβολήν, *kathuperbolḗn* (Gal **1** 13). In the AV בְּעֵבֶר, *beʽēbher*, is occasionally tr[d] "beyond," and when this word is joined to הַיַּרְדֵּן, *ha-yardēn*, "Jordan," as it usually is, it becomes critically important. In ARV, *beʽēbher ha-yardēn* is tr[d] "beyond the Jordan," in Gen **50** 10.11; Dt **3** 20.25; Josh **9** 10; Jgs **5** 17; "on this side Jordan" in Dt **1** 1.5; Josh **1** 14.15; "on the other side Jordan" in Dt **11** 30; Josh **12** 1; **22** 4; **24** 2.8 (cf AV and RV, vs 14.15; see RIVER, THE), Jgs **10** 8; 1 S **31** 7; and "on the side of Jordan" in Josh **5** 1. ARV gives "beyond the Jordan" throughout. מֵעֵבֶר, *mēʽēbher*, is used with *ha-yardēn* in Nu **34** 15; **35** 14; Josh **13** 32; Jgs **7** 25; and עֵבֶר, *ʽēbher*, alone in Dt **4** 49 (AV "on this side"); Josh **13** 27 (AV "on the other side"). It is clear that the phrase may be tr[d] "across Jordan"; that it is used of either side of the Jordan (Dt **3** 8 speaks of the eastern, **3** 20.25 of the western); that "beyond Jordan" may be used of the side of the Jordan on which the writer stands (Josh **5** 1; **9** 1; **12** 7); but from the fact that Dt **1** 1.5; **4** 41. 46.47.49, where statements are made about Moses, the reference is to the country E. of the Jordan, while in Dt **3** 20.25; **11** 30, where Moses is represented as speaking, the W. is indicated, critics have concluded that the author (at least of Dt) must have lived after Moses, being careful to distinguish between himself and the prophet.

FRANK E. HIRSCH

BEZAANANNIM, bḗ-zā-an-an′im (Josh **19** 33 RVm). See ZAANANNIM.

BEZAI, bē′zā-ī (בֵּצָי, *bēçay*, "shining"[?]):

(1) A chief who with Nehemiah sealed the covenant (Neh **10** 18).

(2) The descendants of B. returned with Zerubbabel to Jerus (323, Ezr **2** 17; 324, Neh **7** 23 = Bassai, 1 Esd **5** 16).

BEZALEL, bez′a-lel (בְּצַלְאֵל, *beçal′ēl*, "in the shadow [protection] of 'El [God]"; Βεσελεήλ, *Beseleḗl;* AV **Bezaleel**):

(1) A master workman under Moses; son of Uri, son of Hur, of the tribe of Judah. Jeh gave him especial wisdom and skill for his task, which was, with the aid of Oholiab of the tribe of Dan, to superintend the making of the tabernacle and its furniture (Ex **31** 2; **35** 30; **36** 1.2 (8); **37** 1; **38** 22; 1 Ch **2** 20; 2 Ch **1** 5).

(2) An Israelite of the time of Ezra who put away a foreign wife (Ezr **10** 30). F. K. FARR

BEZEK, bē′zek (בֶּזֶק, *bezeḳ;* Βέζεκ, *Bézek,* B, 'Αβιέζεκ, *Abiézek*):

(1) The city of Adoni-bezek taken by Judah and Simeon (Jgs **1** 4 f), in the territory allotted to Judah. It is somewhat doubtfully identified with *Bezḳah*, about 3 miles N.E. of Gezer.

(2) The place where Saul marshaled his army before marching to the relief of Jabesh-gilead (1 S **11** 8). *Onom* speaks of two villages of this name 17 Rom miles from Shechem, on the way to Scythopolis. No doubt *Khirbet Ibzīḳ* is intended. Here, or on the neighboring height, *Rās Ibzīḳ*, a mountain 2,404 ft. above sea level, the army probably assembled. W. EWING

BEZER, bē′zẽr (בֶּצֶר, *beçer;* Βόσορ, *Bósor,* "strong"):

(1) A city of refuge, set apart by Moses for the Reubenites and located in the "plain country" (or table-land, *Mīshōr*) E. of the Jordan, later assigned to this tribe by Joshua (Dt **4** 43; Josh **20** 8). The same city was assigned by lot as place of residence to the children of Merari of the Levite tribe (Josh **21** 36; 1 Ch **6** 63.78). Driver, *HDB*, suggests the identity of B. with Bozrah (LXX Bosor) (Jer **48** 24). Besheir has been suggested as the present site. According to the MS it was fortified by Mesha.

(2) A son of Zophah of the house of Asher (1 Ch **7** 37). A. L. BRESLICH

BEZETH, bē′zeth (Βηζέθ, *Bēzéth*): A place in the neighborhood of Jerus to which Bacchides withdrew and where he slew several deserters (1 Macc **7** 19). Possibly the same as Bezetha (see JERUSALEM).

BEZETHA, be-zē′tha: Also called by Jos the "New City" (*BJ*, V, iv, 2), certain suburbs of Jerus, N. of the Temple, which were outside the second but included within the third wall. BEZETH (q.v.) may be the same place. See JERUSALEM.

BIATAS, bī′a-tas (Φαλίας, *Phalías;* A, Φιαθάς, *Phiathás*): RV "Phalias," one of the Levites (1 Esd **9** 48) who "taught [the people] the law of the Lord, making them withal to understand it." Called Pelaiah in Neh **8** 7.

BIBLE, bī′b'l, **THE** (βιβλία, *biblía*):

I. THE NAMES
1. Bible
2. Other Designations—Scriptures, etc
3. OT and NT
II. LANGUAGES

General Designation

This word designates the collection of the Scriptures of the OT and NT recognized and in use in the Christian churches. Different religions (such as the Zoroastrian, Hindu, Buddhist, Mohammedan) have their collections of sacred writings, sometimes spoken of as their "Bibles." The Jews acknowledge only the Scriptures of the OT. Christians add the writings contained in the NT. The present art. deals with the origin, character, contents and purpose of the Christian Scriptures, regarded as the depository and authoritative record of God's revelations of Himself and of His will to the fathers by the prophets, and through His Son to the church of a later age (He **1** 1.2). Reference is made throughout to the arts. in which the several topics are more fully treated.

I. The Names.—The word "Bible" is the equivalent of the Gr word *biblia* (dim. from *bíblos*, the inner bark of the papyrus), meaning originally "books." The phrase "the books" (*ta biblia*) occurs in Dnl **9** 2 (LXX) for prophetic writings. In the Prologue to Sir ("the rest of the books") it designates generally the OT Scriptures; similarly in 1 Macc **12** 9 ("the holy books"). The usage passed into the Christian church for OT (2 Clem **14** 2), and by and by (cir 5th cent.) was extended to the whole Scriptures. Jerome's name for the Bible (4th cent.) was "the Divine Library" (*Bibliotheca Divina*). Afterward came an important change from pl. to sing. meaning. "In process of time this name, with many others of Gr origin, passed into the vocabulary of the western church; and in the 13th cent., by a happy solecism, the neut. pl. came to be regarded as a fem. sing., and 'The Books' became by common consent 'The Book' (*biblia*, sing.), in which form the word was passed into the languages of modern Europe" (Westcott, *Bible in the Church*, 5). Its earliest occurrences in Eng. are in *Piers Plowman*, Chaucer and Wycliffe.

1. Bible

2. Other Designations—Scriptures, etc

There is naturally no name in the NT for the complete body of Scripture; the only Scriptures then known being those of the OT. In 2 Pet **3** 16, however, Paul's epistles seem brought under this category. The common designations for the OT books by Our Lord and His apostles were "the scriptures" (writings) (Mt **21** 42; Mk **14** 49; Lk **24** 32; Jn **5** 39; Acts **18** 24; Rom **15** 4, etc), "the holy scriptures" (Rom **1** 2); once "the sacred writings" (2 Tim **3** 15). The Jewish technical division (see below) into "the law," the "prophets," and the "(holy) writings" is recognized in the expression "in the law of Moses, and the prophets, and the psalms" (Lk **24** 44). More briefly the whole is summed up under "the law and the prophets" (Mt **5** 17; **11** 13; Acts **13** 15). Occasionally even the term "law" is extended to include the other divisions (Jn **10** 34; **12** 34; **15** 25; 1 Cor **14** 21). Paul uses the phrase "the oracles of God" as a name for the OT Scriptures (Rom **3** 2; cf Acts **7** 38; He **5** 12; 1 Pet **4** 11).

3. OT and NT

Special interest attaches to the names "Old" and "New Testament," now and since the close of the 2d cent. in common use to distinguish the Jewish and the Christian Scriptures. "Testament" (lit. "a will") is used in the NT (AV) to represent the Gr word *diathḗkē*, in classical usage also "a will," but in the LXX and NT employed to translate the Heb word *b^{e}rīth*, "a covenant." In RV, accordingly, "testament" is, with two exceptions (He **9** 16.17), changed to "covenant" (Mt **26** 28; 2 Cor **3** 6; Gal **3** 15; He **7** 22; **9** 15, etc). Applied to the Scriptures, therefore, "Old" and "New Testament" mean, strictly, "Old" and "New Covenant," though the older usage is now too firmly fixed to be altered. The name is a continuation of the OT designation for the law, "the book of the covenant" (2 K **23** 2). In this sense Paul applies it (2 Cor **3** 14) to the OT law; "the reading of the old testament" (RV "Covenant"). When, after the middle of the 2d cent., a definite collection began to be made of the Christian writings, these were named "the New Testament," and were placed as of equal authority alongside the "Old." The name *Novum Testamentum* (also *Instrumentum*) occurs first in Tertullian (190–220 AD), and soon came into general use. The idea of a Christian Bible may be then said to be complete.

II. Languages.—The OT, it is well known, is written mostly in Heb; the NT is written wholly in Gr. The parts of the OT not in Heb, viz. Ezr **4** 8—**6** 18; **7** 12-26; Jer **10** 11; Dnl **2** 4—**7** 28, are in Aram. (the so-called Chaldee), a related dialect, which, after the Exile, gradually displaced Heb as the spoken language of the Jews (see Aramaic; Language and Text of OT). The ancient Heb text was "unpointed," i.e. without the vowel-marks now in use. These are due to the labors of the Massoretic scholars (after 6th cent. AD).

The Gr of the NT, on which so much light has recently been thrown by the labors of Deissmann and others from the Egyp papyri, showing it to be a form of the "common" (Hellenistic) speech of the time (see Language of NT), still remains, from its penetration by Heb ideas, the influence of the LXX, peculiarities of training and culture in the writers, above all, the vitalizing and transforming power of Christian conceptions in vocabulary and expression, a study by itself. "We speak," the apostle says, "not in words which man's wisdom teacheth, but which the Spirit teacheth" (1 Cor **2** 13). This is not always remembered in the search for parallels in the papyri. (For tr^s^ into other languages, see VERSIONS.)

III. Compass and Divisions.—The story of the origin, collection, and final stamping with canonical authority of the books which compose our present Bible involves many points still keenly in dispute. Before touching on these debatable matters, certain more external facts fall to be noticed relating to the general structure and compass of the Bible, and the main divisions of its contents.

1. Jewish Bible—Josephus

A first step is to ascertain the character and contents of the *Jewish Bible*—the Bible in use by Christ and His apostles. Apart from references in the NT itself, an important aid is here afforded by a passage in Jos (*CAp*, I, 8), which may be taken to represent the current belief of the Jews in the 1st cent. AD. After speaking of the prophets as writing their histories "through the inspiration of God," Jos says: "For we have not myriads of discordant and conflicting books, but 22 only, comprising the record of all time, and justly accredited as Divine. Of these, 5 are books of Moses, which embrace the laws and the traditions of mankind until his own death, a period of almost 3,000 years. From the death of Moses till the reign of Artaxerxes, the successor of Xerxes, king of Persia, the prophets who followed Moses narrated the events of their time in 13 books. The remaining 4 books consist of hymns to God, and maxims of conduct for men. From Artaxerxes to our own age, the history has been written in detail, but it is not esteemed worthy of the same credit, on account of the exact succession of the prophets having been no longer maintained." He goes on to declare that, in this long interval, "no one has dared either to add anything to [the writings], or to take anything from them, or to alter anything," and speaks of them as "the decrees [*dógmata*] of God," for which the Jews would willingly die. Philo (20 BC–cir 50 AD) uses similar strong language about the law of Moses (in Eusebius, *Pr. Ev.*, VIII, 6).

In this enumeration of Jos, it will be seen that the Jewish sacred books—39 in our Bible—are reckoned as 22 (after the no. of letters in the Heb alphabet), viz. 5 of the law, 13 of the prophets and 4 remaining books. These last are Ps, Prov, Cant and Eccl. The middle class includes all the historical and prophetical books, likewise Job, and the reduction in the no. from 30 to 13 is explained by Jgs–Ruth, 1 and 2 S, 1 and 2 K, 1 and 2 Ch, Ezr–Neh, Jer–Lam and the 12 minor prophets, each being counted as one book. In his 22 books, therefore, Jos includes all those in the present Heb canon, and none besides—not the books known as the APOCRYPHA, though he was acquainted with and used some of these.

Other lists and divisions.—The statement of Jos as to the 22 books acknowledged by the Jews is confirmed, with some variation of enumeration, by the lists preserved by Eusebius (*HE*, vi.26) from Melito of Sardis (cir 172 AD) and Origen (186–254 AD), and by Jerome (*Pref to OT*, cir 400) —all following Jewish authorities. Jerome knew also of a rabbinical division into 24 books. The celebrated passage from the Talm (*Bābhā' Bathrā'*, 14*b:* see CANON OF OT; cf Westcott, *Bible in Church*, 35; Driver, *LOT*, vi) counts also 24. This no. is obtained by separating Ruth from Jgs and Lam from Jer. The threefold division of the books, into Law, Prophets, and other sacred Writings (*Hagiographa*), is old. It is already implied in the Prologue to Sir (cir 130 BC), "the law, the prophets, and the rest of the books"; is glanced at in a work ascribed to Philo (*De vita contempl.*, 3); is indicated, as formerly seen, in Lk **24** 44. It really reflects stages in the formation of the Heb canon (see below). The rabbinical division, however, differed materially from that of Jos in reckoning only 8 books of the prophets, and relegating 1 and 2 Ch, Ezr–Neh, Est, Job and Dnl to the Hagiographa, thus enlarging that group to 9 (Westcott, op. cit., 28; *DB*, I, "Canon"). When Ruth and Lam were separated, they were added to the list, raising the no. to 11. Some, however, take this to be the original arrangement. In printed Heb Bibles the books in all the divisions are separate. The Jewish schools further divided the "Prophets" into "the former prophets" (the historical books—Josh, Jgs, S and K), and "the latter prophets" (Isa, Jer, Ezk and the 12 minor prophets as one book).

NT references.—It may be concluded that the above lists, excluding the Apoc, represent the Heb Bible as it existed in the time of Our Lord (the opinion, held by some, that the Sadducees received only the 5 books of the law rests on no sufficient evidence). This result is borne out by the evidence of quotations in Jos and Philo (cf Westcott, op. cit.). Still more is it confirmed by an examination of OT quotations and references in the NT. It was seen above that the main divisions of the OT are recognized in the NT, and that, under the name "Scriptures," a Divine authority is ascribed to them. It is therefore highly significant that, although the writers of the NT were familiar with the LXX, which contained the Apoc (see below), no quotation from any book of the Apoc occurs in their pages. One or two allusions, at most, suggest acquaintance with the Book of Wisdom (e.g. Wisd **5** 18–21 ‖ Eph **6** 13–17). On the other hand, "every book in the Heb Bible is distinctly quoted in the NT with the exception of Josh, Jgs, Ch, Cant, Eccl, Ezr, Neh, Est, Ob, Zeph and Nah" (Westcott). Enumerations differ, but about 178 direct quotations may be reckoned in the Gospels, Acts and Epistles; if references are included, the no. is raised to about 700 (see QUOTATIONS IN NT). In four or five places (Lk **11** 49–51; Jas **4** 5; 1 Cor **2** 9; Eph **5** 14; Jn **7** 38) apparent references occur to sources other than the OT; it is doubtful whether most of them are really so (cf Westcott, op. cit., 46–48; Eph **5** 14 may be from a Christian hymn). An undeniable influence of Apocalyptic literature is seen in Jude, where vs 14.15 are a direct quotation from the Book of Enoch. It does not follow that Jude regarded this book as a proper part of Scripture.

Hitherto we have been dealing with the Heb OT; marked changes are apparent when we turn to the

2. The LXX

Septuagint, or Gr version of the LXX current in the Gr-speaking world at the commencement of the Christian era. The importance of this version lies in the fact that it was practically the OT of the early church. It was used by the apostles and their converts, and is freely quoted in the NT, sometimes even when its renderings vary considerably from the Heb. Its influence was necessarily, therefore, very great.

Origin.—The special problems connected with origin, text and literary relations of the LXX are dealt with elsewhere (see SEPTUAGINT). The version took its rise, under one of the early Ptolemies, from the needs of the Jews in Egypt, before the middle of the 2d cent. BC; was gradually executed, and completed hardly later than cir 100 BC; thereafter spread into all parts. Its renderings reveal frequent divergence in MSS from the present MT, but show also that the translators permitted themselves considerable liberties in enlarging, abbreviating, transposing and otherwise modifying the texts they had, and in the insertion of materials borrowed from other sources.

The Apocrypha.—The most noteworthy differences are in the departure from Jewish tradition in the arrangement of the books (this varies greatly; cf Swete, *Intro to OT in Gr,* II, ch i), and in the inclusion in the list of the other books, unknown to the Heb canon, now grouped as the Apocrypha. These form an extensive addition. They include the whole of the existing Apoc, with the exception of 2 Esd and Pr Man. All are of late date, and are in Gr, though Sir had a Heb original which has been partly recovered. They are not collected, but are interspersed among the OT books in what are taken to be their appropriate places. The Gr fragments of Est, e.g. are incorporated in that book; Sus and Bel form part of Dnl; Bar is joined with Jer, etc. The most important books are Wisd, Sir and 1 Macc (cir 100 BC). The fact that Sir, originally in Heb (cir 200 BC), and of high repute, was not included in the Heb canon, has a weighty bearing on the period of the closing of the latter.

Ecclesiastical use.—It is, as already remarked, singular that, notwithstanding this extensive enlargement of the canon by the LXX, the books just named obtained no Scriptural recognition from the writers of the NT. The more scholarly of the Fathers, likewise (Melito, Origen, Athanasius, Cyr, Jerome, etc), adhere to the Heb list, and most draw a sharp distinction between the canonical books, and the Gr additions, the reading of which is, however, admitted for edification (cf Westcott, op. cit., 135–36, 168, 180, 182–83). Where slight divergencies occur (e.g. Est is omitted by Melito and placed by Athanasius among the Apoc; Origen and Athanasius add Bar to Jer), these are readily explained by doubts as to canonicity or by imperfect knowledge. On the other hand, familiarity with the LXX in writers ignorant of Heb could not but tend to break down the limits of the Jewish canon, and to lend a Scriptural sanction to the additions to that canon. This was aided in the West by the fact that the Old Lat VSS (2d cent.) based on the LXX, included these additions (the Syr Pesh followed the Heb). In many quarters, therefore, the distinction is found broken down, and ecclesiastical writers (Clement, Barnabas, Irenaeus, Tertullian, Clem. Alex., Basil, etc) quote freely from books like Wisd, Sir, Bar, Tob, 2 Esd, as from parts of the OT.

3. The Vulgate, etc (OT)

An important landmark is reached in the *Vulg* or Lat version of Jerome. Jerome, on grounds explained in his Preface, recognized only the Heb Scriptures as canonical; under pressure he executed later a hasty tr of Tob and Jud. Feeling ran strong, however, in favor of the other books, and ere long these were added to Jerome's version from the Old Lat (see Vulgate). It is this enlarged Vulg which received official recognition, under anathema, at the Council of Trent (1543), and, with revision, from Clement VIII (1592), though, earlier, leading Romish scholars (Ximenes, Erasmus, Cajetan) had made plain the true state of the facts. The Gr church vacillated in its decisions, sometimes approving the limited, sometimes the extended, canon (cf Westcott, op. cit., 217–29). The churches of the Reformation (Lutheran, Swiss), as was to be expected, went back to the Heb canon, giving only a qualified sanction to the reading and ecclesiastical use of the Apoc. The early English VSS (Tyndale, Coverdale, etc) include, but separate, the apocryphal books (see English Versions). The Anglican Articles express the general estimate of these books: "And the other books (as Jerome saith) the Church doth read for example of life and instruction of manners; yet doth it not apply them to establish any doctrine" (Art. VIII). Modern Protestant Bibles usually exclude the Apoc altogether.

From this survey of the course of opinion on the compass of the OT, we come to the NT. This admits of being more briefly treated.

4. The NT

It has been seen that a Christian NT did not, in the strict sense, arise till after the middle of the 2d century. Gospels and Epistles had long existed, collections had begun to be made, the Gospels, at least, were weekly read in the assemblies of the Christians (Justin, 1 *Apol.*, 67), before the attempt was made to bring together, and take formal account of, all the books which enjoyed apostolic authority (see Canon of NT). The needs of the church, however, and very specially controversy with gnostic opponents, made it necessary that this work should be done; collections also had to be formed for purposes of tr into other tongues. Genuine gospels had to be distinguished from spurious; apostolic writings from those of later date, or falsely bearing apostolic names. When this task was undertaken, a distinction soon revealed itself between two classes of books, setting aside those recognized on all hands as spurious: (1) books universally acknowledged—those named afterward by Eusebius the *homologoúmena;* and (2) books only partially acknowledged, or on which some doubt rested—the Eusebian *antilegómena* (*HE*, iii.25). It is on this distinction that differences as to the precise extent of the NT turned.

(1) "*Acknowledged books.*"—The "acknowledged" books present little difficulty. They are enumerated by Eusebius, whose statements are confirmed by early lists (e.g. that of Muratori, cir 170 AD), quotations, VSS and patristic use. At the head stand the Four Gospels and the Acts, then come the 13 epistles of Paul, then 1 Pet and 1 Jn. These, Westcott says, toward the close of the 2d cent., "were universally received in every church, without doubt or limitation, as part of the written rule of Christian faith, equal in authority with the Old Scriptures, and ratified (as it seemed) by a tradition reaching back to the date of their composition" (op. cit., 133). With them may almost be placed Revelation (as by Eusebius) and He, the doubts regarding the latter relating more to Pauline authority than to genuineness (e.g. Origen).

(2) "*Disputed books.*"—The "disputed" books were the epistles of Jas, Jude, 2 and 3 Jn and 2 Pet. These, however, do not all stand in the same rank as regards authentication. A chief difficulty is the silence of the western Fathers regarding Jas, 2 Pet and 3 Jn. On the other hand, Jas is known to Origen and is included in the Syr Pesh; the Muratorian Fragment attests Jude and 2 Jn as "held in the Catholic church" (Jude also in Tertullian, Clem. Alex., Origen); none of the books are treated as spurious. The weakest in attestation is 2 Pet, which is not distinctly traceable before the 3d cent. (See Canon of NT; arts. s.v.) It is to be added that, in a few instances, as in the case of the OT Apoc, early Fathers cite as Scripture books not generally accepted as canonical (e.g. Barnabas, Hermas, Apoc of Pet).

The complete acceptance of all the books in our present NT canon may be dated from the Councils of Laodicea (cir 363 AD) and of Carthage (397 AD), confirming the lists of Cyril of Jerus, Jerome and Augustine.

IV. Literary Origin and Growth—Canonicity.—Thus far the books of the OT and NT have been taken simply as given, and no attempt has been made to inquire how or when they were written or compiled, or how they came to acquire the dignity and authority implied in their reception into a sacred canon. The field here entered is one bristling with controversy, and it is necessary to choose one's steps with caution to find a safe way through it. Details in the survey are left, as before, to the special articles.

Attention here is naturally directed, first, to the OT. This, it is obvious, and is on all sides admitted, has a long literary history prior to its final settlement in a canon. As to the course of that history traditional and modern critical views very widely differ. It may possibly turn out that the truth lies somewhere midway between them.

1. The OT

(1) *OT indications.*—If the indications furnished by *the OT itself* be accepted, the results are something like the following:

(*a*) Patriarchal age: No mention is made of writing in the patriarchal age, though it is now known that a high literary culture then prevailed in Babylonia, Egypt and Palestine, and it is not improbable, indeed seems likely, that records in some form came down from that age, and are, in parts, incorporated in the early history of the Bible.

(*b*) Mosaic age: In Mosaic times writing was in use, and Moses himself was trained in the learning of the Egyptians (Ex **2** 10; Acts **7** 22). In no place is the composition of the whole Pent (as traditionally believed) ascribed to Moses, but no inconsiderable amount of written matter is directly attributed to him, creating the presumption that there was more, even when the fact is not stated. Moses wrote "all the words of Jeh" in the "book of the covenant" (Ex **21–23; 24** 4.7). He wrote "the words of this law" of Dt at Moab, "in a book, until they were finished" (Dt **31** 9.24.26). This was given to the priests to be put by the side of the ark for preservation (vs 25.26). Other notices occur of the writing of Moses (Ex **17** 14; Nu **33** 2; Dt **31** 19.22; cf Nu **11** 26). The song of Miriam, and the snatches of song in Nu **21,** the first (perhaps all) quoted from the "book of the Wars of Jeh" (Nu **21** 14 ff), plainly belong to Mosaic times. In this connection it should be noticed that the discourses and law of Dt imply the history and legislation of the critical JE histories (see below). The priestly laws (Lev, Nu) bear so entirely the stamp of the wilderness that they can hardly have originated anywhere else, and were probably then, or soon after, written down. Joshua, too, is presumed to be familiar with writing (Josh **8** 30–35; cf Dt **27** 8), and is stated to have written his farewell address "in the book of the law of God" (Josh **24** 26; cf **1** 7.8). These statements already imply the beginning of a sacred literature.

(*c*) The Judges: The song of Deborah (Jgs **5**) is an indubitably authentic monument of the age of the Judges, and the older parts of Jgs, at least, must have been nearly contemporary with the events which they record. A knowledge of writing among the common people seems implied in Jgs **8** 14 (ARVm). Samuel, like Joshua, wrote "in a book" (1 S **10** 25), and laid it up, evidently among other writings, "before Jehovah."

(*d*) The age of David and Solomon was one of high development in poetical and historical composition: witness the elegies of David (2 S **1** 17 ff; **3** 33.34), and the finely-finished narrative of David's reign (2 S **9–20**), the so-called "Jerusalem-Source," admitted to date "from a period very little later than that of the events related" (Driver, *LOT*, 183). There were court scribes and chroniclers.

David and the Monarchy: David, as befits his piety and poetical and musical gifts (cf on this *POT*, 440 ff), is credited with laying the foundations of a sacred psalmody (2 S **23** 1 ff; see Psalms), and a whole collection of psalms (**1–72,** with exclusion of the distinct collection, **42–50**), once forming a separate book (cf Ps **72** 20), are, with others, ascribed to him by their titles (Pss **1, 2, 10** are untitled). It is hardly credible that a tradition like this can be wholly wrong, and a Davidic basis of the Psalter may safely be assumed. Numerous psalms, by their mention of the "king" (as Pss **2, 18, 20, 21, 28, 33, 45, 61, 63, 72, 101, 110**), are naturally referred to the period of the monarchy (some, as Ps **18** certainly, Davidic). Other groups of psalms are referred to the temple guilds (Sons of Korah, Asaph).

(*e*) Wisdom literature: Solomon is renowned as founder of the Wisdom literature and the author of Proverbs (1 K **4** 32; Prov **1** 1; **10** 1; Eccl **12** 9; Eccl itself appears to be late), and of the Song (Cant **1** 1). The "men of Hezekiah" are said to have copied out a collection of his proverbs (Prov **25** 1; see Proverbs). Here also may be placed the Book of Job. Hezekiah's reign appears to have been one of literary activity: to it, probably, are to be referred certain of the Pss (e.g. Pss **46, 48;** cf Perowne, Delitzsch). In history, during the monarchy, the prophets would seem to have acted as the "sacred historiographers" of the nation. From their memoirs of the successive reigns, as the later books testify (1 Ch **29** 29; 2 Ch **9** 29; **12** 15, etc), are compiled most of the narratives in our canonical writings (hence the name "former prophets"). The latest date in 2 K is 562 BC, and the body of the book is probably earlier.

(*f*) Prophecy: With the rise of written prophecy a new form of literature enters, called forth by, and vividly mirroring, the religious and political conditions of the closing periods of the monarchy in Israel and Judah (see Prophecy). On the older view, Obadiah and Joel stood at the head of the series in the pre-Assyr period (9th cent.), and this seems the preferable view still. On the newer view, these prophets are late, and written prophecy begins in the Assyr period with Amos (Jeroboam II, cir 750 BC) and Hosea (cir 745–735). When the latter prophet wrote, Samaria was tottering to its fall (721 BC). A little later, in Judah, come Isaiah (cir 740–690) and Micah (cir 720–708). Isaiah, in the reigns of Uzziah, Jotham, Ahaz and Hezekiah, is the greatest of the prophets in the Assyr age, and his ministry reaches its climax in the deliverance of Jerus from Sennacherib (2 K **18, 19;** Isa **36, 37**). It is a question whether some oracles of an Isaianic school are not mingled with the prophet's own writings, and most scholars now regard the 2d part of the book (chs **40–66**) as exilian or (in part) post-exilian in date. The standpoint of much in these chs is certainly in the Exile; whether the composition of the whole can be placed there is extremely doubtful (see Isaiah). Nahum, who prophesies against Nineveh, belongs to the very close of this period (cir 660).

The prophets Zephaniah (under Josiah, cir 630 BC) and Habakkuk (cir 606) may be regarded as forming the transition to the next—the Chaldaean—period. The Chaldaeans (unnamed in Zeph) are advancing but are not yet come (Hab **1** 6). The great prophetic figure here, however, is Jeremiah, whose sorrowful ministry, beginning in the 13th year of Josiah (626 BC), extended through the succeeding reigns till after the fall of Jerus (586 BC). The prophet elected to remain with the remnant in the land, and shortly after, troubles having arisen, was forcibly carried into Egypt (Jer **43**). Here also he prophesied (chs **43, 44**). From the reign of Jehoiakim, Jeremiah consistently declared the success of the Chaldaean arms, and foretold the 70 years' captivity (**25** 12–14). Baruch acted as his secretary in writing out and editing his prophecies (chs **36, 45**).

(*g*) Josiah's reformation: A highly important event in this period was Josiah's reformation in his 18th year (621 BC), and the discovery, during repairs of the temple, of "the book of the law," called also "the book of the covenant" and "the law of Moses" (2 K **22** 8; **23** 2.24.25). The finding of this book, identified by most authorities with the Book of Dt, produced an extraordinary sensation. On no side was there the least question that it was a genuine ancient work. Jeremiah, strangely, makes no allusion to this discovery, but his prophecies are deeply saturated with the ideas and style of Dt.

(*h*) Exilian and post-exilian: The bulk of Isa **40–66** belongs, at least in spirit, to the Exile, but the one prophet of the Exile known to us by name is the priestly Ezekiel. Carried captive under Jehoiachin (597 BC), Ezekiel labored among his fellow-exiles for at least 22 years (Ezk **1** 2; **29** 17). A man of the strongest moral courage, his symbolic visions on the banks of the Chebar alternated with the most direct expostulation, exhortation, warning and promise. In the description of an ideal temple and its worship with which his book closes (chs **40–48**), critics think they discern the suggestion of the Levitical code.

(*i*) Daniel: After Ezekiel the voice of prophecy is silent till it revives in Daniel, in Babylon, under Nebuchadnezzar and his successors. Deported in 605 BC, Daniel rose to power, and "continued" until the 1st year of Cyrus (536 BC; Dnl **1** 21). Criticism will have it that his prophecies are a product of the Maccabean age, but powerful considerations on the other side are ignored (see DANIEL). Jonah may have been written about this time, though the prophet's mission itself was pre-Assyr (9th cent.). The rebuilding of the temple after the return, under Zerubbabel, furnished the occasion for the prophecies of Haggai and Zechariah (520 BC). Scholars are disposed to regard only Zec **1–8** as belonging to this period—the remainder being placed earlier or later. Malachi, nearly a cent. after (cir 430), brings up the rear of prophecy, rebuking unfaithfulness, and predicting the advent of the "messenger of the covenant" (Mal **3** 1.2). To this period, or later, belong, besides post-exilian psalms (e.g. Pss **124, 126**), the books of Ezr, Neh, Ch, Est and apparently Eccl.

(*j*) A preëxilic Bible: If, in this rapid sketch, the facts are correctly represented, it will be apparent that, in opposition to prevalent views, a large body of sacred lit. existed (laws, histories, psalms, wisdom-books, prophecies), and was recognized long before the Exile. God's ancient people had "Scriptures"—had a Bible—if not yet in collected form. This is strikingly borne out by the numerous OT passages referring to what appears to be a code of sacred writings in the hands of the pious in Israel. Such are the references to, and praises of, the "law" and "word" of God in many of the Pss (e.g. **1, 19, 119, 12** 6; **17** 4; **18** 21.22), with the references to God's known "words," "ways," "commandments," "statutes," in other books of the OT (Job **8** 8; Hos **8** 12; Dnl **9** 2). In brief, Scriptures, which must have contained records of God's dealings with His people, a knowledge of which is constantly presupposed, "laws" of God for the regulation of the heart and conduct, "statutes," "ordinances," "words" of God, are a postulate of a great part of the OT.

(2) *Critical views*.—The account of the origin and growth of the OT above presented is in marked contrast with that given in the textbooks of the *newer critical schools*. The main features of these critical views are sketched in the art. CRITICISM (q.v.); here a brief indication will suffice. Generally, the books of the OT are brought down to late dates; are regarded as highly composite; the earlier books, from their distance from the events recorded, are deprived of historical worth. Neither histories nor laws in the Pent belong to the Mosaic age: Josh is a "romance"; Jgs may embody ancient fragments, but in bulk is unhistorical. The earliest fragments of Israelitish literature are lyric pieces like those preserved in Gen **4** 23.24; **9** 25–27; Nu **21**; the Song of Deborah (Jgs **5**) is probably genuine. Historical writing begins about the age of David or soon thereafter. The folklore of the Hebrews and traditions of the Mosaic age began to be reduced to writing about the 9th cent. BC.

(*a*) The Pentateuch: Our present Pent (enlarged to a "Hexateuch," including Josh) consists of 4 main strands (themselves composite), the oldest of which (called J, from its use of the name Jehovah) goes back to about 850 BC. This was Judaean. A parallel history book (called E, from its use of the name Elohim, God) was produced in the Northern kingdom about a century later (c 750). Later still these two were united (JE). These histories, "prophetic" in spirit, were originally attributed to individual authors, distinguished by minute criteria of style: the more recent fashion is to regard them as the work of "schools." Hitherto the only laws known were those of the (post-Mosaic) Book of the Covenant (Ex **20–23**). Later, in Josiah's reign, the desire for centralization of worship led to the composition of the Book of Dt. This, secreted in the temple, was found by Hilkiah (2 K **22**), and brought about the reformation of Josiah formerly mentioned. Dt (D), thus produced, is the third strand in the Pentateuchal compilation. With the destruction of the city and temple, under the impulse of Ezekiel, began a new period of law-construction, now priestly in spirit. Old laws and usages were codified; new laws were invented; the history of institutions was recast; finally, the extensive complex of Levitical legislation was brought into being, clothed with a wilderness dress, and ascribed to Moses. This elaborate Priestly Code (PC), with its accompanying history, was brought from Babylon by Ezra, and, united with the already existing JE and D, was given forth by him to the restored community at Jerus (444 BC; Neh **8**) as "the law of Moses." Their acceptance of it was the inauguration of "Judaism."

(*b*) Histories: In its theory of the Pent the newer criticism lays down the determinative positions for its criticism of all the remaining books of the OT. The historical books show but a continuation of the processes of literary construction exemplified in the books ascribed to Moses. The Deuteronomic element, e.g. in Josh, Jgs, 1, 2 S, 1, 2 K, proves them, in these parts, to be later than Josiah, and historically untrustworthy. The Levitical element in 1, 2 Ch demonstrates its pictures of David and his successors to be distorted and false. The same canon applies to the prophets. Joel, e.g. must be post-exilian, because it presupposes the priestly law. The patriarchal and Mosaic histories being subverted, it is not permitted to assume any high religious ideas in early Israel. David, therefore, could not have written the Pss. Most, if not practically all, of these are post-exilian.

(*c*) Psalms and prophets: Monotheism came in—at least first obtained recognition—through Amos and Hosea. The prophets could not have the foresight and far-reaching hopes seen in their writings: these passages, therefore, must be removed. Generally the tendency is to put dates as low as possible and very many books, regarded before as preexilian, are carried down in whole or part, to exilian, post-exilian, and even late Gr times (PC, Psalter, Job, Prov, Cant, Eccl, 2 Isa, Joel, Lam). Dnl is Maccabean and unhistorical (cir 168–167 BC).

It is not proposed here to discuss this theory, which is not accepted in the present art., and is considered elsewhere (see CRITICISM; PENTATEUCH). The few points calling for remark relate to canonical acceptance.

(3) *Formation of the canon.*—The general lines of the completed Jewish canon have already been sketched, and some light has now been thrown on the process by which the several books obtained a sacred authority. As to the actual stages in the *formation of the canon* opinions again widely diverge (see CANON OF THE OT).

(*a*) Critical theory: On the theory at present in favor, no collections of sacred books were made prior to the return from Babylon. The only books that had authority before the Exile were, perhaps, the old Book of the Covenant, and, from Josiah's time, the Book of Dt. Both, after the return, were, on this theory, embodied, with the JE histories, and the PC, in Ezra's completed Book of the Law (with Josh [?]), in which, accordingly, the foundation of a canon was laid. The fivefold division of the law was later. Subsequently, answering to the 2d division of the Jewish canon, a collection was made of the prophetic writings. As this includes books which, on the critical view, go down to Gr times (Jon; Zec **9–14**), its completion cannot be earlier than well down in the 3d cent. BC. Latest of all came the collection of the "Hagiographa"—a division of the canon, on the theory, kept open to receive additions certainly till the 2d cent., some think after. Into it were received such late writings as Eccl, Maccabean Pss, Dnl. Even then one or two books (Eccl, Est) remained subjects of dispute.

(*b*) More positive view: It will appear from the foregoing that this theory is not here accepted without considerable modification. If the question be asked, What constituted a right to a place in the canon? the answer can hardly be other than that suggested by Jos in the passage formerly quoted —a real or supposed inspiration in the author of the book. Books were received if men had the prophetic spirit (in higher or lower degree: that, e.g. of wisdom); they ceased to be received when the succession of prophets was thought to fail (after Mal). In any case the writings of truly inspired men (Moses, the prophets, psalmists) were accepted as of authority. It was sought, however, to be shown above, that such books, many of them, already existed from Moses down, long before the Exile (the law, collections of psalms, of proverbs, written prophecies: to what end did the prophets write, if they did not mean their prophecies to be circulated and preserved?); and such writings, to the godly who knew and used them, had the full value of Scripture. A canon began with the first laying up of the "book of the law" before Jeh (Dt **31** 25.26; Josh **24** 26). The age of Ezra and Nehemiah, therefore, is not that of the beginning, but, as Jewish tradition rightly held (Jos; 2 Macc **2** 13; Talm), rather that of the completion, systematic delimitation, acknowledgment and formal close of the canon. The divisions of "law, prophets, and holy writings" would thus have their place from the beginning, and be nearly contemporaneous. The Samaritans accepted only the 5 books of the law, with apparently Josh (see SAMARITAN PENTATEUCH).

(*c*) Close of the canon: There is no need for dogmatism as to an absolute date for the close of the canon. If inspired voices continued to be heard, their utterances were entitled to recognition. Books duly authenticated *might* be added, but the non-inclusion of such as a book as Sir (Ecclus: in Heb, cir 200 BC) shows that the limits of the canon were jealously guarded, and the onus of proof rests on those who affirm that there were such books. Calvin, e.g. held that there were Maccabean Pss. Many modern scholars do the same, but it is doubtful if they are right. Eccl is thought on linguistic grounds to be late, but it and other books need not be so late as critics make them. Dnl is confidently declared to be Maccabean, but there are weighty reasons for maintaining a Pers date (see DANIEL). As formerly noticed, the threefold division into "the law, the prophets, and the rest [*tá loipá*, a definite number] of the books" is already attested in the Prologue to Sir.

2. The NT

Critical controversy, long occupied with the OT, has again keenly attached itself to *the NT*, with similar disturbing results (see CRITICISM). Extremer opinions may be here neglected, and account be taken only of those that can claim reasonable support. The NT writings are conveniently grouped into the historical books (Gospels and Acts); Epistles (Pauline and other); and a Prophetic book (Rev). In order of writing, the Epistles, generally, are earlier than the Gospels, but in order of subject, the Gospels naturally claim attention first.

(1) *The Gospels and Acts.*—The main facts about the origin of *the Gospels* can perhaps be distinguished from the complicated literary theories which scholars are still discussing (see GOSPELS). The first three Gospels, known as the Synoptics, evidently embody a common tradition, and draw from common sources. The Fourth Gospel—that of John—presents problems by itself.

(*a*) The Synoptics: The former—the Synoptic Gospels (Mt, Mk, Lk)—fall in date well within the apostolic age, and are, in the 2d cent., uniformly connected with the authors whose names they bear. Mark is spoken of as "the interpreter of Peter" (Papias, in *HE* iii.39); Luke is the well-known companion of Paul. A difficulty arises about Matthew, whose Gospel is stated to have been written in Aram. (Papias, ut supra, etc), while the gospel bearing his name is in Gr. The Gr gospel seems at least to have been sufficiently identified with the apostle to admit of the early church always treating it as his.

The older theory of origin assumed an oral basis for all 3 Gospels. The tendency in recent criticism is to distinguish two main sources: (1) Mk, the earliest gospel, a record of the preaching of Peter; (2) a collection of the sayings and discourses of Jesus, attributed to Matthew (the Eusebian *Logia*, now called Q); with (3) a source used by Luke in the sections peculiar to himself—the result of his own investigations (Lk **1** 1–4). Mt and Lk are supposed to be based on Mk and the Logia (Q); in Luke's case with the addition of his special material. Oral tradition furnished what remains. A simpler theory may be to substitute for (1) a Petrine tradition already firmly fixed while yet the apostles were working together in Jerus. Peter, as foremost spokesman, would naturally stamp his own type upon the oral narratives of Christ's sayings and doings (the Mk type), while Matthew's stories, in part written, would be the chief source for the longer discourses. The instruction imparted by the apostles and those taught by them would everywhere be made the basis of careful catechetical teaching, and records of all this, more or less fragmentary, would be early in circulation (Lk **1** 1–4). This would explain the Petrine type of narrative, and the seeming dependence of Mt and Lk, without the necessity of supposing a direct use of Mk. So important a gospel could hardly be included in the "attempts" of Lk **1** 1.

(*b*) The Fourth Gospel: The Fourth Gospel (Jn), the genuineness of which is assumed (see JOHN, GOSPEL OF), differs entirely in character and style. It is less a narrative than a didactic work, written to convince its readers that Jesus is "the Son of God" (Jn **20** 31). The gospel may be presumed to have been composed at Ephesus, in the last years of the apostle's residence there. With this its character corresponds. The other gospels had long been known; John does not therefore traverse the ground already covered by them. He confines himself chiefly to matters drawn from his personal recollections: the Judaean ministry, the visits of Christ to Jerus, His last private discourses to His disciples. John had so often retold, and so long brooded over, the thoughts and words of Jesus, that they had become, in a manner, part of his own thought, and, in reproducing them, he necessarily did so with a subjective tinge, and in a partially paraphrastic and interpretative manner. Yet it is truly the words, thoughts and deeds of his beloved Lord that he narrates. His gospel is the needful complement to the others—the "spiritual" gospel.

(*c*) The Acts: The Acts narrates the origin and early fortunes of the church, with, as its special motive (cf **1** 8), the extension of the gospel to the Gentiles through the labors of Paul. Its author is Luke, Paul's companion, whose gospel it continues (**1** 1). Certain sections—the so-called "we-sections" (**16** 10–17; **20** 5–15; **21** 1–18; **27** 1—**28** 16)—are transcribed directly from Luke's journal of Paul's travels. The book closes abruptly with Paul's 2 years' imprisonment at Rome (**28** 30.31; 60–61 AD), and not a hint is given of the issue of the imprisonment—trial, liberation or death. Does this mean that a 3d "treatise" was contemplated? Or that the book was written while the imprisonment still continued? (thus now Harnack). If the latter, the Third Gospel must be very early.

(2) *The Epistles.*—(*a*) Pauline: Doubt never rested in the early church on the 13 epistles of Paul. Following upon the rejection by the "Tübingen" school of all the epistles but 4 (Rom 1, 2 Cor, Gal), the tide of opinion has again turned strongly in favor of their genuineness. An exception is the Pastoral epistles (1, 2 Tim, Tit), still questioned by some on insufficient grounds (see Pastoral Epistles). The epistles, called forth by actual needs of the churches, are a living outpouring of the thoughts and feelings of the mind and heart of the apostle in relation to his converts. Most are letters to churches he himself had founded (1, 2 Cor, Gal, Eph[?], Phil, 1, 2 Thess): two are to churches he had not himself visited, but with which he stood in affectionate relations (Rom, Col); one is purely personal (Philem); three are addressed to individuals, but with official responsibilities (1, 2 Tim, Tit). The larger number were written during his missionary labors, and reflect his personal situation, anxieties and companionships at the places of their composition; four are epistles of the 1st Rom imprisonment (Eph, Phil, Col, Philem): 2 Tim is a voice from the dungeon, in his 2d imprisonment, shortly before his martyrdom. Doctrine, counsel, rebuke, admonition, tender solicitude, ethical instruction, prayer, thanksgiving, blend in living fusion in their contents. So marvelous a collection of letters, on such magnificent themes, was never before given to the world.

The earliest epistles, in point of date, are generally held to be those to the Thessalonians, written from Corinth (52, 53 AD). The church, newly-founded, had passed through much affliction (1 Thess **1** 6; **2** 14; **3** 3.4, etc), and Paul writes to comfort and exhort it. His words about the Second Coming (**4** 13 ff) led to mistaken expectations and some disorders. These his 2d epistle was written to correct (2 Thess **2** 1–3; **3** 6, etc).

Corinth itself received the next epistles—the 1st called forth by reports received at Ephesus of grave divisions and irregularities (1 Cor **1** 11; **3** 3; **11** 18 ff, etc), joined with pride of knowledge, doctrinal heresy (**15** 12 ff), and at least one case of gross immorality (ch **5**) in the church; the 2d, written at Philippi, expressing joy at the repentance of the offender, and removing the severe sentence that had been passed upon him (2 Cor **2** 1–10; cf 1 Cor **5** 3.4), likewise vindicating Paul's own apostleship (chs **10–13**). The date of both is 57 AD. 1 Cor contains the beautiful hymn on love (ch **13**), and the noble chapter on resurrection (ch **15**).

In the following year (58 BC) Paul penned from Corinth the Epistle to the Romans—the greatest of his doctrinal epistles. In it he develops his great theme of the impossibility of justification before God through works of law (chs **1–3**), and of the Divine provision for human salvation in a "righteousness of God" in Christ Jesus, received through faith. He exhibits first the objective side of this redemption in the deliverance from condemnation effected through Christ's reconciling death (chs **3–5**); then the subjective side, in the new life imparted by the spirit, giving deliverance from the power of sin (chs **6–8**). A discussion follows of the Divine sovereignty in God's dealings with Israel, and of the end of these dealings (chs **9–11**), and the epistle concludes with practical exhortations, counsels to forbearance and greetings (chs **12–16**).

Closely connected with the Epistle to the Romans is that to the Galatians, in which the same truths are handled, but now with a polemical intent in expostulation and reproach. The Galatian churches had apostatized from the gospel of faith to Jewish legalism, and the apostle, sorely grieved, writes this powerful letter to rebuke their faithlessness, and recall them to their allegiance to the truth. It is reasonable to suppose that the 2 epistles are nearly related in place and time. The question is complicated, however, by the dispute which has arisen as to whether the churches intended are those of Northern Galatia (the older view; cf Conybeare and Howson, Lightfoot) or those of Southern Galatia (Sir Wm. Ramsay), i.e. the churches of Derbe, Lystra, Iconium and Antioch, in Paul's time embraced in the Rom province of Galatia (see Galatia; Galatians). If the latter view is adopted, date and place are uncertain; if the former, the epistle may have been written from Ephesus (cir 57 AD).

The 4 epistles of the imprisonment all fall within the years 60, 61 AD. That to the Philippians, warmly praising the church, and exhorting to unity, possibly the latest of the group, was sent by the hand of Epaphroditus, who had come to Rome with a present from the Philippian church, and had there been overtaken by a serious illness (Phil **2** 25–30; **4** 15–18). The remaining 3 epistles (Eph, Col, and Philem) were written at one time, and were carried to their destinations by Epaphras. Eph and Col are twin epistles, similar in thought and style, extolling the preëminence of Christ, but it is doubtful whether the former was not really a "circular" epistle, or even, perhaps, the lost Epistle to the Laodiceans (Col **4** 16; see Epistle to the Laodiceans). The Colossian epistle has in view an early form of gnostic heresy (cf Lightfoot, *Gal*). Philem is a personal letter to a friend of the apostle's at Colossae, whose runaway slave, Onesimus, now a Christian, is being sent back to him with warm commendations. See Captivity Epistles.

Latest from Paul's pen are the Pastoral Epistles (1, 2 Tim, Tit), implying his liberation from his 1st imprisonment, and a new period of missionary labor in Ephesus, Macedonia and Crete (see Pastoral Epistles). Timothy was left at Ephesus (1 Tim **1** 3), Titus at Crete (Tit **1** 5), for the regulation and superintendence of the churches.

The epistles, the altered style of which shows the deep impress of advancing years and changed conditions, contain admonitions to pastoral duty, with warnings as to perils that had arisen or would arise. 1 Tim and Tit were written while the apostle was still at liberty (63 AD); 2 Tim is from his Rom prison, when his case had been partly heard, and the end was impending (2 Tim **4** 6.16.17).

(*b*) Epistle to the Hebrews: These are the Pauline Epistles proper. *The Epistle to the Hebrews*, though ascribed to Paul in the title of the AV, is not really his. It is an early writing (probably before the destruction of Jerus, 70 AD) of some friend of the apostle's (in Italy, cf **13** 23.24), designed, by a reasoned exhibition of the superiority of Jesus to Moses and the Levitical priesthood, and of the fulfilment of OT types and institutions in His person and sacrifice, to remove the difficulties of Jewish Christians, who clung with natural affection to their temple and divinely appointed ritual. It was included by Eusebius, with others in the East (not, however, by Origen), among the epistles of Paul: in the West the Pauline authorship was not admitted. Many, nevertheless, with Origen, upheld a connection with Paul ("the thoughts are Paul's"). Ideas and style suggest an Alexandrian training: hence Luther's conjecture of Apollos as the writer. There can be no certainty on the subject. The value of the Epistle is unimpaired, whoever was the author.

(*c*) Catholic Epistles: Of the 7 so-called "*Catholic*" Epistles, Jas and Jude are by "brethren" of the Lord (James, "the Lord's brother," was head of the church at Jerus, Acts **15** 13; **21** 18; Gal **1** 19, etc); Peter and John, to whom the others were ascribed, were apostles. Jas and 1 Pet are addressed to the Jews of the Dispersion (1 Pet **1** 1; Jas **1** 1). The doubts respecting certain of these writings have already been mentioned. The early date and acceptance of Jas is attested by numerous allusions (Clem. of Rome, Barnabas, Hermas, *Did*). Many regard it as the earliest of the epistles—before Paul's. Its tone is throughout practical. The seeming conflict with Paul on faith and works, which led Luther to speak slightingly of it, is only verbal. Paul, too, held that a dead faith avails nothing (1 Cor **13** 2; Gal **5** 6). 1 Jn, like 1 Pet, was undisputed (if the Fourth Gospel is genuine, 1 Jn is), and, on internal grounds, the shorter epistles (2, 3 Jn) need not be doubted (see Epistles of John). Jude, rugged in style, with allusions to Jewish Apocalypses (vs 9.14), is well attested, and 2 Pet seems to found on it. The last-named epistle must rely for acceptance on its own claim (2 Pet **1** 1.18), and on internal evidence of sincerity. It is to be observed that, though late in being noticed, it never appears to have been treated as spurious. The style certainly differs from 1 Pet; this may be due to the use of an amanuensis. If accepted, it must be placed late in Peter's life (before 65 AD). 1 Pet and Jude, in that case, must be earlier (see Catholic Epistles).

(3) *Prophecy.*—The Book of Revelation: The one prophetic book of the NT—the apocalyptic counterpart of Dnl in the OT—is the *Book of Rev.* The external evidence for the Johannine authorship is strong (see Apocalypse). Tradition and internal evidence ascribe it to the reign of Domitian (cir 95 AD). Its contents were given in vision in the isle of Patmos (Rev **1** 9). The theory which connects it with the reign of Nero through the supposed fitness of this name to express the mystic no. 666 is entirely precarious (cf Salmon, *Intro to NT*, 245–54). The main intent is to exhibit in symbolic form the approaching conflicts of Christ and His church with anti-Christian powers—with secular world-power (Beast), with intellectual anti-Christianism (False Prophet), with ecclesiastical anti-Christianism (Woman)—these conflicts issuing in victory and a period of triumph, preluding, after a sharp, final struggle, the last scenes (resurrection, judgment), and the eternal state. When the visions are taken, not as poetic imaginings, but as true apocalyptic unveilings, the change in style from the gospel, which may be regarded as already written, can readily be understood. These mighty revelations in Patmos brought about, as by volcanic force, a tremendous upheaval in the seer's soul, breaking through all previous strata of thought and feeling, and throwing everything into a new perspective. On the resultant high keynote: "Amen: Come, Lord Jesus" (Rev **22** 20), the NT closes.

(4) *Canonicity.*—The principal steps by which the books now enumerated were gradually formed into *a NT "Canon,"* have been indicated in previous sections. The test of canonicity here, as in the OT, is the presence of inspiration. Some would prefer the word "apostolic," which comes to the same thing. All the writings above reckoned were held to be the works of apostles or of apostolic men, and on this ground were admitted into the list of books having authority in the church. Barnabas (cir 100–120 AD) already quotes Mt **20** 16 with the formula "it is written." Paul quotes as "scripture" (1 Tim **5** 18) a passage found only in Lk (**10** 7). Paul's Epistles are classed with "other scriptures" in 2 Pet **3** 16. Post-apostolic Fathers draw a clear distinction between their own writings and those of apostles like Paul and Peter (Polycarp, Ignatius, Barnabas). The Fathers of the close of the 2d cent. treat the NT writings as in the fullest degree inspired (cf Westcott, *Intro to Study of Gospels*, Append. B). An important impulse to the formation of a definite canon came from the gnostic Marcion (cir 140 AD), who made a canon for himself in 2 parts, "Gospel" and "Apostolicon," consisting of one gospel (a mutilated Lk) and 10 epistles of Paul (excluding Pastorals). A challenge of this kind had to be taken up, and lists of NT writings began to be made (Melito, Muratorian Fragment, etc), with the results previously described. By the commencement of the 4th cent. unanimity had practically been attained as regards even the *Antilegomena*. At the Council of Nicaea (325 AD), Westcott says, "the Holy Scriptures of the Old and New Testaments were silently admitted on all sides to have a final authority" (*Bible in Church*, 155). See Canon of NT.

V. Unity and Spiritual Purpose—Inspiration.—

1. Scripture a Unity

Holy Scripture is not simply a collection of religious books: still less does it consist of mere fragments of Jewish and Christian literature. It belongs to the conception of Scripture that, though originating "by divers portions and in divers manners" (He **1** 1), it should yet, in its completeness, constitute a unity, evincing, in the spirit and purpose that bind its parts together, the Divine source from which its revelation comes. The Bible is the record of God's revelations of Himself to men in successive ages and dispensations (Eph **1** 8–10; **3** 5–9; Col **1** 25.26), till the revelation culminates in the advent and work of the Son, and the mission of the Spirit. It is this aspect of the Bible which constitutes its grand distinction from all collections of sacred writings—the so-called "Bibles" of heathen religions—in the world. These, as the slightest inspection of them shows, have no unity. They are accumulations of heterogeneous materials, presenting, in their collocation, no order, progress, or plan. The reason is, that they embody no historical revelation working out a purpose in consecutive stages from germinal beginnings to perfect close.

The Bible, by contrast, is a single book because it embodies such a revelation, and exhibits such a purpose. The unity of the book, made up of so many parts, is the attestation of the reality of the revelation it contains.

2. The Purpose of Grace

This feature of *spiritual purpose* in the Bible is one of the most obvious things about it (cf *POT*, 30 ff). It gives to the Bible what is sometimes termed its "organic unity." The Bible has a beginning, middle and end. The opening chs of Gen have their counterpart in the "new heaven and new earth" and paradise restored of the closing chapters of Rev (**21, 22**). Man's sin is made the starting-point for disclosures of God's grace. The patriarchal history, with its covenants and promises, is continued in the story of the Exodus and the events that follow, in fulfilment of these promises. Dt recapitulates the lawgiving at Sinai. Josh sees the people put in possession of the promised land. Backsliding, rebellion, failure, do not defeat God's purpose, but are overruled to carry it on to a surer completion. The monarchy is made the occasion of new promises to the house of David (2 S **7**). The prophets root themselves in the past, but, at the very hour when the nation seems sinking in ruin, hold out bright hopes of a greater future in the extension of God's kingdom to the Gentiles, under Messiah's rule. A critical writer, Kautzsch, has justly said: "The abiding value of the OT lies above all in this, that it guarantees to us with absolute certainty the fact and the process of a Divine plan and way of salvation, which found its conclusion and fulfilment in the new covenant, in the person and work of Jesus Christ" (*Bleibende Bedeutung des AT*, 22, 24, 28–29, 30–31).

Fulfilment in Christ.—How truly all that was imperfect, transitional, temporary, in the OT was brought to realization and completion in the redemption and spiritual kingdom of Christ need not here be dwelt upon. Christ is the prophet, priest and king of the New Covenant. His perfect sacrifice, "once for all," supersedes and abolishes the typical sacrifices of the old economy (He **9, 10**). His gift of the Spirit realizes what the prophets had foretold of God's law being written in men's hearts (Jer **31** 31–34; **32** 39.40; Ezk **11** 19.20, etc). His kingdom is established on moveless foundations, and can have no end (Phil **2** 9–11; He **12** 28; Rev **5** 13, etc). In tracing the lines of this redeeming purpose of God, brought to light in Christ, we gain the key which unlocks the inmost meaning of the whole Bible. It is the revelation of a "gospel."

3. Inspiration

"Inspiration" is a word round which many debates have gathered. If, however, what has been said is true of the Bible as the record of a progressive revelation, of its contents as the discovery of the will of God for man's salvation, of the prophetic and apostolic standing of its writers, of the unity of spirit and purpose that pervades it, it will be difficult to deny that a quite peculiar presence, operation, and guidance of the Spirit of God are manifest in its production. The belief in inspiration, it has been seen, is implied in the formation of these books into a sacred canon. The full discussion of the subject belongs to a special art. (see Inspiration).

Biblical claim.—Here it need only be said that the claim for inspiration in the Bible is one made in fullest measure by the Bible itself. It is not denied by any that Jesus and His apostles regarded the OT Scriptures as in the fullest sense inspired. The appeal of Jesus was always to the Scriptures, and the word of Scripture was final with Him. "Have ye not read?" (Mt **19** 4). "Ye do err, not knowing the scriptures, nor the power of God" (Mt **22** 29). This because "God" speaks in them (Mt **19** 4). Prophecies and psalms were fulfilled in Him (Lk **18** 31; **22** 37; **24** 27.44). Paul esteemed the Scriptures "the oracles of God" (Rom **3** 2). They are "God-inspired" (2 Tim **3** 16). That NT prophets and apostles were not placed on any lower level than those of the OT is manifest from Paul's explicit words regarding himself and his fellow-apostles. Paul never faltered in his claim to be "an apostle of Christ Jesus through the will of God" (Eph **1** 1, etc)—"separated unto the gospel of God" (Rom **1** 1)—who had received his message, not from man, but by "revelation" from heaven (Gal **1** 11.12). The "mystery of Christ" had "now been revealed unto his holy apostles and prophets in the Spirit," in consequence of which the church is declared to be "built upon the foundation of the apostles and prophets, Christ Jesus himself being the chief corner stone" (Eph **2** 20; **3** 5).

Marks of inspiration.—It might be shown that these claims made by NT writers for the OT and for themselves are borne out by what the OT itself teaches of prophetic inspiration, of wisdom as the gift of God's spirit, and of the light, holiness, saving virtue and sanctifying power continually ascribed to God's "law," "words," "statutes," "commandments," "judgments" (see above). This is the ultimate test of "inspiration"—that to which Paul likewise appeals—its power to "make wise unto salvation through faith which is in Christ Jesus" (2 Tim **3** 15)—its profitableness "for teaching, for reproof, for correction, for instruction which is in righteousness" (ver 16)—all to the end "that the man of God may be complete, furnished completely unto every good work" (ver 17). Nothing is here determined as to "inerrancy" in minor historical, geographical, chronological details, in which some would wrongly put the essence of inspiration; but it seems implied that at least there is no error which can interfere with or nullify the utility of Scripture for the ends specified. Who that brings Scripture to its own tests of inspiration, will deny that, judged as a whole, it fulfils them?

4. Historical Influence of the Bible

3. The claim of the Bible to a Divine origin is justified by its *historical influence*. Regarded even as lit., the Bible has an unexampled place in history. Ten or fifteen MSS are thought a goodly number for an ancient classic; the MSS of whole or parts of the NT are reckoned by thousands, the oldest going back to the 4th or 5th cent. Another test is tr. The books of the NT had hardly begun to be put together before we find tr[s] being made of them in Lat, Syr, Egyp, later into Gothic and other barbarous tongues (see Versions). In the Middle Ages, before the invention of printing, tr[s] were made into the vernacular of most of the countries of Europe. Today there is not a language in the civilized world, hardly a language among uncivilized tribes, wherever missions have gone, into which this word of God has not been rendered. Thanks to the labors of Bible Societies, the circulation of the Bible in the different countries of the world in recent years outstrips all previous records. No book has ever been so minutely studied, has had so many books written on it, has founded so vast a lit. of hymns, liturgies, devotional writings, sermons, has been so keenly assailed, has evoked such splendid defences, as the Bible. Its spiritual influence cannot be estimated. To tell all the Bible has been and done for the world would be to rewrite in large part the history of modern civilization. Without it, in heathen lands, the arm and tongue of the missionary would be paralyzed. With it, even in the absence of the missionary, wondrous results are often effected.

In national life the Bible is the source of our highest social and national aspirations. Professor Huxley, though an agnostic, argued for the reading of the Bible in the schools on this very ground. "By the study of what other book," he asked, "could children be so much humanized, and made to feel that each figure in that vast historical procession fills, like themselves, but a momentary space in the interval between two eternities, and earns the blessings or the curses of all times, according to its effort to do good and to hate evil, even as they are also earning their payment for their work?" (*Critiques and Addresses*, 61).

VI. Addenda.—A few notes may be added, in closing, on special points not touched in the preceding sections.

1. Chapters and Verses

Already in pre-Talm times, for purposes of reading in the synagogues, the Jews had larger divisions of the law into sections called *Pārāshāhs*, and of the prophets into similar sections called *Haphṭārāhs*. They had also smaller divisions into *Peṣūḳīm*, corresponding nearly with our verses. The division into chapters is much later (13th cent.). It is ascribed to Cardinal Hugo de St Caro (d. 1248); by others to Stephen Langton, archbishop of Canterbury (d. 1227). It was adopted into the Vulg, and from this was transferred by R. Nathan (cir 1440) to the Heb Bible (Bleek, Keil). Verses are marked in the Vulg as early as 1558. They first appear in the NT in Robert Stephens' edition of the Gr Testament in 1551. Henry Stephens, Robert's son, reports that they were devised by his father during a journey on horseback from Paris to Lyons.

2. AV and RV

The AV of 1611, based in part on earlier English VSS, esp. Tyndale's, justly holds rank as one of the noblest monuments of the English language of its own, or any, age. Necessarily, however, the Gr text used by the translators ("Textus Receptus"), resting on a few late MSS, was very imperfect. With the discovery of more ancient MSS, and multiplication of appliances for criticism, the need and call for a revised text and tr became urgent. Finally, at the instance of the Convocation of the Province of Canterbury, the task of revision was undertaken by Committees representing the best English and American scholarship. Their labors resulted in the publication, in 1881, of the Revised NT, and in 1885, of the Revised OT (a revised edition of the Apoc was published in 1896). The preferences of the American Revisers were printed in an appendix, a pledge being given that no further changes should be made for 14 years. The English Companies were disbanded shortly after 1885, but the American Committee, adhering to its own renderings, and believing that further improvements on the English RV were possible, continued its organization and work. This issued, in 1901, in the production of the ARV, which aims at greater consistency and accuracy in a number of important respects, and is supplied, also, with carefully selected marginal references (see AMERICAN REVISED VERSION). Little could be done, in either ERV or ARV, in the absence of reliable data for comparison, with the text of the OT, but certain obvious corrections have been made, or noted in the margin.

3. Helps to Study

In recent years abundant helps have been furnished, apart from Commentaries and Dictionaries, for the intelligent study of the English Bible. Among such works may be mentioned the *Oxford Helps to the Study of the Bible;* the valuable *Aids to Bible Students* (Eyre and Spottiswoode, 1898); Dr. Angus' *Bible Handbook* (revised by Green); A. S. Peake's *Guide to Biblical Study* (1897); W. F. Adeney's *How to Read the Bible* (1896); R. C. Moulton's *The Modern Reader's Bible* (1907); *The Sunday School Teachers' Bible* (1875); The *Variorum Reference Bible* and *Variorum Teachers' Bible* (1880); Weymouth's *NT in Modern Speech* (1909); *The Twentieth Cent. NT* (Westcott and Hort's text, 1904); S. Lloyd's *The Corrected English NT* (Bagster, 1905).

LITERATURE.—Cf arts. in the Bible Dicts., specially Sanday on "Bible," and Dobschütz on "The Bible in the Church," in Hastings' *Enc of Rel. and Ethics*, II; Westcott, *The Bible in the Church* (1875); W. H. Bennett, *A Primer of the Bible* (1897); A. F. Kirkpatrick, *The Divine Library of the OT* (1896); J. Eadie, *The English Bible;* works on Introduction (Driver, etc); books mentioned above under "Helps"; B. B. Warfield in *Princeton Theological Review* (October, 1910); C. A. Briggs, *General Intro to the Study of Holy Scripture* (Scribners, 1899); W. H. Green, *General Intro to the OT* (Scribners, 1899); E. C. Bissell, *The Pent: Its Origin and Structure* (Scribners, 1885); Zahn, *Intro to the NT*.

JAMES ORR

BIBLICAL CRITICISM. See CRITICISM OF BIBLE.

BIBLICAL DISCREPANCIES, bib'li-kal dis-krep'an-siz. See DISCREPANCIES, BIBLICAL.

BIBLICAL THEOLOGY, bib'li-kal thē-ol'ō-ji:

I. As a Science.—Bib. theology seems best defined as the doctrine of Bib. religion. As such it

1. Definition

works up the material contained in the OT and the NT as the product of exegetical study. This is the modern technical sense of the term, whereby it signifies a systematic representation of Bib. religion in its primitive form.

Bib. theology has sometimes been taken to signify not alone this science of the doctrinal declarations of the Scriptures, but the whole group of sciences concerned with the interpretation and exposition of the Scriptures. In that wider view of Bib. theology, the term exegetical theology has been used to define and include the group of sciences already referred to. But the whole weight of preference seems, in our view, to belong to the narrower use of the term Bib. theology, as more strictly scientific.

2. Relation to Dogmatics

This is not to confound the science of Bib. theology with that of dogmatics, for their characters are sharply distinguished. The science of dogmatics is a historico-philosophical one; that of Bib. theology is purely historic. Dogmatics declares what, for religious faith, must be regarded as truth; Bib. theology only discovers what the writers of the OT and the NT adduce as truth. This latter merely ascertains the contents of the ideas put forward by the sacred writers, but is not concerned with their correctness or verification. It is the *what* of truth, in these documentary authorities, Bib. theology seeks to attain. The *why*, or *with what right*, it is so put forward as truth, belongs to the other science, that of dogmatics.

Bib. theology is thus the more objective science; it has no need of dogmatics; dogmatics, on the other hand, cannot be without the aid of Bib. theology.

3. Place and Method of Biblical Theology

The Bib. theologian should be a Christian philosopher, an exegete, and, above all, a historian. For it is in a manner purely historical that Bib. theology seeks to investigate the teaching, in whole, of each of the sacred writers. Each writing it studies in itself, in its relation to the others, and in its place in history taken as a whole. Its method is historical-genetic. The proper place of Bib. theology is at the head of historical theology, where it shines as a center of light. Its ideal as a science is to present a clear, complete and comprehensive survey of the Bib. teachings.

4. Relation to Exegesis

In pursuance of this end, Bib. theology is served by scientific exegesis, whose results it presents in ordered form so as to exhibit the organic unity and completeness of Bib. religion. The importance of Bib. theology lies in the way it directs, corrects and fructifies all moral and dogmatic theology by bringing it to the original founts of truth. Its spirit is one of impartial historical inquiry.

II. History of Biblical Theology.—Bib. theology, in any truly scientific form, dates only from the 18th cent.

1. Its Rise in Scientific Form

Offspring as it was of German rationalism, it has yet been found deserving of cultivation and scientific study by the most orthodox theology. Indeed, Pietism, too, urged its claims as Bib. dogma, over against the too scholastic dogma of orthodoxy.

2. Patristic and Scholastic Periods

The Patristic theology, no doubt, was Bib., and the Alexandrian School deserves special praise. The scholastic theology of the Middle Ages leaned on the Fathers rather than on the Bible. Bib. theology, in spirit, though not in form, found a revival at the Reformation. But this was early followed by a 17th cent. type of scholasticism, polemical and confessional.

3. 17th and 18th Cents.

Even in that cent., however, efforts of a more purely Bib. character were not wanting, as witness those of Schmidt, Witsius and Vitringa. But throughout the entire 18th cent. there were manifest endeavors to throw off the scholastic yoke and return to Bib. simplicity. Haymann (1708), Büsching (1756), Zachariae (1772) and Storr (1793), are examples of the efforts referred to. But it was from the rationalistic side that the first vindication of Bib. theology as a science of independent rank was made. This merit belonged to Gabler (1787), who urged a purely historical treatment of the Bible, and was, later, shared by his colleague, G. L. Bauer, who issued a *Bib. Theology of the NT* (Ger) in four parts (1800–1802). More independent still was the standpoint assumed by C. F. Ammon in his *Biblische Theologie* (2d ed, 1801–2). Ammon does not fail to apprehend the historical character of our science, saying that Bib. theology should deal only with the "materials, fundamental ideas, and results of Bib. teaching, without troubling itself about the connection of the same, or weaving them into an artificial system."

4. OT Theology in First Half of 19th Cent.

The influence of Schleiermacher was hardly a fortunate one, the OT being sundered from the NT, and attention centered on the latter. Kayser (1813) and, still more, De Wette, who died in 1850, pursued the perfecting of our science, particularly in matters of method. Continuators of the work were Baumgarten-Crusius (1828), Cramer (1830) and Cölln, whose work was posthumously presented by D. Schulz in 1836. It was in the second quarter of the 19th cent. that the Bib. theology of the OT began to receive the full attention it deserved. It has been declared the merit of Hegel's philosophy to have taught men to see, in the various Bib. systems of doctrine, a complete development, and Hegel did, no doubt, exert a fertilizing influence on historical inquiry. But it must also be said that the Hegelian philosophy affected Bib. theology in a prejudicial manner, as may be seen in Vatke's a priori construction of history and doctrine in his work, *Die bib. Theologie* (1835), and in Bruno Bauer's *Die Religion des AT* (1838–39), which controverted but did not improve upon Vatke. Steudel (1840), Oehler (1845) and Hävernick (1848) are worthy of particularly honorable mention in this OT connection. In his *Theology of the OT* (3d ed, 1891; Amer. ed, 1883) G. F. Oehler excellently maintained the close connection between the OT and the NT, which Hengstenberg had already emphasized in 1829.

5. NT Theology in the 19th Cent.

The Bib. theology of the NT was furthered by the memorable Neander. In 1832, he first issued his *Planting and Training of the Christian Church*; while his *Life of Jesus* first appeared in 1837. In this latter work, he summarized the doctrine of the Redeemer, while the former presented the doctrinal teaching of the apostolic writers in such wise as to show the different shades of thought peculiar to each of them, pointing out, at the same time, "how, notwithstanding all difference, there was an essential unity beneath, unless one is deceived by the form, and how the form in its diversity is easily explained." C. F. Schmid improved in some respects upon Neander's work in his excellent *Biblical Theology of the NT*, issued (1853) after his death by Weizsäcker (new ed, 1864). In Schmid's work, the Bib. theology of the NT is presented with objectivity, clearness and penetrating sympathy.

Hahn's *Theology of the NT* (1854) came short of doing justice to the diverse types of doctrinal development in the NT. The work of G. V. Lechler on the apostolic and post-apostolic age, was, in its improved form of 1857, much more important. E. Reuss, in 1852, issued his valuable *History of the Christian Theology of the Apostolic Age*, a complete and critical work, but not sufficiently objective in its treatment. The *Prelections on NT Theology* of F. C. Baur, head of the Tübingen school, exemplify both the merits and the defects of the school. They are critical, independent and suggestive, but lacking in impartiality. They were published by his son after his death (1864). A new ed of these lectures on NT theology was issued by Pfleiderer in 1893.

Having first dealt with the teachings of Jesus, Baur then set out the materials of the NT theology in three periods, making Paul well-nigh the founder of Christianity. For him only four epistles of Paul were genuine products of the apostolic age, namely, Romans, the two Corinthians, Galatians, together with the Revelation. To the growth and history of the NT Baur applied the method of the Hegelian dialectic, and, though powerful and profound, displayed a lack of sane, well-balanced judgment. Yet so conservative a scholar as Weiss gave Baur the credit of having "first made it the problem of criticism to assign to each book of the NT its place in the history of the development of primitive Christianity, to determine the relations to which it owes its origin, the object at which it aims, and the views it represents." Among Baur's followers may be noted Pfleiderer, in his *Paulinism* (1873).

The Theology of the NT, by J. J. Van Oosterzee (Eng. ed, 1870), is a serviceable book for students, and the *NT Theology* of A. Immer (1878), already famous for his hermeneutical studies, is noteworthy. Chief among subsequent cultivators of the Bib. theology of the NT must be reckoned B. Weiss, whose work in two volumes (Eng. ed, 1882–83) constitutes a most critical and complete, thorough and accurate treatment of the subject in all its details: W. Beyschlag, whose *NT Theology* (Eng. ed, in 2 vols, 1895) is also valuable; H. Holtzmann, whose treatise on *NT Theology* (1897) dealt in a critical fashion with the doctrinal contents of the NT. Holtzmann's learning and ability are great, but his work is marred by naturalistic presuppositions. The French work on *Theology of the NT*, by J. Bovon (2 vols, 1893–94) is marked by great independence, skill and fairness. *The Theology of the NT*, by W. F. Adeney (1894), and the yet more recent, and very attractively written, work with the same title, by G. B. Stevens (1899), bring us pretty well up to the present state of our science in respect of the NT.

6. OT Theology in Second Half of the 19th Cent.

Coming back to the Bib. theology of the OT in the second half of the 19th cent., we find A. Klostermann's *Investigations into the OT Theology*, which appeared in 1868. The OT theology, no less than that of the NT, was set forth by that great scholar, H. Ewald, in four vols (1871–75; Eng. ed [first part], 1888). His interest in NT theology was due to his strong feeling that the NT is really the second part of the record of Israel's revelation. A. Kuenen dealt with the *Religion of Israel* in two volumes (Eng. ed, 1874–75), writing nobly but with defective insight into, and comprehension of, the higher religious ideas of Israel. F. Hitzig's *Prelections* (1880) deal with the theology of the OT, as part of their contents. H. Schultz treated of the *OT Theology* in two vols (1st ed, 1869; 5th ed, 1896; Eng. ed, 1892), in a careful, mainly just, and, by comparison, well-balanced handling of the development of its religious ideas.

We have not touched upon writers like Smend, for example, in his *History of OT Religion* (1893), and J. Robertson, in his *Early Religion of Israel* (2d ed, 1892), who treat of the Bib. theology of the OT only in a way subsidiary to the consideration of the historico-critical problems. *The Conception of Revelation in the OT* was dealt with by F. E. König in 1882 in a careful and comprehensive manner, and with regard to the order and relation of the documents, revelation in Israel being taken by him in a supranaturalistic sense. Significant also for the progress of OT Bib. theology was *The Theological and the Historical View of the OT*, by C. Siegfried (1890), who insisted on the development of the higher religion of Israel being studied from the elder prophets as starting-point, instead of the law.

Mention should be made of *Biblical Study: Its Principles, Methods and History*, by C. A. Briggs (1883; 4th ed, 1891); of the important *Compendium of the Bib. Theology of the O and the NT* by K. Schlottmann (1889); of E. Riehm's valuable *OT Theology* (1889); and of G. Dalman's *Studies in Bib. Theology*—the Divine name and its history—in 1889. Also, of the *OT Theology* of A. Duff (1891); A. Dillmann's *Handbook of OT Theology*, edited by Kittel (1895); and of Marti's ed of the *Theology of the OT* of A. Kayser (3d ed, 1897).

Of *Theology of the OT*, by A. B. Davidson (1904), it may be said that it does full justice to the idea of a progressive development of doctrine in the OT, and is certainly divergent from the view of those who, like Cheyne, treat the OT writings as so many fragments, from which no theology can be extracted. *Biblical Theology of the OT*, by B. Stade (1905), is the work of a distinguished representative of the modern critical views, already famous for his work on the history of Israel (1887). *The Theology of the OT* by W. H. Bennett (1906) is a clear and useful compendium of the subject.

7. Bearings of Criticism on OT Theology

Recent works like *The Problem of the OT* by James Orr (1905), *OT Critics* by Thomas Whitelaw (1903), and *Essays in Pentateuchal Criticism*, by Harold M. Wiener (1909), deal with the critical questions, and do not concern us here, save to remark that they are not without bearing, in their results, upon the theology of the OT. Such results are, e.g. the insistences, in Orr's work, on the unity of the OT, the higher than naturalistic view of Israel's religious development, the discriminate use of Divine names like Elohim and Jehovah, and so forth; and the express contention in Whitelaw's work, that the critical hypotheses are not such as can yield "a philosophically reasonable theology" (p. 346). Indeed, it must not be supposed that even works, like that of S. R. Driver, *Introduction to the Literature of the OT* (first issued in 1891), are without resultant influence on Bib. theology.

So far from that, the truth is that there is probably no result of the readjustment of the history and lit. of the OT so important as its bearings on the Bib. theology of the OT. For the order and the method of revelation are most surely involved in the order and relation of the books or documents, and the course of the history. The progress of the revelation ran parallel with the work of God in Nature and in the growth of human society. Hence the reconstruction of the historical theology of the OT will take much time and study, that the full value of the OT may be brought out as that of an independent and permanent revelation, with characteristic truths of its own. Meantime, the reality of that revelation, and the teleological character of the OT, have been brought out, in the most signal manner, by theological scholars like Dorner, Dillmann, Kittel, Kautsch, Schultz and others, who feel the inadequacy of natural development or "human reflection" to account for OT theology, and the immediacy of God's contact with man in OT times to be alone sufficient to account for a revelation so weighty, organically connected, dynamically bound together, monotheistic and progressive.

III. Divisions of Biblical Theology.—The divisions of OT theology are matters of grave difficulty.

1. Divergent Views on the OT

For the newer criticism has practically transformed that mode of representing the process of Israel's religious development, which had been customary or traditional. On this latter view, the Patriarchal Age was succeeded by the Mosaic Age, with its law-giving under Moses, followed, after an intercalated period of Judges and monarchy, by the splendid Age of Prophecy. Then there was the Exile preparing the way, after the Return, for the new theocracy, wherein the Law of Moses was sought with more persistent endeavor, though not without darkly legalistic result. Such were the historic bases for OT theology, but the modifications proposed by the new criticism are sufficiently serious. These it will be necessary to indicate, without going beyond the scope of this art. and attempting criticism of either the one view or the other. It is the more necessary to do so, that finality has not been reached by criticism. We are only concerned with the difference which these divergent views make for OT Bib. theology, whose reconstruction is very far from perfected.

That they do mean serious difference has been indicated in the historical part of this art. Most obtrusive of these differences is the proposal to invert the order of law and prophecy, and speak rather of the Prophets and the Law. For the Law is, on the newer view, taken to belong to the post-

2. Law and Prophecy

prophetic period—in short, to the period of the return from the Exile, whereas, in the traditional scheme of the order of revelation, the Law was found in full force both at the Exodus and the Return, with a dead-letter period between. The garment of legalism, the newer criticism asserts, could not have suited the Israelitish nation in its early and undeveloped stage, as it does after the teachings of the prophets and the discipline of the Exile. Against this, the older scheme prefers the objection that an external and legalistic system is made the outcome of the lofty spiritual teaching of the prophets; the letter appears super-imposed upon the spirit. Criticism, however, postulates for the ritual codes of the Pent an influence parallel in time with that of prophetism.

3. Prophetism and Judaism

Besides the adjustments of prophecy and law just referred to, the critical views postulate a primal period in which the religion of the prophets, with their view of Israel's vocation, was inculcated; also, a final period of Judaism, intercalated between the Return and the Maccabees, in which are seen at work the Levitical law, and various anti-legal tendencies. It must be obvious that attempts to integrate the OT theology amid the prevailing uncertainties of criticism must be far from easy or final, even if the need and importance be felt of keeping the religious interest before even the historical in OT study. For the OT writers, religion was primary, history secondary and incidental, we may well believe.

4. Place of Mosaism

We must be content to know less of the remote beginnings and initial stages of Israel's religious development, for, as A. B. Davidson remarked, "in matters like this we never can get at the beginning." J. Robertson deems criticism wrong in not allowing "a sufficient starting-point for the development," by which he means that pure prophetic religion needs "a pure pre-prophetic religion" to explain its more than "germinal or elementary character." It may be noted, too, how much greater place and importance are attached to Mosaism or Moses by critics like Reuss, Schultz, Bredenkamp and Strack, than by Wellhausen, who yet allows a certain substratum of actual and historical fact.

5. Israel's Religious Development

It may be observed, further, that no one is under any compulsion to account for such a transformation, as even Wellhausen allows, in the slow growth from very low beginnings of the idea of Jeh up to pure and perfect monotheism—among a non-metaphysical people—by the simple supposition of naturalistic theory. Evolutionary the critical hypothesis of the religious development of Israel may be, but that development was clearly not so exclusively controlled by human elements or factors as to exclude the presence of supernatural energy or power of revelation. It had God within it—had, in Dorner's phrase, "teleology as its soul." Thus, as even Gunkel declares, "Israel is, and remains, the people of revelation." This is why Israel was able to make—despite all retrograde tendencies—rectilinear progress toward a predestined goal—the goal of being what Ewald styled a "purely immortal and spiritual Israel." OT theology does not seem to have sufficiently realized that the OT really presents us with theologies rather than a theology—with the progressive development of a religion rather than with theological ideas resting on one historic plane.

LITERATURE.—I, OT Literature: B. Stade, *Biblische Theologie des AT*, 1905; H. Schultz, *AT Theologie*, 5th ed, 1896; Eng. ed, 1892; H. Ewald, *Revelation: Its Nature and Record*, Eng. ed, 1884; G F. Oehler, *Theology of the OT*, Eng. ed, 1874; A. Kuenen, *The Religion of Israel to the Fall of the Jewish State*, Eng. ed, 1875; E. Riehm, *AT Theologie*, 1889; S. R. Driver, *An Introduction to the Literature of the OT*, 1st ed, 1891; A. B. Davidson, *Theology of the OT*, 1904; J. Orr, *The Problem of the OT*, 1905; A. Duff, *OT Theology*, 1891; J. Robertson, *Early Religion of Israel*, 2d ed, 1892; W. R. Smith, *The OT in the Jewish Church*, new ed, 1892; W. H. Bennett, *The Theology of the OT*, 1896; T. K. Cheyne, *Founders of OT Criticism*, 1893; T. Whitelaw, *OT Critics*, 1903; W. G. Jordan, *Biblical Criticism and Modern Thought*, 1909; H. M. Wiener, *Essays in Pentateuchal Criticism*, 1909; E. C. Bissell, *The Pentateuch: Its Origin and Structure*, 1885; D. K. v. Orelli, *The OT Prophecy*, Amer. ed, 1885, Eng. ed, 1893; B. Duhm, *Die Theologie der Propheten*, 1875; E. Riehm, *Messianic Prophecy*, 2d Eng. ed, 1891; C. I. Bredenkamp, *Gesetz und Propheten*, 1881; W. R. Smith, *The Prophets of Israel*, 1882; D. K. Schlottmann, *Kompendium der biblischen Theologie des A. u. N. Testaments*, 1889; A. T. Kirkpatrick, *The Divine Library of the OT*, 1891; J. Lindsay, *The Significance of the OT for Modern Theology*, 1896; R. Kittel, *Scientific Study of the OT*, Eng. ed, 1910.

II, NT Literature: W. Beyschlag, *NT Theology*, 2d ed, 1896; Eng. ed, 1895; H. Holtzmann, *Lehrbuch der NT Theologie*, 1897; B. Weiss, *Lehrbuch der biblischen Theologie des NT*, 7th ed, 1903; Eng. ed, 1883; J. J. v. Oosterzee, *Die Theologie des NT*, 2d ed, 1886; Eng. ed, 1870; J. Bovon, *Théologie du Nouveau Testament*, 1893–94; C. F. Schmid, *Biblische Theologie des NT*, new ed, 1864; G. B. Stevens, *The Theology of the NT*, 1899; F. C. Baur, *Vorlesungen über NT Theologie*, 1864; W. F. Adeney, *The Theology of the NT*, 1894; A. C. McGiffert, *A History of Christianity in the Apostolic Age*, 1897; E. Reuss, *History of Christian Theology in the Apostolic Age*, Eng. ed, 1872; H. H. Wendt, *The Teaching of Jesus*, Eng. ed, 1892; A. B. Bruce, *The Kingdom of God*, 1890; J. Moorhouse, *The Teaching of Christ*, 1891; O. Pfleiderer, *Der Paulinismus*, 2d ed, 1890; 2d Eng. ed, 1891; A. Sabatier, *The Apostle Paul*, Eng. ed, 1891; G. B. Stevens, *The Pauline Theology*, 2d ed, 1897; G. Matheson, *The Spiritual Development of St. Paul*, 1890; E. Riehm, *Der Lehrbegriff des Hebräerbriefs*, 1867; B. Weiss, *Der petrinische Lehrbegriff*, 1855; G. B. Stevens, *The Johannine Theology*, 1894; B. Weiss, *Der johanneische Lehrbegriff in seinen Grundzügen untersucht*, 1862.

JAMES LINDSAY

BICHRI, bik'rī (בִּכְרִי, *bikhrī*, "first born"; cf *HPN*, 88, 102): Father of Sheba who rebelled against David. B. is of the house of Benjamin and the word probably means a "descendant of Becher" (2 S **20** 1 ff). Cf BECHER 1.

BID: Variously signifying, according to six Heb and as many Gr originals: (1) "to command" (Nu **14** 10; Mt **1** 24 AV, προστάττω, *prostáttō*); (2) "to prescribe" or "order" (Jn **2** 2); (3) "to consecrate," and so rendered in RV (Zeph **1** 7; cf 1 S **16** 5); (4) εἶπον, *eípon*, "to say" or "tell" (Mt **16** 12); (5) "to call" i.e. "invite" (καλέω, *kaléō*), conspicuously used in this sense in Christ's parables of the Marriage Feast (Mt **22** 3–9) and of the Great Supper (Lk **14** 7–24); (6) "to take leave of," ἀποτάττω, *apotáttō* (Lk **9** 61).

BIDDEN, bid'n: "Called," "invited" (1 S **9** 13).

BIDE, bīd: A variant of "abide" (q.v.); is the rendering of περιμένω, *periménō*, in Wisd **8** 12 (RV "they shall wait for me"). In Acts **1** 4 the same word is tr[d] "wait for."

BIDKAR, bid'kar (בִּדְקַר, *bidhkar;* "son of Deker"[?]; cf *HPN*, 69): A captain in the service of Jehu, formerly his fellow-officer (2 K **9** 25).

BIER, bēr:

(1) Found in the OT only in 2 S **3** 31, "and king David followed *the bier*"; and in the NT in Lk **7** 14, "and he [Jesus] came nigh and touched *the bier*." The Heb word rendered "bier" (*miṭṭāh*) and its Gr equivalent (*sorós*) mean strictly "coffin." The so-called "bier" among the ancient Hebrews was simply an open coffin or a flat wooden frame, on which the body of the dead was carried from the house to the grave.

(2) Closed coffins, so universal now in the West, were unknown to common usage among the Hebrews of olden times, though not unknown to Egyptians, Greeks and Romans.

At the burial of Abner the people were commanded to "rend their clothes" and "gird themselves with sackcloth," and the king himself in token of his grief and royal regard, "followed *the bier*" in the procession to the grave (2 S **3** 31).

(3) Of Jesus, when He met the procession that went out of the gate of the city of Nain, bearing to the grave the only son of the widowed mother, Luke says, "When the Lord saw her, he had compassion on her . . . . and he came nigh and touched *the bier*," and commanded the young man to arise, etc. We should recall that contact with a dead body was forbidden by the law as a source of defilement (Nu **19** 11 f); so Jesus here "came nigh" and "touched the bier" only in raising the young man, thus avoiding any criticism for infraction of the law. In Jn **11** 35, as here, we have a miracle of Jesus which clearly pointed to a higher law—the eternal law of compassion which received its first full expression in the life of Jesus and forms one of the distinctive features of the gospel.

GEO. B. EAGER

BURIAL PROCESSION.

BIGTHA, big'tha (בִּגְתָא, *bigh^{e}thā'*; LXX **Βαραζί**, *Barazí*; B, **Βωραζή**, *Bōrazē*; A, **'Οαρεβωά**, *Oareböá*): One of the seven eunuchs or chamberlains having charge of the harem of King Xerxes ("Ahasuerus") and commanded to bring Vashti to the king's banquet (Est **1** 10).

BIGTHAN, big'than, **BIGTHANA**, big-thā'na (בִּגְתָן, בִּגְתָנָא, *bigh^{e}thān, bigh^{e}thānā'*; LXX omits name): One of the two chamberlains or eunuchs of Xerxes ("Ahasuerus") who conspired against the king's life, the conspiracy being detected by Mordecai and the culprits hanged (Est **2** 21). Possibly these men had been partially superseded by the degradation of Vashti and were thus prompted to take revenge on Xerxes.

BIGVAI, big'vā-ī (בִּגְוַי, *bighway*; **Βαογεί**, *Baogeí*, **Βαγουά**, *Bagouá*):

(1) The head of one of the families who returned from Babylon with Zerubbabel (Ezr **2** 2; Neh **7** 7), having a large number of his retainers (2,056, according to Ezr **2** 14; 2,067, according to Neh **7** 19), besides 72 males later under Ezra (**8** 14).

(2) One of those who subscribed the covenant with Nehemiah (**10** 16).

BIKATH-AVEN, bik-ath-ā'ven (בִּקְעַת־אָוֶן, *biḳ'ath 'āwen*, "valley of vanity" [Am **1** 5 AVm]). See AVEN; BETH-EDEN.

BILDAD, bil'dad (בִּלְדַּד, *bildadh*, "Bel has loved"): The second of the three friends of Job who, coming from distant regions, make an appointment together to condole with and comfort him in his affliction (Job **2** 11). He is from Shuah, an unknown place somewhere in the countries E. and S.E. of Pal (or the designation Shuhite may be intended to refer to his ancestor Shuah, one of Abraham's sons by Keturah, Gen **25** 2), and from his name (compounded with Bel, the name of a Bab deity) would seem to represent the wisdom of the distant East. His three speeches are contained in Job **8**, **18** and **25**. For substance they are largely an echo of what Eliphaz has maintained, but charged with somewhat increased vehemence (cf **8** 2; **18** 3.4) because he deems Job's words so impious and wrathful. He is the first to attribute Job's calamity to actual wickedness; but he gets at it indirectly by accusing his children (who were destroyed, **1** 19) of sin to warrant their punishment (**8** 4). For his contribution to the discussion he appeals to tradition (**8** 8–10), and taking Eliphaz' cue of cause and effect (ver 11) he gives, evidently from the literary stores of wisdom, a description of the precarious state of the wicked, to which he contrasts, with whatever implication it involves, the felicitous state of the righteous (**8** 11–22). His second speech is an intensified description of the wicked man's woes, made as if to match Job's description of his own desperate case (cf **18** 5–21 with **16** 6–22), thus tacitly identifying Job with the reprobate wicked. His third speech (**25**), which is the last utterance of the friends, is brief, subdued in tone, and for substance is a kind of Parthian shot, reiterating Eliphaz' depravity idea, the doctrine that dies hardest. This speech marks the final silencing of the friends.

JOHN FRANKLIN GENUNG

BILEAM, bil'ē-am (בִּלְעָם, *bil'ām*; **'Ιβλαάμ**, *Iblaám*): A town in the territory of Manasseh assigned to the Kohathite Levites (1 Ch **6** 70), probably the same as Ibleam (Josh **17** 11, etc), and identical with the modern *Bel'āmeh*, half a mile S. of *Jenīn*.

BILGAH, bil'ga, **BILGAI**, bil'gā-ī (בִּלְגָּה, *bilgāh*; בִּלְגַּי, *bilgay*, "cheerfulness"): A priest or priestly family in the time of the Return (Neh **12** 5), and (under the form of "Bilgai," Neh **10** 8) in the time of Nehemiah. According to 1 Ch **24** 14, Bilgah is the 15th of the 24 divisions of the priests who officiated in the Temple. In the LXX, the names read **Βελγάι**, *Belgái*, *Belgá* and *Balgás*. The traditional explanation of the name is "rejuvenation"; modern exegetes explain it as "cheerfulness."

BILHAH, bil'ha (person) (בִּלְהָה, *bilhāh;* **Βαλλά,** *Ballá*): A slave girl whom Laban gave to Rachel (Gen **29** 29), and whom the latter gave to Jacob as a concubine (Gen **30** 3.4); the mother of Dan and Naphtali (Gen **30** 4.7; **35** 25; **46** 25; 1 Ch **7** 13); guilty of incest with Reuben (Gen **35** 22).

BILHAH, bil'ha (place) (בִּלְהָה, *bilhāh;* A, **Βαλαά,** *Balaá*; B, **'Αβελλά,** *Abellá*): A city in Simeon (1 Ch **4** 29) = Baalah (Josh **15** 29), Balah (**19** 3), and Baalath (**19** 44). Unidentified.

BILHAN, bil'han (בִּלְהָן, *bilhān;* **Βαλαάν,** *Balaán*):

(1) A Horite chief, son of Ezer (Gen **36** 27; 1 Ch **1** 42).

(2) A descendant of Benjamin, son of Jediael, father of seven sons who were heads of houses in their tribes (1 Ch **7** 10).

BILL, BOND, etc:

(1) In the parable of the Unjust Steward (Lk **16** 6 f) "bill," AV, better "bond," RV, is used to translate the Gr *grámmata,* which is the equivalent of the contemporary Heb legal term *sh^eṭar,* "writing." This "writing," in the usage of the times, was an acknowledgment of the taking over or receiving of goods or money that had to be written and signed by the debtor himself. (See *Bābhā' Bathrā'* **10** 8.) Edersheim's averment that the Gr word was adopted into the Heb (*Life and Times of Jesus the Messiah,* II, 272), is based, according to competent textual critics, upon a false reading. The Gr, according to Tisch., Treg. and WH, is *tá grámmata,* not *tó grámma* (*TR*). The word is indefinite, lit. "the letter," and determines nothing involved in controversy.

(2) A question much discussed is, Was "the bond" (RV) merely an acknowledgment of debt, or was it an obligation to pay a fixed annual rental from the produce of a farm? Edersheim, for instance, holds the former view, Lightfoot the latter. That the obligation is stated in the parable *in kind* —wheat and oil—and *not in money*—seems to bear against the simple debt theory. Edersheim sets down the remissions spoken of as authorized by the steward as amounting in money value to only about £5 and £25 respectively, and thinks they represented not a single but an annual payment (cf Kennedy, 1-vol *HDB,* and Fraser, *DCG,* art. "Bill").

(3) Still another question has arisen: Was the old "bond" simply altered, or was a new one substituted for it? Here again Lightfoot and Edersheim are in the controversy and on opposite sides. The alteration of the old bond is suggested though not demanded by the language here, and, moreover, would be, Edersheim thinks, in accordance with the probabilities of the case. Such bonds were usually written, not on vellum or papyrus, but on wax-covered tablets, and so could be easily erased or altered by the *stylus* with its flat, thick "eraser" (*mōḥēk*).

(4) It is probably safe to conclude: (*a*) that the "bill" or "bond" had to be written and signed by the person assuming the obligation; (*b*) that it was the only formal or legal evidence of the debt incurred; and (*c*) that the supervision of the whole transaction belonged of right to "the steward." Should "the steward" conspire with the debtor against the master, the latter, it would appear, would have no check against the fraud.

LITERATURE.—Lightfoot, *Hor. Heb.,* ed L. and T., II, 268–73; Edersheim, *Life and Times of Jesus the Messiah,* II, 272 ff; crit. comm. in loc.

GEO. B. EAGER

BILL OF DIVORCEMENT, di-vōrs'ment. See DIVORCE IN OT.

BILLOW, bil'o (גַּל, *gal,* "a great rolling wave"): Figuratively, of trouble, "All thy waves and thy billows are gone over me" (Ps **42** 7; cf Jon **2** 3).

BILSHAN, bil'shan (בִּלְשָׁן, *bilshān*): An Israelite who returned with Zerubbabel (Ezr **2** 2 = Neh **7** 7). The name may be explained as "inquirer" (new Heb and Aram.), בלשׁ, *bālash,* the ב (*b*) being an abbreviation of בֶּן, *ben,* as in בִּדְקַר, *bidhḳar,* and בִּמְהָל, *bimhāl.* Bilshan would then be a compound of בֶּן, *ben,* and לָשׁוֹן, *lāshōn.* J. Halévy (*Revue études juives,* X, 3) translates the name "père de la langue," אַב לָשׁוֹן, *'abh lāshōn.* In 1 Esd **5** 8, he is called "Beelsarus," which is akin to the form "Belshar" = "Belshar-uṣṣur" or "O Bel, protect the king." Bilshan points to "Belšun," "his lord." The rabbis take Bilshan as a surname to the preceding Mordecai. H. J. WOLF

BIMHAL, bim'hal (בִּמְהָל, *bimhāl*): A descendant of Asher (1 Ch **7** 33).

BIND, bīnd, **BOUND** (**δέω,** *déō*): There are a number of Heb words used to express this word in its various meanings, *'ālam* (Gen **37** 7), *'āṣar* (**42** 24), *ḳāshar* (Dt **6** 8). It sometimes means "to attach," "to fasten" (Ex **28** 28; Deut **14** 25). It was used also with reference to an agreement in a judicial sense (Nu **30** 2.3), or to make one a prisoner (Jgs **16** 10; Ps **149** 8). It means also "to control" (Job **38** 31).

Figurative: In a fig. sense, to bind heavy and burdensome (extra) so-called religious duties on men (Mt **23** 4). This fig. use of the word in Mt **16** 19 and **18** 18 has given special interest to it. Necessarily certain powers for administration must be conferred on this company of men to carry out the purpose of Christ. That this power was not conferred on Peter alone is evident from the fact that in Mt **18** 18 it is conferred on all the apostles. The use of the word in the NT is to declare a thing to be binding or obligatory (Jn **20** 23). In this sense this authority is used by some denominations in the service in preparation for the Lord's Supper, in which after the confession of sin by the people the ministers say, "I declare to you who have sincerely repented of your sins and believe on the Lord Jesus Christ the entire forgiveness of your sins." This statement is followed by the further declaration that if any have not so repented God will not forgive them, but will retain them and call them to account. The claim of the church of Rome that these statements of Our Lord confer on the priests and bishops, or primarily on the pope, the power to retain or forgive sins, is without historical validity and does violence to the Scriptures. See AUTHORITY; FORGIVENESS; PETER.

JACOB W. KAPP

BINEA, bin'ē-a (בִּנְעָא, *bin'āh*): A name in the genealogy of Benjamin (1 Ch **8** 37 = **9** 43).

BINNUI, bin'ū-ī (בִּנּוּי, *binnūy,* a proper name, "a building up"):

(1) A Levite, living in the time of Ezra (Ezr **8** 33; Neh **10** 9; **12** 8).

(2) One of the *b^enē Paḥath-mō'ābh* who had taken foreign wives (Ezr **10** 30—Balnuus of 1 Esd **9** 31) and one of the *b^enē Bānī* (Ezr **10** 38) who had also intermarried.

(3) The son of Henadad, who built part of the wall of Jerus (Neh **3** 24), and sealed the covenant with Nehemiah (Neh **10** 9). In all probability he is identical with "Bavvai, the son of Henadad" mentioned in **3** 18. "Bavvai" is either a corruption of "Binnui," or is the name of the Levitical house of which Bavvai was the chief representative.

Binnui is mentioned in **10** 9 as a leading Levite, and, besides, the names in these vs are obviously those of priests and Levites; so the former theory is probably correct.

(4) Head of a family who returned with Zerubbabel (Neh **7** 15; Ezr **2** 10). H. J. Wolf

BIRD-CATCHER, bûrd′kach-ẽr. See Fowler.

BIRDS, bûrds (עַיִט, *'ayiṭ;* Gr variously **τὰ πετεινά,** *tá peteiná* [Mt **13** 4], **τὰ ὄρνεα τοῦ οὐρανοῦ,** *tá órnea toú ouranoú* [Rev **19** 17], **ὄρνις,** *órnis* [Mt **23** 37; Lk **13** 34]; Lat *avis;* OE "brid"):

I. Meaning of the Word.—All authorities agree that the exact origin of the word bird, as we apply it to feathered creatures, is unknown.

1. In Early Hebrew

The Heb *'ayiṭ* means to "tear and scratch the face," and in its original form undoubtedly applied to birds of prey. It is probable that no spot of equal size on the face of the globe ever collected such numbers of vultures, eagles and hawks as ancient Pal. The land was so luxuriant that flocks and herds fed from the face of Nature. In cities, villages, and among tent-dwellers incessant slaughter went on for food, while the heavens must almost have been obscured by the ascending smoke from the burning of sacrificed animals and birds, required by law of every man and woman. From all these slain creatures the offal was thrown to the birds. There were no guns; the arrows of bowmen or "throw sticks" were the only protection against them, and these arms made no noise to frighten feathered creatures, and did small damage. So it easily can be seen that the birds would increase in large numbers and become so bold that men were often in actual conflict with them, and no doubt their faces and hands were torn and scratched.

Later, as birds of song and those useful for food came into their lives, the word was stretched to cover all feathered creatures.

2. In Later Usage

In the AV *'ayiṭ* is tr^d^ "fowl," and occurs several times: "And when the fowls came down upon the carcases, Abram drove them away" (Gen **15** 11). "They shall be left together unto the fowls of the mountains, and to the beasts of the earth; and the fowls shall summer upon them, and all the beasts of the earth shall winter upon them" (Isa **18** 6). "There is a path which no fowl knoweth, and which the vulture's eye hath not seen" (Job **28** 7). The ARV changes these and all other references to feathered creatures to "birds," making a long list. The Heb *'ayiṭ* in its final acceptance was used in Pal as "bird" is with us.

Our earliest known form of the word is the OE "brid," but they applied the term to the young of any creature.

3. In Old English

Later its meaning was narrowed to young produced from eggs, and the form changed to "bird."

II. Natural History of Birds.—The first known traces of birds appear in the formation of the Triassic period, and are found in the shape of footprints on the red sandstone of the Connecticut valley.

This must have been an ancient sea bed over which stalked large birds, leaving deeply imprinted impressions of their feet.

1. Earliest Traces and Specimens

These impressions baked in the sun, and were drifted full of fine wind-driven sand before the return of the tide. Thus were preserved to us the traces of 33 species of birds all of which are proven by their footprints to have been much larger than our birds of today. The largest impressions ever found measured 15 in. in length by 10 in width, and were set from 4 to 6 ft. apart. This evidence would form the basis for an estimate of a bird at least four times as large as an ostrich. That a bird of this size ever existed was not given credence until the finding of the remains of the dinornis in New Zealand. The largest specimen of this bird stood $10\frac{1}{2}$ ft. in height. The first complete skeleton of a bird was found in the limestone of the Jurassic period in Solenhofen, Bavaria. This bird had 13 teeth above and 3 below, each set in a separate socket, wings ending in three-fingered claws much longer than the claws of the feet, and a tail of 20 vertebrae, as long as the body, having a row of long feathers down each side of it, the specimen close to the size of a crow. The first preserved likeness of a bird was found frescoed on the inside of a tomb of Maydoon, and is supposed to antedate the time of Moses 3,000 years. It is now carefully preserved in the museum of Cairo. The painting represents six geese, four of which can be recognized readily as the ancestors of two species known today. Scientists now admit that Moses was right in assigning the origin of birds to the water, as their structure is closer reptilian than mammalian, and they reproduce by eggs. To us it seems a long stretch between the reptile with a frame most nearly bird-like and a feathered creature, but there is a possibility that forms making closer connection yet will be found.

The trunk of a bird is compact and in almost all instances boat-shaped. Without doubt prehistoric man conceived his idea of

2. Structural Formation

navigation and fashioned his vessel from the body of a water bird, and then noticed that a soaring bird steered its course with its tail and so added the rudder. The structural formation of a bird is so arranged as to give powerful flight and perfect respiration. In the case of a few birds that do not fly, the wings are beaten to assist in attaining speed in running, as the ostrich, or to help in swimming under the water, as the auk. The skull of a young bird is made up of parts, as is that of man or animal; but with age these parts join so evenly that they appear in a seamless formation. The jaws extend beyond the face, forming a bill that varies in length and shape with species, and it is used in securing food, in defence, feather dressing, nest building—in fact it is a combination of the mouth and hand of man. The spine is practically immovable, because of the ribs attached to the upper half and the bony structure supporting the pelvic joints of the lower. In sharp contrast with this the neck is formed of from 10 to 23 vertebrae, and is so flexible that a bird can turn its head completely around, a thing impossible to man or beast. The breast bone is large, strong, and provided with a ridge in the middle, largest in birds of strong flight, smallest in swimmers, and lacking only in birds that do not fly, as the ostrich. The wings correspond to the arms of man, and are now used in flight and swimming only. Such skeletons as the Archeopteryx prove that the bones now combined in the tip of the wing were once claws. This shows that as birds spread over land and developed wing power in searching longer distances for food or when driven by varying conditions of climate, the wings were used more in flight, and the claws gradually joined in a tip and were given covering that grew feathers, while the bill became the instrument for taking food and for defence. At the same time the long tail proving an incumbrance, it gradually wore away and contracted to the present form. Studied in detail of bony structure, muscle, and complicated arrangement of feathers of differing sizes, the wing of a bird proves one of Nature's marvels. The legs are used in walking or swimming, the thigh joint being so enveloped in the body that the true leg is often mistaken for it. This makes the knee of a man correspond to the heel of a bird, and in young birds of prey especially, the shank or tarsus is used in walking, until the bones harden and the birds are enabled to bear their weight on the feet and straighten the shank. The toes vary with species. Pliny classified birds by them: "The first and principal difference and distinction in birds is taken from their feet; for they have either hooked talons, as Hawkes, or long round claws as Hens, or else they be broad, flat and whole-footed as Geese." Flight is only possible to a bird when both wings are so nearly full-feathered that it balances perfectly. In sleep almost every bird places its head under its wing and stands on one foot. The arrangement by which this is accomplished, without tiring the bird in the least, is little short of miraculous and can be the result only of slow ages of evolution. In the most finished degree this provision for the comfort of the bird is found among cranes and other long-legged water birds. The bone of one part of the leg fits into the bone of the part above, so that it is practically locked into place with no exertion on the part of the bird. At the same time the muscles that work the claws, cross the joints of the leg so that they are stretched by the weight of the bird, and with no effort, it stands on earth or perches on a branch. This explains the question so frequently asked as to why the feet of a perching bird do not become so cramped and tired that it falls.

3. Birds' Food, Blood, etc

Birds feed according to their nature, some on prey taken alive, some on the carrion of dead bodies, some on fish and vegetable products of the water, some on fruit seed, insects and worms of the land. Almost every bird indulges in a combination of differing foods. Their blood is from 12° to 16° warmer than that of the rest of the animal kingdom, and they exhibit a corresponding exhilaration of spirits. Some indulge in hours of sailing and soaring, some in bubbling notes of song, while others dart near earth in playful dashes of flight. Birds are supposed to be rather deficient in the senses of taste and touch, and to have unusually keen vision. They reproduce by eggs that they deposit in a previously selected and prepared spot, and brood for a length of time varying with the species. The young of birds of prey, song birds, and some water birds, remain in the nests for differing lengths of time and are fed by the old birds; while others of the water birds and most of the game birds leave the nest as soon as the down is dry, and find food as they are taught by their elders, being sheltered at night so long as needful.

III. Birds of the Bible.—The birds of the Bible were the same species and form as exist in Pal today. Because of their wonderful coloring, powerful flight, joyous song, and their similarity to humanity in home-making and the business of raising their young, birds have been given much attention, and have held conspicuous place since the dawn of history. When the brain of man was young and more credulous than today he saw omens, signs and miracles in the characteristic acts of birds, and attributed to them various marvelous powers: some were considered of good omen and a blessing, and some were bad and a curse.

1. Earliest Mention

The historians of the Bible frequently used birds in comparison, simile, and metaphor. They are first mentioned in Gen **7** 14.15, "They, and every beast after its kind, and all the cattle after their kind, and every creeping thing that creepeth upon the earth after its kind, and every bird after its kind, every bird of every sort." This is the enumeration of the feathered creatures taken into the ark to be preserved for the perpetuation of species after the flood abated. They are next found in the description of the sacrifice of Abram, where it was specified that he was to use, with the animals slaughtered, a turtle dove and a young pigeon, the birds not to be divided. It is also recorded that the birds of prey were attracted by the carcases as described in Gen **15** 9–11, "And he said unto him, Take me a heifer three years old, and a she-goat three years old, and a ram three years old, and a turtle-dove, and a young pigeon. And he took him all these, and divided them in the midst, and laid each half over against the other: but the birds divided he not. And the birds of prey came down upon the carcasses, and Abram drove them away." Pal abounded in several varieties of "doves" (q.v.) and their devotion to each other, and tender, gentle characteristics had marked them as a loved possession of the land; while the clay cotes of pigeons were reckoned in establishing an estimate of a man's wealth.

2. Used in Sacrifice

In an abandon of gratitude to God these people offered of their best-loved and most prized possessions as sacrifice; and so it is not surprising to find the history of burnt offerings frequently mentioning these birds which were loved and prized above all others. Their use is first commanded in Lev **1** 14–17, "And if his oblation to Jeh be a burnt-offering of birds, then he shall offer his oblation of turtle-doves, or of young pigeons. And the priest shall bring it unto the altar, and wring off its head, and burn it on the altar; and the blood thereof shall be drained out on the side of the altar; and he shall take away its crop with the filth thereof, and cast it beside the altar on the east part, in the place of the ashes." Again in Lev **5** 7–10, we read: "And if his means suffice not for a lamb, then he shall bring his trespass-offering for that wherein he hath sinned, two turtle-doves, or two young pigeons, unto Jeh; one for a sin-offering, and the other for a burnt-offering." Throughout the Bible these birds figure in the history of sacrifice (Lev **12** 8; **14** 4–8; Nu **6** 10, etc).

3. Other References

The custom of weaving cages of willow wands, in which to confine birds for pets, seems to be referred to when Job asks (**41** 5),

> "Wilt thou play with him as with a bird?
> Or wilt thou bind him for thy maidens?"

See Job **12** 7:

> "But ask now the beasts, and they shall teach thee;
> And the birds of the heavens, and they shall tell thee."

David was thinking of the swift homeward flight of an eagle when he wrote:

> "In Jehovah do I take refuge:
> How say ye to my soul,
> Flee as a bird to your mountain?" (Ps **11** 1).

His early days guarding the flocks of his father no doubt suggested to him the statement found in Ps **50** 11:

> "I know all the birds of the mountains;
> And the wild beasts of the field are mine"
> (RVm "in my mind").

In describing Lebanon, the Psalmist wrote of its waters:

> "By them the birds of the heavens have their habitation;
> They sing among the branches" (**104** 12).

He mentioned its trees:

> "Where the birds make their nests:
> As for the stork, the fir-trees are her house" (**104** 17).

See also **78** 27; **148** 10.

The origin of the oft-quoted phrase, "A little bird told me," can be found in Eccl **10** 20: "Revile not the king, no, not in thy thought; and revile not the rich in thy bedchamber: for a bird of the heavens shall carry the voice, and that which hath wings shall tell the matter." In a poetical description of spring in the Song of Solomon, we read:

"The flowers appear on the earth;
The time of the singing of birds is come,
And the voice of the turtle-dove is heard in our land"
(Cant **2** 12).

In his prophecy concerning Ethiopia, Isaiah wrote, "They shall be left together unto the ravenous birds of the mountains, and to the beasts of the earth; and the ravenous birds shall summer upon them, and all the beasts of the earth shall winter upon them" (Isa **18** 6). In foretelling God's judgment upon Babylon, Isaiah (**46** 11) refers to Cyrus as "a ravenous bird [called] from the east, the man of my counsel from a far country"; "probably in allusion to the fact that the griffon was the emblem of Persia; and embroidered on its standard" (*HDB*, I, 632); (see EAGLE). Jer **4** 25 describes the habit of birds, which invariably seek shelter before an approaching storm. In His denunciation of Israel, Jeh questions, in Jer **12** 9, "Is my heritage unto me as a speckled bird of prey? are the birds of prey against her round about?" When Jeremiah threatened the destruction of Jerus, he wrote that Jeh would "cause them to fall by the sword before their enemies, and by the hand of them that seek their life: and their dead bodies will I give to be food for the birds of the heavens" (**19** 7): that is, He would leave them for the carrion eaters. Ezekiel threatens the same fate to the inhabitants of Gog (**39** 4.17). Hosea (**9** 11) prophesies of Ephraim, "Their glory shall fly away like a bird." In the Sermon on the Mount, Jesus mentions the birds, as recorded by Mt **6** 26: "Behold the birds of the heaven, that they sow not, neither do they reap, nor gather into barns; and your heavenly Father feedeth them. Are not ye of much more value than they?" In the sermon from the boat where He spoke the parable of the Sower He again mentioned the birds: "As he sowed, some seeds fell by the way side, and the birds came and devoured them" (**13** 4). Mark describes the same sermon in **4** 4, and ver 32 of the same ch quotes the parable of the Mustard Seed: "Yet when it is sown, [it] groweth up, and becometh greater than all the herbs, and putteth out great branches; so that the birds of the heaven can lodge under the shadow thereof." In **8** 5, Luke gives his version of the parable of the Sower, and in **13** 19 of the Mustard Seed. See also Rev **19** 17.21. These constitute all the important references to birds in the Bible, with the exception of a few that seem to belong properly under such subjects as TRAPS; NETS; CAGES, etc.

GENE STRATTON-PORTER

BIRDS OF ABOMINATION. See ABOMINATION, BIRDS OF.

BIRDS OF PREY, prā: They were undoubtedly the first birds noticed by the compilers of Bib. records. They were camp followers, swarmed over villages and perched on the walls of cities. They were offensive in manner and odor, and of a boldness unknown to us in birds. They flocked in untold numbers, there was small defence against them, and the largest and strongest not only carried away meat prepared for food and sacrifice, but also preyed upon the much-prized house pigeons, newly born of the smaller animals, and even at times attacked young children. See Gen **15** 11, "And the birds of prey came down upon the carcasses, and Abram drove them away." Because they were attracted from above the clouds by anything suitable for food, people recognized that these were birds of unusual vision. When Job wanted to tell how perfectly the path to the gold mine was concealed, he wrote, "That path no bird of prey knoweth" (Job **28** 7). The inference is, that, if it were so perfectly concealed that it escaped the piercing eyes of these birds, it was not probable that man would find it. These birds were so strong, fierce and impudent that everyone feared them, and when the prophets gave warning that people would be left for birds of prey to ravage, they fully understood what was meant, and they were afraid (Isa **18** 6). In His complaint against His heritage, Jeh questions, "Is my heritage unto me as a speckled bird of prey? are the birds of prey against her round about?" (Jer **12** 9). And when he prophesied the destruction of Jerus, Jeremiah painted a dreadful picture, but one no doubt often seen in that land of pillage and warfare: "Their dead bodies will I give to be food for the birds of the heavens, and for the beasts of the earth" (**19** 7). GENE STRATTON-PORTER

BIRDS, UNCLEAN, un-klēn′: The lists of birds forbidden as food are given in Lev **11** 13–19 and Dt **14** 12–18. The names are almost identical, Dt containing one more than Lev and varying the order slightly. In Dt **14** 13 the first name, *hā-rā'āh*, is almost certainly a corruption of *ha-dā'āh*, the first name in Lev **11** 14. In ARV it is tr[d] "kite" in Lev, while in Dt it is tr[d] "glede." The additional one in Dt is *ha-dayyāh*, and is tr[d] "kite." Doubtless the three words, *ha-dā'āh*, *hā-'ayyāh* and *ha-dayyāh*, are generic and refer to different birds of the kite or perhaps falcon family, so it is impossible to give specific meanings to them. There are twenty-one names in all, counting the extra one in Dt. The tr of many of these words is disputed. The ARV gives them as follows: eagle, gier eagle, ospray, kite, falcon, glede, every raven, ostrich, night-hawk, sea-mew, hawk, little owl, cormorant, great owl, horned owl, pelican, vulture, stork, heron, hoopoe and bat. It will be observed that all of them are either carrion-eaters, birds of prey, or water fowl. The names of those birds which may be eaten are not given, the principle of classification is that of elimination. No principle of separation is given as is the case with the animals. The reason for the prohibition doubtless lies in the unsanitary and repulsive nature of the flesh of these birds, the Divine command endorsing the instincts which were repelled by such food. For particulars, see separate arts. on each of these birds. See also ABOMINATION, BIRDS OF. JAMES JOSIAH REEVE

BIRSHA, bûr′sha (בִּרְשַׁע, *birsha'*): King of Gomorrah (Gen **14** 2), who joined the league against Chedorlaomer. The name is probably corrupt; some have tried to explain it as בְּרֶשַׁע, *b[e]resha'*, "with wickedness," a name purposely used by the writer in referring to this king.

BIRTH, bûrth (γένεσις, *génesis*):

(1) It was said by the angel beforehand of John the Baptist, "Many shall rejoice at his *birth*"; and when he was born Elisabeth said, "Thus hath the Lord done unto me . . . . to take away my reproach among men" (Lk **1** 14.25). Among the ancient Hebrews barrenness was a "reproach," and the birth of a child, of a son esp., an occasion for rejoicing.

(2) This, no doubt, was due in part to the Messianic hope inspired and sustained by prophecy (see Gen **3** 15, where it was foretold that the seed of the woman should bruise the serpent's head; and subsequent prophecies too numerous to mention). Cases in point worth studying are found in Gen **4** 1, where Eve rejoices over the birth of her firstborn and cries, "I have gotten a man with the help of

Jeh"; and 1 S **1** 20, where Hannah exults over her firstborn, calling his name "Samuel," "because," she says, "I have asked him of Jeh."

(3) The marvelous passage in Isa **7** 14, "Behold, a virgin shall conceive, and bear a son, and shall call his name Immanuel," must have intensified the longing and hope of every devout Jewish maiden to be a mother, if mayhap, under God, she might be the mother of Messiah—*Immanuel!* (Cf Mt **1** 22. 23; Lk **1** 13 f.) See JESUS CHRIST; VIRGIN BIRTH.

GEO. B. EAGER

BIRTH, NEW. See REGENERATION.

BIRTH, VIRGIN. See VIRGIN BIRTH.

BIRTHDAY, bûrth'dā:

(1) The custom of observing birthdays of great men, esp. of kings, was widespread in ancient times (see Gen **40** 20 f, "the third day, which was Pharaoh's *birthday*," etc; cf 2 Macc **6** 7; and Herod. ix.110; in the NT, Mt **14** 6; Mk **6** 21, "Herod on his *birthday* made a supper to his lords," etc, i.e. Herod Antipas). Here we see the ancient custom reflected in two conspicuous instances cents. apart: (*a*) Pharaoh, on his *birthday* "made a feast unto all his servants," etc, and (*b*) Herod on his *birthday* "made a supper to his lords, and the high captains," etc. The AV (Mt **14** 6) has it "when Herod's *birthday* was kept," etc.

The correct text here (Tisch., HH) has a very peculiar construction, but without material difference of meaning. The locative case gives the time of the principal action, "danced on Herod's birthday, when it occurred." The construction is not unexampled (see Jelf, §699). This need not be called "a case absolute," though it corresponds to the Lat ablative (locative) absolute; and the Gr genitive absolute is itself not really "absolute," i.e. it is not cut loose from the rest of the construction, but gives some event to which the principal action is referred, for the indication of its circumstances.

(2) The term "birthday" (τὰ γενέσια, *tá genésia*) was applied also to the anniversary of a king's accession to the throne (Edersheim); but Wieseler's argument that such is the case here is not conclusive. It is easy to suppose that when Herod's birthday approached he was sojourning at the castle of Machaerus, accompanied by leading military and civil officials of his dominions (Mk **6** 21). Petty ruler as he was, not properly "king" at all, he affected kingly ways (cf Est **5** 3.6; **7** 2).

(3) *Genesia*, which in Attic Gr means the commemoration of the dead, in later Gr is interchangeable with *genéthlia* = "birthday celebrations"; and there is no good reason why the rendering of the AV and RV here, "birthday," should not be right. (See Swete on Mk **6** 21, and *HDB*, s.v.) For date of Christ's birth, etc, see JESUS CHRIST; CALENDAR, etc.

GEO. B. EAGER

BIRTHRIGHT, bûrth'rīt (בְּכֹרָה, *b^e^khōrāh*, from *b^e^khōr*, "firstborn"; **πρωτοτόκια,** *prōtotókia*): Birthright is the right which naturally belonged to the firstborn son. Where there were more wives than one, the firstborn was the son who in point of time was born before the others, apparently whether his mother was a wife or a concubine. Sarah protests against Ishmael being heir along with Isaac, but it is possible that the bestowal of the rights of the firstborn on Isaac was not due to any law, but rather to the influence of a favorite wife (Gen **21** 10). The birthright of the firstborn consisted in the first place of a double portion of what his father had to leave. This probably means that he had a double share of such property as could be divided. We have no certain knowledge of the manner in which property was inherited in the patriarchal age, but it seems probable that the lands and flocks which were the possession of the family as a whole, remained so after the death of the father. The firstborn became head of the family and thus succeeded to the charge of the family property, becoming responsible for the maintenance of the younger sons, the widow or widows, and the unmarried daughters. He also, as head, succeeded to a considerable amount of authority over the other members. Further, he generally received the blessing, which placed him in close and favored covenant-relationship with Jeh. According to the accounts which have come down to us, all these gifts and privileges could be diverted from the firstborn son. This could happen with his own consent, as in the case of Esau, who sold his birthright to Jacob (Gen **25** 29–34), or by the decision of the father, as in the case of Reuben (Gen **48** 22; **49** 3.4; 1 Ch **5** 1.2) and of Shimri (1 Ch **26** 10). In the Deuteronomic version of the law, a provision is made, prohibiting the father from making the younger son the possessor of the birthright, just because his mother was specially beloved (Dt **21** 15–17). The blessing also could be diverted from the eldest son. This was done when Jacob blessed the children of Joseph, and deliberately put the younger before the elder (Gen **48** 13.14.17–19); even when the blessing was obtained by the younger son in a fraudulent manner, it could not be recalled (Gen **27**). Jacob does not appear to have inherited any of the property of his father, although he had obtained both the birthright and the blessing.

In the NT "birthright," *prototokia*, is mentioned only once (He **12** 16), where the reference is to Esau. In various passages where Our Lord is spoken of as the firstborn, as in Col **1** 15–19; He **1** 2, the association of ideas with the OT conception of birthright is easy to trace. See also FIRST-BORN; FAMILY; HEIR; INHERITANCE; LAW.

J. MACARTNEY WILSON

BIRTH-STOOL, bûrth'stōōl: Found only in Ex **1** 16, in connection with Heb women in Egypt when oppressed by Pharaoh. The Heb (*'ŏbhnayīm*) here rendered "birth-stool" is used in Jer **18** 3, and is there rendered "potter's wheel." The word is used in both places in the dual form, which points, no doubt, to the fact that the potter's wheel was composed of two discs, and suggests that the birth-stool was similarly double. See STOOL.

BIRZAITH, bûr-zā'ith, AV **Birzavith,** bûr-zā'vith (בִּרְזָוִת, בִּרְזָיִת, *birzāwith* or *birzāyith;* **Βηζαίθ,** *Bēzaíth*, or **Βερζαίε,** *Berzaíe*): The name of a town in Asher founded by Malchiel (1 Ch **7** 31). It probably corresponds to the modern *Bīr ez-Zait*, "well of olive oil," near Tyre.

BISHLAM, bish'lam (בִּשְׁלָם, *bishlām*, "peaceful" [?]): One of three foreign colonists who wrote a letter of complaint against the Jews to Artaxerxes (Ezr **4** 7=1 Esd **2** 16). In 1 Esd the reading is "Bēlemus." "And in the days of Artaxerxes wrote Bishlam, Mithredath, Tabeel, and the rest of his companions, unto Artaxerxes, king of Persia," etc (Ezr **4** 7). The LXX renders Bishlam *en eirēnē*, "in peace," as though it were a phrase rather than a proper name; this is clearly an error.

BISHOP, bish'up: The word is evidently an abbreviation of the Gr **ἐπίσκοπος,** *episkopos;* Lat *episcopus*.

GENERAL

1. Use in the LXX and Classic Gr

The LXX gives it the generic meaning of "superintendency, oversight, searching" (Nu **4** 16; **31** 14) in matters pertaining to the church, the state, and the army (Jgs **9** 28; 2 K **12** 11; 2 Ch **34** 12.17; 1 Macc **1** 54; Wisd **1** 6). Nor is it unknown to classical Gr. Thus Homer in the *Iliad* applied it to the gods (xxii.255), also Plutarch, *Cam.*, 5. In Athens the governors of conquered states were called by this name.

2. NT Use

The word is once applied to Christ himself, "unto the Shepherd and Bishop of your souls" (1 Pet **2** 25). It abounds in Pauline lit., and is used as an alternative for *presbúteros* or elder (Tit **1** 5.7; 1 Tim **3** 1; **4** 14; **5** 17.19). The earliest ecclesiastical offices instituted in the church were those of elders and deacons, or rather the reverse, inasmuch as the latter office grew almost immediately out of the needs of the Christian community at Jerus (Acts **6** 1–6). The presbyteral constitution of Jerus must have been very old (Acts **11** 30) and was distinct from the apostolate (Acts **15** 2.4.6.22. 23; **16** 4). As early as 50 AD Paul appointed "elders" in every church, with prayer and fasting (Acts **14** 23), referring to the Asiatic churches before established. But in writing to the Philippians (**1** 1) he speaks of "bishops" and "deacons." In the gentile Christian churches this title evidently had been adopted; and it is only in the Pastoral Epistles that we find the name "presbyters" applied. The name "presbyter" or "elder," familiar to the Jews, signifies their age and place in the church; while the other term "bishop" refers rather to their office. But both evidently have reference to the same persons. Their office is defined as "ruling" (Rom **12** 8), "overseeing" (Acts **20** 17.28; 1 Pet **5** 2), caring for the flock of God (Acts **20** 28). But the word *archein*, "to rule," in the hierarchical sense, is never used. Moreover each church had a college of presbyter-bishops (Acts **20** 17.28; Phil **1** 1; 1 Tim **4** 14). During Paul's lifetime the church was evidently still unaware of the distinction between presbyters and bishops.

Of a formal **ordination,** in the later hierarchical sense, there is no trace as yet. The word "ordained" used in the AV (Acts **1** 22) is an unwarrantable interpolation, rightly emended in the RV. Neither the word *cheirotonēsantes* (Acts **14** 23, tr[d] "appointed" ARV) nor *katastēsēs* (Tit **1** 5, tr[d] "appoint" ARV) is capable of this tr. In rendering these words invariably by "ordain," the AV shows a *vitium originis.* No one doubts that the idea of ordination is extremely old in the history of the church, but the laying on of hands, mentioned in the NT (Acts **13** 3; 1 Tim **4** 14; 2 Tim **1** 6; cf Acts **14** 26; **15** 40) points to the communication of a spiritual gift or to its invocation, rather than to the imparting of an official status.

3. Later Development of the Idea

According to Rome, as finally expressed by the Council of Trent, and to the episcopal idea in general, the hierarchical organization, which originated in the 3d cent., existed from the beginning in the NT church. But besides the NT as above quoted, the early testimony of the church maintains the identity of "presbyters" and "bishops." Thus Clement of Rome (*Ep.* 1, chs 42, 44, 57), the *Did*, ch 15; perhaps the *Constitutions*, II, 33, 34, in the use of the pl. form; Irenaeus (*Adv. Haer.*, iii.2, 3), Ambrosiaster (on 1 Tim **3** 10; Eph **4** 11), Chrysostom (Hom 9 in *Ep. ad Tim*), in an unequivocal statement, the "presbyters of old were called bishops . . . . and the bishops presbyters," equally unequivocally Jerome (*Ad Tit*, 1, 7), "the same is the presbyter, who is also the bishop." Augustine and other Fathers of the 4th and 5th cents. hold this view, and even Peter Lombard, who preceded Aquinas as the great teacher of the church of the Middle Ages. Hatch of Oxford and Harnack of Berlin, in the face of all this testimony, maintain a distinction between the presbyters, as having charge of the law and discipline of the church, and the bishops, as being charged with the pastoral care of the church, preaching and worship. This theory is built upon the argument of prevailing social conditions and institutions, as adopted and imitated by the church, rather than on sound textual proof. The distinction between presbyters and bishops can only be maintained by a forced exegesis of the Scriptures. The later and rapid growth of the hierarchical idea arose from the accession of the Ebionite Christian view of the church, as a necessary continuation of the OT dispensation, which has so largely influenced the history of the inner development of the church in the first six cents. of her existence.

HENRY E. DOSKER

ANGLICAN VIEW

I. Episcopacy Defined.—*Episcopacy* is the government in the Christian church by bishops. The rule of the Orthodox churches in the East, of the Roman Catholics, and of the Anglicans is that the consecration of other bishops, and the ordination of priests and deacons can only be by a bishop; and with them, a bishop is one who claims historic descent from apostolic or sub-apostolic times.

II. Offices in the Early Church.—In the NT, the office of bishop is not clearly defined. Indeed there appear to have been many degrees of ministry in the infant church: apostles, prophets, evangelists, teachers, presbyters or elders, bishops or overseers, and deacons.

Due allowance is not generally made for the mental attitude of the apostles and early Christians. They were looking for the speedy return of Christ, and consequently did not organize the church in its infancy, as it was afterward found necessary to do. For this reason, while the different persons who composed the body of Christian ministers did not overlap or infringe on each other's work, yet the relative rank or priority of each minister was not clearly defined.

1. Apostles

The apostles were undoubtedly first, and in them rested the whole authority, and they were the depository of the power committed unto them by Christ.

2. Prophets

Next to the apostles in rank, and first in point of mention (Acts **11** 27), came the prophets. So important were these officers in the early church that they were sent from Jerus to warn the rapidly growing church at Antioch of an impending famine. Then it appears that there were resident prophets at Antioch, men of considerable importance since their names are recorded, Barnabas, Symeon, Lucius, Manaen and Saul (Acts **13** 1). These men received a command from the Holy Spirit to "separate me Barnabas and Saul," on whom they laid their hands and sent them forth on their work. The election is conducted on the same lines as the election by the eleven apostles of St. Matthias, and Barnabas and Paul are hereafter called apostles. It is an ordination to the highest order in the Christian ministry by "prophets and teachers." Whether "prophets and teachers" refers to two distinct ministries, or whether they are terms used for the same one is uncertain. It may be that of the five men mentioned, some were prophets, and others teachers.

In Acts **15** 32 we have given us the names of two other prophets, Judas and Silas. St. Paul tells the Corinthians (1 Cor **12** 28) that God hath set some in his church, first apostles, secondly prophets, thirdly teachers, and writing to the Ephesians he places the prophets in the same rank. "He gave some, apostles; and some, prophets; and some, evangelists; and some, pastors and teachers; for the perfecting of the saints, for the work of the ministry" (Eph **4** 11.12 AV). And again, he says that the mystery of Christ is now "revealed unto his holy apostles and prophets in the Spirit" (Eph

3 5). The same apostle in that wonderful imagery of Christians being built up for a habitation of God, says they are "being built upon the foundation of the apostles and prophets, Christ Jesus himself being the chief corner stone" (Eph **2** 20).

In the case of the ordination of Timothy, which St. Paul says distinctly was by his own laying on of hands and that of the presbytery, it is of great consequence to note that St. Paul says to Timothy that his ordination was "according to the prophecies which went before on thee" (1 Tim **1** 18 AV). From this it would appear that the prophets, as in the case of St. Paul himself, guided by the Holy Ghost, chose Timothy for the overseership or bishopric, or it may be, which is just as likely, that Timothy was set apart by the laying on of hands by some prophets, to the rank of elder or presbyter which did not carry with it the "overseership." It is at any rate evident that in the selection of Timothy St. Paul is insistent on pointing out that it was through the prophets (cf 1 Tim **1** 18; **4** 14; 2 Tim **1** 6).

In Revelation, the term prophet constantly occurs as a term denoting rank equivalent to that of apostle: "ye saints, and ye apostles, and ye prophets" (Rev **18** 20); "blood of prophets and of saints" (Rev **16** 6; **18** 24). The angel calls himself "thy fellow-servant, and of thy brethren the prophets" (Rev **22** 9 AV). The words prophesy and prophesying are used in a general sense, and it does not mean that they were in every case the formal utterances of prophets.

3. Elders or Presbyters

The ministry of the elders of the Christian church was modeled after that of the synagogue in which there were elders and teachers. The Christian elders or presbyters were most likely a council of advice in each local Christian *ecclesia*. They appear to act conjointly and not separately (Acts **15** 4.6.22; **16** 4; **20** 17; Jas **5** 14).

4. Teachers

Teachers were the equivalent of those teachers or catechists of the synagogue before whom Our Lord was found in the temple. Evangelists were persons who probably had the gift of oratory and whose function it was to preach the glad tidings. Philip was one of them (Acts **21** 8). In the instructions

5. Evangelists

to Timothy he is bidden to do the work of an evangelist, that is to say, to preach the gospel. This was to be part of his work in the ministry.

In writing to Timothy, St. Paul twice says that he himself was ordained preacher, and apostle and teacher. This does not mean that he held three grades of the ministry, but that his duties as an apostle were to preach and to teach. The fact that the apostles called themselves elders does not thereby confirm the view that the bishops mentioned by them were not superior to elders, any more than the fact that the apostles called themselves teachers, or preachers, makes for the view that teachers, or preachers, were the equals of apostles.

6. Bishops

Bishops or overseers were probably certain elders chosen out of the body of local elders. Under the Jewish dispensation, the elders stayed at home, that is, they did no ministerial visiting, but it was soon found necessary as the Christian church grew to have someone to attend to outside work to win over by persuasion and exposition of the Scriptures those inclined to embrace Christianity. This necessitated visiting families in their own homes. Then, it became necessary to shepherd the sheep. Someone had to oversee or superintend the general work. The Jewish elders always had a head and in a large synagogue the conditions laid down for its head, or *legatus*, were almost identical with those laid down by St. Paul to Timothy. He was to be a father of a family, not rich or engaged in business, possessing a good voice, apt to teach, etc.

The term *episkopos* was one with which the Hellenistic Jews and Gentiles were well acquainted; and it became thus a fitting term by which to designate the men called out of the body of elders to this special work of oversight. Then, again, the term *episkopos* was endeared to the early Christians as the one applied to Our Lord—"the Shepherd and Bishop of your souls" (1 Pet **2** 25). The duties of elders, or presbyters, are not clearly defined in the NT.

In the Acts, the term is found only twice, one in reference to Judas, "his bishopric [or overseership] let another take" (Acts **1** 20 AV), and in St. Paul's address to the elders of Ephesus, he warns them to feed the church over which they have been made overseers or bishops (Acts **20** 28). It is impossible to say whether this "overseership" refers to all the elders addressed, or to such of those elders as had been made "overseers," or "bishops."

In the epistles, we find the church more clearly organized, and in these writings we find more definite allusions to bishops and their duties (Phil **1** 1; 1 Tim **3** 1.2; Tit **1** 7; 1 Pet **2** 25).

St. Paul tells Timothy, "If a man desire the office of a bishop [or overseer] he desireth a good work." "A bishop [or overseer] must be blameless" (1 Tim **3** 1.2 AV). He tells Titus that "he is to ordain elders in every city" and that a "bishop must be blameless, as the steward of God" (Tit **1** 5.7 AV).

On the other hand, there are numerous texts where elders and their duties are mentioned and where there is no reference whatever to bishopric or oversight. The epistles show that of necessity there had grown to be a more distinct organization of the ministry, and that following the custom of the synagogue to some of the elders had been committed a bishopric or oversight. At the same time the rank of a bishop, or overseer, was not yet one of the highest. St. Paul does not enumerate it in the order of ministry which he gives to the Ephesians—apostles, prophets, evangelists, pastors and teachers.

That Timothy had an oversight over the elders or presbyters is evident from the fact that St. Paul enjoins him to rebuke those that sin: "Against an elder receive not an accusation, except at the mouth of two or three witnesses. Them that sin reprove in the sight of all" (1 Tim **5** 19.20). This, of course, refers to a formal trial by one in authority of persons inferior to him in rank.

It has been asserted that the terms elder and bishop in the NT were equivalent and denoted the same office or grade in the ministry. This assertion seems unwarranted. They do not naturally denote the same grade any more than do apostle and teacher, or angel and prophet.

7. Deacons

The deacons were the seven appointed to take charge of the temporal affairs of the church. Their appointment was perhaps suggested by the alms-collectors of the synagogue. In the NT they do not appear as deacons to have had any part in the sacred ministry, except, in the case of Philip the evangelist, if it be assumed that he was a deacon, which is uncertain. Nowhere is it recorded that they laid hands on anyone, or were considered as capable of bestowing any grace. In the epistles they are mentioned with the bishops—"bishops and deacons" (Phil **1** 1), thus showing the nature of their influence as the helpers of the "bishops" in the management of the growing funds, or properties of the church.

III. Episcopacy according to the NT.—The passages where the Gr word occurs which has been tr[d] either as bishops, or overseers, are so few that they are enumerated: Acts **20** 17.28: the Ephesian elders are stated to be bishops [or overseers] to feed the church; Phil **1** 1: the salutation of Paul and Timothy to bishops [or overseers] and deacons at Philippi; 1 Tim **3** 1.2 and Tit **1** 7 give the exhortation to Timothy and Titus as holding the office of a bishop; 1 Pet **2** 25, where the apostle referring to Christ says, "unto the Shepherd and Bishop of your souls."

IV. The "Didache."—Passing out of the NT, we come to the early Christian writing, the so-called Teaching of the Twelve Apostles. Setting aside the question for what class of Christians this document was intended, the clear fact stands out that at the date of its writing the two highest grades in the Christian ministry were still called apostles and prophets. Various dates have been assigned to this document ranging from 80 to 160 AD.

At the end of ch **10**, which deals with the thanksgiving or eucharist, the remark is made, "But permit the prophets to make thanksgiving as much as they desire." Chs **11** and **13** deal with apostles and prophets. They were to be treated "according to the ordinance of the gospel." An apostle was not to be allowed to stay more than a couple of days at the utmost, and in no case was he to receive any money, else he was to be considered "a false prophet." A prophet could beg on behalf of others, but not for himself; but a prophet could settle among a congregation, and in that case he was to receive the same first-fruits "of money and raiment and of every possession" as the chief priest did under the old dispensation. It is to be noted that in reality the prophets, though placed second in order, were to be treated with the greater respect. If the prophet settles down, he becomes the man of the first rank in that Christian community.

Ch **15** deals with bishops and deacons, and we are told that if appointed they rendered the ministry of prophets and teachers, but the warning is given, "Despise them not, therefore, for they are your honoured ones, together with the prophets and teachers." This shows that bishops were localized; and that while they could be appointed over a community, they were not considered as of equal rank with the prophets.

V. Clement of Rome.—Clement of Rome in his Epistle to the Corinthians says that the apostles preaching through countries and cities appointed the first-fruits of their labors to be bishops and deacons (ch **42**). It is usually said that Clement meant elders by the term "bishops," but it is much more likely that he meant what he said; that according to the tradition received by him, the apostles appointed bishops, that is, appointed bishops out of the elders—mentioned in the Acts. In ch **44** Clement warns against the sin of ejecting from the episcopate those who have presented the offerings, and says, "Blessed are those presbyters who have finished their course."

The reason why the terms apostles and prophets fell into desuetude was, as regards the first, not so much out of respect to the original apostles, but because the apostles in the sub-apostolic age became apparently only wandering evangelists of little standing; while the prophets lowered their great office by descending to be soothsayers, as the Shepherd of Hermas plainly intimates. With the fall of the apostles and the prophets, there rose into prominence the bishops and deacons.

VI. Bishops and Deacons.—The deacons acted as secretaries and treasurers to the bishops. They were their right-hand men, representing them in all secular matters. As the numbers of Christians increased, it was found absolutely necessary for the bishops to delegate some of their spiritual authority to a second order.

VII. Bishops and Presbyters (Priests).—Thus very slowly emerged out of the body of elders the official presbyters or priests. To them the bishop delegated the power to teach, to preach, to baptize, to celebrate the Holy Eucharist; but how slowly is evidenced by the fact that so late as 755 AD the Council of Vern forbade priests to baptize, except by distinct permission of their bishop.

VIII. Ignatian Epistles on the Three Orders.—When we come to the Ignatian epistles written between 110–17 AD, we find a distinct threefold order. We have given us the names of Damas, for bishop, Bassus and Apollonius for presbyters, Zotion for deacon. Throughout these epistles there is no question that the bishop is supreme. Apostles and prophets are not even mentioned. The bishop succeeds to all the powers the apostles and prophets had. On the other hand, as with the Jewish elders, so with the Christian presbyters, they form a council with the bishop. Here we see in clear day what we had all along suspected to be the case in apostolic times: a council of presbyters with a ruler at their head and deacons to attend to money matters.

It is quite immaterial as to whether a bishop had ten or a hundred presbyter-elders under him, whether he was bishop in a small town or in a large city. The question of numbers under him would not affect his authority as has been claimed. The greatness of the city in which he exercised this rule would add dignity to his position, but nothing to his inherent authority.

From this time on it is admitted by all that bishops, priests and deacons have been continuously in existence. Their powers and duties have varied, have been curtailed as one order has encroached on the power of the other, but still there the three orders have been. Gradually the presbyters or priests encroached on the power of the bishop, till now, according to Anglican usage, only the power of ordaining, confirming and consecrating churches is left to them.

IX. Views of Reformers.—At the time of the Reformation there was a great outcry against bishops. This was caused by the fact that under feudalism the bishops had come to be great temporal lords immersed in schemes of political and material aggrandizement, and often actually leading their armies in times of war. Many of the bishops were proud and arrogant, forgetful that their duties as fathers of the children of Christ were to look after those committed to them with fatherly kindness and charity or that as pastors they had to tend the erring sheep with Divine patience and infinite love.

The bulk of the adherents to the Reformed religion, looking upon the bishops as they were and as their fathers had known them, recoiled from retaining the office, although their principal men, like Calvin, deplored the loss of bishops, and hoped that bishops of the primitive order would some day be restored. The present modern Anglican bishop seems to sum up in his person and office the requirements laid down by Calvin.

Conclusion

Thus the claim put forth by the Anglicans in the preface to the Ordinal may be considered as sound: "It is evident unto all men, diligently reading Holy Scripture and ancient Authors, that from the Apostles' time there have been these Orders of Ministers in Christ's Church—Bishops, Priests, and Deacons."

LITERATURE.—Teaching of the Twelve Apostles; Clement of Rome; Shepherd of Hermas; Ignatian epistles; Muratorian Fragment; Works of John Lightfoot; Duchesne, *Origines du Culte Chrétien;* Pellicia, *Polity of the Christian Church;* Bishop MacLean, *Ancient Church Orders;* Cheetham, *Hist of the Christian Church during the First Six Cents.;* Salmon, *Intro to NT;* Elwin, *The Minister of Baptism;* Cruttwell, *Literary Hist of Early Christianity;* Potter, *Church Government;* Lowndes, *Vindication of Anglican Orders;* E. Hatch, *The Organization of the Early Christian Churches;* C. Gore, *The Church and the Ministry;* Thompson, *Historic Episcopate* (Presbyterian); Baird, *Huguenots.*

ARTHUR LOWNDES

CONGREGATIONAL VIEW

1. The NT Church a Spiritual Democracy

As a spiritual and social democracy, Congregationalism finds no warrant or precedent in the NT for the episcopal conception of the words "bishop," "presbyter," and "elder." It interprets ἐπίσκοπος, *epískopos*, lit. as *overseer*—not an ecclesiastical dignitary but a spiritual minister. It finds the Romanist view of Peter's primacy, founded alone on Mt **16** 18, contradicted by the entire trend of Christ's teaching, as e.g. when referring to the Gentiles exercising *lordship* and *authority* Christ says, "Not so shall it be among you" (Mt **20** 26 ff). He set the precedent of official greatness when He said "the Son of man came not to be ministered unto, but to minister," and that "whosoever would become great among you shall be your minister [servant]." Paul's testimony confirms this in suggesting no primacy among the apostles and prophets, but making "Christ . . . . himself . . . . the chief corner stone" (Eph **2** 20). The organization and history of the early Christian church establish this view of its simplicity and democracy. In Acts **1** 20 the RV corrects the rendering "bishopric" (given by the King James translators, who were officers in the Episcopal church) to "office," thus relieving the verse of possible ecclesiastical pretensions.

The church formed on the day of Pentecost was the *spontaneous* coming together of the original 120 disciples and the 3,000 Christian converts, for fellowship, worship and work, under the inspiration and guidance of the Holy Spirit. Its only creed was belief in the risen Christ and the renewing power of the Holy Spirit; its only condition of membership, repentance and baptism.

2. Election of Officers by Popular Vote

The apostles naturally took leadership but, abrogating all authority, committed to the church as a whole the choice of its officers and the conduct of its temporal and spiritual affairs. Judas' place in the apostolate was not filled by succession or episcopal appointment (Acts **1** 23–26). The seven deacons were elected by popular vote (Acts **6** 1–6). One of the seven—Philip—preached and, without protest, administered the rite of baptism (Acts **8** 12.13).

The churches in the apostolic era were independent and self-governing, and the absence of anything like a centralized ecclesiastical authority is seen by the fact that the council at Jerus, called to consider whether the church at Antioch should receive the uncircumcised into membership, was a delegated body, composed in part of lay members, and having only *advisory* power (Acts **15** 1–29).

3. The Epistles not Official Documents

The apostolic letters, forming so large a part of the NT, are not official documents but letters of loving pastoral instruction and counsel. The terms bishops, elders, pastors and teachers are used synonymously and interchangeably, thus limiting the officers of the early church to two orders: pastors and deacons. See also CHURCH GOVERNMENT; DIDACHE.

4. Restoration of Primitive Ideals

Under the spiritual tyrannies of the Church of England, during the reigns of Henry VIII, Edward VI, "bloody" Mary and Queen Elizabeth, the Dissenting bodies, chiefly the Congregationalists, returned to the simplicity and spiritual freedom of the primitive church. The issue was forced by two arbitrary acts of Parliament under Elizabeth: the Act of Supremacy and the Act of Uniformity. Emancipation from the intellectual and religious tyranny of these acts was won at the cost of many martyrdoms. These struggles and persecutions wrought into the successors of Robert Browne, the father of modern Congregationalism, a deep-seated and permanent resentment against all forms of autocratic power in church and state. They challenged, at the cost of life, both the Divine Right of kings, and of bishops. They believed that in Christ Jesus all believers are literally and inalienably made "kings and priests unto God" (Rev **1** 6 AV), actual spiritual sovereigns, independent of all human dictation and control in matters of belief and worship. The Pilgrims expatriated themselves to secure this spiritual liberty; and to their inherent antagonism to inherited and self-perpetuated power, whether civil or ecclesiastical, must be credited the religious freedom and civil democracy of America.

LITERATURE.—For further study see Henry M. Dexter, *Congregationalism*, ch ii; Dunning's *Congregationalists in America*, chs i, ii: Rainy, *The Ancient Catholic Church.*

DWIGHT M. PRATT

BISHOPRICK, bish'up-rik (ἐπισκοπή, *episkopḗ;* Acts **1** 20 AV, quoted from Ps **109** 8): RV "office," m, "overseership." See BISHOP.

BISHOPS' BIBLE. See ENGLISH VERSIONS.

BIT AND BRIDLE, brī'd'l (מֶתֶג־וָרֶסֶן, *methegh wā-reṣen*): The two words occur in conjunction (Ps **32** 9 AV, "Be ye not as the horse, or as the mule, which have no understanding; whose mouth must be held in with *bit* and *bridle*, lest they come near unto thee"; RV "else they will not come near unto thee," m, "that they come not near." *Methegh*, tr[d] "bit" above, is properly a bridle or halter in which the bit was a loop passed round the under jaw of the animal; *reṣen* has a

Bit and Bridle.

similar meaning. The counsel in the ver is that men should render a willing obedience to God and not be like the animals that man has to bridle and curb in order to get them to do his will. Cf Jas **3** 3, where we have "bit" as tr of *chalinós*, "a bit" or "curb," "We put bits [RV "bridles"] in the horses' mouths that they may obey us." "Bridle" occurs separately as tr of *methegh* (2 S **8** 1), "David took Metheg-ammah," AVm "the bridle of Ammah," RV "the bridle of the mother city," m, as AV; the meaning may be that he took the control or dominion of it; "I will put . . . . my bridle in thy lips" (2 K **19** 28; Isa **37** 29); "a bridle for the ass" (Prov **26** 3); of *reṣen* (Job **30** 11), "They have also let loose the bridle before me," RV "and they have cast off the bridle before me" (acted in an unbridled [unrestrained] manner); **41** 13, said of "leviathan" (RV "the hippopotamus"), "Who can come to him with his double bridle?" ARV "within his jaws?" ERV "within his double bridle," others, "into the double row of his teeth"; Isa **30** 28, "a bridle in the jaws of the people causing them to err," RV "a bridle that causeth to err"; of *maḥṣōm*, which means "a muzzle" (Ps **39** 1), "I will keep my mouth with a bridle," AVm "Heb, a bridle, or muzzle for my mouth"; so RVm.

To "bridle" occurs (Jas **1** 26, "bridleth not his tongue"; **3** 2 "able to bridle the whole body"; *chalinagōgéō*, "to lead" or "guide with a bit"). In 1 Esd **3** 6, and 2 Macc **10** 29, we have "bridles of gold" (*chrusochalinós*). W. L. WALKER

BITHIAH, bi-thī'a (בִּתְיָה, *bithyāh;* **Βεθθιά,** *Beththiá;* B, **Γελιά,** *Geliá,* "daughter of Jeh"): The daughter of a Pharaoh who married Mered, a descendant of Judah (1 Ch **4** 18). Whether this Pharaoh was an Egyp king, or whether it was in this case a Heb name, it is difficult to say. The name Bithiah seems to designate one who had become converted to the worship of Jeh, and this would favor the first supposition. If, as the RV reads, the other wife of Mered is distinguished as "the Jewess" (instead of AV "Jehudijah"), this supposition would receive further support.

FRANK E. HIRSCH

BITHRON, bith'ron (הַבִּתְרוֹן, *ha-bithrōn;* **ὅλην τὴν παρατείνουσαν,** *hólēn tēn parateínousan,* lit. "the entire [land] extending"; 2 S **2** 29, "the Bithron," i.e. the gorge or groove): Does not seem to be a proper name; rather it indicates the gorge by which Abner approached Mahanaim. Buhl (*GAP*, 121) favors identification with *Wādy 'Ajlūn*, along which in later times a Rom road connected *'Ajlūn* and Mahanaim. Others (Guthe, *Kurz. bib. Wörterbuch,* s.v.) incline to *Wādy esh Sha'īb.*

BITHYNIA, bi-thin'i-a (**Βιθυνία,** *Bithunía*): A coast province in northwestern Asia Minor on the Propontis and the Euxine. Its narrowest compass included the districts on both sides of the Sangarius, its one large river, but in prosperous times its boundaries reached from the Rhyndacus on the west to and beyond the Parthenius on the east. The Mysian Olympus rose in grandeur to a height of 6,400 ft. in the southwest, and in general the face of Nature was wrinkled with rugged mountains and seamed with fertile valleys sloping toward the Black Sea.

Hittites may have occupied Bithynia in the remote past, for Priam of Troy found some of his stoutest enemies among the Amazons on the upper Sangarius in Phrygia, and these may have been Hittite, and may easily have settled along the river to its mouth. The earliest discernible Bithynians, however, were Thracian immigrants from the European side of the Hellespont. The country was overcome by Croesus, and passed with Lydia under Pers control, 546 BC. After Alexander the Great, Bithynia became independent, and Nicomedes I, Prusias I and II, and Nicomedes II and III, ruled from 278 to 74 BC. The last king, weary of the incessant strife among the peoples of Asia Minor, especially as provoked by the aggressive Mithridates, bequeathed his country to Rome. Nicomedia and Prusa, or Brousa, were founded by kings whose names they bear; the other chief cities, Nicaea and Chalcedon, had been built by Gr enterprise earlier. There were highways leading from Nicomedia and Nicaea to Dorylaeum and to Angora (see Ramsay, *Historical Geography of Asia Minor,* and *The Church in the Rom Empire before A.D. 170*). Under Rome the Black Sea littoral as far as Amisus was more or less closely joined with Bithynia in administration.

Ships Drawn up on Coast of Black Sea.

Paul and Silas essayed to go into Bithynia, but the Spirit suffered them not (Acts **16** 7). Other evangelists, however, must have labored there early and with marked success. Bithynia is one of the provinces addressed in 1 Pet **1** 1.

Internal difficulties and disorders led to the sending of Pliny, the lawyer and literary man, as governor, 111 to 113 AD. He found Christians under his jurisdiction in such numbers that the heathen temples were almost deserted, and the trade in sacrificial animals languished. A memorable correspondence followed between the Rom governor and the emperor Trajan, in which the moral character of the Christians was completely vindicated, and the repressive measures required of officials were interpreted with leniency (see E. G. Hardy, *Pliny's Correspondence with Trajan,* and *Christianity and the Rom Government*). Under this Rom policy Christianity was confirmed in strength and in public position. Subsequently the first Ecumenical Council of the church was held in Nicaea, and two later councils convened in Chalcedon, a suburb of what is now Constantinople. The emperor Diocletian had fixed his residence and the seat of government for the eastern Roman Empire in Nicomedia.

Bithynia was for a thousand years part of the Byzantine Empire, and shared the fortunes and misfortunes of that state. On the advent of the Turks its territory was quickly overrun, and Orchan, sultan in 1326, selected Brousa as his capital, since which time this has been one of the chief Ottoman cities. G. E. WHITE

BITTER, bit'ẽr, **BITTERNESS,** bit'ẽr-nes (מַר, *mar,* or מָרָה, *mārāh*="bitter" [lit. or fig.]; also [noun] "bitterness" or [adv.] "bitterly"; "angry," "chafed," "discontented," "heavy" [Gen **27** 34; Ex **15** 23; Nu **5** 18.19.23.24.27; Est **4** 1; Job **3** 20; Ps **64** 3; Prov **5** 4; **27** 7; Eccl **7** 26; Isa **5** 20; Jer **2** 19; **4** 18; Ezk **27** 31; Am **8** 10; Hab **1** 6]; the derivatives מָרַר, מְרֹר, and מְרֹרָה, *mārar, m^e rōr, m^e rōrāh,* used with the same significance according to the context, are found in Ex **1** 14; **12** 8; Nu **9** 11; Job **13** 26; Isa **24** 9. The derivatives *m^e rī* and *m^e rīrī* occur in Dt **32** 24; Job **23** 2m; and תַּמְרוּר, *tamrūr,* is found in Jer **6** 26; **31** 15. In the NT the verb **πικραίνω,** *pikrainō*="to embitter"; the adj. **πικρός,** *pikrós*

= "bitter," and the noun πικρία, *pikría*, "bitterness," supply the same ideas in Col **3** 19; Jas **3** 11.14; Rev **8** 11; **10** 9.10): It will be noted that the word is employed with three principal spheres of application: (1) the physical sense of taste; (2) a **fig.** meaning in the objective sense of cruel, biting words; intense misery resulting from forsaking God, from a life of sin and impurity; the misery of servitude; the misfortunes of bereavement; (3) more subjectively, bitter and bitterness describe emotions of sympathy; the sorrow of childlessness and of penitence, of disappointment; the feeling of misery and wretchedness, giving rise to the expression "bitter tears"; (4) the ethical sense, characterizing untruth and immorality as the bitter thing in opposition to the sweetness of truth and the gospel; (5) Nu **5** 18 RV speaks of "the water of bitterness that causeth the curse." Here it is employed as a technical term.

FRANK E. HIRSCH

BITTER HERBS, hûrbs, or ûrbs (מְרֹרִים, *m^erōrīm*): Originally in the primitive Passover (Ex **12** 8; Nu **9** 11) these were probably merely salads, the simplest and quickest prepared form of vegetable accompaniment to the roasted lamb. Such salads have always been favorites in the Orient. Cucumbers, lettuce, water-cress, parsley and endive are some of those commonly used. Later on the Passover ritual (as it does today) laid emphasis on the idea of "bitterness" as symbolical of Israel's lot in Egypt. In modern Pal the Jews use chiefly lettuce and endive for the "bitter herbs" of their Passover. In Lam **3** 15 the same word is used: "He hath filled me with bitterness [*m^erōrīm*], he hath sated me with wormwood." Here the parallelism with "wormwood" suggests some plant more distinctly bitter than the mild salads mentioned above, such, for example, as the colocynth (*Citrullus colocynthus*) or the violently irritating squirting cucumber (*Ecballium elaterium*).

E. W. G. MASTERMAN

BITTERN, bit'ẽrn (קִפֹּד, *ḳippōdh;* Lat *Botaurus stellaris;* Gr **ἐχῖνος,** *echínos*): A nocturnal member of the heron family, frequenting swamps and marshy places. Its Heb name means a creature of waste and desert places. The bittern is the most individual branch of the heron (*ardeidae*) family on account of being partially a bird of night. There are observable differences from the heron in proportion, and it differs widely in coloration. It is one of the birds of most ancient history, and as far back as records extend is known to have inhabited Europe, Asia, Africa, Australia and America. The African bird that Bible historians were familiar with was 2½ ft. in length. It had a 4-in. bill, bright eyes and plumage of buff and chestnut, mottled with black. It lived around swamps and marshes, hunting mostly at night, and its food was much the same as that of all members of the heron family, frogs being its staple article of diet. Its meat has not the fishy taste of most members of the heron family, and in former times was considered a great delicacy of food. In the days of falconry it was protected in England because of the sport afforded in hunting it. Aristotle mentions that previous to his time the bittern was called *óknos*, which name indicates "an idle disposition." It was probably bestowed by people who found the bird hiding in swamps during the daytime, and saw that it would almost allow itself to be stepped upon before it would fly. They did not understand that it fed and mated at night. Pliny wrote of it as a bird that "bellowed like oxen," for which reason it was called *Taurus*. Other mediaeval writers called it *botaurus*, from which our term bittern is derived. There seems to be much confusion as to the early form of the name; but all authorities agree that it was bestowed on the bird on account of its voice. Turner states that in 1544 the British called it "miredromble," and "botley bump," from its voice. Rolland says the French called it *Bœuf d'eau*. In later days "bog-bull," "stake-driver" and "thunder-pumper" have attached themselves to it as terms fitly descriptive of its voice. Nuttall says its cry is "like the interrupted bellowing of a bull, but hollower and louder, and is heard at a mile's distance, as if issuing from some formidable being that resided at the bottom of the waters." Tristram says, "Its

Bittern (*Botaurus stellaris*).

strange booming note, disturbing the stillness of night, gives an idea of desolation which nothing but the wail of a hyena can equal." Thoreau thought its voice like the stroke of an ax on the head of a deeply driven stake. In ancient times it was believed the bird thrust its sharp beak into a reed to produce this sound. Later it was supposed to be made by pushing the bill into muck and water while it cried. Now the membrane by which the sound is produced has been located in the lungs of the bird. In all time it has been the voice that attracted attention to the bittern, and it was solely upon the ground of its vocal attainments that it entered the Bible. There are three references, all of which originated in its cry. Isaiah in prophesying the destruction of Babylon (**14** 23 AV) wrote: "I will also make it a possession for the bittern, and pools of water"; in other words he would make of it a desolate and lonely swamp. Again in **34** 11 AV, in pronouncing judgment against Idumaea, he wrote, "But the cormorant and the bittern shall possess it." In the RV, "cormorant" and "bittern" are changed to "pelican" and "porcupine." The change from the cormorant to pelican makes less difference, as both are water birds, and the Heb *shālākh*, which means "a plunging bird," would apply equally to either of them. If they were used to bear out the idea that they would fill the ruins with terrifying sound, then it is well to remember that the cormorant had something of a *voice*, while the pelican is notoriously the most *silent* of birds.

The change from bittern to porcupine is one with which no ornithologist would agree. About 620 BC, the prophet Zephaniah (**2** 14) clearly indicates this bird: "And herds shall lie down in the midst of her, all the beasts of the nations: both the pelican and the porcupine shall lodge in the capitals thereof; their voice shall sing in the windows; desolation shall be in the thresholds: for he hath laid bare the cedar work." This should forever settle the question raised by some modern commentators as to whether a bird or beast is intended by the word *ḳippōdh*. In some instances it seems to have been confounded with *ḳunfudh*, the hedgehog or porcupine. No natural historian ever would agree to this, because these animals are not at home in the conditions that were known to exist here. Even granting that Nineveh was to be made dry, it must be remembered that the marshes of the Tigris lay very close, and the bird is of night, with a voice easily carrying over a mile. Also it was to "sing" and to "lodge" on the "upper lintels" which were the top timbers of the doors and windows. These formed just the location a bittern would probably perch upon when it left its marshy home and went booming through the night in search of a mate. It was without doubt the love song of the bittern that Isaiah and Zephaniah used in completing prophecies of desolation and horror, because with the exception of mating time it is a very quiet bird. For these reasons the change from bittern to porcupine in the RV, of the paragraph quoted, is a great mistake, as is also that of cormorant to pelican.

GENE STRATTON-PORTER

BITTERNESS, bit'ẽr-ness. See BITTER.

BITTERNESS, WATER OF. See ADULTERY (2).

BITTER WATER. See ADULTERY (2); MARAH.

BITUMEN, bi-tū'men. See SLIME.

BIZIOTHIAH, biz-yo-thī'a (בִּזְיוֹתְיָה, *bizyōthᵉyāh;* LXX **αἱ κῶμαι αὐτῶν,** *hai kōmai autōn,* lit. "their villages"; AV **Bizjothjah,** biz-joth'ja, "place of Jah's olives" [Young], or "contempt of Jah" [Strong]): According to MT, a town in the south of Judah, near Beersheba (Josh **15** 28). LXX reads "and her daughters," only one consonant of MT being read differently; and so We, Hollenberg, Di et al. The LXX has probably preserved the original text (cf Neh **11** 27).

BIZTHA, biz'tha (LXX **Μαζάν,** *Mazán;* also *Bazán* and *Bazeá*): One of the seven eunuchs or chamberlains of King Ahasuerus (Xerxes). It is possible that the name is derived from the Pers *besteh,* "bound," hence "eunuch" (Est **1** 10).

BLACK. See COLORS.

BLACKNESS (כִּמְרִירִים, *kimrīrīm,* "obscurations"; קַדְרוּת, *ḳadhrūth,* "darkness"; **γνόφος,** *gnóphos,* "darkness," **ζόφος,** *zóphos,* "blackness"): Terms rarely used but of special significance in picturing the fearful gloom and blackness of moral darkness and calamity. Job, cursing the day of his birth, wishes that it, a *dies ater* ("dead black day"), might be swallowed up in darkness (Job **3** 5). Because of Israel's spiritual infidelity Jeh clothes the heavens with the blackness of sackcloth (Isa **50** 3), the figure being that of the inky blackness of ominous, terrifying thunder clouds. The fearful judgment against sin under the old dispensation is illustrated by the appalling blackness that enveloped smoking, burning, quaking Sinai at the giving of the law (He **12** 18; cf Ex **19** 16–19; **20** 18). The horror of darkness culminates in the impenetrable blackness of the under-world, the eternal abode of fallen angels and riotously immoral and ungodly men (Jude ver 13; see also ver 6 and 2 Pet **2** 4.17). Human language is here too feeble to picture the moral gloom and rayless night of the lost: "Pits [AV "chains"] of darkness" (cf the ninth plague of Egypt, "darkness which may be felt" [Ex **10** 21]). Wicked men are "wandering stars," comets that disappear in "blackness of darkness . . . . reserved for ever." In art this **fig.** language has found majestic and awe-inspiring expression in Doré's illustrations of Dante's *Purgatory* and Milton's *Paradise Lost.*

DWIGHT M. PRATT

BLAINS, blānz (אֲבַעְבֻּעָה, *'ăbhaʻbuʻāh:* only in Ex **9** 9.10): Pustules containing fluid around a boil or inflamed sore. It is an OE word "bleyen," used sometimes as a synonym for boil. Wyclif (1382) uses the expression "stinkende bleyne" for Job's sores. The Heb word is from a root which means that which bubbles up. See BOIL.

BLASPHEMY, blas'fē-mi (**βλασφημία,** *blasphēmía*): In classical Gr meant primarily "defamation" or "evil-speaking" in general; "a word of evil omen," hence "impious, and irreverent speech against God."

(1) In the OT as subst. and vb.: (*a*) (בָּרַךְ, *bārakh*) "Naboth did blaspheme God and the king" (1 K **21** 10.13 AV); (*b*) (גָּדַף, *gādhaph*) of Sennacherib defying Jeh (2 K **19** 6.22=Isa **37** 6.23; also Ps **44** 16; Ezk **20** 27; cf Nu **15** 30), "But the soul that doeth aught with a high hand [i.e. knowingly and defiantly], ... the same blasphemeth [so RV, but AV "reproacheth"] Jehovah; and that soul shall be cut off from among his people." Blasphemy is always in word or deed, injury, dishonour and defiance offered to God, and its penalty is death by stoning; (*c*) (חָרַף, *ḥāraph*) of idolatry as blasphemy against Jeh (Isa **65** 7); (*d*) (נָקַב, *nāḳabh*) "And he that blasphemeth the name of Jeh, he shall surely be put to death" (Lev **24** 11.16); (*e*) (נָאַץ, *nā'aç*) David's sin is an occasion to the enemies of the Lord to blaspheme (2 S **12** 14; also Ps **74** 10.18; Isa **52** 5; cf Ezk **35** 12; 2 K **19** 3 AV; Isa **37** 3).

(2) In the NT blasphemy, subst. and vb., may be (*a*) of evil-speaking generally (Acts **13** 45; **18** 6). The Jews contradicted Paul "and blasphemed," RVm "railed." (So in AV of Mt **15** 19=Mk **7** 22; Col **3** 8, but in RV "railings"; Rev **2** 9 RVm "reviling"; so perhaps in 1 Tim **1** 20; or Hymenaeus and Alexander may have blasphemed Christ by professing faith and living unworthily of it.) (*b*) Speaking against a heathen goddess: the town clerk of Ephesus repels the charge that Paul and his companions were blasphemers of Diana (Acts **19** 37). (*c*) Against God: (*α*) uttering impious words (Rev **13** 1.5.6; **16** 9.11.21; **17** 3); (*β*) unworthy conduct of Jews (Rom **2** 24) and Christians (1 Tim **6** 1; Tit **2** 5, and perhaps 1 Tim **1** 20); (*γ*) of Jesus Christ, alleged to be usurping the authority of God (Mt **9** 3=Mk **2** 7=Lk **5** 21), claiming to be the Messiah, the son of God (Mt **26** 65=Mk **14** 64), or making Himself God (Jn **10** 33.36). (*d*) Against Jesus Christ: Saul strove to make the Christians he persecuted blaspheme their Lord (Acts **26** 11). So was he himself a blasphemer (1 Tim **1** 13; cf Jas **2** 7).

The Unpardonable Sin

(3) Blasphemy against the Holy Spirit: "Every sin and blasphemy shall be forgiven unto men; but the blasphemy against the Spirit shall not be forgiven. And whosoever shall speak a word against the Son of man, it shall be forgiven him; but whosoever shall speak against the Holy Spirit, it shall not be forgiven him, neither in

this world, nor in that which is to come" (Mt **12** 31.32 = Mk **3** 28.29; Lk **12** 10). As in the OT "to sin with a high hand" and to blaspheme the name of God incurred the death penalty, so the blasphemy against the Holy Spirit remains the one unpardonable sin. These passages at least imply beyond cavil the personality of the Holy Spirit, for sin and blasphemy can only be committed against persons. In Mt and Mk a particular case of this blasphemy is the allegation of the Pharisees that Jesus Christ casts out devils by Beelzebub. The general idea is that to attribute to an evil source acts which are clearly those of the Holy Spirit, to call good evil, is blasphemy against the Spirit, and sin that will not be pardoned. "A distinction is made between Christ's other acts and those which manifestly reveal the Holy Spirit in Him, and between slander directed against Him personally as He appears in His ordinary acts, and that which is aimed at those acts in which the Spirit is manifest" (Gould, *Mark* ad loc.). Luke does not refer to any particular instance, and seems to connect it with the denial of Christ, although he, too, gives the saying that "who shall speak a word against the Son of man, it shall be forgiven." But which of Christ's acts are not acts of the Holy Spirit, and how therefore is a word spoken against Him not also blasphemy against the Holy Spirit? John identifies the Holy Spirit with the exalted Christ (Jn **14** 16–18.26.28). The solution generally offered of this most difficult problem is concisely put by Plummer (*Luke* ad loc.): "Constant and consummate opposition to the influence of the Holy Spirit, because of a deliberate preference of darkness to light, render repentance and therefore forgiveness morally impossible." A similar idea is taught in He **6** 4–6, and 1 Jn **5** 16: "A sin unto death." But the natural meaning of Christ's words implies an inability or unwillingness to forgive on the Divine side rather than inability to repent in man. Anyhow the abandonment of man to eternal condemnation involves the inability and defeat of God. The only alternative seems to be to call the kenotic theory into service, and to put this idea among the human limitations which Christ assumed when He became flesh. It is less difficult to ascribe a limit to Jesus Christ's knowledge than to God's saving grace (Mk **13** 32; cf Jn **16** 12.13). It is also noteworthy that in other respects, at least, Christ acquiesced in the view of the Holy Spirit which He found among His contemporaries. See HOLY SPIRIT.
T. REES

BLAST (נְשָׁמָה, *n^{e}shāmāh*, רוּחַ, *rū^{a}ḥ*):

(1) The blowing of the breath of Jeh, expressive of the manifestation of God's power in Nature and Providence. "With the blast of thy nostrils the waters were piled up" (Ex **15** 8), referring to the east wind (**14** 21; cf 2 S **22** 16 and Ps **18** 15). "I will send a blast upon him" (2 K **19** 7 AV; RV "put a spirit in him," i.e. "an impulse of fear" [Dummelow in loc.]; cf Isa **37** 7). "By the blast of his anger are they consumed" (Job **4** 9; cf Isa **37** 36).

(2) The word *rū^{a}ḥ* is used with reference to the tyranny and violence of the wicked (Isa **25** 4).

(3) The blowing of a wind instrument: "When they make a long blast with the ram's horn" (Josh **6** 5).
M. O. EVANS

BLAST, BLASTING, blast'ing (שִׁדָּפוֹן, *shiddāphōn*—root, שָׁדַף, *shādhaph*, lit. "scorching"): This is the effect produced upon grain or other plants by the hot east winds which blow from the desert of Arabia. They usually continue to blow for two or three days at a time. If they occur in the spring near ripening time, the grain is often turned yellow and does not properly mature. The farmers dread this wind. In some localities, if they suspect that the east wind is coming, they set up a great shouting and beating of pans, hoping to drive it off. Sometimes this wind is a double pestilence, when it brings with it a cloud of locusts (2 Ch **6** 28). The writer, while journeying in the northern part of the Arabian desert, the source of these winds, witnessed such a cloud of locusts on their way toward habitable regions. It did not call for a very vivid imagination on the part of the children of Israel to realize the meaning of the curses and all manner of evil which would befall those who would not hearken to the voice of Jeh. Dt **28** 22–24 could easily be considered a poetic description of the east winds (Arab. *howa sharkî'yeh*) which visit Pal and Syria at irregular intervals today. The heat is fiery: it dries up the vegetation and blasts the grain; the sky is hazy and there is a glare as if the sun were reflected from a huge brass tray. Woodwork cracks and warps; the covers of books curl up. Instead of rain, the wind brings dust and sand which penetrate into the innermost corners of the dwellings. This dust fills the eyes and inflames them. The skin becomes hot and dry. To one first experiencing this storm it seems as though some volcano must be belching forth heat and ashes. No other condition of the weather can cause such depression. Such a pestilence, only prolonged beyond endurance, was to be the fate of the disobedient. This word should not be confused with mildew. Since the words blasting and mildew occur together it may be inferred that mildew (lit. "a paleness") must mean the sickly color which plants assume for other causes than the blasting of the east wind, such, as for instance, fungus diseases or parasites (1 K **8** 37; Am **4** 9; Hag **2** 17).
JAMES A. PATCH

BLASTUS, blas'tus (Βλάστος, *Blástos*, "shoot"): The chamberlain of Herod Agrippa I, whose services as an intermediary between them and the king were gained by the people of Tyre and Sidon. These cities were dependent on Pal for corn and other provisions, and when Herod, on the occasion of some commercial dispute, forbade the export of foodstuffs to Tyre and Sidon, they were at his mercy and were compelled to ask for peace. "Having made Blastus the king's chamberlain their friend," probably by means of a bribe, the Phoen embassy was given an opportunity of setting their case before Herod (Acts **12** 20 ff).
S. F. HUNTER

BLAZE, blāz ("to publish"): Found only in AV of Mk **1** 45, for Gr *diaphēmízein*, tr[d] by RV "spread abroad," as in Mt **9** 31; **28** 15.

BLEMISH, blem'ish:

(1) מוּם, *mūm*, מְאוּם, *m^{e}'ūm;* μῶμος, *mōmos:* This word signifies no particular skin disease, as has been supposed; but is used generally for any and all disfiguring affections of the skin, such as eczema, herpes, scabies, etc, even for scratches and scars, as in Lev **24** 19.20; and thence for moral defects, as in Eph **5** 27. The existence of a blemish in a person of priestly descent prevented him from the execution of the priestly office; similarly an animal fit for sacrifice was to be without blemish. In the NT Christ is presented as the antitype of a pure and ritually acceptable sacrifice "as a lamb without blemish and without spot" (He **9** 14; 1 Pet **1** 19), and the disciples are admonished to be blameless, "without blemish" (Eph **5** 27). Rarely the word is used to designate a reprobate person (2 Pet **2** 13).

(2) Blemish in the eye, תְּבַלֻּל, *t^{e}bhallul* (from a root בָּלַל, *bālal*, "to overflow"; Arab. بَلَّ, *balla*,

بلل, *balal*, "to moisten"), cataract, white spots in the eye (Lev **21** 20). H. L. E. LUERING

BLESS (בָּרַךְ, *bārakh*): This word is found more frequently in the OT than in the NT, and is used in different relations.

(1) It is first met in Gen **1** 22 at the introduction of animal life upon the earth, where it is written, "And God blessed them, saying, Be fruitful, and multiply," etc. The context furnishes the key to its meaning, which is the bestowal of good, and in this particular place the pleasure and power of increase in kind. Thus it is generally employed in both Testaments, the context always determining the character of the bestowal; for instance (where man is the recipient), whether the good is temporal or spiritual, or both.

Occasionally, however, a different turn is given to it as in Gen **2** 3 AV, where it is written, "And God blessed the seventh day, and hallowed it." Here the good consists in the setting apart and consecrating of that day for His use.

(2) In the foregoing instances the Creator is regarded as the source of blessing and the creature the recipient, but the order is sometimes reversed, and the creature (man) is the source and the Creator the recipient. In Gen **24** 48, for example, Abraham's servant says, "I bowed my head, and worshipped Jeh, and blessed Jeh, the God of my master Abraham," where the word evidently means to worship God, to exalt and praise Him.

(3) There is a third use where men only are considered. In Gen **24** 60, her relatives "blessed Rebekah, and said unto her, Our sister, be thou the mother of thousands of ten thousands" (AV "millions"), where the word expresses the wish or hope for the bestowal of the good designated. There are also instances where such a blessing of man by man may be taken in the prophetic sense, as when Isaac blessed Jacob (Gen **27** 4.27), putting himself as it were in God's place, and with a sense of the Divine concurrence, pronouncing the good named. Here the word becomes in part a prayer for, and in part a prediction of, the good intended. Balaam's utterances are simply prophetic of Israel's destiny (Nu **23** 9.10.11.23m.24).

Although these illustrations are from the OT the word is used scarcely differently in the NT; "The blessing of bread, of which we read in the Gospels, is equivalent to giving thanks for it, the thought being that good received gratefully comes as a blessing"; cf Mt **14** 19 and **15** 36 with 1 Cor **11** 24 (Adeney, *HDB*, I, 307). See also BENEDICTION. JAMES M. GRAY

BLESSED, bles′ed (בָּרוּךְ, *bārūkh*): Where God is referred to, this word has the sense of "praise," as in 1 S **25** 32, "Blessed be Jeh, the God of Israel." But where man is in mind it is used in the sense of "happy" or "favored," and most frequently so in the Psalms and the Gospels, as for example, "Blessed is the man that walketh not in the counsel of the wicked" (Ps **1** 1); "Blessed art thou among women" (Lk **1** 42); "Blessed are the poor in spirit" (Mt **5** 3). See BEATITUDES.

BLESSEDNESS, bles′ed-nes: This tr of **μακαρισμός**, *makarismós* (a word signifying "beatification" or "the ascription of blessing"), is used but three times, in Rom **4** 6.9, and Gal **4** 15, in AV only. In the first two instances it refers to the happy state or condition of a man to whom Christ's righteousness is imputed by faith, and in the last to a man's experience of that condition. See HAPPINESS.

BLESSING (בְּרָכָה, *berākhāh*; **εὐλογία**, *eulogía*): Sometimes means the form of words used in invoking the bestowal of good, as in Dt **33** 1; Josh **8** 34; and Jas **3** 10. Sometimes it means the good or the benefit itself which has been conferred, as in Gen **27** 36, "Hast thou not reserved a blessing for me?" and Prov **10** 22, "The blessing of Jeh, it maketh rich." "The cup of blessing" (τὸ ποτήριον τῆς εὐλογίας, *tó potḗrion tḗs eulogías*, a special use of the word in 1 Cor **10** 16), means the cup for which we bless God, or which represents to us so much blessing from God.
JAMES M. GRAY

BLESSING, CUP OF (**τὸ ποτήριον τῆς εὐλογίας**, "the consecrated cup," 1 Cor **10** 16): A technical term from the Jewish liturgy transferred to the Lord's Supper, and signifying the cup of wine upon which a blessing was pronounced. The suggestion that it carries with it a higher significance, as a cup that brings blessing, is not without force. The succeeding words, "we bless," are equivalent to "for which we give thanks." It was consecrated by thanksgiving and prayer. See also CUP.

BLESSING, VALLEY OF. See BERACAH.

BLINDFOLD, blīnd′fold (**περικαλύπτω**, *perikalúptō*): A sport common among the children of ancient times, in which the blindfolded were struck on the cheek, then asked who had struck them, and not let go until they had correctly guessed. This treatment was accorded Christ by his persecutors (Lk **22** 64).

BLINDING, blīnd′ing. See PUNISHMENTS.

BLINDNESS, blīnd′ness (עָוַר, *ʽāwar*, and variants; **τυφλός**, *tuphlós*): The word blind is used as a vb., as Jn **12** 40, usually in the sense of obscuring spiritual perception. In reference to physical blindness it is used as a noun frequently or else as an adj. with the noun *man*. There are 54 references to this condition, and there is no reason to believe, as has been surmised, that blindness was any less rife in ancient times than it is now, when defective eyes and bleared, inflamed lids are among the commonest and most disgusting sights in a Pal crowd. In the Papyrus Ebers (1500 BC) there are enumerated a number of diseases of the eye and a hundred prescriptions are given for their treatment. That the disease occurred in children and caused destruction and atrophy of the eyeball is testified to by the occurrence of a considerable number of mummy heads, in which there is marked diminution in size of one orbit. The commonest disease is a purulent ophthalmia, a highly infectious condition propagated largely by the flies which can be seen infesting the crusts of dried secretion undisturbed even on the eyes of infants. (In Egypt there is a superstition that it is unlucky to disturb them.) This almost always leaves the eyes damaged with bleared lids, opacities of the cornea, and sometimes extensive internal injury as well. Like other plagues, this disease was thought to be a Divine infliction (Ex **4** 11). Minor forms of the disease destroy the eyelashes and produce the unsightly *tender-eyes* (in Gen **29** 17 the word *rakh* may mean simply "weak").

Blindness from birth is the result of a form of this disease known as *ophthalmia neonatorum* which sets in a few days after birth. I have seen cases of this disease in Pal. Sometimes ophthalmia accompanies malarial fever (Lev **26** 16). All these diseases are aggravated by sand, and the sun glare, to which the unprotected inflamed eyes are exposed. Most of the extreme cases which one sees are beyond remedy—and hence the giving of sight to the blind is generally put in the front of the mighty works of healing by Our Lord. The methods used by Him in these miracles varied probably according to the degree of faith in the blind man; all were merely tokens, not intended as remedies. The case of the man in Mk **8** 22 whose healing seemed gradual is an instance of the phenomenon met with in cases where, by operation, sight has been given to one congenitally blind, where it takes some time before he can interpret his new sensations.

The blindness of old age, probably from senile cataract, is described in the cases of Eli at 98 years of age (1 S **3** 2; **4** 15), Ahijah (1 K **14** 4), and Isaac (Gen **27** 1). The smiting of Elymas (Acts **13** 11) and the Syrian soldiers (2 K **6** 18) was either a miraculous intervention or more probably a temporary hypnotism; that of Paul (Acts **9** 8) was doubtless a temporary paralysis of the retinal cells from the bright light. The "scales" mentioned were not material but in the restoration of his sight it seemed as if scales had fallen from his eyes. It probably left behind a weakness of the eyes (see THORN IN THE FLESH). That blindness of Tobit (Tob **2** 10), from the irritation of sparrows' dung, may have been some form of conjunctivitis, and the cure by the gall of the fish is paralleled by the account given in Pliny (xxxii.24) where the gall of the fish *Callionymus Lyra* is recommended as an application in some cases of blindness. The hypothesis that the gall was used as a pigment to obscure the whiteness of an opaque cornea (for which Indian ink tattooing has been recommended, not as a cure but to remove the unsightliness of a white spot) has nothing in its favor for thereby the sight would not be restored. The only other reference to medicaments is the **fig.** mention of eyesalve in Rev **3** 18.

Blindness unfitted a man for the priesthood (Lev **21** 18); but care of the blind was specially enjoined in the Law (Lev **19** 14), and offences against them are regarded as breaches of Law (Dt **27** 18).

Figuratively, blindness is used to represent want of mental perception, want of prevision, recklessness, and incapacity to perceive moral distinctions (Isa **42** 16.18.19; Mt **23** 16 ff; Jn **9** 39 ff).

ALEX. MACALISTER

BLINDNESS, JUDICIAL, jū-dish′al, jōō-dish′al: Among the ancient Israelites in the pre-Can. period disputes within the family or clan or tribe would be settled by the natural head of the family or clan or tribe. According to Ex **18** Moses, as the leader of the tribes, settled all disputes. But he was compelled to appoint a body of magistrates—heads of families—to act in conjunction with himself, and under his judicial oversight. These magistrates settled ordinary disputes while he reserved for himself the more difficult cases. After the conquest of Canaan, the conditions of life became so complex, and questions of a difficult nature so constantly arose, that steps were taken (1) to appoint official judges—elders of the city (Josh **8** 33; Jgs **8** 3; 1 K **21** 8); (2) to codify ancient custom, and (3) to place the administration of justice on an organized basis. It is significant that in one of the oldest documents in the Pent—viz. in the Book of the Covenant (Ex **20** 20—**23** 33)—the miscarriage of justice was of such frequent occurrence as to require special mention (**23** 1–3.6–8). In fact the OT abounds with allusions to the corruption and venality of the magisterial bench (Dt **16** 19; Lev **19** 15; Am **5** 12; Mic **3** 11; **7** 3; Isa **1** 23; **5** 23; Zeph **3** 3; Ps **15** 5; Prov **17** 23). According to the Book of the Covenant (Ex **23** 8) 'a bribe blindeth the eyes of the open-eyed.' This descriptive phrase indicates a prolific cause of the miscarriage of justice—an exceedingly common thing in the East, in the present no less than in the past. The prohibition in ver 3, "Neither shalt thou favor a poor man in his cause," is rather remarkable and many scholars are of opinion that "a great man" should be read for "a poor man" as, according to ver 6 AV, the common fault was "wresting the judgment of the poor." The rich alone could offer a satisfactory bribe. But it should be pointed out that Lev (**19** 15) legislates in view of both tendencies—"respecting the person of the poor" and "honoring the person of the mighty." Sympathy with the poor no less than a bribe from the well-to-do might affect the judgment of the bench. Dt (**16** 19) reproduces the words of the Book of the Covenant with a slight alteration—viz. "eyes of the wise" for "eyes of the open-eyed" ("them that have sight"). Both phrases vividly bring out the baneful effect of bribery—a magistrate otherwise upright and honest—open-eyed and wise—may be unconsciously yet effectively influenced in his judicial decisions by a gift sufficiently large. A similar phrase is found in the story of Abraham's life (Gen **20** 16). A gift of a thousand shekels to Abraham was intended to be a "covering of the eyes" for Sarah, i.e. compensation or reparation for the wrong which had been done. For a gift of such magnitude she ought to wink at the injury. Job (**9** 24) declares in his bitterness that God "covereth the faces of the judges"—inflicts judicial blindness on them so that justice in this world is out of the question. Judicial corruption was the burden of the prophets' preaching—"judges loved bribes, and followed after rewards," with the result that "the fatherless" and "the widow" were helpless to have their grievances redressed (Isa **1** 23). A satisfactory reward would always secure the acquittal of the offender (Isa **5** 23). Micah combines judges, priests and prophets under a similar charge; they are all guilty of gross venality (**3** 11). Prov (**17** 23) defines the wicked person as one who is always prepared to take a "bribe out of the bosom, to pervert the ways of justice"; on the other hand the good man is he who will not take a reward against the innocent (Ps **15** 5) or "shaketh his hands from taking a bribe" (Isa **33** 15). In regard to Jeh alone is absolute incorruptibility affirmed—he "regardeth not persons, nor taketh reward" (Dt **10** 17).

T. LEWIS

BLOOD, blud (דָּם, *dām*, probably from אָדַם, *'ādham*, "to be red"; αἷμα, *haíma*): Used in the OT to designate the life principle in either animal or vegetable, as the blood of man or the juice of the grape (Lev **17** 11, et al.); in the NT for the blood of an animal, the atoning blood of Christ, and in both OT and NT in a **fig.** sense for bloodshed or murder (Gen **37** 26; Hos **4** 2; Rev **16** 6).

1. Primitive Ideas

Although the real function of the blood in the human system was not fully known until the fact of its circulation was established by William Harvey in 1615, nevertheless from the earliest times a singular mystery has been attached to it by all peoples. Blood rites, blood ceremonies and blood feuds are common among primitive tribes. It came to be recognized as the life principle long before it was scientifically proved to be. Naturally a feeling of fear, awe and reverence would be attached to the shedding of blood. With many uncivilized peoples scarification of the body until blood flows is practised. Blood brotherhood or blood friendship is established by African tribes by the mutual shedding of blood and either drinking it or rubbing it on one another's bodies. Thus and by the inter-transfusion of blood by other means it was thought that a community of life and interest could be established.

Notwithstanding the ignorance and superstition surrounding this suggestively beautiful idea, it grew to have more than a merely human significance and application. For this crude practice of inter-transference of human blood there came to be a symbolic substitution of animal blood in sprinkling or anointing. The first reference in the OT to blood (Gen **4** 10) is **fig.**, but highly illustrative of the reverential fear manifested upon the shedding of blood and the first teaching regarding it.

2. Heb and OT Customs

The rite of circumcision is an OT form of blood ceremony. Apart from the probable sanitary importance of the act is the deeper meaning in the establishment of a bond of friendship between the one upon whom the act is performed and Jeh Himself. In order that Abraham might become "the friend of God" he was commanded that he should be circumcised as a token of the covenant between him and God (Gen **17** 10–11; see CIRCUMCISION).

It is significant that the eating of blood was prohibited in earliest Bible times (Gen **9** 4). The custom probably prevailed among heathen nations as a religious rite (cf Ps **16** 4). This and its unhygienic influence together doubtless led to its becoming taboo. The same prohibition was made under the Mosaic code (Lev **7** 26; see SACRIFICE).

Blood was commanded to be used also for purification or for ceremonial cleansing (Lev **14** 5–7. 51.52; Nu **19** 4), provided, however, that it be taken from a clean animal (see PURIFICATION).

In all probability there is no trace of the superstitious use of blood in the OT, unless perchance in 1 K **22** 38 (see BATHING); but everywhere it is vested with cleansing, expiatory, and reverently symbolic qualities.

As in the transition from ancient to Heb practice, so from the OT to the NT we see an exaltation of the conception of blood and blood ceremonies. In Abraham's covenant his own blood had to be shed. Later an expiatory animal was to shed blood (Lev **5** 6; see ATONEMENT), but there must always be a shedding of blood. "Apart from shedding of blood there is no remission" (He **9** 22). The exaltation and dignifying of this idea finds its highest development then in the vicarious shedding of blood by Christ Himself (1 Jn **1** 7). As in the OT "blood" was also used to signify the juice of grapes, the most natural substitute for the drinking of blood would be the use of wine. Jesus takes advantage of this, and introduces the beautiful and significant custom (Mt **26** 28) of drinking wine and eating bread as symbolic of the primitive intertransfusion of blood and flesh in a pledge of eternal friendship (cf Ex **24** 6.7; Jn **6** 53–56). This is the climactic observance of blood rites recorded in the Bible.

3. NT Teachings

LITERATURE.—Trumbull, *The Blood Covenant* and *The Threshold Covenant;* Westermarck, *The Origin and Development of the Moral Ideas;* Robertson Smith, *Lectures on the Religion of the Semites.*

WALTER G. CLIPPINGER

BLOOD AND WATER (**αἷμα καὶ ὕδωρ**, *haíma kaí húdōr*): The remarkable passage (Jn **19** 34) from which this expression is taken refers to the piercing of the Saviour's side by the soldier. The evangelist notes here what he, as an eyewitness of the crucifixion, had seen as a surprising fact. Whereon this surprise was founded cannot now be more than guessed at. Nor is it necessary here to discuss the reason or reasons why the apostle mentions the fact at all in his report, whether merely for historical accuracy and completeness, or as a possible proof of the actual death of Christ, which at an early date became a subject of doubt among certain Christian sects, or whether by it he wished to refer to the mystical relation of baptismal cleansing ("water") and the atonement ("blood") as signified thereby. Let it suffice to state that a reference often made to 1 Jn **5** 6.8 is here quite out of place. This passage, though used by certain Fathers of the church as a proof of the last-named doctrine, does not indeed refer to this wonderful incident of the crucifixion story. The argument of 1 Jn **5** 8 concerns the Messiahship of Jesus, which is proved by a threefold witness, for He is the one whom at the baptism of John ("water") God attested as the Messiah by the heavenly voice, "This is my beloved Son," who at the crucifixion ("blood") had the testimony that the Father had accepted His atoning sacrifice, and whose promise of sending the Comforter fulfilled on Pentecost ("spirit") presented us with the final proof of the completed Messianic task. The same expression in 1 Jn **5** 6 refers probably to the same argument with the implied meaning that Jesus came not only by the merely ceremonial water of baptism, but also by the more important, because vivifying, blood of atonement.

The physiological aspect of this incident of the crucifixion has been first discussed by Gruner (*Commentatio de morte Jesu Christi vera*, Halle, 1805), who has shown that the blood released by the spear-thrust of the soldier must have been extravasated before the opening of the side took place, for only so could it have been poured forth in the described manner. While a number of commentators have opposed this view as a fanciful explanation, and have preferred to give the statement of the evangelist a symbolical meaning in the sense of the doctrines of baptism and eucharist (so Baur, Strauss, Reuss and others), some modern physiologists are convinced that in this passage a wonderful phenomenon is reported to us, which, inexplicable to the sacred historian, contains for us an almost certain clue to the real cause of the Saviour's death. Dr. Stroud (*On the Physiological Cause of the Death of Christ*, London, 1847) basing his remarks on numerous postmortems, pronounced the opinion that here we had a proof of the death of Christ being due not to the effects of crucifixion but to "laceration or rupture of the heart" as a consequence of supreme mental agony and sorrow. It is well attested that usually the suffering on the cross was very prolonged. It often lasted two or three days, when death would supervene from exhaustion. There were no physical reasons why Christ should not have lived very much longer on the cross than He did. On the other hand, death caused by laceration of the heart in consequence of great mental suffering would be almost instantaneous. In such a case the phrase "of a broken heart," becomes lit. true. The life blood flowing through the aperture or laceration into the pericardium or caul of the heart, being extravasated, soon coagulates into the red clot (blood) and the limpid serum (water). This accumulation in the heart-sac was released by the spear-thrust of the soldier (which here takes providentially the place of a postmorten without which it would have been impossible to determine the real cause of death), and from the gaping wound there flow the two component parts of blood distinctly visible.

Several distinguished physicians have accepted Dr. Stroud's argument, and some have strengthened it by the observation of additional symptoms. We may mention Dr. James Begbie, fellow and late president of the Royal College of Physicians of Edinburgh, Sir J. Y. Simpson, professor at the University of Edinburgh, and others (see Dr. Hanna, *Our Lord's Life on Earth*, Appendix I). The latter refers to the loud cry, mentioned by the Synoptists (Mt **27** 50; Mk **15** 37; Lk **23** 46), which preceded the actual death of Jesus, as a symptom characteristic of cases of "broken heart." He adds that Dr. Walshe, professor of medicine in University College, London, one of the greatest authorities on the diseases of the heart, says that a "piercing shriek" is always uttered in such cases immediately before the end.

While we may never reach a state of absolute certainty on this subject, there is no valid reason to deny the probability of this view of the death of Christ. It certainly gives a more solemn insight into Christ's spiritual anguish, "the travail of his soul" on our behalf, which weighed upon Him so heavily that long before the usual term of bodily and therefore endurable suffering of crucified persons Christ's loving heart broke, achieving the great atoning sacrifice for all mankind.

H. L. E. Luering

BLOOD, AVENGER OF. See Avenger.

BLOOD, ISSUE, ish'ū, **OF.** See Bloody Flux.

BLOODGUILTINESS, blud-gilt'i-nes: Found in the AV only in Ps **51** 14. RV adds Ex **22** 2.3; 1 S **25** 26.33. Ezk **18** 13 seems to indicate that the phrase does not necessarily signify bloodshed, but any grievous sin which, if it remains, will block God's favor to His land and people (cf Dt **21** 8; Isa **1** 15). Ps **51** is to be interpreted in this light.

BLOOD-REVENGE, blud-rē̆-venj': See Avenger.

BLOODSHEDDING, blud'shed-ing (αἱματεκχυσία, *haimatekchusía*, He **9** 22): In this passage the indispensability of expiating sacrifice is positively set forth.

BLOODTHIRSTY, blud'thûrs-ti (אַנְשֵׁי דָמִים, *'anshē dāmīm*, "men of blood"): This occurs in the AV only in Prov **29** 10; in RV, Ps **5** 6; **55** 23; **59** 2; **139** 19. See Bloody.

BLOODY, blud'i (דָּם, *dām*="blood" of man or an animal; and where the King James translators have rendered with the adj. "bloody," the Heb employs the noun in the construct case, "of blood"): "A bridegroom of blood" (Ex **4** 25.26, AV **bloody husband**). Zipporah, not being an Israelite, probably objected to the circumcision of infants, if not to the rite altogether; apprehending, however, that her husband's life was imperiled possibly through some grievous sickness (**4** 24) because of their disobedience in this particular, she performed the ceremony herself upon her son, saying, "A bridegroom of blood art thou to me."

In RV the expression (AV "bloody") is variously rendered, "man of blood" (2 S **16** 7.8); "men of blood" (Ps **26** 9); "bloodthirsty" (**5** 6; **59** 2; **139** 19). In 2 S **21** 1, "It is for Saul, and for his bloody house," might be rendered "Upon Saul and his house rests bloodshed."

Ezekiel calls Jerus "the bloody city" (Ezk **22** 2; **24** 6; cf **7** 23), referring to those unjustly put to death by the wicked rulers of Jerus. Nineveh also is called "the bloody city" (Nah **3** 1). The capital here virtually stands for the kingdom, and history bears witness to the enormous cruelties perpetrated by the Assyr rulers. It is siege on siege, pools of blood everywhere, the flaying of men alive, "great baskets stuffed with the salted heads of their foes." For two hundred years it is the story of brute force and ruthless cruelty. "The prey departeth not." And now every cruelty which they have visited upon others is to be turned upon themselves (**3** 19).

M. O. Evans

BLOODY FLUX, fluks (πυρετὸς καὶ δυσεντερία, *puretós kaí dusentería*, lit. "fever and dysentery"): The disease by which the father of Publius was afflicted in Malta (Acts **28** 8). RV calls it "dysentery"; a common and dangerous disease which in Malta is often fatal to soldiers of the garrison even at the present day (Aitken, *Pract. of Medicine*, II, 841). It is also prevalent in Pal at certain seasons, and in Egypt its mortality was formerly about 36 per cent. Its older name was due to the discharge of blood from the intestine. Sometimes portions of the bowel become gangrenous and slough, the condition described as affecting Jehoram (2 Ch **21** 19). There seems to have been an epidemic of the disease at the time of his seizure (2 Ch **21** 14.15), and in the case of the king it left behind it a chronic ulcerated condition, ending in gangrene. Somewhat similar conditions of chronic intestinal ulceration following epidemic dysentery I have seen in persons who had suffered from this disease in India.

Alex. Macalister

BLOODY SWEAT, swet (ὡσεὶ θρόμβοι αἵματος, *hōseí thrómboi haímatos*): Described in Lk **22** 44 as a physical accompaniment of Our Lord's agony at Gethsemane (on the passage, which is absent in some MSS, see WH). Many old writers take this to mean that the perspiration dropped in the same manner as clots of blood drop from a wound, regarding the Gr word prefixed as expressing merely a comparison as in Mt **28** 3, where *leukón hōs chiṓn* means "white as snow." Cases of actual exudation of blood are described in several of the mediaeval accounts of stigmatization, and Lefébvre describes the occurrence of something similar in his account of Louise Lateau in 1870. For references to these cases see art. "Stigmatization" in *Enc Brit*, XXII, 550. It is perhaps in favor of the older interpretation that the word used by Aeschylus for drops of blood is *stagṓn* (*Agam.* 1122) and by Euripides *stalagmós*, not *thromboi*. None of the instances given by Tissot (*Traité des nerfs*, 279), or Schenck (*Observ. méd.*, III, 455), can be said to be unimpeachable; but as the agony of Our Lord was unexampled in human experience, it is conceivable that it may have been attended with physical conditions of a unique nature.

Alex. Macalister

BLOOM, blōōm, **BLOSSOM,** blos'um. See Flowers.

BLOT, blot (מוּם, *mūm*, contracted from מְאוּם, *m*e*'ūm*, "spot"): Occurs in the sense of scorn (Prov **9** 7). In Job **31** 7 (AV) it is used **fig.** of a moral defect; RV has "spot." Blot out (מָחָה, *māḥāh*, "to wipe out," ἐξαλείφω, *exaleíphō*, "to smear out"), to obliterate or destroy: "That a tribe be not blotted out" (AV "destroyed," Jgs **21** 17). To blot men out of God's book is to cut them off by an untimely death (Ex **32** 32).

Figuratively: "To blot out sin" is to forgive sin fully (Ps **51** 1.9; Acts **3** 19; Col **2** 14). Not to blot out sin is to reserve for punishment (Neh **4** 5). The names of those who inherit eternal life are not blotted out of the "book of life" (Rev **3** 5). See Book of Life; Book of Remembrance; Forgiveness.

L. Kaiser

BLOW, blō (נָשַׁף, *nāshaph*): Used with reference to the wind (Ex **15** 10; Ps **78** 26; **147** 18; πνέω, *pnéō*, "to breathe," Lk **12** 55; Jn **3** 8; Rev **7** 1); תָּקַע, *tāḳa'*, with reference to trumpet sound (Nu **10** 3.4–10; **31** 6 AV; Jgs **7** 18.20; 1 K **1** 34; 1 Ch **15** 24; Ps **81** 3; Ezk **33** 3.6; Hos **5** 8; Joel **2** 1.15); פּוּחַ, *pū*a*ḥ*, with reference to the strong expulsion of the breath (Ezk **21** 31; **22** 20.21; Hag

1 9; Isa **40** 7; **54** 16; Job **20** 26); נָשַׁף, *nāshaph*, with reference to a forcible slap or stroke with a hand or an instrument (Ps **39** 10; Isa **40** 24; Jer **14** 17 AV). FRANK E. HIRSCH

BLUE, blōō. See COLORS.

BOANERGES, bō-a-nûr′jēz (**Βοανηργές**, *Boanērgés;* בְּנֵי רֶגֶשׁ, *b^e nē reghesh,* "sons of thunder"): The surname bestowed by Jesus upon James and John, the sons of Zebedee, when they were ordained to the apostleship (Mk **3** 17). See JAMES, SON OF ZEBEDEE. It has also been regarded as an equivalent of the "Heavenly Twins," the Sons of Zeus or Thunder. According to this interpretation, the name Boanerges would represent the Dioscuri in some form or other of their varied presentation in the cults of the Mediterranean (cf Professor J. Rendel Harris in *Expos*, ser. vii, III, 146). C. M. KERR

BOAR, bōr (חֲזִיר, *ḥăzīr*): In lamenting the troubled state of the Jewish nation the Psalmist (**80** 13) says: "The boar out of the wood doth ravage it, and the wild beasts of the field feed on it," with evident reference to Israel's enemies, the Assyrians, etc. The wild boar is abundant in certain parts of Pal and Syria, esp. in the thickets which border the lakes and rivers, as about the *Ḥūleh*, the sea of Galilee, the Jordan, and in the deltas of streams flowing into the Dead Sea, as *Ghaur-us-Ṣāfiyeh*. Several fountains in Lebanon bear the name, *'Ain-ul-Ḥazīr*, though *ḥazīr* is not an Arab. word, *khanzīr* being the Arab. for "swine." See SWINE. ALFRED ELY DAY

BOARD, bōrd (קֶרֶשׁ, *ḳeresh*, "a slab or plank," "deck of a ship," "bench," "board"): This word is found in Ex **26** 16–21; **36** 21 ff; its pl. occurs in Ex **26** 15.17–29; **35** 11; **36** 20–34; **39** 33; **40** 18; Nu **3** 36; **4** 31. This word also is used in tr of לוּחַ, *lūaḥ* (Ex **27** 8; **38** 7; Cant **8** 9; Ezk **27** 5 AV)="a tablet" (of stone, wood or metal), "board," "plate," "table"; also of *çēlā'*="rib," hence a "side," "timber," "plank" (1 K **6** 15 f). In 1 K **6** 9, שְׂדֵרָה, *s^e dhērāh*="a rank," "a row," hence, "a range" or "board" is used. In the NT we find the expression "on board" in Acts **27** 44 AV, in tr of ἐπὶ σανίσιν, *epí sanísin*="planks." FRANK E. HIRSCH

BOAST, bōst (הָלַל, *hālal*, "to praise"; **καυχάομαι**, *kaucháomai*, "to vaunt oneself," used both in a good and a bad sense): To praise God: "In God have we made our boast all the day long" (Ps **44** 8); to praise oneself, to vaunt (Ps **10** 3). In the NT the RV frequently translates "glory," where the AV has "boast," in a good sense (2 Cor **7** 14). In the sense of self-righteousness (Eph **2** 9; Rom **2** 17. 23). Boaster (ἀλαζών, *alazṓn*, "a braggart") occurs in AV (Rom **1** 30; 2 Tim **3** 2); RV has "boastful."

BOAT, bōt. See SHIPS.

BOAZ, bō′az (בֹּעַז, *bō'az;* **Βόοζ**, *Bóoz;* "quickness"[?] Ruth **2–4**; 1 Ch **2** 11.12; Mt **1** 5; Lk **3** 32):

(1) A resident of Bethlehem and kinsman of Elimelech, Naomi's husband. In Ruth **2** 1 he is described as a *gibbōr ḥayil*, a phrase which can mean either "a mighty man of valor" or else "a man of position and wealth." The latter is probably the sense in which the phrase is applied to Boaz (cf 1 S **9** 1). He had fields outside the town, and to them Ruth went to glean. Boaz noticed her and extended special kindness and protection to her, bidding her remain with his female workers, and charging the men not to illtreat her, and also giving her of the reapers' food at mealtime. Boaz awoke one night and found Ruth lying at his feet. He praised her virtue, and promised to take charge of her if her dead husband's next-of-kin failed to do so. He laid her case before the next-of-kin, and finally redeemed the family property himself and bought as well the right to take Ruth in marriage.

Field of Boaz.

The son of Boaz and Ruth was Obed, father of Jesse, and grandfather of David. 1 Ch **2** 11.12 makes Boaz a descendant of Hezron, and so probably a chief of the Hezronite clan in Bethlehem. Jewish tradition identifies Boaz with Ibzan (Jgs **12** 8–10).

Boaz "is set before us as a model of piety, generosity and chastity" (H. P. Smith, *OT History*, 398). He found virtue and rewarded it. *HPM*, §§501–8, gives a picture of the life of "a well-to-do landed proprietor of central Pal," much of which could aptly be taken as a description of Boaz.

(2) The name of one of the two bronze pillars erected in front of Solomon's temple, the other being Jachin (1 K **7** 21; 2 Ch **3** 17). See JACHIN AND BOAZ; TEMPLE. DAVID FRANCIS ROBERTS

BOCCAS, bok′as (**Βοκκάς**, *Bokkás*): A priest in the line of Ezra (1 Esd **8** 2) called Bukki in Ezr **7** 4 and Borith in 2 Esd **1** 2.

BOCHERU, bō′kē-rōō (בֹּכְרוּ, *bōkh^e rū*): A son of Azrikam, Saul's descendant (1 Ch **8** 38=**9** 34). For the ending וּ (*ū*), cf the forms גַּשְׁמוּ, *gashmū* (Neh **6** 1.6) and מְלִיכוּ, *m^e līkhū* (**12** 14 AV and RVm).

BOCHIM, bō′kim (הַבֹּכִים, *ha-bōkhīm*): A place on the mountain W. of Gilgal said to have been so named (lit. "the weepers") because Israel wept there at the remonstrance of the angel (Jgs **2** 1.5). No name resembling this has been discovered. Given on the occasion mentioned, it may not have endured. Many, following LXX, identify it with Bethel.

BODY, bod′i:

PHILOLOGICAL

(1) Generally speaking, the OT language employs no fixed term for the human body as an entire organism in exact opposition to "soul" or "spirit." Various terms were employed, each of which denotes only one part or element of the physical nature, such as "trunk," "bones," "belly," "bowels," "reins," "flesh," these parts being used, by synecdoche, for the whole: עֶצֶם, *'eçem*="bone," or "skeleton," hence "body," is found in Ex **24** 10 AV; Lam **4** 7; נֶפֶשׁ, *nephesh*="living organism" (Lev **21** 11; Nu **6** 6.7.11; **19** 11.13.16; Hag **2** 13); נְבֵלָה, *n^e bhēlāh*="a flabby thing," "carcass" (Dt **21** 23; Isa **26** 19; Jer **26** 23; **36**

30); בֶּטֶן, *beṭen*="womb" (Dt **28** 4.11.18.53; **30** 9; Job **19** 17 AV; Ps **132** 11; Mic **6** 7); יָרֵךְ, *yārēkh* = "thigh," "generative parts," "body" (Jgs **8** 30); גְּוִיָּה, *g^ewīyāh* = "a body, whether alive or dead" (1 S **31** 10.12; 2 K **8** 5 AV; Dnl **10** 6); מֵעִים, *mē'īm*, "body" (Cant **5** 14); גּוּפָה, *gūphāh* ="corpse" (1 Ch **10** 12); גֵּוָה, *gēwāh*="the back," i.e. (by extension) "person" (Job **20** 25); שְׁאֵר, *sh^e'ēr*="flesh, as living or for food," "body" (Ezk **10** 12); גֶּשֶׁם, *geshem*="a hard shower of rain," hence "a body" (Dnl **4** 33; **5** 21; **7** 11); נִדְנֶה, *nidhneh*="a sheath," hence the receptacle of the soul, "body" (Dnl **7** 15).

The Gr word which is used almost exclusively for "body" in the NT is σῶμα, *sôma*, Lat *corpus* (Mt **5** 29.30; **6** 22.23.25; **26** 26; Jn **2** 21; Acts **9** 40; 1 Cor **15** 35.37.38.44; Eph **1** 23; **2** 16; **4** 4.12.16; **5** 23.30). χρώς, *chrôs*, signifying primarily the "surface" or "skin," occurs in Acts **19** 12. A compound word with *sōma*, as its base, σύσσωμος, *sússōmos*="a member of the same body," occurs in Eph **3** 6. From the above, it appears that the NT places the body as a whole into opposition to the spirit or the invisible nature. Paul, of course, employs the term also to designate the sublimated substance with which we are to be clothed after the resurrection when he speaks of the "spiritual body" (1 Cor **15** 44). FRANK E. HIRSCH

GENERAL

(2) **σῶμα,** *sôma*, Lat *corpus:* The term "body" is not found in the Heb of the OT in the sense in which it occurs in the Gr.

1. In the OT

"The Heb word for 'body' is גְּוִיָּה, *g^ewīyāh*, which is sometimes used for the 'living' body (Ezk **1** 11), 'bodies of the cherubim' (Gen **47** 18; Neh **9** 37), but usually for the dead body or carcass. Properly speaking the Heb has no term for 'body.' The Heb term around which questions relating to the body must gather is *flesh*" (Davidson, *OT Theol.*, 188). Various terms are used in the OT to indicate certain elements or component parts of the body, such as "flesh," "bones," "bowels," "belly," etc, some of which have received a new meaning in the NT. Thus the OT "belly" (Heb *beṭen*, Gr *koilía*), "Our soul is bowed down to the dust; our belly cleaveth unto the earth" (Ps **44** 25 AV)—as the seat of carnal appetite—has its counterpart in the NT: "They serve . . . . their own belly" (Rom **16** 18). So also the word tr[d] "bowels" (*mē'īm, rahămīm*) in the sense of compassion, as in Jer **31** 20 AV: "Therefore my bowels are troubled for him," is found in more than one place in the NT. Thus in Phil **1** 8 AV, "I long after you all in the bowels *splágchna*] of Christ," and again, "if there be any bowels [*splagchna*] and mercies" (Phil **2** 1 AV).

2. In the NT

"Body" in the NT is largely used in a **fig.** sense, either as indicating the "whole man" (Rom **6** 12; He **10** 5), or as that which is morally corrupt — "the body of this death" (Rom **6** 6; **7** 24). Hence the expression, "buffet my body" (1 Cor **9** 27, *hupōpiázō*, a word adopted from the prize-ring, *palaestra*), the body being considered as the lurking-place and instrument of evil. (Cf Rom **8** 13 AV "Mortify the deeds of the body.")

3. Other Meanings

Between these two the various other meanings seem to range. On the one hand we find the church called "the body of Christ" (Eph **4** 16; 1 Cor **12** 13), with diversity of gifts, enjoying the "unity of the Spirit in the bond of peace." On the other we read of a *spiritual*, incorruptible body, a resurrection-body as opposed to the *natural* body, which is doomed to corruption in death (1 Cor **15** 44). Not only do we find these meanings in the word itself, but also in some of its combinations. On the one hand we read in Eph **3** 6 of the Gentiles as "partakers of the promise in Christ" as "fellow-heirs," and "of the same body" (*sússōma*) in corporate union with all who put their trust in the Redeemer of mankind; on the other, we read of mere "bodily [somatic] exercises," which are not profitable (1 Tim **4** 8)—where "body" evidently is contrasted with "spirit." And again, we read of the Holy Ghost descending in "bodily" (somatic) shape upon the "Son of God" (Lk **3** 22), in whom dwelt the "fulness of the Godhead bodily" (somatically) (Col **2** 9). So, too, the "body" is called a temple of the Holy Ghost: "Know ye not that your body is a temple of the Holy Spirit?" (1 Cor **6** 19).

4. The Body and Sin

From all this it is apparent that the body in itself is not necessarily evil, a doctrine which is taught in Gr philosophy, but nowhere in the OT and NT. The rigid and harsh dualism met with in Plato is absent from St. Paul's writings, and is utterly foreign to the whole of Scripture. Here we are distinctly taught, on the one hand, that the body is subordinated to the soul, but on the other, with equal clearness, that the human body has a dignity, originally conferred upon it by the Creator, who shaped it out of earth, and glorified it by the incarnation of Christ, the sinless One, though born of a woman. Julius Müller has well said: "Paul denies the presence of evil in Christ, who was partaker of our fleshly nature (Gal **4** 4), and he recognizes it in spirits who are not partakers thereof (Eph **6** 12 AV, 'spiritual wickedness in high places'). Is it not therefore in the highest degree probable that according to him evil does not necessarily pertain to man's sensuous nature, and that *sárx* (say *body*) denotes something different from this?" (*The Christian Doctrine of Sin*, I, 321, Eng. ed). He further shows that the derivation of sin from sense is utterly irreconcilable with the central principle of the apostle's doctrine as to the perfect holiness of the Redeemer, and that "the doctrine of the future resurrection—even taking into account the distinction between the *sōma psuchikón* and the *sōma pneumatikón* (1 Cor **15** 44)—is clearly at variance with the doctrine that sin springs from the corporal nature as its source" (318).

5. The First Sin

The very first sin was spiritual in its origin—an act of rebellion against God—the will of the creature in opposition to the will of the Creator (Gen **3**). It was conceived in doubt—"Hath God said?"; it was born in desire—"The tree was good for food"; it was stimulated by a rebellious hankering after equality with God: "Ye shall be as God, knowing good and evil"; it was introduced from without, from the spiritual world, through the agency of a mysterious, supernatural being, employing "a beast of the field more subtle than any which Jehovah God had made." That the serpent in the OT is not identified with Satan, and that the clearest utterance in pre-Christian times on the subject is to be found in the Book of Wisd **2** 24 ("by the envy of the devil death entered into the world"), may be true. That the narrative of the Fall is **fig.** or symbolical may also be granted. But the whole tendency of the early narrative is to connect the first human sin with a superhuman being, employing an agent known to man, and making that agent its representative in the "subtlety" of the great temptation as a prelude to the mighty fall. The NT is clear on this point (Jn **8** 44; **16** 11; 2 Cor **11** 3; 1 Tim **2** 14; He **2** 14; Rev **12** 9). Great historic truths are imbedded in that narrative, whatever we may think of the form which that narrative has assumed. There can be no doubt that the oldest and truest traditions of the human race are to be found there. It is not denied that sin has desecrated the temple of the living God, which is the body. That body indeed has become defiled and polluted by sin. Paul recognizes "an abnormal development of the sensuous in fallen man, and regards sin as having in a special manner entrenched itself in the body, which becomes liable to death on this very account (Rom **6** 23; **7** 24)" (*Enc of Rel. and Ethics*, I, 761). But we may safely say that the theory which connects sin with the physical body, and gives it a purely sensuous origin, is alien to the whole spirit and letter of revelation. J. I. MARAIS

FIGURATIVE

(3) In the NT (σῶμα, *sôma*, "the body" both of men and animals) the word has a rich **fig.** and spiritual use: (1) the temporary home of the soul (2 Cor **5** 6); (2) "the temple of the Holy Spirit" (1 Cor **6** 19); (3) "temple" (Jn **2** 21); (4) "the old man," the flesh as the servant of sin or the sphere in which moral evil comes to outward expression (Rom **6** 6; **7** 7; cf Paul's use of *sárx*, "flesh"); (5) the "church" as Christ's body, the organism through which He manifests His life and in which His spirit dwells (Eph **1** 23; Col **1** 24); (6) the spiritual "unity" of believers, one redeemed society or organism (Eph **2** 16; a *corpus mysticum*, Eph **4** 4); (7) "substance" (spiritual reality or life in Christ) v. "shadow" (Col **2** 17); (8) the ascended and glorified body of Jesus (Phil **3** 21); (9) the resurrection or "spiritual" (v. natural) body of the redeemed in heaven (1 Cor **15** 44); (10) the whole personality, e.g. the spiritual presence, power and sacrificial work of Christ, the mystical meaning of "the body and the blood" symbolized in the bread and cup of the sacrament (1 Cor **11** 27). The term body is exceptionally rich in connection with the self-giving, sacrificial, atoning work of Christ. It was the outward sphere or manifestation of His suffering. Through the physical He revealed the extent of His redeeming and sacrificial love. He "bare our sins in his body upon the tree" (1 Pet **2** 24), thus forever displacing all the ceaseless and costly sacrifices of the old dispensation (He **9** 24–28). Special terms "body of his flesh" (Col **1** 22); "body of sin" (Rom **6** 6); "body of this death" (Rom **7** 24); "body of his glory" (Phil **3** 21).

πτῶμα, *ptôma*, used only of *fallen*, i.e. *dead* bodies (Rev **11** 8.9). DWIGHT M. PRATT

BODY-GUARD, bod′i-gärd: The expression occurs in Apoc (1 Esd **3** 4), "the body-guard that kept the king's person."

BODY OF DEATH, deth (**σῶμα τοῦ θανάτου**, *sôma toú thanátou*): These words are found in Paul's impassioned argument on the reign of the law, which dooms man to continuous disappointment and convinces him of the terrible power of indwelling sin. "O wretched man that I am! who shall deliver me from the body of this death?" (Rom **7** 24 AV). It is the "picture of the still unredeemed man in his relation to the law" (Meyer). The tr, "this body of death," though grammatically possible, is logically impermissible. The picture here before the mind of the apostle is not physical but ethical. Death points to the dominion of sin, to the reign of the law, as revealed in his physical life, from which he is delivered only through regeneration, by faith in Christ. It points to the "I must" and to the "I cannot." It is therefore the bondage under the law of sin, the body as the seat of this conscious and bitter struggle, that the figure points at. And yet the ethical may have a physical background. There may be a distant reference here to the dreadful punishment of the ancients of chaining the living body to a corpse, that the constant corruption of death might extinguish the life of the victim of this exquisite torture. HENRY E. DOSKER

BODY OF HEAVEN: The AV translates the Heb idiom, עֶצֶם הַשָּׁמַיִם, *'eçem ha-shāmayim*, by "the body of heaven" (Ex **24** 10). A more correct rendering is given in the RV, "the very heaven," taking the word *'eçem* in its idiomatic use as an intensive, which is derived from its lit. meaning, "bone," as "strength," "substance," and then as "self" (cf Job **21** 23); the substance of the blue, unclouded sky, hence the clear sky itself.

BODY, SPIRITUAL, spir′it̹-ū-al: Paul describes the body after the resurrection as a *spiritual* body (*sôma psuchikón*) and contrasts it with the natural (psychical body, *sôma pneumatikón*, 1 Cor **15** 44). Our present natural body has for its life-principle the soul (*psuchḗ*) but the resurrection body is adapted and subordinated to the spirit (*pneúma*). See PSYCHOLOGY. The apostle does not argue for a literal and material identity of that future body with the present one, but thinks of it as the counterpart of the present animal organism so conditioned as to be adapted to a state of existence which lies wholly within the sphere of the spirit. Against his Corinthian readers he argues that the resurrection cannot be succeeded by a state of non-existence, nor is he willing to admit a mere etherealized state. There must be a body, but between it and our present body there is a similar difference to that between the first and second Adam. The present body and the first Adam were alike dominated by the soul (*psuchḗ*); but as the second Adam became a life-giving spirit, so will the resurrection body be a spiritual one. Christ became a life-giving spirit through the resurrection (Meyer on 1 Cor **15** 45); and since we are to bear His image (ver 49), it becomes evident that Christ's resurrection-body is the nearest possible approach to a sensible representation of the spiritual body. For this Paul argues more directly when he affirms that our resurrection-body shall be transformed according to the body of His glory (Phil **3** 21; cf 1 Jn **3** 2). The body of Christ after the resurrection was conformed in many respects to the body of His earthly life, yet with some marked differences. He ate (Lk **24** 42.43); He breathed (Jn **20** 22); possessed flesh and bones (Lk **24** 39), and could be apprehended by the bodily senses (Lk **24** 40; Jn **20** 27). His body possessed characteristics which differentiated it entirely from the popular fancy of ghosts or apparitions (Lk **24** 36–43). Yet His body was superior to the usual barriers which restrict human movements. Barred doors and distances did not impede His going (Jn **20** 19–26; Lk **24** 31–36). The context shows that the purpose of His eating was to convince the disciples that it was really He (Lk **24** 41–43), and not to sustain life which His body was probably capable of maintaining in other ways. John speaks of His appearances after His resurrection as "manifestations" (Jn **21** 1–21). A change in His person and appearance had certainly taken place, for those who knew Him best did not at once recognize Him (Lk **24** 16; Jn **20** 14). It is evident therefore that the post-resurrection-body of Jesus was one that had the power of materializing itself to natural senses, or withdrawing itself at will. It was this same body which was taken into the heavens at the ascension, and which remains in heaven (Acts **1** 11; **3** 21). There is no hint that it underwent any change in its removal from earth. Hence the spiritual body of which Paul speaks is not to be unlike the body which Jesus possessed after His resurrection. There is to be an absence of the desires and passions which belong naturally to the present bodily existence (Mt **22** 30; Lk **20** 35.36). WM. CHAS. MORRO

BOHAN, bō'han (בֹּהַן, *bōhan,* "thumb," "stumpy"): A son of Reuben according to Josh **15** 6; **18** 17. No mention is made of B. in the genealogies of Reuben. "The stone of Bohan" (*'ebhen bōhan*) was a boundary mark on the N.E. frontier of Judah, separating it from Benjamin. Site unidentified.

BOIL (noun) (שְׁחִין, *sh^eḥīn;* ἕλκος, *hélkos*): A localized inflamed swelling. The Heb word is derived from a root probably meaning "to burn," and is used as a generic term for the sores in the sixth plague of Egypt (Ex **9** 9–11); for a sore which might be confounded with leprosy (Lev **13** 18–23); for Job's malady (**2** 7) and Hezekiah's disease (2 K **20** 1; Isa **38** 21). Our Eng. word is derived from the vb. "to beal," i.e. to suppurate, now obsolete except as a dialect word in Scotland and Ireland. Wyclif uses the name for Lazarus' sores (Lk **16** 20), "houndis lickeden his bylis." The Egyp word *sḥn* is the name of an abscess, and occurs in the reduplicated form *ḥnḥnt* in Papyr. Ebers, CV. The plague of boils in Egypt came without warning immediately after the insect plagues of *kinnīm* (sandflies) and that of *'ārōbh* or flies, and followed the epizoötic murrain, which is suggestive in the light of the transmission of toxic germs by insects. It has been supposed by some to be elephantiasis, as Pliny says that this disease was peculiar to Egypt (xxvi.5). A stronger case has been made out for its identity with confluent smallpox; but as it is not described as being a fatal disease, it may more probably have been an aggravated form of the ordinary gregarious furuncles or boils, due to the microbe *streptococcus pyogenes.*

Job's body is said to have been covered with itchy, irritating sores which made his face unrecognizable (**2** 12), caused continual burning pain (**3** 24; **6** 4), and which were infested with maggots (**7** 5) and exhaled a nauseous fetor (**19** 17). His sleep was destroyed and his nervous system enfeebled (**3** 26) so that he required assistance to move, as he sat in the ashes (**2** 8). Various diagnoses have been made of his malady, but it is most probable that it was a form of the disease known as "oriental sore," or "Bagdad boil," called in Algeria "Biskra batton," in which the intensely itchy sores are often multiple, affecting the face, hands, and other exposed parts. The cases which I have seen have been very intractable and disfiguring.

Hezekiah's boil was apparently more localized, and the indefinite description would accord with that of a carbuncle. It seems to have rendered him unclean (Isa **38** 22), though the reference may be to the practice referred to in Lev **13** 18 f. The "botch" of Egypt (Dt **28** 27.35 AV) is a tr of the same word, as is "boil" in RV. Botch is an old Eng. name for boil and occurs in *Piers Plowman,* and the adj. "botchy" is used in *Troilus and Cressida* (II, 1, 6). The word is cognate to the old French *boche* or *poche,* a form of our later word "pock." The sores of Lazarus (Lk **16** 20) were probably old varicose ulcers, such as are as common on the legs of the old and poor in the East as they are in the West.

ALEX. MACALISTER

BOIL (verb) (בָּשַׁל, *bāshal,* רָתַח, *rāthaḥ*): "Boil" is the tr of *bāshal,* "to bubble up," "to boil," "to be cooked," Piēl, "to cause to boil," "to cook" (Lev **8** 31; 1 K **19** 21; 2 K **6** 29; Ezk **46** 20.24 *bis*); of *rāthaḥ,* "to be hot," "to boil," "to be made to boil," "to be greatly moved" under strong emotion (the bowels), Hiph. "to cause to boil" (Job **30** 27 AV "My bowels boiled, and rested not," ERV "My bowels boil." ARV "My heart is troubled"; **41** 31, "He maketh the deep to boil like a pot"; Ezk **24** 5, "make it boil well"); of *bā'āh,* "to bubble" or "well up" (Isa **64** 2 [1, in Heb] "The fire causeth the waters to boil"); in AVm of Ps **45** 1 ("My heart is inditing a good matter") we have Heb "boileth" or "bubbleth up" (*rāḥash,* "to boil" or "bubble up," RV text, "My heart overfloweth with a goodly matter").

"Boiling-places," occurs in Ezk **46** 23 as the tr of *m^ebhashsh^elōth,* "hearths," "boiling-places." ARV has "boiling-houses" for "places of them that boil" (Ezk **46** 24), "boil well" for "consume" (**24** 10); ARV has "boiling over" for "unstable" (Gen **49** 4; ERVm "bubbling over").

W. L. WALKER

BOLDNESS, bōld'nes (παρρησία, *parrēsía,* "confidence," "fearlessness," "freedom of speech"): This was one of the results of discipleship (Acts **4** 13.29.31; Eph **3** 12; Phil **1** 20; 1 Tim **3** 13; 1 Jn **4** 17). It was a necessary qualification for the work assigned them. They were not only subject to violent persecutions, but also were the constant subject of ridicule and contempt. Paul uses the word in the sense of plainness in 2 Cor **3** 12. In He **10** 19; 1 Jn **2** 28; **4** 17, it has the sense of freeness resulting from confidence. In Philem ver 8, the reference is to the authority which Paul claims in this case. JACOB W. KAPP

BOLLED, bōld (גִּבְעֹל, *gibh'ōl,* "the calyx of flowers"): Hence "in bloom," and so rendered, in RV, of flowering flax (Ex **9** 31).

BOLSTER, bōl'stẽr: Found in AV only in 1 S **19** 13.16, "Behold, the teraphim was in the bed, with the *pillow* of goat's hair at the head thereof" (AV "for his bolster"), and **26** 7.11.12.16, "Saul lay sleeping . . . . with his spear stuck in the ground at his *head.*" "Bolster" in these passages in AV was used to translate a Heb word whose true significance is "the place of the head," or "the head-place." It will be noted that it has disappeared from the RV, which rightly has throughout "head," instead of "bolster." See CUSHION.

BOLT, bōlt (נָעַל, *nā'al,* "to bind up"): The ancient Hebrews had fastenings of wood or iron for the doors of houses (2 S **13** 17.18; Cant **5** 5), city gates (Neh **3** 3.6.13–15), prison doors, etc (Isa **45** 2), which were in the form of bolts. These were sometimes pushed back from within; but there were others which, by means of a key, could be unfastened and pushed back from without (Jgs **3** 23 ff). These were almost the only form of locks known. See BAR; LOCK.

In Hab **3** 5, *resheph* (a poetic word for "flame") is rendered "fiery bolts" (AV "burning coals"). It seems to denote "the fiery bolts, by which Jeh was imagined to produce pestilence or fever" (Driver, *Dt,* 367). M. O. EVANS

BOND. See BAND; BILL; CHAIN.

BONDAGE, bon'dāj: Used in two senses in Scripture, a literal and a metaphorical sense.

(1) In the former sense it refers (*a*) to the condition of the Hebrews (עֲבֹדָה, *'ăbhōdhāh*) in Egypt (Ex **1** 14 AV; **2** 23 and often) which is frequently called "the house of bondage" ("slaves,"

עֲבָדִים, *'ăbhādhīm*), Ex **13** 3.14; **20** 2; Dt **5** 6 and often. It also refers to the condition of the Hebrews in Babylonia (Isa **14** 3 AV) and in Persia (Ezr **9** 8f), where a slightly different form of the same root (עַבְדוּת, *'abhedhūth*) is used in the original. In both these cases the bondage was not so much personal as national. As a rule individuals were not subject to individuals, but the whole Heb people were subject to the Egyp, Bab and the Pers states. They were forced to labor on public works, and otherwise, and were denied their own freedom when the exigencies of state seemed to demand it. The former word *'ăbhōdhāh* is also used in Neh **5** 18 as descriptive of the subject and depressed conditions of the Hebrews in Pal during the earlier years after their return from captivity, when they were still living under Pers suzerainty. (*b*) The word bondage (*'ăbhādhīm*) is also used to describe the slavery into which the poor Jews were being forced by their more prosperous brethren in the earlier years under the Persians in Pal (Neh **5** 5). Here true personal, though temporary, slavery is meant. (*c*) Marriage is once referred to as a bondage (1 Cor **7** 15) (vb. δουλόω, *doulóō*).

(2) It is used in the metaphorical sense only in NT. ἡ δουλεία, *hē douleía*, "bondage," is the power of physical corruption as against the freedom of life (Rom **8** 21), the power of fear as over against the confidence of Christian faith (Rom **8** 15; He **2** 15), and esp. is it the bondage of the letter, of the elements, of a ceremonial and institutional salvation which must be scrupulously and painfully observed, as contrasted with the freedom of the sons of God, emancipated by faith in Jesus Christ. This bondage is a peculiarly Pauline idea since he was fighting for Christian freedom (Gal **2** 4; **4** 3.9. 24.25; **5** 1). In 2 Pet **2** 19 the idea is essentially different. Libertinism, masquerading under the name of freedom, is branded as bondage, in contrast with the true freedom of righteous living. See SLAVERY.

WILLIAM JOSEPH MCGLOTHLIN

BONDMAID, bond'mād: Occurs but three times in AV (Lev **19** 20; **25** 44; Gal **4** 22 [RV "handmaid"]). The first instance is that of a Heb girl who has by birth, purchase or otherwise come into temporary slavery. The word here is שִׁפְחָה, *shiphḥāh*. It occurs often in the OT, but is elsewhere trd "maid," "handmaid," "woman servant," "maidservant," etc. The other instance (Lev **25** 44) refers to foreign slave girls and has a different word, אָמָה, *'āmāh*, which also occurs a number of times, but is elsewhere trd "handmaid," etc. The NT instance (Gal **4** 22) refers to Hagar, Abraham's Egyp slave girl. The original word παιδίσκη, *paidískē*, occurs several other times, but in AV is elsewhere trd "maid," "damsel," etc. It means a slave girl. See SLAVERY.

WILLIAM JOSEPH MCGLOTHLIN

BONDMAN, bond'man: One of the trs of the word עֶבֶד, *'ebhedh*, very common in the OT. It refers to the ordinary slave, either foreign (Gen **43** 18; **44** 9.33; Lev **25** 44.46) or Heb (Lev **25** 42; 2 K **4** 1). Hebrews were forbidden to enslave Hebrews, but did it nevertheless. It also refers to the Israelites in the bondage of Egypt (Dt **15** 15, and often), and in the exile of Babylonia (Ezr **9** 9). The intended treatment of the men of Judah in Samaria (2 Ch **28** 10) was apparently to sell them into ordinary slavery or bondage. The word is used once in the NT (Rev **6** 15) to translate δοῦλος, *doúlos*, where it evidently means a slave in contrast with a freeman. See SLAVERY.

WILLIAM JOSEPH MCGLOTHLIN

BONDSERVANT, bond'sûr-vant: Appears only once in AV (Lev **25** 39) where it translates עֶבֶד, *'ebhedh*, "a slave": "Thou shalt not cause him to render the service of a bondservant" or slave. RV frequently uses bondservant (δοῦλος, *doúlos*) instead of the word "servant" of AV (Jn **8** 34.35; 1 Cor **7** 21; Gal **4** 7). See SLAVERY.

BONE, bōn, **BONES** (עֶצֶם, *'eçem*, עֹצֶם, *'ōçem*; Aram. גְּרֶם, *gerem*, by extension used for "bony frame," "body," "strength," Ps **35** 10; "the whole man"; Lk **24** 39, "flesh and bones" = the solid and tangible framework of the body; **fig.** the substance, the idea of a thing, the thing, *per se*): **Figurative:** Very often we find the use of these words in metaphorical phrases, in which a disease or a discomfort of the body denotes certain emotions or mental attitudes. Thus the expression "rottenness of the bones" (Prov **12** 4; **14** 30) signifies the feelings of a man whose wife causes him shame and confusion, or is equivalent to "envy," "jealousy." The tr of the LXX in these passages by σκώληξ, *skōlēx*, "worm," and σής, *sēs*, "maggot," "moth," is incorrect. The same phrase is used in Hab **3** 16 for utter dejectedness through the anticipation of approaching evil. Similarly the "shaking of the bones" (Job **4** 14) is expressive of fear, and denotes dejection and sadness in Jer **23** 9. The "burning of the bones" is found as a symptom of Job's disease (Job **30** 30), and stands for grief, depression of spirits in Ps **102** 3 and Lam **1** 13, and also for the feeling of Jeremiah, when he attempted to hold back the Divine message (Jer **20** 9), while "dryness of bones" (Prov **17** 22) is the opposite of "good health." Other similar expressions of mental distress are the "piercing of the bones" (Job **30** 17), the bones are "troubled" (Ps **6** 2), "out of joint" (Ps **22** 14), "consumed" (Ps **31** 10 AV), "wasted away" or "waxed old" (Ps **32** 3), "broken" (Ps **51** 8; Lam **3** 4), "ill at rest" (Ps **38** 3), "bone of my bones," etc (Gen **2** 23), having the same nature, and the nearest relation (2 S **5** 1) and affection (Eph **5** 30). In the last-mentioned passage, RV omits "of his flesh, and of his bones" as an interpolation from Gen **2** 23. The figs. in Mic **3** 2.3 are expressive of the most cruel oppression and murder.

H. L. E. LUERING

BONNET, bon'et: In AV the designation of the special headdress of the rank and file of the priesthood, RV "head-tire" (Ex **28** 40). It consisted of a long swath of fine white linen wound around the head in oriental fashion. The Heb word found in Ex **29** 9 RV, "to bind head-tires," lit. "to wind head-tires," means, in the light of usage, "to form an egg-shaped turban." Cf Jos, *Ant*, III, vii, 3; and see Rich, *Dict. Rom and Gr Ant*, s.v. *pileus*, for illustration of the egg-shaped cap of Ulysses, with which Jerome compared the priestly turban. See DRESS; MITRE, etc.

BOOK, bŏŏk (סֵפֶר, *çēpher*; ἡ βίβλος, *hē bíblos*):

1. Definition
2. Inward Books
3. Publication
   (1) Mechanical Copies
   (2) Personal Copies
4. Oral Transmission
5. MSS
   (1) Epigraphy
   (2) Sphragistics
   (3) Numismatics
   (4) Diplomatics
   (5) Paleography
6. Printed Books
7. Variations
8. Textual Criticism
9. Higher Criticism
10. Literary Criticism
11. Origin of New Forms
12. Survival
13. Book Collections
14. Early History of Books in Bible Lands

LITERATURE

1. Definition

A book is any record of thought in words. It consists of a fixed form of words embodied in some kind of substance. The form of words is the main factor, but it has no existence without the record. The kind of record is indifferent; it may be carved on stone, stamped on clay, written or printed on vellum, papyrus or paper, or only stamped on the mind of author or hearer, if so be it keeps the words in fixed form. Looked on as a form of words the book is called a work, and looked on as a record it is called a volume, document, inscription, etc, as the case may be; but neither volume nor work has any real existence as book save as united.

The Bib. words for book, both Gr and Heb, oscillate in meaning (as they do in all languages) between the two elements, the form of words and the material form. The common words for book in the NT, from which too the word "Bible" comes, refer back to the papyrus plant or the material on which the book is written, just as the Eng. word "book" was long supposed to be derived from the beech tree, on whose bark the book was written. The usual word in the Heb of the OT (*ṣēpher*) may possibly refer to the act of writing, just as the Gr word *grámmata* and the Eng. "writings" do, but

A Writer, His Palette, and a Papyrus Leaf.

more likely, as its other meanings of "numbering" and "narration" or even "missive" indicate, it refers neither to the material nor to the writing process but to the literary work itself. It suggests at least the fact that the earliest books were, indeed, books of tallies. The knot-books and various notch-book tallies are true books. In the King James' version the "word" (*dābhār*) is sometimes tr[d] book, and, although changed in these places in the RV to "acts" or "deeds," it was nevertheless quite properly tr[d] a book, just as the "word" in Gr is used for book, and indeed in Eng. when the Bible is called the Word. Besides these terms commonly tr[d] book in the EV, various book forms are referred to in the Bible as roll or volume (which is the same in origin), tablet, and perhaps rock inscription (Job **19** 23.24).

The fact that the Bible is a book, or indeed a library of many kinds of books, makes necessary that to approach its study one should have some systematic idea of the nature of the book; the origin of new forms and their survival, oral and manuscript transmission, the nature of the inward book and the various kinds of inward books. Apart from the matter of general archaeological use for historical interpretation, the questions of inspiration, the incarnate, creative, and indwelling word and many other doctrines are wholly bound up with this question of the nature of the book, and many phrases, such as the Book of Life, can hardly be understood without knowing with some degree of clearness what a book is.

The archaeology, text criticism and higher criticism of the past few years have revolutionized book history and theory in their respective fields. Above all the young science of experimental psychology has, in its short life, contributed more even than the others to an understanding of the book and The Book, the word of God and the Word of God, the Bible and Jesus Christ.

2. Inward Books

Modern experimental psychology by its study of inward images, inward speech, inward writings and other kinds of inward book forms has, in particular, thrown on Bib. inspiration, higher criticism and text criticism and the various aspects of the doctrine of the word, an unexpected light. Inward books, it appears, are not only real, but of many kinds, visual and auditory, oral and written, sensory and motor, and these different kinds have perhaps a material basis and local habitation in different parts of the brain. At least they have real existence; they are real records which preserve a fixed form of words, to be brought out of the recesses of the mind from time to time for re-shaping, re-study or utterance. (See Dittrich, *Sprachpsychologie*, 1903; LeRoy, *Le langage*, Paris, 1905; Van Ginneken, *Principes de linguistique psychol.*, 1907; A. Marty, *Untersuch. Sprachphilosophie*, 1908; Macnamara, *Human Speech*, 1909; the classical work is Wundt, *Völkerpsychologie: Die Sprache*, Leipzig, 1900.)

Inward books may be originals or copies. Every book is, to begin with, inward. Men sometimes speak of an autograph as the "original," but it is in fact only a first-hand copy of the original, which is inward, and never by any chance becomes or can become outward. Besides these originals there are also inward copies of the books of others. The fact that a book may be memorized is no new thing, but the analysis of the process is. It seems that a book may be inwardly copied through eye or ear or touch or any sense from some outward book; or again it may be copied back and forth within, from sense copy to motor copy, from visual to oral, auditory to inward writing. In reading aloud the visual image is copied over into oral; in taking dictation the auditory image is copied over into inward writing. Many men, even in reading from print, cannot understand unless they translate as they go into oral images or even move their lips. Many others either hearing or reading a French book, e.g. have to translate inwardly into English and have in the end two memory copies, one French and one English, both of which may be recalled. In whatever way they are recorded, these memory impressions are real copies of outward books, and in the case of tribal medicine men, Vedic priests, the ancient minstrels, village gossips, and professional story-tellers of all kinds, the inward collection of books may become a veritable library.

3. Publication

The end for which a book is created is in general to reach another mind. This means the utterance or copying into some outward material and the re-copying by another into memory. The commonest modes of utterance are oral speech and writing; but there are many others, some appealing to eye, some to ear, some to touch: e.g. gesture language of the Indian and the deaf mute, pressure signs for the blind and deaf, signal codes, drum language, the telegraph click, etc. If the persons to be reached are few, a single oral speech or manuscript may be enough to supply all needs of publication, but if there are very many the speech or writing must somehow be multiplied. This may be done by the author himself. Blind Homer, it is alleged, repeated the *Iliad* in many cities; and the modern political orator may repeat the same speech several times in the same evening to different audiences. So too the author may, as many Lat writers did, copy out several autographs. If the audience is still too great to be reached by authors' utterances, the aid of heralds, minstrels, scribes and the printing-press must be called in to copy from the autographs or other author's utterances; and in case of need more help yet is called in, copies

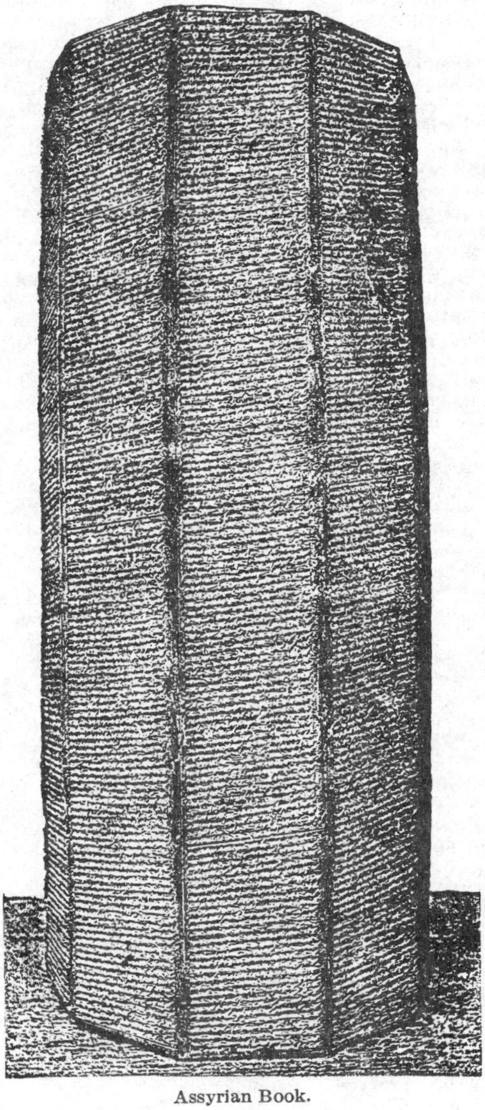

Assyrian Book.

made from these copies, and copies again, and so on to perhaps hundreds of copyings. This process may be represented as $x+x^1+x^2+x^3+x^n$ where x=an original, x^1 a first-hand copy of author's utterance, x^2 a second-hand copy, x^3 a third-hand, etc.

Books may thus be divided into originals, first-hand or authors' copies and re-copies. Re-copies in turn whether at second-, third-, fourth- or nth-hand, may be either mechanical or personal, according as the copy is direct from outward material to outward material or from the outward material to a human memory.

(1) *Mechanical copies* include photographic copies of MSS, or of the lips in speaking, or of gesture, or any other form of utterance which may be photographed. They include also phonographic records, telegraph records, and any other mechanical records of sound or other forms of utterance. Besides photographic and phonograhic processes, mechanical copies include founding, stamping by seal or die, stereographic, electrotype, stencil, gelatine pad and printing-press processes, any processes, in short, which do not pass *via* the human mind, but direct from copy to copy by material means. They do not include composition in movable types or by type-setting machines, typewriting machines and the like, which, like writing, require the interposition of a human mind. These mechanical copies are subject to defects of material, but are free from psychological defects and error, and defect of material is practically negligible.

(2) *Personal copies* include inward copies, or memory books, and the re-uttered copies from these copies, to which latter class belong all copied MSS. The memory copy may be by eye from writing, or from the lips of a speaker in the case of the deaf. Or it may be by ear from oral speech, telegraph key, drum or other sound utterances. Or it may be again from touch, as in the case of finger-tip lip-reading or the reading of raised characters by the blind. Each of these kinds may perhaps be located in a different part of the mind or brain, and its molecular substratum may be as different from other kinds of inward record as a wave of light is different from a wave of sound, or a photograph from the wax roll of a phonograph; but whatever the form or nature, it somehow records a certain fixed form of words which is substantially equivalent to the original. This memory copy, unlike the mechanical copy, is liable to substantial error. This may arise from defects of sense or of the inward processes of record and it is nearly always present. Why this need be so is one of the mysteries of human nature, but that it is, is one of the obvious facts; and when memory copies are re-uttered there is still another crop of errors, "slips of tongue and pen," equally mysterious but equally inevitable. It comes to pass, therefore, that where oral or manuscript transmission exists, there is sure to be a double crop of errors between the successive outward copies. When thus a form of words is frequently re-copied or reprinted *via* the human mind the resulting book becomes more and more unlike the original as to its form of words, until in the late manuscript copies of early works there may often be thousands of variations from the original. Even an inspired revelation would thus be subject to at least one and perhaps two or three sets of errors from copying before it reached even the autograph stage.

Before the knowledge of handwriting became general, oral publication was usual, and it is still not uncommon. The king's laws and proclamations, the works of poets and historians, and the sacred books were anciently published orally by heralds and minstrels and prophets; and these primitive publishers are survived still by town criers, actors, reciters, and Scripture readers.

4. Oral Transmission

Up to the point of the first impression on another mind, oral publication has many advantages. The impression is generally more vivid, and the voice conveys many nice shades of feeling through inflection, stress, and the delicate variations in tone quality which cannot be expressed in writing. When it comes to transmission, however, oral tradition tends to rapid deterioration with each re-copy. It is true that such transmission may be quite exact with enough painstaking and repetition; thus the modern stage affords many examples of actors with large and exact repertories, and the Vedas were, it is alleged, handed down for cents.

by a rigidly trained body of memorizers. The memorizing of Confucian books by Chinese students and of the Koran by Moslem students is very exact. Nevertheless exact *transmission* orally is rare, and exists only under strictly artificial conditions. Ear impressions, to begin with, tend to be less exact than eye impressions, in any event, because they depend on a brief sense impression, while in reading the eye lingers until the matter is understood. Moreover, the memory copy is not fixed and tends to fade away rapidly; unless very rigidly guarded and frequently repeated it soon breaks up its verbal form. This is readily seen by the great variety in the related legends of closely related tribes; and in modern times in the tales of village gossips and after-dinner stories, which soon lose their fixed verbal form, save as to the main point.

There is great difference of opinion as to the part which oral transmission played in the composition of the OT. The prevailing theory of the higher critics of the 19th cent. made this the prime factor of transmission to at earliest the 8th cent. BC, but the recent remarkable revelations of archaeology regarding the use of written documents in Pal at the time of the Exodus and before has changed the situation somewhat. The still more recent developments as to the Sem character of Pal before the invasion of the Israelites, together with the growing evidence of the prevailing use of handwriting all over Pal by not later than the 9th cent., point in the same direction. It is now even asserted (Clay, *Amorites*) that the Sem wave was from the north rather than the south, in which case the only possible ground for ascribing illiteracy to the Hebrews at the time of the conquest, and therefore exclusive oral tradition, would be removed.

Whatever may be the facts, it may be said with some definiteness that the theory which implies two sets of traditions, handed down for several cents. and retaining a considerable amount of verbal likeness, implies written tradition, not oral, for no popular tradition keeps identical verbal forms for so long a time, and there is little ground for supposing artificial transmission by professional memorizers. The schools of the prophets might, indeed, have served as such, but there is no evidence that they did; and it would have been curious if, writing being within easy reach, this should have been done. As in almost all literatures, it is far more likely that the popular traditions are derived from and refreshed by literary sources, than that lit. was compiled from traditions with long oral transmission.

Bib. references to oral publication are found in the references to heralds (see s.v.), to Solomon's wisdom as "spoken" (1 K **4** 32–34), proclamations and edicts, the public reading of the law in the OT, and the reading in the synagogue in the NT. All the oracles, "thus saith the Lord" and "the word of Jeh," to Moses, etc, and all allusions to preaching the word, belong to this class of oral publication and transmission. A direct allusion to oral transmission is found in Ps **44** 1, "We have heard with our ears, O God, our fathers have told us."

5. MSS

The distinction of handwriting as against oral utterance lies first in the permanence of the record, but it has also a curious psychological advantage over speech. The latter reaches the mind through hearing one letter at a time as uttered. With writing, on the other hand, the eye grasps three to six letters at a time, and takes in words as wholes instead of spelling them out. The ear always lags, therefore, the eye anticipates, although it may also linger if it needs to. While therefore impressions from hearing may perhaps be deeper, one may gather many more in the same time from reading.

When it comes to transmission, the advantage of handwriting is obvious. In the first place, even the poorest ink hardly fades as rapidly as memory. Then at best few men reach a hundred years, and therefore no memory copy, while on the other hand the limit to the life of writing has never been reached. We have writings that have lasted 6,000 years, at least; while if the Palermo stone, e.g. had been orally transmitted it must needs have passed through some 200 copyists at least, each producing two sets of errors. The advantage of manuscript transmission over oral tradition in its permanence is thus very great. It is true, of course, that in the case of fragile material like papyrus, paper, or even leather, transmission ordinarily implies many re-copyings and corresponding corruption, but even at worst these will be very much better than the best popular oral tradition.

In the broad sense MSS include all kinds of written books without regard to material, form or instruments used. In the narrowest sense they are limited to rolls and codices, i.e. to literary manuscripts. Inscriptions are properly written matter engraved or inscribed on hard material. Documents, whether private letters or official records, are characteristically folded in pliable material. Literary works again are usually rolls or else codices, which latter is the usual form of the printed books as well. These three classes of written books have their corresponding sciences in epigraphy, diplomatics and paleography.

(1) *Epigraphy* has to do primarily with inscriptions set up for record in public places. These include published laws, inscriptions, biographical memorials like the modern gravestone inscriptions and those on memorial statues, battle monuments and the like. It includes also votive inscriptions, inscriptions on gems, jewels, weights and measures, weapons, utensils, etc. Seals and coins from all points of view belong here and form another division under printing. These have their own sciences in numismatics and sphragistics. The chief Bib. reference is to the "tables of stone" (Ex **24** 12). See TABLE; ALPHABET; WEIGHT; WRITING, etc.

(See Lidzbarski, *Handb. nordsemit. Epigr.*, 1898–.)

(2) *Sphragistics* is the science of seals. Scripture references to the seal or signet (Gen **38** 18; Job **38** 14; Rev **5** 1; etc) are many. See SEAL; SIGNET.

(3) *Numismatics* has to do with inscriptions on coins and medals, and is becoming one of the greatest sources of our knowledge of ancient history, esp. on account of the aid derived from coins in the matter of dating, and because of the vast quantity of them discovered. See MONEY.

(4) *Diplomatics*, or the science of documents, has to do with contracts of sale and purchase (Jer **3** 8; **32** 14), bills of divorce (Dt **24** 1) and certificates of all sorts of the nature of those registered in the modern public records. These may be on clay tablets, as in Babylonia and the neighboring regions, or on *ostraca* as found esp. in Egypt, but everywhere in the ancient Mediterranean world, and notably for Bib. history, in Samaria, as discovered by the Harvard expedition. Multitudes of the Egyp papyri discovered in modern times are of this character as well as the Italian papyri until papyrus was succeeded by vellum. Many are also found on wax, gold, silver, brass, lead tablets, etc. See LETTERS; OSTRACA; PAPYRI.

(5) *Paleography* has to do with volumes or books of considerable bulk, chiefly. It has, therefore, to do mainly with literary works of all sorts, but it shades into diplomatics when official documents, such as collections of laws (e.g. Deuteronomy), treatises, such as the famous treaty between the

Hittites and Egypt, and modern leases are of such bulk as to be best transmitted in volume form. It has to do chiefly with the clay tablets, papyrus, leather, vellum and paper volumes. The clay tablet is mentioned in the OT at various points (see TABLET), the roll in both OT and NT (see ROLL). The leather roll is the traditional form for the Heb Scriptures up to the present day, although the codex or modern volume form had been invented before the conclusion of the NT, and the earliest extant copies are in this form. The books of the OT and NT were all probably first written on rolls. For the different methods of producing these various forms—graving, casting, pressing, pen and ink, etc, see WRITING.

A Reader with a Roll (from a Fresco at Pompeii).

6. Printed Books

Printing differs from writing chiefly in being executed in two dimensions. In writing, a chisel or brush or pen follows a continuous or interrupted line, while printing stamps a letter or a part of a letter, a line, a page, or many pages at a stroke. The die, the wedge for clay tablets, seals, molds, xylographic plates, as well as the typewriter, movable type or electrotype plates, etc, belong properly to printing rather than writing. The wedge stamp, or single-letter die, the typewriter, the matrix and movable type form, however, a sort of transition between the pen point and the printing-press in that they follow letter after letter. Coins and seals, on the other hand, differ little from true printing save in the lengths of the writings; Bab seals and the rotary press are one in principle. Sphragistics, or the science of seals, and numismatics, or the science of coins, medals, etc, belong thus with printing from this point of view, but are more commonly and conveniently classed with epigraphy, on the principle that they depend on the light and shade of incision or relief in one color as distinguished from the color contrasts of ink or paint. Printed books include the xylographic process of Chinese and early European printing, page and form printing from movable type, and all electrotype, stencil, gelatine pad, etc, processes.

The advantage of printing over writing is in the more rapid multiplication of copies, and still more in the accuracy of the copies. The first setting in movable type is as liable to error as any written copy, but all impressions from this are wholly without textual variations. For printed editions of the Bible see TEXT; VERSIONS, etc.

In the natural process of transmission all reprints in movable type, manuscripts or oral repetitions accumulate variations with each re-copying. These are, in general, errors, and the process is one of degeneration.

7. Variations

In oral transmission the average error with each generation is very great, and it is only with incredible pains that the best copies are made equal to even the average manuscript, which in turn at its best only equals the first type-set copy. The same expenditure of care on this type-set copy produces thousands of copies in printing where it produces one in manuscript. The phonograph, the typewriter, type-bar composition, photographic and electrotype methods have reduced the average error in modern books to a very low point. But even after incredible pains on the part of the authors and professional proofreaders, the offered reward of a guinea for each detected error in the Oxford revised version of the Bible brought several errors to light. This version is however about as nearly free from textual error as any large book ever made, and millions of copies of it are now printed wholly without textual variation.

But textual errors are not the only variations. It often happens that the author or someone else undertakes to correct the errors and makes substitutions or additions of one sort or another. The result is a revised edition, which is, in general, an improvement, or evolution upward. Variations are thus of two kinds: involuntary and intentional, corresponding pretty well with the words "copies" and "editions" of a work.

Strictly speaking, every book with intentional changes is a new work, but colloquially it is counted the "same work" until the changes become so great that the resemblance of the form of words to the original is hard to recognize. It is a common thing for a work to be edited and reëdited under a certain author's name (Herzog), then become known by the joint name of the author and editor (Herzog-Plitt or Schaff-Herzog), and finally become known under the name of the latest editor (Hauck). In this case it is often described for a time on a title-page as "founded" on its predecessor, but generally the original author's name is dropped from the title-page altogether when no great portions retain the original verbal form. All editions of a work are recognized in common use in some sense as new works; and in the bookshop or library a man is careful to specify the latest ed of Smith, or Brown's ed of Smith, to avoid getting the older and outdated original work.

Sometimes the original work and the additions, corrections, explanations, etc, are kept quite separate and distinct—additional matter being given in MSS in the margins, or between lines, and in printed books as footnotes or in brackets or parentheses. This is commonly the case with the text-and-comment eds of Bib. books and great writers. Sometimes, as often in ancient MSS, it happens in copying that what were marginal and interlinear notes become run in as an undistinguished part of the text and, still more often, what was indicated as quotation in an original work loses its indications and becomes an undistinguished part of the work. In the case of the paraphrase the comment is intentionally run in with the words of the text; and most editors of scientific works likewise make no attempt to distinguish between the original matter and additions by another hand, the whole responsibility being thrown forward on the editor. Sometimes the original work itself to begin with is largely made up of quotation, or is a mere compilation or collection of works in which the "originality" is confined to title-page or preface or even a mere title, as in the case of the OT, the NT, and the Bible, and the order of arrangement of parts.

Almost all books are thus composite. Even in a manuscript copy of a manuscript, or an oral repetition of an oral tale, two human minds have contributed to the net result, and the work of each may perhaps be distinguished from that of the other. In the case of a new ed by the same author, the result is still composite—a new work composed of old and new material. With all new eds by other authors the compositeness increases until, e.g. an ed of the Bible with textual variants and select comments from various writers becomes the combined work of thousands of writers, each distinguished as to his work from all the rest by his name or some symbol.

The work proper or work unchanged, save for involuntary error, includes thus copies, tr^s, abridgments, selections and quotations; the revised work or work with voluntary changes includes eds and paraphrases (which are simply texts with commentary run into the text), digests, redactions, etc, and perhaps compilations.

These two kinds of variations give rise to the two sciences of text-criticism and higher or historical criticism. The former distinguishes all accidental errors of transmission, the latter all the voluntary changes; the former aims to reconstruct the original, the latter to separate in any given book between the work of the original and each editor.

In this connection it must not be forgotten that the original itself may be a composite work—containing long quotations, made up wholly of selections or even made up of whole works bound together by a mere title. In these cases textual criticism restores not the original of each, but the original text of the whole, while higher criticism takes up the task of separating out the elements first of later eds and redactions of this original, then of the original itself.

The involuntary variations of MSS or oral tradition give rise to the science of text-criticism. The point of the science is to reconstruct exactly the original form of words or text. Formerly the method for this was a mere balancing of probabilities, but since Tregelles it has become a rigid logical process which traces copies to their near ancestors, and these in turn farther back, until a genealogical tree has been formed of actual descent. The law of this is in effect that "like variations point to a common ancestor," the biological law of "homology," and if the groupings reveal as many as three independent lines of copies from the original, the correct text can be constructed with mathematical precision, since the readings of two lines will always be right against the third—granting a very small margin of error in the psychological tendency of habit in a scribe to repeat the same error. The method proceeds (1) to describe all variations of each MS (or equally of each oral or printed copy) from the standard text; (2) to group the MSS which have the most pronounced variations; (3) to unite these groups on the principle of homology into larger and larger groups until authors' utterances have been reached and through these the inward original. The results are expressed in a text and variants—the text being a corrected copy of the original, and the variants showing the exact contribution of each copyist to the MSS which he produced.

8. Textual Criticism

It is carefully to be remembered that text-criticism proper has only to do with a particular form of words. Every tr or ed is a separate problem complete in itself when the very words used by translator and the editor have been reconstructed. These may in turn be useful in reconstructing the original, but care must be had not to amend, tr or ed from the original, and the original in turn, when it contains quotations from other writers, must not be amended from the originals of these writers. The task of textual criticism is to set forth each man's words—each original author, each copyist, each translator, each editor, just as his words were—no more and no less. (See TEXT OF OT; TEXT OF NT.)

Higher criticism has to do with voluntary variations or variations in subject-matter. Like text-criticism it has to do with distinguishing the share of each of several coöperators in a composite work; and like it higher criticism traces the contributions of various authors each to its source. It differs, however, in dealing with original matter. While the variations by officious scribes, or intelligent scribes who correct spelling, grammar, wrong dates and the like, come pretty closely into the region of editing, and on the other hand the redactor is sometimes little more than an officious copyist, still the line of involuntary and voluntary change holds good, whether it be the grafting into an original work by the author of many quotations, or the grafting onto the work by others of the work of themselves or of other authors. It is not the business of the textual critic to separate out either of these (it is expressly his business not to), although his work may greatly help and even furnish results which can be used automatically. The whole of this double field of composite authorship belongs to higher criticism.

9. Higher Criticism

In the case of most modern works the task of the higher critic is a simple one. Quotation marks, a growing ethical feeling against plagiarism, the mechanical conveniences of typographical display, and the like, all contribute to a careful separation of the work of each contributor. Nevertheless, in many cases as, for example, in the editing of textbooks and newspapers, this is not regarded. While the signed article in the encyclopaedia is now nearly universal, the signed review more and more common, the signed editorial is still rare, and the others by no means universal. It is still a matter of interest to many to pick out by his "style" the author of an unsigned article, review or editorial—which is higher criticism.

In ancient lit., where there were few such mechanical conveniences in discriminating, and little or no conscience had been developed about incorporating anything which suited the purpose of the writer in part or as a whole, the result was often a complete patchwork of verbal forms of many writers. The task of higher criticism is to sort out the original and each of its literary variants, and to trace these variants to their originals. The net result in the case of any work does not differ much from an ordinary modern work with quotation marks and footnotes referring to the sources of the quotations. It restores, so to speak, the punctuation and footnotes which the author omitted or later copyists lost. It includes many nice questions of discrimination through style and the historical connection of the fragments with the works from which they were taken; and after these have been analyzed out, many nice questions also of tracing their authorship or at least the time, place and environment of their composition. It includes thus the questions of superhuman authorship and inspiration.

Literary criticism has to do with originals as originals, or, in composite works, the original parts of originals. An original work may include quotations from others or be mainly quotations, and its "originality" consists in part in the way these quotations are introduced and used. By "original," however, is meant in the main new verbal forms. The original work must not plagiarize nor even use stereotyped phrases, although it may introduce

10. Literary Criticism

proverbs or idiomatic phrases. In general, however, originality means that literary food has been digested—reduced to its chemical elements of word or briefest phrase and rebuilt into a wholly new structure in the mind. The building in of old doorways and ornaments may be a part of the literary architect's originality, but they themselves were not "original" with him.

The literary critic has thus to do with a man's originality—the contribution that he has made to the subject, the peculiar quality of this in its fitness to influence other minds which is effected by the "reaction of the whole personality," all his learning and emotioned experience, on every part of his material—what in short we call style. This involves a judgment or comparison with all other works on the same subject as to its contribution of new matter and its readability.

The chief problems of book science may be described in the words of biological science as (1) the origin of new forms, (2) survival.

11. Origin of New Forms

The question of the origin of a new literary work and its survival is so like that of the origin of a new species and its survival that it may be regarded less as analogy than as falling under the same laws of variations, multiplication, heredity and natural selection. The origin of variant forms of the same original through involuntary and voluntary changes has been traced above up to the point where editorial variants overwhelm the original and a new author's name takes the place of the old. After this step has been taken it is a new work, and at bottom the origin of all new works is much the same. The process is most clearly seen in treatises of some branch of science, say physics. A general treatise, say on Heat, is published, giving the state of knowledge on the subject at that time. Then monographs begin to be produced. The monograph may and generally does include, in bibliographical or historical outline, the substance of previous works, and in every event it implies the previous total. The point of the monograph itself is, however, not the summary of common knowledge but the contribution that it makes, or, in the language of natural science, the "useful variant" of the subject which it produces. After some accumulation of these monographs, or useful variants of previous treatises, some author gathers them together and unites them with previous treatises into a new general treatise or textbook, which is in effect the latest previous treatise with all variants developed in the meantime.

In either case a permanent new form has been produced—the old common knowledge with a difference, and the process goes on again: the new work is multiplied by publication into many like individuals; these like individuals develop each its variations; the variations in the same direction unite in some new accepted fact, idea or law, expressed in a monograph; common knowledge with this new variation forms a new general work which again is multiplied, and so on.

And what is true of scientific monographs is just as true in substance of literature, of oral tradition and of the whole history of ideas. It is the perpetual putting together of variations experienced two or more times by one individual or one or more times each by two or more individuals, with the common body of our ideas, and producing thus a new fixed form. Popular proverbs, for example, and all poetry, fiction and the like, come thus to sum up a long human experience.

And carrying the matter still farther back, what is true of the scientific book and of poetry and of folk-literature, is true also of the inward evolution of every thought, even those phrased for conversation or indeed for self-communion—it is the result of a series of variations and integrations. The workings of the scientist's mind in producing a contribution and the workings of the farmer's mind in evolving a shrewd maxim, are alike the result of a long series of these observations, variations and integrations. Repeated observations and the union of observations which vary in the same direction is the history of the thought process all the way along from the simplest perception of the infant, up through the ordinary thinking of the average man, to the most complex concept of the philosopher.

Through all the processes of inward thought and outward expression thus the same process of evolution in the production of a new form holds good: it is the synthesis of all works on a given subject (i.e. any more or less narrow field of reality), the multiplication of this synthetic work, the development of new variations in it and the reunion again of all these variations in a more comprehensive work.

When it comes to the matter of the survival of a new work when it has been produced, the problem is a double one: (1) the survival of

12. Survival

the individual book, and (2) the survival of the work, i.e. any copy of the original whose text does not vary so far that it may not be recognized as the "same" work. The original book is in a man's mind and survives only so long as its author survives. In the same sense that the author dies, the individual book dies. No new book, therefore, survives its author. If, however, by survival is meant the existence of any copy, or copy of a copy of this original, containing much (but never quite) the same form of words, then the book survives in this world, in the same sense that the author survives, i.e. in its descendants; it is the difference between personal immortality and race immortality. At the same time, however, the survival of species depends on the individual. A work or a species is no metaphysical reality, but a sum total of individuals with, of course, their relations to one another.

On the average, the chance of long survival for any individual copy of a book is small. Every new book enters into a struggle for existence; wind and weather, wear and tear conspire to destroy it. On the whole they succeed sooner or later. Some books live longer than others, but however durable the material, and however carefully treated they may be, an autograph rarely lasts a thousand years. If survival depended on permanence of the individual, there would be no Bible and no classics.

The average chance of an individual book for long life depends (1) on the intrinsic durability of its material, or its ability to resist hostile environment, (2) on isolation.

The enemies to which books are exposed are various: wind, fire, moisture, mold, human negligence and vandalism, and human use. Some materials are naturally more durable than others. Stone and metal inscriptions survive better than wood or clay, vellum than papyrus or paper.

On the other hand, however, if isolated or protected from hostile environment, very fragile material may outlast more substantial. Papyrus has survived in the mounds of Egypt, and unbaked clay tablets in the mounds of Babylonia, while millions of stone and metal inscriptions written thousands of years later have already perished. Here the factor of isolation comes in. Fire and pillage, moth and rust and the bookworm destroy for the most part without respect of persons. It is only those books which are out of the way of destructive agencies which survive. An unbaked tablet which has survived 5,000 years under rubbish may crumble to dust in 5 years after it has been dug up and exposed to the air. This isolation may be accidental or "natural," as when tablets and papyri are preserved under ruins, but it may also be artificial and the result of human care. A third factor of survival is therefore the ability of a work to procure for itself human protection, or artificial isolation. In brief this ability is the "value" of a book to its owner. This value may lie in the material, artistic excellence, association or rarity. Any variation in the direction of value which may be expressed financially tends to preserve. In fire or shipwreck, these are the ones saved, in pillage the ones spared. They are the ones for whom fire-proof buildings and special guardians are provided. An exception to this rule is when the material is more valuable for other than book purposes. In times of war the book engraved on gold or lead or paper may be melted down for coin or bullets or torn up for cartridges, while stone and vellum books are spared. The general law is, however, that value tends to preserve, and it has been remarked that all the oldest codices which have survived in free environment are sumptuous copies.

Literary value on the other hand is, on the whole, a factor of destruction for the individual rather than of survival. The better a book is the more it is read, and the more it is read, the faster it wears out. The worthless book on the top shelf outlasts all the rest. In cases of fire or shipwreck an owner will save books which cannot be replaced and the books most easily replaced are those with literary value. A man will sometimes save his favorite books, and does treat them often with a certain reverent care, which tends to preservation but, on the whole, literary value tends to destruction.

When it comes to the survival of the work or race survival, matters are reversed. Literary value is the prime factor. It is the ability of a book to get itself multiplied or re-copied which counts—the quality, whatever it may be, which tends to make a man wish to replace his copy when it is worn out, and to make many men wish to read the work.

This literary interest operates first to produce a large number of copies in order to meet the demand, each of which copies has its chance of survival. It operates also by inducing men to use the very best material, paper, ink, binding, etc, which results in giving each individual book a longer time to produce a new copy.

The modern newspaper published in a million copies is ephemeral, in the first place, because it is printed upon paper which cannot last, save in very favorable conditions of isolation, for more than forty or fifty years. In the second place, it is very rarely reprinted save for an occasional memorial copy. Books like the Bible or Virgil, Dante or Shakespeare, on the other hand, are reprinted in multitudes of editions and in many instances in the most permanent material that art can devise.

It often happens that a book is popular for a short time, but will not survive a changed environment. The newspaper is popular for a few hours, but the time environment changes and interest is gone. It sometimes happens that a book is very popular in one country and wholly fails to interest in another. Millions of copies of *Uncle Tom's Cabin* and *Ben Hur* were required to fill the demand of one generation where a few hundreds may suffice for the next.

All the time popular taste, which is only another name for average human experience, is judging a book. A book survives because it is popular—not necessarily because it is popular with the uneducated majority, but because it appeals continually to the average human experience of some considerable class, good or bad. Survival is, therefore, natural. Skilled critics help popular judgment, and select lists aid, but in the long run the test is simply of its correspondence with human experience; in short, it is because men "like" it that a book survives.

There is thus going on all the time a process of struggle and "natural selection" which in the end is a survival of the fittest in the true evolutionary sense, i.e. books survive because fitted to their environment of human experience or taste. There grows up, therefore, continually in every country a certain class of books which are counted classics. These are those which have survived their tests, and are being still further tested. Some have been tested from remote antiquity, and it is the books which survive the test of many periods of time, many kinds of geographical environment, and many varieties of intellectual environment, i.e. which appeal to many classes of readers, which are the true classics and which, on the other hand, show that they do correspond with the fundamental facts of human experience, simply because they have survived. In general it is the religious books which have survived in all nations, and the only books which have been tested in all lands and ages and appeal to Oriental and Western, ancient and modern alike, are those of the Christian Bible.

It has been noticed above that the process of forming a new work is the bringing together of all works on the same subject in order to unite all their variations in the new work. It is for this purpose that every student brings together the working library on his specialty; it is what the librarian does when he brings together all the books on a subject for the use of students. Every man who reads up on a subject is performing the same task for himself, and likewise every man who does general reading.

13. Book Collections

There are few libraries, however, which attempt to get together all the books on a subject. Most libraries are select libraries containing the best books on the subject: by this is meant all books which have anything new or in short have a useful variation. This is an artificial process of the critical human mind, but in humanity in general it is going on all the time as a natural process. Men are perpetually at work choosing their "five-foot shelves," the collections of the very "best of best books." The reason for this lies in the fact that the average human mind can read and hold only a limited number of books; an unconscious process is all the time going on tending to pick out the small number of books which on the whole contain the greatest amount of human experience to the average page. The mass of world's books, however enormous, is thus boiled down by a natural selection to a few books, which contain the essence of all the rest. The process tends to go on in every country and every language. The most universal example is the Bible, which represents a long process of natural selection through many periods of time and considerable variety of geographical influence. It unites the quintessence of Sem ideas with the corresponding quintessence of Indo-European ideas, each embodied in a correspondingly perfect language—for language itself is in the last analysis the quintessence of the experience of any people in its likeness and unlikeness to other peoples. It is therefore by the mere fact of "survival" and "natural selection" proved to be the "fittest" to survive, i.e. that which corresponds most nearly to universal human experience. Councils do not form the canon of Scripture: they simply set a seal upon a natural process. The Bible is thus the climax of bookmaking as man is of the animal creation. It is as unique among books as man is unique among all living things. See LIBRARIES.

The history of books begins at least with the history of writing. Some of the pictures on the cave walls of the neolithic age (Déchelette, *Man: Archaeol., Prehist.* [1908], 201–37) seem to have the essential characteristics of books and certainly the earliest clay tablets and inscriptions do. These seem to carry back with certainty to at least 4,200 years BC. By a thousand years later, tablet books and inscriptions were common and papyrus books seem to have been well begun. Another thousand years, or some time before Ḥammurabi, books of many sorts were numerous. At the time of Abraham, books were common all over Egypt, Babylonia, Pal, and the eastern Mediterranean as far at least as Crete and Asia Minor. In the time of Moses, whenever that may have been, the alphabet had perhaps been invented, books were common among all priestly and official classes, not only in Babylonia, Assyria and Egypt, but at least in two or three scores of places in Pal, north Syria and Cyprus. In the time of David not only was historical, official and religious lit. common in Egypt and Assyria, but poetry and fiction had been a good deal developed in the countries round about Pal; and very soon after, if not long before, as the Moabitic, Siloam, Zkr, Zenjirli, Baal-Lebanon, Gezer and Samaritan inscriptions show, Sem writing was common all over Pal and its neighborhood.

14. Early History of Books in Bible Lands

LITERATURE.—Articles by Dziatzko on "Buch" and "Bibliotheken," in Pauly-Wissowa, *Real-encyclopädie d. class. Altertumsw.*, V, 5, and his *Antikes Buchwesen*, Leipzig, 1900, are mines of material, and the bibliographical reference thorough. The rapid developments in the history of most ancient books may be followed in Hortzschansky's admirable annual volume, *Bibliographie des Bibliotheks- und Buchwesens*, Leipzig, 1904 ff. For a first orientation the little book of O. Wiese, *Schrift und Buchwesen in alter u. neuer Zeit* (3d ed, Leipzig, 1910), or in English, the respective articles in the *Encyclopaedia Britannica*, are perhaps best. On the scientific side the best introductions are Vol I of Iwan Müller's *Handb. d. klass. Altertumsw.* and T. Birt's *D. antike Buchwesen* (Berlin, 1882). For Bib. aspects of the Book, the best of all, and very adequate indeed, is the long article of E. von Dobschütz on the "Bible in the Church" in the Hastings' *Encyclopaedia of Religion*, II, 579–615, and esp. on account of the bibliographical apparatus at the end of each section. These little bibliographies give a complete apparatus on many of the above subjects. Paragraphs with bibliographies on others of above topics will be found in the W. Sanday article on "Bible," just preceding.

E. C. RICHARDSON

BOOK OF ABRAHAM. See APOCALYPTIC LITERATURE.

BOOK OF ENOCH. See ENOCH, BOOK OF.

BOOK OF JUBILEES. See APOCALYPTIC LITERATURE; APOCRYPHA.

BOOK OF LIFE (סֵפֶר חַיִּים, *ṣēpher ḥayyīm;* ἡ βίβλος τῆς ζωῆς, *hē bíblos tḗs zōḗs*, "book of life"): The phrase is derived from the custom of the ancients of keeping genealogical records (Neh **7** 5.64; **12** 22.23) and of enrolling citizens for various purposes (Jer **22** 30; Ezk **13** 9). So God is represented as having a record of all who are under His special care and guardianship. To be blotted out of the Book of Life is to be cut off from God's favor, to suffer an untimely death, as when Moses pleads that he be blotted out of God's book—that he might die, rather than that Israel should be destroyed (Ex **32** 32; Ps **69** 28). In the NT it is the record of the righteous who are to inherit eternal life (Phil **4** 3; Rev **3** 5; **13** 8; **17** 8; **21** 27). In the apocalyptic writings there is the conception of a book or of books, that are in God's keeping, and upon which the final judgment is to be based (Dnl **7** 10; **12** 1; Rev **20** 12.15; cf Bk Jub **39** 6; **19** 9). See APOCALYPSE; BLOT; BOOK OF REMEMBRANCE; JUDGMENT, LAST. L. KAISER

BOOK OF NOAH. See APOCALYPTIC LITERATURE.

BOOK OF REMEMBRANCE, rē-mem′brans (סֵפֶר זִכָּרוֹן, *ṣēpher zikkārōn*, "book of record"): Is related in meaning to the "Book of Life." It refers to a list of the righteous, recorded in a book that lies before God (Mal **3** 16; cf Dnl **7** 10). See BOOK OF LIFE.

BOOKS OF ADAM. See APOCALYPTIC LITERATURE; ADAM, BOOKS OF.

BOOT, bōōt (סְאוֹן, *ṣ*ᵉ*'ōn;* AV **battle;** ARV "armor"; ARVm "boot"): The word *ṣ*ᵉ*'ōn*, found only in Isa **9** 5 (He **9** 4), is probably a loanword from the Assyr *šênu*, meaning "shoe," "sandal." The root has the same meaning in Aram. and Ethiopic. The passage should be trd "every boot of the booted warrior."

BOOTH, bōōth, bōōth: The Heb word *ṣukkāh* (rendered in the AV "booth" or "booths," eleven times; "tabernacle" or "tabernacles," ten times; "pavilion" or "pavilions," five times; "cottage" once) means a hut made of wattled twigs or branches (Lev **23** 42; Neh **8** 15). In countries where trees are abundant such wattled structures are common as temporary buildings as they can be constructed in a very short time. Cattle were probably housed in them (Gen **33** 17). Such hurriedly-made huts were used by soldiers (2 S **11** 11; 1 K **20** 12) and by harvesters—hence the name feast of "booths" or "tabernacles" (see TABERNACLES, FEAST OF). Job (**27** 18) uses booth (‖ moth's house) as a symbol of impermanence. Similar huts were erected in vineyards, etc, to protect them from robbers and beasts of prey. The isolated condition of Jerus in the time of the prophet Isaiah is compared to a "booth in a vineyard" (Isa **1** 8). T. LEWIS

BOOTHS, FEAST OF. See FEASTS AND FASTS, I, 2.

BOOTY, bōōt′i (בָּז and בַּז, *bāz, baz*): "Booty" is the tr of *bāz* or *baz*, usually rendered "prey" and "spoil" (Jer **49** 32); of *malḳō*ᵃ*ḥ*, "prey," "booty" (Nu **31** 32, "the booty—the rest of the prey," RV "the prey, over and above the booty," *bāz*); of *m*ᵉ*shiṣṣāh*, "spoil" (Hab **2** 7; Zeph **1** 13; RV "spoil"); of *ōphéleia*, "gain" (2 Macc **8** 20). "*Booty* respects what is of personal service to the captor; *spoils* whatever serves to designate his triumph; *prey* includes whatever gratifies the appetite and is to be consumed" (Crabb, *English Synonymes*). *Persons* (for slaves, etc) might be part of the booty. See also SPOIL. W. L. WALKER

BOOZ, bō′oz (*TR*, **Booζ,** *Boóz;* WH, **Boés,** *Boés*): AV, Gr form of Boaz (thus RV) (Mt **1** 5; Lk **3** 32).

BOR-ASHAN, bōr-ash′an: A correction of the MT in ARV in 1 S **30** 30 for AV "Chor-ashan" and ERV "Cor-ashan." Probably the same as ASHAN (Josh **15** 42; 1 Ch **4** 32; **6** 59), which see.

BORDER, bōr′dẽr, **BORDERS:** Indicating in both sing. and pl. the outlines or territory of a country. In the sense of "limits," "boundaries" or "territory," it occurs as a tr of גְּבוּל, *g*ᵉ*bhūl* (and its fem. גְּבוּלָה, *g*ᵉ*bhūlāh*, in Ps **74** 17) in numerous passages in OT, esp. in Josh. יְרֵכָה, *y*ᵉ*rēkhāh* = "the flank," "the side," "the coast," hence "the border" occurs in Gen **49** 13; קָצֶה, *ḳāçeh* = "an extremity," "brim," "brink," "edge" (Ex **16** 35; **19** 12; Josh **4** 19); מִסְגֶּרֶת, *miṣgereth* = something inclosing, i.e. "a margin" (Ex **37** 12.14;

1 K **7** 28 f.31 f.35 f AV; 2 K **16** 17 AV); שָׂפָה or שֶׂפֶת, *sāphāh*, or *sepheth*="the lip" (as a natural boundary) hence "a margin," "brim," "brink," "edge" (Ex **28** 26; **39** 19 AV); קֵץ, *ḳēç*="an extremity," "end" (2 K **19** 23 AV); תּוֹצָאָה, *tōçā'āh* ="exit," hence "boundary" (1 Ch **5** 16); תּוֹר, *tōr* = "a succession," "a string," "row," hence "border" (Cant **1** 11 AV); יָד, *yādh*="hand," used in a great variety of applications, both lit. and **fig.**, proximate and remote; but how it should be tr[d] with "border" in 1 Ch **7** 29 is not clear; better would be: "in the hands of the children of Manasseh." Three Gr words occur for the idea: κράσπεδον, *kráspedon*="a margin," "fringe" (Mt **23** 5; Mk **6** 56; Lk **8** 44); ὅριον, *hórion*="a limit," "a boundary line" (Mt **4** 13); μεθόριος, *methórios* = "contiguous" (neuter pl. as noun, "frontier," "border" in Mk **7** 24). FRANK E. HIRSCH

BORDERER, bor'dẽr-ẽr (**παρακειμένους,** *parakeiménous*): One who dwells on the borders or confines of a country. Only in 2 Macc **9** 25, "The princes that are borderers and neighbors unto my kingdom."

BORE, bōr: According to the Book of the Covenant (Ex **20** 20—**23** 33) a slave whom his master had purchased was to be released after six years. Should he choose to remain in his master's service a religious ceremony was necessary to ratify his decision. "Then his master shall bring him unto God" (better than "unto the judges" of the AV), "and shall bring him to the door, or unto the doorpost; and his master shall *bore* his ear through with an awl" (Ex **21** 6). It is highly improbable that "unto God" means "to a sanctuary"; for there was no special reason for performing this ceremony near the door of a sanctuary. On the other hand the entrance to a private house was a sacred spot. According to primitive thinking near the door dwelt the household gods whose function it was to guard the house and its occupants, e.g. against the entry of disease. It was natural that the ceremony of attaching the slave permanently to the master's household should be performed in the presence of the household gods. "The boring of the ear of slaves was a common practice in antiquity, possibly to symbolize the duty of obedience, as the ear was the organ of hearing" (Bennett). The Deuteronomist (Dt **15** 17) rejects the religious aspect of the ceremony—probably as a relic of Can. religion—and looks upon it as a secular and symbolical operation. According to his view, the awl was thrust through the ear of the slave to the door. The slave in question was permanently attached to the household. T. LEWIS

BORITH, bō'rith: Mentioned in the genealogical table which traces the descent of Esdras (Ezra) from Aaron (2 Esd **1** 2). In 1 Esd **8** 2, his name appears as BOCCAS (q.v.), and in 1 Ch **6** 5.51; Ezr **7** 4, BUKKI (q.v.).

BORN. See BEAR, BORN.

BORN AGAIN. See REGENERATION.

BORNE. See BEAR, BORNE.

BORROWING, bor'ō-ing:

(1) In the OT period loans were not of a commercial nature, i.e. they were not granted to enable a man to start or run a business. They were really a form of charity, and were made by the lender only to meet the pressure of poverty. To the borrower they were esteemed a form of misfortune (Dt **28** 12 f), and by the lender a form of beneficence. Hence the tone of the Mosaic legislation on the subject.

(2) Laying interest upon the poor of Israel was forbidden in all the codes (see Ex **22** 25 [JE]; Dt **23** 19; Lev **25** 36 H), because it was looked upon as making unwarranted profit out of a brother's distress: "If thou lend money to any of my people with thee that is poor, thou shalt not be to him as a creditor; neither shall ye lay upon him interest . . . . and it shall come to pass, when he crieth unto me, that I will hear; for I am gracious."

(3) The Law, however, allowed interest to be taken of a foreigner, or non-Jew (Dt **23** 20: "Unto a foreigner thou mayest lend upon interest"; cf Dt **15** 3); and even among Jews pledges were allowed under limitations, or taken against the law (Dt **24** 10; cf Job **24** 2.3: "There are that remove the landmarks . . . . they take the widow's ox for a pledge"). In Dt **15** 1 ff there is a remarkable law providing a "release" by the creditor every "seven years," a "letting drop of loans" (see Driver in loc.). In Ex **3** 22, AV "shall borrow" is rendered "shall ask" in RV. GEO. B. EAGER

BOSCATH, bos'kath. See BOZKATH.

BOSOM, bŏŏz'um: In the ordinary signification of the anterior upper portion of the trunk of the body, חֹק, חֵיק, *ḥōḳ* or *ḥēḳ*, "inlet, "lap" (Ex **4** 6.7; Nu **11** 12; Dt **13** 6; **28** 54.56; Ruth **4** 16; Ps **74** 11; Isa **65** 6.7; Lam **2** 12). "A present in the bosom" (Prov **21** 14): bribes carried ready for use in the fold of the robe. חֵצֶן, *ḥēçen*="bosom" (with special reference to that portion of the body which is between the arms), occurs in Ps **129** 7; חֹב, *ḥōbh*="a cherisher," hence "the bosom" (Job **31** 33); צַלַּחַת, *çallaḥath*=something advanced or deep, "a bowl"; **fig.** "the bosom" (Prov **19** 24 AV; **26** 15 AV). The Gr employs κόλπος, *kólpos* (Lk **6** 38; Jn **13** 23). For Abraham's bosom, see separate art.

Figurative: In a fig. sense it denotes intimacy and unrestrained intercourse (Gen **16** 5; 2 S **12** 8); tender care and watchfulness (Isa **40** 11); closest intimacy and most perfect knowledge (Jn **1** 18); "into their bosom" (Ps **79** 12) indicates the bosom as the seat of thought and reflection. F. E. HIRSCH

BOSOM, ABRAHAM'S. See ABRAHAM'S BOSOM.

BOSOR, bō'sor (**Βοσόρ,** *Bosór*):

(1) A city named among those taken by Judas Maccabaeus "in the land of Gilead" (1 Macc **5** 26.36). From the towns named it is evident that this phrase is elastic, covering territory beyond what is usually called the land of Gilead. Possibly therefore Bosor may be identical with *Buṣr el-Ḥarīrī*, in the *Luḥf*, S.E. of *el-Lejā'*.

(2) In 2 Pet **2** 15 AV, the Gr form of BEOR (q.v.).

BOSORA, bos'ō-ra (**Βοσορᾶ,** *Bosorá*): One of the strong cities of Gilead taken by Judas Maccabaeus (1 Macc **5** 26.28). It is identical with the Rom Bostra, the city whose extensive ruins lie on the S.E. border of the *Ḥaurān*, on the old Rom road that runs between *Ḍer'ah* and *Ṣalkhad*. The modern name is *Bosra eski-Shām*. It cannot be identified with BOZRAH either (1) or (2), as it lies much too far north. It appears for the first time in history in the passage noted above. The ruins show it to have been a place of great strength and importance. In the time of Herod the Great it was in the hands of the Nabataeans. When Aulus Cornelius Palma conquered these regions, Bostra was made capital of the province under the name of Nova Trajana Bostra, in honor of the emperor

Trajan. This was in 105 AD, from which year the Bostrian era was reckoned. It was taken by the Moslems under Khalid—"the sword of God." It resisted the attack of Baldwin III. Later it fell on evil days. Now, if it be true, as the proverb says, that "the prosperity of *Boṣra* is the prosperity of the *Ḥaurān*," the case of the latter is sad indeed.

W. Ewing

BOSS, bos: Occurs only in the pl. as a tr of גַּב, *gabh*="arch," or "protuberance," referring to the curved ornaments of a shield (Job **15** 26), the central knob of the buckler.

BOTANY, bot'a-ni: On account of the great diversity in the climatic and topographical conditions Pal is peculiarly rich in the variety of its flora—the best authority, Post, distinguishes 3,500 species. The land as a whole belongs to the botanical area known as the "Mediterranean region," a region characterized climatically by very dry, hot summers and fairly mild winters. Plants here grow in spring, rest in the hot, dry season and grow again in autumn; the long-continued, scorching sunlight and the absence of water for five or six months at a time, lead to the destruction of vast quantities of seeds and young plants imported by various natural means and by human agency. Among these xerophile or drought-resisting plants, some of the most characteristic features are a thick, leathery rind admitting of little transpiration, e.g. cactus, stonecrops, etc, and the presence of bulbs, rigid stalks, or fleshy leaves, of which the flora of Pal abounds with examples. Equally characteristic are dry, much-branched spiny trees or shrubs with scanty foliage and small leaves, such as the acacias and the thorny burnet. In connection with this last, it may be mentioned that, next to the strong sunlight and drought, the great enemy of vegetation over a great part of the "Mediterranean region"—emphatically so in Pal—is the goat. He is one of the most destructive of animals, and as he has for long ages been allowed to graze freely all over the hillsides, it is not wonderful that in many spots it is only plants like the thorny burnet with its powerful spines which have survived.

1. General Characteristics of Palestinian Flora

The common plants of Pal will be referred to in order shortly, but among those esp. characteristic of the whole region are the olive and the fig, the ilex oak and the bay laurel, the arbutus and the sumach.

A number of trees and shrubs which have been imported into this region within comparatively recent times have become so acclimatized as to be today among the most noticeable plants. Prominent among these is the well-known opuntia or prickly pear, an introduction from the continent of America; so characteristic is this of modern Pal scenery that it is a common feature in pictures by artists who have painted Scripture scenes in the Holy Land. The common variety, *Opuntia ficus-Indica* with its innumerable sharp prickles makes impenetrable hedges round many of the village gardens, while the *Opuntia cochinillifera*, cultivated specially round *Nablûs* and introduced from tropical America with the cochineal insect, is almost unarmed. The American aloe (*Argave Americana*)—quite a different plant be it noted from either the Aloes (which see) of the Bible or the well-known medicinal aloes—has established itself in many parts as a garden ornament and will doubtless in time become thoroughly indigenous. More important and more recent of introduction is the group of eucalypti or gum trees, of which some half-dozen varieties have been imported. As is well known, they all come from Australia, where they flourish in climatic conditions somewhat similar to those of the Mediterranean region. Seeds of eucalypti were first introduced into Europe in 1854, having been sent from Melbourne to Paris, and from that center they have found their way to all parts. The most common variety is the *Eucalyptus globulus* which is now to be found everywhere in the Mediterranean region. It was introduced into Pal through the late Baron E. de Rothschild of Paris, and great plantations of it have been made specially in the neighborhood of the Jewish colonies. In the marshy plains between *Sammarin* and Caesarea over a million have been planted, and here, and also on the marshy shores of Lake Hûleh, this tree has attained magnificent proportions. Many specimens will be found with trunks two or three feet in circumference and of a height of upward of 100 feet. This size is nothing for a eucalyptus, many of these trees attaining in their native habitat a height of 300, or even 400 ft., but time is required, and it may be that eventually many of the eucalypti of the Holy Land will also acquire giant proportions. That this group of trees has come to stay is evident. Not only in small forests such as those mentioned, but also in isolated groups all over the land they may be found. Their quick growth, fresh, evergreen foliage and their reputed health-giving properties account for their wide cultivation. Concerning this last it may be said that the virtues of the eucalyptus as a prophylactic against malaria have been much exaggerated. The most malignant cases of malaria may sometimes be found in houses shaded by eucalyptus boughs, and the *Anopheles*, or malarial-bearing mosquito, in such situations will be found swarming among its leaves. Probably the beneficial action of the eucalyptus is simply one of drying up marshy lands by absorbing great quantities of water into its deep-running roots.

2. Plants Introduced Since Bible Times

Other trees which have been recently introduced but now flourish even better than the indigenous trees are the locust tree (*Robinia pseudo-acacia*), from America, the "Pride of India" (*Melia Azedaracht*) called in Arab. *zinzilukt*, a stranger from India, very extensively grown, the so-called "Spanish pepper tree" (*Schinus molle*), the *Casuarina stricta* from Australia, the very common *ailanthus* (*A. glandulosus*), a native of China, and many others. Of fruit trees the apricot, mulberry, orange, citron, lemon and prickly pear have all been introduced into Syria within historic times; as have almost all the best varieties of the indigenous fruits.

A question of great interest to Bible students is, How far has the fertility of the land altered in historic times? Two facts are important in answering this:

3. Fertility and Climate in Modern and Ancient Palestine

(1) The general features of the climate have been the same since the days of the patriarchs, probably since the dawn of history. We may gather this from the many Bib. references to the seasonal rain (Lev **26** 4)—the "early" and the "latter" (e.g. Dt **11** 14; Jer **5** 24; Hos **6** 3); to the frequent droughts (e.g. 1 K **17**; Am **4** 6.7); to the grateful mention of the "dew" (Dt **32** 2; 2 S **1** 21; **17** 12; Mic **5** 7, etc); to the repeated mention of the most characteristic products of modern Pal—the olive and fig, the vine and almond, the oak and the terebinth. It is further confirmed by the presence everywhere of the ruins of ancient terraces on the hillsides and of the "broken cisterns" which are found at every site where once cultivation flourished.

(2) It is undeniable that the destruction of forest and thicket all over the land has been immense during the past fifty years. The increasing demands for fires by resident Europeans and the development

of steam mills, the result of European enterprise, are largely responsible. The firewood brought to Jerus comes from ever-increasing distances, as the wood in the neighborhood is consumed, and the destruction has been increasingly ruthless. First the branches are cut, then the trunks are leveled, and finally the very roots are dug out of the soil. At a greater distance, as for example in the once extensive forests E. of the Jordan, a terrible destruction is being wrought by the charcoal burners. Thousands of sacks of charcoal arrive in Jerus during the autumn months, chiefly in the care of Circassian settlers in the E. Jordan lands; but a similar work is pursued by other charcoal burners in the northern parts of upper Galilee. All the tree trunks are soon destroyed and then the rising branches are cut as soon as they reach any size, so that miles of country which, within the memory of many now living, were forest are now either entirely treeless or covered with nothing but brushwood. This last consists of dwarf oak, carob, terebinth, arbutus, wild olive and hawthorn—all capable of development into noble trees. The process having been commenced by the hand of man is assisted by the goats who crop the tender leaves and shoots, and thus keep stunted many of the bushes. Older inhabitants can remember that between Bethlehem and Hebron, where today scarcely a twig is visible, there were trees and brushwood all the way, and in the 7th cent. the pilgrim Arculphus writes of a pine wood as existing S. of Bethlehem. This destruction is common all over the land. The only trees which have any chance of surviving are those which from their near proximity to some sacred *Wely* or grave, or in some case from their own traditional sanctity, have been left uninjured from motives of superstition. Such "holy" trees occur all over the land, sometimes singly, at others in groves; they may be any species of tree. Commonly they are oaks, terebinths, carob, *meis* (nettle tree), *sidr* (zizyphus) or hawthorn.

Besides the wilful destruction of trees for firewood or charcoal another agent has in places been in operation. It is a common thing for the fellahin to clear a large area for ploughing by burning all the vegetation; such fires sometimes extend far beyond the area intended (cf Ps **83** 14). There is a large and almost entirely sterile district, chiefly of bare rock, between *Ṣafed* and *Jebel Jermuk* in Galilee which was swept a few years ago by a raging fire which eyewitnesses state blazed for a week. The destruction of all this vegetation has led to the washing away of almost all the soil, so that now great labor would be required to make this area productive. The removal of the natural vegetation produces sterility in two ways. Firstly, whereas the deep roots of trees and shrubs support the soil even on hillsides of considerable slope, and slowly but surely cause the disintegration of the underlying rocks, while their stems and branches by accumulating decaying leaves and twigs ever make more and richer soil, so the destruction of these plants leads to the washing away of the soil by the torrential winter's rain, until the bare rock—never on the hillslopes very far from the surface—is laid open to the sky. Secondly, the rainfall, which was once largely absorbed by this soil, now rapidly rushes off the denuded rocks and flows away to the valleys. The consequent result of this—combined with the destruction of many miles of the artificial soil-surfaces of terraces—is that a large proportion of the rainfall which once found its way slowly through the soil to the sources of the springs—never very deep in Pal—now rapidly runs down the valley bottoms to the lower grounds. The whole mountain region thus suffers from drought. It is a common saying that "trees bring rain." Probably the truth is simply that vegetation modifies the climate almost entirely by retaining moisture in the soil, and in the surface air near the soil; by preventing rapid evaporation for the surface through the shade they afford, and by increasing the output of the springs in the way described above. Remove the vegetation, and the soil gradually leaves the hillsides and the rainfall is largely wasted. This is what has happened over large districts in the Holy Land, and the consequent diminution of some of the springs even within half a cent. has been scientifically noted.

While therefore, from the permanent climatic conditions, Pal could never have been a land of verdure such, for example, as England, yet we know with certainty that its native vegetation has much diminished within the memory of many now living. But besides this, we have abundant historical evidence that at several periods it was much more productive. This is shown, for example, abundantly in the writings of Jos, and, for later periods, in the accounts of many pilgrims. But indeed the mere fact that for many cents. Pal had a population far greater than today is in itself a proof; for as things are, modern Pal is not able to support a much greater population than at present. Great expenditure of capital and labor on the restoring of ancient terraces, the construction of dams and systems of irrigation and the planting of trees is one essential preparation for any considerable development of the land. For any of these things to be possible a radical change in the attitude of the Turkish government is an essential preliminary.

With regard to Bible evidence it is clear from very many references in the historical books of the OT that "forest" or "woodland" was very plentiful in those days. In a large proportion where the word *ya'ar* (tr^d "forest") occurs it is definitely associated with trees. (For references see FOREST.) Whether these references are always to tall trees or also to the brushwood such as is plentiful in parts of Galilee today, is immaterial, as the latter consists of the same elements as the former, only stunted through the interference of man. It would certainly appear probable that at the time of the arrival of the Hebrews there were considerable forests of trees—oaks, terebinths, pines, etc—over a great part of the higher mountains. In Josh **17** 14–18 we have reference to Joshua's twice-repeated command to the people to cut down the "forest," as the inhabited areas were too narrow for them. In later ages, e.g. in NT times, the cultivation of the land must have been so thorough that, to the W. of the Jordan especially, the area left for forest trees must necessarily have been much circumscribed; but the land then with its millions of olive trees and countless vineyards in the mountains and its great palm groves at Jericho and the coast, not to mention all kinds of imported fruit trees, must have presented a very different appearance from its present comparative barrenness. As a single example we may compare the glowing description by Jos of the extraordinary fertility of Gennesaret with its present condition (Jos, *BJ*, III, x, 8). Two periods in history stand out preëminent in the history of Pal as times of prosperity and fertility: that about and immediately succeeding the rise of Christianity and that of the Lat kingdom of Jerus (see Conder, *The Latin Kingdom of Jerusalem*, 239–41: "The present culture of Pal does not, perhaps, attain to a tenth of that which enriched the Latins in the 1st cent. of their rule"). In both these periods the land was highly cultivated and the population large, in the former more so than the latter. That the blight of the Ottoman Turks is largely responsible for the decay of agriculture and progressive deforestation in recent centuries is undoubted, but it is more than possible that at one if not at both these periods another factor was at work. It is difficult to believe that in the days when Palmyra was a vast city and Petra a great emporium, the home of a highly developed civilization, these sites were not better supplied by springs than at present; at those times great tracts of country E. of the Jordan, now swallowed up by the desert, were sites of flourishing cities whose melancholy and lonely ruins are the wonder of all. No afforestation and no increased cultivation will account for the supplies of water which must have sustained such a development; and it is only reasonable to suppose, and there is much to support such a view, that there must have been then a rainfall somewhat greater or more prolonged than today. It must be remembered the increased rainfall of, say, only one inch per annum over a long series of years, or a sustained extension of the rainfall to two or three inches later in the season, or even a few degrees of greater cold producing heavy snow instead of rain, would, any of them, greatly improve the fertility of the soil and the output of the springs. All the evidence seems to confirm the theory that there have been cycles of greater and of lesser rainfall extending over cents., and that the periods we have mentioned, certainly the Rom period, coincided with one of the former cycles. At the present time there is some evidence that the rainfall has, on the whole, been increasing during the last 50 years and the cultivated area of the land, as contrasted with the natural "forest" land, is also slowly extending.

In dealing briefly with some of the more characteristic and remarkable of the plants of the Holy Land we must recognize at least four distinct plant zones: (1) The coast plains and the western mountains, with a distinctly "Mediterranean flora"; (2) The Jordan valley or *Ghor*, with a very peculiar semi-tropical flora in which a considerable number of African forms occur; (3) The steppe or desert zones, specially those E. of the Jordan and to the south. The higher western slopes to the E. of the Jordan also have a very similar flora; (4) The Lebanon and Anti-Lebanon above 4,000 ft. in which Alpine forms occur, and in the higher regions of which there is a flora entirely distinct from the three other zones. These divisions are necessarily somewhat artificial. Everywhere the western slopes are more fertile than the eastern, so that the land to the E. of the waterparting in western Pal partakes more of the desert flora than that opposite to it on the east. Vegetation in all parts is more abundant on the hill slopes with a northern aspect, as it gets more shade; this is particularly noticeable in the drier areas.

4. Plant Zones in the Holy Land

(1) *The coast-plains and western mountains.*—(*a*) In the maritime plain there is a rich red alluvial soil with abundance of water deep under the surface. The annual mean temperature is 70° F.; frost is extremely rare, and the atmosphere is distinctly humid, though the rainfall is less than in the higher hills. Citrons, oranges and lemons here flourish, palms grow in places on the coast, melons and pomegranates reach perfection. Vines have been extensively planted by Jewish colonists in the neighborhood of Jaffa. Cereals—wheat, barley and Egyp maize (*Sorghum annuum*)—are extensively grown. The wild flora is similar to that of the mountains. The sycamore fig (Arab. *jummeiz*) flourishes around Jaffa—it is a tree which requires a warm climate; it was in Talmudic writings one of the distinctions between "lower" and "upper" Galilee that the sycamore fig flourished in the former and not in the latter. It is evident it was far more plentiful in olden times (see SYCAMORE). A closely allied tree, the mulberry, is common everywhere, though not really indigenous. Two varieties occur, the *Morus nigra* (Arab. *tût-shāmi*) a native of central Asia, cultivated for its delicious fruit, and the *M. alba* (Arab. *tût beledi*) a native of China introduced as food for silk worms. See SYCAMINE. Another tree which reaches perfection only in the warmer regions of the plain—and that too in the Jordan valley—is the tamarisk (Arab. *athl*) of which Post recognizes 9 species. It is characterized by its brittle feathery branches covered by minute scale-like leaves; a bedraggled, wind-torn tamarisk half buried in sea-sand is a characteristic sight all along the Syrian coast. Under favorable conditions some species attain considerable size. See TAMARISK.

(*b*) In the higher mountain regions there is an average temperature of 62° F. and extreme variations between a maximum of 100° or 80° in the shade in the summer and a few degrees of frost in the winter. Here the fig, vine and olive do admirably, their late fruiting corresponding with the "dew"—or clouds of fine mist—which settle over the mountains after sunset, particularly in the north. Apricots, mulberries, quince, apples and pears (chiefly from imported grafts), peaches and plums, almonds and walnuts do well in sheltered spots. Wheat and barley are grown on hill slopes or in valley bottoms all over the mountain region.

In the valleys where there is running water the oleander (*Nerium oleander;* Arab. *difleh*) abounds —a plant beautiful in foliage and flower but poisonous and not uncommonly imparting its poison to the water in which it grows. In similar situations occurs the Vitex (*V. Agnus Castris*), a variety of verbena whose lilac or purple flowers are, whereever they occur, a sure sign of the presence of water on or near the surface.

In similar situations flourishes the oriental plane (*Platanus orientalis;* Arab. *dilb*), a tree which often attains great size (see PLANE TREE), and also the alder (*Alnus orientalis;* Arab. *naght*), a tree of humbler growth. There are some 8 varieties of willow (Arab. *sifsaf*), a tree very common along the water courses (see WILLOW). Poplars (Arab. *ḥaur*) are plentiful in places, esp. near water. Three native varieties are known, but the cylindrical Lombardy poplar, an imported variety, is most widely cultivated (see POPLAR). The southern hackberry or nettle tree (*Celtis australis;* Arab. *mais*) a member of the *Urticaceae* closely allied to the elm, is an indigenous tree which is widely planted; it is not uncommonly seen beside Moslem shrines. It grows to a height of 20 to 30 ft., and yields a close-grained timber taking a high polish. The walnut (*Juglans regia;* Arab. *jauz*) is a valuable timber tree and grows to noble proportions. It flourishes around Damascus, being a water-loving tree: some of the most magnificent specimens occur at *Sheba'*, a village in the lower slopes of Hermon. The walnut is really an imported tree, its native home being Persia and the Himalayas, but it has been long naturalized.

The carob (*Ceratonia siliqua;* Arab. *kharrûb*) is a handsome evergreen tree whose dense, dark glistening foliage renders it everywhere conspicuous. It is widely distributed, esp. in the lower mountain regions. Its pods are the HUSKS (which see) of Lk **15** 16. Oaks are among the most important and characteristic of all the trees and shrubs of Pal: the evergreen oak which forms, it is estimated, two-thirds of all the shrubby vegetation of Carmel and attains noble proportions at some of the Moslem shrines, the Valonica oak, plentiful on the hills E. of Nazareth, and the ilex or holm oak, commonest near the coast, are among the more important. The recent destruction of timber in the Holy Land has esp. fallen upon the oaks, which afford the best of all fuel; as their growth is very slow and there is no attempt to plant young trees this is most regrettable. (For fuller account see OAK.) Closely allied to the oak both in the OT and with the modern inhabitant—though botanically very distinct—is the terebinth or turpentine tree (*Pistacia terebinthus;* Arab. *butm*), one of the finest trees in Pal. Although from a distance superficially like an oak, the foliage is very different. In many spots in Pal where terebinths are for various reasons regarded as "sacred" they have obtained splendid proportions. See TEREBINTH.

Pines, although they flourish on the coast and lower mountain slopes, are, together with cypresses, junipers and cedars, reserved to the discussion of the flora of the fourth division of the country—the Alpine regions.

The hawthorn (*Crataegus;* Arab. *za'rûr*), of which there are 4 varieties, occurs as a shrub or small tree everywhere, its sweet-scented white or pink blossom being much in evidence in the spring.

Among the more important shrubs which make up the thickets over the limestone hills the following may be briefly enumerated:

The sumach (*Rhus conaria*), usually a shrub but occasionally a small tree, grows in considerable quantities in fertile spots in the mountains; from its fruit an acid drink is concocted and the fruit, bark and young leaves are used in tanning.

A plant closely allied to this, and also to the terebinth, is the lentesk (*Pistacia lentiscus;* Arab. *serrês*), a common shrub in the lower mountain region, e.g. on Carmel, which yields mastich, a white gum, thought by many to be the BALM of the OT (which see).

The bay laurel (*Laurus nobilis;* Arab. *el ghār*) occurs in clumps in many places. It is the Daphne of the Greeks and was sacred to Apollo. From its large, leathery, shining leaves were made the laurel crowns of victory in classical times. This, it may be mentioned in passing, is quite a distinct plant from our familiar "cherry laurel," which is allied to the cherry.

The butchers' broom (*Ruscus aculeatus*) is very plentiful. It is a plant peculiar in having its leaf-petioles flattened out like a leaf (phillodia), so that the flower and berry appear to arise from the middle of the midrib of the leaf.

The myrtle (*Myrtus communis;* Arab. *rîhān* or *aās*) is exceedingly common, esp. in northern Pal, and when it grows near water it attains a good size. See MYRTLE.

A showy shrub, which sometimes attains to the dimensions of a tree 20 or 30 ft. high, is the arbutus (Arab. *ḳoṭlib*) or strawberry tree. Two kinds occur, the less common *Arbutus unedo* or true "strawberry tree" which has a rough, warty fruit of a scarlet color, and *Arbutus andrachne* with a smooth, red bark, which when peeled off leaves a reddish inner surface. It has small orange-colored, non-edible berries. The red stems of this arbutus may be seen conspicuous in thickets all over the land, but very few are allowed to come to full growth.

Among some of the more showy shrubs we may mention the oleaster (*Eleagnus hortensis;* Arab. *zaizafân*) with its beautiful silvery leaves and white blossom (see OIL TREE); the styrax (*Styrax officinale;* Arab. *haz* or *'abhar*), a shrub or small tree, with beautiful white flowers, somewhat resembling orange blossoms, the dried juice from whose bark is the officinal STORAX (which see); the Judas tree (*Cercis siliquaestrum;* Arab. *zemzariḳ*), a straggling shrub or tree with very showy pink flowers, and the caper (*Capparis spinosa;* Arab. *el âṣîf*), which is very common on old walls and about ruins (see CAPER BERRY). The beautiful rockrose or *Cistus* (Arab. *ghibrah*) is found on many shrubby hillsides, even on the bare mountain tops. The *C. villosus* has pink and the *C. salviaefolus* white blossoms, the petals being curiously crumpled and falling off almost at once when the flower is picked. From the Cistus is obtained the gum called Ladanum (Arab. *ladhanun;* Heb *lōṭ*) for which see MYRRH. Many of the hill tops near the watershed, which should be clothed by forests of oaks and pines, are now almost bare and support upon the dry and scanty soil nothing but low bushes of thorny burnet, mingled with wild thyme and mint, with, in places, small bushes of the Cistus. This thorny burnet (*Poterium Spinosum;* Arab. *ballân*) is almost ubiquitous; its long thorns and tiny leaves enable it to survive the goats. It is of considerable economic importance, as from masses of this plant the *fellahîn* fire almost all the limekilns in the land; and they use it extensively too for their ovens. It is a common sight in the late summer, after the harvest is gathered in, to see companies of peasants gathering this plant into clumps all over the hillsides, and conveying it on the women's heads in huge masses to the kilns. They pile around the kilns enormous heaps, enough to keep the furnace continually burning for several days. They may well be the "thorns under the pot" of Eccl **7** 6. See THORNS.

Of the myriad spring flowers which make such a brilliant annual display it is impossible here to write in any detail. Earliest after the rains appear the crocuses and the cyclamen, then the narcissi, anemones—scarlet, white and purple—the scarlet ranunculi, gladioli, irises, dwarf orchids, pink and yellow flax, mountain lilies, borage and bugloss, the primrose-colored Pal scabious, and vast numbers of small Compositae all appear in quick succession. When these fade many brilliant thistles continue to add some color to the otherwise dry roadsides, and last of all, in the late summer, numbers of tall stalks of squill, shot from the now leafless bulbs, remain scattered in groups over the dry and leafless ground as last survivors of the season's display. The varieties of flowers are enormous, but those mentioned are almost universally present.

Of cultivated vegetables mention may be made of CUCUMBERS (q.v.), lettuce, onions, GARLIC (q.v.), MELONS (q.v.), cauliflower and cabbage, potatoes (a fairly recent introduction), sweet potatoes, the egg plant (*Melongena badinjān*), artichokes (which also grow wild) and the *bāmieh* (*Hibiscus esculentus*).

(2) *The Jordan valley.*—The flora of this region is of a very special kind, and has affinities to Africa. Several trees and shrubs are of great interest. Firstly, mention may be made of the group of true acacias. One variety, the *'anbar* (*Acacia Farnesiana*), is by no means peculiar to the *Ghor*, but is used for making hedges in many parts of the land; its little yellow, fluffy, scented flowers are a great favorite with the natives; it is usually a shrub rather than a tree. The remaining acacias are desert inhabitants and in many places are the only trees. The seyyal, which includes *A. tortilis* and *A. seyal*, flourishes on the west shores of the Dead Sea, at 'Ain Jidy and southward; from it is obtained the gum arabic of commerce; it probably yielded the wood known in the OT as SHITTIM WOOD (q.v.).

The semitropical *Ghor* is the home of many other thorny trees. Extremely characteristic of the whole region are the jujube trees of which the *nabk* or *sidr* tree (*Zizyphus spina-Christi*), is the most common. It has rounded yellowish fruit; under favorable conditions it develops into a tall and handsome tree. Somewhat less common is the *'ennābh* (*Z. vulgaris*) which bears an edible fruit of the shape and size of an olive. A third kind, the *dôm* (*Z. lotus*), is merely a shrub and has small pea-sized fruit. These various kinds of jujube trees are found in every part of the Jordan depression and of the valleys approaching it. Closely allied botanically to these thorny shrubs is the *samûr* (*Paliurus aculeatus*) or "Christ thorn," widely used for the making of hedges (see BRIERS). Another common shrub, or small tree, in the hotter parts of the *Ghor* near Jericho and the Dead Sea, is the *zaḳḳūm* (*Balanites Ægyptiaca*) from whose oval berries the monks of Jericho extract a resinous substance which they term "Balm of Gilead."

The *dibk* (*Cordia myxa*), a giant borage, which grows to a tree of 7 or 8 ft. high is widely cultivated but grows in the *Ghor* spontaneously. The fruit, which is edible, is used principally for making bird lime.

A very striking tree near Jericho and the Dead Sea is the *'oshr* (*Calotropis procera*), a member of the *N.O. Asclepiadeae*. It has large obovate leaves, cabbage-like in consistence—a great contrast to the small, dry, dull-colored leaves of most of its neighbors. The trunk has a cork-like bark and white, milky juice and the fruit consists of queer apple-like follicles which, though solid looking, are only inflated with air and contain but silk threads and seeds. These have been supposed to be the apples of Sodom of Jos, which he describes as looking like tempting fruit but which on examination prove to contain but dust. A much more likely theory is that he refers to the equally common colocynth (*Citrullus colocynthus*). See WILD GOURD.

Another abundant herb is the *Solanum coagulans* (Arab. *khādak*), whose apple-like fruit has also received (without serious claim) the name of "apple of Sodom."

Then there are in the immediate neighborhood of the Dead Sea a whole group of salt-loving plants which grow in the saline marshes such, for example, as the samphire or glasswort (*Salicornia fructosa* and *S. herbacea*). The latter of these is called the *kali* plant, because it is burnt in order to obtain potash (*el kali*). Another group is included under the name of sea blite or sueda (Arab. *suweid*) of which there are several varieties.

Along the banks of the Jordan willows (*Silex safsaf*) and tamarisks (especially *Tamarix Jordanis*) abound.

At various parts of the Jordan valley, but particularly to the north of Lake Huleh, flourishes the papyrus reed (*Cyperus papyrus*), known in Arab. as *babîr*, the source of the earliest paper.

Of cultivated plants, palms, as we know from history, grow here well, though their cultivation has been neglected; sterile wild palms still occur in some of the warmer valleys, esp. to the E. of the Dead Sea. Many dead palm-tree trunks lie scattered along the shores of the Dead Sea.

In situations well supplied with water, bananas flourish—they are cultivated both near Jericho and near the Lake of Galilee. Oranges, lemons and citrons also grow well. All kinds of ordinary vegetables are grown in various parts of this region. Wheat and barley yield an early and an abundant crop in irrigated regions on both sides of the Jordan; rice and Indian maize are cultivated in irrigated fields N. of Lake Huleh, and cotton at several spots. With scientific irrigation this region might be one of the most productive upon earth.

(3) *The Steppe or "Desert" Zones* are chiefly noticeable for the absence of trees and the stunted condition of the small shrubs and herbs which grow there. Thorny plants like *Poterium*, *Astragalus* (the most characteristic order) and *Cousinea* thistles flourish. With the early rains a rapid growth of dwarf flowers appears which dries up soon after the rainy season ends. Botanically the region stands somewhat distinct by the occurrence of Pers and Indian plant-forms. This region includes the great corn land of the Hauran and Nukra —some of the richest of their kind.

(4) *The flora of the Lebanon and Anti-Lebanon* consists, in the lower slopes, of similar plants to those mentioned under (1). The *Conifera* are specially characteristic of this northern region, the destruction of these trees in Pal proper being in many parts complete. Of the indigenous cypress (Arab. *Saru*) we have one species, the *Cypressus sempervirens*, a handsomer tree than the cylindrical kind —a cultivated variety—planted so frequently in Turkish cemeteries (see CYPRESS). There are 6 varieties of juniper known, and one species of yew. Of pines the two important kinds are—the Aleppo pine (*Pinus Halepensis*), which grows with considerable rapidity and is widely planted, and the handsomer stone pine (*Pinus pinia* the true *snobar* of the Arabs), probably more truly the native tree (see PINE TREE). The most important and characteristic member of this order of trees is the cedar which still flourishes in a very few spots (see CEDAR). On the Lebanon occurs a single species of rhododendron (*R. Ponticum*) and one of heather (*Erica verticillata*). Above the height of 7,000 ft. trees and shrubs disappear and vegetation is chiefly represented by low, rounded, thorny bushes, chiefly varieties of Astragalus; by clumps of *Acantholimon Lebanoticum;* by small procumbent bushes of *Cerasus prostata*—a member of the cherry family—and the *Coloneaster nummularia* with scarlet berries. Even on the summit of Hermon it is astonishing how many tiny flowers are in bloom in the late summer after the snow has melted. The most curious feature of this region is the almost complete absence of Arctic forms such as are found in the Alps and even in the Himalayas.

LITERATURE.—Prof. Ellsworth Huntington, *Pal and Its Transformation;* J. Glaisher (*PEF*); *Meteorological Observations at Jerus;* Rev. G. E. Post, M.D., *Flora of Syria, Pal and Sinai;* Mrs. Hannah Zeller, *Wild Flowers of the Holy Land;* Augusta A. Temple, *Flowers and Trees of Pal;* Tristram, *The Fauna and Flora of Pal* (*PEF Memoirs*); also articles in recent Bible Dictionaries, particularly those by Dr. Post in *HDB*, and by Sir W. T. Thiselton-Dyer, director of Kew Gardens, in *EB*.

E. W. G. MASTERMAN

BOTCH. See BOIL.

BOTRYS, bot'ris (**Βότρυς,** *Bótrus;* mod. *Batrûn*): A town of Phoenicia on the coast some miles N. of Gebal (Byblus) on the southern side of the bold promontory called in classic times Theoprosopon. It is said to have been founded by Ithobal (Ethbaal), king of Tyre, whose daughter married Ahab (Jos, *Ant*, VIII, xiii, 2). The town is not mentioned in Scripture.

BOTTLE, bot''l (חֵמֶת, *ḥēmeth*, נֹאד, *nō'dh*, נֵבֶל, *nēbhel*, בַּקְבֻּק, *baḳbuḳ*, אוֹב, *'ōbh;* **ἀσκός,** *askós*): The most lit. rendering of all the words for b. in EV is "skin," or "wine-skin," RV. The primitive b. among eastern peoples was really a bag made from skins, tanned or untanned, of kid, goat, cow, camel or buffalo—in most cases drawn off of the animal entire, after the legs and head were cut off, and, when filled, grotesquely retaining the shape of the animal. The skins in common use today, as anciently no doubt, for holding water, milk, butter and cheese, have the hair left on and are far from cleanly-looking. Those used for wine and oil are tanned by means of oak bark and seasoning in smoke, a process that gives a peculiar astringency of flavor to the wine kept in them, and gave rise to the parable of Jesus about putting new wine into old wine-skins (Mt **9** 17; Mk **2** 22; Lk **5** 37). The fact that the leather underwent distension once and only once under fermentation, and the further fact that the wine-skins became dried and liable to crack from the smoke and dry heat of the tents and houses, gave point to the parable: "No man putteth new wine into old wine-skins; else the wine will burst the skins, and the wine perisheth, and the skins: but they put new wine into fresh wine-skins." All such "bottles" today are liable to crack and become worthless.

Bottles of Skins.

Pliny Fisk used fresh goat-skins to carry water, but he says this gave the water a reddish color and an exceedingly loathsome taste. Harmer tells of carrying liquids in smoked skin-bottles, which when rent "were mended by putting in a new piece, or by gathering up the piece, or by inserting a flat bit of wood." Burckhardt says he saw Arabs keeping water for their horses on journeys in "large bags made of tanned camel-skin." They would sew the skins up well on four sides, but would leave two openings, one to admit the air, one to let out the water. Two such bags made a good load for a camel. Edwin Wilbur Rice says the leather or skin-bottles are of different sizes and kinds, usually made from the skin of the goat, rarely ever from that of the sheep, as it is not considered strong enough. But sometimes they are made from the skin of the camel, or the ox, which is then prepared by tanning. When leather bags are sewed up the joinings are smeared with grease, as the skin-bottles of all sorts are, as they grow older, lest the water, or other liquid, ooze through.

Water Carriers with Skin Bottles.

Such bottles, being more portable and less breakable than earthenware, were peculiarly well suited to the use of primitive and nomad peoples, as they are to the roving Bedouin of today. The mention of them, however, in such various accounts and connections as those for instance of the story of Hagar (Gen **21** 19), of the Gibeonites (Josh **9** 4), and of David (1 S **25** 18) shows that they were in common use among ancient Orientals, pastoral and peasant alike. Tourists still find that they are admirably suited to travelers in waterless districts, or districts where the water is brackish and bad. One of the characteristic figures even in oriental centers like Damascus today is the water-man who sells from his dripping goat-skin water cooled with the snow of Hermon, flavored with lemon, rose, or licorice, temptingly offered up and down the streets by his clapping his brass cups and crying in the most pleading but pleasing tones, "Drink, drink, thirsty one" (cf Isa **55** 1). But, as Dr. Mackie, of Beirût, says, "While the bottle is thus highly prized, and the water thus kept in it is a grateful necessity, the luxury of the East belongs to the spring itself, to the draught from the fountain of living waters. Hence the comparison Jesus made at Jacob's well (Jn **4** 14), and the one blessed terminus of all, the Shepherd's leading (Rev **7** 17). See *HDB*, s.v.

Of course in the settled life of the Orient water, milk, wine and other liquids are often kept in earthen jars or other receptacles. For such "bottles" see PITCHER; VESSEL. Glass bottles are not mentioned in the Bible; but those now found in tombs, for keeping perfume in, may have been known in OT times.

Assyrian Glass Bottles (from the British Museum Collection).

Figurative: (1) For the clouds (Job **38** 37). (2) For intoxication, through which, because of their headstrong continuance in sin, Israel shall be helpless to resist the enemy's attack (Jer **13** 12). (3) For sorrow: "Put thou my tears into thy bottle" (Ps **56** 8). "The Psalmist's sorrows were so many that they would need a great wine-skin to hold them all. There is no allusion to the little lachrymatories of fashionable and fanciful Romans: it is a robuster metaphor by far; such floods of tears had the Psalmist wept that a leathern bottle would scarce hold them" (*Treasury of David*, III, 39). "God treasures His servants' tears as if they were water or wine." St. Bernard says, "The tears of penitents are the wine of angels" (Dummelow's *Comm.*, 351).

GEO. B. EAGER

BOTTOM, bot'um: Rendered by several Heb words: (1) שֶׁרֶשׁ, *sheresh*, "root"; Chald, שֹׁרֶשׁ, *shōresh* (Job **36** 30, "the b. of the sea"). (2) קַרְקַע, *ḳarḳa'*, "soil," "pavement of *tesserae*" (Am **9** 3). (3) קֶצֶב, *ḳeçebh*, "cutting," "chop," "extremity" (Jon **2** 6, "the bottoms of the mountains"). (4) רְפִידָה, *rᵉphīdhāh*, "railing," "couch" (Cant **3** 10, "the b. thereof of gold"). (5) חֵיק, *ḥēḳ*, "bosom," "lap" (Ezk **43** 13.14.17, RVm "hollow"). (6) מְצֻלָּה, *mᵉçullāh*, "to be dark," "shadowy place," from prim. root *çālal*, "to tumble down," i.e. "settle"; hence the idea of a valley ("the myrtle-trees that were in the bottom," Zec **1** 8 RVm "shady place"). The prophet may have been wont to frequent the myrtle grove in the glen or bottoms, in the neighborhood of Jerus, for meditation and prayer (*BTP*, II, 283). M. O. Evans

BOTTOMLESS, bot'um-les, **PIT** (**τὸ φρέαρ τῆς ἀβύσσου,** *tó phréar tês abússou,* "the pit of the abyss," Rev **9** 1.2 AV): In RV, *hē abussos* (always an adj. in classical authors="bottomless") is uniformly rendered "the abyss" (q.v.) (Lk **8** 31; Rom **10** 7; Rev **9** 11; **11** 7; **17** 8; **20** 1.3).

BOUGH, bou. See Branch.

BOUGHT, bout (תָּוֶךְ, *tāwekh,* "bisection," "middle"): The best part of a sling that contains the stone, "in the midst of the bought of a sling" (1 S **25** 29 AVm, AV "out of the middle," RV "from the hollow").

BOUGHT, bôt (adj. and vb.). See Buying.

BOUND. See Bind.

BOUNDS, boundz: גָּבַל, *gābhal*="to twist" (as a rope), "to make an enclosure" (as by a line) occurs in Ex **19** 12.23; Ps **104** 9. גְּבוּל, *g^ebhūl*="a cord," hence "a boundary," "territory" (Ex **23** 31 AV), with its fem. form גְּבוּלָה, *g^ebhūlāh* (Dt **32** 8; Isa **10** 13); חֹק, *ḥōḳ*="enactment," "appointment" (of time, space, quantity, labor, or usage), hence "commandment," "decree," "ordinance" (Job **14** 5; **26** 10 AV); in the Gr, ὁροθεσία, *horothesía,* in the sense of "a limit," "boundary line," occurs in Acts **17** 26.

BOUNTIFULNESS, boun'ti-fŏŏl-nes, **BOUNTY,** boun'ti (**ἁπλότης,** *haplótēs,* "singleness," "benevolence," 2 Cor **9** 11 AV; טוֹב, *ṭōbh,* "to be good" [Prov **22** 9]; **εὐλογία,** *eulogía,* "good speech," "blessing" [2 Cor **9** 6]; גָּמַל, *gāmal,* "to treat well" [Ps **119** 17]; שׁוֹעַ, *shōa',* "to be liberal" [Isa **32** 5]; יָד, *yādh,* "hand," "power"): Paul speaks of the church at Corinth "being enriched in everything unto all liberality" (AV "bountifulness," 2 Cor **9** 11). The offering of the church at Corinth for the Christians of Judaea is termed a "bounty," a blessing, liberally given: "and not of extortion" (AV "of covetousness," 2 Cor **9** 5.6). The word occurs also in 1 K **10** 13: "Besides that which Solomon gave her of his royal bounty," lit. "according to the hand of King Solomon." L. Kaiser

BOW, bō. See Archery.

BOW, bou, **BOWING,** bou'ing. See Adoration; Attitudes.

BOW, bō, **IN THE CLOUD:** Reference to the promise made to Noah (Gen **9** 13) preserved in the the Constellation figures. See Astronomy, II, 4.

BOWELS, bou'elz (מֵעָה, *mē'āh,* pl. מֵעִים, *mē'īm,* רֶחֶם, *reḥem,* pl. רַחֲמִים, *raḥămīm;* **σπλάγχνον,** *splágchnon*):

(1) **Literal:** The lit. meaning of these words is intestines, then the abdomen, the womb (matrix and uterus). As will be seen there is not much definiteness in the use of these expressions from the standpoint of physiology; but not less so than in modern oriental languages and even in many occidental languages, as popularly used. The remarkable phrases used in 2 Ch **21** 18.19, "Jeh smote him in his bowels" and "His bowels fell out by reason of his sickness," refer to a severe and fatal case of hemorrhoids.

(2) **Figurative:** In fig. language these words denote deep emotions of various kinds. As in physiology we speak of the "nervus sympathicus," the ancients expressed by these terms "affection," "sympathy" and "mercy," feelings of distress and sorrow, as in Job **30** 27 AV; Lam **1** 20 AV; **2** 11 AV. In one passage we have to translate *mē'īm* by "heart," being the seat of affection and devotion (Ps **71** 6): "Thy law is within my heart" (**40** 8). In the NT (RV) the word is only given in Acts **1** 18. H. L. E. Luering

BOWING, bou'ing (נָטָה, *nāṭāh,* "to incline," "bulge"): The Psalmist's assailants expected that he would be "like a leaning [AV "bowing"] wall" (Ps **62** 3) before their united attack, as when an ill-built, bulging wall gives way under a sudden and heavy fall of rain (cf Ezk **13** 11; **38** 22).

BOWL, bōl:

(1) The primitive Hebrews, like the wandering Bedouin of today, probably used bowls of wood, as less breakable than earthenware. Some hollow dish of the sort would be indispensable, even in the lowest stage of nomad life, to receive the milk of the flock, and as the common dish in which to serve the family meal. We have abundant proof, however, that vessels of earthenware of various sorts were in use by the settled peoples of Canaan in the earliest times. Many interesting specimens, characteristic of different peoples and ages, have been found by excavators of the *PEF,* esp. recently by Flinders Petrie and Fred. Bliss at Tell el-Hesy (see *Tell el-Hesy* [Lachish], by Petrie, and *A Mound of Many Cities,* by Bliss) and by Macalister and others at Gezer, Taanach, Megiddo, etc (see *PEFS*).

It was probably in some such dish—"a b. fit for lords" (EV "a lordly dish")—that Jael offered Sisera a draught of sour milk (Jgs **5** 25; cf Arab. *leben*), and the b. into which Gideon wrung the water from his fleece (Jgs **6** 38) is denoted by the same word (סֵפֶל, *ṣēphel;* LXX *lekánē*), though this may have been of earthenware instead of wood. Certainly the *ṣēphel* was a dish of goodly size.

(2) Another word rendered sometimes "bowl" and sometimes "basin" is מִזְרָק, *mizrāḳ.* It is used of the large silver bowls presented by "the princes of the congregation" (Nu **7** 13 f). See Basin. It is also applied by Amos (**6** 6) to the costly bowls used by the nobles of Samaria in their debaucheries.

(3) A still larger b. is mentioned by Jer (**35** 5), AV "pot" (גָּבִיעַ, *gābhī^a'*). This same word is used of Joseph's cup (Gen **44** 2 f): "Put my cup, the silver cup, in the sack's mouth." As used at banquets it corresponds to the *crater,* from which the drinking cups (כּוֹסוֹת, *kōṣōth*) were replenished. The material seems to have been uniformly silver. But see (4).

(4) B. is used in AV to tr גָּבִיעַ, *gābhī^a',* "the bowls made like almonds" (Ex **25** 33 AV), as applied to the "cups" (RV), or calyxes, used to ornament the golden candlestick (see Tabernacle). It seems to have been an elastic term.

(5) The b. of Zec **4** 3 (גֻּלָּה, *gullāh,* found also in **5** 2 correct text), is represented as the receptacle for oil in the candlestick of the prophet's vision. It is likewise used of "the lamp of life" (Eccl **12** 6) and to designate the bowl-shaped capitals of Jachin and Boaz (1 K **7** 41.42; 2 Ch **4** 12.13).

(6) B. is found in Isa **51** 17.22 RV, "b. of the cup" (AV "dregs of the cup"). Some think the second word here (קֻבַּעַת כּוֹס, *ḳubba'ath kōṣ*) is a gloss to explain the unusual preceding word.

(7) In Rev where AV has "vial" (*phiálē*) RV has "bowl." See BASIN. GEO. B. EAGER

BOWMAN, bō'man: Israel seems not to have been equal to the surrounding peoples in the use of the bow. The battle of Gilboa was clearly lost through the superior skill of the Phili bowmen. This seems to have moved David to encourage archery practice in Judah (2 S **1** 18; cf Driver in loc.). It is thought probable that the revival of Israel's military power under Jeroboam, son of Joash, was due to improvement in archery. Hosea, a contemporary, speaks of the bow as the national weapon of Israel (**1** 5.7). The most skilled bowmen of antiquity were the Assyrians (cf Isa **5** 28; **37** 33). From Assyr reliefs it seems that it was their practice to overwhelm their enemies with the bow, and to use sword and spear only when the foe had been demoralized and put to flight. See ARCHERY. GEO. B. EAGER

BOWSHOT, bō'shot: Found only in Gen **21** 16 in the account of Hagar and her child: "And she went, and sat her down over against him a good way off, as it were a bowshot," lit. "stretchings of a bow," a typical oriental way of indicating distance.

BOX: The passages in which this word occurs are 2 K **9** 1.3 (Heb *pakh,* "cruet," "flask," RV vial) and the synoptic passages Mt **26** 7 AV; Mk **14** 3 AV; Lk **7** 37 AV (Gr *alábastron*). "Perfume-boxes" are mentioned in Isa **3** 20; in the NT pas-

Alabaster Boxes.

sages RV renders "alabaster cruse." "Alabaster" was a white stone much used in ornamentation; and out of it small vessels were made for holding precious ointment. "She brake the cruse" (Mk **14** 3), i.e. the seal, not the vessel.

In Isa **41** 19 and **60** 13, "box" is found in connection with "tree," as "box-tree" (q.v.).

BOXING. See GAMES.

BOX-TREE, box'trē (תְּאַשּׁוּר, *t'ashshūr;* Isa **41** 19; **60** 13, "boxwood" Ezk **27** 6): A tree of uncertain identity, which must once have been common in the forests of Lebanon. According to Post (*HDB*, I, 313), "The only species of box found in Bible lands is *Buxus longifolia,* which is a shrub from 2 to 3 ft. high. It does not grow S. of Mt. Cassius and it is unlikely that it did in historical times."

As an alternative to the box the cypress, *Cupressus sempervirens*—known in Arab. as *Sherbīn*—has been suggested. It is a fine tree and was probably once plentiful, but as it seems to answer to the *berosh* (see FIR), it cannot well be the *t'ashshūr.* There is nothing certain to go upon.
E. W. G. MASTERMAN

BOY (יֶלֶד, *yeledh,* "child," נַעַר, *na'ar,* "lad," "youth"; **παῖς, ὁ, ἡ,** *ho* and *hē país*): Refers to a child of any age, and is sometimes used of either sex: Joel **3** 3; Zec **8** 5; Mt **17** 18; Lk **2** 43; **8** 51.54 fem.; **9** 42. In the East the word applies also to an adult who is a servant (Mt **8** 6 RVm). The boy occupied a place of special importance in the family life of all ancient people. In Syria the father even was called by the name of his son. He was known as the father of Joseph, or whatever the name might be. As is true among all oriental people, while the father had absolute control in his case as well as in the case of the rest of the household, yet the boy received a consideration and advantages not accorded to the daughter. In the Jewish family his religious life began at the fourth year. He was expected to learn the Scriptures at five, the Mish at ten, and to fulfil the whole law at thirteen. At twelve years he was expected to learn a trade, and attained to something of independence at that age, though he did not come into full rights as a citizen until he was twenty. Among many nations there was special rejoicing at the birth of the boy, and sometimes a feast. One of the most ancient customs was the planting of a cedar tree on this occasion. See CHILD; FAMILY; SON.
JACOB W. KAPP

BOZCATH, boz'kath (בָּצְקַת, *boçkath*). See BOZKATH.

BOZEZ, bō'zez (בּוֹצֵץ, *bōçēç;* **Βαζές,** *Bazés,* probably from an obsolete root *bāçaç,* corresponding to the Arab. *baṣṣa,* "to shine" or "to ooze"): The name of the northern of the two cliffs that stand one on each side of the gorge of Michmash (1 S **14** 4). It catches the sun during most of the day, while the southern cliff is in the shade. To this circumstance it may owe its name, "shining." "The contrast is surprising and picturesque between the dark coal color of the south side, and the ruddy or tawny tints of the northern cliff, crowned with the gleaming white of the upper chalky strata. The picture is unchanged since the day when Jonathan looked over to the white camping ground of the Philis, and Bozez must have then shone as brightly as it does now, in the full light of an eastern sun" (Conder, *Tent Work,* 256). W. EWING

BOZKATH, boz'kath (בָּצְקַת, *boçkath,* "stony"; LXX **Βασηδώθ,** *Basēdōth*): A town in the Shephelah of Judah named between Lachish and Eglon (Josh **15** 39). It was the birthplace of Adaiah the mother of King Josiah (2 K **22** 1; AV "Boscath"). The site is not identified.

BOZRAH, boz'ra (בָּצְרָה, *boçrāh,* "sheepfold"; **Βοσόρρα,** *Bosórrha,* **Βοσόρ,** *Bosór*):

(1) The capital of Edom, a city of great antiquity (Gen **36** 33; 1 Ch **1** 44; Isa **34** 6; **63** 1; Jer **49** 13; Am **1** 12). It may be identical with *Buṣeirah,* which lies about 7 miles S.W. of *Ṭufīleh,* on the main road to Petra.

(2) A city in Moab mentioned in Jer **48** 24. It is probably identical with **Bezer,** the city of refuge. It may be represented today by *Ḳusūr Bashair,* which towers lie some 15 miles S.E. of Dibon. In this case Beth-gamul would be identical with *Jemail,* 8 miles E. of Dibon, and Beth-meon with *Ma'in,* S.W. of Medebah. W. EWING

BRACELET, brās'let (אֶצְעָדָה, *'eç'ādhāh,* חָח, *ḥāḥ,* צָמִיד, *çāmīdh,* פָּתִיל, *pāthīl,* שֵׁרוֹת, *shērōth*): Used to translate a number of Heb words, only one of which means a band for the arm (*'eç'ādhāh*), as in 2 S **1** 10, "the bracelet that was on his arm." In Ex **35** 22, where both men and women are said to have brought as offerings among other "jewels of gold" "bracelets" (RV "brooches"), another word (*ḥāḥ*) is used, meaning most likely nose-rings (see RINGS). The b. asked of Judah by Tamar as a pledge ("Thy signet, and thy b., and thy staff that is in thy hand," Gen **38** 18.25 AV) was probably the cord of softly-twisted wool for the shepherd's headdress (*pāthīl;* RV "cord"). The bracelets ("two bracelets for her hands of ten shekels weight of gold") which Abraham's servant gave to Rebekah stand for still another word (*çāmīdh*). These "bracelets" are always spoken of as "bracelets for

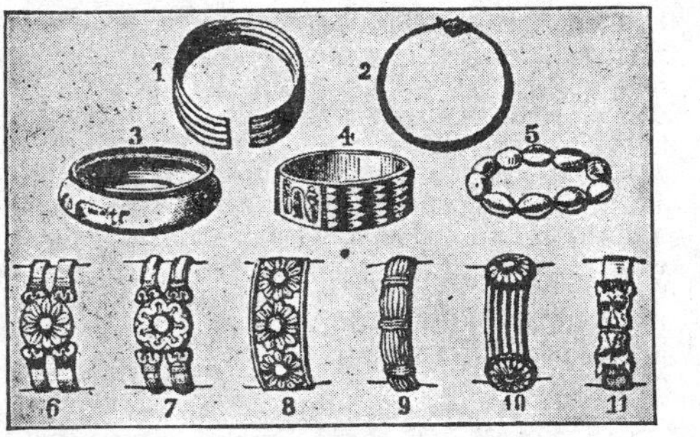

Egyptian and Assyrian Bracelets.

1. Egyptian Silver Bracelet (British Museum). 2. Egyptian Iron Bracelet Set with Cornelian (British Museum). 3. Egyptian Gold Bracelet. 4. Egyptian Inlaid Work (British Museum). 5. Egyptian Bracelet Made of Cowries (British Museum). 6, 7, 8. Assyrian Bracelets from the Sculptures (British Museum). 9, 10, 11. Assyrian Bracelets (from Botta).

the hands," or as "put upon the hands" (Gen **24** 47; cf Ezk **16** 11; **23** 42). Isaiah, predicting the day when Jeh will smite the haughty daughters of Zion, who "walk with outstretched necks and wanton eyes, walking and mincing as they go, and making a tinkling with their feet," says, "In that day the Lord will take away the beauty of their anklets . . . . the *bracelets*" (**3** 19, *shērōth*) etc, where some translate "twisted ornaments," leaving it uncertain as to just what is specifically meant. In 2 S **1** 10 the b. appears with the crown as one of the royal insignia. In 2 K **11** 12, according to Wellhausen, W. R. Smith (*OTJC*², 311n.) and others, we should read, "Then he brought out the king's son, and put the crown upon him and gave him *bracelets*" [הצעדות] for "*testimony*" [העדות]. See *DB*.

Today, as of old, the bracelet is multiform and a favorite ornament in the East. It is made of gold, silver, copper, brass, glass and even enameled earthenware, and in many designs: flat band, plain ring, interlinked rings, as well as of twisted wires, connected squares, solid or perforated, with or without pendants (Mackie).

When owned by women, bracelets had the special recommendation, along with other jewelry, of being inalienable—not to be taken by the husband in case of divorce, nor seized and sold for his debts. "Even now," says Rice (*Orientalisms*, etc, 41), "in Moslem lands a woman may be divorced without legal process, at the freak of her husband, but she can carry away undisputed any amount of gold, silver, jewels, precious stones, or apparel that she has loaded on her person; so she usually wears all her treasures on her person, not knowing when the fateful word may be spoken." GEO. B. EAGER

BRAG (**μεγαλαυχέω**, *megalauchéō*, "proud brags"): Occurs only in the Apoc (2 Macc **15** 32), not being sufficiently dignified to be given a place in the canonical Scriptures by the King James translators (cf Jth **16** 5).

BRAIDED, brād'ed, **BRAIDING**, brād'ing (**τὸ πλέγμα**, *tó plégma*, "that which is plaited," 1 Tim **2** 9; **ἡ ἐμπλοκή**, *hē emplokḗ*, "a plaiting," 1 Pet **3** 3): Used with reference to Christian women in two passages where the apostles emphasized the superiority of good works and spiritual grace over outward adornment. See EMBROIDERY.

BRAMBLE, bram'b'l. See THORNS.

BRAN (**τὰ πίτυρα**, *tá pítura*): The women of Babylon are described as burning "bran for incense" in their unchaste idolatrous worship (Bar **6** 43).

BRANCH, bransh, and **BOUGH**: Represented by very many words in the Heb.

(1) זְמוֹרָה, *zemōrāh*, used esp. of a vine branch. The spies "cut down from thence a branch with one cluster of grapes" (Nu **13** 23). See also Ezk **15** 2; Nah **2** 2. "They put the branch to their nose" (Ezk **8** 17), refers to some unknown idolatrous practice, as does also Isa **17** 10, "thou plantest pleasant plants, and settest it with strange slips," or "vine slips of a strange [god]" RVm.

(2) יוֹנֶקֶת, *yōneḳeth*, lit. "a sucker." "The tender branch thereof will not cease" (Job **14** 7). Used **fig.** of Israel, Ps **80** 11 (RV "shoots"); Ezk **17** 22 AV; Hos **14** 6, and of the wicked, Job **8** 16 (RV "shoots"), **15** 30.

(3) כִּפָּה, *kippāh*, Job **15** 32. Isa **9** 14; **19** 15, RV has "palm-branch," "Therefore Jeh will cut off from Israel head and tail, palm-branch and rush, in one day" (**9** 14).

(4) נֵצֶר, *nēçer* (of the same Heb root, according to many commentators, as Nazareth), lit. "a little shoot springing from the root" ("out of a shoot from her roots," Dnl **11** 7), which may be planted out to grow (Isa **11** 1; **60** 21), or may be rooted out and thrown away (Isa **14** 19).

(5) צֶמַח, *çemaḥ*. The "branch" of Messianic prophecy. See PROPHECY. "In that day shall the branch [m "shoot" or "sprout"] of Jeh be beautiful and glorious" (Isa **4** 2); "a shoot out of the stock of Jesse" (Isa **11** 1); "a righteous branch" (Jer **23** 5; **33** 15): "my servant the Branch" (Zec **3** 8); "the man whose name is the Branch" (Zec **6** 12).

(6) קָנֶה, *ḳānāh*, is used for the "branches" of the golden candlesticks (Ex **25** 32; **37** 18 ff). Lit. *kānāh* means a "reed."

There are a number of words, less frequently used, meaning "branch":

(7) בַּדִּים, *baddīm* (pl. only used; Ezk **17** 6; **19** 14).

(8) דָּלִית, *dālīth* (pl. only used; Jer **11** 16).

(9) מַטֶּה, *maṭṭeh* (Ezk **19** 11).

(10) סָעִיף, *ṣā'īph* (Isa **18** 5; סְעַפָּה, *ṣe'appāh* (pl.) (Ezk **31** 6); סַרְעַפָּה, *ṣar'appāh* (Ezk **31** 5).

(11) עָנָף, *'ānāph* (Mal **4** 1; Ps **80** 11); עֲנַף, *'ănāph* (Dnl **4** 14.21); עָנֵף, *'eneph* (Ezk **36** 8).

(12) פֻּארָה, *pu'rāh*, "a bough" (Isa **10** 33); פֹּארוֹת, *pō'rōth* (pl. only) (Ezk **31** 5.8).

(13) צַמֶּרֶת, *çammereth*, "foliage" or "boughs of trees," lit. "locks" or "fleece" of trees (Ezk **17** 3; **31** 3).

(14) קָצִיר, *ḳāçīr* (collective) (Job **14** 9), "boughs" (Ps **80** 11), "branches."

(15) שִׁבֹּלֶת, *shibbeleth*, the two olive branches of Zec **4** 12.

(16) שׂוֹךְ, *sōkh*, root meaning "to interweave" (Jgs **9** 49); שׂוֹכָה, *sōkhāh* (Jgs **9** 48), "boughs."

(17) שָׂרִיג, *sārīgh* (pl. only, שָׂרִיגִים, *sārīghīm*), "branches" (of the vine) (Gen **40** 10; Joel **1** 7).

Represented in Gr in the NT:
(1) **βαΐον**, *baíon* (Jn **12** 13), "a palm branch."
(2) **κλάδος**, *kládos* (Mt **13** 32; **21** 8; **24** 32; Mk **4** 32; **13** 28; Lk **13** 19; Rom **11** 16.17.18. 19.21).
(3) **κλῆμα**, *klēma*, a slip or cutting of the vine, esp. one cut off to be grafted into another plant (Jn **15** 2.4.5.6).
(4) **στιβάς**, *stibás* (=**στοιβάς**, *stoibás*), a "twig" or "bough" (Mk **11** 8). E. W. G. Masterman

BRAND: In the double signification of an object on fire and of objects used to feed a fire. The first meaning is expressed by אוּד, *'ūdh*, "a bent stick" for stirring fire (Am **4** 11; Zec **3** 2; cf Isa **7** 4); the second by לַפִּיד, *lappīdh*, in Jgs **15** 4.5. A third meaning is found in זִיקָה, *zīḳāh*, indicating the brand as a spreader of fire (Prov **26** 18).

BRANDING. See Punishments.

BRASEN, brā'z'n. See Brass.

BRASS, bras, **BRAZEN** (נְחֹשֶׁת, *neḥōsheth*): The use of the word brass has always been more or less indefinite in its application. At the present time the term brass is applied to an alloy of copper and zinc or of copper, zinc and tin. The word trd "brass" in the AV would be more correctly rendered bronze, since the alloy used was copper and tin (Ex **27** 4). In some passages however copper is meant (Dt **8** 9), as bronze is an artificial product. This alloy was known in Egypt in at least 1600 BC. It was probably known in Europe still earlier (2000 BC), which helps to answer the question as to the source of the tin. Bronze was probably of European origin and was carried to Egypt. At a later period the Egyptians made the alloy themselves, bringing their copper from Sinai, Cyprus or northern Syria (see Copper), and their tin from the Balkan regions or from Spain or the British Isles (see Tin). When the Children of Israel came into the promised land, they found the Canaanites already skilled in the making and use of bronze instruments. This period marked the transition from the bronze age to the iron age in Pal. Museums possessing antiquities from Bible lands have among their collections many and varied bronze objects. Among the most common are nails, lamps, hand mirrors, locks, cutting instruments, etc. Within comparatively recent times brass, meaning an alloy of copper and zinc, has been introduced into Syria. The alloy is made by the native workmen (see Crafts). Sheet brass is now being extensively imported for the making of bowls, vases, etc. Bronze is practically unknown in the modern native arts.

Figurative: "Brass," naturally, is used in Scripture as the symbol of what is firm, strong, lasting; hence "gates of brass" (Ps **107** 16), "hoofs of brass" (Mic **4** 13), "walls of brass" (Jeremiah is made as a "brazen wall," **1** 18; **15** 20), "mountains of brass" (Dnl **2** 35, the Macedonian empire; the arms of ancient times were mostly of bronze). It becomes a symbol, therefore, of hardness, obstinacy, insensibility, in sin, as "brow of brass" (Isa **48** 4); "they are brass and iron" (Jer **6** 28, of the wicked); "all of them are brass" (Ezk **22** 18, of Israel). James A. Patch

BRAVERY, brāv'ẽr-i: תִּפְאָרָה, *tiph'ārāh*, or תִּפְאֶרֶת, *tiph'ereth* = "beauty," "glory," "honor" and "majesty," hence "splendor of bravery." "The bravery of their tinkling ornaments" (Isa **3** 18 AV), "the beauty of their anklets" (ARV). Cf *bravado*, *bravura*.

BRAWLER, brôl'ẽr (Ḳerē מִדְיָנִים, *midhyānīm*; Kethībh מִדְוָנִים, *midhwānīm*, "quarrelsomeness"; **ἄμαχος**, *ámachos*, "not fighting"): Spoken of the quarrelsome woman; "a contentious [AV "brawling"] woman" (Prov **21** 9). He who seeks the office of a bishop should be "no brawler" (*πάροινος*, *pároinos*, AV "given to wine," Tit **1** 7); "not contentious" (AV "not a brawler," 1 Tim **3** 3; Tit **3** 2).

BRAY, brā (נָהַק, *nāhaḳ*, "to bray," of the ass; כָּתַשׁ, *kāthash*, "to pound in a mortar"): This word occurs with two distinct meanings: (*a*) The harsh cry of the ass (Job **6** 5). Job argued that as the sounds instinctively uttered by animals denote their wants, even so his words were but the natural expression of his longing for some adequate explanation of his sufferings, or, failing this, for death itself. Used **fig.** of Job's mockers (Job **30** 7). (*b*) "To beat small in a mortar," "to chastise." Prov **27** 22 refers to a more elaborate process than threshing for separating grain (ERV "corn") from its husk and impurities; used **fig.** of a thorough but useless course of discipline; or still more probably with reference to the Syrian custom of braying meat and bruised corn together in a mortar with a pestle, "till the meat and grain become a uniform indistinguishable pulp" (see *Expos T*, VIII, 521). M. O. Evans

BRAZEN, brā'z'n. See Brass.

BRAZEN SEA. See Sea, The Molten.

BRAZEN SERPENT. See Nehushtan.

BREACH, brēch: Represented by (1) פֶּרֶץ, *pereç* = "a tear," "a rending asunder," "a break," hence **fig.** "enmity," "disruption," "strife" (Gen **38** 29; Jgs **21** 15; 2 S **5** 20; 1 Ch **15** 13; Neh **6** 1; Job **16** 14; Ps **106** 23; Isa **30** 13; **58** 12); (2) שֶׁבֶר, *shebher* = "fracture," "affliction," "bruise," "destruction" (Lev **24** 20; Jer **14** 17; Lam **2** 13; Ps **60** 2); (3) בֶּדֶק, *bedheḳ* = "a gap" or "leak" (in a building or ship) occurring in 2 K **12** 5–8.12; **22** 5; (4) תְּנוּאָה, *tenū'āh* = "alienation," "breach of promise" (Nu **14** 34 AV); (5) מִפְרָץ, *miphrāç* = "a break" (in the shore), and hence "a haven" (Jgs **5** 17, RV "creeks"). Frank E. Hirsch

BREACH, brēch, **OF COVENANT**, kuv'e-nant, kuv'ĕ-nant. See Crimes.

BREACH OF RITUAL, rit'ū-al. See Crimes.

BREACH OF TRUST. See Crimes.

BREAD, bred (לֶחֶם, *leḥem*; **ἄρτος**, *ártos*):

I. Dietary Preëminence
II. Materials
  1. Barley
  2. Wheat
  3. Three Kinds of Flour
III. Bread-Making
  1. Grinding
  2. Kneading
  3. Baking
    (1) Hot Stones
    (2) Baking Pans
  4. Ovens
    (1) The Bowl-Oven
    (2) The Jar-Oven
    (3) The Pit-Oven
  5. Forms of Baked Bread
  6. Work for Women
IV. Sanctity and Symbolism of Bread
  1. Sanctity
  2. Symbolism
Literature

The art of bread-making is very ancient. It was even known to the Egyptians at a very early day (Wilkinson, *Ancient Egyptians*), to the Hebrews of the Exodus (Nowack, *Lehrbuch der hebr. Archäologie*) and, of course, to the Greeks and Romans of a later day. Bread played a large part in the vocabulary and in the life of the ancient Hebrews.

I. Dietary Preëminence.—(1) In the East bread is primary, other articles of food merely accessory; while in the West meat and other things chiefly constitute the meal, and bread is merely secondary. Accordingly "bread" in the OT, from Gen **3** 19 onward, stands for food in general. (2) Moreover in ancient times, as now, most probably, when the peasant, carpenter, blacksmith or mason left home for the day's work, or when the muleteer or messenger set out on a journey, he wrapped other articles of food, if there were any, in the thin loaves of bread, and thus kept them ready for his use as needed. (3) Often the thin, glutinous loaf, puffed out with air, is seen today, opened on one side and used so as to form a natural pouch, in which meat, cheese, raisins and olives are inclosed to be eaten with the bread (see Mackie in *DCG*, art. "Bread"). The loaf of bread is thus made to include everything and, for this reason also, it may fitly be spoken of as synonymous with food in general. To the disciples of Jesus, no doubt, "Give us this day our daily bread" would naturally be a petition for all needed food, and in the case of the miraculous feeding of the multitude it was enough to provide them with "bread" (Mt **14** 15 ff).

II. Materials.—*Barley* was in early times, as it is today, the main bread-stuff of the Pal peasantry (see Jgs **7** 13, where "the cake of barley bread" is said to be "the sword of Gideon"), and of the poorer classes of the East in general (see Jn **6** 13, where the multitude were fed on the miraculous increase of the "five barley loaves," and cf Jos, *BJ*, V, x, 2).

1. Barley

But *wheat*, also, was widely used as a bread-stuff then, as it is now, the wheat of the Syrian plains and uplands being remarkable for its nutritious and keeping qualities.

2. Wheat

Three kinds, or qualities, of flour, are distinguished, according to the way of making: (1) a coarser sort, rudely made by the use of pestle and mortar, the "beaten corn" of Lev **2** 14.16 (RV "*bruised*"); (2) the "flour" or "meal" of ordinary use (Ex **29** 2; Lev **2** 2; **6** 15), and (3) the "fine meal" for honored guests (see Gen **18** 6, where Abraham commands Sarah to "make ready . . . . three measures of fine meal") with which we may compare the "fine flour" for the king's kitchen (1 K **4** 22) and the "fine flour" required for the ritual meal offering, as in Lev **2** 1; **5** 11; **7** 12; **14** 10; **23** 13; **24** 5; etc.

3. Three Kinds of Flour

III. Bread-Making.—After thoroughly sifting and cleaning the grain, the first step in the process was to reduce it to "meal" or "flour" by rubbing, pounding, or grinding. (In Nu **11** 8 it is said of the manna "The people went about, and gathered it, and ground it in mills, or beat it in mortars.") It has been shown that by a process, which is not yet extinct in Egypt, it was customary to rub the grain between two stones, called the "corn-rubbers" or "corn grinders," of which many specimens have been found by Petrie, Bliss, Macalister and others, at Lachish, Gezer and elsewhere (*PEFS*, 1902, 326; 1903, 118; cf Erman, *Egypt*, 180, for illustrations of actual use). For detailed descriptions of the other processes, see MORTAR; MILL.

1. Grinding

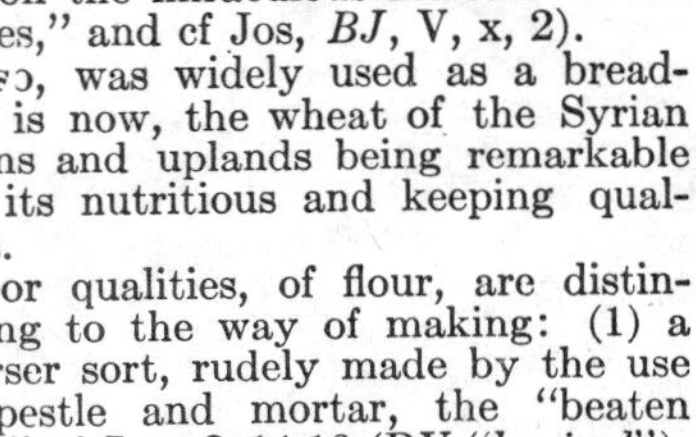

Egyptians Kneading Dough with Their Hands.

The "flour" was then ordinarily mixed simply with water, kneaded in a wooden basin or kneading-trough (Ex **8** 3) and, in case of urgency, at once made into "cakes" and baked. (See Ex **12** 34, "And the people took their dough before it was leavened.") The Hebrews called such cakes *maççōth*, and they were the only kind allowed for use on the altar during Passover, and immediately following the Feast of Unleavened Bread (also called *Maççōth*). Commonly however the process was as follows: a lump of leavened dough of yesterday's baking, preserved for the purpose, was broken up and mixed with the day's "batch," and the whole was then set aside and left standing until it was thoroughly leavened (see LEAVEN).

2. Kneading

Egyptians Kneading Dough with Their Feet.

We find in the OT, as in the practice of the East today, three modes of firing or baking bread: (1) that represented by Elijah's cake baked on the hot stones (1 K **19** 6 RVm; cf "the cakes upon the hearth," Gen **18** 6 AV, and see Robinson, *Researches*, II, 406). The stones were laid together and a fire was lighted upon them. When the stones were well heated the cinders were raked off, and the cakes laid on the stones and covered with ashes. After a while the ashes were again removed and the cake was turned (see Hos **7** 8) and once more covered with the glowing ashes. It was thus cooked on both sides evenly and made ready for eating (cf Vulg, *Panis subcineraris*, and DeLagarde, *Symmicta*, II, 188, where *ἐγκουθία*, *egkouthia*, is referred to as "the hiding" of the cakes under the ashes). Out of these primitive usages of the pastoral tribes and peasants grew other improved forms of baking. (2) An ancient method of baking, prevalent still among the Bedouin of Syria and Arabia, is to employ a heated convex iron plate, or griddle, what we would call a frying pan, in lieu of the heated sand or stones. The Heb "baking-pan" (מַחֲבַת, *maḥăbhath*, Lev **2** 5; **7** 9; cf Ezk **4** 3) must have been of this species of "griddle." The reference in 1 Ch **9** 31 is probably to bread baked in this way. There it is said that one of the sons of the priests "had the office of trust over the things that were baked in *pans*."

3. Baking

תַּנּוּר, *tannūr* (cf Arab.), no doubt were used by the Hebrews, when they settled in Pal, as they were used by the settled populations of the Orient in general, more and more as they approached civilized conditions. These "ovens" were of various kinds: (1) The simplest used by the ancients were hardly more primitive than the kind quite commonly used in Pal today. It may be called the **"bowl-oven."** It consists of a large clay-bowl, which is provided with a movable lid. This bowl is placed inverted upon small stones and then heated with a fuel distinctly oriental, consisting of dried dung heaped over and around it. The bread is baked on the stones, then covered by the inverted oven, which is heated by the firing of the fuel of dung on the outside of the cover. (2) The **jar-oven** is another form of oven found in use there today. This is a large earthenware jar that is heated by fuel of grass (Mt **6** 30),

4. Ovens

stubble (Mal **4** 1), dry twigs or thorns (1 K **17** 12) and the like, which are placed within the jar for firing. When the jar is thus heated the cakes are stuck upon the hot inside walls. (3) The **pit-oven** was doubtless a development from this type. It was formed partly in the ground and partly built up of clay and plastered throughout, narrowing toward the top. The ancient Egyptians, as the monuments and mural paintings show, laid the cakes upon the outside of the oven (Wilkinson, *Ancient Egyptians*); but in Pal, in general, if the customs of today are conclusive, the fire was kindled in the inside of the pit-oven. Great numbers of such ovens have been unearthed in recent excavations, and we may well believe them to be exact counterparts of the oven of the professional bakers in the street named after them in Jerus "the bakers' street" (Jer **37** 21). The largest and most developed form of oven is still the public oven of the town or city of this sort; but the primitive rural types still survive, and the fuel of thorns, and of the grass, "which today is, and tomorrow is cast into the oven," are still in evidence.

5. Forms of Baked Bread

(1) The large pone or thick, light loaf of the West is unknown in the East. The common oriental cake or loaf is proverbially thin. The thin home-made bread is really named both in Heb and Arab. from its thinness as is reflected in the tr "wafer" in Ex **16** 31; **29** 23; Lev **8** 26; Nu **6** 19; 1 Ch **23** 29. Such bread was called in Heb *rāḳīḳ* (רָקִיק, *rāḳīḳ;* cf modern Arab. *warkûk*, from *warak*="foliage," "paper").

(2) It is still significantly customary at a Syrian meal to take a piece of such bread and, with the ease and skill of long habit, to fold it over at the end held in the hand so as to make a sort of spoon of it, which then is eaten along with whatever is lifted by it out of the common dish (cf Mt **26** 23). But this "dipping in the common dish" is so accomplished as not to allow the contents of the dish to be touched by the fingers, or by anything that has been in contact with the lips of those who sit at meat (cf Mackie, *DCG*, art. "Bread").

(3) Such "loaves" are generally today about 7 in. in diameter and from half an inch to an inch thick. Such, probably, were the lad's "barley loaves" brought to Christ at the time of the feeding of the 5,000 (Jn **6** 9.13). Even thinner cakes, of both leavened and unleavened bread, are sometimes made now, as of old, esp. at times of religious festivals. Often they are coated on the upper surface with olive oil and take on a glossy brown color in cooking; and sometimes they are sprinkled over with aromatic seeds, which adhere and impart a spicy flavor. They may well recall to us the "oiled bread" of Lev **8** 26 and "the wafers anointed with oil" of Ex **29** 2 and Lev **2** 4.

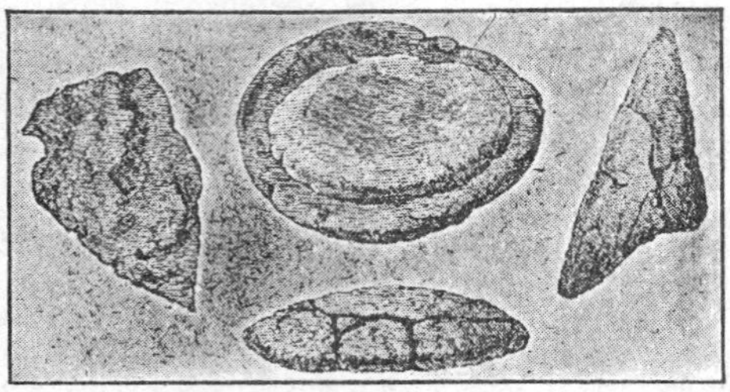

Egyptian Cakes or Loaves of Bread (from Specimens in the British Museum).

(4) Sometimes large discs of dough about 1 in. thick and 8 in. in diameter are prepared and laid in rows on long, thin boards like canoe paddles, and thus inserted into the oven; then, by a quick, deft jerk of the hand, they are slipped off upon the hot pavement and baked. These are so made and baked that when done they are soft and flexible, and for this reason are preferred by many to the thinner cakes which are cooked stiff and brown.

Arab Women Preparing Bread.

(5) The precise nature of the **cracknels** of 1 K **14** 3 (ARV "cakes") is not known. A variety of **bakemeats** (Gen **40** 17, lit. "food, the work of the baker") are met with in the OT, but only in a few cases is it possible or important to identify their nature or forms (see *Enc Bibl*, coll. 460 f). A cake used for ritual purposes (Ex **29** 2 and often) seems, from its name, to have been pierced with holes, like the modern Passover cakes (cf Kennedy, 1-vol *HDB*, art. "Bread").

6. Work for Women

(*a*) Every oriental household of importance seems to have had its own oven, and bread-making for the most part was in the hands of the women. Even when and where baking, as under advancing civilization, became a recognized public industry, and men were the professional bakers, a large part of the baker's work, as is true today, was to fire the bread prepared and in a sense pre-baked by the women at home. (*b*) The women of the East are often now seen taking a hand in sowing, harvesting and winnowing the grain, as well as in the processes of "grinding" (Eccl **12** 3; Mt **24** 41; Lk **17** 35), "kneading" (Gen **18** 6; 1 S **28** 24; 2 S **13** 8; Jer **7** 18) and "baking" (1 S **8** 13), and doubtless it was so in ancient times to an equal extent.

IV. Sanctity and Symbolism of Bread.—It would seem that the sanctity of bread remains as un-

1. Sanctity

changed in the Orient as the sanctity of shrines and graves (cf Mackie, *DCG*, art. "Bread," and Robinson's *Researches*). As in Egypt everything depended for life on the Nile, and as the Nile was considered "sacred," so in Pal, as everything depended upon the wheat and barley harvest, "bread" was in a peculiar sense "sacred." The psychology of the matter seems to be about this: all life was seen to be dependent upon the grain harvest, this in turn depended upon rain in its season, and so bread, the product at bottom of these Divine processes, was regarded as peculiarly "a gift of God," a daily reminder of his continual and often undeserved care (Mt **5** 45 ff; consider in this connection the Lord's Prayer, "Give us this day our daily bread," Mt **6** 11; cf Lk **11** 11). Travelers generally note as a special characteristic of the Oriental of today that, seeing a scrap of bread on the roadside, he will pick it up and throw it to a street dog, or place it in a crevice of the wall, or on a tree-branch where the birds may get it. One thing is settled with him, it must not be trodden under foot in the common dust, for, in the estimation of all, it has in it an element of mystery and sacredness as coming from the Giver of all good.

2. Symbolism

(*a*) In partaking of the hospitality of the primitive peasants of Pal today, east and west of the Jordan, one sees what a sign and symbol of hospitality and friendship the giving and receiving of bread is. Among the Arabs, indeed, it has become a proverb, which may be put into English thus: "Eat salt together, be friends forever." Once let the Arab break bread with you and you are safe. You may find the bread the poorest barley loaf, still marked by the indentations of the pebbles, with small patches of the gray ash of the hearth, and here and there an inlaid bit of singed grass or charred thorn, the result of their primitive process of baking; but it is *bread*, the best that the poor man can give you, "a gift of God," indeed, and it is offered by the wildest Arab, with some sense of its sacredness and with somewhat of the gladness and dignity of the high duty of hospitality. No wonder, therefore, that it is considered the height of discourtesy, yea, a violation of the sacred law of hospitality, to decline it or to set it aside as unfit for use. (*b*) Christ must have been influenced by His knowledge of some such feeling and law as this when, on sending forth His disciples, He charged them to "take no bread with them" (Mk **6** 8). Not to have expected such hospitality, and not to have used what would thus be freely offered to them by the people, would have been a rudeness, not to say an offence, on the part of the disciples, which would have hindered the reception of the good tidings of the Kingdom. (*c*) It has well been pointed out that God's gift of natural food to His people enters in for the praises of the *Magnificat* (Lk **1** 53), and that when Christ called Himself "the bread of life" (Jn **6** 35) He really appealed to all these endeared and indissoluble associations connected in the eastern mind with the meaning and use of bread. Most naturally and appropriately in the inauguration of the New Covenant Christ adopted as His memorial, not a monument of stone or brass, but this humble yet sacred article of food, familiar and accessible to all, to become, with the "wine" of common use, in the Lord's Supper, the perpetual symbol among His disciples of the communion of saints.

LITERATURE.—Wilkinson, *Ancient Egypt*, 1878, II, 34; Erman, *Aegypten und aegyptisches Leben*, 1885, 191 ff; Nowack, *Lehrbuch der hebr. Archäologie*, 1894; Maimonides, *Yadh, Temidhin U-Musaphin*, v, 6–8; Bacher, *Monatsschrift*, 1901, 299; Mishnah B.M., II, 1, 2; Robinson, *Biblical Researches in Palestine*, II, 416; Doughty, *Travels in Arabia Deserta*, I, 131; Jos, *BJ*; and Bible Dicts. on "Bread," "Dietary Laws": "*Maççōth*," "*Ḥallāh*," etc.

GEO. B. EAGER

BREADTH, bredth (רֹחַב, *rōḥabh*, the root idea being to make wide, spacious): A term of expanse or measurement used of the ark (Gen **6** 15); of the tabernacle (Ex **27** 13); of Solomon's temple (1 K **6** 2). πλάτος, *plátos*, "breadth," as of the celestial city (Rev **21** 16). **Figuratively,** of the comprehensiveness of God's law (Ps **119** 96); of the heart (1 K **4** 29, rendered "largeness of heart" EV); of God's immeasurable love (Eph **3** 18).

BREAK, brāk: שָׁבַר, *shābhar* = "break" (down, off, in pieces, up), "destroy," "quench" (Isa **14** 25; Jer **19** 10.11; Ezk **4** 16; Am **1** 5); פָּרַק, *pāraḳ* = "to break off" or "craunch"; **fig.** "to deliver" (Gen **27** 40 AV); עָרַף, *'āraph* = "to break the neck," hence "to destroy" (Ex **13** 13); הָרַס, *hāraṣ* = "to break through" (**19** 21.24); פָּרַץ, *pāraç* = "to break" (forth, away), occurs in **19** 22.24; 1 S **25** 10; "breaking faith," Hos **4** 2; פָּרַח, *pāraḥ* = "to break forth as a bud" (Lev **13** 12); נָתַץ or נָתַק, *nāthaç*, or *nāthaḳ* = "destroy" (Ezk **23** 34 AV, RV "gnaw"; see BREAST); חָלַל, *ḥālal* = "profane," "defile," "stain" (Nu **30** 2; Ps **89** 31.34); בָּקַע, *bāḳa'* = "rip open" (2 K **3** 26; Isa **58** 8); רָעַע, *rā'a'* = "to spoil by breaking to pieces," "to make good for nothing" (Job **34** 24; Ps **2** 9; Jer **15** 12, AV "Shall iron break northern iron?"); פָּצַח, *pāçaḥ* = "to break out" (in joyful sound), "break forth," "make a noise" (Isa **14** 7, the nations rejoice in the peace which follows the fall of the oppressor); נִיר, *nīr* = "to glisten," "gleam" (as of a fresh furrow) (Jer **4** 3; Hos **10** 12); פָּתַח, *pāthaḥ* = "to open wide," "loosen," "have vent" (Jer **1** 14); נָפַץ, *nāphaç* = "to dash to pieces or scatter," "overspread," "scatter" (Jer **48** 12, the work usually done carefully shall be done roughly; **51** 20–23, descriptive of the terrible fate appointed for Babylon); נָאַף, *nā'aph* = "to break wedlock" (Ezk **16** 38); צָלַח, צָלֵחַ, *çālaḥ* or *çālēaḥ* = "break out," "come mightily" (Am **5** 6). The NT employs λύω, *lúō* = "to loosen," "dissolve" (Mt **5** 19); διορύσσω, *diorússō* = "to penetrate burglariously," "break through" (Mt **6** 19.20, Gr "dig through"); ῥήγνυμι or ῥήσσω, *rhḗgnumi* or *rhḗssō* = "to disrupt," "burst," "to utter with a loud voice" (Gal **4** 27); κλάω, *kláō* = "to break" (Acts **20** 7, "to break bread," i.e. to celebrate the Lord's Supper; 1 Cor **10** 16). See also BREACH.

FRANK E. HIRSCH

BREAK OF DAY: אוֹר, *'ōr*, "to be light," "the light breaks" (2 S **2** 32); αὐγή, *augḗ*, "bright light," "radiance" (Acts **20** 11). See DAWN.

BREAST, brest: Signifying the front view of the bust in humans and the corresponding portion of the body in animals. חָזֶה, *ḥāzeh*, occurs in Ex **29** 26.27; Lev **7** 30.31.34; **8** 29; **10** 14.15; Nu **6** 20; **18** 18; and חֲדִי, *ḥădhī*, in Dnl **2** 32. שַׁד or שֹׁד, *shadh*, or, *shōdh* = "breast" in the sense of pap of a woman or animal (Job **24** 9; Cant **8** 1.8.10; Isa **60** 16; Lam **4** 3). Only one word occurs with this signification in the NT: στῆθος, *stḗthos* = "bosom," "chest" (Lk **18** 13; **23** 48; Jn **13** 25; **21** 20). See WAVE-OFFERING.

Figurative: "The breasts of virginity," pressed and bruised (Ezk **23** 3.8 AV), indicative of Ezekiel's belief that Israel practiced idolatry in Egypt (cf **20** 8). "To tear [pluck off] thy breasts" (**23** 34) denotes the anguish of the people in parting with their beloved sin (cf Hos **2** 2). "Its breast of silver" (Dnl **2** 32) is possibly expressive of the humanity and wealth of the Medo-Pers empire.

FRANK E. HIRSCH

BREASTPLATE, brest'plāt. See ARMOR.

BREASTPLATE OF THE HIGH PRIEST, prēst: The Heb word חֹשֶׁן, *ḥōshen*, rendered in AV "breastplate," means really a "pouch" or "bag." The references to it are found exclusively in the Law (Ex **25** 7; **28**; **29** 5; **35** 9.27; **39**; Lev **8** 8). The descriptions of its composition and particularly the directions with regard to wearing it are exceedingly obscure. According to Ezr **2** 63 and Neh **7** 65 the Urim and Thummim, which were carried in the priestly pouch, were lost during the Bab exile. The actual pouch was a "span in length and a span in breadth," i.e. about 9 in. square. It was made, like the ephod, of "gold, of blue, and purple, and scarlet, and fine twined linen" (Ex **28** 15 f). In it were twelve precious stones, in rows of four, representing the twelve tribes of Israel. Apparently the pouch had two rings (perhaps four) through which passed two gold chains by which it was fastened to the ephod supplied for the purpose with ouches or clasps. The pouch was worn by the high priest over his heart when he entered the "holy place" "for a memorial before Jeh." The presence of the high priest, the representative of the people, with the names of the separate tribes on his person, brought each tribe before the notice of Jeh and thereby directed His attention to them. The full designation was *ḥōshen mishpāṭ*, "pouch of judgment" or "decision." It was the distinctive symbol of the priest in his capacity as the giver of oracles. As already suggested the priestly pouch contained the Urim and Thummim which were probably precious stones used as lots in giving decisions. In all probability the restored text of 1 S **14** 41 preserves the true custom. On one side stood Saul and Jonathan, and the people on the other side. If the result was Urim, Saul and Jonathan would be the guilty parties. If the result was Thummim, the guilt would fasten on the people. T. LEWIS

BREATH, breth, **BREATHE,** brēth, **BREATHING,** brēth'ing: In the EV of the OT "breath" is the rendering of נְשָׁמָה, *n^{e}shāmāh*, and of רוּחַ, *rū^{a}ḥ*. These words differ but slightly in meaning, both signifying primarily "wind," then "breath," though the former suggests a gentler blowing, the latter often a blast. As applied to persons there is no very clear distinction between the words. Yet in general one may say that of the two *n^{e}shāmāh* is employed preferably of breath regarded *physiologically:* "vital breath," hence the vital principle, "soul [animal] life" (cf Gen **2** 7; **7** 22; Job **27** 3, where both words occur; Isa **42** 52; Dnl **5** 23); while *rū^{a}ḥ* (though it, too, sometimes signifies "vital breath") is the word generally employed where the breath is regarded *physically*—breath or blast as an *act* or *force*—and so is related to the will or the emotions, whence the meaning "spirit," also sometimes "thought," "purpose" (cf Job **4** 9; **9** 18; Ps **18** 15; **146** 4; Ezk **37** 5.6.8.9.10). The examples cited, however, and other passages reveal a lack of uniformity of usage. Yet generally *rū^{a}ḥ* is the expression, *n^{e}shāmāh*, the principle, of life. Yet when employed of God they of course signify the principle, not of His own life, but of that imparted to His creatures. "Breathe" in EV of the OT requires no remark except at Ps **27** 12 ("such as breathe out cruelty"), from *yāphaḥ*, "to breathe hard," "to snort" (cf Acts **9** 1). In the NT "breath" (πνοή, *pnoē*) occurs once Acts **17** 25 in the plain sense of vital principle, the gift of God. "Breathed" is employed in Jn **20** 22 of Our Lord's concrete symbolism of the giving of the Spirit. In Acts **9** 1 Saul's "breathing threatening and slaughter" is lit. "snorting," etc, and the nouns are partitive genitives, being the element of which he breathed. See also SPIRIT. J. R. VAN PELT

BREECHES, brich'iz, brēch'iz: A garment, extending from the waist to or just below the knee or to the ankle, and covering each leg separately. Breeches are not listed among the garments of an ordinary wardrobe, but the priests in later times (Ex **20** 26) wore a garment resembling modern trousers. These priestly linen breeches, מִכְנְסֵי בַד, *mikhn^{e}ṣē bhadh*, were worn along with the linen coat, the linen girdle and the linen turban by Aaron on the Day of Atonement, when he entered the "holy place." (The word מִכְנְסֵי, *mikhn^{e}ṣē* is derived from a root, כנס, *kānaṣ*=גנז, *gānaz*, "to cover up," "hide.") Ordinary priests also wore them on sacrificial occasions (Ex **28** 42; **39** 28; Lev **6** 10; Ezk **44** 18). Apart from the breeches just referred to, the only reference to a similar garment among the Israelites is found in Dnl **3** 21, where the סַרְבָּל, *ṣarbāl*, RV "hosen," is mentioned. (The AV translates "coats.") The rendering of the AV is the more likely, though the meaning of the Aram. *sarbāl* is obscure (cf the thorough discussion in Ges., *Thesaurus*). In Tg and Talm (cf Levy, *NHWB*, s.v.), and is so taken by the rabbinical commentators. Still, Aq. and Theod. (σαράβαρα, *sarábara*), LXX in ver 27, Symm (*anaxurídes*), Pesh, express the meaning "trousers" (of a looser kind than those worn by us), a garment known (from Herodotus and other sources) to have been worn by the ancient Scythians and Persians, and to have been called by them *sarabara*. The word, with the same connotation, was brought into the Arab. in the form *sirwāl*. In both these senses the word may be originally Pers: in that of mantle, meaning properly (according to Andreas) a "head-covering" (*sarabara*), for which in Persia the peasants often use their mantle; in that of "trousers," corresponding to the mod. Pers *shalwar*, "under-breeches." Cook has pointed out that "mantles, long-flowing robes, and therefore extremely liable to catch the flames," are more likely to be esp. mentioned in this ch than trousers, or (RV) "hosen."

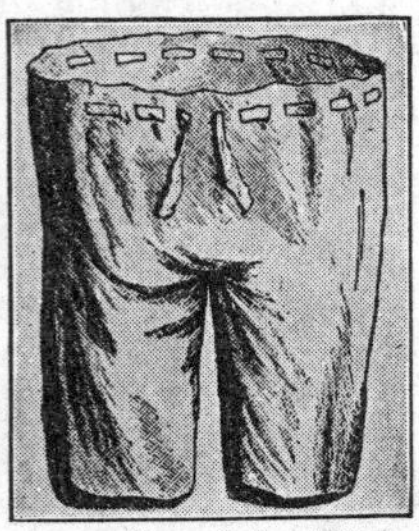
Breeches of the High Priest.

The word פַּטִּישׁ, *paṭīsh* (Dnl **3** 21), is also uncertain. The LXX and Theod. render *tiárai*, "turbans"; Pesh has the same word, which is variously taken by Syrian lexicographers as "tunic," "trousers," or a kind of "gaiter" (Payne Smith, *Thes. Syr.*, col. 3098). (For further discussion of these words, cf commentaries on Dnl of *Jour. Phil.*, XXVI, 307 ff.)

In general, we must remember that a thorough discussion of Israelitish "dress" is impossible, because of the limitations of our sources. H. J. WOLF

BREED, brēd: Found in the past tense in Ex **16** 20 as a tr of רוּם, *rūm*="to bring up," "to rise." In this ver, the manna is said to have arisen, i.e. "become alive" (with worms), to indicate that God's gifts are spoiled by selfish and miserly hoarding. The pres. act. occurs in Gen **8** 17 for שָׁרַץ, *shāraç*="to wriggle," "swarm," "abound," hence "breed abundantly"; and in Dt **32** 14 for בֵּן, *bēn*= "son," "descendant," "child," "colt," "calf," "breed." The pres. part. is found in Zeph **2** 9 AV for מִמְשָׁק, *mimshāḳ*, a derivative of מֶשֶׁק, *meshek* ="possession," "territory," "field." The passage in question should therefore be tr^{d} "field of nettles" (RV "possession of nettles"). FRANK E. HIRSCH

BRETHREN, breth'ren. See BROTHER.

BRETHREN OF THE LORD: In Mt **12** 46 ff; Mk **3** 31 ff; Lk **8** 19 ff, while Jesus was in the midst of an earnest argument with scribes and Pharisees, His mother and brothers sent a message evidently intended to end the discussion. In order to indicate that no ties of the flesh should interfere with the discharge of the duties of His Messianic office, He stretched His hands toward His disciples, and said: "Whosoever shall do the will of my Father who is in heaven, he is my brother, and sister, and mother." In Mt **13** 54 ff; Mk **6** 2 ff, while He was teaching in His own town, Nazareth, His neighbors, who, since they had watched His natural growth among them, could not comprehend the extraordinary claims that He was making, declare in an interrogative form, that they know all about the entire family, mother, brothers and sisters. They name the brothers. Bengel suggests that there is a tone of contempt in the omission of the names of the sisters, as though not worth mentioning. In Jn **2** 12, they are said to have accompanied Jesus and His mother and disciples from the wedding at Cana. In Jn **7** 3 ff, they are described as unbelieving, and ridiculing His claims with bitter sarcasm. This attitude of hostility has disappeared, when, at Jerus, after the resurrection and ascension (Acts **1** 14), in the company of Mary and the Eleven, and the faithful group of women, they "continued steadfastly in prayer," awaiting the promise of the gift of the Holy Spirit. Their subsequent participation in the missionary activity of the apostolic church appears in 1 Cor **9** 5: "Have we no right to lead about a wife that is a believer, even as the rest of the apostles, and the brethren of the Lord, and Cephas?" In Gal **1** 19, James, bishop of the church at Jerus, is designated "the Lord's brother," thus harmonizing with Mt **13** 55, where their names are recorded as James, Joseph, Simon and Judas. When, then, "Jude, ... brother of James" is mentioned (Jude ver 1), the immediate inference is that Jude is another brother of the Lord. In reading these passages, the natural inference is that these "brethren" were the sons of Joseph and Mary, born after Jesus, living with Mary and her daughters, in the home at Nazareth, accompanying the mother on her journeys, and called the "brethren" of the Lord in a sense similar to that in which Joseph was called His father. They were brethren because of their common relationship to Mary. This impression is strengthened by the fact that Jesus is called her *prōtótokos*, "first-born son" (Lk **2** 7), as well as by the very decided implication of Mt **1** 25. Even though each particular, taken separately, might, with some difficulty, be explained otherwise, the force of the argument is cumulative. There are too many items to be explained away, in order to establish any other inference. This view is not the most ancient. It has been traced to Tertullian, and has been more fully developed by Belvidius, an obscure writer of the 4th cent.

Two other views have been advocated with much learning and earnestness. The earlier, which seems to have been prevalent in the first three cents. and is supported by Origen, Eusebius, Gregory of Nyssa and Ambrose, Epiphanius being its chief advocate, regards these "brethren" as the children of Joseph by a former marriage, and Mary as his second wife. Joseph disappears from sight when Jesus is twelve years old. We know nothing of him after the narrative of the child Jesus in the temple. That there is no allusion to him in the account of the family in Mk **6** 3 indicates that Mary had been a widow long before she stood by the Cross without the support of any member of her immediate family. In the Apocryphal Gospels, the attempt is made to supply what the canonical Gospels omit. They report that Joseph was over eighty years of age at his second marriage, and the names of both sons and daughters by his first marriage are given. As Lightfoot (comm. on *Galatians*) has remarked, "they are pure fabrications." Theophylact even advanced the theory that they were the children of Joseph by a levirate marriage, with the widow of his brother, Clopas. Others regard them as the nephews of Joseph whom, after the death of his brother Clopas, he had taken into his own home, and who thus became members of his family, and were accounted as though they were the children of Joseph and Mary. According to this view, Mary excepted, the whole family at Nazareth were no blood relatives of Jesus. It is a Docetic conception in the interest of the dogma of the perpetual virginity of Mary. All its details, even that of the advanced age and decrepitude of Joseph, start from that premise.

Another view, first propounded by Jerome when a very young man, in antagonizing Belvidius, but afterward qualified by its author, was followed by Augustine, the Roman Catholic writers generally, and carried over into Protestantism at the Reformation, and accepted, even though not urged, by Luther, Chemnitz, Bengel, etc, understands the word "brother" in the general sense of "kinsman," and interprets it here as equivalent to "cousin." According to this, these brethren were actually blood-relatives of Jesus, and not of Joseph. They were the children of Alphaeus, otherwise known as Clopas (Jn **19** 25), and the sister of Mary. This Mary, in Mt **27** 56, is described as "the mother of James and Joses," and in Mk **15** 40, "the mother of James the less and of Joses, and Salome." This theory as completely developed points to the three names, James, Judas and Simon found both in the list of the apostles and of the "brethren," and argues that it would be a remarkable coincidence if they referred to different persons, and the two sisters, both named Mary, had found the very same names for their sons. The advocates of this theory argue also that the expression "James the less" shows that there were only two persons of the name James in the circle of those who were most closely connected with Jesus. They say, further, that, after the death of Joseph, Mary became an inmate of the home of her sister, and the families being combined, the presence and attendance of her nephews and nieces upon her can be explained without much difficulty, and the words of the people at Nazareth be understood. But this complicated theory labors under many difficulties. The identity of Clopas and Alphaeus cannot be established, resting, as it does, upon obscure philological resemblances of the Aram. form of the two names (see ALPHAEUS). The most that such argument affords is a mere possibility. Nor is the identity of "Mary the wife of Clopas" with the sister of Mary, the mother of Jesus, established beyond a doubt. Jn **19** 25, upon which it rests, can with equal correctness be interpreted as teaching that four women stood by the cross, of whom "Mary of Clopas" was one, and His mother's sister was another. The decision depends upon the question as to whether "Mary" be in apposition to "sister." If the ver be read so as to present two pairs, it would not be a construction without precedent in the NT, and would avoid the difficulty of finding two sisters with the same name—a difficulty greater yet than that of three cousins with the same name. Nor is the identity of "James the less" with the son of Alphaeus beyond a doubt. Any argument concerning the comparative "less," as above explained, fails when it is found that in the Gr there is no comparative, but only "James the little," the implication being probably that of his stature as considerably below the average, so as to occasion remark. Nor is the difficulty less when it is proposed to identify three of these brethren of Jesus with apostles of the same name. For the "brethren" and the apostles are repeatedly distinguished. In Mt **12** 49, while the former stood without, the latter are gathered around Jesus. In Jn **2** 12, we read: "his mother, and his brethren, and his disciples." In Acts **1** 13 the Eleven, including James the son of Alphaeus, and Simon, and Judas of James, and then it is said that they were accompanied by "his brethren." But the crowning difficulty of this hypothesis of Jerome is the record of the unbelief of the brethren and of their derision of His claims in Jn **7** 3–5.

On the other hand, the arguments against regarding them as sons of Mary and Joseph are not formidable. When it is urged that their attempts to interfere with Jesus indicate a superiority which, according to Jewish custom, is inconsistent with the position of younger brothers, it may be answered that those who pursue an unjustifiable course are not models of consistency. When an argument is sought from the fact that Jesus on the cross commended His mother to John, the implication is immediate that she had no sons of her own to whom to turn in her grief and desolation; the answer need not be restricted to the consideration that unknown domestic circumstances may explain the omission of her sons. A more patent explanation is that as they did not understand their brother, they could not understand their mother, whose whole life and interests were bound up in her first-born. But, on the other hand, no one of the disciples understood Jesus and appreciated His work and treasured up His words as did John. A bond of fellowship had thus been established between John and Mary that was closer than her nearer blood relationship with her own sons, who, up to this time, had regarded the course of Jesus with disapproval, and had no sympathy with His mission. In the home of John she would find consolation for her loss, as the memories of the wonderful life of her son would be recalled, and she would converse with him who had rested on the bosom of Jesus and whom Jesus loved. Even with the conversion of these brethren within a few days into faithful confessors, before the view of Jesus, provision was made for her deeper spiritual communion with her risen and ascended Son through the testimony of Jesus which John treasured in his deeply contemplative spirit. There was much that was alike in the characters of Mary and John. This may have had its ground in relationship, as many regard Salome his mother, the sister of the mother of Jesus mentioned in Jn **19** 25.

Underneath both the stepbrother (Epiphanian) and the cousin (Hieronymian) theories, which coincide in denying that Mary was the actual mother of these brethren, lies the idea of the perpetual virginity of Mary. This theory which has as its watchword the stereotyped expression in liturgy and hymn, *"Maria semper Virgo,"* although without any support from Holy Scripture, pervades the theology and the worship of the ancient and the mediaeval churches. From the Gr and Rom churches it has passed into Protestantism in a modified form. Its plea is that it is repugnant to Christian feeling to think of the womb of Mary, in which the Word, made flesh, had dwelt in a peculiar way, as the habitation of other babes. In this idea there lies the further thought, most prominent in mediaeval theology, of a sinfulness of the act in itself whereby new human lives come into existence, and of the inclination implanted from the creation, upon which all family ties depend. 1 Tim **4** 3.4; He **13** 4 are sufficient answer. The taint of sin lies not in marriage, and the use of that which is included in its institution, and which God has blessed (cf Acts **10** 15), but in its perversion and abuse. It is by an inconsistency that Protestants have conceded this much to the theory of Rome, that celibacy is a holier estate than matrimony, and that virginity in marriage is better than marriage itself. The theory also is connected with the removal of Mary from the sphere of ordinary life and duties as too commonplace for one who is to be surrounded with the halo of a demi-god, and to be idealized in order to be worshipped. The interpretation that they are the Lord's real brethren ennobles and glorifies family life in all its relations and duties, and sanctifies motherhood with all its cares and trials as holier than a selfish isolation from the world, in order to evade the annoyances and humiliations inseparable from fidelity to our callings. Not only Mary, but Jesus with her, knew what it was to grieve over a house divided concerning religion (Mt **10** 35 ff). But that this unbelief and indifference gave way before the clearer light of the resurrection of Jesus is shown by the presence of these brethren in the company of the disciples in Jerus (Acts **1** 14). The reference to His post-resurrection appearance to James (1 Cor **15** 7) is probably connected with this change in their attitude. 1 Cor **9** 5 shows that at least two of these brothers were active as missionaries, undoubtedly within the Holy Land, and to Jews, according to the agreement into which James entered in Gal **2**, and his well-known attitude on questions pertaining to the Gentiles. Zahn regards James as an ascetic and celibate not included in 1 Cor **9** 5, which is limited then to Jude and Simon. Their marriage indicates "the absence in the Holy Family of that pseudo-asceticism which has so much confused the tradition concerning them" (Alford). See also James; Jude.

For fuller discussions, see the extensive arguments of Eadie and Lightfoot, in their commentaries on Gal, the former in favor of the Helvidian, and the latter, with his exhaustive scholarship, of the Epiphanian views; also, on the side of the former, Mayor, *The Ep. of St. James;* Alford, *Gr Test.;* Farrar, *Early Days of Christianity;* Zahn, *Intro to the NT.*

H. E. Jacobs

BRIBERY, brīb′ẽr-i (שֹׁחַד, *shōḥadh,* "a gift," in a corrupt sense, "a bribe"): The Heb law condemns everything that would tend to impair the impartial administration of justice, particularly the giving and receiving of gifts or bribes, in order to pervert judgment (Ex **23** 8). Allusions are frequent to the prevailing corruption of oriental judges and rulers. "And fire shall consume the tents of bribery" (Job **15** 34; 1 S **8** 3; Ps **26** 10; Isa **1** 23; **33** 15; Ezk **22** 12). Samuel speaks of a "ransom" in the sense of a bribe: "Of whose hand have I taken a ransom [כֹּפֶר, *kōpher,* "covering," AV "bribe"] to blind mine eyes therewith?" (1 S **12** 3; Am **5** 12; cf Am **2** 6). See Blindness, Judicial. Crimes; Justice; Punishments.

L. Kaiser

BRICK (לְבֵנָה, *lᵉbhēnāh*): The ancient Egyp word appears in the mod. Egyp Arab. *toob.* In Syria the sun-baked bricks are commonly called *libn* or *lebin,* from the same Sem root as the Heb word.

Bricks are mentioned only a few times in the Bible. The story of how the Children of Israel, while in bondage in Egypt, had their task of brick-making made more irksome by being required to collect their own straw is one of the most familiar of Bible narratives (Ex **1** 14; **5** 7.10–19).

Modern excavations at Pithom in Egypt (Ex **1** 11) show that most of the bricks of which that store-city was built were made of mud and straw baked in the sun. These ruins are chosen as an example from among the many ancient brick structures because they probably represent the work of the very Heb slaves who complained so bitterly of their royal taskmaster. In some of the upper courses rushes had been substituted for straw, and still other bricks had no fibrous material. These variations could be explained by a scarcity of straw at that time, since, when there was a shortage in the crops, all the straw (Arab. *tibn*) was needed for feeding the animals. It may be that when the order came for the workmen to provide their own straw they found it impossible to gather sufficient and still furnish the required number of bricks

(Ex **5** 8). However, the quality of clay of which some of the bricks were made was such that no straw was needed.

Brickmaking in early Egyp history was a government monopoly. The fact that the government pressed into service her Asiatic captives, among whom were the Children of Israel, made it impossible for independent makers to compete. The early bricks usually bore the government stamp or the stamp of some temple authorized to use the captives for brick manufacture. The methods employed by the ancient Egyptians differ in no respect from the modern procedure in that country. The Nile mud is thoroughly slipped or mixed and then rendered more cohesive by the addition of earth. The outer coating of plaster must be renewed from year to year. In some of the villages of northern Syria the brick houses are dome-shaped, looking much like beehives. In the defiant assertion of Isa **9** 10 the superiority of hewn stone over bricks implied a greater difference in cost and stability than exists between a frame house and a stone house in western lands today.

In the buildings of ancient Babylonia burnt bricks were used. These have been found by modern excavators, which confirms the description of Gen **11** 3. Burnt bricks were rarely used in Egypt before the Rom period and in Pal their use for building purposes was unknown. Specimens of partially burnt, glazed bricks have been found in

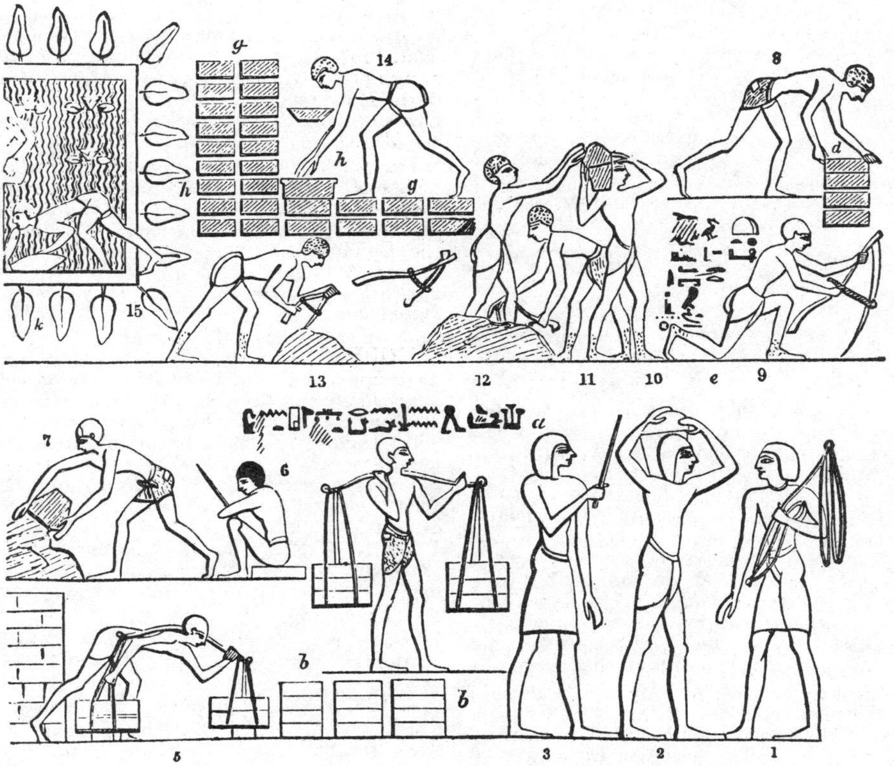

Foreign Captives Employed in Making Bricks at Thebes.

1, 2. Men returning after carrying the bricks. 3, 6. Task-masters. 4, 5. Men carrying bricks. 9, 13. Digging or mixing the mud or clay. 8, 14. Making bricks with wooden moulds, *d*, *h*. 15. Fetching water from tank, *k*. At *e* the bricks (tobi) are said to be made at Thebes

chopped straw or stubble. The pasty mass is next worked into a mould made in the shape of a box without a bottom. If the sides of the mould have been dusted with dry earth it will easily slip off and the brick is allowed to dry in the sun until it becomes so hard that the blow of a hammer is often necessary to break it.

When the children of Israel emigrated to their new country they found the same methods of brickmaking employed by the inhabitants, methods which are still in vogue throughout the greater part of Pal and Syria. In the interior of the country, esp. where the building stone is scarce or of poor quality, the houses are made of sun-baked brick (*libn*). Frequently the west and south walls, which are exposed most to the winter storms, are made of hewn stone and the rest of the structure of bricks. When the brick-laying is finished the house is plastered inside and outside with the same material of which the bricks are made and finally whitewashed or painted with grey- or yellow-colored Babylonia and recently in one of the Hittite mounds of northern Syria. These were probably used for decorative purposes only. If burnt bricks had been generally used in Pal, traces of them would have been found with the pottery which is so abundant in the ruins (see Pottery).

The fact that unburnt bricks were so commonly used explains how the sites of such cities as ancient Jericho could have become lost for so many cents. When the houses and walls fell they formed a heap of earth not distinguishable from the surrounding soil. The wood rotted and the iron rusted away, leaving for the excavator a few bronze and stone implements and the fragments of pottery which are so precious as a means of identification. The "tels" or mounds of Pal and Syria often represent the ruins of several such cities one above the other.

Literature.—H. A. Harper, *The Bible and Modern Discoveries;* Wilkinson, *Manners and Customs of the Ancient Egyptians;* Erman, *Life in Ancient Egypt;* Hilprecht, *Recent Research in Bible Lands.*

James A. Patch

BRICK-KILN, brik′kil, -kiln (מַלְבֵּן, *malbēn*): The Heb word is better tr[d] by "brickmould." In Syria the brickmould is still called *milben.* In Jer **43** 9 the ARV rendering is "brickwork" and the ARVm "pavement." 2 S **12** 31 becomes much clearer if the ARVm is incorporated. Being put to work at the brickmould was considered the task of those taken as slaves. The ancestors of the new taskmasters had themselves been put to similar toil.

BRIDE, brīd. See MARRIAGE.

BRIDE-CHAMBER, brīd′chām-bẽr (νυμφών, *numphṓn*): The room in which the marriage ceremonies were held (Mt **9** 15; Mk **2** 19; Lk **5** 34; cf Mt **22** 10). See CHAMBER; MARRIAGE.

BRIDE-CHAMBER, SONS (CHILDREN) OF THE (οἱ υἱοὶ τοῦ νυμφῶνος, *hoi huioí toú numphōnos*): These were friends or companions of the bridegroom and were usually very numerous (Mt **9** 15; Mk **2** 19; Lk **5** 34). Any wedding guest might be included in the expression, or anyone who took part in the bridal procession and remained for the wedding-feast (see MARRIAGE). In the above passages "the sons of the bride-chamber" are the disciples of Christ.

BRIDEGROOM, brīd′grōōm; **BRIDEGROOM, FRIEND OF.** See MARRIAGE.

BRIDGE, brij (γέφυρα, *géphura*, 2 Macc **12** 13 AV; RV GEPHYRUN): Does not occur in the canonical Scriptures, unless it be indirectly in the proper name Geshur (גְּשׁוּר, *geshūr*, 2 S **3** 3; **13** 37; **15** 8; 1 Ch **2** 23, and others). The so-called Jacob's bridge is said to mark the site where Jacob crossed the upper Jordan on his return from Paddan-aram, but, of course, does not date from the time of the patriarch. There are traces of ancient bridges across the Jordan in the vicinity of the Lake of Gennesaret, over the Arnon and over other rivers which enter the Jordan from the east; but none of them seem to date farther back than the Rom period. Nah **2** 6, in which the Chaldaic paraphrase renders "bridges," evidently refers to dikes or weirs. Judas Maccabaeus is said to have planted a bridge in order to besiege the town of Casphor (2 Macc **12** 13). Jos (*Ant*, V, i, 3) tells us that the Jordan, before the passage of the Israelites, had never been bridged, evidently implying that in his own time bridges had been constructed over it, which was the case, under the Romans. The bridge connecting the temple with the upper part of the city of which Jos speaks (*War*, VI, vi, 2; *Ant*, XV, xi, 5) probably was a viaduct.

FRANK E. HIRSCH

BRIDLE, brī′d'l. See BIT.

BRIER, brī′ẽr. See THORNS.

BRIGANDINE, brig′an-dēn. See ARMS (Defensive, 5); COAT OF MAIL.

BRIGHTNESS, brīt′nes: Used by AV in He **1** 3 for "effulgence of his glory," as in RV and ARV. The Gr *apaúgasma* may mean either "reflection" or "radiation." Patristic usage favors the latter; cf Wisd **7** 26; also the Nicene Creed: "Light of Light," i.e. the Son not only manifests the Father, but is of the same substance. "What emanates from light, must have the nature of light" (Delitzsch).

BRIM: קָצֶה, *ḳāçeh* or קָצֶה, *ḳēçeh*="an extremity" (in a variety of applications and idioms), "border," "edge," "side," "shore" (Josh **3** 15 AV; RV "brink"); also שָׂפָה or שֶׂפֶת, *sāphāh* or *sepheth*="edge," "lip" (1 K **7** 23.24.26; 2 Ch **4** 2.5). In Jn **2** 7, the adv. ἄνω, *ánō*, is used to emphasize the vb. ἐγέμισαν, *egémisan*="to fill," thus giving the idea of "filling to the top."

BRIMSTONE, brim′stōn, brim′stun (גָּפְרִית, *gophrīth;* τὸ θεῖον, *tó theíon*): The word tr[d] "brimstone" probably referred originally to the pitch of trees, like the cypress. By analogy it has been rendered "brimstone" because of the inflammability of both substances. Sulphur existed in Pal in early times and was known by most of the ancient nations as a combustible substance. In the vicinity of the Dead Sea, even at the present time, deposits of sulphur are being formed. Blanckenhorn (*ZDPV*, 1896) believes that this formation is due to the action of bituminous matter upon gypsum, as these two substances are found associated with each other in this district. Travelers going from Jericho to the Dead Sea may pick up lumps of sulphur, which are usually incrusted with crystals of gypsum. Dt **29** 23 well describes the present aspect of this region. That the inhabitants of the land had experienced the terrors of burning sulphur is very probable. Once one of these deposits took fire it would melt and run in burning streams down the ravines spreading everywhere suffocating fumes such as come from the ordinary brimstone match. No more realistic figure could be chosen to depict terrible suffering and destruction. It is not at all unlikely that during some of the disastrous earthquakes which took place in this part of the world, the hot lava sent forth ignited not only the sulphur, but also the bitumen, and added to the horrors of the earthquake the destruction caused by burning pitch and brimstone.

The **figurative** use of the word brimstone to denote punishment and destruction is illustrated by such passages as Dt **29** 23; Job **18** 15; Ps **11** 6; Isa **30** 33; Ezk **38** 22; Lk **17** 29; Rev **9** 17.

JAMES A. PATCH

BRING: דָּשָׁא, *dāshā'*="to sprout," "spring" (Gen **1** 11 AV); שָׁרַץ, *shāraç*="to wriggle," "swarm" (Gen **1** 20 f; **9** 7; Ex **8** 3); יָלַד, *yāladh*="to bear," "beget" (Gen **3** 16; 2 K **19** 3; Job **15** 35; **39** 1.2; "what a day may bring forth," Prov **27** 1; "before the decree bring forth," Zeph **2** 2); עָנַן, *'ānan*="to cloud over," "to darken" (Gen **9** 14); שָׁלַח, *shālah*="to send on," "to escort" (**18** 16); שׁוּב, *shūbh*="to turn back," "bring" (again, back, home again), "fetch," "establish" (**24** 5.6.8; Job **10** 9; Ps **68** 22; "bring him back to see," Eccl **3** 22; Zec **10** 6.10); נָגַשׁ, *nāghash*="present," "adduce" (an argument) (1 S **13** 9; **15** 32; **23** 9; **30** 7; "bring forth your strong reasons," Isa **41** 21.22); עָשָׂה, *'āsāh*="to do," "cause to be," "accomplish" (Ps **37** 5); עָלָה, *'ālāh*="to carry up," "exalt," "restore" (Gen **46** 4; Ex **3** 8.17; **33** 12; Ps **71** 20; Hos **12** 13); נָגַע, *nāgha'*="to touch," "lay hand upon," "reach to" (Lev **5** 7); כָּבַד, *kābhadh*, or כָּבֵד, *kābhēdh*="to be heavy" (causat. "to make weighty"), "to be glorious" (Prov **4** 8); כָּנַע, *kāna'*="to bend the knee," hence "humiliate," "bring" (down, into subjection, under), "subdue" (Dt **9** 3; Isa **25** 5); זָכַר, *zākhar*="to mark," "call to, put (put in) remembrance" (Ps **38** title; **70** title); יָבַל, *yābhal*="to flow," "bring" (esp. with pomp) (**60** 9; **68** 29; **76** 11; Zeph **3** 10); חוּל, *ḥūl*, or חִיל, *ḥīl*="to writhe in pain," "to be in travail" (Isa **66** 8); צָעַד, *çā'adh*="to step regularly," "march," "hurl" (Job **18** 14); הָלַךְ, *hālakh*="to walk," "get" (Hos **2** 14); גָּדַל, *gādhal*="bring up," "increase" (**9** 12).

The NT employs τελεσφορέω, *telesphoréō* = "to bring to maturity," "to ripen" (Lk **8** 14); ὑπομιμνήσκω, *hupomimnḗskō* = "to bring to mind," "suggest," "bring to remembrance" (Jn **14** 26); δουλόω, *doulóō* = "to enslave" (Acts **7** 6); σύντροφος, *súntrophos* = "brought up with" (**13** 1 RV, "the foster-brother of"); διασῴζω, *diasṓzō* = "to save," "to care," "rescue" (**23** 24); ἀθετέω, *athetéō* = "to set aside," "cast off," "bring to naught" (1 Cor **1** 19); καταργέω, *katargéō* = "to abolish," "destroy," "do away," "put away," "make void" (**1** 28); προπέμπω, *propémpō* = "to send forward," "bring forward" (1 Cor **16** 6 AV; Tit **3** 13 AV; 3 Jn ver 6 AV); ἐκτρέφω, *ektréphō* = "to rear up to maturity," "to cherish," "nourish" (Eph **6** 4 AV). FRANK E. HIRSCH

BRINK, brink: שָׂפָה, *sāphāh,* or שֶׂפֶת, *sepheth* = "the lip," "margin," "bank," "edge" (Gen **41** 3; Ex **2** 3; **7** 15); קָצֶה, *ḳāçeh,* or קְצָה, *ḳēçeh* = "an extremity," "border," "brim" (Josh **3** 8.15; Isa **19** 7; Dnl **12** 5). See BRIM.

BROAD, brôd (רֹחַב, *rōḥabh,* "width"; רְחֹב, *reḥōbh,* "a broadway," "street," "court"; εὐρύχωρος, *eurúchōros,* "spacious"): Occurs frequently as a term of dimension (Ex **27** 1; 1 K **6** 6; Ezk **40** 6.43 RV, "handbreadth long") and as indicative of strength (Neh **3** 8; Jer **51** 58). The centers of communal life are called the "broad places," often rendered "streets" (Jer **5** 1; Cant **3** 2; Nah **2** 4). A court before the temple: "the broad place on the east" (AV "the east street," 2 Ch **29** 4); "broad plates" (Nu **16** 38.39, RV "beaten").

Figurative: Relief from distress: "Yea, he would have allured thee out of [Heb "the mouth of"] distress into a broad place" (Job **36** 16); the liberty of obedience or liberty within the law (Ps **119** 96, "broad," "roomy," "at liberty"); the all-sufficiency of God for His people (Isa **33** 21). Jerus could not boast of a river or navy—Jeh's presence with and within her, would more than supply these deficiencies; the road to destruction: "Broad is the way, that leadeth to destruction" (Mt **7** 13); the ostentatious piety of the Pharisees: "They make broad [πλατύνω, *platúnō,* "widen"] their phylacteries" (Mt **23** 5). See CITY; GATE.

L. KAISER

BROAD PLACE. See CITY.

BROIDERED, broid'ẽrd: (1) רִקְמָה, *riḳmāh,* "variegation of color" (Ezk **16** 10.13.18; **26** 16; **27** 7.16.24); (2) תַּשְׁבֵּץ, *tashbēç,* "checkered stuff" (as reticulated). The high priest's garments consisted of "a breastplate, and an ephod, and a robe, and a broidered coat [Ex **28** 4 AV; RV "a coat of checker work"], a miter, and a girdle"; (3) πλέγμα, *plégma,* "twined or plaited work" (1 Tim **2** 9 AV). See BRAIDED; EMBROIDERY.

BROKEN: brō'k'n: Occurs both as past part. of the vb. tr^d "to break" and as an adj. The former use will be dealt with here only so far as vbs. occur which are thus tr^d but do not present the non-participial forms. Such are: מְרוֹחַ, *merōaḥ* = "bruised," "emasculated" (Lev **21** 20); חָתַת, *ḥāthath* = "to frustrate," hence "to break down" either by violence or by confusion and fear (1 S **2** 10; Jer **48** 20.39); דָּכָה, *dākhāh* = "to collapse" (Ps **44** 19; **51** 8); רָצַץ, *rāçaç* = "to crack in pieces," "crush" (Eccl **12** 6); כָּתַת, *kāthath* = "to bruise or violently strike," "break in pieces" (Isa **30** 14); Jer **2** 16 should evidently be rendered: "have grazed on the crown of thy head," instead of AV "have broken," etc, for רָעָה, *rā'āh* = "to tend a flock," "pasture," "graze," but gives no hint of the meaning "to break"; עָלָה, *'ālāh* = "to arise," "depart" (Jer **37** 11); συνθλάω, *sunthláō* = "to dash together," "shatter" (Mt **21** 44); ἐξορύσσω, *exorússo* = "to dig through," "to extract," "remove" (Mk **2** 4). See BREAK. FRANK E. HIRSCH

BROKENFOOTED, brō'k'n-fo͝ot-ed (שֶׁבֶר רֶגֶל, *shebher reghel*): In Lev **21** 19, one of the blemishes which prevented a man of priestly descent from the execution of the priestly office.

BROKENHANDED, brō'k'n-hand-ed (שֶׁבֶר יָד, *shebher yādh*): In Lev **21** 19 one of the blemishes which prevented a man of priestly descent from the execution of the priestly office.

BROKENHEARTED, brō'k'n-här-ted (שְׁבַר לֵב, *shābhar lēbh;* συντετριμμένοι τὴν καρδίαν, *suntetrimménoi tḗn kardían;* Ps **69** 20.21; Isa **61** 1; Lk **4** 18 AV; "of a broken heart," Ps **34** 18; "broken in heart," **147** 3): People who feel their spiritual bankruptcy and helplessness, and who long for the help and salvation of God. Such people are in the right condition to be met and blessed by God. Cf "of contrite spirit" (Ps **34** 18; Isa **66** 2).

BROOCH, brōch (חָח, *ḥāḥ*): Used in pl. by RV (AV "bracelets") for a class of "jewels of gold" brought as offerings by both men and women of Israel (Ex **35** 22). "Brooches," as Mackie says, is unoriental. The Heb word means most likely nose-rings. See BRACELET; RING.

BROOK, bro͝ok (נַחַל, *naḥal,* אָפִיק, *'āphīḳ,* יְאוֹר, *ye'ōr,* מִיכָל, *mīkhāl;* χείμαρρος, *cheímarrhos*): In Pal there are few large streams. Of the smaller ones many flow only during the winter, or after a heavy rain. The commonest Heb word for brook is *naḥal,* which is also used for *river* and for *valley,* and it is not always clear whether the valley or the stream in the valley is meant (Nu **13** 23; Dt **2** 13; 2 S **15** 23). The Arab. *wādi,* which is sometimes referred to in this connection, is not an exact ‖, for while it may be used of a dry valley or of a valley containing a stream, it means the valley and not the stream. *'Āphīḳ* and *ye'ōr* are tr^d both "brook" and "river," *ye'ōr* being generally used of the Nile (Ex **1** 22, etc), though in Dnl **12** 5–7, of the Tigris. *Cheimarrhos,* "winter-flowing," is applied in Jn **18** 1 to the Kidron. Many of the streams of Pal which are commonly called rivers would in other countries be called brooks, but in such a dry country any perennial stream assumes a peculiar importance. ALFRED ELY DAY

BROOK OF EGYPT, THE (נַחַל, *naḥal* = "a flowing stream," "a valley"; best tr^d by the oriental word *wady,* which means, as the Heb word does, both a stream and its valley):

1. Name

The Brook of Egypt is mentioned six times in the OT (Nu **34** 5; Josh **15** 4.47; 1 K **8** 65; Isa **27** 12); once, Gen **15** 18, by another word, נָהָר, *nāhār.* The Brook of E. was not an Egyp stream at all, but a little desert stream near the borderland of Egypt, a *wady* of the desert, and, perhaps, the dividing line between Canaan and Egypt. It is usually identified with the *Wady el 'Arish* of modern geography.

2. Description

The Brook of E. comes down from the plateau *et Tih* in the Sinai peninsula and falls into the Mediterranean Sea at lat. 31 5 N., long. 33 42 E. Its source is at the foot of the central mountain group of the peninsula. The upper portion of the *wady* is some 400 ft. above the sea. Its course, with one sharp bend to the W. in the upper part, runs nearly due N. along the western slope of the plateau. Its whole course of 140 miles lies through the desert. These streams in the Sinai peninsula are usually dry water-courses, which at times become raging rivers, but are very seldom babbling "brooks." The floods are apt to come with little or no warning when cloudbursts occur in the mountain region drained.

WĀDI-UL-'AIN (THE PRESUMED SITE OF GERAR).

3. Archaeology

The use of the Heb word *naḥal* for this *wady* points to a curious and most interesting and important piece of archaeological evidence on the critical question of the origin of the Pent. In the Pent, the streams of Egypt are designated by an Egyp word (יְאֹר, *y^e'ōr*) which belongs to Egypt, as the word *bayou* does to the lower Mississippi valley, while every other stream mentioned, not excepting this desert stream, "the Brook of E.," is designated by one or other of two Heb words, *naḥal* and *nāhār*. Each of these words occurs 13 times in the Pent, but never of the streams of Egypt. The use of *nāhār* in Ex **7** 19 in the account of the plagues is not really an exception for the word is then used generically in contrast with *y^e'ōr* to distinguish between the "flowing streams," *n^ehārōth*, and the sluggish irrigation branches of the Nile, *y^e'ōrīm*, "canals" (cf CANALS) (Isa **19** 6; **33** 21), while *y^e'ōr* occurs 30 times but never of any other than the streams of Egypt. There is thus a most exact discrimination in the use of these various words, a discrimination which is found alike in P, J, and E of the documentary theory, and also where R is supposed to have altered the documents. Such discrimination is scarcely credible on the hypothesis that the Pent is by more than one author, in later than Mosaic times, or that it is by any author without Egyp training. The documentary theory which requires these instances of the use of these various words for "river" to have been recorded by several different authors or redactors, in different ages and all several cents. after the Exodus, far away from Egypt and opportunities for accurate knowledge of its language, seems utterly incompatible with such discriminating use of these words. And even if the elimination of all mistakes be attributed to one person, a final R, the difficulty is scarcely lessened. For as no purpose is served by this discriminating use of words, it is evidently a natural phenomenon. In every instance of the use of *y^e'ōr*, one or other of the usual Heb words, *naḥal* or *nāhār* would have served the purpose of the author, just as any foreign religious writer might with propriety speak of the "streams of Louisiana," though a Louisianian would certainly call them "*bayous*." How does the author come to use *y^e'ōr* even where his native Heb words might have been used appropriately? Why never, where its appropriateness is even doubtful, not even saying *y^e'ōr* for *naḥal* of the "Brook of E."? It is not art, but experience, in the use of a language which gives such skill as to attend to so small a thing in so extensive use without a single mistake. The only time and place at which such experience in the use of Egyp words is to be expected in Israel is among the people of the Exodus not long subsequent to that event.

M. G. KYLE

Dry Wādy in Edom.

BROOM, brōōm: Occurs in 1 K **19** 4m ("broom-tree"); Job **30** 4, and Ps **120** 4m as the tr of the Heb רֹתֶם, *rōthem*, where AV employed "juniper" which is retained in RV text in 1 K **19** 4 and Job **30** 4. Juniper is certainly incorrect and broom is not a particularly happy rendering. The *rōthem* was doubtless the shrub called by the Arabs *ratam*, a shrub which casts so little shadow that it would be used for shade only when there was no other refuge from the desert sun, and would be eaten only in case of the direst necessity, but which could be burned and used for the making of charcoal. See JUNIPER. DAVID FOSTER ESTES

BROTH, broth (מָרָק, *mārāḳ*): Equivalent to our "soup." When Gideon (Jgs **6** 19) made ready a kid, "the flesh he put in a basket," but, it is added, "he put the broth in a pot"; and he is told by the angel to "pour out the broth" (ver 20). Isaiah (**65** 4) makes Jeh speak of rebellious Israel as "a people that provoke me to my face continually sacrificing in gardens," and adds in description "that eat swine's flesh, and broth of abominable things is in their vessels" (*mārāḳ, pārāḳ*). See FOOD.

BROTHER, bruth'ẽr (אָח, *'āḥ;* ἀδελφός, *adelphós* =kin by birth, from the same parents or parent): Used extensively in both OT and NT of other relations and relationships, and expanding under Christ's teaching to include the universal brotherhood of man. Chiefly employed in the natural sense, as of Cain and Abel (Gen **4** 8); of Joseph and his brethren (Gen **42** 3); of Peter and Andrew, of James and John (Mt **10** 2). Of other relationships: (1) Abram's nephew, Lot, is termed "brother" (Gen **14** 14); (2) Moses' fellow-countrymen are "brethren" (Ex **2** 11; Acts **3** 22; cf He **7** 5); (3) a member of the same tribe (2 S **19** 12); (4) an ally (Am **1** 9), or an allied or cognate people (Nu **20** 14); (5) used of common discipleship or the kinship of humanity (Mt **23** 8); (6) of moral likeness or kinship (Prov **18** 9); (7) of friends (Job **6** 15); (8) an equal in rank or office (1 K **9** 13); (9) one of the same faith (Acts **11** 29; 1 Cor **5** 11); (10) a favorite oriental metaphor used to express likeness or similarity (Job **30** 29, "I am a brother to jackals"); (11) a fellow-priest or office-bearer (Ezr **3** 2); Paul called Sosthenes "brother" (1 Cor **1** 1) and Timothy his spiritual son and associate (2 Cor **1** 1); (12) a brother-man, any member of the human family (Mt **7** 3-5; He **2** 17; **8** 11; 1 Jn **2** 9; **4** 20); (13) signifies spiritual kinship (Matt **12** 50); (14) a term adopted by the early disciples and Christians to express their fraternal love for each other in Christ, and universally adopted as the language of love and brotherhood in His kingdom in all subsequent time (2 Pet **3** 15; Col **4** 7.9.15). The growing conception of mankind as a brotherhood is the outcome of this Christian view of believers as a household, a family (Eph **2** 19; **3** 15; cf Acts **17** 26). Jesus has made "neighbor" equivalent to "brother," and the sense of fraternal affection and obligation essential to vital Christianity, and coextensive with the world. The rabbis distinguished between "brother" and "neighbor," applying "brother" to Israelites by blood, "neighbor" to proselytes, but allowing neither title to the Gentiles. Christ and the apostles gave the name "brother" to all Christians, and "neighbor" to all the world (1 Cor **5** 11; Lk **10** 29 ff). The missionary passion and aggressiveness of the Christian church is the natural product of this Christian conception of man's true relation to man. See also FAMILY RELATIONSHIPS. DWIGHT M. PRATT

BROTHERHOOD, bruth'ẽr-hŏŏd: The rare occurrence of the term (only Zec **11** 14 and 1 Pet **2** 17) in contrast with the abundant use of "brother," "brethren," seems to indicate that the sense of the vital relation naturally called for the most concrete expression: "the brethren." But in 1 Pet **2** 17 the abstract is used for the concrete. In the OT the brotherhood of all Israelites was emphasized; but in the NT the brotherhood in Christ is a relation so much deeper and stronger as to eclipse the other. See also BROTHER; BRETHREN.

BROTHER-IN-LAW. See RELATIONSHIPS, FAMILY.

BROTHERLY, bruth'ẽr-li (אָח, *'āḥ*, "brother"; φιλαδελφία, *philadelphia*, "brotherly love"): *Like a brother* in all the large human relationships indicated above; e.g. the early friendly and fraternal alliance between Tyre and Israel as illustrated by "brotherly covenant" between David and Solomon, and Hiram, king of Tyre (2 S **5** 11; 1 K **5** 12), and repudiated in a later generation by the treachery of Tyre (Am **1** 9). See BROTHERLY KINDNESS (LOVE).

BROTHERLY KINDNESS, kīnd'nes (AV 2 Pet **1** 7), or **LOVE** (AV Rom **12** 10; 1 Thess **4** 9; He **13** 1; φιλαδελφία, *philadelphia*): In RV, "love of the brethren" in all places, and so in AV of 1 Pet **1** 22, thus defining the disposition as love, and its objects as brethren. Since God is Father and men are His sons, they are therefore brethren of one another. As sonship is the most essential factor in man's right relation to God, so is brotherhood in his relation to his fellow-man. Brotherhood is first known as the relation between sons of the same parent, a relation of tender affection and benevolence. It becomes gradually extended to kindred, and to members of the same tribe or nation. And the Christian ideal of society is that a similar relation should exist between all men without limit or distinction. *Agápē*, "love" (see CHARITY), is the word in the NT that generally denotes this ideal. "Thou shalt love thy neighbor as thyself" is the whole law of conduct as between man and man (Mt **22** 39.40); and neighbor includes every man within one's reach (Lk **10** 29 ff), even enemies (Mt **5** 44; Lk **6** 35). Without the love of man, the love of God is impossible, but "he that abideth in love abideth in God" (1 Jn **4** 16.20).

1. As Moral Ideal

But man's sonship to God may be potential or actual. He may not respond to God's love or know His Fatherhood. Likewise love to man may not be reciprocated, and therefore may be incomplete. Yet it is the Christian's duty, like God, to maintain his disposition of love and benevolence to those that hate and curse him (Lk **6** 27.28). But within the Christian community, love should respond to love, and find its fulfilment, for there all men are, or should be, God's sons actually, "because the love of God hath been shed abroad in our hearts, through the Holy Spirit which was given unto us" (Rom **5** 5). And this mutual love within the Christian brotherhood (1 Pet **5** 9) is called *philadelphia*.

2. As Actual Between Christians

This twofold ideal of social morality as universal benevolence and mutual affection had been foreshadowed by the STOICS (q.v.). Men as citizens of the world should adopt an attitude of justice and mercy toward all men, even slaves; but within the community of the "wise" there should be the mutual affection of friendship. Christianity succeeded in organizing and realizing in intense

3. Stoic Teaching

and practical fellowship the ideal that remained vague and abstract in the Gr schools: "See how these Christians love one another." It was their Master's example followed, and His commandment and promise fulfilled: "Love one another . . . . as I have loved you . . . .; by this shall all men know that ye are my disciples" (Jn **13** 14.34.35). Paul in his earliest epistle bears witness that the Thessalonians practise love "toward all the brethren that are in all Macedonia," even as they had been taught of God, but urges them to "abound more and more" (1 Thess **4** 9.10). For the healing of differ-

4. Christian Advance on Heathen Thought

ences, and to build up the church in order and unity, he urges the Romans "in love of the brethren (to) be tenderly affectioned one to another" (Rom **12** 10). Christians must even "forbear one another in love" (Eph **4** 2) and "walk in love, even as Christ also loved you" (Eph **5** 2; Phil **2** 1.2). It involves some suffering and sacrifice. The author of the Epistle to the He recognizes the presence of "love of the brethren" and urges that it may continue (He **13** 1). It is the direct result of regeneration, of purity and obedience to the truth (1 Pet **1** 22.23). It proceeds from godliness and issues in love (2 Pet **1** 7). "Love of the brethren" (*agapē*) is the one practical topic of John's epistles. It is the message heard from the beginning, "that we should love one another" (1 Jn **3** 11.23). It is the test of light and darkness (**2** 10); life and death (**3** 14); children of God or children of the devil (**3** 10; **4** 7–12). Without it there can be no knowledge or love of God (**4** 20), but when men love God and obey Him, they necessarily love His children (**5** 2). No man can be of God's family, unless his love extends to all its members.

T. Rees

BROTHER'S WIFE: (יְבֵמֶת, *ybhēmeth*="a sister-in-law," "brother's wife" [Dt **25** 7.9]; אִשָּׁה, *'ishshāh*="a woman," "wife"; אֵשֶׁת אָח, *'ēsheth 'āḥ* ="brother's wife" [Gen **38** 8.9; Lev **18** 16; **20** 21]; **ἡ γυνὴ τοῦ ἀδελφοῦ**, *hē gunḗ toú adelphoú*="the brother's wife" [Mk **6** 18]): A brother's wife occupies a unique position in Heb custom and law, by virtue of the institution of the Levirate. The widow had no hereditary rights in her husband's property, but was considered a part of the estate, and the surviving brother of the deceased was considered the natural heir. The right to inherit the widow soon became a duty to marry her if the deceased had left no sons, and in case there was no brother-in-law, the duty of marriage devolved on the father-in-law or the agnate who inherited, whoever this might be. The first son of the Levirate marriage was regarded as the son of the deceased. This institution is found chiefly among people who hold to ancestral worship (Indians, Persians, Afghans, etc), from which circumstances Benzinger (*New Sch-Herz*, IV, 276) derives the explanation of this institution in Israel. The Levirate marriage undoubtedly existed as a custom before the Israelitish settlement in Canaan, but after this received special significance because of the succession to the property of the first son of the marriage, since he was reckoned to the deceased, inherited from his putative, not from his real father, thus preventing the disintegration of property and its acquirement by strangers, at the same time perpetuating the family to which it belonged. While the law limited the matrimonial duty to the brother and permitted him to decline to marry the widow, such a course was attended by public disgrace (Dt **25** 5 ff). By the law of Nu **27** 8, daughters were given the right to inherit, in order that the family estate might be preserved, and the Levirate became limited to cases where the deceased had left no children at all.

Frank E. Hirsch

BROW, brou: Is found in Isa **48** 4, "thy brow brass" as the tr of מֵצַח, *mēçaḥ*, meaning "to be clear," i.e. conspicuous. In Lk **4** 29 "led him unto the brow of the hill" is the rendering of ὀφρύς, *ophrús*, lit. "the eyebrow," but used throughout Gr lit. as any prominent point or projection of land (cf use of *supercilium* in Verg. *Georg.* i.108).

BROWN. See Colors.

BRUISE, brōōz, **BRUISED,** brōōzd: The noun occurs in Isa **1** 6 AV, "bruises and putrifying sores," as the tr of חַבּוּרָה, *ḥabbūrāh*. The vb. trs a number of Heb words, the principal ones being (1) שׁוּף, *shūph* (Gen **3** 15 [*bis*]); (2) דָּקַק, *dāḳaḳ* (Isa **28** 28 [*bis*] [ARV "ground," "and though the wheel of his cart and his horses scatter it, he doth not grind it" for the AV "nor break it with the wheels of his cart, nor bruise it with his horsemen"]); (3) דָּכָא, *dākhā'*, in the classical passage, Isa **53** 5, "He was bruised for our iniquities," ver 10, "Yet it pleased Jeh to bruise him"; (4) רָצַץ, *rāçaç*, "A bruised reed shall he not break," Isa **42** 3 (quoted in Mt **12** 20).

In the NT bruise is the tr of σπαράσσω, *sparássō*, "to rend" (ARV "bruising him sorely") Lk **9** 39; of συντρίβω, *suntríbō*, "to break to pieces" (Mt **12** 20); "shall bruise Satan under your feet shortly" (Rom **16** 20); of θραύω, *thraúō*, in Lk **4** 18 in the quotation from Isa **58** 6, "to set at liberty them that are bruised" (WH omits the verse).

Arthur J. Kinsella

BRUIT, brōōt (שֵׁמַע, *shēma'*): A word no longer in common use (marked "archaic" and "obsolete" by Murray), signifying a rumor or report. The word occurs in AV Jer **10** 22 (RV "rumour"; ARV "tidings") and AV Nah **3** 19 (RV "bruit," app. "report"; ARV "report").

BRUTE, brōōt, **BRUTISH,** brōōtish (בַּעַר, *ba'ar*, "stupid"; **ἄλογος**, *álogos*, "without speech," hence irrational, unreasonable [Acts **25** 27; 2 Pet **2** 12; Jude ver 10 AV]): The man who denies God acts in an irrational way. Such persons are described as brutish (Ps **49** 10; **92** 6; **94** 8; Jer **10** 14.21; **51** 17). These are stupid, unteachable. This is a graphic description of the atheist. The proverb, "No fool like the learned fool," is esp. true of the ignorance of the unbelievers of the Scriptures. Their objections to the Bible, as a rule, are utterly ridiculous. The word is occasionally used in the sense of thoughtless ignorance. Brutish counsel is counsel that is foolish, unreasonable (Isa **19** 11). The term is used by Agur (Prov **30** 2) to express the low estimate he has of himself and his conscious lack of knowledge.

Jacob W. Kapp

BUBASTIS, bū-bas'tis. See Pi-beseth.

BUCKET, buk'et (דְּלִי, *dlī*): The word is found only in Isa **40** 15; Nu **24** 7, in the latter passage in a **fig.** use. The bucket was doubtless a water-skin with two cross-pieces at the top to fit it for use in drawing water, like those now in use in Pal. The ordinary word for water-skin is a different one (*nō'dh*).

BUCKLE, buk''l (**πόρπη**, *pórpē*): As a mark of favor Jonathan Maccabaeus was presented by Alexander Balas with a buckle of gold (1 Macc **10** 89), the wearing of which was restricted to the blood royal. The buckle was used for fastening the mantle or outer robe on the shoulder or chest.

BUCKLER, buk'lẽr: God is called a "buckler" (RV "shield") to them that trust Him (Ps **18** 2.30; 2 S **22** 31; Prov **2** 7). See Armor.

BUD. See FLOWER.

BUFFALO, buf'a-lō. See CATTLE.

BUFFET, buf'et (κολαφίζω, *kolaphízō*, "to beat with the fist"): Refers to bodily maltreatment and violence: "Then did they spit in his face and buffet him" (Mt **26** 67; Mk **14** 65; 1 Cor **4** 11; 1 Pet **2** 20). Paul speaks of "a thorn in the flesh, a messenger of Satan to buffet me" (2 Cor **12** 7). Used **fig.** of self-control: "I buffet [AV **keep under,** RVm "bruise"] my body, and bring it into bondage" (1 Cor **9** 27). The Gr in this passage reads ὑπωπιάζω, *hupōpiázō*, lit. "to give a blow beneath the eye." In Lk **18** 5 the same word is rendered "wear out": "Lest she wear me out by her continual coming" (AV "weary me," RVm "bruise me") (see Pape's *Lex.*, s.v.).

L. KAISER

BUGEAN, bū-jē'an, bū'jē-an (**Βουγαῖος,** *Bougaíos*): An epithet given to Haman in Apoc, Ad Est (**12** 6, RV; AV has "Agagite").

BUILD, bild, **BUILDING,** bild'ing (בָּנָה, *bānāh*, בִּנְיָה, *binyāh*, once [Ezk **41** 13]; **οἰκοδομέω,** *oikodoméō*): The building conditions ex-

1. Building Conditions isting at the time of the Heb conquest were rude and untutored, and, with the exception of the work of the Solomonic period, there was still little or no effort made to introduce a higher state, until the time when Gr influence began to be felt (cir 3d cent. BC). In localities where stone was not available, mud bricks were used, and their perishable nature being realized, stone slab facing came into use. These slabs were a protection against the weather and had no constructive value. Probably the hand of the "jerry" builder can be seen in an attempt to make such bad construction appear to be solid stone.

In stone localities buildings were of stone, but the class of building was only that of the rude stone waller. Random rubble masonry,

2. Masonry unskilfully laid, was the prevailing characteristic. Occasionally a piece of carefully dressed masonry is found, but it is the exception and is often a re-use of an earlier type akin to "sawed stone" (1 K **7** 9). The remains of Jewish walls of the period of the early kings in Jerus show skill which does not appear to have existed elsewhere. The boss and margin stones, with wide mud joint, were, in part, the actual masonry of the early fortifications, and were re-used and imitated over and over again. The type crops up in feeble imitation at different sites throughout the country, but hammer-picked and rough hammer-dressed stones are also common. The fine comb pick and marginal dressing of the walls of the Temple area belong to the Herodian period (see Bliss and Dickie, "Excavations at Jerusalem," 273 ff, *PEFS*, 1898). The absence of lime is a striking characteristic. There is no distinctive type which can be named exclusively Jewish, although there is good reason for believing that the boss and margin type has a Jewish origin. Wilson (*Golgotha*, 124) points out that the projecting bosses had a defensive value, in breaking the force of the battering-ram, and here again the necessity of defense shows its vitality in the existence of such a well-engineered detail. The absence of the finer qualities of building craft can be traced to the same source.

Foundations of fortifications were usually on rock which was sometimes squared for a bed, but more often leveled up with small stones.

3. Foundations A portion of the S. wall of Jerus, certainly late (5th cent. AD), was laid on a foundation of small rubble resting on débris, accumulated over an earlier wall. (See Plate IV, *Excavations at Jerusalem*, p. 29.) In smaller buildings, the foundations were usually laid on the débris of earlier structures. At Lachish mud brick walls were laid on a foundation of stone. A peculiar method of spreading a layer of sand under the foundations was also noted (see *A Mound of Many Cities*, 125–26).

The native wall of today is less rudely built and is bedded in lime mortar. It is a broad wall usually about 3 ft. thick, with inner and outer

4. Modern Methods faces of large stones, filled in between with small rubble without proper bond, somewhat in the manner of ancient building. To make up for the want of bond, it is a common habit to insert a piece of steel joint across the return angle (see BEAM). The building and hewing methods, in all probability, are the same as they were in early Jewish times. Hewers sit at their work, with the plane of the stone on which they operate, lying obliquely from them. Stones are conveyed from the quarry, if at a distance from the building site, on donkeys, thence on men's backs to the top of the wall, by rude gangways. Every man digs his "own cistern" (Isa **36** 16), which is sunk in the rock under the site of the house, and used as a quarry from which stones for the building are supplied. If water is scarce, the cistern is sunk first, and the winter rains are allowed to collect and provide the necessary water for the building.

To build up is often used in the sense of giving increase and prosperity, or of stablishing and strengthening. Thus in Job **22** 23;

5. Figurative Ps **69** 35; Jer **18** 9. A kindred sense is to restore what was decayed, as in Isa **58** 12. To "build an house" for a person is to grant him children or a numerous posterity (Ruth **4** 11; of David, 2 S **7** 27; 1 Ch **17** 10). Spiritually, the word is used of one's work in life, or of the formation of character and habits. The main thing here is the foundation. Those who build on Christ's word build on rock; those who reject this word build on sand (Mt **7** 24–27). Christ is the sole true foundation; the work which a man builds on this will be tried by fire (1 Cor **3** 9–15). The church is compared to a building (1 Cor **3** 9; 1 Pet **2** 4–6) reared on the foundation of apostles and prophets (their truths or teaching), Jesus Christ Himself being the chief corner-stone (Eph **2** 20–22). Believers are "builded up" in Christ (Col **2** 7), and are exhorted to build themselves up on their most holy faith (Jude ver 20). See ARCHITECTURE; HOUSE; FORTIFICATION.

A. C. DICKIE

BUILDER, bild'ẽr (בָּנָה, *bānāh*; **οἰκοδομέω,** *oikodoméō*, **τεχνίτης,** *technítēs*): "To build," "builder," etc, are in the OT commonly the tr of *bānāh*, "to build," occurring very frequently; see BUILD, BUILDING. The lit. significance leads also to several **fig.** applications, esp. to God as Divine Builder (1) as *establishing*, e.g. the nation (Ps **69** 35; **102** 16; Jer **12** 16), the throne of David (Ps **89** 4), Jerus (**147** 2); (2) in *restoration*—rebuilding (Isa **58** 12; **61** 4; **65** 21; Jer **31** 4.28; **42** 10; Ezk **36** 36; Am **9** 11; cf Acts **15** 16); (3) as establishing in prosperity (Job **22** 23; 1 S **2** 35; Jer **24** 6; cf Gen **16** 2. RVm, Heb, "be builded by her"); (4) the firm establishment of the Divine attributes (Ps **89** 2); (5) Divine opposition (Lam **3** 5, "He hath builded against me"); cf Job **19** 8; (6) the choosing of a *corner-stone* which the builders rejected (Ps **118** 22.23; quoted by Christ [Mt **21** 42; Mk **12** 10; Lk **20** 17]; by Peter [Acts **4** 11; 1 Pet **2** 7]).

In the NT Christians are represented as being (1) built by God (1 Cor **3** 9.16) on Christ as the one foundation (Mt **16** 18, on Jesus as the Christ; 1 Pet **2** 5 f; Acts **9** 31 RVm; Rom **15** 20; 1 Cor

3 10.12.14 [*epoikodoméō*]; Eph **2** 20); (2) as being continuously and progressively built up in their faith and life (Acts **20** 32; 1 Cor **8** 1 RVm, "buildeth up"; **10** 23m, Gr "build up"; **14** 4.17m; 1 Thess **5** 11; cf Jude ver 20); (3) they are "builded together" (*sunoikodoméō*) in Christ (Eph **2** 22; Col **2** 7 [*epoikodomeō*]; cf 1 Cor **3** 9); (4) "builded up" is used in a bad sense (1 Cor **8** 10 AV and RV, "emboldened," RVm "be builded up"); (6) in He **3** 4 God is represented as the *Builder* (establisher) of all things, RVm "established," and in **11** 10 as the Builder (*technítēs*), of the New Jerus; in **9** 11 for "building" RV has "creation" (*ktísis*); (7) in 1 Cor **3** 10–14; Gal **2** 18, *building* represents constructing a system of teaching; Paul speaks of himself as "a wise master-builder" (*sophós architéktōn*).

W. L. Walker

BUKKI, buk'ī (בֻּקִּי, *bukkī*, "mouth of Jah"): (1) A Danite, son of the tribal prince Jogli (Nu **34** 22); he was one of the representative chiefs who assisted in the division of the land.

(2) Son of Abishua and father of Izzi, a priest, fourth in descent from Aaron, in the line of Eleazar (1 Ch **6** 5.51), and ancestor of Ezra (Ezr **7** 4). In 2 Esd **1** 2 the name appears as Borith, and in 1 Esd **8** 2 as Boccas.

BUKKIAH, buk-ī'a (בֻּקִּיָּהוּ, *bukkīyāhū*, "proved of God"): A Levite, son of Heman (1 Ch **25** 4.13). See Bakbukiah.

BUL, bul (בּוּל, *būl*): Name of the 8th month of the Jewish year (1 K **6** 38). It is of Phoen origin and signifies the month of rain, the beginning of the rainy season. See Calendar.

BULL, bo͝ol, **BULLOCK,** bo͝ol'ok. See Cattle.

BULL, WILD. See Antelope; Cattle.

BULLS, JEROBOAM'S. See Calf (Golden).

BULRUSH, bo͝ol'rush. See Reed.

BULRUSHES, ARK OF. See Ark of Bulrushes.

BULWARK, bo͝ol'wark: The word represents several Heb terms (חֵל, *ḥēl*, Isa **26** 1; חֵילָה, *ḥēlāh*, Ps **48** 13; מְצוֹד, *māçōdh*, Eccl **9** 14; מָצוֹר, *māçōr*, Dt **20** 20). In 2 Ch **26** 15 the word is tr[d] in RV "battlements." See Fortification.

BUNAH, bū'na (בּוּנָה, *būnāh*); A son of Jerahmeel (1 Ch **2** 25).

BUNCH, bunsh: Is used of (1) a "bunch of hyssop" (Ex **12** 22, אֲגֻדָּה, *'ăghuddāh*); (2) a "cluster of raisins" (2 S **16** 1 AV; 1 Ch **12** 40 AV צִמּוּק, *çimmūḳ*="something dried or shriveled"); (3) a "camel's hump" (Isa **30** 6 AV דַּבֶּשֶׁת, *dabbesheth*): of obscure etymology.

BUNDLE, bun'd'l: Represents in EV the words *çerōr*, from a vb. meaning "cramp," "bind," etc (Gen **42** 35; 1 S **25** 29; Cant **1** 13); *çebheth*, from a vb. probably meaning "to grasp" (Ruth **2** 16); and δέσμη, *désmē*, from δέω, *déō*, "to tie up," "bind," hence lit. "bundle," just as the Eng. word is derived from "bind" (Mt **13** 30); and πλῆθος, *plēthos*, properly "multitude." The custom of binding up precious things in bundles (cf Cant **1** 13) is the basis of the very interesting metaphor in 1 S **25** 29: "The soul of my lord shall be bound in the bundle of life with Jeh thy God," or perhaps better, "in the bundle of the living in the care of Jeh"—an assurance of perfect safety.

J. R. Van Pelt

BUNNI, bun'ī (בֻּנִּי, *bunnī*, בּוּנִי, *būnī*, בּוּנִּי, *būnnī*; cf Bani):

(1) A Levite (Neh **9** 4). The repetition of Bani's name in this passage is probably a scribal error. The Syr version for the second "Bani" reads "Binnui"; but as, in **10** 9 and **12** 8, Binnui's name comes, as here, between those of Jeshua and Kadmiel, we should substitute Binnui here for the first Bani. The LXX renders all three names as if the Heb in each case had been בְּנֵי, *b*[e]*nē*, "sons of," reducing the proper names in the ver to five. The names probably stand for chief Levitical houses rather than individuals.

(2) Another Levite, one of the overseers of the temple, father of Hashabiah, according to Neh **11** 15; but, according to 1 Ch **9** 14, Hashabiah is "of the sons of Merari." The reading in Neh is a corruption of the one in Ch.

H. J. Wolf

BURDEN, bûr'd'n: In the OT more than one word is rendered "burden."

1. In the OT

(1) מַשָּׂא, *massā'*, from a root נָשָׂא, *nāsā'*, "he lifted up." Thus lit. any load is called *massā'* (Ex **23** 5; Nu **4** 15.24.27 ff; 2 K **5** 17; **8** 9). **Figuratively,** people are a burden (Nu **11** 11.17; Dt **1** 12; 2 S **15** 33; **19** 35). A man may be a burden to himself (Job **7** 20). Iniquities are a burden (Ps **38** 4). Taxes may be a burden (Hos **8** 10).

(2) In both AV and RV *massā'* is tr[d] "burden," as applied to certain prophetic utterances; but both ARVm and RVm have "oracle." Examples are Isa **13** 1; **14** 28, and often; Jer **23** 33.36.38, no marginal reading; Ezk **12** 10; Nah **1** 1; Hab **1** 1; Zec **9** 1; **12** 1; Mal **1** 1. As was natural under the circumstances, such oracles usually denounced judgment upon place or people. Hence probably the tr "burden." But some of these prophetic utterances do not contain denunciation or threat (Zec **12**). The passage in Jer, moreover, implies that the prophet used the term in the sense of "oracle," for scoffers are reproved for perverting the word and giving it the meaning "burden." *Massā'*, therefore, means something taken up with solemnity upon the lips, whether threatening or not, and the rendering, "burden," ought most likely to be given up.

The word מַשְׂאֵת, *mas'ēth*, of the same derivation as *massā'*, is applied to foolish oracles (Lam **2** 14 AV, oracles ARV, burdens ARVm, burdens RV, oracles RVm; Am **5** 11, burdens AV, exactions ARV and RV).

Massā' is used also in Prov **30** 1 and **31** 1, and is variously rendered prophecy (AV), oracle (ARV), burden, or the name of the speaker's country (RVm, ARVm), oracle (RV). The reading is doubtful, but probably the reference is to the speaker's country—"Jakeh, of Massa" (cf Gen **25** 14), "Lemuel king of Massa."

(3) Other words tr[d] "burden" are from the root סָבַל, *ṣābhal*, "to bear a load" (Neh **4** 17; Ps **81** 6; 1 K **11** 28; AVm, charge AV, labor ARV and RV, burden ARVm and RVm, Ex **5** 4.5; **6** 6.7; Isa **10** 27; Isa **14** 25).

In the NT several Gr words mean "burden."

2. In the NT

(1) βάρος, *báros*, "something heavy." Burdens of the day (Mt **20** 12), the burden of duty to be borne, a difficult requirement (Acts **15** 28; Rev **2** 24). The burden of one's moral infirmities (Gal **6** 2).

(2) φορτίον, *phortíon*, "something to be borne." The obligation which Christ imposes (Mt **11** 30); the legal ordinances of the Pharisees (Lk **11** 46); a man's individual responsibility (Gal **6** 5). Whether any clear and consistent distinction can be made between these two words is doubtful. Probably, however, *phortion* refers to the load as

something to be borne, whether heavy or light, whilst *baros* may be an oppressive load. According to Lightfoot *baros* may suggest a load of which a man may rightly rid himself should occasion serve, but *phortion* a burden which he is expected to bear, as every soldier carries his own pack. But most likely too much weight should not be given to these distinctions.

(3) There is also the word γόμος, *gómos*, "the freight" of a ship (Acts **21** 3); cf ὄγκος, *ógkos*, weight or encumbrance which impedes the runner's progress to the goal (He **12** 1), with particular reference to the superfluous flesh which an athlete seeks to get rid of in training (cf 1 Cor **9** 24–27), and **fig.** whatever hinders the full development of Christian manhood. GEORGE HENRY TREVER

BURGLARY, bûr′gla-ri. See CRIMES.

BURIAL, ber′i-al (קְבוּרָה, *ḳ*e*bhūrāh;* cf NT **τὸ ἐνταφιάσαι,** *tó entaphiásai*):

I. IMMEDIATE BURIAL CONSIDERED URGENT
  1. Reasons for This
  2. The Burial of Jesus
  3. The Usual Time
  4. Duties of Next of Kin
II. PREPARATIONS FOR BURIAL
  1. Often Informal and Hasty
  2. Usually with More Ceremony
  3. Contrasts between Jewish Customs and Other Peoples'
    (1) Cremation
    (2) Embalming
III. ON THE WAY TO THE GRAVE
  1. Coffins Unknown
  2. Professional Mourners
IV. AT THE GRAVE
  1. Graves Dug in the Earth
  2. Family Tombs. Later Customs
  3. Sealed Stones
  4. Stated Times of Mourning
  5. Excessive Mourning
  6. Dirge-Songs
V. FAILURE TO RECEIVE BURIAL A CALAMITY OR JUDGMENT
VI. PLACES OF BURIAL: HOW MARKED
LITERATURE

It is well to recall at the outset that there are points of likeness and of marked contrast between oriental and occidental burial customs in general, as well as between the burial customs of ancient Israel and those of other ancient peoples. These will be brought out, or suggested later in this art.

I. Immediate Burial Considered Urgent.—The burial of the dead in the East in general was and

1. Reasons

is often effected in such a way as to suggest to the westerner indecent haste. Dr. Post says that burial among the people of Syria today seldom takes place later than ten hours after death, often earlier; but, he adds, "the rapidity of decomposition, the excessive violence of grief, the reluctance of Orientals to allow the dead to remain long in the houses of the living, explain what seems to us the indecency of haste." This still requires the survivors, as in the case of Abraham on the death of Sarah, to bury their dead out of their sight (Gen **23** 1–4); and it in part explains the quickness with which the bodies of Nadab and Abihu were carried out of the camp (Lev **10** 4), and those of Ananias and Sapphira were hastened off to burial (Acts **5** 1–11). Then, of course, the defilement to which contact with a dead body gave occasion, and the judgment that might come upon a house for harboring the body of one dying under a Divine judgment, further explain such urgency and haste.

2. The Burial of Jesus

It was in strict accordance with such customs and the provision of the Mosaic law (Dt **21** 23; cf Gal **3** 13), as well as in compliance with the impulses of true humanity, that Joseph of Arimathea went to Pilate and begged the body of Jesus for burial on the very day of the crucifixion (Mt **27** 39 ff).

3. The Usual Time

The dead are often in their graves, according to present custom, within two or three hours after death. Among oriental Jews burial takes place, if possible, within twenty-four hours after death, and frequently on the day of death. Likewise Mohammedans bury their dead on the day of death, if death takes place in the morning; but if in the afternoon or at night, not until the following day.

4. Duties of Next of Kin

As soon as the breath is gone the oldest son, or failing him, the nearest of kin present, closes the eyes of the dead (cf Gen **46** 4, "and Joseph shall put his hand upon thine eyes"). The mouth, too, is closed and the jaws are bound up (cf Jn **11** 44, "and his face was bound about with a napkin"). The death is announced, as it was of old, by a tumult of lamentation preceded by a shrill cry, and the weeping and wailing of professional mourners (cf Mk **5** 38 ff). See MOURNING.

II. Preparations for Burial.—These are often informal and hasty. Under the tyranny of such

1. Often Informal and Hasty

customs as those noted, it is often impossible to make them elaborate. Canon Tristram says: "As interments take place at latest on the evening of the day of death, and frequently at night, there can be no elaborate preparations. The corpse, dressed in such clothes as were worn in life, is stretched on a bier with a cloth thrown over it, until carried forth for burial" (*Eastern Customs*, 94). In Acts **5** 6 we read of Ananias, "The young men . . . . wrapped him round, and they carried him out and buried him." "What they did," as Dr. Nicol says, "was likely this: they unfastened his girdle, and then taking the loose under-garment and the wide cloak which was worn above it, used them as a winding-sheet to cover the corpse from head to foot." In other words, there was little ceremony and much haste.

2. Usually with More Ceremony

Usually, however, there was more ceremony and more time taken. Missionaries and natives of Syria tell us that it is still customary to wash the body (cf Acts **9** 37), anoint it with aromatic ointments (cf Jn **12** 7; **19** 39; Mk **16** 1; Lk **24** 1), swathe hands and feet in grave-bands, usually of linen (Jn **11** 44*a*), and cover the face or bind it about with a napkin or handkerchief (Jn **11** 44*b*). It is still common to place in the wrappings of the body aromatic spices and other preparations to retard decomposition. Thus the friends at Bethany prepared the body of Lazarus, and he came forth wrapped in grave-bands and with a napkin bound about his face. And, we are further told that after the burial of Jesus, Nicodemus brought "a mixture of myrrh and aloes, about a hundred pounds," and that they "took the body of Jesus, and bound it in linen cloths with the spices, as the custom of the Jews is to bury," and that Mary Magdalene and two other women brought spices for the same purpose (Jn **19** 39.40; Mk **16** 1; Lk **24** 1). That this was a very old custom is witnessed by such passages as 2 Ch **16** 14, where it is said that Asa, the king, was laid "in the bed which was filled with sweet odors and divers kinds of spices prepared by the perfumers' art" (cf Jn **12** 3.7; Sir **38** 16). From Acts **5** 6; **8** 2 it appears that there was in later times a confraternity of young men whose business it was to attend to these proprieties and preparations on behalf of the dead; but it was probably only in exceptional cases that they were called upon to act. Certainly such ministries ordinarily devolved, as they do now, upon loving relatives and friends, and mostly women, among the Jews as well as among the Greeks. The practice among the Greeks, both by similarity and contrast, affords an interesting illustration. The following instance is aptly cited in *DB* (art. "Burial"): Electra believing Orestes to be dead and his ashes placed in the sepulchral urn (Soph. *Electra* 1136–52), addresses him thus: "Woe is me! These loving hands have not washed or decked thy corpse, nor taken, as was meet, their sad burden from the flaming pyre. At the hands of strangers, hapless one, thou hast had those rites, and so art come to us, a little dust in a narrow urn."

This brings us to note two marked contrasts between customs in Israel and among other peoples.

3. Contrasts between Jewish Customs and Other Peoples'

(1) With the Greeks it was customary to cremate the dead (see CREMATION); but there was nothing in Jewish practice exactly corresponding to this. Tacitus (*Hist.* v.5) expressly says, in noting the contrast with Rom custom, that it was a matter of piety with the Jews "to bury rather than to burn dead bodies." The burning of the bodies of Saul and his sons by the men of Jabesh-Gilead (1 S **31** 11–13) seems to have been rather a case of emergency, than of conformity to any such custom, as the charred bones were buried by the same men under the tamarisk at Jabesh, and later, by David's order, removed and laid to rest in the sepulcher of Kish (2 S **21** 12–14). According to the Mosaic law burning was reserved, either for the living who had been found guilty of unnatural sins (Lev **20** 4; **21** 9), or for those who died under a curse, as in the case of Achan and his family, who after they had been stoned to death were, with all their belongings, burned with fire (Josh **7** 25).

(2) As the burning practised by the Greeks found no place in Jewish law and custom, so embalming, as practised by the Egyptians, was unknown in Israel, the cases of Jacob and Joseph being clearly special, and in conformity to Egyp custom under justifying circumstances. When Jacob died it was Joseph, the Egyp official, who "commanded his servants the physicians to embalm his father" (Gen **50** 2), and it was conventionally the fit thing that when Joseph himself died his body was embalmed and "put in a coffin [sarcophagus] in Egypt" (**50** 26).

III. On the Way to the Grave.—When the preparations were made and the time came, the corpse was carried to the grave on a bier, or litter (מִטָּה, *miṭṭāh*). Coffins were unknown in ancient Israel, as they are among the Jews of the East to this day. The only one mentioned in the Bible is the sarcophagus in which the embalmed body of Joseph was preserved, unless Asa's bed (2 Ch **16** 14) be another, as some think. Moslems, like eastern Jews, never use coffins. The bier sometimes has a pole at each corner by means of which it is carried on the shoulders to the tomb. See BIER.

1. Coffins Unknown

The procession of mourners is made up largely, of course, of relatives and friends of the deceased, but is led by professional mourning women, who make the air resound with their shrieks and lamentations (cf Eccl **12** 5; Jer **9** 17; Am **5** 16). See MOURNING. Am **5** 16 alludes to this custom in describing the mourning that shall be over the desolations of Israel: "Wailing shall be in all the broad ways; and they shall say in all the streets, Alas! alas! and they shall call the husbandman to mourning, and such as are skilful in lamentation to wailing." Jer (**9** 17.18) breaks out: "Call for the mourning women, that they may come; . . . . and let them make haste, and take up a wailing for us, that our eyes may run down with tears, and our eyelids gush out with waters." Dr. Fred. Bliss tells of a mourning delegation at the *mahal*, or mourning house, of a great man. "No matter how gaily they may be chatting as they approach, when they reach the house they rush forward, handkerchiefs to face, sobbing, weeping, with utmost demonstrations of grief, going through them time after time as occasion requires." Amelia B. Edwards gives a vivid account of her first experience with such mourning: "It rose like the far-off wavering sound of many owls. It shrilled, swelled, wavered, dropt, and then died away, like the moaning of the wind at sea. We never heard anything so wild and plaintive." Among some Jews of today, it is said, the funeral procession moves swiftly, because there are supposed to be innumerable evil spirits (*shēdhīm*) hovering about, desirous to attack the soul, which is thought to be in the body until interment takes place and the corpse is actually covered (see *DB*, art. "Burial").

2. Professional Mourners

IV. At the Grave.—When the grave, or place of entombment, is reached ceremonies more or less characteristic and peculiar to the Orient take place. When the body is let down into the ground, the bier, of course, is set aside, and at first a heap of stones only is piled over the shallow grave—to preserve the dead from the dreaded depredations of hyaenas, jackals or thieves.

1. Graves Dug in the Earth

Tombs of the Kings.

Beyond question graves among ancient Jews were often simply dug in the earth, as they are with us, and as they are with Jews at Jerus and elsewhere in the East today.

2. Family Tombs. Later Customs

But originally, it would seem to have been customary for each family to have a family tomb: either a natural cave, prepared with stone shelves to receive the bodies, or else hewn out of rock in the hillside, each tomb, or sepulcher, having many niches or *loculi*, in each one of which a body could be placed (see Gen **25** 10; **49** 31; **50** 13; **35** 19; Josh **24** 32). As Dr. Nicol says, "All among the Israelites who possessed any land, or who could afford it, had their family tombs, hewn out of the rock, each sepulchre containing many niches. Many generations of a family could thus be placed in the ancestral tomb." Countless numbers of such tombs are to be found all over Pal, but Machpelah, of course, is the chief example (Gen **23**). Compare the cases of Joshua buried in his inheritance at Timnath-serah (Josh **24** 30), Samuel in his house at Ramah (1 S **25** 1), Joab in his house in the wilderness (1 K **2** 34), Manasseh in the garden of his house (2 K **21** 18), Josiah in the same tomb, it would seem, as his father and grandfather (2 K **23** 30), and Asa, singled out for special mention (2 Ch **16** 14). According to custom, too, the Jew was not to sell his burying-place, if it was possible for him to hold it. Today in the Orient it is quite different—burying-places of Moslem, Jewish and Christian peoples, while distinct from each other, are community rather than family burying-places.

Interior of Tombs of the Kings.

3. Sealed Stones

When the tomb was a cave, or was dug out from some rock, the entrance was often closed with a large circular stone set up on its edge or rim and rolled in its groove to the front of the mouth of the tomb, so as to close it securely. This stone was then often further secured by a strap, or by sealing. In such case it could easily be seen or known if the tomb had been disturbed. Pilate, it will be recalled, directed that the tomb of Joseph of Arimathea, in which the body of Jesus was laid, should be carefully sealed and made as secure as the officials could make it. "So they went, and made the sepulchre sure, sealing the stone, the guard being with them" (Mt **27** 66).

4. Stated Times of Mourning

In Syria, as elsewhere in the East, it is customary to have stated times after the burial for mourning at the tomb—for example on the third, seventh, and fortieth days, and again on the anniversary of the burial. The relatives or friends then go to the tomb without ornaments, often with hair disheveled; sometimes with head covered and faces blackened with soot, or ashes, or earth, in their oldest and poorest clothing, which is sometimes violently rent, and, sitting or moving in a circle around or near to the tomb, they break out in spells into weird, dirge-like singing or wailing.

Exterior of Garden Tomb.

5. Excessive Mourning

The violence of grief at times leads to lacerations of the body and the shedding of blood. Morier (*Second Journey through Persia*), describing a celebration which takes place annually to commemorate the death of the grandson of Mohammed, says: "I have seen the most violent of them, as they vociferated *Ya Hosein!* walk the streets with their bodies streaming with blood by the voluntary cuts they had given themselves." Such cutting of the flesh in mourning for the dead was specifically forbidden by the Mosaic law (Lev **19** 28; **21** 5; Dt **14** 1). But excessive mourning for the dead is often alluded to in Scripture (see 2 S **1** 11.12; Ps **6** 6; **119** 136; Lam **1** 16; **3** 48; Jer **9** 1).

6. Dirge-Songs

The custom of dirge-songs seems to be alluded to (Mt **9** 23; Mk **5** 38) in the narrative of the healing of the ruler's daughter: "Jesus came into the ruler's house, and saw the flute-players, and the crowd making a tumult." A characteristic oriental funeral procession and burial are vividly pictured in the narrative of the burial of Jacob (Gen **50** 6–13).

V. Failure to Receive Burial Counted a Calamity or a Judgment.—Any lack of proper burial is still regarded in the East, as it was in ancient times, as a great indignity or a judgment from God. It is esteemed the greatest calamity that can befall a person. It gives men still untold distress to think they shall not receive suitable burial, according to the customs of their respective race, or family, or religion—a fact or sentiment that is often alluded or appealed to by way of illustration in the

Interior of Garden Tomb.

Scriptures. For a corpse to remain unburied and become food for beasts of prey was the climax of indignity or judgment (2 S **21** 10.11; 1 K **13** 22; **14** 11; **16** 4; **21** 24; 2 K **9** 37; Jer **7** 33; **8** 1; Ezk **29** 5; Ps **79** 3; Rev **11** 9), and uncovered blood cried for vengeance (Ezk **24** 6 f; **39** 11–16), the idea being the same as among other oriental peoples, that the unburied dead would not only inflict trouble upon his family, but bring defilement also and a curse upon the whole land. It was, therefore, an obligation resting upon all to bury even the dead found by the way (Tob **1** 18; **2** 8). Even malefactors were to be allowed burial (Dt **21** 22.23), and the exceptional denial of it to the sons of Rizpah gave occasion for the touching story of her self-denying care of the dead found in 2 S **21** 10.11.

VI. Places of Burial: How Marked.—Ordinary graves were marked by the heaping of crude stones, but hewn stones and sometimes costly pillars were set up as memorials of the dead (Ezk **39** 15; 2 K **23** 17 RV, "What monument is that which I see?" the reference being to a sepulchral pillar). Jacob set up a pillar over Rachel's grave (Gen **35** 20), and her tomb is marked by a monument to this day. Absalom's grave in the wood of Ephraim had a heap of stones raised over it (2 S **18** 17), but in this case, as in the case of Achan, it was not for honor but for dishonor. In NT times the place of burial was uniformly outside the cities and villages (see Lk **7** 12; Jn **11** 30). There was public provision made for the burial of strangers (Mt **27** 7), as in the closing days of the monarchy there was a public burying-ground at Jerus (Jer **26** 23), probably where it is to this day between the city wall and the Kidron Valley. Thousands of Jewish graves on the sloping sides of the Valley of Jehoshaphat, where the Jews have come from all lands to be buried, bear witness today to the belief that associates the coming of Messiah with a blessed resurrection. Many Jews hold that Messiah, when He comes, will descend upon the Mount of Olives, and will pass through these resting-places of the dead as He enters the Holy City in glory.

Literature.—*HDB*, art. "Burial"; Keil, *Bib. Arch.*, II, 199 f; Nowack, *Heb Arch.*, I, 187 ff; "Burial" and "Tombs" in Kitto, *Cycl.*; Thomson, *LB* (see "Funerals" in Index); Tristram, *Eastern Customs in Bible Lands;* Mackie, *Bible Manners and Customs.*

Geo. B. Eager

BURIER, ber'i-ẽr (קָבַר, *ḳābhar*): "Set up a sign by it, till the buriers have buried it" (Ezk **39** 15). "When the searchers found any human remains as they passed through the land, they were to set up a mark to attract the attention of the buriers, who followed them" (Dummelow's *Comm.*, in loc.). See Burial.

BURN, bûrn, **BURNING,** bûrn'ing: **Figurative:** In addition to the ordinary meaning, burn is used metaphorically in the following passages of the NT:

(1) *καίω, kaíō* (Lk **24** 32), "Was not our heart burning within us," i.e. greatly moved.

(2) *πυρόω, puróō,* used twice, once in the sense of inflamed with sexual desire (1 Cor **7** 9), "For it is better to marry than to burn," and in 2 Cor **11** 29 of the heat of the passions, here of grief, or anger, "Who is offended [ARV "caused to stumble"] and I burn not?" See also Punishments.

BURNT OFFERING. See Sacrifice in the OT and NT.

BURNT SACRIFICE. See Sacrifice in the OT and NT.

BUSH, bo͝osh:

(1) (סְנֶה, *ṣ^{e}neh,* Ex **3** 2–4; Dt **33** 16; **βάτος,** *bátos,* Mk **12** 26; Lk **6** 44, "bramble bush"; **20** 37; Acts **7** 30.35. All the OT references and the NT references, except Lk **6** 44, are to the same "bush," viz. Moses' "burning bush"). From its etymology *ṣ^{e}neh* clearly denotes a "thorny" plant, as does the corresponding *batos* in the LXX and NT. In the Lat VSS *rubus,* i.e. "bramble," is used as equivalent. Several varieties of bramble flourish in Pal, of which the most common is *Rubus discolor,* but this is not an indigenous plant in Sinai. It is stated by Post that a bush of this plant has been planted by the monks of the Convent of St. Catherine at Sinai to the rear of the "Chapel of the Burning Bush." In spite of tradition there is but little doubt that Moses' "burning bush" must actually have been a shrub of one of the various thorny acacias, or allied plants, indigenous in the Sin peninsula.

(2) (שִׂיחַ, *sī^{a}ḥ,* "plant," Gen **2** 5; "shrub," Gen **21** 15; "bush," Job **30** 4.7). In the first reference any kind of plant may be meant, but in the other passages the reference is to the low bushes or scrub, such as are found in the desert.

(3) (נַהֲלֹלִים, *nahălōlīm,* AV **bushes,** RV PASTURES, m "bushes," Isa **7** 19). The meaning appears to be rather a place for watering flocks, the corresponding Arab. root نَهَلَ, *nahal,* having the meaning "to quench one's thirst," and the corresponding noun of place, مَنْهَل, *manhal,* meaning a watering-place in the desert.

E. W. G. Masterman

BUSH, THE BURNING, bûrn'ing: The scene at the burning bush (סְנֶה, *ṣ^{e}neh,* "a bush," LXX *bátos,* "blackberry bush") reveals God to the world in one of the theophanies with fire, of which there are four mentioned in the Bible (Ex **3** 2; **13** 21; **19** 18; also 2 Thess **1** 8 AV, yet to be fulfilled). Many other Divine manifestations were associated with fire. The Burning Bush is mentioned elsewhere in Dt **33** 16; Mk **12** 26; Lk **20** 37; Acts **7** 30.31.

1. Meaning and Use

Exact identification of the particular kind of bush in which God appeared to Moses is impossible. Attempts have been made to identify it with the blackberry bush, as by the LXX and also by the monks of the Convent of St. Catharine on Mount Sinai who grow the blackberry there in token of their tradition. The cassia has also been suggested. Both identifications are failures, the former because the blackberry does not grow in that region unless imported and tended, the latter for philological reasons. Nothing in the language used gives any clue to the species of the bush. The generally accepted view that it was some kind of thorn bush is an assumption with scarcely other ground than that there are so many thorny bushes in that region. This fact does, however, give to the assumption much probability.

2. Identification

The old Jewish commentators have many things to say in explanation of this theophany (cf *Jew Enc*). That one thing which will meet with much response from the Christian heart is that the unconsumed bush with the fire in the midst of it indicated that the Israelites would not be consumed by the afflictions in Egypt. The application of this view to God's people under affliction in all ages is often made by Christian homilists. But this cannot have been the primary meaning of the theophany. Of the many theophanies and other Divine manifestations with fire, the specific signification must be learned from a careful study of the circumstances in each case. The fire does not seem to have any one fundamental meaning running through them all. In addition to the references already given, cf Ps **18** 8–12; **50** 3; Ezk **1** 4; Mic **1** 1–4; Hab **3** 3–6; He **12** 29.

3. Interpretation

The exact meaning of the Burning Bush as a method or medium of revelation may appear as follows: (1) The flame in this bush was not the flame of persecution by God's enemies without, but the flame of God's presence or the presence of His angel within. (2) The idea of burning and yet not being consumed is brought into the narrative by Moses' wonderment in the moment of his ignorance, before he knew that God was in the bush. (3) The real significance of the flame in this case seems to be light and glory and preservation where God manifests Himself graciously. This is the universal idea of revealed religion. The prevailing idea of God in the religions round about was that God dwelt in darkness. The approach to the gods in Egyp temples was through ever-deepening gloom. It was thought that God was very dangerous and apt to be a *destroyer,* so that a priest must always intervene. God as a gracious *Saviour* was the new idea revelation was bringing to the world. This was now first clearly announced, but was not to be fully revealed throughout the time of the long line of priests until the Great High Priest should come and make a "way of approach" that we may come "with boldness unto the throne of grace."

M. G. Kyle

BUSHEL, bo͝osh'el (**μόδιος,** *módios*): A dry measure containing about a peck, but as it is used in the NT (Mt **5** 15; Mk **4** 21; Lk **11** 33) it does not refer to capacity but is used only to indicate a covering to conceal the light.

BUSHY, bo͝osh′i: Found in Cant **5** 11 as the tr of תַּלְתַּל, *tāltāl,* meaning trailing, pendulous (LXX ἐλάται, *elátai,* lit. "ductile"); RVm reads "curly."

BUSINESS, biz′nes: Is the rendering of four Heb words: (1) מְלָאכָה, *m^elā'khāh,* in Gen **39** 11 (ARV "work"); 1 Ch **26** 29.30; 2 Ch **13** 10 (ARV "in their work"); **17** 13 (ARV "many works"); Neh **11** 16.22; **13** 30 (ARV "in his work"); Est **3** 9; Ps **107** 23; Prov **22** 29; Dnl **8** 27. (2) דָּבָר, *dābhār,* lit. "a word," is so tr[d] in Dt **24** 5; Josh **2** 14.20; Jgs **18** 7 (ARV "dealings"); **18** 28 (ARV "dealings"); 1 S **21** 2.8. (3) מַעֲשֶׂה, *ma'ăseh,* "an action" (1 S **20** 19). (4) עִנְיָן, *'inyān,* "employment" (Eccl **5** 3; **8** 16).

In the NT "business" in Lk **2** 49 is the rendering of the phrase ἐν τοῖς τοῦ πατρός μου, *en toís toú patrós mou,* lit. "in the things of my Father," which ARV renders "in my Father's house," with "about my Father's business" as the marginal reading. "Business" is also used in the tr of χρεία, *chreía,* lit. "need," of Acts **6** 3; as the tr of σπουδή, *spoudḗ,* lit. "haste" of Rom **12** 11 (ARV "diligence"); of πρᾶγμα, *prágma,* lit. "thing done," of Rom **16** 2 (ARV "matter"); of πράσσειν τὰ ἴδια, *prássein tá ídia,* lit. "tend to one's own business," of 1 Thess **4** 11. In Acts **19** 24.25 in Paul's account of the riot in Ephesus, ἐργασία, *ergasía,* lit. "working," "performing," is tr[d] "little business" in ver 24 (AV "small gain"), and "by this business" in ver 25 (AV "by this craft").

Arthur J. Kinsella

BUSYBODY, biz′i-bod-i (**περίεργος,** *periergos,* **ἀλλοτριοεπίσκοπος,** *allotrioepískopos*): The word is found twice in Paulinic lit.: 1 Tim **5** 13, "not only idle, but tattlers also and busybodies," and 2 Thess **3** 11, "work not at all, but are busybodies." It is also found in 1 Pet **4** 15 AV (RV "meddler") "or as a busybody in other men's matters." If these passages be coupled with such others as Jas **3** 2–10; **4** 11; Eph **4** 29.31; Tit **3** 2, it becomes evident that sins against the eighth commandment were as common in the apostolic church as they are today. To this day backbiting is a common trait of oriental peoples. And it is this sin which is so repeatedly warned against by the apostles, as in direct conflict with the ethics of Christianity, and in violation of that spirit of brotherly love and mutual trust which Christ has enjoined on His followers, and which is the very marrow of the outward revelation of the Christian faith (1 Cor **13**). Henry E. Dosker

BUTLER, but′lẽr: An officer in households of kings, or other dignitaries, having charge of wines and other potables. מַשְׁקֶה, *mashkeh,* "one who gives drink" (Gen **40** 1–23; **41** 9), rendered "cupbearer" in 1 K **10** 5; 2 Ch **9** 4; Neh **1** 11. The office was one of considerable importance in oriental courts, because of the danger to the king's life through plots of poison, etc. Nehemiah held this position to King Artaxerxes. Wealthy courts, as that of Solomon, usually had more than one (1 K **10** 5); over these cupbearers or butlers was the *sar ha-mashkīm,* or chief butler (Gen **40** 9).

Edward Bagby Pollard

BUTTER. See Food.

BUYING, bī′ing (כָּרָה, *kārāh,* לָקַח, *lākaḥ,* קְנָא, *k^enā',* קָנָה, *kānāh,* שָׁבַר, *shābhar;* **ἀγοράζω,** *agorázō,* **ὠνέομαι,** *ōnéomai,* **ἐμπορεύομαι,** *emporeúomai*):

I. In the Earliest Periods and among Nomads
  1. The Primitive Stage (the "Shop")
  2. In OT Times
  3. In NT Times
II. Oriental Buying a Tedious Process
III. Shops and Bazaars
  1. Oriental Shops
  2. The Market-Place
IV. Buying on Credit
  Paying Cash (Money)
V. Open-Air Markets and Fairs

I. In the Earliest Periods and among Nomads.—Among primitive races and nomads there can be, of course, no organized commerce.

1. The Primitive Stage; the "Shop"

Yet they buy and sell, by barter and exchange, in rude and simple ways. When tribes become settled and live in villages the "shop" is established—usually at first the simple "stall" of the grocer (*bakkal*) where one can buy bread, cheese, salt and dried fish, olives, oil, bundles of wood or charcoal, and even earthenware vessels for the passing traveler. At a later stage the village will have also, according to demand, other shops, as, for instance, those of the baker, the blacksmith, the cobbler, and, today, will be found in many obscure places in the East the butcher's shop, and the coffee house.

These gradations and the gradual rise to the more organized commerce of the Gr-Rom period are indicated in a way by the succession of

2. In OT Times

words for "buying" used in the Bible and the conditions and circumstances pictured and implied in the various accounts of buying and selling. Even as early as Abraham's time, however, there were buying and weighing of silver in exchange. "Hear me," pleads Abraham with the children of Heth, "and entreat for me to Ephron the son of Zohar, that he may give me the cave of Machpelah . . . . which is in the end of his field; for the full price let him give it to me." And Ephron said, "Nay, my lord, hear me: the field give I thee, and the cave that is therein." But Abraham said, "If thou wilt . . . . I will give the price of the field; take it of me, and I will bury my dead there. And Ephron answered . . . ., My lord, hearken unto me: a piece of land worth four hundred shekels of silver, what is that betwixt me and thee? bury therefore thy dead. . . . . And Abraham weighed to Ephron the silver . . . . four hundred shekels of silver, current money with the merchant. So . . . . the field, and the cave, and all the trees that were in the field, ... were made sure unto Abraham for a possession" (Gen **23** 8–18). Other examples of primitive buying are found in Josh **24** 32 ("the parcel

Market-Place at Jaffa.

of ground which Jacob bought of the sons of Hamor the father of Shechem for a hundred pieces of money"); in Ruth **4** 5–9, where Boaz is represented as buying "the parcel of land which was Elimelech's . . . . of the hand of Naomi . . . . and of Ruth the Moabitess, the wife of the dead . . . . all that was Elimelech's"; and in 2 S **24**

21–24, where David is said to have "bought the threshing-floor" of A. at "a price." Such cases, however, are in a sense exceptional; trade in general at that time was by barter and exchange, without intermediary or market-place.

3. In NT Times

In NT times things have so changed that the word most commonly used for buying (*agorazō*) means "to use the market-place," and another (*emporeuomai*) points to a class of traders or merchants who *go on*, from city to city—"continue" here or there "and buy and sell" (Jas **4** 13 AV).

II. Oriental Buying often a Tedious Process.—Something of this is seen even in the fine examples given above. Doubtless, however, eastern buyers and sellers of old haggled over prices with controversy and heat, even as such buyers do today. Everywhere you find them now keen for bargains, but "striking a bargain" is a tedious process. They grow warm and then cool off; they are swept into a frenzy by some new turn of the strife and then calm down; but soon the haggling and arguing begin over again, becoming more heated and seemingly more hopeless than ever, and often they become so excited as to threaten to come to blows. But they don't mean it all, and at last they find a common basis; the sale is made with flattering compliments to one another, and, if we may believe appearances, to the rapturous delight of both parties to the bargain.

Going to Market.

The native Oriental clearly takes pleasure in such exercise, and sees great possibilities before him. He graciously assures you at the outset that the bargain shall be "just as you like it—*just as you like it!*" Is he not a servant of God? What cares he for money? What he most wants is your happiness and good will—that is the sweetest thing in life—the love and favor of brothers. After a while you offer a price. He says, "What is such a trifle between us? Take it for nothing!" But he is far from meaning it, and so the haggling begins and the fire and heat of controversy follow—perhaps for hours.

III. Shops and Bazaars.—Oriental shops are all of a pattern—the workshop and the place to store

1. Oriental Shops

and sell goods is one and the same. It is on the street, of course, and a platform, usually about 2 ft. high, extends along the whole front. A small door opens to a room back, which, as far as such a thing is possible in the Orient, is private. The goods, particularly the best articles, are displayed in front, somewhat as they are in the windows of our department stores. In the center of the platform is a *sejadeh*, a rug or mat. Upon this the keeper sits in true oriental fashion—cross-legged. He is never too busy with his accounts to let the passerby escape his keen eye. He will give up his *nargileh* any time to hail the stranger, display his goods, and coaxingly invite him to look at the special beauty and quality of his articles.

2. The Market-Place

All the shops or storerooms of the oriental village line the "market," which as a rule, is in the center of the village, or on the chief street. This the Arabs call *suk*, *sookh* (cf Mt **20** 3). Here the peasant is found with his donkeys or camels laden with food-stuffs and country produce. The gardener is there with his small fruits, and the fisherman with his latest "catch." All the shopkeepers, too, are on or near to this street or market center. "The *sookh* in a country village," says J. Garrow Duncan, "is one of the most interesting sights of modern Egypt. Formerly the cattle and dry-goods markets were uniformly held in an open space in the center of each village. Now the government compels them to go to a fenced enclosure outside of the town. At Belbeys the ordinary market is still held in the center of the town, but the cattle market is a mile away, across the canal. As in a bazaar, such as the traveler sees in Cairo, the merchants of the various trades dispose themselves here in lanes, all easily accessible from the main street, which is thus left clear. On the left are the dealers in copper utensils, busily plying their trade; next to them the makers of sieves and riddles; then comes a large space filled with pottery ware, and, close by, the vegetable venders. There, jammed in between the pottery space and the coppersmiths, is a lane of gold- and silversmiths—the greatest sharks in the market, their chief prey being the women. On the other side of the main street are the shoemakers' lane, the drapers' lane, the grocers, the seed men, the sweetmeat-sellers, fruit-merchants, dealers in glass and carnelian jewelry and, lastly, the butchers' stalls, all arranged in lanes, and all equally ready to trade or to enjoy a joke at each other's expense. There is apparently little eagerness to trade—except when a tourist appears." To one who is ignorant of the value of his wares, the oriental dealer has no fixed price. This is really regulated by the supposed ignorance of the purchaser. If you choose, you may give him what he asks, and be laughed at all round the *sookh*. If you are wise, you will offer something near to the real value and firmly refuse to vary or haggle, and he will come to terms.

Professor Elihu Grant tells of a shop in a Syrian village—"a small room, 6 to 12 ft. square, with a door, but no window, a counter or bench, and shelves and bins along the sides, where sugar, flour, oil, matches, candies, spice, starch, coffee, rice, dried figs, etc, were found, but no wrapping-paper. The buyer must bring his own dish for liquids; other things he carries away in the ample folds of his skirt or in a handkerchief." "Every considerable Turkish town," says Van Lennep, "has a *bazaar*, *bezesten*, or 'arcade': a stone structure, open at both ends, a narrow alley or street running through it, covered with an arched roof, the sides pierced with openings or windows. This covered street is lined on both sides with shops, narrow and shallow. Dealers in similar goods and articles flock together here, as do the artisans of like trades in all oriental cities." Such shops can yet be seen in quite characteristic form in Damascus, Bagdad, Cairo and Constantinople, as in ancient days they were found in Babylon, Jerus and Noph (see Ezk **27** 13–24).

IV. Buying on Credit.—The shop-keeper does not always get cash from the native buyer. Dr. Post found that debt was well-nigh universal in Syria. The peasant sows "borrowed" seed, in "borrowed" soil, plants and reaps with "borrowed" tools, and lives in a "borrowed" house. Even in case of an abundant harvest the proportion of the crop left by the landlord and the tax-gatherer leaves the man and his family but the barest living at best; at times he can barely pay the debt accumulated in making and gathering in the crop, and sometimes fails in doing this. In the rare cases when the buyer pays cash for his purchases, he makes payment, after a true oriental fashion, in coin of the most various or varying values, or in rings of copper, silver or gold, such as are now common in the market-places of China. This throws light upon some Scriptural passages, as, for example, Gen **43** 21.22, where the language implies that the "rings" or "strings of money" were weighed: "Behold, every man's money was in the mouth of his sack, our money in full weight . . . . and other money have we brought down in our hand to buy food." In Ezr **2** 69, three kinds of currency are mentioned, "darics of gold," "pounds of silver," and "priests' garments," as having been given into the treasury for the house of God. The term rendered "darics of gold," *'ădharkōnīm*, stands for Pers coins, which were similar to the Gr "darics." The Persians are said to have got the idea of coining from Lydia, at the capture of Sardis, 564 BC. Early Lydian coins were of electrum, but Croesus changed this to coins of gold and silver, probably about 568 BC. Examples of these ancient coins are now known (Rice, *Orientalisms in Bible Lands*, 234).

Paying Cash (Money)

V. Open-Air Markets and Fairs.—In inland towns and cities, markets and market-places are often found in the open air, as well as under cover. Great fairs are held thus on certain days of the week. Several towns will agree upon different days as market days and will offer in turn whatever they have for sale: lambs, sheep, cattle, horses, mules, chickens, eggs, butter, cheese, vegetables, fruits, and even jewelry and garments. In such a case it is as if the whole town for the day was turned into a market or exhibition, where everything is for sale. On such days peasants and townspeople come together in much larger numbers than is ordinary, and mingle freely together. The day thus chosen now, as in olden times, is often a holy day—Friday, which is the Moslem Sabbath, or the Christian Sunday, where Christians abound. Such instances form a side-light on such passages as Neh **13** 15–22: "In those days saw I in Judah some men treading winepresses on the sabbath, and bringing in sheaves, and lading asses therewith; as also wine, grapes, and figs, and all manner of burdens, which they brought into Jerus on the sabbath day: and I testified against them." Morier testifies that he attended similar fairs in Persia, where were gathered sellers of all sorts of goods in temporary shops or tents, such as sellers of barley and flour, as it was at the gate of Samaria after the famine (2 K **7**). Layard also speaks of having seen at the gate of the modern town of Mosul, opposite the site of ancient Nineveh, shops for the sale of wheat, barley, bread-stuffs, and drinks for the thirsty. It will be recalled that it was "at the gate" that Boaz (Ruth **4** 1–3) called the elders and people to witness that he had bought all that was Elimelech's. For similar allusions see Job **5** 4; Prov **31** 23; Ps **127** 5; Lam **5** 14. See MONEY; TRADE, etc; also *DB*, *DCG*, etc.

GEO. B. EAGER

BUZ, buz, **BUZI**, bū'zī, **BUZITE**, buz'īt (בּוּז, *būz*):

(1) Second son of Nahor (Gen **22** 21). The word occurs again in Jer **25** 23, by the side of Dedan (Gen **10** 7) and Tema (Gen **25** 15), and is probably, therefore, the name of a people living in the neighborhood of Edom. Būz and Hazo (Gen **22** 22) are probably the countries of *Bâzu* and *Ḥazû* (the former described as full of snakes and scorpions), which Esarhaddon invaded (*KB*, II, 131).

(2) A Gadite (1 Ch **5** 14) (בּוּזִי, *būzī*), "an inhabitant of Buz"), a title given to Elihu, the fourth speaker in the Book of Job (Job **32** 2).

HORACE J. WOLF

BY: In the sense of "against" which survives only in dialectal English (cf Wright, *Dialect Dict.*, I, 470, for examples) is the AV rendering of the dative ἐμαυτῷ, *emautō* of 1 Cor **4** 4 (ARV renders this "against"). In classical Gr the same idiom *sunoída* with dative = "be conscious" or "be cognizant of" a thing.

BY AND BY: In the sense of "immediately" is the AV tr of ἐξαυτῆς, *exautēs*, of Mk **6** 25 (ARV "forthwith"); of εὐθύς, *euthús*, Mt **13** 21 (ARV "straightway"); of εὐθέως, *euthéōs*, Lk **17** 7 (ARV "straightway"); **21** 9 (ARV "immediately"). In Eng. lit. this meaning is obsolete (cf "After you have dyned and supte, laboure not *by and by* after, but make a pause—the space of an howre or more with some pastyme" (*Babees Book*, *EETS*, 247).

BYBLUS, bib'lus. See GEBAL.

BYPATHS, bī'pathz. See BYWAY.

BYSSUS, bis'us. See LINEN.

BYWAY, bī'wā (נְתִיבוֹת, *nethībhōth*): Only in Jgs **5** 6. Cf Jer **18** 15; AV "paths" (RV "bypaths").

BYWORD, bī'wûrd: שַׁמָּה, *shammāh* = "consternation," "astonishment," "waste," "wonderful language," "object of remark" (Dt **28** 37; 1 K **9** 7; 2 Ch **7** 20); מָשָׁל, *māshāl*, or מְשֹׁל, *meshōl* = "a satire," "byword" (Job **17** 6; Ps **44** 14); מִלָּה, *millāh*, or מִלֶּה, *millēh* = "a topic," "object of talk," "byword" (Job **30** 9).

C

CAB. See KAB.

CABBON, kab′on (כַּבּוֹן, *kabbōn;* **Χαβρά,** *Chabrá*): An unidentified place in the Shephelah of Judah near Eglon (Josh **15** 40). It is possibly the same as MACHBENA, which see.

CABIN, kab′in (חֲנֻיּוֹת, *ḥănuyyōth,* "vaults"; Jer **37** 16 RV, "cells"): In the East the prison often consisted of a pit (cf "dungeon-house" RV and "house of the pit" RVm) with vaulted cells around it for the confinement of prisoners. The word is probably a gloss. The phrase "and into the cells" seems superfluous after "into the dungeon-house."

CABUL, kā′bul (כָּבוּל, *kābhūl;* B, **Χωβαμασομέλ,** *Chōbamasomél;* A, **Χαβὼλ ἀπὸ ἀριστερῶν,** *Chabṓl apó aristerōn*):

(1) A city on the boundary between Asher and Zebulun (Josh **19** 27). It corresponds to the Chabolo of Jos (*Vita,* 43, etc), and is represented by the modern village *Kābūl,* about nine miles S.E. of Acre.

(2) A district probably connected with (1), containing 20 cities, given by Solomon to Hiram king of Tyre (1 K **9** 10 ff).

CADDIS, kad′is. See GADDIS.

CADES, kā′dēz. See KEDESH (Apoc).

CADES-BARNE, kā′dēz bär′nē. See KADESH-BARNEA (Apoc).

ÇADHĒ, tsä-thā′ (צ ץ): The eighteenth letter of the Heb alphabet, and as such employed in Ps **119** to designate the 18th part, every verse of which begins with this letter. It is transliterated in this Encyclopaedia as ç (almost *ts*). It came also to be used for the number 90. For name, etc, see ALPHABET; TSADHE.

CAESAR, sē′zar (**Καῖσαρ,** *Kaísar*): Originally the surname of the Julian gens (thus, Caius Julius Caesar); afterward a name borne by the Rom emperors. In the NT the name is definitely applied to Augustus (Lk **2** 1, "Caesar Augustus"), to whom it belonged by adoption, and to Tiberius (Lk **3** 1, "Tiberius Caesar"; cf Mt **22** 17.21). The "Caesar" to whom Paul appealed (Acts **25** 11.12.21) was Nero. The form is perpetuated in "Kaiser" and "Czar."

CAESAREA, ses-a-rē′a, sē-za-rē′a (**Καισαρεία,** *Kaisareía*):

(1) Caesarea Palestina (pal-es-tī′na). The ancient name in the Arab. form *Ḳaisarīyeh* still clings to the ruins on the sea shore, about 30 miles N. of Jaffa. It was built by Herod the Great on the site of Strato's Tower (*Ant,* XIII, xi, 2; XV, ix, 6), and the name Caesarea Sebaste was given it in honor of Augustus (ib, XVI, v, 1). With his usual magnificence Herod lavished adornments on the city. He erected sumptuous palaces and public buildings, a theater, and amphitheater with prospect to the sea; while a spacious system of sewers under the city secured cleanliness and health. But "the greatest and most laborious work of all" was a magnificent harbor "always free from the waves of the sea," which Jos says was not less than the Piraeus: this however is an exaggeration. It was of excellent workmanship, and all the more remarkable because the place itself was not suitable for such noble structures. The whole coast line, indeed, is singularly ill-fitted for the formation of harbors. The mighty breakwater was constructed by letting down stones 50×18×9 ft. in size into twenty fathoms deep. The mole was 200 ft. wide. Part was surmounted by a wall and towers. A promenade and dwellings for mariners were also provided. The work was done in ten or twelve years. It became the residence of the Rom procurator. It passed into the hands of Agrippa I; and here he miserably died (Acts **12** 19.23). Here dwelt Philip the Evangelist (Acts **8** 40; **21** 8). To Caesarea Peter was sent to minister to the Rom centurion Cornelius (Acts **10**). Thrice Paul passed through Caesarea (Acts **9** 30; **18** 22; **21** 8); hither he was sent under guard from Jerus to escape danger from the Jews (**23** 23); and here he was imprisoned till his final departure for Rome.

Riots between Gentiles and Jews in Caesarea gave rise to the war (*BJ,* II, xiii, 7; xiv, 4 f). Terrible cruelties were practised on the Jews under Felix and Florus. Here Vespasian was hailed emperor by his soldiers. Titus here celebrated the birthday of his brother Domitian by setting 2,500 Jews to fight with beasts in the amphitheater. Eusebius was bishop of Caesarea (313–40 AD). In 548 AD a massacre of the Christians was organized and carried out by the Jews and Samaritans. The city passed into Moslem hands in 638. In the time of the Crusades it fell, now to the Christians and now to the Moslems; and was finally overthrown by Sultan Bibars in 1265 AD.

The cathedral stood on the site of a temple built by Herod, where the ruins are seen today; as are also those of two aqueducts which conveyed water from *Nahr ez-Zerḳā.* The landward wall of the Rom city was nearly 3 miles in length.

(2) Caesarea Philippi (fi-lip′ī) (**Καισαρεία ἡ Φιλίππου,** *Kaisareía hē Philíppou*). At the S.W. base of Mt. Hermon, on a rocky terrace, 1,150 ft. above sea-level, between *Wādy Khashabeh* and *Wādy Za'areh,* lie the ruins of the ancient city. It was a center for the worship of Pan: whence the name Paneas, applied not only to the city, but to the whole district (*Ant,* XV, x, 3). It is possible that this may have been the site of ancient Baal-hermon; while Principal G. A. Smith would place Dan here (*HGHL,* 480). The district was given by Augustus to Herod the Great 20 BC, by whom a temple of white marble was built in honor of the emperor. Paneas formed part of the tetrarchy of Philip. He rebuilt and beautified the town, calling it Caesarea as a compliment to Augustus, and adding his own name to distinguish it from Caesarea on the coast of Sharon (*Ant,* XVIII, ii, 1; *BJ,* II, ix, 1). From Bethsaida Jesus and His disciples came hither, and on the way Peter made his famous confession, after which Jesus began to tell them of His coming passion (Mt **16** 13 ff; Mk **8** 27 ff). Some think that on a height near Caesarea Philippi Jesus was transfigured. See TRANSFIGURATION, MOUNT OF. Agrippa II renamed the town Neronias (*Ant,* XX, ix, 4). The ancient name however outlived both Caesarea and Neronias, and survives in the Arab. form *Bāniās.* The modern village, built among the ruins, contains 350 inhabitants. The walls and towers of which the remains are seen date from Crusading times. The castle, *eṣ-Ṣubeibeh,* crowns the hill behind the town, and must have been a place of strength from the earliest

NICHES AND TABLETS AT BANIAS (CAESAREA PHILIPPI)

times. Its possession must always have been essential to the holding of the valley to the west. Immediately to the north of the town, at the foot of a steep crag, the fountain of the Jordan rises. Formerly the waters issued from a cave, *Maghāret rās en-Neba'*, "cave of the fountain head," now filled up with débris. Two niches cut in the face of the rock recall the idolatries practised here in olden times. A shrine of el-Khudr stands on the west of the spring. With the rich soil and plentiful supplies of water, in a comparatively temperate climate, average industry might turn the whole district into a garden. As it is, the surroundings are wonderfully beautiful. W. EWING

CAESAR'S HOUSEHOLD, hous'hold (**οἱ ἐκ τῆς Καίσαρος οἰκίας**, *hoi ek tēs Kaisaros oikias*, "they that are of Caesar's household," Phil **4** 22): These words occur in the epistle which Paul wrote from Rome near the end of his first imprisonment there, probably in the end of 61 AD, to the church in Philippi. They give us most interesting information in regard to the progress made in the propagation of the gospel in Rome.

It is necessary to ask, in the first place, What is meant by the words "Caesar's household"? and when the meaning of that phrase is known, then it is needful to discuss the question which rises at once, In what way did the gospel enter Caesar's household? How is it that the gospel, which at the first chiefly advanced among the poorer classes in the Empire, made its way at a bound into the very palace of the Caesars?

1. What Exactly Was Caesar's Household?

"Caesar's household" meant the whole of the persons, slaves and freemen alike, composing the establishment of the emperor in his palace on the Palatine Hill at Rome. The slaves of the imperial household formed a host in themselves. At a time when many a private citizen in Rome owned several hundreds of slaves, it need not surprise anyone to know that there was a vastly larger number of such persons in the palace of the emperor. This was a period when the city of Rome and the court of the Caesars swarmed with Asiatics, many of whom were Jews, and many of them would be in slavery, or in employment, in the imperial court. It cannot be forgotten that Poppaea, Nero's shameless consort, was a proselyte to Judaism and that she continued to advocate successfully the cause of the Jews before the emperor as occasion arose.

These persons in the emperor's palace would be employed in every conceivable capacity as household servants, cooks, bathmen, gardeners, grooms, kennel-keepers, porters, doorkeepers, messengers, secretaries, amanuenses, teachers, librarians, architects, carpenters, shoemakers, and in all other forms of service. Of course they were not all slaves: there was a very large number of freemen. The *domus* or *familia Caesaris* (represented by the Gr *oikia Kaisaros*) included the whole of the imperial household, the meanest slaves as well as the most powerful courtiers. On the character and constitution of this household we happen to possess more information than perhaps on any other department of social life in Rome. "In Rome itself, if we may judge by these inscriptions, the *domus Augusta* must have formed no inconsiderable fraction of the whole population; but it comprised likewise all persons in the emperor's service, whether slaves or freemen, in Italy and even in the provinces" (Lightfoot, *Comm. on Phil*, 171). In the list of offices filled by members of the imperial household were also such functions as those of keepers of the wardrobe or of the plate-chest; even the "tasters" formed a separate class of servants under a chief of their own. To belong to Caesar's household would secure even to the lowest grade of slaves substantial privileges and immunities, and would give a certain social importance, which made this position a valued one. An office in the emperor's household, however mean, was thought of so highly, that in the monumental inscriptions such a fact is recorded with scrupulous care.

The next inquiry is, How did the gospel win its way into Caesar's household? And, first, there

2. How Did the Gospel Enter into Caesar's Household?

is no need at all to suppose that the gospel was unknown, even in the palace, previous to the arrival of Paul in Rome. For in that numerous household of the emperor there would be Jews, perhaps many of them; and all the Jews were at that time filled with Messianic hopes, and thus were ready to listen to the gospel.

3. The Gospel Known There before Paul's Arrival

As soon therefore as the gospel entered Rome, as soon as it was proclaimed in the many synagogues there, these members of Caesar's household could not fail, equally with the other members of the synagogue, to hear the story of Jesus Christ and of His cross and resurrection. A fact such as this, that the gospel was known in Rome previous to Paul's arrival there, is quite sufficient to account for the other fact, that the gospel was known in Caesar's palace.

But the propagation of the gospel received a great impetus and help forward, when Paul arrived

4. The Gospel Advances in the Palace

in the city. For although he was a "bound prisoner," his wrist fastened by an iron chain, day and night, to the soldier who guarded him, he was able to "preach the kingdom of God and to teach those things which concern the Lord Jesus Christ, with all confidence, no man forbidding him" (Acts **28** 31 AV). And in this way the gospel would again reach members of the emperor's household. Immediately after his arrival in Rome, Paul had put himself in communication with "the chief of the Jews"—probably the rulers of the synagogues in Rome—and many of them came to him in his lodging and conferred with him. Those chief men of the Jews expressed their great desire to hear from him what his thoughts were in regard to the hope of Israel (ver 22); and naturally all the Jews in Rome would be equally desirous to gain this information from a man of the outstanding position and character of Paul. The Jewish community in Rome had for years past been permeated with the hope of the coming of the Messiah; indeed successive rumors of false Christs had kept them in a fever of excitement, which, on one occasion at least, had broken out in tumult, so strong was their hope of His speedy appearing. Thus it would come about, as a matter of course, that the gospel would reach all the Jews in Rome, and from this knowledge of Jesus, whom Paul proclaimed, the Jews who were in the service of the emperor could not possibly be excluded.

But besides this, the fact that Paul was in daily contact and intercourse with the soldiers who

5. The Gospel Carried by Paul's Soldier-Guard

guarded him could not fail to lead to the introduction of the gospel into the regiment. And as part of the Praetorian Guard was quartered in buildings on the Palatine Hill, attached to the emperor's palace there, there was thus one other channel through which the gospel would be made known to some of those who resided in the palace of Caesar. It is thus seen that there is nothing at all surprising in the fact that there were Christians in Caesar's household.

Some of Lightfoot's suggestions and conjectures on this subject are exceedingly interesting. He reviews the names of the persons to whom Paul sends greeting in Rom **16** and compares them with the names of persons who lived at that time, and which have been found in monumental inscriptions on the *columbaria* or places of sepulture exhumed on the Appian Way. Many of the occupants of those *columbaria* were freedmen or slaves of the emperors, and were contemporaries of Paul. The result of Lightfoot's review of the names is that he claims to have established a fair presumption that among the salutations in Rom **16** some members at least of the imperial household are included (*Phil*, 177).

6. Lightfoot's Conjecture

In the household of the emperor there were necessarily many persons of high rank. Perhaps we may find a hint that the gospel had been embraced by some in the higher grades of society, in such strange facts as the execution of Titus Flavius Clemens, a man of consular rank and cousin to the emperor, and also in the fact that Flavia Domitilla, the wife of Flavius Clemens, was banished by Domitian, notwithstanding her near relationship to him, for she was the emperor's niece. Her daughter Portia also shared in the same punishment of exile. The charges brought against all three were atheism and inclination to Jewish customs: surely such charges were sufficiently vague and even self-contradictory. The opinion has been suggested that probably these three persons in the inner circle of the emperor's kinsmen were Christians.

Ramsay (*St. Paul the Traveller*, etc, 353), speaking of Lightfoot's conjectures, already referred to, writes, "In all probability he is right in thinking that all the slaves of Aristobulus (son of Herod the Great) and of Narcissus (Claudius' favorite freedman) had passed into the imperial household, and that members of their two *familiae* are saluted as Christians by Paul (Rom **16** 10 ff)."

7. Aristobulus and Narcissus

The fact of greatest interest in the whole subject is, that in society so profligate and corrupt as the court of Nero, there were "saints," Christian men whose garments were clean and who kept themselves unspotted from the world amid surroundings so dreadful and in temptation so unceasing; that the gospel was known and obeyed and loved, and that hearts and lives were loyal to Christ even in the palace of Nero Caesar. JOHN RUTHERFURD

CAGE, kāj (כְּלוּב, *kelūbh*; **φυλακή**, *phulakē*): The earliest known form of cage made to confine a bird, for the pleasure of its song or the beauty of its coloring, was a crude affair of willows or other pliable twigs. Later cages were made of pottery, and now they are mostly made of wire. References in the Bible make it very clear that people were accustomed to confine in cages such birds as they esp. prized for pets, or to detain them for market purposes. James indicated that cages were common when he wrote (**3** 7): "For every kind of beasts and birds . . . . is tamed, and hath been tamed by mankind." In Job (**41** 5) we find these lines

"Wilt thou play with him as with a bird?
Or wilt thou bind him for thy maidens?"

The only way to play with a bird is to confine it so that it grows accustomed to you and thus loses fear. Jeremiah compared the civil state of Judah to a "cage [crate] full of birds" (**5** 27), "the houses of the rich being stuffed with craftily-obtained wealth and articles of luxury" (*HDB*). The sale of sparrows as an article of food still continues in the eastern markets. Jesus referred to this (Mt **10** 29) and it was He who entered the temple and overthrew "the seats of them that sold the doves" (Mt **21** 12). In Rev **18** 2 we find a reference to "a hold [AV "cage"] of every unclean and hateful bird." See also Ecclus **11** 30.

GENE STRATTON-PORTER

CAIAPHAS, kā'a-fas, kī'a-fas (**Καϊάφας**, *Kaïáphas;* Caiaphas = Kephas [cf Dods in *Expositor's Gr Test*, I, 803], and has also been interpreted as meaning "depression"): Caiaphas was the surname of Joseph, a son-in-law of Annas (cf Jn **18** 13), who filled the post of high priest from about 18–36 AD, when he was deposed by Vitellius (cf Jos, *Ant*, XVIII, ii, 2; iv, 3). He is mentioned by Lk as holding office at the time of John the Baptist's preaching in the wilderness (Lk **3** 2).

Caiaphas took a leading part in the trial and condemnation of Jesus. It was in his court or palace that the chief priests (Sadducees) and Pharisees, who together constituted the Sanhedrin, assembled "that they might take Jesus by subtlety, and kill him" (cf Mt **26** 3.4; Jn **11** 49). The regal claims of the new Messiah and the growing fame of His works had made them to dread both the vengeance of imperial Rome upon their nation, and the loss of their own personal authority and prestige (cf Jn **11** 48). But Caiaphas pointed a way out of their dilemma: let them bide their time till the momentary enthusiasm of the populace was spent (cf Mt **26** 5), and then by the single sacrifice of Jesus they could at once get rid of a dangerous rival and propitiate the frowns of Rome (cf Jn **11** 49.50; **18** 14). The commentary of St. John upon this (Jn **11** 51.52) indicates how the death of Jesus was indeed to prove a blessing not only for Israel but also for all the children of God; but not in the manner which the cold-blooded statecraft of Caiaphas intended. The advice of the high priest was accepted by the Sanhedrin (ver 53), and they succeeded in arresting Jesus. After being led "to Annas first" (**18** 13), Jesus was conducted thence in bonds to Caiaphas (ver 24). According to Mt He was led immediately upon His arrest to Caiaphas (Mt **26** 57). Mk and Lk do not refer to Caiaphas by name. His conduct at this preliminary trial of Jesus (vs 57–68), its time and its procedure, were almost entirely illegal from the standpoint of the then existing Jewish law (cf JESUS CHRIST, TRIAL OF; and A. Taylor Innes, *The Trial of Jesus Christ*). False witnesses were first called, and when Jesus refused to reply to their charges, Caiaphas asked of Him if He were "the Christ, the Son of God" (ver 63). Upon Our Lord's answering "Thou hast said" (ver 64), Caiaphas "rent his garments, saying, He hath spoken blasphemy: what further need have we of witnesses? behold, now ye have heard the blasphemy" (ver 65). Upon this charge was Jesus found "worthy of death" (ver 66). Caiaphas is also mentioned in Acts **4** 6 as being among those who presided over the trial of Peter and John. C. M. KERR

CAIN, kān (קַיִן, *ḳayin*, "spear" or "smith," resembling in sound the root *ḳānāh*, "get," "acquire," Gen **4** 1 RVm, but not necessarily derived from that root; LXX **Κάϊν**, *Káïn*):

1. The Scripture Narrative

(1) In Gen **4** 1–24 Cain is the first son of Adam and Eve. His birth is hailed as a manifestation of Jeh's help. He becomes "a tiller of the ground," and brings to Jeh an offering of the produce of the soil, his brother Abel, the shepherd, bringing at the same time the fat of the firstborn of his own flock. From Cain and from his offering Jeh withholds the sign of acceptance which he grants to Abel. That the ground of this difference of treatment is to be found (so He **11** 4) in

Cain's lack of right disposition toward Jeh is shown by his behavior (see ABEL). Instead of humbling himself he gives signs of strong indignation at Jeh's refusal to favor him. Under the just rebuke of Jeh he hardens his heart and is further confirmed in impenitence. His jealousy of Abel, unrepented of, increases until it culminates in deliberate murder. Deliberate, for in Gen **4** 8 we must restore a clause to the Heb text, all the ancient VSS bearing witness, and read "And Cain said unto Abel his brother, Let us go into the field," etc. In the vain attempt to conceal his crime Cain adds falsehood to his other sins. He is cursed "from," i.e. away from, that soil upon which he poured out his brother's blood, and must become a fugitive and a wanderer, far from the immediate presence of Jeh. Although his remonstrance against the severity of his sentence displays no genuine contrition, still Jeh in pity appoints a "sign" for his protection. Cain takes up his abode in the land of Nod ("wandering"), and there builds a city and becomes the ancestor of a line which includes Jabal, forefather of tent-dwelling cattle-keepers; Jubal, forefather of musicians; Tubal-cain, forefather of smiths; and Lamech, like Cain, a man of violence. In Cain's character we see "a terrible outburst of self-will, pride, and jealousy, leading to a total and relentless renunciation of all human ties and affection." "Among the lessons or truths which the narrative teaches may be instanced: the nature of temptation, and the manner in which it should be resisted; the consequences to which an unsubdued temper may lead a man; the gradual steps by which in the end a deadly crime may be committed; the need of sincerity of purpose lest our offering should be rejected; God's care for the guilty sinner after he has been punished; the interdependence upon one another of members of the human race; and the duties and obligations which we all owe to each other" (Driver). In He **11** 4 Cain's spiritual deficiency is pointed out; 1 Jn **3** 12 observes his envy and jealousy, as "of the wicked one," and Jude ver 11 makes him a very type of the ungodly.

2. Difficulties

With few and bold strokes the story of Cain as it stands paints for us the character of the first of murderers and the scene of his detection and condemnation. To the religious purpose of the narrative all other things are made tributary. But if we cannot refrain from putting the familiar question, Who was Cain's wife? it is also impossible upon close study of Gen **4**, as it stands, to avoid asking what was the nature of the sign of Jeh's acceptance (ver 4), or of the "sign" appointed for Cain (ver 15); or what we are to think of the introduction in the midst of the narrative, without explanation, of such important institutions as sacrifice (vs 3.4) and blood-revenge (ver 14); who were the persons of whom Cain stood in fear (ver 14); who inhabited the city he built (ver 17); how the wanderer and fugitive could become the city-builder; and why the shepherd life should be represented as beginning with Abel (ver 2) and again with Jabal (ver 20); also whether the narrator means that not only the collection of men in cities (ver 17), but also animal husbandry, music and metal-working (ver 20–22) are to be looked upon with disfavor as having sprung from Cain or from his descendants? Most of these questions find their answers in one consideration: the narrative is not exhaustively complete and is not intended to be so. That a large body of racial traditions existed, from which, with the severest condensation, the author of Gen selected his material, is the conclusion forced by close examination of the Gen narrative and comparison of it with the most ancient extant traditions. "In Gen **4** these old stories are not told for their own sakes. The incompleteness and the difficulties left unsolved do not allow this assumption to be made. They form simply the material foundation, to which higher ideas and doctrines are attached" (Dillmann).

3. Critical Theories

Without going outside the Scripture text we may find strong evidence that the narrative under consideration is founded in part upon ancient sources. Let the line of Cain (**4** 17–24) be compared with that of Seth (**5** 1–29):

CAINITE	SETHITE
Adam ("man")	Adam ("man")
	Seth
	Enosh ("man")
Cain	Kenan
Enoch	Mahalalel
Irad	Jared
Mehujael	Enoch
Methushael	Methuselah
Lamech	Lamech
Jabal, Jubal, Tubal-cain	Noah
	Shem, Ham, Japhet

The Heb forms of the names show even more clearly that Cain = Kenan, Irad = Jared, Methushael = Methuselah; a single transposition, that of the first and third names after Cain, brings the two Enochs together, and likewise the similar names Mehujael and Mahalalel. Thus we have six names nearly or quite identical; seven ancestors in one list and ten in the other, ending in both cases with a branching into three important characters. Resemblances equally certain, though not by any means so obvious, exist between the names in this double list and the names of the ten kings of Babylonia who reigned before the Flood, as the latter are given by Berosus, the Babylonian historian of the 3d cent. BC (see Skinner, Driver, Sayce as below). Thus one source of which the author in Gen **4** made use appears to have been an ancient list in genealogical form, by which the first of mankind was linked with the beginnings of civilized institutions and arts. Another part of his material was the story of a brother's murder of a brother (**4** 1–16). Many maintain at this point that the narrative must be based upon the doings of tribes, rather than of individuals. It is true that not seldom in the OT tribal history is related under individual names (cf Gen **49**; Jgs **1**, and the tables of tribes in Gen **25** 1–4; **36**); yet the tribe referred to can hardly be the Kenites of the OT, who appear as the close allies of Israel, not esp. bloodthirsty or revengeful, and haunted by no shadow of early crime against a brother tribe (see KENITES). The indications in **4** 1–16 of a developed state of society and a considerable population may go to show that the narrative of the murder was not originally associated with the sons of the first man. Thus there is room to suppose that in the process of condensation and arrangement Cain, son of Adam; Cain, the murderer; and Cain, city-builder and head of a line of patriarchs, have been made one. The critical conclusions here epitomized are indeed reached by a delicate and difficult process; but it is asserted in their favor that they make possible the removal of difficulties which could be explained in no other manner. The question which will arise with many, What theory of inspiration can be held consistently with the application of such critical processes? is dealt with at length by most modern commentators (see CRITICISM; INSPIRATION).

LITERATURE.—A. Dillmann, *Genesis* (ET); S. R. Driver, *Genesis* ("Westminster Commentaries"); H. E. Ryle, *Early Narratives of Genesis;* J. Skinner, *Genesis* (*ICC*); A. H. Sayce, "Archaeology of the Book of Genesis," *Expos T*, August, 1910, June, 1911.

(2) In Josh **15** 57, RV KAIN, which see. See also KENITES. F. K. FARR

CAINAN, kā′nan, kā̆-ī′nan (**Καϊνάν**, *Kaïnán*): (1) Gr form of Kenan (Lk **3** 37): also AV form in OT (except 1 Ch **1** 2).

(2) A son of Arphaxad (Lk **3** 36), omitted in Gen **10** 24; **11** 12.

CAKE. See BREAD.

CALAH, kā′la (כָּלַח, *kālaḥ;* **Χάλαχ**, *Chálach*, also *Chálak* or *Kálach;* in Assyr *Kalḫu, Kalḫa, Kalḫi, Kalaḫ*): The name of one of the great cities of Nimrod (Gen **10** 11), or rather, Asshur (text), which formed, with Nineveh, Resen between Calah and Nineveh, and Rehoboth-Ir (probably lying more to the N.), Asshur's great fourfold capital. The meaning of the name is unknown, but if a Sumerian etymology be accepted, some such signification as "Holy Gate" (*Ka-laḫ*) or the like—a parallel to *Ka-dingira*=*Bâb-îli*, "Gate of God" (see Babel, Babylon)—might be regarded as possible.

1. Date of the City's Foundation

As Nineveh is mentioned by Ḥammurabi, who reigned about 2000 BC, it is clear that that city was already, in his time, an important place; and the passage in Gen **10** 11 implies, though it does not actually prove, that Calah was of about the same period. The Assyr king Aššur-naṣir-âpli (cir 885 BC) states that Calah was made (probably=founded) by Shalmaneser (I) cir 1300 BC, but this is possibly simply an indication that he rebuilt it. Later on, the site seems to have become neglected, for Aššur-naṣir-âpli states that,

2. Early References to the City

the city having fallen into ruin, he rebuilt it, and it thereafter became practically the capital of the country, for he not only reërected or restored its shrines and temples—the temple of Ninip, with the god's image; the temple of "the Lady of the Land," and the temples of Sin, Gula, and Enlil—but he also received tribute there. Among his other works may be mentioned the water-channel Pati-ḫengala, and the plantations, whose fruits, apparently, he offered to the god Aššur (Asshur), and the temples of the city. It also became a favorite place of residence for the later kings of Assyria, who built palaces, and restored the city's temples from time to time.

3. Its Position

Calah occupied the roughly triangular tract formed by the junction of the Greater Zab (r.) with the Tigris (l.), which latter stream anciently flowed rather closer to the western wall than it does now, and would seem to have separated the small town represented by Selamiyeh from the extensive ruins of Calah, which now bear the name of *Nimroud*. The main ruins are situated on a large, rectangular platform on the bank of the old bed of the Tigris. The most prominent edifice

4. The Temple-Tower

was the great Temple-tower at the N.W. corner—a step-pyramid (*ziqqurat*) like the Bab towers, constructed of brick faced with stone, and rising, in stages, to a height of cir 126 ft., probably with a sanctuary at the top (see Babel, Tower of). A long vault occupies the basement-stage of this structure, and caused Sir A. H. Layard, its discoverer, to regard it as the probable traditional tomb of Ninus, under whose shadow the tragedy of Pyramis and Thisbe took place. Ovid (*Metam.* iv.98) describes the tomb of Ninus as having been situated "at the entrance of Nineveh," and, if this be correct, Calah must have been regarded as the southern portion of that great city, which, on a preaching journey, may well have taken three days (Jon **3** 3) to traverse, provided Khorsabad was in reality its northern extremity.

5. The Temples and Palaces

The platform upon which the temple-tower of Calah was situated measures cir 700×400 yds., and the portion not occupied by that erection afforded space for temples and palaces. In the center of the E. side of this platform lie the remains of the palace of Aššur-naṣir-âpli, the chambers and halls of which were paneled with sculptured and inscribed slabs, the principal doorways being flanked with finely carved winged and human-headed lions and bulls. In the S.E. corner are the remains of the palace of Esarhaddon, built, at least in part, with material taken from the palace of Tiglath-pileser IV, which was situated in the S. portion of the platform. The remains of this last are, as a result of this spoliation, exceedingly meager. The S.W. corner of the platform contains the remains of the last palace built on the site—a very inferior erection constructed for Aššur-êtil-îlâni (cir 626 BC). One of the temples on this platform was that dedicated to Ninip, situated at the S.W. corner of the temple-tower. The left-hand entrance was flanked by man-headed lions, while the sides of the right-hand entrance were decorated with slabs showing the expulsion of the evil spirit from the temple—a spirited sculpture now in the Nimroud Gallery of the British Museum.

6. The Temple of Ninip

On the right-hand side of the entrance was an arch-headed slab with a representation of King Aššur-naṣir-âpli in low relief, standing in the usual conventional attitude. Before it stood a stone tripod altar, implying that Divine honors were paid to this king. (Both these are now in the British Museum.) The remains of another temple were found to the E. of this, and there are traces of further buildings at other points of the platform.

7. The Sculptures of Aššur-naṣir-âpli

The slabs from Aššur-naṣir-âpli's palace show this king's warlike expeditions, but as descriptive lettering is wanting, the campaigns cannot be identified. Notwithstanding this disadvantage, however, they are of considerable importance, showing, as they do, incidents of his various campaigns—the crossing of rivers, the march of his armies, the besieging of cities, the reception of tribute, the life of the camp and hunting the lion and the wild bull. The reliefs from the temples, which are much larger and finer, show the king engaged in various religious ceremonies and ritual acts, and are among the most striking examples of Assyr sculpture. When looking at these works of art, the student's thoughts go back with thankfulness to those Assyrians who, through the generations, cared for and preserved these monuments, though the vandalism of Esarhaddon in dressing off the slabs of Tiglath-pileser IV to carve his own bas-reliefs thereon will ever be regretted.

8. The City Walls

The site is described as being 14 miles S. of Kouyunjik (Nineveh) and consists of an inclosure formed of narrow mounds still having the appearance of walls. Traces of no less than 108 towers, the city's ancient defences, are said to be visible even now on the N. and E., where the walls were further protected by moats. The area which the walls inclose—about 2,331×2,095 yds.—would contain about 1,000 acres.

Layard, *Nineveh and Its Remains*, and *Nineveh and Babylon*, still remain the standard works upon the subject, and his *Monuments of Nineveh* gives the most complete collection of the sculptures found. See also George Smith, *Assyrian Discoveries*, and Rassam, *Asshur and the Land of Nimrod*.

T. G. Pinches

CALAMITY, ka-lam′i-ti (אֵיד, *'ēdh*, "a load" or "burden" under which one is crushed, hence "misfortune"; הַיָּה, *hayyāh*, הַוָּה, *hawwāh*, "fall," "ruin," the latter word used only in pl.; רַע, *ra'*, "evil in essence," hence "adversity," once only, Ps **141** 5, RV "wickedness"): Purely an OT term, signifying adversities—natural, but more often those that result from wickedness or moral evil. Various kinds: (1) *folly*, "a foolish son" (Prov **19** 13); (2) *disease, poverty, bereavement*, as in Job's experience (Job **6** 2; **30** 13); (3) *persecution* (2 S **22** 19; Ps **18** 18); (4) *Divine retribution and judgment* (Dt **32** 35); cf ruin of the wicked (Prov **1** 26, also 27 RV for "destruction" AV); (5) *the devastation of war* (Jer **46** 21); (6) *adversities* of any kind (Prov **27** 10).

Dwight M. Pratt

CALAMOLALUS, kal-a-mol′a-lus, -mol-ā′lus (A, **Καλαμωλάλος,** *Kalamōlálos,* B, **Καλαμωκάλος,** *Kalamōkálos*): This name is corrupt (1 Esd **5** 22). It has evidently arisen through combining the two names Lod and Hadid, in the lists of Ezr (**2** 33) and Neh (**7** 37).

CALAMUS, kal′a-mus. See Reed.

CALCOL, kal′kol, **CHALKOL,** kal′kol (כַּלְכֹּל, *kalkōl*): Mentioned in 1 K **4** 31 as one of the wise men with whom Solomon was compared. The better orthography is **Calcol** which AV gives for the same name in 1 Ch **2** 6. In the former passage, Calcol is the son of Mahol, while in the latter he is called the son of Zerah of the tribe of Judah, and a brother of Heman and Ethan.

CALDRON, kôl′drun (the rendering of קַלַּחַת, *kallaḥath,* סִיר, *ṣīr,* דּוּד, *dūdh,* אַגְמֹן, *'aghmōn*): *Ḳallaḥath* is found only in 1 S **2** 14; Mic **3** 3. It is a pot for cooking, of undefined size and characteristics, in the former passage for sanctuary use, in the latter for domestic. *Ṣīr* is tr[d] caldron in Jer **1** 13(RV); **52** 18 f(AV); Ezk **11** 3.7.11. It was distinctly a large pot, employed both for domestic use and in the sanctuary. *Dūdh* is tr[d] caldron only in 2 Ch **35** 13. It was also a pot for cooking. *'Aghmōn* is tr[d] caldron by AV in Job **41** 20, but it is a mistranslation; RV correctly has "rushes." George Ricker Berry

CALEB, kā′leb (כָּלֵב, *kālēbh;* in the light of the cognate Syr and Arab. words, the meaning is not "dog," which is כֶּלֶב, *kelebh,* in Heb, but "raging with canine madness"; **Χαλέβ,** *Chaléb*): As a person, Caleb, the son of Jephunneh, occurs in the story of the spies (Nu **13** ff). He represents the tribe of Judah as its prince (Nu **13** 6; cf ver 2). While the majority of the men sent out by Moses bring back evil report, Caleb and Hoshea, or Joshua, the son of Nun, are the only ones to counsel the invasion of the promised land (ib, 30; **14** 6 ff). Accordingly, these two alone are permitted to survive (**14** 38; **32** 12). Upon the conquest and distribution of the land by Joshua, Caleb reminds the leader of the promise made by God through Moses, and so he receives Hebron as an inheritance for himself and his descendants (Josh **14** 6–15), after driving out from thence the Anakim who were in possession of the city (**15** 14). In the ‖ account in Jgs **1** 8 ff, the dispossession of the Can inhabitants of Hebron is ascribed to Judah (ver 10). Both accounts agree in mentioning Othniel, a younger brother of Caleb, as the conqueror of Kiriath-sepher or Debir; as his reward he receives the hand of Achsah, Caleb's daughter. Achsah is given by her father a portion of the Southland; but, upon request, she obtains an abundant water supply with upper and nether springs (Josh **15** 15–19; Jgs **1** 12–15).

In 1 S **30** 14 Caleb is undoubtedly the name of a clan which is, moreover, differentiated from Judah. Modern scholars therefore assume that Caleb was originally an independent clan which in historical times merged with Judah. As Caleb is called the son of Kenaz (Jgs **1** 13) or the Kenizzite (Nu **32** 12), it is further believed that the Calebites were originally associated with an Edomite clan named Kenaz (Gen **36** 11), and that they entered their future homes in the southern part of Pal from the south. Their migration up north would then be reflected in the story of the spies.

In the genealogical tables (1 Ch **2**), Caleb is made a descendant of Judah through his father Hezron. He is the brother of Jerahmeel, and the "father" of Hebron and of other towns in Judah. (Chelubai, ver 9, is apparently identical with Caleb.)

Nabal, with whom David had an encounter, is called a Calebite, i.e. one belonging to the house of Caleb (1 S **25** 3). Max L. Margolis

CALEB-EPHRATHAH, kā′leb ef′ra-thä (AV **Caleb-ephratah,** -ef′ra-tä, כָּלֵב אֶפְרָתָה, *kālēbh 'ephrāthāh*): The place where Hezron died (1 Ch **2** 24). Many scholars, however, read with the LXX "after the death of Hezron, Caleb came unto Ephrath, the wife of Hezron, his father." The name does not occur elsewhere, and none resembling it has been recovered.

CALENDAR, kal′en-dar (Lat *calendarium,* "an account book," from *calendae,* "day on which accounts were due"): The Heb or Jewish calendar had three stages of development: the preëxilic, or Bib.; the postexilic, or Talmudic; and the post-Talmudic. The first rested on observation merely, the second on observation coupled with calculation, and the third on calculation only. In the first period the priests determined the beginning of each month by the appearance of the new moon and the recurrence of the prescribed feasts from the vernal and autumnal equinoxes. Thus the month *Abib* (*'ābhībh*), the first month of the year according to the Levitical law, in which the Passover was to be celebrated, was determined by observation (Ex **12** 2; Dt **16**). After the exile more accurate methods of determining the months and seasons came into vogue, and calculation was employed to supplement and correct observations and the calendar was regulated according to the Bab system, as is evidenced by the names of the months which are derived from it. In later times the calendar was fixed by mathematical methods (see art. "Calendar" in *Jew Enc*). The difficulty of ascertaining the first day of the new moon by observation, in the early period, led to the celebration of two days, as seems to be indicated in 1 S **20** 27. We have only four names of months belonging to the preëxilic period, and they are Phoen. Of these *Abib* (*'ābhībh*) was the first month, as already indicated, and it corresponded to *Nisan* (*nīṣān*) in the later calendar. It was the month in which the Exodus occurred and the month of the Passover (Ex **13** 4; **23** 15; **34** 18; Dt **16** 1).

The 2d month of this calendar was *Ziv* (*zīw*) (1 K **6** 1.37); *Ethanim* (*'ēthānīm*) was the 7th (1 K **8** 2), corresponding to *Tishrī* of the later calendar, and *Būl* (*būl*) the 8th, corresponded to *Marḥesvan* (*marḥeshwān*) (1 K **6** 38). There were of course other month names in this old calendar, but they have not come down to us. These names refer to the aspects of the seasons: thus *Abib* (*'ābhībh*) means grain in the ear, just ripening (Lev **2** 14; Ex **9** 31); *Ziv* (*zīw*) refers to the beauty and splendor of the flowers in the spring; *Ethanim* (*'ēthānīm*) means perennial, probably referring to living fountains; and *Būl* (*būl*) means rain or showers, being the month when the rainy season commenced. The full calendar of months used in the postexilic period is given in a table accompanying this art. The names given in the table are not all found in the Bible, as the months are usually referred to by number, but we find *Nīṣān* in Neh **2** 1 and Est **3** 7; *Ṣīwān* in Est **8** 9; *Tammūz* in Ezk **8** 14, although the term as here used refers to a Phoen god after whom the month was named; *'Ĕlūl* occurs in Neh **6** 15; *Kīṣlēw* (ARV "chislev") in Neh **1** 1 and Zec **7** 1; *Ṭēbhēth* in Est **2** 16; *Sh[e]bhāṭ* in Zec **1** 7 and *'Ădhār* in Ezr **6** 15 and several times in Est. These months were lunar and began with the new moon, but their position in regard to the seasons varied somewhat because of the intercalary month about every three years.

The year (שָׁנָה, *shānāh*) originally began in the autumn, as appears from Ex **23** 16 and **34** 22, where it is stated that the feast of Ingathering should be at the end of the year; the Sabbatic year began, also, in the 7th month of the calendar year (Lev **25** 8–10), indicating that this had been the beginning of the year. This seems to have been a reckoning for civil purposes, while the year beginning with *Nīsān* was for ritual and sacred purposes. This resulted from the fact that the great feast of the Passover occurred in this month and the other feasts were regulated by this, as we see from such passages as Ex **23** 14–16 and Dt **16** 1–17. Jos (*Ant*, I, iii, 3) says: "Moses appointed that *Nīsān*, which is the same with *Xanthicus*, should be the first month of their festivals, because he brought them out of Egypt in that month; so that this month began the year as to all solemnities they observed to the honor of God, although he preserved the original order of the months as to selling and buying and other ordinary affairs." A similar custom is still followed in Turkey, where the Mohammedan year is observed for feasts, the pilgrimage to Mecca and other sacred purposes, while the civil year begins in March O.S.

Hebrew		Greek		
Nīṣān	נִיסָן	*Xanthikós*	Ξανθικός	March–April
'Iyyār	אִיָּר	*Artemísios*	'Αρτεμίσιος	April–May
Ṣīwān	סִיוָן	*Daísios*	Δαίσιος	May–June
Tammūz	תַּמּוּז	*Pánemos*	Πάνεμος	June–July
'Ābh	אָב	*Lṓos*	Λῷος	July–August
'Ĕlūl	אֱלוּל	*Gorpiaíos*	Γορπιαῖος	August–September
Tishrī	תִּשְׁרִי	*Huperberetaíos*	'Υπερβερεταῖος	September–October
Marḥeshwān	מַרְחֶשְׁוָן	*Díos*	Δῖος	October–November
Kiṣlēw	כִּסְלֵו	*Apellaíos*	'Απελλαῖος	November–December
Ṭēbhēth	טֵבֵת	*Audunaíos*	Αὐδυναῖος	December–January
Sh^{e}bhāṭ	שְׁבָט	*Perítios*	Περίτιος	January–February
'Ădhār	אֲדָר	*Dústros*	Δύστρος	February–March

CALENDAR OF MONTHS USED IN THE POSTEXILIC PERIOD.

The year was composed of 12 or 13 months according as to whether it was ordinary or leap year. Intercalation is not mentioned in Scripture, but it was employed to make the lunar correspond approximately to the solar year, a month being added whenever the discrepancy of the seasons rendered it necessary. This was regulated by the priests, who had to see that the feasts were duly observed at the proper season. The intercalary month was added after the month of *'Ădhār* and was called the second *'Ădhār* (שֵׁנִי, *shēnī*, וַאֲדָר, *wa-'ădhār*, "*and* Adar"), and, as already indicated, was added about once in 3 years. More exactly, 4 years out of every 11 were leap years of 13 months (*Jew Enc*, art. "Calendar"), this being derived from the Bab calendar. If, on the 16th of the month *Nīṣān*, the sun had not reached the vernal equinox, that month was declared to be the second *'Ădhār* and the following one *Nīṣān*. This method, of course, was not exact and about the 4th cent. of our era the mathematical method was adopted. The number of days in each month was fixed, seven having 30 days, and the rest 29. When the intercalary month was added, the first *'Ădhār* had 30 and the second 29 days. H. PORTER

CALF, käf (עֵגֶל, *'ēghel;* פַּר, *par*, or פָּר, *pār*, often rendered "bullock"): The etymology of both words is uncertain, but the former has a close ‖ in the Arab. *'ijl*, "calf." *Par* is generally used of animals for sacrifice, *'ēghel*, in that and other senses. *'Ēghel* is used of the golden calves and frequently in the expression, *'ēghel marbēḳ*, "fatted calf," or "calf of the stall," the latter being the literal meaning (1 S **28** 24; Jer **46** 21; Am **6** 4; Mal **4** 2).

At the present day beef is not highly esteemed by the people of the country, but mutton is much prized. In the houses of the peasantry it is common to see a young ram being literally stuffed with food, mulberry or other leaves being forced into its mouth by one of the women, who then works the sheep's jaw with one hand. The animal has a daily bath of cold water. The result is deliciously fat and tender mutton. Such an animal is called a *ma'lūf*. From the same root we have *ma'laf*, "manger," suggestive of the Heb *marbēḳ*, "stall."

The calf for sacrifice was usually a male of a year old. Other references to calves are: "to skip like a calf" (Ps **29** 6); "the calf and the young lion and the fatling together" (Isa **11** 6); "a habitation deserted . . . . there shall the calf feed, and there shall he lie down, and consume the branches thereof" (Isa **27** 10). See CATTLE.

ALFRED ELY DAY

CALF, käf, **GOLDEN**, gōl'd'n:

I. THE NAME
II. ANCIENT CALF WORSHIP
 1. Narrative of Aaron's Golden Calf
 2. Jeroboam's Golden Calves
III. ATTITUDE OF ELIJAH TO THE BULL SYMBOLS
IV. ATTITUDE OF AMOS AND HOSEA TO THE BULL SYMBOLS
LITERATURE

I. The Name.—The term עֵגֶל, *'ēghel*, is the ordinary Heb name for a male calf and is as flexible as the Eng. name, applying to any animal from one a year old (Mic **6** 6) or perhaps younger (Lev **9** 3; **12** 6) to one three years old (Gen **15** 9; cf Jer **34** 18.19). It has been thought that the habitual use of this diminutive term for the golden bulls which Aaron and Jeroboam set up—esp. as it is twice made feminine (Hos **10** 5; **13** 2)—was intended to indicate their small size and thus to express contempt for them. This however, though plausible, is by no means certain. It was not their size which made these bulls contemptible in the eyes of the prophets, and besides there were no life-size bulls of molten gold in any surrounding countries so far as known. The reference to female calves that were kissed (**13** 2), presumably at Bethel, may refer not to the worship of the bulls, but to their female counterparts, since in all other countries such female deities invariably accompanied the bull gods. Bethel may be esp. mentioned because it was the "king's sanctuary" (Am **7** 13) or because of the multitude of altars and high places found there (Hos **10** 8; cf **8** 11; Am **5** 26). False worship is also mentioned in connection with Jeroboam's apostasy, at Gilgal and Gilead (Hos **4** 15; **12** 11;

Am **4** 4; **5** 5), Samaria (Hos **8** 6; **10** 5; **13** 2.16); and Beersheba (Am **5** 5; **8** 14) where no bulls had been set up by Jeroboam so far as stated. That these places receive more condemnation than Dan —which is explicitly mentioned in only one passage (**8** 14) though it was a chief center of the bull worship (1 K **12** 30)—may be due to the fact that the worship of the female deity was the more popular. This was certainly true in neighboring countries and also in other cities in Pal, as has recently been proved by the excavations (see below).

II. Ancient Calf Worship.—The origin of animal worship is hidden in obscurity, but reverence for the bull and cow is found widespread among the most ancient historic cults. Even in the prehistoric age the influence of the bull symbol was so powerful that it gave its name to one of the most important signs of the Zodiac, and from early historic times the horns of the bull were the familiar emblem of the rays of the sun, and solar gods were very commonly represented as bull-gods (Jensen, *Kosmologie*, 62–90; Winckler, *Altorientalische Forschungen*, 1901–5, *passim;* Jeremias, *Das Alter der bab. Astronomie*, 1909, *passim*). The Egyptians, close neighbors of the Hebrews, in all eras from that of the Exodus onward, worshipped living bulls at Memphis (not Mendes, as *EB*) and Heliopolis as incarnations of Ptah and Ra, while one of the most elaborate rituals was connected with the life-size image of the Hathor-cow (Naville, *Deir el Bahari*, Part I [1907], 163–67), while the sun was revered as the "valiant bull" and the reigning Pharaoh as "Bull of Bulls." But far more important in this connection is the fact that "calf" worship was almost if not quite universal among all the ancient Sem peoples. If the immediate ancestors of Abraham did not revere this deity, they were certainly quite unlike their relatives, the Babylonians, among whom, according to all tradition, they lived before they migrated to Pal (Gen **11** 28.30; Jos, *Ant*, I, vi, 5), for the Babylonians revered the bull as the symbol of their greatest gods, Anu and Sin and Marduk—the ideograph of a young bullock forming a part of the latter's name—while Hadadrimmon, an important Amorite deity, whose attributes remarkably resemble those of Jeh (see Ward, *AJSL*, XXV, 175–85; Clay, *Amurru* [1909], 87–89), is pictured standing on the back of a bull. In Phoenicia also the bull was a sacred animal, as well as in northern Syria where it ranked as one of the chief Hittite deities, its images receiving devout worship (see further, Sayce, *Enc of Rel. and Ethics*, s.v. "Bull"). Among all these peoples the cow goddess was given at least equal honor. In Babylonia the goddess Ishtar has the cow for her symbol on very ancient seal cylinders, and when this nude or half-nude goddess appears in Pal she often stands on a bull or cow (see William Hayes Ward, *Cylinders and Other Ancient Oriental Seals*), and under slightly different forms this same goddess is revered in Arabia, Moab, Phoenicia, Syria and elsewhere, while among the Sem Canaanites the bull was the symbol of Baal, and the cow of Astarte (see particularly Barton, *Hebraica*, IX, 133–63; X, 1–74, and *Semitic Origins*, ch vii; Driver, "Astarte" in *DB*). Recent excavations in Pal have shown that during all eras no heathen worship was as popular as that of Astarte in her various forms (see S. A. Cook, *Rel. of Ancient Pal*, 1909). That she once is found wearing ram's horns (*PEFS* [1903], 227) only reveals her nature more clearly as the goddess of fertility. Her relation to the sacred fish at Carnion in Gilead and to the doves of Ascalon, as well as to female prostitution and to Nature's "resurrection" and fruitage, had been previously well known, as also her relation to the moon which governs the seasons. Is there any rational *motif* which can account for this widespread "calf" worship? Is it conceivable that this cult could so powerfully influence such intelligent and rather spiritually-minded nations as the Egyptians and Babylonians if it were wholly irrational and contained no spiritual content? And is there no rational explanation behind this constant fusion of the deity which controls the breeding of cattle with the deity which controls vegetation? How did the bull come to represent the "corn spirit," so that the running of a bull through the corn (the most destructive act) came to presage good crops; and how did the rending of a bull, spilling his life blood on the soil, increase fertility? (See Fraser, *Golden Bough*, II, 291–93, 344.) The one real controlling *motif* of all these various representations and functions of the "calf" god may be found in the ancient awe, esp. among the Semites, for the *Mystery of Life*. This seems to offer a sufficient reason why the bull, which is a most conspicuous example of life-giving power, should be so closely connected with the reproductive processes of the animal and vegetable kingdoms and also with the sun, which from earliest historic times was considered as preëminently the "giver of life." Bull worship was not always an exhibition of gross animalism, but, certainly in Bible times, often represented a concept which was the product of reflection upon one of the deepest mysteries of Nature. Few hymns in Egypt or Babylon express higher spiritual knowledge and aspiration than those addressed to the bull gods or to others honored with this title, e.g. this one to the god Sin of Ur, the "heifer of Anu," "Strong young bull, with strong horns, ... with beard of lapis-lazuli color . . . . self-created, full of developed fruit . . . . Mother-womb who has taken up his abode, begetter of all things, exalted habitation among living creatures; O merciful gracious father, in whose hand rests the life of the whole world; O Lord, thy divinity is full of awe like the far-off heaven and the broad ocean!" (Rogers, *Religion of Babylonia and Assyria* [1908], 164). Many modern scholars believe that the primitive Egyptians and Babylonians really thought of their earthly and heavenly gods as animals (see esp. Maspero, *Bulletin critique*, 1886; *Revue de l'histoire des religions*, 1888), but it seems certain that at least as early as the date of the Exodus these stars and beasts were not regarded by all as being themselves deities, but rather as symbols or representations of deity (Davis and Cobern, *Ancient Egypt*, 281–89; Brugsch, *Die Aegyptologie*, I, 135; Chwolsohn, *Die Ssabier u. der Ssabismus*, II, 134).

1. Narrative of Aaron's Golden Calf

The text of Ex **32** is certainly composite (see e.g. Bacon's "Exodus" in loc. and *DB*), and some words and phrases are a verbal duplicate of the narrative of Jeroboam's calf worship (cf Ex **32** 4 with 1 K **12** 28, and see ‖ columns in Driver's *Deuteronomy*). Some Bible critics so analyze the text as to make the entire calf story a later element, without ancient basis, added to some short original statement like Ex **32** 7–11, for the sake of satirizing Jeroboam's bull worship and its non-Levitical priesthood (see e.g. Kuenen, *Hexateuch*). Most recent critics have however accepted the incident as an ancient memory or historic fact attested by the oldest sources, and used thus by the Deuteronomist (Dt **9**), though the verbal form may have been affected by the later editor's scorn of the northern apostasy. It seems clearly unreasonable to suppose that a Heb writer at any era would so fiercely abuse his own ancestors, without any traditional basis for his statements, merely for the sake of adding a little more which cast reproach upon his northern neighbors, and it seems equally unlikely that any such baseless charges would have been accepted as true by the slandered nation. The old expositors, accepting the essential historicity of the account, generally followed Philo and the early Fathers in supposing this calf of gold was an image of the Apis or Mnevis bulls of Egypt, and this is occasionally yet advocated by some Egyptologists (e.g. Steindorf, *Ancient Egypt* [1903], 167; cf also Jeremias, *OT in Light of Ancient East* [1911], II, 138). The objections made to this view by the skeptics of the 18th cent., based on the supposed impossibility of such chemical and mechanical skill being possessed at that era, have mostly been made obsolete by recent discovery. The common modern objection that this could not have been Apis worship because the Apis was a living bull, has much more weight, though images of Serapis are not uncommon and were probably worshipped in the temple itself. It may be added that a renaissance of this worship occurred at this very era. So Erman, *Handbook of Egyp Rel.* (1907), 23–79. Modern Bible scholars, however, are practically unanimous in the opinion that the Golden Calf, if worshipped at all, must have been a representation of a Sem, not an Egyp, deity. In favor of this it may be suggested: (1) It was an era when each deity was considered as the god of a particular country and it would seem impossible that a native Egyp god should be thought of as joining with Egypt's enemies and assisting them to reach a land over which he had no control. (2) The Israelitish religion shows little influence from Egypt, but was immensely influenced from Canaan and Babylon, Apis only being mentioned once (Jer **46** 20 [trd "heifer"]; cf Ezk **20** 7.8, and see Brugsch, *Steininschrift und Bibelwort, passim*, and Robertson, *Early Religion of Israel*, 217). (3) The bull and cow are now known to have been ordinary symbols for the most popular deities which were worshipped by all the race-relatives of the Hebrews and nowhere more devoutly than in Canaan and in the adjoining districts (see above). (4) Some of the chief gods of the pasture land of Goshen, where the Hebrews had resided for centuries (Gen **47** 6; **50** 8), were Sem gods which were worshipped not only by the Edomitic Bedawin and other foreigners living there by the "pools of Pithom" (cf Ex **1** 11) but by the native Egyptians, Ramses II even naming a daughter after one of these. The special god of this district had as its symbol a bull calf, and one inscription actually speaks of the statue of a "golden calf of 600 pounds weight" which it was the custom to dedicate annually to one of these Sem gods, while another inscription mentions a statue of gold "a cubit in height" (Breasted, *Ancient Records of Egypt* [1905], III, 630–38; Naville, *Goshen, Store City of Pithom;* Erman, *Handbook*, 173–74; Brugsch, op. cit.). (5) The chief proof, however, is the statement of the text that the feast in connection with this worship was a "feast to Jehovah" (Ex **32** 5). When Moses disappeared for forty days in the Mount, it was not unnatural that the people should turn back to the visible symbols worshipped by their ancestors, and should give to them the new name or new attributes which had been attached to deity by Moses. The worship was condemned for much the same reason as that of Jeroboam's calves (see next section).

2. Jeroboam's Golden Calves

Though this passage (1 K **12** 26–33; cf 2 Ch **10** 14.15) may have been reëdited later, "there is no reason to infer that any detail of fact is underived from the olden time" (Burney, *Heb Text of Kings* [1902], and *DB*). These calves which Jeroboam set up were doubtless bulls (1 K **12** 28, Heb) but at least as early as Hosea's time it seems probable (see above) that the more licentious worship of the feminine principle had been added to the official worship (Hos **10** 5; **13** 2, Heb). This which elsewhere naturally and universally accompanied the bull worship could most truly be called "the sin of Samaria" (Am **8** 14) and be classed as the "sin of Jeroboam" (1 K **14** 9.16; **16** 26; 2 K **10** 29). There is no sufficient reason for explaining the term "molten" in any other than its most natural and usual sense (Ex **32** 8.24; 2 K **17** 16; Dt **9** 16), for molded metal idols were common in all eras in Pal and the surrounding countries, though the core of the image might be molten or graven of some inferior metal overlaid with gold (Isa **30** 22; **40** 19, Heb; Dt **7** 25; Ex **32** 4). These bull images were undoubtedly intended to represent Jeh (yet cf Robertson, op. cit., and Orr, *Problem of OT* [1906], 145). The text explicitly identifies these images with Aaron's calf (1 K **12** 28), so that nearly all the reasons given above to prove that Aaron's image represented not an Egyp but an ancient Sem deity are equally valid here. To these various other arguments may be added: (1) The text itself states that it is Jeh who brought them from Egypt (Hos **2** 15; **12** 13; **13** 4), whom they call "My lord," and to whom they swear (Hos **2** 16 AVm; **4** 15); and to whom they present their wine offerings, sacrifices and feasts (Hos **8** 13; **9** 4.5, Heb; cf Am **5** 8). (2) Jehu, though he destroyed all Baal idols, never touched these bulls (2 K **10** 28.29). (3) The ritual, though freer, was essentially that of the Jerus temple (1 K **12** 32; Hos **5** 6; Am **4** 5; **5** 22.23; see, Oettli, *Greifswalder Studien* [1895], quoted in *DB*, I, 342). (4) Even the southern prophets recognized that it was Jeh who had given Jeroboam the kingdom (1 K **11** 31; **12** 15.24) and only Jeh worship could have realized Jeroboam's purpose of attaching to the throne by this cult such devout citizens as would otherwise be drawn to Jerus to worship. It was to guard against this appeal which the national sanctuary made to devout souls that this counter worship had been established. As Budde says, "A foreign cult would only have driven the devout Ephraimites the more surely over to Jerusalem" (*Rel. of Israel* [1899], 113). Jeroboam was not attempting to shock the conscience of his religious adherents by making heathenism the state religion, but rather to win these pious worshippers of Jeh to his cause. (5) The places selected for the bull worship were places already sacred to Jeh. This was preëminently true of Bethel which, cents. before Jerus had been captured from the Jebusites, had been identified with special revelations of Jehovah's presence (Gen **13** 3.4; **28** 19; **31** 13; **35** 15; 1 S **7** 16; Hos **12** 4). (6) The history shows that the allegiance of his most pious subjects was retained (1 K **12** 20) and that not even Elijah fled to the Southern, supposing that the Northern Kingdom had accepted the worship of heathen gods as its state religion. Instead of this, Elijah, though the boldest opponent of the worship of Baal, is never reported as uttering one word against the bull worship at Dan and Bethel.

III. Attitude of Elijah to the Bull Symbols.—This surprising silence is variously explained. A few scholars, though without any historic or textual evidence for the charge, are sure that the Bible narratives (though written by southern men) are fundamentally defective at this point, otherwise they would report Elijah's antagonism to this cult. Other few, equally without evidence, are comfortably sure that he fully approved the ancient ancestral calf cult. Others, with more probability, explain his position on the ground that, though he may not have favored the bull symbol—which was never used by the Patriarchs so far as known, and certainly was not used as a symbol of Jeh in the

Southern Kingdom, or Hosea the northern prophet would have spoken of it—yet being himself a northern man of old ideals and simple habits, Elijah may have believed that, even with this handicap, the freer and more democratic worship carried on at the ancient holy places in the N. was less dangerous than the elaborate and luxurious ritual of the aristocratic and exclusive priesthood of the S., which insisted upon political and religious centralization, and was dependent upon such enormous revenues for its support (cf 1 K **12** 10.14). At any rate it is self-evident that if Elijah had turned against Jeroboam and the state religion, it would have divided seriously the forces which needed to unite, in order to oppose with all energy the much fouler worship of Baal which just at this crisis, as never before or afterward, threatened completely to overwhelm the worship of Jeh.

IV. Attitude of Amos and Hosea to the Bull Symbols.—It is easy to see why Hosea might fiercely condemn a ritual which Elijah might rightly tolerate. (1) This calf worship may have deteriorated. Elijah lived closer to the time when the new state ritual was inaugurated and would naturally be at its best. Hosea lived at an era when he could trace the history of this experiment for nearly two cents., and could see clearly that these images had not helped but greatly hindered the development of the ethical and spiritual religion of Jeh. Even if at first recognized as symbols, these images had become common idols (Hos **12** 11; **13** 2, and *passim*). "This thing *became* a sin" (1 K **12** 30; **13** 34). The history of religion shows many such instances where the visible or verbal symbol which in one era had been a real aid to devotion at a later time became positively antagonistic to it (see IMAGES). As Baal was also worshipped under the form of a calf and as Jeh himself was at times called "Baal" (Isa **54** 5; Jer **31** 32; Hos **2** 16 Heb) this unethical tendency would be accelerated, as also by the political antagonism between Judah and Ephraim and the bitter hatred between the two rival priesthoods (cf 2 Ch **11** 15; **13** 9). Certain it is that by the middle of the 8th cent. the worship at Dan and Bethel had extended itself to many other points and had become so closely affiliated with the heathen worship as to be practically indistinguishable—at least when viewed from the later prophetic standpoint. But (2) it cannot be doubted that the prophetic standpoint had changed in 200 years. As the influence of the northern worship had tended toward heathenism, so the influence of the southern worship of an imageless god had tended toward higher spiritual ideals. Elijah could not have recognized the epoch-making importance of an imageless temple. The constant pressure of this idea—God is Spirit—had developed a new spiritual conscience, which by the 8th cent. was so keen that the worship of Jeh under the form of an image was not improperly considered as almost if not quite as bad as out-and-out heathenism, just as the Reformers of the 16th cent. regarded the Roman Catholic images as little better than idols (Hos **8** 5.6; **11** 2; **13** 2; cf 2 K **17** 16.17). The influence of this new conscience is also seen in the fact that it is not simply or perhaps chiefly the "calves" which are condemned, but the spirit of ungodliness and unkindness which also made the orthodox worship in Jerus little if any better than that at Bethel (Hos **6** 4; **5** 12.14). The influence of this theology—God is Spirit—had so filled the souls of these prophets that even the sacrifices had lost their importance when unaccompanied by kindness and spiritual knowledge (Hos **6** 6; **7** 1), and it is the absence of this essential spirit, rather than the form of worship, which Amos and Hosea condemn in the Northern Kingdom (Am **2** 6–8; **3** 10; **4** 1; **5** 7.12–15.21–24; **6** 12; **8** 4–6; Hos **4** 2.3; **9** 1; **10** 12–14). These later prophets could also see, as Elijah could not possibly have seen, that unity of worship was imperatively needed, and that sacrifices in the old sacred "high places" must be discontinued. Only thus could superstitious fanaticism and religious disintegration be avoided. A miscellaneous and unregulated Jeh cult might become almost as bad as heathenism. Indeed it might be worse if it gave the Baal spirit and interpretation to Jeh worship. See also ASTROLOGY, II, 2.

LITERATURE.—Besides references above, see esp. commentaries of Dillmann and Driver on Exodus; Kuenen, *Religion of Israel;* W. R. Smith, *Religion of Semites,* 93–113 and index; König, *Hauptprobleme der altisraelitischen Religionsgeschichte;* Baethgen, *Beitr. zur semit. Religionsgeschichte;* Kittel, *History of Hebrews;* "Baal" and "Ashtoreth" in *Enc of Rel. and Ethics* (full lit.); "Golden Calf" in *Jew Enc* for Rabbinical and Mohammedan lit.

CAMDEN M. COBERN

CALF IMAGE. See IMAGES.

CALITAS, kal'i-tas (**Καλιτάς,** *Kalitás,* or **Καλειταίς,** *Kaleitaís*): One of the Levites who put away their foreign wives at the request of Esdras (Ezra), 1 Esd **9** 23, "Colius, who was called Calitas." It is the Gr form of Heb Kelita (cf ‖ passage, Ezr **10** 23, "Kelaiah, the same is Kelita"). He is also named with those who explained the law when read to the people by Esdras (1 Esd **9** 48; cf Neh **8** 7). It is not certain whether he is to be identified with the Kelita of Neh **10** 10 (one of the Levites who signed the covenant made by Nehemiah). The word probably means "dwarf."

D. MIALL EDWARDS

CALKER, kôk'ẽr. See SHIPS AND BOATS.

CALLING, kôl'ing (**κλῆσις,** *klēsis,* from *kaléō,* "I call"): Is a NT expression. The word is used chiefly by Paul, though the idea and term are found also elsewhere. It has a definite, technical sense, the invitation given to men by God to accept salvation in His kingdom through Jesus Christ. This invitation is given outwardly by the preaching of the gospel, inwardly by the work of the Holy Spirit. With reference to Israel, it is on the part of God irrevocable, not repented of. Having in His eternal counsel called this people, He intrusted them with great gifts, and because He did thus enrich them, He also, in the course of time, summoned them to fulfil the task of initiating the world into the way of salvation, and of preparing salvation for the world. Therefore He will not desert His people, for He will not revoke that call (Rom **11** 29). This calling is high or upward, in Christ, that is, made in heaven by God on account of Christ and calling man to heaven (Phil **3** 14). Similarly it is a heavenly calling (He **3** 1); also a holy calling, holy in aim, means, and end (2 Tim **1** 9). Christians are urged to walk worthy of this calling (Eph **4** 1) (ARV and RV, but AV has "vocation"). In it there is hope; it is the inspirer of hope, and furnishes for hope its supreme object (Eph **4** 4). Men are exhorted so to live that God will count them worthy of their calling (2 Thess **1** 11). They are also urged to make their calling and election sure (2 Pet **1** 10). See ELECTION. There is a somewhat peculiar use of the word in 1 Cor **1** 26 and **7** 20, namely, that condition of life in which men were when God called them, not many of them wise after the flesh, not many mighty, not many noble, some circumcised, some uncircumcised, some bond, some free, some male, some female, some married, some unmarried.

GEORGE HENRY TREVER

CALLISTHENES, ka-lis'the-nēz (**Καλλισθένης,** *Kallisthénēs*): An officer of Nicanor who was charged with the burning of the sacred portals of the temple at the time of the desecration under

Antiochus Epiphanes (168 BC). After the decisive defeat of Nicanor's army at Emmaus (165 BC) the Jews celebrated the victory in the city of their fathers and burned C. who had fled into an outhouse with others who had set the sacred gates on fire, "the meet reward of their impiety" (2 Macc **8** 33).

CALNEH, kal′ne (כַּלְנֵה, *kalnēh;* **Χαλαννή**, *Chalannē*): The name of the fourth city of Nimrod's kingdom (Gen **10** 10), the three preceding it being Babel, Erech, and Accad, i.e. the capital of the realm of Babylonia and the chief cities of three of the principal states. The meaning of the name is unknown, and many regard the identification as uncertain. G. Rawlinson thought it to be the modern *Niffer* (or *Noufar*), comparing the Talmudic (cf *Yoma'*) *Nopher*, which is said to be the same as Calneh. What place-name Calneh corresponds with in cuneiform is doubtful. Fried. Delitzsch (*Wo lag das Paradies?*) compared it with *Kul-unu*, but as we are told to pronounce this group as *Kullaba*, it seems unlikely that there is any connection between the two. The identification proposed by G. Rawlinson, however, may be regarded as being supported by the bilingual Creation-legend, in which Merodach (=Nimrod) is made the founder of Babylon, Erech and Nippur, which would in that case be three of the four cities mentioned in Gen **10** 10.

1. Identified with Nippur

The inscriptions reveal to us Nippur as a city with a glorious past. Sargon of Agadé, Sur-Engur, Dungi and all the more prominent kings of Babylonia in its larger sense interested themselves in the rebuilding and restoration of its renowned temples, so as to gain the favor of their great divinities. The city's earlier divine patrons were Enlil and Ninlil, the older Bel and Beltis, whose shrines were at the great temple-tower called Ê-kura, "the house of the land," and a poetical legend in Sumerian (dialectical) recording their visit to the city, and enumerating its sacred places, still exists (*PSBA*, March, 1911, 85 ff). Later, the chief deities of the city seem to have been Ninip, the son of Enlil, and his spouse Nin-Nipri, "the lady of Nippur." These two divine beings likewise evoked the muse of the city-scribes, who dealt with the glories of the god in a composition extending over several tablets, in which his favor to his spouse Nin-Nipri is extolled; and to whom a career very similar to that of Merodach, the head of the Bab pantheon, is attributed (*PSBA*, December, 1906, 270 ff). The great temple-tower of Niffer, which was dedicated to the god Enlil, was a very striking object among the buildings and temples of the city, and the lower stages are still in an extremely perfect condition. Most interesting, also, are the remains of streets and houses which enable the general conditions of life in ancient Babylonia to be estimated, and suggest that they are similar to those subsisting even at the present day. Our knowledge of the city is almost entirely due to the American excavations at Niffer, inaugurated by Rev. J. P. Peters, which have been most fruitful, and have shed quite a new light on the city's history. See Peters' *Nippur* (2 vols, 1887); the many volumes written or edited by Professor H. V. Hilprecht under the general title *The Babylonian Expedition of the University of Pennsylvania;* and Professor A. T. Clay's *Light on the OT from Babel* (Philadelphia, 1907). T. G. Pinches

2. Nippur's Importance

3. Its Deities and Their Legends

4. Its Ruins Today

CALNEH, kal′ne, **CALNO**, kal′no (כַּלְנֵה, *kalneh* [Am **6** 2], כַּלְנוֹ, *kalnō* [Isa **10** 9]): "Probably the Kulnia (Kullani) associated with Arpad and Hadrach, Syrian cities, in the Assyr 'tribute' list (*Western Asiatic Inscriptions*, II, 53, no. 3); *Kullanhu* about six miles from Arpad" (*HDB*, I, 344, and 1-vol *HDB*, 109).

CALPHI, kal′fī. See Chalphi.

CALVARY, kal′va-ri. See Golgotha.

CALVES, kävz, OF THE LIPS (LXX **καρπὸν χειλέων**, *karpón cheiléōn*): This is the AV rendering of a dubious Heb text in Hos **14** 2 (פָּרִים שְׂפָתֵינוּ, *pārīm sᵉphāthēnū*). The RV runs "So will we render *as* bullocks *the offering* of our lips." Strange as the text is, it may be retained, and it admits of at least a possible explanation. The prophet calls on his contemporaries to return in penitence to Jeh. Their worship should consist not of meaningless dumb ritual, but of "words"—hymns and prayers, expressive of real gratitude and of actual needs—or perhaps pledges of repentance and reform. The people respond and undertake that their worship shall consist of "calves or bullocks of lips," i.e. not of animal offerings, but of promises of reform or vows of obedience. But this explanation is forced and most modern commentators follow the LXX, which presupposes a slightly different Hebrew text, and renders פְּרִי שְׂפָתֵינוּ, *pᵉrī sᵉphāthēnū*, "fruit of our lips," i.e. adoring gratitude or, as the author of the Epistle to the He, who quotes this verse from the LXX, explains it, "sacrifice of praise" (He **13** 15). The same phrase occurs in Isa **57** 19, where it signifies gladsome gratitude. T. Lewis

CAMBYSES, kam-bī′sēz (Aram., כנבוזי; Pers, *Kambujiya;* Assyr, *Kambuzia;* Egyp, *Kambythet;* Susian, *Kanpuziya*): The older son of Cyrus, king of Persia. Some have thought that he is the Ahasuerus of Ezr **4** 6. This seems to be most improbable, inasmuch as the Heb form of Ahasuerus is the exact equivalent of the Old Pers form of Xerxes, and we have no evidence that Cambyses was ever called Xerxes.

Ancient authorities differ as to who was the mother of Cambyses. It is variously said that she was Cassandane, a Pers princess, Amytis, a Median princess, or Nititis, a daughter of Apries king of Egypt. He had one brother, Bardes or Smerdes, whom he put to death secretly shortly after his accession, probably because of an attempted rebellion. Cambyses organized an expedition for the conquest of Egypt, which was rendered successful by internal treachery and by the aid of the Phoen, Cyprian and Gr fleets. During this campaign Cambyses seems to have acted with good generalship and with clemency toward the conquered. After the subjugation of Egypt, Cyrene and Barca, the modern Tripoli, submitted to his sway. He then desired to undertake the conquest of Carthage, but was compelled to give it up, because his Phoen allies, without whose ships it was impossible for him to conduct his army in safety, refused to join in an attack upon a country that had been colonized by them. He is said to have sent an army of 50,000 men against the oasis of Jupiter Ammon. This army is said to have perished in the sands. A little less unsuccessful expedition was made against Ethiopia. After some initial successes, Cambyses was forced to return to Egypt with the shattered remains of his army. He found that the Egyptians were in revolt, led by their king Psammetichus III, whose life he had formerly spared. This revolt was put down with great harshness, the Egyp king being taken and executed, and many of the temples being destroyed. Shortly after this, Cambyses heard that a certain Magian, who claimed to be his brother Smerdes whom he had secretly put to death, had set himself up as king of Persia, and that almost the whole of his Asiatic dominions had acknowledged him as king. With the fragments of his army he started toward Persia to attack the usurper, but on the way was killed by a wound inflicted by himself, it is uncertain whether by accident or with intention. His general and cousin, Darius Hystaspis, soon put down the false Smerdis and reigned in his stead.

For two or more years Cambyses was king of Babylon, while his father was king of the lands. The son was a drunkard and subject to fits of unbridled passion, but seems to have been of good capacity as a general and as an administrator. Many of the tales that have been told against him were doubtless invented by his enemies, and he has left us no records of his own. That he married his own sisters is probable; but it must be remembered that this was the custom of the Egyp kings of that time and may have been of the Pers kings as well. As to his conduct in Egypt, the only contemporary Egyp authority says that he worshipped before the holiness of Neit as all the pious kings had done, that he ordered that the temple of Neit should be purified, and that its revenues should be restored as they had been before they had been confiscated by Akhmes for his Gr troops. He adds also that not merely were the strangers who had taken up their abode in the temple of Neit ejected from her sanctuary, but that their goods were taken away and their houses destroyed. Darius Hystaspis, the only other contemporary source of information, says of him simply that he was the son of Cyrus, of the same father and mother as Bardes, whom he slew secretly at some time before he set out on his Egyp campaign; and that he died by suicide shortly after he had heard of the rebellion of Persia, Media and the other provinces against him, and of the establishment of Gaumata the Magian as king under the claim that he was "Barzia, the son of Cyrus and brother of Cambyses."

The name of Cambyses is found in three of the Elephantine papyri recently published (September, 1911) by Professor Sachau of Berlin. The fragment numbered **59** 1 is so broken that it is impossible to make out the connection or the sense. In papyrus I, we are told that when Cambyses came to Egypt he found in the fortress of Yeb (Elephantine) a temple or synagogue (*'agōra'*), which had been built in the days of the Egyp kings; and that although he had torn down the temples of the Egyp gods, he had allowed no harm to be done to that of Jeh. The third papyrus is so interesting, because of its mention of Bagoas, the Pers governor of Jerus in 407 BC, who had hitherto been known only from Jos, and of Dalayah the son of the Sanballat who opposed the rebuilding of the wall of Jerus in the time of Ezra-Nehemiah, that we shall now give a tr of it in full: "A memorial of that which Bagoas and Dalayah said to me: Thou shalt say in Egypt unto Arsames with regard to the house of the altar of the God of heaven that was built in the fortress of Yeb before the time of Cambyses and which the accursed(?) Waidrang destroyed in the 14th year of Darius the king, that it shall be built again upon its place as it was before, and that meal-offerings and incense-offerings shall be offered upon that altar as they used to be."

Literature.—For further information as to the history of Cambyses see Rawlinson, *Ancient Monarchies;* Prasek, *Geschichte der Meder und Perser;* the Behistun inscr in the edd of the various recensions by Bezold, Spiegel, Weisbach, Thomson, and King; Herodotus; Josephus; the Sachau papyri; and Petrie, *History of Egypt*, III.

R. Dick Wilson

CAMEL, kam'el (גָּמָל, *gāmāl;* κάμηλος, *kámēlos;* בֶּכֶר, *bekher*, and בִּכְרָה, *bikhrāh* [Isa **60** 6; Jer **2** 23: "dromedary," ARVm "young camel"], רֶכֶשׁ, *rekhesh* [1 K **4** 28; see Horse], כִּרְכָּרוֹת, *kirkārōth* [Isa **66** 20, "swift beasts," ARV "dromedaries"); בְּנֵי הָרַמָּכִים, *b^enē hā-rammākhīm* [Est **8** 10, "young dromedaries," ARV "bred of the stud"]; אֲחַשְׁתְּרָנִים, *'ăḥashteránīm* [Est **8** 10.14, AV "camels," ARV "that were used in the king's service"]): There are two species of camel, the Arab. or one-humped camel or dromedary, *Camelus dromedarius*, and the Bactrian or two-humped camel, *Camelus bactrianus*. The latter inhabits the temperate and cold parts of central Asia and is not likely to have been known to Bib. writers. The Arab. camel inhabits southwestern Asia and northern Africa and has recently been introduced into parts of America and Australia. Its hoofs are not typical of ungulates but are rather like great claws.

Young Camels Grazing.

The toes are not completely separated and the main part of the foot which is applied to the ground is a large pad which underlies the proximal joints of the digits. It may be that this incomplete separation of the two toes is a sufficient explanation of the words "parteth not the hoof," in Lev **11** 4 and Dt **14** 7. Otherwise these words present a difficulty, because the hoofs are completely separated though the toes are not. The camel is a ruminant and chews the cud like a sheep or ox, but the stomach possesses only three compartments instead of four, as in other ruminants. The first two compartments contain in their walls small pouches, each of which can be closed by a sphincter muscle. The fluid retained in these pouches may account in part for the power of the camel to go for a relatively long time without drinking.

The Arab. camel is often compared with justice to the reindeer of the Esquimaux. It furnishes hair for spinning and weaving, milk, flesh and leather, as well as being an invaluable means of transportation in the arid desert. There are many Arab. names for the camel, the commonest of which is *jamal* (in Egypt *gamal*), the root being common to Arab., Heb and other Sem languages. From it the names in Lat, Gr, Eng. and various European languages are derived. There are various breeds of camels, as there are of horses. The riding camels or dromedaries, commonly called *hajīn*, can go, even at a walk, much faster than the pack camels. The males are mostly used for carrying burdens, the females being kept with the herds. Camels are used to a surprising extent on the rough roads of the mountains, and one finds in the possession of *fellāḥīn* in the mountains and on the littoral plain larger and stronger pack camels than are often found among the Bedawin. Camels were apparently not much used by the Israelites after the time of the patriarchs. They were taken as spoil of war from the Amalekites and other tribes, but nearly the only reference to their use by the later Israelites was when David was made king over all Israel at Hebron, when camels are mentioned among the animals used for bringing food for the celebration (1 Ch **12** 40). David had a herd of camels, but the herdsman was Obil, an Ishmaelite (1 Ch **27** 30). Nearly all the other Bib. references to

Camels at the Sea of Galilee.

camels are to those possessed by Abraham, Isaac and Jacob, Ishmaelites, Amalekites, Midianites, Hagrites and the "children of the East" (see EAST). Two references to camels (Gen **12** 16; Ex **9** 3) are regarded as puzzling because the testimony of the Egyp monuments is said to be against the presence of camels in ancient Egypt. For this reason, Gen **12** 16, in connection with Abram's visit to Egypt, is turned to account by Canon Cheyne to substantiate his theory that the Israelites were not in Egypt but in a north Arab. land of *Muṣri* (*EB* s.v. "Camel," 4). While the flesh of the camel was forbidden to the Israelites, it is freely eaten by the Arabs.

There are three references to the camel in NT: (1) to John's raiment of camel's hair (Mt **3** 4; Mk **1** 6); (2) the words of Jesus that "it is easier for a camel to go through a needle's eye, than for a rich man to enter into the kingdom of God" (Mt **19** 24; Mk **10** 25; Lk **18** 25); (3) the proverb applied to the Pharisees as blind guides, "that strain out the gnat, and swallow the camel" (Mt **23** 24). Some MSS read *ho kámilos*, "a cable," in Mt **19** 24 and Lk **18** 25.

There are a few unusual words which have been trd "camel" in text or margin of one or the other version. (See list of words at beginning of art.) *Bekher* and *bikhrāh* clearly mean a young animal, and the Arab. root word and derivatives are used similarly to the Heb. *Rākhash*, the root of *rekhesh*, is compared with the Arab. *rakaḍ*, "to run," and, in RV, *rekhesh* is trd "swift steeds." *Kirkārōth*, *rammākhīm* and *'ăḥashtᵉrānīm* must be admitted to be of doubtful etymology and uncertain meaning.

ALFRED ELY DAY

CAMEL'S HAIR (**τρίχες καμήλου**, *tríches kamḗlou*): In Mt **3** 4 and Mk **1** 6 the description of John's raiment is explicit to the extent of telling the kind of hair of which his raiment was made. It is probable that his garment was made of a tawed camel skin, for the more expensive woven camel's hair garment would not be in keeping with the rest of the description. It is still common among the poor in some parts of Syria, when a camel or other animal dies, to remove its skin and, after treating the inner surface to stop decomposition, to make it up into various domestic articles. The writer once saw a peasant dragging a skin along the road which proved to be that of a donkey which had just died on the route. His intention was probably to make it up into a cloak. Some believe that Elijah's mantle was of camel's hair (2 K **1** 8; cf Zec **13** 4). Of that we cannot be sure, for in the East today the hairy garment is usually goat's hair or wool either woven or still clinging to the skin. It was much more likely to have been one of these latter. See SHEEP RAISING. Camel's hair, when woven into fabrics, as in rugs, makes an article of even softer and more glossy texture than wool. See WEAVING.

JAMES A. PATCH

CAMON, kā'mon (קָמוֹן, *ḳāmōn*, "standing-place," Jgs **10** 5 AV). See KAMON.

CAMP. See WAR.

CAMPHIRE, kam'fīr. See HENNA.

CANA, kā'na, **OF GALILEE** (**Κανὰ τῆς Γαλιλαίας**, *Kaná tḗs Galilaías*): This was the scene of Christ's earliest miracle, when, at the marriage feast, He turned water into wine (Jn **2** 1 ff). It was the home of Nathanael (**21** 2). From Cana, after the marriage, Jesus "went down" to Capernaum (**2** 12), and returned at the request of the centurion (**4** 46.51). These are the only notices of Cana in Scripture, and from them we learn merely that it was in Galilee, and in the uplands W. of the lake. Other villages of the same name are mentioned by Jos, but probably this one is intended by the Cana where for a time he dwelt (*Vita*, 16) which he locates in the plain of Asochis (ib, 41). The Gr *kanā* probably transliterates an old Heb *ḳānāh*, "place of reeds." This ancient name survives in *Khirbet Ḳānā*, a ruined site with rock-hewn tombs, cisterns and a pool, on the northern edge of *Sahl el-Baṭṭauf*, the plain of Asochis. Near by are marshy stretches where reeds still abound: the name therefore is entirely appropriate. The name *Ḳānā el-Jelīl*, the exact Arab. equivalent of *Kana tēs Galilaias*, is also heard among the natives. This, however, may have arisen from the suggested identification with Cana of the Gospel. The position agrees well enough with the Gospel data.

Kefr Kennah, a thriving village about 3¾ miles from Nazareth, on the southern edge of *Sahl Tor'ān*, the plain S. of the range of that name, through which the road from Nazareth to Tiberias passes, has also many advocates. This identification is accepted by the Gr and Lat churches, which have both built extensively in the village; the Greeks showing stone jars said to have been used in the miracle, and the traditional house of

Cana of Galilee.

Nathanael being pointed out. A copious spring of excellent water rises W. of the village; and the pomegranates grown here are greatly prized. The change of name, however, from *Ḳānā* to *Kennah*—(note the doubled *n*), is not easy; and there are no reeds in the neighborhood to give the name any appropriateness.

Onom locates Cana in the tribe of Asher toward Great Sidon, probably thinking of *Ḳānā*, a village about 8 miles S. of Tyre. The pilgrims of the

Middle Ages seem to be fairly divided as to the two sites. Saewulf (1102), Brocardius (1183), Marinus Sanutus (1321), Breydenbach (1483) and Anselm (1507) favor the northern site; while on the side of *Kefr Kennah* may be reckoned St. Paula (383), St. Willibald (720), Isaac Chelo (1334) and Quaresimus (1616). It seems pretty certain that the Crusaders adopted the identification with *Khirbet Ḳānā* (Conder, *Tent Work*, 69 f). While no absolute decision is possible, on the available evidence probability points to the northern site.

Col. Conder puts in a claim for a third site, that of *'Ain Ḳānā* on the road from *er-Reineh* (a village about 1½ mile from Nazareth on the Tiberias road) to Tabor (*Tent Work*, 81). W. Ewing

CANAAN, kā'nan, **CANAANITES**, kā'nan-īts (כְּנַעַן, *k^ena'an;* **Χαναάν**, *Chanaán*):

1. Geography
2. Meaning of the Name
3. The Results of Recent Excavations
4. History
   (1) Stone Age
   (2) Bronze Age
   (3) A Babylonian Province
   (4) Jerusalem Founded
   (5) The Hyksos
   (6) Egyptian Conquest
   (7) Tell el-Amarna Tablets
5. The Israelitish Invasion
6. Culture
7. Art
8. Commerce
9. Art of Writing
Literature

Canaan is stated in Gen **10** 6 to have been a son of Ham and brother of Mizraim, or Egypt. This indicates the Mosaic period when the conquerors of the XVIIIth and XIXth Egyp Dynasties made Canaan for a time a province of the Egyp empire. Under the Pharaoh Meneptah, at the time of the Exodus, it ceased to be connected with Egypt, and the Egyp garrisons in the S. of the country were expelled by the Philis, who probably made themselves masters of the larger portion of it, thus causing the name of Philistia or Pal to become synonymous with that of Canaan (see Zeph **2** 5). In the Am Tab, Canaan is written Kinakhna and Kinakhkhi. The latter form corresponds with the Gr Χνᾶ (*Chná*), a name given to Phoenicia (Hecat. *Fragments* 254; Eusebius, *Praep. Ev.*, i.10; ix.17).

1. Geography

In Nu **13** 29 the Canaanites are described as dwelling "by the sea, and along by the side of the Jordan," i.e. in the lowlands of Pal. The name was confined to the country W. of the Jordan (Nu **33** 51; Josh **22** 9), and was esp. applied to Phoenicia (Isa **23** 11; cf Mt **15** 22). Hence Sidon is called the "firstborn" of Canaan (Gen **10** 15, though cf Jgs **3** 3), and the LXX translates "Canaanites" by "Phoenicians" and "Canaan" by the "land of the Phoenicians" (Ex **16** 35; Josh **5** 12). Kinakhkhi is used in the same restricted sense in the Am Tab, but it is also extended so as to include Pal generally. On the other hand, on the Egyp monuments Seti I calls a town in the extreme S. of Pal "the city of Pa-Kana'na" or "the Canaan," which Conder identifies with the modern *Khurbet Kenan* near Hebron.

As in the Am Tab, so in the OT, Canaan is used in an extended sense to denote the whole of Pal W. of the Jordan (Gen **12** 5; **23** 2.19; **28** 1; **31** 18; **35** 6; **36** 2; **37** 1; **48** 7; Ex **15** 15; Nu **13** 2; Josh **14** 1; **21** 2; Ps **135** 11). Thus Jerus which had Amorite and Hittite founders is stated to be of "the land of the Canaanite" (Ezk **16** 3), and Isa (**19** 18) terms Hebrew, which was shared by the Israelites with the Phoenicians and, apparently, also the Amorites, "the language of Canaan." Jabin is called "the king of Canaan" in Jgs **4** 2.23.24; but whether the name is employed here in a restricted or extended sense is uncertain.

2. Meaning of the Name

As the Phoenicians were famous as traders, it has been supposed that the name "Canaanite" is a synonym of "merchant" in certain passages of the OT. The pursuit of trade, however, was characteristic only of the maritime cities of Phoenicia, not of the Canaanitish towns conquered by the Israelites. In Isa **23** 11 we should tr "Canaan" (as LXX) instead of "merchant city" (AV); in Hos **12** 7 (8), "as for Canaan" (LXX), instead of "he is a merchant" (AV); in Zeph **1** 11, "people of Canaan" (LXX), instead of "merchant people" (AV); on the other hand, "Canaanite" seems to have acquired the sense of "merchant," as "Chaldean" did of "astrologer," in Isa **23** 8, and Prov **31** 24, though probably not in Zec **14** 21, and Job **41** 6 (Heb **40** 30).

3. The Results of Recent Excavation

Much light has been thrown upon the history of Canaan prior to the Israelitish occupation by recent excavation, supplemented by the monuments of Babylonia and Egypt. The Pal Exploration led the way by its excavations in 1890–92 at *Tell el-Hesy*, which turned out to be the site of Lachish, first under Professor Flinders Petrie and then under Dr. Bliss. Professor Petrie laid the foundations of Pal archaeology by fixing the chronological sequence of the Lachish pottery, and tracing the remains of six successive cities, the fourth of which was that founded by the Israelites. Between it and the preceding city was a layer of ashes, marking the period when the town lay desolate and uninhabited. The excavations at Lachish were followed by others at *Tell es-Safi*, the supposed site of Gath; at *Tell Sandahanna*, the ancient Marissa, a mile S. of *Bêt Jibrîn*, where interesting relics of the Gr period were found, and at Jerus, where an attempt was made to trace the city walls. Next to Lachish, the most fruitful excavations have been at Gezer, which has been explored by Mr. Macalister with scientific thoroughness and skill, and where a large necropolis has been discovered as well as the remains of seven successive settlements, the last of which comes down to the Seleucid era, the third corresponding with the first settlement at Lachish. The two first settlements go back to the neolithic age. With the third the Sem or "Amorite" period of Canaan begins; bronze makes its appearance; high-places formed of monoliths are erected, and inhumation of the dead is introduced, while the cities are surrounded with great walls of stone. While Mr. Macalister has been working at Gezer, German and Austrian expeditions under Dr. Schumacher have been excavating at *Tell em-Mutesellim*, the site of Megiddo, and under Dr. Sellin first at *Tell Taanak*, the ancient Taanach, and then at Jericho. At Taanach cuneiform tablets of the Mosaic age were found in the house of the governor of the town; at Samaria and Gezer cuneiform tablets have also been found, but they belong to the late Assyr and Bab periods. At Jericho, on the flat roof of a house adjoining the wall of the Canaanitish city, destroyed by the Israelites, a number of clay tablets were discovered laid out to dry before being inscribed with cuneiform characters. Before the letters were written and despatched, however, the town, it seems, was captured and burnt. See Bethel, Cities of the Plain, Beth-shean, Beth-shemesh, Gibeon, Gerar, Gerasa, Kirjath-sepher, Megiddo, Mizpah, Ophel, Samaria, Shechem, Shiloh, Beth-pelet, Hazor, Harosheth of the Gentiles, Abel-beth-maacah.

(1) *The stone age.*—The history of Canaan begins with the palaeolithic age, palaeolithic implements

having been found in the lowlands. Our first knowledge of its population dates from the neolithic period. The neolithic inhabitants of Gezer were of short stature (about 5 ft. 4 in. in height), and lived in caves—at least in the time of the first prehistoric settlement—and burned their dead. Their sacred place was a double cave with which cup-marks in the rock were connected, and their pottery was rude; some of it was ornamented with streaks of red or black on a yellow or red wash. In the time of the second settlement a rude stone wall was built around the town. The débris of the two neolithic settlements is as much as 12 ft. in depth, implying a long period of accumulation.

4. History

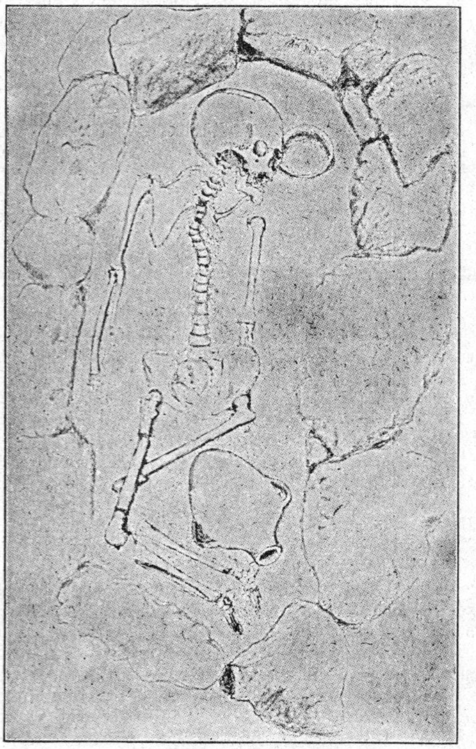

Foundation Sacrifice Found at Gezer.

(2) *The bronze age.*—The neolithic population was succeeded by one of Sem type, which introduced the use of metal, and buried its dead. The name of Amorite has been given to it, this being the name under which the Sem population of Canaan was known to the Babylonians. Gezer was surrounded by a great wall of stone intersected by brick towers; at Lachish the Amorite wall was of crude brick, nearly 29 ft. in thickness (cf Dt **1** 28). A "high-place" was erected at Gezer consisting of 9 monoliths, running from N. to S., and surrounded by a platform of large stones. The second monolith has been polished by the kisses of the worshippers; the seventh was brought from a distance. Under the pavement of the sanctuary lay the bones of children, more rarely of adults, who had been sacrificed and sometimes burnt, and the remains deposited in jars. Similar evidences of human sacrifice were met with under the walls of houses both here and at Taanach and Megiddo. In the Israelitish strata the food-bowl and lamp for lighting the dead in the other world are retained, but all trace of human sacrifice is gone. At Lachish in Israelitish times the bowl and lamp were filled with sand. The second "Amorite" city at Gezer had a long existence. The high-place was enlarged, and an Egyptian of the age of the XIIth Dynasty was buried within its precincts. Egyp scarabs of the XIIth and XIIIth Dynasties are now met with; these give place to scarabs of the Hyksos period, and finally to those of the XVIIIth Dynasty (1600 BC). Hittite painted pottery of Cappadocian type is also found in the later débris of the city as well as seal-cylinders of the Bab pattern.

(3) *A Babylonian province.*—Meanwhile Canaan had for a time formed part of the Bab empire. Gudea, viceroy of Lagas under the kings of the Dynasty of Ur (2500 BC), had brought "limestone" from the "land of the Amorites," alabaster from Mt. Lebanon, cedar-beams from Amanus, and gold-dust from the desert between Pal and Egypt. A cadastral survey was drawn up about the same time by Uru-malik, "the governor of the land of the Amorites," the name by which Syria and Canaan were known to the Babylonians, and colonies of "Amorites" engaged in trade were settled in the cities of Babylonia. After the fall of the Dynasty of Ur, Babylonia was itself conquered by the Amorites who founded the dynasty to which Khammu-rabi, the Amraphel of Gen **14** 1, belonged (see ḤAMMURABI). In an inscription found near Diarbekir the only title given to Khammu-rabi is "king of the land of the Amorites." Bab now became the official, literary and commercial language of Canaan, and schools were established there in which the cuneiform script was taught. Canaanitish culture became wholly Bab; even its theology and gods were derived from Babylonia. The famous legal code of Khammu-rabi (see ḤAMMURABI, CODE OF) was enforced in Canaan as in other parts of the empire, and traces of its provisions are found in Gen. Abram's adoption of his slave Eliezer, Sarai's conduct to Hagar, and Rebekah's receipt of a dowry from the father of the bridegroom are examples of this. So, too, the sale of the cave of Machpelah was in accordance with the Bab legal forms of the Khammu-rabi age. The petty kings of Canaan paid tribute to their Bab suzerain, and Bab officials and "commerical travelers" (*damgari*) frequented the country.

(4) *Jerusalem founded.*—We must ascribe to this period the foundation of Jerus, which bears a Bab name (*Uru-Salim*, "the city of Salim"), and commanded the road to the naphtha springs of the Dead Sea. Bitumen was one of the most important articles of Bab trade on account of its employment for building and lighting purposes, and seems to have been a government monopoly. Hence the rebellion of the Canaanitish princes in the naphtha district (Gen **14**) was sufficiently serious to require a considerable force for its suppression.

(5) *The Hyksos.*—The Amorite dynasty in Babylonia was overthrown by a Hittite invasion, and Bab authority in Canaan came to an end, though the influence of Bab culture continued undiminished. In the N. the Hittites were dominant; in the S., where Egyp influence had been powerful since the age of the XIIth Dynasty, the Hyksos conquest of Egypt united Pal with the Delta. The Hyksos kings bear Canaanitish names, and their invasion of Egypt probably formed part of that general movement which led to the establishment of an "Amorite" dynasty in Babylonia. Egypt now became an appanage of Canaan, with its capital, accordingly, near its Asiatic frontier. One of the Hyksos kings bears the characteristically Canaanitish name of Jacob-el, written in the same way as on Bab tablets of the age of Khammu-rabi, and a place of the same name is mentioned by Thothmes III as existing in southern Pal.

(6) *Egyptian conquest.*—The Pharaohs of the

XVIIIth Dynasty expelled the Hyksos and conquered Pal and Syria. For about 200 years Canaan was an Egyp province. With the Egyp conquest the history of the second Amorite city at Gezer comes to an end. The old wall was partially destroyed, doubtless by Thothmes III (about 1480 BC). A third Amorite city now grew up, with a larger and stronger wall, 14 ft. thick. The houses built on the site of the towers of the first wall were filled with scarabs and other relics of the reign of Amon-hotep III (1440 BC). At Lachish the ruins of the third city were full of similar remains, and among them was a cuneiform tablet referring to a governor of Lachish mentioned in the Am Tab. At Taanach cuneiform tablets of the same age have been discovered, written by Canaanites to one another but all in the Bab script and language.

(7) *Tell el-Amarna tablets*.—In the Am Tab we have a picture of Canaan at the moment when the Asiatic empire of Egypt was breaking up through the religious and social troubles that marked the reign of Amon-hotep IV. The Hittites were attacking it in the N.; in the S. of Canaan the *Khabiri* or "confederate" bands of free-lances were acquiring principalities for themselves. The petty kings and governors had foreign troops in their pay with which they fought one against the other; and their mercenaries readily transferred their allegiance from one paymaster to another, or seized the city they were engaged to defend. Hittites, Mitannians from Mesopotamia, and other foreigners appear as governors of the towns; the Egyp government was too weak to depose them and was content if they professed themselves loyal. At times the Canaanitish princes intrigued with the Assyrians against their Egyp masters; at other times with the Mitannians of "Aram-Naharaim" or the Hittites of Cappadocia. The troops sent by the Egyp Pharaoh were insufficient to suppress the rebellion, and the authority of the Egyp commissioners grew less and less. Eventually the king of the Amorites was compelled to pass openly over to the Hittite king, and Canaan was lost to the Pharaohs.

5. The Israelitish Invasion

Gaza and the neighboring towns, however, still remained in their hands, and with the recovery of Egyptian power under the XIXth Dynasty allowed Seti I to march once more into Canaan and reduce it again to subjection. In spite of Hittite attacks the country on both sides of the Jordan acknowledged the rule of Seti and his son Ramses II, and in the 21st year of the latter Pharaoh the long war with the Hittites came to an end, a treaty being made which fixed the Egyp frontier pretty much where the Israelitish frontier afterward ran. A work, known as *The Travels of the Mohar*, which satirizes the misadventures of a tourist in Canaan, gives a picture of Canaan in the days of Ramses II. With the death of Ramses II Egyp rule in Pal came finally to an end. The Philis drove the Egyp garrisons from the cities which commanded the military road through Canaan, and the long war with the Hittites exhausted the inland towns, so that they made but a feeble resistance to the Israelites who assailed them shortly afterward. The Egyptians, however, never relinquished their claim to be masters of Canaan, and when the Philis power had been overthrown by David we find the Egyp king again marching northward and capturing Gezer (1 K **9** 16). Meanwhile the country had become to a large extent Israelite. In the earlier days of the Israelitish invasion the Canaanitish towns had been destroyed and the people massacred; later the two peoples intermarried, and a mixed race was the result. The portraits accompanying the names of the places taken by Shishak in southern Pal have Amorite features, and the modern *fellahin* of Pal are Canaanite rather than Jewish in type.

6. Culture

Canaanitish culture was based on that of Babylonia, and begins with the introduction of the use of copper and bronze. When Canaan became a Bab province, it naturally shared in the civilization of the ruling power. The religious beliefs and deities of Babylonia were superimposed upon those of the primitive Canaanite. The local Baal or "lord" of the soil made way for the "lord of heaven," the Sun-god of the Babylonians. The "high-place" gradually became a temple built after a Bab fashion. The sacred stone, once the supreme object of Canaanitish worship, was transformed into a Beth-el or shrine of an indwelling god. The gods and goddesses of Babylonia migrated to Canaan; places received their names from Nebo or Nin-ip; Hadad became Amurrû "the Amorite god"; Istar passed into Ashtōreth, and Asirtu, the female counterpart of Asir, the national god of Assyria, became Ashērah, while her sanctuary, which in Assyria was a temple, was identified in Canaan with the old fetish of an upright stone or log. But human sacrifice, and more esp. the sacrifice of the firstborn son, of which we find few traces in Babylonia, continued to be practised with undiminished frequency until, as we learn from the excavations, the Israelitish conquest brought about its suppression. The human victim is also absent from the later sacrificial tariffs of Carthage and Marseilles, its place being taken in them by the ram. According to these tariffs the sacrifices and offerings were of two kinds, the *zau'at* or sin offering and the *shelem* or thank-offering. The sin offering was given wholly to the god; part of the thank-offering would be taken by the offerer. Birds which were not allowed as a sin offering might constitute a thank-offering. Besides the sacrifices, there were also offerings of corn, wine, fruit and oil.

7. Art

What primitive Canaanitish art was like may be seen from the rude sculptures in the *Wadi el-Qana* near Tyre. Under Bab influence it rapidly developed. Among the Can spoil captured by Thothmes III were tables, chairs and staves of cedar and ebony inlaid with gold or simply gilded, richly embroidered robes, chariots chased with silver, iron tent poles studded with precious stones, "bowls with goats' heads on them, and one with a lion's head, the workmanship of the land of Zahi" (the Phoen coast), iron armor with gold inlay, and rings of gold and silver that were used as money. At Taanach, gold and silver ornaments have been found of high artistic merit. To the Israelites, fresh from the desert, the life of the wealthy Canaanite would have appeared luxurious in the extreme.

8. Commerce

The position of Canaan made it the meeting-place of the commercial routes of the ancient world. The fleets of the Phoen cities are celebrated in the Am Tab, and it is probable that they were already engaged in the purple trade. The inland towns of Canaan depended not only on agriculture but also on a carrying trade: caravans as well as "commercial travelers" (*damgari*) came to them from Cappadocia, Babylonia and Egypt. Bronze, silver, lead, and painted ware were brought from Asia Minor, together with horses; naphtha was exported to Babylonia in return for embroidered stuffs; copper came from Cyprus, richly chased vessels of the precious metals from Crete and corn from Egypt. Baltic amber has been found at Lachish, where a furnace with iron slag, discovered in the third Amorite city, shows that the native iron was worked before the age of the Israelitish conquest. The manufacture of glass goes back to the same epoch.

As far back as 2500 BC, alabaster and limestone had been sent to Babylonia from the quarries of the Lebanon.

9. Art of Writing

Long before the age of Abraham the Bab seal-cylinder had become known and been imitated in Syria and Canaan. But it was not until Canaan had been made a Bab province under the Khammu-rabi dynasty that the cuneiform system of writing was introduced together with the Bab language and literature. Henceforward schools were established and libraries or archive-chambers formed where the foreign language and its complicated syllabary could be taught and stored. In the Mosaic age the Taanach tablets show that the inhabitants of a small country town could correspond with one another on local matters in the foreign language and script, and two of the Tell el-Amarna letters are from a Canaanitish lady. The official notices of the name by which each year was known in Babylonia were sent to Canaan as to other provinces of the Bab empire in the cuneiform script; one of these, dated in the reign of Khammurabi's successor, has been found in the Lebanon.

LITERATURE.—H. Vincent, *Canaan d'après l'exploration récente*, 1907; G. A. Smith, *Historical Geography of the Holy Land*, 1894; Publications of the Palestine Exploration Fund; E. Sellin, *Tell Ta'annek* and *Eine Nachlese auf dem Tell Ta'annek*, 1904–5; Schumacher, *Tell Mutesellim*, 1909; Thiersch, *Die neueren Ausgrabungen in Palästina*, 1908.

See, further, ARKITE; ARVADITE; BAAL; GIRGASHITE; HITTITE; HIVITE; JEBUSITE; KADMONITE; KENIZZITE; PALESTINE; PERIZZITE; REPHAIM; SINITE; TEMANITE.

A. H. SAYCE

CANAANITESS, kā'nan-īt-es. See SHUA; BATH-SHUA.

CANALS, ka-nalz' (יְאֹרִים, *y^{e}'ōrīm*): The word "canals" occurs in several places in the RVm (Ex **7** 19; **8** 5; Isa **19** 6; Nah **3** 8). *y^{e}'ōr* is an Egyp word, the designation of the Nile (Brugsch, *Geogr*, I, 8, 78). The proper name of the Nile as a god was Hapi. There were several common designations of the Nile, but the usual one was *y^{e}'ōr*, Heb pl. *y^{e}'ōrīm*. The primary meaning of *y^{e}'ōr* in Egyp is not certain, but its significance in use for the Nile is plain enough. All the waters in Egypt were of the Nile and this word *y^{e}'ōr* was used to denote all of them, the Nile and all its ramifications through the whole irrigating system. Thus *y^{e}'ōrīm*, Niles, came to be used. As only the main channels of the Nile had much current, the *y^{e}'ōrīm* came naturally to convey the idea of sluggishness. In the account of the plagues (Ex **7** 19), names are used descriptively to designate the different waters of Egypt: *n^{e}hārōth*, "flowing streams," for the main channels of the river, and *y^{e}'ōrīm* for other streams, which by contrast must mean, as it should according to its use by the Egyptians, "the sluggish streams," i.e. "canals," as it is rendered by the Revisers. This meaning of the word being thus clearly established, it is appropriately used in the RVm in the other instances of its occurrence in like circumstances.

M. G. KYLE

CANANAEAN, kā-na-nē'an, **CANAANITE,** kā'nan-īt. See SIMON (CANANAEAN).

CANDACE, kan'da-sē (**Κανδάκη,** *Kandákē*): Queen of the Ethiopians (Acts **8** 27). Pliny states that the name Candace had already been borne for many years by the queens of Ethiopia (vi.29). See ETHIOPIA. Her treasurer, "a eunuch of great authority," was baptized by Philip the Evangelist on his return from worshipping in Jerus.

CANALS IN EGYPT.

CANDLE, kan'd'l, **CANDLESTICK,** kan'd'l-stik (נֵר, *nēr;* **λύχνος,** *lúchnos;* מְנוֹרָה, *m^{e}nōrāh;* **λυχνία,** *luchnía*):

(1) "Candle" is found in the OT, AV, as the rendering of *nēr*, and in the NT for *luchnos*. In all places except Jer **25** 10 and Zeph **1** 12 (see m) RV gives the more exact rendering "lamp." See LAMP. Candle, in our sense of the term, was unknown to antiquity.

(2) "Candlestick" stands for what was a common and indispensable article of ancient house furniture, a lamp-stand (*m^{e}nōrāh*). Accordingly we find it mentioned in a case thoroughly representative of the furnishings of an oriental room of the plainer sort, in the account of "the prophet's chamber" given in 2 K **4** 10. Here we find that the furniture consisted of a "bed," a "table," a "seat," and a "candlestick," or lamp-stand. The excavations of Petrie and Bliss at Lachish (*Tell el-Hesy*, 104), not to mention others, help to make it clear that a lamp-stand is meant in passages where the Heb word, *m^{e}nōrāh*, or its Gr equivalent *luchnia*, is used. Accordingly throughout the NT, RV has consistently rendered *luchnia* by "stand" (Mt **5** 15; Mk **4** 21; Lk **8** 16; **11** 33).

(3) The "candlestick" of Dnl **5** 5 is rather the candelabrum (*nebhrashtā'*) of Belshazzar's ban-

queting-hall. The "golden candlestick" of the tabernacle and the temple requires special treatment. See CANDLESTICK (GOLDEN); TABERNACLE.

(4) Certain **figurative** uses of "candle" and "candlestick" in the Bible demand attention. The ancient and still common custom of the East of keeping a house lamp burning night and day gave rise to the figure of speech so universally found in oriental languages by which the continued prosperity of the individual or the family is set forth by the perennially burning lamp (see Job **29** 3: "when his lamp shined upon my head"; Ps **18** 28: "Thou wilt light my lamp"). The converse in usage is seen in many passages—(see Job **18** 6: "His lamp above him shall be put out"; **21** 17: "How oft is it that the lamp of the wicked is put out"; Prov **24** 20: "The lamp of the wicked shall be put out"; Jer **25** 10: "Take from them . . . . the light of the lamp"). The same metaphor is used in Rev **2** 5 to indicate the judgment with which the church of Ephesus was threatened: "I will move thy candlestick out of its place." "The seven golden candlesticks" (Rev **1** 20) which John saw were "the seven churches," the appointed light-bearers and dispensers of the religion of the risen Christ. Hence the significance of such a threat.

GEO. B. EAGER

CANDLESTICK, kan′d'l-stik, **THE GOLDEN,** gold''n (מְנוֹרָה, *mnōrāh*, lit. "lamp-stand"): An important part of the furniture of the tabernacle and temples. See TABERNACLE; TEMPLE; LAMP.

The candlestick is first met with in the descriptions of the tabernacle (Ex **25** 31–39; **37** 17–24).

1. The Tabernacle It was, with the utensils connected with it (snuffers, snuff dishes), to be made of pure beaten gold, of one piece, a talent in weight (Ex **25** 39). It consisted of a pedestal or base, of a central stem (the name "candlestick" is specially given to this), of six curving branches—three on each side—and of seven lamps resting on the tops of the branches and stem. Stem and branches were ornamented

FIG. 1.—Golden Candlestick (from Arch of Titus).

with cups like almond-blossoms, knops and flowers —four of this series on the stem, and three on each of the branches. Some, however, understand the "cup" to embrace the "knop" and "flower" (calyx and corolla). The shape of the pedestal is uncertain. Jewish tradition suggests three small feet; the representation of the candlestick on the Arch of Titus has a solid, hexagonal base (see Fig. 1). The position of the candlestick was on the S. side of the holy place (Ex **40** 24).

In Solomon's temple the single golden candlestick was multiplied to ten, and the position was altered.

2. Temple of Solomon The candlesticks were now placed in front of the Holy of Holies, five on one side, five on the other (1 K **7** 49; 2 Ch **4** 7). Further details are not given in the texts, from which it may be presumed that the model of the tabernacle candlestick was followed.

The second temple reverted to the single golden candlestick. When the temple was plundered by

3. Temple of Zerubbabel Antiochus Epiphanes, the candlestick was taken away (1 Macc **1** 21); after the cleansing, a new one was made by Judas Maccabaeus (**4** 49.50).

The same arrangement of a single golden candlestick, placed on the S. side of the holy place, was continued in Herod's Temple (Jos, *BJ*, V, v, 5).

4. Temple of Herod It was this which, carried away by Titus, was represented on his Arch at Rome.

The immediate object of the candlestick was to give light in the holy place. The lamps were lighted in the evening and burned till the

5. Use and Symbolism morning (Ex **30** 7. 8; Lev **24** 3; 1 S **3** 3; 2 Ch **13** 11), light being admitted into the temple during the day by the upper windows. Jos in his cosmical speculations (*BJ*, V, v, 5) takes the seven lamps to signify the seven planets. In Zechariah's vision of the golden candlestick (**4** 2 ff), the seven lamps are fed by two olive trees which are interpreted to be "the two anointed ones," Zerubbabel and Joshua—the civil and spiritual representatives of the theocracy. The candlestick here, like the seven candlesticks in Rev **1** 20.21, symbolizes the church of God, then in its OT form, the idea conveyed being that God's church is set to be a light-giver in the world. Cf Christ's words (Mt **5** 14.16; Lk **12** 35), and Paul's (Phil **2** 15).

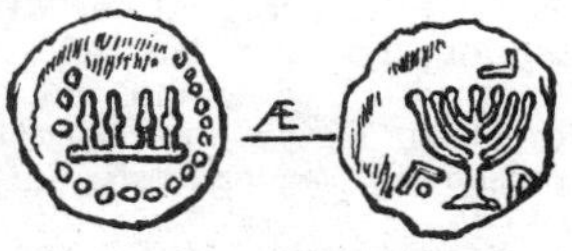

FIG. 2.—Coin of Antigonus (40–37 BC).

The oldest known representation of the seven-branched candlestick is on a coin of Antigonus, cir 40 BC (see Madden's *Coins of the Jews*, 102). For literature see TABERNACLE; TEMPLE.

JAMES ORR

CANE, kān. See REED.

CANKER, kaṇ′kẽr. See GANGRENE.

CANKERED, kaṇ′kẽrd (Jas **5** 3 RV, "rusted").

CANKER-WORM, kaṇ′kẽr-wûrm (יֶלֶק, *yeleḳ*, [Joel **1** 4; **2** 25; Nah **3** 15.16]): The name given to a larval stage of the LOCUST (q.v.). See also CATERPILLAR.

CANNEH, kan′e (כַּנֵּה, *kannēh;* **Χανάα**, *Chanáa*): Mentioned in Ezk **27** 23 in connection with Haran and Eden as one of the places with which Tyre had commercial relations. This is the only reference to the place and the site is unknown. Gesenius and others think it is probably the same as Calneh of Am **6** 2 or of Gen **10** 10, and Calno of Isa **10** 9. According to the Tgs, Eusebius, and Jerome, this place is identical with Ctesiphon, which was situated on the Tigris. One codex of De Rossi has made this identification in the passage in Ezk **27** 23. Cornill thinks Canneh is the Calneh of Am **6** 2, but Cheyne thinks the name is really non-existent. He says the words rendered "and Canneh and Eden" should rather be "and the sons of Eden."

A. W. FORTUNE

CANON, kan′un, OF THE OLD TESTAMENT, THE:

I. Introductory.—The problem of how we came by 39 books known as OT "Scripture" is a purely historical investigation. The question involved is, not who wrote the several books, but who made them into a collection, not their origin or contents, but their history; not God's part, but man's. Our present aim, accordingly, must be to trace the process by which the various writings became "Scripture."

1. The Christian Term "Canon"

The word "canon" is of Christian origin, from the Gr word κανών, *kanōn*, which in turn is probably borrowed from the Heb word, קָנֶה, *ḳāneh*, meaning a reed or measuring rod, hence norm or rule. Later it came to mean a rule of faith, and eventually a catalogue or list. In present usage it signifies a collection of religious writings Divinely inspired and hence authoritative, normative, sacred and binding. The term occurs in Gal **6** 16; 2 Cor **10** 13–16; but it is first employed of the books of Scripture in the technical sense of a standard collection or body of sacred writings, by the church Fathers of the 4th cent.; e.g. in the 59th canon of the Council of Laodicea (363 AD); in the Festal Epistle of Athanasius (365 AD); and by Amphilochius, archbishop of Iconium (395 AD).

2. The Corresponding Heb Expression

How the ancient Hebrews expressed the conception of canonicity is not known; but it is safe to say that the idea, as an idea, existed long before there was any special phrase invented to express it. In the NT the word "Scriptures" conveys unquestionably the notion of sacredness (Mt **21** 42; Jn **5** 39; Acts **18** 24). From the 1st cent. AD and following, however, according to the Talm, the Jews employed the phrase "defile the hands." Writings which were suitable to be read in the synagogue were designated as books which "defile the hands." What this very peculiar oriental expression may have originally signified no one definitely knows. Probably Lev **16** 24 gives a hint of the true interpretation. According to this passage the high priest on the great Day of Atonement washed not only when he put on the holy garments of his office, but also when he put them off. Quite possibly, therefore, the expression "defile the hands" signified that the hands which had touched the sacred writings must first be washed before touching aught else. The idea expressed, accordingly, was one akin to that of *taboo*. That is to say, just as certain garments worn by worshippers in encircling the sacred Kaaba at Mecca are taboo to the Mohammedans of today, i.e. cannot be worn outside the mosque, but must be left at the door as the worshippers quit the sanctuary, so the Heb writings which were fit to be read in the synagogue rendered the hands of those who touched them taboo, defiling their hands, as they were wont to say, so that they must first be washed before engaging in any secular business. This seems to be the best explanation of this enigmatical phrase. Various other and somewhat fanciful explanations of it, however, have been given: for example, to prevent profane uses of worn-out synagogue rolls (Buhl); or to prevent placing consecrated grain alongside of the sacred rolls in the synagogues that it might become holy, as the grain would attract the mice and the mice would gnaw the rolls (Strack, Wildeboer and others); or to prevent the sacred, worn-out parchments from being used as coverings for animals (Graetz); or to "declare the hands to be unclean unless previously washed" (Fürst, Green). But no one of these explanations satisfies. The idea of taboo is more likely imbedded in the phrase.

3. The "Hidden Books" of the Jews

The rabbins invented a special phrase to designate rolls that were worn-out or disputed. These they called *g^enūzīm*, meaning "hidden away." Cemeteries filled with Heb manuscripts which have long been buried are frequently found today in Egypt in connection with Jewish synagogues. Such rolls might first be placed in the *g^enīzāh* or rubbish chamber of the sanctuary. They were not, however, apocryphal or uncanonical in the sense of being extraneous or outside the regular collection. For such the Jews had a special term *ṣ^{e}phārīm ḥīçōnīm*, "books that are outside." These could not be read in the synagogues. "Hidden books" were rather worn-out parchments, or canonical rolls which might by some be temporarily disputed. See Apocrypha.

4. The Determining Principle in the Formation of the Canon

Who had the right to declare a writing canonical? To this question widely divergent answers have been given. According to a certain class of theologians the several books of the OT were composed by authors who were conscious not only of their inspiration but also that their writings were destined to be handed down to the church of future generations as sacred. In other words each writer canonized, as it were, his own writings. For example, Dr. W. H. Green (*Canon*, 35 f, 106, 110) says: "No formal declaration of their canonicity was needed to give them sanction. They were from the first not only eagerly read by the devout but believed to be Divinely obligatory. . . . . Each individual book of an acknowledged prophet of Jeh, or of anyone accredited as inspired by Him to make known His will, was accepted as the word of God immediately upon its appearance. . . . . Those books and those only were accepted as the Divine standards of their faith and regulative of their conduct which were written for this definite purpose by those whom they believed to be inspired of God. It was this which made them canonical. The spiritual profit found in them corresponded with and confirmed the belief in their heavenly origin. And the public official action which further attested, though it did not initiate, their canonicity, followed in the wake of the popular recognition of their Divine authority. . . . . The writings of the prophets, delivered to the people as a declaration of the Divine will, possessed canonical authority from the moment of their appearance. . . . . The canon does not derive its authority from the church, whether Jewish or Christian; the office of the church is merely that of a custodian and a witness." So likewise Dr. J. D. Davis (*Pres. and Ref. Review*, April, 1902, 182).

On the contrary, Dillmann (*Jahrb. für deutsche Theol.*, III, 420) more scientifically claims that "history knows nothing of the individual books having been designed to be sacred from their origin. . . . . These books bore indeed in themselves from the first those characteristics on account of which they were subsequently admitted into the sacred collection, but yet always had first to pass through a shorter or longer period of verification, and make trial of the Divine power resident within them upon the hearts of the church before they were outwardly and formally acknowledged by it as Divine books." As a matter of fact, the books of the OT are still on trial, and ever will be. So far as is known, the great majority of the writers of Holy Scripture did not arbitrarily hand over their productions to the church and expect them to be regarded as canon Scripture. Two parties are involved in the making of canonical Scripture—the original authors and the church—both of whom were inspired by the same Spirit. The authors wrote inspired by the Divine Spirit, and the church ever since—Jewish and Christian alike—has been inspired to recognize the authoritative character of their writings. And so it will be to the end of time. "We cannot be certain that anything comes from God unless it bring us personally something evidently Divine" (Briggs, *The Study of Holy Scripture*, 162).

5. The Tripartite Division of the OT

The Jews early divided the OT writings into three classes: (1) the *Tōrāh*, or Law; (2) the *N^e^bhī'īm*, or Prophets; and (3) the *K^e^thūbhīm*, or Writings, called in Gr the Hagiographa. The *Tōrāh* included the 5 books of the Pentateuch (Gen, Ex, Lev, Nu, Dt), which were called "the Five-fifths of the Law." The *N^e^bhī'īm* embraced (*a*) the four so-called Former Prophets, Josh, Jgs, 1 and 2 S, counted as one book, 1 and 2 K, also counted as one book; and (*b*) the four so-called Latter Prophets, Isa, Jer, Ezk, and the Twelve Minor Prophets, counted as one book; a total of 8 books. The *K^e^thūbhīm*, or Writings, were 11 in all, including Ps, Prov, and Job, the five *M^e^ghillōth* or Rolls (Cant, Ruth, Lam, Eccl, Est), Dnl, Ezr-Neh, counted as one book, and 1 and 2 Ch, also counted as one book; in all 24 books, exactly the same as those of the Protestant canon. This was the original count of the Jews as far as we can trace it back. Later certain Jewish authorities appended Ruth to Jgs, and Lam to Jer, and thereby obtained the number 22, which corresponded to the number of letters in the Heb alphabet; but this manner of counting was secondary and fanciful. Still later others divided S, K, Ch, Ezr-Neh and Jer-Lam into two books each respectively and thereby obtained 27, which they fancifully regarded as equivalent to the 22 letters of the Heb alphabet plus 5, the number of letters having a peculiar final form when standing at the end of a word. Jerome states that 22 is the correct reckoning, but he adds, "Some count both Ruth and Lam among the Hagiographa, and so get 24." 4 Esd, which is the oldest (85–96 AD) witness to the number of books in the OT, gives 24.

6. How Account for the Tripartite Division?

The answer to the question of how to account for the tripartite division involves the most careful investigation of the whole process by which the canon actually took shape. If the entire canon of the OT were formed, as some allege, by one man, or by one set of men, in a single age, then it is obvious that the books must have been separated into three groups on the basis of some material differences in their contents. If, on the other hand, the process of canonization was gradual and extended over several generations, then the various books were separated from one another probably because one section of the canon was closed before certain other books of similar character were written. At any rate it is difficult to see why K and Ch are not included in the same division, and especially strange that Dnl does not stand among the prophets. To explain this mystery, mediaeval Jews were wont to say that "the Prophets were inspired by the spirit of prophecy, whereas the Writings by the Holy Spirit," implying different degrees of inspiration. But this is a distinction without a difference, the Holy Spirit and the spirit of prophecy are one and the same. Modern Protestants distinguish between the *donum propheticum* and the *munus propheticum*, i.e. between the gift and the office of prophecy. They allow that Daniel possessed the gift of prophecy, but they deny that he was Divinely appointed to the office of prophet. But compare Mt **24** 15, which speaks of "Daniel the prophet," and on the other hand, Am **7** 14, in which Amos resents being considered a prophet. Oehler modifies this explanation, claiming that the threefold division of the canon corresponds to the three stages of development in the religion of Israel, namely, Mosaism, Prophetism, and Hebraism. According to Oehler, the Law was the foundation of the entire canon. From it there were two lines of development, one objective, the Prophets, the other subjective, the Writings. But Oehler's theory does not satisfactorily account for Ezr and Neh and Ch, being in the third division; for in what sense can they be said to be more subjective than Jgs, S, and K? The LXX version (250–150 BC) takes no notice of the tripartite division. The true solution probably is that the process was gradual. When all the witnesses have been examined, we shall probably discover that the Law was canonized first, the Prophets considerably later, and the Writings last of all. And it may further become evident that the two last divisions were collected synchronously, and hence that the tripartite divisions of the canon are due to material differences in their contents as well as to chronology.

II. Examination of the Witnesses.—Though the OT does not tell us anything about the processes of its own canonization, it does furnish valuable hints as to how the ancient Hebrews preserved their writings.

1. The OT's Witness to Itself (cir 1450–444 BC)

Thus in Ex **40** 20 it is stated that the "testimony," by which is meant the two tables of the Law containing the Ten Commandments, was put into the Ark of the Covenant for safe-keeping. In Dt **31** 9.24–26, the laws of Dt are said to have been delivered to the sons of Levi, and by them deposited "by the side of the ark . . . . that it may be there for a witness against thee." Such language indicates that the new law-book is regarded "as a standard of faith and action" (Driver, *Dt*, 343). According to 1 K **8** 9, when Solomon brought the Ark up from the city of David to the Temple, the two tables were still its only contents, which continued to be carefully preserved. According to 2 K **11** 12, when Joash was crowned king, Jehoiada the high priest is said to have given (lit. "put upon") him "the testimony," which doubtless contained "the substance of the fundamental laws of the covenant," and was regarded as "the fundamental charter of the constitution" (cf H. E. Ryle, *Canon of the OT*, 45). Likewise in Prov **25** 1, it is stated that a large number of proverbs were copied out by Hezekiah's men. Now all these, and still other passages which might be summoned, witness to the preservation of certain portions of the OT. But preservation is not synonymous with canonization. A writing might easily be preserved without being made a standard of faith and conduct. Nevertheless the two ideas are closely related; for, when religious writings are sedulously preserved it is but natural to infer that their intrinsic value was regarded as correspondingly precious.

Two other passages of paramount importance remain to be considered. The first is 2 K **22** 8 ff, describing the finding of the "Book of the Law," and how Josiah the king on the basis of it instituted a religious reformation and bound the people to obey its precepts. Here is an instance in which the Law, or some portion of it (how much no one can say), is regarded as of normative and authoritative character. The king and his coadjutators recognize at once that it is ancient and that it contains the words of Jeh (2 K **22** 13.18.19). Its authority is undisputed. Yet nothing is said of its "canonicity," or that it would "defile the hands"; consequently there is no real ground for speaking of it as "the beginnings of the canon," for in the same historic sense the beginnings of the canon are to be found in Ex **24** 7. The other passage of paramount importance is Neh **8** 8 f, according to which Ezra is said to have "read in the book, in the law of God, distinctly." Not only did Ezra read the Law; he accompanied it with an interpretation. This seems to imply, almost beyond question, that in Ezra's time (444 BC) the Law, i.e. the Pent, was regarded as canonical Scripture. This is practically all that the OT says about itself, though other passages, such as Zec **7** 12 and Dnl **9** 2 might be brought forward to show the deep regard which the later prophets had for the writings of their predecessors. The former of these is the *locus classicus* in the OT, teaching the inspiration of the Prophets; it is the OT ‖ to 2 Tim **3** 16.

Chronologically the OT is of course our most ancient witness. It brings us down to 444 BC.

2. The Samaritan Pentateuch (cir 432 BC)

The next in order is the Samaritan Pent, the history of which is as follows: About 432 BC, as we know from Neh **13** 28 and Jos (*Ant*, XI, vii, 2—viii, 4), Nehemiah expelled from the Jewish colony in Jerus Manasseh, the polygamous grandson of Eliashib the high priest and son-in-law of Sanballat. Manasseh founded the schismatic community of the Samaritans, and instituted on Mt. Gerizim a rival temple-worship to that at Jerus. Of the Samaritans there still survive today some 170 souls; they reside in Shechem and are known as "the smallest religious sect in the world." It is true that Jos, speaking of this event, confuses chronology somewhat, making Nehemiah and Alexander the Great contemporaries, whereas a cent. separated them, but the time element is of little moment. The bearing of the whole matter upon the history of the formation of the canon is this: the Samaritans possess the Pent only; hence it is inferred that at the time of Manasseh's expulsion the Jewish canon included the Pent and the Pent only. Budde (*EB* col. 659) says: "If alongside of the Law there had been other *sacred writings*, it would be inexplicable why these last also did not pass into currency with the Samaritans." Such a conclusion, however, is not fully warranted. It is an argument from silence. There are patent reasons on the other hand why the Samaritans should have rejected the Prophets, even though they were already canonized. For the Samaritans would hardly adopt into their canon books that glorified the temple at Jerus. It cannot, accordingly, be inferred with certainty from the fact that the Samaritans accept the Pent only, that therefore the Pent at the time of Manasseh's expulsion was alone canonical, though it may be considered a reasonable presumption.

3. The Septuagint Version (cir 250–150 BC)

The LXX version in Gr is the first tr of the OT ever made; indeed the OT is the first book of any note in all lit. to receive the honor of being tr[d] into another tongue. This fact in itself is indicative of the esteem in which it was held at the time. The work of tr was inaugurated by Ptolemy Philadelphus (285–247 BC) and probably continued for well-nigh a cent. (cir 250–150 BC). Aristeas, a distinguished officer of Ptolemy, records how it came about. It appears that Ptolemy was exceedingly fond of books, and set his heart on adding to his famous collection in Alexandria a tr of the Heb Pent. In order to obtain it, so the story goes, the king set free 198,000 Jewish slaves, and sent them with presents to Jerus to ask Eleazar the high priest for their Law and Jewish scholars capable of translating it. Six learned rabbis from each tribe (6×12=72) were sent. They were royally feasted; 70 questions were asked them to test their wisdom, and after 72 days of coöperation and conference they gave the world the OT in the Gr language, which is known as the LXX version. To this fabulous story, Christian tradition adds that the rabbis did the work of translating in 72 (some say 36) separate cells on the island of Pharos, all working independently of each other, and that it was found at the expiration of their seclusion that each had produced a tr exactly word for word alike, hence supernaturally inspired. Justin Martyr of the 2d cent. AD says that he was actually shown by his Alexandrian guide the ruins of these LXX cells. The story is obviously a fable. The kernel of real truth at the bottom of it is probably that Ptolemy Philadelphus about the middle of the 3d cent. BC succeeded in obtaining a tr of the Law. The other books were tr[d] subsequently, perhaps for private use. The lack of unity of plan in the books outside the Law indicates that probably many different hands at different times were engaged upon them. There is a subscription, moreover, at the close of the tr of Est which states that Lysimachus, the son of Ptolemy in Jerus, tr[d] it. But the whole was apparently completed before Jesus ben Sirach the younger wrote his Prologue to Ecclus (cir 132 BC).

Now the LXX version, which was the Bible of Our Lord and His apostles, is supposed to have included originally many of the Apocryphal books. Furthermore, in our present LXX, the canonical and Apocryphal books stand intermingled and in an order which shows that the translators knew nothing of the tripartite division of later Judaism, or if they did they quite ignored it. The order of the books in our English OT is of course derived from the LXX through the Vulg of St. Jerome. The books in the LXX are arranged as follows: Pent, Josh, Jgs, Ruth, 1 and 2 S, 1 and 2 K, 1 and 2 Ch, 1 and 2 Esd, Neh, Tob, Jth, Est, Job, Ps, Prov, Eccl, Wisd, Ecclus, Hos, Am, Mic, Joel, Ob, Jon, Nah, Hab, Zeph, Hag, Zec, Mal, Isa, Jer, Bar, Lam, Ep. Jer, Ezk, Dnl, 1, 2 and 3 Macc. On the basis of the LXX, Catholics advocate what is known as the "larger" canon of the Jews in Alexandria; Protestants, on the other hand, deny the existence of an independent canon in Alexandria in view of the "smaller" canon of the Jews in Pal. The actual difference between the Catholic and Protestant OTs is a matter of 7 complete books and portions of two others: viz. Tob, Jth, Wisd, Ecclus, Bar, 1 and 2 Macc, together with certain additions to Est (**10** 4—**16** 24) and to Dnl (**3** 24–90; Three; Sus ver 13 and Bel ver 14). These Protestants reject as apocryphal because there is no sufficient evidence that they were ever reckoned as canonical by the Jews anywhere. The fact that the present LXX includes them is far from conclusive that the original LXX did, for the following reasons: (1) The design of the LXX was purely literary; Ptolemy and the Alexandrians were interested in building up a library. (2) All the extant MSS of the LXX are of Christian not Jewish origin. Between the actual tr of the LXX (cir 250–150 BC) and the oldest MSS of the LXX extant (cir 350 AD) there is a chasm of fully 500 years, during which it is highly possible that the so-called Apocryphal books crept in. (3) In the various extant MSS of the LXX, the Apocryphal books vary in number and name. For example, the great Vatican MS, which is probably "the truest representative which remains of the Alexandrian Bible," and which comes down to us from the 4th cent. AD, contains no Book of Macc whatever, but does include 1 Esd, which St. Jerome and Catholics generally treat as apocryphal. On the other hand, the Alexandrian MS, another of the great MSS of the LXX, dating from the 5th cent. AD, contains not only the extra-canonical book of 1 Esd, but 3 and 4 Macc, and in the NT the 1st and 2d Epistles of Clement, none of which, however, is considered canonical by Rome. Likewise the great Sinaitic MS, hardly less important than the Vatican as a witness to the LXX and like it dating from the 4th cent. AD, omits Bar (which Catholics consider canonical), but includes 4 Macc, and in the NT the Epistle of Barnabas and the Shepherd of Hermas; all of which are excluded from the canon by Catholics. In other MSS, 3 Macc, 3 Esd and Pr Man are occasionally included. The problem as to how many books the original LXX version actually included is a very complicated one. The probability is that it included no one of these variants. (4) Still another reason for thinking that there never existed in Egypt a separate or "larger" canon is the fact that during the 2d cent. AD, the Alexandrian Jews adopted Aquila's Gr version of the OT in lieu of their own, and it is known that Aquila's text excluded all Apocryphal books. Add to all this the fact that Philo, who lived in Alexandria from cir 20 BC till 50 AD, never quotes from one of these Apocryphal books though he often does from the canonical, and that Origen, who also resided in Alexandria (cir 200 AD), never set his *imprimatur* upon them, and it becomes reasonably convincing that there was no "larger" canon in Alexandria. The value of the evidence derived from the LXX, accordingly, is largely negative. It only indicates that when the tr of the OT into Gr was made in Alexandria, the process of canonization was still incomplete. For had it been actually complete, it is reasonable to suppose that the work of tr would have proceeded according to some well-defined plan, and would have been executed with greater accuracy. As it is, the translators seem to have taken all sorts of liberties with the text, adding to the books of Est and Dnl and omitting fully one-eighth of the text of Jer. Such work also indicates that they were not executing a public or ecclesiastical trust, but rather a private enterprise. Our necessary conclusion, therefore, is that the work of canonization was probably going on in Pal while the work of tr was proceeding in Alexandria.

4. Ecclus, or the Wisdom of Jesus ben Sirach (cir 170 BC)

Our next witness is Jesus ben Sirach who (cir 170 BC) wrote a formidable work entitled Ecclus, otherwise known as Sir. The author lived in Jerus and wrote in Heb. His book is a book of Wisdom resembling Prov; some of his precepts approach the high level of the Gospel. In many respects Ecclus is the most important of all the Apocryphal books; theologically it is the chief monument of primitive Sadduceeism. In chs **44–50**, the author sings a "hymn to the Fathers," eulogizing the mighty heroes of Israel from Enoch to Nehemiah, in fact from Adam to Simon, including the most famous men described in the OT, and making explicit mention of the Twelve Prophets. These facts would indicate that the whole or, at least, the most of the OT was known to him, and that already in his day (180 BC) the so-called Minor Prophets were regarded as a special group of writings by themselves. What the value of Ecclus is as a witness, however, depends upon the interpretation one places on **24** 33, which reads: "I will yet pour out doctrine as prophecy and leave it unto generations of ages." From this it is inferred by some that he feels himself inspired and capable of adding to the canon already in existence, and that, though he knew the full prophetic canon, he did not draw any very definite line of demarkation between his own work and the inspired writings of the prophets. For example, he passes over from the patriarchs and prophets of Israel to Simon the son of Onias, who was probably the high priest in his own time, making no distinction between them. But this may have been partly due to personal conceit; cf **39** 12, "Yet more will I utter, which I have thought upon; and I am filled as the moon at the full." Yet, perhaps, in his day still only the Law and the Prophets were actually canonized, but alongside of these a body of lit. was being gathered and gradually augmented of a nature not foreign to his own writings, and therefore not clearly marked off from literary compositions like his own. Yet to Sirach the Law is everything. He identifies it with the highest wisdom; indeed, all wisdom in his judgment is derived from a study of the Law (cf **19** 20–24; **15** 1–18; **24** 23; **2** 16; **39** 1).

5. The Prologue to Ecclus (cir 132 BC)

The Prologue or Preface to Ecclus is our next witness to the formation of the canon. It was written by the grandson of Jesus ben Sirach, who bore his grandfather's name (cir 132 BC). Jesus ben Sirach the younger tr[d] in Egypt his grandfather's proverbs into Gr, and in doing so added a Preface or Prologue of his own. In this Prologue, he thrice refers to the tripartite division of the OT. In fact the Prologue to Ecclus is the oldest witness we have to the threefold division of the OT books. He says: "Whereas many and great things have been delivered unto us by the Law and the Prophets, and by others, ... my grandfather, Jesus, when he had given himself to the reading of the Law, and the Prophets, and other books of our Fathers, and had gotten therein good judgment (RV "having gained great familiarity therein"), was drawn on also himself to write something pertaining to learning and wisdom. . . . . For the same things uttered in Heb and tr[d] into another tongue, have not the same force in them; and not only these things, but the Law itself, and the Prophets, and the rest of the books, have no small difference, when they are spoken in their own language." These are explicit and definite allusions to the threefold division of the OT writings, yet only the titles of the first and second divisions are the technical names usually employed; the third is especially vague because of his use of the terms, "the other books of the Fathers," and "the rest of the books." However, he evidently refers to writings with religious contents; and, by "the other books of the Fathers," he can hardly be supposed to have meant an indefinite number, though he has not told us which they were or what was their number. From his further statement that his grandfather, having immersed himself in the Law and the Prophets, and other books of the Fathers, felt drawn on also himself to write something for the profit of others, it may be inferred that in his time there was as yet no definite gulf fixed between canonical writings and those of other men, and that the sifting process was still going on (cf W. R. Smith, *OTJC*², 178–79).

6. 1 and 2 Macc (between 125 and 70 BC)

1 Macc was written originally in Heb; 2 Macc in Gr, somewhere between 125 and 70 BC. The author of 1 Macc is acquainted, on the one hand, with the deeds of John Hyrcanus (135 to 105 BC), and knows nothing on the other of the conquest of Pal by Pompey (63 BC). The value of this book as a witness to the history of the canon centers about his allusions to Daniel and the Psalms. In 1 Macc **1** 54, he tells how Antiochus Epiphanes "set up the abomination of desolation" upon the altar at Jerus, referring most likely to Dnl **9** 24–27; and in 1 Macc **2** 59.60 he speaks of Ananias, Azarias and Misael, who by believing were saved from the fiery furnace, and of Daniel, who was delivered from the mouths of the lions (cf Dnl **1** 7; **3** 26; **6** 23). From these allusions, it would seem as though the Book of Dnl was at that time regarded as normative or canonical. This is confirmed by 1 Macc **7** 16.17, which introduces a quotation from Ps **79** 2, with the solemn formula, "According to the words which he wrote"; which would suggest that the Ps also were already canonical.

2 Macc, written cir 124 BC, also contains a couple of passages of considerable importance to us in this investigation. Both, however, are found in a spurious letter purporting to have been sent by the inhabitants of Judaea to their fellow-countrymen residing in Egypt. The first passage (2 Macc **2** 13) tells how Nehemiah, "founding a library, gathered together the acts of the kings, and the prophets, and of David, and the epistles of the kings concerning holy gifts." These words throw no special light upon the formation of the canon, but they do connect with the name of Nehemiah the preservation of public documents and historical records of national interest, and how he, as a lover of books, founded a library. This is in perfect agreement with what we know of Nehemiah's character, for he compiled the genealogy of Neh **7**; besides, collection precedes selection. The other passage (2 Macc **2** 14) reads: "In like manner also Judas gathered together all things that were lost by reason of the war we had, and they remain with us." Though found in a letter, supposed to be spurious, there is every reason for believing this statement to be true. For when Antiochus, the arch enemy of the nation, sought to stamp out the religion of the Jews by destroying their books (cf 1 Macc **1** 56.57), what would have been more natural for a true patriot like Judas than to attempt to re-collect their sacred writings? "This statement, therefore," as Wildeboer says, "may well be worthy of credence" (*The Origin of the Canon of the OT*, 40). Though it yields nothing definite as to the number of the books recovered, it is obvious that the books collected were the most precious documents which the nation possessed. They were doubtless religious, as was the age.

7. Philo (cir 20 BC–50 AD)

Philo is our next witness. He flourished in Alexandria between cir 20 BC and 50 AD, leaving behind him a voluminous literature. Unfortunately, he does not yield us much of positive value for our present purpose. His evidence is largely negative. True, he nowhere mentions the tripartite division of the OT, which is known to have existed in his day. Nor does he quote from Ezk, the Five Megilloth (Cant, Ruth, Lam, Eccl, Est), Dnl, Ch, or from the Twelve Minor Prophets, except Hos, Jon, and Zec. Moreover he held a loose view of inspiration. According to Philo, inspiration was by no means confined to the sacred Scriptures; all truly wise and virtuous men are inspired and capable of expressing the hidden things of God. But as Dr. Green (*Canon*, 130) rightfully contends, "Philo's loose views of inspiration cannot be declared irreconcilable with the acceptance of a fixed canon, unless it is first shown that he places others whom he thinks inspired on a level with the writers of Scripture. This he never does." Philo's reverence for the "Law" was unbounded. In this respect he is the type of other Alexandrians. He quotes predominatingly from the Law. Moses was to him the source of all wisdom, even the wisdom of the Gentiles. Concerning the laws of Moses, he is reported by Eusebius as saying: "They have not changed so much as a single word in them. They would rather die a thousand deaths than detract anything from these laws and statutes." On the other hand, Philo never quotes any of the Apocryphal books. Hence it may safely be assumed that his canon was essentially ours.

8. The NT as a Witness (cir 50–100 AD)

The evidence furnished by the NT is of the highest importance. When summed up, it gives the unmistakable impression that when the NT was written (cir 50–100 AD) there was a definite and fixed canon of OT Scripture, to which authoritative appeal could be made. And first, too much importance can scarcely be attached to the names or titles ascribed to the OT writings by the authors of the NT: thus, "the scripture" (Jn **10** 35; **19** 36; 2 Pet **1** 20), "the scriptures" (Mt **22** 29; Acts **18** 24), "holy scriptures" (Rom **1** 2), "sacred writings" (2 Tim **3** 15), "the law" (Jn **10** 34; **12** 34; **15** 25; 1 Cor **14** 21), "law and prophets" (Mt **5** 17; **7** 12; **22** 40; Lk **16** 16; **24** 44; Acts **13** 15; **28** 23). Such names or titles, though they do not define the limits of the canon, certainly assume the existence of a complete and sacred collection of Jewish writings which are already marked off from all other lit. as separate and fixed. One passage (Jn **10** 35) in which the term "scripture," is employed seems to refer to the OT canon as a whole; "and the scripture cannot be broken." In like manner the expression "law and prophets" is often used in a generic sense, referring to much more than merely the 1st and 2d divisions of the OT; it seems rather to refer to the old dispensation as a whole; but the term "the law" is the most general of all. It is frequently applied to the entire OT, and apparently held in Christ's time among the Jews a place akin to that which the term "the Bible" does with us. For example, in Jn **10** 34; **12** 34; **15** 25, texts from the prophets or even from the Ps are quoted as part of "the Law"; in 1 Cor **14** 21 also, Paul speaks of Isa **28** 11 as a part of "the law." These names and titles, accordingly, are exceedingly important; they are never applied by NT writers to the Apocrypha.

One passage (Lk **24** 44) furnishes clear evidence of the threefold division of the canon. But here again, as in the Prologue of Sir, there is great uncertainty as to the limits of the 3d division. Instead of saying "the law, the prophets and the writings," Luke says, "the law, the prophets and the psalms." But it is obvious enough why the Pss should have been adduced by Jesus in support of His resurrection. It is because they especially testify of Christ; they were, therefore, the most important part of the 3d division for His immediate purpose, and it may be that they are meant to stand *a potiori* for the whole of the 3d division (cf Budde, *EB*, col. 669).

Another passage (Mt **23** 35; cf Lk **11** 51) seems to point to the final order and arrangement of the books in the OT canon. It reads: "That upon you may come all the righteous blood shed on the earth, from the blood of Abel the righteous unto the blood of Zachariah son of Barachiah, whom ye slew between the sanctuary and the altar." Now, in order to grasp the bearing of this ver upon the matter in hand, it must be remembered that in the modern arrangement of the OT books in Heb, Ch stands last; and that the murder of Zachariah is the last recorded instance in this arrangement, being found in 2 Ch **24** 20.21. But this murder took place under Joash king of Judah, in the 9th cent. BC. There is another which is chronologically later, namely, that of Uriah son of Shemaiah who was murdered in Jehoiakim's reign in the 7th cent. BC (Jer **26** 23). Accordingly, the argument is this, unless Ch already stood last in Christ's OT, why did He not say, "from the blood of Abel unto the blood of Uriah"? He would then have been speaking chronologically and would have included all the martyrs whose martyrdom is recorded in the OT. But He rather says, "from the blood of Abel unto the blood of Zachariah," as though He were including the whole range of OT Scripture, just as we would say "from Genesis to Malachi." Hence it is inferred, with some degree of justification also, that Ch stood in Christ's time, as it does today in the Heb Bible of the Massorets, the last book of an already closed canon. Of course, in answer to this, there is the possible objection that in those early days the Scriptures were still written by the Jews on separate rolls.

Another ground for thinking that the OT canon was closed before the NT was written is the numerous citations made in the NT from the OT. Every book is quoted except Est, Eccl, Cant, Ezr, Neh, Ob, Nah, and Zeph. But these exceptions are not serious. The Twelve Minor Prophets were always treated by the Jews *en bloc* as one canonical work; hence if one of the twelve were quoted all were recognized. And the fact that 2 Ch **24** 20.21 is quoted in Mt **23** 35 and Lk **11** 51 presupposes also the canonicity of Ezr-Neh, as originally these books were one with Ch, though they may possibly have already been divided in Jesus' day. As for Est, Eccl, and Cant, it is easy to see why they are not quoted: they probably failed to furnish NT writers material for quotation. The NT writers simply had no occasion to make citations from them. What is much more noteworthy, they never quote from the Apocryphal books, though they show an acquaintance with them. Professor Gigot, one of the greatest of Roman Catholic authorities, frankly admits this. In his *General Introduction to the Study of the Scriptures*, 43, he says: "They never quote them explicitly, it is true, but time and again they borrow expressions and ideas from them." As a matter of fact, NT writers felt free to quote from any source; for example, Paul on Mars' Hill cites to the learned Athenians an astronomical work of the Stoic Aratus of Cilicia, or perhaps from a Hymn to Jupiter by Cleanthes of Lycia, when he says, "For we are also his offspring" (Acts **17** 28). And Jude vs 14.15 almost undeniably quotes from En (**1** 9; **60** 8)—a work which is not recognized as canonical by any except the church of Abyssinia. But in any case, the mere quoting of a book does not canonize it; nor, on the other hand, does failure to quote a book exclude it. Quotation does not necessarily imply sanction; no more than reference to contemporary lit. is incompatible with strict views of the canon. Everything depends upon the manner in which the quotation is made. In no case is an Apocryphal book cited by NT authors as "Scripture," or as the work of the Holy Spirit. And the force of this statement is not weakened by the fact that the authors of NT writings cited the LXX instead of the original Heb; for, "they are responsible only for the inherent truthfulness of each passage in the form which they actually adopt" (Green, *Canon*, 145). As a witness, therefore, the NT is of paramount importance. For, though it nowhere tells us the exact number of books contained in the OT canon, it gives abundant evidence of the existence already in the 1st cent. AD of a definite and fixed canon.

9. 4 Esd (cir 81–96 AD)

4 Esd in Lat (2 Esd in Eng.) is a Jewish apocalypse which was written originally in Greek toward the close of the 1st cent. (cir 81–96 AD). The passage of special interest to us is **14** 19–48 which relates in most fabulous style how Ezra is given spiritual illumination to reproduce the Law which had been burned, and how, at the Divine command, he secludes himself for a period of 40 days, after which he betakes himself with five skilled scribes to the open country. There, a cup of water is offered him; he drinks, and then dictates to his five amanuenses continuously for 40 days and nights, producing 94 books of which 70 are kept secret and 24 published. The section of supreme importance reads as follows: "And it came to pass, when the forty days were fulfilled, that the Most High spake, saying, 'The first that thou hast written, publish openly, that the worthy may read it; but keep the seventy last, that thou mayest deliver them only to such as be wise among the people; for in them is the spring of understanding, the fountain of wisdom, and the stream of knowledge.' And I did so" (4 Esd **14** 45–48). The story is obviously pure fiction. No wonder that a new version of it arose in the 16th cent., according to which the canon was completed, not by Ezra alone, but by a company of men known as the Great Synagogue. From the legend of 4 Esd it is commonly inferred that the 24 books which remain after subtracting 70 from 94 are the canonical books of the OT. If so, then this legend is the first witness we have to the number of books contained in the OT canon. This number corresponds exactly with the usual number of sacred books according to Jewish count, as we saw in § 5 above. The legend, accordingly, is not without value. Even as legend it witnesses to a tradition which existed as early as the 1st Christian cent., to the effect that the Jews possessed 24 specially sacred books. It also points to Ezra as the chief factor in the making of Scripture and intimates that the OT canon has long since been virtually closed.

10. Jos' "Contra Apionem" (cir 100 AD)

Flavius Josephus, the celebrated Jewish historian, was born 37 AD. He was a priest and a Pharisee. About 100 AD, he wrote a controversial treatise, known as *Contra Apionem*, in defence of the Jews against their assailants, of whom Apion is taken as a leading representative. Now Apion was a famous grammarian, who in his life had been hostile to the Jews. He had died some 50 years before *Contra Apionem* was written. Jos wrote in Gr to Greeks. The important passage in his treatise (I, 8) reads as follows: "For it is not the case with us to have vast numbers of books disagreeing and conflicting with one another. We have but twenty-two, containing the history of all time, books that are justly believed in. And of these, five are the books of Moses, which comprise the laws and the earliest traditions from the creation of mankind down to the time of his (Moses') death. This period falls short but by a little of three thousand years. From the death of Moses to the reign of Artaxerxes, king of Persia, the successor of Xerxes, the prophets who succeeded Moses wrote the history of the events that occurred in their own time; in thirteen books. The remaining four documents comprise hymns to God and practical precepts to men. From the days of Artaxerxes to our own time every event has indeed been recorded. But these recent records have not been deemed worthy of equal credit with those which preceded them, because the exact succession of the prophets ceased. But what faith we have placed in our own writings is evident by our conduct; for though so great an interval of time (i.e. since they were written) has now passed, not a soul has ventured either to add, or to remove, or to alter a syllable. But it is instinctive in all Jews at once from their very birth to regard them as commands of God, and to abide by them, and, if need be, willingly to die for them."

The value of this remarkable passage for our study is obviously very great. In the first place Jos fixes the number of Jewish writings which are recognized as sacred at 22, joining probably Ruth to Jgs and Lam to Jer. He also classifies them according to a threefold division, which is quite peculiar to himself: 5 of Moses, 13 of the prophets, and 4 hymns and maxims for human life. The 5 of Moses were of course the Pent; the 13 of the prophets probably included the 8 regular *N^{e}bhī'īm* plus Dnl, Job, Ch, Ezr-Neh, and Est; the "4 hymns and maxims" would most naturally consist of Ps, Prov, Cant and Eccl. There is little doubt that his 22 books are those of our present Heb canon.

Another very remarkable fact about Jos' statement is the standard he gives of canonicity, namely, antiquity; because, as he says, since Artaxerxes' age the succession of prophets had ceased. It was the uniform tradition of Jos' time that prophetic inspiration had ceased with Malachi (cir 445–432 BC). Hence, according to him, the canon was closed in the reign of Artaxerxes (465–425 BC). He does not pause to give any account of the closing of the canon; he simply assumes it, treating it as unnecessary. Prophecy had ceased, and the canon was accordingly closed; the fact did not require to be officially proclaimed. As remarked above, the value of Jos as a witness is very great. But just here an important question arises: How literally must we interpret his language? Was the OT canon actually closed before 425 BC? Were not there books and parts of books composed and added to the canon subsequent to his reign? Dr. Green seems to take Jos literally (*Canon*, 40, 78). But Jos is not always reliable in his chronology. For example, in his *Antiquities* (XI, vi, 13) he dates the story of Esther as occurring in the reign of Artaxerxes I (whereas it belongs to Xerxes' reign), while in the same work (XI, v, 1) he puts Ezra and Nehemiah under Xerxes (whereas they belong to the time of Artaxerxes). On the whole, it seems safer on internal grounds to regard Jos' statements concerning the antiquity of the Jewish canon as the language not of a careful historian, but of a partisan in debate. Instead of expressing absolute fact in this case, he was reflecting the popular belief of his age. Reduced to its lowest terms, the element of real truth in what he says was simply this, that he voiced a tradition which was at that time universal and undisputed; one, however, which had required a long period, perhaps hundreds of years, to develop. Hence we conclude that the complete OT canon, numbering 22 books, was no new thing 100 AD.

11. The Councils of Jamnia (90 and 118 AD)

According to the traditions preserved in the Mish, two councils of Jewish rabbis were held (90 and 118 AD respectively) at Jabne, or Jamnia, not far S. of Joppa, on the Mediterranean coast, at which the books of the OT, notably Eccl and Cant, were discussed and their canonicity ratified. Rabbi Gamaliel II probably presided. Rabbi Akiba was the chief spirit of the council. What was actually determined by these synods has not been preserved to us accurately, but by many authorities it is thought that the great controversy which had been going on for over a cent. between the rival Jewish schools of Hillel and Shammai was now brought to a close, and that the canon was formally restricted to our 39 books. Perhaps it is within reason to say that at Jamnia the limits of the Heb canon were officially and finally determined by Jewish authority. Not that official sanction created public opinion, however, but rather confirmed it.

12. The Talm (200–500 AD)

The Talm consists of two parts: (1) The Mish (compiled cir 200 AD), a collection of systematized tradition; and (2) the Gemara, *G^{e}mārā* (completed about 500 AD), a "vast and desultory commentary on the Mish." A Baraitha', or unauthorized gloss, known as the *Bābhā' Bathrā'* 14 b, a Talmudic tractate, relates the "order" of the various books of the OT and who "wrote" or edited them. But it says nothing of the formation of the canon. To write is not the same as to canonize; though to the later Jews the two ideas were closely akin. As a witness, therefore, this tractate is of little value, except that it confirms the tripartite division and is a good specimen of rabbinic speculation. For the full text of the passage, see Ryle, *Canon of the OT*, 273 ff.

13. Jewish Doubts in the 2d Cent. AD

During the 2d cent. AD, doubts arose in Jewish minds concerning four books, Prov, Cant, Eccl, and Est. In a certain Talmudic tractate it is related that an attempt was made to withdraw (*gānaz*, "conceal," "hide") the Book of Prov on account of contradictions which were found in it (cf **26** 4.5), but on deeper investigation it was not withdrawn. In another section of the Talmud, Rabbi Akiba is represented as saying concerning Cant: "God forbid that any man of Israel should deny that the Song of Songs defileth the hands, for the whole world is not equal to the day in which the Song of Songs was given to Israel. For all Scriptures are holy, but the Song of Songs is the holiest of the holy." Such extravagant language inclines one to feel that real doubt must have existed in the minds of some concerning the book. But the protestations were much stronger against Eccl. In one tractate it is stated: "The wise men desired to hide it because its language was often self-contradictory (cf Eccl **7** 3 and **2** 2; **4** 2 and **9** 4), but they did not hide it because the beginning and the end of it consist of words from the Torah (cf **1** 3; **12** 13.14)." Likewise Est was vigorously disputed by both the Jerus and Bab Gemaras, because the name of God was not found in it; but a Rabbi Simeon ben Lakkish (cir 300 AD) defended its canonicity, putting Esther on an equality with the Law and above the Prophets and the other Writings. Other books, for example, Ezekiel and Jonah, were discussed in post-Talmudic writings, but no serious objections were ever raised by the Jews against either. Jonah was really never doubted till the 12th cent. AD. In the case of no one of these disputed books were there serious doubts; nor did scholastic controversies affect public opinion.

This brings us to the end of our examination of the witnesses. In our survey we have discovered (1) that the OT says nothing about its canonization, but does emphasize the manner in which the Law was preserved and recognized as authoritative;

(2) that to conclude that the Jews possessed the Law only, when the renegade Manasseh was expelled by Nehemiah from Jerus, because the Samaritans admit of the Law alone as the true canon, is unwarrantable; (3) that the LXX version as we know it from the Christian MSS extant is by no means a sufficient proof that the Alexandrians possessed a "larger" canon which included the Apoc; (4) that Jesus ben Sirach is a witness to the fact that the Prophets in his day (180 BC) were not yet acknowledged as canonical; (5) that his grandson in his Prologue is the first witness to the customary tripartite division of OT writings, but does not speak of the 3d division as though it were already closed; (6) that the Books of Macc seem to indicate that the Ps and Dnl are already included in the canon of the Jews; (7) that Philo's testimony is negative, in that he witnesses against the Apocryphal books as an integral part of Holy Scripture; (8) that the NT is the most explicit witness of the series, because of the names and titles it ascribes to the OT books which it quotes; (9) that 4 Esd is the first witness to the number of books in the OT canon—24; (10) that Jos also fixes the number of books, but in arguing for the antiquity of the canon speaks as an advocate, voicing popular tradition, rather than as a scientific historian; (11) that the Councils of Jamnia may, with some ground, be considered the official occasion on which the Jews pronounced upon the limits of their canon; but that (12) doubts existed in the 2d cent. concerning certain books; which books, however, were not seriously questioned.

14. Summary and Conclusion

From all this we conclude, that the Law was canonized, or as we would better say, was recognized as authoritative, first, cir 444 BC; that the Prophets were set on an even footing with the Law considerably later, cir 200 BC; and that the Writings received authoritative sanction still later, cir 100 BC. There probably never were three separate canons, but there were three separate classes of writings, which between 450 and 100 BC doubtless stood on different bases, and only gradually became authoritative. There is, therefore, ground for thinking, as suggested above (§ 6), that the tripartite division of the OT canon is due to material differences in the contents as well as to chronology.

III. The Canon in the Christian Church.—In making the transition from the Jewish to the Christian church, we find the same canon cherished by all. Christians of all sects have always been disposed to accept without question the canon of the Jews. For cents. all branches of the Christian church were practically agreed on the limits set by the Jews, but eventually the western church became divided, some alleging that Christ sanctioned the "larger" canon of Alexandria, including the Apocrypha, while others adhered, as the Jews have always done, to the canon of the Jews in Pal. Taking the eastern or oriental church first, the evidence they furnish is as follows: The Pesh, or Syr version, dating from cir 150 AD, omits Ch; Justin Martyr (164 AD) held to a canon identical with that of the Jews; the Canon of Melito, bishop of Sardis, who (cir 170 AD) made a journey to Pal in order carefully to investigate the matter, omits Est. His list, which is the first Christian list we have, has been preserved to us by Eusebius in his *Eccl. Hist.*, IV, 26; Origen (d. 254 AD), who was educated in Alexandria, and was one of the most learned of the Gr Fathers, also set himself the task of knowing the "Heb verity" of the OT text, and gives us a list (also preserved to us by Eusebius, *Eccl. Hist.*, VI, 5) in which he reckons the number of books as 22 (thus agreeing with Jos). Inadvertently he omits the Twelve Minor Prophets, but this is manifestly an oversight on the part of either a scribe or of Eusebius, as he states the number of books is 22 and then names but 21. The so-called Canon of Laodicea (cir 363 AD) included the canonical books only, rejecting the Apocrypha. Athanasius (d. 365 AD) gives a list in which Est is classed as among the non-canonical books, but he elsewhere admits that "Est is considered canonical by the Hebrews." However, he included Bar and the Epistle of Jeremiah with Jeremiah. Amphilochius, bishop of Iconium (cir 380 AD), speaks of Est as received by some only. Cyril, bishop of Jerus (d. 386 AD), gives a list corresponding with the Heb canon, except that he includes Bar and the Epistle of Jeremiah. Gregory of Nazianzus in Cappadocia (d. 390 AD) omits Est. But Anastasius, patriarch of Antioch (560 AD), and Leontius of Byzantium (580 AD) both held to the strict Jewish canon of 22 books. The Nestorians generally doubted Est. This was due doubtless to the influence of Theodore of Mopsuestia (cir 390–457 AD) who disputed the authority of Ch, Ezr, Neh, Est and Job. The oriental churches as a whole, however, never canonized the Apocrypha.

1. In the Eastern or Oriental Church

Between 100 and 400 AD, the NT writings became canonical, occupying in the Christian church a place of authority and sacredness equal to those of the OT. The tendency of the period was to receive everything which had been traditionally read in the churches. But the transference of this principle to the OT writings produced great confusion. Usage and theory were often in conflict. A church Father might declare that the Apocryphal books were uninspired and yet quote them as "Scripture," and even introduce them with the accepted formula, "As the Holy Ghost saith." Theologically they held to a strict canon, homiletically they used a larger one. But even usage was not uniform. 3 and 4 Esd and the Book of En are sometimes quoted as "Holy Writ," yet the western church never received these books as canonical. The criterion of usage, therefore, is too broad. The theory of the Fathers was gradually forgotten, and the prevalent use of the LXX and other versions led to the obliteration of the distinction between the undisputed books of the Heb canon and the most popular Apocryphal books; and being often publicly read in the churches they finally received a quasi-canonization.

2. In the Western Church

Tertullian of Carthage (cir 150–230 AD) is the first of the Lat Fathers whose writings have been preserved. He gives the number of OT books as 24, the same as in the Talm. Hilary, bishop of Poitiers in France (350–368 AD), gives a catalogue in which he speaks of "Jeremiah and his epistle," yet his list numbers only 22. Rufinus of Aquileia in Italy (d. 410 AD) likewise gives a complete list of 22 books. Jerome also, the learned monk of Bethlehem (d. 420 AD), gives the number of canonical books as 22, corresponding to the 22 letters of the Heb alphabet, and explains that the five double books (1 and 2 S, 1 and 2 K, 1 and 2 Ch, Ezr-Neh, Jer-Lam) correspond to the five final letters of the Heb alphabet. In his famous *Prologus Galeatus* or "Helmed Preface" to the books of S and K, he declares himself for the strict canon of the Jews; rejecting the authority of the deuterocanonical books in the most outspoken manner, even distinguishing carefully the apocryphal additions to Est and to Dnl. As the celebrated Catholic writer, Dr. Gigot, very frankly allows, "Time and again this illustrious doctor [Jerome] of the Lat church rejects the authority of the deuterocanonical books in the most explicit manner" (*General Intro*, 56).

Contemporaneous with Jerome in Bethlehem lived Augustine in North Africa (353–430 AD). He was the bishop of Hippo; renowned as thinker, theologian and saint. In the three great Councils of Hippo (393) and Carthage (397 and 419 AD), of which he was the leading spirit, he closed, as it were, the great debate of the previous generations on the subject of how large shall be the Bible. In his essay on *Christian Doctrine*, he catalogues the books of Scripture, which had been transmitted by the Fathers for public reading in the church, giving their number as 44, with which he says "the authority of the OT is ended." These probably correspond with the present canon of Catholics. But it is not to be supposed that Augustine made no distinction between the proto- and deutero-canonical books. On the contrary, he limited the term "canonical" in its strict sense to the books which are inspired and received by the Jews, and denied that in the support of doctrine the books of Wisd and Ecclus were of unquestioned authority, though long custom had entitled them to respect. And when a passage from 2 Macc was urged by his opponents in defence of suicide, he rejected their proof by showing that the book was not received into the Heb canon to which Christ was witness. At the third Council of Carthage (397 AD), however, a decree was ratified, most probably with his approval, which in effect placed all the canonical and deutero-canonical books on the same level, and in the course of time they actually became considered by some as of equal authority (see DEUTERO-CANONICAL BOOKS). A few years later, another council at Carthage (419 AD) took the additional step of voting that their own decision concerning the canon should be confirmed by Boniface, the bishop of Rome; accordingly, thereafter, the question of how large the Bible should be became a matter to be settled by authority rather than by criticism.

From the 4th to the 16th cent. AD the process of gradually widening the limits of the canon continued. Pope Gelasius (492–496 AD) issued a decretal or list in which he included the OT apocrypha. Yet even after this official act of the papacy the sentiment in the western church was divided. Some followed the strict canon of Jerome, while others favored the larger canon of Augustine, without noting his cautions and the distinctions he made between inspired and uninspired writings. Cassiodorus (556 AD) and Isidore of Seville (636 AD) place the lists of Jerome and Augustine side by side without deciding between them. Two bishops of North Africa, Primasius and Junilius (cir 550 AD) reckon 24 books as strictly canonical and explicitly state that the others are not of the same grade. Popular usage, however, was indiscriminate. Outside the Jews there was no sound Heb tradition. Accordingly, at the Council of Florence (1442 AD), "Eugenius IV, with the approval of the Fathers of that assembly, declared all the books found in the Lat Bibles then in use to be inspired by the same Holy Spirit, without distinguishing them into two classes or categories" (cf Gigot, *General Intro*, 71). Though this bull of Eugenius IV did not deal with the canonicity of the Apocryphal books, it did proclaim their *inspiration*. Nevertheless, down to the Council of Trent (1546 AD), the Apocryphal books possessed only inferior authority; and when men spoke of canonical Scripture in the strict sense, these were not included.

Luther, the great Saxon Reformer of the 16th cent., marks an epoch in the history of the Christian OT canon. In translating the Scriptures into German, he gave the deutero-canonical books an intermediate position between the OT and the NT. The Lutheran church, also, while it does not expressly define the limits of the canon, yet places the Apocryphal writings by themselves as distinct and separate from Holy Scripture. This indeed was the attitude of all the early Reformers. In the Zürich Bible of 1529, as in the Genevan version in English of 1560, the Apocryphal books were placed apart with special headings by themselves. Thus the early Reformers did not entirely reject the Apocryphal writings, for it was not an easy task to do so in view of the usage and traditions of centuries.

Rome had vacillated long enough. She realized that something must be done. The Reformers had sided with those who stood by Jerome. She therefore resolved to settle the matter in an ecclesiastical and dogmatic manner. Accordingly the Council of Trent decreed at their fourth sitting (April 8, 1546), that the Apocryphal books were equal in authority and canonical value to the other books of sacred Scripture; and to make this decree effective they added: "If, however, anyone receive not as sacred and canonical the said books entire with all their facts, and as they have been used to be read in the Catholic church, and as they are contained in the Old Lat Vulg ed . . . . let him be anathema." The decree was the logical outcome of the ever-accumulating snowball tendency in the western church. The historical effect of it upon the church is obvious. It closed forever the field of Bib. study against all free research. Naturally, therefore, the Vatican Council of 1870 not only reiterated the decree but found it easy to take still another step and canonize tradition.

Repeated endeavors were made during the 16th and 17th cents. to have the Apocryphal books removed from the Scriptures. The Synod of Dort (1618–19), Gomarus, Deodatus and others, sought to accomplish it, but failed. The only success achieved was in getting them separated from the truly canonical writings and grouped by themselves, as in the Gallican Confession of 1559, the Anglican Confession of 1562, and the Second Helvetic Confession of 1566. The Puritan Confession went farther, and declared that they were of a purely secular character. The various continental and Eng. versions of the Bible then being made likewise placed them by themselves, apart from the acknowledged books, as a kind of appendix. For example, the Zürich Bible of 1529, the French Bible of 1535, Coverdale's English tr of 1536, Matthew's of 1537, the second ed of the Great Bible, 1540, the Bishops' of 1568, and the AV of 1611. The first Eng. version to omit them altogether was an ed of King James's Version published in 1629; but the custom of printing them by themselves, between the OT and the NT, continued until 1825, when the Edinburgh Committee of the British and Foreign Bible Society protested that the Society should no longer translate these Apocryphal writings and send them to the heathen. The Society finally yielded and decided to exclude them (May 3, 1827). Since then, Protestants in Great Britain and America have given up the practice of publishing the Apoc as a part of sacred Scripture. In Europe, also, since 1850, the tendency has been in the same direction. The Church of England, however, and the American Episcopal church, do not wholly exclude them; certain "readings" being selected from Wisd, Ecclus and Bar, and read on week days between October 27 and November 17. Yet, when the ERV appeared in 1885, though it was a special product of the Church of England, there was not so much as a reference to the Apocryphal writings. The Irish church likewise removed them; and the ARV ignores them altogether.

LITERATURE.—G. Wildeboer, *The Origin of the Canon of the OT*, trd by B. W. Bacon, London, Luzac & Co.,

1895; H. E. Ryle, *The Canon of the OT*, London and New York, Macmillan, 1892; F. Buhl, *Canon and Text of the OT*, trd by John MacPherson, Edinburgh, T. & T. Clark, 1892; W. H. Green, *General Intro to the OT, The Canon*, New York, Scribner, 1898; W. Robertson Smith, *The OT in the Jewish Church*, 2d ed, London, A. & C. Black, 1895; F. E. Gigot, *General Intro to the Holy Scriptures*, 3d ed, New York, Cincinnati and Chicago, Benziger Bros., 1903; B. F. Westcott, *The Bible in the Christian Church*, London and New York, Macmillan, 1901; C. A. Briggs, *General Intro to the Study of Holy Scripture*, New York, Scribner, 1899; A. F. Kirkpatrick, *The Divine Library of the OT*, London and New York, Macmillan, 1892; Hastings, *DB*, III, 1900, art. "OT Canon" by F. H. Woods; Cheney and Black's *EB*, I, 1899, art. "Canon" by K. Budde; The *New Schaff-Herzog Enc of Religious Knowledge*, II, 1908, art. "Canon of Scripture" by H. L. Strack; *Jour. of Bib. Lit.*, 1893, 118-28, art. "The Alleged Triple Canon of the OT," by W. J. Beecher; Abbé A. Loisy, *Histoire du canon de l'ancien testament*, Paris, 1890; J. Fürst, *Der Kanon des AT*, Leipzig, 1868; E. Reuss, *Histoire du canon des saintes écritures dans l'église chrétienne*, Strassburg, 1864, Eng. tr, Edinburgh, 1891.

GEORGE L. ROBINSON

CANON, kan'un, OF THE NEW TESTAMENT, THE:

I. Two Preliminary Considerations
 1. Early Christians Had the OT
 2. No Intention of Writing the NT
II. Three Stages of the Process
 1. From the Apostles to 170 AD
  (1) Clement of Rome; Ignatius; Polycarp
  (2) Forces Increasing Value of Writings
   (a) Apologists. Justin Martyr
   (b) Gnostics. Marcion
 2. From 170 AD to 220 AD
  (1) Irenaeus
  (2) Muratorian Fragment
 3. 3d and 4th Cents.
  (1) Origen
  (2) Dionysius
  (3) Cyprian
  (4) Eusebius
  (5) Athanasius
  (6) Council of Carthage. Jerome; Augustine
Literature

I. Two Preliminary Considerations.—The canon is the collection of 27 books which the church (generally) receives as its NT Scriptures. The history of the canon is the history of the process by which these books were brought together and their value as sacred Scriptures officially recognized. That process was gradual, furthered by definite needs, and, though unquestionably continuous, is in its earlier stages difficult to trace. It is always well in turning to the study of it to have in mind two considerations which bear upon the earliest phases of the whole movement. These are:

1. Early Christians Had the OT

(1) The early Christians had in their hands what was a Bible to them, viz. the OT Scriptures. These were used to a surprising extent in Christian instruction. For a whole cent. after the death of Jesus this was the case. These Scriptures were read in the churches, and there could be at first no idea of placing beside them new books which could for a moment rank with them in honor and authority. It has been once and again discussed whether Christianity from the first was a "book-religion." The decision of the matter depends upon what is referred to by the word "book." Christianity certainly did have from the very beginning a book which it reverenced—the OT—but years passed before it had even the beginnings of a book of its own. What has been called "the wealth of living canonical material," namely, prophets and teachers, made written words of subordinate value. In this very teaching, however, with its oral traditions lay the beginnings of that movement which was ultimately to issue in a canon of writings.

2. No Intention of Writing the NT

(2) When the actual work of writing began no one who sent forth an epistle or framed a gospel had before him the definite purpose of contributing toward the formation of what we call "the Bible." All the NT writers looked for "the end" as near. Their words, therefore, were to meet definite needs in the lives of those with whom they were associated. They had no thought of creating a new sacred lit. And yet these incidental occasional writings have come to be our choicest Scripture. The circumstances and influences which brought about this result are here briefly set forth.

II. Three Stages of the Process.—For convenience of arrangement and definiteness of impression the whole process may be marked off in three stages: (1) that from the time of the apostles until about 170 AD; (2) that of the closing years of the 2d cent. and the opening of the 3d (170–220 AD); (3) that of the 3d and 4th cents. In the first we seek for the evidences of the growth in appreciation of the peculiar value of the NT writings; in the second we discover the clear, full recognition of a large part of these writings as sacred and authoritative; in the third the acceptance of the complete canon in the East and in the West.

1. From the Apostles to 170 AD

(1) *The first period extending to 170 AD.*—It does not lie within the scope of this art. to recount the origin of the several books of the NT. This belongs properly to NT Introduction (q.v.). By the end of the 1st cent. all of the books of the NT were in existence. They were, as treasures of given churches, widely separated and honored as containing the word of Jesus or the teaching of the apostles. From the very first the authority of Jesus had full recognition in all the Christian world. The whole work of the apostles was in interpreting Him to the growing church. His sayings and His life were in part for the illumination of the OT; wholly for the understanding of life and its issues. In every assembly of Christians from the earliest days He was taught as well as the OT. In each church to which an epistle was written that epistle was likewise read. Paul asked that his letters be read in this way (1 Thess **5** 27; Col **4** 16). In this attentive listening to the exposition of some event in the life of Jesus or to the reading of the epistle of an apostle began the "authorization" of the traditions concerning Jesus and the apostolic writings. The widening of the area of the church and the departure of the apostles from earth emphasized increasingly the value of that which the writers of the NT left behind them. Quite early the desire to have the benefit of all possible instruction led to the interchange of Christian writings. Polycarp (110 AD ?) writes to the Philippians, "I have received letters from you and from Ignatius. You recommend me to send on yours to Syria; I shall do so either personally or by some other means. In return I send you the letter of Ignatius as well as others which I have in my hands and for which you made request. I add them to the present one; they will serve to edify your faith and perseverance" (Epistle to Phil, XIII). This is an illustration of what must have happened toward furthering a knowledge of the writings of the apostles. Just when and to what extent "collections" of our NT books began to be made it is impossible to say, but it is fair to infer that a collection of the Pauline epistles existed at the time Polycarp wrote to the Phil and when Ignatius wrote his seven letters to the churches of Asia Minor, i.e. about 115 AD. There is good reason to think also that the four Gospels were brought together in some places as early as this. A clear distinction, however, is to be kept in mind between "collections" and such recognition as we imply in the word "canonical." The gathering of books was one of the steps preliminary to this. Examination of the testimony to the NT in this early time indicates also that it is given with

no intention of framing the canonicity of NT books. In numerous instances only "echoes" of the thought of the epistles appear; again quotations are incomplete; both showing that Scripture words are used as the natural expression of Christian thought. In the same way the Apostolic Fathers refer to the teachings and deeds of Jesus. They witness "to the substance and not to the authenticity of the Gospels." That this all may be more evident let us note in more detail the witness of the subapostolic age.

Clement of Rome, in 95 AD, wrote a letter in the name of the Christians of Rome to those in Corinth. In this letter he uses material found in Mt, Lk, giving it a free rendering (see chs **46** and **13**); he has been much influenced by the Epistle to the He (see chs **9, 10, 17, 19, 36**). He knows Rom, Cor, and there are found echoes of 1 Tim, Tit, 1 Pet and Eph.

The Epistles of Ignatius (115 AD) have correspondences with our gospels in several places (Eph **5**; Rom **6, 7**) and incorporate language from nearly all of the Pauline epistles. The Epistle to Polycarp makes large use of Phil, and besides this cites nine of the other Pauline epistles. Ignatius quotes from Mt, apparently from memory; also from 1 Pet and 1 Jn. In regard to all these three writers—Clement, Polycarp, Ignatius—it is not enough to say that they bring us reminiscences or quotations from this or that book. Their thought is tinctured all through with NT truth. As we move a little farther down the years we come to "The Teaching of the Twelve Apostles" (cir 120 AD in its present form; see DIDACHE); the Epistle of Barnabas (cir 130 AD) and the Shepherd of Hermas (cir 130 AD). These exhibit the same phenomena as appear in the writings of Clement, Ignatius and Polycarp as far as references to the NT are concerned. Some books are quoted, and the thought of the three writings echoes again and again the teachings of the NT. They bear distinct witness to the value of "the gospel" and the doctrine of the apostles, so much so as to place these clearly above their own words. It is in the Epistle of Barnabas that we first come upon the phrase "it is written," referring to a NT book (Mt) (see *Epis.*, iv.14). In this deepening sense of value was enfolded the feeling of authoritativeness, which slowly was to find expression. It is well to add that what we have so far discovered was true in widely separated parts of the Christian world as e.g. Rome and Asia Minor.

The lit. of the period we are examining was not, however, wholly of the kind of which we have been speaking. Two forces were calling out other expressions of the singular value of the writings of the apostles, whether gospels or epistles. These were (*a*) *the attention of the civil government* in view of the rapid growth of the Christian church and (*b*) *heresy.* The first brought to the defence or commendation of Christianity the *Apologists,* among whom were Justin Martyr, Aristides, Melito of Sardis and Theophilus of Antioch. By far the most important of these was Justin Martyr, and his work may be taken as representative. He was born about 100 AD at Shechem, and died as a martyr at Rome in 165 AD. His two Apologies and the Dialogue with Trypho are the sources for the study of his testimony. He speaks of the "Memoirs of the Apostles, called Gospels" (*Ap.*, i.66) which were read on Sunday interchangeably with the prophets (i.67). Here emerges that equivalence in value of these "Gospels" with the OT Scriptures which may really mark the beginning of canonization. That these Gospels were our four Gospels as we now have them is yet a disputed question; but the evidence is weighty that they were. (See Purves, *Testimony of Justin Martyr to Early Christianity,* Lect V.) The fact that Tatian, his pupil, made a harmony of the Gospels, i.e. of our four Gospels, also bears upon our interpretation of Justin's "Memoirs." (See Hemphill, *The Diatessaron of Tatian.*) The only other NT book which Justin mentions is the Apocalypse; but he appears to have known the Acts, six epistles of Paul, He and 1 Jn, and echoes of still other epistles are perceptible. When he speaks of the apostles it is after this fashion: "By the power of God they proclaimed to every race of men that they were sent by Christ to teach to all the Word of God" (*Ap.*, i.39). It is debatable, however, whether this refers to more than the actual preaching of the apostles. The beginning of the formation of the canon is in the position and authority given to the Gospels.

While the Apologists were busy commending or defending Christianity, *heresy* in the form of Gnosticism was also compelling attention to the matter of the writings of the apostles. From the beginning gnostic teachers claimed that Jesus had favored chosen ones of His apostles with a body of esoteric truth which had been handed down by secret tradition. This the church denied, and in the controversy that went on through years the question of what were authoritative writings became more and more pronounced. Basilides e.g., who taught in Alexandria during the reign of Hadrian (AD 117–38), had for his secret authority the secret tradition of the apostle Matthias and of Glaucias, an alleged interpreter of Peter, but he bears witness to Mt, Lk, Jn, Rom, 1 Cor, Eph, and Col in the effort to recommend his doctrines, and, what is more, gives them the value of Scripture in order to support more securely his teachings. (See *Philosophoumena* of Hippolytus, VII, 17). Valentinus, tracing his authority through Theodas to Paul, makes the same general use of NT books, and Tertullian tells us that he appeared to use the whole NT as then known.

The most noted of the Gnostics was *Marcion,* a native of Pontus. He went to Rome (cir 140 AD), there broke with the church and became a dangerous heretic. In support of his peculiar views, he formed a canon of his own which consisted of Luke's Gospel and ten of the Pauline epistles. He rejected the Pastoral Epistles, He, Mt, Mk, Jn, the Acts, the Catholic epistles and the Apocalypse, and made a recension of both the gospel of Lk and the Pauline epistles which he accepted. His importance, for us, however, is in the fact that he gives us the first clear evidence of the canonization of the Pauline epistles. Such use of the Scriptures inevitably called forth both criticism and a clearer marking off of those books which were to be used in the churches opposed to heresy, and so "in the struggle with Gnosticism the canon was made." We are thus brought to the end of the first period in which we have marked the collection of NT books in greater or smaller compass, the increasing valuation of them as depositions of the truth of Jesus and His apostles, and finally the movement toward the claim of their authoritativeness as over against perverted teaching. No sharp line as to a given year can be drawn between the first stage of the process and the second. Forces working in the first go on into the second, but results are accomplished in the second which give it its right to separate consideration.

2. From 170 AD to 220 AD

(2) *The period from 170 AD to 220 AD.*—This is the age of a voluminous theological literature busy with the great issues of church canon and creed. It is the period of the great names of Irenaeus, Clement of Alexandria, and Tertullian, representing respectively Asia Minor, Egypt and North Africa. In passing into it we come into

the clear light of Christian history. There is no longer any question as to a NT canon; the only difference of judgment is as to its extent. What has been slowly but surely shaping itself in the consciousness of the church now comes to clear expression.

Irenaeus.—That expression we may study in Irenaeus as representative of the period. He was born in Asia Minor, lived and taught in Rome and became afterward bishop of Lyons. He had, therefore, a wide acquaintance with the churches, and was peculiarly competent to speak concerning the general judgment of the Christian world. As a pupil of Polycarp, who was a disciple of John, he is connected with the apostles themselves. An earnest defender of the truth, he makes the NT in great part his authority, and often appeals to it. The four Gospels, the Acts, the epistles of Paul, several of the Catholic epistles and the Apocalypse are to him Scripture in the fullest sense. They are genuine and authoritative, as much so as the OT ever was. He dwells upon the fact that there are four gospels, the very number being prefigured in the four winds and the four quarters of the earth. Every attempt to increase or diminish the number is heresy. Tertullian takes virtually the same position (*Adv. Marc.*, iv.2), while Clement of Alexandria quotes all four gospels as "Scripture." By the end of the 2d cent. the canon of the gospels was settled. The same is true also of the Pauline epistles. Irenaeus makes more than two hundred citations from Paul, and looks upon his epistles as Scripture (*Adv. Haer.*, iii.12, 12). Indeed, at this time it may be said that the new canon was known under the designation "The Gospel and the Apostles" in contradistinction to the old as "the Law and the Prophets." The title "New Testament" appears to have been first used by an unknown writer against Montanism (cir 193 AD). It occurs frequently after this in Origen and later writers. In considering all this testimony two facts should have emphasis: (1) its wide extent: Clement and Irenaeus represent parts of Christendom which are widely separated; (2) the relation of these men to those who have gone before them. Their lives together with those before them spanned nearly the whole time from the apostles. They but voiced the judgment which silently, gradually had been selecting the "Scripture" which they freely and fully acknowledged and to which they made appeal.

The Muratorian Fragment.—Just here we come upon the Muratorian Fragment, so called because discovered in 1740 by the librarian of Milan, Muratori. It dates from some time near the end of the 2d cent., is of vital interest in the study of the history of the canon, since it gives us a list of NT books and is concerned with the question of the canon itself. The document comes from Rome, and Lightfoot assigns it to Hippolytus. Its list contains the Gospels (the first line of the fragment is incomplete, beginning with Mk, but Mt is clearly implied), the Acts, the Pauline epistles, the Apocalypse, 1 and 2 Jn (perhaps by implication the third) and Jude. It does not mention He, 1 and 2 Pet, Jas. In this list we have virtually the real position of the canon at the close of the 2d cent. Complete unanimity had not been attained in reference to all the books which are now between the covers of our NT. Seven books had not yet found a secure place beside the gospel and Paul in all parts of the church. The Palestinian and Syrian churches for a long time rejected the Apocalypse, while some of the Catholic epistles were in Egypt considered doubtful. The history of the final acceptance of these belongs to the third period.

3. 3rd and 4th Cents.

(3) *The period included by the 3d and 4th cents.*—It has been said that "the question of the canon did not make much progress in the course of the 3d cent." (Reuss, *History of the Canon of Holy Scripture*, 125). We have the testimony of a few notable teachers mostly from one center, Alexandria. Their consideration of the question of the disputed book serves just here one purpose. By far the most distinguished name of the 3d cent. is *Origen.* He was born in Alexandria about 185 AD, and before he was seventeen became an instructor in the school for catechumens. In 203 he was appointed bishop, experienced various fortunes, and died in 254. His fame rests upon his ability as an exegete, though he worked laboriously and successfully in other fields. His testimony is of high value, not simply because of his own studies, but also because of his wide knowledge of what was thought in other Christian centers in the world of his time. Space permits us only to give in summary form his conclusions, esp. in regard to the books still in doubt. The Gospels, the Pauline epistles, the Acts, he accepts without question. He discusses at some length the authorship of He, believes that "God alone knows who wrote it," and accepts it as Scripture. His testimony to the Apocalypse is given in the sentence, "Therefore John the son of Zebedee says in the Revelation." He also gives sure witness to Jude, but wavers in regard to Jas, 2 Pet, 2 and 3 Jn.

Another noted name of this cent. is *Dionysius of Alexandria*, a pupil of Origen (d. 265). His most interesting discussion is regarding the Apocalypse, which he attributes to an unknown John, but he does not dispute its inspiration. It is a singular fact that the western church accepted this book from the first, while its position in the East was variable. Conversely the Epistle to the He was more insecure in the West than in the East. In regard to the Catholic epistles Dionysius supports Jas, 2 and 3 Jn, but not 2 Pet or Jude.

In the West the name of *Cyprian*, bishop of Carthage (248–58 AD), was most influential. He was much engaged in controversy, but a man of great personal force. The Apocalypse he highly honored, but he was silent about the Epistle to the He. He refers to only two of the Catholic epistles, 1 Pet and 1 Jn.

These testimonies confirm what was said above, viz. that the end of the 3d cent. leaves the question of the full canon about where it was at the beginning. 1 Pet and 1 Jn seem to have been everywhere known and accepted. In the West the five Catholic epistles gained recognition more slowly than in the East.

In the early part of the 4th cent. *Eusebius* (270–340 AD), bishop of Caesarea before 315, sets before us in his *Church History* (III, chs iii–xxv) his estimate of the canon in his time. He does not of course use the word canon, but he "conducts an historical inquiry into the belief and practice of earlier generations." He lived through the last great persecution in the early part of the 4th cent., when not only places of worship were razed to the ground, but also the sacred Scriptures were in the public market-places consigned to the flames (*HE*, VIII, 2). It was, therefore, no idle question what book a loyal Christian must stand for as his Scripture. The question of the canon had an earnest, practical significance. Despite some obscurity and apparent contradictions, his classification of the NT books was as follows: (1) The acknowledged books. His criteria for each of these was authenticity and apostolicity and he placed in this list the Gospels, Acts, and Paul's epistles, including He. (2) The disputed books, i.e. those which had obtained only partial recognition, to which he assigned Jas, Jude, 2 Pet and 2 Jn. About the Apocalypse also he was not sure. In this testimony there is not much advance over that of the 3d cent. It is virtually the canon of Origen. All this makes evident the fact that as yet no official decision nor uniformity of usage in the church gave a completed canon. The time, however, was drawing on when various forces at work were to bring much nearer this unanimity and enlarge the list of acknowledged books. In the second half of the 4th cent. repeated efforts were made to put an end to uncertainty. *Athanasius* in one of his pastoral letters in connection with the publishing of the ecclesiastical calendar gives a list of the books comprising Scripture, and in the NT portion are included all the 27 books which we now recognize. "These are the wells of salvation," he writes, "so that he who thirsts may be satisfied with the sayings in these. Let no one add to these. Let nothing be taken away." Gregory of Nazianzen (d. 390 AD) also published a list omitting Rev, as did Cyril of Jerus (d. 386), and quite at the end of the cent. (4th) Isidore of Pelusium speaks of the "canon of truth, the Divine Scriptures." For a considerable time the Apocalypse was not accepted in the Palestinian or Syrian churches. Athanasius helped toward its acceptance in the church of Alexandria. Some differences of opinion, however, continued. The Syrian church did not accept all of the Catholic epistles until much later.

The Council of Carthage in 397, in connection with its decree "that aside from the canonical Scriptures nothing is to be read in church under the name of Divine Scriptures," gives a list of the books of the NT. After this fashion there was an endeavor to secure unanimity, while at the same time differences of judgment and practice continued. The books which had varied treatment through these early cents. were He, the Apocalypse and the five minor Catholic epistles. The advance of Christianity under Constantine had much to do with the reception of the whole group of books in the East. The task which the emperor gave to Eusebius to prepare "fifty copies of the Divine Scriptures" established a standard which in time gave recognition to all doubtful books. In the West, Jerome and Augustine were the controlling factors in its settlement of the canon. The publication of the Vulg virtually determined the matter.

In conclusion let it be noted how much the human element was involved in the whole process of forming our NT. No one would wish to dispute a providential overruling of it all. Also it is well to bear in mind that all the books have not the same clear title to their places in the canon as far as the history of their attestation is concerned. Clear and full and unanimous, however, has been the judgment from the beginning upon the Gospels, the Acts, the Pauline epistles, 1 Pet and 1 Jn.

LITERATURE.—Reuss, *History of the Canon of Holy Scriptures;* E. C. Moore, *The NT in the Christian Church;* Gregory, *Canon and Text of the NT;* Introductions to NT of Jülicher, Weiss, Reuss; Zahn, *Geschichte des Neutest. Kanons;* Harnack, *Das NT um das Jahr 200; Chronologie der altchristlichen Literatur;* Westcott, *The Canon of the NT;* Zahn, *Forschungen zur Gesch. des neutest. Kanons.*

J. S. RIGGS

CANOPY, kan'ŏ-pi (חֻפָּה, *ḥuppāh*, from a root meaning "to inclose" or "cover"): Isa **4** 5 AV has "defence," ERV "canopy," ARV "covering," the last being best, though "canopy" has much in its favor. In Ps **19** 5 (He **19** 6) *ḥuppāh* is used of the bridegroom's chamber and in Joel **2** 16 of the bride's. Among the Hebrews the *ḥuppāh* was originally the chamber in which the bride awaited the groom for the marital union. In Jth **10** 21; **13** 9.15; **16** 19 the word canopy occurs as the Eng. equivalent of the Gr κωνωπεῖον, *kōnōpeíon*, which was primarily a mosquito-net and then a canopy over a bed, whether for useful or for decorative purposes. JOHN RICHARD SAMPEY

CANTICLES, kan'ti-k'lz. See SONG OF SONGS.

CAPERBERRY, kā'pĕr-ber-i (אֲבִיּוֹנָה, *'ăbhīyōnāh;* κάππαρις, *kápparis;* Eccl **12** 5 RVm): The tr "the caperberry shall fail" (RV "burst") instead of "desire shall fail" (AV) has the support of the LXX and of some Talmudic writers (see G. F. Moore, *JBL*, X, 55–64), but it is doubtful.

The caperberry is the fruit of the thorny caper, *Capparis spinosa* (N.O. *Capparidaceae*), a common Pal plant with pretty white flowers and brightly colored stamens. Largely on account of its habit of growing out of crevasses in old walls it has been identified by some with the HYSSOP (q.v.). The familiar "capers" of commerce are the young buds, but the berries were the parts most used in ancient times; their repute as excitants of sexual desire is ancient and widespread. Various parts of this plant are still used for medical purposes by the modern peasants of Pal.

E. W. G. MASTERMAN

CAPERNAUM, ka-pĕr'na-um (Καπερναούμ [TR], Καφαρναούμ [B א D, etc], *Kapernaoúm, Kapharnaoúm*): The woe spoken by the Master against this great city has been fulfilled to the uttermost (Mt **11** 23; Lk **10** 15). So completely has it perished that the very site is a matter of dispute today. In Scripture Capernaum is not mentioned outside the Gospels. When Jesus finally departed from Nazareth, He dwelt in Capernaum (Mt **4** 13) and made it the main center of His activity during a large part of His public ministry. Near by He called the fishermen to follow Him (Mk **1** 16), and the publican from the receipt of custom (Mt **9** 9, etc). It was the scene of many "mighty works" (Mt **11** 23; Mk **1** 34). Here Jesus healed the centurion's son (Mt **8** 5, etc), the nobleman's son (Jn **4** 46), Simon Peter's mother-in-law (Mk **1** 31, etc), and the paralytic (Mt **9** 1, etc); cast out the unclean spirit (Mk **1** 23, etc); and here also, probably, He raised Jairus' daughter to life (Mk **5** 22, etc). In Capernaum the little child was used to teach the disciples humility, while in the synagogue Jesus delivered His ever-memorable discourse on the bread of life (Jn **6**).

From the notices in the Gospels we gather that Capernaum was a city of considerable importance. Some think that the words "shalt thou be exalted," etc (Mt **11** 23; Lk **10** 15), mean that it stood on an elevated site. Perhaps more naturally they refer to the excessive pride of the inhabitants in their city. It was a customs station, and the residence of a high officer of the king (Mt **9** 9; Jn **4** 46, etc). It was occupied by a detachment of Rom soldiers, whose commander thought the good will of the people worth securing at the expense of building for them a synagogue (Mt **8** 5; Lk **7** 5). It stood by the sea (Mt **4** 13) and from Jn **6** 17 ff (cf Mt **14** 34; Mk **6** 53), we see that it was either in or near the plain of Gennesaret.

Jos twice mentions Capernaum. It played no great part in the history of his time, and seems to have declined in importance, as he refers to it as a "village." And now the work of the German monks under the direction of Père Orfali has settled beyond reasonable dispute the site of Capernaum as certainly at the place now called *Tell Ḥūm*. The position of Capernaum at this point, "exalted unto heaven," though it be on a comparatively flat shore, immediately impresses one standing at the ruins and looking south. There is before him the most magnif-

TELL HUM—TRADITIONAL CAPERNAUM

icant view afforded by any spot around the whole lake. The land juts out a little into the lake at this point, and the whole panorama of that incomparable little sea is seen as from a reviewing stand. Certainly also the denunciation pronounced by our Lord has fallen upon the city.

The excavations have not yet extended to the whole city, but the strange, and minutely detailed, description of the approach to the "synagogue of our Lord" written by the pilgrim Sylvia 385 AD is found exactly to conform to the street leading up from the quay directly to the remains of the great synagogue. This synagogue is found to be probably of the 4th cent., but on the ruins of one of the 1st cent., most probably the very one erected by the centurion mentioned by Luke (**7** 5). The "chief seats" along the side of the synagogue are still to be seen and, more remarkable still, the carved manna-pot from the lintel of the door is in accord with the well-known practice of placing the manna-pot in that position. This confronted the pulpit and reading desk of the synagogue and may thus have suggested the text from which Christ preached the sermon on the "true bread come down from heaven," which is recorded in the gospel (Jn **6** 48–59). To stand in that pulpit is deeply impressive and should solemnize all one's future preaching.

The two chief rivals for the honor of representing Capernaum are *Tell Ḥūm*, a ruined site on the lake shore, nearly 2½ miles W. of the mouth of the Jordan; and *Khān Minyeh*, fully 2½ miles farther west, at the N.E. corner of the plain of Gennesaret. Dr. Tristram suggested *'Ain El-Madowwerah*, a large spring inclosed by a circular wall, on the western edge of the plain. But it stands about a mile from the sea; there are no ruins to indicate that any considerable village ever stood here; and the water is available for only a small part of the plain.

In favor of *Tell Ḥūm* is *Onom*, which places Chorazin 2 miles from Capernaum. If *Kerāzeh* is Chorazin, this suits *Tell Ḥūm* better than *Khān Minyeh*. To this may be added the testimony of Theodosius (cir 530), Antoninus Martyr (600), and John of Würtzburg (1100). Jewish tradition speaks of *Tankhum*, in which are the graves of Nahum and Rabbi Tankhum. Identifying *Kefr Nahum* with *Tankhum*, and then deriving *Tell Ḥūm* from *Tankhum*, some have sought to vindicate the claims of this site. But every link in that chain of argument is extremely precarious. A highway ran through *Tell Ḥūm* along which passed the caravans to and from the E.; but the place was not in touch with the great north-and-south traffic.

There is also no fountain near *Tell Ḥūm* answering the description of Jos. Of recent advocates of *Tell Ḥūm*, it is sufficient to name Schürer (*HJP*, IV, 71) and Buhl (*GAP*, 224 f). In this connection it may be interesting to note that the present writer, when visiting the place recently (1911), drew his boatman's attention to a bit of ruined wall rising above the greenery W. of the lagoon, and asked what it was called. *Kanīset el Kufry*, was the reply, which may be freely rendered, "church of the infidels." This is just the Arab. equivalent of the Jewish "church of the *mīnīm*."

For *Khān Minyeh* it may be noted that Gennesaret corresponds to *el-Ghuweir*, the plain lying on the N.W. shore, and that *Khān Minyeh* stands at the N.E. extremity of the plain; thus answering, as *Tell Ḥūm* cannot do, the description of the Gospels. The copious fountains at *eṭ-Ṭābigha*, half a mile to the E., supplied water which was conducted round the face of the rock toward *Khān Minyeh* at a height which made it possible to water a large portion of the plain. If it be said that Jos must have been carried to *Tell Ḥūm* as being nearer the scene of his accident—see however, the comment above—it does not at all follow that he was taken to the nearest place. Arculf (1670) described Capernaum as on a "narrow piece of ground between the mountain and the lake." This does not apply to *Tell Ḥūm;* but it accurately fits *Khān Minyeh*. Isaac Chelo (1334) says that Capernaum, then in ruins, had been inhabited by *Mīnīm*, that is, Jewish converts to Christianity. The name *Minyeh* may have been derived from them. Quaresimus (1620–26) notes a *Khān* called Menieh which stood by the site of Capernaum. Between the ruined *Khān* and the sea there are traces of ancient buildings. Here the road from the E. united with that which came down from the N. by way of *Khān Jubb Yusif*, so that this must have been an important center, alike from the military point of view, and for customs. This is the site favored by, among others, G. A. Smith (*HGHL*, 456 f; *EB*, s.v.) and Conder. Sanday argued in favor of *Khān Minyeh* in his book, *The Sacred Sites of the Gospel*, but later, owing to what the present writer thinks a mistaken view of the relation between *Tell Ḥūm* and the fountain at *eṭ-Ṭābigha*, changed his mind (*Expos T*, XV, 100 ff). There is no instance of a fountain 2 miles distant being called by the name of a town. *Tell Ḥūm*, standing on the sea shore, was independent of this fountain, whose strength also was spent in a westward direction, away from *Tell Ḥūm*.

The balance of evidence was therefore heavily in favor of *Khān Minyeh* until Professor R. A. S. Macalister published the results of his researches. He seems to be wrong in rejecting the name *Tell Ḥūm* in favor of *Talḥum;* and he falls into a curious error regarding the use of the word *tell*. No one who speaks Arab., he says, "would ever think of applying the word *Tell*, 'mound,' to this flat widespread ruin." In Egyp Arab., however, *tell* means "ruin"; and Rev. Asad Mansur, a man of education whose native language is Arab., writes: "I do not understand what the objectors mean by the word 'tell.' In Arab. 'tell' is used for any heap of ruins, or mound. So that the ruins of *Tell Ḥūm* themselves are today a 'tell'" (*Expos*, April, 1907, 370). Professor Macalister is on surer ground in discussing the pottery found on the rival sites. At *Khān Minyeh* he found nothing older than the Arab. period, while at *Tell Ḥūm* pottery of the Rom period abounds—"exactly the period of the glory of Capernaum" (*PEFS*, April and July, 1907). If this be confirmed by further examination, it disposes of the claim of *Khān Minyeh*. Important Rom remains have now been found between the ruined *Khān* and the sea. It is no longer open to doubt that this was the site of a great Rom city. The Rom period however covers a long space. The buildings at *Tell Ḥūm* are by many assigned to the days of the Antonines. Is it possible from the remains of pottery to make certain that the city flourished in the time of the Herods? If the city at *Tell Ḥūm* had not yet arisen in the days of Christ, those who dispute its claim to be Capernaum are under no obligation to show which city the ruins represent. They are not the only extensive ruins in the country of whose history we are in ignorance.

REVISED BY M. G. K. W. EWING

CAPH. See KAPH.

CAPHARSALAMA, kaf-ar-sal′a-ma, kaf-ar-sa-lā′ma (**Χαφαρσαλαμά,** *Chapharsalamá*): The site of an indecisive skirmish between Judas Maccabaeus and Nicanor, an officer of the king of Syria and governor of Judaea. The situation cannot be precisely fixed but it must have been in the neighborhood of Jerus, for Nicanor, after losing 5,000 men, retired with the remainder to "the city of

David" (1 Macc **7** 26–32). The first part of the word, "Caphar," means village or hamlet; the last part has been identified with Siloam and also with *Khirbet Deir Sellām,* about 12½ miles W. of Jerus.

CAPHENATHA, ka-fen′a-tha. See CHAPHENATHA.

CAPHIRA, ka-fī′ra (A, **Καφιρά,** *Kaphirá,* B, **Πειρά,** *Peirá*): A town whose inhabitants returned from Babylon with Zerubbabel (1 Esd **5** 19). It corresponds to CHEPHIRAH (Ezr **2** 25), which see.

CAPHTHORIM, kaf′thō-rim (כַּפְתֹּרִים, *kaphtōrīm*). See CAPHTORIM.

CAPHTOR, kaf′tor, **CAPHTORIM,** kaf′tor-im (כַּפְתּוֹר, *kaphtōr,* כַּפְתֹּרִים, *kaphtōrīm;* **Καππαδοκία,** *Kappadokía,* **Γαφθοριείμ,** *Gaphtorieím,* **Καφθοριείμ,** *Kaphtorieím*): The country and people whence came the Philis (Gen **10** 14 = 1 Ch **1** 12 [here the clause "whence went forth the Philis" should probably come after Caphtorim]; Dt **2** 23; Jer **47** 4; Am **9** 7). Jer (loc. cit.) calls it an "island"; there is evidence of ancient connection between Crete and Philistia; and the Philis are called Cherethites, which may mean Cretans (see CHERETHITES). These considerations have led many to identify Caphtor with the important island of Crete. It should be noted, however, that the word אִי, *'ī,* used by Jeremiah, denotes not only "isle," but also "coastland."

1. First Theory: Crete

Ebers (*Aegypten und die Bücher Moses,* 130 ff) thought that Caphtor represented the Egyp *Kaft-ur,* holding that Kaft was the Egyp name for the colonies of Phoenicians in the Delta, extended to cover the Phoenicians in the north and their colonies. *Kaft-ur,* therefore, would mean "Greater Phoenicia." But the discovery of Kaptar among the names of countries conquered by Ptolemy Auletes in an inscription on the Temple of Kom Ombo is fatal to this theory.

2. Second Theory: Phoenicia

A third theory would identify Caphtor with the *Kafto* of the Egyp inscriptions. As early as the time of Thotmes III the inhabitants of this land, the *Kafti,* are mentioned in the records. In the trilingual inscription of Canopus the name is rendered in Gr by *Phoinikē,* "Phoenicia." This seems to be an error, as the Kafti portrayed on the monuments have no features in common with the Semites. They certainly represent a western type. It is held that the Egyp Kafto is a district in Asia Minor, probably Cilicia. The sea-pirates, the *purasati,* whom Rameses III subdued (cir 1200 BC), entered Syria from the north. The *r* in the name is the Egyp equivalent of the Semitic *l.* Therefore *Purasatī* = Pilishtī, "Philistines." And so it is proposed to identify Caphtor with Cilicia. A serious objection to this theory is the absence of the final "r" in *Kafto.* McCurdy's suggestion (*HDB*) that it represents a Heb *waw,* written as a vowel-letter in an original *Kafto,* does not carry conviction.

3. Third Theory: Cilicia

It is impossible to give a certain decision; but the balance of probability seems still inclined to the first theory. W. EWING

CAPPADOCIA, kap-a-dō′shi-a (**ἡ Καππαδοκία,** *hē Kappadokía*): An extensive province in eastern Asia Minor, bounded by the Taurus mountains on the S., the Anti-Taurus and the Euphrates on the E., and, less definitely, by Pontus and Galatia on the N. and W. Highest mountain, Argaeus, over 13,000 ft. above sea-level; chief rivers, the Pyramus now Jihan, Sarus now Sihon, and Halys now the Kuzul; most important cities, Caesarea Mazaca, Comana, Miletene now Malatia, and Tyana now Bor. At Malatia the country unrolls itself as a fertile plain; elsewhere the province is for the most part composed of billowy and rather barren uplands, and bleak mountain peaks and pastures.

Coin of Ariarathes V, Philometor, King of Cappadocia, 163–130 BC.

The Gr geographers called Cappodax the son of Ninyas, thereby tracing the origin of Cappadocian culture to Assyria. Cuneiform tablets from Kul Tepe (Kara Eyuk), deciphered by Professors Pinches and Sayce, show that in the era of Khammurabi (see ḤAMMURABI) this extensive ruin on the ox-bow of the Halys and near Caesarea Mazaca, was an outpost of the Assyr-Bab Empire. A Hittite civilization followed, from about 2000 BC onward. Malatia, Gurun, Tyana and other old sites contain important and undoubted Hittite remains, while sporadic examples of Hittite art, architecture and inscriptions are found in many places, and the number is being steadily increased by fresh discovery. After the Hittites fade from sight, following the fall of Carchemish, about 718 BC, Cappadocia emerges as a satrapy of Persia. At the time of Alexander the Great it received a top-dressing of Gr culture, and a line of native kings established an independent throne, which lasted until Cappadocia was incorporated in the Rom Empire, 17 AD. Nine rulers bore the name of Ariarathes (RV Arathes) the founder of the dynasty, and two were named Ariobarzanes. One of these kings is referred to in 1 Macc **15** 22. The history of this Cappadocian kingdom is involved, obscure and bloody.

Pagan religion had a deep hold upon the population prior to the advent of Christianity. Comana was famous for its worship of the great goddess Ma, who was served, according to Strabo, by 6,000 priestesses, and only second to this was the worship paid to Zeus at Venasa.

Representatives from Cappadocia were present at Pentecost (Acts **2** 9), and Peter includes the converts in this province in the address of his letter (1 Pet **1** 1). Caesarea became one of the most important early centers of Christianity. Here the Armenian youth of noble blood, Krikore, or Gregory the Illuminator, was instructed in the faith to which he afterward won the formal assent of his whole nation. Here Basil governed the churches of his wide diocese and organized monasticism. His brother, Gregory of Nyssa, and Gregory Nazianzen, lived and labored not far away. Cappadocia passed with the rest of Asia Minor into the Byzantine Empire, but from its exposed position early fell under the domination of the Turks, having been conquered by the Seljukians in 1074. G. E. WHITE

CAPTAIN, kap′tin: In AV there are no fewer than 13 Heb words, and 4 different Gr words, which are rendered by this one Eng. word. In the RV some of these are rendered by other Eng. words, and so we find for "captain": "marshal" (Jer **51** 27; Nah **3** 17), "prince" (1 S **9** 16), "governor" (Jer **51** 23.28), while in the case of one of these

Heb words a different construction is found altogether (Jer **13** 21).

Of Heb words in the OT rendered by "captain" (1) the most frequent is שַׂר, *sar*, which denotes "a military commander," whether of thousands or hundreds or fifties (Nu **31** 48; 1 S **8** 12 and many other places). *Sar* is the chief officer of any department, civil and religious, as well as military—captain of the guard AV and RV, chief of the executioners RVm (Gen **37** 36); chief butler (Gen **40** 9); chief baker (Gen **40** 16); chief of a district (Neh **3** 15); chiefs of tribes (Naphtali; Zebulun, Ps **68** 27); chiefs over gangs of slaves (Ex **1** 11); chiefs of the priests and the Levites (Ezr **8** 29). (2) רַב, *rabh*, later Heb for chief of the executioners or captain of the guard, a title always given to Nebuzar-adan (2 K **25** 8 ff; Jer **39** 9 ff) and to Arioch (Dnl **2** 14). Compare also Rab-mag, chief of the magicians (Jer **39** 13), and Ashpenaz, chief of the eunuchs (Dnl **1** 3). (3) רֹאשׁ, *rō'sh*, "head" over a host (Israel in the wilderness, Nu **14** 4), over tribes (Dt **29** 10, where RV renders "heads"), over thousands (1 Ch **12** 20). Abijah, king of Judah, before joining battle against Jeroboam, claimed "God himself is with us for our captain" AV, "with us at our head" RV (2 Ch **13** 12). (4) שָׁלִישׁ, *shālīsh*, originally the third man in the chariot, who, when the chief occupant was the king, or commander-in-chief, was of the rank of captain (2 K **7** 2; **9** 25), the term "third man" being generalized to mean "a captain" in 2 K **10** 25; 2 Ch **8** 9, where "chief of his captains" combines (1) and (4). (5) נָגִיד, *nāghīdh*, leader by Divine appointment: of Saul (1 S **9** 16, "captain," AV, "prince" RV **10** 1); of David (2 S **5** 2); of Hezekiah (2 K **20** 5); with a charge in connection with the temple (2 Ch **31** 13). It is the word used of Messiah "the prince" (Dnl **9** 25), who is also Prince of the Covenant (**11** 22). (6) נָשִׂיא, *nāsī'*, rendered "captain" in AV Nu **2** 3.5.7 only, there in RV and in other places, both AV and RV, rendered "prince." In 1 Ch **7** 40 "chief of the princes" combines (3) and (6). (7) פֶּחָה, *peḥāh*, is found almost entirely in a foreign title denoting "governor," and belongs to the later history of Israel (Neh **2** 7.9; Ezr **8** 36; Hag **1** 1), rendered "captain" in exclusively foreign associations (1 K **20** 24; 2 K **18** 24; Dnl **3** 27 f). (8) קָצִין, *ḳāçīn* (from root of *ḳadi*, Arab. for "judge"), denotes "dictator," almost "usurper," and is found in "rulers of Sodom" AV and RV, "judges of Sodom" RVm (Isa **1** 10), used of Jephthah in sense of "captain" AV, "chief" RV (Jgs **11** 6), found combined with (3), "head and captain" (AV, "head and chief" RV Jgs **11** 11). In Josh **10** 24 it denotes commanders of troops, AV "captains of the men of war," RV "chiefs of the men of war." (9) כַּר, *kar*, in Ezk **21** 22 "to set captains" AV, is trd "to set battering rams" RV. (10) בַּעַל, *ba'al*, only once in "captain of the ward" (Jer **37** 13). (11) טִפְסַר, *ṭiphṣar*, a dignitary belonging to an oriental court, in AV rendered "captain," in RV "marshal" (Nah **3** 17; Jer **51** 27). (12) שַׁלִּיט, *shallīṭ*, in Dnl **2** 15 of Arioch, the king's captain; in Eccl **8** 8 "having power over," and in **7** 19 used of "mighty men" (RV "rulers").

1. In the OT

Of Gr words rendered by "captain" in NT there are the following: (1) ἀρχηγός, *archēgós*, rendered "captain" in He **2** 10 AV but relegated to the margin in RV, where "author" (of their salvation) is preferred, this being the rendering of He **12** 2 AV and RV, "author" (and finisher of our faith), "captain" being still retained in RVm. Cf Acts **3** 15 and **5** 31, where the same Gr word is rendered "Prince," the RVm of the former passage giving "Author." In the Risen and Ascended Christ the various conceptions thus expressed are found to blend. (2) χιλίαρχος, *chilíarchos*, the Lat *tribunus militum* of which there were six to a legion, commanding the six cohorts of which it was composed. In its lit. acceptation it would be "commander of a thousand," and it is so used in Acts **22** 28 where it designates the commander of the Rom garrison in Jerus, consisting of a cohort, and is rendered "chief captain" (Jn **18** 12; Acts **21** 31; **22** 24; **24** 22). It is used more vaguely in the sense of "military officer" in Mk **6** 21; Rev **6** 15; **19** 18. (3) στρατηγός, *stratēgós*, used only by St. Luke in the NT, and almost exclusively of (*a*) officials in charge of the Temple (Lk **22** 4.52; Acts **4** 1; **5** 24.26). The captain of the Temple had the superintendence of the Levites and priests who were on guard in and around the Temple, and under him were *stratēgoi*, who were also captains of the Temple police, although they took their instruction from him as their head. He was not only a priest, but second in dignity only to the high priest himself; (*b*) the exception to St. Luke's general usage is where the word is used of the chief authorities in civil affairs at Philippi; where "the magistrates," as the word is rendered (Acts **16** 20 f), called themselves "praetors" (*stratēgoi*). In the case of Paul and Silas they placed themselves in peril of removal from their office by ordering them to be beaten, being Romans and uncondemned. (4) στρατοπεδάρχης, *stratopedárchēs*, the captain of the guard to whom Julius of the Augustan band (according to the TR, Acts **28** 16) delivered St. Paul and his fellow-prisoners. The word has disappeared from RV, but the passage in which it occurs has attestation which satisfies Blass, Sir William Ramsay, and other scholars. It was supposed that this was the captain of the Praetorian guard, but Mommsen and Ramsay believe him to be the *princeps peregrinorum castrorum*. See AUGUSTAN BAND; ARMY, ROMAN.

2. In the NT

T. NICOL

CAPTIVE, kap'tiv (שְׁבִי, *shebhī*, גָּלָה, *gālāh*; **αἰχμάλωτος**, *aichmálōtos* and its derivatives): The frequent references in the OT to captives as men forcibly deported (from the Heb root שָׁבָה, *shābhāh*) or inhabiting a land foreign to them (from Heb גָּלָה, *gālāh*) reflect the universal practice of the ancient world. The treatment of captives was sometimes barbarous (2 S **8** 2) but not always so (2 K **6** 21. 22). See further under ASSIR and WAR.

Figurative: Except in Job **42** 10 the fig. use of the idea is confined to the NT, where reference is made to the triumphal reign of the Lord Jesus (Lk **4** 18; Eph **4** 8), or, on the other hand, to the power of the devil (2 Tim **2** 26), or of false teachers (**3** 6); cf also Rom **7** 23; 2 Cor **10** 5. See CAPTIVITY.

F. K. FARR

CAPTIVITY, kap-tiv'i-ti (גּוֹלָה, *gōlāh*, גָּלוּת, *gālūth*, שְׁבוּת, *sh^ebhūth*, שִׁבְיָה, *shibhyāh*; **μετοικεσία**, *metoikesía*):

I. OF THE NORTHERN KINGDOM (THE WORK OF ASSYRIA)
  1. Western Campaigns of Shalmaneser II, 860–825 BC
  2. Of Rimmon-nirari III, 810–781 BC
  3. Of Tiglath-pileser III, 745–727 BC
  4. Of Shalmaneser IV, 727–722 BC—Siege of Samaria
  5. Samaria Captured by Sargon, 722 BC
  6. Depopulation and Repopulation of Samaria
  7. The Ten Tribes in Captivity

II. OF JUDAH (THE WORK OF THE CHALDAEAN POWER) Southern Kingdom and House of David
  1. Break-up of Assyria
  2. Downfall of Nineveh, 606 BC
  3. Pharaoh Necoh's Revolt

I. Of the Northern Kingdom.—The captivity of the Northern Kingdom was the work of the great Assyr power having its seat at Nineveh on the Tigris. The empire of Assyria, founded nearly 2000 BC, had a long history behind it when its annals begin to take notice of the kingdoms of Israel and Judah.

1. Western Campaigns of Shalmaneser II, 860-825 BC

The reign of Shalmaneser II (860–825 BC) marks the first contact between these powers. This is not the Shalmaneser mentioned in 2 K **17** and **18,** who is the fourth of the name and flourished more than a cent. later. Shalmaneser II was contemporary during his long reign with Jehoshaphat, Jehoram, Ahaziah and Joash, kings of Judah; with Ahab, Ahaziah, Jehoram and Jehu, kings of Israel; with Hazael and Benhadad II, kings of Syria at Damascus, and with Mesha, king of Moab. The Assyr authorities for his reign are an inscription engraved by himself on the rocks of Armenia; the Black Obelisk brought by Layard from Nimroud, now in the British Museum; and the texts engraved on the bronze gates of Balawât, discovered by Hormuzd Rassam in 1878, and recognized as the swinging gates of Shalmaneser's palace. From these authorities we learn that in his 6th year he encountered the combined forces of Damascus, Hamath, Israel, and other states which had united to oppose his progress westward, and completely routed them in the battle of Karkar (854 BC). The danger which threatened the western states in common had brought Syria and Israel together; and this is in accord with the Scripture narrative which tells of a covenant, denounced by God's prophet, between Ahab and Benhadad (1 K **20** 34 ff), and mentions a period of three years when there was no war between Syria and Israel. The defeat of the allies seems, however, to have broken up the confederacy, for, soon after, Ahab is found, with the aid of Jehoshaphat of Judah, attempting unsuccessfully, and with fatal result to himself, to recover from the weakened power of Syria the city of Ramoth-gilead (1 K **22**). In another campaign to the West, which likewise finds no record in Scripture, Shalmaneser received the tribute of Tyre and Sidon, and of "Yahua of Khumri," that is, of Jehu, of the land of Omri, as Israel is called on the monuments.

The next Assyrian monarch who turned his arms against the West was Rimmon-nirari III (810–781 BC), grandson of Shalmaneser II. Although he is not mentioned by name in Scripture, his presence and activity had their influence upon contemporary events recorded in 2 K. He caused Syria to let go her hold of Israel; and although he brought Israel into subjection, the people of the Northern Kingdom would rather have a ruler exercising a nominal sovereignty over them in distant Nineveh than a king oppressing them in Damascus. Hence Rimmon-nirari has been taken for the saviour whom God gave to Israel, "so that they went out from under the hand of the Syrians" (2 K **13** 5; cf ver 23).

2. Of Rimmon-nirari III, 810-781 BC

With the death of Rimmon-nirari in 781 BC, the power of Assyria received a temporary check, and on the other hand the kingdom of Judah under Uzziah and the kingdom of Israel under Jeroboam II reached the zenith of their political prosperity. In 745 BC, however, a usurper, Pul, or Pulu, ascended the throne of Assyria, and reigned as Tiglath-pileser III. It is by the former name that he is first mentioned in the Scripture narrative (2 K **15** 19; 1 Ch **5** 26), and by the latter that he is mentioned on the monuments. That the two names belong to one man is now held to be certain (Schrader, *COT*, I, 230 f).

3. Of Tiglath-pileser III, 745-727 BC

Tiglath-pileser was one of the greatest monarchs of antiquity. He was the first to attempt to consolidate an empire in the manner to which the world has become accustomed since Rom times. He was not content to receive tribute from the kings and rulers of the states which he conquered. The countries which he conquered became subject provinces of his empire, governed by Assyr satraps and contributing to the imperial treasury. Not long after he had seated himself on the throne, Tiglath-pileser, like his predecessors, turned his attention to the West. After the siege of Arpad, northward of Aleppo, the Assyr forces made their way into Syria, and putting into operation the Assyr method of deportation and repopulation, the conqueror annexed Hamath which had sought the alliance and assistance of Azariah, that is Uzziah, king of Judah. Whether he then refrained from molesting Judah, or whether her prestige was broken by this campaign of the Assyr king, it is not easy to say. In another campaign he certainly subjected Menahem of Israel with other kings to tribute. What is stated in a word or two in the Annals of Tiglath-pileser is recorded at length in the Bible history (2 K **15** 19 ff): "There came against the land Pul the king of Assyria; and Menahem gave Pul a thousand talents of silver, that his hand might be with him to confirm the kingdom in his hand. And Menahem exacted the money of Israel, even of all the mighty men of wealth, of each man 50 shekels of silver, to give to the king of Assyria. So the king of Assyria turned back, and stayed not there in the land." In the reign of Pekah, under his proper name of Tiglath-pileser, he is recorded to have raided the northern parts of Israel, and carried the inhabitants away into the land of Assyria (2 K **15** 29). We next hear of Ahaz, king of Judah, appealing to the Assyrians for help against "these two tails of smoking firebrands," Rezin of Syria and Pekah, the son of Remaliah (Isa **7** 4). To secure this help he took the silver and gold of the house of the Lord, and sent it as a present to the king of Assyria (2 K **16** 8). Meanwhile Tiglath-pileser was setting out on a new campaign to the West. He carried fire and sword through Syria and the neighboring lands as far as Gaza, and on his return he captured Samaria, without, however, razing it to the ground. Pekah having been slain by his own people, the Assyr monarch left Hoshea, the leader of the conspiracy, on the throne of Israel as the vassal of Assyria.

In 727 BC Tiglath-pileser III died and was succeeded by Shalmaneser IV. His reign was short

4. Of Shalmaneser IV, 727-722 BC

and no annals of it have come to light. In 2 K **17** and **18**, however, we read that Hoshea, relying upon help from the king of Egypt, thought the death of Tiglath-pileser a good opportunity for striking a blow for independence. It was a vain endeavor, for the end of the kingdom of Israel was at hand. The people were grievously given over to oppression and wickedness, which the prophets Amos and Hosea vigorously denounced. Hosea, in particular, was "the prophet of Israel's decline and fall." Prophesying at this very time he says: "As for Samaria, her king is cut off, as foam upon the water. The high places also of Aven, the sin of Israel, shall be destroyed: the thorn and the thistle shall come up on their altars; and they shall say to the mountains, Cover us; and to the hills, Fall on us" (Hos **10** 7.8; cf vs 14.15). No less stern are the predictions by Isaiah and Micah of the doom that is to overtake Samaria: "Woe to the crown of pride of the drunkards of Ephraim, and to the fading flower of his glorious beauty, which is on the head of the fat valley of them that are overcome with wine" (Isa **28** 1). "For the transgression of Jacob is all this, and for the sins of the house of Israel. What is the transgression of Jacob? is it not Samaria? . . . . Therefore I will make Samaria as a heap of the field, and as places for planting vineyards" (Mic **1** 5.6). No help came from Egypt. With the unaided and enfeebled resources of his kingdom Hoshea had to face the chastising forces of his sovereign. He was made prisoner outside Samaria and was most likely carried away to Nineveh. Meanwhile the land was overrun and the capital doomed to destruction, as the prophets had declared.

Not without a stubborn resistance on the part of her defenders did "the fortress cease from

5. Samaria Captured by Sargon, 722 BC

Ephraim" (Isa **17** 3). It was only after a three years' siege that the Assyrians captured the city (2 K **17** 5). If we had only the record of the Hebrew historian we should suppose that Shalmaneser was the monarch to whom fell the rewards and honors of the capture. Before the surrender of the city Shalmaneser had abdicated or died, and Sargon, only once mentioned in Scripture (Isa **20** 1), but one of the greatest of Assyr monarchs, had ascended the throne. From his numerous inscriptions, recovered from the ruins of Khorsabad, we learn that he, and not Shalmaneser, was the king who completed the conquest of the revolted kingdom and deported the inhabitants to Assyria. "In the beginning [of my reign]," says Sargon in his Annals, "the city Samaria [I took] with the help of Shamash, who secures victory to me [. . . . 27,290 people inhabiters of it] I took away captive; 50 chariots the property of my royalty, which were in it I appropriated. [. . . . the city] I restored, and more than before I caused it to be inhabited; people of the lands conquered by my hand in it [I caused to dwell. My governor over them I appointed, and tribute] and imposts just as upon the Assyrians I laid upon them." The Assyr Annals and the Scripture history support and supplement each other at this point. The sacred historian describes the deportation as follows: "The king of Assyria took Samaria, and carried Israel away into Assyria, and placed them in Halah, and on the Habor, the river of Gozan, and in the cities of the Medes . . . . because they obeyed not the voice of Jeh their God, but transgressed

his covenant, even all that Moses, the servant of Jeh, commanded, and would not hear it, nor do it" (2 K **17** 6.7; **18** 11.12). The re-

6. Depopulation and Repopulation of Samaria

population of the conquered territory is also described by the sacred historian: "And the king of Assyria brought men from Babylon, and from Cuthah, and from Avva, and from Hamath and Sepharvaim, and placed them in the cities of Samaria instead of the children of Israel; and they possessed Samaria, and dwelt in the cities thereof" (2 K **17** 24). The fact that Sargon introduced foreign settlers taken in war into Samaria is attested by inscriptions. That there were various episodes of deportation and repopulation in connection with the captivity of the Northern Kingdom appears to be certain. We have seen already that Tiglath-pileser III deported the population of the northern tribes to Assyria and placed over the depopulated country governors of his own. And at a time considerably later, we learn that Sargon's grandson Esarhaddon, and his great-grandson Ashur-bani-pal, "the great and noble Osnappar," imported to the region of Samaria settlers of nations conquered by them in the East (Ezr **4** 2.10). Of the original settlers, whom a priest, carried away by the king of Assyria but brought back to Bethel, taught "the law of the god of the land," it is said that "they feared Jehovah, and served their own gods, after the manner of the nations from among whom they had been carried away" (2 K **17** 33). The hybrid stock descended from those settlers is known to us in later history and in the Gospels as the Samaritans.

We must not suppose that a clean sweep was made of the inhabitants of the Northern Kingdom. No

7. The Ten Tribes in Captivity

doubt, as in the Bab captivity, "the poorest of the land were left to be vinedressers and husbandmen" (2 K **25** 12). The numbers actually deported were but a moiety of the whole population. But the kingdom of the Ten Tribes was now at an end. Israel had become an Assyr province, with a governor established in Samaria. As regards the Golah—the captives of Israel in the cities of the Medes—it must not be supposed that they became wholly absorbed in the population among whom they were settled. We can well believe that they preserved their Israelitish traditions and usages with sufficient clearness and tenacity, and that they became part of the Jewish dispersion so widespread throughout the East. It is quite possible that at length they blended with the exiles of Judah carried off by Nebuchadrezzar, and that then Judah and Ephraim became one nation as never before. The name Jew, therefore, naturally came to include members of what had earlier been the Northern Confederacy of Israel as well as those of the Southern Kingdom to which it properly belonged, so that in the post-exilic period, Jehudi, or Jew, means an adherent of Judaism without regard to local nationality.

II. Of the Southern Kingdom (Judah).—The captivity of Judah was the work of the great Chaldaean power seated at Babylon on the Euphrates. While the Northern Kingdom had new dynasties to rule it in quick succession, Judah and Jerus remained true to the House of David to the end. The Southern Kingdom rested on a firmer foundation, and Jerus with its temple and priesthood secured the throne against the enemies who overthrew Samaria for nearly a cent. and a half longer.

Sargon, who captured Samaria in 722 BC, was followed by monarchs with a great name as conquerors and builders and patrons of lit., Sennacherib, Esarhaddon, Ashurbanipal. When Ashurbanipal died in 625 BC, the dissolution of the Assyr Empire was not far off. Its hold over the West had greatly slackened, and the tributary peoples were breaking out into revolt. Bands of Scythians, a nomad Aryan race, from the region between the Caucasus and the Caspian, were sweeping through the Assyr Empire as far as Pal and Egypt, and the prophecies of Jeremiah and Zephaniah reflect their methods of warfare and fierce characteristics. They were driven back, however, at the frontier of Egypt, and appear to have returned to the North without invading Judah.

1. Break-up of Assyria

From the North these hordes were closing in upon Nineveh, and on all sides the Assyr power was being weakened. In the "Burden of Nineveh," the prophet Nahum foreshadows the joy of the kingdom of Judah at the tidings of its approaching downfall: "Behold, upon the mountains the feet of him that bringeth good tidings, that publisheth peace! Keep thy feasts, O Judah, perform thy vows; for the wicked one shall no more pass through thee; he is utterly cut off" (Nah **1** 15; cf **3** 8–11). The Medes regained their independence and under their king, Cyaxares, formed an alliance with the Chaldaeans, who soon afterward revolted under the leadership of Nabopolassar, viceroy of Babylon. Rallying these various elements to his standard Nabopolassar laid siege to the Assyr capital, and in 606 BC, Nineveh, which had been the capital city of great conquerors, and had "multiplied [her] merchants above the stars of heaven" (Nah **3** 16), fell before the combined forces of the Medes and Chaldaeans, fell suddenly and finally, to rise no more. Of the new Bab Empire upon which the Chaldaeans now entered, Nebuchadrezzar, whose father Nabopolassar had associated him with him on the throne, was the first and most eminent ruler.

2. Downfall of Nineveh, 606 BC

That the people of Judah should exult in the overthrow of Nineveh and the empire for which it stood we can well understand. Jerus herself had by God's mercy remained unconquered when Sennacherib nearly a cent. before had carried off from the surrounding country 200,150 people and had devastated the towns and fortresses near. But the hateful Assyr yoke had rested upon Judah to the end, and not upon Judah only but even upon Egypt and the valley of the Nile. In 608 BC Pharaoh Necoh revolted from his Assyr suzerain and resolved upon an eastern campaign. He had no desire to quarrel with Josiah of Judah, through whose territory he must pass; but in loyalty to his Assyr suzerain Josiah threw himself across the path of the Egyp invader and perished in the battle of Megiddo. The Pharaoh seems to have returned to Egypt, taking Jehoahaz the son of Josiah with him, and to have appointed his brother Jehoiakim king of Judah, and to have exacted a heavy tribute from the land.

3. Pharaoh Necoh's Revolt

But he did not desist from his purpose to win an eastern empire. Accordingly he pressed forward till he reached the Euphrates, where he was completely routed by the Bab army under Nebuchadrezzar in the decisive battle of Carchemish, 604 BC. The battle left the Chaldaeans undisputed masters of Western Asia, and Judah exchanged the yoke of Assyria for that of Babylon.

4. Defeat at Carchemish, 604 BC

So far as cruelty was concerned, there was little to choose between the new tyrants and the old oppressors. Of the Chaldaeans Habakkuk, who flourished at the commencement of the new Empire, says: "They are terrible and dreadful. . . . . Their horses also are swifter than leopards, and are more fierce than the evening wolves; and their horsemen spread themselves: yea, their horsemen come from far; they fly as an eagle that hasteth to devour" (Hab **1** 7.8 ARVm). Over Western Asia, including Judah, Nebuchadrezzar since the battle of Carchemish was supreme. It was vain for Judah to coquet with Egypt when Nebuchadrezzar had a long and powerful arm with which to inflict chastisement upon his disloyal subjects.

5. The New Babylonian Empire under Nebuchadrezzar, 604–562 BC

The mission of Jeremiah the prophet in this crisis of the history of Judah was to preach obedience and loyalty to the king of Babylon, and moral reformation as the only means of escaping the Divine vengeance impending upon land and people. He tells them in the name of God of the great judgment that was to come at the hand of the Chaldaeans on Jerus and surrounding peoples. He even predicts the period of their subjection to Chaldaean domination: "And this whole land shall be a desolation, and an astonishment; and these nations shall serve the king of Babylon seventy years" (Jer **25** 11). This preaching was unpalatable to the partisans of Egypt and to those who believed in the inviolability of Jerus. But with stern rebuke and with symbolic action he proclaims the doom of Jerus, and in the face of persecution and at the risk of his life, the prophet fulfils his ministry.

Jehoiakim, who was first the vassal of Pharaoh Necoh, and then of Nebuchadrezzar, was in corruption and wickedness too faithful a representative of the people. Jeremiah charges him with covetousness, the shedding of innocent blood, oppression and violence (Jer **22** 13–19). The fourth year of Jehoiakim was the first year of Nebuchadrezzar, who, fresh from the victory of Carchemish, was making his sovereignty felt in the western world. The despicable king of Judah became Nebuchadrezzar's vassal and continued in his allegiance three years, after which he turned and rebelled against him. But he received neither encouragement nor help from the neighboring peoples. "Jehovah sent against him bands of the Chaldeans, and bands of the Syrians, and bands of the Moabites, and bands of the children of Ammon, and sent them against Judah to destroy it, according to the word of Jehovah, which he spake by his servants the prophets" (2 K **24** 2). The history of the latter part of Jehoiakim's reign is obscure. The Heb historian says that after a reign of eleven years he slept with his fathers, from which we infer that he died a natural death. From Daniel we learn that in the third year of Jehoiakim, Nebuchadrezzar came up against Jerus and besieged it, and carried off, along with vessels of the house of God, members of the seed royal, and of the nobility of Judah, among whom was Daniel the prophet. That Jehoiakim was included in what seems to be a first instalment of the captivity of Judah is expressly affirmed by the Chronicler who says: "Against him [Jehoiakim] came up Nebuchadnezzar . . . . and bound him in fetters, to carry him to Babylon" (2 Ch **36** 6). However the facts really stand, the historian adds to the record of the death of Jehoiakim and of the succession of Jehoiachin the significant comment: "And the king of Egypt came not again any more out of this land; for the king of Babylon had taken, from the brook of Egypt unto the river Euphrates, all that pertained to the king of Egypt" (2 K **24** 7).

6. Revolt and Punishment of Jehoiakim, 608–597 BC

Jehoiachin who succeeded Jehoiakim reigned only three months, the same length of time as his unfortunate predecessor Jehoahaz (2 K **23** 31). The captivity of Jehoahaz in Egypt and the captivity of Jehoiachin in Babylon are lamented in a striking elegy by Ezekiel, who compares them to young lions, the offspring of the mother lioness Israel, which learned to catch their prey and devoured men, but were taken in the pit of the nations and put in rings, so that their roar was no more heard in the mountains of Israel (Ezk **19** 1–9). Nebuchadrezzar came in person while his servants were besieging Jerus, and Jehoiachin surrendered at discretion. So the king and his mother and his servants and his princes and his officers were carried off with the mighty men of valor, even ten thousand captives. 'None remained, save the poorest sort of the people of the land. He carried out thence all the treasures of the house of Jehovah, and the treasures of the king's house, and cut in pieces all the vessels of gold, which Solomon king of Israel had made in the temple of Jehovah, as Jehovah had said. And all the men of might, even seven thousand, and the craftsmen and the smiths a thousand, all of them strong and apt for war, even them the king of Babylon brought captive to Babylon. And the king of Babylon made Mattaniah, Jehoiachin's father's brother, king in his stead, and changed his name to Zedekiah' (2 K **24** 10–17). From Jehoiachin dates the carrying away into Babylon, the year being 597 BC. The unfortunate monarch lived in exile in Babylon 38 years, and seems to have retained the respect and loyalty of the exiles among whom he dwelt.

7. Siege and Surrender of Jerusalem under Jehoiachin, 597 BC

8. First Deportation, 597 BC

It was with reference to the deportation of the princes and craftsmen and smiths that Jeremiah had his vision of the baskets of figs—one containing figs very good, like the first ripe figs; the other very bad, so bad they could not be eaten (Jer **24** 1–3). The good figs were the captives of Judah carried away into the land of the Chaldaeans for good; the bad figs were the king Zedekiah and his princes and the residue of Jerus, upon whom severe judgments were yet to fall till they were consumed from off the land (vs 4–10).

Among the captives thus carried to Babylon and placed on the banks of the Chebar was the priest-prophet Ezekiel. Five years after the captivity he began to have his wonderful "visions" of God, and to declare their import to the exiles by the rivers of Babylon. To the desponding captives who were engrossed with thoughts of the kingdom of Judah, not yet dissolved, and of the Holy City, not yet burned up with fire, Ezekiel could only proclaim by symbol and allegory the destruction of city and nation, till the day when the distressing tidings reached them of its complete overthrow. Then to the crushed and despairing captives he utters no lamentations like those of Jeremiah, but rather joyful predictions of a rebuilt city, of a reconstituted kingdom, and of a renovated and glorious temple.

9. The Ministry of Ezekiel, 592-570 BC

Although the flower of the population had been carried away into Babylon and the Temple had been despoiled of its treasures, Jerus and the Temple still stood. To the inhabitants who were left behind, and to the captives in Babylon, Jeremiah had a message. To the latter he offered counsels of submission and contentment, assured that the hateful and repulsive idolatries around them would throw them back upon the law of their God, and thus promote the work of moral and spiritual regeneration within them. 'Thus saith Jeh, I will give them a heart to know me, that I am Jehovah: and they shall be my people, and I will be their God; for they shall return unto me with their whole heart' (Jer **24** 5.7). To "the residue of Jerus" his counsels and predictions were distasteful, and exposed him to the suspicion of disloyalty to his people and his God. None of his warnings was more impressive than that symbolically proclaimed by the bands and bars which the prophet was to put upon his neck to send to the kings of Edom and Moab and Ammon and Tyre and Sidon, who seem to have had ideas of forming an alliance against Nebuchadrezzar. Zedekiah was also urged to submit, but still entertained hopes that the king of Babylon would allow the captives of Judah to return. He even himself went to Babylon, perhaps summoned thither by his suzerain (Jer **51** 59). With an Egyp party in Jerus urging an alliance with Egypt, and with a young and warlike Pharaoh on the throne, Hophra (Apries), Zedekiah deemed the opportunity favorable for achieving independence, and entered into an intrigue with the Egyp king. So Zedekiah rebelled against the king of Babylon (2 K **24** 20).

10. Jeremiah's Ministry in Jerusalem, 597-588 BC

It was a bold throw, but Nebuchadrezzar would brook no such disloyalty from his vassals. He marched at once to the West, and committed to Nebuzaradan the task of capturing Jerus, while he himself established his headquarters at Riblah, in Syria, on the Orontes. Meanwhile the Pharaoh with his army crossed the frontier to the help of his allies, and compelled the Chaldaeans to raise the siege of Jerus and meet him in the field (Jer **37** 5). But here his courage failed him, and he retired in haste without offering battle. Nebuzaradan now led back his army and the siege became closer than before.

11. Zedekiah's Rebellion and the Siege of Jerusalem, 588-586 BC

During the breathing-space afforded by the withdrawal of the Chaldaeans, Jeremiah was going out of the city to his native Anathoth, some 4 miles to the N.E. across the ridge, on family business (Jer **37** 11–15). His departure was observed, and he was charged with falling away to the Chaldaeans, and cast into an improvised dungeon in the house of Jonathan the scribe. While there the king sent for him and asked, "Is there any word from Jehovah?" And Jeremiah answered fearlessly, "There is. Thou shalt be delivered into the hand of the king of Babylon." For a time Jeremiah, by the favor of Zedekiah, enjoyed after this a greater measure of freedom; but as he continued to urge in hearing of all the people the duty of surrender, his enemies vowed that he should be put to death, and had him cast into a foul empty cistern, where he ran the risk of being choked or starved to death. Once again the king sought an interview with the prophet, giving him private assurance that he would not put him to death nor allow his enemies to do so. Again the prophet counseled surrender, and again he was allowed a measure of freedom.

But the end of the doomed city was at hand. In the 11th year of Zedekiah, 586 BC, in the 4th month, the 9th day of the month, a breach was made in the city (Jer **39** 1.2), and the final assault completed the work that had been done by months of famine and want. Zedekiah and his men of war do not seem to have waited for the delivery of the last assault. They fled from the city by night "by the way of the king's garden, through the gate betwixt the two walls," and made eastward for the Arabah. But the army of the Chaldaeans pursued them, and overtook Zedekiah in the plains of Jericho. They took him prisoner and brought him to Nebuchadrezzar at Riblah, where the king of Babylon first slew the son of Zedekiah, and then put out his eyes. With

12. Destruction of Jerusalem, 586 BC

the sons of the captured monarch were slain all the nobles of Judah. This time neither city nor temple nor palace was spared. Nebuzaradan "burnt the house of Jeh, and the king's house; and all the houses of Jerus, even every great house, burnt he with fire" (2 K **25** 9). His soldiers, too, broke down the walls of Jerus round about. The treasure and the costly furnishings of the Temple, in so far as they had escaped the former spoliation, were carried away to Babylon. The ruin of Jerus was complete. The Book of Lamentations utters the grief and shame and penitence of an eyewitness of the captures and desolation of the Holy City: "Jehovah hath accomplished his wrath, he hath poured out his fierce anger; and he hath kindled a fire in Zion, which hath devoured the foundations thereof. The kings of the earth believed not, neither all the inhabitants of the world, that the adversary and the enemy would enter into the gates of Jerus. Woe unto us! for we have sinned. For this our heart is faint; for these things our eyes are dim; for the mountain of Zion, which is desolate: the foxes walk upon it" (Lam **4** 11.12; **5** 16.18).

13. Second Deportation of Inhabitants, 586 BC

"So Judah," says the prophet who had been through the siege and the capture (if not rather the editor of his prophecies), "was carried away captive out of his land" (Jer **52** 27). The statements of the numbers carried away are, however, conflicting. In Jer (**52** 28–30) we read of three deportations: that of 597 BC when 3,023 Jews were carried off; that of 586 BC when Nebuchadrezzar carried off 832 persons; and one later than both in 581 BC, when Nebuzaradan carried away captive of the Jews 745 persons—a total of 4,600.

14. Third Deportation, 581 BC

In 2 K **24** 15.16 it is said that in 597 Nebuchadrezzar carried to Babylon 8,000 men. Dr. George Adam Smith taking all the data together estimates that the very highest figures possible are 62,000 or 70,000 men, women and children, less than half of the whole nation (*Jerusalem*, II, 268–70). In 597 BC, Nebuchadrezzar carried off the princes and nobles and craftsmen and smiths, leaving behind the poorest sort of the people of the land (2 K **24** 14). In 586 BC Nebuzaradan carried off the residue of the people that were left in the city, but he "left of the poorest of the land to be vinedressers and husbandmen" (2 K **25** 12). "They were, as the Bib. narratives testify, the *poorest of the land*, from whom every man of substance and energy had been sifted; mere groups of peasants, without a leader and without a center; disorganized and depressed; bitten by hunger and compassed by enemies; uneducated and an easy prey to the heathenism by which they were surrounded. We can appreciate the silence which reigns in the Bible regarding them, and which has misled us as to their numbers. They were a negligible quantity in the religious future of Israel: without initiative or any influence except that of a dead weight upon the efforts of the rebuilders of the nation, when these at last returned from Babylonia" (*Jerusalem*, II, 269–70).

15. Gedaliah, Governor of Judah

Over those who were left behind, Gedaliah was appointed governor, with his residence at Mizpah, where also a Bab contingent remained on guard. Jeremiah had the choice of being taken to Babylon or of remaining in Judah. He preferred to remain with the residue of the people under the care of Gedaliah. With the murder of Gedaliah by Ishmael, a traitorous scion of the royal house, who in turn had to flee and made good his escape, it looked as if the last trace of the former kingdom of Judah was wiped out. Against the counsel of Jeremiah, the remnant, led by Johanan the son of Kareah, resolved to take refuge in Egypt and insisted that Jeremiah and his friend Baruch should accompany them. It is in Egypt, amid disappointment and misrepresentation which he had to endure, that we have our last glimpse of the prophet of the downfall of Judah. Of the descendants of those settlers in Egypt remarkable remains have been discovered within the last few years. They consist of Aram. papyri which were found at Assouan, the ancient Syene, and which belong to a time not more than a cent. after the death of Jeremiah. The documents are accounts and contracts and deeds of various kinds, from which we gather that in the 5th cent. BC there were Jews keeping themselves apart as they do still, worshipping Jeh, and no other God, and even having a temple and an altar of sacrifice to which they brought offerings as their fathers did at Jerus before the destruction of the Temple. These papyri give us valuable glimpses of the social condition and religious interest of the settlers. See DISPERSION.

16. The Exiles in Babylon

Of the Jewish captives carried off by Nebuchadrezzar and settled by the rivers of Babylon, we learn something from the prophecies of Daniel which are now generally believed to belong to the Maccabean period, and much from the prophecies of Ezekiel, from the Psalms of the Captivity, and from the Second Isaiah, whose glowing messages of encouragement and comfort were inspired by the thought of the Return. From Haggai and Zechariah we see how the work of rebuilding the Temple was conceived and carried out. Of the social condition of the Exiles an interesting revelation is given by the excavations at Nippur. From cuneiform tablets, now in the Imperial Ottoman Museum at Constantinople, preserved among the business archives of the wealthy firm of Murashu, sons of Nippur, in the reign of Artaxerxes I and Darius II (464–405 BC), there can be read quite a number of Jewish names. And the remarkable thing is that many of the names are those known to us from the genealogical and other lists of the Books of K and Ch and Ezr and Neh. Professor Hilprecht (*The Babylonian Expedition*, IX, 13 ff) infers from an examination of these that a considerable number of the Jewish exiles, carried away by Nebuchadrezzar after the destruction of Jerus, were settled in Nippur and its neighborhood. Of this fact there are various proofs. The Talmudic tradition which identifies Nippur with Calneh (Gen **10** 10) gains new force in the light of these facts. And "the river Khebar in the land of the Chaldeans," by which Ezekiel saw his vision, is now known from inscriptions to be a large navigable canal not far from Nippur (ib, 27.28).

17. The Rise and Development of Judaism

The influence of the Captivity as a factor in the development of Judaism can hardly be overestimated. "The captivity of Judah," says Dr. Foakes-Jackson (*Biblical History of the Hebrews*, 316) "is one of the greatest events in the history of religion. . . . . With the captivity the history of Israel ends, and the history of the Jews commences." Placed in the midst of heathen and idolatrous surroundings the Golah recoiled from the abominations of their neighbors and clung to the faith of their fathers in the God of Abraham. Exposed to the taunts and the scorn of nations that despised them, they formed an inner circle of their own, and cultivated that exclusiveness which has marked them ever since. Being without a country, without a ritual system, without any material basis for their life as a people, they learned as never before to prize those spiritual possessions which had come down to them from the past. They built up their nationality in their new surroundings upon the foundation of their religion. Their prophets, Jeremiah and Ezekiel, had encouraged and stimulated them with the assurance of spiritual blessings, and the promise of restoration. For their whole social and domestic and spiritual life there was needed some steady and continuous regulative principle or scheme. The need of this threw their leaders and thinkers back upon the Law of Moses. The rabbi and the scribe took the place of the sacrificing priest. The synagogue and the Sabbath came to occupy a new place in the religious practice of the people. These and other institutions of Judaism only attained to maturity after the Return, but the Captivity and the Exile created the needs they were meant to supply. While the prophets were clear and explicit in setting forth the Captivity, they were not less so in predicting the Return. Isaiah with his doctrine of the Remnant, Micah, Zephaniah, Jeremiah, Ezekiel and others gifted with the vision of God, cheered the nation, each in their day, with the hope of restoration and return, not for Judah only but for Israel as well. Vineyards were to be planted again upon the mountains of Samaria as well as in the valleys of Judah. Jeremiah had even predicted the length of the period of the Exile, when he declared that the inhabitants of the land should serve the king of Babylon for seventy years (Jer **25** 12; **29** 10).

18. The Return by Permission of Cyrus, 538 BC

It was in Cyrus, who brought about the fall of Babylon and ended the New Babylonian Empire in 539 BC, that the hopes of the exiles came to be centered. He was "the battle-axe" with which Jeh was to shatter Babylon (Jer **51** 20), and as he proceeded on his path of victory the unknown Seer whom we call the Second Isaiah welcomed him as the liberator of his people. "Thus saith Jehovah . . . . of Jerus, She shall be inhabited; and of the cities of Judah, They shall be built, and I will raise up the waste places thereof; that saith to the deep, Be dry, and I will dry up thy rivers; that saith of Cyrus, He is my shepherd, and shall perform all my pleasure, even saying of Jerus, She shall be built; and of the temple, Thy foundation shall be laid" (Isa **44** 26–28).

19. Rebuilding of the Temple, 536 BC

Within a year of the entry of Cyrus into Babylon an edict was issued (2 Ch **36** 22.23; Ezr **1** 1 ff), granting permission to the exiles to return and build a house for the Lord in Jerus. He also brought forth the vessels of the Temple which Nebuchadrezzar had carried away and handed them over to Sheshbazzar, the prince of Judah; and Sheshbazzar brought them with him when they of the Captivity were brought up from Babylon unto Jerus.

Particulars of the Return are given in the Books of Ezr and Neh, and in the prophecies of Haggai and Zechariah. Of the exiles 42,360 returned under Sheshbazzar, besides slaves; and under Jeshua the son of Jozadak the priest, and Zerubbabel, the son of Shealtiel, first an altar was built and then the foundations of the Temple were laid. In consequence of the opposition of the Samaritans, who were refused any share in the restoration of the Temple, the work of rebuilding was greatly hindered, and came to a stop. It was then that Haggai and Zechariah urged the resumption of the work and partly by denouncing the niggardliness of the people and partly by foreshadowing the glorious future in store for the Temple, hastened forward the enterprise. At length in the month Adar, in the 6th year of Darius (515 BC) the work was completed and the Passover celebrated within the courts of the restored Sanctuary (Ezr **6** 15–18).

20. Reforms and Labors of Ezra and Nehemiah

For some decades the history is silent, and it was in 458 BC that Ezra set out for Jerus taking 1,800 Jews along with him. He found that the returned Jews had become allied in marriage with the people of the land and were in danger of losing their racial characteristics by absorption among the heathen (Ezr **9**). It was due no doubt to his efforts and those of Nehemiah, supported by the searching and powerful utterances of Malachi, that this peril was

Terra-Cotta Cylinder Containing the History of the Capture of Babylon by Cyrus the Great.

averted. Thirteen years later (445 BC) Nehemiah, the cupbearer of Artaxerxes, having heard of the desolate condition of the Holy City, the place of his fathers' sepulchers, obtained leave of his master to visit Jerus. With letters to the governors on the route and to the keeper of the king's forest, he set out, and came safely to Jerus. Having himself inspected the walls he called the people to the work of repairing the ruins, and despite the taunts and calumny and active hostility of the Sam opposition he had the satisfaction of seeing the work completed, the gates set up and the city repeopled. Nehemiah and Ezra then gathered the people together to hear the words of the Law, and at a solemn convocation the Law was read and explained to the assembly. Thereafter a covenant was entered into by the people that they would observe the Law of Moses and not intermarry with the heathen nor traffic on the Sabbath, but would pay a third of a shekel annually for the services of the Temple and would bring first-fruits and tithes (Neh **10** 28 ff).

21. Modern Theories of the Return

The course of the history as here set forth has been disputed by some modern scholars, who hold that there was no return of the exiles under Cyrus and that the rebuilding of the Temple was the work of the Jews who remained behind in Judah and Jerus (*EB*, art. "Ezra-Nehemiah"). This view, held by the late Professor Kosters of Leyden and supported by Professor H. P. Smith and other scholars, proceeds largely upon the rejection of the historical character of the Book of Ezr-Neh. The historical difficulties which are found in the book are by no means such as to warrant us in denying the fact of the Return and the work of Ezra in connection with Nehemiah. As regards the Return, the course of the narrative is too well supported by documents which bear upon them the stamp of historical truth to be rashly disputed. Moreover, it seems highly improbable that an enterprise requiring such energy and skill and faith should have been undertaken, without stimulus from without, by the residue of the people. We have already seen how little initiative was to be expected of the poorest of the people; and the silence of Haggai, on the subject of the Return, is no argument against it. That the Judaism of Pal required invigoration by an infusion of the zeal and enthusiasm which grew up in the Judaism of Bab, is manifest from the story of the Captivity.

22. Importance of the Period Ezra-Nehemiah

From the age of Nehemiah and the period immediately preceding it came influences of the utmost moment for the future. "Within these hundred years," says the late Dr. P. Hay Hunter in *After the Exile* (I, xvi), "the teaching of Moses was established as the basis of the national life, the first steps were taken toward the formation of a canon of Scripture. Jewish society was moulded into a shape which succeeding cents. modified, but did not essentially change. During this period the Judaea of the days of Our Lord came into being. Within this period the forces which opposed Christ, the forces which rallied to His side, had their origin. This cent. saw the rise of parties, which afterward became sects under the names of Pharisees and Sadducees. It laid the foundation of Rabbinism. It fixed the attitude of the Jews toward the Gentiles. It put the priesthood in the way to supreme authority. It gave birth to the Samaritan schism."

Figurative uses. See CAPTIVE.

LITERATURE.—Schrader, *COT*, I; McCurdy, *HPM*, I, 281 ff, II, 249 ff, III; C. F. Burney, *Notes on Heb Text of Bks of Kings;* Foakes-Jackson, *Bib. Hist of the Hebrews*, 260–412; G. A. Smith, *Jerusalem*, II, 223–349; *Cambridge Biblical Essays*, 93–135; P. Hay Hunter, *The Story of Daniel* and *After the Exile; EB*, art. "Ezra-Nehemiah"; Nicol, *Recent Archaeology and the Bible*, 239–78; H. P. Smith, *OT Hist*, 219–412; Kittel, *Hist of the Hebrews*, II, 329 ff.

T. NICOL

CAPTIVITY EPISTLES. See PHILEMON.

CAR. See PALANQUIN.

CARABASION, kar-a-bā'zi-on (Ῥαβασίων, *Rhabasiōn*, **Καραβασίων**, *Karabasiōn;* **Marimoth**): One of the sons of Baani (1 Esd **9** 34) who had married foreign wives, during the captivity. The name is allowed to be corrupt; it seems to be represented by Meremoth in the list of Ezr **10** 36.

CARAVAN, kar'a-van, kar-a-van' (אֹרַח, *'ōraḥ*): This word is not found in AV, but RV employs it three times, viz. in Job **6** 18.19 (*'orḥōth*), where AV renders "paths" (ver 18) and "troops" (ver 19); in Isa **21** 13 (*'ōr^ehōth*), where AV and EV give "travelling companies," and in Ezk **27** 25 (*shārōth*), where AV gives a totally different tr. The Heb text in Ezk is dubious, but in Isa and Job "caravan" is undoubtedly a correct rendering of the Heb (cf also Gen **37** 25). The inhabitants of Pal were familiar with the caravans—the goods trains of the Sem world—which traveled between Babylon and Syria on the one hand to Arabia and on the other to Egypt. The main routes between these countries passed through Canaan. Isaiah refers to "caravans of Jedanites"—a trading Arab. tribe who conveyed their wares to Babylon. Job compares his would-be friends to a deceitful brook, full in the rainy season, but dry in summer, which entices caravans to turn aside from the main route in the hope of a plentiful supply of water, but which fails the thirsty travelers when they need it most. T. LEWIS

CARAVANSARY, kar-a-van'sa-ri. See INN.

CARBUNCLE, kär'buṇ-k'l. See STONES, PRECIOUS.

CARCAS, kär'kas (כַּרְכַּס, *karkaṣ*): One of seven chamberlains, ordered to summon Queen Vashti before King Ahasuerus (Est **1** 10). The Targ allegorizes the first five of the names.

CARCASS, CARCASE, kär'kas: The dead body of a beast; used sometimes in a contemptuous way of the dead body of a human being. The use of the word as applied to a living body is not found in either OT or NT. (1) It occurs as a tr of the Heb פֶּגֶר, *pegher*, in Gen **15** 11; this Heb word is also tr^d "dead body" in Nu **14** 29; 1 S **17** 46; Isa **34** 3; **66** 24; Ezk **6** 5; **43** 7.9, and "corpse" in Nah **3** 3. (2) The Heb נְבֵלָה, *n^ebhēlāh*, is also tr^d "carcass" in Lev **5** 2; **11** 8.11; Jer **16** 18, but as "dead body" in Dt **28** 26 ("body," Josh **8** 29; 1 K **13** 22.29; 2 K **9** 37); Isa **5** 25; Jer **7** 33; **16** 4; **19** 7. (3) In Jgs **14** 8 the word מַפָּלָה, *mappēlāh*, from נָפַל, *nāphal*, "to incline" or "fall," is also tr^d "carcass." (4) In Mt **24** 28 the word "carcase" (not "carcass") is used to render the Gr πτῶμα, *ptōma*, the reference probably being here to the dead body of an animal For the body of a human being the Gr is tr^d "corpse" (Mt **14** 12; Mk **6** 29; **15** 45), and "dead bodies" (Rev **11** 8.9). W. N. STEARNS

CARCHEMISH, kär'ke-mish (כַּרְכְּמִישׁ, *kark^emīsh;* **Χαρμεῖς**, *Charmeīs*, **Καρχαμεῖς**, *Karchameīs*): An exceedingly ancient Hittite city on the banks of the Euphrates, identified with Jerablus (Hierapolis) about 23 hours from Aleppo, between *Birejik* and *Membij*. The Assyr form of the name is *Kargamiš* or *Gargamiš*, but its meaning is doubtful, the interpretation "Fort of the god Chemosh" having been suggested before it was known that the Assyr-Bab form of Chemosh was not *Kamish* or *Gamish*, but *Kammusu* (*Kammosu*). Systematic excavations on the site have apparently only just been made, those undertaken by Consul J. Henderson, after the death of G. Smith the Assyriologist, having been mainly devoted to the excavation of sculptures, etc. The site has vast walls and palace-mounds about 8,000 ft. in circumference.

The earliest occurrence of the name is in an adjectival form, namely, *Karkamisū*, "Carchemishite," applied to a vase or measure of 200 *qa*, in a list of property at Sippar in the reign of Ammi-ṣaduga (cir 1900 BC). Later on, the Egyp poet known as Pentaur refers to the people of Carchemish (*Qarqameša*) as forming, with the men of Arvad, Aleppo and Gozan, part of "the host of the miserable king of the Hittites" (*Ḫattu-šil*), who fought against Rameses II at the battle of Kadesh. The first Assyr king to mention Carchemish is Tiglath-pileser I (cir 1268 BC), who states that he plundered "from the neighborhood of the land of Suḫu [the Shuhites] as far as Carchemish of the land of Ḫattu" in one day.

1. Evidence of the City's Early Existence

Later, the city attracted the attention of the Assyr king Aššur-naṣir-âpli, who started on the 8th of Iyyar, about the year 870 BC, to the conquest of the district, and received tribute from the son of Bît-Baḫiani; and, a little later, from Sangara of Carchemish, who is described as king of the Hittites. This tribute consisted of 20 talents of silver, various objects of gold, 100 talents of copper, 250 talents of iron, furniture, chariots and horses—an enormous treasure. Shalmaneser II, son of Aššur-naṣir-âpli, also took tribute from the king of Carchemish here referred to. On the first occasion when the two monarchs met, Sangara was in alliance with the Sam'alians, Patinians, and Til-Bursip. After the capture of Šazabē (858 BC), a strong city of Sangara of Carchemish, all the opposing princes submitted. The tribute paid by the Hittite king on this occasion is depicted on strip F of the bronze coverings of the gates of Balawât, which has four representations of the place—two in the upper and two in the lower row of reliefs. The Kurkh monolith states that the tribute consisted of "2 talents of gold, 70 talents of silver, 80 talents of bronze, 100 talents of iron, 30 talents of purple stuff, 500 weapons, his daughter with a dowry, and 100 daughters of his great men, 500 oxen, and 5,000 sheep." A yearly tax was also imposed. The reliefs show two long trains of tribute-bearers, that in the lower row escorting the princess, who, apparently accompanied by her father, goes to meet the Assyr king. Šamši-Adad, Shalmaneser II's son, merely mentions Carchemish as being on the western limits of his empire.

2. Its Later History

In the time of Tiglath-pileser IV, the city was ruled by King Pisiri(s), who paid tribute as an Assyr vassal. On the accession of Sargon of Assyria, however, Pisiris tried to throw off the Assyr yoke, and made alliance with Meta of Moschi (Mesech) and other rulers, but was taken prisoner in the operations which followed. In the subsequent plundering of the city, those who suffered most were the inhabitants of the city who had been most active against Assyria. These were carried captive, and their places filled, as was the custom, by Assyr settlers. The city's importance under Assyr rule continued, the "mana of Carchemish" being one of the standard weights in use at Nineveh. After incorporation into the Assyr empire it was ruled by Assyr governors, one of whom, Bêl-êmuranni, was eponym for the year 691 BC (reign of Sennacherib). The OT gives later details. In the time of Josiah, Pharaoh Necoh marched to fight against the city, and the Jewish king went out to meet him, but lost his life at Megiddo (2 Ch **35** 20 ff). Four years later (605 BC), the Egyp king was himself defeated by Nebuchadrezzar under the walls of the city (Jer **46** 2) in the battle which decided the fate of Western Asia.

3. Tiglath-pileser IV Receives Its Tribute, and Sargon of Assyria Incorporates It

The art of Carchemish was that of the Hittite nation to which the city belonged, but it was strongly influenced by the style of the Assyrians, and exhibits a mannerism if anything more pronounced. The inscriptions found on the site are in the usual Hittite style—boldly carved natural objects and implements in relief arranged in boustrophedon-bands between division-lines. It is not improbable, however, that cuneiform was also used, and texts in Phoen characters may, by chance, be found. The patron-deity of the city was the Asiatic goddess Atargatis, whose worship, when the place lost its importance, was removed to the new Hierapolis now represented by *Membij*. See HITTITES.

4. Sculpture and Inscriptions Found at Carchemish

T. G. PINCHES

CARE, kâr, **CAREFULNESS**, kâr'fŏŏl-ness, **CAREFUL**, kâr'fŏŏl: The Eng. word "care" has such a variety of meanings, and so many Heb and Gr words in the Bible are tr[d] by this Eng. expression and its compounds, that it is difficult to organize them into a single brief article. We may do so, however, by remembering that into our word are really woven two strands, one Teutonic and one Lat. The former element implies a measure of trouble or sorrow, as the pain from a blow, a throb, a distress in the mind; the latter, from Lat *cura*, implies a stretching forward, attention to some person or thing. We can often discern these two senses side by side in the Bible, and sometimes they almost run into one another. This is so esp. in the AV. We can treat the subject best by keeping separate, as far as possible, these two senses.

I. In the Sense of Anxiety, Solicitude.—In the OT several words are tr[d] "care," in this sense. "Thy father hath left off caring for the asses," concern about them lit. "matters of the asses" (דִּבְרֵי, *dibhrē*, 1 S **10** 2). "They shall eat bread by weight, and with care" (דְּאָגָה, *de'āghāh*, "carefulness" RV; "fearfulness" ARV, Ezk **4** 16). The same word is rendered carefulness (AV and RV; "fearfulness," ARV, Ezk **12** 18–19); and "fear" (AV; "carefulness," RV and ARV, Josh **22** 24). Again, "heaviness" (AV, RV and ARV), but "care" (RVm and ARVm, Prov **12** 25). Once more, "sorrow" (AV, RV and ARV), but "care" (RVm and ARVm, Jer **49** 23). There is also the word חֲרָדָה, *ḥărādhāh*, "trembling," "fear," "anxiety." It is rendered "trembling" (Gen **27** 33 AV). But "thou hast been careful for us with all this care" ("showed us all this reverence," RVm, ARVm, 2 K **4** 13).

1. Substantives

In the NT care, in the sense of anxiety, is the meaning given to μέριμνα, *mérimna*, the condition of being drawn mentally in different directions, distraction of mind. "Care of the world" (Mt **13** 22; Mk **4** 19; Lk **8** 14, "c. of this life," Lk **21** 34); "care of all the churches" (2 Cor **11** 28) ("anxiety," RV and ARV); "casting all your care upon him" ("anxiety," RV, ARV, 1 Pet **5** 7). Also in the Apoc, "My heart faileth for care" (1 Macc **6** 10); "Care bringeth old age before the time" (Sir **30** 24). To these may be added the adj. *amérimnos*, "I would have you without carefulness" (AV; "free from cares," RV and ARV, 1 Cor **7** 32).

In the OT (דָּאַג, *dā'agh*, "to have concern or anxiety for"). "Not be careful in the year of drought" (Jer **17** 8). (שׂוּם לֵב, *sūm lēbh*, "to set the heart upon"), "If we flee away, they will not care for us" ("set their heart upon us" AVm, 2 S **18** 3).

2. Verbs

In the NT (μεριμνάω, *merimnáō*), "Thou art careful and troubled" ("anxious" RV and ARV, Lk **10** 41). "He that is unmarried careth for things that belong to the Lord" ("is careful for," RV and ARV, 1 Cor **7** 32–34). "Members should have the same care one for another" (1 Cor **12** 25). "Who will naturally care [ARV "care truly"] for your state" (Phil **2** 20). "Be careful for nothing" ("in nothing be anxious," RV and ARV, Phil **4** 6). The Apoc has "careful" (Bar **3** 18) and the RV has "be not careful overmuch," where a distinction is plainly made between care in the sense of anxiety and of attention, for a person cannot be too attentive, but he may be too anxious (2 Esd **2** 27).

The impersonal vb. (μέλει, *mélei*), though not quite so strong as *merimnaō*, always implies a degree of concern higher than is felt in mere attention. "Carest thou not that we perish?" (Mk **4** 38). "Carest not for anyone" (AV "no man," Mt **22** 16; Mk **12** 14). "Dost thou not care that my sister did leave me to serve alone?" (Lk **10** 40). "Careth not for the sheep" (Jn **10** 13). "Cared for the poor" (Jn **12** 6). "Gallio cared for none of these things" (Acts **18** 17). "Care not for it" (1 Cor **7** 21). "He careth for you" (1 Pet **5** 7). "Doth God care for oxen?" (better, "Is it for the oxen that God careth?" RV and ARV, 1 Cor **9** 9).

II. In the Sense of Attention.—In the sense of attention, with the flavor of earnestness added from the original Teutonic meaning of the word care, we have the tr of σπουδή, *spoudḗ*, "speed," "earnest care." "What carefulness it wrought in you" ("earnest care," RV, ARV, 2 Cor **7** 11). "Our care for you in the sight of God" ("earnest care," RV, ARV, 2 Cor **7** 12). "Put the same care into the heart of Titus" ("earnest care," RV, ARV, 2 Cor **8** 16). We have also φρονεῖν, *phroneín*, the infin. used as a subst. "Your care for me hath flourished" ("thought," RV, ARV, Phil **4** 10). Also φροντίς, *phrontís*, "thought" ("care" ARV, Wisd **6** 17; **7** 4).

1. Substantives

"A land which Jehovah thy God careth for" (דָּרַשׁ, *dārash*, "seek after") ("seeketh after," RVm, ARVm, Dt **11** 12). "No man careth for my soul" ("sought" AVm, Ps **142** 4; חָשָׁה, *ḥāshah*). "We are not careful to answer" (AV, AVm, ARVm; "We have no need to answer," RV, ARV, Dnl **3** 16). In the NT ἐπιμελέομαι, *epimeléomai*, "Take care of him" (Lk **10** 34.35). "How shall he take care of the church of God?" (1 Tim **3** 5). φροντίζω, *phrontízō*, "to be thoughtful or mindful of," "may be careful to maintain good works" (Tit **3** 8). G. H. Trever

2. Verbs

CAREAH, ka-rē'a. See Kareah.

CAREFUL, CAREFULNESS. See Care.

CAREFULLY, kâr'fo͝ol-i: The same two strands of anxiety and of attention appear in this word as in care. Several words in the Heb and Gr are thus rendered in the Eng. VSS. "Anxiously" is the thought in "The inhabitants of Maroth waited carefully for good" (חָלָה, *ḥālāh*, "to be in pain," "was grieved" AVm, "waiteth anxiously" RV, ARV, "is in travail" RVm, ARVm, Mic **1** 12).

In the sense of *attentively*, the Heb emphatic expression, the infinite absolute with the finite vb. is rendered "carefully" in, "Thou shalt carefully hearken" (lit. "hearing, thou shalt hear," "diligently hearken" RV, ARV, Dt **15** 5). The same Heb is rendered "diligently hearken" AV; "hearken diligently" RV, ARV (Dt **11** 13; **28** 1).

In the NT σπουδαιοτέρως, *spoudaiotérōs*, "I sent him the more carefully" ("diligently" RV, ARV, Phil **2** 28). The vb. (ἐκζητέω, *ekzētéō*, "I seek out," is trd "seek carefully": "though he sought it carefully with tears" ("diligently" RV, ARV, He **12** 17). RV adds others (ἀκριβόω, *akribóō*, "I ascertain exactly"), "learned of them carefully" RV ("diligently" AV; "exactly" ARV, Mt **2** 7.16). The adv. *akribôs*, "search out carefully" RV ("diligently" AV; "exactly" ARV, Mt **2** 8). "Taught carefully" RV ("diligently" AV; "accurately" ARV, Acts **18** 25). "More carefully" RV ("more perfectly" AV, "more accurately" ARV, Acts **18** 26). Ἐπισκοπέω, *episkopéō*, "I oversee," is rendered "look carefully" (RV, ARV, "look diligently" AV, He **12** 15).

In the Apoc *merimnáō* is trd "carefully," as "We should carefully think of thy goodness" ("ponder" RV, Wisd **12** 22). G. H. Trever

CARELESS, kâr'les, **CARELESSLY,** kâr'les-li: These words always mean, "without anxiety," the confidence springing from a sense of security. There is both the vb. בָּטַח, *bāṭah*, "he trusted," and the noun בֶּטַח, *beṭah*, "Ye careless daughters" (RVm "confident") (Isa **32** 9–11). People dwelt careless ("in security" RV, ARV, Jgs **18** 7); "careless Ethiopians" (Ezk **30** 9). "Thou that dwellest carelessly" ("sittest securely" RV, ARV, Isa **47** 8). "Thou that dwellest carelessly" ("securely" RV, ARV, "confidently" AVm, Ezk **39** 6). "The city that dwelt carelessly" (Zeph **2** 15). ARV and RV add בָּזָה, *bāzāh*, "he despised," using the participle in "He that is careless of his ways shall die," "despiseth" AV, ARVm, RVm (Prov **19** 16). G. H. Trever

CAREM, kā'rem (**Καρέμ**, *Karém*): A city of Judah interpolated by the LXX (Josh **15** 59). Probably Beth-haccherem (q.v.).

CARIA, kā'ri-a (**Καρία**, *Karía*): A country in the S.W. of Asia Minor which extended on the N. to Lydia, on the E. to Phrygia, on the S. to Lycia, and the W. to the Aegean Sea. Its borders, however, like those of most of the ancient countries of Asia Minor, were never definitely fixed; hence the difficulty presented by the study of the political divisions. The general surface of the country is rugged, consisting of mountainous ridges running across it, and terminating as promontories jutting into the sea. Its history consists chiefly of that of its practically independent cities of which Miletus (Acts **20** 15–20) and Cnidus (Acts **27** 7) are the chief. For some time previous to 168 BC it had lost its independence, and belonged to the island of Rhodes, but in that year Rome made it again free. According to 1 Macc **15** 23, Caria was one of several places to which the Rom senate in 139–138 BC sent letters in favor of the Jews, a fact showing that its population was mixed. Its coast cities, however, were peopled chiefly by Greeks. In 129 BC Caria became a part of the Rom province of Asia, and from that date its history coincides with that of the province. Though Paul and others of the apostles traversed Caria in their missionary journeys, only its cities are mentioned by name in that connection. E. J. Banks

CARITES, kar'i-tēz (כָּרִי, *kārī*, "one ready," "life-guardsman"): A body of troops mentioned in 2 K **11** 4.19 (AV "captains"). Instead of Cherethites (q.v.), the Kethibh of 2 S **20** 23 offers the reading *Carites*.

CARMANIANS, kär-mā'ni-anz. See Carmonians.

CARME, kär'mē. See Charme.

CARMEL, kär′mel (כַּרְמֶל, or, with art., הַכַּרְמֶל, *karmel,* "fruit garden," or *ha-karmel;* Jos, **ὁ Κάρμηλος,** *ho Kármēlos,* **Καρμήλιον ὄρος,** *Karmēlion óros*):

(1) A beautifully wooded mountain range running for about 13 miles in a south-easterly direction from the promontory which drops on the shore of the Mediterranean near Haifa, at the southern extremity of the plain of Acre, to the height of *el-Maḥraḳah* which overlooks the plain of Esdraelon. On the top of the promontory, at a height of 500 ft. the monastery of St. Elias stands. From this point there is a gradual ascent until the greatest height is reached at *Esfīyeh* (1,742 ft.), the peak at *el-Maḥraḳah* being only some 55 ft. lower. The mountain—usually named with the art., "the Carmel"—still justifies its name, "the garden with fruit trees." The steep slopes on the N. and E., indeed, afford little scope for cultivation, although trees and brushwood grow abundantly. But to the S. and W. the mountain falls away to the sea and the plain in a series of long, fertile valleys, where the "excellency" of Carmel finds full illustration today. There are a few springs of good water; but the main supply is furnished by the winter rains, which are caught and stored in great cisterns. The villages on the slopes have a look of prosperity not too often seen in Syria, the rich soil amply rewarding the toil of the husbandmen. Oak and pine, myrtle and honeysuckle, box and laurel flourish; the sheen of fruitful olives fills many a hollow; and in the time of flowers Carmel is beautiful in a garment of many colors. Evidences of the ancient husbandry which made it famous are found in the cisterns, and the oil and wine presses cut in the surface of the rock. There is probably a reference to the vine culture here in 2 Ch **26** 10. In the **fig.** language of Scripture it appears as the symbol of beauty (Cant **7** 5), of fruitfulness (Isa **35** 2), of majesty (Jer **46** 18), of prosperous and happy life (ib, **50** 19). The languishing of Carmel betokens the vengeance of God upon the land (Nah **1** 4); and her decay, utter desolation (Am **1** 2; Isa **33** 9).

Roughly triangular in form, with plains stretching from its base on each of the three sides, the mountain, with its majestic form and massive bulk, is visible from afar.

Asylum and Sanctuary

Its position deprived it of any great value for military purposes. It commanded none of the great highways followed by armies: the passes between Esdraelon and Sharon, to the E. of Carmel, furnishing the most convenient paths. But the mountain beckoned the fugitive from afar, and in all ages has offered asylum to the hunted in its caves and wooded glens. Also its remote heights with their spacious outlook over land and sea; its sheltered nooks and embowering groves have been scenes of worship from old time. Here stood an ancient altar of Jeh (1 K **18** 30). We may assume that there was also a sanctuary of Baal, since the worshippers of these deities chose the place as common ground for the great trial (1 K **18**). The scene is traditionally located at *el-Maḥraḳah,* "the place of burnt sacrifice," which is still held sacred by the Druzes. A Lat chapel stands near, with a great cistern. A good spring is found lower down the slope. Just below, on the N. bank of the Kishon stands the mound called *Tell el-ḳissīs,* "mound of the priest." From the crest of Carmel Elijah descried the coming storm, and, descending the mountain, ran before the chariot of Ahab to the gate of Jezreel (1 K **18** 42 ff). Under the monastery on the western promontory is a cave, said to be that of Elijah. An older tradition locates the cave of the prophet at *ed-Deir,* near *'Ain es-Sīh.* It may have been the scene of the events narrated in 2 K **1** 9 ff. Elisha also was a familiar visitor to Mt. Carmel. It was within the territory allotted to Asher; in later times it passed into the hands of Tyre (*BJ,* III, iii, 1).

(2) A city of Judah, in the uplands near Hebron, named with Maon and Ziph (Josh **15** 55). Here Saul for some reason not stated set up a monument or trophy (1 S **15** 12; lit. "hand"). It was the

Carmel of Judah.

home of Nabal the churlish and drunken flockmaster, whose widow Abigail David married (1 S **25**); and also of Hezro, one of David's mighty men (2 S **23** 35; 1 Ch **11** 37). It is represented by the modern *el-Karmil,* about 10 miles to the S.E. of Hebron. *Karmil* is the pronunciation given me by several natives this spring. There are considerable ruins, the most outstanding feature being a square tower dating from the 12th cent., now going swiftly to ruin. There are also caves, tombs and a large reservoir. W. Ewing

CARMELITE, kär′mel-īt (כַּרְמְלִי, *karmᵉlī;* **Καρμήλιος,** *Karmēlios,* **Καρμηλίτης,** *Karmēlítēs*): A native of the Judaean Carmel. Those who are thus named are Nabal, the husband of Abigail (1 S **30** 5, etc), and Hezro (AV Hezrai), one of David's mighty men (2 S **23** 35). In 2 S **3** 3 LXX reads *tēs Abigaías tēs Karmēlías,* "of Abigail the Carmelitess" (1 S **27** 3; 1 Ch **3** 1). See following art., Carmelitess.

CARMELITESS, kär′mel-īt-es, kär-mel-ī′tes (כַּרְמְלִית, *karmᵉlīth;* **Καρμήλια,** *Karmēlia*): A name applied only to Abigail, the wife of Nabal, and subsequently of David, a native of Carmel in Judah (1 S **27** 3; 1 Ch **3** 1).

CARMI, kär′mī (כַּרְמִי, *karmī,* "fruitful," "noble"):

(1) A son of Reuben who came to Egypt with Jacob (Gen **46** 9; Ex **6** 14; 1 Ch **5** 3). Also the name of a family of which Carmi was the head (Nu **26** 6).

(2) A Judahite (1 Ch **2** 7), son of Zabdi, according to Josh **7** 1, and father of Achan, who is given the name of "Achar" in 1 Ch **2** 7. This last form "Achar" is preferred to the usual "Achan" in order to bring out the play on the Heb word for "troubler." The Heb runs עָכָר עֹכֵר יִשְׂרָאֵל, *'ākhār 'ōkhēr yisrā'ēl,* "Achar, the troubler of Israel." As regards the phrase "the sons of Carmi" (1 Ch **2** 7), Carmi is probably to be taken as the son of Zimri (=Zabdi, Josh **7** 1). The Tg, however, has "Carmi who is Zimri." The LXX identifies Zimri and Zabdi.

(3) In 1 Ch **4** 1, Carmi, elsewhere called son of Zabdi or Zimri, is made son of Judah; but Wellhausen correctly changes "Carmi" to "Chelubai" (cf 1 Ch **2** 9). Horace J. Wolf

CARMONIANS, kär-mō'ni-anz; AV **Carmanians:** A people mentioned in one of the visions —"an horrible vision" (2 Esd **15** 30 ff)—of the "Apocalypse of Esdras." Their country, Carmania, was an extensive province of Asia lying between Parthia and Ariana and the N. side of the Pers Gulf, and extending to Drangiana and Gedrosia on the E. and to the river Bagradas and Persis on the W. It is frequently mentioned by the ancient writers, among others by Strabo and Arrian, who describe the inhabitants as closely resembling the Medians and Persians in manners and customs. In the passage cited they are intended to denote a fierce and warlike people, being described as "raging in wrath as wild boars of the wood" and associated with the "dragons of Arabia." J. Hutchison

CARNAIM, kär-nā'im, kär'nā-im (**Καρνείν,** *Karneín,* 1 Macc **5** 26, **Καρναίν,** *Karnaín,* vs 43 f, **τὸ Κάρνιον,** *tó Kárnion,* 2 Macc **12** 21.26): One of the strong cities besieged and captured by Judas Maccabaeus in his campaign E. of the Jordan (1 Macc **5** 26.43 f). In the temple of Atargatis, which was situated here, those who fled from the city were put to death. It is apparently identical with Ashteroth Karnaim. It is called Carnion in 2 Macc **12** 21.

CARNAL, kär'nal: In the OT there is an expression which indicates sexual intercourse (שִׁכְבַת זֶרַע, *shikh^ebhath zera'*, "lying of seed," Lev **18** 20; **19** 20; Nu **5** 13). In the NT the words rendered "carnal" are derived from σάρξ, *sárks,* "flesh." This refers to the flesh as opposed to the *pneúma,* "spirit," and denotes, in an ethical sense, mere human nature, the lower side of man as apart from the Divine influence, and therefore estranged from God and prone to sin; whatever in the soul is weak and tends toward ungodliness (see Flesh). Thus one may be carnal (σάρκινος, *sárkinos*), sold under sin (Rom **7** 14). Christians may be carnal (*sarkinos,* 1 Cor **3** 1; *sarkikós,* 1 Cor **3** 3); the lower side of their being is dominant and not the spirit, hence they fall into sins of envy and strife. The weapons of the Christian warfare are not carnal, not merely human (of the flesh RV, ARV), but spiritual (2 Cor **10** 4); "not after the law of a carnal commandment" (He **7** 16); "The carnal mind is enmity against God" ("mind of the flesh" RV, ARV, Rom **8** 7). So, "to be carnally minded is death" ("mind of the flesh" RV, ARV, Rom **8** 6). There are "carnal ordinances," in contrast to the spiritual ones of the gospel (He **9** 10); "Minister unto them in carnal things," those that pertain to the body in contrast to spiritual things (Rom **15** 27; 1 Cor **9** 11). The same expressions are elsewhere rendered "fleshly" (2 Cor **1** 12; **3** 3 RV "hearts of flesh"; 1 Pet **2** 11).

Is there any difference between *sarkinos* and *sarkikos?* The former more definitely denotes the material of which an object is made. It may express with emphasis the idea of *sarkikos,* the spiritual given up as it were to the flesh. See Man (The Natural). G. H. Trever

CARNION, kär'ni-on. See Carnaim.

CAROUSINGS, ka-rouz'ingz (**πότοις,** *pótois,* dative pl. of *pótos*): This word is found only in ARV and once only (1 Pet **4** 3). The AV translates it "banquetings." It is one of the gentile excesses of fleshly indulgence against which the Christians are warned by Peter.

CARPENTER, kär'pen-tẽr (חָרָשׁ, *ḥārāsh;* **τέκτων,** *téktōn*): This word, which is a general word for a graver or craftsman, is tr[d] "carpenter" in 2 K **22** 6; 2 Ch **24** 12; Ezr **3** 7; Isa **41** 7. The same word is rendered "craftsman" in the ARV of Jer **24** 1 and **29** 2 and "smith" in the ARV of Zec **1** 20. In 2 S **5** 11; 2 K **12** 11; 1 Ch **14** 1; and Isa **44** 13, *ḥārāsh* occurs with *'ēç* (wood), and is more exactly tr[d] "carpenter" or "worker in wood." *Tektōn,* the corresponding Gr word for artificer, is tr[d] "carpenter" in Mt **13** 55 and Mk **6** 3. See Carving; Crafts.

CARPUS, kär'pus (**Κάρπος,** *Kárpos*): A name but once mentioned in the NT (2 Tim **4** 13), "the cloak that I left at Troas with Carpus." These words were written from the dungeons, where Paul was confined during his second imprisonment. The name, common enough in Paul's day, signifies "fruit" (Young) or "wrist" (Davis). The words indicate that Paul must have been very well acquainted with the family of Carpus. He was presumably one of his converts; and the apostle must have lodged with him and also have had considerable confidence in him, since he committed to his care not only the comparatively valueless "cloak," but esp. the priceless "books and parchments." It is idle to attempt to find out the identity of Carpus, but one cannot help wondering what were the contents of these books and parchments for which the apostle longed in his bitter second imprisonment. Henry E. Dosker

CARRIAGE, kar'ij (כְּלִי, *k^elī,* כְּבוּדָּה, *k^ebhuddāh,* נְשׂוּאָה, *n^esū'āh;* **ἐπισκευασάμενοι,** *episkeuasámenoi;* RV "We took up our baggage"; ARVm "made ready"): One or the other of the above words occurs in six different places and all have been tr[1] in the AV by "carriage" in its obsolete meaning (Jgs **18** 21; 1 S **17** 22 [twice]; Isa **10** 28; **46** 1; Acts **21** 15). In the RV and ARV these are tr[1] by the more modern expressions "goods," "baggage," or "the things that you carried." In 1 S **17** 20 AVm "place of the carriage" occurs as the equivalent of "trench." The Heb *ma'gālāh* may mean "the place of wagons" as tr[d] in RV, as it is not at all improbable that the encampment was surrounded by the baggage train. James A. Patch

CARRY, kar'i (נָשָׂא, *nāsā',* נָהַג, *nāhagh*): The EV rendering of a number of Heb and Gr words, and it has several shades of meaning, of which the following are the most important:

(1) "To take up," "to bear," "to transport from one place to another," as, "to carry away handkerchiefs" (Acts **19** 12), "to carry a corpse" (Gen **50** 13), and "to be carried away by the wind" (Dnl **2** 35).

(2) "To cause to go" or "come," "to lead," "to drive," as, "to be carried away to Babylon" (2 K **20** 17), "to be carried away to Pilate" (Mk **15** 1), "to carry away cattle" (Gen **31** 18), and "to carry away daughters" (Gen **31** 26).

(3) "To uphold," or "sustain," "and even to hoar hairs will I carry you" (Isa **46** 4).

(4) "To bear," or "endure," as, "to carry sorrows" (Isa **53** 4).

(5) "To overwhelm," "to bear away," "to destroy," as, "to carry away as with a flood" (Ps **90** 5).

(6) "To influence," "to move," as, "to carry away with dissimulation" (Gal **2** 13), "to carry away with error" (2 Pet **3** 17), "to be carried away by strange teachings" (He **13** 9). A. W. Fortune

CARSHENA, kär'shē-na, kar-shē'na (כַּרְשְׁנָא, *karsh^enā'*): The first named among the "seven princes of Persia and Media" under Ahasuerus (Est **1** 14). See Princes, The Seven.

CART, kärt (עֲגָלָה, *'ăghālāh*): The Heb word has been trd in some passages "cart," and in others "wagon." In one ver only has it been trd "chariot." The context of the various passages indicates that a distinction was made between vehicles which were used for carrying baggage or produce and those used for carrying riders (chariots), although in their primitive form of construction they were much the same (cf Eng. "cart" and "carriage").

Egyptian Cart (with Two Wheels).

Carts, like "chariots" (q.v.), were of Assyr origin. They were early carried to Egypt where the flat nature of the country readily led to their adoption. From Egypt they gradually found their way among the people of the Palestinian plains. In the hills of Judaea and Central Pal, except where highways were built (1 S **6** 12), the nature of the country prevented the use of wheeled vehicles. 1 S **6** 7.8.10.11.14 show that the people of the plains used carts. The men of Kiriath-jearim found it easier to carry the ark (1 S **7** 1). Their attempt to use a cart later (2 S **6** 3.6; 1 Ch **13** 7) proved disastrous and they abandoned it for a safer way (2 S **6** 13).

Modern Cart.

That carts were used at a very early date is indicated by Nu **7** 3.7.8. That these vehicles were not the common mode of conveyance in Pal is shown in Gen **45**. Pharaoh commanded that Joseph's brethren should return to their father with their beasts of burden (**45** 21) and take with them Egyp wagons (**45** 19.21; **46** 6) for bringing back their father and their families. The very unusual sight of the wagons was proof to Jacob of Joseph's existence (**45** 27).

Bible descriptions and ancient Bab and Egyp pictures indicate that the cart was usually two-wheeled and drawn by two oxen.

With the Arabian conquests and subsequent ruin of the roads wheeled vehicles disappeared from Syria and Pal. History is again repeating itself. The Circassians, whom the Turkish government has settled near Caesarea, Jerash (Gerasa) and Ammān (Philadelphia), have introduced a crude cart which must be similar to that used in OT times. The two wheels are of solid wood. A straight shaft is joined to the wooden axle, and to this a yoke of oxen is attached. On the Philistian plains may be seen carts of present-day Egyp origin but of a pattern many cents. old. With the establishment of government roads during the last 50 years, European vehicles of all descriptions are fast coming into the country.

One **figurative** reference is made to the cart (Isa **5** 18), but its meaning is obscure.

James A. Patch

CARVING, kärv'ing: Carving, or engraving, was extensively used among the peoples of Bible lands. There were no materials used in the arts which were not subjected to the graver's skill. Carved objects of wood, stone, ivory, clay, bronze, gold, silver and glass discovered today show how skilful the ancient carvers were. Carving was principally done in bas-relief, although Ex **28** 11 shows that incised lines were also used. The signets and scarabs are examples of this class of carving. Several Heb words have been trd "carved" in the AV. *Peṣel* or *peṣīl* is found in Jgs **18** 18; 2 Ch **33** 7.22; **34** 3.4; *ḥāḳah* in 1 K **6** 35. The tr "graven" appears in the RV of all these passages. In 1 K **6** 29.32.35, *ḳāla'* appears; in 1 K **6** 18.32, *miḳla'ath;* in 1 K **6** 29 and Ps **74** 6, *pittūaḥ;* in Ex **31** 5; **35** 33, *ḥărōsheth* (see Carpenter); *ḥăṭūbhāh* in Prov **7** 16 is better trd "striped" as in the RV. For further notes on carving, see Crafts. James A. Patch

CASDIM, kaz'dim. See Chesed.

CASE, kās: Ordinarily to describe the circumstances or condition of things; sometimes, juridically (**αἰτία**, *aitia*, Mt **19** 10; Acts **25** 14), as that for which a reckoning has to be given, as frequently the Lat *rēs.* In Ex **5** 19, "they were in evil case," is interpreted by RV as "were set on mischief."

CASEMENT, kās'ment. See House.

CASIPHIA, ka-sif'i-a, ka-sif-ē'a (כָּסִפְיָא, *kāṣiphyā'*): An unidentified place in North Babylonia, near the river Ahava, to which Ezra sent for "ministers for the house of our God" (Ezr **8** 17). Some have thought the name to be connected with *keṣeph,* "silver" or "money." LXX renders *argurīō toú tópou,* as in 1 Esd **8** 45, "the place of the treasury."

CASLUHIM, kas'lū-him, kas-lū'him (כַּסְלֻחִים, *kaṣlūḥīm;* **Χασμωνιείμ**, *Chasmōnieím*): The name of a people mentioned in Gen **10** 14; 1 Ch **1** 12 as descended from Mizraim. The parenthesis should probably follow Caphtorim. From them, it is said, sprang the Philistines, which see.

CASPHON, kas'fon. See Casphor.

CASPHOR, kas'for (AV **Casphon**; **Κασφώρ**, *Kasphōr,* 1 Macc **5** 26; **Χασφών**, *Chasphōn,* **Χασφώθ**, *Chasphōth,* ver 36; **Κασπείν**, *Kaspein,* 2 Macc **12** 13): A city E. of the Jordan captured by Judas Maccabaeus (1 Macc **5** 36). It is probably identical with Caspis of 2 Macc **12** 13. It was a fortress of great strength, with a lake near it. This has led some to think it may be represented by *el-Muzērīb,* an important station on the pilgrim route to Mecca. The ancient name of this city, however, has not been discovered. See Ashtaroth.

CASPIN, kas'pin, **CASPIS,** kas'pis. See Casphor.

CASSIA, kash'a: Two Heb words, (1) קִדָּה, *ḳiddāh,* which is mentioned, along with myrrh, cinnamon, calamus and olive oil, as one of the ingredients of the "holy anointing oil" (Ex **30** 24); it was, too, one of the wares in which Vedan and Javan traded with Tyre (Ezk **27** 19); it is identified in the Pesh and the Tg with (2). (2) קְצִיעוֹת, *ḳᵉçī'ōth* (plur. only, probably referring to the strips of bark), a word from which is derived the Gr **κασία,** *kasía,* and hence cassia (Ps **45** 8). It is probable that both (1) and (2) refer to *Cassia lignea,* the inner bark of *Cinnamomum cassia,* a plant growing in eastern Asia closely allied to that which yields the cinnamon of commerce. It is a fragrant, aromatic bark and was probably used in a powdered form. Both as an ingredient in unguents and as one of the perfumes at funerals, cassia, like cinnamon, was much used by the Romans. The cassia of Scripture must be clearly distinguished from the entirely distinct *Cassia lanceolata* and *C. obovata* which yield the familiar senna. The proper name Keziah (q.v.) is the sing. form of *ḳᵉçī'ōth.*

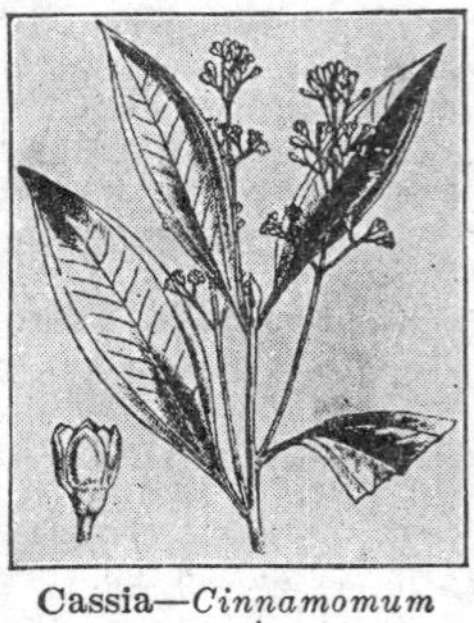

Cassia—*Cinnamomum cassia.*

E. W. G. Masterman

CAST: In general "to throw," with various degrees of violence; usually, with force, but not so necessarily, as e.g. in "cast a net," "cast lots." When applied to molten metal, as in Eng., first, "to let run into molds," with reference to their descent by gravity, and, then, "to form," as in Ex **25** 12, etc. Usually in the NT for βάλλω, *bállō,* but not always. Thus, in Lk **1** 29 "cast in her mind" means "considered" (διελογίζετο, *dielogízeto*); "cast reproach" for Gr ὠνείδιζον, *ōneídizon,* "reproached" (Mt **27** 44); "casting down" for καθαιρέω, *kathairéō,*" "demolishing" (2 Cor **10** 4); "casting all anxiety upon" (1 Pet **5** 7), a still stronger term, as in Lk **17** 2 AV; Acts **27** 19. As a fundamental Gr word, it is compounded with many prepositions, "about," "away," "down," "forth," "in," "into," "off," "out," "up," "upon." "Cast down" in 2 Cor **4** 9 AV is used in a military sense of one prostrated, but not killed in battle. Cf Ps **42** 5 with RVm. "Castaway" of AV in 1 Cor **9** 27, is in RV "rejected" (cf He **6** 8), ἀδόκιμος, *adókimos,* i.e. what the application of a test shows to be counterfeit, or unfit; trᵈ "reprobate" in Rom **1** 28; 2 Cor **13** 5. 6.7, etc.

H. E. Jacobs

CASTANETS, kas'ta-nets, kas-ta-nets' (מְנַעַנְעִים, *mᵉna'an'īm*): Are mentioned in 2 S **6** 5 among the musical instruments upon which David and the house of Israel played at the time of the bringing up of the ark out of the house of Abinadab. This word is incorrectly trᵈ "cornets" in the AV. The castanet was probably about the same kind of instrument as the Egyp *sistrum,* and the RV has "sistra" in the margin of 2 S **6** 5. The *sistrum* was a loop-shaped metal frame through which were passed loose rods at the ends of which were rings. The instrument was held by a long handle and was rattled during songs and dances. It was used in Egypt in religious worship or to scare away evil influences. There is only the one reference to this instrument in the Bible.

A. W. Fortune

CASTAWAY, kast'a-wā (**ἀδόκιμος,** *adókimos,* from *dokimázō,* "I test," "I approve after testing," hence approved after being tested): This word is rendered "castaway" only in AV: "I myself should be a castaway" ("rejected" RV, ARV, 1 Cor **9** 27). But the same word occurs a number of times usually trᵈ "reprobate" (Rom **1** 28; 2 Cor **13** 5–7; 2 Tim **3** 8; Tit **1** 16); "rejected" (He **6** 8).

CASTLE, kas''l. See Fortification.

CASTOR, kas'tẽr, **AND POLLUX,** pol'uks. See Dioscuri; Astronomy.

CAT (**αἴλουρος,** *aílouros*): The only mention of this animal is in Bar **6** 22. It is not mentioned in the canonical Scriptures, though Bochart (*Hieroz.,* 862) gives "wild cats" as the equivalent of *çīyīm* in Isa **13** 21; **34** 14; Jer **50** 39; Ps **74** 19, where EV gives "wild beasts of the desert." Mention is, however, made of cats, *cathod,* in the Welsh Bible (Isa **34** 14). The only mention of the *catta* in classical Lat writers is in Martial xiii.69. How the cat was regarded in Egypt is described in Herod. ii.66 and Rawlinson's notes. In Bar **6** 22 cats are mentioned with "bats, swallows and birds" as sitting with impunity on the images of the heathen gods which are unable to drive them off. See also Zoology.

J. Hutchison

CATECHIST, kat'ē-kist, **CATECHUMEN,** kat-ē-kū'men (**κατηχίζειν,** *katēchízein,* "to resound," "to teach," "to instruct"): A catechist is a teacher who instructs his pupils in the elements of his own religion. In the OT he teaches them the rudiments of OT truth; in the NT he teaches the principles of the Christian faith. A catechumen, one whom the catechist instructs or catechizes, in preparation for the ceremony of baptism.

The words are derived from κατηχεῖν, *katēchein,* meaning "to give a sound," "to answer," "to echo." Classically it was used of the sounding down of rushing water, of the falling of music from a ship to the sea. Then it came to signify the sounding down of words of command or instruction. The preposition *katá* strengthens the meaning, bringing out more emphatically the back or return sound, the echo, the answer. So it came to mean familiar verbal instruction, a free informal discussion between teacher and pupil. Luke informs Theophilus (Lk **1** 4) that he intends to give him a succinct and orderly account of those things which he had previously received by word of mouth (*perí hōn katēchḗthēs*). See also the Gr in Acts **18** 25 and **21** 21; Rom **2** 18; 1 Cor **14** 19; Gal **6** 6. In all these passages the Gr vb. is "catechised."

We do not find in the NT an organized catechumenate, such as we find in the 3d and 4th cents. The apostles preached mainly to synagogue-instructed Jews who were familiar with the law and the prophets and the Psalms, or to Gentiles who had learned from the Jews and had become "proselytes" (q.v.). The first apostolic preaching and teaching was to convince the hearers that Jesus was the promised Messiah, the Saviour of the world As believers multiplied, the contrast between them and those who rejected the teaching became more and more marked. Opposition, scorn and persecution became more bold and bitter. The Christians were compelled to set forth and defend their beliefs more clearly. They had to meet and answer keen and persistent objections. And so the necessity for clear, systematic and organized teaching grew more and more into the form of an ordered catechumenate. The Apos Consts, from the latter part of the 3d cent., show the institution in a fair state of development. A Jew, pagan, or heretic of good moral standing, upon application to the deacon, presbyter, or bishop, was admitted into the state of catechumen by the sign of the cross and the imposition of hands (*Sch-Herz* s.v.).

The basis for the Christian catechumenate we find in the great commission (Mt **28** 19.20). The aim of this commission was to make disciples, i.e. believing followers. The means for this discipling are baptizing and teaching. The result of using the means is that those who have become disciples are to observe all things whatsoever Christ has commanded.

Jesus Himself at twelve years of age had become a child of the law, a catechumen. He increased in wisdom and learned obedience. He became the great Catechist instructing His disciples, other private individuals and the multitudes. See an example of His catechizing in Mt **16** 13 ff.

Paul was a master in method. See examples of use of the modern pedagogical method of apperception in Acts **14** 14 ff; **17** 16 ff; **19** 8.9. The catechetical method is frequently found in the epistles (see 1 Cor **3** 1.2; He **5** 11.14; **6** 1.2; 1 Pet **2** 2; 1 Jn **2** 13), and so the idea of religious nurture and instruction is found all through the NT. The catechist and the catechumen are there. It was not something new in the NT. Its roots lie back and run through the OT. The narrative of God's first communication with man, inside the gates of Eden, concerning commandment, law, sin, its consequences, its remedy, takes a catechetical form. The importance of systematic instruction, both public and private, is emphasized throughout the OT and NT, although it might not always take the form of catechizing in the modern pedagogical sense. In the patriarchal age the father was the prophet, the teacher, the catechist, in his house, which often included several families with their servants (see Gen **18** 19). Matthew Henry explains thus: "Abraham not only took care of his children, but his whole household, including his servants, were catechized" (see also Ex **12** 26; Dt **6** 1–9; Josh **4** 6.7; **24** 15; Ps **34** 11). Priests and Levites in addition to their sacerdotal functions were catechists (instructors) among the people (Lev **10** 11; Dt **33** 10; 2 Ch **15** 3; Ezk **44** 23). In later times the synagogues had regular instruction in the law and the prophets. See Education; Instruction; Teacher.

G. H. Gerberding

CATERPILLAR, kat'ẽr-pil-ẽr (חָסִיל, *ḥāṣīl* [Ps **78** 46; Joel **1** 4, etc]; יֶלֶק, *yeleḳ* [Ps **105** 34 AV, ARV "grasshopper"; Jer **51** 14.27 AV; elsewhere "canker-worm"]): A name given to a larval stage of the Locust (q.v.).

CATHOLIC, kath'ō-lik, **EPISTLES** (**ἐπιστολαὶ καθολικαί**, *epistolaí katholikaí*): In distinction from the apostolic or Pauline epistles which were addressed to individual churches or persons, the term "catholic," in the sense of universal or general, was applied by Origen and the other church Fathers to the seven epistles written by James, Peter, John and Jude. As early as the 3d cent. it came to be used in the sense of "encyclical," "since," as Theodoret says, "they are not addressed to single churches, but generally [*kathólou*] to the faithful, whether to the Jews of the Dispersion, as Peter writes, or even to all who are living as Christians under the same faith." Three other explanations of the term have been given, viz. (1) that it was intended to indicate a common apostolic authorship (only a few support this view); (2) that it signifies that the seven epistles were universally received as genuine; (3) that it refers to the catholicity of their doctrine, i.e. orthodox and authoritative versus heretical epistles whose teachings were in harmony with Christian truth. By some misconception of the word "catholic" the Western Church interpreted it as signifying "canonical" and sometimes called these epistles *epistolae canonicae*. That it was originally used in the sense of "general" epistles is now commonly received.

This is evident from their form of address. St. James wrote to all Jews, "of the Dispersion," who had embraced the Christian faith. In his first epistle St. Peter addressed the same Christians, including also gentile converts, resident in five provinces of Asia Minor: "elect who are sojourners of the Dispersion." His second epistle is to all Christians everywhere. St. John's first letter was evidently written to a cycle of churches and intended for universal use. St. Jude also had in mind all Christians when he said "to them that are called beloved in God," etc. The seeming exceptions are 2 and 3 Jn, addressed to individuals, but included with the catholic epistles as properly belonging with St. John's first epistle and of value to the general reader. The character and contents of these seven epistles are treated under their various heads. The letters of St. James and St. Jude belong to the Judaic school of Christianity; those of St. Peter to a broad and non-partisan type of faith that both includes and mediates between the Judaists and Paulinists. St. John's letters were written after the internal doctrinal controversies of the church had ceased, and the pressure of opposition and error from without tended to unite his "little children" in a new community of love and spiritual life.

Dwight M. Pratt

CATHUA, ka-thū'a (**Καθουά**, *Kathouá*; B, **Κουά**, *Kouá*): Head of a family of temple-servants who returned from the captivity with Zerubbabel (1 Esd **5** 30); corresponds to Giddel in Ezr **2** 47.

CATTLE, kat''l (בְּהֵמָה, *behēmāh*, "a dumb beast"; מִקְנֶה, *miḳneh*, "a possession," from קָנָה, *ḳānāh*, "to acquire" [cf Arab. *ḳana'*, "to acquire," and Gr **κτῆνος**, *ktēnos*, "beast," and pl. **κτήνεα**, *ktēnea*, "flocks," from **κτάομαι**, *ktáomai*, "to acquire," flocks being both with the Homeric peoples and with the patriarchs an important form of property; cf Eng. "fee"]; צֹאן, *çō'n*, "small cattle," "sheep" or goats [cf Arab. *ḍa'n*, "sheep"]; שֶׂה, *seh*, a single sheep or goat [cf Arab. shāh]; מְלָאכָה, *melā'khāh*, "property," from לָאַךְ, *lā'akh*, "to minister" [cf Arab. *malākah* and *mulk*, "property," from *malak*, "to possess"]; מְרִיא, *merī'*, "fatling" [1 K **1** 9]; **θρέμμα**, *thrémma* [Jn **4** 12], "cattle," i.e. "that which is nourished," from **τρέφω**, *tréphō*, "to nourish"; בָּקָר, *bāḳār*, "kine," "oxen" [cf Arab. *baḳar*, "cattle"]; שׁוֹר, *shōr*, תּוֹר, *tōr* [Dnl **4** 25], **ταῦρος**, *taúros* [Mt **22** 4], "ox" or "bull"; **βοῦς**, *boús*, "ox" [Lk **13** 15]; אֶלֶף, *'eleph*, only in pl., אֲלָפִים, *'ălāphīm*, "oxen" [Ps **8** 7]): From the foregoing and by examination of the many references to "cattle," "kine" or "oxen," it is apparent that there are important points of contact in derivation and usage in the Heb, Gr and Eng. terms. It is evident that neat cattle were possessed in abundance by the patriarchs and later Israelites, which is far from being the case in Pal at the present day. The Bedawin usually have no cattle. The *fellāḥīn* in most parts of the country keep them in small numbers, mostly for plowing, and but little for milk or for slaughtering. Travelers in the Holy Land realize that goat's milk is in most places easier to obtain than cow's milk. The commonest cattle of the *fellāḥīn* are a small black breed. In the vicinity of Damascus are many large, fine milch cattle which furnish the delicious milk and cream of the Damascus bazaars. For some reason, probably because they are not confined and highly fed, the bulls of Pal are meek creatures as compared with their European or American fellows.

In EV the word "cattle" is more often used in a wide sense to include sheep and goats than to denote merely neat cattle. In fact, *bāḳār*, which distinctively denotes neat cattle, is often rendered "herds," as *çō'n*, lit. "sheep," is in a large number of instances trd "flocks." A good illustration is found in Gen **32** 7: "Then Jacob . . . . divided the people [*'ām*] that were with him, and the flocks [*çō'n*], and the herds [*bāḳār*], and the camels [*gᵉmallīm*], into two companies [*maḥănōth*]." For the last word AV has "drove" in Gen **33** 8, RV "company."

Cattle.

Next to *çō'n*, the word most commonly rendered "flock" in EV is *'ēdher*, from root "to arrange," "to set in order." *'Ēdher* is rendered "herd" in Prov **27** 23, and in Joel **1** 18 it occurs twice, being rendered "herds of cattle," *'edhrē bāḳār*, and "flocks of sheep," *'edhrē ha-çō'n*. *Miḳneh* is rendered "flock" in Nu **32** 26, "herd" in Gen **47** 18, and "cattle" in a large number of passages. Other words rendered "flock" are: *mar'īth* (r. *rā'āh* [Arab. *ra'a*], "to pasture"), once in Jer **10** 21; *'ashtᵉrōth çō'n*, "flocks of thy sheep," RV "young of thy flock," in Dt **7** 13, etc, *'ashtārōth* being pl. of *'ashtōreth*, or Ashtoreth; *ḥăsīph*, once in 1 K **20** 27: "The children of Israel encamped before them [the Syrians] like two little flocks of kids," *ḥăsīph* signifying "something stripped off or separated," from root *ḥāsaph*, "to strip" or "to peel," like the Arab. *ḳaṭī'*, "flock," from root *ḳaṭa'*, "to cut off"; ποίμνη, *poímnē* (Mt **26** 31): "The sheep of the flock shall be scattered," and (Lk **2** 8): "keeping watch by night over their flock"; ποίμνιον, *poímnion* (Lk **12** 32): "Fear not, little flock," and (1 Pet **5** 2): "Tend the flock of God which is among you."

Figurative: Not only *poimnē* and *poimnion* but also *'ēdher* and *çō'n* are used fig. of God's people; e.g. Isa **40** 11: "He will feed his flock [*'ēdher*] like a shepherd"; Zec **10** 3: "Jeh of hosts hath visited his flock [*'ēdher*], the house of Judah"; Isa **65** 10: "And Sharon shall be a fold of flocks" (*çō'n*); Jer **23** 2: "Ye have scattered my flock" (*çō'n*); Ezk **34** 22: "Therefore will I save my flock" (*çō'n*); Mic **7** 14: "Feed . . . . the flock [*çō'n*] of thy heritage."

The wild ox or wild bull, RV "antelope" (*tᵉ'ō* or *tō'* of Dt **14** 5 and Isa **51** 20), is considered by the writer to be probably the Arabian oryx, and in this he is in agreement with Tristram (*NHB*). Tristram however thinks that the unicorn (*rēm* or *rᵉ'ēm*), RV "wild ox," was the aurochs, while the present writer believes that this also may well have been the oryx, which at the present day has at least three names in Arab., one of which, *baḳar-ul-waḥsh*, means "wild ox." See ANTELOPE.

Our domestic cattle are believed by some of the best authorities to be of the same species as the ancient European wild ox or aurochs, *Bos taurus*, which is by others counted as a distinct species under the title of *Bos primigenius*. The aurochs was widely spread over Europe in Rom times, but is now extinct. Some degenerate wild cattle are preserved in some British parks, but these according to Lydekker in the *Royal Natural History* are probably feral descendants of early domestic breeds. Tristram cites the occurrence in the Dog River bone breccia of teeth which may be those of the aurochs, but this is a deposit accumulated by prehistoric man of an unknown antiquity to be variously estimated according to the predilections of the geologist at a few thousands or a few score of thousands of years, and is far from proving that this animal existed in Pal in Bible times or at any time.

The European bison (*Bos* or *Bison bonassus*) is thought by some to be the wild ox of the Bible. This is a forest-dwelling species and is now confined to the forests of Lithuania and the Caucasus. It was formerly more widely distributed, but there is no certain evidence that it ever lived as far S. as Pal, and there have probably never existed in Pal forests suitable to be the haunts of this animal.

About the Sea of Tiberias and the Jordan valley and in the plain of Coele-Syria there exist today Indian buffaloes (*Bos bubalus*), some feral and some in a state of domestication, which are believed to have been introduced in comparatively recent times. See BEAST; CALF.

ALFRED ELY DAY

CAUDA, kô'da (**Καῦδα**, *Kaúda;* also called **Κλαῦδα**, *Klaúda;* AV **Clauda**; the modern Gr name Gaudho supports the form Cauda): An island 23 miles W. of Cape Matala. It is a small island, and can never have supported a large population, or have been of any importance. Its elevation to the rank of a bishopric in Byzantine times must have been due to its association with the voyage of St. Paul. The ship with Paul on board was driven under the lee of Cauda (Acts **27** 16); in the calm water south of the island the crew succeeded in hauling in the boat, undergirding the ship and slackening sail. W. M. CALDER

CAUL, kôl:

(1) יֹתֶרֶת, *yōthereth* (Ex **29** 13), the large lobe or flap of the liver, which is usually mentioned together with the kidneys and the fat as the special portions set aside for the burnt offering (Lev **3** 4.10.15; **4** 9; **7** 4; **8** 16.25; **9** 10.19).

(2) סְגוֹר, *ṣᵉghōr* (from the root *ṣāghar*, "to inclose," "shut up"), Hos **13** 8, lit. the inclosure or covering of the heart, the caul or pericardium, or perhaps the chest as surrounding the heart. It must not be forgotten, however, that the expression may be taken in the sense of "mailcoat of the heart," i.e. hardened heart, which is shut to the influence of God's grace. So Luther and many modern translators and commentators.

H. L. E. LUERING

CAUSE, kôs: In both AV and RV "for this cause" (AV "*cause*") occurs in Ex **9** 16 as the rendering of בַּעֲבוּר זֹאת, *ba'ăbhūr zō'th*="in order that"; "to the end that"; so also in Dnl **2** 12 for כָּל־קֳבֵל דְּנָה, *kol-ḳ^{e}bhēl d^{e}nāh,* and in 2 Ch **32** 20 AV for עַל־זֹאת, *'al-zō'th,* where RVS read "because of." In the NT the word is used adverbially in the tr of several Gr phrases: ἕνεκα τούτου, *héneka toútou* (Mt **19** 5; Mk **10** 7); διὰ τοῦτο, *diá toúto,* Jn **12** 27; Rom **1** 26; **13** 6; **15** 9 (RV "therefore"); 1 Cor **11** 30; 1 Thess **2** 13; 2 Thess **2** 11; 1 Tim **1** 16; He **9** 15; εἰς τοῦτο, *eis toúto,* Jn **18** 37 (where AV varying the phraseology reads "to this end," "for this cause"); 1 Pet **4** 6 AV; τούτου χάριν, *toútou chárin,* Eph **3** 14. Unusual renderings occur, as "for his cause" (="because of"), 2 Cor **7** 12; as ="affair," "thing," obs. in AV 1 K **12** 15; 2 Ch **10** 15, where the word occurs as a paraphrase of נְסִבָּה, *n^{e}ṣibbāh* (="turn of affairs"). In 1 S **25** 31 (AV, RV) "causeless" (=without cause ARV) occurs arbitrarily in adv. sense.

W. N. Stearns

CAUSEWAY, kôz'wā (more correctly **CAUSEY,** kô'zi): This word occurs in 1 Ch **26** 16.18 for the Heb מְסִלָּה, *m^{e}ṣillāh;* LXX παστοφόριον τῆς ἀναβάσεως, *pastophorion tēs anabáseōs.* In 2 Ch **9** 11 the word is tr^d "terraces" (LXX ἀναβάσεις, *anabáseis*). Cf *BDB,* s.v., where מְסִלּוֹת, *m^{e}ṣillōth,* is an error for מִסְעָדוֹת, *miṣ'ādhōth* (1 K **10** 12). In all the above passages reference is made to a series or flight of steps leading up into the temple. The word also signifies a prepared, traveled road, as in Nu **20** 19; Jgs **20** 31 f.45; 1 S **6** 12; 2 S **20** 12 f; 2 K **18** 17 (Isa **36** 2); Isa **7** 3; **11** 16; **19** 23; **33** 8; **40** 3; **49** 11; Jer **31** 21.

Figurative: In Isa **59** 7 the word (*m^{e}ṣillāh*) occurs in a fig. sense, so also in Jgs **5** 20; Prov **16** 17.

W. N. Stearns

CAVE, kāv (מְעָרָה, *m^e'ārāh* [cf Arab. *maghārah*], חוֹר, *ḥōr* [Job **30** 6 AV], מְחִלּוֹת, *m^{e}ḥillōth* [Isa **2** 19]; ὀπή, *opē* [He **11** 38], σπήλαιον, *spēlaion* [Jn **11** 38]; *ḥōr,* more often rendered "hole," is akin to Arab. *khaur,* "gulf" or "inlet," but is also related to *m^e'ārāh* [cf also Arab. *ghaur* "low-land," esp. of the Jordan valley and Dead Sea]. *M^{e}ḥillōth* [r. *ḥālal,* "to pierce" (cf Arab. *khall,* "to pierce")]

Cave in Lebanon Converted into a Shrine.

occurs only in Isa **2** 19, where AV has "caves" and translates *m^e'ārōth* in the same ver by "holes." In RV these words are very properly changed about. *Spēlaion* is a common Gr word for "cave"; *opē* means rather "hole"): In Pal as in other limestone countries, caves are of frequent occurrence,

Natural Bridge at Lebanon.

and not a few of large size are known. Water from the rain and snow, seeping down through cracks, enlarges the passages through which it goes by dissolving away the substance of the rock. Just as upon the surface of the land the trickling streams unite to form brooks and rivers, so many subterranean streams may come together in a spacious channel, and may issue upon the surface as a bold

Stream Issuing from Cave at 'Afka, Lebanon.

spring. The cave of the Dog River near *Beirût* and that of *'Afḳa* (perhaps Aphek [Josh **13** 4]) in Lebanon are excellent examples of this. Not infrequently after forming a cave the stream of water may find some lower outlet by a different route, leaving its former course dry. In some cases the hinder part of the roof of the cave may fall in, leaving the front part standing as a natural bridge. Numerous shallow caves, esp. in the faces of cliffs, are formed not by seeping water, but by atmospheric erosion, a portion of a relatively soft stratum of rock being hollowed out, while harder strata above and below it are but little worn away. Many of the hermits' caves originated in this way and were artificially enlarged and walled up at the mouth. The principal caves mentioned in the Bible are those of Machpelah, Makkedah and Adullam (q.v.). See Den.

Alfred Ely Day

CEASE, sēs: A remarkable array of 20 Heb and 6 Gr words is so tr^d. In the AV 15 of the former and 3 of the latter are used only once with this rendering. The originals most frequently in use are חָדַל, *ḥādhal*, "to leave off"; שָׁבַת, *shābhath*, "to rest from" (labor); παύομαι, *paúomai*, "to make to cease." Few words illustrate better the fertility of the Heb in expressing limitless shades of meaning, impoverished by the use of one Eng. word. This extensive variety is, however, well expressed by "cease": i.e. *stop, come to an end*, e.g. ceasing of *tears* (Jer **14** 17); *work* (Ezr **4** 24); *grinders* (Eccl **12** 3); *thunder* (Ex **9** 29); *the wicked* (Job **3** 17); *anger* (Ps **37** 8). The significance of *shābhath* lies in its being the Heb for Sabbath, implying complete cessation: as of *manna* (Josh **5** 12); *strife and ignominy* (Prov **22** 10); occurs with negative to show the *ceaseless* Providence of God in Nature: "summer and winter . . . . shall not c." (Gen **8** 22). In the NT it illustrates Christ's power over *Nature;* wind and raging sea ceased (Lk **8** 24); over a sinner's *heart:* "not ceased to kiss my feet" (διαλείπω, *dialeípō*) (Lk **7** 45); *devotion* of the early disciples, "ceased not to teach and to preach Jesus as the Christ" (Acts **5** 42); the eternity and blessedness of the believer's sabbatic rest (ἀπολείπω, *apoleípō*) (He **4** 10 AV). DWIGHT M. PRATT

CEDAR, sē′dar, sē′dẽr (אֶרֶז, *'erez*, from Heb root meaning "to be firm"; **κέδρος**, *kédros*): The *'erez* was in almost all the OT references the true cedar, *Cedrus libani*, but the name may have been applied in a loose way to allied trees, such as junipers and pines. In Nu **24** 6—"as cedar-trees beside the waters"—the reference must, as is most probable, be purely poetical (see ALOES) or the *'ărāzīm* must signify some other kind of tree which flourishes beside water.

Cedar is twice mentioned as a substance for ritual cleansing. In Lev **14** 4 the cleansed leper was sprinkled with the blood of a "clean bird" into which had been put "cedar-wood, and scarlet, and hyssop." In Nu **19** 6 "cedar-wood, and hyssop, and scarlet" were to be cast into the holocaust of the red heifer. (For the symbolical meaning see CLEAN.) Here it is very generally considered that the cedar could not have been the wood of *Cedrus libani*, which so far as we know never grew in the wilderness, but that of some species of juniper—according to Post, *Juniperis phoenicea*, which may still be found in the wilderness of Edom.

1. Cedar for Ritual Cleansing

Cedar trees are everywhere mentioned with admiration in the OT. Solomon made the cedar the first of trees (1 K **4** 33). They are the "glory of Lebanon" (Isa **35** 2; **60** 13). The most boastful threat of Sennacherib was that he would cut down the tall cedars of Lebanon (Isa **37** 24). They were strong, as is implied in—

2. Cedar Trees in the OT

> "The voice of Jeh is powerful; . . . .
> The voice of Jeh breaketh the cedars;
> Yea, Jeh breaketh in pieces the cedars of Lebanon"
> (Ps **29** 4.5).

The cedars are tall—"whose height was like the height of the cedars"—(Am **2** 9; 2 K **19** 23); majestic (2 K **14** 9), and excellent (Cant **5** 15). The Assyr power is compared to—"a cedar in Lebanon with fair branches, and with a forest-like shade, and of high stature; and its top was among the thick boughs . . . . its stature was exalted above all the trees of the field; and its boughs were multiplied, and its branches became long" (Ezk **31** 3–5). They are in particular God's trees—

> "The trees of Jeh are filled with moisture,
> The cedars of Lebanon, which he hath planted" (Ps **104** 16).

Doubtless as a reminiscence of this the Syrians today call the cedar *'ars er rubb*, "the cedar of the Lord." The growth of the cedar is typical of that of the righteous man (Ps **92** 12).

That cedars were once very abundant in the Lebanon is evident (1 K **6** 9–18; **10** 27). What they contributed to the glory and beauty of that district may be seen in Zec **11** 1–2:

> "Open thy doors, O Lebanon, that the fire may devour thy cedars.
> Wail, O fir-tree, for the cedar is fallen, because the glorious [RVm] ones are destroyed:
> Wail, O ye oaks of Bashan, for the strong forest is come down."

Cedars of Lebanon at the Besherri Grove.

The wood of the cedar has always been highly prized—much more so than the sycamore (1 K **10** 27; Isa **9** 10). David had a house of cedar built for him by Hiram, king of Tyre (2 S **5** 11), and he prepared "cedar-trees without number" for the temple which his son was to build (1 Ch **22** 4). Cedar timber was very much used in the construction of Solomon's temple and palace, the trees being cut in the Lebanon by Sidonians by orders of the king of Tyre—"Hiram gave Solomon timber of cedar and timber of fir according to all his desire" (1 K **5** 6–10). One of Solomon's most important buildings was known as "the house of the forest of Lebanon" (1 K **7** 2; **10** 17; 2 Ch **9** 16), on account of the source of its materials. While cedar was well adapted for beams (1 K **6** 9; Cant **1** 17), boards (Cant **8** 9), pillars (1 K **7** 2) and ceilings (Jer **22** 14), it was suited as well for carved work, such as idols (Isa **44** 14.15). It was also used for ships' masts (Ezk **27** 5).

3. Cedar Timber

The *Cedrus libani* still survives in the mountains of Syria and flourishes in much greater numbers in the Taurus mountains. "There are groves of cedars above *el-Ma'āṣir, Barûk, 'Ain Zehaltah, Hadith, Besherri,* and *Sîr*" (Post, *Flora*, 751). Of these the grove at Besherri is of world-wide renown. It consists of a group of about 400 trees, among them some magnificent old patriarchs, which lies on the bare slopes of the Lebanon

4. Cedars in Modern Syria

some 6,000 ft. above the sea. Doubtless they are survivors of a forest which here once covered the mountain slopes for miles. The half a dozen highest specimens reach a height of between 70 and 80 ft., and have trunks of a circumference of 40 ft. or more. It is impossible to estimate with any certainty their age, but they may be as much as 800, or even 1,000, years old. Though magnificent, these are by no means the largest of their kind. Some of the cedars of Amanus are quite 100 ft. high and the Himalayan cedar, *Cedrus deodara*, a variety of *Cedrus libani*, reaches a height of 150 ft. The impressiveness of the cedar lies, however, not so much in its height and massive trunk, as in the wonderful lateral spread of its branches, which often exceeds its height. The branches grow out horizontally in successive tiers, each horizontal plane presenting, when looked at from above, the appearance of a green sward. The leaves are about an inch long, arranged in clusters; at first they are bright green, but they change with age to a deeper tint with a glaucous hue; the foliage is evergreen, the successive annual growths of leaves each lasting two years. The cones, 4 to 6 in. long, are oval or oblong-ovate, with a depression at times at the apex; they require two years to reach maturity and then, unlike other conifers, they remain attached to the tree, dropping out their scales bearing the seeds.

The wood of the cedar, specially grown under the conditions of its natural habitat, is hard, close grained, and takes a high polish. It is full of resin (Ps **92** 14) which preserves it from rot and from worms. Cedar oil, a kind of turpentine extracted from the wood, was used in ancient times as a preservative for parchments and garments.

E. W. G. Masterman

CEDRON, sē′dron. See Kidron.

CEILAN, sē′lan. See Kilan.

CEILED, sēld, **CEILING,** sēl′ing (AV and ERV **Cieled, Cieling;** the Heb words for "ceiled" are חָפָה, *ḥippāh*, סָפַן, *ṣāphan*, שְׂחִיף, *sāḥīph;* for "ceiling," סִפֻּן, *ṣippun*): Ceiling occurs only in 1 K **6** 15. It comes from the root *ṣāphan*, meaning "to cover." It has its common meaning of the upper surface of a room; there is, however, some doubt of the text. Ceiled is found in 2 Ch **3** 5 ([*ḥippāh*]; Jer **22** 14; Hag **1** 4 [*ṣāphan* in both]; Ezk **41** 16 [*sāḥīph*]), the text of the last passage being doubtful. In none of these cases does "ceiled" refer to the upper surface of a room, but to the covering or paneling of the inner walls of a house with cedar or other costly wood. This is in accordance with a common early use of the Eng. word, no longer frequent. George Ricker Berry

CELEBRATE, sel′ĕ-brāt: Of the three Heb words so rendered הָלַל, *hālal*, "to praise," is preeminently significant. It is an onomatopoetic word meaning "to give a clear, sharp sound," as in vocal rejoicing, celebration. Its equivalent in Ethiopic is *ellell*, Ger. *hallen*, Eng. *halloo*, and appears in the great choral word *Hallelujah* of the Heb religion. Passing into Christian use it has become the term most expressive of majestic praise. Pss **113–118** and **136** are called *Hallel psalms*. Found in Hezekiah's psalm of praise for his miraculous recovery: "Death cannot *celebrate* thee" (Isa **38** 18). חָגַג, *ḥāghagh*, root meaning "to move in a circle," hence "to keep a festival" by sacred leaping and dancing; "celebrate [RV "keep"] a feast" (Lev **23** 41); שָׁבַת, *shābhath*, "to rest," i.e. keep or observe a holy day; "celebrate [RV "keep"] your sabbath" (Lev **23** 32).

Dwight M. Pratt

CELESTIAL, sē-les′chal (ἐπουράνιος, *epouránios*, "above the sky," "heavenly"): Peculiar to Paul's majestic argument on the resurrection: celestial vs terrestrial bodies (1 Cor **15** 40) with reference possibly to sun and moon, etc, but more probably to the bodies of angels in distinction from those of beasts and mortal men (cf Christ's words, Mt **22** 30; Lk **20** 36); including also doubtless in the apostle's thought the resurrection-body of Jesus and of the saints already taken into glory. Light is thrown on its meaning by the rendering of the same Gr original as "heavenly places" (Eph **1** 3.20; **2** 6; **3** 10); "heavenly" (1 Cor **15** 48). Hence "celestial" as used by Paul indicates the soul's continued life beyond the grave, the spiritual body of the redeemed in heaven, who, in Christ, have put on immortality. Dwight M. Pratt

CELLAR, sel′ẽr, sel′ar (κρύπτη, *krúptē;* אוֹצָר, *'ōçār*): *Kruptē* is found only in Lk **11** 33, and is rendered "cellar" in RV; AV has "secret place." In this passage it doubtless means a cellar beneath a house. Etymologically the Gr word means "a covered place," and in classical Gr its usage includes vaults and crypts as well as cellars. It seems evident that it was only the larger houses in Pal in which cellars were used with any frequency. It is shown by the excavations that in rebuilding a town which was in ruins the old houses were sometimes utilized as cellars for the new. *'ōçār*, is rendered cellar only in 1 Ch **27** 27 f. It is an erroneous rendering, the correct meaning being stores, or supplies, of wine and oil. George Ricker Berry

CELOSYRIA, sē-lo-sir′i-a. See Coele-syria.

CENCHREAE, sen′krĕ-ē (Κεγχρεαί, *Kegchreaí*, WH *Kenchreaí;* AV incorrectly **Cenchrea**): A seaport of Corinth on the eastern side of the isthmus (see Corinth). Here according to Acts **18** 18, St. Paul had his hair shorn before sailing for Syria, since he had a vow. A local church must have been established there by St. Paul, since Phoebe, the deaconess of Cenchreae, was intrusted with the Epistle to the Romans, and was commended to them in the highest terms by the apostle, who charged them to "assist her in whatsoever matter she may have need" (Rom **16** 1.2).

CENDEBAEUS, sen-de-bē′us (Κενδεβαῖος, *Kendebaíos;* AV **Cendebeus**): A general of Antiochus VII who was appointed "captain of the seacoast" of Pal (1 Macc **15** 38 ff) after the defeat of Tryphon by Antiochus 138 BC. He fortified Kedron and harassed the Jews in various ways. As Simon Maccabaeus was too old to attack C. in person he sent his two eldest sons, Judas and John, who defeated him with great loss at Modin (1 Macc **16** 1–10).

CENSER, sen′sẽr: In AV censer is used as a tr of two Heb words, viz. מַחְתָּה, *maḥtāh*, and מִקְטֶרֶת, *miḳtereth*. The former word is generally rendered "censer," sometimes "firepan," and in three cases (Ex **25** 38; **37** 23; Nu **4** 9) "snuffdish" It denoted a bowl-shaped vessel used for different purposes, viz. (1) a censer, in which incense was burnt (Lev **10** 1); (2) a firepan, made of bronze, used in connection with the altar of burnt offering (Ex **27** 3); (3) a snuffdish, i.e. a receptacle to hold pieces of burnt lamp-wick removed by the tongs or snuffers (Ex **25** 38). Probably in all these cases the same kind of vessel was meant, viz. a bowl-shaped utensil with a handle, not unlike a saucepan. The other Heb word (derived from the same root as the word for "incense") denoted a vessel for conveying incense (Ezk **8** 11; 2 Ch **26**

19). The Gr word θυμιατήριον, *thumiatērion*, by which the LXX rendered *miḳtereth*, is used also in He **9** 4, where AV gives "censer," but ARV is

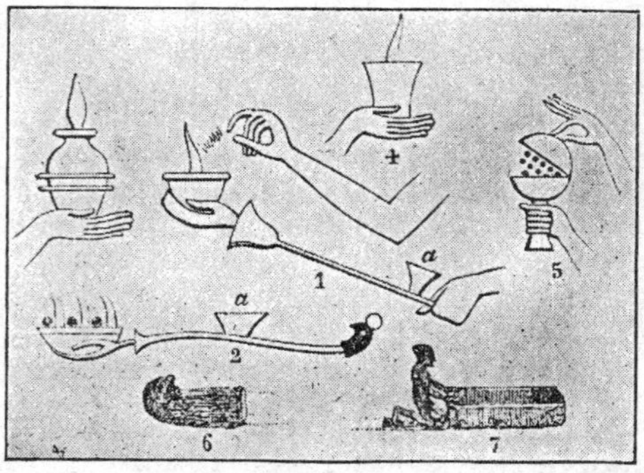

Censers.

1. Throwing incense on flame. 2. Balls of incense burning. *aa.* Boxes for holding incense.—*Rosellini.* 3, 4. Censers of different forms.—*Wilkinson.* 5. Box or cup for incense.—*Wilkinson.* 6, 7. Head of handle and pan of censers in bronze.—*Brit.Mus.*

probably more correct, viz. "altar of incense" (see Commentaries s.v.). Cf also Rev **8** 3.5, where λιβανωτός, *libanōtós*, properly the adj. of "frankincense," is tr^d "censer." T. LEWIS

CENSUS, sen'sus. See DAVID; QUIRINIUS.

CENTURION, sen-tū'ri-un: As the name implies, **ἑκατοντάρχης** or **-ος,** *hekatontárchēs* or *-os;* **κεντυρίων,** *kenturíōn,* Lat *centurio,* was the commander of a hundred men, more or less, in a Rom legion. St. Matthew and St. Luke use the Gr word while St. Mark prefers the Lat form, as he does in the case of other words, seeing that he wrote primarily for Rom readers. The number of centurions in a legion was 60, that being at all epochs the number of centuries, although the number varied in the cohort or *speira.* The ordinary duties of the centurion were to drill his men, inspect their arms, food and clothing, and to command them in the camp and in the field. Centurions were sometimes employed on detached service the conditions of which in the provinces are somewhat obscure. Men like Cornelius and Julius (Acts **10** 1; **27** 1) may have been separated from the legion to which they properly belonged for the discharge of special duties. They and other centurions mentioned in the Gospels and the Acts (Mt **8** 5; Mk **15** 39.44.45; Lk **23** 47) are represented by the sacred writers in a favorable light. See AUGUSTAN BAND. T. NICOL

CEPHAS, sē'fas. See PETER (SIMON).

CERAS, sē'ras (**Κηράς,** *Kērás;* RV KERAS [q.v.]).

CERTAIN, sẽr'tin, **CERTAINLY,** sẽr'tin-li, **CERTAINTY,** sẽr'tin-ti: The rendering of some Heb words and forms expressive of what is definitely settled or determined.

(1) Tr of the Heb נָכוֹן, *nākhōn,* "to be established" or "fixed," as in Dt **13** 14 (Heb 15); **17** 4; 1 S **23** 23 (cf Ex **16** 4, "a certain rate every day" AV). In the NT it is the rendering of ἀσφαλής, *asphalēs,* ἀσφάλεια, *aspháleia,* from "a" privative and *sphallein,* "to shake" or "move"; as in Lk **1** 4, "the certainty of those things" = actual circumstances; Acts **21** 34; **22** 30; **25** 26.

(2) The word "c." is also employed in the OT to bring out the force of the absolute infinitive form used with the finite vb. to express emphasis or to strengthen the idea of the main vb. (Kautzsch-Gesenius, *Heb Grammar,* tr Collins-Cowley, 357, 3). Such usage occurs in Gen **18** 10; Josh **9** 24; Lev **5** 19; **24** 16; 1 S **20** 3 AV; 1 K **2** 37; Jer **26** 15; **36** 29; **42** 19.22; **44** 17.

(3) The word "c." is also made auxiliary to bring out the force of such expressions as the Heb יְצַב, *yāçabh,* "to be firm," as in Dan **2** 8; also in the NT, of the vb. ἀστατεῖν, *astatein,* as in 1 Cor **4** 11, "have no certain dwelling-place."

(4) Mention might be made also of "c." as the rendering of sundry words, as אַךְ, *'akh,* in Lam **2** 16; כִּי, *kī,* in Ex **3** 12; and ὄντως, *óntōs,* in Lk **23** 47, all being expressions for what is sure, beyond doubt. W. N. STEARNS

CERTIFY, sẽr'ti-fī: Occurs in (1) 2 S **15** 28 (הַגִּיד, *haggīdh,* "to show," "announce," from נָגַד, *nāghadh*); (2) Ezr **4** 14.16; **5** 10; **7** 24 (הוֹדַע, *hō-dha',* "to make known," from יְדַע, *y^edha';* Aram. for יָדַע, *yādha'*); (3) Est **2** 22 AV (אָמַר, *'āmar,* "to say," "tell," so RV); and (4) Gal **1** 11 AV (γνωρίζω, *gnōrízō,* "to make to know," so RV). In the EV, accordingly, the word has not the strong, specific sense of "to make certain," but only the broader sense of "to make to know." Cf Ps **39** 5 (Prayer Book version), "that I may be certified how long I have to live."

CETAB, sē'tab. See KETAB.

CHABRIS, kā'bris (**'Αβρίς,** *Abrís,* **Χαβρείς,** *Chabreís*): Son of Gothoniel, one of the three rulers of Bethulia in the time of Judith (Jth **6** 15; **8** 10; **10** 6).

CHADIAS, kā'di-as, **THEY OF** (RV CHADIASAI, kā'di-a-sī; A, **Χαδάσαι,** *Chadásai;* B, **οἱ Χαδιάσαι,** *hoi Chadiásai*): The inhabitants of the city here referred to returned with Zerubbabel, along with the Ammidioi (1 Est **5** 20). The name is not found in Ezr and Neh. The Chadiasai have been taken for the people of Kadesh and the Ammidioi for the people of Humtah (Josh **15** 54). Possibly the place is identical with Kedesh of Josh **15** 23.

CHAEREAS, kē'rē-as (**Χαιρέας,** *Chairéas;* AV **Chereas**): Brother of Timotheus, the Ammonite leader against Judas Maccabaeus (1 Macc **5** 6). He held the fortress of Gazara (the "Jazer" of 1 Macc **5** 8) to which Timotheus fled from Judas. The latter pursued him and captured the fortress after a vigorous siege. In the slaughter which followed the two brothers, Ch. and Tim., were killed (2 Macc **10** 32.37).

CHAFE, chāf (מַר, *mar,* "bitter"; hence bitter of soul, deadly, destructive, ferocious, "as a bear robbed of her whelps"): Occurs only in 2 S **17** 8; used by Hushai to characterize David's supposedly fierce mood at the time of Absalom's armed rebellion.

CHAFF, chaf: Four different words have been tr^d "chaff" in the OT:

(1) מוֹץ, *mōç,* is found in Job **21** 18; Ps **1** 4; **35** 5; Isa **17** 13; **29** 5; **41** 15; Hos **13** 3; Zeph **2** 2.

(2) חֲשַׁשׁ, *ḥăshash,* occurs in two vs (Isa **5** 24 and **33** 11). Cf "*ḥashīsh,*" an Arab. word which, as commonly used, denotes grass either standing or cut, green or dry, although, strictly speaking, dry or cut grass alone. In RV Isa **5** 24 the tr is "dry grass."

(3) תֶּבֶן, *tebhen,* is tr^d "chaff" in AV (Jer **23** 28). The same word is rendered "straw" in RV (cf Arab. *tibn*).

(4) אוּר, *'ūr*, a Chald word, occurs in Dnl **2** 35. In the NT ἄχυρον, *áchuron*, is found in Mt **3** 12 and Lk **3** 17.

In the process of winnowing, as it has been carried on in the East for thousands of years, the grain is tossed into the air so that the wind may cause a separation of chaff and straw. The light husks from the wheat and fine particles of straw are dispersed by the wind in the form of a fine dust; the heavier straw which has been broken into short pieces by the threshing process falls near at hand on the edge of the threshing-floor, while the grain falls back upon the pile. In Syria and Pal, that which falls near at hand as cut straw is called *tibn*. This word occurs in the Arab. tr of Mt **3** 12 and Lk **3** 17. This straw is ordinarily saved and fed as "roughage" to the animals. It could easily be gathered and burned, as indicated in the above-mentioned vs, while the chaff is blown away beyond recovery, a strong figure to depict complete annihilation (Job **21** 18; Isa **29** 5; **41** 16; Hos **13** 3, Dnl **2** 35). See AGRICULTURE; STRAW; WINNOWING.

JAMES A. PATCH

CHAIN, chān, **CHAINS,** chānz: Chains were used by the Hebrews:

(1) As ornaments: אֶצְעָדָה, *'eç'ādhāh*, נְטִיפָה, *n^eṭīphāh*, עֲנָק, *'ānāḳ*, רָבִיד, *rābhīdh*, שַׁרְשְׁרָה, *sharsh^erāh*, רַתּוֹק, *rattōḳ*. As ornaments for the person they were worn about the ankles (Nu **31** 50; Isa **3** 20) and about the neck (Cant **4** 9; Ezk **16** 11). They were used as ornaments for the ephod and breastplate of the high priest (Ex **28** 14; **39** 15). These chains were of pure gold. Solomon placed chains before the oracle in the temple (1 K **6** 21), and these were also of pure gold. They were used as ornaments for graven images (Isa **40** 19) and around the necks of prized animals. This was true of the camels taken from the Midianites by Gideon (Jgs **8** 21.26).

(2) As marks of distinction: רָבִיד, *rābhīdh*, הָמוּנֵךְ (הַמְנִיךְ) *hămūnēkh* (*hamnīkh*): That seems to be true of the chain which Pharaoh placed about the neck of Joseph (Gen **41** 42), and of the one which the king of Babylon promised to the wise men (Dnl **5** 7).

(3) As means of confining prisoners: נְחֹשֶׁת, *n^ehōsheth*; ἅλυσις, *hálusis*: A number of passages that were tr[d] "chains" in the AV are tr[d] "fetters" in the RV (see Jgs **16** 21; 2 S **3** 34). Among the Romans the prisoner was chained to one or two guards (Acts **12** 6.7; **21** 33; Eph **6** 20; 2 Tim **1** 16). These chains were perhaps made of copper or an alloy of copper and tin.

(4) As a **figurative** expression: עֲנָק, *'ānāḳ*. The Psalmist likens pride to a chain about the neck (**73** 6), and in Prov it is stated that the young man who hears the instruction of his father and forsakes not the law of his mother shall find that they are chains about his neck (**1** 9). In Rev **20** 1 the angel is described as descending with a great chain in his hand. According to the AV Peter speaks of the fallen angels as having been delivered into "chains of darkness" (2 Pet **2** 4), σειρά, *seirá*, and Jude speaks of them as being reserved in "everlasting chains" (Jude ver 6, RV "bonds"), δεσμός, *desmós*. See also PUNISHMENTS.

A. W. FORTUNE

CHAIR, châr. See SEAT; SEATS, CHIEF.

CHALCEDONY, kal-sed'ō-ni, kal'sē-dō-ni. See STONES, PRECIOUS.

CHALCOL, kal'kol. See CALCOL.

CHALDEA, kal-dē'a, **CHALDEANS,** kal-dē'anz (כַּשְׂדִּים, *kasdīm*, אֶרֶץ כַּשְׂדִּים, *'ereç kasdīm*; **Χαλδαία,** *Chaldaía*, **Χαλδαῖοι,** *Chaldaíoi*):

1. Geographical Position
   Seats of the Chaldeans
2. Originally Sumero-Akkadian
3. History of the Chaldean Tribes
4. Merodach-baladan and Sargon of Assyria
5. Šûzubu
6. Mušêzib-Marduk
7. Merodach-baladan's Son
8. Na'id-Marduk
9. Palîa
10. Nabû-bêl-šumâti and Others
    His Tragic End
11. The Chaldeans Forge Ahead
12. Nabopolassar's Revolt against Assyria
13. The Chaldeans as Learned Men

"*Kasdīm*," "land of *Kasdīm*" or "the Chaldeans," is the usual designation, in the OT, for the land and the people (Jer **50** 10; **51** 24; **24** 5; **25** 12). The corresponding Gr form with *l* for *s* follows the Assyr-Bab *Kaldu*, *mât Kaldi*, "Chaldean, land of the Chaldeans." *Kasdim* is possibly connected with the name of Kesed (*Kesedh*), nephew of Abraham (Gen **22** 22), and may be derived from the Assyr-Bab root *kašādu*, "to capture," suggesting that the Chaldeans were originally tribes of nomadic plunderers (cf Job **1** 17).

1. Geographical Position

In its widest acceptation, Chaldea is the name of the whole of Babylonia, owing to the fact that the Chaldeans had given more than one king to the country. In the strict sense, however, their domain was the tract at the N.W. end of the Pers Gulf, which was often called by the Assyro-Babylonians *mât Tâmtim*, "the Land of the Sea," a province of unknown extent. When these tribes migrated into Babylonia is uncertain, as is also their original home; but as they are closely related to the Aramaeans, it is possible that their first settlements lay in the neighborhood of the Aramaean states bordering on the Holy Land. Tiglath-pileser IV (742 BC) speaks of the *ra'asāni* or chiefs of the *Kaldu*, and the mention of numerous Aramaean tribes in Babylonia itself shows that their example of settling there soon found imitators, as did the Anglo-Saxons when they invaded Britain. Among the Chaldean tribes in Babylonia may be mentioned Bît Amukkâni, whose capital was Sapia; Bît Yakîn, which furnished the dynasty to which Merodach-baladan II belonged; and probably also Bît Dakkuri, as all three lay near the Pers Gulf. Sargon of Assyria excludes Bît-Amukkâni and Bît-Dakkuri, and speaks of "the whole of the land of Chaldea, as much as there is; the land of Bît-Yâkîni, on the shore of the Salt River [the Pers Gulf], to the border of Tilmun" (the island of Bahrein and the adjacent mainland) (*Pavement Inscr.*, IV, ll. 82, 83, 85, 86). It was probably the influence of the Babylonians among whom they settled which changed these nomads into city-dwellers. Sennacherib refers to 75 (var. 89) strong cities and fortresses of Chaldea, and 420 (var. 800) smaller towns which were around them; and there were also Chaldeans (and Aramaeans) in Erech, Nippur (Calneh), Kis, Ḫursag-kalama, Cuthah, and probably Babylon.

2. Originally Sumero-Akkadian

The "land of the sea" (*mât Tâmtim*) is mentioned in the chronicle of the early Bab kings (rev. 14) as being governed by Êa-gamil, contemporary of Samsu-ṭitana (cir 1900 BC), but at that period it was apparently one of the original Sumero-Akkadian states of Babylonia. It is doubtful whether, at that early date, the Chaldeans had entered Babylonia and founded settlements there, though the record mentions Aramaeans somewhat later on.

One of the earliest references to the Chaldeans is that of Shalmaneser II of Assyria, who, on invading Babylonia in the eponymy of Bêl-

3. History of the Chaldean Tribes bunaya (851 BC), captured the city Baqâni, which belonged to Adini of the Chaldean tribe of Dakuri. After plundering and destroying the place, Shalmaneser attacked Enzudi, the capital, whereupon Adini submitted and paid tribute. On this occasion Yâkîni, of "the Land of the Sea," also paid tribute, as did Mušallim-Marduk, son of Amukkāni (the *Bît-Amukkāni* mentioned above). The next Assyr ruler to mention the country is Adadnirari III (810 BC), who speaks of all the kings of the Chaldeans, which evidently refers to the various states into which the Chaldean tribes were divided. Later on, Sargon of Assyria, in his 12th year, decided to break the power of Merodach-baladan, who had made himself master of Babylon. To effect this, he first defeated the Gambulians, who were the Chaldean king's supporters, and the Elamites, his allies over the border. The Chaldean, however, did not await the Assyr king's attack, but escaped to Yatburu in Elam, leaving considerable spoil behind him. Though extensive operations

4. Merodach-baladan and Sargon of Assyria were carried out, and much booty taken, the end of the campaign seems only to have come two years later, when Dûr-Yâkîn was destroyed by fire and reduced to ruins. In the "Annals of Hall XIV" Sargon claims to have taken Merodach-baladan prisoner, but this seems doubtful. Merodach-baladan fled, but returned and mounted the throne again on Sargon's death in 705 BC. Six months later Sennacherib, in his turn, attacked him, and he again sought safety in flight. A Chaldean chief named Šûzubu, however, now came forward, and

5. Šûzubu proclaimed himself king of Babylon, but being defeated, he likewise fled. Later on, Sennacherib attacked the Chaldeans at Nagîtu and other settlements in Elamite-territory which Merodach-baladan and his followers had founded. After the death of Merodach-baladan, yet another Chaldean, whom Sennacherib calls likewise Šûzubu, but whose full name was Mušêzib-Marduk, mounted the

6. Mušêzib-Marduk Babylonian throne. This ruler applied for help against Sennacherib of Assyria to Umman-menanu, the king of Elam, who, taking the bribe which was offered, supported him with an armed force, and a battle was fought at Ḥalulê on the Tigris, in which Sennacherib claims the victory—probably rightly. Mušêzib-Marduk reigned 4 years, and was taken prisoner by his whilom ally, Umman-menanu, who sent him to Assyria.

In the reign of Esarhaddon, Nabû-zêr-napišti-lîšir, one of the sons of Merodach-baladan, gathered

7. Merodach-baladan's Son an army at Larsa, but was defeated by the Assyrians, and fled to Elam. The king of that country, however, wishing to be on friendly terms with Esarhaddon, captured him and put him to death. This prince had a brother named Na'id-Marduk, who, not feeling himself safe in the country which had acted treacherously toward his house, fled, and made submission to Esarhaddon, who received him

8. Na'id-Marduk favorably, and restored to him the dominion of the "Land of the Sea." This moderation secured the fidelity of the Chaldeans, and when the Elamite Urtaku sent inviting them to revolt against their suzerain, they answered to the effect that Na'id-Marduk was their lord, and they were the servants of the king

of Assyria. This took place probably about 650 BC, in the reign of Esarhaddon's son Aššur-banî-âpli (see Osnappar).

Hostility to Assyria, however, continued to exist in the tribe, Palîa, grandson of Merodach-baladan, being one of the prisoners taken by

9. Palîa Aššur-banî-âpli's troops in their operations against the Gambulians (a Babylonian, and perhaps a Chaldean tribe) later on. It was only during the struggle of Šamaš-šum-ukîn (Saosduchimos), king of Babylon, Aššur-banî-âpli's brother, however, that they took sides against Assyria as a nationality. This change was due to the invitation of the Bab king—who may have been regarded, rather than Aššur-banî-âpli, as their overlord. The chief of the Chaldeans was at that time another grandson of Merodach-baladan, Nabû-bêl-šumāti, who seized the As-

10. Nabû-bêl-šumāti syrians in his domain, and placed them in bonds. The Chaldeans suffered, with the rest, in the great defeat of the Bab and allied forces, when Babylon and the chief cities of the land fell. Mannu-kî-Babîli of the Dakkurians, Êa-šum-ikîša of Bît-Amukkāni, with other Chaldean states, were punished for their complicity in Šamaš-šum-ukîn's revolt, while Nabû-bêl-šumāti fled and found refuge at the court of Indabigaš, king of Elam. Aššur-banî-âpli at once demanded his surrender, but civil war in Elam broke out, in which Indabigaš was slain, and Umman-aldāš mounted the throne. This demand was now renewed, and Nabû-bêl-šumāti, fearing that he would be surrendered, decided to end his life. He therefore directed his armor-bearer to dispatch him, and each ran the other through with his sword. The prince's corpse, with the head of his armor-bearer, were then sent, with some of the Chaldean fugitives, to Assyria, and presented to the king. Thus ended, for a time, Chaldean ambition in Babylonia and in the domain of eastern politics.

With the death of Aššur-banî-âpli, which took place about 626 BC, the power of Assyria fell, his

11. The Chaldeans Forge Ahead successors being probably far less capable men than he. This gave occasion for many plots against the Assyr empire, and the Chaldeans probably took part in the general movement. In the time of Saracus (Sin-šarra-iškun of Assyria, cir 620 BC) Busalossor would seem to have been appointed general of the forces in Babylonia in consequence of an apprehended invasion of barbarians from the sea (the Pers Gulf) (Eusebius, *Chronicon*, book i). The new general, however, revolted against the Assyrians, and made himself master of Babylonia. As, in other cases, the Assyrians seem to have been exceedingly faithful to their king, it has been thought possible that

12. Nabopolassar's Revolt against Assyria this general, who was none other than Nabopolassar, the father of Nebuchadrezzar, was not really an Assyrian, but a Babylonian, and probably a Chaldean. This theory, if correct, would explain how Babylonia, in its fullest sense, obtained the name of Chaldea, and was no longer known as the land of Shinar (Gen 10 10). The reputation of Merodach-baladan, the contemporary of Hezekiah, may have been partly responsible for the change of name.

It was not in the restricted sense, but as a synonym of Babylonian, that the name Chaldean obtained the signification of "wise man." That the Chaldeans in the restricted and correct sense were more learned than, or even as learned as, the Babylonians in general, is unlikely. Moreover, the native inscriptions give no indication that this was the case. The Babylonians in general, on the other

hand, were enthusiastic students from very early times. From their inscriptions, it is certain that among their centers of learning may be classed Sippar and Larsa, the chief seats of sun-worship; Nippur, identified with the Calneh of Gen **10** 10; Babylon, the capital; Borsippa in the neighborhood of Babylon; Ur of the Chaldees; and Erech. There is, also, every probability that this list could be extended, and will be extended, when we know more; for wherever an important temple existed, there was to be found also a priestly school. "The learning of the Chaldeans" (Dnl **1** 4; **2** 2; **4** 7; **5** 7.11) comprised the old languages of Babylonia (the two dialects of Sumerian, with a certain knowledge of Kassite, which seems to have been allied to the Hittite; and other languages of the immediate neighborhood); some knowledge of astronomy and astrology; mathematics, which their sexagesimal system of numeration seems to have facilitated; and a certain amount of natural history. To this must be added a store of mythological learning, including legends of the Creation, the Flood (closely resembling in all its main points the account in the Bible), and apparently also the Temptation and the Fall. They had likewise a good knowledge of agriculture, and were no mean architects, as the many celebrated buildings of Babylonia show—compare not only the descriptions of the Temple of Belus (see Babel, Tower of) and the Hanging Gardens, but also the remains of Gudea's great palace at Lagaš (*Tel-loh*), where that ruler, who lived about 2500 BC, is twice represented as an architect, with plan and with rule and measure. (These statues are now in the Louvre.) That their architecture never attained the elegance which characterized that of the West, is probably due to the absence of stone, necessitating the employment of brick as a substitute (Gen **11** 3). See Babylonia; Shinar.

13. The Chaldeans as Learned Men

T. G. Pinches

CHALKSTONE, chôk'stōn (אַבְנֵי־גִר, *'abhnēghir* [cf Eben-ezer, אֶבֶן הָעֶזֶר, *'ebhen hā-'ezer*, "stone of the help," 1 S **7** 12]): In Isa **27** 9 we have: "Therefore by this shall the iniquity of Jacob be forgiven, and this is all the fruit of taking away his sin: that he maketh all the stones of the altar as chalkstones that are beaten in sunder, so that the Asherim and the sun-images shall rise no more." *'Abhnē-ghir* is compounded of *'ebhen*, "stone," which occurs in many passages, and *gir* or *gīr*, "lime" (cf Arab. *jīr*, "gypsum" or "quicklime"), which occurs only here and in Dnl **5** 5: "wrote . . . . upon the plaster [*gīr*] of the wall of the king's palace." Nearly all the rock of Pal is limestone. When limestone is burned, it is converted into lime, which is easily broken into pieces, and, if allowed to remain open to the air, becomes slaked by the moisture of the atmosphere and crumbles into dust. The reference is to the destruction of the altar. It may mean that the altar will be burned so that the stones will become lime, or, more probably, that the stones of the altar will be broken as chalkstones (i.e. lumps of quicklime) are broken. There is no doubt that lime was known to the Egyptians, Assyrians and Hebrews, though clay, with or without straw, was more commonly used in building. Even bitumen ("slime") appears to have been used for mortar. See Clay; Lime; Slime. Alfred Ely Day

CHALLENGE, chal'enj: Only in Ex **22** 9, where AV has taken Heb *'āmar*, "say," in the sense of "claim." RV "whereof one saith, This is it," points more definitely to the idea of identification of the stolen personal property.

CHALPHI, kal'fī (Χαλφί, *Chalphí;* AV **Calphi**): Father of Judas, who, along with Mattathias, steadily supported Jonathan at the battle of Gennesar when the hosts of Demetrius' princes were routed (1 Macc **11** 70).

CHAMBER, chām'bēr (the tr of the following Heb words: חֶדֶר, *ḥedher*, חֻפָּה, *ḥuppāh*, יָצִיעַ, *yāçīaʿ*, יָצוּעַ, *yāçūaʿ*, לִשְׁכָּה, *lishkāh*, נִשְׁכָּה, *nishkāh*, עֲלִיָּה, *'ălīyāh*, צֵלָע, *çēlā'*, and the Aram. word עִלִּית, *'illīth*): For the most part the word chamber is the expression of an idea which would be adequately expressed by the Eng. word "room," in accordance with an earlier use of the word, now little employed. For the arrangement of rooms in a Heb house, see House. *Ḥedher* is a word of frequent occurrence, and designates a private room. *Ḥuppāh* is trd "chamber" only in Ps **19** 5, where it is used in connection with "bridegroom," and means a bridal chamber. The same Heb word used of the bride in Joel **2** 16 is rendered "closet." *Yāçīaʿ* and *yāçūaʿ* are found only in 1 K **6** 5.6.10 (AV only in all the passages), *yāçūaʿ* being the reading of Kethībh and *yāçīaʿ* of Ḳerē in each case. Here the meaning is really "story," as given in RV, except in ver 6, where doubtless the text should be changed to read *ha-çēlā'*, "the side-chamber." *Lishkāh*, a frequent word, and the equivalent *nishkāh*, infrequent, are used ordinarily of a room in the temple utilized for sacred purposes, occasionally of a room in the palace. *'Ălīyāh* and the equivalent Aram. *'illīth* signify "a roof chamber," i.e. a chamber built on the flat roof of a house. *Çēlā'*, when used of a chamber, designates a side-chamber of the temple. It is usually rendered "side-chamber," but "chamber" in 1 K **6** 5.8 (AV), where RV has "side-chamber."

George Ricker Berry

CHAMBER, ROOF. See Chamber.

CHAMBERING, chām'bēr-ing: Illicit intercourse; the rendering in EV since Tyndale of κοίταις, *koítais* (lit. "beds," Rom **13** 13). The Gr usage is paralleled in classic authors and the LXX; like the Eng. participle, it denotes repeated or habitual acts. The word is not recorded elsewhere in Eng. lit. as vb. or participle in this sense; in *Othello*, iii, 3, a chamberer is an intriguer, male wanton, in Byron, *Werner*, IV, 1, 404, a gallant or carpet knight, and in Chaucer, *Clerk's Tale*, 766, a concubine.

CHAMBERLAIN, chām'bēr-lin: In the OT the word rendered chamberlain, סָרִיס, *ṣārīṣ*, is more properly "eunuch," an officer which oriental monarchs placed over their harems (Est **1** 10.12.15; **2** 3.14.21; **4** 4 f; **6** 2.14; **7** 9; 2 K **23** 11). This officer seems also to have had other duties. See under Eunuch. In the NT (1) οἰκονόμος, *oikonómos*, lit. manager of the household, apparently the "treasurer" as in RV "Erastus the treasurer of the city saluteth you" (Rom **16** 23). Cf adapted use as applied to Christian apostles and teachers, bishops, and even to individual members; in which cases, rendered "stewards" (1 Cor **4** 1; Tit **1** 7; 1 Pet **4** 10). (2) In Acts **12** 20, "Blastus the king's chamberlain" (*ho epí toú koitōnos toú basiléōs*, "he who is over the king's bed-chamber"), not treasure-chamber, as above; here *praefectus cubiculo*, or chief *valet de chambre* to the royal person, a position involving much honor and intimacy.

Edward Bagby Pollard

CHAMBERS IN THE HEAVENS. See Astronomy; Dial of Ahaz.

CHAMBERS IN THE SOUTH. See Astronomy; South, Chambers of.

CHAMBERS OF IMAGERY, im'āj-ri, im'ā-jẽr-i (מַשְׂכִּית, *maskīth*): The reference (Ezk **8** 12) is to chambers in the temple where the elders of Israel were wont to assemble and practise rites of an idolatrous character. What the imagery consisted of, we may gather from ver 10: symbolic representations of beasts and reptiles and "detestable things." It is thought that these symbols were of a zodiacal character. The worship of the planets was in vogue at the time of the prophet among the degenerate Israelites.

CHAMELEON, ka-mē'lḗ-un (כֹּחַ, *kō^{a}ḥ*, RV LAND CROCODILE [Lev **11** 30]; תִּנְשֶׁמֶת, *tinshemeth*, AV **mole,** RV CHAMELEON [Lev **11** 30]):

Kō^{a}ḥ, which in the AV is rendered "chameleon" and in the RV "land crocodile," means also "strength" or "power," as in Gen **4** 12; 1 S **2** 9; Ps **22** 15; Isa **40** 29, and many other passages. The LXX has χαμαιλέων, *chamailéōn*, but on account of the

Chameleon—*Chamaeleo vulgaris.*

ordinary meaning of the word, *kō^{a}ḥ*, it has been thought that some large lizard should be understood here. The desert monitor, *Varanus griseus*, one of the largest of lizards, sometime attaining the length of 4 ft., is common in Pal and may be the animal here referred to. The name "monitor" is a tr of the German *warnen*, "to warn," with which has been confused the Arab. name of this animal, *waran* or *waral*, a word of uncertain etymology.

The word *tinshemeth* in the same verse is rendered in AV "mole" and in RV "chameleon." The LXX has ἀσπάλαξ, *aspálax* (=*spálax*, "mole"). *Tinshemeth* also occurs in the lists of unclean birds in Lev **11** 18 and Dt **14** 16, where it is rendered: AV "swan"; RV "horned owl"; LXX πορφυρίων, *porphuríōn* (i.e. "coot" or, acc. to some, "heron"); Vulg *cygnus*, "swan." It appears to come from the root *nāsham*, "to breathe"; cf *n^{e}shāmāh*, "breath" (Gen **2** 7; Job **27** 3 AV, etc). It has therefore in Lev **11** 30 been referred to the chameleon on account of the chameleon's habit of puffing up its body with air and hissing, and in the other passages to the pelican, on account of the pelican's great pouched bill.

The common chameleon is abundant in Pal, being found also in North Africa and in Spain. The other species of chameleons are found principally in Africa and Madagascar. It is not only a harmless but a decidedly useful creature, since it feeds upon insects, esp. flies. Its mode of capturing its prey is most interesting. It slowly and cautiously advances until its head is from 4 to 6 in. from the insect, which it then secures by darting out its tongue with great rapidity. The pigment cells in its skin enable it to change its color from pale yellow to bright green, dark green and almost black, so that it can harmonize very perfectly with its surroundings. Its peculiar toes and prehensile tail help to fit it for its life in the trees. Its prominent eyes with circular lids, like iris diaphragms, can be moved independently of each other, and add to its striking appearance. See LAND CROCODILE; MOLE; SWAN; HORNED OWL; PELICAN.

ALFRED ELY DAY

CHAMOIS, sham'i, sha-mwä', sha-moi' (זֶמֶר, *zemer;* **καμηλοπάρδαλις,** *kamēlopárdalis*): Occurs only once in the Bible, i.e. in the list of clean animals in Dt **14** 5. Gesenius refers to the vb. *zāmar*, "to sing," and suggests the association of dancing or leaping, indicating thereby an active animal. M'Lean in *EB* cites the rendering of the Tgs *dīṣa'*, or "wild goat." Now there are two wild goats in Pal. The better known is the ibex of the S., which may well be the *ya'ēl* (EV "wild goat"; Job **39** 1; Ps **104** 18; 1 S **24** 2), as well as the *'akkō* (EV "wild goat," Dt **14** 5). The other is the pasang or Pers wild goat which ranges from the N.E. of Pal and the Syrian desert to Persia, and which

From *Roy. Nat. Hist.*, by permission.

Chamois: Persian Wild Goat or Pasang—*Capra aegagrus.* (This may be the *zemer*, EV chamois, of Dt **14** 5.)

may be the *zemer* (EV "chamois"). The accompanying illustration, which is taken from the *Royal Natural History*, shows the male and female and young. The male is distinguished by its larger horns and goatee. The horns are in size and curvature very similar to those of the ibex (see GOAT, sec. 2), but the front edge is like a nicked blade instead of being thick and knotty as in the ibex. Like the ibex it is at home among the rocks, and climbs apparently impossible cliffs with marvelous ease.

Tristram (*NHB*) who is followed by Post (*HDB*) suggests that *zemer* may be the Barbary sheep (*Ovis tragelaphus*), though the latter is only known to inhabit the Atlas Mountains, from the Atlantic to Tunis. Tristram supports his view by reference to a *kebsh* ("ram") which the Arabs say lives in the mountains of Sinai, though they have apparently neither horns nor skins to show as trophies, and it is admitted that no European has seen it. The true chamois (*Rupicapra tragus*) inhabits the high mountains from the Pyrenees to the Caucasus, and there is no reason to suppose that it was ever found in Syria or Pal. ALFRED ELY DAY

CHAMPAIGN, sham-pān', sham'pān (עֲרָבָה, *'ărābhāh*, בִּקְעָה, *bik'āh*): A champaign is a flat open country, and the word occurs in Dt **11** 30 AV (RV "the Arabah") as a tr of *'ărābhāh*, for which AV has in most places "the plain," and RV "the Arabah," when it is used with the art. and denotes a definite region, i.e. the valley of the Jordan from the Sea of Galilee to the Dead Sea (Dt **2** 8; **3** 17; **4** 49; Josh **3** 16; **8** 14; **11** 16; **12** 1.3.8; 2 S **2** 29; **4** 7; 2 K **14** 25; **25** 4; Jer **39** 4; **52** 7), and also the valley running southward from the Dead Sea to the Gulf of Akabah (Dt **1** 1). Ezk **47** 8 has for *hā-'ărābhāh* "the desert," AVm "plain," RV "the Arabah." The pl. is used in Josh **5** 10; 2 K **25** 5, "the plains of Jericho," and in Nu **22** 1 and **26** 3, "the plains of Moab." Elsewhere *'ărābhāh* is rendered in EV "desert" or "wilderness" (Job **24** 5; **39** 6; Isa **33** 9; **35** 1.6; **40** 3; **41** 19; **51** 3; Jer **2** 6; **17** 6; **50** 12). At the present day, the Jordan valley is called the *Ghaur* (cf Heb *'ūr*, "to dig," *m^e'ārāh*, "cave," and Arab. *maghārah*, "cave"). This name is also applied to the deltas of streams flowing into the Dead Sea from the E., which are clothed with thickets of thorny trees and shrubs, i.e. *Ghaur-ul-Mezra'ah*, at the mouths of *Wādi-Kerak* and *Wādi-Beni-Ḥammād*, *Ghaur-uṣ-Ṣāfiyeh*, at the mouth of *Wādi-ul-Ḥisa*. The name "Arabah" (Arab. *al-'Arabah*) is now confined to the valley running southward from the Dead Sea to the Gulf of Akabah, separating the mountains of Edom from Sinai and the plateau of *at-Tīh*. See ARABAH.

Ezk **37** 2 AVm has "champaign" for *biḳ'āh*, which is elsewhere rendered "vale" or "valley." *Biḳ'āh* seems to be applied to wide, open valleys, as: "the valley of Jericho" (Dt **34** 3), "the valley of Megiddo" (2 Ch **35** 22; Zec **12** 11), "the valley of Lebanon" (Josh **11** 17). If Baal-Gad be *Ba'albeḳ* and "the valley of Lebanon" be Coele-syria, the present name of Coele-syria, *al-Biḳā'* (pl. of *buḳ'ah*, "a low, wet place or meadow"), may be regarded as a survival of the Heb *biḳ'āh*.

ALFRED ELY DAY

CHAMPION, cham'pi-un (אִישׁ־הַבֵּנַיִם, *'īsh ha-bēnayim*): In 1 S **17** 4.23 this unusual expression occurs in the description of Goliath. It means lit. "the man of the two spaces," "spaces," or "space between," and is perhaps to be explained by the fact that there was a brook flowing through the valley separating the two armies. In 1 S **17** 51 the word champion is the rendering of the Heb *gibbōr*, "mighty man."

CHANAAN, kā'nan, kā'nā-an (**Χαναάν**, *Chanaán*) **Chanaanite**, kā'nan-īt, AV in the Apoc (Jth **5** 3.16) and NT (Acts **7** 11; **13** 19) for RV CANAAN, CANAANITE (q.v.).

CHANCE, chans: The idea of chance in the sense of something wholly fortuitous was utterly foreign to the Heb creed. Throughout the whole course of Israel's history, to the Heb mind, law, not chance, ruled the universe, and that law was not something blindly mechanical, but the expression of the personal Jeh. Israel's belief upon this subject may be summed up in the couplet,

> "The lot is cast into the lap;
> But the whole disposing thereof is of Jeh"
> (Prov **16** 33).

A number of Heb and Gr expressions have been tr[d] "chance," or something nearly equivalent, but it is noteworthy that of the classical words for chance, *συντυχία*, *suntuchía*, and *τύχη*, *túchē*, the former never occurs in the Bible and the latter only twice in the LXX.

The closest approach to the idea of chance is found in the statement of the Philis that if their device for ascertaining the cause of their calamities turned out a certain way they would call them a chance, that is, bad luck (מִקְרֶה, *miḳreh*, 1 S **6** 9). But note that it was a heathen people who said this. We have the same Heb noun and the vb., from which the noun is taken, a number of times, but variously rendered into Eng.: Uncleanness that "chanceth him by night" (Dt **23** 10). "Her hap was to light on the portion of the field" (Ruth **2** 3). "Something hath befallen him" (1 S **20** 26). "One event happeneth to them all" (Eccl **2** 14.15); "that which befalleth the sons of men" ("sons of men are a chance," ERVm) (Eccl **3** 19). "There is one event to the righteous and to the wicked" (Eccl **9** 2.3). Here the idea certainly is not something independent of the will of God, but something unexpected by man.

There is also קָרָא, *ḳārā'*, "If a bird's nest chance to be before thee in the way" (Dt **22** 6). Both the above Heb words are combined in the statement "As I happened by chance upon Mount Gilboa" (2 S **1** 6). "And Absalom chanced to meet the servants of David" ("met the servants," **18** 9, AV). "And there happened to be there a base fellow" (2 S **20** 1).

We have also פֶּגַע, *pegha'*, "Time and chance happeneth to them all," meaning simply occurrence (Eccl **9** 11). "Neither adversary, nor evil occurrence" (1 K **5** 4).

In the NT we have *συγκυρία*, *sugkuría*, "coincidence," a meeting apparently accidental, a coincidence. "By chance a certain priest was going down that way" (Lk **10** 31). Also *εἰ τύχοι*, *ei túchoi*. "It may chance of wheat, or of some other kind," i.e. we cannot tell which (1 Cor **15** 37). "It may be" (1 Cor **14** 10).

If we look at the LXX we find *tuchē* used twice. "And Leah said, [*En tuchē*] With fortune" ("a troop cometh," AV; "fortunate," RV; "with fortune," RVm, Gen **30** 11). Note, it was no Israelite, but Leah who said this. "That prepare a table for Fortune, and that fill up mingled wine unto Destiny" ("fate," Isa **65** 11). In this passage *tuchē* stands for the Heb מְנִי, *m^enī*, the god of destiny, and Fortune is for Gad, the old Sem name for the god of fortune found in inscriptions, private names, etc. Note here, however, also, that the prophet was rebuking idolatrous ones for apostasy to heathen divinities.

We have also in the Apoc, "these things which have chanced," RV "to be opened unto thee" (2 Esd **10** 49). See also GAD; MENI.

GEORGE HENRY TREVER

CHANCELLOR, chan'sel-ẽr: The rendering in Ezr **4** 8.9.17 of the Heb בְּעֵל־טְעֵם, *b^e'ēl ṭ^e'ēm;* LXX *Βάαλ*, *Báal* (9), *Βαλγάμ*, *Balgám* (17), the latter being an incorrect tr of Heb ע. In 1 Esd **2** 16.25, *Βεέλτεθμος*, *Beéltethmos* (cf Ezr **4** 8) occurs as a corruption, doubtless of בְּעֵל־טְעֵם, *b^e'ēl ṭ^e'ēm*. The term in question designates an Assyr office, viz. that of the "master or lord of official intelligence," or "postmaster" (Sayce).

CHANGE, chānj: A word which seeks to express the many shades of meaning contained in 13 variations of 9 Heb words and 5 Gr. These signify, in turn, "to change," "to exchange," "to turn," "to put or place," "to make other" i.e. "alter," "to disguise oneself." חָלַף, *ḥālaph*, and its derivatives, occurring often, indicates "to pass away," hence alter, renew, e.g. (1) "changes of raiment" (Gen **45** 22; Jgs **14** 12.13.19); (2) "changed my wages ten times" (Gen **31** 7.41); (3) heavens changed "as a vesture" (Ps **102** 26); (4) "changes and warfare" (Job **10** 17), i.e. relays of soldiers as illustrated in 1 K **5** 14 (RVm "host after host is against me"); (5) "till my change come" (RV "release"), i.e. death (Job **14** 14); (6) "changed the ordinances" (ARV "violated the statutes"), i.e. disregarded law (Isa **24** 5); (7) change of mind

(Hab **1** 11 AV). Used also of change of character, הָפַךְ, *hāphakh*: (1) of leprosy, "changed unto white" (Lev **13** 16); (2) **fig.** of the moral life, "Can the Ethiopian change his skin?" (Jer **13** 23); so also מוּר, *mūr*, and derivatives, "changed their gods" and "their glory," etc (Ps **106** 20; Jer **2** 11; Hos **4** 7). Other words used to indicate change of name (2 K **24** 17); of day and night (Job **17** 12); of times and seasons (Dnl **2** 21); of countenance (Dnl **7** 28); of behavior (1 S **21** 13); God's unchangeableness, "I, Jeh, change not" (Mal **3** 6).

In the NT the word has to do chiefly with spiritual realities: (1) μετατίθημι, *metatíthēmi*, of the necessary change of the priesthood and law under Christ (He **7** 12); (2) ἀλλάττω, *alláttō*, of His changing the customs of Moses (Acts **6** 14); (3) of moral change, e.g. debasement (Rom **1** 23.25.26); (4) of bodily change at the resurrection (1 Cor **15** 51.52; μετασχηματίζω, *metaschēmatízō*, Phil **3** 21 AV); (5) μεταβάλλω, *metabállō*, of change of mind in presence of a miracle (Acts **28** 6); (6) of the change to come over the heavens at the great day of the Lord (He **1** 12; cf 2 Pet **3** 10.12).

Figurative uses indicated separately in the course of the article. DWIGHT M. PRATT

CHANGE OF RAIMENT, rā'ment. See DRESS.

CHANGER, chān'jēr (**κολλυβιστής,** *kollubistḗs*, "money-changer," and so rendered Mt **21** 12; Mk **11** 15): A banker or other person who changes money at a fixed rate. Indignant at the profane traffic in the temple Jesus "poured out the changers' money" (Jn **2** 15). So used only here. For fuller treatment see BANK; MONEY-CHANGERS.

CHANNEL, chan'el (אָפִיק, *'āphīḳ* [r. אָפַק, *'āphaḳ*, "to hold or contain," "to be strong"; cf Arab. *'afaḳ*, "to overcome," and *'āfiḳ*, "preëminent"]; שִׁבֹּלֶת, *shibbōleth* [r. שָׁבַל, *shābhal*, "to go," "to go up or grow," "to flow"; cf Arab. *'asbal*, "to flow," "to rain," "to put forth ears"; *sabalat*, "an ear of grain"; *sabīl*, "a road," "a public fountain"]): In Job **12** 21; **40** 18; **41** 15 we have *'āphīḳ* in the sense of "strong" (but cf **40** 18, RV "tubes" [of brass]). Elsewhere it is trd "river," "brook," "stream," "channel" or "watercourse." *Shibbōleth* (in the dialect of Ephraim *ṣibbōleth* [Jgs **12** 6]) means "an ear of grain" (Gen **41** 5 ff; Ruth **2** 2; Isa **17** 5) or "a flood of water" (Ps **69** 2.15; Isa **27** 12). In 2 S **22** 16 (cf Ps **18** 15) we have:

"Then the channels of the sea appeared,
The foundations of the world were laid bare,
By the rebuke of Jeh,
At the blast of the breath of his nostrils."

This is reminiscent of "fountains of the deep" (Gen **7** 11; **8** 2; Prov **8** 28). It is a question how far we should attribute to these ancient writers a share in modern notions of oceanography, but the idea seems to be that of a withdrawal of the water of the ocean, and the laying bare of submarine declivities and channels such as we know to exist as the result of erosion during a previous period of elevation, when the given portion of ocean floor was dry land.

The fact that many streams of Pal flow only during the rainy season seems to be referred to in Job **6** 15; and perhaps also in Ps **126** 4. See BROOK; RIVER. ALFRED ELY DAY

CHANT (פָּרַט, *pāraṭ*): Occurs only once in AV in Am **6** 5, and the meaning of the Heb is uncertain. *Pāraṭ* corresponds to an Arab. root meaning to anticipate. It may therefore signify to improvise, to sing without care or preparation. RV "to sing idle songs" suits the context. See Driver, *Joel and Amos*.

CHANUNEUS, ka-nun'ē-us (**Χανουναῖος,** *Chanounaíos*; AV **Channuneus**): A Levite in the list of 1 Esd **8** 48, probably corresponding to "Merari" in Ezr **8** 19.

CHAPEL, chap'el (מִקְדָּשׁ, *miḳdāsh*, "a holy place"; RV SANCTUARY, q.v.): "It is the king's chapel" (Am **7** 13 AV), an expression indicative of the dependence of this sanctuary on the court.

CHAPHENATHA, ka-fen'a-tha (**Χαφεναθά,** *Chaphenathá*; AV **Caphenatha**): A name apparently given to part of the eastern wall of Jerus or a fort in that neighborhood which is said (1 Macc **12** 37) to have been repaired by Jonathan Maccabaeus. The place cannot now be identified. Various speculations have been made as to the origin of the name, but they can hardly be said to throw any light on the passage cited.

CHAPITER, chap'i-tēr. See ARCHITECTURE; JACHIN AND BOAZ; TEMPLE, II, 4.

CHAPMAN, chap'man (pl. אַנְשֵׁי הַתָּרִים, *'anshē ha-tārīm*): Word used only once in AV (2 Ch **9** 14, ARV "the traders"; cf also 1 K **10** 15 RV, where the Heb uses the same expression). The Eng. word means "merchant"; cf the vb. "to chaffer," and the Germ. *Kaufmann*. The Heb means "those who go about" as merchants.

CHAPT (חָתַת, *ḥāthath*): The Heb term *ḥāthath* means "broken," "terrified" or "dismayed." This term as it occurs in Jer **14** 4 is rendered "chapt" in EV, "cracked" in ARV, and "dismayed" in RVm. Inasmuch as the Heb term means "broken," it is not incorrectly rendered "chapt" or "chapped," which means to be cracked open.

CHARAATHALAN, kar-a-ath'a-lan (**Χαρααθαλάν,** *Charaathalán*; AV **Charaathalar** [1 Esd **5** 36]): Most probably a corruption of the text. The names "Cherub, Addan, and Immer" in the lists of Ezr **2** 59 and Neh **7** 61 are presented in the text cited as "Charaathalan leading them, and Allar."

CHARACA, kar'a-ka. See CHARAX.

CHARASHIM, kar'a-shim (חֲרָשִׁים, *ḥărāshīm*, "craftsmen"). See GE-HARASHIM.

CHARAX, kār'ax (**εἰς τὸν Χάρακα,** *eis tón Cháraka*; AV **Characa,** kar'a-ka; **Χάραξ,** *Chárax*): A place mentioned only in 2 Macc **12** 17. It lay E. of the Jordan and is said to be 750 stadia from Caspis, and to be inhabited by Jews called Tubieni, that is, of Tobie (Tob) in Gilead (1 Macc **5** 9.13; 2 Macc **12** 17). There is no clue as to the direction in which Ch. lay from Caspis. Possibly Kerak (Kir-moab), in post-Bib. times called Charamōba and Mōboucharax, may represent the place. It lay about 100 miles S. of el-Mezerib, S.E. of the Dead Sea.

CHARCHEMISH, kär'ke-mish. See CARCHEMISH.

CHARCHUS, kär'kus. See BARCHUS.

CHAREA, kā'rē-a (**Χαρέα,** *Charéa*): Head of a family of temple-servants (1 Esd **5** 32); called "Harsha" in Ezr **2** 52; Neh **7** 54.

CHARGE, chärj, **CHARGEABLE,** chär'ja-b'l (from Lat *carrus*, "a wagon," hence "to lay or put a load on or in," "to burden, or be a burden"):

Figurative: (1) of a special duty (מִשְׁמֶרֶת, *mishmereth*, "thing to be watched"), "the c. of Jeh"

(Lev **8** 35), the injunctions given in Ex **29**; "the c. of the tabernacle" (Nu **1** 53); "the c. of the sons of Gershon" (**3** 25); (2) of the burden of expense (כָּבֵד, *kābhēdh*, "to be, or make heavy"; ἀδάπανος, *adápanos*, "without expense"), "lest we be chargeable unto thee" (2 S **13** 25 AV, RV "burdensome"); "The former governors . . . . were c. unto the people" (Neh **5** 15 m "laid burdens upon"); "that . . . . I may make the gospel without c." (1 Cor **9** 18; see CHARGES); (3) of oversight, care, custody, "Who gave him a c. over the earth?" (Job **34** 13); "to have the c. of the gate" (2 K **7** 17); "c. of the vessels of service" (1 Ch **9** 28); "cause ye them that have c. [פְּקֻדּוֹת, *pᵉkuddōth*, "inspectors"] over the city" (Ezk **9** 1); "who had the c. of all her treasure" (Acts **8** 27 AV, RV "was over"); (4) of a command, injunction, requirement, "He gave him a c." (Gen **28** 6); "His father charged the people with the oath" (1 S **14** 27); "Jesus strictly [m "sternly"] charged them" (Mt **9** 30); "I charge you by the Lord" (1 Thess **5** 27 AV, RV "adjure"); "having received such a c." (Acts **16** 24, παραγγελία, *paraggelía*, "private or extra message"); "This c. I commit unto thee" (1 Tim **1** 18); (5) of blame, responsibility, reckoning, "Lord, lay not this sin to their c." (Acts **7** 60); "nothing laid to his c." (**23** 29); "Who shall lay anything to the c. of God's elect?" (Rom **8** 33). M. O. EVANS

CHARGER, chär'jẽr (ARV "platter"): A word which meant in the older Eng. speech a flat dish or platter. It is used in the Bible as the tr (1) of קְעָרָה, *kᵉʿārāh*, which in Nu **7** 19 AV (RV "platter") and repeatedly in that chapter denotes one of the gifts made by the several princes at the dedication of the tabernacle; (2) of אֲגַרְטָל, *'ăghartāl*, a word of uncertain derivation used in Ezr **1** 9 (AV) twice to designate certain temple vessels which might better be called "libation bowls"; (3) of πίναξ, *pínax*, used Mt **14** 8.11; Mk **6** 25.28 (EV) for the dish in which the head of John the Baptist was presented. DAVID FOSTER ESTES

CHARGES, chär'jiz (δαπανάω, *dapanáō*, "to spend"): "Be at charges for them" (Acts **21** 24, AV "with them"), i.e. pay the sacrificial expenses of these poorer Nazirites (cf Jos, *Ant*, XIX, xvi, 1).

CHARIOT, char'i-ot (מֶרְכָּב, *merkābh*, מֶרְכָּבָה, *merkābhāh*, "riding-chariot," רֶכֶב, *rekhebh*, "war-chariot"; ἅρμα, *hárma*):

1. Chariots of Egypt
2. " of the Canaanites
3. " of Solomon and Later Kings
4. " of the Assyrians
5. " of Chaldaeans, Persians, Greeks
6. In the NT
7. Figurative Use

LITERATURE

1. Chariots of Egypt

It is to the chariots of ancient Egypt that reference is first made in Scripture. Joseph was honored by being made to ride in the second chariot of King Pharaoh (Gen **41** 43). Joseph paid honor to his father on his arrival in Goshen by meeting him in his chariot (Gen **46** 29). In the state ceremonial with which the remains of Jacob were escorted to Canaan, chariots and horsemen were conspicuous (Gen **50** 9). In the narrative of the departure of the Israelites from Egypt and of Pharaoh's futile attempts to detain them the chariots and horsemen of Pharaoh figure largely (Ex **14** 17.18.23.25; **15** 4.19). It was with the Hyksos invasion, some cents. before the Exodus, that the horse, and subsequently the chariot, were introduced for purposes of war into Egypt; and it may have been the possession of chariots that enabled those hated shepherd warriors to overpower the native Egyptians. The Egyp chariot was distinguished by its lightness of build. It was so reduced in weight that it was possible for a man to carry his chariot on his shoulders without fatigue. The ordinary chariot was made of wood and leather, and had only two occupants, the fighting man and his shield-bearer. The royal chariots were ornamented with gold and silver, and in the battle of Megiddo Thothmes III is represented as standing in his chariot of electrum like the god of war, brandishing his lance. In the battle the victorious Egyptians captured 2,041 horses and 924 chariots from the Syrian allies.

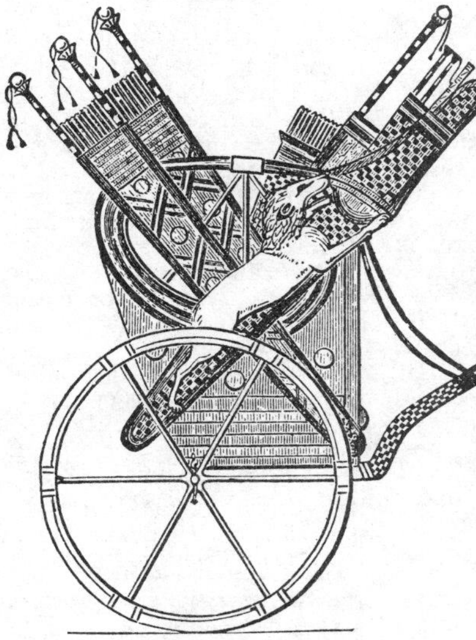

Egyptian War-Chariot.

2. Chariots of the Canaanites

The Canaanites had long been possessed of horses and chariots when Joshua houghed their horses and burnt their chariots with fire at the waters of Merom (Josh **11** 6.9). The chariots of iron which the Canaanites could manoeuvre in the plains and valleys proved a formidable obstacle to the complete conquest of the land (Jgs **1** 19). Jabin had 900 chariots of iron, and with them he was able to oppress the children of Israel twenty years (Jgs **4** 3). The Philis of the low country and the maritime plain, of whom we read in Jgs and S, were a warlike people, were disciplined and well armed and their possession of chariots gave them a great advantage over the Israelites. In the war of Michmash they put into the field the incredible number of 30,000 chariots and 6,000 horsemen, only in the end to suffer a grievous defeat (1 S **13** 5; **14** 20). In the battle of Gilboa, however, the chariots and horsemen of the Philis bore down all opposition, and proved the destruction of Saul and his house. Of these chariots there have come down to us no detailed description and no representation. But we cannot be far wrong in turning to the chariot of the Hittites as a type of the Canaanite and Phili chariot. It is not from the monuments of the Hittites themselves, however, but from the representations of the Kheta of the Egyp monuments, that we know what their chariots were like. Their chariotry was their chief arm of offence. The Hittite chariot was used, too, for hunting; but a heavier car with paneled sides was employed for war. The Egyp monuments represent three Hittites in each car, a practice which differed from that of Egypt and attracted attention. Of the three, one guided the chariot, another did the fighting with sword and lance, and the third was the shield-bearer.

3. Chariots of Solomon and Later Kings

The Israelites living in a mountainous country were tardy in adopting the chariot for purposes of war. David houghed all the chariot horses of Hadadezer, king of Zobah, and "reserved of them for a hundred chariots" (2 S **8** 4), and Adonijah prepared for himself chariots and horsemen with a view to contest the throne of his father (1 K **1** 5). But Solomon was the first in Israel to acquire chariots and horses on a national scale, and to build cities for their accommodation (1 K **9** 19). In MT of the OT we read that Solomon had agents who received droves of horses from Egypt, and it is added: "And a chariot came up and went out of Egypt for 600 shekels of silver, and a horse for 150; and so for all the kings of the Hittites, and for the kings of Syria, did they bring them out by their means" (1 K **10** 29). On the strength of a warrantable emendation of the text it is now proposed to read the preceding (ver 28): "And Solomon's import of horses was from Muṣri and from Kuë; the king's traders received them from Kuë at a price"—where Muṣri and Kuë are North Syria and Cilicia. No doubt it was Egypt out of which the nation was forbidden by the Deuteronomic law to multiply horses (Dt **17** 16), but on the other hand the statement of Ezk (**27** 14) that Israel derived horses, chargers and mules not from Egypt but from Togarmah—North Syria and Asia Minor—agrees with the new rendering (Burney, *Notes on Hebrew Text of the Books of Kings*, in loc.). From Solomon's time onward chariots were in use in both kingdoms. Zimri, who slew Elah, son of Baasha, king of Israel, was captain of half his chariots (1 K **16** 9). It was when sitting in his chariot in disguise beside the driver that Ahab received his fatal wound at Ramoth-gilead (1 K **22** 34). The floor of the royal chariot was a pool of blood, and "they washed the chariot by the pool of Samaria" (vs 35.38). It was in his war-chariot that his servants carried Josiah dead from the fatal field of Megiddo (2 K **23** 30). The chief pieces of the Heb chariot were (1) the pole to which the two horses were yoked, (2) the axle—resting upon two wheels with six or eight spokes (1 K **7** 33)—into which the pole was fixed, (3) a frame or body open behind, standing upon the axle and fitted by a leather band to the pole. The chariots of iron of which we read (Jgs **4** 3) were of wood strengthened or studded with iron. Like that of the Hittite, the Heb chariot probably carried three men, although in the chariot of Ahab (1 K **22** 34) and in that of Jehu (2 K **9** 24 f) we read of only two.

Assyrian Chariot.

4. Chariots of the Assyrians

In the later days when the Assyrians overran the lands of the West, the Israelites had to face the chariots and the hosts of Sennacherib and of the kings (2 K **19** 23). And they faced them with chariots of their own. An inscription of Shalmaneser II of Assyria tells how in the battle of Karkar (854 BC) Ahab of the land of Israel had put into the field 2,000 chariots and 10,000 soldiers. But the Assyr chariotry was too numerous and powerful for Israel. The Assyr chariot was larger and heavier than the Egyp or the Heb: it had usually three and sometimes four occupants (Maspéro, *Life in Ancient Egypt and Assyria*, 322). When we read in Nahum's prophecy of "chariots flashing with steel," "rushing to and fro in the broad ways" (Nah **2** 3.4), it is of the Assyr chariots that we are to think being hastily got together for the defence of Nineveh.

5. Chariots of Chaldaeans, Persians, Greeks

In early Bab inscriptions of the 3d millennium before Christ there is evidence of the use of the war-chariots, and Nebuchadrezzar in his campaigns to the West had chariots as part of his victorious host (Jer **47** 3). It was the Persians who first employed scythed chariots in war; and we find Antiochus Eupator in the Seleucid period equipping a Gr force against Judaea which had 300 chariots armed with scythes (2 Macc **13** 2).

6. In the NT

In the NT the chariot is only twice mentioned. Besides the chariot in which the Ethiopian eunuch was traveling when Philip the evangelist made up to him (Acts **8** 28.29.38), there is only the mention of the din of war-chariots to which the onrush of locusts in Apocalyptic vision is compared (Rev **9** 9).

7. Figurative Use

In the fig. language of Scripture, the chariot has a place. It is a tribute to the powerful influence of Elijah and Elisha when they are separately called "the chariots of Israel and the horsemen thereof" (2 K **2** 12; **13** 14). The angelic hosts are declared to be God's chariots, twice ten thousand, thousands upon thousands (Ps **68** 17). But chariots and horses themselves are a poor substitute for the might of God (Ps **20** 7). God Himself is represented as riding upon His chariots of salvation for the defence of His people (Hab **3** 8). In the Book of Zec, the four chariots with their horses of various colors have an apocalyptic significance (Zec **6**). In the worship of the host of heaven which prevailed in the later days of the kingdom of Judah, "the chariots of the sun" (see art.) were symbols which led the people into gross idolatry and King Josiah burnt them with fire (2 K **23** 11).

LITERATURE.—Nowack, *Heb Arch.*, I, 366 f; Garstang, *Land of the Hittites*, 363 f; Maspéro, *Struggle of the Nations* and *Life in Ancient Egypt and Assyria;* Rawlinson, *Five Great Monarchies*, II, 1–21.

T. NICOL

CHARIOTS OF THE SUN (מַרְכְּבוֹת הַשֶּׁמֶשׁ, *markᵉbhōth ha-shemesh*): These, together with "horses of the sun," are mentioned in 2 K **23** 11. They are said to have stood in the temple, a gift of the kings of Judah. Josiah removed the horses from the precincts of the temple and burned the chariots. Among the Greeks, Helios was endowed with horses and chariots. Thus the course of the sun as he sped across the skies was understood by the mythological mind of antiquity. The Bab god Shamash (=Heb *Shemesh*) likewise had his chariot and horses as well as his charioteer. The cult of the sun and other heavenly bodies which was particularly in vogue during the latter days of the Judaean monarchy (cf 2 K **23** 5; Ezk **8** 16 f; Dt **17** 3; Jer **8** 2) seems to have constituted an element of the Canaanitish religion (cf the names of localities like Beth-shemesh and the like). The chariots of the sun are also referred to in En **72** 5.37; **75** 4, and Gr Apoc of Bar **6**.

MAX L. MARGOLIS

CHARITABLY, char′i-ta-bli (**κατὰ ἀγάπην**, *katá agápēn*): The RV, which substitutes "love" for "charity" regularly, removing the latter word from the vocabulary of Scripture, makes a like change in Rom **14** 15, the only occurrence of "charitably" in AV; RV "in love." See CHARITY.

CHARITY, char'i-ti (**ἀγάπη,** *agápē*):

1. A New Word
2. A New Ideal
3. An Apostolic Term
4. Latin Equivalents
5. English Translation
6. Inward Motive
7. Character
8. Ultimate Ideal
9. Almsgiving
10. Tolerance

In AV in 26 places from 1 Cor **8** 1 onward. The same Gr word, which appears in the NT 115 times, is elsewhere tr[d] by "love."

The subst. *agapē* is mainly, if not exclusively, a Bib. and ecclesiastical word (see Deissmann, *Bible Studies,* 198 ff), not found in profane writings, although the vb. *agapā́n,* from which it is derived, is used in classical Gr in the sense of "love, founded in admiration, veneration, esteem, like the Lat *diligere*" (Grimm-Thayer), rather than natural emotion (Lat *amare*). It is a significant evidence of the sense of a new ideal and principle of life that permeated the Christian consciousness of the earliest communities, that they should have made current a new word to express it, and that they should derive that word, not from the current or philosophical language of Gr morality, but from the LXX.

1. A New Word

2. A New Ideal

In the NT the word is apostolic, and appears first and predominantly in the Pauline writings. It is found only twice in the Synoptics (Mt **24** 12; Lk **11** 42), and although it is in both places put in the mouth of the Saviour, it can easily be understood how the language of a later time may have been used by the narrator, when it is considered that these gospels were compiled and reduced to writing many years after the spread of the Pauline epistles. The word is not found in Jas, Mk or Acts, but it appears in Paul 75 times, in Jn 30 times, in Pet 4 times, in Jude twice and in He twice. Jesus Christ gave the thing and the spirit in the church, and the apostles (probably Paul) invented the term to express it. When Jerome came to translate the Gr testament into Lat, he found in that language no word to represent *agapē*. *Amor* was too gross, and he fell back on *dilectio* and *caritas,* words which, however, in their original meanings were too weak and colorless to represent *agapē* adequately. No principle seems to have guided him in the choice of the one word or the other in particular places. *Caritas* in Eng. became "charity," and was taken over by the Eng. translators from the Vulg, though not with any regularity, nor as far as can be judged, according to any definite principle, except that it is used of *agapē* only in man, never as it denotes a quality or action of God, which is always tr[d] by "love." When *agapē* is tr[d] by "charity" it means either (1) a disposition in man which may qualify his own character (1 Cor **8** 1) and be ready to go forth to God (1 Cor **8** 3) or to men; or (2) an active and actual relation with other men, generally within the church (Col **3** 14; 1 Thess **3** 6; 2 Thess **1** 3; 1 Tim **1** 5; **4** 12; 1 Pet **4** 8; **5** 14), but also absolutely and universally (1 Cor **13**). In the earlier epistles it stands first and unique as the supreme principle of the Christian life (1 Cor **13**), but in the later writings, it is enumerated as one among the Christian virtues (1 Tim **2** 15; 2 Tim **2** 22; **3** 10; Tit **2** 2; 2 Pet **1** 7; Rev **2** 19). In Paul's psalm of love (1 Cor **13**) it is set forth as an innermost principle contrasted with prophecy and knowledge, faith and works, as the motive that determines the quality of the whole inner life, and gives value to all its activities. If a man should have all gifts of miracles and intellect, and perform all the works of goodness and devotion, "and have not love, it profiteth nothing," for they would be purely external and legal, and lacking in the quality of moral choice and personal relation which give life its value (vs 1–3). Love itself defines men's relation to men as generous, tolerant and forgiving. "Love suffereth long, and is kind; love envieth not" (ver 4). It determines and defines a man's own character and personality. It is not boastful and arrogant, but dignified, pure, holy, courageous and serene. Evil cannot provoke it nor wrong delight it. It bears cheerfully all adversity and follows its course in confident hope (vs 4–7). It is final virtue, the ultimate ideal of life. Many of life's activities cease or change, but "love never faileth." To it all other graces and virtues are subordinated. "Now abideth faith, hope, love, these three; and the greatest of these is love" (vs 8–13). In one passage only in the NT (3 Jn ver 6) *agapē* seems to have a meaning that comes near to the later, ecclesiastical meaning of *charity* as almsgiving. With the growing legalism of the church and the prevalence of monastic ideals of morality, *caritas* came to mean the very opposite of Paul's *agapē*—just "the giving of goods to feed the poor," which "without love profiteth nothing." At present the word means either liberality to the poor, or tolerance in judging the actions of others, both qualities of love, but very inadequate to express its totality. The Revisers have therefore accurately dropped the word and substituted "love" for it in all passages. It is interesting to note that in Welsh the reverse process has occurred: *cariad* (from Lat *caritas*) was used throughout to translate *agapē*, with the result that in both religious and ordinary speech the word has established itself so firmly as almost to oust the native word *serch.*

3. An Apostolic Term

4. Latin Equivalents

5. English Translation

6. Inward Motive

7. Character

8. Ultimate Ideal

9. Almsgiving

10. Tolerance

T. REES

CHARM, chärm: *Definition.*—The word charm is derived from the Latin *carmen,* "a song," and denotes strictly what is sung; then it comes to mean a magical formula chanted or recited with a view to certain desired results. Charm is distinguished from amulet in this, that the latter is a material object having as such a magical potency, though it is frequently an inscribed formula on it that gives this object its power (see AMULET). The word charm stands primarily for the incantation, though it is often applied to an inscribed amulet.

A charm may be regarded as having a positive or a negative effect. In the first case it is supposed to secure some desired object or result (see AMULET). In the second, it is conceived as having the power of warding off evils, as the evil eye, the inflictions of evil spirits and the like. In the last, its negative meaning, the word "countercharm" (German, *Gegenzauber*) is commonly used.

Charms are divisible into two general classes according as they are written (or printed) or merely spoken:

(1) *Written charms.*—Of these we have examples in the phylacteries and the *m[e]zūzāh* noticed in the art. AMULET. In Acts **19** 13–20 we read of written charms used by the Ephesians, such as are elsewhere called ἐφέσια γράμματα (*ephésia grámmata*). Such magical formulae were written generally on leather, though sometimes on papyrus, on lead, and

even on gold. Those mentioned in the above passage must have been inscribed on some very valuable material, gold perhaps, or they could not have cost £2,000 (=50,000 drachmas). Charms of the kind have been dug up from the ruins of Ephesus. In modern Egypt drinking-bowls are used, inscribed with passages from the Koran, and it is considered very lucky to drink from such a "lucky bowl," as it is called. Parts of the Koran and often complete miniature copies are worn by Egyptians and esp. by Egyp soldiers during war. These are buried with the dead bodies, just as the ancient Egyptians interred with their dead portions of the Book of the Dead or even the whole book, and as the early Abyssinians buried with dead bodies certain magical texts. Jos (*Ant*, VIII, ii, 5) says that Solomon composed incantations by which demons were exorcised and diseases healed.

(2) *Spoken charms* are at least as widespread as those inscribed. Much importance was attached by the ancients (Egyp, Bab, etc) to the manner in which the incantations were recited, as well as to the substance of the formulae. If beautifully uttered, and with sufficient frequency, such incantations possessed unlimited power. The stress laid on the mode of reciting magical charms necessitated the existence of a priestly class and did much to increase the power of such a class. The binding force of the uttered word is implied in many parts of the OT (see Josh **9** 20). Though the princes of Israel had promised under false pretences to make a covenant on behalf of Israel with the Gibeonites, they refused to break their promise because the word had been given. The words of blessing and curse were believed to have in themselves the power of self-realization. A curse was a means of destruction, not a mere realization (see Nu **22–24,** Balaam's curses; Jgs **5** 23; Job **31**). In a similar way the word of blessing was believed to insure its own realization. In Gen **48** 8–22 the greatness of Ephraim and Manasseh is ascribed to the blessing of Jacob upon them (see further Ex **12** 32; Jgs **17** 2; 2 S **21** 3). It is no doubt to be understood that the witch of Endor raised Samuel from the dead by the recitation of some magical formula (1 S **28** 7 ff).

The uttering of the *tetragrammaton* was at a very early time (at latest 300 BC) believed to be magically potent, and hence its ordinary use was forbidden, so that instead of Jeh, the Jews of the time, when the earliest part of the LXX was trd, used for this Divine name the appellative *'ădhōnāi*= "Lord." In a similar way among the Jews of post-Bib. and perhaps of even Bib. times, the pronunciation of the Aaronic blessing (Nu **6** 24–26) was supposed to possess great efficacy and to be a means of certain good to the person or persons involved. Evil spirits were exorcised by Jews of Paul's day through the use of the name of the Lord Jesus (Acts **19** 13). In the Talm (*Peṣāḥīm* 110*a*) it is an instruction that if a man meets a witch he should say, "May a pot of boiling dung be stuffed into your mouth, you ugly witch," and her power is gone.

For literature see AMULET.

T. WITTON DAVIES

CHARME, kär'mē (so RV; AV **Carme; Χαρμή,** *Charmḗ*): A Gr transliteration of Heb *ḥārim*. The name of a priestly family in the list of those who returned from the Exile (1 Esd **5** 25=Harim in Ezr **2** 39=Neh **7** 42).

CHARMIS, kär'mis (**Χάρμεις,** *Chármeis*, **Χαρμείς,** *Charmeís*, A, **Χαλμείς,** *Chalmeís*): The son of Melchiel, one of the three elders or rulers of the town of Bethulia (Jth **6** 15; **8** 10; **10** 6).

CHARRAN, kar'an (**Χαῤῥάν,** *Charrhán*): Gr form of HARAN (q.v.) (Acts **7** 2.4).

CHASE, chās. See HUNTING.

CHASEBA, kas'ē-ba (**Χασεβά,** *Chasebá*): The name of a family of temple-servants in the list of those who returned from Babylon (1 Esd **5** 31). The name is not given in the ∥ passages in Ezr and Neh.

CHASTE, chāst, **CHASTITY,** chas'ti-ti. See CRIMES; MARRIAGE.

CHASTENING, chās''n-ing, **CHASTISEMENT,** chas'tiz-ment: These two words corresponding to Heb מוּסָר, *mūṣār*, and Gr παιδεία, *paideía*, are distinguished in Eng. use, in that "chastisement" is applied to the infliction of pain, either as a punishment or for recalling to duty, while "chastening" is a wider term, indicating the discipline or training to which one is subjected, without, as in the other term, referring to the means employed to this end. The narrower term occurs in RV but once in the NT and then in its verbal form, Lk **23** 16: "I will therefore chastise him." AV uses it also in He **12** 8.

The meaning of the word *paideia* grows with the progress of revelation. Its full significance is unfolded in the NT, when reconciliation through Christ has brought into prominence the true fatherhood of God (He **12** 5.10). In the OT, where it occurs about 40 times, the radical meaning is that simply of training, as in Dt **8** 5: "As a man chasteneth his son, so Jeh thy God chasteneth thee." But, as in a dispensation where the distinguishing feature is that of the strictest justice, retributive punishment becomes not only an important, but a controlling factor in the training, as in Lev **26** 28: "I will chastise you seven times for your sins." In this sense, it is used of chastisements inflicted by man even unjustly: "My father chastised you with whips, but I will chastise you with scorpions" (1 K **12** 11). As, therefore, the thought of the suffering inflicted, or that of the end toward which it is directed, preponderates, the Psalmist can pray: "Neither chasten me in thy hot displeasure" (Ps **6** 1), and take comfort in the words: "Blessed is the man whom thou chastenest" (Ps **94** 12). Hence it is common in both AV and RV to find the Heb *mūṣār*, and Gr *paideia* trd as "instruction." Illustrations are most numerous in Prov.

In the NT the Gr *paideia* is used with a variety similar to its corresponding Heb in the OT. Examples of the fundamental idea, viz. that of "training," are found in such passages as Acts **7** 22; **22** 3, where Moses and Paul are said to have been "instructed," and 2 Tim **3** 16, where Scripture is said to be "profitable . . . . for instruction" (cf 1 Tim **1** 20; 2 Tim **2** 25; Tit **2** 12; Rom **2** 20). A similar, but not identical, thought, is found in Eph **6** 4: "Nurture them in the chastening and admonition of the Lord." But when *paideia* is described as bringing pain, the mystery of suffering, which in the OT is most fully treated in the Book of Job, at last finds its explanation. The child of God realizes that he cannot be beneath God's wrath, and hence that the chastening which he endures is not destructive, but corrective (1 Cor **10** 13; **11** 32; 2 Cor **6** 9; Rev **3** 19). In He **12** 5–11, such consolation is afforded, not, as in the above passages, by incidental allusions, but by a full argument upon the basis of Prov **3** 11 f, an OT text that has depth and richness that can be understood and appropriated only by those who through Christ have learned to recognize the Omnipotent Ruler of heaven and earth, as their loving and considerate Father. On the basis of this passage, a distinction is often drawn between punishment and chastisement; the former, as an act of justice, revealing wrath, and the latter, as an act of mercy, love. Since to them that are in Christ Jesus, there is no condemnation (Rom **8** 1) they can suffer no punishment, but only chastisement. Where there is guilt, there is punishment; but where guilt has been removed, there can be no punishment. There being no degrees of justification, no one can be forgiven in part, with a partial guilt still set to his account for which he must yet give a reckoning, either here or hereafter. If, then, all the righteousness of Christ belongs to him, and no sin whatever remains to be forgiven, either in whole or in part, all life's sorrows are remedial agencies against danger and to train for the kingdom of heaven. H. E. Jacobs

CHATTER, chat'ẽr (צָפַף, *çāphaph*): This word, which means to "peep," "twitter," or "chirp," as small birds do, is tr[d] "chatter" only in Isa **38** 14, "Like a swallow or a crane, so did I chatter." See Chirp.

CHAVAH, kā'va (LXX **Ζωή,** *Zōḗ*): A transliteration of the Heb חַוָּה, *ḥawwāh* or *ḥavvāh*, which means "life giver," "living," and appears in our Eng. VSS as Eve (Gen **3** 20 AVm).

CHEBAR, kē'bär (כְּבָר, k^e*bhār*, "joining" [Young], "length" [Strong]; **Χοβάρ,** *Chobár*): The river by the side of which his first vision was vouchsafed to Ezekiel (**1** 1). It is described as in "the land of the Chaldaeans," and is not, therefore, to be sought in northern Mesopotamia. This rules out the Habor, the mod. Chabour, with which it is often identified. The two names are radically distinct: חָבוֹר could not be derived from כְּבָר. One of the great Bab canals is doubtless intended. Hilprecht found mention made of (*nāru*) *kabaru*, one of these canals large enough to be navigable, to the E. of Nippur, "in the land of the Chaldaeans." This "great canal" he identifies with the mod. *shaṭṭ en-Nīl*, in which probably we should recognize the ancient Chebar. W. Ewing

CHECK (מוּסָר, *mūşār*): Occurs in Job **20** 3 AV, "I have heard the check of my reproach" (RV "the reproof which putteth me to shame"), i.e. a check or reproof, such as that which closes the last speech of Job (ch **19**), and intended to put Zophar to shame.

CHECKER-WORK, chek'ẽr-wûrk (**NETWORK**) (שְׂבָכָה, s^e*bhākhāh*): This was a kind of ornamentation used on the tops of the pillars of Jachin and Boaz before the porch of the Temple (1 K **7** 17). Its exact form is not known. See Temple. For "a broidered coat" (Ex **28** 4 AV), RV gives "a coat of checker work." See Broidered; Embroidery.

CHEDORLAOMER, ked-ŏr-lȧ-ō'mẽr, ked-ôr-lā'o-mẽr (כְּדָרְלָעֹמֶר, k^e*dhorlā'ōmer;* **Χοδολλογόμορ,** *Chodollogómor*):

1. Was He the Elamite King Kudur-laḫgumal?
2. Kudur-laḫgumal and the Babylonians
3. The Son of Eri-Ekua
4. Durmaḫ-îlâni, Tudḫul(a) and Kudur-laḫmal
5. The Fate of Sinful Rulers
6. The Poetical Legend
7. Kudur-laḫgumal's Misdeeds
8. The Importance of the Series

The name of the Elamite overlord with whom Amraphel, Arioch and Tidal marched against Sodom and Gomorrah, and the other cities of the plain (Gen **14** 1 ff). The Gr (LXX) form of the name is *Chodollogomor*, implying a different vocalization, the assimilation of *r* with *l*, and the pronunciation of *'o* as *gho* (*Codorlaghomer*). This suggests that the Elamite form, in cuneiform, would be *Kudur-lagamar*, the second element being the name of a god, and the whole therefore meaning "servant of La'omer" (Lagamar), or the like. A Bab deity worshipped at Dilmu, *Lagamal*, may be the same as the Elamite *Lagamar*. This name is not found in the cuneiform inscriptions, unless it be, as is possible, the fancifully-written *Kudur-laḫ[gu]mal* (or *Kodorlaḫgomal*) of three late Bab legends, one of which is in poetical form. Besides this Elamite ruler, two of these tablets mention also a certain *Eri-Aku* or *Eri-Akua*, son of *Durmaḫ-îlâni*, and one of them refers to *Tudḫul[a]* or Tidal. See Eri-aku, 4.

1. Was He the Elamite King Kudur-laḫgumal?

Objections have been made to the identification of Chedorlaomer with the Kudur-laḫ[gu]mal of these texts, some Assyriologists having flatly denied the possibility, while others expressed the opinion that, though these names were respectively those with which they have been identified, they were not the personages referred to in Gen **14**, and many have refrained from expressing an opinion at all. The main reason for the identification of Kudur-laḫ[gu]mal[?] with Chedorlaomer is its association with the names Eri-Eaku and Tudḫul[a] found on two of the documents. No clear references to the expedition against the Cities of the Plain, however, have been found in these texts.

2. Kudur-laḫgumal and the Babylonians

The longer of the two prose compositions (*Brit. Mus.*, Sp. II, 987) refers to the bond of heaven [extended?] to the four regions, and the fame which he (Merodach?) set for [the Elamites] in Babylon, the city of [his] glory. So [?the gods], in their faithful (or everlasting) counsel, decreed to Kudur-laḫgumal, king of Elam, [their favor?]. He came down, and [performed] what was good to them, and exercised dominion in Babylon, the city of Kar-Duniaš (Babylonia). When in power, however, he acted in a way which did not please the Babylonians, for he loved the winged fowl, and favoured the dog which crunched the bone. "What(?) king of Elam was there who had (ever) [shown favor to?] the shrine of Ê-saggil?" (Ê-sagila, the great temple of Belus at Babylon).

3. The Son of Eri-Ekua

A letter from Durmaḫ-îlâni son of Eri-Ekua (?Arioch) is at this point quoted, and possibly forms the justification for the sentences which had preceded, giving, as they do. reasons for the intervention of the native ruler. The mutilation of the inscription, however, makes the sense and sequence very difficult to follow.

4. Durmaḫ-îlâni, Tudḫul(a) and Kudur-laḫmal

The less perfect fragment (Sp. III, 2) contains, near the beginning, the word *ḫammu*, and if this be, as Professor F. Hommel has suggested, part of the name Ḫammurabi (Amraphel), it would in all probability place the identification of Kudur-laḫgumal(?) with Chedorlaomer beyond a doubt. This inscription states, that Merodach, in the faithfulness of his heart, caused the ruler not supporting [the temples of Babylonia] to be slain with the sword. The name of Durmaḫ-îlâni then occurs, and it seems to be stated of him that he carried off spoil, and Babylon and the temple Ê-saggil were inundated. He, however, was apparently murdered by his son, and old and young [were slain] with the sword. Then came Tudḫul[a] or Tidal, son of Gazzā[ni?], who also carried off spoil, and again the waters devastated Babylon and Ê-saggil. But to all appearance Tudḫul[a], in his turn, was overtaken by his fate, for "his son shattered his head with the weapon of his hands." At this point there is a reference to Elam, to the city Aḫḫêa(?), and to the land of Rabbātu^m, which he (? the king of Elam) had spoiled. Whether this refers to some expedition to Palestine or not is uncertain, and probably unlikely, as the next phrase speaks of devastation inflicted in Babylonia. But an untoward fate overtook this ruler likewise,

5. The Fate of Sinful Rulers

for Kudur-laḫmal (=laḫgumal), his son, pierced his heart with the steel sword of his girdle. All these references to violent deaths are apparently cited to show the dreadful end of certain kings, "lords of sin," with whom Merodach, the king of the gods, was angry.

The third text is of a poetical nature, and refers several times to "the enemy, the Elamite"—apparently Kudur-laḫgu[mal]. In this

6. The Poetical Legend

noteworthy inscription, which, even in its present imperfect state, contains 78 lines of wedge-written text, the destruction wrought by him is related in detail. He cast down the door (of the temple) of Ištar; entered Du-maḫ, the place where the fates were declared (see BABEL, BABYLON), and told his warriors to take the spoil and the goods of the temple. He was afraid, however, to proceed to extremities, as the god of the place

7. Kudur-laḫgumal's Misdeeds

"flashed like lightning, and shook the [holy] places." The last two paragraphs state that he set his face to go down to Tiamtu (the seacoast; see CHALDEA), whither Ibi-Tutu, apparently the king of that district, had hastened, and founded a pseudo-capital. But the Elamite seems afterward to have taken his way north again, and after visiting Borsippa near Babylon, traversed "the road of darkness—the road to Mešku" (?Mesech). He destroyed the palace, subdued the princes, carried off the spoil of all the temples and took the goods [of the people] to Elam. At this point the text breaks off.

Where these remarkable inscriptions came from there ought to be more of the same nature, and if these be found, the mystery of Chedor-

8. The Importance of the Series

laomer and Kudur-laḫgumal will probably be solved. At present it can only be said, that the names all point to the early period of the Elamite rulers called Kudurides, before the land of Tiamtu or Tâmdu was settled by the Chaldaeans. Evidently it was one of the heroic periods of Babylonian history, and some scribe of about 350 BC had collected together a number of texts referring to it. All three tablets were purchased (not excavated) by the British Museum, and reached that institution through the same channel. See the *Journal of the Victoria Institute*, 1895–96, and Professor Sayce in *PSBA* (1906), 193 ff, 241 ff; (1907), 7 ff. T. G. PINCHES

CHEEK, chēk, **CHEEKBONE,** chēk'bōn:

(1) לְחִי, *lᵉḥī; σιαγών, siagṓn,* "the jaw," "jawbone," "side of the face." The Heb word denotes originally freshness and rounded softness of the cheek, a sign of beauty in youth and maiden (Cant **1** 10; **5** 13). The oriental guards with jealous care his cheek from touch or defilement, therefore a stroke on the cheek was, and is to this day, regarded as an act of extreme rudeness of behavior, a deadly affront. Our Saviour, however, teaches us in Mt **5** 39 and Lk **6** 29 that even this insult is to be ignored and pardoned.

Jawbones of animals have been frequently used as tools and weapons among primitive people. We see this sufficiently proven from cave deposits in many parts of the world, and from recent ethnological researches, esp. in Australia. In the light of this evidence it is interesting to note that Samson used a jawbone of an ass with success against his enemies the Philis (Jgs **15** 15).

(2) מַלְקוֹחַ, *malḳōaḥ* (Ps **22** 15), is a dual form indicative of the two jaws, to which a parched tongue seems to cleave.

(3) מְתַלְּעָה, *methallᵉ'āh* (Job **29** 17), better "cheek teeth" (q.v.). H. L. E. LUERING

CHEEK TEETH (מְתַלְּעָה, *methallᵉ'āh,* transposed from מַלְתָּעָה, *maltā'āh* [only in Ps **58** 6], lit. "the biter," "crusher," "molar," "jaw-teeth," "great teeth" [Job **29** 17 m; Joel **1** 6]).

Figurative: The word is used as a synonym of reckless strength and cruelty.

CHEER, chēr, **CHEERFULNESS,** chēr'fo͝ol-nes: The Eng. word "cheer" meant (1) originally face, countenance (Gr *κάρα, kára,* "head," through OFr. *chere,* "face"), (2) then the expression on the face, esp. (3) the expression of good spirits, and finally (4) good spirits, without any reference to the facial expression. The noun "cheer" in EV is only found with adj. "good" (except 1 Esd **9** 54, "great cheer"), the word not having quite lost its earlier neutral character (*any* face expression, whether joyous or otherwise). In OT, טוֹב, *ṭōbh,* is tr[d] "cheer," "let thy heart cheer thee" (see GOOD); שָׂמֵחַ, *sāmēaḥ,* "to rejoice" is so tr[d] in Dt **24** 5, "shall cheer his wife" (AV "cheer up his wife"), and Jgs **9** 13, "wine, which cheereth God [*'ĕlōhīm*] and man." The phrase "of good cheer" occurs in OT in Job **9** 27 (AV "comfort"); in Apoc, 1 Esd **9** 54; Wisd **18** 6; Bar **4** 5.30; Sir **18** 32 AV (RV "luxury"); in NT for Gr *euthuméō, eúthumos,* in Acts **27** 22.25.36, and for *tharséō* in Mt **9** 2.22 (AV "comfort"); **14** 27; Mk **6** 50; **10** 49 (RV; "comfort" in AV); Jn **16** 33; Acts **23** 11. "Cheer" as vb. trans. occurs in Eccl **11** 9; Deut **24** 5; Jgs **9** 13.

Cheerful occurs in Prov **15** 13.15 (AV "merry"); Zec **8** 19; **9** 17 AV; Sir **30** 25; 2 Cor **9** 7.

Cheerfully, Acts **24** 10.

Cheerfulness, Rom **12** 8. D. MIALL EDWARDS

CHEESE, chēz. See FOOD; MILK.

CHELAL, kē'lal (כְּלָל, *kᵉlāl,* "perfection"): One of the *bᵉnē Paḥath-Mō'ābh* who took "strange wives" (Ezr **10** 30).

CHELCIAS, kel'si-as. See HELKIAS; HILKIAH.

CHELLIANS, kel'i-anz: The people of "Chellus" (Jth **2** 23) (q.v.).

CHELLUH, kel'ū. See CHELUHI.

CHELLUS, kel'us (**Χελλούς,** *Chelloús*), a place named (Jth **1** 9) among those W. of the Jordan to which Nebuchadnezzar sent his summons. It is mentioned along with "Kades," and as it lay N. of the "children of Ishmael" it may with some probability be taken as lying S.W. of Jerus. It has been conjectured that it may be Chalutzah (Reland, *Pal,* 717), a place under the form Elusa well known to the ancient geographers.

CHELOD, kē'lod (**Χελεούδ,** *Cheleoúd,* **Χελεούλ,** *Cheleoúl*): In Jth **1** 6 it is said that "many nations of the sons of C. assembled themselves to the battle." They are mentioned as obeying the summons of Nebuchadnezzar to his war against Arphaxad. No very probable suggestion has been made as to the meaning of Chelod.

CHELUB, kē'lub:

(1) כְּלוּב, *kᵉlūbh,* father of Mehir (1 Ch **4** 11); the name is probably a variation of Caleb. Well-

hausen (*De gentibus et familiis Judaeis*) reads כָּלֵב בֶּן חֶזְרוֹן, *kālēbh ben ḥezrōn*.

(2) Father of Ezri (1 Ch **27** 26), one of the officers of David. See Genealogy.

CHELUBAI, ke-lōō'bī (כְּלוּבַי, *kelūbhāy*): Another form of Caleb used in 1 Ch **2** 9; cf **2** 18.42. Caleb is here described as the brother of Jerahmeel, and son of Hezron, a remote ancestor, instead of as the son of Jephunneh. See Caleb.

CHELUHI, kel'ōō-hī (כְּלוּהִי, *kelūhī*, Kt.; כְּלוּהוּ, *kelūhū*, Ḳerē; RVm Cheluhu; AV **Chelluh**): Mentioned in the list of persons with foreign wives (Ezr **10** 35=1 Esd **9** 34).

CHEMARIM, kem'a-rim (כְּמָרִים, *kemārīm*, a pl. whose sing. *kōmer* is not found in the OT): Occurs only once in the text of EV (Zeph **1** 4, AV **Chemarims**), though the Heb word is found also in 2 K **23** 5 (EV "idolatrous priests") and Hos **10** 5 (EV "priests," EVm, however, having "Chemarim" in both places). Some regard the word as an interpolation in Zeph **1** 4, since the LXX omits it and its presence disturbs the parallelism. The word, which is of Aram. origin (*kumra*, priest), is used in the OT only in an unfavorable sense, its origin and associations naturally suggesting Syr affinities. In the Syr, however, no such connotation is involved. In the Pesh version of the OT it is used indifferently of idolatrous priests and of priests of Jeh, while in the same version of the NT it is used of the Levitical priests and of Our Lord (e.g. He **2** 17; **3** 1; **4** 14.15, and often) and in Acts **19** 35 it is the rendering of *neōkóros* (RV "temple-keeper," AV "worshipper"). The question of the root idea of the word remains unsettled. The traditional supposition, which finds some support even among modern scholars, is that the verbal form means "to be black," the priests being supposed to have been clad in black. But it is doubtful whether the root had this meaning. Another conjecture takes the root to mean "to be sad," the priest being a man of a sad countenance, an ascetic. Cheyne would relate the word to the Assyr *kummaru*, having the sense of "a clean vesture." It is at all events probable that the priests, both in Israel and in the surrounding nations, employed white vestments, rather than black, when in the performance of their official functions. According to Mish, *Middōth*, v.4, a Levitical priest who had become disqualified for service put on black garments and departed, while the others put on white garments and went in and ministered. The reference to the Baal worship in 2 K **10** 22 seems more congruous with this view; hence probably black-robed priests (Chemarim) of Baal and the unfaithful priests of Jeh shall be cut off together. G. A. Smith (*BTP*, II, 56) reads "the priestlings with the priests."

J. R. Van Pelt

CHEMOSH, kē'mosh (כְּמוֹשׁ, *kemōsh*; Χαμώς, *Chamṓs*):

1. Moabites the People of Chemosh
2. Solomon and Chemosh Worship
3. Josiah Putting Down Chemosh Worship
4. Chemosh and Ammonites
5. Moabite Stone
6. Mesha''s Inscription and OT
7. Chemosh in the Inscription
8. Parallels between Inscription and OT Record
9. Ethical Contrast

Literature

The national God of the Moabites, as Baal of the Zidonians, or Milcom (Moloch, Malcam) of the Ammonites. The Moabites are apostrophized in an old Heb song as the "people of Chemosh" (Nu **21** 29). Jeremiah in his oracle of doom upon Moab has recourse to the same old song and calls the people "the people of Chemosh." The impotence of the god to deliver his people is described by the prophet in figures representing him as going into captivity with them, his priests and princes together, and Moab is to be ashamed of him as Israel was of the Golden Calf of Bethel, which did not avail to save the Northern Kingdom from the conquering Assyr power (Jer **48** 7.13.46).

1. Moabites the People of Chemosh

For Chemosh, "the abomination of Moab," as for Moloch, "the abomination of the children of Ammon," Solomon, under the influence of his idolatrous wives, built a high place in the mount before Jerus (1 K **11** 7). It was natural that they should desire to worship still after the manner of the gods of their native land, but although the effect of all this was seen in the moral and spiritual deterioration of Solomon himself there is no indication that the immoralities and cruelties associated with such worship were then practised in Jerus. In the days of Ahaz and Manasseh, even as early as the days of Abijam of Judah, they were (1 K **15** 12.13). Josiah found these abominations of alien worship, which had been introduced by Solomon and added to by Ahaz and Manasseh, flourishing when he came to the throne. Moved by the prohibitions of the Book of the Law (Dt **12** 29–31; **18** 10), Josiah pulled down and defiled the high places and the altars, and in order to make a clean sweep of the idolatrous figures, "he brake in pieces the pillars," or obelisks, "and cut down the Asherim," or sacred poles, "and filled their places with the bones of men" (2 K **23** 1–20).

2. Solomon and Chemosh Worship

3. Josiah Putting Down Chemosh Worship

There is one passage where Chemosh is designated the god of the Ammonites (Jgs **11** 24). Jephthah is disputing the right of the Ammonites to invade territory which belongs to Israel because Jeh has given it to them by conquest. And he asks: 'Shouldst thou not possess the territory of those whom Chemosh, thy god, dispossesses, and we the territory of all whom Jeh, our god, dispossesses?' It may be that he is called here the god of the Ammonites by a mere oversight of the historian; or that Moab and Ammon being kindred nations descended from a common ancestor, Lot, Chemosh may in a sense belong to both. We notice, however, that Jephthah's argument in meeting the claim preferred by the king of Ammon passes on to Israel's relation to the Moabites and makes mention only of well-known Moabite cities. Chemosh is accordingly named because of his association with Moab, the cities of which are being spoken of, although strictly and literally Milcom should have been named in an appeal addressed as a whole to the Ammonites (vs 12–28; cf Moore ad loc.).

4. Chemosh and Ammonites

The discovery of the Moabite Stone in 1868 at Dibon has thrown light upon Chemosh and the relations of Moab to its national god. The monument, which is now one of the most precious treasures of the Louvre in Paris, bears an inscription which is the oldest specimen of Sem alphabetic writing extant, commemorating the successful effort made about 860 or 850 BC by Mesha', king of Moab, to throw off the yoke of Israel. We know from the OT record that Moab had been reduced to subjection by David (2 S **8** 2); that it paid a heavy tribute to Ahab, king of Israel (2 K **3** 4); and that, on the death of Ahab, Mesha' its king rebelled against Israelite rule (2 K **3** 5). Not till the reign of Jehoram was any

5. Moabite Stone

effort made to recover the lost dominion. The king of Israel then allied himself with the kings of Judah and Edom, and marching against Moab by the way of the Red Sea, inflicted upon Mesha' a defeat so decisive that the wrath of his god, Chemosh, could be appeased only by the sacrifice of his son (2 K **3** 6 ff).

The historical situation described in the OT narrative is fully confirmed by Mesha''s inscription.

6. Mesha''s Inscription and the OT

There are, however, divergences in detail. In the Book of K the revolt of Mesha' is said to have taken place after the death of Ahab. The inscription implies that it must have taken place by the middle of Ahab's reign. The inscription implies that the subjection of Moab to Israel had not been continuous from the time of David, and says that 'Omri, the father of Ahab, had reasserted the power of Israel and had occupied at least a part of the land.

It is with what the inscription says of Chemosh that we are chiefly concerned. On the monument

7. Chemosh in the Inscription

the name appears twelve times. Mesha' is himself the son of Chemosh, and it was for Chemosh that he built the high place upon which the monument was found. He built it because among other reasons Chemosh had made him to see his desire upon them that hated him. It was because Chemosh was angry with his land that 'Omri afflicted Moab many days. 'Omri had taken possession of the land of Medeba and Israel dwelt in it his days and half his son's days, but Chemosh restored it in Mesha''s days. Mesha' took 'Ataroth which the king of Israel had built for himself, slew all the people of the city, and made them a gazing-stock to Chemosh and to Moab. Mesha' brought thence the altar-hearth of Dodo, and dragged it before Chemosh in Kerioth. By command of Chemosh, Mesha' attacked Nebo and fought against Israel, and after a fierce struggle he took the place, slaying the inhabitants *en masse*, 7,000 men and women and maidservants, devoting the city to 'Ashtor-Chemosh and dragging the altar vessels of Jeh before Chemosh. Out of Jahaz, too, which the king of Israel had built, Chemosh drove him before Mesha'. At the instigation of Chemosh, Mesha' fought against Horonaim, and, although the text is defective in the closing paragraph, we may surmise that Chemosh did not fail him but restored it to his dominions.

Naturally enough there is considerable obscurity in local and personal allusions. Dodo may have

8. Parallels between Inscription and OT Record

been a local god worshipped by the Israelites E. of the Jordan. Ashtor-Chemosh may be a compound divinity of a kind not unknown to Sem mythology, Ashtor representing possibly the Phoen Ashtoreth. What is of importance is the recurrence of so many phrases and expressions applied to Chemosh which are used of Jeh in the OT narratives. The religious conceptions of the Moabites reflected in the inscription are so strikingly like those of the Israelites that if only the name of Jeh were substituted for that of Chemosh we might think we were reading a chapter of the Books of K. It is not in the inscriptions, however, but in the OT narrative that we find a reference to the demand of Chemosh for human sacrifice. "He took his eldest son," says the Heb annalist, "that should have reigned in his stead, and offered him for a burnt-offering upon the wall. And there was great wrath against Israel: and they departed from him, and returned to their own land" (2 K **3** 27). This appears to indicate that the Israelites had to give up their purpose to fasten the yoke of bondage again upon Mesha' and that they returned empty-handed to their own land. But this fortunate result for Moab was due to the favor of Chemosh, and in particular to the human sacrifice by which he was propitiated.

If we find in these representations of Chemosh in the OT narrative and in Mesha''s inscription a

9. Ethical Contrast

striking similarity to the Heb conception of Jeh, we cannot fail to notice the lack of the higher moral and spiritual elements supplied to the religion of Israel by the prophets and indeed from Moses and Abraham downward. "Chemosh," says W. Baudissin, "is indeed the ruler of his people whom he protects as Yahweh the Israelites, whom he chastises in his indignation, and from whom he accepts horrible propitiatory gifts. But of a God of grace whose long-suffering leads back even the erring to Himself, of a Holy God to whom the offering of a pure and obedient heart is more acceptable than bloody sacrifices, of such a God as is depicted in Israel's prophets and sweet singers there is no trace in the Moabite picture of Chemosh. While Mesha' is represented as offering up his own son in accordance with the stern requirements of his religion, OT law-givers and prophets from the beginning condemned human sacrifice" (*RE*³, art. "Kemosh").

Literature.—*RE*³, art. "Kemosh"; Cooke, *Text-Book of North-Semitic Inscriptions*, "*Moabite Stone*," 1–14; W. Robertson Smith, *Prophets of Israel*, 49 ff; Sayce, *HCM*, 364 ff.

T. Nicol

CHENAANAH, kē-nā'a-na (כְּנַעֲנָה, *k^e na'ănāh*, fem. form of "Canaan," though others explain it as "toward Canaan"): The name of two men:

(1) The fourth-named of the seven sons of Bilham, son of Jediael, of the tribe of Benjamin, a leading warrior in the time of David (1 Ch **7** 10).

(2) Father of the false prophet Zedekiah, who encouraged Ahab against Micaiah (1 K **22** 11.24; 2 Ch **18** 10.23).

CHENANI, kē-nā'nī (כְּנָנִי, *k^e nānī*, "planted"): One of the names mentioned in Neh **9** 4, in connection with the constitution of "congregation." If the names represent houses or families, eight Levitical houses probably sang some well-known psalm on this occasion. If they are names of individual representatives, they were probably deputed to recite or chant some special prayer in order to lead the worship of the people.

CHENANIAH, ken-a-nī'a (כְּנַנְיָהוּ, *k^e nanyāhū*, and כְּנַנְיָה, *k^e nanyāh*, lit. "established by God"): Chief of the Levites who was over "the songs," or "the carrying" (viz. "of the ark") from the house of Obed-edom to Jerus (1 Ch **15** 22.27; **26** 29).

CHEPHAR-AMMONI, kē-fär-am'ō-nī (AV **Chephar-haammoni**; כְּפַר הָעַמּוֹנִי, *k^e phar hā'ammōnī;* B, **Κεφειρὰ καὶ Μονεί**, *Kepheirá kaí Moneí;* A, **Καφηραμμίν**, *Kaphērammín*, "village of the Ammonites"): A place in the territory of Benjamin (Josh **18** 24). It may be identical with *Kefr 'Āna*, a ruined site about two miles to the N.E. of Bethel.

CHEPHAR-HAAMONI, kē-fär-ha-am'ō-nī. See Chephar-ammoni.

CHEPHIRAH, ke-fī'ra (הַכְּפִירָה, *ha-k^e phīrāh;* B, **Καφειρά**, *Kapheirá* [Josh **9**]; A has *Chepheirá*, B has **καὶ Φειρά**, *kaí Pheirá* [Josh **18**]): One of the cities of the Hivites who by guile made alliance with Israel (Josh **9** 17). It was in the lot of Benjamin (**18** 26), and was reoccupied after the return from Babylon (Ezr **2** 25; Neh **7** 29). It is represented by the modern *Kefīreh*, to the S.W. of Gibeon, and N. of *Ḳaryat el-'Anab*. It stands on high ground, with many ancient remains.

CHERAN, kē'ran (כְּרָן, *k^{e}rān*): A Horite clan-name, occurring in the genealogy of Seir, the Horite (Gen **36** 26), and in the ‖ list in 1 Ch **1** 41. Dillmann derives it from *kar*, "a lamb."

CHERETHITES, ker'ē-thīts (כְּרֵתִים, הַכְּרֵתִי, *k^{e}rēthīm, ha-k^{e}rēthī;* **Χελεθί,** *Chelethí* "executioners," "life-guardsmen"): A people in South Pal whose territory bordered upon that of Judah (1 S **30** 14). In ver 16 this land is apparently identified with that of the Philis. In Ezk **25** 16 the Philis and the Cherethites are threatened together; while in Zeph **2** 5 the Cherethites are evidently the dwellers in "the land of the Philis," "the inhabitants of the seacoast." LXX in both Ezk and Zeph renders the name "Cretans." The translators may have been "guided only by the sound." But Zeus Cretagenes in Gaza suggests a connection with the island of Crete. See, however, CAPHTOR. It may be taken as certain that the Cherethites were a Phili clan. In conjunction with the Pelethites they are frequently named as forming the guard of David (2 S **8** 18, etc). It was the custom of many ancient monarchs to have a guard of foreign mercenaries. W. EWING

CHERISH, cher'ish (סָכַן, *ṣākhan;* **θάλπω,** *thálpō*): *Ṣākhan*, "to act the friend," "to be useful," is tr^{d} "cherish" (1 K **1** 2.4); *thalpō*, "to warm," "to make warm," "to foster" (Eph **5** 29), said of the regard the husband should have for his wife, even as his own flesh which he "nourisheth and *cherisheth*, even as Christ also the church," and in 1 Thess **2** 7, of Paul amongst his converts, "as when a nurse cherisheth her own children."

CHERITH, kē'rith, **THE BROOK** (נַחַל כְּרִית, *naḥal k^{e}rīth;* **Χειμάῤῥους Χοῤῥάθ,** *Cheimárrhous Chorrháth*): The place where Elijah hid and was miraculously fed, after announcing the drought to Ahab

Traditional Site of Brook Cherith.

(1 K **17** 3). It is described as being "before Jordan." As the prophet was with Ahab when he received this direction, "before" would naturally be only on the west side of Jordan. Elijah certainly would not be sent to Gilead, where Ahab would be sure to search.

CHERUB, kē'rub (כְּרוּב, *k^{e}rūbh;* **Χερούβ,** *Cheroúb,* **Χαρούβ,** *Charoúb*): A place in Babylonia from which people whose genealogies had fallen into confusion went up at the return from exile (Ezr **2** 59; Neh **7** 61); unidentified. In 1 Esd **5** 36 we read "Charaathalan leading them, and Allar," a phrase that seems to have arisen through confusion of the names in the passages cited above.

CHERUBIC, che-rōō'bik, **FORMS IN THE CONSTELLATIONS.** See ASTRONOMY.

CHERUBIM, cher'ū-bim, cher'ŏŏ-bim (כְּרוּבִים, *k^{e}rūbhīm*, pl. of cherub, כְּרוּב, *k^{e}rūbh*): Through the influence of the Sept, "cherubim" was used in the earlier Eng. VSS, also as a sing., hence the pl. was made to sound "cherubims." The etymology of the word cannot be ascertained.

1. As Guardians of Paradise

In Gen **3** 24 the cherubim are placed by God, after the expulsion of Adam from the garden of Eden, at the east thereof, together with the flaming sword "to keep the way of the tree of life." In their function as guardians of Paradise the cherubim bear an analogy to the winged bulls and lions of Babylonia and Assyria, colossal figures with human faces standing guard at the entrance of temples (and palaces), just as in Egypt the approaches to the sanctuaries are guarded by sphinxes. But the Bab colossi go by the name of *lamassu*, or *shedu;* no designation at all approaching the Heb *k^{e}rūbh* has so far been found in the Assyr language. Nor are thus named the winged figures, half human and half animal, which in Bab and Pers art are found on both sides of the "sacred tree." Thus a Bab origin of the Heb cherubim is neither proved nor disproved. If we look for further analogies which, of course, do not indicate a borrowing on the part of the Hebrews, we may mention the fabulous griffins (*γρύπες, grúpes*), usually represented as having the heads and wings of an eagle and the body and hind quarters of a lion; they were believed by the Greeks to inhabit Scythia, and to keep jealous watch over the gold of that country.

2. The Garden as the Abode of the Gods

If we read between the lines of the Paradise account in Gen (cf **3** 8), the garden of Eden, the primeval abode of man, reveals itself as more than that: it was apparently the dwelling-place of God. In the polytheistic story of the creation of the world and early life of man, which, while in several respects analogous (cf **3** 22), is devoid of the more spiritual notions of Hebraism, the garden was the abode of the gods who alone had access to the tree of life from the fruit of which they derived their immortality. Adam, before the fall, is conceived as a superhuman being; for while he is forbidden to taste of the fruit of the tree of knowledge, the way to immortality is open to him; for it is only after transgressing the Divine command that he merits death and becomes mortal. The choice of immortal innocence and mortal knowledge lay before him; he elected death with knowledge.

3. The Cherubim as Attendants of the Deity

The symbolical elements of the Paradise story are more patent in Ezk **28** 13 ff, where the fall of the king of Tyre is likened to that of primeval man. The garden is situated on a holy mountain of Elohim (=God to Ezekiel, but gods in the primitive source), the 'mountain of assembly' of Isa **14** 13, high above the stars in the recesses of the North. It is a wonderful place, adorned with all manner of precious stones. There man, perfect from the day he was created, resplendent with beauty, excelling in wisdom, walks among the fiery stones, like a cherub with outstretched wings. The cherubs are apparently the attendants of the Deity, beauteous angels, of whom man was to be one: but he fell from glory and was hurled from the sanctuary which he had polluted. Some of the angelic attendants of the Deity within are placed in Gen without, to do service as guardians of the unapproachable holy garden.

4. As Bearers of the Throne

As attendants of God, they bear the throne upon which He descends from His high abode. Thus in the description of a theophany in Ps **18**, we read:

> "He bowed the heavens also, and came down;
> And thick darkness was under his feet.
> And he rode upon a cherub, and did fly;
> Yea, he soared upon the wings of the wind"
> (vs 9 and 10).

Hence the Lord, or, as the fuller title goes, the Lord of Hosts, is repeatedly styled "He that sitteth [throned] above the cherubim" (Ps **80** 1; **99** 1; 1 S **4** 4, and elsewhere). There is certainly no trace here of bull figures: bulls do not fly. The underlying conception is, it seems, rather that of the storm cloud. Cf Ps **104** 3:

> "Who maketh the clouds his chariot;
> Who walketh upon the wings of the wind."

The Heb for "chariot" is רְכוּב, *r^ekhūbh*, a sort of inverted *k^erūbh*.

5. In the Vision of Ezekiel

But the function of the cherubim as bearers and movers of the Divine throne is brought out most clearly in the vision of Ezekiel (ch **1**, with which cf ch **10**). In ch **1** the prophet designates them as "living creatures" (*ḥayyōth*); but upon hearing God's words addressed to the "man clothed in linen" (**10** 2) he perceives that the living creatures which he saw in the first vision were cherubim (ver 20); hence in **9** 3 the chariot or throne, from which the glory of God went up, is spoken of as a cherub. The following is a description in detail of the cherubim as seen by Ezekiel. They are represented as four living creatures, each with four faces, man, lion, ox (replaced in the ‖ ch by cherub), and eagle (**1** 10; **10** 14), having the figure and hands of men (**1** 5.8), and the feet of calves (ver 7). Each has four wings, two of which are stretched upward (ver 11), meeting above and sustaining the "firmament," that is, the bottom of the Divine throne (**1** 22; **10** 1), while two are stretched downward, conformable the one to the other, so as to cover their bodies (**1** 11.23). In appearance, the living creatures resemble coals of fire (cf **10** 2.6 f, where the "man clothed in linen" is bidden fill both his hands with coals of fire from between the cherubim), burning like torches, the fire flashing up and down among the creatures, a bright fire out of which lightning goes forth (**1** 13). Thus the creatures run and vanish as the appearance of a flash of lightning (ver 14). The cherubim do not turn as they change direction, but always go straight forward (**1** 9.17; **10** 11), as do the wheels of the cherubic chariot with rings full of eyes round about (**1** 18; **10** 12). The cherubim represent the spirit, or will, in the wheels: at the direction of the spirit, the wheels are lifted up from the bottom and the chariot moves upward (**1** 19 f; **10** 16 f). The cherubim are thus the moving force of the vehicle.

6. Relation to Seraphim and Other Angels

Ezekiel's cherubim are clearly related to the seraphim in Isaiah's inaugural vision (Isa **6**). Like the cherubim, the seraphim are the attendants on God as He is seated upon a throne high and exalted; they are also winged creatures: with twain they cover their faces, and with twain they cover their feet, and with twain they fly. Like the Levites in the sanctuary below, they sing a hymn of adoration: "Holy, holy, holy, is Jeh of hosts: the whole earth is full of his glory." In the Book of Enoch, the cherubim, seraphim, and ophannim (wheels), and all the angels of power constitute the "host of God," the guardians of His throne, the singers of praise ascribing blessedness to "the Lord of Spirits," with the archangel Gabriel at their head (see **20** 7; **40**; **61** 10 f; **71** 7). And so in the Jewish daily liturgy the seraphim, ophannim, and "living creatures" constitute the heavenly choir who, the elect ministers of the Living God, ready to do the will of their maker with trembling, intone in sweet harmony the Thrice-holy. In the Talm, the cherubim are represented as having the likeness of youths (with a fanciful etymology, כְּ+רוּב, *k^e+rūbh*, "like a youth"; *Ṣukk* 5*b*; *Ḥag* 13*b*), while, according to the Midr, they have no definite shape, but appear indifferently as men or women, or as spirits and angelic beings (*Gen rabbā'* **21**).

7. In Rev 4

The "four living creatures" of Rev **4** 6 ff are clearly modeled upon Ezekiel, with supplementary touches from Isaiah. Full of eyes before and behind, they are in the midst of the throne, and round about it. One resembles a lion, the other a calf, and the third a man, and the fourth a flying eagle. Each of the creatures has six wings. "They have no rest day and night, saying, Holy, holy, holy, is the Lord God, the Almighty, who was and who is and who is to come."

8. Ornamental Cherubim in the Temple of Solomon

In the temple of Solomon, two gigantic cherubic images of olive-wood plated with gold, ten cubits high, stood in the innermost sanctuary (the *d^ebhīr*) facing the door, whose wings, five cubits each, extended, two of them meeting in the middle of the room to constitute the throne, while two extended to the walls (1 K **6** 23–28; **8** 6.7; 2 Ch **3** 10–13; **5** 7.8). The Chronicler represents them as the chariot of the Lord (1 Ch **28** 18). There were also images of the cherubim carved on the gold-plated cedar planks which constituted the inner walls of the temple, and upon the olive-wood doors (1 K **6** 29.35; 2 Ch **3** 7); also on the bases of the portable lavers, interchanging with lions and oxen (1 K **7** 29–36). According to the Chronicler, they were also woven in the veil of the Holy of Holies (2 Ch **3** 14).

9. In the Temple of Ezekiel

Ezekiel represents the inner walls of the temple as carved with alternating palm trees and cherubim, each with two faces, the lion looking on one side, the man on the other (Ezk **41** 18–25).

10. In the Tabernacle

In the Tabernacle, there were two cherubim of solid gold upon the golden slab of the "lid," or "mercy-seat," facing each other, with wings outstretched above, so as to constitute a throne on which the glory of the Lord appeared, and from which He spake (Ex **25** 18–22; **37** 7–9; Nu **7** 89; He **9** 5). There were also cherubim woven into the texture of the inner curtain of the Tabernacle and the veil (Ex **26** 1.31; **36** 8.35). There were no cherubim in the temple of Herod, but the walls were painted with figures of them (see Talm *Yōmā'* 54*a*). In the times of Jos no one knew what the Scriptural cherubim looked like (*Ant*, VIII, iii, 3).

LITERATURE.—*BDB*, s.v.; *KAT*³, 529 f, and references; commentaries on Gen and Ezk.

MAX L. MARGOLIS

CHERUBIM. The cherubic forms in the constellation figures. See ASTRONOMY, II, 8.

CHESALON, kes'a-lon (כְּסָלוֹן, *k^eṣālōn;* **Χασλών**, *Chaslōn*, **Χασαλών**, *Chasalōn*): One of the cities on the N. boundary of Judah (Josh **15** 10). In the 4th cent. it was a "very large village." It is now *Keslā*, 2,087 ft. above sea-level, a small village perched on a mountain ridge to the S. of *Wady el Humār*. See *PEF*, III, 25, 26; Sh XVII.

CHESED, kē'sed, kes'ed (כֶּשֶׂד, *kasdīm;* **Χάσζαδ,** *Chászad*): One of the sons of Nahor and Milcah (Gen **22** 22); was probably the father of the Casdim. The early Bab form *Kašdu* appears in Assyr as Kaldu or Kaldû. EV follows the Assyr and Gr style of writing the name and uses Chaldees or Chaldaeans instead of Casdim. The Chaldaeans dwelt in the lower valley of the Euphrates, at the head of the Pers Gulf. Abram came from Ur of the Chaldees (Gen **11** 28.31; **15** 7; Neh **9** 7). In Job **1** 17 the Casdim are described as invading the land of Uz, the eldest brother of Chesed (Gen **22** 21.22). In the days of Nebuchadrezzar the Casdim overran Syria and Pal and carried the people of Judah in successive deportations into captivity (2 K **24** 1 f.10 ff; **25** 1 ff). In Dnl **2** 2.5 the Casdim are named with the magicians and astrologers as a learned class, skilled in interpretations. Casdim is sometimes used in Heb for the land of Chaldaea (Ezk **23** 15 f; **11** 24). JOHN RICHARD SAMPEY

CHESIL, kē'sil, kes'il (כְּסִיל, *kᵉṣīl;* A, **Χασείρ,** *Chaseír*): A town in the extreme S. of Judah named with Eltolad, Hormah and Ziklag (Josh **15** 30). The name does not occur again. In Josh **19** 4 it is replaced by Bethul (LXX Βαιθήλ, *Baithḗl*), and in 1 Ch **4** 30 by Bethuel. "Chesil" may have arisen from a misreading of the text.

CHESNUT, ches'nut. See CHESTNUT.

CHEST, chest (אֲרוֹן, *'ārōn,* גְּנָזִים, *gᵉnāzīm;* **κιβωτός,** *kibōtós*):

(1) The ark of the covenant in OT is invariably denoted by the word *'ārōn*, elsewhere rendered AV and RV "chest." See ARK.

(2) *'Ārōn* is also the word rendered "coffin" (Gen **50** 26: "and he was put in a coffin in E."). See COFFIN.

(3) In K and Ch (2 K **12** 9.10; 2 Ch **24** 8.10. 11) *'ārōn* stands uniformly for a money chest. It is the "chest" that Jehoiada, the priest, placed in the court "beside the altar" and "bored a hole in the lid of" that the priests might "put therein all the money that was brought into the house of Jeh" (2 K **12** 9); and "the chest" that King Joash commanded to be made and set "without at the gate of the house of Jeh" to receive "the tax that Moses the servant of God laid upon Israel" (2 Ch **24** 8.10.11). One feature is common to the thing meant in all these applications—the c. was rectangular in shape, and, most probably in every instance, made of wood.

(4) Jos (*Ant*, VI, 1.2) uses the equivalent of the word to denote the "coffer" (1 S **6** 8 ff EV), or small chest, in which the princes of Philistia deposited the gold mice.

(5) In NT times the "chests" that were provided in the court of the women, in the temple of Herod, to receive the various kinds of money gifts had the exceptional shape of a trumpet (if *Shᵉḳālīm*, vi.5 may be trusted)—wide at the bottom and gradually narrowing toward the top, hence called שׁוֹפָרוֹת, *shōphārōth*. It was into these that the Master was watching the multitude casting in their money when He saw the poor widow cast in her two mites (Mk **12** 41.42).

(6) In Ezk **27** 24, where the prophet is giving an inventory of the merchandise of Tyre, another word entirely is used (*gᵉnāzīm*), and it is rendered in AV and RV "chests" ("chests of rich apparel, bound with cords and made of cedar"). According to Cornill, Davidson, Smend and others this rendering is without sufficient support (see *DB* and comm. in loc.). GEO. B. EAGER

CHESTNUT, ches'nut, **TREE.** See PLANE TREE.

CHESULLOTH, ke-sul'ōth (הַכְּסֻלּוֹת, *ha-kᵉṣullōth;* B, **Χασαλώθ,** *Chasalōth,* A, **'Αχεσαλώθ,** *Achesalōth*): A town on the border of Zebulun (Josh **19** 18), the same as Chisloth-tabor (**19** 12). It is represented by the modern village *Iksāl* on the northern edge of Esdraelon, cir 3 miles W. of Mt. Tabor.

CHETH, khāth. See ḤETH.

CHETTIIM, ket'i-im, ket-ī'im (כִּתִּים, *kittīm*). See KITTIM.

CHEW, chōō, chū, **CUD** (מַעֲלֵה גֵרָה, *ma'ălēh gērāh*, lit. "bringing up" [ARVm], i.e. "chewing the cud," from *gārar*, "to roll," "ruminate"): One of the marks of cleanliness, in the sense of fitness for food, of a quadruped, given in Lev **11** 3 and Dt **14** 6, is the chewing of the cud. Among the animals considered clean are therefore included the ox, the sheep, the goat, the hart, the gazelle, the roebuck, the wild goat, the pygarg, the antelope and the chamois. Several of the forbidden animals are expressly named in the passages, e.g. the camel, the rock-badger, the hare and the swine. In addition to the distinctions between clean and unclean animals mentioned in the Bible, the Talm points out that the clean animals have no upper teeth, that their horns are either forked, or if not forked they are clear of splinters, notched with scales and round, and that certain portions of the meat of clean animals tear lengthwise as well as across. Many theories have been advanced as to the reasons for the distinctions with regard to the chewing of the cud and the cloven hoof. See *Jew Enc*, s.v. "Clean." The most obvious is that ruminating animals and animals without claws were apparently cleaner-feeding animals than the others.
NATHAN ISAACS

CHEZIB, kē'zib. See ACHZIB (1).

CHICKEN, chik''n, chik'in (AS *cīcen* or *cȳcen;* Lat *Gallus ferrugineus;* **ἀλεκτρυών,** *alektruōn*, masc. and fem.): A barnyard fowl of any age. The record is to be found in the books of the disciples, but Jesus is responsible for the only direct mention of chickens in the Bible. Mt **23** 37, contains this: "O Jerusalem, Jerusalem, that killeth the prophets, and stoneth them that are sent unto her! how often would I have gathered thy children together, even as a hen gathereth her chickens under her wings, and ye would not!" Luke's version of the same scene says: "Even as a hen gathereth her own brood under her wings" (**13** 34). There is no reference to chickens in the OT sufficiently clear to specify our common domestic bird. The many references to "fatted fowl" in these older records, in accordance with the text and the history of the other nations, were pigeons, guineas, ducks, geese and swans. The importation of peafowl by Solomon is mentioned. The cock and hen are distinctive birds and would have been equally a marvel worth recording had they been introduced at that time. From the history of the bird in other countries it is a safe estimate to place their entrance into Pal between five and six hundred years BC. That would allow sufficient time for them to increase and spread until they would be well known and common enough to be used effectively in the ministry of Jesus Christ. Every historical fact and indication points to the capture and domestication of the red jungle fowl in Burmah. The Chinese records prove that they first secured imported fowl from the West in 1400 BC. Their use for food dated from 1200 to 800 BC, in the Book of Manu, but it was specified that only those that ran wild were to be eaten. From these countries they were imported to Greece and Italy, and from there carried south into Pal. Homer (Δ 10; cf also *alektruōn*, P 602) names a man Cock, *aléktōr*, which seems to indicate that he knew the bird. Pindar gives them slight mention; Aristophanes wrote of them as "Pers birds," which indicates that they worked their way westward by importation. I cannot find them in the records of Aristotle, but Aristophanes advanced the idea that not the gods, but the birds were rulers of men in ancient times, and compared the comb of the cock with the crown of a king, and pointed out that when he "merely crows at dawn all jump up to their work" (*Aves*, 489–90). They were common in Italy in the days of Pliny, who was ten years old at the time of the crucifixion of Christ. Pliny gave many rules for raising chickens, proving that much was known of their habits in his time. Yet so credulous was he and so saturated with superstition, that, mixed with his instructions for preserving eggs, brooding and raising chickens, is the statement that on account of the fighting power of the cocks the lions feared them. He wrote that a man named Galerius in the time of the consuls, Lepidus and Catulus, owned a barnyard fowl that spoke. He names Lenius Strabo as the first man to devise a "coupe" to keep fowl in and "cram" them to fatness. He gave the laws governing the use of fowl at table and recorded that in Egypt eggs were hatched in manure beds, which is conclusive proof that birds had been carried across the Mediterranean several cents. previous. The records of Babylon, 600 BC, contain figures undoubtedly intended for cocks, and they were reproduced in marble in Lycia at that time. In all these reproductions the birds have the drooping tail of the wild, and there is no record of the date at which they erected the tail, lifted the head and assumed the upright bearing of today.

GENE STRATTON-PORTER

CHIDE, chīd: Only in the OT, translating Heb רִיב, *rībh*, a word which is more frequently rendered "strive." Since in Gen **31** 36; Jgs **8** 1; Ps **103** 9, the strife is one of words, it means in these passages, "scold," or "sharply censure," and is applied either to mutinous protests and reproaches of inferiors to a superior, or, as in the last of these passages, to rebukes administered by a superior to inferiors.

CHIDON, kī'don, **THE THRESHING-FLOOR OF** (גֹּרֶן כִּידֹן, *gōren kīdhōn;* LXX B, omits; A has **Χειλώ**, *Cheilō*): The place where Uzza perished because he touched the ark (1 Ch **13** 9). In 2 S **6** 6 it is called the threshing-floor of Nachon. No name resembling either of these has been discovered.

CHIEF, chēf: The Eng. word is in AV of OT the tr of some 17 different Heb words, most frequently of *rō'sh*, "head," *sar*, "prince," and *rē'shīth*, "beginning." The principal changes made by RV are: (1) Heb *bēth 'ābh*, "house of a father," being recognized as a technical term denoting a subdivision of a tribe, *rō'sh* is rendered lit. "head," when it occurs in connection with this phrase, so that "chief fathers" (Num **31** 26) and "chief of the fathers" (Ezr **1** 5) become "heads of fathers' houses"; (2) Heb *nāghīdh* and *nāsī'* are more accurately tr[d] "prince" in such passages as 1 Ch **5** 2; Nu **3** 32; (3) the misinterpretations which brought about the tr "chief" for *'ăçīlīm*, "corners," Isa **41** 9, and for *ma'ăleh*, "ascent," in 2 Ch **32** 33, are corrected.

In the NT "chief" is in most of its appearances the tr of Gr *prōtos*, "first"; the RV reads "first" for AV "chief," "chiefest," in Mt **20** 27; Mk **10** 44; Acts **16** 12. The reading in the latter passage is a difficult one, but the AV "Philippi, which is the chief city of that part of Macedonia," seems to imply a political authority which Philippi did not possess; RV "a city of Macedonia, the first of the district." Gr *árchōn*, "prince," "ruler," is rendered by AV "chief," by RV "prince," in Lk **11** 15; AV "chief Pharisees," RV "rulers of the Pharisees," in Lk **14** 1.

The original meaning of "chief" having been weakened, the comparative and superlative were admitted into English, the latter only appearing in AV or RV: 1 S **2** 29; Cant **5** 10; 2 Cor **11** 5, etc.

On "chief of Asia" (Acts **19** 31 AV) see ASIARCH.

F. K. FARR

CHIEF FRIENDS, GOOD, MEN. See FRIENDS, CHIEF; GOOD, CHIEF; CHIEF.

CHIEF MUSICIAN, mū-zish'an. See ASAPH.

CHIEF SEATS, chēf sēts (**πρωτοκαθεδρία**, *prōtokathedría*): It was one of the reproaches urged by Our Lord against the scribes and Pharisees that they loved the chief seats in the synagogues (Mt **23** 6; Mk **12** 39; Lk **11** 43; **20** 46). These were special seats set in front of the ark containing the Scriptures and of the reader's platform, and facing the congregation. They were specially reserved for those who were held in the highest honor in the congregation. There were seventy-one such seats in the great synagogue of Alexandria, which were occupied by the members of the great Council in that city (see SYNAGOGUE).

J. MACARTNEY WILSON

CHILD, chīld, **CHILDREN,** chil'dren (בֵּן, *bēn*, "son," יֶלֶד, *yeledh*, "child", נַעַר, *na'ar*, "lad"; **τέκνον**, *téknon*, **παιδίον**, *paidíon*): The Hebrews regarded the presence of children in the family as a mark of Divine favor and greatly to be desired (Gen **15** 2; **30** 1; 1 S **1** 11.20; Ps **127** 3; Lk 1 7.28). The birth of a male child was esp. a cause for rejoicing (Ps **128** 3, Heb); more men, more defenders for the tribe. If there were no sons born to a household, that family or branch became lost. If the wife proved childless, other wife or wives might be added to the family (Gen **16** f). Further, each Jewish mother, at least in later times, hoped that her son might prove to be the Messiah. The custom of Levirate marriage, which was not limited to the Heb people, rested on the principle that if a man died childless his brother should marry his widow, the children of such union being considered as belonging to the brother whose name and line were thus preserved from extinction (Dt **25** 5; Gen **38** 26; Mt **22** 24).

Children were sometimes dedicated to God, even before their birth (1 S **1** 11). Names often were significant: Moses (Ex **2** 10); Samuel (1 S **1** 20); Ichabod (**4** 21; cf Gen **30**) (see PROPER NAMES). The firstborn son belonged to God (Nu **3** 44 ff). The ceremony of redeeming the firstborn occurred on the thirtieth day. Friends of the family were invited to a feast, the rabbi also being present. The child was placed in the hands of the priest. The father carried some gold or silver in a cup or vessel. The priest asked the mother whether this was her firstborn, and, on being answered in the affirmative, claimed the child as Jehovah's. The father offered the redemption money, which was accepted in exchange for the child (cf 1 Pet **1** 18). See FIRSTBORN. Other stages in the life of the child were celebrated with fitting ceremonies. In the fourth year, in Pal, on the second day of the Passover occurred the ceremony of the first cutting of the boy's hair, the friends sharing the privilege. Sometimes, as in the case of the wealthy, the weight of the child in currency was given as a donation to the poor. In common with the custom of other eastern peoples, male children were circumcised (Gen **17** 12), the rite being performed on the eighth day.

Early education was cared for in the home, the children growing up more or less with the mother (Prov **6** 20; **31** 1; 2 Tim **1** 5; **3** 14.15), and the girl continuing with her mother until her marriage. In wealthier families tutors were employed (1 Ch **27** 32). Schools for children are first mentioned by Jos (*Ant*, XV, x, 5). According to the Talm the first school for children was established about 100 BC, but in the time of Jesus such schools were common. Children were taught to read and to write even in families of moderate means, these arts being widely diffused as early as 600 BC, if not earlier (Isa **8** 1; **10** 19). Great stress was laid on the Torah, i.e. the law of Moses. Boys were trained also in farming, the tending of cattle, and in the trades. The religious training of the boy began in his fourth year, as soon as he could speak distinctly. The religious life of the girl also began early. In later times at least children took part in the Sabbath and Passover festivals and boys attended synagogue and school regularly.

Children were subject to the father (Neh **5** 5 marks the extreme), who in turn was bound to protect them, though he himself had the power of life and death (Lev **18** 21; **20** 2 ff). Respect for and obedience to parents were stoutly upheld by public opinion (Ex **20** 12; Dt **5** 16; cf Prov **6** 20; Mic **7** 6; Dt **21** 18–21; Ex **21** 15).

Both the OT and NT afford abundant evidence of the strength of the bond that bound the Heb family together (Gen **21** 16; 2 S **18** 33; 1 K **3** 23 ff; 2 K **4** 19; Isa **8** 4; Job **29** 5; Mt **19** 13; **20** 20; Mk **9** 24; Lk **2** 48; Jn **4** 47; He **2** 13; **11** 23). The gift of a son from Jeh was the height of joy; the loss of a child marked the depth of woe. A hint occurs in the custom of naming a man as the father of his firstborn son (*HDB*, I, 382), or even the use of the father's name as a surname (Bar-jonah, Bartimaeus) and such continues in Syria at the present day. This idea is further instanced in the use, in both OT and NT, of the terms to express the relation between God and men (Ex **4** 22; Dt **14** 1; **32** 6; Jer **3** 4; Zec **12** 10; Mal **1** 6). See also FAMILY RELATIONSHIPS; SONS.

LITERATURE.—Benzinger, *Hebräische Archäologie*, 2d ed, 1907, 112–23; for rabbinical lore, Friedenberg in *Jew Enc*, IV, 27 f.

W. N. STEARNS

Figurative: Child is the EV rendering of the Gr τέκνον, *téknon*. The corresponding Heb words (בֵּן, *bēn*, and יֶלֶד, *yeledh*, are usually tr^d "son," but they have practically the same significance in the fig. use of the term. Child is used fig. to describe:

(1) An affectionate greeting. Jesus addressed the sick of the palsy as "child" (Mk **2** 5 RVm).

(2) The disciples, or followers, of a teacher. Jesus addressed His disciples as children (Mk **10** 24). Paul referred to Timothy as his child (1 Tim **1** 2), and also to Onesimus (Philem ver 10). John also designated the disciples to whom he was writing as his children (2 Jn ver 4). The same use of "children" or "sons" is common in the OT (see 1 K **20** 35; 2 K **2** 3.5.7; **4** 38). As a term of special endearment, disciples are sometimes called "little children" (τεκνία, *teknía*). Jesus thus addressed His disciples when He was speaking about His departure (Jn **13** 33). Paul thus addressed the Galatians (Gal **4** 19), and that was a favorite expression with John (see 1 Jn **2** 1; **4** 4; **5** 21). A term that was even more endearing was *paidía*, which means "little ones" or "babes." Jesus used this term once in addressing His disciples after His resurrection (Jn **21** 5), and John also used this term occasionally in saluting those to whom he was writing (1 Jn **2** 18).

(3) Those who belong to God. Children of God is a common expression in both the OT and the NT. It is based on the relation between parents and children, and in general describes God's affection for His own, and their dependence upon Him, and moral likeness to Him. The term is sometimes used of those who are disloyal to God, and they are designated as "rebellious children" (see Isa **30** 1). See CHILDREN OF GOD.

(4) Those who belong to the devil. Those who are like the devil in thought and action are designated as "children of the devil" (1 Jn **3** 10).

(5) One's relation to something to which he belongs, or by which he is dominated in his affection for it. Thus we have (*a*) the children of a city or country (see Jer **2** 16; Mt **23** 37), and this designates those who belong to that particular city or country; (*b*) children of wisdom (Mt **11** 19 AV; Lk **7** 35), and these are the ones whose lives are dominated by wisdom. WH adopted *érgon* for *teknon* in Mt **11** 19, but this seems to be without any good reason; (*c*) children of obedience (1 Pet **1** 14), and these are the ones who are eager to obey; (*d*) children of light (Eph **5** 8), and this designates those whose souls are illumined by the light.

(6) Those who are liable to some particular fate. Thus we have (*a*) children of cursing, or those who are exposed to cursing (2 Pet **2** 14), and (*b*) children of wrath or those who are exposed to wrath (Eph **2** 3).

(7) Moral likeness or spiritual kinship (Gal **3** 7 AV; cf Jn **8** 39; "the children of Abraham"). See secs. (3), (4).

A. W. FORTUNE

CHILD-BEARING, child'bâr-ing: Only in 1 Tim **2** 15: "She shall be saved through her [m "the"] child-bearing" (διὰ τῆς τεκνογονίας, *diá tḗs teknogonías*). The reference is to the calling of woman as wife and mother, as her ordinary lot in life, and to the anxieties, pains and perils of maternity, as the culmination and representation of the penalties woman has incurred because of the Fall (Gen **3** 16). "She shall be saved by keeping faithfully and simply to her allotted sphere as wife and mother" (Dummelow). The preposition *dia* is not used here instrumentally, as though child-bearing were a means of her salvation, but locally, as in 1 Cor **3** 15, "saved so as through fire," where life is saved by rushing through the flames. The explanation by reference to the incarnation, with an appeal to Gal **4** 4, favored by Ellicott and others, seems very mechanical.

H. E. JACOBS

CHILDHOOD, chīld'ho͝od, **GOSPELS OF THE.** See APOCRYPHAL GOSPELS.

CHILDREN OF EDEN, ē'd'n (בְּנֵי עֶדֶן, *b^enē 'edhen*): In 2 K **19** 12; Isa **37** 12 "the children of Eden that were in Telassar" are mentioned in connection with "Gozan, and Haran, and Rezeph" as having been destroyed by the Assyrians who were before the time of Sennacherib. The expression, "the c. of E. that were in T.," undoubtedly referred to a tribe which inhabited a region of which Telassar was the center. Telassar means "the hill of Asshur" and, according to Schrader, it was a name that might have been given to any place where a temple had been built to Asshur. Inasmuch as

Gozan, and Haran, and Rezeph were in Mesopotamia it would seem probable that "the c. of E. that were in T." belonged to the same locality. The "c. of E." is quite probably to be identified with the *Bît 'Adini* of the inscriptions and this referred to a district on the middle Euphrates. According to the inscriptions Gozan, Haran, Rezeph, and Bît 'Adini were destroyed by Sennacherib's forefathers, and this is in accord with the account in 2 K and Isa.

The "Eden" of Ezk **27** 23 is usually taken as the name of a place in Mesopotamia with which Tyre had commercial relations, and probably belongs to the region of "the c. of E.," discussed above.

Some writers think the "Beth-eden" of Am **1** 5 RVm [ARV "*Aven*"] is to be identified with the *Bît 'Adini* of the inscriptions and hence with "the c. of E.," but this is doubtful. This was perhaps in Syria in the neighborhood of Damascus.

A. W. Fortune

CHILDREN OF GOD:

Introduction: Meaning of Terms
I. OT Teaching
1. Mythological Survivals
2. Created Sonship
3. Israel's Collective Covenant Sonship
4. Individual and Personal Relation
5. Universalizing the Idea
II. NT Teaching
1. Physical and Limited Sonship Disappears
2. As Religious Experience, or Psychological Fact
(1) Filial Consciousness of Jesus
(2) Communicated to Men
3. As Moral Condition, or Ethical Fact
4. As State of Being, or Ontological Fact
(1) Essence of Christ's Sonship
(2) And of Men's
5. As Relation to God, or Theological Fact
(1) Eternal Generation
(2) The Work of Grace

Meaning of Terms

Children (Sons and Daughters) of God (בְּנֵי and בְּנוֹת אֱלֹהִים, *b^e^nē* and *b^e^nōth 'ĕlōhīm*, lit. "sons and daughters of God"; **τέκνα θεοῦ**, *tékna theoú*, and **υἱοί θεοῦ**, *huioí theoú*): so AV; but RV translates the latter Gr phrase more accurately "sons of God." *Tekna* contains the idea of origin or descent, but also that of personal relation, and is often used metaphorically of "that intimate and reciprocal relationship formed between men by the bonds of love, friendship, trust, just as between parents and children" (Grimm-Thayer). *Huioi*, too, conveys the ideas of origin, and of personal relation, but the latter in the fuller form in which it appears in mature age. "The difference between *huios* and *teknon* appears to be that whereas *teknon* denotes the natural relationship of child to parent, *huios* implies in addition to this the recognized status and legal privileges reserved for sons" (Sanday and Headlam, on Rom **8** 14). This difference obtains, however, only in a very general sense.

The above phrases denote the relation in which men are conceived to stand to God, either as deriving their being from Him and depending upon Him, or as standing in that personal relation of intimate trust and love toward Him which constitutes the psychological fact of sonship. The exact significance of the expression depends upon the conception of God, and particularly of His Fatherhood, to which it corresponds. It therefore attains to its full significance only in the NT, and its meaning in the OT differs considerably, even though it marks stages of development up to the NT idea.

I. OT Teaching.—The most primitive form of the idea appears in Gen **6** 1–4, where the sons of God by marrying the fair daughters of men become the fathers of the giants. These were a subordinate order of Divine beings or demi-gods, and the title here may mean no more, although it was probably a survival of an earlier idea of the actual descent of these gods from a higher God. The idea of a heavenly court where the sons of God come to present themselves before Jeh is found in quite late lit. (Job **1** 6; **2** 1; **38** 7; Ps **29** 1; **89** 6). In all these cases the phrase implies a certain kinship with God and dependence upon Him on the part of the Divine society around Him. But there is no evidence to show whether the idea of descent of gods from God survived to any extent, nor is there any indication of a very close personal relationship. A more resonable interpretation of the phrases, "sons of God" and "daughters of men," is that they mean "the godly and the ungoldy." The mingling of the good and the bad always results in an immediate apparent improvement which later becomes a deterioration.

1. Mythological Survivals

The idea of creation has taken the place of that of procreation in the OT, but without losing the sense of sonship. "Saith Jeh, the Holy One of Israel, and his Maker: Ask me . . . . concerning my sons, and concerning the work of my hands" (Isa **45** 11). Israel acknowledges the absolute sovereignty of God as her Father and Maker (Isa **64** 8). Israel's Maker is also her Husband, and by inference the Father of her children (Isa **54** 5). Since all Israel has one Father, and one God created her, the tribes owe brotherly conduct to one another (Mal **2** 10). Jeh upbraids His sons and daughters whom He as their Father bought, made and established. "He forsook God who made him, and lightly esteemed the Rock of his salvation. . . . . Of the Rock that begat thee thou art unmindful, and hast forgotten God that gave thee birth" (Dt **32** 6.15.18 ff). These passages reveal the transition from the idea of original creation to that of making and establishing Israel as a nation. All things might be described as children of God if creation alone brought it to pass, but Israel stands in a unique relation to God.

2. Created Sonship

The covenant relation of God with Israel as a nation is the chief form in which man's sonship and God's fatherhood appear in the OT. "Israel is my son, my firstborn" (Ex **4** 22); "When Israel was a child, then I loved him, and called my son out of Egypt" (Hos **11** 1). And to be children of God involves the obligation to be a holy people (Dt **14** 1.2). But Israel has proved unworthy of her status: "I . . . . have brought up children, and they have rebelled against me" (Isa **1** 2.4; **30** 1.9). Yet He will have pity upon them: "for I am a father to Israel, and Ephraim is my firstborn" (Jer **31** 9.20). Israel's unworthiness does not abolish the relation on God's side; she can therefore return to Him again and submit to His will (Isa **63** 16; **64** 8); and His pity exceeds a mother's love (Isa **49** 15). The filial relation of Israel to God is summed up and symbolized in a special way in the Davidic king: "I will be his father, and he shall be my son" (2 S **7** 14=1 Ch **17** 13; cf 1 Ch **22** 10; **28** 6; Ps **2** 7).

3. Israel's Collective Covenant Sonship

God's fatherhood to collective Israel necessarily tends to develop into a *personal relation* of father and son between Him and individual members of the nation. The children of Israel, whatever their number, shall be called "the sons of the living God" (Hos **1** 10). Jeh's marriage relation with Israel as a nation made individual Israelites His children (Hos **2** 19.20; Jer **3** 14.22; cf Isa **50** 1; Ezk **16** 20.21; **23** 37), and God's ownership of His children, the individual members of the nation, is asserted (cf Ps **127** 3). Chastisement and pity alike God deals forth as Father to His children (Dt **1** 31; **8** 5; Ps **103** 13), and these are intimate personal relations which can only obtain between individuals.

4. Individual and Personal Relation

5. Universalizing the Idea

In another direction the idea of God as the father of Israel tends to be modified by the inclusion of the Gentiles. The word "first-born" (in Ex **4** 22 and Jer **31** 9.20) may be only an emphatic form of expressing sonship, or it may already suggest the possibility of the adoption of the Gentiles. If that idea is not present in words, it is an easy and legitimate inference from several passages, that Gentiles would be admitted some day into this among the rest of Israel's privileges (Isa **19** 25; **65** 1; Zec **14** 16).

II. NT Teaching.—As the doctrine of Divine fatherhood attains its full spiritual and moral significance in the NT, so does the experience and idea of sonship. All traces of physical descent have disappeared. Paul's quotation from a heathen poet: "For we are also his offspring" (Acts **17** 28), whatever its original significance, is introduced by the apostle for the purpose of enforcing the idea of the spiritual kinship of God and men. The phrase "Son of God" applied to Christ by the Rom centurion (Mt **27** 54; Mk **15** 39) may or may not, in his mind, have involved the idea of physical descent, but its utterance was the effect of an impression of similarity to the gods, produced by the exhibition of power attending His death. The idea of creation is assumed in the NT, but generally it is not prominent in the idea of sonship. The virgin birth of Jesus, however, may be understood as implying either the creative activity of the Holy Spirit, or the communication of a preëxistent Divine being to form a new human personality, but the latter idea also would involve creative activity in the physical realm (cf Lk **3** 38: "Adam [son] of God"). The limitations of the OT conception of sonship as national and collective disappear altogether in the NT; God is father of all men, and of every man. In potentiality at least every man and all men are sons of God. The essence of sonship consists in a personal experience and moral likeness which places man in the most intimate union and communion with God.

1. Physical and Limited Sonship Disappears

2. As Religious Experience, or Psychological Fact

(1) *The filial consciousness of Jesus.*—Divine sonship was first realized and made manifest in the consciousness of Jesus (Mt **11** 27). For Him it meant unbroken personal knowledge of God and communion with Him, and the sense of His love for Him and of His satisfaction and delight in Him (Mt **3** 17; **17** 5; Mk **1** 11; **9** 7; Lk **3** 22; **9** 35). Whether the "voice out of the heavens saying, This is my beloved Son, in whom I am well pleased" was objective or not, its message always dwelt in the filial consciousness of Jesus. The Father's love was to Him a source of knowledge and power (Jn **5** 20), the reward of His self-sacrifice (**10** 17) and the inspiration of His love for men (**15** 9).

Sonship meant for Him His Messianic mission (Mt **16** 16.17). It involved His dependence on the Father and His obedience to Him (Jn **5** 19.30; **8** 29), and a resulting confidence in His mission (**5** 36; **10** 36.37). It filled Him with a sense of dignity, power and glory which the Father gave Him, and would yet give in larger measure (Mt **26** 63.64; **16** 27; Jn **17** 5).

(2) *Communicated to men.*—Jesus communicated His own experience of God to men (Jn **14** 9) that they also might know the Father's love and dwell in it (Jn **17** 26). Through Him and through Him alone can they become children of God in fact and in experience (Jn **1** 12; **14** 6; Mt **11** 27). It is therefore a distinctively Christian experience and always involves a relation of faith in Christ and moral harmony with Him. It differs from His experience in one essential fact, at least in most men. It involves an inner change, a change of feeling and motive, of ideal and attitude, that may be compared to a new birth (Jn **3** 3). Man must turn and return from disobedience and alienation through repentance to childlike submission (Lk **15** 18–20). It is not the submission of slaves, but the submission of sons, in which they have liberty and confidence before God (Gal **4** 6), and a heritage from Him for their possession (Gal **4** 6.7; Rom **8** 17). It is the liberty of self-realization. As sons they recognize their kinship with God, and share his mind and purpose, so that His commands become their pleasure: "For this is the love of God, that we keep his commandments: and his commandments are not grievous" (1 Jn **5** 3). They have boldness and access to God (Eph **2** 18; **3** 12). With this free union of love with God there comes a sense of power, of independence of circumstances, of mastery over the world, and of the possession of all things necessary which become the heirs of God (Mt **6** 26.32; **7** 11). "For whatsoever is begotten of God overcometh the world" (1 Jn **5** 4). They learn that the whole course and destiny of creation is for the "revealing of the sons of God" (Rom **8** 19.21).

3. As Moral Condition, or Ethical Fact

Christ's sonship involved His moral harmony with the Father: "I have kept my Father's commandments, and abide in his love" (Jn **15** 10; **8** 53). He accomplished the work which the Father gave Him to do (Jn **17** 4; **5** 19), "becoming obedient even unto death, yea, the death of the cross" (Phil **2** 8). And sonship makes the same demand upon men. The peacemakers and those who forgive like God are His children (Mt **5** 9.45; Lk **6** 35). "For as many as are led by the Spirit of God, these [and these only] are sons of God" (Rom **8** 14). God will be Father to the holy (2 Cor **6** 18). The test and mark of the children of God is that they do righteousness and love the brethren (1 Jn **3** 10). They are blameless and harmless, without blemish, in the midst of a crooked and perverse generation (Phil **2** 15). Therefore their ideal of life is to be "imitators of God" and to walk in love even as Christ did (Eph **5** 1). Sonship grows to its consummation as the life grows in the likeness of Christ, and the final destiny of all sons is to be ever like Him (1 Jn **3** 2).

4. As State of Being, or Ontological Fact

Sonship is properly and primarily a relation, but it may so dominate and transform the whole of a man's life, thought and conduct as to become his essential being, the most comprehensive category under which all that he is may be summed up.

(1) *Essence of sonship in Christ.*—It is so that the NT comprehends the person of Christ. Everything that He did, He did as God's son, so that He is *the* Son, always and ever Son. In the beginning, in the bosom of the Father, He is the ONLY BEGOTTEN (q.v.) Son (Jn **1** 1.18). He is born a Son of God (Lk **1** 35). He begins life in the things of His Father (Lk **2** 49). His whole life is that of the beloved Son (Mt **3** 17; **17** 5). As Son of God He dies (Mt **26** 63; Lk **22** 70; Mt **27** 40.43; cf Jn **5** 18). In His resurrection He was declared to be the Son of God with power (Rom **1** 4); as Jesus the Son of God He is our great high priest in heaven (He **4** 14), and in the glory of His father He will come to judge in the last day (Mt **16** 27).

(2) *Men's sonship.*—Unlike Him, men's moral sonship is neither eternal nor universal. Are they therefore sons in any sense always and everywhere? All children are heirs of the kingdom of

God and objects of the Father's care (Lk **18** 16; Mt **18** 10). But men may turn away from the Father and become unworthy to be called His sons (Lk **15** 13.19). They may become children of the devil (1 Jn **3** 10; Jn **8** 44), and children of wrath (Eph **2** 3). Then they lose the actuality, but not the potentiality, of sonship. They have not the experience or character of sons, but they are still moral and rational beings made in the image of God, open to the appeal and influence of His love, and able to "rise and go to their Father." They are objects of God's love (Jn **15** 13; Rom **5** 8) and of His gracious search and seeking (Lk **15** 4; Jn **11** 52). But they are actual sons only when they are led by the Spirit of God (Rom **8** 14); and even so their sonship will only be consummated in the resurrection (Rom **8** 23; Lk **20** 36).

In the relation of father and son, fatherhood is original and creative. That does not necessarily mean priority in time.

5. As Relation to God, or Theological Fact

(1) *Eternal generation.*—Origen's doctrine of the eternal generation of Christ, by which is meant that God and Christ always stood in the relation of Father and Son to one another, is a just interpretation of the NT idea that the Son "was in the beginning with God" (*prós tón Theón*). But Jesus was conscious of His dependence upon the Father and that His sonship was derived from Him (Jn **5** 19.36). Still more manifest is it that men derive their sonship from God. He made them for Himself, and whatever in human nature qualifies men to become sons of God is the free gift of God. But men in their sin and disobedience could not come to a knowledge of the Father, had He not "sent forth his Son . . . . that we might receive the adoption of sons" (Gal **4** 4.5): "Behold what manner of love the Father hath bestowed upon us, that we should be called children of God" (1 Jn **3** 1); "God so loved the world, that he gave his only begotten son" (q.v.) who gave men "the right to become children of God, even to them that believe on his name" (Jn **3** 16; **1** 12). It is not the children of the flesh but the children of the promise who are children of God (Rom **9** 4). The mere act of birth does not constitute men into children of God, but His covenant of free grace must be added. God being essentially Father made men and the universe, sent His Son and His Spirit, "for the revealing of the sons of God." But they can only know the Father, and realize their sonship when they respond to His manifestation of fatherly love, by faith in God and obedience to Him.

(2) *The work of grace.*—The question whether sonship is natural and universal or conditional upon grace working through faith, does not admit of a categorical answer. The alternatives are not strict antitheses. God does all things as Father. To endow man with rational and moral nature capable of his becoming a son was an act of love and grace, but its whole purpose can be communicated only in response to faith in Christ. But a natural sonship which is not actual is meaningless. A man's moral condition and his attitude toward God are the most essential elements of his nature, for a man's nature is just the sum total of his thoughts, acts and states. If these are hostile or indifferent to God, there is nothing left that can have the reality or bear the name of son. For if the word son be used of mere creaturehood and potentiality, that is to give it a meaning entirely different from NT usage. All men by nature are potential sons, because God has made them for sonship and does all things to win them into their heritage. Men may be sons of God in a very imperfect and elementary manner. The sharp transitions of Pauline and Johannine theology are rather abstract distinctions for thought than actual descriptions of spiritual processes. But Paul and John also contemplate a growth in sonship, "till we all attain unto the unity of the faith, and of the knowledge of the Son of God, unto a fullgrown man, unto the measure of the stature of the fulness of Christ" (Eph **4** 13). See SONS OF GOD.

For lit. and further discussion, see special arts. on ADOPTION; GOD; JESUS CHRIST. T. REES

CHILDREN OF ISRAEL, iz'rā-el (בְּנֵי יִשְׂרָאֵל, *b^enē yisrā'ēl*): A very common term in both the OT and the NT, and it refers to the Israelites as the descendants of a common ancestor, Jacob, whose name was changed to Israel (see Gen **32** 24–32). It was customary to designate the members of the various tribes as the children of the one from whom the tribe originated (see Nu **1** 20–43; Ezr **2** 3–61), and it was natural that the people who boasted of Israel as their ancestor should be designated as his children. The first reference to the descendants of Jacob is found in the account of the changing of Jacob's name to Israel, and the purpose is to connect them with the experience in Jacob's life which led to the change in his name: "Therefore the children of Israel eat not the sinew of the hip, which is upon the hollow of the thigh, unto this day: because he touched the hollow of Jacob's thigh in the sinew of the hip." At the time when this was written "the c. of I." was a term that was commonly applied to the Israelites. In 2 K **17** 34 they are called "the children of Jacob," and this occurs in connection with the account of the changing of Jacob's name to Israel and is intended to connect them closely with their father Jacob, who was favored of God.

After a time, it is quite likely that the term "c. of I." lost its peculiar significance and was simply one of the popular terms designating the inhabitants of Pal, but at first it was intended to connect these people with their ancestor Jacob whose name was changed to Israel. The Jews of the NT times connected themselves with Abraham rather than with Jacob (see Jn **8** 39; Rom **9** 7; Gal **3** 7, τέκνα, *tékna*, or υἱοὶ 'Αβραάμ, *huioí Abraám*).

A. W. FORTUNE

CHILDREN OF THE BRIDECHAMBER. See BRIDECHAMBER, SONS OF THE.

CHILDREN OF THE EAST, ēst (בְּנֵי קֶדֶם, *b^enē ḳedhem*): A term which in a general way designated the inhabitants of the country E. of Pal. The Hebrews thought of their own country as occupying the central place, and of the other parts of the world in relation to this. They spoke of the "queen of the south" (Mt **12** 42), and of the "king of the south" (Dnl **11** 5.6). They spoke of people coming from "the east and the west" and sitting down with the patriarchs (Mt **8** 11).

The term "children of the east" seems to have been applied to the inhabitants of any part of the country E. of Pal. It is stated that Jacob, when he fled from Esau, "came to the land of the children of the east" (Gen **29** 1), and the place to which he came was Haran in Mesopotamia. In Jer **49** 28 the inhabitants of Kedar are called "the children of the east," and in later Jewish lit. Kedar is identified with the Arabs (see KEDAR). Job was designated as "the greatest of all the children of the east" (Job **1** 3), and the land of Uz was mentioned as his home (Job **1** 1). While it is impossible absolutely to locate the land of Uz, it must have been on the edge of the desert which was E. of Pal. The children of the east seem to have been famous for their wisdom. It is said that "Solomon's wisdom excelled the wisdom of all the children of the east" (1 K **4** 30), and "Wise-men from the east" came to

Jerus seeking the one that was born king of the Jews (Mt **2** 1).

Many of the inhabitants of the east country were regarded as descending from Abraham (see Gen **25** 6), and hence they were related to Israel.

A. W. Fortune

CHILEAB, kil'ē-ab (כִּלְאָב, *kil'ābh;* **Δαλουιά,** *Dalouiá,* "restraint of father"): A son of David, born to him at Hebron. His mother was Abigail, whom David married after the death of her husband Nabal, the Carmelite (2 S **3** 3). In the corresponding account (1 Ch **3** 1) he is called "Daniel," the meaning of which name ("God is my judge") points to its having been given in order to commemorate God's judgment upon Nabal (1 S **25** 39; cf Gen **30** 6). Some suppose that he bore both names, but the LXX reading here *Dalouia* (1 Ch *Damniēl*), and the identity of the last three letters of the Heb word "Chileab" with the first three of the following word, seems to indicate that the text of Samuel is corrupt.

Horace J. Wolf

CHILION, kil'i-on (כִּלְיוֹן, *kilyōn,* "pining," "wasting away"): One of the two sons of Elimelech and Naomi, "Mahlon and Chilion, Ephrathites of Beth-lehem-judah" (Ruth **1** 2). With his mother and brother he came into Moab and there both married Moabitish women, Orpah being the name of Chilion's wife and Ruth that of the wife of Mahlon (**4** 9. 10). Both died early and Orpah remained in Moab while Ruth accompanied Naomi back to Bethlehem. When Boaz married Ruth he "bought all that was Elimelech's, and all that was Chilion's, and Mahlon's, of the hand of Naomi" (**4** 9).

W. L. Walker

CHILMAD, kil'mad (כִּלְמַד, *kilmadh;* **Χαρμάν,** *Charmán*): A city or district mentioned after Sheba and Asshur as supplying merchandise to Tyre (Ezk **27** 23). By changing *m* into *w* (common in Assyr-Bab) this has been compared with *Kalwādha* near Bagdad (G. Smith, *TSBA*, I, 61; Delitzsch, *Paradies*, 206), but the identification seems improbable. Though regarded as the name of a country in the LXX and the Vulg (*Charman; Chelmad*), there is some doubt whether this view of the word is correct. The Tg substitutes *Madhai,* "Media," and on this account Mez (Stadt *Harran*, 24) amends to *Kōl Madhai,* "all Media." The absence of the copula "and" has caused others to further modify the vocalization, and by reading *kᵉlimmūdh* instead of Chilmad, the sense "Asshur was as the apprentice of thy trading" (Ḳimḥi, Hitzig, Cornill) is obtained, but is not satisfactory. Probably both text and tr are susceptible of improvement.

T. G. Pinches

CHIMHAM, kim'ham (כִּמְהָם, *kimhām* [2 S **19** 37.38] or כִּמְהָן, *kimhān* [2 S **19** 40] or כְּמוֹהָם, *kᵉmōhem* [Jer **41** 17 Kt.]; this reading, however, may probably be safely ignored): One of the sons of Barzillai the Gileadite, who supported David while the latter was in exile in Mahanaim (2 S **19** 37). After the death of Absalom, Barzillai was invited to spend the remainder of his life with the king; but he refused, and sent his son Chimham in his stead. From the mention of "the habitation of Chimham, which is by Beth-lehem" (Jer **41** 17 AV), it has been inferred that Chimham received a grant of land from David's patrimony at Bethlehem, which retained his name for at least four cents. It has been suggested that his name was probably Ahinoam (אֲחִינֹעַם, *'ăḥīnō'am*).

Horace J. Wolf

CHIMNEY, chim'ni. See House.

CHINNERETH, kin'ē-reth (כִּנֶּרֶת, *kinnereth* [Dt **3** 17; Josh **19** 35, etc]) or **CHINNEROTH,** kin'ē-roth (כִּנֲּרוֹת, *kinărōth;* B, **Κενερέθ,** *Kenerḗth,* A, **Χενερόθ,** *Chenerṓth* [Josh **11** 2]). At the N.E. corner of the plain of Bethsaida rises a lyre-shaped hill whose summit is covered with ancient ruins of the Bronze Age. The modern name, *Tel ‘Oreimeh,* means "harp," or "lyre." This place is now generally accepted.

CHIOS, kē'os, kī'os (**Χίος,** *Chíos*): An island belonging to Turkey in the Aegaean Sea, S. of Lesbos, and very near the mainland of Asia Minor. St. Paul's vessel passed it on his last voyage to Jerus (Acts **20** 15). The channel here is very picturesque. From St. Luke's expression, "we came the following day over against Chios," it has been conjectured that they were becalmed; more probably it simply means that, because of the dark moon, they lay at anchor for the night on the Asian coast opposite the island (*HDB*, s.v.). Herod, when on his way to Agrippa at the Bosphorus, "continued many days at Chios" and conferred many royal benefactions upon the inhabitants (Jos, *Ant*, XVI, ii, 2).

The soil is sterile (though well cultivated), the climate mild. Earthquakes are frequent. In the mountains (highest 4,000 ft.) beautiful blue marble with white veins, and excellent potter's clay, were quarried in antiquity. In modern times large quantities of ochre are mined. The chief industry is the culture of the silkworm, the cocoons being sent to Lyons. Oranges, lemons, almonds, brandy, anise, mastich and leather are also exported. The inhabitants, who are almost entirely Greeks, number about 60,000. The capital, Castro, has a population of 15,000. The place where Homer is said to have collected his pupils around him is still pointed out to the traveler at the foot of Mt. Epos, near the coast. It is in reality (probably) a very old sanctuary of Cybele, the Mother of the Gods. The tragic poet Ion, the historian Theopompus and the sophist Theocritus were natives of Chios. The Chians were especially famous for their skill in telling stories, and for their levity. A familiar proverb says that "it is easier to find a green horse than a sober-minded Sciot" (Conybeare and Howson, XX, 549).

The oldest inhabitants of the island were Leleges, Cretans and Carians, who were conquered by the Ionians. The latter made Chios one of the most flourishing states in Ionia. When the Persians overran Asia Minor and oppressed the Gr colonies, the Chians showed a Pan-Hellenic spirit. They surrendered, however, to Cyrus in 546 BC. Nevertheless, 46 years later they joined in the rebellion of Aristagoras against the Persians. In the naval engagement off the island Lade they fought with 100 ships and displayed great bravery. Again they fell into the power of Persia; but after the battle of Mycale (479) the Chians joined the Athenian confederacy. In 412 they sided with the Peloponnesians, in the 19th year of the war which Athens had been waging against Sparta and her allies. For this act of treason the Athenians devastated the island. At the end of the war the Chians revolted from Sparta and, after the battle of Naxos (376), became an ally of Athens once more. Oppressed now by Athens, as she had been by Sparta, Chios made an alliance with Thebes in 363 and defended herself successfully against the Athenian general, Chares; and in 355 Athens was forced to recognize the island's independence. Later the Chians became friends of the Romans and in the war with Mithridates were obliged to surrender their ships to the Pontic king and in addition pay him 2,000 talents.

In 1307 AD Turkish pirates subjugated and laid waste the island. The Turks themselves became masters of Chios in 1566. In the war of the Gr revolution the Chians joined the Greeks (Feb. 1821) but were overpowered by the Turks. The Pasha decreed that the island should be utterly devastated; 23,000 Chians were massacred and 47,000 sold into slavery. Only 5,000 escaped. A second attempt to regain their freedom was made in 1827, but met with failure. When the kingdom of Greece was established two years later, Chios was not included. On April 3, 1881, the island was visited by a terrible earthquake, the city of Castro being almost entirely destroyed.

LITERATURE.—Conybeare and Howson, *The Life and Epistles of St. Paul;* W. M. Ramsay, *St. Paul the Traveller;* G. H. Gilbert, *The Student's Life of Paul* (chiefly concerned with the chronology and order of events in Paul's life); Eckenbrecher, *Die Insel Chios* (1845); Pauli, id (in the *Mitteilungen der Geogr. Gesellschaft in Hamburg,* 1880–81).

J. E. HARRY

CHIRP, chẽrp (צָפַף, *çāphaph*): "Chirp" occurs in the AVm and RVm of Isa **29** 4, "Thy voice shall be as of one that hath a familiar spirit, out of the ground, and thy speech shall whisper [m, "chirp"] out of the dust." The reference is to "the sounds made by wizards and ventriloquists, who imitated the chirping of the bats which was supposed to proceed from the lower world"; hence for "peep" of AV in Isa **8** 19 we have "chirp"—"wizards, that chirp and that mutter."

Figurative: We have also in Isa **10** 14 RV, in a fig. allusion to young birds, "chirped" instead of "peeped." See CHATTER. W. L. WALKER

CHISLEU, kis′lū, **CHISLEV,** kis′lev. See KISLEV.

CHISLON, kis′lon, kiz′lon (כִּסְלוֹן, *kiṣlōn*, "strength"): A prince of Benjamin, the father of Elidad (Nu **34** 21).

CHISLOTH-TABOR, kis-loth-tā′bor, kiz′lōth-. See CHESULLOTH.

CHITLISH, kit′lish (כִּתְלִישׁ, *kithlīsh*, "separation"; AV **Kithlish,** ERV "Chithlish," kith′lish): An unidentified town named with Lahman and Gederoth in the Shephelah of Judah (Josh **15** 40).

CHITTIM, kit′im. See KITTIM.

CHIUN, kī′un: Thus Heb כִּיּוּן, *kīyūn*, is transliterated in Am **5** 26 AV. The vowels represent an assimilation to some such word as *shiḳḳūç*, "detestable thing," or *gillūl*, "idol" (properly "a filthy thing"), in consonance with the well-known habit of the punctuators (cf מֹלֶךְ, *mōlekh*, Molech with the vowels of *bōsheth*, בֹּשֶׁת, "shame"). The Syr VS has preserved the correct vocalization; apparently also the Sept, albeit the consonants have suffered corruption (so particularly in the Gr MSS of Acts **7** 43). There can be no doubt that we should vocalize כֵּיוָן, *kēwān*=the Assyr Kai(a)-wanu=Kaiamanu by which at least in late Bab Saturn was indicated. The passage in Amos refers to the Saturn worship which appears to have been in vogue in the prophet's days. The Israelites shall carry with them into exile the images of their gods (render with the m of RV: "Yea, ye shall take up," etc). The received vocalization is as old as Aquila and Symmachus. MAX L. MARGOLIS

CHIUN, kī′un (Am **5** 26 AV): Called in Acts **7** 43 "Rephan" (Ῥεμφάν, *Rhemphán*), the planet Saturn. See ASTROLOGY.

CHLOE, klō′ē (Χλόη, *Chlóē*, "a tender shoot"): A woman, presumably a Christian, mentioned only in 1 Cor **1** 11. She was a resident either of Corinth or of Ephesus. Paul had been informed by some of her household, probably Christian slaves, of the dissensions in the church at Corinth. Nothing more is known of her.

CHOBA, kō′ba, **CHOBAI,** kō′bā-ī (Χωβά, *Chōbá*, Jth **4** 4; Χωβαί, *Chōbaí*, **15** 4 f): A place named along with Jericho, Aesora, and the valley of Salem (Jth **4** 4; **15** 4 f). Reland's (*Pal*, 721) suggestion of Choabis, which the Peutinger Tables give as 12 Rom miles from Scythopolis, seems probable. It may be identical with *el-Mekhubby*, about 11 miles from *Beisān* (Scythopolis), and 3 miles from *Ṭūbās*.

CHOENIX, kē′niks (χοῖνιξ, *choínix*): A Gr dry measure, almost equal to one quart. Mentioned in the NT only in Rev **6** 6, where RVm would read "choenix" instead of the indefinite tr "measure." The ver is then obviously a threat of famine.

CHOICE, chois. See CHOOSE; WILL.

CHOKE, chōk (πνίγω, *pnígō*, and its compounds): Is used in its primary sense of "to strangle," or "to suffocate," in describing the fate of the swine (Lk **8** 33 AV). The RV has "drowned," but "choked" is the correct rendering of the Gr word.

Figurative: It is used in the sense of "to strangle" "smother," "suffocate," as if by depriving of breath, in describing the fate of the young grain growing in the midst of thorns (Mt **13** 7). The fig. is carried a little farther still in describing the way the word, planted in the heart, is overcome by the care of the world, and the deceitfulness of riches (Mt **13** 22). A. W. FORTUNE

CHOLA, kō′la (Χωλά, *Chōlá*; AV Cola): This names occurs only with that of Chobai (see CHOBA) in Jth **15** 4. It may be identical with the modern *Kā'un*, between *el-Mekhubby* and *Beisān*.

CHOLER, kol′ẽr: Lit. "bile," is used in the sense of a disease (χολέρα, *choléra*) (Sir **31** 20; **37** 30), and in the sense of bitter anger (מָרַר, *mārar*) (Dnl **8** 7; **11** 11 EV, ARV "anger").

CHOOSE, chōōz, **CHOSEN,** chō′z′n (בָּחַר, *bāḥar*, קָבַל, *kābhal*, בָּרָא, *bārā'*, בָּרָה, *bārāh*; ἐκλέγω, *eklégō*):

I. IN THE OT
   1. Human Choice
   2. God Chooses King of Israel
   3. God Chooses Jerusalem
   4. Election of Israel
   5. Jehovah's Grace
      (1) An Act of Sovereignty
      (2) For Mankind's Sake
II. IN THE NT
   1. Various Meanings
   2. Of God's Free Grace
   3. Ultimate Antinomies
   4. Election Corresponds to Experience

The words denote an act of comparison of two or more objects or persons, the preference and selection of one, or of a few out of a larger number for a certain purpose, function, position or privilege.

I. In the OT.—For *bāḥar* and its derivatives: men choosing wives (Gen **6** 2); Lot choosing the cities of the Plain (Gen **13** 11); often of kings and generals choosing soldiers for their prowess (e.g. Ex **17** 9; Josh **8** 3; 1 S **13** 2; 2 S **10** 9; **17** 1). The word *bāḥar* is often used for "young men," as being choice, in the prime of manhood. The most important uses of *bāḥar* are these: of Israel choosing a king (1 S **8** 18; **12** 13); of moral and religious choice: choosing Jeh as God (Josh **24** 15.22), or other gods (Jgs **5** 8; **10** 14); the way of truth (Ps **119** 30); to refuse the evil and choose the good (Isa **7** 15.16); cf David's choice of evils (2 S **24** 12). A leading idea is that of God choosing Moses as leader (Nu **16** 5.7; **17** 5); the Levites to the priesthood (1 S **2** 28; 2 Ch **29** 11); Saul as king (1 S **10** 24), David (2 S **6** 21; 1 K

1. Human Choice

2. God Chooses King of Israel

11 34), Solomon (1 Ch **28** 5). All this follows from the theocratic idea that God rules personally over Israel as His chosen people. A more important, but still subsidiary, idea is that of Jeh choosing Jerus as the place of His habitation and worship (Dt **12** 5; and 20 other times, Josh **9** 27; 1 K **8** 44.48; Ps **132** 13; Zec **1** 17; **2** 12; **3** 2). This was the ruling idea of Josiah's reformation which was instrumental in putting down polytheistic ideas and idolatrous practices in Israel, and was therefore an important factor in the development of Heb monotheism; but it was an idea that Heb monotheism had to transcend and reject to attain its full growth. "The hour cometh, when neither in this mountain, nor in Jerusalem, shall ye worship the Father" (Jn **4** 21).

3. God Chooses Jerusalem

But the fundamental idea of choosing, which governs all others in the OT, is that of God choosing Israel to be His peculiar people. He chose Abraham, and made a covenant with him, to give him the land of Canaan (Neh **9** 7 ff): "For thou art a holy people unto Jeh thy God: Jeh thy God hath chosen thee to be a people for his own possession, above all peoples that are upon the face of the earth .... because Jeh loveth you, and because he would keep the oath which he sware unto your fathers" (Dt **7** 6–8). Historically this idea originated in the old conception of Jeh as the tribal God of Israel, bound to her by natural and indissoluble ties (see God). But as their conception of Jeh became more moral, and the idea of His righteousness predominated, it was recognized that there was no natural and necessary relation and harmony between Israel and Jeh that accounted for the favor of a righteous God toward her, for Israel was no better than her neighbors (Am **1, 2**). Why then was Jeh Israel's God, and Israel His people? It was by an act of free choice and sovereign grace on God's part. "You only have I known of all the families of the earth" (Am **3** 2). In Hos the relation is described under the figure of a marriage tie. Jeh is Israel's husband: and to realize the force of the figure, it is necessary to recall what ancient and oriental marriage customs were. Choice and favor were almost entirely made by the husband. The idea of the covenant which Jeh out of His free grace made with Israel comes to the forefront in Dt and Jer. Because He loved her, and for no other reason, He has chosen Israel to be His peculiar people. In Isa **40–66** the idea is carried farther in two directions: (1) Jeh's gracious choice of Israel rests ultimately on His absolute sovereignty: "O Jacob my servant, and Israel, whom I have chosen: thus saith Jeh that made thee, and formed thee from the womb" (**44** 1.2; cf Isa **29** 16; Jer **18** 6; Isa **64** 8). For Israel's deliverance Cyrus and his world-empire are in Jeh's hands as clay in the potter's hands (Isa **45** 9.10). (2) "Israel is elect for the sake of mankind." This is the moral interpretation of a choice that otherwise appears arbitrary and irrational. God's purpose and call of salvation are unto all mankind. "Look unto me, and be ye saved, all the ends of the earth; for I am God, and there is none else" (Isa **45** 22). And Israel is His servant, chosen, the messenger He sends, "to bring forth justice to the Gentiles" (Isa **42** 1.19; **43** 10.12). The idea is further developed in the conception of the Servant of Jeh (q.v.) as the faithful few (or one) formed "from the womb to be his servant, to bring Jacob again to him," "for a light to the Gentiles," God's "salvation unto the end of the earth" (Isa **49** 1–6; **52** 13—**53** 12) (cf Isaiah's doctrine of the Remnant: Shearjashub; also, the righteous, the godly, the meek, in Pss; and see Skinner, *Isaiah*, II, xxx ff). As the conception of personality and of individual relation and responsibility to God developed from Ezk onward, together with the resulting doctrine of personal immortality, the conditions were prepared for the application of the idea of election to individuals (cf Ps **65** 4).

4. Election of Israel

5. Jehovah's Grace

Coördinate with the idea of God choosing Israel runs the complementary idea that Israel should prove faithful to the covenant, and worthy of the choice. God has chosen her, not for any merit in her, but of His free grace, and according to His purpose of salvation, but if Israel fails to respond by faithful conduct, fitting her to be His servant and messenger, He may and will cast her off, or such portion of her as proves unworthy. See Oehler, *OT Theol.*, I, 256 ff, 287 f.

Three other Heb words expressing choice in minor matters are: *ḳābhal*, for David's choice of evils (1 Ch **21** 11); *bārā'*, to mark out a place (Ezk **21** 19), to select singers and porters for the temple (1 Ch **9** 22; **16** 41); *bārāh*, to choose a man to represent Israel against Goliath (1 S **17** 8).

II. In the NT.—The whole conception of God, of His relation to Israel, and of His action in history indicated above, constituted the religious heritage of Jesus Christ and His disciples. The national conciousness had to a considerable extent given place to that of the individual; and salvation extended beyond the present life into a state of blessedness in a future world. But the central ideas remain, and are only modified in the NT in so far as Jesus Christ becomes the Mediator and Agent of God's sovereign grace. *Eklegō* and its derivatives are the words that generally express the idea in the NT. They are used (1) of the general idea of selecting one out of many (Lk **14** 7); (2) of choosing men for a particular purpose, e.g. of the church choosing the seven (Acts **6** 5); of the choice of delegates from the Council of Jerus (Acts **15** 22.25; cf 2 Cor **8** 19), *cheirotonéō;* choose by vote (RV "appoint") (cf Acts **10** 41), *procheirotonéō;* (3) of moral choice (Mk **13** 20): "Mary hath chosen the good part" (Lk **10** 42); (4) of Christ as the chosen Messiah of God (Lk **23** 35; 1 Pet **2** 4 AV); (5) of Christ choosing His apostles (Lk **6** 13; Jn **6** 70; **13** 18; **15** 16.19; Acts **1** 2.24); Paul (Acts **9** 15; cf **22** 14 AV), *procheirízomai;* Rufus (Rom **16** 13); and Paul chose Silas (Acts **15** 40), *epilégō;* (6) of God (*a*) choosing Israel (Acts **13** 17; cf Rom **9** 11), (*b*) choosing the Christian church as the new Israel (1 Pet **2** 9 AV), (*c*) choosing the members of the church from among the poor (Jas **2** 5), the foolish, weak and despised (1 Cor **1** 27–28), (*d*) choosing into His favor and salvation a few out of many: "Many are called, but few are chosen" (Mt **20** 16 [omitted in RV]; **22** 14); God shortens the days of the destruction of Jerus "for the elect's sake, whom he chose" (Mk **13** 20).

1. Various Meanings

In Eph **1** 4–6 every phrase tells a different phase of the conception: (1) God chose (and foreordained) the saints in Christ before the foundation of the world; (2) according to the good pleasure of His will; (3) unto adoption as sons through Jesus Christ unto Himself; (4) to be holy and without blemish before Him in love; (5) to the praise of the glory of His grace; (6) which He freely bestowed on them in the Beloved. And in Rev **17** 14, the triumphant church in heaven is described as "called and chosen and faithful." God's sovereign choice governs the experience and testing of the saints at every point from beginning to end.

2. Of God's Free Grace

Thus in the NT as in the OT (1) God's covenant of grace is free and unconditional. It is unto all men, now as individuals rather than nations, and without distinction of race or class. It is no less free and sovereign, because it is a father's grace. (2) Israel is still a chosen race for a special purpose. (3) The church and the saints that constitute it are chosen to the full experience and privileges of sonship. (4) God's purpose of grace is fully revealed and realized through Jesus Christ.

3. Ultimate Antinomies

This doctrine raises certain theological and metaphysical difficulties that have never yet been satisfactorily solved. (1) How can God be free if all His acts are preordained from eternity? This is an antinomy which indeed lies at the root of all personality. It is of the essence of the idea of personality that a person should freely determine himself and yet act in conformity with his own character. Every person in practice and experience solves this antinomy continually, though he may have no intellectual category that can coördinate these two apparently contradictory principles in all personality. (2) How can God be just, if a few are chosen and many are left? And (3) How can man be free if his moral character proceeds out of God's sovereign grace? It is certain that if God chose all or left all He would be neither just nor gracious, nor would man have any vestige of freedom. The doctrine describes accurately (*a*) the moral fact, that some accept salvation and others reject it; (*b*) the religious fact

4. Election Corresponds to Experience

that God's sovereign and unconditional love is the beginning and cause of salvation. The meeting-point of the action of grace, and of man's liberty as a moral and responsible being, it does not define. Nor has the category as yet been discovered wherewith to construe and coördinate these two facts of religious experience together, although it is a fact known in every Christian experience that where God is most sovereign, man is most free.

For other passages, and the whole idea in the NT, see ELECTION. T. REES

CHOP (פָּרַשׂ, *pāras*):

Figurative: This word, meaning "to cut in pieces," "to distribute," often trd "spread," is rendered "chop" in Mic **3** 3, they "chop them in pieces, as for the pot," fig. for the destruction of God's people through the cruel exactions of their rulers.

CHORASHAN, kôr-ash'an, kŏ-rā'shan. See CORASHAN.

CHORAZIN, kŏ-rā'zin (**Χοραζίν**, *Chorazín*, Mt **11** 21; **Χωραζίν**, *Chōrazín*, Lk **10** 13; WH **Χοραζείν**, *Chorazeín*): A city whose name appears only in the woe pronounced against it by Christ (Mt **11** 21; Lk **10** 13). Its appearance there, however, shows that it must have been a place of some importance, and highly privileged by the ministry of Jesus. It was already deserted in the time of Eusebius, who places it 2 miles from Capernaum (*Onom*, s.v.). We can hardly doubt that it is represented by the extensive ruins of *Kerāzeh*, on the heights to the north of *Tell Ḥūm*. It is utterly desolate: a few carved stones being seen among the heaps. There are traces of a Rom road which connected the ancient city with the great highway between north and south which touched the lake shore at *Khān Minyeh*. W. EWING

CHORBE, kôr'bē (**Χορβέ**, *Chorbé*; AV **Corbe**): Head of a family which returned with Zerubbabel (1 Esd **5** 12). The name apparently corresponds to Zaccai in Ezr **2** 9 and Neh **7** 14.

CHOSAMAEUS, kos-a-mē'us (A, **Σίμων Χοσαμαῖος**, *Símōn Chosamaíos*; B, **Χοσάμαος**, *Chosámaos*): Occurs in 1 Esd **9** 32 as the name of one of the sons of Annas. But in the ‖ passage (Ezr **10** 31) the name is simply *Shimeon*, followed by "Benjamin, Malluch, Shemariah," which are omitted in 1 Esd. The LXX of Ezr **10** 31 has Σεμεών, *Semeôn*, followed by the three omitted names. The difference may have arisen from a mistake of a copyist, or from the use of an imperfect MS.

CHOSEN, chō'z'n. See CHOOSE.

CHOZEBA, kŏ-zē'ba (כֹּזֵבָא, *kōzēbhā'*, "deceitful"): Same as ACHZIB and CHEZIB (q.v.).

CHRIST AS KING, PRIEST, PROPHET. See under several titles; also CHRIST, OFFICES OF.

CHRIST, JESUS. See JESUS CHRIST.

CHRIST, THE EXALTATION, egz-ôl-tā'shun, **OF:**

I. THE RESURRECTION
  1. Its Glorification of Christ
  2. Resurrection Body—Identity, Change, Present Locality
  3. The Agent of the Resurrection
II. ASCENSION OF OUR LORD
  1. Its Actuality
  2. General Doctrine
  3. Lutheran Doctrine
  4. Relation to Doctrine of Existence-Form
  5. Necessity
III. EXALTATION TO THE RIGHT HAND OF GOD
  1. Its Significance
  2. Its Essential Necessity
IV. THE SECOND ADVENT
  1. Reality
  2. Judgment

This term is given to that condition of blessedness, glory and dominion into which Our Lord entered after the completion of His earthly career of humiliation and suffering, and which is to be regarded as the reward of His meritorious obedience, and the issue of His victorious struggle, and at the same time the means of His prosecution and completion of His work as Redeemer and Saviour of the world. The classic passage of Scripture, rich in suggestion, and the source of much controversy in the development of Christian theology, is Phil **2** 5–11. The word "exalted" of ver 9, ὑπερυψόω, *huperupsóō*, occurs only in this place in the NT and, like its Lat representative, is limited to ecclesiastical use. Cf Rom **14** 9; Eph **1** 19–23; 1 Pet **3** 21.22.

Christ's Exaltation includes His Resurrection, Ascension, Session at the right hand of God, and Advent as Judge and Consummator of the world's redemption.

I. The Resurrection.—The historic place and validity of this event will be found under other heads; our concern is with the event

1. Its Glorification of Christ

as it relates to the glorification of Our Lord. (1) It revealed His power over death. (2) It confirms all His claims to Divine Sonship. (3) It attests His acceptance and that of His work by God. (4) It crowns the process of the redemption of the world. (5) It forms the beginning of that new creation which is life eternal, and over which death can have no power. (6) It is the entrance of the Son of God into the power and glory of the New Kingdom, or the restored Kingdom of the Sovereign Ruler of the Universe. The following Scriptures among many others may be consulted: Rev **1** 18; Acts **2** 24; Rom **1** 4; 1 Cor **15** 20; Jn **5** 25; Rom **4** 25; Rom **6** 4.5; Col **2** 12; Phil **3** 10; Rom **6** 9.

An interesting and important question arises in connection with Christ's exaltation, relating to the nature of the body of the risen Lord.

2. Christ's Resurrection Body

It was clearly identical with that of His natural life. It was recognized by the marks which were upon it: Lk **24** 39.40; Jn **20** 24–29. It received food: Lk **24** 43 (cf **24** 30; Jn **21** 12.13;

Acts **10** 41). Nevertheless it was changed. After the resurrection, it was not at once recognized: Jn **20** 15; **21** 7; Lk **24** 31. It appeared under apparently new conditions of relation to material substance: Jn **20** 19; Lk **24** 36. It suddenly became visible, and as suddenly vanished. These facts suggest what reverently may be surmised as to its exalted condition. The apostle's declaration as to the resurrection-body of the redeemed furnishes some hints: 1 Cor **15** 35–49; cf Phil **3** 21. We may cautiously, from the history of the resurrection and the Pauline doctrine, conclude, that Our Lord still possesses a human body. It is of material substance, with new properties. It occupies space. It was seen by Paul, by Stephen, by the seer of the Apocalypse. It is glorious, incorruptible, spiritual.

3. The Agent of the Resurrection

By whom was the resurrection effected? It is referred by some Scriptures to God. See Ps **16** 10 (cf Acts **2** 27.31); and the distinct affirmation by Peter (Acts **2** 32). Paul declares that Christ was "raised . . . . through the glory of the Father" (Rom **6** 4). In Eph **1** 19.20, it was the mighty power of God which was wrought in Christ "when he raised him from the dead." Elsewhere it is ascribed to Christ Himself. He declared: "Destroy this temple, and in three days I will raise it up" (Jn **2** 19). In Jn **10** 17.18, Our Lord declares: "I lay down my life, that I may take it again. No one taketh it away from me, but I lay it down of myself. I have power to lay it down, and I have power to take it again." The efficient agent is said, according to the generally received reading of Rom **8** 2, to have been the Spirit of God, and thus the resurrection is referred to each person of the Godhead. The doctrine of the Lutheran church refers the act to the human power of the Lord Himself, which by incarnation had been endowed with attributes of Deity. This view consists with their teaching of the omnipresence of the body of Jesus (see below on the section "Ascension").

II. The Ascension of Our Lord.—The exaltation of Christ consisted further in His ascension.

1. Its Actuality

Some have held that the resurrection and ascension of Jesus ought to be regarded as aspects of the same event. But Mary saw the *risen* Lord, though she was forbidden to touch Him, for "I am not yet *ascended* unto the Father: but go unto my brethren, and say to them, I *ascend*," etc (Jn **20** 17). This, compared with the invitation to Thomas to touch Him, eight days later, suggests something in the ascension added to that which the resurrection implied, and the general thought of the church has consistently regarded the latter as a further step in the exaltation of the Lord.

2. General Doctrine of the Church

The fact of ascension is recorded in Mk **16** 19, and Lk **24** 50.51, and with greater detail in Acts **1** 9–11. According to these accounts, the ascension was seen by the disciples, and this suggests that heaven is a locality, where are the angels, who are not ubiquitous, and where Christ's disciples will find the place which He declared He was going to prepare for them (Jn **14** 2). Heaven is also undoubtedly referred to as a state (Eph **2** 6; Phil **3** 20), but Christ's body must be in some place, and where He is, there is Heaven.

This is certainly the doctrine of the church in general, and seems to be consistent with the Scriptural teaching.

3. Lutheran Doctrine

But the Lutherans have maintained that the ascension of the Lord merely involved a change of state in the human nature of Christ. He possessed during His life on earth the Divine attributes of omnipresence, omnipotence and omniscience, but He voluntarily abstained from their exercise. But at His ascension He returned to the full use of these powers. The ascension is Christ's return to immensity. The community of natures gave these Divine qualities to the humanity of Jesus, which Luther declared involved its ubiquity, and that as He was at the right hand of God, and God was everywhere, so Christ in His human personality was in no specific place but everywhere. This omnipresence is not of the infinite extension of the body of the Lord, but He is present as God is everywhere present in knowledge and power.

4. Theory of Laying aside the Existence-Form of God

Another theory of the ascended humanity of the Lord depends upon the conception of the Son of God laying aside at incarnation the "existence-form of God," and while affirming that Christ's body is now in a definite place, it proceeds to hold that at the ascension the accidental and variable qualities of humanity were laid aside, and that He dwells in heaven as a glorified man. Ebrard says: "He has laid aside forever the existence form of God, and assumed that of man in perpetuity, in which form by His Spirit He governs the church and the world. He is thus dynamically present to all His people." This form of doctrine seems to involve as the result of the incarnation of the Son of God His complete and sole humanity. He is no more than a man. The Logos is no longer God, and as the ascension did not involve the reassumption of the "existence-form of God," Christ in glory is only a glorified man.

5. Its Necessity

The ascension was necessary, in conformity with the spiritual character of the kingdom which Christ founded. Its life is that of faith, not sight. A perpetual life of even the resurrected Christ on earth would have been wholly inconsistent with the spiritual nature of the new order. The return of Christ to the special presence of God was also part of His high-priestly service (see Christ, Offices of) and His corporal absence from His people was the condition of that gift of the Spirit by which salvation was to be secured to each believer and promulgated throughout the world, as declared by Himself (Jn **16** 7). Finally, the ascension was that physical departure of the Lord to the place which He was to prepare for His people (Jn **14** 2.3). The resurrection was this completion of the objective conditions of redemption. The ascension was the initial step in the carrying out of redemptive work in the final salvation of mankind.

III. Exaltation Completed at the Right Hand of God.—The term "the right hand of God" is

1. Its Significance

Scriptural (Acts **7** 55.56; Rom **8** 34; Eph **1** 20; He **1** 3; **10** 12; **12** 2; 1 Pet **3** 22) and expresses the final step in the Lord's exaltation. Care must be taken in the use of the expression. It is a figure to express the association of Christ with God in glory and power. It must not be employed as by Luther to denote the relation of the body of Christ to space, neither must it be limited to the Divine nature of the Logos reinstated in the conditions laid aside in incarnation. Christ thus glorified is the God-man, the theanthropic person, Divine and human. This exaltation is based upon the essential glory of the Son of God, who "being

2. Its Essential Necessity

the brightness of his glory and the express image of his person . . . . sat down on the right hand" (He **1** 3 AV). It is the claim which the Lord makes for Himself in His prayer (Jn **17** 4.5), and is thus specifically declared in Phil **2** 6–11: "God highly exalted Him." But in His glory Christ received the power universal and Divine. In Eph **1** 20–22 His supreme dignity and power are affirmed "far above . . . . every name," "all things . . . . under His feet" (cf He **2** 8; 1 Cor **15** 27; 1 Pet **3** 22). Christ at the "right hand of God" is the highly suggestive picture of His universal dominion asserted by Himself (Mt **28** 18): "All authority hath been given unto me in heaven and on earth." It is vain to speculate upon the relation of Christ's nature in this exalted state. We cannot distinguish between the human and Divine. We can only believe in, and trust and submit to the One Glorified Person who thus administers the kingdom in perfect harmony with its Divine laws in all the ages, and His own revelation of the will of God, as given to man in His own earthly career: pitiful, tender, serving, helping, restoring, saving, triumphant. The exaltation is for His mediatorial and finally saving work. He is the Head of His church; He is the Lord of angels and men; He is the Master of the ages.

IV. The Second Advent.—The exaltation of Christ is to be completed by His coming again at the close of the dispensation, to complete His redemptive work and judge the world, and so to establish the final Kingdom of God. This belief has found a place in all the ecumenical symbols. Theology has ever included it in its eschatology. It is clear that the apostles and the early church expected the second coming of the Lord as an immediate event, the significance of which, and especially the effect of the nonfulfilment of which expectation, does not fall within the province of this article to consider. The various theories of the Parousia, the different ideas as to the time and the form of the second Advent, do not concern its relation to the exaltation of the Lord. Whenever and however He may return; whether He is ever coming to the church and to the world, His visible or His spiritual presence, do not affect the fact that He has been exalted to the position of ultimate Lord and final judge of men. We may therefore define this crowning condition of exaltation as:

1. Reality

(1) *An advent,* real, personal and visible. We must guard against the extremes of limiting this advent on the one side to a final particular event, on the other to those critical and catastrophic movements in world history which have led to the extension of God's kingdom and a virtual judgment of men. The Lord is ever coming, and also He will return. See Acts **1** 11; Lk **17** 24; Mt **24** 30; **25** 31; Lk **19** 12; Mt **13** 40.41.49; Lk **18** 8; Jn **5** 28.29; **6** 40.54; **21** 22; Acts **3** 20; 2 Thess **1** 10; He **9** 28; Jas **5** 8; Jude ver 14; 1 Jn **2** 28; Rev **1** 7. The reality and visibility of the advent depend upon the personal and abiding relation of the Lord to the world-redemption. Christianity is not merely a spiritual dynamic drawn from a series of past events. It is the living relation of the complete humanity of the redeemed to the God-man, and must therefore be consummated in a spiritual and material form. The ultimate of Christianity is no more docetic than was its original. A reverent faith will be satisfied with the fact of the glory whenever it shall arrive. The form and time are unrevealed. Preparation and readiness are better than speculation and imaginary description.

2. Judgment

(2) *The Judgment* is clearly taught by Scripture. Our Lord declares that He is appointed Judge (Jn **5** 22; **9** 39). Paul teaches that we must "all stand before the judgment-seat of God" (Rom **14** 10). Here again there is the suggestion of the judgment which is ever being made by the Lord in His office as Sovereign and Administrator of the kingdom; but there is also the expectation of a definite and final act of separation and discernment. Whatever may be the form of this judgment (and here again a wise and reverent silence as to the unrevealed is a becoming attitude for the believer), we are sure that He who will make it, is the glorified Word incarnate, and it will be the judgment of a wisdom and justice and love that will be the complete glory of the Christ. See also ASCENSION; JUDGMENT; PAROUSIA; RESURRECTION.

LL. D. BEVAN

CHRIST, HUMANITY OF. See HUMANITY OF CHRIST.

CHRIST, INTERCESSION OF. See INTERCESSION OF CHRIST.

CHRIST, OFFICES, of'is-is, **OF:**

General Titles of Our Lord
I. CHRIST'S MEDIATION EXPRESSED IN THE SPECIFIC OFFICES
History of the Theory
II. THE THREEFOLD OFFICE IN THE OT
The Failure of the Offices to Secure Their Desired Ends
III. THE PROPHET
The Forecast of the True Prophet
IV. CHRIST THE PROPHET
1. Christ's Manner of Teaching
2. Christ as Prophet in His Church
V. THE PRIESTHOOD OF CHRIST
1. Judaic Priesthood
2. Sacrificial Relations of Christ in the Gospels
3. Christ's Ethical Teaching Affected by Sacrificial Ideas
4. Mutual Confirmations of the Synoptics
5. The Dual Outgrowth of Sacrifice, the Victim and Sacrificer
6. Christ's Priesthood in the Apostolic Ministry and Epistles
7. The Crowning Testimony of the Epistle to the Hebrews
8. Christ's Relation to Sin Expressed in Sacrificial Terms
VI. CHRIST'S KINGLY OFFICE
The Breakdown of the Secular Monarchy
VII. THE MESSIANIC BASIS OF THE THREEFOLD OFFICE OF THE LORD
LITERATURE

This term has been used by theologians to describe the various characters of Our Lord's redemptive work. Many appellative and metaphorical titles are found in Scripture for Christ, designative of His Divine and human natures and His work: God (Jn **20** 28); Lord (Mt **22** 43.44); Word (Jn **1** 1.14); Son of God (Mt **3** 17; Lk **1** 35; Col **1** 15; 1 Jn **5** 20); Firstborn from the dead (Col **1** 18); Beginning of the Creation of God (Rev **3** 14); Image of God (2 Cor **4** 4); Express Image of His Person (He **1** 3 AV); Alpha and Omega (Rev **1** 8; **22** 13); Son of Man (Mt **8** 20; Jn **1** 51; Acts **7** 56); Son of David (Mt **9** 27; **21** 9); Last Adam (1 Cor **15** 45.47); Captain of Salvation (He **2** 10 m); Saviour (Lk **2** 11; Jn **4** 42; Acts **5** 31); Redeemer (Isa **59** 20; Tit **2** 14); Author and Perfecter of Faith (He **12** 2); Light of the World (Jn **8** 12); Lamb of God (Jn **1** 29.36); Creator of all things (Jn **1** 3.10); Mediator (1 Tim **2** 5); Prophet (Dt **18** 15; Lk **24** 19); Great High Priest (He **4** 14); King (Lk **1** 33; Rev **17** 14; **19** 16); Way, Truth and Life (Jn **14** 6). These and many others express the mediatorial office of the Lord. As mediator, He stands between God and Man, revealing the Father to man, and expressing the true relation of man to God. The term (Gr μεσίτης, *mesítēs*), moreover, signifies messenger, interpreter, advocate, surety or pledge in Gal **3** 19.20, where a covenant is declared to be assured by the hand of one who intervenes. Thus the covenant is confirmed and fulfilled by Him who secures that its stipulations should be carried out, and harmony is restored where before there had been difference and separation (1 Tim **2** 5; He **8** 6; **9** 15; **12** 24). Thus is expressed the purpose of God to redeem mankind by mediation.

General Titles of Our Lord

I. Christ's Mediation Expressed in the Specific Offices.—In presenting a systematic idea of this Redemptive Work of Christ by Mediation, Christian thought gave to it a harmonious character by choosing the most general and familiar titles of the Lord as the most inclusive categories expressive of the mode of Redemption. These were prophetic, priestly and regal.

Historical Review of the Theory

The first trace of this division is found in Euseb. *HE*, I, 3, and his *Demonstratio Evangelica*, IV, 15. It was accepted very largely in the Gr church, and continues to be used by Russian ecclesiastical writers. The Rom church has not so generally followed it, though it is found in the writings of many Rom theologians. The earlier reformers, especially Lutheran, ignored it. But Gerhard employed it and the Lutheran theologians followed his example, although some of these repudiated it, as Ernesti, Döderlein and Knapp. Calvin employed the division in his *Institutes*, II, 15. It was incorporated in the Heidelberg Catechism and has been adopted by most theologians of the Reformed church and by Eng. and American divines. In Germany most theological writers, such as De Wette, Schleiermacher, Tholuck, Nitzsch, Ebrard, adopt it, affirming it as expressive of the essential quality of the work of redemption, and the most complete presentment of its contents. The justification of this position is found in the important place occupied in the progress of revelation by those to whom were intrusted the duties of teaching and leading men in relation to God in the offices of priest, prophet and king. Even the modern development of Christian thought which extends the view of Divine dealing with man over the entire race and its religious history, not excluding those who would find in the most recent conditions of the world's life the outworking of the will of God in the purposes of human salvation, cannot discover any better form of expressing Christ's relation to man than in terms of the prophetic, the priestly and the governmental offices. The prophet is the instrument of teaching; the priest expresses the ethical relation of man to God; while the king furnishes the typical form of that exercise of sovereign authority and Providential direction which concerns the practical life of the race.

II. The Threefold Office as Presented in the OT.—From the close relation which Jesus in both His person and work bore to the OT dispensation, it is natural to turn to the preparatory history of the early Scriptures for the first notes of these mediatorial offices. That the development of the Jewish people and system ever moved toward Christ as an end and fulfilment is universally acknowledged. The vague and indeterminate conditions of both the religious and national life of Israel manifest a definite movement toward a clearer apprehension of man's relationship to God. Nothing is more clear in Israel's history than the gradual evolution of official service both of church and state, as expressed in the persons and duties of the prophet, the priest and the king. The early patriarch contained in himself the threefold dignity, and discharged the threefold duty. As the family became tribal, and the tribe national, these duties were divided. The order of the household was lost for a while in the chaos of the larger and less homogeneous society. The domestic altar was multiplied in many "high places." Professional interpreters of more or less religious value began to be seers, and here and there, prophets. The leadership of the people was occasional, ephemeral and uncertain. But the men of Divine calling appeared from time to time; the foundation work of Moses was built on; the regular order of the worship of Jeh, notwithstanding many lapses, steadily prevailed. Samuel gave dignity to his post as judge, and he again beheld the open vision of the Lord; he offered the appointed sacrifices; he established the kingly office; and although he was not permitted to see the family of David on the throne, like Moses he beheld afar off the promised land of a Divinely appointed kingdom. With the accession of the Davidic house, the three orders of God's service were completely developed. The king was seated on the throne, the priest was ministering at the one altar of the nation, the prophet with the Divine message was ever at hand to teach, to guide and to rebuke.

The Failure of the Threefold Offices to Secure Their Desired Ends

Notwithstanding this growth of the special institutions—prophet, priest and king—the religious and national condition was by no means satisfactory. The kingdom was divided; external foes threatened the existence of the nation; idolatry was not extinguished, and the prophets who were true to Jeh were compelled to warn and rebuke the sins of the rulers and the people, and even to testify against the priests for their unfaithfulness to the truth and purity of the religion which they professed. The best hopes of Israel and the Divine promises seem thus to be contradicted by the constant failure of the people to realize their best ideals. Hence slowly arose a vague expectation of reform. The idea of the better condition which was coming grew ever more distinct, and settled down at length to Israel's Messianic hope, expressed in various forms, finally converging to the looking for of one who should in some mysterious way gather into himself the ideas which belonged especially to the three great offices.

***III. The* Prophet.**—In this art. we are concerned only with the offices as they tend to their fulfilment in Christ. For the more general treatment of each office, reference must be made to the special arts.

The Forecast of the True Prophet

The first appearance of the idea of the special prophet of Jeh is in Dt **18** 15. Moses had been sent by the people to hear the Lord's words on their behalf (Ex **20** 19; Dt **5** 27); and this incident in the later passage of Dt **18** 15–22 is connected with the promise of a prophet, while at the same time reference is made to the general fact of prophecy and the conditions of its validity and acceptance. Here we find the germ of the expectation of *the* Prophet, which occupied so large a place in the mind of Israel. In the act of the people sending Moses to receive the word, and Jeh's promise to send a prophet whom they would accept, we see also the suggestion of a distinction between the first dispensation and the latter. The Divine promise was to the effect that what was given by Moses God would consummate in a prophetic revelation through a person. The conception of this personality is found in the second part of Isa (**40–66**). Isaiah's mission was vain, Isa **49** 4, but the coming one shall prevail, **49–53** (*passim*). But the success of this servant of Jeh was not to be only as a prophet, but by taking on himself the penalty of sin (**53** 5), and by being made an offering for sin; and as Mighty Victor triumphing over all foes (**53** 10–12), the dignities of whose kingship are set forth in various parts of the prophetic writings. Thus the general effect of the course of the earlier revelation may be summed up in this prophetic ministry with which has been combined a priestly and a royal character. It was an ever-advancing manifestation of the nature and will of God, delivered by inspired men who spake at sundry times and in divers manners, but whose message was perfected and extended by Jesus Christ (He **1** 1), who thus became *the* Prophet of the Lord.

IV. Christ, the Prophet.—Christ's ministry illustrates the prophetic office in the most extensive and exalted sense of the term. He was designed and appointed by the Father (Isa **61** 1.2; cf Lk **4** 16–21; Mt **17** 5). In 1 Cor **1** 30, Christ is declared to be made to us wisdom. His intimate knowledge of God (Jn **1** 18; Mt **11** 27; Jn **16** 15), the qualities of His teaching dependent upon His nature, both Divine and human (Jn **3** 34); His authority (Jn **1** 9.17.18; Lk **4** 18–21); His knowledge of God (Mk **12** 29; Jn **4** 24; Mt **11** 25; Jn **17** 11.25; Mt **18** 35)—these all peculiarly fitted Christ to be the Revealer of God. Besides His doctrine of God, His ministry included the truth concerning Himself, His nature, claims, mission, the doctrine of the Holy Spirit, and the religious life of man. He taught as none other the foundation of religion, the facts on which it was based, the essence of Divine service, the nature of sin, the grace of God, the means of atonement, the laws of the kingdom of God and the future state. By the acknowledgment of even those who have denied His Divine nature and redemptive work, He has been recognized as the Supreme Moral Teacher of the world. His claim to be *the* Prophet is seen in that He is the source of the ever-extending revelation of the eternal. His own words and works He declared were only part of the fuller knowledge which would be furnished by the system which He established (Lk **9** 45; **18** 34; Jn **12** 16; **14** 26; **15** 26; **16** 12.13.14).

1. Christ's Manner of Teaching

How remarkable was His method of teaching! Parable, proverb, absolute affirmation, suggestion, allusion to simple objects, practical life—these all made His teaching powerful, easily understood, living; sometimes His action was His word—and all with a commanding dignity and gracious winsomeness, that was felt by His hearers and has ever been recognized (Mt **7** 29). So perfect and exalted was the teaching of Jesus that many have supposed that revelation ceased with Him, and the immediate followers whom He especially inspired to be His witnesses and interpreters. Certainly in Him the prophetic ministry culminated.

2. Christ as Prophet in His Church

An important aspect of Christ's prophetic office is that of His relation to the church as the source, through the instrumentality of His Spirit, of ever-enlarging knowledge of Divine truth which it has been able to gain. This is the real significance of the claim which some churches make to be the custodians and interpreters of the tradition of faith, with which has also gone the theory of development—not as a human act but as a ministration of the Lord through His Spirit, which is granted to the church. Even those who hold that all Divine truth is to be found in the sacred Scriptures have yet maintained that God has much truth still to bring out of His word by the leading and direction of the Spirit of Jesus. The Scripture itself declares that Christ was the light which lighteth every man that cometh into the world (Jn **1** 9). He Himself promised that the Spirit which He would give would guide His followers into all truth (Jn **16** 13). The apostles claimed to receive their teaching and direction of the church from the Lord (1 Cor **11** 23). The testimony of Jesus is definitely declared to be the spirit of prophecy (Rev **19** 10). Indeed, all the apostolic writings in almost every line affirm that what they teach is received from the Spirit, who is the Spirit of the Lord.

V. The Priesthood of Christ.—For the history of the development of the priesthood of Israel on which Our Lord's High-Priesthood is ideally based, reference must be made to the art. esp. dealing with that subject. The bearings of that institution upon the work of Jesus as Redeemer alone fall under this section.

1. Judaic Priesthood

Judaism like all religions developed an extensive system of priestly service. As the moral sense of the people enlarged and became more distinct, the original simplicity of sacrifice, especially as a commensal act, in which the unity of the celebrants with each other and with God was expressed, was expanded into acts regularly performed by officials, in which worship, thanksgiving, covenant and priestly expiation and atonement were clearly and definitely expressed. The progress of sacrifice may be seen in the history of the OT from Cain and Abel's (Gen **4** 3.4), Noah's (Gen **8** 20), Abraham's covenant (Gen **15** 9–18), etc, to the elaborate services of the Mosaic ritual set forth in Lev, the full development of which is found only in the later days of Israel. When Christ appeared, the entire sacerdotal system had become incorporated in the mind, customs and language of the people. They had learned more or less distinctly the truth of man's relation to God in its natural character, and esp. in that aspect where man by his sin had separated himself from God and laid himself open to the penalty of law. The conception of priesthood had thus grown in the consciousness of Israel, as the necessary instrument of mediation between man and God. Priestly acts were performed on behalf of the worshipper. The priest was to secure for man the Divine favor. This could only be gained by an act of expiation. Something must be done in order to set forth the sin of man, his acknowledgment of guilt, the satisfaction of the law, and the assurance of the Divine forgiveness, the restored favor of God and finally the unity of man and God.

2. Sacrificial Relations of Christ in the Gospels

That the work of Christ partook of the nature of priestly service is already indicated by references in the Gospels themselves. He was called "Jesus; for it is he that shall save his people from their sins" (Mt **1** 21). Salvation from sin, in the habit of thought at which the Jew had arrived, must have expressed itself most clearly in the symbolic signification of the sacrifices in the temple. Thus in the very name which Our Lord received His priesthood is suggested. The frankincense of the Magi's offering is not without its mystical meaning (Mt **2** 11). Some may find in the Baptist's words, "baptize you in the Holy Spirit and in fire" (Mt **3** 11), a suggestion of priestly action, for the understanding of John's declaration must be found in the conventional ideas of the Jewish thought of the period, determined as they undoubtedly were by the history of priestly service in the past and the fully developed ritual of the temple. The baptizing of the proselyte was not necessarily a priestly act, as indeed we cannot be certain that the baptism was always necessary at the introduction of a proselyte into the Jewish church. But the association of circumcision with the initiation of the proselyte certainly introduced the priest, and the sprinkling of the congregation by the priest was a familiar part of his official duties. It is quite probable therefore that John's use of the expression carried with it something of the sacerdotal idea.

3. Christ's Ethical Teaching Affected by Sacrificial Ideas

The spirit of Our Lord's teaching, as seen in the Sermon on the Mount, etc, as it reflects the thought of the Galilean ministry, may be regarded as prophetic rather than priestly. Still the end of the teaching was righteousness, and it was impossible for a Jew to conceive of the securing of righteousness without some reference to priestly administration and influence. The contrast of the effect of Christ's teaching with that of the scribes (Mt **7** 29) keeps us in the vicinity of the law as applied through the sacerdotal service of which the scribes were the interpreters and teachers, and surely therefore a hint of Our Lord's relation to priesthood may have found its way into the minds of His immediate hearers. He was careful to recognize the authority of the priest (Mt **8** 4).

The doctrine of sacrifice emerges somewhat more distinctly in the reference to the cross, which Our Lord associates with the thought of finding life by losing it (Mt **16** 24.25), and when the taking up the cross is interpreted by following Christ, and this hint is soon followed by Christ's distinct reference to His coming sufferings (Mt **17** 9.12), more definitely referred to in vs 22.23. Now the object of the work of the Lord takes clearer form. The Son of Man is come to save that which was lost (Mt **18** 11 ARVm). As the time of the catastrophe drew nearer, the Lord became still more distinct in His references to His coming death (Mt **20** 18.19), and at length declares that "the Son of man came . . . . to give his life a ransom for many" (Mt **20** 28). Our Lord's quotations (Mt **21** 42; **23** 39) concerning the rejected "corner stone," and the Blessed One "that cometh in the name of the Lord" (Ps **118** 22.26), are drawn from a psalm filled with the spirit of the priestly service of the temple, and in their reference to Himself again illustrate the ever-increasing recognition of His priesthood. He also uses the official term "Christ" (Messiah, the anointed one) more frequently (Mt **24** 5.23.24). On the eve of the betrayal and trial the crucifixion is clearly foretold (Mt **26** 2); and the death (**26** 12). The full significance of the death is asserted at the institution of the Lord's Supper. The bread is "my body," the wine is "my blood of the new covenant," and it is declared to be "poured out for many unto remission of sins" (Mt **26** 26–28 m).

4. Mutual Confirmation of the Synoptics

A similar succession of ideas of Our Lord's priestly work may be found in the other gospels (see Mk **1** 8.44; **8** 29; see below on the significance of the term Christ; **8** 31.34; **9** 9.10). The inability of the disciples to understand the life that was to follow death here is indicated —the truth of the gospel of death and resurrection so closely bound up with the conception of sacrifice, where the blood is the life which given becomes the condition of the new union with God, being thus revealed by Christ as the initial doctrine to be continuously enlarged (**9** 31; **10** 21.33.34.45; **11** 9; **12** 10; **13** 21.22; **14** 8.22–25.61.62). In Lk the priestly "atmosphere" is introduced in the earliest part of the narrative, the history of Zacharias and Elisabeth giving emphasis to the setting of John's own mission (Lk **1**). The name Jesus (Lk **1** 31); the special relation of the new kingdom to sin, necessarily connected with sacrifice in the mind of a priest, found in Zacharias' psalm (Lk **1** 77.78); the subtle suggestion of the Suffering One in the "also" of **2** 35 AV (ARV omits) shows that the third Gospel is quite in line with the two other Synoptics (see also Lk **3** 3; **5** 14). The claim to forgive sins must have suggested the sacrificial symbol of remission (Lk **5** 24; **9** 23; **13** 35; **14** 27; **18** 31; **20** 14; **22** 19.20; **24** 7.26. 46.47). In the Fourth Gospel, we have the word of the Baptist, "Behold, the Lamb of God" (Jn **1** 29.36), where Christ's relation to sin is distinctly expressed (see LAMB OF GOD)—the baptism in the Spirit (**1** 33). It is highly probable that the apostle John was the "other" of the two disciples, (**1** 40) and, having heard the Baptist's words, is the only evangelist who records them, thus introducing from his personal knowledge the sacrificial idea earlier into his history than the Synoptics. Christ declares that He will give His life for the life of the world (**6** 51). The entire passage (vs 47–65) is suffused with the conception of "life for life," one of the elements constituting the conception of the sacrificial act. In **8** 28 (cf **3** 14; **12** 32) Christ predicts His crucifixion. The Good Shepherd gives His life for the sheep (**10** 15). In vs 17.18, Christ claims the power to lay down His life and to take it again. He is the sacrifice and the Sacrificer.

5. The Dual Outgrowth of Sacrifice, Victim and Sacrificer

Here appears for the first time the double relation of Christ to the sacrificial idea, worked out in the later thought of the church into the full significance of Our Lord's priestly office. In **11** 25.26 Christ is the source of life, and life after death. It is hardly possible that this conception should not have, even if remotely suggested, some reference to the significance of sacrifice; for in the sacrifices the Divine claim for the blood, as specially to be set apart as the Divine portion, was ever present. God ever claimed the blood as His; for to Him the life was forfeited by sin. And moreover He alone possesses life and gives it. Of that forfeit and that Divine sovereignty of life, sacrifice is the expression. This is fully realized and made actual in Christ's life and death for man, in which man shares by His unity with Christ. Man at once receives the penalty of sin in dying with Christ, and rises again into the new life which Our Lord opened, and of which He is the ceaseless energy and power through the spirit of God. The emergence of this idea is illustrated by the evangelist in the sayings of Caiaphas, where as the high priest of the nation he gives, though unconsciously, a significant expression to the truth that it was "expedient" that Jesus 'should die for the nation and for the children of God everywhere scattered' (**11** 47–52). Here the symbolic significance of sacrifice is practically realized: death in the place of another and the giving of life to those for whom the sacrifice was offered. The vitalizing power of Christ's death is asserted in the discourse following the visit of the Greeks (**12** 24–33). The idea of life from the dying seed is associated with the conception of the power of attraction and union by the cross. The natural law of life through death is thus in harmony with the gift of life through sacrifice involving death. That sacrifice may be found much more widely than merely in death, is shown by the law of service illustrated in the washing of the disciples' feet (**13** 14–17); and this is declared to spring out of love (**15** 13). For the priestly ideas of Our Lord's prayer (Jn **17**) see INTERCESSION; INTERCESSION OF CHRIST; PRAYERS OF CHRIST.

6. Christ's Priesthood in the Apostolic Ministry and Epistles

Christ's priestly office finds illustration in the Acts of the Apostles, in the apostolic declaration of Christ's Messianic office, not only Lord, but also Christ the Anointed One (Acts **2** 36). Peter's reference to the stone which completed the temple, the service of which was essentially sacrificial, as the Symbol of Christ, the Crown of that Spiritual Temple (Acts **4** 11); Philip's application of the passage in Isa of the sheep led to the slaughter (Isa **53** 7.8) to Our Lord (Acts **8** 32.35); Peter's discourse to Cornelius, culminating in the remission of sins through Christ (Acts **10** 43)—all indicates the steady growth in the apostolic ministry of the conception of Our Lord's priestly office. The idea takes its most distinct form in Paul's sermon at Antioch (Acts **13** 38.39). The necessity of Christ's death and resurrection was the essence of Paul's message (Acts **17** 3). And in the address to the elders, the church is declared to have been purchased by God with His own blood (Acts **20** 28).

As the epistles express the more elaborated thought of the apostolic ministry, the sacrifice of Our Lord naturally finds more definite exposition, and inasmuch as He was both active and passive in the offering of Himself, the conception of sacrifice branches into the twofold division, the object offered, and the person offering. It must never be forgotten, however, that the thought of Christ's sacrifice even when thus separated into its two great divisions necessarily involves in each conception the suggestion of the other: God setting Him forth as a propitiation through faith in His blood (Rom **3** 25). He was delivered for our offences and raised for our justification (Rom **4** 25). Through Him we have access to the conditions of justification and peace (Rom **5** 2). Christ died for the ungodly, and we are justified by His blood (Rom **5** 8.9). The conception of life both as forfeit from man and gift by God, expressed by sacrifice, runs through the reasoning of Rom **8** (see esp. 11.32–34, where Christ who died for man rises from the dead, and becomes the intercessor; the victim and the High Priest are thus united in the Lord, and thus He becomes full expression and supplier of the love of God which is the perfect life). In 1 Cor **1** 23 Paul affirms the preaching of the cross as the center of his message. The subject of his teaching was not merely Christ, but Christ and Him crucified (1 Cor **2** 2). In 1 Cor **5** 7 Christ is declared to be the Passover, and sacrificed for us (1 Cor **10** 16–18). The manifestation of the death of the Lord by the bread and wine is given in the account of the institution of the Supper (1 Cor **11** 26). In 1 Cor **15** 3 Christ is said expressly to have died for our sins. Christ's sacrifice lies at the basis of all the thought of the Galatian epistle (**1** 4; **2** 20; **3** 13).

In Eph we have the definite statement of redemption through the blood of Christ (Eph **1** 7). Christ's humiliation to the cross is given in Phil **2** 8; community with Christ's death, one of the important elements of sacrifice, in Phil **3** 10.11. Forgiveness, the essence of redemption, is declared to be through the blood of Christ (Col **1** 14). Peace is secured through the blood of the cross, and reconciliation (Col **1** 20); the presentation of us in Christ's flesh through death, holy and unblamable and unreprovable to God (Col **1** 22). The community of sacrifice sets forth the oneness of believers with Christ (Col **3** 1–4). Christ is declared to be the one Mediator between God and man, who gave Himself a ransom for all (1 Tim **2** 5.6).

7. The Crowning Testimony of the Epistle to the Hebrews

The chief source of the priestly conception of Our Lord is the Epistle to the He. Christ is declared to have by Himself purged our sins (He **1** 3); to taste of death for every man (He **2** 9); that He might be a merciful and faithful High Priest to make reconciliation for the sins of the people (He **2** 17; cf He **3** 1); the community of sacrifice (He **3** 14); our great High Priest has passed into the heavens (He **4** 14); His pitifulness (**4** 15); the authority and power of Christ's priesthood fully set forth (He **5**). Christ was made a High Priest after the order of Melchizedek (He **5** 6). The priesthood of Christ being of the order of Melchizedek is more excellent than the Aaronic priesthood (He **7**). Christ's priesthood being eternal, that of the Aaronic is abolished (He **8**). Christ's high-priesthood is made effectual by His own blood; and He entered once for all into the holy place, and has become the Mediator of a New Covenant (He **9** 11–15). Christ is forever the representative of man in heaven (He **9** 24–28). Christ by the sacrifice of Himself forever takes away sin, and has consecrated the new and living way to God (He **10**). He is the Mediator of the New Covenant (He **12** 24). The entire Epistle is steeped in the conception of Christ's priesthood.

In 1 Pet **1** 2 the sacrificial element appears in the "sprinkling of the blood of Jesus Christ." The sufferings of the Lord were prophesied, the spirit of the Anointed One signifying what the prophets desired to know (**1** 11); the redemption by the precious blood of Christ is of "a lamb without blemish and without spot" (**1** 19); the priesthood of believers was *through* Christ (**2** 5), who carried up our sins in his body to the tree (**2** 24 RVm).

In the Johannine writings we have the cleansing from sin by the blood of Jesus Christ (1 Jn **1** 7). Christ is said to have laid down His life for us (1 Jn **3** 16). The sacrifice as well as the teaching of Christ is insisted on in the coming by blood as well as by water (**5** 6).

The appearance of Christ in Rev **1** 13 is high-priestly; His robe is the *talar*, the high-priestly garment. The sacrificial place of Christ is indicated by "a Lamb . . . . as though it had been slain" (Rev **5** 6.9.12). The repeated title of Christ throughout the Apocalypse is The Lamb.

8. Christ's Relation to Sin Expressed in Sacrificial Terms

This review of the Scripture teaching on priesthood clearly indicates the development of thought which led to the affirmation of Our Lord's priestly office. He came to put away sin. The doctrine of sin was intimately associated with the priestly service of the temple. The sacrifices were in some cases sin offerings, and in these there ever appeared, by the function of the blood which is the life, the fatal loss of life by sin, the punishment of which was the withdrawal of the Divine gift of life. The life was always in the sacrifice reserved for God. It was natural therefore when Christ appeared that His work in taking away sin should have been interpreted in the light of sacrificial thought. We find the idea steadily developed in the NT. He was the sacrifice, the Lamb of God. The question as to who offered the sacrifice was answered—Himself. Then He became in the conception of apostolic teaching, esp. emphasized in the Epistle to the He, the priest as well as the sacrifice. This was at length completely defined in the theology of the church, and has generally been accepted as setting forth an important aspect of Our Lord's redemptive work.

VI. Christ's Kingly Office.—The association of rule with the redemption of mankind was early found in Divine revelation. It is in the *Protevangelium* of Gen **3** 15; the covenant with Abraham contains it (Gen **22** 17.18); the blessing of Jacob reflects it (Gen **49** 10). After the successive attempts to establish a visible and earthly monarchy, its settlement in the family of David was associated with Divine premonitions of continued and gracious royalty (2 S **7** 18–29; **23** 1–7; Pss **2, 45, 72, 110**). The failure of the earthly monarchy and the fatal experiences of the kingdom turned the thought of the devout, esp. guided by prophetic testimony, to a coming king who should restore the glory of the Davidic house and the people of Israel. Here and there the conception appears of the more extended reign of the Coming One, and the royal authority finds a growing place in the prophetic Scriptures (Isa **2** 1–4; **9** 6.7; **11** 1–10; **42** 1–4; **52** 13–15; **53** 12; **60**; Jer **23** 5.6; **30** 18–24; Dnl **2** 44; **7** 9–14.27; Mic **5** 1–4; Zec **3**). The postexilic conception of the king became one of the supreme and most active ideas in the Jewish mind. The reign of the Messiah was to be earthly, and all nations were to be subject to the Jew. The Jews of Pal seem to have retained the more patriotic and the more

The Breakdown of the Secular Monarchy

material form of the idea (see 1 Macc **14** 41), while the Egyptian and dispersed Jews began to regard the more spiritual character of the coming Messiah. References to the future blessedness of Israel under the restored royalty do not appear so largely in the Apoc writings which it must be remembered reflect chiefly their Egyp-Jewish sources. Still there are some passages of interest (Bar **4** 21–5; Tob **13**; Ecclus **35** 18.19; **36** 11–16; **47** 11.22). In the NT we have references to the strong expectation of the restored royalty and kingdom (Jn **1** 49; **6** 15; **12** 12–15; Acts **1** 6). Christ's kingship was speedily recognized by those who saw His works of power, and acknowledged His authority. He Himself clearly claimed this authority (Mt **22** 43–45; Jn **18** 36.37). It was however not a kingdom based upon material and external power and rule, but on the foundation of truth and righteousness. The Kingdom of Heaven or of God is familiar to every reader of the words of Jesus. It was thus He described the new order which He had come to establish, of which He was to be the Lord and Administrator; not an earthly dominion after the fashion of this world's kingdoms; it was to be the rule of mind and of spirit. It was to be extended by ethical forces, and the principle of its authority was centered in Christ Himself. It was to be developed on earth but perfected in the future and eternal life. Some divines have distinguished Christ's regal power as that of nature, that of grace, that of glory. Many believe that there is to be a personal visible reign of Christ upon the earth. Some hold that this will be produced by His advent prior to an age of millennial glory. Other views regard the advent as the close of earthly conditions and the final judgment.

VII. The Messianic Basis of the Threefold Office of the Lord.—That the developments of Jewish thought centered round what may conveniently be called the idea of the Messiah is plain to any student of the OT and other Jewish writings. They sprang from the ethical and theological ideas of this people, interpreted by and expressed in their political and religious forms, and continually nurtured by their experiences in the varied course of their national life. The essence of Messianic belief was a personal deliverer. Jewish history had always been marked by the appearance and the exploits of a great man. The capacity of the production of exceptional and creative individuals has been the characteristic of the race in all its ages. A judge, a lawgiver, a teacher, a seer, a king—each had helped, or even saved the people in some critical period. Each had added to the knowledge of God, whether received or rejected by the people. The issues of such service had remained, enshrined in a growing lit., or made permanent in a finally centralized and unified ritual, recorded in chronicle and lyric. The hope of Israel at one time did not take the completely personal form; indeed, it is probably easy to exaggerate the Messianic element as we look back from the perfect realization of it, in the Christian revelation and history. Much that has been called Messianic has been the result of reading into the OT what has been derived from Christian thought and experience. Zeph has been described as a picture of Israel's restoration and triumph. Yet apparently it has no reference to the personal element. Still the "Messiah" begins to appear in the prophetic writings (see above), esp. in the royal elements of His office. It is at this point that the meaning of the term is to be considered. "Jeh's anointed" is found as applied to a king, and is familiar in this use in the OT. But anointing belonged to the priesthood and to the prophetic order, if not actually, at least metaphorically, as setting apart (see 1 K **19** 16; Ps **105** 15; Isa **61** 1). And the word Messiah (Christ) the Anointed, came to be used for that conception of a person, perhaps first employed definitely (Dnl **9** 24–26), who should be the Deliverer of the Jews and even still more widely, a Redeemer. In the age immediately preceding the Christian, the idea had taken possession not only of the Jews, but also of the Samaritans (Jn **4** 25); and was not altogether unknown in gentile thought; e.g. Sib Or, iii.97; Virgil *Ecl.* iv. It involves certainly the prophetic and royal offices and, in the idea of a Suffering Servant, was closely allied to the objects of the sacrificial order.

The claim of Jesus to be the Christ, and the recognition of this claim by His followers and apostles, gave a new meaning to the teaching of the OT, and the writings lying outside the canon, but which were familiar to the people. Especially was the suffering and death of the Lord and its relation to sin the occasion of a new understanding of the Mosaic and later-developed sacrificial system. Jesus as the Offerer of Himself perfected the function of the priest, as He became the Lamb of God who taketh away the sins of the world. He thus completed the threefold ministry of the Messiah as the Prophet who reveals, the Priest who offers and intercedes, the King who rules. In Him the offices are commingled. He rules by His sacrifice and His teaching; He reveals by His Kingship and His offering. The offices spring from both His person and His work, and are united in the final issue of the salvation of the world. See also EXALTATION OF CHRIST; INTERCESSION OF CHRIST.

LITERATURE.—Euseb., *HE*, I,3; Aug., *De civ. Dei*, x. 6; Catech. Council of Trent; Calvin, *Instit.*, II, 15; Heidelb. Catech. Ans. 31 and Reformed Liturg; Thanksgiving aft. Inft. Bapt.; J. Gerhard, *Loci Theolog;* Spener, *Catechism.;* Ernesti, *De officio Christi triplici;* Knapp, *Theology*, sec. 107; Ebrard, *Herzog Realencyc.*, s.v. Further discussion is found in the standard theologies, as Pye Smith, *First Lines*, and *Scrip. Testim. to the Messiah;* Hodge, Shedd, Weiss, *Bib. Theol. of the NT*, Van Oosterzee, *Christian Dogmatics*. See also Higginson, *Ecce Messias;* Moule's brief but suggestive statement in *Outlines of Christian Doctrine;* Ritschl, *A Critical History of the Christian Doctrine of Justification and Reconciliation*, esp. Introduction; Dorner, *The Development of the Doctrine of the Person of Christ.*

LL. D. BEVAN

CHRIST, PERSON OF. See PERSON OF CHRIST.

CHRIST, TEMPTATION OF. See TEMPTATION OF CHRIST.

CHRISTIAN, kris'chan, kris'ti-an (**Χριστιανός**, *Christianós*):

1. Historicity of Acts 11 26
2. Of Pagan Origin
3. The Christian Attitude to the Name
4. Was Christian the Original Form?
5. The Christians and the Empire
6. Social Standing of the Early Christians
7. Christian Self-Designations

LITERATURE

The word Christian occurs only three times in the NT (Acts **11** 26; **26** 28; and 1 Pet **4** 16). The first passage, Acts **11** 26, gives the origin of the term, "The disciples were called Christians first in Antioch." The older generation of critical scholars disputed the historicity of this statement.

1. Historicity of Acts 11:26

It was argued that, had the term originated so early, it must have been found far more frequently in the records of early Christianity; sometimes also that the termination *-ianus* points to a Lat origin. But there is general agreement now that these objections are groundless. The historicity of the Lukan account is upheld not only by Harnack, but by the more radical Knopf in *Die Schriften des NT*, edited by Johannes Weiss. In early imperial times, the adjectival termination *-ianos* was widely diffused throughout the whole empire. Originally applied to the slaves belonging to the great households, it had passed into regular use to denote the adherents of an individual or a party. A Christian is thus simply an adherent of Christ. The name belongs, as Ramsay says, to the popular slang, as indeed sect and party names generally do. It is only after a considerable interval, and very often under protest, that such names are accepted as self-designations.

2. Of Pagan Origin

The name, then, did not originate with the Christians themselves. Nor would the Jews have applied it to the followers of Jesus, whose claim to be the Christ they opposed so passionately. They spoke of the Christians as "the sect of the Nazarenes" (Acts **24** 5); perhaps also as "Galíleans," a term which the emperor Julian attempted later vainly to revive. The word must have been coined by the heathen population of Antioch, as the church emerged from the synagogue, and a Christianity predominantly gentile took its place among the religions of the world.

3. The Christian Attitude to the Name

Perhaps the earliest occurrence of *Christian* as a self-designation is in *Did* **12** 4. In the Apologists and Ignatius on the other hand the word is in regular use. 1 Pet simply takes it over from the anti-Christian judicial procedure of the law courts, without in any way implying that the Christians used it among themselves. There is every probability, however, that it was the danger which thus began at an early date to attach to the name which commended it to the Christians themselves as a title of honor. Deissmann (*Licht vom Osten*, 286) suggests that *Christian* means *slave of Christ*, as *Caesarian* means *slave of Caesar*. But the word can scarcely have had that fulness of meaning till the Christians themselves had come to be proud of it.

According to tradition, Luke himself belonged to Antioch. In Acts **11** 27.28 Codex D reads "There was much rejoicing, and when we had assembled, there stood up," etc. In view of the greater authority now so frequently accorded to the so-called Western text, we cannot summarily dispose of such a reading as an interpolation. If the historian was not only an Antiochene, but a member of the original gentile Christian church, we have the explanation alike of his interest in the origin of the name Christian, and of the detailed precision of his information.

4. Was Christian the Original Form?

In all three NT passages the uncorrected Codex ℵ reads "Chrestian." We know from many sources that this variant was widely current in the 2d cent. Blass in his ed of Acts not only consistently reads Chrestian, but conjectures that Chrestian is the correct reading in Tacitus (*Annals*, xv.44), the earliest extra-Biblical testimony to the word. The Tacitus MS has since been published in facsimile. This has shown, according to Harnack (*Mission and Expansion*, ET, I, 413, 414), that "Chrestian" actually was the original reading, though the name "Christ" is correctly given. Harnack accordingly thinks that the Lat historian intended to correct the popular appellation of cir 64 AD, in the light of his own more accurate knowledge. "The common people used to call them 'Chrestians,' but the real name of their founder was Christ." Be this as it may, a confusion between "Christos" and the familiar Gr slave name "Chrestos" is more intelligible at an early date than later, when Christianity was better known. There must have been a strong tendency to conform the earlier witnesses to the later, familiar, and etymologically correct, usage. It is all the more remarkable, therefore, that ℵ* retains "Chrestian." On the whole it seems probable that this designation, though bestowed in error, was the original one.

5. The Christians and the Empire

The fuller discussion of this subject more appropriately falls under the arts. dealing with the relation of the church and empire. Suffice it here to say that Paul apparently hoped that by his acquittal the legal position of Christianity as a *religio licita* would be established throughout the empire, and that 1 Pet belongs to a time when the mere profession of Christianity was a crime in the eyes of the state, but that in all probability this was a new position of affairs.

6. Social Standing of the Early Christians

That early Christianity was essentially a movement among the lower non-literary classes has been rightly emphasized—above all by Deissmann. This is a circumstance of the utmost importance for the correct understanding of the early history of our faith, though probably Deissmann in some degree exaggerates and misplaces the significance. Is it correct to say, for example, that "primitive Christianity was relatively indifferent to politics, not as Christianity, but as a movement of the humbler folks, whose lot on the whole had certainly been lightened by the Empire" (*Licht vom Osten*, 254)? Very probably however the difficulties of the Pauline gentile mission were appreciably increased by the fact that he touched a lower social stratum than that of the original Jewish Christianity of Pal. No class more resents being associated in any way with the "submerged masses" than the self-respecting peasant or artisan, who seems to have formed the backbone of the Pal church. The apostle had consequently to fight against social, no less than racial and religious, prejudices.

7. Christian Self-Designations

The Christians originally called themselves "Disciples," a term afterward restricted to personal hearers of the Lord, and regarded as a title of high distinction. The ordinary self-designations of the apostolic age are "believers" (Acts **5** 14; 1 Tim **4** 12), "saints" (Acts **9** 13.32.41; Rom **1** 7), "brethren" (Acts **6** 3; **10** 23, etc), "the elect" (Col **3** 12; 2 Tim **2** 10), "the church of God" (Acts **20** 28 m), "servants [slaves] to God" (Rom **6** 22; 1 Pet **2** 16). The apostolic authors refer to themselves as "servants [slaves] of Christ Jesus" (Phil **1** 1). Other expressions are occasionally met with, of which perhaps the most significant is: Those "that call upon the name of the Lord" (Acts **9** 14; Rom **10** 12.13; 1 Cor **1** 2). Cf Pliny's report to Trajan (*Epistles*, X, 97): "They affirmed that . . . . they had been wont to assemble and address a hymn to Christ as to a god."

LITERATURE.—The most recent discussion of the names of Christian believers, including "Christian," is in Harnack's *Mission and Expansion of Christianity*, ET (2d ed, 1908), I, 399 ff. See also *EB*, *HDB*, *DCG*, with the lit. there cited. On the social status of the early Christians, cf Orr's *Neglected Factors in the Study of the Early Progress of Christianity;* on the religious significance of the name, see CHRISTIANITY.

JOHN DICKIE

CHRISTIANITY, kris-chan′i-ti, kris-chi-an′i-ti, kris-ti-an′i-ti (**Χριστιανισμός**, *Christianismós*):

I. IN PRINCIPLE AND ESSENCE
1. Early Use of Term
2. NT Implications: Messiahship—Resurrection—Redemption
   Pauline Summaries
3. Did Jesus Claim to Be Christ?
4. The Resurrection
   Its Evidence
5. Two Contrasted Estimates of Our Lord's Person
   (1) The Non-Believing Estimate—not Truly Historical
   (2) The Believing Estimate—Relation to Experience
6. Christianity an Experience of Salvation
7. Jesus and the Gospel

I. In Principle and Essence.—Unlike "Christian" (AV), the term "Christianity," so far as is known, was first used by the Christians themselves, but does not occur in the NT. It is exactly parallel to *Judaism* ("the Jews' religion"), found not only in Gal **1** 13.14, but in 2 Macc **2** 21, etc. Our earliest authority for the word "Christianism" is Ignatius of Antioch. Christian is now a title of honor, and the Christian's glory is "to live according to Christianism" (Ignatius, *Ad magnes*, 10).

1. Early Use of Term

While, however, the name is foreign to the NT, the NT is by universal consent our most important source of information regarding the thing. Christianity arose out of the life and work of Jesus of Nazareth, who claimed to be "the Christ." During Jesus' lifetime this claim was admitted by a circle of adherents, in whose view, afterwards, it was triumphantly vindicated by His resurrection from the dead. By resurrection He "was declared to be the Son of God with power" (Rom **1** 4). With this was united from the first the recognition of Christ as the God-sent Redeemer, through whom has come to the world forgiveness, reconciliation with God and Divine spiritual power.

2. NT Implications: Messiahship—Resurrection—Redemption

Pauline summaries.—One of the oldest summaries of Christianity is that of Paul in 1 Cor **15** 3.4: "For I delivered unto you first of all that which also I received: that Christ died for our sins according to the scriptures; . . . . and that he hath been raised on the third day according to the scriptures." Of similar purport are the apostle's words in 2 Cor **5** 18.19: "God, who reconciled us to himself through Christ, and gave unto us the ministry of reconciliation; to wit, that God was in Christ, reconciling the world unto himself, not reckoning unto them their trespasses." From this reconciliation springs the new life of believers (Rom **6**; 2 Cor **5** 14–17).

More recently some have denied that Jesus advanced any such claim to Messiahship, but always upon purely arbitrary and subjective grounds. On the one hand these writers have been profoundly impressed by the grandeur of Jesus' character; on the other they have looked upon the claim to stand in such a unique relation to God and man as unfounded or meaningless. They have sought, accordingly, to escape the difficulty by denying that Jesus regarded Himself as the Anointed of the Lord (thus, e.g. Wrede). Sometimes they have gone the length even of affirming that Jesus was not so regarded by His personal disciples. Divine honors were accorded Him only gradually, as the memory of what He actually was faded away, and an idealization begotten of Christian faith took its place. The notion of Messiah is merely a piece of Jewish folklore. This position in its distinctively modern form has been answered, it seems to us, with absolute conclusiveness, by Professor James Denney in his *Jesus and the Gospel.* In a historical point of view, nothing in Jesus' life is more certain than that He regarded Himself as the Christ, the culmination and fulfilment of the Divine revelation given to Israel. This conviction of His is the point round which His whole message revolves. The most recent NT theology, that, e.g. of Dr. Paul Feine (1910), rightly starts from Jesus' Messianic consciousness, and seeks to understand His whole teaching in the light of it. Doubtless, like everything else which Jesus touched, the concept of Messiahship becomes transmuted and glorified in His hands. Our Lord was in no way dependent upon current beliefs and expectations for the content of His Messianic consciousness. But is it likely that His followers, without His authority, would have attributed Messiahship to one so utterly unlike the Messiah of popular fancy?

3. Did Jesus Claim to Be the Christ?

The NT proves not only that the Christians from the very outset were fully persuaded, on what they regarded as adequate grounds in history and experience, that their Lord had risen from the dead, but also that this conviction mastered them, giving direction and purpose to their whole lives. Historical Christianity was erected on the foundation of a Risen Lord.

4. The Resurrection

Its evidence.—On this point Professor Denney says (*Jesus and the Gospel,* 111): "The real historical evidence for the resurrection is the fact that it was believed, preached, propagated, and produced its fruit and effect in the new phenomenon of the Christian church, long before any of our gospels were written. . . . . Faith in the resurrection was not only prevalent but immensely powerful before any of our NT books were written. Not one of them would ever have been written but for that faith. It is not this or that in the NT—it is not the story of the empty tomb, or of the appearing of Jesus in Jerus or in Galilee—which is the primary evidence for the resurrection: it is the NT itself. The life that throbs in it from beginning to end, the life that always fills us again with wonder, as it beats upon us from its pages, is the life which the Risen Saviour has quickened in Christian souls. The evidence for the resurrection of Jesus is the existence of the church in that extraordinary spiritual vitality which confronts us in the NT. This is its own explanation of its being."

The best Christian thought of our day has no more difficulty than had the apostles in holding and establishing what Principal Forsyth fitly calls "the superhistoric finality of Christ." In the very nature of the case, wherever the problem of Our Lord's person has been seriously faced, there have always been two distinct estimates of His value, that of assured faith, based upon personal experience of His redemptive power, and that of mere externalism.

5. Two Contrasted Estimates of Our Lord's Person

(1) *The latter or non-believing estimate* has no more right now to call itself "historical" or "scientific," than it had, nearly nineteen hundred years ago, to crucify the Lord of glory. The priests

doubtless thought that they understood Jesus better than the ignorant, deluded Galileans. Yet the boldest champion of "the religio-historic method" would scarcely claim that theirs was the correct judgment. As a matter of fact, the so-called critical school are no more free from presuppositions than is the most thoroughgoing traditionalist. Nor have they a monopoly either of historical knowledge or of critical acumen. No truths are accessible to them which are not equally available for the Christian believer. No proof exists, beyond their own unsupported assertions, that they are better interpreters of the common truth. On the other hand, that whole range of experience and conviction in which the Christian believer finds the supreme assurance of the truth of his religion is to them a sealed book. Surely, then, it is the height of absurdity to maintain that the external, non-believing, estimate of Our Lord's person is likely to be the more correct one. From the standpoint of Christian faith, such an external estimate is necessarily inadequate, whether it finds expression in a mechanical acceptance of the whole ecclesiastical Christology, or in the denial that such a person as Jesus of Nazareth ever lived.

(2) *The believing estimate* of Our Lord's person is the essence of Christianity as a historical religion. But according to the NT this estimate is itself Divinely inwrought and Divinely attested (Mt **16** 17; 1 Cor **12** 3; 1 Jn **4** 2.3). It presupposes the perfect objective self-manifestation of God in Jesus Christ on the one hand, and the subjective appropriation of this revelation by faith on the other. No argument against the reality of the revelation can be built upon the fact, generally acknowledged by Christian theologians nowadays, that the Deity of Our Lord and the supernatural origin of our religion can neither be proved nor disproved independently of one's personal attitude to Christianity. This follows necessarily from the nature of the apprehension of Divine truth. Spiritual things are spiritually discerned. There can be no impersonal knowledge of religious, any more than of ethical and aesthetic, truth. In these realms another's knowledge has no real meaning for anyone till he has felt its power and tested it in his own experience. Evangelical Christians do not accept the Deity of the Lord as the cardinal article of their religious faith on any merely external authority whether of Scripture or of tradition, or even of His own recorded words apart from experience of Christ. They accept it precisely as they accept the authority of Scripture itself, because of the witness of the Spirit with their spirits. The combined testimony of Scripture and tradition is confirmed in their religious life, when by receiving Jesus as Our Lord and Saviour they experience the Christian power. This power is the great experienced reality in the light of which alone the other realities become intelligible. "One thing I know, that, whereas I was blind, now I see" (Jn **9** 25). "Lord, to whom shall we go? thou hast the words of eternal life" (Jn **6** 68).

6. Christianity an Experience of Salvation

The true church of Christ consists of all who have experienced the power of Christ, delivering them from the guilt, the stain, and the dominion of sin and bringing the peace of God into their souls. Nothing less than this is either the gospel of Our Lord and Saviour Jesus Christ, or the historic faith of Christendom, or a religion adequate to human need. The Christian doctrine is partly the assertion of the reality of this power, partly its interpretation. Facts of history and theological propositions are vital to our faith, just in proportion as they are vitally related to this power. The Christian essentials are those elements, historical and dogmatic, without which Christianity would lose in whole or in part its living power to reconcile sinful man to the all-righteous, loving God.

7. Jesus and the Gospel

Thus Jesus Himself belongs to His gospel. He is the heart and core of it. Christianity is both a rule of life and a doctrine. But in its inmost nature and being it is neither an ethic, nor a theology, but a religion—a new relation to God and man, Divinely mediated through Jesus Christ in His life, death and resurrection. As many as receive Him, to them gives He the right to become children of God, even to them that believe on His name, who are born not of blood, nor of the will of the flesh, nor of the will of man, but of God (Jn **1** 12). He brings man to God by bringing God to man, and the power of God into man's sin-stained life.

8. NT Types of Doctrines

It can scarcely be claimed that NT Christianity was in a theological point of view absolutely homogeneous. Various types can be distinguished with more or less clearness; even the ordinary reader feels a difference of theological atmosphere between e.g. Rom and Jas. This is inevitable, and need occasion no perplexity to Christian faith. All theology is partly interpretation—the relation of universal and eternal reality to personal thought. Hofmann rightly says that genuine Christian faith is one and the same for all, but that everyone must have his own theology, if he is to have any at all. In all genuine serious thought there is a personal element not precisely the same for any two individuals. It is possible to find in the NT foreshadowings of all the great distinctive types of historic Christianity. But the essential purpose of the NT is to make Christ real to us, to proclaim reconciliation to God through Him, and to convey the Christian power to our lives. The NT everywhere exhibits the same Christ, and bears witness to the same redeeming, life-transforming power.

9. Naturalistic Interpretations—the Religio-Historic School

The attempt has often been made to explain Christianity as the natural product of contemporary forces intellectual and religious—most recently by the so-called "religio-historic school." But at most they have only shown that the form in which the religious concepts of primitive Christianity found articulate expression was to some extent influenced *ab extra*, and that the earliest Christians were in their general intellectual outlook the children of their own time. They have not proved that the distinctive content of Christianity was derived from any external source. They have not even realized what they have to prove, in order to make good their contention. They have done nothing to account for the Christian power on their principles.

LITERATURE.—See the NT Theologies, especially that of Feine (1910); Seeberg, *Fundamental Truths of the Christian Religion* (ET very incorrect, 1908); Seeberg's *Lehrbuch d. Dogmengeschichte*, 2d ed, I, 1908; Brown, *Essence of Christianity*, New York, 1902; W. N. Clarke, *What Shall We Think of Christianity?* New York, 1899; above all Denney, *Jesus and the Gospel* (1909), and Forsyth, *Person and Place of Jesus Christ* (1909).

JOHN DICKIE

II. Historical and Doctrinal.—In its historical and doctrinal relations, developments, and influence, and its connection with the successive phases of human thought, Christianity presents many points of interest, only the more prominent of which can here briefly be touched upon.

A convenient starting-point is the well-known distinction of Lessing (Fragment in *Works*, XI,

242 ff) between "the religion of Christ" and "the Christian religion"—a distinction which still exactly marks the attitude to Christianity of the modern so-called "historical" school. By "the religion of Christ" is meant the religion which Christ Himself acknowledged and practised as man; by "the Christian religion" is meant the view which regards Christ as more than man, and exalts Him as an object of worship. From this standpoint the problem for the historian is to show how the religion of Christ came to develop into the Christian religion—in modern speech, how the "Jesus of history" became the "Christ of faith."

1. "Religion of Christ" and "The Christian Religion"

(1) *The historical Jesus is supernatural.*—It has already been pointed out (under I above) that the view of Jesus on which the assumed contrast rests is not one truly historical. The fallacy lies in regarding the Jesus of history as simply a man among men—holier, diviner in insight, but not essentially distinguished from the race of which He was a member. This is not the Christ of apostolic faith, but as little is it the picture of the historical Jesus as the Gospels actually present it. There, in His relations alike to God and to man, in His sinlessness, in His origin, claims, relation to OT revelation, judgeship of the world, in His resurrection, exaltation, and sending of the Spirit, Jesus appears in a light which it is impossible to confine within natural or purely human limits. He is the Saviour who stands over against the race He came to save. It is the same fallacy which underlies the contrast frequently sought to be drawn between the religious standpoints of Christ and Paul. Paul never for an instant dreamt of putting himself on the same plane with Christ. Paul was sinner; Christ was Saviour. Paul was disciple; Christ was Lord. Paul was weak, struggling man; Christ was Son of God. Jesus achieved redemption; Paul appropriated it. These things involved the widest contrasts in attitude and speech.

(2) *Essence of Christianity in redemption.*—Though, therefore, Christ, in His relations of love and trust to the Father, and perfection of holy character, necessarily ever remains the Great Exemplar to whose image His people are to be conformed (Rom **8** 29), in whose steps they are to follow (1 Pet **2** 21), it is not correct to describe Christianity simply as the religion which Christ practised. Christianity takes into account also the work which Christ came to do, the redemption He achieved, the blessings which, through Him, are bestowed on those who accept Him as their Saviour, and acknowledge Him as their Lord. Essentially Christianity is a religion of redemption; not, therefore, a religion practised by Jesus for Himself, but one based on a work He has accomplished for others. Experimentally, it may be described as consisting, above all, in the joyful consciousness of redemption from sin and reconciliation to God through Jesus Christ, and in the possession of a new life of sonship and holiness through Christ's Spirit. Everything in the way of holy obedience is included here. This, at least, reduced to its simplest terms, is undeniably what Christianity meant for its first preachers and teachers, and what historically it has meant for the church ever since.

Definitions of Christianity are as numerous as the writers who treat of the subject; but one or two definitions may be glanced at as illustrative of the positions above assumed. As modern types, Schleiermacher and Ritschl may be selected in preference to writers of more conspicuous orthodoxy.

2. Modern Definitions

(1) *Schleiermacher*, in his *Der Christliche Glaube*, has an interesting definition of Christianity. Christianity he speaks of as "a form of monotheistic faith, of the teleological order of religion (i.e. in which the natural is subordinated to the moral), the peculiarity of which, in distinction from other religions of this type, essentially is, that in it everything is referred to the redemption accomplished through Jesus of Nazareth" (sec. 11). As, in general, Schleiermacher's merit is recognized to lie in his bringing back, in a time of religious decay, the person of Christ to a central place in His religion, so here his true religious feeling is manifested in his fixing on the reference to redemption by Christ as the distinctive thing in Christianity.

(2) *Ritschl's* definition is more complicated, and need not here be cited in full (cf his *Justif. and Recon.*, III; ET, 13). The important point is that, like Schleiermacher, Ritschl gives, together with the idea of the kingdom of God, an essential place to the idea of redemption in the conception of Christianity. "Christianity," he says, "so to speak, resembles not a circle described from a single centre, but an ellipse which is determined by two *foci*" (*Jb.*, 11). The idea of the kingdom of God furnishes the teleological, the idea of redemption the religious, element in Christianity. There is truth in this; only it is to be remembered that the kingdom of God, as representing the end, can only, in a world of sin, be brought into existence through a redemption. Redemption, therefore, still remains the basal conception.

In the enlarged view of modern knowledge, Christianity can be no longer regarded in isolation, but is seen to take its place in the long series of historical religions. It appears, like these other religions, in a historical context; has, like some of them, a personal founder; claims, as they also do, or did, the allegiance of multitudes of the population of the world; presents in externals (e.g. the possession of Scriptures), sometimes in ideas, analogies to features in these religions. For this reason, an influential modern school is disposed to treat Christianity, as before it, the religion of Israel, as simply one of these historical religions—"nothing less, but also nothing more"—explaining it from the inherent laws of religious development, and rejecting the idea of any special, authoritative revelation. Sacred books are pitted against sacred books; moral codes against moral codes; Jesus against founders of other religions; gospel stories against legends of the Buddha; ideas like those of the virgin birth, the incarnation, the resurrection, against seeming parallels on other soils. For examination of the principal of these alleged resemblances, see COMPARATIVE RELIGION.

3. Place in Historical Religions

(1) *This place unique.*—Here it is desirable to look at the place of Christianity in the series of historical religions in certain of its wider aspects. The uniqueness of Christ's religion, and justification of its claim to a special, Divine origin, will only appear the more clearly from the comparison. In general, it need only be remarked that no other religion in the world has ever even *professed* to present a plain, historically developed, progressive revelation, advancing through successive stages in the unfolding of a Divine purpose of grace, till it culminates in the appearance of a person, life, character and work, like that of Jesus Christ; not in one single instance.

(2) *Universality of Christianity.*—A distinction is commonly made between *national* and *universal* religions, and Christianity is classed as one of the three universal religions—the other two being Buddhism and Mohammedanism (cf e.g. Kuenen's Hibbert Lectures on *National Religions and Universal Religions*). There is certainly agreement in the fact that the two religions named with Chris-

tianity are not "national" religions; that they are "universal," in the sense in which Christianity is, may be denied. Neither Buddhism nor Mohammedanism has any fitness to become a religion for the world, nor, with all their remarkable extension, have they succeeded in establishing themselves, as Christianity has done, in East and West, in Old World and in New. *Mohammed* boasted that he would plant his religion wherever the palm tree grew (Palgrave), and this still marks very nearly the range of its conquests. It is not a revivifying influence, but a blight on all higher civilization. It degrades woman, perpetuates slavery, fosters intolerance, and brings no real healing for the spiritual woes of mankind. *Buddhism*, again, notwithstanding its wide spread in China and neighboring lands, has in it no real spring of moral progress, and is today withering up at the root. Its system of "salvation"—attainment of *Nirvana*—is not for the many but the few. It has not a message for all men alike. Buddha does not profess that all can accept his method, or ought to be asked to do so. For the multitude it is impossible of attainment. In practice, therefore, instead of one, he has three codes of duty—one for the laity, who continue to live in the world; one for the monks, who do not aspire to Arahatship or sainthood: and one for those who would reach the goal of Nirvana. These last are very few; only two cases are specified, besides Buddha himself, of success in this endeavor. In contrast with these Christianity approves itself as a strictly universal religion—the only religion of its kind in the world. In its doctrines of the one God and Father, and of the brotherhood of all mankind; its teaching on universal need through sin, and universal provision for salvation in Christ; its gospel of reconciliation addressed to all; its pure spirituality in worship and morality; its elevating and emancipating tendency in all the relations of human life, it approves itself as a religion for all sections and races of mankind, for all grades of civilization and stages of culture, appealing to that which is deepest in man, capable of being understood and received by all, and renewing and blessing each one who accepts and obeys it. The history of missions, even among the most degraded races, in all parts of the globe, is the demonstration of this truth. (On the universalism of Christianity, cf Baur, *Church Hist of the First Three Cents.*, I, Pt 1.)

(3) *The absolute religion.*—It is the custom, even in circles where the full supernatural claims of Christianity are not admitted, to speak of Christ's religion as, in comparison with others, "the *absolute* religion," meaning by this that in Christianity the true idea of religion, which in other faiths is only striven after, attains to complete and final expression. Hegel, e.g. speaks of Christianity as the "Absolute or Revealed Religion" in the sense that in it the idea is discovered of the essential unity of God and man (thus also T. H. Green, E. Caird, etc); others (e.g. Pfleiderer) in the meaning that it expresses the absolute "principle" of religion—a Divine sonship. Christianity also claims for itself, though in a more positive way, to be the absolute religion. It is the final and perfect revelation of God for which not only revelation in Israel, but the whole providential history of the race, was a Divinely ordained preparation (Gal **4** 4). It is absolute in the sense that a larger and fuller revelation than Christ has given is not needed, and is not to be looked for. Not only in this religion is all truth of Nature about God's being, attributes and character, with all truth of OT revelation, purely gathered up and preserved, but in the person and work of the incarnate Son a higher and more complete disclosure is made of God's Fatherly love and gracious purposes to mankind, and a redemption is presented as actually accomplished adequate to all the needs of a sinful world. Mankind can never hope to attain to a higher idea of God, a truer idea of man, a profounder conception of the end of life, of sin, of duty, a Diviner provision for salvation, a more perfect satisfaction in fellowship with God, a grander hope of eternal life, than is opened to it in the gospel. In this respect again, Christianity stands alone (cf W. Douglas Mackenzie, *The Final Faith, a Statement of the Nature and Authority of Christianity as the Religion of the World*).

(4) *Religion of redemption.*—A third aspect in which Christianity as a historical religion is sometimes regarded is as a religion of *redemption.* In this light a comparison is frequently instituted between it and Buddhism, which also in some sort is a religion of redemption. But the comparison brings out only the more conspicuously the unique and original character of the Christian system. Buddhism starts from the conception of the inherent evil and misery of existence, and the salvation it promises as the result of indefinitely prolonged striving through many successive lives is the eternal rest and peace of non-being; Christianity, on the other hand, starts from the conception that everything in its original nature and in the intent of its Creator is good, and that the evil of the world is the result of wrong and perverted development—holds, therefore, that redemption from it is possible by use of appropriate means. And redemption here includes, not merely deliverance from existing evils, but restoration of the Divine likeness which has been lost by man, and ultimate blessedness of the life everlasting. Dr. Boyd Carpenter sums up the contrast thus: "In Buddhism redemption comes from below; in Christianity it is from above; in Buddhism it comes from man; in Christianity it comes from God" (*Permanent Elements in Religion*, Intro, 34).

4. Development and Influence

Christianity, as an external magnitude, has a long and chequered history, into the details of which it is not the purpose of this art. to enter. Ecclesiastical developments are left untouched. But a little may be said of its outward expansion, of the influences that helped to mould its doctrinal forms, and of the influence which it in turn has exercised on the thought and life of the peoples into whose midst it came.

(1) *Expansion of Christianity.*—From the first Christianity aimed at being a *world-conquering* principle. The task it set before itself was stupendous. Its message was not one likely to commend it to either Jew or Greek (1 Cor **1** 23). It renounced temporal weapons (in this a contrast with Mohammedanism); had nothing to rely on but the naked truth. Yet from the beginning (Acts **2**) it had a remarkable reception. Its universal principle was still partially veiled in the Jewish-Christian communities, but with Paul it freed itself from all limitations, and entered on a period of rapid and wide diffusion.

(*a*) The apostolic age: It is the peculiarity of the Pauline mission, as Professor W. M. Ramsay points out, that it followed the great lines of Rom communication, and aimed at establishing itself in the large cities—the centers of civilization (*Church in Roman Empire*, 147, etc). The Book of Acts and the Epistles show how striking were the results. Churches were planted in all the great cities of Asia Minor and Macedonia. In Rome Tacitus testifies that by the time of Nero's persecution (64 AD) the Christians were a "great multitude" ("*ingens multitudo*" [*Annals* xv.44]).

(*b*) Succeeding period: Our materials for estimating the progress of Christianity in the post-apostolic age are scanty, but they suffice to show us the church pursuing its way, and casting its spell alike on East and West, in centers of civilization and dim regions of barbarism. In the last quarter of the 2d cent. great churches like those of Carthage and Alexandria burst into visibility, and reveal how firm a hold the new religion was taking of the empire. Deadly persecution could not stop this march of the church to victory. From the middle of the 3d cent. there is no question that it was progressing by leaps and bounds. This is the period in which Harnack puts its great expansion (*Expansion*, II, 455, ET). On the back of the most relentless persecution it had yet endured, the Diocletian, it suddenly found itself raised by the arms of Constantine to a position of acknowledged supremacy. By this time it had penetrated into all ranks of society, and reckoned among its adherents many of noblest birth.

(*c*) Modern missions: It is unnecessary to trace the subsequent course of Christianity in its conquest of the northern nations. For a time the zeal for expansion slumbered, but, with the revival of the missionary spirit at the close of the 18th cent., a new forward movement began, the effects of which in the various regions of the heathen world are only now beginning to be realized. It is impossible to read without a thrill what was accomplished by the pioneers of Christian missions in the South Seas and other early fields; now the tidings of what is being done in India, China, Japan, Korea, Africa and elsewhere, by Christian preaching and education, awaken even more astonishment. Countries long closed against the gospel are now opened, and the standard of the cross is being carried into all. The church is arousing to its missionary obligations as never before. Still, with all this progress, immense obstacles remain to be overcome. Including all the populations of nominally Christian lands, the adherents of the Christian religion are reckoned to amount only to some 560,000,000, out of a total of over 1,600,000,000 of the population of the world (Hickmann). This looks discouraging, but it is to be remembered that it is the Christian peoples that represent the really progressive portion of the human race.

(2) *The doctrinal shaping* of Christianity has taken place largely as the result of conflict with opposing errors. First, as was inevitable, its conflict was waged with that narrowest section of the Jewish-Christian community—the Ebionites of early church history—who, cleaving to circumcision, disowned Paul, and insisted that the Gentiles should observe the law (Gal **5** 13.14; see EBIONITES). These, as a party of reaction, were soon left behind, and themselves fell under heretical (Essenian) influences.

(*a*) Gnosticism: A more formidable conflict was that with Gnosticism—the distinctive heresy of the 2d cent., though its beginnings are already within the apostolic age (cf Lightfoot, *Colossians*). This strange compound of oriental theosophy and ideas borrowed from Christianity (see GNOSTICISM) would have dissolved Christ's religion into a tissue of phantasies, and all the strength and learning of the Church were needed to combat its influence. Its opposition was overruled for good in leading to a fixing of the earliest creed (see APOSTLES' CREED), the formation of an authoritative NT canon (see BIBLE; CANON), and the firm assertion of the reality of Christ's humanity.

(*b*) Monarchianism: Christianity had now entered the world of Gr thought, and ere long had contests to sustain within its own borders. First came assaults (3d cent.) on the idea of the Trinity in what are known as the Monarchian heresies—the assertion that the Father Himself was incarnate and suffered in Christ (Patripassianism), or that the Trinity consisted only in "modes" of the Divine self-revelation (Sabellianism).

(*c*) Arianism: These were hardly repelled when a yet greater danger overtook the church in the outbreak (318 AD) of the violent Arian controversy, the Son Himself being now declared to be a creature, exalted, before all worlds, but not truly of the nature of God. The commotion produced by this controversy led to the summoning of the first ecumenical council—that of Nicaea (325 AD), and the framing of the Nicene Creed, affirming the full deity of the Son. A like controversy about the Spirit (the Macedonian, 4th cent.), led to the confirming of this creed, and adoption of additional clauses, at the Council of Constantinople (381 AD).

(*d*) Sin and grace: The doctrine of the Trinity was now settled, but new controversies speedily sprang up—in the West on sin and grace (Pelagius and Augustine) (411–18 AD), and in the East in the long series of controversies known as the Christological, bearing on the right apprehension of the person of Christ (4th to 7th cents.): as against Pelagius, who denied original sin, and affirmed man's natural ability to keep the whole law of God, Augustine vindicated the complete dependence of man on the grace of God for his salvation.

(*e*) Person of Christ: And as against errors successively denying the reality of a human soul in Jesus (Appollinarianism), dissolving the unity of His person (Nestorianism, condemned at Ephesus, 431 AD), or conversely, fusing together the Divine and human into one nature (Eutychianism, Monophysitism), the church maintained, and embodied in a Creed at Chalcedon (451 AD), the integrity of the two natures, Divine and human, in the one Divine person of the Lord. These decisions are upheld by all branches of the church—Gr, Lat, Protestant.

(*f*) The atonement: The mediaeval scholastic period made one great advance in the attempt of Anselm in his *Cur Deus Homo* (1089) to lay deep the foundations of a doctrine of atonement in the idea of the necessity of a satisfaction for human sin: Abelard, on the other hand, denied the need of satisfaction, and became the representative of what are known as moral theories of the atonement. It was reserved for the Protestant Reformers, however, to bring this doctrine to its true bearing, as furnishing the ground for man's free justification before God in his union with Christ, who had made full satisfaction for his guilt. There have been many theories of atonement, but the idea that Christ has "satisfied Divine justice" is too firmly imbedded in all the Reformation creeds, and has too profound a Scriptural support, to be removed.

(*g*) The 16th cent. Reformation, on its outward side, was a revolt against the errors and corruptions of the papacy, but in its positive aspect it may be described as the reassertion of the sole mediatorship of Christ (as against priestly intervention), the sole authority of Scripture (as against tradition), and justification by faith alone (as against salvation by works of merit). The schism meant a separation of the great Protestant communities and nations from the church of Rome, which, by its claim of papal supremacy, had already separated from itself the great Gr communion.

(*h*) Lutheran and Reformed: Within Protestantism itself a difference of genius between the Swiss and German Reformers, with divergences of view on the sacraments, led to the formation of two main types—the Lutheran (German) and the Reformed (Swiss)—and between these two, as respects theology and church order, later Protestantism has mostly been divided. Luther represented the one; Calvin for long was the chief name in the other. With the rise of Arminianism and other forms of dissent from the peculiarities of Calvinism, the aspect of Protestantism became more variegated. Of the later divisions, producing the numerous modern sects which yet own allegiance to the common head (Presbyterians, Episcopalians, Methodists, Baptists, Congregationalists, etc), it is not necessary here to speak. The unity of spirit revealed in creed, worship and combined endeavors in Christ's service goes deeper than all outward differences.

(3) *Its influence.*—Christianity preaches a kingdom of God, or supremacy of God's will in human hearts and human affairs, by which is meant, on its earthly side, nothing less than a complete reconstruction of society on the two great bases of love to God and love to man—"Thy will be done, as in heaven, so on earth" (Mt **6** 10). The influence of Christianity is paramount in all the great advances that have been made in the moral and social amelioration of the state of mankind.

(*a*) The ancient world: It was so undoubtedly in the ancient world. The world into which Christianity came was one fast sinking into dissolution through the weight of its own corruptions. Into that world Christianity brought a totally new idea of man as being of infinite dignity and immortal worth. It restored the well-nigh lost sense of responsibility and accountability to God; breathed into the world a new spirit of love and charity, and created that wealth of charitable and beneficent institutions with which Christian lands are now full (Lecky speaks of it as "covering the globe with countless institutions of mercy, absolutely unknown in the whole pagan world," *Hist of Morals*, II, 91); set up a new moral ideal and standard of integrity which has acted as an elevating force on moral conceptions till the present hour; restored woman to her rightful place as man's helpmeet and equal; created the Christian home; gave the slave an equal place with his master in the kingdom of God, and struck at the foundations of slavery by its doctrines of the natural brotherhood and dignity of man; created self-respect, and a sense of duty in the use of one's powers for self-support and the benefit of others; urged to honest labors; and in a myriad other ways, by direct teaching, by the protest of holy lives, and by its general spirit, struck at the evils, the malpractices, the cruelties of the time.

(*b*) The modern world: Despite many failures, and gross backslidings in the church itself, these ideas, implanted in the world, and liberating other forces, have operated ever since in advancing the progress of the race. They exist and operate far beyond the limits of the church. They have been taken up and contended for by men outside the church—by unbelievers even—when the church itself had become unfaithful to them. None the less they are of Christian parentage. They lie at the basis of our modern assertion of equal rights, of justice to the individual in social and state arrangements, of the desire for brotherhood, peace and amity among classes and nations. It is Christian love which is sustaining the best, purest and most self-sacrificing efforts for the raising of the fallen, the rescue of the drunkard, the promotion of enlightenment, virtues, social order and happiness. It is proving itself the grand civilizing agency in other regions of the world. Christian missions, with their benign effects in the spread of education, the checking of social evils and barbarities, the creation of trade and industry, the change in the status of women, the advance in social and civilized life, generally, is the demonstration of it (see Dennis, *Christian Missions and Social Progress*).

(*c*) Testimony of Huxley: Professor Huxley will not be regarded as a biased witness on behalf of Christianity. Yet this is what he writes on the influence of the Christian Scriptures, and his words may be a fitting close to this article: "Throughout the history of the western world," he says, "the Scriptures, Jewish, and Christian, have been the great instigators of revolt against the worst forms of clerical and political despotism. The Bible has been the Magna Charta of the poor, and of the oppressed; down to modern times no state has had a constitution in which the interests of the people are so largely taken into account, in which the duties, so much more than the privileges, of rulers are insisted upon, as that drawn up for Israel in Dt and Lev; nowhere is the fundamental truth that the welfare of the State, in the long run, depends upon the uprightness of the citizen so strongly laid down. Assuredly the Bible talks no trash about the rights of man; but it insists upon the equality of duties, on the liberty to bring about that righteousness which is somewhat different from struggling for 'rights'; on the fraternity of taking thought for one's neighbor as for one's self."

LITERATURE.—See works cited in Part I above; also Kuenen, Hibbert Lectures for 1882, *National Religions and Universal Religions;* W. M. Ramsay, *The Church in the Roman Empire;* M. Dods, *Mohammed, Buddha, and Christ;* on early expansion of Christianity, Harnack, *Mission and Expansion of Christianity,* and Orr, *Neglected Factors in the Study of the Early Progress of Christianity;* on the essence of Christianity, W. Douglas Mackenzie, *The Final Faith;* on the influence of Christianity, C. L. Brace, *Gesta Christi;* Uhlhorn, *Christian Charity in the Ancient Church;* C. Schmidt, *Social Results of Early Christianity;* Lecky, *History of European Morals;* Dennis, *Christian Missions and Social Progress; Reports of World Miss. Conference,* 1910.

JAMES ORR

CHRISTOLOGY, kris-tol′o-ji. See PERSON OF CHRIST.

CHRISTS, krīsts. See CHRISTS, FALSE; MESSIAH.

CHRISTS, FALSE, fôls (ψευδόχριστοι, *pseudóchristoi*): In His discourse on the last things, uttered by Him on the Tuesday of the week of His Passion, Jesus solemnly forewarned His disciples that many would come in His name, saying "I am the Christ," who would deceive many; that there would arise false Christs and false prophets, who would show great signs and wonders, so as to lead astray, if possible, even the elect; that, therefore, if any man said to them, "Lo, here is the Christ," or "Lo, there," they were not to believe it (Mt **24** 5.11.23-25; Mk **13** 6.21-23; Lk **21** 8).

1. Christ's Warnings

The warning was needed. De Wette, Meyer, and others have, indeed, pointed out that there is no historical record of anyone expressly claiming to be the Christ prior to the destruction of Jerus. This, however, is probably only in appearance (cf Lange, *Comm.* on Mt **24** 3). Edersheim remarks: "Though in the multitude of impostors, who, in the troubled time between the rule of Pilate and the destruction of Jerus, promised Messianic deliverance to Israel, few names and claims of this kind have been specially recorded, yet the hints in the NT, and the references, however guarded, in the Jewish historian, imply the appearance of many such seducers" (*Jesus the Messiah*, V, ch vi; in 1906 ed, II, 446). The revolts in this period were generally connected with religious pretensions in the leaders (Jos, *BJ*, II, xiii, 4—"deceived and deluded the people under pretense of Divine inspiration"), and, in the fevered state of Messianic expectation, can hardly have lacked, in some instances, a Messianic character. Judas of Galilee (Acts **5** 37; Jos, *Ant*, XVIII, i, 1, 6; *BJ*, II, viii, 1) founded a numerous sect (the Gaulonites)

2. Early Notices

by many of whom, according to Origen (*Hom on Lk*, **25**), he was regarded as the Messiah (cf *DB*, s.v.). The Theudas of Acts **5** 36, "giving himself out to be somebody," may or may not be the same as the Theudas of Jos (*Ant*, XX, v, 1), but the latter, at least, made prophetic claims and deluded many. He promised to divide the river Jordan by a word. Another instance is the "Egyptian" for whom Paul was mistaken, who had made an "uproar" (Acts **21** 38; RV "sedition")—one of a multitude of "impostors and deceivers," Jos tells us, who persuaded multitudes to follow them into the wilderness, pretending that they would exhibit wonders and signs (*Ant*, XX, viii, 6). This Egyptian was to show them that, at his command, the walls of Jerus would fall down (*BJ*, II, xiii, 5). Of another class was the Samaritan Dositheus, with whom Simon Magus was said to be connected (see refs to Eusebius, Origen, Hippolytus, Clementine writings, etc, in *DB*, s.v.). He is alleged to have been regarded as "the prophet like unto Moses," whom God was to raise up.

3. Bar-Cochba

The most celebrated case of a false Christ is that of Bar-Cochba (to give the name its usual form), the leader of the great insurrection under Hadrian in 132 AD (Eus., *HE*, IV,6; for Jewish and other authorities, see the full account in Schürer, *HJP*, I, 2, pp. 297 ff, ET). The insurrection was on a scale which it required the whole force of the Rom empire to put down (cf Schürer). The leader's own name was Simon, but the title, "Bar-Cochba" ("son of a star"), was given him with reference to the prophecy in Nu **24** 17 of the star that should come out of Jacob. Rabbi Akiba, the most celebrated doctor of his time, applied this prophecy, with that in Hag **2** 6.7, to Simon, and announced him as the Messiah. He is commonly known in Jewish lit. as Barcosiba, probably from his birthplace. Immense multitudes flocked to his standard, and the Christians in Pal were severely persecuted. Coins were issued in his name. After tremendous efforts the rebellion was crushed, and Jerus was converted into a Rom colony (*Aelia Capitolina*), which Jews were forbidden to enter.

4. Jewish Pseudo-Messiahs

Among the Jews themselves, in later times, many pseudo-Messiahs have arisen. An interesting account of some of these is given by Mr. Elkan Adler in his Introduction to the volume, *Aspects of the Heb Genius* (London, Routledge, 1910). "Such there had been," this writer says, "from time to time ever since the destruction of the Temple." In the 16th and 17th cents., however, the belief in pseudo-Messiahs took new and remarkable shapes. Among the names mentioned is that of David Reubeni, or David of the tribe of Reuben (1524), who ultimately fell a sacrifice to the Inquisition. Under his influence a Portuguese royal secretary, Diego Pires, adopted the Jewish faith, changed his name to Solomon Molko, and finally proclaimed himself the Messiah. In 1529 he published some of his addresses under the title of *The Book of Wonder*. He was burned at the stake at Mantua. "Other Kabbalists, such as Isaac Luria and Chajim Vital and Abraham Shalom, proclaimed themselves to be Messiahs or forerunners of the Messiah, and their works and MSS are still piously studied by many oriental Jews." The chief of all these false Messiahs was Sabbatai Zevi, born at Smyrna in 1626. "His adventures," it is said, "created a tremendous stir in western Europe." He ultimately became an apostate to Islam; notwithstanding which fact he had a line of successors, in whom the sect of Donmeh, in Salonica, continue to believe. Another mentioned is Jacob Frank, of Podolia, who revealed himself in 1755 as the Holy Lord, in whom there dwelt the same Messiah-soul that had dwelt in David, Elijah, Jesus, Mohammed, Sabbatai Zevi, and his followers. Jewish lit. in the 18th cent. is full of controversial writing connected with Sabbatianism. As a special source of information on modern false Messiahs among the Jews, Lange mentions the serial *Dibhrē 'emeth*, or *Words of Truth* (Breslau, 1853–54).

JAMES ORR

CHRONICLES, kron'i-k'ls, **BOOKS OF** (דִּבְרֵי הַיָּמִים, *dibhrē ha-yāmīm*, "The Words of the Days"; LXX **Παραλειπομένων**, *paraleipoménōn*):

1. The Name
2. The Position of Chronicles in the OT
3. Two Books, or One?
4. The Contents
5. Sources Biblical and Extra-Biblical
6. Nehemiah's Library
7. The Way of Using the Biblical Sources
8. Additions by the Chronicler
9. Omissions by the Chronicler
10. The Extra-Biblical Sources
11. The Object in Writing the Books of Chronicles
12. The Text
13. Critical Estimates
14. Date and Authorship
15. Evidence as to Date and Authorship
Arguments for a Later Date
16. Truthfulness and Historicity
(1) Alleged Proofs of Untruthfulness
(2) Truthfulness in the Various Parts
17. The Values of the Chronicles
LITERATURE

1. The Name

The analogy of this title to such Eng. words as diary, journal, chronicle, is obvious. The title is one which frequently appears in the Heb of the OT. It is used to denote the records of the Medo-Pers monarchy (Est **2** 23; **6** 1; **10** 2), and to denote public records, either Pers or Jewish, made in late postexilian times (Neh **12** 23), and to denote public records of King David (1 Ch **27** 24). But its most common use is to denote the Judahite and Israelite records referred to in the Books of K as sources (1 K **14** 19; **15** 7 and about 30 other places). The references in K are not to our present Books of Ch, for a large proportion of them are to matters not mentioned in these. Either directly or indirectly they refer the reader to public archives.

As applied to our present Books of Ch this title was certainly not intended to indicate that they are strictly copies of public documents, though it may indicate that they have a certain official character distinguishing them from other contemporary or future writings. The Gr title is *Paraleipomenōn*, "Of Things that have been Left Untold." Some copies add "concerning the kings of Judah," and this is perhaps the original form of the title. That is, the Gr translators thought of Ch as a supplement to the other narrative Scriptural books. Jerome accepted the Gr title, but suggested that the Heb title would be better represented by a derivative from the Gr word *chrónos*, and that this would fit the character of the book, which is a chronicle of the whole sacred history. Jerome's suggestion is followed in the title given to the book in the Eng. and other languages.

2. The Position of Chronicles in the OT

In most of the VSS, as in the Eng., the Books of Ch are placed after the Books of K, as being a later account of the matters narrated in K; and Ezr and Neh follow Ch as being continuations of the narrative. In the Heb Bibles the Books of Ezr and Neh and 1 and 2 Ch are placed last. By common opinion, based on proof that is entirely sufficient, the three books constitute a single literary work or group of works, by one author or school of authors. It is convenient to use the term "the Chronicler" to designate the author, or the authors if there were more than one.

3. Two Books, or One?

It is the regulation thing to say that 1 and 2 Ch were originally one book, which has been divided into two. The fact is that Ch is counted as one book in the count which regards the OT as 22 or 24 books, and as two books in the count which regards the whole number of books as 39; and that both ways of counting have been in use as far back as the matter can be traced. Both ways of counting appear in the earliest Christian lists, those of Origen and Melito, for example. 1 Ch closes with a summary which may naturally be regarded as the closing of a book.

4. The Contents

With respect to their contents the Books of Ch are naturally divided into three parts. The first part is preliminary, consisting mostly of genealogical matters with accompanying facts and incidents (1 Ch **1–9**). The second part is an account of the accession and reign of David (1 Ch **10–29**). The third part is an account of the events under David's successors in the dynasty (2 Ch).

The genealogies begin with Adam (1 Ch **1** 1) and extend to the latest OT times (1 Ch **9;** cf Neh **11,** and the latest names in the genealogical lines, e.g. 1 Ch **3** 19 ff). The events incidentally mentioned in connection with them are more numerous and of more importance than the casual reader would imagine. They are some dozens in number. Some of them are repeated from the parts of the OT from which the Chronicler draws as sources—for example, such statements as that Nimrod was a mighty one, or that in the time of Peleg the earth was divided, or the details concerning the kings of Edom (1 Ch **1** 10.19.43 ff; cf Gen **10**,8.25; **36** 31 ff). Others are instances which the Chronicler has taken from other sources than the OT—for instance, the story of Jabez, or the accounts of the Simeonite conquests of the Meunim and of Amalek (1 Ch **4** 9.10.38–43).

The account in Ch of the reign of David divides itself into three parts. The first part (1 Ch **10–21**) is a series of sections giving a general view, including the death of Saul, the crowning of David over the twelve tribes, his associates, his wars, the bringing of the ark to Jerus, the great Davidic promise, the plague that led to the purchase of the threshing-floor of Ornan the Jebusite. The second part (1 Ch **22—29** 22*a*) deals with one particular event and the preparations for it. The event is the making Solomon king, at a great public assembly (1 Ch **23** 1; **28** 1 ff). The preparations for it include arrangements for the site and materials and labor for the temple that is to be built, and the organizing of Levites, priests, singers, doorkeepers, captains, for the service of the temple and the kingdom. The third part (1 Ch **29** 22*b*–30) is a brief account of Solomon's being made king "a second time" (cf 1 K **1**), with a summary and references for the reign of David.

The history of the successors of David, as given in 2 Ch, need not here be commented upon.

5. Sources Biblical and Extra-Biblical

The sources of the Books of Ch classify themselves as Biblical and extra-Biblical. Considerably more than half the contents come from the other OT books, especially from S and K. Other sources mentioned in the Books of Ch are the following:

(1) The Book of the Kings of Judah and Israel (2 Ch **16** 11; **25** 26; **28** 26; **32** 32).

(2) The Book of the Kings of Israel and Judah (2 Ch **27** 7; **35** 27; **36** 8).

(3) The Book of the Kings of Israel (2 Ch **20** 34).

(4) The Book of the Kings (2 Ch **24** 27).

It is possible that these may be four variant forms of the same title. It is also possible that they may be references to our present Books of K, though in that case we must regard the formulas of reference as conventional rather than exact.

(5) The Book of the Kings of Israel (1 Ch **9** 1), a genealogical work.

(6) The Midr of the Book of the Kings (2 Ch **24** 27).

(7) The Words of the Kings of Israel (2 Ch **33** 18), referred to for details concerning Manasseh.

Observe that these seven are books of Kings, and that the contents of the last three do not at all correspond with those of our Biblical books. In the seventh title and in several of the titles that are yet to be mentioned it is commonly understood that "Words" is the equivalent of "acts" or "history"; but it is here preferred to retain the form "Words," as lending itself better than the others to the syntactical adjustments.

(8) The Words of Samuel the Man of Vision and the Words of Nathan the Prophet and the Words of Gad the Seer (1 Ch **29** 29) are perhaps to be counted as one work, and identified with our Books of Jgs and S.

(9) The Words of Nathan the Prophet (2 Ch **9** 29; cf 1 K **11** 41–53). Source concerning Solomon.

(10) The Prophecy of Ahijah the Shilonite (2 Ch **9** 29; cf 1 K **11** 29 ff; **14** 2 ff, etc). Solomon.

(11) The Visions of Jedo the Seer (2 Ch **9** 29; cf 1 K **13**). Solomon.

(12) The Words of Shemaiah the Prophet (2 Ch **12** 15; cf 1 K **12** 22 ff). Rehoboam.

(13) "Shemaiah wrote" (1 Ch **24** 6). David.

(14) Iddo the Seer in Reckoning Genealogies (2 Ch **12** 15). Rehoboam.

(15) "The Words [The History] of Jehu the son of Hanani, which is inserted in the Book of the Kings of Israel" (2 Ch **20** 34; cf 1 K **16** 1.7.12). Jehoshaphat.

(16) "The rest of the acts of Uzziah, first and last, did Isaiah the Prophet, the son of Amoz, write" (2 Ch **26** 22; cf Isa **1** 1; **6**).

(17) "The Vision of Isaiah . . . . in the Book of the Kings of Judah and Israel" (2 Ch **32** 32; cf 2 K **18–20;** Isa **36–39,** etc). Hezekiah.

(18) The Words of the Seers (2 Ch **33** 19 m). Manasseh.

(19) References to "Lamentations," and to "Jeremiah," etc (2 Ch **35** 25). Josiah.

(20) The Midr of the Prophet Iddo (2 Ch **13** 22). Abijah.

These numbers, from 12 to 20, are referred to as works of prophets. At first thought there is plausibility in the idea that the references may be to the sections in S and K where these several prophets are mentioned; but in nearly all the cases this explanation fades out on examination. The Chronicler had access to prophetic writings not now known to be in existence.

(21) Liturgical writings of David and Solomon (2 Ch **35** 4; cf Ezr **3** 10). Josiah.

(22) Commandments of David and Gad and Nathan (2 Ch **29** 25). Hezekiah.

(23) The Commandment of David and Asaph and Heman and Jeduthun (2 Ch **35** 15). Josiah.

(24) Chronicles of King David (1 Ch **27** 24).

(25) Last Words of David (1 Ch **23** 27).

Add to these many mentions of genealogical works, connected with particular times, those for example of David, Jotham, Jeroboam II (1 Ch **9** 22; **5** 17), and mentions of matters that imply record-keeping, from Samuel and onward (e.g. 1 Ch **26** 26–28). Add also the fact that the Chronicler had a habit, exhibited in Ezr and Neh, of using and quoting what he represents to be public documents, for example, letters to and from Cyrus and Artaxerxes and Darius and Artaxerxes Longimanus (Ezr **1** 1;

6 3; **4** 7.17; **5** 6; **6** 6; **7** 11; Neh **2** 7). It is no exaggeration to say that the Chronicler claims to have had a considerable library at his command.

If such a library as this existed we should perhaps expect to find some mention of it somewhere. Such a mention I think there is in the much discussed passage in 2 Macc **2** 13–15. It occurs in what purports to be a letter written after 164 BC by the Maccabean leaders in Jerus to Aristobulus in Egypt. The letter has a good deal to say concerning Nehemiah, and among other things this: "And how he, founding a library, gathered together the books about the kings and prophets, and the [books] of David, and letters of kings about sacred gifts." It says that these writings have been scattered by reason of the war, but that Judas has now gathered them again, and that they may be at the service of Aristobulus and his friends.

6. Nehemiah's Library

This alleged letter contains statements that seem fabulous to most modern readers, though they may not have seemed so to Judas and his compatriots. Leaving out of view, however, the intrinsic credibility of the witness, the fitting of the statement into certain other traditions and into the phenomena presented in Chronicles is a thing too remarkable to neglect. In the past, men have cited this passage as an account of the framing of a canon of Scripture—the canon of the Prophets, or of the Prophets and the Hagiographa. But it purports to be an account of a library, not of a body of Scripture; and its list of contents does not appear to be that of either the Prophets or the Hagiographa or both. But it is an exact list of the sources to which the author (or authors) of Ch and Ezr and Neh claim to have access—"books about the kings" (see above, Nos. 1–7), "and prophets" (Nos. 8–20), "and of David" (Nos. 21–25 ff), "and letters of kings about sacred gifts" (those cited in Ezr and Neh). The library attributed to Neh corresponds to the one which the Chronicler claims to have used; and the two independent pieces of evidence strongly confirm each the other.

The method in which the Biblical sources are used in Ch presents certain remarkable features. As a typical instance study 1 Ch **10** in comparison with 1 S **31**. In verses 1–12 the passage in Chronicles is just a transcription, with slight changes, of the passage in S. A large part of Ch is thus made up of passages transcribed from S and K. The alternative is that the Chronicler transcribed from sources which had earlier been transcribed in S and K, and this alternative may in some cases be the true one.

7. The Way of Using the Biblical Sources

This phenomenon is interesting for many reasons. It has its bearings on the trustworthiness of the information given; a copy of an ancient document is of higher character as evidence than a mere report of the contents of the document. It has a bearing on questions concerning the text; are the texts in K and Ch to be regarded as two recensions? It is especially interesting as illustrating the literary processes in use among the writers of our Scriptures.

It is sometimes said that they used their sources not by restating the contents as a modern compiler would do, but by just copying. It would be more correct to say that they do this part of the time. In 1 Ch **10** the copying process ceases with the 12th ver. In vs 13 and 14 the Chronicler condenses into a sentence a large part of the contents of 1 S; one clause in particular is a condensation of 1 S **28**. So it is with other parts. 1 Ch **1** 1–4 is abridged from Gen **5** at the rate of a name for a section; so is 1 Ch **1** 24–27 from Gen **11** 10–26. In the various parts of Ch we find all the methods that are used by any compiler; the differentiating fact is simply that the method of transcribing is more used than it would be by a modern compiler.

In the transcribed passages, almost without exception, there has been a systematic editorial revision. Words and clauses have been pruned out, and grammatical roughness smoothed away. Regularly the text in Chronicles is somewhat briefer, and is more fluent than in S or K. If we give the matter careful attention we will be sure that this revisional process took place, and that it accounts for most of the textual differences between Ch and the earlier writings, not leaving many to be accounted for as corruptions.

Of course the most significant changes made by the Chronicler are those which consist in additions and omissions. It is a familiar fact that the added passages in Ch which bulk largest are those which deal with the temple and its worship and its attendants—its priests, Levites, musicians, singers, doorkeepers. Witness for example the added matter in connection with the bringing of the ark to Jerus, the preparations for the temple, the priests' joining Rehoboam, the war between Abijah and Jeroboam, the reforms under Asa and Jehoshaphat, details concerning Uzziah, Hezekiah's passover, the reform of Manasseh, the passover of Josiah (1 Ch **15–16, 22–29**; 2 Ch **11** 13–17; **13**; **14**; **15**; **17**; **19**; **20**; **26** 16–21; **29–31**; **33** 10–20; **35**). It has been less noticed than it should be that while the Chronicler in these passages magnifies the ceremonial laws of Moses, he magnifies those of David yet more.

8. Additions by the Chronicler

Next in bulk comes the added genealogical and statistical matter, for example, the larger part of the preliminary genealogies, details as to David's followers, Rehoboam's fortified cities and family affairs with details concerning the Shishak invasion, Asa's military preparations and the invasion by Zerah, with numbers and dates, Jehoshaphat's military arrangements, with numbers, Jehoram's brothers and other details concerning him, Uzziah's army and his business enterprises (1 Ch **2–9**; **12**; **27**; 2 Ch **11** 5–12.18–23; **12** 3–9; **14** 3–15; **17** 1–5.10–19; **21**; **26** 6–15).

The Chronicler is sometimes spoken of as interested in priestly affairs, and not in the prophets. That is a mistake. He takes particular pains to magnify the prophets (e.g. 2 Ch **20** 20; **36** 12.16). He uses the word "prophet" 30 times, and the two words for "seer" (*ḥōzeh* and *rō'eh*) respectively 5 and 11 times. He gives us additional information concerning many of the prophets—for example, Samuel, Gad, Nathan, Ahijah, Shemaiah, Hanani, Jehu, Elijah, Isaiah, Jeremiah. He has taken pains to preserve for us a record of many prophets concerning whom we should otherwise be ignorant—Asaph, Heman, Jeduthun, Jedo (2 Ch **9** 29), Iddo, the Oded of Asa's time, Jahaziel the son of Zechariah, Eliezer the son of Dodavah, two Zechariahs (2 Ch **24** 20; **26** 5), unnamed prophets of the time of Amaziah (2 Ch **25** 5–10.15.16), Oded of the time of Ahaz (2 Ch **28** 9).

In addition, however, to the materials that can be thus classified, it is the method of the Chronicler to preserve interesting incidents of all kinds by working them into his narrative. When he reaches Jair in his genealogical list, he finds himself in possession of a bit of information not contained in the older writings, and he inserts it (1 Ch **2** 21 ff). He is interested to keep alive the memory of the "families of scribes which dwelt at Jabez" (1 Ch **2** 55). He has found items concerning craftsmen, and concerning a linen industry, and a potters' industry, and he connects these with names in his list (1 Ch **4** 14.21.23). He has come across a bit of a hymn in the name of Jabez, and he attaches the hymn to his list of names as an annotation (1 Ch **4** 9.10). There are matters concerning the sickness and the burial of Asa, and concerning the bad conduct of Joash after the death of Jehoiada, and concerning constructions by Hezekiah (2 Ch **16** 12.13; **24** 15–27; **32** 27–30), that seem to the Chronicler worth preserving, though they are not recorded in the earlier writings. The fruits of the habit appear, in many scores of instances, in all parts of the Books of Ch.

9. Omissions by the Chronicler

As the Books of Ch thus add matters not found in the older books, so they leave out much that is contained in the Books of S and K. Here, however, the question should rather be as to what the Chronicler has retained from his sources than as to what he has omitted. He writes for readers whom he assumes to be familiar with the earlier books, and he retains so much of the older narrative as seems to him necessary for defining the relations of his new statements of fact to that narrative. From the point where the history of David begins he has omitted everything that is not strictly connected with David or his dynasty—the history of northern Israel as such, the long narratives concerning the prophets, such distressing affairs as those of Amnon and Absalom and Adonijah and the faithlessness of Solomon, and a multitude of minor particulars. We have already noticed his systematic shortening of the passages which he transcribes.

10. The Extra-Biblical Sources

There are two marked phenomena in the parts of Ch which were not taken from the other canonical books. They are written in later Heb of a pretty uniform type; many parts of them are fragmentary. The Heb of the parts that were copied from S and K is of course the classical Heb of those books, generally made more classical by the revision to which it has been subjected. The Heb of the other parts is presumably that of the Chronicler himself. The difference is unmistakable. An obvious way of accounting for it is by supposing that the Chronicler treated his Scriptural sources with especial respect, and his other sources with more freedom. We will presently consider whether this is the true account.

There are indications that some of the non-Biblical sources were in a mutilated or otherwise fragmentary condition when the Chronicler used them. Broken sentences and passages and constructions abound. In the trs these are largely concealed, the translators having guessed the meanings into shape, but the roughnesses are palpable in the Heb. They appear less in the long narratives than in the genealogies and descriptive passages. They are sometimes spoken of as if they were characteristic of the later Heb, but there is no sense in that.

For example, most of the genealogies are incomplete. The priestly genealogies omit some of the names that are most distinguished in the history, such names as those of Jehoiada and two Azariahs (2 K **11** 9, etc; 2 Ch **26** 17; **31** 10). Many of the genealogies are given more than once, and in variant forms, but with their incompleteness still palpable. There are many breaks in the lists. We read the names of one group, and we suddenly find ourselves in the midst of names that belong to another group, and with nothing to call attention to the transition. The same phenomena appear in the sections in 1 Ch **23** 2—**27**. These contain a succession of matters arranged in absolutely systematic order in classes and subclasses, while many of the statements thus arranged are so fragmentary as to be hardly intelligible. The most natural explanation of these phenomena assumes that the writer had a quantity of fragments in writing—clay tablets, perhaps, or pottery or papyrus, or what not, more or less mutilated, and that he copied them as best he could, one after another. A modern writer, doing such work, would indicate the lacunae by dots or dashes or other devices. The ancient copyist simply wrote the bits of text one after another, without such indications. In regard to many of the supposable lacunae in Ch scholars would differ, but there are a large number in regard to which all would agree. If some one would print a text of Ch in which these should be indicated, he would make an important contribution to the intelligibility of the books.

11. The Object in Writing the Books of Chronicles

On the basis of these phenomena what judgment can we form as to the purposes for which the books of Ch were written? There are those who find the answer to this question a very simple one. They say that the interests of the writer were those of the temple priesthood, that it seemed to him that the older histories did not emphasize these interests as they ought, and that he therefore wrote a new history, putting into it the views and facts which he thought should be there. If this statement were modified so as not to impugn the good faith of the Chronicler, it would be nearly correct as a statement of part of his purpose. His purpose was to preserve what he regarded as historical materials that were in danger of being lost, materials concerning the temple-worship, but also concerning a large variety of other matters. He had the historian's instinct for laying hold of all sorts of details, and putting them into permanent form. His inspiration from God (we do not here discuss the nature of that inspiration) led him this way. He wanted to save for the future that which he regarded as historical fact. The contents of the book, determined in part by his enthusiasm for the temple, were also determined in part by the nature of the materials that were providentially at his disposal. There seems also to have been present in his consciousness the idea of bringing to completion the body of sacred writings which had then been accumulating for centuries.

As we have seen, the Gr translators gave to the Books of Ch a title which expressed the idea they had of the work. They regarded it as the presentation of matters which had been omitted in the earlier Scriptures, as written not to supersede the older books, but to supplement them, as being, along with Ezr and Neh, a work that brought the Scriptures up to date, and made them complete.

12. The Text

The text of the Books of Ch has been less carefully preserved than that of some other parts of the OT. Witness for example the numbers 42 and 8 for the ages of Ahaziah and Jehoiachin (2 Ch **22** 2; cf 2 K **8** 26; 2 Ch **36** 9; cf 2 K **24** 8). There is no proof, however, of important textual corruption. As we have seen, the fragmentary character of certain parts is probably in the main due to exactness in following fragmentary sources, and not to bad text; and the differences between S or K and Ch, in the transcribed passages, are mostly due to intended revision rather than to text variations.

13. Critical Estimates

In critical discussions less semblance of fair play has been accorded to Ch than even to most of the other Scriptures. It is not unusual to assume that the Chronicler's reference to sources is mere make-believe, that he "has cited sources simply to produce the impression that he is writing with authority." Others hurry to the generalization that the Books of K mentioned in Ch (see Nos. 1–7 above) are all one work, which must therefore have been an extensive Midr (commentary, exegetical and anecdotal) on the canonical Books of K; and that the references to prophetic writings are to sections in this Midr; so that practically the Chronicler had only two sources, the canonical books and this midrashic history of Israel; and that "it is impossible to determine" whether he gathered any bits of information from any other sources.

Into the critical theories concerning Ch enters a hypothesis of an earlier Book of K that was more extensive than our present canonical books. And in recent publications of such men as Büchler, Benzinger and Kittel are theories of an analysis of Ch into documents—for example, an earlier writing that made no distinction between priests and Levites, or an earlier writing which dealt freely with the canonical books; and the later writing of the Chronicler proper.

What we know in the matter is that three sets of authors combined in producing the Books of Ch—first, the men who produced the canonical sources, second, the men who produced the other sources, and third, the man or men who directly or indirectly put the contents of these sources together into the book which we have. We have no means of knowing what most of the intermediate processes were, and it is superlatively useless to guess. It is gratuitous to say that the mention of sources in Ch is not made in good faith. It is probable that among the sources were Midrashim that were nearly contemporaneous. It is exceedingly improbable that none of the sources mentioned were genuine and ancient. All probabilities agree to the effect that the returned exiles and their near descendants were likely to study the ancient history of their race, and to gather materials for that purpose. As we have seen, the phenomena of the book indicate the presence of an antiquarian motive which was sure to be interested in genuine items of evidence from the remote past.

14. Date and Authorship

The current opinion sixty years ago was that the Books of Ch and the whole OT were completed about 404 BC, near the time when Artaxerxes Mnemon succeeded Darius Nothus. The statement now fashionable is that the Books of Ch were completed not later than about 250 BC, and this constantly degenerates into the statement that they were written about 250 BC or later. In fact, they were completed within the lifetime of Nehemiah, not later or not much later than 400 BC.

In discussing this we cannot ignore the fact that Ch and Ezr and Neh are one work, or, if you prefer, one series. The closing vs of 2 Ch duplicate the opening vs of Ezr. This is not, probably, an inadvertent repetition. The Books of Ch were written later than the other parts of the series. The closing vs are the Chronicler's notification to his readers that he has brought up the earlier history to the point at which he had previously begun the narrative in Ezr.

The testimony concerning Ezra and the "men of the Great Synagogue" and Nehemiah and their work on the Scriptures does not deserve the contempt with which some persons treat it. We know nothing concerning the Great Synagogue as an organization, but we know much concerning the succession of men, from Daniel to Simon the Just, who are called the men of the Great Synagogue. The old traditions do not say that Ezra was the founder of the succession, but they make him the typical person in it. Two bits of tradition are not necessarily inconsistent if one attributes work to Ezra which the other attributes to the men of the Great Synagogue. The regulation remark that tradition attributes Biblical work to Ezra and not to Nehemiah is untrue. Nehemiah was one of the men of the Great Synagogue, and prominent as such. He is introduced to us as a handsome boy, a king's favorite, coming to Jerus in 444 BC. In 433 BC he returned to the king. After an unknown interval of time he came back to Judaea, and presumably spent the remainder of his long life there, dying some years or some decades after 400 BC.

15. Evidence as to Date and Authorship

The placing of the work of the Ch at the close of the Heb Scriptures is in itself of the nature of testimony. The men who placed it there testify thereby to their belief that these are the latest writings of the OT aggregate. We are familiar with the testimony of *Bābhā' Bathrā'* to the effect that most of the later books of the OT were due to the men of the Great Synagogue and to Ezra, but that Nehemiah completed the Books of Ch. We cannot avoid including the Ch among the 22 books which Jos says were written before the death of Artaxerxes Longimanus (*CAp*, I, 8). Of course the limit of time here really intended by Jos is not the death of Artaxerxes, but the lifetime of men who were contemporary with him—that of Nehemiah, for example. We have already noted the testimony concerning Nehemiah's library (2 Macc **2** 13–15). The time when the library was being gathered was the most likely time for it to be used as the Chronicler has used it. Add the recapitulation in Ecclus (**44–49**), which mentions Nehemiah latest in its list of OT worthies.

Internal marks, also, justify the conclusion that the work of the Chronicler was complete before Nehemiah died. The abundant presence of Pers words and facts, with the absence of Gr words and facts, seems conclusive to the effect that the work was done before the conquests of Alexander rendered the Gr influence paramount. In some of the sections (e.g. Ezr **7** 28 ff; Neh *passim*) Ezra and Nehemiah speak in the first person. The whole work makes the impression of being written up to date. The latest situation in Ch is the same with that in Neh (1 Ch **9**; cf Neh **11** 3—**12** 26). The latest event mentioned is the differentiating of the Samaritan schism. A certain enrolment was made (Neh **12** 22–26) in the reign of Darius, up to the high-priesthood of Johanan (elsewhere called Jonathan and John), but including Jaddua the son of Johanan in the high-priestly succession. Ezra and Nehemiah were still in office (Neh **12** 26). This enrolment naturally connects itself with the expulsion of Jaddua's brother Manasseh for marrying into the family of Sanballat (Neh **13** 28; Jos, *Ant*, XI, 7–8). Jaddua belongs to the fifth generation from Jeshua, who was high priest 538 BC. Jos says that Sanballat held a commission from Darius. He mentions a certain Bagoas, "general of another Artaxerxes' army," as in relations with the high priest John.

Arguments for a later date.—Jos, however, apparently regards the Darius who commissioned Sanballat as the last of the kings of that name, and says that Jaddua was contemporary with Alexander the Great, thus dating the Samaritan schism a little before 331 BC. All scholars reject these statements when they are used for dating the Samaritan schism, but some scholars eagerly accept them for the purpose of proving the late date of the last books of the Heb Bible. The argument never was valid, and it is completely exploded by the Aram. papyri recently discovered in Egypt, which show that Bagoas and the high priest Johanan and the sons of Sanballat were contemporaries in 407 BC, the 17th year of Darius Nothus, and for some years earlier.

Dr. Driver (*LOT*, ed 1897, 518) expresses an opinion very commonly held concerning the Chronicles: "The only positive clue which the book contains as to the date at which it was composed is the genealogy in 1 Ch **3** 17–24, ... carried down to the *sixth* generation after Zerubbabel. This would imply a date not earlier than about 350 BC." Turn to the passage and do your own arithmetic on it. Jeconiah was born 614 BC (2 K **24** 8). If as an average each of the sons in the succession was born when his father was about 25 years old, that would bring the first birth in the 6th generation from Zerubbabel to about 414 BC, and not 350 BC. This is not an improbable showing.

Dr. Driver suggests, however, that in ver 21 we should follow the Gr reading instead of the Heb. This would give us: "And the sons of Hananiah: Pelatiah, and Jeshaiah his son, Rephaiah his son, Arnan his son, Obadiah his son, Shecaniah his son." The meaning here is ambiguous. It may be understood to be that each of the six men named after Hananiah was the son of the man named before him (cf vs 10–14, or 1 Ch **6** 20–30.50–53); or as counting the six as the sons of Hananiah (cf **3** 16; **7** 20.21, etc). Understanding it in the first of these two ways the number of generations after Zerubbabel would be increased to eleven. So many generations before the early decades of the 4th cent. BC would be exceptional, though not impossible. But the statement that there were 11 generations is weak, being based on a conjectural interpretation of an unproved text emendation, and standing unconfirmed in opposition to credible proof.

16. Truthfulness and Historicity

"The Books of Ch are a tendency writing of little historical value"; "a distorted picture in the interest of the later institutions of postexilic Judaism"; "some ancient facts, having trickled down through oral or written tradition, are doubtless preserved. . . . . They are few indeed compared with the products of the imagination, and must be sifted like kernels of wheat from a mass of chaff." These statements, taken at random from the book that happens to be handiest, fairly represent the opinion held by many. They regard the Ch as a fabrication made in the interest of a religious party, a fabrication in which the history has been intentionally falsified.

A principal motive for this opinion is to discredit the testimony of Ch against certain critical theories, the said testimony being more full and detailed than that in S and K and the prophets. But on the whole question the testimony of Ch is to the same effect with that of the other books. The testimony of the other books supports that of the Ch. The discrediting of Ch is part of a theory which denies the historical trustworthiness of practically all parts of the OT and NT.

(1) *Alleged proofs of untruthfulness.*—Against the Ch it is alleged that they sometimes contradict the older books; but nearly all the instances are capable of satisfactory solution. The large numerals in Ch, for example those concerning the armies of David, Abijah, Jeroboam, Asa, Zerah, Jehoshaphat, Amaziah, Uzziah, are adduced as extravagant and incredible. Most of the difficulty in connection with such numbers, whether in Ch or Ex or Nu or Jgs or S, disappears when we observe that they clearly belong to an artificial way of counting. These numbers are given in even thousands or even hundreds (even fifties or tens in a very few instances), which would not be the case if the hundreds and thousands were merely numerical. It is alleged that the Chronicler views the glories of the past as on a larger scale than that in which they are presented in the earlier books, but this is not uniformly the case. On the basis of these allegations the Chronicler is charged with an extravagance that is inconsistent with sober truthfulness, but this charge follows the fate of the others. It is said that the Chronicler lacked trustworthy sources, but that is a thing to be proved, not taken for granted, and we have seen that it is improbable. It is alleged that the text is in such bad shape as to render the contents unreliable. This may be balanced against the counter conjecture that, since the Books of Ch have not been so often copied as the Books of K, their text is in the transcribed passages to be preferred to that of K. In fine, the reasons alleged against the historicity of Ch dwindle on examination, though there remain some problems that cannot be so easily disposed of.

(2) *Truthfulness in the various parts.*—Different parts of the Ch have their own separate problems of historicity. Take the genealogies, for example. If anyone had fabricated them, he would not have put them into their present fragmentary form, in which they have no story interest, and are of no direct use to anybody. On the other hand it is reasonable to account for their present form by the hypothesis that the writer used such materials as he had. This hypothesis is not derogatory to the inspiration of the writer. Deity saw fit to have these materials placed in the Scriptures, and to this end He influenced men of different generations through providential leadings and through impulses of the Spirit. No one thinks that the Spirit-guided man who put the genealogies in their final form received them as miraculous revelations. He received them as the product of effort in study—his own efforts and those of his predecessors. He is entitled to be counted as truthful if he used good judgment and fidelity in selecting and recording his materials.

Similar statements would be true in regard to the other statistical matter, and in regard to the many incidents that are mentioned in connection with the genealogies and other matters. To think of them as inventions by the Chronicler is not congruous with human experience. They are too brief and broken to have interest by themselves as stories. You can assign no possible reason that one could have for inventing them. They bear the marks of being genuine antiquarian discoveries. The final writer believed that he had come across facts which would be of interest if put into connection with the history as currently narrated. These matters are much more reasonably accounted for as facts than as inventions. And furthermore, a good many of them, first and last, have been corroborated by exploration. Take, for example, Manasseh's being carried to Babylon by the captains of the king of Assyria, or the account of Uzziah's military greatness (2 Ch **33** 11; **26** 6 ff), or the references to industries in 1 Ch **4** 14–23 (cf *PEFS*, 1905, 243, 328; or *Bible Sidelights from Gezer*, 150 ff).

Possibly on a different footing is such a passage as the account of Abijah and Jeroboam (2 Ch **13** 3–18). It says that Abijah had 400,000 men and Jeroboam 800,000, of whom 500,000 were slain in the battle. One might plausibly argue that these numbers were intended as a notice to the reader that he is to understand the story, not as fact, but as a work of the imagination, a religious parable, a midrashic narrative sermon, taken from the Midr of Iddo (ver 22). Whether or no one finds this argument convincing, anyone can see that it does not accuse the Books of Ch of being untruthful. If the passage is a parable it is true in the sense in which it was intended to be understood. A similar case is the account of Jehoshaphat's peril from the invading nations and his wonderful rescue (2 Ch **20**).

On still a different footing are such narratives as those concerning the bringing up of the ark, the first making of Solomon king, the reforms under

Asa, Jehoshaphat, Hezekiah, Josiah. These are sober narratives, with nothing in them to suggest flights of the imagination. Probably no one doubts that the Chronicler intended them to be understood as historical fact. If one is under bondage to the modern tradition which dates Dt from the time of Josiah and the priestly laws from after the exile, he must needs count these parts of Ch as falsified history; but if he is free from that bondage he will see no strong reason for counting them so.

17. The Values of the Chronicles

In fine men are correct when they say that the greatest values of the Books of Ch lie in their availability for vividly illustrating the great truths of religion. They are correct when they assign great value to these books as depicting the ideas of the time when they were written. But they are none the less of great value as repeating from the other Scriptures the outline of the history of the religion of Jeh, and presenting additional material for the filling in of that outline.

Literature.—Among the older commentaries on Ch see that of Keil in the Keil-Delitzsch series, published in Eng. in 1872; that of Zöckler in the Lange series, 1876; that of Barker in the *Pulpit Commentary*, after 1880. Among more recent works, from the point of view which denies the historicity of Ch, see R. Kittel in the *Polychrome Bible*, 1895, and Curtis and Masden in the *International Critical Commentary*, 1910. A brilliant characterization from that point of view is that by Torrey, "The Chronicler as Editor and as Independent Narrator" in *AJSL*, January, 1909, and subsequent numbers. On the other side see Beecher, *Reasonable Biblical Criticism*, 1911, chs xviii and xxii; "Is the Chronicler a Veracious Historian?" in *Bible Student* (October, 1899 and subsequent numbers), is a defense of the historicity. All works on OT Introduction discuss the questions concerning Ch. In view of the many proper names in Ch, such a book as Gray, *Studies in Heb Proper Names*, has its uses. For the chronological facts, especially in connection with the closing of the OT history, see Beecher, *Dated Events of the OT*, 1907. For the Egyp papyri see *Drei Aramäische Papyrusurkunden aus Elephantine*, Sachau, Berlin, 1907, or the Appendix to Toffteen, *Historic Exodus*. Also Sprengling's art. in *AJSL*, April, 1911. As to light on the Ch from explorations, see "The Excavations of Gezer, 1902–5, and 1907–9," *PEF*; or *Bible Sidelights from the Mounds of Gezer*, 1906. For other books see the lists in *EB* and *HDB*.

Willis J. Beecher

CHRONOLOGY, krō-nol′ō-ji, OF THE OLD TESTAMENT:

I. Introductory.—For evident reasons the student of Biblical chronology must meet many difficulties, and must always be severely handicapped.

1. Difficulties of the Subject

First of all, the OT is not purely nor intentionally a book of history. Nor does it present a formulated system of chronology, its many numbers and dates being used principally with a view to the spiritual facts and truths with which the authors were concerned. We are not, therefore, to expect to find a perfectly arranged order of periods and dates, though happily for us in our investigation we shall indeed find many accurately dated events, frequent consecutions of events, and orderly successions of officials; as, for example, the numerous genealogical tables, the succession of judges and the lists of kings.

Furthermore, there is not to be found in the OT one particular and definitely fixed era, from which all of its events are dated, as is the case in Christian history. The points of departure, or reckoning, are found to vary in different periods of the advancing history; being at one stage the Creation, at another the migration of Abraham, or the Exodus, or again the disruption of the kingdom. Ordinarily dates and all time-allusions are comparative, i.e. they are related to the reign of some contemporary monarch, as the vision of Isaiah "in the year that king Uzziah died" (Isa **6** 1), or to some unusual occurrence, historical or natural, as the great earthquake (Am **1** 1; Zec **14** 5). Only occasional reference is found to some event, which marks an era-beginning; such as the Exodus (Jgs **11** 16. 26; 1 K **6** 1).

The general lack of uniformity among writers on Bib. chronology contributes further toward increase of the already perplexing confusion. It is almost possible to say that no two writers agree; and proposed harmonies are with each other most inharmonious. The two arts. on OT chronology in a recent work (Murray, *Illus. Bible Dictionary*, 1908), for example, are several hundred years apart at certain points. Wide diversity of opinion exists about the most prominent events, such as the call of Abraham and the age of his famous contemporary Ḥammurabi, the year of the Exodus, and the beginning of Solomon's temple. Naturally there is less variance of opinion about later dates, some of which, e.g. the fall of Samaria and the destruction of Jerus, may be considered as fixed. A like wide range of opinion prevails among archaeologists with regard to events in contemporaneous history, the difference between Goodspeed and Hommel in the dates of early Bab history being five hundred years, and the beginning and extent of the Hyksos period in Egypt varying in different "authorities" by hundreds of years. Nor should the difference in the various and total numbers of the Heb, Samaritan and LXX texts of the pre-Abrahamic ages be left out of sight in any statement of the difficulties attending the discussion of this subject.

2. Plan of Treatment

These difficulties, and others as serious, have determined the plan of this article. The usual method of development has been to begin with the sources of OT history, and to follow its course downward. While such a system may have its advantages, there is, however, this serious disadvantage connected with it: that the least certain dates are confessedly those at the beginning of the records, and the use of them at the foundation renders the whole structure of the discussion more or less uncertain. Archaeology and comparative history have done much to fix dates from the Exodus downward, bringing these later cents. by discovery and translation almost into the position of attested history. But the ages before the Exodus, and particularly before Abraham, still lie from the very nature of the case in great obscurity. And thus any system beginning with the indistinct early past, with its compacted numbers and their uncertain interpretation, is much like a chain hung on thin air. The writer purposes, therefore, beginning with certain familiar, important and pivotal dates, to gather around and relate to these the events and persons of the OT. Such accepted dates are: the completion of the Second Temple in 516, the fall of Jerusalem in 586, the fall of Samaria in 721, tribute to Shalmanezer II from Jehu in 842, and from a member of Omri's dynasty in 854. Such OT events as mark the beginning of eras are the Disruption, Solomon's temple, the Exodus and Abraham's Call. The material and the plan, then, almost necessarily require that we begin at the end of the history and work logically backward to the earlier stages, at which we may hope to arrive with firm ground under our feet for the disposition of the more uncertain problems. It is hoped that on this plan the system of chronology will not be mere speculation, nor a personal theory, but of some certainty and affording some assurance in days of wild assertion and free manipulation.

It should be remembered that this is a study of Bible chronology, and therefore full value will be given to the explicit and positive statements of the Bible. Surely the time has come, when all fair-minded men should recognize that a clear and straightforward declaration of the Sacred Scriptures is not to be summarily rejected because of its apparent contradiction by some unknown and irresponsible person, who could stamp clay or chisel stone. It has been all too common that archaeological and critical adventurers have doubted and required accurate proof of every Bible statement, but have been ready enough to give credence to any statement from ancient pagan sources. We assume, as we have every reason to do, the trustworthiness of the Bible records, which have been corroborated in countless instances; and we shall follow their guidance in preference to any other. The help of contemporaneous history and the witness of archaeology can be used to advantage, but should not be substituted for the plain facts of the Scriptures, which are full worthy of our trust and regard. The province of a chronology of the Bible is properly to present in system the dates therein given, with an honest effort to harmonize the difficulties, using the external helps, but ever regardful of Scripture authority and rights.

3. The Bible to Be Regarded as Highest Authority

II. The Ages between the Testaments.—Between the coming of Christ and the end of OT history there lie in round numbers four hundred years. But while these were extra-Biblical ages, they were neither barren nor uneventful years; for in them will be found much of the highest value in the development of Jewish life, and in the preparation for the Messiah. And thus they have their proper place in Bible chronology (see BETWEEN THE TESTAMENTS). The birth of Jesus could not have been later than 4 BC, since Herod the Great died in April of that year. Herod became king of Judaea in 37 BC. Pal had been conquered and Jerus entered by the Romans under Pompey in 56 BC, the Jews coming in this way under the power of Rome. The Rom age was preceded by the government of priest-kings, with which the Idumaean Antipater became identified by marriage, so that Herod, whom Rome made king, was both Jew and alien.

The period of the Maccabees, which ended in 39 BC with the removal of Antigonus by the Romans in favor of Herod, began 168 BC with Judas. Antipater, who had been appointed procurator of Judaea in 47, was assassinated in 43 BC. The period of the Seleucidae stretches from its close with the regency of Antiochus VII in 128 back to its founder, Seleucus, 312 BC. The most notable of these monarchs from the Jewish point of view was Antiochus Epiphanes, who reigned from 175 to 164, and in 168 gave occasion to the rise of the Maccabees by his many acts of impiety and oppression, particularly the desecration of the Jerus temple. In 203 BC Antiochus the Great, who had become king of Syria in 223, took Jerus, and later, in 198, annexed Judaea to Syria. Previous to this Judaea had been an Egyp dependency, as after the death of Alexander the Great, 323 BC, and the division of his empire, it had been annexed by Ptolemy Soter to Egypt. Ptolemy Philadelphus, becoming king 280 BC, encouraged the tr of the Heb Scriptures into Gr, the result being the LXX version, and all it meant by way of preparation for the spread of Christianity. Alexander's defeat of Darius III, or Codomannus, at Arbela in 331 brought the Pers empire to an end, fulfilling the long-cherished ambition of the Greeks for mastery of Asia. The long reign of the Biblical king of Persia, Artaxerxes Longimanus, extended from 465 to 424 BC, and in reaching his reign we find ourselves in the region of the OT history. Reversing the order of this brief review and setting out from OT point of view, we have the following table for the cents. between the Testaments:

Death of Artaxerxes I, and succession of Darius II	424
Accession of Darius III, last of Pers monarchs	336
Alexander succeeds Philip as king of Macedonia	336
Alexander visits Jerus	332
Battle of Arbela and overthrow of Persia	331
Death of Alexander and division of his empire	323
Ptolemy Soter attaches Judaea to Egypt	320
Seleucid era begins with accession of Seleucus I	312
Ptolemy Philadelphus reigns in Egypt	283
Traditional date of beginning of LXX version	cir 250
Antiochus the Great, king of Syria	223
He annexes Judaea to Syria	198
Antiochus Epiphanes ascends the throne	175
He makes Jason high priest, removing Onias	174
Desecration of Temple by Ant. Epiph	168
Resistance of Mattathias and rise of Maccabees	168
Judas Maccabaeus victorious	166
Judas dies, succeeded by Jonathan	160
Jonathan slain, succeeded by Simon	143
Simon becomes high priest	142
Succeeded by John Hyrcanus	135
Aristobulus I becomes high priest	106
Alexander Jannaeus	105
Jerus taken by Pompey	63
Antipater appointed procurator of Judaea	47
Antipater murdered	43
Antigonus, last Maccabean, put on throne	40
Slain by Herod, who becomes king of Judaea	37
Augustus made Rom emperor	31
Restoration of Temple begun	19
Birth of Jesus Christ in Bethlehem	cir 5
Death of Herod the Great	4

III. The Persian Period.—Entering now the last period of OT history, which may be called the Pers period, we find that the activities of Ezra, Nehemiah and other Jewish leaders are dated by the regnal years of the kings of Persia (e.g. Hag **1** 1; Zec **1** 1; Ezr **1** 1; Neh **2** 1); and consequently the difficulties in the chronology of this period are not great. Recently a fanciful effort has been made to place the events narrated in Esther, Ezra and Nehemiah in the time of the Bab Captivity, claiming Scripture warrant from the occurrence of these names, with Mordecai, in Ezr **2** 2 and Neh **7** 7; but altogether without success (see *Prince of Judah, or Days of Nehemiah Redated*). These names were doubtless of common occurrence, and their appearance among those returning with Zerubbabel is not sufficient to affect the historical evidence for the accepted dates of Ezra and Nehemiah. The attempt to move back these dates into the 6th cent., to associate Nehemiah with Daniel and Mordecai and to place his work before Zerubbabel may be dismissed as pure fancy and impossible of reconciliation with the OT narrative.

Artaxerxes I began his reign, which gives date

to Ezra and Nehemiah, in 465 BC. In his 7th year, 458, Ezra went from Babylon to Jerus by the king's decree (Ezr **7** 7), taking back with him the vessels of the Temple and much besides for the worship at Jerus, accompanied also by a great company of returning Jews. Nehemiah followed from Shushan in the 20th year of the king (Neh **1** 1), having heard of and being distressed by the partial failure of Ezra's efforts. Under his wise and courageous leadership, the city walls were speedily restored, and many reforms accomplished. He returned after twelve years (433) to the service of the king in Shushan (Neh **13** 6), but in a short time, hearing evil tidings from Jerus, went back to complete his reforms, and apparently spent the rest of his life in that work. Although the Bible is silent, such is the testimony of Jos. The Book of Mal, reflecting the difficulties and evils of this time, is evidently to be placed here, but not with exactness, as it might have been written as early as 460 or as late as 420.

The period from the return under Ezra (458) back to the completion of the Temple in the reign of Darius I (516) is, with the exception of incidental references and the assignment of undated books and incidents, practically a blank. Here belong, we believe, the Book of Est, possibly Mal, some of the Pss, and those social and religious tendencies among the returned exiles, which made the vigorous reforms of Ezra and Nehemiah so necessary. But the OT does not draw the curtain from the mystery of that half-century, that we may know the happenings and watch the development. Beyond this blank we come again to explicit dates. The second temple, begun with the Return under Zerubbabel, was completed in the 6th year of Darius, i.e. 516. The building of it, which had been early abandoned for selfish reasons, was resumed in the 2d year of Darius under the exhortation of the prophets Haggai and Zechariah (Hag **1** 1; Zec **1** 1). Darius the Great began his reign in 521. Cambyses succeeded Cyrus in 527. Babylon was taken by the Persians in 538, and shortly after the Jews, under the edict of Cyrus, began their return to Jerus, reaching their destination by 536 at the latest. Cyrus overthrew Lydia in 545, the Medes five years earlier, and must have come to the Pers throne not later than 555. His conquest of Asia Minor opened the contest between Persia and Greece for supremacy, to be continued by Darius and Xerxes, resulting finally at Arbela (331) in Gr triumph under Alexander, and the inauguration of a new age.

The table for the Pers period of OT history, following the stream upward, is therefore as follows:

Death of Nehemiah	cir 400
Death of Artaxerxes I	424
Nehemiah comes second time to Jerus	432
Nehemiah returns to Persia (Neh **13** 6)	433
First coming of Neh and repairing of walls	445
Book of Malachi, possibly	cir 450
Return of Ezra and his company	458
Accession of Artaxerxes I	465
Events of Book of Esther	cir 480
Accession of Xerxes (Ahasuerus)	486
Defeat of Darius at Marathon	490
Completion of the Temple	516
Ministry of Haggai and Zechariah	520
Darius Hystaspis becomes king	521
Death of Cyrus and accession of Cambyses	527
Arrival of Jews in Jerus under edict of Cyrus	536
Capture of Babylon by Persians	538
Croesus of Lydia defeated by Cyrus	545
Persia and Media united	cir 550
Supremacy of Cyrus over Elam and Persia	cir 556
Birth of Cyrus, supposed to be in	600

IV. Babylonian Period.—Just preceding the Pers is the Bab period of OT chronology, overlapping, of course, the former, and finally superseded by it in Cyrus' conquest of Babylonia. This period may properly be said to begin with the death in 626 BC of Asshurbanipal, the last great ruler of Assyria. At this time Nabopolassar had been made governor of Babylonia, subject to the supremacy of Assyria. With Asshurbanipal's death Nabopolassar became independent sovereign of Babylonia, and shortly entered into league with the Medes to overthrow the rule of Assyria, and then to divide its empire between them. This was accomplished in the fall of Nineveh (606) which brought the end of the mighty Assyr empire, the last king being Sinsharishkun (the historic Saracus), a son of Asshurbanipal. Some years before his death in 604 Nabopolassar associated with him on the throne of Babylonia his son Nebuchadnezzar, most illustrious ruler of the new Bab empire, and intimately connected with the history of Judah in the last years of that kingdom. His long reign came to an end in 562.

While the conflict, which brought Assyria to its end, and the attendant confusion, were absorbing the attention of Mesopotamian countries, Egypt under a new and virile dynasty was reviving her ambitions and intrigues for dominion in Asia. Pharaoh-necoh II taking advantage of the confusion and helplessness of Assyria invaded Pal in 609, intending to march on through Pal to attack Mesopotamia. King Josiah in loyalty to his Assyr overlord opposed him, but was defeated and slain at the battle of Megiddo, after a reign of 31 years; apparently an unnecessary and foolish opposition on Josiah's part, as the plan of Necoh's march shows that Judah was not directly affected. After the victory at Megiddo, Necoh continued his march north-eastward, subduing Syria and hoping to have a hand in Mesopotamian affairs. But in 606 or 607 BC he was defeated at Carchemish and driven back to Egypt by Nebuchadnezzar, fresh from victory over Nineveh. In the same year Nebuchadnezzar marched against Egypt, receiving the submission of Jerus as he passed through Pal, and sending noble hostages back to Babylon, among whom were Daniel and his three friends. The death of his father and his endangered succession recalled Nebuchadnezzar suddenly to Babylon, where he became sole ruler in 604. It appears that Necoh must have returned to Egypt after Megiddo and before the battle of Carchemish, as he made Jehoiakim king in place of Jehoahaz, whom he carried captive to Egypt. Nebuchadnezzar's victory at Carchemish and his march southward brought Judah in close relations with Babylon, and opened up the dramatic chapter of Jerusalem's fall and exile. These historic events fix the dates of the last kings and the closing incidents of the kingdom of Judah, as shown in the following table:

Fall of Babylon and death of Belshazzar	538
Co-regency of Belshazzar with his father (Dnl **8** 1)	542
Accession of Nabonidus, father of Belshazzar	555
Death of Nebuchadnezzar, and succession of Evil-Merodach	561
Jehoiachin released from prison (Jer **52** 31)	561
Last dated prophecy of Ezk (**40** 1)	572
Murder of Gedaliah and flight of Jews to Egypt	585
Fall of Jerus and Third Deportation	586
Beginning of Ezekiel's prophetic activity (Ezk **1** 1)	592
Accession of Zedekiah, last king of Judah	597
Brief reign of Jehoiachin, his removal to Babylon; Second Deportation of captives including Ezekiel	597

Revolt and death of Jehoiakim; invasion of Nebuchadnezzar	598
Death of Nabopolassar and accession of Nebuchadnezzar	604
Nebuchadnezzar invades Pal; First Deportation, including Daniel	606
Battle of Carchemish and route of Necoh	607
Fall of Nineveh	607
Jehoiakim made king by Necho	608
Death of Josiah and brief reign of Jehoahaz	609
Accession of Pharaoh Necho	610
Nabopolassar, king of Bab on death of Asshurbanipal	626

V. Assyrian Period and Judah after Fall of Samaria.—This section, which may for convenience be treated as a division, is the chronology of Judah under Assyria after the fall of the Northern Kingdom in 721. As the Scripture time-references are frequent and explicit, and the contemporaneous Assyr records are full, and explicit also, the problems of this period are neither many nor insoluble. One difficulty is found in the fact that the aggregate years of the reigns of Hezekiah, Manasseh, Amon and Josiah fall one or two years short of the period between Hezekiah's accession in 726 and Josiah's death in 609. But there is evidence of anarchical conditions at the close of Amon's reign (2 K **21** 23.24), and it is probable that at least a year should be counted for the interregnum. The chief difficulty is with the invasions of Sennacherib in Hezekiah's reign. The confusion is caused by the *apparent* dating of Sennacherib's famous and disastrous invasion of 701 in the 14th year of Hezekiah's reign (2 K **18** 13). Various attempts at reconciliation have been made; one attempt has been to place the beginning of Hezekiah's reign in 715, which is out of the question entirely, as it disregards the exact terms in which the beginning of his reign is placed before the fall of Samaria (2 K **18** 10). Another suggestion has been that "24th" be read instead of "14th"; but this is pure conjecture. There is a simple and satisfactory solution: in the chapters which contain the record (2 K **18** and Isa **36**) it is evident that *two* invasions are described. Frequently in the Scriptures records are topical rather than chronological, and just so in this instance the topic is Sennacherib's menace of Judah, and the ultimate deliverance by Jeh. The story includes two invasions: the *first* in the 14th year of Hezekiah (713) when Sennacherib led the armies of his father Sargon, the end of which, so far as Jerus was concerned, was the payment of tribute by Hezekiah, as is accurately stated in 2 K **18** 16. The *second* invasion, the description of which begins with the following ver (17), was the more serious, and is probably identified as that of 701, when Sennacherib had become king. The necessary insertion of a paragraph indicator between vs 16 and 17 satisfies every demand for harmony.

From 609 BC, the year of Josiah's death, we count back 31 years to the beginning of his reign in 639; he attained his majority in the 8th year (632; 2 Ch **34** 3); the reformation in his 12th year, at the time of the Scythian irruption, would fall in 628 (2 Ch **34** 3); in the following year Jeremiah began to prophecy; and in Josiah's 18th year (621) the temple was cleansed and the Book of the Law found (2 Ch **34** 8). Allowing a year of confusion, Amon began his short reign in 642, and Manasseh his long reign of 55 years in 697, Hezekiah's reign of 29 years dating back to 726. Some fixed important dates of contemporaneous history are: death of Asshurbanipal, Assyria's last great king, in 626, with the consequent independence of Babylon and beginning of the 2d Bab empire. Asshurbanipal's long reign began in 668 on the death of his father Esarhaddon; who succeeded his father Sennacherib in 681. Sargon usurped the Assyr throne in 722, and died in 705. Shalmanezer IV, successor of Tiglath-pileser III, reigned for the brief space between 727 and 722. In Egypt the XXVth, or Ethiopian Dynasty, was in power from cir 720 to 667, two of its kings, So and Tirhakah, having mention in the OT (2 K **17** 4; **19** 9; Isa **37** 9), and after this the XXVIth (a native) Dynasty appeared, Pharaoh-necoh being one of its kings. The dates of this period we may summarize in the following table:

Death of Josiah after reign of 31 years	609
Pharaoh-necho begins to reign	610
Josiah purifies temple; Book of the Law found	621
Death of Asshurbanipal, and revival of Babylon	626
Jeremiah enters upon his ministry	627
Reformation in 12th year of Josiah	628
Scythian invasion of Western Asia	cir 630
Majority of Josiah; good beginning of actual reign	632
Josiah proclaimed king at 8 years of age	639
Assassination of Amon; ensuing confusion	640
Death of Manasseh	642
Manasseh carried to Babylon	cir 650
Asshurbanipal succeeds Esarhaddon	668
Esarhaddon invades Egypt	670
Probable settlement of foreigners in Samaria	672
Assassination of Sennacherib	681
Death of Isaiah, probably about	680
Death of Hezekiah and accession of Manasseh	697
Sennacherib's campaign against Egypt, siege of Jerus, and his disastrous rout	701
Sargon dies and Sennacherib succeeds	705
Embassy of Merodach-baladan to Hezekiah	711
Sickness of Hezekiah	712
First invasion of Pal by Sennacherib	cir 713
Sabako, or So, is king of Egypt	715
Palestine invaded by Sargon; Ashdod taken (Isa **20** 1)	720
Fall of Samaria; end of Northern Kingdom	721
Sargon takes Assyr throne	722
Revolt of Hoshea, and siege of Samaria begun	724
Hezekiah's reign begins	726
Shalmanezer IV succeeds Tiglath-pileser III	727

VI. Period of Divided Kingdom.—The most complex, but most interesting, problems of OT chronology are found in the period of the Divided Kingdom. In the lit. of this period are found a larger number of dates and historical references than in that of any other. We have the assistance of several important sources and factors in arranging these dates: (1) The ‖ records of the kingdoms of Israel and Judah serve as checks to each other, since the accession and death of the kings in each nation are fixed by reference to reigns of those of the other. Many other events are similarly related. (2) The history of the two kingdoms, or parts of it, at least, is given in three ‖ authorities: the Books of K, of Ch, and of the Prophets. (3) The Assyr records are fullest and are practically continuous in this period, the *limu* lists extending unbroken from 893 to 650 BC.

1. Causes of Variation in Systems

But while this apparently should be the most satisfactory field for the chronologist, it has been found impossible to arrive at anything approaching certainty, and consequently there is considerable divergence among individuals and schools. One cause of variation is the difference between the Assyr royal lists and the total of the OT numbers for this period, the OT aggregate being 51 years greater then the Assyr lists. Two common methods of harmonizing this difference have been adopted: (1) to accept the OT aggregate as correct and to assume that the 51 years have been omitted from the Assyr lists (see W. J. Beecher, *Dated Events of OT*, 18, 19); (2) to harmonize the OT numbers with the Assyr lists by taking into account the overlapping of reigns of kings who were, for brief periods, associated on the throne. Instances of such overlapping are the co-regency of Uzziah and Jotham in Judah (2 K **15** 5), and possibly the reign of Pekah contemporaneously with Menahem and Pekahiah in Israel (2 K **15** 23–28). The latter method yields the most satisfactory results, and will be adopted in this article. The chief point of difference will be the age of Solomon and the foundation-laying of the Temple. This may be found according to the former method by adding 51 years to the dates as given below. That the method of following the aggregate of the OT numbers must *assume* arbitrarily that there have been omissions from the Assyr lists, and that it also must resort to some overlapping and adjustment of the numbers as they are given in the text, are sufficient reasons against its adoption. And in meeting the difficulties of this period it should always be borne in mind that the OT is not a book of annals merely, and that dates are given not for any special interest in them, but to correlate and emphasize events. Ordinarily dates are given with reference to local situations and contemporary persons, and not as fixed by some great epoch-marking event; e.g. Uzziah's reign is fixed not with reference to the Disruption nor the Temple building, but by relation to his Israelite contemporary, Jeroboam II.

However, there are some fixed dates, which are so by reason of their international significance, and upon these we may rest with reasonable assurance. Such are the fall of Samaria (721 BC); the accession of Tiglath-pileser III (745); tribute paid to Shalmaneser II by Jehu in 842, and by Ahab, or one of his dynasty, in 854; and the invasion of Judah by Pharaoh-shishak in the fifth year of Rehoboam (1 K **14** 25). There are also certain coincident dates, fixed with fair accuracy, in the ‖ history of the two kingdoms, which serve both as starting-points and as checks upon each other. The most prominent of these are: the beginning of Hezekiah's reign, 5 years before the fall of Samaria (2 K **18** 10); the synchronism of the reigns of Jeroboam II and Jotham (1 Ch **5** 17), Jotham's accession being used as a basis of calculation for the reigns of Israelite kings (2 K **15** 30); the coincidence of the end of the Omri Dynasty and the death of Ahaziah, king of Judah (2 K **9**), Jehu and Athaliah therefore beginning their reigns at the same time; and, primarily, the division of the kingdom and the synchronous beginning of the reigns of Jeroboam I and Rehoboam. Using these fixed dates and coincidences, we must find the summaries of the reigns of Israelite and Jewish kings between 721, the 9th year of Hoshea and the 6th of Hezekiah, and 843, the beginning of the reigns of Jehu and Athaliah, to be 122 years each; and likewise the summaries from 843 back to the Disruption to be the same.

2. Some Important and Pivotal Dates

The most serious difficulties are found near the end of the period, when conditions in the Northern Kingdom were becoming anarchical, and, also evident coregencies, the extent of which is not evident, occurred in the Southern Kingdom. Pekah is said to have reigned 20 years (2 K **15** 27); and yet Menahem paid tribute to Assyria in 738, and he was succeeded for two years by his son Pekahiah, from whom Pekah seized the kingdom. This would allow Pekah only 6 years of sovereignty. The explanation lies in the context: in the confusion which followed the death of Jeroboam, Pekah established his authority over the section E. of the Jordan, and to that year the numbers in 2 K **15** 27.32; 2 K **16** 1 refer. Uzziah was leprous the last 16 years of his life, and Jotham his son was over the kingdom (2 K **15** 5). The length of Jotham's reign was just 16 years, not additional to the 16 of the coregency, as this would result in the absurdity of making him coregent at the age of 9 years (2 K **15** 33). Therefore nearly his whole reign is included in the 52 years of his father. For some reason Ahaz was associated with his father Jotham before the death of the latter, since the 16 years of his reign plus the 5 of Hezekiah before the fall of Samaria bring his accession before the death of Uzziah and Jotham, i.e. in 741. So that for approximately 6 years the three reigns were contemporaneous. That these 6 years may not be accounted for by a coregency with Hezekiah at the other end of Ahaz' reign is evident from the age of Hezekiah at his accession (2 K **18** 2), and from the radical difference in the policy of the two kings. Isa **7** 1 may suggest that Uzziah and Jotham died about the same time, and that Ahaz was regarded as succeeding both directly.

3. Difficulties to Be Removed

Another difficulty is found at the beginning of Uzziah's reign, where he is said to have succeeded his father Amaziah at the age of 16, but is also said to have accomplished certain notable things after his father's death (2 K **14** 21.22). Evidently, then, he became king before the death of Amaziah. When did this coregency begin? No better time is suggested than Amaziah's ignominious defeat by Jehoash of Israel in the 15th year of his reign, after which the people arose and put Uzziah in his place, Amaziah living on for 15 years (2 K **14** 17), so that 15 of Amaziah's 29 years were contemporaneous with Uzziah. Further, in the last years of Joash of Judah there may have been a coregency, since he was "very sick" in those years (2 Ch **24** 25). Thus the totals of 146 years for the reigns of the kings of Israel and of 165 for the reigns of the kings of Judah between 721 and 842 are reduced to the actual 121 by the overlappings, which are suggested in the narrative itself.

For the first division of this period, from the rise of Jehu, cir 843, to the division of the kingdom, the totals of the reigns of the kings of Israel is 98 years, and of the kings of Judah is 95. But there must be some overlappings. The interval between Ahab and Jehu, as shown by mention of them in the Assyr records, is 12 years; but the two sons of Ahab reigned 14 years, Ahaziah 2 and Jehoram 12. Evidently the last year of Ahab, in which came the defeat at Karkar, was the 1st of Ahaziah, and the 2d of Ahaziah, who suffered in that year serious accident (2 K **1** 2), was the first of Jehoram. It is probable that the long reign of Asa closed with Jehoshaphat as coregent (1 K **15** 23), so the above totals of both kingdoms must be reduced to some extent, probably to 90 years, and the disruption of the kingdom placed about 933 BC. Shishak, founder of the XXIId Dynasty, invaded Pal in the 5th year of Rehoboam (1 K **14** 25), and in, or shortly before, the 21st year of his own reign, so that he must have become sovereign of Egypt about 950 BC. Jeroboam fled to Egypt after Solomon had reigned more than 20 years, as is shown by the connection of Jeroboam with the building of Millo; and so Jeroboam's flight must have been about the beginning of Shishak's reign. This is in accord with the OT records, since the hostile Shishak Dynasty must have arisen in the reign of Solomon, the dynasty which was ruling at the beginning of his reign having been in alliance with him. So

4. Overlappings

we place the accession of Shishak about 950, his invasion of Judah in 929, and the Disruption in 933 BC.

An interesting instance of coregency in this period is that of Jehoshaphat and Jehoram, for while Ahaziah of Israel began to reign in the 17th year of Jehoshaphat (1 K **22** 51) and died in the 2d year of Jehoram (2 K **1** 17), the year of his death since the precocious Jewish sovereigns attained their majority at 15 years of age (cf 2 Ch **34** 3). The coregency for 2 years of Joash and Amaziah (2 Ch **24** 25) brings the aggregate years of the reigns of the kings of both kingdoms down to the accession of Jeroboam II, three years before Uzziah's accession, into exact accord. Finally, the difference of three years in the totals of reigns in

A HARMONY OF THE CHRONOLOGY OF THE NORTHERN AND SOUTHERN KINGDOMS

Israel	BC	Judah
Fall of Samaria; end of Kingdom of Israel	721	6th year of Hezekiah (2 K **18** 10)
Siege of Samaria begun; 7th year of Hoshea	723	4th year of Hezekiah (2 K **18** 9)
	726	Accession of Hezekiah (2 K **18** 1)
Hoshea made king by Tiglath-pileser (2 K **17** 1)	729	12th year of Ahaz, counting coregency
Death of Pekah (2 K **15** 30)	730	20th year from beginning of Jotham's coregency
Pekah and Rezin invade Judah (Isa **7** 1)	734	Jotham dies, Ahaz reigns alone (2 K **16** 1)
2d year of Pekah over all Israel (2 K **15** 32)	735	Death of Uzziah (2 K **15** 2); vision of Isaiah (**6** 1) Jotham reigns alone for short time
Pekah becomes king, killing Pekahiah (2 K **15** 25.27)	736	52d year of Uzziah
Pekahiah succeeds; Menahem dies (2 K **15** 22.23)	738	50th year of Uzziah
Menahem pays tribute to Assyria (2 K **15** 19)	741	Ahaz becomes coregent (2 K **15** 30; **17** 1)
Menahem kills Shallum and reigns (2 K **15** 13–17)	748	39th year of Uzziah
Zechariah succeeds Jeroboam II (2 K **15** 8)	749	Regency of Jotham began (2 K **15** 5.32)
Era of political confusion; Pekah usurped authority in Gilead (2 K **15** 8–16 ff) Hosea the Prophet (Hos **1** 1)	750	Leprosy of Uzziah (2 Ch **26** 16–21) The great earthquake (Am **1** 1; Zec **14** 5)
Amos the Prophet (Am **1** 1; **7** 9.10)	752	
	764	Uzziah frees Judah from vassalage to Israel (2 K **15** 1)
Jonah the Prophet (2 K **14** 25; Jon **1** 1)	cir 775	Death of Amaziah (2 K **14** 17; 2 Ch **25** 25)
4th year of Jeroboam II (2 K **15** 8)	787	Uzziah made king by the people (2 K **14** 21.22)
Death of Joash; Jeroboam succeeds (2 K **14** 16.23)	790	Humiliating defeat of Amaziah by Joash (2 K **14** 8–14)
	803	Death of Joash (2 K **12** 1.21)
Death of Jehoahaz (2 K **13** 1)	804	Amaziah coregent (2 K **14** 1; **13** 10; 2 Ch **24** 25)
Joash becomes coregent (2 K **13** 1.10)	806	37th year of Joash
Death of Jehu (2 K **10** 35.36)	816	
Jehoahaz coregent in old age of Jehu (2 K **13** 1)	820	23d year of Joash
7th year of Jehu	837	Overthrow of Athaliah (2 K **11** 21) Joash seven years old (2 K **12** 1)
Jehu pays tribute to Assyria	842	
Jehu destroys dynasty of Omri, and reigns (2 K **10** 36)	843	Athaliah usurps throne on death of Ahaziah (2 K **11** 1.3)
Jehoram slain by Jehu (2 K **9** 24)	843	Ahaziah slain by Jehu (2 K **9** 27) in 1st year of his reign 2 K **8** 25
11th year of Jehoram	844	Ahaziah coregent with his father (2 K **9** 29)
5th year of Jehoram	850	Death of Jehoshaphat; sole reign of Jehoram (2 K **8** 16)
Jehoram succeeds Ahaziah; fatal accident to Ahaz; death of Ahab (1 K **22** 37; 2 K **1** 2.17)	854	18th year of Jehoshaphat, and 2d of Jehoram (2 K **1** 17; **3** 1)
Battle of Ḳarḳar, tribute to Assyria		Jehoshaphat aids Ahab against Syria (1 K **22** 1 ff)
Coregency of Ahaziah (1 K **22** 51)	855	Jehoram becomes coregent
Naboth robbed and murdered by Jezebel (1 K **21** 1)	cir 856	
Wars with Syria	867–857	
Elijah the Prophet appears (1 K **17** 1)	cir 870	
4th year of Ahab	872	Asa dies and Jehoshaphat reigns alone (1 K **22** 41)
	874	Jehoshaphat coregent in Asa's 39th year (2 Ch **16** 12)
Ahab succeeds on death of Omri (1 K **16** 29)	875	38th year of Asa
Omri builds Samaria, having overcome all opposition to his reign (1 K **16** 23.24)	881	31st year of Asa
Zimri's brief reign after murder of Elah; people divided between Omri and Tibni (1 K **16**)	886	27th year of Asa
Elah succeeds on death of Baasha (1 K **16** 6.7)	887	26th year of Asa
Baasha begins building Ramah (1 K **15** 17)	896	War with Baasha in the 17th year of Asa
		Hanani the Prophet
	898	War with Zerah; Azariah the prophet (2 Ch **14** 9; **15** 1)
Baasha founds new dynasty (1 K **15** 33)	910	3d year of Asa
Death of Jeroboam I, succession of Nadab	911	2d year of Asa
20th year of Jeroboam	913	Death of Abijah, succession of Asa (1 K **15** 9)
18th year of Jeroboam	915	Rehoboam dies; Abijah succeeds (1 K **15** 1)
	929	Invasion of Shishak (1 K **14** 25)
Jeroboam king over Israel	933	Rehoboam king over Judah

was also the 18th of Jehoshaphat, so that the father and son reigned together about 5 years. It is evident also that Jehoshaphat ruled before his father's death, as the total of his reign is counted from the coregency's beginning (1 K **22** 41), but certain events are dated from his sole reign on the death of Asa (1 K **22** 51; 2 K **3** 1). It is probable that the 6 years of Athaliah were included in the 40 years of the reign of Joash, the legitimate king. The age of his son, Amaziah, at his accession (2 Ch **25** 1) does not operate against this probability, the two kingdoms from Jehu to the Disruption is explained by the fact that in Israel the first year of a king was coincident with the last of his predecessor, whereas in Judah, certainly at the beginning of this period, the first year of a king followed the death of his predecessor; e.g. while Asa began to reign in the 20th year of Jeroboam (1 K **15** 9), Jeroboam, who reigned 22 years, died *three* years later in the *second* year of Asa (1 K **15** 25). Observation of this principle in the accessions of the first three kings after Jeroboam removes the difference, the long numbers of the reign of Asa being found to corroborate. The preceding table will illustrate these facts of the records, as harmonizing the dates of the two contemporaneous kingdoms.

VII. From the Disruption to the Exodus.—The period now to be considered extends from the disruption of the kingdom back to the Exodus. The reasons for combining the Biblical events within these widely separated dates into one period of such length are evident, viz. (1) the regular sequence of the history; (2) the occurrence of comprehensive numbers for the period as a whole, e.g. Jgs **11** 26 and 1 K **6** 1; the chronological data of the Book of Jgs, which lead directly up to the developments in the time of the united kingdom, e.g. the narrative of Ruth preparing the way for the reign of David. Characteristic of this period is the frequent occurrence of the general numbers 80, 40 and 20, which (Acts **13** 21), are given as 40 years each; and here there may be some overlapping, Solomon, e.g. becoming king before David's death (1 K **1** 43–48). We are rather surprised to find that there is no statement of the length of Samuel's ministry, such as its important place in the national life would lead us to expect. The probable reason for this is that his life was paralleled largely by the reign of Saul and the administration of Eli. A period of 40 years is assigned to Eli (1 S **4** 18); the aggregate of numbers given for the Judges is 410 years; Joshua ruled for 40 years (Jgs **2** 8); and finally the wilderness wanderings covered another 40-year period. The sum total of all these numbers is 670—far beyond the comprehensive reckonings of Jgs **11** 26; 1 K **6** 1, and Acts **13** 19. It is evident from Jgs **10** 7.8; **13** 1 that the periods of Ammonite and Phili oppression were either con-

	Long or Consecutive Numbers		Shortened Nos., Synchronisms Reckoned	
	No. Years	BC	No. Years	BC
Death of Solomon, followed by Disruption	...	933	...	933
Jeroboam a refugee in Egypt	16	cir 948	16	cir 948
Shishak rules Egypt	1	cir 949	1	cir 949
Foundation of Temple laid	20	969	20	969
Death of David, in coregency of Solomon	2	971	2	971
Solomon made king (1 K 1)	1	972	1	972
David reigns over all Israel	32	1004	32	1003
David reigns over Judah	7	1011	7	1010
David anointed by Samuel	...	1024	...	1023
Birth of David	...	1041	...	1040
Beginning of Saul's reign; Samuel still judge	40	1051	*39	1049
Samuel's administration (1 S 7 2.15) certainly	20	1071	20	1069
Eli began to judge	40	1111	39	1108
Samson (contemporary with Eli; Jgs **13** 1) began	20	1131	0	1108
Oppression by Philistines	40	1171	0	....
Abdon began to judge in Ephraim	8	1179	7	1115
Elon began to judge in Zebulun	10	1189	9	1124
Ibzan began to judge contemporaneous with Elon	8	1197	0	1124
Jephthah's judgeship	6	1203	5	1129
Oppression by Ammonites (Jgs **12**)	18	1221	0	....
Jair began to judge (including oppression of Ammon)	22	1243	21	1150
Tola began to judge	23	1266	22	1172
Abimelech's usurpation	3	1269	0	....
Gideon's judgeship, including Abimelech	40	1300	39	1211
Oppression by Midian (Jgs **6** 1)	7	1316	0	....
Deborah and Barak co-judges	40	1356	39	1250
Oppression by Canaanites (Jgs **4** 3)	20	1376	0	....
Period under Ehud and Shamgar (Jgs **3** 30.31· **4** 1)	80	1456	79	1329
Oppression by Moab (Jgs **3** 14)	18	1474	0	....
Othniel of Judah judges	40	1514	39	1368
Oppression by Cushan-rishathaim (Jgs **3** 8)	8	1522	0	....
Entrance into Canaan under Joshua	40	1562	40	1408
Death of Moses	...	1563	...	1409
Death of Aaron	...	1564	...	1410
Israel at Kadesh, 2d time	...	1564	...	1410
Israel at Sinai	...	1601	...	1447
Exodus from Egypt, led by Moses	40	1602	40	cir 1448
	670		517	

* One year will be subtracted from each long administration for overlapping with predecessor.

are not necessarily to be taken always as exact, but possibly at times indicating a round, or generation, number. In order to get the time limits of this period, it is necessary to count back 37 years from the end of Solomon's reign in 933 BC, and this brings us to that epoch-marking event, the laying of the foundations of the Temple in 969 or 970, the 4th year of his reign (1 K **6** 1); and from this event we are brought by the addition of the comprehensive number 479, given in the same verse, back to the year of the Exodus, approximately 1448 BC, making the total length of the period about 516 years.

Indications of Overlapping

But the addition of the numbers given for the various reigns and administrations of the period yields a total which is much greater than 516, and therefore one must seek in the text indications of overlapping, which will bring the narrative into harmony with itself. The reigns of Solomon (1 K **11** 42), David (1 K **2** 11) and Saul temporaneous or very near together, and therefore that the comprehensive number, 300 years, of Jgs **11** 26, reaches from the entrance into Canaan under Joshua down to the age of Samson, as well as of Jephthah. The administrations of Ibzan, Elon and Abdon (Jgs **12** 8–13) should then be regarded as practically synchronous with Jephthah and Samson, and the number of their years should, in part at least, be left out of account. The numbers from Samson and Eli to Solomon are approximately fixed, 20 to Samson, 40 to Eli, 40 to Saul and 40 to David; and their total accords with the 300 before Jephthah, and the 40 of wilderness wanderings in making up the grand total (1 K **6** 1) from Solomon to the Exodus. This proportion before and after Jephthah, or Samson, and the Phili oppression, approximately 330 and 150 years, is in agreement with the genealogies of Ruth **4** 18–22; 1 S **14** 3; **22** 9; 1 Ch **2, 6, 24**. The shortening therefore of the excessive aggregate of 670 years must be sought in the records from Samson back to Joshua. Assuming that the oppressions may be synchronous with the administrations of preceding or succeeding judges, that Abimelech's abortive attempt to become king (Jgs **9**) should be included in Gideon's 40 years, and that parallelings are possible in the three judges just after Jephthah (Jgs **12** 8–13) and the two just before (Jgs **10** 1–5), it is possible to bring the detailed time-references of the Books of Jgs into satisfactory agreement with the comprehensive numbers. That the period of the Judges is shorter than the aggregate of the numbers assigned to each is further indicated by the manner in which the brief narratives at the end of the book—the migration of the Danites, the sin and punishment of Benjamin—and the Book of Ruth, bring the earlier generations into close touch with the later; cf the genealogy of David (Ruth **4** 18–22).

The preceding table (p. 641) shows the dates of events according to the longer reckoning, and also according to the suggested shortening by taking into account the possible synchronisms. It should be remembered that these figures are not indisputable, but merely tentative and suggestive.

VIII. From the Exodus to the Birth of Abraham.—The period of OT chronology now to receive our attention is that which extends from the Exodus in cir 1448 BC back to the call and migration of Abraham. This may be called the period of the patriarchal wanderings, the formative or infancy period of the nation, and therefore of the highest interest historically and religiously. But it is not possible to fix its dates with indisputable accuracy, since, with rare exceptions, the events of the OT record are not related in their narration to eras or definite persons of the contemporary nations; and since also the chronology of these nations is much in dispute among historians and archaeologists, with variations of hundreds of years.

Main Points at Issue

The chief points at issue here for determination of the chronological problems are the time of the Exodus, the duration of Israel's sojourn in Egypt and the date of Ḥammurabi. Considering these in their order: (1) As to the Exodus, opinions have been divided among the XVIIIth, XIXth and XXth dynasties as the time of the Oppression and Exodus of Israel, and there are plausible arguments for, and serious objections to, each of these periods. When all things have been considered it seems best to fix upon the XVIIIth Dynasty as the age of the Oppression and Exodus, Thothmes III as the Pharaoh of the Oppression, and the years immediately following his death as the time of the Exodus, for the following reasons: (*a*) This is in harmony with the time-reckoning from the Temple of Solomon back to the Exodus (1 K **6** 1), and fully satisfies the Biblical numbers for the intervening period, as shown above; while either later dynastic period would necessitate either unnatural cramping or ruthless rejection of the Biblical numbers. To place the Exodus so late as Ramses III, after 1200 BC, is in the light of the Biblical reckoning an evident absurdity. (*b*) In the XVIIIth Dynasty we can look best for the Pharaoh "that knew not Joseph," as it was the leader of this dynasty, Ahmes I, who conquered and drove out the Hyksos, and left to his followers as a legacy cordial hatred of the Asiatics. (*c*) Thothmes III was a great builder, and the heavy tasks of the Hebrews would fit well into his reign. He was also the champion of Amon, the god of Thebes, having been a priest of that god; therefore the religious significance of the Exodus and the struggle preceding it were most natural in his age. (*d*) An inscription of Menephthah, son of Ramses II, indicates that Israel was in Pal in his time, therefore he could not have been the Pharaoh of the Exodus, nor his father the oppressor. (*e*) The objection that Pharaohs of the XIXth and XXth dynasties invaded and claimed sovereignty over Pal is of little consequence, since these invasions usually involved only the sea-plain, and any city or district might secure immunity and maintain its *status quo* by payment of tribute. In later cents. many foreign invasions swept through Israel without disturbing the national integrity. As for the objection that the cities Ramses and Pithom indicate the age of Ramses II, it is altogether probable that they were built long before his time, and only restored by him. For these reasons the earlier date is assigned to the Exodus. (2) Whether the duration of the sojourn in Egypt was 430 or 215 years will depend upon the interpretation of the comprehensive 430, or roundly 400, which is of frequent occurrence in the Bible as indicating the extent of the period of the Hebrews' wanderings among, and oppression by, the nations (Gen **15** 13; Ex **12** 40; Acts **7** 6; Gal **3** 17). These passages have been, and may properly be, interpreted as indicating the time of the actual sojourn in Egypt, or the time from the entrance of Abraham into Canaan to the Exodus. Modern archaeological discoveries and the logical conclusions from them, our better knowledge of the history and conditions of contemporaneous Egypt, the shortening of the Hyksos period, as by Meyer, Mahler and Breasted, and the acceptance of a later date for Ḥammurabi, all seem to favor the shorter, or 215-year, view of the sojourn. The remaining 215 years cover the period from Jacob's descent into Egypt back to the migration of Abraham. The shorter period is adopted here for the reasons already given; but by the addition of 215 the dates from the death of Joseph backward may be conformed to the theory of the longer period. (3) Accepting the almost universal and well-grounded judgment that the Amraphel of Gen **14** is the famous Ḥammurabi of the 1st Bab Dynasty, we should have assistance in determining the date of his Biblical contemporary Abraham, if the opinions of scholars about the age of Ḥammurabi were not so divergent. Goodspeed (*Hist Bab. and Assyr.*) places his reign at 2297–2254 BC; Hommel (art. on "Babylonia," *HDB*) fixes the probable date at 1772–1717, an astonishing divergence of 500 years, and suggestive of the spendthrift manner in which chronologists are accustomed to dispose of the past ages of man. The difference in this instance is caused by the disposition of the IId Bab Dynasty, Goodspeed making its more than 360 years follow the Ḥammurabi Dynasty, and adding the years of the two; Hommel on the other hand regarding the IId, or Southern, Dynasty as contemporaneous with the Ist, or Northern. But it is more probable that the truth lies between these extremes, since the IId Dynasty must have had some independent standing, and must have ruled alone for a time, in order to secure consideration as a dynasty. This moderate reckoning is now commonly adopted, Breasted placing Ḥammurabi at 1900 BC, Davis (in *DB*) about 1975, and Pinches (in Murray's *Illus. B. Dict.*) later than 2000 BC. It is in accord with the Bible numbers, as the following table shows, and does not vary materially from the reckoning of Ussher, which was based upon those numbers. Therefore the age of Ḥammurabi and Abraham may be considered as about 1900 BC, or 2100, if one estimates the sojourn in Egypt at 430 years. The former is more reasonable. The Am Tab, preserving correspondence of the 14th and 15th cents. between the Pharaohs of the XVIIIth Dynasty and Pal and Babylon, by showing the contemporary sovereigns of the empires of the Nile and the Euphrates, contribute confirmation to the Biblical reckoning. It is possible that increased knowledge of the Hittite empire and its dealings with Egypt, Pal and Bab may in the near future contribute further confirmation. The foregoing conclusions may be summarized in the following table:

	BC	Addition of 215 Years for Longer Sojourn in Egypt
The Exodus from Egypt.....	cir 1448	....
Jehovah appeared to Moses at Horeb..................	1449	....
Flight of Moses from Egypt...	1488	....
Birth of Moses..............	1528	....
Birth of Aaron..............	1532	....
Death of Levi (approximation)	1570	1785
*Possible date of Amram's birth	1587	....
Death of Joseph.............	cir 1594	1809
Death of Jacob, aged 147.....	1647	1862
*Birth of Kohath, possibly	1647	....
Jacob and his sons go down to Egypt...................	1664	1879
Joseph exalted over Egypt, 10 years estimated for 7 years of plenty and part of years of famine................	1674	1889
Joseph sold by his brethren...	1687	1902
Birth of Benjamin, death of Rachel..................	1698	....
Jacob left Paddan-Aram, meeting with Esau.............	1699	....
Birth of Joseph.............	1704	1919
†Birth of Levi, probably......	1708	1923
Jacob marries Leah and Rachel	1711	....
His flight from Hebron to Haran..................	1718	....
Death of Abraham..........	1780	1995
Birth of Esau and Jacob	1795	2010
Marriage of Isaac and Rebekah	1815	....
Death of Sarah (Gen **24** 67)..	1816	....
Birth of Isaac..............	1855	2070
Destruction of Sodom and Gomorrah................	cir 1856	....
Birth of Ishmael............	1869	....
Invasion by Chedorlaomer and Amraphel...............	cir 1875	2090
Abraham's sojourn in Egypt..	cir 1878	....
His migration from Haran to Canaan................	1880	2095
Birth of Sarah..............	1939	....
Birth of Abraham..........	cir 1955	2170
Birth of his father Terah.....	2025	2240

* The age of Kohath at birth of Amram is estimated at 60 years; similarly the age of Amram at Aaron's birth.

† If Joseph was born 6 years before Jacob returned from Paddan-Aram, Levi was about 4 years older.

IX. From Abraham to the Creation.—One other general period of OT chronology remains for consideration: from the age of Abraham back to the creation of the world, about which in the nature of the case there can be no absolute certainty, and in which there is neither reason nor need for inflexible accuracy. The system, or succession, of numbers in the early chapters of Gen (**5** and **11** 10–26) has given rise, in the effort to explain these numbers, to several theories.

(1) The literal interpretation, the best known advocate of which was Archbishop Ussher (d. 1656), whose literal arrangement was introduced into the margin of the AV after his death. This theory takes the birth- and death-numbers just as they are, and by addition of the time intervals between the birth of the various patriarchs, together with Adam's age at the birth of Seth, shows that 1,656 years elapsed from the Creation to the Flood, and 290 years from the Flood to Abraham's birth, according to the MT. But it must be apparent at the very outset, that, on the most liberal arrangement of the numbers and the most conservative geological and anthropological estimate, this reckoning is not sufficiently long to satisfy the known facts of the age of the earth, of the life of man upon the earth, and of established historic dates. Even the conservative system of Professor Breasted (*Anc. Egypt*) places the first certain date of Egyp history, viz. the introduction of the Sothic calendar, as early as 4241 BC, which is more than two cents. beyond Ussher's beginning of the world. Moreover, at that time an astronomical basis of reckoning time was in existence, implying an age of culture already gone before. This difficulty was appreciated by the earliest interpreters, as indicated by the variations of the Sam and LXX texts, the latter increasing the total of the age about 1,500 years and inserting a new name into the genealogical list of Gen **11**. An interesting commentary on the literal method is that it makes Noah live until Abraham was seventy years old, and prolongs the life of Shem to within the lifetime of Jacob.

(2) A second theory is the dynastic: that the long number of a patriarch's lifetime indicates the era during which his house or dynasty prevailed, to be followed by the long number of the next dynasty; e.g. the 930 years of Adam were followed by the 912 of Seth, and so on until the period is stretched to cover thousands of years. But there are evident objections to this view: it does not account for the invariable origin of each succeeding dynasty so near the beginning of its predecessor, and it disregards the manifest plan of the inspired author to narrate the descent of the human race through families and not by eras or empires.

(3) By others it has been conjectured that the units of time have been different in the ancient ages of man; that originally the time-unit was the lunar cycle, by which the 969 lunar cycles of Methuselah's life really should be reduced to a little more than 80 years of more recent times; and that in the days of Abraham a year measured from equinox to equinox had superseded the lunar time-measurement. It is possible that the LXX variations were based upon this idea, since it increased the age at which every father begat a son to at least 162 in the generations before the Flood. But even this expedient would not remove all difficulties from the physical side; nor have we the slightest indication of the points at which these radical changes of the time-units were made. On the contrary the decrease of man's years seems to have come by somewhat gradual process, and not by sharp and tremendous breaks.

(4) Others have thought to meet the difficulties by suggesting the omission of links in the chain of descent, in accordance with Heb custom of omitting inconsequential names from a genealogical list. The omission by Matthew of certain names from his genealogy of Jesus Christ, in order to preserve his symmetrical scheme of fourteens (Mt **1** 8), is an illustration in point. As corroborative of this it might be urged that the LXX does insert a name between Arpachshad and Shelah (Gen **11** 12). It may be said confidently that whatever theory of the genealogies before Abraham one may adopt, it is altogether reasonable to suppose that one name, or many, may have been omitted from the line of descent.

The dates resulting from the literal and exact interpretation of the genealogical lists of Gen **5** and **11** may be tabulated as follows:

Death of Eber..........................	1716 BC
Death of Shem.........................	1745
Death of Shelah........................	1777
Death of Arpachshad.................	1806
Death of Terah.........................	1820
Death of Serug.........................	1854
Death of Reu...........................	1877
Death of Noah.........................	1885
Death of Nahor........................	1907
Death of Peleg.........................	1907

BIRTH OF ABRAHAM	**1955**
Birth of Terah	2025
Birth of Nahor	2054
Birth of Serug	2084
Birth of Reu	2116
Birth of Peleg	2146
Birth of Eber	2180
Birth of Shelah	2210
(Here LXX inserts Kainan with 130 years)	
Birth of Arpachshad	2245
Death of Methuselah	2245
Year of the Flood	2245
Death of Lamech	2250
Birth of Shem	2345
Birth of Noah	2845
Death of Adam	2971
Birth of Lamech	3027
Birth of Methuselah	3214
Birth of Enoch	3274
Birth of Jared	3441
Birth of Mahalaleel	3506
Birth of Kenan	3576
Birth of Enosh	3666
Birth of Seth	3771
Creation of Adam	3901

If the 130 years of Kainan, whom the LXX inserts between Shelah and Arpachshad, be added, the date for Adam's creation is increased to 4031 BC. The exhibit of this table is most interesting and suggestive. Noah, Shem, Arpachshad, Shelah, Eber, Peleg were contemporaries of Abraham. Shem, Shelah and Eber were living after Jacob's birth. Adam, Enoch, Methuselah and Lamech were contemporary; and Methuselah's long life came to an end in the year of the Flood.

A Suggested Interpretation

These genealogical lists of the early chapters of Gen appear therefore not to have been given as an exact and exclusive system of chronology; but it is more probable that they were written to present a general, compact, or mere outline statement of the origin, early experience and apostasy of the human race, given without the purpose of recording every possible link in the chain of descent, or every incident in the early racial experience. There are many indications, or suggestions at least, that this is the sensible and Divinely intended interpretation, some of which have been stated: the variant items and summaries of the MT, LXX and Sam; the frequent omission in Heb genealogies of one or more generations, the third, or later, descendant being truly regarded as a son; the age of the world; the comparative antiquity of man; and the more ancient dates disclosed by archaeology. It should be noticed further that the inspired writer gives *ten* generations from Adam to the Flood, and ten also from the Flood to Abraham, as if by the use of the decimal, or representatively human, number he would indicate to us that he is dealing with comprehensively complete numbers and not with those that are minutely complete, arranging in symbolic form the account of man's descent. See ANTEDILUVIAN PATRIARCHS.

But while the age of man may be greater than the mechanical and exact sum of the Gen numbers, we should not be deluded into the belief that it is so great as some anthropologists and geologists, who are prodigal of their numbers, would have us think. The numbers of Gen are much nearer the facts than these dreary stretches and wastes of time. The formation of the Nile and the Euphrates valleys, which furnished historic man's first home, is quite recent, possibly not antedating 7000 BC; the account of the Flood is the record of a great cataclysm which came upon historic man within these millenniums; we have the records of the presence of intelligent man in these fertile and recently formed centers without traces of his origin and development in, and movement from, other homes. Archaeology and ancient history bring civilized man upon us with somewhat of suddenness, well established in homelands of recent formation. Whence came these peoples whose great works and thoughts are found near the beginning of an era so clearly limited by history and geography? If they came from elsewhere and developed tediously, why have they left no trail of their movement and no trace of the evolution? So late as the 3d millennium BC Mesopotamia was sparsely settled, and Pal in the first half of the 2d millennium was still thinly settled. It is a legitimate conclusion, then, that intelligent man's life on the earth does not extend far beyond the total of the Bible numbers (see ANTEDILUVIANS; DELUGE). At the same time it is far from necessary to force a literal and exact interpretation on these numbers, which were given rather to trace lineage, keep relationships, show development under the Divine purpose, and fix responsibility, than to mark particular years.

X. *Peculiarities and Characteristics.*

1. Peculiarities

—A narrative recounting some of the peculiarities of Oriental chronology in Bible lands, where the modern facilities and conveniences of life are much wanting, especially where time pieces and calendars are practically unknown, together with analytical grouping of the characteristics of OT chronology as they appear upon close scrutiny, will greatly help the student in understanding the strange puzzle of OT chronology.

(1) In 1892 a small party of student travelers was making arrangements for the overland journey from Egypt to Mt. Sinai and return. A German missionary to the Bedouin of that region was adviser in the making of arrangements. It was suggested by one of the party that a clause should be written into the agreement to the effect that, if the travelers desired to stop for a few days and examine antiquities by the way, it would not be put forward as a claim for additional pay for the expedition. "Oh," said the missionary, "that is quite unnecessary; the Bedouin will not count the time. They have no way of counting time, have neither clocks nor calendars. They consider only the event, the journey. They agree to take you to Mt. Sinai and return for so much money. You may take three weeks or three months to the journey, as you please. That will make no difference in the pay. They will go to their flocks and their families, while you tarry, and return when you are ready to go on. Besides, time is what they have more of than anything else." Here the Occidental learns in the ancient Orient that without clocks and calendars they reckon by events. (2) In the same year one of these desert travelers went with a missionary friend to visit one of the 10,000 mud villages in the valley of the Nile. The night was not a restful one in a native home. The next morning the traveler wished to return as soon as possible to the boat on the Nile. The missionary however, knowing the demands of courtesy, insisted that they must not go until after breakfast, but expressed the hope that breakfast might be expedited. "Oh," said the host, "breakfast is just ready." One hour and a half after that time by the traveler's watch, a match was struck to kindle the fire to cook the breakfast. And sometime later still, a cow was driven into the court of the house to be milked to provide the milk to cook the rice to make the breakfast. Was the host untruthful? Not at all; he did not reckon by time, but by events. He

had no way of determining the passage of time. When he said "Breakfast is just ready," he meant it was the next thing in the household economy, that they would do nothing else until that thing was done, and that everything done was to that end. That is to say he reckoned only by events. Thus Jacob could say, "Few and evil have the days of the years of my life been." Though he had lived 130 years, he felt that there was not much worth counting in his life, and many things he did not care to remember. Likewise the promise to the godly man in the 91st Psalm, "With long life will I satisfy him," becomes quite intelligible, though one die at an early age. For is not a life filled with good deeds satisfactory whatever be its years? So, even after the Roman reckoning of time had come in, the old habit of reckoning by events clung in the speech of the people. Our Lord said to John on Patmos, "Behold, I come quickly." It is near 2,000 years since that time and he has not come yet, but his coming was the next event in his kingdom; *and it still is.*

(3) Another peculiarity of OT chronology may best be observed in the Scripture itself. In the record of the reigns of the kings of Judah and Israel this peculiarity appears most clearly. The chronological formula in these historical records runs thus: In such and such a year in the reign of so and so King of Judah began so and so to reign at Samaria and reigned so many years. This was the usual method instead of the ordinary chronological method with which we are familiar in modern books of history giving the date of the beginning of the reign with reference to an epoch in the past: in most modern lands it is the birth of Christ. These Biblical records dated the beginning of a reign by looking round about and comparing it with contemporaneous persons and events. So familiar are Bible readers with this Biblical method of the chronology of reigns that ordinarily they do not notice it, and especially so when a date BC is volunteered in the margin of the Bible by the publisher. When set in contrast with our modern method of chronology, the peculiarity of the Biblical method becomes at once apparent.

(4) There are still other peculiarities of OT chronology which, by their very character, are also serious difficulties in the way of any attempt to prepare a chronology of the OT similar to a chronology of modern history. All modern records are dated from some epoch; in ancient Rome the epoch used was the founding of the city; in all Christian lands the birth of Christ is made the epoch; in Mohammedan lands the Hegeira is used in the same way. Naturally the attempt to present a chronology of the OT proceeds along the same line and endeavors to date all the events BC. But no such epoch, nor any other general epoch, is found in the OT. The Exodus is used as an epoch in two instances, the time of the judgeship of Jephthah and the building of the temple by Solomon. But, in general, events were not recorded epochally at all. The people had no epoch and no one round about them had an epoch. There is but one event recorded epochally in the whole history of Egypt, the tablet of Seti erected by Rameses the Great, which is dated in the 400th year of King Nubti. The ancient Oriental world did not think epochally and so the epochal method of recording history has no place in their record. It is no wonder that the attempt to put an epoch into the Biblical record meets with such difficulty as that no two chronologists agree, and no two editions of the same chronology, while the author is still alive and able to revise his work.

(5) Still another difficulty arises from the using of the genealogies of the Bible as a basis for chronology. Many chronologies have been constructed upon the assumption that the genealogies might be so used. The careful scrutiny of the genealogies and the use made, or not made, of them in the Bible reveals that they may never be so used as a means of constructing chronology. At the very threshold of the subject it is most suggestive that the Biblical writers, who present the genealogies, never make them the basis of chronology; they never add up the genealogies in any way to get their sum total. If they had intended the genealogies as a basis for chronology, surely they would have so used them. Then, an examination of some of the genealogies, as of Moses (Ex **6** 16–20) and that of our Lord (Mt **1**: cf Ks and Chs) makes it perfectly clear that genealogies give the line of descent, but do not always include each step in the descent. In accord with the method of reckoning by events, the man that did nothing or who lived an unworthy life is apt to be dropped out, as are the descendants of the detested queen Athaliah in the genealogy of our Lord. Then the words "son" and "daughter" and "beget" and "bare" do not, as usually with us, denote immediate descent, but any point in the descent however remote (Ex **6** 20; Nu **26** 59; Gen **46** 16–18; Dt **4** 25; Isa **51** 2). Even the lists of the patriarchs, both antediluvian and postdiluvian, may not be added together to construct chronology, but denote the record of great world-rulers, such as in later history are called dynastic heads. Each birth recorded merely notes the time at which a line went off in which sometime, it may have been the tenth generation, the next dynastic head arose (Green, *Bibliotheca Sacra*, 1890, 285 ff).

After such illustrations of the peculiarities of OT chronology, indeed of chronology anywhere, when not assisted by clocks and calendars, it will be comparatively easy to detect the characteristics of OT chronology. They are as follows:

2. Characteristics

(1) OT chronology chronicles events rather than the flight of time, man's relation to life rather than his relation to time. Historical examples of this characteristic abound. Moses (Dt) in recounting the history of Israel in his exhortations of the people gives but little hint of the flight of time. The events of their history are mentioned in order, but no estimate of the time elapsing between the events is given. Only the most general remarks are inserted in passing, as "afterwards" or "after a long time." Joshua (**24** 1–13) follows the same method. The Hebrew word translated "after" or "afterwards" is exceedingly indefinite and ofttimes logical, rather than temporal, in its significance. Yet such expressions are only indications of passing time. They give no indication of the duration of time. Even Stephen, in the long speech which he made while the mob held stones in their hands for killing him, still followed the same method, though at that time the Roman reckoning had come in. The people in common speech still continued to use the old Hebrew method of reckoning by events. In individual lives, it was the sum of events, especially those worthy to be counted, rather than the span of years, that was counted to make up a life. So Jacob told Pharaoh of his age (Gen **47** 9), and so the Psalmist promised long life to the godly man.

(2) OT chronology considered events on the plane of contemporaneity rather than in the line of succession. We use both methods now, but the determining principle is succession. OT chronology also used both methods, but the formative principle was contemporaneity. The general historical plan followed in the Books of Ks and Chs fully illustrates this method. Sometimes there was a look backward, and in the prophets forward, but for the most part they looked round about and took account of history on the plane on which they lived it.

(3) In so far as OT chronology looks backward

and forward it considers perspective rather than duration. Before the invention of the microscope and the telescope, the minute and far-reaching conception of things which these give did not enter into the conception of events then as it now does. Our scrutiny has been almost infinitely magnified by the microscope, and we in imagination now attain to the utmost reaches of the telescope. Thus, what we are pleased to denominate the prophetic method, which looks forward and sees things in perspective, seeing one event after and through another intervening event, they also applied in some measure to history. They sometimes saw things rather in perspective than in duration. The speeches of Moses, Joshua, and Stephen, already studied, illustrate this principle, as do also the historical statements in the Book of Job. The greatest difference of opinion exists concerning the time to which that book looks back.

(4) Order, synchronism, and proportion are the determining factors in OT chronology. Events are usually recorded in chronological order. Synchronism is apparent everywhere. But proportion is sometimes allowed to modify order in the OT as in the Gospels; the matter is at times arranged topically. Thus ofttimes little events of world-history are made to be seen in their greatness in redemption history. Note thus the place given Israel in the Bible compared with her place in the political history of the world of that time, or the importance given to the story of Abraham and Lot in comparison with the great events of world-history in the military events of the four kings of Gen **14**.

(5) OT chronology is not scientific, but simply natural, as life is lived everywhere. We constantly speak of a thing that happened "six months ago" or "last week" or "two hours ago," but only, when we have to date a document or give testimony in court, do we consult a calendar or look at the clock and make mathematically precise statements.

(6) OT chronology may be compared with our modern system thus: (*a*) Modern chronology is purely mathematical, OT chronology introduces a moral element. The man who did nothing and the year in which nothing happened are apt to be passed over in silence. (*b*) Modern chronology considers passing events from a fixed point in the past, the birth of Christ. OT chronology reckons always from the moving point of the present, looking round about on that plane.

OT chronology is not yet fully understood in all of its details, but there is no reason to think that it is not correct when completely understood. Chronological systems prepared to fit the Bible are all estimated according to our system, and that too from data prepared on principles entirely different from those used in the Bible. Such systems are to be used for our convenience, but never for the purpose of correcting Biblical data. We must ask a man what he means, not tell him. So we must ask the Bible for its chronological method and not attempt to force ours upon it. The rise of the science of pottery in Bible lands is now giving hope that very soon a cultural chronology for the land will be completely and accurately worked out. It is most reassuring that wherever it is possible to lay this alongside of the Biblical events, the narrative of the events is corroborated. This fact is most reassuring concerning the historicity of the narratives of the OT; only a narrative of real events can thus be paralleled by the remains of it dug up in the field of Biblical history. Witnesses may speak falsely; material evidence, the "exhibit" in a case in court, tells the truth. Folklore and legends and myths cannot thus be confirmed by cultural chronology; they may illustrate manners and customs, but their events are largely imaginary and leave nothing to be dug up in the field. It will soon be possible to arrange a pottery chronology with a possible error of not more than fifty years, instead of the three hundred years now between the disputants concerning the date of the Exodus and the Conquest. When all the principal events of OT history have been paralleled by the cultural dates and thus certified in exact order, and the date BC determined within fifty years, there will be a very great advance from the present confusion concerning OT Chronology.

This pottery chronology has already determined the beginnings of civilization in the Jordan Valley as occurring very early in the Early Bronze Age (in the 4th millennium BC; see Civilization in the Jordan Valley) with the occupation of Yenoamam (north), Gennesaret, and Beth-yerah; the great break in the civilization of the Jordan Valley as occurring near the end of the Early Bronze Age (see Cities of the Plain) and lasting until after the end of OT history and well into NT history; has fixed also the Exodus and the Conquest at the beginning of Early Iron I (see Kiriath-sepher); and the occupation of Beth-shean by the Philistines under Egypt suzerainty until the time of Saul near the end of Early Iron I; and has given an exact date in the short reign of Jehoiachin toward the end of Early Iron II.

Literature.—Ussher, *Chronologia Sacra;* G. Smith, *Assyr Eponym Canon;* Maspero, *The Dawn of Civilization; The Struggle of the Nations; The Passing of the Empires;* Goodspeed, *A History of the Babylonians and Assyrians;* Breasted, *Ancient Egypt; Hist. of Egypt, Mesopotamia and Israel* in *Hist. of World;* Hommel, *Ancient Heb Tradition;* L. W. King, *Chronology of the Bab Kings;* Beecher, *Dated Events of OT;* Auchinloss, *Chronology of the Holy Bible;* various commentaries; Driver, *Bk of Genesis;* Skinner, *Genesis;* Moore, *Comm. on Judges;* G. A. Smith, "Isaiah" in *Expositor's Bible*, etc. Magazines: James Orr, "Assyr and Heb Chronology" in *Presbyterian Review*, 1889; "Israel and the Exodus" in *Expositor*, 1897; J. D. Davis, "Chronology of the Divided Kingdom" in *Presbyterian and Reformed Review*, 1891. Bible Dictionaries: J. D. Davis in *Dict. of the Bible*, Westminster Press; Hommel, arts. on "Assyria" and "Babylonia" in *HDB*. Of interest also, Franke Parker, *Chronology*, 1858.

Revised by M. G. K. Edward Mack

CHRONOLOGY OF THE NEW TESTAMENT:

I. Chronology of the Life of Jesus
  1. Birth of Jesus
    (1) Death of Herod
    (2) Census of Quirinius
    (3) Star of the Magi
    (4) Course of Abijah
    (5) Day and Month
    (6) Summary
  2. Baptism of Jesus
  3. First Passover
  4. Death of John the Baptist
  5. Length of Jesus' Ministry
  6. Death of Jesus
  7. Summary of Dates
Literature
II. Chronology of the Apostolic Age
  1. Paul's Conversion
  2. Death of Herod Agrippa I
  3. Famine under Claudius
  4. Sergius Paulus
  5. Edict of Claudius
  6. Gallio
  7. Festus
  8. Relative Chronology of Acts
  9. Pauline Epistles
  10. Release and Death of Paul
  11. Death of Peter
  12. Death of James the Just
  13. The Synoptic Gospels, etc.
  14. Death of John
  15. Summary of Dates
Literature

The current Christian era is reckoned from the birth of Jesus and is based upon the calculations of Dionysius (6th cent.). Subsequent investigation has shown that the Dionysian date is at least four years too late. Several eras were in use in the time of Jesus; but of these only the Varronian will be used coördinately with the Dionysian in the discussion of the chronology of the life of Jesus, 753 A.U.C. being synchronous with 1 BC and 754 A.U.C. with 1 AD.

I. Chronology of the Life of Jesus.—Jesus was born before the death of Herod the Great (Mt **2** 1 ff) at the time of a census or enrolment made in the territory of Herod in accordance with a decree of Augustus when Quirinius (RV, Cyrenius AV) was exercising authority in the Rom province of Syria (Lk **2** 1 f). At the time of Jesus' birth a star led the Magi of the East to seek in Jerus the infant whom they subsequently found in Bethlehem (Mt **2** 1 ff). John the Baptist was six months older than Jesus (Lk **1** 36) and he was born in the days of Herod (Lk **1** 5; cf **2** 1) after his father, Zacharias, of the priestly course of Abijah, had been performing the functions of his office in the temple.

1. Birth of Jesus

(1) *Death of Herod.*—The death of Herod the Great occurred in the spring of 750/4.* He ruled from his appointment in Rome 714/40 (*Ant*, XIV, xiv, 4–5, in the consulship of Caius Domitius Calvinus and Caius Asinius Pollio) 37 years, and from his accession in Jerus after the capture of the city 717/37 (*Ant*, XIV, xvi, 1–3; *BJ*, I, xvii, 9; I, xviii, 1–3; Dio Cassius xlix.22; cf. Schürer, *GJV*³, I, 358, n. 11) 34 years (*Ant*, XVII, xviii, 1; *BJ*, I, xxxiii, 7–8; cf Schürer, op. cit., I, 415, n. 167 where it is shown that Jos reckons a year too much, probably counting from Nisan 1 and including partial years). Just before Herod's death there was an eclipse of the moon (*Ant*, XVII, vi, 4). According to astronomical calculations an eclipse was visible in Pal on March 23 and September 15, 749/5, March 12, 750/4, and January 9, 753/1. Of these the most probable is that of March 12, 750/4. Soon after the eclipse Herod put to death his son Antipater and died five days later (*Ant*, XVII, vii; *BJ*, I, xxxiii, 7). Shortly after Herod's death the Passover was near at hand (*Ant*, XVII, vi, 4—ix, 3). In this year Passover (Nisan 15) fell on April 11; and as Archelaus had observed seven days of mourning for his father before this, Herod's death would fall between March 17 and April 4. But as the 37th (34th) year of his reign was probably reckoned from Nisan 1 or March 28, his death may be dated between March 28 and April 4, 750/4.

This date for Herod's death is confirmed by the evidence for the duration of the reigns of his three sons. Archelaus was deposed in 759/6 (Dio Cassius lv.27 in the consulship of Aemilius Lepidus and Lucius Arruntius) in the 10th year of his reign (*Ant*, XVII, xiii, 2; cf *BJ*, II, vii, 3 which gives the year as the 9th). Antipas was deposed most probably in the summer of 792/39 (*Ant*, XVIII, vii, 1–2; cf XVIII, vi, 11; XIX, viii, 2; *BJ*, II, ix, 6; Schürer, op. cit., I, 448, n. 46 and 416, n. 167). There are coins of Antipas from his 43d year (Madden, *Coins of the Jews*, 121 ff). The genuineness of a coin from the 44th year is questioned by Schürer but accepted by Madden. The coin from the 45th year is most probably spurious (Schürer, op. cit., I, 417, n. 167). Philip died after reigning 37 years, in the 20th year of Tiberius—August 19, 786/33–787/34 (*Ant*, XVIII, iv, 6). There is also a coin of Philip from his 37th year (Madden, op. cit., 126). Thus Archelaus, Antipas and Philip began to reign in 750/4.

(2) *Census of Quirinius.*—The census or enrolment, which, according to Lk **2** 1 f, was the occasion of the journey of Joseph and Mary to Bethlehem where Jesus was born, is connected with a decree of Augustus embracing the Gr-Rom world. This decree must have been carried out in Pal by Herod and probably in accordance with the Jewish method —each going to his own city—rather than the Rom (*Dig.* 15, 4, 2; Zumpt, *Das Geburtsjahr Christi*, 195; Kenyon, *Greek Papyri in the British Museum*, III, 124 f; Schürer, *Theol. Ztg*, 1907, 683 f; and on the other hand, Ramsay, *Expositor*, 1908, I, 19, n.). Certainly there is no intimation of an insurrection such as characterized a later census (Acts **5** 37; *Ant*, XVIII, i, 1; *BJ*, II, xvii, 7; cf Tac. *Ann.* vi.41; Livy *Epit.* cxxxvi, cxxxvii; Dessau, *Inscrip. lat. Sel.* no. 212, col. ii, 36) and this may have been due in no small measure to a difference in method. Both Jos and Luke mention the later census which was made by Quirinius on the deposition of Archelaus, together with the insurrection of Judas which accompanied it. But while Jos does not mention the Herodian census—although there may be some intimation of it in *Ant*, XVI, ix, 3; XVII, ii, 4; cf. Sanclemente, *De vulg. aerae emend.*, 438 f; Ramsay, *Was Christ Born at Beth.*¹, 178 ff—Luke carefully distinguishes the two, characterizing the census at the time of Jesus' birth as "first," i.e. first in a series of enrolments connected either with Quirinius or with the imperial policy inaugurated by the decree of Augustus. The Gr-Rom writers of the time do not mention this decree and later writers (Cassiodor, Isidor and Suidas) cannot be relied upon with certainty as independent witnesses (Zumpt, *Geburtsjahr*, 148 ff). Yet the geographical work of Agrippa and the preparation of a *breviarium totius imperii* by Augustus (Tac. *Ann.* i.11; Suet. Aug. 28 and 101; Dio Cassius liii.30; lvi.33; cf Mommsen, *Staatsrecht*, II, 1025, n. 3), together with the interest of the emperor in the organization and finances of the empire and the attention which he gave to the provinces (Marquardt, *Röm. Staatsverwaltung*, II, 211 f; cf 217), are indirectly corroborative of Luke's statement. Augustus himself conducted a census in Italy in 726/28, 746/8, 767/14 (Mommsen, *Res Ges.*, 34 ff) and in Gaul in 727/27 (Dio Cassius liii.22, 5; Livy *Epit.* cxxxiv) and had a census taken in other provinces (Pauly-Wissowa, *Realencyc.*, s.v. "Census," 1918 f; Marquardt, op. cit., II, 213). For Egypt there is evidence of a regular periodic census every 14 years extending back to 773/20 (Ramsay, op. cit., 131 ff; Grenfell and Hunt, *Oxy. Papyri*, II, 207 ff; Wilcken, *Griech. Ostraka*, I, 444 ff) and it is not improbable that this procedure was introduced by Augustus (Schürer, op. cit., I, 515). The inference from Egyp to similar conditions in other provinces must indeed be made cautiously (Wilcken, op. cit., 449; Marquardt, op. cit., 441); yet in Syria the regular *tributum capitis* seems to imply some such preliminary work (*Dig.* l. 15, 3; Appian, *Syr.*, 50; Marquardt, op. cit., II, 200, n. 2; Pauly-Wissowa, op. cit., 1921; Ramsay, op. cit., 154). The time of the decree is stated only in general terms by Luke, and it may have been as early as 727/27 (Zumpt, op. cit., 159; Marquardt, op. cit., II, 212) or later in 746–8 (Huschke, *Census*, 34; Ramsay, op. cit., 158 ff), its execution in different provinces and subject kingdoms being carried out at different times. Hence Luke dates the census in the kingdom of Herod specifically by connecting it with the administrative functions of Quirinius in Syria. But as P. Quintilius Varus was the legate of Syria just before and after the death of Herod from 748/6–750/4 (*Ant*, XVII, v, 2; XVII, ix, 3; XVII, x, 1 and 9; XVII, xi, 1; Tac. *Hist.* v.9; and coins in Eckhel, *Doctr. num. vet.*, III, 275) and his predecessor was C. Sentius Saturninus from 745/9–748/6 (*Ant*, XVI, ix, 1; x, 8; xi, 3; XVII, i, 1; ii, 1; iii, 2), there seems to be no place for Quirinius during the closing years of Herod's reign. Tertullian indeed speaks of Saturninus as legate at the time of Jesus' birth (*Adv. Marc.*, iv.9). The interpretation of Luke's statement as indicating a date for the census before Quirinius was legate (Wieseler, *Chron. Syn.*, 116; Lagrange, *Revue Biblique*, 1911, 80 ff) is inadmissible. It is possible that the connection of the

* The alternative numbers are BC or AD, i.e. 750 A.U.C. = 4 BC, etc.

census with Quirinius may be due to his having brought to completion what was begun by one of his predecessors; or Quirinius may have been commissioned especially by the emperor as *legatus ad census accipiendos* to conduct a census in Syria and this commission may have been connected temporally with his campaign against the Homonadenses in Cilicia (Tac. *Ann.* iii.48; cf Noris, *Cenotaph. Pis.*, 320 ff; Sanclemente, op. cit., 426 *passim;* Ramsay, op. cit., 238). It has also been suggested by Bour (*L'Inscription de Quirinius*, 48 ff) that Quirinius may have been an imperial procurator specially charged with authority in the matter of the Herodian census. The titulus Tiburtinus (*CIL*, XIV, 3613; Dessau, *Inscr. Lat. Sel.*, 918)—if rightly assigned to him—and there seems to be no sufficient reason for questioning the conclusiveness of Mommsen's defence of this attribution (cf Liebenam, *Verwaltungsgesch.*, 365)—proves that he was twice legate of Syria, and the titulus Venetus (*CIL*, III, 6687; Dessau, op. cit., 2683) gives evidence of a census conducted by him in Syria. His administration is dated by Ramsay (op. cit., 243) in 747/7; by Mommsen in the end of 750/4 or the beginning of 751/3 (op. cit., 172 ff). Zahn (*Neue kirch. Zeitschr.*, 1893, IV, 633 ff), followed by Spitta (*Zeitschr. f. d. neutest. Wiss.*, 1906, VII, 293 ff), rejects the historicity of the later census connected by Jos with the deposition of Archelaus, basing his view on internal grounds, and assigns the Lucan census to a time shortly after the death of Herod. This view however is rendered improbable by the evidence upon which the birth of Jesus is assigned to a time before the death of Herod (Mt **2** 1 ff; Lk **1** 5; **2** 1 f); by the differentiation of the census in Lk **2** 1 f and Acts **5** 37; by the definite connection of the census in Jos with Syria and the territory of Archelaus (cf also the tit. Venet.); and by the general imperial policy in the formation of a new province (Marquardt, op. cit., II, 213). Moreover there seems to be no adequate ground for identifying the Sabinus of Jos with Quirinius as urged by Weber, who regards the two accounts (*Ant*, XVII, viii, 1 ff and XVII, iv, 5; XVIII, i, 2; ii, 1 ff) as due to the separation by Jos of ‖ accounts of the same events in his sources (*Zeitschr. f. d. neutest. Wiss.*, 1909, X, 307 ff)—the census of Sabinus-Quirinius being assigned to 4 BC, just after the death of Herod the Great. The synchronism of the second census of Quirinius with the periodic year of the Egyp census is probably only a coincidence, for it was occasioned by the deposition of Archelaus; but its extension to Syria may be indicative of its connection with the imperial policy inaugurated by Augustus (Tac. *Ann.* vi.41; Ramsay, op. cit., 161 f).

(3) *Star of the Magi.*—The identification of the star of the Magi (Mt **2** 2; cf **2** 7.9.16; Macrobius, *Sat.*, II, 4; Sanclemente, op. cit., 456; Ramsay, op. cit., 215 ff) and the determination of the time of its appearance cannot be made with certainty, although it has been associated with a conjunction in 747/7 and 748/6 of Saturn and Jupiter in the sign of Pisces—a constellation which was thought to stand in close relation with the Jewish nation (Ideler, *Handbuch d. math. u. tech. Chron.*, II, 400 ff). When the Magi came to Jerus, however, Herod was present in the city; and this must have been at least several months before his death, for during that time he was sick and absent from Jerus (*Ant*, XVII, vi, 1 ff; *BJ*, I, xxxiii, 1 ff).

(4) *Course of Abijah.*—The chronological calculations of the time of the service of the priestly course of Abijah in the temple, which are made by reckoning back from the time of the course of Jehoiarib which, according to Jewish tradition, was serving at the time of the destruction of Jerus by Titus, are uncertain (Schürer, op. cit., II, 337, n. 3; cf Lewin, *Fasti Sacri*, 836).

(5) *Day and month.*—The day and month of Jesus' birth are also uncertain. December 25 was celebrated by the church in the West as early as the 2d cent.—if the date in Hippolytus on Dan., IV, 23, be genuine (cf Ehrhardt, *Altchr. Lit.*, 1880–1900, 383); but January 6 was celebrated in the East as the anniversary both of the birth and of the baptism. The fact that shepherds were feeding their flocks at night when Jesus was born (Lk **2** 8) makes it improbable that the season of the year was winter.

(6) *Summary.*—The birth of Jesus may therefore be assigned to the period 747/7 to 751/5, before the death of Herod, at the time of a census made by Herod in accordance with a decree of Augustus and when Quirinius was exercising extraordinary authority in Syria—Varus being the regular legate of the province, i.e. probably in 748/6. See JESUS CHRIST.

2. Baptism of Jesus

The Synoptic Gospels begin their description of the public ministry of Jesus with an account of the ministry of John the Baptist (Mt **3** 1 ff; Mk **1** 1 ff; Lk **3** 1 ff; cf Jn **1** 19 ff; **4** 24; Jos, *Ant*, XVIII, iii, 3) and Luke definitely dates the baptism of Jesus by John in the 15th year of Tiberius. Luke also designates this event as the beginning of Jesus' ministry, and by stating Jesus' age approximately brings it into connection with the date of His birth. If Luke reckoned the reign of Tiberius from the death of Augustus, August 19, 767/14, the 15th year would extend from August 19, 781/28 to August 18, 782/29; and if Jesus was about thirty years old at this time, His birth would fall in 751/3 to 752/2—or sometime after the death of Herod, which is inconsistent with Luke's own and Matthew's representation. This indeed was one of the common modes of reckoning the imperial reigns. The mode of reckoning from the assumption of the tribunician power or from the designation as imperator is altogether unlikely in Luke's case and intrinsically improbable, since for Tiberius the one began in 748/6 and the other in 743/11 (Dio Cassius lv.9; liv.33; Vell. ii.99; Suet. *Tib.* ix.11). But if, as seems likely, the method of reckoning by imperial years rather than by the yearly consuls was not definitely fixed when Luke wrote, it is possible that he may have counted the years of Tiberius from his appointment in 764/11 or 765/12 to equal authority with Augustus in the provinces (Vell. ii 121; Suet. *Tib.* xx.21; Tac. *Ann.* i.3). This method seems not to have been employed elsewhere (Lewin, op. cit., 1143 f; cf Ramsay, op. cit., 202 f). The coins of Antioch in which it is found are regarded as spurious (Eckhel, op. cit., III, 276), the genuine coins reckoning the reign of Tiberius from the death of Augustus (ib, III, 278). If Luke reckoned the reign of Tiberius from 764/11 or 765/12, the 15th year would fall in 778/25 or 779/26, probably the latter, and Jesus' birth about thirty years earlier, i.e. about 748/6 or 749/5.

3. First Passover

At the time of the first Passover in Jesus' ministry the Herodian temple had been building 46 years (Jn **2** 20). Herod began the temple in the 18th year of his reign (*Ant*, XV, xi, 1, which probably corrects the statement in *BJ*, I, xxi, 1 that it was the 15th year; cf Schürer, op. cit., I, 369 f, n. 12). As Jos reckons from the accession of Herod in 717/37, the 18th year would be 734/20 to 735/21 and 46 years later would be 780/27 to 781/28. The interval implied in John between this Passover and the beginning of Jesus' ministry agrees well with the Lucan dating of the baptism in 779/26.

The imprisonment of John the Baptist, which preceded the beginning of Jesus' Galilean work, was continued for a time (Mt **11** 2–19; Lk **7** 18–35) but was finally terminated by beheading at the order of Herod Antipas. Announcement of the death was made to Jesus while in the midst of His Galilean ministry (Mt **14** 3–12; Mk **6** 14–29; Lk **9** 7–9). Jos reports that the defeat of Antipas by Aretas, in the summer of 789/36, was popularly regarded as a Divine punishment for the murder of John (*Ant*, XVIII, v, 2). But although Jos mentions the divorce of Aretas' daughter by Antipas as one of the causes of hostilities, no inference can be drawn from this or from the popular interpretation of Antipas' defeat, by which the interval between John's death and this defeat can be fixed (Schürer, op. cit., I, 443 f).

4. Death of John the Baptist

The Synoptic Gospels mention the Passion Passover at which Jesus' ministry was terminated, but they contain no data by which the interval between the imprisonment of John the Baptist and this Passover can be fixed with certainty. Yet indications are not wanting that the interval consisted of at least two years. The Sabbath controversy broke out in Galilee when the grain was still standing in the fields (Mt **12** 1; Mk **2** 23; Lk **6** 1) and the condition of the grass when the Five Thousand were fed (Mt **14** 15; Mk **6** 39; Lk **9** 12) points to the springtime, the Passion Passover marking the return of still another springtime (cf also Lk **13** 7; Mt **23** 37). But the Gospel of John mentions explicitly three Passovers (**2** 23; **6** 4; **11** 55) and probably implies a fourth (**5** 1), thus necessitating a ministry of at least two years and making probable a ministry of three years after the first Passover. The Passover of **6** 4 cannot be eliminated on textual grounds, for the documentary evidence is conclusive in its favor and the argument against it based on the statements of certain patristic writers is unconvincing (cf Turner, *HDB*, I, 407 f; Zahn, *Kom.*, IV, 708 ff). The indications of time from **6** 4—the Passover when the Five Thousand were fed in Galilee—to **11** 55—the Passion Passover—are definite and clear (**7** 2; **10** 22). But the interval between the first Passover (**2** 23) and the Galilean Passover (**6** 4) must have been one and may have been two years. The following considerations favor the latter view: Jesus was present in Jerus at a feast (**5** 1) which is not named but is called simply "a" or "the" feast of the Jews. The best authorities for the text are divided, some supporting the insertion, others the omission of the definite art. before "feast." If the art. formed part of the original text, the feast may have been either Tabernacles—from the Jewish point of view—or Passover—from the Christian point of view. If the art. was wanting in the original text, the identification of the feast must be made on contextual and other grounds. But the note of time in **4** 35 indicates the lapse of about nine months since the Passover of **2** 23 and it is not likely that the Galilean ministry which preceded the feeding of the Five Thousand lasted only about three months. In fact this is rendered impossible by the condition of the grain in the fields at the time of the Sabbath controversy. The identification of the feast of Jn **5** 1 with Purim, even if the art. be not genuine, is extremely improbable; and if so, a Passover must have intervened between **2** 23 and **6** 4, making the ministry of Jesus extend over a period of three years and the months which preceded the Passover of **2** 23. While the identification cannot be made with certainty, if the feast was Passover the subject of the controversy with the Jews in Jerus as well as the season of the year would harmonize with the Synoptic account of the Sabbath controversy in Galilee which probably followed this Passover (cf the variant reading in Lk **6** 1).

5. Length of Jesus' Ministry

Jesus was put to death in Jerus at the time of the Passover when Pontius Pilate was procurator of Judaea (Mt **27** 2 ff; Mk **15** 1 ff; Lk **23** 1 ff, Jn **18** 29 ff; **19** 1 ff; Acts **3** 13; **4** 27; **13** 28; 1 Tim **6** 13; Tac. *Ann.* xv.44), Caiaphas being the high priest (Mt **26** 3.57; Jn **11** 49; **18** 13 ff) and Herod Antipas the tetrarch of Galilee and Perea (Lk **23** 7 ff). Pilate was procurator from 779/26 to 789/36 (*Ant*, XVIII, iv, 3; v, 3; cf Schürer, op. cit., I, 487, n. 141); Caiaphas was high priest from 771/18 to 789/36 (*Ant*, XVIII, ii, 2; iv, 3; cf Schürer, op. cit., II, 271) and Antipas was tetrarch from 750/4 to 792/39. If the first Passover of Jesus' ministry was in 780/27, the fourth would fall in 783/30. The gospels name Friday as the day of the crucifixion (Mt **27** 62; Mk **15** 42; Lk **23** 54; Jn **19** 14.31.42) and the Synoptic Gospels represent this Friday as Nisan 15—the day following (or according to Jewish reckoning from sunset to sunset, the same day as) the day on which the paschal supper was eaten (Mt **26** 17 ff; Mk **14** 12 ff; Lk **22** 7 ff). But the Fourth Gospel is thought by many to represent the paschal meal as still uneaten when Jesus suffered (**18** 28; cf **13** 29); and it is held that the Synoptic Gospels also contain traces of this view (Mt **26** 5; Mk **14** 2; **15** 21; Lk **23** 26). Astronomical calculations show that Friday could have fallen on Nisan 14 or 15 in 783/30 according to different methods of reckoning (von Soden, *EB*, I, 806; cf Bacon, *Journal of Biblical Literature*, XXVIII, 2, 1910, 130 ff; Fotheringham, *Jour. of Theol. Studies*, October, 1910, 120 ff), but the empirical character of the Jewish calendar renders the result of such calculations uncertain (Schürer, op. cit., I, 749 f). In the year 783/30 Friday, Nīṣān 15, would fall on April 7. There is an early patristic tradition which dates the death of Jesus in the year 782/29, in the consulship of the Gemini (Turner, *HDB*, I, 413 f), but its origin and trustworthy character are problematical.

6. Death of Jesus

7. Summary of Dates

1. Birth of Jesus, 748/6.
2. Death of Herod the Great, 750/4.
3. Baptism of Jesus, 779/26.
4. First Passover of Jesus' ministry, 780/27.
5. Death of Jesus, 783/30.

Literature.—Schürer, *Geschichte des Jüdischen Volkes im Zeitalter Jesu Christi*, 3. und 4. Aufl., 1901–9, 3 vols, Eng. tr of the 2d ed, in 5 vols, 1885–94; Ideler, *Handbuch der mathematischen und technischen Chronologie*, 1825–26, 2 vols; Wieseler, *Chronologische Synopse der Evangelien*, 1843, Eng. tr; Lewin, *Fasti Sacri*, 1865; Turner, art. "Chronology of the NT" in *HDB*, 1900, I, 403–25; von Soden, art. "Chronology" in Cheyne and Black, *EB*, 1899, I, 799–819; Ramsay, *Was Christ Born at Bethlehem?* 1898; F. R. Montgomery Hitchcock, art. "Dates" in *DCG*; Mommsen, *Res Gestae Divi Augusti*².

II. Chronology of the Apostolic Age.—The chronology of the apostolic age must be based on the data in Acts and the epistolary lit. of the NT which afford contacts with persons or events of the Gr-Rom world. From the fixed points thus secured a general outline of the relative chronology may be established with reasonable probability.

1. Paul's Conversion

Paul was converted near Damascus (Acts **9** 3 ff; **22** 5 ff; **26** 12 ff; Gal **1** 17). After a brief stay in that city (Acts **9** 19 ff) he went to Arabia and then came again to Damascus (Gal **1** 17). When he left Damascus the second time, he returned to Jerus after an absence of three years (Gal **1** 18). The flight of Paul from Damascus (Acts **9** 24) probably terminated his second visit to the city. At that time the ethnarch of Aretas, the king of the Nabathaeans, acting with the resident Jews (Acts **9** 23 f), guarded the city to seize him (2 Cor **11** 32). Aretas IV succeeded Obodas about 9 BC, and reigned until about 40 AD. Damascus was taken by the Romans in 62 BC and probably continued under their control until the death of Tiberius (March 37 AD). Rom coins of Damascus exist from the time of Augustus, Tiberius and Nero, but there are no such coins from the time of Caligula and Claudius (Schürer, op. cit., I, 737; II, 153). Moreover the relations of Aretas to Augustus and Tiberius make it extremely improbable that he held Damascus during their reign as part of his kingdom or acquired it by conquest. The statement of Paul however seems to imply Nabathaean control of the city, and this is best explained on the supposition that Damascus was given to Aretas by Caligula, the change in the imperial attitude being due perhaps to the influence primarily of Agrippa and possibly also of Vitellius (Steinmann, *Aretas IV*, 1909, 34 ff). But if Paul's escape from Damascus was not earlier than 37 AD, his conversion cannot be placed earlier than 34 or 35 AD, and the journey to Jerus 14 years later (Gal **2** 1) not earlier than 50 or 51 AD.

2. Death of Herod Agrippa I

Herod Agrippa I died in Caesarea shortly after a Passover season (Acts **12** 23; cf **12** 3.19). Caligula had given him the tetrarchy of Philip and of Lysanias in 37 AD—the latter either at this time or later—with the title of king (*Ant*, XVIII, vi, 10; *BJ*, II, ix, 6) and this was increased in 40 AD by the tetrarchy of Antipas (*Ant*, XVIII, vii, 1 f; *BJ*, II, ix, 6). Claudius gave him also Judaea and Samaria (*Ant*, XIX, v, 1; *BJ*, II, xi, 5) thus making his territory even more extensive than that of his grandfather, Herod the Great. Agrippa reigned over "all Judaea" for three years under Claudius (*Ant*, XIX, viii, 2; *BJ*, II, xi, 6), his death falling in the spring of 44 AD, in the 7th year of his reign. The games mentioned by Jos in this connection are probably those that were celebrated in honor of the return of Claudius from Britain in 44 AD. There are coins of Agrippa from his 6th year, but the attribution to him of coins from other years is questioned (Schürer, op. cit., 560, n. 40; Madden, op. cit., 132).

3. Famine under Claudius

The prophecy of a famine and its fulfilment under Claudius (Acts **11** 28) are associated in Acts with the death of Herod Agrippa I (**11** 30; **12** 23). Famines in Rome during the reign of Claudius are mentioned by Suetonius (*Claud.* xviii), Dio Cassius (lx.11), Tacitus (*Annals* xii.43), and Orosius (vii.6). Jos narrates in the time of Fadus the generosity of Helena during a famine in Pal (*Ant*, XX, ii, 5), but subsequently dates the famine generally in the time of Fadus and Alexander. The famine in Pal would fall therefore at some time between 44 and 48 (Schürer, op. cit., I, 567, n. 8).

4. Sergius Paulus

When Paul visited Cyprus with Barnabas the island was administered by Sergius Paulus (Acts **13** 7 ff), a propraetor with the title proconsul (Marquardt, op. cit., I, 391). There is an inscription from Cyprus (Cagnat, *Inscr. graec. ad res rom. pertin.*, III, 930) dating from the 1st cent., and probably from the year 53 (Zahn, *Neue kirch. Zeitschr.*, 1904, XV, 194) in which an incident in the career of a certain Apollonius is dated in the proconsulship of Paulus (ἐπὶ Παύλου [ἀνθ]υπάτου, *epí Paúlou* [*anth*]-*upátou*). From another inscription (*CIG*, 2632), dated in the 12th year of Claudius, it appears that L. Annius Bassus was proconsul in 52. If the Julius Cordus mentioned by Bassus was his immediate predecessor, the proconsulship of Sergius Paulus may be dated at some time before 51.

5. Edict of Claudius

When Paul came to Corinth for the first time he met Aquila and Priscilla, who had left Rome because of an edict of Claudius expelling the Jews from the city (Acts **18** 2). Suetonius mentions an expulsion of the Jews from Rome by Claudius but gives no date (*Claud.* xxv; cf Dio Cassius lx.6). Orosius however dates the edict in the 9th year of Claudius or 49 AD (*Hist.* vii.6, 15); and although Jos, from whom he quotes, does not mention this edict but records the favor shown by Claudius to the Jews and to Herod Agrippa I (*Ant*, XIX, v, 1–3; cf Dio Cassius lx.6, 6, 9, 10; 8, 2), it is not improbable that the date is approximately accurate (Schürer, op. cit., III, 62, n. 92).

6. Gallio

During Paul's first sojourn in Corinth the apostle was brought before the proconsul Gallio (Acts **18** 12). This could not have been earlier than the year 44 when Claudius gave Achaia back to the Senate and the province was administered by a propraetor with the title of proconsul (Dio Cassius lx.24; Marquardt, op. cit., I, 331 f; Ramsay, *Expos.*, 1897, I, 207). Moreover the career of Seneca makes it improbable that his brother would be advanced to this position before 49 or 50 (Harnack, *Chron.*, I, 237; Wieseler, *Chron. d. apos. Zeitalters*, 119). There is a fragmentary inscription from Delphi containing a letter from the emperor Claudius in which mention is made of Gallio. The inscription is dated by the title of the emperor which contains the number 26. This is referred naturally to the *acclammatio* as "*imperator*" and dated in the year 52 before August, after which time the number 27 occurs in the title of Claudian inscriptions. Gallio may therefore have been proconsul from the spring or summer of the year 51–52 or 52–53. The latter seems the more probable time (cf Aem. Bourguet, *De rebus Delphicis*, 1905, 63 f; Ramsay, *Expos.*, 1909, I, 467 f; *Princeton Theological Review*, 1911, 290 f; 1912, 139 f; Deissmann, *Paulus*, 1911, 159–177; Lietzmann, *Zeitschrift für wissenschaftliche Theologie*, 1911, 345–54).

7. Festus

When Paul had been for two years a prisoner in Caesarea Felix was succeeded by Festus as procurator of Judaea (Acts **24** 27). The accession of Festus, which is placed by Eusebius in the Church History in the reign of Nero (*HE*, II, 22, 1), is dated in the Chronicle in the version of Jerome in the 2d year of Nero, 56 AD, and in the Armenian version in the 14th year of Claudius, 54 AD. The excerpts from the Chronicle in Syncellus apparently follow the text underlying the version of Jerome, but state simply that Festus was sent as successor of Felix by Nero (ed. Schoene, II, 154). After his removal from office Felix was tried in Rome, but escaped punishment through the influence of his brother Pallas, who, according to Jos, was in favor with Nero at that time (*Ant*, XX, viii, 9). Pallas was removed from office before February 13, 55 AD (Tac. *Ann.* xiii.14, 1; cf 15, 1), but apparently continued to have influence with the emperor; for he fixed the terms of his removal and was permitted to enjoy his fortune for several years (Tac. *Ann.* xiii.14, 1 f; 23, 1–3). His death occurred in 62 AD (Tac. *Ann.* xiv.65, 1). The trial of Felix must therefore have occurred before 62; but it is impossible to place it before the removal of Pallas, for this would necessitate the removal of Felix in 54 AD, and this is excluded by the fact that the first summer of Nero's reign fell in 55 AD. But if Eusebius reckoned the imperial years from September 1st after the accession (Turner, *Jour. of Theol. Studies*, 1902, 120 f; *HDB*, I, 418 f), the summer of the second year of Nero would fall in 57. In any event the removal and trial of Felix must have fallen after the removal of Pallas. The date of the Eusebian Chronicle is thus without support from Tacitus or Jos, and its value depends on the character of the source from which it was obtained—if there was such a source, for it is at least possible that the definite date owes its origin solely to the necessities imposed on Eusebius by the form of the Chronicle. It is not unlikely that the error of 5 years made by Eusebius in the reign of Agrippa II may be the source of a similar error in regard to Festus in spite of the fact that the framework of the Chronicle is generally furnished not by the years of the Jewish kings but by the imperial years (Erbes in Gebhardt u. Harnack, *Texte und Untersuchungen*, N.F., IV, 1, 1899; *Die Todestage d. Apos. Paulus u. Petrus;* Turner, *Jour. of Theol. Studies*, 1902, III, 120 f; Ramsay, *Pauline and Other Studies*, 1906, 350 ff). There is evidence however in Acts **21** 38 that Paul's arrest could not have been earlier than the spring of 55 AD. For Paul was supposed by the chief captain to be the Egyptian who had led an insurrection that had been suppressed by Felix during the reign of Nero (*Ant*, XX, viii, 6; *BJ*, II, 13, 5). Thus the accession of Festus, two years later (Acts **24** 27), could not have been earlier than 57 AD.

But if the summer of 57 AD is the earliest date possible for the accession of Festus, the summer of 60 AD is the latest date that is possible. Albinus, the successor of Festus, was present in Jerus in October, 62 AD (*Ant*, XX, ix, 1 ff), and while the administration of Festus was probably shorter than that of Felix (cf *Ant*, XX, viii, 9–11; *BJ*, II, xiv, 1 with *Ant*, XX, vii, 1–8, 8; *BJ*, II, 12–13), it is not likely that it lasted less than two years. But as between 57 AD and 60 AD, probability favors the latter. For greater justice is thus done to the words of Paul to Felix: "Forasmuch as I know that thou hast been of many years a judge unto this nation," etc (Acts **24** 10). Felix was appointed by Claudius in 52 AD (Tac. *Ann.* xii. 54; *Ant*, XX, v, 2) and was continued in office by Nero. Most of the events of his administration are narrated by Jos under Nero (*Ant*, XX, viii, 5 ff); and although Tacitus mentions an administration of Felix in Samaria when Cumanus was administering Galilee (*Ann.* xii.54), the omission of any direct reference to Judaea, the unusual character of such a double administration and the explicit statement of Jos that Claudius sent Felix as successor of Cumanus, make it unlikely that Paul's statement is to be understood of an administration beginning earlier than 52 AD. If Festus succeeded in the summer of 60 AD, Paul's arrest would fall in 58 and the "many years" of Felix' administration would cover a period of 6 years, from 52 AD to 58 AD (cf Schürer, op. cit., I, 577 f, n. 38). Ramsay argues in favor of 57 AD as the year of Paul's arrest and 59 AD as the year of the accession of Festus (*Pauline and Other Studies*, 1906, 345 ff).

8. Relative Chronology of Acts

If Festus succeeded Felix in the summer of 60 AD, Paul would reach Rome in the spring of 61 AD, and the narrative in Acts would terminate in 63 AD (**28** 30). Paul's arrest in Jerus 2 years before the accession of Festus (**24** 27) would fall in the spring of 58 AD. Previous to this Paul had spent 3 months in Corinth (**20** 3) and 3 years in Ephesus (**20** 31; cf **19** 10), which would make the beginning of the third missionary journey fall about 54 AD. There was an interval between the second and the third journeys (**18** 23), and as Paul spent 18 months at Corinth (**18** 11) the beginning of the second journey would fall about 51 AD. The Apostolic Council preceded the second journey and may be dated about 50 AD —14 years subsequent to Paul's first visit to Jerus (37 AD) in the third year after his conversion in 35 AD. The first missionary journey was made after the visit of Paul and Barnabas to Jerus with the alms from the church at Antioch (**11** 30; **12** 25), about the time of the death of Herod Agrippa I, and would fall between 44 AD and 50 AD. The growth of the early church in Jerus previous to Paul's conversion would thus extend over a period of about 5 years from 30 AD to 35 AD.

9. Pauline Epistles

Ten of the thirteen Pauline epistles were written during a period of about ten years between Paul's arrival in Corinth and the close of his first Rom imprisonment. These epistles fall into three groups, each possessing certain distinctive characteristics; and although each reflects the difference in time and occasion of its production, they all reveal an essential continuity of thought and a similarity of style which evidences unity of authorship. The earliest group consists of the Thessalonian epistles, both of which were written from Corinth on the second missionary journey about 52 or 53 AD, while Silas (Silvanus) was still in Paul's company and shortly after Paul's visit to Athens (1 Thess **1** 1; **3** 1.2.6; 2 Thess **1** 1). The major epistles belong to the third missionary journey. 1 Cor was written from Ephesus about 55 AD; Gal probably from Ephesus, either before or after 1 Cor, for Paul had been twice in Galatia (Gal **4** 13); 2 Cor from Macedonia about 57 AD; and Rom from Corinth about 57 or 58 AD. The imprisonment epistles were written from Rome: Col, Eph and Philem about 62 AD, and Phil about 63 AD.

10. Release and Death of Paul

When Paul wrote to Philemon (Philem ver 22) and to the Philippians (Phil **2** 24; cf **1** 25), he expected a favorable issue of his trial in Rome and was looking forward to another visit to the East. Before his arrest he had planned a journey to Spain by way of Rome (Rom **15** 28), and when he bade farewell to the Ephesian elders at Miletus (Acts **20** 25) he must have had in mind not only the dangers of his journey to Jerus, but also his determination to enter another field of labor. 1 Clement **5**, the Muratori Canon and the Apocryphal Acts of Peter (Zahn, *Einltg.*[3], I, 444 f) witness to the Spanish journey, and the Pastoral Epistles to a journey to the East and to another imprisonment in Rome. The two lines of evidence for Paul's release are independent and neither can be explained as derived merely from the statement of Paul's intention in Rom and in Philem and Phil. The historical situation implied in the Pastoral Epistles can be charged with artificiality only on the hypothesis that Paul was not released from his first Rom imprisonment. The data of these epistles cannot be fitted into any period of Paul's life previous to his imprisonment. But these data are embodied in just those parts of the Pastoral Epistles which are admitted to be Pauline by those who regard the epistles as containing only genuine fragments from Paul but assign the epistles in their present form to a later writer. On any hypothesis of authorship, however, the tradition which these epistles contain cannot be much later than the first quarter of the 2d cent. It is highly probable therefore that Paul was released from his first Rom imprisonment; that he visited Spain and the East; and that he was imprisoned a second time in Rome where he met his death in the closing years of Nero's reign, i.e. in 67 or 68 AD. According to early tradition Paul suffered martyrdom by beheading with the sword (Tert., *De praescr. haer.*, xxxvi), but there is nothing to connect his death with the persecution of the Christians in Rome by Nero in 64 AD.

Little is known of Peter beside what is recorded of him in the NT. The tradition of his bishopric of 20 or 25 years in Rome (cf Harnack, *Gesch. d. altchr. Lit.*, II; *Die Chronologie*, I, 243 f) accords neither with the implications of Acts and Gal nor with Paul's silence in Rom. But 1 Pet was probably written from Rome (**5** 13; cf Euseb., *HE*, ii.15, 2) and the testimony to Peter's martyrdom (implied in Jn **21** 18 f) under Nero in Rome by crucifixion (Tert., *De praes. haer.*, xxxvi; cf 1 Clem **5** 1 ff) is early and probably trustworthy. Tradition also associates Peter and Paul in their Rom labors and martyrdom (Dionysius in Euseb., *HE*, ii.25, 8; Iren., *Adv. haer.*, iii.1, 2; iii.3, 1). The mention of the Vatican as the place of Peter's interment (Caius in Euseb., *HE*, ii.25, 6 f) may indicate a connection of his martyrdom with the Neronian persecution in 64 AD; but this is not certain. Peter's death may therefore be dated with some probability in Rome between 64 and 67 AD. His two epistles were written at some time before his death, probably the First about 64 and the Second at some time afterward and subsequent to the Epistle of Jude which it apparently uses. (The arguments against the Rom sojourn and martyrdom of Peter are stated fully by Schmiedel in the *EB*, s.v. "Simon Peter," esp. col. 458 ff; on the other hand cf Zahn, *Einleitung*³, II, 17 ff, Eng. tr, II, 158 ff.)

11. Death of Peter

12. Death of James the Just

James the Just, the brother of the Lord, was prominent in the church of Jerus at the time of the Apostolic Council (Acts **15** 13 ff; Gal **2** 9; cf **1** 19; **2** 12) and later when Paul was arrested he seems still to have occupied this position (Acts **21** 18 ff), laboring with impressive devotion for the Jewish people until his martyrdom about the year 66 AD (*Ant*, XX, ix, 1; Euseb., *HE*, ii.23, 3 ff; *HRE*³, VIII, 581; Zahn, *Einltg.*³, I, 76). The Epistle of Jas contains numerous indications of its early origin and equally clear evidence that it was not written during the period when the questions which are discussed in the major epistles of Paul were agitating the church. It is probably the earliest book of the NT, written before the Apostolic Council.

13. The Synoptic Gospels

In the decade just preceding the fall of Jerus, the tradition of the life and teaching of Jesus was committed to writing in the Synoptic Gospels. Early tradition dates the composition of Matthew's Gospel in the lifetime of Peter and Paul (Iren., *Adv. haer.*, iii.1, 1; Eusebius, *HE*, v.8, 2 ff), and that of the Gospel of Mark either just before or after Peter's death (Clement in Euseb., *HE*, vi.14, 7; cf ii.15; and Irenaeus, *Adv. haer.*, iii.11, 1; Presbyter of Papias in Euseb., *HE*, iii. 39, 15; cf also 2 Pet **1** 15). The Lucan writings —both the Gospel and Acts—probably fall also in this period, for the Gospel contains no intimation that Jesus' prophecy of the destruction of Jerus had been fulfilled (cf Lk **21** 21; Acts **11** 28), and the silence of Acts about the issue of Paul's trial is best explained on the hypothesis of an early date (Jerome, *De vir. illustr.*, vii; Harnack, *Neue Untersuch. zur Apostelgesch.*, 1911; cf also Lk **10** 7; 1 Tim **5** 18). To this period belong also the Epistle of Jude and the Epistle to the He (if addressed to Jewish Christians of Pal; but later, about 80 AD, if addressed to Jewish Christians of Rome [Zahn, *Einltg.*³, II, 152]), the former being used in 2 Pet and the latter in 1 Clem.

14. Death of John

Early tradition connects John with Ephesus and mentions his continuing in life until the time of Trajan (Irenaeus, *Adv. haer.*, ii.22, 5 [Eusebius, *HE*, v.24]; iii.1, 1; v.30, 3; v.33, 4; Clement in Eusebius, *HE*, iii.23, 5–19; Polycrates in Eusebius, *HE*, iii.31, 3; v.24, 3; Justin, *Dialogue*, lxxxi; cf Rev **1** 1.4.9; **22** 8; Jn **21** 22.23.24; **19** 35). He died probably about the end of the 1st cent. There is another but less well-attested tradition of martyrdom based chiefly on the De Boor fragment of Papias (*Texte u. Unters.*, 1888), a Syr Martyrology of the 4th cent. (Wright, *Jour. of Sacred Lit.*, 1865–66, VIII, 56 ff, 423 ff), the Codex Coislinianus 305 of Georgius Hamartolus. This tradition, it is thought, finds confirmation in Mk **10** 35–40; Mt **20** 20–23 (cf Bousset, *Theologische Rundschau*, 1905, 225 ff, 277 ff). During the closing years of his life John wrote the Revelation, the Fourth Gospel and the three Epistles.

15. Summary of Dates

Conversion of Paul		35
Death of James, son of Zebedee		44
Death of Herod Agrippa I		44
Famine under Claudius		44–48
Epistle of James	before	50
First missionary journey		45–49
Edict of Claudius		49–50
Proconsulship of Sergius Paulus	before	51
Apostolic Council		50
Second missionary journey		50–53
1 and 2 Thess from Corinth		52/53
Proconsulship of Gallio		52/53
Third missionary journey		54–58
Paul in Ephesus		54–57
1 Cor and Gal from Ephesus		55–57
2 Cor from Macedonia		57
Rom from Corinth		57/58
Arrest of Paul in Jerus		58
Accession of Festus—not before		57
probably		60
First Rom imprisonment of Paul		61–63/4
Col, Eph, Philem, from Rome		62
Phil from Rome		63
Release of Paul and journeys in West and East		64–67
1 Tim and Tit from Macedonia		65–66
2 Tim from Rome		67
Death of Paul in Rome		67/8
Synoptic Gospels, Acts, Jude and He,	before	67
1 and 2 Pet from Rome		64–67
Death of Peter in Rome		64–67
Death of James the Just	about	66
Fourth Gospel, Revelation, Epistles of John from Ephesus	before	100
Death of John		98–100

LITERATURE.—In addition to the lit. mentioned in sec. 8: Anger, *De temporum in actis apostolorum ratione*, 1833; Wieseler, *Chronologie des apos. Zeitalters*, 1848: Hoennicke, *Die Chronologie des Lebens des Apostels Paulus*, 1903; Harnack, *Gesch. d. altchr. Lit. bis Euseb.*, II, 1, *Die Chronologie bis Iren.*, 1897; Lightfoot, *Biblical Essays*, 1893; Zahn, *Einleitung*, II, 1907 (Eng. tr, 1909).

W. P. ARMSTRONG

CHRYSOLITE, kris′o-līt. See STONES, PRECIOUS.

CHRYSOPRASE, kris′o-praz, **CHRYSOPRASUS**, kri-sop′ra-sus. See STONES, PRECIOUS.

CHUB, chub (כּוּב, *kūbh*). See CUB.

CHUN, chun (כּוּן, *kūn*, "founding"). See CUN.

CHURCH, chûrch:

The word "church," which is derived from κυριακός, *kuriakós*, "of or belonging to the Lord," represents in the EV of the NT the Gr ἐκκλησία, *ekklēsía*, Lat *ecclesia*. It is with the signification of this word *ekklēsia* as it meets us in the NT, and with the nature of the society which the word is there used to describe, that the present art. is concerned.

I. Pre-Christian History of the Term.—Although *ekklēsia* soon became a distinctively Christian word, it has its own pre-Christian history; and to those, whether Jews or Greeks, who first heard it applied to the Christian society it would come with suggestions of familiar things. Throughout the Gr world and right down to NT times (cf Acts **19** 39), *ekklēsia* was the designation of the regular assembly of the whole body of citizens in a free city-state, "called out" (Gr *ek*, "out," and *kalein*, "to call") by the herald for the discussion and decision of public business. The LXX translators, again, had used the word to render the Heb *ḳāhāl*, which in the OT denotes the "congregation" or community of Israel, esp. in its religious aspect as the people of God. In this OT sense we find *ekklēsia* employed by Stephen in the Book of Acts, where he describes Moses as "he that was in the church [RVm "congregation"] in the wilderness" (Acts **7** 38). The word thus came into Christian history with associations alike for the Greek and the Jew. To the Greek it would suggest a self-governing democratic society; to the Jew a theocratic society whose members were the subjects of the Heavenly King. The pre-Christian history of the word had a direct bearing upon its Christian meaning, for the *ekklēsia* of the NT is a "theocratic democracy" (Lindsay, *Church and Ministry in the Early Cents.*, 4), a society of those who are free, but are always conscious that their freedom springs from obedience to their King.

II. Its Adoption by Jesus.—According to Mt **16** 18 the name *ekklēsia* was first applied to the Christian society by Jesus Himself, the occasion being that of His benediction of Peter at Caesarea Philippi. The authenticity of the utterance has been called in question by certain critics, but on grounds that have no textual support and are made up of quite arbitrary presuppositions as to the composition of the First Gospel. It is true that Jesus had hitherto described the society He came to found as the "kingdom of God" or the "kingdom of heaven," a designation which had its roots in OT teaching and which the Messianic expectations of Israel had already made familiar. But now when it was clear that He was to be rejected by the Jewish people (cf ver 21), and that His society must move on independent lines of its own, it was natural that He should employ a new name for this new body which He was about to create, and thus should say to Peter, on the ground of the apostle's believing confession, "Upon this rock I will build my church." The adoption of this name, however, did not imply any abandonment of the ideas suggested by the conception of the kingdom. In this very passage (ver 19) "the kingdom of heaven" is employed in a manner which, if it does not make the two expressions church and kingdom perfectly synonymous, at least compels us to regard them as closely correlative and as capable of translation into each other's terms. And the comparative disuse by the apostolic writers of the name "kingdom," together with their emphasis on the church, so far from showing that Christ's disciples had failed to understand His doctrine of the kingdom, and had substituted for it the more formal notion of the church, only shows that they had followed their Master's guidance in substituting for a name and a conception that were peculiarly Jewish, another name whose associations would enable them to commend their message more readily to the world at large.

III. Its Use in the NT.—Apart from the passage just referred to, the word *ekklēsia* occurs in the Gospels on one other occasion only (Mt **18** 17). Here, moreover, it may be questioned whether Our Lord is referring to the Christian church, or to Jewish congregations commonly known as synagogues (see RVm) The latter view is more in keeping with the situation, but the promise immediately given to the disciples of a power to bind and loose (ver 18) and the assurance "Where two or three are gathered together in my name, there am I in the midst of them" (ver 20) are evidently meant for the people of Christ. If, as is probable, the *ekklēsia* of ver 17 is the Christian *ekklesia* of which Christ had already spoken to Peter, the words show that He conceived of the church as a society possessing powers of self-government, in which questions of discipline were to be decided by the collective judgment of the members.

1. In the Gospels

In Acts the *ekklēsia* has come to be the regular designation for the society of Christian believers, but is employed in two distinct senses. First in a *local* sense, to denote the body of Christians in a particular place or district, as in Jerus (**5** 11; **8** 1), in Antioch (**13** 1; **15** 22), in Caesarea (**18** 22)—a usage which reappears in the Apocalypse in the letters to the Seven Churches. Then in a wider and what may be called a universal sense, to denote the sum total of existing local churches (**9** 31 RV), which are thus regarded as forming one body.

2. In Acts

In the Pauline Epistles both of these usages are frequent. Thus the apostle writes of "the church of the Thessalonians" (1 Thess **1** 1), "the church of God which is at Corinth" (1 Cor **1** 2; 2 Cor **1** 1). Indeed he localizes and particularizes the word yet further by applying it to a single Christian household or to little groups of believers who were accustomed to assemble in private houses for worship and fellowship (Rom **16** 5; 1 Cor **16** 19; Col **4** 15; Philem ver 2)—an employment of the word which recalls the saying of Jesus in Mt **18** 20. The *universal* use, again, may be illustrated by the contrast he draws between Jews and Greeks on the one hand and the church of God on the other (1 Cor **10** 32), and by the declaration that God has set in the church apostles, prophets, and teachers (**12** 28).

3. In the Pauline Epistles

But Paul in his later epistles has another use of *ekklēsia* peculiar to himself, which may be described as the *ideal* use. The church, now, is the body of which Christ is the head (Eph **1** 22 f; Col **1** 18.24). It is the medium through which God's manifold wisdom and eternal purpose are to be made known not only to all men, but to the principalities and powers in the heavenly places (Eph **3** 9–11). It is the bride of whom He is the heavenly Bridegroom, the bride for whom in His love He gave Himself up, that He might cleanse and sanctify her and might present her to Himself a glorious church, a church without blemish, not having spot or wrinkle or any such thing (**5** 25 ff). This church clearly is not the actual church as we know it on earth, with its divisions, its blemishes, its shortcomings in faith and love and obedience. It is the holy and catholic church that is to be when the Bridegroom has completed the process of lustration, having fully "cleansed it by the washing of water with the word." It is the ideal which the actual church must keep before it and strive after, the ideal up to which it shall finally be guided by that Divine in-working power which is able to conform the body to the head, to make the bride worthy of the Bridegroom, so that God may receive in the church the glory that is His (Eph **3** 21).

IV. The Notes of the Church.—Although a systematic doctrine of the church is neither to be found nor to be looked for in the NT, certain characteristic notes or features of the Christian society are brought before us from which we can form some conception as to its nature. The fundamental note is *faith.* It was to Peter confessing his faith in Christ that the promise came, "Upon this rock I will build my church" (Mt **16** 18). Until Jesus found a man full of faith He could not begin to build His church; and unless Peter had been the prototype of others whose faith was like his own, the walls of the church would never have risen into the air. Primarily the church is a society not of thinkers or workers or even of worshippers, but of believers. Hence we find that "believers" or "they that believed" is constantly used as a synonym for the members of the Christian society (e.g. Acts **2** 44; **4** 32; **5** 14; 1 Tim **4** 12). Hence, too, the rite of baptism, which from the first was the condition of entrance into the apostolic church and the seal of membership in it, was recognized as preëminently the sacrament of faith and of confession (Acts **2** 41; **8** 12.36; Rom **6** 4; 1 Cor **12** 13). This church-founding and church-building faith, of which baptism was the seal, was much more than an act of intellectual assent. It was a personal laying hold of the personal Saviour, the bond of a vital union between Christ and the believer which resulted in nothing less than a new creation (Rom **6** 4; **8** 1.2; 2 Cor **5** 17).

1. Faith

If faith in Christ is the fundamental note of the Christian society, the next is *fellowship* among the members. This follows from the very nature of faith as just described; for if each believer is vitally joined to Christ, all believers must stand in a living relation to one another. In Paul's favorite figure, Christians are members one of another because they are members in particular of the body of Christ (Rom **12** 5; 1 Cor **12** 27). That the Christian society was recognized from the first as a fellowship appears from the name "the brethren," which is so commonly applied to those who belong to it. In Acts the name is of very frequent occurrence (**9** 30, etc), and it is employed by Paul in the epistles of every period of his career (1 Thess **4** 10, etc). Similar testimony lies in the fact that "the *koinōnía*" (EV "fellowship") takes its place in the earliest meetings of the church side by side with the apostles' teaching and the breaking of bread and prayers (Acts **2** 42). See COMMUNION. The *koinōnia* at first carried with it a community of goods (Acts **2** 44; **4** 32), but afterward found expression in the fellowship of ministration (2 Cor **8** 4) and in such acts of Christian charity as are inspired by Christian faith (He **13** 16). In the Lord's Supper, the other sacrament of the primitive church, the fellowship of Christians received its most striking and most sacred expression. For if baptism was esp. the sacrament of faith, the Supper was distinctively the sacrament of love and fellowship—a communion or common participation in Christ's death and its fruits which carried with it a communion of hearts and spirits between the participants themselves.

2. Fellowship

Although local congregations sprang up wherever the gospel was preached, and each of these enjoyed an independent life of its own, the *unity* of the church was clearly recognized from the first. The intercourse between Jerus and Antioch (Acts **11** 22; **15** 2), the conference held in the former city (**15** 6 ff), the right hand of fellowship given by the elder apostles to Paul and Barnabas (Gal **2** 9), the untiring efforts made by Paul himself to forge strong links of love and mutual service between gentile and Jewish Christians (2 Cor **8**)—all these things serve to show how fully it was realized that though there were many churches, there was but one church. This truth comes to its complete expression in the epistles of Paul's imprisonment, with their vision of the church as a body of which Christ is the head, a body animated by one spirit, and having one Lord, one faith, one baptism, one God and Father of all (Eph **4** 4 ff; Col **1** 18; **3** 11). And this unity, it is to be noticed, is conceived of as a visible unity. Jesus Himself evidently conceived it so when He prayed for His disciples that they all might be one, so that the world might believe (Jn **17** 21). And the unity of which Paul writes and for which he strove is a unity that finds visible expression. Not, it is true, in any uniformity of outward polity, but through the manifestation of a common faith in acts of mutual love (Eph **4** 3.13; 2 Cor **9**).

3. Unity

Another dominant note of the NT church lay in the *consecration* of its members. "Saints" is one of the most frequently recurring designations for them that we find. As thus employed, the word has in the first place an objective meaning; the sainthood of the Christian society consisted in its separation from the world by God's electing grace; in this respect it has succeeded to the prerogatives of Israel under the old covenant. The members of the church, as Peter said, are "an elect race, a royal priesthood, a holy nation, a people for God's own possession" (1 Pet **2** 9). But side by side with this sense of an outward and priestly consecration, the name "saints" carried within it the thought of an ethical holiness—a holiness consisting, not merely in a status determined by relation to Christ, but in an actual and practical saintliness, a consecration to God that finds expression in character and conduct. No doubt the members of the church are called saints even when the living evidences of sainthood are sadly lacking. Writing to the Corinthian church in which he found so much to blame, Paul addresses its members by this title (1 Cor **1** 2; cf **6** 11). But he does so for other than formal reasons—not only because consecration to God is their outward calling and status as believers, but also because he is assured that a work of real sanctification is going on, and must continue to go on, in their bodies and their spirits which are His. For those who are in Christ are a new creation (2 Cor **5** 17), and those to whom has come the separating and consecrating call (2 Cor **6** 17) must cleanse themselves from all filthiness of the flesh and spirit, perfecting holiness in the fear of God (**7** 1). Paul looks upon the members of the church, just as he looks upon the church itself, with a prophetic eye; he sees them not as they are, but as they are to be. And in his view it is "by the washing of water with the word," in other words by the progressive sanctification of its members, that the church itself is to be sanctified and cleansed, until Christ can present it to Himself a glorious church, not having spot or wrinkle or any such thing (Eph **5** 26.27).

4. Consecration

Yet another note of the church was spiritual *power.* When the name *ekklēsia* was given by Jesus to the society He came to found, His promise to Peter included the bestowal of the gift of power (Mt **16** 18.19). The apostle was to receive the "power of the keys," i.e. he was to exercise the privilege of opening the doors of the kingdom of heaven to the Jew (Acts **2** 41) and to the Gentile (**10** 34–38; **15** 7). He was further to have the power of

5. Power

binding and loosing, i.e. of forbidding and permitting; in other words he was to possess the functions of a legislator within the spiritual sphere of the church. The legislative powers then bestowed upon Peter personally as the reward of his believing confession were afterward conferred upon the disciples generally (Mt **18** 18; cf ver 1 and also vs 19.20), and at the conference in Jerus were exercised by the church as a whole (Acts **15** 4.22). The power to open the gates of the kingdom of heaven was expanded into the great missionary commission, "Go ye therefore, and make disciples of all the nations" (Mt **28** 19)—a commission that was understood by the apostolic church to be addressed not to the eleven apostles only, but to all Christ's followers without distinction (Acts **8** 4, etc). To the Christian society there thus belonged the double power of legislating for its own members and of opening the kingdom of heaven to all believers. But these double functions of teaching and government were clearly recognized as delegated gifts. The church taught the nations because Christ had bid her go and do it. She laid down laws for her own members because He had conferred upon her authority to bind and to loose. But in every exercise of her authority she relied upon Him from whom she derived it. She believed that Christ was with her alway, even unto the end of the world (Mt **28** 20), and that the power with which she was endued was power from on high (Lk **24** 49).

V. The Organization of the Church.—It seems evident from the NT that Jesus gave His disciples no formal prescriptions for the organization of the church. In the first days after Pentecost they had no thought of separating themselves from the religious life of Israel, and would not realize the need of any distinct organization of their own. The temple-worship was still adhered to (Acts **2** 46; **3** 1), though it was supplemented by apostolic teaching, by prayer and fellowship, and by the breaking of bread (**2** 42.46). Organization was a thing of gradual growth suggested by emerging needs, and the differentiation of function among those who were drawn into the service of the church was due to the difference in the gifts bestowed by God upon the church members (1 Cor **12** 28). At first the Twelve themselves, as the immediate companions of Jesus throughout His ministry and the prime witnesses of the Christian facts and esp. of the resurrection (cf Acts **1** 21.22), were the natural leaders and teachers of the community. Apart from this, the earliest evidence of anything like organization is found in the distinction drawn by the Twelve themselves between the ministry of the word and the ministry of tables (Acts **6** 2.4)—a distinction which was fully recognized by Paul (Rom **12** 6.8; 1 Cor **1** 17; **9** 14; **12** 28), though he enlarged the latter type of ministry so as to include much more than the care of the poor. The two kinds of ministry, as they meet us at the first, may broadly be distinguished as the general and prophetic on the one hand, the local and practical on the other.

1. The General and Prophetic Ministry

From Acts **6** 1 ff we see that the Twelve recognized that they were Divinely called as apostles to proclaim the gospel; and Paul repeatedly makes the same claim for himself (1 Cor **1** 17; **9** 16; 2 Cor **3** 6; **4** 1; Col **1** 23). But apostleship was by no means confined to the Twelve (Acts **14** 14; Rom **16** 7; cf *Did* **11** 4 ff); and an itinerant ministry of the word was exercised in differing ways by prophets, evangelists, and teachers, as well as by apostles (1 Cor **12** 28.29; Eph **4** 11). The fact that Paul himself is variously described as an apostle, a prophet, a teacher (Acts **13** 1; **14** 14; 1 Tim **2** 7; 2 Tim **1** 11) appears to show that the prophetic ministry was not a ministry of stated office, but one of special gifts and functions. The apostle carried the good tidings of salvation to the ignorant and unbelieving (Gal **2** 7.8), the prophet (in the more specific sense of the word) was a messenger to the church (1 Cor **14** 4.22); and while the teacher explained and applied truth that was already possessed (He **5** 12), the prophet was recognized by those who had spiritual discernment (1 Cor **2** 15; **14** 29; 1 Jn **4** 1) as the Divinely employed medium of fresh revelations (1 Cor **14** 25.30.31; Eph **3** 5; cf *Did* **4** 1).

2. The Local and Practical Ministry

The earliest examples of this are the Seven of Jerus who were intrusted with the care of the "daily ministration" (Acts **6** 1 ff). With the growth of the church, however, other needs arose, and the local ministry is seen developing in two distinct directions. First there is the presbyter or elder, otherwise known as the bishop or overseer, whose duties, while still local, are chiefly of a spiritual kind (Acts **20** 17.28.35; 1 Tim **3** 2.5; Jas **5** 14; 1 Pet **5** 2). See BISHOP. Next there are the deacon and the deaconess (Phil **1** 1; 1 Tim **3** 8–13), whose work appears to have lain largely in house to house visitation and a practical ministry to the poor and needy (1 Tim **5** 8–11). The necessities of government, of discipline, and of regular and stated instruction had thus brought it to pass that within NT times some of the functions of the general ministry of apostles and prophets were discharged by a local ministry. The general ministry, however, was still recognized to be the higher of the two. Paul addresses the presbyter-bishops of Ephesus in a tone of lofty spiritual authority (Acts **20** 17 ff). And according to the *Did*, a true prophet when he visits a church is to take precedence over the resident bishops and deacons (*Did* **10** 7; **13** 3). See CHURCH GOVERNMENT.

LITERATURE.—Hort, *The Christian Ecclesia;* Lindsay, *The Church and the Ministry in the Early Cents.*, lects I–V; Hatch, *Bampton Lectures;* Gwatkin, *Early Church History to AD 313;* Köstlin, art. "Kirche" in *RE;* Armitage Robinson, art. "Church" in *EB;* Fairbairn, *Christ in Modern Theology*, 513–34; Dargan, *Ecclesiology;* Denney, *Studies in Theology*, ch viii.

J. C. LAMBERT

CHURCH GOVERNMENT, guv'ẽrn-ment:

I. APPROACH TO SUBJECT
   1. The General Sense
   2. The Local Sense
II. INTERNAL ORDER
   1. Subjects of Admission
   2. Definite Organizations
   3. Ministers
      (1) General
      (2) Local
   4. Ecclesiastical Functions
      (1) Control of Membership
      (2) Selection of Officers, etc
      (3) Observations of Ordinances
   5. Independent (Autonomous) Organizations
III. EXTERNAL AUTHORITY
IV. COÖPERATIVE RELATIONS
LITERATURE

The object here sought is to discover what kind of church government is mirrored in the NT. To do this with perfect definiteness is, no doubt, quite impossible. Certain general features, however, may clearly be seen.

I. Approach to the Subject.—The subject is best approached through the Gr word *ekklēsia*, tr[d] "church." Passing by the history of this word, and its connection with the Heb words *'ēdhāh* and *ḳāhāl* (which the LXX sometimes renders by ἐκκλησία, *ekklēsia*), we come at once to the NT usage. Two perfectly distinct senses are found, viz. a general and a local.

Christ is "head over all things to the church, which is his body . . . . " (Eph **1** 22); "the general assembly and church of the firstborn who are enrolled in heaven" (He **12** 23). Here we have "church" in the broadest sense, including all the redeemed in earth and heaven, and in all ages (see also Eph **1** 22; **3** 10; **5** 22–27; Col **1** 24; He **12** 23).

1. The General Sense

Here the Scripture passages are very numerous. In some cases, the word is used in the sing., and in others the pl.; in some it is used with reference to a specified church, and in others without such specification. In all cases the sense is local. In Acts **11** 26, it is said that Paul and Barnabas were "gathered together with the church," where the church at Antioch is meant. In Acts **14** 23, Paul and Barnabas are said to have "appointed elders in every church," that is, churches which they had planted. In Rev **2** and **3** the seven churches of Asia Minor are addressed. In Acts **16** 5 we are told that the churches "were strengthened in the faith." On the local sense see, further, Acts **8** 1; **15** 4; **16** 5; **20** 17; Rom **16** 4; 1 Cor **1** 2; **6** 4; **11** 16; Gal **1** 2.22, and many other places.

2. The Local Sense

There are a few passages that do not seem exactly to fit into either of the above categories. Such, for example, are Mt **18** 17 and 1 Cor **12** 28, where it seems best to understand a generic sense. Such, also, are passages like Acts **9** 31, and 1 Cor **10** 32, where a collective sense best suits the cases.

Church government in the NT applies only to the local bodies.

II. Internal Order.—With respect to the constitution and life of these NT churches, several points may be made out beyond reasonable doubt.

They were composed of persons who professed faith in Christ, and who were believed to have been regenerated, and who had been baptized. See Acts **2** 41.44.47 (RV "added to them"); **8** 12; Rom **1** 8; **6** 4; **10** 9.10; 1 Cor **1** 2; Col **1** 2.4; 1 Tim **6** 12, and others, where they are called "saints," "sons of God," "faithful brethren," "sanctified in Christ Jesus."

1. Subjects of Admission

They are definitely and permanently organized bodies, and not temporary and loose aggregations of individuals. It is quite impossible, for example, to regard the church at Antioch as a loose aggregation of people for a passing purpose. The letters of Paul to the churches at Rome, Corinth, Philippi, Thessalonica, cannot be regarded as addressed to other than permanent and definitely organized bodies.

2. Definite Organizations

They were served by two classes of ministers—one general, the other local.

(1) *General.*—At the head of these is the "apostle" (1 Cor **12** 28; Eph **4** 11). His official relation to the churches was general. He did not necessarily belong to the group of the original Eleven. Besides Matthias (Acts **1** 26), Paul and Barnabas (1 Cor **9** 5.6), James, the Lord's brother (Gal **1** 19), Andronicus and Junias (Rom **16** 7) are reckoned as "apostles." The one invariable and necessary qualification of an apostle was that he should have seen the Lord after the Resurrection (Acts **1** 22; 1 Cor **9** 1). Another qualification was to have wrought "the signs of an apostle" (2 Cor **12** 12; cf 1 Cor **9** 2). He was to bear witness to what he had seen and heard, to preach the gospel of the kingdom (Acts **1** 8; 1 Cor **1** 17), to found churches and have a general care of them (2 Cor **11** 28). From the nature of his chief qualification, his office was temporary.

3. Ministers

Next comes the "prophet." His relation to the churches, also, was general. It was not necessary that he should have seen the Lord, but it appertained to his spiritual function that he should have revelations (Eph **3** 5). There is no indication that his office was in any sense administrative.

After the "prophet" come the "evangelist" and "teacher," the first, a traveling preacher, the second, one who had special aptitude for giving instruction.

After the "teacher" and "evangelist" follow a group of special gifts of "healing," "helps," "governments," "tongues." It may be that "helps" and "governments" are to be identified with "deacons" and "bishops," to be spoken of later. The other items in this part of Paul's list seem to refer to special *charismata.*

(2) *Local.*—There were two clearly distinct offices of a local and permanent kind in the NT churches. Paul (Phil **1** 1) addresses "all the saints in Christ Jesus that are at Philippi, with the bishops and deacons." See BISHOP; DEACON.

The most common designation of the first of these officers is "elder" (πρεσβύτερος, *presbúteros*). In one passage (Eph **4** 11) he is called "pastor" (ποιμήν, *poimḗn*). In Acts **20** 17–28, it becomes clear that the office of elder, bishop, and pastor was one; for there the apostle charges the elders of the church at Ephesus to feed (pastor) the church in which the Holy Spirit has made them bishops (cf Titus **1** 5.7; 1 Pet **5** 1.2).

The function of the elders was, in general, spiritual, but involved an oversight of all the affairs of the church (1 Tim **3** 2; **5** 17).

As to the second of the local church officers, it has to be said that little is given us in the NT. That the office of deacon originated with the appointment of the Seven in Acts **6** is not certain. If we compare the qualifications there given by the apostles with those given by Paul in 1 Tim **3** 8–13, it seems quite probable that the necessity which arose at Jerus, and which led to the appointment of the Seven was really the occasion for originating the office of deacon in the churches. The work assigned the Seven was secular, that is to say, the "service of tables." They were to relieve the apostles of that part of the work. A similar relation to the work of the elders seems to have been borne by that of the deacons.

Again, they exercised the highest ecclesiastical functions.

(1) *They had control of membership.*—In Mt **18** 17, Our Lord, by anticipation, lodges final action, in the sphere of church discipline, with the church. When the church has taken action, the matter is ended. There is no direction to take it to a higher court. In the church at Corinth, there was a man who was guilty of an infamous offence against purity. With regard to the case, Paul urged the most summary discipline (1 Cor **5** 5). If the church should act upon the judgment which he communicated to them, they would act when "gathered together"; that is to say, action would be taken in conference of the church. In 2 Cor **2**, a reference to the case shows that they had acted upon his advice, and that the action was taken by the majority ("the many," the more, 2 Cor **2** 6). In 2 Cor **2** he counsels restoration of this excluded member now repentant. Exclusion and restoration of members were to be effected by a church. This, of course, carried with it the reception of members in the first instance.

4. Ecclesiastical Functions

(2) *They selected their officers and other servants.*—This was true in case of the Seven (Acts **6** 3–13; see other cases in Acts **15** 22; 1 Cor **16** 3; 2 Cor **8** 1 ff; Phil **2** 25). Acts **14** 23 and Titus **1** 5

seem, at first, to offset the passages just given. In one of these, Paul and Barnabas are said to have "appointed" (χειροτονήσαντες, *cheirotonḗsantes*) elders in the churches which they had planted. But scholars of first quality, though themselves adhering to Presbyterial or Episcopal forms of church government, maintain that Paul and Barnabas ordained the elders whom the churches selected—that they "appointed" them in the usual way, by the suffrages of the members of the churches concerned. The word rendered "appoint" in Tit **1** 5 (καταστήσῃς, *katastḗsēs*) is more easily understood as referring to ordination instead of selection.

(3) *They observed the ordinances.*—Paul gives direction (1 Cor **11** 20–34) to the church at Corinth about the observance of the Lord's Supper. These directions are given, not to any officer or set of officers, but to the church. Ecclesiastically, of course, the two ordinances are on the same level; and, if one of them had been committed to the custody, so to say, of the churches, so must the other.

5. Independent (Autonomous) Organizations

The management of their business was in their own hands. Paul wrote the church at Corinth: "Let all things be done decently and in order" (1 Cor **14** 40). In that comprehensive injunction, given to a church, is implied control of its affairs by the church.

III. External Authority.—The investigation up to this point places us in position to see that there is in the NT no warrant for ecclesiastical grades in the ministry of the churches, by which there may be created an ascending series of rulers who shall govern the churches merged into one vast ecclesiastical organization called "the church." So, also, we are in position to see that there is no warrant for an ascending series of courts which may review any "case" that originates in a local church. We may see, on the contrary, that to each local church has been committed by Christ the management of its own affairs; and that He had endowed every such church with ecclesiastical competency to perform every function that any ecclesiastical body has a right to perform.

As the churches are not to be dominated by any external ecclesiastical authority, so they are not to be interfered with, in their church life, by civil government. Jesus taught that Christians should be good citizens (Mt **22** 15–22); so did the apostles (Rom **13** 1–7; 1 Pet **2** 13–16). Jesus also taught the spirituality of His Kingdom: "My kingdom is not of this world" (Jn **18** 36). It follows that only where the life of a church touches the civic life of the community has the civil authority any right to interfere.

IV. Coöperative Relations.—While each local church, according to the NT, is independent of every other in the sense that no other has jurisdiction over it, yet coöperative relations were entered into by NT churches. Examples and indications of that may be found in Rom **15** 26.27; 2 Cor **8, 9**; Gal **2** 10; Rom **15** 1; 3 Jn ver 8. The principle of coöperation effective in those cases is susceptible of indefinite expansion. Churches may properly coöperate in matters of discipline, by seeking and giving counsel, and by respecting each other's disciplinary measures. In the great, paramount business of evangelizing and teaching the nations, they may coöperate in a multitude of ways. There is no sphere of general Christian activity in which the churches may not voluntarily and freely coöperate for the betterment of the world, the salvation of humanity.

For other standpoints see BISHOP; GOVERNMENT; MINISTRY, etc.

LITERATURE.—Hort, *The Christian Ecclesia;* Hatch, *Organization of the Early Christian Churches;* Whitley, *Church, Ministry and Sacraments in the NT;* Lindsay, *The Church and the Ministry in the Early Cents.;* French, *Synonyms of NT;* Vitringa, *De Synagoga Vetere;* Holzinger, *ZAW;* Schürer, *HJP*, II; Driver, *LOT;* Thayer, *NT Lex.*, and Cremer, *Bib. Theol. Lex.*, s.v., "*ekklēsia*" and "*sunagōgē*"; Neumann, *Röm. Staat und die allgemeine Kirche;* Ramsay, *Church in Rom Emp.;* Lightfoot, "The Christian Ministry," in *Comm. on Philippians;* Harvey, *The Church;* Dagg, *Church Order;* Hovey, *Religion and the State;* Owen, *Church Government;* Ladd, *Principles of Church Polity;* Dexter, *Congregationalism;* Hodge, *Discussions in Church Polity;* Abbey, *Ecclesiastical Constitutions;* Hooker, *Ecclesiastical Polity;* Jacob, *Ecclesiastical Polity;* Bore, *The Church and Its Ministry;* Dollinger, *The Church and The Churches;* Stanley, *Lectures on the Eastern Church;* Dargan, *Ecclesiology.*

E. J. FORRESTER

CHURCHES, chûrch′iz, **ROBBERS OF.** See ROBBERS OF TEMPLES.

CHURCHES, SEVEN. See ANGELS OF THE SEVEN CHURCHES.

CHURL, chûrl (כִּילַי or כֵּלַי, *kīlay* or *kēlay*): The Heb word occurs only in Isa **32** 5.7, in the latter ver in a form slightly modified so as to produce a pleasing assonance with the word immediately following. The word probably means "crafty" or "miserly," both ideas being suitable to the context, though "miserly" accords with the setting in Isa somewhat better.

In 1 S **25** 3 the Heb *ḳāsheh* which means "hard," "severe," "rough," is rendered "churlish." In Saxon, churl, as the name for the lowest order of freemen, came to be used of persons boorish in manner. The rough and ill-mannered Nabal is aptly described as churlish. JOHN RICHARD SAMPEY

CHUSHAN-RISHATHAIM, kū-shan-rish-a-thā′im. See CUSHAN-RISHATHAIM.

CHUSI, kū′sī, kū′si (Χούς, *Choús*): A place only named in Jth **7** 18, as near Ekrebel on the brook Mochmur. It was in central Pal, and has with some probability been identified with *Ḳūzah*, a village 5½ miles S. of Nablus and 5 miles W. of Agrabeh (Ekrebel).

CHUZAS, kū′zas, chū′zas (Χουζᾶς, *Chouzás;* AV **Chuza**): The steward of Herod Antipas. In Lk **8** 3 we read that his wife Joanna, "and Susanna, and many others," ministered to Christ and His disciples. See JOANNA (Lk **24** 10).

CICCAR, sik′är (כִּכָּר, *kikkār*, "circle"): Used of the circle of the Jordan (Gen **13** 10, Heb). See PLAIN; CITIES OF THE PLAIN.

CIELED, sēld, **CIELING,** sēl′ing. See CEILED; CEILING.

CILICIA, si-lish′i-a (ἡ Κιλικία, *hē Kilikía*): An important province at the S.E. angle of Asia Minor, corresponding nearly with the modern Turkish *vilayet* of Adana; enfolded between the Taurus mountains and the Mediterranean Sea, with the Amanus range on the E. and Pamphylia on the W.; chief rivers, the Pyramus, Sarus, Cydnus and Calycadnus. The character of Cilician history has been largely determined by the physical features of the province. It is divided by nature into a mountainous part to the W., called Tracheia, and a broad, alluvial plain, hot and fertile, toward the E., termed Campestris or Pedias. Cilicia has always been isolated from its neighbors by land by its encircling mountains, save for its two famous mountain passes, the "Syrian Gates," which offer an easy road to Antioch and the S., and the wonderful "Cilician Gates," which open a road to central and western Asia Minor. Through these passes the armies and the pilgrims, the trade and the travel of the cents. have made their way. Alexander was one of the most renowned leaders of such expeditions, and at Issus he met and shattered the power of the Pers empire.

The early settlers of Cilicia are held to have been Sem Syrians and Phoenicians, but in the still earlier days the inhabitants must have been Hittites. While few Hittite remains have been brought to light in Cilicia proper, the province was so surrounded by Hittites, and such important works of Hittite art and industry remain on the outskirts of the province, as at Ivriz, Marash, Sinjirli and Sakche Geuzi, that the intervening territory could hardly fail to be overspread with the same civilization and imperial power. See Professor John Garstang's *The Land of the Hittites*.

Cilicia appears as independent under Syennesis, a contemporary of Alyattes of Lydia, 610 BC. Later it passed under the Pers sway, but retained its separate line of kings. After Alexander the Seleucid rulers governed Cilicia from Antioch. The disturbances of the times enabled the pirates so to multiply and establish themselves in their home base, in Cilicia, Tracheia, that they became the scourge of the Mediterranean until their power was broken by Pompey (67–66 BC). Cilicia was by degrees incorporated in the Rom administration, and Cicero, the orator, was governor (51–50 BC).

The foremost citizen of the province was Saul of Tarsus (Acts **21** 39; **22** 3; **23** 34). Students or pilgrims from Cilicia like himself disputed with Stephen (Acts **6** 9). Some of the earliest labors of the great apostle were near his home, in Syria and Cilicia (Gal **1** 21; Acts **15** 23.41). On his voyage to Rome he sailed across the sea which is off Cilicia (Acts **27** 5). Constantinople and Antioch may be regarded as the front and back door of Asia Minor, and as the former was not founded till the 4th cent., Asia Minor may be regarded as fronting during apostolic days on Antioch. Cilicia was intimately connected with its neighbor province on the S. The first Christian apostles and evangelists followed the great highways, through the famous mountain passes, and carried the religion of Jesus to Asia Minor from Antioch as a base.

Armenians migrating from the N. founded a kingdom in Cilicia under Roupen which was terminated by the overthrow of King Levon, or Leo, by the conquering Turks in 1393. A remnant of this kingdom survives in the separate Armenian catholicate of Sis, which has jurisdiction over a few bishoprics, and Armenians are among the most virile of the present inhabitants of the province.

G. E. White

CINNAMON, sin'a-mun (קִנָּמוֹן, *kinnāmōn;* **κιννάμωμον**, *kinnámōmon*): Mentioned, like cassia, as a perfume. In Ex **30** 23 it is one of the ingredients of the "holy anointing oil"; in Prov **7** 17 it is, along with myrrh and aloes, a perfume for a bed; in Cant **4** 14 it is a very precious spice. Cinnamon is (Rev **18** 13) part of the merchandise of "Babylon the great."

Cinnamon is the product of *Cinnamomum zeylanicum*, a laurel-like plant widely cultivated in Ceylon and Java. It has a profuse white blossom, succeeded by a nut from which the fragrant oil is obtained. The wood is the inner bark from branches which have reached a diameter of from 2 to 3 inches; the epidermis and pulpy matter are carefully scraped off before drying. In commerce the cheaper *Cassia ligra* of China is sometimes substituted for true cinnamon, and it is thought by some authorities that this was the true cinnamon of the ancients. See, however, Cassia.

E. W. G. Masterman

CINNEROTH, sin'e-rōth (כִּנְּרוֹת, *kinn^erōth*). See Chinnereth.

CIRAMA, si-rā'ma, sir'a-ma. See Kirama.

CIRCLE, sûr'k'l: Is used with reference to the vault of the heavens (חוּג, *hūgh*) in Isa **40** 22, and in a similar sense in Wisd **13** 2 (RVm), "circle of stars" (*κύκλος ἄστρων*, *kúklos ástrōn*). It is also used in the sense of surrounding territory, as in the expression "circle of Jordan" (Gen **13** 10 RVm). See also Ciccar; Astronomy, III, 1.

CIRCUIT, sûr'kit, "a going around": Used to represent several Heb words in several senses, e.g. the sun's orbit (תְּקוּפָה, *t^ekūphāh*), Ps **19** 6; the vault of the heavens (חוּג, *hūgh*), Job **22** 14 AV; the circuit of the winds (סָבִיב, *ṣābhībh*), Eccl **1** 6 (see Astronomy); Samuel's visiting of communities (סָבַב, *ṣābhabh*), 1 S **7** 16. In the RV the idea of encircling or "fetching a compass" (AV) is expressed by the phrase "to make a circuit" (הָסֵב, *hāṣēbh*), 2 S **5** 23; 2 K **3** 9; and in the RVm it indicates a plain (הַכִּכָּר, *ha-kikkār*), Neh **3** 22. The Gr *perielthóntes* is tr^d in the same way (Acts **28** 13), but RVm reads "cast loose," following the WH reading *perielóntes*.

Nathan Isaacs

CIRCUMCISION, sûr-kum-sizh'un (מוּל, *mūl*, מוּלֹת, *mūlōth;* **περιτομή**, *peritomḗ*): The removal of the foreskin is a custom that has prevailed, and prevails, among many races in different parts of the world—in America, Africa and Australia. It was in vogue among the western Semites—Hebrews, Arabians, Moabites, Ammonites, Edomites, Egyptians, but was unknown among the Semites of the Euphrates. In Canaan the Philis were an exception, for the term "uncircumcised" is constantly used in connection with them. Generally speaking, the rite of circumcision was a precondition of the enjoyment of certain political and religious privileges (Ex **12** 48; Ezk **44** 9); and in view of the fact that in the ancient world religion played such an important rôle in life, it may be assumed that circumcision, like many other strange customs whose original significance is no longer known, originated in connection with religion. Before enumerating the different theories which have been advanced with regard to the origin and original significance of circumcision, it may be of advantage to consider some of the principal references to the rite in the OT.

1. Circumcision in the OT

In the account of the institution of the covenant between Yahweh and Abraham which is given (Gen **17**), circumcision is looked upon as the ratification of the agreement. Yahweh undertook to be the God of Abraham and of his descendants. Abraham was to be the father of a multitude of nations and the founder of a line of kings. He and his descendants were to inherit Canaan. The agreement thus formed was permanent; Abraham's posterity should come within the scope of it. But it was necessary to inclusion in the covenant that every male child should be circumcised on the 8th day. A foreigner who had attached himself as a slave to a Heb household had to undergo the rite—the punishment for its non-fulfilment being death or perhaps excommunication. According to Ex **12** 48 also no stranger could take part in the celebration of the Passover unless he had been circumcised. In the Book of Josh (**5** 2–9) we read that the Israelites were circumcised at Gilgal ("Rolling"), and thus the "reproach of Egypt" was "rolled away." Apparently circumcision in the case of the Hebrews was prohibited during the Egyp period—circumcision being a distinctive mark of the ruling race. It is noticeable that flint knives were used for the purpose. This use of an obsolete instrument is one of many proofs of conservatism in religion. According to the strange and obscure account of the circumcision by Zipporah of her eldest son (Ex **4** 25) the performance of the rite in the case of the son apparently possesses a vicarious value, for thereby Moses becomes a "bridegroom of blood." The marriage bond is ratified by the rite of blood (see 4 below). But it is possible that the author's meaning is that owing to the fact that Moses had not been circumcised (the "reproach of Egypt") he was not fit to enter the matrimonial estate (see 3 below).

The different theories with regard to the origin of circumcision may be arranged under four heads:

2. Theories of Origin

(1) Herodotus (ii.37), in dealing with circumcision among the Egyptians, suggests that it was a sanitary operation. But all suggestions of a secular, i.e. non-religious, origin to the rite, fail to do justice to the place and importance of religion in the life of primitive man.

(2) It was a tribal mark. Tattooed marks frequently answered the purpose, although they may have been originally charms. The tribal mark enabled one member of the tribe to recognize another and thus avoid injuring or slaying a fellow-tribesman. It also enabled the tribal deity to recognize a member of the tribe which was under his special protection. A mark was placed on Cain to indicate that he was under the special protection of Yahweh (Gen **4** 15). It has been suggested, in the light of Isa **44** 5 RVm, that the employer's mark was engraved (tattooed) on the slave's hand. The prophet represents Jews as inscribing on their hands that they belong to Yahweh. The walls of Jerus are engraved on Yahweh's palms (Isa **49** 16). On the other hand "cuttings in the flesh" are prohibited in Lev **19** 28 because they were common in the case of the non-Jewish religions. Such tattooed marks might be made in conspicuous places when it was necessary that they should be easily seen, but there might be reason for secrecy so that the marks might be known only to the members of the tribe in question.

(3) It was a rite which celebrated the coming of age of the person. It signified the attainment of puberty and of the right to marry and to enjoy full civic privileges.

(4) As human sacrifices began to be done away with, the sacrifice of the most easily removed portion of the anatomy provided a vicarious offering.

(5) It was a sacramental operation. "The shedding of blood" was necessary to the validity of any covenant between tribes or individuals. The rite of blood signifies the exchange of blood on the part of the contracting parties, and therefore the establishment of physical affinity between them. An alliance based on blood-relationship was inviolable. In the same way the tribal god was supposed to share in the blood of the sacrificed animal, and a sacred bond was established between him and the tribe. It is not quite obvious why circumcision should be necessary in connection with such a ceremony. But it may be pointed out that the process of generation excited the wonder and awe of primitive man. The prosperity of the tribe depended on the successful issue of the marriage bond, and a part of the body which had so much to do with the continuation and numerical strength of the tribe would naturally be fixed upon in connection with the covenant of blood. In confirmation of the last explanation it is urged that in the case of the covenant between Jeh and Abraham circumcision was the rite that ratified the agreement. In opposition to (3) it has been urged that among the Hebrews circumcision was performed in infancy—when the child was 8 days old. But this might have been an innovation among the Hebrews, due to ignorance of the original significance of the rite. If circumcision conferred upon the person circumcised the right to the enjoyment of the blessings connected with membership in the tribe it was natural that parents should be anxious that such an initiatory act should be performed early in life. The question of adult and infant baptism is capable of similar explanation. When we examine explanations (2), (3), (4), (5), we find that they are really different forms of the same theory. There can be no doubt that circumcision was originally a religious act. Membership in the tribe, entrance upon the rights of citizenship, participation in the religious practices of the tribe—these privileges are interdependent. Anyone who had experienced the rite of blood stood within the scope of the covenant which existed between the tribe and the tribal god, and enjoyed all the privileges of tribal society. It is easily understood why the historian carefully relates the circumcision of the Israelites by Joshua on their arrival in Canaan. It was necessary, in view of the possible intermingling of the conquerors and the conquered, that the distinctive marks of the Abrahamic covenant should be preserved (Josh **5** 3).

3. Spiritual Significance

In Jer **9** 25 and Dt **30** 6 we find the spiritual significance of circumcision. A prophet like Jeremiah was not likely to attach much importance to an external act like circumcision. He bluntly tells his countrymen that they are no better than Egyptians, Edomites, Moabites and Ammonites. They are uncircumcised in heart. Paul uses the term *concision* for this outward circumcision unaccompanied by any spiritual change (Phil **3** 2). The question of circumcision occasioned a protracted strife among the early Christians. Judaizing Christians argued for the necessity of circumcision. It was a reminiscence of the unrelenting particularism which had sprung up during the prolonged oppression of the Gr and Rom period. According to their view salvation was of the Jews and for the Jews. It was necessary to become a Jew in order to become a Christian. Paul consented to circumcision in the case of Timothy "because of the Jews" (Acts **16** 3). But he saw that a principle was at stake and in most of his epistles he points out the sheer futility of the contention of the Judaizers. (See commentaries on Rom and Gal.)

4. Figurative Uses

In a few suggestive passages we find a **fig.** application of the term. For three years after the settlement in Canaan the "fruit of the land" was to be considered as "uncircumcised" (Lev **19** 23), i.e. it was the property of the Baalim, the gods of Pal. The fruit of the fourth year belonged to Yahweh. Moses with characteristic humility describes himself as a man of "uncircumcised lips" (Ex **6** 30). Jeremiah charges his contemporaries with having their ear uncircumcised (Jer **6** 10) and their heart (**9** 26). "An uncircumcised heart is one which is, as it were, closed in, and so impervious to good influences and good impressions, just as an uncircumcised ear (Jer **6** 10) is an ear which, from the same cause, hears imperfectly; and uncircumcised lips (cf Ex **6** 12.30) are lips which open and speak with difficulty" (Driver on Dt **10** 16).

T. Lewis

CIS, sis (**Κείς**, *Keis*): The form given in Acts **13** 21 AV for Kish, the father of Saul the first king of Israel (1 Sam **9** 1 f).

CISAI, sī'sā-ī. See Kiseus.

CISTERN, sis'tẽrn, **WELL, POOL, AQUEDUCT**:

Use of Terms
1. General
2. Wells or Cylindrical Cisterns
3. Private Cisterns
4. Public Cisterns
5. Pools and Aqueducts
6. Figurative Uses
Literature

Several words are rendered by "cistern," "well," "pool," the relations of which in AV and RV are as follows:

Use of Terms

"Cistern," בֹּאר, *bō'r* (Jer **2** 13, etc), or בּוֹר, *bōr* (2 K **18** 31). The latter word is frequently in AV tr^d "well." RV in these cases changes to "cistern" in text (Dt **6** 11; 2 Ch **26** 10; Neh **9** 25) or m (1 S **19** 22, etc). The words גֶּבֶא, *gebhe'* (Isa **30** 14), גֵּב, *gēbh* (Jer **14** 3), rendered "pit" in AV are changed to "cistern" RV (the latter in ARV only).

The proper Heb word for "well" is בְּאֵר, *be'ēr* (seen in Beer-sheba, "well of the oath," Gen **21** 31), but other terms are thus rendered in AV, as עַיִן, *'ayin* (Gen **24** 13.16, etc, and frequently), מַעְיָן, *ma'yān* (Josh **18** 15), מָקוֹר, *māḳōr* (Prov **10** 11). In these cases RV usually changes to "fountain"; in Ex **15** 27, however, it renders *'ayin* by "springs," and in Ps **84** 6, *ma'yān* by "place of springs."

"Pool," אֲגַם, *'ăgham* (Isa **14** 23, etc; in AV, Ex **7** 19; **8** 5, rendered "ponds"); more frequently בְּרֵכָה, *berēkhāh* (2 S **2** 13; **4** 12, etc). In Ps **84** 6 the cognate בְּרָכָה, *berākhāh*, is changed to "blessing."

In the NT "well" represents the two words: πηγή, *pēgḗ* (Jn **4** 6.14; in RVm "spring"; 2 Pet **2** 17; RV renders "springs"), and φρέαρ, *phréar* (Jn **4** 11.12). "Pool" is κολυμβήθρα, *kolumbḗthra*, in Jn **5** 2.4.7; **9** 7.11.

1. General

The efforts made to supplement the natural water supply, both in agricultural and in populated areas, before as well as after the Conquest, are clearly seen in the innumerable cisterns, wells and pools which abound throughout Pal. The rainy season, upon which the various storage systems depend, commences at the end of October and ends in the beginning of May. In Jerus, the mean rainfall in 41 years up to 1901 was 25.81 in., falling in a mean number of 56 days (see Glaisher, *Meteorological Observations*, 24). Toward the end of summer, springs and wells, where they have not actually dried up, diminish very considerably, and cisterns and open reservoirs become at times the only sources of supply. Cisterns are fed from surface and roof drainage. Except in the rare instances where springs occur, wells depend upon percolation. The great open reservoirs or pools are fed from surface drainage and, in some cases, by aqueducts from springs or from more distant collecting pools. In the case of private cisterns, it is the custom of the country today to close up the inlets during the early days of the rain, so as to permit of a general

Fig. 1.—"The Great Sea" under the Temple.

wash down of gathering surfaces, before admitting the water. Cisterns, belonging to the common natives, are rarely cleansed, and the inevitable scum which collects is dispersed by plunging the pitcher several times before drawing water. When the water is considered to be bad, a somewhat primitive cure is applied by dropping earth into the cistern, so as to sink all impurities with it, to the bottom. The accumulation often found in ancient cisterns probably owes some of its presence to this same habit.

2. Wells

It is necessary to include wells under the head of cisterns, as there appears to be some confusion in the use of the two terms. Wells, so called, were more often deep cylindrical reservoirs, the lower part of which was sunk in the rock and cemented, the upper part being built with open joints, to receive the surface percolation. They were often of great depth. Job's well at Jerus, which is certainly of great antiquity, is 125 ft. deep (see *PEF*, "Jerus," 371).

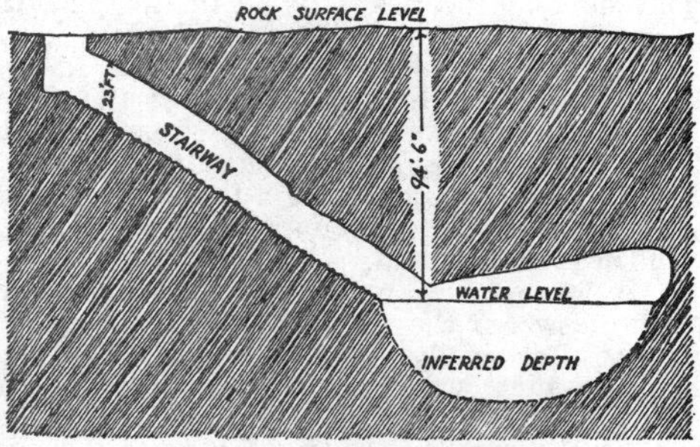

Fig. 2.—Reservoir at Gezer.

The discovery of "living water" when digging a well, recorded in Gen **26** 19 m, appears to have been an unusual incident. Uzziah hewed out many cisterns in the valley for his cattle (2 Ch **26** 9.10 RV), and he built towers, presumably to keep watch over both cattle and cisterns. Isaac "digged again the wells" which had been filled in by the Philis (Gen **26** 18). Wells were frequently dug in the plain, far from villages, for flocks and herds, and rude stone troughs were provided nearby. The well was usually covered with a stone, through which a hole was pierced sufficiently large to allow of free access for the pitchers. A stone was placed over this hole (Gen **29** 10) when the well was not in use. The great amount of pottery found in ancient cisterns suggests that clay pots were used for drawing water (see *Bible Sidelights*, 88). Jos (*Ant*, IV, viii, 37) elucidates the passage in Ex **21** 33 requiring the mouth of a "pit" or "well" to be covered with planks against accidents. This would seem to apply to wide-mouthed wells which had not been narrowed over to receive a stone cover. It may have been a well or cistern similar to these into which Joseph was cast (Gen **37** 24). In fact, dry-wells and cisterns formed such effective dungeons, that it is very probable they were often used for purposes of detention. From earliest times, wells have been the cause of much strife. The covenant between Abimelech and Abraham at Beersheba (Gen **21** 32) was a necessity, no less pressing then than it is now. The well, today, is a center of life in the East. Women gather around it in pursuit of their daily duties, and travelers, man and beast, divert their course thereto, if needs be, for refreshment; and news of the outer world is carried to and from the well. It is, in fact, an all-important center, and daily presents a series of characteristic Bible scenes. The scene between Rebekah and the servant of Abraham (Gen **24** 11 ff) is one with frequent parallels. The well lies usually at some little distance from the village or city. Abraham's servant made his "camels to kneel down without the city by the well of water at the time of the evening, the time that women go out to draw water." Saul and his servant found young maidens going out of the city to draw water (1 S **9** 11). Moses helped the daughters of the priest of Midian at the well, which was evidently at some distance from habitation (Ex **2** 16 ff).

Private cisterns must be distinguished from public

ARCHES OF ANCIENT AQUEDUCT AT ANTIOCH

cisterns or wells. They were smaller and were sunk in the rocks within private boundaries, each owner having his own cistern (2 K **18** 31; Prov **5** 15). Ancient sites are honeycombed with these cisterns. A common type in Jerus seems to have been bottle-shaped in section, the extended bottom part being in the softer rock, and the narrow neck in the hard upper stratum. Many irregularly shaped cisterns occur with rock vaults supported by rock or masonry piers. Macalister tells of the discovery at Gezer of a small silt catch-pit attached to a private cistern, and provided with an overflow channel leading to the cistern. It is an early instance of a now well-known method of purification. The same device and a trap in an aqueduct were found by Xenia Seminary and American School of Oriental Research at Kirjath-Sepher. The "broken cisterns" (Jer **2** 13) probably refer to insufficiently sealed cisterns.

3. Private Cisterns

Besides private cisterns there were huge public rock-cut cisterns within the city walls. The great water caverns under the Temple area at Jerus show a most extensive system of water storage (see *Recovery of Jerus*, ch vii). There are 37 of these described in *PEF*, "Jerus," 217 ff, and the greatest is an immense rock-cut cavern the roof of which is partly rock and partly stone, supported by rock piers (see Fig. 1, *PEF*). It is 43 ft. deep with a storage capacity of over two million gallons and there are numerous access manholes. This cistern is fed by an aqueduct from Solomon's Pools about 10 miles distant by road, and is locally known as *Bahar el Kebîr*, the "Great Sea." One of the most recent and one of the most interesting rock-cut reservoirs yet discovered is that at Gezer. (See *PEFS*, 1908, 96 ff.) In this example, the pool of spring water is reached by a great rock-tunnel staircase which descends 94 ft. 6 in. from the surface. The staircase diminishes in size as it descends, and at its greatest, it is 23 ft. high and 12 ft. 10 in. wide (see section Fig. 2). These proportions may seem unnecessarily large, but may be accounted for by the necessity for providing light at the water level. As a matter of fact, the brink of the pool receives the light from above. The work dates back to pre-Israelite times.

4. Public Cisterns

Open pools were common in every city. They were cut out of the rock and were built and cemented at points where occasion demanded. They were often of great size. The pool outside Jerus known as *Birket es Sultan* measures 555 ft.×220 ft.×36 ft. deep, and the so-called Hezekiah's Pool within the walls, is 240 ft.×144 ft.×about 20 ft. deep. The latter probably owes its

5. Pools and Aqueducts

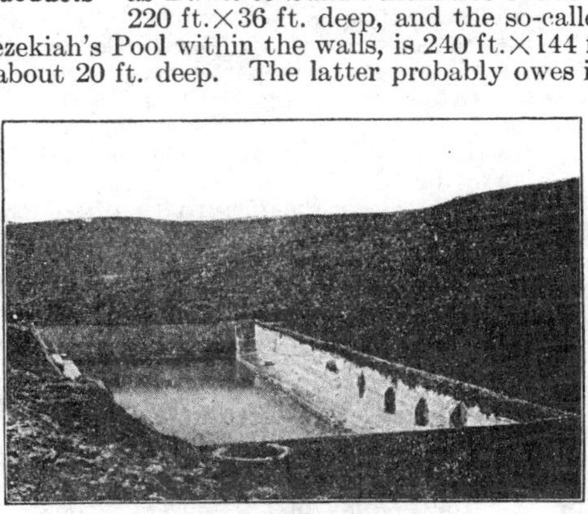

Fig. 3.—Pools of Solomon.

origin to the rock-cut fosse of early Jewish date. The *Birket es Sultan*, on the other hand, probably dates from the time of the Turkish occupation. They may, however, be taken as examples, which, if somewhat larger, are still in accord with the pool system of earlier history. Pools were usually fed by

Fig. 4.—Rock-cut Aqueduct.

surface drainage, and in some cases by aqueducts from springs at some distance away. They seem to have been at the public service, freely accessible to both man and beast. Pools situated outside the city walls were sometimes connected by aqueducts with pools within the city, so that the water could be drawn within the walls in time of siege. The so-called Pools of Solomon, three in number (see Fig. 3), situated about 10 miles by road from Jerus, are of large proportions and are fed by surface water and by aqueducts from springs. The water from these pools is conveyed in a wonderfully engineered course, known as the lower-level aqueduct, which searches the winding contours of the Judaean hills for a distance of about 15 miles, before reaching its destination in "the great sea" under the Temple area (Fig. 1). This aqueduct is still in use, but its date is uncertain (see G. A. Smith, *Jerus*, 131, where the author finds reason for ascribing it to the period of Herod). The course and destination of another aqueduct known as the high-level aqueduct is less definite. These aqueducts are of varying dimensions. The low-level aqueduct at a point just before it enters the Temple area was found to measure 3 ft. high×2 ft. 3 in. wide, partly rock-cut and partly built, and rendered in smooth-troweled cement, with well-squared stone covers (see *PEF*, *Excavations at Jerus*, 53 ff). There are many remains of rock-cut aqueducts throughout Pal (see Fig. 4) which seem to indicate their use in early Heb times, but the lack of OT references to these works is difficult to account for, unless it is argued that in some cases they date back to pre-Israelite times. The great tunnel and pool at Gezer lends a measure of support to this hypothesis. On the other hand, a plea for a Heb origin is also in a measure strengthened by the very slight reference in the OT to such a great engineering feat as the cutting of the Siloam tunnel, which is doubtless the work of Hezekiah. The pool of Siloam was originally a simple rock-cut reservoir within the walls, and was constructed by Hezekiah (2 Ch **32** 30). It measures 75 ft.×71 ft. It is the upper pool of Isa **7** 3. A lower overflow pool existed immediately beyond, contained by the city wall across the Tyropœon valley. The aqueduct which supplies the upper pool takes a tortuous course of about 1,700 ft. through the solid rock from the Virgin's fountain, an intermittent spring on the E. slope of the hill. The water reaches the pool on the S.W. of the spur of Ophel, and it was in the rock walls of this aqueduct that the famous Siloam inscription recording the completion of the work was discovered.

Herod embellished the upper pool, lining it with stone and building arches around its four sides (see *PEF*, *Excavations at Jerus*, 154 ff), and the pool was most likely in this condition in the time of Christ (Jn **9** 6.7). There are numerous other pools, cisterns and aqueducts in and around Jerus, which provide abundant evidence of the continual struggle after water, made by its occupants of all times (see G. A. Smith, *Jerus*, ch v, vol I). See also Pit; Well, etc.

6. Figurative Uses

Good wives are described as cisterns (Prov **5** 15 ff). "The left ventricle of the heart, which retains the blood till it be redispersed through the body, is called a cistern" (Eccl **12** 6). Idols, armies and material objects in which Israel trusted were "broken cisterns" (Jer **2** 13, see above) "soon emptied of all the aid and comfort which they possess, and cannot fill themselves again."

Literature.—G. A. Smith, *Jerusalem; PEF Memoirs*, Jerusalem vol; Wilson, *The Recovery of Jerusalem;* Macalister, *Bible Sidelights; PEFS;* Bliss and Dickie, *Excavations at Jerusalem;* Josephus.

Arch. C. Dickie

CITADEL, sit'a-del (1 Macc **1** 33; **3** 45). See Fortification.

CITHERN, sith'ẽrn (κιθάρα, *kithára;* 1 Macc **4** 54 AV, *kithárais kaí kinúrais* is trd "citherns and harps"; RV "harps and lutes"; cf guitar, zither): As 1 Macc was originally written in Heb, it is natural to suppose that these two Gr words stand for Heb *nebhālīm* and *kinnōrōth;* but to this it may be objected that *kithara* and *kinura* are not used elsewhere together to represent two different instruments. On the contrary we have either *kinura kai nabla* or *kithara kai psaltērion.* The most probable explanation of the unusual collocation of these two words in 1 Macc is that *kithara* was a gloss meant to explain the obsolescent *kinura.* See Music.

James Millar

CITIES, LEVITICAL. See Levitical Cities; City.

CITIES OF REFUGE. See Refuge, Cities of.

CITIES, sit'iz, **OF THE PLAIN,** plān, **CICCAR** (כִּכַּר הַיַּרְדֵּן, *kikkar ha-yardēn*): Included Sodom, Gomorrah, Admah, Zeboiim and Zoar. The locality is first referred to in Gen **13** 10, where it is said that Lot "lifted up his eyes, and beheld all the Plain of the Jordan, that it was well watered every where, before Jeh destroyed Sodom and Gomorrah, like the garden of Jeh, like the land of Egypt, as thou goest unto Zoar." The word trd plain is *kikkār,* "circle." In this ver, and in the 11th, as well as in 1 K **7** 46 and Mt **3** 5, we have the full phrase "circle of the Jordan." Elsewhere (Gen **13** 12; **19** 17.29; Dt **34** 3; 2 S **18** 23) the word for "circle" is used alone with the art. Until recently the traditional view that this circle of the Jordan was at the south end of the Dead Sea was universally maintained. The arguments in favor of this view are: (1) The name of Sodom is preserved in Jebel Usdum—Usdum having the same consonants with Sodom; moreover, the name is known to have referred to a place in that region as early as the days of Galen (*De Simpl. medic. Facult.,* 4.19) who describes certain "salts of Sodom" from the mountains surrounding the lake which are called Sodom. (2) Zoar seems to have been represented in the Middle Ages by a place which the Crusaders called Segore, and Arab. writers Zoghar. Under the name Zughar or Sughar the place is often referred to by mediaeval Arabian geographers as situated 1° S. of Jericho "at the end of the Dead Sea" and as a station on the route between the Gulf of Akabah and Jericho, two days' journey from Jericho. Ptolemy (v.17.5) reckons Zoar as belonging to Arabia Petrea. Eusebius (*Onom,* 261) describes the Dead Sea as lying between Jericho and Zoar. Jos (*Ant,* I, xi, 4) makes the Dead Sea extend 580 stadia "as far as Zoar of Arabia" (*Wars,* IV, viii, 4). These references would locate Zoar at the base of the mountains just S.E. of the Dead Sea, and, as it was within easy reach of Sodom, from which Lot fled, would fix the Cities of the Plain in that locality. Jerome (Comm. on Isa **15** 5) says that Zoar was in the borders of Moab.

On the other hand, it is maintained that the "kikkar of the Jordan" lay N. of the Dead Sea for the following reasons: (1) That is the region which is visible from the heights of Bethel (Gen **13** 10). (2) Zoar was said to be in the range of Moses' vision from the top of Pisgah (Dt **34** 1–3). (3) In Gen **14** the four Kings coming up from Kadesh attacked the Amorites that dwelt in Hazezon-tamar before reaching Sodom. Hazezon-tamar is to be identified with En-gedi. (4) The region south of the Dead Sea is described "as the garden of the Lord." Explorations of the geologists, Wright and Blanckenkorn, and especially now recent researches at the lower end of the Dead Sea by the expedition of Xenia Seminary and American School of Oriental Research have made further discussion of the location of the Cities of the Plain superfluous.

1. Civilization

The Canaanite civilization represented in the story of Abraham and Lot as being upon the Plain was actually there. The great High Place of the Plain, its greatness indicated by the great fortress protecting it, was found. Beside the temple was a camping place where the people gathered from time to time, as at Gilgal, to worship. At the side of this camping place was a cemetery. From the graves came the unmistakable pottery of the Early Bronze Age, the time of Abraham and Lot. A careful search of the Plain for 20 miles revealed the fact that for 2,500 years from this time there was no civilization of any kind on the Plain. In accord with this is the silence of the Scriptures concerning any history of the Plain onward to the end of the Biblical record (*Bibliotheca Sacra,* July, 1924). "As pointed out above, the pottery from Bab-ed-Dra' is all older than the 18th cent. BC at the latest, since none of the characteristic Middle Bronze, or Hyksos, types appear, and everything is 'first Semitic.' The date we have fixed for the catastrophe of Sodom and Gomorrah, about the early part of the 18th cent. BC, seems to be exceedingly probable" (Albright, *Annual of American School of Oriental Research,* VI).

2. Description

The description of this region (Gen **13** 10) "As the garden of the Lord," is the only correct description since the "captivity of Sodom" has been restored (Ezk **16** 53). Three little rivers of fresh water flow through the Plain and the rains of many centuries have washed the salt and sulphur out of the soil so that, with proper irrigation, 10,000 acres could be turned into a tropical garden.

3. Catastrophe

The catastrophe did take place as recorded (Gen **19**). The Biblical record is prepared from the standpoint of divine providence. It relates only the miraculous elements, the holding of the powers of destruction in leash until Lot be gotten out, and the exact timing and control of these powers of destruction. On the other hand the geologists can only tell us what took place as shown by the remains still existing there. A stratum of salt 150 ft. thick underlies the mountain here. Over it is a stratum of marl mingled with free sulphur. This is now a *burned out* region of oil and asphalt. Moreover, a great rupture in the strata completes the story. At sometime, somehow, God kindled the gases, which always collect where there is oil; a great explosion took place and the salt and sulphur were carried up into the heavens red hot so that it literally rained fire and brimstone over the whole Plain.

4. Location

The exact location of the Cities of the Plain is determined by the location of the remains of the catastrophe; the remains certainly have not moved around. They are right here around *Jebel Usdum*. In classical and NT times they were visible (Tac. *Hist*. v. 7; Strabo *Geog;* Jos. *Bel. Jud.* iv, viii. 4). In later times the sea has risen.

5. Moab

Pottery at the Moabite temple of Eder on the side of the mounain east of the Plain reveals a transition period from the Early Bronze of the time of Abraham and Lot to the Middle Bronze immediately succeeding (Albright, *Annual of American School of Oriental Research*, VI; *Bibliotheca Sacra*, July, 1924; Kyle, *Explorations at Sodom*).

LITERATURE.—Authorities favoring the south end of the Dead Sea: Dillmann, *Genesis*, 111 f; Robinson, *BRP*², II, 187 ff; G. A. Smith, *HGHL*, 505 ff; Baedeker-Socin, *Pal*, III, 146; Buhl, *GAP*, 117, 271, 274; see also esp. Samuel Wolcott, "Site of Sodom," *Bibliotheca Sacra*, XXV, 112–51.. Favoring the north end: Sir George Grove in various arts. in *DB;* Canon Tristram, *Land of Moab*, 330 ff; Selah Merrill, *East of the Jordan*, 232–39; W. M. Thomson, *The Land and the Book*.

REVISED BY M. G. K. GEORGE FREDERICK WRIGHT

CITIES, STORE, stōr. See CITY.

CITIMS, sit′imz. See CHITTIM (1 Macc **8** 5 AV).

CITIZENSHIP, sit′i-zen-ship: All the words in use connected with this subject are derived from πόλις, *pólis*, "city." These words, with the meanings which they have in the Bible, are the nouns, πολίτης, *polítēs*, "citizen"; πολιτεία, *politeía*, "citizenship"; πολίτευμα, *políteuma*, "commonwealth"; συμπολίτης, *sumpolítēs*, "fellow-citizen"; and the verb, πολιτεύω, *politeúō*, "to behave as a citizen." Each will be considered more fully in its proper place.

1. Philological

2. Civil

(1) *The word for citizen* is sometimes used to indicate little if anything more than the inhabitant of a city or country. "The citizens of that country" (Lk **15** 15); "His citizens hated him" (Lk **19** 14). Also the quotation from the LXX, "They shall not teach every man his fellow-citizen" (He **8** 11; cf Jer **31** 34). So also in the Apoc (2 Macc **4** 50; **5** 6; **9** 19).

(2) *Roman citizenship*.—This is of especial interest to the Bible student because of the apostle Paul's relation to it. It was one of his qualifications as the apostle to the Gentiles. Luke shows him in Acts as a Rom citizen, who, though a Jew and a Christian, receives, for the most part, justice and courtesy from the Rom officials, and more than once successfully claims its privileges. He himself declares that he was a citizen of Tarsus (Acts **21** 39). He was not only born in that city but had a citizen's rights in it. See PAUL; TARSUS.

But this citizenship in Tarsus did not of itself confer upon Paul the higher dignity of Rom citizenship. Had it done so, Claudius Lysias would not have ordered him to be scourged, as he did, after having learned that he was a citizen of Tarsus (Acts **21** 39; cf **22** 25). So, over and above this Tarsian citizenship, was the Rom one, which availed for him not in one city only, but throughout the Rom world and secured for him everywhere certain great immunities and rights. Precisely what all of these were we are not certain, but we know that, by the Valerian and Porcian laws, exemption from shameful punishments, such as scourging with rods or whips, and esp. crucifixion, was secured to every Rom citizen; also the right of appeal to the emperor with certain limitations. This sanctity of person had become almost a part of their religion, so that any violation was esteemed a sacrilege. Cicero's oration against Verres indicates the almost fanatical extreme to which this feeling had been carried. Yet Paul had been thrice beaten with rods, and five times received from the Jews forty stripes save one (2 Cor **11** 24.25). Perhaps it was as at Philippi before he made known his citizenship (Acts **16** 22.23), or the Jews had the right to whip those who came before their own tribunals. Rom citizenship included also the right of appeal to the emperor in all cases, after sentence had been passed, and no needless impediment must be interposed against a trial. Furthermore, the citizen had the right to be sent to Rome for trial before the emperor himself, when charged with capital offences (Acts **16** 37; **22** 25–29; **25** 11).

How then had Paul, a Jew, acquired this valued dignity? He himself tells us. In contrast to the *parvenu* citizenship of the chief captain, who seems to have thought that Paul also must have purchased it, though apparently too poor, Paul quietly says, "But I was free born" (AV; "a Roman born" RV, Acts **22** 28). Thus either Paul's father or some other ancestor had acquired the right and had transmitted it to the son.

3. Metaphorical and Spiritual

What more natural than that Paul should sometimes use this civic privilege to illustrate spiritual truths? He does so a number of times. Before the Sanhedrin he says, in the words of our Eng. VSS, "I have lived before God in all good conscience" (Acts **23** 1). But this tr does not bring out the sense. Paul uses a noticeable word, *politeuō*, "to live as a citizen." He adds, "to God" (τῷ Θεῷ, *tō Theō*). That is to say, he had lived conscientiously as God's citizen, as a member of God's commonwealth. The day before, by appealing to his Rom citizenship, he had saved himself from ignominious whipping, and now what more natural than that he should declare that he had been true to his citizenship in a higher state? What was this higher commonwealth in which he has enjoyed the rights and performed the duties of a citizen? What but the theocracy of his fathers, the ancient church, of which the Sanhedrin was still the ostensible representative, but which was really continued in the kingdom of Christ without the national restrictions of the older one? Thus Paul does not mean to say simply, "I have lived conscientiously before God," but "I have lived as a citizen to God, of the body of which He is the immediate Sovereign." He had lived theocratically as a faithful member of the Jewish church, from which his enemies claimed he was an apostate. Thus Paul's conception was a kind of blending of two ideas or feelings, one of which came from the old theocracy, and the other from his Rom citizenship.

Later, writing from Rome itself to the Philippians, who were proud of their own citizenship as members of a *colonia*, a reproduction on a small scale of the parent commonwealth, where he had once successfully maintained his own Rom rights, Paul forcibly brings out the idea that Christians are citizens of a heavenly commonwealth, urging them to live worthy of such honor (Phil **1** 27 m).

A similar thought is brought out when he says, "For our commonwealth [*politeuma*] is in heaven" (Phil **3** 20 m). The state to which we belong is heaven. Though absent in body from the heavenly commonwealth, as was Paul from Rome when he asserted his rights, believers still enjoy its civic privileges and protections; sojourners upon earth, citizens of heaven. The OT conception, as in Isa **60–62,** would easily lend itself to this idea, which appears in He **11** 10.16; **12** 22–24; **13** 14; Gal **4** 26, and possibly in Rev **21**. See also ROME.

G. H. TREVER

CITRON, sit′run. See APPLE.

form a casing to the earthen ramparts, with which the site was afterwards surrounded and which served as a protection against the intrusion of enemies. Later Sem intruders occupied the site, stone houses were built, and high stone defence walls were substituted for the earthen stone-cased ramparts. These later walls were much higher and stronger

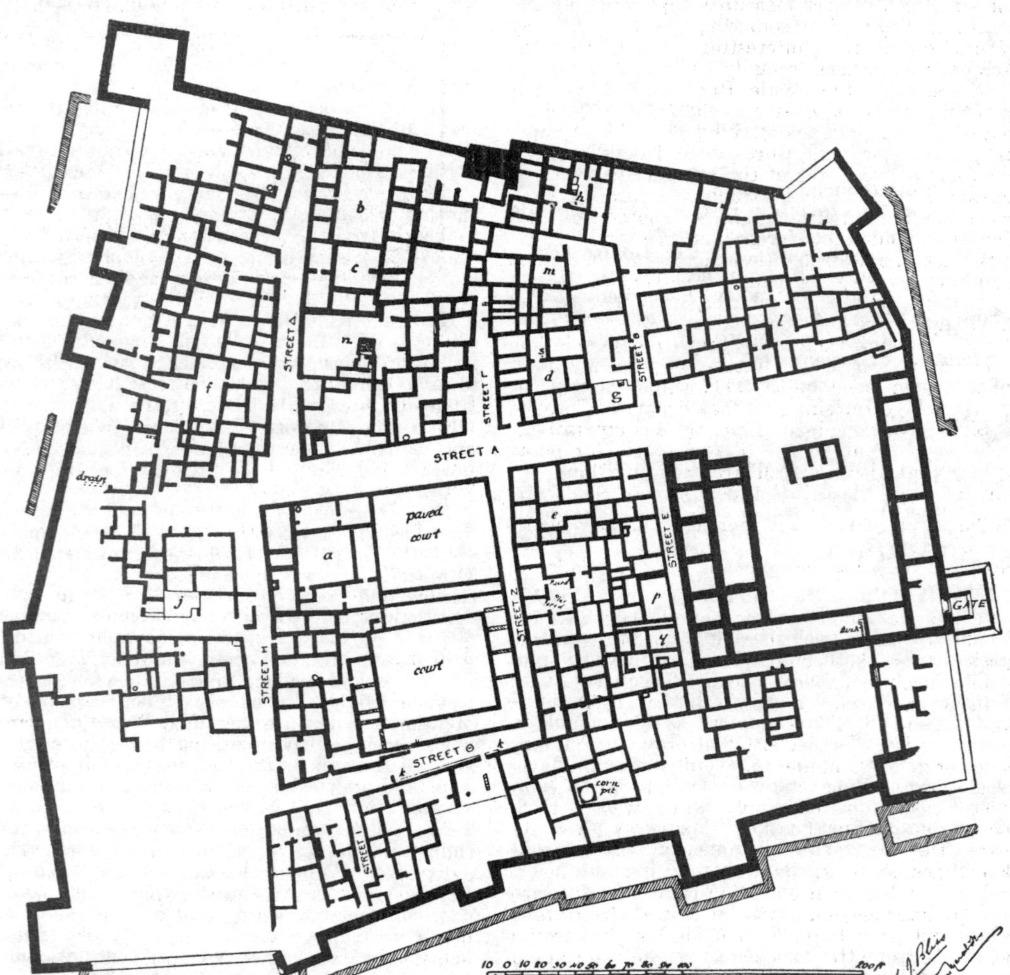

FIG. 1.—TELL SANDAHANNAH.

CITY, sit′i (עִיר, ʽīr, קִרְיָה, *ḳiryāh;* **πόλις,** *pólis*):

I. THE CANAANITE CITY
  1. Origin
  2. Extent
  3. Villages
  4. Sites
  5. External Appearance
  6. General
II. THE CITY OF THE JEWISH OCCUPATION
  1. Tower
  2. High Place
  3. Broad Place
  4. Streets
  5. General Characteristics
III. STORE CITIES
IV. LEVITICAL CITIES
LITERATURE

I. Canaanite City.—The development of the Can. city has been traced by Macalister in his report on the excavation at Gezer (*PEFS*, 1904, 108 ff). It originated on the slopes of a bare rocky spur, in which the Neolithic Troglodytes quarried their habitations out of the solid rock, the stones therefrom being used to

1. Origin

than those of the Neolithic occupation and were the walls seen by the Israelites when they viewed the country of their promise.

"The people that dwell in the land are strong, and the cities are fortified, and very great" (Nu **13** 28) was the report of the spies sent by Moses to spy out the land of Canaan, to see "what cities they are that they dwell in, whether in camps, or in strongholds" (Nu **13** 19.20). The difficulties of the task set before the advancing Israelites and their appreciation of the strength of the cities, is here recorded, and also in Dt **1** 28: "The people are greater and taller than we; the cities are great and fortified up to heaven; and moreover we have seen the sons of the Anakim there." This assessment of greatness was based upon comparative ignorance of such fortifications and the want of war experience and the necessary implements of assault. It need not, therefore, be supposed that the cities were

2. Extent

"great" except by comparison in the eyes of a tent-dwelling and pastoral people. On the contrary, most recent exploration has proved that they were small (see Père Vincent, *Canaan*, 27, n. 3, and Pl. I, where comparative measurements of the areas of ancient cities show that, in nine cities compared, Tell Sandahannah [barely 6 acres] is the smallest). Gezer measures approximately 22¼ acres and Tell el-Hesy somewhat greater. By way of illustration, it is interesting to note that the Acropolis at Athens, roughly computed, measures 7¼ acres, while the Castle Rock at Edinburgh is about 6 acres, or the same as the whole Seleucidan city of Tell Sandahannah (see Fig. 1). The Acropolis at Tell Zakarîya measures about 2 acres or nearly one-fourth of the area of the whole city (about 8½ acres). It is unlikely that Jebus (Jerusalem) itself was an exception, although in Solomonic and later times it extended to a far greater area.

3. Villages

Besides the walled cities there were "unwalled [country] towns a great many" (Dt **3** 5), "villages," unfortified suburbs, lying near to and under the protection of the walled cities and occupied by the surplus population.

4. Sites

The almost incredible number of cities and their villages mentioned in the OT, while proving the clannishness of their occupants, proves, at the same time, their comparatively small scale. Traces of similar populations that rise and fall are seen in China and Japan today. As a little poem says of Karakura:

"Where were palaces and merchants and the blades of warriors,
Now are only the cicadas and waving blades of grass."

"Cities that stood on their mounds" (Josh **11** 13; Jer **30** 18) as at Lachish and Taanach are distinguished from those built on natural hills or spurs of hills, such as Jebus, Gezer, Tell es Safi (Gath?), Bethshemesh (see Vincent, *Canaan*, 26 ff). The Arab. name "Tell" is applied to all mounds of ancient cities, whether situated on a natural eminence or on a plain, and the word is common in the geographical nomenclature of Pal. Sites were chosen near a water supply, which was ever the most essential qualification. For purposes of defence, the nearest knoll or spur was selected. Sometimes these knolls were of no great height and their subsequent elevation is accounted for by the gradual accumulation of debris from town refuse and from frequent demolitions; restoration being effected after a leveling up of the ruins of the razed city (see Fig. 2: Tell el-Hesy, *PEF*,

Fig. 2.—Tell el-Hesy.

which shows a section of the Tell from which the levels of the successive cities in distinct stratification were recovered). Closely packed houses, in narrow alleys, with low, rude mud, brick, or stone and mud walls, with timber and mud roofs, burned readily and were easily razed to the ground (Josh **8** 1 ff; **11** 11).

5. External Appearance

It would seem that, viewed from the outside, these cities had the appearance of isolated forts, the surrounding walls being strengthened at frequent intervals, with towers. The gates were approached by narrow roads, which mounted the slopes of the mound at the meeting-point of the meandering paths on the plain below (see Fig. 3). The walls of Tell ej-Judeideh were strengthened by towers in the inside, and presented an unbroken circuit of wall to the outside view (see Fig. 4, *PEF*). Houses on the wall (Josh **2** 15; 2 Cor **11** 33) may have been seen from the outside; but it is unlikely that any

Fig. 3.—Approaches to a City.

building within the walls was visible, except possibly the inner tower or stronghold. The whole of the interior of the early Jerus (Jebus) was visible from the hills to the E., but this peculiarity of position is uncommon. Strong and high walls, garrisoned by men-at-arms seen only through the battlements, showed no weakness, and the gates, with their narrow and steep approaches and projecting defence towers, looked uninviting traps (Fig. 5). The mystery of these unseen interiors could therefore be easily conjured into an exaggeration of strength.

6. General

The inhabitants of the villages (בָּנוֹת, *bānōth*, "daughters," Nu **32** 42 m) held feudal occupation and gave service to their lord of the city (אֵם, *'ēm*, "mother," 2 S **20** 19), in defence of their own or in attacks on their neighbor's property. Such were the cities of the truculent, marauding kings of Canaan, whose broken territories lent themselves to the upkeep of a condition, of the weakness of which, the Israelites, in their solid advance, took ready advantage.

II. Jewish Occupation.—After the conquest, and the abandonment of the pastoral life for that of agriculture and general trade, the condition of the cities varied but little, except that they were, from time to time, enlarged and strengthened. Solomon's work at Jerus was a step forward, but there is little evidence that, in the other cities which he is credited with having put his hands to, there was any embellishment. Megiddo and Gezer at least show nothing worthy of the name. Greek influence brought with it the first real improvements in city building; and the later work of Herod raised cities to a grandeur which was previously undreamt of among the Jews. Within the walls, the main points considered in the "layout" were, the Tower or Stronghold, the High Place, the Broad Place by the Gate, and the Market-Place.

1. The Tower or Stronghold

The Tower or Stronghold was an inner fort which held a garrison and commander, and was provisioned with "victuals, and oil and wine" (2 Ch **11** 11), to which the defenders of the city when hard pressed betook themselves, as a last resource. The men of the tower of Shechem held out against Abimelech (Jgs **9** 49) who was afterward killed by a stone thrown by a woman from the Tower of Thebez "within the city" (Jgs **9** 51.53). David took the stronghold of Zion, "the same is the city of David" (2 S **5** 7), which name (Zion) was afterward applied to the whole city. It is not unlikely that the king's house was included in the stronghold. Macalister (*PEFS*, 1907, 192 ff) reports the discovery of a Canaanite castle with enormously thick walls abutting against the inside of the city wall. The strongholds at Taanach and Tell el-Hesy are similarly placed; and the Acropolis at Tell Zakarîya lies close to, but independent of, the city wall.

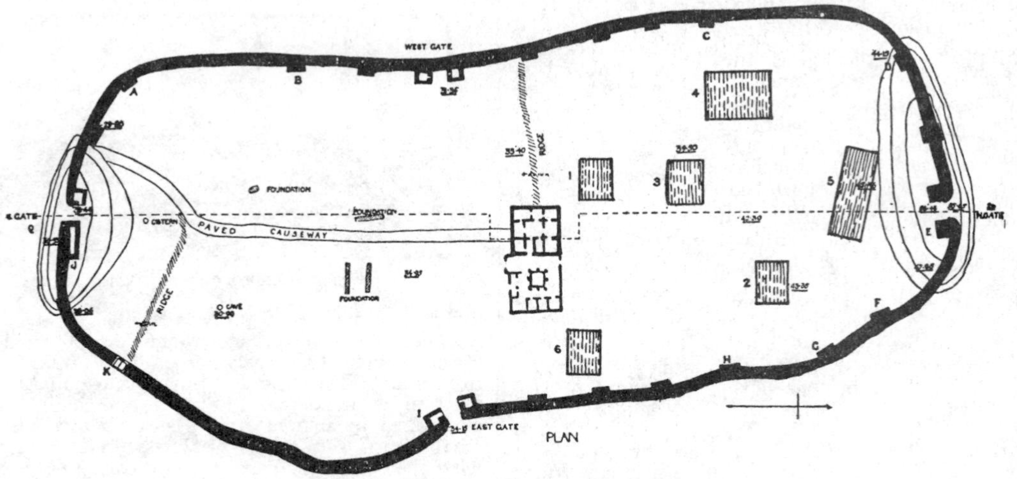

Fig. 4.—Walls of Tell ej-Judeideh.

2. The High Place

The High Place was an important feature in all Can. cities and retained its importance long after the conquest (1 S **9** 12 ff; 1 K **3** 2; Am **7** 9). It was a sanctuary, where sacrifices were offered and feasts were held, and men did "eat before Jeh" (Dt **14** 26). The priests, as was their custom, received their portion of the flesh (1 S **2** 12 ff). The High Place discovered at Gezer (*Bible Sidelights*, ch iii) is at a lower level than the city surrounding it, and lies N. and S. It is about 100 ft. in length, and when complete consisted of a row of ten rude undressed standing stones, of which eight are still remaining, the largest being 10 ft. 6 in. high, and the others varying to much smaller sizes. See High Place.

3. The Broad Place

The Broad Place (Neh **8** 1.3.16; Jer **5** 1) seems to have been, usually, immediately inside the city gate. It was not, in early Jewish cities, an extensive open area, but simply a widening of the street, and was designated "broad" by comparison with the neighboring alleys, dignified by the name of street. It took the place of a general exchange. Justice was dispensed (Ruth **4** 2) and punishment was administered. Jeremiah was put in "the stocks that were in the upper gate of Benjamin" (Jer **20** 2), proclamations were read, business was transacted, and the news and gossip of the day were exchanged. It was a place for all classes to congregate (Job **29** 7 m; Prov **31** 23), and was also a market-place (2 K **7** 1). In later times, the market-place became more typically a market square of the Gr agora plan, with an open area surrounded by covered shelters. The present market-place at Haifa resembles this. Probably it was this type of market-place referred to in Mt **11** 16; **20** 3 and Lk **7** 32; **11** 43. The street inside the Damascus gate of Jerus today is, in many ways, similar to the Broad Place, and retains many of its ancient uses. Here, Bedouin and Fellahîn meet from the outlying districts to barter, to arbitrate, to find debtors and to learn the news of the day. Lying as it did immediately inside the gate, the Broad Place had a defensive value, in that it admitted of concentration against the forcing of the gate. There does not seem to have been any plan of either a Can. or early Jewish city, in which this question of defence did not predominate. Open areas within the city were "waste places" (Isa **58** 12) and were not an integral part of the plan.

4. The Streets

The streets serving these quarters were not laid out on any fixed plan. They were, in fact, narrow, unpaved alleys, all seeming of equal importance, gathering themselves crookedly to the various centers. Having fixed the positions of the City Gates, the Stronghold and the High Place, the inhabitants appear to have been allowed to situate themselves the best way they could, without restriction of line or frontage. Houses were of modest proportions and were poorly built; planned, most often, in utter disregard of the square, and presenting to the street more or less dead walls, which were either topped by parapets or covered with projecting wood and mud roofs (see Architecture, Fig. 1; House).

Fig. 5.—City Gate.

The streets, as in the present day in Pal, were allocated to separate trades: "bakers' street" (Jer **37** 21), place "of the merchants" (Neh **3** 31.32 AV), "goldsmiths," etc. The Valley of the Cheesemakers was a street in the Tyropœon Valley at Jerus.

For a discussion of the subject of "cisterns," see the separate art. s.v.

The people pursued the industries consequent upon their own self-establishment. Agriculture claimed first place, and was their most highly esteemed occupation. The king's lands were farmed by his subjects for his own benefit, and considerable tracts of lands belonged to the aristocracy. The most of the lands, however, belonged to the cities and villages, and were allotted among the free husbandmen. Various cereals were raised, wheat and barley being most commonly cultivated. The soil was tilled and the crops reaped and threshed in much the same manner and with much the same implements as are now used in Syria. Cities lying in main trade routes developed various industries more quickly than those whose positions were out of touch with foreign traffic. Crafts and trades, unknown to the early Jews, were at first monopolized by foreigners who, as a matter of course, were elbowed out as time progressed. Cities on the seaboard of Phoenicia depended chiefly on maritime trade. Money, in the form of ingots and bars of precious metals, "weighed out" (2 K **12** 11), was current in preëxilic times, and continued in use after foreign coinage had been introduced. The first native coinage dates from the Maccabean period (see Madden, *Jewish Coinage*, ch iv). Slavery was freely trafficked in, and a certain number of slaves were attached to the households of the more wealthy. Although they were the absolute property of their masters, they enjoyed certain religious privileges not extended to the "sojourners" or "strangers" who sought the protection of the cities, often in considerable numbers.

5. General Characteristics

The king's private property, from which he drew full revenue, lay partly within the city, but to a greater extent beyond it (1 S **8** 15.16). In addition to his private property, he received tithes of fields and flocks, "the tenth part of your seed." He also drew a tax in the shape of certain "king's mowings" (Am **7** 1). Vassal kings paid tribute; Mesha, king of Moab, rendered wool "unto the king of Israel" (2 K **3** 4).

See G. A. Smith, *Jerusalem*, I, chs v–x, for detailed account of the conditions of Jewish city life. For details of government, see ELDER; JUDGES; SANHEDRIN.

III. Store Cities.—These were selected by Solomon and set aside for stores of victuals, chariots, horsemen, etc (1 K **9** 19). Jehoshaphat "built in Judah castles and cities of store" (2 Ch **17** 12). Twelve officers were appointed by Solomon to provision his household, each officer being responsible for the supply in one month in the year (1 K **4** 7). There were also "storehouses in the fields, in the cities, and in the villages" (1 Ch **27** 25 AV).

IV. The Levitical Cities.—These were apportioned 13 to the children of Aaron, 10 to Kohath, 13 to Gershon, 12 to Merari, 48 cities in all (Josh **21** 13 ff), 6 of which were cities of Refuge (Nu **35** 6); see REFUGE, CITIES OF. For further details see ARCHITECTURE; HOUSE.

LITERATURE.—*PEFS;* Bliss and Dickie, *Excavations at Jerusalem;* Macalister, *Excavation at Gezer;* Bliss and Macalister, *Excavations in Pal;* Sellin, *Excavation at Taanach;* Schumacher, *Excavation at Tell Mutesellim;* Macalister, *Bible Sidelights;* G. A. Smith, *Jerusalem; Historical Geography of the Holy Land;* Bliss, *Mounds of Many Cities;* Vincent, *Canaan.*

ARCH. C. DICKIE

CITY OF CONFUSION, kon-fū'zhun (קִרְיַת־תֹּהוּ, *kiryath-tōhū*): A name applied to Jerus (Isa **24** 10 AV).

CITY OF DAVID. See ZION.

CITY OF DESTRUCTION, dē-struk'shun (עִיר הַהֶרֶס, *'īr ha-hereṣ;* LXX **Βασεδέκ,** *Basedék*): In his prediction of the future return of Egypt to Jeh, Isaiah declares, "In that day there shall be five cities in the land of Egypt that speak the language of Canaan, and swear to Jeh of hosts; one shall be called The city of destruction" (Isa **19** 18). The name *'īr ha-hereṣ*, "the city of overthrow," is evidently a play upon *'īr ha-ḥereṣ*, "city of the sun," a designation of Heliopolis (same meaning; cf the name for this city, Beth-shemesh, Jer **43** 13), in Egyptian, On (Gen **41** 45), which last name Ezekiel, by a similar play on sound, changes into Aven. See ON. Some codices, however, as the RVm notes, read here *'īr ha-ḥereṣ*, the actual name of the city.

JAMES ORR

CITY, GOLDEN. See GOLDEN CITY.

CITY OF PALM TREES, päm' trēz (עִיר הַתְּמָרִים, *'īr ha-t^emārīm*). See JERICHO (Dt **34** 3; Jgs **1** 16; **3** 13; 2 Ch **28** 15).

CITY OF SALT. See SALT, CITY OF.

CITY OF WATERS. See RABBAH.

CITY, ROYAL. See RABBAH.

CITY, RULERS, rōōl'ẽrz, **OF:** The EV rendering of the πολιτάρχαι, *politárchai*, of Thessalonica, before whom Jason and the other Christians were dragged by the mob (Acts **17** 6.8). The term distinguishes the magistrates of a free Gr city from the ordinary Rom officials. It primarily denotes "rulers of the citizens," and hence was used only of magistrates of free cities. The term seems to have been confined largely to Macedonia, although there have been found a few inscriptions elsewhere in which it is used. The use of this term well illustrates the accuracy of the author of the Book of Acts, for while *politarchai* is not used by classical authors, this form is attested by a number of Macedonian inscriptions. Much work has been done in this field in recent years and the results throw light on the reference in Acts. Of the inscriptions that have been found at least five belong to Thessalonica (see art. by Professor Burton, in the *AJT* of 1898, "The Politarchs").

"The rulers" of Philippi, before whom Paul and Silas were brought, is the EV rendering of ἄρχοντες, *árchontes*, which is commonly used in the NT (Acts **16** 19). This is the ordinary term for "rulers" and is not the same as "rulers of the city."

A. W. FORTUNE

CLAP: An emphatic expression of joy, "They clapped their hands [*nākhāh*], and said, Long live [AV "God save"] the king" (2 K **11** 12); "Oh clap your hands [*tāḳa'*], all ye peoples" (Ps **47** 1); or exultation (*ṣāphaḳ*, Lam **2** 15; *māḥā'*, Ezk **25** 6; *tāḳa'*, Nah **3** 19); or repudiation (*ṣāphaḳ*, Job **27** 23; **34** 37).

Figurative: To denote Nature's "sympathy" with God's people. "Let the floods clap [*māḥā'*] their hands" (Ps **98** 8); "All the trees of the field shall clap their hands" (Isa **55** 12; cf Jgs **5** 20).

CLASPS, klasps (קֶרֶס, *ḳereṣ*): The word occurs nine times in Ex **26, 36,** and **39,** which record the specifications for the erection of the tabernacle and their subsequent carrying out. In each of these passages the AV renders "taches"—an early Eng. word of French origin now embodied in our "attachment." 50 clasps or taches of gold were ordered to be used in connecting together the two sets of inner tapestry curtains (10 in number) of the tabernacle (Ex **26** 6), and 50 clasps of brass (bronze) were similarly to be used in joining the two sets of goats' hair curtains (11 in number) which formed the outer covering (**26** 11). See TABERNACLE. As to the nature of the clasp itself, it seems to have belonged to a double set of loops, opposite to each other, to one of which in each set, required to be of blue cord, a gold or brass button or pin was attached, which, being inserted into the loop opposite, kept the curtain in position (**26** 4–6).

A difficulty arises from the direction in Ex **26** 33 that the veil which divided the "dwelling" into two parts—the holy place and the most holy—was to be suspended "under the clasps." If the clasps are supposed to be midway in the total length of the tabernacle, this would make the two holy places to be of equal size, contrary to the usual assumption that the outer was twice the length of the inner. The term "under" must therefore be used with some latitude, or the ordinary conception of the arrangement of the curtains, or of the size of the holy places will have to be revised (the dimensions are not actually given in the description).

W. SHAW CALDECOTT

CLAUDA, klô′da. See CAUDA.

CLAUDIA, klô′di-a (**Κλαυδία,** *Klaudía*): A member of the Christian congregation at Rome, who, with other members of that church, sends her greetings, through Paul, to Timothy (2 Tim **4** 21). More than this concerning her cannot be said with certainty. The *Apostolical Constitutions* (VII, 21) name her as the mother of Linus, mentioned subsequently by Irenaeus and Eusebius as bishop of Rome. An ingenious theory has been proposed, upon the basis of the mention of Claudia and Pudens as husband and wife in an epigram of Martial, that they are identical with the persons of the same name here mentioned. A passage in the *Agricola* of Tacitus and an inscription found in Chichester, England, have been used in favor of the further statement that this Claudia was a daughter of a British king, Cogidubnus. See argument by Alford in the Prolegomena to 2 Tim in his *Gr Testament.* It is an example of how a very few data may be used to construct a plausible theory. If it be true, the contrast between their two friends, the apostle Paul, on the one hand, and the licentious poet, Martial, on the other, is certainly unusual. If in 2 Tim **4** 21, Pudens and Claudia be husband and wife, it is difficult to explain how Linus occurs between them. See argument against this in Lightfoot, *The Apostolic Fathers.*

H. E. JACOBS

CLAUDIUS, klô′di-us (**Κλαύδιος,** *Klaúdios*): Fourth Rom emperor. He reigned for over 13 years (41–54 AD), having succeeded Caius (Caligula) who had seriously altered the conciliatory policy of his predecessors regarding the Jews and, considering himself a real and corporeal god, had deeply offended the Jews by ordering a statue of himself to be placed in the temple of Jerus, as Antiochus Epiphanes had done with the statue of Zeus in the days of the Maccabees (2 Macc **6** 2). Claudius reverted to the policy of Augustus and Tiberius and marked the opening year of his reign by issuing edicts in favor of the Jews (*Ant,* XIX, 5), who were permitted in all parts of the empire to observe their laws and customs in a free and peaceable manner, special consideration being given to the Jews of Alexandria who were to enjoy without molestation all their ancient rights and privileges. The Jews of Rome, however, who had become very numerous, were not allowed to hold assemblages there (Dio LX, vi, 6), an enactment in full correspondence with the general policy of Augustus regarding Judaism in the West. The edicts mentioned were largely due to the intimacy of Claudius with Herod Agrippa, grandson of Herod the Great, who had been living in Rome and had been in some measure instrumental in securing the succession for Claudius. As a reward for this service, the Holy Land had a king once more. Judaea was added to the tetrarchies of Philip and Antipas; and Herod Agrippa I was made ruler over the wide territory which had been governed by his grandfather. The Jews' own troubles during the reign of Caligula had given "rest" (ARV "peace") to the churches "throughout all Judaea and Galilee and Samaria" (Acts **9** 31). But after the settlement of these troubles, "Herod the king put forth his hands to afflict certain of the church" (Acts **12** 1). He slew one apostle and "when he saw that it pleased the Jews, he proceeded to seize" another (Acts **12** 3). His miserable death is recorded in Acts **12** 20–23, and in *Ant,* XIX, 8. This event which took place in the year 44 AD is held to have been coincident with one of the visits of Paul to Jerus. It has proved one of the chronological pivots of the apostolic history.

Whatever concessions to the Jews Claudius may have been induced out of friendship for Herod Agrippa to make at the beginning of his reign, Suetonius records (*Claud.* ch 25) "Judaeos impulsore Chresto assidue tumultuantes Roma expulit," an event assigned by some to the year 50 AD, though others suppose it to have taken place somewhat later. Among the Jews thus banished from Rome were Aquila and Priscilla with whom Paul became associated at Corinth (Acts **18** 2). With the reign of Claudius is also associated the famine which was foretold by Agabus (Acts **11** 28). Classical writers also report that the reign of Claudius was, from bad harvest or other causes, a period of general distress and scarcity over the whole world (Dio LX, 11; Suet. *Claud.* xviii; Tac. *Ann.* xi. 4; xiii.43; see Mommsen, *Provinces of the Rom Empire,* ch ix; and Conybeare and Howson, *Life and Epistles of St. Paul,* I).

J. HUTCHISON

CLAUDIUS LYSIAS, klô′di-us lis′i-as (**Κλαύδιος Λυσίας,** *Klaúdios Lysías*): A chief captain who intervened when the Jews sought to do violence to Paul at Jerus (Acts **21** 31; **24** 22). Lysias, who was probably a Greek by birth (cf **21** 37), and who had probably assumed the Rom forename Claudius (**23** 26) when he purchased the citizenship (**22** 28), was a military tribune or chiliarch (i.e. leader of 1,000 men) in command of the garrison stationed in the castle overlooking the temple at Jerus. Upon learning of the riot instigated by the Asiatic Jews, he hastened down with his soldiers, and succeeded in rescuing Paul from the hands of the mob. As Paul was the apparent malefactor, Lysias bound him with two chains, and demanded to know who he was, and what was the cause of the disturbance. Failing amid the general tumult to get any satisfactory reply, he conducted Paul to the castle, and there questioned him as to whether he was the "Egyptian," an impostor that had lately been defeated by Felix (Jos, *BJ,* II, xiii, 5; *Ant,* XX, viii, 6). Upon receiving the answer of Paul that he was a "Jew of Tarsus," he gave him permission to address the people from the stairs which connected the castle and the temple. As the speech of Paul had no pacifying effect, Lysias purposed examining him by scourging; but on learning that his prisoner was a Rom citizen, he desisted from the attempt and released him from his bonds. The meeting of the Sanhedrin which Lysias then summoned also ended in an uproar, and having rescued Paul with difficulty he conducted him back to the castle. The news of the plot against the life of one whom he now knew to be a Rom citizen decided for Lysias that he could not hope to cope alone with so grave a situation. He therefore dispatched Paul under the protection of a bodyguard to Felix at Caesarea, along with a letter explaining the circumstances (**23** 26–30. The genuineness of this letter has been questioned by some, but without sufficient reason.) In this letter he took care to safeguard his own conduct, and to shield his hastiness in binding Paul. There is evidence (cf Acts **24** 22) that Lysias was also summoned to Caesarea at a later date to give his testimony, but no mention is made of his arrival there. It is probable, however, that he was among the chief captains who attended the trial of Paul before King Agrippa and Festus (cf **25** 22). For the reference to him in the speech of Tertullus (see **24** 7 RVm), see TERTULLUS. C. M. KERR

CLAW, klô (פַּרְסָה, *parṣāh*, lit. "hoof"): One of the marks of a "clean" animal is stated thus: "Every beast that parteth the hoof, and cleaveth the cleft into two claws, ye shall eat" (Dt **14** 6 AV; RV "hath the hoof cloven in two"). See CHEW; CUD. AV uses the word "claws" where RV supplies "hoofs" in Zec **11** 16, "and will tear their hoofs in pieces," as the sheep are being overdriven. In the only other passage containing the word (Dnl **4** 33) there is no Heb equivalent in the original—"his nails like birds' [claws]."

CLAY, klā (חֹמֶר, *ḥōmer*, חֲסַף, *ḥăṣaph*, טִיט, *ṭīṭ*, מֶלֶט, *meleṭ*, עָבִי, *'ăbhī*, מַעֲבֶה, *ma'ăbheh*, עַבְטִיט, *'abhṭīṭ;* πηλός, *pēlós*, "wet clay," "mud"): True clay, which is a highly aluminous soil, is found in certain localities in Pal, and is used in making pottery. The Heb and Gr words, as well as the Eng. "clay," are, however, used loosely for any sticky mud. In making mud bricks, true clay is not always used, but ordinary soil is worked up with water and mixed with straw, molded and left to dry in the sun. *Ḥōmer* (cf *ḥemār*, "slime" or "bitumen") is rendered both "clay" and "mortar." *Ṭīṭ* is rendered "clay" or "mire." In Isa **41** 25 we have: "He shall come upon rulers as upon mortar [*ḥōmer*], and as the potter treadeth clay" (*ṭīṭ*). In Nah **3** 14, "Go into the clay [*ṭīṭ*], and tread the mortar [*ḥōmer*]; make strong the brickkiln" (i.e. make the walls ready to withstand a siege). *Ḥăṣaph* is the clay of the image in Nebuchadnezzar's dream (Dnl **2** 33 ff). *Meleṭ* occurs only in Jer **43** 9, where we find: AV, "Take great stones . . . . and hide them in the clay in the brickkiln"; RV, "hide them in mortar in the brickwork"; RVm, "lay them with mortar in the pavement." In Hab **2** 6, *'abhṭīṭ* (found only here) is rendered in AV "thick clay," as if from *'ăbhī* and *ṭīṭ*, but RV has "pledges," referring the word to r. *'ābhaṭ*, "to give a pledge." In 1 K **7** 46, *ma'ăbheh hā-'ădhāmāh* (cf 2 Ch **4** 17, *'ăbhī hā-'ădhāmāh*) is the compact or clayey soil in the plain of Jordan between Succoth and Zarethan, in which Hiram cast the vessels of brass for Solomon's temple. In Jn **9** 6.11.14, Thayer gives "made mud of the spittle"; in Rom **9** 21, "wet clay." ALFRED ELY DAY

CLEAN, klēn (Anglo-Saxon *clæne*, "clear," "pure"): Rendering four Heb roots: בַּר, *bar*, etc, "purify," "select," "make shining"; זַךְ, *zakh*, etc, "bright," "clean," "pure"; נָקִי, *nāḳī*, "free from," "exempt"; טָהֵר, *ṭāhēr*, "clean," "pure," "empty," "bright"(?) the principal root, rendered "clean" 80 times (AV): occurring in all its forms in various renderings about 200 times; also one Gr root, καθαρός, *katharós*, etc, akin to *castus*, "chaste," "free from admixture or adhesion of anything that soils, adulterates, corrupts" (Thayer's *Lexicon*). The physical, ritual, ethical, spiritual, figurative uses continually overlap, esp. the last four.

1. Physical

The physical use is infrequent: "Wash . . . . with snow water, and make my hands never so clean" (*zākhakh*, Job **9** 30; **figurative** also); "clean provender" (*hāmīç*, RV "savory"; RVm "salted"); "Cleanse . . . . inside of the cup and of the platter, that the outside thereof may become clean also" (*katharos*, Mt **23** 26); "arrayed in fine linen, clean [*katharón*] and white" (Rev **19** 8; ARV "bright and pure").

2. Ceremonial

The principal use was the ceremonial; applied to persons, places or things, "undefiled," "not causing defilement," or "from which defilement has just been removed"; *ṭāhēr*, almost exclusively ceremonial, being the chief Heb root. *Katharos* (NT), or derivatives, has this use clearly in Mk **1** 44; Lk **5** 14: "Offer for thy cleansing the things which Moses," etc; He **9** 13.22.23: "the cleanness of the flesh," etc. "Clean" is applied to animals and birds: "of every clean beast" (Gen **7** 2); "of all clean birds" (Dt **14** 11); (for list of unclean creatures see Lev **1** 4–20); to places: "Carry forth . . . . unto a clean place" (**4** 12); to buildings: "Make atonement for the house; and it shall be clean" (**14** 53); to persons: "A clean person shall take hyssop" (Nu **19** 18); to clothing: "garment . . . . washed the second time, and shall be clean" (Lev **13** 58); and to objects of all sorts, free or freed from defilement.

3. Ethical or Spiritual

The ethical or spiritual meaning, either directly or figuratively, is found in the OT chiefly in Job, Pss, the Prophets, whose interest is ethico-religious, rather than ritual, but the predominant uses are found in the NT: "Cleanse yourselves [*bārar*], ye that bear the vessels of Jeh" (Isa **52** 11); "How can he be clean [*zākhāh*] that is born of a woman?" (Job **25** 4) (principally moral, perhaps with allusion to the ceremonial defilement of childbirth); "The fear of Jeh is clean" (Ps **19** 9), that is, the religion of Jeh is morally undefiled, in contrast to heathen religions; "He that hath clean [*nāḳī*] hands, and a pure heart" (Ps **24** 4); "Purify me with hyssop, and I shall be clean" (*ṭāhēr*, Ps **51** 7); "Therefore said he, Ye are not all clean" (*katharos*, Jn **13** 11). Here, as in Ps **51** 7 and many others, the ritual furnishes a **figure** for the spiritual, illustrating the Divine purpose in the ritual, to impress, prefigure and prepare for the spiritual. A somewhat similar **figurative** moral use is found in Acts **18** 6: "Your blood be upon your own heads; I am clean" (*katharos*, "guiltless," "unstained"). See also UNCLEAN; PURIFICATION; DEFILEMENT.

Clean.—Adverb (in one case adj.): "utterly," "wholly"; usually rendering an intensive use of the Heb vb. as Joel **1** 7: "He hath made it clean bare" (lit. "stripping he will strip"); Zec **11** 17: "Arm . . . . clean dried up"; Isa **24** 19 AV: "Earth is clean dissolved." Twice it renders a principal vb.: Josh **3** 17: "Passed clean over the Jordan" (lit. "finished with regard to J."); Lev **23** 22 AV: "Shall not make a clean riddance" (lit. "shall not finish the corners"; ARV "shalt not wholly reap"). Once it renders a noun: Ps **77** 8: "Is his lovingkindness clean gone for ever?" ("end," *he-'āphēṣ*, "has his lovingkindness come to an end?"); and once an advb., "clean [ὄντως, *óntōs*, "actually," "really"] escaped" (2 Pet **2** 18); but ARV, following the reading "*olígōs*," "a little," "scarcely," renders "just escaping." PHILIP WENDELL CRANNELL

CLEANSE, klenz: "Make clean," "purify" being a frequent rendering of the original. It is found often (ARV) instead of "purge," "purify" (AV), renders nearly the same roots, and has the same overlapping phases, as "clean."

1. Physical

Physical cleansing, often **figuratively** used: "Stripes that wound cleanse away [*tamrīḳ*] evil" (Prov **20** 30); "A hot wind

. . . . not to winnow, nor to cleanse" (*bārar*, Jer **4** 11); "Straightway his leprosy was cleansed" (*katharízō*, Mt **8** 3).

In the ceremonial sense: (1) With a very strong religious aspect: to purify from sin by making atonement (*ḥāṭā'*); e.g. the altar, by the sin offering (Ex **29** 36); the leprous house (Lev **14** 48–53); the people, by the offering of the Day of Atonement (Lev **16** 30); the sanctuary, by the blood of the sin offering (Ezk **45** 18 ff). (2) To expiate (*kāphar*, "cover," "hide"); sin (in this case blood-guiltiness): "The land cannot be cleansed of the blood" (AV Nu **35** 33; ARV "no expiation can be made for the land"). (3) To remove ceremonial defilement, the principal use, for which the chief root is *ṭāhēr:* "Take the Levites . . . . and cleanse them" (Nu **8** 6); "and she shall be cleansed [after childbirth] from the fountain of her blood" (Lev **12** 7); "Cleanse it, and hallow it [the altar] from the uncleannesses of the children of Israel" (**16** 19), etc. This use is infrequent in the NT, except **figuratively**. Clear instances are Mk **1** 44: "Offer for thy cleansing [*katharismós*] . . . . for a testimony unto them" (also Lk **5** 14); He **9** 22.23: "necessary therefore that the copies of the things in the heavens should be cleansed with these." Physical, ritual, and **figurative** uses are combined in Mt **23** 25: "Ye cleanse the outside of the cup and of the platter." Acts **10** 15: "What God hath cleansed, make not thou common" uses the figure of the ritual to declare the complete abolition of ceremonial defilement and hence of ceremonial cleansing. For the elaborate system of ceremonial cleansing see esp. Lev **12–17,** also arts. Unclean; Purification. Its principal agencies were water, alone, as in minor or indirect defilements, like those produced by contact with the unclean (Lev **15** 5–18, etc); or combined with a sin offering and burnt offering, as with a woman after childbirth (**12** 6–8); fire, as with gentile booty (Nu **31** 23; by water, when it would not endure the fire); the ashes of a red heifer without spot, mingled with running water, for those defiled by contact with the dead (Nu **19** 2 ff). For the complex ceremonial in cases of leprosy, combining water, cedar, hyssop, crimson thread, the blood and flight of birds, the trespass **offering,** sin offering, burnt offering, see **Lev 14.** Blood, the vehicle and emblem of life, plays a large part in the major cleansings, in which propitiation for sin, as well as the removal of ceremonial defilement, is prominent, as of the temple, altar, etc: "According to the law, I may almost say, all things are cleansed with blood" (He **9** 22).

2. Ceremonial

In the ethical and spiritual sense, using the symbolism chiefly of 2. This embodies two phases: (1) the actual removal of sin by the person's own activity, "Wherewith shall a young man cleanse [*zākhāh*] his way?" (Ps **119** 9); "Cleanse your hands, ye sinners" (Jas **4** 8); "Let us cleanse ourselves from all defilement" (2 Cor **7** 1); (2) God's removal of the guilt and power of sin, as by discipline or punishment: "He cleanseth it" (Jn **15** 2, AV "purgeth"); "I have cleansed thee" (Ezk **24** 13); or in forgiveness, justification, sanctification. In these latter cases the exculpatory idea is sometimes the prominent, although the other is not absent: "I will cleanse [*ṭāhēr*] them from all their iniquity, whereby they have sinned against me; and I will pardon all their iniquities" (Jer **33** 8); "Wash me thoroughly from mine iniquity, and cleanse [*ṭāhēr*, "declare me clean"] me from my sin" (Ps **51** 2). "Cleanse [*nakkēh;* ARV "clear"] thou me from hidden faults" (Ps **19** 12), while formally to be understood "hold innocent," really connotes forgiveness. In Eph **5** 26, it is hard to determine whether pardon or God-given holiness is predominant: "That he might sanctify it [the church], having cleansed it by the washing of water with the word." In 1 Jn **1** 7, the sanctificatory meaning seems almost wholly to absorb the other: "The blood of Jesus his Son cleanseth us ["is purifying, sanctifying"] from all sin"; but in ver 9 it is again hard to determine the predominance: "He is faithful and righteous to forgive us our sin, and to cleanse us from all unrighteousness." The uncertainty lies in that the second clause may not, as in our speech, add a distinct idea, but may be Heb synonymous parallelism. Perhaps it is not wise to seek too curiously to disentangle the two ideas, since they cannot be separated. God never "clears" where he has not begun to "cleanse," and never "cleanses" by the Spirit without "clearing" through the blood.

3. Ethical and Spiritual

Philip Wendell Crannell

CLEAR, klēr, **CLEARNESS,** klēr'nes (בַּר, *bar;* **διαβλέπω,** *diablépō*): Equivalent of several Heb and Gr words for bright, unclouded, shining without obstruction, distinct, brilliant; "clearer than the noonday" (Job **11** 17): "clear as the sun" (Cant **6** 10); "clear shining after rain" (2 S **23** 4); "clear heat in sunshine" (Isa **18** 4); "clear as crystal" (Rev **21** 11). Advb. "clearly," for distinctly (Mt **7** 5; Mk **8** 25; Rom **1** 20). Noun, "clearness," for brilliancy, in Ex **24** 10, "as the very heaven for clearness."

From this physical, it is applied, in a moral sense, to character, as spotless and free from guilt, or charge, or obligation, "from oath" (Gen **24** 8); "from transgression" (Ps **19** 13). Hence the vb. "to clear" means juridically to declare or prove innocent, to vindicate (Gen **44** 16; Ex **34** 7; Nu **14** 18; cf *hágnos*, 2 Cor **7** 11, RV "pure"). "Be clear when thou judgest" (Ps **51** 4) refers to the proof and vindication of the righteousness of God.

H. E. Jacobs

CLEAVE, klēv: Is used in the Bible in two different senses:

(1) בָּקַע, *bāḳaʿ*, "to split," or "to rend." We are told that Abraham "clave the wood for the burnt-offering" (Gen **22** 3), and that "they clave the wood of the cart" (1 S **6** 14). The Psalmist speaks of Jeh cleaving fountain and flood (**74** 15), and the plowman cleaving the earth (**141** 7). For other examples see Jgs **15** 19; Eccl **10** 9; Ps **78** 15; Hab **3** 9.

(2) דָּבַק, *dābhaḳ;* κολλάω, *kolláō*, "to adhere to," or "to join one's self to." This meaning is the reverse of the preceding. The Psalmist speaks of his tongue cleaving to the roof of his mouth (**137** 6). We are told that a man should cleave unto his wife (Gen **2** 24; Mt **19** 5). It is said that Ruth clave unto her mother-in-law (Ruth **1** 14), and that certain men clave unto Paul (Acts **17** 34; cf **4** 23; **11** 23 m).

"Cleave" is also used in this sense to describe one's adherence to principles. Paul admonished the Romans to cleave to that which is good (Rom **12** 9).

A. W. Fortune

CLEFT, kleft, **CLIFF,** klif, **CLIFT,** klift: The first of these words, from cleave, "to split," is a crevice or narrow opening, as "of the ragged rocks" (Isa **2** 21); "under the clefts of the rocks" (Isa **57** 5). "Clift" is an obsolete form of cleft, found in AV Ex **33** 22; Isa **57** 5, but not in RV. "Cliff," an abrupt, precipitous, towering rock, is not in RV, but is found in AV 2 Ch **20** 16, RV "ascent," Job **30** 6.

CLEMENCY, klem'en-si (**ἐπιείκεια,** *epieíkeia*, "fairness," "sweet reasonableness," Acts **24** 4): The Gr word is rendered elsewhere "gentleness," 2 Cor **10 1;** Tit **3** 2, "meekness"; Jas **3** 17; 1 Pet **2** 18.